The IUCN Species Survival Cor

1997 IUCN Red List of
Threatened
Plants

Edited by
Kerry S. Walter (Royal Botanic Garden Edinburgh) and
Harriet J. Gillett (World Conservation Monitoring Centre)

The IUCN Species Survival Commission

1997 IUCN Red List of
Threatened Plants

Edited by
Kerry S. Walter (Royal Botanic Garden Edinburgh) and
Harriet J. Gillett (World Conservation Monitoring Centre)

Compiled by
The World Conservation Monitoring Centre

In association with
Association for Biodiversity Information
National Botanical Institute
Royal Botanic Garden Edinburgh
Royal Botanic Gardens, Kew
Smithsonian Institution
The Nature Conservancy
The New York Botanical Garden
Wildlife Australia

Foreword by
Brian Huntley

IUCN – The World Conservation Union
1998

The designation of geographical entities in this book, and the presentation of the material, do not imply the expression of any opinion whatsoever on the part of IUCN or other participating organizations concerning the legal status of any country, territory, or area, or of its authorities, or concerning the delimitation of its frontiers or boundaries.

The views expressed in this publication do not necessarily reflect those of IUCN or other participating organizations.

Published by: IUCN, Gland, Switzerland and Cambridge, UK

The World Conservation Union

Copyright: © 1998 International Union for Conservation of Nature and Natural Resources

Reproduction of this publication for educational and other non-commercial purposes is authorised without prior written permission from the copyright holder provided the source is fully acknowledged.

Reproduction of this publication for resale or other commercial purposes is prohibited without prior written permission of the copyright holder.

Citation: Walter, K.S. and Gillett, H.J. [eds] (1998). *1997 IUCN Red List of Threatened Plants*. Compiled by the World Conservation Monitoring Centre. IUCN – The World Conservation Union, Gland, Switzerland and Cambridge, UK. lxiv + 862pp.

ISBN: 2-8317-0328-X

Cover photo: *Elaeocarpus bojeri*, a critically endangered tree endemic to the island of Mauritius: Wendy Strahm.

Produced by: IUCN Publications Services Unit

Camera-ready copy of the List, data sources and index were provided by the World Conservation Monitoring Centre, 219 Huntingdon Road, Cambridge CB3 0DL, UK.

Printed by: Page Bros (Norwich) Ltd

Available from: IUCN Publications Services Unit
219c Huntington Road, Cambridge CB3 0DL, UK
Tel: +44 1223 277894, Fax +44 1223 277175
E-mail: iucn-psu@wcmc.org.uk
http://www.iucn.org
A catalogue of IUCN publications is also available.

The text of this book is printed on 90 gsm Fineblade Cartridge made from low-chlorine pulp.

Contributions to the IUCN Species Survival Commission and the *1997 IUCN Red List of Threatened Plants*

The Species Survival Commission gratefully recognizes its extensive network of volunteers and partner organisations who make products like the IUCN Red Lists possible. Those individuals who have contributed time and expertise are listed in the Acknowledgements. SSC also wishes to acknowledge those donors whose major financial contributions support a wide variety of SSC activities, as well as development and publication of the *1997 IUCN Red List of Threatened Plants.*

The Sultanate of Oman established the Peter Scott IUCN/SSC Action Plan Fund in 1990. The Fund supports Action Plan development and implementation; to date, more than 80 grants have been made from the Fund to Specialist Groups. As a result, the Action Plan Programme has progressed at an accelerated level and the network has grown and matured significantly. The SSC is grateful to the Sultanate of Oman for its confidence in and support for species conservation worldwide.

The Chicago Zoological Society (CZS) provides significant in-kind and cash support to the SSC, including grants for special projects, editorial and design services, staff secondments and related support services. The mission of CZS is to help people develop a sustainable and harmonious relationship with nature. The Zoo carries out its mission by informing and inspiring 2,000,000 annual visitors, serving as a refuge for species threatened with extinction, developing scientific approaches to manage species successfully in zoos and the wild, and working with other zoos, agencies, and protected areas around the world to conserve habitats and wildlife.

The Council of Agriculture (COA), Taiwan has awarded major grants to the SSC's Wildlife Trade Programme and Conservation Communications Programme. This support has enabled SSC to continue its valuable technical advisory service to the Parties to CITES as well as to the larger global conservation community. Among other responsibilities, the COA is in charge of matters concerning the designation and management of nature reserves, conservation of wildlife and their habitats, conservation of natural landscapes, coordination of law enforcement efforts as well as promotion of conservation education, research and international cooperation.

The World Wide Fund For Nature (WWF) provides significant annual operating support to the SSC. WWF's contribution supports the SSC's minimal infrastructure and helps ensure that the voluntary network and Publications Programme are adequately supported. WWF aims to conserve nature and ecological processes by: (1) preserving genetic, species, and ecosystem diversity; (2) ensuring that the use of renewable natural resources is sustainable both now and in the longer term; and (3) promoting actions to reduce pollution and the wasteful exploitation and consumption of resources and energy. WWF is one of the world's largest independent conservation organizations with a network of National Organizations and Associates around the world and over 5.2 million regular supporters. WWF continues to be known as World Wildlife Fund in Canada and in the United States of America.

The National Wildlife Federation (NWF) made significant annual contributions to the SSC Conservation Communications Fund and SSC's southeast Asia programme during the mid-1990s. NWF is the largest non-governmental, non-profit conservation-education and advocacy organization in the United States. It emphasizes assisting individuals and organizations of all cultures, in the United States and abroad, to conserve wildlife and other natural resources and to protect the earth's environment to assure a peaceful, equitable, and sustainable future.

IUCN also wishes to thank the **Norcross Wildlife Foundation** for supporting publication of this book.

Contributors to the *1997 IUCN Red List of Threatened Plants*

The *1997 IUCN Red List of Threatened Plants* represents a partnership among several NGO and government institutions. Contributions of major data sets made this publication possible; these contributions and the institutions that made them are described below. Of special note is the role played by the World Conservation Monitoring Centre,

which undertook the massive and challenging task of bringing the widely divergent data sources together.

WCMC – World Conservation Monitoring Centre

The World Conservation Monitoring Centre (WCMC), based in Cambridge, UK, is a joint-venture between the three partners in the *World Conservation Strategy* and its successor *Caring for the Earth*: IUCN – The World Conservation Union, UNEP – United Nations Environment Programme and WWF – World Wide Fund For Nature. The Centre provides information services on the conservation and sustainable use of species and ecosystems and supports others in the development of their own information systems.

WCMC has developed global overview databases that include threatened plant and animal species, habitats of conservation concern, critical sites, protected areas of the world, and the utilisation of and trade in wildlife species and products. Drawing on these databases, WCMC provides an information service to the conservation and development communities, governments and the United Nations agencies, scientific institutions, the business and commercial sector, and the media. WCMC produces a wide variety of specialist outputs and reports based upon analyses of data integrated from many sources. It is also actively involved, particularly in developing countries, in building the capacities of other institutions for promoting and planning the conservation and sustainable use of their own biological resources.

TNC – The Nature Conservancy

The Nature Conservancy (TNC) is an international non-governmental organization dedicated exclusively to biodiversity protection. With more than 900,000 members, the Conservancy owns and manages over 1,600 reserves, the largest private system of nature sanctuaries in the world. Internationally the Conservancy works to support in-country organizations and agencies that share its focus on the protection of biological diversity. The Conservancy has helped establish a network of Natural Heritage Programs and Conservation Data Centers, based in state and national agencies and private organizations throughout the United States, Canada, Latin America, and the Caribbean. Together with this network of data centers, the Conservancy develops and maintains biodiversity databases for use in informing conservation and development activities. The conservation status and geographic distribution of many western

hemisphere plants have been assessed and documented by this multi-institutional effort, including a comprehensive listing of threatened plants of the United States and Canada. This western hemisphere data set forms a major contribution to the *1997 IUCN Red List of Threatened Plants*.

ABI (formerly BIN) – associated with TNC

The Association for Biodiversity Information (ABI) was established in 1994 to advance the goals of Natural Heritage Programs, Conservation Data Centers and associated organizations whose mission is to provide information on the distribution, abundance, and conservation needs of rare species and natural communities. ABI seeks to assist its members to operate as a network by sharing technologies, facilitating the exchange of knowledge and experiences, and facilitating the development of multijurisdictional information products and services. Most Natural Heritage data centers that provided state-level U.S. conservation status assessments as part of The Nature Conservancy's contribution to this volume are constituent members of ABI.

National Botanical Institute (NBI), South Africa

The mission of the NBI is to promote the sustainable use, conservation, appreciation and enjoyment of the exceptionally rich plant life of South Africa, for the benefit of all its people. The NBI grows more than 10,000 indigenous plant species in eight National Botanical Gardens, located country-wide, providing an exceptional amenity and educational focus for local and overseas visitors alike. The research activities of the Institute, which focus on the systematics, ecology, conservation, ethnobotany and horticulture of southern Africa's plants, are conducted from three research centres. These centres include three herbaria which together house 1.8 million specimens. The Institute also develops and maintains databases on plant diversity for use in conservation and development activities.

Smithsonian Institution

The Smithsonian Institution, founded in 1846 by an Act of Congress, counts among its most important missions the discovery, identification and understanding of the world around us. Personnel and research support for the North America, Middle America and South America sections of the *1997 IUCN Red List of Threatened Plants* were provided by the Department of Botany, National Museum of Natural History, Smithsonian Institution with support from other sources. Its cadre of research scientists, which includes a large number of biologists specialising in taxonomy, systematics and evolutionary studies, is contributing to the global inventory of species and to the revision of our view of natural systems. The production of the data for this volume is but one of the efforts to provide accurate information for the use of resource managers and planners and as an educational tool for future generations.

Wildlife Australia

Wildlife Australia deals with wildlife issues that were formerly the concern of the Australian National Parks and Wildlife. It manages or co-manages with the Aboriginal traditional owners seventeen parks, reserves and other land and marine protected areas. Nature reserves, marine parks and botanic gardens, including the Australian National Botanic Garden, are also managed by Wildlife Australia. In areas of Australia's Commonwealth responsibility, Wildlife Australia manages endangered species and marine wildlife. International agreements to which Australia is a party and which are administered under the aegis of Wildlife Australia cover the regulation of whaling, trade in endangered species, protection of migratory and endangered species, and the conservation of nature in the South Pacific. Wildlife Australia is part of Environment Australia which incorporates the environment programmes of the Australian Department of Environment, Sport and Territories, and supports scientific research to document Australia's flora and fauna.

RBGE – Royal Botanic Garden Edinburgh

Founded in 1670 as a Physic Garden in Scotland's capital city, the Royal Botanic Garden Edinburgh is one of the oldest botanic gardens in the world and is, after Oxford, the second oldest in the United Kingdom. In the ensuing 327 years, it has become one of the world's major botanic gardens, with extensive research, conservation, and education programmes spanning the globe. Today the institution encompasses four gardens across Scotland, each affording distinct conditions for the cultivation of plants, and together attracting up to 1 million visitors each year.

RBGE is primarily a research institution devoted to the study of plants and fungi. Its world-famous living collections (58,000 accessions representing 21,000 taxa – 6% of the world's known vascular plants), herbarium (2 million specimens), and library (300,000 books, journals, illustrations and archives) underpin the Garden's research programme in taxonomy (both monographic and floristic), horticulture, molecular systematics, genetic conservation, and both phanerogamic and cryptogamic biodiversity studies; these well documented living and herbarium collections serve as biological standards, and provide the taxonomic framework to enable publications such as this to be produced.

RBGE grows 1,386 species (581 genera, 152 families) of threatened plants listed in this book, including 13 that are extinct in the wild, and is discovering the horticultural and ecological parameters under which they grow, with the eventual aim of re-introduction and re-establishment when appropriate.

The Royal Botanic Gardens, Kew

The mission of the Royal Botanic Gardens, Kew is to ensure better management of the Earth's environment by increasing knowledge and understanding of the plant kingdom. The Kew Herbarium is one of the world's largest and houses an encyclopaedic collection of over six million specimens of vascular plants and fungi from every country in the world. The Jodrell Laboratory carries out fundamental research in plant biochemistry, physiology, anatomy, cytology and molecular systematics. The library, with its collection of over 750,000 books and journals is a resource for all of Kew's research work. The living collections are the world's largest with 79,600 accessions representing 35,900 species; one in ten of all vascular plants. In addition Kew has the largest seed bank of wild plants containing over 4,000 species.

NYBG – The New York Botanical Garden

An international leader in botanical research, The New York Botanical Garden is at the forefront of the battle to preserve the world's plant life. Since 1891 its scientists have conducted over 1,000 research expeditions worldwide to discover and document plants. Today it operates one of the world's most active research programs in systematic and economic botany. NYBG's staff of more than 100 researchers and technicians, including Ph.D. botanists, concentrates on exploring tropical regions where plant diversity is rapidly vanishing. The institution is also active in training the next generation of botanists through graduate programs here and field research abroad.

Contents

Foreword x

Editors' note xi

Acknowledgements xii

Acronyms xvi

Introduction xvii
   Purpose xvii
   History of the threatened plants list xviii
   Data coverage and quality xix

Organisation of information xxi
   Names xxi
   Conservation Status xxii
   Distribution xxiii
   Data sources xxv
   Statistics xxv

Analysis of the list xxvi
   Species counts xxvi
   Geographic analysis xxvi
   Taxonomic analysis xxxiv
   Plant extinctions xlvi

Global Red Lists – where next? xlvii

Appendix I: IUCN Red List Categories il
   IUCN Red List Categories as used in this
     List (pre-1994) il
   1994 IUCN Red List Categories il

Appendix II: Threatened Plants Database
     management liii
   Bibliographic information liii
   Taxon information liii
   Distribution information liii

Appendix III: The Nature Conservancy
     and Wildlife Australia status ranks lvii
   Interpretation of The Nature Conservancy
     status ranks lvii
   Interpretation of Wildlife Australia status
     ranks lviii

References lxi

Navigating the List lxiv

1997 IUCN Red List of Threatened
Plants 1–752

Data sources 755–824

Index 827–862

List of Tables
   Table 1. Major taxa included in this
      Red List xxi
   Table 2. Taxonomic levels of CITES
      listings displayed in this Red List . . . xxiii
   Table 3. BRUs (Biological Recording
      Units) xxiv
   Table 4. Comparison of potential methods
      of counting threatened plants xxvi
   Table 5. Globally threatened vascular
      plants: IUCN Category by
      country xxvii
   Table 6. Countries with at least 5% of
      their native species threatened xxxiii
   Table 7. Globally threatened taxa of
      vascular plants: IUCN Categories
      by country-level endemism xxxv
   Table 8. Globally threatened taxa of
      vascular plants: IUCN Categories
      by major taxa and families xxxv
   Table 9. Vascular plant families listed
      with at least 50% of their species
      threatened xlv
   Table 10. Number of families and genera
      containing globally threatened
      vascular plants for each IUCN Red
      List Category xlv
   Table 11. Major tables used in the
      Threatened Plants Database liv
   Table 12. Type of data records suppressed
      from the Red List lv
   Table 13. Conversion of TNC ranks to
      IUCN Categories lviii

List of Figures
   Figure 1. Percentage of the world's
      vascular plant species threatened at
      a global scale xvii

Foreword

The closing decades of this century have witnessed an unprecedented interest in the future of planet earth. The alarming loss of natural habitats, and the species and ecosystem processes dependent on them, has stimulated conservationists around the globe to share knowledge and resources to document, monitor and attempt to reverse the deterioration of the planet's health. This book provides a snap-shot of the state of the world's plant diversity at the end of the second millennium. It presents a shocking picture of nearly 34,000 species, or 12.5 per cent of the world's flora, facing extinction.

This book is the first comprehensive listing of threatened plants at a global scale. As a synthesis of numerous data sets of varying vintage and quality, it inevitably contains errors, redundancies and omissions. Its strength lies in the decision to go forward and publish what can at best be a first approximation. It is at once both a stimulus and a challenge to botanists and conservationists around the world to evaluate every statement and record included in this volume – and to contribute to a revised edition in the near future. The power and accessibility of the Internet and future information technologies will make possible a rapid advance in exchange and integration of threatened plant information, and the appearance of the second edition of this list in electronic as well as hard copy format.

Red Data Books are as relevant today as they were thirty years ago when the concept was introduced to the world by the late Sir Peter Scott, then Chairman of IUCN's Species Survival Commission. While viewed by some as antiquated artefacts of the pre-electronic age, RDBs have served conservation well, most especially in developing countries where knowledge on the biota is often incomplete and where authoritative RDB lists, even in stagnant hard copy form, are an invaluable aid to drawing the attention of decision makers to biodiversity conservation priorities.

The Convention on Biological Diversity is the most important international instrument for conservation yet created, and its implementation will be dependent on the availability of the kinds of information provided in this book. The Convention focuses on the responsibility of sovereign nations regarding biodiversity conservation and its sustainable use, and it is pertinent to note that a staggeringly high 91 per cent of the species listed in this book as threatened are limited in their geographical distribution to single countries. Thus the future of no fewer than 33,798 species listed in the book falls within the direct responsibility of individual nations – the majority of these signatories to the Convention. The Convention calls upon signatories to prepare national biodiversity action plans by mid 1997, setting a tight timetable for positive measures to address the conservation needs of the vast majority of species listed in the book. This volume's utility to the implementation of the CBD is thus of direct relevance.

What the book does not address, nor is it meant to address, is the global need for capacity building in plant conservation biology, and most particularly in plant taxonomy, the Cinderella of the biosciences. The Convention on Biological Diversity will fail in all its noble goals if the taxonomic expertise of all countries, but most especially developing countries, is not rapidly reinforced. Fortunately, initiatives stimulated and supported by such financial mechanisms as the Global Environmental Facility, through UNEP and UNDP, offer new opportunities for capacity building and institutional strengthening. Motivated by the urgency of needs documented by books such as this and the actions resulting from the CBD, one can look to the near millennium with a cautious measure of optimism.

Professor Brian Huntley
National Botanical Institute, South Africa

Editors' note

Please read the Introduction to this book before consulting the Red List. It is important to understand the data-gathering, compiling, and management processes involved in preparing the list in order to draw reasonable conclusions from the data presented. The Threatened Plants Database from which this list was produced has been developed over many years and is dependent on the contribution of data from vastly diverse sources throughout the world. As this Red List is the result of merging several regional databases, two of which do not follow the IUCN Categories of threat, particularly detailed explanations of the conversion of threat categories are included.

There are many challenges arising from the management of such a large data set, some of which are evident in this list. We appeal to users of this Red List to appreciate the complexity of managing the data, and the many issues that arise in attempting to create a harmonised and consistent list, particularly with regard to the following issues:

- Only vascular plants have been included in this book. Much work is being done today to assess the number of threatened non-vascular plants, and hopefully these will be reported in the next edition of the Red List.

- This Red List shows a distinct regional bias, partly due to the merging of three regional databases with the Threatened Plants Database, and partly because there are vast areas of the world for which floristic and conservation status data are incomplete, particularly in Africa, Asia, the Caribbean, and South America.

- Publication of this list has been made possible due to the generosity of The Nature Conservancy, Wildlife Australia and the National Botanical Institute in making their extensive data sets available in electronic format. Anyone interested in obtaining further details for North America, Australia or South Africa should contact the relevant organisation directly for the most current information about the conservation status of plants in these regions.

- Known synonyms have been suppressed from this list, although some do appear either due to lack of information, or differences in taxonomic opinion.

- Most plant author names appear as they were originally provided by the data source. Ideally, we follow the standard established by Brummitt and Powell (1992) for plant authorities. However, due to the long history of the database, the many sources of data, and the size of the data holdings, it has not been possible to bring all existing records in line with this standard.

- Great efforts have been taken to ensure that credit is given for the origin of all data, both published and unpublished, by providing a comprehensive list of data sources. The data sources also provide an extremely important indication of the date of publication and, therefore, the currency of the conservation data. It has not been possible to go back to 'old' sources for updated information, and some data in this list are inevitably out of date.

- Finally, despite our best efforts to adhere to strict guidelines concerning interpretation of conflicting sources of information, it was inevitable that editorial control had to be exerted in many instances, particularly in deciding on criteria for inclusion in this published list. Whilst great effort has been made to ensure the accuracy of the data presented, given the size of the list, it is inevitable that some records will prove to be inaccurate. As editors we accept final responsibility for the data presented here, but emphasise that a list such as this simply provides a view of the data as it existed on the Threatened Plants Database on 22 May 1997, and will always require further additions, alterations and improvements. Comments on, and additions to the list are always welcomed, and provide a vital input to improving further listings.

Acknowledgements

Collation of the information presented in this IUCN Red List has only been possible with the support of an enormous number of people throughout the world. The extent of this support is evident by referring to the list of 2,091 data sources which follows the main list. Not only do these entries indicate the source of the data, they also allow credit to be given to the primary data gatherers, without whom production of compendia such as this is not feasible.

Many people supplied particularly large amounts of information and/or useful advice. At the risk of providing only an incomplete list, these include: J. Abrahamsen, C.D. Adams, E. Adjanohoun, J.M. Aguilar Cumes, L. Aké Assi, J.R. Akeroyd, D.M. A. Alanen, D.M. Al-Eisawi, A.H. Al-Khayar, R.M. Alfaro, S.I. Ali, T. Almeida, R. Alvaro, K. Ammann, S. Andrews, A.L. Antohiou, G. W. Argus, B. von Arx, E.O.A. Asibey, P.S. Ashton, G.G. Aymonin, J.A. Bacone, M.M.J. van Balgooy, M.J. Balick, P. Bamps, C. Barclay, W.T. Barker, T.M. Barkley, T. Baytop, H.E. Beaty, S. Beck, L.J. Beloussova, D. Benkert, G. Benl, P. Berry, R.W. Boden, P. Boniface, I. Bonnelly de Calventi, J. Bonnet, A. Borhidi, J. Bosser, M. Boydak, L. Brako, D. Bramwell, F.J. Breteler, J.D. Briggs, P. Broussalis, R.E. Brown, R.K. Brummitt, W. Burger, W. Burley, R. Burton, B. Burtt, R. Bye, L.J.T. Cadet, M. Lisete Caixinhas, J.E. Canfield, S. Carter-Holmes, J. Cerovsky, J.D. Chapman, A.O. Chater, M.N. Chaudhri, A.S. Cheke, S. Cheng-kui, M. Chilcott, V.I. Chopik, E.A. Christenson, G.L. Church, S. Cochrane, M. Cohen, N.H.A. Cole, J.B. Comber, P. Condy, M. Conrad, M.J.E. Coode, C.D.K. Cook, T.A. Cope, F. Corbetta, B. Corrias, J. Cortes, R.A. Countryman, P. Coyne, P.J. Cribb, J.R. Croft, Q. Cronk, B.S. Croxall, K. Curry- Lindahl, T. Curtis, S.K. Czerepanov, W. d'Arcy, P.H. Davis, J.-P. d'Huart, E. d'Souza, M. Damanakis, A. Danin, G. Davidse, B. de Winter, R.A. DeFilipps, H. Dernirez, G. Dennis, G. Dihoru, M. Dillon, M.G. Diamini, C.H. Dodson, D.D. Doone, L.E. Dorr, F. Dowsett-Lernaire, J. Dransfield, S. Dransfield, A.M. Dray, R.L. Dressler, B. Dummond, R.W Dwyer, J. Dwyer, I.D. Edwards, E. Einarsson, T. Ekim, J.M. Engel, H. Ern, I. Escobar, A. Escudeiro, S. Estenssoro, R. Faden, P. Fairburn, A. Farjon, L. Farrell, J.M. Fay, A. Federov, J. Feilberg, K. Ferguson, L.F. Ferguson, A.A. Ferrar, S. Filipello, H. Fink, M.A. Fischer, J.J. Floret, E. Forero, L.L. Forman, B. Fredskild, J.D. Freeman, F. Friedmann,

I. Friis, F.R. Fosberg, E. Gabrielian, F. Garbari, M.F. Gardner, Z.O. Gbile, C. Geerling, D. Geltman, A.H. Gentry, A. George, B. Gibbs- Russell, M.G. Gilbert, J.B. Gillett, D.R. Given, H.C. Gjerlaug, L. Godical, E.E. Gogina, C. Goldberg, P. Goldblatt, P. Golz, P.L. Gorchakovsky, S. Peccenini Gordini, N. Goulandris, L.D. Gómez, C. Gómez-Campo, J.-J. de Granville, M.H. Grayum, P. Gregerson, W. Greuter, C. Grey-Wilson, V.I. Grubov, C.V.S. Gunatilleke, I.A.U.N. Gunatilleke, M.N. el Hadidi, E. Hágsater, W.J. Hahn, T.V. Hall, N. Hallé, O. Hamann, H. Hamburger, L. Hämet-Ahti, B.E. Hammel, A.C. Hamilton, A. Hansen, W.Z. Hao, R.M. Harley, I. Hedberg, O. Hedberg, I.C. Hedge, D. Henderson, A.J. Hepburn, F.N. Hepper, D. Herbst, J.E. Hernández- Bermejo, V.H. Heywood, C. Hilton-Taylor, F.-C. Ho, E. Hogan, K. Høiland, L. Holm-Nielsen, S. Holt, R.E. Holttum, J. Holub, M. Houser, K.S. Hsu, T.C. Huang, O. Huber, C.J. Humphries, H.G. Hundley, D.R. Hunt, J. Hunziker, T. Ingelög, K. Iwatsuki, H. Jacques-Félix, P. Jaeger, S.K. Jain, J. Jalas, H. Jasiewicz, C. Jeffrey, J. Jensen, J. Jérémie, C. Jermy, R. Jenkins, R. Johns, D.V. Johnson, M.C. Johnston, J.-C. Jolinon, B. Jonsell, L.D. Jornez, C. Kabuye, M.G. Karrer, K. Kartawinata, S. Keel, D.L. Kelly, H. Keng, R. Kiesling, R. Kiew, Kim Yong- Shik, R.A. King, R.B. de Klee, S. Knees, E. Köhler, J. Kornas, R. Kral, I. Kryukova, B.A. Kuzmanov, R. Kwok, M. Laínz, E. Landolt, E. Lanfranco, T. Lamb, J. Lambinon, P. Lantz, S.E. Lauzon, A. Lawalrée, C.C. Lay, J.-P. Lebrun, T.B. Lee, Y.N. Lee, J.H. Leigh, D.B. Lellinger, J.Y. Lesouëf, F. Le Sueur, R. Letouzey, G.P. Lewis, R.W. Lichvar, J.C. Lindeman, H.P. Linder, A.H. Liogier, J.M. Lock, B. Løjtnant, D. Long, A.H. Lot, J. Lovett, C.A. Luer, J.L. Luteyn, H.E. Luther, S. Lyster, P.J.M. Maas, B. MacBryde, H.S. MacKee, J. MacKnight, D.A. Madulid, J. Malato- Beliz, W. Marais, F. Markgraf, C. Martin, G. Martinelli, P.C. Martinelli, B. Mathew, M. Maunder, E. Mayer, S.J. Mayo, D. McClintock, B.R. McDonald, L.R. McMahan, R. McVaugh, R.D. Meikle, J.E. Mendes Ferrão, J. Mennema, H. Meusel, R. Mill, J. Miller, T.G. Miller, N.A. Minyaev, M.J. Mitchell, N. Mohner, D. Money, T. Monod, F. Monterroso, B. de Montmollin, D.M. Moore, H.E. Moore, W.H. Moore, R.C. Moran, Ph. Morat, S.A. Mori, N. Morin, L.E. Morse, T. Müller, M. Muñoz Schick, D.F. Murray, F. Näscher, C. Nelson S., F. Németh, E. Ni Lamha, O. Nilsson, D.H. Nicolson, H. Niklfeld, H. Nishida, R. Nordhagen, C. Norquist, M. Numata,

C. Ochoa, H. Ohba, J.C. Okafor, R. Olaczek, L. Olivier, P. Olwell, S. Orzell, R.T. Pace, C.N. Page, J. Page, G. Palacios, C. Pannell, A. Pelaez Goycochea, F.H. Perring, Phan Ke Loc, D. Philcox, B.R. Philips, A. Phillipps, D. Phitos, R.E.G. Pichi-Sermolli, J. Pickard, S. Pignatti, G.E. Pilz, U. Pinborg, E. Pingitore, A.R. Pinto da Silva, A. Pinzl, J. J. Pipoly, M. Plotkin, A.C. Podzorski, R.M. Polhill, D.M. Porter, D.A. Powell, R. Press, G. Proctor, S. Price, A. Radcliffe-Smith, F. Raimondo, T.P. Ramamoorthy, M.H. Ramos Lopes, V. Randrianasolo, A.L. Rao, W. Rauh, P.H. Raven, R.W. Read, L. Reichling, S.A. Renvoize, S. Rivas-Martínez, S.A. Robertson, W.A. Rodgers, J.A. Rodrigues de Paiva, M. Romeril, W. Rossi, J.H. Rumely, H. Runemark, J. Rzedowski, M.-H. Sachet, M.S. Khan, M.J.S. Sands, C. Sargent, A.R.K. Sastry, M. Scannell, J. Van Scheepen, C. Scheepers, F.M. Schlegel, M. Schmid, J. Schwegman, J.W. Scott, P. Scott, K. Scriven, R.R. Sears, K. Segnestam, J. Seyani, K.H. Sheikh, G. Sheppard, T. Shimizu, A. Shmida, G. Sfikas, S. Siwatibau, P. Skoberne, L.E. Skog, A.C. Smith, L.B. Smith, W.A. Smith, T. Smitinand, B.E. Smythies, S. Snogerup, J.C. Solomon, G.V. Somner, B.A. Sorrie, M. Soto, R. Spichiger, W.T. Stearn, W.D. Stevens, D.W. Stevenson, J. Stewart, J. Steyermark, C. Stirton, A.L. Stoffers, W.A. Strahm, H.E. Strang, A. Strid, A.M. Studart da Fonseca Vaz, T.F. Stuessy, H.-J. Su, A. Sugden, H. Sukopp, J. Sultana, J. Suominen, J.D. Supthut, D. Sutton, W.R. Sykes, W. Tai, A.L. Takhtajan, E. Tanner, N.P. Taylor, Y. Te-Tsun, J.P. Theurillat, P. Thomas, A.D. Thompson, G. Thor, D. Van Tien, V.N. Tikhomirov, V.M. Toledo, C.C. Townsend, H. Trass, G. Traxler, G. Troupin, C. Tyndeman, N.W. Uhl, P. Uotila, B. Valdes, T. Vasconcelos, B. Verdcourt, C. Villamil, D.E. Viney, K. Vollesen, A.P. Vovides, S. Vuokko, M. Wadhwa, F.H. Wadsworth, W.H. Wagner, W.L. Wagner, S. Wahlberg, M.G. Walters, S.M. Walters, D.C. Wasshausen, D.A. Webb, L. Webb, E.J. Weeda, E. Weinert, O. Weiskirchner, D.W. Weller, T. Wendt, H. Van der Werff, M. Werkhoven, W.A. Whistler, F. White, T.C. Whitmore, G.E. Wickens, S.R. Wilbur, R.T. Winterbottom, J.R.I. Wood, K. Woolliams, T. Wraber, A. Wünschmann, J.J. Wurdack, P. Wyse Jackson, F. Yaltirik, J. Zaffran, T. Zanoni, E. Zardini, J.L. Zarruchi, C. Zimmer, A. Zimmermann, E.M. van Zinderen Bakker, and G. Zizka.

The many staff of the Threatened Plants Unit (TPU) over the years are especially to be thanked for their work in data gathering, validation, and manipulation. They include Ronald Melville, Hugh Synge, Sara Oldfield, Christine Leon, Stephen Davis, Charlie Jarvis, Jana Zantovska, Stephen Droop, Robert Madams, and Vernon Heywood. Special thanks also go to Jane Villa-Lobos of the Latin American Plants Program at the Smithsonian Institution, and Olga Herrera-MacBryde, who have tirelessly gathered and reviewed conservation data for Mexico, Central and South America.

Special mention needs to be made of the three organisations that generously made their national data sets available in electronic format:

The Nature Conservancy (TNC), USA, provided data on approximately 11,000 plants for the United States, Canada, and Latin America, representing the largest single data contribution to this list. This data exchange has involved a great deal of effort on the part of TNC's Lynn S. Kutner, Larry E. Morse, Shirley Keel, and Bruce Stein, as well as the members of the Natural Heritage and Conservation Data Center Network, the Association for Biodiversity Information, and John T. Kartesz of the North Carolina Botanical Garden. Sincere thanks are due to them all for their work in providing this important Western Hemisphere data set to this project.

Wildlife Australia supplied data on approximately 5,000 plant taxa native to Australia. The data were compiled for *Rare or Threatened Australian Plants,* the fourth revision of which was compiled in 1995 and published the following year (Briggs and Leigh, 1996). That revision gathered the knowledge of specialists in all states and territories of Australia as well as some overseas workers. Special thanks are due to John Briggs, John Leigh, and Lyn Meredith for their assistance in making this valuable information available in electronic format.

The National Botanical Institute (NBI), South Africa, provided data on approximately 3,435 threatened plant taxa which occur in southern Africa (the area including Namibia, Botswana, Swaziland, Lesotho, and South Africa). This information was obtained as part of a collaborative project on threatened plants in southern Africa co-ordinated by Craig Hilton-Taylor, the initial results of which were recently published as the *Red Data List of Southern African Plants* (Hilton-Taylor, 1996). A large number of professional and amateur botanists contributed to this project and they are fully acknowledged in the above publication. The following people, however, deserve special mention because of the pivotal role they played in providing data and helping to check all the information received: Tania Anderson, Wayne Boyd, Kate Braun, Patricia Craven, Johann du Preez, Craig Hilton-Taylor, Gillian Maggs, Pete Phillipson,

Ruida Pool, Rob Scott-Shaw, Marianne Strohbach, and Sumitra Talukdar. Sincere thanks are also due to Tony Hall, Steve Fourie, Dave Everard, and their co-workers for laying the impressive foundations on which most of the threatened plants work in southern Africa is based.

Although many botanic gardens and herbaria around the world have made substantial contributions to the information in this List, several (including their library staff) deserve special mention – the Royal Botanic Gardens, Kew, the National Museum of Natural History of the Smithsonian Institution, the Natural History Museum (UK), the Royal Botanic Garden Edinburgh, The New York Botanical Garden, Missouri Botanical Garden, and the Arnold Arboretum of Harvard University. The Royal Botanic Garden Edinburgh has played a crucial role in the completion of this book by allowing one of the editors (KSW) to continue work on it after he left WCMC in 1993.

For a period of several years in the 1980s, the IUCN/WWF Plant Advisory Group (PAG) met regularly and provided vital advice and guidance on plant conservation issues. PAG members included Laurent Aké Assi, Peter S. Ashton, Robert Boden, Enrique Forero, Arturo Gómez-Pompa, Ole Hamann, He Shan An, Kuswata Kartawinata, T.N. Khoshoo, Nañuza Luiza da Menezes, Ghillean T. Prance, Pierre Quézel, Voara Randrianasolo, Peter Raven, Richard Schultes, Armen Takhtajan, Eddy van der Maarel, and Wang Xian-pu.

Thanks are given to Wendy Strahm, the current IUCN Plants Officer, and her predecessors, along with the Chairs and many members of SSC plant Specialist Groups throughout the world who have played a key role in collating and checking data, including: Conifers (Aljos Farjon and Chris Page), Cacti and Succulents (Ted Anderson, David Hunt, Sara Oldfield and Nigel Taylor), Cycads (Cynthia Giddy and Dennis Stevenson), Europe (Klaus Ammann), Ferns (Clive Jermy), Mediterranean Islands (Bertrand de Montmollin), North America (Robert Mohlenbrock), Orchids (Eric Hágsater), Palms (Michael Balick, John Dransfield and Dennis Johnson), South America (Enrique Forero and Carlos Villamil), and Temperate Broadleaved Trees (David Hunt). These groups have been responsible for drawing up and annotating a great many lists over the years.

Credit is given to the people involved with establishing and managing the Threatened Plants Database as well as to those responsible for entering, editing, and managing its ever-expanding data holdings. The database was originally established under Grenville Lucas of the Royal Botanic Gardens, Kew, and implemented and managed for many years by Hugh Synge, followed by Chris Leon. Thanks are due to those who were most involved in developing the early databases used to track the information shown in this book – Duncan Mackinder, Nick Phillips, Eddie Wymer, Pete Rooney, Mike Crosby, Jeremy Harrison, Al Blake, and Steve Luckcock. In addition to these people, Robert Jenkins, Keith Carr, and Larry Morse of The Nature Conservancy and Ian Barnes and Duncan Bennett of WCMC played an indirect but pivotal role in the further development of the current Threatened Plants Database by Kerry Walter, who headed WCMC's plant activities from 1991–1993, followed by Harriet Gillett.

Manual data entry has been undertaken by too many people to list comprehensively. However, WCMC staff involved in recent years include Pete Atkinson, Kevin Burgess, Rob Cubey, Karen Headley, Neil Jenking, David Kirk, Beverley Lewis, Jim Lucas, Sarah Skinner, Maria Toal, Jon White, and volunteers Lorna Hall and Peter Richardson. Charlotte Jenkins, Sara Oldfield and Amy Mackinven, working on a WCMC/SSC project on the Conservation and Sustainable Management of Trees, have also been involved with updating tree data. The contributions of former TPU staff members, while less recent than those listed above, are no less appreciated or important – Katherine Barnes, Margaret Beyer, Penny Croucher, Jane Flood, Deb Goodenough, Patrick Gregerson, Louise Henson, Erica Kiess, Heather Macleod, Vicki Morgan, Noel McGough, Nicky Powell, Judy Sheppard, Rosemary Simpson and Winifred Worth.

As any database manager will know, the process of checking data can appear to produce as many problems as it solves, and a special mention is due to Johanna Sidey, Donna Smith, and Simon Reeve for bearing the onerous burden of cleaning up the data following the electronic data merges prior to publication, and still managing a smile at the end of the day!

Thanks are due to Tim Johnson and Simon Stuart who provided management support. Steven Mugeridge, Julie Reay and Rose Warwick provided invaluable technical and administrative assistance. Over the years useful discussions have taken place with many colleagues within IUCN and WCMC, including Mark Collins, Mary Cordiner, Brian

Groombridge, Martin Jenkins, Jeremy Harrison, Jo Taylor, Sue Wells, and Lissie Wright. RBGE staff Rob Cubey and Martin Pullan provided assistance with data transfers.

External financial support for the Threatened Plants Database and its outputs has come from a range of sources either as direct funding or as indirect support for a range of WCMC projects and programmes and is hereby gratefully acknowledged: CITES Secretariat; Council of Europe; Darwin Initiative for the Survival of Species; European Economic Community; International Tropical Timber Organisation (ITTO); IUCN – The World Conservation Union; Government of the Netherlands; National Museum of Natural History, Smithsonian Institution; U.K. Natural Environment Research Council (NERC) on behalf of the European Research Councils, co-ordinated through the European Science Foundation; United Nations Environment Programme (UNEP) under their Global Environment Monitoring System (GEMS); World Wide Fund For Nature (WWF); and WWF-US.

The New York Botanical Garden has generously supported this project by publicising and distributing this book to its network. Although they have not been involved as an institution in the compilation and production of this Red List, their researchers have long been contributors to the database, and they recognise the importance of publishing this first edition of the Red List.

Finally we would like to thank both friends and families for their tolerance and support, particularly over the final months of preparation: Martin Gardner, Sabina Knees, Mike O'Neal, and Phil, Eli and Ned Trathan.

Kerry S. Walter
Royal Botanic Garden Edinburgh

Harriet J. Gillett
World Conservation Monitoring Centre
September, 1997

Acronyms

ANZECC	Australia and New Zealand Environment and Conservation Council
BCIS	Biodiversity Conservation Information System
BRU	Biological Recording Unit (also known as Basic Recording Unit)
CDC	Conservation Data Centers
CITES	Convention on International Trade in Endangered Species of Fauna and Flora
ISO	International Standards Organisation
IUCN	The World Conservation Union
NBI	National Botanical Institute
NHCD	Natural Heritage Central Database
NHP	National Heritage Program
NYBG	New York Botanical Garden
ROTAP	*Rare or Threatened Australian Plants*
SSC	Species Survival Commission
TDWG	International Working Group on Taxonomic Databases for Plant Sciences
TNC	The Nature Conservancy
TPU	Threatened Plants Unit
UNDP	United Nations Development Programme
UNEP	United Nations Environment Programme
WCMC	World Conservation Monitoring Centre
WWF	World Wide Fund For Nature

Introduction

The *1997 IUCN Red List of Threatened Plants* represents a milestone in the history of Red Data books and lists, providing, as it does, the first-ever published list of vascular plants (ferns and fern allies, gymnosperms including conifers and cycads, and flowering plants) recorded as globally Rare, Vulnerable, Endangered or Extinct. The current volume lists 33,798 species (see species counts, p.xxvi) as threatened. Compared to an estimated global flora of 270,000 species this results in the grim statistic that over 12.5% of the world's vascular flora is threatened at the global scale (Figure 1). These threatened plants are to be found in 369 families, scattered throughout 200 countries.

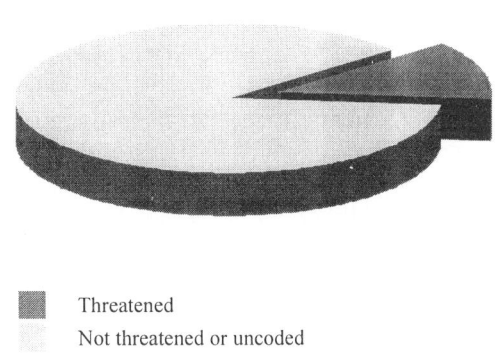

■ Threatened
  Not threatened or uncoded

Figure 1. Percentage of the world's vascular plant species threatened at a global scale.

It must be stressed that although over 12.5% of the world's flora has now been identified as globally threatened, this is just the tip of the iceberg for several reasons. Despite data drawn from thousands of sources, much information is still lacking, due to gaps in either taxonomic knowledge or on-the-ground fieldwork. Secondly, information was often only available to indicate that a species was threatened in part of its range. Although suspected to merit listing as globally threatened, these species were not included in this list as the distribution data were incomplete and therefore did not satisfy the strict conditions for listing (see "Interpreting and assigning the global threat status", p. xxiii). Finally, data presented here are assessed at the *species*, *subspecies,* or *varietal* level. When the unit being assessed is the *population* within a species or the genetic erosion within these species and populations, the conservation situation becomes much worse (Gaston, 1996; Harper & Hawksworth,

1994). This concern about genetic erosion and diminishing genetic diversity at the population level is particularly important in the areas of plant genetic resources and wild relatives of cultivated plants (Falk & Holsinger, 1991; Falk *et al.* 1996; Frankel *et al.* 1995; Heywood, 1995).

The major message of this global compilation is that the number of threatened plant species that we know of is enormous, but as more information becomes available, the situation will be shown to be even worse; thus increased conservation action for plants is desperately needed. We hope that this list will help governments, non-government organisations, and individuals to understand better the scale and urgency of the problems surrounding threats to plants on a global scale, and use this information to promote and guide actions to conserve plant biodiversity in all of its incredible richness.

This Red List is the result of years of data collection by researchers throughout the world and provides a unique overview of the conservation status of the world's vascular plants, following the pre-1994 IUCN Red List Categories (Appendix I). It has been compiled by the World Conservation Monitoring Centre (WCMC) in close collaboration with the many partners noted in the acknowledgements, and was generated directly from the Threatened Plants Database on 22 May, 1997. The database underlying this list continues to be updated on a daily basis and we remain as eager as ever to receive comments and additional information on any aspect of this book.

Purpose

International IUCN Red Data Books were conceived by Peter Scott in 1963 as *'a register of threatened wildlife that includes definitions of degrees of threat'* (Scott *et al.*, 1987). This concept generated enormous interest throughout the world, demonstrated by the production of many national Red Books and Lists for a wide range of plant and animal taxa. However, unlike Red Data Books, Red Data Lists lack detailed information for each species, providing instead a summary view. Five IUCN Red Lists of Threatened Animals have been compiled by WCMC in the past decade (IUCN, 1996), the most recent listing all globally threatened birds and mammals, plus some reptiles, fish, amphibians, and invertebrates. The task of publishing a list of the world's threatened vascular plants – containing more than six times the number of species as in the *1996 IUCN Red List of Threatened Animals* – proved to be such a major challenge that it is only now being achieved for the first time. However as more and more work is being undertaken on threatened plants, and as more accurate and detailed information is generated, we hope that the publication of revised and much improved volumes will become standard practice.

Red Lists serve a wide variety of purposes. In *"The reasons for Red Data Books"*, Collar (1996) gives a comprehensive account of ethical, economical, educational, practical and institutional reasons for the production of International Red Lists in particular. Based on the assumptions that species are the principal unit of concern, and that priorities are to be determined based on their level of threat, then five issues are important:

Priority setting
To help identify key regions and taxonomic groups for targeted funding and concerted public policy.

Comprehensiveness
To provide a comprehensive primary source of data, based on scientific expertise, laying the foundation for biodiversity databases and repatriation of data.

Objectivity
To produce a work based on a global standard of threat assessment, thereby placing evidence of the conservation status of vascular flora in the public domain.

Motivation
To motivate people to participate in conservation networks, actions, and educational programmes.

Monitoring
To provide a baseline for the measurement of conservation progress (or further deterioration).

Many of the ecosystem approaches to conservation rely on the concept of indicator species or flagship species. This list does not provide details on what these species should be, but does provide a major argument for making decisions about which species are likely to be in greatest need of conservation activity, and where in the world they occur.

As Collar (1996) comments: *"Red Data Books are (seemingly) big and slow to grow and expensive to keep going; but so are rhinos, so are pandas, so are condors. Those who expect the discipline of biodiversity priority-setting to be satisfied by short-term on-site consultancies involving the scanning of forest-cover maps and protected-area species inventories may well think of Red Data Books as dinosaurs that have had their day. Those who recognise the multitude of benefits that steadily accrue from focused and painstaking data assembly and analysis will appreciate Red Data Books as the unspectacular but indispensable root system from which true judgement and real conservation can grow."*

It is our sincere hope that this list of globally threatened plants will serve as that root system and also that it will be taken for no more or no less than it is – a first attempt at summarising the conservation status on a global level of some of the most important organisms on Earth. Together with other major data compilations such as: *Global Biodiversity: Status of the Earth's Living Resources* (Groombridge, 1992), *Global Biodiversity Assessment* (Heywood, 1995) and *Centres of Plant Diversity, A Guide and Strategy for their Conservation* (WWF & IUCN, 1994–1997), the *1997 IUCN Red List of Threatened Plants* will help provide the information needed to support the global plant conservation information needs outlined in *Caring for the Earth. A Strategy for Sustainable Living* (IUCN/UNEP/WWF, 1991) and *The Botanic Gardens Conservation Strategy* (IUCN/BGCS, 1989).

History of the threatened plants list

This list of threatened plants has a long history. Work began in the late 1960s, when Sir Peter Scott, then Chairman of the IUCN Species Survival Commission (SSC), invited Ronald Melville, a retired botanist at the Royal Botanic Gardens Kew, to compile a Red Data Book on Angiosperms to match the famous loose-leaf books on threatened animal groups. By 1971, Melville had been able to publish two sets of loose-leaf sheets covering 118 plants in all. But, as a result of the work, he had come up with the prediction – startling at the time – that 20,000 flowering plant species could be in danger. The prediction galvanised the SSC to consider how to cover plants and to realise that a Red Data Book, with pages on each threatened species, would not be practical.

In 1973 Jack Heslop-Harrison, then Director of Kew, agreed that the work would be carried forward as a joint project of Kew and IUCN. The SSC Threatened Plants Committee was created, and Gren

Lucas was appointed to run the programme with Hugh Synge as Research Assistant, funded by the World Wildlife Fund (WWF). The first project was to prepare a list of threatened plants of Europe for the Council of Europe. Involving hundreds of taxonomic experts, this list was published in 1977, covering some 2,000 threatened species, and was the first continent-wide list of its kind to be produced. In the following year, *The IUCN Plant Red Data Book* was published (Lucas & Synge, 1978) using these and other data. This book provided details on the conservation status of 250 species of plants – 1% of the then estimated 25,000 threatened species – chosen to represent the types of threats facing plants, as well as to highlight at least some plants from virtually all parts of the globe. As hoped, this book stimulated many other countries to produce their own Red Data books. The booklet *How to use the IUCN Red Data Categories*, produced by the Threatened Plants Committee Secretariat (1981) provided valuable guidance in applying the Categories.

During the 1980s, the work of the renamed Threatened Plants Unit (TPU) expanded, and the team reached over 10 staff at its peak. During this period many TPU staff developed excellent contacts in their designated geographic area, a model that proved particularly successful. During this time TPU produced its *Threatened Plants Newsletter,* sending it to nearly 5,000 people world-wide. In late 1979 arrangements were made for the Smithsonian Institution to gather data on threatened plants in Latin America, and Jane Villa-Lobos was appointed to carry out the work. From her office nearly 160 issues of the *Biological Conservation Newsletter* have been produced. In addition to being widely distributed throughout the world and now available on the Internet, this newsletter has supplied a great many data sources for the Threatened Plants Database.

This work spawned a range of major initiatives supporting *in situ* and *ex situ* plant conservation. Most significant was the joint IUCN/WWF Plants Conservation Programme, which ran from 1984 to 1990. The early work in cataloguing which threatened plants in the database were being grown in botanic gardens led in 1987 to the creation of the Botanic Gardens Conservation Secretariat, later renamed Botanic Gardens Conservation International (BGCI), now an extremely effective organisation in its own right, linking more than 500 botanic gardens in the world that provide vital support to *ex situ* conservation. The need to track literature references led to the building of the foremost bibliographic database on plant conservation, much of which was published in the *World Plant Conservation Bibliography* (Anon, 1990), and available as part of the Threatened Plants Database on which this list is based.

Part of TPU's message in the 1970s and the 1980s was that each country should prepare its own Plant Red Data Book as the best way of assembling information and stimulating action, particularly for *in situ* plant conservation. This approach proved very successful and many countries in the developed world have now prepared such works. The Unit's book *Plants in Danger: What Do We Know?* (Davis *et al.,* 1986) summarised the state of knowledge about plant conservation issues country-by-country and showed what had been achieved.

In 1990, the Threatened Plants Unit moved from Kew to WCMC in Cambridge. At the same time, all the data were transferred to a different database system (*BG-BASE*, described in Appendix II), from which this list is directly produced. However, many of the entries on the list presented here are direct electronic descendants of the original index cards and hand-written species sheets gathered since the late 1960s. WCMC now maintains the Threatened Plants Database, with information continuing to be provided by a global network of botanists and institutions, and increasingly in electronic form.

Data coverage and quality

This Red List includes records for 33,798 threatened or extinct species – roughly 12.5% of the world's total vascular plants – threatened on a global level. Despite this large figure, a data set such as this will always be incomplete, and the quality of data will vary considerably depending upon the region and taxonomic group under consideration. We can say with some confidence that data for North America, Australia, South Africa and Europe should prove to be reasonably robust. In addition several taxonomic groups (e.g. ferns, conifers, cycads, palms, cacti) have received particular attention and should provide a reasonably accurate picture.

We are aware that data, in particular for many parts of Africa, Asia, the Caribbean, and South America, are either patchy or lacking. This is true for both taxonomic as well as conservation data, as confirmed by a recent gap analysis study on the availability of botanical information for biodiversity conservation (Olson *et al.*, 1996). We therefore apologise for the gaps in the current list. However, by emphasising these areas of data deficiency we hope that concerted efforts will be made in the near future to fill in these gaps to better understand the conservation status of plants in these biologically rich areas. However to do this we need stronger plant specialist networks and better ways of managing this massive amount of data. These will be developed under the Biodiversity Conservation Information System (BCIS) (see Global Red Lists – where next, p. xlvii).

Information provided in this Red List represents only a subset of the data held in the Threatened Plants Database at WCMC. Particularly relevant additional data, not published here, include synonyms, common names, habit (tree, shrub, etc.), use, presence in protected areas and presence in cultivation (information maintained by Botanic Gardens Conservation International, a copy of which is periodically merged with the Threatened Plants Database).

Organisation of information

The Red List is arranged by major taxa as seen in Table 1: fern allies, true ferns, gymnosperms (gnetophytes, conifers, *Ginkgo*, and cycads), and angiosperms (dicotyledons and monocotyledons). Within each of these major taxa, families and their respective genera and species are listed alphabetically. Following the taxonomic data list is a list of all relevant data sources, arranged numerically, and finally an index to the genera, families, and major taxa is included. For each family statistics are provided on the total number of genera, species and threatened taxa.

Table 1
Major taxa included in this Red List

Fern allies	Lycopodiopsida
True ferns	Pteridopsida
Gymnosperms	Gnetopsida (gnetophytes)
	Pinopsida (conifers),
	Ginkopsida *(Ginkgo)*
	Cycadopsida (cycads)
Angiosperms	Magnoliopsida (dicotyledons)
	Liliopsida (monocotyledons)

This list is a global catalogue of those vascular plant taxa that have been assessed in some degree, and fall within the pre-1994 IUCN categories as globally threatened or extinct. Interpretation of the list and summary tables requires an understanding of the process involved in drawing up the list, an appreciation of how comprehensive the data may or may not be (especially where the gaps occur), and knowledge of how the data are managed. Each of these topics is taken up below.

Names

Managing the taxonomy of a global dataset at the species and infraspecific level, with data provided from diverse sources over a period of more than two decades, presents many problems. The aim in managing the Threatened Plants Database has been to maintain a reasonably coherent taxonomy, sufficiently accurate for the purposes of plant conservation, within existing funding and time constraints rather than a totally rigorous taxonomic check list. This lack of complete taxonomic and nomenclatural rigour will undoubtedly upset some readers, and it will result in some taxa either not being listed under their correct name, or listed under more than one name. Ensuring input from the relevant taxonomic experts is a major part of the work involved in managing the data and further advice on taxonomy is always welcome.

Where available, regional floras (particularly *Flora Europaea*, *Flora Mesoamericana* and *Flora Neotropica*) have been followed in preference to national floras. All plant name records imported electronically from TNC, Wildlife Australia, NBI and *Flora Europaea* were treated as taxonomically accepted (see Appendix II, Taxon information).

Despite the clear preference for following these regional authorities, plant names have of necessity been incorporated from an extensive range of sources, all of which are listed in the DATA SOURCES section following the main list. The data source(s) provided after each name is the source from which the particular plant name was first recorded in the database. No attempt has been made to list the original publication of the name.

Although the database allows users to track multiple common names (vernacular names, trade names, timber names, etc.) in different languages, these common names have been excluded from this list due to lack of space.

Genera and families follow *Vascular Plant Families and Genera* (Brummitt, 1992).

Synonyms

Records considered to be synonyms are linked to the accepted name in the database, and have been suppressed from this list. Inevitably, some names not yet recorded on the database as synonyms will have been included in this list, so a taxon may, unfortunately, be included under more than one name.

Authors

Authors of plant names – at both the species and infraspecific level – have been incorporated according to the source from which the name was obtained. Where possible, authors names have been standardised according to Brummitt & Powell (1992). Please note, however, that due to limitations of time and staff resources, an author may well be cited in disparate ways throughout this list, and some authors are missing.

Species vs. infraspecies

Plant names are recorded at the taxonomic level at which they are provided to WCMC, with data on subspecies or varieties held in addition to information at the species level. For example, *Wendlandiella gracilis* Dammer, *W. gracilis* Dammer var. *gracilis*, *W. gracilis* Dammer var. *polyclada* (Burret) Henderson, and *W. gracilis* Dammer var. *simplicifrons* (Burret) Henderson are all to be found on this list, as some information has come at the species level and other information at the infraspecific level. This of necessity complicates the list and occasionally results in inconsistent data sets, but we felt it best to present the data in a way that most closely represented the information provided to us. The taxonomic counts, both in the Red List itself and the data summary in this introduction, are for species (see p. xxvi).

Although this book covers only vascular plants, much work has been undertaken on non-vascular plants and fungi. All relevant data on nonvascular plants and on fungi available to WCMC have been omitted from this publication although have been incorporated into the Threatened Plants Database. There is a clear need to include global listings for these groups in future Red Lists.

Conservation Status

Data on conservation status are presented in this list following the pre-1994 IUCN threat categories (Appendix I). These categories have been widely applied to thousands of taxa of plants and animals, referring to the conservation status of an organism in the wild.

The current list, using the pre-1994 IUCN Categories, is important as a baseline for future work, even as various groups of specialists are beginning to re-code plants using the 1994 IUCN Categories.

The IUCN Red List Categories system was revised in 1994 to incorporate quantitative criteria for each Category. These criteria can be consistently applied across all taxa, thus allowing meaningful comparisons of threat between species in different orders. The 1994 Red List Categories will be used in future listings. Details of the pre-1994 and 1994 IUCN Red List Categories are given in Appendix I.

Finally, please note that as this list uses the pre-1994 system, not all "Endangered", "Vulnerable" or "Rare" Categories are comparable between plant taxa. Given the huge variation in population dynamics, breeding strategies and life cycles exhibited by vascular plants – from a sedge to a monkey-puzzle tree – this is not surprising, but it must not be ignored by those trying to make global comparisons based on the statistics and information provided in this Red List.

Sources of conservation status data

Data are presented in this list for both local (national and subnational) and global status. Data on national conservation status have been provided by a wide range of organisations and individuals throughout the world, with data sets relating to either a geographical area or a taxonomic group. Major sources have been national Red Data books or lists that have been produced by countries throughout the world. Data have also been provided by SSC Specialist Groups. In addition, a great deal of information has been supplied by individual botanists and conservationists. Often these workers have provided updated information or completely new information about taxa of conservation concern, and we hope to bring them into the SSC network.

A major portion of the list comes from electronic data sets from The Nature Conservancy (TNC), Wildlife Australia, National Botanical Institute (NBI), and *Flora Europaea*. This list therefore represents a mixture of various 'official' status reports as well as individual opinion; by referring to the data source it is possible to determine the source of virtually all data in this list.

WCMC's role is essentially one of compiling the outputs of these distributed data sets, and assigning global threat categories based on the collective local threat status information. WCMC makes no value judgement during the process, other than validating, as far as possible, the source of the supplied national threat status data.

Interpreting threat status

In many cases, national/subnational threat status is given in published national Red Data books or lists, with threat status given according to IUCN Categories. Where different schemes have been followed, every effort has been made by WCMC to assign the appropriate IUCN threat category based on the definitions given by the data providers (see Appendix III). Where electronic data sets are concerned, detailed discussions have been held prior to the data being merged into the global database. Although the constraints of space in this volume prevent the display of these "non-IUCN" threat categories, they are maintained in the database.

Interpreting and assigning the global threat status

The global threat status recorded for each taxon in the Threatened Plants Database is assigned at WCMC on the basis of the combined national/subnational data. For a taxon to be listed as globally threatened, information is needed on the local threat status throughout its natural range. Global threat status is assigned only once the full distribution for the taxon in question is known. A "lowest common denominator" approach is followed meaning, for example, that a species listed as Rare within part of its range but Endangered throughout the rest of its range, will be listed as Rare globally. A species listed as Endangered globally will be either Endangered or Extinct throughout its range, and so on.

Many taxa have had to be omitted from this Red List due to insufficient information on distribution and/or status, despite being listed as threatened at the national level in one or more countries. These records are available in the Threatened Plants Database, and it is hoped that these data, representing information for over 14,000 more taxa, will be evaluated in the future.

Exceptions to assigning the global threat status

In some instances data provided to WCMC have given global rather than, or in addition to, national/subnational threat status. This is particularly true for large data sets that have been provided electronically, notably from The Nature Conservancy (data sources 20850 and 20883) and Wildlife Australia (data source 20681). If global but not local threat status has been provided, a local rank of Indeterminate has been assigned by WCMC.

CITES listing

The Threatened Plants Database includes data concerning all taxa listed on CITES (Convention on International Trade in Endangered Species of Fauna and Flora) Appendices I and II current as of the ninth meeting of the Conference of the Parties to CITES (WCMC, 1996). Two species, *Orothamus zeyheri* and *Protea odorata*, were downlisted from Appendix I to Appendix II at the 1997 tenth Conference of the Parties. CITES listing is at the level of species, genus or family, and records on the database are flagged at the appropriate taxonomic level. They are displayed in this list as indicated in the following table.

Table 2
Taxonomic levels of CITES listings displayed in this Red List

Family	I or II (underlined)
Genus	*I or II* (italicised)
Species or infraspecies	I or II (normal type)

Note that not all taxa within genera and families that have blanket listings under CITES are shown in this list. Only those taxa that have been assessed and found to be threatened throughout their range are included.

Distribution

Distribution information is recorded following the standard of Biological Recording Unit (BRU) (Hollis & Brummitt, 1992), endorsed as an international data standard by the Taxonomic Database Working Group. This standard provides a four-tier hierarchical scheme, ranging from near-continents (level 1) to larger countries and islands being subdivided into geopolitical areas (level 4). Wherever possible, we have tried to record distributional data at "level 4", although in some cases data has had to be recorded at a higher level (for example, as "Indonesia" rather than "Kalimantan"). In total, the 238 countries recognised by ISO (ISO, 1993) are divided into 1004 BRUs at these four levels (see Table 3).

Data are recorded at the finest scale possible within the BRU scheme. For example, if data are provided on the threat status of a plant within individual states of Mexico, then this is the scale at which the data are recorded in the database. However, if data are only provided for a particular plant in Mexico as a whole, then the data can only be recorded in the database at the national level. This unavoidably leads to some inconsistencies and data sets that are not directly comparable, but as discussed under 'Species vs. infraspecies' above, we feel that it is important to present the data with the most detail possible.

Since BRUs are geopolitically based, they do not cross national boundaries. All BRU units are linked to the appropriate ISO country code, allowing country-level queries to be made even though the data are often stored at a lower level. Some modifications have been made at WCMC to the BRU scheme to take into account political changes since the standard was published.

There is also a free-text "geographic qualifier" available in the database, which appears in this list as bracketed information following the name of the BRU. This qualifier provides additional information about the distribution of the taxon within the BRU – for example, a mountain range. Please note

Table 3
BRUs (Biological Recording Units)[1]

Level 1 Areas	Level 4 Areas
Europe	55 areas in 42 countries[2], of which 7 are subdivided: Greece (2), Italy (3), Spain (2), Russia (6), Ukraine (2), France (2), and the United Kingdom (3).
Africa	76 areas in 59 countries, of which 11 are subdivided: Angola (2), Equatorial Guinea (3), Mauritius (2), Namibia (2), Portugal (3), Réunion (2), Seychelles (2), St Helena (2), São Tomé and Principe (2), South Africa (5), and Spain (3).
Asia – Temperate	90 areas in 35 countries, of which 6 are subdivided: China (27), Japan (2), Taiwan (3), Yemen (2), Georgia (4), and Russia (23).
Asia – Tropical	70 areas in 24 countries, of which 4 are subdivided: India (37), Indonesia (8), Malaysia (3), and Papua New Guinea (2).
Australasia	17 areas in 2 countries, both of which are subdivided: Australia (12) and New Zealand (5).
Pacific	40 areas in 26 countries, of which 6 are subdivided: Cook Islands (2), French Polynesia (4), Japan (3), Kiribati (3), Solomon Islands (2), and US islands (6).
Northern America	99 areas in 5 countries, of which 3 are subdivided: Canada (15), Mexico (30), and the United States (52).
Southern America	127 areas in 47 countries, of which 13 are subdivided: Argentina (23), Brazil (29), Chile (16), Colombia (3), Costa Rica (2), Ecuador (2), Guadaloupe (2), Honduras (2), Mexico (5), Nicaragua (2), Puerto Rico (2), Venezuela (3) and Netherlands Antilles (2).
Antarctic	12 areas in 8 countries, of which 2 are subdivided: Falkland Islands (3), and French Southern Territories (3).

[1] Hollis, S. and Brummitt, R.K. (1992).

[2] ISO Standard 3166 is used by Hollis and Brummitt to define political countries. The units in the ISO standard are countries, dependencies and other areas of special interest for purposes of international exchange, without indicating any expression of opinion whatever concerning the legal status of any country or territory or of its authorities or concerning the delimitation of its frontiers.

that this information is in many cases not comprehensive, and is not always from the BRU data source listed.

Data sources

A critically important feature of the Threatened Plants Database is the linkage maintained between many data fields and their data sources. Considerable effort is made to ensure that the source of plant names, distribution and conservation status is tracked, ensuring that credit is given to the primary sources of data and that users can judge the validity of the data provided. A complete list of all the data sources used in the production of this Red List is included following the main list. Here over 2,000 of the 19,067 records in the data source file are listed, approximately 10,000 of which were published in the *World Plant Conservation Bibliography* (Anon, 1990).

The list of DATA SOURCES demonstrates the wide variety of sources of information drawn upon by WCMC in the development of the Threatened Plants Database. These include official Red Data Books, published floras and monographs, journal articles, electronic lists, annotations made by specialists to WCMC printouts, and personal communications. Please note that some of the information in this list dates from data sources that are 10–15 years old, and

updates to these particular records are clearly desirable. In this publication multiple data sources for the name are sometimes shown, thus allowing users to track multiple and/or conflicting data. However we have listed only one conservation status as the primary or current view, and have displayed the data that seem most appropriate.

The current practice while entering data into the database is to require the relevant data source number for all new plant names, distribution or threat data. However, prior to the 1990 adoption of *BG-BASE*, the practice was slightly different, and not all of these fields were mandatory. Although efforts have been made to fill in missing fields during the preparation of this list, time and resources have not permitted all missing data sources to be checked and updated from the original card index system.

Statistics

Summary statistics are given in the list at the beginning of each family. These comprise an estimate of the number of genera and species in the family. These figures are derived from numerous sources with Brummitt (1992) and Cronquist (1981) being the main sources. The figure for recorded threatened species is calculated from the data as explained in the analysis. Please note that species recorded as Extinct are not included in this count.

Analysis of the list

Estimates for the global number of vascular plant species commonly range from 250,000–270,000. In this book, analyses are made against the estimate of 270,000 thereby under- rather than over-estimating the figure for percent species threatened. Figures for the number of genera per family are mainly taken from Brummitt (1992) or from Cronquist (1981). Figures for number of species per genus and number of species per country are taken from a wide range of sources whose data sources were not able to be shown in this list. Undoubtedly, there may be other, equally or more valid, estimates for many of these figures.

Species counts

The manipulation of any large data set such as this, which is a compilation of many other lists, is fraught with difficulty and requires careful interpretation. In particular the many differences of opinion as to what constitutes a species, subspecies, or variety in the plant kingdom make it difficult to decide which unit is most appropriate to present in summary tables.

Given the data included in the list, three options for providing summary counts are available. The first is to provide counts for all taxa listed (*taxa count*). This will provide a slight overestimate since some taxa are listed at both the specific and infraspecific level. The second option is to count only taxa listed at the specific level (*species count-low)*, which will provide an underestimate, as

some taxa are only listed at the infraspecific level, and information was not available to assess the species as a whole. The third and middle option (*species count)* is to count as threatened all those taxa listed as threatened at the species level, plus all those species of which at least one component part (i.e. subspecies or variety) is listed as threatened. The results of the three different methods of counting are summarised in Table 4.

The difference between the highest and lowest estimates for total figures is 11.7%. Even the 'best' case scenario indicates that at least 11.5% (31,195 out of an estimated 270,000 species) of the world's vascular flora is under threat. However it must be recognised that irrespective of the figures used, the situation in reality is much worse due to the major gaps of knowledge about plants, from different regions or taxonomic groups, as well as a conservation point of view. This is particularly accentuated in the tropics.

In the tables that follow a breakdown by threat category for each country and for each family is given according to the **species count** figure.

Geographic analysis

The number of threatened species recorded for each country, and the percentage this represents of their national flora, are given in Table 5. Note that a relatively high figure of threatened species for a

Table 4
Comparison of potential methods of counting threatened plants

	Ex	Ex/E	E	V	R	I	Total (threatened and extinct)	% decrease from taxa count	% world flora threatened[1]
Taxa count	396	400	6,951	8,387	14,998	4,187	35,319	–	13.1%
Species count[2]	**380**	**371**	**6,522**	**7,951**	**14,504**	**4,070**	**33,798**	**4.3**	**12.5%**
Species count – low	368	348	6,100	7,309	13,276	3,794	31,195	11.7	11.5%

[1] Calculated against a world flora of 270,000.

[2] The figures used in geographical and country analyses below.

particular country may only reflect the effort that has been made by that country in collating data, while a low figure for another country may reflect that similar efforts have not yet been undertaken in that country. On the other hand, some countries clearly have greater conservation problems than others due to a variety of reasons.

It is of interest to note that the three countries providing complete electronic data sets are also listed as having the highest percentage of their national floras threatened.

Table 5
Globally threatened vascular plants: IUCN Category by country[1]

Country	Ex	Ex/E	E	V	R	I	Total no. threatened[2]	No.species	% threatened
Afghanistan			1	1	2		4	4,000	0.1
Albania	1	3	1		73	2	79	3,031	2.6
Algeria			31	22	80	8	141	3,164	4.5
American Samoa				1	8		9	471	1.9
Angola				2	13	15	30	5,185	0.6
Antigua & Barbuda			1		2		3	845	0.4
Argentina	3		61	31	136	19	247	9,372	2.6
Armenia						31	31		
Australia	71		246	630	1,366	3	2,245	15,638	14.4
Austria	1		1	1	20	1	23	3,100	0.7
Azerbaijan		1	1		2	24	28		
Bahamas		2		2	4	23	31	1,111	2.8
Bangladesh		1		21	1	1	24	5,000	0.5
Barbados			2				2	572	0.3
Belarus						1	1		
Belgium		1	1				2	1,550	0.1
Belize			5	9	37	6	57	2,894	2.0
Benin				2	1	1	4	2,201	0.2
Bermuda	3		5		5		10	167	6.0
Bhutan		1	1	6	10	5	23	5,468	0.4
Bolivia	1		90	38	88	11	227	17,367	1.3
Bosnia & Herzegovina	1			3	59	2	64		
Botswana					6	1	7	2,151	0.3
Brazil	5	10	406	280	596	66	1,358	56,215	2.4
British Indian Ocean Ter.						1	1	101	1.0

Country	Ex	Ex/E	E	V	R	I	Total no. threatened[2]	No.species	% threatened
Brunei Darussalam				11	6	8	25	6,000	0.4
Bulgaria		1	1	14	84	6	106	3,572	3.0
CIS [3]	5		16	17	158	18	209	22,281	0.9
Cambodia			1	4			5		
Cameroon			2	34	17	36	89	8,260	1.1
Canada	2	3	58	110	106	1	278	3,270	8.5
Cape Verde				1			1	774	0.1
Cayman Islands		1	6	2	2	2	13	539	2.4
Central African Republic						1	1	3,602	0.0
Chad					12		12	1,600	0.8
Chile	6	1	102	107	107	12	329	5,284	6.2
China	2	1	86	108	102	15	312	32,200	1.0
Christmas Island		1	1	2	10	1	15	411	3.6
Colombia	3	1	208	137	294	72	712	51,220	1.4
Comoros			2	1		1	4	721	0.6
Congo				1	2		3	6,000	0.1
Cook Islands			9	2		1	12	284	4.2
Costa Rica	2	3	103	179	217	25	527	12,119	4.3
Côte d'Ivoire	2		14	56	9	15	94	3,660	2.6
Croatia				2	4		6	3,000	0.2
Cuba	23		330	319	163	76	888	6,522	13.6
Cyprus			9	13	23	6	51	1,682	3.0
Czechoslovakia (former) [3]	2		4	20	25	32	81	2,590	3.1
Denmark					2		2	1,450	0.1
Djibouti			1			1	2	641	0.3
Dominica			6	4	26	21	57	1,228	4.6
Dominican Republic			27	17	45	47	136	5,657	2.4
Ecuador	4		121	214	439	50	824	19,362	4.3
Egypt	2		19	8	45	10	82	2,076	3.9
El Salvador			7	12	18	5	42	2,911	1.4
Equatorial Guinea				3	8		11	3,250	0.3
Estonia			1			1	2		
Ethiopia		3	69	31	46	14	163	6,603	2.5

Country	Ex	Ex/E	E	V	R	I	Total no. threatened[2]	No.species	% threatened
Falkland Islands			2		4		6	165	3.6
Fiji		7	18	25	22	2	74	1,518	4.9
Finland				1	4	1	6	1,102	0.5
France	7	3	21	81	83	7	195	4,630	4.2
French Guiana		1	15	15	67		98	5,625	1.7
French Polynesia	12		45	27	46	69	187	959	19.5
Gabon				6	40	45	91	6,651	1.4
Gambia					1		1	974	0.1
Georgia					2	27	29		
Germany	3		3	2	5	4	14	2,682	0.5
Ghana		1	30	63	5	4	103	3,725	2.8
Gibraltar				3	1		4		
Greece	6	1	28	80	430	32	571	4,992	11.4
Greenland				1	4		5	529	0.9
Grenada			1	1	6		8	1,068	0.7
Guadeloupe			5	5	13	3	26	1,400	1.9
Guam			7	2	4	5	18	330	5.5
Guatemala		4	42	74	165	70	355	8,681	4.1
Guinea				12	25	2	39	3,000	1.3
Guyana			27	26	99		152	6,409	2.4
Haiti		1	29	12	35	23	100	5,242	1.9
Honduras	1	2	16	23	40	15	96	5,680	1.7
Hong Kong			2	1	5	1	9	1,984	0.5
Hungary			3	7	16	4	30	2,214	1.4
Iceland					1		1	377	0.3
India	19	41	152	102	251	690	1,236	16,000	7.7
Indonesia	1	4	24	73	102	61	264	29,375	0.9
Iran					2		2	8,000	0.0
Ireland					1		1	950	0.1
Israel		2	7	7	13	3	32	2,317	1.4
Italy	1		29	80	190	12	311	5,599	5.6
Jamaica			142	220	334	48	744	3,308	22.5
Japan	5	3	63	171	435	35	707	5,565	12.7
Jordan			1	1	6	1	9	2,100	0.4
Kazakhstan		6			30	35	71		

Country	Ex	Ex/E	E	V	R	I	Total no. threatened[2]	No.species	% threatened
Kenya		3	31	79	97	30	240	6,506	3.7
Kyrgyzstan				1	5	28	34		
Laos					2		2		
Lebanon	1		2		1	2	5	3,000	0.2
Lesotho			1	2	14	4	21	1,591	1.3
Liberia			3	20		2	25	2,200	1.1
Libya			4	18	30	5	57	1,825	3.1
Liechtenstein			1		1	1	3	1,410	0.2
Lithuania	1					1	1		
Luxembourg			1				1	1,246	0.1
Madagascar		19	91	57	85	54	306	9,505	3.2
Malawi			1	3	54	3	61	3,765	1.6
Malaysia	3	3	84	146	144	113	490	15,500	3.2
Mali			2	1	11	1	15	1,741	0.9
Malta	1			1	10	4	15	914	1.6
Martinique		4	8	7	19	6	44	1,287	3.4
Mauritania					3		3	1,100	0.3
Mauritius	47	6	118	72	96	2	294	750	39.2
Mexico	11	5	234	443	801	110	1,593	26,071	6.1
Micronesia			1	1	1	1	4	1,194	0.3
Moldova					2	3	5		
Mongolia							0	2,272	0.0
Montserrat			1		1		2	671	0.3
Morocco	1		3	3	157	23	186	3,675	5.1
Mozambique			5	8	58	18	89	5,692	1.6
Myanmar			3	7	14	8	32	7,000	0.5
Namibia			4	5	56	10	75	3,174	2.4
Nepal			2	5	10	3	20	6,973	0.3
Netherlands				1			1	1,221	0.1
Netherlands Antilles			1		1		2		
New Caledonia	5	5	160	214	91	10	480	3,322	14.4
New Zealand	7		42	42	115	12	211	2,382	8.9
Nicaragua		2	19	32	37	8	98	7,590	1.3
Nigeria			18	16	1	2	37	4,715	0.8
Niue				1			1	178	0.6
Norfolk Island	2		11	7	21	1	40	445	9.0

Country	Ex	Ex/E	E	V	R	I	Total no. threatened[2]	No.species	% threatened
North Korea					4		4	2,898	0.1
Northern Mariana Islands			5	1	2	3	11	315	3.5
Norway				3	9		12	1,715	0.7
Oman			2	13	1	14	30	1,204	2.5
Pakistan	2		2	2	5	5	14	4,950	0.3
Panama			602	420	217	63	1,302	9,915	13.1
Papua New Guinea			2	9	58	23	92	11,544	0.8
Paraguay			21	25	79	4	129	7,851	1.6
Peru	3	4	354	218	290	40	906	18,245	5.0
Philippines		4	5	60	47	244	360	8,931	4.0
Pitcairn			2	11		1	14	76	18.4
Poland	1	1	1	10	10	5	27	2,450	1.1
Portugal	2		46	113	98	12	269	5,050	5.3
Puerto Rico		4	97	71	40	11	223	2,493	8.9
Réunion	6	1	29	40	24	5	99	546	18.1
Romania			11	14	67	7	99	3,400	2.9
Russian Federation [3]	1	3	3	18	96	94	214		
St. Vincent & Grenadines			3		5	1	9	1,166	0.8
São Tomé & Príncipe		1		1	1		3	895	0.3
Saudi Arabia				5	1	1	7	2,028	0.3
Senegal					28	3	31	2,086	1.5
Seychelles		5	21	30	11	11	78	250	31.2
Sierra Leone			2	15	11	1	29	2,090	1.4
Singapore	1		4	7	8	10	29	2,168	1.3
Slovenia				2	11		13	3,175	0.4
Solomon Islands				3	33	6	42	3,172	1.3
Somalia			7	23	58	15	103	3,028	3.4
South Africa	53		226	368	1,264	357	2,215	23,420	9.5
South Korea	1		9	2	55		66	2,898	2.3
Spain	3	3	185	272	484	41	985	5,050	19.5
Sri Lanka	1	1	69	68	81	236	455	3,314	13.7
St Kitts & Nevis			3		1		4	659	0.6

Country	Ex	Ex/E	E	V	R	I	Total no. threatened[2]	No.species	% threatened
St Lucia			5		1		6	1,028	0.6
St. Helena	11	3	22	2	27	14	68	165	41.2
St. Pierre & Miquelon				2	2	1	5		
Sudan			1	3	1	5	10	3,137	0.3
Suriname			13	10	79	1	103	5,018	2.1
Swaziland		1	9	9	17	6	42	2,715	1.5
Sweden				3	10		13	1,750	0.7
Switzerland	1		4		21	5	30	3,030	1.0
Syria	2		5		3		8	3,000	0.3
Taiwan			19	32	251	23	325	3,568	9.1
Tajikistan	1	3			2	45	50		
Tanzania	1		14	63	103	256	436	10,008	4.4
Thailand			27	21	33	304	385	11,625	3.3
Togo				4			4	2,201	0.2
Tonga				1	1		2	463	0.4
Trinidad & Tobago			2	3	5	11	21	2,259	0.9
Tunisia			1		18	5	24	2,196	1.1
Turkey	10	1	47	167	1,608	53	1,876	8,650	21.7
Turkmenistan		2			1	14	17		
Turks & Caicos Islands					2		2	448	0.4
USA	22	181	1,178	1,783	1,495	32	4,669	16,108	29.0
Uganda			2	8	3	2	15	5,406	0.3
Ukraine		1	7	2	14	28	52		
United Kingdom	1		1	3	14		18	1,623	1.1
Uruguay			9	2	4		15	2,278	0.7
Uzbekistan		3			3	35	41		
Vanuatu			3	1	20	2	26	870	3.0
Venezuela			135	65	212	14	426	21,073	2.0
Viet Nam		2	6	25	301	7	341	10,500	3.2
Virgin Islands (British)			4	3	6	1	14		
Virgin Islands (USA)		1	10	12	15	2	40		
Western Samoa					17	1	18	737	2.4
Yemen		1	33	28	55	32	149	1,650	9.0

Country	Ex	Ex/E	E	V	R	I	Total no. threatened[2]	No.species	% threatened
Yugoslavia (former)[3]	1		1	6	143	5	155	5,351	2.9
Zaire			2	5	67	4	78	11,007	0.7
Zambia			2		9	1	12	4,747	0.3
Zimbabwe			4	11	58	27	100	4,440	2.3

[1] "Country" in this table refers to either a country or subset of a country (e.g. an island dependency such as Réunion).

[2] Total number threatened includes Ex/E, E, V, R and I, but excludes Ex.

[3] Figures for the former Czechoslovakia, former USSR and former Yugoslavia have only been partially rationalised to bring them in line with current political boundaries.

Table 6
Countries[1] with at least 5% of their native species threatened

Country[1]	Ex	Ex/E	E	V	R	I	Total no. threatened[2]	No. species	% threatened
St. Helena[3]	11	3	22	2	27	14	68	165	41.2
Mauritius	47	6	118	72	96	2	294	750	39.2
Seychelles		5	21	30	11	11	78	250	31.2
USA	22	181	1,178	1,783	1,495	32	4,669	16,108	29.0
Jamaica			142	220	334	48	744	3,308	22.5
Turkey	10	1	47	167	1,608	53	1,876	8,650	21.7
French Polynesia	12		45	27	46	69	187	959	19.5
Spain	3	3	185	272	484	41	985	5,050	19.5
Pitcairn			2	11		1	14	76	18.4
Réunion	6	1	29	40	24	5	99	546	18.1
Australia	71		246	630	1,366	3	2,245	15,638	14.4
New Caledonia	5	5	160	214	91	10	480	3,322	14.4
Sri Lanka	1	1	69	68	81	236	455	3,314	13.7
Cuba	23		330	319	163	76	888	6,522	13.6
Panama			602	420	217	63	1,302	9,915	13.1
Japan	5	3	63	171	435	35	707	5,565	12.7
Greece	6	1	28	80	430	32	571	4,992	11.4
South Africa	53		226	368	1,264	357	2,215	23,420	9.5
Taiwan			19	32	251	23	325	3,568	9.1
Yemen		1	33	28	55	32	149	1,650	9.0
New Zealand	7		42	42	115	12	211	2,382	8.9
Puerto Rico		4	97	71	40	11	223	2,493	8.9
Canada	2	3	58	110	106	1	278	3,270	8.5
India	19	41	152	102	251	690	1,236	16,000	7.7
Chile	6	1	102	107	107	12	329	5,284	6.2

Country[1]	Ex	Ex/E	E	V	R	I	Total no. threatened[2]	No. species	% threatened
Mexico	11	5	234	443	801	110	1,593	26,071	6.1
Italy	1		29	80	190	12	311	5,599	5.6
Guam			7	2	4	5	18	330	5.5
Portugal	2		46	113	98	12	269	5,050	5.3
Morocco	1		3	3	157	23	186	3,675	5.1
Peru	3	4	354	218	290	40	906	18,245	5.0
Bermuda	3		5		5		10	167	6.0

[1] "Country" in this table refers to either a country or subset of a country (e.g. an island dependency such as Réunion).
[2] Total no. threatened includes Ex/E,E,V,R and I, but excludes Ex.
[3] St Helena comprises St Helena, Ascension Island and Tristan da Cunha Islands.

Endemism and threat

Figures for threatened species endemism at the country or a sub-set of the country are given in Table 7. The vast majority (91%) of the plants listed in this book are recorded as single-country endemics. This is partly, but not entirely, due to the greater risks to survival that plants with a restricted range face, compared to risks faced by widely distributed species. The prominence on this list of island endemics is demonstrated by the inclusion of seven islands or island groups in the top ten areas listed according to percentage of its flora under threat: St. Helena, Mauritius, Seychelles, Jamaica, French Polynesia, Pitcairn, and Réunion (Table 6).

However Table 6 must be treated with care, as in cases where threatened species data are well-known (e.g. the USA, Australia, and South Africa), the more complete the information on threatened species, the greater percentage of the flora is known to be globally threatened. Therefore once more information is collected in South America, Africa, and Asia, it is highly likely that many other countries will have much more than 5% of their flora threatened at a global level.

In addition, while it would be expected that a high percentage of this list would constitute single-country endemics, the actual percentage of single-country endemics reported here is known to be artificially high due to the process of assigning global threat status for the following reason: taxa are assigned a threatened global status, and therefore listed in this book, **only** if full distribution and conservation data are available. Due to this rigorous process, many species with populations that cross political boundaries which would otherwise seem appropriate for inclusion in this list have unfortunately had to be excluded due to incomplete distribution and conservation data. An example of such a species is *Swietenia mahagoni* (Mahogany), a widespread Caribbean species. Threatened by logging throughout its natural range, this species was listed on Appendix II of CITES in 1992. However as conservation status information for each of its range countries was not available, this species is not included in this list (although it will be included in future lists when the 1994 IUCN threat categories are used). An additional *c.*14,000 taxa might well be listed if full conservation and distribution data of these taxa were known. These data are available in the Threatened Plants Database.

Taxonomic analysis

In the Red List, statistics are given for each family of the number of species listed as threatened (excluding extinct species). A total of 372 families out of an estimated 511 families of vascular plants (Brummitt, 1992) contain globally extinct and/or threatened species (Table 8). Not surprisingly, the largest families contain the largest number of threatened species.

Table 7
Globally threatened taxa of vascular plants: IUCN Categories by country – level endemism [1]

	Ex	Ex/E	E	V	R	I	Total No. (threatened and extinct)
Single country[2]	382	388	6,629	7,616	13,371	3,856	32,242
two countries	11	11	268	616	1,209	253	2,368
> two countries	3	1	54	155	418	78	709
Total	396	400	6,951	8,387	14,988	4,187	35,319

[1] This table can only be generated against the **taxon count** (see Table 4). The discrepancy between species and taxon count is 4.3%.

[2] "Country" in this table refers to either a country or subset of a country (e.g. an island dependency such as Réunion).

Table 8
Globally threatened taxa of vascular plants: IUCN Categories by major taxa and families

Family	Ex	Ex/E	E	V	R	I	Total no. threatened[1]	Total no. species	% threatened
Fern allies									
Isoetaceae	2		11	4	22	2	39	79	49.7
Lycopodiaceae	1		3	6	11	3	23	519	4.4
Psilotaceae			1		1		2	7	30.8
Selaginellaceae	1		3	5	9	6	23	713	3.2
TOTAL	**4**	**0**	**18**	**15**	**43**	**11**	**87**	**1,318**	**6.6**
True ferns									
Adiantaceae		1	6	4	16	11	38	712	5.3
Aspleniaceae		3	12	3	25	3	46	711	6.5
Blechnaceae			2	2	11	2	17	238	7.1
Cyatheaceae		1	10	36	100	55	202	623	32.4
Davalliaceae			1				1	130	0.8
Dennstaedtiaceae			1	1	9	4	15	486	3.1
Dicksoniaceae				3		1	4	41	9.8
Dryopteridaceae	2	5	12	10	41	7	75	464	16.2
Gleicheniaceae				1	3		4	140	2.9
Grammitidaceae			2	2	39	22	65	500	13.0
Hymenophyllaceae			4	4	18	1	27	600	4.5
Lomariopsidaceae			4	1	12		17	615	2.8
Loxsomataceae			1	1			2	4	50.0
Marattiaceae			3	1	6	1	11	204	5.4
Marsileaceae			3	2	1	2	8	67	11.9

Family	Ex	Ex/E	E	V	R	I	Total no. threatened[1]	Total no. species	% threatened
Oleandraceae				2			2	91	2.2
Ophioglossaceae			6	5	12		23	81	28.4
Osmundaceae				1		1	2	18	11.1
Parkeriaceae					1		1	4	25.0
Plagiogyriaceae					2		2	36	5.6
Polypodiaceae	1	1	3	6	12	4	26	1,068	2.4
Pteridaceae			3	3	8	5	19	259	7.3
Schizaeaceae				1	1	1	3	143	2.1
Thelypteridaceae	1		9	5	19	8	41	1,000	4.1
Vittariaceae					2		2	113	1.8
Woodsiaceae	1	2	3	3	17	5	30	705	4.3
TOTAL	5	13	85	97	356	133	683	9,053	7.5
Gnetopsida (gnetophytes)									
Ephedraceae					1		1	40	2.5
TOTAL	0	0	0	0	1	0	1	40	2.5
Pinopsida (conifers)									
Araucariaceae			5	11	13	1	30	38	78.9
Cephalotaxaceae			1	3		1	5	7	71.4
Cupressaceae	1	1	17	19	21	6	64	130	49.2
Pinaceae			17	50	62	4	133	250	53.2
Podocarpaceae			5	28	33	4	70	125	56.0
Taxaceae			4	7	3	1	15	20	75.0
Taxodiaceae			2	4	4		10	16	62.5
TOTAL	1	1	51	122	136	17	327	586	55.8
Ginkopsida (ginkgo)									
Ginkgoaceae					1		1	1	100.0
TOTAL	0	0	0	0	1	0	1	1	100.0
Cycadopsida (cycads)									
Cycadaceae	1		5	11	4		20	35	57.1
Stangeriaceae					1		1	1	100.0
Zamiaceae	2		39	50	36	3	128	144	88.9
TOTAL	3	0	44	61	41	3	149	180	82.8
Dicotyledons									
Acanthaceae	7	1	63	67	192	106	429	2,500	17.2
Aceraceae			2	2	7	3	14	112	12.5
Actinidiaceae			2	1	1	1	5	300	1.7
Aizoaceae	7		16	20	86	41	163	2,500	6.5
Alzateaceae					1		1	1	100.0

Family	Ex	Ex/E	E	V	R	I	Total no. threatened[1]	Total no. species	% threatened
Amaranthaceae	4	1	9	4	24	6	44	900	4.9
Anacardiaceae		1	12	19	39	15	86	600	14.3
Ancistrocladaceae			1	1			2	18	11.4
Anisophylleaceae					2		2	40	5.0
Annonaceae		2	24	36	91	59	212	2,300	9.2
Apocynaceae	5	1	33	31	70	14	149	2,000	7.5
Aquifoliaceae	1	1	6	4	18	8	37	370	10.0
Araliaceae			30	22	36	19	107	700	15.3
Aristolochiaceae			5	3	23	4	35	600	5.8
Asclepiadaceae	9	3	72	60	199	86	420	2,000	21.0
Balanopaceae					1		1	9	11.1
Balanophoraceae			1	1	3		5	45	11.1
Balsaminaceae	1	3	5		12	49	69	450	15.3
Basellaceae			1	1	3		5	18	28.6
Begoniaceae	1	1	14	8	28	13	64	1,020	6.3
Berberidaceae			5	12	15	11	43	650	6.6
Betulaceae			2	1	8	2	13	125	10.4
Bignoniaceae			34	43	73	5	155	800	19.4
Bombacaceae			11	3	7	3	24	200	12.0
Boraginaceae	8	6	43	82	211	36	378	2,000	18.9
Bretschneideraceae					1		1	1	100.0
Brunelliaceae			29	19	9		57	62	91.9
Bruniaceae	4		3	2	8	4	17	75	22.7
Buddlejaceae				2	10	2	14	150	9.3
Burseraceae			9	9	58	4	80	600	13.3
Buxaceae			4	8	4	5	21	60	35.0
Cactaceae	6	1	89	173	253	65	581	1,500	38.7
Callitrichaceae			1	3	1		5	35	14.3
Calycanthaceae			1	1	1		3	5	60.0
Calyceraceae					1		1	60	1.7
Campanulaceae	5	22	103	62	200	41	428	2,000	21.4
Canellaceae			1	1	3	2	7	20	35.0
Capparaceae		1	9	11	19	10	50	800	6.3
Caprifoliaceae			3	9	19	1	32	400	8.0
Caricaceae			1	3	4		8	30	26.7
Caryocaraceae			4	2	5		11	23	47.8
Caryophyllaceae	2	7	67	87	304	55	520	2,000	26.0
Casuarinaceae			4	6	4		14	50	28.0
Cecropiaceae			15	12	14		41	276	14.9
Celastraceae	1	3	25	15	28	22	93	800	11.6
Ceratophyllaceae						1	1	6	16.7

Family	Ex	Ex/E	E	V	R	I	Total no. threatened[1]	Total no. species	% threatened
Chenopodiaceae	1		15	30	37	6	88	1,500	58.7
Chloranthaceae			4	7	8	1	20	75	26.7
Chrysobalanaceae			80	54	86	5	225	450	50.0
Cistaceae			16	8	15	4	43	200	21.5
Clethraceae				1	2	1	4	65	6.2
Cochlospermaceae				1	1		2	15	13.3
Columelliaceae				1			1	4	25.0
Combretaceae			6	8	53	6	73	400	18.3
Compositae	21	23	475	606	1,258	191	2,553	20,000	12.8
Connaraceae			18	6	21	6	51	350	14.6
Convolvulaceae	2	1	26	31	50	26	134	1,500	8.9
Cornaceae			2	2	5		9	100	9.0
Corylaceae			2	3	4	1	10	22	45.5
Corynocarpaceae					1		1	5	20.0
Crassulaceae	4	1	31	42	137	16	227	900	25.2
Crossosomataceae			2		2		4	10	40.0
Cruciferae	10	6	126	196	383	36	747	3,000	24.9
Crypteroniaceae				1			1	7	14.3
Cucurbitaceae	1	1	11	7	34	21	74	700	10.6
Cunoniaceae		1	1	13	10		25	350	7.1
Cyrillaceae				2			2	14	14.3
Daphniphyllaceae				1	1		2	35	5.7
Datiscaceae				1			1	4	25.0
Davidsoniaceae			1				1	1	100.0
Degeneriaceae					1		1	1	100.0
Diapensiaceae				3	2		5	18	27.8
Dichapetalaceae			17	10	11	7	45	235	19.1
Didiereaceae					3		3	11	27.3
Dilleniaceae			7	4	14	5	30	350	8.6
Dioncophyllaceae						1	1	3	33.3
Dipsacaceae		1	3	8	40	10	62	260	23.8
Dipterocarpaceae		7	30	70	23	65	195	600	32.5
Droseraceae			2	4	7	1	14	100	14.0
Ebenaceae			15	38	12	16	81	450	18.0
Elaeagnaceae			1	3	5		9	50	18.0
Elaeocarpaceae			4	9	29	2	44	400	11.0
Elatinaceae				1	4		5	40	12.5
Epacridaceae	3		7	14	38	1	60	400	15.0
Eremolepidaceae				1			1	12	8.3
Ericaceae	7		127	142	205	35	509	3,500	14.5
Erythroxylaceae	1	1	22	18	20	8	69	200	34.5

Family	Ex	Ex/E	E	V	R	I	Total no. threatened[1]	Total no. species	% threatened
Escalloniaceae			2	3	8	2	15	170	8.8
Eucommiaceae					1		1	1	100.0
Eucryphiaceae					1		1	6	16.7
Euphorbiaceae	11	4	192	263	318	156	933	7,500	12.4
Fagaceae		1	13	21	36	25	96	800	12.0
Flacourtiaceae		1	67	46	70	12	196	800	24.5
Fouquieriaceae				1	2	2	5	11	45.5
Frankeniaceae	3		1	1	4		6	80	7.5
Geissolomataceae					1		1	1	100.0
Gentianaceae			16	21	60	14	111	1,000	11.1
Geraniaceae		1	13	11	50	10	85	700	12.1
Gesneriaceae		10	57	53	79	66	265	2,500	10.6
Globulariaceae			3	1	5		9	300	3.0
Goetzeaceae			1				1	7	14.3
Gomortegaceae			1				1	1	100.0
Goodeniaceae	1		3	11	18	1	33	300	11.0
Greyiaceae					1		1	3	33.3
Grossulariaceae	1		4	6	4	3	17	180	9.4
Grubbiaceae					1		1	3	33.3
Gunneraceae			2	1	1	1	5	50	10.0
Guttiferae			16	31	78	27	152	1,200	12.7
Gyrostemonaceae	1		1				1	17	5.9
Halophytaceae						1	1	1	100.0
Haloragaceae	1		6	5	12	3	26	100	26.0
Hamamelidaceae			3		17	2	22	100	22.0
Hernandiaceae	1		4		5	2	11	60	18.3
Hippocastanaceae				1			1	16	6.3
Hoplestigmataceae						1	1	2	50.0
Humiriaceae				1	3		4	50	8.0
Hydnoraceae			1				1	10	10.0
Hydrangeaceae				10	6	2	18	170	10.6
Hydrophyllaceae	2		14	30	38		82	250	32.8
Icacinaceae			8	10	10	5	33	400	8.3
Idiospermaceae					1		1	1	100.0
Illecebraceae			4	10	32	3	49	117	41.9
Illiciaceae			1	1	1		3	40	7.5
Ixonanthaceae				1			1	30	3.3
Juglandaceae			3	4	4	1	12	60	20.0
Krameriaceae				1	2		3	15	20.0
Labiatae	9	25	100	132	432	44	733	3,200	22.9
Lacistemataceae			1	2	4		7	20	35.0

Family	Ex	Ex/E	E	V	R	I	Total no. threatened[1]	Total no. species	% threatened
Lactoridaceae				1			1	1	100.0
Lardizabalaceae					3	2	5	30	16.7
Lauraceae	1		65	57	105	32	259	2,000	13.0
Lecythidaceae			54	39	49		142	400	35.5
Leeaceae					2	3	5	70	7.1
Leguminosae	22	14	392	506	1,063	231	2,206	13,100	16.8
Leitneriaceae					1		1	1	100.0
Lennoaceae					2		2	5	44.4
Lentibulariaceae			2	5	7	10	24	200	12.0
Limnanthaceae			2	3	3		8	11	72.7
Linaceae			9	10	27	2	48	220	21.8
Loasaceae	1		5	13	7		25	200	12.5
Loganiaceae	1		10	11	9	7	37	500	7.4
Loranthaceae	2	2	12	7	14	5	40	700	5.7
Lythraceae			6	6	36	9	57	500	11.4
Magnoliaceae	1		13	10	15	5	43	220	19.5
Malesherbiaceae			1		3		4	25	16.0
Malpighiaceae			36	34	30	9	109	1,200	9.1
Malvaceae	3	13	53	44	102	21	233	1,250	18.6
Marcgraviaceae			1	1	3		5	100	5.0
Medusagynaceae			1				1	1	100.0
Medusandraceae						1	1	1	100.0
Melastomataceae		4	99	84	228	72	487	4,000	12.2
Meliaceae			29	34	39	7	109	550	19.8
Melianthaceae				1		1	2	22	9.1
Meliosmaceae			6	3	6	1	16	27	59.3
Menispermaceae	1		9	2	9	18	38	400	9.5
Menyanthaceae			1	1	3	1	6	33	18.5
Molluginaceae			3	4	4	1	12	100	12.0
Monimiaceae			5	5	13		23	450	5.1
Montiniaceae			1				1	3	33.3
Moraceae		3	30	23	38	16	110	1,000	11.0
Morinaceae					1	1	2	13	15.4
Moringaceae					1	1	2	10	20.0
Myoporaceae	1		7	12	12	1	32	125	25.6
Myricaceae			1	1	3		5	50	10.0
Myristicaceae			7	6	3	3	19	300	6.3
Myrsinaceae	1	1	30	48	50	62	191	1,000	19.1
Myrtaceae	4	5	147	218	326	51	747	3,000	24.9
Nepenthaceae		1	3	5	6	4	19	75	25.3
Nesogenaceae	1	1	1			1	3	7	42.9

Family	Ex	Ex/E	E	V	R	I	Total no. threatened[1]	Total no. species	% threatened
Nyctaginaceae	1	1	15	13	18	2	49	300	16.3
Nymphaeaceae				3	1		4	50	8.0
Ochnaceae	1		5	3	6	1	15	400	3.8
Olacaceae			18	11	25	5	59	250	23.6
Oleaceae			16	17	18	19	70	600	11.7
Oliniaceae						2	2	8	25.0
Onagraceae	2	1	20	36	61	1	119	675	17.6
Opiliaceae					1		1	50	2.0
Oxalidaceae			1	11	12	7	31	900	3.4
Paeoniaceae			1	4	3	3	11	30	36.7
Papaveraceae			10	18	48	8	84	200	42.0
Parnassiaceae					2	1	3	16	18.8
Passifloraceae	1		14	6	18	10	48	650	7.4
Pedaliaceae			1		2		3	80	3.8
Pellicieraceae						1	1	1	100.0
Penaeaceae			1	3	10		14	20	70.0
Pentaphragmataceae					1	1	2	30	6.7
Phytolaccaceae			1	2	2		5	125	4.0
Piperaceae	3	2	83	15	50	12	162	1,700	9.5
Pittosporaceae	1		12	12	9	3	36	200	18.0
Plantaginaceae			7	9	14	3	33	254	13.0
Plumbaginaceae	3	1	34	55	80	10	180	400	45.0
Podostemaceae			8	4	3	5	20	200	10.0
Polemoniaceae		1	17	42	42		102	300	34.0
Polygalaceae		1	13	22	35	21	92	750	12.3
Polygonaceae		3	43	81	87	14	228	1,000	22.8
Portulacaceae			15	12	25		52	500	10.4
Primulaceae		2	16	25	45	24	112	1,000	11.2
Proteaceae	5	1	73	91	183	5	353	1,000	35.3
Quiinaceae			2	2	2		6	40	15.0
Rafflesiaceae			1	2	5	1	9	50	18.0
Ranunculaceae	2	2	38	82	143	29	294	2,000	14.7
Resedaceae					14	1	15	70	21.4
Rhabdodendraceae			1				1	3	33.3
Rhamnaceae		2	28	54	78	9	171	900	19.0
Rhizophoraceae		1	5	3	2	1	12	100	12.0
Rhoipteleaceae					1		1	1	100.0
Rhynchocalycaceae				1			1	1	100.0
Roridulaceae					1		1	2	50.0
Rosaceae	2	22	82	119	156	40	419	3,000	14.0
Rubiaceae	22	13	223	275	369	240	1,120	6,500	17.2

Family	Ex	Ex/E	E	V	R	I	Total no. threatened[1]	Total no. species	% threatened
Rutaceae	10	9	95	91	163	24	382	1,500	25.5
Sabiaceae					2	1	3	30	10.0
Salicaceae			2	18	19	2	41	340	12.1
Santalaceae	4		6	11	16	2	35	400	8.8
Sapindaceae	2	1	38	35	64	6	144	1,500	9.6
Sapotaceae		2	126	75	135	23	361	800	45.1
Sarraceniaceae				1	4		5	15	33.3
Saxifragaceae	1	1	6	29	60	6	102	588	17.4
Schisandraceae					1	2	3	50	6.0
Scrophulariaceae	8	13	160	259	478	59	969	4,000	24.2
Scytopetalaceae				1	2		3	20	15.0
Simaroubaceae			1	11	8	1	21	150	14.0
Solanaceae	5	3	41	71	72	31	218	2,800	7.8
Sphenostemonaceae						1	1	7	14.3
Stachyuraceae				1			1	6	18.2
Stackhousiaceae					2		2	23	8.9
Staphyleaceae					2	1	3	50	6.0
Sterculiaceae	7	1	24	27	32	22	106	1,000	10.6
Stilbaceae					1		1	12	8.3
Stylidiaceae			2	2	5		9	155	5.8
Styracaceae			4	3	5	2	14	150	9.3
Surianaceae					1		1	6	16.7
Symplocaceae			6	10	23	4	43	350	12.3
Tamaricaceae				1	3		4	100	4.0
Theaceae		1	16	12	27	17	73	600	12.2
Theligonaceae					1		1	3	33.3
Theophrastaceae			5	8	5	3	21	100	21.0
Thymelaeaceae	1	3	13	16	32	8	72	500	14.4
Tiliaceae		1	4	3	15	4	27	450	6.0
Tovariaceae				1			1	2	50.0
Trapaceae				1			1	15	6.7
Tremandraceae	2		3	4	2		9	28	32.1
Trigoniaceae			7	5	5		17	26	65.4
Trimeniaceae			1				1	5	20.0
Tropaeolaceae			1		3		4	92	4.3
Turneraceae			2	1	4	1	8	120	6.7
Ulmaceae			7	7	4		18	150	12.0
Umbelliferae	3	8	56	98	238	70	470	3,000	15.7
Urticaceae	2	2	32	35	40	8	117	700	16.7
Vahliaceae					1		1	5	20.0
Valerianaceae			1	3	23	4	31	300	10.3

Family	Ex	Ex/E	E	V	R	I	Total no. threatened[1]	Total no. species	% threatened
Verbenaceae	1	3	22	27	40	30	122	2,600	4.7
Violaceae	1	1	31	20	44	14	110	800	13.8
Viscaceae	1		11	6	6	16	39	350	11.1
Vitaceae			6	4	14	12	36	700	5.1
Vochysiaceae			1	1		1	3	200	1.5
Winteraceae			2	4	5		11	100	11.0
Zygophyllaceae	1		2		10	1	13	250	5.2
TOTAL	**272**	**284**	**4,925**	**6,000**	**11,335**	**2,980**	**25,524**	**167,224**	**15.3**
Monocotyledons									
Agavaceae			13	14	35	6	68	380	17.9
Alismataceae			2	2	6		10	75	13.3
Alliaceae	1	4	19	40	86	15	164	832	19.7
Aloaceae			36	65	84	21	206	700	29.4
Alstroemeriaceae			3		1	1	5	152	3.3
Amaryllidaceae	7		38	42	79	17	176	700	25.1
Anthericaceae			4	4	11	3	22	481	4.6
Aponogetonaceae			1	2	3	1	7	40	17.5
Araceae	3		27	65	59	72	223	1,800	12.4
Asparagaceae			2	1	6	4	13	55	23.6
Asphodelaceae	1	2	5	6	27	8	48	319	15.0
Asteliaceae			3	2	4		9	34	26.5
Blandfordiaceae					1		1	4	25.0
Bromeliaceae	1		277	111	76	16	480	2,000	24.0
Burmanniaceae		5		1	3	5	14	130	10.8
Calectasiaceae				1			1	1	100.0
Cannaceae				1			1	50	2.0
Centrolepidaceae			1	2	3		6	35	17.1
Colchicaceae			3	11	19	1	34	106	32.1
Commelinaceae	1		3	6	10	10	29	700	4.1
Convallariaceae		1	1	7	12	4	25	172	14.5
Costaceae			1	8	8		17	150	11.3
Cyanastraceae						1	1	6	16.7
Cyclanthaceae			2		2	2	6	180	3.3
Cyperaceae	5	4	54	62	115	45	280	4,000	7.0
Dioscoreaceae	1		28	20	15	9	72	630	11.4
Dracaenaceae	1		4	14	2		20	156	12.8
Eriocaulaceae	4	2	11	15	22	13	63	1,200	5.3
Eriospermaceae					35	1	36	90	40.0
Gramineae	17	8	139	141	358	130	776	8,000	9.7
Haemodoraceae			1	11	3		15	100	15.0
Heliconiaceae			14	14	15		43	100	43.0

Family	Ex	Ex/E	E	V	R	I	Total no. threatened[1]	Total no. species	% threatened
Hostaceae			1	1	2		4	40	10.0
Hyacinthaceae	3		19	21	77	17	134	654	20.5
Hydatellaceae	1			1	1		2	7	28.6
Hydrocharitaceae		1	1	4	6	2	14	100	14.0
Hypoxidaceae			1	1	2	2	6	142	4.2
Iridaceae	9	3	90	70	276	45	484	1,500	32.3
Juncaceae			2	5	11	4	22	300	7.3
Juncaginaceae				1			1	20	5.0
Lemnaceae					1	2	3	31	9.7
Liliaceae	6	1	27	42	62	17	149	460	32.4
Limnocharitaceae					3		3	10	31.6
Lomandraceae				1	5		6	42	14.3
Lowiaceae					1		1	6	16.7
Marantaceae			5	1	1	4	11	400	2.8
Melanthiaceae			4	4	8	1	17	146	11.6
Musaceae	1			1	1		2	42	4.8
Orchidaceae	21	16	325	529	646	263	1,779	30,000	5.9
Palmae	2	25	204	258	262	120	869	3,000	29.0
Pandanaceae	7		6	10	16	9	41	732	5.6
Philydraceae					1		1	5	20.0
Phormiaceae					3	1	4	36	11.1
Pontederiaceae					1		1	30	3.3
Potamogetonaceae			5	1	3		9	100	9.0
Restionaceae	1		5	19	27	7	58	400	14.5
Ruscaceae				2	2		4	8	50.0
Smilacaceae				3	7	1	11	330	3.3
Stemonaceae				1	1		2	30	6.7
Strelitziaceae					1	1	2	7	28.6
Tecophilaeaceae	1				3		3	42	7.1
Trilliaceae			2	2	11	1	16	52	30.8
Triuridaceae			2	1	4	4	11	70	15.7
Velloziaceae			1		1	3	5	250	2.0
Xanthorrhoeaceae				2	1		3	15	20.0
Xyridaceae			3	3	12	1	19	200	9.5
Zannichelliaceae					1		1	8	13.3
Zingiberaceae	1	1	4	4	31	36	76	1,000	7.6
Zosteraceae					1		1	18	5.6
TOTAL	95	73	1,399	1,656	2,592	926	6,646	63,611	10.4
GRAND TOTAL	380	371	6,522	7,951	14,505	4,070	33,418	242,013	13.8

[1] Total number threatened includes EX/E, E, V, R and I but excludes Ex.

Table 9
Vascular plant families listed with at least 50% of their species threatened[1]

Taxon[2]	Family	Ex	Ex/E	E	V	R	I	Total no. threatened[3]	No. species	% threatened
D	Brunelliaceae			29	19	9		57	62	91.9
G4	Zamiaceae	2		39	50	36	3	128	144	88.9
G2	Araucariaceae			5	11	13	1	30	38	78.9
G2	Taxaceae			4	7	3	1	15	20	75.0
D	Limnanthaceae			2	3	3		8	11	72.7
G2	Cephalotaxaceae			1	3		1	5	7	71.4
D	Penaeaceae			1	3	10		14	20	70.0
D	Trigoniaceae			7	5	5		17	26	65.4
G2	Taxodiaceae			2	4	4		10	16	62.5
D	Calycanthaceae			1	1	1		3	5	60.0
D	Meliosmaceae			6	3	6	1	16	27	59.3
G4	Cycadaceae	1		5	11	4		20	35	57.1
G2	Podocarpaceae			5	28	33	4	70	125	56.0
G2	Pinaceae			17	50	62	4	133	250	53.2
D	Chrysobalanaceae			80	54	86	5	225	450	50.0
D	Hoplestigmataceae						1	1	2	50.0
F	Loxsomataceae			1	1			2	4	50.0
D	Roridulaceae					1		1	2	50.0
M	Ruscaceae				2	2		4	8	50.0
D	Tovariaceae				1			1	2	50.0

[1] Excluding monotypic families: Alzataceae, Bretschneideraceae, Calectasiaceae, Davidsoniaceae, Degeneriaceae, Eucommiaceae, Geissolomataceae, Ginkgoaceae, Gomortegaceae, Halopytaceae, Idiospermaceae, Lactoridaceae, Leitneriaceae, Medusagynaceae, Medusandraceae, Pellicieraceae, Rhoipteleaceae, Rhynchocalycaceae, Stangeriaceae.

[2] Major taxa: D: Dicotyledons; F: Ferns; G2 Pinopsida; G4 Cycadopsida; M Monocotyledons.

[3] Total number threatened includes Ex/E, E,s V, R and I but excludes Ex.

Table 10
Number of families and genera containing globally threatened vascular plants for each IUCN Red List Category

	World Total	Ex	Ex/E	E	V	R	I	Total[1]
Families	511[2]	103	89	267	289	326	235	369
Genera	21,900[3]	297	227	2,146	2,459	3,532	1,612	5,555

[1] Total figures are not simply summations of Ex, Ex/E, E, V, R and I, but the total number of families or genera listed which contain threatened species.

[2] Brummitt (1992).

[3] Approximate figure – mainly following Cronquist (1981).

It is interesting to note which families have the highest percentage of threatened species. Excluding nineteen monotypic families with one threatened species (and therefore 100% threatened), 20 families are listed with at least 50% of their species threatened (see Table 9). Of these, eight are gymnosperms. The prominence of the gymnosperms may be due to the fact that they are a well-known and relatively small group, and substantial effort has been made to assess their conservation status. At the same time, the gymnosperms include many species that are widely exploited both for timber and horticultural purposes, which has lead to decreasing populations. Also, gymnosperms are an ancient group of species, and may not be adapting well to the rapidly changing times that we live in. In contrast, the ferns as a group appear to face relatively low levels of threat. This may be due in part to the fact that fern spores travel relatively easily with the result that many species are widely distributed. At the same time, many fern species have not been included due to incomplete conservation assessments and complicated taxonomic issues.

Threatened species are distributed throughout the plant kingdom. Table 10 shows the number of families and genera which contain threatened taxa, by IUCN category. Families not represented on this list (*c.* 42 families) are mostly very small, comprising less than ten species. Thus it can be clearly stated that about a quarter of the estimated number of genera of vascular plants contain threatened taxa.

Plant extinctions

One surprising figure in this book is the relatively low number of species which are recorded as having become Extinct in the wild: 380 species, plus 371 species listed as Ex/E (see Table 8). Given the often quoted predictions in the popular and scientific press of extremely high extinction rates, the numbers in this book will seem very low. While this may in part be due to lack of data and the fact that plant extinctions have only been recently recorded, at the same time it may be that we are still at the brink of a far more serious wave of extinction. The grim statistic that at least 6,522 species are Endangered, and that these are likely to join the Extinct list in the near future, should be taken as a warning that the situation will get far worse unless vastly increased conservation action is taken now.

Global Red Lists – where next?

Throughout the history of the Threatened Plants Database, datasets have been provided, either as hard copy, or more recently in electronic format, in support of plant conservation initiatives world-wide. By putting data on nationally threatened plants into a global context, regional *in situ* and *ex situ* conservation needs become more apparent. These demand a range of solutions, from the development of protected areas systems (IUCN, 1992) to safeguard whole populations, to the development of cultivation techniques for plants that are already extinct in the wild. Increasingly, botanic garden living collection policies focus on plants of conservation importance (IUCN & BGCS, 1989). In many cases, the living collections of botanic gardens contain large numbers of threatened and extinct species. The Royal Botanic Garden Edinburgh for example has 1387 such taxa alive in its collections (Walter *et al.*, 1995). In addition, botanic gardens are now undertaking activities that bridge the gap between *in situ* and *ex situ* conservation, with the living collections being used as source material for reintroduction programmes (Atkinson *et al.*, 1995; Bramwell, 1991).

The large demand for the data needed to underpin these activities made provision of information in book format a clear objective, in particular to ensure the data are accessible to as many people as possible. Also, by publishing the information in this book, a record of what is known in 1997 is provided, a view that will inevitably become quickly outdated as further conservation information is gathered and as conservation activities take place.

The *1997 IUCN Red List of Threatened Plants* provides a snapshot of the Threatened Plants Database maintained by WCMC as it stood on 22 May 1997. Global databases must be kept constantly updated so as to make new knowledge accessible as rapidly as possible.

Data continue to be incorporated at WCMC on a daily basis, to keep pace with the data produced world wide. A joint WCMC/SSC project on the conservation and sustainable use of trees will include the production of a world list of threatened trees following the 1994 IUCN Categories of threat (see Appendix I). Work is also underway in many SSC Specialist Groups to update the threat category of their respective taxa. New and active members of these Groups are always welcome, and should contact the SSC Plants Officer at IUCN. Funding permitting, a global list of threatened plants following the 1994 IUCN Categories will be produced. This will provide an important component of the Biodiversity Conservation Information System (BCIS), a consortium of organisations including IUCN and WCMC whose mission includes the provision of data to support environmentally sound decision-making and actions affecting the status of biodiversity.

Appendix I
IUCN Red List Categories

The *1997 IUCN Red List of Threatened Plants* is based on the pre-1994 IUCN Categories, drawn up by the IUCN Species Survival Commission. These have since been revised (IUCN, 1994). Subsequent listings will be made using the 1994 Categories and criteria. Details of both systems are given below.

IUCN Red List Categories as used in this List (pre-1994)

EXTINCT (Ex)
Taxa not definitely located in the wild during the past 50 years.

EXTINCT/ENDANGERED (Ex/E)
Taxa that are suspected of having recently become Extinct.

ENDANGERED (E)
Taxa in danger of extinction and whose survival is unlikely if the causal factors continue operating. Included are taxa whose numbers have been reduced to a critical level or whose habitats have been so drastically reduced that they are deemed to be in immediate danger of extinction. Also included are taxa that may be extinct but have definitely been seen in the wild in the past 50 years.

VULNERABLE (V)
Taxa believed likely to move into the 'Endangered' category in the near future if the causal factors continue operating. Included are taxa of which most or all the populations are decreasing because of over-expioitation, extensive destruction of habitat or other environmental disturbance; taxa with populations that have been seriously depleted and whose ultimate security has not yet been assured; and taxa with populations that are still abundant but are under threat from severe adverse factors throughout their range.

RARE (R)
Taxa with small world populations that are not at present 'Endangered' or 'Vulnerable', but are at risk. These taxa are usually localised within restricted geographical areas or habitats or are thinly scattered over a more extensive range.

INDETERMINATE (I)
Taxa that are known to be Endangered, Vulnerable or Rare but where there is not enough information to say which of the three categories is appropriate.

The word 'threatened' has no official definition within the IUCN Red List Categories; it is generally understood, however, to include taxa that are Endangered, Vulnerable, Rare or Indeterminate. It should not be confused with the use of the same term by the U.S. Fish and Wildlife Service, and in other countries, where it has a legal definition.

Additional categories recorded in the Threatened Plants Database, but excluded from this list, comprise: nt (not threatened), ? (no information), O (out of danger), K (insufficiently known).

1994 IUCN Red List Categories

EXTINCT (EX)
A taxon is Extinct when there is no reasonable doubt that the last individual has died.

EXTINCT IN THE WILD (EW)
A taxon is Extinct in the wild when it is known only to survive in cultivation, in captivity or as a naturalised population (or populations) well outside the past range. A taxon is presumed Extinct in the Wild when exhaustive surveys in known and/or expected habitat, at appropriate times (diurnal, seasonal, annual), throughout its historic range have failed to record an individual. Surveys should be over a time frame appropriate to the taxon's life cycle and life form.

CRITICALLY ENDANGERED (CR)
A taxon is Critically Endangered when it is facing an extremely high risk of extinction in the wild in the immediate future, as defined by any of the criteria (A to E) on pages l and li.

ENDANGERED (EN)
A taxon is Endangered when it is not Critically Endangered but is facing a very high risk of extinction in the wild in the near future, as defined by any of the criteria (A to E) on page li.

VULNERABLE (VU)

A taxon is Vulnerable when it is not Critically Endangered or Endangered but is facing a high risk of extinction in the wild in the medium-term future, as defined by any of the criteria (A to E) on page lii.

LOWER RISK (LR)

A taxon is Lower Risk when it has been evaluated, does not satisfy the criteria for any of the categories Critically Endangered, Endangered or Vulnerable. Taxa included in the Lower Risk category can be separated into three subcategories:

1. **Conservation Dependent (cd).** Taxa which are the focus of a continuing taxon-specific or habitat-specific conservation programme targeted towards the taxon in question, the cessation of which would result in the taxon qualifying for one of the threatened categories above within a period of five years.

2. **Near Threatened (nt).** Taxa which do not qualify for Conservation Dependent, but which are close to qualifying for Vulnerable.

3. **Least Concern (lc).** Taxa which do not qualify for Conservation Dependent or Near Threatened.

DATA DEFICIENT (DD)

A taxon is Data Deficient when there is inadequate information to make a direct, or indirect, assessment of its risk of extinction based on its distribution and/or population status. A taxon in this category may be well studied, and its biology well known, but appropriate data on abundance and/or distribution are lacking. Data Deficient is therefore not a category of threat or Lower Risk. Listing of taxa in this category indicates that more information is required and acknowledges the possibility that future research will show that threatened classification is appropriate. It is important to make positive use of whatever data are available. In many cases great care should be exercised in choosing between DD and threatened status. If the range of a taxon is suspected to be relatively circumscribed, if a considerable period of time has elapsed since the last record of the taxon, threatened status may well be justified.

NOT EVALUATED (NE)

A taxon is Not Evaluated when it is has not yet been assessed against the criteria.

THE CRITERIA FOR CRITICALLY ENDANGERED, ENDANGERED AND VULNERABLE

CRITICALLY ENDANGERED (CR)

A taxon is Critically Endangered when it is facing an extremely high risk of extinction in the wild in the immediate future, as defined by any of the following criteria (A to E):

A) **Population reduction in the form of either of the following:**

1. An observed, estimated, inferred or suspected reduction of at least 80% over the last 10 years or three generations, whichever is the longer, based on (and specifying) any of the following:

   a) direct observation

   b) an index of abundance appropriate for the taxon

   c) a decline in area of occupancy, extent of occurrence and/or quality of habitat

   d) actual or potential levels of exploitation

   e) the effects of introduced taxa, hybridisation, pathogens, pollutants, competitors or parasites.

2. A reduction of at least 80%, projected or suspected to be met within the next 10 years or three generations, whichever is the longer, based on (and specifying) any of (b), (c), (d) or (e) above.

B) **Extent of occurrence estimated to be less than 100km^2 or area of occupancy estimated to be less than 10km^2, and estimates indicating any two of the following:**

1. Severely fragmented or known to exist at only a single location.

2. Continuing decline, observed, inferred or projected, in any of the following

   a) extent of occurrence

   b) area of occupancy

   c) area, extent and/or quality of habitat

   d) number of locations or sub-populations

   e) number of mature individuals.

3. Extreme fluctuations in any of the following:

    a) extent of occurrence

    b) area of occupancy

    c) number of locations or subpopulations

    d) number of mature individuals.

C) **Population estimated to number less than 250 mature individuals and either:**

1. An estimated continuing decline of at least 25% within three years or one generation, whichever is longer or

2. A continuing decline, observed, projected, or inferred, in numbers of mature individuals and population structure in the form of either:

    a) severely fragmented (i.e. No subpopulation estimated to contain more than 50 mature individuals)

    b) all individuals are in a single subpopulation.

D) **Population estimated to number less than 50 mature individuals.**

E) **Quantitative analysis showing the probability of extinction in the wild is at least 50% within 10 years or three generations, whichever is the longer.**

ENDANGERED (EN)

A taxon is Endangered when it is not Critically Endangered but is facing a very high risk of extinction in the wild in the near future, as defined by any of the following criteria (A to E):

A) **Population reduction in the form of either of the following:**

1. An observed, estimated, inferred or suspected reduction of at least 50% over the last 10 years or three generations, whichever is the longer, based on (and specifying) any of the following:

    a) direct observation

    b) an index of abundance appropriate for the taxon

    c) a decline in area of occupancy, extent of occurrence and/or quality of habitat

    d) actual or potential levels of exploitation

    e) the effects of introduced taxa, hybridisation, pathogens, pollutants, competitors or parasites.

2. A reduction of at least 50%, projected or suspected to be met within the next 10 years or three generations, whichever is the longer, based on (and specifying) any of (b), (c), (d), or (e) above.

B) **Extent of occurrence estimated to be less than 5000km^2 or area of occupancy estimated to be less than 500km^2, and estimates indicating any two of the following:**

1. Severely fragmented or known to exist at no more than five locations.

2. Continuing decline, inferred, observed or projected, in any of the following:

    a) extent of occurrence

    b) area of occupancy

    c) area, extent and/or quality of habitat

    d) number of locations or sub-populations

    e) number of mature individuals.

3. Extreme fluctuations in any of the following:

    a) extent of occurrence

    b) area of occupancy

    c) number of locations or sub-populations

    d) number of mature individuals.

C) **Population estimated to number less than 2500 mature individuals and either:**

1. An estimated continuing decline of at least 20% within five years or two generations, whichever is longer, or

2. A continuing decline, observed, projected, or inferred, in numbers of mature individuals and population structure in the form of either:

    a) severely fragmented (i.e. No subpopulation estimated to contain more than 250 mature individuals)

    b) all individuals are in a single subpopulation.

D) **Population estimated to number less than 250 mature individuals.**

E) **Quantitative analysis showing the probability of extinction in the wild is at least 10% within 100 years.**

VULNERABLE (VU)

A taxon is Vulnerable when it is not Critically Endangered or Endangered but is facing a high risk of extinction in the wild in the medium-term future, as defined by any of the following criteria (A to E):

A) Population reduction in the form of either of the following:

1. An observed, estimated, inferred or suspected reduction of at least 20% over the last 10 years or three generations, whichever is the longer, based on (and specifying) any of the following:

    a) direct observation

    b) an index of abundance appropriate for the taxon

    c) a decline in area of occupancy, extent of occurrence and/or quality of habitat

    d) actual or potential levels of exploitation

    e) the effects of introduced taxa, hybridisation, pathogens, pollutants, competitors or parasites.

2. A reduction of at least 20%, projected or suspected to be met within the next ten years or three generations, whichever is the longer, based on (and specifying) any of (b), (c), (d) or (e) above.

B) Extent of occurrence estimated to be less than 20,000km^2 or area of occupancy estimated to be less than 2000km^2, and estimates indicating any two of the following:

1. Severely fragmented or known to exist at no more than ten locations.

2. Continuing decline, inferred, observed or projected, in any of the following:

    a) extent of occurrence

    b) area of occupancy

    c) area, extent and/or quality of habitat

    d) number of locations or subpopulations

    e) number of mature individuals

3. Extreme fluctuations in any of the following:

    a) extent of occurrence

    b) area of occupancy

    c) number of locations or subpopulations

    d) number of mature individuals

C) Population estimated to number less than 10,000 mature individuals and either:

1. An estimated continuing decline of at least 10% within 10 years or three generations, whichever is longer, or

2. A continuing decline, observed, projected, or inferred, in numbers of mature individuals and population structure in the form of either:

    a) severely fragmented (i.e. no subpopulation estimated to contain more than 1000 mature individuals)

    b) all individuals are in a single subpopulation

D) Population very small or restricted in the form of either of the following:

1. Population estimated to number less than 1000 mature individuals.

2. Population is characterised by an acute restriction in its area of occupancy (typically less than 100km^2) or in the number of locations (typically less than five). Such a taxon would thus be prone to the effects of human activities (or stochastic events whose impact is increased by human activities) within a very short period of time in an unforeseeable future, and is thus capable of becoming Critically Endangered or even Extinct in a very short period.

E) Quantitative analysis showing the probability of extinction in the wild is at least 10% within 100 years.

1. Population estimated to number less than 1000 mature individuals.

2. Population is characterised by an acute restriction in its area of occupancy (typically less than 100km^2) or in the number of locations (typically less than five). Such a taxon would thus be prone to the effects of human activities (or stochastic events whose impact is increased by human activities) within a very short period of time in an unforeseeable future, and is thus capable of becoming Critically Endangered or even Extinct in a very short period.

Appendix II
Threatened Plants Database management

Plant data are managed at WCMC using *BG-BASE*, a variable-length field, relational database management system built using Advanced Revelation, and widely adopted by botanical institutions throughout the world. The database is externally dynamic with over 100 changes and additions made per day; all records are date-stamped and initialled so that changes to records can be easily tracked. Full-word, partial-word, and phonetic searches are available to streamline data entry and retrieval.

Managing plant data on a global scale is a complex task, especially given the range of diverse uses that the database serves at WCMC, for instance, production of the plant data are found in the *Checklist of CITES Species* (WCMC, 1996) and *World Plant Bibliography* (Anon, 1990). Therefore, the database management system used is large and incorporates many more features than would be necessary simply to produce this list. For maximum efficiency, *BG-BASE* data are managed in a series of database tables (or files) whose constituent records are related to one another through shared fields. *BG-BASE* has over 4,200 fields spread across approximately 200 database files, of which WCMC uses a relatively small percentage. The major *BG-BASE* tables used by WCMC are shown below.

Bibliographic information

When plant information is received by WCMC, the first step taken is to create a data source record in the DS table (19,076 records) for that information. These data source records are mostly books, journal articles, proceedings, and other published work, but they can also be conversations, and annotations made to WCMC lists, etc. The location of each data source is coded so that it may be found quickly; full citation details can be output as camera-ready bibliographies. The key field in this table is DS. NUM, the number shown throughout this book and in the DATA SOURCES section following the main list.

Taxon information

The Threatened Plants Database already contains information on nearly half of all known vascular plants. When "new" taxa are added, a record is created in the NAMES table, which handles information on the scientific name, common names, and languages and synonymy. Accepted names and synonyms are linked and indexed together so that any name searched for, automatically brings up all relevant records.

If the nomenclatural and taxonomic status of a name has not been verified, the name is coded as "unchecked" (note such names have **not** been suppressed from this List). Information about the taxon's habit (tree, shrub, herbaceous, etc.) and uses (timber, wild crop relative, etc.) is also collected where possible. Selections of data from the NAMES table are periodically downloaded to BGCI allowing conservation audits of botanic gardens world-wide to be undertaken, an example of which is given in the Utrecht University catalogue of plant collections (Wollenberg *et al.*, 1992). Further tables allow inventory data for protected areas to be stored (Murray *et al.*, 1992).

Each NAMES record is linked to a record in the GENERA table, where records are in turn linked to the FAMILIES table. CITES information is stored in all three of these tables, as appropriate, depending on what taxonomic level is listed.

Distribution information

For each area of the world in which a plant is said to occur, a separate record is created in the DISTRIBUTIONS table. These records, besides holding pointers to the name of the plant and the name of the area (stored in the BRUs table), contain information on the geographic area to which the plant may be restricted, the data source for the distribution information, the conservation status (IUCN category and the status as given if the data source is not using IUCN Categories), and the data source for this conservation information. Other fields which exist but which are relatively infrequently used by WCMC include: number of individuals and/or populations of the taxon known to exist in the area, date(s) when the taxon was last seen in the area, threat(s) to the taxon in the area, legal status of the taxon in the area, presence in conservation areas, and habitats occupied by this taxon. Other fields used include Occurrence and Introduced flags, as specified in the POSS (Plant

Occurrence Status Scheme) adopted by TDWG (Threatened Plants Unit, *in press*). All introduced records have been suppressed from this list.

Further details on the structure of *BG-BASE* can be found on the Internet at http://www.rbge.org.uk/bgbase. Examples of database records that were excluded from this list are shown in Table 12.

Table 11
Major tables used in the Threatened Plants Database

Table	No. records	Table contents
NAMES	139,719	Information on scientific names of species and infraspecies (broken into 30 fields in order to be compatible with standards for storing scientific names of both naturally occurring and cultivated plants, see Walter *et al.*, 1995), data source(s) for name, status of the name (accepted, invalid, orthographic variant, synonym, pro parte synonym, sensu synonym, not found in literature, tentatively accepted name, unchecked names), synonymy (multiple alternate names/synonyms can be linked to an accepted name), data source for the synonymy, vernacular names (as many as necessary, including language and data source), global IUCN conservation status, TNC global rank, presence on CITES Appendices (if listed at the species or infraspecies level), habit (tree, shrub, vine/liana, herbaceous, succulent etc.), use, and a flag for complete/incomplete distribution. By links to the GENERA table, full upper-level taxonomic information is available to each NAMES record. There are index links from the DISTRIBUTIONS table that allow instant queries on all distributions of a taxon.
DISTRIBUTIONS	191,100	Information on distribution (at BRU level 3 or 4, see Table 3), free-text area qualifier specifying area(s) in the BRU to which the taxon is restricted, introduced flag, occurrence flag, data source for distribution information, flag for existence of a distribution map in that data source, local threat status, data source for threat status, status as given (for storing non-IUCN threat status categories), numbers of individuals and/or populations known of this taxon in this BRU, date taxon was last seen in this BRU, threats to the taxon in this BRU, legal status of this taxon in this BRU, protected areas within this BRU in which the taxon occurs (linked to the WCMC Protected Areas database of 40,000 records), habitat types occupied by this taxon in this BRU, and general data sources concerning this taxon in this BRU.
DATA SOURCES	19,076	Information on the published and unpublished sources of information for data in all other tables; fields include type of data source (book, journal article, chapter in book, unpublished, etc.), author(s), publication date(s), title, subtitle, journal name, volume, number, pages, publisher, place of publication, citation notes, location of reference, language of reference and of abstract, relevance codes, countries mentioned, families mentioned, genera mentioned, species mentioned, abstract, accuracy of citation, and access type. Bibliographies published from this include Anon. (1990) and Atkinson *et al.*, (1995).
GENERA	27,101	Information on all genera of vascular plants and many non-vascular plants; fields include genus, author, family placement (link to FAMILIES table), synonymy, status of the name (as under NAMES above), presence on CITES Appendices (if listed at the generic level).
FAMILIES	956	Family statistics (number of genera, number of species, number of threatened species), as well as global range are also stored here. Information on all vascular plant families and many non-vascular families; fields include family, preferred name (for family pairs such as Asteraceae/Compositae), major taxon, synonymy, vernacular name, number of species, number of genera, distribution, and phylogenetic placement according to various systems of classification.

Table	No. records	Table contents
COUNTRIES	243	Information on all countries of the world, including international abbreviation (see ISO, 1993). English name, official name, synonyms, land area, size of flora (numbers of pteridophytes, gymnosperms, angiosperms, and vascular plants, along with corresponding data sources), number and percent of endemic plant species along with corresponding data sources. Although *BG-BASE* does not code distributions at the country level, country-level queries can be done through calculations automatically performed by the BRUS table.
BRUs	1076	Information on all Biological Recording Units (see Table 3) including fields for level (1–4), level 1–4 codes and names (for tracking hierarchical nesting), BRU name, political name, English name, French name, German name, Spanish name, keyword (for spelling variants), land area, latitude/longitude, sorting order (for sorting the distributions under a taxon in this List). There are index links from the DISTRIBUTIONS table that allow instant queries for all taxa within a BRU.

Table 12 Type of data records suppressed from the Red List

Type of data suppressed	Rationale
Fungi and non-vascular plants	The amount and quality of the data for fungi and non-vascular plants groups such as bryophytes and lichens in the Threatened Plants Database, while substantial, are not yet adequate to give a reasonable global overview.
Synonyms, unpublished, invalid, and doubtful names	Lack of space prevents the inclusion of synonyms in this list.
Taxa lacking threat status in one or more countries	Since WCMC does not assign a global threat category to plants without knowing the category within each area where the plant is native, such information cannot be included in this list. **Special exceptions**: Data provided by TNC (data sources 20850 and 20883), flagged as globally threatened, but with a ? at the national level have been treated as a special case, and **are** included (see Appendix III).
Taxa for which complete distribution is not known	Since WCMC does not assign a global threat status until the full distribution of a taxon has been ascertained, taxa for which a complete distribution is not yet available cannot be included. *c.*14,000 additional records may have appeared as part of this book if this rule had been relaxed.
Distribution records where the taxon was introduced or assumed to be introduced	WCMC holds data on introduced as well as native plants; however, such introduced plants fall outside the scope of the IUCN Red Data Book categories used in this List, and were therefore suppressed.

Appendix III
The Nature Conservancy and Wildlife Australia status ranks

Interpretation of The Nature Conservancy status ranks

The single largest outside data set contributed to this project derived from The Nature Conservancy (USA), which provided status and distribution data for approximately 11,000 globally threatened plants of the United States, Canada, and Latin America (TNC, 1996a; TNC, 1996b). The conservation status of each plant was assessed using the ranking system developed by TNC and its collaborators in the Natural Heritage and Conservation Data Center Network. Since these TNC status ranks were developed independently of and differ from the IUCN threat categories used in this publication, a conversion protocol was developed for their translation to IUCN Categories and incorporation into this publication.

Over the past twenty years TNC has helped establish a network of Natural Heritage Programs and Conservation Data Centers based in more than 85 state and national agencies and private organisations throughout the western hemisphere. Consistent methods for the assessment and documentation of species status have been developed for use in the biodiversity inventory and information management activities of these centres. These conservation status ranks provide an approximation of the risk of extinction for a particular taxon. As indicated in Table 13 below, rarity, as measured by number and size of populations or occurrences, is a principal extinction risk factor used in assessing status, but other criteria also considered include breadth of overall distribution, known population trends, and known and inferred threats (Master, 1991). The TNC conservation status ranking system follows a one-through-five scale, ranging from critically imperilled (Gl) to demonstrably secure (G5); extinct or possibly extinct species are tracked independently (Stein *et al.*, 1995; Stein & Chipley, 1996). This one-through-five ranking is applied at global (i.e., range-wide), national, and sub-national (i.e., state or provincial) levels, indicated by the prefix G, N, or S.

Assigning status ranks is a collaborative effort shared by TNC and the Natural Heritage Programs (NHP) and Conservation Data Centers (CDC). In general, sub-national and national status is assessed and documented by the relevant state or national data centre; with assessment of global status co-ordinated by TNC based on national and sub-national ranks and other information. While ranks are developed in a decentralised network arrangement, a summary of the current global, national, and sub-national ranks is maintained by TNC in the Natural Heritage Central Database (NHCD) at its Arlington, Virginia headquarters.

Information sources used by TNC, NHP, and CDC biologists to assess species status include herbarium collections, published reports in the scientific literature, other documented sightings, targeted field inventories, and population censuses. Distribution data in the NHCD derive from a variety of sources. For the United States and Canada, much of the state and province-level distribution data have been developed by the Biota of North America Program of the North Carolina Botanical Garden. For Latin America, major sources for national and province-level distribution data include the *Flora Neotropica* monograph series, and electronic databases of the Missouri Botanical Garden.

To contribute to this publication, the NHCD was queried for all plant taxa with global ranks of G3 (globally vulnerable) or rarer. National and sub-national distributions and status ranks for these 11,000 taxa were then output for transfer to WCMC and incorporation into its Threatened Plants Database. Within the NHCD, the rank of a particular taxon maybe expressed as a range (e.g., G2G3), indicating uncertainty about the plant's conservation status; for this publication, such "range ranks" were converted to a single rank value according to an algorithm developed for this purpose. The original TNC ranks were stored in *BG-BASE*, and the TNC ranks were then converted by WCMC to the IUCN threat categories used in this publication according to the protocol described in Table 13.

Table 13
Conversion of TNC ranks to IUCN Categories

TNC category[1234]	Definition	IUCN equivalent
GX, NX, SX	presumed extinct (not located despite extensive searches)	Ex
GH, NH, SH	historical occurrence (still some hope of discovery)	Ex/E
G1, N1, S1	critically imperilled (typically five or fewer occurrences or 1,000 or fewer individuals)	E
G2, N2, S2	imperilled (typically six to twenty occurrences or 1,000–3,000 individuals)	V
G3, N3, S3	vulnerable (rare; typically 21 to 100 occurrences or 3,000 to 10,000 individuals)	R
NR, SR N?, S?	Recorded within nation or state, but local status not available; when combined with global rank of G1 to G3, local status is given in this book as Indeterminate	I
G4, N4, S4	Apparently secure (uncommon but not rare; some cause for long-term concern, usually more than 100 occurrences and 10,000 individuals)	(not transferred)
G5, N5, S5	Secure (common, widespread and abundant)	(not transferred)

[1] "G" codes refer to rankings made at the global level; "N" codes refer to rankings made at a national level; and "S" codes refer to rankings made at the sub-regional level (US state, Canadian province, or similar units).

[2] See Stein *et al.*, 1995; Stein and Chipley, 1996.

[3] TNC ranks of 4 and 5 generally do not imply priorities for conservation concern, and do not correspond to any of the IUCN threatened categories (see Appendix III); therefore, they were not included in this data transfer.

[4] TNC ranks of NE are excluded from this list. These indicate exotic plants.

Interpretation of Wildlife Australia status ranks

Data for approximately 5,000 taxa of Australian native plants (of a total national vascular flora of *c.* 18,000–20,000) were compiled for a revision of *Rare or Threatened Australian Plants* – ROTAP (Briggs & Leigh, 1996). The list included a number of undescribed taxa for which it was possible to assign a conservation ranking, but these have been omitted from this publication. However, their inclusion in ROTAP as a conservation tool for Australia is essential as many of these may be under imminent threat and deserve as much attention as do described taxa.

The national list of Australian plants at risk was first compiled in 1981 for the Australian National Parks and Wildlife Service. Revisions of that list were published in 1988 and 1996. Rare or Threatened Australian Plants (ROTAP) had no legal status, but the early editions were the only nationally recognised threatened plants list at that time. In 1993 the Australian and New Zealand Environment and Conservation Council (ANZECC) issued a list, based on ROTAP, that was endorsed by all of Australia's state and territory conservation agencies. In 1992 the Commonwealth of Australia proclaimed the Endangered Species Protection Act and a schedule to the Act included a version of ROTAP and the ANZECC plants list.

In 1996 responsibility for maintenance of the national list of threatened plants was taken by the Threatened Species and Communities Section of Wildlife Australia, within the federal environment department. Details of threatened Australian plants will be compiled as the National Threatened Flora Database and will be endorsed by ANZECC agencies. Whilst this list will have no legal status it will be used as a basis for entries to the schedules of the Endangered Species Protection Act.

ROTAP uses a binary coding system developed and refined over several years but based on the IUCN Categories used in this List. While the ROTAP codes X, E, V, R, and K use definitions close to those of the IUCN Categories, the ROTAP system uses other indicators to supply additional information to users of the list. For example, the ROTAP code for *Dawinia collina* is 2VCit. This indicates that this plant is Vulnerable (V), that its geographic range is less than 100km (2), that there is at least one population reserved in a national park or other protected area (C), that fewer than 1,000 plants are known to occur within the reserve (i) and that the total known population is conserved (t). A full discussion of these terms may be found in Briggs & Leigh (1996). In this Red List only the 'top level' codes for Australian taxa are used.

It should be noted that each of Australia's states and territories compiles lists of threatened taxa based on state boundaries. These state lists are used in the compilation of the national ROTAP list. Thus, a plant that grows in more than one state may be classed as Endangered in one state and Vulnerable in another state, but on a national assessment the plant may be rated Vulnerable. Within the Australian context the state and national lists are complementary.

References

Anon. 1990. *World Plant Conservation Bibliography*. Compiled by Royal Botanic Gardens, Kew and Threatened Plants Unit, World Conservation Monitoring Centre. 645pp.

Atkinson, P., Maunder, M. & Walter, K.S. 1995. *A reference list for plant re-introductions, recovery plans and restoration programmes.* Royal Botanic Gardens, Kew. 36pp. (also available electronically: http://www.rbgkew.org.uk/conservation).

Bramwell, D. 1991. Botanic gardens in conservation: reintroduction into the wild. Pp. 209–216 in Heywood, V.H. and Wyse Jackson, P.S. (Eds.). *Tropical Botanic Gardens. Their Role in Conservation and Development.* San Diego: Academic Press.

Briggs, J. & Leigh, J. 1996. *Rare or Threatened Australian Plants.* CSIRO, Melbourne. 466pp.

Brummitt, R.K. (comp.). 1992. *Vascular Plant Families and Genera.* A listing of the genera of vascular plants of the world according to their families, as recognised in the Kew Herbarium, with an analysis of relationships of the flowering plant families according to eight systems of classification. Royal Botanic Gardens, Kew. 804pp.

Brummitt, R.K. & Powell, C.E. (eds.). 1992. *Authors of Plant Names.* A list of authors of scientific names of Plants, with recommended standard forms of their names, including abbreviations. Royal Botanic Gardens, Kew. 732pp.

Collar, N.J. 1996. The reasons for Red Data Books. *Oryx* 30 (2): 121–130.

Cronquist, A. 1981. *An Integrated System of Classification of Flowering Plants.* Columbia University Press, New York. 1262pp.

Davis, S., Droop, S., Gregerson, P., Henson, L., Leon, C., Villa-Lobos, J., Synge, H. & Zantovska, J. (1986). *Plants in Danger. What Do We Know?* International Union for Conservation of Nature and Natural Resources, Gland, Switzerland & Cambridge, UK. 461pp.

Falk, D.A. & Holsinger, K.E. 1991. *Genetics and Conservation of Rare Plants.* Center for Plant Conservation. Oxford University Press, Oxford, UK. 283pp.

Falk, D.A., Olwell, M. & Millar, C. 1996. *Restoring Diversity.* Island Press. Columbia, USA. 505pp.

Frankel, O.H., Brown, A.H.D. & Burdon, J.J. 1995. *The Conservation of Plant Biodiversity.* Cambridge University Press, Cambridge, UK. 299pp.

Gaston, K.J. (ed). 1996. *Biodiversity: a Biology of Numbers and Difference.* Blackwell Science Ltd., Oxford, UK. 396pp.

Groombridge, B. (ed.). 1992. *Global Biodiversity: Status of the Earth's Living Resources.* Compiled by the World Conservation Monitoring Centre. Chapman & Hall, London. 594pp.

Harper, J.L. & Hawksworth D.L. 1994. Biodiversity: measurement and estimation. *Phil. Trans. Roy. Soc. Lond. B.* 345: 5–12.

Heywood, V. (ed.). 1995. *Global Biodiversity Assessment.* Published for the United Nations Environment Programme. Cambridge University Press, Cambridge, UK. 1140pp.

Hilton-Taylor, C. 1996. *Red Data List of Southern African Plants.* National Botanical Institute, Pretoria, South Africa. 117pp.

Hollis, S. & Brummitt, R.K (eds). 1992. *World Geographical Scheme for Recording Plant Distributions. Plant Taxonomic Database Standards No. 2.* Hunt Institute for Botanical Documentation, Pittsburgh. 105pp.

ISO. 1993, with amendments. *Codes for the Representation of Names of Countries.* International Standards Organization. ISO 3166. Maintenance Agency Secretariat, Berlin. 60pp.

IUCN. 1992. *Protected Areas of the World: A Review of National Systems.* Vols. 1–4. IUCN, Gland, Switzerland and Cambridge, UK.

IUCN. 1994. *IUCN Red List Categories.* As Approved by the 40th Meeting of the IUCN Council. IUCN Gland, Switzerland. 22pp.

IUCN. 1996. *IUCN Red List of Threatened Animals.* IUCN, Gland, Switzerland. 368pp.

IUCN & BGCS, 1989. *The Botanic Gardens Conservation Strategy.* WWF & IUCN, Gland, Switzerland. 60pp.

IUCN, UNEP & WWF. 1991. *Caring for the Earth. A Strategy for Sustainable Living*. Gland, Switzerland. 228pp.

Lucas, G. & Synge, H. 1978. *The IUCN Plant Red Data Book*. IUCN, Switzerland. 540pp.

Master, L.L. 1991. Assessing threats and setting priorities for conservation. *Conservation Biology* 5:559–563.

Murray, M.G., Green, M.J.B. & Walter, K.S. 1992. Status of Plant and Animal Inventories for Protected Areas in the Tropics. A Contribution to the ODA Strategy Programme for Research on Forestry and Agroforestry Implemented by the Oxford Forestry Institute under its Forestry Research Programme. WCMC, Cambridge, UK. 106pp. (unpublished)

Olson, D. Dinerstein, E, Castro, G. and Maravi, E. (eds.) 1996. *Identifying gaps in botanical information for Biodiversity Conservation in Latin America and the Caribbean*. Proceedings of a workshop on April 7–9, 1996 in Washington, DC and consultations with regional experts. WWF Washington DC, USA.

Scott, P., Burton, J.A. and Fitter, R. 1987. Red Data Books: the historical background. Pp.1–5 *in* Fitter, R. and Fitter, M. (eds.). *The Road to Extinction*. IUCN, Gland, Switzerland.

Stein, B.A., Master, L.L., Morse, L.E., Kutner, L.S. & Morrison, M. 1995. Status of US Species: Setting Conservation Priorities. Pp. 399-400 *in* E.T. LaRoe, G.S. Farris, C.E. Puckett, P.D. Doran, &. Mac, M. (eds.) *Our Living Resources*. A Report to the Nation on the Distribution, Abundance, and Health of US Plants, Animals, and Ecosystems. US Dept. of the Interior – National Biological Service, Washington, DC.

Stein, B.A. & Chipley, R.M. (eds.). 1996. *Priorities for Conservation: 1996 Annual Report Card for U.S. Plant and Animal Species*. The Nature Conservancy, Arlington, Virginia, USA. 18pp.

Threatened Plants Committee Secretariat. 1981. *How to Use the IUCN Red Data Book Categories*. Threatened Plants Committee, Kew, UK. 9pp.

Threatened Plants Unit. In press. Plant Occurrence and Status Scheme (POSS). A standard for recording the relationship between a plant and a place. Gillett, H.J., Leon, C., Mackinder, D., Rooney, P., Synge, H., and Walter, K.S (eds.). Plant Taxonomic Database Standard XX, International Working Group on Taxonomic Databases for Plant Sciences. 26pp. (also available electronically: http://www.wcmc.org.uk/poss).

TNC. 1996a. Natural Heritage Central Database. (Status and distribution data on North American plants, developed in collaboration with the Association for Biodiversity Information, U.S. and Canadian Natural Heritage Programs and Conservation Data Centers, and North Carolina Botanical Garden Biota of North America Program.)

TNC. 1996b. Natural Heritage Central Database. (Status and distribution data on Latin American plants, developed in collaboration with Latin American Conservation Data Centers and Missouri Botanical Garden).

Walter, K.S., *et al*. 1995. *Catalogue of Plants Growing at the Royal Botanic Garden Edinburgh*. Royal Botanic Garden Edinburgh, Edinburgh, UK. 477pp.

WCMC. 1996. *Checklist of CITES Species*. A Reference to the Appendices to the Convention on International Trade in Endangered Species of Wild Fauna and Flora. CITES Secretariat and World Conservation Monitoring Centre, Geneva, Switzerland and Cambridge, UK. 400pp.

Wollenberg, B.J.W. van den, Tolsma, J., Vos, J., Lukkien, V.P.A., & Oudijk, A. (eds.). 1992. *Utrecht University Catalogue of Plant Collections*. Botanic Gardens, Utrecht, The Netherlands, 548pp.

WWF & IUCN. *1994–7. Centres of Plant Diversity. A Guide and Strategy for Their Conservation*. 3 volumes. IUCN Publications Unit, Cambridge, UK.

1997 IUCN Red List of
Threatened Plants

Navigating the list

This Red List provides data on globally threatened vascular plants, arranged in the following order:

Fern allies	• Lycopodiopsida
True ferns	• Pteridopsida
Gymnosperms	• Ginkopsida (*Ginkgo*)
	• Cycadopsida (cycads)
	• Gnetopsida (gnetophytes)
	• Pinopsida (conifers),
Angiosperms	• Magnoliopsida (dicotyledons)
	• Liliopsida (monocotyledons)

Within each of these major taxa, families are listed alphabetically.

Example of a record
[with corresponding description]

Cycadopsida
[Major taxon]

Zamiaceae
[Family]

Number of genera: 8

Number of species: 144

Recorded threatened species: 128 (88%)

Africa; Australia; America
[Geographic Range]

E	I	*Ceratozamia euryphyllidia* **Vazquez-Torres, Sabato & D. Stevenson**	*20883, 11119*
[global threat status]	[CITES listing where relevant]	[Scientific name and authority]	[data source(s) for scientific name]
	V	*20016* Mexico - Veracruz *20016*	
	[local threat status]	[data source for local threat status] [distribution] [distribution data source]	

Please see introduction for fuller explanations.

Lycopodiopsida

Isoetaceae

Number of genera: 1-2
Number of species: 77-80
Recorded threatened species: 39   (49%)

Temperate and tropical.

E   *Isoetes alcalophila* Halloy *16336*
    E   *20176* Argentina - Tucuman *20176*

R   *Isoetes andicola* (Pfeiffer) L.D. Gomez *17371*
    R   *12468* Peru *12468*

R   *Isoetes asiatica* (Makino) Makino *5942*
    E   *11552* Russia (Far East) - Kamchatka *5942*
    I   *5942* Russia (Far East) - Kurilskye Is. *5942*
    I   *5942* Russia (Far East) - Primorye *5942*
    I   *5942* Russia (Far East) - Sakhalin *5942*
    I   *19216* China (Mongolia) *19216*
    R   *11163* Japan *11163*

E   *Isoetes azorica* Durieu ex Milde *12032, 20171*
    E   *19216* Portugal - Azores *12032*

I   *Isoetes beringensis* Komarov *5942*
    I   *5942* Russia (Far East) - Kamchatka (Komandorskije) *5942*

R   *Isoetes bilaspurensis* Panigr. *11350*
    R   *11350* India - Madhaya Pradesh *11350*

R   *Isoetes bolanderi* Engelm. *19002*
    R   *19850* Mexico *19850*

E   *Isoetes boomii* N.Luebke & W.C.Taylor *20850*
    E   *20850* U.S. - Georgia *20850*

V   *Isoetes boryana* Durieu *8000, 20171*
    V   *20528* France (south-west coast) *20528*

R   *Isoetes brochonii* Moteley *8000, 20171*
    R   *19216* France (east Pyrenees) *8000*

I   *Isoetes capensis* A.V.Duthie var. *stephanseniae*
    (A.V.Duthie) Schelpe & N.C.Anthony *20604*
    I   *20604* South Africa - Cape Province *20604*

E   *Isoetes castillonii* H.P.Fuchs *16336*
    E   *16336* Argentina *16336*

Ex   *Isoetes dixitii* Shende *11352*
    Ex   *11352* India - Maharashtra (Panchghani) *11352*

R   *Isoetes elatior* F.Muell. ex A.Braun *20681*
    R   *20681* Australia - Tasmania *20681*

E   *Isoetes escondidensis* Halloy *16336*
    E   *16336* Argentina *16336*

R   *Isoetes flaccida* Shuttlw. ex A.Braun *20850*
    R   *20850* U.S. - Florida *20850*
    R   *20850* U.S. - Georgia *20850*

R   *Isoetes habbemensis* Alston *19594*
    R   *19216* Indonesia - Irian Jaya *19594*
    R   *19216* Papua New Guinea *19594*

V   *Isoetes heldreichii* Wettst. *8000, 20171*
    V   *19216* Greece (Pindhios Mountains) *8000*

E   *Isoetes hieroglyphica* A.A.Eat. *20850, 14480*
    E   *20850* Canada - New Brunswick *20850*
    I   *20850* Canada - Nova Scotia *20850*
    I   *20850* Canada - Ontario *20850*
    I   *20850* Canada - Quebec *20850*
    I   *20850* U.S. - Maine *20850*
    I   *20850* U.S. - Vermont *20850*
    I   *20850* U.S. - Wisconsin *20850*

R   *Isoetes humilior* F.Muell. ex A.Braun *20681*
    R   *20681* Australia - Tasmania *20681*

V   *Isoetes lithophila* N.E.Pfeiffer *20850*
    V   *20850* U.S. - Texas *20850*

E   *Isoetes louisianensis* Thieret *20850, 14511*
    E   *20850* U.S. - Louisiana *20850*

E   *Isoetes malinverniana* Ces.& De Not. *8000, 20171*
    E   *18264* Italy (Piemonte & Lombardia) *19997*

R   *Isoetes melanotheca* Alston *7926*
    R   Guinea *7926*

R   *Isoetes neoguineensis* Baker *19594*
    R   *19216* Papua New Guinea *19594*

R   *Isoetes pallida* Hickey *12001*
    R   *19216* Mexico - Oaxaca *12001*

R   *Isoetes piedmontana* (N.E.Pfeiffer) C.F.Reed *20850*
    V   *20850* U.S. - Alabama *20850*
    R   *20850* U.S. - Georgia *20850*
    E   *20850* U.S. - North Carolina *20850*
    V   *20850* U.S. - South Carolina *20850*
    E   *20850* U.S. - Virginia *20850*

R   *Isoetes pringlei* Underw. *9001*
    R   *19216* Mexico - Chiapas *9001*

V   *Isoetes prototypus* D.M.Britt. *20850*
    I   *20850* Canada - New Brunswick *20850*
    I   *20850* Canada - Nova Scotia *20850*
    I   *20850* U.S. - Maine *20850*

R   *Isoetes rhodesiana* Alston *7749*
    R   Zimbabwe *7749*

Ex   *Isoetes sampathkumarnii* L.N.Rao *11353*
    Ex   *11353* India - Karnataka *11353*

R   *Isoetes savatieri* Franchet *16336*
    R   *19448* Argentina *21305*
    R   *21305* Chile *21305*

R   *Isoetes sinensis* Palmer *17617*
    E   *17617* China - Anhui (Xiuning; Dongxi) *11139*
    E   *17617* China - Jiangsu (Nanjing) *11139*
    E   *17617* China - Zhejiang *11139*
    R   *11163* Japan *11163*

R   *Isoetes spinulospora* Jermy & Schelpe
    R   Equatorial Guinea - Bioko

R   *Isoetes stevensii* Croft *19594*
    R   *19216* Papua New Guinea *19594*

R   *Isoetes storkii* Palmer *9034*
    R   *9593* Costa Rica *9034*
    R   *19216* Panama *11714*

E   *Isoetes taiwanensis* DeVol *20511*
    E   *20511* Taiwan *20511*

E   *Isoetes tegetiformans* Rury *20850*
    E   *20850* U.S. - Georgia *20850*

R   *Isoetes tenuifolia* Jermy *6072*
    R   *19216* Ghana *6072*
    E   Kenya

R   *Isoetes velata* A.Braun ssp. *asturicense* (M.Laínz)
    Rivas Mart. & Prada *20171*
    R   *20874* Spain (Hercynian massif) *20874*

V   *Isoetes velata* A.Braun ssp. *tenuissima* (Boreau)
    O.Bolòs & Vigo *20171*
    V   *20528* France (central) *20528*

E   *Isoetes wormaldii* Sim *20604*
    E   *20604* South Africa - Cape Province *20604*

Lycopodiaceae

Number of genera: 4
Number of species: 450-587
Recorded threatened species: 23   (4%)

Cosmopolitan.

R   *Diphasiastrum madeirense* (J.H.Wilce) Holub *12032, 20171*
       R   Portugal - Azores *12032*
       R   Portugal - Madeira *12032*

R   *Huperzia deminuens* (Herter) B. Ollg. *21282*
       R   *21282*   Brazil *21282*

R   *Huperzia eremorum* (Rolleri) Holub *21282*
       R   *21282*   Colombia *21282*

R   *Huperzia fuegiana* (Roiv.) Holub *21305*
       R   *21305*   Falkland Is. *21305*
       R   *21305*   Chile - Tierra del Fuego *21305*

V   *Huperzia lockyeri* (D.Jones & B.Gray) Holub *20681*
       V   *20681*   Australia - Queensland *20681*

V   *Huperzia mannii* (Hbd.) Kartesz & Gandhi *20850*
       V   *20850*   U.S. - Hawaii *20850*

V   *Huperzia marsupiiformis* (D.Jones & B.Gray) Holub *20681*
       V   *20681*   Australia - Queensland *20681*

E   *Huperzia nutans* (Brack.) Rothm. *20850, 14662*
       E   *20850*   U.S. - Hawaii *20850*

V   *Huperzia polytrichoides* (Kaulfuss) Trevisan *20850*
       I   *20850*   U.S. - Hawaii *20850*

R   *Huperzia pruinosa* (Herter) Holub *21282*
       R   *21282*   Peru *21282*

R   *Huperzia regnellii* (Maxon) B.Ollg. & P.G.Windisch *21282*
       R   *21282*   Brazil - Minas Gerais *21282*

E   *Huperzia sulcinervia* (Spring) Trevisan *20850*
       E   *20850*   U.S. - Hawaii *20850*

R   *Lycopodiella limosa* Chinnock *20681*
       R   *20681*   Australia - Queensland *20681*

V   *Lycopodiella margueriteae* J.G.Bruce, W.H.Wagner & Beitel *20850*
       I   *20850*   U.S. - Michigan *20850*
       E   *20850*   U.S. - Virginia *20850*

V   *Lycopodiella subappressa* J.G.Bruce, W.H.Wagner & Beitel *20850*
       E   *20850*   U.S. - Indiana *20850*
       E   *20850*   U.S. - Michigan *20850*

I   *Lycopodium aberdaricum* Chiov.
       I   Kenya

I   *Lycopodium axillare* Roxb. *18997*
       Ex/E   *19213*   Ascension Is. *19213*
       V   *18997*   St Helena *18997*
       I   Tristan da Cunha

I   *Lycopodium ceylanicum* Spring *10251*
       I   *16162*   Sri Lanka *10251*

R   *Lycopodium chonoticum* Philippi *5595*
       R   *19534*   Chile *5595*

R   *Lycopodium halconense* Copel. *10278*
       R   Philippines *10278*

E   *Lycopodium phlegmaria* L. var. *longiflorum* Spring *20819*
       E   *20819*   North Mariana Is. (Rota) *20819*

       E   *20819*   U.S. - Guam *20819*

R   *Lycopodium phlegmaria* L. var. *longifolium* Spring *18338*
       R   *18338*   U.S. - Guam *18338*

R   *Lycopodium pseudovarium* Brownlie
       R   *19216*   New Caledonia *19216*

R   *Lycopodium setaceum* Lam. ssp. *galapagense* Hamann *11117*
       R   Ecuador - Galapagos *11117*

Ex   *Urostachys rubrus* (Cham.) Hert *19539*
       Ex   *19539*   Brazil - Minas Gerais *19539*

Psilotaceae

Number of genera: 2
Number of species: 3-10
Recorded threatened species: 2   (28%)

Tropical and warm temperate.

E   *Psilotum nudum* L. var. *molesworthiae* Iranzo, Prada & Salvo *19818*
       E   *19818*   Spain (Ibérica, Cádiz, Sierra de Algibe) *20661*

R   *Tmesipteris norfolkensis* P. Green *10604*
       R   *19108*   Australia - Norfolk Is. *10604*

Selaginellaceae

Number of genera: 1
Number of species: 700-725
Recorded threatened species: 23   (3%)

Widespread (mainly tropical).

E   *Selaginella adunca* A. Br. ex Hieron. *11494*
       E   India - Himachal Pradesh (Janusar, Simla) *11358*
       E   India - Uttar Pradesh *11358*

R   *Selaginella atimonanensis* Tan & Jermy *10278*
       R   Philippines (Quezon NP) *11305*

E   *Selaginella balfourii* Baker *5852*
       E   *5852*   Mauritius - Rodrigues *5852*

I   *Selaginella calostachya* (Hook. & Grev.) Alston *10251*
       I   *16162*   Sri Lanka *10251*

E   *Selaginella cataractarum* Alston *11494*
       E   India - Kerala *11359*
       Ex   *18228*   India - Tamil Nadu (Silver Cascade, Kodaikanal) *11359*

I   *Selaginella cochleata* (Hook. & Grev.) Spring *10251*
       I   *16162*   Sri Lanka *10251*

V   *Selaginella eatonii* Hieron. ex Small *20850*
       V   *20850*   U.S. - Florida *20850*

I   *Selaginella firmuloides* Warb.
       I   *19216*   New Caledonia *19216*

V   *Selaginella gigantea* Steyermark & A. R. Smith *20883*
       I   *20883*   Venezuela *20883*

R   *Selaginella leucobryoides* Maxon *20850*
       V   *20850*   U.S. - Arizona *20850*
       I   *19216*   U.S. - California *20850*
       I   *20850*   U.S. - Nevada *20850*

R   *Selaginella lineariformis* Jermy *9283*
       R   *19216*   Malaysia - Sarawak (G. Mulu NP) *9283*

R   *Selaginella molleri* Hieron *7926*
       R   Equatorial Guinea - Bioko *11607*

I	*Selaginella neocaledonica* Baker	
	I	*19216* New Caledonia *19216*
Ex	*Selaginella orizabensis* Hieron. *9019*	
	Ex	*11119* Mexico - Veracruz *9019*
I	*Selaginella praetermissa* Alston *10251*	
	I	*16162* Sri Lanka *10251*
R	*Selaginella pricei* Tan & Jermy *10278*	
	R	Philippines *10278*
I	*Selaginella protensa* Alston *7926*	
	I	Côte d'Ivoire *7926*
V	*Selaginella pulcherrima* Liebm. ex Fourn. *9015*	
	V	*9425* Mexico - Veracruz *9015*
R	*Selaginella raynaliana* Tard.	
	R	Cameroon (Ebolowa & Akoakas)
R	*Selaginella subisophylla* Jermy	
	R	*19216* Zambia *19216*
R	*Selaginella tama-montana* Serizawa *11163*	
	R	*11163* Japan *11163*
R	*Selaginella tortipila* A.Braun *20850*	
	V	*20850* U.S. - Georgia *20850*
	R	*20850* U.S. - North Carolina *20850*
	I	*20850* U.S. - South Carolina *20850*
V	*Selaginella utahensis* Flowers *20850*	
	Ex/E	*20850* U.S. - Nevada *20850*
	V	*20850* U.S. - Utah *20850*
V	*Selaginella viridissima* Weatherby *20883, 20850*	
	E	*20850* U.S. - Texas *20850*
	I	*20883* Mexico *20883*

Pteridopsida

Adiantaceae

Number of genera:	33-38
Number of species:	712
Recorded threatened species:	38 (5%)

Cosmopolitan.

E	*Adiantum gertrudis* Espin. *5595*	
	E	*21305* Chile *5595*
I	*Adiantum imbricatum* R.Tryon	
	I	*12468* Peru *12468*
I	*Adiantum macrocladum* Klotzsch	
	I	*12468* Peru *12468*
R	*Adiantum mindanaense* Copel. *10278*	
	R	Philippines *10278*
R	*Adiantum mochaenum* Kunkel *19534*	
	R	*19534* Chile *19534*
V	*Adiantum ogasawarense* Tagawa *19134*	
	V	*19134* Japan - Kazan Retto *19134*
	V	*19134* Japan - Ogasawara-shoto *19134*
E	*Adiantum pearcei* Philippi *19534*	
	E	*21305* Chile *19534*
I	*Adiantum poeppigianum* (Kuhn) Hieron.	
	I	*12468* Peru *12468*
E	*Adiantum reniforme* L. var. *sinense* Y.X. Lin *11139*	
	E	*17617* China - Sichuan (Wanxian; Shizhu) *11139*
I	*Adiantum ruizianum* Klotzsch	
	I	*12468* Peru *12468*
I	*Adiantum scalare* R. Tryon	

	I	*12468* Peru *12468*
I	*Adiantum sessilifolium* Hook.	
	I	*12468* Peru *12468*
E	*Adiantum viridimontanum* Paris *20850*	
	I	*20850* Canada - Quebec *20850*
	V	*20850* U.S. - Vermont *20850*
E	*Adiantum vivesii* Proctor *20883, 19002*	
	I	*20883* Puerto Rico *20883*
Ex/E	*Anogramma ascensionis* (Hook.) Diels *3204*	
	Ex/E	*3204* Ascension Is. *3204*
R	*Cheilanthes arizonica* (Maxon) Mickel *20883, 20850*	
	V	*20850* U.S. - Arizona *20850*
	I	*20883* Mexico *20883*
R	*Cheilanthes cantangensis* (Tryon) Tryon *17371*	
	R	*17371* Peru *17371*
R	*Cheilanthes cooperae* D.C. Eat. *20850*	
	I	*20850* U.S. - California *20850*
R	*Cheilanthes depauperata* Baker *20604*	
	R	*20604* South Africa - Cape Province *20604*
I	*Cheilanthes fractifera* R.Tryon	
	I	*12468* Peru *12468*
R	*Cheilanthes krameri* Franchet & Sav. *11163*	
	R	*11163* Japan *11163*
R	*Cheilanthes kunzei* Mett. *20604*	
	R	*20604* Namibia *20604*
	R	*20604* South Africa - Cape Province *20604*
R	*Cheilanthes lonchophylla* (Tryon) R.Tryon & A.F.Tryon *17371*	
	R	*17371* Peru *17371*
R	*Cheilanthes valdiviana* Philippi *5595*	
	R	*5595* Chile *5595*
R	*Cheilanthes viscida* Davenport *20850*	
	I	*20850* U.S. - California *20850*
E	*Coniogramme gracilis* Ogata *11163*	
	E	*11163* Japan *11163*
R	*Coniogramme indica* Fee *11266*	
	R	India - Manipur (Hongua Hill, Ukhrul) *11266*
	R	India - Meghalaya *11266*
R	*Doryopteris allenae* Tryon	
	R	Malaysia - Peninsular Malaysia (Perak; Selangor)
I	*Eriosorus accrescens* A.F. Tryon	
	I	*12468* Peru *12468*
I	*Eriosorus lechleri* (Kuhn) A.F. Tryon	
	I	*12468* Peru *12468*
I	*Eriosorus stuebelii* (Hieron.) A.F. Tryon	
	I	*12468* Peru *12468*
V	*Notholaena chilensis* (E.J. Remy) Sturm *19116, 21305*	
	V	*21305* Chile - Juan Fernandez Is. *19116*
I	*Pellaea boivini* Hook. *16162*	
	I	*16162* Sri Lanka *16162*
V	*Pellaea lyngholmii* Windham *20850*	
	I	*20850* U.S. - Arizona *20850*
R	*Pellaea myrtillifolia* Mett. ex Kuhn *19534*	
	R	*21305* Chile *19534*
R	*Pellaea rufa* A.F.Tryon *20604*	
	R	*20604* South Africa - Cape Province *20604*
V	*Pentagramma pallida* (Weatherby) Yatskievych, Windham & Wollenweber *20850*	

I	20850	U.S. - California *20850*

R   *Sinopteris grevilleoides* (Christ) C. Chr. & Ching *11139*

R	17617	China - Sichuan (Qingchuan; Maoweng) *11139*
R	17617	China - Yunnan *11139*

Aspleniaceae

Number of genera: 9-14
Number of species: 711
Recorded threatened species: 46   (6%)

Pantropical; subtropical; some temperate.

R   *Asplenium adamsii* Alston

R		Cameroon (Cameroon mt)

R   *Asplenium adulterinum* Milde *14526, 20171*

R		Austria
R	21091	Bosnia & Herzegovina *21091*
E	2050	Czech Republic *2050*
V	20673	Finland *8000*
V	20640	Germany *20640*
V	17832	Norway *17832*
V	19366	Poland (Sudetes, Sudetic foothills) *7897*
R	19949	Romania *19949*
I	19321	Slovakia *19321*
R	13662	Slovenia (central) *13662*
V	18216	Sweden *18216*
R	18154	Switzerland *18154*

R   *Asplenium aemilii-guineae* Alston *7926*

R		Equatorial Guinea - Bioko (Moka) *7926*

R   *Asplenium aethiopicum* (Burm.f.) Bech *20681, 18996*

R	20681	Australia - Western Australia *20681*
R	18996	St Helena *18996*

R   *Asplenium ascensionis* S.Watson *3204*

R	3204	Ascension Is. *3204*

R   *Asplenium athertonense* S.B.Andrews *20681*

R	20681	Australia Queensland *20681*

R   *Asplenium balearicum* Shivas *18264, 20171*

V	20528	France - Corsica *15080*
E	18264	Italy (Tuscany, Lazio) *18264*
E	18264	Italy - Sardinia *18264*
E	18264	Italy - Sicily (Pantelleria I.) *18264*
R	20821	Spain - Balearic Is. (Menorca) *11562*

R   *Asplenium bourgaei* Boiss. ex Milde *20171*

R		Greece

E   *Asplenium cardiophyllum* (Hance) Bak. *19134*

E	19134	China - Hainan Is. *19134*
E	19134	Japan (Kita Daito-jima) *19134*
E	19134	Japan - Ogasawara-shoto *19134*

Ex/E   *Asplenium centrifugale* Baker *881*

Ex/E	14224	Australia - Christmas Is. *881*

E   *Asplenium chondrophyllum* Bertero ex Colla *19116*

E	19125	Chile - Juan Fernandez Is. *19116*

R   *Asplenium compressum* Sw. *18997*

R	19213	St Helena *18997*

R   *Asplenium creticum* Lovis, Reichst. & Zaffran *20171*

R	20730	Greece - Crete *20730*

I   *Asplenium disjunctum* Sledge *10251*

I	16162	Sri Lanka *10251*

R   *Asplenium eberhardtii* Tard. *6057*

R		Vietnam *6057*

R   *Asplenium insolitum* A. Reid Smith *9003*

R	9003	Mexico *12007*

R   *Asplenium isabelense* Brause *7926*

R		Equatorial Guinea - Bioko *7926*

R   *Asplenium jahandiezii* (Litard.) Rouy *8000, 20171*

R	20528	France (Gorges du Verdon) *8000*

Ex/E   *Asplenium leucostegioides* Baker *20850, 14662*

Ex/E	20850	U.S. - Hawaii *20850*

I   *Asplenium longipes* Fee *10251*

I	16162	Sri Lanka *10251*

E   *Asplenium macrosorum* Bertero ex Colla *19116*

E	19125	Chile - Juan Fernandez Is. *19116*

R   *Asplenium majoricum* Litard. *8000, 20171*

V	20692	Spain (Valencian region) *20692*
R		Spain - Balearic Is.

I   *Asplenium micantifrons* (Tuy.) Tuy. ex H. Ohba *8622*

I	19134	Japan - Kazan Retto (Minami-Iwojima) *8622*
I	19134	Japan - Ogasawara-shoto *8622*

V   *Asplenium pauperequitum* *19305*

V	19305	New Zealand - North Is. *19305*

E   *Asplenium petrarchae* (Guérin) DC. ssp. *bivalens* (D.E.Meyer) Lovis & Reichst. *19818, 20171*

E	19818	Spain (Sierra de Grazalema) *19818*

R   *Asplenium platybasis* Kunze ex Mett. var. *platybasis* *18997*

R	18997	St Helena *18997*

I   *Asplenium platybasis* Kunze ex Mett. var. *subnudum* C. Chr. *19938*

I		Tristan da Cunha (Gough, Inaccessible, Nightingale Is.) *19938*

R   *Asplenium protractum* Tard. *6057*

R		Vietnam *6057*

R   *Asplenium rehmanniana* Engl. var. *longicuneata* R. & A. Fernandes *7749*

R		Mozambique *7749*

E   *Asplenium reuteri* Milde *12840*

E	12840	Turkey *12840*

E   *Asplenium rhomboideum* Brack. *20850*

E	20850	U.S. - Hawaii *20850*

E   *Asplenium schizophyllum* C. Christens. *20850*

E	20850	U.S. - Hawaii *20850*

R   *Asplenium schweinfurthii* Baker *15534*

R	15534	Yemen - Socotra *15534*

R   *Asplenium scolopendrium* (Fern.) comb.nov. var. *americanum* (Fern.) Kartesz & Gandhi *20850*

I	20850	Canada - New Brunswick *20850*
R	20850	Canada - Ontario *20850*
E	20850	U.S. - Alabama *20850*
I	20850	U.S. - Maryland *20850*
E	20850	U.S. - Michigan *20850*
V	20850	U.S. - New York *20850*
E	20850	U.S. - Tennessee *20850*

E   *Asplenium stellatum* Colla *19116*

E	19125	Chile - Juan Fernandez Is. *19116*

R   *Asplenium subaequilaterale* (Baker) Hieron *7926*

R		Equatorial Guinea - Bioko *7926*

R   *Asplenium trigonopterum* Kunze *11163*

R	11163	Japan *11163*

R   *Asplenium vespertinum* Maxon *20850*

I	20850	U.S. - California *20850*

V   *Asplenium wildii* Bailey *20681*

V	20681	Australia - Queensland *20681*

R   *Ceterach cordatum* Sw. var. *haughtonii* C.

Chr. *18997*

R   *18997* St Helena *18997*

E   ***Diellia erecta*** Brack. *20850, 19095*

    E   *20850* U.S. - Hawaii (all islands) *20850*

E   ***Diellia falcata*** Brack. *20850, 19095*

    E   *20850* U.S. - Hawaii (Oahu) *20850*

E   ***Diellia laciniata*** (Hbd.) Diels *20850*

    E   *20850* U.S. - Hawaii *20850*

Ex/E   ***Diellia mannii*** (D.C. Eat.) Robins. *20850*

    Ex/E   *20850* U.S. - Hawaii *20850*

E   ***Diellia unisora*** W.H. Wagner *20850, 19095*

    E   *20850* U.S. - Hawaii (Oahu) *20850*

R   ***Phyllitis hybrida*** (Milde) C.Chr. *20171*

    I   *20852* Croatia *20852*
    R   (former) Yugoslavia

V   ***Phyllitis scolopendrium*** (L.) Newman var. *americana*
    Fern. *16059*

    V   *16059* Canada - Ontario *16059*
    V   *16059* U.S. - Alabama (Jackson & Morgan Co.)
        16059
    V   *16059* U.S. - Michigan (Mackinac Co.) *16059*
    V   *16059* U.S. - New York (Madison & Onondaga Co.)
        16059
    V   *16059* U.S. - Tennessee (Marion Co.) *16059*

Blechnaceae

Number of genera: 8 - 9
Number of species: 238
Recorded threatened species: 17   (7%)

Cosmopolitan.

R   ***Blechnum corralense*** Espin. *5595*

    R   *19534* Chile *5595*

R   ***Blechnum fullagarii*** (F. Muell.) C. Chr.

    R   *14225* Australia - NSW - Lord Howe Is. *14225*

R   ***Blechnum gregsonii*** (Watts) Tindale *20681*

    R   *20681* Australia - New South Wales *20681*

I   ***Blechnum longicauda*** C. Chr. *19116*

    I   *19125* Chile - Juan Fernandez Is. *19116*

E   ***Blechnum mochaenum*** Kunkel var. *fernandeziana*
    (Looser) De la Sota *19116, 21305*

    E   *19116* Chile - Juan Fernandez Is. *19116*

I   ***Blechnum obtusatum*** (Labill.) Mett. var. *francii*
    (Rosenstock) Brownlie

    I   New Caledonia

V   ***Blechnum schottii*** (Colla) C. Chr. *19116*

    V   *19125* Chile - Juan Fernandez Is. *19116*

R   ***Doodia brackenridgei*** Carr.

    R   Fiji

R   ***Doodia gracilis*** Copel.

    R   New Caledonia

E   ***Doodia lyonii*** O. Deg. *20850*

    E   *20850* U.S. - Hawaii *20850*

R   ***Doodia marquesensis*** E. Brown

    R   French Polynesia - Marquesas Is

R   ***Doodia mollis*** Parris

    R   New Zealand - North Is.

V   ***Doodia paschalis*** C. Chr. *17912*

    V   *17912* Chile - Easter Is. *17912*

R   ***Doodia scaberula*** Parris

    R   Papua New Guinea

R   ***Doodia squarrosa*** Colenso

    R   New Zealand - North Is.

R   ***Steenisioblechnum acuminatum*** (White & Goy)
    Hennipman *20681*

    R   *20681* Australia - Queensland *20681*

R   ***Struthiopteris castanea*** Nakai *11163*

    R   *11163* Japan *11163*

Cyatheaceae

Number of genera: 1 - 4
Number of species: 623
Recorded threatened species: 202   (32%)

Pantropical to warm temperate.

E   II   ***Alsophila amintae*** Conant *20883, 19002*

    E   *20883* Puerto Rico *20883*

V   II   ***Alsophila polystichoides*** Christ *14244*

    V   *14244* Costa Rica *14244*
    V   *16317* Panama *14244*

R   II   ***Cnemidaria glandulosa*** Stolze *14244*

    R   *14244* Panama *14244*

V   II   ***Cnemidaria stolzeana*** L.D. Gómez *14244*

    V   *16317* Panama *14244*

R   II   ***Cnemidaria suprastrigosa*** R.C. Moran *14244*

    R   *14244* Panama *14244*

R   II   ***Cnemidaria tryoniana*** Stolze

    R   Colombia

R   II   ***Cnemidaria varians*** R.C. Moran *14244*

    R   *14244* Panama *14244*

R   II   ***Cyathea abbottii*** Maxon *12491*

    R   *12616* Dominican Republic *12616*
    R   *12616* Haiti *12616*

R   II   ***Cyathea aciculosa*** Copel. *14803*

    V   Papua New Guinea - Bismarck Arch.
    R   *14803* Solomon Is. - South *14803*

V   II   ***Cyathea acuminata*** Copel. *20093*

    V   Philippines (Panay) *20093*

R   II   ***Cyathea akawaiorum*** P.J. Edwards *12349*

    R   Guyana (Mt Roraima) *12349*

R   II   ***Cyathea alatissima*** (Stolze) *12491*

    R   *12616* Peru *12625*

I   II   ***Cyathea albida*** Tard.

    I   *6963* Madagascar

R   II   ***Cyathea albomarginata*** R.C. Moran *14244*

    R   *14244* Costa Rica *14244*
    R   *14244* Panama *14244*

V   II   ***Cyathea albosetacea*** (Beddome) Copel. *14708*

    V   *13883* India - Nicobar Is. (Great Nicobar, Kamotra
        Is.) *11273*

V   II   ***Cyathea alleniae*** Holttum

    V   Malaysia - Peninsular Malaysia

R   II   ***Cyathea alstonii*** R. Tryon *12612*

    R   *12616* Colombia (Macarena) *12612*

I   II   ***Cyathea alticola*** (Tard.) Tindale

    I   *6963* Madagascar

V   II   ***Cyathea annae*** (Alderw.) Domin

    V   Indonesia - Moluccas

I   II   ***Cyathea apoensis*** Copel *20093*

    I   Philippines *20093*

I   II   ***Cyathea appendiculata*** Baker

	I		6963		Madagascar
I	II	*Cyathea approximata* Bonap. var. *approximata*			
	I		6963		Madagascar
I	II	*Cyathea approximata* Bonap. var. *sorisquamata* Tardieu			
	I		6963		Madagascar
R	II	*Cyathea arfakensis* Gepp			
	R				Papua New Guinea
I	II	*Cyathea aristata* Domin *12491*			
	I		9114		Mexico - Oaxaca *12625*
	I		9114		Mexico - Veracruz *9114*
V	II	*Cyathea arthropoda* Copel.			
	V				Malaysia - Sarawak
I	II	*Cyathea ascendens* Domin			
	I				Papua New Guinea
R	II	*Cyathea assurgens* R. Tryon *10538*			
	R		12616		Colombia *10538*
	R		12616		Ecuador *10538*
R	II	*Cyathea atrospinosa* Holttum			
	R				Papua New Guinea
I	II	*Cyathea auriculata* Tard.			
	I		6963		Madagascar
V	II	*Cyathea australis* (R. Br.) Domin ssp. *norfolkensis* Holttum			
	V				Australia - Norfolk Is.
R	II	*Cyathea baileyana* (Domin) Domin *20681*			
	R		20681		Australia - Queensland *20681*
I	II	*Cyathea ballardii* Tard.			
	I		6963		Madagascar
I	II	*Cyathea bellisquamata* Bonap. var. *basilobata* C. Chr.			
	I		6963		Madagascar
I	II	*Cyathea bellisquamata* Bonap. var. *bellisquamata*			
	I		6963		Madagascar
R	II	*Cyathea binuangensis* Alderw. *10278*			
	R				Philippines *10278*
R	II	*Cyathea bipinnata* (R. Tryon) *12491*			
	R		12616		Ecuador *10538*
I	II	*Cyathea boivini* Mett. var. *boivini*			
	I		6963		Madagascar
I	II	*Cyathea boivini* Mett. var. *concava* Tard.			
	I		6963		Madagascar
I	II	*Cyathea boivini* Mett. var. *humblotii* C. Chr.			
	I		6963		Madagascar
R	II	*Cyathea boliviana* R. Tryon *12612*			
	R		12616		Bolivia *12612*
I	II	*Cyathea borbonica* Desv. var. *laevigata* Bonap.			
	I		6963		Madagascar
I	II	*Cyathea borbonica* Desv. var. *pesvilleana* C. Chr.			
	I		6963		Madagascar
I	II	*Cyathea borbonica* Desv. var. *simulans* (Baker) C. Chr.			
	I		6963		Madagascar
V	II	*Cyathea brevipinna* Baker			
	V		14227		Australia - NSW - Lord Howe Is. *14227*
V	II	*Cyathea brownii* Domin *19108*			
	V				Australia - Norfolk Is.
V	II	*Cyathea bunnemeijerii* Alderw.			
	V				Malaysia - Sarawak
V	II	*Cyathea caracasana* (Klotzsch) Domin var. *maxonii* (Maxon) R. Tryon *12612*			
	V		14244		Costa Rica *14244*
	V		16317		Panama *16317*
R	II	*Cyathea carrii* Holttum			
	R				Papua New Guinea
I	II	*Cyathea catillifera* Holttum			
	I				Papua New Guinea
R	II	*Cyathea christii* Copel.			
	R				Philippines
R	II	*Cyathea cicatricosa* Holttum			
	R				New Caledonia
R	II	*Cyathea cinerea* Copel. *10278*			
	R				Philippines *10278*
V	II	*Cyathea coactilis* Holttum			
	V				Papua New Guinea
V	II	*Cyathea cocleana* Stolze *12491*			
	V		16317		Panama *12625*
R	II	*Cyathea concinna* (Baker ex Jenman) Jenman *12491*			
	R		12616		Jamaica (Blue Mts.) *12615*
I	II	*Cyathea costalisora* Copel.			
	I				Papua New Guinea
I	II	*Cyathea costularis* Bonap.			
	I		6963		Madagascar
I	II	*Cyathea costulisora* Domin			
	I				Indonesia - Sumatra
R	II	*Cyathea cuatrecasasii* (R. Tryon) *12491*			
	R		12616		Colombia (central) *12619*
R	II	*Cyathea curranii* Copel. *10278*			
	R				Philippines *10278*
R	II	*Cyathea cyclopodium* (R. Tryon) Lellinger *12111*			
	R		12616		Venezuela *12111*
I	II	*Cyathea decrescens* Mett. var. *decrescens*			
	I		6963		Madagascar
I	II	*Cyathea decrescens* Mett. var. *hirsutifolia* C. Chr.			
	I		6963		Madagascar
I	II	*Cyathea deminuens* Holttum			
	I				Indonesia - Sumatra
R	II	*Cyathea demissa* (C. Morton) A.R. Smith ex Lell. var. *demissa* *12111*			
	R				Venezuela *12111*
R	II	*Cyathea demissa* (C. Morton) A.R. Smith ex Lell. var. *thysanolepis* (D. Barrington) *12491*			
	R				Venezuela *11211*
I	II	*Cyathea dicksonioides* Holttum			
	I				Papua New Guinea
I	II	*Cyathea dimorpha* (Christ) Copel.			
	I				Indonesia - Sulawesi
R	II	*Cyathea dissoluta* Baker ex Jenman *12612*			
	R		12616		Jamaica *12612*
V	II	*Cyathea doctersii* Alderw.			
	V				Indonesia - Sumatra
I	II	*Cyathea dregei* Kunze var. *polyphlebia* C.			

		Chr.	
I		6963	Madagascar

I II *Cyathea dregei* Kunze var. *segregata* C.
     Chr.
 I   6963 Madagascar

I II *Cyathea dryopteroides* Maxon *12491*
 I   8058 Puerto Rico *8058*

R II *Cyathea dudleyi* R. Tryon *12612*
 R 12616 Peru *12612*

R II *Cyathea edanoi* Copel.
 R   Philippines

R II *Cyathea estelae* (Riba) Proctor *12491*
 R 12616 Jamaica *12622*

V II *Cyathea excavata* Holttum
 V   Malaysia - Peninsular Malaysia

E II *Cyathea exilis* Holttum *20681, 9282*
 E 20681 Australia - Queensland *9282*

R II *Cyathea falcata* (Kuhn) Domin *12111*
 R 14244 Panama *14244*
 R 12111 Colombia *12111*

R II *Cyathea ferruginea* Christ
 R   Philippines

R II *Cyathea fusca* Baker
 R   Papua New Guinea

I II *Cyathea glaberrima* Holttum
 I   Papua New Guinea (D'entrecasteaux Is.)

V II *Cyathea gregaria* (Brause) Domin
 V   Papua New Guinea

E II *Cyathea hainanensis* Ching
 E   China

R II *Cyathea halconensis* Christ *20093*
 R   Philippines *20093*

R II *Cyathea haughtii* (Maxon) R. Tryon *12612*
 R 12616 Colombia *12612*

R II *Cyathea heliophila* R. Tryon *10538*
 R 10538 Ecuador *10538*

V II *Cyathea hodgeana* Proctor *12491*
 V 12616 Dominica *8767*

R II *Cyathea hookeri* Thwaites *10251*
 R 16162 Sri Lanka *10251*

R II *Cyathea horridula* Copel.
 R   Papua New Guinea

R II *Cyathea hotteana* C. Chr. & Ekman *12491*
 R 12616 Dominican Republic *10569*
 R 12616 Haiti *10569*

V II *Cyathea howeana* Domin
 V 14227 Australia - NSW - Lord Howe Is. *14227*

I II *Cyathea humbertiana* Domin
 I   6963 Madagascar

I II *Cyathea imbricata* Alderw.
 I   Papua New Guinea

V II *Cyathea impar* R. Tryon *12612*
 V 10538 Panama *12612*

R II *Cyathea inaequalis* Holttum
 R   Papua New Guinea

V II *Cyathea incisoserrata* Copel.
 V   Malaysia - Peninsular Malaysia
 V   Malaysia - Sarawak

V II *Cyathea insulana* Holttum

V   Papua New Guinea (D'entrecasteaux Is.)

V II *Cyathea insularum* Holttum
 V   Papua New Guinea (Louisiade Arch.)

R II *Cyathea intramarginalis* (Wind.) Lellinger *12111*
 R 12616 Venezuela *12111*

I II *Cyathea isaloensis* C. Chr.
 I   6963 Madagascar

E II *Cyathea kermadecensis* Oliver *19106*
 E 19305 New Zealand - Kermadec Is. *19106*

R II *Cyathea klossii* Ridley
 R   Papua New Guinea

I II *Cyathea lastii* Baker
 I   6963 Madagascar

V II *Cyathea latevagans* (Baker) Domin *12111*
 V   Colombia *11211*

R II *Cyathea latipinnula* Copel. *10278*
 R   Philippines *10278*

R II *Cyathea lepifera* (J. Smith) Copel. *20015*
 R 17617 China - Fujian (Xiamen) *11139*
 R 17617 Taiwan *11139*
 R   Philippines *17617*
 R 20017 Japan (Ryukyu Islands) *20017*

Ex/E II *Cyathea leprieurii* (Kunze) Domin *12491*
 Ex/E 12616 French Guiana *12625*

I II *Cyathea leptochlamys* Baker
 I   6963 Madagascar

I II *Cyathea ligulata* Baker
 I   6963 Madagascar

I II *Cyathea loerzingii* Holttum
 I   Indonesia - Sumatra

I II *Cyathea longipinnata* Bonap.
 I   6963 Madagascar

R II *Cyathea macarthurii* (F. Muell.) Baker
 R 14225 Australia - NSW - Lord Howe Is. *14225*

R II *Cyathea macropoda* Domin *14665*
 R   Indonesia - Sumatra

I II *Cyathea madagascarica* Bonap.
 I   6963 Madagascar

V II *Cyathea magnifolia* Alderw.
 V   Indonesia - Sumatra

I II *Cyathea marattioides* Willd.
 I   6963 Madagascar

R II *Cyathea marginata* (Brause) Domin
 R   Papua New Guinea

R II *Cyathea masapilidensis* Copel.
 R   Philippines

R II *Cyathea media* Wagn. & Grether
 R   Papua New Guinea

I II *Cyathea melanocaula* Desv.
 I   6963 Madagascar

I II *Cyathea melleri* (Baker) Domin
 I   6963 Madagascar

R II *Cyathea microchlamys* Holttum *10278*
 R   Philippines *10278*

I II *Cyathea micropelidota* Copel.
 I   Fiji

R II *Cyathea microphylla* Mett. *12612*
 R   Peru (south) *12612*

Pteridopsida: Cyatheaceae: *Cyathea*

R II *Cyathea modesta* (Baker) Copel.
    R   Indonesia - Sumatra

V II *Cyathea moseleyi* Baker
    V   Papua New Guinea - Bismarck Arch.

R II *Cyathea mucilagina* R.C. Moran *14244*
    R   *14244* Costa Rica *14244*
    R   *14244* Ecuador *14244*
    R   *14244* Peru *14244*

R II *Cyathea multisegmenta* R. Tryon *12612*
    R   *12616* Peru *12612*

R II *Cyathea nanna* (D. Barrington) Lellinger *12111*
    R   *12616* Guyana *11211*

R II *Cyathea negrosiana* Christ
    R   Philippines

I II *Cyathea nigropaleata* Holttum
    I   Papua New Guinea

E II *Cyathea nilgirensis* Holttum *14708*
    E   India - Kerala (Palghat; Silent Valley)
                11347
    E   India - Tamil Nadu *11347*

R II *Cyathea nockii* Jenman *12491*
    R   *12616* Jamaica *12617*

R II *Cyathea nodulifera* R.C. Moran *14244*
    R   *14244* Costa Rica *14244*
    R   *14244* Panama *14244*

V II *Cyathea obliqua* Copel. *20093*
    V   Philippines *20093*

V II *Cyathea ogurae* (Hayata) Domin *11163*
    V   *19134* Japan - Ogasawara-shoto (Chichizima I.)
                11163

I II *Cyathea orthogonalis* Bonap.
    I   *6963* Madagascar

V II *Cyathea pallidipaleata* Holttum
    V   Indonesia - Sulawesi

R II *Cyathea papuana* (Ridley) Alderw.
    R   Papua New Guinea

R II *Cyathea parianensis* (Wind.) Lellinger *12111*
    R   *12616* Venezuela (Paria Peninsula) *12621*

V II *Cyathea parvipinna* Holttum
    V   Papua New Guinea

I II *Cyathea patellifera* Alderw.
    I   Indonesia - Sumatra

E II *Cyathea pectinata* Ching & S.H. Wu
    E   China

R II *Cyathea peladensis* (Hieron.) Domin *10538*
    R   *12616* Colombia *12612*
    R   *10538* Ecuador *10538*

I II *Cyathea perpunctulata* (Alderw.) Domin
    I   Indonesia - Sumatra

I II *Cyathea perrieriana* C. Chr.
    I   *6963* Madagascar

E II *Cyathea petiolulata* Ching & S.H. Wu
    E   China

R II *Cyathea phalaenolepis* (C. Chr.) Domin *12111*
    R   *20035* Colombia (Pacific coasts) *11211*
    R   *20035* Ecuador (Pacific coasts) *11211*

R II *Cyathea phegopteroides* (Hook.) Domin *12111*
    R   Peru *11211*

R II *Cyathea physolepidota* Alston
    R   Papua New Guinea

I II *Cyathea pilosula* Tard.
    I   *6963* Madagascar

I II *Cyathea plagiostegia* Copel.
    I   Fiji

R II *Cyathea pruinosa* Rosenstock
    R   Papua New Guinea

E II *Cyathea pseudogigantea* Ching & S.H. Wu
    E   China

R II *Cyathea pseudomuelleri* Holttum
    R   Papua New Guinea

V II *Cyathea pseudonanna* (L.D. Gómez) Lellinger *11714*
    V   *16317* Panama *11714*

R II *Cyathea punctulata* Alderw.
    R   Indonesia - Sumatra

R II *Cyathea pycnoneura* Holttum
    R   Papua New Guinea

I II *Cyathea quadrata* Baker var. *ivohibensis* C. Chr.
    I   *6963* Madagascar

I II *Cyathea quadrata* Baker var. *quadrata*
    I   *6963* Madagascar

I II *Cyathea recurvata* (Brause) Domin
    I   Papua New Guinea

R II *Cyathea robinsonii* Copel. *20093*
    R   Philippines *20093*

R II *Cyathea robusta* (C. Moore) Holttum
    R   *14225* Australia - NSW - Lord Howe Is. *14225*

R II *Cyathea roraimensis* Domin (Domin) *12349*
    R   *12616* Guyana *12349*

R II *Cyathea rufescens* Domin *12111*
    R   *12616* Peru *12618*

R II *Cyathea rufopannosa* Christ
    R   Philippines

R II *Cyathea rupestris* Maxon *12111*
    R   *12616* Colombia *10569*

R II *Cyathea saccata* Christ
    R   Indonesia - Sulawesi

R II *Cyathea sagittifolia* (Hook.) Domin *12491*
    R   Trinidad & Tobago

R II *Cyathea sarasinorum* Holttum
    R   Indonesia - Sulawesi

I II *Cyathea scandens* (Brause) Domin
    I   Papua New Guinea

R II *Cyathea schlechteri* (Brause) Domin
    R   Papua New Guinea

I II *Cyathea schliebenii* Reim.
    I   Tanzania

V II *Cyathea sechellarum* Mett.
    V   Seychelles (granitic)

R II *Cyathea senex* Alderw.
    R   Indonesia - Sumatra

I II *Cyathea serratifolia* Baker
    I   *6963* Madagascar

R II *Cyathea setifera* Holttum
    R   Indonesia - Moluccas

R II *Cyathea setulosa* Copel.
    R   Philippines

V II *Cyathea sibuyanensis* Copel. *20093*

	V		Philippines *20093*	
I	II	*Cyathea similis* C. Chr.		
		I	*6963* Madagascar	
R	II	*Cyathea simplex* R. Tryon *12612*		
		R	*12616* Venezuela *12612*	
R	II	*Cyathea singularis* (Stolze) *12491*		
		R	*12616* Colombia (Putamayo) *12625*	
R	II	*Cyathea sinuata* Hook. & Grev. *10251*		
		R	*16162* Sri Lanka *10251*	
R	II	*Cyathea sipapoensis* (R. Tryon) Lellinger *12111*		
		R	*12616* Venezuela *12621*	
I	II	*Cyathea stelligera* Holttum		
		I	New Caledonia	
R	II	*Cyathea steyermarkii* R. Tryon *12612*		
		R	*12616* Venezuela *12612*	
V	II	*Cyathea strigillosa* (Maxon) Domin *12491*		
R	II	*Cyathea strigosa* Christ		
		R	Indonesia - Sulawesi	
I	II	*Cyathea subincisa* C. Chr.		
		I	*6963* Madagascar	
R	II	*Cyathea tenuicaulis* Domin		
		R	Papua New Guinea	
V	II	*Cyathea ternatea* Alderw.		
		V	Indonesia - Moluccas	
R	II	*Cyathea teysmannii* Copel.		
		R	Indonesia - Sulawesi	
E	II	*Cyathea tinganensis* Ching & S.H. Wu		
		E	China	
R	II	*Cyathea trachypoda* Alderw.		
		R	Indonesia - Sumatra	
V	II	*Cyathea tripinnatifida* Roxb.		
		V	Indonesia - Moluccas	
E	II	*Cyathea tsangii* Ching & S.H. Wu		
		E	China	
I	II	*Cyathea tsaratananensis* Tard.		
		I	*6963* Madagascar	
I	II	*Cyathea tsilotsilensis* Tard.		
		I	*6963* Madagascar	
R	II	*Cyathea tuyamae* H. Ohba *8622*		
		R	*19135* Japan - Kazan Retto (Minami-Iwojima) *8622*	
R	II	*Cyathea urbanii* Brause *12491*		
		R	*12616* Dominican Republic *10569*	
R	II	*Cyathea vandeusenii* Holttum		
		R	Papua New Guinea	
R	II	*Cyathea venezuelensis* A. Reid Smith ex Lellinger *12111*		
		R	Venezuela *11211*	
R	II	*Cyathea verrucosa* Holttum		
		R	Indonesia - Sumatra	
I	II	*Cyathea viguieri* Tard.		
		I	*6963* Madagascar	
R	II	*Cyathea vilhelmii* Domin *12612*		
		R	*12616* Peru *12612*	
R	II	*Cyathea weatherbyana* (C. Morton) C. Morton *11117*		
		R	*11117* Ecuador - Galapagos *11117*	
R	II	*Cyathea wendlandii* (Mett. ex Kuhn) Dominnn *12111*		
		V	*12111* Costa Rica *11211*	

	R		*12111* Panama *11211*	
R	II	*Cyathea williamsii* (Maxon) Domin *12111*		
		R	Venezuela *11211*	
I	II	*Cyathea zakamenensis* Tard.		
		I	*6963* Madagascar	
R	II	*Cyathea zamboangana* Copel.		
		R	Philippines	

Davalliaceae

Number of genera:	6-10	
Number of species:	130	
Recorded threatened species:	1	(< 1%)

Pantropical and temperate.

E		*Davallia puketi* *19305*	
	E	*19305* New Zealand - North Is. *19305*	

Dennstaedtiaceae

Number of genera:	18	
Number of species:	486	
Recorded threatened species:	15	(3%)

Pantropical.

R		*Lindsaea kawabatae* Kurata *11163*	
	R	*20511* Taiwan *20511*	
	R	*11163* Japan *11163*	
I		*Lindsaea latifrons* Kramer *17371*	
	I	*12468* Peru *12468*	
R		*Lindsaea malabarica* (Beddome) Baker ex C. Chr. *11494*	
	R	*13883* India - Kerala (Peermade; Silent Valley) *11355*	
	R	*13883* India - Madhaya Pradesh (Bastar) *11355*	
	R	*13883* India - Tamil Nadu (Salem; Yercaud; Shevaroy) *11355*	
R		*Lindsaea repanda* Kunze *11163*	
	R	*11163* Japan *11163*	
E		*Lindsaea repens* (Bory) Thwaites var. *macraeana* (Hook. & Arn.) Mett. ex Kuhn *20850*	
	E	*20850* U.S. - Hawaii *20850*	
R		*Lindsaea securifolia* Presl var. *kusukusensis* (Hayata) Shieh *20511*	
	R	*20511* Taiwan *20511*	
I		*Lindsaea spruceana* Kuhn *17371*	
	I	*12468* Peru *12468*	
R		*Lindsaea tenera* Dryander *5376*	
	R	India - Andaman Is. (South & Little Andamans) *11356*	
	R	India - Nicobar Is. (Katchal & Great Nicobar) *11356*	
R		*Microlepia calvescens* (Wall.) Presl var. *intramarginalis* (Tagawa) Sheih *20511*	
	R	*20511* Taiwan *20511*	
I		*Microlepia majuscula* (Lowe) T. Moore *10251*	
	I	*16162* Sri Lanka *10251*	
R		*Microlepia taiwaniana* Tagawa *20511*	
	R	*20511* Taiwan *20511*	
I		*Paesia taiwanensis* Shieh *20511*	
	I	*20511* Taiwan *20511*	
R		*Sphenomeris clavata* (L.) Maxon *20850*	
	V	*20850* U.S. - Florida *20850*	
	I	*20883* Puerto Rico *20883*	
	I	*20883* USA - Virgin Is. *20883*	

V   *Sphenomeris minutula* Kurata *11163*
    V   *11163* Japan *11163*

R   *Tapeinidium acuminatum* Kramer *10278*
    R   Philippines *10278*

Dicksoniaceae

Number of genera: 3 - 7
Number of species: 41
Recorded threatened species: 4   (9%)

Montane tropical and temperate.

I   II   *Cibotium cumingii* Kunze *12238*
       I   *12238* Philippines *12238*

V   II   *Dicksonia berteriana* (Colla) Hook. *20883*
       V   *20883* Chile *20883*

V   II   *Dicksonia externa* Skottsb. *19116*
       V   *19125* Chile - Juan Fernandez Is. *19116*

V   II   *Thyrsopteris elegans* Kunze *20045*
       V   *19125* Chile - Juan Fernandez Is. *19116*

Dryopteridaceae

Number of genera: 20 - 47
Number of species: 464
Recorded threatened species: 75   (16%)

Temperate; tropical.

R   *Acrorumohra subreflexipinna* (Ogata) H.Ito *20511*
    R   *20511* Taiwan *20511*

R   *Arachniodes carvifolia* (Kunze) Ching *20850*
    I   *20850* U.S. - Hawaii *20850*

V   *Arachniodes dimorphophylla* (Hayata) Ching *11163*
    V   *11163* Japan *11163*

R   *Arachniodes hekiana* Kurata *11163*
    R   *11163* Japan *11163*

R   *Arachniodes pseudorepens* Nakaike *11163*
    R   *11163* Japan *11163*

R   *Arachniodes repens* Kurata *11163*
    R   *11163* Japan *11163*

E   *Ctenitis canacae* Holttum *20776*
    E   *20771* Mauritius (Brise Fer) *10720*

E   *Ctenitis cumingii* Holtum *19185*
    E   *19185* Pitcairn (Pitcairn Island) *19185*

R   *Ctenitis dubia* (Copel.) Copel. *11269*
    R   Philippines (Leyte Forest, Mahagnao) *11269*

R   *Ctenitis iriomotensis* (H. Ito) Nakaike *11163*
    R   *11163* Japan *11163*

R   *Ctenitis lorenceii* Holtt. *5852*
    R   *5852* Mauritius - Rodrigues *5852*

E   *Ctenitis mearnsii* Copel. *11272*
    E   Philippines (Pauai & Mt Pulog, Benguet) *11272*

R   *Ctenitis microlepigera* (Nakai) Ching *11163*
    R   *11163* Japan *11163*

Ex/E   *Ctenitis paleolata* Copel. *11270*
    Ex/E   Philippines (Pauai, Benguet Province) *11270*

R   *Ctenitis pleiosorus* (Hook.f.) C. Morton *11117*
    R   Ecuador - Galapagos *11117*

R   *Ctenitis psamalensis* A. Reid Smith *9001*

    R   *9001* Guatemala *9001*
    R   *9001* Mexico *9001*

R   *Ctenitis sinii* (Ching) Ching *11163*
    R   *11163* Japan *11163*

E   *Ctenitis squamigera* (Hook. & Arn.) Copeland *20850*
    E   *20850* U.S. - Hawaii *20850*

V   *Cyrtomium microindusium* Kurata *11163*
    V   *11163* Japan *11163*

I   *Cyrtomium taiwanense* Tagawa *20511*
    I   *20511* Taiwan *20511*

R   *Dryopteris ardechensis* Fraser-Jenkins *20528*
    R   *20528* France (south) *20528*

Ex/E   *Dryopteris ascensionis* (Hook.) Kuntze *3204*
    Ex/E   *3204* Ascension Is. *3204*

E   *Dryopteris cognata* (C. Presl) Kuntze *18997*
    E   *18997* St Helena *18997*

I   *Dryopteris corleyi* Fraser-Jenk. *10270, 20171*
    I   *20874* Spain (Cantabrian coast) *10270*

R   *Dryopteris crinalis* (Hook. & Arn.) C. Christens. *20850*
    R   *20850* U.S. - Hawaii *20850*

I   *Dryopteris enneaphylla* (Bak.) C. Chr. var. *pseudosieboldii* (Hayata) Tagaw *20511*
    I   *20511* Taiwan *20511*

V   *Dryopteris gamblei* (Hope) C. Chr. *14708*
    V   *14708* Bhutan *14708*
    V   *14708* India - Meghalaya *14708*
    V   *14708* India - Uttar Pradesh *14708*
    V   *14708* India - West Bengal *14708*

R   *Dryopteris hadanoi* Kurata *11163*
    R   *11163* Japan *11163*

R   *Dryopteris insularis* Kodama *11163*
    R   *11163* Japan *11163*

R   *Dryopteris napoleonis* (Bory) Kuntze
    R   *18997* St Helena *18997*

R   *Dryopteris pallida* (Bory) C.Chr. ex Maire & Petitm. ssp. *balearica* (Litard.) Fraser Jenkins *20171*
    R   Spain - Balearic Is.

V   *Dryopteris rossii* C. Christens. *20850*
    E   *20850* U.S. - Arizona *20850*
    I   *20850* U.S. - Michigan *20850*

E   *Dryopteris sandwicensis* (Hook. & Arn.) C. Christens. *20850*
    I   *20850* U.S. - Hawaii *20850*

R   *Dryopteris shiroumensis* Kurata & Nakamura *11163*
    R   *11163* Japan *11163*

R   *Dryopteris sparsa* (D.Don) Kuntze *20681*
    R   *20681* Australia - Queensland *20681*

Ex   *Dryopteris speluncae* (L.) Underwood
    Ex   Bermuda

R   *Dryopteris squamiseta* (Hook) Kuntze *7926*
    R   Equatorial Guinea - Bioko

R   *Dryopteris tsugiwoi* Kurata *11163*
    R   *11163* Japan *11163*

V   *Dryopteris tsutuiana* Kurata *11163*
    V   *11163* Japan *11163*

R   *Lastreopsis calantha* (Endl.) Tind. *11649*
    R   *19108* Australia - Norfolk Is. *14288*

R   *Lastreopsis grayi* D.L.Jones *20681*

	R	20681	Australia - Queensland *20681*
R	***Lastreopsis nephrodioides*** (Baker) Tind.		
	R	*14225*	Australia - NSW - Lord Howe Is. *14225*
R	***Lastreopsis silvestris*** D.A.Smith ex Tindale *20681*		
	I	*20681*	Australia - New South Wales *20681*
	I	*20681*	Australia - Queensland *20681*
R	***Lastreopsis tinarooensis*** Tindale *20681*		
	R	*20681*	Australia - Queensland *20681*
V	***Lastreopsis walleri*** Tindale *20681*		
	V	*20681*	Australia - Queensland *20681*
Ex	***Lastreopsis wattii*** (Beddome) Tagawa *11494*		
	Ex	*11494*	India - Manipur *11494*
R	***Polybotrya sorbifolia*** Mett. ex Kuhn *11714*		
	R	*9426*	Costa Rica *11714*
	R	*14244*	Brazil *14244*
	R	*14244*	Colombia *14244*
	R	*14244*	Venezuela *14244*
E	***Polystichum aleuticum*** C. Christens. *20850, 21309*		
	E	*20850*	U.S. - Alaska *20850*
I	***Polystichum anomalum*** (Hook. & Arn.) J. Smith *10251*		
	I	*16162*	Sri Lanka *10251*
E	***Polystichum calderonense*** Proctor *20883, 19002*		
	I	*20883*	Puerto Rico *20883*
E	***Polystichum drepanum*** (Swartz) C. Presl *17891*		
	E		Portugal - Madeira *17891*
V	***Polystichum dudleyi*** Maxon *20850*		
	I	*20850*	U.S. - California *20850*
E	***Polystichum falcinellum*** (Swartz) C. Presl		
	E		Portugal - Madeira
R	***Polystichum haleakalense*** Brack. *20850*		
	I	*20850*	U.S. - Hawaii *20850*
R	***Polystichum hillebrandii*** Carruthers *20850, 8328*		
	I	*20850*	U.S. - Hawaii *20850*
Ex/E	***Polystichum kwakiutlii*** D.H. Wagner *20850*		
	I	*20850*	Canada - British Columbia *20850*
R	***Polystichum moorei*** Christ *19108*		
	R	*14223*	Australia - NSW - Lord Howe Is. *14223*
R	***Polystichum munchii*** (Christ) C. Chr. *9001*		
	R	*9001*	Guatemala *9001*
	R	*9001*	Mexico *9001*
E	***Polystichum obai*** Tagawa *11163*		
	E	*11163*	Japan *11163*
R	***Polystichum ohmurae*** Kurata *11163*		
	R	*11163*	Japan *11163*
R	***Polystichum otomasui*** Kurata *11163*		
	R	*11163*	Japan *11163*
R	***Polystichum setigerum*** (K. Presl) K. Presl *20850, 10701*		
	E	*20850*	Canada - British Columbia *20850*
	V	*20850*	U.S. - Alaska *20850*
R	***Polystichum shimurae*** Kurata *11163*		
	R	*11163*	Japan *11163*
V	***Polystichum tetragonum*** Fée *19116, 21305*		
	V	*19125*	Chile - Juan Fernandez Is. *19116*
Ex/E	***Polystichum wattii*** (Bedd.) C. Chr. *14708*		
	Ex/E	*14708*	India - Manipur *14708*
R	***Polystichum whiteleggei*** Watts		
	R	*14225*	Australia - NSW - Lord Howe Is. *14225*
R	***Polystichum yaeyamense*** (Makino) Makino *11163*		

	R	*11163*	Japan *11163*
I	***Pteridrys syrmatica*** (Willd.) C. Chr. & Ching *16162*		
	I	*16162*	Sri Lanka *16162*
I	***Pteridrys zeylanica*** Ching *16162*		
	I	*16162*	Sri Lanka *16162*
V	***Rumohra berteroana*** (Colla) R.A. Rodr. *19116, 21305*		
	V	*19125*	Chile - Juan Fernandez Is. *19116*
R	***Sorolepidium glaciale*** Christ *11139*		
	R	*17617*	China - Sichuan (Muli; Daocheng) *11139*
	R	*17617*	China - Xizang Zizhiqu (Bemi) *11139*
	R	*17617*	China - Yunnan (Lijiang, Zhongdian) *11139*
Ex/E	***Tectaria amesiana*** A.A. Eat. *20850*		
	I	*20850*	U.S. - Florida *20850*
V	***Tectaria chattagramica*** (C.B. Clarke) Ching *14872*		
	V	*14872*	Bangladesh *14872*
E	***Tectaria estremeriana*** Proctor & A.M. Evans *20883*		
	I	*20883*	Puerto Rico *20883*
I	***Tectaria thwaitesii*** (Beddome) Ching *10251*		
	I	*16162*	Sri Lanka *10251*
R	***Tectaridium primitivum*** Copel.		
	R		Philippines
R	***Triplophyllum fraternum*** (Mett.) Holttum var. *elongatum* Holttum *11612*		
	R		Sao Tome & Principe *11612*

Gleicheniaceae

Number of genera:	2-4
Number of species:	140
Recorded threatened species:	4 (2%)

Pantropical.

V	***Dicranopteris linearis*** (Burm. f.) Underw. var. *sebastiana* Panigr. & Dixit *14782*		
	V	*14782*	India - Tamil Nadu *14782*
R	***Gleichenia abscida*** Rodway *20681*		
	R	*20681*	Australia - Tasmania *20681*
R	***Gleichenia litoralis*** (Philippi) C. Chr. *5595*		
	R	*5595*	Chile *5595*
R	***Gleichenia weatherbyi*** Fosb.		
	R		Micronesia - Caroline Is. (Ponape, Kusaie)

Grammitidaceae

Number of genera:	14
Number of species:	500
Recorded threatened species:	65 (13%)

Pantropical and South temperate.

E	***Adenophorus periens*** Bishop *20850*		
	E	*20850*	U.S. - Hawaii *20850*
I	***Ctenopteris glandulosa*** J. Smith *10251*		
	I	*16162*	Sri Lanka *10251*
V	***Ctenopteris malayana*** Parris *9280*		
	V	*14876*	Malaysia - Peninsular Malaysia (G. Ulu Kali) *9280*
R	***Ctenopteris nhatrangensis*** (C. Chr.) Tard. *6057*		
	R		Vietnam *6057*
R	***Ctenopteris sakaguchiana*** (Koidz.) H. Ito *11163*		
	R	*11163*	Japan *11163*
I	***Ctenopteris thwaitesii*** (Beddome) Sledge *10251*		
	I	*16162*	Sri Lanka *10251*

V	*Ctenopteris walleri* (Maiden & Betche) *20681*	
	V	*20681* Australia - Queensland *20681*
I	*Grammitis ahenobarba* Parris	
	I	Indonesia - Irian Jaya
R	*Grammitis albosetosa* (Bailey) Parris *20681*	
	R	*20681* Australia - Queensland *20681*
R	*Grammitis alepidota* M. Price *10278*	
	R	Philippines (Mt Banahaw & Mt Canloon) *10278*
R	*Grammitis ceratocarpa* Copel.	
	R	Indonesia - Irian Jaya (Mt Carstensz & Wilhelmina)
	R	Papua New Guinea (Huon & Mt Wilhelm)
R	*Grammitis clavipila* Parris	
	R	Papua New Guinea
R	*Grammitis collina* Parris	
	R	Papua New Guinea (Western Highlands)
I	*Grammitis coredrosora* (Alderw.) Copel.	
	I	Indonesia - Irian Jaya
R	*Grammitis crenulata* Parris	
	R	Papua New Guinea (Mt Dayman & Mt Suckling)
I	*Grammitis crinifera* Parris	
	I	Indonesia - Irian Jaya (Mt Helling)
R	*Grammitis curtipila* Parris	
	R	Papua New Guinea
	R	*14803* Solomon Is. - South *14803*
R	*Grammitis demissa* Parris	
	R	Papua New Guinea - Bismarck Arch.
I	*Grammitis dictymioides* Copel.	
	I	Indonesia - Irian Jaya
R	*Grammitis diminuta* (Baker) Copel.	
	R	*14225* Australia - NSW - Lord Howe Is. *14225*
I	*Grammitis ebenina* (Maxon) Tard. *18997*	
	E	*18997* St Helena *18997*
	I	*19213* Tropical Africa *19213*
I	*Grammitis excelsa* Parris	
	I	Indonesia - Irian Jaya (Ilim Valley)
R	*Grammitis fabaespora* (Copel.) Seymour *9012*	
	R	*19757* Panama *9012*
I	*Grammitis glossophylla* Parris	
	I	Papua New Guinea (Rossel I.)
I	*Grammitis habbemensis* Copel.	
	I	Indonesia - Irian Jaya
I	*Grammitis hispida* Copel.	
	I	Indonesia - Irian Jaya
R	*Grammitis imberbis* Parris	
	R	Papua New Guinea (Mt Scorpion, Star Mts)
I	*Grammitis inconstans* (Alderw.) Copel.	
	I	Indonesia - Irian Jaya
R	*Grammitis knightii* (Copel.) Seymour *9012*	
	R	*19757* Costa Rica *9012*
I	*Grammitis meijer-dreesii* Copel.	
	I	Indonesia - Irian Jaya
R	*Grammitis merrillii* (Copel.) Copel.	
	R	Indonesia - Irian Jaya (Waigeo)
	R	Indonesia - Moluccas
	R	Philippines (Palawan)
I	*Grammitis mesocarpa* (Alderw.) Copel.	
	I	Indonesia - Irian Jaya
I	*Grammitis montana* Parris	

	I	Papua New Guinea (Mt Sarawaket)
R	*Grammitis murrayana* (C. Chr.) Copel.	
	R	Papua New Guinea
R	*Grammitis nigropaleata* Copel.	
	R	Papua New Guinea (Morobe Province)
R	*Grammitis nipponica* Tagawa & Iwatsuki *11163*	
	R	*11163* Japan *11163*
R	*Grammitis nudicarpa* Copel.	
	R	*14225* Australia - NSW - Lord Howe Is. *14225*
I	*Grammitis papuensis* (Alderw.) Parris	
	I	Indonesia - Irian Jaya (Mt Carstensz)
R	*Grammitis podocarpa* (Maxon) Seymour *9012*	
	R	*19757* Panama *9012*
R	*Grammitis pseudolocellata* Parris	
	R	Papua New Guinea (Mt Dayman)
R	*Grammitis rawlingsii* Parris	
	R	*19305* New Zealand - North Is. *19305*
I	*Grammitis reducta* (Alderw.) Copel.	
	I	Indonesia - Irian Jaya (Mt Doorman Top)
I	*Grammitis reptans* Parris	
	I	Indonesia - Irian Jaya (Mt Wilhelmina)
I	*Grammitis rupestris* Parris	
	I	Papua New Guinea (Laloki R.)
R	*Grammitis salticola* Parris	
	R	Papua New Guinea (Mt Giluwe)
R	*Grammitis silvicola* Parris	
	R	Papua New Guinea (Mt Piora)
I	*Grammitis subreticulata* (Copel.) Copel.	
	I	Papua New Guinea
R	*Grammitis taeniophylla* Parris	
	R	Papua New Guinea (Mt Hunstein, E. Sepik)
E	*Grammitis tenuis* Parris	
	E	Papua New Guinea (Ekuti Range)
R	*Grammitis tmesipteris* (Copel.) Seymour *9012*	
	R	*9426* Costa Rica *9012*
R	*Grammitis tomaculosa* Parris	
	R	Indonesia - Irian Jaya
	R	Papua New Guinea
R	*Grammitis torricelliana* (Brause) Parris	
	R	Papua New Guinea
	R	Philippines
R	*Grammitis trichopoda* (F. Muell. & Baker) Copel.	
	R	Papua New Guinea
R	*Grammitis trogophylla* Copel.	
	R	Papua New Guinea
R	*Grammitis tuberculata* Parris	
	R	Papua New Guinea (W. Highlands & Enga Prov.)
R	*Grammitis tuyamae* H. Ohba *8622*	
	R	*19134* Japan - Kazan Retto (Minami-Iwojima) *8622*
I	*Grammitis viridula* (Alderw.) Parris	
	I	Indonesia - Irian Jaya
	I	Indonesia - Java
	I	Indonesia - Sulawesi
	I	Indonesia - Sumatra
	I	Papua New Guinea
I	*Grammitis wallii* (Beddome) Copel. *10251*	
	I	*16162* Sri Lanka *10251*
R	*Grammitis wattsii* Copel.	

	R	*14225* Australia - NSW - Lord Howe Is. *14225*
R	*Grammitis zurquina* (Maxon ex Copel.) Seymour *9012*	
	V	*20895* Vietnam *20985*
	R	*19757* Costa Rica *9012*
R	*Lellingeria isidrensis* (Maxon ex Cople.) A. Reid Smith & R. Moran *14244*	
	R	*9426* Costa Rica *14244*
R	*Xiphopteris ascensionensis* (Hieron.) Cronk *9997*	
	R	*3204* Ascension Is. *3204*
R	*Xiphopteris exilis* Parris *9280*	
	R	*14876* Malaysia - Peninsular Malaysia (G. Belumut, Johor) *9280*
R	*Xiphopteris sparsipilosa* (Holttum) Holttum *9280*	
	R	*14876* Malaysia - Peninsular Malaysia (Perak; Pahang; Selangor) *9280*
R	*Xiphopteris villosissima* (Hook.) Alston var. *laticellulata* Benl *10672*	
	R	Cameroon (Cameroon Mt) *10672*

Hymenophyllaceae

Number of genera:	5-10
Number of species:	600
Recorded threatened species:	27 (4%)

Mostly tropical montane and South temperate.

R	*Abrodictyum boninense* Tagawa & Iwatsuki *8037*	
	R	*19134* Japan - Kazan Retto *8622*
	E	*19134* Japan - Ogasawara-shoto *8037*
R	*Callistopteris bauerana* (Endl.) Copel. *19108*	
	R	Australia - NSW - Lord Howe Is.
	R	*19108* Australia - Norfolk Is. *19108*
E	*Crepidomanes boninense* (Tagawa & Iwatsuki) Iwatsuki *11163*	
	E	*11163* Japan *11163*
R	*Crepidomanes majoriae* (Watts) Wakef. *20681*	
	R	*20681* Australia - Queensland *20681*
R	*Crepidomanes subclathratum* (Iwatsuki) Iwatsuki *11163*	
	R	*11163* Japan *11163*
R	*Hymenophyllum capillaceum* Roxb. *18997*	
	R	*18997* St Helena *18997*
R	*Hymenophyllum capurroi* de la Sota *16336*	
	R	*16336* Argentina *16336*
	R	*20176* Argentina - Tucuman *20176*
V	*Hymenophyllum cuneatum* Kunze var. *cuneatum* *19116, 21305*	
	V	*21305* Chile - Juan Fernandez Is. (R.Crusoe & A.Selkirk Is.) *19116*
	V	*21305* Chile *21305*
R	*Hymenophyllum eboracense* Croxall *20681*	
	R	*20681* Australia - Queensland *20681*
R	*Hymenophyllum gracilescens* Domin *20681*	
	R	*20681* Australia - Queensland *20681*
R	*Hymenophyllum howense* Brownlie	
	R	*14225* Australia - NSW - Lord Howe Is. *14225*
R	*Hymenophyllum kerianum* Watts *20681*	
	R	*20681* Australia - Queensland *20681*
R	*Hymenophyllum moorei* Baker	
	R	*14225* Australia - NSW - Lord Howe Is. *14225*
R	*Hymenophyllum poilanei* Tard. & C. Chr. *6057*	
	R	Vietnam *6057*
R	*Hymenophyllum pumilum* Hook. & Baker *20681*	

	R	*20681* Australia - New South Wales *20681*
V	*Hymenophyllum rugosum* C. Chr. & Skottsb. *19116*	
	V	*21305* Chile - Juan Fernandez Is. *19116*
E	*Hymenophyllum tayloriae* Farrar & Raine *20850*	
	I	*20850* U.S. - Alabama *20850*
	E	*20850* U.S. - North Carolina *20850*
	I	*20850* U.S. - South Carolina *20850*
R	*Hymenophyllum whitei* Goy *20681*	
	R	*20681* Australia - Queensland *20681*
R	*Reediella endlicheriana* (Presl) Pichi-Serm. *20681*	
	R	*20681* Australia - Queensland *20681*
V	*Serpyllopsis caespitosa* (Gaudich.) C. Chr var. *fernandeziana* C. Chr & Skottsb. *19116, 21305*	
	V	*21305* Chile - Juan Fernandez Is. (R.Crusoe & A.Selkirk Is.) *19116*
R	*Trichomanes draytonianum* Brack. *20850*	
	R	*20850* U.S. - Hawaii *20850*
V	*Trichomanes exsectum* Kunze *19116, 21305*	
	V	*21305* Chile - Juan Fernandez Is. (R.Crusoe & A.Selkirk Is.) *19116*
	V	*21305* Chile *21305*
E	*Trichomanes ingae* C. Chr. *19116, 21305*	
	E	*19116* Chile - Juan Fernandez Is. *19116*
E	*Trichomanes philippianum* Sturm *19116, 21305*	
	E	*19116* Chile - Juan Fernandez Is. *19116*
R	*Trichomanes ridleyi* Copel.	
	R	*14876* Malaysia - Peninsular Malaysia *14876*
R	*Trichomanes speciosum* Willd. *8000, 20171*	
	E	*20528* France *20528*
	R	*11495* Ireland (south-west) *11495*
	V	*19806* Italy (Toscana - Apuan Alps) *19997*
	R	*20874* Spain (Cádiz & Atlantic coast) *8000*
	V	*20587* United Kingdom *19232*
	I	Portugal - Azores *12032*
	V	*14161* Portugal - Madeira *12032*
	R	*19806* Spain - Canary Is. *12032*
I	*Trichomanes wallii* Thwaites ex Trimen *10251*	
	I	*16162* Sri Lanka *10251*

Lomariopsidaceae

Number of genera:	7-8
Number of species:	615
Recorded threatened species:	17 (2%)

Pantropical to warm temperate.

R	*Bolbitis simplex* R.C. Moran *14244*	
	R	*14244* Panama *14244*
R	*Edanyoa difformis* Copel.	
	R	Philippines
R	*Elaphoglossum beddomei* Sledge *13883*	
	R	*13883* India - Tamil Nadu (Nilgiri and Anamally mountains) *13883*
R	*Elaphoglossum calanasanicum* Holttum *10278*	
	R	Philippines *10278*
E	*Elaphoglossum dimorphum* (Hook. & Grev.) T. Moore *18997*	
	E	*19213* St Helena *18997*
R	*Elaphoglossum drakensbergense* Schelpe *20604*	
	R	*20604* South Africa - Natal *20604*
	R	*20604* South Africa - Orange Free State *20604*
R	*Elaphoglossum insulare* C. Chr.	
	R	*19941* Tristan da Cunha (Gough Is.) *19941*

R   *Elaphoglossum negrosensis* Holttum *10278*
   R   Philippines *10278*

E   *Elaphoglossum nervosum* (Bory) Christ *18997*
   E   *19213*   St Helena *18997*

E   *Elaphoglossum nilgiricum* Kraj. ex Sledge *11494*
   E   *11494*   India - Kerala (Silent Valley) *11494*
   E   *11494*   India - Tamil Nadu (Nilgiri Hills) *11494*

R   *Elaphoglossum pellucidum* Gaud. *20850*
   I   *20850*   U.S. - Hawaii *20850*

R   *Elaphoglossum pendulifolium* Tagawa *20511*
   R   *20511*   Taiwan *20511*

E   *Elaphoglossum serpens* Maxon & Morton ex Maxon *20883, 19002*
   I   *20883*   Puerto Rico *20883*

V   *Elaphoglossum stigmatolepis* (Fee) Moore *13883*
   V   *13883*   India (Nilgiri & Pulney Hills) *13883*

R   *Elaphoglossum tosaense* (Yatabe) Makino *11163*
   R   *11163*   Japan *11163*

R   *Elaphoglossum yoshinagae* (Yatabe) Makino *11163*
   R   *11163*   Japan *11163*

R   *Microstaphyla furcata* (L.f.) Fee *18997*
   R   *18997*   St Helena *18997*

Loxsomataceae

Number of genera: 2
Number of species: 4
Recorded threatened species: 2   (50%)

New World tropical; New Zealand.

V   *Loxsoma cunninghamii* R. Br. ex Cunn. *86*
   V   New Zealand - North Is.

E   *Loxsomopsis costaricensis* Christ *9593*
   E   *9593*   Costa Rica *9593*

Marattiaceae

Number of genera: 4
Number of species: 204
Recorded threatened species: 11   (5%)

Tropical and warm.

E   *Angiopteris chauliodonta* Copel. *8049*
   E   *19185*   Pitcairn (Pitcairn Island) *8049*

R   *Angiopteris magna* Ching ex Tard. & C. Chr. *6057*
   R   Vietnam *6057*

R   *Archangiopteris cadieri* Tard. & C. Chr. *6057*
   R   Vietnam *6057*

E   *Archangiopteris henryi* Christ & Giesenh. *11139*
   E   *17617*   China - Yunnan (Jinping & Pingbian) *11139*

R   *Archangiopteris henryi* Christ & Gies. var. *somai* (Hayata) Tagawa *20511*
   R   *20511*   Taiwan *20511*

E   *Archangiopteris itoi* Shieh *20511*
   E   *20511*   Taiwan *20511*

R   *Archangiopteris subintegra* Hayata *6057*
   R   *20985*   Vietnam *6057*

V   *Christensenia assamica* (Griffith) Ching *13883*
   V   *20756*   China - Yunnan (south) *20756*
   V   *5374*   India - Arunachal Pradesh *5374*
   V   *13883*   India - Assam *13883*

R   *Danaea carillensis* Christ *9026*

   R   *11992*   Costa Rica *9026*

R   *Danaea plicata* Christ *11714*
   R   *12111*   Costa Rica *11714*

I   *Marattia boninensis* Nakai *8037*
   I   Japan - Kazan Retto *8622*
   V   *19134*   Japan - Ogasawara-shoto *8037*

R   *Marattia purpurascens* Vriese *3204*
   R   *3204*   Ascension Is. *3204*

Marsileaceae

Number of genera: 3
Number of species: 67
Recorded threatened species: 8   (11%)

Temperate and tropical.

E   *Marsilea azorica* Launert & Paiva *12032, 20171*
   E   Portugal - Azores *12032*

I   *Marsilea batardae* Launert *17891, 20171*
   V   *20076*   Portugal *12032*
   I   *20874*   Spain *20648*

V   *Marsilea botryocarpa* Ballard
   V   Kenya

E   *Marsilea glomerata* Launert
   E   Kenya

I   *Marsilea megalomania* Launert
   I   Kenya

V   *Marsilea schelpeana* Launert *20604*
   V   *20604*   South Africa - Cape Province *20604*

R   *Marsilea vestita* Hook & Grev. ssp. *tenuifolia* (Engelm. ex A. Braun) D.M. Johnson *20850*
   V   *20850*   U.S. - Texas *20850*

E   *Marsilea villosa* Kaulfuss *20850*
   E   *20850*   U.S. - Hawaii *20850*

Oleandraceae

Number of genera: 4
Number of species: 91
Recorded threatened species: 2   (2%)

Tropical to warm temperate.

V   *Arthropteris altescandens* (Colla) J. Em. *19116*
   V   *19125*   Chile - Juan Fernandez Is. *19116*

V   *Oleandra ejurana* C.J. Adams *7926*
   V   *6072*   Ghana *7926*

Ophioglossaceae

Number of genera: 3
Number of species: 81
Recorded threatened species: 23   (28%)

Temperate with some tropical.

E   *Botrychium acuminatum* W.H. Wagner *20850, 15826*
   E   *20850*   Canada - Ontario *20850*
   E   *20850*   U.S. - Michigan *20850*

R   *Botrychium atrovirens* (Sahashi) *11163*
   R   *11163*   Japan *11163*

R   *Botrychium campestre* W.H. Wagner & Farrar ex W.H. & F. Wagner *20850, 15827*
   E   *20850*   Canada - Alberta *20850*
   I   *20850*   Canada - New Brunswick *20850*
   E   *20850*   Canada - Ontario *20850*
   E   *20850*   Canada - Quebec *20850*

E   *20850*   Canada - Saskatchewan *20850*
E   *20850*   U.S. - Colorado *20850*
V   *20850*   U.S. - Iowa *20850*
V   *20850*   U.S. - Michigan *20850*
V   *20850*   U.S. - Minnesota *20850*
I   *20850*   U.S. - Montana *20850*
I   *20850*   U.S. - Nebraska *20850*
Ex/E   *20850*   U.S. - New York *20850*
E   *20850*   U.S. - North Dakota *20850*
E   *20850*   U.S. - Oregon *20850*
I   *20850*   U.S. - South Dakota *20850*
E   *20850*   U.S. - Wisconsin *20850*
E   *20850*   U.S. - Wyoming *20850*

V   *Botrychium echo* **W.H. Wagner** *20850*
   I   *20850*   U.S. - Arizona *20850*
   V   *20850*   U.S. - Colorado *20850*
   E   *20850*   U.S. - Utah *20850*

E   *Botrychium gallicomontanum* **Farrar &**
   Johnson-Groh *20850*
   I   *20850*   U.S. - Minnesota (Frenchman's Bluff)
       20850

R   *Botrychium hesperium* **(Maxon & Clausen) W.H. Wagner &**
   Lellinger *20850, 14352*
   E   *20850*   Canada - Alberta *20850*
   E   *20850*   Canada - British Columbia *20850*
   E   *20850*   Canada - Ontario *20850*
   E   *20850*   Canada - Saskatchewan *20850*
   I   *20850*   U.S. - Arizona *20850*
   V   *20850*   U.S. - Colorado *20850*
   E   *20850*   U.S. - Michigan *20850*
   E   *20850*   U.S. - Montana *20850*
   E   *20850*   U.S. - Utah *20850*
   I   *20850*   U.S. - Wyoming *20850*

E   *Botrychium lineare* **W.H. Wagner** *20850*
   I   *20850*   Canada - New Brunswick *20850*
   V   *19095*   Canada - Ontario *19095*
   I   *20850*   Canada - Quebec *20850*
   I   *20850*   U.S. - California *20850*
   E   *20850*   U.S. - Colorado *20850*
   I   *20850*   U.S. - Idaho *20850*
   E   *20850*   U.S. - Montana *20850*
   I   *20850*   U.S. - Oregon *20850*
   E   *20850*   U.S. - Utah *20850*

R   *Botrychium microphyllum* **(Sahashi)** *11163*
   R   *11163*   Japan *11163*

R   *Botrychium minus* **(Hara)** *11163*
   R   *11163*   Japan *11163*

R   *Botrychium montanum* **W.H. Wagner** *20850, 14352*
   E   *20850*   Canada - British Columbia *20850*
   V   *20850*   U.S. - California *20850*
   V   *20850*   U.S. - Montana *20850*
   E   *20850*   U.S. - Oregon *20850*
   R   *20850*   U.S. - Washington *20850*

R   *Botrychium mormo* **W.H. Wagner** *20850*
   I   *20850*   Canada - Quebec *20850*
   E   *20850*   U.S. - Michigan *20850*
   R   *20850*   U.S. - Minnesota *20850*
   E   *20850*   U.S. - Wisconsin *20850*

V   *Botrychium pallidum* **W.H. Wagner** *20850*
   I   *20850*   Canada - Manitoba *20850*
   E   *20850*   Canada - Ontario *20850*
   Ex/E   *20850*   Canada - Quebec *20850*
   I   *20850*   Canada - Saskatchewan *20850*
   V   *20850*   U.S. - Colorado *20850*
   I   *20850*   U.S. - Maine *20850*
   V   *20850*   U.S. - Michigan *20850*
   I   *20850*   U.S. - Minnesota *20850*

V   *Botrychium paradoxum* **W.H. Wagner** *20850, 13153*
   E   *20850*   Canada - Alberta *20850*
   E   *20850*   Canada - British Columbia *20850*

I   *20850*   Canada - Saskatchewan *20850*
E   *20850*   U.S. - Colorado *20850*
E   *20850*   U.S. - Montana *20850*
E   *20850*   U.S. - Oregon *20850*
E   *20850*   U.S. - Utah *20850*
E   *20850*   U.S. - Washington *20850*

E   *Botrychium pseudopinnatum* **W.H. Wagner** *20850, 15826*
   E   *20850*   Canada - Ontario *20850*

V   *Botrychium pumicola* **Coville ex Underwood** *20850,*
   19095
   V   *20850*   U.S. - Oregon *20850*

R   *Botrychium rugulosum* **W.H. Wagner** *20850, 14352*
   V   *20850*   Canada - Ontario *20850*
   I   *20850*   Canada - Prince Edward Is. *20850*
   V   *20850*   Canada - Quebec *20850*
   I   *20850*   U.S. - Connecticut *20850*
   R   *20850*   U.S. - Michigan *20850*
   I   *20850*   U.S. - Minnesota *20850*
   E   *20850*   U.S. - New York *20850*
   V   *20850*   U.S. - Vermont *20850*
   V   *20850*   U.S. - Wisconsin *20850*

E   *Botrychium simplex* **E. Hitchc. var.** *compositum*
   (Lasch) Milde *20850*
   I   *20850*   U.S. - California *20850*
   I   *20850*   U.S. - Pennsylvania *20850*
   Ex/E   *20850*   U.S. - Wyoming *20850*

V   *Ophioglossum concinnum* **Brack.** *20850, 11878*
   V   *20850*   U.S. - Hawaii *20850*

E   *Ophioglossum fernandezianum* **C. Chr.** *19116*
   E   *19125*   Chile - Juan Fernandez Is. *19116*

R   *Ophioglossum kawamurae* **Tagawa** *11163*
   R   *11163*   Japan *11163*

R   *Ophioglossum lineare* **Schltr. & Brause** *20681*
   R   *20681*   Australia - Northern Territory *20681*

R   *Ophioglossum namegatae* **Nishida & Kurita** *11163*
   R   *11163*   Japan *11163*

R   *Ophioglossum parvum* **Nishida & Kurita** *11163*
   R   *11163*   Japan *11163*

Osmundaceae

Number of genera:	3	
Number of species:	18	
Recorded threatened species:	2	(11%)

Temperate and tropical.

V   *Leptopteris moorei* **(Baker) Christ**
   V   *14226*   Australia - NSW - Lord Howe Is. *14226*

I   *Osmunda collina* **Sledge** *10251*
   I   *16162*   Sri Lanka *10251*

Parkeriaceae

Number of genera:	1	
Number of species:	4	
Recorded threatened species:	1	(25%)

Pantropical.

R   *Ceratopteris gaudichaudii* **Brongn.**
   R   *18338*   U.S. - Guam *18338*

Plagiogyriaceae

Number of genera: 1
Number of species: 36
Recorded threatened species: 2   (5%)

Tropical and subtropical, excluding Africa.

R   *Plagiogyria japonica* Nakai var. *pseudojaponica*
         (Nakaike) Iwatsuki *11163*
         R   *11163* Japan *11163*

R   *Plagiogyria yakumonticola* Nakaike *11163*
         R   *11163* Japan *11163*

Polypodiaceae

Number of genera: 40-47
Number of species: 1,068
Recorded threatened species: 26   (2%)

Cosmopolitan especially tropical.

R   *Colysis elegans* Kurata *11163*
         R   *11163* Japan *11163*

R   *Colysis evrardii* Tard. *6057*
         R   Vietnam *6057*

I   *Crypsinus okamotoi* (Tagawa) Tagawa *20511*
         I   *20511* Taiwan *20511*

V   *Crypsinus yakuinsularis* Tagawa *11163*
         V   *11163* Japan *11163*

E   *Dendroglossa minutula* (Fee) Copel. *11494*
         E   *11494* India - Meghalaya (Khasi hills) *11494*

V   *Drynaria meeboldii* Rosenst. *13883*
         V   *13883* India - Manipur *13883*

E   *Holcosorus bisulcatus* (Hook.) Ching *14708*
         E   India - Arunachal Pradesh *11258*

R   *Lepisorus boninensis* (Ching) Ching *11163*
         R   *11163* Japan *11163*

R   *Lepisorus mikawanus* Kurata *11163*
         R   *11163* Japan *11163*

I   *Leptochilus wallii* (Baker) C. Chr. *10251*
         I   *16162* Sri Lanka (Deniyaya, Morawak Korale)
                  10251

I   *Loxogramme confertifolia* Nakai *20511*
         I   *20511* Taiwan *20511*

R   *Microsorium pappei* (Mett. ex Kuhn) Tardieu *20604*
         R   *20604* Mozambique *20604*
         R   *20604* Zimbabwe *20604*
         R   *20604* South Africa - Cape Province *20604*
         R   *20604* South Africa - Natal *20604*

R   *Microsorum baithoensis* Tu *6057*
         R   *15734* Vietnam *6057*

R   *Microsorum membranifolium* (R.Br.) Ching *20681*
         R   *20681* Australia - Queensland *20681*

R   *Microsorum takhtajanii* Tu *6057*
         R   *15734* Vietnam *6057*

V   *Neocheiropteris palmatopedata* (Baker) Christ *11139*
         V   *17617* China - Guizhou *11139*
         V   *17617* China - Sichuan *11139*
         V   *17617* China - Yunnan *11139*

R   *Neocheiropteris sapaensis* Tu *6057*
         R   *15734* Vietnam *6057*

Ex/E   *Platycerium grande* (J. Smith ex Fee) Presl *10278*
         Ex/E *12238* Philippines (Mt San Cristobal, Quezon)

11271

Ex   *Platycerium ridleyi* *20099*
         Ex   *20099* Indonesia - Kalimantan *20099*
         Ex   *20099* Indonesia - Sumatra *20099*
         Ex   *20099* Malaysia - Peninsular Malaysia *20099*
         Ex   *20099* Singapore *20099*

R   *Pleopeltis nicklesii* (Tard.) Alston *7926*
         R   Guinea (Keniekounde) *7926*

V   *Polypodium amamianum* Tagawa *11163*
         V   *11163* Japan *11163*

E   *Polypodium espinosae* Weath. *19536, 21305*
         E   *21305* Chile *21305*

V   *Polypodium intermedium* Colla ssp.
         intermedium *19116, 21305*
         V   *19125* Chile - Juan Fernandez Is. *19116*

I   *Polypodium viridulum* Alderw.
         I   Indonesia - Irian Jaya

R   *Pyrrosia liebuschii* (Hieron.) Schelpe *5926*
         R   *5926* Tanzania (east Usambaras Mts.) *5926*

V   *Synammia intermedia* (Colla) Kunkel
         V   Chile - Juan Fernandez Is.

R   *Thayeria cornucopia* Copel. *10149*
         R   Philippines (north) *10196*

Pteridaceae

Number of genera: 6-7
Number of species: 259
Recorded threatened species: 19   (7%)

Pantropical.

E   *Pteris adscensionis* Sw. *3204*
         E   *3204* Ascension Is. *3204*

I   *Pteris bakeri* C. Chr. *17371*
         I   *12468* Peru *12468*

R   *Pteris barombiensis* Hieron.
         R   Cameroon (Barombi)

V   *Pteris berteroana* Agardh *19116, 21305*
         V   *21305* Chile - Juan Fernandez Is. (R.Crusoe & A.Selkirk
                  Is.) *19116*

R   *Pteris boninensis* H. Ohba *11163*
         R   *11163* Japan *11163*

I   *Pteris confusa* T. Walker *10251*
         I   *16162* Sri Lanka *10251*

R   *Pteris ekemae* Benl *10672*
         R   Cameroon (Cameroon mt) *10672*

I   *Pteris gongalensis* T. Walker *10251*
         I   *16162* Sri Lanka *10251*

R   *Pteris kawabatae* Kurata *11163*
         R   *11163* Japan *11163*

R   *Pteris kidoi* Kurata *11163*
         R   *20511* Taiwan *20511*
         R   *11163* Japan *11163*

R   *Pteris kingiana* Endl. *19108*
         R   *19108* Australia - Norfolk Is. (Coastal cliffs)
                  14288

E   *Pteris lidgatei* (Baker) Christ *20850*
         E   *20850* U.S. - Hawaii *20850*

V   *Pteris nakasimae* Tagawa *11163*
         V   *11163* Japan *11163*

V   *Pteris paleacea* Roxb. *18997*

V		*19213* St Helena *18997*	

I	*Pteris praetermissa* T. Walker *10251*
	I *16162* Sri Lanka *10251*

I	*Pteris reptans* T. Walker *10251*
	I *16162* Sri Lanka *10251*

R	*Pteris yakuinsularis* Kurata *11163*
	R *11163* Japan *11163*

E	*Pteris yamatensis* Tagawa *11163*
	E *11163* Japan *11163*

R	*Pteris zahlbruckneriana* Endl. *19108*
	R *19108* Australia - Norfolk Is. *19108*

Schizaeaceae

Number of genera:	4 - 5
Number of species:	143
Recorded threatened species:	3 (2%)

Pantropical and southern warm temperate.

R	*Anemia bartlettii* Mickel *9009*
	R *19758* Belize *9009*

V	*Anemia wrightii* Baker *20850*
	V *20850* U.S. - Florida *20850*

I	*Schizaea pusilla* Pursh *20883, 20850*
	I *20850* Canada - New Brunswick *20850*
	I *20850* Canada - Nova Scotia *20850*
	I *20883* France - St Pierre & Miquelon *20883*
	E *20850* U.S. - Delaware *20850*
	R *20850* U.S. - New Jersey *20850*
	E *20850* U.S. - New York *20850*
	E *20883* Peru *20883*

Thelypteridaceae

Number of genera:	30
Number of species:	1,000
Recorded threatened species:	41 (4%)

Pantropical; some subtropical and temperate.

I	*Amauropelta hakgalensis* Holttum *10251*
	I *16162* Sri Lanka *10251*

I	*Amauropelta odontosora* (Bonap.) Holttum
	I Côte d'Ivoire

E	*Chingia australis* Holttum *20681*
	E *20681* Australia - Queensland *20681*

R	*Chingia pricei* Holttum *10278*
	R Philippines *10278*

R	*Chingia urens* Holttum *10278*
	R Philippines *10278*

V	*Christella clarkei* (Bedd.) Holtt. *14782*
	V *14782* India - Sikkim *14782*

V	*Christella kaumaunica* Holttum *14782*
	V *14782* India - Uttar Pradesh *14782*

R	*Coryphopteris didymochlaenoides* (Clarke) Holtt. *14782*
	R *14782* India - Meghalaya *14782*

R	*Cyclogramma squamaestipes* (Clarke) Tagawa *14782*
	R *14782* India - Sikkim *14782*

E	*Goniopteris bermudiana* (Baker) Gilbert
	E Bermuda

R	*Haplodictyum bulusanicum* Holttum *10278*
	R Philippines *10278*

R	*Metathelypteris decipiens* (Clarke) Ching *14782*

R	*14782* India - Meghalaya (Khasi hills) *14782*	
R	*14782* India - West Bengal (Darjeeling Himalayas) *14782*	

R	*Oreopteris elwesii* (Bak.) Holttum *13883*
	R *13883* India - Sikkim (near Lachen) *13883*

R	*Pneumatopteris oppositifolia* (Hook.) Holttum
	R Equatorial Guinea - Bioko *11610*
	R Equatorial Guinea - Pagalu *11610*

R	*Pneumatopteris venulosa* (Hook.) Holttum
	R Equatorial Guinea
	R Equatorial Guinea - Bioko
	R Equatorial Guinea - Pagalu

I	*Pronephrium gardneri* Holttum *10251*
	I *16162* Sri Lanka *10251*

I	*Pronephrium longipetiolatum* (K. Iwats.) Holtt. *20511*
	I *20511* Taiwan *20511*

E	*Pseudocyclosorus gamblei* Holttum & Grimes *14782*
	E *14782* India - Tamil Nadu (Nilgiri & Palni Hills) *14782*

E	*Pseudocyclosorus griseus* (Baker) Holttum & Grimes *14782*
	E *14782* India - Tamil Nadu *14782*

R	*Pseudophegopteris dianae* (Hook.) Holttum *18997*
	R *18997* St Helena *18997*

V	*Stenogramma himalaica* (Ching) K. Iwats. *14782*
	V *14782* India (NW Himalayas) *14782*

R	*Thelypteris albicaulis* (Fée) A.R. Smith *9016*
	R *19757* Mexico *9016*

Ex	*Thelypteris altissima* (Holttum) Vorster *20604*
	Ex *20604* South Africa - Natal *20604*

R	*Thelypteris banaensis* C. Chr. *6057*
	R Vietnam *6057*

R	*Thelypteris boninensis* (Kodama ex Koidz.) Iwatsuki *11163*
	R *11163* Japan *11163*

E	*Thelypteris boydiae* (Eat.) K. Iwats. *20850*
	E *20850* U.S. - Hawaii *20850*

R	*Thelypteris crassiuscula* (C. Chr. & Maxon) Lellinger *11714*
	R *11992* Costa Rica *11714*

R	*Thelypteris ensiformis* (C. Chr.) R. Tryon *11714*
	R *11992* Costa Rica *11714*

E	*Thelypteris inabonensis* Proctor *20883, 19002*
	E *20883* Puerto Rico *20883*

R	*Thelypteris knysnaensis* N.C.Anthony & Schelpe *20604*
	R *20604* South Africa - Cape Province *20604*

V	*Thelypteris mombachensis* L.D. Gómez *9025*
	V *9426* Nicaragua *9025*

V	*Thelypteris oroniensis* L.D. Gómez *9017*
	V *9426* Costa Rica *9017*

E	*Thelypteris pilosa* (M. Martens & Galeotti) Crawf. var. *alabamensis* Crawford *20850, 14704*
	V *20850* U.S. - Alabama *20850*

R	*Thelypteris puberula* A.R. Sm. var. *sonorensis* A.R. Sm. *20883, 20850, 19002*
	V *20850* U.S. - Arizona *20850*
	V *20850* U.S. - California *20850*
	R *20883* Mexico *20883*

R	*Thelypteris sclerophylla* (Poepp. ex Spreng.) Morton *20850*

E	20850	U.S. - Florida *20850*
I	20883	Puerto Rico *20883*

R   *Thelypteris tuerckheimii* (J.D. Smith) Reed *9016*
     R   *19757* Guatemala *9016*
     R   *19757* Mexico *9016*

E   *Thelypteris verecunda* Proctor *20883, 19002*
     E   *20883* Puerto Rico *20883*

E   *Thelypteris yaucoensis* Proctor *20883, 19002*
     I   *20883* Puerto Rico *20883*

I   *Trigonospora angustifrons* Sledge *10251*
     I   *16162* Sri Lanka *10251*

I   *Trigonospora glandulosa* Sledge *10251*
     I   *16162* Sri Lanka *10251*

I   *Trigonospora obtusiloba* Sledge *10251*
     I   *16162* Sri Lanka *10251*

I   *Trigonospora zeylanica* (Ching) Sledge *10251*
     I   *16162* Sri Lanka *10251*

Vittariaceae

Number of genera:		8-9
Number of species:		113
Recorded threatened species:		2 (1%)

Pantropical to warm temperate.

R   *Antrophyum annetii* (Jeanp.) Tard.
     R   Cameroon

R   *Vittaria schaeferi* Hieron.
     R   Cameroon (Manengouba & Ebolowa)

Woodsiaceae

Number of genera:		18-20
Number of species:		705
Recorded threatened species:		30 (4%)

Temperate to montane tropics.

E   *Athyrium atratum* Beddome *11494*
     E   *11494* India - Manipur *11494*

R   *Athyrium christensenii* Tard. *6057*
     R   Vietnam *6057*

R   *Athyrium duthei* (Bedd.) *14708*
     R   *14708* India - Sikkim *14708*
     R   *14708* India - Uttar Pradesh *14708*

R   *Athyrium excelsius* Nakai *15957*
     R   *15923* Korea, South (Mt. Chiri, Mt. Paekyang, Yangdeog) *15957*

R   *Athyrium masamunei* Serizawa *11163*
     R   *11163* Japan *11163*

R   *Athyrium nikkoense* Makino *11163*
     R   *11163* Japan *11163*

R   *Athyrium viridescentipes* Kurata *11163*
     R   *11163* Japan *11163*

R   *Athyrium yakusimense* Kurata *11163*
     R   *11163* Japan *11163*

R   *Cystoathyrium chinense* Ching *11139*
     R   *17617* China - Sichuan (Erlangshan) *11139*

V   *Cystopteris douglasii* Hook. *20850*
     V   *20850* U.S. - Hawaii *20850*

R   *Deparia bonincola* (Nakai) M. Kato *8622*
     R   *19134* Japan - Kazan Retto (Minami-Iwojima) *8622*
     R   *19134* Japan - Ogasawara-shoto *8622*

Ex/E   *Deparia kaalaana* (Copeland) M. Kato *20850*
     Ex/E   *20850* U.S. - Hawaii *20850*

V   *Deparia minamitanii* (Serizawa) Kato *11163*
     V   *11163* Japan *11163*

V   *Deparia otomasui* (Kurata) Kato *11163*
     V   *11163* Japan *11163*

I   *Deparia polyrhizon* (Baker) Sledge *10251*
     I   *16162* Sri Lanka *10251*

R   *Diplazium amamianum* Tagawa *11163*
     R   *11163* Japan *11163*

I   *Diplazium cognatum* (Hieron) Sledge *10251*
     I   *16162* Sri Lanka *10251*

Ex   *Diplazium laffanianum* (Baker) C. Chr.
     Ex   Bermuda

R   *Diplazium lonchophyllum* Kunze *20850*
     E   *20850* U.S. - Louisiana *20850*

E   *Diplazium longicarpum* Kodama *8037*
     E   *19134* Japan - Ogasawara-shoto *8037*

R   *Diplazium melanochlamys* (Hook.) T. Moore *14225*
     R   *14225* Australia - NSW - Lord Howe Is. *14225*

E   *Diplazium molokaiense* Robins. *20850*
     E   *20850* U.S. - Hawaii *20850*

R   *Diplazium nigropaleaceum* Kunze *18997*
     R   *19213* St Helena *18997*

I   *Diplazium paradoxum* Fee *10251*
     I   *16162* Sri Lanka *10251*

I   *Diplazium prescottianum* (Wallich ex Hook.) Beddome *1144*
     I   *20099* Singapore *20099*

R   *Diplazium tetsuyamanakae* Kurata *11163*
     R   *11163* Japan *11163*

I   *Diplazium zeylanicum* (Hook.) T. Moore *10251*
     I   *16162* Sri Lanka *10251*

R   *Gymnocarpium appalachianum* Pryer *20850*
     I   *20850* U.S. - Maryland *20850*
     E   *20850* U.S. - North Carolina *20850*
     Ex/E   *20850* U.S. - Ohio *20850*
     E   *20850* U.S. - Pennsylvania *20850*
     R   *20850* U.S. - Virginia *20850*
     E   *20850* U.S. - West Virginia *20850*

Ex/E   *Woodsia andersonii* (Beddome) Christ *11262*
     Ex/E   India - Uttar Pradesh (Kali Valley, Kumaon) *11262*

R   *Woodsia cochisensis* Windham *20850*
     I   *20850* U.S. - Arizona *20850*
     E   *20850* U.S. - New Mexico *20850*
     I   *20883* Mexico *20883*

R   *Woodsia kitadakensis* Ohwi *11163*
     R   *11163* Japan *11163*

Gnetopsida

Ephedraceae

Number of genera:		1
Number of species:		40
Recorded threatened species:		1 (2%)

Warm temperate North and South America; warm temperate Eurasia.

R   *Ephedra californica* S.Watson *20883, 20850, 19002*
     I   *20850* U.S. - Arizona *20850*

I		20850	U.S. - California 20850
I		20850	U.S. - Nevada 20850
I		20883	Mexico 20883

R **Ephedra californica** S.Wats. var.
  californica 20850

I		20850	U.S. - Arizona 20850
I		20850	U.S. - California 20850
I		20883	Mexico 20883

V **Ephedra californica** S.Wats. var. *funerea* (Coville
  & Morton) L. Benson 20850

E		20850	U.S. - Arizona 20850
V		20850	U.S. - California 20850
V		20850	U.S. - Nevada 20850

Pinopsida

Araucariaceae

Number of genera:	2
Number of species:	38
Recorded threatened species:	30 (78%)

Southern Hemisphere (excluding Africa) to Indochina and the Philippines.

R **Agathis atropurpurea** B.Hyland 20681, 20316

R		20681	Australia - Queensland 20374

V **Agathis corbassonii** de Laub. 20329

V		20893	New Caledonia 20329

R **Agathis endertii** Meijer Drees 19727

V		18270	Indonesia - Kalimantan 19727
R		18270	Malaysia - Sabah 19727
R		18270	Malaysia - Sarawak 19727

V **Agathis flavescens** Ridley 19727

V		20761	Malaysia - Peninsular Malaysia 19727

V **Agathis kinabaluensis** de Laub. 19727

V		20761	Malaysia - Sabah (Mt Kinabalu) 19727

R **Agathis lanceolata** Lindley ex Warb. 20329

R		20893	New Caledonia 20329

V **Agathis lenticula** de Laub. 19727

V		18270	Malaysia - Sabah (Mt Kinabalu) 19727

I **Agathis macrophylla** (Lindl.) Mast. 20482

I		8836	Solomon Is. - South (Santa Cruz, Utupua & Vanikoro) 20482
I		21021	Vanuatu 20482

R **Agathis microstachya** J.F.Bailey & C.White 20681, 17718

R		20681	Australia - Queensland 20681

V **Agathis montana** de Laub. 20329

V		20913	New Caledonia (Mt Panié) 20437

V **Agathis moorei** (Lindl.) Mast. 20329

V		20893	New Caledonia 20329

V **Agathis orbicula** de Laub. 19727

V		18270	Malaysia - Sabah 19727
V		18270	Malaysia - Sarawak 19727

R **Agathis ovata** (Moore ex Vieill.) Warb. 20329

R		20893	New Caledonia (south) 20329

R **Agathis silbae** de Laub. 20333

R		18270	Vanuatu 20333

R **Agathis spathulata** de Laub. 19727

R		18270	Papua New Guinea (east highlands) 19727

R **Agathis vitiensis** (Seemann) Benth. & Hook.f. 10253

R		18270	Fiji 10253

R **Araucaria angustifolia** (Bertol.) Kuntze 20883, 20438

E		20176	Argentina - Misiones (northeast) 20176
		20883	Bolivia 20883
V		17746	Brazil - Minas Gerais 17746
V		17746	Brazil - Parana 13928
V		20761	Brazil - Rio de Janeiro 10370
V		17746	Brazil - Rio Grande do Sul 13928
V		17746	Brazil - Santa Catarina 13928
V		17746	Brazil - Sao Paulo 17746
V		20761	Paraguay 20883

R I **Araucaria araucana** (Mol.) K. Koch 20883, 15088

V		20176	Argentina - Neuquen 20176
R		20883	Chile 20883

R **Araucaria bernieri** Buchh. 20329

R		20893	New Caledonia 20329

R **Araucaria biramulata** Buchh. 20329

R		20893	New Caledonia 20329

V **Araucaria heterophylla** (Salisb.) Franco 20464

V		20761	Australia - Norfolk Is. (Norfolk and Philip Islands) 20464

V **Araucaria humboldtensis** Buchh. 20329

V		20761	New Caledonia 20329

R **Araucaria laubenfelsii** Corbasson 20329

R		20893	New Caledonia 20329

E **Araucaria luxurians** (Brongn. & Gris) de Laub. 20329

E		20893	New Caledonia 20329

V **Araucaria muelleri** (Carriere) Brongn. & Gris 20329

V		20913	New Caledonia 18270

E **Araucaria nemorosa** de Laub. 20329

E		20893	New Caledonia (Port Boisé) 20329

E **Araucaria rulei** F. Muell. 20329

E		20893	New Caledonia 20329

V **Araucaria schmidii** de Laub. 20329

V		20761	New Caledonia (Mt Panié) 20329

E **Araucaria scopulorum** de Laub. 20329

E		20893	New Caledonia (local on coast) 20329

E **Wollemia noblei** W.Jones & K.Hill ms. 20681

E		20681	Australia - New South Wales 20681

Cephalotaxaceae

Number of genera:	1
Number of species:	7
Recorded threatened species:	5 (71%)

Eastern Himalayas to Japan.

V **Cephalotaxus hainanensis** Li 20358

V		19703	China - Hainan Is. 17617
R		20985	Vietnam 20985

I **Cephalotaxus lanceolata** K.M.Feng 20358

I		20761	China - Yunnan (Gongshan) 11139
I		20761	Myanmar (north) 19703

V **Cephalotaxus mannii** Hook.f. 17617

V		18270	China - Guangdong (Xinyi) 11139
V		18270	China - Guangxi (Rongxian) 11139
E		18270	China - Xizang Zizhiqu (Metue; Zizhiqu) 11139
V		18270	China - Yunnan 11139
V		20761	India - Assam (Mishmi Hills) 18270
V		18270	India - Meghalaya (Khasi Hills; Jaintia Hills) 18270
V		18270	India - Nagaland (Naga Hills) 18270
V		20761	Thailand (north) 19703
V		18270	Vietnam 6057

V **Cephalotaxus oliveri** Masters 17617

V		18270	China - Guangdong (north) 11139

V	*18270*	China - Guangxi *11139*
V	*20761*	China - Guizhou *11139*
V	*18270*	China - Hubei *11139*
V	*18270*	China - Hunan *11139*
V	*18270*	China - Jiangxi *11139*
V	*18270*	China - Sichuan *11139*
V	*18270*	China - Yunnan *11139*
V	*20761*	India (eastern) *20761*
V	*20761*	Vietnam (northern) *6057*

E   *Cephalotaxus wilsoniana* Hayata *20018*

    E   *20761*   Taiwan (north & central) *18270*

Cupressaceae

Number of genera: 18-19
Number of species: 130
Recorded threatened species: 64   (49%)

Cosmopolitan.

V   *Austrocedrus chilensis* (D. Don) Pichi-Serm. & Bizzarri *15088*

    V   *20761*   Argentina (Questrihue) *18270*
    V   *13875*   Chile - Biobio *20761*

R   *Callitris baileyi* C.White *20681, 20318*

    I   *20681*   Australia - New South Wales *18270*
    I   *20681*   Australia - Queensland *18270*

R   *Callitris monticola* J.Garden *20681, 20318*

    I   *20681*   Australia - New South Wales *20316*
    I   *20681*   Australia - Queensland *20316*

V   *Callitris neocaledonica* Dümmer *20329*

    V   *20913*   New Caledonia *20329*

V   *Callitris oblonga* A.Rich. & Rich. *20681, 20316*

    V   *20681*   Australia - New South Wales *20681*

E   *Callitris sulcata* (Parl.) Schltr. *20329*

    E   *20893*   New Caledonia *20329*

V   *Calocedrus formosana* (Florin) Florin *20018*

    V   *20511*   Taiwan (north and central) *20018*

V   *Calocedrus macrolepis* Kurz *11139*

    V   *18270*   China - Hainan Is. *11139*
    V   *18270*   China - Guangxi *11139*
    V   *18270*   China - Guizhou *11139*
    V   *18270*   China - Yunnan *11139*
    V   *18270*   Myanmar (north-east) *18270*
    E   *20985*   Vietnam *6057*

R   *Chamaecyparis formosensis* Matsum. *20018*

    R   *20761*   Taiwan (central and northern parts of Zhongyang Range) *17617*

R   *Chamaecyparis lawsoniana* (A. Murr.) Parl. *20850, 20171*

    I   *20850*   U.S. - California (coastal) *20850*
    R   *20850*   U.S. - Oregon (south-west) *20850*

V   *Chamaecyparis obtusa* Sieb. & Zucc. var. *formosana* (Hayata) Hayata *20018*

    V   *20761*   Taiwan *18270*

R   *Chamaecyparis thyoides* (L.) Britten, Sterns & Poggenburg var. *henryae* (H. L. Li) Little *20346*

    R   *18270*   U.S. - Alabama *18270*
    R   *18270*   U.S. - Florida *18270*
    R   *18270*   U.S. - Mississippi *18270*

V   *Cupressus arizonica* Greene var. *montana* (Wiggins) Little *20346*

    V   *20761*   Mexico - Baja California Peninsula *20457*

R   *Cupressus arizonica* Greene var. *nevadensis* (Abrams) Little *19002*

    R   *18270*   U.S. - California (Piute Mts) *20457*

V   *Cupressus arizonica* Greene var. *stephensonii* (C.B. Wolf) Little *20346*

    V   *18270*   U.S. - California (Cuyamaca Mts) *20457*

E   *Cupressus atlantica* Gaussen *18270*

    E   *20761*   Morocco (southern, near Tizi-n-Test) *10370*

V   *Cupressus bakeri* Jepson *20850*

    V   *20850*   U.S. - California *20850*
    E   *20850*   U.S. - Oregon *20850*

V   *Cupressus cashmeriana* Royle ex Carrière *8477*

    V   *19723*   Bhutan *8477*

V   *Cupressus chengiana* S.Y. Hu *18270*

    V   *17617*   China - Gansu (southern (Min River drainage): Zhouqu; Wudu; Wengxian) *11139*
    V   *17617*   China - Sichuan (north-west) *11139*

E   *Cupressus chengiana* S.Y. Hu var. *jiangeensis* (N. Chao) C.T. Kuan *18270*

    E   *18270*   China - Sichuan *18270*

R   *Cupressus duclouxiana* Hickel *18270*

    R   *18270*   China - Sichuan (southwestern) *18270*
    R   *18270*   China - Xizang Zizhiqu (southeastern) *18270*
    R   *18270*   China - Yunnan *18270*

E   *Cupressus dupreziana* A. Camus *20389*

    E   *18270*   Algeria *20389*

V   *Cupressus gigantea* W. C. Cheng & L.K. Fu *17617*

    V   *20761*   China - Xizang Zizhiqu (southeastern, Tsangpo River valley) *11139*

E   *Cupressus goveniana* Gord. *20850*

    E   *20850*   U.S. - California *20850*

E   *Cupressus goveniana* Gord. var. *abramsiana* (C.B. Wolf) Little *20346, 7996*

    E   *20761*   U.S. - California (San Mateo & Santa Cruz mountains) *20346*

E   *Cupressus goveniana* Gord. var. *pygmaea* Lemmon *20346*

    E   *20850*   U.S. - California (Mendocino Co.) *20346*

V   *Cupressus guadalupensis* S.Watson var. *forbesii* (Jepson) Little *20346*

    V   *19723*   U.S. - California (southwestern) *20457*
    V   *19723*   Mexico - Baja California Peninsula *20457*

E   *Cupressus guadalupensis* S.Watson var. *guadalupensis* *18270*

    E   *18270*   Mexico - Guadelupe *18270*

R   *Cupressus lusitanica* Mill. var. *benthamii* (Endl.) Carrière *20344*

    R   *18270*   Mexico - Hidalgo *20344*
    R   *18270*   Mexico - Puebla *20344*
    R   *18270*   Mexico - Veracruz *20344*

R   *Cupressus macnabiana* A. Murr. *20850*

    I   *20850*   U.S. - California *20850*

R   *Cupressus sargentii* Jepson *20850*

    I   *20850*   U.S. - California *20850*

R **I** *Fitzroya cupressoides* (Molina) I. M. Johnston *20883, 15088*

    E   *20761*   Argentina *20883*
    E   *20176*   Argentina - Chubut *20176*
    E   *20176*   Argentina - Neuquen *20176*
    E   *20176*   Argentina - Rio Negro *20176*
    E   *20761*   Chile *20883*

R   *Fokienia hodginsii* (Dunn) Henry & Thomas *11139*

    V   *17617*   China - Fujian (west and northwest)

Pinopsida: Cupressaceae: Fokienia

17617

V	*17617*	China - Guangdong (northern)	*17617*
V	*17617*	China - Guangxi (northeast and south)	*17617*
V	*17617*	China - Guizhou (southeast and northwest)	*17617*
V	*17617*	China - Hunan (Dupang Shan)	*17617*
V	*17617*	China - Jiangxi (east and southwest)	*17617*
V	*17617*	China - Sichuan (south, south-east)	*17617*
V	*17617*	China - Yunnan (southeastern & central)	*17617*
V	*17617*	China - Zhejiang (southern)	*17617*
V	*18270*	Laos (northern)	*17940*
K	*20985*	Vietnam	*18270*

E   *Juniperus barbadensis* **L.** *18270*

E   *18270*   St Lucia (Petit Piton) *18270*

E   *Juniperus bermudiana* **L.** *19407*

E   *18270*   Bermuda *19407*

I   *Juniperus blancoi* **Martínez** *9018*

I   *20761*   Mexico - Durango (El Salto) *9018*
I   *20761*   Mexico - Mexico State (Carmona) *9018*
I   *20761*   Mexico - Sonora (north-east) *9018*

E   *Juniperus brevifolia* **(Seub.) Antoine** *18270, 20171*

E   *20761*   Portugal - Azores *18270*

E   *Juniperus cedrus* **Webb & Berthel.** *18270*

E   *20761*   Portugal - Madeira *18270*
E   *20761*   Spain - Canary Is. (Tenerife, Palma) *18270*

R   *Juniperus centrasiatica* **Komarov** *18270*

R   *18270*   China - Xinjiang Uygur Zizhiqu (Kuen Luen Mts.) *18270*

V   *Juniperus comitana* **Martínez** *9004*

V   *18270*   Guatemala (north) *9004*
V   *18270*   Mexico - Chiapas (Columbretes Is.) *9018*

E   *Juniperus communis* **L. var.** *megistocarpa* **Fern. & St. John** *20850*

I   *20850*   Canada - New Brunswick *20850*
I   *20850*   Canada - Nova Scotia *20850*

R   *Juniperus convallium* **Rehder & Wilson** *18270*

R   *18270*   China - Sichuan (north-west) *18270*
R   *18270*   China - Xizang Zizhiqu (south-east) *18270*

R   *Juniperus convallium* **Rehder & Wilson var.** *microsperma* **(Cheng & Fu) Silba** *18270*

R   *18270*   China - Xizang Zizhiqu (south-east) *18270*

I   *Juniperus deppeana* **Steud. var.** *patoniana* **(Martínez) T.A. Zanoni** *9018*

I   *20761*   Mexico - Durango *9018*

I   *Juniperus deppeana* **Steud. var.** *zacatecensis* **Martínez** *9018*

I   *20761*   Mexico - Durango *9018*
I   *20761*   Mexico - Zacatecas (west) *9018*

V   *Juniperus durangensis* **Martínez** *18270*

V   *18270*   Mexico - Aguascalientes *18270*
V   *18270*   Mexico - Chihuahua *18270*
V   *18270*   Mexico - Durango *18270*
V   *18270*   Mexico - Jalisco *18270*
V   *18270*   Mexico - Sonora *18270*
V   *18270*   Mexico - Zacatecas *18270*

Ex/E   *Juniperus ekmanii* **Florin** *18270*

Ex/E   *18270*   Haiti (Morne la Selle; Morne la Visite) *19407*

V   *Juniperus gamboana* **Martínez** *18270*

V	*20761*	Guatemala (Huehuetenango)	*9018*
V	*20761*	Mexico - Chiapas	*9018*

R   *Juniperus gaussenii* **Cheng** *18270*

R   *18270*   China - Yunnan *18270*

E   *Juniperus gracilior* **Pilg.** *18270*

E   *20761*   Dominican Republic (Constanza) *9018*

E   *Juniperus jaliscana* **Martínez** *20344*

E   *20761*   Mexico - Durango (south) *18270*
E   *20761*   Mexico - Jalisco (north-west) *18270*

R   *Juniperus komarovii* **Florin** *18270*

R   *18270*   China - Sichuan (north) *18270*

I   *Juniperus lucayana* **Britton** *18270*

V   *18270*   Bahamas *19407*
I   *20990*   Cuba (Isla de Pinos) *18270*
Ex   *18270*   Haiti *18270*
V   *18270*   Jamaica *18270*

R   *Juniperus martinezii* **Perez de la Rosa** *20344*

R   *20761*   Mexico - Aguascalientes *20344*
R   *20761*   Mexico - Guanajuato *20344*
R   *20761*   Mexico - Jalisco *9027*

R   *Juniperus pingii* **Cheng ex Y. de Ferré** *18270*

R   *20761*   China - Sichuan (west) *18270*
R   *20761*   China - Yunnan (north-west) *18270*

R   *Juniperus przewalskii* **Komarov** *18270*

R   *20761*   China - Gansu *18270*
R   *20761*   China - Qinghai (east) *18270*
R   *20761*   China - Sichuan (north) *18270*

V   *Juniperus recurva* **Buch-Ham. ex D. Don var.** *coxii* **(Jacks.) Melville** *18270*

V   *18270*   China - Yunnan (north-west) *18270*
V   *20761*   Myanmar (north-west) *20761*

I   *Juniperus standleyi* **Steyerm.** *9004*

I   *20822*   Guatemala *18270*
I   *20822*   Mexico - Chiapas (Tacana volcano) *9018*

I   *Juniperus taxifolia* **Hook. & Arn.** *8038*

I   *20761*   Japan (Ryukyu Is.) *18270*
I   *20761*   Japan - Ogasawara-shoto (Bonin Is.) *8038*

E   *Juniperus urbaniana* **Pilg. & Ekman** *18270*

E   *18270*   Haiti (Pic la Selle) *19407*

V   *Libocedrus austro-caledonica* **Brongn. & Gris** *20329*

V   *20913*   New Caledonia *20409*

E   *Libocedrus chevalieri* **Buchh.** *20329*

E   *20893*   New Caledonia (Mt Humboldt, Mt Kouakoué) *20409*

V   *Libocedrus plumosa* **(D. Don) Sarg.** *18270*

V   *20761*   New Zealand *20326*

E   *Libocedrus yateensis* **Guillaumin** *20329*

E   *20913*   New Caledonia (Yaté river, Ouinné river) *20409*

I   *Microbiota decussata* **Komarov** *5942*

I   *5942*   Russia (Far East) - Khabarovsk *5942*
I   *5942*   Russia (Far East) - Primorye *5942*

E   *Neocallitropsis pancheri* **(Carriere) de Laub.** *20329*

E   *20913*   New Caledonia (South east) *20409*

V   I   *Pilgerodendron uviferum* **(Don) Florin** *10260*

V   *20761*   Argentina (Andes to Tierra del Fuego) *20489*
E   *20176*   Argentina - Chubut *20176*
E   *20176*   Argentina - Neuquen *20176*
E   *20176*   Argentina - Rio Negro *20176*
E   *20176*   Argentina - Santa Cruz *20176*
V   *18270*   Chile (Region X to Tierra del Fuego) *20418*

R	*Platycladus orientalis* (L.f.) Franco *18270*		
	I	5942	Tajikistan *5942*
	I	5942	Uzbekistan *5942*
	R	18270	China - Gansu (south) *18270*
	R	18270	China - Hebei *18270*
	R	18270	China - Henan *18270*
	R	18270	China - Shaanxi (south) *18270*
	R	18270	China - Shanxi *18270*
	R	20761	Iran *20761*

R   *Tetraclinis articulata* (Vahl) Mast. *13351, 20171*

	E	13351	Malta (Maqluba - Qrendi) *13351*
	E	18270	Spain (Cartagena) *20406*
	R	18270	Algeria (north) *20430*
	V	18270	Morocco (north) *20430*
	R	20761	Tunisia *20430*

R   *Thuja koraiensis* Nakai *11139*

	V	17617	China - Jilin (Changbaishan) *11139*
	I	20761	Korea, North (Kogen & south Kankeyo) *20497*
	R	15923	Korea, South (Mt Sorak, Mt Taebaek) *15923*

Ex   *Thuja sutchuenensis* Franchet *11139*

	Ex	18270	China - Sichuan (north-east, near Chengkou) *11139*

E   *Widdringtonia cedarbergensis* Marsh *20604, 20377*

	E	20604	South Africa - Cape Province (Cedarberg Mts.) *20604*

E   *Widdringtonia schwarzii* (Marloth) Mast. *20604, 18270*

	E	20604	South Africa - Cape Province (Willowmore District) *20604*

Pinaceae

Number of genera:	10-12
Number of species:	250
Recorded threatened species:	133 (53%)

Northern Hemisphere, south to Sumatra, Java, Central America and West Indies.

E   *Abies beshanzuensis* M.H. Wu *17617*

	E	18038	China - Zhejiang *8051*

R   *Abies bracteata* (D. Don) D. Don ex Poit. *18270*

	R	18270	U.S. - California *18270*

I   *Abies chengii* Rushforth *18270*

	I	20761	China - Yunnan (north-west) *18270*

V   *Abies chensiensis* Van Tieghem ssp. *chensiensis* *18270*

	V	18270	China - Gansu (south-east) *18270*
	V	19723	China - Henan (Nexiang) *11139*
	V	18270	China - Hubei (west) *18270*
	V	18270	China - Shaanxi (south) *18270*

I   *Abies chensiensis* Van Tieghem ssp. *yulongxueshanensis* Rushforth *18270*

	I	20761	China - Yunnan *2050*

V   *Abies durangensis* Martínez var. *coahuilensis* (I.M. Johnston) Martínez *18270*

	V	20761	Mexico - Coahuila *18270*

E   *Abies fanjingshanensis* W.L. Huang, Y.L. Tu & S.Z. Fang *17617*

	E	18270	China - Guizhou (north-east) *18270*

I   *Abies forrestii* C. Coltm. Rogers var. *georgei* (Orr) Farjon *18270*

	I	20761	China - Sichuan *18270*
	I	20761	China - Xizang Zizhiqu *18270*
	I	20761	China - Yunnan *18270*

V   *Abies fraseri* (Pursh) Poir. *20850, 18270*

	V	20850	U.S. - North Carolina (west) *20850*
	V	20850	U.S. - Tennessee (east) *20850*
	E	20850	U.S. - Virginia (south-west) *20850*

V   *Abies guatemalensis* Rehder *20883*

	V	20883	El Salvador *20883*
	V	20883	Guatemala *20883*
	V	20883	Honduras *20883*
	V	20883	Mexico *20883*

V   I   *Abies guatemalensis* Rehder var. *guatemalensis* *18270*

	V	20761	El Salvador *20376*
	V	20761	Guatemala (west) *20376*
	V	20761	Honduras *20376*
	V	20761	Mexico (south) *20376*

I   I   *Abies guatemalensis* Rehder var. *jaliscana* Martínez *18270*

	I	20761	Mexico - Jalisco *20376*

I   I   *Abies guatemalensis* Rehder var. *tacanensis* (Lundell) Martínez *20344*

	I	20761	Mexico - Chiapas (north) *2790*

V   *Abies hickelii* Flous & Gaussen var. *hickelii* *18270*

	V	20761	Mexico - Chiapas *20344*
	V	20761	Mexico - Guerrero *20344*
	V	20761	Mexico - Oaxaca *20344*

V   *Abies hickelii* Flous & Gaussen var. *oaxacana* (Martínez) Farjon & Silba *18270*

	V	20761	Mexico - Guerrero *2790*
	V	20761	Mexico - Oaxaca *2790*

R   *Abies hidalgensis* Debreczy, Rácz & Guizar *21253*

	R	21253	Mexico - Hidalgo *21253*

R   *Abies koreana* Wilson *15957*

	R	20761	Russian Federation *15957*
	R	20761	Korea, South *15957*

R   *Abies lowiana* (Gord.) A. Murr. var. *viridula* Debreczy & Rácz *21253*

	R	21253	Mexico - Chihuahua *21253*

E   *Abies nebrodensis* (Lojac.) Mattei *10370, 20171*

	E	18270	Italy - Sicily *10370*

V   *Abies numidica* de Lannoy ex Carrière *18270*

	V	18270	Algeria (Mt Babor, Mt Tababor) *10487*

R   *Abies pinsapo* Boiss. var. *marocana* (Trabut) Ceballos & Bolanos *18270*

	R	20761	Morocco (Rif Mts) *18270*

R   *Abies pinsapo* Boiss. var. *pinsapo* *19432*

	R	20761	Spain *20660*

V   *Abies pinsapo* Boiss. var. *tazaotana* (Cozar ex Hug. del Vill.) Pourtet *18270*

	V	18270	Morocco (Mt Tazaot) *18270*

V   *Abies recurvata* Masters var. *recurvata* *18270*

	V	20761	China - Sichuan (Songpan) *18270*

V   *Abies sibirica* Ledeb. ssp. *semenovii* (B.A. Fedtschenko) Farjon *18270*

	V	18270	Kyrgyzstan *18270*
	V	20761	China *20761*

V   *Abies squamata* Masters *18270*

	V	18270	China - Gansu (south) *18270*
	V	18270	China - Qinghai (south) *18270*
	V	18270	China - Sichuan (west) *18270*
	V	18270	China - Xizang Zizhiqu *18270*

R   *Abies veitchii* Lindl. var. *sikokiana* (Nakai) Kusaka *18270*

	R	18270	Japan (Shikoku) *18270*

V	*Abies vejarii* Martínez ssp. *mexicana* (Martínez) Farjon *16386*		
	V	20761	Mexico - Coahuila (south-east) *18270*
	V	20761	Mexico - Nuevo Leon *18270*
E	*Abies yuanbaoshanensis* Y.J. Lu & L.K. Fu *17617*		
	E	18270	China - Guangxi *11139*
R	*Abies zapotekensis* Debreczy, Rácz & Ramírez *21253*		
	R	21253	Mexico - Oaxaca *21253*
E	*Abies ziyuanensis* L.K. Fu & S.L. Mo *17617*		
	E	18270	China - Guangxi (Ziyuan) *11139*
	E	18270	China - Hunan *11139*
R	*Cathaya argyrophylla* Chun & Kuang *11139*		
	R	20761	China - Guangxi (Longsheng, Jinxiu) *11139*
	R	20761	China - Guizhou (Daozheng, Tongxing, Tongxi) *10439*
	R	20761	China - Hunan (Luohandong, Bamianshan) *17617*
	R	20761	China - Sichuan *10439*
V	*Cedrus brevifolia* (Hook.f.) Henry *18270*		
	V	18270	Cyprus (Mt. Triphylos) *20761*
R	*Keteleeria fortunei* (Andr. Murr) Carrière *11139*		
	R	20761	China - Fujian *11139*
	R	20761	China - Guangdong *11139*
	R	20761	China - Guangxi *11139*
	R	20761	China - Guizhou *20761*
	R	20761	China - Hunan *20761*
	R	20761	China - Jiangxi *20761*
	R	20761	China - Yunnan *20761*
	R	20761	China - Zhejiang *20761*
	R	20761	Vietnam *20761*
V	*Larix chinensis* Beissner *17617*		
	V	17617	China - Shanxi (Qingling) *11139*
R	*Larix decidua* Mill. ssp. *polonica* (Racib.) Domin *20171*		
	V	18270	Poland (Carpathian Mts.) *18270*
	R	19947	Romania (Carpathian Mts.) *20650*
	E	20655	Ukraine (Carpathian Mts.) *20650*
R	*Larix griffithiana* Hook. var. *speciosa* (Cheng & Law) Silba *18270*		
	R	20761	China - Sichuan *19703*
	R	18270	China - Xizang Zizhiqu (south-east) *18270*
	R	18270	China - Yunnan (north-west) *18270*
	R	20761	Myanmar (North) *19703*
V	*Larix mastersiana* Rehder & E. Wilson *17617*		
	V	20761	China - Sichuan (west) *8482*
V	*Larix potaninii* Batalin var. *himalaica* (Cheng & Fu) Farjon & Silba *18270*		
	V	18270	China - Xizang Zizhiqu (south (himalaya)) *18270*
	V	20761	Nepal *20761*
V	*Nothotsuga longibracteata* (Cheng) Hu ex C. N. Page *18270*		
	E	18270	China - Fujian (south) *8482*
	E	18270	China - Guangdong (north) *8482*
	E	18270	China - Guangxi (north-east) *8482*
	E	18270	China - Guizhou (north-east) *8482*
	E	18270	China - Hunan (south-west) *8482*
	V	11139	China - Jiangxi *11139*
V	*Picea alcoquiana* (Veitch ex Lindl.) Carrière var. *acicularis* (Shirasawa) Fitschen *18270*		
	V	18270	Japan (central (Yatsugadake mountains)) *20501*
R	*Picea alcoquiana* (Veitch ex Lindl.) Carrière var. *alcoquiana* *18270*		

	R	18270	Japan (central) *20501*
R	*Picea alcoquiana* (Veitch ex Lindl.) Carrière var. *reflexa* (Shirasawa) Fitschen *18270*		
	R	18270	Japan (central: Akaishi Range) *20501*
E	*Picea aurantiaca* Masters *17617*		
	E	18270	China - Sichuan (Kangding, Zheduo Shan) *8482*
V	*Picea brachytyla* (Franch.) Pritzel *11139*		
	V	18270	China - Gansu (Zhueni; Zhouqu) *11139*
	V	17617	China - Henan (Xixia) *11139*
	V	18270	China - Hubei (West) *17617*
	V	18270	China - Shaanxi (Pingli; Langao; Fengxian) *11139*
	V	18270	China - Sichuan (east & north) *17617*
	V	18270	China - Xizang Zizhiqu *18270*
	V	18270	China - Yunnan (north-west) *18270*
V	*Picea brachytyla* (Franch.) Pritzel var. *complanata* (Masters) Cheng ex Rehder *18270*		
	V	18270	China - Sichuan (west) *17617*
	V	18270	China - Yunnan (north-west) *17617*
	V	18270	India (north-east) *18270*
	V	18270	India - Arunachal Pradesh *16386*
	V	18270	Myanmar (north) *16386*
R	*Picea breweriana* S.Watson *20850*		
	I	20850	U.S. - California (Siskiyou Mts) *20850*
	R	20850	U.S. - Oregon (south-west) *20850*
V	*Picea chihuahuana* Martínez *19894*		
	V	18270	Mexico - Chihuahua (south-west) *10600*
	V	18270	Mexico - Durango (south) *10600*
	V	18270	Mexico - Nuevo Leon *20480*
V	*Picea engelmannii* Parry ex Engelm. ssp. *mexicana* (Martínez) P. Schmidt *16386*		
	V	18270	Mexico - Chihuahua *20475*
	V	18270	Mexico - Nuevo Leon *19894*
E	*Picea farreri* C.N. Page & Rushforth *20507*		
	E	18270	Myanmar (Feng-Shui-Ling Valley) *20507*
R	*Picea jezoensis* (Sieb. et Zucc.) Carrière var. *komarovii* (V.N. Vasiljev) Cheng & Fu *18270*		
	R	18270	China - Jilin *16386*
	R	18270	Korea, North *16386*
R	*Picea koraiensis* Nakai var. *koraiensis* *18270*		
	R	18270	Russian Federation (Ussuri River) *16386*
	R	18270	China - Jilin *16386*
	R	18270	Korea, North *16386*
R	*Picea koraiensis* Nakai var. *pungsanensis* (Uyeki ex Nakai) Schmidt-Vogt ex Farjon *18270*		
	R	18270	Korea, North (Mt Pungsan) *15957*
E	*Picea koyamae* Shirasawa *18270*		
	E	18270	Japan (Yatsuga-take, Nagano) *20501*
V	*Picea likiangensis* (Franch.) Pritzel var. *hirtella* (Rehder & Wilson) Cheng ex Chen *18270*		
	V	18270	China - Sichuan (west) *18270*
	V	18270	China - Xizang Zizhiqu (south-east) *18270*
E	*Picea likiangensis* (Franch.) Pritzel var. *montigena* (Masters) Cheng ex Chen *18270*		
	E	18270	China - Sichuan (south-west) *18270*
V	*Picea likiangensis* (Franch.) Pritzel var. *rubescens* Rehder & Wilson *18270*		
	V	18270	China - Qinghai (south) *18270*
	V	18270	China - Sichuan (west) *18270*
	V	18270	China - Xizang Zizhiqu (south-east) *18270*
V	*Picea maximowiczii* Masters var. *maximowiczii* *18270*		

V   20761   Japan (Yatsugadake Mountains, Fuji-san)
20501

V   *Picea maximowiczii* Masters var. *senanensis*
Hayashi *18270*

     V   20761   Japan (Yatsugadake Mountains, Fuji-san?)
20501

R   *Picea meyeri* Rehder & Wilson *18270*

     R   18270   China - Gansu *18270*
     R   18270   China - Hebei *18270*
     R   18270   China - Nei Monggol Zizhiqu *18270*
     R   18270   China - Shaanxi *18270*
     R   18270   China - Shanxi *18270*

V   *Picea neoveitchii* Masters *11139*

     V   18270   China - Gansu (Tianshu; Huixian; Mingshan)
11139
     E   18270   China - Henan (Neixiang) *18270*
     V   18270   China - Hubei (Xingshan; Badong) *11139*
     V   18270   China - Shaanxi (south) *11139*
     V   18270   China - Shanxi (Wutai Shan) *11139*
     V   18270   China - Sichuan *18270*

V   *Picea omorika* (Pancic) Purk. *8000, 20171*

     R   21091   Bosnia & Herzegovina *21091*

V   *Picea purpurea* Masters *18270*

     V   18270   China - Gansu *18270*
     V   18270   China - Qinghai (east) *18270*
     V   18270   China - Sichuan *18270*

R   *Picea retroflexa* Masters *18270*

     R   18270   China - Sichuan (west) *18270*

R   *Picea spinulosa* (Griffith) Henry *18270*

     R   18270   China - Xizang Zizhiqu (south-east)
18270
     R   18270   Bhutan *10777*
     R   18270   India - Sikkim (east Himalaya) *10777*

R   *Picea torano* (K. Koch) Koehne *18270*

     R   18270   Japan (Honshu, Kyushu, Shikoku) *20502*

R   *Picea wilsonii* Masters *18270*

     R   18270   China - Gansu *18270*
     R   18270   China - Hebei *18270*
     R   18270   China - Hubei *18270*
     R   18270   China - Shaanxi *18270*
     R   18270   China - Shanxi *18270*
     R   18270   China - Sichuan (west) *18270*

V   *Pinus amamiana* Koidzumi *18270*

     V   18270   Japan (Yakushima, Tanegashima) *10370*

R   *Pinus aristata* Engelm. *20850, 20171*

     V   20850   U.S. - Arizona *20850*
     I   20850   U.S. - Colorado *20850*
     I   20850   U.S. - New Mexico *20850*

R   *Pinus arizonica* Martinez var. *cooperi* (C.E.Blanco)
Farjon *20761*

     R   20883   Mexico *20883*

R   *Pinus arizonica* Martinez var. *stormiae*
Martinez *20850*

     I   20850   U.S. - Arizona *20850*
     I   20850   U.S. - Texas *20850*
     R   20883   Mexico *20883*

R   *Pinus armandii* Franch. var. *mastersiana* (Hayata)
Hayata *18270*

     R   18270   Taiwan *18270*

R   *Pinus ayacahuite* var. *veitchii* Shaw *20883*

     R   20883   Mexico *20883*

V   *Pinus balfouriana* Grev. & Balf. *20850, 19002*

     I   20850   U.S. - California *20850*

R   *Pinus balfouriana* Jeffrey ex Andr. Murray ssp.
austrina R. Mastrogiuseppe & J. Mastrogiuseppe *18270*

R   18270   U.S. - California (Tulare, Fresno and Inyo
counties) *18270*

R   *Pinus balfouriana* Jeffrey ex Andr. Murray ssp.
balfouriana *20761*

     R   20761   U.S. - California (Klamath Mnts.) *20761*

V   *Pinus bhutanica* Grierson, Long & Page *18270*

     V   18270   Bhutan *10777*

R   *Pinus brutia* Ten. var. *eldarica* (Medw.)
Silba *18270*

     V   18270   Azerbaijan (Georgian border) *18270*
     R   18270   Afghanistan *18270*
     R   18270   Iran *18270*

V   *Pinus brutia* Ten. var. *pityusa* (Stev.)
Silba *18270*

     V   18270   Syria *18270*
     V   11552   Russian Federation (Caucasus) *11552*
     V   18270   Georgia (Black Sea coast) *18270*
     V   18270   Ukraine - Crimea *20654*

V   *Pinus bungeana* Zucc. ex Endl. *18270*

     V   18270   China - Gansu (south) *18270*
     V   18270   China - Hebei *18270*
     V   18270   China - Henan *18270*
     V   18270   China - Hubei (Badong Xian) *18270*
     V   18270   China - Shaanxi *18270*
     V   18270   China - Shanxi *18270*
     V   18270   China - Sichuan (north) *18270*

R   *Pinus canariensis* Sweet ex Spreng. *18270, 20171*

     R   18270   Spain - Canary Is. *18270*

V   *Pinus catarinae* M.-F. Robert-Passini *20883, 14279*

     V   20883   Mexico *20883*

V   *Pinus cembroides* Zucc. ssp. *lagunae* (M.-F.
Passini) D.K. Bailey *14279*

     V   18270   Mexico - Baja California Sur (Sierra de la
Laguna) *20465*

R   *Pinus cembroides* Zucc. ssp. *orizabensis* D.K.
Bailey *20883, 18270*

     R   20883   Mexico *20883*
     R   18270   Mexico - Puebla *20465*
     R   18270   Mexico - Tlaxcala *20465*
     R   18270   Mexico - Veracruz *20465*

R   *Pinus chihuahuana* Engelm. *18270*

     R   18270   U.S. - Arizona (south) *18270*
     R   18270   U.S. - New Mexico (south-west) *18270*
     R   18270   Mexico (Sierra Madre Occidental) *18270*
     R   18270   Mexico - Chihuahua *20344*
     R   18270   Mexico - Durango *20344*
     R   18270   Mexico - Jalisco *20344*
     R   18270   Mexico - Nayarit *20344*
     R   18270   Mexico - Sonora *20344*
     R   18270   Mexico - Zacatecas *20344*

R   *Pinus clausa* (Chapman ex Engelm.) Vasey ex
Sarg. *20850, 18270*

     R   18270   U.S. - Alabama (Baldwin County) *20850*
     I   20850   U.S. - Florida *20850*

V   *Pinus contorta* Dougl. ex Loud. var. *bolanderi*
(Parl.) Vasey *20850, 18270*

     V   20850   U.S. - California (Mendocino County)
20850

I   *Pinus contorta* Doug. ex Loud. var. *murrayana*
(Balf.) Critchfield *20346*

     I   19848   Mexico *19848*

R   *Pinus coulteri* D. Don *10167*

     R   18270   U.S. - California *18270*
     I   19848   Mexico *19848*
     V   16360   Mexico - Baja California Peninsula
10167

V		*Pinus culminicola* Andresen & Beaman *20883, 10567*	
	E	*18270*	Mexico - Coahuila *20479*
	E	*18270*	Mexico - Nuevo Leon *20479*
E		*Pinus dabeshanensis* W.C.Cheng & Y.W.Law *11139*	
	E	*17617*	China - Anhui *11139*
	E	*17617*	China - Henan *11139*
	E	*17617*	China - Hubei *11139*
E		*Pinus dalatensis* Y. de Ferré *18270*	
	R	*20985*	Vietnam (Mountains north of Dalat) *20456*

V   *Pinus densiflora* Sieb. & Zucc. var. *funebris* (Komarov) Liou & Wang *18270*

	V	*18270*	Russian Federation (maritime province) *20497*
	R	*18270*	Korea, North *20497*
R		*Pinus durangensis* Mart. *20883*	
	R	*20883*	Mexico *20883*
V		*Pinus fenzeliana* Hand.-Mazz. *18270*	
	V	*18270*	China - Hainan Is. *18270*
	V	*18270*	Vietnam *18270*
R		*Pinus gerardiana* Wallich ex D.Don *18270*	
	R	*18270*	China - Xizang Zizhiqu (south) *18270*
	R	*18270*	Afghanistan (east) *10483*
	R	*18270*	India - Jammu & Kashmir *18270*
	R	*18270*	Pakistan (north) *20456*
R		*Pinus greggii* Engelm. *20883, 18270*	
	R	*14279*	Mexico - Coahuila (south) *20376*
	R	*14279*	Mexico - Hidalgo *20376*
	R	*14279*	Mexico - Nuevo Leon *20458*
	R	*14279*	Mexico - San Luis Potosi *20376*

V   *Pinus halepensis* Miller var. *ceciliae* Llorens

	V		Spain - Balearic Is.

V   *Pinus heldreichii* H.Christ var. *heldreichii* *8000, 20171*

	V	*18270*	Greece (Olimbos) *8000*

R   *Pinus heldreichii* H.Christ var. *leucodermis* (Ant.) Markgraf ex Fitschen *8000, 20171*

	R	*18270*	Albania *18270*
	R	*18270*	Greece *18270*
	R	*18264*	Italy (Basilicata; Campania) *18264*
	R	*18270*	(former) Yugoslavia (south) *18270*
R		*Pinus herrerae* Martínez *18270*	
	R	*18270*	Mexico (south-west) *20376*
	R	*18270*	Mexico - Colima *20344*
	R	*18270*	Mexico - Durango *20344*
	R	*18270*	Mexico - Guerrero *20344*
	R	*18270*	Mexico - Jalisco *20344*
	R	*18270*	Mexico - Michoacan *20344*
	R	*18270*	Mexico - Sinaloa *20344*
V		*Pinus jaliscana* Perez de la Rosa *20883, 18270*	
	V	*18270*	Mexico - Jalisco (west) *14279*
R		*Pinus johannis* M.-F. Robert *9021*	
	R	*18270*	Mexico - Coahuila *14279*
	R	*18270*	Mexico - Nuevo Leon *14279*
	R	*18270*	Mexico - Zacatecas *9021*
E		*Pinus krempfii* Lecomte *6057*	
	R	*20985*	Vietnam (Khanh Hoa, Lam Dong) *15160*
V		*Pinus kwangtungensis* Chun Tsiang *17617*	
	V	*17617*	China - Guangdong (north) *11139*
	V	*17617*	China - Hainan Is. (Mt. Wuzhi) *17617*
	V	*17617*	China - Guangxi (south & north-east) *11139*
	V	*17617*	China - Guizhou (Dushan) *19728*
	V	*17617*	China - Hunan (southwest) *11139*
	V	*20985*	Vietnam *20454*
R		*Pinus latteri* Mason *18270*	
	R	*18270*	China - Guangdong *18270*
	R	*18270*	China - Hainan Is. *18270*
	R	*18270*	China - Guangxi *18270*
	R	*18270*	Myanmar (east) *18270*
	R	*18270*	Vietnam (north) *18270*
R		*Pinus lawsonii* Roezl ex Gordon & Glend. *18270*	
	R	*18270*	Mexico (south) *18270*
	R	*18270*	Mexico - Guerrero *14279*
	R	*18270*	Mexico - Jalisco *14279*
	R	*18270*	Mexico - Mexico State *14279*
	R	*18270*	Mexico - Michoacan *14279*
	R	*18270*	Mexico - Oaxaca *14279*
	R	*18270*	Mexico - Puebla *14279*

R   *Pinus lawsonii* Roezl var. *gracilis* Debreczy & Rácz *21253*

	R	*21253*	Mexico - Oaxaca *21253*
R		*Pinus longaeva* D.K. Bailey *20850, 18270*	
	V	*20850*	U.S. - California (east) *20850*
	R	*20850*	U.S. - Nevada (south) *20850*
	I	*20850*	U.S. - Utah *20850*
R		*Pinus luchuensis* Mayr *18270*	
	R	*18270*	Japan (Luchu) *18128*
R		*Pinus lumholtzii* Robinson & Fernald *18270*	
	R	*18270*	Mexico (west) *18128*
	R	*18270*	Mexico - Aguascalientes *20344*
	R	*18270*	Mexico - Durango *20344*
	R	*18270*	Mexico - Guanajuato *20344*
	R	*18270*	Mexico - Jalisco *20344*
	R	*18270*	Mexico - Nayarit *20344*
	R	*18270*	Mexico - Sinaloa *20344*
	R	*18270*	Mexico - Sonora *20344*
	R	*18270*	Mexico - Zacatecas *20344*
R		*Pinus martinezii* Larsen *20883, 14279*	
	V	*18270*	Mexico - Jalisco (west) *18270*
	V	*18270*	Mexico - Michoacan *14279*

E   *Pinus massoniana* Lambert var. *hainanensis* W.C.Cheng & L.K. Fu *11139*

	E	*17617*	China - Hainan Is. (Yajiadaling) *18270*
E		*Pinus maximartinezii* Rzedowski *20883, 9019*	
	E	*20883*	Mexico *20883*
	E	*18270*	Mexico - Zacatecas *20509*

V   *Pinus michoacana* Mart. var. *quevedoi* Mart. *20883*

	V	*20883*	Mexico *20883*
R		*Pinus morrisonicola* Hayata *18270*	
	R	*18270*	Taiwan (central mountains) *20018*
V		*Pinus muricata* D. Don *20883, 20850, 18270*	
	R	*18270*	U.S. - California (Santa Cruz, Santa Rosa Is.) *20850*
	I	*20883*	Mexico *20883*
	R	*18270*	Mexico - Baja California Peninsula *20456*
E		*Pinus muricata* D. Don var. *muricata* *20850*	
	I	*20850*	U.S. - California *20850*
R		*Pinus nelsonii* Shaw *20883, 18270*	
	R	*20883*	Mexico *20883*
	R	*14279*	Mexico - Coahuila (Carmen Mts) *18270*
	R	*14279*	Mexico - Nuevo Leon *18270*
	R	*14279*	Mexico - San Luis Potosi *14279*
	R	*14279*	Mexico - Tamaulipas *14279*
I		*Pinus nigra* ssp. *banatica* *17823*	
	I	*17823*	Czech Republic *17823*
	I	*17823*	Slovakia *17823*

R   *Pinus nigra* J.F.Arnold ssp. *dalmatica* (Visiani) Franco *8000, 20171*

R   *14279*   (former) Yugoslavia (Dalmatia) *10567*

R   *Pinus oaxacana* (Mart.) Mirov var. *diversiformis* Debeczy & Rácz *21253*

R   *21253*   Mexico - Oaxaca *21253*

V   *Pinus occidentalis* Sw. *18270*

V   *18270*   Dominican Republic *20460*

R   *Pinus oocarpa* Mart. var. *trifoliata* Mart. *20883*

R   *20883*   Mexico *20883*

V   *Pinus patula* Schltdl. & Cham. ssp. *tecunumanii* (Eguiluz & Perry) Styles *18270*

E   *10370*   Belize *20445*
V   *18270*   El Salvador *10370*
V   *18270*   Guatemala *10370*
V   *18270*   Honduras *20471*
V   *18270*   Mexico - Chiapas *20445*
V   *18270*   Mexico - Oaxaca *18270*
E   *10370*   Nicaragua *10370*

R   *Pinus peuce* Griseb. *18270, 20171*

E   *20178*   Albania *10370*
R   *18270*   Bulgaria (west) *10370*
R   *18270*   Greece (extreme north) *10370*
R   *18270*   (former) Yugoslavia (south) *10370*

R   *Pinus pinceana* Gord. *20883, 18270*

R   *20761*   Mexico - Coahuila *14279*
R   *20761*   Mexico - Hidalgo *14279*
R   *20761*   Mexico - Queretaro *14279*
R   *20761*   Mexico - San Luis Potosi *18270*
R   *20761*   Mexico - Zacatecas *14279*

R   *Pinus pseudostrobus* Mart. var. *apulcensis* (Lindley) A.R.Shaw *20883*

R   *20883*   Mexico *20883*

R   *Pinus pseudostrobus* Lindl. var. *estevesii* Martínez *18270*

R   *14279*   Mexico - Coahuila *14279*
R   *14279*   Mexico - Nuevo Leon *14279*
R   *14279*   Mexico - Tamaulipas *14279*

R   *Pinus quadrifolia* Parl. ex Sudworth *20883, 20850, 18270*

R   *18270*   U.S. - California (south) *20850*
R   *20883*   Mexico *20883*
R   *18270*   Mexico - Baja California Peninsula *18270*

E   *Pinus radiata* D. Don var. *binata* (Engelm.) Lemn. *20883, 14279*

E   *20883*   Mexico *20883*

E   *Pinus radiata* D. Don var. *radiata* D.Don *20883, 20850, 20171*

E   *20850*   U.S. - California (south) *20850*

R   *Pinus reflexa* Engelm. *19850*

R   *19850*   Mexico *19850*

R   *Pinus remota* (Little) D.K. Bailey & Hawksworth *18270*

R   *18270*   U.S. - Texas (south-west) *18270*
R   *18270*   Mexico - Chihuahua (east) *18270*
R   *18270*   Mexico - Coahuila *18270*
R   *18270*   Mexico - Nuevo Leon (west) *18270*

E   *Pinus rzedowskii* Madrigal et Caballero *20883, 14279*

E   *19850*   Mexico - Michoacan (west) *20344*

V   *Pinus strobus* L. var. *chiapensis* Martínez *20761*

V   *20761*   Guatemala (El Quiché) *20883*
V   *20761*   Mexico *9004*
V   *20761*   Mexico - Chiapas *20376*
V   *20761*   Mexico - Guerrero *14279*
V   *20761*   Mexico - Oaxaca *20376*
V   *20761*   Mexico - Puebla *20376*

V   *20761*   Mexico - Veracruz *20376*

I   *Pinus sylvestris* L. var. *cretacea* (Kalen.) Komarov *5942, 20171*

I   *5942*   Ukraine *5942*

V   *Pinus sylvestris* L. var. *mongolica* Litv. *11139*

V   *18270*   China - Heilongjiang *11139*
V   *17617*   China - Nei Monggol Zizhiqu (Datlinggan Shan) *17617*
V   *18270*   Mongolia (Greater & lesser Hinggan Ling) *17617*

V   *Pinus sylvestris* ssp. *nevadensis* (Christ) Heyw. *15398*

V   *15398*   Spain (Sierra Nevada) *15398*

V   *Pinus sylvestris* L. var. *sylvestriformis* (Taken.) Cheng ex C.D. Chu *18270*

V   *18270*   China - Jilin (Changbaishan) *17617*

R   *Pinus tabuliformis* Carrière var. *henryi* (Mast.) C.T. Kuan *18270*

R   *18270*   China - Hubei *18270*
R   *18270*   China - Shaanxi *18270*
R   *18270*   China - Sichuan *18270*

R   *Pinus taiwanensis* Hayata var. *damingshanensis* W.C. Cheng & L.K. Fu *18270*

R   *18270*   China - Guangxi (Daming Shan) *18270*
R   *18270*   China - Guizhou *18270*

E   *Pinus torreyana* Parry ex Carr. *20850, 18270*

E   *20850*   U.S. - California *20850*

E   *Pinus torreyana* Parry ex Carr. ssp. *insularis* Haller *20850*

E   *20850*   U.S. - California *20850*

E   *Pinus torreyana* Parry ex Carr. ssp. *torreyana* *20850*

E   *20850*   U.S. - California *20850*

E   *Pinus wangii* Hu & Cheng *18270*

E   *17617*   China - Yunnan *11139*

V   *Pinus washoensis* Mason & Stockwell *20850, 18270*

I   *20850*   U.S. - California (north-east) *20850*
V   *20850*   U.S. - Nevada (Washoe Co.) *20850*
V   *20850*   U.S. - Oregon *20850*

R   *Pinus yunnanensis* Franch. var. *tenuifolia* W.C. Cheng & Y.W. Law *18270*

R   *18270*   China - Guangxi *18270*
R   *18270*   China - Guizhou *18270*

R   *Pseudolarix amabilis* (Nelson) Rehder *18270*

R   *17617*   China - Anhui (south) *19728*
E   *18270*   China - Fujian (north) *18270*
R   *17617*   China - Henan (Gushi) *17617*
R   *17617*   China - Hubei (Lichuan) *19728*
E   *18270*   China - Hunan *18270*
R   *17617*   China - Jiangsu *19728*
E   *18270*   China - Jiangxi (north) *18270*
R   *17617*   China - Sichuan (Wanxian) *19728*
E   *18270*   China - Zhejiang (north) *18270*

V   *Pseudotsuga brevifolia* W.C. Cheng & L.K. Fu *17617*

V   *17617*   China - Guangxi (southwest & northwest) *17617*
V   *17617*   China - Guizhou (Libe, Anlong) *17617*

R   *Pseudotsuga flahaultii* Flous *19850*

R   *19850*   Mexico *19850*

V   *Pseudotsuga forrestii* Craib *17617*

V   *17617*   China - Sichuan (Mianning; Xichang) *11139*
V   *17617*   China - Xizang Zizhiqu (Chayu) *11139*

V   *17617*   China - Yunnan (northwest) *11139*

V   *Pseudotsuga gaussenii* Flous *17617*
- V   *17617*   China - Anhui (southeast) *11139*
- V   *17617*   China - Fujian (Jianning) *11139*
- V   *17617*   China - Jiangxi (Dexing) *11139*
- E   *18270*   China - Sichuan *18270*
- V   *17617*   China - Zhejiang (north & northwest) *11139*

R   *Pseudotsuga guinieri* Flous *19850*
- R   *19850*   Mexico *19850*

V   *Pseudotsuga japonica* (Shiras.) Beissner *18270*
- V   *18270*   Japan (Honshu, Kyushu, Shikoku) *20501*

R   *Pseudotsuga macrocarpa* (Vasey) Mayr *20850, 18270*
- R   *18270*   U.S. - California (south) *20850*

R   *Pseudotsuga menziesii* (Mirb.) Franco var. *oaxacana* Debreczy & Rácz *21253*
- R   *21253*   Mexico - Oaxaca *21253*

R   *Pseudotsuga rehderi* Flous *19848*
- R   *19848*   Mexico *19848*

V   *Pseudotsuga sinensis* Dode *17617*
- V   *17617*   China - Guizhou *11139*
- V   *17617*   China - Hubei *11139*
- V   *17617*   China - Hunan *11139*
- V   *17617*   China - Shaanxi (Zhengping) *11139*
- V   *17617*   China - Sichuan *11139*
- V   *19723*   China - Xizang Zizhiqu *19723*
- V   *17617*   China - Yunnan *11139*

R   *Pseudotsuga wilsoniana* Hayata *20018*
- R   *20511*   Taiwan *20018*

R   *Tsuga caroliniana* Engelm. *20850, 18270*
- E   *20850*   U.S. - Georgia *20850*
- R   *20850*   U.S. - North Carolina *20850*
- I   *20850*   U.S. - South Carolina *20850*
- V   *20850*   U.S. - Tennessee *20850*
- I   *20850*   U.S. - Virginia *20850*

V   *Tsuga chinensis* (Franch.) Pritzel var. *oblongisquamata* W.C.Cheng & L.K.Fu *18270*
- V   *18270*   China - Gansu (Zhouqu) *19728*
- V   *18270*   China - Hubei (west) *19728*
- V   *18270*   China - Sichuan (northeast, west & north) *19728*

V   *Tsuga chinensis* (Franch.) Pritzel var. *robusta* W.C.Cheng & L.K.Fu *18270*
- V   *18270*   China - Hubei *18270*
- V   *18270*   China - Sichuan (Yalong valley) *18270*

V   *Tsuga chinensis* (Franchet) Pritzel var. *tchekiangensis* (Flous) Cheng & L.K. Fu *17617*
- V   *17617*   China - Anhui (Huangshan) *11139*
- V   *17617*   China - Fujian (Wuzi Shan) *19728*
- V   *17617*   China - Guangdong (Ruyuan) *11139*
- V   *17617*   China - Guangxi (Dayao Shan) *17617*
- V   *17617*   China - Guizhou (Guiyiang) *11139*
- V   *17617*   China - Hunan (Lingxian, Guidong) *11139*
- V   *17617*   China - Jiangxi (Qianshan) *11139*
- V   *17617*   China - Yunnan (Maguan, Malipo) *11139*
- V   *17617*   China - Zhejiang (northwest & southern) *11139*

V   *Tsuga forrestii* Downie *17617*
- V   *18270*   China - Guizhou (Fanjinshen) *18270*
- V   *18270*   China - Sichuan (south-west) *11139*
- V   *18270*   China - Yunnan (north-west) *11139*

R   *Tsuga mertensiana* (Bong.) Carrière ssp. *mertensiana* var. *jeffreyi* (Henry) Schneider *18270*
- R   *18270*   Canada - British Columbia (Vancouver Island) *18270*
- R   *18270*   U.S. - Washington (north) *18270*

Podocarpaceae

Number of genera:	6-17
Number of species:	125
Recorded threatened species:	70 (56%)

Mostly Southern Hemisphere, extending north to Japan, Central America, and West Indies.

E   *Acmopyle sahniana* Buchh. & N.E. Gray *10253*
- E   *20761*   Fiji (Viti Levu) *10253*

I   *Afrocarpus usambarensis* (Pilg.) C.N. Page *20342*
- I   *20761*   Tanzania (Mbulu & Lushoto) *18270*

R   *Dacrycarpus kinabaluensis* (Wasscher) de Laub. *19727*
- R   *20761*   Malaysia - Sabah (Mt Kinabalu) *19727*

R   *Dacrycarpus steupii* (Wasscher) de Laub. *19727*
- R   *20761*   Indonesia - Irian Jaya *18270*
- Ex   *19723*   Indonesia - Kalimantan (nr Balikpapan) *19727*
- E   *19723*   Indonesia - Sulawesi (Latimodjong Mts) *19727*

I   *Dacrydium comosum* Corner *19727*
- I   *20761*   Malaysia - Peninsular Malaysia *20452*

R   *Dacrydium cornwalliana* de Laub. *19727*
- R   *18270*   Indonesia - Irian Jaya *19727*
- R   *18270*   Papua New Guinea *19727*

V   *Dacrydium ericioides* de Laub. *19727*
- V   *18270*   Malaysia - Sarawak (Merurong plateau) *19727*

R   *Dacrydium gibbsiae* Stapf *19727*
- R   *18270*   Malaysia - Sabah (Mt Kinabalu) *20477*

V   *Dacrydium gracilis* de Laub. *19727*
- V   *18270*   Malaysia - Sabah (Mt Kinabalu) *20477*

E   *Dacrydium guillauminii* Buchh. *20329*
- E   *20893*   New Caledonia *20329*

V   *Dacrydium leptophyllum* (Wasscher) de Laub. *19727*
- V   *18270*   Indonesia - Irian Jaya (Mt Goliath) *19727*

V   *Dacrydium lycopodioides* Brongn. & Gris *20329*
- V   *20913*   New Caledonia (south-east) *20329*

V   *Dacrydium nausoriense* de Laub. *10253*
- V   *18270*   Fiji (Viti Levu) *10253*

R   *Dacrydium spathoides* de Laub. *19727*
- R   *18270*   Indonesia - Irian Jaya *19727*

R   *Falcatifolium angustum* de Laub. *19727*
- R   *18270*   Malaysia - Sarawak (Two locations on the coast.) *19727*

R   *Falcatifolium gruezoi* de Laub. *19727*
- R   *18270*   Indonesia - Moluccas *19727*
- R   *18270*   Indonesia - Sulawesi *19727*
- R   *18270*   Philippines *19727*

V   *Halocarpus kirkii* (F. Muell. ex Parl.) Quinn *20328*
- V   *20761*   New Zealand - North Is. (between Hokiana and Manukau Harbour) *18270*

V   *Lepidothamnus fonkii* Phil. *20328*
- E   *16336*   Argentina *20489*
- E   *20176*   Argentina - Chubut *20489*
- E   *20176*   Argentina - Neuquen *20489*
- E   *20176*   Argentina - Rio Negro *20489*
- V   *18270*   Chile (Valdivia, Cordillera Pelado, Chiloé Island) *20427*

E   *Microstrobos fitzgeraldii* (F.Muell.) J.Garden & L.A.S.Johnson *20681, 20051*
- E   *20681*   Australia - New South Wales *20681*

R   *Microstrobos niphophilus* J.Garden & L.A.S.Johnson 20681, 20316
- R   *18270*   Australia - Tasmania *20372*

V   *Nageia fleuryi* (Hickel) de Laub. *20367*
- V   *18270*   China - Guangdong (Gaoyao; Longmen & Zengcheng) *17617*
- V   *18270*   China - Guangxi (Hepu) *17617*
- V   *18270*   China - Yunnan (Mengzi; Pingbian) *17617*
- V   *18270*   Kampuchea *18270*
- V   *20985*   Vietnam *18270*

R   *Nageia formosensis* (Dümmer) C.N.Page *20018*
- R   *18270*   Taiwan (south) *18270*

R   *Nageia maximus* (de Laub.) de Laub. *19727*
- R   *18270*   Malaysia - Sarawak *20367*

R   *Podocarpus affinis* Seemann *10253*
- R   *18270*   Fiji (Vitu Levu, Namosi, Voma Peak) *10253*

I   *Podocarpus angustifolius* Griseb. *20368*
- I   *20990*   Cuba (Las Villas, Pinar del Rio) *20368*

R   *Podocarpus annamiensis* N.E. Gray *20454*
- V   *19703*   China - Hainan Is. *11139*
- R   *18270*   Myanmar (east) *18270*
- V   *15734*   Vietnam *6057*

R   *Podocarpus atjehensis* (Wasscher) de Laub. *19727*
- R   *18270*   Indonesia - Sumatra (Gajo Lands) *19727*
- R   *18270*   Papua New Guinea (Wissel Lakes) *19727*

R   *Podocarpus borneensis* de Laub. *19727*
- R   *18270*   Indonesia - Kalimantan (incl. Karimata Island) *19727*
- R   Malaysia - Sabah *14184*

V   *Podocarpus capuronii* de Laub. *20419*
- V   *18270*   Madagascar (Mt. Ambatomenaloha) *20352*

V   *Podocarpus costalis* C. Presl *10278*
- E   *20511*   Taiwan (Orchis Is.) *20018*
- V   *20761*   Philippines (Luzon strait Is.) *20443*

V   *Podocarpus costaricensis* de Laub. *20356*
- V   *18270*   Costa Rica (San Marcos de Irazu) *20353*
- V   *18270*   Panama *20353*

E   *Podocarpus decumbens* N.E. Gray *20329*
- E   *20913*   New Caledonia *20329*

R   *Podocarpus deflexus* Ridley *19727*
- R   *18270*   Indonesia - Sumatra (Gajo Lands) *19727*
- R   *18270*   Malaysia - Peninsular Malaysia *19727*

R   *Podocarpus dispermus* C.White *20681, 20316*
- R   *20681*   Australia - Queensland *20681*

R   *Podocarpus fasciculus* de Laub. *20018*
- R   *18270*   Taiwan *20118*
- R   *18270*   Japan (Ryukyu Islands) *18270*

V   *Podocarpus gibbsii* N.E. Gray *19727*
- V   *18270*   Malaysia - Sabah (Mt Kinabalu) *20477*

R   *Podocarpus globulus* de Laub. *19727*
- R   *18270*   Indonesia - Kalimantan (northern (Mt Kinabalu, Mt Salim)) *19727*

V   *Podocarpus hispaniolensis* de Laub. *20343*
- V   *18270*   Dominican Republic (Cordillera central) *20365*

V   *Podocarpus humbertii* de Laub. *20352*
- V   *18270*   Madagascar *20352*

R   *Podocarpus laubenfelsii* Tiong *20481*
- R   *18270*   Indonesia - Kalimantan *19727*

V   *Podocarpus longifoliolatus* Pilg. *19748*
- V   *20913*   New Caledonia *20329*

V   *Podocarpus lophatus* de Laub. *20443*
- V   *18270*   Philippines (Mt Tapulao) *20443*

R   *Podocarpus lucienii* de Laub. *20329*
- R   *20913*   New Caledonia *20329*

I   *Podocarpus macrophyllus* (Thunberg ex Murray) D.Don var. *piliramulus* Z.X.Chen & Z.Q.Li *19728*
- I   *19728*   China - Hubei (Zhoushan) *19728*

R   *Podocarpus madagascariensis* Baker *20362*
- R   *6963*   Madagascar *20352*

V   *Podocarpus madagascariensis* Baker var. *procerus* de laub. *20352*
- V   *18270*   Madagascar (Fort Dauphin) *20352*

R   *Podocarpus monteverdeensis* de Laub. *20353*
- R   *18270*   Costa Rica (Cordillera de Tilarán, Monteverde Res.) *20366*

V   *Podocarpus nubigenus* Lindl. *10553*
- E   *20176*   Argentina - Neuquen *20176*
- V   *19536*   Chile - Aisen *20761*

R   *Podocarpus pallidus* N.E. Gray *20485*
- R   *18270*   French Polynesia (Tongan Is.) *20485*

V   I   *Podocarpus parlatorei* Pilg. *12379*
- V   *18270*   Argentina *18270*
- V   *18270*   Bolivia *20416*
- V   *18270*   Peru *12379*

R   *Podocarpus pendulifolius* Buchh. & N.E. Gray *20350*
- R   *18270*   Venezuela *20350*

V   *Podocarpus polyspermus* de Laub. *19727*
- V   *20893*   New Caledonia *20329*

V   *Podocarpus purdieanus* Hook. *20368*
- V   *18270*   Jamaica (Mt Diablo) *20368*

R   *Podocarpus roraimae* Pilg. *20350*
- R   *18270*   Venezuela *20493*

V   *Podocarpus rostratus* Laurent *20352*
- V   *18270*   Madagascar *20352*

R   *Podocarpus rotundus* de Laub. *20443*
- R   *18270*   Indonesia - Kalimantan (Mt Beratus) *20093*
- R   *18270*   Philippines (Mt Banajo, Lucban) *20093*

R   *Podocarpus rusbyi* Buchh. & N.E. Gray *20354*
- R   *18270*   Bolivia (Mapiri, Cocopunco) *20354*

R   *Podocarpus salicifolius* Klotzsch & Karsten ex Endl. *20350*
- R   *18270*   Venezuela (northern) *20350*

V   *Podocarpus salignus* D. Don *16436*
- V   *20761*   Chile - Maule *20761*

R   *Podocarpus spathoides* de Laub. *19727*
- R   *18270*   Indonesia - Moluccas (Morotai) *19727*
- R   *18270*   Malaysia (Mt Ophir) *19727*
- R   *18270*   Papua New Guinea (Rossel Island) *19727*
- R   *18270*   Solomon Is. - South *20487*

R   *Podocarpus subtropicalis* de Laub. *18270*
- R   *18270*   China - Sichuan (Mt Omei) *18270*
- R   *18270*   China - Yunnan *18270*

V   *Podocarpus tixieri* Gaussen *18270*
- V   *18270*   Kampuchea (Elephant Mts.) *18270*
- V   *18270*   Thailand *18270*

V   *Podocarpus transiens* (Pilg.) de Laub. *20377*
- V   *18270*   Brazil (Serra do Cipó) *20337*

V   *Podocarpus trinitensis* N.E. Gray *18270*
- V   *18270*   Trinidad & Tobago (summit of El Tucuche) *18270*

V	***Podocarpus urbanii*** Pilg. *20368*	
	V	*18270* Jamaica (Blue Mts.) *20072*
R	***Prumnopitys andina*** (Poepp. ex Endl.) de Laub. *20883*	
	R	*20883* Chile *20883*
R	***Prumnopitys ladei*** (Bailey) Laubenf. *20681, 14223*	
	R	*20681* Australia - Queensland *20681*
V	***Prumnopitys standleyi*** (Buchholz & Gray) de Laubenfels *20883, 20353*	
	V	*20883* Costa Rica *20883*
E	***Retrophyllum minor*** (Carrière) C.N. Page *20342*	
	E	*20893* New Caledonia (south-eastern) *20329*
R	***Retrophyllum piresii*** (Silba) C.N. Page *20342*	
	R	*18270* Brazil - Rondonia (Serra Pacas Novos) *18270*
V	***Saxegothaea conspicua*** Lindl. *19448*	
	V	*19448* Argentina *19448*
	E	*20176* Argentina - Chubut *20176*
	E	*20176* Argentina - Neuquen *20176*
	E	*20176* Argentina - Rio Negro *20176*
	V	*19534* Chile *20427*

Taxaceae

Number of genera:	5
Number of species:	20
Recorded threatened species:	15 (75%)

Northern Hemisphere, south to Celebes and Mexico; one species in New Caledonia.

V	***Amentotaxus argotaenia*** (Hance) Pilg. *18270*	
	V	*18270* China - Fujian *18270*
	V	*18270* China - Gansu *18270*
	V	*18270* China - Guangdong *18270*
	V	*18270* China - Guangxi *18270*
	V	*18270* China - Hubei *18270*
	V	*18270* China - Hunan *18270*
	V	*18270* China - Jiangsu *18270*
	V	*18270* China - Jiangxi *18270*
	V	*18270* China - Sichuan *18270*
	V	*18270* China - Xizang Zizhiqu *18270*
	V	*18270* China - Zhejiang *18270*
V	***Amentotaxus argotaenia*** (Hance) Pilg. var. *brevifolia* K.M. Lan & F.H. Zhang *9155*	
	V	*18270* China - Guizhou *9155*
V	***Amentotaxus assamica*** D.K. Ferguson *20495*	
	V	*20761* China (Medog) *20761*
	V	*18270* India - Arunachal Pradesh *20495*
E	***Amentotaxus formosana*** Li *20018*	
	E	*20761* Taiwan (south-east) *20511*
V	***Amentotaxus poilanei*** (De Ferré & Rouane) D.K. Ferguson *19703*	
	I	*20985* Vietnam (south) *20496*
V	***Amentotaxus yunnanensis*** Li *17617*	
	V	*20761* China - Guizhou (Xingyi) *11139*
	V	*20761* China - Yunnan (Wengshanzhou) *11139*
	I	*20985* Vietnam (Ha Tuyen) *20454*
E	***Pseudotaxus chienii*** (W.C. Cheng) W.C. Cheng *11139*	
	E	*20761* China - Guangdong (Ruyian) *11139*
	E	*20761* China - Guangxi *11139*
	E	*20761* China - Hunan *11139*
	E	*20761* China - Jiangxi (Dexing; Jinggangshan) *11139*
	E	*20761* China - Zhejiang (Longgun, Shuichang, Jiyun) *11139*
R	***Taxus brevifolia*** Nutt. *18270*	
	R	*18270* Canada - Alberta *18270*
	R	*18270* Canada - British Columbia *18270*
	R	*19723* U.S. - Idaho *19723*
	R	*18270* U.S. - Montana *18270*
	R	*18270* U.S. - Oregon *18270*
	R	*19723* U.S. - Washington *19723*
V	***Taxus floridana*** Nutt. ex Chapman *20850, 18270*	
	V	*20850* U.S. - Florida (Apalachicola River hills) *20850*
R	***Taxus globosa*** Schltr. *9004*	
	R	*20761* Guatemala *3260*
	R	*20761* Honduras *20468*
	R	*18270* Mexico *9004*
	R	*18270* Mexico - Chihuahua *20480*
V	***Taxus yunnanensis*** W.C. Cheng & L.K. Fu *18270*	
	V	*18270* China - Sichuan (south west) *9004*
	V	*18270* China - Xizang Zizhiqu (south east) *9004*
	V	*18270* China - Yunnan (north west to west) *9004*
	V	*20761* Myanmar (north) *19703*
R	***Torreya californica*** Torr. *20850, 18270*	
	R	*20761* U.S. - California (coast ranges, Sierra Nevada) *20850*
V	***Torreya fargesii*** Franch. *18270*	
	V	*18270* China - Hubei (west) *18270*
	V	*20761* China - Jiangxi *19703*
	V	*20761* China - Shaanxi (south) *19703*
	V	*18270* China - Sichuan (north east & Emei Shan) *19703*
E	***Torreya jackii*** Chun *17617*	
	E	*18270* China - Fujian (Taining; Puchen) *11139*
	E	*18270* China - Zhejiang *11139*
E	***Torreya taxifolia*** Arn. *20850, 18270*	
	E	*20850* U.S. - Florida (north-west) *20850*
	E	*20850* U.S. - Georgia (south-west) *20850*
I	***Torreya yunnanensis*** Cheng & L.K. Fu *17617*	
	I	*20761* China - Yunnan *19703*

Taxodiaceae

Number of genera:	10
Number of species:	16
Recorded threatened species:	10 (62%)

Eastern Asia; Tasmania; North America.

R	***Cryptomeria japonica*** (L. f.) D. Don var. *japonica* *18270*	
	R	*19723* Japan *17882*
V	***Cunninghamia konishii*** Hayata *18270*	
	V	*18270* Taiwan (northern central) *19703*
E	***Cunninghamia unicanaliculata*** D.Y. Wang & H.L. Liu *17617*	
	E	*17617* China - Sichuan (Dechang, Miyi, Yieyu) *18270*
R	***Glyptostrobus pensilis*** (Staunton) K. Koch *18270*	
	R	*17617* China - Fujian (northern and southern) *17617*
	R	*17617* China - Guangdong (southern) *17617*
	R	*17617* China - Hainan Is. *18270*
	R	*17617* China - Guangxi *18270*
	R	*17617* China - Jiangxi *18270*
	R	*17617* China - Sichuan *19703*
	R	*17617* China - Yunnan (southeastern (Pingbian)) *17617*
	E	*20985* Vietnam *6057*
E	***Metasequoia glyptostroboides*** Hu & Cheng *17617*	
	E	*17617* China - Hubei (Lichuan) *11139*
	E	*17617* China - Hunan (Longshan & Sangzhi)

11139
E   *17617*   China - Sichuan (Shizhu) *11139*

V   *Sciadopitys verticillata* (Thunb. ex J.A. Murray) Sieb. & Zucc. *18270*
    V   *19723*   Japan (south) *18270*

V   *Sequoiadendron giganteum* (Lindl.) Buchh. *20850, 20171*
    V   *20761*   U.S. - California *20850*

V   *Taiwania cryptomerioides* Hayata *18270*
    V   *20511*   Taiwan (Zhongyang Range) *17617*

R   *Taiwania flousiana* Gaussen *17617*
    R   *17617*   China - Sichuan (southeast) *19703*
    R   *17617*   China - Yunnan *11139*
    V   *18270*   Myanmar (north) *18270*

R   *Taxodium mucronatum* Ten. *18270*
    R   *18270*   U.S. - Texas (south) *18270*
    R   *18270*   Guatemala (Huehuetenango) *9004*
    R   *18270*   Mexico *20369*

Ginkgopsida

Ginkgoaceae

Number of genera: 1
Number of species: 1
Recorded threatened species: 1   (100%)

China.

R   *Ginkgo biloba* L. *11139*
    R   *17617*   China - Zhejiang (Xitianmushan) *11139*

Cycadopsida

Cycadaceae

Number of genera: 1
Number of species: 35
Recorded threatened species: 20   (57%)

Madagascar; eastern and Southeast Asia; Indomalaysia; Australia; Polynesia.

E I   *Cycas beddomei* Dyer *11494*
    E   *20016*   India - Andhra Pradesh *11494*

R II   *Cycas brunnea* K.Hill *20681, 20016*
    I   *20681*   Australia - Northern Territory *20016*
    I   *20681*   Australia - Queensland *20016*

V II   *Cycas cairnsiana* F.Muell. *20681, 13882*
    V   *20681*   Australia - Queensland *13882*

R II   *Cycas celebica* Miq.
    R   Indonesia - Sulawesi

V II   *Cycas chamberlainii* W.H. Brown & Kienholz *17674*
    V   *20016*   Philippines *17674*

V II   *Cycas conferta* Chirgwin *20681, 13882*
    V   *20681*   Australia - Northern Territory *13882*

R II   *Cycas couttsiana* K.Hill *20681, 20016*
    R   *20681*   Australia - Queensland *20016*

    Cycas guizhouensis K. Lan & R. Zhou *21390, 20016*
    V   *20016*   China *20016*

V II   *Cycas hainanensis* C.J. Chen & C.Y. Chen
    V   *20016*   China - Hainan Is. *15015*

E II   *Cycas hongheensis* Yang & Yang *20894*
    E   *20894*   China - Yunnan *20894*

V II   *Cycas megacarpa* K.Hill *20681, 20016*
    V   *20681*   Australia - Queensland *20016*

E II   *Cycas micholitzii* Thisteton-Dyer *17617*
    E   *20894*   China - Guangxi (Longzhou) *8243*
    V   *20985*   Vietnam *10241*

E II   *Cycas multipinnata* C.J. Chen & S.Y. Yang *20894*
    E   *20894*   China - Yunnan *20894*

V II   *Cycas ophiolitica* K.Hill *20681, 20016*
    V   *20681*   Australia - Queensland *20681*

V II   *Cycas platyphylla* K.Hill *20681, 20016*
    V   *20681*   Australia - Queensland *20016*

R II   *Cycas seemannii* A. Br. *20016*
    R   *20016*   Pacific Is. (southwest) *20016*
    R   *20016*   Fiji *15015*
    R   *20016*   Tonga *15015*
    R   *20016*   Vanuatu *15015*

V II   *Cycas silvestris* K.Hill *20681, 20016*
    V   *20681*   Australia - Queensland *20016*

Ex II   *Cycas szechuanensis* C. Cheng & L.K. Fu *20016*
    Ex   *20016*   China *20016*

V II   *Cycas taitungensis* Shen. Hill. Tsod & Ohen *20511*
    V   *20511*   Taiwan *20511*

V II   *Cycas taiwaniana* Carruth. *11139*
    V   *20016*   China - Hainan Is. *11139*
    E   *20854*   Taiwan (Taidong; Taizhong) *11139*

E II   *Cycas wadei* Merr.
    E   *20016*   Philippines (Palawan) *13833*

Stangeriaceae

Number of genera: 1
Number of species: 1
Recorded threatened species: 1   (100%)

South Africa.

R I   *Stangeria eriopus* (Kunze) Baill. *20604, 14011*
    E   *20604*   Swaziland *20604*
    R   *20604*   South Africa - Cape Province (east Cape & Transkei) *20604*
    R   *20604*   South Africa - Natal *20604*

Zamiaceae

Number of genera: 8
Number of species: 144
Recorded threatened species: 128   (88%)

Africa; Australia; America.

E I   *Ceratozamia euryphyllidia* Vazquez-Torres, Sabato & D. Stevenson *20883, 11119*
    E   *20016*   Mexico - Veracruz *20016*

E I   *Ceratozamia hildae* Landry & M. Wilson *20883, 9114*
    E   *20883*   Mexico *20883*
    E   *20016*   Mexico - Queretaro *9114*
    E   *20016*   Mexico - San Luis Potosi *9114*

V I   *Ceratozamia kuesteriana* Regel *20883, 9114*
    V   *20883*   Mexico *20883*
    V   *20016*   Mexico - Tamaulipas *20016*

V I   *Ceratozamia latifolia* Miq. *20883, 11988*
    V   *20883*   Mexico *20883*
    V   *20016*   Mexico - Hidalgo *20016*
    V   *20016*   Mexico - Queretaro *20016*
    V   *20016*   Mexico - San Luis Potosi *20016*

R I   *Ceratozamia matudae* Lundell *20883, 9114*
    V   *20016*   Guatemala *20883*
    V   *20016*   Mexico - Chiapas *9114*
    V   *20016*   Mexico - Oaxaca *20016*

I I   *Ceratozamia mexicana* Brongn. *20883, 11988*

I		*19850*	Mexico - Hidalgo *20016*
I		*19850*	Mexico - Puebla *20016*
I		*19850*	Mexico - San Luis Potosi *9114*
I		*19850*	Mexico - Veracruz *9114*
E	*I*	*Ceratozamia microstrobila* Vovides & Rees *20883, 9114*	
	V	*20883*	Mexico *20883*
	V	*20016*	Mexico - San Luis Potosi *9114*
V	*I*	*Ceratozamia miqueliana* H. Wendl. *20883, 9019*	
	V	*20883*	Mexico *20883*
	V	*20016*	Mexico - Veracruz *9114*
V	*I*	*Ceratozamia norstogii* D. Stevenson *20883, 9114*	
	V	*20883*	Mexico *20883*
	V	*20016*	Mexico - Chiapas *9114*
R	*I*	*Ceratozamia robusta* Miq. *20883, 11988*	
	R	*20016*	Belize *20883*
	R	*20016*	Guatemala *20883*
	R	*19850*	Mexico - Chiapas *9114*
	R	*19850*	Mexico - Veracruz *9114*
V	*I*	*Ceratozamia sabatoi* Vovides et al. *19850*	
	V	*20016*	Mexico - Hidalgo *20016*
	V	*20016*	Mexico - Queretaro *20016*
E	*I*	*Ceratozamia zaragozae* Medellin-Leal *20883, 9114*	
	E	*20883*	Mexico *20883*
	E	*20016*	Mexico - San Luis Potosi *9114*
E	*I*	*Chigua bernalii* D. Stevenson *20883, 15015*	
	E	*20016*	Colombia *20883*
E	*I*	*Chigua restrepoi* D. Stevenson *20883, 15015*	
	E	*20016*	Colombia *20883*
E	*II*	*Dioon califanoi* De Luca & Sabato *20883, 9019*	
	V	*20883*	Mexico *20883*
	V	*20016*	Mexico - Oaxaca *9114*
	V	*20016*	Mexico - Puebla *20016*
E	*II*	*Dioon caputoi* De Luca, Sabato & Vazquez-Torres *20883, 9019*	
	E	*20883*	Mexico *20883*
	E	*20016*	Mexico - Puebla *9114*
R	*II*	*Dioon edule* Lindley *20883*	
	R	*20883*	Mexico *20883*
R	*II*	*Dioon edule* Lindley var. *angustifolium* (Miq.) Miq. *20883, 20016*	
	R	*20883*	Mexico *20883*
	R	*20016*	Mexico - Nuevo Leon *15015*
	R	*20016*	Mexico - San Luis Potosi *15015*
	R	*20016*	Mexico - Tamaulipas *15015*
V	*II*	*Dioon holmgrenii* De Luca, Sabato & Vazquez-Torres *20883, 20016*	
	E	*20016*	Mexico - Oaxaca *19850*
V	*II*	*Dioon mejiae* Standley & L.O. Williams *20883, 20016*	
	R	*20016*	Honduras (North) *20883*
	R	*20016*	Nicaragua *20883*
V	*II*	*Dioon merolae* De Luca, Sabato & Vazquez-Torres *20883, 20016*	
	V	*20883*	Mexico *20883*
	V	*20016*	Mexico - Chiapas *19850*
V	*II*	*Dioon purpusii* Rose *20883, 9019*	
	V	*20883*	Mexico *20883*
	V	*20016*	Mexico - Oaxaca *9114*
	R	*16360*	Mexico - Puebla *9114*
V	*II*	*Dioon rzedowskii* De Luca, A. Moretti, Sabato & Vazquez-Torres *20883, 9019*	
	E	*20016*	Mexico - Oaxaca *9114*
R	*II*	*Dioon spinulosum* Dyer *20883, 9019*	
	R	*20883*	Mexico *20883*
	R	*20016*	Mexico - Oaxaca *9114*

	R	*20016*	Mexico - Veracruz *9114*
	I	*16360*	Mexico - Yucatan *9114*
R	*II*	*Dioon tomasellii* De Luca, Sabato & Vazquez-Torres var. *sonorense* DeLuca, Sabato, V. Torres *20883, 9020*	
	V	*20016*	Mexico (North West coast) *20883*
R	*II*	*Dioon tomasellii* De Luca, Sabato & Vazquez-Torres var. *tomasellii* *20883, 9020*	
	R	*20016*	Mexico (South West Coast) *20883*
E	*I*	*Encephalartos aemulans* Vorster *20604, 20016*	
	E	*20604*	South Africa - Natal (North) *20604*
V	*I*	*Encephalartos altensteinii* Lehm. *20604, 14695*	
	V	*20604*	South Africa - Cape Province (east Cape, Ciskei & Transkei) *20604*
E	*I*	*Encephalartos arenarius* R.A.Dyer *20604*	
	E	*20604*	South Africa - Cape Province *20604*
E	*I*	*Encephalartos brevifoliolatus* P.Vorster *20847*	
	E	*20895*	South Africa - Transvaal *20847*
V	*I*	*Encephalartos bubalinus* Melville *20057*	
	V	*20057*	Kenya (Tanzania border) *19109*
	V	*20057*	Tanzania (Kenya border) *17435*
V	*I*	*Encephalartos caffer* (Thunb.) Lehm. *20604*	
	V	*20604*	South Africa - Cape Province *20604*
E	*I*	*Encephalartos cerinus* Lavranos & D.L.Goode *20604, 20016*	
	E	*20604*	South Africa - Natal (kwaZulu) *20604*
E	*I*	*Encephalartos chimanimaniensis* R.A.Dyer & I.Verd. *20604, 6088*	
	E	*20604*	Mozambique *20604*
	E	*20604*	Zimbabwe *20604*
E	*I*	*Encephalartos concinnus* R.A.Dyer & I.Verd. *20604, 6088*	
	E	*20604*	Zimbabwe *20604*
E	*I*	*Encephalartos cupidus* R.A.Dyer *20604, 17458*	
	E	*20807*	South Africa - Transvaal (east) *20604*
V	*I*	*Encephalartos cycadifolius* (Jacq.) Lehm. *20604*	
	V	*20604*	South Africa - Cape Province (east) *20604*
V	*I*	*Encephalartos delucanus* Malaisse, Sclavo & Croisiers *20016*	
	V	*20894*	Tanzania *20016*
E	*I*	*Encephalartos dolomiticus* Lavranos & D.L.Goode *20604, 17458*	
	E	*20604*	South Africa - Transvaal (east) *20604*
E	*I*	*Encephalartos dyerianus* Lavranos & D.L.Goode *20604, 20016*	
	E	*20604*	South Africa - Transvaal (east) *20604*
I	*I*	*Encephalartos equatorialis* P.J.H.Hurter & H.F.Glen *20807*	
	I	*20847*	Uganda (Lake Victoria) *20847*
V	*I*	*Encephalartos eugene-maraisii* I.Verd. *20604, 20016*	
	V	*20604*	South Africa - Transvaal (west) *20604*
R	*I*	*Encephalartos ferox* Bertol.f. *20604, 20016*	
	R	*20745*	Mozambique *20604*
	V	*20604*	South Africa - Natal *20604*
V	*I*	*Encephalartos friderici-guilielmi* Lehm. *20604, 20016*	
	V	*20604*	South Africa - Cape Province (east Cape & Transkei) *20604*
	V	*20604*	South Africa - Natal *20604*
V	*I*	*Encephalartos ghellinckii* Lem. *20604, 20016*	
	V	*20604*	South Africa - Cape Province (Transkei) *20604*

	V	20604	South Africa - Natal *20604*

V *I* *Encephalartos gratus* Prain *20604*
  V 20604 Malawi *20604*
  V 20604 Mozambique *20604*

E *I* *Encephalartos heenanii* R.A.Dyer *20604, 18023*
  E 20604 Swaziland *20604*
  E 20604 South Africa - Transvaal *20604*

R *I* *Encephalartos hildebrandtii* A. Braun & Bouche var. *dentatus* Melville *19007*
  R   Tanzania
  E 19007 Uganda *19007*

V *I* *Encephalartos hirsutus* P.J.H.Hurter & H.F.Glen *20847*
  V 20895 South Africa - Transvaal *20847*

V *I* *Encephalartos horridus* (Jacq.) Lehm. *20604, 20016*
  V 20604 South Africa - Cape Province *20604*

V *I* *Encephalartos humilis* I.Verd. *20604, 20016*
  V 20604 South Africa - Transvaal *20604*

E *I* *Encephalartos inopinus* R.A.Dyer *20604, 17458*
  E 20604 South Africa - Transvaal *20604*

V *I* *Encephalartos kisambo* Faden & Bentje *20057*
  V 20057 Kenya (Maungu Hills, Kasigau, Kisambo) *20057*

E *I* *Encephalartos laevifolius* Stapf & Burtt Davy *20604, 18023*
  E 20604 Swaziland *20604*
  E 20604 South Africa - Natal *20604*
  E 20604 South Africa - Transvaal *20604*

R *I* *Encephalartos lanatus* Stapf & Burtt Davy *20604, 20016*
  R 20604 South Africa - Transvaal *20604*

E *I* *Encephalartos latifrons* Lehm. *20604, 20016*
  E 20604 South Africa - Cape Province (east) *20604*

R *I* *Encephalartos laurentianus* De Wild. *20604, 20016*
  R 20016 Angola *20016*
  R 20016 Zaire *20016*

R *I* *Encephalartos lebomboensis* I.Verd. *20604, 5914*
  V 20745 Mozambique *20604*
  V 20604 Swaziland *20604*
  R 20604 South Africa - Natal *20604*
  R 20604 South Africa - Transvaal *20604*

R *I* *Encephalartos lehmannii* Lehm. *20604, 20016*
  R 20604 South Africa - Cape Province (east) *20604*

V *I* *Encephalartos longifolius* (Jacq.) Lehm. *20604, 15976*
  V 20604 South Africa - Cape Province *20604*

R *I* *Encephalartos manikensis* (Gilliland) Gilliland *20604, 6088*
  R 20604 Mozambique *20604*
  R 20604 Zimbabwe *20604*

E *I* *Encephalartos marunguensis* Devred
  E 20016 Zaire *6086*

E *I* *Encephalartos middelburgensis* Vors., Robb. & S.van der Westh. *20604, 20016*
  E 20604 South Africa - Transvaal (central) *20604*

E *I* *Encephalartos msinganus* Vorster *20016*
  E 20016 South Africa - Natal (kwaZulu) *20016*

E *I* *Encephalartos munchii* R.A.Dyer & I.Verd. *20604, 7922*
  E 20604 Mozambique *20604*

R *I* *Encephalartos natalensis* R.A.Dyer & I.Verd. *20604, 20016*
  R 20604 South Africa - Natal (kwaZulu) *20604*

V *I* *Encephalartos ngoyanus* I.Verd. *20604, 18023*
  V 20604 Swaziland *20604*
  V 20604 South Africa - Natal (north & kwaZulu) *20604*
  V 20604 South Africa - Transvaal (South East) *20604*

E *I* *Encephalartos nubimontanus* P.J.H.Hurter *20847*
  E 20847 South Africa - Transvaal *20847*

V *I* *Encephalartos paucidentatus* Stapf & Burtt Davy *20604, 18023*
  E 20604 Swaziland *20604*
  V 20604 South Africa - Transvaal (east) *20604*

V *I* *Encephalartos powysorum* Beentje *20057*
  V 20057 Kenya *19109*

V *I* *Encephalartos princeps* R.A.Dyer *20604, 20016*
  V 20604 South Africa - Cape Province *20604*

E *I* *Encephalartos pterogonus* R.A.Dyer & I.Verd. *20604, 7922*
  E 20604 Mozambique *20604*

E *I* *Encephalartos schmitzii* Malaisse *19624*
  E 20016 Zaire *20016*
  E 20016 Zambia *20016*

R *I* *Encephalartos sclavoi* De Luca, D. Stevenson & Moreti *20016*
  R 20016 Tanzania *20016*

R *I* *Encephalartos tegulaneus* Melville *20057*
  R 20057 Kenya *19109*

R *I* *Encephalartos transvenosus* Stapf & Burtt Davy *20604*
  R 20604 South Africa - Transvaal *20604*

V *I* *Encephalartos trispinosus* (Hook.) R.A.Dyer *20604*
  V 20604 South Africa - Cape Province (east & Ciskei) *20604*

E *I* *Encephalartos turneri* Lavranos & D.L.Goode *20604, 20016*
  E 20604 Mozambique *20604*

V *I* *Encephalartos umbeluziensis* R.A.Dyer *20604, 18023*
  V 20604 Mozambique *20604*
  E 20604 Swaziland *20604*

E *I* *Encephalartos venetus* Vorster *20604*
  E 20604 South Africa - Natal (north) *20016*
  E 20604 South Africa - Transvaal (east) *20016*

E *I* *Encephalartos whitelockii* P.J.H.Hurter *20847*
  E 20847 Uganda (Mpanga River Falls) *20847*

Ex *I* *Encephalartos woodii* Sander *20604, 3774*
  Ex 20604 South Africa - Natal (kwaZulu) *20604*

V *II* *Macrozamia conferta* D.L.Jones & P.I.Forster *20681*
  V 20681 Australia - Queensland *20681*

R *II* *Macrozamia crassifolia* P.I.Forster & D.L.Jones *20681*
  R 20681 Australia - Queensland *20681*

V *II* *Macrozamia fearnsidei* D.L.Jones *20681, 20016*
  V 20681 Australia - Queensland *20681*

R *II* *Macrozamia johnsonii* D.Jones & K.Hill *20681, 20016*
  R 20681 Australia - New South Wales *20681*

E *II* *Macrozamia lomandroides* D.L.Jones *20681, 20016*
  E 20681 Australia - Queensland *20681*

V *II* *Macrozamia macdonnellii* (Miq.) A.DC. *20681, 20016*
  V 20681 Australia - Northern Territory *20681*

R *II* *Macrozamia machinii* P.I.Forster & D.L.Jones *20681*
  R 20681 Australia - Queensland *20681*

V *II* *Macrozamia occidua* D.L.Jones & P.I.Forster *20681*

	V	20681 Australia - Queensland 20681	
R	II	*Macrozamia parcifolia* P.I.Forster & D.L.Jones 20681	
	R	20681 Australia - Queensland 20681	
E	II	*Macrozamia platyrhachis* Bailey 20681	
	E	20681 Australia - Queensland 20681	
V	II	*Macrozamia viridis* D.L.Jones & P.I.Forster 20681	
	V	20681 Australia - Queensland 20681	
V	I	*Microcycas calocoma* (Miq.) A. DC. 20883, 5607	
	E	20016 Cuba (Piñar del Río) 20883	
R	II	*Zamia acuminata* Oerst. ex Dyer in Hemsl. 20883, 11988	
	V	20883 Costa Rica 20883	
	R	20883 Nicaragua 20883	
	R	20883 Panama 20883	
R	II	*Zamia amplifolia* Hort. ex Masters 20883, 20016	
	V	20016 Colombia (Choco) 20883	
	V	20883 Ecuador 20883	
R	II	*Zamia angustifolia* Jacq. 20883, 11989	
	V	20016 Bahamas (Eleuthera) 20883	
	V	20016 Cuba (east, mainly Oriente Prov.) 20883	
V	II	*Zamia angustissima* Miq. 20883	
	V	20883 Cuba 20883	
R	II	*Zamia boliviana* (Brongn.) A. DC. 20883, 11988	
	R	20883 Bolivia 20883	
R	II	*Zamia chigua* Seem. 20883, 11988	
	V	20016 Panama 20883	
	V	20016 Colombia (Choco) 20883	
V	II	*Zamia cremnophila* Vovides, Schutzman & Dehgan 20883, 12471	
	V	20883 Mexico 20883	
	V	20016 Mexico - Tabasco 12471	
V	II	*Zamia cunaria* Dressler & D. Stevenson 20883, 20016	
	R	20894 Panama 20883	
E	II	*Zamia dressleri* D. Stevenson 20883, 20016	
	V	20894 Panama 20883	
V	II	*Zamia fischeri* Miq. 20883, 9019	
	V	20016 Mexico - Nuevo Leon 20016	
	V	20016 Mexico - Queretaro 9114	
	V	20016 Mexico - San Luis Potosi 9114	
	V	20016 Mexico - Veracruz 20016	
V	II	*Zamia furfuracea* L.f. in Aiton 20883, 9019	
	V	20883 Mexico 20883	
	V	9425 Mexico - Veracruz 9019	
R	II	*Zamia herrerae* Calderon & Standley 20883, 19850	
	E	20016 El Salvador 20883	
	E	20016 Guatemala 20883	
	E	20016 Honduras 20883	
	E	20016 Mexico - Chiapas 20016	
V	II	*Zamia inermis* Vovides, Rees & Vazquez-Torres 20883, 9114	
	E	9425 Mexico - Veracruz 9114	
V	II	*Zamia ipetiensis* D. Stevenson 20883, 20016	
	V	20883 Panama 20883	
R	II	*Zamia kickxii* Miq. 20883	
	R	20894 Cuba 20883	
R	II	*Zamia manicata* Linden ex Regel 20883, 11988	
	R	20883 Panama 20883	
	V	20883 Colombia 20883	
V	II	*Zamia montana* A. Br. 20883, 11967	
	V	20883 Colombia 20883	
Ex	II	*Zamia monticola* Chamberlain 11988	
	Ex	19763 Mexico 11988	

R	II	*Zamia muricata* Willd. 20883, 11988	
	I	20883 Colombia 20883	
	R	20016 Venezuela 20883	
I	II	*Zamia obliqua* A. Br. 20883, 11988	
	V	16317 Panama 20883	
	R	20883 Colombia (Choco) 20883	
R	II	*Zamia paucijuga* Wieland 19850	
	R	20016 Mexico 19850	
R	II	*Zamia picta* Dyer 20883, 11988	
	R	16319 Belize 16319	
	R	11988 Guatemala 11988	
	V	20883 Mexico 20883	
	R	11988 Mexico - Chiapas 15015	
V	II	*Zamia portoricensis* Urban 20883, 11989	
	V	20883 Puerto Rico (Susua Forest) 20883	
V	II	*Zamia pseudomonticola* L.D. Gomez 20883, 20016	
	R	20894 Costa Rica (west) 20883	
V	II	*Zamia pseudoparasitica* Yates in Seem. 20883, 11988	
	V	20883 Panama 20883	
E	II	*Zamia purpurea* Vovides, Rees & Vazquez-Torres 20883, 11988	
	E	20016 Mexico - Oaxaca 11988	
	E	20016 Mexico - Veracruz 11988	
R	II	*Zamia pygmaea* Sims 20883, 11989	
	R	20883 Cuba 20883	
R	II	*Zamia roezlii* Linden ex Regel 20883, 20807	
	V	20016 Panama 20883	
	V	20016 Colombia (Choco) 11988	
	V	20016 Ecuador 20016	
R	II	*Zamia skinneri* Dietr. 20883, 9006	
	V	20016 Costa Rica 20883	
	V	20016 Nicaragua 20883	
	V	20016 Panama 20883	
	V	19763 Colombia 11988	
V	II	*Zamia soconuscensis* Schutzman, Vovides & Dehgan 20883, 12471	
	V	20883 Mexico 20883	
	V	20016 Mexico - Chiapas 12471	
E	II	*Zamia spartea* A. DC. 20883, 20016	
	E	20883 Mexico 20883	
	V	20016 Mexico - Oaxaca 20016	
V	II	*Zamia splendens* Schutzman 20883, 9114	
	V	20883 Mexico 20883	
	V	20016 Mexico - Chiapas 9114	
R	II	*Zamia standleyi* Schutzman 20883, 20016	
	R	20016 Honduras 20883	
E	II	*Zamia sylvatica* Chamberlain 20883, 19850	
	E	20883 Mexico 20883	
	V	19850 Mexico - Oaxaca 15015	
R	II	*Zamia tuerckheimii* J.D. Smith 20883, 9004	
	?	Belize 9004	
	I	20883 Guatemala 20883	
	I	20883 Honduras 20883	
E	II	*Zamia vasquezii* D. Stevenson 19850	
	E	20016 Mexico - Veracruz 20016	
E	II	*Zamia verschaffeltii* Miq. 20894	
	E	20894 Mexico - Chiapas 20894	
V	II	*Zamia wallisii* A. Br. 20883, 11988	
	V	20883 Colombia 20883	

Magnoliopsida (dicots)

Acanthaceae

Number of genera:	228-250
Number of species:	2,500
Recorded threatened species:	429 (17%)

Tropical, with only a few species in temperate regions.

R   *Acanthus dioscoridis* L. var. *brevicaulis* (Freyn) A. Hossain *12840*
     R   *12840*   Turkey *12840*

R   *Acanthus dioscoridis* L. var. *laciniatus* Freyn *12840*
     R   *12840*   Turkey *12840*

R   *Acanthus dioscoridis* L. var. *perringii* (Siehe) A. Hossain *12840*
     R   *12840*   Turkey *12840*

R   *Acanthus latisepalus* C.B. Clarke
     R   Gabon

E   *Adhatoda beddomei* C.B. Clarke *20263*
     E   *20263*   India - Kerala (Travancore Hills) *20263*

I   *Andrographis beddomei* C.B. Clarke
     I   India - Andhra Pradesh

R   *Andrographis glomeruliflorum* Bremek. *19120*
     R   *19120*   Thailand *19120*

R   *Andrographis rosulata* Brem. *19120*
     R   *19120*   Thailand *19120*

I   *Andrographis stellata* Clarke *2268*
     I   India - Tamil Nadu (Nilgiri Hills) *2268*

R   *Angkalanthus oligophylla* Balf. f. *15534*
     R   *15534*   Yemen - Socotra *15534*

E   *Angkalanthus paucifolius* Balf. f.
     E   Yemen - Socotra

R   *Anisacanthus andersonii* T. Daniel *9045*
     R   *11620*   Mexico *9045*

R   *Anisacanthus tetracaulis* Leonard *9035*
     R   *11620*   Honduras *9035*

R   *Anisotes diversifolius* Balf. f. *15534*
     R   *15534*   Yemen - Socotra *15534*

E   *Apassalus parvulus* Alain & Leonard *5607*
     E   *19105*   Cuba (Guantanamo) *5607*

R   *Aphelandra adscendens* Leonard *9036*
     R   *9036*   Colombia *9036*

R   *Aphelandra albert-smithii* Leonard *9036*
     R   *9036*   Colombia *9036*

R   *Aphelandra arisema* Leonard *9036*
     R   *9036*   Colombia *9036*

R   *Aphelandra bahiensis* (Nees) Wassh. *9036*
     R   *11620*   Brazil *9036*

R   *Aphelandra benoistii* Wassh. *9036*
     R   *11620*   Ecuador *9036*

R   *Aphelandra botanodes* Leonard *9036*
     R   *9036*   Colombia *9036*

R   *Aphelandra chaponensis* Leonard *9036*
     R   *9036*   Colombia *9036*

R   *Aphelandra chrysantha* Wassh. *9036*
     R   *11620*   Ecuador *9036*

R   *Aphelandra cinnabarina* Wassh. *9036*

     R   *11620*   Ecuador *9036*

R   *Aphelandra claussenii* Wassh. *9036*
     R   *11620*   Brazil *9036*

R   *Aphelandra colorata* (Vell. Conc.) Wassh. *9036*
     R   *11620*   Brazil *9036*

R   *Aphelandra crenata* Leonard *9036*
     R   *9036*   Colombia *9036*

R   *Aphelandra crispata* Leonard *9036*
     R   *11620*   Colombia *9036*
     R   *11620*   Ecuador *9036*

R   *Aphelandra cuscoensis* Wassh. *18200*
     R   *11620*   Peru *18200*

E   *Aphelandra darienensis* Wassh. *20883, 9006*
     R   *11620*   Panama *20883*

R   *Aphelandra dichyla* Leonard *9036*
     R   *9036*   Colombia *9036*

R   *Aphelandra dielsii* Mildbr. *9036*
     R   *11620*   Ecuador *9036*

R   *Aphelandra dodsonii* Wassh. *9036*
     R   *11620*   Ecuador *9036*

R   *Aphelandra dunlapiana* Standley & L.O. Williams *9036*
     R   *11620*   Honduras *9036*

R   *Aphelandra eurystoma* Mildbr. *18200*
     R   *11620*   Peru *18200*

E   *Aphelandra ferreyrae* Wassh. *18200*
     E   *11620*   Peru *18200*

R   *Aphelandra flammea* Wassh. *9036*
     R   *11620*   Ecuador *9036*

R   *Aphelandra galba* Wassh. *9036*
     R   *11620*   Ecuador *9036*

V   *Aphelandra gracilis* Leonard *20883, 9006*
     I   *20883*   Panama *20883*

R   *Aphelandra hapala* Wassh. *18200*
     R   *11620*   Peru *18200*

I   *Aphelandra harleyi* Wassh. *9036*
     I   *11620*   Brazil *9036*

R   *Aphelandra hintonii* Wassh. *9053*
     R   *11620*   Mexico *9053*

R   *Aphelandra huilensis* Leonard *9036*
     R   *9036*   Colombia *9036*

I   *Aphelandra ignea* (Schrader) Nees ex Steudel *9036*
     I   *11620*   Brazil *9036*

R   *Aphelandra juninensis* Wassh. *18200*
     R   *11620*   Peru *18200*

R   *Aphelandra kolobantha* Lindau *9036*
     R   *9036*   Bolivia *9036*

E   *Aphelandra latibracteata* Wassh. *18200*
     E   *11620*   Peru *18200*

E   *Aphelandra laxa* Durkee *20883, 9006*
     R   *11620*   Panama *20883*

R   *Aphelandra limbatifolia* Lindau *18200*
     R   *11620*   Peru *18200*

R   *Aphelandra marginata* Nees & Martius *9036*
     R   *11620*   Brazil *9036*

I   *Aphelandra maximiliana* (Nees) Benth. *9036*
     I   *11620*   Brazil *9036*

R   *Aphelandra micans* Moritz ex Vatke *9036*
     R   *11620*   Venezuela *9036*

R *Aphelandra montis-scalaris* Lindau ex Pilger *18200*
   R   *11620* Peru *18200*

E *Aphelandra mucronata* (Ruiz Lopez & Pavon) Nees *18200*
   E   *11620* Peru *18200*

R *Aphelandra neesiana* Wassh. *9036*
   R   *11620* Brazil *9036*

I *Aphelandra nemoralis* Nees *9036*
   I   *11620* Brazil *9036*

R *Aphelandra nephoica* Wassh. *9036*
   R   *9036* Colombia *9036*

R *Aphelandra nuda* Nees *9036*
   R   *11620* Brazil *9036*

I *Aphelandra obtusa* (Nees) Wassh. *9036*
   I   *11620* Brazil *9036*

I *Aphelandra obtusifolia* (Nees) Wassh. *9036*
   I   *11620* Brazil *9036*

R *Aphelandra paulensis* Wassh. *9036*
   R   *11620* Brazil *9036*

E *Aphelandra pepe-parodii* Wassh. *18200*
   E   *11620* Peru *18200*

R *Aphelandra phrynioides* Lindau *9036*
   R   *11620* Brazil *9036*

R *Aphelandra pinarotricha* Leonard *9036*
   R   *9036* Colombia *9036*

R *Aphelandra quadrifaria* Leonard *9036*
   R   *9036* Colombia *9036*

R *Aphelandra reticulata* Wassh. *9036*
   R   *11620* Venezuela *9036*

I *Aphelandra rigida* Glaziou ex Mildbr. *9036*
   I   *11620* Brazil *9036*

R *Aphelandra seibertii* Leonard *9037*
   R   *11620* Costa Rica *9037*
   R   *11620* Panama *9037*

R *Aphelandra speciosa* Brandegee *9004*
   R   *11620* Guatemala *9004*
   I   *11620* Mexico *9004*

I *Aphelandra stephanophysa* Nees *9036*
   I   *11620* Brazil *9036*

I *Aphelandra steyermarkii* Wassh. *9036*
   I   *11620* Venezuela *9036*

V *Aphelandra storkii* Leonard *9037*
   V   *11620* Costa Rica *9037*

I *Aphelandra sulphurea* Hook.
   I   Ecuador

R *Aphelandra superba* Lindau
   R   Ecuador

R *Aphelandra terryae* Standl. *20883*
   R   *20883* Panama *20883*
   I   *20883* Colombia *20883*

I *Aphelandra tessmannii* Mildbr. *18200*
   I   *11620* Peru *18200*

R *Aphelandra tillettii* Wassh. *18200*
   R   *11620* Peru *18200*

R *Aphelandra tonduzii* Leonard *9037*
   R   *11620* Costa Rica *9037*
   R   *11620* Panama *9006*

E *Aphelandra verticellata* Nees ex Hemsley *9036*
   E   *11620* Mexico *9036*

E *Aphelandra viscosa* Mildbr. *18200*
   E   *11620* Peru *18200*

R *Aphelandra weberbaueri* Mildbr. *18200*
   R   *11620* Peru *18200*

R *Aphelandra wurdackii* Wassh. *18200*
   R   *9036* Peru *9036*

E *Barleria aculeata* Balf. f. *15534*
   E   *15534* Yemen - Socotra *15534*

V *Barleria argillicola* Oberm. *20604*
   V   *20604* South Africa - Natal *20604*

R *Barleria dolomiticola* M. & K.Balkwill *20604*
   R   *20604* South Africa - Transvaal *20604*

R *Barleria gibsonioides* Blatt. et McC. *13883*
   R   *13883* India - Maharashtra (Panchgani, Satara Dist.) *13883*

V *Barleria greenii* M. & K.Balkwill *20604*
   V   *20604* South Africa - Natal *20604*

R *Barleria lancifolia* T. Anderson var. *charlesii* Benoist
   R   Mauritania

R *Barleria megalosiphon* Mildbr.
   R   Namibia

R *Barleria molensis* Wild *7752*
   R   Zimbabwe *7752*

Ex *Barleria natalensis* Lindau *20604*
   Ex   *20604* South Africa - Natal *20604*

E *Barleria observatrix* Bosser & Heine *10082*
   E   *20771* Mauritius *10082*

E *Barleria popovii* Verdc. *15534*
   E   *15534* Yemen - Socotra *15534*

I *Barleria prionitis* L. var. *diacantha* Blatter & Hallberg *7771*
   I   India - Rajasthan *7771*

R *Barleria schmittii* Benoist *7926*
   R   Mauritania *7926*

V *Blechum killipii* Leonard *20883, 19221*
   R   *13336* Jamaica *20883*

R *Blepharis attenuata* Napper *8895*
   R   Israel *8895*

V *Blepharis spiculifolia* Balf. f. *15534*
   V   *15534* Yemen - Socotra *15534*

R *Bravaisia grandiflora* J.D. Smith *9004*
   R   *11620* Belize *9004*
   R   *11620* Guatemala *9004*
   R   *11620* Mexico *9004*

V *Carlowrightia albiflora* Daniel *20883, 9038*
   V   *20883* Mexico *20883*
   R   *9038* Mexico - Tamaulipas *9038*

R *Carlowrightia hapalocarpa* Robinson & Greenman *9038*
   R   *11550* Mexico - San Luis Potosi *9038*

V *Carlowrightia henricksonii* Daniel *20883, 9038*
   E   *20883* Mexico *20883*
   R   *9038* Mexico - Tamaulipas *9038*

R *Carlowrightia hintonii* Daniel *20883*
   R   *20883* Mexico *20883*

V *Carlowrightia lesueurii* Henrickson & Daniel *20883*
   E   *20883* Mexico *20883*

R *Carlowrightia mcvaughii* Daniel *20883, 9038*
   I   *20883* Mexico *20883*

V *Carlowrightia ovata* A. Gray *20883, 9038*

E	20883	Mexico *20883*
R	9038	Mexico - Chihuahua *9038*

R *Carlowrightia pectinata* Brandegee *20883, 9038*

I	20883	Mexico *20883*

R *Carlowrightia pringlei* Robinson & Greenman *20883, 9038*

V	20883	Mexico *20883*
R	11620	Mexico - Oaxaca *9038*
R	11620	Mexico - Puebla *9038*

R *Carlowrightia trichocarpa* Daniel *20883, 9038*

R	20883	Mexico *20883*
V	11620	Mexico - Tamaulipas *9038*

R *Chamaeranthemum tonduzii* Lindau *9037*

R	9420	Costa Rica *9037*

E *Dicliptera abuensis* Blatter *11494*

E	11494	India - Rajasthan (Mt Abu, Dhobi Ghats) *11494*

R *Dicliptera albocostata* Brem. *19120*

R	19120	Thailand *19120*

R *Dicliptera antidysenterica* A. Molina *9039*

R	11620	Honduras *9039*

R *Dicliptera australis* (Nees) R.M.Barker *20681*

R	20681	Australia - Northern Territory *20681*

I *Dicliptera beddomei* C.B. Clarke

I		India - Andhra Pradesh (Nallamalai Hills; Kurnool)

I *Dicliptera clavata* (J.G.Forster) A.L.Jussieu *20845*

Ex	20845	French Polynesia - Society Is. (Tahiti) *20845*

I *Dicliptera debilis* Leonard *9004*

I	11620	Guatemala *9004*

E *Dicliptera dodsonii* Wassh. *6155*

E	6155	Ecuador *6155*

R *Dicliptera effusa* Balf. f. *15534*

R	15534	Yemen - Socotra (Socotra and Abd al Kuri) *15534*

Ex *Dicliptera falcata* (Lam.) Bosser & Heine *10082*

Ex	20771	Mauritius *10082*

I *Dicliptera forsteriana* C.Nees *20845*

I	20845	French Polynesia - Society Is. *20845*
I	20845	French Polynesia - Tubuai Is. (Rapa) *20845*

R *Dicliptera fragilis* Brem. *19120*

R	19120	Thailand *19120*

I *Dicliptera ghatica* Sant. *13883*

I	13883	India - Maharashtra (Meroli, Khandala ghats, Pune Dist.) *13883*

E *Dicliptera gracilis* Leonard *20883, 9006*

I	11620	Panama *20883*

I *Dicliptera guttata* Standley & Leonard *9004*

I	11620	Guatemala *9004*

R *Dicliptera imbricata* Leonard *9417*

R	9420	Costa Rica *9417*

I *Dicliptera inutilis* Leonard *9004*

I	11620	Guatemala *9004*

E *Dicliptera krugii* Urban *20883, 15106*

I	20883	Puerto Rico *20883*

V *Dicliptera maclearii* Hemsley *881*

V	14224	Australia - Christmas Is. *881*

V *Dicliptera membranacea* Leonard *9004*

V	11620	Guatemala *9004*
V	11620	Mexico *9004*

R *Dicliptera pallida* Leonard *9037*

R	9420	Costa Rica *9037*

R *Dicliptera paposana* Philippi *5595*

R	19534	Chile *5595*

R *Dicliptera skutchii* Leonard *9039*

R	9420	Costa Rica *9037*

R *Dicliptera syringifolia* Merxm. *7769*

R		Zimbabwe (Rusape) *7769*

I *Dicliptera trianae* Leonard *16887*

I	19353	Colombia *16887*

I *Didyplosandra andersonii* (Beddome) Bremek.

I		India - Tamil Nadu

R *Dipteracanthus orthocaulus* Brem. *19120*

R	19120	Thailand *19120*

R *Dipteracanthus subulatua* (Imlay) Brem. *19120*

R	19120	Thailand *19120*

V *Drejerella maestrensis* Urban *5607*

V	19105	Cuba (Santiago de Cuba) *5607*

V *Dyschoriste angusta* (Gray) Small *20850*

V	20850	U.S. - Florida *20850*

R *Dyschoriste hondurensis* Leonard *9035*

R	11620	Honduras *9035*

I *Ecbolium striatum* Balf. f. *15534*

I	15534	Yemen - Socotra *15534*
I	15534	Kenya *15534*
I	15534	Somalia *15534*

I *Ecbolium striatum* Balf. f. var. *minor* Balf. f. *15534*

I	15534	Yemen - Socotra *15534*

V *Elytraria bissei* H. Dietrich *11840*

V	19105	Cuba (Guantanamo) *11840*

V *Elytraria caroliniensis* (Walter ex J. Gmelin) Pers. var. *angustifolia* (Fern.) Blake *20850*

V	20850	U.S. - Florida *20850*

V *Elytraria filicaulis* Borh. & Muniz *5607*

V	19105	Cuba (Holguin; Guantanamo) *5607*

R *Elytraria macrophylla* Leonard *11550*

R	11550	Mexico *11550*

V *Elytraria spathulifolia* Borh. & Muniz *5607*

V	19105	Cuba (Guantanamo) *5607*

V *Graptophyllum balansae* Heine *20893*

V	20893	New Caledonia *20893*

R *Graptophyllum excelsum* (F.Muell.) Druce *20681*

R	20681	Australia - Queensland *20681*

V *Graptophyllum ilicifolium* (F.Muell.) F.Muell. *20681*

V	20681	Australia - Queensland *20681*

V *Graptophyllum ophiolithicum* Heine *20893*

V	20893	New Caledonia *20893*

E *Graptophyllum reticulatum* A.R.Bean & Sharpe *20681*

E	20681	Australia - Queensland *20681*

R *Gymnostachyum glomeruliflorum* Brem. *19120*

R	19120	Thailand *19120*

I *Gymnostachyum pictum* Elm. *13833*

I	13833	Philippines (Palawan) *13833*

I *Gymnostachyum thwaitesii* T. Anderson *10252*

I	16162	Sri Lanka *10252*

R *Gypsacanthus nelsonii* Lott, Jaramillo & Rzed. *9488*

R	11620	Mexico - Guerrero *9488*
R	11620	Mexico - Puebla *9488*

R	*Habracanthus azureus* D. Gibson *9004*	
	R	*11620* Guatemala *9004*
R	*Habracanthus lamprus* Leonard *10166*	
	R	*19538* Colombia *10166*
R	*Habracanthus latilabris* D. Gibson *9004*	
	R	*11620* Guatemala *9004*
R	*Habracanthus luteus* Durkee *9420*	
	R	*9420* Costa Rica *9420*
R	*Habracanthus ruberrimus* D. Gibson *9004*	
	R	*11620* Guatemala *9004*
I	*Hallieracantha addisoniensis* (Elm.) Merr. *13833*	
	I	*13833* Philippines (low altitude) *13833*
I	*Hallieracantha aequifolia* (C.B. Clarke) Merr. *13833*	
	I	*13833* Philippines (low altitude) *13833*
I	*Hallieracantha elmeri* Merr. *13833*	
	I	*13833* Philippines (low altitude) *13833*
I	*Hallieracantha pulgarensis* Elm. *13833*	
	I	*13833* Philippines *13833*
V	*Hansteinia reflexiflora* Leonard *20883, 9006*	
	I	*20883* Panama *20883*
V	*Hansteinia sessilifolia* (Oersted) Durkee *9037*	
	V	*9420* Costa Rica *9037*
E	*Hemigraphis neocaledonica* Heine *20893*	
	E	*20893* New Caledonia *20893*
I	*Henrya gualanensis* (H. Robinson & Bartlett) Happ *9004*	
	I	*11620* Guatemala *9004*
E	*Henrya tuberculosperma* T. F. Daniel *20883, 9046*	
	I	*20883* Mexico *20883*
	R	*11620* Mexico - Jalisco *9046*
R	*Herpetacanthus panamensis* Leonard *20883, 9006*	
	I	*20883* Costa Rica *20883*
	V	*20883* Panama *20883*
R	*Holographis anisophylla* T. Daniel *9048*	
	R	*11620* Mexico - Colima *9048*
R	*Holographis argyrea* (Leonard) T. Daniel *9040*	
	R	*19848* Mexico *19848*
	R	*16360* Mexico - Guerrero *9040*
R	*Holographis hintonii* (Leonard) T. Daniel *9048*	
	R	*11620* Mexico - Guerrero *9048*
R	*Holographis ilicifolia* Brandegee *9048*	
	R	*11620* Mexico *9048*
R	*Holographis pallida* Leonard & H. Gentry *9048*	
	R	*11620* Mexico *9048*
R	*Holographis parayana* Miranda *9048*	
	R	*11620* Mexico *9048*
R	*Holographis peloria* (Leonard) T. Daniel *9049*	
	R	*11620* Mexico - Durango *9049*
R	*Holographis pueblensis* T. Daniel *9048*	
	R	*11620* Mexico - Puebla *9048*
R	*Hoverdenia speciosa* Nees *11550*	
	R	*11550* Mexico *11550*
R	*Hygrophila chevalieri* Benoist *7926*	
	R	Mali *8003*
	R	Senegal *8003*
R	*Hygrophila micrantha* (Nees) T. Anderson *7926*	
	R	Mali *7926*
	R	Senegal *8003*
I	*Hygrophila pinnatifida* (Dalz.) Sreemadh.	

I		India - Karnataka
E	*Hygrophila pogonocalyx* Hayata *20511*	
	E	*20511* Taiwan *20511*
V	*Hypoestes andamanensis* Thoth. *14782*	
	V	*14782* India - Andaman Is. *14782*
Ex	*Hypoestes inconspicua* Balf.f. *10082*	
	Ex	*5852* Mauritius - Rodrigues *5852*
R	*Hypoestes lanata* Dalz. *14782*	
	R	*14782* India *14782*
I	*Hypoestes larsenii* Brem. *19120*	
	I	*19120* Thailand *19120*
I	*Hypoestes merrillii* Clarke ex Elm. *13833*	
	I	*13833* Philippines (low altitude) *13833*
I	*Hypoestes palawanensis* Clarke *13833*	
	I	*13833* Philippines (Palawan) *13833*
I	*Hypoestes pubescens* Balf. f. *15534*	
	I	*15534* Yemen - Socotra *15534*
Ex	*Hypoestes rodriguesiana* Balf.f. *10082*	
	Ex	*5852* Mauritius - Rodrigues (Mont Malartic) *5852*
Ex	*Hypoestes serpens* (Vahl) R.Br. *10082*	
	Ex	*20771* Mauritius *10082*
E	*Isoglossa eranthemoides* (F.Muell.) R.M.Barker *20681*	
	E	*20681* Australia - New South Wales *20681*
I	*Isoglossa nervosa* C.B. Clarke	
	I	Cameroon (Mt Cameroon)
R	*Justicia agria* Alain & Leonard *5607*	
	R	*19105* Cuba (Granma) *5607*
E	*Justicia allenii* (Leonard) Durkee *20883, 9006*	
	R	*11620* Panama *20883*
V	*Justicia angusta* (Chapman) Small *20850*	
	V	*20850* U.S. - Florida *20850*
I	*Justicia bartlettii* (Leonard) D. Gibson *9004*	
	I	*11620* Belize *9004*
	I	*11620* Guatemala *9004*
V	*Justicia blechoides* (Lindau) Stearn *20883, 19221*	
	R	*13336* Jamaica *20883*
R	*Justicia bolusii* C.B.Clarke *20604*	
	R	*20604* South Africa - Cape Province *20604*
V	*Justicia borinquensis* Britt. *20883, 8058*	
	I	*20883* Puerto Rico *20883*
R	*Justicia borrerae* (Hemsley) T.F. Daniel *9001*	
	R	*11620* Guatemala *9001*
	R	*11620* Mexico *9001*
Ex	*Justicia brachystachya* Thouars ex Schultz *15112*	
	Ex	*15112* Mauritius *15112*
R	*Justicia brenesii* (Leonard) D. Gibson *9420*	
	R	*9420* Costa Rica *9420*
R	*Justicia breteleri* Wasshausen *21279*	
	R	*21279* Venezuela *21279*
I	*Justicia calliantha* Leonard *9039*	
	I	*11620* Honduras *9039*
R	*Justicia ciliata* (Yamamoto) Hsieh & Huang *20511*	
	R	*20511* Taiwan *20511*
V	*Justicia coahuilana* T. Daniel *9041*	
	V	*11620* Mexico *9041*
E	*Justicia cooleyi* Monachino & Leonard *20850, 17890*	
	E	*20850* U.S. - Florida *20850*

R   *Justicia costaricana* Leonard *9037*
     R   *9420*   Costa Rica *9037*

V   *Justicia crassifolia* (Chapman) Chapman ex **Small** *20850*
     V   *20850* U.S. - Florida *20850*

E   *Justicia culebritae* Urban *20883*
     I   *20883* Puerto Rico (Culebrita) *20883*
     I   *20883* British Virgin Is. (Virgin Gorda) *20883*
     ?   *19002* USA - Virgin Is. *19002*

R   *Justicia ensiflora* (Standley) D. Gibson *9004*
     R   *11620* Belize *9004*
     R   *11620* Honduras *9004*

R   *Justicia graciliflora* (Standl.) D. Gibson *20883, 9006*
     I   *20883* Panama *20883*

R   *Justicia grandifolia* D. Gibson *9004*
     R   *11620* Guatemala *9004*

E   *Justicia hepperi* Heine *7926*
     E   Nigeria *7926*

R   *Justicia hyssopifolia* L. *15105*
     R   *15105* Spain - Canary Is. *15105*

I   *Justicia ianthina* Wassh. *6155*
     I   *11620* Ecuador *6155*

V   *Justicia jamaicensis* (Britton) Stearn *20883, 19221*
     R   *13336* Jamaica *20883*

R   *Justicia lindeniana* (Nees) Macbr. *9004*
     R   *11620* Guatemala *9004*
     R   *11620* Mexico *9004*

R   *Justicia linearis* Robinson & Greenman *9041*
     R   *11550* Mexico *9041*

R   *Justicia macrantha* Bentham var. *piliformis* D. Gibson *9004*
     R   *11620* Guatemala *9004*

E   *Justicia mckenleyi* Proctor *20883, 13336*
     E   *13336* Jamaica *20883*

V   *Justicia metallica* Lindau *9037*
     V   *11620* Costa Rica *9037*
     V   *11620* Panama *9037*

I   *Justicia microcarpa* Ridley
     I   Malaysia - Peninsular Malaysia (Selangor)

R   *Justicia minima* A.Meeuse *20604*
     R   *20604* South Africa - Transvaal *20604*

R   *Justicia montana* (Standley & Leonard) D. Gibson *9004*
     R   *11620* Guatemala *9004*

V   *Justicia multicaulis* J.D. Smith *9004*
     V   *11620* Guatemala *9004*

R   *Justicia nemorosa* Sw. *20883*
     R   *20883* Jamaica *20883*

E   *Justicia nigerica* S. Moore *7926*
     E   Nigeria *7926*

R   *Justicia niokolo-kobae* Berhaut *8003*
     R   Mali (Keniaba) *8003*
     R   Senegal (Niokolo-Koba) *8003*

I   *Justicia novogranatensis* Leonard *16887*
     I   *19353* Colombia *16887*

V   *Justicia oreophila* Clarke *14872*
     V   *14872* Bangladesh *14872*

R   *Justicia orosiensis* Durkee *9420*
     R   *9420*   Costa Rica *9420*

E   *Justicia panamense* Durkee *20883, 9006*

     I   *11620* Panama *20883*

R   *Justicia pectoralis* Jacq. var. *ovata* Wassh. *6155*
     R   *11620* Ecuador *6155*

R   *Justicia pedicellata* D. Gibson *9004*
     R   *11620* Guatemala *9004*

E   *Justicia pinensis* S. Moore *20893*
     E   *20893* New Caledonia *20893*

R   *Justicia pittieri* Lindau *9037*
     R   *11620* Costa Rica *9037*
     R   *11620* Panama *9417*

I   *Justicia preussii* (Lindau) C.B. Clarke
     I   Cameroon (Buea, Mimbia)

R   *Justicia procumbens* L. var. *hayatai* (Yamamoto) Ohwi *20511*
     R   *20511* Taiwan *20511*

R   *Justicia procumbens* L. var. *linearifolia* Yamamoto *20511*
     R   *20511* Taiwan *20511*

Ex   *Justicia psychotrioides* Thouars ex Schultz *15112*
     Ex   *15112* Mauritius *15112*

R   *Justicia refulgens* Leonard *9037*
     R   *11620* Panama *9037*

V   *Justicia rigida* Balf. f. *15534*
     V   *15534* Yemen - Socotra *15534*

R   *Justicia riopalenquensis* Wassh.
     R   Ecuador

R   *Justicia robinsonii* Ridley
     R   Malaysia - Peninsular Malaysia (Langkawi, Kedah)

V   *Justicia runyonii* Small *20883, 20850, 8058*
     V   *20850* U.S. - Texas *20850*
     I   *20883* Mexico *20883*

I   *Justicia rupestris* Ridley
     I   Malaysia - Peninsular Malaysia

I   *Justicia salsoloides* T. Anderson
     I   India - Karnataka (Carnatic & Mysore)

E   *Justicia sarapiquensis* McDade *20883, 9044*
     R   *11620* Costa Rica *20883*

R   *Justicia sericea* Ruiz Lopez & Pavon *18200*
     R   *11620* Peru *18200*

R   *Justicia silvicola* D. Gibson *9004*
     R   *11620* Guatemala *9004*

I   *Justicia skutchii* Leonard *9037*
     I   *9420*   Costa Rica *9037*

V   *Justicia sonorae* Wassh. *9052*
     V   *11550* Mexico *9052*

V   *Justicia stenophylla* Urban & Britton *5607*
     V   *19105* Cuba (Camaguey) *5607*

I   *Justicia steyermarkii* Standley & Leonard *9004*
     I   *11620* Guatemala *9004*

I   *Justicia subalternans* C.B. Clarke
     I   Malaysia - Peninsular Malaysia

V   *Justicia sulfurea* (J.D. Smith) D. Gibson *9004*
     V   *11620* Guatemala *9004*

V   *Justicia tonduzii* Lindau *9037*
     V   *9420*   Costa Rica *9037*

R   *Justicia urophylla* (Lindau) D. Gibson *9006*
     R   *11620* Costa Rica *9006*
     I   *11620* Panama *9006*

I	*Justicia valida* Ridley		
	I		Malaysia - Peninsular Malaysia
R	*Justicia warnockii* B.L. Turner *20850*		
	R	*20850*	U.S. - Texas *20850*
V	*Justicia wrightii* Gray *20850*		
	V	*20850*	U.S. - New Mexico *20850*
	V	*20850*	U.S. - Texas *20850*
I	*Kudoacanthus albo-nervosa* Hosok. *20511*		
	I	*20511*	Taiwan *20511*
I	*Lepidagathis amaranthoides* Elm. *13833*		
	I	*13833*	Philippines (low altitude) *13833*
R	*Lepidagathis barberi* Gamble *14782*		
	R	*14782*	India (Southern Peninsular India) *14782*
R	*Lepidagathis brevispica* Brem. *19120*		
	R	*19120*	Thailand *19120*
I	*Lepidagathis chiangraiensis* Brem. *19120*		
	I	*19120*	Thailand *19120*
I	*Lepidagathis diffusa* Clarke *14782*		
	I	*14782*	India *14782*
I	*Lepidagathis palawanensis* Merr. *13833*		
	I	*13833*	Philippines (low altitude) *13833*
R	*Lepidagathis stenophylla* Clarke ex Hayata *20511*		
	R	*20511*	Taiwan *20511*
R	*Lophostachys guatemalensis* J.D. Smith *9004*		
	R	*11620*	El Salvador *9004*
	R	*11620*	Guatemala *9004*
E	*Lophostachys zungiae* C. Nelson *20050*		
	E	*20050*	Honduras *20050*
R	*Louteridium chartaceum* Leonard *9004*		
	R	*11620*	Belize *9004*
R	*Louteridium mexicanum* (Baillon) Standley *9004*		
	R	*11620*	Guatemala *9004*
	R	*19848*	Mexico *19848*
E	*Louteridium rzedowskii* T. F. Daniel *20883, 9046*		
	I	*20883*	Mexico *20883*
R	*Mackenziea caudata* (T. And.) Ramam. *13883*		
	R	*13883*	India - Karnataka (South Canara; Coorg) *13883*
	R	*13883*	India - Kerala (Wynaad & Travancore, southwestern Ghats) *13883*
I	*Mananthes tenuispica* Brem. *19120*		
	I	*19120*	Thailand *19120*
V	*Megalostoma viridescens* Leonard *9004*		
	V	*11620*	Guatemala *9004*
R	*Mendoncia costaricana* Oersted *9037*		
	R	*9420*	Costa Rica *9037*
	R	*11620*	Panama *9037*
R	*Mendoncia hoffmannseggiana* Nees *8679*		
	R	*8679*	French Guiana *8679*
	R	*19954*	Guyana *19954*
	R	*8679*	Suriname *8679*
E	*Metarungia galpinii* (Baden) Baden *20604*		
	E	*20604*	South Africa - Cape Province *20604*
R	*Mexacanthus mcvaughii* T. Daniel *9043*		
	R	*11550*	Mexico *9043*
V	*Mirandea huastecensis* T. Daniel *9042*		
	V	*11550*	Mexico *9042*
R	*Monechma saxatile* Munday *20604*		
	R	*20604*	South Africa - Cape Province *20604*
R	*Neriacanthus grandiflorus* Leonard *9006*		

	R	*11620*	Panama *9006*
	R	*11620*	Colombia *9006*
R	*Neriacanthus purdieanus* Benth. *20883, 13336*		
	R	*13336*	Jamaica *20883*
I	*Neuracanthus aculeatus* Balf. f. *15534*		
	I	*15534*	Yemen - Socotra *15534*
I	*Neuracanthus capitatus* Balf. f. *15534*		
	I	*15534*	Yemen - Socotra *15534*
	I	*15534*	Somalia *15534*
Ex/E	*Neuracanthus neesianus* Clarke *13883*		
	Ex/E	*13883*	India - Tamil Nadu *13883*
I	*Nilgirianthus campanulatus* (Wight) Bremek.		
	I		India - Karnataka (Coorg)
I	*Nilgirianthus papillosus* (T. Anders.) Bremek. *2268*		
	I		India - Tamil Nadu (Nilgiri Hills) *2268*
I	*Odontonema brevipes* Urb. *5932*		
	I	*5932*	Trinidad & Tobago (Tobago) *5932*
V	*Odontonema microphyllus* Durkee *20883, 9006*		
	I	*20883*	Panama *20883*
V	*Oplonia acicularis* (Sw.) Stearn *20883*		
	V	*20883*	Jamaica *20883*
V	*Oplonia acunae* Borh. *5607*		
	V	*19105*	Cuba (Sancti Spiritus; Granma; Santiago de Cuba) *5607*
R	*Oplonia armata* (Sw.) Stearn var. *armata* *20883*		
	R	*20883*	Jamaica *20883*
R	*Oplonia armata* (Sw.) Stearn var. *pallidior* Stearn *20883*		
	R	*20883*	Jamaica *20883*
R	*Oplonia hutchisonii* Wassh. *18200*		
	R	*11620*	Peru *18200*
R	*Oplonia jamaicensis* (Lindau) Stearn *20883*		
	R	*20883*	Jamaica *20883*
V	*Oplonia moana* Borh. *5607*		
	V	*19105*	Cuba (Holguin; Guantanamo) *5607*
R	*Peristrophe brassii* R.M.Barker *20681*		
	R	*20681*	Australia - Queensland *20681*
I	*Peristrophe cliffordii* K.Balkwill *20604*		
	I	*20604*	South Africa - Transvaal *20604*
I	*Peristrophe gillilandiorum* K.Balkwill *20604*		
	I	*20604*	Zimbabwe *20604*
	I	*20604*	South Africa - Transvaal *20604*
R	*Peristrophe namibiensis* K.Balkwill ssp. *brandbergensis* K.Balkwill *20604*		
	R	*20604*	Namibia *20604*
R	*Peristrophe namibiensis* K.Balkwill ssp. *namibiensis* *20604*		
	R	*20604*	Namibia *20604*
R	*Phidiasia lindavii* Urban *11840*		
	R	*19105*	Cuba (Holguin) *11840*
I	*Phlebophyllum canaricum* (Beddome) Bremak.		
	I		India - Karnataka (South Canara)
E	*Phlebophyllum jeyporensis* (Beddome) Bremek. *11494*		
	E	*11494*	India - Andhra Pradesh *11494*
	E	*11494*	India - Madhaya Pradesh (Bastar) *11494*
	E	*11494*	India - Orissa (Kalahandi & Koraput) *11494*
I	*Phlebophyllum lanatum* (Nees) Bremak.		
	I		India - Karnataka (Mysore)

I   India - Tamil Nadu (Sispara, Nilgiri Hills)

E   *Physacanthus talbotii* S. Moore *7926*
     E   Nigeria *7926*

I   *Plegmatolemma leucostachyum* Brem. *19120*
     I   *19120* Thailand *16120*

I   *Plegmatolemma minus* Brem. *19120*
     I   *19120* Thailand *19120*

E   *Poikilacanthus capitatus* (Leonard) Ramamoorthy *20883*
     I   *20883* Mexico *20883*

V   *Poikilacanthus pansamalanus* (J.D. Smith) D. Gibson *9004*
     V   *11620* Guatemala *9004*

R   *Poikilacanthus setiferus* Standley & Steyerm. *9004*
     R   *11620* Guatemala *9004*
     R   *11620* Mexico *9004*

R   *Poikilacanthus skutchii* D. Gibson *9004*
     R   *11620* Guatemala *9004*

I   *Polytrema cupreum* Ridley
     I   Malaysia - Peninsular Malaysia (near Ipoh, Perak)

V   *Pseuderanthemum incisum* Benoist *20802*
     V   *20893* New Caledonia *20802*

R   *Pseuderanthemum longistylum* Imlay *19120*
     R   *19120* Thailand *19120*

I   *Pseuderanthemum micranthum* Leonard *16887*
     I   *19353* Colombia *16887*

I   *Pseuderanthemum minutiflorum* (Elm.) Merr. *13833*
     I   *13833* Philippines (low altitude) *13833*

R   *Pseuderanthemum pittieri* Leonard *9037*
     R   *9420* Costa Rica *9037*

E   *Pseuderanthemum tunicatum* (Afzel.) Milne-Redh. *19181*
     E   *19181* Seychelles (Silhouette) *14296*

R   *Psiloesthes elongata* Benoist *6057*
     I   *20985* Vietnam *6057*

V   *Pulchranthus adenostachyus* (Lindau) Baum *20883*
     I   *20883* Brazil *20883*
     I   *20883* Colombia *20883*
     I   *20883* Peru *20883*

E   *Pulchranthus congestus* (Lindau) Baum, Reveal, & Nowicke *20883*
     I   *20883* Brazil *20883*

E   *Pulchranthus surinamensis* (Bremek.) Baum *20883*
     I   *20883* Suriname *20883*

E   *Pulchranthus variegatus* (Aublet) Baum *20883*
     I   *20883* Brazil *20883*
     I   *20883* French Guiana *20883*

E   *Razisea wilburii* McDade *20883, 9417*
     R   *11620* Costa Rica *20883*

V   *Rhaphidospora bonneyana* (F.Muell.) R.M.Barker *20681*
     Ex/E *20681* Australia - New South Wales *20681*
     V   *20681* Australia - Queensland *20681*

I   *Rhaphidospora lanceolata* Brem. *19120*
     I   *19120* Thailand *19120*

R   *Rhinacanthus pulcher* Milne-Redh. *17435*
     R   *17435* Kenya *17435*

R   *Rhinacanthus scoparius* Balf. f. *15534*
     R   *15534* Yemen - Socotra *15534*

I   *Rhyticalymma kerrii* (Imlay) Brem. *19120*
     I   *19120* Thailand *19120*

R   *Rhyticalymma longipetiolatum* Brem. *19120*

R   *19120* Thailand *19120*

R   *Rhyticalymma trichocarpum* (Imlay) Brem. *19120*
     R   *19120* Thailand *19120*

I   *Rostellularia bankaoensis* Brem. *19120*
     I   *19120* Thailand *19120*

I   *Rostellularia elegans* Brem. *19120*
     I   *19120* Thailand *19120*

I   *Rostellularia rachaburiensis* Brem. *19120*
     I   *19120* Thailand *19120*

V   *Ruellia anthracina* Leonard *20883, 9006*
     R   *11620* Panama *20883*

I   *Ruellia barbillana* Cuf. *9037*
     I   *9420* Costa Rica *9037*

I   *Ruellia carnea* Balf. f. *15534*
     I   *15534* Saudi Arabia *15534*
     I   *15534* Yemen - Socotra *15534*
     I   *15534* Ethiopia *15534*
     I   *15534* Somalia *15534*

E   *Ruellia colonensis* Wassh. *20883, 9006*
     R   *11620* Panama *20883*

R   *Ruellia cordata* Brandegee *9002*
     R   *11620* Mexico *9002*

R   *Ruellia dioscoridis* Napper *15534*
     R   *15534* Yemen - Socotra *15534*

R   *Ruellia macrosolen* Lillo ex Ezcurra *20883*
     I   *20883* Argentina *20883*
     I   *20883* Bolivia *20883*
     I   *20883* Paraguay *20883*

V   *Ruellia noctiflora* (Nees) Gray *20850*
     E   *20850* U.S. - Alabama *20850*
     V   *20850* U.S. - Florida *20850*
     E   *20850* U.S. - Georgia *20850*
     E   *20850* U.S. - Louisiana *20850*
     V   *20850* U.S. - Mississippi *20850*

I   *Ruellia nudispica* Clarke *13833*
     I   *13833* Philippines (low altitude) *13833*

I   *Ruellia obtusata* S.F. Blake *9004*
     I   *11620* Belize *9004*

V   *Ruellia pedunculata* Torr. ex Gray ssp. *pinetorum* (Fern.) R.W. Long *20850*
     I   *20850* U.S. - Alabama *20850*
     E   *20850* U.S. - Florida *20850*
     I   *20850* U.S. - Louisiana *20850*
     I   *20850* U.S. - Mississippi *20850*
     I   *20850* U.S. - South Carolina *20850*
     I   *20850* U.S. - Texas *20850*
     I   *20850* U.S. - Virginia *20850*

I   *Ruellia philippinensis* Elm. *13833*
     I   *13833* Philippines (low altitude) *13833*

E   *Ruellia praeclara* Standl. *20883, 9006*
     R   *11620* Costa Rica *9417*
     R   *11620* Panama *20883*

E   *Ruellia tarapotana* Lindau *18200*
     E   *11620* Peru *18200*

R   *Ruellia tubiflora* Kunth var. *tubiflora* *9006*
     R   *11620* Panama *9006*

R   *Ruellia williamsii* Leonard *9035*
     R   *11620* Honduras *9035*

I   *Rungia linifolia* Nees
     I   India - Karnataka

I   *Rungia minutifolia* C.B. Clarke
     I   Malaysia - Peninsular Malaysia

I	*Salpinctium natalense* (C.B.Clarke) T.J.Edwards *20604*	
	I	20604 South Africa - Natal *20604*
R	*Salpixantha coccinea* Hook. *20883*	
	R	20883 Jamaica *20883*
E	*Sanchezia aurantiaca* Leonard & Lyman B. Smith *18200*	
	E	11620 Peru *18200*
E	*Sanchezia aurea* Leonard & Lyman B. Smith *18200*	
	E	11620 Peru *18200*
E	*Sanchezia dasia* Leonard & Lyman B. Smith *18200*	
	E	11620 Peru *18200*
E	*Sanchezia ferreyrae* Leonard & Lyman B. Smith *18200*	
	E	11620 Peru *18200*
E	*Sanchezia klugii* Leonard & Lyman B. Smith *18200*	
	E	11620 Peru *18200*
E	*Sanchezia lasia* Leonard & Lyman B. Smith *18200*	
	E	11620 Peru *18200*
E	*Sanchezia villosa* Leonard & Lyman B. Smith *18200*	
	E	11620 Peru *18200*
E	*Santapaua madurensis* Balakr. ex Subram. *13883*	
	E	13883 India - Tamil Nadu *13883*
R	*Sapphoa ekmanii* Borh. *5607*	
	R	19105 Cuba (Guantanamo) *5607*
R	*Sarojusticia kempeana* (F.Muell.) Bremek. ex H.Eichler ssp. kempeana *20681*	
	R	20681 Australia - Northern Territory *20681*
I	*Sericocalyx thailandicus* Brem. *19120*	
	I	19120 Thailand *19120*
V	*Siphonoglossa durangensis* Henrickson & Hilsenbeck *14294*	
	V	14294 Mexico - Durango *14294*
V	*Siphonoglossa linearifolia* Henrickson & Hilsenbeck *14294*	
	V	14294 Mexico - Durango *14294*
V	*Siphonoglossa mexicana* Hilsenbeck *20883*	
	I	20883 Mexico *20883*
R	*Siphonoglossa nkandlaensis* Immelman *20604*	
	R	20604 South Africa - Cape Province *20604*
	R	20604 South Africa - Natal *20604*
E	*Siphonoglossa ramosa* var. *discolor* (S. F. Blake) Hilsenbeck *20883*	
	I	20883 Guatemala *20883*
V	*Siphonoglossa ramosa* var. *hondurensis* (Standley & Steyermark) Hilsenbeck *20883*	
	I	20883 Costa Rica *20883*
	I	20883 Guatemala *20883*
	I	20883 Honduras *20883*
R	*Spathacanthus hoffmannii* Lindau *9037*	
	R	9420 Costa Rica *9037*
V	*Spathacanthus simplicifolius* (J.D. Smith) Leonard *9004*	
	V	11620 Guatemala *9004*
R	*Staurogyne agrestis* Leonard *20883, 9006*	
	I	20883 Costa Rica *20883*
	V	20883 Panama *20883*
I	*Staurogyne bella* Brem. *19120*	
	I	19120 Thailand *19120*
I	*Staurogyne densiflora* Brem. *19120*	
	I	19120 Thailand *19120*
I	*Staurogyne expansa* Brem. *19120*	

	I	19120 Thailand *19120*
I	*Staurogyne latifolia* Brem. *19120*	
	I	19120 Thailand *19120*
I	*Staurogyne longiciliata* Brem. *19120*	
	I	19120 Thailand *19120*
I	*Staurogyne multiflora* Brem. *19120*	
	I	19120 Thailand *19120*
I	*Staurogyne polycaulis* Brem. *19120*	
	I	19120 Thailand *19120*
I	*Staurogyne singularis* Brem. *19120*	
	I	19120 Thailand *19120*
R	*Staurogynopsis maiana* Mangenot & Ake Assi	
	R	Côte d'Ivoire
V	*Stenandrium arnoldii* H. Dietrich *11840*	
	V	19105 Cuba (Holguin) *11840*
R	*Stenandrium chameranthemoideum* Oersted *9050*	
	R	11620 Mexico *9050*
V	*Stenandrium ekmanii* Urban *5607*	
	V	19105 Cuba (Santiago de Cuba) *5607*
E	*Stenandrium manchonense* T. Daniel *9050*	
	E	11620 Mexico - Guerrero *9050*
E	*Stenandrium nanum* (Standley) T. Daniel *9050*	
	E	11620 Mexico - Yucatan *9050*
V	*Stenandrium pallidum* H. Dietrich *11840*	
	V	19105 Cuba (Guantanamo) *11840*
E	*Stenandrium pilosulum* (Blake) T. Daniel *9050*	
	E	11620 Mexico - Chihuahua *9050*
	E	11620 Mexico - Sonora *9050*
R	*Stenandrium subcordatum* Standley *9004*	
	R	11620 Guatemala *9004*
	R	11620 Mexico *9004*
E	*Stenandrium verticillatum* Brandegee *9050*	
	E	11620 Mexico *9050*
I	*Stenosiphonium setosum* T. Anderson	
	I	India - Karnataka (Mysore)
R	*Stenostephanus glabrus* (Oersted) T.F. Daniel *9001*	
	R	9001 Mexico - Chiapas *9001*
R	*Stenostephanus lobeliiformis* Nees *19560*	
	R	19560 Brazil (Serra dos Orgaos) *19560*
R	*Stenothyrsus ridleyi* C.B. Clarke	
	R	Malaysia - Peninsular Malaysia (near Ipoh, Perak)
R	*Streblacanthus cordatus* Lindau *11620*	
	R	11620 Panama *11620*
	R	11620 Ecuador
I	*Streblacanthus longiflorus* Cuf. *9037*	
	I	9420 Costa Rica *9037*
V	*Streblacanthus macrophyllus* Lindau *9037*	
	V	11620 Costa Rica *9037*
V	*Streblacanthus parviflorus* Leonard *9004*	
	V	11620 Guatemala *9004*
I	*Strobilanthes andamanensis* Bor *7771*	
	I	India - Andaman Is. *7771*
I	*Strobilanthes gardnerana* (Nees) T. Anderson *10252*	
	I	16162 Sri Lanka *10252*
E	*Strobilanthes hallbergii* Blatter *11494*	
	E	11494 India - Rajasthan (Mt Abu, Dhobi Ghats) *11494*
V	*Strobilanthes japonica* (Thunb.) Miq. *10573*	
	V	10573 Japan *10573*

R	*Strobilanthes leucopogon* Ridley		
	R		Malaysia - Peninsular Malaysia (Langkawi, Kedah)
I	*Strobilanthes nigrescens* T. Anderson *10252*		
	I	*16162*	Sri Lanka *10252*
I	*Strobilanthes nockii* Trimen *10252*		
	I	*16162*	Sri Lanka *10252*
I	*Strobilanthes pachyphyllus* C.B. Clarke		
	I		Malaysia - Peninsular Malaysia
I	*Strobilanthes palawanensis* Elm. *13833*		
	I	*13833*	Philippines (Palawan) *13833*
	Ex	*20099*	Singapore *20099*
I	*Strobilanthes punctata* Nees *10252*		
	I	*16162*	Sri Lanka *10252*
I	*Strobilanthes rhytisperma* C.B. Clarke *10252*		
	I	*16162*	Sri Lanka *10252*
I	*Strobilanthes stenodon* C.B. Clarke *10252*		
	I	*16162*	Sri Lanka *10252*
I	*Strobilanthes thwaitesii* T. Anderson *10252*		
	I	*16162*	Sri Lanka *10252*
I	*Strobilanthes urceolaris* Gamble		
	I		India - Tamil Nadu (Nilgiri & Palani Hills)
I	*Strobilanthes zeylanica* T. Anderson *10252*		
	I	*16162*	Sri Lanka *10252*
R	*Suessenguthia vargasii* Wassh. *18200*		
	R	*11620*	Peru *18200*
R	*Tetramerium butterwickianum* T. Daniel *10559*		
	R	*11550*	Mexico - Michoacan *10559*
R	*Tetramerium crenatum* T. Daniel *10559*		
	R	*11550*	Mexico - Oaxaca *10559*
R	*Tetramerium diffusum* Rose *10559*		
	R	*11550*	Mexico *10559*
R	*Tetramerium emilyanum* T. Daniel *10559*		
	R	*11550*	Mexico - Michoacan *10559*
V	*Tetramerium guerrerense* T. Daniel *10559*		
	V	*11620*	Mexico - Guerrero *10559*
R	*Tetramerium macvaughii* T. Daniel *10559*		
	R	*11550*	Mexico - Colima *10559*
R	*Tetramerium oaxacanum* T. Daniel *10559*		
	R	*11620*	Mexico - Oaxaca *10559*
E	*Tetramerium obovatum* T. Daniel *10559*		
	E	*11620*	Mexico - Oaxaca *10559*
R	*Tetramerium ochoterenae* (Miranda) T. Daniel *10559*		
	R	*11620*	Mexico *10559*
I	*Tetramerium rubrum* Happ *10559*		
	I	*11620*	Mexico *10559*
R	*Tetramerium rzedowskii* T. Daniel *10559*		
	R	*11550*	Mexico - Michoacan *10559*
R	*Tetramerium tetramerioides* (Lindau) T. Daniel *10559*		
	R	*11620*	Mexico - Oaxaca *10559*
V	*Tetramerium yaquianum* T. Daniel *10559*		
	V	*11620*	Mexico - Sonora *10559*
I	*Thunbergia bicolor* (Wight) Lindau		
	I		India - Tamil Nadu (Nilgiri Hills)
R	*Thunbergia venosa* C.B.Clarke *20604*		
	R	*20604*	South Africa - Natal *20604*
V	*Trybliocalyx pyramidatus* Lindau *9004*		
	V	*11620*	Guatemala *9004*
E	*Xerothamnella herbacea* R.M.Barker *20681*		
	E	*20681*	Australia - Queensland *20681*
V	*Xerothamnella parvifolia* C.White *20681*		
	I	*20681*	Australia - New South Wales *20681*
	I	*20681*	Australia - Queensland *20681*
	I	*20681*	Australia - South Australia *20681*
E	*Yeatesia mabryi* Hilsenbeck *20883*		
	I	*20883*	Mexico *20883*

Aceraceae

Number of genera:	2
Number of species:	112
Recorded threatened species:	14 (12%)

Temperate and subtropical, especially Malesia; China. T.

E	*Acer buergerianum* Miq. ssp. *formosanum* (Hayata) Murray & Lauener *21069, 20511,*		
	E	*20854*	Taiwan *20511*
V	*Acer caesium* Wallich ex Brandis *7731*		
	V	*11494*	India - Himachal Pradesh *11494*
	V	*11494*	India - Jammu & Kashmir *11494*
	V	*11494*	India - Uttar Pradesh *11494*
	V		Nepal *7731*
R	*Acer cappadocicum* Gleditsch var. *stenocaryum* Yalt. *12840*		
	R	*20618*	Turkey *20618*
R	*Acer erythranthum* Gagnepain *6057*		
	R		Vietnam *6057*
I	*Acer heldreichii* Orph. ex Boiss. ssp. *visianii* H. Maly *6062, 20171*		
	R	*21091*	Bosnia & Herzegovina *21091*
	I	*6062*	Bulgaria (west) *8000*
	I	*6062*	(former) Yugoslavia *8000*
R	*Acer hyrcanum* Fischer & Meyer ssp. *sphaerocaryum* Yaltirik *20618*		
	R	*20618*	Turkey *20618*
I	*Acer molle* Paxton		
	I		India (West Himalaya)
R	*Acer monspessulanum* L. ssp. *oksalinum* Yalt. *12840*		
	R	*20618*	Turkey *20618*
R	*Acer negundo* L. ssp. *mexicanum* (DC.) Standley *9114*		
	?		Guatemala *21069*
	R	*19848*	Mexico - Veracruz *9114*
E	*Acer oblongum* Wallich ex DC. var. *membranaceum* Banerji *11494*		
	E	*11494*	India - Uttar Pradesh *11494*
E	*Acer oblongum* Wallich ex DC. var. *microcarpum* Hiern *11494*		
	E	*11494*	India - Arunachal Pradesh *11494*
V	*Acer pycnanthum* K. Koch *10572, 21069*		
	V	*10572*	Japan (Nagano, Aichi, Gifu of Honshu Is.) *20626*
I	*Acer undulatum* Pojark. *12840*		
	I	*20618*	Turkey *20618*
R	*Dipteronia dyeriana* Henry *17617*		
	R	*17617*	China - Yunnan (Wengshan; Mengzhi) *11139*
R	*Dipteronia sinensis* Oliver *17617*		
	R	*17617*	China - Gansu *11139*
	R	*17617*	China - Guizhou (Yingjiang) *11139*
	R	*17617*	China - Henan *11139*
	R	*17617*	China - Hubei *11139*

R	*17617*	China - Hunan (Shimeng; Shangzhi; Dayun) *11139*	
R	*17617*	China - Shaanxi *11139*	
R	*17617*	China - Sichuan *11139*	

Actinidiaceae

Number of genera:	3
Number of species:	300
Recorded threatened species:	5 (1%)

Warm temperate Asia to Queensland, Fiji, tropical America.

V   *Saurauia chaparensis* Soejarto *20883*
    V   *20883*   Bolivia *20883*

I   *Saurauia griffithii* Dyer
    I   India - Arunachal Pradesh
    I   India - Sikkim

E   *Saurauia molinae* Soejarto *20883*
    I   *20883*   Honduras *20883*

E   *Saurauia oroquensis* Soejarto *20883*
    I   *20883*   Colombia *20883*
    I   *20883*   Venezuela *20883*

R   *Saurauia serrata* DC. *10088*
    R   *19850*   Mexico *10088*

Aizoaceae

Number of genera:	12-128
Number of species:	2,500
Recorded threatened species:	163 (6%)

South Africa; Australia.

R   *Aloinopsis acuta* L.Bolus *20604*
    R   *20604*   South Africa - Cape Province *20604*

R   *Aloinopsis jamesii* L.Bolus *20604*
    R   *20604*   South Africa - Cape Province *20604*

R   *Aloinopsis loganii* (L.Bolus) L.Bolus *20604*
    R   *20604*   South Africa - Cape Province *20604*

R   *Aloinopsis setifera* (L.Bolus) L.Bolus *20604*
    R   *20604*   South Africa - Cape Province *20604*

R   *Aloinopsis villetii* (L.Bolus) L.Bolus *20604*
    R   *20604*   South Africa - Cape Province *20604*

R   *Astridia citrina* (L.Bolus) L.Bolus *20604*
    R   *20604*   Namibia *20604*
    R   *20604*   South Africa - Cape Province *20604*

I   *Astridia speciosa* L.Bolus *20604*
    E   *20604*   Namibia *20604*
    I   *20604*   South Africa - Cape Province *20604*

I   *Bijlia tugwelliae* (L.Bolus) L.Bolus *20604*
    I   *20604*   South Africa - Cape Province *20604*

R   *Braunsia stayneri* (L.Bolus) L.Bolus *20604*
    R   *20604*   South Africa - Cape Province *20604*

R   *Braunsia vanrensburgii* (L.Bolus) L.Bolus *20604*
    R   *20604*   South Africa - Cape Province *20604*

R   *Caryotophora skiatophytoides* Leistner *20604*
    R   *20604*   South Africa - Cape Province *20604*

V   *Cephalophyllum fulleri* L.Bolus *20604*
    V   *20604*   South Africa - Cape Province *20604*

Ex   *Cephalophyllum parvulum* (Schltr.) H.E.K.Hartmann *20604*
    Ex   *20604*   South Africa - Cape Province *20604*

R   *Cephalophyllum pulchellum* L.Bolus *20604*
    R   *20604*   South Africa - Cape Province *20604*

I   *Cephalophyllum pulchrum* L.Bolus *20604*
    I   *20604*   South Africa - Cape Province *20604*

R   *Cephalophyllum staminodiosum* L.Bolus *20604*
    R   *20604*   South Africa - Cape Province *20604*

V   *Cephalophyllum tetrastichum* H.E.K.Hartmann *20604*
    V   *20604*   South Africa - Cape Province *20604*

I   *Cheiridopsis alata* L.Bolus *20604*
    I   *20604*   South Africa - Cape Province *20604*

R   *Cheiridopsis delphinoides* S.A.Hammer *20604*
    R   *20604*   South Africa - Cape Province *20604*

V   *Cheiridopsis pearsonii* N.E.Br. *20604*
    V   *20604*   South Africa - Cape Province *20604*

V   *Cheiridopsis peculiaris* N.E.Br. *20604*
    V   *20604*   South Africa - Cape Province *20604*

I   *Cheiridopsis rudis* L.Bolus *20604*
    I   *20604*   South Africa - Cape Province *20604*

V   *Cheiridopsis umdausensis* L.Bolus *20604*
    V   *20604*   South Africa - Cape Province *20604*

I   *Cheiridopsis velox* S.A.Hammer *20604*
    I   *20604*   South Africa - Cape Province *20604*

Ex   *Circandra serrata* (L.) N.E.Br. *20604*
    Ex   *20604*   South Africa - Cape Province *20604*

R   *Cleretum lyratifolium* Ihlenf. & Struck *20604*
    R   *20604*   South Africa - Cape Province *20604*

R   *Conophytum achabense* S.A.Hammer *20604*
    R   *20604*   South Africa - Cape Province *20604*

V   *Conophytum acutum* L.Bolus *20604*
    V   *20604*   South Africa - Cape Province *20604*

R   *Conophytum armianum* S.A.Hammer *20604*
    R   *20604*   South Africa - Cape Province *20604*

R   *Conophytum auriflorum* Tischer ssp. *auriflorum* *20604*
    R   *20604*   South Africa - Cape Province *20604*

R   *Conophytum bicarinatum* L.Bolus *20604*
    R   *20604*   South Africa - Cape Province *20604*

R   *Conophytum blandum* L.Bolus *20604*
    R   *20604*   South Africa - Cape Province *20604*

V   *Conophytum burgeri* L.Bolus *20604*
    V   *20604*   South Africa - Cape Province *20604*

R   *Conophytum carpianum* L.Bolus *20604*
    R   *20604*   South Africa - Cape Province *20604*

R   *Conophytum concavum* L.Bolus *20604*
    R   *20604*   South Africa - Cape Province *20604*

R   *Conophytum ernstii* S.A.Hammer ssp. *ernstii* *20604*
    R   *20604*   South Africa - Cape Province *20604*

R   *Conophytum frutescens* Schwantes *20604*
    R   *20604*   South Africa - Cape Province *20604*

R   *Conophytum herreanthus* S.A.Hammer ssp. *herreanthus* *20604*
    R   *20604*   Namibia *20604*
    E   *20604*   South Africa - Cape Province *20604*

R   *Conophytum khamiesbergense* (L.Bolus) Schwantes *20604*
    R   *20604*   South Africa - Cape Province *20604*

R   *Conophytum klinghardtense* Rawe ssp. *baradii* (Rawe) S.A.Hammer *20604*
    R   *20604*   Namibia *20604*

R   *Conophytum loeschianum* Tischer *20604*

R		20604 Namibia *20604*
R		20604 South Africa - Cape Province *20604*
R	*Conophytum phoeniceum* S.A.Hammer *20604*	
R		20604 South Africa - Cape Province *20604*
R	*Conophytum regale* Lavis *20604*	
R		20604 South Africa - Cape Province *20604*
R	*Conophytum ricardianum* Loesch & Tischer ssp. *ricardianum 20604*	
R		20604 Mozambique *20604*
Ex	*Conophytum ricardianum* Loesch & Tischer ssp. *rubriflorum* Tischer *20604*	
Ex		20604 Namibia *20604*
R	*Conophytum rugosum* S.A.Hammer ssp. *rugosum 20604*	
R		20604 South Africa - Cape Province *20604*
R	*Conophytum schlechteri* Schwantes *20604*	
R		20604 South Africa - Cape Province *20604*
Ex	*Conophytum semivestitum* L.Bolus *20604*	
Ex		20604 South Africa - Cape Province *20604*
E	*Conophytum smorenskaduense* De Boer ssp. *hermarium* S.A.Hammer *20604*	
E		20604 South Africa - Cape Province *20604*
R	*Conophytum swanepoelianum* Rawe ssp. *swanepoelianum 20604*	
R		20604 South Africa - Cape Province *20604*
R	*Conophytum taylorianum* (Dinter & Schwantes) N.E.Br. ssp. *taylorianum 20604*	
R		20604 Namibia *20604*
V	*Conophytum uviforme* (Haw.) N.E.Br. ssp. *subincanum* (Tischer) S.A.Hammer *20604*	
V		20604 South Africa - Cape Province *20604*
R	*Conophytum vanheerdei* Tischer *20604*	
R		20604 South Africa - Cape Province *20604*
R	*Conophytum velutinum* Schwantes ssp. *velutinum 20604*	
R		20604 South Africa - Cape Province *20604*
E	*Cypselea rubriflora* Urban *5607*	
E		19105 Cuba (Matanzas; Cienfuegos) *5607*
V	*Delosperma napiforme* (N.E.Br.) Schwantes *10082*	
V		14234 Réunion *10082*
R	*Delosperma oehleri* (Engl.) Herre *19498*	
R		5926 Tanzania (Masai district) *5926*
I	*Delosperma pondoense* L.Bolus *20604*	
I		20604 South Africa - Cape Province *20604*
I		20604 South Africa - Natal *20604*
I	*Delosperma steytlerae* L. Bolus *7749*	
I		Zimbabwe *7749*
I	*Delosperma subpetiolatum* L.Bolus *20604*	
I		20604 South Africa - Natal *20604*
I	*Delosperma suttoniae* Lavis *20604*	
I		20604 South Africa - Natal *20604*
I	*Delosperma velutinum* L.Bolus *20604*	
I		20604 South Africa - Natal *20604*
V	*Didymaotus lapidiformis* (Marloth) N.E.Br. *20604*	
V		20604 South Africa - Cape Province *20604*
R	*Dinteranthus microspermus* (Dinter & Derenb.) Schwantes ssp. *microspermus 20604*	
R		20604 Namibia *20604*
I	*Dinteranthus pole-evansii* (N.E.Br.) Schwantes *20604*	

I		20604 South Africa - Cape Province *20604*
V	*Dinteranthus vanzylii* (L.Bolus) Schwantes *20604*	
V		20604 South Africa - Cape Province *20604*
R	*Dinteranthus wilmotianus* L. Bolus ssp. *impunctatus* N. Sauer *20604*	
R		20604 South Africa - Cape Province *20604*
R	*Diplosoma lueckhoffii* (L.Bolus) Schwantes ex Ihlenf. *20604*	
R		20604 South Africa - Cape Province *20604*
E	*Diplosoma retroversum* (Kensit) Schwantes *20604*	
E		20604 South Africa - Cape Province *20604*
R	*Drosanthemum bellum* L.Bolus *20604*	
R		20604 South Africa - Cape Province *20604*
R	*Drosanthemum hallii* L.Bolus *20604*	
R		20604 South Africa - Cape Province *20604*
R	*Drosanthemum micans* (L.) Schwantes *20604*	
R		20604 South Africa - Cape Province *20604*
R	*Drosanthemum thudichumii* L.Bolus var. *gracilius* L.Bolus *20604*	
R		20604 South Africa - Cape Province *20604*
I	*Ectotropis alpina* N.E.Br. *20604*	
I		20604 South Africa - Cape Province *20604*
E	*Erepsia brevipetala* L.Bolus *20604*	
E		20604 South Africa - Cape Province *20604*
R	*Erepsia dubia* Liede *20604*	
R		20604 South Africa - Cape Province *20604*
I	*Erepsia hallii* L.Bolus *20604*	
I		20604 South Africa - Cape Province *20604*
R	*Erepsia insignis* (Schltr.) Schwantes *20604*	
R		20604 South Africa - Cape Province *20604*
R	*Erepsia patula* (Haw.) Schwantes *20604*	
R		20604 South Africa - Cape Province *20604*
V	*Erepsia pentagona* (L.Bolus) L.Bolus *20604*	
V		20604 South Africa - Cape Province *20604*
I	*Erepsia pillansii* (Kensit) Liede *20604*	
I		20604 South Africa - Cape Province *20604*
E	*Erepsia polita* (L.Bolus) L.Bolus *20604*	
E		20604 South Africa - Cape Province *20604*
R	*Erepsia polypetala* (A.Berger & Schltr.) L.Bolus *20604*	
R		20604 South Africa - Cape Province *20604*
Ex	*Erepsia promontorii* L.Bolus *20604*	
Ex		20604 South Africa - Cape Province *20604*
I	*Erepsia steytlerae* L.Bolus *20604*	
I		20604 South Africa - Cape Province *20604*
V	*Erepsia villiersii* L.Bolus *20604*	
V		20604 South Africa - Cape Province *20604*
V	*Faucaria tigrina* (Haw.) Schwantes *20604*	
V		20604 South Africa - Cape Province *20604*
R	*Fenestraria rhopalophylla* (Schltr. & Diels) N.E.Br ssp. *aurantiaca* (N.E.Br) H.E.H.Hartmann *20604*	
R		20604 Namibia *20604*
R		20604 South Africa - Cape Province *20604*
R	*Frithia pulchra* N.E.Br. var. *pulchra 20604*	
R		20803 South Africa - Transvaal *20604*
Ex	*Gibbaeum esterhuyseniae* L.Bolus *20604, 3774*	
Ex		20604 South Africa - Cape Province *20604*
I	*Gibbaeum schwantesii* Tischer *20604*	

Magnoliopsida (dicots): Aizoaceae: *Gibbaeum*

I	20604	South Africa - Cape Province	20604

R **Gunniopsis kochii** (W.Wagner) Chinn. 20681
  R 20681 Australia - South Australia 20681

E **Hydrodea cryptantha** (Hook.f.) N.E. Br. 18996
  E 18996 St Helena 18996

R **Jacobsenia hallii** L.Bolus 20604
  R 20604 South Africa - Cape Province 20604

R **Jordaaniella clavifolia** (L.Bolus)
    H.E.K.Hartmann 20604
  R 20604 South Africa - Cape Province 20604

I **Jordaaniella uniflora** (L.Bolus) H.E.K.Hartmann 20604
  I 20604 South Africa - Cape Province 20604

R **Lampranthus algoensis** L.Bolus 20604
  R 20604 South Africa - Cape Province 20604

I **Lampranthus dunensis** (Sond.) L.Bolus 20604
  I 20604 South Africa - Cape Province 20604

R **Lampranthus fugitans** L.Bolus 20604
  R 20604 South Africa - Cape Province (Transkei)
        20604
  K 20604 South Africa - Natal 20604

R **Lampranthus rustii** (A.Berger) N.E.Br. 20604
  R 20604 South Africa - Cape Province 20604

V **Lampranthus scaber** (L.) N.E.Br. 20604
  V 20604 South Africa - Cape Province 20604

R **Lithops aucampiae** L.Bolus ssp. *euniciae* (De Boer)
    D.T.Cole var. *euniciae* 20604
  R 20604 South Africa - Cape Province 20604

R **Lithops aucampiae** L.Bolus ssp. *euniciae* (De Boer)
    D.T.Cole var. *fluminalis* D.T.Cole 20604
  R 20604 South Africa - Cape Province 20604

I **Lithops bromfieldii** L.Bolus var. *glaudinae* (De
    Boer) D.T.Cole 20604
  I 20604 South Africa - Cape Province 20604

V **Lithops coleorum** S.A.Hammer & R.Uijs 20604
  V 20604 South Africa - Transvaal 20604

E **Lithops comptonii** L. Bolus var.
    comptonii 20604
  E 20604 South Africa - Cape Province 20604

R **Lithops comptonii** L.Bolus var. *weberi* (L.Bolus)
    B.Fearn 20604
  R 20604 South Africa - Cape Province 20604

I **Lithops divergens** L. Bolus var. *amethystina* De
    Boer 20604
  I 20604 South Africa - Cape Province 20604

V **Lithops divergens** L. Bolus var.
    divergens 20604
  V 20604 South Africa - Cape Province 20604

V **Lithops dorotheae** Nel 20604
  V 20604 South Africa - Cape Province 20604

R **Lithops fulviceps** (N.E.Br.) N.E.Br. var. *lactinea*
    D.T.Cole 20604
  R 20604 Namibia 20604

I **Lithops gesineae** De Boer var. *annae* (De Boer)
    D.T.Cole 20604
  I 20604 Namibia 20604

E **Lithops gesineae** De Boer var. *gesineae* 20604
  E 20604 Namibia 20604

R **Lithops geyeri** Nel 20604
  R 20604 South Africa - Cape Province 20604

R **Lithops gracilidelineata** Dinter ssp. *brandbergensis*
    (De Boer) D.T.Cole 20604
  R 20604 Namibia 20604

R **Lithops helmutii** L.Bolus 20604
  R 20604 South Africa - Cape Province 20604

R **Lithops hookeri** (A.Berger) Schwantes var. *susannae*
    (D.T.Cole) D.T.Cole 20604
  R 20604 South Africa - Cape Province 20604

R **Lithops lesliei** (N.E.Br.) N.E.Br. ssp. *burchellii*
    D.T.Cole 20604
  R 20604 Lesotho 20604

R **Lithops meyeri** L.Bolus 20604
  R 20604 South Africa - Cape Province 20604

R **Lithops naureeniae** D.T.Cole 20604
  R 20604 South Africa - Cape Province 20604

R **Lithops olivacea** L.Bolus var. *nebrownii*
    D.T.Cole 20604
  R 20604 South Africa - Cape Province 20604

R **Lithops otzeniana** Nel 20604
  R 20604 South Africa - Cape Province 20604

R **Lithops pseudotruncatella** (A.Berger) N.E.Br. ssp.
    pseudotruncatella var. *elisabethae* (Dinter) de Boer &
    Boom 20604
  R 20604 Namibia 20604

R **Lithops pseudotruncatella** (A.Berger) N.E.Br. ssp.
    pseudotruncatella var. *riehmerae*
    D.T.Cole 20604
  R 20604 Namibia 20604

R **Lithops pseudotruncatella** (A.Berger) N.E.Br. ssp.
    volkii (Schwantes ex de Boer & Boom) D.T.Cole 20604
  R 20604 Namibia 20604

V **Lithops salicola** N.E.Br. 20604
  V 20604 South Africa - Cape Province 20604
  V 20604 South Africa - Orange Free State 20604

R **Lithops schwantesii** Dinter ssp. *schwantessi* var.
    rugosa (Dinter) de Boer & Boom 20604
  R 20604 Namibia 20604

R **Lithops viridis** C.A.Lückh. 20604
  R 20604 South Africa - Cape Province 20604

I **Maughaniella luckhoffii** (L. Bolus) L. Bolus
  I   Southern Africa

E **Mesembryanthemum gaussenii** Leredde 10488
  E 14958 Algeria 10488

R **Mitrophyllum abbreviatum** L.Bolus 20604
  R 20604 South Africa - Cape Province 20604

I **Mitrophyllum roseum** L.Bolus 20604
  I 20604 South Africa - Cape Province 20604

R **Mossia intervallaris** (L.Bolus) N.E.Br. 20604
  R 20604 South Africa - Transvaal 20604

E **Muiria hortenseae** N.E.Br. 20604
  E 20604 South Africa - Cape Province 20604

I **Nelia pillansii** (N.E.Br.) Schwantes 20604
  I 20604 South Africa - Cape Province 20604

R **Nelia schlechteri** Schwantes 20604
  R 20604 South Africa - Cape Province 20604

R **Neohenricia spiculata** S.A.Hammer 20604
  R 20604 South Africa - Cape Province 20604

I **Odontophorus marlothii** N.E.Br. 20604
  I 20604 South Africa - Cape Province 20604

R   *Ophthalmophyllum villetii* L.Bolus *20604*
     R   *20604*   South Africa - Cape Province *20604*

E   *Orthopterum coegana* L.Bolus *20604*
     E   *20604*   South Africa - Cape Province *20604*

R   *Pleiospilos compactus* (Aiton) Schwantes ssp. *minor*
     (L.Bolus) H.E.K.Hartmann & Leide *20604*
     R   *20604*   South Africa - Cape Province *20604*

I   *Pleiospilos nelii* Schwantes *20604*
     I   *20604*   South Africa - Cape Province *20604*

E   *Pleiospilos simulans* (Marloth) N.E.Br. *20604*
     E   *20604*   South Africa - Cape Province *20604*

I   *Rabiea jamesii* (L.Bolus) L.Bolus *20604*
     I   *20604*   South Africa - Cape Province *20604*

I   *Rhinephyllum inaequale* L.Bolus var. *latipetalum*
     L.Bolus *20604*
     I   *20604*   South Africa - Cape Province *20604*

R   *Ruschia amicorum* (L.Bolus) Schwantes *20604*
     R   *20604*   South Africa - Cape Province *20604*

I   *Ruschia filamentosa* (L.) L.Bolus *20604*
     I   *20604*   South Africa - Cape Province *20604*

R   *Ruschia firma* L.Bolus *20604*
     R   *20604*   South Africa - Cape Province *20604*

E   *Ruschia leipoldtii* L.Bolus *20604*
     E   *20604*   South Africa - Cape Province *20604*

E   *Ruschia promontorii* L.Bolus *20604*
     E   *20604*   South Africa - Cape Province *20604*

I   *Ruschia rubricaulis* (Haw.) L.Bolus *20604*
     I   *20604*   South Africa - Cape Province *20604*

E   *Saphesia flaccida* (Jacq.) N.E.Br. *20604*
     E   *20604*   South Africa - Cape Province *20604*

I   *Schwantesia acutipetala* L.Bolus *20604*
     I   *20604*   South Africa - Cape Province *20604*

V   *Schwantesia borcherdsii* L.Bolus *20604*
     V   *20604*   South Africa - Cape Province *20604*

I   *Schwantesia triebneri* L.Bolus *20604*
     I   *20604*   South Africa - Cape Province *20604*

R   *Scopelogena verruculata* (L.) L.Bolus nom.
     inval. *20604*
     R   *20604*   South Africa - Cape Province *20604*

R   *Sesuvium ayresii* Marais *10082*
     R   *5852*   Mauritius *10082*
     R   *5852*   Mauritius - Rodrigues *5852*

E   *Sesuvium trianthemoides* Correll *20850, 14662*
     E   *20850*   U.S. - Texas *20850*

I   *Stomatium geoffreyi* L.Bolus *20604*
     I   *20604*   South Africa - Cape Province *20604*

I   *Stomatium ronaldii* L.Bolus *20604*
     I   *20604*   South Africa - Cape Province *20604*

R   *Tanquana archeri* (L.Bolus) H.E.K.Hartmann &
     Liede *20604*
     R   *20604*   South Africa - Cape Province *20604*

R   *Tanquana hilmarii* (L.Bolus) H.E.K.Hartmann &
     Liede *20604*
     R   *20604*   South Africa - Cape Province *20604*

E   *Tetragonia crystallina* L'Her. *18200*
     E   *9446*   Peru *18200*

I   *Tetragonia pentandra* Balf. f. *15534*
     I   *15534*   Yemen - Socotra *15534*

V   *Tetragonia vestita* I.M. Johnston *18200*
     V   *12468*   Peru *18200*

Ex   *Trianthema cypseleoides* (Fenzl) Benth. *20681*
     Ex   *20681*   Australia - New South Wales *20681*

R   *Trianthema megasperma* A.Prescott *20681*
     R   *20681*   Australia - Northern Territory *20681*

I   *Trichodiadema aureum* L.Bolus *20604*
     I   *20604*   South Africa - Cape Province *20604*

R   *Trichodiadema burgeri* L.Bolus *20604*
     R   *20604*   South Africa - Cape Province *20604*

R   *Trichodiadema hallii* L.Bolus *20604*
     R   *20604*   South Africa - Cape Province *20604*

I   *Trichodiadema obliquum* L.Bolus *20604*
     I   *20604*   South Africa - Cape Province *20604*

I   *Trichodiadema peersii* L.Bolus *20604*
     I   *20604*   South Africa - Cape Province *20604*

R   *Trichodiadema pygmaeum* L.Bolus *20604*
     R   *20604*   South Africa - Cape Province *20604*

I   *Trichodiadema rogersiae* L.Bolus *20604*
     I   *20604*   South Africa - Cape Province *20604*

I   *Trichodiadema rupicolum* L.Bolus *20604*
     I   *20604*   South Africa - Cape Province *20604*

R   *Vlokia ater* S.A.Hammer *20604*
     R   *20604*   South Africa - Cape Province *20604*

Ex   *Zeuktophyllum suppositum* (L.Bolus) N.E.Br. *20604*
     Ex   *20604*   South Africa - Cape Province *20604*

Alzateaceae

Number of genera:	1	
Number of species:	1	
Recorded threatened species:	1	(100%)

Peru, Bolivia.

R   *Alzatea verticellata* Ruiz Lopez & Pavon ssp.
     verticellata 11371
     R   Bolivia *11371*
     R   *19960*   Peru *18200*

Amaranthaceae

Number of genera:	65-70	
Number of species:	900	
Recorded threatened species:	44	(4%)

Tropical and subtropical.

E   *Achyranthes arborescens* R. Br. *11649*
     E   *11649*   Australia - Norfolk Is. *11649*

E   *Achyranthes aspera* L. var. *borbonica* (Willd. ex
     Schultes) Townsend
     E   *14220*   Réunion *14220*

Ex/E   *Achyranthes atollensis* St. John *20850, 14301*
     Ex/E *20850*   U.S. - Hawaii *20850*

R   *Achyranthes coynei* Sant. *13883*
     R   *13883*   India - Maharashtra (Khandala, Pune)
        13883

I   *Achyranthes diandra* Roxb. *8021*
     I   *16162*   Sri Lanka *8021*

Ex   *Achyranthes mangarevica* Suesseng. *20845*
     Ex   *20845*   French Polynesia - Tuamotu Is. *20845*

I   *Achyranthes marchionica* F.Brown *20845*
     I   *20845*   French Polynesia - Marquesas Is *20845*

E	*Achyranthes mutica* **Gray** *20850, 14209*	
	E	*20850* U.S. - Hawaii (Kauai, Hawaii) *20850*
V	*Achyranthes splendens* **Mart. ex Moq.** *20850, 14209*	
	I	*20850* U.S. - Hawaii *20850*
E	*Achyranthes splendens* **Mart. ex Moq. var.** *rotundata* **Hbd.** *20850*	
	E	*20850* U.S. - Hawaii *20850*
V	*Achyranthes splendens* **Mart. ex Moq. var.** *splendens* *20850*	
	V	*20850* U.S. - Hawaii *20850*
E	*Aerva congesta* **Balf.f.** *10082*	
	E	*20771* Mauritius *5852*
	Ex	*5852* Mauritius - Rodrigues *5852*
R	*Aerva microphylla* **Moq.** *15534*	
	R	*15534* Yemen - Socotra *15534*
R	*Aerva revoluta* **Balf. f.** *15534*	
	R	*15534* Yemen - Socotra *15534*
I	*Aerva wightii* **Hook.f.** *14782*	
	I	*14782* India - Kerala (Tirunelveli hills) *18341*
	I	*14782* India - Tamil Nadu (Tirunelveli Hills) *18341*
E	*Alternanthera crassifolia* **(Standley) Alain** *5607*	
	E	*19105* Cuba (Santiago de Cuba) *5607*
R	*Alternanthera filifolia* **(Hook.f.) J. Howell ssp.** *glauca* **J. Howell** *11117*	
	R	Ecuador - Galapagos (Tortuga) *5670*
R	*Alternanthera filifolia* **(Hook.f.) J. Howell ssp.** *microcephala* **Eliasson** *11117*	
	R	Ecuador - Galapagos *11117*
R	*Alternanthera filifolia* **(Hook.f.) J. Howell ssp.** *pintensis* **Eliasson** *11117*	
	R	Ecuador - Galapagos (Pinta) *11117*
R	*Alternanthera filifolia* **(Hook.f.) J. Howell ssp.** *rabidensis* **Eliasson** *11117*	
	R	Ecuador - Galapagos (Rabida) *11117*
R	*Alternanthera galapagensis* **(A. Stewart) J. Howell** *11117*	
	R	Ecuador - Galapagos *11117*
R	*Alternanthera helleri* **(Robinson) J. Howell** *11117*	
	R	Ecuador - Galapagos (Darwin, Wolf) *11117*
R	*Alternanthera maritima* **(Mart.) St.-Hil.** *20850*	
	I	*20850* U.S. - Florida *20850*
	I	*20850* U.S. - Louisiana *20850*
E	*Alternanthera nesiotes* **I.M. Johnston** *11117*	
	E	Ecuador - Galapagos (Floreana) *11117*
R	*Alternanthera snodgrassii* **(Robinson) J. Howell** *11117*	
	R	Ecuador - Galapagos *11117*
E	*Amaranthus brownii* **Christoph. & Caum** *20850, 14209*	
	E	*20850* U.S. - Hawaii (Nihoa) *20850*
R	*Amaranthus floridanus* **(S.Watson) Sauer** *20850*	
	R	*20850* U.S. - Florida *20850*
R	*Amaranthus furcatus* **J. Howell** *11117*	
	R	Ecuador - Galapagos *11117*
V	*Amaranthus pumilus* **Raf.** *20850, 15978*	
	Ex/E	*20850* U.S. - Connecticut *20850*
	Ex/E	*20850* U.S. - Delaware *20850*
	Ex/E	*20850* U.S. - Maryland *20850*
	Ex	*20850* U.S. - Massachusetts *20850*
	Ex/E	*20850* U.S. - New Jersey *20850*
	E	*20850* U.S. - New York *20850*
	V	*20850* U.S. - North Carolina *20850*

	Ex/E	*20850* U.S. - Rhode Is. *20850*
	E	*20850* U.S. - South Carolina *20850*
	Ex/E	*20850* U.S. - Virginia *20850*
E	*Amaranthus urceolatus* **Bentham** *18200*	
	E	*9446* Peru *18200*
Ex	*Blutaparon rigidum* **(Robinson & Greenman) Mears** *11117*	
	Ex	Ecuador - Galapagos (Santiago) *11117*
R	*Celosia taitoensis* **Hayata** *20511*	
	R	*20511* Taiwan *20511*
E	*Charpentiera densiflora* **Sohmer** *20850, 14209*	
	E	*20850* U.S. - Hawaii (Kua`i) *20850*
I	*Cyathula ceylanica* **Hook.f.** *8021*	
	I	*16162* Sri Lanka (Uma Oya, Kandy District) *8021*
R	*Froelichia juncea* **Robinson & Greenman ssp.** *alata* **J. Howell** *11117*	
	R	Ecuador - Galapagos (Santa Cruz) *11117*
R	*Froelichia juncea* **Robinson & Greenman ssp.** *juncea* *11117*	
	R	Ecuador - Galapagos (Isabela) *11117*
R	*Froelichia nudicaulis* **Hook.f. ssp.** *curta* **J. Howell** *11117*	
	R	Ecuador - Galapagos (Pinzon) *11117*
R	*Froelichia nudicaulis* **Hook.f. ssp.** *nudicaulis* *11117*	
	R	Ecuador - Galapagos *11117*
I	*Hermbstaedtia capitata* **Schinz** *20604*	
	I	*20604* South Africa - Transvaal *20604*
R	*Iresine arrecta* **Standley** *9037*	
	R	*19754* Costa Rica *9037*
R	*Iresine costaricensis* **Standley** *9037*	
	R	*19754* Costa Rica *9037*
R	*Lithophila radicata* **(Hook.f.) Standley** *11117*	
	R	Ecuador - Galapagos *11117*
R	*Lithophila subscaposa* **(Hook.f.) Standley** *11117*	
	R	Ecuador - Galapagos (Pinzon; Santiago; Floreana) *11117*
V	*Nototrichium humile* **Hbd.** *20850*	
	V	*20850* U.S. - Hawaii *20850*
E	*Nototrichium humile* **Hillebrand var.** *humile* *14209*	
	E	*14209* U.S. - Hawaii *14209*
R	*Pleuropetalum darwinii* **Hook.f.** *11117*	
	R	Ecuador - Galapagos *11117*
R	*Pleuropetalum pleiogynum* **(Kuntze) Standl.** *20883*	
	I	*20883* Costa Rica *20883*
	R	*20883* Panama *20883*
I	*Psilotrichum aphyllum* **C.C. Townsend** *15534*	
	I	*15534* Yemen - Socotra *15534*
R	*Ptilotus aristatus* **Benl** *20681*	
	I	*20681* Australia - Northern Territory *20681*
	I	*20681* Australia - South Australia *20681*
V	*Ptilotus beckerianus* **(F.Muell.) J.Black** *20681*	
	V	*20681* Australia - South Australia *20681*
R	*Ptilotus comatus* **Benl** *20681*	
	R	*20681* Australia - Northern Territory *20681*
Ex	*Ptilotus fasciculatus* **Fitzg.** *20681, 14223*	
	Ex	*20681* Australia - Western Australia *20681*
R	*Ptilotus maconochiei* **Benl** *20681*	
	R	*20681* Australia - Queensland *20681*

R   *Ptilotus pseudohelipteroid* Benl *20681*
     R   *20681* Australia - Queensland *20681*

Ex   *Ptilotus pyramidatus* (Moq.) F.Muell. *20681, 14223*
     Ex   *20681* Australia - Western Australia *20681*

R   *Ptilotus remotiflorus* Benl *20681*
     R   *20681* Australia - Queensland *20681*

Anacardiaceae

Number of genera: 60-80
Number of species: 600
Recorded threatened species: 86   (14%)

Tropical and subtropical, few temperate species.

R   *Anacardium corymbosum* Barbosa Rodrigues *20883*
     I   *20883* Brazil *20883*

R   *Anacardium fruticosum* Mitchell & S.A.Mori *20883*
     I   *20883* Guyana *20883*

V   *Astronium gracile* var. *acuminatum* (Chodat &
     Hassler)F. Barkley *21001, 20883*
     V   *20883* Paraguay *20883*

I   *Astronium urundeuva* (Allemâo) Engl. *19951*
     E   Argentina *12382*
     V   *20176* Argentina - Jujuy *20176*
     V   *20176* Argentina - Salta *20176*
     E   Bolivia *12382*
     V   *17746* Brazil - Bahia *17248*
     V   *17746* Brazil - Goias *17248*
     V   *17746* Brazil - Maranhao *17248*
     V   *17746* Brazil - Mato Grosso *17248*
     V   *17746* Brazil - Minas Gerais *17248*
     V   *17746* Brazil - Piaui *17248*
     E   Brazil - Sao Paulo *17248*
     I   Paraguay *20103*

R   *Astronium urundeuva* (Fr. Allem) Engler var.
     candollei (Engl.) Hassler *21056*
     R   *20883* Argentina *20883*
              Brazil *21056*
     R   *20883* Paraguay *20883*

R   *Bouea poilanei* Evrard *6057*
     R   Vietnam *6057*

E   *Buchanania barberi* Gamble *13883*
     E   *13883* India - Kerala (Travancore) *13883*

I   *Buchanania lanceolata* Wight
     I   India - Kerala (Quilon, Travancore)

I   *Buchanania platyneura* Kurz *14782*
     I   *14782* India - Andaman Is. *14782*
     I   *14782* India - Nicobar Is. *14782*

V   *Campnosperma seychellarum* Marchand *14296*
     V   *19181* Seychelles *14296*

R   *Campnosperma zeylanicum* Thwaites *8021*
     R   *12838* Sri Lanka *8021*

R   *Choerospondias axillaris* (Roxb.) B.L. Burtt & A.W. Hill
     var. *japonica* (Ohwi) Ohwi *10572*
     R   *10572* Japan *10572*

R   *Comocladia cordata* Britton *20883, 13336*
     R   *13336* Jamaica *20883*

E   *Comocladia parvifolia* Britton *20883*
     E   *20883* Jamaica *20883*

Ex/E   *Comocladia undulata* Urban *19001*
     Ex/E *19001* Martinique *19001*

R   *Comocladia velutina* Britton *20883*
     R   *20883* Jamaica *20883*

V   *Cyrtocarpa caatingae* Mitchell & Daly *20883, 21345*
     I   *20883* Brazil *20883*

R   *Dracontomelon petelotii* Tard. *6057*
     R   Vietnam *6057*

R   *Dracontomelon schmidii* Tard. *6057*
     R   Vietnam *6057*

R   *Euleria tetramera* Urban *5607*
     R   *19105* Cuba *5607*

V   *Euroschinus aoupiniensis* Hoff *20893*
     V   *20893* New Caledonia *20893*

V   *Euroschinus jaffrei* Hoff *20893*
     V   *20893* New Caledonia *20893*

R   *Gluta compacta* Evrard *6057*
     R   Vietnam *6057*

R   *Gluta megalocarpa* (Evrard) Tard. *6057*
     R   Vietnam *6057*

V   *Haplorhus peruviana* Engler *20883, 13875*
     V   *20883* Chile (Ariza Region) *21089*
     R   *12468* Peru (south) *21089*

V   *Lannea transulta* (Balf. f.) A.R. Smith *15534*
     V   *15534* Yemen - Socotra *15534*

V   *Mangifera andamanica* King *7739*
     V   *14782* India - Andaman Is. *7739*

E   *Mangifera flava* Evrard *7739*
     E   Kampuchea *7739*
     E   Vietnam *7739*

I   *Mangifera khasiana* Pierre *7739*
     I   India - Assam (Khasi hills) *7739*

E   *Mangifera lambii* Kosterm. *10582*
     E   Malaysia - Sabah (Tenom) *10582*

R   *Mangifera minutifolia* Evrard *7739*
     R   Vietnam *7739*

V   *Mangifera monandra* Merr. *7739*
     V   Philippines *7739*

E   *Mangifera superba* Hook.f. *7739*
     E   Malaysia - Peninsular Malaysia *7739*

I   *Mangifera torquenda* Kosterm. *10582*
     I   Indonesia - Kalimantan *10597*
     E   Malaysia - Sabah *10582*

I   *Mangifera whitmorei* Kochummen *10592*
     I   Malaysia - Peninsular Malaysia (along Rekam R., N.
              Perak) *10592*

R   *Mangifera zeylanica* (Blume) Hook.f. *7739*
     R   *12838* Sri Lanka *7739*

I   *Melanochyla nitida* King *19209*
     I   *19209* Malaysia - Peninsular Malaysia (Pulau Pinang/Penang &
              Prai, Perak) *19209*

E   *Nothopegia aureo-fulva* Beddome ex Hook.f. *13883*
     E   *13883* India - Tamil Nadu (Tirunelveli Hills)
              13883

I   *Nothopegia colebrookiana* (Wight) Blume
     I   India - Tamil Nadu

R   *Orthopterygium huancui* (Gray) Hemsley *18200*
     R   *12468* Peru *18200*

R   *Ozoroa namaquensis* (Sprague) Von Teichman & A.E.van
     Wyk *20604*
     R   *20604* Namibia *20604*
     R   *20604* South Africa - Cape Province *20604*

R   *Pistacia coccinea* Collett & Hemsley
     R   Myanmar (Shan Hills)

Magnoliopsida (dicots): Anacardiaceae: *Pistacia*

R	*Pistacia malayana* M.R. Henderson		
	R		Malaysia - Peninsular Malaysia
E	*Poupartia borbonica* Gmelin *10082*		
	E	20771	Réunion *10082*
	E	20771	Mauritius *10082*
E	*Poupartia castanea* (Baker) Engl. *10082*		
	E	5852	Mauritius - Rodrigues *5852*
E	*Poupartia pubescens* (Baker) Engl. *10082*		
	E	20771	Mauritius *10082*
R	*Rhus albomarginata* Sond. *20604*		
	R	20604	South Africa - Cape Province *20604*
R	*Rhus batophylla* Codd *20604*		
	R	20604	South Africa - Transvaal *20604*
I	*Rhus glutinosa* A.Rich. ssp. *glutinosa* var. *unifoliolata* Cufodontis *20907*		
	I	20907	Ethiopia (Gojam) *20907*
R	*Rhus kwazuluana* Moffett *20604*		
	R	20604	South Africa - Natal *20604*
R	*Rhus maricoana* Moffett *20604*		
	R	20604	South Africa - Transvaal *20604*
V	*Rhus michauxii* Sarg. *20850*		
	E	20850	U.S. - Georgia *20850*
	V	20850	U.S. - North Carolina *20850*
	Ex	20850	U.S. - South Carolina *20850*
	E	20850	U.S. - Virginia *20850*
R	*Rhus monticola* Meikle *7749*		
	R		Malawi (Mt. Mlanje) *7749*
R	*Rhus rhodesiensis* R. & A. Fernandes *7750*		
	R		Zimbabwe *7750*
R	*Rhus rudatisii* Engl. *20604*		
	R	20604	South Africa - Natal *20604*
R	*Rhus sekhukhuniensis* Moffett *20604*		
	R	20604	South Africa - Transvaal *20604*
R	*Rhus wildii* R. & A. Fernandes *7749*		
	R		Zimbabwe *7749*
I	*Schinopsis haenkeana* Engl. *10007*		
	V	19448	Argentina *19448*
	I	20176	Argentina - Cordoba *20176*
	I	20176	Argentina - San Juan *20176*
	I	20176	Argentina - San Luis *20176*
	V	19354	Bolivia *19354*
R	*Schinus longifolius* (Lindl.) Spreg. var. *paraguariensis* (Hassler) F. Barkley *21056*		
	I	20883	Argentina *20883*
			Brazil *21056*
	V	20883	Paraguay *20883*
	V	20883	Uruguay *20883*
I	*Schinus patagonicus* (Philippi) I.M. Johnston *16336*		
	I	16336	Argentina *16336*
	I	20176	Argentina - Chubut *20176*
	I	20176	Argentina - Neuquen *20176*
	I	20176	Argentina - Rio Negro *20176*
R	*Schinus terebinthifolius* Raddi *20883*		
	I	20883	Ecuador *20883*
R	*Sclerocarya gillettii* Kokwaro *20057*		
	R	20057	Kenya *20057*
I	*Semecarpus auriculata* Beddome *5379*		
	I		India - Kerala (Western Ghats) *5379*
	I		India - Tamil Nadu (Muthukuzhivayal) *5379*
R	*Semecarpus caudata* Pierre *6057*		
	R		Vietnam *6057*

R	*Semecarpus gardneri* Thwaites *8021*		
	R	12838	Sri Lanka *8021*
V	*Semecarpus marginata* Thwaites *8021*		
	V	12838	Sri Lanka (Gilimale FoR) *8021*
I	*Semecarpus moonii* Thwaites *8021*		
	I	16162	Sri Lanka (Kottawa Arboretum, Galle) *8021*
R	*Semecarpus myriocarpa* Evrard & Tard. *6057*		
	R		Vietnam *6057*
I	*Semecarpus obovata* Moon *8021*		
	I	16162	Sri Lanka *8021*
V	*Semecarpus ochracea* Alston *12838*		
	V	12838	Sri Lanka *12838*
V	*Semecarpus parvifolia* Thwaites *8021*		
	V	12838	Sri Lanka *8021*
I	*Semecarpus paucinervius* Merr. *13833*		
	I	13833	Philippines (Palawan) *13833*
E	*Semecarpus pubescens* Thwaites *8021*		
	E	12838	Sri Lanka *8021*
E	*Semecarpus riparia* Virot *20893*		
	E	20893	New Caledonia *20893*
R	*Semecarpus subpeltata* Thwaites *8021*		
	R	12838	Sri Lanka *8021*
V	*Semecarpus supanduriformis* Wallich *14872*		
	V	14872	Bangladesh *14872*
R	*Semecarpus walkeri* Hook.f. *8021*		
	R	12838	Sri Lanka *8021*
R	*Swintonia minuta* Evrard *6057*		
	R		Vietnam *6057*
V	*Tapirira bethanniana* Mitchell *20883, 21344*		
	I	20883	French Guiana *20883*
R	*Thyrsodium bolivianum* Mitchell & Daly *20883, 21343*		
	I	20883	Bolivia *20883*
	I	20883	Brazil *20883*
	I	20883	Peru *20883*
V	*Trichoscypha albiflora* Engl. *7926*		
	V	20858	Ghana *6072*
	V	20858	Liberia
V	*Trichoscypha atropurpurea* Engl. *20274*		
	V	20858	Ghana *20274*
	V	20858	Liberia *7926*
	V	20858	Nigeria *20274*
V	*Trichoscypha beguei* Aubrev. & Pellegr. *20274*		
	V	20858	Côte d'Ivoire *7926*
	V	20858	Ghana *20274*
	V	20858	Liberia *7926*
V	*Trichoscypha cavalliensis* Aubrev. & Pellegr. *20274*		
	V	20858	Côte d'Ivoire *7926*
	V	20858	Ghana *20274*
	V	20858	Liberia *7926*
E	*Trichoscypha chevalieri* Aubrev. & Pellegr. *20274*		
	E	20858	Côte d'Ivoire *20274*
	E	20858	Ghana *20274*
R	*Trichoscypha liketensis* Veken *19358*		
	R	19358	Zaire (Forestier Central) *19358*
R	*Trichoscypha parvifoliolata* Veken *19358*		
	R	19358	Zaire (Kasai) *19358*

Ancistrocladaceae

Number of genera:	1
Number of species:	15-20
Recorded threatened species:	2 (11%)

Tropics.

V   *Ancistrocladus robertsoniorum* **Leonard** *7959*
      V   *20057* Kenya (Mwele; Gongoni; Buda Forest) *7959*

E   *Ancistrocladus uncinatus* **Hutch. & Dalz.** *7926*
      E   *20749* Nigeria (Eket) *7926*

Anisophylleaceae

Number of genera:	4
Number of species:	40
Recorded threatened species:	2 (5%)

Tropical or subtropical forests, mostly Africa and Indomalaysia; South America.

R   *Anisophyllea cinnamomoides* (**Gardner & Champ.**) **Alston** *8021*
      R   *12838* Sri Lanka *8021*

R   *Anisophyllea obtusifolia* **Engl. & Brehmer** *20556*
      R   *5926* Tanzania (east Usambara mountains) *5926*

Annonaceae

Number of genera:	125-130
Number of species:	2,300
Recorded threatened species:	212 (9%)

Mainly tropical, rarely warm temperate.

I   *Alphonsea hortensis* **H. Huber** *8021*
      I   *16162* Sri Lanka *8021*

I   *Alphonsea keithii* **Ridl.** *19120*
      I   *19120* Thailand *19120*

I   *Alphonsea zeylanica* **Hook.f. & Thomson** *8021*
      I   *16162* Sri Lanka *8021*

R   *Anaxagorea floribunda* **Timmerman** *13769*
      R   *13713* Peru *13769*

R   *Anaxagorea macrantha* **R.E. Fries** *13769*
      R   *13713* Brazil *13769*

R   *Anaxagorea manausensis* **Timmerman** *13769*
      R   *13713* Brazil *13769*

R   *Anaxagorea pachypetala* (**Diels**) **R.E. Fries** *13769*
      R   *13713* Peru *13769*

R   *Anaxagorea rheophytica* **P. Maas & Westra** *13771*
      R   *13713* Venezuela *13771*

V   *Anaxagorea silvatica* **R. E Fries** *13769*
      V   *13713* Brazil *13769*

R   *Ancana hirsuta* **Jessup** *20681*
      R   *20681* Australia - Queensland *20681*

V   *Annona acuminata* **Saff.** *20883, 9006*
      V   *20883* Panama *20883*

R   *Annona campestris* **R. E. Fries** *20883*
      I   *20883* Paraguay *20883*

V   *Annona coriacea* var. *cuneata* **R. E. Fries** *20883*
      I   *20883* Paraguay *20883*

I   *Annona domingensis* **R.E.Fries** *21008*
      I   *21008* Dominican Republic (around Santo Domingo) *21008*

I   *Annona ekmanii* **R.E. Fries** *5607*
      I   *19105* Cuba (Holguin) *5607*

V   *Annona elliptica* **R.E. Fries** *5607*
      V   *19105* Cuba (Pinar del Rio) *5607*

R   *Annona glaucophylla* **R. E. Fries** *20883, 19951*
      I   *20883* Paraguay *20883*

E   *Annona havanensis* **R.E. Fries** *5607*
      E   *19105* Cuba (Ciud. Habana; Matanzas) *5607*

V   *Annona hayesii* **Standl.** *20883, 10747*
      V   *20883* Panama *20883*

V   *Annona jamaicensis* **Sprague** *20883*
      R   *20883* Jamaica *20883*

E   *Annona moaensis* **Leon & Alain** *5607*
      E   *19105* Cuba (Holguin) *5607*

R   *Annona oblongifolia* **R.E. Fries** *5607*
      R   *19105* Cuba (Santiago de Cuba; Holguin) *5607*

V   *Annona paraguayensis* **R. E. Fries** *20883, 19951*
      I   *20883* Paraguay *20883*

V   *Annona phaeoclados* **C. Martius** *20883, 19951*
      I   *20883* Paraguay *20883*

R   *Annona praetermissa* **F. & R.** *20883, 13336*
      R   *13336* Jamaica *20883*

V   *Annona spraguei* **Saff.** *20883, 9006*
      V   *20883* Panama *20883*

I   *Artabotrys brevipes* **Craib** *19120*
      I   *19120* Thailand *19120*

R   *Artabotrys fragrans* **Ast** *6057*
      R   Vietnam *6057*

R   *Artabotrys hispidus* **Sprague & Hutch.** *7926*
      R   Sierra Leone *7926*

R   *Artabotrys le-testui* **Pellegrin**
      R   Gabon

R   *Artabotrys modestus* **Diels** ssp. *modestus* *19499*
      R   *5926* Tanzania (Lindi) *5926*

R   *Artabotrys nicobaricus* **D. Das** *7771*
      R   *14782* India - Nicobar Is. *14782*

I   *Artabotrys oblanceolatus* **Craib** *19120*
      I   *19120* Thailand *19120*

I   *Artabotrys sponosus* **Craib** *19120*
      I   *19120* Thailand *19120*

R   *Artabotrys vanprukii* **Craib** *19120*
      R   *19120* Thailand *19120*

I   *Artabotrys vidaliana* **Elm.** *13833*
      I   *13833* Philippines (Palawan) *13833*

R   *Asimina obovata* (**Willd.**) **Nash** *20850*
      I   *20850* U.S. - Florida *20850*
      I   *20850* U.S. - Georgia *20850*

E   *Asimina tetramera* **Small** *20850*
      E   *20850* U.S. - Florida *20850*

R   *Asteranthe trollii* **Diels** *5926*
      R   *5926* Tanzania (Uluguru mountains) *5926*

R   *Bocageopsis pleiosperma* **P. Maas** *13713*
      R   *13713* Brazil *13713*

I   *Cyathostemma longipes* **Craib** *19120*
      I   *19120* Thailand *19120*

E   *Cymbopetalum torulosum* **G. E. Schatz** *20883, 11312*
      I   *20883* Costa Rica *20883*

I   20883 Panama 20883

R *Dasymaschalon evrardii* Ast *6057*
   R   Vietnam *6057*

I *Dasymaschalon scandens* Elm. *13833*
   I *13833* Philippines (low and medium altitudes)
      13833

E *Deeringothamnus pulchellus* Small *20850*
   E 20850 U.S. - Florida *20850*

E *Deeringothamnus rugelii* (B.L. Robins.) Small *20850*
   E 20850 U.S. - Florida *20850*

V *Dennettia tripetala* Bak.f. *20274*
   V 20858 Tropical Africa (Guinea-wide) *20858*
   V 20858 Ghana *20274*
   V 20858 Nigeria *18326*

I *Desmos palawanensis* (Elm.) Merr. *13833*
   I *13833* Philippines (low and medium altitudes)
      13833

E *Desmos viridiflorus* (Beddome) Saff. *11494*
   E *11494* India - Kerala *11494*
   E *11494* India - Tamil Nadu *11494*

R *Duckeanthus grandiflorus* R.E. Fries *13774*
   R *13713* Brazil *13774*

V *Enantia kummeriae* Engl. & Diels *19499*
   V 5926 Tanzania (East Usambara & Udzungwa Mts.)
      5926

V *Enicosanthum acuminata* (Thwaites) Airy Shaw *8021*
   V *12838* Sri Lanka (south-west) *8021*

E *Friesodielsia obanensis* (Baker f.) van Steenis *7926*
   E   Nigeria (Oban) *7926*

I *Goniothalamus expansus* Craib *19120*
   I *19120* Thailand *19120*

V *Goniothalamus hookeri* Thwaites *8021*
   V *12838* Sri Lanka (Sinharaja; Reigam Korale)
      8021

R *Goniothalamus rhynchantherus* Dunn *11494*
   R *11494* India - Kerala (Trivandrum District)
      11494
   R *11494* India - Tamil Nadu (Tirunelveli District)
      11494

I *Goniothalamus simonsii* Hook.f. & Thomson
   I   India - Meghalaya

R *Goniothalamus takhtajanii* Ban *6057*
   R 20985 Vietnam *6057*

I *Goniothalamus thomsonii* Thwaites *8021*
   I *16162* Sri Lanka (Hinidumkanda, Kanneliya) *8021*

I *Goniothalamus wynaadensis* Beddome
   I   India - Tamil Nadu

R *Greenwayodendron suaveolens* (Engl. & Diels) Verdc. ssp.
    usambaricum Verdc. *19499*
   R 5926 Tanzania (east Usambara Mts.) *5926*

I *Guatteria cargadero* Triana & Planchon *19353*
   I *19352* Colombia *19353*

V *Guatteria jefensis* Barringer *20883, 9077*
   I 20883 Panama *20883*

E *Guatteria panamensis* R.E. Fries *20883, 9006*
   I 20883 Panama *20883*

R *Guatteriella campinensis* Morawetz & P. Maas *13776*
   R *13713* Brazil *13776*

R *Guatteriella tomentosa* R.E. Fries *13777*
   R *13713* Brazil *13777*

R *Guatteriopsis kuhlmannii* R.E. Fries *13781*
   R *13713* Brazil *13781*

R *Haplostichanthus johnsonii* F.Muell. *20681*
   R 20681 Australia - Queensland *20681*

R *Heteropetalum brasiliense* Benth. *13782*
   R   Brazil *13783*

R *Heteropetalum spruceanum* R.E. Fries *13782*
   R   Brazil *13783*

R *Hexalobus mossambicensis* N. Robson *7749*
   R   Mozambique (north) *20886*

R *Hornschuchia alba* (A. St. Hil.) R.E. Fries *11309*
   R *13713* Brazil *11309*

R *Hornschuchia cauliflora* P. Maas & van Setten *13773*
   R *13713* Brazil *13773*

R *Hornschuchia myrtillus* Nees *11309*
   R *13713* Brazil *11309*

R *Hornschuchia obliqua* P. Maas & van Setten *13773*
   R *13713* Brazil *13773*

R *Hornschuchia polyantha* P. Maas *13713*
   R *13713* Brazil *13713*

V *Isolona cauliflora* Verdc. *19499*
   V *19109* Kenya (Makadara & Mangea forest) *19109*
   V 5926 Tanzania (east Usambara Mts.) *5926*

V *Isolona deightonii* Keay *20274*
   V 20858 Ghana *20274*
   V 20858 Sierra Leone *20767*

R *Malmea costaricensis* R.E. Fries *9037*
   R 9426 Costa Rica *9037*

I *Melodorum fuscum* Craib *19120*
   I *19120* Thailand *19120*

V *Miliusa nilagirica* Beddome *13883*
   V *13883* India - Tamil Nadu *13883*

R *Miliusa parviflora* Ridley
   R   Malaysia - Peninsular Malaysia (Perlis; Kedah)

I *Miliusa tectona* Hutch. ex Parkinson *7771*
   I 7771 India - Andaman Is. *7771*

I *Miliusa zeylanica* Gardner ex Hook.f. & Thomson *8021*
   I *16162* Sri Lanka (Reigam Korale; Bentota) *8021*

I *Mitrephora alba* Craib *19120*
   I *19120* Thailand *19120*

R *Mitrephora andamanica* Thoth. & Das *7771*
   R *14782* India - Andaman Is. *14782*

I *Mitrephora caudata* Merr. *13833*
   I *13833* Philippines *13833*

V *Mitrephora collinsae* Craib *19120*
   V *19120* Thailand *19120*

I *Mitrephora fragrans* Merr. *13833*
   I *13833* Philippines (low altitude) *13833*

V *Mitrephora keithii* Ridl. *19120*
   V *19120* Thailand *19120*

I *Mitrephora lanota* (Blanco) Merr. *13780*
   I *15960* Philippines *13780*

V *Mitrephora winitii* Craib *19120*
   V *19120* Thailand *19120*

V *Monanthotaxis capea* (E.G. Camus) Verdc. *11631*
   V 20887 Côte d'Ivoire (Mudjika forest) *11631*

I *Monanthotaxis dictyoneura* (Diels) Verdc. *19499*
   I 5926 Tanzania (Ulanga district) *5926*

I   *Monanthotaxis discolor* (Diels) Verdc. *19499*
    I   *5926*   Tanzania (Njombe district) *5926*

I   *Monanthotaxis faulknerae* Verdc. *19499*
    I   *5926*   Tanzania (Tanga district) *5926*

I   *Monanthotaxis trichantha* (Diels) Verdc. *19499*
    I   *5926*   Tanzania (Lindi) *5926*

E   *Monocyclanthus vignei* Keay *6072*
    E   *20858*   Ghana *6072*
    E   *20858*   Liberia *20274*

V   *Neostenanthera hamata* (Benth.) Exell *20274*
    V   *20858*   Côte d'Ivoire *7926*
    V   *20858*   Ghana *20274*
    V   *20858*   Liberia *7926*
    V   *20858*   Sierra Leone *7926*

R   *Neostenanthera robsonii* Le Thomas
    R   Gabon (Lastoursville & Moumba)

E   *Oncodostigma hainanensie* (Merr.) Tsiang & P.T. Li *17617*
    E   *17617*   China - Hainan Is. *11139*
    E   *17617*   China - Guangxi (Hepu) *11139*

I   *Ophrypetalum odoratum* Diels ssp. *longipedicellatum* Verdc. *19499*
    I   *5926*   Tanzania (Morogoro district) *5926*

R   *Orophea hirsuta* King
    R   Malaysia - Peninsular Malaysia

I   *Orophea palawanensis* Elm. *13833*
    I   *13833*   Philippines (low and medium altitudes) *13833*

I   *Orophea salicifolia* Hutch. *7771*
    I   *7771*   India - Andaman Is. *7771*

I   *Orophea submaculata* Elm. *13833*
    I   *13833*   Philippines (Palawan) *13833*

I   *Orophea thomsoni* Beddome
    I   India - Tamil Nadu

I   *Orophea torulosa* Hutch. *7771*
    I   *7771*   India - Andaman Is. *7771*

I   *Orophea uniflora* Hook.f. & Thomson *13883*
    I   India - Karnataka
    I   India - Kerala
    I   India - Tamil Nadu

R   *Oxandra maya* Miranda *9058*
    R   *19755*   Mexico *9058*

V   *Phaeanthus malabaricus* Beddome *14782*
    V   *14782*   India - Kerala *14782*

I   *Phoenicanthus coriacea* (Thwaites) H. Huber *8021*
    I   *16162*   Sri Lanka (south-west) *8021*

I   *Phoenicanthus obliqua* (Hook.f. & Thomson) Alston *8021*
    I   *16162*   Sri Lanka *8021*

V   *Piptostigma fugax* A.Chev. ex Hutch. & Dlaz. *20274*
    V   *20858*   Côte d'Ivoire *7926*
    V   *20858*   Ghana *20274*
    V   *20858*   Liberia *7926*

R   *Piptostigma oyemense* Pellegrin
    R   Gabon (Oyem)

Ex/E   *Polyalthia angustifolia* *19472*
    Ex/E   *19472*   Fiji (Mt Korombamba) *19472*

I   *Polyalthia elmeri* Merr. *13833*
    I   *13833*   Philippines (Palawan) *13833*

R   *Polyalthia michaelii* C.White *20681*
    R   *20681*   Australia - Queensland *20681*

R   *Polyalthia minima* Ast *6057*
    R   Vietnam *6057*

I   *Polyalthia moonii* Thwaites *8021*
    I   *16162*   Sri Lanka (Reigam Korale, Kalutara) *8021*

I   *Polyalthia palawanensis* Merr. *13833*
    I   *13833*   Philippines (low altitude) *13833*

I   *Polyalthia persicaefolia* (Hook.f. & Thomson) Thwaites *8021*
    I   *16162*   Sri Lanka *8021*

R   *Polyalthia rufescens* Hook.f. & Thomson *14782*
    R   *14782*   India - Kerala *14782*
    R   *14782*   India - Tamil Nadu *14782*

E   *Polyceratocarpus scheffleri* Engl. & Diels *19499*
    E   *5926*   Tanzania (Usambara, Uluguru, Udzungwa Mts.) *20921*

R   *Popowia beddomeana* Hook.f. & Thomson *11494*
    R   *11494*   India - Kerala *11494*
    R   *11494*   India - Tamil Nadu *11494*

I   *Popowia parvifolia* Kurz *7771*
    I   India - Nicobar Is. *7771*

I   *Popowia velutina* King
    I   Malaysia - Peninsular Malaysia (Gopeng, Perak)

R   *Pseudephedranthus fragans* (R.E.Fries) Aristeg. *13713*
    R   *13713*   Venezuela (Amazonia) *13713*

R   *Pseudoxandra pacifica* P. Maas *13713*
    R   *13713*   Colombia *13713*

R   *Pseuduvaria froggattii* (F.Muell.) Jessup *20681*
    R   *20681*   Australia - Queensland *20681*

I   *Pseuduvaria galeata* J. Sincl. *19209*
    I   *19209*   Malaysia - Peninsular Malaysia (Johor) *19209*

R   *Pseuduvaria hylandii* Jessup *20681*
    R   *20681*   Australia - Queensland *20681*

R   *Pseuduvaria mulgraveana* Jessup var. *glabrescens* Jessup *20681*
    R   *20681*   Australia - Queensland *20681*

R   *Pseuduvaria prainii* (King) Merr. *14782*
    R   *14782*   India - Andaman Is. *14782*
    R   *14782*   India - Nicobar Is. *14782*

R   *Pseuduvaria villosa* Jessup *20681*
    R   *20681*   Australia - Queensland *20681*

R   *Reedrollinsia cauliflora* J.W. Walker *11311*
    R   *11306*   Mexico - Chiapas *11311*

V   *Rollinia amazonica* R. E. Fries *20883, 13783*
    R   *13713*   Colombia (Amazonas) *21009*

R   *Rollinia andicola* P. Maas & Westra *20883*
    I   *20883*   Ecuador (Chimborazo) *21009*
    I   *20883*   Peru (Amazonas; Pasco) *21009*

E   *Rollinia bahiensis* P. Maas & Westra *20883, 13713*
    I   *20883*   Brazil *20883*
    R   *13713*   Brazil - Bahia *9097*

E   *Rollinia boliviana* R. E. Fries *20883, 13785*
    R   *13713*   Bolivia (La Paz) *21009*

E   *Rollinia calcarata* R. E. Fries *20883, 13781*
    I   *20883*   Brazil *20883*
    R   *21009*   Brazil - Acre *21009*

V   *Rollinia centrantha* R. E. Fries *20883*
    I   *20883*   Ecuador (Pastaza) *21009*
    I   *20883*   Peru *20883*

R	*Rollinia chrysocarpa* P. Maas & Westra *20883, 16347*		
	R	*21009* Ecuador (Napo) *21009*	
	R	*21009* Peru (Amazonas) *21009*	
R	*Rollinia danforthii* Standley *20883, 9037*		
	I	*20883* Costa Rica *20883*	
	I	*20883* Colombia (Antioquia) *21009*	
R	*Rollinia dolichopetala* R. E. Fries *20883, 16347*		
	I	*20883* Ecuador (Morona-Santiago; Pastaza) *21009*	
V	*Rollinia ecuadorensis* R. E. Fries *20883, 13777*		
	R	*13713* Ecuador (Napo) *21009*	
R	*Rollinia fendleri* R. E. Fries *20883*		
	I	*20883* Venezuela *20883*	
E	*Rollinia ferruginea* (R. E. Fries) P. Maas & Westra *20883, 13784*		
	I	*20883* Brazil *20883*	
	R	*21009* Brazil - Rio de Janeiro *21009*	
R	*Rollinia fosteri* P. Maas & Westra *20883*		
	I	*20883* Ecuador (Guayas) *21009*	
	I	*20883* Peru (Amazonas; Madre de Dios) *21009*	
E	*Rollinia helosioides* P. Maas & Westra *20883, 13784*		
	R	*13713* Brazil *13784*	
	I	*20883* Ecuador (Napo) *21009*	
R	*Rollinia herzogii* R. E. Fries *20883*		
	R	*20883* Bolivia (Santa Cruz) *21009*	
	I	*20883* Peru (Madre de Dios) *21009*	
R	*Rollinia mammifera* P. Maas & Westra *20883*		
	I	*20883* Brazil *20883*	
	?	Brazil - Acre *21009*	
	I	*20883* Peru (San Martín) *21009*	
V	*Rollinia pachyantha* P. Maas & Westra *20883*		
	I	*20883* Colombia (El Valle) *21009*	
R	*Rollinia parviflora* A. F. C. P. de Saint-Hilaire *20883*		
	I	*20883* Brazil *20883*	
	?	Brazil - Rio de Janeiro *21009*	
R	*Rollinia pickelii* Diels *20883, 13774*		
	I	*20883* Brazil *20883*	
	?	Brazil - Paraiba *21009*	
	?	Brazil - Pernambuco *21009*	
E	*Rollinia rufinervis* Triana & Planchon *20883, 13774*		
	R	*13713* Colombia (Antioquia) *21009*	
R	*Rollinia ubatubensis* P. Maas & Westra *20883, 13784*		
	I	*20883* Brazil *20883*	
	?	Brazil - Sao Paulo (Ubatuba) *21009*	
R	*Rollinia velutina* van Marle *20883*		
	I	*20883* Colombia (Boyacá) *21009*	
	I	*20883* Venezuela (Apure) *21009*	
R	*Rollinia xylopiifolia* (A. F. C. P. de Saint-Hilaire & Tulasne) R. E. Fries *20883*		
	I	*20883* Brazil *20883*	
	I	*20883* Brazil - Espirito Santo *21009*	
	I	*20883* Brazil - Rio de Janeiro *21009*	
	I	*20883* Brazil - Sao Paulo *21009*	
I	*Saccopetalum arboreum* Elm. *13833*		
	I	*13833* Philippines (low altitude) *13833*	
R	*Saccopetalum prolificum* (Chun & How) Tsiang *17617*		
	R	*17617* China - Hainan Is. *11139*	
Ex/E	*Sageraea grandiflora* Dunn *11494*		
	Ex/E	*11494* India - Kerala *11494*	
I	*Sageraea laurifolia* (Grah.) Blatter		
	I	India - Karnataka (Concan)	
	I	India - Kerala	
	I	India - Tamil Nadu	

I	*Sageraea listeri* King var. *andamanica* Chatterjee *7771*		
	I	India - Andaman Is. *7771*	
I	*Sageraea reticulata* Craib *19120*		
	I	*19120* Thailand *19120*	
V	*Sageraea thwaitesii* Hook.f. & Thomson *8021*		
	V	*12838* Sri Lanka *8021*	
I	*Stelechocarpus longipes* Craib *19120*		
	I	*19120* Thailand *19120*	
I	*Stenanona panamensis* Standl. *20883, 9006*		
	I	*20883* Panama *20883*	
R	*Tetrameranthus globuliferus* Westre *13786*		
	R	*13713* Ecuador *13786*	
R	*Tetrameranthus macrocarpus* R.E. Fries *13786*		
	R	*13713* Colombia *13786*	
R	*Tetrameranthus umbellatus* Westre *13786*		
	R	*13713* Peru (Amazonia) *13713*	
I	*Toussaintia orientalis* Verdc. *19499*		
	I	*5926* Tanzania (Uzaramo & Ulanga districts) *5926*	
V	*Tridimeris hahniana* (Baillon) Baillon *11309*		
	V	*11306* Mexico *11309*	
E	*Trivalvaria kanjilalii* D. Das *11494*		
	E	*11494* India - Meghalaya *11494*	
I	*Unona longiflora* Roxb.		
	I	India - Meghalaya (Tura Peak & Nongkhyllem R)	
R	*Unona tiebaghiensis* Daniker		
	R	New Caledonia	
R	*Unonopsis angustifolia* (Benth.) R.E. Fries *13781*		
	R	*13713* Brazil *13781*	
E	*Unonopsis panamensis* R.E. Fries *20883, 9006*		
	I	*20883* Panama *20883*	
R	*Unonopsis riedeliana* R.E. Fries *13781*		
	R	*13713* Brazil *13781*	
R	*Unonopsis rigida* R.E. Fries *13787*		
	R	*13713* Brazil *13787*	
R	*Unonopsis umbilicata* (Dunal) R.E. Fries ssp. *umbilicata* *13781*		
	R	Grenada *13781*	
R	*Unonopsis velutina* P. Maas *13713*		
	R	*13713* Venezuela *13713*	
R	*Uvaria clavata* Pierre ex Engl. & Diels		
	R	Gabon	
I	*Uvaria decidua* Diels *19499*		
	I	*5926* Tanzania (Lindi) *5926*	
E	*Uvaria eucincta* Beddome ex Dunn *13883*		
	E	*13883* India - Orissa *7771*	
R	*Uvaria flexuosa* Ast *6057*		
	R	Vietnam *6057*	
I	*Uvaria gabonensis* Engl. & Diels		
	I	Gabon (Libreville)	
I	*Uvaria hamiltonii* Hook. F. & Th. var. *kurzii* King *7771*		
	I	India - Andaman Is. *7771*	
R	*Uvaria klainei* Pierre ex Engl. & Diels		
	R	Gabon (Libreville)	
I	*Uvaria lurida* Hook.f. & Thomson		
	I	India - Meghalaya	

R	*Uvaria nicobarica* Raiz. & Sahni *7771*	
	R	*14782* India - Nicobar Is. *14782*
I	*Uvaria nudistellata* Elm. *13833*	
	I	*13833* Philippines (medium altitude) *13833*
I	*Uvaria semecarpifolia* Hook.f. & Thomson *8021*	
	I	*16162* Sri Lanka *8021*
R	*Uvaria sofa* Scott Elliot *7926*	
	R	Guinea *7926*
R	*Uvaria thomasii* Sprague & Hutch. *8003*	
	R	Senegal (Basse Casamance) *8003*
	R	Sierra Leone (Sendugu) *8003*
V	*Uvaria tortilis* A. Chev. ex Hutch. *7926*	
	V	Côte d'Ivoire (Bingerville) *7926*
R	*Uvariodendron anisatum* Verdc. *7959*	
	R	*20057* Kenya (THika; Karura, Meru & Emali forests) *17435*
E	*Uvariodendron gorgonis* Verdc. *19499*	
	E	*20057* Kenya (Kwale) *19499*
	E	*20057* Tanzania (Morogoro) *19499*
V	*Uvariodendron occidentale* Le Thomas *20274*	
	V	*20858* Cameroon *18326*
	V	*20858* Côte d'Ivoire *20274*
	V	*20858* Ghana *20274*
	V	*20858* Liberia *18326*
	V	*20858* Nigeria *18326*
R	*Uvariopsis le-testui* Pellegrin	
	R	Gabon (Lastoursville)
V	*Xylopia acunae* Borh. & Risco *5607*	
	V	*19105* Cuba (Sancti Spiritus) *5607*
E	*Xylopia amplexicaulis* (Lam.) Baillon *10082, 21329*	
	E	*20771* Mauritius *10082*
R	*Xylopia championii* Hook.f. & Thomson *8021*	
	R	*12838* Sri Lanka (south-west) *8021*
R	*Xylopia ekmanii* R.E. Fries *5607*	
	R	*19105* Cuba (Guantanamo) *5607*
V	*Xylopia elliotii* Engl. *20274*	
	V	*20858* Côte d'Ivoire *20858*
	V	*20858* Ghana *20274*
R	*Xylopia hastarum* M.L. Green *20883*	
	R	*20883* Jamaica *20883*
E	*Xylopia lamarckii* Baillon *10082, 21329*	
	E	*20771* Mauritius *10082*
V	*Xylopia latipetala* Verdc. *19499*	
	V	*20885* Tanzania (Rondo Plateau) *20885*
R	*Xylopia longifolia* DC. *20883*	
	V	*20883* Panama *20883*
I	*Xylopia nigricans* Hook.f. & Thomson *8021*	
	I	*16162* Sri Lanka (Ritigala FoR) *8021*
R	*Xylopia torrei* N. Robson *7749*	
	R	Mozambique *7749*
V	*Xylopiastrum taiense* Aubrév.	
	V	Côte d'Ivoire (Tai)

Apocynaceae

Number of genera: 168-200
Number of species: 2,000
Recorded threatened species: 149 (7%)

Tropics, particularly rain forest regions.

I	*Aganosma montana* Kerr *19120*	
	I	*19120* Thailand *19120*

R	*Aganosma petelotii* Ly *6057*	
	R	*15734* Vietnam *6057*
I	*Alstonia curtisii* King & Gamble *19120*	
	I	*19120* Thailand *19120*
R	*Alstonia marquisensis* M.Grant *20845*	
	R	*20845* French Polynesia - Marquesas Is *20845*
R	*Alstonia quaternava* Van Heurck *20893*	
	R	*20893* New Caledonia *20893*
R	*Alstonia saligna* S.Moore *20893*	
	R	*20893* New Caledonia *20893*
R	*Alyxia angustifolia* Ridley	
	R	Malaysia - Peninsular Malaysia
R	*Alyxia divaricata* Pitard *6057*	
	R	Vietnam *6057*
R	*Alyxia gynopogon* Roemer & Schultes *19108*	
	R	*19108* Australia - Norfolk Is. *14288*
R	*Alyxia ilicifolia* F.Muell. ssp. *magnifolia* (F.M.Bailey) P.I.Forster *20681*	
	R	*20681* Australia - Queensland *20681*
R	*Alyxia insularis* Kaneh. & Sas.	
	R	Taiwan (Lan Yu & Is. Lutao)
R	*Alyxia integricarpa* Boit. *20893*	
	R	*20893* New Caledonia *20893*
R	*Alyxia lindii* F. Muell.	
	R	*14225* Australia - NSW - Lord Howe Is. *14225*
R	*Alyxia orophila* Domin *20681*	
	R	*20681* Australia - Queensland *20681*
R	*Alyxia sharpei* P.Forster *20681*	
	R	*20681* Australia - Queensland *20681*
R	*Alyxia spathulata* Guillaumin	
	R	New Caledonia
R	*Alyxia squamulosa* C. Moore & F. Muell. *14223*	
	R	*14223* Australia - NSW - Lord Howe Is. *14223*
R	*Alyxia taiwanensis* Lu & Yang *20511*	
	R	*20854* Taiwan *20511*
R	*Alyxia torresiana* Gaudich.	
	R	*18338* North Mariana Is. (Rota, Saipan, Tinian) *18338*
	R	*18338* U.S. - Guam *18338*
R	*Alyxia vieillardii* Boit.	
	R	New Caledonia
R	*Ambelania duckei* Markgraf *20883*	
	R	*20883* Brazil *20883*
	V	*20883* Peru *20883*
R	*Ambelania occidentalis* Zarruchi *20883*	
	V	*20883* Brazil *20883*
	E	*20883* Colombia *20883*
	R	*20883* Peru *20883*
V	*Amsonia fugatei* S.P. McLaughlin *20850*	
	V	*20850* U.S. - New Mexico *20850*
V	*Amsonia grandiflora* Alexander *20883, 20850, 8058*	
	V	*20850* U.S. - Arizona *20850*
	E	*20883* Mexico *20883*
R	*Amsonia hubrichtii* Woods. *20850*	
	R	*20850* U.S. - Arkansas *20850*
	E	*20850* U.S. - Oklahoma *20850*
E	*Amsonia kearneyana* Woods. *20883, 20850, 19002*	
	E	*20850* U.S. - Arizona *20850*
	I	*20883* Mexico *20883*
R	*Amsonia ludoviciana* Vail *20850*	

V	20850	U.S. - Georgia	20850
R	20850	U.S. - Louisiana	20850
Ex/E	20850	U.S. - Mississippi	20850
I	20850	U.S. - South Carolina	20850

R *Amsonia peeblesii* Woods. *20850*

R	20850	U.S. - Arizona	20850

V *Amsonia rigida* Shuttlw. ex Small *20850*

E	20850	U.S. - Alabama	20850
I	20850	U.S. - Florida	20850
I	20850	U.S. - Georgia	20850
I	20850	U.S. - Louisiana	20850

E *Amsonia tharpii* Woods. *20850*

E	20850	U.S. - New Mexico	20850
E	20850	U.S. - Texas	20850

I *Anodendron nervosum* Kerr *19120*

I	19120	Thailand	19120

V *Anodendron rhinosporum* Thwaites *8021*

V	12838	Sri Lanka (Ritigala SNR)	8021

R *Apocynum venetum* L. var. *basikurmon*
Hara *10573*

R	10573	Japan	10573

R *Aspidosperma camporum* Muell. Arg. in Mart. *20883, 19951*

I	20883	Brazil	20883
R	20883	Paraguay	20883

E *Aspidosperma chodatii* Hassler ex Mark. *20883*

E	20883	Paraguay	20883

E *Aspidosperma darienense* Dwyer *20883, 9006*

I	20883	Panama	20883

R *Aspidosperma polyneuron* Muell. Arg. *20883, 10370*

E	5462	Argentina	20883
I	20176	Argentina - Misiones	20176
I	20883	Bolivia	20883
I	20883	Brazil	20883
E	19352	Colombia	20883
V	20883	Paraguay	20883
E	10370	Peru	20883

R *Aspidosperma quirandy* Hassler *20883*

R	20883	Paraguay	20883

R *Aspidosperma riedelii* Muell. Arg. *20883*

I	20883	Brazil	20883
R	20883	Paraguay	20883

R *Aspidosperma triternatum* Rojas Acosta *20883*

I	20883	Argentina	20883
R	20883	Paraguay	20883

E *Cameraria microphylla* Britton *5607*

E	19105	Cuba (Ciego de Avila; Camaguey)	5607

E *Carissa edulis* (Forssk.) Vahl. var. *sechellensis*
(Baker) Pichon *14981*

E	14981	Seychelles (Silhouette)	14981

V *Carissa xylopicron* Thouars *10082*

E	14234	Réunion	14234
E	5852	Mauritius	5852
V	5852	Mauritius - Rodrigues	5852

I *Catharanthus coriaceus* Markgraf *19940*

I	19940	Madagascar	10368

R *Cerbera dumicola* P.Forster *20681*

R	20681	Australia - Queensland	20681

R *Cerbera inflata* S.T.Blake *20681*

R	20681	Australia - Queensland	20681

E *Cerberiopsis neriifolia* (S. Moore) Boit. *20893*

E	20893	New Caledonia	20893

V *Cerberiopsis obtusifolia* (Van Heurck & F. Muell.)
Boit. *20893*

V	20893	New Caledonia	20893

R *Chilocarpus alyxifolius* Pierre *6057*

R		Vietnam	6057

R *Couma catingae* Ducke *20883*

R	20883	Brazil	20883

V *Cycladenia humilis* Benth. var. *jonesii* (Eastw.)
Welsh & Atwood *20850*

E	20850	U.S. - Arizona	20850
V	20850	U.S. - Utah (south-east)	20850

R *Ervatamia chilangensis* Ly *6057*

R	15734	Vietnam (Lang Son)	6057

V *Forsteronia domatiella* Proctor *20883*

V	20883	Jamaica	20883

R *Forsteronia myriantha* J.D. Sm. *20883, 9096*

I	20883	Guatemala	20883
V	20883	Panama	20883

R *Forsteronia viridescens* Blake *20883*

I	20883	Belize	20883
I	20883	Guatemala	20883
V	20883	Panama	20883

E *Forsteronia wilsonii* (Griseb.) Woodson *20883, 13336*

E	13336	Jamaica	20883

Ex *Holarrhena pubescens* (Buch.-Ham.) Wall ex G.
Don *18102*

Ex	18102	Pakistan	18102

E *Hunteria ghanensis* J. Hall & Leeuwenb. *20274*

E	20858	Ghana	20274

E *Ichnocarpus microcalyx* Pitard *19120*

E	19120	Thailand	19120

R *Kopsia cochinchinensis* Kuntze *6057*

R		Vietnam	6057

R *Landolphia owariensis* Beauv. var. *leiocalyx*
(Pichon) H. Huber *7926*

R		Guinea (Fouta Djalon)	7926

R *Landolphia utilis* (A. Chev.) Pichon *7926*

R		Côte d'Ivoire	7926

E *Lepinia taitensis* Decne. *20845*

E	20845	French Polynesia - Society Is. (Moorea, Tahiti)	20845

V *Malouetia isthmica* Markgr. *20883, 10747*

V	20883	Panama	20883
		Colombia (San José del Palmar)	21093

E *Mandevilla campanulata* Markgr. *20883, 10747*

I	20883	Panama	20883

R *Melodinus angustifolius* Hayata *20511*

R	20511	Taiwan	20511

R *Melodinus baccellianus* (F.Muell.) S.T.Blake *20681*

R	20681	Australia - Queensland	20681

R *Melodinus baueri* Endl. *19108*

R	19108	Australia - Norfolk Is.	14288

R *Melodinus cochinchinensis* (Lour.) Merr. *6057*

R		Vietnam	6057

E *Melodinus insulae-pinorum* Boit. *20893*

E	20893	New Caledonia	20893

R *Melodinus minutiflorus* Pitard *6057*

R		Vietnam	6057

V *Melodinus reticulatus* Boit. *20893*

V	20893	New Caledonia	20893

V	*Melodinus tiebaghiensis* Boit. *20893*	
	V	20893 New Caledonia *20893*
E	*Mortoniella pittieri* Woodson *11967*	
	Ex/E	11967 Costa Rica *11967*
	E	11967 Nicaragua *11967*
V	*Mucoa pantchenkoana* Markgraf *20883*	
	V	20883 Venezuela *20883*
V	*Neisosperma brevituba* (Boit.) Boit. *20893*	
	V	20893 New Caledonia *20893*
Ex	*Neisosperma brownii* Fosberg & Sachet *20845*	
	Ex	20845 French Polynesia - Marquesas Is (Nuku Hiva) *20845*
E	*Neisosperma kilneri* (F.Muell.) Fosb. *20681*	
	E	20681 Australia - Queensland *20681*
E	*Neisosperma sevenetii* (Boit.) Boit. *20893*	
	E	20893 New Caledonia *20893*
E	*Neisosperma thiollierei* (Montr.) Boit. *20893*	
	E	20893 New Caledonia *20893*
R	*Neobracea acunaiana* Lippold *5607*	
	R	19105 Cuba (Holguin; Guantanamo) *5607*
E	*Neobracea martiana* Borh. & Muniz *5607*	
	E	19105 Cuba (Santiago de Cuba) *5607*
V	*Neobracea susannina* Borh. *5607*	
	V	19105 Cuba (Santiago de Cuba) *5607*
R	*Nouettea cochinchinensis* Pierre *6057*	
	R	Vietnam *6057*
V	*Ochrosia borbonica* J. Gmelin *10082*	
	V	14234 Réunion *10082*
	E	20771 Mauritius *10082*
Ex	*Ochrosia fatuhivensis* Fosberg & Sachet *20845*	
	Ex	20845 French Polynesia - Marquesas Is (Fatu Hiva) *20845*
V	*Ochrosia grandiflora* Boit. *20893*	
	V	20893 New Caledonia *20893*
E	*Ochrosia haleakalae* St. John *20850, 10260*	
	E	20850 U.S. - Hawaii (Maui & Hawai`i) *20850*
R	*Ochrosia hexandra* Koidz. *19134*	
	R	19135 Japan - Kazan Retto *8622*
E	*Ochrosia inventorum* L.Allorge *20802*	
	E	20893 New Caledonia (Pointe Maa) *20802*
E	*Ochrosia kauaiensis* St. John *20850, 14209*	
	E	20850 U.S. - Hawaii (Kaua`i) *20850*
Ex/E	*Ochrosia kilaueaensis* St. John *20850, 14209, 21348, 21356*	
	Ex/E	20850 U.S. - Hawaii (Kilauea) *20850*
E	*Ochrosia moorei* (F.Muell.) Benth. *20681*	
	I	20681 Australia - New South Wales *20681*
	I	20681 Australia - Queensland *20681*
Ex	*Ochrosia nukuhivensis* Fosberg & Sachet *20845*	
	Ex	20845 French Polynesia - Marquesas Is (Nuku Hiva) *20845*
Ex	*Ochrosia tahitensis* Lanessan ex Pichon *20845*	
	Ex	20845 French Polynesia - Society Is. (Tahiti) *20845*
E I	*Pachypodium ambongense* L. Poisson *10368*	
	E	19879 Madagascar (Mahajunga) *20578*
R I	*Pachypodium baronii* Constantin & Bois var. *baronii* *10368*	
	R	19879 Madagascar (Mahajunga) *20578*
E I	*Pachypodium baronii* Constantin & Bois var. *windsori*	

		(L. Poisson) Pichon *10368*
	E	20578 Madagascar (Antsiranana) *20578*
E I	*Pachypodium decaryi* L. Poisson *10368*	
	E	20578 Madagascar (Mahajunga) *20578*
R II	*Pachypodium densiflorum* Baker var. *brevicalyx* H. Perrier *10368*	
	R	19879 Madagascar (Antananarivo) *20578*
R II	*Pachypodium horombense* Pichon *10368*	
	R	19879 Madagascar
R II	*Pachypodium lamerei* Drake var. *ramosum* (Costantin & Bois) Pichon *10368*	
	R	19879 Madagascar (Toliara) *20578*
V II	*Pachypodium namaquanum* (Wyley ex Harv.) Welw. *20604*	
	V	20604 Namibia *20604*
	V	20604 South Africa - Cape Province *20604*
R II	*Pachypodium rosulatum* Baker var. *rosulatum* *10368*	
	R	19879 Madagascar (Mahajunga) *20578*
R	*Parabarium chevalieri* Pitard *6057*	
	R	Vietnam *6057*
E	*Parahancornia krukovii* Monschino *20883*	
	V	20883 Brazil *20883*
V	*Parahancornia oblonga* Monachino *20883*	
	E	20883 Brazil *20883*
	E	20883 Venezuela *20883*
V	*Parahancornia peruviana* Monachino *21102, 17462*	
	V	20883 Peru *20883*
R	*Parsonsia alboflavescens* (Dennst.) Mabb. *20681*	
	R	20681 Australia - Northern Territory *20681*
V	*Parsonsia densivestita* C.White *20681*	
	V	20681 Australia - Queensland *20681*
V	*Parsonsia dorrigoensis* J.B.Williams ms. *20681*	
	V	20681 Australia - New South Wales *20681*
V	*Parsonsia larcomensis* J.B.Williams ms. *20681*	
	V	20681 Australia - Queensland *20681*
R	*Parsonsia largiflorens* (Benth.) S.T.Blake *20681*	
	I	20681 Australia - New South Wales *20681*
	I	20681 Australia - Queensland *20681*
V	*Parsonsia rupestris* J.B.Williams ms. *20681*	
	V	20681 Australia - Queensland *20681*
R	*Parsonsia siamensis* Kerr *19120*	
	R	19120 Thailand *19120*
R	*Parsonsia tenuis* S.T.Blake *20681*	
	I	20681 Australia - New South Wales *20681*
	I	20681 Australia - Queensland *20681*
I	*Petchia ceylanica* (Wight) Livera *8021*	
	I	16162 Sri Lanka *8021*
E	*Prestonia lenticellata* A. Gentry *20883, 10747*	
	I	20883 Panama *20883*
V	*Prestonia obovata* Standl. *20883, 9006*	
	V	20883 Panama *20883*
E	*Prestonia remediorum* Woods. *20883, 9006*	
	I	20883 Panama *20883*
E	*Prestonia tysonii* A. Gentry *20883, 10747*	
	I	20883 Panama *20883*
E	*Prestonia wedelii* Woods. *20883, 10747*	
	I	20883 Panama *20883*
E	*Pteralyxia kauaiensis* Caum *20850, 14209, 21349*	
	E	20850 U.S. - Hawaii (Kaua`i) *20850*

V	*Pteralyxia macrocarpa* (Hbd.) K. Schum. *20850, 14209*	
	V	20850 U.S. - Hawaii *20850*
R	*Rauvolfia beddomei* Hook.f.	
	R	*18228* India - Kerala (Travancore Hills) *18228*
	I	India - Tamil Nadu (Tirunelveli Hills)
R	*Rauvolfia chaudocensis* Pierre ex Pitard *6057*	
	R	Vietnam *6057*
V	*Rauvolfia linearifolia* Britton & P. Wilson *5607*	
	V	*19105* Cuba (Santiago de Cuba; Holguin) *5607*
E	*Rauvolfia sachetiae* Fosberg *20845*	
	E	20845 French Polynesia - Marquesas Is (Hiva Oa, Nuku Hiva) *20845*
E	*Rauvolfia sevenetii* Boit. *20893*	
	E	20893 New Caledonia *20893*
R	*Rauvolfia spathulata* Boit. *20893*	
	R	20893 New Caledonia *20893*
I	*Rhazya greissii* Tackh. & Boulos	
	I	Egypt
I	*Secondatia macnabii* (Urb.) Woodson *20883, 13336*	
	I	*13336* Jamaica *20883*
R	*Spongiosperma longilobum* Markgraf *20883*	
	R	20883 Brazil *20883*
R	*Spongiosperma riparium* Monachino *20883*	
	E	20883 Colombia *20883*
	V	20883 Venezuela *20883*
I	*Stemmadenia brasiliensis* Leeuwenberg *20831*	
	I	20831 Brazil - Pará *20831*
V	*Stephanostema stenocarpum* Schumann *5926*	
	V	5926 Tanzania *5926*
V	*Strempeliopsis arborea* Urb. *20883, 13336*	
	V	*13336* Jamaica *20883*
R	*Strophanthus annamensis* Tsiang *6057*	
	R	Vietnam *6057*
V	*Strophanthus zimmermannianus* Monach. *20057*	
	V	20057 Kenya (Shimba hills) *20057*
I	*Tabernaemontana capuronii* Leeuwenberg *20832*	
	I	20832 Madagascar (Foulpointe) *20832*
I	*Tabernaemontana granulosa* Pitard *20832*	
	I	20832 Vietnam *20832*
R	*Tabernaemontana ochroleuca* Urb. *20883, 13336*	
	R	*13336* Jamaica *20883*
E	*Tabernaemontana ovalifolia* Urb. *20883, 13336*	
	E	*13336* Jamaica *20883*
V	*Tabernaemontana persicariifolia* Jacq. *20832*	
	E	*14234* Réunion *14234*
	V	20771 Mauritius *10936*
R	*Tabernaemontana wullschlaegelii* Griseb. *20883*	
	R	20883 Jamaica *20883*
R	*Thevetia bicornuta* Muell. Arg. *20883*	
	R	20883 Paraguay *20883*
R	*Trachelospermum formosanum* Liu & Ou *20511*	
	R	20511 Taiwan *20511*
I	*Urceola laevis* (Elm.) Merr. *13833*	
	I	*13833* Philippines (Palawan) *13833*
I	*Vallaris macrantha* Ridl. *19120*	
	I	*19120* Thailand *19120*
R	*Vallesia flexuosa* Woodson *9037*	
	R	9426 Costa Rica *9037*
R	*Vallesia spectabiilis* *19848*	

	R	*19848* Mexico *19848*
I	*Wrightia dolichocarpa* Bahadur & Bennet	
	I	India - Goa, Daman & Diu (Nagar Haveli)
I	*Wrightia flavido-rosea* Trimen *8021*	
	I	*16162* Sri Lanka (Doluwakanda, Kurungala) *8021*
V	*Wrightia pubescens* R. Br. ssp. *lanitii* (Blanco) Ngan *10278*	
	V	Philippines *10278*
R	*Wrightia versicolor* S.T.Blake *20681*	
	R	20681 Australia - Queensland *20681*

Aquifoliaceae

Number of genera:	2-4
Number of species:	320-420
Recorded threatened species:	37 (10%)

Nearly cosmopolitan.

R	*Ilex arisanensis* Yam. *20511*	
	R	20854 Taiwan *20511*
V	*Ilex beecheyi* (Loes.) Makino *8037*	
	V	*19134* Japan - Ogasawara-shoto *20626*
R	*Ilex bioritsensis* Hayata *20511*	
	R	20511 Taiwan *20511*
I	*Ilex cassine* L. ssp. *mexicana* (Turcz.) E. Murray *11733*	
	I	11733 Mexico - Veracruz *11733*
R	*Ilex collina* Alexander *20850*	
	E	20850 U.S. - North Carolina *20850*
	V	20850 U.S. - Virginia *20850*
	R	20850 U.S. - West Virginia *20850*
E	*Ilex cookii* Britt. & Wilson *20883, 8058*	
	I	20883 Puerto Rico (Cerro de Punta) *20883*
E	*Ilex dimorphophylla* Koidz. *20626*	
	E	20626 Japan (Ryukyu) *20626*
I	*Ilex embeloides* Hook.f.	
	I	India - Meghalaya (Khasi hills)
R	*Ilex florifera* F. & R. *20883, 13336*	
	R	*13336* Jamaica *20883*
R	*Ilex formosae* (Loes.) Li	
	R	Taiwan (south)
Ex/E	*Ilex gardneriana* Wight *14782*	
	Ex/E	*14782* India - Tamil Nadu (Sispara, Nilgiri) *14782*
R	*Ilex harrisii* Loes. *20883*	
	R	20883 Jamaica *20883*
V	*Ilex jamaicana* Proctor *20883, 13336*	
	V	*19890* Jamaica (Portland) *20883*
E	*Ilex khasiana* Purakaystha	
	E	India - Meghalaya (Khasi hills) *7771*
R	*Ilex loeseneri* Tard. *6057*	
	R	Vietnam *6057*
R	*Ilex lonicerifolia* var. *matsudai* *20854*	
	R	20854 Taiwan *20854*
V	*Ilex maingayi* Hook. f. *7730*	
	V	20099 Malaysia - Peninsular Malaysia (west coast & southern regions) *19209*
R	*Ilex matanoana* *18128*	
	R	*19136* Japan - Ogasawara-shoto *18128*
I	*Ilex micrantha* Triana & Planchon *19352*	

I		*19352* Colombia *19352*	
I	***Ilex mitis*** (L.) Radlk. var. *schliebenii* Loes. *19501*		
	I	*5926* Tanzania (Uluguru mountains) *5926*	
R	***Ilex moana*** Borh. & Muniz *5607*		
	R	*19105* Cuba (Guantanamo) *5607*	
V	***Ilex nannophylla*** Borh. & Muniz *5607*		
	V	*19105* Cuba (Santiago de Cuba) *5607*	
R	***Ilex opaca*** Sol. var. *arenicola* (Ashe) Ashe *20850, 17890*		
	R	*20850* U.S. - Florida *20850*	
I	***Ilex palawanica*** Lossn. ex Elm. *13833*		
	I	*13833* Philippines (Mt. Pulgar) *13833*	
R	***Ilex perado*** Aiton ssp. *perado* *20171*		
	R	Portugal - Madeira	
E	***Ilex perado*** Aiton ssp. *platyphylla* (Webb & Berthel.) Tutin *15105*		
	E	*15105* Spain - Canary Is. *15105*	
R	***Ilex percoriacea*** Tuy. *8038*		
	R	*19134* Japan - Ogasawara-shoto (Chichijima) *8038*	
E	***Ilex praetermissa*** Kiew		
	E	Malaysia - Peninsular Malaysia (Klang Gates Ridge)	
R	***Ilex puberula*** Proctor *13336*		
	R	*13336* Jamaica *13336*	
I	***Ilex rarasanensis*** Sasaki *20511*		
	I	*20511* Taiwan *20511*	
R	***Ilex rubrinervis*** Tard. *6057*		
	R	Vietnam *6057*	
R	***Ilex sideroxyloides*** (Sw.) Griseb. var. *occidentalis* (Macfad.) Loes. *20883*		
	R	*20883* Jamaica *20883*	
	I	*20883* Puerto Rico *20883*	
E	***Ilex sintenisii*** (Urban) Britt. *20883*		
	V	*20883* Puerto Rico *20883*	
I	***Ilex subtriflora*** Griseb. *20883, 13336*		
	I	*13336* Jamaica *20883*	
Ex	***Ilex ternatiflora*** (C. Wright) R.A. Howard *15112*		
	Ex	*19105* Cuba (Pinar del Rio) *15112*	
R	***Ilex tsugitakayamensis*** Sas. *20511*		
	R	*20511* Taiwan *20511*	
R	***Ilex urbaniana*** Loes. *15107*		
	R	*15107* Puerto Rico *15107*	
	R	*15107* British Virgin Is. *15107*	
E	***Ilex vaccinioides*** Loes. *20883*		
	E	*20883* Jamaica *20883*	
I	***Ilex venulosa*** Hook.f.		
	I	India - Arunachal Pradesh (Khasi hills)	

Araliaceae

Number of genera:	47-70	
Number of species:	700	
Recorded threatened species:	107	(15%)

Tropical and subtropical; some in temperate regions.

R	***Acanthopanax baviensis*** R. Viguier *6057*		
	R	Vietnam *6057*	
R	***Apiopetalum velutinum*** Baillon *20893*		
	R	*20893* New Caledonia *20893*	
R	***Aralia macdowallii*** F.Muell. *20681*		

	R	*20681* Australia - Queensland *20681*	
R	***Aralia soratensis*** Marchal *18200*		
	R	*12468* Peru *18200*	
I	***Arthrophyllum pulgarense*** Elm. *13833*		
	I	*13833* Philippines (upper Mt. Pulgar) *13833*	
V	***Astrotricha crassifolia*** Blakely *20681*		
	V	*20681* Australia - New South Wales *20681*	
R	***Astrotricha parvifolia*** Wakef. *20681*		
	R	*20681* Australia - Victoria *20681*	
V	***Astrotricha roddii*** R.Makinson *20681*		
	I	*20681* Australia - New South Wales *20681*	
	I	*20681* Australia - Queensland *20681*	
R	***Brassaiopsis gaussenii*** Bui *6057*		
	R	Vietnam *6057*	
E	***Cheirodendron dominii*** Krajina *20850, 14209*		
	E	*20850* U.S. - Hawaii (Kaua`i) *20850*	
V	***Cheirodendron forbesii*** (Sherff) Lowry *20850, 14209*		
	I	*20850* U.S. - Hawaii (Kaua`i - Makaleha Mts) *20850*	
I	***Cheirodendron marquesense*** F. Brown		
	I	French Polynesia - Marquesas Is	
V	***Cussonia bancoensis*** Aubrev. & Pellegr. *15970*		
	V	*20858* Ghana *15970*	
R	***Cussonia gamtoosensis*** Strey *20604*		
	R	*20604* South Africa - Cape Province *20604*	
I	***Cussonia kirkii*** Seem. var. *bracteata* Tennant *19502*		
	I	*5926* Tanzania (Lindi) *5926*	
I	***Cussonia kirkii*** Seem. var. *quadripetala* Tennant *19502*		
	I	*5926* Tanzania (Songea district) *5926*	
R	***Cussonia ostinii*** Chiov. *19704*		
	R	*19704* Ethiopia (Gonder, Gojam, Welega, Kefa.) *19704*	
V	***Dendropanax blakeanus*** Britton *20883, 19890*		
	R	*19890* Jamaica *20883*	
R	***Dendropanax caloneurus*** (Harms) Merr. *6057*		
	R	*15734* Vietnam *6057*	
E	***Dendropanax cordifolius*** Britton *20883, 13336*		
	E	*20883* Jamaica *20883*	
E	***Dendropanax darienensis*** Seem. *20883, 9006*		
	I	*20883* Panama *20883*	
E	***Dendropanax filipes*** Britton *20883, 13336*		
	E	*20883* Jamaica *20883*	
E	***Dendropanax grandiflorus*** Britton *20883, 13336*		
	E	*20883* Jamaica *20883*	
E	***Dendropanax grandis*** Britton *20883, 13336*		
	E	*20883* Jamaica *20883*	
E	***Dendropanax morbifera*** Lev. *15957*		
	E	*15923* Korea, South (Chejudo) *15957*	
R	***Dendropanax nutans*** (Sw.) Decne. & Planch. *20883*		
	I	*20883* Jamaica *20883*	
R	***Dendropanax nutans*** (Sw.) Decne. & Planch. var. *nutans* *20883*		
	R	*20883* Jamaica *20883*	
R	***Dendropanax nutans*** Adams var. *obtusifolius* C.D. Adams *20883, 15911*		
	I	*20883* Jamaica *20883*	
E	***Dendropanax ovalifolius*** (F. & R.) Adams *20883, 15911*		

Magnoliopsida (dicots): Araliaceae: *Dendropanax*

R		*13336* Jamaica *20883*	

R   *Dendropanax pendulus* (Sw.) Decne. & Planch. *20883*
     R   *20883* Jamaica *20883*

R   *Dendropanax portlandianus* Proctor *20883, 13336*
     R   *13336* Jamaica *20883*

E   *Dendropanax sessiliflorus* (Standl. & A.C. Sm.) A.C. Sm. *20883, 9006*
     I   *20883* Panama *20883*

R   *Dendropanax swartzii* (F. & R.) A.C. Smith *20883, 13336*
     R   *13336* Jamaica *20883*

R   *Echinopanax horridum* Kom. *15957*
     R   *15923* Korea, South (Mt Sorak) *15957*

R   *Fatsia oligocarpella* Koidz. *19135*
     R   *19135* Japan - Kazan Retto (Minami-Iwojima) *8622*
     R   *19134* Japan - Ogasawara-shoto *8622*

V   *Gastonia crassa* (Hemsley) Friedm. *14296*
     V   *19181* Seychelles *14296*

E   *Gastonia lionnetii* F. Friedmann *14981*
     E   *14981* Seychelles *14981*

E   *Gastonia mauritiana* Marais *10082*
     E   *20771* Mauritius *10082*

E   *Gastonia rodriguesiana* Marais *10082*
     E   *5852* Mauritius - Rodrigues *5852*

E   *Gastonia sechellarum* (Baker) Harms var. *sechellarum* *14296*
     E   Seychelles (granitic) *14296*

E   *Gastonia sechellarum* (Baker) Harms var. *contracta* F. Friedmann *14981*
     E   *14981* Seychelles (granitic) *14981*

E   *Gastonia sechellarum* (Baker) Harms var. *curiosae* F. Friedmann *14981*
     E   *14981* Seychelles (granitic) *14981*

E   *Megalopanax rex* Ekman *5607*
     E   *19105* Cuba *5607*

I   *Merrilliopanax cordifolia* Sastry
     I   India - Arunachal Pradesh (Subansiri)

V   *Meryta angustifolia* (Endl.) Seemann *19108*
     V   *11649* Australia - Norfolk Is. *14288*

I   *Meryta brachypoda* Harms *10169*
     E   *19185* French Polynesia - Tubuai Is. *10169*
     E   *19185* Pitcairn (Henderson Is.) *10169*

V   *Meryta choristantha* Harms *20845*
     V   *20845* French Polynesia - Tubuai Is. (Rapa) *20845*

I   *Meryta drakeana* Nadeaud *20845*
     I   *20845* French Polynesia - Society Is. (Tahiti) *20845*

R   *Meryta lanceolata* J.G.Forster *20845*
     R   *20845* French Polynesia - Society Is. (Moorea, Tahiti) *20845*

E   *Meryta latifolia* (Endl.) Seemann *11649*
     E   *11649* Australia - Norfolk Is. *11649*

V   *Meryta lucida* J.Moore *20845*
     V   *20845* French Polynesia - Society Is. (Raiatea) *20845*

R   *Meryta malietoa* P. Cox *7925*
     R   Western Samoa (Savaii) *7925*

I   *Meryta mauruensis* Nadeaud *20845*

     I   *20845* French Polynesia - Society Is. (Tahiti) *20845*

I   *Meryta raiateensis* J.Moore *20845*
     I   *20845* French Polynesia - Society Is. *20845*

E   *Meryta salicifolia* J.Moore *20845*
     E   *20845* French Polynesia - Society Is. (Tahiti) *20845*

R   *Meryta sinclairii* *19305*
     R   *19305* New Zealand - North Is. *19305*

V   *Meryta sonchifolia* Linden & André *20893*
     V   *20893* New Caledonia *20893*

E   *Munroidendron racemosum* (Forbes) Sherff *20850, 21349*
     E   *20850* U.S. - Hawaii *20850*

V   *Myodocarpus angustialatus* Lowry ined. *20893*
     V   *20893* New Caledonia *20893*

I   *Oreopanax dussii* Krug & Urban ex Duss *10200*
     I   Dominica (only from high peaks) *10200*
     I   Guadeloupe (only from high peaks) *10200*
     E   *19001* Martinique (Morne Piquet, Piton Dumanué, Piton Boucher) *19001*

R   *Oreopanax lempiranus* Hazlett *9098*
     R   *9730* Honduras *9098*

V   *Oreopanax nicaraguensis* M. J. Cannon & J. F. M. Cannon *20883*
     I   *20883* Costa Rica *20883*
     I   *20883* Nicaragua *20883*
     I   *20883* Panama *20883*

E   *Osmoxylon mariannense* (Kaneh.) Fosb. & Sachet *20818*
     E   *20825* North Mariana Is. (Rota) *20825*

E   *Panax vietnamensis* Ha & Grushv. *6057*
     E   *20985* Vietnam *6057*

E   *Panax zingiberensis* C.Y. Wu & K.M. Feng *17617*
     E   *17617* China - Yunnan *11139*

R   *Pentapanax castanopsisicola* Hayata *20511*
     R   *20854* Taiwan *20511*

R   *Pentapanax warmingianus* (Marchal) Harms *20883, 20311*
     I   *20883* Argentina *20883*
     I   *20883* Brazil *20883*
     ?   Brazil - Rio Grande do Sul *20311*
     R   *20883* Paraguay *20883*

E   *Polyscias aemiliguineae* Bernardi *10082*
     E   *14234* Réunion *10082*

R   *Polyscias bellendenkerensis* (Bailey) Philipson *20681*
     R   *20681* Australia - Queensland *20681*

R   *Polyscias cissodendron* (C. Moore & F. Muell.) Harms
     R   *14225* Australia - NSW - Lord Howe Is. *14225*

V   *Polyscias dichroostachya* Baker *10082*
     V   *20771* Mauritius *10082*

R   *Polyscias farinosa* (Del.) Harms *19704*
     R   *19704* Ethiopia (Tigray Upland, Gonder, Shewa Upland, Kefa.) *19704*

E   *Polyscias gracilis* Marais *10082*
     E   *20771* Mauritius *10082*

R   *Polyscias kikuyuensis* Summerh. *7959*
     R   *20057* Kenya (central) *7959*

V   *Polyscias mauritiana* Marais *10082*
     V   *20771* Mauritius *10082*

E   *Polyscias neraudiana* (Drake) R. Viguier *10082*
     E   *20771* Mauritius *10082*

V   *Polyscias nothisii* Lowry ined. *20893*
     V   *20893* New Caledonia *20893*

V   *Polyscias paniculata* (DC.) Baker *10082*
     V   *20771*   Mauritius *10082*

E   *Polyscias rivalsii* Bernardi *10082*
     E   *14234*   Réunion *10082*

I   *Polyscias stuhlmannii* Harms var. *inarticulata*
     Tennant *19502*
     I   *5926*   Tanzania (West Usambara mts) *5926*

R   *Polyscias stuhlmannii* Harms var.
     stuhlmannii *20057*
     R   *20057*   Kenya (Taita hills) *20057*
     R   *20057*   Tanzania (Usambara, Ukaguru & Uluguru Mnts.) *17435*

I   *Polyscias tahitensis* (Nadeaud) Harms *20845*
     I   *20845*   French Polynesia - Society Is. (Raiatea, Tahiti) *20845*

R   *Polyscias willmottii* (F.Muell.) Philipson *20681*
     R   *20681*   Australia - Queensland *20681*

R   *Pseudopanax gunnii* (Hook.f.) K.Koch *20681*
     R   *20681*   Australia - Tasmania *20681*

V   *Pseudopanax scopoliae* (Baillon) Philipson *20893*
     V   *20893*   New Caledonia *20893*

V   *Pseudosciadium balansae* Baillon *20893*
     V   *20893*   New Caledonia *20893*

R   *Reynoldsia sandwicensis* Gray *20850, 14209*
     R   *20850*   U.S. - Hawaii *20850*

I   *Schefflera agamae* Merr. *13833*
     I   *13833*   Philippines (low altitude) *13833*

I   *Schefflera albido-bracteata* Elm. *13833*
     I   *13833*   Philippines (Palawan) *13833*

V   *Schefflera apioidea* Baillon *20893*
     V   *20893*   New Caledonia *20893*

I   *Schefflera bourdillonii* Gamble *21173*
     I   India - Kerala (Travancore Hills)

R   *Schefflera brenesii* A.C. Sm. *20883*
     I   *20883*   Costa Rica *20883*
     V   *20883*   Panama *20883*

R   *Schefflera chapana* Harms *6057*
     R   Vietnam *6057*

I   *Schefflera curranii* Merr. *13833*
     I   *13833*   Philippines (Palawan) *13833*

E   *Schefflera epiphytica* A.C. Sm. *20883, 9006*
     I   *20883*   Panama *20883*

I   *Schefflera foxworthyi* Merr. *13833*
     I   *13833*   Philippines (low and medium altitudes) *13833*

E   *Schefflera gleasonii* (Britt. & Wilson) Alain *20883*
     I   *20883*   Puerto Rico *20883*

R   *Schefflera kontumensis* Bui *6057*
     R   Vietnam *6057*

I   *Schefflera lukwangulensis* (Tenn.) Bernardi *19502*
     I   *5926*   Tanzania (Uluguru, Southern Nguru & Usambara Mts.) *20921*

E   *Schefflera musangensis* M.R. Henderson *21173*
     E   Malaysia - Peninsular Malaysia (Kelantan, Selangor)

I   *Schefflera palawanensis* Merr. *13833*
     I   *13833*   Philippines (low altitude) *13833*

R   *Schefflera palmiformis* Grushv. & N. Skvortsova *6057*
     R   *15734*   Vietnam *6057*

E   *Schefflera procumbens* (Hemsley) Frodin *14296*
     E   Seychelles (granitic) *14296*

V   *Schefflera stearnii* Howard & Proctor *20883, 13336*
     V   *13336*   Jamaica *20883*

I   *Schefflera stolzii* Harms *19502*
     I   *5926*   Tanzania (Rungwe district) *5926*

E   *Schefflera subracemosa* (King) R. Viguier *21173*
     E   Malaysia - Peninsular Malaysia (Perak)

V   *Schefflera troyana* (Urb.) A.C.Sm. *20883, 19890*
     R   *19890*   Jamaica (Clarendon, Peckham woods) *20883*

R   *Schefflera urbaniana* (Marchal) Frodin *19001*
     R   *19001*   Martinique (Pitons du Carbet) *19001*

R   *Schefflera veillonorum* Bernardi *21173, 20893*
     R   *20893*   New Caledonia *20893*

V   *Sinopanax formosana* (Hayata) Li *20511*
     V   *20854*   Taiwan *20311*

R   *Stilbocarpa lyallii* J. Armstr. *86*
     R   *19305*   New Zealand - South Is. *19305*

R   *Stilbocarpa robusta* (Kirk) Cockayne *86*
     R   *19305*   New Zealand - South Is. (Snares Island) *19305*

E   *Tetraplasandra gymnocarpa* (Hbd.) Sherff *20850, 21357*
     E   *20850*   U.S. - Hawaii *20850*

E   *Tetraplasandra gymnocarpa* (Hillebrand) Sherff var. *gymnocarpa* *14209*
     E   *14209*   U.S. - Hawaii (O`ahu - Ko`olau Mts.) *14209*

Aristolochiaceae

Number of genera: 8-10
Number of species: 600
Recorded threatened species: 35   (5%)

Tropical to warm temperate.

I   *Apama barberi* Gamble
     I   India - Tamil Nadu

R   *Aristolochia bodamae* Dingler *20171*
     R   Greece

I   *Aristolochia brevilabris* Bornm. *12840*
     I   *12840*   Turkey *12840*

R   *Aristolochia cilicica* Davis & Khan *12840*
     R   *12840*   Turkey *12840*

R   *Aristolochia cucurbitifolia* Hayata *20511*
     R   *20511*   Taiwan *20511*

I   *Aristolochia helix* Phuphat *19120*
     I   *19120*   Thailand (Khao Phangnga, Khao Khanap Nam) *19277*

R   *Aristolochia kankauensis* Sasaki *20511*
     R   *20511*   Taiwan *20511*

R   *Aristolochia kaoi* Liu & Lai *20511*
     R   *20511*   Taiwan *20511*

R   *Aristolochia krausei* Davis *12840*
     R   *12840*   Turkey *12840*

R   *Aristolochia lycica* Davis & Khan *12840*
     R   *12840*   Turkey *12840*

E   *Aristolochia pfeiferi* Barringer *20883, 9105*
     I   *20883*   Panama *20883*

R   *Aristolochia poluninii* Davis & Khan *12840*
     R   *12840*   Turkey *12840*

R   *Aristolochia rechingeriana* Kit Tan & Sorger *12840*
     R   *12840*   Turkey *12840*

E   *Aristolochia samsunensis* Davis *12840*
    E   *12840*   Turkey *12840*

R   *Aristolochia sicula* Tineo *20171*
    R   *19164*   Italy - Sicily (central and notheastern part) *19164*

R   *Aristolochia stenosiphon* Davis & Khan *12840*
    R   *12840*   Turkey *12840*

R   *Aristolochia tyrrhena* E.Nardi & Arrigoni *20171*
    V   *20528*   France - Corsica *20528*
    R   *20805*   Italy - Sardinia *20528*

R   *Aristolochia weberbaueri* O.C. Schmidt *18200*
    R   *12468*   Peru *18200*

R   *Asarum caudatum* Lindl. var. *viridiflorum* M.E. Peck *20850*
    R   *20850*   U.S. - Oregon *20850*

I   *Asarum epigynum* Hayata *20511*
    I   *20511*   Taiwan *20511*

R   *Asarum hypogynum* Hayata *20511*
    R   *20511*   Taiwan *20511*

R   *Heterotropa kurosawae* (Sugim.) F. Maek. *10572*
    R   *10572*   Japan *10572*

E   *Heterotropa minamitaniana* (Hatus.) F. Maek. *10572*
    E   *10572*   Japan *10572*

R   *Heterotropa nomadakensis* (Hatus.) F. Maek. *10572*
    R   *10572*   Japan *10572*

R   *Heterotropa savatieri* (Franchet) F. Maek. *10572*
    R   *10572*   Japan *10572*

R   *Heterotropa stellata* F. Maek. *10572*
    R   *10572*   Japan *10572*

R   *Heterotropa trigyna* (Araki) F. Maek. *10572*
    R   *10572*   Japan *10572*

R   *Hexastylis contracta* Blomquist *20850*
    E   *20850*   U.S. - Kentucky *20850*
    E   *20850*   U.S. - North Carolina *20850*
    R   *20850*   U.S. - Tennessee *20850*

R   *Hexastylis naniflora* Blomquist *20850*
    V   *20850*   U.S. - North Carolina *20850*
    V   *20850*   U.S. - South Carolina *20850*

V   *Hexastylis rhombiformis* Gaddy *20850*
    V   *20850*   U.S. - North Carolina *20850*

R   *Hexastylis shuttleworthii* Gaddy var. *harperi* Gaddy *20850*
    V   *20850*   U.S. - Alabama *20850*
    R   *20850*   U.S. - Georgia *20850*

V   *Hexastylis speciosa* Harper *20850*
    V   *20850*   U.S. - Alabama *20850*

E   *Pararistolochia talbotii* (S. Moore) Keay *7926*
    E   Nigeria *7926*

E   *Pararistolochia tenuicauda* (S. Moore) Keay *7926*
    E   Nigeria (Oban) *7926*

V   *Thottea barberi* (Gamble) Ding Hou *13883*
    V   *13883*   India - Tamil Nadu (Tirunelveli) *13883*

Asclepiadaceae

Number of genera: 250-315
Number of species: 2,000
Recorded threatened species: 420   (21%)

Tropical and subtropical, especially Africa, with relatively few species in temperate regions.

R   *Amblystigma cionophorus* (Griseb.) Fourn. *16336*

    R   *16336*   Argentina *16336*
    R   *20176*   Argentina - Jujuy *20176*
    R   *20176*   Argentina - Tucuman *20176*

E   *Aphanostelma tubatum* Malme *16336*
    E   *20176*   Argentina - Tucuman *20176*

I   *Asclepias atroviolacea* Woodson *14294*
    I   *14294*   Mexico - Durango *14294*

Ex   *Asclepias bicuspis* N.E.Br. *20604*
    Ex   *20604*   South Africa - Natal *20604*

I   *Asclepias compressidens* (N.E.Br.) Nicholas *20604*
    I   *20604*   South Africa - Cape Province *20604*

E   *Asclepias concinna* (Schltr.) Schltr. *20604*
    E   *20604*   South Africa - Cape Province *20604*
    E   *20604*   South Africa - Natal *20604*

I   *Asclepias cooperi* N.E.Br. *20604*
    I   *20604*   South Africa - Cape Province *20604*

R   *Asclepias cultriformis* Harv. ex Schltr. *20604*
    R   *20604*   Swaziland *20604*
    R   *20604*   South Africa - Cape Province *20604*
    R   *20604*   South Africa - Natal *20604*
    R   *20604*   South Africa - Transvaal *20604*

R   *Asclepias curtissii* Gray *20850*
    R   *20850*   U.S. - Florida *20850*

R   *Asclepias cutleri* Woods. *20850*
    R   *20850*   U.S. - Arizona *20850*
    V   *20850*   U.S. - Utah *20850*

V   *Asclepias disparilis* N.E.Br. *20604*
    V   *20604*   South Africa - Cape Province *20604*
    V   *20604*   South Africa - Natal *20604*

I   *Asclepias dissona* N.E.Br. *20604*
    I   *20604*   South Africa - Transvaal *20604*

I   *Asclepias expansa* (E.Mey.) Schltr. *20604*
    I   *20604*   South Africa - Cape Province *20604*

R   *Asclepias fallax* (Schltr.) Schltr. *20604*
    R   *20604*   South Africa - Transvaal *20604*

V   *Asclepias gordon-grayae* Nicholas *20604*
    V   *20604*   South Africa - Natal *20604*

V   *Asclepias labriformis* M.E. Jones *20850*
    R   *20850*   U.S. - Utah *20850*

R   *Asclepias lemmonii* Gray *20850*
    V   *20850*   U.S. - Arizona *20850*

V   *Asclepias meadii* Torr. ex Gray *20850*
    V   *20850*   U.S. - Illinois *20850*
    Ex   *20850*   U.S. - Indiana *20850*
    E   *20850*   U.S. - Iowa *20850*
    V   *20850*   U.S. - Kansas *20850*
    V   *20850*   U.S. - Missouri *20850*
    Ex   *20850*   U.S. - Wisconsin *20850*

R   *Asclepias monticola* N.E.Br. *20604*
    R   *20604*   South Africa - Cape Province *20604*

I   *Asclepias nana* I.Verd. *20604*
    I   *20604*   South Africa - Transvaal *20604*

R   *Asclepias oreophila* Nicholas *20604*
    R   *20604*   South Africa - Cape Province *20604*
    R   *20604*   South Africa - Natal *20604*

V   *Asclepias patens* N.E.Br. *20604*
    V   *20604*   South Africa - Cape Province *20604*

V   *Asclepias peltigera* (E.Mey.) Schltr. *20604*
    V   *20604*   South Africa - Cape Province *20604*
    V   *20604*   South Africa - Natal *20604*

I   *Asclepias praemorsa* Schltr. *20604*

V	20604	South Africa - Cape Province *20604*
I	20604	South Africa - Natal *20604*

E *Asclepias prostrata* Blackwell *20883, 20850, 8058*

E	20850	U.S. - Texas *20850*
I	20883	Mexico *20883*

V *Asclepias rzedowskii* W. D. Stevens *20883*

I	20883	Mexico *20883*

R *Asclepias sanjuanensis* Heil, J.M. Porter & Welsh *20850*

V	20850	U.S. - New Mexico *20850*

E *Asclepias schlechteri* (K.Schum.) N.E.Br. *20604*

E	20604	South Africa - Cape Province *20604*
E	20604	South Africa - Natal *20604*

R *Asclepias solanoana* Woods. *20850*

R	20850	U.S. - California *20850*

R *Asclepias uncialis* Greene *20850*

E	20850	U.S. - Arizona *20850*
V	20850	U.S. - Colorado *20850*
I	20850	U.S. - Nevada *20850*
V	20850	U.S. - New Mexico *20850*
I	20850	U.S. - Oklahoma *20850*
Ex/E	20850	U.S. - Wyoming *20850*

R *Asclepias uncialis* Greene ssp. *ruthiae* (Maguire) Kartesz & Gandhi *20850*

I	20850	U.S. - Arizona *20850*
I	20850	U.S. - Nevada *20850*
V	20850	U.S. - New Mexico *20850*
R	20850	U.S. - Utah *20850*

V *Asclepias uncialis* Greene ssp. *uncialis 20850*

I	20850	U.S. - Arizona *20850*
I	20850	U.S. - Colorado *20850*
E	20850	U.S. - New Mexico *20850*
I	20850	U.S. - Oklahoma *20850*

V *Asclepias velutina* (Schltr.) Schltr. *20604*

V	20604	South Africa - Transvaal *20604*

V *Asclepias viridula* Chapman *20850, 19734*

V	20850	U.S. - Florida *20850*
I	20850	U.S. - Georgia *20850*

E *Asclepias welshii* N.& P. Holmgren *20850*

E	20850	U.S. - Arizona *20850*
E	20850	U.S. - Utah (Coorg, south Canara) *20850*

I *Asclepias woodii* (Schltr.) Schltr. *20604, 18023*

I	20039	Swaziland *20039*
E	20604	South Africa - Natal *20604*

R *Asclepias xysmalobioides* Hilliard & B.L.Burtt *20604*

R	20604	Lesotho *20604*
R	20604	South Africa - Natal *20604*

I *Aspidoglossum delagoense* (Schltr.) Kupicha *20604*

I	20604	Mozambique *20604*
I	20604	South Africa - Natal *20604*

E *Aspidoglossum demissum* Kupicha *20604*

E	20604	South Africa - Natal *20604*

I *Aspidoglossum difficile* Hilliard *20604*

I	20604	South Africa - Natal *20604*

V *Aspidoglossum flanaganii* (Schltr.) Kupicha *20604*

V	20604	South Africa - Cape Province *20604*

I *Aspidoglossum uncinatum* (N.E.Br.) Kupicha *20604*

I	20604	South Africa - Cape Province *20604*

V *Aspidoglossum xanthosphaerum* Hilliard *20604*

V	20604	South Africa - Natal *20604*

R *Aspidonepsis cognata* (N.E.Br.) Nicholas & Goyder *20604*

R	20604	South Africa - Cape Province *20604*
V	20604	South Africa - Natal *20604*
R	20604	South Africa - Orange Free State *20604*

R *Aspidonepsis reenensis* (N.E.Br.) Nicholas & Goyder *20604*

R	20604	South Africa - Natal *20604*
R	20604	South Africa - Orange Free State *20604*
R	20604	South Africa - Transvaal *20604*

V *Aspidonepsis shebae* Nicholas & Goyder *20604*

V	20604	South Africa - Transvaal *20604*

I *Bidaria cuspidata* (Thunb.) H. Huber *8021*

I	16162	Sri Lanka (Lankagama, Sinharaja) *8021*

R *Brachystelma asmarensis* Chiov. *6087*

R	6087	Ethiopia *6087*

I *Brachystelma australe* R.A.Dyer *20604*

I	20604	South Africa - Cape Province *20604*
I	20604	South Africa - Natal *20604*

I *Brachystelma bournea* Gamble

I	India - Tamil Nadu (Madurai)

I *Brachystelma caffrum* (Schltr.) N.E.Br. *20604*

I	20604	South Africa - Cape Province *20604*

I *Brachystelma campanulatum* N.E.Br. *20604*

I	20604	South Africa - Cape Province *20604*

I *Brachystelma cathcartense* R.A.Dyer *20604*

I	20604	South Africa - Cape Province *20604*

I *Brachystelma comptum* N.E.Br. *20604*

I	20604	South Africa - Cape Province *20604*

R *Brachystelma constrictum* J. Hall *6072*

R		Chad (Bediol)
E	6072	Ghana *6072*

I *Brachystelma delicatum* R.A.Dyer *20604*

I	20604	South Africa - Cape Province *20604*

I *Brachystelma dimorphum* R.A.Dyer ssp. *dimorphum 20604*

I	20604	South Africa - Cape Province *20604*
I	20604	South Africa - Orange Free State *20604*

I *Brachystelma dimorphum* R.A.Dyer ssp. *gratum* R.A.Dyer *20604*

I	20604	South Africa - Orange Free State *20604*

R *Brachystelma discoideum* R.A.Dyer *20604*

I	20604	Zimbabwe *20604*
I	20604	Botswana *20604*
R	20604	South Africa - Transvaal *20604*

I *Brachystelma franksiae* N.E.Br. *20604*

I	20604	South Africa - Natal *20604*

I *Brachystelma glenense* R.A.Dyer *20604*

I	20604	South Africa - Orange Free State *20604*

R *Brachystelma gracillimum* R.A.Dyer *20604*

R	20604	South Africa - Transvaal *20604*

I *Brachystelma incanum* R.A.Dyer *20604*

I	20604	South Africa - Transvaal *20604*

E *Brachystelma keniense* Schweinf. *6073*

E	6073	Kenya *6073*

I *Brachystelma lankana* Dassan. & Jayas. *8021*

I	16162	Sri Lanka (Dikpatana, Matale) *8021*

I *Brachystelma linearis* A. Rich. *6087*

I	6087	Ethiopia *6087*

R *Brachystelma longifolium* (Schltr.) N.E.Br. *20604*

R	20604	South Africa - Transvaal *20604*

R *Brachystelma meyerianum* Schltr. *20604*

R	20604	South Africa - Cape Province	20604

I   *Brachystelma micranthum* E.Mey. 20604
    I   20604   South Africa - Cape Province   20604

R   *Brachystelma minimum* R.A.Dyer 20604
    R   20604   South Africa - Cape Province   20604

R   *Brachystelma minor* E.A.Bruce 20604, 17458
    R   20604   South Africa - Transvaal   20604

I   *Brachystelma montanum* R.A.Dyer 20604
    I   20604   South Africa - Cape Province   20604

E   *Brachystelma natalense* (Schltr.) N.E.Br. 20604
    E   20604   South Africa - Natal   20604

E   *Brachystelma ngomense* R.A.Dyer 20604
    E   20604   South Africa - Natal   20604

Ex   *Brachystelma occidentale* Schltr. 20604
    Ex   20604   South Africa - Cape Province   20604

I   *Brachystelma parvulum* R.A.Dyer 20604, 17458
    I   20604   South Africa - Transvaal   20604

R   *Brachystelma perditum* R.A.Dyer 20604
    R   20604   Lesotho   20604
    R   20604   South Africa - Natal   20604
    R   20604   South Africa - Orange Free State   20604

R   *Brachystelma petraeum* R.A.Dyer 20604
    R   20604   South Africa - Natal   20604

R   *Brachystelma pilosum* R.A.Dyer 20604
    R   20604   Zimbabwe   20604
    R   20604   South Africa - Transvaal   20604

I   *Brachystelma schoenlandianum* Schltr. 20604
    I   20604   South Africa - Cape Province   20604

I   *Brachystelma tabularium* R.A.Dyer 20604
    I   20604   South Africa - Cape Province   20604

V   *Brachystelma tenellum* R.A.Dyer 20604
    V   20604   South Africa - Natal   20604

I   *Brachystelma tenue* R.A.Dyer 20604
    I   20604   South Africa - Natal   20604

R   *Brachystelma vahrmeijeri* R.A.Dyer 20604
    R   20604   South Africa - Natal   20604

Ex   *Caralluma arenicola* N.E. Brown 6180
    Ex   6180   South Africa - Cape Province   6180

V   *Caralluma aucheriana* (Decne) N.E. Br. 20146
    V   20146   Oman (northern)   20146

V   *Caralluma burchardii* N.E. Brown 17891
    V   15105   Spain - Canary Is.   15105

I   *Caralluma diffusa* (Wight) N.E. Br.
    I   India - Kerala (Travancore Hills)
    I   India - Tamil Nadu (Coimbatore Hills)

E   *Caralluma distincta* E.A. Bruce
    E   Kenya
    E   Tanzania

V   *Caralluma dodsoniana* Lavr. 20146
    E   20146   Oman   20146
    V   20146   Yemen, Democratic   20146
    V   20146   Somalia   20146

V   *Caralluma hexagona* Lavranos 20146
    E   20146   Oman (foothills of Jabal al Samhan) 20146
    V   20146   Saudi Arabia   20146
    V   20146   Yemen, Democratic (southeast)   20146

I   *Caralluma joannis* Maire
    I   Morocco

R   *Caralluma sacculata* N.E. Br. 6087

R	6087	Ethiopia	6087

R   *Caralluma sinaica* (Decne.) A. Berger
    E   Egypt
    R   Israel
    I   Jordan

E   *Caralluma tubiformis* E.A. Bruce & Bally
    E   Kenya

V   *Caralluma venenosa* Maire 10488
    V   14958   Algeria   10488

E   *II Ceropegia achtenii* De Wild. ssp. *togoensis* H. Huber 7926
    E   6072   Ghana   7926

R   *II Ceropegia affinis* Vatke 20202
    R   20211   Ethiopia   20202
    R   20211   Somalia   20202

R   *II Ceropegia albisepta* Jum. & H. Perrier var. *albisepta* 10368
    R   20211   Madagascar (Toliara)   20578

R   *II Ceropegia albisepta* Jum. & H. Perrier var. *bruceana* H. Huber 20064
    R   20211   Kenya   20202
    R   20211   Tanzania   20202
    R   20211   Uganda   20202

R   *II Ceropegia albisepta* Jum. & H. Perrier var. *robynsiana* (Werdermann) H. Huber 20064
    R   20211   Zaire   20228

E   *II Ceropegia ampliata* E. Meyer ssp. *madagascariensis* Lavranos 20273
    E   20211   Madagascar (Fianarantsoa)   20578

I   *II Ceropegia ampliata* E. Meyer ssp. *oxyloba* H. Huber 20206
    I   5926   Tanzania (Dar es Salaam)   5926

V   *II Ceropegia angustifolia* Wight 13883
    V   13883   Bangladesh   13883
    V   13883   India - Meghalaya   13883
    V   13883   Nepal   13883

Ex   *II Ceropegia antennifera* Schltr. 20604, 20207
    Ex   20604   South Africa - Natal   20604

R   *II Ceropegia aridicola* W.W. Smith 10260
    R   20211   China

E   *II Ceropegia armandii* Rauh 20213
    E   20211   Madagascar (Toliara)   20578

R   *II Ceropegia attenuata* Hook. 11494
    R   20211   India - Karnataka   11494
    R   20211   India - Maharashtra (Thane; Raigadh; Pune Dist.)   11494

R   *II Ceropegia ballyana* Bullock 20206
    R   20273   Kenya   20206

I   *II Ceropegia barbata* R.A.Dyer 20604, 20064
    I   20604   South Africa - Cape Province   20604

E   *II Ceropegia barnesii* Bruce & Chatterjee 11494
    E   20211   India - Karnataka (South Canara)   11494
    E   20211   India - Tamil Nadu (Nilgiri Hills)   11494

R   *II Ceropegia beddomei* Hook.f. 11494
    R   20211   India - Kerala (Trivandrum; Ponmudi; Idukki)   11494

I   *II Ceropegia bhutanica* Hara 20064
    I   20211   Bhutan   20211

E   *II Ceropegia bosseri* Rauh & Buchloh 20213
    E   20211   Madagascar (Fianarantsoa)   20578

Magnoliopsida (dicots): Asclepiadaceae: *Ceropegia*

R	*II*	*Ceropegia botrys* K. Schum. *20212*	
	R	*20211* Saudi Arabia *20212*	
	R	*20211* Yemen *20212*	
	R	*20211* Somalia *20212*	

R *II Ceropegia brevirostris* Bally & Field *20064*
    R *20211* Tanzania *19976*

V *II Ceropegia bulbosa* Roxb. *20202*
    V *20273* Oman (southwest) *20202*
    V *20273* Yemen *20202*
    V *20273* India (Punjab, West Peninsula) *8754*
    V *20273* India - Uttar Pradesh *8754*
    E *20273* Pakistan (Punjab) *8754*
    V *20273* Ethiopia *20202*
    V *20273* Somalia *20202*

R *II Ceropegia cancellata* Rchb. *20604, 20207*
    R *20604* South Africa - Cape Province (including Transkei) *20604*

I *II Ceropegia candelabrum* L. var. *biflora* (L.) M. Ansari *20064*
    I *16162* Sri Lanka *16162*

E *II Ceropegia ceratophora* Svent. *15105*
    E *20750* Spain - Canary Is. *15105*

R *II Ceropegia chipiaensis* Stopp *20064*
    R *20211* Angola *20206*

I *II Ceropegia chrysochroma* Huber *20064*
    I *5926* Tanzania *5926*

E *II Ceropegia cycniflora* R.A.Dyer *20604, 20064*
    E *20604* South Africa - Natal *20604*

I *II Ceropegia decaisneana* Wight var. *brevicollis* (Hook.f.) H. Huber *20064*
    I India - Kerala
    I India - Tamil Nadu

R *II Ceropegia decidua* E.A. Bruce ssp. *pretoriensis* R.A. Dyer *20211*
    R *20211* South Africa - Transvaal *20207*

R *II Ceropegia deightonii* Hutch. & Dalz. ssp. *deightonii* *10260*
    R *20211* Ghana *7855*
    R *20211* Nigeria *7855*

R *II Ceropegia dichotoma* Haw. ssp. *dichotoma* *15105*
    R *15105* Spain - Canary Is. *15105*

R *II Ceropegia dimorpha* Humbert *20213*
    R *20211* Madagascar (Fianarantsoa) *20578*

E *II Ceropegia dinteri* Schlechter *20207*
    E *20211* Namibia *20207*

R *II Ceropegia dorjei* C.E.C. Fischer *20211*
    R *20211* Bhutan

I *II Ceropegia elegans* Wallich var. *gardneri* (Thwaites) H. Huber *8021*
    I *16162* Sri Lanka *8021*

E *II Ceropegia evansii* McCann *11494*
    E *20211* India - Maharashtra (Khandala, Pune) *11494*

E *II Ceropegia fantastica* Sedgw. *11494*
    E *20211* India - Goa, Daman & Diu *11494*
    E *20211* India - Karnataka (Sulgeri, North Kanara) *11494*

R *II Ceropegia filiformis* (Burch.) Schltr. *20604, 10260*
    R *20604* South Africa - Cape Province *20604*
    V *20604* South Africa - Orange Free State *20604*

R *II Ceropegia fimbriata* E. Mey. ssp.

---

    fimbriata *10260*
    R *20211* South Africa - Cape Province *20207*

R *II Ceropegia fimbriifera* Beddome *11494*
    R *20211* India - Karnataka *11494*
    R *20211* India - Kerala (Travancore Hills) *10178*
    R *20211* India - Tamil Nadu *11494*

R *II Ceropegia floribunda* N.E. Br. *10260*
    R *20211* Botswana *20207*
    R *20211* Namibia *20207*

R *II Ceropegia fusca* Bolle *15105*
    R *15105* Spain - Canary Is. *15105*

R *II Ceropegia hians* Svent. var. *hians* *20064*
    R *15105* Spain - Canary Is. *15105*

R *II Ceropegia hians* Svent. var. *striata* Sventenius *20064*
    R *15105* Spain - Canary Is. *15105*

E *II Ceropegia hofstaetteri* Rauh *20213*
    E *20211* Madagascar (Mahajunga) *20578*

E *II Ceropegia hookeri* Clarke ex Hook. f. var. *hookeri* *10260*
    E *13883* China - Xizang Zizhiqu *13883*
    E *13883* India - Sikkim *13883*
    E *13883* Nepal *13883*

E *II Ceropegia huberi* Ansari *11494*
    E *20211* India - Maharashtra (Varadha Ghat; Susale Island; Amba Ghat) *20266*

R *II Ceropegia humbertii* H. Huber *20213*
    R *20211* Madagascar (Antsiranana) *20578*

I *II Ceropegia intermedia* Wight. var. *wightii* Hook.f. *10260*
    I India - Tamil Nadu

R *II Ceropegia jainii* Ansari & Kulk. *10511*
    R *20211* India - Maharashtra *10511*

R *II Ceropegia kachinensis* Prain *20211*
    R *20211* Myanmar

V *II Ceropegia krainzii* Svent. *15105*
    V *15105* Spain - Canary Is. *15105*

R *II Ceropegia kundelunguensis* F. Malaisse *20064*
    R *20211* Zaire *20228*

R *II Ceropegia langkawiensis* Rintz *10260*
    R *20211* Malaysia - Peninsular Malaysia

E *II Ceropegia lawii* Hook.f. *11494*
    E *20211* India - Maharashtra (Konkan, Harishchandragad) *11494*

E *II Ceropegia leroyi* Rauh & Marn.-Lap. *20213*
    E *20211* Madagascar (Fianarantsoa) *20578*

R *II Ceropegia lindenii* Lavranos *20064*
    R *20211* Somalia *20064*

R *II Ceropegia maccannii* Ansari *10512*
    R *20211* India - Maharashtra *10512*

Ex/E *II Ceropegia maculata* Bedd. *13883*
    Ex/E *13883* India - Kerala *13883*
    Ex/E *13883* India - Tamil Nadu *13883*
    Ex/E *13883* Sri Lanka *13883*

R *II Ceropegia madagascariensis* Decne. *20213*
    R *20211* Madagascar (Mahajunga) *20578*

R *II Ceropegia mafekingensis* (N.E.Br.) R.A.Dyer *20604, 20064*
    R *20211* Namibia - Caprivi Strip *20276*
    R *20604* South Africa - Cape Province *20604*
    R *20211* South Africa - Natal *20207*

R   20604   South Africa - Transvaal *20604*

E   *II*   *Ceropegia mahabalei* Hem. & Ans. *20064*
    E   20211   India - Maharashtra *13883*

R   *II*   *Ceropegia maiuscula* Huber *20064*
    R   20211   Tanzania *20206*

E   *II*   *Ceropegia mayottae* H. Huber *20064*
    E   20211   Comoros *20212*

R   *II*   *Ceropegia media* (Huber) M.Y. Ansari *20064*
    R   20211   India - Maharashtra *20204*

R   *II*   *Ceropegia muzingana* F. Malaisse *20064*
    R   20211   Zaire *20228*

R   *II*   *Ceropegia ngoyana* F. Malaisse *20064*
    R   20211   Zaire *20228*

R   *II*   *Ceropegia noorjahaniae* Ansari *20064*
    R   20211   India *13883*
    R   20211   India - Maharashtra (Panchgani Ghat, Satara
         District) *13883*

R   *II*   *Ceropegia nuda* Hutch. & Bruce *20212*
    R   20211   Somalia *20212*

V   *II*   *Ceropegia occidentalis* R.A.Dyer *20604, 20064*
    V   20604   South Africa - Cape Province *20604*

R   *II*   *Ceropegia oculata* Hook. var. *occulta* *20064*
    R   11494   India - Maharashtra (Pune; Ratnagiri; Raigad)
         11494

E   *II*   *Ceropegia odorata* Nimmo ex Hook.f. *10171*
    E   20211   India - Gujarat (Pavagadh Hill) *11494*
    E   20211   India - Maharashtra (Melghat) *11494*
    E   20211   India - Rajasthan (Mt Abu) *11494*

E   *II*   *Ceropegia omissa* Huber *11494*
    E   20211   India - Tamil Nadu (Sengalteri, Tirunelvelly)
         11494

E   *II*   *Ceropegia panchganiensis* Blatter & McCann *10506*
    E   20211   India - Maharashtra (Panchgani; Lingmala)
         10506

R   *II*   *Ceropegia paricyma* N.E. Brown *20207*
    R   20211   Malawi *7855*
    R   20211   Mozambique *7855*
    R   20211   Tanzania *20228*
    R   20211   Zambia *20228*
    R   20211   Zimbabwe *7855*
    R   20211   Namibia - Caprivi Strip *20207*

I   *II*   *Ceropegia parviflora* Trimen *8021*
    I   20211   Sri Lanka (Anuradhapura) *8021*

E   *II*   *Ceropegia petignatii* Rauh *20213*
    E   20211   Madagascar (Toliara) *20578*

R   *II*   *Ceropegia praetermissa* Raynal & A. Raynal *8003*
    R   Senegal *8003*

I   *II*   *Ceropegia purpurascens* K. Schum. ssp. *thysanotos*
    (Wederm.) Huber *20064*
    I   5926   Tanzania *5926*

R   *II*   *Ceropegia pusilla* Wight & Arn. *11494*
    R   20211   India - Karnataka (Mysore District)
         11494
    R   20211   India - Tamil Nadu *11494*

I   *II*   *Ceropegia racemosa* N.E. Br. ssp. *glabra* H.
    Huber *20213*
    I   Madagascar (centre & north) *20213*

I   *II*   *Ceropegia racemosa* N.E. Br. ssp.
    racemosa *10368*
    I   Madagascar

R   *II*   *Ceropegia radicans* Schltr. ssp.
    radicans *20211, 20604*

R   20211   South Africa - Cape Province (east &
         Transkei) *20207*

E   *II*   *Ceropegia razafindratsirana* (Rauh & Buchloh)
    Rauh *20213*
    E   20211   Madagascar (Fianarantsoa) *20578*

R   *II*   *Ceropegia rollae* Hemadri *20211*
    R   20211   India - Maharashtra *13883*

V   *II*   *Ceropegia rudatisii* Schltr. *20604, 20207*
    V   20604   South Africa - Natal (coastal) *20604*

I   *II*   *Ceropegia rupicola* Defl. var. *stictantha* N.P.
    Taylor *20064*
    I   20212   Yemen *20212*

E   *II*   *Ceropegia sahyadrica* Ansari & Kulk. *20211*
    E   20211   India - Maharashtra (Pune & Sindhudurg
         District) *11494*

R   *II*   *Ceropegia santapaui* Wadh. & Ans. *20064*
    R   20211   India - Maharashtra (Pune; Satara; Ratnagiri)
         13883

R   *II*   *Ceropegia saxatilis* Jumelle & H. Perrier *20213*
    R   20211   Madagascar (Mahajunga) *20578*

R   *II*   *Ceropegia scabra* Jumelle & H.Perrier *20213*
    R   20211   Madagascar (Toliara) *20578*

R   *II*   *Ceropegia scabriflora* N.E.Br. *20604, 20207*
    V   20604   South Africa - Natal *20604*
    R   20211   South Africa - Transvaal *20207*

E   *II*   *Ceropegia simoneae* Rauh *20578*
    E   20211   Madagascar (Toliara) *20578*

I   *II*   *Ceropegia sobolifera* N.E. Br. var. *nephroloba*
    Huber *20064*
    I   5926   Tanzania *5926*

R   *II*   *Ceropegia spiralis* Wight *11494*
    R   20211   India - Andhra Pradesh *11494*
    R   20211   India - Karnataka *11494*
    R   20211   India - Kerala *11494*
    R   20211   India - Tamil Nadu *11494*

R   *II*   *Ceropegia stentiae* E.A.Bruce *20604, 20202*
    R   20604   South Africa - Transvaal (Pietersburg
         Plateau) *20604*

R   *II*   *Ceropegia swaziorum* D.V. Field *20064*
    R   20211   Swaziland *19976*

R   *II*   *Ceropegia taprobanica* H. Huber *8021*
    R   20211   Sri Lanka (Rangala, Kandy; Gilimale)
         8021

R   *II*   *Ceropegia ugeni* C.E.C. Fischer *19976*
    R   20211   Bhutan *7855*

R   *II*   *Ceropegia verruculosa* (R.A.Dyer) D.V.Field *20604,*
    20064
    R   20604   South Africa - Transvaal *20604*

E   *II*   *Ceropegia vincaefolia* Hook. *20206*
    E   20211   India - Maharashtra (Thane; Pune; Satara)
         19976

R   *II*   *Ceropegia viridis* Choux var. *truncata* (H. Huber)
    H. Huber *20213*
    R   20211   Madagascar *20213*

R   *II*   *Ceropegia viridis* Choux var. *viridis* *20213*
    R   20211   Madagascar (Toliara) *20578*

R   *Cryptolepis grayi* P.Forster *20681*
    R   20681   Australia - Queensland *20681*

I   *Curroria macrophylla* A.R. Smith *15534*
    I   15534   Yemen - Socotra *15534*

R   *Cynanchum austrokiusianum* Koidz. *10573*

R   *10573*   Japan *10573*

R   *Cynanchum calcareum* Ohashi *10573*
     R   *10573*   Japan *10573*

R   *Cynanchum chirindense* S. Moore *7872*
     R   *6088*   Zimbabwe *7872*

R   *Cynanchum christineae* P.Forster *20681*
     R   *20681*   Australia - Northern Territory *20681*

R   *Cynanchum compactum* Choux var. *compactum 10368*
     R   *20578*   Madagascar (Fianarantsoa) *20578*

V   *Cynanchum doianum* Koidz. *10573*
     V   *10573*   Japan *10573*

I   *Cynanchum ekmanii* Alain *5607*
     I   *19105*   Cuba (Holguin) *5607*

E   *Cynanchum elegans* (Benth.) Domin *20681*
     E   *20681*   Australia - New South Wales *20681*

R   *Cynanchum fawcettii* (Schltr.) Stearn *20883*
     R   *20883*   Jamaica *20883*

R   *Cynanchum filisepalum* (Standley) L.O. Williams *9037*
     R   *9099*   Costa Rica *9037*

R   *Cynanchum harrisii* (Schltr.) Stearn *20883*
     R   *20883*   Jamaica *20883*

R   *Cynanchum hartii* (Schlechter) Proctor *20883*
     R   *20883*   Jamaica *20883*

V   *Cynanchum infimicola* L.O. Wms. *20883*
     V   *20883*   Panama *20883*

I   *Cynanchum jamaicense* (Griseb.) Woodson *20883, 13336*
     I   *13336*   Jamaica *20883*

R   *Cynanchum katsi* Ohwi *10573*
     R   *10573*   Japan *10573*

R   *Cynanchum krameri* (Franchet & Sav.) Matsum. *10573*
     R   *10573*   Japan *10573*

R   *Cynanchum lanhsuense* Yamazaki *20511*
     R   *20511*   Taiwan *20511*

R   *Cynanchum liebiana* (F.Muell.) P.Forster *20681*
     R   *20681*   Australia - Northern Territory *20681*

R   *Cynanchum macrolobum* Jum. & H. Perrier *10368*
     R   *20578*   Madagascar (Toliara) *20578*

R   *Cynanchum magdalenicum* Dugand *20883*
     V   *20883*   Panama *20883*
     I   *20883*   Colombia *20883*

R   *Cynanchum marnieranum* Rauh *10368*
     R   *20578*   Madagascar (Toliara) *20578*

V   *Cynanchum monense* (Britt.) Alain *20883*
     I   *20883*   Puerto Rico (Mona) *20883*

V   *Cynanchum multinerve* (Franchet & Sav.) Matsum. *10573*
     V   *10573*   Japan *10573*

R   *Cynanchum pachylobum* Choux *10368*
     R   *20578*   Madagascar (Toliara) *20578*

R   *Cynanchum priorii* (Rendle) Stearn *20883, 13336*
     R   *13336*   Jamaica *20883*

R   *Cynanchum rauhianum* Descoings *10368*
     R   *20578*   Madagascar (Fianarantsoa) *20578*

R   *Cynanchum rendlei* Stearn *20883*
     R   *20883*   Jamaica *20883*

E   *Cynanchum rossii* Rauh *10368*
     E   *20578*   Madagascar (Toliara) *20578*

R   *Cynanchum utahense* (Engelm.) Woods. *20850*

     E   *20850*   U.S. - Arizona *20850*
     I   *20850*   U.S. - California *20850*
     I   *20850*   U.S. - Nevada *20850*
     V   *20850*   U.S. - Utah *20850*

I   *Cynanchum virens* D.Dietr. *20604*
     E/V   *20604*   Lesotho *20604*
     I   *20604*   South Africa - Cape Province *20604*
     V   *20604*   South Africa - Orange Free State *20604*
     I   *20604*   South Africa - Transvaal *20604*

R   *Cynanchum yamanakae* Ohwi & Ohasi *10573*
     R   *10573*   Japan *10573*

V   *Cynanchum zeyheri* Schltr. *20604*
     V   *20604*   South Africa - Cape Province *20604*

I   *Dischidia rafflesiana* Wallich
     I   India - Assam

E   *Dischidia scortechinii* King & Gamble
     E   Malaysia - Peninsular Malaysia

E   *Dischidia tomentella* Ridley
     E   Malaysia - Peninsular Malaysia

R   *Dregea formosana* Yamazaki *20511*
     R   *20511*   Taiwan *20511*

R   *Duvalia parviflora* N.E.Br. *20604*
     R   *20604*   South Africa - Cape Province *20604*

E   *Duvaliandra dioscoridis* (Lav.) Gilbert *15534*
     E   *15534*   Yemen - Socotra *15534*

I   *Echidnopsis insularis* Lavranos *15534*
     I   *15534*   Yemen - Socotra *15534*

V   *Echidnopsis scutellata* (defl. A. Berger ssp. *dhofarensis* Bruyns *20146*
     V   *20146*   Oman (Dhofar) *20146*

R   *Emplectanthus cordatus* N.E.Br. *20604*
     R   *20604*   South Africa - Natal *20604*

R   *Emplectanthus gerrardii* N.E.Br. *20604*
     R   *20604*   South Africa - Natal *20604*

R   *Fanninia caloglossa* Harv. *20604*
     R   *20604*   South Africa - Cape Province *20604*
     R   *20604*   South Africa - Natal *20604*

E   II   *Frerea indica* Dalz. *11494*
     E   *11494*   India - Maharashtra (Junnar & Purandhar hills) *11494*

R   *Gongylosperma lanuginosum* Ridley
     R   Malaysia - Peninsular Malaysia (Langkawi, Kedah)

V   *Gonolobus allenii* Woods. *20883, 9006*
     V   *20883*   Panama *20883*

E   *Gonolobus chiriquensis* (Woods.) Woods. *20883, 9006*
     I   *20883*   Panama *20883*

E   *Gonolobus fuscoviolaceus* Woods. *20883, 9006*
     I   *20883*   Panama *20883*

R   *Gonolobus inaequalis* L.O. Wms. *20883*
     V   *20883*   Panama *20883*
     I   *20883*   Colombia *20883*

R   *Gonolobus jamaicensis* Rendle *20883, 13336*
     R   *13336*   Jamaica *20883*

E   *Gonolobus lewisii* L.O. Wms. *20883*
     I   *20883*   Panama *20883*

E   *Gonolobus ophioglossa* Woods. *20883, 9006*
     I   *20883*   Panama *20883*

I   *Gonolobus pubescens* Griseb. *20883, 13336*
     I   *13336*   Jamaica *20883*

R   *Gonolobus rhamnifolius* Griseb. *20883, 13336*

R   *13336*   Jamaica *20883*

V   *Gonolobus stapelioides* Desv. *20883, 19890*
    R   *19890*   Jamaica *20883*

V   *Gonolobus stellatus* Griseb. *20883*
    V   *20883*   Jamaica *20883*

V   *Gymnema brevifolium* Benth. *20681*
    V   *20681*   Australia - Queensland *20681*

I   *Gymnema elegans* Wight & Arn.
    I   India - Tamil Nadu

R   *Gymnema khandalense* Santapan *14782*
    R   *14782*   India - Maharashtra *14782*

R   *Gymnema muelleri* Benth. *20681*
    R   *20681*   Australia - Northern Territory *20681*

I   *Gymnema rotundatum* Thwaites *8021*
    I   *16162*   Sri Lanka (Nalanda; Hanguranketha) *8021*

R   *Heterostemma brownii* Hayata *20511*
    R   *20511*   Taiwan *20511*

R   *Hoodia dregei* N.E.Br. *20604*
    R   *20604*   South Africa - Cape Province *20604*

R   *Hoodia officinalis* (N.E.Br.) Plowes ssp. *delaetiana*
     (Dinter) Bruyns *20604*
    R   *20604*   Namibia *20604*

R   *Hoodia pilifera* (L.f.) Plowes ssp. *annulata*
     (N.E.Br.) Bruyns *20604*
    R   *20604*   South Africa - Cape Province *20604*

R   *Hoodia pilifera* (L.f.) Plowes ssp.
     pilifera *20604*
    R   *20604*   South Africa - Cape Province *20604*

V   *Hoodia pilifera* (L.f.) Plowes ssp. *pillansii*
     (N.E.Br.) Bruyns *20604*
    V   *20604*   South Africa - Cape Province *20604*

I   *Hoya lobii* Hook.f.
    I   India - Meghalaya

R   *Hoya macgillivrayi* Bailey *20681*
    R   *20681*   Australia - Queensland *20681*

R   *Hoya parasitica* Wall. ex Traill *20099, 10260*
    R   *20099*   Singapore *20099*

I   *Huernia boleana* M. Gilbert *6087*
    I   *6087*   Ethiopia *6087*

I   *Huernia echidnopsioides* (L.C.Leach) L.C.Leach *20604*
    I   *20604*   South Africa - Cape Province *20604*

R   *Huernia hislopii* Turrill ssp. *robusta* Leach &
     Plowes *7889*
    R   Zimbabwe *7889*

R   *Huernia humilis* (Masson) Haw. *20604*
    R   *20604*   South Africa - Cape Province *20604*

V   *Huernia hystrix* (Hook.f.) N.E.Br. var. *parvula*
     L.C.Leach *20604*
    V   *20604*   South Africa - Natal *20604*

V   *Huernia kennedyana* Lavranos *20604*
    V   *20604*   South Africa - Cape Province *20604*

R   *Huernia longii* Pillans *20604*
    R   *20604*   South Africa - Cape Province *20604*

I   *Huernia longituba* N.E. Br. ssp. *cashelensis* Leach
     & Plowes *7889*
    I   Zimbabwe *7889*

E   *Huernia nouhuysii* I.Verd. *20604*
    E   *20604*   South Africa - Transvaal *20604*

I   *Huernia occulta* Leach & Plowes *7889*
    I   Zimbabwe *7889*

I   *Huernia pendula* E.A.Bruce *20604*
    I   *20604*   South Africa - Cape Province *20604*

R   *Huernia praestans* N.E.Br. *20604*
    R   *20604*   South Africa - Cape Province *20604*

Ex   *Huernia thudichumii* L.C.Leach *20604*
    Ex   *20604*   South Africa - Cape Province *20604*

Ex   *Huernia witzenbergensis* C.A.Lückh. *20604*
    Ex   *20604*   South Africa - Cape Province *20604*

E   *Jacaima costata* (Urb.) Rendle *20883*
    I   *20883*   Jamaica *20883*

V   *Jacaima costata* (Urb.) Rendle var.
     costata *20883, 13336*
    V   *13336*   Jamaica (St. Andrew, St. Catherine)
          20883

E   *Jacaima costata* (Urb.) Rendle var. *goodfriendii*
     Proctor *20883, 13336*
    E   *19890*   Jamaica *20883*

E   *Jacaima parvifolia* Proctor *20883, 13336*
    E   *19890*   Jamaica (Clarendon) *20883*

E   *Karimbolea verrucosa* Descoings *10368*
    E   *20578*   Madagascar (Toliara) *20578*

Ex   *Marsdenia araujacea* F.Muell. *20681*
    Ex   *20681*   Australia - Queensland *20681*

R   *Marsdenia balansae* Baillon
    R   New Caledonia

V   *Marsdenia coronata* Benth. *20681, 14223*
    V   *20681*   Australia - Queensland *20681*

I   *Marsdenia dusii* Schltr. *10200*
    I   Dominica *10200*
    I   Martinique *10200*

V   *Marsdenia elliptica* Dcne. *20883*
    I   *20883*   Puerto Rico *20883*

R   *Marsdenia hemiptera* Rchb. *20681*
    I   *20681*   Australia - New South Wales *20681*
    I   *20681*   Australia - Northern Territory *20681*
    I   *20681*   Australia - Queensland *20681*

R   *Marsdenia liisae* J.Williams *20681*
    R   *20681*   Australia - New South Wales *20681*

R   *Marsdenia longiloba* Benth. *20681*
    I   *20681*   Australia - New South Wales *20681*
    I   *20681*   Australia - Queensland *20681*

R   *Marsdenia macfadyenii* Rendle *20883*
    R   *20883*   Jamaica *20883*

E   *Marsdenia margaritaria* Foster *20883, 9006*
    I   *20883*   Panama *20883*

E   *Marsdenia panamensis* Spellman *20883, 9006*
    I   *20883*   Panama *20883*

R   *Marsdenia raziana* Yog. et Subr. *13883*
    R   *13883*   India - Karnataka (Chikmagalur dist.)
          13883

V   *Marsdenia troyana* Urb. *20883, 13336*
    V   *13336*   Jamaica *20883*

Ex   *Marsdenia tubulosa* F. Muell. *15112*
    Ex   *15112*   Australia - NSW - Lord Howe Is. *15112*

E   *Matelea acuminata* (Griseb.) Woods.
    E   *19105*   Cuba *19105*

V   *Matelea alabamensis* (Vail) Woods. *20850*
    E   *20850*   U.S. - Alabama *20850*

E	20850	U.S. - Florida 20850
E	20850	U.S. - Georgia 20850

Ex/E *Matelea balbisii* (Dcne.) Woods. 20850, 14662
    Ex/E 20850 U.S. - Arizona 20850

V *Matelea baldwyniana* (Sweet) Woods. 20850
    Ex/E 20850 U.S. - Alabama 20850
    I   20850 U.S. - Arkansas 20850
    E   20850 U.S. - Florida 20850
    I   20850 U.S. - Georgia 20850
    I   20850 U.S. - Missouri 20850
    I   20850 U.S. - Oklahoma 20850

R *Matelea brevicoronata* (B.L. Robins.) Woods. 20850
    R   20850 U.S. - Texas 20850

I *Matelea correllii* Spellman
    I   17672 Bahamas 17672

R *Matelea decumbens* W. D. Stevens 20883, 9110
    I   20883 Mexico 20883

R *Matelea edwardsensis* Correll 20850
    R   20850 U.S. - Texas 20850

R *Matelea flavidula* (Chapman) Woods. 20850
    I   20850 U.S. - Alabama 20850
    E   20850 U.S. - Florida 20850
    I   20850 U.S. - Georgia 20850
    I   20850 U.S. - Mississippi 20850
    I   20850 U.S. - North Carolina 20850
    I   20850 U.S. - South Carolina 20850
    I   20850 U.S. - Tennessee 20850

V *Matelea floridana* (Vail) Woods. 20850
    V   20850 U.S. - Florida 20850
    I   20850 U.S. - Georgia 20850

E *Matelea grisebachiana* (Schltr.)
    E   19105 Cuba 19105

E *Matelea panamensis* Spellman & Dwyer 20883, 9006
    I   20883 Panama 20883

E *Matelea pittieri* (Standl.) Woods. 20883, 9006
    I   20883 Panama 20883

E *Matelea radiata* Correll 20850, 14662
    E   20850 U.S. - Texas 20850

E *Matelea texensis* Correll 20850
    E   20850 U.S. - Texas 20850

E *Matelea tigrina* (Griseb.) Woods.
    E   19105 Cuba 19105

E *Matelea tristis* (Seem.) Spellman 20883, 9006
    I   20883 Panama 20883

I *Miraglossum davyi* (N.E.Br.) Kupicha 20604
    I   20604 South Africa - Transvaal 20604

I *Miraglossum pilosum* (Schltr.) Kupicha 20604
    I   20604 South Africa - Cape Province 20604
    I   20604 South Africa - Natal 20604

E *Mitolepis arbuscula* A.R. Smith 15534
    E   15534 Yemen - Socotra 15534

R *Mitolepis intricata* Balf. f. 15534
    R   15534 Yemen - Socotra 15534

R *Mitostigma caudatum* Malme 16336
    R   20176 Argentina - Tucuman 20176

R *Mitostigma mitophorus* (Griseb.) Meyer 16336
    R   20176 Argentina - Tucuman (Valle de Tafí) 20176

R *Mitostigma tucumanense* Meyer 16336
    R   20176 Argentina - Tucuman 20176

R *Notechidnopsis columnaris* (Nel) Lavranos &

Bleck 20604
    R   20604 South Africa - Cape Province 20604

I *Oianthus beddomei* Hook.f.
    I   India - Karnataka
    I   India - Kerala (Wynaad)

Ex/E *Oianthus deccanensis* W.A. Talbot 11494
    Ex/E 11494 India - Maharashtra 11494

I *Oianthus disciflorus* Hook.f. 1170
    I   India - Andhra Pradesh (Kurnool) 1170
    I   India - Karnataka (North Canara) 1170

I *Orbea macloughlinii* (I.Verd.) L.C.Leach 20604
    I   20604 South Africa - Cape Province 20604

I *Orbea pulchella* (Masson) L.C.Leach 20604
    I   20604 South Africa - Cape Province 20604

V *Orbea speciosa* L.C.Leach 20604
    V   20604 South Africa - Natal 20604

R *Orbea umbracula* (M.D. Henderson) Leach 7749
    R   Zimbabwe 7749

R *Orbea woodii* (N.E.Br.) L.C.Leach 20604
    R   20604 South Africa - Natal 20604

V *Orbeanthus conjunctus* (A.C.White & B.Sloane) L.C.Leach 20604
    V   20604 South Africa - Transvaal 20604

R *Orbeanthus gerstneri* (Letty) Leach ssp. *elongata* (R.A. Dyer) Leach 20803
    R   South Africa - Transvaal

R *Orbeanthus gerstneri* (Letty) Leach ssp. *gerstneri* 20803
    R   South Africa - Natal

V *Orbeanthus hardyi* (R.A.Dyer) L.C.Leach 20604
    V   20604 South Africa - Transvaal 20604

R *Orbeanthus paradoxa* (Verdoorn) Leach 20803
    R   South Africa - Natal
    R   South Africa - Transvaal

R *Orbeopsis gerstneri* (Letty) L.C.Leach ssp. *elongata* (R.A.Dyer) L.C.Leach 20604
    R   20604 South Africa - Transvaal 20604

I *Pachycarpus graminifolius* Wild 7754
    I   Zimbabwe (Chimanimani) 7754

R *Pachycarpus lebomboensis* D.M.N.Sm. 20604
    R   20604 South Africa - Natal 20604

I *Pachycarpus mackenii* (Harv.) N.E.Br. 20604
    I   20604 South Africa - Natal 20604

V *Pachycarpus rostratus* N.E.Br. 20604
    V   20604 South Africa - Natal 20604

E *Pachycarpus stelliceps* N.E.Br. 20604, 20039
    E   20604 Swaziland 20604

I *Pachycarpus stenoglossus* (E.Mey.) N.E.Br. 20604
    I   20604 South Africa - Cape Province 20604

R *Pachycarpus suaveolens* (Schltr.) Nicholas & Goyder 20604
    R   20604 South Africa - Transvaal 20604

R *Pachycymbium lancasteri* Lavranos 20604
    R   20604 South Africa - Transvaal 20604

V *Pachycymbium luntii* (N.E. Br.) Gilbert 20146
    E   20146 Oman (Dhofar) 20146
    V   20146 Yemen, Democratic 20146

R *Pectinaria articulata* (Aiton) Haw. ssp. *articulata* 20604

R		20604 South Africa - Cape Province 20604	

R Pectinaria articulata (Aiton) Haw. ssp. *borealis* Bruyns 20604
  R   20604 South Africa - Cape Province 20604

R Pectinaria longipes (N.E.Br.) Bruyns 20604
  R   20604 South Africa - Cape Province 20604

E Philibertia campanulata (Lindl.) Nichols. 20176
  E   20176 Argentina - Catamarca 20176
  E   20176 Argentina - Jujuy 20176
  E   20176 Argentina - La Rioja 20176
  E   20176 Argentina - Salta 20176
  E   20176 Argentina - Santiago del Estero 20176

R Piaranthus barrydalensis Meve 20604
  R   20604 South Africa - Cape Province 20604

R Quaqua armata (N.E.Br.) Bruyns ssp. *arenicola* (N.E.Br.) Bruyns 20604
  E   20604 South Africa - Cape Province 20604

R Quaqua armata (N.E.Br.) Bruyns ssp. *maritima* Bruyns 20604
  R   20604 South Africa - Cape Province 20604

R Quaqua framesii (Pillans) Bruyns 20604
  R   20604 South Africa - Cape Province 20604

R Quaqua inversa (N.E.Br.) Bruyns var. *cincta* (C.A.Lückh.) Bruyns 20803
  R   20803 South Africa - Cape Province 20803

R Quaqua inversa (N.E.Br.) Bruyns var. *inversa* 20803
  R   20803 South Africa - Cape Province 20803

R Quaqua linearis (N.E.Br.) Bruyns 20803
  R   20604 South Africa - Cape Province 20604

R Quaqua multiflora (R.A.Dyer) Bruyns 20604
  R   20604 South Africa - Cape Province 20604

R Quaqua parviflora (Masson) Bruyns ssp. *bayeriana* Bruyns 20604
  R   20604 South Africa - Cape Province 20604

R Quaqua pruinosa (Masson) Bruyns 20803
  R   20604 Namibia 20604
  R   20604 South Africa - Cape Province 20604

V Raphionacme arabica A.G. Miller & J.A. Biagi 20146
  E   20146 Oman (Dhofar) 20146
  V   20146 Yemen, Democratic 20146

I Raphionacme elsana Venter & R.L.Verh. 20604
  I   20604 South Africa - Natal 20604

R Raphionacme lobulata Venter & R.L.Verh. 20604
  R   20604 South Africa - Cape Province 20604

E Rhytidocaulon fulleri Lavranos & Mortimer 20146
  E   20146 Oman (Dhofar) 20146

I Rhytidocaulon paradoxum Bally 6087
  I   6087 Ethiopia 6087

I Riocreuxia alexandrina (H.Huber) R.A.Dyer 20604, 20207
  I   20604 South Africa - Natal 20604

I Riocreuxia bolusii N.E.Br. 20604
  I   20604 South Africa - Cape Province 20604

I Riocreuxia flanaganii Schltr. 20604, 20207
  I   20604 South Africa - Cape Province (including Transkei) 20604

Ex Riocreuxia woodii N.E.Br. 20604, 20207
  Ex   20604 South Africa - Natal 20604

I Sarcostemma socotranum Lavranos 15534
  I   15534 Yemen - Socotra 15534

R Schizoglossum montanum R.A.Dyer 20604
  R   20604 Lesotho 20604
  R   20604 South Africa - Natal 20604
  R   20604 South Africa - Orange Free State 20604

V Schizoglossum rubiginosum Hilliard 20604
  V   20604 South Africa - Natal 20604

V Schizoglossum singulare Kupicha 20604
  V   20604 South Africa - Natal 20604

R Secamone rodriguesiana F.Friedmann 10082
  R   5852 Mauritius - Rodrigues 5852

R Secamone socotrana Balf. f. 15534
  R   15534 Yemen - Socotra 15534

R Seshagiria sahyadrica Ansari & Hemadri 13883
  R   13883 India - Maharashtra 13883

V Sisyranthus fanniniae N.E.Br. 20604
  V   20604 South Africa - Natal 20604

V Socotranthus socotranus (Balf. f.) Kuntze 15534
  V   15534 Yemen - Socotra 15534

R Spirella robinsonii Cost. 6057
  R   Vietnam 6057

R Stapelia baylissii L.C.Leach 20604
  R   20604 South Africa - Cape Province 20604

V Stapelia clavicorona I.Verd. 20604
  V   20604 South Africa - Transvaal 20604

V Stapelia divaricata Masson 20604
  V   20604 South Africa - Cape Province 20604

R Stapelia erectiflora N.E.Br. var. *prostratiflora* L.C.Leach 20604
  R   20604 South Africa - Cape Province 20604

I Stapelia glabricaulis N.E.Br. 20604
  I   20604 South Africa - Cape Province 20604

V Stapelia immelmaniae Pillans 20604
  V   20604 South Africa - Cape Province 20604

I Stapelia obducta L.C.Leach 20604
  I   20604 South Africa - Cape Province 20604

R Stapelia paniculata Willd. 20604
  R   20604 South Africa - Cape Province 20604

R Stapelia peglerae N.E.Br. 20604
  R   20604 South Africa - Cape Province 20604

R Stapelia praetermissa L.C.Leach var. *luteola* L.C.Leach 20604
  R   20604 South Africa - Cape Province 20604

R Stapelia praetermissa L.C.Leach var. *praetermissa* L.C.Leach 20604
  R   20604 South Africa - Cape Province 20604

R Stapelia rubiginosa Nel 20604
      20604 South Africa - Cape Province 20604

V Stapelia scitula L.C.Leach 20604
  V   20604 South Africa - Cape Province 20604

R Stapelia tsomoensis N.E.Br. 20604
  R   20604 South Africa - Cape Province 20604

I Stapelia villetiae Lückh. 20803
  I   South Africa - Cape Province

R Stapelianthus arenarius Bosser & Morat 10368
  R   20578 Madagascar (Toliara) 20578

R Stapelianthus decaryi Choux 10368
  R   20578 Madagascar (Toliara) 20578

R   *Stapelianthus hardyi* Lavranos *10368*
    R   *20578*   Madagascar (Toliara) *20578*

R   *Stapelianthus insignis* Descoings var.
      insignis 10368
    R   *20578*   Madagascar (Toliara) *20578*

R   *Stapelianthus keraudreniae* Bosser & Morat *20578*
    R   *20578*   Madagascar (Toliara) *20578*

R   *Stapelianthus madagascariensis* (Choux) Choux *10368*
    R   *20578*   Madagascar (Toliara) *20578*

R   *Stapelianthus montagnacii* (Boiteau) Boiteau &
      A.Bertrand *10368*
    R   *20578*   Madagascar (Toliara) *20578*

R   *Stapelianthus pilosus* (Choux) Lavranos & Hardy *10368*
    R   *20578*   Madagascar (Toliara) *20578*

V   *Stapeliopsis breviloba* (R.A.Dyer) Bruyns *20604*
    V   *20604*   South Africa - Cape Province *20604*

R   *Stapeliopsis exasperata* (Bruyns) Bruyns *20604*
    R   *20604*   South Africa - Cape Province *20604*

E   *Stapeliopsis neronis* Pillans *20604*
    E   *20604*   Namibia *20604*
    E   *20604*   South Africa - Cape Province *20604*

R   *Stapeliopsis pillansii* (N.E.Br.) Bruyns *20604*
    R   *20604*   South Africa - Cape Province *20604*

V   *Stapeliopsis saxatilis* (N.E.Br.) Bruyns ssp.
      stayneri (M.B.Bayer) Bruyns *20604*
    V   *20604*   South Africa - Cape Province *20604*

I   *Streptocaulon kleinii* Wight & Arn.
    I   India (Deccan Peninsula)

R   *Tanulepis sphenophylla* Balf.f. *5852*
    R   *5852*   Mauritius - Rodrigues *5852*

R   *Toxocarpus beddomei* Gamble *14782*
    R   *14782*   India - Kerala (Palghat Hills) *14782*
    R   *14782*   India - Tamil Nadu *14782*

E   *Toxocarpus longistigma* (Roxb.) Wight & Arn. ex
      Steud. *11494*
    E   *11494*   India - Andhra Pradesh *11494*

V   *Toxocarpus palghatensis* Gamble
    V   *13883*   India - Kerala (Palghat Hills) *13883*

R   *Toxocarpus pauciflorus* M.R. Henderson
    R   Malaysia - Peninsular Malaysia

E   *Toxocarpus schimperianus* Hemsley *14296*
    E   *14981*   Seychelles (Mahé, Praslin, Curieuse)
       14296

R   *Trachycalymma fimbriatum* (Weimarck) Bullock *7871*
    R   Zimbabwe *7871*

I   *Tridentea choanantha* (Lavranos & Hall) Leach
    I   Southern Africa

I   *Tridentea pachyrrhiza* (Dinter) L.C.Leach *20604*
    I   *20604*   Namibia *20604*
    I   *20604*   South Africa - Cape Province *20604*

R   *Tridentea virescens* (N.E.Br.) L.C.Leach *20604*
    R   *20604*   Namibia *20604*
    R   *20604*   South Africa - Cape Province *20604*

I   *Tromotriche herrei* (Nel) Bruyns *20604*
    I   *20604*   South Africa - Cape Province *20604*

R   *Tromotriche longii* (C.A.Lückh.) Bruyns *20604*
    R   *20604*   South Africa - Cape Province *20604*

R   *Tromotriche ruschiana* (Dinter) Bruyns *20604*
    R   *20604*   Namibia *20604*
    R   *20604*   South Africa - Cape Province *20604*

R   *Tromotriche thudichumii* (Pillans) L.C.Leach *20604*
    R   *20604*   South Africa - Cape Province *20604*

R   *Tylophora calcicola* M.R. Henderson
    R   Malaysia - Peninsular Malaysia (Kelantan, Pahang)

R   *Tylophora coriacea* Marais *10082*
    R   Mauritius *10082*
    E   *14981*   Seychelles *14981*

R   *Tylophora lanyuensis* Liu & Lu *20511*
    R   *20511*   Taiwan *20511*

E   *Tylophora linearis* P.Forster *20681*
    E   *20681*   Australia - New South Wales *20681*
    E   *20681*   Australia - Queensland *20681*

E   *Tylophora rupicola* P.Forster *20681*
    E   *20681*   Australia - Queensland *20681*

V   *Tylophora williamsii* P.Forster *20681*
    V   *20681*   Australia - Queensland *20681*

E   *Tylophora woollsii* Benth. *20681*
    E   *20681*   Australia - New South Wales *20681*

I   *Tylophora zeylanica* Decne. *8021*
    I   *16162*   Sri Lanka (Hantana, Wattegoda, Kandy)
       8021

E   *Utleria salicifolia* Beddome *14782*
    E   *14782*   India - Kerala *14782*
    E   *14782*   India - Tamil Nadu *14782*

R   *Vincetoxicum creticum* Browicz *20731*
    R   *20731*   Greece - Crete *20731*

V   *Vincetoxicum pannonicum* (Borhidi) Holub *8000, 20171*
    V   *20686*   Hungary *8000*

R   *Vincetoxicum rossicum* (Kleopow) Barbar. *20171*
    R   former European USSR *8000*

E   *White-sloanea crassa* (N.E. Br.) Chiov.
    E   Somalia

R   *Woodia mucronata* (Thunb.) N.E.Br. *20604*
    R   *20604*   South Africa - Cape Province *20604*
    R   *20604*   South Africa - Natal *20604*

R   *Woodia singularis* N.E.Br. *20604*
    R   *20604*   Swaziland *20604*
    R   *20604*   South Africa - Transvaal *20604*

R   *Woodia verruculosa* Schltr. *20604*
    R   *20604*   South Africa - Cape Province *20604*
    R   *20604*   South Africa - Natal *20604*

R   *Xysmalobium gerrardii* Scott-Elliot *20604*
    R   *20604*   South Africa - Cape Province *20604*
    R   *20604*   South Africa - Natal *20604*

I   *Xysmalobium pearsonii* L.Bolus *20604*
    I   *20604*   South Africa - Cape Province *20604*

R   *Xysmalobium tysonianum* (Schltr.) N.E.Br. *20604*
    I   *20604*   Lesotho *20604*
    I   *20604*   South Africa - Cape Province *20604*
    R   *20604*   South Africa - Natal *20604*

Balanopaceae

Number of genera: 1
Number of species: 9
Recorded threatened species: 1   (11%)

Southwest Pacific, especially New Caledonia.

R   *Balanops balansae* Baillon *20893*
    R   *20893*   New Caledonia *20893*

Balanophoraceae

Number of genera:	19
Number of species:	45
Recorded threatened species:	5 (11%)

Tropical and subtropical.

R **Balanophora kiusiana** Ohwi *10572*
   R *10572* Japan *10572*

E **Balanophora wilderi** Setchell *19473*
   E *19473* Cook Is.(Southern group) (Rarotonga) *19473*

R **Balanophora yakusimensis** Masam. *10572*
   R *10572* Japan *10572*

V **Dactylanthus taylorii** Hook.f. *86*
   V *19305* New Zealand - North Is. *19305*

R **Helosis cayennensis** (Swartz) Spreng var. **cayennensis** *10200*
   R Dominica *10200*
   V *17079* Brazil *17079*
   V *17746* Brazil - Amazonas *17079*
   V *17746* Brazil - Rio Grande do Sul *17079*
   V *17746* Brazil - Rondonia *17079*
   V *17746* Brazil - Roraima *17079*
   V *17746* Brazil - Santa Catarina *17079*
   R *18200* Peru *18200*

Balsaminaceae

Number of genera:	2
Number of species:	450
Recorded threatened species:	69 (15%)

Tropical Asia and Africa, some in temperate regions; India to Java.

I **Impatiens acaulis** Arn.
   I India - Karnataka (Concan)
   I India - Kerala (Malabar)
   I India - Tamil Nadu (Nilgiri)

I **Impatiens aliciae** C. Fischer
   I India - Kerala (Travancore)

Ex/E **Impatiens anaimudica** C. Fischer *14782*
   Ex/E *14782* India - Kerala (Anaimudi) *14782*

I **Impatiens barberi** Hook.f.
   I India - Karnataka (Cadamany)

I **Impatiens cochinica** Hook.f.
   I India - Kerala (Kavalay, Cochin)

I **Impatiens coelotropis** C. Fischer
   I India - Kerala (Anaimudi)

I **Impatiens concinna** Hook.f.
   I India - Kerala (Malabar)

I **Impatiens crenata** Beddome
   I India - Tamil Nadu

Ex **Impatiens cryptoneura** Hook.f. *20742*
   Ex *20742* Malaysia - Peninsular Malaysia *20742*

I **Impatiens dassysperma** Wight
   I India - Karnataka (Mysore hills)
   I India - Tamil Nadu (Courtallum, Tirunelveli)

I **Impatiens debilis** Turcz. *2268*
   I India - Tamil Nadu (Nilgiri Hills) *2268*

I **Impatiens dendricola** C. Fischer
   I India - Karnataka (Thandiadumolu, Coorg)

I **Impatiens digitata** Warb. ssp. **digitata** Grey-Wilson *19503*

I *5926* Tanzania (Mt Kilimanjaro) *5926*

I **Impatiens digitata** Warb. ssp. **ngorongorensis** Grey-Wilson *19503*
   I *5926* Tanzania *5926*

I **Impatiens elegantissima** Gilg. ssp. **nov.** *5926*
   I *5926* Tanzania *5926*

I **Impatiens engleri** Gilg ssp. **engleri** *19503*
   I *5926* Tanzania (Lushoto & Morogoro) *19503*

R **Impatiens flanaganiae** Hemsl. *20604*
   R *20604* South Africa - Cape Province *20604*
   R *20604* South Africa - Natal *20604*

R **Impatiens gongolana** Halle
   R Gabon (Monts de Cristal)

E **Impatiens gordonii** Horne ex Baker *14296*
   E *14981* Seychelles (Mahé) *14296*

I **Impatiens grandisepala** Grey-Wilson
   I Cameroon (Cameroon mt)

I **Impatiens harrissii** Hook.f.
   I India (W. Himalaya)

I **Impatiens janthina** Thwaites *8021*
   I *16162* Sri Lanka *8021*

Ex/E **Impatiens johnii** Barnes *14782*
   Ex/E *14782* India - Kerala (Kalaar valley, Idikki) *14782*

E **Impatiens jurpioides** T. Shimizu *19120*
   E *19120* Thailand *19120*

I **Impatiens keilii** Gilg ssp. **keilii** *19503*
   I *5926* Tanzania (Morogoro, Iringa) *19503*

I **Impatiens kentrodonta** Gilg *19503*
   I *5926* Tanzania (Kilosa & Morogoro) *19503*

I **Impatiens kilimanjari** Oliv. *19503*
   I *5926* Tanzania (Mt Kilimanjaro) *5926*

I **Impatiens laticornis** C. Fischer *4988*
   I India - Tamil Nadu (Kundha, Nilgiri hills) *4988*

I **Impatiens lawii** Hook.f. & Thomson
   I India - Kerala

I **Impatiens lawsonii** Hook.f. *2268*
   I India - Tamil Nadu (Nilgiri Hills) *2268*

I **Impatiens leptura** Hook.f.
   I India - Kerala (Travancore)

I **Impatiens letestuana** Halle
   I Gabon

I **Impatiens letouzeyi** Grey-Wilson
   I Cameroon (Kumba)

I **Impatiens leucantha** Thwaites *8021*
   I *16162* Sri Lanka *8021*

I **Impatiens lucida** Heyne
   I India - Karnataka (South Canara)
   I India - Kerala (Travancore)

Ex/E **Impatiens macrocarpa** Hook.f. *14782*
   Ex/E *14782* India - Kerala (Travancore Hills) *14782*

I **Impatiens meeboldii** Hook.f.
   I India - Jammu & Kashmir

E **Impatiens munnarensis** Barnes *14782*
   E *14782* India - Kerala (Munnar, Idikki) *14782*

I **Impatiens munronii** Wight
   I India - Tamil Nadu (Sispara, Nilgiri)

I **Impatiens nataliae** Hook.f.

I		India - Karnataka (Kumsi, Shimoga)
E	***Impatiens neo-barnesii*** C. Fischer *4988*	
E	*13883*	India - Tamil Nadu (Kundha, Nilgiri hills) *4988*
E	***Impatiens nilagirica*** C. Fischer *13883*	
E	*13883*	India - Tamil Nadu (Kundha, Nilgiri hills) *4988*
R	***Impatiens nzoana*** A. Chev. ssp. ***bennae*** (Jacq.-Fel.) Grey-Wilson	
R		Guinea
R	***Impatiens oumina*** Halle	
R		Gabon (Ayoumba)
I	***Impatiens pahalgamensis*** Hook.f.	
I		India - Jammu & Kashmir
I	***Impatiens pallide-rosea*** Gilg var. ***pallide-rosea*** Grey-Wilson *19503*	
I	*5926*	Tanzania (Uluguru mts) *19503*
I	***Impatiens pallidiflora*** Hook.f.	
I		India - Kerala (Devicolam, Idikki)
R	***Impatiens pandata*** Barnes *14782*	
R	*14782*	India - Kerala *14782*
I	***Impatiens platyadena*** C. Fischer	
I		India - Kerala (Anaimudi)
I	***Impatiens polhillii*** Grey-Wilson ined. *19503*	
I	*5926*	Tanzania (Iringa) *5926*
R	***Impatiens quisqualis*** Launert *7749*	
R		Malawi *7749*
I	***Impatiens repens*** Moon *8021*	
I	*16162*	Sri Lanka *8021*
R	***Impatiens ridleyi*** Hook.f.	
R		Malaysia - Peninsular Malaysia (Selangor; Pahang)
I	***Impatiens rivulicola*** Hook.f.	
I		India - Kerala (Puraiar Valley, Travancore)
R	***Impatiens rubromaculata*** Warb. ssp. ***schulziana*** (Launert) Grey-Wilson *7856*	
R		Malawi *7856*
I	***Impatiens rufescens*** Benth. ex Wight & Arn. *2268*	
I		India - Tamil Nadu *2268*
I	***Impatiens setosa*** Hook.f.	
I		India - Tamil Nadu
R	***Impatiens shirensis*** Baker f. *7749*	
R		Malawi *7749*
I	***Impatiens stocksii*** Hook.f.	
I		India - Karnataka
I	***Impatiens subcordata*** Arn. *8021*	
I	*16162*	Sri Lanka (Ramboda; Hakgala; Hewaheta) *8021*
R	***Impatiens talbotii*** Hook. f. *14782*	
R	*14782*	India - Karnataka *14782*
I	***Impatiens taprobanica*** Hiern *8021*	
I	*16162*	Sri Lanka *8021*
R	***Impatiens tayemonii*** Hayata *20511*	
R	*20511*	Taiwan *20511*
I	***Impatiens teitensis*** Grey-Wilson ssp. ***teitensis*** Grey-Wilson *19109*	
I	*19109*	Kenya *19109*
I	***Impatiens tipusensis*** M.R. Henderson	
I		Malaysia - Peninsular Malaysia (Gua Tipus, Pahang)
R	***Impatiens tuberosa*** H. Perrier *10368*	

R	*20578*	Madagascar (Antsiranana) *20578*
I	***Impatiens ulugurensis*** Warb. *19503*	
I	*5926*	Tanzania (Uluguru mts) *5926*
I	***Impatiens verucunda*** Hook.f.	
I		India - Kerala (Periakanal & Devicolam)
I	***Impatiens viridiflora*** Wight	
I		India - Tamil Nadu
I	***Impatiens walkeri*** Hook. *8021*	
I	*16162*	Sri Lanka *8021*
I	***Impatiens wightiana*** Beddome	
I		India - Tamil Nadu

Basellaceae

Number of genera:	4
Number of species:	15-20
Recorded threatened species:	5 (27%)

Tropical and subtropical, mostly New World.

E	***Anredera aspera*** Sperling *20883*	
E	*20883*	Bolivia *20883*
R	***Anredera densiflora*** Sperling *20883*	
E	*20883*	Ecuador *20883*
R	*20883*	Peru *20883*
V	***Anredera krapovickasii*** (Villa C.) Sperling *20883*	
E	*20883*	Argentina *20883*
V	*20883*	Bolivia *20883*
R	***Anredera tucumanensis*** (Lillo & Hauman) Sperling *20883*	
R	*20883*	Argentina *20883*
E	*20883*	Bolivia *20883*
V	*20883*	Brazil *20883*
R	***Tournonia hookeriana*** Moquin-Tandon, in DC *20883*	
E	*20883*	Colombia *20883*
R	*20883*	Ecuador *20883*

Begoniaceae

Number of genera:	3-5
Number of species:	1,020
Recorded threatened species:	64 (6%)

Tropical, especially northern South America.

R	***Begonia aborensis*** Dunn *14782*	
R	*14782*	India - Arunachal Pradesh *14782*
R	***Begonia aggeloptera*** Halle	
R		Gabon
E	***Begonia aliciae*** C. Fischer *14782*	
E	*14782*	India - Kerala (Travancore Hills) *14782*
E	***Begonia anamalayana*** Bedd. *14782*	
E	*14782*	India (southwestern Ghats) *14782*
R	***Begonia austrotaiwanensis*** Chen & Peng *20511*	
R	*20511*	Taiwan *20511*
V	***Begonia bissei*** J. Sierra *11840*	
V	*19105*	Cuba (Guantanamo) *11840*
R	***Begonia brevibracteata*** Kupicha *7749*	
R		Malawi *7749*
Ex/E	***Begonia brevicaulis*** DC. *14782*	
Ex/E	*14782*	India - Meghalaya *14782*
E	***Begonia brevicyma*** C. DC. *20883, 9006*	
I	*19577*	Panama *20883*
R	***Begonia buimontana*** Yamamoto *20511*	
R	*20511*	Taiwan *20511*

Magnoliopsida (dicots): Begoniaceae: *Begonia*

R	***Begonia burkillii*** Dunn *14782*		
	R	*14782* India - Arunachal Pradesh *14782*	
I	***Begonia canarana*** Miq. *14782*		
	E	*14782* India - Karnataka (South Canara) *14782*	
	E	*14782* India - Kerala (Malabar) *14782*	
	I	*19215* Malaysia - Sabah *19215*	
R	***Begonia carletonii*** Standley *9037*		
	R	*19760* Costa Rica *9037*	
	R	*19577* Panama *9037*	
R	***Begonia copeyana*** C. DC. *9037*		
	R	*19761* Costa Rica *9037*	
R	***Begonia cordifolia*** (Wight) Thwaites *14782*		
	R	*14782* India - Kerala (Malabar) *14782*	
	R	*14782* India - Tamil Nadu (Tirunelveli Hills) *14782*	
Ex	***Begonia cowellii*** Nash *5607*		
	Ex	*19105* Cuba (Granma) *5607*	
V	***Begonia cubensis*** Hassk. *11840*		
	V	*19105* Cuba (Santiago de Cuba) *11840*	
E	***Begonia davidsoniae*** Sm. & Schubert *20883, 9006*		
	I	*19577* Panama *20883*	
R	***Begonia dregei*** Otto & A.Dietr. *20604*		
	R	*20604* South Africa - Cape Province *20604*	
	R	*20604* South Africa - Natal *20604*	
I	***Begonia ferramica*** Halle		
	I	Gabon	
I	***Begonia ficifolia*** Halle		
	I	Gabon	
R	***Begonia formosana*** (Hayata) Masamune forma *albomaculata* Liu & Lai *20511*		
	R	*20511* Taiwan *20511*	
E	***Begonia garagarana*** C. DC. *20883, 9006*		
	I	*19577* Panama *20883*	
E	***Begonia geraniifolia*** Hook. *18200*		
	E	*9446* Peru *18200*	
R	***Begonia homonyma*** Steud. *20604, 15013*		
	R	*20604* South Africa - Cape Province *20604*	
	R	*20604* South Africa - Natal *20604*	
I	***Begonia ignorata*** Irmscher		
	I	Malaysia - Peninsular Malaysia (Kota Glanggi, Pahang)	
R	***Begonia kingiana*** Irmscher		
	R	Malaysia - Peninsular Malaysia	
E	***Begonia leivae*** J. Sierra *11840*		
	E	*19105* Cuba (Santiago de Cuba) *11840*	
I	***Begonia lethomasiae*** R. Wilczek		
	I	Gabon	
V	***Begonia libanensis*** Urban *11840*		
	V	*19105* Cuba (Guantanamo) *11840*	
E	***Begonia lomensis*** Britton & P.Wilson *11840*		
	E	*19105* Cuba (Santiago de Cuba) *11840*	
R	***Begonia lushaiensis*** C.E. C. Fischer *14782*		
	R	*14782* India - Mizoram *14782*	
E	***Begonia maestrensis*** Urban *11840*		
	E	*19105* Cuba (Santiago de Cuba) *11840*	
R	***Begonia minutifolia*** Halle		
	R	Gabon	
E	***Begonia mucronistipula*** C. DC. *20883, 10747*		
	I	*20883* Panama *20883*	
I	***Begonia nicolai-hallei*** R. Wilczek		
	I	Gabon	
R	***Begonia nurii*** Irmscher		
	R	Malaysia - Peninsular Malaysia (Kelantan, Pahang)	
R	***Begonia nyassensis*** Irmscher *7749*		
	R	Malawi *7749*	
E	***Begonia octopetala*** L'Her. ssp. *octopetala* *18200*		
	E	*9446* Peru *18200*	
V	***Begonia opuliflora*** Putz. *9006*		
	V	*16317* Panama *9006*	
I	***Begonia palawanensis*** Mart. *13833*		
	I	*13833* Philippines (low altitude) *13833*	
R	***Begonia phoeniogramma*** Ridley		
	R	Malaysia - Peninsular Malaysia	
R	***Begonia phrixophylla*** Blatt. et McC. *13883*		
	R	*13883* India - Maharashtra *13883*	
I	***Begonia purdieana*** A. DC. *20883, 13336*		
	I	*13336* Jamaica *20883*	
E	***Begonia rajah*** Ridley; Ridley *12936, 10260*		
	E	*12936* Malaysia *12936*	
R	***Begonia rubro-venia*** Hook. var. *meisneri* Clarke *14782*		
	R	*14782* India - Meghalaya *14782*	
R	***Begonia rumpiensis*** Kupicha *7749*		
	R	Malawi *7749*	
E	***Begonia salisburyana*** Irmsch *7926*		
	E	Nigeria (Okomu) *7926*	
R	***Begonia satrapis*** Clarke *14782*		
	R	*14782* India - Sikkim *14782*	
I	***Begonia scintillans*** Dunn *14782*		
	I	*14782* India - Arunachal Pradesh *14782*	
R	***Begonia scutata*** Wall. ex DC. *14782*		
	R	*14782* India *14782*	
	R	*14782* India - Sikkim *14782*	
	R	*14782* India - West Bengal *14782*	
	R	*19218* Nepal *14782*	
V	***Begonia seychellensis*** Hemsley *14296*		
	V	*19181* Seychelles *14296*	
V	***Begonia socotrana*** Hook. f. *14908*		
	V	*15534* Yemen - Socotra (Haijir Mts.) *14908*	
R	***Begonia subpeltata*** Wight *14782*		
	R	*14782* India (South Deccan Peninsula and Western Ghats) *14782*	
	E	*14782* Sri Lanka *14782*	
R	***Begonia taiwaniana*** Hayata *20511*		
	R	*20511* Taiwan *20511*	
I	***Begonia tessaricarpa*** Clarke *14782*		
	I	*14782* India - Assam *14782*	
V	***Begonia trichocarpa*** Dalz. *14782*		
	V	*14782* India (Western Ghats and southwest India) *14782*	
R	***Begonia triflora*** Irmscher var. *caloskiadia* Halle		
	R	Gabon	
R	***Begonia vestita*** C. DC. *9004*		
	R	*19760* Costa Rica *9037*	
	I	*19577* Panama *9006*	
I	***Begonia vittariifolia*** Halle		
	I	Gabon	
E	***Begonia watti*** Clarke *14782*		
	E	*14782* India - Nagaland *14782*	

I   *Begonia wengeri* C.E. C. Fischer *14782*
    I   *14782* India - Mizoram *14782*

I   *Begonia woodii* Merr. *13833*
    I   *13833* Philippines (Palawan) *13833*

V   *Begonia wrightiana* A. DC *11840*
    V   *19105* Cuba (Guantanamo) *11840*

R   *Hillebrandia sandwicensis* D. Oliver *20850, 14209*
    I   *20850* U.S. - Hawaii *20850*

Berberidaceae

Number of genera: 13
Number of species: 650
Recorded threatened species: 43   (6%)

Widespread, especially temperate Northern Hemisphere.

R   *Achlys japonica* Maxim. *10572*
    R   *10572* Japan *10572*

R   *Berberis affinis* Don *11494*
    R   *11494* India - Uttar Pradesh (Kumaon) *11494*

R   *Berberis alpicola* Schneider *20511*
    R   *20511* Taiwan *20511*

R   *Berberis apiculata* Ahrendt *13883*
    R   *13883* India - Himachal Pradesh (Simla) *13883*

R   *Berberis bicolor* Lev. *20511*
    R   *20511* Taiwan *20511*

V   *Berberis cliffortioides* Diels *18200*
    V   *12468* Peru *18200*

V   *Berberis corymbosa* Hook. & Arn. *19116*
    V   *19125* Chile - Juan Fernandez Is. *19116*

V   *Berberis everestiana* Ahrendt var. *ventosa*
    Ahrendt *7731*
    V   Nepal *7731*

V   *Berberis harrisoniana* Kearney & Peebles *20850*
    V   *20850* U.S. - Arizona *20850*

R   *Berberis hayatana* Mizush. *20511*
    R   *20511* Taiwan *20511*

I   *Berberis huegeliana* Schneider *11494*
    I   *11494* India - Jammu & Kashmir (Kashmir) *11494*

R   *Berberis iliensis* Popov *5942*
    R   *5942* Kazakhstan (south-east) *5942*

R   *Berberis karkaralensis* Kornilova & Potapov *5942*
    R   *5942* Kazakhstan (east) *5942*

R   *Berberis kashmiriana* Ahrendt *11494*
    R   *11494* India - Jammu & Kashmir (Mantnar valley, nr Desu) *11494*

V   *Berberis lambertii* R. Parker *11494*
    V   *11494* India - Uttar Pradesh *11494*

E   *Berberis litoralis* Philippi *15088*
    E   *13875* Chile *13875*

V   *Berberis maderensis* Lowe *14166*
    V   *14166* Portugal - Madeira *14177*

E   *Berberis masafuerana* Skottsb. *19116*
    E   *19125* Chile - Juan Fernandez Is. *19116*

V   *Berberis nilghiriensis* Ahrendt *2268*
    V   *18228* India - Tamil Nadu (Nilgiri Hills) *2268*

I   *Berberis orthobotrys* Bien. ex Aitch. var.
    sinthanensis Ahrendt
    I   India - Jammu & Kashmir (only Kashmir)

R   *Berberis osmastonii* Dunn *11494*

    R   *11494* India - Uttar Pradesh (Garhwal) *11494*

I   *Berberis petiolaris* Wallich ex G. Don var.
    garhwalana Ahrendt
    I   India - Uttar Pradesh (Garhwal; Kumaun)

R   *Berberis poluninii* Ahrendt *7731*
    R   Nepal *7731*

I   *Berberis pseudoumbellata* R. Parker
    I   India - Himachal Pradesh (Chamba, Simla)
    I   India - Jammu & Kashmir (only Kashmir)
    I   India - Uttar Pradesh (Garhwal)

I   *Berberis royleana* Ahrendt
    I   India - Jammu & Kashmir (only Kashmir)

V   *Dysosma versipellis* (Hance) M. Cheng *17617*
    V   *17617* China - Anhui *11139*
    V   *17617* China - Fujian *11139*
    V   *17617* China - Guangxi *11139*
    V   *17617* China - Guizhou *11139*
    V   *17617* China - Henan *11139*
    V   *17617* China - Hubei *11139*
    V   *17617* China - Hunan *11139*
    V   *17617* China - Jiangxi *11139*
    V   *17617* China - Shaanxi *11139*
    V   *17617* China - Sichuan *11139*
    V   *17617* China - Yunnan *11139*
    V   *17617* China - Zhejiang *11139*

I   *Epimedium colchicum* (Boiss.) Trautv. *5942*
    I   *5942* Russia - North Caucasus *5942*
    I   *5942* Georgia (Black Sea coast) *5942*

R   *Epimedium grandiflorum* Morr. var. *coelestre*
    Shimizu *10572*
    R   *10572* Japan *10572*

V   *Epimedium perralderianum* Coss. *10487*
    V   *14958* Algeria *10487*

R   *Gymnospermium altaicum* (Pallas) Spach ssp. *odessanum*
    (DC.) E. Mayer & Pulevic *10270*
    R   *19121* Albania *19121*
    E   *14155* Greece (Peloponnisos) *20731*
    E   *19949* Romania *8000*

I   *Gymnospermium darwasicum* (Regel) Takht. *5942*
    I   *5942* Tajikistan *5942*

I   *Gymnospermium odessanum* (DC.) Takht. *5942*
    I   *5942* Ukraine *5942*

I   *Gymnospermium smirnowii* (Trautv.) Takht. *5942*
    I   *5942* Ukraine *5942*

V   *Mahonia amplectens* Eastw. *20850*
    I   *20850* U.S. - California *20850*

E   *Mahonia higginsiae* (Munz) Ahrendt *20883, 19002*
    E   *20850* U.S. - California *20850*
    E   *20883* Mexico *20883*

I   *Mahonia jaunsarensis* Ahrendt
    I   India - Uttar Pradesh (Chakrata)

V   *Mahonia nervosa* (Pursh) Nutt. var. *mendocinensis*
    (J.B. Roof) J.B. Roof *20850*
    I   *20850* U.S. - California *20850*

V   *Mahonia nevinii* (Gray) Fedde *20850*
    V   *20850* U.S. - California *20850*

R   *Mahonia oiwakensis* Hayata *20511*
    R   *20854* Taiwan *20511*

E   *Mahonia pinnata* (Lag.) Fedde ssp. *insularis* (Munz)
    J.B. Roof *20850*
    E   *20850* U.S. - California *20850*

E   *Mahonia sonnei* Abrams *20850*

E   *20850*   U.S. - California *20850*

R   **Mahonia swaseyi** (Buckl. ex Young) Fedde *20850*
     R   *20850*   U.S. - Texas *20850*

I   **Ranzania japonica** Ito *10572*
     I   *10572*   Japan *10572*

Betulaceae

Number of genera: 6
Number of species: 120-130
Recorded threatened species: 13   (10%)

Mainly temperate and cool Northern Hemisphere.

R   **Alnus glutinosa** (L.) Gaertner ssp.
       betuloides *20618*
     R   *20618*   Turkey *20618*

R   **Alnus hakkodensis** Hayashi *10572*
     R   *10572*   Japan *10572*

R   **Alnus maritima** (Marsh.) Muhl. ex Nutt. *20850*
     R   *20850*   U.S. - Delaware *20850*
     R   *20850*   U.S. - Maryland *20850*
     V   *20850*   U.S. - Oklahoma *20850*

V   **Betula apoiensis** Nakai *10572*
     V   *20626*   Japan (Mt Apoi) *20626*

R   **Betula browicziana** Guner *12840*
     R   *20618*   Turkey *20618*

R   **Betula chichibuensis** Hara *10572*
     R   *10572*   Japan *10572*

R   **Betula ermani** Cham. var. **saitoana**
       Hatus. *15957*
     R   *15923*   Korea, South (Mt. Halla, Mt. Chiri)
                 15957

R   **Betula globispica** Shirai
     R   Japan (central)

E   **Betula halophila** Ching ex P.C. Li *17617*
     E   *17617*   China - Xinjiang Uygur Zizhiqu (Artai)
                 11139

I   **Betula megrelica** Sosn. *5942*
     I   *5942*   Georgia *5942*

E   **Betula murrayana** Barnes & Dancik *20850*
     E   *20850*   U.S. - Michigan *20850*

R   **Betula parvibracteata** Peinado, Morena & Velasco
     R   Spain

I   **Betula raddeana** Trautv. *5942*
     I   *5942*   Russia - North Caucasus *5942*
     I   *5942*   Georgia *5942*

Bignoniaceae

Number of genera: 100
Number of species: 800
Recorded threatened species: 155   (19%)

Mainly tropical, especially tropical America.

E   **Amphitecna costata** A. Gentry *20883, 9089*
     E   *12472*   Guatemala *20883*

R   **Amphitecna isthmica** (A. Gentry) A. Gentry *20883*
     I   *20883*   Costa Rica *20883*
     I   *20883*   Panama *20883*
     I   *20883*   Colombia *20883*

E   **Amphitecna macrophylla** (Seemann) Miers ex
       Baillon *20883, 9089*
     E   *20883*   Mexico *20883*
     Ex/E *12472*   Mexico - Veracruz *9089*

V   **Amphitecna megalophylla** (Donnell Smith) A.
       Gentry *20883*
     I   *20883*   Guatemala *20883*

E   **Amphitecna parviflora** A. Gentry *20883, 9089*
     V   *12472*   Panama *20883*

R   **Amphitecna regalis** (Linden) A. Gentry *20883*
     I   *20883*   Mexico *20883*

R   **Amphitecna sessilifolius** (J.D. Sm.) L.O. Wms. *20883*
     I   *20883*   Costa Rica *20883*
     I   *20883*   Panama *20883*

V   **Amphitecna silvicola** L. O. Williams *20883, 9006*
     V   *12472*   Guatemala *20883*
     V   *12472*   Mexico *20883*

E   **Amphitecna spathicalyx** (A. Gentry) A. Gentry *20883,*
       9089
     E   *12472*   Panama *20883*

V   **Amphitecna steyermarkii** (A. Gentry) A. Gentry *20883*
     I   *20883*   Guatemala *20883*
     I   *20883*   Mexico *20883*

E   **Amphitecna tuxtlensis** A. Gentry *20883, 9089*
     V   *12472*   Mexico *20883*

R   **Argylia adscendens** var. **viridis** (Philippi) Gleisner &
       Ricardi *20883*
     I   *20883*   Chile *20883*

V   **Argylia bifrons** Philippi *20883*
     I   *20883*   Chile *20883*

R   **Argylia checoensis** (Meyen) Johnston *20883*
     I   *20883*   Chile *20883*

V   **Argylia farnesiana** Gleisner & Ricardi *20883*
     I   *20883*   Chile *20883*

R   **Argylia geranioides** A. de Candolle *20883*
     I   *20883*   Chile *20883*

V   **Argylia glutinosa** Philippi *20883*
     I   *20883*   Chile *20883*

R   **Argylia potentillifolia** A. de Candolle *20883*
     I   *20883*   Chile *20883*

R   **Argylia robusta** Sandwith *20883, 16336*
     V   *16336*   Argentina *20883*
     V   *20176*   Argentina - Neuquen *20176*
     V   *20176*   Argentina - Mendoza *20176*

R   **Argylia tomentosa** Philippi *20883*
     I   *20883*   Chile *20883*

R   **Catalpa brevipes** Urban *20883, 5607*
     V   *19105*   Cuba (Granma) *20883*
     I   *20883*   Dominican Republic (Azua (south west))
                 20074
     I   *20883*   Haiti (Massif de la Hotte) *20074*

R   **Catalpa purpurea** Grisebach *20883*
     I   *20883*   Cuba *20883*
     I   *20883*   Haiti (La Gonâve) *21008*

V   **Colea colei** (Bojer ex Hook.) M.L.Green *10082*
     V   *20771*   Mauritius *10082*

I   **Colea seychellarum** Seemann *14296*
     I   *19181*   Seychelles (granitic) *14296*

E   **Crescentia mirabilis** Ekman ex Urban *20883, 5607*
     E   *19105*   Cuba (Camaguey) *20883*

E   **Crescentia portoricensis** Britt. *20883, 8058*
     E   *20883*   Puerto Rico (western) *20883*

R   **Cuspidaria weberbaueri** (Sprague) A. Gentry *18200*
     R   *12468*   Peru *18200*

Magnoliopsida (dicots): Bignoniaceae: *Cuspidaria*

R   *Delostoma dentatum* D. Don *20883*
     I   *20883*   Peru *20883*

E   *Delostoma gracile* A. Gentry *20883, 12472*
     E   *12472*   Peru *20883*

R   *Digomphia ceratophora* A. Gentry *20883*
     I   *20883*   Colombia *20883*
     I   *20883*   Venezuela *20883*

V   *Ekmanianthe actinophylla* (Grisebach) Urban *20883, 20513*
     I   *20883*   Cuba *20883*

V   *Ekmanianthe longiflora* (Grisebach) Urban *20883*
     I   *20883*   Cuba *20883*
     I   *20883*   Dominican Republic (Barahona) *20074*
     I   *20883*   Haiti (Gonaïves) *20074*

V   *Fernandoa lutea* (Verdcourt) Bidgood *20885*
     V   *20885*   Tanzania (Rondo) *20900*

R   *Haplophragma serratum* Dop *6057*
     R   Vietnam *6057*

I   *Hexaneurocarpon brilletii* Dop *6057*
     I   *15734*   Vietnam *6057*

V   *Jacaranda acutifolia* Kunth *18200*
     V   *12468*   Peru *18200*

R   *Jacaranda arborea* Urban *20883*
     I   *20883*   Cuba *20883*

R   *Jacaranda bracteata* Bureau & K. Schumann *20883*
     I   *20883*   Brazil *20883*

E   *Jacaranda bullata* A. Gentry *20883*
     I   *20883*   Brazil *20883*

R   *Jacaranda campinae* A. Gentry & Morawetz *20883*
     I   *20883*   Brazil *20883*

E   *Jacaranda carajasensis* A. Gentry *20883*
     I   *20883*   Brazil *20883*

R   *Jacaranda caucana* A. Gentry ssp. *calycina* A. Gentry *20883, 12472*
     V   *12472*   Colombia *20883*

R   *Jacaranda caucana* ssp. *glabrata* A. Gentry *20883*
     I   *20883*   Venezuela *20883*

R   *Jacaranda cowellii* Britton & Wilson *20883*
     I   *20883*   Cuba *20883*

E   *Jacaranda crassifolia* Morawetz *20883*
     I   *20883*   Brazil *20883*

V   *Jacaranda egleri* Sandwith *20883*
     I   *20883*   Brazil *20883*

V   *Jacaranda ekmanii* Alain *20883*
     I   *20883*   Dominican Republic (Pedernales, Barahona) *20074*
     I   *20883*   Haiti (south) *20074*

V   *Jacaranda grandifoliolata* A. Gentry *20883*
     I   *20883*   Brazil *20883*

V   *Jacaranda intricata* A. Gentry & W. Morawetz *20883*
     I   *20883*   Brazil *20883*

R   *Jacaranda irwinii* A. Gentry *20883*
     I   *20883*   Brazil *20883*

R   *Jacaranda macrocarpa* Bureau & K. Schumann *20883*
     I   *20883*   Brazil *20883*
     I   *20883*   Colombia *20883*
     I   *20883*   Peru *20883*

R   *Jacaranda microcalyx* A. Gentry *20883*
     I   *20883*   Brazil *20883*

R   *Jacaranda mimosifolia* D. Don *10747*
     R   *20074*   Argentina *10747*
     I   *20176*   Argentina - Catamarca *20176*
     I   *20176*   Argentina - Jujuy *20176*
     I   *20176*   Argentina - Salta *20176*
     R   *20074*   Bolivia *12379*

V   *Jacaranda montana* Morawetz *20883*
     I   *20883*   Brazil *20883*

R   *Jacaranda morii* A. Gentry *20883*
     I   *20883*   Brazil *20883*

R   *Jacaranda orinocensis* Sandwith *20883*
     I   *20883*   Venezuela *20883*

R   *Jacaranda praetermissa* Sandwith *20883*
     I   *20883*   Brazil *20883*

R   *Jacaranda pulcherrima* Morawetz *20883*
     I   *20883*   Brazil *20883*

R   *Jacaranda racemosa* Chamisso *20883*
     I   *20883*   Brazil *20883*

E   *Jacaranda rugosa* A. Gentry *20883*
     I   *20883*   Brazil *20883*

V   *Jacaranda selleana* Urban *20883*
     I   *20883*   Dominican Republic (Pedernales) *20074*
     I   *20883*   Haiti (Massif de la Selle) *20074*

V   *Jacaranda sparrei* A. Gentry *20883, 18200*
     I   *20883*   Ecuador *20883*
     I   *12468*   Peru *20883*

V   *Jacaranda subalpina* Morawetz *20883*
     I   *20883*   Brazil *20883*

R   *Niedzwedzkia semiretschenskia* B. Fedtsch. *5942*
     R   *5942*   Kazakhstan (south-east) *5942*
     R   *5942*   Uzbekistan *5942*

E   *Paratecoma peroba* (Record & Mell) Kuhlmann *20883, 13928*
     E   *20883*   Brazil *20883*
     ?   Brazil - Bahia *13928*
     ?   Brazil - Rio de Janeiro *13928*

R   *Parmentiera cereifera* Seem. *20883, 10747*
     I   *20883*   Panama *20883*

V   *Parmentiera dressleri* A. Gentry *10747*
     V   *16317*   Panama *10747*

R   *Parmentiera millspaughiana* L. O. Williams *20883, 9089*
     I   *20883*   Mexico *20883*

E   *Parmentiera morii* A. Gentry *20883, 9089*
     V   *12472*   Panama *20883*

R   *Parmentiera parviflora* Lundell *20883, 9004*
     I   *20883*   Guatemala *20883*
     I   *20883*   Mexico *20883*

V   *Parmentiera stenocarpa* Dugand & L. B. Smith *20883*
     I   *20883*   Colombia *20883*

E   *Parmentiera trunciflora* Standley & L. Williams *20883, 9089*
     I   *20883*   Nicaragua *20883*

E   *Parmentiera valerii* Standley *20883, 9089*
     E   *12472*   Costa Rica *20883*

R   *Pseudocatalpa caudiculata* (Standley) A. Gentry *9004*
     R   *9004*   Belize *9004*
     R   *9004*   Guatemala *9004*

R   *Radermachera poilanei* Dop *6057*
     R   Vietnam *6057*

R   *Radermachera tonkinensis* Dop *6057*

R		Vietnam *6057*	
V	*Romeroa verticillata* Dugand *20883*		
I		*20883* Colombia *20883*	
E	*Sparattosperma catingae* A. Gentry *20883*		
I		*20883* Brazil *20883*	
R	*Spathodeopsis collignonii* Dop *6057*		
R		Vietnam *6057*	
R	*Spirotecoma apiculata* (Britton) Alain *20883*		
I		*20883* Cuba *20883*	
R	*Spirotecoma holguinensis* (Britton) Alain *20883*		
I		*20883* Cuba *20883*	
R	*Spirotecoma rubriflora* (Leonard) Alain *20883*		
I		*20883* Cuba *20883*	
I		*20883* Dominican Republic (Barahona, Samaná, El Seibo) *20074*	
I		*20883* Haiti (Massif du Nord, Massif de la Selle) *20074*	
V	*Spirotecoma spiralis* (Wright ex Grisebach) Pichon *20883*		
I		*20883* Cuba *20883*	
E	*Synapsis ilicifolia* Griseb. *5607*		
E		*19105* Cuba (Santiago de Cuba) *5607*	
E	*Tabebuia acunana* Borh. & Muniz *5607*		
E		*19105* Cuba (Santiago de Cuba) *5607*	
V	*Tabebuia anafensis* Urban *5607*		
V		*19105* Cuba (Ciud. Habana; Matanzas) *5607*	
V	*Tabebuia arianeae* A. Gentry *20883*		
I		*20883* Brazil *20883*	
R	*Tabebuia arimaoensis* Britton *20883*		
I		*20883* Cuba *20883*	
V	*Tabebuia bibracteolata* (Grisebach) Britton *20883*		
V		*19105* Cuba (Santiago de Cuba) *20883*	
R	*Tabebuia billbergii* ssp. *ampla* A. Gentry *20883*		
I		*20883* Ecuador *20883*	
I		*20883* Peru *20883*	
V	*Tabebuia botelhensis* A. Gentry *20883*		
I		*20883* Brazil *20883*	
R	*Tabebuia brooksiana* Britton *20883*		
I		*20883* Cuba *20883*	
V	*Tabebuia buchii* (Urban) Britton *20883*		
I		*20883* Haiti (north) *20074*	
R	*Tabebuia bullata* A. Gentry *20883*		
I		*20883* Dominican Republic (central: Peravia, La Vega & Santiago) *20074*	
V	*Tabebuia bureavii* Sandwith *20883*		
I		*20883* Brazil *20883*	
V	*Tabebuia caleticana* A. Gentry & D. Albert *20883*		
I		*20883* Cuba *20883*	
V	*Tabebuia capotei* Borh. *5607*		
V		*19105* Cuba (Pinar del Rio) *5607*	
R	*Tabebuia cassinoides* (Lamarck) A. P. de Candolle *20883, 20310*		
I		*20883* Brazil *20883*	
?		Brazil - Santa Catarina *20310*	
R	*Tabebuia catarinensis* A. Gentry *20883*		
I		*20883* Brazil *20883*	
E	*Tabebuia clementis* Alain *20883*		
I		*20883* Cuba *20883*	
E	*Tabebuia conferta* Urban *20883, 15229*		

I		*15229* Haiti (Massif de la Hotte) *20074*	
R	*Tabebuia coralibe* Standley *20883*		
I		*20883* Colombia *20883*	
R	*Tabebuia crispiflora* Alain *20883*		
I		*20883* Cuba *20883*	
I		*20883* Dominican Republic (south west & central) *20074*	
V	*Tabebuia cristata* A. Gentry *20883*		
I		*20883* Brazil *20883*	
V	*Tabebuia del-riscoi* Borh. *5607*		
V		*19105* Cuba (Pinar del Rio; Holguin) *5607*	
V	*Tabebuia dominguensis* (Urban) Britton *20883*		
I		*20883* Dominican Republic (north Barahona peninsula) *20074*	
R	*Tabebuia dubia* (C. Wright ex Sauvalle) Britton ex Seibert *20883*		
I		*20883* Cuba *20883*	
V	*Tabebuia elegans* Urban *20883*		
I		*20883* Cuba *20883*	
E	*Tabebuia elongata* Urban *20883*		
I		*20883* Cuba *20883*	
I	*Tabebuia furfuracea* Urban *5607*		
I		*19105* Cuba (Santiago de Cuba; Holguin) *5607*	
E	*Tabebuia geronensis* Britton *5607*		
E		*19105* Cuba (Juventud Is.) *5607*	
E	*Tabebuia glaucescens* Urban *20883*		
I		*20883* Cuba *20883*	
R	*Tabebuia haemantha* (Bertol. ex Spreng.) DC. *20883*		
I		*20883* Puerto Rico *20883*	
R	*Tabebuia hypoleuca* (Wright ex Sauvalle) Urban *20883*		
I		*20883* Cuba *20883*	
R	*Tabebuia inaequipes* Urban *20883*		
I		*20883* Cuba *20883*	
V	*Tabebuia jackiana* Ekman ex Urban *20883, 5607*		
I		*19105* Cuba (Pinar del Rio) *20883*	
I	*Tabebuia jojoana* Britton & P. Wilson *5607*		
I		*19105* Cuba (Guantanamo) *5607*	
R	*Tabebuia lapacho* (K. Schumann) Sandwith *20883, 20176*		
I		*20883* Argentina *20883*	
E		*20176* Argentina - Jujuy *20176*	
E		*20176* Argentina - Salta *20176*	
I		*20883* Bolivia *20883*	
R	*Tabebuia linearis* Alain *20883, 5607*		
E		*19105* Cuba (Holguin) *20883*	
R	*Tabebuia maxonii* Urban *20883*		
I		*20883* Dominican Republic (Samaná Bay) *20074*	
R	*Tabebuia moaensis* Britton *20883*		
I		*20883* Cuba *20883*	
E	*Tabebuia multinervis* Urban & Ekman *20883*		
I		*20883* Haiti (Massif de la Selle) *20074*	
V	*Tabebuia ophiolitica* Alain *20883*		
I		*20883* Dominican Republic (north) *20074*	
R	*Tabebuia orinocensis* (Sandwith) A. Gentry *20883*		
I		*20883* Colombia *20883*	
I		*20883* Venezuela *20883*	
E	*Tabebuia paniculata* Leonard *20883*		
E		*20883* Dominican Republic (Samaná peninsula) *20074*	
R	*Tabebuia pedicellata* (Bureau & K. Schumann) A. Gentry *20883*		

I 20883 Brazil 20883

E *Tabebuia pergracilis* Britton & P. Wilson 5607
    E 19105 Cuba (Sancti Spiritus) 5607

I *Tabebuia picotensis* Urban 5607
    I 5607 Cuba 5607

V *Tabebuia pinetorum* Britton 20883
    I 20883 Cuba 20883

R *Tabebuia platyantha* (Griseb.) Britton 20883
    R 20883 Jamaica 20883

E *Tabebuia polyantha* Urban & Ekman 20883
    I 20883 Dominican Republic (north and central Cordilleras) 20074
    I 20883 Haiti (Massif du Nord, Massif de la Hotte) 20074

E *Tabebuia polymorpha* Urban 20883
    I 20883 Cuba 20883

V *Tabebuia pulverulenta* Urban 20883, 5607
    I 19105 Cuba (Santiago de Cuba; Holguin) 20883

R *Tabebuia pumila* A. Gentry 20883
    I 20883 Brazil 20883

V *Tabebuia reticulata* A. Gentry 20883
    I 20883 Brazil 20883

R *Tabebuia revoluta* (Urban) Britton 20883
    I 20883 Dominican Republic (Jarabacoa) 20074

R *Tabebuia rigida* Urban 20883
    I 20883 Puerto Rico 20883

V *Tabebuia riodocensis* A. Gentry 20883
    I 20883 Brazil 20883

V *Tabebuia sauvallei* Britton 20883
    I 20883 Cuba 20883

E *Tabebuia saxicola* Britton 5607
    E 19105 Cuba (Villa Clara) 5607

R *Tabebuia schumanniana* Urban 20883
    I 20883 Puerto Rico 20883

E *Tabebuia selachidentata* A. Gentry 20883
    I 20883 Brazil 20883

R *Tabebuia shaferi* Britton 20883
    I 20883 Cuba 20883

R *Tabebuia striata* A. Gentry 20883, 9006
    R 12472 Panama 20883
    R 12472 Colombia 20883

R *Tabebuia vinosa* A. Gentry 20883
    I 20883 Dominican Republic (Cordillera Central) 20074

E *Tabebuia zanonii* A. Gentry 20883
    I 20883 Dominican Republic (Los Haitises) 20074

V *Tabebuia zolyomiana* Borh. 5607
    V 19105 Cuba (Holguin) 5607

R *Tecoma cochabambensis* (Herzog) Sandwith 20883
    I 20883 Bolivia 20883

R *Tecoma fulva* (Cavanilles) D. Don 20883
    I 20883 Chile 20883
    I 20883 Peru 20883

R *Tecoma guarume* A. de Candolle 20883
    I 20883 Peru 20883

E *Tecoma tanaeciiflora* (Kränzlin) Sandwith 20883
    I 20883 Bolivia 20883
    I 20883 Peru 20883

R *Tecoma weberbaueriana* (Kränzlin) Melchior 20883,

18200
    I 20883 Ecuador 20883
    R 12468 Peru 20883

R *Tecomanthe hillii* (F.Muell.) Steenis 20681
    R 20681 Australia - Queensland 20681

E *Tecomanthe speciosa* W. Oliver 86
    E 13378 New Zealand - North Is. (Three Kings Is.) 13378

R *Tynnanthus croatianus* A. Gentry 9006
    R 12472 Panama 9006
    R 12472 Colombia 12472

R *Tynnanthus macranthus* L.O. Williams 9037
    R 9426 Costa Rica 9037
    V 12472 Panama 10747

Bombacaceae

Number of genera: 20-30
Number of species: 200
Recorded threatened species: 24   (12%)

Tropical, especially Central and South America.

R *Adansonia za* Baillon 10368
    R   Madagascar

I *Bombax insigne* Wall. var. *polystemon* Prain 7771
    I 14782 India - Nicobar Is. 7771

V *Ceiba glaziovii* (Kuntze) Schum. 11597
    V 11597 Brazil 11597

    Ceiba insignis (Kunth) Gibbs & Semir 16401
    I 16401 Panama 9006

V *Ceiba jasminodora* (St. Hil.) Schum. 11597
    V 11597 Brazil 11597

E *Ceiba pubiflora* var. *glabriflora* Hassler 20883
    E 20883 Paraguay 20883

E *Ceiba rosea* (Seem.) Schum. 20883
    I 20883 Panama 20883

R *Ceiba trischistandra* (Gray) Bakh. 11597
    V   Ecuador 11597
    R 19962 Peru 11597

R *Cullenia ceylanica* (Gardner) Schumann 8021
    R 12838 Sri Lanka 8021

R *Cullenia rosayroana* Kosterm. 8021
    R 12838 Sri Lanka 8021

E *Durio macrantha* Kosterm. 15943
    E 15943 Indonesia - Sumatra (north) 15943

R *Eriotheca gracilipes* (K. Schum.) 20883
    I 20883 Bolivia 20883
    I 20883 Brazil 20883
    V 20883 Paraguay 20883

E *Gyranthera darienensis* Pitt. 20883, 9006
    V 19577 Panama 20883

E *Matisia exalata* Alverson 20883
    I 20883 Panama 20883

E *Pseudobombax argentinum* (Fries) Robyns 21056
    E 16336 Argentina 16336
    E 20176 Argentina - Jujuy 20176
    E 20176 Argentina - Salta 20176
            Bolivia 21056
            Brazil - Sao Paulo 21056
            Paraguay 21056

R *Pseudobombax marginatum* (St. Hil.) A. Robyns 20883

I	20883	Bolivia *20883*
I	20883	Brazil *20883*
V	20883	Paraguay *20883*
I	20883	Peru *20883*

R   *Pseudobombax tomentosum* (Mart. & Zucc.) A. Robyns *20883*

I	20883	Bolivia *20883*
I	20883	Brazil *20883*
R	20883	Paraguay *20883*

E   *Quararibea aurantiocalyx* Alverson *20883*

I	20883	Costa Rica *20883*
I	20883	Panama *20883*

V   *Quararibea costaricensis* Alverson *20883*

V	20883	Costa Rica *20883*

E   *Quararibea dolichopoda* A. Robyns *20883, 9092*

I	20883	Panama *20883*

E   *Quararibea gomeziana* Alverson *20883*

I	20883	Costa Rica *20883*
I	20883	Panama *20883*

E   *Quararibea pendula* Alverson *20883*

I	20883	Costa Rica *20883*
I	20883	Panama *20883*

E   *Quararibea santaritensis* Alverson *20883*

I	20883	Panama *20883*

I   *Spirotheca rhodostyla* Cuatrec. *19353*

I	19353	Colombia *19353*

Boraginaceae

Number of genera:	100	
Number of species:	2,000	
Recorded threatened species:	378	(18%)

Cosmopolitan, especially western North America and Mediterranean region; east into Asia.

I   *Alkanna amana* Rech. f. *12840*

I	12840	Turkey *12840*

I   *Alkanna areolata* Boiss. var. *areolata* *12840*

I	12840	Turkey *12840*

I   *Alkanna areolata* Boiss. var. *sublaevis* Huber-Mor. *12840*

I	12840	Turkey *12840*

R   *Alkanna attilae* Davis *12840*

R	12840	Turkey *12840*

R   *Alkanna aucherana* A. DC *12840*

R	12840	Turkey *12840*

R   *Alkanna calliensis* Heldr. ex Boiss. *20171*

R		Greece

R   *Alkanna cappadocica* Boiss. & Bal. *12840*

R	12840	Turkey *12840*

R   *Alkanna froedinii* Rech. f. *12840*

R	12840	Turkey *12840*

I   *Alkanna haussknechtii* Bornm. *12840*

I	12840	Turkey *12840*

R   *Alkanna hispida* Huber-Mor. *12840*

R	12840	Turkey *12840*

R   *Alkanna incana* Boiss. *12840*

R	12840	Turkey *12840*

V   *Alkanna macrophylla* Boiss. & Heldr. *12840*

V	12840	Turkey *12840*

V   *Alkanna macrosiphon* Boiss. & Heldr. *12840*

V	12840	Turkey *12840*

I   *Alkanna methanaea* Hausskn. *20171*

I		Greece

R   *Alkanna noneiformis* Griseb. *20171*

R		(former) Yugoslavia

R   *Alkanna oreodoxa* Huber-Mor. *12840*

R	12840	Turkey *12840*

R   *Alkanna orientalis* (L.) Boiss var. *leucantha* (Bornm.) Huber-Mor. *12840*

R	12840	Turkey *12840*

R   *Alkanna pamphylica* Huber-Mor. & Reese *12840*

R	12840	Turkey *12840*

R   *Alkanna pelia* (Halácsy) Rech.f. *20171*

R		Greece

R   *Alkanna phrygia* Bornm. *12840*

R	12840	Turkey *12840*

V   *Alkanna pinardii* Boiss. *12840*

V	12840	Turkey *12840*

R   *Alkanna primulifolia* Griseb.

R		Bulgaria
R		Greece

R   *Alkanna pulmonaria* Griseb. *20171*

R		(former) Yugoslavia

R   *Alkanna punctulata* Huber-Mor. *12840*

R	12840	Turkey *12840*

I   *Alkanna sartoriana* Boiss. & Heldr. *20171*

I		Greece

R   *Alkanna saxicola* Huber-Mor. *12840*

R	12840	Turkey *12840*

I   *Alkanna shattuckia* (Post) Post *12840*

I	12840	Turkey *12840*

R   *Alkanna sieberi* DC. *20171*

R	20730	Greece - Crete *19121*

R   *Alkanna sieheana* Rech. f. *12840*

R	12840	Turkey *12840*

R   *Alkanna stribrnyi* Velen. *5204, 20171*

V	19426	Bulgaria (south) *5204*
R		(former) Yugoslavia

R   *Alkanna verecunda* Huber-Mor. *12840*

R	12840	Turkey *12840*

I   *Alkanna viscidula* Boiss. *12840*

I	12840	Turkey *12840*

V   *Amsinckia carinata* A. Nels. & J.F. Macbr. *20850*

V	20850	U.S. - Oregon *20850*

R   *Amsinckia furcata* Suksdorf *20850*

R	20850	U.S. - California *20850*

E   *Amsinckia grandiflora* (Kleeb. ex Gray) Kleeb. ex Greene *20850*

E	20850	U.S. - California (SW San Joaquin Valley) *20850*

R   *Anchusa cespitosa* Lam. *20171*

R	20730	Greece - Crete *19121*

V   *Anchusa crispa* Viv. *8000, 20171*

E	15080	France - Corsica *12844*
V	18264	Italy - Sardinia (northern Sardegna) *8001*

R   *Anchusa macrosyrinx* Rech.f. *20171*

R		Greece

R   *Anchusa phocidica* L.-A. Gustavsson

R		Greece

R	***Anchusa rechingeri*** Riedl	
	R	Greece
R	***Anchusa sartorii*** Heldr. ex Gusul. *20171*	
	R	Greece
R	***Anchusa serpentinicola*** Rech.f. *20171*	
	R	Greece
	R	(former) Yugoslavia
I	***Anchusa spruneri*** Boiss. *20171*	
	I	Greece
R	***Anchusa subglabra*** Caball. *20171*	
	R	Spain
E	***Arnebia benthamii*** Benth. *14768*	
	E	India - Jammu & Kashmir *14768*
R	***Arnebia purpurea*** Erik & Sumbul *12840*	
	R	*12840* Turkey *12840*
I	***Borago longifolia*** Poiret	
	V	Algeria
	I	Tunisia
R	***Bourreria baccata*** Raf. *20883*	
	R	*20883* Jamaica *20883*
R	***Bourreria mollis*** Standley *9004*	
	R	*11181* Belize *9004*
	R	*11181* Guatemala *11181*
	R	*11181* Honduras *11181*
	R	*11181* Mexico *11181*
	R	*11181* Nicaragua *11181*
	Bourreria panamensis I.M. Johnst. *20883*	
	I	*20883* Panama *20883*
V	***Bourreria radula*** (Poir.) G. Don *20883, 19002*	
	E	*20850* U.S. - Florida *20850*
	I	*20883* Puerto Rico *20883*
R	***Bourreria rekoi*** Standley *11183*	
	R	*11181* Mexico *11183*
E	***Bourreria rubra*** E. J. Lott & J. S. Miller *20883, 11181*	
	R	*11181* Mexico *20883*
R	***Bourreria superba*** I.M. Johnston *11181*	
	R	*11181* Mexico *11181*
V	***Bourreria velutina*** (DC.) Gurke *20883, 13336*	
	V	*19890* Jamaica (St. Catherine) *20883*
I	***Brunnera sibirica*** Steven *5942*	
	I	*5942* Russia (Siberia) - Altai *5942*
R	***Buglossoides gastonii*** (Benth.) I.M.Johnst. *20171*	
	V	France
	R	Spain
I	***Buglossoides glandulosa*** (Velen.) R.Fern. *5204, 20171*	
	V	*19426* Bulgaria (south) *5204*
	I	*19417* Romania *19417*
I	***Coldenia procumbens*** L. var. *aristata* Merr. *13833*	
	I	*13833* Philippines (low altitude) *13833*
E	***Cordia acunae*** (Mold.) Alain *5607*	
	E	*19105* Cuba (Holguin) *5607*
R	***Cordia anisophylla*** J.S. Miller *13866*	
	R	*11181* Panama *13866*
V	***Cordia bellonis*** Urban *20883*	
	I	*20883* Puerto Rico *20883*
V	***Cordia borinquensis*** Urban *20883*	
	I	*20883* Puerto Rico *20883*
R	***Cordia clarendonensis*** (Britton) Stearn *20883, 13336*	

	R	*13336* Jamaica (Clarendon, Trelawny) *20883*
R	***Cordia colimensis*** I.M. Johnston *11181*	
	R	*11181* Mexico *11181*
V	***Cordia corallicola*** Urban *5607*	
	V	*19105* Cuba (Granma) *5607*
R	***Cordia cordiformis*** I.M. Johnston *11181*	
	R	*11181* Guatemala *11181*
	R	*11181* Mexico - Chiapas *11181*
	?	Mexico - Colima *21204*
R	***Cordia correae*** J.S. Miller *11675*	
	R	*11181* Panama *11675*
R	***Cordia croatii*** J.S. Miller *11675*	
	R	*11181* Costa Rica *11675*
	R	*11181* Panama *11675*
V	***Cordia decandra*** Hook. & Arn. *15088*	
	V	*13875* Chile *13875*
R	***Cordia dumosa*** Alain *5607*	
	R	*19105* Cuba (Las Tunas, Guantanamo) *5607*
R	***Cordia elliptica*** Sw. *20883*	
	R	*20883* Jamaica *20883*
R	***Cordia globulifera*** I.M. Johnston *11181*	
	R	*11181* Mexico *11181*
R	***Cordia guerkiana*** Loes. *11183*	
	R	*11181* Mexico - Oaxaca *11183*
E	***Cordia harrisii*** Urb. *20883, 13336*	
	E	*20883* Jamaica (Trelawny, Hanover) *20883*
V	***Cordia iberica*** Urban *5607*	
	V	*19105* Cuba (Guantanamo) *5607*
R	***Cordia igualensis*** Bartlett *11183*	
	R	*11181* Mexico - Guerrero *11183*
V	***Cordia intricata*** C. Wright *5607*	
	V	*19105* Cuba (Sancti Spiritus) *5607*
E	***Cordia lasiocalyx*** Pitt. *20883, 9006*	
	I	*20883* Panama *20883*
I	***Cordia lauta*** I.M. Johnston *11183*	
	I	*11181* Mexico *11183*
E	***Cordia leslieae*** J.S. Miller *11675*	
	E	*11181* Panama *11675*
R	***Cordia liesneri*** J.S. Miller *13866*	
	R	*11181* Costa Rica *13866*
E	***Cordia macvaughii*** James S. Miller *20883, 11181*	
	R	*11181* Mexico *20883*
I	***Cordia marchionica*** Drake	
	I	French Polynesia - Marquesas Is
R	***Cordia obovata*** Balf. f. *20884*	
	R	*20884* Oman *20884*
	R	*20884* Yemen - Socotra *20884*
	R	*20884* Somalia (north-east) *20884*
I	***Cordia octandra*** A. DC.	
	I	India - Kerala (Travancore Hills)
E	***Cordia rupicola*** Urban *20883, 15106*	
	I	*20883* Puerto Rico *20883*
	I	*20883* British Virgin Is. (Anegada) *20883*
R	***Cordia scouleri*** Hook.f. *11117*	
	R	Ecuador - Galapagos *11117*
I	***Cordia skutchii*** I.M. Johnston *9004*	
	I	*11181* Guatemala *9004*
R	***Cordia suckertii*** Chiov. *20884*	
	R	*20884* Ethiopia *20884*

R		20884 Somalia (central) *20884*	
V	***Cordia suffruticosa*** Borh. *5607*		
	V	*19105* Cuba (Holguin) *5607*	
R	***Cordia tacarcunensis*** J.S. Miller *11675*		
	R	*11181* Panama *11675*	
R	***Cordia tinifolia*** Willd. ex Roemer & Schultes *11183*		
	R	*11181* Mexico - Guerrero *11183*	
V	***Cordia troyana*** Urb. *20883, 13336*		
	V	*20883* Jamaica *20883*	
E	***Cordia van-hermannii*** Alain *5607*		
	E	*19105* Cuba (Holguin) *5607*	
E	***Cordia wagnerorum*** Howard *20883, 8058*		
	V	*19002* Puerto Rico *20883*	
V	***Cryptantha abata*** I.M. Johnston *20850*		
	I	*20850* U.S. - Arizona *20850*	
	I	*20850* U.S. - Nevada *20850*	
	V	*20850* U.S. - Utah *20850*	
R	***Cryptantha atwoodii*** Higgins *20850*		
	R	*20850* U.S. - Arizona *20850*	
V	***Cryptantha barnebyi*** I.M. Johnston *20850*		
	V	*20850* U.S. - Utah *20850*	
R	***Cryptantha caespitosa*** (A. Nels.) Payson *20850*		
	V	*20850* U.S. - Colorado *20850*	
	E	*20850* U.S. - Idaho *20850*	
	V	*20850* U.S. - Utah *20850*	
	R	*20850* U.S. - Wyoming *20850*	
V	***Cryptantha cinerea*** Higgins & Welsh var. ***arenicola*** Higgins & Welsh *20850*		
	E	*20850* U.S. - Arizona *20850*	
	V	*20850* U.S. - Utah *20850*	
V	***Cryptantha clevelandii*** Greene *20850*		
	I	*20850* U.S. - California *20850*	
E	***Cryptantha clevelandii*** Greene var. ***dissita*** (I.M. Johnston) Jepson & Hoover *20850*		
	E	*20850* U.S. - California *20850*	
V	***Cryptantha compacta*** Higgins *20850*		
	V	*20850* U.S. - Utah *20850*	
R	***Cryptantha corollata*** (I.M. Johnston) I.M. Johnston *20850*		
	I	*20850* U.S. - California *20850*	
E	***Cryptantha crassipes*** I.M. Johnston *20850*		
	E	*20850* U.S. - Texas *20850*	
V	***Cryptantha creutzfeldtii*** Welsh *20850*		
	V	*20850* U.S. - Utah *20850*	
E	***Cryptantha crinita*** Greene *20850*		
	E	*20850* U.S. - California *20850*	
R	***Cryptantha dumetorum*** (Greene ex Gray) Greene *20850*		
	I	*20850* U.S. - Arizona *20850*	
	I	*20850* U.S. - California *20850*	
	I	*20850* U.S. - Nevada *20850*	
	E	*20850* U.S. - Utah *20850*	
R	***Cryptantha elata*** (Eastw.) Payson *20850*		
	V	*20850* U.S. - Colorado *20850*	
	V	*20850* U.S. - Utah *20850*	
V	***Cryptantha ganderi*** I.M. Johnston *20883, 20850, 8058*		
	E	*20850* U.S. - Arizona *20850*	
	E	*20850* U.S. - California *20850*	
		20883 Mexico *20883*	
R	***Cryptantha glomeriflora*** Greene *20850*		
	I	*20850* U.S. - California *20850*	
R	***Cryptantha grahamii*** I.M. Johnston *20850*		

R		20850 U.S. - Utah *20850*	
R	***Cryptantha hoffmannii*** I.M. Johnston *20850*		
	I	*20850* U.S. - California *20850*	
	I	*20850* U.S. - Nevada *20850*	
R	***Cryptantha inaequata*** I.M. Johnston *20850*		
	I	*20850* U.S. - Arizona *20850*	
	I	*20850* U.S. - California *20850*	
	I	*20850* U.S. - Nevada *20850*	
	E	*20850* U.S. - Utah *20850*	
V	***Cryptantha incana*** Greene *20850*		
	I	*20850* U.S. - California *20850*	
Ex/E	***Cryptantha insolita*** (J.F. Macbr.) Payson *20850, 14662*		
	Ex/E	*20850* U.S. - Nevada *20850*	
E	***Cryptantha johnstonii*** Higgins *20850*		
	E	*20850* U.S. - Utah *20850*	
V	***Cryptantha jonesiana*** (Payson) Payson *20850*		
	V	*20850* U.S. - Utah *20850*	
R	***Cryptantha leiocarpa*** (Fisch. & C.A. Mey.) Greene *20850*		
	I	*20850* U.S. - California *20850*	
	I	*20850* U.S. - Oregon *20850*	
V	***Cryptantha leucophaea*** (Dougl. ex Lehm.) Payson *20850*		
	I	*20850* Canada - British Columbia *20850*	
	Ex/E	*20850* U.S. - Oregon *20850*	
	V	*20850* U.S. - Washington *20850*	
R	***Cryptantha longiflora*** (A. Nels.) Payson *20850*		
	I	*20850* U.S. - Colorado *20850*	
	V	*20850* U.S. - Utah *20850*	
R	***Cryptantha mensana*** (M.E. Jones) Payson *20850*		
	E	*20850* U.S. - Colorado *20850*	
	R	*20850* U.S. - Utah *20850*	
R	***Cryptantha microstachys*** (Greene ex Gray) Greene *20850*		
	I	*20850* U.S. - California *20850*	
R	***Cryptantha milo-bakeri*** I.M. Johnston *20850*		
	I	*20850* U.S. - California *20850*	
	I	*20850* U.S. - Oregon *20850*	
R	***Cryptantha mohavensis*** (Greene) Greene *20850*		
	I	*20850* U.S. - California *20850*	
R	***Cryptantha muricata*** (Hook. & Arn.) A. Nels. & J.F. Macbr. *20850*		
	I	*20850* U.S. - Arizona *20850*	
	I	*20850* U.S. - California *20850*	
	I	*20850* U.S. - Nevada *20850*	
E	***Cryptantha muricata*** (Hook. & Arn.) A.Nels. & J.F.Macbr. var. ***clokeyi*** (I.M.Johnston) *20850*		
	?	*20850* U.S. - California *20850*	
R	***Cryptantha nemaclada*** Greene *20850*		
	I	*20850* U.S. - California *20850*	
R	***Cryptantha nubigena*** (Greene) Payson *20850*		
	Ex/E	*20850* Canada - British Columbia *20850*	
	I	*20850* U.S. - California *20850*	
E	***Cryptantha ochroleuca*** Higgins *20850*		
	E	*20850* U.S. - Utah *20850*	
R	***Cryptantha osterhoutii*** (Payson) Payson *20850*		
	I	*20850* U.S. - Arizona *20850*	
	E	*20850* U.S. - Colorado *20850*	
	V	*20850* U.S. - Utah *20850*	
R	***Cryptantha oxygona*** (Gray) Greene *20850*		
	I	*20850* U.S. - California *20850*	
	I	*20850* U.S. - Nevada *20850*	

R   *Cryptantha paradoxa* (A. Nels.) Payson *20850*
- I   20850   U.S. - Colorado *20850*
- V   20850   U.S. - New Mexico *20850*
- R   20850   U.S. - Utah *20850*

R   *Cryptantha paysonii* (J.F. Macbr.) I.M. Johnston *20850*
- R   20850   U.S. - New Mexico *20850*
- E   20850   U.S. - Texas *20850*

V   *Cryptantha roosiorum* Munz *20850*
- V   20850   U.S. - California *20850*

R   *Cryptantha salmonensis* (A. Nels. & J.F. Macbr.) Payson *20850*
- R   20850   U.S. - Idaho *20850*

E   *Cryptantha schoolcraftii* Tiehm *20850*
- R   20850   U.S. - Nevada *20850*

R   *Cryptantha scoparia* A. Nels. *20850*
- I   20850   U.S. - California *20850*
- I   20850   U.S. - Colorado *20850*
- I   20850   U.S. - Idaho *20850*
- E   20850   U.S. - Montana *20850*
- I   20850   U.S. - Nevada *20850*
- I   20850   U.S. - Oregon *20850*
- E   20850   U.S. - Utah *20850*
- I   20850   U.S. - Washington *20850*
- E   20850   U.S. - Wyoming *20850*

V   *Cryptantha semiglabra* Barneby *20850*
- V   20850   U.S. - Arizona *20850*
- E   20850   U.S. - Utah *20850*

R   *Cryptantha similis* Mathew & Raven *20850*
- I   20850   U.S. - California *20850*

R   *Cryptantha sobolifera* Payson *20850*
- I   20850   U.S. - California *20850*
- I   20850   U.S. - Idaho *20850*
- V   20850   U.S. - Montana *20850*
- I   20850   U.S. - Nevada *20850*
- I   20850   U.S. - Oregon *20850*

R   *Cryptantha sparsiflora* (Greene) Greene *20850*
- I   20850   U.S. - California *20850*

R   *Cryptantha stricta* (Osterhout) Payson *20850*
- I   20850   U.S. - Colorado *20850*
- R   20850   U.S. - Utah *20850*
- V   20850   U.S. - Wyoming *20850*

E   *Cryptantha subcapitata* Dorn & Lichvar *20850*
- E   20850   U.S. - Wyoming *20850*

V   *Cryptantha traskiae* I.M. Johnston *20850*
- V   20850   U.S. - California *20850*

E   *Cryptantha welshii* Thorne & Higgins *20850*
- R   20850   U.S. - Nevada *20850*

R   *Cynoglossum borbonicum* Bory *10082*
- R   10082   Réunion *10082*
- Ex   20771   Mauritius *10082*

R   *Cynoglossum sphacioticum* Boiss. & Heldr. *20171*
- R   20730   Greece - Crete *20730*

V   *Cynoglossum troodi* Lindb.f. *14230*
- V   19164   Cyprus (Troodos) *14230*

V   *Dasynotus daubenmirei* I.M. Johnston *20850*
- V   20850   U.S. - Idaho *20850*

V   *Echiostachys spicatus* (Burm.f.) Levyns *20604*
- V   20604   South Africa - Cape Province *20604*

V   *Echium acanthocarpum* Svent. *15358*
- V   20750   Spain - Canary Is. *19174*

E   *Echium auberianum* Webb & Berthel. *17530*
- E   15105   Spain - Canary Is. *15105*

V   *Echium bethencourtii* Santos *15105*
- V   15105   Spain - Canary Is. *15105*

V   *Echium callithyrsum* Webb ex Bolle *15105*
- V   15105   Spain - Canary Is. *15105*

V   *Echium cantabricum* (Lainz) Fernandez Casas & Lainz *11496*
- V   11496   Spain *11496*

R   *Echium canum* Emberger & Maire
- R   Morocco

V   *Echium decaisnei* Webb ssp. *purpuriense* Bramwell
- V   Spain - Canary Is. *5314*

V   *Echium gentianoides* Webb ex Coincy *14166*
- V   20750   Spain - Canary Is. *15105*

V   *Echium giganteum* L.f. *15105*
- V   15105   Spain - Canary Is. *15105*

V   *Echium handiense* Svent. *15105*
- V   20750   Spain - Canary Is. *15105*

V   *Echium hierrense* Webb ex Bolle *15105*
- V   20750   Spain - Canary Is. *15105*

V   *Echium leucophaeum* Webb ex Sprague & Hutch. *15105*
- V   20750   Spain - Canary Is. *15105*

V   *Echium onosmifolium* Webb ssp. *spectabile* Kunkel
- V   Spain - Canary Is.

V   *Echium pininana* Webb & Berthel. *15105*
- V   20750   Spain - Canary Is. *15105*

E   *Echium saetabense* Peris, Figuerola & Stübing *20692*
- E   20692   Spain (near Ayora, Valencia province) *20692*

R   *Echium scaettae* Pampan.
- R   Libya

V   *Echium simplex* DC. *15105*
- V   15105   Spain - Canary Is. *15105*

V   *Echium strictum* L.f. ssp. *exasperatum* (Webb ex Coincy) Bram.
- V   Spain - Canary Is.

R   *Echium strictum* L.f. ssp. *gomeraeum* (Svent.) Bram.
- R   Spain - Canary Is.

V   *Echium sventenii* D. Bramwell *15105*
- V   20750   Spain - Canary Is. *15105*

V   *Echium triste* Svent. ssp. *nivariense* (Svent.) Bram.
- V   Spain - Canary Is.

V   *Echium triste* Svent. ssp. *triste* *15105*
- V   15105   Spain - Canary Is. *15105*

R   *Echium virescens* DC. *15105*
- R   15105   Spain - Canary Is. *15105*

R   *Echium webbii* Coincy *15105*
- R   15105   Spain - Canary Is. *15105*

R   *Echium wildpretii* H. Pearson ex Hook.f. *17530*
- R   20750   Spain - Canary Is. *15105*

V   *Echium wildpretii* H. Pearson ex Hook.f. ssp. *trichosiphon* (Svent.) Bram. *15105*
- V   15105   Spain - Canary Is. *15105*

V   *Ehretia glandulosissima* Verdc. *20556*
- V   20885   Tanzania (Lindi Region) *20556*

R   *Ehretia grahamii* Randell *20681*

R		20681	Australia - Queensland *20681*

I *Ehretia wightiana* **Wallich ex G. Don**

    I   India - Tamil Nadu (Tirunelveli District)

I *Eritrichium nanum* **(L.) Schrad. ex Gaudin ssp.** *jankae* *17823, 20171*

    I   *17823*   Czech Republic *17823*
    I   *17823*   Slovakia *17823*

E *Gyrocaryum oppositifolium* **Valdés** *19818*

    E   *19818*   Spain (Sierra Norte de Sevilla) *19818*

V *Hackelia brevicula* **(Jepson) J.L. Gentry** *20850*

    V   *20850*   U.S. - California *20850*

R *Hackelia ciliata* **(Dougl. ex Lehm.) I.M. Johnston** *20850, 14430*

    I   *20850*   Canada - Alberta *20850*
    E   *20850*   Canada - British Columbia *20850*
    I   *20850*   U.S. - Idaho *20850*
    I   *20850*   U.S. - Washington *20850*

V *Hackelia cronquistii* **J.L. Gentry** *20850*

    E   *20850*   U.S. - Idaho *20850*
    I   *20850*   U.S. - Nevada *20850*
    V   *20850*   U.S. - Oregon *20850*

R *Hackelia davisii* **Cronq.** *20850*

    R   *20850*   U.S. - Idaho *20850*

V *Hackelia diffusa* **(Dougl. ex Lehm.) I.M. Johnston var.** *diffusa* *20850, 14430*

    V   *20850*   Canada - British Columbia *20850*
    I   *20850*   U.S. - Idaho *20850*
    V   *20850*   U.S. - Oregon *20850*
    V   *20850*   U.S. - Washington *20850*

V *Hackelia gracilenta* **(Eastw.) I.M. Johnston** *20850*

    V   *20850*   U.S. - Colorado *20850*

R *Hackelia hispida* **R.L. Carr var.** *disjuncta* **R.L. Carr** *20850*

    R   *20850*   U.S. - Washington *20850*

E *Hackelia ibapensis* **L.& J. Shultz** *20850*

    E   *20850*   U.S. - Utah *20850*

R *Hackelia ophiobia* **R.L. Carr** *20850*

    V   *20850*   U.S. - Idaho *20850*
    V   *20850*   U.S. - Nevada *20850*
    E   *20850*   U.S. - Oregon *20850*

V *Hackelia patens* **J.L. Gentry var.** *harrisonii* **J.L. Gentry** *20850*

    V   *20850*   U.S. - Utah *20850*

E *Hackelia venusta* **(Piper) St. John** *20850*

    E   *20850*   U.S. - Washington *20850*

R *Halacsya sendtneri* **(Boiss.) Dörfl.** *20178, 20171*

    R   *20178*   Albania *20178*
    R   *21091*   Bosnia & Herzegovina *21091*
    R   (former) Yugoslavia

R *Harpagonella palmeri* **Gray var.** *palmeri* *20850*

    I   *20850*   U.S. - Arizona *20850*
    V   *20850*   U.S. - California *20850*

V *Heliotropium anderssonii* **Robinson** *11117*

    V   Ecuador - Galapagos (Santa Cruz) *11117*

R *Heliotropium anomalum* **Hook. & Arn.** *20850*

    I   *20850*   U.S. - Hawaii *20850*

I *Heliotropium bacciferum* **Forsk. var.** *suberosum* **(Clark) Bhandari** *7771*

    I   India - Gujarat (Kutch. north-east Rajastan) *7771*
    I   Pakistan (Sind) *7771*

V *Heliotropium dentatum* **Balf. f.** *15534*

V		15534	Yemen - Socotra *15534*

V *Heliotropium ferreyrae* **I.M. Johnston** *18200*

    V   *9446*   Peru *18200*

I *Heliotropium ferrugineogriseum* **Nab.** *12840*

    I   *12840*   Turkey *12840*

V *Heliotropium guanicense* **Urban** *20883, 8058*

    I   *20883*   Puerto Rico *20883*

R *Heliotropium haussknechtii* **Bunge** *12840*

    R   *12840*   Turkey *12840*

V *Heliotropium marchionicum* **Decne.** *20845*

    V   *20845*   French Polynesia - Marquesas Is (Eiao, Nuku Hiva) *20845*

R *Heliotropium myriophyllum* **Urban** *5607*

    R   *19105*   Cuba (Camaguey) *5607*

R *Heliotropium odorum* **Balf. f.** *15534*

    R   *15534*   Yemen - Socotra *15534*

Ex *Heliotropium pannifolium* **Burchell ex Hemsley** *18996*

    Ex   *18996*   St Helena *18996*

V *Heliotropium pilosum* **Ruiz Lopez & Pavon** *18200*

    V   *9446*   Peru *18200*

R *Heliotropium serpylloides* **Griseb.** *5607*

    R   *19105*   Cuba (SC; Gu) *5607*

R *Lappula echinophora* **(Pall.) Kuntze** *20171*

    R   former European USSR

R *Lappula glabrata* **Popov**

    R   former USSR *6930*

R *Lepidocordia williamsii* **(I.M. Johnston) J.S. Miller** *16826*

    R   *16826*   Nicaragua *16826*

Ex *Lindelofia angustifolia* **(Schrenk) A. Brand.** *6930*

    Ex   *6930*   former USSR *6930*

E *Lithodora nitida* **(Ern) R.Fern.** *8000, 20171*

    E   *19174*   Spain (Sierra Magina) *11496*

R *Lithodora zahnii* **(Heldr. ex Halácsy) I.M.Johnst.** *20171*

    R   Greece

V *Lithospermum confine* **I.M. Johnston** *20850*

    I   *20850*   U.S. - Arizona *20850*
    I   *20850*   U.S. - New Mexico *20850*
    I   *20850*   U.S. - Texas *20850*

R *Lithospermum goulandriorum* **Rech.f.**

    R   Greece

E *Lobostemon bolusii* **Levyns** *20604*

    E   *20604*   South Africa - Cape Province *20604*

V *Lobostemon capitatus* **(L.) H.Buek** *20604*

    V   *20604*   South Africa - Cape Province *20604*

R *Lobostemon collinus* **Schltr. ex C.H.Wright** *20604*

    R   *20604*   South Africa - Cape Province *20604*

V *Lobostemon hottentoticus* **Levyns** *20604*

    V   *20604*   South Africa - Cape Province *20604*

R *Lobostemon regulareflorus* **(Ker Gawl.) Buys** *20604*

    R   *20604*   South Africa - Cape Province *20604*

E *Macromeria alba* **Nesom** *20883*

    E   *20883*   Mexico *20883*

R *Mattiastrum lithospermifolium* **(Lam.) Brand** *20171*

    R   Greece

V *Mertensia cusickii* **Piper** *20850*

    I   *20850*   U.S. - California *20850*
    I   *20850*   U.S. - Idaho *20850*

V	20850	U.S. - Nevada 20850
I	20850	U.S. - Oregon 20850

V *Mertensia drummondii* (Lehm.) G. Don 20850, 6796, 21309

E	20850	Canada - Franklin 20850
I	20850	Canada - Yukon Territory 20850
V	20850	U.S. - Alaska 20850

R *Mertensia macdougalii* Heller 20850

I	20850	U.S. - Arizona 20850

R *Mertensia paniculata* (Ait.) G. Don var. *eastwoodiae* (J.F. Macbr.) Hulten 20850

I	20850	Canada - Mackenzie 20850
R	20850	U.S. - Alaska 20850

V *Mertensia platyphylla* Heller 20850

I	20850	Canada - British Columbia 20850
I	20850	U.S. - Oregon 20850
I	20850	U.S. - Washington 20850

R *Mertensia pterocarpa* (Turcz.) Tatew. & Ohwi 10573

R	10573	Japan 10573

R *Moltkia doerfleri* Wettst. 20178, 20171

R	20178	Albania 20178

R *Moltkia suffruticosa* (L.) Brand 18264, 20171

R	18264	Italy (Veneto, Tuscany) 18264

R *Myosotidium hortensia* (Decne.) Baillon 86

R	19305	New Zealand - Chatham Is. 19106

E *Myosotis albo-sericea* Hook.f. 86

E	19305	New Zealand - South Is. 19305

R *Myosotis amabilis* Cheeseman

R		New Zealand - North Is.

R *Myosotis ambigens* (Bég.) Grau 20171

R		Italy

R *Myosotis azorica* H.C.Watson 8000, 20171

R		Portugal - Azores 8000

V *Myosotis colensoi* (Kirk) J.F. Macbr. 86

V	19305	New Zealand - South Is. 19305

R *Myosotis concinna* Cheeseman 19305

R	19305	New Zealand - South Is. 19305

I *Myosotis czekanowskii* (Trautv.) Kamelin & V. Tikhom. 5942

I	5942	Russia (Siberia) - Yakutiya (north) 5942

R *Myosotis gallica* Vestergr. 20171

R		France (south-east)

R *Myosotis laeta* Cheeseman 19305

R	19305	New Zealand - South Is. 19305

V *Myosotis lusitanica* R.Schust. 8000, 20171

V	20076	Portugal 8000

R *Myosotis macrosiphon* Font Quer & Maire

R		Morocco

R *Myosotis matthewsii* L. Moore 19305

R	19305	New Zealand - North Is. 19305

V *Myosotis oreophila* Petrie 19305

V	19305	New Zealand - South Is. 19305

Ex *Myosotis petiolata* Hook.f. var. *pottsiana* L. Moore

Ex		New Zealand - North Is.

R *Myosotis platyphylla* Boiss. 12840

R	12840	Turkey 12840

E *Myosotis rehsteineri* Wartm. 14229, 20171

E		Austria
E	20640	Germany 20644

E	18264	Italy (Piedmont, Lombardy) 19997
E	14229	Liechtenstein 14229
E	18154	Switzerland 18154

E *Myosotis retusifolia* R. Afonso 20076

E	20076	Portugal 20076

E *Myosotis ruscinonensis* Rouy 14166, 20171

E	14188	France (south) 14188

E *Myosotis solange* Grenter & Zaffan 19121

E	20730	Greece - Crete 20730

R *Myosotis transsylvanica* Porcius 8000, 20171

R	19607	Romania 8000

Ex *Myosotis traversii* Hook.f. var. *cinerascens* (Petrie) L. Moore 19305

Ex	19305	New Zealand - South Is. 19305

E *Nesocaryum stylosum* (Philippi) I.M. Johnston 5595

E	19534	Chile - Islas Desventurados 5595

R *Nomosa rosei* I.M. Johnston 11181

R	11181	Mexico - Durango 11181

I *Nonea anomala* Hausskn. & Bornm. 12840

I	12840	Turkey 12840

I *Nonea karsensis* M. Popov 12840

I	12840	Turkey 12840

R *Nonea pulmonarioides* Boiss. & Bal. 12840

R	12840	Turkey 12840

R *Nonea vivianii* A. DC. 10270

R		Egypt (W.Med. coast) 10269
R		Libya 10270

R *Omphalodes brassicifolia* (Lag.) Sweet 20171

R	20660	Spain (Cádiz, Málaga) 20661

R *Omphalodes chiangii* Higgins 9094

R	9094	Mexico - Coahuila 9094

I *Omphalodes commutata* G. Lopez 20660

I	20660	Spain (Cádiz, Málaga) 20661

R *Omphalodes davisana* Kit Tan & Sorger 12840

R	12840	Turkey 12840

R *Omphalodes laevisperma* Nakai 10573

R	10573	Japan 10573

V *Omphalodes littoralis* Lehm. 20171

V	20528	France (west coast) 20528

E *Omphalodes littoralis* Lehm. ssp. *gallaecica* M. Lainz 10270

E	20874	Spain (north-west) 10270

R *Omphalodes pavoniana* Boiss. 20171

R		Spain

V *Omphalodes prolifera* Ohwi 10573

V	10573	Japan 10573

R *Omphalodes ripleyana* Davis 12840

R	12840	Turkey 12840

Ex *Onosma affine* Hausskn. ex H. Riedl 12840

Ex	12840	Turkey 12840

R *Onosma angustissimum* Hausskn. & Bornm. 12840

R	12840	Turkey 12840

R *Onosma arcuatum* H. Riedl 12840

R	12840	Turkey 12840

R *Onosma argentatum* Huber-Mor. 12840

R	12840	Turkey 12840

R *Onosma bozakmanii* H. Riedl 12840

R	12840	Turkey 12840

R *Onosma briquetii* Czecz. 12840

R		12840	Turkey	*12840*

R *Onosma bubanii* Stroh *20171*
    R   Spain

R *Onosma caespitosum* Kotschy *14230*
    R   *19164*   Cyprus (Northern Range) *14230*

R *Onosma cappadocicum* Siehe ex H. Riedl *12840*
    R   *12840*   Turkey *12840*

R *Onosma cyrenaicum* E. Dur. & G. Barratte
    R   Libya

R *Onosma davisii* H. Reidl *12840*
    R   *12840*   Turkey *12840*

Ex *Onosma discedens* Hausskn. ex Bornm. *12840*
    Ex   *12840*   Turkey *12840*

V *Onosma elegantissima* Rech.f. & Goulimy *20171*
    V   *19121*   Greece - Crete *19121*

R *Onosma euboica* Rech.f. *20171*
    R   Greece

R *Onosma fastigiata* (Braun-Blanq.) Braun-Blanq. ex
    Lacaita *8000, 20171*
    R   France (south) *8000*
    R   Italy (north-west) *8000*

E *Onosma fastigiata* (Br.-Bl.) Lacaita ssp. *atlantica*
    Br.-Bl. ex Kerguélen *20528, 20528*
    E   *20528*   France (west) *20528*

V *Onosma halophilum* Boiss. & Heldr. *12840*
    V   *12840*   Turkey *12840*

R *Onosma helleri* Greuter & Burdet *12840*
    R   *12840*   Turkey *12840*

R *Onosma intertextum* Huber-Mor. *12840*
    R   *12840*   Turkey *12840*

R *Onosma leptantha* Heldr. *20171*
    R   Greece

I *Onosma linearilobum* Hausskn. ex H. Riedl *12840*
    I   *12840*   Turkey *12840*

R *Onosma liparioides* DC. *12840*
    R   *12840*   Turkey *12840*

R *Onosma lycaonicum* Huber-Mor. *12840*
    R   *12840*   Turkey *12840*

R *Onosma neglectum* H. Reidl *12840*
    R   *12840*   Turkey *12840*

R *Onosma nigricaula* H. Riedl *12840*
    R   *12840*   Turkey *12840*

R *Onosma obtusifolium* Hausskn. & Sint. ex Bornm. *12840*
    R   *12840*   Turkey *12840*

I *Onosma papillosum* H. Riedl. *12840*
    I   *12840*   Turkey *12840*

R *Onosma polyanthum* DC. *12840*
    R   *12840*   Turkey *12840*

I *Onosma polyphylla* Ledeb. *5942, 20171*
    I   *5942*   Russia - North Caucasus (north) *5942*
    I   *5942*   Ukraine - Crimea *5942*

R *Onosma proballantherum* Rech.f. *12840*
    R   *12840*   Turkey *12840*

E *Onosma proponticum* Aznav. *12840*
    E   *12840*   Turkey *12840*

V *Onosma psammophila* Rech.f. & Riedl
    V   Greece

E *Onosma pseudarenaria* Schur *8000, 20171*

    E   *8000*   Romania *8000*

R *Onosma pseudoarenaria* Schur ssp. *delphinensis*
    (Br.-Bl.) P. Fourn. *20528*
    R   *20528*   Italy *20528*

R *Onosma pulchrum* H. Riedl *12840*
    R   *12840*   Turkey *12840*

R *Onosma rhodopea* Velen.
    I   Bulgaria
    R   Greece

R *Onosma rutilum* Huber- Mor. *12840*
    R   *12840*   Turkey *12840*

R *Onosma sieheanum* Hayek *12840*
    R   *12840*   Turkey *12840*

R *Onosma sintenisii* Hausskn. ex Bornm. *12840*
    R   *12840*   Turkey *12840*

R *Onosma sorgeri* Teppner var. *sorgeri* *12840*
    R   *12840*   Turkey *12840*

R *Onosma strigosissimum* Boiss. *12840*
    R   *12840*   Turkey *12840*

R *Onosma subulifolium* Riedl *12840*
    R   *12840*   Turkey *12840*

I *Onosma taygetea* Boiss. & Heldr. *20171*
    I   Greece

I *Onosma tornensis* Jáv. *8000, 20171*
    E   *19710*   Hungary (north) *6951*
    I   *19710*   Slovakia (south-east) *6951*

R *Onosma troodi* Kotschy *14230*
    R   *19164*   Cyprus (Troodos) *14230*

I *Onosma tschichatschevii* Popov *12840*
    I   *12840*   Turkey *12840*

R *Onosma velutinum* Boiss. *12840*
    R   *12840*   Turkey *12840*

R *Onosmodium helleri* Small *20850*
    R   *20850*   U.S. - Texas *20850*

R *Onosmodium molle* Michaux ssp. *bejariense* (DC. ex
    A. DC.) Cochrane *20850*
    R   *20850*   U.S. - Texas *20850*

R *Onosmodium molle* Michaux ssp. *molle* *20850*
    V   *20850*   U.S. - Alabama *20850*
    I   *20850*   U.S. - Illinois *20850*
    E   *20850*   U.S. - Kentucky *20850*
    I   *20850*   U.S. - Missouri *20850*
    R   *20850*   U.S. - Tennessee *20850*

R *Paracaryum amani* (Rchb.f.) R. Mill *12840*
    R   *12840*   Turkey *12840*

R *Paracaryum artvinense* R. Mill *12840*
    R   *12840*   Turkey *12840*

I *Paracaryum coelastinum* (Lindley) Benth.
    I   India - Karnataka

R *Paracaryum corymbiforme* (DC. & A. DC.) Boiss. *12840*
    R   *12840*   Turkey *12840*

R *Paracaryum erysimifolium* Boiss. *12840*
    R   *12840*   Turkey *12840*

R *Paracaryum kurdistanicum* (Brand) R. Mill *12840*
    R   *12840*   Turkey *12840*

I *Paracaryum leptophyllum* (A. DC.) Boiss. *12840*
    I   *12840*   Turkey *12840*

R *Paracaryum lithospermifolium* (Lam.) Grande var.
    erectum R. Mill. *12840*
    R   *12840*   Turkey *12840*

I	*Paracaryum malabaricum* C.B. Clarke	
	I	India - Karnataka (Canara & Mysore)
R	*Paracaryum paphlagonicum* (Bornm.) R. Mill *12840*	
	R	*12840* Turkey *12840*
R	*Paracaryum polycarpum* (Rech.f.) R. Mill *12840*	
	R	*12840* Turkey *12840*
R	*Paracaryum reuteri* Boiss. & Hausskn. *12840*	
	R	*12840* Turkey *12840*
R	*Paracaryum shepardii* Post & Beauv. *12840*	
	R	*12840* Turkey *12840*
R	*Paracaryum stenolophum* Boiss. *12840*	
	R	*12840* Turkey *12840*
R	*Paraskevia cesatiana* (Fenzl & Friedr.) W. & G. Sauer	
	R	Greece
R	*Perittostema pinetorum* I.M. Johnston *11181*	
	R	*11181* Mexico *11181*
R	*Plagiobothrys chorisianus* (Cham.) I.M. Johnston *20850*	
	I	*20850* U.S. - California *20850*
V	*Plagiobothrys chorisianus* (Cham.) I.M. Johnston var. *chorisianus* *20850*	
	V	*20850* U.S. - California *20850*
Ex	*Plagiobothrys diffusus* (Greene) I.M. Johnston *20850, 14662*	
	Ex	*20850* U.S. - California *20850*
R	*Plagiobothrys distantiflorus* (Piper) I.M. Johnston ex M.E. Peck *20850*	
	I	*20850* U.S. - California *20850*
E	*Plagiobothrys figuratus* (Piper) I.M. Johnston ex M.E. Peck ssp. *corallicarpus* (Piper) Chambers *20850*	
	E	*20850* U.S. - Oregon *20850*
Ex/E	*Plagiobothrys glaber* (Gray) I.M. Johnston *20850*	
	I	*20850* U.S. - Arizona *20850*
	Ex/E	*20850* U.S. - California *20850*
V	*Plagiobothrys glomeratus* Gray *20850*	
	V	*20850* U.S. - California *20850*
	I	*20850* U.S. - Nevada *20850*
Ex/E	*Plagiobothrys glyptocarpus* (Piper) I.M. Johnston var. *modestus* I.M. Johnston *20850*	
	Ex/E	*20850* U.S. - California *20850*
E	*Plagiobothrys hirtus* (Greene) I.M. Johnston *20850*	
	E	*20850* U.S. - Oregon *20850*
V	*Plagiobothrys humistratus* (Greene) I.M. Johnston *20850*	
	I	*20850* U.S. - California *20850*
Ex/E	*Plagiobothrys hystriculus* (Piper) I.M. Johnston *20850*	
	Ex/E	*20850* U.S. - California *20850*
Ex/E	*Plagiobothrys lamprocarpus* (Piper) I.M. Johnston *20850, 14662*	
	Ex/E	*20850* U.S. - Oregon *20850*
Ex/E	*Plagiobothrys lithocaryus* (Greene ex Gray) I.M. Johnston *20850*	
	Ex/E	*20850* U.S. - California *20850*
Ex	*Plagiobothrys mollis* (A. Gray) I.M. Johnston var. *vestitus* (Greene) I.M. Johnston *20850*	
	Ex	*20850* U.S. - California *20850*
R	*Plagiobothrys parishii* I.M. Johnston *20850*	
	I	*20850* U.S. - California *20850*
R	*Plagiobothrys scriptus* (Greene) I.M. Johnston *20850*	
	E	*20850* U.S. - California *20850*
E	*Plagiobothrys strictus* (Greene) I.M. Johnston *20850*	
	E	*20850* U.S. - California *20850*
V	*Plagiobothrys uncinatus* J.T. Howell *20850*	
	V	*20850* U.S. - California *20850*
I	*Podonosma galalensis* Schweinf. ex Boiss. *16168*	
	I	*16168* Egypt (Galala Desert) *16168*
R	*Procopiania circinalis* (Runemark) Pawl.	
	R	Greece
R	*Procopiania insularis* Pawl. *20731*	
	R	Greece
R	*Pulmonaria filarszkyana* Jáv. *17762, 20171*	
	R	*20631* Romania *20631*
	V	former European USSR
R	*Rindera graeca* (A.DC.) Boiss. & Heldr. *20171*	
	R	Greece
R	*Rindera gymnandra* (Coss.) Guerke *10488*	
	R	*14958* Algeria *10488*
R	*Rochefortia acrantha* Urb. *20883, 13336*	
	R	*13336* Jamaica *20883*
V	*Rochefortia oblongata* Urban & Ekman *5607*	
	V	*19105* Cuba (Santiago de Cuba) *5607*
V	*Selkirkia berteroi* (Colla) Hemsley *19116*	
	V	*19125* Chile - Juan Fernandez Is. *19116*
R	*Solenanthus albanicus* (Degen & Bald.) Degen & Bald. *8000, 20171*	
	R	*20178* Albania *8000*
	E	Greece *8000*
R	*Solenanthus atlanticus* Pitard	
	R	Morocco
R	*Solenanthus formosus* R. Mill *12840*	
	R	*12840* Turkey *12840*
R	*Solenanthus pindicus* Alden	
	R	Greece
E	*Solenanthus reverchonii* Degen *19818, 20171*	
	E	*19818* Spain (Jaén & Granada) *19818*
R	*Solenanthus scardicus* Bornm. *20178, 20171*	
	V	*20178* Albania *20178*
	R	(former) Yugoslavia
R	*Solenanthus tubiflorus* Murb.	
	R	Algeria
	R	Tunisia
E	*Symphytum cycladense* Pawl *8000, 20171*	
	E	Greece (S. Aegean region) *8000*
R	*Symphytum davisii* Wickens *20171*	
	R	Greece
R	*Symphytum gussonei* F.W.Schultz *20171*	
	R	*19164* Italy - Sicily *19164*
R	*Symphytum icaricum* Pawl.	
	R	Greece
R	*Symphytum longipetiolatum* Wickens *12840*	
	R	*12840* Turkey *12840*
R	*Symphytum longisetum* Huber-Mor. & Wickens *12840*	
	R	*12840* Turkey *12840*
R	*Symphytum naxicola* Pawl *20171*	
	R	Greece
V	*Symphytum pseudobulbosum* Asnav *12840*	
	V	*12840* Turkey *12840*

R   *Symphytum savvalense* Kurtto *12840*
    R   *12840* Turkey *12840*

R   *Symphytum sylvaticum* Boiss. *12840*
    R   *12840* Turkey *12840*

I   *Tianschaniella umbellulifera* B. Fedtsch. ex
        Popov *5942*
    I   *5942* Kyrgyzstan *5942*

E   *Tiquilia ferreyrae* (I.M. Johnston) A.
        Richardson *18200*
    E   *9446* Peru *18200*

E   *Tournefortia arborescens* Lam. *10082*
    E   *14234* Réunion *10082*

E   *Tournefortia bojeri* A. DC. *10082*
    E   *14234* Réunion *14234*
    Ex   *20771* Mauritius *10082*

R   *Tournefortia brenesii* Standley *9037*
    R   *11181* Costa Rica *9037*
    R   *11181* Panama *10747*

R   *Tournefortia longispica* J.S. Miller *11675*
    R   *11181* Panama *11675*

R   *Tournefortia multiflora* J.S. Miller *11675*
    R   *11181* Panama *11675*

V   *Tournefortia roxburghii* Clarke *14872*
    V   *14872* Bangladesh *14872*

V   *Tournefortia smaragdina* Proctor *20883, 13336*
    V   *13336* Jamaica *20883*

R   *Tournefortia staminea* Griseb. *20883*
    R   *20883* Jamaica *20883*

R   *Tournefortia urceolata* J.S. Miller *11675*
    R   *11181* Panama *11675*

V   *Trichodesma scottii* Balf.f. *15534*
    V   *15534* Yemen - Socotra (Hajhir & Majhah) *15534*

R   *Trigonotis ikumae* Makino *10573*
    R   *10573* Japan *10573*

R   *Trigonotis nankotaizanensis* (Sasaki) Masamune & Ohwi ex
        Masamune *20511*
    R   *20511* Taiwan *20511*

I   *Wellstedia socotrana* Balf. f. *15534*
    I   *15534* Yemen - Socotra *15534*
    I   *15534* Somalia *15534*

Bretschneideraceae

Number of genera: 1
Number of species: 1
Recorded threatened species: 1   (100%)

Mountains of western and southwestern China.

R   *Bretschneidera sinensis* Hemsley *17617*
    R   *17617* China - Fujian *11139*
    R   *17617* China - Guangdong *11139*
    R   *17617* China - Guangxi *11139*
    R   *17617* China - Guizhou *11139*
    R   *17617* China - Hubei *11139*
    R   *17617* China - Hunan *11139*
    R   *17617* China - Jiangxi *11139*
    R   *17617* China - Sichuan *11139*
    R   *17617* China - Yunnan *11139*
    R   *17617* China - Zhejiang *11139*
    R   Taiwan (Taibei) *11139*
    I   *20985* Vietnam (Lai Chau) *6057*

Brunelliaceae

Number of genera: 1
Number of species: 62
Recorded threatened species: 57   (91%)

Tropical America.

E   *Brunellia acostae* Cuatrecasas *20883*
    I   *20883* Ecuador *20883*

E   *Brunellia almaguerensis* Cuatrecasas *20883, 19353*
    I   *19352* Colombia *20883*

V   *Brunellia antioquensis* (Cuatrecasas)
        Cuatrecasas *20883*
    I   *20883* Colombia *20883*

R   *Brunellia boliviana* Britton ex Rusby *20883*
    I   *20883* Bolivia *20883*

E   *Brunellia boliviana* Britton ex Rusby var.
        boliviana *20883*
    I   *20883* Bolivia *20883*

R   *Brunellia boliviana* Britton ex Rusby var. *brittonii*
        Cuatrecasas *20883*
    I   *20883* Bolivia *20883*

E   *Brunellia boqueronensis* Cuatrecasas *20883*
    I   *20883* Colombia *20883*

E   *Brunellia briquetii* Baehni *20883*
    I   *20883* Peru *20883*

E   *Brunellia brunnea* Macbride *20883*
    I   *20883* Peru *20883*

V   *Brunellia bullata* Cuatrecasas *20883*
    I   *20883* Colombia *20883*

E   *Brunellia carpishensis* Cuatrecasas *20883*
    I   *20883* Peru *20883*

V   *Brunellia cayambensis* Cuatrecasas *20883*
    I   *20883* Ecuador *20883*

E   *Brunellia comocladifolia* Humb. & Bonpl. ssp.
        boyacensis Cuatrecasas *20883*
    I   *20883* Colombia *20883*

R   *Brunellia comocladifolia* Humb. & Bonpl. ssp.
        comocladifolia *20883*
    I   *20883* Colombia *20883*
    I   *20883* Ecuador *20883*

R   *Brunellia comocladifolia* Humb. & Bonpl. ssp.
        cubensis Cuatrecasas *20883*
    I   *20883* Cuba *20883*

V   *Brunellia comocladifolia* Humb. & Bonpl. ssp.
        cundinamarcensis Cuatrecasas *20883*
    I   *20883* Colombia *20883*

R   *Brunellia comocladifolia* Humb. & Bonpl. ssp.
        domingensis Cuatrecasas *20883*
    I   *20883* Dominican Republic *20883*
    I   *20883* Haiti *20883*
    I   *20883* Puerto Rico *20883*
            Mexico *21008*
            Peru *21008*

E   *Brunellia comocladifolia* Humb. & Bonpl. ssp.
        guadalupensis Cuatrecasas *20883*
    I   *20883* Guadeloupe *20883*

V   *Brunellia comocladifolia* Humb. & Bonpl. ssp.
        josephensis Cuatrecasas *20883*
    I   *20883* Costa Rica *20883*

V   *Brunellia comocladifolia* Humb. & Bonpl. ssp.

     ptariana (Steyermark) Cuatrecasas *20883*
I   *20883* Venezuela *20883*

E **Brunellia coroicoana** Cuatrecasas *20883*
I   *20883* Bolivia *20883*

E **Brunellia cuatrecasana** Orozco *20883, 19353*
I   *19353* Colombia *20883*

E **Brunellia cutervensis** Cuatrecasas *20883*
I   *20883* Peru *20883*

E **Brunellia cuzcoensis** Cuatrecasas *20883*
I   *20883* Peru *20883*

V **Brunellia darienensis** Cuatr. & Porter *20883*
I   *20883* Panama *20883*
?   Colombia (Cordillera del Darién) *21093*

E **Brunellia dichapetaloides** Macbride *20883*
I   *20883* Peru *20883*

E **Brunellia diversifolia** Orozco *20883, 19353*
I   *19353* Colombia *20883*

V **Brunellia dulcis** Macbride *20883*
I   *20883* Peru *20883*

E **Brunellia ecuadoriensis** Cuatrecasas *20883*
I   *20883* Ecuador *20883*

E **Brunellia elliptica** Cuatrecasas *20883*
I   *20883* Colombia *20883*

E **Brunellia espinalii** Cuatrecasas *20883*
I   *20883* Colombia *20883*

V **Brunellia farallonensis** Cuatrecasas *20883*
I   *20883* Colombia *20883*

E **Brunellia foreroi** Orozco *20883, 19353*
I   *19353* Colombia *20883*

E **Brunellia gentryi** Cuatrecasas *20883*
I   *20883* Colombia *20883*

E **Brunellia glabra** Cuatrecasas *20883*
I   *20883* Colombia *20883*

R **Brunellia goudotii** Tulasne *20883*
I   *20883* Colombia *20883*

E **Brunellia hexasepala** Loesener *20883*
I   *20883* Peru *20883*

E **Brunellia hiltyana** Cuatrecasas *20883, 19353*
I   *19353* Colombia *20883*

E **Brunellia hygrothermica** Cuatrecasas *20883*
I   *20883* Colombia *20883*

R **Brunellia inermis** Ruíz & Pavón *20883*
I   *20883* Peru *20883*

V **Brunellia integrifolia** ssp. *mollis* (Cuatrecasas)
    Cuatrecasas *20883*
I   *20883* Colombia *20883*

E **Brunellia latifolia** Cuatrecasas *20883*
I   *20883* Colombia *20883*

V **Brunellia littlei** Cuatrecasas *20883*
I   *20883* Colombia *20883*

E **Brunellia littlei** Cuatrecasas ssp. *caucana*
    Cuatrecasas *20883*
I   *20883* Colombia *20883*

V **Brunellia littlei** Cuatrecasas ssp.
    littlei *20883*
I   *20883* Colombia *20883*

V **Brunellia macrophylla** Killip & Cuatrecasas *20883*
I   *20883* Colombia *20883*

V **Brunellia morii** Cuatrecasas *21093*
I   *20883* Panama *20883*

V **Brunellia occidentalis** Cuatrecasas *20883, 19353*
E   *19352* Colombia *20883*

E **Brunellia oliveri** Britton *20883*
I   *20883* Bolivia *20883*

R **Brunellia ovalifolia** Humboldt & Bonpland *20883*
I   *20883* Ecuador *20883*

V **Brunellia pallida** Cuatrecasas *20883*
I   *20883* Colombia *20883*

E **Brunellia penderiscana** Cuatrecasas *20883*
I   *20883* Colombia *20883*

V **Brunellia pitayensis** Cuatrecasas *20883, 19353*
I   *19353* Colombia *20883*

R **Brunellia propinqua** Humboldt, Bonpland & Kunth *20883*
I   *20883* Colombia *20883*

R **Brunellia propinqua** Humboldt, Bonpland & Kunth ssp.
    propinqua *20883*
I   *20883* Colombia *20883*

V **Brunellia propinqua** Humboldt, Bonpland & Kunth ssp.
    susaconensis Cuatrecasas *20883*
I   *20883* Colombia *20883*

V **Brunellia putumayensis** Cuatrecasas *20883*
I   *20883* Colombia *20883*

V **Brunellia racemifera** Tulasne *20883*
I   *20883* Colombia *20883*

E **Brunellia rhoides** Rusby *20883*
I   *20883* Bolivia *20883*

E **Brunellia rufa** Killip & Cuatrecasas *20883*
I   *20883* Colombia *20883*

R **Brunellia sibundoya** ssp. *sebastopola*
    Cuatrecasas *20883*
I   *20883* Colombia *20883*

R **Brunellia sibundoya** ssp. *sibundoya* *20883*
I   *20883* Colombia *20883*

V **Brunellia standleyana** Cuatrecasas *20883, 9426*
I   *20883* Costa Rica *20883*

R **Brunellia stenoptera** Diels *20883*
I   *20883* Ecuador *20883*

V **Brunellia stuebelii** Hieronymous *20883*
I   *20883* Colombia *20883*

V **Brunellia subsessilis** Killip & Cuatrecasas *20883*
I   *20883* Colombia *20883*

V **Brunellia trianae** Cuatrecasas *20883*
I   *20883* Colombia *20883*

R **Brunellia trigyna** Cuatrecasas *20883*
I   *20883* Colombia *20883*
I   *20883* Venezuela *20883*

E **Brunellia velutina** Cuatrecasas *20883*
I   *20883* Colombia *20883*

R **Brunellia weberbaueri** Loesener *20883*
I   *20883* Peru *20883*

E **Brunellia zamorensis** Steyermark *20883*
I   *20883* Ecuador *20883*

Bruniaceae

Number of genera:	12-18,289
Number of species:	75
Recorded threatened species:	17 (22%)

South Africa and Natal.

V   *Audouinia capitata* (L.) Brongn. *20604*
    V   *20604* South Africa - Cape Province *20604*

R   *Berzelia dregeana* Colozza *20604*
    R   *20604* South Africa - Cape Province *20604*

R   *Berzelia ecklonii* Pillans *20604*
    R   *20604* South Africa - Cape Province *20604*

R   *Brunia macrocephala* Willd. *20604*
    R   *20604* South Africa - Cape Province *20604*

I   *Lonchostoma esterhuyseniae* Strid *20604*
    I   *20604* South Africa - Cape Province *20604*

R   *Lonchostoma purpureum* Pillans *20604*
    R   *20604* South Africa - Cape Province *20604*

R   *Pseudobaeckea stokoei* Pillans *20604*
    R   *20604* South Africa - Cape Province *20604*

I   *Raspalia barnardii* Pillans *20604*
    I   *20604* South Africa - Cape Province *20604*

R   *Raspalia schlechteri* Dummer *20604*
    R   *20604* South Africa - Cape Province *20604*

E   *Raspalia trigyna* (Schltr.) Dummer *20604, 18289*
    E   *20604* South Africa - Cape Province *20604*
    E   *20604* South Africa - Natal (sandstone region in southern
                Natal) *20604*

Ex   *Staavia brownii* Dummer *20604*
    Ex   *20604* South Africa - Cape Province *20604*

R   *Staavia dodii* Bolus *20604*
    R   *20604* South Africa - Cape Province *20604*

E   *Staavia dregeana* C.Presl *20604*
    E   *20604* South Africa - Cape Province *20604*

R   *Staavia glutinosa* (L.) Dahl *20604*
    R   *20604* South Africa - Cape Province *20604*

Ex   *Staavia phylicoides* Pillans *20604*
    Ex   *20604* South Africa - Cape Province *20604*

I   *Staavia verticillata* (L.f.) Pillans *20604*
    I   *20604* South Africa - Cape Province *20604*

E   *Staavia zeyheri* Sond. *20604*
    E   *20604* South Africa - Cape Province *20604*

Ex   *Thamnea depressa* Oliv. *20604, 6180*
    Ex   *20604* South Africa - Cape Province *20604*

I   *Thamnea gracilis* (Kuntze) Oliv. *20604*
    I   *20604* South Africa - Cape Province *20604*

V   *Thamnea hirtella* Oliv. *20604*
    V   *20604* South Africa - Cape Province *20604*

Ex   *Thamnea uniflora* Sol. ex Brongn. *20604, 6180*
    Ex   *20604* South Africa - Cape Province *20604*

Buddlejaceae

Number of genera:	10
Number of species:	150
Recorded threatened species:	14 (9%)

Mainly tropical and subtropical.

I   *Adenoplusia uluguruensis* Melchior *7959*
    I   *5926* Tanzania (Morogoro Distr.) *7959*

R   *Buddleja chaplana* Robinson *11981*
    R   *20155* Mexico - Jalisco *20155*

R   *Buddleja corrugata* Jones *11981*
    R   *11981* Mexico *11981*

V   *Buddleja formosana* Hatusima *20854*
    V   *20854* Taiwan *20854*

I   *Buddleja ibarrensis* Norman *11351*
    I   *19556* Ecuador *11351*

R   *Buddleja jamesonii* Benth. *11351*
    R   *19556* Ecuador *11351*

R   *Buddleja lanata* Benth. *11351*
    R   *19556* Ecuador *11351*

R   *Buddleja lojensis* Norman *11351*
    R   *19556* Ecuador *11351*

V   *Buddleja longifolia* Hunt.,bonpl.& Kunth. *11351*
    V   *19556* Ecuador *19556*
    V   *19556* Peru *18200*

R   *Buddleja polycephala* Kunth *11351*
    R   *18200* Peru *18200*

R   *Emorya suaveolens* Torr. *20850*
    E   *20850* U.S. - Texas *20850*

R   *Nuxia glomerulata* (C.A.Sm.) I.Verd. *20604*
    R   *20604* South Africa - Transvaal *20604*

R   *Peltanthera floribunda* Benth. *11351*
    R   *11351* Costa Rica *11351*
    R   *11351* Panama *11351*
    R   *11351* Bolivia *11351*
    R   *11351* Colombia *11351*
    R   Ecuador
    R   *18200* Peru *11351*

R   *Sanango racemosum* (Ruiz Lopez & Pavon)
    Barringer *11351*
    R   *18200* Peru *11351*

Burseraceae

Number of genera:	16-20
Number of species:	600
Recorded threatened species:	80 (13%)

Pantropical, especially tropical America and Northeast
Africa.

R   *Beiselia mexicana* Forman *10168*
    R   *10168* Mexico - Michoacan *10168*

E   *Boswellia nana* Hepper *15534*
    E   *15534* Yemen - Socotra *15534*

E   *Boswellia ogadensis* Vollesen *19704*
    E   *19704* Ethiopia (Harerge) *19704*

I   *Boswellia ovalifoliolata* Balakr. & A.N. Henry
    I   India - Andhra Pradesh

R   *Boswellia pirottae* Chiov. *19704*
    R   *19704* Ethiopia (Gonder, Gojam, Wello Upland, Shewa Upland,
                Kefa.) *19704*

V   *Bursera arborea* (Rose) Riley *9114*
    ?   Mexico - Colima *21232*
    ?   Mexico - Durango *21232*
    ?   Mexico - Michoacan *21232*
    ?   Mexico - Nayarit *21232*
    ?   Mexico - Oaxaca *21232*
    V   *19850* Mexico - Sinaloa *11559*

R   *Bursera aromatica* Proctor *20883, 13336*
    R   *13336* Jamaica *20883*

E   *Bursera hollickii* (Britton) F. & R. *13336*

-89-

E		13336 Jamaica *13336*	

R   *Bursera lunanii* (Spreng) Adams & Dandy *20883*
     R   20883 Jamaica *20883*

R   *Bursera malacophylla* Robinson *11117*
     R   Ecuador - Galapagos *11117*

R   *Canarium harveyi* Seem. var. *novaehebridense* *14800*
     R   14800 Solomon Is - Santa Cruz Is *14800*
     R   14800 Vanuatu (Banks group) *14800*

I   *Canarium luzonicum* (Blume) A.Gray *20676, 13780*
     I   Philippines *13780*

V   *Canarium paniculatum* (Lam.) Benth. *10082*
     V   20771 Mauritius *10082*

I   *Canarium perlisanum* Leenh.
     I   Malaysia - Peninsular Malaysia (Perlis)

E   *Canarium whitei* Guillaumin *20893*
     E   20893 New Caledonia *20893*

V   *Canarium zeylanicum* Blume *10276*
     V   12838 Sri Lanka *10276*

R   *Commiphora alata* Chiov. *20884*
     R   20884 Somalia (south) *20884*

R   *Commiphora chaetocarpa* J.B.Gillett *20087*
     R   20087 Kenya *20057*
     R   20884 Somalia (central) *17435*

R   *Commiphora ciliata* Vollesen *20087*
     R   20057 Ethiopia (southern) *17435*
     R   20057 Kenya *20057*
     R   20884 Somalia (central & south) *20884*

R   *Commiphora corrugata* J.B.Gillett & K.Vollesen *20884*
     R   20884 Ethiopia *20884*
     R   20884 Kenya *20884*
     R   20884 Somalia (central & south) *20884*

E   *Commiphora monoica* Vollesen *20087*
     E   19704 Ethiopia (Bale) *19704*

R   *Commiphora obovata* Chiov. *20556*
     R   20884 Ethiopia *20556*
     R   20884 Kenya *20556*
     R   20884 Somalia (north & central) *20556*

R   *Commiphora planifrons* (Balf. f.) Engl. *15534*
     R   15534 Yemen - Socotra *15534*

R   *Commiphora pseudopaolii* J.B.Gillett *20087*
     R   20884 Kenya *20057*
     R   20884 Somalia (central & south) *20884*

R   *Commiphora sulcata* Chiov. *20884*
     R   20884 Somalia (north & central) *20884*

R   *Commiphora swynnertonii* B.D.Burtt *20087*
     R   20057 Kenya *20057*
     R   20057 Tanzania (Mkinke river; Mpwapwa, Kilimalindi) *17435*

R   *Commiphora unilobata* J.B.Gillett & K.Vollesen *20884*
     R   20884 Ethiopia *20884*
     R   20884 Kenya *20884*
     R   20884 Somalia (central & south) *20884*

V   *Crepidospermum cuneifolium* (Cuatrec.) Daly *11559*
     V   11559 Colombia *11559*

V   *Crepidospermum multijugum* Swart *11559*
     V   11559 Peru *11559*

R   *Dacryodes acutipyrena* Cuatrec. *11559*
     R   11559 Colombia *11559*

R   *Dacryodes belemensis* Cuatrec. *11559*
     R   11559 Brazil *11559*

R   *Dacryodes colombiana* Cuatrec. *11559*
     R   11559 Colombia *11559*

R   *Dacryodes cupularis* Cuatrec. *11559*
     R   11559 Colombia *11559*

E   *Dacryodes cuspidata* (Cuatrec.) Daly *20883, 11559*
     I   20883 Brazil *20883*
     R   11559 Colombia *11559*
     I   20883 Venezuela *20883*

R   *Dacryodes glabra* (Steyerm.) Cuatrec. *11559*
     R   11559 Venezuela *11559*

R   *Dacryodes granatensis* Cuatrec. *11559*
     R   11559 Colombia *11559*

R   *Dacryodes kukachkana* L.O. Williams *11559*
     R   11559 Brazil *11559*
     R   11559 Peru *11559*

R   *Dacryodes olivifera* Cuatrec. *11559*
     R   11559 Colombia *11559*

R   *Dacryodes paraensis* Cuatrec. *11559*
     R   11559 Brazil *11559*

R   *Dacryodes roraimensis* Cuatrec. *11559*
     R   11559 Venezuela *11559*

R   *Dacryodes steyermarkii* Sandw. *11559*
     R   11559 Venezuela *11559*

R   *Protium amplum* Cuatrec. *11559*
     R   11559 Colombia *11559*

R   *Protium araguense* Cuatrec. *11559*
     R   11559 Venezuela *11559*

R   *Protium buenaventurense* Cuatrec. *11559*
     R   11559 Colombia *11559*

R   *Protium carolense* Daly *11559*
     R   11559 Brazil *11559*
     R   11559 Venezuela *11559*

I   *Protium connarifolium* (Perk.) Merr. *13833*
     I   13833 Philippines (low altitude) *13833*

R   *Protium crassipetalum* Cuatrec. *11559*
     R   11559 Guyana *11559*
     R   11559 Venezuela *11559*

R   *Protium demerarense* Sandw. *11559*
     R   11559 Brazil *11559*
     R   11559 French Guiana *11559*
     R   11559 Guyana *11559*

R   *Protium gigantum* Engl. var. *crassifolium* (Engl.) Daly *11559*
     R   11559 Brazil *11559*
     R   11559 French Guiana *8679*
     R   11559 Suriname *8679*

R   *Protium glomerulosum* Cuatrec. *11559*
     R   11559 Colombia *11559*

R   *Protium guacayanum* Cuatrec. *11559*
     R   11559 Colombia *11559*

R   *Protium icicariba* (DC.) Marchand *11559*
     R   11559 Brazil *11559*

E   *Protium inconforme* Pitt. *20883, 9006*
     I   20883 Panama *20883*

R   *Protium kleinii* Cuatrec. *11559*
     R   11559 Brazil *11559*
     I   11559 Brazil - Rio Grande do Sul *20311*
     I   11559 Brazil - Santa Catarina *20310*

R   *Protium laxiflorum* Engl. *11559*
     R   11559 Brazil *11559*

R   *Protium llanorum* Cuatrec. *11559*

	R	*11559* Colombia *11559*	

R   *Protium macrocarpum* Cuatrec. *11559*
- R   *11559* Colombia *11559*
- R   *11559* Ecuador *11559*

R   *Protium macrophyllum* (Kunth) Engl. *11559*
- R   *11559* Colombia *11559*
- R   *11559* Peru *11559*
- R   *11559* Venezuela *11559*

R   *Protium macrosepalum* Swart *11559*
- R   *11559* Venezuela *11559*

E   *Protium melinonis* Engl. *11559*
- E   *11559* French Guiana *11559*

R   *Protium minutiflorum* Cuatrec. *11559*
- R   *11559* Colombia *11559*

R   *Protium montanum* Swart *11559*
- R   *11559* Bolivia *11559*

R   *Protium nervosum* Cuatrec. *11559*
- R   *11559* Colombia *11559*

V   *Protium nitidifolium* (Cuatrec.) Daly *20883*
- I   *20883* Brazil *20883*
- I   *20883* Peru *20883*

R   *Protium opacum* Swart ssp. *exagerratum* Daly *11559*
- R   *11559* Venezuela *11559*

V   *Protium pilosum* (Cuatrec.) Daly *20883*
- I   *20883* Brazil *20883*

R   *Protium pittieri* (Rose) Engl. *11559*
- R   *11559* Costa Rica *11559*
- R   *11559* Panama *11559*

R   *Protium ptarianum* Steryerm. *11559*
- R   *11559* Venezuela *11559*

R   *Protium puncticulatum* Macbr. *11559*
- R   *11559* Bolivia *11559*
- R   *11559* Brazil *11559*
- R   *11559* Peru *11559*

R   *Protium reticulatum* Engl.
- R   Brazil
- R   Venezuela

V   *Protium tenuifolium* ssp. *meleodii* (I. M. Johnst.) D. M. Porter *21093*
- V   *20883* Panama *20883*

R   *Protium tenuifolium* ssp. *sessiliflorum* (Rose) D. M. Porter *21093*
- ?   Costa Rica *21093*
- ?   Honduras *21093*
- ?   Nicaragua *21093*
- R   *20883* Panama *20883*

R   *Protium veneralense* Cuatrec. *11559*
- R   *11559* Colombia *11559*

E   *Protium vestitum* (Cuatrec.) Daly *20883, 11559*
- R   *11559* Colombia *20883*

R   *Protium widgrenii* Engl. *11559*
- R   *11559* Brazil *11559*

R   *Tetragastris breviacuminata* Swart *11559*
- R   *11559* Brazil *11559*

R   *Tetragastris catuaba* Soares da Cunha *11559*
- R   *11559* Brazil *11559*

V   *Tetragastris occhionii* (Rizzini) Daly *20883, 11559*
- I   *20883* Brazil *20883*

R   *Trattinnickia ferruginea* Kuhlm. *11559*
- R   *11559* Brazil *11559*

R   *Trattinnickia laxiflora* Swart *21102*
- R   *11559* Peru *11559*

R   *Trattinnickia multiflora* Cuatrec. *11559*
- R   *11559* Colombia *11559*

Buxaceae

Number of genera:	5
Number of species:	60
Recorded threatened species:	21 (35%)

Nearly cosmopolitan.

V   *Buxus acuminata* (Griseb.) Muell. Arg. *5607*
- V   *19105* Cuba (Guantanamo) *5607*

E   *Buxus acunae* Borh. & Muniz *5607*
- E   *19105* Cuba (Holguin) *5607*

V   *Buxus arborea* Proctor *20883, 13336*
- V   *13336* Jamaica *20883*

V   *Buxus baracoensis* Borh. & Muniz *5607*
- V   *19105* Cuba (Guantanamo) *5607*

R   *Buxus citrifolia* (Willd.) Sprengel *9006*
- R   *19577* Panama *9006*

I   *Buxus colchica* Pojark. *5942*
- I   *5942* Russia - North Caucasus *5942*
- I   *5942* Azerbaijan *5942*
- I   *5942* Georgia *5942*

I   *Buxus cubana* Baill. *5607*
- I   *19105* Cuba (Guantanamo) *5607*

E   *Buxus heterophylla* Urban *5607*
- E   *19105* Cuba (Holguin) *5607*

I   *Buxus holttumiana* Hatus.
- I   Malaysia - Peninsular Malaysia (Kaki Bukit, Perlis)

R   *Buxus microphylla* Sieber & Zucc. var. *intermedia* (Kaneh.) Li *20511*
- R   *20511* Taiwan *20511*

V   *Buxus moana* Alain *5607*
- V   *19105* Cuba (Holguin) *5607*

E   *Buxus muelleriana* Urban
- E   *19105* Cuba *19105*

I   *Buxus nyasica* *21097*
- I   *20890* Malawi (Mt. Chese & Mt. Soche) *20890*

V   *Buxus obtusifolia* (Mildbr.) Hutch. *20057*
- V   *10900* Kenya (coastal) *17435*
- V   *10900* Tanzania (Tanga & coast) *17435*

V   *Buxus revoluta* (Britton) Alain *5607*
- V   *19105* Cuba (Holguin; Guantanamo) *5607*

V   *Buxus rotundifolia* (Britton) Mathou *5607*
- V   *19105* Cuba (Holguin, Guantanamo) *5607*

I   *Buxus rupicola* Ridley
- I   Malaysia - Peninsular Malaysia (Langkawi, Kedah)

R   *Buxus subcolumnaris* Muell. Arg. *19001*
- R   *19001* Martinique *19001*

V   *Buxus vaccinioides* (Britton) Urban *5607*
- V   *19105* Cuba (SC; Ho; Gu) *5607*

E   *Buxus vahlii* Baill. *20883, 7984*
- I   *20883* Jamaica *20883*
- E   *20883* Puerto Rico *20883*
- I   *20883* USA - Virgin Is. (St Croix) *20883*

R   *Pachysandra axillares* Fr. var. *tricarpa* Hayata *20511*
- R   *20511* Taiwan *20511*

Cactaceae

Number of genera: 30-200
Number of species: 1,000-2,000
Recorded threatened species: 581 (38%)

American deserts.

V II *Acanthocereus brasiliensis* Britton & Rose *15964*
     V   *15964* Brazil *15964*

R II *Aporocactus flagelliformis* (L.) Lemaire *12469*
     R   *19850* Mexico - Hidalgo *14255*
     R   *16360* Mexico - Oaxaca *9114*
     R   *19850* Mexico - Puebla *14255*

E I *Ariocarpus agavoides* (Castaneda) E.F. Anderson *15964*
     E   *20067* Mexico - Tamaulipas *9114*

E I *Ariocarpus bravoanus* H.M. Hern & E.F. Anderson *20067*
     E   *20067* Mexico - San Luis Potosi *20067*

V II *Ariocarpus fissuratus* (Engelm.) K. Schum. var.
      hintonii Stuppy & N.P. Taylor *20067*
     V   *20067* Mexico - San Luis Potosi *20067*

V II *Ariocarpus fissuratus* (Engelm.) Britton & Rose var.
      lloydii (Rose) W.T. Marsh *12437*
     V   *20067* Mexico - Coahuila *12437*
     V   *20067* Mexico - Durango *12437*
     V   *20067* Mexico - Zacatecas *12529*

V I *Ariocarpus scaphirostris* Böedeker *15964*
     V   *20067* Mexico - Nuevo Leon *9114*

V I *Ariocarpus trigonus* (F.A.C. Weber) K. Schum. *21384,*
     15964
     V   *20067* Mexico - Nuevo Leon *9114*
     V   *20067* Mexico - Tamaulipas *9114*

I II *Arrojadoa bahiensis* *21307*
     I   *21307* Brazil *21307*

I II *Arrojadoa dinae* ssp. *dinae* *15964, 21307*
     I   *21307* Brazil *15964*

I II *Arrojadoa dinae* ssp. *eriocaulis* *21307*
     I   *21307* Brazil *21307*

I II *Arthrocereus glaziovii* *15964*
     I   *21307* Brazil *15964*

I II *Arthrocereus melanurus* ssp. *melanurus* *21307*
     I   *21307* Brazil *21307*

I II *Arthrocereus melanurus* ssp. *odorus* *21307*
     I   *21307* Brazil *21307*

R II *Arthrocereus odorus* F. Ritter *15964*
     R   *15964* Brazil *15964*

I II *Arthrocereus rondonianus* *15964*
     I   *21307* Brazil *15964*

I II *Arthrocereus spinosissimus* (Buining & Brederoo) F.
      Ritter *15964*
     I   *15964* Brazil *15964*

E I *Astrophytum asterias* (Zucc.) Lem. *20883, 20850,*
     15964
     E   *20850* U.S. - Texas (Rio Grande valley) *20850*
     E   *20883* Mexico *20883*
     E   *20067* Mexico - Nuevo Leon *12469*
     E   *20067* Mexico - Tamaulipas *12469*

V II *Astrophytum capricorne* (A. Dietr.) Britton & Rose var.
      capricorne *12469*
     V   *9114* Mexico - Coahuila *9114*
     V   *21263* Mexico - Nuevo Leon *21263*

E II *Astrophytum capricorne* (A. Dietr.) Britton & Rose var.
      niveum (K. Kayser) Oken *12437*

E   *16360* Mexico - Coahuila *12437*

E II *Astrophytum myriostigma* Lemaire var. *coahuilense*
      (K. Kayser) Borg *12437*
     E   *12437* Mexico - Coahuila *12437*

V II *Astrophytum myriostigma* Lemaire var. *cuadricostatum*
      C. Glass & R. Foster *14257*
     V   *14257* Mexico - Tamaulipas *14257*

V II *Astrophytum myriostigma* Lemaire var.
      myriostigma *12469*
     V   *9114* Mexico - Coahuila *9114*
     V   *14280* Mexico - San Luis Potosi *14280*
     V   *21263* Mexico - Tamaulipas *21263*

I II *Astrophytum ornatum* (DC.) A. Weber *15964*
     I   *9114* Mexico - Coahuila *9114*
     I   *21263* Mexico - Guanajuato *21263*
     I   *21263* Mexico - Hidalgo *21263*
     I   *9114* Mexico - Queretaro *9114*
     I   *21263* Mexico - San Luis Potosi *21263*

E II *Austrocactus hibernus* F. Ritter *15964*
     E   *15964* Chile *15964*

R II *Austrocactus philippii* (regel & Schmidt) Buxbaum &
      Ritter *15964*
     R   *19034* Chile *19034*

R II *Austrocactus spiniflorus* (Phil.) Ritter *15964*
     R   *15964* Chile *19034*

R I *Aztekium ritteri* (Böedeker) Böedeker *15964*
     R   *20067* Mexico - Nuevo Leon *9114*

R II *Bergerocactus emoryi* (Engelm.) Engelm. *20850, 15964*
     V   *20850* U.S. - California *20850*
     ?   Mexico *15964*

R II *Brachycereus nesioticus* (Schumann) Backeb. *15964*
     R   *15964* Ecuador - Galapagos *11117*

R II *Brasilicereus markgrafii* Backeb. & Voll *15964*
     R   *15964* Brazil *15964*

V II *Browningia candelaris* (Meyen) Britton et Rose *20883,*
     15964
     V   *20883* Chile *20883*
     R   *15964* Peru *20883*

R II *Cephalocereus apicicephalium* E.Y. Dawson *15964*
     R   *12787* Mexico - Oaxaca *12787*

R II *Cephalocereus nizandensis* (H. Bravo & Macdougall) F.
      Buxb. *15964*
     R   *19850* Mexico *19850*

V II *Cephalocereus senilis* (Haw.) Pfeiffer *15964*
     V   *15964* Mexico - Hidalgo *9114*

I II *Cereus mirabella* *15964*
     I   *21307* Brazil *15964*

V II *Cereus quadricostatus* Bello *8058*
     V   *19002* Puerto Rico *8058*

I II *Cipocereus bradei* *15964*
     I   *21307* Brazil *15964*

R II *Cipocereus crassisepalus* *15964*
     R   *15964* Brazil *15964*

I II *Cipocereus minensis* ssp. *pleurocarpus* *21307*
     I   *21307* Brazil *21307*

R II *Cipocereus pleurocarpus* Ritter *15964*
     R   *15964* Brazil *15964*

R II *Cipocereus pusilliflorus* (Ritter) D.C. Zappi & N.P.
      Taylor *15964*
     R   *15964* Brazil *15964*

V II *Cleistocactus acanthurus* (Vaupel) D. Hunt *15964*
   V *15964* Peru *18200*

R II *Coleocephalocereus pluricostatus* Buining &
      Brederoo *15964*
   R *15964* Brazil *15964*

R II *Coleocephalocereus purpureus* (Buining & Brederoo)
      Ritter *15964*
   R *15964* Brazil *15964*

R II *Copiapoa bridgesii* (Pfeiff.) Backeb. *15964*
   R *15964* Chile *15964*

R II *Copiapoa calderana* F. Ritten *15964*
   R *19535* Chile *15964*

R II *Copiapoa chaniaralensis* Ritter *15964*
   R *19034* Chile *19034*

R II *Copiapoa coquimbana* (Karwinsky) Britton & Rose *15964*
   R *15964* Chile *19034*

E II *Copiapoa desertorum* Ritter *15964*
   E *15964* Chile *19034*

R II *Copiapoa desertorum* Ritter var. *hornilloensis*
      (Ritter) A. Hoffmann *19034*
   R *19034* Chile *19034*

R II *Copiapoa desertorum* Ritter var. *rubriflora*
      (Ritter) A. Hoffmann *19034*
   R *19034* Chile *19034*

V II *Copiapoa desertorum* Ritter var. *rupestris* (Ritter)
      A. Hoffmann *19034*
   V *19034* Chile *19034*

R II *Copiapoa fiedleriana* (K. Schum.) Backeb. *15964*
   R *19535* Chile *15964*

V II *Copiapoa humilis* (Philippi) Hutch. *15964*
   V *16430* Chile *15964*

R II *Copiapoa humilis* (Philippi) Hutchinson var.
      esmeraldana (Ritter) A. Hoffmann *19034*
   R *19034* Chile *19034*

V II *Copiapoa humilis* (Philippi) Hutchinson var.
      longispina (Ritter) A. Hoffmann *19034*
   V *19034* Chile *19034*

R II *Copiapoa hypogaea* Ritter *15964*
   R *19034* Chile *19034*

V II *Copiapoa krainziana* Ritter *15964*
   V *19034* Chile *19034*

R II *Copiapoa laui* L. Diers *15964*
   R *15964* Chile *15964*

R II *Copiapoa longistaminea* Ritter *15964*
   R *15964* Chile *19034*

R II *Copiapoa malletiana* (Lem. ex Salm-Dyck)
      Backeb. *15964*
   R *15964* Chile *19535*

R II *Copiapoa marginata* (Salm-Dyck.) Britton & Rose *15964*
   R *19535* Chile *15964*

V II *Copiapoa megarhiza* Britton & Rose var. *echinata*
      (Ritter) *19034*
   V *19034* Chile *19034*

E II *Copiapoa megarhiza* Britton & Rose var.
      megarhiza *19034*
   E *19535* Chile *15964*

E II *Copiapoa rupestris* Ritter *15964*
   E *15964* Chile *15964*

V II *Copiapoa solaris* (Ritter) Ritter *15964*

V *19034* Chile *19034*

E II *Copiapoa tenuissima* Ritter *15964*
   E *15964* Chile *15964*

E II *Copiapoa tocopillana* Ritter *15964*
   E *15964* Chile *19034*

R II *Copiapoa variispinata* Ritter *15964*
   R *15964* Chile *15964*

R II *Corryocactus brevistylus* (Schumann) Britton &
      Rose *15964*
   V *19034* Chile *19034*
   R *18200* Peru *19034*

V II *Coryphantha asperispina* Boedeker *12437*
   V *12437* Mexico - Coahuila *12437*
   V *12437* Mexico - Nuevo Leon *12437*

I II *Coryphantha dasyacantha* (Engelm.) Orc. var.
      dasyacantha *8058*
   I *8058* U.S. - Texas *8058*
   I *8058* Mexico *8058*

R II *Coryphantha durangensis* (Runge) Britton & Rose *15964*
   R *19850* Mexico *12469*

V II *Coryphantha elephantidens* (Lemaire) Lemaire *15964*
   V *9114* Mexico - Morelos *9114*

V II *Coryphantha glanduligera* (Otto ex Dietrich)
      Lemaire *15964*
   V *16360* Mexico *16360*

E II *Coryphantha gracilis* L. Bremer & Lau *15964*
   E *9114* Mexico - Chihuahua *9114*

R II *Coryphantha grata* L. Bremer *15964*
   R *19850* Mexico *19850*

I II *Coryphantha longicornis* Boedeker *15964*
   I *19850* Mexico *12469*

V II *Coryphantha macromeris* (Britt. & Rose) L. Benson var.
      runyonii (Britt. & Rose) L. Benson *20850*
   V *20850* U.S. - Texas *20850*

R II *Coryphantha maiz-tablasensis* Backeb. *15964*
   R *14262* Mexico - San Luis Potosi *14262*

R II *Coryphantha melleospina* H. Bravo-Holl. *15964*
   R *15964* Mexico *12469*

R II *Coryphantha odorata* Boedeker *15964*
   R *15964* Mexico *15964*

V II *Coryphantha poselgeriana* (A. Dietr.) Britton & Rose var.
      poselgeriana *12469*
   V *9114* Mexico *9114*

I II *Coryphantha poselgeriana* (A. Dietr.) Britton & Rose var.
      saltillensis (Poselger) Bremer *12469*
   I *15964* Mexico *12469*

R II *Coryphantha pseudoechinus* Boedeker *15964*
   R *15964* Mexico *12469*

V II *Coryphantha pulleineana* (Backeb.) C. Glass *15964*
   V *15964* Mexico *12469*

R II *Coryphantha radians* (DC.) Britton & Rose *15964*
   R *19850* Mexico *12469*

V II *Coryphantha ramillosa* Cutak *20883, 20850, 15964*
   V *20850* U.S. - Texas *20850*
   I *20883* Mexico *20883*
   V *19848* Mexico - Coahuila *9114*

R II *Coryphantha recurvata* (Engelm.) Britt. & Rose *20883,*
   20850, 15964
   V *20850* U.S. - Arizona *20850*
   I *20883* Mexico *20883*

R II *Coryphantha retusa* Britton & Rose var. *mellospina*
(H.Bravo-Hollis) H.Bravo-Hollis *15964*
     R *19850* Mexico *19850*

R II *Coryphantha scheeri* Lemaire var. *robustispina*
(Schott ex Engelm.) L. Benson *20883, 20850, 8058*
     R *20850* U.S. - Arizona (Pima & Santa Cruz Co.)
20850
     E *20850* U.S. - Texas *20850*
     E *20883* Mexico *20883*
     E *19123* Mexico - Sonora (north) *19123*

R II *Coryphantha scheeri* Lemaire var. *uncinata* L.
Benson *20850*
     I *20850* U.S. - New Mexico *20850*
     R *20850* U.S. - Texas *20850*

I II *Coryphantha strobiliformis* (Poselger) Moran var.
durispina (Quehl) L. Benson *8058*
     I *8058* U.S. - Texas *8058*
     I *8058* Mexico *8058*

V II *Coryphantha sulcata* (Engelm.) Britton & Rose var.
nickelsiae (K. Brandeg.) L. Benson *20883, 20850, 9114*
     Ex/E *20850* U.S. - Texas *20850*
     I *20883* Mexico *20883*
     V *19850* Mexico - Coahuila *12437*
     V *19850* Mexico - Nuevo Leon *9114*
     V *15964* Mexico - Tamaulipas *12437*

V II *Coryphantha valida* (J.A. Purpus) L. Bremer *15964*
     V *19860* Mexico *12469*

E I *Coryphantha werdermannii* Boedeker *15964*
     E *15964* Mexico - Coahuila *9114*

V II *Dendrocereus nudiflorus* (Engelm.) Britton &
Rose *15964*
     V *19105* Cuba *15964*

R I *Discocactus bahiensis* Britton & Rose *15964*
     R *15964* Brazil (eastern) *14964*

Discocactus boomianus Buining & Brederoo *21384,
15964*
     V *15964* Brazil *15964*

Discocactus buenekeri W.R. Abraham *21384, 15964*
     I *15964* Brazil *14964*

E I *Discocactus horstii* Buin. & Bred. *15964*
     E *15964* Brazil *14964*

I I *Discocactus placentiformis* (Lehm.) Schum. *15964*
     I *21307* Brazil (eastern) *14964*

R I *Discocactus pseudoinsignis* Tayl. & Zapp. *15964*
     R *15964* Brazil (eastern) *14964*

Discocactus subviridigriseus Buining ex J.
Theunissen *21384, 15964*
     E *15964* Brazil (eastern) *14964*

V I *Discocactus zehntneri* Britton & Rose *15964*
     V *15964* Brazil (eastern) *14964*

I I *Discocactus zehntneri* Britton & Rose ssp. *boomianus*
(Buin & Bred) Tayl & Zapp *21384, 21307*
     I *21307* Brazil *21307*

I I *Discocactus zehntneri* ssp. *zehntneri* *21307*
     I *21307* Brazil *21307*

R II *Disocactus ackermannii* (Lindley) Barthlott *15964*
     R *16385* Mexico - Chiapas *16385*
     V *16385* Mexico - Oaxaca *16385*
     V *16385* Mexico - Veracruz *16385*

R II *Disocactus biformis* (Lindley in Edwards)
Lindley *15964*
     R *15964* Guatemala *15964*

     R *15964* Honduras *15964*

R II *Disocactus eichlamii* (Weingard) Britton & Rose *15964*
     R *15964* Guatemala *14247*

R II *Disocactus kimnachii* Rowley *15964*
     R *14248* Costa Rica *15964*

R I *Disocactus macdougallii* (Alexander) Barthlott *15964*
     R *19850* Mexico - Chiapas *14248*

R II *Disocactus macranthus* (Alex.) Kimnach &
Hutchinson *15964*
     R *19860* Mexico - Chiapas *16385*
     R *19860* Mexico - Oaxaca *16385*
     R *19860* Mexico - Veracruz *16385*

V II *Disocactus phyllanthoides* (DC.) Barthlott *15964*
     V *19850* Mexico - Puebla *14248*
     V *19850* Mexico - Veracruz *9114*

I II *Disocactus quezaltecus* (Standley & Steyerm.)
Kimnach *15964*
     I *14258* Guatemala *14258*

E II *Echinocactus grusonii* Hildm. *15964*
     E *9114* Mexico - Hidalgo *9114*
     E *9114* Mexico - Queretaro *9114*

V II *Echinocactus horizonthalonius* Lemaire var. *nicholii*
L. Benson *20883, 20850, 20079*
     V *20850* U.S. - Arizona *20850*
     I *20883* Mexico *20883*

V II *Echinocactus parryi* Engelm. *15964*
     V *19850* Mexico - Chihuahua *12437*

V II *Echinocactus platyacanthus* Link & Otto *15964*
     V *15964* Mexico *12469*

V II *Echinocereus adustus* Engelm. var.
adustus *12107*
     V *15964* Mexico - Chihuahua (Cusihuiriac) *12107*

V II *Echinocereus adustus* Engelm. var. *schwarzii* (A.
Lau) N.P. Taylor *12107*
     V *15964* Mexico - Durango (Guanaceui & Canantlan)
12107

V II *Echinocereus bristolii* W. Marshall var.
bristolii *12107*
     V *15964* Mexico - Sonora *12107*

R II *Echinocereus bristolii* W. Marshall var.
pseudopectinatus N.P. Taylor *12107*
     V *12107* U.S. - Arizona (south-east) *12107*
     R *19850* Mexico - Sonora (north-east) *12107*

V II *Echinocereus chisoensis* W.T. Marsh. *20850*
     I *20850* U.S. - Texas *20850*

E II *Echinocereus chisoensis* W. Marshall var.
chisoensis *20883, 20850, 12107*
     E *20850* U.S. - Texas (Chisos Mts) *20850*
     I *20883* Mexico *20883*

E II *Echinocereus chloranthus* (Engelm.) Hort.Haage var.
neocapillus Weniger *20850, 12107*
     E *20850* U.S. - Texas (Brewster Co.) *20850*

V II *Echinocereus coccineus* var. *arizonicus* (Rose ex
Orcutt) Ferguson *20850*
     V *20850* U.S. - Arizona *20850*
     I *20850* U.S. - New Mexico *20850*

R II *Echinocereus coccineus* var. *paucispinus* (Engelm.)
Ferguson *20850*
     R *20850* U.S. - Texas *20850*

I II *Echinocereus engelmannii* (Parry ex Engelm.) Lemaire var.
armatus L. Benson *12107*

	I	*15964*	U.S. - California *12107*
	I	*15964*	U.S. - Nevada (Mojavean Desert) *12107*

I II *Echinocereus engelmannii* (Parry ex Engelm.) Lemaire var. *chrysocentrus* (Engelm. & Bigelow) Ruempler *12107*

	I	*15964*	U.S. - Arizona (north & west) *12107*
	I	*15964*	U.S. - California *12107*
	I	*15964*	U.S. - Nevada (south & east) *12107*
	I	*15964*	U.S. - Utah (west) *12107*

E II *Echinocereus engelmannii* (Parry ex Engelm.) Lemaire var. *howei* L. Benson *20850, 12107*

	E	*20850*	U.S. - California (southernmost Mojave Desert) *20850*
	I	*20850*	U.S. - Nevada *20850*

I II *Echinocereus engelmannii* (Parry ex Engelm.) Lemaire var. *munzii* (Parish) Pierce & Fosb. *12107*

	I	*12107*	U.S. - California (south) *12107*
	I	*12107*	Mexico - Baja California Peninsula (Sierra Juarez, east slopes) *12107*

V II *Echinocereus engelmannii* (Parry ex Engelm.) Lemaire var. *nicholii* (L. Benson) D. Parfitt *12107*

	V	*12107*	U.S. - Arizona (central south; Sonoran D.) *12107*
	V	*12107*	Mexico - Sonora (north-west; Sonoran Desert) *12107*

I II *Echinocereus engelmannii* (Parry ex Engelm.) Lemaire var. *purpureus* L. Benson *12107*

	I	*19002*	U.S. - Utah (near St George) *12107*

I II *Echinocereus engelmannii* (Parry ex Engelm.) Lemaire var. *variegatus* (Engelm. & Bigelow) Ruempler *12107*

	I	*15964*	U.S. - Arizona (north-west) *12107*
	I	*15964*	U.S. - Utah (south-east) *12107*

E II *Echinocereus fendleri* (Engelm.) Ruempler var. *kuenzleri* (Castetter, Pierce & Schwerin) L. Benson *20850, 12107*

	E	*20850*	U.S. - New Mexico (Otero Co.) *20850*
	I	*12107*	Mexico - Chihuahua (north) *12107*

E I *Echinocereus ferreirianus* H. Gates ssp. *lindsayi* (J. Meyrán) N.P. Taylor *21384, 12107*

	E	*20067*	Mexico - Baja California Peninsula *12107*

V II *Echinocereus freudenbergeri* G. Frank *15964*

	V	*19850*	Mexico - Coahuila (central & south) *12496*

V II *Echinocereus knippelianus* Liebner var. *knippelianus* *12107*

	V	*20067*	Mexico - Coahuila (south-east) *12107*

E II *Echinocereus knippelianus* Liebner var. *kruegeri* C. Glass & R. Foster *12107*

	E	*12107*	Mexico - Nuevo Leon (south) *12107*

V II *Echinocereus laui* G. Frank *12107*

	V	*15964*	Mexico - Sonora (near Yecora) *12107*

R II *Echinocereus leucanthus* N.P. Taylor *15964*

	R	*19850*	Mexico - Sinaloa *12107*
	R	*19850*	Mexico - Sonora *12107*

V II *Echinocereus lloydii* Britt. & Rose *20850, 20079*

	Ex/E	*20850*	U.S. - New Mexico *20850*
	V	*20850*	U.S. - Texas *20850*

V II *Echinocereus longisetus* (Engelm.) Lemaire var. *delaetii* (Gurke) N.P. Taylor *12496*

	V	*19850*	Mexico - Coahuila (central-south & south-east) *12496*

I II *Echinocereus maritimus* (M.E. Jones) Schumann var. *hancockii* (E. Dawson) N.P. Taylor *12107*

	I	*12107*	Mexico - Baja California Peninsula (Cedros Is.) *12107*

	I	*12107*	Mexico - Baja California Sur *12107*

V II *Echinocereus nicholii* (L. Benson) Parfitt *20850, 15964*

	I	*20850*	U.S. - Arizona *20850*
	?		Mexico *15964*

R II *Echinocereus nivosus* C. Glass & R. Foster *15964*

	R	*20067*	Mexico - Coahuila (Sierra Madre Oriental) *12107*

E II *Echinocereus palmeri* Britton & Rose *15964*

	E	*19848*	Mexico - Chihuahua (central & south) *12107*

I II *Echinocereus pamanesiorum* A. Lau *12107*

	I	*15964*	Mexico - Zacatecas (Rio Huaynamuta valley) *12107*

R II *Echinocereus papillosus* Linke ex Rumpl. *20850*

	R	*20850*	U.S. - Texas *20850*

E II *Echinocereus papillosus* Linke ex Ruempler var. *angusticeps* (Clover) W.T. Marsh. *20850, 12107*

	E	*20850*	U.S. - Texas (Hidalgo Co.) *20850*

R II *Echinocereus pensilis* (K. Brandegee) J.A. Purpus *12107*

	R	*15964*	Mexico - Baja California Sur (Cape region) *12107*

E II *Echinocereus pulchellus* (C. Martius) Schumann var. *pulchellus* *12107*

	E	*20067*	Mexico - Hidalgo *12107*
	E	*20067*	Mexico - Oaxaca (north) *12107*
	E	*20067*	Mexico - Puebla *12107*
	E	*20067*	Mexico - Queretaro (south-east) *12107*

E II *Echinocereus pulchellus* (C. Martius) Schumann var. *sharpii* N.P. Taylor *20067*

	E	*20067*	Mexico - Nuevo Leon *20067*

V II *Echinocereus pulchellus* (C. Martius) Schumann var. *weinbergii* (Weing.) N.P. Taylor *12107*

	V	*15964*	Mexico - Zacatecas (west) *12107*

R II *Echinocereus rayonesensis* N.P. Taylor *15964*

	R	*12496*	Mexico - Nuevo Leon (valley of Rayones) *12496*

E II *Echinocereus reichenbachii* (Tersch. ex Walp.) Hort.Haage var. *albertii* L. Benson *20850, 8058*

	E	*20850*	U.S. - Texas (Rio Grande Plain) *20850*

R II *Echinocereus reichenbachii* (Tersch. ex Walp.) Hort.Haage var. *baileyi* (Rose) N.P. Taylor *20850, 12107*

	I	*20850*	U.S. - New Mexico *20850*
	I	*20850*	U.S. - Oklahoma (south) *20850*
	E	*20850*	U.S. - Texas (Childress Co.) *20850*

I II *Echinocereus reichenbachii* (Tersch. ex Walp.) Hort. Haage var. *fitchii* (Britton & Rose) L. Benson *12107*

	I	*15964*	U.S. - Texas (south) *12107*
	V	*19850*	Mexico - Nuevo Leon (north) *12107*
	V	*19850*	Mexico - Tamaulipas (north) *12107*

E I *Echinocereus schmollii* (Weing.) N.P. Taylor *15964*

	E	*19848*	Mexico - Queretaro (south-east) *12107*

I II *Echinocereus sciurus* (K. Brandegee) Dams var. *floresii* (Backeb.) N.P. Taylor *12107*

	I	*12107*	Mexico - Sinaloa (Topolobampa vicinity) *12107*

R II *Echinocereus sciurus* (K. Brandegee) Britton & Rose var. *sciurus* *12107*

	R	*19848*	Mexico - Baja California Sur (South Cape) *12107*

R II *Echinocereus stoloniferus* W. Marshall var. *stoloniferus* *12107*

R   19850 Mexico - Sonora (south-east) *12107*

R II *Echinocereus subinermis* Salm-Dyck ex Scheer var. **subinermis** *12107*

    R   19850 Mexico - Chihuahua (south-west) *12107*
    R   19850 Mexico - Sinaloa *12107*
    R   19850 Mexico - Sonora *12107*

I II *Echinocereus triglochidiatus* Engelm. var. *paucispinus* (Engelm.) W. Marshall *12107*

    I   19002 U.S. - Texas (south) *12107*

V II *Echinocereus viereckii* Werderm. var. *morricalii* (Riha) N.P. Taylor *12107*

    V   12107 Mexico - Nuevo Leon *12107*

V II *Echinocereus viridiflorus* Engelm. var. *correllii* L. Benson *20850, 12107*

    V   20850 U.S. - Texas (Pecos Co.; Brewster Co.) *20850*

E II *Echinocereus viridiflorus* Engelm. var. *davisii* (A.D. Houghton) W.T. Marsh. *20850, 12107*

    E   20850 U.S. - Texas (Brewster Co.) *20850*

R II *Echinopsis chrysantha* Werderm. *15964*

    R   15964 Argentina *15964*

V II *Echinopsis deserticola* (Werd.) Friedrich & G.D. Rowley *15964*

    V   19034 Chile *15964*

R II *Echinopsis glauca* (Ritter) Friedrich & G.D. Rowley *15964*

    R   19034 Chile *15964*
    R   18200 Peru *15964*

V II *Echinopsis litoralis* (Joh.) Friedrich & Rowley *15964*

    V   19534 Chile *15964*

R II *Echinopsis skottsbergii* (Backeb.) Friedrich & G.D. Rowley *15964*

    R   15964 Chile *19034*

E II *Echinopsis smrziana* Backeb. *15964*

    E   20176 Argentina - Salta *20176*

V II *Echinopsis spinibarbis* (Otto) A. Hoffmann *19034*

    V   19034 Chile *19034*

V II *Echinopsis uebelmanniana* (Lembcke & Backeb.) A. Hoffmann *15964*

    V   15964 Chile *19034*

V II *Epiphyllum anguliger* (Lemaire) G. Don *15964*

    V   14249 Mexico - Guerrero *14249*
    ?   Mexico - Jalisco *21204*
    V   14249 Mexico - Mexico State *12469*
    V   14249 Mexico - Michoacan *14249*
    V   14249 Mexico - Oaxaca *14249*

I II *Epiphyllum caudatum* Britton & Rose *15964*

    I   15964 Mexico - Tabasco *14260*

R II *Epiphyllum grandilobum* (A. Weber) Britton & Rose *15964*

    R   14249 Costa Rica *15964*
    V   14249 Panama *15964*

I II *Epiphyllum lauii* Kimnach *15964*

    I   15964 Mexico *15964*

V II *Epithelantha bokei* L. Benson *15964*

    E   15964 U.S. - Texas *12437*
    V   19850 Mexico *12437*

I II *Epithelantha micromeris* Britton & Rose var. *greggii* (Engelm.) Borg *12469*

    I   19860 Mexico *12469*

E II *Epithelantha micromeris* Britton & Rose var.

pachyrhiza Marshall *12469*

    E   19860 Mexico *12469*

V II *Epithelantha micromeris* Britton & Rose var. *polycephala* (Backeb.) C. Glass & R. Foster *12437*

    V   12437 Mexico - Coahuila *12437*

V II *Eriosyce rodentiophila* Ritter *15964*

    V   19034 Chile *19034*

V II *Eriosyce sandillon* (Remy) Philippi *15964*

    V   19034 Chile *19034*

R II *Escobaria aguirreana* (C. Glass & R. Foster) N.P. Taylor *15964*

    R   9114 Mexico - Coahuila *9114*

V II *Escobaria albicolumnaria* Hester *20850, 15964*

    V   20850 U.S. - Texas *20850*

V II *Escobaria asperispina* (Boedeker) D.R. Hunt *15964*

    V   19850 Mexico *15964*

V II *Escobaria chaffeyi* Britton & Rose *14280*

    V   14280 Mexico - Coahuila *14280*
    V   14280 Mexico - San Luis Potosi *14280*

E II *Escobaria cubensis* (Britton & Rose) D.R. Hunt *15964*

    E   19105 Cuba *19105*

I II *Escobaria dasyacantha* Britton & Rose *15964*

    I   15964 U.S. - Texas *8058*
    I   8058 Mexico *15964*

V II *Escobaria dasyacantha* Britton & Rose var. *chaffeyi* (Britt. & Rose) N.P.Taylor *20850*

    E   20850 U.S. - Texas *20850*

R II *Escobaria dasyacantha* Britton & Rose var. *dasyacantha* *20850*

    I   20850 U.S. - New Mexico *20850*
    V   20850 U.S. - Texas *20850*
    I   20883 Mexico *20883*

R II *Escobaria dasyacantha* Britton & Rose var. *duncanii* (Hester) N.P.Taylor *20850*

    E   20850 U.S. - New Mexico *20850*
    E   20850 U.S. - Texas *20850*

E II *Escobaria guadalupensis* Brack & Heil *20850, 15964*

    I   20850 U.S. - New Mexico *20850*
    E   20850 U.S. - Texas *20850*

R II *Escobaria laredoi* (C. Glass & R. Foster) N.P. Taylor *15964*

    R   20067 Mexico - Coahuila *11419*

V II *Escobaria leei* (Rose) Bodeker *15964*

    V   20079 U.S. - New Mexico *20079*

E I *Escobaria minima* (Baird) D.R. Hunt *20850, 15964*

    E   20850 U.S. - Texas *20850*

E II *Escobaria missouriensis* (Clover) D.R. Hunt var. *marstonii* (Clover) D.R. Hunt *20850*

    I   20850 U.S. - Arizona *20850*
    I   20850 U.S. - Oklahoma *20850*
         20850 U.S. - Utah *20850*

R II *Escobaria orcuttii* Bodecker *20883, 20850, 15964*

    I   20850 U.S. - Arizona *20850*
    R   20850 U.S. - New Mexico *20850*
    I   20883 Mexico *20883*

V II *Escobaria organensis* (A.D. Zimmerman) Castetter, Pierce & Schwerin *20850, 15964*

    V   20850 U.S. - New Mexico *20850*

E II *Escobaria robbinsiorum* (W.H. Earle) D.R. Hunt *20883, 20850*

    E   20850 U.S. - Arizona *20850*

	I		20883 Mexico 20883

R II *Escobaria robbinsorum* (W. Earle) D. Hunt *15964*
    V   *15964* U.S. - Arizona (Cochise Co.) *4115*
    R   *14252* Mexico - Sonora *14252*

R II *Escobaria roseana* (Boedeker) Backeb. *12469*
    R   *19850* Mexico *12469*

V II *Escobaria sandbergii* Castetter, Pierce &
    Schwerin *20850, 15964*
    V   *20850* U.S. - New Mexico *20850*

V I *Escobaria sneedii* Britt. & Rose *20850, 15964*
    V   *20850* U.S. - New Mexico *20850*
    I   *20850* U.S. - Texas *20850*

V II *Escobaria sneedii* Britt. & Rose var. *leei* (Rose ex
    Bodecker) D.R.Hunt *20850*
    V   *20850* U.S. - New Mexico *20850*

V II *Escobaria sneedii* Britt. & Rose var.
    sneedii *20850*
    V   *20850* U.S. - New Mexico *20850*
    V   *20850* U.S. - Texas *20850*

V II *Escobaria villardii* Castetter, Pierce &
    Schwerin *20850, 15964*
    I   *20850* U.S. - California *20850*
    V   *20850* U.S. - New Mexico *20850*

R II *Escobaria vivipara* var. *rosea* (Clokey) D.R.
    Hunt *20850*
    E   *20850* U.S. - Arizona *20850*
    V   *20850* U.S. - California *20850*
    R   *20850* U.S. - Nevada *20850*

R II *Espostoopsis dybowskii* (Roland-Goss) F. Buxb. *15964*
    R   *15964* Brazil *15964*

E II *Eulychnia aricensis* Ritt. *15964*
    E   *19535* Chile *15964*

R II *Eulychnia iquiquensis* (Schumann) Britton &
    Rose *15964*
    R   *15964* Chile *19034*

V II *Eulychnia procumbens* Backeb. *15964*
    V   *5598* Chile *15964*

R II *Facheiroa ulei* (Gurke) Werderm. *15964*
    R   *15964* Brazil *15964*

R II *Ferocactus alamosanus* Britton & Rose *15964*
    R   *15964* Mexico *15964*
    R   *15964* Mexico - Sonora

I II *Ferocactus chrysacanthus* (Orcutt) Britton &
    Rose *12469*
    I   *19850* Mexico - Baja California Peninsula *14264*

I II *Ferocactus cylindraceus* Orcutt. var.
    cylindraceus *15964*
    I   *15964* U.S. - Arizona *8058*
    I   *15964* U.S. - California *8058*
    I   *19850* Mexico - Sonora *9114*

V II *Ferocactus emoryi* (Engelm.) Orcutt *20850, 15964*
    I   *20850* U.S. - Arizona *20850*
    V   *16360* Mexico *15964*

R II *Ferocactus haematacanthus* (A. Weber) Backeb. & F.
    Knuth *15964*
    R   *14264* Mexico - Puebla *9114*
    R   *14264* Mexico - Veracruz *14264*

R II *Ferocactus johnstonianus* Britton & Rose *12469*
    R   *19848* Mexico *9019*

E II *Ferocactus peninsulae* (F.A.C. Weber) Britton & Rose var.
    santa-maria (Britton & Rose) N.P. Taylor *20067*

	E		20067 Mexico - Baja California Sur 20067

V II *Ferocactus pilosus* (Salm-Dyck) Werderm. *15964*
    V   *19850* Mexico *19850*

V II *Ferocactus recurvus* (Miller) Borg var. *greenwoodii*
    C. Glass *9114*
    V   *9114* Mexico - Oaxaca *9114*

R II *Ferocactus reppenhagenii* G. Unger *15964*
    R   *19850* Mexico *15964*

V II *Ferocactus townsendianus* Britton & Rose *15964*
    V   *19850* Mexico *9114*

I II *Ferocactus viridescens* (Nutt.) Britton & Rose *15964*
    I   *15964* U.S. - California *9114*
    V   *9114* Mexico - Baja California Peninsula *9114*

Ex/E II *Frailea matoana* Buining & Brederoo *15964*
    Ex/E   *15964* Brazil *15964*

V II *Haageocereus australis* Backeb *15964*
    V   *19034* Chile *19034*
    V   *18200* Peru *19034*

R II *Haageocereus chilensis* Ritt. *5598*
    R   *5598* Chile *5598*

V II *Haageocereus fascicularis* (Meyen) Ritter *15964*
    V   *19034* Chile *19034*

E II *Haageocereus limensis* (Salm-Dyck) F. Ritter *15964*
    E   *12468* Peru *18200*

E II *Haageocereus multangularis* (Willd.) F. Ritter *15964*
    E   *12468* Peru *18200*

I II *Harrisia aboriginum* *15964*
    I   *15964* United States of America *15964*

V II *Harrisia earlei* Britton & Rose *15964*
    V   *19105* Cuba (Pinar del Rio) *5607*

R II *Harrisia fernowii* Britton *15964*
    R   *19105* Cuba *19105*

E II *Harrisia fragrans* Small *20850, 15964*
    E   *20850* U.S. - Florida *20850*

E II *Harrisia portoricensis* Britt. *20883, 15964*
    E   *20883* Puerto Rico (Mona; Desecheo) *20883*

V II *Harrisia simpsonii* Small *20850, 15964*
    I   *15964* United States of America *15964*
    V   *20850* U.S. - Florida *20850*

V II *Harrisia taetra* *15964*
    V   *19105* Cuba (Pinar del Rio) *19105*

V II *Harrisia taylori* Britton *15964*
    V   *19105* Cuba *19105*

R II *Hatiora epiphylloides* *15964*
    R   *15964* Brazil *15964*

I II *Hatiora epiphylloides* ssp. *bradei* *21307*
    I   *21307* Brazil *21307*

I II *Hatiora epiphylloides* ssp. *epiphylloides* *21307*
    I   *21307* Brazil *21307*

I II *Hatiora gaertneri* *15964*
    I   *15964* Brazil *15964*

V II *Hatiora herminiae* *15964*
    V   *15964* Brazil *15964*

I II *Hatiora rosea* *15964*
    I   *15964* Brazil *15964*

R II *Helianthocereus atacamensis* (Phil.) Backeb. *20883*
    R   *20883* Chile *20883*

R II *Heliocereus speciosus* (Cavan.) Britton & Rose var.
    amecamensis (Heese) Weing. ex A. Berger *12469*

	R	16385	Mexico - Michoacan *16385*

I   II   *Heliocereus speciosus* (Cavan.) Britton & Rose var. **elegantissimus** (Britton & Rose) *12469*
     I   15964   Mexico *12469*

E   II   *Heliocereus speciosus* (Cavan.) Britton & Rose var. **serratus** (Weing.) Borg *12469*
     E   16385   Guatemala *16385*
     E   16385   Mexico *12469*

I   II   *Heliocereus speciosus* (Cavan.) Britton & Rose var. **speciosus** *12469*
     I   15964   Mexico *12469*

E   II   *Heliocereus speciosus* (Cavan.) Britton & Rose var. **superbus** (Ehrenbg.) A. Berger *12469*
     E   19860   Mexico *12469*

R   II   *Horridocactus garaventae* *15964*
     R   19535   Chile *15964*

R   II   *Hylocereus calcaratus* (A. Weber) Britton & Rose *15964*
     R   14255   Costa Rica *16385*

R   II   *Hylocereus stenopterus* (A. Weber) Britton & Rose *15964*
     R   14255   Costa Rica *14255*
     V   14255   Panama (Chiriquí) *10747*

R   II   *Jasminocereus thouarsii* (F.A.C. Weber) Backeb. var. **delicatus** (E. Dawson) E.F. Anders. & Walk. *11117*
     R   11117   Ecuador - Galapagos *11117*

R   II   *Jasminocereus thouarsii* (F.A.C. Weber) Backeb. var. **sclerocarpus** (Schumann) E.F. Anders. & Walk. *11117*
     R   11117   Ecuador - Galapagos *11117*

R   II   *Jasminocereus thouarsii* (F.A.C. Weber) Backeb. var. **thouarsii** *11117*
     R   11117   Ecuador - Galapagos *11117*

V   II   *Leptocereus arboreus* Britton & Rose *15964*
     V   19105   Cuba *5607*

R   II   *Leptocereus assurgens* (C. Wright) Britton & Rose *15964*
     R   19105   Cuba *19105*

E   II   *Leptocereus ekmanii* (Werderm.) Knuth *15964*
     E   19105   Cuba (Pinar del Rio) *5607*

E   II   *Leptocereus grantianus* Britt. *20883, 15964*
     I   20883   Puerto Rico (including Culebra Is.) *20883*

R   II   *Leptocereus maxonii* Britton & Rose *15964*
     R   19105   Cuba (SC; Gu) *5607*

V   II   *Leptocereus prostratus* Britton & Rose *15964*
     V   19105   Cuba (Pinar del Rio) *5607*

E   II   *Leptocereus quadricostatus* (Bello) Britt. & Rose *20883, 15964*
     I   20883   Puerto Rico *20883*

R   II   *Leptocereus sylvestris* Britton & Rose *15964*
     R   19105   Cuba (Granma) *5607*

Ex   II   *Leptocereus wrightii* León *15964*
     Ex   19105   Cuba (Ciud. Habana) *5607*

R   II   *Leuchtenbergia principis* Hooker *15964*
     R   20067   Mexico - Coahuila *9114*
     R   21263   Mexico - Durango *21263*
     R   20067   Mexico - Hidalgo *20067*
     R   20067   Mexico - Nuevo Leon *9114*
     R   20067   Mexico - San Luis Potosi *9114*
     R   21263   Mexico - Tamaulipas *21263*
     R   21263   Mexico - Zacatecas *21263*

Ex   II   *Lobivia vatteri* Krainz *16336*
     Ex   16336   Argentina *16336*

R   II   *Lophophora diffusa* (Croizat) H. Bravo-Hollis *15964*
     R   20067   Mexico - Queretaro *20067*

E   II   *Mammillaria aff.* Salm-Dyck *20883*
     E   20883   Jamaica *20883*

R   II   *Mammillaria albicans* A. Berger *1058*
     R   19848   Mexico *1058*

V   II   *Mammillaria albicoma* Boedeker *9114*
     V   19848   Mexico - Tamaulipas *9114*

R   II   *Mammillaria angelensis* R.T. Craig *1058*
     R   19848   Mexico *1058*

R   II   *Mammillaria anniana* C. Glass & R. Foster *1058*
     R   19848   Mexico *1058*

V   II   *Mammillaria aureiceps* Lemaire *15964*
     V   19848   Mexico - Mexico D.F. *9114*

V   II   *Mammillaria aureilanata* Backeb. *1058*
     V   20067   Mexico - San Luis Potosi *20067*

R   II   *Mammillaria aurihamata* Boedeker *1058*
     R   14271   Mexico - San Luis Potosi *1058*

R   II   *Mammillaria backebergiana* Buchenau var. **backebergiana** *1058*
     R   14271   Mexico - Mexico State *1058*

R   II   *Mammillaria backebergiana* Buchenau var. *ernestii* (Fittkau) C. Glass & R. Foster *14271*
     R   14271   Mexico *14271*

R   II   *Mammillaria baumii* Boedeker *1058*
     R   15964   Mexico - Tamaulipas *1058*

R   II   *Mammillaria beiselii* Diers *1058*
     R   15964   Mexico *1058*

R   II   *Mammillaria bella* Backeb. *1058*
     R   15964   Mexico *1058*

R   II   *Mammillaria blossfeldiana* Boedeker *1058*
     R   19850   Mexico *1058*

V   II   *Mammillaria bocasana* Poselger *9114*
     V   19848   Mexico - San Luis Potosi *9114*

V   II   *Mammillaria bocensis* R.T. Craig *19850*
     V   19850   Mexico *15964*

R   II   *Mammillaria bombycina* Quehl *1058*
     R   19850   Mexico *1058*

R   II   *Mammillaria boolii* G. Lindsay *1058*
     R   19850   Mexico *1058*

I   II   *Mammillaria candida* Scheidw. *9114*
     I   19850   Mexico - Chihuahua *9114*
     I   19850   Mexico - Coahuila *9114*
     I   19850   Mexico - Nuevo Leon *9114*
     I   19850   Mexico - Tamaulipas *9114*
     I   19850   Mexico - Zacatecas *9114*

R   II   *Mammillaria capensis* (H. Gates) R.T. Craig *1058*
     R   19848   Mexico *1058*

E   II   *Mammillaria carmenae* Castaneda & Nunez *9114*
     E   19848   Mexico - Tamaulipas *9114*

V   II   *Mammillaria carretii* Rebut *1058*
     V   15964   Mexico *1058*

R   II   *Mammillaria cerralboa* (Britton & Rose) Orcutt *12469*
     R   19848   Mexico *12469*

V   II   *Mammillaria coahuilensis* (Boedeker) Moran *9114*
     V   19848   Mexico - Coahuila *9114*

R   II   *Mammillaria crucigera* Martius *9114*

R		19850 Mexico - Oaxaca *9114*	

R II *Mammillaria deherdtiana* Farwig var. *deherdtiana* *1058*
  R 19850 Mexico - Oaxaca *14271*

R II *Mammillaria diguetii* (A. Weber) D.R. Hunt *1058*
  R 15964 Mexico *1058*

R II *Mammillaria dixanthocentron* Backeb. *9058*
  R 19850 Mexico *9058*

R II *Mammillaria duoformis* R.T. Craig & E. Dawson *1058*
  R 19848 Mexico *1058*

V II *Mammillaria erectacantha* Foerster *1058*
  V 19848 Mexico *1058*

V II *Mammillaria esperanzaensis* Boedeker *9114*
  V 16360 Mexico - Puebla *9114*

R II *Mammillaria estebanensis* G. Lindsay *1058*
  R 15964 Mexico *1058*

R II *Mammillaria evermanniana* (Britton & Rose) Orcutt *1058*
  R 19848 Mexico *1058*

R II *Mammillaria fittkaui* C. Glass & R. Foster *1058*
  R 14265 Mexico - Jalisco *14265*

R II *Mammillaria fuauxiana* Backeb. *1058*
  R 15964 Mexico *15964*

R II *Mammillaria glareosa* Boedeker *1058*
  R 19850 Mexico *1058*

R II *Mammillaria glassii* R. Foster var. *ascensionis* (Reppenhagen) C. Glass & R. Foster *1058*
  R 14271 Mexico - Nuevo Leon *14271*

R II *Mammillaria goodridgei* Scheer var. *goodridgei* *15964*
  R 15964 Mexico - Guadelupe *10339*
  R 15964 Mexico - Baja California Peninsula (I. Cedros) *10339*

V II *Mammillaria goodridgei* Scheer var. *rectispina* E. Dawson *12469*
  V 19860 Mexico - Baja California Peninsula (Cedros Is.) *12469*

R II *Mammillaria grusonii* Runge *1058*
  R 19848 Mexico *1058*

V II *Mammillaria guelzowiana* Werderm. *1058*
  V 19848 Mexico *1058*

R II *Mammillaria guerreronis* (H. Bravo-Holl.) Backeb. *9114*
  R 19848 Mexico - Guerrero *9114*

V II *Mammillaria hahniana* Werderm. *1058*
  V 19850 Mexico *1058*

V II *Mammillaria halei* T.S. Brandegee *1058*
  V 20067 Mexico - Baja California Sur (Isla Magdalena, Isla Santa Margarita) *20067*

R II *Mammillaria heidiae* Krainz *9114*
  R 19850 Mexico - Puebla *9114*

R II *Mammillaria hernandezii* C. Glass & R. Foster *19850*
  R 19850 Mexico *19848*

V II *Mammillaria herrerae* Werderm. *1058*
  V 19848 Mexico *1058*

R II *Mammillaria hertrichiana* R.T. Craig *1058*
  R 19848 Mexico *1058*

R II *Mammillaria huajuapensis* H. Bravo-Holl. *1058*
  R 15964 Mexico *1058*

V II *Mammillaria huitzilopochtli* D.R. Hunt *1058*
  V 15964 Mexico *1058*

V II *Mammillaria humboldtii* Ehrenb. *9114*
  V 19850 Mexico - San Luis Potosi *9114*

R II *Mammillaria insularis* H. Gates *1058*
  R 19848 Mexico *1058*

R II *Mammillaria johnstonii* (Britton & Rose) Orcutt *1058*
  R 19848 Mexico *1058*

V II *Mammillaria klissingiana* Boedeker *9114*
  V 19848 Mexico - Tamaulipas *9114*

R II *Mammillaria knippeliana* Quehl *1058*
  R 15964 Mexico *1058*

V II *Mammillaria kraehenbuehlii* Krainz *1058*
  V 19848 Mexico *1058*

I II *Mammillaria laui* D.Hunt forma *dasyacantha* D.Hunt *19850*
  I 19850 Mexico *19850*

I II *Mammillaria laui* D. Hunt var. *discata* D. Hunt *19850*
  I 19850 Mexico *19850*

I II *Mammillaria laui* D. Hunt. var. *laui* *19850*
  I 19850 Mexico - Tamaulipas *9114*

V II *Mammillaria lenta* K. Brandegee *1058*
  V 19848 Mexico *1058*

R II *Mammillaria lindsayi* R.T. Craig *1058*
  R 19848 Mexico *1058*

V II *Mammillaria longiflora* (Britton & Rose) A. Berger *1058*
  V 19848 Mexico *1058*

R II *Mammillaria magnifica* Buchenau *1058*
  R 19848 Mexico *1058*

R II *Mammillaria maritima* G. Lindsay *1058*
  R 19848 Mexico *1058*

R II *Mammillaria marksiana* Krainz *1058*
  R 19848 Mexico *1058*

V II *Mammillaria mathildae* Krahenb. & Krainz *1058*
  V 19848 Mexico *1058*

R II *Mammillaria matudae* H. Bravo-Holl. *1058*
  R 19848 Mexico *1058*

V II *Mammillaria melaleuca* Karw. *1058*
  V 15964 Mexico *1058*

R II *Mammillaria mercadensis* Patoni *9114*
  R 19850 Mexico - Durango *9114*

R II *Mammillaria meyranii* H. Bravo-Holl. *1058*
  R 19850 Mexico *1058*

R II *Mammillaria microhelia* Werderm. *9114*
  R 19850 Mexico - San Luis Potosi *9114*

R II *Mammillaria miegiana* Earle *1058*
  R 15964 Mexico *1058*

R II *Mammillaria moelleriana* Boedeker *1058*
  R 15964 Mexico *1058*

R II *Mammillaria multidigitata* G. Lindsay *1058*
  R 15964 Mexico *1058*

R II *Mammillaria nana* Backeb. *1058*
  R 21263 Mexico - Guanajuato *21263*
  R 21263 Mexico - Queretaro *21263*

V II *Mammillaria napina* J.A. Purpus *9114*
  V 19850 Mexico - Puebla *9114*

Magnoliopsida (dicots): Cactaceae: *Mammillaria*

R   II   *Mammillaria nejapensis* R.T. Craig & F. Dawson *1058*
    R   *15964* Mexico *1058*

R   II   *Mammillaria neopalmeri* R.T. Craig *1058*
    R   *15964* Mexico *1058*

V   II   *Mammillaria oteroi* C. Glass & R. Foster *1058*
    V   *19850* Mexico *1058*

R   II   *Mammillaria painteri* Rose *9114*
    R   *15964* Mexico - Queretaro *9114*

R   II   *Mammillaria parkinsonii* Ehrenb. *1058*
    R   *15964* Mexico *1058*

E   I   *Mammillaria pectinifera* (Rümpler) A. Weber *9114*
    E   *20067* Mexico - Oaxaca *9114*
    E   *20067* Mexico - Puebla *9114*

R   II   *Mammillaria peninsularis* (Britton & Rose) Orcutt *1058*
    R   *15964* Mexico *1058*

R   II   *Mammillaria pennispinosa* Krainz var. *nazasensis* C. Glass & R. Foster *1058*
    R   *1058* Mexico *1058*

R   II   *Mammillaria pennispinosa* Krainz var. *pennispinosa* *12469*
    R   *21263* Mexico - Coahuila *21263*
    R   *21263* Mexico - Durango *21263*

R   II   *Mammillaria perezdelarosae* H. Bravo-Holl. & Scheinvar *1058*
    R   *19850* Mexico - Jalisco *1058*

R   II   *Mammillaria petrophila* K. Brandegee *1058*
    R   *15964* Mexico *1058*

R   II   *Mammillaria pilcayensis* H. Bravo-Holl. *15964*
    R   *15964* Mexico *15964*

R   II   *Mammillaria pilispina* J.A. Purpus *9114*
    R   *15964* Mexico - San Luis Potosi *9114*

I   II   *Mammillaria plumosa* A. Weber *9114*
    I   *19848* Mexico - Coahuila *9114*
    I   *19848* Mexico - Nuevo Leon *9114*

R   II   *Mammillaria pondii* Greene *1058*
    R   *19848* Mexico *1058*

R   II   *Mammillaria pringlei* (J. Coulter) K. Brandegee *9114*
    R   *19850* Mexico - Mexico D.F. *9114*

R   II   *Mammillaria pubispina* Boedeker *1058*
    R   *15964* Mexico *1058*

R   II   *Mammillaria reppenhagenii* D.R. Hunt *1058*
    R   *15964* Mexico *1058*

R   II   *Mammillaria rettigiana* Boedeker *1058*
    R   *15964* Mexico *1058*

R   II   *Mammillaria roseoalba* Boedeker *9114*
    R   *15964* Mexico - Nuevo Leon *12437*
    R   *15964* Mexico - Tamaulipas *9114*

R   II   *Mammillaria rubrograndis* Lau & Reppenhagen *1058*
    R   *15964* Mexico *1058*

V   II   *Mammillaria saboae* C. Glass var. *goldii* C. Glass & R. Foster *1058*
    V   *15964* Mexico - Sonora *12437*

V   II   *Mammillaria saboae* C. Glass var. *saboae* *1058*
    V   *15964* Mexico *1058*

E   II   *Mammillaria san-angelensis* Sanchez-Mej. *9114*
    E   *15964* Mexico - Mexico D.F. *9114*

E   II   *Mammillaria sanchez-mejoradae* R. Gonzalez G. *20067*
    E   *20067* Mexico - Nuevo Leon *20067*

V   II   *Mammillaria schiedeana* Ehrenb. var. *dumetorum* (J.A. Purpus) C. Glass & R. Foster *12469*
    V   *14267* Mexico - San Luis Potosi *14267*

V   II   *Mammillaria schiedeana* Ehrenb. var. *schiedeana* *1058*
    V   *14267* Mexico - Hidalgo *14267*
    V   *14267* Mexico - Queretaro *14267*

R   II   *Mammillaria schwarzii* Shurly *1058*
    R   *14269* Mexico - Guanajuato *14269*

V   II   *Mammillaria senilis* Lodd. *1058*
    V   *19850* Mexico *1058*

R   II   *Mammillaria setispina* Coulter *1058*
    R   *16360* Mexico *1058*

R   II   *Mammillaria slevinii* (Britton & Rose) Boedeker *1058*
    R   *15964* Mexico *1058*

E   I   *Mammillaria solisioides* Backeb. *9114*
    E   *20067* Mexico - Oaxaca *20067*
    E   *20067* Mexico - Puebla *9114*

R   II   *Mammillaria stella-de-tacubaya* Heese *1058*
    R   *15964* Mexico *1058*

V   II   *Mammillaria supertexta* C. Martius *1058*
    V   *15964* Mexico *1058*

R   II   *Mammillaria surculosa* Boedeker *1058*
    R   *15964* Mexico *1058*

I   II   *Mammillaria swinglei* (Britton & Rose) Boedeker *1058*
    I   *15964* Mexico *1058*

R   II   *Mammillaria tayloriorum* C. Glass & R. Foster *1058*
    R   *15964* Mexico *1058*

R   II   *Mammillaria tepexicensis* J. Meyrán *19850*
    R   *19850* Mexico *19850*

V   II   *Mammillaria theresae* Cutak *9114*
    V   *16360* Mexico - Durango *9114*

V   II   *Mammillaria tonalensis* D.R. Hunt *1058*
    V   *19850* Mexico *1058*

R   II   *Mammillaria varieaculeata* Buchenau *1058*
    R   *19850* Mexico *1058*

V   II   *Mammillaria weingartiana* Boedeker *1058*
    V   *15964* Mexico *1058*

R   II   *Mammillaria wiesingeri* Boedeker *1058*
    R   *15964* Mexico *1058*

R   II   *Mammillaria wrightii* Engelm. var. *wrightii* *20850*
    E   *20850* U.S. - Arizona *20850*
    R   *20850* U.S. - New Mexico *20850*
    E   *20850* U.S. - Texas *20850*

R   II   *Mammillaria xaltianguensis* Sánchez-Mej. *1058*
    R   *15964* Mexico *1058*

R   II   *Mammillaria yaquensis* R.T. Craig *9114*
    R   *15964* Mexico - Sonora *9114*

R   II   *Mammillaria yucatanensis* (Britton & Rose) Orcutt *15964*
    R   *19850* Mexico - Yucatan *9114*

R   II   *Mammillaria zeilmanniana* Boedeker *1058*
    R   *19850* Mexico *1058*

V   II   *Mammillaria zephyranthoides* Scheidw. *9114*
    V   *21263* Mexico - Guanajuato *21263*
    V   *19850* Mexico - Oaxaca *9114*

I   II   *Mammillaria zeyeriana* W. Haage *1058*
    I   *15964* Mexico *1058*

V II *Matucana aurantiaca* 15964
   V   15964 Peru 15964

V II *Matucana formosa* F. Ritter 15964
   V   12468 Peru 18200

V II *Matucana krahnii* (Donald) Bregman 15964
   V   15964 Peru 12468

E II *Matucana madisoniorum* (Hutchinson) G. Rowley 15964
   E   15964 Peru 12468

V II *Matucana paucicostata* F. Ritter 15964
   V   15964 Peru 18200

V II *Matucana tuberculata* (Donald) Bregman 15964
   V   12468 Peru 18200

V II *Melocactus azureus* 15964
   V   15964 Brazil 15964

I II *Melocactus azureus* ssp. *ferreophilus* 21307
   I   21307 Brazil 21307

E I *Melocactus conoideus* Buining & Brederoo 15964
   E   15964 Brazil (Vitoria da Conquista) 14964

E II *Melocactus curvispinus* Pfeiffer ssp. *dawsonii* (H. Bravo-Holl.) N.P. Taylor 15964
   E   20067 Mexico - Jalisco 20067

V I *Melocactus deinacanthus* Buing & Brederoo 15964
   V   15964 Brazil 14964

V II *Melocactus ferreophilus* 15964
   V   15964 Brazil 15964

V I *Melocactus glaucescens* Buining & Brederoo 15964
   V   15964 Brazil 14964

E II *Melocactus harlowii* (Britton & Rose) Vaupel 15964
   E   19105 Cuba (Guantanamo) 5607

E II *Melocactus holguinensis* Areces 15964
   E   19105 Cuba (Holguin) 5607

V II *Melocactus margaritaceus* 15964
   V   15964 Brazil 15964

E II *Melocactus matanzanus* Leon 15964
   E   19105 Cuba (Guantanamo; Matanzas) 5607

V II *Melocactus oaxacensis* (Britton & Rose) Backeb. 9114
   V   9114 Mexico - Oaxaca 9114

V II *Melocactus pachyacanthus* 15964
   V   15964 Brazil 15964

I II *Melocactus pachyacanthus* ssp. *viridis* 21307
   I   21307 Brazil 21307

V I *Melocactus paucispinus* G. Heimen & R. Paul 15964
   V   15964 Brazil 14964

V II *Melocactus violaceus* 15964
   V   15964 Brazil 15964

I II *Micranthocereus albicephalus* 15964
   I   21307 Brazil 15964

R II *Micranthocereus auriazureus* 15964
   R   15964 Brazil 15964

V II *Micranthocereus dolichospermaticus* 15964
   V   15964 Brazil 15964

R II *Micranthocereus polyanthus* 15964
   R   15964 Brazil 15964

V II *Micranthocereus streckeri* 15964
   V   15964 Brazil 15964

R II *Micranthocereus violaciflorus* 15964
   R   15964 Brazil 15964

E II *Mila caespitosa* Britton & Rose 15964

   E   12468 Peru 12468

I II *Neobesseya cubensis* (Britton & Rose) Hest. 5607
   I   5607 Cuba 5607

V II *Neobuxbaumia euphorbioides* (Haw.) F. Buxb. 15964
   V   15964 Mexico - Tamaulipas 12437
   V   15964 Mexico - Veracruz 12787

I II *Neobuxbaumia macrocephala* (A. Weber) Dawson 15964
   I   15964 Mexico - Puebla 12787

R II *Neobuxbaumia polylopha* (DC.) Backeb. 12469
   R   15964 Mexico - Hidalgo 12787
   R   15964 Mexico - Queretaro 12787

R II *Neoporteria andreaeana* 15964
   R   15964 Argentina 15964

R II *Neoporteria aricensis* (Ritter) Don & G.D. Rowley 15964
   R   15964 Chile 19034

Ex II *Neoporteria aspillagae* 15964
   Ex   19034 Chile 15964

R II *Neoporteria bulbocalyx* 15964
   R   15964 Argentina 15964

V II *Neoporteria carrizalensis* (Ritter) A. Hoffmann var. *carrizalensis* 19034
   V   19034 Chile 19034

V II *Neoporteria carrizalensis* (Ritter) A. Hoffmann var. *totoralensis* (Ritter) A. Hoffmann 19034
   V   19034 Chile 19034

E II *Neoporteria chilensis* (Hildmann) Britton & Rose 15964
   E   15964 Chile 19034

V II *Neoporteria clavata* (Soehr.) Werdermann var. *nigrihorrida* (Backeb.) A. Hoffmann 19034
   V   19034 Chile 19034

R II *Neoporteria confinis* 15964
   R   15964 Chile 15964

R II *Neoporteria crispa* (F.Ritter) Donald & Rowley 15964
   R   15964 Chile 15964

V II *Neoporteria curvispina* (Bert.) Don & G.D. Rowley 15964
   V   19034 Chile 19034

V II *Neoporteria eriosyzoides* (Ritter) Don & G.D. Rowley 15964
   V   19034 Chile 19034

V II *Neoporteria horrida* (Reny ex Gay) Hunt var. *armata* (Ritter) A. Hoffmann 19034
   V   19034 Chile 19034

V II *Neoporteria horrida* (Reny ex Gay) Hunt var. *coliguayensis* (Ritter) A. Hoffmann 19034
   V   19034 Chile 19034

V II *Neoporteria horrida* (Reny ex Gay) Hunt var. *horrida* 19034
   V   19034 Chile 19034

V II *Neoporteria horrida* (Reny ex Gay) Hunt var. *limariensis* (Ritter) A. Hoffmann 19034
   V   19034 Chile 19034

V II *Neoporteria horrida* (Reny ex Gay) Hunt var. *odoriflora* (Ritter) A. Hoffmann 19034
   V   19034 Chile 19034

I II *Neoporteria islayensis* (Forst.) Donald & Rowley 15964
   I   19034 Chile 19034

E   *12468* Peru *15964*

V   II   *Neoporteria jussieui* (Monville) Britton & Rose var. *chaniarensis* (Ritter) A. Hoffmann *19034*
    V   *19034* Chile *19034*

I   II   *Neoporteria jussieui* (Monville) Britton & Rose var. *chorosensis* (Ritter) A. Hoffmann *19034*
    I   *19034* Chile *19034*

V   II   *Neoporteria jussieui* (Monville) Britton & Rose var. *dimorpha* (Ritter) A. Hoffmann *19034*
    V   *19034* Chile *19034*

I   II   *Neoporteria jussieui* (Monville) Britton & Rose var. *huascensis* (Ritter) A. Hoffmann *19034*
    I   *19034* Chile *19034*

V   II   *Neoporteria jussieui* (Monville) Britton & Rose var. *jussieui* *19034*
    V   *19034* Chile *19034*

I   II   *Neoporteria jussieui* (Monville) Britton & Rose var. *setosiflora* (Ritter) A. Hoffmann *19034*
    I   *19034* Chile *19034*

I   II   *Neoporteria jussieui* (Monville) Britton & Rose var. *wagenknechtii* (Ritter) A. Hoffmann *19034*
    I   *19034* Chile *19034*

I   II   *Neoporteria kunzei* (Foerster) Backeb. var. *confinis* (Ritter) A. Hoffmann *19034*
    I   *19034* Chile *19034*

V   II   *Neoporteria kunzei* (Foerster) Backeb. var. *kunzei* *19034*
    V   *15964* Chile *19034*

R   II   *Neoporteria napina* (Phil.) Backeb. & Dolz *15964*
    R   *15964* Chile *19034*

E   II   *Neoporteria nidus* (Soehr.) Werdermann var. *coimasensis* (Ritter) A. Hoffmann *19034*
    E   *15964* Chile *19034*

E   II   *Neoporteria nidus* (Soehr.) Werdermann var. *gerocephala* (Ito) Ritter *19034*
    E   *15964* Chile *19034*

E   II   *Neoporteria nidus* (Ritter) A. Hoffmann var. *multicolor* *19034*
    E   *15964* Chile *19034*

E   II   *Neoporteria nidus* (Soehr.) Britton & Rose var. *nidus* *19034*
    E   *15964* Chile *19034*

E   II   *Neoporteria occulta* (Schumann) *15964*
    E   *15964* Chile *19034*

E   II   *Neoporteria odieri* (Salm Dyck) *15964*
    E   *15964* Chile *19034*

R   II   *Neoporteria pilispina* *15964*
    R   *15964* Chile *15964*

E   II   *Neoporteria recondita* (Ritter) Don & G.D. Fowley *15964*
    E   *15964* Chile *19034*

E   II   *Neoporteria simulans* (Ritter) Don & G.D. Fowley *15964*
    E   *15964* Chile *19034*

R   II   *Neoporteria sociabilis* *15964*
    R   *15964* Chile *15964*

R   II   *Neoporteria strausiana* *15964*
    R   *15964* Argentina *15964*

V   II   *Neoporteria taltalensis* Hutchinson *15964*

    V   *19034* Chile *19034*

R   II   *Neoporteria umadeave* *15964*
    R   *15964* Argentina *15964*

V   II   *Neoporteria vallenarensis* *15964*
    V   *15964* Chile *15964*

R   II   *Neoporteria villicumensis* *15964*
    R   *15964* Argentina *15964*

R   I   *Obregonia denegrii* Fric *15964*
    R   *20067* Mexico - Tamaulipas *9114*

R   II   *Opuntia anteojoensis* D.J. Pinkava *15964*
    R   *19848* Mexico *15964*

E   II   *Opuntia atacamensis* Phil. *15964*
    E   *19535* Chile *15964*

E   II   *Opuntia aureispina* (Brack & Heil) Pinkava & Parfitt *20850, 15964*
    E   *20850* U.S. - Texas *20850*

R   II   *Opuntia basilaris* Engelm. & Bigelow var. *aurea* (E.M. Baxter) W.T. Marsh. *20850, 14662*
    R   *20850* U.S. - Arizona *20850*
    I   *20850* U.S. - Utah *20850*

E   II   *Opuntia basilaris* Engelm. & Bigelow var. *brachyclada* (Griffiths) Munz *20850*
    E   *20850* U.S. - California *20850*
    I   *20850* U.S. - Nevada *20850*

E   II   *Opuntia basilaris* Engelm. & Bigelow var. *heilii* Welsh & Neese *20850*
    E   *20850* U.S. - Utah *20850*

V   II   *Opuntia basilaris* Engelm. & Bigelow var. *treleasei* (Coult.) Coult. ex Toumey *20850*
    I   *20850* U.S. - Arizona *20850*
    V   *20850* U.S. - California *20850*
    E   *20850* U.S. - Utah *20850*

V   II   *Opuntia basilaris* Engelm. & Bigelow var. *woodburyi* W.H. Earle *20850, 14662*
       20850 U.S. - Utah *20850*

R   II   *Opuntia bigelovii* Engelm. *20850, 14662*
    I   *20850* U.S. - Arizona *20850*
    I   *20850* U.S. - California *20850*
    I   *20850* U.S. - Nevada *20850*
    ?   Mexico *15964*

V   II   *Opuntia bigelovii* Engelm. var. *hoffmannii* Fosberg *20850*
    I   *20850* U.S. - California *20850*

I   II   *Opuntia borinquensis* Britt. & Rose *15964*
    I   *15106* Puerto Rico *14662*

I   II   *Opuntia brachyclada* *15964*
    I   *15964* United States of America *15964*

R   II   *Opuntia bravoana* E. Baxter *12469*
    R   *15964* Mexico *12469*

R   II   *Opuntia camachoi* *15964*
    R   *15964* Chile *15964*

R   II   *Opuntia chaffeyi* Britton & Rose *12469*
    R   *19850* Mexico *12469*

R   II   *Opuntia clavarioides* *15964*
    R   *15964* Argentina *15964*

R   II   *Opuntia clavata* Engelm. *20850, 15964*
    I   *20850* U.S. - Arizona *20850*
    I   *20850* U.S. - New Mexico *20850*

I   II   *Opuntia echios* J. Howell var. *barringtonensis* E. Dawson *11117*
    I   *15964* Ecuador - Galapagos (Santa Fe) *11117*

I   <u>II</u> *Opuntia echios* J. Howell var. *echios* *11117*
   I   *15964* Ecuador - Galapagos *11117*

I   <u>II</u> *Opuntia echios* J. Howell var. *gigantea* (J. Howell)
      D. Porter *11117*
   I   *15964* Ecuador - Galapagos (Santa Cruz) *11117*

I   <u>II</u> *Opuntia echios* J. Howell var. *inermis* E.
      Dawson *11117*
   I   *15964* Ecuador - Galapagos (V. Sierra Negra, Isabela)
        11117

I   <u>II</u> *Opuntia echios* J. Howell var. *zacana* (J. Howell)
      E.F. Anders. & Walk. *11117*
   I   *15964* Ecuador - Galapagos (Floreana) *11117*

E   <u>II</u> *Opuntia engelmannii* (Griffiths) Parfitt & Pinkava var.
      flexospina (Griffiths) Parfitt & Pinkava *20850*
   E   *20850* U.S. - Texas *20850*

E   <u>II</u> *Opuntia engelmannii* (Griffiths) Parfitt & Pinkava var.
      linguiformis (Griffiths) Parfitt & Pinkava *20850*
   E   *20850* U.S. - Texas *20850*

R   <u>II</u> *Opuntia excelsa* Sanchez-Mej. *12469*
   R   *19850* Mexico - Jalisco *16385*

I   <u>II</u> *Opuntia flexospina* *15964*
   I   *15964* United States of America *15964*

I   <u>II</u> *Opuntia fosbergii* *15964*
   I   *15964* United States of America *15964*

R   <u>II</u> *Opuntia fulgida* Engelm. *20850, 14662*
   I   *20850* U.S. - Arizona *20850*
   I   *20850* U.S. - New Mexico *20850*
   ?   Mexico *15964*

V   <u>II</u> *Opuntia fuliginosa* Griffiths *12469*
   V   *16385* Mexico - Morelos *16385*

I   <u>II</u> *Opuntia galapageia* Henslow var.
      galapageia *11117*
   I   *15964* Ecuador - Galapagos *11117*

I   <u>II</u> *Opuntia galapageia* Henslow var. *macrocarpa* E.
      Dawson *11117*
   I   *15964* Ecuador - Galapagos (Pinzon) *11117*

I   <u>II</u> *Opuntia galapageia* Henslow var. *profusa* E.F.
      Anderson & Walkington *11117*
   I   *15964* Ecuador - Galapagos (Rabida) *11117*

V   <u>II</u> *Opuntia gosseliniana* A. Weber *20850*
   I   *20850* U.S. - Arizona *20850*

V   <u>II</u> *Opuntia heacockiae* Arp *20850, 15964*
   I   *20850* U.S. - Colorado *20850*

R   <u>II</u> *Opuntia helleri* Schumann *11117*
   R   *15964* Ecuador - Galapagos *11117*

E   <u>II</u> *Opuntia imbricata* Haw. var. *argentea*
      Anthony *20850*
   E   *20850* U.S. - Texas *20850*

R   <u>II</u> *Opuntia insularis* A. Stewart *11117*
   R   *15964* Ecuador - Galapagos *11117*

E   <u>II</u> *Opuntia jamaicensis* Britton & Harris *20883, 15964*
   E   *13336* Jamaica *20883*

Ex <u>II</u> *Opuntia linguiformis* *15964*
   Ex *15964* United States of America *15964*

R   <u>II</u> *Opuntia littoralis* (Engelm.) Cockerell *20850, 15964*
   I   *20850* U.S. - Arizona *20850*
   I   *20850* U.S. - California *20850*
   ?   Mexico *15964*

V   <u>II</u> *Opuntia macracantha* *15964*
   V   *19105* Cuba *19105*

V   <u>II</u> *Opuntia martiniana* (L. Benson) Parfitt *20850, 15964*
   I   *20850* U.S. - Arizona *20850*
   I   *20850* U.S. - California *20850*
   I   *20850* U.S. - Nevada *20850*
   I   *20850* U.S. - Utah *20850*

V   <u>II</u> *Opuntia megarhiza* Rose *12469*
   V   *19850* Mexico - San Luis Potosi *19850*

V   <u>II</u> *Opuntia megasperma* J. Howell var.
      megasperma *11117*
   V   *14980* Ecuador - Galapagos (Champion; Floreana)
        5670

R   <u>II</u> *Opuntia megasperma* J. Howell var. *mesophytica*
      Lundh *11117*
   R   *15964* Ecuador - Galapagos *11117*

R   <u>II</u> *Opuntia megasperma* J. Howell var. *orientalis* (J.
      Howell) D. Porter *11117*
   R   *15964* Ecuador - Galapagos *11117*

R   <u>II</u> *Opuntia microdasys* (J. Lehm.) Pfeiffer var.
      albispina Fobe *12469*
   R   *14290* Mexico - San Luis Potosi *14290*

R   <u>II</u> *Opuntia molinensis* *15964*
   R   *15964* Argentina *15964*

I   <u>II</u> *Opuntia multigeniculata* *15964*
   I   *15964* United States of America *15964*

E   <u>II</u> *Opuntia munzii* C.B. Wolf *20850, 15964*
   E   *20850* U.S. - California *20850*

R   <u>II</u> *Opuntia oricola* Philbrick *20850, 14662*
   I   *20850* U.S. - California *20850*
   ?   Mexico *15964*

E   <u>II</u> *Opuntia pachypus* Schumann *12468*
   E   *15964* Peru *12468*

R   <u>II</u> *Opuntia parryi* Engelm. *20850*
   I   *20850* U.S. - California *20850*

R   <u>II</u> *Opuntia polyacantha* Haw. var. *juniperina* (Britt. &
      Rose) L. Benson *20850*
   I   *20850* U.S. - Arizona *20850*
   I   *20850* U.S. - Colorado *20850*
   I   *20850* U.S. - New Mexico *20850*
   I   *20850* U.S. - Utah *20850*
   E   *20850* U.S. - Wyoming *20850*

I   <u>II</u> *Opuntia pusilla* (Haw.) Nutt. *15964*
   I   *19002* U.S. - North Carolina *14662*

R   <u>II</u> *Opuntia rosarica* G. Lindsay *16385*
   R   *19848* Mexico - Baja California Peninsula
        16385

E   <u>II</u> *Opuntia sanguinea* Proctor *20883, 13336*
   E   *13336* Jamaica *20883*

R   <u>II</u> *Opuntia santamaria* (Baxter) H. Bravo-Holl. *16385*
   R   *19848* Mexico - Baja California Sur *16385*

V   <u>II</u> *Opuntia santa-rita* (Griffiths & Hare) Rose *20850,*
      15964
   I   *20850* U.S. - Arizona *20850*
   I   *20850* U.S. - New Mexico *20850*
   I   *20850* U.S. - Texas *20850*

R   <u>II</u> *Opuntia saxicola* J. Howell *11117*
   R   *15964* Ecuador - Galapagos (V. Cerro Azul, Isabela)
        11117

R   <u>II</u> *Opuntia spinosissima* P. Mill. *20883, 20850, 15964*
   E   *20850* U.S. - Florida *20850*
   R   *20883* Jamaica *20883*
   R   *20883* Puerto Rico *20883*
   R   *20883* British Virgin Is. (Green Cay) *20883*
   R   *20883* USA - Virgin Is. *20883*

V   II   *Opuntia stenopetala* Engelm. var. *inerme* H. Bravo-Holl. *16385*
- V   *16385*   Mexico - Hidalgo *16385*
- V   *16385*   Mexico - Queretaro *16385*

R   II   *Opuntia tarapacana* Phil. *15964*
- R   *19535*   Chile *15964*

V   II   *Opuntia tetracantha* Toumey *20883, 20850, 15964*
- I   *20850*   U.S. - Arizona *20850*
- I   *20883*   Mexico *20883*

I   II   *Opuntia treleasei* Coult. *14662*
- I   *15964*   U.S. - California *14662*

I   II   *Opuntia werneri* *21307*
- I   *21307*   Brazil *21307*

V   II   *Opuntia whipplei* Engelm. & Bigelow *20850, 14662*
- I   *20850*   U.S. - Arizona *20850*
- I   *20850*   U.S. - Colorado *20850*
- V   *20850*   U.S. - Nevada *20850*
- I   *20850*   U.S. - New Mexico *20850*
- V   *20850*   U.S. - Utah *20850*

E   II   *Opuntia whipplei* Engelm. & Bigelow var. *multigeniculata* (Clokey) L. Benson *20850*
- I   U.S. - Arizona
- E   *20850*   U.S. - Nevada *20850*

R   II   *Opuntia wigginsii* L. Benson *20850, 15964*
- I   *20850*   U.S. - Arizona *20850*
- E   *20850*   U.S. - California *20850*

E   II   *Opuntia yanganucensis* (Rauh & Backeb.) G. Rowley *15964*
- E   *12468*   Peru *15964*

V   II   *Oreocereus australis* *15964*
- V   *15964*   Chile *15964*

R   II   *Oreocereus hempelianus* (Guerke) D. Hunt *15964*
- V   *15964*   Chile *5598*
- R   *18200*   Peru *15964*

V   II   *Ortegocactus macdougallii* Alex. *12469*
- V   *15964*   Mexico *12469*

R   II   *Pachycereus fulviceps* (F.A.C. Weber ex Schumann) D. Hunt *15964*
- R   *19850*   Mexico *19850*

E   II   *Pachycereus gaumeri* Britton & Rose *15964*
- E   *19848*   Mexico - Chiapas *16385*
- E   *19848*   Mexico - Yucatan *16385*

E   I   *Pediocactus bradyi* L. Benson *20850, 15964*
- E   *20850*   U.S. - Arizona *20850*

V   I   *Pediocactus despainii* Welsh & Goodrich *20850, 15964*
- V   *20850*   U.S. - Utah *20850*

E   I   *Pediocactus knowltonii* L. Benson *20850, 15964*
- E   *20850*   U.S. - Colorado *20850*
- E   *20850*   U.S. - New Mexico *20850*

V   I   *Pediocactus paradinei* B.W. Benson *20850, 15964*
- V   *20850*   U.S. - Arizona *20850*

V   II   *Pediocactus peeblesianus* (Croizat) L. Benson *20850*
- V   *20850*   U.S. - Arizona *20850*

V   I   *Pediocactus peeblesianus* (Croizat) L. Benson var. *fickeiseniae* L. Benson *20850*
- V   *20850*   U.S. - Arizona *20850*

E   I   *Pediocactus peeblesianus* (Croizat) L. Benson var. *peeblesianus* *20850, 20079*
- E   *20850*   U.S. - Arizona *20850*

R   I   *Pediocactus sileri* (Engelm.) L. Benson *20850, 19582*
- R   *20850*   U.S. - Arizona *20850*

    E   *20850*   U.S. - Utah *20850*

R   II   *Pediocactus simpsonii* (Engelm.) Britt. & Rose var. *minor* (Engelm.) Cockerell *20850*
- I   *20850*   U.S. - Colorado *20850*
- R   *20850*   U.S. - New Mexico *20850*
- I   *20850*   U.S. - Utah *20850*
- I   *20850*   U.S. - Wyoming *20850*

E   I   *Pediocactus winkleri* Heil *20850, 15964*
- E   *20850*   U.S. - Utah *20850*

R   I   *Pelecyphora aselliformis* Ehrenb. *15964*
- R   *20067*   Mexico - San Luis Potosi *9114*

V   I   *Pelecyphora strobiliformis* (Werderm.) Fric & Schelle *15964*
- V   *20067*   Mexico - Nuevo Leon *12437*
- E   *20067*   Mexico - Tamaulipas *9114*

R   II   *Peniocereus cuixmalensis* Sánchez-Mej. *15964*
- R   *19850*   Mexico *15964*

R   II   *Peniocereus fosterianus* Cutak var. *fosterianus* *12469*
- R   *15964*   Mexico *12469*

I   II   *Peniocereus fosterianus* Cutak var. *multitepalus* Sánchez-Mej.
- I   *15964*   Mexico *15964*

R   II   *Peniocereus fosterianus* Cutak var. *nizandensis* Sánchez-Mej. *14255*
- R   *15964*   Mexico - Chiapas *14255*
- R   *15964*   Mexico - Oaxaca *14255*

R   II   *Peniocereus greggii* Britton & Rose *15964*
- I   *15964*   U.S. - Arizona *8058*
- I   *8058*   U.S. - California *8058*
- I   *8058*   U.S. - New Mexico *8058*
- I   *8058*   U.S. - Texas *8058*
- R   *19850*   Mexico *8058*

V   II   *Peniocereus greggii* var. *greggii* *20850*
- I   *20850*   U.S. - Arizona *20850*
- I   *20850*   U.S. - New Mexico *20850*
- V   *20850*   U.S. - Texas *20850*

R   II   *Peniocereus lazaro-cardenasii* (Contereras) D. Hunt *15964*
- R   *19850*   Mexico *19850*

R   II   *Peniocereus maculatus* (Weing.) Cutak *12469*
- R   *15964*   Mexico - Guerrero *16385*

R   II   *Peniocereus marianus* (Gentry) Sánchez-Mej. *12469*
- R   *15964*   Mexico - Sinaloa *16385*
- R   *15964*   Mexico - Sonora *16385*

I   II   *Peniocereus rosei* G. Ortega *12469*
- I   *15964*   Mexico *12469*

R   II   *Peniocereus striatus* (Brandegee) F. Bauxhaum *15964*
- R   *19893*   U.S. - Arizona *19893*
- R   *19893*   Mexico *19893*

R   II   *Peniocereus tepalcatepecanus* Sánchez-Mej. *12469*
- R   *15964*   Mexico - Michoacan *16385*

R   II   *Peniocereus zopilotensis* (J. Meyrán) F. Buxham *15964*
- R   *15964*   Mexico - Guerrero *12787*

R   II   *Pereskia aureiflora* Ritter *20883, 15964*
- R   *20883*   Brazil *20883*

R   II   *Pereskia bahiensis* Gurke *20883, 15964*
- R   *20883*   Brazil *20883*

R   II   *Pereskia diaz-romeroana* Cárdenas *20883, 15964*
- R   *20883*   Bolivia *20883*

V   II   *Pereskia grandifolia* Haw. var. *violacea* Leuenberger *20883*

R   20883 Brazil *20883*

V II *Pereskia humboldtii* Britton & Rose var. *humboldtii 20883*

    V   *20883* Peru *20883*

V II *Pereskia humboldtii* Britton & Rose var. *rauhii* (Backeberg) Leuenber *20883*

    V   *20883* Peru *20883*

R II *Pereskia portulacifolia* (Linnaeus) De Candolle *20883, 5642*

    V   *20883* Dominican Republic *20883*

    R   *20883* Haiti *20883*

E II *Pereskia quisqueyana* Liogier *20883, 15964*

    E   *20883* Dominican Republic *20883*

V II *Pereskia weberiana* K. Schumann. *20883, 15964*

    V   *20883* Bolivia *20883*

R II *Pereskia zinniiflora* De Candolle *20883, 15964*

    R   *20883* Cuba *20883*

I II *Pilosocereus aurisetus* ssp. *aurilanatus 21307*

    I   *21307* Brazil *21307*

I II *Pilosocereus floccosus* ssp. *quadricostatus 21307*

    I   *21307* Brazil *21307*

R II *Pilosocereus fulvilanatus 15964*

    R   *15964* Brazil *15964*

I II *Pilosocereus robinii* (L.) Byles & Rowley *20883, 20850, 19718*

    I   *20850* U.S. - Florida *20850*

    V   *15964* Cuba *15964*

    I   *20883* Puerto Rico *20883*

    I   *20883* USA - Virgin Is. *20883*

E II *Pilosocereus robinii* var. *deeringii* (Small) Kartesz & Gandhi *20850*

    E   *20850* U.S. - Florida *20850*

I II *Pilosocereus robinii* (L.) Byles & Rowley var. *robinii 20883, 20850*

    E   *20850* U.S. - Florida *20850*

    I   *20883* Cuba *20883*

    I   *20883* Puerto Rico *20883*

    I   *20883* USA - Virgin Is. *20883*

R II *Pilosocereus rosae 15964*

    R   *15964* Brazil *15964*

R II *Pilosocereus tehuacanus* (Weing.) Byles & Rowl. *15964*

    R   *12787* Mexico - Puebla *12787*

R II *Pilosocereus ulei 15964*

    R   *15964* Brazil *15964*

R II *Pilosocereus vilaboensis 15964*

    R   *15964* Brazil *15964*

V II *Pseudorhipsalis alata* (Swartz) Britton & Rose *15964*

    V   *13336* Jamaica *15964*

R II *Pseudorhipsalis lankesteri* (Kimnach) W. Barthlott *15964*

    R   *15964* Costa Rica *15964*

R II *Pyrrhocactus duripulpa* Ritt. *5598*

    R   *5598* Chile *5598*

E II *Pyrrhocactus esmeraldana* Ritt. *5598*

    E   *5598* Chile *5598*

E II *Pyrrhocactus fankhauseri* Ritt. *5598*

    E   *5598* Chile *5598*

V II *Pyrrhocactus fulva* Ritt. *5598*

    V   *5598* Chile *5598*

R II *Pyrrhocactus hypogea* Ritt. *5598*

    R   *5598* Chile *5598*

E II *Pyrrhocactus imitans* Backeb. *5598*

    E   *5598* Chile *5598*

E II *Pyrrhocactus krausii* Ritt. *15964*

    E   *19535* Chile *15964*

E II *Pyrrhocactus laniceps* Ritt. *5598*

    E   *5598* Chile *5598*

R II *Pyrrhocactus limariensis 15964*

    R   *15964* Chile *15964*

Ex II *Pyrrhocactus longirama* Ritt. *5598*

    Ex   *5598* Chile *5598*

E II *Pyrrhocactus malleota* Ritt. *5598*

    E   *5598* Chile *5598*

E II *Pyrrhocactus napinus* Philippi *5598*

    E   *5598* Chile *5598*

R II *Pyrrhocactus nigriscoparia* Backeb. *5598*

    R   *5598* Chile *5598*

Ex II *Pyrrhocactus nuda* Ritt. *5598*

    Ex   *5598* Chile *5598*

E II *Pyrrhocactus odieri* Ritt. *5598*

    E   *5598* Chile *5598*

R II *Pyrrhocactus olivana* Ritt. *19534*

    R   *19534* Chile *19534*

E II *Pyrrhocactus pseudoreichei* Lembcke & Backeb. *5598*

    E   *19535* Chile *5598*

E II *Pyrrhocactus reichei* Schumann *5598*

    E   *19535* Chile *5598*

E II *Rebutia neumanniana 15964*

    E   *16336* Argentina *16336*

    E   *20185* Argentina - Jujuy (Humahuaca) *20175*

I II *Rhipsalis baccifera* ssp. *hileiabaiana 21307*

    I   *21307* Brazil *21307*

I II *Rhipsalis burchellii 15964*

    I   *21307* Brazil *15964*

I II *Rhipsalis cereoides 15964*

    I   *21307* Brazil *15964*

I II *Rhipsalis mesembryanthoides 15964*

    I   *21307* Brazil *15964*

I II *Rhipsalis pacheo-leonis* ssp. *pacheo-leonis 21307*

    I   *21307* Brazil *21307*

I II *Rhipsalis pilocarpa 15964*

    I   *21307* Brazil *15964*

R II *Schlumbergera kautskyi 15964*

    R   *15964* Brazil *15964*

E II *Schlumbergera orssichiana 15964*

    E   *15964* Brazil *15964*

V II *Schlumbergera truncata 15964*

    V   *15964* Brazil *15964*

E II *Sclerocactus blainei* Welsh & Thorne *20850*

    E   *20850* U.S. - Nevada *20850*

R II *Sclerocactus erectocentrus* (Coult.) N.P. Taylor *20850*

    R   *20850* U.S. - Arizona *20850*

    I   *20850* U.S. - New Mexico *20850*

    I   *20883* Mexico *20883*

E I *Sclerocactus erectocentrus* var. *acunensis* (W.T. Marsh) H. Bravo *20883*

V	20078	U.S. - Arizona 20078
I	20883	Mexico 20883
I	20078	Mexico - Sonora 9114

R I *Sclerocactus glaucus* (J.A. Purpus ex K. Schum.) L. Benson 20850, 15964

R	20850	U.S. - Colorado 20850
R	20850	U.S. - Utah 20850

V I *Sclerocactus mariposensis* (Hester) N.P. Taylor 20883, 20850, 15964

V	20850	U.S. - Texas 20850
I	20883	Mexico 20883
V	19850	Mexico - Coahuila 8058

V I *Sclerocactus mesae-verdae* (Boissevain ex Boissevain & C. Davids.) L. Benson 20850, 15964

V	20850	U.S. - Colorado 20850
V	20850	U.S. - New Mexico 20850

V I *Sclerocactus papyracanthus* (Engelm.) N.P. Taylor 20883, 20850, 15964

V	20850	U.S. - Arizona 20850
V	20850	U.S. - New Mexico 20850
E	20850	U.S. - Texas 20850
I	20883	Mexico 20883

R II *Sclerocactus parviflorus* Clover & Jotter var. *intermedius* (Peebles) Woodruff & L. Benson 20850

I	20850	U.S. - Arizona 20850
I	20850	U.S. - Colorado 20850
R	20850	U.S. - New Mexico 20850
I	20850	U.S. - Utah 20850

E II *Sclerocactus schlesseri* Heil & Welsh 20850

E	20850	U.S. - Nevada 20850

V II *Sclerocactus spinosior* (Engelm.) Woodruff & L. Benson 20850

E	20850	U.S. - Arizona 20850
I	20850	U.S. - Colorado 20850
V	20850	U.S. - Utah 20850

R II *Sclerocactus unguispinus* (Engelm.) N.P. Taylor 15964

R	19850	Mexico - San Luis Potosi 15964

R II *Sclerocactus whipplei* (Eng. & Bigel.) Britton & Rose var. *heilii* Castetter, Pierce & Schwerin 20850

R	20850	U.S. - New Mexico 20850

E I *Sclerocactus wrightiae* L. Benson 20850, 15964

E	20850	U.S. - Utah 20850

V II *Selenicereus anthonyanus* (Alex.) D.R. Hunt 15964

V	14253	Mexico - Chiapas 12469

R II *Selenicereus atropilosus* Kimnach 16390

R	16385	Mexico - Jalisco 16385

R II *Selenicereus brevispinus* Britton & Rose 5607

R	15964	Cuba (Camaguey) 5607

V II *Selenicereus chrysocardium* (Alexander) Kimnach 15964

V	19850	Mexico - Chiapas 14249
V	19850	Mexico - Tabasco 14249

R II *Selenicereus donkelaarii* (Salm-Dyck) Britton & Rose 15964

R	14254	Mexico - Yucatan 12469

R II *Selenicereus hamatus* (Scheidw.) Britton & Rose 12469

R	15964	Mexico 12469

I II *Selenicereus innesii* Kimnach 5607

I	15964	St Vincent (near Owia) 8767

R II *Stenocactus coptonogonus* (Lemaire) A. Berger 19850 Mexico 15964

R II *Stenocactus sulphureus* (Dietrich) H. Bravo-Hollis 19850

R	19850	Mexico 15964

R II *Stenocereus chacalapensis* (H. Bravo-Holl. & Macdougall) F. Buxb.

R	12787	Mexico - Oaxaca 12787

V II *Stenocereus eruca* (K. Brandegee) Gibson & Horak 12787

E	20067	Mexico - Baja California Peninsula 12437
V	20067	Mexico - Baja California Sur 20067

R II *Stenocereus martinezii* (G. Ortega) H. Bravo-Holl.

R	19848	Mexico - Sinaloa 12787

R II *Tacinga braunii* 15964

R	15964	Brazil 15964

V II *Thelocactus bicolor* (Pfeiffer) Britton & Rose var. *bolaensis* (Runge) A. Berger 12437

V	12437	Mexico - Coahuila 12437

V II *Thelocactus bicolor* (Pfeiffer) Britton & Rose var. *flavidispinus* Backeberg 20883, 20850, 19002

V	20850	U.S. - Texas 20850
I	20883	Mexico 20883

V II *Thelocactus bicolor* (Pfeiffer) Britton & Rose var. *schwarzii* (Backeberg) E.F. Anderson 20067

V	20067	Mexico - Tamaulipas 20067

V II *Thelocactus conothelos* (Regel & Klein) Backeberg & Knuth var. *argenteus* C. Glass & R. Foster 14281

V	20067	Mexico - Nuevo Leon 20067

V II *Thelocactus conothelos* (Regel & Klein) Backeberg & Knuth var. *aurantiacus* C. Glass & R. Foster 11419

V	20067	Mexico - Nuevo Leon 11419

V II *Thelocactus hastifer* (Werderm. & Bodecker) F.M. Knuth 15964

V	20067	Mexico - Queretaro 20067

R II *Thelocactus heterochromus* (A. Weber) V. Oosten 15964

R	19850	Mexico 15964

R II *Thelocactus leucacanthus* (Zucc.) Britton & Rose var. *ehrenbergii* (Pfeiffer) H. Bravo-Holl. 19850

R	19850	Mexico 15964

V II *Thelocactus macdowellii* (Rebut ex Quehl) C. Glass 12529

V	20067	Mexico - Coahuila 12437

R II *Thelocactus rinconensis* (Poselger) Britton & Rose var. *nidulans* (Quehl) Glass & R. Foster 19850

R	19850	Mexico 19850

V II *Thelocactus tulensis* (Poselger) Britton & Rose 15964

V	15964	Mexico 12469

V II *Thelocactus tulensis* (Poselger) Britton & Rose var. *matudae* (Sánchez-Mejorada & A. Lau) E.F. Anderson 14281

V	20067	Mexico - Nuevo Leon 15964

E II *Thelocephala krausii* 15964

E	15964	Chile 15964

E II *Trichocereus atacamensis* (Philippi) Marshall & Bock 11748

E	19534	Chile 11748

V I *Turbinicarpus gielsdorfianus* (Werderm.) John & Riha 15964

V	19850	Mexico - San Luis Potosi 9114
V	21263	Mexico - Tamaulipas 21263

V I *Turbinicarpus hoferi* J.M. Luthy & A.B. Lau 21384, 19850

V	19850	Mexico 19850

R   I *Turbinicarpus knuthianus* (Boed.) John & Riha *15964*
    R   *12469* Mexico - San Luis Potosi *15964*

V   I *Turbinicarpus laui* C. Glass & R. Foster *9114*
    V   *20067* Mexico - San Luis Potosi *9114*

V   I *Turbinicarpus lophophoroides* (Werderm.) F. Buxb. &
    Backeb. *14273*
    V   *16360* Mexico - San Luis Potosi *14273*

V   I *Turbinicarpus mandragora* (Berger) A. Zimmerman *15964*
    V   *19850* Mexico - Coahuila *9114*

V   I *Turbinicarpus pseudomacrochele* (Backeb.) F. Buxb. &
    Backeb. *20067*
    V   *20067* Mexico - Queretaro *9114*

I   I *Turbinicarpus saueri* (Boedeker) John & Riha *15964*
    I   *19850* Mexico - Coahuila *9114*
    I   *19850* Mexico - Tamaulipas *14273*

E   I *Turbinicarpus schmiedickeanus* (Bödeker) F. Buxb. & Backeb.
    var. *flaviflorus* (G. Frank) C. Glass & R. Foster *14273*
    E   *14273* Mexico - Nuevo Leon *14273*
    E   *14273* Mexico - San Luis Potosi *14273*
    E   *14273* Mexico - Tamaulipas *14273*

V   I *Turbinicarpus schmiedickeanus* (Bödeker) F. Buxb. & Backeb.
    var. *gracilis* (C. Glass & R. Foster) C. Glass & R.
    Foster *14273*
    V   *14273* Mexico - Nuevo Leon *14273*

V   I *Turbinicarpus schmiedickeanus* (Bödeker) F. Buxb. & Backeb.
    var. *klinkerianus* (Backeberg & H.J. Jacobsen) C. Glass & R.
    Foster *14273*
    V   *20067* Mexico - San Luis Potosi *14273*

V   I *Turbinicarpus schmiedickeanus* (Bödeker) F. Buxb. & Backeb.
    var. *macrochele* (Werderm.) C. Glass & R. Foster *14273*
    V   *20067* Mexico - San Luis Potosi *14273*

V   I *Turbinicarpus schmiedickeanus* (Bödeker) F. Buxb. & Backeb.
    var. *schmiedickeanus* *9019*
    V   *20067* Mexico - Tamaulipas *14273*

V   I *Turbinicarpus schmiedickeanus* (Bödeker) F. Buxb. & Backeb.
    var. *schwarzii* (Shurly) C. Glass & R. Foster *14273*
    V   *20067* Mexico - San Luis Potosi *14273*

V   I *Turbinicarpus schwarzii* (Shurly) Backeb. *21384,
    15964*
    V   *21263* Mexico - Tamaulipas *21263*

V   I *Turbinicarpus subterraneus* (Backeb.) A. Zimmerman var.
    zaragosae (Glass & Foster) A. Zimmerman *20067*
    V   *20067* Mexico - Nuevo Leon *20067*

V   I *Turbinicarpus swobodae* L. Diers *21384, 19850*
    V   *19850* Mexico *19850*

V   I *Turbinicarpus ysabelae* (K. Schlange) John &
    Riha *21384, 15964*
    V   *19850* Mexico *15964*

E   I *Uebelmannia buiningii* Donald *14964*
    E   *15964* Brazil - Minas Gerais (east) *14964*

    Uebelmannia flavispina Buining & Brederoo *21384,
    14964*
    R   *15964* Brazil - Minas Gerais (east) *14964*

V   I *Uebelmannia gummifera* (Backeb. & Voll) Buining *14964*
    V   *15964* Brazil - Minas Gerais (east) *14964*

I   I *Uebelmannia pectinifera* Buin ssp. *flavispina*
    (Buin. & Bred.) Braun & Est *21307*
    I   *21307* Brazil *21307*

V   I *Uebelmannia pectinifera* Buin. ssp. *horrida* (Braun)
    Braun & Est *21384, 14964*

    V   *15964* Brazil - Minas Gerais (east) *14964*

V   I *Uebelmannia pectinifera* Buining var.
    pectinifera *14964*
    V   *15964* Brazil - Minas Gerais (east) *14964*

V   I *Uebelmannia pectinifera* Buining var.
    pseudopectinifera *14964*
    V   *15964* Brazil - Minas Gerais *14964*

R   II *Weberocereus bradei* (Britton & Rose) Rowley *15964*
    R   *14260* Costa Rica *15964*

R   II *Weberocereus imitans* (Kimnach & Hutch.) D.
    Hunt *15964*
    R   *14260* Costa Rica *15964*

E   II *Weberocereus rosei* *15964*
    E   *15964* Ecuador *15964*

I   II *Weberocereus tonduzii* (A. Weber) Rowley *15964*
    I   *14253* Costa Rica *15964*
    V   *14253* Panama *14253*

R   II *Weberocereus trichophorus* Johnson & Kimnach *14255*
    R   *14255* Costa Rica *14255*

Callitrichaceae

Number of genera: 1
Number of species: 35
Recorded threatened species: 5 (14%)

Cosmopolitan, centered in temperate zones.

R   *Callitriche brachycarpa* Hegelm. *20681*
    I   *20681* Australia - Tasmania *20681*
    I   *20681* Australia - Victoria *20681*

V   *Callitriche cyclocarpa* Hegelm. *20681*
    I   *20681* Australia - New South Wales *20681*
    I   *20681* Australia - Victoria *20681*

E   *Callitriche fassettii* Schotsman *20850*
    I   *20850* U.S. - Oregon *20850*

V   *Callitriche longipedunculata* Morong *20850*
    I   *20850* U.S. - California *20850*

V   *Callitriche trochlearis* Fassett *20850*
    I   *20850* U.S. - California *20850*
    I   *20850* U.S. - Oregon *20850*

Calycanthaceae

Number of genera: 3
Number of species: 5
Recorded threatened species: 3 (60%)

China; North America.

E   *Calycanthus brockiana* Ferry & Ferry *20850*
    I   *20850* U.S. - Georgia *20850*

V   *Calycanthus chinensis* Cheng & S.Y. Chang *17617*
    V   *17617* China - Zhejiang (Lingan, Tiantai)
    11139

R   *Calycanthus occidentalis* Hook. & Arn. *20850*
    I   *20850* U.S. - California *20850*

Calyceraceae

Number of genera: 6
Number of species: 60
Recorded threatened species: 1 (1%)

Central and South America.

R   *Nastanthus falklandicus* David Moore
    R   Falkland Is.

Campanulaceae

Number of genera: 70
Number of species: 2,000
Recorded threatened species: 428   (21%)

Cosmopolitan.

V *Adenophora hatsusimae* Kitam. *10573*
    V *10573* Japan *10573*

I *Adenophora jacutica* Fed. *5942*
    I *5942* Russia (Far East) - Khabarovsk *5942*

V *Adenophora maximowicziana* Makino *10573*
    V *10573* Japan *10573*

R *Adenophora takedae* Makino var. *howozana*
    Sugimoto *10573*
    R *10573* Japan *10573*

R *Adenophora tashiroi* Makino & Nakai *10573*
    R *10573* Japan *10573*

R *Adenophora taurica* (Sukaczev) Juz. *8000, 20171*
    R former European USSR *8000*

R *Adenophora teramotoi* Hurusawa & Yamaz. *10573*
    R *10573* Japan *10573*

R *Adenophora triphylla* A. DC. var. *puellaris*
    Hara *10573*
    R *10573* Japan *10573*

I *Apetahia longistigmata* (F. Brown) F. Wimmer *20845*
    I *20845* French Polynesia - Marquesas Is *20845*

R *Apetahia margaretae* (F.Brown) F.Wimmer *20845*
    E *20845* French Polynesia - Tubuai Is. (Rapa)
    20845

E *Apetahia raiateensis* Baillon *20845*
    E *20845* French Polynesia - Society Is. (Raiatea)
    20845

R *Asyneuma babadaghensis* Yildiz & Kit Tan *12840*
    R *12840* Turkey *12840*

R *Asyneuma comosiforme* Hayek & Janch. *20178, 20171*
    R *20178* Albania *20178*

R *Asyneuma compactum* (Boiss. & Heldr.) Damboldt *12840*
    R *12840* Turkey *12840*

R *Asyneuma davisianum* Yildiz & Kit Tan *12840*
    R *12840* Turkey *12840*

R *Asyneuma ekimianum* Kit Tan & Yikdiz *12840*
    R *12840* Turkey *12840*

V *Asyneuma giganteum* (Boiss.) Bornm. *17891*
    V *20731* Greece - East Aegean Is *20731*

R *Asyneuma ilgazensis* Yildiz & Kit Tan *12840*
    R *12840* Turkey *12840*

R *Asyneuma isauricum* Contandr. & al. *12840*
    R *12840* Turkey *12840*

R *Asyneuma linifolium* (Boiss. & Heldr.) Bornm. ssp.
    eximium (Rech.f.) Damboldt *12840*
    R *12840* Turkey *12840*

V *Asyneuma linifolium* (Boiss. & Heldr.) Bornm. ssp.
    glabrum Kit Tan & Yildiz *12840*
    V *12840* Turkey *12840*

V *Asyneuma linifolium* (Boiss. & Heldr.) Bornm. ssp.
    nallihanicum Kit Tan & Yildiz *12840*
    V *12840* Turkey *12840*

R *Asyneuma lycium* (Boiss.) Bornm. *12840*
    R *12840* Turkey *12840*

R *Asyneuma pulvinatum* Davis *12840*
    R *12840* Turkey *12840*

R *Asyneuma rigidum* (Willd.) Grossh. ssp. *graminifolium*
    Huber-Mor. *12840*
    R *12840* Turkey *12840*

R *Asyneuma trichostegium* (Boiss.) Bornm. *12840*
    R *12840* Turkey *12840*

V *Azorina vidalii* (H.C.Watson) Feer *8000, 20171*
    V *19174* Portugal - Azores *19174*

V *Berenice arguta* Tul. *10082*
    V *14234* Réunion *14234*

E *Brighamia insignis* Gray *20850, 14209*
    E *20850* U.S. - Hawaii (Kaua`i, Ni`ihau) *20850*

E *Brighamia rockii* St. John *20850, 14209*
    E *20850* U.S. - Hawaii (Moloka`i) *20850*

E *Burmeistera darienensis* Wilbur *20883, 9006*
    I *20883* Panama *20883*

E *Burmeistera dendrophila* F. Wimmer *20883, 9006*
    I *20883* Panama *20883*

E *Burmeistera dukei* Wilbur *20883, 9006*
    I *20883* Panama *20883*

V *Burmeistera glauca* (F. Wimmer) Gleason *20883, 9006*
    I *20883* Panama *20883*

E *Burmeistera hammelii* Wilbur *20883, 10747*
    I *20883* Panama *20883*

E *Burmeistera kirkbridei* Wilbur *20883, 9006*
    I *20883* Panama *20883*

E *Burmeistera mcvaughii* Wilbur *20883*
    I *20883* Panama *20883*

E *Burmeistera morii* Wilbur *20883, 9006*
    I *20883* Panama *20883*

E *Burmeistera panamensis* Wilbur *20883, 9006*
    I *20883* Panama *20883*

E *Burmeistera pinnatisecta* Luteyn *20883*
    I *20883* Colombia *20883*

E *Burmeistera pirrensis* Wilbur *20883, 9006*
    I *20883* Panama *20883*

R *Burmeistera resupinata* Zahlbr. var. *heilbornii*
    Wimm. *11351*
    R *11351* Ecuador *11351*

E *Burmeistera toroensis* Wilbur *20883, 9006*
    I *20883* Panama *20883*

V *Burmeistera utleyi* Wilbur *20883, 9006*
    I *20883* Panama *20883*

I *Campanula abietina* Griseb. *19321, 20171*
    I *19321* Slovakia *19321*

R *Campanula adsurgens* Leresche & Levier *20171*
    R Spain

R *Campanula aghrica* Kit Tan & Sorger *12840*
    R *12840* Turkey *12840*

I *Campanula aizoon* Boiss. & Spruner ssp. *aizoides*
    (Zaffran) Fedorov *8000, 20171*
    I *20731* Greece (Mt Chelmos) *8000*

V *Campanula aizoon* Boiss. & Spruner ssp.
    aizoon *8000, 20171*
    V *14155* Greece (Parnassos; Giona) *8000*

I *Campanula akhdarensis* Miller & Whitcombe *20146*
    I *20146* Oman (northern) *20146*

Magnoliopsida (dicots): Campanulaceae: *Campanula*

R	*Campanula alata* Desf.		
	R	Algeria	
	R	Tunisia	
R	*Campanula albicans* (Buser) Engler *20528*		
	R	20528 France (Alpes-Maritimes) *20528*	
R	*Campanula alphonsii* Wall. ex DC. *13883*		
	R	13883 India (Nilgiris and Palany Hills and Western Ghats) *13883*	
V	*Campanula angustiflora* Eastw. *20850*		
	I	20850 U.S. - California *20850*	
R	*Campanula antalyensis* Ayasligil & Kit Tan *12840*		
	R	12840 Turkey *12840*	
R	*Campanula antiatlantica* Maire M. Weiller & Wilczek		
	R	Morocco	
R	*Campanula apennina* (Podlech) Podlech *20171*		
	R	Italy	
I	*Campanula ardonensis* Rupr. *5942*		
	I	5942 Russia - North Caucasus *5942*	
R	*Campanula argentea* Lam. *12840*		
	R	12840 Turkey *12840*	
R	*Campanula atlantica* Coss. & Durieu		
	R	Algeria	
	R	Tunisia	
I	*Campanula aurasiaca* (Battand. & Trabut) Ozenda *10488*		
	I	14958 Algeria *10488*	
I	*Campanula autraniana* Albov *5942*		
	I	5942 Russia - North Caucasus *5942*	
E	*Campanula barborensis* Quezel *10488*		
	E	14958 Algeria *10488*	
R	*Campanula beckiana* Hayek *20171*		
	I	Austria	
	R	(former) Yugoslavia	
R	*Campanula bipinnatifida* Davis *12840*		
	R	12840 Turkey *12840*	
V	*Campanula bohemica* Hruby *8000, 20171*		
	V	2050 Czech Republic (Sudeten mountains) *8000*	
R	*Campanula bornmuelleri* Nab. *12840*		
	R	12840 Turkey *12840*	
R	*Campanula californica* (Kellogg) Heller *20850*		
	R	20850 U.S. - California *20850*	
R	*Campanula carpatha* Halácsy *20171*		
	R	20730 Greece - Crete *20730*	
R	*Campanula choruhensis* Kit Tan & Sorger *12840*		
	R	12840 Turkey *12840*	
R	*Campanula columnaris* Contandr. et al		
	R	Greece (Vardousia)	
R	*Campanula constantini* Beauverd & Topali *20171*		
	R	Greece	
R	*Campanula coriacea* Davis *12840*		
	R	12840 Turkey *12840*	
R	*Campanula cretica* (ADC.) D. Dietr. *19121*		
	R	20730 Greece - Crete *20730*	
R	*Campanula creutzburgii* Greuter *20171*		
	R	20730 Greece - Crete *20730*	
R	*Campanula cymaea* Phitos *20171*		
	R	Greece	
E	*Campanula damboldtiana* Davis & Sorger *12840*		
	E	14197 Turkey *12840*	
R	*Campanula davisii* Turrill *12840*		

	R	12840 Turkey *12840*	
R	*Campanula delicatula* Boiss. *20171*		
	R	20731 Greece - East Aegean Is *20731*	
I	*Campanula dolomitica* E. Busch *5942*		
	I	5942 Russia - North Caucasus *5942*	
R	*Campanula ekimiana* Guner *12840*		
	R	12840 Turkey *12840*	
R	*Campanula elatinoides* Moretti *20171*		
	R	Italy	
I	*Campanula engurensis* Charadze *5942*		
	I	5942 Russia - North Caucasus *5942*	
	I	5942 Georgia *5942*	
R	*Campanula euboica* Phitos *20171*		
	R	Greece	
R	*Campanula exigua* Rattan *20850*		
	R	20850 U.S. - California *20850*	
R	*Campanula fenestrellata* Feer *20171*		
	I	20852 Croatia *20852*	
	R	(former) Yugoslavia	
V	*Campanula forsythii* (Arcang.) Podlech *20171*		
	V	Italy - Sardinia	
R	*Campanula fruticulosa* (Schwarz & Davis) Damboldt *12840*		
	R	12840 Turkey *12840*	
E	*Campanula gelida* Kovanda *8000, 20171*		
	E	2050 Czech Republic (northern Moravia) *6951*	
R	*Campanula goulimyi* Turrill *20171*		
	R	Greece	
R	*Campanula hagielia* Boiss.		
	R	Greece	
R	*Campanula hakkarica* Davis *12840*		
	R	12840 Turkey *12840*	
R	*Campanula hedgei* Davis *12840*		
	R	12840 Turkey *12840*	
V	*Campanula hercegovina* Degen & Fiala *20171*		
	R	21091 Bosnia & Herzegovina *21091*	
	V	(former) Yugoslavia	
R	*Campanula heterophylla* L. *20171*		
	R	Greece	
R	*Campanula hierapetrae* Rech.f. *20171*		
	R	20730 Greece - Crete *20730*	
R	*Campanula incurva* Aucher ex A.DC. *20171*		
	R	Greece	
R	*Campanula isaurica* Contandr. et al. *12840*		
	R	12840 Turkey *12840*	
V	*Campanula isophylla* Moretti *18264, 20171*		
	V	18264 Italy *18264*	
R	*Campanula jacquinii* (Sieber) A.DC. *20730*		
	R	20730 Greece - Crete *20730*	
R	*Campanula jaubertiana* Timb.-Lagr. *20171*		
	R	France	
	R	Spain	
I	*Campanula karakuschensis* Grossh. *5942*		
	I	5942 Armenia *5942*	
R	*Campanula keniensis* Thulin		
	R	Kenya (Masai distr.) *7959*	
I	*Campanula komarovii* Maleev *5942*		
	I	5942 Russia - North Caucasus *5942*	
I	*Campanula kryophila* Rupr. *5942*		

	I	5942	Russia - North Caucasus *5942*
R	*Campanula laciniata* L. *20171*		
	I	20731	Greece (Cyclades) *20731*
R	*Campanula lanata* Friv. *19709, 20171*		
	R	19709	Bulgaria *19709*
R	*Campanula latiloba* A. DC. ssp. *rizeensis* Guner *12840*		
	R	12840	Turkey *12840*
R	*Campanula lavrensis* (Tocl & Rohlena) Phitos *20171*		
	R		Greece
R	*Campanula ledebouriana* Trautv. *12840*		
	R	12840	Turkey *12840*
R	*Campanula legionensis* Pau		
	R		Spain
R	*Campanula leucosiphon* Boiss. & Heldr. *12840*		
	R	12840	Turkey *12840*
R	*Campanula longisepala* Podlech *20171*		
	R		France (south-east/Mt. Ventoux)
E	*Campanula lycica* Kit Tan & Sorger *12840*		
	E	12840	Turkey *12840*
R	*Campanula macrostyla* Boiss. & Heldr. *12840*		
	R	12840	Turkey *12840*
I	*Campanula makaschvilii* E. Busch *5942*		
	I	5942	Georgia *5942*
I	*Campanula merxmuelleri* Phitos *20171*		
	I		Greece
I	*Campanula mirabilis* Albov *5942*		
	I	5942	Russia - North Caucasus *5942*
R	*Campanula moravica* (Spitzn.) Kovanda *8000, 20171*		
	I	2050	Czech Republic *2050*
	R	20686	Hungary *20686*
	V	19321	Slovakia *19321*
R	*Campanula morettiana* Rchb. *8000, 20171*		
	R	18264	Italy (Trentino-Alto Adige, Veneto & Friuli-Venezia Giulia) *8000*
R	*Campanula munzurensis* Davis *12840*		
	R	12840	Turkey *12840*
R	*Campanula myrtifolia* Boiss. & Heldr. *12840*		
	R	12840	Turkey *12840*
R	*Campanula nisyria* Papatsou & Phitos		
	R	20731	Greece - East Aegean Is *20731*
R	*Campanula numidica* Durieu *10488*		
	R	14958	Algeria *10488*
Ex	*Campanula oligosperma* Damboldt *12840*		
	Ex	12840	Turkey *12840*
I	*Campanula ossetica* M. Bieb. *5942*		
	I	5942	Russia - North Caucasus *5942*
R	*Campanula papillosa* Halácsy *20171*		
	R		Greece
I	*Campanula paradoxa* Kolak. *5942*		
	I	5942	Russia - North Caucasus *5942*
R	*Campanula peshmenii* Guner *12840*		
	R	12840	Turkey *12840*
R	*Campanula pindicola* Alden		
	R		Greece
R	*Campanula pinnatifida* Huber-Mor. *12840*		
	R	12840	Turkey *12840*
V	*Campanula piperi* T.J. Howell *20850*		
	I	20850	U.S. - Washington *20850*

R	*Campanula portenschlagiana* Schult. *20171*		
	R	21091	Bosnia & Herzegovina *21091*
	I	20852	Croatia *20852*
	R		(former) Yugoslavia
R	*Campanula poscharskyana* Degen *20171*		
	I	20852	Croatia *20852*
	R	19174	(former) Yugoslavia *19174*
R	*Campanula primulifolia* Brot. *20076, 20171*		
	E	20076	Portugal *20076*
	R		Spain
R	*Campanula pseudostenocodon* Lacaita *20171*		
	R		Italy
R	*Campanula psilostachya* Boiss. & Kotschy *12840*		
	R	12840	Turkey *12840*
R	*Campanula ptarmicifolia* Lam. var. *capitellata* Damboldt *12840*		
	R	12840	Turkey *12840*
R	*Campanula pterocaula* Hausskn. *12840*		
	R	12840	Turkey *12840*
R	*Campanula pubicalyx* (Davis) Damboldt *12840*		
	R	12840	Turkey *12840*
R	*Campanula pulvinaris* Hausskn. & Bornm. *12840*		
	R	12840	Turkey *12840*
R	*Campanula quercetorum* Huber-Mor. & Simon *12840*		
	R	12840	Turkey *12840*
I	*Campanula radula* Fischer ex Tchich. *5942*		
	I	5942	Armenia *5942*
R	*Campanula raineri* Perp. *18264, 20171*		
	R	18264	Italy *18264*
V	*Campanula raveyi* Boiss. *12840*		
	V	12840	Turkey *12840*
R	*Campanula rechingeri* Phitos *20171*		
	R		Greece
R	*Campanula reiseri* Halácsy *20171*		
	R	20731	Greece (West Aegean islands) *20731*
V	*Campanula reverchonii* Gray *20850*		
	V	20850	U.S. - Texas *20850*
R	*Campanula rimarum* Boiss. *12840*		
	R	12840	Turkey *12840*
E	*Campanula robinsiae* Small *20850*		
	E	20850	U.S. - Florida *20850*
V	*Campanula romanica* Savul *17823, 20171*		
	V	19949	Romania *20631*
I	*Campanula rosmarinifolia* Kerr *19120*		
	I	19120	Thailand *19120*
R	*Campanula rotundifolia* L. ssp. *aitanica* Pau ex O.Bolòs *20692*		
	R	20692	Spain (east) *20692*
I	*Campanula rotundifolia* L. ssp. *sudetica* (Hruby) Soó *2050, 20171*		
	I	2050	Czech Republic *2050*
R	*Campanula rupestris* Sibth. & Sm. *20171*		
	R		Greece
R	*Campanula rupicola* Boiss. & Spruner *20171*		
	R		Greece
V	*Campanula sabatia* De Not. *8000, 20171*		
	V	18264	Italy (Liguria) *19997*
R	*Campanula sartorii* Boiss. & Heldr. *20171*		
	R		Greece

V	*Campanula saxatilis* **L.** *20171*	
	V	*20730* Greece - Crete *20730*
R	*Campanula sciathia* **Phitos** *20171*	
	R	Greece
R	*Campanula scoparia* **(Boiss. & Hausskn.)** **Damboldt** *12840*	
	R	*12840* Turkey *12840*
R	*Campanula scopelia* **Phitos** *20171*	
	R	Greece
E	*Campanula secundiflora* **Vis. & Pancic** *20171*	
	E	(former) Yugoslavia
R	*Campanula seraglio* **Kit Tan & Sorger** *12840*	
	R	*12840* Turkey *12840*
E	*Campanula sharsmithiae* **Morin** *20850*	
	E	*20850* U.S. - California *20850*
V	*Campanula shetleri* **Heckard** *20850*	
	V	*20850* U.S. - California *20850*
V	*Campanula sorgerae* **Phitos** *12840*	
	V	*12840* Turkey *12840*
R	*Campanula sporadum* **Feer**	
	R	Greece
R	*Campanula stricta* **L. var.** *alidagensis* **Damboldt** *12840*	
	R	*12840* Turkey *12840*
R	*Campanula strigillosa* **Boiss.** *12840*	
	R	*12840* Turkey *12840*
R	*Campanula telephioides* **Boiss. & Hausskn.** *12840*	
	R	*12840* Turkey *12840*
R	*Campanula telmessii* **Huber-Mor. & Phitos** *12840*	
	R	*12840* Turkey *12840*
R	*Campanula teucrioides* **Boiss.** *12840*	
	R	*12840* Turkey *12840*
R	*Campanula tomentosa* **Lam.** *12840, 20171*	
	R	*12840* Turkey *12840*
R	*Campanula trachyphylla* **Schott & Kotschy** *12840*	
	R	*12840* Turkey *12840*
R	*Campanula transsilvanica* **Schur ex Andrae** *5204, 20171*	
	R	*5204* Bulgaria (Southern and Western - three sites) *5204*
	V	*19949* Romania *20631*
R	*Campanula troegerae* **Damboldt** *12840*	
	R	*12840* Turkey *12840*
R	*Campanula viciosoi* **Cav.** *20692*	
	R	*20692* Spain (Valencian region and peripheral sites) *20692*
R	*Campanula wattiana* **Nayar et Babu** *13883*	
	R	*13883* India - Himachal Pradesh *13883*
	R	*13883* India - Uttar Pradesh *13883*
I	*Campanula wiedmanii* **Podl.**	
	I	Spain
V	*Campanula wilkinsiana* **Greene** *20850*	
	V	*20850* U.S. - California *20850*
R	*Campanula willkommii* **Witasek** *11496*	
	R	*11496* Spain (Granada) *11496*
R	*Campanula xylocarpa* **Kovanda** *8000, 20171*	
	R	*20686* Hungary *6951*
	V	*19321* Slovakia (Muránska Vyosocina mountains, Slovensky Krasand) *6951*
R	*Campanula yildirimlii* **Kit Tan & Sorger** *12840*	
	R	*12840* Turkey *12840*

V	*Canarina canariensis* **(L.) Vatke** *15105*	
	V	*15105* Spain - Canary Is. *15105*
E	*Centropogon amplicorollinus* **(F.Wimmer) B.A.Stein** *20883*	
	E	*20883* Colombia *20883*
	E	*20883* Peru *20883*
R	*Centropogon baezanus* **Jeppesen** *20883*	
	R	*20883* Ecuador *20883*
E	*Centropogon darienensis* **Wilbur** *20883, 9006*	
	I	*20883* Panama *20883*
V	*Centropogon densiflorus* **Bentham** *20883*	
	V	*20883* Ecuador *20883*
E	*Centropogon escobarae* **B.A.Stein ined.** *20883*	
	E	*20883* Colombia *20883*
E	*Centropogon eurystomus* **F. Wimmer** *20883*	
	E	*20883* Ecuador *20883*
V	*Centropogon floricomus* **McVaugh** *20883, 9006*	
	I	*20883* Panama *20883*
V	*Centropogon gesneriiformis* **Drake** *20883*	
	V	*20883* Ecuador *20883*
	E	*20883* Peru *20883*
E	*Centropogon hirtus* **(Cav.) Presl** *20883*	
	E	*20883* Peru *20883*
E	*Centropogon latifolius* **F. Wimmer** *20883*	
	E	*20883* Peru *20883*
E	*Centropogon leucocarpus* **McVaugh** *20883, 9006*	
	I	*20883* Panama *20883*
V	*Centropogon luteynii* **Wilbur** *20883, 9006*	
	I	*20883* Panama *20883*
R	*Centropogon macrophyllus* **(G. Don) F. Wimmer** *20883*	
	R	*20883* Bolivia *20883*
	R	*20883* Peru *20883*
R	*Centropogon panamensis* **Wilbur** *20883, 9006*	
	I	*20883* Panama *20883*
E	*Centropogon papillosus* **F. Wimmer** *20883*	
	E	*20883* Ecuador *20883*
V	*Centropogon pulcher* **Zahlbr.** *20883, 19002*	
	V	*20883* Peru *20883*
E	*Centropogon quebradanus* **F. Wimmer** *20883*	
	E	*20883* Ecuador *20883*
E	*Centropogon reflexus* **Presl** *20883, 19002*	
	E	*20883* Peru *20883*
R	*Centropogon roseus* **Rusby** *20883*	
	E	*20883* Bolivia *20883*
	R	*20883* Peru *20883*
R	*Centropogon sciaphilus* **Zahlbr.** *20883*	
	R	*20883* Peru *20883*
E	*Centropogon silvaticus* **F. Wimmer** *20883*	
	E	*20883* Peru *20883*
R	*Centropogon trachyanthus* **F. Wimmer** *20883*	
	R	*20883* Ecuador *20883*
E	*Centropogon uncialis* **McVaugh** *20883*	
	E	*20883* Colombia *20883*
I	*Cephalostigma flexuosum* **Hook.f. & Thomson**	
	I	India - Karnataka
	I	India - Tamil Nadu (north Coimbatore Hills)
R	*Clermontia arborescens* **(Mann) Hbd.** *20850, 14209*	
	I	*20850* U.S. - Hawaii *20850*
E	*Clermontia arborescens* **(Mann) Hbd. ssp.**	

arborescens 20850
E   20850 U.S. - Hawaii 20850

E   *Clermontia calophylla* F. Wimmer 20850, 14209
E   20850 U.S. - Hawaii (Hawai`i - Kohala Mts.)
20850

E   *Clermontia drepanomorpha* Rock 20850, 14209, 21355
E   20850 U.S. - Hawaii (Big Island - Kohala Mts.)
20850

R   *Clermontia grandiflora* Gaud. 20850
I   20850 U.S. - Hawaii 20850

R   *Clermontia hawaiiensis* (Hbd.) Rock 20850
R   20850 U.S. - Hawaii 20850

E   *Clermontia lindseyana* Rock 20850, 14209, 21348
E   20850 U.S. - Hawaii (east Maui & Hawai`i)
20850

R   *Clermontia micrantha* (Hbd.) Rock 20850, 14209
I   20850 U.S. - Hawaii (West Maui, Lana`i) 20850

Ex/E *Clermontia multiflora* Hbd. 20850, 14209
Ex/E 20850 U.S. - Hawaii (O`ahu, West Maui) 20850

E   *Clermontia oblongifolia* Gaud. 20850
I   20850 U.S. - Hawaii 20850

E   *Clermontia oblongifolia* Gaud. ssp. *brevipes* (F.
Wimmer) Lammers 20850, 14209, 21358
E   20850 U.S. - Hawaii (Moloka`i) 20850

E   *Clermontia oblongifolia* Gaud. ssp. *mauiensis*
(Rock) Lammers 20850, 14209
E   20850 U.S. - Hawaii (Maui, Lana`i) 20850

E   *Clermontia peleana* Rock 20850, 14209, 21348, 21356
E   20850 U.S. - Hawaii (east Maui & Hawai`i)
20850

E   *Clermontia peleana* Rock ssp. *peleana* 20850
E   20850 U.S. - Hawaii 20850

Ex/E *Clermontia peleana* Rock ssp. *singuliflora* (Rock)
T.G.Lammers 20850
Ex/E 20850 U.S. - Hawaii 20850

R   *Clermontia persicifolia* Gaud. 20850, 14209
I   20850 U.S. - Hawaii (O`ahu) 20850

E   *Clermontia pyrularia* Hbd. 20850, 14209, 21348, 21356
E   20850 U.S. - Hawaii (Mauna Kea, Mauna Loa)
20850

E   *Clermontia samuelii* Forbes 20850, 14209
I   20850 U.S. - Hawaii (East Maui) 20850

E   *Clermontia samuelii* Forbes ssp. *hanaensis* (St.
John) Lammers 20850
E   20850 U.S. - Hawaii 20850

E   *Clermontia samuelii* Forbes ssp.
samuelii 20850
E   20850 U.S. - Hawaii 20850

E   *Clermontia tuberculata* Forbes 20850, 14209
E   20850 U.S. - Hawaii 20850

E   *Clermontia waimeae* Rock 20850
E   20850 U.S. - Hawaii 20850

R   *Codonopsis affinis* Hook. f. et Thoms. 13883
R   13883 India - Sikkim (darjeeling) 13883

R   *Cryptocodon monocephalus* (Trautv.) Fed. 5942
R   5942 Kazakhstan 5942
R   5942 Tajikistan 5942
I   5942 Uzbekistan 5942

R   *Cyananthus integra* Wall. ex Benth. 13883
R   13883 India (Kumoan - Tehri Garhwal Himalayas.)

13883

R   *Cyanea aculeatiflora* Rock 20850, 14209
R   20850 U.S. - Hawaii (East Maui) 20850

E   *Cyanea acuminata* (Gaud.) Hbd. 20850
E   20850 U.S. - Hawaii 20850

Ex/E *Cyanea arborea* Hbd. 20850
Ex/E 20850 U.S. - Hawaii 20850

Ex   *Cyanea arborea* (H. Mann) Hillebrand var.
arborea 14209
Ex   14209 U.S. - Hawaii 14209

E   *Cyanea asarifolia* St. John 20850, 14209
E   20850 U.S. - Hawaii (Kaua`i) 20850

Ex   *Cyanea asplenifolia* (H. Mann) Hillebr. 14209
Ex   14209 U.S. - Hawaii (north-west Maui) 14209

Ex/E *Cyanea aspleniifolia* (Mann) Hbd. 20850
Ex/E 20850 U.S. - Hawaii 20850

Ex/E *Cyanea comata* Hbd. 20850, 14209
Ex/E 20850 U.S. - Hawaii (east Maui) 20850

E   *Cyanea copelandii* Rock 20850, 14209
I   20850 U.S. - Hawaii (East Maui, Hawai`i)
20850

Ex/E *Cyanea copelandii* Rock ssp. *copelandii* 20850
Ex/E 20850 U.S. - Hawaii 20850

E   *Cyanea copelandii* Rock ssp. *haleakalaensis* (St.
John) Lammers 20850
I   20850 U.S. - Hawaii (Maui) 20850

R   *Cyanea coriacea* (Gray) Hbd. 20850
I   20850 U.S. - Hawaii 20850

E   *Cyanea dunbarii* Rock 20850, 14209
E   20850 U.S. - Hawaii (Moloka`i - Waihanau)
20850

Ex/E *Cyanea giffardii* Rock 20850, 14209
Ex/E 20850 U.S. - Hawaii (Glenwood) 20850

E   *Cyanea glabra* (F. Wimmer) St. John 20850, 14301
E   20850 U.S. - Hawaii (east Maui) 20850

V   *Cyanea grimesiana* Gaud. 20850
I   20850 U.S. - Hawaii 20850

Ex/E *Cyanea grimesiana* Gaudich. ssp. *cylindrocalyx*
(Rock) Lammers 20850, 14209
Ex/E 20850 U.S. - Hawaii (Waipi`o Valley) 20850

V   *Cyanea grimesiana* Gaudich. var.
grimesiana 14209
V   14209 U.S. - Hawaii 14209

E   *Cyanea grimesiana* Gaud. ssp. *obatae* (St. John)
Lammers 20850, 14209
E   20850 U.S. - Hawaii (O`ahu - Wai`anae Mts.)
20850

R   *Cyanea hamatiflora* Rock 20850, 14209
I   20850 U.S. - Hawaii (East Maui) 20850

E   *Cyanea hamatiflora* Rock ssp. *carlsonii* (Rock)
Lammers 20850, 14209, 21348, 21356
E   20850 U.S. - Hawaii 20850

V   *Cyanea hardyi* Rock 20850, 14209
I   20850 U.S. - Hawaii (Kaua`i) 20850

V   *Cyanea horrida* (Rock) O. Deg. & Hosaka 20850, 14209
V   20850 U.S. - Hawaii (East Maui) 20850

V   *Cyanea kunthiana* (Gaud.) Hbd. 20850, 14209
V   20850 U.S. - Hawaii (Maui) 20850

V   *Cyanea leptostegia* Gray 20850

V   *20850*   U.S. - Hawaii *20850*

E   *Cyanea lindseyana* Rock *20850*

     I   *20850*   U.S. - Hawaii *20850*

E   *Cyanea linearifolia* Rock *20850, 14209*

     E   *20850*   U.S. - Hawaii (Kaua`i) *20850*

Ex/E   *Cyanea lobata* Mann *20850*

     Ex/E   *20850*   U.S. - Hawaii *20850*

E   *Cyanea lobata* H. Mann var. *lobata* *14209*

     E   *14209*   U.S. - Hawaii (Lana`i, west Maui) *14209*

Ex/E   *Cyanea longissima* (Rock) St. John *20850, 14209*

     Ex/E   *20850*   U.S. - Hawaii (east Maui) *20850*

E   *Cyanea macrostegia* Hillebr. ssp. *gibsonii* (Hbd.) Lammers *20850, 14209*

     E   *20850*   U.S. - Hawaii (Lana`i) *20850*

E   *Cyanea macrostegia* Hillebrand var. *parvibracteata* Rock *14209*

     E   *14209*   U.S. - Hawaii *14209*

E   *Cyanea mannii* (Brigham) Hbd. *20850, 14209*

     E   *20850*   U.S. - Hawaii (Moloka`i) *20850*

Ex/E   *Cyanea marksii* Rock *20850, 14209*

     Ex/E   *20850*   U.S. - Hawaii (Hawai`i) *20850*

E   *Cyanea mceldowneyi* Rock *20850, 14209*

     E   *20850*   U.S. - Hawaii (east Maui) *20850*

E   *Cyanea membranacea* Rock *20850, 14209*

     E   *20850*   U.S. - Hawaii (O`ahu - Waianae Mts.) *20850*

Ex/E   *Cyanea obtusa* (Gray) Hbd. *20850, 14209*

     Ex/E   *20850*   U.S. - Hawaii *20850*

E   *Cyanea pinnatifida* (Cham.) F. Wimmer *20850, 14209*

     E   *20850*   U.S. - Hawaii (O`ahu) *20850*

E   *Cyanea platyphylla* (Gray) Hbd. *20850, 14209*

     E   *20850*   U.S. - Hawaii (Hawai`i) *20850*

Ex/E   *Cyanea pohaku* Lammers *20850, 14209*

     Ex/E   *20850*   U.S. - Hawaii (east Maui) *20850*

E   *Cyanea procera* Hbd. *20850, 14209, 21358*

     E   *20850*   U.S. - Hawaii (east Moloka`i) *20850*

Ex/E   *Cyanea profuga* Forbes *20850, 14209*

     Ex/E   *20850*   U.S. - Hawaii (Molokai) *20850*

Ex/E   *Cyanea pycnocarpa* (Hbd.) F. Wimmer *20850, 14209*

     Ex/E   *20850*   U.S. - Hawaii (Kohala Mts.) *20850*

Ex/E   *Cyanea quercifolia* (Hbd.) F. Wimmer *20850*

     Ex/E   *20850*   U.S. - Hawaii *20850*

Ex   *Cyanea quercifolia* (Hillebrand) F.E. Wimmer var. *quercifolia* *14209*

     Ex   *14209*   U.S. - Hawaii (east Maui) *14209*

E   *Cyanea recta* (Wawra) Hbd. *20850, 14209*

     E   *20850*   U.S. - Hawaii (north-east Kaua`i) *20850*

E   *Cyanea scabra* Hbd. *20850*

     E   *20850*   U.S. - Hawaii *20850*

Ex/E   *Cyanea shipmanii* Rock *20850, 14209*

     Ex/E   *20850*   U.S. - Hawaii (Mauna Kea) *20850*

E   *Cyanea solanacea* Hbd. *20850, 14209*

     E   *20850*   U.S. - Hawaii *20850*

V   *Cyanea solenocalyx* Hbd. *20850*

     V   *20850*   U.S. - Hawaii *20850*

E   *Cyanea stictophylla* Rock *20850, 21348, 21356*

     E   *20850*   U.S. - Hawaii *20850*

E   *Cyanea stictophylla* Rock var.

stictophylla *14209*

     E   *14209*   U.S. - Hawaii *14209*

E   *Cyanea superba* (Cham.) Gray *20850*

     I   *20850*   U.S. - Hawaii *20850*

Ex/E   *Cyanea superba* (Cham.) A.Gray ssp. *regina* (Wawra) Lammers *20850, 14209*

     Ex/E   *20850*   U.S. - Hawaii (O`ahu - Ko`olau Mts.) *20850*

E   *Cyanea superba* (Cham.) Gray ssp. *superba* (Cham.) Gray *20850*

     E   *20850*   U.S. - Hawaii *20850*

V   *Cyanea tritomantha* Gray *20850*

     V   *20850*   U.S. - Hawaii *20850*

V   *Cyanea tritomantha* A.Gray var. *tritomantha* *14209*

     V   *14209*   U.S. - Hawaii *14209*

E   *Cyanea truncata* (Rock) Rock *20850*

     E   *20850*   U.S. - Hawaii *20850*

E   *Cyanea truncata* Rock var. *truncata* *14209*

     E   *14209*   U.S. - Hawaii (Oahu) *14209*

E   *Cyanea undulata* Forbes *20850, 14209*

     E   *20850*   U.S. - Hawaii (Kaui`i - Wahiawa Bog) *20850*

R   *Cyphia corylifolia* Harv. *20604*

     R   *20604*   South Africa - Natal *20604*

R   *Cyphia ranunculifolia* E.Wimm. *20604*

     R   *20604*   South Africa - Cape Province *20604*

Ex/E   *Delissea fallax* Hbd. *20850, 14209*

     Ex/E   *20850*   U.S. - Hawaii (Hamakua & Hilo) *20850*

Ex/E   *Delissea laciniata* Hbd. *20850*

     Ex/E   *20850*   U.S. - Hawaii *20850*

Ex   *Delissea laciniata* Hbd. var. *laciniata* *14209*

     Ex   *14209*   U.S. - Hawaii (O`ahu) *14209*

Ex/E   *Delissea lauliiana* Lammers *20850, 14209*

     Ex/E   *20850*   U.S. - Hawaii (O`ahu) *20850*

Ex/E   *Delissea parviflora* Hbd. *20850, 14209*

     Ex/E   *20850*   U.S. - Hawaii (Kohala Mts, Mauna Kea) *20850*

E   *Delissea rhytidosperma* Mann *20850, 14209*

     E   *20850*   U.S. - Hawaii (Kaua`i) *20850*

E   *Delissea rivularis* (Rock) F. Wimmer *20850, 14209*

     E   *20850*   U.S. - Hawaii (Kaua`i) *20850*

Ex/E   *Delissea sinuata* Hbd. *20850*

     Ex/E   *20850*   U.S. - Hawaii *20850*

Ex/E   *Delissea sinuata* Hbd. ssp. *lanaiensis* (Rock) Lammers *20850, 14209*

     Ex/E   *20850*   U.S. - Hawaii *20850*

Ex/E   *Delissea sinuata* Hbd. ssp. *sinuata* *20850*

     Ex/E   *20850*   U.S. - Hawaii *20850*

E   *Delissea subcordata* Gaud. *20850*

     E   *20850*   U.S. - Hawaii *20850*

E   *Delissea undulata* Gaud. *20850, 14209*

     E   *20850*   U.S. - Hawaii *20850*

Ex/E   *Delissea undulata* Gaud. ssp. *kauaiensis* Lammers *20850, 21351*

     Ex/E   *20850*   U.S. - Hawaii *20850*

Ex/E   *Delissea undulata* Gaud. ssp. *niihauensis* (St. John) Lammers *20850, 21351*

     Ex/E   *20850*   U.S. - Hawaii *20850*

E   *Delissea undulata* Gaud. ssp. *undulata* 20850,
          21351, 21356
          E   20850   U.S. - Hawaii 20850

V   *Downingia bella* Hoover 20850
          I   20850   U.S. - California 20850

E   *Downingia concolor* Greene var. *brevior*
          McVaugh 20850
          E   20850   U.S. - California 20850

R   *Downingia cuspidata* (Greene) Greene ex Jepson 20850
          I   20850   U.S. - California 20850

R   *Downingia montana* Greene 20850
          I   20850   U.S. - California 20850
          I   20850   U.S. - Oregon 20850

V   *Downingia ornatissima* Greene 20850
          I   20850   U.S. - California 20850

R   *Downingia pulchella* (Lindl.) Torr. 20850
          I   20850   U.S. - California 20850
          I   20850   U.S. - Oregon 20850

R   *Downingia pusilla* (G. Don) Torr. 20850
          V   20850   U.S. - California 20850

R   *Edraianthus dalmaticus* (A.DC.) A.DC. 20171
          V   21091   Bosnia & Herzegovina 21091
          R   (former) Yugoslavia

R   *Edraianthus dinaricus* (A.Kern.) Wettst. 20171
          R   (former) Yugoslavia

I   *Edraianthus owerinianus* Rupr. 5942
          I   5942   Russia - North Caucasus 5942

V   *Edraianthus pumilio* (Port.) A.DC. 20171
          V   (former) Yugoslavia

R   *Edraianthus wettsteinii* Halácsy & Bald. 20178, 20171
          R   20178   Albania 20178
          R   (former) Yugoslavia

R   *Githopsis pulchella* Vatke 20850
          I   20850   U.S. - California 20850

E   *Githopsis tenella* Morin 20850
          I   20850   U.S. - California 20850

R   *Hanabusaya asiatica* Nakai 15947
          R   5767   Korea, South (north to Mt Sorak) 15957

V   *Heterochaenia borbonica* Badre & Cadet 10082
          V   14234   Réunion 14234

V   *Heterochaenia ensifolia* (Lam.) DC. 10082
          V   20771   Réunion 10082
          Ex   20771   Mauritius 10082

V   *Heterochaenia rivalsii* Badré & Cadet 10082
          V   14234   Réunion 14234

V   *Howellia aquatilis* Gray 20850
          Ex/E 20850   U.S. - California 20850
          E   20850   U.S. - Idaho 20850
          V   20850   U.S. - Montana 20850
          Ex   20850   U.S. - Oregon 20850
          E   20850   U.S. - Washington 20850

Ex   *Hypsela sessiliflora* E.Wimmer 20681, 14223
          Ex   20681   Australia - New South Wales 20681

R   *Isotoma luticola* Carolin 20681
          R   20681   Australia - Northern Territory 20681

R   *Jasione bulgarica* Stoj. & Stef. 19709, 20171
          R   19709   Bulgaria 19709

V   *Jasione crispa* (Pourr.) Samp. ssp. *arvernensis*
          Tutin 20171
          V   20528   France (Pay-de-Dôme) 20813

V   *Jasione crispa* (Pourr.) Samp. ssp. *serpentinica*
          Pinto da Silva 8000, 20171
          V   20076   Portugal (north east) 8000

R   *Jasione crispa* (Pourr.) Samp. ssp. *tomentosa* (DC.)
          Rivas Mart. 20171
          R   Spain

E   *Jasione heldreichii* Boiss. & Orph var. *papillosa*
          J. Parnel 12840
          E   12840   Turkey 12840

R   *Jasione idaea* Stoy. 12840
          R   12840   Turkey 12840

R   *Jasione laevis* Lam. ssp. *gredensis* Rivas Mart. &
          Sancho
          R   Spain

I   *Jasione lusitanica* A.DC. 8000, 20171
          V   14155   Portugal 8000
          I   14155   Spain 14198

R   *Jasione mansanetiana* R.Rosselló & Peris 20692
          R   20692   Spain (Villahermosa Valley, Castellón
                        province) 20692

R   *Jasione penicillata* Boiss. 20171
          R   Spain

R   *Jasione supina* Sieber ssp. *akmanii*
          Damboldt 12840
          R   12840   Turkey 12840

R   *Jasione supina* Sieber ssp. *supina* 12840
          R   12840   Turkey 12840

R   *Jasione supina* Sieber ssp. *tmolea* (Stoj.)
          Damboldt 12840
          R   12840   Turkey 12840

R   *Laurentia bicolor* (Battand.) Maire & Steph. 10488
          R   Algeria 10488

E   *Laurentia canariensis* DC.
          E   Spain - Canary Is.

V   *Legenere limosa* (Greene) McVaugh 20850
          V   20850   U.S. - California 20850

V   *Lobelia alticaulis* Proctor 20883, 13336
          V   20883   Jamaica 20883

R   *Lobelia bambuseti* R.E. & T.C.E. Fries 20057
          R   20057   Kenya (Mt. Kenya; Nyandurua; Aberdares)
                        20057

R   *Lobelia beaugleholei* D.E.Albrecht 20681
          I   20681   Australia - South Australia 20681
          I   20681   Australia - Victoria 20681

V   *Lobelia boninensis* Koidz. 8038
          V   19134   Japan - Ogasawara-shoto 8038

V   *Lobelia boykinii* Torr. & Gray ex A. DC. 20850
          V   20850   U.S. - Alabama 20850
          Ex/E 20850   U.S. - Delaware 20850
          I   20850   U.S. - Florida 20850
          V   20850   U.S. - Georgia 20850
          E   20850   U.S. - New Jersey 20850
          E   20850   U.S. - North Carolina 20850
          I   20850   U.S. - South Carolina 20850

R   *Lobelia bridgesii* Hook. & Arn. 13875
          R   13875   Chile 13875

E   *Lobelia caledoniana* Adams 20883, 15911
          V   13336   Jamaica 20883

R   *Lobelia caudata* (Griseb.) Urb. 20883, 13336
          R   19890   Jamaica 20883

V   *Lobelia digitalifolia* (Griseb.) Urban var.

	guadeloupensis (Urban) McVaugh *5710*
V	*5710* Guadeloupe (Mateliane etc.) *5710*
E	*Lobelia dressleri* Wilbur *20883, 9037*
I	*20883* Panama *20883*
E	*Lobelia dunbarii* Rock *20850, 14209*
E	*20850* U.S. - Hawaii (Moloka`i) *20850*
R	*Lobelia dunbarii* Rock ssp. *paniculata* (Rock) Lammers *14209*
R	*14209* U.S. - Hawaii (Moloka`i) *14209*
R	*Lobelia fawcettii* Urb. *20883*
R	*20883* Jamaica *20883*
R	*Lobelia gaudichaudii* A. DC. *20850*
I	*20850* U.S. - Hawaii *20850*
E	*Lobelia gaudichaudii* DC. ssp. *koolauensis* (Hosaka & Fosberg) Lammers *20850, 14209*
E	*20850* U.S. - Hawaii (O`ahu - Ko`olau Mts) *20850*
R	*Lobelia gloria-montis* Rock *20850, 14209*
R	*20850* U.S. - Hawaii (Moloka`i) *20850*
R	*Lobelia grandifolia* Britton *20883*
R	*20883* Jamaica *20883*
E	*Lobelia harrisii* Urb. *20883, 13336*
E	*20883* Jamaica *20883*
I	*Lobelia hosseusii* E. Wimm. *19120*
I	*19120* Thailand *19120*
E	*Lobelia hypoleuca* Hbd. *20850*
E	*20850* U.S. - Hawaii *20850*
R	*Lobelia innominata* Rendle *20883*
R	*20883* Jamaica *20883*
V	*Lobelia kauaensis* (Gray) Heller *20850, 14209*
I	*20850* U.S. - Hawaii (Kaua`i) *20850*
I	*Lobelia leucantha* Kerr *19120*
I	*19120* Thailand *19120*
R	*Lobelia lobata* E. Wimmer *7749*
R	Zimbabwe *7749*
R	*Lobelia longisepala* Engl.
R	Tanzania
R	*Lobelia loochooensis* Koidz. *10573*
R	*10573* Japan *10573*
R	*Lobelia lukwangulensis* Engl.
R	Tanzania (Uluguru)
R	*Lobelia martagon* (Griseb.) Hitchc. *20883*
R	*20883* Jamaica *20883*
E	*Lobelia monostachya* (Rock) Lammers *20850, 14209*
E	*20850* U.S. - Hawaii (O`ahu - Ko`olau Mts.) *20850*
V	*Lobelia niihauensis* St. John *20850*
V	*20850* U.S. - Hawaii *20850*
R	*Lobelia niihauensis* St. John var. *niihauensis* *14209*
R	*14209* U.S. - Hawaii *14209*
E	*Lobelia oahuensis* Rock *20850, 14209*
E	*20850* U.S. - Hawaii (O`ahu - Ko`olau Mts.) *20850*
Ex/E	*Lobelia remyi* Rock *20850, 14209*
	Ex/E *20850* U.S. - Hawaii (O`ahu) *20850*
I	*Lobelia salicina* Lam. var. *brachyantha* Urban *5642*
I	Dominican Republic (Prov. Barahona, Paraiso)

	5642
I	*Lobelia sancta* H. Thulin *10260*
I	Tanzania (Ukaguru)
E	*Lobelia serpens* Lam. var. *puberula* E. Wimm. *10082*
E	*20771* Mauritius *10082*
R	*Lobelia trullifolia* Hemsley var. *saliensis* (E. Wimmer) E. Wimmer *7849*
R	Malawi *7849*
E	*Lobelia vagans* Balf.f. *10082*
E	*5852* Mauritius - Rodrigues *5852*
I	*Lobelia valida* L.Bolus *20604*
I	*20604* South Africa - Cape Province *20604*
R	*Lobelia villosa* (Rock) St. John & Hosaka *20850, 14209*
I	*20850* U.S. - Hawaii (Kaua`i) *20850*
V	*Lobelia yuccoides* Hbd. *20850, 14209*
V	*20850* U.S. - Hawaii (Kaua`i, O`ahu) *20850*
V	*Lobelia zwartkopensis* E.Wimm. *20604*
V	*20604* South Africa - Cape Province *20604*
R	*Michauxia thyrsoidea* Boiss. & Heldr. *12840*
R	*12840* Turkey *12840*
R	*Musschia aurea* (L.f.) DC. *14166*
R	Portugal - Madeira
E	*Musschia wollastonii* Lowe *17891*
E	Portugal - Madeira *17891*
V	*Nemacladus gracilis* Eastw. *20850*
I	*20850* U.S. - Arizona *20850*
I	*20850* U.S. - California *20850*
I	*20850* U.S. - Nevada *20850*
V	*Nemacladus montanus* Greene *20850*
I	*20850* U.S. - California *20850*
R	*Nemacladus pinnatifidus* Greene *20850*
I	*20850* U.S. - California *20850*
R	*Nemacladus ramosissimus* Nutt. *20850*
I	*20850* U.S. - California *20850*
R	*Nemacladus secundiflorus* G.T. Robbins *20850*
I	*20850* U.S. - California *20850*
E	*Nemacladus twisselmannii* J.T. Howell *20850*
E	*20850* U.S. - California *20850*
E	*Nesocodon mauritianus* (I. Richardson) Thulin *10082*
E	*20771* Mauritius *10082*
I	*Ostrowskia magnifica* Regel *5942*
I	*5942* Kazakhstan *5942*
I	*5942* Tajikistan *5942*
I	*5942* Uzbekistan *5942*
R	*Parishella californica* Gray *20850*
I	*20850* U.S. - California *20850*
R	*Physoplexis comosa* (L.) Schur *8000, 20171*
R	*14155* Austria *8000*
R	*18264* Italy (Alps) *19997*
R	(former) Yugoslavia *8000*
R	*Phyteuma cordatum* Balb. *18264, 20171*
R	*20528* France (Alpes-Maritime) *20528*
R	*18264* Italy (Piedmont, Liguria) *18264*
R	*Phyteuma gallicum* Rich.Schulz *20171*
R	France (south-central)
R	*Phyteuma humile* Schleich. ex Gaudin *20171*
?	France
R	*8623* Italy (Aosta valley, Piedmont) *20804*

R   18154   Switzerland *18154*

R   *Phyteuma pseudorbicularis* Pant. *20178*
     R   20178   Albania *20178*
     R   (former) Yugoslavia

R   *Pratia gelida* (F.Muell.) Benth. *20681*
     R   20681   Australia - Victoria *20681*

R   *Prismatocarpus cordifolius* Adamson *20604*
     R   20604   South Africa - Cape Province *20604*

R   *Prismatocarpus spinosus* Adamson *20604*
     R   20604   South Africa - Cape Province *20604*

I   *Roella goodiana* Adamson *20604*
     I   20604   South Africa - Cape Province *20604*

R   *Roella rhodantha* Adamson *20604*
     R   20604   South Africa - Cape Province *20604*

E   *Rollandia angustifolia* (Hbd.) Rock *20850*
     E   20850   U.S. - Hawaii (Oahu, Koolau Mts) *20850*

E   *Rollandia crispa* Gaud. *20850*
     E   20850   U.S. - Hawaii *20850*

R   *Rollandia crispa* Gaudich. var. *crispa 14209*
     R   14209   U.S. - Hawaii (O`ahu - Ko`olau Mts.) *14209*

E   *Rollandia humboldtiana* Gaud. *20850, 14209*
     E   20850   U.S. - Hawaii (O`ahu) *20850*

R   *Rollandia lanceolata* Gaud. *20850*
     I   20850   U.S. - Hawaii *20850*

E   *Rollandia lanceolata* Gaud ssp. *calycina* (Cham.) Lammers *20850, 14209*
     E   20850   U.S. - Hawaii (O`ahu) *20850*

R   *Rollandia lanceolata* Gaud. ssp. *lanceolata 20850*
     R   20850   U.S. - Hawaii *20850*

E   *Rollandia longiflora* Wawra *20850, 14209*
     E   20850   U.S. - Hawaii (O`ahu) *20850*

Ex/E   *Rollandia parvifolia* Forbes *20850, 14209*
     Ex/E   20850   U.S. - Hawaii (Kaua`i) *20850*

Ex/E   *Rollandia purpurellifolia* Rock *20850, 14209*
     Ex/E   20850   U.S. - Hawaii (O`ahu) *20850*

E   *Rollandia St.-Johnii* Hosaka *20850, 14209*
     E   20850   U.S. - Hawaii *20850*

E   *Sclerotheca arborea* (J.G.Forster) A.L.DC. *20845*
     E   20845   French Polynesia - Society Is. (Tahiti) *20845*

I   *Sclerotheca forsteri* Drake *20845*
     I   20845   French Polynesia - Society Is. (Moorea, Tahiti) *20845*

V   *Sclerotheca joyorum* J.Raynal *20845*
     V   20845   French Polynesia - Society Is. (Tahiti) *20845*

V   *Sclerotheca oreades* F.Wimmer *20845*
     V   20845   French Polynesia - Society Is. (Tahiti) *20845*

E   *Sclerotheca viridiflora 19471*
     E   19473   Cook Is.(Southern group) (Rarotonga) *19471*

E   *Siphocampylus albiguttur* McVaugh *20883, 9006*
     I   20883   Panama *20883*

R   *Siphocampylus argentinus* (Griseb.) Hieron. var. *cuspidatus* F. Wimmer
     R   20176   Argentina *20176*

I   *Siphocampylus caudatus 15229*

     I   15229   Haiti (La Visite & Macaya National Parks) *15229*

E   *Siphocampylus darienensis* Wilbur *20883, 9006*
     I   20883   Panama *20883*

V   *Siphocampylus impressus* Urban *5607*
     V   19105   Cuba (Guantanamo) *5607*

E   *Siphocampylus libanensis* Urban *5607*
     E   19105   Cuba (Guantanamo) *5607*

V   *Siphocampylus maxonis* F. Wimmer *20883, 9006*
     I   20883   Panama *20883*

E   *Siphocampylus oscitans* B.A.Stein *20883*
     I   20883   Peru *20883*

V   *Siphocampylus undulatus* Urban *5607*
     V   19105   Cuba *5607*

E   *Siphocampylus yumuriensis* Kirouac *5607*
     E   19105   Cuba (Guantanamo) *5607*

R   *Solenopsis minuta* C. Presl. ssp. *annua* Greuter, Matthäs & Risse *20731*
     R   20731   Greece - Crete *20731*

I   *Specularia juliani* Battand. *10488*
     I   14958   Algeria *10488*

R   *Symphyandra cretica* A.DC. *20171*
     R   Greece

R   *Symphyandra hofmannii* Pant. *20171*
     R   21091   Bosnia & Herzegovina *20852*
     R   (former) Yugoslavia

R   *Symphyandra lazica* Boiss. & Bal. *12840*
     R   12840   Turkey *12840*

V   *Symphyandra samothracica* (Degen) Halacsy
     V   Greece

R   *Symphyandra sporadum* Halacsy *20171*
     R   Greece

E   *Symphyandra zangezura* Lipsky
     E   former USSR *6930*

V   *Trachelium asperuloides* Boiss. & Orph. *19174, 20171*
     V   19174   Greece *19174*

R   *Trachelium jacquinii* (Sieber) Boiss. *5204, 20171*
     R   5204   Bulgaria (south) *5204*
     R   Greece
     R   19873   Turkey *19873*

E   *Trematolobelia grandifolia* (Rock) O. Deg. *20850*
     E   20850   U.S. - Hawaii *20850*

E   *Trematolobelia singularis* St. John *20850, 14209*
     E   20850   U.S. - Hawaii *20850*

E   *Trimeris scaevolifolia* (Roxb.) Mabb. *18996*
     E   18996   St Helena *18996*

R   *Wahlenbergia angustifolia* (Roxb.) A. DC. *18996*
     R   18996   St Helena *18996*

I   *Wahlenbergia annuliformis* Brehmer *20604*
     I   20604   South Africa - Cape Province *20604*

E   *Wahlenbergia bernardi* Leredde *10488*
     E   14958   Algeria *10488*

V   *Wahlenbergia berteroi* Hook. & Arn. *19116*
     V   19125   Chile - Juan Fernandez Is. *15983*

I   *Wahlenbergia brachycarpa* Schltr. *20604*
     I   20604   South Africa - Cape Province *20604*

R   *Wahlenbergia brockeii* J. Hay
     R   New Zealand - South Is.

I   *Wahlenbergia brockiei 19305*

I		*19305* New Zealand *19305*
Ex	*Wahlenbergia burchellii* A. DC. *18996*	
	Ex	*18996* St Helena *18996*
R	*Wahlenbergia buseriana* Schltr. & Brehmer *20604*	
	R	*20604* South Africa - Cape Province *20604*
I	*Wahlenbergia debilis* H.Buek *20604*	
	I	*20604* South Africa - Cape Province *20604*
R	*Wahlenbergia doleritica* Hilliard & B.L.Burtt *20604*	
	R	*20604* Lesotho *20604*
	V	*20604* South Africa - Natal *20604*
R	*Wahlenbergia glabra* P.J.Smith *20681*	
	I	*20681* Australia - New South Wales *20681*
	I	*20681* Australia - Queensland *20681*
E	*Wahlenbergia grahamae* Hemsley *19116*	
	E	*19125* Chile - Juan Fernandez Is. *15983*
R	*Wahlenbergia insulae-howei* Loth. *14223*	
	R	*14223* Australia - NSW - Lord Howe Is. *14223*
R	*Wahlenbergia islensis* P.J.Smith *20681*	
	R	*20681* Australia - Queensland *20681*
E	*Wahlenbergia larrainii* (Bertero ex Colla) Skottsb. *15983*	
	E	*15983* Chile - Juan Fernandez Is. *15983*
E	*Wahlenbergia linifolia* (Roxb.) A. DC. *18996*	
	E	*18996* St Helena *18996*
V	*Wahlenbergia masafuerae* (Philippi) Skottsb. *19125*	
	V	*19125* Chile - Juan Fernandez Is. *15983*
R	*Wahlenbergia polycephala* (Mildbr.) Thulin *7959*	
	R	Tanzania *7959*
Ex	*Wahlenbergia roxburghii* A. DC. *18996*	
	Ex	*18996* St Helena *18996*
R	*Wahlenbergia scopulicola* Carolin ex P.J.Smith *20681*	
	I	*20681* Australia - New South Wales *20681*
	I	*20681* Australia - Queensland *20681*
I	*Wahlenbergia simpsonii* J. Hay *19305*	
	I	*19305* New Zealand - South Is. *19305*
I	*Wahlenbergia songeana* Thulin *7959*	
	I	Tanzania (Songea Distr.) *7959*
I	*Wahlenbergia tetramera* Thulin *20604*	
	I	*20604* South Africa - Natal *20604*

Canellaceae

Number of genera: 6
Number of species: 20
Recorded threatened species: 7 (35%)

Tropical Africa; Madagascar; South America.

R	*Cinnamodendron corticosum* Miers *20883, 13336*	
	R	*13336* Jamaica *20883*
R	*Cinnamodendron cubense* Urban *11840*	
	R	*19105* Cuba (Oriente) *11840*
R	*Cinnamodendron tenuifolium* Uittien *8679*	
	R	*8679* Suriname *8679*
E	*Pleodendron macranthum* (Baill.) v. Tiegh. *20883, 10197*	
	E	*20883* Puerto Rico *20883*
I	*Warburgia elongata* Verdc. *19510*	
	I	*5926* Tanzania (Uzaramo) *19510*
V	*Warburgia salutaris* (Bertol.f.) Chiov. *20604, 6088*	
	E	*20745* Mozambique (Lebombo Mnts.) *20886*
	E	*20909* Zimbabwe (eastern) *20572*

	V	*20604* Swaziland *20604*
	E	*20604* South Africa - Natal *20604*
	E	*20604* South Africa - Transvaal *20604*
I	*Warburgia stuhlmannii* Engl. *19510*	
	V	*20057* Kenya (Kwale) *19510*
	I	*20057* Tanzania (Msubugwe forest) *17435*

Capparaceae

Number of genera: 45
Number of species: 800
Recorded threatened species: 50 (6%)

Tropical and subtropical.

R	*Boscia foetida* Schinz ssp. *minima* Toelken *20604*	
	R	*20604* Botswana *20604*
	R	*20604* South Africa - Cape Province *20604*
	R	*20604* South Africa - Transvaal *20604*
R	*Boscia keniensis* Beentje *20057*	
	R	*19109* Kenya *19109*
I	*Boscia rotundifolia* Pax *5926*	
	I	*5926* Tanzania (Dodoma) *19512*
Ex/E	*Cadaba parvula* Polhill *10584*	
	Ex/E	*20057* Kenya *10584*
E	*Capparis antonensis* Woods. *20883, 9006*	
	I	*20883* Panama *20883*
R	*Capparis braianensis* Gagnepain *6057*	
	R	Vietnam *6057*
E	*Capparis carolinensis* Kaneh.	
	E	Micronesia - Caroline Is. (Peliliu)
E	*Capparis chiriquensis* Woods. *20883, 9006*	
	I	*20883* Panama *20883*
I	*Capparis cinerea* Jacobs *13883*	
	I	*13883* India - Manipur *13883*
E	*Capparis crotonantha* Standl. *20883, 9006*	
	I	*20883* Panama *20883*
V	*Capparis diversifolia* Wight & Arn. *11494*	
	V	*11494* India - Kerala *11494*
	V	*11494* India - Tamil Nadu *11494*
R	*Capparis fusifera* Dunn *11494*	
	R	*11494* India - Kerala (Travancore) *11494*
	R	*11494* India - Tamil Nadu *11494*
I	*Capparis klossii* Ridl. *19120*	
	I	*19120* Thailand *19120*
R	*Capparis lankesteri* Standley *9037*	
	R	*19793* Costa Rica *9037*
E	*Capparis mirifica* Standl. *20883, 9006*	
	I	*20883* Panama *20883*
I	*Capparis monantha* Jacobs *19120*	
	I	*19120* Thailand *19120*
V	*Capparis neocaledonica* Vieill. ex Schltr. *20802*	
	V	*20893* New Caledonia *20802*
I	*Capparis nitida* Ruiz Lopez & Pavon *18200*	
	I	*18200* Peru *18200*
R	*Capparis nobilis* (Endl.) Benth. *19108*	
	R	*19108* Australia - Norfolk Is. *14288*
V	*Capparis pachyphylla* Jacobs *13883*	
	V	*14782* India - Arunachal Pradesh *14782*
E	*Capparis panamensis* Iltis *20883, 10337*	
	R	*19793* Panama *20883*

R   *Capparis prisca* J.F. Macbr. *18200*
- R   9446   Peru *18200*

R   *Capparis rheedii* DC. *11494*
- R   11494   India - Goa, Daman & Diu *11494*
- R   11494   India - Karnataka (North Kanara; South Kanara) *11494*
- R   11494   India - Kerala *11494*
- R   11494   India - Tamil Nadu (Tirunelveli District) *11494*

I   *Capparis rosanowiana* B. Fedtsch. *5942*
- I   5942   Tajikistan *5942*
- I   5942   Uzbekistan (south-east) *5942*

V   *Capparis sandwichiana* DC. *20850*
- V   20850   U.S. - Hawaii *20850*

V   *Capparis shevaroyensis* Sund. *11494*
- V   11494   India - Tamil Nadu *11494*

V   *Capparis thozetiana* (F.Muell.) F.Muell. *20681*
- V   20681   Australia - Queensland *20681*

R   *Capparis viburnifolia* Gagnepain *6057*
- R   Vietnam *6057*

I   *Cleome burmanni* Wight et Arn. *13883*
- I   13883   India - Kerala *13883*
- I   13883   India - Tamil Nadu *13883*

R   *Cleome densifolia* C.H. Wright *7749*
- R   Malawi (Mlanje) *7749*

E   *Cleome gamboensis* Urban *5607*
- E   19105   Cuba (Las Tunas, Granma) *5607*

I   *Cleome gynandra* L. var. *nana* (Blatter & Hallberg) Bhandari *7771*
- I   India - Rajasthan (Jaiselmer, Jodhpur) *7771*

V   *Cleome multicaulis* DC. *20883, 20850, 8058*
- V   20850   U.S. - Arizona *20850*
- V   20850   U.S. - Colorado *20850*
- E   20850   U.S. - New Mexico *20850*
- E   20850   U.S. - Texas *20850*
- E   20850   U.S. - Wyoming *20850*
- I   20883   Mexico *20883*

R   *Cleome oligandra* Kers *19512*
- R   Tanzania *19512*

R   *Cleome parvula* R.A. Graham *19512*
- R   Tanzania (Mpwapwpa) *19512*

R   *Cleome schlechteri* Briq. *20604*
- R   20604   South Africa - Natal *20604*
- R   20604   South Africa - Transvaal *20604*

E   *Cleome tenuicaulis* Urban *5607*
- E   19105   Cuba (Camaguey; Las Tunas) *5607*

V   *Cleomella brevipes* S.Watson *20850*
- I   20850   U.S. - California *20850*
- I   20850   U.S. - Nevada *20850*

V   *Cleomella macbrideana* Payson *20850*
- I   20850   U.S. - Idaho *20850*

R   *Cleomella parviflora* Gray *20850*
- I   20850   U.S. - Arizona *20850*
- I   20850   U.S. - California *20850*
- I   20850   U.S. - Idaho *20850*
- I   20850   U.S. - Nevada *20850*

V   *Forchhammeria polyandra* (Griseb.) Alain *5607*
- V   19105   Cuba (Holguin; Guantanamo) *5607*

R   *Maerua andradae* Wild *7749*
- R   Mozambique *7749*

R   *Maerua salicifolia* Wild *7749*

R   Zimbabwe *7749*

R   *Maerua scandens* (Klotzsch) Gilg *7749*
- R   Mozambique *7749*

V   *Oceanopapaver neocaledonicum* Guillaumin *20893*
- V   20893   New Caledonia *20893*

R   *Oxystylis lutea* Torr. & Frem. *20850*
- I   20850   U.S. - California *20850*
- I   20850   U.S. - Nevada *20850*

R   *Polanisia erosa* Iltis ssp. *breviglandulosa* Iltis *20850*
- R   20850   U.S. - Texas *20850*

E   *Steriphoma macranthum* Standl. *20883, 9006*
- I   20883   Panama *20883*

I   *Thylachium alboviolaceum* Gilg *19512*
- I   5926   Tanzania (Morogoro district) *5926*

I   *Thylachium macrophyllum* Gilg *19512*
- I   5926   Tanzania (Morogoro) *19512*

Caprifoliaceae

Number of genera: 15
Number of species: 400
Recorded threatened species: 32   (8%)

Mostly North temperate and boreal regions; also tropical mountains.

R   *Abelia insularis* Nakai *15957*
- R   Korea, South (Dagelet Is.) *15957*

R   *Diervilla rivularis* Gattinger *20850*
- I   20850   U.S. - Alabama *20850*
- R   20850   U.S. - Georgia *20850*
- E   20850   U.S. - North Carolina *20850*
- V   20850   U.S. - Tennessee *20850*

V   *Heptacodium miconioides* Rehder *17617*
- V   17617   China - Anhui (Jingxian, Xuancheng) *11139*
- V   17617   China - Hubei (Xingshan) *11139*
- V   17617   China - Zhejiang *11139*

R   *Kolkwitzia amabilis* Graebner *17617*
- R   17617   China - Anhui (Jingshai, Hueshan, Guichi) *11139*
- R   17617   China - Gansu (Tianshui; Huixian) *11139*
- R   17617   China - Hebei (Pingshuen) *11139*
- R   17617   China - Henan *11139*
- R   17617   China - Hubei (Yixi; Jiunxian; Fangxian) *11139*
- R   17617   China - Shaanxi (Huaying, Shanyang) *11139*
- R   17617   China - Shanxi *11139*

R   *Lonicera alpigera* L. var. *viridissima* Nakai *10573*
- R   10573   Japan *10573*

R   *Lonicera cerasoides* Nakai *15957*
- R   15923   Korea, South (Mt Chiri) *15957*

V   *Lonicera demissa* Rehder var. *borealis* Hara & Kikuchi *10573*
- V   10573   Japan *10573*

R   *Lonicera kabylica* Rehder *10488*
- R   14958   Algeria *10488*

R   *Lonicera karataviensis* Pavlov *5942*
- R   5942   Kazakhstan (near the border of Kirgistan) *5942*

R   *Lonicera kawakamii* *20854*
- R   20854   Taiwan *20854*

V *Lonicera linderifolia* Maxim. var. *konoi* (Makino) Okuy. *10573*
  V *10573* Japan *10573*

V *Lonicera linderifolia* Maxim. var. *linderifolia* *10573*
  V *10573* Japan *10573*

R *Lonicera mochizukiana* Makino var. *filiformis* Koidz. *10573*
  R *10573* Japan *10573*

R *Lonicera nummulariifolia* Jaub. & Spach ssp. *glandulifera* (Huber-Mor.) Chamb. *12840*
  R *20618* Turkey *20618*

V *Lonicera oiwakensis* Hayata *20511*
  V *20854* Taiwan *20511*

I *Lonicera paradoxa* Pojark. *5942*
  I *5942* Kyrgyzstan *5942*
  I *5942* Tajikistan *5942*

V *Lonicera pyrenaica* L. ssp. *majoricensis* (Gand.) O. Browicz *20171*
  V *20645* Spain - Balearic Is. *20645*

R *Lonicera stabiana* Guss. ex Pasq. *18264, 20171*
  R *18264* Italy (Campania) *18264*

R *Sambucus lanceolata* R. Br.
  R Portugal - Madeira

E *Sambucus palmensis* Link *15358*
  E *15105* Spain - Canary Is. *17891*

E *Sambucus tigranii* Troitsky
  E former USSR

E *Symphoricarpos guadalupensis* Correll *20850*
  E *20850* U.S. - Texas *20850*

V *Viburnum arboreum* Britton *20883*
  V *20883* Jamaica *20883*

R *Viburnum boninsimae* Koidz. *8622*
  R *19134* Japan - Kazan Retto *8622*
  R *19134* Japan - Ogasawara-shoto *8622*

R *Viburnum brachyandrum* Nakai *10573*
  R *10573* Japan *10573*

V *Viburnum bracteatum* Rehd. *20850*
  E *20850* U.S. - Alabama *20850*
  E *20850* U.S. - Georgia *20850*
  E *20850* U.S. - Tennessee *20850*

V *Viburnum carlesii* Hemsley var. *bitchiuense* Nakai *10573*
  V *10573* Japan *10573*

R *Viburnum dispar* C. Morton *10341*
  R *19755* Mexico - Jalisco *10341*

R *Viburnum parvifolium* Hayata *20511*
  R *20511* Taiwan *20511*

V *Viburnum plicatum* var. *formosanum* *20854*
  V *20854* Taiwan *20854*

R *Viburnum tinus* L. ssp. *rigidum* (Vent.) P. Silva *15105*
  R *15105* Spain - Canary Is. *15105*

R *Viburnum villosum* Griseb. var. *glabrescens* Griseb. *20883, 13336*
  R *13336* Jamaica *20883*

V *Viburnum villosum* Griseb. var. *subdentatum* Griseb. *20883, 13336*
  V *13336* Jamaica *20883*

R *Weigela subsessilis* (Nakai) Bailey *15957*

R *15923* Korea, South (Mt Chiri) *15957*

Caricaceae

Number of genera:	4
Number of species:	30
Recorded threatened species:	8 (26%)

Tropical and subtropical America; Africa.

R *Carica candicans* Gray *18200*
  R *19964* Peru *18200*

V *Carica chilensis* (Planchon ex A. DC.) Solms-Laub *15088*
  V *13875* Chile *13875*

V *Carica cnidoscoloides* Lorence & Torres *20883*
  I *20883* Mexico *20883*

E *Carica horovitziana* Badillo *11351*
  E *19569* Ecuador *11351*

V *Carica jamaicensis* Urb. *20883*
  V *20883* Jamaica *20883*

R *Carica omnilingua* Badillo *11351*
  R *19569* Ecuador *11351*

R *Carica papaya* L. var. *bady* Ake Assi
  R Côte d'Ivoire

R *Carica sprucei* Badillo *11351*
  R *19569* Ecuador *11351*

Caryocaraceae

Number of genera:	2
Number of species:	23
Recorded threatened species:	11 (47%)

Tropical America, especially Amazon basin.

E *Anthodiscus klugii* Standl. ex Prance *20883, 11589*
  R *19964* Peru *20883*

E *Anthodiscus montanus* Gleason *20883, 19352*
  I *19352* Colombia *20883*

R *Anthodiscus peruanus* Baillon *20883*
  I *20883* Peru *20883*

R *Anthodiscus trifoliatus* G. F. W. Meyer *20883, 8679*
  R *20883* Guyana *20883*

E *Caryocar amygdaliforme* G. Don *20883*
  I *20883* Peru *20883*

R *Caryocar coriaceum* Wittmack *20883*
  I *20883* Brazil *20883*

V II *Caryocar costaricense* J.D. Sm. *20883, 9037*
  E *20883* Costa Rica *20883*
  I *20883* Panama *20883*
  I *20883* Colombia *20883*

R *Caryocar dentatum* Gleason *20883*
  I *20883* Bolivia *20883*
  I *20883* Brazil *20883*

V *Caryocar edule* Casaretto *20883*
  I *20883* Brazil *20883*

E *Caryocar glabrum* ssp. *album* Prance & Freitas da Silva *20883*
  E *20883* Guyana *20883*

R *Caryocar montanum* Prance *20883*
  I *20883* Brazil *20883*
  I *20883* Guyana *20883*
  I *20883* Venezuela *20883*

Caryophyllaceae

Number of genera:	75
Number of species:	2,000
Recorded threatened species:	520 (26%)

Widespread, especially North America.

I   *Agrostemma gracilis* Boiss. *20171*
     I   Greece

I   *Allochrusa gypsophiloides* (Regel) Schischk. *5942*
     I   *5942*   Kazakhstan *5942*
     I   *5942*   Kyrgyzstan *5942*
     I   *5942*   Tajikistan *5942*
     I   *5942*   Uzbekistan *5942*

I   *Allochrusa tadshikistanica* Schischkin *5942*
     I   *5942*   Tajikistan *5942*

E   *Alsinidendron lychnoides* (Hbd.) Sherff *20850, 14209*
     E   *20850*   U.S. - Hawaii (Kaua`i) *20850*

E   *Alsinidendron obovatum* Sherff *20850, 14209*
     E   *20850*   U.S. - Hawaii (O`ahu) *20850*

E   *Alsinidendron trinerve* Mann *20850, 14209*
     E   *20850*   U.S. - Hawaii (O`ahu) *20850*

E   *Alsinidendron viscosum* (Mann) Sherff *20850, 14209*
     E   *20850*   U.S. - Hawaii (Kaua`i) *20850*

R   *Arenaria alfacarensis* Pamp. *11496*
     R   *11496*   Spain (Jaén, Granada & Albacete) *11496*

R   *Arenaria angustifolia* Mc.Neill *12840*
     R   *12840*   Turkey *12840*

R   *Arenaria angustijolioides* Kit Tan & Sorger *12840*
     R   *12840*   Turkey *12840*

R   *Arenaria angustisepala* McNeill *12840*
     R   *12840*   Turkey *12840*

R   *Arenaria arundana* Gallego
     R   *20662*   Spain *20662*

R   *Arenaria bisulca* (Bartl.) Rohr *16336*
     R   *19448*   Argentina *19448*
     R   *20176*   Argentina - Catamarca *20176*
     R   *20176*   Argentina - Salta *20176*
     R   *20176*   Argentina - Tucuman *20176*

R   *Arenaria capillipes* (Boiss.) Boiss. *11496*
     R   *11496*   Spain (Málaga: Sierra bermeja, Sierra de Tolox) *20662*

R   *Arenaria cariensis* A. Carlstrom *12840*
     R   *12840*   Turkey *12840*

R   *Arenaria catamarcensis* Pax. *16336*
     R   *16336*   Argentina *16336*
     R   *20176*   Argentina - Catamarca *20176*
     R   *20176*   Argentina - Jujuy *20176*
     R   *20176*   Argentina - La Rioja *20176*
     R   *20176*   Argentina - Salta *20176*

V   *Arenaria cinerea* DC. *20171*
     V   *20528*   France (Haute) *20528*

R   *Arenaria conica* Boiss. *20171*
     R   Spain

R   *Arenaria controversa* Boiss. *20171*
     V   France
     R   Spain

E   *Arenaria curvifolia* Majumdar *11494*
     E   *11494*   India - Uttar Pradesh (Garwhal Himalaya) *11494*

R   *Arenaria davisii* McNeill *12840*
     R   *12840*   Turkey *12840*

R   *Arenaria deflexa* Dec. ssp. *microcephala* McNeill *12840*
     R   *12840*   Turkey *12840*

R   *Arenaria eliasiana* Kit Tan & Sorger *12840*
     R   *12840*   Turkey *12840*

E   *Arenaria ferruginea* Duthie ex Williams *11494*
     E   *11494*   India - Uttar Pradesh (Kali/Dhauki Valley, Kumaon) *11494*

I   *Arenaria foliacea* Turrill *19509*
     I   *5926*   Tanzania (West Usambara mountains) *5926*

R   *Arenaria fragillima* Rech.f. *20171*
     R   *20730*   Greece - Crete *20730*

Ex/E   *Arenaria franklinii* Douglas ex Hook var. *thompsonii* M.E.Peck *20850*
     Ex/E   *20850*   U.S. - Oregon *20850*

R   *Arenaria gionae* Gustavsson *20171*
     R   Greece

E   *Arenaria grandiflora* L. ssp. *bolosii* (Canig.) Kupffer *20645*
     E   *20647*   Spain - Balearic Is. (Mallorca) *20821*

R   *Arenaria guicciardii* Heldr. ex Boiss. *20171*
     R   *20731*   Greece - East Aegean Is *10270*

R   *Arenaria halacsyi* Bald. *20171*
     E   *21091*   Bosnia & Herzegovina *21091*
     R   (former) Yugoslavia

I   *Arenaria hispida* L. *20171*
     V   France
     I   Spain

R   *Arenaria huteri* A.Kern. *20171*
     R   Italy

R   *Arenaria isauricaa* Boiss. *12840*
     R   *12840*   Turkey *12840*

V   *Arenaria katoana* Makino *10572*
     V   *10572*   Japan *10572*

V   *Arenaria kingii* (S.Watson) M.E.Jones ssp. *rosea* Maguire *20850*
     V   *20850*   U.S. - Nevada *20850*

R   *Arenaria ledebouriana* Fenzl var. *armeniaca* McNeill *12840*
     R   *12840*   Turkey *12840*

R   *Arenaria ledebouriana* Fenzl var. *grandiflora* Hartvig & Strid *12840*
     R   *12840*   Turkey *12840*

I   *Arenaria litoralis* Phitos, non Salisb. *20171*
     I   Greece

E   *Arenaria livermorensis* Correll *20850*
     E   *20850*   U.S. - Texas *20850*

R   *Arenaria luschanii* McNeill *12840*
     R   *12840*   Turkey *12840*

V   *Arenaria macradenia* S.Watson var. *kuschei* (Eastw.) Maguire *20850*
     I   *20850*   U.S. - California *20850*

V   *Arenaria merckioides* Maxim. var. *chokaiensis* (Yatabe) Okuy. *10572*
     V   *10572*   Japan *10572*

R   *Arenaria mons-cragus* Kit Tan ex Sorger *12840*
     R   *12840*   Turkey *12840*

I   *Arenaria neelgerrensis* Wight & Arn.
     I   India - Jammu & Kashmir
     I   India - Tamil Nadu

E   *Arenaria nevadensis* Boiss. & Reut. *15398, 20171*
     E   *15398*   Spain (Sierra Nevada) *15398*

E   *Arenaria norvegica* Gunnerus ssp. *anglica*
     G.Halliday *20171*
     E   *20587*   United Kingdom *20587*

E   *Arenaria paludicola* B.L. Robins. *20850*
     E   *20850*   U.S. - California *20850*
     I   *20850*   U.S. - Oregon *20850*
     Ex   *20850*   U.S. - Washington *20850*

V   *Arenaria pamphylica* sensu Hayek *12840, 20171*
     V   *12840*   Turkey *12840*

R   *Arenaria peloponnesiaca* Rech.f.
     R   Greece

I   *Arenaria phitosiana* Greuter & Burdet *20171*
     I   *20731*   Greece *20731*

I   *Arenaria pomeli* Munby
     I   *20662*   Spain (Cádiz, Málaga) *20662*

R   *Arenaria provincialis* Chater & G.Halliday *8000, 20171*
     R   *20528*   France (nr Marseille & Toulon) *8000*

R   *Arenaria pseudoacantholimon* Bornm. *12840*
     R   *12840*   Turkey *12840*

R   *Arenaria racemosa* Willk. *11496*
     R   *11496*   Spain (Malaga) *11496*

V   *Arenaria rhodia* Boiss. ssp. *macropetala*
     McNeill *12840*
     V   *12840*   Turkey *12840*

R   *Arenaria rigida* M.Bieb. *8001, 20171*
     R   *5204*   Bulgaria (north-east) *5204*
     E   *19949*   Romania *20631*
     R   former European USSR *8001*

R   *Arenaria sabulinea* Gris. ex Fenzl *12840*
     R   *12840*   Turkey *12840*

R   *Arenaria saponarioides* Boiss. & Balansa ssp. *saponarioides* *12840, 20171*
     R   *12840*   Turkey *12840*

R   *Arenaria scariosa* Boiss. *12840*
     R   *12840*   Turkey *12840*

R   *Arenaria serpentini* A.K.Jacks. *20171*
     R   *20178*   Albania *20178*

R   *Arenaria sivasica* Kit Tan ex Sorger *12840*
     R   *12840*   Turkey *12840*

R   *Arenaria speluncarum* McNeill *12840*
     R   *12840*   Turkey *12840*

E   *Arenaria stenomeres* Eastw. *20850*
     E   *20850*   U.S. - Nevada *20850*

R   *Arenaria tenuis* Gay
     R   Spain

V   *Arenaria thangoensis* W. Smith *11494*
     V   *11494*   India - Sikkim (Thango; Chugya) *11494*

R   *Arenaria tomentosa* Willk. *11496*
     R   *11496*   Spain (Almeria & Granada) *11496*

R   *Arenaria uninervia* McNeill *12840*
     R   *12840*   Turkey *12840*

V   *Arenaria ursina* B.L. Robins. *20850*
     V   *20850*   U.S. - California *20850*

R   *Bolanthus cherlerioides* (Bornm.) Bark. *12840*
     R   *12840*   Turkey *12840*

R   *Bolanthus creutzburgii* Greuter *20731*

R   *20730*   Greece - Crete *20730*

R   *Bolanthus frankenioides* (Boiss.) Bark. var. *fasciculatus* (Boiss. & Heldr.) Bark. *12840*
     R·   *12840*   Turkey *12840*

R   *Bolanthus frankenioides* (Boiss.) Bark. var. *frankenioides* *12840*
     R   *12840*   Turkey *12840*

R   *Bolanthus fruticulosus* (Bory & Chaub.) Barkoudah *20171*
     R   *20731*   Greece (Peloponnisos) *20731*

R   *Bolanthus laconicus* (Boiss.) Barkoudah *20171*
     R   *20731*   Greece (Peloponnisos) *20731*

R   *Bolanthus spergulifolius* (Jaub. & Spach) Huber-Mor. *12840*
     R   *12840*   Turkey *12840*

R   *Bolanthus stenopetalum* Hartvig & Strid *12840*
     R   *12840*   Turkey *12840*

R   *Bolanthus thymoides* Huber-Mor. *12840*
     R   *12840*   Turkey *12840*

V   *Bufonia chevallieri* Battand. *10487*
     V   *14958*   Algeria *10487*

E   *Bufonia multiceps* Decne. *16168*
     E   *16168*   Egypt (Sinai) *16168*

R   *Bufonia perennis* Pourr. *20171*
     R   France (south)

R   *Bufonia stricta* (Sibth. & Sm.) Gürke ssp. *cecconia* (Bald.) Rech. fil. *20730*
     R   *20730*   Greece - Crete *20730*

V   *Bufonia teneriffae* Christ *15105*
     V   *15105*   Spain - Canary Is. *15105*

R   *Cerastium aleuticum* Hulten *20850*
     R   *20850*   U.S. - Alaska *20850*

V   *Cerastium alpinum* ssp. *babiogorense* *16721*
     V   *17821*   Czech Republic *17821*
     V   *19615*   Slovakia *19321*

E   *Cerastium alsinifolium* Tausch *8000, 20171*
     E   *2050*   Czech Republic (Mariánské Lázne) *6951*

R   *Cerastium araraticum* Rupr. *12840*
     R   *12840*   Turkey *12840*

V   *Cerastium arvense* L. ssp. *glandulosum* (Kit.) Soó *19266, 20171*
     V   *19321*   Slovakia *19266*

V   *Cerastium arvense* L. var. *ovatum* (Miyabe) E. Miki *10572*
     V   *10572*   Japan *10572*

R   *Cerastium azoricum* Hochst. ex Seub. *20171*
     R   Portugal - Azores

E   *Cerastium beeringianum* ssp. *terrae-novae* (Fern. & Wieg.) Hulten *20850*
     I   *20850*   Canada - Alberta *20850*
     I   *20850*   Canada - Labrador *20850*
     E   *20850*   Canada - Newfoundland *20850*
     I   *20850*   Canada - Quebec *20850*
     I   *20850*   Canada - Saskatchewan *20850*

V   *Cerastium brachypetalum* Pers. ssp. *doerfleri* (Halácsy ex Hayek) P.D.Sell & Whitehead *20171*
     V   *20730*   Greece - Crete *20730*

R   *Cerastium dominici* Kit Tan & R. Mill *12840*
     R   *12840*   Turkey *12840*

Ex/E   *Cerastium fischerianum* Ser. var. *molle*

Ohwi *10572*
Ex/E *10572* Japan *10572*

I   *Cerastium formosanum* Ohwi *20511*
   I   *20511* Taiwan *20511*

R   *Cerastium haussknechtii* Boiss. *12840*
   R   *12840* Turkey *12840*

R   *Cerastium krylovii* Schischk. & Gortschak.
   R   former European USSR

R   *Cerastium ligusticum* Viv. ssp. *palustre* (Moris) P.D.Sell & Whitehead *20171*
   R   *18264* Italy - Sardinia *18264*

R   *Cerastium macranthum* Boiss. *12840*
   R   *12840* Turkey *12840*

R   *Cerastium maximum* L. *20850, 20171*
   I   *20850* Canada - Mackenzie *20850*
   I   *20850* Canada - Yukon Territory *20850*
   V   *20850* U.S. - Alaska *20850*

R   *Cerastium parvipetalum* Hosok. *20511*
   R   *20511* Taiwan *20511*

R   *Cerastium pisidicum* Ayasligil & Kit Tan *12840*
   R   *12840* Turkey *12840*

I   *Cerastium runemarkii* Möschl & Rech.f. *20171*
   I   Greece

R   *Cerastium saccardoanum* Dirat *12840*
   R   *12840* Turkey *12840*

R   *Cerastium schizopetalum* Maxim. var. *bifidum* Takeda *10572*
   R   *10572* Japan *10572*

I   *Cerastium smolikanum* Hartvig *20171*
   I   Greece

R   *Cerastium subpilosum* Hayata *20511*
   R   *20511* Taiwan *20511*

V   *Cerastium sventenii* Jalas *15105*
   V   *15105* Spain - Canary Is. *15105*

R   *Cerastium theophrasti* Merxm. & Strid *20171*
   R   Greece

I   *Cerastium thomsoni* Hook.f.
   I   India (W. Himalaya)

R   *Cerastium transsilvanicum* Schur *17823, 20171*
   R   *19949* Romania *20631*

R   *Cerastium vagans* Lowe *20171*
   R   Portugal - Madeira

R   *Cerastium vourinense* Möschl & Rech.f. *20171*
   R   Greece

R   *Colobanthus curtisiae* J.G.West *20681*
   R   *20681* Australia - Tasmania *20681*

R   *Colobanthus nivicola* M.Gray *20681*
   R   *20681* Australia - New South Wales *20681*

R   *Colobanthus pulvinatus* F.Muell. *20681*
   R   *20681* Australia - New South Wales *20681*

I   *Dianthus absconditus* Fernandez Casas
   I   Spain

R   *Dianthus aciphyllus* Sieber ex Ser. *20171*
   R   Greece

I   *Dianthus andronakii* Woron. ex Schischk. *12840*
   I   *12840* Turkey *12840*

V   *Dianthus arenarius* L. ssp. *bohemicus* (F. A. Novak) *2050*
   E   *17807* Czech Republic (Cepal - district Litomerice)

2050
   V   *19615* Slovakia *19615*

R   *Dianthus brevicaulis* Fenzl var. *setaceus* Reeve *12840*
   R   *12840* Turkey *12840*

R   *Dianthus callizonus* Schott & Kotschy *17823, 20171*
   R   *19949* Romania (Craiului Mts.) *20631*

I   *Dianthus carthusianorum* L. ssp. *sudeticus* Kovanda *19711*
   I   *19711* Czech Republic (Hruby Jesenik Mts.) *19711*

V   *Dianthus charidemii* Pau *20171*
   V   *17778* Spain *17778*

R   *Dianthus chimanimaniensis* Hooper *7749*
   R   Mozambique *7749*

R   *Dianthus cibrarius* Clem. *12840*
   R   *12840* Turkey *12840*

V   *Dianthus cintranus* Boiss. & Reut. ssp. *cintranus* *8000, 20171*
   V   *20076* Portugal (central) *8000*

R   *Dianthus costae* Willk. *20171*
   R   Spain

V   *Dianthus cyprius* A.K. Jackson & Turrill *14230*
   V   *19164* Cyprus *14230*

V   *Dianthus diutinus* Kit. *17786, 20171*
   V   *20686* Hungary *17786*
   Ex   *19417* Romania *19417*

R   *Dianthus eldivenus* Czecz. *12840*
   R   *12840* Turkey *12840*

R   *Dianthus elegans* Urv. var. *actinopetalus* (Fenzl) Reeve *12840*
   R   *12840* Turkey *12840*

R   *Dianthus engleri* Hausskn. & Bornm. *12840*
   R   *12840* Turkey *12840*

R   *Dianthus eretmopetalus* Stapf *12840*
   R   *12840* Turkey *12840*

R   *Dianthus erinaceus* Boiss. *12840*
   R   *12840* Turkey *12840*

R   *Dianthus freynii* Vandas *6951, 20171*
   V   *21091* Bosnia & Herzegovina *21091*
   I   Bulgaria *6951*
   R   (former) Yugoslavia *6951*

R   *Dianthus fruticosus* L. *20171*
   R   *19121* Greece - Crete *20730*

V   *Dianthus fruticosus* L. ssp. *amorginus* Runemark *20730*
   V   *20808* Greece (Cyclades) *20808*

V   *Dianthus fruticosus* L. ssp. *carpathus* Runemark *20730*
   V   *20730* Greece - Crete *20730*

R   *Dianthus fruticosus* L. ssp. *creticus* (Tausch.) Runemark *20730*
   R   *20730* Greece - Crete *20730*

V   *Dianthus fruticosus* L. ssp. *occidentalis* Runemark *20730*
   V   *20808* Greece *20808*

V   *Dianthus fruticosus* L. ssp. *sitiacus* Runemark *20730*
   V   *20730* Greece - Crete *20730*

V   *Dianthus furcatus* Balb. ssp. *gyspergerae* (Rouy)

      Briq. *8000, 20171*

V   20726 France - Corsica *20528*

R   ***Dianthus gallicus*** Pers. *8000, 20171*
   V   *14166* France (west coast) *8000*
   V   *14166* Spain (north coast) *8000*
   R   *19937* United Kingdom - Channel Is. (Jersey) *19937*

R   ***Dianthus giganteus*** d'Urv. ssp. ***banaticus*** (Heuffel) Tutin *17823, 20171*
   R   *19947* Romania *20631*

R   ***Dianthus glacialis*** Haenke ssp. ***gelidus*** (Schott, Nyman & Katschy) Tutin *17823, 20171*
   R   *19949* Romania (eastern Alps and Carpathians) *20631*

R   ***Dianthus goerkii*** Hartvig & Strid *12840*
   R   *12840* Turkey *12840*

R   ***Dianthus graniticus*** Jord. *20171*
   R   France (Auvergne, Cevennes)

R   ***Dianthus gredensis*** Pau ex Caball. *20171*
   R   Spain

E   ***Dianthus guessfeldtianus*** Muschler
   E   Egypt

I   ***Dianthus hypanicus*** Andrz. *5942, 20171*
   I   *5942* Ukraine (west) *5942*

R   ***Dianthus juniperinus*** Sm. *20171*
   R   *19121* Greece - Crete *20730*

V   ***Dianthus juniperinus*** Sm. ssp. ***aciphyllus*** (Sieber ex Ser.) Turland *20730*
   V   *20730* Greece - Crete *20730*

V   ***Dianthus juniperinus*** Sm. ssp. ***bauhinorum*** (Greuter) Turland *20730*
   V   *20730* Greece - Crete *20730*

V   ***Dianthus juniperinus*** Sm. ssp. ***heldreichii*** Greuter *20171*
   V   *20730* Greece - Crete *20730*

V   ***Dianthus juniperinus*** Sm. ssp. ***idaeus*** Turland *20730*
   V   *20730* Greece - Crete *20730*

V   ***Dianthus juniperinus*** Sm. ssp. ***juniperinus*** *20171*
   V   *20730* Greece - Crete *20730*

V   ***Dianthus juniperinus*** Sm. ssp. ***kavusicus*** Turland *20730*
   V   *20730* Greece - Crete *20730*

V   ***Dianthus juniperinus*** Sm. ssp. ***pulviniformis*** (Greuter) Turland *20730*
   V   *20730* Greece - Crete *20730*

R   ***Dianthus kamisbergensis*** Sond. *20604*
   R   *20604* South Africa - Cape Province *20604*

R   ***Dianthus knappii*** (Pant.) Asch. & Kanitz ex Borbás *20171*
   V   *21091* Bosnia & Herzegovina *21091*
   R   (former) Yugoslavia

R   ***Dianthus lanceolatus*** Steven ex Rchb. *8000, 20171*
   R   former European USSR *8000*

V   ***Dianthus langeanus*** Willk. *20171*
   V   Spain

I   ***Dianthus mercurii*** Heldr. *20171*
   I   Greece

R   ***Dianthus merinoi*** M. Lainz *11496*

R   *11496* Spain *11496*

I   ***Dianthus minimus*** Javeid
   I   India - Jammu & Kashmir

V   ***Dianthus moravicus*** Kovanda *19266, 20171*
   V   *19615* Czech Republic (southern) *19266*

E   ***Dianthus morisianum*** Valsecchi *18264*
   E   *18264* Italy - Sardinia *18264*

R   ***Dianthus muschianus*** Kotschy & Boiss. *12840*
   R   *12840* Turkey *12840*

R   ***Dianthus myrtinervius*** Griseb. *20171*
   R   Greece
   R   (former) Yugoslavia

R   ***Dianthus nardiformis*** Janka *19266, 20171*
   R   *5204* Bulgaria (north & east) *5204*
   V   *19608* Romania *8000*

V   ***Dianthus nitidus*** Waldst. & Kit. *19266, 20171*
   Ex   *19266* Poland (Pieniny Mts.) *19266*
   V   *19321* Slovakia (west Carpathians) *19266*

R   ***Dianthus pallidiflorus*** Ser. *20171*
   R   Bulgaria
   I   former European USSR

E   ***Dianthus plumarius*** ssp. ***lumnitzeri*** *20720*
   E   *20720* Hungary *20720*

I   ***Dianthus plumarius*** L. ssp. ***praecox*** Domin *20686*
   E   *20686* Hungary *20686*
   I   *20720* Slovakia *20720*

E   ***Dianthus plumarius*** ssp. ***regis stephani*** *20720*
   E   *20720* Hungary *20720*

I   ***Dianthus praecox*** W.K. *6951*
   I   *6369* Poland (Tatry & Pieniny Mts.) *20798*
   V   *19321* Slovakia *6951*

V   ***Dianthus praecox*** Kit. ssp. ***lumnitzeri*** (Wiesb.) Kmetova *19321*
   V   *19321* Slovakia *19321*

V   ***Dianthus pulviniformis*** Greuter *20171*
   V   *20731* Greece - Crete *20731*

R   ***Dianthus recognitus*** Schischk. *12840*
   R   *12840* Turkey *12840*

R   ***Dianthus rhodius*** Rech.f.
   R   Greece

R   ***Dianthus robustus*** Boiss. & Kotschy *12840*
   R   *12840* Turkey *12840*

V   ***Dianthus serotinus*** Waldst. & Kit., *19266, 20171*
   Ex   *19417* Romania *19417*
   V   *19321* Slovakia *19321*

R   ***Dianthus sessiliflorus*** Boiss. *12840*
   R   *12840* Turkey *12840*

V   ***Dianthus sinaicus*** Boiss. *8895*
   E   Egypt
   V   Israel *8895*

R   ***Dianthus sphacioticus*** Boiss. & Heldr. *20171*
   R   *20730* Greece - Crete *20730*

R   ***Dianthus spiculifolius*** Schur *17823, 20171*
   R   *19949* Romania *20631*

R   ***Dianthus stamatiadae*** Rech.f. *20171*
   R   Greece

I   ***Dianthus subbaeticus*** Fernandez Casas
   I   *11496* Spain *11496*

V   ***Dianthus xylorrizus*** Boiss. & Heldr. *20171*

	V		20730 Greece - Crete *20730*
R	*Dianthus zederbaueri* Vierh. *12840*		
	R		*12840* Turkey *12840*
R	*Drymaria malachioides* Briq. *9661*		
	R		*19755* Mexico *9661*
R	*Drymaria monticola* J. Howell *11117*		
	R		Ecuador - Galapagos (Santa Cruz) *11117*
I	*Eremogone cephalotes* (M. Bieb.) Fenzl *5942*		
	I		*5942* Ukraine *5942*
I	*Gastrolychnis soczaviana* (Schischkin) Tolm. & Kozhanczikov *5942*		
	I		*5942* Russia (Far East) - Magadan *5942*
	I		*5942* Russia (Siberia) - Yakutiya *5942*
R	*Gastrolychnis triflora* (R .Br.) Tolm. et Kozhancz. ssp. *wrangelica* Jurtz. *20085, 21309*		
	R		*20085* Russia (E.Europe) - North *20085*
R	*Gypsophila achaia* Bornm. *20171*		
	R		*20731* Greece (Sterea Ellas, Peloponnisos) *20731*
R	*Gypsophila adenophylla* Bark. *12840*		
	R		*12840* Turkey *12840*
R	*Gypsophila aucheri* Boiss. *12840*		
	R		*12840* Turkey *12840*
I	*Gypsophila aulieatensis* B. Fedtsch. *5942*		
	I		*5942* Kazakhstan (southern) *5942*
R	*Gypsophila baytopiorum* Kit Tan *12840*		
	R		*12840* Turkey *12840*
R	*Gypsophila bitlisensis* Bark. *12840*		
	R		*12840* Turkey *12840*
R	*Gypsophila brachypetala* Trautv. *12840*		
	R		*12840* Turkey *12840*
R	*Gypsophila briquetiana* Schischk. *12840*		
	R		*12840* Turkey *12840*
R	*Gypsophila confertifolia* Huber-Mor. *12840*		
	R		*12840* Turkey *12840*
R	*Gypsophila curvifolia* Fenzl *12840*		
	R		*12840* Turkey *12840*
R	*Gypsophila davisii* Bark. *12840*		
	R		*12840* Turkey *12840*
R	*Gypsophila festucifolia* Huber-Mor. *12840*		
	R		*12840* Turkey *12840*
V	*Gypsophila germanicapolitana* Huber-Mor. *12840*		
	V		*12840* Turkey *12840*
R	*Gypsophila glomerata* auct., non Pall. ex Adams *12840, 20171*		
	R		*12840* Turkey *12840*
R	*Gypsophila graminifolia* Bark. *12840*		
	R		*12840* Turkey *12840*
R	*Gypsophila hakkiarica* Kit Tan *12840*		
	R		*12840* Turkey *12840*
I	*Gypsophila heteropoda* Freyn & Sint. ssp. *minutiflora* Bark. *12840*		
	I		*12840* Turkey *12840*
I	*Gypsophila lepidioides* Boiss. *12840*		
	I		*12840* Turkey *12840*
R	*Gypsophila leucochlaena* Huber-Mor. *12840*		
	R		*12840* Turkey *12840*
R	*Gypsophila macedonica* Vandas *20171*		
	R		(former) Yugoslavia

V	*Gypsophila montserratii* Fern.Casas *11496, 20171*		
	V		*11496* Spain *11496*
R	*Gypsophila nodiflora* (Boiss.) Bark. *12840*		
	R		*12840* Turkey *12840*
V	*Gypsophila oblanceolata* Bark. *12840*		
	V		*12840* Turkey *12840*
R	*Gypsophila paniculata* L. var. *araratica* Huber-Mor. *12840*		
	R		*12840* Turkey *12840*
V	*Gypsophila papillosa* Porta *8000, 20171*		
	V		*18264* Italy (Veneto) *19997*
R	*Gypsophila parva* Bark. *12840*		
	R		*12840* Turkey *12840*
R	*Gypsophila perfiolata* L. var. *araratica* Kit Tan *12840*		
	R		*12840* Turkey *12840*
R	*Gypsophila peshmenii* A. Guner *12840*		
	R		*12840* Turkey *12840*
V	*Gypsophila pilulifera* Boiss. & Heldr. *12840*		
	V		*12840* Turkey *12840*
R	*Gypsophila pinifolia* Boiss. & Hausskn. *12840*		
	R		*12840* Turkey *12840*
V	*Gypsophila simonii* Huber-Mor. *12840*		
	V		*12840* Turkey *12840*
R	*Gypsophila simulatrix* Bornm. & Woron. *12840*		
	R		*12840* Turkey *12840*
R	*Gypsophila sphaerocephala* Fenzl ex Tchihat. var. *syriaca* (Sch.) Huber-Mor. *12840*		
	R		*12840* Turkey *12840*
R	*Gypsophila tuberculosa* Huber-Mor. *12840*		
	R		*12840* Turkey *12840*
R	*Gypsophila uralensis* Less. ssp. *pinegensis* (Perf.) R. Kam. *8001*		
	R		*11552* Russian Federation (north western) *11552*
V	*Holosteum umbellatum* L. ssp. *hirsutum* (Mutel) Breistr. *20171*		
	V		*20528* France (south-east) *20528*
R	*Krauseola gilletti* Turrill		
	R		Kenya (Northern Frontier Province) *7959*
I	*Krauseola mosambicina* (Moss) Pax & K. Hoffm. *7749*		
	I		Mozambique *7749*
V	*Loeflingia squarrosa* Nutt. ssp. *artemisiarum* Barneby & Twisselman *20883, 20850, 19002*		
	V		*20850* U.S. - California *20850*
	I		*20850* U.S. - Oregon *20850*
	E		*20850* U.S. - Wyoming *20850*
	I		*20883* Mexico *20883*
I	*Lychnis lagrangei* Coss.		
	I		Morocco
V	*Lychnis nivalis* Kit. *19266, 20171*		
	V		*20631* Romania (east Carpathians) *19266*
I	*Melandrium astrachanicum* Pacz. *5942, 20171*		
	I		*5942* Russia (E.Europe) - South (Astrakhan) *5942*
R	*Minuartia anatolica* (Boiss.) Woron. var. *lanuginosa* McNeill *12840*		
	R		*12840* Turkey *12840*
R	*Minuartia anatolica* (Boiss.) Woron. var. *phrygia* (Bornm.) McNeill *12840*		

R   *12840*   Turkey *12840*

R   *Minuartia anatolica* (Boiss.) Woron var.
    scleranthoides (Boiss. & Noe) McNeill *12840*
    R   *12840*   Turkey *12840*

R   *Minuartia anatolica* (Boiss.) Woron var. *tetrastiche*
    McNeill *12840*
    R   *12840*   Turkey *12840*

R   *Minuartia baldaccii* (Halácsy) Mattf. ssp.
    skutariensis Hayek. *20178, 20171*
    R   *20178*   Albania *20178*

I   *Minuartia bilykiana* Klokov *8000, 20171*
    I   former European USSR *8000*

E   *Minuartia corymbulosa* (Boiss. & Bal.) McNeill var.
    breviflora (Boiss.) McNeill *12840*
    E   *12840*   Turkey *12840*

R   *Minuartia corymbulosa* (Boiss. & Bal.) McNeill var.
    gypsophiloides McNeill *12840*
    R   *12840*   Turkey *12840*

V   *Minuartia cumberlandensis* (B.E. Wofford & Kral)
    McNeill *20850*
    E   *20850*   U.S. - Kentucky *20850*
    V   *20850*   U.S. - Tennessee *20850*

E   *Minuartia decumbens* T.W. & J.P. Nelson *20850*
    E   *20850*   U.S. - California *20850*

R   *Minuartia dianthifolia* (Boiss.) Hand.-Mazz. ssp.
    cataonica McNeill *12840*
    R   *12840*   Turkey *12840*

R   *Minuartia dianthifolia* (Boiss.) Hand.-Mazz. ssp.
    dianthifolia *12840*
    R   *12840*   Turkey *12840*

E   *Minuartia glaucina* Dvoráková *19842*
    E   *19321*   Slovakia *19321*

E   *Minuartia godfreyi* (Shinners) McNeill *20850, 10260*
    E   *20850*   U.S. - Alabama *20850*
    E   *20850*   U.S. - Arkansas *20850*
    E   *20850*   U.S. - Florida *20850*
    I   *20850*   U.S. - Georgia *20850*
    E   *20850*   U.S. - North Carolina *20850*
    Ex   *20850*   U.S. - South Carolina *20850*
    E   *20850*   U.S. - Tennessee *20850*

R   *Minuartia gracilis* McNeill *12840*
    R   *12840*   Turkey *12840*

E   *Minuartia graminifolia* (Ard.) Jáv. ssp.
    graminifolia *20171*
    E   *19949*   Romania *20631*

I   *Minuartia grignensis* (Rchb.) Mattf. *20171*
    I   Italy

R   *Minuartia handelii* Mattf. *20171*
    E   *21091*   Bosnia & Herzegovina *21091*
    R   (former) Yugoslavia

I   *Minuartia helmii* (Ser.) Schischk. *11552, 20171*
    I   *5942*   Russia (E.Europe) - East (Ural mountains)
               5942
    I   *5942*   Russia (E.Europe) - North (Ural mountains)
               5942
    I   *5942*   Russia (Siberia) - West (Ural mountains)
               5942

R   *Minuartia herniarioides* (Rion) Hess & Landolt *18154,*
    I   Italy *8000*
    R   *18154*   Switzerland *18154*

E   *Minuartia hirsuta* (M.Bieb.) Hand.-Mazz. ssp.
    frutescens (Kit.) Hand.-Mazz. *20171*

    E   *19949*   Romania *20631*

R   *Minuartia issaurica* McNeill *12840*
    R   *12840*   Turkey *12840*

R   *Minuartia krascheninnikovii* Schischk. *8000, 20171*
    R   *11552*   Russian Federation (Ural Mts) *11552*

I   *Minuartia langii* (Reuss) Holub *19321*
    I   *19321*   Slovakia *19321*

R   *Minuartia macrocarpa* (Pursh) Ostenf. var. *jooi*
    (Makino) Hara *10572*
    R   *10572*   Japan *10572*

E   *Minuartia marcescens* (Fenzl) House *20850, 5567*
    E   *20850*   Canada - Newfoundland *20850*
    E   *20850*   Canada - Quebec *20850*
    E   *20850*   U.S. - Vermont *20850*

R   *Minuartia mesogitana* (Boiss.) Hand.-Mazz. ssp. *lydia*
    (Boiss.) McNeill *12840*
    R   *12840*   Turkey *12840*

V   *Minuartia mesogitana* (Boiss.) Hand.-Mazz. ssp.
    macrocarpa McNeill *12840*
    V   *12840*   Turkey *12840*

R   *Minuartia nifensis* McNeill *12840*
    R   *12840*   Turkey *12840*

R   *Minuartia pestalozzae* (Boiss.) Bornm. *12840*
    R   *12840*   Turkey *12840*

R   *Minuartia pichleri* (Boiss.) Maire & Petitm. *20171*
    R   Greece

R   *Minuartia platyphylla* (Gay ex Christ) McNeill *15105*
    R   *15105*   Spain - Canary Is. *15105*

R   *Minuartia recurva* (All.) Schinz. & Thell. ssp.
    carica McNeill *12840*
    R   *12840*   Turkey *12840*

R   *Minuartia rimarum* (Boiss. & Bal.) Mattf. var.
    multiflora McNeill *12840*
    R   *12840*   Turkey *12840*

R   *Minuartia senneniana* Maire & Mauricio
    R   Morocco

R   *Minuartia stojanovii* (Kit.) Kozuharov &
    Kuzmanov *5204*
    R   *5204*   Bulgaria (south-west) *5204*
    R   Greece

E   *Minuartia stolonifera* T.W. & J.P. Nelson *20850*
    I   *20850*   Canada - Labrador *20850*
    I   *20850*   Canada - Ontario *20850*
    E   *20850*   U.S. - California *20850*

R   *Minuartia taurica* (Steven) Graebn. *8000, 20171*
    R   former European USSR *8000*

R   *Minuartia trichocalycina* (Ten. & Guss.)
    Grande *18264, 20171*
    R   *18264*   Italy (Abruzzi) *18264*

R   *Minuartia umbellulifera* (Boiss.) McNeill ssp.
    fimbriata McNeill *12840*
    R   *12840*   Turkey *12840*

R   *Minuartia umbellulifera* (Boiss.) McNeill var.
    kurdica McNeill *12840*
    R   *12840*   Turkey *12840*

R   *Minuartia umbellulifera* (Boiss.) McNeill ssp.
    pontica (Bornm.) McNeill *12840*
    R   *12840*   Turkey *12840*

R   *Minuartia umbellulifera* (Boiss.) McNeill ssp.
    salbacica McNeill *12840*

	R	12840 Turkey *12840*

R *Minuartia valedictionis* McNeill *12840*
    R 12840 Turkey *12840*

R *Minuartia valentina* (Pau) Sennen *20648*
    R 20692 Spain (Castellón & Valencia provinces) *20692*

R *Minuartia velenovski* (Rohlena) Hayek *20178*
    R 20178 Albania *20178*
    R (former) Yugoslavia

R *Minuartia verna* (L.) Hiern ssp. *brevipetala* Hartvig & Strid *12840*
    R 12840 Turkey *12840*

E *Minuartia wettsteinii* Mattf. *20171*
    E 20730 Greece - Crete *20730*

R *Moehringia dielsiana* Mattf. *18264, 20171*
    R 18264 Italy (Lombardy) *18264*

R *Moehringia fontqueri* Pau *8000, 20171*
    R Spain (south east (Almeria)) *8000*

I *Moehringia hypanica* Grynj & Klokov *5942, 20171*
    I 5942 Ukraine *5942*

R *Moehringia intermedia* (Loisel.) Panizzi *20171*
    R 20171 France *20171*

R *Moehringia jankae* Griseb. ex Janka *19266, 20171*
    R 5204 Bulgaria *19266*
    V 19949 Romania (Dolurogea) *19266*

R *Moehringia lebrunii* Merxm. *18264, 20171*
    R 20528 France (Alpes-Maritimes) *20528*
    R 18264 Italy (Liguria) *18264*

R *Moehringia markgrafii* Merxm. & Gutermann *18264, 20171*
    R 18264 Italy *18264*

R *Moehringia minutiflora* Bornm. *20171*
    R (former) Yugoslavia

R *Moehringia papulosa* auct., non Bertol. *18264, 20171*
    R France
    R 18264 Italy (marches) *18264*

R *Moehringia sedoides* (Pers.) Cumino ex Loisel. *20171*
    R 20528 France (Alpes-Maritimes) *20528*
    R 20528 Italy *20528*

R *Moehringia stellarioides* Coss. *10487*
    R 14958 Algeria *10487*

R *Moehringia tommasinii* Marches. *8000, 20171*
    V 18264 Italy (Friuli-Venezia Giulia) *19997*
    R 13662 Slovenia (south western) *13662*

I *Petrocoma hoefftiana* (Fischer) Rupr. *5942*
    I 5942 Russia - North Caucasus *5942*

R *Petrocoptis crassifolia* Rouy *8000, 20171*
    R 19174 Spain (Pyrenees) *11496*

V *Petrocoptis grandiflora* Rothm. *8000, 20171*
    V 19174 Spain (north-west) *8000*

R *Petrocoptis pardoi* Pau *8000, 20171*
    R 20874 Spain (Castellon province) *11496*

V *Petrocoptis pseudoviscosa* Fern.Casas *17891, 20171*
    V 20874 Spain *20874*

V *Petrocoptis viscosa* Rothm. *20171*
    V Spain

R *Petrorhagia dianthoides* (Sm.) P.W.Ball & Heywood *20171*
    R 20731 Greece - Crete *20731*

V *Petrorhagia hispidula* (Boiss. & Heldr.) Ball &

    Heyw. *12840*
    V 12840 Turkey *12840*

R *Petrorhagia lycica* (Davis) Ball & Heyw. *12840*
    R 12840 Turkey *12840*

V *Petrorhagia pamphylica* (Boiss. & Ball.) Ball. & Heyw. *12840*
    V 12840 Turkey *12840*

R *Petrorhagia peroninii* (Boiss. Ball. & Heyw. *12840*
    R 12840 Turkey *12840*

R *Petrorhagia rhiphaea* (Pau & al) P.W. Ball & Heywood
    R Morocco

R *Petrorhagia rupestris* Brullo & Furnari
    R Libya

R *Phryna ortegioides* (Fisch. & Mey.) Pax & Hoffm. *12840*
    R 12840 Turkey *12840*

V *Pinosia glandulosa* Alain *5607*
    V 19105 Cuba (Guantanamo) *5607*

R *Polycarpaea carnosa* C. Smith ex Buch *15105*
    R 15105 Spain - Canary Is. *15105*

V *Polycarpaea diffusa* Wight & Arnott *14782*
    V 14782 India - Tamil Nadu *14782*

I *Polycarpaea gamopetala* R. Berhaut *8003*
    I Senegal *8003*

R *Polycarpaea gomerensis* Burchard
    R Spain - Canary Is.

R *Polycarpaea incana* I.D.Cowie *20681*
    R 20681 Australia - Northern Territory *20681*

I *Polycarpaea jazirensis* R.A. King *20146*
    I 20146 Oman (central) *20146*

I *Polycarpaea linearifolia* (DC.) DC. var. *racemosa* Berhaut *8003*
    I Senegal *8003*

V *Polycarpaea robusta* (Pitard) Kunkel *15105*
    V 20750 Spain - Canary Is. *15105*

R *Polycarpaea smithii* Link *15105*
    R 20750 Spain - Canary Is. *15105*

R *Polycarpaea staminodina* F.Muell. *20681*
    R 20681 Australia - Northern Territory *20681*

R *Polycarpaea tenuis* Webb ex Christ *15105*
    R 15105 Spain - Canary Is. *15105*

R *Polycarpon prostratum* (Forssk.) Asch. & Schweinf. var. *littorale* J. Raynal & A. Raynal *8003*
    R Senegal (Tanma) *8003*

R *Psammosilene tunicoides* W.C. Wu & C.Y. Wu *17617*
    R 17617 China - Guizhou (Wening) *11139*
    R 17617 China - Sichuan *11139*
    R 17617 China - Xizang Zizhiqu (Lingze, Mangkang) *11139*
    R 17617 China - Yunnan *11139*

R *Pseudostellaria okamotoi* Ohwi *15957*
    R 15923 Korea, South (Mt Chiri) *15957*

R *Sanctambrosia manicata* Skottsb. ex Kuschel *5595*
    R 19534 Chile - Islas Desventurados *5595*

R *Saponaria cypria* Boiss. *14230*
    R 19164 Cyprus (Troodos area) *14230*

R *Saponaria dalmasiia* Boissieu *12840*
    R 12840 Turkey *12840*

E *Saponaria halophila* Hedge & Huber-Mor. *12840*

E		*12840* Turkey *12840*
R	*Saponaria lutea* L. *18154, 20171*	
	R	*20528* France (Savoie) *20528*
	I	Italy *8000*
	R	*18154* Switzerland *18154*
R	*Saponaria pamphylica* Boiss. & Heldr. *12840*	
	R	*12840* Turkey *12840*
R	*Saponaria picta* Boiss. *12840*	
	R	*12840* Turkey *12840*
R	*Saponaria pinetorum* Hedge *12840*	
	R	*12840* Turkey *12840*
I	*Saponaria syriaca* Boiss. *12840*	
	I	*12840* Turkey *12840*
E	*Schiedea adamantis* St. John *20850, 14209*	
	E	*20850* U.S. - Hawaii (Oahu) *20850*
Ex/E	*Schiedea amplexicaulis* Mann *20850, 14209*	
	Ex/E	*20850* U.S. - Hawaii (Kaua`i) *20850*
E	*Schiedea apokremnos* St. John *20850, 14209*	
	E	*20850* U.S. - Hawaii (Kaua`i) *20850*
V	*Schiedea diffusa* Gray *20850*	
	V	*20850* U.S. - Hawaii *20850*
V	*Schiedea globosa* Mann *20850*	
	V	*20850* U.S. - Hawaii *20850*
E	*Schiedea haleakalensis* O. Deg. & Sherff *20850, 14209*	
	E	*20850* U.S. - Hawaii (east Maui) *20850*
E	*Schiedea helleri* Sherff *20850, 14209*	
	E	*20850* U.S. - Hawaii (Kaua`i) *20850*
E	*Schiedea hookeri* Gray *20850*	
	E	*20850* U.S. - Hawaii *20850*
R	*Schiedea hookeri* A.Gray var. *hookeri* *14209*	
	R	*14209* U.S. - Hawaii (O`ahu, Maui) *14209*
Ex/E	*Schiedea implexa* (Hbd.) Sherff *20850, 14209*	
	Ex/E	*20850* U.S. - Hawaii (east Maui) *20850*
E	*Schiedea kaalae* Wawra *20850*	
	E	*20850* U.S. - Hawaii *20850*
E	*Schiedea kaalae* Wawra var. *kaalae* *14209*	
	E	*14209* U.S. - Hawaii (O`ahu) *14209*
E	*Schiedea kealiae* Caum & Hosaka *20850, 14209*	
	E	*20850* U.S. - Hawaii (O`ahu - Wai`anae Mts.) *20850*
V	*Schiedea ligustrina* Cham. & Schlecht. *20850*	
	V	*20850* U.S. - Hawaii *20850*
E	*Schiedea lydgatei* Hbd. *20850*	
	E	*20850* U.S. - Hawaii *20850*
R	*Schiedea lydgatei* Hillebrand var. *lydgatei* *14209*	
	R	*14209* U.S. - Hawaii (Moloka`i) *14209*
V	*Schiedea mannii* St. John *20850, 14209*	
	V	*20850* U.S. - Hawaii (O`ahu - Wai`anae Mts.) *20850*
E	*Schiedea membranacea* St. John *20850, 14209*	
	E	*20850* U.S. - Hawaii (Kaua`i) *20850*
V	*Schiedea menziesii* Hook. *20850*	
	V	*20850* U.S. - Hawaii *20850*
R	*Schiedea menziesii* Hook. var. *menziesii* *14209*	
	R	*14209* U.S. - Hawaii *14209*
E	*Schiedea nuttallii* Hook. *20850*	
	E	*20850* U.S. - Hawaii *20850*
R	*Schiedea nuttallii* Hook. var. *nuttallii* *14209*	
	R	*14209* U.S. - Hawaii (O`ahu - Wai`anae Mts.) *14209*
V	*Schiedea pubescens* Hbd. *20850*	
	I	*20850* U.S. - Hawaii *20850*
E	*Schiedea pubescens* Hillebrand var. *pubescens* *20850, 14209*	
	E	*20850* U.S. - Hawaii *20850*
V	*Schiedea pubescens* Hillebrand var. *purpurascens* Sherff *20850, 14209*	
	V	*20850* U.S. - Hawaii *20850*
E	*Schiedea salicaria* Hbd. *20850, 14209*	
	E	*20850* U.S. - Hawaii (West Maui) *20850*
E	*Schiedea spergulina* Gray *20850*	
	I	*20850* U.S. - Hawaii *20850*
E	*Schiedea spergulina* A. Gray var. *leiopoda* Sherff *20850, 14209*	
	E	*20850* U.S. - Hawaii *20850*
E	*Schiedea spergulina* A. Gray var. *spergulina* *20850, 14209*	
	E	*20850* U.S. - Hawaii (Kaua`i) *20850*
E	*Schiedea stellarioides* Mann *20850*	
	E	*20850* U.S. - Hawaii *20850*
Ex	*Schiedea stellarioides* H. Mann var. *stellarioides* *14209*	
	Ex	*14209* U.S. - Hawaii (Kaua`i) *14209*
E	*Schiedea verticillata* F. Br. *20850, 14209*	
	E	*20850* U.S. - Hawaii (Nihoa) *20850*
I	*Silene adscendens* Lag. *20171*	
	I	Spain (Almeria coast)
I	*Silene akinfievii* Schmalh. *5942*	
	I	*5942* Russia - North Caucasus *5942*
	I	*5942* Georgia *5942*
R	*Silene akmaniana* Ekim & Celik *12840*	
	R	*12840* Turkey *12840*
E	*Silene alexandri* Hbd. *20850, 14209*	
	E	*20850* U.S. - Hawaii (east Moloka`i) *20850*
R	*Silene almolae* J.Gay *20171*	
	R	Spain
V	*Silene ammophila* Boiss. & Heldr. *20171*	
	V	*20731* Greece - Crete (inc. Karpathos, Kasos) *20731*
R	*Silene anatolica* Melzheimer & Baytop *12840*	
	R	*12840* Turkey *12840*
I	*Silene aomorensis* Mizush. *10572*	
	I	*10572* Japan *10572*
V	*Silene aperta* Greene *20850*	
	I	*20850* U.S. - California *20850*
R	*Silene araratica* Schischk. *12840*	
	R	*12840* Turkey *12840*
R	*Silene argaea* Fisch. & Mey. *12840*	
	R	*12840* Turkey *12840*
R	*Silene aristidis* Pomel *10487*	
	R	*14958* Algeria *10487*
R	*Silene armena* Boiss. var. *serrulata* (Boiss.) Coode & Cullen *12840*	
	R	*12840* Turkey *12840*
V	*Silene articulata* Viv.	

V   Libya

R   *Silene azirensis* Coode & Cullen *12840*
    R   *12840* Turkey *12840*

R   *Silene barbara* Humbert & Maire
    R   Morocco

R   *Silene barbeyana* Heldr. ex Boiss. *20171*
    R   Greece

R   *Silene bernardina* S.Watson *20850*
    I   *20850* U.S. - California *20850*
    I   *20850* U.S. - Nevada *20850*
    I   *20850* U.S. - Oregon *20850*

R   *Silene berthelotiana* Webb *15105*
    R   *15105* Spain - Canary Is. *15105*

I   *Silene biafrae* Hook.f.
    I   Cameroon (Cameroon mt)

R   *Silene biappendiculata* Rohrb.
    R   Egypt
    R   Libya

R   *Silene birandiana* Ekim *12840*
    R   *12840* Turkey *12840*

R   *Silene bolanthoides* Quezel,Coutaud & A. Pamukc. *12840*
    R   *12840* Turkey *12840*

R   *Silene bourgeaui* Webb ex Christ *15105*
    R   *15105* Spain - Canary Is. *15105*

R   *Silene brachypoda* Rouy *20171*
    R   France (south)

R   *Silene brevicalyx* Hartwig & Strid *12840*
    R   *12840* Turkey *12840*

R   *Silene campanula* Pers. *20171*
    R   France
    R   Italy

E   *Silene campanulata* S.Watson ssp. *campanulata* *20850*
    E   *20850* U.S. - California *20850*

I   *Silene canariensis* Willd. *15105*
    I   *15105* Spain - Canary Is. *15105*

R   *Silene capillipes* Boiss. & Heldr. *12840*
    R   *12840* Turkey *12840*

R   *Silene caramanica* Boiss. & Heldr. *12840*
    R   *12840* Turkey *12840*

R   *Silene cariensis* Boiss. *12840*
    R   *12840* Turkey *12840*

R   *Silene cartilaginea* Huber-Mor. *12840*
    R   *12840* Turkey *12840*

R   *Silene caryophlloides* (Poiret.) Otth ssp. *echinus* (Bois. & Held.) Coode & Cullen *12840*
    R   *12840* Turkey *12840*

R   *Silene caryphylloides* (Poiret) Otth ssp. *stentoria* (Fenzl) Coode & Cullen *12840*
    R   *12840* Turkey *12840*

R   *Silene cerastoides* L. *20171*
    R   *20731* Greece - Crete *20731*

E   *Silene cintrana* Rothm. *8000, 20171*
    E   *20076* Portugal (Cintra) *8000*

E   *Silene cirtensis* Pomel *10487*
    E   *14958* Algeria *10487*

R   *Silene claryi* Battand. *10487*
    R   *14958* Algeria *10487*

E   *Silene clokeyi* C.L. Hitchc. & Maguire *20850*
    E   *20850* U.S. - Nevada *20850*

R   *Silene cordifolia* All. *20171*
    R   France
    R   Italy

I   *Silene cretacea* Fisch. ex Spreng. *5942, 20171*
    I   *5942* Russia (E.Europe) - South *5942*

Ex/E *Silene cryptopetala* Hbd. *20850, 14209*
    Ex/E *20850* U.S. - Hawaii (east Maui) *20850*

R   *Silene cythnia* (Halácsy) Walters *20171*
    R   Greece

R   *Silene damboldtiana* Greuter & Melzh. *20171*
    R   Greece

Ex/E *Silene degeneri* Sherff *20850, 14209*
    Ex/E *20850* U.S. - Hawaii (east Maui) *20850*

R   *Silene delicatula* Boiss. ssp. *pisidica* Coode & Cullen *12840*
    R   *12840* Turkey *12840*

V   *Silene diclinis* (Lag.) M.Laínz *19174, 20171*
    V   *19174* Spain (La Safor, Valencia) *20692*

R   *Silene dictaea* Rech.f. *20171*
    R   *20731* Greece - Crete *20731*

R   *Silene dinarica* Spreng. *17823, 20171*
    R   *19949* Romania *20631*

R   *Silene dionysii* Stoj. & Jordanov *20171*
    R   Greece

R   *Silene dissecta* Litard. & Maire
    R   Morocco

E   *Silene douglasii* Hook. var. *oraria* (M.E. Peck) C.L. Hitchc. & Maguire *20850*
    E   *20850* U.S. - Oregon *20850*

R   *Silene echinosperma* Boiss. & Heldr. *20171*
    R   Greece

R   *Silene echinospermoides* Huber-Mor. *20731*
    R   *20731* Greece - East Aegean Is *20731*

V   *Silene elegans* Link ex Brot. *20171*
    V   *8322* Portugal *8322*

R   *Silene elisabetha* Jan *20171*
    R   Italy

R   *Silene elisabethae* Jan *18264, 20171*
    R   *18264* Italy *18264*

R   *Silene ermenekensis* M. Vural & Kit Tan *12840*
    R   *12840* Turkey *12840*

R   *Silene fraudatrix* Meikle *14230*
    R   *19164* Cyprus *14230*

I   *Silene fruticosa* L. ssp. *cyrenaica* Beguinot & Vaccari *13988*
    I   *13988* Egypt (westernmost part of Mediterranean coast) *13988*
    I   Libya

V   *Silene furcata* Raf. ssp. *angustiflora* (Rupr.) Walters *14526, 20171*
    E   *20673* Finland *8000*
    V   *17832* Norway *14166*
    V   *20083* Sweden *18216*

R   *Silene gaditana* Talavera & Bocquet *20171*
    R   *20661* Spain (Cádiz, Málaga) *20661*

R   *Silene ghiarensis* Battand. *10487*
    R   *14958* Algeria *10487*

R   *Silene giraldii* Guss. *20171*
    R   Italy
    R   Italy - Sardinia

V   *Silene glaberrima* Faure & Maire *10487*
    V   *14958* Algeria *10487*

R   *Silene goulimyi* Turrill *19174, 20171*
    R   *19174* Greece *19174*

I   *Silene guicciardii* Boiss. & Heldr. *20171*
    I   Greece

R   *Silene haradjianii* Chowdh. *12840*
    R   *12840* Turkey *12840*

V   *Silene haussknechtii* Heldr. ex Hausskn. *8000, 20171*
    V   Greece

E   *Silene hawaiiensis* Sherff *20850*
    E   *20850* U.S. - Hawaii *20850*

R   *Silene hawaiiensis* Sherff var.
    hawaiiensis *14209*
    R   *14209* U.S. - Hawaii *14209*

I   *Silene hellmannii* Claus *8000, 20171*
    I   *11552* Russian Federation (western, Ural Mts)
        11552

E   *Silene hicesiae* Brullo & Signor. *17891, 20171*
    E   *18264* Italy - Sicily *17891*

I   *Silene hidakaalpina* (Miy. & Tatew.) Ohwi &
    Ohashi *10572*
    I   *10572* Japan *10572*

V   *Silene hifacensis* Rouy ex Willk. *8000, 20171*
    E   *20692* Spain (east - Alicante Province) *8000*
    V   *11496* Spain - Balearic Is. (Ibiza) *8000*

V   *Silene holzmannii* Heldr. ex Boiss. *20171*
    V   *20731* Greece - East Aegean Is *20731*

R   *Silene inclinata* Huber & Mor. *12840*
    R   *12840* Turkey *12840*

R   *Silene insularis* Barbey *20171*
    R   *20731* Greece - Crete (Karpathos) *20731*

R   *Silene integripetala* Bory & Chaub. ssp. *greuteri*
    (Phitos) Akeroyd *19121, 20171*
    R   *20731* Greece - Crete *20731*

R   *Silene isaurica* Contandr. & Quezel *12840*
    R   *12840* Turkey *12840*

R   *Silene ispartensis* Ghazanfar *12840*
    R   *12840* Turkey *12840*

R   *Silene jailensis* N.I.Rubtzov *20171*
    E   *20655* Ukraine - Crimea *20653*
    R   former European USSR

I   *Silene khasiana* Rohrb. *14782*
    I   *14782* India - Meghalaya *14782*

R   *Silene kumaonensis* F. Williams *13883*
    R   *13883* India - Uttar Pradesh (Garhwal Himalaya)
        13883

R   *Silene kunawarensis* Royle *13883*
    R   *13883* India - Himachal Pradesh *13883*
    R   *13883* India - Jammu & Kashmir *13883*
    R   *13883* Pakistan *13883*

R   *Silene laconica* Boiss. & Orph. *20171*
    R   Greece

V   *Silene lagunensis* C. Smith *15105*
    V   *15105* Spain - Canary Is. *15105*

E   *Silene lanceolata* Gray *20850*
    E   *20850* U.S. - Hawaii *20850*

E   *Silene lanceolata* A.Gray var.
    lanceolata *14209*
    E   *14209* U.S. - Hawaii *14209*

R   *Silene leucophylla* Boiss.
    R   Egypt

V   *Silene longicilia* (Brot.) Otth *8000, 20171*
    V   *20076* Portugal *8000*

R   *Silene lucida* Chowdh. ssp. *glandulosa* T.
    Ekim *12840*
    R   *12840* Turkey *12840*

R   *Silene lycaonica* Chowdh. *12840*
    R   *12840* Turkey *12840*

R   *Silene macrantha* (Pancic) H.Neumayer *20178, 20171*
    R   *20178* Albania *20178*
    R   (former) Yugoslavia

V   *Silene mariana* Pau *17891, 20171*
    V   *20660* Spain (Clórde, Sevilla, Málaga) *11496*

I   *Silene marmarica* Beguinot & Vaccari
    I   Libya

E   *Silene marmorensis* Kruckeberg *20850*
    E   *20850* U.S. - California *20850*

R   *Silene morrisonmontana* (Hayata) Ohwi & Ohashi var.
    glabella (Ohwi) & Ohashi *20511*
    R   *20511* Taiwan *20511*

V   *Silene nachlingerae* Tiehm *20850*
    V   *20850* U.S. - Nevada *20850*

V   *Silene nevadensis* Boiss. *20171*
    V   Spain

R   *Silene niederi* Heldr. ex Boiss. *20171*
    R   Greece

E   *Silene nocteolens* Webb & Berthel. *15105*
    E   *20750* Spain - Canary Is. *15105*

R   *Silene oligantha* Boiss. & Heldr. *20171*
    R   Greece

Ex   *Silene oligotricha* Huber-Mor. *12840*
    Ex   *12840* Turkey *12840*

R   *Silene oreades* Boiss. & Heldr. *12840*
    R   *12840* Turkey *12840*

E   *Silene orphanidis* Boiss. *8000, 20171*
    E   Greece (north (Athos)) *8000*

R   *Silene ovata* Pursh *20850*
    E   *20850* U.S. - Alabama *20850*
    V   *20850* U.S. - Arkansas *20850*
    E   *20850* U.S. - Georgia *20850*
    E   *20850* U.S. - Kentucky *20850*
    E   *20850* U.S. - Mississippi *20850*
    V   *20850* U.S. - North Carolina *20850*
    I   *20850* U.S. - South Carolina *20850*
    E   *20850* U.S. - Tennessee *20850*
    E   *20850* U.S. - Virginia *20850*

R   *Silene paphlagonica* Bornm. *12840*
    R   *12840* Turkey *12840*

R   *Silene parishii* S.Watson *20850*
    I   *20850* U.S. - California *20850*

E   *Silene parishii* S.Wats var. *parishii* *20850*
    I   *20850* U.S. - California *20850*

R   *Silene pentelica* Boiss. *20171*
    R   Greece

E   *Silene perlmanii* W.L. Wagner, Herbst & Sohmer *20850,*
    14209

E	20850	U.S. - Hawaii (O`ahu, Wai`anae Mts.) 20850

R   *Silene petersonii* Maguire *20850*

    R   20850   U.S. - Utah *20850*

E   *Silene petersonii* Maguire var. *minor* C.L. Hitchc. & Maguire *20850*

    20850   U.S. - Utah *20850*

V   *Silene petersonii* Maguire var. *petersonii 20850*

    20850   U.S. - Utah *20850*

R   *Silene pindicola* Hausskn. *19174, 20171*

    R   20178   Albania *20178*
    R   19174   Greece *19174*

R   *Silene pinetorum* Boiss. & Heldr. *20171*

    R   20731   Greece - Crete *20731*

R   *Silene plankii* C.L. Hitchc. & Maguire *20850*

    R   20850   U.S. - New Mexico *20850*
    E   20850   U.S. - Texas *20850*

R   *Silene pogonocalyx* (Svent.) D. Bramwell in press *15105*

    R   15105   Spain - Canary Is. *15105*

V   *Silene polypetala* (Walt.) Fern. & Schub. *20850, 16273*

    E   20850   U.S. - Florida *20850*
    V   20850   U.S. - Georgia *20850*

E   *Silene pompeiopolitana* J.Gay ex Boiss. *12840, 20171*

    E   12840   Turkey *12840*

E   *Silene pseudovestita* Battand. *10487*

    E   14958   Algeria *10487*

E   *Silene rectiramea* B.L. Robins. *20850, 14662*

    E   20850   U.S. - Arizona *20850*

E   *Silene reeseana* Maire

    E   Morocco

R   *Silene regia* Sims *20850*

    V   20850   U.S. - Alabama *20850*
    V   20850   U.S. - Arkansas *20850*
    E   20850   U.S. - Georgia *20850*
    E   20850   U.S. - Illinois *20850*
    V   20850   U.S. - Indiana *20850*
    Ex/E   20850   U.S. - Kansas *20850*
    E   20850   U.S. - Kentucky *20850*
    R   20850   U.S. - Missouri *20850*
    V   20850   U.S. - Ohio *20850*
    E   20850   U.S. - Oklahoma *20850*
    Ex/E   20850   U.S. - Tennessee *20850*

I   *Silene repens* Patrin var. *apoiensis* Hara *10572*

    I   10572   Japan *10572*

R   *Silene reticulata* Desf. *14958*

    R   Algeria
    I   Tunisia

R   *Silene retzdorffiana* (K.Maly) H.Neumayer *20171*

    V   21091   Bosnia & Herzegovina *21091*
    R   (former) Yugoslavia

V   *Silene reverchoni* Battand. *10487*

    V   14958   Algeria *10487*

R   *Silene rhiphaena* Pau & Font Quer

    R   Morocco

R   *Silene rosulata* Soy.-Will. & Godron *10487, 20171*

    R   14958   Algeria *10487*

R   *Silene rosulta* Soyer-Willemet & Godron ssp. *sanctae-therasiae* (Jeanmonod) Jeanmonod *18264*

R	18264	Italy - Sardinia *18264*

E   *Silene rothmaleri* P.Silva *8000, 20171*

    E   20706   Portugal (south west) *8000*

V   *Silene sabinosae* Pitard *15105*

    V   20750   Spain - Canary Is. *15105*

V   *Silene salsuginea* Huber-Mor. *12840*

    V   12840   Turkey *12840*

V   *Silene sangaria* Coode & Cullen *12840, 20171*

    V   19873   Turkey *12840*

R   *Silene scabrida* Soy.-Will. & Godron

    R   Algeria
    I   Tunisia

V   *Silene schimperiana* Boiss. *16168*

    V   16168   Egypt *16168*

R   *Silene schmuckeri* Wettst. *20171*

    R   (former) Yugoslavia

R   *Silene schwarzenbergeri* Halácsy *19174, 20171*

    R   19174   Albania *19174*
    R   19174   Greece *19174*

R   *Silene scythicina* Coode & Cullen *12840*

    R   12840   Turkey *12840*

E   *Silene seelyi* Morton & J.W. Thompson *20850*

    E   20850   U.S. - Washington *20850*

E   *Silene sessionis* Battand. *10487*

    E   14958   Algeria *10487*

R   *Silene sipylea* O. Schwarz *12840*

    R   12840   Turkey *12840*

V   *Silene sordida* Huber-Mor. & Reese *12840*

    V   12840   Turkey *12840*

V   *Silene spaldingii* S.Watson *20850*

    E   20850   Canada - British Columbia *20850*
    E   20850   U.S. - Idaho *20850*
    E   20850   U.S. - Montana *20850*
    E   20850   U.S. - Oregon *20850*
    V   20850   U.S. - Washington *20850*

R   *Silene splendens* Boiss. *12840*

    R   12840   Turkey *12840*

R   *Silene squamigera* Boiss. ssp. *vesiculifera* (Gay ex Boiss.) Coode & Cullen *12840*

    R   12840   Turkey *12840*

R   *Silene stenocalycina* Rech.f. *20171*

    R   Greece

E   *Silene stockenii* Chater *19174, 20171*

    E   19174   Spain (Cádiz) *11496*

R   *Silene subciliata* B.L. Robins. *20850*

    E   20850   U.S. - Louisiana *20850*
    R   20850   U.S. - Texas *20850*

R   *Silene succulenta* Forssk. *20171*

    V   Greece
    R   20805   Italy - Sardinia *20805*

V   *Silene succulenta* Forssk. ssp. *corsica* (DC.) Nyman *15080, 20171*

    V   20726   France - Corsica *15080*
    V   18264   Italy - Sardinia *15080*

R   *Silene surculosa* Huber-Mor. *12840*

    R   12840   Turkey *12840*

Ex/E   *Silene telavivensis* Zoh. & Plitm. *8895*

    Ex/E   Israel (last seen 1960) *8896*

R   *Silene tempskyana* Freyn & Sint. *20171*

    R   Greece

R   *Silene tunicoides* Boiss. *12840*
  R   *12840* Turkey *12840*

E   *Silene uralensis* (Rupr.) Bocquet ssp. *ogilviensis*
    (Porsild) Brunton *20850, 1034*
  E   *20850* Canada - Yukon Territory *20850*
  I   *20850* U.S. - Alaska *20850*

I   *Silene vagans* Clarke *14782*
  I   *14782* India - Nagaland *14782*

V   *Silene velutina* Pourr. ex Loisel. *8000, 20171*
  V   *19174* France - Corsica (south-eastern) *19174*
  E   *18264* Italy - Sardinia (rocks of northern Sardegna.)
        19997

R   *Silene velutinoides* Pomel *10487, 20171*
  R   *14958* Algeria *10487*

V   *Silene verecunda* S.Watson ssp.
    verecunda *20850*
  V   *20850* U.S. - California *20850*

R   *Silene vidaliana* Pau & Font Quer
  R   Morocco

R   *Silene viscariopsis* Bornm. *20171*
  R   (former) Yugoslavia

I   *Silene volubilitana* Braun-Blanquet & Maire
  I   Morocco

R   *Silene wrightii* Gray *20850*
  R   *20850* U.S. - New Mexico *20850*

R   *Silene zawadzkii* Herbich *17823, 20171*
  R   *19947* Romania *19949*
  I   *5942* Ukraine (Carpathian Mts.) *5942*

V   *Spergula arvensis* L. ssp. *gracilis* (E. Petit)
    Briq. *8001, 20171*
  V   *20726* France - Corsica *19164*

V   *Spergula fontenellei* Maire *10487*
  V   *14958* Algeria *10487*

R   *Spergula viscosa* Lag. ssp. *viscosa*
  R   Spain

V   *Spergularia azorica* (Kindb.) Lebel *8000, 20171*
  V   *19174* Portugal - Azores *8000*

E   *Spergularia collina* I.M. Johnston *18200*
  E   *9446* Peru *18200*

E   *Spergularia congestifolia* I.M. Johnston *18200*
  E   *9446* Peru *18200*

R   *Spergularia fallax* Lowe
  R   Portugal - Madeira
  I   Portugal - Salvage Is.
  R   Spain - Canary Is.

V   *Spergularia fasciculata* Philippi *18200*
  V   *9446* Peru *18200*

R   *Spergularia lyciaularia* Mounnier & Quezel *12840*
  R   *12840* Turkey *12840*

V   *Spergularia masafuerana* Skottsb. *19116*
  V   *19125* Chile - Juan Fernandez Is. *19116*

R   *Spergularia pycnorrhiza* (Maire) Monnier *10487*
  R   *14958* Algeria *10487*

R   *Spergularia tenuifolia* Pomel *10488*
  R   *14958* Algeria *10488*

V   *Stellaria alaskana* Hulten *20850, 1034*
  I   *20850* Canada - British Columbia *20850*
  E   *20850* Canada - Yukon Territory *20850*
  V   *20850* U.S. - Alaska *20850*

R   *Stellaria aphanantha* Griseb. *16336*

R   *16336* Argentina *16336*
R   *20176* Argentina - Catamarca *20176*

R   *Stellaria decipiens* var. *angustata* *19106*
  R   *19305* New Zealand - Antipodes Is. *19106*

I   *Stellaria depressa* Schmid
  I   India - Jammu & Kashmir

R   *Stellaria dicranoides* (Cham. & Schlecht.) Fenzl *1034*
  E   *20850* Canada - Yukon Territory *20850*
  R   *20850* U.S. - Alaska *20850*

Ex *Stellaria elatinoides* Hook. f. *15135*
  Ex *15135* New Zealand - North Is. *15135*

V   *Stellaria fontinalis* (Short & Peter) B.L.
    Robins. *20850*
  E   *20850* U.S. - Kentucky *20850*
  V   *20850* U.S. - Tennessee *20850*

R   *Stellaria longipes* Goldie ssp. *arenicola* (Raup)
    Chinnappa & J.K. Morton *20850*
  E   *20850* Canada - Alberta *20850*
  R   *20850* Canada - Saskatchewan *20850*

R   *Stellaria nipponica* Ohwi var. *yezoensis*
    Hara *10572*
  R   *10572* Japan *10572*

E   *Stellaria porsildii* Chinnappa *20850*
  E   *20850* U.S. - Arizona *20850*
  E   *20850* U.S. - New Mexico *20850*

R   *Stellaria pterosperma* Ohwi *10572*
  R   *10572* Japan *10572*

V   *Stellaria ruscifolia* Hulten ssp. *aleutica*
    Hulten *20850*
  V   *20850* U.S. - Alaska *20850*

R   *Thurya capitata* Boiss. & Bal. *12840*
  R   *12840* Turkey *12840*

R   *Uebelinia crassifolia* T.C.E. Fries
  R   Kenya (Mt. Kenya & Aberdare Mts.) *7959*

R   *Velezia hispida* Boiss. *12840*
  R   *12840* Turkey *12840*

V   *Velezia pseudorigida* Huber-Mor. *12840*
  V   *12840* Turkey *12840*

V   *Velezia tunicoides* Davis *12840*
  V   *12840* Turkey *12840*

Casuarinaceae

Number of genera:	1	
Number of species:	50	
Recorded threatened species:	14	(28%)

Australia, Pacific islands, Asia.

R   *Allocasuarina crassa* L.A.S.Johnson *20681*
  R   *20681* Australia - Tasmania *20681*

E   *Allocasuarina defungens* L.A.S.Johnson *20681*
  E   *20681* Australia - New South Wales *20681*

V   *Allocasuarina duncanii* L.A.S.Johnson &
    D.I.Morris *20681*
  V   *20681* Australia - Tasmania *20681*

E   *Allocasuarina emuina* L.A.S.Johnson *20681*
  E   *20681* Australia - Queensland *20681*

V   *Allocasuarina fibrosa* (C.Gardner)
    L.A.S.Johnson *20681*
  V   *20681* Australia - Western Australia *20681*

R   *Allocasuarina filidens* L.A.S.Johnson *20681*

R		20681 Australia - Queensland *20681*
E	*Allocasuarina glareicola* L.A.S.Johnson *20681*	
E		20681 Australia - New South Wales *20681*
E	*Allocasuarina portuensis* L.A.S.Johnson *20681*	
E		20681 Australia - New South Wales *20681*
R	*Allocasuarina rupicola* L.A.S.Johnson *20681*	
I		20681 Australia - New South Wales *20681*
I		20681 Australia - Queensland *20681*
V	*Allocasuarina simulans* L.A.S.Johnson *20681*	
V		20681 Australia - New South Wales *20681*
V	*Allocasuarina thalassoscopica* L.A.S.Johnson *20681*	
V		20681 Australia - Queensland *20681*
V	*Allocasuarina tortiramula* E.M.Bennett *20681*	
V		20681 Australia - Western Australia *20681*
R	*Gymnostoma australianum* L.A.S.Johnson *20681*	
R		20681 Australia - Queensland *20681*
V	*Gymnostoma leucodon* (Poisson) L.Johnson *20893*	
V		20893 New Caledonia *20893*

Cecropiaceae

Number of genera:	6
Number of species:	276
Recorded threatened species:	41 (14%)

Tropical.

R	*Cecropia granvilleana* C.C. Berg *11120*	
R	11120 French Guiana *11120*	
V	*Cecropia longipes* Pitt. *20883, 9006*	
V	20883 Panama *20883*	
E	*Cecropia maxonii* Pitt. *20883, 9006*	
I	20883 Panama *20883*	
R	*Cecropia pittieri* Robinson *9037*	
R	11120 Costa Rica *9037*	
E	*Coussapoa arachnoidea* Akkermans & Berg *20883*	
E	20883 Brazil *20883*	
V	*Coussapoa argentea* Akkermans & Berg *20883*	
I	20883 Venezuela *20883*	
E	*Coussapoa batavorum* Akkermans & Berg *20883, 11120*	
E	20883 Colombia *20883*	
R	*Coussapoa brevipes* Pitt. *20883, 9006*	
I	20883 Panama *20883*	
E	*Coussapoa chocoensis* Cuatrecasas *20883, 11120*	
E	20883 Colombia *20883*	
E	*Coussapoa cinnamomea* Cuatrecasas *20883*	
E	20883 Colombia *20883*	
E	*Coussapoa cupularis* Akkermans & Berg *20883, 11120*	
E	20883 Brazil *20883*	
R	*Coussapoa curranii* Blake *20883, 11120*	
I	20883 Brazil (south-east and south) *21022*	
V	*Coussapoa echinata* Akkermans & Berg *20883, 9991*	
R	9991 Panama *20883*	
V	*Coussapoa ferruginea* Trécul *20883*	
I	20883 Brazil *20883*	
I	20883 French Guiana *20883*	
E	*Coussapoa floccosa* Akkermans & Berg *20883, 11120*	
E	20883 Brazil *20883*	
I	21022 Brazil - Minas Gerais *21022*	
E	*Coussapoa fulvescens* Berg *20883*	
E	20883 Colombia *20883*	

R	*Coussapoa glaberrima* Burger *20883, 9037*	
I	20883 Costa Rica *20883*	
I	20883 Nicaragua *20883*	
I	20883 Panama *20883*	
R	*Coussapoa longepedunculata* Akkermans & Berg *20883*	
I	20883 Ecuador *20883*	
I	20883 Peru *20883*	
E	*Coussapoa macerrima* Akkermans & Berg *20883, 9991*	
E	20883 Costa Rica *20883*	
E	*Coussapoa manuensis* Berg *20883, 12468*	
R	9991 Peru *20883*	
V	*Coussapoa napoensis* Akkermans & Berg *20883*	
I	20883 Colombia *20883*	
I	20883 Ecuador *20883*	
V	*Coussapoa nymphaeifolia* Standley *20883*	
I	20883 Costa Rica *20883*	
E	*Coussapoa pachyphylla* Akkermans & Berg *20883, 11120*	
I	20883 Brazil *20883*	
E	*Coussapoa scabra* Akkermans & Berg *20883, 11120*	
E	20883 Brazil *20883*	
E	*Coussapoa tolimensis* Berg *20883*	
E	20883 Colombia *20883*	
V	*Coussapoa valaria* Berg *20883*	
I	20883 Colombia *20883*	
R	*Pourouma acuminata* Martius ex Miquel *20883*	
I	20883 Brazil *20883*	
I	20883 Peru *20883*	
R	*Pourouma bicolor* (Standley) C.C. Berg & van Heusden ssp. *chocoana* (Standley) C.C. Berg & Heusolen *20883, 9006*	
I	20883 Panama *20883*	
I	20883 Colombia *20883*	
R	*Pourouma bicolor* ssp. *tessmannii* (Mildbraed) C.C. Berg & van Heusden *20883*	
I	20883 Peru *20883*	
E	*Pourouma bolivarensis* C. C. Berg *20883*	
I	20883 Venezuela *20883*	
V	*Pourouma elliptica* Standley *20883*	
V	20883 Brazil *20883*	
R	*Pourouma ferruginea* Standley *20883*	
I	20883 Brazil *20883*	
R	*Pourouma formicarum* Ducke *20883*	
R	20883 Brazil *20883*	
R	*Pourouma guianensis* ssp. *venezuelensis* (Cuatrecasas) C.C. Berg & van Heusden *20883*	
V	20883 Venezuela *20883*	
V	*Pourouma herrerensis* Berg *20883*	
I	20883 Peru *20883*	
R	*Pourouma hirsutipetiolata* Mildbraed *20883*	
I	20883 Colombia *20883*	
I	20883 Ecuador *20883*	
V	*Pourouma hirsutipetiolata* Mildbraed ssp. *hirsutipetiolata* *20883*	
I	20883 Colombia *20883*	
R	*Pourouma hirsutipetiolata* Mildbraed ssp. *hispida* (Standley & Cuatrecasas) C. C. Berg & van Heusden *20883*	
E	20883 Colombia *20883*	
I	20883 Ecuador *20883*	
R	*Pourouma melinonii* ssp. *glabrata* C.C. Berg & van Heusden *20883*	
I	20883 Panama *20883*	
I	20883 Colombia *20883*	

V	*Pourouma napoensis* Berg 20883, 11120
	V	11120	Ecuador 20883
V	*Pourouma oraria* Standl. & Cuatr. 20883, 9006
	I	20883	Panama 20883
	V	11120	Colombia 20883
V	*Pourouma phaeotricha* Mildbraed 20883
	I	20883	Brazil 20883
	I	20883	Peru 20883
E	*Pourouma stipulaceae* C.C. Berg 20883
	I	20883	Guyana 20883
R	*Pourouma tomentosa* ssp. *essequiboensis* (Standley)
	C.C. Berg & van Heusden 20883
	I	20883	Brazil 20883
	I	20883	Guyana 20883
R	*Pourouma tomentosa* ssp. *maroniensis* (Benoist) C.C.
	Berg & van Heusden 20883
	I	20883	Brazil 20883
	I	20883	French Guiana 20883
	I	20883	Suriname 20883

Celastraceae

Number of genera:	50
Number of species:	800
Recorded threatened species:	93 (11%)

Pantropical, some in temperate regions.

E	*Anthodon panamense* A.C. Sm. 20883, 10747
	I	20883	Panama 20883
E	*Apatophyllum constablei* McGillivray 20681
	E	20681	Australia - New South Wales 20681
V	*Apatophyllum olsenii* McGillivray 20681
	V	20681	Australia - Queensland 20681
R	*Bhesa ceylanica* (Arn.) Ding Hou 12838
	R	12838	Sri Lanka 12838
E	*Bhesa nitidissima* Kosterm. 10283
	E	12838	Sri Lanka 10283
E	*Bhesa sinica* (H.T. Chang & S.Y. Liang) H.T. Chang & S.Y.
	Liang 17617
	E	17617	China - Guangxi (Nankan) 17617
R	*Campylostemon nigrisilvae* Halle 7927
	R		Côte d'Ivoire
V	*Catha abbottii* A.E.van Wyk & M.Prins 20604
	V	20604	South Africa - Cape Province 20604
	V	20604	South Africa - Natal 20604
E	*Celastrus panamensis* Lund. 20883, 9006
	R	19577	Panama 20883
V	*Crossopetalum ekmanii* (Urban) Alain 5607
	V	19105	Cuba (Sancti Spiritus) 5607
R	*Crossopetalum ilicifolium* (Poir.) Kuntze 20850
	V	20850	U.S. - Florida 20850
R	*Crossopetalum panamense* Lundell 10303
	R	19577	Panama 10303
E	*Crossopetalum rostratum* (Urban) Rothm. 5607
	E	19105	Cuba (Pinar del Rio) 5607
E	*Cuervea hawkesii* Proctor 20883, 13336
	E	13336	Jamaica 20883
R	*Cuervea jamaicensis* Proctor 20883
	R	20883	Jamaica 20883
R	*Denhamia moorei* Jessup 20681
	R	20681	Australia - New South Wales 20681

V	*Denhamia parvifolia* L.S.Smith 20681
	V	20681	Australia - Queensland 20681
R	*Denhamia viridissima* Bailey & F.Muell. 20681
	R	20681	Australia - Queensland 20681
E	*Elaeodendron gomenense* Virot 20893
	E	20893	New Caledonia 20893
R	*Elaeodendron laneanum* A.H. Moore
	R		Bermuda
E	*Elaeodendron vieillardii* Guillaumin 20893
	E	20893	New Caledonia 20893
E	*Euonymus angulatus* Wight 11494
	E	11494	India - Karnataka (Coorg) 11494
	E	11494	India - Kerala (Palghat Dt) 11494
	E	11494	India - Tamil Nadu (Nilgiri Hills) 11494
E	*Euonymus assamicus* Blakelock 11494
	E	11494	India - Assam (Delei Valley) 11494
E	*Euonymus boninensis* Koidz. 8037
	E	19134	Japan - Ogasawara-shoto 8037
I	*Euonymus bullatus* Wallich ex Lindley
	I		India - Assam
	I		India - Meghalaya
R	*Euonymus globularis* Ding Hou 20681
	R	20681	Australia - Queensland 20681
I	*Euonymus koopmannii* Lauche 5942
	I	5942	Kazakhstan 5942
	I	5942	Kyrgyzstan 5942
R	*Euonymus latifolius* (L.) Miller ssp. *cauconis*
	Coode & Cullen 12840
	R	20618	Turkey 20618
R	*Euonymus mexicanus* Benth. 10295
	R	19755	Mexico - Hidalgo 10295
E	*Euonymus morrisonensis* Kaneh. & Sas. 20511
	E	20854	Taiwan (Mt Alishan & Mt Yushan) 20511
E	*Euonymus pallidifolia* Hayata 20511
	E	20854	Taiwan (P'ing-tung; Heng-ch'un) 20511
I	*Euonymus paniculatus* Wight ex M. Lawson
	I		India - Tamil Nadu
Ex/E	*Euonymus serratifolius* Beddome 11494
	Ex/E	11494	India - Tamil Nadu 11494
I	*Euonymus thwaitesii* Lawson 10252
	I	16162	Sri Lanka 10252
R	*Euonymus walkeri* Wight 12838
	R	12838	Sri Lanka 12838
I	*Glyptopetalum palawanense* Merr. 13833
	I	13833	Philippines (Palawan) 13833
R	*Gyminda orbicularis* Borh. & Muniz 5607
	R	19105	Cuba (Guantanamo) 5607
V	*Hexaspora pubescens* C.White 20681, 5465
	V	20681	Australia - Queensland 20681
R	*Hippocratea andamanica* King 7771
	R	14782	India - Andaman Is. 7771
I	*Hippocratea graciliflora* Oliv. var. *newalensis*
	Blakelock 5926
	I	5926	Tanzania 5926
I	*Hippocratea nicobarica* Kurz 7771
	I		India - Nicobar Is. 7771
R	*Hypsophila halleyana* F.Muell. 20681
	R	20681	Australia - Queensland 20681

I   *Kokoona coriacea* King *7609*
   I   *13926*   Malaysia - Peninsular Malaysia (Perak) *7609*

I   *Kokoona sessilis* Ding Hou *7609*
   I   *13926*   Malaysia - Peninsular Malaysia *7609*

I   *Loeseneriella bourdillonii* (Gamble) Raju
   I   India - Kerala

V   *Maytenus abbottii* A.E.van Wyk *20604*
   V   *20604*   South Africa - Cape Province *20604*
   V   *20604*   South Africa - Natal *20604*

R   *Maytenus acuminata* (L. f.) Loes var. *uva-ursi* Brenan *7749*
   R   Malawi *7749*

E   *Maytenus addat* (Loes.) Sebsebe *19704*
   E   *19704*   Ethiopia (Shewa Upland, Arsi, Sidamo, Bale, Gamo Gofa.) *19704*

R   *Maytenus bachmannii* (Loes.) Marais *20604*
   R   *20604*   South Africa - Cape Province *20604*
   R   *20604*   South Africa - Natal *20604*

I   *Maytenus buxifolius* Triana & Planchon *19352*
   I   *19352*   Colombia *19352*

V   *Maytenus clarendonensis* Britton *20883*
   V   *20883*   Jamaica *20883*

E   *Maytenus cortii* (Pichi-Serm.) Cuf. *19704*
   E   *19704*   Ethiopia (Gonder) *19704*

R   *Maytenus crassipes* Urb. *20883*
   R   *20883*   Jamaica *20883*

R   *Maytenus cymosa* Krug & Urban *20883*
   I   *20883*   Puerto Rico (Piñeros; Vieques) *20883*
   I   *20883*   British Virgin Is. (Virgin Gorda) *20883*
   I   *20883*   USA - Virgin Is. (St. Croix; St. Thomas) *20883*

V   *Maytenus dryandri* (Lowe) Loes.
   V   Portugal - Madeira

V   *Maytenus elongata* (Urban) Britt. *20883*
   V   *20883*   Puerto Rico *20883*

I   *Maytenus fruticosa* (Thwaites) Loes. *10252*
   I   *16162*   Sri Lanka *10252*

V   *Maytenus harenensis* Sebsebe *19704*
   V   *19704*   Ethiopia (Bale) *19704*

I   *Maytenus harrisii* Krug & Urb. *20883, 13336*
   I   *13336*   Jamaica *20883*

E   *Maytenus jefeana* Lund. *20883, 10747*
   I   *20883*   Panama *20883*

R   *Maytenus keniensis* Robson ined. *17435*
   R   *17435*   Kenya (Mt. Kenya) *17435*

Ex   *Maytenus lineata* C. Wright *5607*
   Ex   *15112*   Cuba (Pinar del Rio) *5607*

Ex/E   *Maytenus lucayana* Britton *4650*
   Ex/E   *4650*   Bahamas (Grand Bahama) *4650*

R   *Maytenus microcarpa* F. & R. *20883, 13336*
   R   *13336*   Jamaica *20883*

I   *Maytenus mossambicensis* (Kl.) Blakelock var. *stlozii* Robson *5926*
   I   *5926*   Tanzania *5926*

R   *Maytenus oleosa* A.E.van Wyk & R.H.Archer *20604*
   R   *20604*   South Africa - Cape Province *20604*
   R   *20604*   South Africa - Natal *20604*

E   *Maytenus pertinax* N.Hallé & Florence *20845*
   E   *20845*   French Polynesia - Tubuai Is. (Rapa) *20845*

E   *Maytenus ponceana* Britt. *20883, 8058*
   I   *20883*   Puerto Rico *20883*

I   *Maytenus richardsiae* Robson *5926*
   I   *5926*   Tanzania *5926*

R   *Maytenus vanwykii* R.H.Archer *20604*
   R   *20604*   South Africa - Cape Province *20604*
   R   *20604*   South Africa - Natal *20604*

I   *Microtropis deniflora* Wight
   I   India - Tamil Nadu

R   *Monimopetalum chinense* Rehder *17617*
   R   *17617*   China - Anhui *11139*
   R   *17617*   China - Jiangxi *11139*

V   *Paxistima canbyi* Gray *20850*
   V   *20850*   U.S. - Kentucky *20850*
   E   *20850*   U.S. - Maryland *20850*
   E   *20850*   U.S. - Ohio *20850*
   E   *20850*   U.S. - Pennsylvania *20850*
   E   *20850*   U.S. - Tennessee *20850*
   V   *20850*   U.S. - Virginia *20850*
   V   *20850*   U.S. - West Virginia *20850*

R   *Pleurostylia leucocarpa* Baker *10082*
   R   *20771*   Mauritius *10082*

R   *Pleurostylia putamen* Marais *10082*
   R   *5852*   Mauritius - Rodrigues *5852*

I   *Pristimera monilensis* (Hallé) Hallé *7927*
   I   *7927*   Gabon *7927*

V   *Pseudosalacia streyi* Codd *20604*
   V   *20604*   South Africa - Cape Province (Transkei) *20604*
   V   *20604*   South Africa - Natal *20604*

R   *Salacia beddomei* Gamble *13883*
   R   *13883*   India - Tamil Nadu *13883*

I   *Salacia cymosa* Elm. *13833*
   I   *13833*   Philippines (low altitude) *13833*

R   *Salacia gagnepainiana* Tard. *6057*
   R   Vietnam *6057*

E   *Salacia jenkinsii* Kurz *11494*
   E   *11494*   India - Assam *11494*

I   *Salacia lehmbachii* Loes. var. *uregaensis* (Wilczek) Hallé *21073*
   I   *21073*   Zaire (District Forestier Central) *21073*

I   *Salacia macrosperma* Wight
   I   India - Karnataka (Concan)
   I   India - Tamil Nadu (Wynaad, Nilgiri)

Ex/E   *Salacia malabarica* Gamble *11494*
   Ex/E   *11494*   India - Karnataka (Coorg) *11494*
   Ex/E   *11494*   India - Kerala (Travancore Hills) *11494*

I   *Salacia marginata* Ding Hou *13833*
   I   *13833*   Philippines (low altitude) *13833*

V   *Salacia miegei* Halle *20887*
   V   *20887*   Côte d'Ivoire *20887*

E   *Salacia wrightii* Urban *5607*
   E   *19105*   Cuba (Guantanamo) *5607*

E   *Schaefferia lottiae* Lundell *20883*
   I   *20883*   Mexico *20883*

V   *Schaefferia obovata* Urb. *20883, 13336*
   V   *13336*   Jamaica *20883*

E   *Schaefferia ovatifolia* Lundell *20883*
   I   *20883*   Mexico *20883*

V	*Tetrasiphon jamaicensis* Urb. *20883, 13336*	
	V	*13336* Jamaica *20883*
E	*Wimmeria caudata* Lundell *20883*	
	I	*20883* Mexico *20883*
I	*Wimmeria sternii* Lund. *20883, 9690*	
	V	*11967* Nicaragua *9690*
	I	*20883* Panama *20883*
E	*Zinowiewia micrantha* Lund. *20883, 10747*	
	I	*20883* Panama *20883*

Ceratophyllaceae

Number of genera: 1
Number of species: 6
Recorded threatened species: 1   (16%)

Cosmopolitan.

I	*Ceratophyllum tanaiticum* Sapjegin *8000, 20171*	
	I	*11552* Russian Federation (western) *11552*

Chenopodiaceae

Number of genera: 100
Number of species: 1,500
Recorded threatened species: 88   (5%)

Cosmopolitan, especially deserts and semideserts.

V	*Aphanisma blitoides* Nutt. ex Moq. *20883, 20850*	
	V	*20850* U.S. - California *20850*
	V	*20883* Mexico *20883*
V	*Atriplex bonnevillensis* C.A. Hanson *20850*	
	I	*20850* U.S. - Nevada *20850*
	V	*20850* U.S. - Utah *20850*
E	*Atriplex canescens* (Pursh)Nutt. var. *gigantea* Welsh & Stutz *20850*	
	E	*20850* U.S. - Utah *20850*
R	*Atriplex chapinii* I.M. Johnston *5595*	
	R	*19534* Chile - Islas Desventurados *5595*
V	*Atriplex cordulata* Jepson *20850*	
	V	*20850* U.S. - California *20850*
R	*Atriplex coronata* S.Watson var. *coronata* *20850*	
	R	*20850* U.S. - California *20850*
E	*Atriplex coronata* Jepson var. *notatior* Jepson *20850*	
	E	*20850* U.S. - California *20850*
V	*Atriplex coulteri* (Moq.) D. Dietr. *20850*	
	V	*20850* U.S. - California *20850*
V	*Atriplex drymarioides* Standl. *20850*	
		20850 U.S. - Alaska *20850*
R	*Atriplex eichleri* Aellen *20681*	
	R	*20681* Australia - South Australia *20681*
R	*Atriplex foliolosa* Philippi *5595*	
	R	*19534* Chile - Islas Desventurados *5595*
R	*Atriplex fruticulosa* Jepson *20850*	
	I	*20850* U.S. - California *20850*
R	*Atriplex griffithsii* Standl. *20850*	
	R	*20850* U.S. - Arizona *20850*
	V	*20850* U.S. - New Mexico *20850*
V	*Atriplex infrequens* Paul G.Wilson *20681*	
	V	*20681* Australia - New South Wales *20681*
V	*Atriplex klebergorum* M.C. Johnston *20850*	
	V	*20850* U.S. - Texas *20850*

V	*Atriplex parishii* S.Watson *20850*	
	Ex/E	*20850* U.S. - California *20850*
R	*Atriplex parryi* S.Watson *20850*	
	I	*20850* U.S. - California *20850*
	I	*20850* U.S. - Nevada *20850*
V	*Atriplex patula* L. ssp. *spicata* (S.Watson) Hall & Clements *20850*	
	V	*20850* U.S. - California *20850*
I	*Atriplex plebeja* Carmich. *19938*	
	I	*19938* Tristan da Cunha (Nightingale, Tristan) *19938*
R	*Atriplex repanda* Phil. *20883, 10370*	
	R	*20883* Chile *20883*
V	*Atriplex serenana* A. Nels. var. *davidsonii* (Standl.) Munz *20850*	
	V	*20850* U.S. - California *20850*
R	*Atriplex spinifera* J.F. Macbr. *20850*	
	I	*20850* U.S. - California *20850*
R	*Atriplex tatarica* L. var. *constantinopolitana* Aellen *12840*	
	R	*12840* Turkey *12840*
R	*Atriplex tatarica* L. var. *pseudo-ornata* Aellen *12840*	
	R	*12840* Turkey *12840*
E	*Atriplex tularensis* Coville *20850*	
	E	*20850* U.S. - California *20850*
E	*Atriplex vallicola* Hoover *20850*	
	E	*20850* U.S. - California *20850*
R	*Atriplex wardii* Standl. *20850*	
	R	*20850* U.S. - Texas *20850*
V	*Atriplex welshii* C.A. Hanson *20850*	
	V	*20850* U.S. - Utah *20850*
E	*Bassia saxicola* (Guss.) A.J.Scott *18264, 20171*	
	E	*18264* Italy *18264*
	E	*20738* Italy - Sicily *17891*
V	*Beta adanensis* Pamukç. ex Aellen *12840, 20171*	
	V	*12840* Turkey *12840*
R	*Beta nana* Boiss. & Heldr. *20171*	
	R	Greece
R	*Beta patula* Aiton *17891*	
	R	Portugal - Madeira *17891*
E	*Beta trojana* (Pamuk.) Aellen *12840*	
	E	*12840* Turkey *12840*
R	*Beta webbiana* (Moq.) Webb & Berthel.	
	R	Spain - Canary Is.
I	*Chenopodium ambrosioides* L. var. *tomentosum* (Thouars) Aellen *19938*	
	I	*19938* Tristan da Cunha *19938*
E	*Chenopodium crusoeanum* Skottsb. *19116*	
	E	*19125* Chile - Juan Fernandez Is. *19116*
Ex	*Chenopodium helenense* Aellen *10260*	
	Ex	*18996* St Helena *18996*
R	*Chenopodium hircinum* Schrader var. *catamarcense* Allen *16336*	
	R	*16336* Argentina *16336*
	R	*20176* Argentina - Catamarca *20176*
	R	*20176* Argentina - La Rioja *20176*
	R	*20176* Argentina - Tucuman *20176*
V	*Chenopodium moquinianum* Aellen	
	V	Egypt

E   *Chenopodium nesodendron* Skottsb. *19116*
     E   *19125*   Chile - Juan Fernandez Is. *19116*

E   *Chenopodium sanctae-clarae* Johow *19116*
     E   *19125*   Chile - Juan Fernandez Is. *19116*

R   *Chenopodium sancti-ambrosii* Skottsb. *5595*
     R   *19534*   Chile - Islas Desventurados *5595*

R   *Chenopodium subglabrum* (S.Watson) A. Nels. *20850, 2063*
     E   *20850*   Canada - Alberta *20850*
     I   *20850*   Canada - Manitoba *20850*
     I   *20850*   Canada - Ontario *20850*
     E   *20850*   Canada - Saskatchewan *20850*
     I   *20850*   U.S. - Colorado *20850*
     I   *20850*   U.S. - Idaho *20850*
     I   *20850*   U.S. - Michigan *20850*
     I   *20850*   U.S. - Missouri *20850*
     E   *20850*   U.S. - Montana *20850*
     E   *20850*   U.S. - Nebraska *20850*
     I   *20850*   U.S. - Nevada *20850*
     E   *20850*   U.S. - North Dakota *20850*
     I   *20850*   U.S. - Oregon *20850*
     I   *20850*   U.S. - South Dakota *20850*
     I   *20850*   U.S. - Washington *20850*
     E   *20850*   U.S. - Wyoming *20850*

R   *Corispermum algidum* Iljin *8000, 20171*
     R   former European USSR *8000*

R   *Cremnophyton lanfrancoi* Brullo & Pavone *13351, 20171*
     R   *13351*   Malta (SW Malta and W Gozo) *13351*

R   *Cyathobasis fruticulosa* (Bunge) Aellen *12840*
     R   *12840*   Turkey *12840*

I   *Darniella melitensis* (Botschantzev) Brullo *13351*
     I   *13351*   Malta *13351*

R   *Goerziella minima* (Standley) Urban *5607*
     R   *19105*   Cuba (Pinar del Rio) *5607*

V   *Halosarcia bulbosa* Paul G.Wilson *20681*
     V   *20681*   Australia - Western Australia *20681*

R   *Halosarcia entrichoma* Paul G.Wilson *20681*
     R   *20681*   Australia - Western Australia *20681*

V   *Halosarcia flabelliformis* Paul G.Wilson *20681*
     I   *20681*   Australia - South Australia *20681*
     I   *20681*   Australia - Victoria *20681*

E   *Kalidiopsis wagenitzii* Aellen *12840*
     E   *12840*   Turkey *12840*

R   *Kochia californica* S.Watson *20850*
     I   *20850*   U.S. - California *20850*
     I   *20850*   U.S. - Nevada *20850*

V   *Maireana cheelii* (R.Anderson) Paul G.Wilson *20681*
     I   *20681*   Australia - New South Wales *20681*
     I   *20681*   Australia - Victoria *20681*

V   *Maireana melanocarpa* Paul G.Wilson *20681*
     V   *20681*   Australia - South Australia *20681*

R   *Maireana rohrlachii* (Paul G.Wilson) Paul G.Wilson *20681*
     I   *20681*   Australia - South Australia *20681*
     I   *20681*   Australia - Victoria *20681*

V   *Microcnemum coralloides* (Loscos & J.Pardo) Buen *8000, 20171*
     V   Spain *8000*
     E   Turkey *8001*
     E   former USSR *6930*

E   *Microcnemum coralloides* (Loscos et Parda) Font-Quer ssp. *anatolicum* Wagenitz *17781*
     E   *17781*   Turkey *17781*

E   *Nitrophila mohavensis* Munz & Roos *20850*
     E   *20850*   U.S. - California *20850*
     E   *20850*   U.S. - Nevada (Ash Meadows, Nye Co.) *20850*

R   *Oreobliton thesioides* Durieu & Moq.
     R   Algeria
     E   Tunisia

V   *Petrosimonia nigdeensis* Aellen *12840*
     V   *12840*   Turkey *12840*

R   *Proatriplex pleiantha* (W.A. Weber) Stuz & Chu *20850*
     E   *20850*   U.S. - Colorado *20850*
     R   *20850*   U.S. - New Mexico *20850*
     E   *20850*   U.S. - Utah *20850*

V   *Rhagodia acicularis* Paul G.Wilson *20681*
     V   *20681*   Australia - Western Australia *20681*

I   *Rhaphidophyton regelii* (Bunge) Iljin *5942*
     I   *5942*   Kazakhstan *5942*

V   *Roycea pycnophylloides* C.Gardner *20681*
     V   *20681*   Australia - Western Australia *20681*

E   *Salicornia borealis* Wolff & Jefferies *20850, 21309*
     I   *20850*   Canada - Manitoba *20850*

V   *Salicornia emericii* Duval-Jouve var. *vicensis* (J. Duvigneaud) J. Duvigneaud *20528*
     V   *20528*   France (Moselle) *20528*

R   *Salicornia senegalensis* A. Chev. *7926*
     R   Senegal *8003*

E   *Salicornia veneta* Pignatti & Lausi *17891, 20171*
     E   *18264*   Italy (Veneto, Friuli-Venezia Giulia, Emilia-Romagna) *19997*

V   *Salsola anatolica* Aellen *12840*
     V   *12840*   Turkey *12840*

R   *Salsola carpatha* P.H.Davis *20171*
     R   Greece

E   *Salsola chiwensis* Popov *6930*
     E   Asiatic U.S.S.R. *6930*

I   *Salsola hispanica* Botsch. *20171*
     I   Spain

R   *Salsola masclansii* D. Gomez & G. Monts. Marti
     R   Spain

V   *Salsola papillosa* (Coss.) Willk. *20171*
     V   Spain

V   *Salsola prostrata* Pall. ssp. *anatolica* Aellen *12840*
     V   *12840*   Turkey *12840*

R   *Salsola stenoptera* Wagenitz *12840*
     R   *12840*   Turkey *12840*

I   *Salsola tamamschjanae* Iljin *5942*
     I   *5942*   Armenia *5942*

V   *Sclerolaena blakei* (Ising) A.J.Scott *20681*
     V   *20681*   Australia - Queensland *20681*

R   *Sclerolaena everistiana* (Ising) A.J.Scott *20681*
     R   *20681*   Australia - Queensland *20681*

V   *Sclerolaena napiformis* Paul G.Wilson *20681*
     I   *20681*   Australia - New South Wales *20681*
     I   *20681*   Australia - Victoria *20681*

V   *Sclerolaena walkeri* (C.White) A.J.Scott *20681*
     V   *20681*   Australia - Queensland *20681*

R   *Suaeda arctica* Jurtzev & Petrosky *21309*
     R   *21309*   Russia (E.Europe) - North *21309*
     E   former USSR *6930*

E **Suaeda californica** S.Watson *20850*
   E   *20850* U.S. - California *20850*

E **Suaeda cucullata** Aellen *12840*
   E   *14155* Turkey *12840*

V **Suaeda esteroa** Ferren & Whitmore *20850*
   I   *20850* U.S. - California *20850*

R **Suaeda malacosperma** Hara *10572*
   R   *10572* Japan *10572*

R **Suaeda nesophila** I.M. Johnston *5595*
   R   *19534* Chile - Islas Desventurados *5595*

R **Suaeda pelagica** Bartolo, Brullo & Pavone *18264, 20171*
   R   *18264* Italy - Sicily *18264*

V **Suaeda pruinosa** Lange var. **kochii** (Guss. ex Todaro) Marie & Weiller *18264*
   V   *18264* Italy - Sicily *18264*

R **Tegicornia uniflora** Paul G.Wilson *20681*
   R   *20681* Australia - Western Australia *20681*

R **Zuckia brandegei** Standl. var. **arizonica** (Standl.) Welsh *20850*
   I   *20850* U.S. - Arizona *20850*
   E   *20850* U.S. - Utah *20850*

Chloranthaceae

Number of genera:	5	
Number of species:	75	
Recorded threatened species:	20	(26%)

Tropical America, E Asia, Pacific.

R **Ascarina marquesensis** A.C.Smith *20845*
   R   *20845* French Polynesia - Marquesas Is *20845*

I **Ascarina subfalcata** J.Moore *20845*
   I   *20845* French Polynesia - Society Is. (Raiatea) *20845*

V **Hedyosmum burgerianum** D'Arcy & Liesner *20883, 11534*
   V   *19570* Panama *20883*

R **Hedyosmum colombianum** Cuatrecasas *20883*
   I   *20883* Colombia *20883*

R **Hedyosmum correanum** D'Arcy & Liesner *20883, 11534*
   V   *19570* Panama *20883*

R **Hedyosmum costaricense** Wood *20883, 9037*
   I   *20883* Costa Rica *20883*
   I   *20883* Panama *20883*

V **Hedyosmum domingense** var. **cubense** (Urban) Todzia & Wood *20883*
   I   *20883* Cuba *20883*

E **Hedyosmum goudotianum** var. **mombachanum** Todzia *20883*
   I   *20883* Nicaragua *20883*

V **Hedyosmum huascari** Macbride *20883, 11534*
   R   *18200* Peru *20883*

V **Hedyosmum leonis** Kirouac *5607*
   V   *5607* Cuba *5607*

E **Hedyosmum maximum** (O. Kuntze) K. Schumann *20883, 11534*
   R   *11534* Bolivia *20883*
   I   *20883* Peru *20883*

V **Hedyosmum neblinae** Todzia *20883, 11534*
   I   *20883* Brazil *20883*
   I   *20883* Venezuela *20883*

R **Hedyosmum parvifolium** Cordemoy *20883*
   I   *20883* Colombia *20883*
   I   *20883* Venezuela *20883*

R **Hedyosmum peruvianum** Todzia *20883*
   I   *20883* Peru *20883*

R **Hedyosmum pseudoandromeda** Solms-Laubach *20883*
   I   *20883* Venezuela *20883*

V **Hedyosmum pungens** Todzia *20883, 11534*
   V   *11534* Colombia *20883*

E **Hedyosmum purpurascens** Todzia *20883, 11534*
   R   *19570* Ecuador *20883*

E **Hedyosmum steinii** Todzia *20883, 11534*
   R   *11534* Colombia *20883*

R **Hedyosmum strigosum** Todzia *20883*
   I   *20883* Colombia *20883*
   I   *20883* Ecuador *20883*

V **Hedyosmum subintegrum** Urban *20883, 5607*
   V   *19105* Cuba (Holguin, Guantanamo) *20883*

Chrysobalanaceae

Number of genera:	17	
Number of species:	450	
Recorded threatened species:	225	(50%)

Pantropical, especially New World.

I **Acioa cinerea** Engl. ex De Wild.
   I   Cameroon (Bipindi)

E **Acioa dichotoma** De Wild. *7926*
   E   *20749* Nigeria (Eket) *7926*

E **Acioa eketensis** De Wild. *7926*
   E   *20749* Nigeria (Eket) *7926*

R **Acioa laevis** Pierre ex De Wild.
   R   Gabon (Libreville)

R **Acioa pierrei** De Wild. *7927*
   R   Gabon (Libreville & Tchibanga) *7927*

R **Acioa schultesii** Maguire *20883*
   I   *20883* Brazil *20883*
   I   *20883* Venezuela *20883*

V **Acioa somnolens** Maguire *20883, 11589*
   R   *19954* French Guiana *20883*

I **Atuna travancorica** (Bedd.) Kosterm. *13883*
   I   *13883* India - Tamil Nadu (Travancore) *18341*

R **Chrysobalanus stuhlmanni** Dammer *7959*
   R   *5926* Tanzania (Dodoma) *7959*

V **Chrysobalanus venezuelanus** Prance *20883, 11589*
   R   *11589* Venezuela *20883*

R **Couepia amaralae** Prance *20883*
   I   *20883* Brazil *20883*

R **Couepia belemii** Prance *20883*
   I   *20883* Brazil *20883*

E **Couepia bondarii** Prance *20883, 11589*
   I   *20883* Brazil *20883*

R **Couepia canescens** (Gleason) Prance *20883*
   I   *20883* Venezuela *20883*

E **Couepia carautae** Prance *20883, 11589*
   I   *20883* Brazil *20883*

E **Couepia caryophylloides** ssp. **glabra** Prance *20883*
   I   *20883* Brazil *20883*

R **Couepia cidiana** Prance *20883*
  I   *20883* Brazil *20883*

V **Couepia coarctata** Prance *20883*
  I   *20883* Brazil *20883*

V **Couepia cognata** var. **major** Prance *20883*
  I   *20883* Guyana *20883*

V **Couepia cognata** var. **membranacea**
      Prance *20883*
  I   *20883* Guyana *20883*

R **Couepia comosa** Bentham *20883, 8679*
  I   *20883* Guyana *20883*
  I   *20883* Venezuela *20883*

E **Couepia exflexa** Fanshawe & Maguire *20883*
  I   *20883* Guyana *20883*

R **Couepia foveolata** Prance *20883*
  I   *20883* Brazil *20883*
  I   *20883* Guyana *20883*
  I   *20883* Venezuela *20883*

R **Couepia froesii** Prance *20883, 11589*
  I   *20883* Brazil *20883*

V **Couepia glabra** Prance *20883, 11589*
  I   *20883* Brazil *20883*

R **Couepia impressa** ssp. **cabraliae**
      Prance *20883*
  I   *20883* Brazil *20883*

V **Couepia insignis** Fritsch *20883*
  I   *20883* Brazil *20883*

R **Couepia krukovii** Standley *20883*
  I   *20883* Bolivia *20883*
  I   *20883* Brazil *20883*

E **Couepia longipetiolata** Prance *20883, 11589*
  I   *20883* Brazil *20883*

R **Couepia magnoliifolia** Bentham ex Hooker f. *20883*
  I   *20883* Brazil *20883*

R **Couepia maguirei** Prance *20883*
  I   *20883* Brazil *20883*
  I   *20883* Venezuela *20883*

R **Couepia marleneae** Prance *20883*
  I   *20883* Brazil *20883*

E **Couepia martinii** Prance *20883, 11589*
  I   *11589* French Guiana *20883*

E **Couepia meridionalis** Prance *20883*
  I   *20883* Brazil *20883*

E **Couepia monteclarensis** Prance *20883*
  I   *20883* Brazil *20883*

R **Couepia multiflora** Bentham *20883*
  I   *20883* Brazil *20883*
  I   *20883* Guyana *20883*

E **Couepia nutans** Prance *20883, 11589*
  E   *11589* Colombia *20883*

R **Couepia paraensis** var. **cerradoana**
      Prance *20883*
  I   *20883* Brazil *20883*

E **Couepia parvifolia** Prance *20883, 11589*
  I   *20883* Brazil *20883*

V **Couepia pernambucensis** Prance *20883*
  I   *20883* Brazil *20883*

V **Couepia platycalyx** Cuatrecasas *20883, 11589*
  E   *9518* Colombia *20883*
  E   *9518* Venezuela *20883*

E **Couepia recurva** Spruce ex Prance *20883, 9518*
  E   *11589* Ecuador *20883*

E **Couepia reflexa** Ducke *20883*
  I   *20883* Brazil *20883*

R **Couepia sandwithii** Prance *20883*
  I   *20883* Guyana *20883*
  I   *20883* Venezuela *20883*

R **Couepia schottii** Fritsch *20883, 17079*
  I   *20883* Brazil *20883*
  V   *1746* Brazil - Bahia *17079*
  V   *17746* Brazil - Espirito Santo *17746*
  V   *17746* Brazil - Rio de Janeiro *17079*

E **Couepia scottmorii** Prance *20883, 11589*
  E   *9518* Panama *20883*

V **Couepia steyermarkii** Maguire *20883, 11589*
  R   *11589* Venezuela *20883*

V **Couepia stipularis** Ducke *20883, 11589*
  I   *20883* Brazil *20883*

R **Couepia venosa** Prance *20883*
  I   *20883* Brazil *20883*

V **Dactyladenia dinklagei** (Engl.) Prance &
      F.White *20274*
  V   *20858* Tropical Africa (Upper Guinea) *20274*
  V   *20858* Ghana *20274*

E **Dactyladenia hirsuta** (A.Chev.) Prance &
      F.White *20274*
  E   *20887* Côte d'Ivoire *20274*
  E   *20858* Ghana *20274*

E **Exellodendron gracile** (Hooker f.) Prance *20883,
      11589*
  I   *20883* Brazil *20883*

R **Hirtella adderleyi** Prance *20883*
  I   *20883* Venezuela *20883*

V **Hirtella adenophora** Cuatrecasas *20883, 11589*
  R   *11589* Colombia *20883*

R **Hirtella angustissima** Sandwith *20883*
  I   *20883* Guyana *20883*

R **Hirtella araguariensis** Prance *20883*
  I   *20883* Brazil *20883*

E **Hirtella aramangensis** Prance *20883, 9518*
  E   *11589* Brazil *11589*

R **Hirtella arenosa** Prance *20883*
  I   *20883* Brazil *20883*

R **Hirtella bahiensis** Prance *20883*
  I   *20883* Brazil *20883*

E **Hirtella barnebyi** Prance *20883*
  I   *20883* Brazil *20883*

E **Hirtella barrosoi** Prance *20883*
  I   *20883* Brazil *20883*

R **Hirtella caduca** Fanshawe & Maguire *20883*
  I   *20883* Guyana *20883*
  I   *20883* Venezuela *20883*

E **Hirtella conduplicata** Prance *20883*
  I   *20883* Brazil *20883*

E **Hirtella confertiflora** Prance *20883, 11589*
  R   *11589* Venezuela *20883*

V **Hirtella cordifolia** Prance *20883, 11589*
  R   *11589* Venezuela *20883*

V **Hirtella corymbosa** Chamisso & Schlechtendal *20883,
      11589*

I   *20883* Brazil *20883*

R   *Hirtella couepiiflora* Prance *20883*
   I   *20883* Brazil *20883*
   I   *20883* Guyana *20883*

R   *Hirtella cowanii* Prance & Maguire *20883*
   I   *20883* Venezuela *20883*

R   *Hirtella deflexa* Maguire *20883*
   I   *20883* Brazil *20883*
   I   *20883* Guyana *20883*
   I   *20883* Venezuela *20883*

R   *Hirtella dorvalii* Prance *20883*
   I   *20883* Brazil *20883*

E   *Hirtella enneandra* Cuatrecasas *20883, 11589*
   R   *11589* Colombia *20883*

R   *Hirtella fasciculata* Prance *20883*
   I   *20883* Brazil *20883*

V   *Hirtella floribunda* Chamisso & Schlechtendal *20883*
   I   *20883* Brazil *20883*

V   *Hirtella glaziovii* Taubert *20883*
   I   *20883* Brazil *20883*

R   *Hirtella guyanensis* (Fritsch) Sandwith *20883*
   I   *20883* Guyana *20883*
   I   *20883* Venezuela *20883*

R   *Hirtella insignis* Briquet ex Prance *20883, 17079*
   I   *20883* Brazil *20883*
   E   *17746* Brazil - Bahia *17079*

V   *Hirtella juruensis* Pilger *20883, 11589*
   I   *20883* Brazil *20883*

R   *Hirtella kuhlmannii* Pilger *20883, 11589*
   I   *20883* Brazil *20883*

R   *Hirtella latifolia* Prance *20883, 9518*
   I   *20883* Panama *20883*

R   *Hirtella lemsii* L. O. Williams & Prance *20883, 9518*
   I   *20883* Costa Rica *20883*

E   *Hirtella liesneri* Prance *20883*
   I   *20883* Venezuela *20883*

E   *Hirtella longifolia* Bentham ex Hooker f. *20883, 11589*
   I   *20883* Brazil *20883*

R   *Hirtella magnifolia* Prance *20883*
   I   *20883* Brazil *20883*
   I   *20883* Peru *20883*

R   *Hirtella margae* Prance *20883*
   I   *20883* Guyana *20883*
   I   *20883* Suriname *20883*

V   *Hirtella orbicularis* Prance *20883*
   I   *20883* Venezuela *20883*

V   *Hirtella parviunguis* Prance *20883, 17079*
   I   *20883* Brazil *20883*
   E   *17746* Brazil - Bahia *17746*
   E   *17079* Brazil - Espirito Santo *17079*

V   *Hirtella pauciflora* Little *20883*
   I   *20883* Ecuador *20883*

R   *Hirtella pimichina* Lasser & Maguire *20883*
   I   *20883* Brazil *20883*
   I   *20883* Venezuela *20883*

V   *Hirtella racemosa* Lamark var. *glandipedicellata*
     Prance *20883*
   I   *20883* Colombia *20883*

V   *Hirtella racemosa* Lamark var. *hispida*

Prance *20883*
   I   *20883* Brazil *20883*
   I   *20883* French Guiana *20883*

E   *Hirtella radamii* Prance *20883*
   I   *20883* Brazil *20883*

R   *Hirtella rasa* Standley *20883*
   I   *20883* Brazil *20883*
   I   *20883* Peru *20883*

R   *Hirtella revillae* Prance *20883*
   I   *20883* Peru *20883*

R   *Hirtella rugosa* Thuill. ex Pers. *20883*
   I   *20883* Puerto Rico *20883*

E   *Hirtella santosii* Prance *20883, 11589*
   I   *20883* Brazil *20883*
   E   *17746* Brazil - Bahia *17746*

E   *Hirtella scaberula* Spruce ex Hooker f. *20883, 11589*
   I   *20883* Brazil *20883*

R   *Hirtella standleyi* Baehni & Macbride *20883*
   I   *20883* Peru *20883*

E   *Hirtella subglanduligera* Pilgar *20883, 9518*
   E   *11589* Peru *20883*

R   *Hirtella subscandens* Spruce ex Hooker f. *20883*
   I   *20883* Brazil *20883*
   I   *20883* Venezuela *20883*

E   *Hirtella vesiculosa* Suessenguth *20883, 11589*
   R   *11589* Colombia *20883*

E   *Hunga cordata* Prance *20893*
   E   *20893* New Caledonia *20893*

V   *Hunga gerontogea* (Schltr.) Prance *20893*
   V   *20893* New Caledonia *20893*

V   *Hunga guillauminii* Prance *20893*
   V   *20893* New Caledonia *20893*

V   *Hunga mackeeana* Prance *20893*
   V   *20893* New Caledonia *20893*

R   *Licania albiflora* Fanshawe & Maguire *20883, 11589*
   R   *11589* French Guiana *20883*
   R   *11589* Guyana *20883*
   R   *11589* Suriname *20883*

R   *Licania amapaensis* Prance *20883*
   I   *20883* Brazil *20883*
   I   *20883* French Guiana *20883*

V   *Licania angustata* Prance *20883, 11589*
   I   *20883* Brazil *20883*
   R   *9518* Peru *20883*

E   *Licania anneae* Prance *20883, 11589*
   I   *20883* Brazil *20883*

V   *Licania apiculata* Prance *20883, 11589*
   I   *20883* Brazil *20883*

E   *Licania aracaensis* Prance *20883, 17746*
   I   *20883* Brazil *20883*
   R   *17746* Brazil - Amazonas *17746*

R   *Licania arachnoidea* Fanshawe & Maguire *20883, 11589*
   I   *20883* Brazil *20883*
   R   *11589* French Guiana *11589*
   R   *11589* Guyana *20883*
   R   *11589* Peru *20883*
   R   *11589* Suriname *11589*

V   *Licania araneosa* Taubert *20883, 11589*
   I   *20883* Brazil *20883*

E   *Licania arianeae* Prance *20883, 11589*
   I   *20883* Brazil *20883*

E   *Licania bahiensis* Prance *20883, 11589*
     I   *20883* Brazil *20883*

R   *Licania belemii* Prance *20883*
     I   *20883* Brazil *20883*

E   *Licania bellingtonii* Prance *20883, 17746*
     I   *20883* Brazil *20883*
     E   *17746* Brazil - Rondonia *17746*

E   *Licania boliviensis* Prance *20883, 11589*
     R   *11589* Bolivia *20883*

R   *Licania boyanii* Tutin *20883*
     I   *20883* Guyana *20883*
     I   *20883* Venezuela *20883*

V   *Licania buxifolia* Sandwith *20883*
     I   *20883* Guyana *20883*

E   *Licania cabrerae* Prance *20883, 11589*
     R   *11589* Colombia *20883*

E   *Licania caldasiana* Cuatrecasas *20883, 9518*
     R   *11589* Colombia *20883*

V   *Licania calvescens* Cuatrecasas *20883, 9518*
     I   *20883* Colombia *20883*

V   *Licania cecidiophora* Prance *20883*
     I   *20883* Peru *20883*

V   *Licania chiriquiensis* Prance *20883, 9518*
     R   *9518* Panama *20883*

R   *Licania chocoensis* Cuatrecasas *20883, 9518*
     I   *20883* Colombia *20883*

E   *Licania compacta* Fritsch *20883, 11589*
     R   *11589* Guyana *20883*

R   *Licania cordata* Prance *20883*
     I   *20883* Brazil *20883*
     I   *20883* Venezuela *20883*

E   *Licania costaricensis* Standley & Steyermark *20883, 9518*
     R   *9518* Costa Rica *20883*

V   *Licania couepiifolia* Prance *20883*
     I   *20883* Guyana *20883*
     I   *20883* Suriname *20883*

V   *Licania crassivenia* Spruce ex Hooker f. *20883, 11589*
     I   *20883* Brazil *20883*
     R   *9518* Venezuela *20883*

V   *Licania cuatrecasasii* Prance *20883*
     I   *20883* Colombia *20883*

R   *Licania cuprea* Sandwith *20883, 8679*
     I   *20883* Guyana *20883*

E   *Licania cuspidata* (Rusby) Prance *20883, 9518*
     R   *11589* Colombia *20883*
     R   *9518* Venezuela *9518*

R   *Licania cyathodes* R. Benoist *20883*
     I   *20883* French Guiana *20883*

R   *Licania cymosa* Fritsch *20883*
     I   *20883* Brazil *20883*

E   *Licania dodsonii* Prance *20883, 11589*
     E   *11589* Ecuador *20883*

R   *Licania durifolia* Cuatrecasas *20883, 11351*
     I   *20883* Colombia *20883*
     I   *20883* Ecuador *20883*
     I   *20883* Peru *20883*

E   *Licania fasciculata* Prance *20883, 10747*
     I   *20883* Panama *20883*

E   *Licania filomenoi* Prance *20883, 11589*
     R   *11589* Peru *20883*

R   *Licania foldatsii* Prance *20883*
     I   *20883* Venezuela *20883*

V   *Licania foveolata* Prance *20883, 11589*
     R   *11589* Guyana *20883*

R   *Licania fritschii* Prance *20883, 11589*
     I   *20883* Brazil *20883*
     R   *11589* Peru *11589*

E   *Licania fuchsii* Prance *20883, 9518*
     R   *11589* Colombia *20883*

E   *Licania furfuracea* Prance *20883, 11589*
     R   *11589* Venezuela *20883*

E   *Licania gentryi* Prance *20883, 9518*
     R   *11589* Colombia *20883*

R   *Licania glauca* Cuatrecasas *20883, 9518*
     I   *20883* Colombia *20883*

E   *Licania glazioviana* Warming *20883, 11589*
     I   *20883* Brazil *20883*

V   *Licania gonzalezii* Miranda *20883, 9518*
     I   *20883* Mexico *20883*

V   *Licania grandibracteata* Prance *20883*
     I   *20883* Ecuador *20883*

E   *Licania guatemalensis* Lundell *20883, 10299*
     R   *9518* Guatemala *20883*

R   *Licania heteromorpha* Benth var. **perplexans** Sandwith *20883*
     I   *20883* Guyana *20883*
     I   *20883* Suriname *20883*

E   *Licania heteromorpha* Benth var. **revoluta** Prance *20883*
     I   *20883* Brazil *20883*

R   *Licania heteromorpha* Benth var. **subcordata** Fritsch *20883*
     I   *20883* Brazil *20883*

E   *Licania hispida* Prance *20883, 11589*
     R   *11589* Venezuela *20883*

E   *Licania hitchcockii* Maguire *20883, 11589*
     R   *11589* Venezuela *20883*

V   *Licania hypoleuca* Prance var. *foveolata* Prance *20883, 11589*
     I   *20883* Brazil *20883*

V   *Licania indurata* Pilger *20883, 11589*
     I   *20883* Brazil *20883*
     E   *17079* Brazil - Sao Paulo *11589*

R   *Licania irwinii* Prance *20883, 8679*
     I   *20883* French Guiana *20883*
     I   *20883* Suriname *20883*
     I   *20883* Venezuela *20883*

R   *Licania jefensis* Prance *20883, 10747*
     I   *20883* Panama *20883*

R   *Licania jimenezii* Prance *20883, 8679*
     I   *20883* Guyana *20883*
     I   *20883* Suriname *20883*

E   *Licania joseramosii* Prance *20883, 11589*
     I   *20883* Brazil *20883*

V   *Licania kallunkiae* Prance *20883, 11589*
     R   *9518* Costa Rica *20883*
     R   *9518* Panama *20883*

V   *Licania klugii* Prance *20883, 9518*
     R   *11589* Peru *20883*

R   *Licania laevigata* Prance *20883, 11589*
    I   *20883*   Brazil *20883*
    R   *11589*   Suriname *20883*

E   *Licania lamentanda* Prance *20883, 11589*
    I   *20883*   Brazil *20883*

R   *Licania latistipula* Prance *20883*
    I   *20883*   French Guiana *20883*
    I   *20883*   Venezuela *20883*

E   *Licania littoralis* Kuhlmann var. *cuneata*
      Kuhlm. *20883, 11589*
    I   *20883*   Brazil *20883*

V   *Licania longipedicellata* Ducke *20883, 11589*
    I   *20883*   Brazil *20883*
    R   *9518*   Peru *20883*

V   *Licania maguirei* Prance *20883, 11589*
    I   *20883*   Brazil *20883*

E   *Licania maranhensis* Prance *20883, 11589*
    I   *20883*   Brazil *20883*

V   *Licania maritima* Prance *20883, 9518*
    I   *20883*   Colombia *20883*

E   *Licania marleneae* Prance *20883, 11589*
    I   *20883*   Brazil *20883*

V   *Licania maxima* Prance *20883, 11589*
    I   *20883*   Brazil *20883*
    I   *20883*   French Guiana *20883*

E   *Licania mexicana* Lundell *20883, 10299*
    I   *20883*   Mexico *20883*
    R   *11589*   Mexico - Sinaloa *10299*

E   *Licania microphylla* Fanshawe & Maguire *20883, 11589*
    R   *11589*   Guyana *20883*

E   *Licania miltonii* Prance *20883*
    I   *20883*   Brazil *20883*

E   *Licania minuscula* Cuatrecasas *20883, 11589*
    R   *11589*   Colombia *20883*

E   *Licania montana* Prance *20883, 11589*
    R   *11589*   Venezuela *20883*

E   *Licania morii* Prance *20883, 10747*
    R   *9518*   Panama *20883*

V   *Licania naviculistipula* Prance *20883, 11589*
    I   *20883*   Brazil *20883*

E   *Licania nelsonii* Prance *20883*
    I   *20883*   Brazil *20883*

E   *Licania niloi* Prance *20883, 11589*
    I   *20883*   Brazil *20883*

E   *Licania obtusifolia* Fritsch *20883, 11589*
    R   *11589*   French Guiana *20883*

V   *Licania occultans* Prance *20883*
    I   *20883*   Brazil *20883*

R   *Licania operculipetala* Standley & L. O.
      Williams *20883, 9518*
    R   *20883*   Costa Rica *20883*

R   *Licania orbicularis* Spruce ex Hooker f. *20883*
    I   *20883*   Brazil *20883*
    I   *20883*   Venezuela *20883*

R   *Licania ovalifolia* Kleinhoonte *20883, 8679*
    I   *20883*   Brazil *20883*
    I   *20883*   French Guiana *20883*
    I   *20883*   Suriname *20883*

E   *Licania pakaraimensis* Prance *20883*
    I   *20883*   Venezuela *20883*

R   *Licania paraensis* Prance *20883*
    I   *20883*   Bolivia *20883*
    I   *20883*   Brazil *20883*

R   *Licania persaudii* Fanshawe & Maguire *20883, 20513*
    I   *20883*   Guyana *20883*

R   *Licania piresii* Prance *20883, 9518*
    I   *20883*   Brazil *20883*
    R   *9518*   Guyana *20883*

R   *Licania pruinosa* Benoist *20883*
    I   *20883*   Brazil *20883*
    I   *20883*   French Guiana *20883*

E   *Licania retifolia* Blake *20883, 9518*
    I   *20883*   El Salvador *20883*
    E   *11589*   Mexico *20883*

E   *Licania riedelii* Prance *20883, 11589*
    I   *20883*   Brazil *20883*

R   *Licania robusta* Sagot *20883*
    I   *20883*   Brazil *20883*
    I   *20883*   French Guiana *20883*
    I   *20883*   Suriname *20883*

E   *Licania roraimensis* Standley *20883, 11589*
    R   *11589*   Guyana *20883*

R   *Licania rufescens* Klotzsch ex Fritsch *20883*
    I   *20883*   Brazil *20883*
    I   *20883*   Guyana *20883*
    I   *20883*   Suriname *20883*
    I   *20883*   Venezuela *20883*

E   *Licania salicifolia* Cuatrecasas *20883, 9518*
    R   *11589*   Colombia *20883*

R   *Licania salzmanii* (Hooker f.) Fritsch *20883*
    I   *20883*   Brazil *20883*

E   *Licania sandwithii* Prance *20883, 11589*
    R   *11589*   Guyana *20883*
    R   *9518*   Venezuela *9518*

E   *Licania santosii* Prance *20883*
    I   *20883*   Brazil *20883*

E   *Licania silvatica* Glaziou ex Prance *20883, 11589*
    I   *20883*   Brazil *20883*

V   *Licania spicata* Hooker f. *20883*
    I   *20883*   Brazil *20883*

R   *Licania stewardii* Prance *20883*
    I   *20883*   Brazil *20883*

E   *Licania stricta* Kleinhoonte *20883, 11589*
    R   *11589*   Suriname *20883*

R   *Licania subarachnophylla* Cuatrecasas *20883, 11589*
    R   *9518*   Colombia *20883*
    R   *9518*   Venezuela *20883*

R   *Licania subrotundata* Maguire *20883*
    I   *20883*   Venezuela *20883*

E   *Licania tachirensis* Prance *20883, 11589*
    R   *11589*   Venezuela *20883*

E   *Licania tambopatensis* Prance *20883, 11589*
    R   *11589*   Peru *20883*

E   *Licania teixeirae* Prance *20883, 11589*
    I   *20883*   Brazil *20883*

E   *Licania tepuiensis* Prance *20883, 11589*
    R   *11589*   Venezuela *20883*

R   *Licania tocantina* Prance *20883*
    I   *20883*   Brazil *20883*

E   *Licania trigonioides* Macbride *20883, 9518*
    E   *11589*   Peru *20883*

R   *Licania turbinata* Bentham *20883*
     I   *20883* Brazil *20883*

V   *Licania velata* Cuatrecasas *20883, 9518*
     I   *20883* Colombia *20883*

R   *Licania veneralensis* Cuatrecasas *20883, 9518*
     I   *20883* Colombia *20883*

V   *Magnistipula butayei* De Wild. var. *sargosii*
     (Pellegrin) F.White *20274*
     V   *20858* Ghana *7926*

R   *Maranthes panamensis* (Standl.) Prance & White *20883*
     V   *20883* Costa Rica *20883*
     I   *20883* Nicaragua *20883*
     V   *20883* Panama *20883*

V   *Parinari alvimii* Prance *20883*
     I   *20883* Brazil *20883*

V   *Parinari brasiliensis* (Schott) Hooker f. *20883, 11589*
     I   *20883* Brazil *20883*
     E   *17746* Brazil - Minas Gerais *17079*
     E   *17746* Brazil - Rio de Janeiro *17079*

R   *Parinari cardiophylla* Ducke *20883, 11589*
     I   *20883* Brazil *20883*

V   *Parinari chocoensis* Prance *20883, 9518*
     I   *20883* Colombia *20883*

I   *Parinari euadenia* Kosterm *19120*
     I   *19120* Thailand *19120*

I   *Parinari indicum* Beddome
     I   India - Tamil Nadu (Nilgiri Hills)

V   *Parinari littoralis* Prance *20883*
     I   *20883* Brazil *20883*

R   *Parinari maguirei* Prance *20883*
     I   *20883* Guyana *20883*
     I   *20883* Venezuela *20883*

R   *Parinari parvifolia* Sandwith *20883*
     I   *20883* Brazil *20883*
     I   *20883* Guyana *20883*

R   *Parinari romeroi* Prance *20883*
     I   *20883* Colombia *20883*
     I   *20883* Ecuador *20883*

I   *Parinari travancoricum* Beddome
     I   India - Kerala (Travancore)
     I   India - Tamil Nadu (Tirunelveli District)

Cistaceae

Number of genera: 8
Number of species: 200
Recorded threatened species: 43   (21%)

Mostly in temperate and warm temperate.

R   *Cistus albanicus* E.F.Warb. ex Heywood *20178, 20171*
     R   *20178* Albania *20178*
     R   Greece

E   *Cistus heterophyllus* Desf. ssp. *carthaginensis*
     (Pau) M.B.Crespo & Mateo *20648*
     E   *20692* Spain *20692*

V   *Cistus osbeckiafolius* Webb ex Christ *10260*
     V   *20750* Spain - Canary Is. *14155*

V   *Cistus palhinhae* Ingram *8000, 20171*
     V   *20076* Portugal (south-west) *8000*

R   *Fumana paradoxa* Heywood *20171*
     R   Spain

R   *Fumana trisperma* Huber-Mor. & Reese *12840*
     R   *20618* Turkey *20618*

E   *Halimium verticillatum* (Brot.) Sennen *8000, 20171*
     E   *20076* Portugal *8000*

V   *Helianthemum alypoides* Losa & Rivas Goday *17891*
     V   *11496* Spain (Almería) *17891*

R   *Helianthemum antitauricum* Davis et Coode *19873*
     R   *20618* Turkey *20618*

I   *Helianthemum arcticum* (Grosser) Janchen *5942, 20171*
     I   *5942* Russia (E.Europe) - North (north - Kolskiy) *5942*

R   *Helianthemum arenicola* Chapman *20850*
     E   *20850* U.S. - Alabama *20850*
     R   *20850* U.S. - Florida *20850*
     E   *20850* U.S. - Mississippi *20850*

E   *Helianthemum bramwelliorum* Marrero *20750*
     E   *20750* Spain - Canary Is. *20750*

R   *Helianthemum broussonetii* Dunal ex DC. *20750*
     R   *20750* Spain - Canary Is. *20750*

E   *Helianthemum bystropogophyllum* Svent. *14166*
     E   *15105* Spain - Canary Is. *17891*

E   *Helianthemum cirae* Santos *20750*
     E   *20750* Spain - Canary Is. *20750*

R   *Helianthemum cyrenaicum* (Grosser) Brullo & Furnari
     R   Libya

R   *Helianthemum dumosum* (Bickn.) Fern. *20850*
     Ex/E   *20850* U.S. - Connecticut *20850*
     R   *20850* U.S. - Massachusetts *20850*
     V   *20850* U.S. - New York *20850*
     E   *20850* U.S. - Rhode Is. *20850*

R   *Helianthemum eriocephalum* Pomel *10488*
     R   *14958* Algeria *10488*

R   *Helianthemum geniorum* Maire *10488*
     R   *14958* Algeria *10488*

E   *Helianthemum gonzalezferrari* Marrero *20750*
     E   *20750* Spain - Canary Is. *20750*

V   *Helianthemum greenei* B.L. Robins. *20850*
     V   *20850* U.S. - California *20850*

I   *Helianthemum grosii* Pau & Font Quer
     I   Morocco

E   *Helianthemum inaguae* Marrero, G.Martin & G.Artiles *20750*
     E   *20750* Spain - Canary Is. *20750*

E   *Helianthemum juliae* Wildpret *17530*
     E   *19174* Spain - Canary Is. *19174*

E   *Helianthemum lini* Santos *20750*
     E   *20750* Spain - Canary Is. *20750*

R   *Helianthemum maritimum* Pomel *10488*
     R   *14958* Algeria *10488*

V   *Helianthemum nashii* Britt. *20850*
     I   *20850* U.S. - Florida *20850*

V   *Helianthemum origanifolium* (Lam.) Pers. ssp. *serrae*
     (Camb.) Guinea & Heywood *20171*
     V   Spain - Balearic Is.

R   *Helianthemum pannosum* Boiss. *11496, 20171*
     R   *11496* Spain *11496*

I   *Helianthemum salicifolium* (L.) Miller var. *glabrum*
     Meikle *14230*
     I   *19164* Cyprus *14230*

I   *Helianthemum schweinfurthii* Grosser *10270*

I		16168 Egypt (Gebel El Shallufa) *16168*

R   *Helianthemum soongoricum* Schrenk *17617*
- R   17617 China - Gansu (Mingle) *11139*
- R   17617 China - Nei Monggol Zizhiqu (Xierdoeshi) *11139*
- R   17617 China - Xinjiang Uygur Zizhiqu (Yining; Gongliou; Gongnais) *11139*

E   *Helianthemum teneriffae* Coss. *15105*
- E   20750 Spain - Canary Is. *15105*

R   *Helianthemum tholiforme* D. Bramwell & al. *15105*
- R   20750 Spain - Canary Is. *15105*

V   *Helianthemum thymiphyllum* Svent. *15105*
- V   15105 Spain - Canary Is. *15105*

E   *Hudsonia montana* Nutt. *20850*
- E   20850 U.S. - North Carolina *20850*

R   *Lechea cernua* Small *20850*
- R   20850 U.S. - Florida *20850*

V   *Lechea divaricata* Shuttlw. ex Britt. *20850*
- I   20850 U.S. - Alabama *20850*
- V   20850 U.S. - Florida *20850*

E   *Lechea intermedia* Legget ex Britt. var. *depauperata* Hodgdon *20850, 2063*
- I   20850 Canada - Manitoba *20850*
- E   20850 Canada - Saskatchewan *20850*

E   *Lechea lakelae* Wilbur *20850*
- E   20850 U.S. - Florida *20850*

E   *Lechea maritima* Leggett var. *subcylindrica* Hodgdon *20850, 14393*
- E   20850 Canada - New Brunswick *20850*
- E   20850 Canada - Prince Edward Is. *20850*

R   *Lechea maritima* Leggett var. *virginica* Hodgdon *20850*
- I   20850 U.S. - Delaware *20850*
- I   20850 U.S. - Maryland *20850*
- E   20850 U.S. - North Carolina *20850*
- R   20850 U.S. - Virginia *20850*

E   *Lechea mensalis* Hodgdon *20883, 20850, 8058*
- E   20850 U.S. - Texas *20850*
- I   20883 Mexico *20883*

E   *Tuberaria major* (Willk.) P.Silva & Rozeira *8000, 20171*
- E   20076 Portugal (south) *8000*

Clethraceae

Number of genera: 1
Number of species: 65
Recorded threatened species: 4   (6%)

Tropical America; southeastern United States; Southeast Asia; East Indies.

R   *Clethra alexandri* Griseb. *20883*
- R   20883 Jamaica *20883*

V   *Clethra nicaraguensis* C. Hamilton *10353*
- V   11967 Nicaragua *10353*

I   *Clethra pulgarensis* Elm. *13833*
- I   13833 Philippines (Mt. Pulgar) *13833*

R   *Clethra tonkinensis* Dop *6057*
- R   Vietnam *6057*

Cochlospermaceae

Number of genera:
Number of species: 15
Recorded threatened species: 2   (13%)

Tropical, often in drier regions.

V   *Amoreuxia gonzalezii* Sprague & Riley *20883, 20850*
- E   20850 U.S. - Arizona *20850*
-    20883 Mexico *20883*

R   *Cochlospermum tetraporum* Hallier *20883, 16336*
- E   16336 Argentina *20883*
- E   20176 Argentina - Jujuy *20176*
- E   20176 Argentina - Salta *20176*
- I   20883 Bolivia *20883*

Columelliaceae

Number of genera: 1
Number of species: 4
Recorded threatened species: 1   (25%)

Colombia to Bolivia.

V   *Columellia obovata* Ruiz Lopez & Pavon *18200*
- V   12468 Peru *18200*

Combretaceae

Number of genera: 20
Number of species: 400
Recorded threatened species: 73   (18%)

Tropical and subtropical, especially Africa.

I   *Anogeissus sericea* Brandis var. *nummularia* King ex Duthie *7771*
- I   India - Gujarat *7771*
- I   India - Punjab *7771*
- I   India - Rajasthan (west) *7771*

R   *Buchenavia amazonia* A.R.A. Alwan Al-Mayah & C.A. Stace *10260*
- R   11543 Brazil *11543*
- R   11543 Colombia *11543*
- R   11543 Peru *11543*

R   *Buchenavia congesta* Ducke *11543*
- R   11543 Brazil *11543*
- R   11543 Colombia *11543*

R   *Buchenavia fanshawei* Exell & Maguire *8679*
- R   11543 Brazil *11543*
- R   11543 Guyana *8679*

R   *Buchenavia guianensis* (Aublet) Alwan & Stace
- R   11543 Brazil *11543*
- R   11543 French Guiana *11543*

R   *Buchenavia hoehneana* N. Mattos *11543*
- R   11543 Brazil *11543*

R   *Buchenavia megalophylla* Van Heurck & Mueller *11543*
- R   11543 Brazil *11543*
- R   11543 Guyana *11543*

R   *Buchenavia nitidissima* (Rich.) Alwan & Stace *11543*
- R   11543 French Guiana *11543*

R   *Buchenavia ochroprumna* Eichler *11543*
- R   11543 Brazil *11543*

R   *Buchenavia pallidovirens* Cuatrec. *18200*
- R   11543 Brazil *11543*
- R   11543 Colombia *11543*
- R   11543 Peru *11543*

R   *Buchenavia pulcherrima* Exell & Stace *11543*

R   11543   Guyana *11543*

R   ***Buchenavia sericocarpa*** Ducke *11543*
R   11543   Brazil *11543*
R   11543   Colombia *11543*
I   18200   Peru *11543*

R   ***Buchenavia suaveolens*** Eichler *11543*
R   11543   Brazil *11543*
R   11543   Colombia *11543*
R   11543   Venezuela *11543*

R   ***Buchenavia tomentosa*** Eichler *11543*
R   11543   Brazil *11543*

R   ***Bucida macrostachya*** Standley *9004*
R   11543   Belize *11543*
R   11543   Guatemala *11543*
R   11543   Mexico *11543*
R   11543   Nicaragua *11543*

R   ***Bucida molineti*** (M. Gomez) Alwan *11543*
R   11543   Belize *11543*
R   11543   Guatemala *11543*

I   ***Combretum batesii*** Exell
I   Cameroon (Cameroon mt)

R   ***Combretum brevistylum*** Eichler *11543*
R   11543   Brazil *11543*
R   11543   Venezuela *11543*

R   ***Combretum caudatisepalum*** Exell & Garcia *7749*
R   Mozambique *7749*

R   ***Combretum chionanthoides*** Engl. & Diels *20057*
R   19109   Kenya *19109*

R   ***Combretum discolor*** Taub *11543*
R   11543   Brazil *11543*
R   11543   Paraguay *11543*

R   ***Combretum frangulifolium*** Kunth *11543*
R   11543   Colombia *11543*
R   11543   Venezuela *11543*

R   ***Combretum hilarianum*** D. Dietr. *11543*
R   11543   Brazil *11543*

R   ***Combretum labiocarpum*** Engl. & Diels *7749*
R   Mozambique *7749*

E   ***Combretum laxum*** (Pitt.) Croat var. ***epiphyticum*** (Pittier) Croat *20883, 10747*
I   20883   Panama *20883*

R   ***Combretum llewelynii*** J.F. Macbr. *18200*
R   11543   Brazil *11543*
R   11543   Ecuador *11543*
R   11543   Peru *11543*

R   ***Combretum mkuzense*** Carr & Retief *20604*
R   20604   South Africa - Natal *20604*

R   ***Combretum monetaria*** Martius *11543*
R   11543   Brazil *11543*

R   ***Combretum petrophilum*** Retief *20604, 17458*
R   20604   South Africa - Transvaal *20604*

R   ***Combretum pisonioides*** Taub *11543*
R   11543   Brazil *11543*

R   ***Combretum rohrii*** Exell
R   11543   Brazil *11543*
R   11543   French Guiana *11543*

R   ***Combretum rupicola*** Ridley *11543*
R   11543   Brazil *11543*

R   ***Combretum sprucei*** Eichler *11543*
R   11543   Venezuela *11543*

R   ***Combretum stocksii*** Sprague *7749*

R   Mozambique *7749*

V   ***Combretum tanaense*** Jessie J. Clark *6073*
V   19109   Kenya *7959*

E   ***Combretum tenuipetiolatum*** Wickens *20057*
E   20057   Kenya (coastal) *19109*
E   20057   Tanzania (Tanga) *20057*

I   ***Combretum trochainii*** Berhaut *8003*
I   Senegal *8003*

R   ***Combretum ulei*** Exell *11543*
R   11543   Brazil *11543*

R   ***Combretum vernicosum*** Rusby *11543*
R   11543   Bolivia *11543*
R   11543   Brazil *11543*

R   ***Dansiea elliptica*** Byrnes *20681*
R   20681   Australia - Queensland *20681*

R   ***Dansiea grandiflora*** Pedley *20681*
R   20681   Australia - Queensland *20681*

R   ***Macropteranthes fitzalanii*** F.Muell. *20681*
R   20681   Australia - Queensland *20681*

R   ***Macropteranthes leiocaulis*** P.I.Forster *20681*
R   20681   Australia - Queensland *20681*

V   ***Macropteranthes montana*** (F.Muell.) F.Muell. *20681*
V   20681   Australia - Queensland *20681*

R   ***Pteleopsis barbosae*** Exell *7749*
R   Mozambique *7749*

E   ***Pteleopsis habeensis*** Aubrev. ex Keay *11751*
E   20858   Ghana *15970*
E   20858   Mali (Bandiagara) *11751*
E   20858   Nigeria (Yankari game reserve) *20274*

R   ***Pteleopsis tetraptera*** Wickens *10583*
R   19109   Kenya (Mombasa, Kilifi) *19508*
R   20057   Tanzania (Tanga) *19508*

R   ***Ramatuela argentea*** Kunth *11543*
R   11543   Brazil *11543*
R   11543   Colombia *11543*
R   11543   Venezuela *11543*

R   ***Ramatuela crispialata*** Ducke *11543*
R   11543   Brazil *11543*
R   11543   Colombia *11543*
R   11543   Venezuela *11543*

R   ***Ramatuela virens*** Spruce ex Eichler *11543*
R   11543   Brazil *11543*
R   11543   Colombia *11543*
R   11543   Venezuela *11543*

V   ***Terminalia arbuscula*** Sw. *20883, 13336*
V   13336   Jamaica *20883*

R   ***Terminalia bentzoë*** (L.) L. f. ssp. ***bentzoë*** *10082*
R   Réunion *10082*
R   20771   Mauritius *10082*

V   ***Terminalia bentzoë*** (L.) L.f. ssp. ***rodriguesensis*** Wickens *10082*
V   5852   Mauritius - Rodrigues *5852*

R   ***Terminalia capitanea*** A.C. Smith *19427*
R   19630   Fiji (Viti Levu) *19427*

E   ***Terminalia cherrieri*** McKee *20802*
E   20893   New Caledonia (Poya area) *20802*

R   ***Terminalia crebrifolia*** A.C. Smith *19427*
R   19630   Fiji (Vanua Levu) *19427*

V   ***Terminalia eriostachya*** A. Rich. *11840*
V   20990   Cuba *11840*

R	*Terminalia gatopensis* **Guillaumin**	
	R	New Caledonia
R	*Terminalia glabrata* **J.G.Forster var.** *brownii* **Fosberg & Sachet** *20845*	
	R	*20845* French Polynesia - Marquesas Is *20845*
E	*Terminalia glabrata* **J.G.Forster var.** *glabrata* *20845*	
	E	*20845* French Polynesia - Society Is. (Tahiti) *20845*
I	*Terminalia glabrata* **J.G.Forster var.** *haroldii* **(Exell) Fosberg & Sachet** *20845*	
	I	*20845* French Polynesia - Tubuai Is. *20845*
I	*Terminalia glabrata* **J.G.Forster var.** *koariki* **(Exell) Fosberg & Sachet** *20845*	
	I	*20845* French Polynesia - Tuamotu Is. (Gambier) *20845*
I	*Terminalia hararensis* **Engl. ex Diels** *20924*	
	I	*20924* Ethiopia (Bale, Harerge) *20924*
I	*Terminalia hecistocarpa* **Engl. ex Diels** *20924*	
	I	*20924* Ethiopia (Bale) *20924*
R	*Terminalia intermedia* **(A. Rich.) Urban** *11840*	
	R	*19105* Cuba (Or; LV; LH; PR) *11840*
R	*Terminalia latifolia* **Sw.** *11543*	
	R	*11543* Jamaica *11543*
	R	*11543* Guatemala *11543*
V	*Terminalia luteola* **A.C. Smith** *19427*	
	V	*19630* Fiji (west-central Vanua Levu) *10253*
V	*Terminalia novocaledonica* **Däniker** *20893*	
	E	*20893* New Caledonia *20893*
R	*Terminalia pachystyla* **Borh.** *5607*	
	R	*19105* Cuba (Holguin) *5607*
V	*Terminalia parviflora* **Thwaites** *12838*	
	V	*12838* Sri Lanka *12838*
I	*Terminalia pellucida* **Presl.** *13780*	
	I	*15960* Philippines *13780*
E	*Terminalia psilantha* **A.C. Smith** *19630*	
	E	*19630* Fiji (Vanua Levu) *19630*
R	*Terminalia quintalata* **Maguire** *11543*	
	R	*11543* Brazil *11543*
	R	*11543* Guyana *11543*
	R	*11543* Venezuela *11543*
E	*Terminalia simulans* **A.C. Smith** *19427*	
	E	*19630* Fiji (Vanua Levu) *19427*
R	*Terminalia strigillosa* **A.C. Smith** *19427*	
	R	*19630* Fiji (Vanua Levu) *19427*
V	*Terminalia vitiensis* **A.C. Smith** *19427*	
	V	*19630* Fiji (Vitu Levu) *19427*
R	*Terminalia yapacana* **Maguire** *11543*	
	R	*11543* Colombia *11543*
	R	*11543* Venezuela *11543*

Compositae

Number of genera: 1,100-1,509
Number of species: 20,000
Recorded threatened species: 2553 (12%)

Cosmopolitan, especially temperate and subtropical regions.

V	*Abrotanella crassipes* **Skottsb.** *19116*	
	V	*19125* Chile - Juan Fernandez Is. *19116*
R	*Abrotanella nivigena* **(F.Muell.) F.Muell.** *20681*	
	I	*20681* Australia - New South Wales *20681*

	I	*20681* Australia - Victoria *20681*
R	*Acamptopappus shockleyi* **Gray** *20850*	
	I	*20850* U.S. - California *20850*
	I	*20850* U.S. - Nevada *20850*
Ex	*Acanthocladium dockeri* **F.Muell.** *20681, 14223*	
	Ex	*20681* Australia - New South Wales *20681*
	Ex	*20681* Australia - South Australia *20681*
V	*Acanthodesmos distichus* **Adams & duQuesnay** *20883, 13336*	
	V	*13336* Jamaica *20883*
R	*Achillea absinthoides* **Halácsy** *20171*	
	R	Greece
R	*Achillea alpina* **L. ssp.** *subcartilaginea* **(Heimerl) Kitam.** *10573*	
	R	*10573* Japan *10573*
R	*Achillea armenorum* **Boiss. & Hausskn.** *12840*	
	R	*12840* Turkey *12840*
R	*Achillea barbeyana* **Heldr. & Heimerl** *20171*	
	R	Greece
R	*Achillea brachyphylla* **Boiss. & Hausskn.** *12840*	
	R	*12840* Turkey *12840*
R	*Achillea fraasii* **Shultes Bip. var.** *troiana* **Aschers. & Heimerl** *12840*	
	R	*12840* Turkey *12840*
R	*Achillea goniocephala* **Boiss. & Bal.** *12840*	
	R	*12840* Turkey *12840*
R	*Achillea gypsicola* **Huber-Mor.** *12840*	
	R	*12840* Turkey *12840*
E	*Achillea horanszkyi* **Ujhelyi** *17786*	
	E	*20619* Hungary *17786*
R	*Achillea kotschyi* **Boiss. ssp.** *canescens* **Bassler** *12840*	
	R	*12840* Turkey *12840*
R	*Achillea lucana* **Pignatti** *18264*	
	R	*18264* Italy (Basilicata, Calabria) *18264*
R	*Achillea magnifica* **Huber-Mor.** *12840*	
	R	*12840* Turkey *12840*
I	*Achillea maura* **Humbert**	
	I	Morocco
E	*Achillea millefolium* **L. var.** *megacephala* **(Raup) Boivin** *20850, 2063*	
	I	*20850* Canada - Alberta *20850*
	I	*20850* Canada - Mackenzie *20850*
	E	*20850* Canada - Saskatchewan *20850*
R	*Achillea multifida* **(DC.) Boiss.** *12840, 20171*	
	R	*12840* Turkey *12840*
R	*Achillea nobilis* **L. ssp.** *denissima* **(O. Schwarz ex Bassler)** *12840*	
	R	*12840* Turkey *12840*
R	*Achillea nobilis* **L. ssp.** *kurdica* **Huber-Mor.** *12840*	
	R	*12840* Turkey *12840*
R	*Achillea oxyloba* **(DC.) Sch.Bip. ssp.** *schurii* **(Sch.Bip.) Heimerl** *20171*	
	R	*19947* Romania *17823*
	I	*5942* Ukraine *5942*
R	*Achillea pseudoaleppica* **Hub.- Mor.** *12840*	
	R	*12840* Turkey *12840*
R	*Achillea ptarmica* **L. var.** *yezoensis* **Kitam.** *10573*	

R		10573 Japan *10573*

R   *Achillea sieheana* Stapf *12840*
R   12840 Turkey *12840*

R   *Achillea sintenisii* Hub.-Mor. *12840*
R   12840 Turkey *12840*

R   *Achillea sipikorensis* Hausskn. & Bornm. *12840*
R   12840 Turkey *12840*

R   *Achillea sipinulifolia* Fenzl ex Boiss. *12840*
R   12840 Turkey *12840*

R   *Achillea taygetea* Boiss. & Heldr. *19174, 20171*
R   19174 Greece *19174*

R   *Achillea thracica* Velen. *5204, 20171*
R   5204 Bulgaria (central) *5204*

R   *Achnophora tatei* F.Muell. *20681*
R   20681 Australia - South Australia *20681*

R   *Acomis acoma* (F.Muell.) Druce *20681*
I   20681 Australia - New South Wales *20681*
I   20681 Australia - Queensland *20681*

R   *Acourtia acevedoi* Gonz. Eliz. *11384*
R   14294 Mexico - Durango *11384*

R   *Acourtia montana* (Rose) Reveal & R. King var.
     intermedia (Bacigal.) Reveal & R. King *14294*
R   14294 Mexico - Durango *14294*

V   *Adenophyllum wrightii* Gray *20850*
I   20850 U.S. - Arizona *20850*
Ex/E   20850 U.S. - New Mexico *20850*

R   *Ageratina altissima* var. *roanensis* (Small) Clewell &
     Woot. *20850*
I   20850 U.S. - Alabama *20850*
I   20850 U.S. - Georgia *20850*
I   20850 U.S. - Kentucky *20850*
R   20850 U.S. - North Carolina *20850*
V   20850 U.S. - Tennessee *20850*
I   20850 U.S. - Virginia *20850*
I   20850 U.S. - West Virginia *20850*

E   *Ageratina chiriquensis* (Rob.) K. & R. *20883, 9522*
I   20883 Panama *20883*

E   *Ageratina croatii* K. & R. *20883, 9006*
I   20883 Panama *20883*

R   *Ageratina durangensis* (H. Robinson) R. King & H.
     Robinson *10836*
R   14294 Mexico - Durango *10836*

R   *Ageratina gonzalezorum* B. Turner *9524*
R   14294 Mexico - Durango *9524*

R   *Ageratina grashoffii* B. Turner *12516*
R   14294 Mexico - Durango *12516*

R   *Ageratina luciae-brauniae* (Fern.) King & H.E.
     Robins. *20850*
V   20850 U.S. - Kentucky *20850*
E   20850 U.S. - South Carolina *20850*
V   20850 U.S. - Tennessee *20850*

V   *Ageratina shastensis* (Taylor & Stebbins) King & H.E.
     Robins. *20850*
V   20850 U.S. - California *20850*

R   *Ageratina sundbergii* B. Turner *12516*
R   14294 Mexico - Durango *12516*

E   *Ageratum chiriquense* (Rob.) K. & R. *20883, 9006*
I   20883 Panama *20883*

I   *Ageratum houstonianum* Mill. *15211, 20171*
I   India - Tamil Nadu (Nilgiri & Palani Hills)

V   *Ageratum littorale* Gray *20850*

I		20850 U.S. - Florida *20850*

E   *Ageratum oliveri* K. & R. *20883, 9006*
I   20883 Panama *20883*

V   *Ageratum panamense* Rob. *20883, 10836*
I   20883 Panama *20883*

R   *Agoseris lackschewitzii* D. Henderson & R.
     Moseley *20850*
E   20850 Canada - British Columbia *20850*
V   20850 U.S. - Idaho *20850*
V   20850 U.S. - Montana *20850*
V   20850 U.S. - Wyoming *20850*

R   *Ainsliaea dissecta* Franchet & Sav. *10573*
R   10573 Japan *10573*

R   *Ainsliaea faurieana* Beauv. *10573*
R   10573 Japan *10573*

R   *Ainsliaea macroclinidioides* Hayata *20511*
R   20511 Taiwan *20511*

R   *Ainsliaea macroclinidioides* Hayata var. *secudiflora*
     (Hayata) Kitamura *20511*
R   20511 Taiwan *20511*

R   *Ainsliaea paucicapitata* Hayata *20511*
R   20511 Taiwan *20511*

E   *Aldama mesoamericana* N. A. Harriman *20883*
I   20883 Nicaragua *20883*

V   *Allagopappus viscosissimus* Bolle *15105*
V   20750 Spain - Canary Is. *15105*

E   *Alloispermum insuetum* Fernández, Urbatsch &
     Sullivan *20883*
I   20883 Colombia *20883*

V   *Ambrosia cheiranthifolia* Gray *20883, 20850, 8058*
V   20850 U.S. - Texas *20850*
I   20883 Mexico *20883*

E   *Ambrosia dentata* (Cabrera) Dillon *18200*
E   9446 Peru *18200*

V   *Ambrosia linearis* (Rydb.) Payne *20850*
V   20850 U.S. - Colorado *20850*

R   *Ambrosia pumila* (Nutt.) Gray *20850*
V   20850 U.S. - California *20850*

V   *Ammobium craspedioides* Benth. *20681*
V   20681 Australia - New South Wales *20681*

V   *Amphoricarpos elegans* Albov *5942*
V   11552 Russia - North Caucasus (Caucasus)
         11552

R   *Amphoricarpos exsul* O. Schwarz *12840*
R   12840 Turkey *12840*

R   *Amphoricarpos praedictus* Ayasligil & Grierson *12840*
R   12840 Turkey *12840*

Ex   *Anacyclus alboranensis* Esteve Chueca & Varo *19818*
Ex   19818 Spain (Isla de Alborán) *19818*

R   *Anacyclus capillifolius* Maire
R   Morocco

I   *Anacyclus exalatus* Murb.
I   Morocco

V   *Anacyclus latealatus* Hub.-Mor. *12840*
V   12840 Turkey *12840*

E   *Anaphalis barnesii* C. Fischer *11494*
E   11494 India - Kerala (High Range, Idukki)
         11494

I   *Anaphalis beddomei* Hook.f.
I   India - Tamil Nadu (Palani Hills)

I	*Anaphalis fruticosa* Hook.f. *8021*	
	I	*16162* Sri Lanka *8021*
R	*Anaphalis horaimontana* Masamune *20511*	
	R	*20511* Taiwan *20511*
I	*Anaphalis pelliculata* Trimen *8021*	
	I	*16162* Sri Lanka (Nuwara Eliya District) *8021*
V	*Anaphalis sinica* Hance var. *pernivea* Shimizu *10573*	
	V	*10573* Japan *10573*
V	*Anaphalis sinica* Hance var. *viscosissima* (Honda) Kitam. *10573*	
	V	*10573* Japan *10573*
V	*Anaphalis sinica* Hance var. *yakusimensis* (Masam.) Yahara *10573*	
	V	*10573* Japan *10573*
I	*Anaphalis thwaitesii* C.B. Clarke var. *glabrescens* Grierson *8021*	
	I	*16162* Sri Lanka (Nuwara Eliya District) *8021*
R	*Anaphalis transnokoensis* Sasaki *20511*	
	R	*20511* Taiwan *20511*
R	*Anaxeton brevipes* Lundgren *20604*	
	R	*20604* South Africa - Cape Province *20604*
R	*Anaxeton ellipticum* Lundgren *20604*	
	R	*20604* South Africa - Cape Province *20604*
R	*Anaxeton hirsutum* (Thunb.) Less. *20604*	
	R	*20604* South Africa - Cape Province *20604*
V	*Andryala crithmifolia* Aiton *17891*	
	V	Portugal - Madeira *17891*
E	*Andryala levitomentosa* (Nyár.) P.D.Sell *8000, 20171*	
	E	*19417* Romania *20631*
R	*Andryala nigricans* Poiret *10488*	
	R	*14958* Algeria *10488*
R	*Andryala webbii* Schultz Bip. ex Christ *15105*	
	R	*15105* Spain - Canary Is. *15105*
R	*Anisopappus paucidentatus* Wild *7754*	
	R	Zimbabwe (Chimanimani) *7754*
V	*Antennaria affinis* Fern. *20850*	
	I	*20850* Canada - Newfoundland *20850*
V	*Antennaria arcuata* Cronq. *20850*	
	E	*20850* U.S. - Idaho *20850*
	E	*20850* U.S. - Nevada *20850*
	I	*20850* U.S. - Oregon *20850*
	V	*20850* U.S. - Wyoming *20850*
R	*Antennaria densifolia* Porsild *20850*	
	I	*20850* Canada - Mackenzie *20850*
	I	*20850* Canada - Yukon Territory *20850*
	E	*20850* U.S. - Alaska *20850*
	E	*20850* U.S. - Montana *20850*
V	*Antennaria eucosma* Fern. & Wieg. *20850, 15814*	
	I	*20850* Canada - Newfoundland *20850*
	R	*20850* Canada - Quebec *20850*
V	*Antennaria pulchella* Greene *20850*	
	V	*20850* U.S. - California *20850*
	I	*20850* U.S. - Nevada *20850*
E	*Antennaria soliceps* Blake *20850*	
	E	*20850* U.S. - Nevada *20850*
R	*Anthemis abrotanifolia* (Willd.) Guss. *20171*	
	R	*20730* Greece - Crete *19121*
R	*Anthemis adonidifolia* Boiss. *12840*	
	R	*12840* Turkey *12840*

R	*Anthemis ammanthus* Greuter *20171*	
	R	*20808* Greece (Cyclades) *20808*
V	*Anthemis amophila* Boiss. & Heldr. *12840*	
	V	*12840* Turkey *12840*
R	*Anthemis anthemiformis* (Freyn & Sint.) Grierson *12840*	
	R	*12840* Turkey *12840*
R	*Anthemis antitaurica* Grierson *12840*	
	R	*12840* Turkey *12840*
R	*Anthemis arenicola* Boiss. var. *arenicola* *12840*	
	R	*12840* Turkey *12840*
V	*Anthemis argyrophylla* (Halácsy & T.Georgiev) Velen. *8000, 20171*	
	V	*5204* Bulgaria (south) *5204*
V	*Anthemis bourgaei* Boiss. & Reut. *20171*	
	V	Spain
E	*Anthemis brachycarpa* Eig *8895*	
	E	Israel *8895*
R	*Anthemis calcarea* Sosn. *12840*	
	R	*12840* Turkey *12840*
R	*Anthemis carpatica* Willd. ssp. *pyrethriformis* (Schur) Beldie *17823, 20171*	
	R	*19949* Romania *19840*
R	*Anthemis cretica* L. ssp. *argaea* (Boiss. & Bal.) Grierson *12840*	
	R	*12840* Turkey *12840*
R	*Anthemis cuneata* Hub.-Mor. & Reese *12840*	
	R	*12840* Turkey *12840*
R	*Anthemis davisii* Yavin *12840*	
	R	*12840* Turkey *12840*
R	*Anthemis dipsacea* Bornm. *12840*	
	R	*12840* Turkey *12840*
V	*Anthemis filicaulis* (Boiss. & Heldr.) Greuter *20171*	
	V	*20730* Greece - Crete *19121*
R	*Anthemis fimbriata* Boiss. *12840*	
	R	*12840* Turkey *12840*
I	*Anthemis gaudium-solis* Velen. *5204, 20171*	
	I	Bulgaria
V	*Anthemis gerardiana* Jord. *20171*	
	V	France (south-east)
E	*Anthemis glaberrima* (Rech.f.) Greuter *17891, 20171*	
	E	*20730* Greece - Crete *17891*
V	*Anthemis halophila* Boiss. & Bal. *12840*	
	V	*12840* Turkey *12840*
R	*Anthemis hydruntina* H.Groves *18264, 20171*	
	R	*18264* Italy (Basilicata, Calabria) *18264*
V	*Anthemis ismelia* Lojac. *18264, 20171*	
	V	*18264* Italy - Sicily (Mt. Gallo) *18264*
R	*Anthemis lithuanica* (DC.) Besser ex Trautv. *8000, 20171*	
	R	former European USSR *8000*
R	*Anthemis macrantha* Heuff. *5204, 20171*	
	R	*5204* Bulgaria (west) *5204*
	R	*19947* Romania *20631*
R	*Anthemis melanoloma* Trautv. ssp. *trapezuntica* Grierson *12840*	
	R	*12840* Turkey *12840*
R	*Anthemis meteorica* Hausskn. *20171*	

R		Greece	
R		(former) Yugoslavia	

R **Anthemis orbelica** Pancic *5204, 20171*
    R   *5204* Bulgaria (south and west) *5204*

R **Anthemis oxylepis** (Boiss.) Boiss. *12840*
    R   *12840* Turkey *12840*

R **Anthemis panachaica** Halácsy *20171*
    R   Greece

R **Anthemis pauciloba** Boiss. var. *sieheana* (Eig) Grierson *12840*
    R   *12840* Turkey *12840*

R **Anthemis pestalozzae** Boiss. *12840*
    R   *12840* Turkey *12840*

R **Anthemis pindicola** Heldr. ex Halácsy *20171*
    R   Greece

R **Anthemis pungens** Yavin *12840*
    R   *12840* Turkey *12840*

R **Anthemis regis-borisii** Stoj. & Acht. *5204, 20171*
    R   *5204* Bulgaria (east) *5204*

R **Anthemis rhodensis** Boiss. *20731*
    R   *20731* Greece - East Aegean Is *20731*

V **Anthemis rosea** Sm. ssp. *rosea* *20731*
    V   *20731* Greece - East Aegean Is (Samos) *20731*

R **Anthemis rumelica** (Velen.) Stoj. & Acht. *5204, 20171*
    R   *5204* Bulgaria (south & east) *5204*

I **Anthemis saguramica** Sosn. *5942*
    I   *5942* Georgia *5942*

R **Anthemis sancti-johannis** Turrill *5204, 20171*
    R   *5204* Bulgaria *5204*

R **Anthemis sibthorpii** Griseb. *20171*
    R   Greece

V **Anthemis sterilis** Steven *8000, 20171*
    V   former European USSR *8000*

R **Anthemis stribrnyi** Velen. *5204, 20171*
    R   *5204* Bulgaria (south) *5204*

I **Anthemis tinctoria** L. ssp. *fussii* (Griseb.) Beldie *17823*
    I   *20631* Romania *20631*

R **Anthemis tinctoria** L. var. *virescens* Bornm. *12840*
    R   *12840* Turkey *12840*

R **Anthemis tomentella** Greuter *20171*
    R   *20730* Greece - Crete *19121*

R **Anthemis tricornis** Big *12840*
    R   *12840* Turkey *12840*

R **Anthemis trotzkiana** Claus ex Bunge *5942, 20171*
    I   *5942* Russia (E.Europe) - South *5942*
    R   *5942* Kazakhstan *5942*

R **Anthemis virescens** Velen. *5204, 20171*
    R   *5204* Bulgaria (south & east) *5204*

R **Anthemis wallii** Hub.-Mor. & Reese *12840*
    R   *12840* Turkey *12840*

I **Anthemis werneri** Stoj. & Acht. *20171*
    I   Greece

R **Antithrixia flavicoma** DC. *20604*
    R   *20604* South Africa - Cape Province *20604*

R **Anvilleina platycarpa** Maire
    R   Morocco

E **Archibaccharis jacksonii** Sundberg *20883*
    I   *20883* Costa Rica *20883*

I **Arctotheca forbesiana** (DC.) Lewin *20604*
    I   *20604* South Africa - Cape Province *20604*

Ex **Argentipallium spiceri** (F.Muell.) Paul G.Wilson *20681*
    Ex *20681* Australia - Tasmania *20681*

R **Argyranthemum adauctum** (Link) Humpheries ssp. *dugorii* (Bolle) Humphries
    R   Spain - Canary Is.

E **Argyranthemum adauctum** (Link) Humphries ssp. *erythrocarpon* (Svent.) Humphries
    E   Spain - Canary Is.

E **Argyranthemum adauctum** (Link) Humphries ssp. *jacobaeifolium* (Schultz Bip.) Humphries
    E   Spain - Canary Is.

E **Argyranthemum adauctum** (Link) Humphries ssp. *palmensis* Santos
    E   Spain - Canary Is.

V **Argyranthemum broussonetii** (Pers.) Humphries ssp. *broussonetii* *15105*
    V   *15105* Spain - Canary Is. *15105*

V **Argyranthemum broussonetii** (Pers.) Humphries ssp. *gomerensis* Humphries
    V   Spain - Canary Is.

V **Argyranthemum callichrysum** (Svent.) Humphries *15105*
    V   *15105* Spain - Canary Is. *15105*

V **Argyranthemum coronopifolium** (Willd.) Humphries *3434*
    V   *15105* Spain - Canary Is. *15105*

R **Argyranthemum dissectum** (Lowe) Lowe
    R   Portugal - Madeira

V **Argyranthemum escarrei** (Svent.) Humphries *15105*
    V   *20750* Spain - Canary Is. *15105*

V **Argyranthemum filifolium** (Schultz Bip.) Humphries *15105*
    V   *20750* Spain - Canary Is. *15105*

R **Argyranthemum foeniculaceum** (Willd.) Webb ex Schultz Bip. *15105*
    R   *15105* Spain - Canary Is. *15105*

R **Argyranthemum frutescens** (L.) Schultz Bip. ssp. *foeniculaceum* (Pitard & Proust) Humphries
    R   Spain - Canary Is.

V **Argyranthemum frutescens** (L.) Schultz Bip. ssp. *pumilum* Humphries
    V   Spain - Canary Is.

V **Argyranthemum haemotomma** (Lowe) Lowe
    V   Portugal - Madeira

V **Argyranthemum hierrense** Humphries *15105*
    V   *15105* Spain - Canary Is. *15105*

E **Argyranthemum lemsii** Humphries *15105*
    E   *20750* Spain - Canary Is. *15105*

E **Argyranthemum lidii** Humphries *14166*
    E   *15105* Spain - Canary Is. *17891*

V **Argyranthemum maderense** (D. Don) Humphries *15105*
    V   *15105* Spain - Canary Is. *15105*

E **Argyranthemum pinnatifidum** (L.f.) Lowe ssp. *succulentum* (Lowe) Humphries *17891*
    E   Portugal - Madeira *17891*

E **Argyranthemum sundingii** Borgen *15105*

E	20750	Spain - Canary Is.	*15105*

V **Argyranthemum sventenii** Humphries & Aldridge *15105*
   V   *15105*   Spain - Canary Is. *15105*

R **Argyranthemum tenerifae** C.J.Humphries *10260*
   R   20750   Spain - Canary Is. *15105*

E **Argyranthemum thalassophytum** (Svent.)
   Humphries *17891*
   E   Portugal - Salvage Is. *17891*

E **Argyranthemum vincentii** Santos & Feria *20750*
   E   20750   Spain - Canary Is. *20750*

R **Argyranthemum webbii** Schultz Bip. *20750*
   R   15105   Spain - Canary Is. *15105*

V **Argyranthemum winterii** (Svent.) Humphries *17891*
   V   20750   Spain - Canary Is. *17891*

E **Argyroxiphium caliginis** Forbes *20850, 14209*
   E   20850   U.S. - Hawaii (West Maui) *20850*

R **Argyroxiphium grayanum** (Hbd.) O. Deg. *20850, 14209*
   R   20850   U.S. - Hawaii *20850*

E **Argyroxiphium kauense** (Rock & Neal) O.& I.
   Deg. *20850, 14209*
   E   20850   U.S. - Hawaii *20850*

V **Argyroxiphium sandwicense** DC. *20850*
   I   20850   U.S. - Hawaii *20850*

E **Argyroxiphium sandwicense** DC. ssp. *sandwicense*
   Hbd. *20850*
   E   20850   U.S. - Hawaii *20850*

E **Argyroxiphium virescens** Hbd. *20850*
   E   20850   U.S. - Hawaii *20850*

Ex **Argyroxiphium virescens** Hillebrand var.
   virescens *14301*
   Ex   14209   U.S. - Hawaii (east Maui) *14209*

V **Arnaldoa coccinosantha** (Muschler) Ferreyra *18200*
   V   9446   Peru *18200*

V **Arnaldoa macbrideana** Ferreyra *18200*
   V   9446   Peru *18200*

V **Arnica frigida** ssp. *griscomii* (Fern.) S.R.
   Downie *20850*
   I   20850   Canada - Newfoundland *20850*
   E   20850   Canada - Quebec *20850*

R **Arnica lanceolata** Nutt. *20850*
   I   20850   Canada - New Brunswick *20850*
   R   20850   Canada - Quebec *20850*
   V   20850   U.S. - Maine *20850*
   E   20850   U.S. - New Hampshire *20850*
   E   20850   U.S. - New York *20850*
   Ex   20850   U.S. - Vermont *20850*

R **Arnica lonchophylla** Greene ssp. *arnoglossa*
   (Greene) Maguire *20850*
   I   20850   U.S. - Montana *20850*
   I   20850   U.S. - South Dakota *20850*
   I   20850   U.S. - Wyoming *20850*

R **Arnica louiseana** Farr *20850*
   I   20850   Canada - Alberta *20850*

E **Arnicastrum guerrerense** Villaseñor *20883, 9749*
   I   20883   Mexico *20883*
   R   19850   Mexico - Guerrero *9749*

V **Arnoglossum diversifolium** (Torr. & Gray) H.E.
   Robins. *20850*
   E   20850   U.S. - Alabama *20850*
   V   20850   U.S. - Florida *20850*
   E   20850   U.S. - Georgia *20850*

   I   20850   U.S. - Louisiana *20850*

E **Artemisia aleutica** Hulten *20850, 21309*
   E   20850   U.S. - Alaska *20850*

R **Artemisia arctica** Less. ssp. *arctica* *20085,*
   21309
   R   20085   Russia (E.Europe) - North *20085*
   R   20085   Canada *20085*
   R   21309   U.S. - Alaska *21309*

V **Artemisia arctica** Less. ssp. *beringensis* (Hulten)
   Hulten *20850*
   V   20850   U.S. - Alaska *20850*

V **Artemisia argentea** L'Herit.
   V   Portugal - Madeira

E **Artemisia biennis** Willd. var. *diffusa*
   Dorn *20850*
   E   20850   U.S. - Wyoming *20850*

R **Artemisia campestris** L. ssp. *bottnica* A.L.
   Lundström ex Kindb. *14526, 20171*
   V   20673   Finland *8000*
   R   18216   Sweden *18216*

V **Artemisia cantabrica** (M. Lainz) M. Lainz *11496*
   V   11496   Spain *11496*

I **Artemisia cina** Berg ex Polj. *5942*
   E   5942   Kazakhstan (south-east) *5942*
   E   5942   Kyrgyzstan *5942*
   I   5942   Uzbekistan *5942*

R **Artemisia congesta** Kitam. *10573*
   R   10573   Japan *10573*

R **Artemisia densiflora** Viv. *18264*
   R   18264   Italy - Sardinia *18264*

I **Artemisia dolichocephala** Pampan.
   I   India - Jammu & Kashmir

R **Artemisia flahaultii** Emberger & Maire
   R   Morocco

R **Artemisia flava** Jurtz. *20085, 21309*
   R   20085   Russia (E.Europe) - North *20085*

R **Artemisia gilvescens** Miq. *10573*
   R   10573   Japan *10573*

R **Artemisia globularia** Hult. var. *lutea* *19002,*
   21309
   V   19002   U.S. - Alaska *19002*

E **Artemisia granatensis** Boiss. *15398, 20171*
   E   15398   Spain (Province of Granada y Almería)
            15398

V **Artemisia hololeuca** M.Bieb. ex Besser *8000, 20171*
   V   11552   Russian Federation (west) *11552*

Ex **Artemisia insipida** Vill. *20171*
   Ex   France (south-west Alps/north-west of Gap)

R **Artemisia kitadakensis** Hara & Kitam. *10573*
   R   10573   Japan *10573*

R **Artemisia lagopus** Fisch. ex Bess. ssp. *abbreviata*
   Krash. Ex. Korobk. *20085, 21309*
   R   20085   Russia (E.Europe) - North *20085*

R **Artemisia lagopus** Fisch. et Bess ssp. *trinana*
   (Bess.) Korobk. *20085, 21309*
   R   20085   Russia (E.Europe) - North *20085*

R **Artemisia legionensis** Lainz
   R   Spain

V **Artemisia ludoviciana** Nutt. ssp. *estesii*
   Chambers *20850*

V   20850 U.S. - Oregon *20850*

V   *Artemisia mauiensis* (Gray) Skottsberg *20850*
    V   20850 U.S. - Hawaii *20850*

E   *Artemisia molinieri* Quézel, M.Barbero &
      R.J.Loisel *20171*
    E   20528 France (Provence) *20528*

R   *Artemisia momiyamae* Kitam. *10573*
    R   10573 Japan *10573*

R   *Artemisia nesiotica* Raven *20850*
    I   20850 U.S. - California *20850*

R   *Artemisia niitakayamensis* Hayata *20511*
    R   20511 Taiwan *20511*

R   *Artemisia niitakayamensis* Hayata var. *tsugitakaensis*
      Kitamura *20511*
    R   20511 Taiwan *20511*

R   *Artemisia nitida* Bertol. *13662, 20171*
    R   Austria *8000*
    R   Italy *8000*
    R   13662 Slovenia (eastern) *13662*

I   *Artemisia nivalis* Braun-Blanq. *18154*
    I   Italy (Monte Rosa)
    E   18154 Switzerland *18154*

R   *Artemisia oelandica* (Besser) Kom. *18216, 20171*
    R   20083 Sweden *18216*

R   *Artemisia packardiae* J. Grimes & Ertter *20850*
    R   20850 U.S. - Idaho *20850*
    V   20850 U.S. - Nevada *20850*
    R   20850 U.S. - Oregon *20850*

V   *Artemisia palmeri* Gray *20850*
    V   20850 U.S. - California *20850*

R   *Artemisia pancicii* (Janka) Ronniger *2050, 20171*
    V   Austria
    E   2050 Czech Republic *2050*
    E   Czech & Slovak Federal Republic
    R   (former) Yugoslavia

R   *Artemisia papposa* Blake & Cronq. *20850*
    R   20850 U.S. - Idaho *20850*
    V   20850 U.S. - Nevada *20850*
    V   20850 U.S. - Oregon *20850*

R   *Artemisia pattersonii* Gray *20850*
    I   20850 U.S. - Colorado *20850*
    I   20850 U.S. - New Mexico *20850*
    E   20850 U.S. - Wyoming *20850*

V   *Artemisia petrosa* (Baumg.) Jan ssp. *eriantha*
      (Ten.) Giacomini & Pignatti *18264*
    V   18264 Italy *18264*

V   *Artemisia porteri* Cronq. *20850*
    V   20850 U.S. - Wyoming *20850*

R   *Artemisia ramosa* C. Smith ex Link
    R   15105 Spain - Canary Is. *15105*

V   *Artemisia rupestris* L. ssp. *woodii*
      Neilson *20850, 1034*
    V   20850 Canada - Yukon Territory *20850*

R   *Artemisia salsoloides* Willd. *8000, 20171*
    R   11552 Russian Federation (west Caucasus, west
         Siberia) *11552*

R   *Artemisia samojedorum* Pamp. *20085, 21309*
    R   20085 Russia (E.Europe) - North *20085*

R   *Artemisia senjavinensis* Bess. *20850, 5942*
    R   11552 Russia (Far East) - Magadan (Bering Straits)
         19118
    V   20850 U.S. - Alaska (Bering Straits) *20850*

R   *Artemisia somai* Hayata var. *batakensis* (Hayata)
      Kitamura *20511*
    R   20511 Taiwan *20511*

R   *Artemisia tilesii* Ledeb. ssp. *unalaschcensis*
      (Bess.) Hulten *20850*
    I   20850 Canada - British Columbia *20850*
    I   20850 Canada - Mackenzie *20850*
    I   20850 Canada - Saskatchewan *20850*
    R   20850 U.S. - Alaska *20850*
    I   20850 U.S. - Idaho *20850*
    I   20850 U.S. - Montana *20850*
    I   20850 U.S. - Nevada *20850*
    I   20850 U.S. - Oregon *20850*

R   *Artemisia trifurcata* Steph. var. *pedunculosa*
      (Koidz.) Kitam. *10573*
    R   10573 Japan *10573*

V   *Artemisia vulgaris* L. var. *kamtschatica*
      Besser *20850*
    V   20850 U.S. - Alaska *20850*

I   *Aspilia grazielae* Santos *12079*
    I   17079 Brazil - Mato Grosso do Sul (Urucum)
         17079

R   *Aspilia paraensis* (Huber) Santos *12079*
    R   17079 Brazil - Pará (Alto Ariramba) *17079*

I   *Aspilia pohlii* Baker *12079*
    I   17079 Brazil *17079*

R   *Aspilia procumbens* Baker *12079*
    R   17079 Brazil - Rio Grande do Norte *17079*

R   *Aster albanicus* Degen ssp. *paparistoi*
      Qosja *20178*
    R   20178 Albania *20178*

R   *Aster altaicus* Willd. var. *taitoensis*
      Kitamura *20511*
    R   20511 Taiwan *20511*

R   *Aster avitus* Alexander *20850*
    R   20850 U.S. - Georgia *20850*
    Ex   20850 U.S. - North Carolina *20850*
    E   20850 U.S. - South Carolina *20850*

V   *Aster bracei* Britt. *20850*
    I   20850 U.S. - Florida *20850*

R   *Aster brickellioides* Greene var. *glabratus*
      Greene *20850*
    I   20850 U.S. - California *20850*
    I   20850 U.S. - Oregon *20850*

V   *Aster chapmanii* Torr. & Gray *20850*
    E   20850 U.S. - Alabama *20850*
    V   20850 U.S. - Florida *20850*

R   *Aster chingshuiensis* Y.C.Liu et C.H.Ou *20511*
    R   20511 Taiwan *20511*

R   *Aster curtus* Cronq. *20850, 10701*
    V   20850 Canada - British Columbia *20850*
    V   20850 U.S. - Oregon *20850*
    R   20850 U.S. - Washington *20850*

V   *Aster defoliatus* Parish *20850*
    I   20850 U.S. - California *20850*

V   *Aster depauperatus* Fern. *20850*
    I   20850 U.S. - Delaware *20850*
    E   20850 U.S. - Maryland *20850*
    V   20850 U.S. - Pennsylvania *20850*
    I   20850 U.S. - Virginia *20850*

R   *Aster elatus* (Greene) Cronq. *20850*
    I   20850 U.S. - California *20850*

V   *Aster georgianus* Alexander *20850*

V	20850	U.S. - Alabama	20850
I	20850	U.S. - Florida	20850
V	20850	U.S. - Georgia	20850
V	20850	U.S. - North Carolina	20850
I	20850	U.S. - South Carolina	20850

V   *Aster glaucescens* (A.Gray) Blake 20850

I	20850	U.S. - Oregon	20850
I	20850	U.S. - Washington	20850

R   *Aster gormanii* (Piper) Blake 20850

R	20850	U.S. - Oregon	20850

E   *Aster grisebachii* Britton 5607

E	19105	Cuba (Pinar del Rio; I. Juventud)	5607

I   *Aster itsunboshi* Kitamura 20511

I	20511	Taiwan	20511

V   *Aster jessicae* Piper 20850

V	20850	U.S. - Idaho	20850
V	20850	U.S. - Washington	20850

V   *Aster jonesiae* Lamboy 20850

I	20850	U.S. - Alabama	20850
I	20850	U.S. - Georgia	20850

V   *Aster kantoensis* Kitam. 10573

V	10573	Japan	10573

R   *Aster kingii* D.C. Eat. 20850

R	20850	U.S. - Utah	20850

E   *Aster kingii* D.C. Eat. var. *barnebyana* (Welsh & Goodrich) Welsh 20850

E	20850	U.S. - Utah	20850

V   *Aster kingii* D.C. Eat. var. *kingii* 20850

V	20850	U.S. - Utah	20850

V   *Aster laevis* A.G. Jones var. *guadalupensis* A.G. Jones 20850

V	20850	U.S. - New Mexico	20850
E	20850	U.S. - Texas	20850

V   *Aster lentus* Greene 20850

V	20850	U.S. - California	20850

V   *Aster linosyris* (L.) Bernh. ssp. *armoricanus* (Rouy) Kerguélen 20528

V	20528	France	20528

V   *Aster mirabilis* Torr. & Gray 20850

V	20850	U.S. - North Carolina	20850
I	20850	U.S. - South Carolina	20850

V   *Aster mollis* Rydb. 20850

V	20850	U.S. - Wyoming	20850

R   *Aster morrisonensis* Hayata 20511

R	20511	Taiwan	20511

E   *Aster nahanniensis* Cody 20850, 6796

E	20850	Canada - Mackenzie	20850

V   *Aster paludicola* Piper 20850

I	20850	U.S. - California	20850
I	20850	U.S. - Oregon	20850

R   *Aster peirsonii* C.W. Sharsmith 20850

I	20850	U.S. - California	20850

V   *Aster puniceus* L. var. *scabricaulis* (Shinn.) A.G. Jones 20850

V	20850	U.S. - Texas	20850

R   *Aster rugulosus* Maxim. var. *shibukawaensis* Kitam. & Murata 10573

R	10573	Japan	10573

E   *Aster saxicastellii* J.N. Campbell & M. Medley 20850

E	20850	U.S. - Kentucky	20850
E	20850	U.S. - Tennessee	20850

R   *Aster sibiricus* L. var. *pygmaeus* (Lindl.) Cody 20850

I	20850	Canada - Mackenzie	20850
E	20850	U.S. - Alaska	20850

R   *Aster sohayakiensis* Koidz. 10573

R	10573	Japan	10573

R   *Aster sorrentinii* (Tod.) Lojac. 17891

R	18264	Italy - Sicily (north centre & central parts)	20738

E   *Aster spinulosus* Chapman 20850

E	20850	U.S. - Florida	20850

E   *Aster subulatus* Michx. var. *obtusifolius* Fern. 20850

E	20850	Canada - New Brunswick	20850

R   *Aster takasagomontanus* Sasaki 20511

R	20511	Taiwan	20511

R   *Aster tarbagatensis* (K.Koch) Merxm. 8000, 20171

R		Russia (E.Europe) - South (South-East)	8000

R   *Aster tenuipes* Makino 10573

R	10573	Japan	10573

V   *Aster vialis* (Bradshaw) Blake 20850

V	20850	U.S. - Oregon	20850

V   *Aster wasatchensis* (M.E.Jones) Blake 20850

I	20850	U.S. - Arizona	20850
I	20850	U.S. - Utah	20850

V   *Aster yakushimensis* (Kitam.) Soejima & Yahara 10573

V	10573	Japan	10573

E   *Aster yukonensis* Cronq. 20850, 6796

E	20850	Canada - Mackenzie	20850
E	20850	Canada - Yukon Territory	20850
E	20850	U.S. - Alaska	20850

R   *Asteriscus pinifolius* Maire & Wilczek

R		Morocco	

E   *Asteriscus schultzii* (Bolle) Pitard & Proust

E	15105	Spain - Canary Is.	15105

I   *Athanasia capitata* (L.) L. 20604

I	20604	South Africa - Cape Province	20604

R   *Athanasia grandiceps* Hilliard & B.L.Burtt 20604

R	20604	South Africa - Natal	20604

V   *Athanasia rugulosa* E.Mey. ex DC. 20604

V	20604	South Africa - Cape Province	20604

I   *Athrixia fontinalis* Wild 7754

I		Zimbabwe (Chimanimani)	7754

R   *Athrixia subsimplex* Brenan 7849

R		Malawi	7849

E   *Atractylis arbuscula* Svent. & Michaelis 14166

E	15105	Spain - Canary Is.	17891

R   *Atractylis boulosii* Tackh.

R		Egypt	

I   *Atractylis caerulea* Battand. 10488

I	14958	Algeria	10488

E   *Atractylis preauxiana* Schultz Bip. 14166

E	15105	Spain - Canary Is.	17891

R   *Atractylis tutinii* Franco 20171

R		Spain	

E   *Axiniphyllum durangense* B. Turner 20883

I	20883	Mexico	20883

R   *Axiniphyllum durangensis* B. Turner 14294

R	14294	Mexico - Durango	14294

I   *Baccharis barragensis* Cuatrec. *19352*
    I   *19352* Colombia *19352*

I   *Baccharis floribundoides* Cuatrec. *19352*
    I   *19352* Colombia *19352*

I   *Baccharis grandiflora* Kunth ssp. *farallonensis*
     Cuatrec. *19352*
    I   *19352* Colombia *19352*

V   *Baccharis kingii* Cuatr. *20883*
    I   *20883* Peru *20883*

E   *Baccharis libertadensis* (S. B. Jones) H.
     Robinson *20883*
    I   *20883* Peru *20883*

I   *Baccharis macrantha* Kunth ssp. *caucanensis*
     Cuatrec. *19352*
    I   *19352* Colombia *19352*

R   *Baccharis orientalis* (Alain) Borh. *5607*
    R   *19105* Cuba (Las Tunas) *5607*

I   *Baccharis paramicola* Cuatrec. *19352*
    I   *19352* Colombia *19352*

R   *Baccharis solomonii* H. Robinson *20883*
    I   *20883* Bolivia *20883*

R   *Baccharis steetzii* Andersson *11117*
    R   Ecuador - Galapagos *11117*

E   *Baccharis vanessae* Beauchamp *20850*
    E   *20850* U.S. - California *20850*

V   *Bafutia tenuicaulis* C. Adams
    V   Cameroon

V   *Balduina atropurpurea* Harper *20850*
    E   *20850* U.S. - Alabama *20850*
    E   *20850* U.S. - Florida *20850*
    V   *20850* U.S. - Georgia *20850*
    Ex/E *20850* U.S. - North Carolina *20850*
    I   *20850* U.S. - South Carolina *20850*

R   *Balsamorhiza macrolepis* Sharp *20850*
    I   *20850* U.S. - California *20850*
    I   *20850* U.S. - Nevada *20850*
    I   *20850* U.S. - Oregon *20850*

V   *Balsamorhiza macrolepis* Sharp var.
     macrolepis *20850*
    V   *20850* U.S. - California *20850*

R   *Barnadesia macbridei* Ferreyra *18200*
    R   *12468* Peru *18200*

R   *Barnadesia wurdackii* Ferreyra *18200*
    R   *12468* Peru *18200*

E   *Barrosoa atlantica* R. M. King & H. Robinson *20883*
    I   *20883* Brazil *20883*

E   *Bartlettina chiriquensis* K. & R. *20883, 9706*
    I   *20883* Panama *20883*

E   *Bartlettina maxonii* (Rob.) K. & R. *20883, 9006*
    I   *20883* Panama *20883*

E   *Bartlettina tamaulipana* (B. L. Turner) R. M. King & H.
     Robinson *20883*
    I   *20883* Mexico *20883*

V   *Basedowia tenerrima* (F.Muell. & Tate) J.Black *20681*
    V   *20681* Australia - South Australia *20681*

I   *Bellis azorica* Hochst. *20171*
    I   *19174* Portugal - Azores *19174*

V   *Bellium crassifolium* Moris *20171*
    V   *20805* Italy - Sardinia *20805*

R   *Berardia subacaulis* Vill. *18264, 20171*

    R   France *8000*
    V   *18264* Italy (Piedmont) *18264*

R   *Berkheya draco* Roessler *20604*
    R   *20604* South Africa - Natal *20604*

R   *Berkheya dregei* Harv. *20604*
    R   *20604* South Africa - Cape Province *20604*

R   *Berkheya francisci* Bolus *20604*
    R   *20604* South Africa - Cape Province *20604*

R   *Berkheya johnstoniana* Britten *7757*
    R   Malawi (Mlanje) *7757*

R   *Berkheya leucaugeta* Hilliard *20604*
    R   *20604* South Africa - Natal *20604*

R   *Berlandiera subacaulis* (Nutt.) Nutt. *20850*
    R   *20850* U.S. - Florida *20850*

I   *Bidens ahnnei* Sherff
    I   French Polynesia - Marquesas Is

R   *Bidens amplectens* Sherff *20850*
    R   *20850* U.S. - Hawaii *20850*

R   *Bidens amplissima* Greene *20850, 14362*
    R   *20850* Canada - British Columbia *20850*

E   *Bidens aoraiensis* J.Grant ex Sherff *20845*
    E   *20845* French Polynesia - Society Is. (Tahiti) *20845*

R   *Bidens asymmetrica* (Levl.) Sherff *20850*
    I   *20850* U.S. - Hawaii *20850*

I   *Bidens australis* K.P. Sprengel *20845*
    I   *20845* French Polynesia - Society Is. *20845*

R   *Bidens bidentoides* (Nutt.) Britt. *20850*
    E   *20850* U.S. - Delaware *20850*
    R   *20850* U.S. - Maryland *20850*
    V   *20850* U.S. - New Jersey *20850*
    R   *20850* U.S. - New York *20850*
    E   *20850* U.S. - Pennsylvania *20850*

I   *Bidens bipontina* Sherff *20845*
    I   *20845* French Polynesia - Marquesas Is *20845*

V   *Bidens campylotheca* Schultz-Bip. *20850*
    I   *20850* U.S. - Hawaii *20850*

V   *Bidens campylotheca* Schultz-Bip. ssp.
     campylotheca *20850, 14209*
    V   *20850* U.S. - Hawaii *20850*

V   *Bidens campylotheca* Schultz-Bip. ssp. *pentamera*
     (Sherff) Ganders & Nagata *20850, 14209*
    V   *20850* U.S. - Hawaii *20850*

E   *Bidens campylotheca* Schultz-Bip. ssp. *waihoiensis*
     St.John *20850, 14209*
    E   *20850* U.S. - Hawaii (east Maui) *20850*

R   *Bidens cervicata* Sherff *20850, 14209*
    R   *20850* U.S. - Hawaii *20850*

E   *Bidens clarendonensis* Britton *20883, 13336*
    E   *13336* Jamaica *20883*

I   *Bidens collina* Degener & Sherff *20845*
    I   *20845* French Polynesia - Marquesas Is (Hiva Oa) *20845*

E   *Bidens conjuncta* Sherff *20850, 14209*
    E   *20850* U.S. - Hawaii (West Maui) *20850*

R   *Bidens conjunctata* Sherff *14209*
    R   *14209* U.S. - Hawaii (West Maui) *14209*

E   *Bidens cordifolia* Schultz-Bip. *20845*
    E   *20845* French Polynesia - Marquesas Is (Nuka Hiva) *20845*

Magnoliopsida (dicots): Compositae: *Bidens*

V   ***Bidens cosmoides*** (Gray) Sherff *20850, 14209*
    I   *20850* U.S. - Hawaii *20850*

I   ***Bidens deltoidea*** J.Moore *20845*
    I   *20845* French Polynesia - Society Is. (Raiatea) *20845*

V   ***Bidens dissecta*** (O.E. Schultz) Sherff *20883, 13336*
    V   *13336* Jamaica *20883*

V   ***Bidens eatonii*** Fern. *20850, 5567*
    V   *20850* Canada - Quebec *20850*

E   ***Bidens forbesii*** Sherff ssp. ***kahiliensis*** Ganders & Nagata *20850, 14209*
    E   *20850* U.S. - Hawaii (Kaua`i) *20850*

I   ***Bidens glandulifera*** M.Grant ex Sherff *20845*
    I   *20845* French Polynesia - Society Is. (Bora Bora) *20845*

V   ***Bidens hendersonensis*** Sherff var. ***hendersonensis*** *8050*
    V   *19185* Pitcairn (Henderson Is.) *17673*

Ex/E   ***Bidens hendersonensis*** Sherff var. ***oenoensis*** Sherff *8616*
    Ex/E   *19185* Pitcairn (Oeno) *8616*

I   ***Bidens hendersonensis*** Sherff var. ***subspathulata*** Sherff *8050*
    I   *17673* Pitcairn (Henderson Is.) *8050*

I   ***Bidens henryi*** Sherff *20845*
    I   *20845* French Polynesia - Marquesas Is (Hiva Oa) *20845*

V   ***Bidens heterodoxa*** (Fern.) Fern. & St. John *20850, 5567*
    E   *20850* Canada - Prince Edward Is. *20850*
    V   *20850* Canada - Quebec *20850*
    Ex/E   *20850* U.S. - Connecticut *20850*
    I   *20850* U.S. - New Jersey *20850*
    I   *20850* U.S. - Wyoming *20850*

R   ***Bidens hillebrandiana*** (Drake) O. Deg. *20850, 14209*
    I   *20850* U.S. - Hawaii *20850*

V   ***Bidens hivaoana*** O.Degener & Sherff *20845*
    V   *20845* French Polynesia - Marquesas Is (Hiva Oa) *20845*

I   ***Bidens jardinii*** Schultz-Bip. *20845*
    I   *20845* French Polynesia - Marquesas Is *20845*

V   ***Bidens mathewsii*** Sherff *19184*
    V   *19185* Pitcairn (Pitcairn Island) *19186*

R   ***Bidens mauiensis*** (Gray) Sherff *20850*
    R   *20850* U.S. - Hawaii *20850*

E   ***Bidens micrantha*** Gaudich ssp. ***ctenophylla*** (Sherff) Nagata & Ganders *20850, 14209*
    E   *20850* U.S. - Hawaii *20850*

E   ***Bidens micrantha*** (Sherff) ssp. ***kalealaha*** Nagata & Ganders *20850, 14209*
    E   *20850* U.S. - Hawaii (Maui, Lana`i) *20850*

E   ***Bidens molokaiensis*** (Hbd.) Sherff *20850, 14209*
    E   *20850* U.S. - Hawaii (O`ahu, Molokai) *20850*

E   ***Bidens orofenensis*** M.Grant ex Sherff *20845*
    E   *20845* French Polynesia - Society Is. (Tahiti) *20845*

R   ***Bidens polycephala*** Schultz-Bip.
    R   *20845* French Polynesia - Marquesas Is *20845*

E   ***Bidens populifolia*** Sherff *20850, 14209*
    E   *20850* U.S. - Hawaii (O`ahu - Ko`olau Mts.) *20850*

R   ***Bidens reptans*** var. ***tomentosa*** O.E. Schultz *20883*
    R   *20883* Jamaica *20883*

E   ***Bidens saint-johniana*** Sherff *20845*
    E   *20845* French Polynesia - Tubuai Is. (Marotiri) *20845*

E   ***Bidens sandvicensis*** Less ssp. ***confusa*** Nagata & Ganders *20850, 14209*
    E   *20850* U.S. - Hawaii (Kaua`i) *20850*

I   ***Bidens serrulata*** (Schultz-Bip.) Sherff
    I   French Polynesia - Marquesas Is

R   ***Bidens teikiteetinii*** Florence & Stuessy *20845*
    R   *20845* French Polynesia - Marquesas Is (Nukua Hiva) *20845*

V   ***Bidens trelawniensis*** Proctor *20883, 13336*
    V   *13336* Jamaica *20883*

I   ***Bidens uapensis*** (F. Brown) Sherff
    I   *20845* French Polynesia - Marquesas Is *20826*

R   ***Bidens valida*** Sherff *20850, 14209*
    R   *20850* U.S. - Hawaii (Kaua`i) *20850*

E   ***Bidens wiebkei*** Sherff *20850, 14209*
    E   *20850* U.S. - Hawaii (Moloka`i) *20850*

R   ***Bigelowia nuttallii*** L.C. Anders. *20850*
    V   *20850* U.S. - Alabama *20850*
    E   *20850* U.S. - Florida *20850*
    R   *20850* U.S. - Georgia *20850*
    I   *20850* U.S. - Louisiana *20850*
    R   *20850* U.S. - Texas *20850*

V   ***Blennosperma bakeri*** Heiser *20850*
    V   *20850* U.S. - California *20850*

E   ***Blennosperma nanum*** (Hook.)Blake var. ***robustum*** J.T. Howell *20850*
    E   *20850* U.S. - California *20850*

E   ***Blepharizonia plumosa*** (Kellogg) Greene ssp. ***plumosa*** *20850*
    E   *20850* U.S. - California *20850*

I   ***Blumea angustifolia*** Thwaites *8021*
    I   *16162* Sri Lanka *8021*

I   ***Blumea crinita*** Arn. *8021*
    I   *16162* Sri Lanka *8021*

R   ***Blumea formosana*** Kitamura *20511*
    R   *20511* Taiwan *20511*

R   ***Blumea linearifolia*** Peng & Leu. *20511*
    R   *20511* Taiwan *20511*

V   ***Boltonia apalachicolensis*** L.C. Anders. *20850*
    V   *20850* U.S. - Florida *20850*

V   ***Brachanthemum baranovii*** (Kraschen. & Polj.) Kraschen. *5942*
    V   *11552* Russia (Siberia) - West (southern) *20627*

R   ***Brachycome humile*** G. Simpson & J. Thomson
    R   New Zealand - South Is.

R   ***Brachycome linearis*** (Petrie) Druce
    R   New Zealand - South Is.

V   ***Brachycome neocaledonica*** Guillaumin *20893*
    V   *20893* New Caledonia *20893*

V   ***Brachycome sarasinii*** Däniker *20893*
    V   *20893* New Caledonia *20893*

R   ***Brachycome segmentosa*** C. Moore & F. Muell.
    R   *14225* Australia - NSW - Lord Howe Is. *14225*

R **Brachyglottis arborescens** W. Oliver *86*
   R   *19305* New Zealand - North Is. (Three Kings Island) *19305*

R **Brachyglottis brunonis** (Hook.f.) B.Nord. *20681*
   R   *20681* Australia - Tasmania *20681*

R **Brachyglottis compacta** (Kirk) Nordenstam *19305*
   R   *19305* New Zealand - North Is. *19305*

R **Brachyglottis huntii** (Muell.) Nordenstam *19305*
   R   *20625* New Zealand - Chatham Is. *19305*

R **Brachyglottis pentacopa** (Drury) Nordenstam *19305*
   R   *19305* New Zealand - North Is. *19305*

I **Brachyglottis saxifragoides** (Hook fil.)
    Nordenstam *19305*
   I   *19305* New Zealand *19305*

R **Brachyscome ascendens** G.Davis *20681*
   I   *20681* Australia - New South Wales *20681*
   I   *20681* Australia - Queensland *20681*

R **Brachyscome eriogona** (J.Black) G.Davis *20681*
   I   *20681* Australia - Queensland *20681*
   I   *20681* Australia - South Australia *20681*

R **Brachyscome humilis** *19305*
   R   *19305* New Zealand - South Is. *19305*

R **Brachyscome linearis** *19305*
   R   *19305* New Zealand - South Is. *19305*

E **Brachyscome muelleri** Sonder *20681*
   E   *20681* Australia - South Australia *20681*

V **Brachyscome muelleroides** G.Davis *20681*
   I   *20681* Australia - New South Wales *20681*
   I   *20681* Australia - Victoria *20681*

V **Brachyscome papillosa** G.Davis *20681*
   V   *20681* Australia - New South Wales *20681*

R **Brachyscome petrophila** G.Davis *20681*
   R   *20681* Australia - Victoria *20681*

R **Brachyscome riparia** G.Davis *20681*
   R   *20681* Australia - Victoria *20681*

R **Brachyscome sieberi** DC. var. *gunnii*
    DC. *20681*
   R   *20681* Australia - Tasmania *20681*

R **Brachyscome stolonifera** G.Davis *20681*
   R   *20681* Australia - New South Wales *20681*

R **Brachyscome xanthocarpa** D.Cooke *20681*
   R   *20681* Australia - South Australia *20681*

V **Brickellia baccharidea** Gray *20883, 20850*
   I   *20850* U.S. - Arizona *20850*
   I   *20850* U.S. - New Mexico *20850*
   E   *20850* U.S. - Texas *20850*
   E   *20883* Mexico *20883*

V **Brickellia brachyphylla** (A.Gray) A.Gray var.
    hinckleyi (Standl.) Flyr *20850*
   V   *20850* U.S. - Texas *20850*

Ex/E **Brickellia brachyphylla** (A.Gray) A.Gray var.
    terlinguensis Flyr *20850*
   Ex/E *20850* U.S. - Texas *20850*

Ex/E **Brickellia chenopodina** (Greene) B.L. Robins. *20850,*
    14662
   Ex/E *20850* U.S. - New Mexico *20850*

V **Brickellia cordifolia** Ell. *20850*
   V   *20850* U.S. - Alabama *20850*
   V   *20850* U.S. - Florida *20850*
   E   *20850* U.S. - Georgia *20850*

R **Brickellia dentata** (DC.) Schultz-Bip. *20850, 8058*
   R   *20850* U.S. - Texas *20850*
   ?   Mexico *10836*

E **Brickellia eupatorioides** (L.) Shinners var.
    floridana (R.W.Long) B.L.Turner *20850*
   E   *20850* U.S. - Florida *20850*

R **Brickellia eupatorioides** (L.) Shinners var.
    gracillima (Gray) B.L.Turner *20883, 20850*
   R   *20850* U.S. - Texas *20850*
   I   *20883* Mexico *20883*

R **Brickellia parvula** Gray *20850*
   I   *20850* U.S. - Arizona *20850*
   E   *20850* U.S. - Texas *20850*

E **Brickellia viejensis** Flyr *20850*
   E   *20850* U.S. - Texas *20850*

R **Bubonium longiradiatum** Maire
   R   Morocco

R **Buphthalmum inuloides** Moris *8000, 20171*
   R   *18264* Italy - Sardinia (extreme north) *8000*

R **Cacalia amagiensis** Kitam. *10573*
   R   *10573* Japan *10573*

R **Cacalia kiushiana** Makino *10573*
   R   *10573* Japan *10573*

R **Cacalia nokoensis** Masamune & Susuki *20511*
   R   *20511* Taiwan *20511*

R **Cacalia peltifolia** Makino *10573*
   R   *10573* Japan *10573*

R **Cacalia pseudo-taimingasa** Nakai *15957*
   R   *15923* Korea, South (Mt Chiri, Mt Tokyu) *15957*

R **Cacalia shikokiana** Makino *10573*
   R   *10573* Japan *10573*

R **Cacalia yakusimense** Masam. *10573*
   R   *10573* Japan *10573*

E **Cadiscus aquaticus** E.Mey. *20604*
   E   *20604* South Africa - Cape Province *20604*

E **Calea bucaramangensis** Pruski & Urbatsch *20883*
   I   *20883* Colombia *20883*

E **Calea crocinervosa** Wussow, Urbatsch, & G.A.
    Sullivan *20883, 12020*
   I   *20883* Mexico *20883*

R **Calea fluviatilis** S.F. Blake *9004*
   R   *12020* Belize *9004*

V **Calea fruticosa** (Gardner) Urbatsch, Zlotsky &
    Pruski *20883*
   I   *20883* Brazil *20883*

V **Calea sickii** (Barroso) Urbastsch, Zlotsky &
    Pruski *20883*
   I   *20883* Brazil *20883*

V **Calea ternifolia** (Robinson) Wussow, Urbatsch, & G. A.
    Sullivan var. *calyculata* (Rob.) Wussow, Urb. & G.A.
    Sul. *20883, 12020*
   I   *20883* Mexico *20883*

V **Calea urticifolia** Wussow, Urbatsch, & G. A. Sullivan var.
    yucatanensis Wussow, Urb.,& G.A. Sullivan *20883, 12020*
   I   *20883* Mexico *20883*

I **Calendula exilis** Font Quer & Sennen
   I   Spain

V **Calendula maderensis** DC. *17891*
   V   Portugal - Madeira *17891*

V   *Calendula suffruticosa* Vahl ssp. *maritima* (Guss.)
      Meikle *18264, 20171*
      V   *18264*   Italy - Sicily *18264*

I   *Calendula vidalii* Pau
      I   Morocco

R   *Callilepis leptophylla* Harv. *20039*
      R   *20039*   Southern Africa *20039*
      I   *20039*   Swaziland *20039*

V   *Calotis glandulosa* F.Muell. *20681*
      V   *20681*   Australia - New South Wales *20681*

V   *Calotis moorei* P.S.Short *20681*
      V   *20681*   Australia - New South Wales *20681*

R   *Calotis suffruticosa* Domin *20681*
      R   *20681*   Australia - Queensland *20681*

V   *Calycadenia fremontii* Gray *20850*
      V   *20850*   U.S. - California *20850*

R   *Calycadenia hispida* (Greene) Greene *20850*
      I   *20850*   U.S. - California *20850*

R   *Calycadenia hooveri* G.D.Carr *20850*
      R   *20850*   U.S. - California *20850*

R   *Calycadenia mollis* Gray *20850*
      I   *20850*   U.S. - California *20850*

R   *Calycadenia pauciflora* Gray *20850*
      I   *20850*   U.S. - California *20850*

R   *Calycadenia spicata* (Greene) Greene *20850*
      I   *20850*   U.S. - California *20850*

E   *Calycadenia truncata* DC. ssp. *microcephala* Hall ex
      Keck *20850*
      E   *20850*   U.S. - California *20850*

E   *Calycadenia villosa* DC. *20850*
      E   *20850*   U.S. - California *20850*

R   *Camchaya eberhardtii* (Gagnepain) Kitam. *6057*
      R   Vietnam *6057*

R   *Cancriniella krascheninnikovii* (Rubtzov)
      Tzvelev *5942*
      R   *5942*   Kazakhstan (south-east) *5942*

R   *Carduncellus araneosus* Boiss. & Reuter ssp.
      pseudomitissimus Rivas Goday & Rivas Mart.
      R   Spain

R   *Carduncellus dianius* Webb *11496*
      R   *19174*   Spain (north-east Alicante) *20692*
      R   *11496*   Spain - Balearic Is. (Ibiza) *11496*

E   *Carduncellus ilicifolius* Pomel *10488*
      E   *14958*   Algeria *10488*

R   *Carduncellus strictus* (Pomel) Hanelt *10504*
      R   *14958*   Algeria *10504*

R   *Carduus acanthoides* L. ssp. *sintenisii*
      Kazmi *12840*
      R   *12840*   Turkey *12840*

R   *Carduus adpressus* C.A.Mey. *8000, 20171*
      R   *5204*   Bulgaria (Southern - two sites only)
              5204

V   *Carduus aurosicus* Vill. *20171*
      V   *20528*   France (southeastern) *20528*

V   *Carduus baeocephalus* Webb
      V   *15105*   Spain - Canary Is. *15105*

V   *Carduus bourgaei* Kazmi *10260*
      V   *15105*   Spain - Canary Is. *15105*

R   *Carduus cronicus* Boiss et Heldr. ssp. *baldaccii*

      Kazmi *20178*
      R   *20178*   Albania *20178*

R   *Carduus kerneri* Simonk. ssp. *lobulatiformis*
      (Csürrs & E.J. Nyárády) Soó *17823, 20171*
      R   *19949*   Romania *20631*

R   *Carduus nutans* L. ssp. *falcato-incurvus*
      Davis *12840*
      R   *12840*   Turkey *12840*

R   *Carduus nutans* L. ssp. *trojanus*
      Davis *12840*
      R   *12840*   Turkey *12840*

R   *Carduus onopordioides* Fisch. ex Bieb. ssp. *turcicus*
      (Kazmi) Davis *12840*
      R   *12840*   Turkey *12840*

R   *Carduus paui* Devesa & Talav. *11496*
      R   *11496*   Spain (Iberian Mts.) *20692*

R   *Carduus ramosissimus* Pancic *20178, 20171*
      R   *20178*   Albania *20178*
      K   *21091*   Bosnia & Herzegovina *21091*
      R   (former) Yugoslavia

R   *Carduus rechingeranus* Kazmi *12840*
      R   *12840*   Turkey *12840*

V   *Carduus squarrosus* (DC.) Lowe
      V   Portugal - Madeira

R   *Carduus thracicus* (Velen.) Hayek *5204, 20171*
      R   *5204*   Bulgaria (Southern and eastern - five sites)
              5204

R   *Carlina barnebiana* B.L.Burtt & P.H.Davis *20171*
      R   *20730*   Greece - Crete *20730*

V   *Carlina canariensis* Pitard *20750*
      V   *20750*   Spain - Canary Is. *15105*

I   *Carlina cirsioides* Klokov *20171*
      I   *5942*   Ukraine *5942*

V   *Carlina diae* (Rech.f.) Meusel & Kästner *20171*
      V   *20730*   Greece - Crete *20730*

R   *Carlina fiumensis* Simonk. *20171*
      R   (former) Yugoslavia

R   *Carlina oligocephala* Boiss. & Kotschy ssp.
      pallescens (Wettst.) Muesel & Kastner *12840*
      R   *12840*   Turkey *12840*

V   *Carlina onopordifolia* Besser ex Szafer, Kulcz. &
      Pawl. *5942, 20171*
      V   *18216*   Poland (south) *20800*
      I   *5942*   Ukraine *5942*

V   *Carlina sitiensis* Rech.f. *20171*
      V   *20730*   Greece - Crete (inc. Kasos) *20730*

R   *Carlina texedae* Marrero *20750*
      R   *20750*   Spain - Canary Is. *20750*

E   *Carminatia alvarezii* Rzedowski & Calderón *20883*
      I   *20883*   Mexico *20883*

R   *Carthamus rhiphaeus* Font Quer & Pau
      R   Morocco

R   *Cassinia amoena* Cheeseman
      R   New Zealand - North Is.

R   *Cassinia collina* C.White *20681*
      R   *20681*   Australia - Queensland *20681*

V   *Cassinia rugata* N.G.Walsh *20681*
      V   *20681*   Australia - Victoria *20681*

R   *Cassinia tenuifolia* Benth.

R 14225 Australia - NSW - Lord Howe Is. *14225*

V **Catamixis baccharoides** Thomson *11494*

   V *11494* India - Uttar Pradesh (Siwalik & Tehri, Garwhal) *11494*

E **Celmisia adamsii** Kirk var. *adamsii* *86*

   E New Zealand - North Is.

V **Celmisia adamsii** Kirk var. *rugosula* Cheeseman *19305*

   V *19305* New Zealand - North Is. *19305*

R **Celmisia cordatifolia** Buchan. var. *similis* W. Martin

   R New Zealand - South Is.

E **Celmisia macmahonii** Kirk var. *macmahonii* *19305*

   E *19305* New Zealand - South Is. *19305*

R **Celmisia morganii** Cheeseman *19305*

   R *19305* New Zealand - South Is. *19305*

R **Celmisia philocremna** Given *5815*

   R *5815* New Zealand - South Is. *5815*

R **Celmisia sericophylla** J.H.Willis *20681*

   R *20681* Australia - Victoria *20681*

R **Celmisia spedeni** G. Simpson *19305*

   R *19305* New Zealand - South Is. *19305*

R **Celmisia thomsonii** Cheeseman *19305*

   R *19305* New Zealand - South Is. *19305*

I **Cenia duckittiae** L.Bolus *20604*

   I *20604* South Africa - Cape Province *20604*

R **Centaurea achaia** Boiss. & Heldr. *20171*

   R Greece

V **Centaurea akamantis** T. Georgiades & G. Chatzikyriakou *20007*

   V *20710* Cyprus (Akamas) *18271*

E **Centaurea alba** L. ssp. *heldreichii* (Halacsy) Dostal *8000, 20171*

   E Greece (west) *8000*

E **Centaurea alba** L. ssp. *princeps* (Boiss. & Heldr.) Gugler *8000, 20171*

   E Greece *17891*

R **Centaurea amaena** Boiss. & Bal. *12840*

   R *12840* Turkey *12840*

R **Centaurea amanicola** Hub.-Mor. *12840*

   R *12840* Turkey *12840*

R **Centaurea androssovii** Iljin *8001*

   R former USSR *6930*

R **Centaurea anthemifolia** Hub.-Mor. *12840*

   R *12840* Turkey *12840*

R **Centaurea antiochia** Boiss. *12840*

   R *12840* Turkey *12840*

R **Centaurea antitauria** Hayek *12840*

   R *12840* Turkey *12840*

R **Centaurea aphrodisea** Boiss. *12840*

   R *12840* Turkey *12840*

R **Centaurea aplolepa** Moretti ssp. *aeolica* (Guss. ex Lojac.) Dostál *20171*

   R *20171* France *20171*

R **Centaurea argecillensis** Gredilla *20171*

   R Spain

R **Centaurea arguta** Nees *10198*

   R Spain - Canary Is. *10198*

R **Centaurea arifolia** Boiss. *12840*

   R *12840* Turkey *12840*

R **Centaurea arpensis** (Czerep.) Wagentiz *8001*

   R former USSR *6930*

V **Centaurea ascalonica** Bornm. *8895*

   V Israel *8895*

R **Centaurea aucherana** DC. *12840*

   R *12840* Turkey *12840*

R **Centaurea austro-anatolica** Hub.-Mor. *12840*

   R *12840* Turkey *12840*

I **Centaurea bagadensis** Woronow *5942*

   I *5942* Russia - North Caucasus *5942*

   I *5942* Transcaucasus *5942*

V **Centaurea balbisiana** Soldano ssp. *aemilii* (Briq.) Kerguélen *20528*

   V *20528* France (Alpes-Maritimes) *20528*

R **Centaurea balbisiana** Soldano ssp. *jordaniana* (Gren. & Godron) Kerguélen *20528*

   R *20528* France (Alpes-de-Haute-Provence) *20528*

V **Centaurea balbisiana** Soldano ssp. *verguinii* (Briq. & Cavill.) Kerguélen *20528*

   V *20528* France (Alpes-Maritimes) *20528*

V **Centaurea baldaccii** Degen ex Baldacci *20171*

   V *20730* Greece - Crete *20730*

R **Centaurea balearica** Rodr. *8000, 20171*

   R *20645* Spain - Balearic Is. *8000*

I **Centaurea barbeyi** (Albov) Sosn. *5942*

   I *5942* Transcaucasus *5942*

R **Centaurea biokovensis** Teyber *20171*

   R (former) Yugoslavia

I **Centaurea boissieri** DC. ssp. *spachii* (Sch.Bip. ex Willk.) Dostál *20171*

   I *20874* Spain (Albacete & Valencia) *8000*

R **Centaurea bombycina** Boiss. ex DC. *11496*

   R *11496* Spain (Málaga, Granada) *11496*

E **Centaurea borjae** Valdes-Berm. & Rivas Goday *17891*

   E *11496* Spain (La Coruña) *17891*

R **Centaurea bourgaei** Boiss. *12840*

   R *12840* Turkey *12840*

I **Centaurea bovina** Velen. *20171*

   I Bulgaria

R **Centaurea brevifimbriata** Hub.-Mor. *12840*

   R *12840* Turkey *12840*

R **Centaurea calcitrapa** L. ssp. *cilicica* (Boiss. & Bal.) Wagenitz *12840*

   R *12840* Turkey *12840*

R **Centaurea candelabrum** Hayek & Kosanin *20178, 20171*

   R *20178* Albania *20178*

R **Centaurea cariensiformis** Hub.-Mor. *12840*

   R *12840* Turkey *12840*

R **Centaurea cariensis** Boiss. *12840*

   R *12840* Turkey *12840*

R **Centaurea cariensis** Boiss. ssp. *maculiceps* (O.Schwarz) Wagenitz *20731*

   R *20731* Greece - East Aegean Is *20731*

R **Centaurea carpatica** (Porcius) Porcius *20171*

   R *19947* Romania *8001*

   R *5942* Ukraine *5942*

R **Centaurea carpatica** (Porc.) Porc. ssp. *rarauensis*

	(Prodan) Cioc. *19955*		
R	19947 Romania *20631*		
R	*Centaurea carratracensis* Lange *11496*		
R	11496 Spain (Málaga, Sierra Carratrata) *11496*		
I	*Centaurea castellanoides* Talav.		
I	Spain		
R	*Centaurea cataonica* Boiss. & Hausskn. *12840*		
R	12840 Turkey *12840*		
R	*Centaurea chalcidicaea* Hayek *20171*		
R	Greece		
R	*Centaurea chaldaeorum* Nab. *12840*		
R	12840 Turkey *12840*		
R	*Centaurea cheirolepidoides* Wagenitz *12840*		
R	12840 Turkey *12840*		
R	*Centaurea chrysantha* Wagenitz *12840*		
R	12840 Turkey *12840*		
R	*Centaurea chrysocephala* Phitos & Georgiadis		
R	Greece		
R	*Centaurea citricolor* Font Quer *17891*		
R	20874 Spain (Sierra Morena) *20874*		
R	*Centaurea clementei* Boiss. ex DC. *20171*		
R	Spain		
R	*Centaurea corcubionensis* M. Lainz *11496*		
R	11496 Spain *11496*		
R	*Centaurea cordubiensis* Font Quer		
R	20660 Spain (Córdoba, Sevilla, Badajot) *11496*		
R	*Centaurea corinthia* Boiss. & Heldr. *20731*		
R	20731 Greece (Sterea Ellas) *20731*		
V	*Centaurea corymbosa* Pourr. *8000, 20171*		
V	20528 France (Aude) *20528*		
R	*Centaurea crithmifolia* Vis. *20171*		
R	(former) Yugoslavia		
R	*Centaurea cuspidata* Vis. *20171*		
R	(former) Yugoslavia		
V	*Centaurea cyrenaica* Beguinot & Vaccari		
V	Libya		
R	*Centaurea cytherea* Rech.f. *20171*		
R	Greece		
R	*Centaurea dalmatica* A.Kern. *20171*		
R	(former) Yugoslavia		
R	*Centaurea davisii* Wagenitz *12840*		
R	12840 Turkey *12840*		
V	*Centaurea deflexa* Wagenitz *12840*		
V	12840 Turkey *12840*		
R	*Centaurea demirizii* Wagenitz *12840*		
R	12840 Turkey *12840*		
R	*Centaurea derderiifolia* Wagenitz *12840*		
R	12840 Turkey *12840*		
V	*Centaurea dichroa* Boiss. & Heldr. *12840*		
V	12840 Turkey *12840*		
R	*Centaurea drabifolioides* Hub.-Mor. *12840*		
R	12840 Turkey *12840*		
R	*Centaurea dubjanskii* Iljin		
R	former European USSR		
R	*Centaurea ducellieri* Battand.		
R	Morocco		
R	*Centaurea ebenoides* Heldr. ex S.Moore *20171*		
R	Greece		

R	*Centaurea emigrantis* Bubani *11496*
R	11496 Spain *11496*
R	*Centaurea ensiformis* Davis *12840*
R	12840 Turkey *12840*
R	*Centaurea eriosiphon* Emberger & Maire
R	Morocco
R	*Centaurea exarata* Boiss. ex Coss. *20171*
E	20076 Portugal *20076*
R	Spain
V	*Centaurea forojulensis* (Poldini) Poldini *18264*
V	18264 Italy (Friuli-Venezia-Giulia) *18264*
V	*Centaurea fraylensis* Sch.Bip. ex Nyman *8000, 20171*
V	20076 Portugal *20076*
R	*Centaurea friderici* Vis. *20171*
R	(former) Yugoslavia
R	*Centaurea gadorensis* G. Blanca *17891*
R	20874 Spain (Sierra de Gador, Almería, Granada) *11496*
R	*Centaurea germanicopolitana* Bornm. *12840*
R	12840 Turkey *12840*
R	*Centaurea glaberrima* Tausch *20171*
R	21091 Bosnia & Herzegovina *21091*
R	(former) Yugoslavia
R	*Centaurea gracillima* Wagenitz *12840*
R	12840 Turkey *12840*
R	*Centaurea grbavacensis* (Rohl.) Stoy. & Acht. *20171*
R	Greece
R	(former) Yugoslavia
R	*Centaurea guilhelmi* (Pau & Sennen) Maire
R	Morocco
R	*Centaurea haenseleri* (Boiss.) Boiss. *11496*
R	11496 Spain *11496*
R	*Centaurea hakkariensis* Wagenitz *12840*
R	12840 Turkey *12840*
V	*Centaurea halophila* Hub.-Mor. *12840*
V	12840 Turkey *12840*
V	*Centaurea hanryi* Jordan ssp. *shuttleworthii* (Rouy) Kerguélen *20528*
V	20528 France (south-east) *20528*
R	*Centaurea haradjianii* Wagenitz *12840*
R	12840 Turkey *12840*
R	*Centaurea hedgei* Wagenitz *12840*
R	12840 Turkey *12840*
V	*Centaurea hermannii* F.Herm. *17781, 20171*
V	17781 Turkey *17781*
R	*Centaurea hierapolitana* Boiss. *12840*
R	12840 Turkey *12840*
R	*Centaurea holtzii* Wagenitz *12840*
R	12840 Turkey *12840*
V	*Centaurea horrida* Badarò *8000, 20171*
V	18264 Italy - Sardinia *19997*
R	*Centaurea huber-morathii* Wagenitz *12840*
R	12840 Turkey *12840*
R	*Centaurea huljakii* J.Wagner *20171*
R	Greece
R	*Centaurea incompta* Vis. *20171*
R	21091 Bosnia & Herzegovina *21091*
R	(former) Yugoslavia
R	*Centaurea ipsaria* Stoj. & Kitanov *20171*

R   Greece

R   *Centaurea jaennensis* Degen & Debeaux *11496, 20171*
   R   *11496* Spain (Jaen & Granada) *11496*

R   *Centaurea janeri* Graells *15846, 20171*
   R   *15846* Spain *15846*

E   *Centaurea jankae* D.Brândza *8000, 20171*
   E   *19417* Romania (Dolrogea) *20631*

E   *Centaurea kalambakensis* Freyn & Sint. *8000, 20171*
   E   Greece (central - near Kalabaka) *8000*

R   *Centaurea karduchorum* Boiss. *12840*
   R   *12840* Turkey *12840*

R   *Centaurea kartschiana* Scop. *8000, 20171*
   V   *18264* Italy (Friuli-Venezia Giulia) *19997*
   R   (former) Yugoslavia (north west) *8000*

R   *Centaurea kernerana* Janka *5204, 20171*
   R   *5204* Bulgaria (central & west) *5204*

V   *Centaurea kilaea* Boiss. *12840, 20171*
   V   *12840* Turkey *12840*

R   *Centaurea koniensis* Hub.-Mor. *12840*
   R   *12840* Turkey *12840*

R   *Centaurea kosaninii* Hayek *20178, 20171*
   R   *20178* Albania *20178*

R   *Centaurea kotschyi* (Boiss. & Heldr.) Hayek var. *decumbens* Wagenitz *12840*
   R   *12840* Turkey *12840*

R   *Centaurea laconica* Boiss. *20171*
   R   *20731* Greece (Peloponissos) *20731*

E   *Centaurea lactiflora* Halácsy *8000, 20171*
   E   Greece (central - Koniskos, NE of Kalabaka) *8000*

R   *Centaurea lactucifolia* Boiss.
   R   *20731* Greece - East Aegean Is (Rhodes) *20731*

R   *Centaurea lainzii* Fernandez Casas *11496*
   R   *11496* Spain (Sierra Bermeja, Malaga) *11496*

R   *Centaurea laureotica* Heldr. ex Halácsy *20171*
   R   Greece

R   *Centaurea leucadea* Lacaita *18264*
   R   *18264* Italy (Puglia) *18264*

Ex/E   *Centaurea leucophaea* Jord. ssp. *biformis* (Timb.-Lagr.) Dostál *20171*
   Ex/E   *20813* France (Pyrénées-Orientales) *20528*

V   *Centaurea leucophaea* Jord. ssp. *pseudocoerulescens* (Briq.) Dostál *20171*
   V   *20528* France (south-east) *20528*

E   *Centaurea linaresii* Lázaro Ibiza *8000, 20171*
   E   *14155* Spain (north-west) *8000*

R   *Centaurea litochorea* Georgiadis & Phitos
   R   Greece

R   *Centaurea longifimbriata* Wagenitz *12840*
   R   *12840* Turkey *12840*

R   *Centaurea loscosii* Willk. *20171*
   R   Spain

R   *Centaurea luschaniana* Heimerl *12840*
   R   *12840* Turkey *12840*

R   *Centaurea lycica* Boiss. *12840*
   R   *12840* Turkey *12840*

R   *Centaurea lycopifolia* Boiss. & Kotschy *12840*
   R   *12840* Turkey *12840*

R   *Centaurea lydia* Boiss. *12840*
   R   *12840* Turkey *12840*

R   *Centaurea macrorrhiza* Willk. *11496*
   R   *11496* Spain (Almeria & Murcia) *11496*

E   *Centaurea maculosa* Lam. ssp. *albida* (Lecoq & Lamotte) Dostál *20171*
   E   *20528* France (south) *20528*

R   *Centaurea maireana* Emberger
   R   Morocco

R   *Centaurea mannagettae* Podp. ssp. *pirinica* (D. Jord.) Koz. *19709*
   R   *19709* Bulgaria *19709*

V   *Centaurea margaritacea* Ten. *20171*
   V   former European USSR

I   *Centaurea mariana* Nyman *11496*
   I   *11496* Spain (Murcia, Almeria) *11496*

R   *Centaurea mathiolifolia* Boiss. *12840*
   R   *12840* Turkey *12840*

R   *Centaurea micracantha* Dufour *20171*
   R   Spain

V   *Centaurea micrantha* Hoffmanns. & Link ssp. *herminii* (Rouy) Dostal *8000, 20171*
   V   *20076* Portugal (north central - Serra da Estrêla) *8000*

R   *Centaurea microcarpa* Coss. & Durieu
   R   Algeria
   I   Tunisia

V   *Centaurea monticola* Boiss. ex DC. *11496*
   V   *11496* Spain (Granada, Jaen) *11496*

R   *Centaurea murbeckii* Hayek *20171*
   V   *21091* Bosnia & Herzegovina *21091*
   R   (former) Yugoslavia

R   *Centaurea musakii* Georgiadis *20731*
   R   *20731* Greece *20731*

R   *Centaurea musarum* Boiss. & Orph. *20171*
   R   Greece

R   *Centaurea mykalea* Hub.-Mor. *12840*
   R   *12840* Turkey *12840*

R   *Centaurea nicolai* Bald. *20178, 20171*
   R   *20178* Albania *20178*
   R   *21091* Bosnia & Herzegovina *21091*
   R   (former) Yugoslavia

E   *Centaurea niederi* Heldr. *8000, 20171*
   E   Greece (west - north of Mesolongion) *8000*

R   *Centaurea nydeggeri* Hub.-Mor *12840*
   R   *12840* Turkey *12840*

R   *Centaurea odyssei* Wagenitz *12840*
   R   *12840* Turkey *12840*

R   *Centaurea olympica* C. Koch. *12840*
   R   *12840* Turkey *12840*

R   *Centaurea omphalotricha* Coss. & Durieu ex Batt. *20171*
   R   Algeria
   I   Tunisia

I   *Centaurea ossaea* Halácsy *20171*
   I   Greece

V   *Centaurea pamphylica* Boiss. & Heldr. *12840*
   V   *12840* Turkey *12840*

R   *Centaurea pangaea* Greuter & Papanic.

R		Greece

V *Centaurea paniculata* L. ssp. *esterellensis*
    (Burnat) Dostál *20171*

V	20528	France (Var, Alpes-Maritimes) *20528*

R *Centaurea paphlagonica* (Bornm.) Wagenitz *12840*

R	12840	Turkey *12840*

R *Centaurea pawlowskii* Phitos & Damboldt

R		Greece

V *Centaurea paxorum* Phitos & Georgiadis *20731*

V	20731	Greece *20731*

R *Centaurea pecho* Albow *12840*

R	12840	Turkey *12840*

R *Centaurea pestalozzae* Boiss. *12840*

R	12840	Turkey *12840*

E *Centaurea peucedanifolia* Boiss. & Orph. *8000, 20171*

E		Greece (north-east - Athos) *8000*

R *Centaurea phaeolepis* Coss. *10488*

R	14958	Algeria *10488*

V *Centaurea pinetorum* Hub.-Mor. *12840*

V	12840	Turkey *12840*

R *Centaurea pinnatifida* Schur *19266, 20171*

R	19949	Romania (S & E Carpathians) *19266*

V *Centaurea poculatoris* Greuter *20171*

V	20730	Greece - Crete *20730*

R *Centaurea poluninii* Wagenitz *12840*

R	12840	Turkey *12840*

R *Centaurea polymorpha* Lag. *20171*

R		Spain

E *Centaurea pontica* Prodán & Nyár. *8000, 20171*

E	19417	Romania (Danube delta) *20631*

R *Centaurea prespana* Rech.f.

R		Greece

R *Centaurea procumbens* Balb. *20171*

R		France
R		Spain

Ex *Centaurea psephelloides* Freyn & Sint. *12840*

Ex	19873	Turkey *12840*

R *Centaurea pseudocadmea* Wagenitz *20171*

R	20731	Greece (Sterea Ellas - Mt Kithaeron) *20731*

R *Centaurea pseudokotschyi* Wagenitz *12840*

R	12840	Turkey *12840*

E *Centaurea pseudoleucolepis* Kleopow *5942, 20171*

E	20655	Ukraine (south-east) *5942*

R *Centaurea pseudophygia* C.A. Meyer ssp. *retezatensis*
    (Pradau) Cire *17823*

R	19949	Romania *20631*

R *Centaurea pseudoreflexa* Hayek *12840*

R	12840	Turkey *12840*

R *Centaurea psilacantha* Boiss. & Heldr. *20171*

R	20731	Greece (Sterea Ellas) *20731*

R *Centaurea ptarmicifolia* Halácsy ex Hayek *20171*

R		Greece

R *Centaurea ptosimopappa* Hayek *12840*

R	12840	Turkey *12840*

R *Centaurea ptosimopappoides* Wagenitz *12840*

R	12840	Turkey *12840*

R *Centaurea pulcherrima* Willd. var. *freynii* (int.)

		Wagenitz *12840*
R	12840	Turkey *12840*

R *Centaurea pulvinata* (G. Blanca) G. Blanca *17891*

R	20874	Spain *11496*

R *Centaurea pumilio* L. *20171*

R	20730	Greece - Crete *20730*

R *Centaurea rechingeri* Phitos *20171*

R	20731	Greece - East Aegean Is *20731*

R *Centaurea redempta* Heldr. ssp.
    redempta *20731*

R	20731	Greece - Crete *20731*

R *Centaurea reuterana* Boiss. var.
    reuterana *12840*

R	12840	Turkey *12840*

R *Centaurea rhizocalathium* (C. Koch.) Tchihat. *12840*

R	12840	Turkey *12840*

R *Centaurea ropalon* Pomel

R		Algeria
I		Tunisia

V *Centaurea rothmalerana* (Arènes) Dostál *15846, 20171*

V	20076	Portugal *20076*

R *Centaurea rufidula* Bornm. *20171*

R		(former) Yugoslavia

R *Centaurea rupestris* ssp. *parnonia* (Hal.) Routsi &
    Georgiadis *20731*

R	20731	Greece *20731*

R *Centaurea sadlerana* Janka *20171*

R		Austria *8000*
R		Czech & Slovak Federal Republic *8000*
R		Hungary *8000*

R *Centaurea sagredoi* G. Blanca *11496*

R	11496	Spain *11496*

R *Centaurea scannensis* (Anzalone) Pignatti *18264*

R	18264	Italy (Abruzzi) *18264*

R *Centaurea schischkinii* Tzvelev. *12840*

R	12840	Turkey *12840*

R *Centaurea schousboei* Lange *20171*

V	20076	Portugal *20076*
R		Spain

R *Centaurea scopulorum* Boiss. & Heldr. *12840*

R	12840	Turkey *12840*

R *Centaurea sericea* Wagenitz *12840*

R	12840	Turkey *12840*

R *Centaurea sipylea* Wagenitz *12840*

R	12840	Turkey *12840*

R *Centaurea sivasica* Wagenitz *12840*

R	12840	Turkey *12840*

R *Centaurea solstitialis* L. ssp. *carneola* (Boiss.)
    Wagenitz *12840*

R	12840	Turkey *12840*

R *Centaurea solstitialis* L. ssp. *pyracantha* (Boiss.)
    Wagenitz *12840*

R	12840	Turkey *12840*

R *Centaurea soskae* Hayek ex Kosanin *20178, 20171*

R	20178	Albania *20178*
V		(former) Yugoslavia

R *Centaurea spinosociliata* Seenus *20171*

R		(former) Yugoslavia

V *Centaurea spinosociliata* Seenus ssp. *tommasinii*
    (A. Kerner) Dostál *18264, 20171*

	V	18264 Italy *18264*	

R *Centaurea spruneri* Boiss. & Heldr. ssp. *minoa* (Heldr. ex Boiss.) Dostal *20730, 20171*
    R   20730 Greece - Crete *20730*

R *Centaurea stapfiana* (Hand.-Mazz.) Wagenitz *12840*
    R   12840 Turkey *12840*

R *Centaurea straminicephala* Hub.-Mor. *12840*
    R   12840 Turkey *12840*

I *Centaurea taliewii* Kleopow *11552, 20171*
    I   5942 Russia (E.Europe) - South *5942*
    I   5942 Kazakhstan *5942*
    I   5942 Ukraine - Crimea *5942*

R *Centaurea tananica* Maire
    R   Morocco

R *Centaurea tardiflora* Wagenitz *12840*
    R   12840 Turkey *12840*

R *Centaurea tauromenitana* Guss. *18264, 20171*
    R   18264 Italy - Sicily (Taormina) *20738*

E *Centaurea tchihatcheffii* Fisch. & Mey. *12840*
    E   12840 Turkey *12840*

R *Centaurea theryi* Emberger & Maire
    R   Morocco

R *Centaurea tossiensis* Freyn & Sint. *12840*
    R   12840 Turkey *12840*

R *Centaurea transiens* Halácsy *20171*
    R   Greece

R *Centaurea triamularia* Alden
    R   Greece

R *Centaurea trichocephala* M.Bieb. ex Willd. ssp. *simonkaiana* (Hayek) Dostál *17823, 20171*
    R   19949 Romania *2050*

Ex *Centaurea tuntasia* Heldr. ex Halácsy *20171*
    Ex 20731 Greece *20731*

R *Centaurea vermiculigera* Hub.-Mor. *12840*
    R   12840 Turkey *12840*

V *Centaurea wagenittzii* Hub.-Mor. *12840*
    V   12840 Turkey *12840*

R *Centaurea wettsteinii* Degen & Dörfl. *20171*
    R   (former) Yugoslavia

R *Centaurea wiedemanniana* Fisch. & Mey. *12840*
    R   12840 Turkey *12840*

R *Centaurea woronowii* Bornm. *12840*
    R   12840 Turkey *12840*

V *Centaurea xylobasis* Rech.f. *20731*
    V   20731 Greece - East Aegean Is *20731*

V *Centaurea zeybekii* Wagenitz *12840*
    V   12840 Turkey *12840*

I *Centaurea zlatarskyana* Urum. & J.Wagner *20171*
    I   Bulgaria

E *Centaurodendron dracaenoides* Johow *19116*
    E   19125 Chile - Juan Fernandez Is. *19116*

E *Centaurodendron palmiforme* Skottsb. *19116*
    E   19125 Chile - Juan Fernandez Is. *19116*

I *Centratherum courtallense* (Wight) Benth.
    I   India - Kerala (Travancore Hills)
    I   India - Tamil Nadu

I *Centratherum mayurii* C. Fischer
    I   India - Karnataka (Kemmangundi hills)

I *Centratherum ritchiei* Hook.f.

    I   India - Karnataka (Canara & Concan)

I *Centratherum tenue* C.B. Clarke
    I   India - Karnataka (Concan)

R *Chaenactis alpigena* C.W. Sharsmith *20850*
    I   20850 U.S. - California *20850*
    I   20850 U.S. - Nevada *20850*

R *Chaenactis artemisiifolia* (Harvey & Gray ex Gray) Gray *20850*
    I   20850 U.S. - California *20850*

E *Chaenactis carphoclinia* Gray var. *peirsonii* (Jepson) Munz *20850*
    E   20850 U.S. - California *20850*

V *Chaenactis cusickii* Gray *20850*
    E   20850 U.S. - Idaho *20850*
    V   20850 U.S. - Oregon *20850*

R *Chaenactis glabriuscula* DC. *20850*
    I   20850 U.S. - California *20850*

R *Chaenactis nevadensis* (Kellogg) Gray *20850*
    I   20850 U.S. - California *20850*
    I   20850 U.S. - Nevada *20850*

V *Chaenactis santolinoides* Greene *20850*
    I   20850 U.S. - California *20850*

R *Chaenactis suffrutescens* Gray *20850*
    R   20850 U.S. - California *20850*

V *Chaenactis thompsonii* Cronq. *20850*
    V   20850 U.S. - Washington *20850*

V *Chaetanthera chiquianensis* Ferreyra *18200*
    V   12468 Peru *18200*

V *Chaetanthera cochlearifolia* H. Robinson *18200*
    V   12468 Peru *18200*

R *Chaetanthera peruviana* Gray *18200*
    R   12468 Peru *18200*

R *Chaetanthera stuebelii* Hieron. var. *abreviata* Cabrera *16336*
    R   19448 Argentina *16336*
    R   20176 Argentina - Jujuy *20176*
    R   20176 Argentina - Tucuman *20176*

R *Chaetopappa effusa* (Gray) Shinners *20850*
    R   20850 U.S. - Texas *20850*

V *Chaetopappa elegans* Soreng & Spellenberg *20850*
    V   20850 U.S. - New Mexico *20850*

R *Chaetopappa hersheyi* Blake *20850*
    R   20850 U.S. - New Mexico *20850*
    V   20850 U.S. - Texas *20850*

V *Chaptalia comptonioides* Britton & P. Wilson *5607*
    V   19105 Cuba (Granma) *5607*

R *Chaptalia cordata* Hieron. *18200*
    R   12468 Peru *18200*

I *Chaptalia eggersii* Urban *5642*
    I   Dominican Republic (Constanza; Valle Nuevo) *5642*

V *Chaptalia ekmanii* Urban *5607*
    V   19105 Cuba (Pinar del Rio) *5607*

V *Chaptalia turquinensis* Borh. & Muniz *5607*
    V   19105 Cuba (Santiago de Cuba) *5607*

I *Chaptalia vegaensis* Urban & Ekman *5642*
    I   Dominican Republic (Bonao) *5642*

E *Cheirolophus anagensis* Santos *20750*
    E   20750 Spain - Canary Is. *20750*

E *Cheirolophus arboreus* (Webb) Holub *20750*

E   *15105* Spain - Canary Is. *15105*

R   ***Cheirolophus argutus*** (Nees) Holub *15105*
    R   *15105* Spain - Canary Is. *15105*

R   ***Cheirolophus canariensis*** (Brouss. ex Willd.)
    Holub *20750*
    R   *15105* Spain - Canary Is. *15105*

E   ***Cheirolophus duranii*** (Burchard) Holub *14166*
    E   *15105* Spain - Canary Is. *17891*

E   ***Cheirolophus falcisectus*** Montelongo & Moraleda *20750*
    E   *15105* Spain - Canary Is. *15105*

E   ***Cheirolophus ghomerythus*** (Svent.) Holub *14166*
    E   *14166* Spain - Canary Is. (La Gomera) *14166*

E   ***Cheirolophus junonianus*** (Svent.) Holub *14166*
    E   *15105* Spain - Canary Is. *17891*

E   ***Cheirolophus lagunae*** Olivares, Peris, Stübing &
    Martin *20700*
    E   *20700* Spain (near Jávea, Valencia province)
        20700

E   ***Cheirolophus massonianus*** (Lowe) Hansen &
    Sunding *17891*
    E   Portugal - Madeira *17891*

E   ***Cheirolophus metlesicsii*** Montelongo *20750*
    E   *15105* Spain - Canary Is. *15105*

E   ***Cheirolophus puntallanensis*** Santos *20750*
    E   *20750* Spain - Canary Is. *20750*

E   ***Cheirolophus santosabreui*** Santos *20750*
    E   *15105* Spain - Canary Is. *15105*

E   ***Cheirolophus satarataensis*** (Svent.) Holub *20750*
    E   *20750* Spain - Canary Is. *20750*

E   ***Cheirolophus satarataensis*** (Svent.) Holub ssp.
    dariasi (Svent.) G.Kunkel *20750*
    E   Spain - Canary Is.

R   ***Cheirolophus sventenii*** (Santos) Kunkel ssp. *gracilis*
    Santos *20750*
    R   *20750* Spain - Canary Is. *15105*

V   ***Cheirolophus sventenii*** (Santos) Kunkel ssp.
    sventenii
    V   *15105* Spain - Canary Is. *15105*

E   ***Cheirolophus tagananensis*** (Svent.) Holub *10260*
    E   *14155* Spain - Canary Is. *10260*

V   ***Cheirolophus webbianus*** (Schultz Bip.) Holub *20750*
    V   *15105* Spain - Canary Is. *15105*

V   ***Chiliadenus lopadusanus*** Brullo *18264*
    V   *18264* Italy - Sicily *18264*

R   ***Chondrilla setulosa*** Charke ex Hook. f. *14782*
    R   *14782* India - Jammu & Kashmir *14782*

R   ***Chondrilla spinosa*** Lamond et Matthews *12840*
    R   *12840* Turkey *12840*

E   ***Chresta harleyi*** H. Robinson *20883*
    I   *20883* Brazil *20883*

R   ***Chromolaena heteroclinia*** (Griseb.) R. King & H.
    Robinson *20883*
    R   *20883* Jamaica *20883*

R   ***Chrysanthemum morii*** Hayata *20511*
    R   *20511* Taiwan *20511*

R   ***Chrysanthemum nivellei*** Braun-Blanquet
    R   Morocco

R   ***Chrysanthemum zawadskii*** Herbich ssp. *coreanum*
    (Nakai) Y.N. Lee

R   Korea, South (Mt Halla, Chejudo) *17577*

R   ***Chrysanthemum zawadskii*** Herbich ssp. *lucidum*
    (Nakai) Y.N. Lee
    R   Korea, South (Ulnungdo) *17577*

R   ***Chrysophthalmum dichotomum*** Boiss. & Heldr. *12840*
    R   *12840* Turkey *12840*

E   ***Chrysopsis floridana*** Small *20850*
    E   *20850* U.S. - Florida (Hillsborough & Pinellas Co)
        20850

V   ***Chrysopsis godfreyi*** Semple *20850*
    E   *20850* U.S. - Alabama *20850*
    V   *20850* U.S. - Florida *20850*

V   ***Chrysopsis gossypina*** (Dress) Semple ssp. *cruiseana*
    (Dress) Semple *20850*
    E   *20850* U.S. - Alabama *20850*
    V   *20850* U.S. - Florida *20850*

E   ***Chrysothamnus eremobius*** L.C. Anders. *20850*
    E   *20850* U.S. - Nevada *20850*

R   ***Chrysothamnus humilis*** Greene *20850*
    I   *20850* U.S. - California *20850*
    E   *20850* U.S. - Idaho *20850*
    I   *20850* U.S. - Nevada *20850*
    I   *20850* U.S. - Oregon *20850*

R   ***Chrysothamnus molestus*** (Blake) L.C. Anders. *20850*
    R   *20850* U.S. - Arizona *20850*

E   ***Chrysothamnus nauseosus*** (Cronq.) Keck ssp. *iridis*
    L.C. Anders. *20850*
    E   *20850* U.S. - Utah *20850*

E   ***Chrysothamnus nauseosus*** (Cronq.) Keck ssp.
    psilocarpus (Blake) L.C.Anders. *20850*
    E   *20850* U.S. - Utah *20850*

V   ***Chrysothamnus nauseosus*** (Cronq.) Keck ssp. *texensis*
    L.C.Anders. *20850*
    V   *20850* U.S. - New Mexico *20850*
    E   *20850* U.S. - Texas *20850*

E   ***Chrysothamnus parryi*** L.C. Anders. ssp. *montanus*
    L.C. Anders. *20850*
    E   *20850* U.S. - Idaho *20850*
    E   *20850* U.S. - Montana *20850*

R   ***Chrysothamnus parryi*** ssp. *salmonensis* L.C.
    Anders. *20850*
    R   *20850* U.S. - Idaho *20850*

R   ***Chrysothamnus spathulatus*** L.C. Anders. *20850*
    R   *20850* U.S. - New Mexico *20850*
    V   *20850* U.S. - Texas *20850*

V   ***Chuquiraga erinacea*** Don *16322*
    V   *19448* Argentina *16322*

R   ***Chuquiraga johnstonii*** Tovar *18200*
    R   *12468* Peru *18200*

R   ***Chuquiraga jussieuii*** Gmelin *18200*
    R   *18200* Peru *18200*

R   ***Chuquiraga weberbaueri*** Tovar *18200*
    R   *12468* Peru *18200*

R   ***Cicerbita brevirostris*** (Schu.-Bip.exVis.&Panc) C.
    Jeffr *12840*
    R   *12840* Turkey *12840*

V   ***Ciceronia chaptalioides*** Urban *5607*
    V   *19105* Cuba (Holguin) *5607*

R   ***Cineraria hederifolia*** Cron *20604*
    R   *20604* South Africa - Transvaal *20604*

R   ***Cirsium aduncum*** Fisch. & Mey. ex DC. ssp.

      bashkalense Davis & Parris *12840*
  R   *12840* Turkey *12840*

R *Cirsium aidzuense* Nakai *10573*
  R   *10573* Japan *10573*

R *Cirsium alatum* (Gmelin) Bobrov ssp. *pseudocreticum*
    Davis & Parris *12840*
  R   *12840* Turkey *12840*

R *Cirsium albescens* Kitamura *20511*
  R   *20511* Taiwan *20511*

R *Cirsium alpis-lunae* Br.-catt. & Gubell. *18264*
  R   *18264* Italy (Tuscany) *18264*

E *Cirsium araneans* Rydb. *20850*
  I   *20850* U.S. - Colorado *20850*

R *Cirsium arisanense* Kitamura forma *purpurescens*
    Kitamura *20511*
  R   *20511* Taiwan *20511*

R *Cirsium barnebyi* Welsh & Neese *20850*
  R   *20850* U.S. - Colorado *20850*
  V   *20850* U.S. - Utah *20850*
  E   *20850* U.S. - Wyoming *20850*

R *Cirsium baytopae* P.H.Davis & Parris *12840, 20171*
  R   *12840* Turkey *12840*

R *Cirsium boluense* Davis & Parris *12840*
  R   *12840* Turkey *12840*

V *Cirsium boninense* Koidz. *8037*
  V   *19134* Japan - Ogasawara-shoto *8037*

R *Cirsium boujartii* (Piller & Mitterp.)
    Sch.Bip. *17823, 20171*
  R   *20178* Albania *20178*
  Ex *20686* Hungary *20686*
  R   *19947* Romania *20631*

R *Cirsium bourgaeanum* Willk. *20171*
  R   Spain

V *Cirsium campylon* H.K. Sharsmith *20850*
  V   *20850* U.S. - California *20850*

V *Cirsium carniolicum* Scop. ssp. *rufescens* (Raymond
    ex DC.) P.Fourn. *20171*
  V   *20528* France (Pyrénées-Atlantiques) *20528*

R *Cirsium cassium* Davis & Parris *12840*
  R   *12840* Turkey *12840*

R *Cirsium chanroenicum* Nakai *15957*
  R   *15923* Korea, South (Mt Chiri, Mt Kaya, Mt Choryong, Mt
       Sorak) *15957*

R *Cirsium chikushiense* Koidz. var.
    chikushiense 10573
  R   *10573* Japan *10573*

R *Cirsium chikushiense* Koidz. var. *yakusimense*
    (Masam.) Yahara *10573*
  R   *10573* Japan *10573*

R *Cirsium chokaiense* Kitam. *10573*
  R   *10573* Japan *10573*

R *Cirsium ciliolatum* (Henderson) J.T. Howell *20850*
  E   *20850* U.S. - California *20850*
  R   *20850* U.S. - Oregon *20850*

R *Cirsium clavatum* (M.E. Jones) Petrak *20850*
  V   *20850* U.S. - Utah *20850*

V *Cirsium clokeyi* Blake *20850*
  V   *20850* U.S. - Nevada *20850*

R *Cirsium confertissimum* Nakai *10573*
  R   *10573* Japan *10573*

V *Cirsium crassicaule* (Greene) Jepson *20850*
  V   *20850* U.S. - California *20850*

R *Cirsium creticum* (Lam.) D'Urv. ssp. *dictaeum*
    Greuter, Matthäs & Risse *19121*
  R   *20730* Greece - Crete *20730*

R *Cirsium davisianum* Kit Tan & Sorger *12840*
  R   *12840* Turkey *12840*

R *Cirsium ducellieri* Maire
  R   Morocco

E *Cirsium eatonii* Welsh var. *harrisonii*
    Welsh *20850*
  E   *20850* U.S. - Utah *20850*

V *Cirsium eatonii* Welsh var. *murdockii*
    Welsh *20850*
  V   *20850* U.S. - Utah *20850*

R *Cirsium edule* Nutt. *20850*
  I   *20850* Canada - British Columbia *20850*
  E   *20850* U.S. - Alaska *20850*
  I   *20850* U.S. - Idaho *20850*
  I   *20850* U.S. - Oregon *20850*
  I   *20850* U.S. - Washington *20850*

R *Cirsium eliasianum* Kit Tan & Sorger *12840*
  R   *12840* Turkey *12840*

R *Cirsium ellenbergii* Bornm. *12840*
  R   *12840* Turkey *12840*

R *Cirsium epiroticum* Petr. *20171*
  R   Greece

R *Cirsium eriophorum* (L.) Scop. ssp. *chodati* Rivas
    Mart., Diaz et al.
  R   Spain

V *Cirsium fontinale* (Greene) Jepson *20850*
  I   *20850* U.S. - California *20850*

E *Cirsium fontinale* (Greene) Jepson var.
    fontinale 20850
  E   *20850* U.S. - California *20850*

E *Cirsium fontinale* (Greene) Jepson var. *obispoense*
    J.T. Howell *20850*
  E   *20850* U.S. - California *20850*

V *Cirsium gaditanum* Talav. & B. Valdes *20850*
  V   *20664* Spain (Cádiz, Málaga) *20664*

R *Cirsium ganjuense* Kitam. *10573*
  R   *10573* Japan *10573*

V *Cirsium griseum* (Rydb.) K. Schum. *20850*
  I   *20850* U.S. - Colorado *20850*

R *Cirsium hakkiaricum* Davis & Parris *12840*
  R   *12840* Turkey *12840*

R *Cirsium hillii* (Canby) Fern. *20850, 14352*
  R   *20850* Canada - Ontario *20850*
  E   *20850* U.S. - Illinois *20850*
  E   *20850* U.S. - Indiana *20850*
  I   *20850* U.S. - Iowa *20850*
  R   *20850* U.S. - Michigan *20850*
  R   *20850* U.S. - Minnesota *20850*
  I   *20850* U.S. - New York *20850*
  E   *20850* U.S. - Ohio *20850*
  V   *20850* U.S. - Wisconsin *20850*

R *Cirsium hosokawae* Kitamura *20511*
  R   *20511* Taiwan *20511*

E *Cirsium hydrophilum* (Greene) Jepson *20850*
  I   *20850* U.S. - California *20850*

E *Cirsium hydrophilum* (Greene) Jepson var.

	hydrophilum 20850		
E	20850	U.S. - California	20850

E   *Cirsium hydrophilum* (Greene) Jepson var. *vaseyi* (Gray) J.T. Howell 20850

E	20850	U.S. - California	20850

R   *Cirsium inudatum* Makino var. *homolepis* (Nakai) Kitam. 10573

R	10573	Japan	10573

R   *Cirsium japonicum* DC. var. *takaoense* Kitamura 20511

R	20511	Taiwan	20511

R   *Cirsium kamtschaticum* Ledeb. ssp. *apoiense* (Nakai) Kitam. 10573

R	10573	Japan	10573

R   *Cirsium kirbense* Pomel 10488

R	14958	Algeria	10488

V   *Cirsium latifolium* Lowe 17891

V		Portugal - Madeira	17891

V   *Cirsium loncholepis* Petrak 20850

V	20850	U.S. - California	20850

V   *Cirsium longistylum* Moore & Frankton 20850

V	20850	U.S. - Montana	20850

V   *Cirsium lucens* Kitam. var. *opacum* Kitam. 10573

V	10573	Japan	10573

R   *Cirsium magofukui* Kitam. 10573

R	10573	Japan	10573

R   *Cirsium mairei* Halácsy 20171

R		Greece	

V   *Cirsium modestum* (Osterhout) Cockerell 20850

I	20850	U.S. - Colorado	20850

V   *Cirsium mohavense* (Greene) Petrak 20850

I	20850	U.S. - California	20850
I	20850	U.S. - Nevada	20850

R   *Cirsium morinifolium* Boiss. & Heldr. 20171

R	20730	Greece - Crete	20730

V   *Cirsium occidentale* (Nutt.) Jepson var. *compactum* Hoover 20850

V	20850	U.S. - California	20850

V   *Cirsium oreophilum* (Rydb.) K. Schum. 20850

I	20850	U.S. - Colorado	20850
I	20850	U.S. - Nevada	20850

V   *Cirsium osterhoutii* (Rydb.) Petrak 20850

I	20850	U.S. - Colorado	20850

R   *Cirsium ownbeyi* Welsh 20850

V	20850	U.S. - Colorado	20850
E	20850	U.S. - Utah	20850
E	20850	U.S. - Wyoming	20850

E   *Cirsium parryi* C. Schaack & G. Goodwin ssp. *mogollonicum* C. Schaack & G. Goodwin 20850

E	20850	U.S. - Arizona	20850

R   *Cirsium pastoris* J.T. Howell 20850

I	20850	U.S. - California	20850
I	20850	U.S. - Nevada	20850
I	20850	U.S. - Oregon	20850

R   *Cirsium perplexans* (Rydb.) Petrak 20850

E	20850	U.S. - Colorado	20850

R   *Cirsium pitcheri* (Torr. ex Eat.) Torr. & Gray 20850, 15046

E	15046	Canada	15046

V	20850	Canada - Ontario	20850
Ex	20850	U.S. - Illinois	20850
V	20850	U.S. - Indiana	20850
R	20850	U.S. - Michigan	20850
V	20850	U.S. - Wisconsin	20850

R   *Cirsium poluninii* Davis & Parris 12840

R	12840	Turkey	12840

V   *Cirsium polycephalum* DC. 12840, 20171

V	12840	Turkey	12840

R   *Cirsium pubigerum* (Desf.) DC. var. *paphlabonicum* Petrak 12840

R	12840	Turkey	12840

R   *Cirsium quercetorum* (Gray) Jepson 20850

I	20850	U.S. - California	20850

V   *Cirsium rhinoceros* Nakai forma *albiflorum* Sakata 15957

V		Korea, South (Mt Halla)	15957

V   *Cirsium rhothophilum* Blake 20850

V	20850	U.S. - California	20850

R   *Cirsium rosulatum* Talav. & B. Valdes

R	11496	Spain	11496

E   *Cirsium rusbyi* (Greene) Petrak 20850

I	20850	U.S. - Arizona	20850

V   *Cirsium scapanolepis* Petrak 20850

I	20850	U.S. - Colorado	20850

V   *Cirsium scopulorum* (Greene) Cockerell ex Daniels 20850

E	20850	U.S. - Colorado	20850
I	20850	U.S. - New Mexico	20850
E	20850	U.S. - Utah	20850

R   *Cirsium setidens* Nakai 15957

R	15923	Korea, South (Mt Pukhan, Mt Namsan, Inchon)	15957

R   *Cirsium sieboldii* Miq. ssp. *austrokiushianum* Kitam. 10573

R	10573	Japan	10573

R   *Cirsium simplex* C.A. Meyer ssp. *satdaghense* Davis & Parris 12840

R	12840	Turkey	12840

R   *Cirsium sipyleum* O. Schwarz 12840

R	12840	Turkey	12840

R   *Cirsium tioganum* (Congd.) Petrak 20850

I	20850	U.S. - Arizona	20850
I	20850	U.S. - California	20850
I	20850	U.S. - Colorado	20850
I	20850	U.S. - Nevada	20850
I	20850	U.S. - New Mexico	20850
I	20850	U.S. - Utah	20850
V	20850	U.S. - Wyoming	20850

Ex   *Cirsium toyoshimae* Koidz. 8038

Ex	19134	Japan - Ogasawara-shoto	8038

V   *Cirsium vinaceum* Woot. & Standl. 20850

V	20850	U.S. - New Mexico (Sacramento Mts, Otero Co.) 20850

V   *Cirsium virginense* Welsh 20850

E	20850	U.S. - Arizona	20850
E	20850	U.S. - Utah	20850

R   *Cirsium wheeleri* (Gray) Petrak 20850

I	20850	U.S. - Arizona	20850
I	20850	U.S. - Nevada	20850
I	20850	U.S. - New Mexico	20850
R	20850	U.S. - Utah	20850

V   *Cirsium wrightii* Gray 20850

E	20850	U.S. - Arizona	*20850*
I	20850	U.S. - New Mexico	*20850*

I   *Cladochaeta candidissima* (M. Bieb.) DC. *8001*

I	5942	Russia - North Caucasus	*5942*
I	5942	Azerbaijan	*5942*

E   *Clibadium pilonicum* Stuessy *20883, 9006*

R	9006	Panama	*20883*

E   *Clibadium rimachii* H. Robinson *20883*

I	20883	Peru	*20883*

E   *Clibadium subauriculatum* Stuessy *20883, 9006*

I	20883	Panama	*20883*

E   *Clibadium zaruchii* H. Robinson *20883*

I	20883	Colombia	*20883*

R   *Colobogyne langbianensis* Gagnepain *6057*

R	20985	Vietnam	*6057*

R   *Comborhiza longipes* (K.Bremer) Anderb. & K.Bremer *20604*

R	20604	South Africa - Cape Province	*20604*

Ex   *Commidendrum burchellii* (Hook.f.) Hemsley *18996*

Ex	18996	St Helena	*18996*

R   *Commidendrum robustum* DC. *10260*

R	18996	St Helena	*18996*

Ex   *Commidendrum rotundifolium* (Roxb.) DC. *15112*

Ex	18996	St Helena	*18996*

R   *Commidendrum rugosum* DC. *10260*

R	18996	St Helena	*18996*

E   *Commidendrum spurium* DC. *10260*

E	18996	St Helena	*18996*

E   *Coreocarpus parthenioides* var. *involutus* (E. L. Greene) E. B. Smith *20883*

I	20883	Mexico	*20883*

R   *Coreopsis bigelovii* (Gray) Hall *20850*

I	20850	U.S. - California	*20850*

R   *Coreopsis calliopsidea* (DC.) Gray *20850*

I	20850	U.S. - California	*20850*

V   *Coreopsis cuneifolia* Greenman *9706*

V	14294	Mexico - Durango	*14294*

R   *Coreopsis douglasii* (DC.) Hall *20850*

I	20850	U.S. - Arizona	*20850*
I	20850	U.S. - California	*20850*

V   *Coreopsis hamiltonii* (Elmer) H.K. Sharsmith *20850*

V	20850	U.S. - California	*20850*

E   *Coreopsis integrifolia* Poir. *20850*

E	20850	U.S. - Florida	*20850*
E	20850	U.S. - Georgia	*20850*
I	20850	U.S. - South Carolina	*20850*

R   *Coreopsis intermedia* Sherff *20850*

E	20850	U.S. - Louisiana	*20850*
R	20850	U.S. - Texas	*20850*

R   *Coreopsis latifolia* Michx. *20850*

E	20850	U.S. - Georgia	*20850*
R	20850	U.S. - North Carolina	*20850*
E	20850	U.S. - South Carolina	*20850*
E	20850	U.S. - Tennessee	*20850*

R   *Coreopsis maritima* (Nutt.) Hook. f. *20850*

R	20850	U.S. - California	*20850*

V   *Coreopsis pulchra* Boynt. *20850*

V	20850	U.S. - Alabama	*20850*
I	20850	U.S. - Georgia	*20850*

R   *Coreopsis rosea* Nutt. *20850, 3064*

V	20850	Canada - Nova Scotia	*20850*
E	20850	U.S. - Delaware	*20850*
I	20850	U.S. - Georgia	*20850*
E	20850	U.S. - Maryland	*20850*
R	20850	U.S. - Massachusetts	*20850*
I	20850	U.S. - Mississippi	*20850*
V	20850	U.S. - New Jersey	*20850*
R	20850	U.S. - New York	*20850*
Ex	20850	U.S. - Pennsylvania	*20850*
V	20850	U.S. - Rhode Is.	*20850*
V	20850	U.S. - South Carolina	*20850*

R   *Coreopsis stillmanii* (Gray) Blake *20850*

I	20850	U.S. - California	*20850*

V   *Corethrogyne californica* DC. *20850*

I	20850	U.S. - California	*20850*
I	20850	U.S. - Oregon	*20850*

E   *Corethrogyne filaginifolia* (Hook. & Arn.) Nutt. var. *incana* (Nutt.) Canby *20850*

E	20850	U.S. - California	*20850*

E   *Corethrogyne filaginifolia* (Hook. & Arn.) Nutt. var. *linifolia* Hall *20850*

E	20850	U.S. - California	*20850*

I   *Corymbium theileri* Markötter *20604*

I	20604	South Africa - Cape Province	*20604*

Ex   *Cosmos atrosanguineus* Stapf *19605*

Ex	19605	Mexico	*19605*

R   *Cosmos linearifolius* (Schultz-Bip.) Hemsley var. *magnificus* Sherff *14294*

R	14294	Mexico - Durango	*14294*

R   *Cotula albida* D. Lloyd

R		New Zealand - South Is.	

R   *Cotula calcarea* D. Lloyd

R		New Zealand - South Is.	

E   *Cotula dioica* Hook.f. ssp. *monoica* D. Lloyd

E		New Zealand - North Is.	

R   *Cotula dispersa* D. Lloyd ssp. *rupestris* D. Lloyd

R		New Zealand - North Is.	

E   *Cotula featherstonii* F. Muell. ex Hook.f. *86*

E		New Zealand - Chatham Is.	

V   *Cotula filiformis* Hook.f.

V		New Zealand - South Is.	

I   *Cotula intermedia* D. Lloyd

I		New Zealand - South Is.	

I   *Cotula myriophylloides* Harv. *20604*

I	20604	South Africa - Cape Province	*20604*

E   *Cotula nana* D. Lloyd *86*

E		New Zealand - South Is.	

R   *Cotula pyrethrifolia* Hook.f. var. *linearifolia* Cheeseman

R		New Zealand - South Is.	

E   *Cotula rotundata* (Cheeseman) D. Lloyd *86*

E		New Zealand - North Is.	

R   *Cousinia agelocephala* Tscherneva

R		former USSR	*6930*

R   *Cousinia androssovii* Juz.

R		former USSR	*6930*

R   *Cousinia aucheri* DC. *12840*

R	12840	Turkey	*12840*

I   *Cousinia badhysi* Kult. *5942*

I	5942	Turkmenistan	5942

R **Cousinia cataonica** Boiss. & Hausskn. *12840*
  R *12840* Turkey *12840*

R **Cousinia cirsioides** Boiss. & Bal. *12840*
  R *12840* Turkey *12840*

R **Cousinia davisiana** Hub.-Mor. *12840*
  R *12840* Turkey *12840*

R **Cousinia decolorans** Freyn & Sint. *12840*
  R *12840* Turkey *12840*

R **Cousinia eleonorae** Hub.-Mor. *12840*
  R *12840* Turkey *12840*

R **Cousinia ermenekensis** Hub.-Mor. *12840*
  R *12840* Turkey *12840*

R **Cousinia euphratica** Hub.-Mor. *12840*
  R *12840* Turkey *12840*

I **Cousinia falconeri** Hook.f.
  I   India - Jammu & Kashmir

R **Cousinia grandifolia** Kult. *5942*
  R *5942* Kazakhstan (south) *5942*

R **Cousinia hakkarica** Hub.-Mor. *12840*
  R *12840* Turkey *12840*

V **Cousinia halysensis** Hub.-Mor. *12840*
  V *12840* Turkey *12840*

V **Cousinia intertexta** Freyn & Sint. *12840*
  V *12840* Turkey *12840*

R **Cousinia margiana** Juz.
  R   former USSR *6930*

R **Cousinia nabelekii** Bornm. *12840*
  R *12840* Turkey *12840*

E **Cousinia platystegia** Tscherneva
  E   former USSR *6930*

E **Cousinia pseudolanata** Popov & Tscherneva
  E   former USSR *6930*

R **Cousinia satdagensis** Hub.-Mor. *12840*
  R *12840* Turkey *12840*

R **Cousinia sintenisii** Freyn *12840*
  R *12840* Turkey *12840*

R **Cousinia sivasica** Hub.-Mor. *12840*
  R *12840* Turkey *12840*

R **Cousinia vanensis** Hub.-Mor. *12840*
  R *12840* Turkey *12840*

R **Cousinia vavilovii** Kult. *5942*
  R *5942* Kazakhstan (south-east border with Kyrgyzstan) *5942*
  R *5942* Kyrgyzstan (border with Kazakhstan) *5942*

R **Cousinia woronowii** Bornm. *12840*
  R *12840* Turkey *12840*

R **Craspedia alba** Everett & Thompson *20681*
  I *20681* Australia - New South Wales *20681*
  I *20681* Australia - Victoria *20681*

R **Craspedia leucantha** F.Muell. *20681*
  R *20681* Australia - New South Wales *20681*

E **Cremanthodium arnicoides** (Wallich) ex DC.) R. Good *14768*
  E   India - Jammu & Kashmir (Apharwat) *14768*

Ex **Crepidiastrum ameristophyllum** (Koidz.) Nakai *8037*
  Ex *15112* Japan - Ogasawara-shoto *8037*

Ex **Crepidiastrum grandicollum** (Koidz.) Nakai *8037*
  Ex *15112* Japan - Ogasawara-shoto *8037*

R **Crepidiastrum lanceolatum** (Houtt.) Nakai forma **batakanensis** (Kitamura) Kitamura *20511*
  R *20511* Taiwan *20511*

V **Crepidiastrum linguaefolium** (Gray) Nakai *8048*
  V *19134* Japan - Ogasawara-shoto *8048*

R **Crepis albanica** (Jáv.) Babc. *20178, 20171*
  R *20178* Albania *20178*
  R   (former) Yugoslavia

R **Crepis albescens** Kuv. et Demid. *20085, 21309*
  R *20085* Russia (E.Europe) - North *20085*

R **Crepis amanica** Bobcock *12840*
  R *12840* Turkey *12840*

R **Crepis athoa** Boiss. *20171*
  R   Greece

R **Crepis aurea** (L.) Cass. ssp. **olympica** (C. Koch) Lamond *12840*
  R *12840* Turkey *12840*

V **Crepis bakeri** Babcock & Stebbins ssp. **idahoensis** Babcock & Stebbins *20850*
  V *20850* U.S. - Idaho *20850*

R **Crepis baldaccii** Halácsy *20178, 20171*
  R *20178* Albania *20178*
  R   Greece

R **Crepis bertiscea** Jáv. *20178, 20171*
  R *20178* Albania *20178*

R **Crepis bithynica** Boiss. *5204, 20171*
  R *5204* Bulgaria (Southern - two sites) *5204*

V **Crepis canariensis** (Schultz Bip.) Babc. *20750*
  V *15105* Spain - Canary Is. *15105*

E **Crepis claryi** Battand. *10488*
  E *14958* Algeria *10488*

E **Crepis crocifolia** Boiss. & Heldr. *8000, 20171*
  E   Greece (south - Taiyetos) *8000*

R **Crepis divaricata** (Lowe) F.W. Schultz *20171*
  R   Portugal - Madeira
  I   Portugal - Salvage Is.

E **Crepis faureliana** Maire *10488*
  E *14958* Algeria *10488*

R **Crepis fontiana** Babc.
  R   Morocco

V **Crepis granatensis** (Willk.) G. Blanca & M. Cueto *17891*
  V *11496* Spain (Mts of Jaén & Granada) *17891*

R **Crepis guioliana** Babc. *20171*
  R   Greece

R **Crepis hakkarica** Lamond *12840*
  R *12840* Turkey *12840*

R **Crepis heldreichiana** (Kuntze) Greuter
  R   Greece

R **Crepis hookeriana** Ball
  R   Morocco

I **Crepis libyca** (Pampan.) Babc.
  I   Egypt
  V   Libya

R **Crepis litardierei** Emberger
  R   Morocco

R **Crepis monticola** Coville *20850*
  I *20850* U.S. - California *20850*
  I *20850* U.S. - Oregon *20850*

R   *Crepis noronhaea* Babc.
      R   Portugal - Madeira

R   *Crepis pawlowskii* Strid
      R   Greece

R   *Crepis pusilla* (Sommier) Merxm. *13351, 20171*
      R   Greece
      R   *13351*   Malta *13351*
      R   *20076*   Portugal *20076*
      R   Spain - Balearic Is.

R   *Crepis suffreniana* (DC.) J.Lloyd *20171*
      I   France
      R   Italy

E   *Cronquistianthus loxensis* R. M. King & H.
       Robinson *20883*
      I   *20883*   Ecuador *20883*

R   *Cullumia pectinata* (Thunb.) Less. *20604*
      R   *20604*   South Africa - Cape Province *20604*

R   *Cyathocline lutea* Law ex Wight *14782*
      R   *14782*   India - Karnataka *14782*
      R   *14782*   India - Maharashtra *14782*

E   *Cylindrocline commersonii* Cass. *10082*
      E   *20771*   Mauritius *10082*

E   *Cylindrocline lorencei* A.J. Scott *10082*
      E   *20771*   Mauritius *10082*

V   *Dahlia rupicola* Sorensen *9553*
      V   *14294*   Mexico - Durango *9553*

R   *Dahlia scapigera* (A. Dietr.) Knowl. & Westc. *9553*
      R   *19755*   Mexico *9553*

R   *Dahlia tenuicaulis* Sorensen *9553*
      R   *19850*   Mexico (north eastern) *9553*

E   *Damnxanthodium calvum* (Greenman) Strother *20883*
      I   *20883*   Mexico *20883*

V   *Darwiniothamnus alternifolius* Lawesson &
       Adsersen *12250*
      V   *14980*   Ecuador - Galapagos *12250*

R   *Darwiniothamnus lancifolius* (Hook.f.) Harling ssp.
       glabrisculus Lawesson & Adsersen *11117*
      R   Ecuador - Galapagos (V. Sierra Negra, Isabela)
             11117

I   *Darwiniothamnus tenuifolius* (Hook.f.) Harling *11117*
      I   Ecuador - Galapagos *11117*

R   *Dasyphyllum excelsum* (D. Don) Cabr. *20883, 15088*
      I   *20883*   Chile *20883*

I   *Delilia inelegans* (Hook.f.) Kuntze *11117*
      I   Ecuador - Galapagos (Floreana) *11117*

R   *Dendranthema japonicum* (Makino) Kitam. var.
       wakasaense (Shimotomai) Kitam. *10573*
      R   *10573*   Japan *10573*

I   *Dendranthema sinuatum* (Ledeb.) Tsvelev *5942*
      I   *5942*   Russia (Siberia) - Altai *5942*
      I   *5942*   Russia (Siberia) - Tuva *5942*

R   *Dendranthema yoshinaganthum* (Makino & Kitam.)
       Kitam. *10573*
      R   *10573*   Japan *10573*

V   *Dendrocacalia crepidifolia* Nakai *8038*
      V   *19134*   Japan - Ogasawara-shoto *8038*

E   *Dendroseris berteriana* Hook. & Arn. *19116*
      E   *19125*   Chile - Juan Fernandez Is. *19116*

E   *Dendroseris gigantea* Johow *19116*
      E   *19125*   Chile - Juan Fernandez Is. *19116*

V   *Dendroseris litoralis* Skottsb. *20883, 19116*
      E   *19125*   Chile - Juan Fernandez Is. *19116*
      V   *20883*   Chile *20883*

E   *Dendroseris macrantha* (Bertero ex Decne.)
       Skottsb. *19116*
      E   *19125*   Chile - Juan Fernandez Is. *19116*

E   *Dendroseris macrophylla* D. Don *19116*
      E   *19125*   Chile - Juan Fernandez Is. *19116*

V   *Dendroseris marginata* (Bert. ex Decne.) Hook. &
       Arn. *19116*
      V   *19125*   Chile - Juan Fernandez Is. *19116*

V   *Dendroseris micrantha* Hook. et Arn. *19116*
      V   *19116*   Chile - Juan Fernandez Is. *19116*

E   *Dendroseris neriifolia* (Dcne.) H. et A. *20883, 19116*
      E   *19125*   Chile - Juan Fernandez Is. *19116*
      E   *20883*   Chile *20883*

E   *Dendroseris pinnata* Hook. et Arn. *19116*
      E   *19125*   Chile - Juan Fernandez Is. *19116*

V   *Dendroseris pruinata* Skottsb. *19116*
      V   *19125*   Chile - Juan Fernandez Is. *19116*

E   *Dendroseris regia* Skottsb. *19116*
      E   *19125*   Chile - Juan Fernandez Is. *19116*

I   *Desmanthodium hondurense* A. Molina *9039*
      I   *9730*   Honduras *9039*

V   *Dicoma cana* Balf. f. *15534*
      V   *15534*   Yemen - Socotra *15534*

V   *Dicoma niccolifera* Wild *6088*
      V   *6088*   Zimbabwe *6088*

V   *Dicoria wetherillii* Eastw. *20850*
      I   *20850*   U.S. - Utah *20850*

E   *Diplostephium santamartae* Cuatr. *20883*
      I   *20883*   Colombia *20883*

E   *Diplostephium serratifolium* Cuatr. *20883*
      I   *20883*   Peru *20883*

V   *Distephanus populifolia* (Lam.) Cass. *10082*
      V   *20771*   Mauritius *10082*

R   *Doronicum balansae* Cavill. *12840*
      R   *12840*   Turkey *12840*

R   *Doronicum bithynicum* Edmondson *12840*
      R   *12840*   Turkey *12840*

R   *Doronicum cacaliifolium* Boiss. & Heldr. *12840*
      R   *12840*   Turkey *12840*

R   *Doronicum cataractarum* Widder *20171*
      R   Austria

R   *Doronicum haussknechtii* Cavill. *12840*
      R   *12840*   Turkey *12840*

R   *Doronicum macrolepis* Freyn & Sint. *12840*
      R   *12840*   Turkey *12840*

V   *Doronicum plantagineum* L. ssp.
       tournefortii *17891*
      V   *20076*   Portugal *20076*

R   *Doronicum reticulatum* Boiss. *12840*
      R   *12840*   Turkey *12840*

R   *Doronicum tobeyi* J.R. Edmondson *12840*
      R   *12840*   Turkey *12840*

E   *Dresslerothamnus angustiradiatus* Rob. *20883, 10747*
      I   *20883*   Panama *20883*

E   *Dresslerothamnus gentryi* H. Robinson *20883*
      I   *20883*   Colombia *20883*

E **Dresslerothamnus peperomioides** H. Robinson *20883*
   I *20883* Panama *20883*

E **Dubautia arborea** (Gray) Keck *20850, 14209*
   E *20850* U.S. - Hawaii *20850*

V **Dubautia dolosa** (O. Deg. & Sherff) G.D. Carr *20850, 14209*
   I *20850* U.S. - Hawaii (East Maui) *20850*

E **Dubautia herbstobatae** G.D. Carr *20850, 14209*
   E *20850* U.S. - Hawaii (O`ahu - Wai`anae Mts.) *20850*

E **Dubautia imbricata** St. John & G.D. Carr *20850, 14209*
   I *20850* U.S. - Hawaii (Kaua`i) *20850*

E **Dubautia imbricata** St. John & G.D. Carr ssp. **acronaea** G.D. Carr *20850, 14209*
   E *20850* U.S. - Hawaii (Kaua`i) *20850*

E **Dubautia imbricata** St. John & G.D. Carr ssp. **imbricata** *20850*
   E *20850* U.S. - Hawaii *20850*

V **Dubautia knudsenii** Hbd. *20850*
   I *20850* U.S. - Hawaii *20850*

E **Dubautia knudsenii** Hillebr. ssp. *filiformis* G.D. Carr *20850, 14209*
   E *20850* U.S. - Hawaii (Kaua`i) *20850*

E **Dubautia knudsenii** Hillebr. ssp. **knudsenii** *20850*
   E *20850* U.S. - Hawaii *20850*

E **Dubautia knudsenii** Hillebr. ssp. *nagatae* (St. John) G.D. Carr *20850, 14209*
   E *20850* U.S. - Hawaii (Kaua`i) *20850*

E **Dubautia laevigata** Gray *20850*
   E *20850* U.S. - Hawaii *20850*

E **Dubautia latifolia** (Gray) Keck *20850, 14209*
   E *20850* U.S. - Hawaii (Kaua`i) *20850*

R **Dubautia linearis** (Gaud.) D. Keck ssp. *hillebrandii* (Mann) G.D. Carr *20850, 14209*
   I *20850* U.S. - Hawaii *20850*

E **Dubautia microcephala** Skottsberg *20850*
   E *20850* U.S. - Hawaii *20850*

R **Dubautia microcephala** Skottsb. var. **microcephala** *14209*
   R *14209* U.S. - Hawaii (Kaua`i) *14209*

R **Dubautia paleata** Gray *20850, 14209*
   I *20850* U.S. - Hawaii (Kaua`i) *20850*

E **Dubautia pauciflorula** St. John & G.D. Carr *20850, 14209*
   E *20850* U.S. - Hawaii (kaua`i) *20850*

E **Dubautia plantaginea** Gaud. ssp. *humilis* G. Carr *20850, 14209*
   E *20850* U.S. - Hawaii (West Maui) *20850*

V **Dubautia platyphylla** (Gray) Keck *20850, 14209*
   I *20850* U.S. - Hawaii (Maui) *20850*

V **Dubautia raillardioides** Hbd. *20850, 14209*
   I *20850* U.S. - Hawaii (Kaua`i) *20850*

V **Dubautia reticulata** (Sherff) Keck *20850, 14209*
   V *20850* U.S. - Hawaii (Maui) *20850*

E **Dubautia sherffiana** Fosberg *20850, 14209*
   E *20850* U.S. - Hawaii (O`ahu - Wai`anae Mts.) *20850*

E **Dubautia waialealae** Rock *20850*

E *20850* U.S. - Hawaii *20850*

R **Dymondia margaretae** Compton *20604*
   R *20604* South Africa - Cape Province *20604*

R **Dyssodia gentryi** M. Johnston *14294*
   R *14294* Mexico - Durango *14294*

R **Eastwoodia elegans** Brandeg. *20850*
   I *20850* U.S. - California *20850*

V **Echinacea laevigata** (C.L. Boynt. & Beadle) Blake *20850, 15014*
   Ex *15014* U.S. - Alabama *15014*
   Ex *15014* U.S. - Arkansas *15014*
   E *20850* U.S. - Georgia (Stephens Co.) *20850*
   Ex *15014* U.S. - Maryland *15014*
   E *20850* U.S. - North Carolina (Durham & Granville Co.) *20850*
   Ex *20850* U.S. - Pennsylvania *20850*
   E *20850* U.S. - South Carolina (Oconee Co.) *20850*
   V *20850* U.S. - Virginia (Pulaski, Montgomery, Campbell & Gran Counties) *20850*

E **Echinacea paradoxa** Britton var. *neglecta* R.L. McGregor *20850*
   E *20850* U.S. - Oklahoma *20850*

R **Echinacea paradoxa** Britton var. **paradoxa** *20850*
   V *20850* U.S. - Arkansas *20850*
   I *20850* U.S. - Missouri *20850*

R **Echinacea simulata** R.L. McGregor *20850*
   I *20850* U.S. - Indiana *20850*
   I *20850* U.S. - Kentucky *20850*
   I *20850* U.S. - Missouri *20850*
   I *20850* U.S. - Tennessee *20850*

E **Echinacea tennesseensis** (Beadle) Small *20850*
   E *20850* U.S. - Tennessee *20850*

R **Echinops emiliae** O. Schwarz ex Davis *12840*
   R *12840* Turkey *12840*

R **Echinops melitenensis** Hedge & Hub.-Mor. *12840*
   R *12840* Turkey *12840*

R **Echinops onopordum** Davis *12840*
   R *12840* Turkey *12840*

R **Echinops pungens** Trautv. var. *adenoclados* Hedge *12840*
   R *12840* Turkey *12840*

R **Echinops saissanicus** (B. Keller) Bobrov *5942*
   R *5942* Kazakhstan (east) *5942*

R **Echinops spinosus** sensu Hayek, non L. *20171*
   R Italy - Sicily

R **Echinops vaginatus** Boiss. & Hausskn. *12840*
   R *12840* Turkey *12840*

V **Ekmania lepidota** (Griseb.) Gleas. *5607*
   V *19105* Cuba (Guantanamo) *5607*

R **Elachanthus glaber** Paul G. Wilson *20681*
   I *20681* Australia - South Australia *20681*
   I *20681* Australia - Victoria *20681*

E **Elephantopus arenarius** Britton & P. Wilson *5607*
   E *19105* Cuba (Pinar del Rio; I. Juventud) *5607*

R **Elytropappus hispidus** (L.f.) Druce *20604*
   R *20604* South Africa - Cape Province *20604*

V **Embergeria grandifolia** (Kirk) Boulos *86*
   V *19305* New Zealand - Chatham Is. *19106*

R **Encelia hispida** Andersson *11117*
   R Ecuador - Galapagos *11117*

R   *Encelia scaposa* (Gray) Gray *20850*
    I   *20850* U.S. - New Mexico *20850*
    E   *20850* U.S. - Texas *20850*

V   *Enceliopsis covillei* (A. Nels.) Blake *20850*
    V   *20850* U.S. - California *20850*
    I   *20850* U.S. - Nevada *20850*

V   *Enceliopsis nudicaulis* (A.Gray) Nelson var.
    corrugata Cronq. *20850*
    V   *20850* U.S. - Nevada *20850*

E   *Epaltes mattfeldii* Urban *5607*
    E   *19105* Cuba (Pinar del Rio) *5607*

E   *Eremanthus argenteus* MacLeish & Schumacher *20883*
    I   *20883* Brazil *20883*

E   *Eremanthus auriculatus* MacLeish & Schumacher *20883*
    I   *20883* Brazil *20883*

V   *Eremanthus graciellae* MacLeish & Schumacher *20883*
    I   *20883* Brazil *20883*

V   *Eremanthus rondoniensis* MacLeish & Schumacher *20883*
    I   *20883* Brazil *20883*

E   *Eremanthus seidelii* MacLeish & Schumacher *20883*
    I   *20883* Brazil *20883*

V   *Eremanthus uniflorus* MacLeish & Schumacher *20883*
    I   *20883* Brazil *20883*

V   *Ericameria cervina* (S.Watson) Rydb. *20850*
    V   *20850* U.S. - Arizona *20850*
    V   *20850* U.S. - Utah *20850*

V   *Ericameria crispa* (L.C. Anders.) Nesom *20850*
    V   *20850* U.S. - Utah *20850*

V   *Ericameria cuneata* (Gray) McClatchie var.
    macrocephala Urbatsch *20850*
    V   *20850* U.S. - California *20850*

V   *Ericameria discoidea* var. *linearis* (Rydb.)
    Nesom *20850*
    R   *20850* U.S. - Montana *20850*
    V   *20850* U.S. - Wyoming *20850*

R   *Ericameria ericoides* (Less.) Jepson *20850*
    I   *20850* U.S. - California *20850*

V   *Ericameria fasciculata* (Eastw.) J.F. Macbr. *20850*
    V   *20850* U.S. - California *20850*

V   *Ericameria gilmanii* (Blake) Nesom *20850*
    V   *20850* U.S. - California *20850*

V   *Ericameria palmeri* (Gray) Hall var. *palmeri*
    Gray *20883, 20850*
    E   *20850* U.S. - California *20850*
    I   *20883* Mexico *20883*

V   *Ericameria pinifolia* (Gray) Hall *20850*
    I   *20850* U.S. - California *20850*

E   *Ericameria riskindii* Turner & Langford *20883, 10349*
    I   *20883* Mexico *20883*
    ?   Mexico - Coahuila *10349*

V   *Ericameria zionis* (L.C. Anders.) Nesom *20850*
    V   *20850* U.S. - Utah *20850*

E   *Erigeron abajoensis* Cronq. *20850*
    E   *20850* U.S. - Utah *20850*

E   *Erigeron acomanus* Spellenberg & P. Knight *20850*
    E   *20850* U.S. - New Mexico *20850*

V   *Erigeron aequifolius* Hall *20850*
    V   *20850* U.S. - California *20850*

V   *Erigeron algidus* Jepson *20850*
    I   *20850* U.S. - California *20850*

    I   *20850* U.S. - Nevada *20850*

R   *Erigeron allocotus* Blake *20850*
    R   *20850* U.S. - Montana *20850*
    R   *20850* U.S. - Wyoming *20850*

V   *Erigeron anchana* Nesom *20850*
    V   *20850* U.S. - Arizona *20850*
    I   *20850* U.S. - New Mexico *20850*

V   *Erigeron arenarioides* (D.C. Eat. ex Gray) Gray ex
    Rydb. *20850*
    V   *20850* U.S. - Utah *20850*

E   *Erigeron arizonicus* Gray *20850*
    E   *20850* U.S. - Arizona *20850*
    I   *20850* U.S. - New Mexico *20850*

E   *Erigeron awapensis* Welsh *20850*
    E   *20850* U.S. - Utah *20850*

R   *Erigeron barbellulatus* Greene *20850*
    I   *20850* U.S. - California *20850*

E   *Erigeron basalticus* Hoover *20850*
    E   *20850* U.S. - Washington *20850*

V   *Erigeron blochmaniae* Greene *20850*
    V   *20850* U.S. - California *20850*

R   *Erigeron breweri* Gray var. *jacinteus* (Hall)
    Cronq. *20850*
    R   *20850* U.S. - California *20850*

R   *Erigeron cabrerae* Dittrich *17530*
    R   *20750* Spain - Canary Is. *15105*

R   *Erigeron candidus* Widder *20171*
    R   Austria

E   *Erigeron carringtoniae* Welsh *20850*
    E   *20850* U.S. - Utah *20850*

R   *Erigeron compositus* Pursh *11552*
    I   *5942* Russia (Far East) - Kamchatka *5942*
    I   *5942* Russia (Far East) - Magadan *5942*
    R   *20085* Russia (E.Europe) - North *20085*

R   *Erigeron consimilis* Cronq. *20850*
    I   *20850* U.S. - Arizona *20850*
    I   *20850* U.S. - Colorado *20850*
    I   *20850* U.S. - New Mexico *20850*
    I   *20850* U.S. - Utah *20850*
    V   *20850* U.S. - Wyoming *20850*

V   *Erigeron cronquistii* Maguire *20850*
    I   *20850* U.S. - Idaho *20850*
    V   *20850* U.S. - Utah *20850*

R   *Erigeron darrellianus* Hemsley
    R   Bermuda

E   *Erigeron decumbens* Nutt. var.
    decumbens *20850*
    E   *20850* U.S. - Oregon *20850*

I   *Erigeron domingensis* Urban *5642*
    I   Dominican Republic *5642*

R   *Erigeron eatonii* Strother & Ferlatte var. *lavandulus*
    Strother & Ferlatte *20850*
    R   *20850* U.S. - Idaho *20850*
    I   *20850* U.S. - Oregon *20850*

R   *Erigeron elatior* (Gray) Greene *20850*
    R   *20850* U.S. - Colorado *20850*
    I   *20850* U.S. - New Mexico *20850*
    E   *20850* U.S. - Utah *20850*
    V   *20850* U.S. - Wyoming *20850*

V   *Erigeron engelmannii* (Cronq.) Cronq. var. *davisii*
    (Cronq.) Cronq. *20850*
    V   *20850* U.S. - Idaho *20850*

Magnoliopsida (dicots): Compositae: *Erigeron*

E		20850 U.S. - Oregon 20850
R	*Erigeron flettii* G.N. Jones 20850	
I		20850 U.S. - Washington 20850
V	*Erigeron frigidus* Boiss. ex DC. 15398, 20171	
V		20874 Spain (Sierra Nevada) 15398
I	*Erigeron fuertesii* Urban 5642	
I		Dominican Republic 5642
V	*Erigeron garrettii* A. Nels. 20850	
V		20850 U.S. - Utah 20850
R	*Erigeron gilensis* Woot. & Standl. 20850	
I		20850 U.S. - Arizona 20850
E	*Erigeron goodrichii* Welsh 20850	
E		20850 U.S. - Utah 20850
V	*Erigeron heliographis* Nesom 20850	
V		20850 U.S. - Arizona 20850
I		20850 U.S. - New Mexico 20850
E	*Erigeron hessii* Nesom 20850	
E		20850 U.S. - New Mexico 20850
V	*Erigeron howellii* Gray 20850	
V		20850 U.S. - Oregon 20850
E		20850 U.S. - Washington 20850
E	*Erigeron hultenii* Spongberg 20850	
E		20850 U.S. - Alaska 20850
E	*Erigeron hyssopifolius* Michx. var. *villicaulis*	
	Fern. 20850, 1034	
E		20850 Canada - Newfoundland (Island) 20850
E		20850 Canada - Quebec 20850
R	*Erigeron incertus* (Urv.) Skottsb.	
R		Falkland Is.
E	*Erigeron ingae* Skottsb. 19116	
E		19125 Chile - Juan Fernandez Is. 19116
V	*Erigeron jonesii* Cronq. 20850	
I		20850 U.S. - Idaho 20850
I		20850 U.S. - Nevada 20850
V		20850 U.S. - Utah 20850
V	*Erigeron kachinensis* Welsh & Moore 20850	
E		20850 U.S. - Colorado 20850
V		20850 U.S. - Utah 20850
E	*Erigeron kuschei* Eastw. 20850	
E		20850 U.S. - Arizona 20850
R	*Erigeron lanatus* Hook. 20850	
I		20850 Canada - Alberta 20850
V		20850 Canada - British Columbia 20850
I		20850 Canada - Yukon Territory 20850
E		20850 U.S. - Colorado 20850
R		20850 U.S. - Montana 20850
E		20850 U.S. - Wyoming 20850
R	*Erigeron lassenianus* Greene 20850	
I		20850 U.S. - California 20850
V	*Erigeron latus* (A. Nels. & J.F. Macbr.) Cronq. 20850	
V		20850 U.S. - Idaho 20850
E		20850 U.S. - Nevada 20850
R	*Erigeron leibergii* Piper 20850, 10701	
E		20850 Canada - British Columbia 20850
I		20850 U.S. - Washington 20850
E	*Erigeron lemmonii* Gray 20850	
E		20850 U.S. - Arizona 20850
V	*Erigeron libanensis* Urban 5607	
V		19105 Cuba (Guantanamo) 5607
V	*Erigeron maguirei* Cronq. 20850	
V		20850 U.S. - Utah 20850

E	*Erigeron maguirei* Cronq. var. *harrisonii*	
	Welsh 20850, 11630	
	20850 U.S. - Utah 20850	
E	*Erigeron maguirei* Cronq. var. *maguirei* 20850	
	20850 U.S. - Utah 20850	
R	*Erigeron major* (Boiss.) Vierh. 20171	
R		Spain
V	*Erigeron mancus* Rydb. 20850	
V		20850 U.S. - Utah 20850
Ex/E	*Erigeron mariposanus* Congdon 20850	
Ex/E		20850 U.S. - California 20850
R	*Erigeron melanocephalus* (A. Nels.) A. Nels. 20850	
R		20850 U.S. - Colorado 20850
I		20850 U.S. - New Mexico 20850
E		20850 U.S. - Utah 20850
V		20850 U.S. - Wyoming 20850
V	*Erigeron mimegletes* Shinners 20850	
V		20850 U.S. - Texas 20850
R	*Erigeron miyabeanus* Tatew. & Kimura 10573	
R		10573 Japan 10573
V	*Erigeron muirii* Gray 20850, 1034, 21309	
E		20850 Canada - Yukon Territory 20850
V		20850 U.S. - Alaska 20850
E	*Erigeron multiceps* Greene 20850	
E		20850 U.S. - California 20850
R	*Erigeron nanus* Schur 8000, 20171	
R		Czech Republic 8000
R		18216 Poland (Tatry Mts.) 18216
R		19947 Romania 19417
V		19321 Slovakia 19321
R	*Erigeron nematophyllus* Rydb. 20850	
I		20850 U.S. - Colorado 20850
E		20850 U.S. - Utah 20850
R		20850 U.S. - Wyoming 20850
R	*Erigeron ochroleucus* Nutt. var.	
	ochroleucus 20850	
I		20850 Canada - Alberta 20850
I		20850 U.S. - Colorado 20850
R		20850 U.S. - Montana 20850
I		20850 U.S. - South Dakota 20850
R		20850 U.S. - Wyoming 20850
I	*Erigeron ocoensis* Urban 5642	
I		Dominican Republic 5642
R	*Erigeron oreganus* Gray 20850	
R		20850 U.S. - Oregon 20850
E		20850 U.S. - Washington 20850
E	*Erigeron ovinus* Cronq. 20850	
V		20850 U.S. - Nevada 20850
E	*Erigeron oxyphyllus* Greene 20850	
I		20850 U.S. - Arizona 20850
V	*Erigeron pallens* Cronq. 20850	
I		20850 Canada - Alberta 20850
I		20850 Canada - British Columbia 20850
I		20850 Canada - Mackenzie 20850
V	*Erigeron paolii* Gamisans 15080	
V		15080 France - Corsica 15080
V	*Erigeron parishii* Gray 20850	
V		20850 U.S. - California 20850
V	*Erigeron paucilobus* Urban 5607	
V		19105 Cuba (Pinar del Rio) 5607
V	*Erigeron peregrinus* (Blake ex J.W. Thompson) Cronq. var.	
	thompsonii (Blake ex J.W. Thompson) Cronq. 20850	

V 20850 U.S. - Washington *20850*

E **Erigeron philadelphicus** (Victorin & Rouss.) Boivin var.
  provancheri (Victorin & Rouss.) Boivin *20850*
 I 20850 Canada - Ontario *20850*
 E 20850 Canada - Quebec *20850*
 I 20850 U.S. - New York *20850*
 I 20850 U.S. - Vermont *20850*

R **Erigeron pinnatisectus** (Gray) A. Nels. *20850*
 R 20850 U.S. - Colorado *20850*
 I 20850 U.S. - New Mexico *20850*
 V 20850 U.S. - Wyoming *20850*

V **Erigeron piperianus** Cronq. *20850*
 V 20850 U.S. - Washington *20850*

E **Erigeron piscaticus** Nesom *20850*
 E 20850 U.S. - Arizona *20850*

R **Erigeron pringlei** Gray *20850*
 R 20850 U.S. - Arizona *20850*

V **Erigeron proselyticus** Nesom *20850*
 V 20850 U.S. - Utah *20850*

I **Erigeron psilocaulis** Urban *5642*
 I Dominican Republic *5642*

E **Erigeron pulchellus** Michaux var. *tolsteadii*
  Cronq. *20850*
  20850 U.S. - Minnesota *20850*

R **Erigeron pygmaeus** (Gray) Greene *20850*
 I 20850 U.S. - California *20850*
 I 20850 U.S. - Nevada *20850*

R **Erigeron radicatus** Hook. *20850, 2063*
 E 20850 Canada - Alberta *20850*
 V 20850 Canada - Saskatchewan *20850*
 R 20850 U.S. - Idaho *20850*
 R 20850 U.S. - Montana *20850*
 E 20850 U.S. - North Dakota *20850*
 E 20850 U.S. - Wyoming *20850*

I **Erigeron rapensis** F.Brown *20845*
 I 20845 French Polynesia - Tubuai Is. (Rapa)
  20845

V **Erigeron religiosus** Cronq. *20850*
 V 20850 U.S. - Utah *20850*

V **Erigeron rhizomatus** Cronq. *20850*
 V 20850 U.S. - New Mexico (McKinley & Catron Co.)
  20850

E **Erigeron rupicola** Philippi *19116*
 E 19125 Chile - Juan Fernandez Is. *19116*

R **Erigeron rybius** Nesom *20850*
 R 20850 U.S. - New Mexico *20850*

V **Erigeron salishii** G.W. Douglas & Packer *20850, 14410*
 E 20850 Canada - British Columbia *20850*
 V 20850 U.S. - Washington *20850*

V **Erigeron salmonensis** S.J. Brunsfeld & Nesom *20850*
 V 20850 U.S. - Idaho *20850*

V **Erigeron saxatilis** Nesom *20850*
 V 20850 U.S. - Arizona *20850*

R **Erigeron setosus** (Benth.) M.Gray *20681*
 R 20681 Australia - New South Wales *20681*

V **Erigeron sionis** Cronq. *20850*
 V 20850 U.S. - Utah *20850*

I **Erigeron subalpinus** Urban *5642*
 I Dominican Republic *5642*

R **Erigeron subglaber** Cronq. *20850*
 R 20850 U.S. - New Mexico *20850*

E **Erigeron supplex** Gray *20850*
 E 20850 U.S. - California *20850*

E **Erigeron taylori** Britton & P. Wilson *5607*
 E Cuba (Santiago de Cuba) *5607*

R **Erigeron thunbergii** A.Gray var. *angustifolius*
  (Tatew.) Hara *10573*
 R 10573 Japan *10573*

V **Erigeron trifidus** Hook. *20850, 15882*
 V 20850 Canada - Alberta *20850*
 E 20850 Canada - British Columbia *20850*
 I 20850 Canada - Saskatchewan *20850*

I **Erigeron tuerckheimii** Urb. *19408, 10260*
 I 19408 Dominican Republic *19408*

R **Erigeron uncialis** (Blake) Cronq. ssp. *conjugans*
  (Blake) Cronq. *20850*
 R 20850 U.S. - Nevada *20850*

E **Erigeron untermannii** Welsh & Goodrich *20850, 11630*
 E 20850 U.S. - Utah *20850*

R **Erigeron utahensis** Gray var. *sparsifolius* (Eastw.)
  Cronq. *20850*
 I 20850 U.S. - Arizona *20850*
 I 20850 U.S. - Colorado *20850*
 I 20850 U.S. - New Mexico *20850*
 V 20850 U.S. - Utah *20850*

I **Erigeron vegaensis** Urb. *19408, 10260*
 I 19408 Dominican Republic *19408*

E **Erigeron wilkenii** O'Kane *20850*
 E 20850 U.S. - Colorado *20850*

E **Erigeron zothecinus** Welsh *20850*
 E 20850 U.S. - Utah *20850*

R **Eriophyllum ambiguum** (Gray) Gray *20850*
 I 20850 U.S. - California *20850*
 I 20850 U.S. - Nevada *20850*

V **Eriophyllum congdonii** Brandeg. *20850*
 V 20850 U.S. - California *20850*

E **Eriophyllum lanatum** (Pursh) James Forbes var. *hallii*
  Constance *20850*
 E 20850 U.S. - California *20850*

R **Eriophyllum lanatum** (Pursh) Forbes var. *obovatum*
  (Greene) Hall *20850*
 I 20850 U.S. - California *20850*

E **Eriophyllum latilobum** Rydb. *20850*
 E 20850 U.S. - California *20850*

V **Eriophyllum mohavense** (I.M. Johnston) Jepson *20850*
 V 20850 U.S. - California *20850*

V **Eriophyllum nevinii** Gray *20850*
 V 20850 U.S. - California *20850*

V **Eriophyllum nubigenum** Greene ex Gray *20850*
 V 20850 U.S. - California *20850*

R **Eriophyllum tanacetiflorum** Greene *20850*
 I 20850 U.S. - California *20850*

R **Erlangea westii** Wild *7754*
 R Zimbabwe (Chimanimani) *7754*

I **Erythrocephalum niasssae** Wild *7923*
 I Mozambique *7923*

V **Eupatorium anomalum** Nash *20850*
 I 20850 U.S. - Alabama *20850*
 I 20850 U.S. - Florida *20850*
 I 20850 U.S. - Georgia *20850*
 E 20850 U.S. - North Carolina *20850*
 I 20850 U.S. - South Carolina *20850*

R	*Eupatorium atroglandulosum* **Alain** *5607*	
	R	*19105* Cuba (Sancti Spiritus) *5607*
R	*Eupatorium betonicifolium* **P. Mill.** *20850*	
	R	*20850* U.S. - Texas *20850*
E	*Eupatorium bigelovii* **Gray** *20883, 20850*	
	I	*20850* U.S. - Arizona *20850*
	I	*20883* Mexico *20883*
V	*Eupatorium borinquense* (**Britt.**) **B.L. Robins.** *20883*	
	I	*20883* Puerto Rico *20883*
V	*Eupatorium breviflorum* **Alain** *5607*	
	V	*19105* Cuba (Pinar del Rio) *5607*
E	*Eupatorium chalceorithales* **Robins.**	
	E	*19105* Cuba *19105*
I	*Eupatorium constanzae* **Urban** *5642*	
	I	Dominican Republic (Constanza) *5642*
V	*Eupatorium contortum* **C.D. Adams** *13336*	
	V	*13336* Jamaica *13336*
I	*Eupatorium cordifolium* **Sw.** *13336*	
	I	*13336* Jamaica *13336*
I	*Eupatorium correlliorum* **Plettman**	
	I	*4650* Bahamas *4650*
V	*Eupatorium critoniforme* **Urb. var.** *pubescens* **C.D.Adams** *13336*	
	V	*13336* Jamaica *13336*
V	*Eupatorium dolphini* **Urb.** *13336*	
	V	*13867* Jamaica (Hanover, Dolphin Head) *13336*
Ex/E	*Eupatorium droserolepis* **B.L. Robins.** *20883, 14662*	
	I	*20883* Puerto Rico *20883*
V	*Eupatorium frustratum* **B.L. Robins.** *20850*	
	I	*20850* U.S. - Florida *20850*
R	*Eupatorium hammatocladum* **Robins. & Britton** *13336*	
	R	*13336* Jamaica *13336*
V	*Eupatorium hardwarense* **Proctor ex Adams** *13336*	
	V	*13336* Jamaica *13336*
V	*Eupatorium hartii* **Urb.** *13336*	
	V	*13336* Jamaica *13336*
I	*Eupatorium heterosquameum* **Urban** *5642*	
	I	Dominican Republic (Jimani) *5642*
I	*Eupatorium imbricatum* (**Griseb.**) **Urban** *5607*	
	I	*19105* Cuba (Guantanamo) *5607*
E	*Eupatorium leucolepis* (**DC.**) **Torr. & A.Gray var.** *novae-angliae* **Fern.** *20850*	
	E	*20850* U.S. - Massachusetts *20850*
	I	*20850* U.S. - New York *20850*
	E	*20850* U.S. - Rhode Is. *20850*
I	*Eupatorium nervosum* **Sw.** *13336*	
	I	*13336* Jamaica *13336*
V	*Eupatorium oligadenium* **Alain** *5607*	
	V	*19105* Cuba (Guantanamo) *5607*
E	*Eupatorium oteroi* **Monachino** *20883*	
	I	*20883* Puerto Rico (Mona) *20883*
R	*Eupatorium platychaetum* **Urb.** *13336*	
	R	*13336* Jamaica *13336*
R	*Eupatorium resinosum* **Torr. ex DC.** *20850*	
	Ex/E	*20850* U.S. - Delaware *20850*
	V	*20850* U.S. - New Jersey *20850*
	Ex	*20850* U.S. - New York *20850*
	V	*20850* U.S. - North Carolina *20850*
	I	*20850* U.S. - South Carolina *20850*
R	*Eupatorium rigidum* **Sw.** *13336*	

	R	*13336* Jamaica *13336*
V	*Eupatorium schizanthum* **Griseb.** *13336*	
	V	*19890* Jamaica (John Crow Peak) *19389*
V	*Eupatorium tetranthum* **Griseb.** *13336*	
	V	*13336* Jamaica *13336*
R	*Eupatorium yakushimense* **Masam. & Kitam.** *10573*	
	R	*10573* Japan *10573*
R	*Euryops brevilobus* **Compton** *20604*	
	R	*20604* South Africa - Cape Province *20604*
R	*Euryops brevipes* **B.Nord.** *20604*	
	R	*20604* South Africa - Natal *20604*
I	*Euryops ciliatus* **B.Nord.** *20604*	
	I	*20604* South Africa - Cape Province *20604*
R	*Euryops decipiens* **Schltr.** *20604*	
	R	*20604* South Africa - Cape Province *20604*
R	*Euryops dentatus* **B.Nord.** *20604*	
	R	*20604* South Africa - Cape Province *20604*
I	*Euryops hypnoides* **B.Nord.** *20604*	
	I	*20604* South Africa - Cape Province *20604*
R	*Euryops indecorus* **B.Nord.** *20604*	
	R	*20604* South Africa - Cape Province *20604*
R	*Euryops integrifolius* **B.Nord.** *20604*	
	R	*20604* South Africa - Cape Province *20604*
I	*Euryops lasiocladus* (**DC.**) **B.Nord.** *20604*	
	I	*20604* South Africa - Cape Province *20604*
R	*Euryops latifolius* **B.Nord.** *20604*	
	R	*20604* South Africa - Cape Province *20604*
R	*Euryops linearis* **Harv.** *20604*	
	R	*20604* South Africa - Cape Province *20604*
R	*Euryops marlothii* **B.Nord.** *20604*	
	R	*20604* South Africa - Cape Province *20604*
V	*Euryops mirus* **B.Nord.** *20604*	
	V	*20604* South Africa - Cape Province *20604*
E	*Euryops muirii* **C.A.Sm.** *20604*	
	E	*20604* South Africa - Cape Province *20604*
R	*Euryops pectinatus* (**L.**) **Cass. ssp.** *lobulatus* **B. Nordenstam** *20604*	
	R	*20604* South Africa - Cape Province *20604*
I	*Euryops pleiodontus* **B.Nord.** *20604*	
	I	*20604* South Africa - Cape Province *20604*
I	*Euryops polytrichoides* (**Harv.**) **B.Nord.** *20604*	
	I	*20604* South Africa - Cape Province *20604*
R	*Euryops rosulatus* **B.Nord.** *20604*	
	R	*20604* South Africa - Cape Province *20604*
R	*Euryops subcarnosus* **DC. ssp.** *minor* **B. Nordenstam** *20604*	
	R	*20604* South Africa - Cape Province *20604*
I	*Euryops ursinoides* **B.Nord.** *20604*	
	I	*20604* South Africa - Cape Province *20604*
R	*Euryops virgatus* **B.Nord.** *20604*	
	R	*20604* South Africa - Cape Province *20604*
R	*Euthamia tenuifolia* (**Pursh**) **Greene var.** *pycnocephala* (**Fern.**) **C.& J. Taylor** *20850*	
	R	*20850* Canada - Nova Scotia *20850*
	E	*20850* U.S. - Maine *20850*
	E	*20850* U.S. - Massachusetts *20850*
	I	*20850* U.S. - New Hampshire *20850*
	I	*20850* U.S. - New York *20850*
I	*Evax longilanata* **Maire & Wilczek**	

I		Morocco
R	***Evax rotundata*** Moris *8000, 20171*	
R	*15080* France - Corsica *15080*	
R	*18264* Italy - Sardinia *18264*	
R	***Ewartia sinclairii*** (Hook.f.) Cheeseman	
R		New Zealand - South Is.
R	***Farfugium hiberniflorum*** (Makino) Kitam. *10573*	
R	*10573* Japan *10573*	
R	***Faujasia flexuosa*** (Lam.) C.Jeffrey ssp. ***erecta*** C.Jeffrey *20771*	
R	*20771* Mauritius *20771*	
E	***Faujasia reticulata*** (Vahl) C.Jeffrey *20771*	
E	*20771* Mauritius *10710*	
I	***Faujasia squamosa*** (Bory) C.Jeffrey *10082*	
I	*14234* Réunion *10082*	
R	***Feddea cubensis*** Urban *5607*	
R	*19105* Cuba (Holguin; Guantanamo) *5607*	
Ex	***Felicia annectens*** (Harv.) Grau *20604, 6180*	
Ex	*20604* South Africa - Cape Province *20604*	
I	***Felicia dentata*** (A. Rich.) Dandy in F.W. Andrews ssp. ***nubica*** Grau	
I	*5908* Sudan (Djebel Marra) *5908*	
R	***Felicia diffusa*** (DC.) Grau ssp. ***khamiesbergensis*** Grau *20604*	
R	*20604* South Africa - Cape Province *20604*	
V	***Felicia elongata*** (Thunb.) O.Hoffm. *20604*	
V	*20604* South Africa - Cape Province *20604*	
R	***Felicia esterhuyseniae*** Grau *20604*	
R	*20604* South Africa - Cape Province *20604*	
R	***Felicia fruticosa*** (L.) G.Nicholson ssp. ***brevipedunculata*** (Hutch.) Grau *20604*	
R	*20604* South Africa - Transvaal *20604*	
R	***Felicia tsitsikamae*** Grau *20604*	
R	*20604* South Africa - Cape Province *20604*	
R	***Felicia wrightii*** Hilliard & B.L.Burtt *20604*	
R	*20604* South Africa - Natal *20604*	
E	***Femeniasia balearica*** (Rodr.) Susanna *20645*	
E	*20874* Spain - Balearic Is. (north Menorca) *20656*	
V	***Ferreyranthus rugosus*** (Ferreyra) H. Robinson&Brettell *18200*	
V	*12468* Peru *18200*	
I	***Filago bolivari*** Caballero	
I		Morocco
I	***Filago duriaei*** Coss. ex Lange *20171*	
I		Spain
I	***Filago evaciformis*** Maire & G. Samuelsson	
I		Morocco
E	***Fitchia cordata*** M.Grant & Carlquist *20845*	
E	*20845* French Polynesia - Society Is. (Bora Bora) *20845*	
E	***Fitchia cuneata*** J.Moore ssp. ***cuneata*** *20845*	
E	*20845* French Polynesia - Society Is. (Raiatea) *20845*	
Ex	***Fitchia mangarevensis*** F.Brown *20845*	
Ex	*20845* French Polynesia - Tuamotu Is. (Gambier, Taravai) *20845*	
V	***Fitchia nutans*** J.Hooker *20845*	
V	*20845* French Polynesia - Society Is. (Tahiti) *20845*	

E	***Fitchia speciosa*** Cheesem. *19473*	
E	*19473* Cook Is.(Southern group) (Rarotonga) *19473*	
V	***Fitchia tahitensis*** Nadeaud *20845*	
V	*20845* French Polynesia - Society Is. (Tahiti) *20845*	
R	***Flaveria floridana*** J.R. Johnston *20850*	
I	*20850* U.S. - Florida *20850*	
V	***Flaveria macdougalii*** Theroux, Pinkava & Keil *20850*	
V	*20850* U.S. - Arizona *20850*	
E	***Fleischmannia allenii*** K. & R. *20883, 9006*	
I	*20883* Panama *20883*	
E	***Fleischmannia chiriquensis*** K. & R. *20883, 9006*	
I	*20883* Panama *20883*	
E	***Fleischmannia croatii*** K. & R. *20883, 9006*	
I	*20883* Panama *20883*	
E	***Fleischmannia panamensis*** K. & R. *20883, 9006*	
I	*20883* Panama *20883*	
E	***Fleischmannia tysonii*** K. & R. *20883, 9006*	
I	*20883* Panama *20883*	
R	***Flourensia microphylla*** (A.Gray) S.F. Blake *10358*	
R	*10358* Mexico - Coahuila *10358*	
R	***Flourensia solitaria*** S.F. Blake *10358*	
R	*10358* Mexico - Coahuila *10358*	
R	***Fontquera paui*** (Font Quer) Maire	
R		Morocco
V	***Fulcaldea laurifolia*** (Kunth) Poiret *18200*	
V	*12468* Peru *18200*	
E	***Gaillardia aestivalis*** (Cory) B.L. Turner var. ***winkleri*** (Cory) B.L. Turner *20850*	
E	*20850* U.S. - Texas *20850*	
R	***Gaillardia cabrera*** Covas *16336*	
R	*20176* Argentina - La Pampa (Sierras de Lihué Calel) *20176*	
V	***Gaillardia flava*** Rydb. *20850*	
V	*20850* U.S. - Utah *20850*	
V	***Gaillardia parryi*** Greene *20850*	
I	*20850* U.S. - Arizona *20850*	
V	*20850* U.S. - Utah *20850*	
R	***Galatella saxatilis*** Novopokr. *8001*	
R	former USSR (Tien Shan) *6930*	
R	***Galinsoga spellenbergii*** B. Turner *12029*	
R	*14294* Mexico - Durango *12029*	
R	***Gerbera aurantiaca*** (Cass.) Sch.Bip. *20604*	
V	*20604* South Africa - Natal *20604*	
R	***Gerbera wrightii*** Harv. *20604*	
R	*20604* South Africa - Cape Province *20604*	
E	***Glossarion bilabiatum*** (Maguire) Pruski *20883*	
I	*20883* Venezuela *20883*	
R	***Glossogyne integrifolia*** Gagnep. *19120*	
R	*19120* Thailand *19120*	
V	***Gnaphalium arizonicum*** Gray *20883, 20850*	
I	*20850* U.S. - Arizona *20850*	
I	*20883* Mexico *20883*	
R	***Gnaphalium griquense*** Hilliard & B.L.Burtt *20604*	
R	*20604* Lesotho *20604*	
R	*20604* South Africa - Natal *20604*	
R	***Gnaphalium helleri*** Britt. var. ***helleri*** *20850*	
I	*20850* U.S. - Alabama *20850*	
I	*20850* U.S. - Arkansas *20850*	

I	*20850*	U.S. - Florida	*20850*
I	*20850*	U.S. - Georgia	*20850*
I	*20850*	U.S. - Louisiana	*20850*
I	*20850*	U.S. - Maryland	*20850*
I	*20850*	U.S. - Michigan	*20850*
I	*20850*	U.S. - Mississippi	*20850*
I	*20850*	U.S. - New Jersey	*20850*
V	*20850*	U.S. - North Carolina	*20850*
I	*20850*	U.S. - Oklahoma	*20850*
I	*20850*	U.S. - South Carolina	*20850*
I	*20850*	U.S. - Tennessee	*20850*
I	*20850*	U.S. - Texas	*20850*
I	*20850*	U.S. - Virginia	*20850*

R *Gnaphalium helleri* Britt. var. *micradenium* (Weatherby) Mahler *20850*

I	*20850*	U.S. - Georgia	*20850*
I	*20850*	U.S. - Indiana	*20850*
Ex/E	*20850*	U.S. - Kentucky	*20850*
I	*20850*	U.S. - Louisiana	*20850*
I	*20850*	U.S. - Maine	*20850*
I	*20850*	U.S. - Maryland	*20850*
I	*20850*	U.S. - Massachusetts	*20850*
I	*20850*	U.S. - Michigan	*20850*
I	*20850*	U.S. - Minnesota	*20850*
I	*20850*	U.S. - Missouri	*20850*
I	*20850*	U.S. - New Hampshire	*20850*
I	*20850*	U.S. - New Jersey	*20850*
Ex/E	*20850*	U.S. - New York	*20850*
E	*20850*	U.S. - North Carolina	*20850*
I	*20850*	U.S. - Pennsylvania	*20850*
I	*20850*	U.S. - South Carolina	*20850*
I	*20850*	U.S. - Tennessee	*20850*
I	*20850*	U.S. - Virginia	*20850*
I	*20850*	U.S. - Wisconsin	*20850*

R *Gnaphalium leucopilinum* Schott & Kotschy ex Boiss. *12840*

R	*12840*	Turkey	*12840*

E *Gnaphalium obtusifolium* L. var. *saxicola* (Fassett) & Cronq. *20850*

E	*20850*	U.S. - Wisconsin	*20850*

I *Gnaphalium rosillense* Urban *5642*

I		Dominican Republic (La Vega, Loma Rosilla) *5642*

R *Gnaphalium sandwicensium* Gaud. *20850*

I	*20850*	U.S. - Hawaii	*20850*

R *Gnaphalium sandwicensium* Gaud. var. *hawaiiense* (O. Deg. & Sherff) W.L. Wagner, Herbst & Sohmer *20850*

R	*20850*	U.S. - Hawaii	*20850*

R *Gnaphalium sandwicensium* Gaudich. var. *sandwicensium* *20850*

R	*20850*	U.S. - Hawaii	*20850*

R *Gnaphalium simii* (Bolus) Hilliard & B.L.Burtt *20604*

R	*20604*	South Africa - Cape Province	*20604*

E *Gochnatia ekmanii* (Urban) Jervis & Alain *5607*

E	*19105*	Cuba (Pinar del Rio)	*5607*

E *Gochnatia gomezii* (Leon) Jervis & Alain *5607*

E	*19105*	Cuba (Holguin)	*5607*

V *Gochnatia intertexta* (C. Wright) Jervis & Alain *5607*

V	*19105*	Cuba (Pinar del Rio)	*5607*

V *Gochnatia maisiana* (Leon) Jervis & Alain *5607*

V	*19105*	Cuba (Guantanamo)	*5607*

E *Gochnatia mantuensis* (C. Wright) Jervis & Alain *5607*

E	*19105*	Cuba (Pinar del Rio)	*5607*

V *Gochnatia montana* (Britton) Jervis & Alain *5607*

V	*19105*	Cuba (Pinar del Rio)	*5607*

V *Gochnatia parvifolia* (Britton) Jervis & Alain *5607*

V	*19105*	Cuba (Holguin)	*5607*

E *Gochnatia wilsoni* (Britton) Jervis & Alain *5607*

E	*19105*	Cuba (Sancti Spiritus)	*5607*

R *Gonospermum canariense* Less. *15105*

R	*20750*	Spain - Canary Is.	*20750*

R *Gonospermum elegans* (Cass.) DC.

R	*15105*	Spain - Canary Is.	*15105*

V *Gonospermum gomerae* Bolle *19174*

V	*19174*	Spain - Canary Is.	*15105*

R *Gratwickia monochaeta* F.Muell. *20681*

R	*20681*	Australia - South Australia	*20681*

V *Grindelia fastigiata* Greene *20850*

I	*20850*	U.S. - Colorado	*20850*
V	*20850*	U.S. - Utah	*20850*

V *Grindelia fraxinopratensis* Reveal & Beatley *20850*

E	*20850*	U.S. - California	*20850*
V	*20850*	U.S. - Nevada	*20850*

R *Grindelia howellii* Steyermark *20850*

E	*20850*	U.S. - Idaho	*20850*
V	*20850*	U.S. - Montana	*20850*

V *Grindelia laciniata* Rydb. *20850*

I	*20850*	U.S. - Arizona	*20850*
E	*20850*	U.S. - Utah	*20850*

E *Grindelia latifolia* Kellogg *20850*

I	*20850*	U.S. - California	*20850*

V *Grindelia oolepis* Blake *20850*

V	*20850*	U.S. - Texas	*20850*

E *Grindelia paludosa* Greene *20850*

I	*20850*	U.S. - California	*20850*

R *Grindelia procera* Greene *20850*

I	*20850*	U.S. - California	*20850*

R *Grindelia pygmaea* Cabrera *16336*

R	*20176*	Argentina - Rio Negro (Meseta de Somuncurá) *20176*	

R *Grindelia robusta* Nutt. *20850*

I	*20850*	U.S. - California	*20850*
I	*20850*	U.S. - Massachusetts	*20850*

V *Guardiola platyphylla* Gray *20883*, *20850*

I	*20850*	U.S. - Arizona	*20850*
I	*20883*	Mexico	*20883*

I *Gundlachia domingensis* (Spreng.) A. Grey *5642*

I		Dominican Republic (San Jose de Ocoa) *5642*

I *Gundlachia ocoana* Urban & Ekman *5642*

I		Dominican Republic (San Jose de Ocoa) *5642*

V *Gutierrezia petradoria* (Welsh & Goodrich) Welsh *20850*

V	*20850*	U.S. - Utah	*20850*

V *Gynoxys laurifolia* (Kunth) Cass

V		Ecuador

E *Gynoxys rimachiana* Cuatr. *20883*

I	*20883*	Peru	*20883*

R *Gynura elliptica* Yabe & Hayata *20511*

R	*20511*	Taiwan	*20511*

I *Gynura hispida* Thwaites *8021*

I	*16162*	Sri Lanka (Nuwara Eliya District)	*8021*

I *Gynura sechellensis* (Baker) Hemsley *14296*

I	*19181*	Seychelles (granitic)	*14296*

E *Gynura truncata* Kerr *19120*

I   *Gynura zeylanica* Trimen *8021*
    E   *19120* Thailand *19120*
    I   *16162* Sri Lanka *8021*

R   *Haeckeria cassiniiformis* F.Muell. *20681*
    R   *20681* Australia - South Australia *20681*

R   *Haploesthes greggii* A.Gray var. *greggii 9567*
    R   *19755* Mexico - Coahuila *9567*

E   *Haplopappus rigidus* Philippi *16336*
    E   *20176* Argentina - Salta *20176*
    E   *20176* Chile (Montañas de Antofagasta y Atacama) *19634*

E   *Haplopappus thiniicola* Rzedowski et Ezcurra *20883*
    I   *20883* Mexico *20883*

E   *Haplostephium passerina* Mart. ex DC. *20883*
    I   *20883* Brazil *20883*

V   *Hartwrightia floridana* Gray ex S.Watson *20850*
    V   *20850* U.S. - Florida *20850*
    E   *20850* U.S. - Georgia *20850*

V   *Hazardia cana* (Gray) Greene *20883, 20850, 8058*
    V   *20850* U.S. - California *20850*
    I   *20883* Mexico *20883*

E   *Hazardia orcuttii* (Gray) Greene *20883, 20850, 8058*
    E   *20850* U.S. - California *20850*
    I   *20883* Mexico *20883*

R   *Hazardia stenolepis* (Hall) Hoover *20850*
    I   *20850* U.S. - California *20850*

E   *Hebeclinium knappii* K. & R. *20883*
    I   *20883* Panama *20883*

E   *Hebeclinium reedii* K. & R. *20883, 9006*
    I   *20883* Panama *20883*

R   *Helenium arizonicum* Blake *20850*
    R   *20850* U.S. - Arizona *20850*

E   *Helenium scaposum* Britton *5607*
    E   *19105* Cuba (Juventud Is.) *5607*

V   *Helenium thurberi* Gray *20883, 20850*
    I   *20850* U.S. - Arizona *20850*
    I   *20883* Mexico *20883*

V   *Helenium virginicum* Blake *20850*
    V   *20850* U.S. - Virginia *20850*

V   *Helianthella castanea* Greene *20850*
    V   *20850* U.S. - California *20850*

V   *Helianthus agrestis* Pollard *20850*
    I   *20850* U.S. - Florida *20850*
    Ex/E   *20850* U.S. - Georgia *20850*

E   *Helianthus carnosus* Small *20850*
    E   *20850* U.S. - Florida *20850*

R   *Helianthus debilis* Nutt. ssp. *tardiflorus* Heiser *20850*
    I   *20850* U.S. - Alabama *20850*
    I   *20850* U.S. - Florida *20850*
    I   *20850* U.S. - Georgia *20850*
    I   *20850* U.S. - Mississippi *20850*

V   *Helianthus debilis* Nutt. ssp. *vestitus* (E.E. Wats.) Heiser *20850*
    V   *20850* U.S. - Florida *20850*

V   *Helianthus deserticola* Heiser *20850*
    I   *20850* U.S. - Arizona *20850*
    V   *20850* U.S. - Nevada *20850*
       20850 U.S. - Utah *20850*

V   *Helianthus eggertii* Small *20850*
    E   *20850* U.S. - Alabama *20850*
    V   *20850* U.S. - Kentucky *20850*
    V   *20850* U.S. - Tennessee *20850*

R   *Helianthus glaucophyllus* D.M. Sm. *20850*
    Ex/E   *20850* U.S. - Alabama *20850*
    I   *20850* U.S. - Georgia *20850*
    R   *20850* U.S. - North Carolina *20850*
    I   *20850* U.S. - South Carolina *20850*
    E   *20850* U.S. - Tennessee *20850*

R   *Helianthus longifolius* Pursh *20850*
    E   *20850* U.S. - Alabama *20850*
    V   *20850* U.S. - Georgia *20850*
    E   *20850* U.S. - North Carolina *20850*

V   *Helianthus neglectus* Heiser *20850*
    I   *20850* U.S. - New Mexico *20850*
    V   *20850* U.S. - Texas *20850*

R   *Helianthus niveus* (Benth.) Brandegee ssp. *tephrodes* (Gray) Heiser *20883, 20850, 8058*
    E   *20850* U.S. - Arizona *20850*
    E   *20850* U.S. - California *20850*
    I   *20883* Mexico *20883*

Ex/E   *Helianthus nuttallii* Torr. & A.Gray ssp. *parishii* (Gray) Heiser *20850*
    Ex/E   *20850* U.S. - California *20850*

V   *Helianthus occidentalis* Riddell ssp. *plantagineus* (Torr. & Gray) Shinners *20850*
    E   *20850* U.S. - Arkansas *20850*
    I   *20850* U.S. - Louisiana *20850*
    ?   *20850* U.S. - Mississippi *20850*
    I   *20850* U.S. - Texas *20850*

V   *Helianthus paradoxus* Heiser *20850*
    I   *20850* U.S. - Indiana *20850*
    R   *20850* U.S. - New Mexico *20850*
    E   *20850* U.S. - Texas *20850*

E   *Helianthus praecox* Torr. & A.Gray ssp. *hirtus* (Heiser) Heiser *20850*
    E   *20850* U.S. - Texas *20850*

V   *Helianthus praecox* Torr. & A.Gray ssp. *praecox 20850*
    V   *20850* U.S. - Texas *20850*

Ex/E   *Helianthus praetermissus* E.E. Wats. *20850, 14662*
    Ex/E   *20850* U.S. - New Mexico *20850*

V   *Helianthus schweinitzii* Torr. & Gray *20850*
    V   *20850* U.S. - North Carolina *20850*
    E   *20850* U.S. - South Carolina *20850*

R   *Helianthus smithii* Heiser *20850*
    V   *20850* U.S. - Alabama *20850*
    Ex/E   *20850* U.S. - Georgia *20850*
    E   *20850* U.S. - Tennessee *20850*

R   *Helichrysum acervatum* S. Moore *7754*
    R   Zimbabwe (Chimanimani) *7754*

R   *Helichrysum aciculare* Balf. f. *15534*
    R   *15534* Yemen - Socotra *15534*

I   *Helichrysum alticolum* Bolus *20604*
    I   *20604* South Africa - Cape Province *20604*

E   *Helichrysum alucense* G.Casanova, Scholz & Hernández *20750*
    E   *20750* Spain - Canary Is. *20750*

R   *Helichrysum amorginum* Boiss. & Orph. *20171*
    R   *20731* Greece (Cyclades) *20731*

R   *Helichrysum amplectens* Hilliard *20604*
    R   *20604* South Africa - Natal *20604*

R   *Helichrysum artvinense* Davis & Kupicha *12840*
    R   *12840* Turkey *12840*

I **Helichrysum aureum** (Houtt.) Merr. var. *argenteum*
    Hilliard *20604*
    I   20604 South Africa - Natal *20604*
    I   20604 South Africa - Transvaal *20604*

I **Helichrysum biafranum** Hook.f.
    I   Cameroon (Cameroon mt & Buea)

R **Helichrysum brassii** Brenan var. *tenellum*
    Brenan *7849*
    R   Malawi *7849*

R **Helichrysum bullulatum** S. Moore *7757*
    R   Malawi (Mlanje) *7757*

V **Helichrysum chasmolycicum** Davis *12840*
    V   12840 Turkey *12840*

E **Helichrysum citricephalum** Hilliard & B.L.Burtt *20604*
    E   20604 South Africa - Natal *20604*

R **Helichrysum compactum** Boiss. *12840*
    R   12840 Turkey *12840*

R **Helichrysum cutchicum** (C.B. Clarke) R. Rao & Deshp.
    R   13883 India - Gujarat *13883*

R **Helichrysum dichroolepis** Brenan *7849*
    R   Malawi *7849*

E **Helichrysum dimorphum** Cockayne *86*
    E   19305 New Zealand - South Is. *19305*

V **Helichrysum doerfleri** Rech.f. *20171*
    V   20730 Greece - Crete *20730*

R **Helichrysum flammeiceps** Brenan *7849*
    R   Malawi *7849*

I **Helichrysum fourcadei** Hilliard *20604*
    I   20604 South Africa - Cape Province *20604*

V **Helichrysum gossypinum** Soh. Bip. *10260*
    V   15105 Spain - Canary Is. *10260*

I **Helichrysum haygarthii** Bolus *20604*
    I   20604 South Africa - Natal *20604*
    I   20604 South Africa - Orange Free State *20604*

V **Helichrysum heldreichii** Boiss. *20171*
    V   20730 Greece - Crete *20730*

R **Helichrysum heywoodianum** Davis *12840*
    R   12840 Turkey *12840*

R **Helichrysum incarnatum** DC. *20604*
    R   20604 South Africa - Cape Province *20604*

I **Helichrysum ingomense** Hilliard *20604*
    I   20604 South Africa - Natal *20604*

R **Helichrysum jubilatum** Hilliard *20604*
    R   20604 South Africa - Cape Province *20604*

R **Helichrysum lindsayanum** Domin *20681*
    R   20681 Australia - Queensland *20681*

R **Helichrysum maestum** Wild *7754*
    R   Zimbabwe (Chimanimani) *7754*

R **Helichrysum mauritianum** A.J. Scott *10082*
    R   20771 Mauritius *10082*

R **Helichrysum monizii** Lowe
    R   Portugal - Madeira

V **Helichrysum monogynum** B.L. Burtt & Sunding *20750*
    V   20750 Spain - Canary Is. *20750*

R **Helichrysum montelinasanum** Schmid *18264*
    R   18264 Italy - Sardinia *18264*

R **Helichrysum nimmoanum** Oliver & Hiern *15534*
    R   15534 Yemen - Socotra *15534*

I **Helichrysum outeniquense** Hilliard *20604*
    I   20604 South Africa - Cape Province *20604*

R **Helichrysum perlanigerum** Gamble *11494*
    R   11494 India - Tamil Nadu *11494*

E **Helichrysum peshmenianum** Erik *12840*
    E   12840 Turkey *12840*

R **Helichrysum rosulatum** Oliver & Hiern *15534*
    R   15534 Yemen - Socotra *15534*

I **Helichrysum saxicola** Hilliard *20604*
    I   20604 South Africa - Cape Province *20604*

R **Helichrysum selago** (Hook. f.) Benth & Hook. f. var. *tumidum* Cheeseman
    R   New Zealand - South Is.

V **Helichrysum sibthorpii** Rouy *8000, 20171*
    V   Greece (north east - Athos) *8000*

E **Helichrysum sonogynum** B. L. Burtt. & Sunding *15105*
    E   15105 Spain - Canary Is. *15105*

R **Helichrysum sordidum** S. Moore *7757*
    R   Malawi (Mlanje) *7757*

R **Helichrysum taenari** Rothm. *8000, 20171*
    R   Greece (north-east) *8000*

I **Helichrysum tricostatum** (Thunb.) Less. *20604*
    I   20604 South Africa - Cape Province *20604*

R **Helichrysum whyteanum** Britten *7757*
    R   Malawi *7757*

I **Helichrysum wightii** Clarke ex Hook.f. *2268*
    I   India - Tamil Nadu *2268*

R **Helichrysum woodii** N.E.Br. *20604*
    R   20604 South Africa - Natal *20604*

R **Helichrysum yuccifolium** (Lam.) DC. *10082*
    R   20771 Mauritius *10082*

I **Heliocauta atlanticus** (Litard. & Maire) Humphries
    I   Morocco *9204*

E **Heliomeris soliceps** (Barneby) Yates *20850*
    E   20850 U.S. - Utah *20850*

E **Hemizonia arida** Keck *20850*
    E   20850 U.S. - California *20850*

V **Hemizonia australis** (Keck) Keck *20850*
    V   20850 U.S. - California *20850*
    ?   Mexico *20883*

V **Hemizonia calyculata** (Babcock & Hall) Keck *20850*
    I   20850 U.S. - California *20850*

V **Hemizonia congesta** DC. *20850*
    I   20850 U.S. - California *20850*

V **Hemizonia congesta** DC. ssp. *vernalis* (Keck) Tanowitz *20850*
    V   20850 U.S. - California *20850*

E **Hemizonia conjugens** Keck *20850*
    E   20850 U.S. - California *20850*

R **Hemizonia corymbosa** (DC.) Torr. & Gray *20850*
    I   20850 U.S. - California *20850*

R **Hemizonia floribunda** Gray *20883, 20850, 8058*
    V   20850 U.S. - California *20850*
    I   20883 Mexico *20883*

E **Hemizonia halliana** Keck *20850*
    E   20850 U.S. - California *20850*

E **Hemizonia increscens** Tanowitz ssp. *villosa* Tanowitz *20850*
    E   20850 U.S. - California *20850*

V *Hemizonia laevis* (Keck) Keck *20850*
  I *20850* U.S. - California *20850*

V *Hemizonia minthornii* Jepson *20850*
  V *20850* U.S. - California *20850*

E *Hemizonia mohavensis* Keck *20850, 14662*
  E *20850* U.S. - California *20850*

E *Hemizonia parryi* Greene ssp. *congdonii* (Robins. & Greenm.) Keck *20850*
  E *20850* U.S. - California *20850*

V *Hemizonia pentactis* (Keck) Keck *20850*
  I *20850* U.S. - California *20850*

V *Hemizonia tracyi* (Babcock & Hall) Keck *20850*
  I *20850* U.S. - California *20850*

E *Heptanthus brevipes* C. Wright *5607*
  E *19105* Cuba (Pinar del Rio) *5607*

V *Heptanthus cochlearifolius* Griseb. *5607*
  V *19105* Cuba (Pinar del Rio; I. Juventud) *5607*

V *Heptanthus yumuriensis* Borh. *5607*
  V *19105* Cuba (Guantanamo) *5607*

R *Herrickia horrida* Woot. & Standl. *20850*
  E *20850* U.S. - Colorado *20850*
  V *20850* U.S. - New Mexico *20850*

V *Hesperevax caulescens* (Benth.) Gray *20850*
  I *20850* U.S. - California *20850*

E *Hesperomannia arborescens* Gray *20850, 21357*
  E *20850* U.S. - Hawaii *20850*

E *Hesperomannia arborescens* A.Gray ssp. *arborescens* *14209*
  E *14209* U.S. - Hawaii (O`ahu, Moloka`i) *14209*

E *Hesperomannia arbuscula* Hbd. *20850*
  E *20850* U.S. - Hawaii *20850*

E *Hesperomannia arbuscula* Hillebrand ssp. *arbuscula* *14209*
  E *14209* U.S. - Hawaii (O`ahu, Maui) *14209*

E *Hesperomannia lydgatei* Forbes *20850, 14209*
  E *20850* U.S. - Hawaii (Kaua`i) *20850*

R *Heteropappus hispidus* (Thunb.) Less. ssp. *insularis* (Makino) Kitam. *10573*
  R *10573* Japan *10573*

R *Heteropappus koidzumianus* Kitam. *10573*
  R *10573* Japan *10573*

R *Heteropappus leptocladus* Matsum. *10573*
  R *10573* Japan *10573*

R *Heteroplexis microcephala* Y.L. Chen *17617*
  R *17617* China - Guangxi (Yangsu) *11139*

R *Heteroplexis sericophylla* Y.L. Chen *11139*
  R China - Guangxi (Yangsu) *11139*

R *Heteroplexis vernonioides* C.C. Chang *11139*
  R China - Guangxi (Longzhou) *11139*

V *Heterotheca barbata* (Rydb.) Semple *20850*
  I *20850* U.S. - Idaho *20850*
  I *20850* U.S. - Washington *20850*

V *Heterotheca bolanderi* (Gray) Harms *20850*
  I *20850* U.S. - California *20850*

V *Heterotheca camphorata* (Eastw.) Harms *20850*
  I *20850* U.S. - California *20850*

V *Heterotheca jonesii* (Blake) Welsh & Atwood *20850*
  V *20850* U.S. - Utah *20850*

V *Heterotheca rutteri* (Rothrock) Shinners *20850*
  V *20850* U.S. - Arizona *20850*

V *Heterotheca villosa* (Pursh) Shinners var. *depressa* (Rydb.) Harms *20850*
  I *20850* U.S. - Montana *20850*
  V *20850* U.S. - Wyoming *20850*

V *Heterotheca viscida* (Gray) Harms *20850*
  I *20850* U.S. - Arizona *20850*
  I *20850* U.S. - New Mexico *20850*
  I *20850* U.S. - Oregon *20850*
  I *20850* U.S. - Texas *20850*

V *Heterotheca zionensis* Semple *20850*
  E *20850* U.S. - Utah *20850*

V *Hieracium argutum* Nutt. *20850*
  I *20850* U.S. - California *20850*

R *Hieracium argyrocomum* (Fr.) Zahn *20171*
  R Spain

E *Hieracium chaunotrichum* (Bornm. et Zahn) Holub *2050*
  E *2050* Czech Republic *2050*

V *Hieracium eriophorum* St.-Amans *20171*
  V *20528* France (south-west) *20528*

R *Hieracium fredesianum* Mateo *20699*
  R *20692* Spain (Puertos Torosa and Beciete) *20692*

E *Hieracium irasuense* Benth. *20883, 10747*
  I *20883* Panama *20883*

E *Hieracium lemmonii* Gray *20850*
  I *20850* U.S. - Arizona *20850*
  I *20850* U.S. - New Mexico *20850*

R *Hieracium morii* Hayata *20511*
  R *20511* Taiwan *20511*

R *Hieracium pinanense* Kitamura *20511*
  R *20511* Taiwan *20511*

Ex *Hieracium purkynei* Celak *19839*
  Ex *2050* Czech Republic *2050*
  Ex *6936* Slovakia *6936*

E *Hieracium robinsonii* (Zahn) Fern. *20850*
  I *20850* Canada - New Brunswick *20850*
  I *20850* Canada - Newfoundland *20850*
  I *20850* Canada - Nova Scotia *20850*
  I *20850* Canada - Prince Edward Is. *20850*
  E *20850* Canada - Quebec *20850*
  Ex/E *20850* U.S. - Maine *20850*
  E *20850* U.S. - New Hampshire *20850*

V *Hieracium rusbyi* Greene *20850*
  E *20850* U.S. - Arizona *20850*
  I *20850* U.S. - New Mexico *20850*

E *Hieracium scabrum* Michx. var. *leucocaule* Fern. & St. John *20850, 14394*
  E *20850* Canada - Nova Scotia *20850*

E *Hieracium texedense* Pau
  E *19818* Spain (Málaga, Sierra de Tejeda) *11496*

I *Hieracium vahlii* Froel. *20171*
  I Spain

R *Hieracium valentinum* Arv.-Touv. & E.Rev. ex Willk. *19174, 20171*
  R *19174* Spain (east) *20692*

E *Holocarpha macradenia* (DC.) Greene *20850*
  E *20850* U.S. - California *20850*

V *Holocarpha virgata* (Gray) Keck ssp. *elongata* Keck *20850*
  V *20850* U.S. - California *20850*

V *Hulsea brevifolia* Gray *20850*

I   *20850* U.S. - California *20850*

V   *Hulsea californica* Torr. & Gray *20850*

   I   *20850* U.S. - California *20850*

R   *Hulsea vestita* Gray ssp. *callicarpha* (Hall)
     Wilken *20850*

   R   *20850* U.S. - California *20850*

R   *Hulsea vestita* Gray ssp. *gabrielensis*
     Wilken *20850*

   R   *20850* U.S. - California *20850*

V   *Hulsea vestita* Gray ssp. *inyoensis* (Keck)
     Wilken *20850*

   I   *20850* U.S. - California *20850*
   E   *20850* U.S. - Nevada *20850*

R   *Hulsea vestita* Gray ssp. *parryi* (Gray)
     Wilken *20850*

   R   *20850* U.S. - California *20850*

R   *Hydropectis stevensii* McVaugh *10354*

   R   *19755* Mexico *10354*

V   *Hymenopappus carrizoanus* B.L. Turner *20850*

   V   *20850* U.S. - Texas *20850*

V   *Hymenostemma pseudanthemis* (Kunze) Willk. *17891, 20171*

   V   *11496* Spain (Malaga, Cádiz) *20664*

R   *Hymenothrix loomisii* Blake *20850*

   I   *20850* U.S. - Arizona *20850*
   I   *20850* U.S. - California *20850*
   I   *20850* U.S. - Nevada *20850*

V   *Hymenothrix wislizeni* Gray *20850*

   I   *20850* U.S. - Arizona *20850*
   I   *20850* U.S. - New Mexico *20850*
   I   *20850* U.S. - Texas *20850*

V   *Hymenoxys acaulis* (Pursh) K. Parker var. *glabra*
     (Gray) K. Parker *14352*

   V   *13967* Canada - Ontario *10764*
   Ex   *13967* U.S. - Illinois *10764*
   E   *19002* U.S. - Ohio *10764*

R   *Hymenoxys brachyactis* Woot. & Standl. *20850*

   R   *20850* U.S. - New Mexico *20850*

R   *Hymenoxys helenioides* (Rydb.) Cockerell *20850*

   I   *20850* U.S. - Arizona *20850*
   E   *20850* U.S. - Colorado *20850*
   I   *20850* U.S. - Nevada *20850*
   I   *20850* U.S. - New Mexico *20850*
   R   *20850* U.S. - Utah *20850*

E   *Hymenoxys lapidicola* Welsh & Neese *20850*

   E   *20850* U.S. - Colorado *20850*
   E   *20850* U.S. - Utah *20850*

R   *Hymenoxys lemmonii* (Greene) Cockerell *20850*

   I   *20850* U.S. - Arizona *20850*
   I   *20850* U.S. - California *20850*
   I   *20850* U.S. - Nevada *20850*
   E   *20850* U.S. - Oregon *20850*
   E   *20850* U.S. - Utah *20850*

V   *Hymenoxys texana* (Coult. & Rose) Cockerell *20850*

   V   *20850* U.S. - Texas (nr Houston, Harris Co.) *20850*

V   *Hymenoxys vaseyi* (Gray) Cockerell *20850*

   V   *20850* U.S. - New Mexico *20850*

R   *Hyoseris taurina* (Pamp.) Martinoli *20171*

   R   Italy - Sardinia

V   *Hypochoeris claryi* Battand. *10488*

   V   *14958* Algeria *10488*

R   *Hypochoeris crepidioides* Tatew. & Kitam. *10573*

   R   *10573* Japan *10573*

E   *Hypochoeris oligocephala* (Svent. & D. Bramwell)
     Lack *14166*

   E   *15105* Spain - Canary Is. *15105*

R   *Hypochoeris rutea* Talav.

   R   *11496* Spain (Cordoba) *11496*

R   *Hypochoeris saldensis* Battand. *10488*

   R   *14958* Algeria *10488*

R   *Hysterionica aconquijana* Lillo *16336*

   R   *16336* Argentina *16336*

V   *Ichthyothere granvillei* H. Robinson *20883*

   I   *20883* Guyana *20883*

I   *Ifloga obovata* Bolle

   I   *15105* Spain - Canary Is. *15105*

R   *Inula fragilis* Boiss. & Hausskn. *12840*

   R   *12840* Turkey *12840*

R   *Inula helenium* L. ssp. *vanensis*
     Grierson *12840*

   R   *12840* Turkey *12840*

R   *Inula helvetica* Weber *20171*

   I   France
   V   Germany
   R   Italy
   V   Spain
   V   *18154* Switzerland *18154*

R   *Inula kalapani* C.B. Clarke *11494*

   R   *11494* India - Meghalaya (Khasi hills) *11494*

R   *Inula macrocephala* Boiss. & Kotschy ex Boiss. *12840*

   R   *12840* Turkey *12840*

R   *Inula oxylepis* Hausskn. *20171*

   R   Greece

R   *Inula pseudolimonella* (Rech.f.) Rech.f. *20171*

   R   *20730* Greece - Crete *20730*

V   *Inula racemosa* Hook. f. *13883*

   V   *13883* India - Jammu & Kashmir *13883*

R   *Inula rotundifolia* (Halácsy) Greuter *20171*

   R   Greece

R   *Inula sarana* Boiss. *12840*

   R   *12840* Turkey *12840*

V   *Inula sechmenii* Hardvig & Strid *12840*

   V   *12840* Turkey *12840*

R   *Inula serpentinica* Rech.f. & Goulimy *20171*

   R   Greece

R   *Inula subfloccosa* Rech.f. *20171*

   R   Greece

E   *Ionactis caelestis* Leary & Nesom *20850*

   E   *20850* U.S. - Nevada *20850*

R   *Iostephane trilobata* Hemsley *9004*

   R   *19755* Mexico *9004*

R   *Iphiona maris-mortui* Feinbrun *8896*

   R   Israel (Dead Sea area) *8896*

V   *Isocarpha glabrata* Blake *5607*

   V   *19105* Cuba (Camaguey) *5607*

E   *Isocoma arguta* Greene *20850*

   E   *20850* U.S. - California *20850*

E   *Isocoma humilis* Nesom *20850*

   E   *20850* U.S. - Utah *20850*

V   *Isocoma pluriflora* (Torr. & Gray) Greene *20850*

I	20850	U.S. - Arizona	20850
I	20850	U.S. - Colorado	20850
I	20850	U.S. - New Mexico	20850
I	20850	U.S. - Texas	20850

R *Iva nevadensis* **M.E. Jones** 20850
I	20850	U.S. - California	20850
I	20850	U.S. - Nevada	20850

V *Iva texensis* **R.C. Jackson** 20850
I	20850	U.S. - Texas	20850

V *Ixeris dentata* **Nakai ssp.** *kitayamensis* **Murata** 10573
V	10573	Japan 10573

E *Ixeris dentata* **Nakai ssp.** *nipponica* **Kitam.** 10573
E	10573	Japan 10573

V *Ixeris longirostrata* **(Hayata) Nakai** 8038
V	19134	Japan - Ogasawara-shoto 8038

I *Ixeris reparia* **(Kerr) Stebbins** 19120
I	19120	Thailand 19120

R *Ixeris tamagawaensis* **(Makino) Kitam.** 10573
R	10573	Japan 10573

R *Ixeris transnokoensis* **(Sasaki) Kitamura** 20511
R	20511	Taiwan 20511

R *Ixiolaena pluriseta* **Haegi** 20681
R	20681	Australia - South Australia 20681

V *Ixodia achillaeoides* **R.Br. ssp.** *arenicola* **Copley** 20681
I	20681	Australia - South Australia 20681
I	20681	Australia - Victoria 20681

E *Jaegeria bellidiflora* **(Moc. & Ses.) Torres & Beaman** 9571
E	9571	Mexico 9571

R *Jamesianthus alabamensis* **Blake & Sherff** 20850
R	20850	U.S. - Alabama 20850

R *Jasonia hesperia* **Maire & Wilczek**
R		Morocco

R *Jurinea brevicaulis* **Boiss.** 12840
R	12840	Turkey 12840

V *Jurinea cypria* **Boiss.** 14230
V	19164	Cyprus (Troodos) 14230

R *Jurinea elegantissima* **Iljin**
R		former USSR 6930

R *Jurinea eximia* **Tek.** 5942
R	5942	Kazakhstan (south) 5942

I *Jurinea fedtschenkoana* **Iljin** 5942
I	5942	Kazakhstan (west) 5942

V *Jurinea fontqueri* **Cuatrec.** 8000, 20171
V	20874	Spain (Sierra de Mágina) 20874

I *Jurinea glycacantha* **(Sibth. & Sm.) DC.** 20171
I	19321	Slovakia 19321

I *Jurinea karatavica* **Iljin**
I		former USSR 6930

R *Jurinea lydiae* **Iljin**
R		former USSR 6930

R *Jurinea mollis* **(L.) Reichenb. ssp.** *transsilvanica* **(Sprengel) Hayek** 17823
R	19949	Romania 20631

Ex/E *Jurinea mugodsharica* **Iljin** 5942
Ex/E	5942	Kazakhstan (west) 5942

R *Jurinea robusta* **Schrenk** 5942
R	5942	Kazakhstan (south-east) 5942

R *Jurinea taygetea* **Halácsy** 20171
V	19426	Bulgaria 19426
R		Greece

R *Kalimeris shimadai* **(Kitamura) Kitamura** 20511
R	20511	Taiwan 20511

V *Kleinia saginata* **P. Halliday** 20146
V	20146	Oman (Dhofar) 20146

I *Kleinia scottii* **(Balf. f.) Chiov.** 15534
I	15534	Yemen - Socotra 15534

E *Koanophyllon dolphinii* **(Urban) R. King & H. Robinson** 20883
E	20883	Jamaica 20883

E *Koanophyllon dukei* **K. & R.** 20883, 9006
I	20883	Panama 20883

V *Koanophyllon gracilipes* **(Urban) R. King & H. Robinson** 20883
V	20883	Jamaica 20883

R *Koanophyllon simile* **(Proctor) R. King & H. Robinson** 20883
R	20883	Jamaica 20883

V *Koehneola repens* **(Griseb.) Urban** 5607
V	19105	Cuba (Santiago de Cuba; Holguin) 5607

R *Krigia montana* **(Michx.) Nutt.** 20850
R	20850	U.S. - Georgia 20850
R	20850	U.S. - North Carolina 20850
I	20850	U.S. - South Carolina 20850
E	20850	U.S. - Tennessee 20850

E *Lachanodes arborea* **(Roxb.) Nordenstam** 18996
E	18996	St Helena 18996

E *Lactuca benthamii* **C.B. Clarke** 11494
E	11494	India - Jammu & Kashmir (Kashmir) 11494

E *Lactuca cooperi* **Anthony** 11494
E	11494	India - Sikkim 11494

E *Lactuca filicina* **Duthie ex Stebb.** 11494
E	11494	India - Uttar Pradesh (Kali Valley, Kumaon) 11494

I *Lactuca herbanica* **Burchard**
I	15105	Spain - Canary Is. 15105

R *Lactuca livida* **Boiss. & Reut.** 20171
R		Spain

R *Lactuca longidentata* **Moris ex DC.** 20171
R		Italy - Sardinia

R *Lactuca mira* **Pavlov** 8001
R		Asiatic U.S.S.R. (Tien Shan) 6930

V *Lactuca palmensis* **Bolle** 20750
V	15105	Spain - Canary Is. 15105

R *Lactuca perennis* **L. var.** *granatensis* **Charpin & Fernandez Casas** 15398
R		Spain

I *Lactuca takhtadzhianii* **Sosn.** 5942
I	5942	Armenia 5942

E *Lactuca terrae-novae* **Fern.** 20850, 14366
E	20850	Canada - Newfoundland 20850

V *Lactuca tetrantha* **B.L. Burtt & P.H. Davis** 14230
V	19164	Cyprus (Troodos) 14230

E *Lactuca undulata* **Ledeb.** 11494
E	11494	India - Jammu & Kashmir (Kashmir) 11494

R   *Lactuca watsoniana* Trel. *8000, 20171*
     R   *19174*   Portugal - Azores *8000*

V   *Lactucosonchus webbii* (Schultz Bip.) Svent. *20750*
     V   *20750*   Spain - Canary Is. *15105*

V   *Laennecia eriophylla* (Gray) Nesom *20850*
     V   *20850*   U.S. - Arizona *20850*

E   *Lagenifera erici* Forbes *20850, 14209*
     E   *20850*   U.S. - Hawaii (Kaua`i) *20850*

E   *Lagenifera helenae* Forbes & Lydgate *20850, 14209*
     E   *20850*   U.S. - Hawaii (kaua`i) *20850*

V   *Lagenifera maviensis* Mann *20850, 14209*
     V   *20850*   U.S. - Hawaii *20850*

E   *Lagenifera minuscula* Cuatr. *20883*
     I   *20883*   Panama *20883*

E   *Lagenifera panamensis* Blake *20883*
     I   *20883*   Panama *20883*

E   *Lagenifera sakirana* Cuatr. *20883*
     I   *20883*   Costa Rica *20883*

E   *Lagenifera westonii* Cuatr. *20883*
     I   *20883*   Costa Rica *20883*

V   *Lagenophora neocaledonica* S.Moore *20893*
     V   *20893*   New Caledonia *20893*

E   *Lagoseris purpurea* (Willd.) Boiss. *5942, 20171*
     E   *20655*   Ukraine - Crimea *5942*

I   *Lamyropappus schakaptaricus* (B. Fedtsch.) Knorr. & Tamam. *5942*
     I   *5942*   Kazakhstan *5942*
     I   *5942*   Kyrgyzstan *5942*
     I   *5942*   Uzbekistan *5942*

R   *Lamyropsis carpini* Greuter
     R   Greece

R   *Lamyropsis lycia* Kupicha *12840*
     R   *12840*   Turkey *12840*

E   *Lamyropsis microcephala* (Moris) Dittrich & Greuter *8000, 20171*
     E   *18264*   Italy - Sardinia (Mte Bruncu Spinu) *19997*

V   *Lantanopsis tomentosa* Borh. & Moncada *5607*
     V   *19105*   Cuba (Granma; Santiago de Cuba) *5607*

R   *Lapsana takasei* (Sasaki) Kitamura *20511*
     R   *20511*   Taiwan *20511*

E   *Lasianthaea nowickeana* D'Arcy *20883, 9006*
     I   *20883*   Panama *20883*

R   *Lasiopogon minutus* (B.Nord.) Hilliard & B.L.Burtt *20604*
     R   *20604*   South Africa - Cape Province *20604*

E   *Lasthenia burkei* (Greene) Greene *20850*
     E   *20850*   U.S. - California *20850*

R   *Lasthenia chrysantha* (Greene ex Gray) Greene *20850*
     I   *20850*   U.S. - California *20850*

E   *Lasthenia conjugens* Greene *20850*
     E   *20850*   U.S. - California *20850*

R   *Lasthenia debilis* (Greene ex Gray) Ornduff *20850*
     I   *20850*   U.S. - California *20850*

V   *Lasthenia glabrata* Lindl. ssp. *coulteri* (Gray) Ornduff *20850*
     V   *20850*   U.S. - California *20850*

R   *Lasthenia leptalea* (Gray) Ornduff *20850*
     R   *20850*   U.S. - California *20850*

V   *Lasthenia macrantha* (A.Gray) Greene ssp. *prisca* Ornduff *20850*
     V   *20850*   U.S. - Oregon *20850*

R   *Lasthenia maritima* (Gray) Ornduff *20850*
     V   *20850*   Canada - British Columbia *20850*
     R   *20850*   U.S. - California *20850*
     I   *20850*   U.S. - Oregon *20850*
     I   *20850*   U.S. - Washington *20850*

R   *Lasthenia platycarpha* (Gray) Greene *20850*
     I   *20850*   U.S. - California *20850*

V   *Launaea anomala* (Battand.) Maire *10488*
     V   *14958*   Algeria *10488*

I   *Launaea viminea* (Battand.) Maire
     I   Morocco

E   *Layia carnosa* (Nutt.) Torr. & Gray *20850*
     E   *20850*   U.S. - California *20850*

V   *Layia discoidea* (Keck) Keck *20850*
     V   *20850*   U.S. - California *20850*

Ex/E   *Layia heterotricha* (DC.) Hook. & Arn. *20850*
     Ex/E   *20850*   U.S. - California *20850*

V   *Layia hieracioides* (DC.) Hook. & Arn. *20850*
     I   *20850*   U.S. - California *20850*

E   *Layia jonesii* Gray *20850*
     E   *20850*   U.S. - California *20850*

E   *Layia leucopappa* Keck *20850*
     E   *20850*   U.S. - California *20850*

R   *Layia munzii* Keck *20850*
     V   *20850*   U.S. - California *20850*

R   *Layia paniculata* Keck *20850*
     I   *20850*   U.S. - California *20850*

R   *Layia pentachaeta* Gray *20850*
     I   *20850*   U.S. - California *20850*

V   *Layia septentrionalis* Keck *20850*
     V   *20850*   U.S. - California *20850*

V   *Layia ziegleri* Munz *20850*
     I   *20850*   U.S. - California *20850*

E   *Lecocarpus darwinii* Adsersen *5670*
     E   *14980*   Ecuador - Galapagos (San Cristobal) *11117*

E   *Lecocarpus lecocarpoides* (Rob. & Gr.) Cronq. & Stuessy *5670*
     E   *14980*   Ecuador - Galapagos (incl. Espanola) *11117*

V   *Lecocarpus pinnatifidus* Decne. *11117*
     V   *14980*   Ecuador - Galapagos (Floreana) *11117*

V   *Lembertia congdonii* (Gray) Greene *20850*
     V   *20850*   U.S. - California *20850*

R   *Leontodon eriopus* Emberger & Maire
     R   Morocco

R   *Leontodon farinosus* Merino & Pau *20171*
     R   Spain

R   *Leontodon garnironii* Emberger & Maire
     R   Morocco

R   *Leontodon microcephalus* (Boiss. ex DC.) Boiss. *8000, 20171*
     R   *20874*   Spain (Granada, Sierra Nevada) *20660*

R   *Leontopodium fauriei* Hand.-Mazz. var. *angustifolium* Hara *10573*
     R   *10573*   Japan *10573*

R *Leontopodium fauriei* Hand.-Mazz. var.
  fauriei 10573
  R 10573 Japan 10573

R *Leontopodium hayachinense* Hara & Kitam. var.
  hayachinense 10573
  R 10573 Japan 10573

R *Leontopodium hayachinense* Hara & Kitam. var.
  miyabeanum Watan. 10573
  R 10573 Japan 10573

R *Leontopodium japonicum* Miq. var. *perniveum*
  Kitam. 10573
  R 10573 Japan 10573

R *Leontopodium shinanense* Kitam. 10573
  R 10573 Japan 10573

I *Lepidolopha fedtschenkoana* Knorr. 5942
  I 5942 Turkmenistan 5942
  I 5942 Uzbekistan 5942

R *Lepidolopha karatavica* Pavlov 5942
  R 5942 Kazakhstan (south) 5942

V *Lepidospartum burgessii* B.L. Turner 20850
  E 20850 U.S. - New Mexico 20850
  E 20850 U.S. - Texas 20850

R *Leptinella albida* 19305
  R 19305 New Zealand - South Is. 19305

E *Leptinella dioica* ssp. *monoica* 19305
  E 19305 New Zealand - North Is. 19305

V *Leptinella featherstonii* 19305
  V 19305 New Zealand - Chatham Is. 19305

E *Leptinella nana* 19305
  E 19305 New Zealand - North Is. 19305
  E 19305 New Zealand - South Is. 19305

R *Leptinella pyrethrifolia* var.
  linearifolia 19305
  R 19305 New Zealand - South Is. 19305

R *Leptinella rotundata* 19305
  R 19305 New Zealand - North Is. 19305

V *Leptorhynchos gatesii* (Williamson) J.H.Willis 20681,
  5465
  V 20681 Australia - Victoria 20681

E *Lessingia germanorum* Cham. 20850
  E 20850 U.S. - California 20850

E *Lessingia germanorum* Cham. var.
  germanorum 20850
  E 20850 U.S. - California 20850

V *Lessingia glandulifera* A.Gray var. *tomentosa*
  (Greene) Ferris 20850
  E 20850 U.S. - California 20850

R *Lessingia hololeuca* Greene 20850
  R 20850 U.S. - California 20850

R *Lessingia lemmonii* Gray 20850
  I 20850 U.S. - Arizona 20850
  I 20850 U.S. - California 20850
  I 20850 U.S. - Nevada 20850

V *Lessingia micradenia* Greene var. *glabrata* (Keck)
  Ferris 20850
  V 20850 U.S. - California 20850

V *Lessingia micradenia* Greene var.
  micradenia 20850
  V 20850 U.S. - California 20850

R *Lessingia ramulosa* Gray 20850

  I 20850 U.S. - California 20850

R *Lessingia virgata* Gray 20850
  I 20850 U.S. - California 20850

V *Leucanthemum burnatii* Briq. & Cavill. 20171
  V 20528 France (Alps) 20528

R *Leucanthemum chloroticum* A.Kern. & Murb. 20171
  R 21091 Bosnia & Herzegovina 21091
  R (former) Yugoslavia

V *Leucanthemum corsicum* (Lessing) DC. ssp. *fenzlii*
  Gamisans 20528
  V 20528 France - Corsica 20528

R *Leucanthemum hosmariense* (Ball) Font Quer
  R Morocco

E *Leucochrysum albicans* (Cunn.) Paul G.Wilson var.
  tricolor (DC.) Paul G.Wilson 20681
  E 20681 Australia - Tasmania 20681

R *Leucochrysum graminifolium* (Paul G.Wilson) Paul
  G.Wilson 20681
  R 20681 Australia - New South Wales 20681

E *Leuzea longifolia* Hoffmanns. & Link 8000, 20171
  E 20076 Portugal 8000

V *Leuzea rhaponticoides* Graells 15846, 20171
  E 20076 Portugal 20076
  V 15846 Spain 15846

V *Liabum amplexicaule* Poeppig 18200
  V 9446 Peru 18200

V *Liatris bracteata* Gaiser 20850
  V 20850 U.S. - Texas 20850

V *Liatris cymosa* (H. Ness) K. Schum. 20850
  V 20850 U.S. - Texas 20850

V *Liatris garberi* Gray 20850
  I 20850 U.S. - Florida 20850

E *Liatris helleri* Porter 20850
  E 20850 U.S. - North Carolina 20850

R *Liatris ohlingerae* (Blake) B.L. Robins. 20850, 17890
  R 20850 U.S. - Florida (Polk & Highland Co.)
    20850

V *Liatris provincialis* Godfrey 20850
  I 20850 U.S. - Alabama 20850
  V 20850 U.S. - Florida 20850

R *Liatris scariosa* (L.) Willd. var. *novae-angliae*
  Lunell 20850
  I 20850 U.S. - Arkansas 20850
  V 20850 U.S. - Connecticut 20850
  E 20850 U.S. - Maine 20850
  I 20850 U.S. - Massachusetts 20850
  I 20850 U.S. - Michigan 20850
  E 20850 U.S. - New Hampshire 20850
  Ex/E 20850 U.S. - New Jersey 20850
  V 20850 U.S. - New York 20850
  Ex/E 20850 U.S. - Pennsylvania 20850
  E 20850 U.S. - Rhode Is. 20850
  I 20850 U.S. - West Virginia 20850

V *Liatris tenuis* Shinners 20850
  E 20850 U.S. - Louisiana 20850
  V 20850 U.S. - Texas 20850

R *Liatris turgida* Gaiser 20850
  I 20850 U.S. - Alabama 20850
  I 20850 U.S. - Georgia 20850
  Ex/E 20850 U.S. - Maryland 20850
  E 20850 U.S. - North Carolina 20850
  I 20850 U.S. - Virginia 20850
  E 20850 U.S. - West Virginia 20850

R	*Ligularia kojimae* Kitamura *20511*	
	R	*20511* Taiwan *20511*
R	*Ligularia taquetii* Nakai *15957*	
	R	*15923* Korea, South (Jejudo) *15957*
Ex/E	*Lipochaeta bryanii* Sherff *20850, 14209*	
	Ex/E	*20850* U.S. - Hawaii *20850*
R	*Lipochaeta connata* (Gaudich.) DC. var. *connata* *20850, 14209*	
	I	*20850* U.S. - Hawaii *20850*
Ex/E	*Lipochaeta degeneri* Sherff *20850, 14209*	
	Ex/E	*20850* U.S. - Hawaii (Molokai) *20850*
E	*Lipochaeta fauriei* Levl. *20850, 14209*	
	E	*20850* U.S. - Hawaii (Kaua`i) *20850*
V	*Lipochaeta heterophylla* A.Gray *20850*	
	I	*20850* U.S. - Hawaii *20850*
E	*Lipochaeta kamolensis* O. Deg. & Sherff *20850, 14209*	
	E	*20850* U.S. - Hawaii (Maui) *20850*
V	*Lipochaeta lobata* (Gaud.) DC. *20850*	
	I	*20850* U.S. - Hawaii *20850*
E	*Lipochaeta lobata* (Gaudich.) DC. var. *leptophylla* O. Deg. & Sherff *20850, 14209*	
	E	*20850* U.S. - Hawaii (O`ahu - Wai`anae Mts.) *20850*
V	*Lipochaeta lobata* (Gaudich.) DC. var. *lobata* *20850, 14209*	
	V	*20850* U.S. - Hawaii *20850*
E	*Lipochaeta micrantha* (Nutt.) Gray *20850, 14209*	
	I	*20850* U.S. - Hawaii (Kaua`i) *20850*
E	*Lipochaeta micrantha* (Nutt.) A.Gray var. *exigua* (O. Deg. & Sherff) R.C. Gardner *20850, 14209*	
	E	*20850* U.S. - Hawaii (Kaua`i) *20850*
E	*Lipochaeta micrantha* (Nutt.) A.Gray var. *micrantha* *20850*	
	E	*20850* U.S. - Hawaii *20850*
Ex/E	*Lipochaeta ovata* R.C. Gardner *20850, 14301*	
	Ex/E	*20850* U.S. - Hawaii (Oahu) *20850*
Ex/E	*Lipochaeta perdita* Sherff *20850, 14209*	
	Ex/E	*20850* U.S. - Hawaii (Ni'ihau - Kawaihoa Pt) *20850*
E	*Lipochaeta remyi* Gray *20850, 14209*	
	E	*20850* U.S. - Hawaii (O`ahu - Wai`anae Mts.) *20850*
R	*Lipochaeta rockii* Sherff *20850*	
	R	*20850* U.S. - Hawaii *20850*
R	*Lipochaeta subcordata* Gray *20850, 14209*	
	I	*20850* U.S. - Hawaii *20850*
R	*Lipochaeta succulenta* (Hook. & Arn.) DC. *20850*	
	R	*20850* U.S. - Hawaii *20850*
E	*Lipochaeta tenuifolia* Gray *20850, 14209*	
	E	*20850* U.S. - Hawaii (O`ahu) *20850*
V	*Lipochaeta tenuis* O. Deg. & Sherff *20850*	
	V	*20850* U.S. - Hawaii *20850*
V	*Lipochaeta tenuis* Degener & Sherff var. *tenuis* *14209*	
	V	*14209* U.S. - Hawaii (O`ahu - Wai`anae Mts.) *14209*
E	*Lipochaeta venosa* Sherff *20850, 14209*	
	E	*20850* U.S. - Hawaii *20850*
E	*Lipochaeta waimeaensis* St. John *20850, 14209*	

	E	*20850* U.S. - Hawaii (Kaua`i) *20850*
Ex/E	*Logfia neglecta* (Soy.-Will.) Holub *8000, 20171*	
	Ex	*20593* Belgium *8000*
	Ex	*20528* France *20528*
	Ex/E	*20726* France - Corsica *8000*
R	*Lomatozona artemisiaefolia* Baker *17079*	
	R	*17079* Brazil - Goias (Serra Dourade em Campos) *17079*
R	*Lopholaena whyteana* (Britten) Phillips & C.A. Smith *7757*	
	R	Malawi (Mlanje) *7757*
R	*Lordhowea insularis* (Benth.) R. Nordenstam *14225*	
	R	*14225* Australia - NSW - Lord Howe Is. *14225*
V	*Lugoa revoluta* DC. *5410*	
	V	*20750* Spain - Canary Is. *15105*
V	*Luina serpentina* Cronq. *20850*	
	V	*20850* U.S. - Oregon *20850*
E	*Lundellianthus breedlovei* (B. Turner) Strother *20883*	
	I	*20883* Mexico *20883*
E	*Lundellianthus harrimanii* Strother *20883*	
	I	*20883* Nicaragua *20883*
E	*Lundellianthus steyermarkii* (S. F. Blake) Strother *20883*	
	I	*20883* Guatemala *20883*
E	*Lychnophora bishopii* H. Robinson *20883*	
	I	*20883* Brazil *20883*
E	*Lychnophora jeffreyi* H. Robinson *20883*	
	I	*20883* Brazil *20883*
V	*Lychnophora morii* H. Robinson *20883*	
	I	*20883* Brazil *20883*
V	*Lychnophora regis* H. Robinson *20883*	
	I	*20883* Brazil *20883*
E	*Lygodesmia doloresensis* S. Tomb *20850*	
	E	*20850* U.S. - Colorado *20850*
	E	*20850* U.S. - Utah *20850*
E	*Lygodesmia entrada* Welsh & Goodrich *20850*	
	E	*20850* U.S. - Utah *20850*
V	*Machaeranthera arida* B.L. Turner & Horne *20883, 19002*	
	I	*20850* U.S. - Arizona *20850*
	I	*20850* U.S. - California *20850*
	E	*20850* U.S. - Nevada *20850*
	I	*20883* Mexico *20883*
V	*Machaeranthera asteroides* (Keck) B.L. Turner var. *lagunensis* (Keck) B.L. Turner *20850*	
	E	*20850* U.S. - California *20850*
V	*Machaeranthera aurea* (Gray) Shinners *20850*	
	V	*20850* U.S. - Texas *20850*
R	*Machaeranthera bigelovii* (Gray) Greene var. *mucronata* (Greene) B.L. Turner *20850*	
	R	*20850* U.S. - Arizona *20850*
E	*Machaeranthera canescens* (Pursh) A.Gray var. *ziegleri* (Munz) B.L. Turner *20850*	
	E	*20850* U.S. - California *20850*
V	*Machaeranthera coloradoensis* (Gray) Osterhout *20850*	
	V	*20850* U.S. - Colorado *20850*
	I	*20850* U.S. - Nevada *20850*
	E	*20850* U.S. - Wyoming *20850*
R	*Machaeranthera grindelioides* (Maguire) Cronq. & Keck var *depressa* (Maguire) Cronq. & Keck *20850*	
	I	*20850* U.S. - Arizona *20850*

R	20850	U.S. - Nevada	20850
R	20850	U.S. - Utah	20850

E *Machaeranthera gypsitherma* Nesom, Vorobik & Hartman *20883, 20850*

	20850	U.S. - New Mexico	20850
I	20883	Mexico	20883

V *Machaeranthera heterocarpa* R.L. Hartman & M.A. Lane *20850*

V	20850	U.S. - Texas	20850

V *Machaeranthera mexicana* B.L. Turner & Horne *20850*

V	20850	U.S. - Arizona	20850

V *Machaeranthera viscida* (Woot. & Standl.) R.L. Hartman *20850*

I	20850	U.S. - New Mexico	20850
E	20850	U.S. - Texas	20850

R *Macowania hamata* Hilliard & B.L.Burtt *20604*

R	20604	South Africa - Natal	20604

R *Madia anomala* Greene *20850*

I	20850	U.S. - California	20850

V *Madia citrigracilis* Keck *20850*

I	20850	U.S. - California	20850

E *Madia doris-nilesiae* T.W. & J.P. Nelson *20850*

E	20850	U.S. - California	20850

V *Madia hallii* Keck *20850*

I	20850	U.S. - California	20850

R *Madia nutans* (Greene) Keck *20850*

V	20850	U.S. - California	20850

V *Madia radiata* Kellogg *20850*

V	20850	U.S. - California	20850

R *Madia rammii* Greene *20850*

I	20850	U.S. - California	20850

V *Madia stebbinsii* T.W. & J.P. Nelson *20850*

V	20850	U.S. - California	20850

V *Madia subspicata* Keck *20850*

I	20850	U.S. - California	20850

V *Madia yosemitana* Parry ex Gray *20850*

V	20850	U.S. - California	20850

E *Malacothrix indecora* Greene *20850*

E	20850	U.S. - California	20850

V *Malacothrix phaeocarpa* W.S. Davis, sp. nov. ined. *20850*

I	20850	U.S. - California	20850

V *Malacothrix saxatilis* (Nutt.) Torr. & A.Gray var. arachnoidea (McGregor) E. Williams *20850*

V	20850	U.S. - California	20850

V *Malacothrix similis* W.S. Davis & Raven *20850*

I	20850	U.S. - California	20850

R *Malacothrix sonorae* W.S. Davis & Raven *20850*

I	20850	U.S. - Arizona	20850
I	20850	U.S. - New Mexico	20850

E *Malacothrix squalida* Greene *20850*

I	20850	U.S. - California	20850

I *Marasmodes duemmeri* Bolus ex. Hutch *10260, 20604*

I	20604	South Africa - Cape Province	20604

E *Marasmodes undulata* Compton *20604, 3774*

E	20604	South Africa - Cape Province	20604

V *Marshallia grandiflora* Beadle & F.E. Boynt. *20850*

E	20850	U.S. - Kentucky	20850
I	20850	U.S. - Maryland	20850
Ex/E	20850	U.S. - North Carolina	20850

E	20850	U.S. - Pennsylvania	20850
I	20850	U.S. - South Carolina	20850
V	20850	U.S. - Tennessee	20850
V	20850	U.S. - West Virginia	20850

V *Marshallia ramosa* Beadle & F.E. Boynt. *20850*

E	20850	U.S. - Florida	20850
V	20850	U.S. - Georgia	20850

R *Marshallia trinervia* (Walt.) Trel. *20850*

V	20850	U.S. - Alabama	20850
I	20850	U.S. - Georgia	20850
R	20850	U.S. - Mississippi	20850
Ex/E	20850	U.S. - North Carolina	20850
I	20850	U.S. - South Carolina	20850
V	20850	U.S. - Tennessee	20850
I	20850	U.S. - Virginia	20850

E *Mecomischus pedunculatus* (Coss. & Durieu) Maire *10488*

E	14958	Algeria	10488

V *Melampodium longicorne* Gray *20850*

I	20850	U.S. - Arizona	20850

R *Melanodendron integrifolium* (Roxb.) DC. *18996*

R	18996	St Helena	18996

V *Melanthera ligulata* Small *20850*

I	20850	U.S. - Florida	20850

V *Melanthera parvifolia* Small *20850*

V	20850	U.S. - Florida	20850

R *Metalasia erectifolia* Pillans *20604*

R	20604	South Africa - Cape Province	20604

R *Metalasia luteola* Karis *20604*

R	20604	South Africa - Cape Province	20604

R *Metalasia umbelliformis* Karis *20604*

R	20604	South Africa - Cape Province	20604

R *Microderis filii* Hochst. *20171*

R		Portugal - Azores	

R *Microderis rigens* (Aiton) DC. *20171*

R		Portugal - Azores	

V *Microseris decipiens* Chambers *20850*

V	20850	U.S. - California	20850

V *Microseris douglasii* (Gray) Schultz-Bip. ssp. platycarpha (Gray) Chambers *20850*

V	20850	U.S. - California	20850

R *Microseris howellii* Gray *20850*

I	20850	U.S. - California	20850
R	20850	U.S. - Oregon	20850

V *Microseris laciniata* Chambers ssp. *detlingii* Chambers *20850*

V	20850	U.S. - Oregon	20850

R *Microseris paludosa* (Greene) J.T. Howell *20850*

I	20850	U.S. - California	20850

R *Microseris sylvatica* (Benth.) Schultz-Bip. *20850*

I	20850	U.S. - California	20850

R *Microspermum debile* Benth. var. *arsenei* Rzed. *9581*

R	19755	Mexico	9581

V *Microspermum flaccidum* P.G. Wilson *9581*

V	19755	Mexico	9581

R *Microspermum gonzalezii* Rzed. *9582*

R	19755	Mexico - Jalisco	9582

R *Microspermum gracillimum* Rzed. *9582*

R	19755	Mexico - Jalisco	9582

V *Microspermum hintonii* Rzed. *9581*

V   *19755*   Mexico *9581*

R   **Microspermum tenue** P.G. Wilson *9581*
    R   *19755*   Mexico *9581*

V   **Mikania brachycarpa** Urb. *20883*
    V   *20883*   Jamaica *20883*

V   **Mikania brachycarpa** Urb. var.
      brachycarpa *20883*
    V   *20883*   Jamaica *20883*

E   **Mikania brachycarpa** Urb. var. *purdieana*
      Urb. *20883*
    E   *20883*   Jamaica *20883*

E   **Mikania cuatrecasasii** W. Holmes *20883*
    I   *20883*   Colombia *20883*

E   **Mikania jamaicensis** Robins. *20883*
    E   *20883*   Jamaica *20883*

V   **Mikania longicarpa** W. Holmes *20883*
    I   *20883*   Colombia *20883*

E   **Mikania macdanielii** W. Holmes *20883*
    I   *20883*   Peru *20883*

E   **Mikania maxonii** Proctor *20883*
    E   *20883*   Jamaica *20883*

E   **Mikania montverdensis** Proctor *20883*
    E   *20883*   Jamaica *20883*

E   **Mikania perhirta** R. M. King & H. Robinson *20883*
    I   *20883*   Brazil *20883*

E   **Mikania stevensiana** Britt. *20883*
    I   *20883*   Puerto Rico *20883*

E   **Mikania tristachya** W. Holmes *20883*
    I   *20883*   Colombia *20883*

R   **Mikania troyana** Urb. *20883, 19890*
    R   *19890*   Jamaica *20883*

E   **Mikania tysonii** K. & R. *20883, 10836*
    I   *20883*   Panama *20883*

E   **Mikania zonensis** K. & R. *20883, 9006*
    I   *20883*   Panama *20883*

R   **Miricacalia makineana** (Yatabe) Kitam. *10573*
    R   *10573*   Japan *10573*

E   **Monactis andersonii** H. Robinson *20883*
    I   *20883*   Ecuador *20883*

R   **Monolopia stricta** Crum *20850*
    I   *20850*   U.S. - California *20850*

R   **Montanoa laskowskii** McVaugh *9628*
    R   *9628*   Mexico *9628*

R   **Montanoa revealii** H. Robinson *9604*
    R   *19755*   Mexico *9604*

E   **Munnozia angusta** Ruiz Lopez & Pavon *18200*
    E   *12468*   Peru *18200*

E   **Mutisia linearifolia** Cav. *5462*
    E   *20176*   Argentina - Neuquen *20176*
    E   *20176*   Argentina - Mendoza *20176*
    E   *20176*   Chile (central) *20176*

V   **Mutisia magnifica** C. Ulloa & P.M. Jorgensen *21272*
    V   *21272*   Ecuador *21272*

I   **Mutisia retrorsa** Cav. *5462*
    I   *16336*   Argentina *5462*
    I   *20176*   Argentina - La Pampa *20176*
    I   *20176*   Argentina - Chubut *20176*
    I   *20176*   Argentina - Neuquen *20176*
    I   *20176*   Argentina - Rio Negro *20176*
    I   *20176*   Argentina - Santa Cruz *20176*

I   *20176*   Argentina - Mendoza *20176*

R   **Mutisia spectabilis** Philippi *19534*
    R   *19534*   Chile *19534*

R   **Myopordon thiebautii** (Gently) Wagenitz *12840*
    R   *12840*   Turkey *12840*

R   **Myriactis japonensis** Koidz. *10573*
    R   *10573*   Japan *10573*

I   **Myriactis wightii** DC. var. *bellidioides*
      Hook.f.
    I   India - Tamil Nadu (Sispara, Nilgiri Hills)

V   **Nananthea perpusilla** (Loisel.) DC. *15080, 20171*
    V   *15080*   France - Corsica *20528*
    V   *18264*   Italy - Sardinia *18264*

R   **Nanothamnus sericeus** Rhoma. *14782*
    R   *14782*   India - Karnataka *14782*
    R   *14782*   India - Maharashtra *14782*

E   **Neocuatrecasia feuereri** R. M. King & H.
      Robinson *20883*
    I   *20883*   Bolivia *20883*

E   **Neomirandea chiriquensis** K. & R. *20883, 9006*
    I   *20883*   Panama *20883*

E   **Neomirandea croatii** K. & R. *20883, 9006*
    I   *20883*   Panama *20883*

E   **Neomirandea folsomiana** Dillon & D'Arcy *20883, 9586*
    I   *20883*   Panama *20883*

E   **Neomirandea gracilis** K. & R. *20883, 9006*
    I   *20883*   Panama *20883*

E   **Neomirandea panamensis** K. & R. *20883, 9006*
    I   *20883*   Panama *20883*

E   **Neomirandea pseudopsoralea** K. & R. *20883, 9006*
    I   *20883*   Panama *20883*

E   **Neomirandea tenuipes** K. & R. *20883, 10836*
    I   *20883*   Panama *20883*

E   **Neomirandea ternata** K. & R. *20883, 10836*
    I   *20883*   Panama *20883*

R   **Neurolaena intermedia** Rydb. *9004*
    R   *9004*   Guatemala *9004*

R   **Nicolletia occidentalis** Gray ex Torr. *20850*
    I   *20850*   U.S. - California *20850*

R   **Nidorella resedifolia** DC. ssp. *serpentinicola*
      Wild *7853*
    R   Zimbabwe *7853*

R   **Nipponanthemum nipponicum** (Franchet ex Maxim.)
      Kitam. *10573*
    R   *10573*   Japan *10573*

I   **Notonia shevaroyensis** Fyson
    I   India - Tamil Nadu (Shevaroy Hills, Salem Dist)

R   **Notoptera hirsuta** (Sw.) Urb. *20883*
    R   *20883*   Jamaica *20883*

R   **Nouelia insignis** Franchet *17617*
    R   *17617*   China - Sichuan *11139*
    R   *17617*   China - Yunnan *11139*

R   **Odixia achlaena** (D.Morris) Orch. *20681*
    R   *20681*   Australia - Tasmania *20681*

R   **Odixia angusta** (Wakef.) Orch. *20681*
    R   *20681*   Australia - Tasmania *20681*

R   **Odontocline fadyenii** (Griseb.) Nordenstam *20883*
    R   *20883*   Jamaica *20883*

R   **Odontocline glabra** (Sw.) Nerdenstam *20883*

	R 20883 Jamaica 20883
R	*Odontocline laciniata* (Sw.) Nordenstam 20883, 13336
	R 13336 Jamaica 20883
R	*Odontocline tercentenariae* (Proctor) Nordenstam 20883, 13336
	R 13336 Jamaica 20883
R	*Oedera conferta* (Hutch.) Anderb. & K.Bremer 20604
	R 20604 South Africa - Cape Province 20604
R	*Oedera foveolata* (K.Bremer) Anderb. & K.Bremer 20604
	R 20604 South Africa - Cape Province 20604
R	*Oedera nordenstamii* (K.Bremer) Anderb. & K.Bremer 20604
	R 20604 South Africa - Cape Province 20604
R	*Oedera resinifera* (K.Bremer) Anderb. & K.Bremer 20604
	R 20604 South Africa - Cape Province 20604
R	*Oedera silicicola* (K.Bremer) Anderb. & K.Bremer 20604
	R 20604 South Africa - Cape Province 20604
V	*Oedera steyniae* (L.Bolus) Anderb. & K.Bremer 20604
	V 20604 South Africa - Cape Province 20604
R	*Oldenburgia grandis* (Thunb.) Baill. 20604
	R 20604 South Africa - Cape Province 20604
R	*Oldenburgia papionum* DC. 20604
	R 20604 South Africa - Cape Province 20604
R	*Olearia adenophora* (F.Muell.) F.Muell. ex Benth. 20681
	R 20681 Australia - Victoria 20681
R	*Olearia allenderae* J.H.Willis 20681
	R 20681 Australia - Victoria 20681
R	*Olearia archeri* Lander 20681
	R 20681 Australia - Tasmania 20681
V	*Olearia astroloba* Lander & N.G.Walsh 20681
	V 20681 Australia - Victoria 20681
R	*Olearia ballii* (F. Muell.) Hemsley 14223
	R 14223 Australia - NSW - Lord Howe Is. 14223
R	*Olearia chathamica* 19305
	R 19305 New Zealand - Chatham Is. 19305
V	*Olearia cordata* Lander 20681
	V 20681 Australia - New South Wales 20681
R	*Olearia ericoides* (Steetz) Wakef. 20681
	R 20681 Australia - Tasmania 20681
E	*Olearia flocktoniae* Maiden & Betche 20681, 5465
	E 20681 Australia - New South Wales 20681
R	*Olearia fragrantissima* 19305
	R 20625 New Zealand - South Is. (eastern) 20625
R	*Olearia frostii* (F.Muell.) J.H.Willis 20681
	R 20681 Australia - Victoria 20681
E	*Olearia hectorii* 19305
	E 20625 New Zealand - North Is. 20625
	E 19305 New Zealand - South Is. 19305
R	*Olearia heterocarpa* S.T.Blake 20681
	I 20681 Australia - New South Wales 20681
	I 20681 Australia - Queensland 20681
R	*Olearia hookeri* (Sonder) Benth. 20681
	R 20681 Australia - Tasmania 20681
E	*Olearia hygrophila* (DC.) Benth. 20681
	E 20681 Australia - Queensland 20681
R	*Olearia lasiophylla* Lander 20681

	R 20681 Australia - New South Wales 20681
V	*Olearia macdonnellensis* D.A.Cooke 20681
	V 20681 Australia - Northern Territory 20681
E	*Olearia microdisca* J.Black 20681
	E 20681 Australia - South Australia 20681
R	*Olearia montana* Lander 20681
	R 20681 Australia - New South Wales 20681
R	*Olearia mooneyi* (F. Muell.) Hemsley 14223
	R 14223 Australia - NSW - Lord Howe Is. 14223
Ex	*Olearia oliganthema* F.Muell. 20681, 14223
	Ex 20681 Australia - New South Wales 20681
V	*Olearia pachyphylla* Cheeseman 86
	V 19305 New Zealand - North Is. 19305
R	*Olearia pannosa* Hook. ssp. *cardiophylla* (F.Muell.) D.Cooke 20681
	R 20681 Australia - South Australia 20681
V	*Olearia pannosa* Hook. ssp. *pannosa* 20681
	I 20681 Australia - South Australia 20681
	I 20681 Australia - Victoria 20681
E	*Olearia polita* 19305
	E 19305 New Zealand - South Is. (Nelson) 20625
R	*Olearia pomahaka* 20625
	R 20625 New Zealand - South Is. (Otago; Southland) 20625
R	*Olearia quercifolia* DC. 20681
	R 20681 Australia - New South Wales 20681
R	*Olearia rhizomatica* Lander ms. 20681
	I 20681 Australia - Capital Territory 20681
	I 20681 Australia - New South Wales 20681
R	*Olearia semidentata* Decne. ex Hook.f.
	R New Zealand - Chatham Is. 19106
R	*Olearia stilwelliae* Blakely 20681
	R 20681 Australia - New South Wales 20681
R	*Olearia traversii* (F. Muell.) Hook.f. 19305
	R 19305 New Zealand - Chatham Is. 19106
R	*Omalotheca sylvatica* ssp. *carpetana* 15846
	R 15846 Spain 15846
E	*Onopordum algeriense* (Munby) Pomel 10488
	E 14958 Algeria 10488
V	*Onopordum bracteatum* L. var. *arachnoideum* Erik & Sumbul 12840
	V 12840 Turkey 12840
V	*Onopordum carduelinum* Bolle 14166
	V 20750 Spain - Canary Is. 17891
R	*Onopordum caricum* Hub.-Mor. 12840
	R 12840 Turkey 12840
E	*Onopordum cyrenaicum* Maire & M. Weiller
	E Libya
I	*Onopordum majorii* Beauverd 20731
	I Greece
R	*Onopordum mesatlanticum* Emberger & Maire
	R Morocco
E	*Onopordum nogalesii* Svent. 14166
	E 15105 Spain - Canary Is. 17891
I	*Onopordum rhodense* Boiss. ex Rech.f.
	I Greece
V	*Onoseris humboldtiana* Ferreyra 18200
	V 12468 Peru 18200
R	*Onoseris macbridei* Ferreyra 18200

R   *12468*   Peru   *18200*

V   *Oonopsis engelmannii* (Gray) Greene *20850*
   I   *20850*   U.S. - Colorado *20850*
   E   *20850*   U.S. - Kansas *20850*

V   *Oonopsis foliosa* (Gray) Greene *20850*
   I   *20850*   U.S. - Colorado *20850*
   I   *20850*   U.S. - Kansas *20850*
   I   *20850*   U.S. - Wyoming *20850*

V   *Oonopsis foliosa* (Gray) Greene var.
     foliosa *20850*
   I   *20850*   U.S. - Colorado *20850*
   I   *20850*   U.S. - Kansas *20850*
   I   *20850*   U.S. - Wyoming *20850*

V   *Oonopsis foliosa* (Gray) Greene var. *monocephala*
     (A. Nels.) Kartesz & Gandhi *20850*
   V   *20850*   U.S. - Colorado *20850*

V   *Oonopsis wardii* (Gray) Greene *20850*
   V   *20850*   U.S. - Wyoming *20850*

V   *Oparanthus albus* (F. Brown) Sherff
   V   French Polynesia - Marquesas Is

R   *Oparanthus coriaceus* (F.Brown) Sherff *20845*
   R   *20845*   French Polynesia - Tubuai Is. (Rapa)
       20845

R   *Oparanthus rapensis* (F.Brown) Sherff *20845*
   R   *20845*   French Polynesia - Tubuai Is. (Rapa)
       20845

R   *Oritrophium blepharophyllum* (Blake) Cuatrec. *12473*
   R   *19537*   Venezuela *12473*

R   *Oritrophium nevadense* (Wedd.) Cuatrec. *12473*
   R   *19537*   Venezuela *12473*

R   *Oritrophium venezuelense* (Steyerm.) Cuatrec. *12473*
   R   *19537*   Venezuela *12473*

R   *Ormenis flahaultii* Emberger
   R   Morocco

R   *Orochaenactis thysanocarpha* (Gray) Coville *20850*
   I   *20850*   U.S. - California *20850*

R   *Osteospermum aciphyllum* DC. *20604*
   R   *20604*   South Africa - Cape Province *20604*

R   *Osteospermum elsieae* Norl. *20604*
   R   *20604*   South Africa - Cape Province *20604*

R   *Osteospermum hafstroemii* Norl. *20604*
   R   *20604*   South Africa - Cape Province *20604*

Ex   *Osteospermum hirsutum* Thunb. *20604, 6180*
   Ex   *20604*   South Africa - Cape Province *20604*

I   *Osteospermum hispidum* Harvey var. *virile*
     Norl. *20604*
   I   *20604*   South Africa - Cape Province *20604*

R   *Osteospermum nyikense* T. Norlindh
   R   Malawi

E   *Osteospermum sanctae-helenae* Norlindh *18996*
   E   *18996*   St Helena *18996*

R   *Othonna armiana* Van Jaarsv. *20604*
   R   *20604*   South Africa - Cape Province *20604*

I   *Othonna cakilefolia* DC. *20604*
     20604   South Africa - Cape Province *20604*

R   *Othonna gypsicola* R.Bates *20681*
   R   *20681*   Australia - South Australia *20681*

R   *Othonna hallii* B.Nord. *20604*
   R   *20604*   South Africa - Cape Province *20604*

R   *Othonna pteronioides* Harv. *20604*

R   *20604*   South Africa - Cape Province *20604*

I   *Othonna rechingeri* B.Nord. *20604*
   I   *20604*   South Africa - Cape Province *20604*

R   *Ozothamnus costatifructus* (R.V.Smith)
     A.Anderb. *20681*
   R   *20681*   Australia - Tasmania *20681*

V   *Ozothamnus eriocephalus* (J.H.Willis) A.Anderb. *20681*
   V   *20681*   Australia - Queensland *20681*

R   *Ozothamnus expansifolius* (Morris & Willis)
     A.Anderb. *20681*
   R   *20681*   Australia - Tasmania *20681*

R   *Ozothamnus gunnii* Hook.f. *20681*
   R   *20681*   Australia - Tasmania *20681*

R   *Ozothamnus lycopodioides* Hook.f. *20681*
   R   *20681*   Australia - Tasmania *20681*

Ex   *Ozothamnus selaginoides* Sonder & F.Muell. *20681*
   Ex   *20681*   Australia - Tasmania *20681*

V   *Ozothamnus tesselatus* (Maiden & R.Baker)
     A.Anderb. *20681*
   V   *20681*   Australia - New South Wales *20681*

R   *Ozothamnus vagans* (C.White) A.Anderb. *20681*
   I   *20681*   Australia - New South Wales *20681*
   I   *20681*   Australia - Queensland *20681*

R   *Ozothamnus whitei* (N.Burb.) A.Anderb. *20681*
   I   *20681*   Australia - New South Wales *20681*
   I   *20681*   Australia - Queensland *20681*

R   *Pachystegia rufa* *19305*
   R   *19305*   New Zealand - South Is. *19305*

R   *Palaeocyanus crassifolius* (Bertol.) Dostál *13351,*
   20171
   R   *13351*   Malta (Malta & Gozo) *13351*

R   *Palafoxia arida* B. Turner * M. Morris var. *gigantea*
     (M.E. Jones) B.L. Turner & Morris *20883, 20850*
   E   *20850*   U.S. - Arizona *20850*
   V   *20850*   U.S. - California *20850*
     20883   Mexico *20883*

E   *Parafaujasia mauritiana* C.Jeffrey *20771*
   E   *20771*   Mauritius *20771*

R   *Paraixeris yoshinoi* Nakai *10573*
   R   *10573*   Japan *10573*

R   *Parantennaria uniceps* (F.Muell.) Beauverd *20681*
   I   *20681*   Australia - Capital Territory *20681*
   I   *20681*   Australia - New South Wales *20681*
   I   *20681*   Australia - Victoria *20681*

R   *Parthenice mollis* Gray *20850*
   I   *20850*   U.S. - Arizona *20850*
   I   *20850*   U.S. - New Mexico *20850*

R   *Parthenium alpinum* (Nutt.) Torr. & Gray *20850*
   E   *20850*   U.S. - Colorado *20850*
   I   *20850*   U.S. - New Mexico *20850*
   R   *20850*   U.S. - Wyoming *20850*

R   *Parthenium integrifolium* Mears var. *mabryanum*
     Mears *20850*
   R   *20850*   U.S. - North Carolina *20850*
   I   *20850*   U.S. - South Carolina *20850*
   I   *20850*   U.S. - Virginia *20850*

R   *Parthenium ligulatum* (M.E. Jones) Barneby *20850*
   V   *20850*   U.S. - Colorado *20850*
   R   *20850*   U.S. - Utah *20850*

R   *Parthenium radfordii* Mears *20850*
   V   *20850*   U.S. - North Carolina *20850*
   I   *20850*   U.S. - South Carolina *20850*

V   *Parthenium tetraneuris* Barneby 20850
>   V   20850   U.S. - Colorado   20850

E   *Pectis havanensis* Urban 5607
>   E   19105   Cuba (Ciud. Habana)   5607

R   *Pectis imberbis* Gray 20883, 20850
>   V   20850   U.S. - Arizona   20850
>   I   20883   Mexico   20883

E   *Pectis juniperina* Rydb. 5607
>   E   19105   Cuba (Pinar del Rio)   5607

E   *Pectis leonis* Rydb. 5607
>   E   19105   Cuba (Sancti Spiritus)   5607

E   *Pectis pinosia* Urban 5607
>   E   19105   Cuba (Juventud Is.)   5607

E   *Pectis ritlandii* Howard & Briggs 5607
>   E   19105   Cuba (Cienfuegos)   5607

R   *Pectis rusbyi* Greene ex Gray 20850
>   R   20850   U.S. - Arizona   20850

R   *Pegolettia dubiefiana* Quezel 10488
>   R   14958   Algeria   10488

E   *Pentacalia carpishensis* (Cuatrec.) Cuatrec. 18200
>   E   9446   Peru   18200

E   *Pentacalia guadalupe* ssp. *caucana* (Cuatr.) Cuatr. 20883
>   I   20883   Colombia   20883

V   *Pentacalia inornata* H. Robinson 20883, 13336
>   V   13336   Jamaica   20883

R   *Pentacalia subdiscolor* H. Robinson 20883, 13336
>   R   13336   Jamaica   20883

E   *Pentachaeta bellidiflora* Greene 20850
>   E   20850   U.S. - California   20850

E   *Pentachaeta exilis* (A. Gray) A. Gray ssp. *aeolica* Van Horn & Ornduff 20850
>   E   20850   U.S. - California   20850

R   *Pentachaeta fragilis* Brandeg. 20850
>   I   20850   U.S. - California   20850

E   *Pentachaeta lyonii* Gray 20850
>   E   20850   U.S. - California   20850

V   *Perezia cirsiifolia* Wedd. 18200
>   V   12468   Peru   18200

V   *Pericallis multiflora* (L'Hér.) B.Nord. 20750
>   V   20750   Spain - Canary Is.   20750

R   *Perityle aglossa* Gray 20850
>   R   20850   U.S. - Texas   20850

E   *Perityle ajoensis* T.K. Todsen 20883, 20850, 11630
>   E   20850   U.S. - Arizona   20850
>   20883   Mexico   20883

V   *Perityle bisetosa* (Torr. ex Gray) Shinners 20850
>   V   20850   U.S. - Texas   20850

V   *Perityle bisetosa* (Torr. ex Gray) Shinners var. *appressa* A.Powell 20850
>   V   20850   U.S. - Texas   20850

E   *Perityle bisetosa* (Torr. ex Gray) Shinners var. *bisetosa* (Torrey) Shinn. 20850
>   E   20850   U.S. - Texas   20850

E   *Perityle bisetosa* (Torr. ex Gray) Shinners var. *scalaris* A.Powell 20850
>   E   20850   U.S. - Texas   20850

E   *Perityle cernua* (Greene) Shinners 20850
>   E   20850   U.S. - New Mexico   20850

V   *Perityle ciliata* (L.H. Dewey) Rydb. 20850
>   I   20850   U.S. - Arizona   20850

V   *Perityle cinerea* (Gray) A. Powell 20850
>   V   20850   U.S. - Texas   20850

E   *Perityle cochisensis* (Niles) A. Powell 20850
>   E   20850   U.S. - Arizona   20850

E   *Perityle congesta* (M.E. Jones) Shinners 20850
>   I   20850   U.S. - Arizona   20850
>   I   20850   U.S. - Nevada   20850

V   *Perityle coronopifolia* Gray 20850
>   I   20850   U.S. - Arizona   20850
>   I   20850   U.S. - New Mexico   20850

V   *Perityle dissecta* (Torr.) Gray 20850
>   I   20850   U.S. - Arizona   20850
>   I   20850   U.S. - New Mexico   20850
>   V   20850   U.S. - Texas   20850

E   *Perityle fosteri* A. Powell 20850
>   E   20850   U.S. - Texas   20850

R   *Perityle gilensis* (M. E. Jones) J. F. MacBr. var. *gilensis* 20850
>   R   20850   U.S. - Arizona   20850

V   *Perityle gilensis* A. Powell var. *salensis* A. Powell 20850
>   V   20850   U.S. - Arizona   20850

V   *Perityle gracilis* (M.E.Jones) Rydb. 20850
>   I   20850   U.S. - Arizona   20850
>   I   20850   U.S. - Nevada   20850

E   *Perityle huecoensis* A. Powell 20850
>   E   20850   U.S. - Texas   20850

Ex/E   *Perityle inyoensis* (Ferris) A. Powell 20850, 14662
>   Ex/E   20850   U.S. - California   20850

R   *Perityle megalocephala* (S.Watson) J.F. Macbr. 20850
>   I   20850   U.S. - California   20850
>   R   20850   U.S. - Nevada   20850

V   *Perityle megalocephala* (S.Watson) J. F. Macbr. var. *intricata* (Brandeg.) A. Powell 20850
>   V   20850   U.S. - Nevada   20850

R   *Perityle megalocephala* (S.Watson) J. F. Macbr. var. *megalocephala* 20850
>   I   20850   U.S. - California   20850
>   R   20850   U.S. - Nevada   20850

R   *Perityle rupestris* A. Powell var. *albiflora* A. Powell 20850
>   R   20850   U.S. - Texas   20850

R   *Perityle rupestris* (Gray) Shinners var. *rupestris* 20850
>   R   20850   U.S. - Texas   20850

V   *Perityle saxicola* (Eastw.) Shinners 20850
>   V   20850   U.S. - Arizona   20850

E   *Perityle specuicola* Welsh & Neese 20850
>   E   20850   U.S. - Utah   20850

V   *Perityle staurophylla* (Barneby) Shinners var. *homoflora* T.K. Todsen 20850
>   V   20850   U.S. - New Mexico   20850

V   *Perityle tenella* (M.E.Jones) J.F.Macbr. 20850
>   I   20850   U.S. - Arizona   20850
>   I   20850   U.S. - Nevada   20850
>   I   20850   U.S. - Utah   20850

E   *Perityle villosa* (Blake) Shinners 20850, 14662
>   E   20850   U.S. - California   20850

E   *Perityle vitreomontana* Warnock 20850

	E	20850 U.S. - Texas *20850*

E   *Perityle warnockii* A. Powell *20850*

	E	20850 U.S. - Texas *20850*

I   *Perymenium wilburorum* McVaugh *10354*

	E	21204 Mexico - Jalisco *21204*

R   *Petasites doerfleri* Hayek *20178, 20171*

	R	20178 Albania *20178*
	V	21091 Bosnia & Herzegovina *21091*

E   *Peteravenia cyrili-nelsonii* (A. Molina) R. King & H. Robinson *10836*

	E	20050 Honduras *10836*

E   *Petrobium arboreum* R. Br. ex Sprengel *18996*

	E	18996 St Helena *18996*

R   *Phagnalon bennettii* Lowe *17891*

	R	Portugal - Madeira

I   *Phagnalon garamantum* Maire *10488*

	I	14958 Algeria *10488*

R   *Phagnalon iminouakense* Emberger

	R	Morocco

R   *Phagnalon latifolium* Maire

	R	Morocco

R   *Phagnalon metlesicsii* Pignatti *18264, 20171*

	R	18264 Italy - Sicily *18264*

R   *Phagnalon umbelliforme* DC. *15105*

	R	15105 Spain - Canary Is. *15105*

R   *Phalacrocarpum hoffmannseggii* (Samp.) M.Laínz *20171*

	E	20076 Portugal *20076*
	R	Spain

R   *Phoebanthus tenuifolius* (Torr. & Gray) Blake *20850*

	E	20850 U.S. - Alabama *20850*
	R	20850 U.S. - Florida *20850*

I   *Phymaspermum villosum* (Hilliard) Källersjö *20604*

	I	20604 South Africa - Cape Province *20604*
	I	20604 South Africa - Natal *20604*

V   *Picris algarbiensis* Franco *8000, 20171*

	V	8322 Portugal *8000*

R   *Picris campylocarpa* Boiss. & Heldr. *12840*

	R	12840 Turkey *12840*

R   *Picris cyrenaica* (Pampan.) Lack

	R	Libya

V   *Picris evae* Lack *20681*

	I	20681 Australia - New South Wales *20681*
	I	20681 Australia - Queensland *20681*

R   *Picris pitardiana* Gandoger

	R	Morocco

R   *Picris willkommii* (Sch.Bip.) Nyman *8000, 20171*

	E	20705 Portugal (south east) *8000*
	R	Spain (south west) *8000*

R   *Pinaropappus parvus* Blake *20850*

	R	20850 U.S. - New Mexico *20850*
	R	20850 U.S. - Texas *20850*

R   *Piqueriopsis michoacana* R. King *9595*

	R	9595 Mexico *9595*

R   *Pityopsis flexuosa* (Nash) Small *20850*

	R	20850 U.S. - Florida *20850*
	I	20850 U.S. - Georgia *20850*

V   *Pityopsis oligantha* (Chapman ex Torr. & Gray) Small *20850*

	I	20850 U.S. - Alabama *20850*
	I	20850 U.S. - Florida *20850*

	I	20850 U.S. - Georgia *20850*
	I	20850 U.S. - Louisiana *20850*
	I	20850 U.S. - Oklahoma *20850*

E   *Pityopsis ruthii* (Small) Small *20850*

	E	20850 U.S. - Tennessee (Polk County) *20850*

E   *Pladaroxylon leucadendron* (Forster f.) Hook.f. *18996*

	E	18996 St Helena *18996*

R   *Plagius flosculosus* (L.) Alavi & Heywood *15080, 20171*

	V	15080 France - Corsica *15080*
	R	20805 Italy - Sardinia *15080*

R   *Pleurocarpaea fasciculata* Dunlop *20681*

	R	20681 Australia - Northern Territory *20681*

V   *Pleuropappus phyllocalymmeus* F.Muell. *20681*

	V	20681 Australia - South Australia *20681*

E   *Pluchea aromatica* Balf. f. *15534*

	E	15534 Yemen - Socotra *15534*

R   *Pluchea lanceolata* (DC.) Oliver & Hiern *8003*

	R	Chad *8003*
	R	Senegal *8003*

V   *Pluchea longifolia* Nash *20850*

	I	20850 U.S. - Florida *20850*

E   *Pluchea obovata* Balf. f. *15534*

	E	15534 Yemen - Socotra *15534*

R   *Podolepis monticola* R.J.Henderson *20681, 8560*

	I	20681 Australia - New South Wales *20681*
	I	20681 Australia - Queensland *20681*

E   *Polymnia cossatotensis* A.B. Pittman & V. Bates *20850*

	E	20850 U.S. - Arkansas *20850*

R   *Polymnia laevigata* Beadle *20850*

	V	20850 U.S. - Alabama *20850*
	E	20850 U.S. - Florida *20850*
	E	20850 U.S. - Georgia *20850*
	E	20850 U.S. - Kentucky *20850*
	Ex	20850 U.S. - Missouri *20850*
	R	20850 U.S. - Tennessee *20850*

E   *Porophyllum pygmaeum* Keil & J. Morefield *20850*

	E	20850 U.S. - Nevada *20850*

I   *Prenanthes amabilis* Balf. f. *15534*

	I	15534 Yemen - Socotra *15534*

R   *Prenanthes barbata* (Torr. & Gray) Milstead *20850*

	V	20850 U.S. - Alabama *20850*
	E	20850 U.S. - Arkansas *20850*
	E	20850 U.S. - Georgia *20850*
	E	20850 U.S. - Kentucky *20850*
	E	20850 U.S. - Louisiana *20850*
	V	20850 U.S. - Tennessee *20850*
	V	20850 U.S. - Texas *20850*

V   *Prenanthes boottii* (DC.) Gray *20850*

	E	20850 U.S. - Maine *20850*
	E	20850 U.S. - New Hampshire *20850*
	E	20850 U.S. - New York *20850*
	E	20850 U.S. - Vermont *20850*

R   *Prenanthes glareosa* (Scho.&Kotsc. ex Bois.) C. Jeff. *12840*

	R	12840 Turkey *12840*

R   *Prenanthes roanensis* (Chickering) Chickering *20850*

	R	20850 U.S. - North Carolina *20850*
	V	20850 U.S. - Tennessee *20850*
	V	20850 U.S. - Virginia *20850*

R   *Psacalium nanum* Pippen *9554*

	R	19755 Mexico *9554*

V   *Pseudobahia bahiifolia* (Benth.) Rydb. *20850*

V		20850 U.S. - California 20850	

V   *Pseudobahia peirsonii* Munz 20850
- V   20850 U.S. - California 20850

R   *Pseudoclappia arenaria* Rydb. 20850
- R   20850 U.S. - New Mexico 20850
- E   20850 U.S. - Oklahoma 20850
- V   20850 U.S. - Texas 20850

E   *Pseudoclappia watsonii* Powell & B.L. Turner 20850
- E   20850 U.S. - Texas 20850

R   *Psiadia arguta* (Pers.) Voiget 10082
- R   20771 Mauritius 10082

V   *Psiadia canescens* A.J. Scott 10082
- V   20771 Mauritius 10082

E   *Psiadia cataractae* A.J. Scott 10082
- E   20771 Mauritius 10082

R   *Psiadia lithospermifolia* (Lam.) Cordem. 10082
- R   20771 Mauritius 10082

Ex   *Psiadia mauritiana* A.J. Scott 10082
- Ex   Mauritius 10082

R   *Psiadia melastomoides* (Lam.) A.J. Scott 10082
- R   10082 Réunion 10082

R   *Psiadia penninervia* DC. 10082
- R   20771 Mauritius 10082

R   *Psiadia pollicina* A.J. Scott 10082
- R   20771 Mauritius 10082

V   *Psiadia retusa* (Lam.) DC. 10082
- V   14234 Réunion 10082

R   *Psiadia rivalsii* A.J. Scott 10082
- R   10082 Réunion 10082

V   *Psiadia rodriguesiana* Balf.f. 10082
- V   5852 Mauritius - Rodrigues 5852

R   *Psiadia salaziana* Cordem. 10082
- R   10082 Réunion 10082

R   *Psiadia terebinthina* A.J. Scott 10082
- R   20771 Mauritius 10082

V   *Psilocarphus brevissimus* Nutt. var. *multiflorus* Cronq. 20850
- V   20850 U.S. - California 20850

R   *Pteronia diosmifolia* Brusse 20604
- R   20604 South Africa - Cape Province 20604

R   *Pterothrix tecta* Brusse 20604
- R   20604 South Africa - Cape Province 20604

R   *Ptilostemon abylensis* (Maire) Greuter
- R   Morocco

R   *Ptilostemon leptophyllus* (Pau & Font Quer) Greuter
- R   Morocco

R   *Ptilostemon niveus* (C.Presl) Greuter 18264, 20171
- R   18264 Italy (Basilicata, Calabria) 18264
- R   Italy - Sicily

R   *Pulicaria armena* (Boiss.) Kotschy 12840
- R   12840 Turkey 12840

E   *Pulicaria burchardii* Hutch. 15105
- E   15105 Spain - Canary Is. 15105

E   *Pulicaria canariensis* Bolle 15105
- E   15105 Spain - Canary Is. 15105

E   *Pulicaria elegans* Camel-Edlin 15534
- E   15534 Yemen - Socotra 15534

E   *Pulicaria filaginoides* Pomel 10488
- E   14958 Algeria 10488

I   *Pulicaria glandulosa* Caball.
- I   Morocco

E   *Pulicaria lanata* Camal-Eldin 15534
- E   15534 Yemen - Socotra 15534

I   *Pulicaria omanensis* ssp. *milleri* Gamal-Eldin 20146
- I   20146 Oman (Dhofar) 20146

I   *Pulicaria pulvinata* Gamal-Eldin 20146
- I   20146 Oman (central) 20146

I   *Pulicaria rajputanae* Blatter & Hallberg 7771
- I   India - Rajasthan 7771

I   *Pulicaria vieraeoides* Balf. f. 15534
- I   15534 Yemen - Socotra 15534

Ex/E   *Pyrethrum kelleri* (Krylov & Plotn.) Kraschen. 5942
- Ex/E 5942 Kazakhstan (east) 5942

I   *Pyrethrum mikeschinii* Tzvelev
- I   5942 Kyrgyzstan 5942
- I   5942 Tajikistan 5942

V   *Pyrrocoma carthamoides* var. *subsquarrosa* (Greene) G. Brown & Keil 20850
- V   20850 U.S. - Montana 20850
- V   20850 U.S. - Wyoming 20850

V   *Pyrrocoma crocea* var. *genuflexa* (Greene) Mayes ex G. Brown & Keil 20850
- I   20850 U.S. - Arizona 20850

R   *Pyrrocoma hirta* var. *sonchifolia* (Greene) Kartesz & Gandhi 20850
- E   20850 U.S. - Idaho 20850
- I   20850 U.S. - Oregon 20850
- I   20850 U.S. - Washington 20850

R   *Pyrrocoma insecticruris* Heller 20850
- R   20850 U.S. - Idaho 20850

V   *Pyrrocoma liatriformis* Greene 20850
- V   20850 U.S. - Idaho 20850
- V   20850 U.S. - Washington 20850

V   *Pyrrocoma lucida* (Keck) Kartesz & Gandhi 20850
- V   20850 U.S. - California 20850

R   *Pyrrocoma radiata* Nutt. 20850
- I   20850 U.S. - California 20850
- R   20850 U.S. - Idaho 20850
- I   20850 U.S. - Nevada 20850
- V   20850 U.S. - Oregon 20850
- I   20850 U.S. - Utah 20850

V   *Pyrrocoma uniflora* var. *gossypina* (Greene) Kartesz & Gandhi 20850
- V   20850 U.S. - California 20850

V   *Raillardella pringlei* Greene 20850, 14662
- V   20850 U.S. - California 20850

V   *Raillardiopsis muirii* (Gray) Rydb. 20850
- V   20850 U.S. - California 20850

R   *Raillardiopsis scabrida* (Eastw.) Rydb. 20850
- R   20850 U.S. - California 20850

E   *Raoulia cinerea* Petrie 86
- E   New Zealand - South Is.

R   *Reichardia crystallina* (Schultz Bip.) D. Bramwell 15105
- R   15105 Spain - Canary Is. 15105

R   *Reichardia famarae* D. Bramwell & Kunkel 15105
- R   20750 Spain - Canary Is. 15105

E   *Relhania rotundifolia* Less. 20604
- E   20604 South Africa - Cape Province 20604

R   *Relhania spathulifolia* **K.Bremer** *20604*
    R   *20604*   South Africa - Cape Province *20604*

E   *Remya kauaiensis* **Hbd.** *20850*
    E   *20850*   U.S. - Hawaii *20850*

E   *Remya kauaiensis* **Hillebrand var.**
     kauaiensis *14209*
    E   *14209*   U.S. - Hawaii (Kaua`i) *14209*

E   *Remya mauiensis* **Hbd.** *20850, 14209*
    E   *20850*   U.S. - Hawaii (West Maui) *20850*

E   *Remya montgomeryi* **W.L. Wagner & Herbst** *20850, 14209*
    E   *20850*   U.S. - Hawaii (Kaua`i) *20850*

R   *Revealia macrocephala* **(Paray) R. King & H.**
     Robinson *10836*
    R   *10836*   Mexico *10836*

Ex/E   *Rhamphogyne rhynchocarpa* **(Balf.f.) S. Moore** *10082*
    Ex/E   *5852*   Mauritius - Rodrigues *10082*

R   *Rhaponticum aulieatense* **Iljin** *5942*
    R   *5942*   Kazakhstan (southern border with Kyrgystan) *5942*
    R   *5942*   Kyrgyzstan (border with Kazakhstan) *5942*

E   *Rhaponticum canariensis* **DC.**
    E   Spain - Canary Is.

E   *Rhodogeron coronopifolius* **Griseb.** *5607*
    E   *19105*   Cuba (Villa Clara) *5607*

E   *Robinsonia berterii* *19116*
    E   *19116*   Chile - Juan Fernandez Is. *19116*

V   *Robinsonia evenia* **Philippi** *19116*
    V   *19125*   Chile - Juan Fernandez Is. *19116*

V   *Robinsonia gayana* **Decne.** *19116*
    V   *19125*   Chile - Juan Fernandez Is. *19116*

V   *Robinsonia gracilis* **Decne.** *19116*
    V   *19125*   Chile - Juan Fernandez Is. *19116*

E   *Robinsonia macrocephala* *19116*
    E   *19116*   Chile - Juan Fernandez Is. *19116*

V   *Robinsonia masafuerae* **Skottsb.** *19116*
    V   *19125*   Chile - Juan Fernandez Is. *19116*

E   *Robinsonia thurifera* **Decne.** *19116*
    E   *19125*   Chile - Juan Fernandez Is. *19116*

E   *Rothmaleria granatensis* **(Boiss. ex DC.) Font**
     Quer *15398, 20171*
    E   *19818*   Spain (Granada) *19818*

E   *Rudbeckia auriculata* **(Perdue) Kral** *20850*
    E   *20850*   U.S. - Alabama *20850*

V   *Rudbeckia graminifolia* **(Torr. & Gray) C.L.Boynt &**
     Beadle *20850*
    I   *20850*   U.S. - Florida *20850*
    I   *20850*   U.S. - Georgia *20850*

V   *Rudbeckia heliopsidis* **Torr. & Gray** *20850*
    V   *20850*   U.S. - Alabama *20850*
    E   *20850*   U.S. - Georgia *20850*
    I   *20850*   U.S. - Louisiana *20850*
    E   *20850*   U.S. - North Carolina *20850*
    E   *20850*   U.S. - South Carolina *20850*
    E   *20850*   U.S. - Virginia *20850*

V   *Rudbeckia nitida* **Nutt. var.** *nitida* *20850*
    E   *20850*   U.S. - Alabama *20850*
    E   *20850*   U.S. - Florida *20850*
    R   *20850*   U.S. - Georgia *20850*

V   *Rudbeckia scabrifolia* **L.E. Brown** *20850*
    V   *20850*   U.S. - Louisiana *20850*
    V   *20850*   U.S. - Texas *20850*

V   *Rudbeckia triloba* **L. var.** *pinnatiloba* **Torr. &**
     Gray *20850*
    V   *20850*   U.S. - Alabama *20850*
    E   *20850*   U.S. - Florida *20850*
    E   *20850*   U.S. - North Carolina *20850*
    E   *20850*   U.S. - Virginia *20850*

R   *Rugelia nudicaulis* **Shuttlw. ex Chapman** *20850*
    R   *20850*   U.S. - North Carolina *20850*
    V   *20850*   U.S. - Tennessee *20850*

R   *Rumfordia revealii* **H. Robinson** *9604*
    R   *19755*   Mexico *9604*

V   *Rutidosis heterogama* **Philipson** *20681*
    V   *20681*   Australia - New South Wales *20681*

E   *Rutidosis lanata* **A.E.Holland** *20681*
    E   *20681*   Australia - Queensland *20681*

V   *Rutidosis leiolepis* **F.Muell.** *20681*
    V   *20681*   Australia - New South Wales *20681*

E   *Rutidosis leptorrhynchoides* **F.Muell.** *20681*
    I   *20681*   Australia - Capital Territory *20681*
    I   *20681*   Australia - New South Wales *20681*
    I   *20681*   Australia - Victoria *20681*

R   *Sabazia gonzalezae* **B. Turner** *10357*
    R   *14294*   Mexico - Durango *10357*

V   *Sachsia polycephala* **Griseb.** *20850*
    E   *20850*   U.S. - Florida *20850*

E   *Sachsia tricephala* **Griseb.** *5607*
    E   *19105*   Cuba (Pinar del Rio) *5607*

I   *Salmea caleoides* **Griseb.** *5607*
    I   *19105*   Cuba (Pinar del Rio) *5607*

I   *Salmea glaberrima* **C. Wright**
    I   *19105*   Cuba (Pinar del Rio) *19105*

I   *Salmea sessilifolia* **Griseb.** *20883, 13336*
    I   *13336*   Jamaica *20883*

I   *Salmea umatilis* **Robins.** *5607*
    I   *19105*   Cuba (Pinar del Rio) *5607*

R   *Santolina ascensionis* **Sennen**
    R   Morocco

V   *Santolina elegans* **Boiss. ex DC.** *15398, 20171*
    V   Spain *15398*

V   *Santolina impressa* **Hoffmanns. & Link** *8000*
    V   *20076*   Portugal *20076*

R   *Santolina ligustica* **Arrigoni** *18264*
    R   *18264*   Italy (Liguria) *18264*

R   *Santolina neapolitana* **Jordan & Fourr.** *18264*
    R   *18264*   Italy (Campania) *18264*

V   *Santolina semidentata* **Hoffmanns. & Link** *8000*
    V   *20076*   Portugal *20076*

R   *Santolina viscosa* **Lag.** *20171*
    R   Spain (gypsum soils)

V   *Sarcanthemum coronopus* **(Lam.) Cass.** *10082*
    V   *5852*   Mauritius - Rodrigues *10082*

V   *Sartwellia gypsophila* **Powell & B.L. Turner** *20850, 9651*
    I   *20850*   U.S. - Texas *20850*
    ?   Mexico - Chihuahua *9651*

R   *Saussurea alpicola* **Kitamura** *15957*
    R   *15923*   Korea, South (north to Mt Nangrim) *15957*

I   *Saussurea atkinsoni* **C.B. Clarke**
    I   India - Himachal Pradesh

	I	India - Jammu & Kashmir

R *Saussurea bracteata* Decne.

R	13883	India - Himachal Pradesh *13883*
R	13883	India - Jammu & Kashmir *13883*
R	13883	India - Uttar Pradesh *13883*
R	13883	Pakistan *13883*

R *Saussurea chinophylla* Takeda *10573*

R	10573	Japan *10573*

R *Saussurea clarkei* Hook.f. *11494*

R	11494	India - Jammu & Kashmir (Kashmir Himalaya) *11494*

E ı *Saussurea costus* (Falc.) Lipsch. *7955*

E	13883	India - Himachal Pradesh *13883*
E	13883	India - Jammu & Kashmir *13883*
E	13883	Pakistan *13883*

R *Saussurea diamantiaca* Nakai *15957*

R	15923	Korea, South *15957*

I *Saussurea foliosa* Edgew.

I		India - Uttar Pradesh (Garhwal; Kumaun)

R *Saussurea franchetii* Koidz. *10573*

R	10573	Japan *10573*

R *Saussurea inaensis* Kitam. *10573*

R	10573	Japan *10573*

R *Saussurea insularis* Kitam. *10573*

R	10573	Japan *10573*

R *Saussurea involucrata* Karelin & Kir. ex Maxim. *17617*

V	17617	China - Xinjiang Uygur Zizhiqu *11139*
R		former USSR *6930*

R *Saussurea kanzanensis* Kitamura *20511*

R	20511	Taiwan *20511*

R *Saussurea kiraisiensis* Masamune *20511*

R	20511	Taiwan *20511*

I *Saussurea kitamurana* Miyabe & Tatew. *5942*

I	5942	Russia (Far East) - Khabarovsk (south) *5942*
I	5942	Russia (Far East) - Primorye *5942*
I	5942	Russia (Far East) - Sakhalin *5942*

R *Saussurea riederi* Herder ssp. *kudoana* Kitam. *10573*

R	10573	Japan *10573*

I *Saussurea roylei* (DC.) Schultz Bip.

I		India - Himachal Pradesh
I		India - Jammu & Kashmir
I		India - Uttar Pradesh

R *Saussurea sovietica* Komarov *5942*

R	5942	Russia (Far East) - Primorye *5942*

R *Saussurea yakusimensis* Masam. *10573*

R	10573	Japan *10573*

R *Saussurea yoshinagae* Kitam. *10573*

R	10573	Japan *10573*

R *Scalesia affinis* Hook.f. *11117*

R		Ecuador - Galapagos *11117*

R *Scalesia aspera* Andersson *11117*

R		Ecuador - Galapagos (Eden, Santa Cruz) *5670*

E *Scalesia atractyloides* Arn. var. *atractyloides* *11117*

E	14980	Ecuador - Galapagos (west Santiago) *9389*

E *Scalesia atractyloides* Arn. var. *darwinii* (Hook.f.) Eliasson *11117*

E		Ecuador - Galapagos (west Santiago) *9389*

R *Scalesia baurii* Robinson & Greenman ssp. *baurii* *11117*

R		Ecuador - Galapagos (Pinta; Rabida; Wolf) *11117*

R *Scalesia baurii* Robinson & Greenman ssp. *hopkinsii* (Robinson) Eliasson *11117*

R		Ecuador - Galapagos (Pinta; Wolf) *11117*

R *Scalesia cordata* A. Stewart *11117*

R		Ecuador - Galapagos (V.Sierra Negra; Cerro Azul) *11117*

R *Scalesia crockeri* J. Howell *11117*

R		Ecuador - Galapagos *11117*

R *Scalesia divisa* Andersson *11117*

R		Ecuador - Galapagos (San Cristobal) *11117*

V *Scalesia gordilloi* Hamann & Wium-Anders. *7747*

V	14980	Ecuador - Galapagos *7747*

R *Scalesia helleri* Robinson ssp. *helleri* *11117*

R		Ecuador - Galapagos (Santa Cruz; Santa Fe) *11117*

E *Scalesia helleri* Robinson ssp. *santacruziana* Harling *11117*

E	14980	Ecuador - Galapagos (south-east Santa Cruz) *9389*

R *Scalesia incisa* Hook.f. *11117*

R		Ecuador - Galapagos (San Cristobal) *11117*

E *Scalesia retroflexa* Hemsley *11117*

E	14980	Ecuador - Galapagos (Punta Nunnez, Santa Cruz) *9389*

V *Scalesia stewartii* Riley *11117*

V	14980	Ecuador - Galapagos *9389*

R *Scalesia villosa* A. Stewart *11117*

R		Ecuador - Galapagos (incl. Floreana) *11117*

R *Scariola tetrantha* (B.L. Burtt & P. Davis) Sojak *14230*

R	19164	Cyprus (Khionistra, Kryos Potamos) *14230*

E *Schistocarpha croatii* H.E. Rob. *20883, 9006*

I	20883	Panama *20883*

E *Sciadocephala dressleri* K. & R. *20883, 9006*

I	20883	Panama *20883*

I *Scorzonera argyria* Boiss. *12840*

I	12840	Turkey *12840*

R *Scorzonera aucheriana* DC. *12840*

R	12840	Turkey *12840*

R *Scorzonera boissieri* Lipschitz *12840*

R	12840	Turkey *12840*

R *Scorzonera davisii* Lipschitz *12840*

R	12840	Turkey *12840*

E *Scorzonera drarii* Tackh.

E		Egypt

V *Scorzonera hieracifolia* Hayek *12840*

V	12840	Turkey *12840*

R *Scorzonera idaea* (Gand.) Lipsch. *20171*

R	20731	Greece - Crete *20731*

R *Scorzonera inaequiscapa* Boiss. *12840*

R	12840	Turkey *12840*

R *Scorzonera lacera* Boiss. & Bal. *12840*

R		12840 Turkey *12840*
R	*Scorzonera lasiocarpa* Chamb. *12840*	
R		12840 Turkey *12840*
R	*Scorzonera mirabilis* Lipschitz *12840*	
R		12840 Turkey *12840*
R	*Scorzonera pisidica* Huber-Mor. *12840*	
R		12840 Turkey *12840*
R	*Scorzonera pygmaea* Sibth. & Sm. *12840*	
R		12840 Turkey *12840*
R	*Scorzonera rhodantha* Hausskn. *20171*	
R		Greece
R	*Scorzonera sandrasica* Hartvig & Strid *12840*	
R		12840 Turkey *12840*
R	*Scorzonera scyria* M.A.Gust. & Snogerup *20171*	
R		Greece
R	*Scorzonera serpentinica* Rech.f. *20171*	
R		Greece
R	*Scorzonera suberosa* C. Koch. ssp. *cariensis* (Boiss.) Chamb. *12840*	
R		12840 Turkey *12840*
I	*Scorzonera tau-saghyz* Lipsch. & Bosse *5942*	
I		5942 Kazakhstan *5942*
I		5942 Kyrgyzstan *5942*
I		5942 Tajikistan *5942*
I		5942 Uzbekistan *5942*
R	*Scorzonera violacea* Chamb. *12840*	
R		12840 Turkey *12840*
R	*Senecio aconquijae* Cabrera *19448*	
R		20176 Argentina - Tucuman *20176*
V	*Senecio actinella* Greene *20850*	
I		20850 U.S. - Arizona *20850*
I		20850 U.S. - New Mexico *20850*
V	*Senecio appendiculatus* (L. f.) Schultz Bip. *15105*	
V		15105 Spain - Canary Is. *15105*
R	*Senecio astephanus* Greene *20850*	
I		20850 U.S. - California *20850*
R	*Senecio austromontanus* Hilliard *20604*	
R		20604 Lesotho *20604*
R		20604 South Africa - Cape Province *20604*
R		20604 South Africa - Natal *20604*
R	*Senecio azulensis* Alain *5607*	
R		19105 Cuba (Guantanamo) *5607*
E	*Senecio behrianus* Sonder & F.Muell. *20681, 14223*	
Ex/E		20681 Australia - New South Wales *20681*
Ex/E		20681 Australia - South Australia *20681*
E		20681 Australia - Victoria *20681*
V	*Senecio bernardinus* Greene *20850*	
V		20850 U.S. - California *20850*
R	*Senecio bicolor* (Willd.) Tod. ssp. *nebrodensis* (Guss.) Chater *18264, 20171*	
R		18264 Italy - Sicily *18264*
R	*Senecio bifistulosus* Hook.f.	
R		New Zealand - South Is.
R	*Senecio blochmaniae* Greene *20850*	
I		20850 U.S. - California *20850*
V	*Senecio bollei* Sunding & Kunkel *15105*	
V		15105 Spain - Canary Is. *15105*
I	*Senecio boluangensis* H. Koyama *19120*	
I		19120 Thailand *19120*
E	*Senecio boquetensis* Standl. *20883, 9006*	

I		20883 Panama *20883*
E	*Senecio caespitosus* Brot. *19488*	
E		20076 Portugal *20076*
R	*Senecio cambrensis* Rosser *8000*	
R		5387 United Kingdom (North Wales) *5387*
R	*Senecio canaliculatus* Bojer ex DC. *10368*	
R		20578 Madagascar (Antananarivo) *20578*
R	*Senecio capillifolius* Hook.f. *20681*	
R		20681 Australia - Tasmania *20681*
R	*Senecio cardamine* Greene *20850*	
V		20850 U.S. - Arizona *20850*
R		20850 U.S. - New Mexico *20850*
R	*Senecio cariensis* Boiss. *12840*	
R		12840 Turkey *12840*
V	*Senecio carinatus* Greenman *5607*	
V		19105 Cuba (Holguin) *5607*
I	*Senecio carlomasonii* B.L. Turner & T.M. Barkl. *20850*	
I		20850 U.S. - Arizona *20850*
I		20883 Mexico *20883*
R	*Senecio carpetanus* Boiss. & Reut. *20171*	
R		20692 Spain (central & Iberic Mts.) *20692*
R	*Senecio cedrorum* Raynal *10368*	
R		20578 Madagascar (Toliara) *20578*
R	*Senecio chalchaquinus* Cabrera *16336*	
R		19448 Argentina *16336*
R	*Senecio chalureaui* Humbert	
R		Morocco
E	*Senecio coincyi* Rouy *15846, 20171*	
E		15846 Spain *15846*
R	*Senecio coleophyllus* Turcz. *20604*	
R		20604 South Africa - Cape Province *20604*
R	*Senecio compactus* Kirk	
R		New Zealand - North Is.
I	*Senecio craibianus* Hosseus	
I		Thailand
R	*Senecio crocatus* Rydb. *20850*	
I		20850 U.S. - Colorado *20850*
I		20850 U.S. - Montana *20850*
I		20850 U.S. - Utah *20850*
Ex/E		20850 U.S. - Wyoming *20850*
R	*Senecio cylindrocephalus* Cabrera *16336*	
R		19448 Argentina *16336*
R		20176 Argentina - Catamarca *20176*
R		20176 Argentina - Tucuman *20176*
I	*Senecio dalzellii* C.B. Clarke	
I		India - Karnataka
R	*Senecio davisii* Matthews *12840*	
R		12840 Turkey *12840*
V	*Senecio dimorphophyllus* T. Barkley & Beauch. var. *intermedius* T.M. Barkl. *20850*	
E		20850 U.S. - Colorado *20850*
V		20850 U.S. - Utah *20850*
V	*Senecio doronicum* (L.) L. ssp. *ruthenensis* (Mazuc & Timb.-Lagr.) Nyman *20171*	
V		20171 France *20171*
E	*Senecio elodes* Boiss. ex DC. *15398, 20171*	
E		15398 Spain (Sierra Nevada) *11496*
R	*Senecio eriopus* Willk. *20171*	
R		Spain

E   *Senecio ertterae* T.M. Barkl. *20850*
     E   *20850* U.S. - Oregon *20850*

R   *Senecio eubaeus* Boiss. & Heldr. *20171*
     R   Greece

V   *Senecio eurycephalus* Torr. & Gray ex Gray var. *lewisrosei* (J.T. Howell) T.M. Barkl. *20850*
     V   *20850* U.S. - California *20850*

I   *Senecio exuberans* R.A.Dyer *20604*
     I   *20604* South Africa - Natal *20604*

R   *Senecio farfarifolius* Boiss. & Kotschy *12840, 20171*
     R   *12840* Turkey *12840*

R   *Senecio flaccidus* var. *douglasii* (DC.) B.L. Turner & T.M. Barkl. *20850*
     I   *20850* U.S. - California *20850*
     I   *20850* U.S. - Nevada *20850*

I   *Senecio flagellifolius* Cabrera *16336*
     I   *16336* Argentina *16336*
     I   *20176* Argentina - Tucuman *20176*

I   *Senecio foeniculoides* Harv. *20604*
     I   *20604* South Africa - Cape Province *20604*

R   *Senecio formosanus* (Sasaki) Kitamura *20511*
     R   *20511* Taiwan *20511*

E   *Senecio franciscanus* Greene *20850*
     E   *20850* U.S. - Arizona (Coconino Nat. Forest) *20850*

E   *Senecio furusei* Kitam. *10573*
     E   *10573* Japan *10573*

R   *Senecio gallerandianus* Coss. & Durieu *10488*
     R   *14958* Algeria *10488*

V   *Senecio ganderi* T.M. Barkl. & Beauchamp *20850*
     V   *20850* U.S. - California *20850*

I   *Senecio gardneri* (Thwaites) C.B. Clarke *8021*
     I   *16162* Sri Lanka (Kandy) *8021*

V   *Senecio garlandii* Belcher *20681*
     V   *20681* Australia - New South Wales *20681*

Ex   *Senecio georgianus* DC. *20681, 5465*
     Ex   *20681* Australia - New South Wales *20681*
     Ex   *20681* Australia - South Australia *20681*
     Ex   *20681* Australia - Victoria *20681*

R   *Senecio glaucus* L. ssp. *cyprius* Meikle *14230*
     R   *19164* Cyprus *14230*

R   *Senecio gnaphalodes* Sieber *20171*
     R   *20731* Greece - Crete (inc. Saria, Karpathos) *20731*

R   *Senecio greenei* Gray *20850*
     I   *20850* U.S. - California *20850*

E   *Senecio hadrosomus* Svent. *15105*
     E   *15105* Spain - Canary Is. *15105*

E   *Senecio hansenii* Kunkel *15105*
     E   *15105* Spain - Canary Is. *15105*

E   *Senecio hansweberi* Cuatr. *20883, 9641*
     I   *20883* Costa Rica *20883*

E   *Senecio hermosae* Pitard *15105*
     E   *19174* Spain - Canary Is. *14155*

V   *Senecio hesperius* Greene *20850*
     V   *20850* U.S. - Oregon *20850*

R   *Senecio hieronymi* Grisebach *20176*
     R   *20176* Argentina - Cordoba *20176*
     R   *20176* Argentina - Catamarca *20176*

     R   *20176* Argentina - Jujuy *20176*
     R   *20176* Argentina - La Rioja *20176*
     R   *20176* Argentina - Mendoza *20176*
     R   *20176* Argentina - Salta *20176*
     R   *20176* Argentina - Santiago del Estero *20176*
     R   *20176* Argentina - San Luis *20176*

E   *Senecio huachucanus* Gray *20883, 8058*
     V   *19002* U.S. - Arizona *8058*
     E   *20883* Mexico *20883*

V   *Senecio huntii* F. Muell.
     V   New Zealand - Chatham Is.

R   *Senecio hyperborealis* Greenm. ssp. *wrangelica* Jurtz., Korobk. & Petrovsky *21309*
     R   *21309* Russia (E.Europe) - North *21309*

R   *Senecio hypochionaeus* Boiss. var. *hypochionaeus* *12840*
     R   *12840* Turkey *12840*

R   *Senecio insubricus* Hess & Landolt *18154, 20678*
     I   Italy *8000*
     R   *18154* Switzerland *18154*

V   *Senecio integerrimus* Nutt. var. *ochroleucus* (Gray) Cronq. *20850, 14409*
     I   *20850* Canada - Alberta *20850*
     Ex/E   *20850* Canada - British Columbia *20850*
     I   *20850* U.S. - California *20850*
     I   *20850* U.S. - Idaho *20850*
     I   *20850* U.S. - Montana *20850*
     I   *20850* U.S. - Oregon *20850*
     I   *20850* U.S. - Washington *20850*

R   *Senecio jacobaea* L. ssp. *gotlandicus* (Neuman) Sterner *18216*
     R   *18216* Sweden *18216*

R   *Senecio johnstonii* Oliv. ssp. *battiscombei* (R.E. & T.C.E. Fr.) Mabberley var. *battiscombei* *20057*
     R   *17435* Kenya (Mt. Kenya; Nyandarua;Aberdares) *20057*

V   *Senecio johnstonii* Oliv. ssp. *battiscombei* (R.E. & T.C.E. Fr.) Mabberley var. *cherenganiensis* Cotton & Blakel. *20057*
     V   *20057* Kenya (Cherengani hills) *20057*

V   *Senecio johnstonii* Oliv. ssp. *battiscombei* (R.E. & T.C.E. Fr.) Mabberley var. *dalei* (Cotton & Blakelock) C. Jeffrey *20057*
     V   *20057* Kenya (Marakwet) *20057*

R   *Senecio johnstonii* Oliv. ssp. *elgonensis* (T.C.E. Fr.) Mabberley var. *elgonensis* *20057*
     R   *20057* Kenya (Mt. Elgon) *20057*
     R   *20057* Uganda (Mt. Elgon) *20057*

R   *Senecio johnstonii* Oliv. ssp. *elgonensis* (T.C.E. Fr.) Mabberley var. *ligulatus* (Cotton & Blakel.) C. Jeffrey *20057*
     R   *20057* Kenya (Mt. Elgon) *20057*
     R   *20057* Uganda (Mt. Elgon) *20057*

R   *Senecio jurineifolius* Boiss. & Bal. *12840*
     R   *12840* Turkey *12840*

R   *Senecio kalingenwae* Hilliard & B.L.Burtt *20604*
     R   *20604* South Africa - Natal *20604*

R   *Senecio karelinoides* Winkler *8001*
     R   Asiatic U.S.S.R. (Pamir-Alai) *6930*

R   *Senecio keniensis* Bak. ssp. *brassiciformis* (R.E. & T.C.E. Fr.) C. Jeffrey *20057*
     R   *20057* Kenya (Nyandarua; Aberdares) *20057*

R   *Senecio keniensis* Bak. ssp. *keniensis* *20057*

R   *20057* Kenya (Mt. Kenya) *20057*

R   ***Senecio keniodendron*** R.E. & T.C.E. Fries *20057*
    R   *20057* Kenya (Mt. Kenya; Nyandarua; Aberdares)
            20057

E   ***Senecio kuhbieri*** Cuatr. *20883, 9641*
    I   *20883* Costa Rica *20883*

E   ***Senecio kundaicus*** C. Fischer *11494*
    E   *11494* India - Tamil Nadu *11494*

E   ***Senecio lagascanus*** DC. ssp. *lusitanicus* (P.Cout)
    Pinto da Silva *20076*
    E   *20076* Portugal *17891*

E   ***Senecio lamarckianus*** Bullock *10260*
    E   *20771* Mauritius *10082*

V   ***Senecio laticostatus*** Belcher *20681*
    V   *20681* Australia - Victoria *20681*

R   ***Senecio lautus*** Forst.f. ex Willd. var. *esperensis*
    Sykes *19106*
    R   *19305* New Zealand - Kermadec Is. *19106*

V   ***Senecio layneae*** Greene *20850*
    V   *20850* U.S. - California *20850*

R   ***Senecio lazicus*** Boiss. & Bal. *12840*
    R   *12840* Turkey *12840*

R   ***Senecio lemmonii*** Gray *20850*
    I   *20850* U.S. - Arizona *20850*

R   ***Senecio leucoglossus*** F.Muell. *20681*
    R   *20681* Australia - Western Australia *20681*

V   ***Senecio lopezii*** Boiss. *20171*
    E   *20076* Portugal *20076*
    V   Spain

E   ***Senecio lyonii*** Gray *20850*
    I   *20850* U.S. - California *20850*

R   ***Senecio macranthus*** A.Rich. *20681*
    R   *20681* Australia - New South Wales *20681*

V   ***Senecio macrocarpus*** Belcher *20681*
    I   *20681* Australia - South Australia *20681*
    Ex/E *20681* Australia - Tasmania *20681*
    I   *20681* Australia - Victoria *20681*

R   ***Senecio malacitanus*** Huter ssp. *frigidus* (Boiss.)
    S. Rivas-martinez, A. Asensi, J. Molero Mesa & f. Valle *20874*
    R   *20874* Spain (Sierra Nevada) *20874*

R   ***Senecio malvifolius*** (L'Hér.) DC. *19174, 20171*
    R   *19174* Portugal - Azores *19174*

R   ***Senecio marotiri*** *19305*
    R   *19305* New Zealand - North Is. *19305*

R   ***Senecio mayurii*** C. Fischer *14782*
    R   *14782* India - Karnataka *14782*

V   ***Senecio megaglossus*** F.Muell. *20681*
    V   *20681* Australia - South Australia *20681*

R   ***Senecio meuselii*** Rauh *10368*
    R   *20578* Madagascar (Fianarantsoa) *20578*

V   ***Senecio millefolium*** Torr. & Gray *20850*
    E   *20850* U.S. - Georgia *20850*
    V   *20850* U.S. - North Carolina *20850*
    V   *20850* U.S. - South Carolina *20850*
    E   *20850* U.S. - Virginia *20850*

V   ***Senecio mishmi*** Clarke *14782*
    V   *14782* India - Meghalaya *14782*

V   ***Senecio moaensis*** Alain *5607*
    V   *19105* Cuba (Holguin) *5607*

R   ***Senecio moldenkei*** Greenman *5607*

R   *19105* Cuba (Holguin) *5607*

R   ***Senecio morrisonensis*** Hayata *20511*
    R   *20511* Taiwan *20511*

I   ***Senecio multidentatus*** var. *huachucanus* (Gray) T.M.
    Barkl. *20883, 20850*
    E   *20850* U.S. - Arizona *20850*
    I   *20883* Mexico *20883*

V   ***Senecio multiflorus*** (L'Herit.) Schultz Bip. *15105*
    V   *15105* Spain - Canary Is. *15105*

R   ***Senecio murrayi*** Bornm. *15105*
    R   *15105* Spain - Canary Is. *15105*

R   ***Senecio neomexicanus*** (Greene) T.M. Barkl. var.
    toumeyi (Greene) T.M. Barkl. *20850*
    V   *20850* U.S. - Arizona *20850*

V   ***Senecio neowebsteri*** Blake *20850*
    ?   *20850* U.S. - Washington *20850*

V   ***Senecio nevadensis*** Boiss. & Reut. *8000, 20171*
    V   Spain *11496*

R   ***Senecio newcombei*** Greene *20850, 10701*
    R   *20850* Canada - British Columbia *20850*

R   ***Senecio olympicus*** Boiss. *12840*
    R   *12840* Turkey *12840*

I   ***Senecio otopterus*** Philippi *16336*
    I   *16336* Argentina *16336*
    I   *20176* Argentina - Jujuy *20176*
    I   *20176* Argentina - Tucuman *20176*

R   ***Senecio ovatifolius*** Boiss. *12840*
    R   *12840* Turkey *12840*

R   ***Senecio pachylepis*** Greenman *5607*
    R   *19105* Cuba (Holguin, Guantanamo) *5607*

R   ***Senecio palmensis*** (C. Smith ex Nees) Link *15105*
    R   *15105* Spain - Canary Is. *15105*

R   ***Senecio papillosus*** F.Muell. *20681*
    R   *20681* Australia - Tasmania *20681*

R   ***Senecio peltophorus*** Brenan *7849*
    R   Malawi *7849*

R   ***Senecio pentacopus*** D. Drury
    R   New Zealand - North Is.

R   ***Senecio perdicioides*** Hook.f.
    R   New Zealand - North Is.

R   ***Senecio persoonii*** De Not. *20171*
    R   Italy

R   ***Senecio petraeus*** Boiss. & Reut. *20171*
    R   Spain

R   ***Senecio platyphyllus*** DC. var. *glandulosus*
    Mathews *12840*
    R   *12840* Turkey *12840*

R   ***Senecio primulifolius*** F.Muell. *20681*
    R   *20681* Australia - Tasmania *20681*

V   ***Senecio quaerens*** Greene *20850*
    E   *20850* U.S. - Arizona *20850*
    E   *20850* U.S. - New Mexico *20850*

V   ***Senecio quercetorum*** Greene *20850*
    I   *20850* U.S. - Arizona *20850*

R   ***Senecio quinqueradiatus*** Boiss. ex DC. *20171*
    R   Spain

R   ***Senecio radiolatus*** F. Muell.
    R   New Zealand - Chatham Is.

R   ***Senecio radiolatus*** ssp. *antipodus* *19106*

R		*19106* New Zealand - Antipodes Is. *19106*

R *Senecio rhabdos* Clarke *14782*

| R | *14782* India - Manipur *14782* |
| R | *14782* India - Nagaland *14782* |

R *Senecio roripaefolius* Cabrera *16336*

R	*16336* Argentina *16336*
R	*20176* Argentina - Catamarca *20176*
R	*20176* Argentina - La Rioja *20176*
R	*20176* Argentina - Tucuman *20176*

V *Senecio rosinae* Gamisans *15080*

| V | *15080* France - Corsica *15080* |

R *Senecio sacramentanus* Woot. & Standl. *20850*

| R | *20850* U.S. - New Mexico *20850* |

R *Senecio sandrasicus* Davis *12840*

| R | *12840* Turkey *12840* |

R *Senecio saniensis* Hilliard & B.L.Burtt *20604*

| R | *20604* Lesotho *20604* |
| R | *20604* South Africa - Natal *20604* |

V *Senecio saugetii* Alain *5607*

| V | *19105* Cuba (Guantanamo) *5607* |

R *Senecio saxifragoides* Hook.f.

| R | New Zealand - South Is. |

V *Senecio scaberulus* *19305*

| V | *19305* New Zealand - North Is. *19305* |
| V | *19305* New Zealand - South Is. *19305* |

R *Senecio sciadophilus* Raoul

| R | New Zealand - South Is. |

E *Senecio smithianus* Cabrera *18200*

| E | *9446* Peru *18200* |

V *Senecio spellenbergii* T.M. Barkl. *20850*

| E | *20850* U.S. - New Mexico *20850* |

R *Senecio steetzii* Bolle *15105*

| R | *15105* Spain - Canary Is. *15105* |

R *Senecio streptanthifolius* Greene var. *laetiflorus* (Greene) J.F. Bain *20850*

I	*20850* U.S. - California *20850*
E	*20850* U.S. - Idaho *20850*
I	*20850* U.S. - Nevada *20850*
I	*20850* U.S. - Oregon *20850*

R *Senecio taitoensis* Hayata *20511*

| R | *20511* Taiwan *20511* |

R *Senecio takedanus* Kitam. *10573*

| R | *10573* Japan *10573* |

R *Senecio tauricolus* Matthews *12840*

| R | *12840* Turkey *12840* |

I *Senecio teneriffae* Schultz Bip.

| I | Spain - Canary Is. |

R *Senecio traversii* F. Muell.

| R | New Zealand - South Is. |

I *Senecio tucumanensis* Cabrera *16336*

| I | *16336* Argentina *16336* |

R *Senecio turneri* Cheeseman

| R | New Zealand - North Is. |

R *Senecio uniflorus* (All.) All., non Retz. *18154*

R	*20528* France *20528*
I	Italy *20528*
R	*18154* Switzerland *18154*

R *Senecio villifructus* Hilliard *20604*

| R | *20604* South Africa - Natal *20604* |

R *Senecio violaefolius* Cabrera *12468*

| R | *12468* Peru *12468* |

R *Senecio warnockii* Shinners *20850*

| I | *20850* U.S. - New Mexico *20850* |
| R | *20850* U.S. - Texas *20850* |

R *Senecio whyteanus* Britten *7757*

| R | Malawi (Mlanje) *7757* |

R *Serratula bulgarica* Acht. & Stoj. *8000, 20171*

| R | *5204* Bulgaria (north-east) *5204* |
| V | *19608* Romania (eastern) *8000* |

R *Serratula cichoracea* (L.) DC. ssp. *cretica* Turrill *20171*

| R | *20731* Greece - Crete *20731* |

R *Serratula flavescens* (L.) Poir. *20171*

| R | Spain |

R *Serratula hakkiarica* Davis *12840*

| R | *12840* Turkey *12840* |

R *Serratula lasiocephala* Bornm. *12840*

| R | *12840* Turkey *12840* |

R *Serratula lycopifolia* (Vill.) A.Kern. *8000, 20171*

V	Austria
V	*21091* Bosnia & Herzegovina *21091*
V	Czech & Slovak Federal Republic
E	*20528* France *20528*
V	*20686* Hungary *20686*
V	*19366* Poland (south east) *18216*
I	*19947* Romania *20631*
V	*19615* Slovakia *19615*
R	*13662* Slovenia (south western) *13662*

I *Serratula tanaitica* P.A.Smirn. *5942, 20171*

| I | *5942* Russia (E.Europe) - South *5942* |

V *Silphium brachiatum* Gattinger *20850*

V	*20850* U.S. - Alabama *20850*
I	*20850* U.S. - Georgia *20850*
I	*20850* U.S. - Kentucky *20850*
V	*20850* U.S. - Tennessee *20850*

R *Silphium perfoliatum* L. var. *connatum* (L.) Cronq. *20850*

I	*20850* U.S. - Kentucky *20850*
I	*20850* U.S. - Maryland *20850*
	20850 U.S. - North Carolina *20850*
I	*20850* U.S. - Virginia *20850*
E	*20850* U.S. - West Virginia *20850*

R *Silphium pinnatifidum* Ell. *20850*

E	*20850* U.S. - Alabama *20850*
R	*20850* U.S. - Georgia *20850*
E	*20850* U.S. - Illinois *20850*
I	*20850* U.S. - Indiana *20850*
I	*20850* U.S. - Kentucky *20850*
I	*20850* U.S. - Ohio *20850*
V	*20850* U.S. - Tennessee *20850*

V *Silphium reverchonii* Bush *20850*

| I | *20850* U.S. - Texas *20850* |

R *Silphium terebinthinaceum* Jacq. var. *luciae-brauniae* Steyermark *20850*

I	*20850* U.S. - Illinois *20850*
R	*20850* U.S. - Kentucky *20850*
I	*20850* U.S. - Mississippi *20850*
I	*20850* U.S. - Ohio *20850*

R *Simsia jamaicensis* Blake *20883, 13336*

| R | *13336* Jamaica *20883* |

E *Simsia panamensis* Rob. & Brett. *20883, 9006*

| I | *20883* Panama *20883* |

E *Sipolisia lanuginosa* Glaz. *2358*

| E | *2358* Brazil - Minas Gerais *2358* |

V *Solidago albopilosa* E.L. Braun *20850*

| V | *20850* U.S. - Kentucky *20850* |

V	*Solidago deamii* Fern. *20850*		
	V	20850 U.S. - Indiana *20850*	
V	*Solidago dumetorum* Lunell *20850*		
	I	20850 Canada - Saskatchewan *20850*	
	I	20850 U.S. - North Dakota *20850*	
Ex/E	*Solidago durangensis* Nesom *14294*		
	Ex/E	14294 Mexico - Durango *14294*	
R	*Solidago gattingeri* Chapman *20850*		
	I	20850 U.S. - Arkansas *20850*	
	I	20850 U.S. - Missouri *20850*	
	E	20850 U.S. - Tennessee *20850*	
	I	20850 U.S. - Texas *20850*	
R	*Solidago glomerata* Michx. *20850*		
	R	20850 U.S. - North Carolina *20850*	
	V	20850 U.S. - Tennessee *20850*	
V	*Solidago guiradonis* Gray *20850*		
	V	20850 U.S. - California *20850*	
R	*Solidago houghtonii* Torr. & Gray ex Gray *20850, 14352*		
	V	20850 Canada - Ontario *20850*	
	I	20850 U.S. - Illinois *20850*	
	R	20850 U.S. - Michigan *20850*	
	E	20850 U.S. - New York (Genesee Co.) *20850*	
I	*Solidago macrorrhiza* Lange *20171*		
	I	France	
	I	Spain	
R	*Solidago minutissima* (Makino) Kitam. *10573*		
	R	10573 Japan *10573*	
R	*Solidago mollis* Shinners var. *angustata* Shinners *20850*		
	I	20850 U.S. - Oklahoma *20850*	
	V	20850 U.S. - Texas *20850*	
R	*Solidago ouachitensis* C.& J. Taylor *20850*		
	R	20850 U.S. - Arkansas *20850*	
	E	20850 U.S. - Oklahoma *20850*	
E	*Solidago plumosa* Small *20850*		
	E	20850 U.S. - North Carolina *20850*	
Ex/E	*Solidago porteri* Small *20850, 14662*		
	Ex/E	20850 U.S. - Georgia *20850*	
	Ex	14662 U.S. - North Carolina *14662*	
R	*Solidago pulchra* Small *20850*		
	R	20850 U.S. - North Carolina *20850*	
E	*Solidago shortii* Torr. & Gray *20850*		
	E	20850 U.S. - Indiana *20850*	
	E	20850 U.S. - Kentucky (Robertson County) *20850*	
E	*Solidago simplex* var. *chlorolepis* (Fern.) Kartesz & Gandhi *20850*		
	E	20850 Canada - Quebec *20850*	
V	*Solidago simplex* var. *ontarioensis* (Ringius) Ringius *20850*		
	I	20850 Canada - Manitoba *20850*	
	R	20850 Canada - Ontario *20850*	
	I	20850 U.S. - Michigan *20850*	
	I	20850 U.S. - Wisconsin *20850*	
V	*Solidago simulans* Fern. *20850*		
	I	20850 U.S. - Georgia *20850*	
	E	20850 U.S. - North Carolina *20850*	
E	*Solidago spithamaea* M.A. Curtis *20850*		
	E	20850 U.S. - North Carolina (Avery Co.) *20850*	
	E	20850 U.S. - Tennessee (Carter Co.) *20850*	
R	*Solidago verna* M.A. Curtis *20850*		
	R	20850 U.S. - North Carolina *20850*	
	E	20850 U.S. - South Carolina *20850*	
V	*Solidago virgaurea* L. ssp. *rupicola* (Rouy) Lambinon *20528*		
	V	20528 France (south-west) *20528*	
R	*Sonchus acaulis* Dum. Cours. *15105*		
	R	15105 Spain - Canary Is. *15105*	
E	*Sonchus arboreus* DC.		
	E	Spain - Canary Is.	
V	*Sonchus bornmuelleri* Pitard *15105*		
	E	15105 Spain - Canary Is. *15105*	
V	*Sonchus bourgeaui* Schultz Bip. *15105*		
	V	15105 Spain - Canary Is. *15105*	
R	*Sonchus brachylobus* Webb & Berthel. *15105*		
	R	15105 Spain - Canary Is. *15105*	
V	*Sonchus canariensis* (Schultz Bip.) Boulos *15105*		
	V	15105 Spain - Canary Is. *15105*	
V	*Sonchus erzincanicus* Matthews *12840*		
	V	12840 Turkey *12840*	
V	*Sonchus fauces-orci* Knoche *15105*		
	V	20750 Spain - Canary Is. *15105*	
R	*Sonchus filifolius* Svent. *20750*		
	R	20750 Spain - Canary Is. *20750*	
E	*Sonchus gandogeri* Pitard *15105*		
	E	20750 Spain - Canary Is. *15105*	
R	*Sonchus gonzalezpadronii* Svent. *15105*		
	R	15105 Spain - Canary Is. *15105*	
R	*Sonchus gummifer* Link *15105*		
	R	20750 Spain - Canary Is. *15105*	
V	*Sonchus imbricatus* Svent. *15105*		
	V	15105 Spain - Canary Is. *15105*	
R	*Sonchus leptocephalus* Cass. ssp. *capillaris* (Svent.) Aldridge		
	R	Spain - Canary Is.	
R	*Sonchus ortunoi* Svent. *15105*		
	R	15105 Spain - Canary Is. *15105*	
R	*Sonchus pinnatus* Aiton		
	R	Portugal - Madeira	
E	*Sonchus pinnatus* Aiton. ssp. *canariensis* (Schultz Bip.) Aldridge		
	E	Spain - Canary Is.	
R	*Sonchus platylepis* Webb ex Schultz Bip.		
	R	Spain - Canary Is.	
V	*Sonchus radicatus* Aiton ssp. *gummifer* (Link) Aldridge		
	V	Spain - Canary Is.	
E	*Sonchus radicatus* Aiton ssp. *tectifolius* (Svent.) Aldridge		
	E	Spain - Canary Is.	
R	*Sonchus regis-jubae* Pitard		
	R	Spain - Canary Is.	
V	*Sonchus tectifolius* Svent. *15105*		
	V	15105 Spain - Canary Is. *15105*	
R	*Sonchus tuberifer* Svent. *15105*		
	R	15105 Spain - Canary Is. *15105*	
V	*Sonchus ustulatus* Lowe ssp. *maderensis* Aldr., in press		
	V	Portugal - Madeira	
R	*Sonchus ustulatus* Lowe ssp. *ustulatus*		
	R	Portugal - Madeira	

E **Sonchus wildpretii** U. et A. Reifenberger *19464*
    E   *19464* Spain - Canary Is. (Gomera) *19464*

V **Spaniopappus ekmanii** Robins. *5607*
    V   *19105* Cuba (Guantanamo) *5607*

R **Sphaeromeria argentea** Nutt. *20850*
    I   *20850* U.S. - Colorado *20850*
    I   *20850* U.S. - Idaho *20850*
    R   *20850* U.S. - Montana *20850*
    I   *20850* U.S. - Nevada *20850*
    V   *20850* U.S. - Wyoming *20850*

R **Sphaeromeria capitata** Nutt. *20850*
    E   *20850* U.S. - Colorado *20850*
    V   *20850* U.S. - Montana *20850*
    E   *20850* U.S. - Utah *20850*
    R   *20850* U.S. - Wyoming *20850*

V **Sphaeromeria compacta** (Hall) Holmgren, Shultz & Lowrey *20850*
    V   *20850* U.S. - Nevada *20850*

V **Sphaeromeria ruthiae** Holmgren, Shultz & Lowrey *20850*
    V   *20850* U.S. - Utah *20850*

E **Sphaeromeria simplex** (A. Nels.) Heller *20850*
    E   *20850* U.S. - Wyoming *20850*

R **Staehelina fruticosa** (L.) L. *20171*
    R   Greece

I **Steirodiscus schlechteri** Bolus ex Schltr. *20604*
    I   *20604* South Africa - Cape Province *20604*

V **Steirodiscus speciosus** (Pillans) B.Nord. *20604*
    V   *20604* South Africa - Cape Province *20604*

V **Stemmacantha australis** (Gaudich.) Dittrich *20681*
    Ex/E *20681* Australia - New South Wales *20681*
    V   *20681* Australia - Queensland *20681*
    Ex/E *20681* Australia - Victoria *20681*

E **Stemmacantha cynaroides** Cass. *8000, 20171*
    E   *19174* Spain - Canary Is. *19174*

V **Stenotus borealis** Rydb. *20850*
    V   *20850* Canada - Yukon Territory *20850*

V **Stephanomeria blairii** Munz & Johnston *20850*
    V   *20850* U.S. - California *20850*

V **Stephanomeria diegensis** Gottlieb *20850*
    I   *20850* U.S. - California *20850*

E **Stephanomeria malheurensis** Gottlieb *20850*
    E   *20850* U.S. - Oregon *20850*

V **Stephanomeria schottii** Gray *20883, 20850*
    V   *20850* U.S. - Arizona *20850*
           20883 Mexico *20883*

E **Stephanomeria tenuifolia** (Torr.) Hall var. *uintensis* Goodrich & Welsh *20850*
    E   *20850* U.S. - Utah *20850*

R **Stephanomeria wrightii** Gray *20850*
    I   *20850* U.S. - New Mexico *20850*
    V   *20850* U.S. - Texas *20850*

I **Steptorhamphus czerepanovii** Kirpiczn. *5942*
    I   *5942* Armenia *5942*
    I   *5942* Azerbaijan *5942*

R **Steptorhamphus singularis** (Wilmott) Fernandes Casas
    R   Spain

R **Stevia cruzii** Grashoff *9613*
    R   *19755* Mexico *9613*

R **Stevia heptachaeta** DC. *16747*
    R   *16747* Brazil - Goias (Serra Doucada) *16747*

V **Stevia lemmonii** (Gray) Gray *20850*

I   *20850* U.S. - Arizona *20850*

V **Stevia lemmonii** (Gray) Gray *20883, 20850*
    I   *20883* Mexico *20883*

R **Stevia perfoliata** Cronq. *9618*
    R   *19755* Mexico *9618*

R **Stevia plummerae** Gray *20850*
    I   *20850* U.S. - Arizona *20850*
    I   *20850* U.S. - New Mexico *20850*

R **Stevia rzedowskii** McVaugh *9532*
    R   *19755* Mexico *9532*

R **Stevia seemannioides** Grashoff *9613*
    R   *19755* Mexico *9613*

R **Stevia talpensis** Grashoff *9613*
    R   *19755* Mexico *9613*

V **Stoebe gomphrenoides** (Lam.) P.J.Bergius *20604*
    V   *20604* South Africa - Cape Province *20604*

R **Stoebe humilis** Levyns *20604*
    R   *20604* South Africa - Cape Province *20604*

R **Stoebe muirii** Levyns *20604*
    I   *20604* South Africa - Cape Province *20604*

V **Stoebe salteri** Levyns *20604*
    V   *20604* South Africa - Cape Province *20604*

E **Stomatochaeta acuminata** Pruski *20883*
    I   *20883* Venezuela *20883*

R **Strotheria gypsophila** B. Turner *9615*
    R   *19755* Mexico *9615*

E **Stylocline sonorensis** Wiggins *20850*
    I   *20850* U.S. - Arizona *20850*
    E   *20850* U.S. - California *20850*

V **Sventenia bupleuroides** Font Quer *14166*
    V   *20750* Spain - Canary Is. (Gran Canaria) *14166*

V **Syncarpha recurvata** (L.f.) B.Nord. *20604*
    V   *20604* South Africa - Cape Province *20604*

Ex/E **Syneilesis aconitifolia** Maxim. var. *longilepis* Kitam. *10573*
    Ex/E *10573* Japan *10573*

V **Syneilesis intermedia** (Hayata) Kitamura *20511*
    V   *20511* Taiwan *20511*

R **Syneilesis subglabrata** (Yamamoto & Sasaki) Kitamura *20511*
    R   *20511* Taiwan *20511*

R **Syneilesis tagawae** Kitam. *10573*
    R   *10573* Japan *10573*

R **Synosma suaveolens** (L.) Raf. ex Britt. *20850*
    Ex/E *20850* U.S. - Connecticut *20850*
    I   *20850* U.S. - Delaware *20850*
    I   *20850* U.S. - District of Columbia *20850*
    E   *20850* U.S. - Florida *20850*
    I   *20850* U.S. - Georgia *20850*
    V   *20850* U.S. - Illinois *20850*
    I   *20850* U.S. - Indiana *20850*
    V   *20850* U.S. - Iowa *20850*
    I   *20850* U.S. - Kentucky *20850*
    I   *20850* U.S. - Maine *20850*
    E   *20850* U.S. - Maryland *20850*
    I   *20850* U.S. - Massachusetts *20850*
    I   *20850* U.S. - Michigan *20850*
    E   *20850* U.S. - Minnesota *20850*
    I   *20850* U.S. - Missouri *20850*
    Ex   *20850* U.S. - New Jersey *20850*
    E   *20850* U.S. - New York *20850*
    Ex/E *20850* U.S. - North Carolina *20850*
    V   *20850* U.S. - Ohio *20850*

R	20850	U.S. - Pennsylvania	20850
I	20850	U.S. - Rhode Is.	20850
V	20850	U.S. - Tennessee	20850
V	20850	U.S. - Virginia	20850
E	20850	U.S. - West Virginia	20850
I	20850	U.S. - Wisconsin	20850

I *Synotis simonsii* (Clarke) Jeffrey & Chen *14782*
  I   *14782* India - Assam *14782*

R *Syntrichopappus lemmonii* (Gray) Gray *20850*
  I   20850 U.S. - California *20850*

V *Taeckholmia arborea* (DC.) Boulos
  V   20750 Spain - Canary Is. *15105*

R *Taeckholmia canariensis* Boulos
  R   *15105* Spain - Canary Is. *15105*

R *Taeckholmia capillaris* (Svent.) Boulos
  R   *15105* Spain - Canary Is. *15105*

E *Taeckholmia heterophylla* Boulos *20750*
  E   20750 Spain - Canary Is. *20750*

R *Taeckholmia microcarpa* Boulos
  R   20750 Spain - Canary Is. *15105*

I *Tanacetum akinfievii* (Alexeenko) Tzvel. *5942, 20627*
  I   *5942* Transcaucasus *5942*

R *Tanacetum albipannosum* Huber-Mor. & Grierson *12840*
  R   *12840* Turkey *12840*

R *Tanacetum alyssifolium* (Bornm.) Grierson *12840*
  R   *12840* Turkey *12840*

R *Tanacetum argenteum* (Lam.) Willd. ssp. *canum* (C. Koch) Grierson *12840*
  R   *12840* Turkey *12840*

R *Tanacetum argenteum* (Lam.) Willd. ssp. *flabellifolium* (Boiss. & Heldr.) Grierson *12840*
  R   *12840* Turkey *12840*

R *Tanacetum cappadocicum* (DC.) Schultz Bip. *12840*
  R   *12840* Turkey *12840*

R *Tanacetum densum* (Lab.) Schultz Bip. ssp. *laxum* Grierson *12840*
  R   *12840* Turkey *12840*

R *Tanacetum densum* (Lab.) Schultz Bip. ssp. *sivasicum* Hub.-Mor. & Grierson *12840*
  R   *12840* Turkey *12840*

R *Tanacetum eginense* (Hausskn. ex Bornm.) Grierson *12840*
  R   *12840* Turkey *12840*

R *Tanacetum ferulaceum* (Webb) Schultz Bip. *20750*
  R   *15105* Spain - Canary Is. *15105*

I *Tanacetum funkii* Sch.Bip. ex Willk. *20171*
  I   Spain

R *Tanacetum germanicopolitanum* (Bornm. & Heimerl) Grierson *12840*
  R   *12840* Turkey *12840*

R *Tanacetum haradjanii* (Rech.fil.) Grierson *12840*
  R   *12840* Turkey *12840*

R *Tanacetum haussknechtii* (Bornm.) Grierson *12840*
  R   *12840* Turkey *12840*

R *Tanacetum heterotomum* (Bornm.) Grierson *12840*
  R   *12840* Turkey *12840*

V *Tanacetum mucronulatum* (Hoffmanns. & Link) Heywood *20171*
  V   20076 Portugal *20076*

R *Tanacetum oltense* (Sosn.) Grierson *12840*

R	*12840*	Turkey	*12840*

R *Tanacetum oxtstegium* (Sosn.) Grierson *12840*
  R   *12840* Turkey *12840*

R *Tanacetum paczoskii* (Zefir.) Tzvelev *20171*
  R   former European USSR

R *Tanacetum praeteritum* (Horwood) Heywood *12840*
  R   *12840* Turkey *12840*

V *Tanacetum ptarmiciflorum* (Webb) Schultz Bip. *17891*
  V   20750 Spain - Canary Is. *17891*

R *Taraxacum aristum* Hagl. & Markl. *20681*
  I   *20681* Australia - Capital Territory *20681*
  I   *20681* Australia - New South Wales *20681*
  I   *20681* Australia - Tasmania *20681*
  I   *20681* Australia - Victoria *20681*

V *Taraxacum californicum* Munz & Johnston *20850*
  V   20850 U.S. - California *20850*

V *Taraxacum cygnorum* Hand.-Mazz. *20681*
  I   *20681* Australia - Tasmania *20681*
  I   *20681* Australia - Victoria *20681*
  Ex/E *20681* Australia - Western Australia *20681*

R *Taraxacum czaunense* Jurtz. & Tzvel. *21309*
  R   *21309* Russia (E.Europe) - North *21309*

R *Taraxacum czukoticum* Jurtz. *21309*
  R   *21309* Russia (E.Europe) - North *21309*

R *Taraxacum dovrense* (Dahlst.) Dahlst. *17832, 20171*
  R   *17832* Norway *17832*

R *Taraxacum glaciale* A.Huet ex Hand.-Mazz. *18264, 20171*
  R   *18264* Italy (Abruzzi, Lazio) *18264*

R *Taraxacum holmboei* Lindb.f. *14230*
  R   *19164* Cyprus (Troodos, Platania, Prodromos, Chionistra) *14230*

R *Taraxacum jurtzevii* Tzvel. *21309*
  R   *21309* Russia (E.Europe) - North *21309*

R *Taraxacum leucocarpum* Jurtz. & Tzvel. *21309*
  R   *21309* Russia (E.Europe) - North *21309*

R *Taraxacum petrovskyi* Tzvel. var. *petrovskyi* Tzvel. *21309*
  R   *21309* Russia (E.Europe) - North *21309*

R *Taraxacum pseudoplatylepium* Jurtz. *21309*
  R   *21309* Russia (E.Europe) - North *21309*

R *Taraxacum semitubulosum* Jurtz. *21309*
  R   *21309* Russia (E.Europe) - North *21309*

R *Taraxacum taimyrense* Tzvel. *21309, 21309*
  R   *21309* Russia (E.Europe) - North *21309*

R *Taraxacum turiense* N.I.Orlova *20171*
  R   former European USSR

R *Taraxacum uschakovii* Jurtz. *21309*
  R   *21309* Russia (E.Europe) - North *21309*

R *Taraxacum wrangelicum* Tzvel. *21309*
  R   *21309* Russia (E.Europe) - North *21309*

R *Taraxacum yuparense* H. Koidz. *10573*
  R   *10573* Japan *10573*

Telanthophora arborescens (Steetz) H.E. Rob. & Brett. *20883, 10747*
  I   20883 Panama *20883*

R *Telekia speciosissima* (L.) Less. *20171*
  R   Italy

V *Tephroseris helenitis* (L.) B. Nordenstam ssp. *candida* (Corb.) B. Nordenstam *20528*

V   *20528*   France (Normandy) *20528*

V   ***Tephroseris helenitis*** (L.) B. Nordenstam ssp.
     macrochaeta (Willk. & Lange) B. Nordenstam *20528*
    E   *20528*   France (Pyrénées-Atlantiques) *20528*
    V   *20528*   Spain *20528*

R   ***Tephroseris integrifolia*** (L.) Holub. ssp. ***karsianus***
     Mathews *12840*
    R   *12840*   Turkey *12840*

I   ***Tephroseris integrifolia*** (L.) Holub. ssp. ***serpentini***
     (G. Gayer) S. Javorka *20171*
    I   Austria

I   ***Tephroseris longifolia*** (Jacq.) Griseb. et Schenk ssp.
     moravica Holub *2050*
    I   *19711*   Czech Republic *2050*
    I   *17821*   Slovakia *17821*

R   ***Tetradymia argyraea*** Munz & Roos *20850*
    E   *20850*   U.S. - Arizona *20850*
    I   *20850*   U.S. - California *20850*
    I   *20850*   U.S. - Nevada *20850*

E   ***Tetramolopium arenarium*** (Gray) Hbd. *20850*
    I   *20850*   U.S. - Hawaii *20850*

E   ***Tetramolopium arenarium*** (A.Gray) Hillebrand var.
     arenarium *20850, 14209*
    E   *20850*   U.S. - Hawaii (Maui, Hawai`i) *20850*

Ex/E   ***Tetramolopium arenarium*** (A.Gray) Hillebrand var.
     confertum Sherff *20850, 14209*
    Ex/E   *20850*   U.S. - Hawaii *20850*

Ex/E   ***Tetramolopium arenarium*** (A.Gray) Hillebr. ssp. ***laxum***
     Lowrey *20850, 14209*
    I   *20850*   U.S. - Hawaii (east Maui) *20850*

E   ***Tetramolopium capillare*** (Gaud.) St. John *20850,*
     14209
    E   *20850*   U.S. - Hawaii (West Maui) *20850*

E   ***Tctramolopium consanguineum*** (Gray) Hbd. *20850*
    I   *20850*   U.S. - Hawaii *20850*

Ex/E   ***Tetramolopium consanguineum*** (Gray) Hbd. ssp.
     consanguineum *20850, 14209*
    Ex/E   *20850*   U.S. - Hawaii *20850*

E   ***Tetramolopium consanguineum*** (Gray) Hbd. var. ***kauense***
     Lowrey *20850*
    E   *20850*   U.S. - Hawaii *20850*

E   ***Tetramolopium consanguineum*** (Gray) Hbd. var.
     leptophyllum Sherff *20850*
    E   *20850*   U.S. - Hawaii *20850*

V   ***Tetramolopium consanguineum*** (Gray) Hbd. ssp.
     leptophyllum (Sherff) Lowrey var. ***kauense***
     Sherff *14301*
    V   *14301*   U.S. -Hawaii *14301*

Ex/E   ***Tetramolopium conyzoides*** (Gray) Hbd. *20850, 14209*
    Ex/E   *20850*   U.S. - Hawaii *20850*

E   ***Tetramolopium filiforme*** Sherff *20850, 14209*
    I   *20850*   U.S. - Hawaii (O`ahu - Wai`anae Mts.)
     20850

E   ***Tetramolopium filiforme*** Sherff var.
     filiforme *20850*
    E   *20850*   U.S. - Hawaii *20850*

E   ***Tetramolopium filiforme*** Sherff var. ***polyphyllum***
     (Sherff) Lowrey *20850, 14209*
    E   *20850*   U.S. - Hawaii *20850*

R   ***Tetramolopium humile*** (Gray) Hbd. *20850*

I   *20850*   U.S. - Hawaii *20850*

E   ***Tetramolopium humile*** (Gray) Hbd. var. ***sublaeve***
     Sherff *20850, 14209*
    E   *20850*   U.S. - Hawaii (Hawai`i) *20850*

E   ***Tetramolopium lepidotum*** (Less.) Sherff *20850*
    I   *20850*   U.S. - Hawaii *20850*

Ex/E   ***Tetramolopium lepidotum*** (Less.) Sherff ssp.
     arbusculum (Gray) Lowrey *20850, 10260*
    Ex/E   *20850*   U.S. - Hawaii (east Maui) *20850*

E   ***Tetramolopium lepidotum*** (Less.) Sherff ssp.
     lepidotum *20850*
    E   *20850*   U.S. - Hawaii *20850*

E   ***Tetramolopium lepidotum*** (Less.) Sherff var.
     lepidotum *14209*

E   ***Tetramolopium remyi*** (Gray) Hbd. *20850, 14209*
    E   *20850*   U.S. - Hawaii (Lana`i) *20850*

E   ***Tetramolopium rockii*** Sherff *20850, 14209*
    I   *14209*   U.S. - Hawaii (Moloka`i) *20850*

E   ***Tetramolopium rockii*** Sherff var. ***calcisabulorum***
     (St. John) Lowrey *20850*
    E   *20850*   U.S. - Hawaii *20850*

E   ***Tetramolopium rockii*** Sherff var.
     rockii *20850*
    E   *20850*   U.S. - Hawaii *20850*

V   ***Tetramolopium sylvae*** Lowrey *20850, 14209*
    E   *19473*   Cook Is.(Southern group) (Mitiaro)
     14209
    V   *20850*   U.S. - Hawaii (Molokai & Maui) *20850*

Ex/E   ***Tetramolopium tenerrimum*** (Less.) Nees *20850, 14209*
    Ex/E   *20850*   U.S. - Hawaii (Oahu - Ko'olau Mts)
     20850

V   ***Tetramolopium vagans*** Pedley *20681*
    V   *20681*   Australia - Queensland *20681*

E   ***Tetraneuris depressa*** (Torr. & Gray ex Gray)
     Greene *20850*
    I   *20850*   U.S. - Colorado *20850*
       20850   U.S. - Utah *20850*

V   ***Tetraneuris herbacea*** Greene *20850*
    V   *20850*   Canada - Ontario *20850*
    E   *20850*   U.S. - Illinois *20850*
    V   *20850*   U.S. - Ohio *20850*

R   ***Tetraneuris turneri*** (Parker) Parker *20850*
    R   *20850*   U.S. - Texas *20850*

E   ***Tetraperone bellioides*** (Griseb.) Urban *5607*
    E   Cuba (Pinar del Rio) *5607*

R   ***Thaminophyllum latifolium*** Bond. *20604*
    R   *20604*   South Africa - Cape Province *20604*

R   ***Thaminophyllum mundii*** Harv. *20604*
    R   *20604*   South Africa - Cape Province *20604*

R   ***Thaminophyllum mundtii*** Harvey
    R   South Africa - Cape Province

E   ***Thelesperma caespitosum*** Dorn
    E   *20850*   U.S. - Utah *20850*
    E   *20850*   U.S. - Wyoming *20850*

V   ***Thelesperma curvicarpum*** T.E. Melchert *20850*
    V   *20850*   U.S. - Texas *20850*

E   ***Thelesperma pubescens*** Dorn *20850*
    E   *20850*   U.S. - Colorado *20850*
    E   *20850*   U.S. - Wyoming *20850*

E   ***Thelesperma subnudum*** A.Gray var. ***alpinum***
     Welsh *20850, 11630*

E	20850	U.S. - Utah	20850

V   *Thurovia triflora* Rose 20850

V	20850	U.S. - Texas	20850

E   *Thymophylla tephroleuca* (Blake) Strother 20850, 14621

E	20850	U.S. - Texas (Zapata Co.)	20850

E   *Thymopsis polyantha* (Urban) Borh. & Muniz 5607

E	19105	Cuba (Matanzas; Villa Clara)	5607

R   *Tolpis azorica* (Nutt.) P.Silva 19174, 20171

R	19174	Portugal - Azores	19174

V   *Tolpis crassiuscula* Svent. 20750

V	15105	Spain - Canary Is.	15105

E   *Tolpis glabrescens* Kammer 20750

E	20750	Spain - Canary Is.	15105

R   *Tolpis macrorhiza* (Lowe ex Hook.) DC.

R		Portugal - Madeira	

R   *Tomanthea daralghezica* (Fomin) Takht.

R		former USSR	6930

R   *Tonestus aberrans* (A. Nels.) Nesom & Morgan 20850

R	20850	U.S. - Idaho	20850
E	20850	U.S. - Montana	20850

V   *Tonestus alpinus* (L.C. Anders. & Goodrich) Nesom & Morgan 20850

V	20850	U.S. - Nevada	20850

E   *Tonestus graniticus* (Tiehm & L. Shultz) Nesom & Morgan 20850

E	20850	U.S. - Nevada	20850

R   *Tonestus peirsonii* (Keck) Nesom & Morgan 20850

I	20850	U.S. - California	20850

V   *Townsendia alpigena* Piper var. *caelilinensis* (Welsh) Kartesz & Gandhi 20850

V	20850	U.S. - Utah	20850

V   *Townsendia alpigena* Piper var. *minima* (Eastw.) Dorn 20850

V	20850	U.S. - Utah	20850

E   *Townsendia aprica* Welsh & Reveal 20850

E	20850	U.S. - Utah (Sevier, Wayne & Emery Co.) 20850	

V   *Townsendia condensata* (Heiser) Dorn var. *anomala* (Heiser) Dorn 20850

V	20850	U.S. - Wyoming	20850

V   *Townsendia formosa* Greene 20850

I	20850	U.S. - Arizona	20850
I	20850	U.S. - New Mexico	20850

E   *Townsendia jonesii* (Beaman) Reveal var. *jonesii* 20850

E	20850	U.S. - Nevada	20850
E	20850	U.S. - Utah	20850

E   *Townsendia jonesii* (Beaman) Reveal var. *lutea* Welsh 20850

E	20850	U.S. - Utah	20850

V   *Townsendia jonesii* (Beaman) Reveal var. *tumulosa* Reveal 20850

V	20850	U.S. - Nevada	20850

R   *Townsendia mensana* M.E.Jones 20850

R	20850	U.S. - Utah	20850

R   *Townsendia nuttallii* Dorn 20850

V	20850	U.S. - Montana	20850
R	20850	U.S. - Wyoming	20850

V   *Townsendia rothrockii* Gray ex Rothrock 20850

I	20850	U.S. - Colorado	20850
E	20850	U.S. - New Mexico	20850

V   *Townsendia smithii* L. Shultz & A. Holmgren 20850

V	20850	U.S. - Arizona	20850

R   *Townsendia spathulata* Nutt. 20850

I	20850	Canada - Alberta	20850
R	20850	U.S. - Montana	20850
R	20850	U.S. - Wyoming	20850

E   *Tracyina rostrata* Blake 20850, 14662

E	20850	U.S. - California	20850

R   *Tragopogon albinervis* Freyn & Sint 12840

R	12840	Turkey	12840

R   *Tragopogon collinus* DC. 8895

R		Egypt	
E		Israel	8895
R		Jordan	8937

V   *Tragopogon cretaceus* S.A.Nikitin 20171

V		former European USSR	

R   *Tragopogon fibrosus* Freyn & Sint. ex Freyn 12840

R	19873	Turkey	12840

V   *Tragopogon lassithicus* Rech.f. 20171

V	20731	Greece - Crete	20731

R   *Tragopogon oligolepis* Hartvig & Strid 12840

R	12840	Turkey	12840

R   *Trichanthemis aulieatensis* (B. Fedtsch.) Kraschen. 5942

R	5942	Kazakhstan	5942

R   *Trichanthemis aurea* Kraschen. 8001

R		Asiatic U.S.S.R.	6930

V   *Trichanthodium baracchianum* (Ewart & J.W.White) P.S.Short 20681

V	20681	Australia - Victoria	20681

E   *Trichocline beckeri* H. Robinson 20883

I	20883	Peru	20883

R   *Tridax durangensis* A. Garcia 14294

R	14294	Mexico - Durango	14294

V   *Tripleurospermum baytopianum* E. Hossain 12840

V	12840	Turkey	12840

R   *Tripleurospermum corymbosum* E. Hossain 12840

R	12840	Turkey	12840

R   *Tripleurospermum fissurale* (Sosn.) E. Hossain 12840

R	12840	Turkey	12840

R   *Tripleurospermum hygrophilum* (Bornm.) Bornm. 12840

R	12840	Turkey	12840

R   *Tripleurospermum kotschyi* (Boiss.) E. Hossain 12840

R	12840	Turkey	12840

R   *Tripleurospermum rosellum* (Boiss. & Orph.) Hayek var. *album* E. Hossain 12840

R	12840	Turkey	12840

R   *Troglophyton acocksianum* Hilliard 20604

R	20604	South Africa - Cape Province	20604

R   *Tugarinovia mongolica* Iljin 17617

R	17617	China - Nei Monggol Zizhiqu	11139

E   *Tuxtla pittieri* (Greenman in W. W. Jones) Villaseñor & Strother 20883

I	20883	Costa Rica	20883
I	20883	Mexico	20883

R   *Uechtritzia armena* Freyn & Sint. 12840

R	12840	Turkey	12840

R   *Urbananthus critoniformis* (Urb.) R. King & H.

Robinson *20883*

R   *20883* Jamaica *20883*

R   *Urbananthus critoniformis* (Urb.) R. King & H. Robinson
var. *critoniformis* *20883*

R   *20883* Jamaica *20883*

V   *Urbananthus critoniformis* (Urb.) R. King & H. Robinson
var. *pubescens* Adams *20883*

V   *20883* Jamaica *20883*

I   *Urmenetea atacamensis* Philippi *20176*

I   *20176* Argentina - Catamarca *20176*

I   *20176* Argentina - Jujuy *20176*

I   *20176* Argentina - Salta *20176*

I   *20176* Chile - Antofagasta *20176*

R   *Urmenetea calchaquina* *16336*

R   *19448* Argentina *16336*

R   *Ursinia coronopifolia* (Less.) N.E.Br. *20604*

R   *20604* South Africa - Cape Province *20604*

R   *Ursinia subflosculosa* (DC.) Prassler *20604*

R   *20604* South Africa - Cape Province *20604*

R   *Vanclevea stylosa* (Eastw.) Greene *20850*

I   *20850* U.S. - Arizona *20850*

V   *20850* U.S. - Utah *20850*

R   *Vellereophyton felinum* Hilliard *20604*

R   *20604* South Africa - Cape Province *20604*

R   *Vellereophyton gracillimum* Hilliard *20604*

R   *20604* South Africa - Cape Province *20604*

R   *Vellereophyton lasianthum* (Schltr. & Moeser)
Hilliard *20604*

R   *20604* South Africa - Cape Province *20604*

R   *Vellereophyton pulvinatum* Hilliard *20604*

R   *20604* South Africa - Cape Province *20604*

E   *Verbesina angulata* Urban *5607*

E   *19105* Cuba (Ciud. Habana) *5607*

V   *Verbesina aristata* (Ell.) Heller *20850*

Ex/E *20850* U.S. - Alabama *20850*

I   *20850* U.S. - Florida *20850*

I   *20850* U.S. - Georgia *20850*

V   *Verbesina aspera* Blake *20883, 13336*

V   *13336* Jamaica *20883*

E   *Verbesina baruensis* Hammel & D'Arcy *20883, 10747*

I   *20883* Panama *20883*

V   *Verbesina caymanensis* Proctor *19712*

V   *19434* Cayman Is. (Spot Bay, Cayman Brac.)
19434

V   *Verbesina chapmanii* J.R. Coleman *20850, 2232*

V   *20850* U.S. - Florida *20850*

R   *Verbesina corral-diazii* B. Turner *14294*

R   *14294* Mexico - Durango *14294*

R   *Verbesina dissita* Gray

E   *20850* U.S. - California *20850*

R   *Verbesina durangensis* B. Turner *14294*

R   *14294* Mexico - Durango *14294*

E   *Verbesina fuscasiccans* D'Arcy *20883, 9006*

I   *20883* Panama *20883*

E   *Verbesina harlingii* H. Robinson *20883*

I   *20883* Ecuador *20883*

V   *Verbesina heterophylla* (Chapman) Gray *20850*

V   *20850* U.S. - Florida *20850*

V   *Verbesina karsticola* Proctor *20883, 13336*

V   *13336* Jamaica *20883*

R   *Verbesina nervosa* Blake *20883, 13336*

R   *13336* Jamaica *20883*

R   *Verbesina petrobioides* (Griseb.) Blake *20883*

R   *20883* Jamaica *20883*

R   *Verbesina portlandiana* Proctor *20883, 13336*

R   *13336* Jamaica *20883*

V   *Verbesina propinqua* (Britton) Blake *20883, 13336*

V   *13336* Jamaica *20883*

V   *Verbesina rupestris* (Urb.) Blake *20883*

V   *20883* Jamaica *20883*

V   *Verbesina villonacoensis* H. Robinson *20883*

I   *20883* Ecuador *20883*

R   *Vernonia accomodata* Wild *7752*

R   Zimbabwe *7752*

Ex   *Vernonia africana* (Sond.) Druce *20604, 3774*

Ex   *20604* South Africa - Natal *20604*

I   *Vernonia anceps* C.B. Clarke *8021*

I   *16162* Sri Lanka *8021*

R   *Vernonia andamanica* Balakr. & Nair *10177*

R   *14782* India - Andaman Is. (Saddle Peak, N.
Andamans) *10177*

R   *Vernonia angusta* (Gleason) Standley *9004*

R   *9004* Guatemala *9004*

V   *Vernonia aronifolia* Gleas. *5607*

V   *19105* Cuba (Pinar del Rio) *5607*

I   *Vernonia beddomei* Hook.f.

I   India - Kerala

R   *Vernonia blodgettii* Small *20850*

R   *20850* U.S. - Florida *20850*

V   *Vernonia borinquensis* Urban *20883*

I   *20883* Puerto Rico *20883*

I   *Vernonia bourdillonii* Gamble

I   India - Kerala (Travancore Hills; Chemungi)
9315

I   India - Tamil Nadu (Tirunelveli Dist.)
9315

E   *Vernonia cajamarcensis* H. Robinson *20883*

I   *20883* Peru *20883*

R   *Vernonia cockburniana* Balf. f. *15534*

R   *15534* Yemen - Socotra *15534*

R   *Vernonia cristalensis* Alain *5607*

R   *19105* Cuba (Holguin) *5607*

R   *Vernonia djalonensis* A. Chev. ex Hutch. & Dalz. *7926*

R   Guinea *7926*

R   *Vernonia elsieae* Stutts *11585*

R   *11585* Brazil *11585*

R   *Vernonia eylesii* *6088*

R   *6088* Zimbabwe *6088*

R   *Vernonia fischeri* O. Hoffm. *20057*

R   *20057* Kenya (Mwingi; Makueni) *20057*

I   *Vernonia fysoni* Calder

I   India - Tamil Nadu (Palani Hills)

V   *Vernonia garrettiana* Craib *19120*

V   *19120* Thailand *19120*

E   *Vernonia guerreroana* S. B. Jones *20883*

I   *20883* Mexico *20883*

V   *Vernonia harrisii* S. Moore *20883, 13336*

V   *13336* Jamaica *20883*

E   *Vernonia heringeri* H. Robinson *20883*

	I	20883 Brazil *20883*

I   *Vernonia heynii* Beddome ex Gamble
     I   India - Kerala (Travancore Hills)

R   *Vernonia kawoziensis* Davies *7749*
     R   Malawi

I   *Vernonia kerrii* Craib *19120*
     I   *19120* Thailand *19120*

R   *Vernonia leonis* Alain *5607*
     R   *19105* Cuba (Guantanamo) *5607*

V   *Vernonia maestralis* Ekman & Urban *5607*
     V   *19105* Cuba (Granma; Santiago de Cuba) *5607*

I   *Vernonia membranacea* Beddome ex S. Moore
     I   India - Kerala (Trivandrum District)
     I   India - Tamil Nadu (Sispara, Nilgiri Hills)

E   *Vernonia multibracteata* Gamble *11494*
     E   *11494* India - Kerala (Peermade, Idukki District) *11494*

R   *Vernonia nepetifolia* Wild
     R   Zimbabwe (Chimanimani) *7749*

I   *Vernonia peninsularis* (Cl.) Hook.f.
     I   India - Tamil Nadu

R   *Vernonia pluvialis* Gleason *20883*
     R   *20883* Jamaica *20883*

I   *Vernonia principes* Gagnep. *19120*
     I   *19120* Thailand *19120*

V   *Vernonia proctori* L.E. Urbatsch *19002*
     ?   Puerto Rico *18767*

E   *Vernonia proctorii* L. E. Urbatsch *20883*
     I   *20883* Puerto Rico *20883*

R   *Vernonia pulchella* Small *20850*
     R   *20850* U.S. - Georgia *20850*
     I   *20850* U.S. - South Carolina *20850*

E   *Vernonia pulneyensis* Gamble *11494*
     E   *11494* India - Tamil Nadu (Pulney Hills, W. Ghats) *11494*

I   *Vernonia ramasamii* Hutch. *9315*
     I   India - Kerala (Trivandrum Dist.) *9315*
     I   India - Tamil Nadu *9315*

Ex/E   *Vernonia recurva* Beddome ex S. Moore *11494*
     Ex/E   *11494* India - Tamil Nadu *11494*

E   *Vernonia reedii* Ekman & Urban *5607*
     E   *19105* Cuba (Sancti Spiritus) *5607*

E   *Vernonia rigida* Sw. *20883, 13336*
     E   *19890* Jamaica (Trelawny) *20883*

I   *Vernonia saligna* DC. var. *nilghirensis* Hook.f.
     I   India - Kerala (Wynaad)
     I   India - Tamil Nadu (Nilgiri Hills)

I   *Vernonia salvifolia* Wight
     I   India - Kerala (Travancore)
     I   India - Tamil Nadu (Courtallum Hills)

I   *Vernonia sangka* Kerr *19120*
     I   *19120* Thailand *19120*

Ex/E   *Vernonia seychellensis* Baker *14296*
     Ex/E   *14981* Seychelles *14981*

V   *Vernonia thomsoni* Hook.f. *14872*
     V   *14872* Bangladesh *14872*

I   *Vernonia thwaitesii* C.B. Clarke *8021*
     I   *16162* Sri Lanka *8021*

V   *Vernonia verticillata* Proctor *20883, 13336*
     V   *13336* Jamaica *20883*

E   *Vernonia viminalis* Gleas.
     E   *19105* Cuba *19105*

V   *Vernonia yunquensis* Gleas. *5607*
     V   *19105* Cuba (Guantanamo) *5607*

R   *Vieraea laevigata* (Brouss. ex Willd.) Webb *20750*
     R   *15105* Spain - Canary Is. *15105*

E   *Viguiera eriophora* ssp. *poblana* Panero & Schilling *20883*
     I   *20883* Mexico *20883*

E   *Viguiera guerrerana* Panero & Schilling *20883*
     I   *20883* Mexico *20883*

E   *Viguiera mirandae* Panero & Schilling *20883*
     I   *20883* Mexico *20883*

E   *Viguiera phenax* Blake *20850*
     E   *20850* U.S. - Texas *20850*

R   *Viguiera puruana* Paray *9550*
     R   *19755* Mexico *9550*

V   *Viguiera reticulata* S.Watson *20850*
     I   *20850* U.S. - California *20850*
     I   *20850* U.S. - Nevada *20850*

E   *Viguiera sharpii* Panero & Schilling *20883*
     I   *20883* Mexico *20883*

V   *Viguiera splendens* Panero & Schilling *20883*
     I   *20883* Mexico *20883*

E   *Viguiera weberbaueri* Blake *18200*
     E   *9446* Peru *18200*

R   *Vittadinia sericea* N.Burb. *20681*
     R   *20681* Australia - Queensland *20681*

R   *Volutaria belouini* (Humbert) Maire
     R   Morocco

V   *Volutaria bollei* (S.B. ex Bolle) Hans. & Kunk. *20750*
     V   *15105* Spain - Canary Is. *15105*

R   *Volutaria saharae* (A. Chev.) Quezel & Santa *10488*
     R   *14958* Algeria *10488*

V   *Wagenitzia lancifolia* (Sieber ex Spreng.) Dostál *8000, 20171*
     V   *20731* Greece - Crete *8000*

V   *Wedelia inconstans* D'Arcy *20883, 9006*
     I   *20883* Panama *20883*

R   *Werneria ciliolata* A.Gray *18200*
     R   *9446* Peru *18200*

E   *Westoniella lanuginosa* Cuatr. *20883, 9640*
     I   *20883* Costa Rica *20883*
     I   *20883* Panama *20883*

V   *Whitneya dealbata* Gray *20850*
     I   *20850* U.S. - California *20850*

E   *Wilkesia hobdyi* St. John *20850, 14209*
     E   *20850* U.S. - Hawaii (Kaua`i) *20850*

V   *Wyethia reticulata* Greene *20850*
     V   *20850* U.S. - California *20850*

V   *Xylorhiza cognata* (Hall) T.J. Wats. *20883, 20850, 19002*
     V   *20850* U.S. - California *20850*
     I   *20883* Mexico *20883*

E   *Xylorhiza confertifolia* (Cronq.) T.J. Wats. *20850*
     E   *20850* U.S. - Utah *20850*

E   *Xylorhiza cronquistii* Welsh & Atwood *20850*

E		20850	U.S. - Utah 20850

E   *Xylorhiza glabriuscula* **T.J. Wats.** var. *linearifolia*
T.J. Wats. 20850

	E	20850	U.S. - Utah 20850

R   *Xylorhiza orcuttii* (**Vasey & Rose**) **Greene** 20883, 20850, 8058

	V	20850	U.S. - California 20850
	I	20883	Mexico 20883
	?		Mexico - Baja California Peninsula 8058

R   *Xylorhiza wrightii* (**Gray**) **Greene** 20850

	R	20850	U.S. - Texas 20850

E   *Youngia nilagiriensis* **Babc.** 11494

	E	11494	India - Tamil Nadu (Sispara, Nilgiri Hills) 11494

R   *Youngia yoshinoi* (**Makino**) **Kitam.** 10573

	R	10573	Japan 10573

E   *Yunquea tenzii* **Skottsb.** 19116

	E	19125	Chile - Juan Fernandez Is. 19116

E   *Zaluzania megacephala* var. *cohauilensis*
Olsen 20883

	I	20883	Mexico 20883

R   *Zinnia citrea* **Torres** 9627

	R	19755	Mexico 9627

Connaraceae

Number of genera: 16-24
Number of species: 300-400
Recorded threatened species: 51   (14%)

Tropical, especially Old World.

R   *Connarus beyrichii* **Planchon** 20883

	I	20883	Brazil 20883

R   *Connarus blanchetti* **Planchon** 20883

	I	20883	Brazil 20883

V   *Connarus blanchetti* **Planchon** var. *blanchetti* 20883

	I	20883	Brazil 20883

R   *Connarus blanchetti* **Planchon** var. *laurifolius*
(**Baker**) **Forero** 20883

	I	20883	Brazil 20883

V   *Connarus brachybotryosus* **Donnell-Smith** 20883

	I	20883	Guatemala 20883
	I	20883	Honduras 20883

E   *Connarus bracteoso-villosus* **Forero** 20883

	I	20883	Peru 20883

V   *Connarus celatus* **Forero** 20883

	I	20883	Brazil 20883

E   *Connarus costaricensis* **Schellenberg** 20883, 12059

	I	20883	Costa Rica 20883

I   *Connarus culionensis* **Merr.** var. *culionensis* 13833

	I	13833	Philippines (low altitude) 13833

I   *Connarus culionensis* **Merr.** var. *stellatus*
Leenh. 13833

	I	13833	Philippines (Palawan) 13833

E   *Connarus cuneifolius* **Baker** 20883

	E	20883	Brazil 20883

E   *Connarus detersoides* **Schellenberg** 20883

	E	20883	Brazil 20883

E   *Connarus ecuadorensis* **Schellenberg** 20883

	I	20883	Ecuador 20883

R   *Connarus elsae* **Forero** 20883

	I	20883	Peru 20883

E   *Connarus guggenheimii* **Forero** 20883

	I	20883	Colombia 20883

R   *Connarus incomptus* **Planchon** 8679

	R		Guyana 8679

E   *Connarus jaramilloi* **Forero** 20883

	I	20883	Colombia 20883

V   *Connarus marginatus* **Planchon** 20883

	I	20883	Brazil 20883

V   *Connarus megacarpus* **S. F. Blake** 20883

	I	20883	Guyana 20883

I   *Connarus nicobaricus* **King** 7771

	I		India - Nicobar Is. (Gt. Nicobar is.) 7771

R   *Connarus nodosus* **Baker** 20883

	I	20883	Brazil 20883

E   *Connarus oblongus* **Schellenberg** 20883

	E	20883	Brazil 20883

R   *Connarus ovatifolius* (**Martius ex Baker**)
Schellenberg 20883

	I	20883	Brazil 20883

E   *Connarus perturbatus* **Forero** 20883

	I	20883	Colombia 20883

V   *Connarus popenoei* **Standley** 20883, 12059

	I	20883	Honduras 20883

E   *Connarus portosegurensis* **Forero** 20883

	I	20883	Brazil 20883

R   *Connarus schultesii* **Standley ex R. E. Schultes** 20883

	I	20883	Mexico 20883

R   *Connarus silvanensis* **Cuatr.** 20883

	I	20883	Panama 20883
	I	20883	Colombia 20883

R   *Connarus stenophyllus* **Standley & L. O. Williams ex A.
Molina** 20883, 12059

	I	20883	Mexico 20883

E   *Connarus subpeltatus* **Schellenberg** 20883

	E	20883	Brazil 20883

R   *Connarus turczaninowii* **Triana** 20883, 9006

	I	20883	Panama 20883

R   *Connarus williamsii* **Britt.** 20883

	I	20883	Panama 20883

V   *Connarus williamsii* (**Steyerm.**) **Forero** var. *allenii*
(**Steyerm.**) **Forero** 20883, 10747

	E	20883	Panama 20883
	I	20883	Colombia 20883

R   *Connarus williamsii* **Britt.** var. *williamsii* 20883

	I	20883	Panama 20883
	I	20883	Colombia 20883

R   *Connarus wurdackii* **Prance** 20883

	I	20883	Brazil 20883
	I	20883	Peru 20883

I   *Ellipanthus calophyllus* **Kurz** 7771

	I		India - Andaman Is. 7771

R   *Ellipanthus hemandradenioides* **Brenan** 20057

	R	20057	Kenya (Kwale, Kilifi) 7959
	R	20057	Tanzania (Tanga, Utete & Lindi) 20900

I   *Ellipanthus madagascariensis* (**Schellenb.**) **Capuron ex**

Keraudren *21043*

I   *21043* Madagascar *21043*

I   **Ellipanthus neglectus** Gamble

     I   India - Kerala (Travancore Hills)

     I   India - Tamil Nadu (Tirunelveli Hills)

E   **Hemandradenia chevalieri** Stapf *21043*

     E   *20858* Côte d'Ivoire *7926*

     E   *20858* Ghana *20858*

I   **Jollydora pierrei** Gilg *21043*

     ?   Gabon (Libreville) *21043*

E   **Pseudoconnarus agelaefolius** Cuatrecasas *20883, 19352*

     I   *19352* Colombia *20883*

E   **Pseudoconnarus agelaeoides** (Schellenberg)

     Forero *20883*

     I   *20883* Peru *20883*

R   **Pseudoconnarus subtriplinervis** (Radlkofer)

     Schellenberg *20883*

     I   *20883* Brazil *20883*

     I   *20883* Guyana *20883*

     I   *20883* Suriname *20883*

V   **Rourea blanchetiana** (Progel) Kuhlmann *20883*

     I   *20883* Brazil *20883*

R   **Rourea brachyandra** F.Muell. *20681*

     R   *20681* Australia - Queensland *20681*

E   **Rourea cuspidata** var. *multijuga*

     Forero *20883*

     I   *20883* Brazil *20883*

R   **Rourea cuspidata** var. *pedicellata*

     Baker *20883*

     I   *20883* Brazil *20883*

     I   *20883* Colombia *20883*

     I   *20883* Venezuela *20883*

R   **Rourea glabra** var. *jamaicensis* Forero *20883*

     I   *20883* Jamaica *20883*

E   **Rourea laurifolia** Schellenberg *20883*

     I   *20883* Brazil *20883*

R   **Rourea martiana** Baker *20883*

     I   *20883* Brazil *20883*

R   **Rourea neglecta** var. *brevipes* Forero *20883*

     I   *20883* Colombia *20883*

R   **Rourea omissa** Forero *20883*

     I   *20883* Peru *20883*

E   **Rourea prancei** Forero *20883*

     I   *20883* Brazil *20883*

E   **Rourea pseudospadicea** Schellenberg *20883*

     I   *20883* Brazil *20883*

R   **Rourea pubescens** (De Candolle) Radlkofer *20883*

     I   *20883* Brazil *20883*

     I   *20883* French Guiana *20883*

     I   *20883* Suriname *20883*

E   **Rourea pubescens** (De Candolle) Radlkofer var.

     pubescens *20883*

     E   *20883* French Guiana *20883*

R   **Rourea revoluta** Planchon *21043, 8679*

     I   *20883* Brazil *20883*

     I   *20883* Guyana *20883*

V   **Rourea revoluta** Planchon var. *glabra*

     Baker *20883*

     I   *20883* Brazil *20883*

     I   *20883* Guyana *20883*

R   **Rourea revoluta** Planchon var. *revoluta* *20883*

     I   *20883* Brazil *20883*

     I   *20883* Guyana *20883*

Convolvulaceae

Number of genera: 50

Number of species: 1,500

Recorded threatened species: 134   (8%)

Nearly cosmopolitan, especially tropical and subtropical.

E   **Argyreia hancorniifolia** Gardner *8021*

     E   *16162* Sri Lanka (Kandy) *8021*

R   **Argyreia queenslandica** Domin *20681*

     R   *20681* Australia - Queensland *20681*

Ex   **Argyreia soutteri** (Bailey) Domin *20681*

     Ex   *20681* Australia - Queensland *20681*

I   **Astripomoea cephalantha** (Haller f.) Verdc. *19514*

     I   *5926* Tanzania (Mwanza) *5926*

I   **Astripomoea polycephala** (Haller f.) Verdc. *19514*

     I   *5926* Tanzania (Handeni) *19514*

R   **Bonamia dietrichiana** H.Hallier *20681*

     R   *20681* Australia - Queensland *20681*

V   **Bonamia elliptica** (Smith & Schubert) Myint &

     Ward *9657*

     V   *9658* Mexico - Chihuahua *9657*

R   **Bonamia grandiflora** (Gray) Hallier f. *20850, 10260*

     R   *20850* U.S. - Florida *20850*

V   **Bonamia menziesii** Gray *20850, 14107*

     V   *20850* U.S. - Hawaii *20850*

V   **Bonamia multicaulis** (Brandegee) House *9657*

     V   *9658* Mexico *9657*

E   **Bonamia ovalifolia** (Torr.) Hallier f. *20883, 20850,*

     9657

     E   *20850* U.S. - Texas *20850*

     I   *20883* Mexico *20883*

R   **Calystegia affinis** Endl. *11649*

     E   *19108* Australia - NSW - Lord Howe Is. *19108*

     R   *19108* Australia - Norfolk Is. *11649*

R   **Calystegia catesbiana** Pursh *20850*

     I   *20850* U.S. - Alabama *20850*

     E   *20850* U.S. - Florida *20850*

     E   *20850* U.S. - Georgia *20850*

     V   *20850* U.S. - North Carolina *20850*

     I   *20850* U.S. - South Carolina *20850*

     I   *20850* U.S. - Virginia *20850*

V   **Calystegia catesbiana** Pursh ssp.

     catesbiana *20850*

     E   *20850* U.S. - Georgia *20850*

     I   *20850* U.S. - North Carolina *20850*

     I   *20850* U.S. - South Carolina *20850*

     I   *20850* U.S. - Virginia *20850*

V   **Calystegia catesbiana** Pursh ssp. *sericata* (House)

     Brummitt *20850*

     V   *20850* U.S. - Georgia *20850*

     V   *20850* U.S. - North Carolina *20850*

     I   *20850* U.S. - South Carolina *20850*

R   **Calystegia collina** (Greene) Brummitt *20850*

     I   *20850* U.S. - California *20850*

V   **Calystegia collina** (Greene) Brummitt ssp. *oxyphylla*

     Brummitt *20850*

     V   *20850* U.S. - California *20850*

R   **Calystegia collina** (Greene) Brummitt ssp. *venusta*

     Brummitt *20850*

R 20850 U.S. - California 20850

R *Calystegia longipes* (S.Watson) Brummitt 20850
I 20850 U.S. - Arizona 20850
I 20850 U.S. - California 20850
I 20850 U.S. - Nevada 20850
E 20850 U.S. - Utah 20850

V *Calystegia macrostegia* (Greene) Brummitt 20850
I 20850 U.S. - California 20850

V *Calystegia macrostegia* (Greene) Brummitt ssp. *amplissima* Brummitt 20850
I 20850 U.S. - California 20850

R *Calystegia occidentalis* (Gray) Brummitt 20850
I 20850 U.S. - California 20850
I 20850 U.S. - Oregon 20850

R *Calystegia occidentalis* (Gray) Brummitt var. *occidentalis* 20850
I 20850 U.S. - California 20850
I 20850 U.S. - Oregon 20850

R *Calystegia peirsonii* (Abrams) Brummitt 20850
R 20850 U.S. - California 20850

R *Calystegia purpurata* (Greene) Brummitt 20850
I 20850 U.S. - California 20850

E *Calystegia sepium* (L.) R. Br. ssp. *binghamiae* (Greene) Brummitt 20850
I 20850 Canada - Nova Scotia 20850
E 20850 U.S. - California 20850

E *Calystegia stebbinsii* Brummitt 20850
E 20850 U.S. - California 20850

R *Calystegia subacaulis* Hook. & Arn. 20850
I 20850 U.S. - California 20850

E *Calystegia subacaulis* Hook. & Arn. ssp. *episcopalis* Brummitt 20850
I 20850 U.S. - California 20850

E *Convolvulus argyrothamnus* Greuter 20171
E 20731 Greece - Crete 20731

I *Convolvulus auricomus* (A. Rich.) Bhandari var. *ferruginosus* Bhandari 7771
I India - Rajasthan (west) 7771

I *Convolvulus blatteri* Bhandari 7771
I India - Rajasthan (Jaisalmer) 7771

V *Convolvulus canariensis* L.
V 19174 Spain - Canary Is. 19174

R *Convolvulus caput-medusae* Lowe 14166
R 19174 Spain - Canary Is. 17891

V *Convolvulus diversifolius* Mendoza-Heuer
V Spain - Canary Is.

E *Convolvulus fernandesii* Pinto da Silva & Teles 20076
E 20076 Portugal 17891

I *Convolvulus flavus* Willd.
I India - Tamil Nadu

R *Convolvulus fruticulosus* Desr. 20750
R 20750 Spain - Canary Is. 20750

R *Convolvulus glandulosus* (Webb) Hallier 20750
R 20750 Spain - Canary Is. 20750

R *Convolvulus holosericeus* Bieb. ssp. *macrocalycinus* Hausskn. & Bornm. ex Bornm. 12840
R 12840 Turkey 12840

E *Convolvulus lopezsocasii* Svent. 20750
E 20750 Spain - Canary Is. 17891

I *Convolvulus maireanus* Pampan.

I Libya

E *Convolvulus massonii* A. Dietr. 14166
E Portugal - Madeira 17891

R *Convolvulus ocellatus* Hook. var. *plicinervis* Verdc. 7760
R Zimbabwe 7760

V *Convolvulus perraudieri* Coss.
V Spain - Canary Is.

R *Convolvulus phrygius* Bornm. 12840
R 12840 Turkey 12840

V *Convolvulus pulvinatus* Sa'ad 12840
V 12840 Turkey 12840

V *Convolvulus simulans* Perry 20850
V 20850 U.S. - California 20850

V *Convolvulus subauriculatus* (Burchard) Lindinger 20750
V 20750 Spain - Canary Is. 20750

V *Convolvulus volubilis* Link in Burch. 20750
V 20750 Spain - Canary Is. 20750

I *Cuscuta atrans* Feinbrun 20171
I 20730 Greece - Crete 20730

V *Cuscuta attenuata* Waterfall 20850
I 20850 U.S. - Kansas 20850
E 20850 U.S. - Oklahoma 20850
V 20850 U.S. - Texas 20850

V *Cuscuta brachycalyx* (Yuncker) Yuncker 20850
I 20850 U.S. - California 20850

V *Cuscuta cozumeliensis* Yuncker 9004
V 9004 Guatemala 9004
V 9004 Mexico 9004

E *Cuscuta dentatasquamata* Yuncker 20850
I 20850 U.S. - Arizona 20850

R *Cuscuta exaltata* Engelm. 20850
I 20850 U.S. - Florida 20850
R 20850 U.S. - Texas 20850

V *Cuscuta harperi* Small 20850
V 20850 U.S. - Alabama 20850
E 20850 U.S. - Georgia 20850

Ex/E *Cuscuta indecora* Choisy var. *warneri* (Yuncker) T. Beliz, comb. nov. ined. 20850
Ex/E 20850 U.S. - Arizona 20850
Ex/E 20850 U.S. - Utah 20850

R *Cuscuta jalapensis* Schltr. 9004
R 9658 Guatemala 9004
R 9658 Mexico 9004

V *Cuscuta jepsonii* Yuncker 20850
I 20850 U.S. - California 20850

R *Cuscuta maroccana* Trabut
R Morocco

E *Cuscuta mitriformis* Engelm. 20850
I 20850 U.S. - Arizona 20850
I 20850 U.S. - New Mexico 20850
I 20883 Mexico 20883

V *Cuscuta nevadensis* I.M. Johnston 20850
I 20850 U.S. - Arizona 20850
I 20850 U.S. - California 20850
I 20850 U.S. - Nevada 20850

V *Cuscuta obtusata* (Engilmann) Trabut 12840
V 12840 Turkey 12840

E *Cuscuta odontolepis* Engelm. 20850
I 20850 U.S. - Arizona 20850

R   *Cuscuta odontolepis* Engelm. var. *fimbriata*
     Yuncker *9037*
- R   *9658*   Costa Rica *9037*
- R   *9658*   Mexico *9037*

R   *Cuscuta plattensis* A. Nels. *20850*
- I   *20850*   U.S. - Washington *20850*
- E   *20850*   U.S. - Wyoming *20850*

R   *Cuscuta rugosiceps* Yuncker *9004*
- R   *9658*   Guatemala *9004*
- R   *9658*   Mexico *9004*

R   *Cuscuta suksdorfii* Yuncker *20850*
- I   *20850*   U.S. - California *20850*
- I   *20850*   U.S. - Oregon *20850*
- I   *20850*   U.S. - Washington *20850*

R   *Cuscuta tinctoria* Martius ex Engelm. var. *kellermaniana* Yuncker *9004*
- R   *9658*   Guatemala *9004*

E   *Cuscuta woodsonii* Yuncker *20883, 9006*
- V   *9658*   Panama *20883*

V   *Cuscuta yucatana* Yuncker *9004*
- V   *9658*   Guatemala *9004*
- V   *9658*   Mexico *9004*

R   *Dichondra occidentalis* House *20850*
- R   *20850*   U.S. - California *20850*
- I   *20850*   U.S. - Oregon *20850*

I   *Erycibe fecunda* Kerr *19120*
- I   *19120*   Thailand *19120*

I   *Erycibe hololuba* Kerr *19120*
- I   *19120*   Thailand *19120*

I   *Erycibe noei* Kerr *19120*
- I   *19120*   Thailand *19120*

E   *Evolvulus siliceus* Britton & P. Wilson *5607*
- E   *19105*   Cuba (Juventud Is.) *5607*

R   *Ipomoea antonschmidii* R.W.Johnson *20681*
- R   *20681*   Australia - Queensland *20681*

R   *Ipomoea barbatisepala* Gray *20850*
- I   *20850*   U.S. - Arizona *20850*
- I   *20850*   U.S. - New Mexico *20850*
- E   *20850*   U.S. - Texas *20850*

I   *Ipomoea cairica* (L.) Sweet var. *semine-glabra* (Blatter & Hallberg) Bhandari
- I   India - Rajasthan

V   *Ipomoea carmesina* Proctor *20883, 13336*
- V   *13336*   Jamaica *20883*

E   *Ipomoea cavalcantei* D. Austin *9658*
- E   *17746*   Brazil - Pará *17746*

R   *Ipomoea chamelana* Mcdonald *21220*
- R   *21220*   Mexico - Guerrero *21220*
- R   *21220*   Mexico - Jalisco *21220*

E   *Ipomoea chiriquiensis* Standl. *20883, 9006*
- V   *9658*   Panama *20883*

R   *Ipomoea clarkei* Hook.f. *14782*
- R   *14782*   India - Uttar Pradesh (Western Ghats in Thane, Pune and Nasik Districts) *14782*

V   *Ipomoea clewelii* C. Nelson *20050*
- V   *20050*   Honduras *20050*

I   *Ipomoea consimilis* Schulze-Menz *19514*
- I   *5926*   Tanzania (Lindi) *5926*

R   *Ipomoea cyanantha* Griseb. *20883*
- R   *20883*   Jamaica *20883*

R   *Ipomoea ephemera* Verdc. *7760*

- R   Mozambique *7760*

I   *Ipomoea erosa* Urban *5607*
- I   *19105*   Cuba (Holguin) *5607*

E   *Ipomoea excisa* Urban *5607*
- E   *19105*   Cuba (Prov. Habana) *5607*

R   *Ipomoea expansa* McDonald *10546*
- R   *11911*   Mexico - Guerrero *10546*

E   *Ipomoea flavo-purpurea* Urban *5607*
- E   *19105*   Cuba (Sancti Spiritus) *5607*

I   *Ipomoea hylophila* Kerr *19120*
- I   *19120*   Thailand *19120*

I   *Ipomoea jucunda* Thwaites *8021*
- I   *16162*   Sri Lanka (Ritigala SNR; Kandy Dist.) *8021*

I   *Ipomoea kilwaensis* Pilger *19514*
- I   *5926*   Tanzania (Kilwa) *19514*

V   *Ipomoea krugii* Urban *20883, 8058*
- I   *20883*   Puerto Rico *20883*

I   *Ipomoea lapathifolia* Haller f. var. *bussei* (Pilger) Verdc. *19514*
- I   *5926*   Tanzania (Kilwa) *19514*

R   *Ipomoea lineolata* Urb. *20883*
- R   *20883*   Jamaica *20883*

I   *Ipomoea macrosepala* Brenan *19514*
- I   *5926*   Tanzania (Shinyanga District) *19514*

R   *Ipomoea mcvaughii* McPherson *9659*
- R   *11911*   Mexico *9659*

I   *Ipomoea microcalyx* Schulze-Menz *19514*
- I   *5926*   Tanzania (Ulanga District) *19514*

E   *Ipomoea nationis* (Hook.) Nichols. *9446*
- E   *9446*   Peru *9446*

R   *Ipomoea noctulifolia* McPherson *9659*
- R   *11911*   Mexico - Jalisco *21204*

R   *Ipomoea perpartita* McPherson *9659*
- R   *11911*   Mexico *9659*

V   *Ipomoea praematura* Eckenwalder *20883*
- I   *20883*   Grenada *20883*
- I   *20883*   Trinidad & Tobago *20883*
- I   *20883*   Colombia *20883*
- I   *20883*   Guyana *20883*

R   *Ipomoea rubella* House *20883*
- R   *20883*   Jamaica *20883*

R   *Ipomoea saintronanensis* R.W.Johnson *20681*
- R   *20681*   Australia - Queensland *20681*

E   *Ipomoea saxicola* Proctor *20883, 13336*
- E   *20883*   Jamaica *20883*

E   *Ipomoea sinaica* Tackh. & Boulos
- E   Egypt

I   *Ipomoea stellaris* Baker *19514*
- I   *5926*   Tanzania (Mikindani) *19514*

E   *Ipomoea tabascana* J.A.McDonald & D. Austin *19812*
- E   *19812*   Mexico - Tabasco (south border) *19812*

R   *Ipomoea tastensis* Brandegee *13791*
- R   *13791*   Mexico - Baja California Sur *13791*

R   *Ipomoea tenuifolia* (Vahl.) Urb. *20883, 13336*
- R   *13336*   Jamaica *20883*

V   *Ipomoea tenuissima* Choisy *20883, 19002, 20850*
- E   *20850*   U.S. - Florida *20850*
- I   *20883*   Puerto Rico *20883*

R	***Ipomoea teotitlanica*** McPherson *9659*	
	R	*11911* Mexico *9659*
V	***Ipomoea thurberi*** Gray *20850*	
	I	*20850* U.S. - Arizona *20850*
R	***Ipomoea tuboides*** O. Deg. & van Ooststr. *20850, 14209*	
	I	*20850* U.S. - Hawaii *20850*
R	***Ipomoea venosa*** (Desr.) Roem. & Schultes var. ***obtusifolia*** Verdc. *7761*	
	R	Mozambique *7761*
R	***Ipomoea verrucisepala*** Verdc. *7761*	
	R	Zimbabwe *7761*
I	***Ipomoea villifera*** House *9004*	
	I	*9658* Guatemala *9004*
I	***Ipomoea zanzibarica*** Verdc. *19514*	
	I	*5926* Tanzania (Zanzibar) *5926*
R	***Itzaea sericea*** Standley & Steyerm. *9658*	
	R	*10544* Belize *9658*
	R	*10544* Guatemala *10544*
	R	*10544* Honduras *10544*
V	***Jacquemontia curtissii*** Peter ex Small *20850*	
	V	*20850* U.S. - Florida *20850*
V	***Jacquemontia pinetorum*** Standley & Steyerm. *9004*	
	V	*9658* Guatemala *9004*
E	***Jacquemontia reclinata*** House *20850*	
	E	*20850* U.S. - Florida *20850*
E	***Maripa lewisii*** Austin *20883, 10747*	
	I	*20883* Panama *20883*
R	***Maripa longifolia*** Sagot *8679*	
	R	*8679* French Guiana *8679*
R	***Merremia dissecta*** (Jacq.) Hallier f. *20604*	
	R	*20604* South Africa - Natal *20604*
R	***Merremia hemmingiana*** Verdc. *7959*	
	R	Kenya (Northern Frontier Province) *7959*
R	***Merremia maypurensis*** Hallier f. *10544*	
	R	Venezuela *10544*
Ex	***Merremia palmata*** H. Hall vel aff. *18102*	
	Ex	*18102* Pakistan (Margallas) *18102*
E	***Metaporana obtusa*** (Balf. f.) Staples *15534*	
	E	*15534* Yemen - Socotra *15534*
I	***Neuropeltis racemosa*** Wallich ex Roxb.	
	I	India - Kerala (Tambracheri Ghat, Malabar)
	V	*20099* Singapore *20099*
I	***Operculina triquetra*** (Vahl) Macbride	
	I	*15106* USA - Virgin Is. (St Croix; St Thomas) *8058*
I	***Rivea clakeana*** Craib *19120*	
	I	*19120* Thailand *19120*
V	***Seddera fastigiata*** (Balf. f.) Verdc. *15534*	
	V	*15534* Yemen - Socotra *15534*
V	***Seddera spinosa*** (Vierh.) Verdc. *15534*	
	V	*15534* Yemen - Socotra (Abd al Kuri) *20746*
I	***Stictocardia lutambensis*** (Schulze-Menz) Verdc. *19514*	
	I	*5926* Tanzania (Morogoro & Lindi Districts) *19514*
V	***Stylisma abdita*** Myint *20850*	
	V	*20850* U.S. - Florida *20850*
V	***Stylisma pickeringii*** (M.Curtis) A.Gray var. ***pickeringii*** *20850*	
	I	*20850* U.S. - Alabama *20850*
	V	*20850* U.S. - Georgia *20850*

	E	*20850* U.S. - New Jersey *20850*
	V	*20850* U.S. - North Carolina *20850*
	E	*20850* U.S. - South Carolina *20850*
E	***Turbina inopinata*** Heine *20802*	
	E	*20893* New Caledonia *20802*
R	***Turbina longiflora*** Verdc. *7761*	
	R	Mozambique *7761*
E	***Turbina wrightii*** (House) Alain	
	E	*19105* Cuba *19105*

Cornaceae

Number of genera:	11
Number of species:	100
Recorded threatened species:	9 (9%)

North temperate; irregularly tropical and South temperate.

R	***Cornus florida*** L. var. ***urbiniana*** (Rose) Wangerin *9019*	
	R	*9019* Mexico - Nuevo Leon *9019*
	R	*9019* Mexico - Veracruz *9019*
V	***Cornus kousa*** Buerg. var. ***yaeyamensis*** Hatus. *20626*	
	V	*20626* Japan (Ryukyu) *20626*
R	***Cornus sessilis*** Torr. ex Dur. *20850*	
	I	*20850* U.S. - California *20850*
R	***Davidia involucrata*** Baillon var. ***involucrata*** *17617*	
	R	*17617* China - Guizhou *11139*
	R	*17617* China - Hubei *11139*
	R	*17617* China - Hunan *11139*
	R	*17617* China - Shaanxi *11139*
	R	*17617* China - Sichuan *11139*
	R	*17617* China - Yunnan *11139*
R	***Davidia involucrata*** Baillon var. ***vilmoriniana*** (Dode) Wanger *11139*	
	R	China - Guizhou *11139*
	R	China - Hubei *11139*
	R	China - Hunan *11139*
	R	China - Shaanxi (Zhengping) *11139*
	R	China - Sichuan *11139*
	R	China - Yunnan *11139*
V	***Mastixia nimali*** Kosterm. *12838*	
	V	*12838* Sri Lanka *12838*
R	***Mastixia poilanei*** Tard. *6057*	
	R	Vietnam *6057*
R	***Mastixia tetrandra*** (Wight ex Thwaites) C.B. Clarke *10276*	
	R	*12838* Sri Lanka *10276*
E	***Nyssa yunnanensis*** W.C. Yin *17617*	
	E	*17617* China - Yunnan (Jinghong) *11139*
E	***Swida darvasica*** (Pojark.) Sojak	
	E	former USSR *6930*

Corylaceae

Number of genera:	4
Number of species:	22
Recorded threatened species:	10 (45%)

North temperate.

R	***Carpinus hebestroma*** Yamamoto *20511*	
	R	*20511* Taiwan *20511*
R	***Carpinus minutiserrata*** Hayata *20511*	
	R	*20511* Taiwan *20511*

E   *Carpinus putoensis* Cheng *17617*
     E   *18038* China - Zhejiang (Putuo Temple, Putuo Shan) *11139*

V   *Carpinus rankanensis* Hayata var. *rankanensis*
     V   Taiwan (north & central)

I   *Carpinus shensiensis* Hu *11815*
     I   China - Shaanxi *11815*

R   *Carpinus tropicales* (J. D. Smith) Lundell *20883*
     I   *20883* El Salvador *20883*
     I   *20883* Guatemala *20883*
     I   *20883* Honduras *20883*
     I   *20883* Mexico *20883*
     I   *20883* Nicaragua *20883*

E   *Carpinus tropicales* (J. D. Smith) Lundell ssp.
      mexicana Furlow *20883*
     I   *20883* Mexico *20883*

R   *Carpinus tschonoskii* Maxim. var. *eximia*
      Hatus. *15957*
     R   *15923* Korea, South (Mt Chiri) *15957*

V   *Corylus chinensis* Franchet *17617*
     V   *17617* China - Henan *11139*
     V   *17617* China - Hubei *11139*
     V   *17617* China - Hunan *11139*
     V   *17617* China - Shaanxi *11139*
     V   *17617* China - Sichuan *11139*
     V   *17617* China - Yunnan *11139*

E   *Ostrya rehderiana* Chun *17617*
     E   *18038* China - Zhejiang (Tianmu Mt) *11139*

Corynocarpaceae

Number of genera: 1
Number of species: 5
Recorded threatened species: 1   (20%)

New Zealand; northeastern Australia; New Guinea.

R   *Corynocarpus rupestris* Guymer ssp.
      arborescens *20681*
     I   *20681* Australia - New South Wales *20681*
     I   *20681* Australia - Queensland *20681*

V   *Corynocarpus rupestris* Guymer ssp. *rupestris*
      Guymer *20681*
     V   *20681* Australia - New South Wales *20681*

Crassulaceae

Number of genera: 25
Number of species: 900
Recorded threatened species: 227   (25%)

Cosmopolitan, except Australia and Polynesia.

I   *Adromischus diabolicus* Toelken *20604*
     I   *20604* South Africa - Cape Province *20604*

I   *Adromischus fallax* Toelken *20604*
     I   *20604* South Africa - Cape Province *20604*

R   *Adromischus liebenbergii* Hutchison *20604*
     R   *20604* South Africa - Cape Province *20604*

R   *Adromischus mammillaris* (L.f.) Lem. *20604*
     R   *20604* South Africa - Cape Province *20604*

R   *Adromischus nanus* (N.E.Br.) Poelln. *20604*
     R   *20604* South Africa - Cape Province *20604*

R   *Adromischus schuldtianus* (Poelln.) Poelln. ssp.
      juttae (Poelln.) Toelken *20604*
     R   *20604* Namibia *20604*

R   *Adromischus subviridis* Toelken *20604*

     R   *20604* South Africa - Cape Province *20604*

V   *Aeonium balsamiferum* Webb & Berthel. *20750*
     V   *20750* Spain - Canary Is. *20750*

R   *Aeonium castello-paivae* Bolle
     R   Spain - Canary Is.

V   *Aeonium ciliatum* (Willd.) Webb & Berthel. *20750*
     V   *20750* Spain - Canary Is. *20750*

V   *Aeonium cuneatum* Webb & Berthel.
     V   *20750* Spain - Canary Is. *20750*

V   *Aeonium gomeraense* Praeger *14166*
     V   *20750* Spain - Canary Is. *19174*

R   *Aeonium goochiae* Webb & Berthel. *20750*
     R   *20750* Spain - Canary Is. *20750*

R   *Aeonium haworthii* Salm-Dyck ex Webb & Berthel. *20750*
     R   *20750* Spain - Canary Is. *20750*

E   *Aeonium mascaense* Bram. *20750*
     E   *20750* Spain - Canary Is. *20750*

V   *Aeonium nobile* Praeger *20750*
     V   *20750* Spain - Canary Is. *20750*

R   *Aeonium pseudourbicum* Bañares *20750*
     R   *20750* Spain - Canary Is. *20750*

V   *Aeonium rubrolineatum* Svent. *20750*
     V   *20750* Spain - Canary Is. *20750*

V   *Aeonium saundersii* Bolle *14166*
     V   *20750* Spain - Canary Is. *20750*

V   *Aeonium sedifolium* (Webb ex Bolle) Pit. &
      Proust *20750*
     V   *20750* Spain - Canary Is. *20750*

V   *Aeonium smithii* (Sims) Webb & Berthel. *20750*
     V   *20750* Spain - Canary Is. *20750*

R   *Aeonium tabulaeforme* (Haw.) Webb. & Berth. *10260*
     R   *20750* Spain - Canary Is. *20750*

V   *Aeonium valverdense* Praeger *20750*
     V   *20750* Spain - Canary Is. *20750*

R   *Aeonium vestitum* Svent.
     R   Spain - Canary Is.

R   *Aeonium virgineum* Webb ex Christ
     R   Spain - Canary Is.

V   *Afrovivella simensis* A. Berger *6087*
     V   Ethiopia (Mt. Buahit) *6087*

E   *Aichryson bethencourtianum* Bolle *20750*
     E   *20750* Spain - Canary Is. *20750*

R   *Aichryson bollei* Webb ex Bolle *20750*
     R   *20750* Spain - Canary Is. *20750*

V   *Aichryson dumosum* (Lowe) Praeger *17891*
     V   Portugal - Madeira *17891*

E   *Aichryson pachycaulon* Bolle ssp. *gonzalezhernandezii*
      (Kunkel) Bramwell
     E   Spain - Canary Is.

V   *Aichryson pachycaulon* Bolle. ssp. *immaculatum*
      (Webb ex Christ) Bram.
     V   Spain - Canary Is.

E   *Aichryson pachycaulon* Bolle ssp. *pachycaulon*
     E   Spain - Canary Is.

V   *Aichryson pachycaulon* Bolle ssp. *parviflorum*
      (Bolle) Bram.
     V   Spain - Canary Is.

V   *Aichryson pachycaulon* Bolle ssp. *praetermisum*

Bram.

V   Spain - Canary Is.

R   *Aichryson palmense* Webb ex Bolle *19174*
    R   *20750* Spain - Canary Is. *19174*

R   *Aichryson tortuosum* (Aiton) Webb & Berthel. *20750*
    R   *20750* Spain - Canary Is. *20750*

R   *Aichryson villosum* (Aiton) Webb & Berthel. *20171*
    R   Portugal - Azores
    R   Portugal - Madeira

R   *Cotyledon orbiculata* L. var. *flanaganii* (schönland & Baker f.) Toelken *20803*
    R   *20803* South Africa - Cape Province *20803*

R   *Cotyledon tomentosa* Harv. ssp. *ladismithiensis* (Poelln.) Toelken *20803*
    R   *20604* South Africa - Cape Province *20604*

Ex   *Crassula alcicornis* Schönland *20604, 6180*
    Ex   *20604* South Africa - Cape Province *20604*

R   *Crassula arborescens* (Mill.) Willd. ssp. *undulatifolia* Toelken *20803*
    R   *20803* South Africa - Cape Province *20803*

R   *Crassula ausensis* Hutchison ssp. *giessii* (Friedrich) Toelken *20604*
    R   *20604* Namibia *20604*

R   *Crassula barbata* Thunb. ssp. *broomii* (Schonl.) Toelken *20604*
    R   *20604* South Africa - Cape Province *20604*

V   *Crassula brevifolia* Harv. ssp. *psammophila* Toelken *20604*
    V   *20604* South Africa - Cape Province *20604*

R   *Crassula cordifolia* Baker *10368*
    R   *20578* Madagascar (Antananarivo) *20578*

R   *Crassula decidua* Schönland *20604*
    R   *20604* South Africa - Cape Province *20604*

R   *Crassula elsieae* Toelken *20604*
    R   *20604* South Africa - Cape Province *20604*

R   *Crassula erecta* (hook. & Arn.) Berger *10701*
    R   *20137* Argentina - Buenos Aires *20137*

R   *Crassula exillis* Harv. ssp. *exillis* *20604*
    R   *20604* South Africa - Cape Province *20604*

R   *Crassula garibina* Marloth & Schönland ssp. *glabra* Toelken *20604*
    R   *20604* South Africa - Cape Province *20604*

R   *Crassula humbertii* Descoings *10368*
    R   *20578* Madagascar (Toliara) *20578*

V   *Crassula hunua* Druce *19305*
    V   *19305* New Zealand - North Is. *19305*
    V   *19305* New Zealand - South Is. *19305*

R   *Crassula multiceps* Harv. *20604*
    R   *20604* South Africa - Cape Province *20604*

R   *Crassula namaquensis* Schonl. & E.G. Baker ssp. *comptonii* (Hutch. & Pillans) Toelken *20604*
    R   *20604* South Africa - Cape Province *20604*

R   *Crassula pellucida* L. ssp. *spongiana* Toelken *20604*
    R   *20604* South Africa - Cape Province *20604*

V   *Crassula planifolia* Schönland *20604*
    V   *20604* South Africa - Cape Province (Transkei) *20604*

I   *Crassula plegmatoides* Friedrich *20604*

    20604 Namibia *20604*
    20604 South Africa - Cape Province *20604*

R   *Crassula roggeveldii* Schönland *20604*
    R   *20604* South Africa - Cape Province *20604*

R   *Crassula ruamahanga* Druce *19305*
    R   *19305* New Zealand - North Is. *19305*
    R   *19305* New Zealand - South Is. *19305*

R   *Crassula rupestris* Thunb. ssp. *marnieriana* (H.E.Huber & H.Jacobsen) Toelken *20604*
    R   *20604* South Africa - Cape Province *20604*

R   *Crassula sericea* Schönland var. *velutina* (Friedr.) Toelken *20604*
    R   *20604* Namibia *20604*
    R   *20604* South Africa - Cape Province *20604*

R   *Crassula sladenii* Schönland *20604*
    R   *20604* Namibia *20604*
    R   *20604* South Africa - Cape Province *20604*

R   *Crassula socialis* Schönland *20604*
    R   *20604* South Africa - Cape Province *20604*

R   *Crassula streyi* Toelken *20604*
    R   *20604* South Africa - Cape Province *20604*
    R   *20604* South Africa - Natal *20604*

R   *Crassula subacaulis* Schönland & Baker f. ssp. *subacaulis* *20604*
    R   *20604* South Africa - Cape Province *20604*

Ex   *Crassula subulata* L. var. *hispida* Toelken *6180, 20604*
    Ex   *6180* South Africa - Cape Province *6180*

I   *Crassula susannae* Rauh & Friedrich *20604*
    I   *20604* South Africa - Cape Province *20604*

R   *Crassula thunbergiana* Schult. ssp. *minutiflora* (schönland & Baker f.) *20604*
    R   *20604* Namibia *20604*
    R   *20604* South Africa - Cape Province *20604*

R   *Crassula vestita* Thunb. *20604*
    R   *20604* South Africa - Cape Province *20604*

R   *Dudleya abramsii* Rose *20850*
    I   *20850* U.S. - California *20850*

E   *Dudleya abramsii* Rose ssp. *affinis* K. Nakai *20850*
    E   *20850* U.S. - California *20850*

V   *Dudleya abramsii* Rose ssp. *calcicola* (Bartel & Shevock) K. Nakai *20850*
    I   *20850* U.S. - California *20850*

V   *Dudleya abramsii* Rose ssp. *murina* (Eastw.) Moran *20850*
    V   *20850* U.S. - California *20850*

V   *Dudleya abramsii* Rose ssp. *parva* (Rose & A. Davids.) Bartel *20850*
    V   *20850* U.S. - California *20850*

V   *Dudleya attenuata* (Rose) Moran ssp. *orcuttii* (Rose) Moran *20850*
    E   *20850* U.S. - California *20850*

R   *Dudleya blochmaniae* (Eastw.) Moran *20850*
    I   *20850* U.S. - California *20850*

V   *Dudleya blochmaniae* (Eastw.) Moran ssp. *blochmaniae* *20850*
    V   *20850* U.S. - California *20850*

E   *Dudleya blochmaniae* (Eastw.) Moran ssp. *insularis* (Moran) Moran *20850*

	E	20850 U.S. - California 20850
E	*Dudleya brevifolia* (Moran) Moran 20850	
	E	20850 U.S. - California 20850
R	*Dudleya candelabrum* Rose 20850	
	V	20850 U.S. - California 20850
R	*Dudleya cespitosa* (Haw.) Britt. & Rose 20850	
	I	20850 U.S. - California 20850
V	*Dudleya cymosa* (Lem.) Britt. & Rose ssp. *costafolia* Bartel & Shevock 20850	
	V	20850 U.S. - California 20850
E	*Dudleya cymosa* (Lem.) Britt. & Rose ssp. *crebrifolia* K. Nakai & Verity 20850	
	E	20850 U.S. - California 20850
V	*Dudleya cymosa* (Lemaire) Britton & Rose ssp. *marcescens* Moran 20850	
	V	20850 U.S. - California 20850
V	*Dudleya cymosa* (Lem.) Britt. & Rose ssp. *ovatifolia* (Britt.) Moran 20850	
	V	20850 U.S. - California 20850
E	*Dudleya cymosa* (Lem.) Britt. & Rose ssp. *setchellii* (Jepson) Moran 20850	
	E	20850 U.S. - California 20850
E	*Dudleya densiflora* (Rose) Moran 20850	
	E	20850 U.S. - California 20850
R	*Dudleya edulis* (Nutt.) Moran 20850	
	I	20850 U.S. - California 20850
R	*Dudleya greenei* Rose 20850	
	R	20850 U.S. - California 20850
E	*Dudleya hassei* (Rose) Moran 20850	
	I	20850 U.S. - California 20850
R	*Dudleya lanceolata* (Nutt.) Britt. & Rose 20850	
	I	20850 U.S. - California 20850
V	*Dudleya multicaulis* (Rose) Moran 20850	
	V	20850 U.S. - California 20850
E	*Dudleya nesiotica* (Moran) Moran 20850	
	E	20850 U.S. - California 20850
V	*Dudleya palmeri* (S. Watts.) Britt. & Rose 20850	
	I	20850 U.S. - California 20850
R	*Dudleya pulverulenta* (Nutt.) Britt. & Rose 20850	
	I	20850 U.S. - California 20850
	R	20850 U.S. - Nevada 20850
V	*Dudleya saxosa* (M.E. Jones) Britton & Rose ssp. *saxosa* 20850	
	I	20850 U.S. - California 20850
E I	*Dudleya stolonifera* Moran 20850	
	E	20850 U.S. - California 20850
E I	*Dudleya traskiae* (Rose) Moran 20850	
	E	20850 U.S. - California (Santa Barbara Is.) 20850
V	*Dudleya variegata* (S.Watson) Moran 20883, 20850, 8058	
	V	20850 U.S. - California 20850
	I	20883 Mexico 20883
E	*Dudleya verityi* K. Nakai 20850	
	E	20850 U.S. - California 20850
E	*Dudleya virens* (Rose) Moran 20850	
	E	20850 U.S. - California 20850
V	*Dudleya viscida* (S.Watson) Moran 20850	
	V	20850 U.S. - California 20850

R	*Echeveria amphoralis* Walth. 19850	
	R	19850 Mexico 19850
I	*Echeveria elegans* Rose 19850	
	I	19850 Mexico 19850
I	*Echeveria laui* Moran & Meyrán 9019	
	I	19850 Mexico - Oaxaca 9019
V	*Echeveria longissima* Walth. var. *aztatlensis* J. Meyrán 19850	
	V	19850 Mexico 19850
V	*Echeveria longissima* Walth. var. *longissima* 19850	
	V	19850 Mexico 19850
R	*Echeveria moranii* E. Walther 19850	
	R	19850 Mexico 19850
I	*Echeveria purpusorum* Berger 19850	
	I	19850 Mexico 19850
I	*Echeveria setosa* Rose & Purpus var. *ciliata* Moran 19850	
	I	19850 Mexico 19850
I	*Echeveria setosa* Rose & Purpus var. *deminuta* J. Meyrán 19850	
	I	19850 Mexico 19850
I	*Echeveria setosa* Rose & Purpus var. *minor* Berger 19850	
	I	19850 Mexico 19850
I	*Echeveria setosa* Rose & Purpus var. *oteroi* 19850	
	I	19850 Mexico 19850
R	*Echeveria setosa* Rose & Purpus var. *setosa* 19850	
	R	19850 Mexico 19850
E	*Graptopetalum bellum* (Moran & Meyran) D.R. Hunt 9662	
	E	9662 Mexico - Chihuahua 9662
I	*Graptopetalum macdougallii* Alexander 19850	
	I	19850 Mexico 19850
V	*Greenovia aizoon* Bolle 17534	
	V	Spain - Canary Is. 17534
V	*Greenovia dodrentalis* (Willd.) Webb & Berthel. 17534	
	V	20750 Spain - Canary Is. 17534
V	*Hylotelephium cauticolum* (Praeger) H. Ohba 10572	
	V	10572 Japan 10572
E	*Hylotelephium sielbodii* (Sweet ex Hook.) H. Ohba var. *ettyuense* (Tomida) H. Ohba 10572	
	E	10572 Japan 10572
V	*Hylotelephium tsugaruense* (Hara) H. Ohba 10572	
	V	10572 Japan 10572
V	*Hypagophytum abyssinicum* 19704	
	V	19704 Ethiopia (Tigray Upland, Gonder, Shewa Upland.) 19704
R	*Jovibarba allionii* (Jord. & Fourr.) D.A.Webb 20171	
	R	France
	R	Italy
I	*Jovibarba hirta* (L.) Opiz ssp. *glabrescens* (Sabr.) Holub 8000, 20171	
	I	19321 Slovakia 19321
I	*Jovibarba hirta* (L.) Opiz ssp. *tatrensis* (Domin) A. Love et D. Love 8000	
	I	19321 Slovakia 19321
Ex/E	*Kalanchoe angustifolia* A. Rich 19704	

	Ex/E	19704 Ethiopia (Tigray Upland) *19704*
R	*Kalanchoe beharensis* Drake var. *aureo-aeneus* H.J. Jacobsen *10368*	
	R	Madagascar
R	*Kalanchoe beharensis* Drake var. *subnuda* H.J. Jacobsen *10368*	
	R	Madagascar
I	*Kalanchoe bitteri* Raym.-Hamet *10368*	
	I	Madagascar
R	*Kalanchoe crundallii* I.Verd. *20604*	
	R	*20604* South Africa - Transvaal *20604*
I	*Kalanchoe fadenorum* Raadts	
	I	Kenya
R	*Kalanchoe faustii* Font Quer	
	R	Morocco
R	*Kalanchoe garambiensis* Kudo *20511*	
	R	*20511* Taiwan *20511*
R	*Kalanchoe olivacea* Dalz. & Gibson *14782*	
	R	*14782* India - Tamil Nadu *14782*
R	*Kalanchoe robusta* Balf. f. *15534*	
	R	*15534* Yemen - Socotra *15534*
E	*Kalanchoe roseus* Clarke *14782*	
	E	*14782* India - Manipur *14782*
	E	*14782* India - Nagaland *14782*
R	*Kalanchoe schimperiana* A. Rich. *19704*	
	R	*19704* Ethiopia (West Eritrea, Tigray Upland, Gamo Gofa, Shewa Upland, Bale) *19704*
R	*Kalanchoe stenosiphon* Britten *19704*	
	R	*19704* Ethiopia (West Eritrea, Tigray Upland) *19704*
R	*Kalanchoe viguieri* Raym.-Hamet & H. Perrier *10368*	
	R	*10368* Madagascar *10368*
E	*Monanthes adenoscepes* Svent. *20750*	
	E	*20750* Spain - Canary Is. *20750*
R	*Monanthes amydros* Svent.	
	R	Spain - Canary Is.
V	*Monanthes anagensis* Praeger	
	V	*20750* Spain - Canary Is. *20750*
E	*Monanthes dasyphylla* Svent.	
	E	Spain - Canary Is.
R	*Monanthes lowei* (Paiva) D. Bramwell in press	
	R	Portugal - Salvage Is.
V	*Monanthes minima* Bolle *20750*	
	V	*20750* Spain - Canary Is. *20750*
R	*Monanthes muralis* (Webb ex Bolle) Christ	
	R	Spain - Canary Is.
E	*Monanthes niphophila* Svent. *17530*	
	E	*20750* Spain - Canary Is. *20750*
R	*Monanthes pallens* Webb ex Christ	
	R	Spain - Canary Is.
R	*Monanthes polyphylla* Haw.	
	R	Spain - Canary Is.
R	*Monanthes silensis* (Praeger) Svent.	
	R	Spain - Canary Is.
E	*Monanthes wildpretii* *17891*	
	E	*20750* Spain - Canary Is. *17891*
R	*Orostachys iwarenge* Makino var. *boehmeri* Ohwi *10572*	
	R	*10572* Japan *10572*

I	*Rosularia aizoon* (Fenzl) A. Berger *5942*	
	I	*5942* Armenia *5942*
R	*Rosularia davisii* Muirhead *12840*	
	R	*12840* Turkey *12840*
R	*Rosularia haussknechtii* Boiss. & Reuter *12840*	
	R	*12840* Turkey *12840*
E	*Rosularia semiensis* (A. Rich) Ohba *19704*	
	E	*19704* Ethiopia (Gonder) *19704*
R	*Rosularia serpentinica* (Werdermann) Muirhead *12840*	
	R	*12840* Turkey *12840*
E	*Sedella leiocarpa* H.K. Sharsmith *20850*	
	E	*20850* U.S. - California *20850*
R	*Sedella pentandra* H.K. Sharsmith *20850*	
	I	*20850* U.S. - California *20850*
R	*Sedella pumila* (Benth.) Britt. & Rose *20850*	
	I	*20850* U.S. - California *20850*
V	*Sedum albomarginatum* Clausen *20850*	
	V	*20850* U.S. - California *20850*
E	*Sedum baleensis* M. Gilbert *19704*	
	E	*19704* Ethiopia (Bale) *19704*
R	*Sedum barcense* Maire & M. Weiller	
	R	Libya
V	*Sedum boninense* Tuy. *8038*	
	V	*19134* Japan - Ogasawara-shoto *8038*
V	*Sedum borissovae* Balk. *20171*	
	V	former European USSR
R	*Sedum borschii* (Clausen) Clausen *20850*	
	V	*20850* U.S. - Idaho *20850*
	I	*20850* U.S. - Montana *20850*
	I	*20850* U.S. - Oregon *20850*
	I	*20850* U.S. - Washington *20850*
R	*Sedum bracteatum* Viv.	
	R	Libya
R	*Sedum brissemoretii* Raymond-Hamet *17891*	
	R	Portugal - Madeira *17891*
R	*Sedum campanulatum* (Willk.) Fern.Gonz. & Cantó *15846, 20171*	
	R	*15846* Spain *15846*
R	*Sedum caroli-henrici* Kit Tan *12840*	
	R	*12840* Turkey *12840*
R	*Sedum cilicicum* Kit Tan & Vural *12840*	
	R	*12840* Turkey *12840*
R	*Sedum cyprium* A.K. Jackson & Turrill *14230*	
	R	*19164* Cyprus (Troodos) *14230*
R	*Sedum cyrenaicum* Brullo & Furnari	
	R	Libya
E	*Sedum drymarioides* Hance var. *toyamae* Hara *10572*	
	E	*10572* Japan *10572*
I	*Sedum duthie* Frod.	
	I	India - Uttar Pradesh (Kumaun)
V	*Sedum epidendron* A. Rich. *19704*	
	V	*19704* Ethiopia (Gonder, Gojam, Shewa Upland, Arsi.) *19704*
R	*Sedum farinosum* Lowe	
	R	Portugal - Madeira
I	*Sedum frutescens* Rose *19850*	
	I	*19850* Mexico *19850*
R	*Sedum gattefossei* Battand.	

R		Morocco

V   *Sedum glomerifolium* M. Gilbert *19704*
     V   *19704*   Ethiopia (Bale) *19704*

V   *Sedum havardii* Rose *20850*
     V   *20850*   U.S. - Texas *20850*

R   *Sedum hewittii* Chamb. *12840*
     R   *12840*   Turkey *12840*

R   *Sedum hierapetrae* Rech.f. *20171*
     R   *20731*   Greece - Crete *20731*

R   *Sedum hillebrandtii* Fenzl *2050, 20171*
     E   *2050*   Czech Republic *2050*
     R   *20686*   Hungary *20686*

R   *Sedum hispanicum* L. var. *planifolium*
     Chamb. *12840*
     R   *12840*   Turkey *12840*

E   *Sedum integrifolium* (Raf.) Nels. ssp. *leedyi*
     (Rosendahl & Moore) Clausen *20850, 14774*
     E   *20850*   U.S. - Minnesota (Fillmore & Olmsted Co.) *20850*
     E   *20850*   U.S. - New York (Yates County) *20850*

R   *Sedum kostovii* Stef. *5204, 20171*
     R   *5204*   Bulgaria (south) *5204*

V   *Sedum lagascae* Pau *20171*
     V   Spain

R   *Sedum lancerottense* R.P. Murray *20750*
     R   *20750*   Spain - Canary Is. *20750*

E   *Sedum laxum* (Britton) A. Berger ssp. *eastwoodiae*
     (Britt.) Clausen *20850*
     E   *20850*   U.S. - California *20850*

R   *Sedum laxum* (Britton) A. Berger ssp. *flavidum*
     Denton *20850*
     R   *20850*   U.S. - California *20850*

R   *Sedum laxum* (Britton) A. Berger ssp. *heckneri*
     (M.E. Peck) Clausen *20850*
     V   *20850*   U.S. - California *20850*
     R   *20850*   U.S. - Oregon *20850*

R   *Sedum maurum* Humbert & Maire
     R   Morocco

R   *Sedum microstachyum* (Kotschy) Boiss. *14230*
     R   *19164*   Cyprus (Troodos, Chionistra) *14230*

E   *Sedum mooneyi* M. Gilbert *19704*
     E   *19704*   Ethiopia (Arsi, Bale.) *19704*

E   *Sedum moranii* Clausen *20850*
     E   *20850*   U.S. - Oregon *20850*

V   *Sedum nevii* Gray *20850*
     V   *20850*   U.S. - Alabama *20850*
     E   *20850*   U.S. - Georgia *20850*
     I   *20850*   U.S. - North Carolina *20850*
     E   *20850*   U.S. - Tennessee *20850*

E   *Sedum nudum* Aiton ssp. *lancerottense* (Murray) A.
     Hansen & Sunding
     E   Spain - Canary Is.

R   *Sedum oblanceolatum* Clausen *20850*
     E   *20850*   U.S. - California *20850*
     V   *20850*   U.S. - Oregon *20850*

E   *Sedum obtusatum* A. Gray ssp. *paradisum*
     Denton *20850*
     E   *20850*   U.S. - California *20850*

R   *Sedum platyphyllum* Alexander *19850*
     R   *19850*   Mexico *19850*

Ex   *Sedum polystriatum* R.T. Clausen *12840*
     Ex   *12840*   Turkey *12840*

R   *Sedum pruinatum* Link ex Brot. *19174, 20171*
     R   *19174*   Portugal *19174*

R   *Sedum pusillum* Michx. *20850*
     I   *20850*   U.S. - Alabama *20850*
     R   *20850*   U.S. - Georgia *20850*
     E   *20850*   U.S. - North Carolina *20850*
     V   *20850*   U.S. - South Carolina *20850*

R   *Sedum radiatum* Clausen ssp. *depauperatum*
     Clausen *20850*
     I   *20850*   U.S. - California *20850*
     R   *20850*   U.S. - Oregon *20850*

E   *Sedum satsumense* Hatus. *10572*
     E   *10572*   Japan *10572*

R   *Sedum sekiteiense* Yamomoto *20511*
     R   *20511*   Taiwan *20511*

R   *Sedum serpentini* Janch. *20178, 20171*
     R   *20178*   Albania *20178*
     R   *21091*   Bosnia & Herzegovina *21091*
     R   Greece *20178*

R   *Sedum sikokianum* Maxim. *10572*
     R   *10572*   Japan *10572*

R   *Sedum sorgerae* Kit Tan & Chamberlain *12840*
     R   *12840*   Turkey *12840*

E   *Sedum suaveolens* Kimnach *9019*
     E   *11119*   Mexico - Durango *9019*

R   *Sedum torulosum* R.T. Clausen *19850*
     R   *19850*   Mexico *19850*

V   *Sedum tosaense* Makino *10572*
     V   *10572*   Japan *10572*

R   *Sedum tymphaeum* *20171*
     R   Greece

R   *Sedum wilczekianum* Font Quer
     R   Morocco

R   *Sedum willkommianum* R.Fern. *20171*
     R   *8322*   Portugal *8322*

R   *Sempervivum andreanum* Wale *20171*
     R   Spain

I   *Sempervivum arboreum* L. *20171*
     I   Morocco

R   *Sempervivum armenum* Boiss. & Huet var. *insigne*
     Muirhead *12840*
     R   *12840*   Turkey *12840*

R   *Sempervivum ballsii* Wale *20171*
     R   Greece

R   *Sempervivum brevipetalum* Kit Tan & Sorger *12840*
     R   *12840*   Turkey *12840*

R   *Sempervivum dolomiticum* Facchini *18264, 20171*
     R   *18264*   Italy *18264*

R   *Sempervivum furseorum* Muirhead *12840*
     R   *12840*   Turkey *12840*

R   *Sempervivum gillianii* Muirhead *12840*
     R   *12840*   Turkey *12840*

R   *Sempervivum giuseppii* Wale *20171*
     R   Spain

R   *Sempervivum glabrifolium* Boiss. *12840*
     R   *12840*   Turkey *12840*

R   *Sempervivum globiferum* L. ssp. *aghricum* Kit Tan &
     Sorger *12840*

R	12840 Turkey *12840*	

R **Sempervivum ispartae** Muirhead *12840*
> R   12840 Turkey *12840*

V **Sempervivum juvanii** Strgar *13662, 20171*
> V   13662 Slovenia (eastern) *13662*

R **Sempervivum kindingeri** Adamovic *20171*
> R   Greece
> R   (former) Yugoslavia

R **Sempervivum kosaninii** Praeger *20171*
> R   (former) Yugoslavia

R **Sempervivum macedonicum** Praeger *20171*
> R   (former) Yugoslavia

R **Sempervivum minus** Turrill s.l. *12840*
> R   12840 Turkey *12840*

V **Sempervivum montanum** L. ssp. *carpaticum* Wettst. ex Hayek *8000, 20171*
> V   19751 Poland *19751*
> V   19321 Slovakia *19321*

R **Sempervivum octopodes** Turrill *20171*
> R   (former) Yugoslavia

R **Sempervivum pisidicum** H. Pesmen & A. Guner *12840*
> R   12840 Turkey *12840*

R **Sempervivum pittonii** Schott, Nyman & Kotschy *20171*
> R   Austria

R **Sempervivum staintonii** Muirhead *12840*
> R   12840 Turkey *12840*

R **Sempervivum thompsonianum** Wale *20171*
> R   (former) Yugoslavia

Ex **Tacitus bellus** Moran & Meyran *9114*
> Ex   9114 Mexico - Chihuahua *9114*

R **Tylecodon albiflorus** Bruyns *20604*
> R   20604 South Africa - Cape Province *20604*

R **Tylecodon atropurpureus** Bruyns *20604*
> R   20604 South Africa - Cape Province *20604*

R **Tylecodon bayeri** Van Jaarsv. *20604*
> R   20604 South Africa - Cape Province *20604*

R **Tylecodon boddleyae** Van Jaarsv. *20604*
> R   20604 South Africa - Cape Province *20604*

R **Tylecodon decipiens** Toelken *20604*
> R   20604 South Africa - Cape Province *20604*

R **Tylecodon ellaphieae** Van Jaarsv. *20604*
> R   20604 South Africa - Cape Province *20604*

V **Tylecodon fragilis** (R.A.Dyer) Toelken *20604*
> V   20604 South Africa - Cape Province *20604*

R **Tylecodon hirtifolius** (W.F.Barker) Toelken *20604*
> R   20604 South Africa - Cape Province *20604*

R **Tylecodon kritzingeri** Van Jaarsv. *20604*
> R   20604 South Africa - Cape Province *20604*

E **Tylecodon singularis** (R.A.Dyer) Toelken *20604*
> E   20604 Namibia *20604*
> E   20604 South Africa - Cape Province *20604*

R **Tylecodon suffultus** Bruyns ex Toelken *20604*
> R   20604 South Africa - Cape Province *20604*

R **Tylecodon sulphureus** (Toelken) Toelken *20604*
> R   20604 South Africa - Cape Province *20604*

R **Tylecodon tenuis** (Toelken) Bruyns *20604*
> R   20604 South Africa - Cape Province *20604*

R **Tylecodon torulosus** Toelken *20604*
> R   20604 South Africa - Cape Province *20604*

Crossosomataceae

Number of genera:	3
Number of species:	10
Recorded threatened species:	4 (40%)

Arid western United States and adjacent Mexico.

R **Apacheria chiricahuensis** C.T. Mason *20850*
> V   20850 U.S. - Arizona *20850*
> R   20850 U.S. - New Mexico *20850*

E **Glossopetalon clokeyi** (Ensign) St. John *20850*
> V   20850 U.S. - Nevada *20850*

R **Glossopetalon spinescens** var. *meionandrum* (Koehne) Trel. *20850*
> I   20850 U.S. - Colorado *20850*
> R   20850 U.S. - Utah *20850*
> E   20850 U.S. - Wyoming *20850*

E **Glossopetalon texense** (Ensign) St. John *20850*
> E   20850 U.S. - Texas *20850*

Cruciferae

Number of genera:	350
Number of species:	3,000
Recorded threatened species:	747 (24%)

Cool temperate or warm temperate Northern or Southern Hemisphere.

R **Aethionema carlsbergii** Strid & Papan. *20171*
> R   Greece (Mt Taygetos)

V **Aethionema cordatum** (Desf.) Boiss. *20171*
> V   Greece

R **Aethionema cordatum** (Desf.) ssp. *pichleri* (Boiss.) Hardvig & Strid *12840*
> R   12840 Turkey *12840*

R **Aethionema demirizii** Davis & Hedge *12840*
> R   12840 Turkey *12840*

R **Aethionema froedinii** Rech. fil. *12840*
> R   12840 Turkey *12840*

R **Aethionema huber-morathli** Davis & Hedge *12840*
> R   12840 Turkey *12840*

R **Aethionema lepidioides** Hub.-Mor. *12840*
> R   12840 Turkey *12840*

R **Aethionema lycium** I.A. Anderson ex al. *12840*
> R   12840 Turkey *12840*

R **Aethionema marashicum** Davis *12840*
> R   12840 Turkey *12840*

R **Aethionema munzurense** Davis & Yildirimli *12840*
> R   12840 Turkey *12840*

R **Aethionema orbiculatum** (Boiss.) Hayek *20171*
> R   Greece

R **Aethionema papillosum** Davis *12840*
> R   12840 Turkey *12840*

R **Aethionema retsina** Phitos & Snogerup *20171*
> R   20731 Greece (west Aegean) *20731*

R **Aethionema speciosum** Boiss. & Huet ssp. *compactum* Hardvig & Strid *12840*
> R   12840 Turkey *12840*

R **Aethionema subulatum** (Boiss. & Heldr.) Boiss. *12840*
> R   12840 Turkey *12840*

V **Aethionema thesiifolium** Boiss. & Heldr. *12840*
> V   12840 Turkey *12840*

V **Aethionema thomasianum** J.Gay *18264, 20171*
  E   *20528* France *20528*
  V   *18264* Italy (Aosta Valley) *18264*

V **Alyssum akamasicum** B.L. Burtt *14230*
  V   *20710* Cyprus (Akamas peninsula) *14230*

R **Alyssum anatolicum** Hausskn. ex Nyar *12840*
  R   *12840* Turkey *12840*

R **Alyssum antiatlanticum** Emberger & Maire
  R   Morocco

R **Alyssum argyrophyllum** Schott & Kotschy *12840*
  R   *12840* Turkey *12840*

R **Alyssum artvinense** Busch *12840*
  R   *12840* Turkey *12840*

R **Alyssum aurantiacum** Boiss. *12840*
  R   *12840* Turkey *12840*

R **Alyssum bornmuelleri** Hausskn. ex Degen *12840*
  R   *12840* Turkey *12840*

R **Alyssum caespitosum** Baumg. *12840*
  R   *12840* Turkey *12840*

R **Alyssum calycocarpum** Rupr. *20171*
  R   former European USSR

V **Alyssum caricum** Dudley & Hub.-Mor. *12840*
  V   *12840* Turkey *12840*

R **Alyssum chondrogynum** B.L. Burtt *14230*
  R   *19164* Cyprus *14230*

R **Alyssum cilicicum** Boiss. & Bal. *12840*
  R   *12840* Turkey *12840*

I **Alyssum crenulatum** Boiss. *12840*
  I   *12840* Turkey *12840*

R **Alyssum davisianum** Dudley *12840*
  R   *12840* Turkey *12840*

R **Alyssum densistellatum** T.R.Dudley *20171*
  R   Greece

R **Alyssum discolor** Dudley & Hub.-Mor. *12840*
  R   *12840* Turkey *12840*

R **Alyssum doerfleri** Degen *20171*
  R   Greece
  R   (former) Yugoslavia

I **Alyssum dubertretii** Gomb *12840*
  I   *12840* Turkey *12840*

R **Alyssum eriophyllum** Boiss. & Hausskn. *12840*
  R   *12840* Turkey *12840*

R **Alyssum euboeum** Halácsy *20171*
  R   Greece

R **Alyssum fallacinum** Hausskn. *20171*
  R   Greece

E **Alyssum fastigiatum** Heywood *8000, 20171*
  E   *14155* Spain (Sierra Nevada) *8000*

R **Alyssum flahaultianum** Emberger
  R   Morocco

V **Alyssum fragillimum** (Baldacci) Rech.f. *20171*
  V   *20730* Greece - Crete *19121*

R **Alyssum fulvescens** Sibth. & Sm. var. *stellatocarpum*
     Hub.-Mor. *12840*
  R   *12840* Turkey *12840*

R **Alyssum giosnanum** Nyar *12840*
  R   *12840* Turkey *12840*

R **Alyssum haussknechtii** Boiss. *12840*

  R   *12840* Turkey *12840*

R **Alyssum heldreichii** Hausskn. *20171*
  R   Greece

R **Alyssum huber-morathii** Dudley *12840*
  R   *12840* Turkey *12840*

R **Alyssum idaeum** Boiss. & Heldr. *20171*
  R   *20730* Greece - Crete *19121*

V **Alyssum lassiticum** Halácsy *20171*
  V   *20730* Greece - Crete *19121*

R **Alyssum lepidoto-stellatum** (Hausskn. & Bornm.)
     Dudley *12840*
  R   *12840* Turkey *12840*

R **Alyssum lesbiacum** (Candargy) Rech.f.
  R   Greece

R **Alyssum leucadeum** Guss. *8000, 20171*
  V   Italy *8000*
  R   (former) Yugoslavia *8000*

R **Alyssum lycaonicum** (Schulz) Dudley *12840*
  R   *12840* Turkey *12840*

R **Alyssum macropodum** Boiss. & Bal. var. *heterotrichum*
     Hub.-Mor. *12840*
  R   *12840* Turkey *12840*

R **Alyssum markgrafii** O.E.Schulz *20171*
  R   *20178* Albania *20178*
  R   (former) Yugoslavia

R **Alyssum moellendorfianum** Asch. ex Beck *20171*
  E   *21091* Bosnia & Herzegovina *20852*
  R   (former) Yugoslavia

R **Alyssum montanum** L. ssp. *brymii*
     Dostál *19839*
  R   *20686* Hungary *20686*
  I   *19751* Poland *19751*
  V   *19321* Slovakia *19321*

R **Alyssum nebrodense** Tineo ssp.
     nebrodense *18264, 20171*
  R   *19164* Greece *19164*
  R   *18264* Italy - Sicily *18264*

I **Alyssum niveum** Dudley *12840*
  I   *12840* Turkey *12840*

V **Alyssum pinifolium** (Nyar) Dudley *12840*
  V   *12840* Turkey *12840*

V **Alyssum pintodasilvae** T.R. Dudley *17891*
  V   *20076* Portugal *20076*

R **Alyssum praecox** Boiss. & Bal. var. *albiflorum*
     Dudley *12840*
  R   *12840* Turkey *12840*

R **Alyssum pterocarpum** Dudley *12840*
  R   *12840* Turkey *12840*

R **Alyssum purpureum** Lag. & Rodr. *11496*
  R   *11496* Spain (Granada & Sierra Nevada) *11496*

V **Alyssum robertianum** Bernard ex Gren. & Godr. *15080,*
     20171
  V   *20528* France - Corsica *15080*
  V   *20805* Italy - Sardinia *19164*

R **Alyssum smolikanum** Nyár. *20171*
  R   *20178* Albania *20178*
  R   Greece

V **Alyssum sphacioticum** Boiss. & Heldr. *20171*
  V   *20730* Greece - Crete *19121*

R **Alyssum taygeteum** Heldr. *20171*

	R		Greece	
R	*Alyssum tenium* Halácsy *20171*			
	R		Greece	
R	*Alyssum tetrastemon* Boiss. *12840*			
	R	*12840*	Turkey *12840*	
R	*Alyssum thymops* (Hub.-Mor. & Reese) Dudley *12840*			
	R	*12840*	Turkey *12840*	
R	*Alyssum trapeziforme* Bornm. ex Nyar *12840*			
	R	*12840*	Turkey *12840*	
R	*Alyssum trichocarpum* Dudley & Hub.-Mor. *12840*			
	R	*12840*	Turkey *12840*	
R	*Alyssum wulfenianum* Bernh. *20171*			
	R		Austria	
	R		(former) Yugoslavia	
R	*Anchonium elichrysifolium* (DC.) Boiss. ssp. *canescens* (Hausskn. & Bornm.) Coode & Cullen *12840*			
	R	*12840*	Turkey *12840*	
R	*Anchonium elichrysifolium* (DC.) Boiss. ssp. *glandulosum* Coode & Cullen *12840*			
	R	*12840*	Turkey *12840*	
R	*Anchonium elichrysifolium* (DC.) Boiss. ssp. *villosum* Cullen & Coode *12840*			
	R	*12840*	Turkey *12840*	
R	*Aphragmus eschscholtzianus* Andrz. ex DC. *20850, 1034*			
	E	*20850*	Canada - British Columbia *20850*	
	E	*20850*	Canada - Yukon Territory *20850*	
	V	*20850*	U.S. - Alaska *20850*	
R	*Arabidopsis bursifolia* (DC.) Botsch. s.str. var. *beringensis* Jurtz. *20085, 21309*			
	R	*20085*	Russia (E.Europe) - North *20085*	
V	*Arabidopsis kneuckeri* (Bornm.) O. Schulz			
	V		Egypt	
I	*Arabidopsis tschuktschorum* (Jurtzev) Jurtzev *5942, 21309*			
	I	*5942*	Russia (Far East) - Magadan (north) *5942*	
R	*Arabis abietina* Bornm. *12840*			
	R	*12840*	Turkey *12840*	
R	*Arabis androsacea* Fenzl. *12840*			
	R	*12840*	Turkey *12840*	
R	*Arabis aubrietioides* Boiss. *12840*			
	R	*12840*	Turkey *12840*	
V	*Arabis beckwithii* S.Watson *20850*			
	I	*20850*	U.S. - Nevada *20850*	
		20850	U.S. - Utah *20850*	
V	*Arabis bodiensis* Rollins *20850*			
	E	*20850*	U.S. - California *20850*	
	V	*20850*	U.S. - Nevada *20850*	
E	*Arabis breweri* S.Watson var. *pecuniaria* Rollins *20850*			
	E	*20850*	U.S. - California *20850*	
R	*Arabis carduchorum* Boiss. *12840*			
	R	*12840*	Turkey *12840*	
R	*Arabis cebennensis* DC. *20171*			
	R		France (mountains in south)	
V	*Arabis constancei* Rollins *20850*			
	V	*20850*	U.S. - California *20850*	
R	*Arabis demissa* Rollins var. *languida* Rollins *20850*			
	I	*20850*	U.S. - Colorado *20850*	
	E	*20850*	U.S. - Montana *20850*	
	I	*20850*	U.S. - Nevada *20850*	
	V	*20850*	U.S. - Wyoming *20850*	
R	*Arabis dispar* M.E. Jones *20850*			
	R	*20850*	U.S. - California *20850*	
	V	*20850*	U.S. - Nevada *20850*	
R	*Arabis doumetii* Coss. *10487*			
	R	*14958*	Algeria *10487*	
R	*Arabis drabiformis* Boiss. *12840*			
	R	*12840*	Turkey *12840*	
E	*Arabis falcatoria* Rollins *20850*			
	E	*20850*	U.S. - Nevada *20850*	
	E	*20850*	U.S. - Utah *20850*	
E	*Arabis falcifructa* Rollins *20850*			
	E	*20850*	U.S. - Nevada *20850*	
V	*Arabis fecunda* Rollins *20850*			
	V	*20850*	U.S. - Montana *20850*	
R	*Arabis fendleri* (S. Wats.) Greene var. *spatifolia* (Rydb.) Rollins *20850*			
	E	*20850*	U.S. - Colorado *20850*	
	I	*20850*	U.S. - New Mexico *20850*	
	I	*20850*	U.S. - Utah *20850*	
	V	*20850*	U.S. - Wyoming *20850*	
R	*Arabis ferdinandi-coburgi* Kellerer & Sünd. *5204, 20171*			
	R	*5204*	Bulgaria *5204*	
R	*Arabis fernaldiana* Rollins var. *fernaldiana* *20850*			
	V	*20850*	U.S. - Colorado *20850*	
	R	*20850*	U.S. - Nevada *20850*	
V	*Arabis fernaldiana* Rollins var. *stylosa* (S.Watson) Rollins *20850*			
	I	*20850*	U.S. - California *20850*	
	V	*20850*	U.S. - Nevada *20850*	
Ex/E	*Arabis fructicosa* A. Nels. *20850, 14662*			
	I	*20850*	U.S. - Montana *20850*	
	Ex/E	*20850*	U.S. - Wyoming *20850*	
V	*Arabis georgiana* Harper *20850*			
	V	*20850*	U.S. - Alabama *20850*	
	E	*20850*	U.S. - Georgia *20850*	
R	*Arabis glaucovalvula* M.E. Jones *20850*			
	I	*20850*	U.S. - California *20850*	
	I	*20850*	U.S. - Nevada *20850*	
R	*Arabis graellsiformis* Hedge *12840*			
	R	*12840*	Turkey *12840*	
R	*Arabis gunnisoniana* Rollins *20850*			
	I	*20850*	U.S. - Colorado *20850*	
Ex/E	*Arabis hastatula* Greene *20850*			
	I	*20850*	U.S. - Oregon *20850*	
E	*Arabis hoffmannii* (Munz) Rollins *20850*			
	E	*20850*	U.S. - California *20850*	
R	*Arabis inyoensis* Rollins *20850*			
	I	*20850*	U.S. - California *20850*	
	I	*20850*	U.S. - Nevada *20850*	
V	*Arabis johnstonii* Munz *20850*			
	V	*20850*	U.S. - California *20850*	
E	*Arabis kennedyae* Meikle *14230*			
	E	*19164*	Cyprus (Troodos) *14230*	
E	*Arabis koehleri* Howell var. *koehleri* *20850*			
	E	*20850*	U.S. - Oregon *20850*	
R	*Arabis koehleri* Howell var. *stipitata* Rollins *20850*			

E		20850 U.S. - California *20850*	
R		20850 U.S. - Oregon *20850*	

E   *Arabis lasiocarpa* Rollins *20850*
    I   20850 U.S. - Idaho *20850*
    E   20850 U.S. - Utah *20850*

R   *Arabis lusitanica* Boiss. *20171*
    R   8322 Portugal *8322*

V   *Arabis macdonaldiana* Eastw. *20850*
    V   20850 U.S. - California *20850*
    E   20850 U.S. - Oregon *20850*

E   *Arabis macloviana* (Urv.) Hook.f.
    E   Falkland Is.

V   *Arabis modesta* Rollins *20850*
    V   20850 U.S. - California *20850*
    V   20850 U.S. - Oregon *20850*

E   *Arabis ophira* Rollins *20850*
    E   20850 U.S. - Nevada *20850*

V   *Arabis oxylobula* Greene *20850*
    I   20850 U.S. - Colorado *20850*

V   *Arabis parishii* S.Watson *20850*
    V   20850 U.S. - California *20850*

R   *Arabis pedemontana* Boiss. *20171*
    R   20804 Italy *20804*

R   *Arabis pendulina* Greene var. *russeola* (Rollins)
        Rollins *20850*
    I   20850 U.S. - Colorado *20850*
    I   20850 U.S. - Utah *20850*
    R   20850 U.S. - Wyoming *20850*

E   *Arabis perstellata* E.L. Braun *20850*
    I   20850 U.S. - Alabama *20850*
    V   20850 U.S. - Kentucky *20850*
    E   20850 U.S. - Tennessee *20850*

E   *Arabis perstellata* E.Braun var. *ampla*
        Rollins *20850*
    E   20850 U.S. - Tennessee *20850*

E   *Arabis perstellata* E.Braun var.
        perstellata *20850*
    I   20850 U.S. - Alabama *20850*
    V   20850 U.S. - Kentucky *20850*

E   *Arabis pinzliae* Rollins *20850*
    E   20850 U.S. - California *20850*
    E   20850 U.S. - Nevada *20850*

E   *Arabis pusilla* Rollins *20850*
    E   20850 U.S. - Wyoming *20850*

R   *Arabis rigidissima* Rollins *20850*
    E   20850 U.S. - California *20850*
    V   20850 U.S. - Nevada *20850*

E   *Arabis rigidissima* Rollins var. *demota*
        Rollins *20850*
    E   20850 U.S. - California *20850*
    E   20850 U.S. - Nevada *20850*

E   *Arabis rigidissima* Rollins var.
        rigidissima *20850*
    E   20850 U.S. - California *20850*

V   *Arabis sadina* (Samp.) Cout. *8000, 20171*
    V   20076 Portugal (central) *8000*

V   *Arabis schistacea* Rollins *20850*
    I   20850 U.S. - Nevada *20850*
    E   20850 U.S. - Utah *20850*

V   *Arabis serotina* Steele *20850*
    V   20850 U.S. - Virginia *20850*
    E   20850 U.S. - West Virginia *20850*

R   *Arabis shockleyi* Munz *20850*
    I   20850 U.S. - California *20850*
    R   20850 U.S. - Nevada *20850*
    R   20850 U.S. - Utah *20850*

R   *Arabis sparsiflora* Nutt. var. *atrorubens* (Suksdorf
        ex Greene) Rollins *20850*
    I   20850 U.S. - Washington *20850*

R   *Arabis stenocarpa* Boiss. & Reuter
    R   Spain

I   *Arabis stewartiana* Jafri
    I   India (W. Himalaya)

R   *Arabis subflava* B.M.G.Jones *20171*
    R   Greece
    R   (former) Yugoslavia

E   *Arabis suffrutescens* S.Watson var. *horizontalis*
        (Greene) Rollins *20850*
    I   20850 U.S. - California *20850*
    E   20850 U.S. - Oregon *20850*

E   *Arabis tanakana* Makino *10572*
    E   10572 Japan *10572*

I   *Arabis tenuirostris* O. Schulz
    I   India - Jammu & Kashmir

E   *Arabis tiehmii* Rollins *20850*
    E   20850 U.S. - California *20850*
    E   20850 U.S. - Nevada *20850*

V   *Arabis tricornuta* Rollins *20850*
    V   20850 U.S. - Arizona *20850*

R   *Arabis werneri* Emberger & Maire
    R   Morocco

R   *Arabis williamsii* Rollins *20850*
    I   20850 U.S. - Idaho *20850*
    I   20850 U.S. - Montana *20850*
    R   20850 U.S. - Wyoming *20850*

V   *Arabis williamsii* Rollins var. *saximontana*
        (Rollins) Rollins *20850*
    I   20850 U.S. - Idaho *20850*
    I   20850 U.S. - Montana *20850*
    V   20850 U.S. - Wyoming *20850*

R   *Arabis williamsii* Rollins var.
        williamsii *20850*
    R   20850 U.S. - Wyoming *20850*

R   *Aubrieta anamasica* H. Pesmen & A. Guner *12840*
    R   12840 Turkey *12840*

R   *Aubrieta erubescens* Griseb. *20171*
    R   Greece

R   *Aubrieta olympica* Boiss. *12840*
    R   12840 Turkey *12840*

I   *Aubrieta scyria* Halácsy *20171*
    I   5409 Greece (Skiros) *5409*

R   *Aubrieta thessala* Boissieu *20171*
    R   Greece

R   *Aurinia leucadea* (Guss.) K.Koch *18264, 20171*
    R   18264 Italy (Puglia) *18264*
    R   20804 (former) Yugoslavia *8000*

E   *Ballantinia antipoda* (F.Muell.) E.Shaw *20681*
    Ex   20681 Australia - Tasmania *20681*
    E   20681 Australia - Victoria *20681*

R   *Barbarea auriculata* Hausskn. ex Bornm. s.l. *12840*
    R   12840 Turkey *12840*

E   *Barbarea australis* Hook.f. *20681*
    E   20681 Australia - Tasmania *20681*

R **Barbarea bosniaca** Murb. *20171*
  R   *21091* Bosnia & Herzegovina *21091*
  R   (former) Yugoslavia

R **Barbarea conferta** Boiss. & Heldr. *20171*
  R   Greece

I **Barbarea lepuznica** Nyár. *17823, 20171*
  I   *19949* Romania *20631*

R **Barbarea lutea** Cullen & Coode *12840*
  R   *12840* Turkey *12840*

R **Barbarea minor** C. Koch var. *anfiactroza* Hartvig & Strid *12840*
  R   *12840* Turkey *12840*

R **Barbarea othocera** Ledeb. var. *formosana* Kitamura *20511*
  R   *20511* Taiwan *20511*

R **Barbarea platycarpa** Hausskn. ex Bornm. *12840*
  R   *12840* Turkey *12840*

V **Barbarea sicula** C.Presl *8000, 20171*
  V   Greece
  V   Italy
  E   *20738* Italy - Sicily *19164*

R **Barbarea taiwaniana** Ohwi *20511*
  R   *20511* Taiwan *20511*

R **Berteroa gintlii** Rohl. *20171*
  R   (former) Yugoslavia

V **Biscutella arvernensis** Jord. *20171*
  V   *20528* France (Massif Central) *20528*

R **Biscutella brevicaulis** Jord. *20171*
  R   *20528* France (French Alps) *20528*

E **Biscutella divionensis** Jord. *20171*
  E   *20528* France (east-central near Dijon) *20528*

V **Biscutella elbensis** Chrtek
  V   Egypt

R **Biscutella foliosa** Mach.-Laur. *20171*
  R   Spain

R **Biscutella gredensis** Guinea *20171*
  R   Spain

V **Biscutella incana** Ten. *18264, 20171*
  V   *18264* Italy (Campania) *18264*

V **Biscutella lamottii** Jord. *20171*
  V   *20528* France (Monts d'Auvergne) *20528*

V **Biscutella neustriaca** Bonnet *8000, 20171*
  V   *20528* France (Normandy) *20528*

V **Biscutella rotgesii** Foucaud *20171*
  V   *19174* France - Corsica *12844*

R **Biscutella sclerocarpa** Revel *20171*
  R   France (south)

V **Biscutella variegata** Boiss. & Reut. *20171*
  V   Spain

V **Biscutella vincentina** (Samp.) Rothm. ex Guinea *8000, 20171*
  V   *20076* Portugal (south west - Cabo de S. Vicente) *8000*

R **Boleum asperum** (Pers.) Desv. *8000, 20171*
  R   *20874* Spain (Ebro basin) *8000*

V **Boreava aptera** Boiss. & Heldr. *12840*
  V   *12840* Turkey *12840*

R **Bornmuellera cappadocica** (DC.) Cullen & Dudley *12840*
  R   *12840* Turkey *12840*

R **Bornmuellera dieckii** Degen *20171*
  R   (former) Yugoslavia

R **Bornmuellera glabrescens** (Boiss. & Bal.) Cullen & Dudley *12840*
  R   *12840* Turkey *12840*

I **Borodinia baicalensis** N. Busch. *5942*
  I   *5942* Russia (Siberia) - Buryatiya *5942*
  I   *5942* Russia (Siberia) - Chita *5942*
  I   *5942* Russia (Siberia) - Irkutsk *5942*

R **Botschantzevia karatavica** (Lipsch. & Pavlov) Nabiev
  R   former USSR *6930*

R **Brassica balearica** Pers. *11496*
  R   *11496* Spain - Balearic Is. *11496*

E **Brassica bourgeaui** (Webb ex Christ) Kuntze
  E   Spain - Canary Is.

R **Brassica cadmea** Heldr. ex O.E. Schulz *20171*
  R   Greece

R **Brassica desnottesii** Emberger & Maire
  R   Morocco

R **Brassica dimorpha** Coss. & Durieu *10487*
  R   *14958* Algeria *10487*

V **Brassica glabrescens** Poldini *17891, 20171*
  V   *18264* Italy (Friuli-Venezia Giulia) *17891*

V **Brassica hilarionis** Post *14230*
  V   *19164* Cyprus *14230*

R **Brassica integrifolia** (West) O.E. Schulz *7926*
  R   Côte d'Ivoire (Man) *7926*

E **Brassica macrocarpa** Guss. *8000, 20171*
  E   *18264* Italy - Sicily (Isola Marettimo & Isola Favignana) *8000*

R **Brassica nivalis** Boiss. & Heldr. ssp. *jordanoffii* O. E. Schulz *8000, 20171*
  R   *5204* Bulgaria (south-west) *8000*

V **Brassica repanda** (Willd.) DC. ssp. *galissieri* (Giraudias) Heywood *20171*
  V   *20528* France (Pyrénées) *20528*

V **Brassica spinescens** Pomel *10487*
  V   *14958* Algeria *10487*

I **Brassica sylvestris** (L.) Mill. ssp. *taurica* Tzvelev *5942*
  I   *5942* Ukraine - Crimea *5942*

R **Brassica villosa** Biv. *20171*
  R   Italy - Sicily

V **Braya fernaldii** Abbe *20850, 14366*
  V   *20850* Canada - Newfoundland (Island) *20850*

E **Braya glabella** Richards. var. *prostata* *13967*
  E   *13967* Canada *13967*

E **Braya longii** Fern. *20850, 14366*
  E   *20850* Canada - Newfoundland (Island) *20850*

Ex/E **Braya pilosa** Hook. *20850, 14438*
  I   *20085* Russia (E.Europe) - North *20085*
  Ex *20850* Canada - Keewatin *20850*
  I   *20850* Canada - Yukon Territory *20850*

V **Cakile edentula** (Bigelow) Hook. ssp. *harperi* (Small) Rodman *20850*
  V   *20850* U.S. - Florida *20850*
  I   *20850* U.S. - Georgia *20850*
  I   *20850* U.S. - North Carolina *20850*
  I   *20850* U.S. - South Carolina *20850*

I **Camelina anomala** Boiss. & Hausskn. *12840*

I		*12840* Turkey *12840*
R	*Camelina stiefelhagenii* **Bornm.** *12840*	
	R	*12840* Turkey *12840*
V	*Capsella bursa-pastoris* (L.) **Medik. ssp.** *thracica*	
	(Velen.) **Stoj. & Stefanov** *19266, 20171*	
	V	*5204* Bulgaria (south) *19266*
V	*Cardamine arakiana* **Koidz.** *10572*	
	V	*10572* Japan *10572*
R	*Cardamine balnearia* **Standley & Steyerm.** *9004*	
	R	*9666* Guatemala *9004*
R	*Cardamine caldeirarum* **Guthnick** *20171*	
	R		Portugal - Azores
R	*Cardamine californica* **Greene var.**	
	californica *20850*	
	I	*20850* U.S. - California *20850*
V	*Cardamine clematitis* **Shuttlw. ex Gray** *20850*	
	I	*20850* U.S. - Alabama *20850*
	I	*20850* U.S. - Georgia *20850*
	V	*20850* U.S. - North Carolina *20850*
	I	*20850* U.S. - South Carolina *20850*
	V	*20850* U.S. - Tennessee *20850*
	V	*20850* U.S. - Virginia *20850*
R	*Cardamine constancei* **Detling** *20850*	
	R	*20850* U.S. - Idaho *20850*
V	*Cardamine cuneata* **Greene** *20850*	
	I	*20850* U.S. - California *20850*
R	*Cardamine eremita* **Standley & Steyerm.** *9004*	
	R	*9666* Guatemala *9004*
R	*Cardamine flagellifera* **O.E. Schulz** *20850*	
	I	*20850* U.S. - Georgia *20850*
	R	*20850* U.S. - North Carolina *20850*
	I	*20850* U.S. - South Carolina *20850*
	V	*20850* U.S. - Tennessee *20850*
	E	*20850* U.S. - Virginia *20850*
	E	*20850* U.S. - West Virginia *20850*
R	*Cardamine gemmata* **Greene** *20850*	
	V	*20850* U.S. - California *20850*
	V	*20850* U.S. - Oregon *20850*
	I	*20850* U.S. - Washington *20850*
R	*Cardamine jejuna* **Standley & Steyerm.** *9004*	
	R	*9666* Guatemala *9004*
R	*Cardamine kiusiana* **Hara** *10572*	
	R	*10572* Japan *10572*
E	*Cardamine kruesselii* **Johow** *19116*	
	E	*19125* Chile - Juan Fernandez Is. *19116*
R	*Cardamine longii* **Fern.** *20850*	
	E	*20850* U.S. - Delaware *20850*
	V	*20850* U.S. - Maine *20850*
	E	*20850* U.S. - Maryland *20850*
	E	*20850* U.S. - Massachusetts *20850*
	Ex/E	*20850* U.S. - New Hampshire *20850*
	Ex/E	*20850* U.S. - New Jersey *20850*
	V	*20850* U.S. - New York *20850*
	E	*20850* U.S. - North Carolina *20850*
	I	*20850* U.S. - Rhode Is. *20850*
	R	*20850* U.S. - Virginia *20850*
R	*Cardamine macrocarpa* **Brandeg.** *20883, 20850, 19002*	
	V	*20850* U.S. - Texas *20850*
	I	*20883* Mexico *20883*
V	*Cardamine macrocarpa* **Rollins var.** *texana*	
	Rollins *20850*	
	V	*20850* U.S. - Texas *20850*
E	*Cardamine micranthera* **Rollins** *20850*	
	E	*20850* U.S. - North Carolina *20850*

V	*Cardamine pattersonii* **Henderson** *20850*	
	V	*20850* U.S. - Oregon *20850*
R	*Cardamine reniformis* **Hayata** *20511*	
	R	*20511* Taiwan *20511*
R	*Cardamine rupicola* (O.E. Schulz) **C.L. Hitchc.** *20850*	
	R	*20850* U.S. - Montana *20850*
I	*Cardamine sphenophylla* **Jurtzev** *5942, 21309*	
	I	*5942* Russia (Far East) - Magadan (north) *5942*
R	*Cardamine trifida* (Lam. ex Poir.) **B.M.G.Jones** *20171*	
	R	former European USSR
R	*Cardamine tumensis* **Nakai** *10572*	
	R	*10572* Japan *10572*
R	*Cardamine yezoensis* **Maxim.** *10572*	
	R	*10572* Japan *10572*
E	*Caulanthus amplexicaulis* **S.Watson var.** *barbarae*	
	(J.T. Howell) **Munz** *20850*	
	E	*20850* U.S. - California *20850*
V	*Caulanthus barnebyi* **Rollins & P. Holmgren** *20850*	
	V	*20850* U.S. - Nevada *20850*
R	*Caulanthus coulteri* **S.Watson** *20850*	
	I	*20850* U.S. - California *20850*
V	*Caulanthus flavescens* (Hook.) **Payson** *20850*	
	I	*20850* U.S. - California *20850*
V	*Caulanthus glaucus* **S.Watson** *20850*	
	I	*20850* U.S. - California *20850*
	I	*20850* U.S. - Nevada *20850*
V	*Caulanthus hallii* **Payson** *20850*	
	I	*20850* U.S. - California *20850*
R	*Caulanthus inflatus* **S.Watson** *20850*	
	I	*20850* U.S. - California *20850*
E	*Caulanthus lemmonii* **S.Watson** *20850*	
	I	*20850* U.S. - California *20850*
R	*Caulanthus major* (M.E. Jones) **Payson** *20850*	
	I	*20850* U.S. - California *20850*
	I	*20850* U.S. - Nevada *20850*
	E	*20850* U.S. - Oregon *20850*
	I	*20850* U.S. - Utah *20850*
V	*Caulanthus simulans* **Payson** *20850*	
	V	*20850* U.S. - California *20850*
E	*Caulostramina jaegeri* (Rollins) **Rollins** *20850*	
	E	*20850* U.S. - California *20850*
R	*Cheesemania radicata* (Hook.f.) **O.Schulz** *20681*	
	R	*20681* Australia - Tasmania *20681*
V	*Chrysochamela draboides* **Woronow** *20171*	
	V	former European USSR
R	*Chrysochamela noeana* (Boiss.) **Boiss.** *12840*	
	R	*12840* Turkey *12840*
R	*Clypeola ciliata* **Boiss.** *12840*	
	R	*12840* Turkey *12840*
I	*Clypeola raddeana* **Albow** *12840*	
	I	*12840* Turkey *12840*
R	*Cochlearia amana* **Contandr. & Quezel** *12840*	
	R	*12840* Turkey *12840*
R	*Cochlearia aragonensis* **H.J.Coste & Soulié** *20171*	
	R	*11496* Spain *11496*
R	*Cochlearia formosana* **Hayata** *20511*	
	R	*20511* Taiwan *20511*
R	*Cochlearia micacea* **E.S.Marshall** *5387, 20171*	

	R	5387	United Kingdom (Perthshire, Angus & Ross) *19232*
Ex/E	*Cochlearia polonica* A.Fröhl. *19266, 20171*		
	Ex/E	20798	Poland (south, nr Olkusz) *7897*
E	*Cochlearia sessilifolia* Rollins *20850*		
	E	20850	U.S. - Alaska *20850*
R	*Cochlearia tatrae* Borbás *7897, 20171*		
	R	18216	Poland (Tatry Mts.) *7897*
	I	19321	Slovakia (Vysoké Tatry, Vel'ka Fatra & Nízke Tatry) *6951*
V	*Coincya leptocarpa* (Gonz.Albo) Greuter & Burdet *8001, 20171*		
	V	11496	Spain *11496*
E	*Coincya rupestris* Porta & Rigo ex Rouy *19266, 20171*		
	E	14155	Spain (Alcarat, Sierra de Alcarez) *11496*
E	*Coincya rupestris* Porta & Rigo ex Rouy ssp. *rupestris 20171*		
	E	20874	Spain (Sierra de Alcaraz) *20874*
R	*Coincya wrightii* (O.E.Schulz) Stace *19701, 20171*		
	R	5387	United Kingdom (south west - Lundy Island) *19232*
R	*Conringia grandiflora* Boiss. & Heldr. *12840*		
	R	12840	Turkey *12840*
E	*Coronopus navasii* Pau *8000, 20171*		
	E	19174	Spain (Sierra de Gádor) *8000*
E	*Crambe arborea* Webb ex Christ *14166*		
	E	19174	Spain - Canary Is. *17891*
R	*Crambe fruticosa* L.f.		
	R		Portugal - Madeira
V	*Crambe gigantea* (Ceball. & Ortuno) D. Bramwell *20750*		
	V	20750	Spain - Canary Is. *20750*
V	*Crambe gomeraea* Webb ex Christ		
	V	20750	Spain - Canary Is. *20750*
V	*Crambe laevigata* DC. ex Christ *14166*		
	V	20750	Spain - Canary Is. *17891*
V	*Crambe microcarpa* Santos *20750*		
	V	20750	Spain - Canary Is. *20750*
R	*Crambe pritzelii* Bolle *20750*		
	R	20750	Spain - Canary Is. *20750*
R	*Crambe scaberrima* Webb ex D. Bramwell *20750*		
	R	19174	Spain - Canary Is. *19174*
R	*Crambe scoparia* Svent. *20750*		
	R	20750	Spain - Canary Is. *20750*
I	*Crambe steveniana* Rupr. *5942, 20171*		
	I	5942	Russia - North Caucasus *5942*
	I	5942	Transcaucasus *5942*
	I	5942	Ukraine - Crimea *5942*
E	*Crambe sventenii* B. Petters. ex Bramw. & Sunding *14166*		
	E	20750	Spain - Canary Is. *17891*
R	*Crambe tataria* Sebeok var. *parviflora* (H.-Mor. Reese) Hedge & H.-Mor. Reese *12840*		
	R	12840	Turkey *12840*
R	*Crambella teretifolia* (Battand.) Maire		
	R		Morocco
R	*Cusickiella quadricostata* (Rollins) Rollins *20850*		
	V	20850	U.S. - California *20850*
	V	20850	U.S. - Nevada *20850*
V	*Degenia velebitica* (Degen) Hayek *20171*		
	I	20852	Croatia *20852*

	V		(former) Yugoslavia
R	*Descurainia artemisioides* Svent. *20750*		
	R	20750	Spain - Canary Is. *20750*
R	*Descurainia gilva* Svent. *20750*		
	R	19174	Spain - Canary Is. *19174*
V	*Descurainia gonzalezii* Svent.		
	V		Spain - Canary Is.
E	*Descurainia ramosissima* Rollins *20850*		
	I	20850	U.S. - Colorado *20850*
E	*Descurainia torulosa* Rollins *20850*		
	E	20850	U.S. - Wyoming *20850*
R	*Dictyophragmus punensis* (Romanczuk) Al-Shehbaz *21276*		
	R	21276	Argentina *21276*
R	*Diplotaxis acris* Boiss. var. *tibestica* Chevassut & Quezel		
	R		Chad
R	*Diplotaxis ibicensis* (Pau) Gómez-Campo *17891, 20171*		
	R	20874	Spain (Alicante) *20692*
	R	20874	Spain - Balearic Is. *20874*
Ex	*Diplotaxis siettiana* Maire *17891, 20171*		
	Ex	19818	Spain (Isla de Alborán) *17891*
V	*Diplotaxis vicentina* (Cout.) Rothm. *8000, 20171*		
	V	20076	Portugal *8000*
V	*Dithyrea maritima* (A. Davids.) A. Davids. *20850*		
	V	20850	U.S. - California *20850*
R	*Draba acaulis* Boiss. *12840*		
	R	12840	Turkey *12840*
V	*Draba aleutica* Ekman ex Hulten *20850, 21309*		
	V	20850	U.S. - Alaska *20850*
R	*Draba aprica* Beadle *20850*		
	V	20850	U.S. - Arkansas *20850*
	V	20850	U.S. - Georgia *20850*
	I	20850	U.S. - Kentucky *20850*
	V	20850	U.S. - Missouri *20850*
	E	20850	U.S. - Oklahoma *20850*
R	*Draba argyraea* Rydb. *20850*		
	R	20850	U.S. - Idaho *20850*
V	*Draba arida* C.L. Hitchc. *20850*		
	V	20850	U.S. - Nevada *20850*
R	*Draba asprella* Greene var. *asprella 20850*		
	R	20850	U.S. - Arizona *20850*
V	*Draba asprella* Greene var. *zionensis* (C.L. Hitchc.) Welsh & Reveal *20850*		
	V	20850	U.S. - Utah *20850*
V	*Draba asterophora* Payson var. *asterophora 20850*		
	E	20850	U.S. - California *20850*
	E	20850	U.S. - Nevada *20850*
E	*Draba asterophora* Payson var. *macrocarpa* C.L. Hitchc. *20850*		
	E	20850	U.S. - California *20850*
V	*Draba borealis* (Hulten) Welsh var. *maxima* (Hulten) Welsh *20850*		
	V	20850	U.S. - Alaska *20850*
E	*Draba brachystylis* Rydb. *20850*		
	I	20850	U.S. - Nevada *20850*
	E	20850	U.S. - Utah *20850*
R	*Draba breweri* S.Watson *20850*		
	I	20850	U.S. - California *20850*
	I	20850	U.S. - Nevada *20850*

R **Draba bruniifolia** Stev. ssp. *armeniaca* Coode &
  Cullen *12840*
   R   *12840* Turkey *12840*

R **Draba cacuminum** E.Ekman *17832, 20171*
   R   *17832* Norway *17832*
   V   *20083* Sweden *18216*

V **Draba californica** (Jepson) Rollins & Price *20850*
   V   *20850* U.S. - California *20850*

V **Draba carnosula** O.E. Schulz *20850*
   V   *20850* U.S. - California *20850*

E **Draba chamissonis** G. Don *20850*
   I   *20850* U.S. - Alaska *20850*

E **Draba corrugata** S.Watson *20850*
   I   *20850* U.S. - California *20850*

R **Draba crassa** Rydb. *20850*
   V   *20850* U.S. - Colorado *20850*
   R   *20850* U.S. - Montana *20850*
   E   *20850* U.S. - Utah *20850*
   V   *20850* U.S. - Wyoming *20850*

V **Draba crassifolia** Graham var. *nevadensis* C.L.
  Hitchc. *20850*
   V   *20850* U.S. - Nevada *20850*

E **Draba cruciata** Payson *20850*
   E   *20850* U.S. - California *20850*

E **Draba cruciata** Payson var. *cruciata* *20850*
   I   *20850* U.S. - California *20850*

E **Draba cruciata** Payson var. *integrifolia* C.L.
  Hitchc. & C.W. Sharsmith *20850*
   E   *20850* U.S. - California *20850*

V **Draba cusickii** Robinson ex Schulz var. *pedicellata*
  Rollins & Price *20850*
   V   *20850* U.S. - Nevada *20850*

R **Draba cuspidata** M.Bieb. *20171*
   R   former European USSR

I **Draba dasyastra** Gilg & O. Schulz
   I   India - Jammu & Kashmir

R **Draba daviesiae** (C.L. Hitchc.) Rollins *20850*
   R   *20850* U.S. - Montana *20850*

E **Draba dorneri** Heuff. *20171*
   E   *19949* Romania *19417*

E **Draba dubia** Suter ssp. *nevadensis* (Pau) Molero
  Mesa & Pérez Rava *15398*
   E   *15398* Spain (Sierra Nevada) *15398*

R **Draba elegans** Boiss. *12840*
   R   *12840* Turkey *12840*

V **Draba exunguiculata** (O.E. Schulz) C.L. Hitchc. *20850*
   V   *20850* U.S. - Colorado *20850*

V **Draba graminea** Greene *20850*
   V   *20850* U.S. - Colorado *20850*

V **Draba grayana** (Rydb.) C.L. Hitchc. *20850*
   V   *20850* U.S. - Colorado *20850*

V **Draba haynaldii** Stur *17762, 20171*
   V   *19949* Romania *20631*

E **Draba hidalgensis** Calderon *9663*
   E   *9666* Mexico *9663*

V **Draba hispanica** Boiss. ssp. *lebrunii*
  Monts.
   V   Spain

I **Draba igarashii** Watan. *10572*

I   *10572* Japan *10572*

V **Draba jaegeri** Munz & Johnston *20850*
   V   *20850* U.S. - Nevada *20850*

R **Draba japonica** Maxim. *10572*
   R   *10572* Japan *10572*

R **Draba kamtschatica** (Ledeb.) N. Busch *20850*
   I   *20850* Canada - British Columbia *20850*
   V   *20850* U.S. - Alaska *20850*

E **Draba kassii** Welsh *20850*
   E   *20850* U.S. - Utah *20850*

R **Draba kitadakensis** Koidz. *10572*
   R   *10572* Japan *10572*

E **Draba kluanei** Mulligan *20850, 1034*
   E   *20850* Canada - Yukon Territory *20850*

R **Draba ladina** Braun-Blanq. *20171*
   R   *18154* Switzerland *18154*

R **Draba lemmonii** S.Watson var. *cyclomorpha* (Payson)
  O.E. Schulz *20850*
   R   *20850* U.S. - Oregon *20850*

V **Draba loiseleurii** Boiss. *15080, 20171*
   V   *15080* France - Corsica *15080*

R **Draba lonchocarpa** Rydb. var. *vestita* O.E.
  Schulz *20850, 10701*
   V   *20850* Canada - British Columbia *20850*
   I   *20850* U.S. - Alaska *20850*

R **Draba macounii** O.E. Schulz *20850*
   I   *20850* Canada - Alberta *20850*
   R   *20850* Canada - British Columbia *20850*
   I   *20850* Canada - Mackenzie *20850*
   I   *20850* Canada - Yukon Territory *20850*
   I   *20850* U.S. - Alaska *20850*
   I   *20850* U.S. - Colorado *20850*
   E   *20850* U.S. - Montana *20850*

V **Draba maguirei** C.L. Hitchc. *20850*
   V   *20850* U.S. - Utah *20850*

E **Draba maguirei** C.L. Hitchc. var. *burkei* C.L.
  Hitchc. *20850*
   E   *20850* U.S. - Utah *20850*

V **Draba maguirei** C.L. Hitchc. var.
  maguirei *20850*
   V   *20850* U.S. - Utah *20850*

R **Draba mogollonica** Greene *20850*
   R   *20850* U.S. - New Mexico *20850*

E **Draba monoensis** Rollins & Price *20850*
   E   *20850* U.S. - California *20850*

V **Draba murrayi** Mulligan *20850, 1034*
   E   *20850* Canada - Yukon Territory *20850*
   V   *20850* U.S. - Alaska *20850*

R **Draba nakaiana** Hara *10572*
   R   *10572* Japan *10572*

R **Draba oblongata** R. Br. ex DC. *20850, 20171*
   I   *20850* Canada - Franklin *20850*
   I   *20850* U.S. - Alaska *20850*

I **Draba odudiana** Lipsky *5942*
   I   *5942* Tajikistan *5942*

V **Draba ogilviensis** Hulten *20850, 1034*
   V   *20850* Canada - Yukon Territory *20850*

R **Draba oiana** Honda *10572*
   R   *10572* Japan *10572*

E **Draba oreibata** J. F. Macbr. & Payson var. *serpentina*
  Tiehm & P. Holmgren *20850*

	E	20850	U.S. - Nevada *20850*
E	*Draba paucifructa* Clokey & C.L. Hitchc. *20850*		
	E	20850	U.S. - Nevada *20850*
E	*Draba pectinipila* Rollins *20850*		
	I	20850	U.S. - Colorado *20850*
	E	20850	U.S. - Wyoming *20850*
V	*Draba pennellii* Rollins *20850*		
	V	20850	U.S. - Nevada *20850*
R	*Draba porsildii* Mulligan *20850*		
	I	20850	Canada - Alberta *20850*
	E	20850	Canada - British Columbia *20850*
	I	20850	Canada - Mackenzie *20850*
	I	20850	Canada - Yukon Territory *20850*
	E	20850	U.S. - Alaska *20850*
	E	20850	U.S. - Colorado *20850*
	E	20850	U.S. - Montana *20850*
	V	20850	U.S. - Wyoming *20850*
V	*Draba pterosperma* Payson *20850*		
	I	20850	U.S. - California *20850*
E	*Draba pycnosperma* Fern. & Knowlt. *20850*		
	E	20850	Canada - Newfoundland *20850*
	E	20850	Canada - Nova Scotia *20850*
	E	20850	Canada - Quebec *20850*
E	*Draba ramulosa* Rollins *20850*		
	E	20850	U.S. - Utah *20850*
R	*Draba rectifructa* C.L. Hitchc. *20850*		
	I	20850	U.S. - Arizona *20850*
	I	20850	U.S. - Colorado *20850*
	I	20850	U.S. - New Mexico *20850*
	V	20850	U.S. - Utah *20850*
V	*Draba ruaxes* Payson & St. John *20850, 1034*		
	V	20850	Canada - British Columbia *20850*
	E	20850	Canada - Yukon Territory *20850*
	V	20850	U.S. - Alaska *20850*
	I	20850	U.S. - Washington *20850*
R	*Draba sakuraii* Makino *10572*		
	R	10572	Japan *10572*
E	*Draba scotteri* Mulligan *20850, 1034*		
	E	20850	Canada - Yukon Territory *20850*
R	*Draba sekiyana* Ohwi *20511*		
	R	20511	Taiwan *20511*
R	*Draba shiroumana* Makino *10572*		
	R	10572	Japan *10572*
V	*Draba sierrae* C.W. Sharsmith *20850*		
	I	20850	U.S. - California *20850*
V	*Draba simonkaiana* Jáv. *17823, 20171*		
	V	19949	Romania *20631*
R	*Draba smithii* Gilg ex O.E. Schulz *20850*		
	V	20850	U.S. - Colorado *20850*
V	*Draba sobolifera* Rydb. *20850*		
	V	20850	U.S. - Utah *20850*
R	*Draba spectabilis* Greene *20850*		
	I	20850	U.S. - Arizona *20850*
	I	20850	U.S. - Colorado *20850*
	I	20850	U.S. - New Mexico *20850*
	E	20850	U.S. - Utah *20850*
	E	20850	U.S. - Wyoming *20850*
R	*Draba spectabilis* Greene var. *oxyloba* (Greene) Gilg & Schulz ex O.E. Schulz *20850*		
	R	20850	U.S. - Colorado *20850*
	E	20850	U.S. - Wyoming *20850*
R	*Draba standleyi* J.F. Macbr. & Payson *20850*		
	E	20850	U.S. - Arizona *20850*

	E	20850	U.S. - New Mexico *20850*
	E	20850	U.S. - Texas *20850*
V	*Draba stenopetala* Trautv. *20850, 1034*		
	E	20850	Canada - Yukon Territory *20850*
	V	20850	U.S. - Alaska *20850*
R	*Draba streptobrachia* Price *20850*		
	R	20850	U.S. - Colorado *20850*
R	*Draba subalpina* Goodman & C.L. Hitchc. *20850*		
	R	20850	U.S. - Utah *20850*
R	*Draba subcapitata* Simm. *20850, 20171*		
	I	20850	Canada - Franklin *20850*
V	*Draba subumbellata* Rollins & Price *20850*		
	V	20850	U.S. - California *20850*
	E	20850	U.S. - Nevada *20850*
R	*Draba taimyrensis* Tolm. *20085, 21309*		
	R	20085	Russia (E.Europe) - North *20085*
R	*Draba thylacocarpa* (Nab.) Hedge *12840*		
	R	12840	Turkey *12840*
V	*Draba trichocarpa* Rollins *20850*		
	V	20850	U.S. - Idaho *20850*
R	*Draba tucumanensis* O. Schulz *16336*		
	R	19448	Argentina *16336*
	R	20176	Argentina - Tucuman (Tafí) *20176*
R	*Draba ventosa* Gray *20850, 1034*		
	E	20850	Canada - Alberta *20850*
	E	20850	Canada - Yukon Territory *20850*
	E	20850	U.S. - Colorado *20850*
	E	20850	U.S. - Utah *20850*
	R	20850	U.S. - Wyoming *20850*
E	*Draba weberi* Price & Rollins *20850*		
	E	20850	U.S. - Colorado *20850*
E	*Draba yukonensis* Porsild *20850, 1034*		
	E	20850	Canada - Yukon Territory *20850*
R	*Drabastrum alpestre* (F.Muell.) O.Schulz *20681*		
	I	20681	Australia - Capital Territory *20681*
	I	20681	Australia - New South Wales *20681*
	I	20681	Australia - Victoria *20681*
I	*Erophila tenerrima* (O. Schulz) Jafri		
	I		India - Jammu & Kashmir
E	*Erucastrum palustre* (Pirona) Vis. *8000, 20171*		
	E	18264	Italy (Fruili-Venezia Giulia) *19997*
I	*Erysimum amasianum* Hausskn. & Bornm. *12840*		
	I	12840	Turkey *12840*
V	*Erysimum ammophilum* Heller *20850*		
	V	20850	U.S. - California *20850*
V	*Erysimum arbuscula* (Lowe) Snogerup		
	V		Portugal - Madeira
R	*Erysimum candicum* Snogerup ssp. *carpathum* Snogerup *20171*		
	R	20730	Greece - Crete (Karpathos, Saria) *20730*
E	*Erysimum capitatum* (Douglas ex Hook) Greene var. *angustatum* (Greene) G. Rossb. *20850*		
	E	20850	U.S. - California *20850*
R	*Erysimum caricum* Boiss. *12840*		
	R	12840	Turkey *12840*
R	*Erysimum deflexum* Cullen *12840*		
	R	12840	Turkey *12840*
V	*Erysimum degenianum* Aznav. *12840*		
	V	19873	Turkey *12840*
R	*Erysimum echinellum* Hand.-Mazz. *12840*		

	R	*12840* Turkey *12840*	
R	*Erysimum favargeri* Polatschek *11496, 20171*		
	R	*11496* Spain (Jaen) *11496*	
V	*Erysimum franciscanum* G. Rossb. *20850*		
	V	*20850* U.S. - California *20850*	
	I	*20850* U.S. - Oregon *20850*	
V	*Erysimum franciscanum* Rossberg var. *franciscanum* *20850*		
	I	*20850* U.S. - California *20850*	
	I	*20850* U.S. - Oregon *20850*	
R	*Erysimum ghiesbreghtii* J.D. Smith *9004*		
	R	*9666* Guatemala *9004*	
	R	*9666* Mexico *9004*	
V	*Erysimum inconspicuum* (S.Watson) MacM. var. *coarctatum* (Fern.) G. Rossb. *20850, 5567*		
	E	*20850* Canada - New Brunswick *20850*	
	E	*20850* Canada - Newfoundland (Island) *20850*	
	I	*20850* Canada - Nova Scotia *20850*	
	V	*20850* Canada - Quebec *20850*	
R	*Erysimum insulare* Greene *20883, 20850, 8058*		
	I	*20850* U.S. - California *20850*	
	I	*20883* Mexico *20883*	
R	*Erysimum leptocarpum* Gay *12840*		
	R	*12840* Turkey *12840*	
R	*Erysimum leptostylum* DC. *20171*		
	R	former European USSR	
V	*Erysimum menziesii* (Hook.) Wettst. *20850*		
	I	*20850* U.S. - California *20850*	
	I	*20850* U.S. - Oregon *20850*	
E	*Erysimum menziesii* (Hook.) Wettst. ssp. *eurekense* Price *20850*		
	E	*20850* U.S. - California *20850*	
V	*Erysimum menziesii* (Hook.) Wettst. ssp. *menziesii* Wettst. *20850*		
	V	*20850* U.S. - California *20850*	
E	*Erysimum menziesii* (Hook.) Wettst. ssp. *yadonii* Price *20850*		
	E	*20850* U.S. - California *20850*	
R	*Erysimum naxense* Snogerup *20171*		
	R	Greece	
R	*Erysimum olympicum* Boiss. *20171*		
	R	Greece	
R	*Erysimum pallidum* Boiss. *12840*		
	R	*12840* Turkey *12840*	
R	*Erysimum penyalarense* (Pau) Polatschek *15846*		
	R	*15846* Spain *15846*	
I	*Erysimum rechingeri* Jáv. *20171*		
	I	Greece	
R	*Erysimum rhodium* Snogerup		
	R	Greece	
E	*Erysimum suffrutescens* G. Rossb. var. *lompocense* G. Rossb. *20850*		
	E	*20850* U.S. - California *20850*	
V	*Erysimum teretifolium* Eastw. *20850*		
	V	*20850* U.S. - California *20850*	
R	*Erysimum thomsonii* Hook. f. *13883*		
	R	*13883* India - Himachal Pradesh *13883*	
V	*Erysimum torulosum* Hub.-Mor. *12840*		
	V	*12840* Turkey *12840*	
R	*Erysimum ucranicum* J.Gay *20171*		

	R	former European USSR	
I	*Erysimum vagicum* Holub *19321*		
	I	*19321* Slovakia *19321*	
I	*Eutrema cordifolium* Turcz. ex Ledeb. *5942*		
	I	*5942* Russia (Siberia) - Irkutsk *5942*	
E	*Eutrema penlandii* Rollins *20850, 13640*		
	E	*20850* U.S. - Colorado (Continental divide) *20850*	
V	*Eutrema tenuis* (Miq.) Makino var. *okinosimensis* (Taken.) Hara *10572*		
	V	*10572* Japan *10572*	
R	*Euzomodendron bourgaeanum* Coss. *20171*		
	R	*19818* Spain (Province of Almeria) *19818*	
I	*Farsetia macrantha* Blatter & Hallberg *7771*		
	I	India - Rajasthan (Mataji's Temple, Barmer) *7771*	
I	*Farsetia socotrana* B.L. Burtt *15534*		
	I	*15534* Yemen - Socotra *15534*	
R	*Graellsia chitralensis* O.E. Schulz		
	R	Pakistan	
R	*Graellsia davisiana* Poilter *12840*		
	R	*12840* Turkey *12840*	
R	*Halimolobos diffusa* (Gray) O. E. Schulz var. *jaegeri* (Munz) Rollins *20850*		
	I	*20850* U.S. - California *20850*	
	I	*20850* U.S. - Nevada *20850*	
R	*Halimolobos mollis* (Hook.) Rollins *20850,*		
	I	*20850* Canada - British Columbia *20850*	
	I	*20850* Canada - Manitoba *20850*	
	I	*20850* Canada - Franklin *20850*	
	I	*20850* Canada - Yukon Territory *20850*	
	I	*20850* U.S. - Alaska *20850*	
R	*Halimolobos perplexa* (L. Henderson) Rollins var. *perplexa* *20850*		
	R	*20850* U.S. - Idaho *20850*	
R	*Halimolobus minutiflora* Rollins *9664*		
	R	*9666* Mexico *9664*	
R	*Halimolobus pedicellata* Rollins *9664*		
	R	*9666* Mexico *9664*	
R	*Hedinia czukotica* (Botsch. et Petrovsky) Jurtz. Korobk. et Baland. *20085, 21309*		
	R	*20085* Russia (E.Europe) - North *20085*	
V	*Heldreichia atalayi* Kit Tan *12840*		
	V	*12840* Turkey *12840*	
R	*Heldreichia bourgaei* Boiss. *12840*		
	R	*12840* Turkey *12840*	
R	*Heliophila arenaria* Sond. var. *agtertuinensis* (O.E.Schulz) Marais *20604*		
	R	*20604* South Africa - Cape Province *20604*	
R	*Heliophila cedarbergensis* Marais *20604*		
	R	*20604* South Africa - Cape Province *20604*	
R	*Heliophila cinerea* Marais *20604*		
	R	*20604* South Africa - Cape Province *20604*	
R	*Heliophila collina* O.E.Schulz *20604*		
	R	*20604* South Africa - Cape Province *20604*	
R	*Heliophila cornellsbergia* B.J.Pienaar & Nicholas *20604*		
	R	*20604* South Africa - Cape Province *20604*	
V	*Heliophila cuneata* Marais *20604*		
	V	*20604* South Africa - Cape Province *20604*	

R   *Heliophila eximia* Marais *20604*
    R   *20604* Namibia *20604*
    R   *20604* South Africa - Cape Province *20604*

R   *Heliophila filicaulis* Marais *20604*
    R   *20604* South Africa - Cape Province *20604*

R   *Heliophila laciniata* Marais *20604*
    R   *20604* South Africa - Cape Province *20604*

I   *Heliophila leptophylla* Schltr. *20604*
    I   *20604* South Africa - Cape Province *20604*

I   *Heliophila obibensis* Marais *20604*
    I   *20604* Namibia *20604*

R   *Heliophila patens* Oliv. *20604*
    R   *20604* South Africa - Cape Province *20604*

R   *Heliophila rimicola* Marais *20604*
    R   *20604* South Africa - Cape Province *20604*

R   *Heliophila schulzii* Marais *20604*
    R   *20604* South Africa - Cape Province *20604*

R   *Heliophila tabularis* Wolley-Dod *20604*
    R   *20604* South Africa - Cape Province *20604*

R   *Heliophila tricuspidata* Schltr. *20604*
    R   *20604* South Africa - Cape Province *20604*

R   *Hemicrambe fruticulosa* Webb
    R   Morocco

E   *Hemicrambe townsendii* Gomez-Campo *15534*
    E   *15534* Yemen - Socotra *15534*

R   *Hesperis aintabica* Post *12840*
    R   *12840* Turkey *12840*

R   *Hesperis bottae* Fourn. *12840*
    R   *12840* Turkey *12840*

R   *Hesperis breviscapa* Boiss. *12840*
    R   *12840* Turkey *12840*

R   *Hesperis campicarpa* Boiss. *12840*
    R   *12840* Turkey *12840*

R   *Hesperis hedgei* Davis *12840*
    R   *12840* Turkey *12840*

R   *Hesperis kitiana* Davis *12840*
    R   *12840* Turkey *12840*

R   *Hesperis matronalis* L. ssp. *cilicica* (Siehe ex Bornm.) Cullen *12840*
    R   *12840* Turkey *12840*

I   *Hesperis matronalis* L. ssp. *moniliformis* (Schur) Bauza *17823*
    I   *20631* Romania *20631*

V   *Hesperis oblongifolia* Schur *19266, 20171*
    V   *19949* Romania *20631*

R   *Hesperis pisidica* Hub.-Mor. *12840*
    R   *12840* Turkey *12840*

R   *Hesperis rechingeri* F.Dvorák *20171*
    R   Greece

R   *Hesperis schischkinii* Tzvelev *12840*
    R   *12840* Turkey *12840*

R   *Hesperis stellata* Dvorak *12840*
    R   *12840* Turkey *12840*

R   *Hesperis verroiana* F.Dvorák *20171*
    R   Greece

V   *Hesperis vrabelyiana* (Schur) Borbás *19266, 20171*
    V   Hungary *19266*

R   *Hirschfeldia rostrata* (Balf. f.) O.E. Schulz *15534*

    R   *15534* Yemen - Socotra *15534*

R   *Hormathophylla cadevalliana* (Pau) T.R.Dudley *20171*
    R   *11496* Spain *11496*

V   *Hormathophylla pyrenaica* (Lapeyr.) Cullen & Dudley *14166*
    V   *20528* France (east Pyrenees) *20528*

R   *Hormathophylla reverchonii* (D. & H.) Cullen & Dudley
    R   *11496* Spain *11496*

Ex   *Hutchinsia tasmanica* Hook. *20681, 14223*
    Ex   *20681* Australia - Tasmania *20681*

R   *Iberis aperta* Barb.-Gamp.
    R   Spain

V   *Iberis aurosica* Chaix ssp. *aurosica* *20171*
    V   *20528* France (south-east) *20528*

R   *Iberis carica* Bornm. *12840*
    R   *12840* Turkey *12840*

V   *Iberis embergeri* Serve *15398*
    V   *14155* Spain (Sierra Nevada) *15398*

R   *Iberis fontqueri* Pau *20171*
    R   *19174* Spain (Málaga, Sierra Bermeja) *11496*

R   *Iberis grosii* Pau *19174*
    R   *19174* Spain (Málaga: Sierra Tejeda, Sierra Almijara) *11496*

V   *Iberis linifolia* L. ssp. *violletii* (Soy.-Will. ex Godr.) Valdés *20171*
    V   *20528* France (Meuse) *20528*

V   *Iberis procumbens* Lange ssp. *microcarpa* Franco & Pinto da Silva *8000, 20171*
    V   *20076* Portugal *8000*

E   *Iberis runemarkii* Greuter & Burdet *10270*
    E   *10270* Greece - East Aegean Is *10270*

V   *Iberis sampaioana* Franco & P.Silva *19266, 20171*
    V   *20076* Portugal *20076*

R   *Iberis semperflorens* L. *20171*
    R   Italy
    R   *19164* Italy - Sicily (north-west includes islands) *19164*
    R   Tunisia

V   *Ionopsidium acaule* (Desf.) Reichenb. *8000*
    V   *20076* Portugal *8000*

R   *Ionopsidium savianum* (Caruel) Ball ex Arcang. *8000*
    R   *19997* Italy (Toscana, Umbria, & Lazio) *19997*

R   *Irenepharsus magicus* Hewson *20681*
    I   *20681* Australia - New South Wales *20681*
    I   *20681* Australia - Victoria *20681*

R   *Irenepharsus phasmatodes* Hewson *20681*
    R   *20681* Australia - South Australia *20681*

R   *Irenepharsus trypherus* Hewson *20681*
    R   *20681* Australia - New South Wales *20681*

E   *Isatis arenaria* Azn. *12840, 20171*
    E   *19174* Turkey *12840*

Ex   *Isatis arnoldiana* N. Busch. *6930*
    Ex   *6930* former USSR *6930*

R   *Isatis athoa* Boiss. *20171*
    R   Greece

R   *Isatis aucheri* Boiss. *12840*
    R   *19174* Turkey *12840*

R   *Isatis bitlisica* Davis *12840*
    R   *19174* Turkey *12840*

R **Isatis callifera** Boiss. & Bal. *12840*
    R   *19174* Turkey *12840*

R **Isatis candolleana** Boiss. *12840*
    R   *19174* Turkey *12840*

R **Isatis cappadocica** Desv. ssp. *alyssifolia* (Boiss.)
    Davis *12840*
    R   *12840* Turkey *12840*

R **Isatis cappadocica** Desv. ssp. *nurihakensis*
    Davis *12840*
    R   *12840* Turkey *12840*

R **Isatis constricta** Davis *12840*
    R   *12840* Turkey *12840*

E **Isatis davisiana** Misirdali *12840*
    E   *12840* Turkey *12840*

R **Isatis demiriziana** Misirdali *12840*
    R   *12840* Turkey *12840*

R **Isatis erzurumica** Davis *12840*
    R   *12840* Turkcy *12840*

R **Isatis frigida** Boiss. & Kotschy *12840*
    R   *12840* Turkey *12840*

R **Isatis huber-morathii** Davis *12840*
    R   *12840* Turkey *12840*

R **Isatis jacutensis** (N. Busch) N. Busch. *20085*
    R   *20085* Russia (E.Europe) - North *20085*

R **Isatis lockmanniana** Kotschy & Boiss. *12840*
    R   *19174* Turkey *12840*

V **Isatis lusitanica** L. *20171*
    V   Greece

V **Isatis mardinensis** Davis & Misirdali *12840*
    V   *12840* Turkey *12840*

E **Isatis pinnatiloba** Davis *12840*
    E   *19174* Turkey *12840*

R **Isatis sivasica** Davis *12840*
    R   *12840* Turkey *12840*

R **Isatis spatella** Davis *12840*
    R   *19174* Turkey *12840*

R **Isatis spectabilis** Davis *12840*
    R   *12840* Turkey *12840*

R **Isatis undulata** Aucher ex Boiss. *12840*
    R   *19873* Turkey *12840*

I **Iskandera hissarica** N. Busch *5942*
    I   *5942* Tajikistan *5942*
    I   *5942* Uzbekistan *5942*

R **Iti lacustris** *19305*
    R   *19305* New Zealand - South Is. *19305*

E **Lachnocapsa spathulata** Balf. f. *15534*
    E   *15534* Yemen - Socotra *15534*

R **Leavenworthia alabamica** Rollins *20850*
    I   *20850* U.S. - Alabama *20850*

R **Leavenworthia alabamica** Rollins var.
    alabamica 20850
    I   *20850* U.S. - Alabama *20850*

V **Leavenworthia alabamica** Rollins var. *brachystyla*
    Rollins *20850*
    I   *20850* U.S. - Alabama *20850*

V **Leavenworthia aurea** Torr. *20850*
    V   *20850* U.S. - Oklahoma *20850*

E **Leavenworthia crassa** Rollins *20850*

V   *20850* U.S. - Alabama *20850*

E **Leavenworthia crassa** Rollins var.
    crassa 20850
    I   *20850* U.S. - Alabama *20850*

E **Leavenworthia crassa** Rollins var. *elongata*
    Rollins *20850*
    I   *20850* U.S. - Alabama *20850*

R **Leavenworthia exigua** Rollins var.
    exigua 20850
    V   *20850* U.S. - Georgia *20850*
    R   *20850* U.S. - Tennessee *20850*

E **Leavenworthia exigua** Rollins var. *laciniata*
    Rollins *20850*
    E   *20850* U.S. - Kentucky *20850*

E **Leavenworthia exigua** Rollins var. *lutea*
    Rollins *20850*
    E   *20850* U.S. - Alabama *20850*
    E   *20850* U.S. - Tennessee *20850*

E **Leavenworthia texana** Mahler *20850*
    E   *20850* U.S. - Texas *20850*

I **Leiospora exscapa** (C. Meyer) Dvorak *5942*
    I   *5942* Russia (Siberia) - Altai *5942*
    I   *5942* Kazakhstan *5942*

R **Lepidium alluaudii** Maire
    R   Morocco

E **Lepidium arbuscula** Hbd. *20850, 14209*
    E   *20850* U.S. - Hawaii (O`ahu - Wai`anae Mts.)
       20850

V **Lepidium aschersonii** Thell. *20681*
    I   *20681* Australia - New South Wales *20681*
    I   *20681* Australia - Victoria *20681*
    Ex/E *20681* Australia - Western Australia *20681*

E **Lepidium banksii** Kirk *19305*
    E   *19305* New Zealand - South Is. *19305*

E **Lepidium barnebyanum** Reveal *20850*
    E   *20850* U.S. - Utah *20850*

V **Lepidium bidentatum** Mont. var. *owaihiense* (Cham. &
    Schlecht.) Fosberg *20850*
    V   *20850* U.S. - Hawaii *20850*

Ex/E **Lepidium bidentatum** Mont. var. *remyi* (Drake)
    Fosberg *20850, 14209*
    Ex/E *20850* U.S. - Hawaii *20850*

V **Lepidium caespitosum** Desv. *12840*
    V   *12840* Turkey *12840*

E **Lepidium cardamines** L. *8000, 20171*
    E   *14155* Spain (central) *8000*

R **Lepidium carrerasii** Rodriguez
    R   Spain - Balearic Is.

E **Lepidium catapycnon** Hewson *20681*
    E   *20681* Australia - Western Australia *20681*

R **Lepidium davisii** Rollins *20850*
    R   *20850* U.S. - Idaho *20850*
    I   *20850* U.S. - Nevada *20850*
    E   *20850* U.S. - Oregon *20850*

Ex **Lepidium drummondii** Thell. *20681, 14223*
    Ex *20681* Australia - Western Australia *20681*

V **Lepidium flavum** Torr. var. *felipense* C.L.
    Hitchc. *20850*
    E   *20850* U.S. - California *20850*

R **Lepidium horstii** Johow *19534*
    R   *19534* Chile *19534*

V	*Lepidium howei-insulae* Thell.		
	V	*14225*	Australia - NSW - Lord Howe Is. *14225*
V	*Lepidium integrifolium* var. *integrifolium* *20850*		
	I	*20850*	U.S. - Arizona *20850*
	I	*20850*	U.S. - Utah *20850*
	E	*20850*	U.S. - Wyoming *20850*
R	*Lepidium inyangense* Jonsell *7892*		
	R		Zimbabwe *7892*
E	*Lepidium jaredii* Brandeg. *20850*		
	I	*20850*	U.S. - California *20850*
E	*Lepidium kawarau* Petrie *86*		
	E	*86*	New Zealand *86*
E	*Lepidium kirkii* Petrie *19305*		
	E	*19305*	New Zealand - South Is. *19305*
R	*Lepidium lasiocarpum* C.L. Hitchc. var. *rotundum* C.L. Hitchc. *20850*		
	R	*20850*	U.S. - Texas *20850*
E	*Lepidium matau* Petrie *86*		
	E		New Zealand - South Is.
V	*Lepidium meyenii* Walp. *18200*		
	V	*12468*	Peru *18200*
R	*Lepidium meyeri* Claus *5942, 20171*		
	I	*5942*	Russia (E.Europe) - South *5942*
	R	*5942*	Kazakhstan (north western) *5942*
	I	*5942*	Ukraine *5942*
E	*Lepidium monoplocoides* F.Muell. *20681*		
	I	*20681*	Australia - New South Wales *20681*
	Ex/E	*20681*	Australia - South Australia *20681*
	I	*20681*	Australia - Victoria *20681*
E	*Lepidium montanum* Nutt. var. *alpinum* S.Watson *20850*		
	E	*20850*	U.S. - Utah *20850*
V	*Lepidium montanum* Nutt. var. *neeseae* Welsh & Reveal *20850*		
	V	*20850*	U.S. - Utah *20850*
V	*Lepidium montanum* Nutt. var. *stellae* Welsh & Reveal *20850, 19002*		
	V	*20850*	U.S. - Utah *20850*
R	*Lepidium nanum* S.Watson *20850*		
	R	*20850*	U.S. - Nevada *20850*
Ex	*Lepidium obtusatum* Kirk *86*		
	Ex	*15135*	New Zealand - North Is. *15135*
V	*Lepidium* *19305*		
	V	*19305*	New Zealand - South Is. *19305*
E	*Lepidium ostleri* Welsh & Goodrich *20850*		
	E	*20850*	U.S. - Utah *20850*
V	*Lepidium papilliferum* (Henderson) A. Nels. & J.F. Macbr. *20850*		
	V	*20850*	U.S. - Idaho *20850*
Ex	*Lepidium peregrinum* Thell. *20681, 14223*		
	Ex	*20681*	Australia - New South Wales *20681*
V	*Lepidium pseudopapillosum* Schinz *20681*		
	I	*20681*	Australia - Capital Territory *20681*
	Ex/E	*20681*	Australia - New South Wales *20681*
	I	*20681*	Australia - South Australia *20681*
	I	*20681*	Australia - Victoria *20681*
R	*Lepidium puberulum* Bunge *20681*		
	R	*20681*	Australia - Western Australia *20681*
E	*Lepidium serra* Mann *20850, 14209*		
	E	*20850*	U.S. - Hawaii (Kaua`i) *20850*

V	*Lepidium sisymbrioides* ssp. *kawarau* *19305*		
	V	*19305*	New Zealand - South Is. *19305*
E	*Lepidium sisymbrioides* ssp. *matau* *19305*		
	E	*19305*	New Zealand - South Is. *19305*
E	*Lepidium solomonii* Al-Shehbaz *20883*		
	I	*20883*	Bolivia *20883*
R	*Lepidium turczaninowii* Lipsky *20654*		
	R	*20650*	Ukraine - Crimea *8001*
V	*Lepidium villarsii* Gren. & Godr. *20171*		
	V	*20528*	France (south-east) *20528*
V	*Lepidium virginicum* L. var. *robinsonii* (Thellung) C.L. Hitchc. *20850*		
	V	*20850*	U.S. - California *20850*
R	*Lesquerella angustifolia* (Nutt. ex Torr. & Gray) S.Watson *20850*		
	I	*20850*	U.S. - Arkansas *20850*
	I	*20850*	U.S. - Maryland *20850*
	I	*20850*	U.S. - Missouri *20850*
	R	*20850*	U.S. - Oklahoma *20850*
	E	*20850*	U.S. - Texas *20850*
V	*Lesquerella arenosa* Rollins & Shaw var. *argillosa* Rollins & Shaw *20850*		
	E	*20850*	U.S. - Colorado *20850*
	V	*20850*	U.S. - Nebraska *20850*
	I	*20850*	U.S. - South Dakota *20850*
	E	*20850*	U.S. - Wyoming *20850*
R	*Lesquerella arizonica* S.Watson *20850*		
	I	*20850*	U.S. - Arizona *20850*
	V	*20850*	U.S. - Utah *20850*
V	*Lesquerella aurea* Woot. *20850*		
	V	*20850*	U.S. - New Mexico *20850*
R	*Lesquerella calchaquina* *19448*		
	R	*19448*	Argentina *19448*
V	*Lesquerella calcicola* Rollins *20850*		
	I	*20850*	U.S. - Colorado *20850*
	R	*20850*	U.S. - New Mexico *20850*
V	*Lesquerella calderi* Mulligan & Porsild *20850*		
	I	*20850*	Canada - Mackenzie *20850*
	I	*20850*	Canada - Yukon Territory *20850*
V	*Lesquerella cinerea* S.Watson *20850*		
	I	*20850*	U.S. - Arizona *20850*
E	*Lesquerella congesta* Rollins *20850*		
	E	*20850*	U.S. - Colorado *20850*
V	*Lesquerella cordiformis* (Rollins) Rollins & Shaw *20850*		
	I	*20850*	U.S. - Nevada *20850*
R	*Lesquerella densipila* Rollins *20850*		
	V	*20850*	U.S. - Alabama *20850*
	R	*20850*	U.S. - Tennessee *20850*
E	*Lesquerella filiformis* Rollins *20850*		
	E	*20850*	U.S. - Missouri *20850*
V	*Lesquerella fremontii* Rollins & Shaw *20850*		
	V	*20850*	U.S. - Wyoming *20850*
V	*Lesquerella garrettii* Payson *20850*		
	V	*20850*	U.S. - Utah *20850*
V	*Lesquerella globosa* (Desv.) S.Watson *20850*		
	E	*20850*	U.S. - Indiana *20850*
	V	*20850*	U.S. - Kentucky *20850*
	I	*20850*	U.S. - Ohio *20850*
	V	*20850*	U.S. - Tennessee *20850*
E	*Lesquerella hemiphysaria* Welsh & Reveal var. *lucens* Welsh & Reveal *20850*		

E	20850	U.S. - Utah	20850

V   *Lesquerella hitchcockii* Munz 20850

V	20850	U.S. - Nevada	20850
I	20850	U.S. - Utah	20850

E   *Lesquerella humilis* Rollins 20850

E	20850	U.S. - Montana	20850

V   *Lesquerella kaibabensis* Rollins 20850

V	20850	U.S. - Arizona	20850

E   *Lesquerella kingii* S.Watson ssp. *bernardina* (Munz) Munz 20850

E	20850	U.S. - California	20850

R   *Lesquerella kingii* S.Watson var. *cobrensis* Rollins & Shaw 20850

R	20850	U.S. - Idaho	20850
I	20850	U.S. - Nevada	20850

R   *Lesquerella kingii* S.Watson ssp. *diversifolia* (Greene) Rollins & Shaw 20850

I	20850	U.S. - Idaho	20850
R	20850	U.S. - Oregon	20850

R   *Lesquerella klausii* Rollins 20850

R	20850	U.S. - Montana	20850

E   *Lesquerella lata* Woot. & Standl. 20850

E	20850	U.S. - New Mexico	20850

E   *Lesquerella lyrata* Rollins 20850

E	20850	U.S. - Alabama	20850

V   *Lesquerella macrocarpa* A. Nels. 20850

V	20850	U.S. - Wyoming	20850

R   *Lesquerella mcvaughiana* Rollins 20850

R	20850	U.S. - Texas	20850

R   *Lesquerella multiceps* Maguire 20850

E	20850	U.S. - Idaho	20850
E	20850	U.S. - Utah	20850
E	20850	U.S. - Wyoming	20850

E   *Lesquerella pallida* (Torr. & Gray) S.Watson 20850

E	20850	U.S. - Texas	20850

V   *Lesquerella parviflora* Rollins 20850

R	20850	U.S. - Colorado	20850

R   *Lesquerella paysonii* Rollins 20850

E	20850	U.S. - Idaho	20850
E	20850	U.S. - Montana	20850
R	20850	U.S. - Wyoming	20850

E   *Lesquerella perforata* Rollins 20850

E	20850	U.S. - Tennessee	20850

R   *Lesquerella prostrata* A. Nels. 20850

I	20850	U.S. - Idaho	20850
E	20850	U.S. - Utah	20850
E	20850	U.S. - Wyoming	20850

V   *Lesquerella pruinosa* Greene 20850

V	20850	U.S. - Colorado	20850

V   *Lesquerella rubicundula* Rollins 20850

I	20850	U.S. - Nevada	20850
V	20850	U.S. - Utah	20850

E   *Lesquerella stonensis* Rollins 20850

E	20850	U.S. - Tennessee	20850

R   *Lesquerella subumbellata* Rollins 20850

I	20850	U.S. - Colorado	20850
R	20850	U.S. - Utah	20850
I	20850	U.S. - Wyoming	20850

E   *Lesquerella thamnophila* Rollins & Shaw 20850

E	20850	U.S. - Texas	20850

E   *Lesquerella tumulosa* (Barneby) Reveal 20850

E	20850	U.S. - Utah	20850

R   *Lesquerella utahensis* Rydb. 20850

R	20850	U.S. - Utah	20850

V   *Lesquerella valida* Greene 20850

V	20850	U.S. - New Mexico	20850
E	20850	U.S. - Texas	20850

R   *Lobularia maritima* (L.) Desv. ssp. *columbretensis* R.Fern. 20648

R	20692	Spain (Columbretes Is.)	20692

R   *Lunaria telekiana* Jáv. 20178, 20171

R	20178	Albania	20178

R   *Malcolmia heterophylla* Caball.

R		Morocco	

V   *Malcolmia lacera* (L.) DC. ssp. *graccilima* (Samp.) Franco 17891

V	20076	Portugal	17891

R   *Mancoa henricksonii* Rollins 9664

R	9666	Mexico	9664

R   *Mancoa laxa* Rollins 9664

R	9666	Mexico	9664

R   *Mancoa rollinsiana* Calderon 9665

R	9666	Mexico	9665

R   *Mancoa stylosa* Rollins 9665

R	9666	Mexico	9665

V   *Maresia malcolmioides* (Coss. & Durieu) Pomel 10488

V	14958	Algeria	10488

R   *Matthiola anchoniifolia* Hub.-Mor. 12840

R	12840	Turkey	12840

R   *Matthiola incana* (L.) R. Brown ssp. *melitensis* Brullo, Lanfranco, Pavone & Ronsisvalle 13351

R	13351	Malta	13351

R   *Matthiola masguindalii* Pau

R		Morocco	

V   *Matthiola parviflora* (Schousb.) R.Br. 20171

V	20732	Spain - Balearic Is.	20732

E   *Megacarpaea bifida* Benth. 14768

E		India - Jammu & Kashmir (Apharwat) 14768

R   *Megacarpaea schugnanica* B. Fedtsch.

R		former USSR	6930

I   *Megadenia bardunovii* Popov 11552

I	5942	Russia (Siberia) - Irkutsk (south)	5942

Ex   *Menkea draboides* (Hook.f.) Benth. 20681, 14223

Ex	20681	Australia - Western Australia	20681

V   *Microlepidium alatum* (J.Black) E.Shaw 20681

V	20681	Australia - South Australia	20681

R   *Moricandia foetida* Bourg. ex Coss. 20171

R		Spain	

V   *Moricandia foleyi* Battand. 10487

V	14958	Algeria	10487

V   *Murbeckiella pinnatifida* (Lam.) Rothm. ssp. *herminii* (Rivas Martinez) Greuter & Burdet 20076

V	20076	Portugal	17891

E   *Murbeckiella sousae* Rothm. 8000, 20171

E	20076	Portugal	8000

V   *Noccaea arenaria* (Duby) F.K. Meyer 20528

V	20528	France (south-west)	20528

E   *Ornithocarpa fimbriata* Rose 9666

E	9666	Mexico - Jalisco	9666

R   *Ornithocarpa torulosa* Rollins *9667*
    R   *9666*   Mexico *9667*

E   *Otocarpus virgatus* Durieu *10487*
    E   *14958*   Algeria (t) *10487*

E   *Parolinia aridanae* Santos *20750*
    E   *20750*   Spain - Canary Is. *20750*

V   *Parolinia filifolia* Svent. ex Kunkel *17534*
    V   *20750*   Spain - Canary Is. *17534*

V   *Parolinia intermedia* Svent. & Bramw. *17534*
    V   *20750*   Spain - Canary Is. *17534*

V   *Parolinia platypetala* Kunkel *20750*
    V   *20750*   Spain - Canary Is. *20750*

E   *Parolinia schizogynoides* Svent. *17534*
    E   *20750*   Spain - Canary Is. *17534*

R   *Parrya arctica* R. Br. *20850*
    I   *20850*   Canada - Franklin *20850*
    I   *20850*   Canada - Yukon Territory *20850*

E   *Parrya nudicaulis* Hulten var. *grandiflora* Hulten *20850*
    E   *20850*   U.S. - Alaska *20850*

R   *Peltariopsis grossheimii* N. Busch.
    R   former USSR *6930*

R   *Pennellia hunnewellii* Rollins *9668*
    R   *9666*   Guatemala *9668*
    R   *9666*   Mexico *9668*

R   *Pennellia juncea* (Schulz) Rollins *9668*
    R   *9666*   Mexico *9668*

E   *Pennellia robinsonii* Rollins *9668*
    E   *9666*   Mexico *9668*

Ex   *Phlegmatospermum drummondii* (Benth.) O.Schulz *20681, 14223*
    Ex   *20681*   Australia - Western Australia *20681*

V   *Physaria acutifolia* Rydb. var. *purpurea* Welsh & Reveal *20850*
    V   *20850*   U.S. - Utah *20850*

V   *Physaria alpina* Rollins *20850*
    I   *20850*   U.S. - Colorado *20850*

R   *Physaria bellii* Mulligan *20850*
    R   *20850*   U.S. - Colorado *20850*

E   *Physaria chambersii* Welsh var. *sobolifera* Welsh *20850*
    E   *20850*   U.S. - Utah *20850*

V   *Physaria condensata* Rollins *20850*
    V   *20850*   U.S. - Wyoming *20850*

V   *Physaria didymocarpa* (Hook.) Gray var. *lanata* A. Nels. *20850*
    I   *20850*   U.S. - Montana *20850*
    V   *20850*   U.S. - Wyoming *20850*

E   *Physaria didymocarpa* (Hook.) A. Gray var. *lyrata* C.L. Hitchc. *20850*
    E   *20850*   U.S. - Idaho *20850*

E   *Physaria dornii* Lichvar *20850*
    E   *20850*   U.S. - Wyoming *20850*

V   *Physaria eburniflora* Rollins *20850*
    V   *20850*   U.S. - Wyoming *20850*

E   *Physaria grahamii* Morton *20850*
    E   *20850*   U.S. - Utah *20850*

V   *Physaria integrifolia* Lichvar var. *monticola* Lichvar *20850*
    E   *20850*   U.S. - Idaho *20850*
    V   *20850*   U.S. - Wyoming *20850*

V   *Physaria lepidota* var. *membranacea* (Rollins) Rollins *20850*
    V   *20850*   U.S. - Utah *20850*

V   *Physaria obcordata* Rollins *20850*
    V   *20850*   U.S. - Colorado *20850*

V   *Physaria repanda* Rollins *20850*
    I   *20850*   U.S. - Utah *20850*

R   *Physaria saximontana* Rollins *20850*
    I   *20850*   U.S. - Montana *20850*
    V   *20850*   U.S. - Wyoming *20850*

V   *Physaria saximontana* Rollins var. *dentata* Rollins *20850*
    I   *20850*   U.S. - Montana *20850*

V   *Physaria saximontana* Rollins var. *saximontana* *20850*
    V   *20850*   U.S. - Wyoming *20850*

V   *Physaria stylosa* Rollins *20850*
    I   *20850*   U.S. - Utah *20850*

R   *Physocardamum davisii* Hedge *12840*
    R   *12840*   Turkey *12840*

R   *Physoptychis haussknechtii* Bornm. *12840*
    R   *12840*   Turkey *12840*

E   *Polyctenium williamsiae* Rollins *20850*
    E   *20850*   U.S. - Nevada *20850*

I   *Prionotrichon gaudanense* (Litv.) Botsch. *5942*
    I   *5942*   Turkmenistan (west) *5942*

I   *Pseudovesicaria digitata* (C. Meyer) Rupr. *5942*
    I   *5942*   Russia - North Caucasus *5942*
    I   *5942*   Armenia *5942*
    I   *5942*   Azerbaijan (Caucasus Mts.) *5942*
    I   *5942*   Georgia (Caucasus Mts.) *5942*

R   *Ptilotrichum macrocarpum* (DC.) Boiss. *20171*
    R   France (south)

R   *Ptilotrichum purpureum* (Lag. & Rodr.) Boiss. *20171*
    R   Spain

R   *Raphanorhyncha crassa* Rollins *9664*
    R   *9666*   Mexico *9664*

I   *Redowskia sophiifolia* Cham. & Schlecht. *5942*
    I   *5942*   Russia (Far East) - Khabarovsk *5942*

R   *Rhizobotrya alpina* Tausch *18264, 20171*
    R   *18264*   Italy (Trentino-Alto Adige, Veneto) *18264*

E   *Rhynchosinapis johnstonii* (Samp.) Heywood *17781, 20171*
    E   *8322*   Portugal *8322*

R   *Rhynchosinapis nivalis* (Boiss. & Heldr.) Heywood *20171*
    R   Greece

R   *Ricotia davisiana* Burtt *12840*
    R   *12840*   Turkey *12840*

V   *Ricotia isatoides* (Barbey) B.L. Burtt *20171*
    V   *20731*   Greece - Crete (Karpathos) *20731*

V   *Ricotia tenuifolia* Sibth. & Sm. *12840*
    V   *12840*   Turkey *12840*

R   *Ricotia varians* Burtt *12840*
    R   *12840*   Turkey *12840*

R   *Robeschia schimperi* (Boiss.) O. Schulz *10269*
    R   Egypt (Sinai) *10270*

R	*Romanschulzia costaricensis* (Standley) Rollins *9006*		
	R	*9666*	Costa Rica *9006*
	R	*19577*	Panama *9006*
R	*Romanschulzia guatemalensis* (Standley) Rollins *9004*		
	R	*9666*	Guatemala *9004*
R	*Rorippa aurea* (Boiss. & Heldr.) Hub.-Mor. *12840*		
	R	*12840*	Turkey *12840*
R	*Rorippa calycina* (Engelm.) Rydb. *20850*		
	E	*20850*	Canada - Mackenzie *20850*
	I	*20850*	U.S. - Idaho *20850*
	E	*20850*	U.S. - Montana *20850*
	I	*20850*	U.S. - Nebraska *20850*
	Ex/E	*20850*	U.S. - North Dakota *20850*
	V	*20850*	U.S. - Washington *20850*
	R	*20850*	U.S. - Wyoming *20850*
Ex	*Rorippa coloradensis* R. Stuckey *20850, 14662*		
	Ex	*20850*	U.S. - Colorado *20850*
R	*Rorippa columbiae* Suksdorf ex T.J. Howell *20850*		
	E	*20850*	U.S. - California *20850*
	R	*20850*	U.S. - Oregon *20850*
	V	*20850*	U.S. - Washington *20850*
V	*Rorippa divaricata* *19305*		
	V	*19305*	New Zealand - North Is. *19305*
E	*Rorippa gambelii* (S.Watson) Rollins & Al-Shehbaz *20883, 20850*		
	E	*20850*	U.S. - California *20850*
	Ex/E	*20883*	Mexico *20883*
R	*Rorippa icarica* Rech.f.		
	R		Greece
V	*Rorippa nikkoensis* Hara *10572*		
	V	*10572*	Japan *10572*
V	*Rorippa ramosa* Rollins *20850*		
	E	*20850*	U.S. - Texas *20850*
E	*Rorippa subumbellata* Rollins *20850*		
	E	*20850*	U.S. - California *20850*
	E	*20850*	U.S. - Nevada *20850*
I	*Rytidocarpus moricandioides* Coss.		
	I		Morocco
R	*Schivereckia berteroides* Fisch. ex M.I.Alex. *8000, 20171*		
	R		former European USSR (Ural Mountains)
I	*Schivereckia podolica* (Besser) Andrz. *8000, 20171*		
	E	*19949*	Romania (eastern) *8000*
	I	*5942*	Russia (E.Europe) - East *5942*
	I	*5942*	Russia (E.Europe) - South *5942*
	I	*5942*	Russia (Siberia) - West *5942*
	I	*5942*	Kazakhstan (north east) *5942*
	E	*20655*	Ukraine (Podolia) *20649*
E	*Schoenocrambe argillacea* (Welsh & Atwood) Rollins *20850, 19124*		
	E	*20850*	U.S. - Utah (south central Uinta basin) *20850*
E	*Schoenocrambe barnebyi* (Welsh & Atwood) Rollins *20850, 19124*		
	E	*20850*	U.S. - Utah (San Rafael Swell and Capitol Reef national park) *20850*
V	*Schoenocrambe suffrutescens* (Rollins) Welsh & Chatterley *19124*		
	V	*19124*	U.S. - Utah (Uinta basin) *19124*
V	*Sibara deserti* (M.E. Jones) Rollins *20850*		
	I	*20850*	U.S. - California *20850*
	I	*20850*	U.S. - Nevada *20850*
E	*Sibara filifolia* (Greene) Greene *20850*		

	E	*20850*	U.S. - California *20850*
R	*Sibara rosulata* Rollins *20850*		
	I	*20850*	U.S. - California *20850*
V	*Sinapidendron angustifolium* (DC.) Lowe		
	V		Portugal - Madeira
R	*Sinapidendron frutescens* (Aiton) Lowe		
	R		Portugal - Madeira
I	*Sinapidendron palmense* (Kuntze) O.E. Schulz		
	I		Spain - Canary Is.
V	*Sinapidendron rupestre* Lowe *17891*		
	V		Portugal - Madeira *17891*
R	*Sinapis allionii* Jacq.		
	R		Egypt
I	*Sinapis aucheri* (Boiss.) O. Schulz		
	I		Egypt
R	*Sinapis turgida* Delile		
	R		Egypt
R	*Sisymbrium cavanillesianum* Castrov. & Valdés Berm. *17891, 20171*		
	R	*20874*	Spain *20874*
R	*Sisymbrium matritense* P.W.Ball & Heywood, non Pau *20171*		
	R		Spain
R	*Sisymbrium maurum* Maire		
	R		Morocco
V	*Smelowskia calycina* (Steph. ex Willd.) C.A. Mey var. *porsildii* Drury & Rollins *20850, 1034*		
	E	*20850*	Canada - Yukon Territory *20850*
	V	*20850*	U.S. - Alaska *20850*
V	*Smelowskia holmgrenii* Rollins *20850*		
	V	*20850*	U.S. - Nevada *20850*
R	*Smelowskia inopinata* (Kom.) Kom. *11552, 11552*		
	R	*11552*	Russian Federation (extreme east) *11552*
E	*Smelowskia ovalis* Jones var. *congesta* Rollins *20850*		
	E	*20850*	U.S. - California *20850*
V	*Smelowskia pyriformis* Drury & Rollins *20850*		
	V	*20850*	U.S. - Alaska *20850*
R	*Sobolewskia sibirica* (Willd.) P.W.Ball *20171*		
	R		former European USSR
E	*Stanfordia californica* S.Watson *20850*		
	E	*20850*	U.S. - California *20850*
V	*Stanleya albescens* M.E. Jones *20850*		
	I	*20850*	U.S. - Arizona *20850*
	I	*20850*	U.S. - Colorado *20850*
	I	*20850*	U.S. - New Mexico *20850*
R	*Sterigmostemum sulphureum* (Banks & Sol.) Bornm. ssp. *glandulosum* Hub.-Mor. & Reese *12840*		
	R	*12840*	Turkey *12840*
V	*Streptanthus albidus* Greene *20850*		
	I	*20850*	U.S. - California *20850*
E	*Streptanthus albidus* E. Greene ssp. *albidus* *20850*		
	E	*20850*	U.S. - California *20850*
V	*Streptanthus albidus* Greene ssp. *peramoenus* (Greene) Kruckeberg *20850*		
	V	*20850*	U.S. - California *20850*
R	*Streptanthus barbiger* Greene *20850*		
	I	*20850*	U.S. - California *20850*

E   *Streptanthus batrachopus* J.L. Morrison *20850*
    E   *20850*   U.S. - California   *20850*

V   *Streptanthus bernardinus* (Greene) Parish *20850*
    V   *20850*   U.S. - California   *20850*

V   *Streptanthus brachiatus* F.W. Hoffmann *20850*
    I   *20850*   U.S. - California   *20850*

E   *Streptanthus brachiatus* F. W. Hoffman ssp. *brachiatus* Dolan & Lapre *20850*
    E   *20850*   U.S. - California   *20850*

E   *Streptanthus brachiatus* F.W. Hoffman ssp. *hoffmanii* Dolan & Lapre *20850*
    E   *20850*   U.S. - California   *20850*

V   *Streptanthus bracteatus* Gray *20850*
    V   *20850*   U.S. - Texas   *20850*

E   *Streptanthus callistus* J.L. Morrison *20850*
    E   *20850*   U.S. - California   *20850*

V   *Streptanthus campestris* S.Watson *20850*
    V   *20850*   U.S. - California   *20850*

E   *Streptanthus cordatus* Nutt. var. *piutensis* J.T. Howell *20850*
    E   *20850*   U.S. - California   *20850*

V   *Streptanthus cutleri* Cory *20850*
    V   *20850*   U.S. - Texas   *20850*

V   *Streptanthus drepanoides* Kruckeberg & Morrison *20850*
    R   *20850*   U.S. - California   *20850*

V   *Streptanthus fenestratus* (Greene) J.T. Howell *20850*
    V   *20850*   U.S. - California   *20850*

Ex/E   *Streptanthus glandulosus* Hook. var. *hoffmanii* Kruckeberg *20850*
    Ex/E   *20850*   U.S. - California   *20850*

E   *Streptanthus glandulosus* Hook ssp. *pulchellus* (Greene) Kruckeberg *20850*
    E   *20850*   U.S. - California   *20850*

E   *Streptanthus hispidus* Gray *20850*
    E   *20850*   U.S. - California   *20850*

V   *Streptanthus howellii* S.Watson *20850*
    E   *20850*   U.S. - California   *20850*
    V   *20850*   U.S. - Oregon   *20850*

E   *Streptanthus insignis* Jepson ssp. *lyonii* Kruckeberg & Morrison *20850, 10260*
    E   *20850*   U.S. - California   *20850*

R   *Streptanthus maculatus* Nutt. *20850*
    I   *20850*   U.S. - Arkansas   *20850*
    I   *20850*   U.S. - Oklahoma   *20850*
    V   *20850*   U.S. - Texas   *20850*

V   *Streptanthus morrisonii* F.W. Hoffmann *20850*
    I   *20850*   U.S. - California   *20850*

V   *Streptanthus morrisonii* F.W. Hoffmann ssp. *elatus* F.W. Hoffmann *20850*
    V   *20850*   U.S. - California   *20850*

E   *Streptanthus morrisonii* F.W. Hoffmann ssp. *hirtiflorus* F.W. Hoffmann *20850*
    E   *20850*   U.S. - California   *20850*

E   *Streptanthus morrisonii* F. W. Hoffmann ssp. *kruckebergii* Dolan & Lapre *20850*
    E   *20850*   U.S. - California   *20850*

V   *Streptanthus morrisonii* F. W. Hoffmann ssp. *morrisonii* *20850*
    V   *20850*   U.S. - California   *20850*

E   *Streptanthus niger* Greene *20850*
    E   *20850*   U.S. - California   *20850*

R   *Streptanthus oliganthus* Rollins *20850*
    V   *20850*   U.S. - California   *20850*
    V   *20850*   U.S. - Nevada   *20850*

V   *Streptanthus sparsiflorus* Rollins *20850*
    V   *20850*   U.S. - New Mexico   *20850*
    V   *20850*   U.S. - Texas   *20850*

R   *Streptanthus squamiformis* Goodman *20850*
    V   *20850*   U.S. - Arkansas   *20850*
    E   *20850*   U.S. - Oklahoma   *20850*

Ex   *Stroganowia sagittata* Karelin & Kir. *6930*
    Ex   *6930*   Asiatic U.S.S.R.   *6930*

E   *Stroganowia tiehmii* Rollins *20850*
    E   *20850*   U.S. - Nevada   *20850*

V   *Syrenia talijevii* Klokov *20171*
    V   former European USSR

R   *Thelypodiopsis alpina* (Standley & Steyerm.) Rollins *9664*
    R   *9666*   Guatemala   *9664*

V   *Thelypodiopsis ambigua* (S. Watts.) Al-Shehbaz *20850*
    I   *20850*   U.S. - Arizona   *20850*
    E   *20850*   U.S. - Utah   *20850*

V   *Thelypodiopsis ambigua* (S. Wats.) Al-Shehbaz var. *ambigua* *20850*
    I   *20850*   U.S. - Arizona   *20850*

V   *Thelypodiopsis ambigua* (S. Wats.) Al-Shehbaz var. *erecta* Rollins *20850*
    I   *20850*   U.S. - Arizona   *20850*
    I   *20850*   U.S. - Utah   *20850*

R   *Thelypodiopsis arcuata* (Rollins) Rollins *9664*
    R   *9666*   Mexico   *9664*

R   *Thelypodiopsis divaricata* (Rollins) Welsh & Reveal *20850*
    R   *20850*   U.S. - Utah   *20850*

R   *Thelypodiopsis incisa* Rollins *9664*
    R   *9666*   Mexico   *9664*

R   *Thelypodiopsis retrofracta* (Rollins) Rollins *9664*
    R   *9666*   Mexico   *9664*

R   *Thelypodiopsis versicolor* (Brandegee) Rollins *9664*
    R   *9666*   Mexico   *9664*

R   *Thelypodiopsis wootonii* (H. Robinson) Rollins *9664*
    R   *9666*   Mexico   *9664*

R   *Thelypodium brachycarpum* Torr. *20850*
    I   *20850*   U.S. - California   *20850*
    V   *20850*   U.S. - Oregon   *20850*

V   *Thelypodium eucosmum* B.L. Robins. *20850*
    V   *20850*   U.S. - Oregon   *20850*

E   *Thelypodium howellii* (M.E. Peck) Al-Shehbaz ssp. *spectabilis* (M.E. Peck) Al-Shehbaz *20850*
    E   *20850*   U.S. - Oregon   *20850*

R   *Thelypodium longipes* (Rollins) Rollins *9664*
    R   *9666*   Mexico   *9664*

R   *Thelypodium repandum* Rollins *20850*
    R   *20850*   U.S. - Idaho   *20850*

V   *Thelypodium rollinsii* Al-Shehbaz *20850*
    V   *20850*   U.S. - Utah   *20850*

V   *Thelypodium sagittatum* (Nutt.) Endl. ex Walp. ssp. *ovalifolium* (Rydb.) Al-Shehbaz *20850*
    V   *20850*   U.S. - Nevada   *20850*

E		20850 U.S. - Utah *20850*
E	*Thelypodium stenopetalum* S.Watson *20850*	
	E	20850 U.S. - California *20850*
R	*Thelypodium texanum* (Cory) Rollins *20850*	
	R	20850 U.S. - Texas *20850*
R	*Thlaspi aghricum* Davis & Tan *12840*	
	R	12840 Turkey *12840*
R	*Thlaspi aileeniae* Rollins *20850*	
	R	20850 U.S. - Idaho *20850*
R	*Thlaspi arcticum* Porsild *20850, 1034, 21309*	
	I	20850 Canada - British Columbia *20850*
	E	20850 Canada - Mackenzie *20850*
	V	20850 Canada - Yukon Territory *20850*
	R	20850 U.S. - Alaska *20850*
R	*Thlaspi bornmuelleri* (Rech.) Hedge *12840*	
	R	12840 Turkey *12840*
R	*Thlaspi bulbosum* Spruner ex Boiss. *20171*	
	R	Greece
V	*Thlaspi caerulescens* J. & C. Presl. ssp. *tatrense* (Zapal) Dvorakova *19321*	
	V	19321 Slovakia *19321*
E	*Thlaspi cariense* A. Carlstrom *12840*	
	E	12840 Turkey *12840*
R	*Thlaspi cilicicum* (Boiss.) Hayek *12840*	
	R	12840 Turkey *12840*
R	*Thlaspi corymbosum* (Gay) Reichb. *18154*	
	I	Italy *8000*
	R	18154 Switzerland *8000*
R	*Thlaspi crassum* Davis *12840*	
	R	12840 Turkey *12840*
R	*Thlaspi dacicum* Heuff. ssp. *banaticum* (Uechtz.) Jár *17823, 20171*	
	R	19949 Romania *20631*
R	*Thlaspi densiflorum* Boiss. & Kotschy *12840*	
	R	12840 Turkey *12840*
V	*Thlaspi dolichocarpum* (Zohary) Greuter & Burdet *12840*	
	V	12840 Turkey *12840*
R	*Thlaspi eigii* (Zohary) Greuter & Burdet *12840*	
	R	12840 Turkey *12840*
R	*Thlaspi elegans* Boiss. *12840*	
	R	12840 Turkey *12840*
R	*Thlaspi epirotum* Halácsy *20171*	
	R	Greece
R	*Thlaspi jankae* A.Kern. *19266, 20171*	
	R	21091 Bosnia & Herzegovina *21091*
	R	Hungary
	R	19417 Romania *17762*
	V	19615 Slovakia *6951*
R	*Thlaspi japonicum* H. Boissieu *10572*	
	R	10572 Japan *10572*
E	*Thlaspi montanum* L. var. *californicum* (S.Watson) P. Holmgren *20850*	
	E	20850 U.S. - California *20850*
R	*Thlaspi montanum* L. var. *siskiyouense* P. Holmgren *20850*	
	R	20850 U.S. - Oregon *20850*
R	*Thlaspi nevadense* Boiss. & Reut. *20171*	
	R	Spain
R	*Thlaspi papillosum* Boiss. *12840*	

	R	12840 Turkey *12840*
R	*Thlaspi parviflorum* A. Nels. *20850*	
	I	20850 U.S. - Idaho *20850*
	V	20850 U.S. - Montana *20850*
	R	20850 U.S. - Wyoming *20850*
V	*Thlaspi schudichii* Soó et Kárp *17786*	
	V	20686 Hungary *17786*
R	*Thlaspi sintenisii* Hausskn. ex Bornm. *12840*	
	R	12840 Turkey *12840*
R	*Thlaspi watsonii* Davis *12840*	
	R	12840 Turkey *12840*
V	*Thlaspi zaffranii* (F.K.Mey.) Greuter & Burdet *20731*	
	V	20731 Greece - Crete *20731*
E	*Thysanocarpus conchuliferus* Greene *20850*	
	E	20850 U.S. - California *20850*
V	*Torularia aculeolata* (Desf.) O.E. Schulz	
	V	Egypt
R	*Trachystoma aphanoneurum* Maire & M. Weiller	
	R	Morocco
Ex/E	*Tropidocarpum capparideum* Greene *20850, 14662*	
	Ex/E	20850 U.S. - California *20850*
V	*Vella lucentina* M.B.Crespo *20648*	
	V	20692 Spain (near Alicante city) *20692*
E	*Warea amplexifolia* (Nutt.) Nutt. *20850, 17890*	
	E	20850 U.S. - Florida *20850*
E	*Warea carteri* Small *20850, 7983*	
	E	20850 U.S. - Florida *20850*
E	*Wasabia koreana* Nakai *15957*	
	E	Korea, South (Dagelet Is.) *15957*

Crypteroniaceae

Number of genera:	1
Number of species:	4-10
Recorded threatened species:	1 (14%)

India, Philippines, Malay Archipelago.

V	*Axinandra zeylanica* Thwaites *10276*	
	V	12838 Sri Lanka *10276*

Cucurbitaceae

Number of genera:	90
Number of species:	700
Recorded threatened species:	74 (10%)

Tropical and subtropical; rarely temperate or cool temperate.

R	*Apatzingania arachoidea* Dieterle *9669*	
	R	11367 Mexico *9669*
E	*Apodanthera ferreyrana* R.M. Crovetto *18200*	
	E	9446 Peru *18200*
I	*Bryonia lappifolia* Vassilcz. *5942*	
	I	5942 Tajikistan *5942*
	I	5942 Uzbekistan *5942*
R	*Bryonia melanocarpa* Nabiev *5942*	
	R	5942 Kazakhstan (southern) *5942*
E	*Cayaponia denticulata* Jeffrey *20883, 10747*	
	I	20883 Panama *20883*
R	*Chalema synanthera* Dieterle *9670*	
	R	11367 Mexico *9670*
I	*Coccinia subglabra* C. Jeffrey *7749*	

I		Mozambique *7749*

I   *Coccinia ulugurensis* **Harms** *19519*
    I   5926   Tanzania (Uluguru and Ukaguru Mts.) *19519*

I   *Corallocarpus gracillipes* (**Naudin) Cogn.**
    I   India - Tamil Nadu (Pondicherry, Carnatic)

R   *Cremastopus minimus* (**S.Watson) P.G. Wilson** *11367*
    R   11367   Mexico *11367*

R   *Cremastopus rostratus* **P.G. Wilson** *11367*
    R   11367   Mexico *11367*

I   *Cucumella aetheocarpa* **Jeffrey** *19519*
    I   5926   Tanzania (Tunduru) *19519*

R   *Cucumis globosus* **C. Jeffrey** *19519*
    R   5926   Tanzania (Mbeya Distr.) *19519*

E   *Cucurbita okeechobeensis* (**Small) Bailey** *20850, 16110*
    E   20850   U.S. - Florida (L. Okeechobee) *20850*

E   *Cucurbita okeechobeensis* **Bailey ssp.**
    okeechobeensis *20850*
    E   20850   U.S. - Florida *20850*

R   *Cyclanthera bourgeana* **Naudin** *11367*
    R   11367   Mexico *11367*

E   *Cyclanthera mathewsii* **Arn.** *18200*
    E   9446   Peru *18200*

V   *Dendrosicyos socotrana* **Balf. f.** *15534*
    V   15534   Yemen - Socotra *15534*

I   *Diplocyclos leiocarpus* (**Gilg) C. Jeffrey** *19519*
    I   5926   Tanzania (Lindi) *19519*

R   *Elaterium carthagenense* **Jacq. var.** *cordatum*
    (**Hook.f.) Svenson** *11117*
    R   Ecuador - Galapagos (V. Alcedo; Pinta;
         Santiago) *11117*

R   *Eureiandra balfourii* **Cogn.** *15534*
    R   15534   Yemen - Socotra *15534*

E   *Frantzia panamensis* **Wunderlin** *20883, 9006*
    I   20883   Panama *20883*

I   *Gerrardanthus grandiflorus* **Cogn.** *19519*
    I   20057   Kenya (Buda forest) *20057*
    I   5926   Tanzania (Lushoto) *19519*

R   *Gerrardanthus tomentosus* **Hook.f.** *20604*
    R   20604   South Africa - Natal *20604*

R   *Hanburia parviflora* **J.D. Smith** *9004*
    R   11367   Guatemala *9004*
    R   11367   Mexico *9004*

R   *Ibervillea sonorae* (**S.Watson) Greene** *11367*
    R   11367   Mexico *11367*

I   *Luffa umbellata* (**Klein) M. Roemer**
    I   India - Kerala (Travancore coast)

R   *Marah guadelupensis* (**S.Watson) Greene** *11367*
    R   11367   Mexico *11367*

R   *Marah watsonii* (**Cogn.) Greene** *20850*
    I   20850   U.S. - California *20850*

I   *Melothria amplexicaulis* (**M. Lawson) Cogn.**
    I   India - Tamil Nadu

I   *Melothria domingensis* **Cong.** *5642*
    I   Dominican Republic (Cienaga-Culata, Constanza)
         5642

I   *Melothria guamensis* **Merr.** *20818*
    I   20818   North Mariana Is. (Saipan) *18035*
    V   20818   U.S. - Guam *18338*

I   *Momordica glabra* **Zimm.** *19519*
    I   5926   Tanzania (east Usambara Mts & Tanga)
         19519

I   *Momordica leiocarpa* **Gilg** *19519*
    I   5926   Tanzania (Lushoto) *19519*

I   *Momordica pycnantha* **Harms** *19519*
    I   5926   Tanzania (Lindi) *5926*

I   *Momordica subangulata* **Blume**
    I   India - Karnataka (South Canara)
    I   India - Kerala (Wynaad)

R   *Nothoalsomitra suberosa* (**Bailey) Telford** *20681*
    R   20681   Australia - Queensland *20681*

R   *Parasicyos maculatus* **Dieterle** *9004*
    R   11367   Guatemala *9004*

I   *Penelopeia suburceolata* **Cogn.** *19408*
    I   19408   Dominican Republic *19408*

I   *Peponium leucanthum* (**Gilg) Cogn.** *19519*
    I   5926   Tanzania (Lindi) *19519*

E   *Peponium sublitorale* **C. Jeffrey & J.S. Page** *14981*
    E   14981   Seychelles - Coralline Is. *14981*

R   *Peponopsis adhaerens* **Naudin** *11367*
    R   11367   Mexico *11367*

V   *Psiguria sp* **Britt.1** *20883*
    I   20883   Puerto Rico *20883*

R   *Pterosicyos laciniatus* **Brandegee** *9004*
    R   11367   Guatemala *9004*
    R   11367   Mexico *9004*

R   *Sechiopsis galeottii* **Cogn.** *11367*
    R   11367   Guatemala *11367*
    R   11367   Mexico *11367*

R   *Sechiopsis tetraptera* **Dieterle** *9670*
    R   11367   Mexico *9670*

R   *Sechium hintonii* (**P.G. Wilson) C. Jeffrey** *11368*
    R   11367   Mexico *11368*

R   *Sechium talamancensis* (**Wunderlin) C. Jeffrey** *11368*
    R   11367   Costa Rica *11368*

R   *Sechium villosa* (**Wunderlin) C. Jeffrey** *11368*
    R   11367   Costa Rica *11368*

R   *Sicyocaulis pentagonus* **Wiggins** *11117*
    R   Ecuador - Galapagos (V.Alcedo, Isabela; S.
         Cruz) *11117*

R   *Sicyos alba* (**St. John) Telford** *14209*
    R   14209   U.S. - Hawaii *14209*

E   *Sicyos albus* (**St. John) Telford** *20850*
    E   20850   U.S. - Hawaii *20850*

R   *Sicyos ampelophyllus* **Woot. & Standl.** *20850*
    I   20850   U.S. - Arizona *20850*
    I   20850   U.S. - New Mexico *20850*
    E   20850   U.S. - Texas *20850*

E   *Sicyos chiriquensis* **Hammel & D'Arcy** *20883*
    I   20883   Panama *20883*

E   *Sicyos cucumerinus* **Gray** *20850, 14209*
    E   20850   U.S. - Hawaii (Moloka`i, Maui, Hawai`i)
         20850

V   *Sicyos erostratus* **St. John** *20850, 14209*
    V   20850   U.S. - Hawaii (O`ahu, Moloka`i) *20850*

R   *Sicyos glaber* **Woot.** *20850*
    E   20850   U.S. - New Mexico *20850*
    R   20850   U.S. - Texas *20850*

V   *Sicyos herbstii* (**St. John) Telford** *20850*

	I	20850	U.S. - Hawaii 20850
Ex/E	*Sicyos hillebrandii* St. John 20850, 14209		
	Ex/E	20850	U.S. - Hawaii (east Maui) 20850
V	*Sicyos lasiocephalus* Skottsb. 14209		
	R	20850	U.S. - Hawaii (Hawai`i) 20850
E	*Sicyos macrophyllus* Gray 20850, 14209		
	E	20850	U.S. - Hawaii (Mauna Kea, Maun Loa) 20850
R	*Sicyos maximowiczii* Cogn. 20850		
	R	20850	U.S. - Hawaii 20850
E	*Sicyos semitonsus* St. John 20850, 14209		
	I	20850	U.S. - Hawaii (Laysan) 20850
Ex	*Sicyos villosa* Hook.f. 11117		
	Ex		Ecuador - Galapagos (Floreana) 11117
V	*Sicyos waimanaloensis* St. John 20850, 14209		
	V	20850	U.S. - Hawaii 20850
V	*Sicyos weberbaueri* Harms 18200		
	V	9446	Peru 18200
R	*Siraitia taiwaniana* (Hay.) C. Jeffrey ex Lu & Zheng 20511		
	R	20511	Taiwan 20511
R	*Tecunumania quetzalteca* Standley & Steyerm. 11367		
	R	11367	Guatemala 11367
	R	11367	Mexico 11367
R	*Trichosanthes baviensis* Gagnepain 6057		
	R		Vietnam 6057
R	*Trichosanthes boninensis* Nakai ex Tuy. 8622		
	R	19134	Japan - Ogasawara-shoto (Chichijima) 8622
I	*Trichosanthes lepiniana* (Naudin) Cogn.		
	I		India - Tamil Nadu (Nilgiri Hills)
I	*Trichosanthes perrottetiana* Cogn.		
	I		India - Tamil Nadu (Pondicherry, Carnatic)
R	*Trichosanthes subvelutina* F.Muell. 20681		
	I	20681	Australia - New South Wales 20681
	I	20681	Australia - Queensland 20681
I	*Trichosanthes villosula* Cogn.		
	I		India - Tamil Nadu (Nilgiri Hills)
R	*Vaseyanthus brandegei* (Cogn.) Rose 11367		
	R	11367	Mexico 11367
I	*Zanonia clarkei* King		
	I		Malaysia - Peninsular Malaysia (Selangor; Perak)

Cunoniaceae

Number of genera:	25
Number of species:	350
Recorded threatened species:	25 (7%)

Southern Hemisphere, especially Australia, New Guinea and New Caledonia; also Mexico and West Indies.

V	*Acrophyllum australe* (Cunn.) Hoogl. 20681		
	V	20681	Australia - New South Wales 20681
V	*Acsmithia vitiense* (A.Gray) Hoogl. 10253, 19630		
	V	19630	Fiji 19630
R	*Ceratopetalum corymbosum* C.White 20681		
	R	20681	Australia - Queensland 20681
R	*Ceratopetalum macrophyllum* Hoogl. 20681		
	R	20681	Australia - Queensland 20681
R	*Ceratopetalum virchowii* C.White 20681		
	R	20681	Australia - Queensland 20681

V	*Cunonia aoupiniensis* Hoogl. ined. 20893		
	V	20893	New Caledonia 20893
V	*Cunonia ouaiemensis* Guillaumin & Virot 20893		
	V	20893	New Caledonia 20893
R	*Cunonia rotundifolia* Däniker 20893		
	R	20893	New Caledonia 20893
V	*Geissois imthurnii* Turrill 10253		
	V	19630	Fiji (Viti Levu) 19630
V	*Geissois stipularis* A.C. Smith 19630		
	V	19630	Fiji (Viti Levu) 19630
V	*Geissois superba* Gillespie 19630		
	V	19630	Fiji (Viti Levu) 19630
R	*Geissois ternata* A.Gray var. *minor* 19630		
	R	19630	Fiji (Viti Levu, Vanua Levu) 19630
E	*Geissois ternata* A.Gray var. *serrata* 19630		
	E	19630	Fiji 19630
R	*Pancheria humboldtiana* Guillaumin 20893		
	R	20893	New Caledonia 20893
R	*Pancheria multijuga* Guillaumin 20893		
	R	20893	New Caledonia 20893
R	*Pancheria robusta* Guillaumin 20893		
	R	20893	New Caledonia 20893
R	*Schizomeria whitei* J.Mattf. 20681		
	R	20681	Australia - Queensland 20681
V	*Spiraeanthemum graeffei* Seemann 19630		
	V	19630	Fiji (Viti Levu) 19630
V	*Spiraeanthemum serratum* Gillespie 19630		
	V	19630	Fiji (Viti Levu, Taveuni) 19630
V	*Weinmannia exigua* A.C. Smith 19630		
	V	19630	Fiji (Vanua Levu) 19630
E	*Weinmannia laurina* (Woods.) Bernardi var. *pseudolaurina* (Woodson) Bernardi 20883, 10747		
	I	20883	Panama 20883
V	*Weinmannia ouaiemensis* Virot 20893		
	V	20893	New Caledonia 20893
V	*Weinmannia portlandiana* Howard & Proctor 20883, 13336		
	V	13336	Jamaica 20883
R	*Weinmannia raiateensis* J.Moore 20845		
	R	20845	French Polynesia - Society Is. (Raiatea) 20845
Ex/E	*Weinmannia spiraeoides* A.Gray 19630		
	Ex/E	19630	Fiji (Ovalau) 19630
V	*Weinmannia vitiensis* Seemann 19630		
	V	19630	Fiji (Viti Levu, Taveuni, Kanavu, Moala) 19630

Cyrillaceae

Number of genera:	3
Number of species:	14
Recorded threatened species:	2 (14%)

Northern South America; Central America; West Indies; southeastern United States.

V	*Purdiaea ekmanii* Kirouac 5607		
	V	19105	Cuba (Santiago de Cuba; Holguin) 5607
V	*Purdiaea microphylla* Britton & P. Wilson 5607		
	V	19105	Cuba (Holguin; Guantanamo) 5607

Daphniphyllaceae

Number of genera:	1
Number of species:	35
Recorded threatened species:	2 (5%)

Asia and Malay Archipelago.

R   *Daphniphyllum glaucescens* var. *lanyuense* Huang. *20511*
     R   *20511* Taiwan *20511*

V   *Daphniphyllum humile* Maxim. ex Franchet & Savat. *5942*
     V   *11552* Russia (Far East) - Kurilskye Is. *5942*

Datiscaceae

Number of genera:	3
Number of species:	4
Recorded threatened species:	1 (25%)

Malesia; Asia; western North America.

V   *Datisca cannabina* L. *20171*
     V   *20731* Greece - East Aegean Is *20731*

Davidsoniaceae

Number of genera:	1
Number of species:	1
Recorded threatened species:	1 (100%)

Northeastern Australia.

E   *Davidsonia pruriens* F.Muell. var. *jerseyana* Bailey *20681*
     E   *20681* Australia - New South Wales *20681*

Degeneriaceae

Number of genera:	1
Number of species:	1
Recorded threatened species:	1 (100%)

Fiji.

R   *Degeneria roseiflora* J.M.Miller *10253, 19630*
     R   *19630* Fiji (Vanua Levu, Taveuni) *19630*

Diapensiaceae

Number of genera:	6
Number of species:	18
Recorded threatened species:	5 (27%)

Arctic & North temperate; south to Himalayas.

V   *Pyxidanthera brevifolia* Wells *20850*
     I   *20850* U.S. - New York *20850*
     V   *20850* U.S. - North Carolina *20850*
     V   *20850* U.S. - South Carolina *20850*

R   *Schizocodon ilicifolius* Maxim. var. *minus* (Makino) Yamaz. *10573*
     R   *10573* Japan *10573*

R   *Schizocodon intercedens* (Ohwi) Yamaz. *10573*
     R   *10573* Japan *10573*

V   *Shortia galacifolia* Torr. & Gray *20850*
     E   *20850* U.S. - Georgia *20850*
     V   *20850* U.S. - North Carolina *20850*
     V   *20850* U.S. - South Carolina *20850*

E   II   *Shortia galacifolia* Torr. & Gray var. *brevistyla* Davies *20850*
     E   *20850* U.S. - North Carolina *20850*

V   II   *Shortia galacifolia* Torr. & Gray var. *galacifolia* *20850*
     E   *20850* U.S. - Georgia *20850*
     V   *20850* U.S. - North Carolina *20850*
     V   *20850* U.S. - South Carolina *20850*

V   *Shortia rotundifolia* Makino *10573*
     V   *10573* Japan *10573*

Dichapetalaceae

Number of genera:	3
Number of species:	235
Recorded threatened species:	45 (19%)

Throughout the tropics, one S. African species.

R   *Dichapetalum asplundeanum* Prance *11589*
     R   *11589* Ecuador *11589*

R   *Dichapetalum barbosae* Torre *7749*
     R   Mozambique *7749*

I   *Dichapetalum braunii* Engl. & Krause *19521*
     I   *5926* Tanzania (Lindi & Kilwa) *19521*

E   *Dichapetalum bullatum* Standley & Steyermark *20883, 9004*
     R   *11589* Guatemala *20883*

E   *Dichapetalum coelhoi* Prance *20883*
     I   *20883* Brazil *20883*

E   *Dichapetalum fadenii* Breteler *20057*
     E   *20057* Kenya (Cha Simba, Mangea) *20057*

V   *Dichapetalum foreroi* Prance *20883*
     I   *20883* Colombia *20883*

I   *Dichapetalum gassitae* Breteler *21044*
     I   *21044* Gabon *21044*

I   *Dichapetalum gelonoides* (Roxb.) Engl. ssp. *andamanicum* (King) Leenh. *7771*
     I   India - Andaman Is. (South) *7771*

E   *Dichapetalum gentryi* Prance *20883, 9676*
     R   *11589* Panama *20883*

R   *Dichapetalum mendoncae* Torre *7749*
     R   Mozambique *7749*

R   *Dichapetalum nevermannianum* Standl. & Valerio *20883, 9037*
     I   *20883* Costa Rica *20883*
     I   *20883* Panama *20883*

I   *Dichapetalum nyangense* Pellegrin *21044*
     I   *21044* Gabon *21044*

R   *Dichapetalum pauper* Rizzini *20883*
     I   *20883* Brazil *20883*

I   *Dichapetalum staminellatum* Breteler *21044*
     I   *21044* Zaire (central) *21044*

E   *Dichapetalum steyermarkii* Prance *20883*
     I   *20883* Venezuela *20883*

V   *Dichapetalum stipulatum* Macbride *20883*
     I   *20883* Peru *20883*

I   *Dichapetalum trichocephalum* Breteler
     I   *21044* Gabon (Lecala) *21044*

R   *Dichapetalum zambesianum* Torre *7749*
     R   Mozambique *7749*

E   *Stephanopodium angulatum* (Little) Prance *20883*
     I   *20883* Ecuador *20883*

E   *Stephanopodium aptotum* Wheeler *20883, 11589*
     R   *11589* Colombia *20883*

V   *Stephanopodium blanchetianum* Baillon *20883*
    I   *20883* Brazil *20883*

V   *Stephanopodium engleri* Baillon *20883*
    I   *20883* Brazil *20883*

E   *Stephanopodium estrellense* Baillon *20883*
    I   *20883* Brazil *20883*

V   *Stephanopodium organense* (Rizzini) Prance *20883, 11589*
    I   *20883* Brazil *20883*

E   *Stephanopodium sessile* Rizzini *20883, 11589*
    I   *20883* Brazil *20883*

E   *Stephanopodium venezuelanum* Prance *20883, 11589*
    R   *11589* Venezuela *20883*

R   *Tapura acreana* (Ule) Rizzini *20883*
    I   *20883* Brazil *20883*
    I   *20883* Peru *20883*

V   *Tapura amazonica* var. *manausensis* Prance *20883*
    I   *20883* Brazil *20883*

E   *Tapura bullata* Standley *20883, 19352*
    I   *19352* Colombia *20883*

E   *Tapura colombiana* Cuatrecasas *20883, 19352*
    I   *20883* Panama *20883*
    I   *19352* Colombia *20883*

R   *Tapura coriacea* Macbride *20883*
    I   *20883* Peru *20883*

V   *Tapura cubensis* ssp. *minor* Prance *20883*
    I   *20883* Cuba *20883*

E   *Tapura ferreyrae* Prance *20883*
    I   *20883* Peru *20883*

E   *Tapura haitiensis* Urban & Ekman *20883*
    I   *20883* Haiti (Massif de la Hotte) *21008*

V   *Tapura ivorensis* Breteler *20274*
    V   *20858* Côte d'Ivoire *20274*
    V   *20858* Ghana *6072*

E   *Tapura juliani* Macbride *20883*
    I   *20883* Peru *20883*

V   *Tapura lanceolata* (Ducke) Rizzini *20883*
    I   *20883* Brazil *20883*

R   *Tapura latifolia* Bentham *20883*
    I   *20883* *20883*
    I   *20883* Dominica *20883*
    I   *20883* Guadeloupe *20883*
    I   *20883* Martinique *20883*
    I   *20883* St Kitts - Nevis *20883*

R   *Tapura mexicana* Prance *9677*
    R   *11589* Mexico *9677*

I   *Tapura neglecta* Halle & Heine *21044, 7927*
    I   *21044* Gabon *7927*

V   *Tapura orbicularis* Ekman ex Urban *20883, 5607*
    R   *19105* Cuba (Holguin) *20883*

E   *Tapura panamensis* Prance *20883, 12042*
    R   *11589* Panama *20883*

R   *Tapura peruviana* Krause *20883*
    I   *20883* Ecuador *20883*
    I   *20883* Peru *20883*

V   *Tapura peruviana* Krause var. *peruviana* *20883*
    I   *20883* Peru *20883*

R   *Tapura peruviana* Krause var. *petioliflora* Prance *20883*

    I   *20883* Ecuador *20883*
    I   *20883* Peru *20883*

E   *Tapura tessmannii* (Krause) Prance *20883*
    I   *20883* Peru *20883*

Didiereaceae

Number of genera:	4
Number of species:	11
Recorded threatened species:	3 (27%)

Dry parts of Madagascar.

R   *Alluaudia montagnacii* Rauh *10368*
    R   *19878* Madagascar *10368*

R   *Alluaudiopsis fiherenensis* Humbert & Choux *10368*
    R   *19878* Madagascar *10368*

R   *Alluaudiopsis marnieriana* Rauh *10368*
    R   *19878* Madagascar *10368*

Dilleniaceae

Number of genera:	10
Number of species:	350
Recorded threatened species:	30 (8%)

Tropical and subtropica, especially Australia.

I   *Acrotrema dissectum* Thwaites ex Hook.f. *10252*
    I   *16162* Sri Lanka *10252*

I   *Acrotrema lyratum* Thwaites ex Hook.f. *10252*
    I   *16162* Sri Lanka *10252*

I   *Acrotrema thwaitesii* Hook.f. & Thomson *10252*
    I   *16162* Sri Lanka *10252*

I   *Dillenia bussei* Gilg *19522*
    I   *5926* Tanzania *19522*

R   *Dillenia ferruginea* (Baillon) Gilg *14296*
    R   *19181* Seychelles (granitic) *14296*

V   *Dillenia fischeri* Merr. *12983*
    V   *15960* Philippines *12983*

I   *Dillenia luzoniensis* (Vid.) Martelli *13780*
    I   *15960* Philippines *13780*

V   *Dillenia megalantha* Merr. *12983*
    V   *15960* Philippines *12983*

V   *Dillenia philippinensis* Rolfe *12983*
    V   *15960* Philippines *12983*

E   *Doliocarpus olivaceus* Standl. *20883, 9006*
    I   *20883* Panama *20883*

E   *Hibbertia bouletii* Veillon *20893*
    E   *20893* New Caledonia *20893*

V   *Hibbertia crispula* J.Black *20681*
    V   *20681* Australia - South Australia *20681*

R   *Hibbertia elata* Maiden & Betche *20681*
    I   *20681* Australia - New South Wales *20681*
    I   *20681* Australia - Queensland *20681*

E   *Hibbertia favieri* Veillon *20893*
    E   *20893* New Caledonia *20893*

R   *Hibbertia hermanniifolia* DC. *20681*
    I   *20681* Australia - New South Wales *20681*
    I   *20681* Australia - Victoria *20681*

R   *Hibbertia hexandra* C.White *20681*
    I   *20681* Australia - New South Wales *20681*
    I   *20681* Australia - Queensland *20681*

R   *Hibbertia humifusa* F.Muell. *20681*
    R   *20681* Australia - Victoria *20681*

R   *Hibbertia kaputarensis* Conn *20681*
   R   *20681*   Australia - New South Wales *20681*

E   *Hibbertia margaretae* Veillon *20893*
   E   *20893*   New Caledonia *20893*

R   *Hibbertia miniata* C.Gardner *20681*
   R   *20681*   Australia - Western Australia *20681*

R   *Hibbertia montana* Steudel *20681*
   R   *20681*   Australia - Western Australia *20681*

R   *Hibbertia monticola* Stanley *20681*
   R   *20681*   Australia - Queensland *20681*

R   *Hibbertia nitida* Benth. *20681*
   R   *20681*   Australia - New South Wales *20681*

R   *Hibbertia paeninsularis* J.Black *20681*
   R   *20681*   Australia - South Australia *20681*

E   *Hibbertia rubescens* Veill. ex Guillaumin *20893*
   E   *20893*   New Caledonia *20893*

R   *Hibbertia silvestris* Diels *20681*
   R   *20681*   Australia - Western Australia *20681*

R   *Hibbertia spathulata* Wakef. *20681*
   R   *20681*   Australia - Victoria *20681*

E   *Schumacheria ahnifolia* Vahl *10276*
   E   *20013*   Sri Lanka *10276*

E   *Schumacheria angustifolia* Hook.f. & Thoms.
   E   *20013*   Sri Lanka *12838*

R   *Wormia triquetra* Rottb. *10276*
   R   *20013*   Sri Lanka *10276*

Dioncophyllaceae

Number of genera: 3
Number of species: 3
Recorded threatened species: 1   (33%)

Rain forests of tropical Africa.

I   *Triphyophyllum peltatum* (Hutch. & Dalz.) Airy Shaw
   I   Côte d'Ivoire
   I   Liberia
   I   Sierra Leone

Dipsacaceae

Number of genera: 10
Number of species: 260
Recorded threatened species: 62   (23%)

Eurasia and Africa, especially Mediterranean region.

R   *Cephalaria amana* Rech. fil. *12840*
   R   *12840*   Turkey *12840*

R   *Cephalaria baetica* Boiss.
   R   Spain

I   *Cephalaria calcarea* Albov
   I   former USSR *6930*

R   *Cephalaria dirmilensis* Hub.-Mor. *12840*
   R   *12840*   Turkey *12840*

R   *Cephalaria elmaliensis* Hub.-Mor. *12840*
   R   *12840*   Turkey *12840*

R   *Cephalaria hakkiarica* Matthews *12840*
   R   *12840*   Turkey *12840*

R   *Cephalaria isaurica* Matthews *12840*
   R   *12840*   Turkey *12840*

I   *Cephalaria litvinovii* Bobrov *5942, 20171*
   I   *5942*   Russia (E.Europe) - South *5942*

R   *Cephalaria lycica* Matthews *12840*
   R   *12840*   Turkey *12840*

R   *Cephalaria paphlagonica* Bobrov *12840*
   R   *12840*   Turkey *12840*

R   *Cephalaria radiata* Griseb. & Schenk *17823, 20171*
   R   *20631*   Romania *20631*

I   *Cephalaria salicifolia* Post *12840*
   I   *12840*   Turkey *12840*

I   *Cephalaria scoparia* Contandr. ex Quezel *12840*
   I   *12840*   Turkey *12840*

R   *Cephalaria sparsipilosa* Matthews *12840*
   R   *12840*   Turkey *12840*

V   *Cephalaria squamiflora* (Sieber) Greuter ssp.
    mediterranea (Viv.) Pignatti *20645*
   V   *20645*   Spain - Balearic Is. *20645*

R   *Cephalaria taurica* Szabo *12840*
   R   *12840*   Turkey *12840*

R   *Cephalaria uralensis* (Murray) Roemer & Schulter ssp.
    multifida (Roman) Roman & Beldie *17823*
   R   *19947*   Romania *20631*

V   *Dipsacus cephalarioides* Matthews & Kupicha *12840*
   V   *12840*   Turkey *12840*

V   *Dipsacus narcisseanus* Lawalree
   V   Cameroon (Bamboutos mts)

I   *Knautia baldensis* A.Kern. ex Borbás *20171*
   I   Italy (Venteto, Trentino) *20804*

I   *Knautia basaltica* Chass. & Szabó *20171*
   I   France (south-central mountains)

R   *Knautia dalmatica* Beck *20171*
   R   (former) Yugoslavia

R   *Knautia foreziensis* Chass. & Szabo *20171*
   R   France (Monts du Forez)

R   *Knautia kitaibelii* (Schult.) Borbás ssp. *tomentella*
    (Szabó) Baksay *20171*
   R   *20686*   Hungary *20686*

E   *Knautia lebrunii* Prudhomme *20528*
   E   *20528*   France (Pyrénées-Orientales) *20528*

R   *Knautia lucana* Lacaita & Szabó *20171*
   R   Italy (Basilicata) *20804*

V   *Knautia nevadensis* (M.Winkl. ex Szabó) Szabó *20171*
   V   *20076*   Portugal *20076*
   V   Spain

R   *Knautia norica* Ehrendorfer
   R   Austria

R   *Knautia pancicii* Szabó *20171*
   R   (former) Yugoslavia

I   *Knautia persicina* A.Kern. *20171*
   I   Italy (Veneto, Trentino) *20804*

R   *Knautia sarajevensis* (Beck) Szabó *20171*
   V   *21091*   Bosnia & Herzegovina *20852*
   R   (former) Yugoslavia

E   *Knautia tatarica* (L.) Szabó *20171*
   E   former European USSR

R   *Knautia travnicensis* (Beck) Szabo *20171*
   R   *21091*   Bosnia & Herzegovina *21091*
   R   (former) Yugoslavia

I   *Knautia velutina* Briq. *18154, 20171*
   I   Italy (Veneto, Lombary, Trentino) *8000*
   E   *18154*   Switzerland *18154*

R	*Pterocephalus arabicus* Boiss. *16168*	
	R	*16168* Egypt (Sinai) *16168*
V	*Pterocephalus dumetorum* (Brouss. ex Willd.) Coulter *20750*	
	V	*20750* Spain - Canary Is. *20750*
Ex/E	*Pterocephalus fructiculosus* Korovin *5942*	
	Ex/E	*5942* Turkmenistan *5942*
V	*Pterocephalus porphyranthus* Svent. *20750*	
	V	*20750* Spain - Canary Is. *20750*
E	*Pterocephalus virens* Berthel.	
	E	Spain - Canary Is.
R	*Scabiosa albocincta* Greuter *20171*	
	R	*20731* Greece - Crete *20731*
R	*Scabiosa camelorum* Coss. & Durieu *10488*	
	R	*14958* Algeria *10488*
R	*Scabiosa cartenniana* Pons & Quezel *10488*	
	R	*14958* Algeria *10488*
R	*Scabiosa columbaria* L. ssp. *paphlagonica* (Bornm.) Matthews *12840*	
	R	*12840* Turkey *12840*
R	*Scabiosa cyprica* Boiss. *14230*	
	R	*19164* Cyprus (Troodos) *14230*
R	*Scabiosa eremophila* Boiss.	
	R	Egypt
	R	Libya
R	*Scabiosa fumarioides* Vis. & Pancic *20171*	
	V	*21091* Bosnia & Herzegovina *21091*
	R	(former) Yugoslavia
R	*Scabiosa hololeuca* Bornm. *12840*	
	R	*12840* Turkey *12840*
R	*Scabiosa kurdica* Post *12840*	
	R	*12840* Turkey *12840*
R	*Scabiosa limonifolia* Vahl *18264, 20171*	
	R	*18264* Italy - Sicily *18264*
R	*Scabiosa minoana* (P.H.Davis) Greuter *20171*	
	R	*20731* Greece - Crete *20731*
I	*Scabiosa olgae* Albov *5942*	
	I	*5942* Russia - North Caucasus *5942*
R	*Scabiosa paucidentata* Hub.-Mor. *12840*	
	R	*12840* Turkey *12840*
R	*Scabiosa pseudobanatica* (Schur) Chstek ssp. *barbata* (E.J. Nyárády) Chstek *17823*	
	R	*19949* Romania *20635*
R	*Scabiosa pseudobanatica* (Schur) Chstek ssp. *pseudobanatica* (E.J. Nyárády) Chstek *17823*	
	R	*19949* Romania *17823*
R	*Scabiosa pseudograminifolia* Hub.-Mor. *12840*	
	R	*12840* Turkey *12840*
V	*Scabiosa pulsatilloides* Boiss. *15398, 20171*	
	V	*15398* Spain (Sierra Nevada) *15398*
R	*Scabiosa rhodopensis* Stoj. & Stef. *5204, 20171*	
	R	*5204* Bulgaria (Southern - two areas) *5204*
R	*Scabiosa roberti* Barratte	
	R	Tunisia
R	*Scabiosa saxatilis* Cav. ssp. *saxatilis* *20171*	
	R	*20692* Spain (Valencia and Alicante provinces) *20692*
R	*Scabiosa sulphurea* Boiss. & Huet *12840*	
	R	*12840* Turkey *12840*

I	*Scabiosa thysdrusiana* Le Houer.	
	I	Tunisia
V	*Succisa trichotocephala* Baksay	
	V	Cameroon
R	*Succisella carvalhoana* (Mariz) Baksay *20171*	
	R	*8322* Portugal *8322*

Dipterocarpaceae

Number of genera:	16
Number of species:	600
Recorded threatened species:	195 (32%)

Centered in tropical rain forests of Malaysia.

I	*Anisoptera reticulata* Ashton *7730*	
	V	Brunei Darussalam *13845*
	I	Malaysia - Sabah *13845*
	I	Malaysia - Sarawak (north east) *13845*
I	*Cotylelobium lewisianum* (Trimen ex Hook.f.) P. Ashton *8021*	
	I	Sri Lanka *8021*
E	*Cotylelobium scabriusculum* (Thwaites) Brandis *8021*	
	E	*12838* Sri Lanka *8021*
V	*Dipterocarpus baudii* Korth. *7730*	
	E	Kampuchea *13845*
	E	Myanmar *12848*
	V	*13845* Thailand (southeastern & peninsular regions) *19257*
	V	Vietnam *13845*
	E	Indonesia - Sumatra *13845*
	V	Malaysia (Peninsular) *13845*
R	*Dipterocarpus bourdilloni* Brandis *12848*	
	R	India (Kerala) *12848*
I	*Dipterocarpus chartaceus* Sym. *7730*	
	I	*16087* Thailand (peninsular region) *19257*
	V	*13926* Malaysia - Peninsular Malaysia *13845*
Ex/E	*Dipterocarpus cinereus* Sloot. *7730*	
	Ex/E	Indonesia - Sumatra (west) *13845*
V	*Dipterocarpus concavus* Foxw. *7730*	
	Ex/E	Indonesia - Sumatra (P. Singkep) *13845*
	V	*13926* Malaysia - Peninsular Malaysia (Pahang; Perak) *13845*
E	*Dipterocarpus conformis* Sloot. ssp. *conformis* *7730*	
	E	Indonesia - Sumatra (northwest) *13845*
I	*Dipterocarpus cuspidatus* Ashton *7730*	
	I	Malaysia - Sarawak (central north) *13845*
R	*Dipterocarpus eurynchus* Miq. *7730*	
	R	*13845* Brunei Darussalam *7730*
	I	*13845* Indonesia - Kalimantan (western) *7730*
	E	*13845* Indonesia - Sumatra *7730*
	R	*13845* Malaysia - Peninsular Malaysia (Terengganu, Johore) *7730*
	I	*13845* Malaysia - Sarawak *7730*
	V	*13845* Philippines *7730*
E	*Dipterocarpus glandulosus* Thwaites *8021*	
	E	*12838* Sri Lanka *8021*
R	*Dipterocarpus hasseltii* Blume *7730*	
	V	*13845* Thailand (Peninsular Thailand) *13845*
	V	*15734* Vietnam *13845*
	E	*13845* Indonesia - Java (Jemba, Janlappa) *13845*
	I	*13845* Indonesia - Kalimantan (south & east) *13845*
	V	*13845* Indonesia - Sumatra *13845*

V	13926	Malaysia - Peninsular Malaysia (central & north) *13845*
E	13845	Malaysia - Sabah (south-east) *13845*
V	13845	Philippines *13845*

V   *Dipterocarpus hispidus* Thwaites *8021*

    V   12838   Sri Lanka *8021*

E   *Dipterocarpus insignis* Thwaites *8021*

    E   12838   Sri Lanka (south-west) *8021*

V   *Dipterocarpus kerrii* King *7730*

V		Myanmar (Mergui - Victoria Point) *12848*
V	13845	Thailand (Peninsula) *13845*
V	13845	Indonesia - Kalimantan (northeast) *13845*
V		Indonesia - Sumatra (east) *13845*
V	13926	Malaysia - Peninsular Malaysia *19209*
E	13845	Philippines *13845*
V	13845	India - Andaman Is. (Goplakabang, Mt Harriet) *12848*

I   *Dipterocarpus lamellatus* Hook.f. *7730*

    I   13845   Malaysia - Sabah (Labuan,) *13845*

I   *Dipterocarpus littoralis* Blume *7730*

    I   Indonesia - Java (Banjumas) *13845*

I   *Dipterocarpus perakensis* Ashton *7730*

    I   Malaysia - Peninsular Malaysia (Penang; Dindings; Pangkor) *13845*

V   *Dipterocarpus rotundifolius* Foxw. *7609*

    V   13926   Malaysia - Peninsular Malaysia (Perak, Trengganu, Pahang) *7609*

V   *Dipterocarpus sublamellatus* Foxw. *7730*

E		Indonesia - Sumatra *13845*
V		Malaysia - Peninsular Malaysia (Johor) *19209*
V		Malaysia - Sarawak *13845*
V	20099	Singapore *20099*

E   *Dipterocarpus zeylanicus* Thwaites *8021*

    E   12838   Sri Lanka *8021*

R   *Hopea aequalis* Ashton *7730*

    I   Malaysia - Sabah *13845*
    R   Malaysia - Sarawak *13845*

I   *Hopea andersonii* Ashton ssp. *basalticola* Ashton *7730*

    I   Malaysia - Sabah *13845*
    I   Malaysia - Sarawak *13845*

I   *Hopea apiculata* Sym. *7730*

I	13845	Myanmar *13845*
I	13845	Thailand *13845*
E		Malaysia - Peninsular Malaysia *13845*

I   *Hopea aptera* Ashton *7730*

    I   Papua New Guinea (west, north) *7730*

V   *Hopea auriculata* Foxw. *7730*

    V   13926   Malaysia - Peninsular Malaysia (NE Johor; E. Pahang) *13845*

V   *Hopea bancana* (Boerl.) Sloot. *7730*

    V   Indonesia - Sumatra (Bangka) *7730*

I   *Hopea basilanica* Foxw. *7730*

    I   13845   Philippines (Mindanao, Basilan) *7730*

I   *Hopea bilitonensis* Ashton *7730*

    E   Indonesia - Sumatra (Belitung, Bangka) *13845*
    I   Malaysia - Peninsular Malaysia *13845*

Ex/E   *Hopea brachyptera* (Foxw.) Sloot. *7730*

    Ex/E   13845   Philippines (Mindanao) *13845*

V   *Hopea brevipetiolaris* (Thwaites) Ashton *8021*

    V   Sri Lanka (Kurunegala) *8021*

V   *Hopea cagayanensis* (Foxw.) Sloot. *7730*

    V   13845   Philippines (N.E. Luzon) *13845*

V   *Hopea celebica* Burck *7730*

    V   Indonesia (Sulawesi) *13845*

V   *Hopea chinensis* Hand.-Mazz. *17617*

    E   17617   China - Guangxi (Shiwandashan) *11139*
    V   Vietnam *12850*

I   *Hopea cordata* Vidal *7730*

    I   20985   Vietnam *13845*

R   *Hopea cordifolia* (Thwaites) Trimen *8021*

    R   16162   Sri Lanka *8021*

R   *Hopea depressinerva* P. Ashton *7730*

    R   13845   Malaysia - Sarawak *13845*

E   *Hopea discolor* Thwaites *8021*

    E   12838   Sri Lanka (Hiniduma, Ratnapura) *8021*

V   *Hopea enicosanthoides* Ashton *7730*

    V   Malaysia - Sarawak *13845*

Ex/E   *Hopea erosa* (Beddome) van Slooten

    Ex/E   India - Tamil Nadu

V   *Hopea exalata* Lin, Yang & Hsue *17617*

    V   17617   China - Hainan Is. *11139*

Ex/E   *Hopea foxworthyi* Elm. *7730*

    Ex/E   13845   Philippines (Sibayan) *13845*

V   *Hopea glabrifolia* C.T. White *7730*

    V   Papua New Guinea (Incl. the Louisiade Archipelago) *13845*

V   *Hopea glaucescens* Sym. *7730*

    V   13926   Malaysia - Peninsular Malaysia *7730*

V   *Hopea gregaria* Sloot. *7730*

    V   Indonesia (Sulawesi, Moluccas) *13845*

E   *Hopea hainanensis* Merr. & Chun *17617*

    E   17617   China - Hainan Is. *11139*
    K   20985   Vietnam *12850*

I   *Hopea hongayanensis* Tardieu *13845*

    I   Vietnam

I   *Hopea inexpectata* Ashton *7730*

    I   Papua New Guinea (south) *13845*

R   *Hopea jacobi* C. Fischer *14782*

    R   14782   India - Karnataka (Coorg) *14782*

V   *Hopea johorensis* Sym. *7730*

    V   13926   Malaysia - Peninsular Malaysia (east Johor) *13845*

R   *Hopea jucunda* Thwaites *12838*

    R   12838   Sri Lanka *12838*

V   *Hopea kerangasensis* Ashton *7730*

    E   Indonesia - Sumatra (east) *13845*
    V   Malaysia - Peninsular Malaysia *13845*
    V   Malaysia - Sarawak *13845*

V   *Hopea longirostrata* Ashton *7730*

    V   Malaysia - Sarawak *13845*

V   *Hopea mesuoides* Ashton *7730*

    V   Brunei Darussalam *13845*
    V   Malaysia - Sarawak *13845*

I   *Hopea mindanensis* Foxw. *7730*

    I   13845   Philippines (Mindanao) *13845*

I   *Hopea nigra* Burck *7730*

    I   Indonesia - Sumatra (east, Belitung, Bangka) *13845*

V   *Hopea nutans* Ridley *7730*

    E   Brunei Darussalam *13845*

V		Indonesia - Kalimantan *13845*	
V	*13926*	Malaysia - Peninsular Malaysia *13845*	
V		Malaysia - Sabah *13845*	
V		Malaysia - Sarawak *13845*	

I   *Hopea oblongifolia* Dyer *12848*
- I   Myanmar (S. Tenasserim, Vict Pt) *12848*
- I   *13845*   Thailand *12947*

I   *Hopea paucinervis* Parijs *7730*
- I   Indonesia - Sumatra (southeast) *13845*

Ex/E   *Hopea polyalthioides* Sym. *7730*
- Ex/E   Malaysia - Peninsular Malaysia (south Johor) *13845*

V   *Hopea pubescens* Ridley *7730*
- V   *13926*   Malaysia - Peninsular Malaysia *13845*

I   *Hopea reticulata* Tardieu *7730*
- I   Thailand
- I   Vietnam

E   *Hopea samarensis* Gutierrez *7730*
- E   *13845*   Philippines (Samar) *13845*

I   *Hopea scabra* Ashton *7730*
- I   Papua New Guinea *13845*

V   *Hopea sphaerocarpa* (Heim) Ashton *7730*
- V   Indonesia - Kalimantan (northwest) *13845*
- V   Malaysia - Sarawak *13845*

I   *Hopea subalata* Sym. *7730*
- I   Malaysia - Peninsular Malaysia (Kanching FoR, Selangor) *13845*

I   *Hopea sublanceolata* Sym. *7730*
- I   *13926*   Malaysia - Peninsular Malaysia *13845*

I   *Hopea sulcata* Sym. *7730*
- I   Malaysia - Peninsular Malaysia *13845*

I   *Hopea tenuivervula* Ashton *7730*
- V   Brunei Darussalam *13845*
- I   Malaysia - Sabah *13845*
- V   Malaysia - Sarawak *13845*

I   *Hopea ultima* Ashton *7730*
- I   Papua New Guinea (southeast) *13845*

I   *Hopea vaccinifolia* Ridl. ex Ashton *7730*
- V   Brunei Darussalam *13845*
- I   Malaysia - Sarawak (north-east) *13845*

V   *Hopea wightiana* Wall. *12848*
- V   *13845*   India - Karnataka (N. Kanara) *12848*
- V   *13845*   India - Kerala *12848*
- V   *13845*   India - Tamil Nadu (Tirunelveli) *12848*

V   *Monotes lutambensis* Verdc. *20556*
- V   *20885*   Tanzania *20556*

V   *Parashorea aptera* Sloot. *7730*
- V   Indonesia - Sumatra (east) *13845*

R   *Parashorea buchananii* Fischer, C.
- R   *13845*   Myanmar (Tagwin chaung in Myitkyina) *12848*

R   *Parashorea chinensis* Wang Hsie *17617*
- R   *17617*   China - Guangxi *11139*
- R   *17617*   China - Yunnan (Mengla; Maguan; Hehong) *11139*
- K   *20985*   Vietnam *12850*

V   *Parashorea densiflora* Slooten & Sym. *7730*
- V   *13926*   Malaysia - Peninsular Malaysia *13845*

V   *Parashorea globosa* Sym. *7730*
- E   Indonesia - Sumatra *13845*
- V   *13926*   Malaysia - Peninsular Malaysia *13845*

V   *Parashorea lucida* (Miq.) Kurz *7730*

V	*13845*	Indonesia - Kalimantan *7730*	
V	*13845*	Indonesia - Sumatra (central Sumatra) *7730*	
V	*13845*	Malaysia - Sarawak *7730*	

V   *Parashorea macrophylla* Wyatt-Smith ex Ashton *7730*
- V   Brunei Darussalam *13845*
- V   Malaysia - Sarawak *13845*

V   *Shorea acuminatissima* Sym. *7730*
- V   Indonesia - Kalimantan (northeast) *13845*
- V   Malaysia - Sabah (east) *13845*

R   *Shorea affinis* (Thwaites) P. Ashton *8021*
- R   *12838*   Sri Lanka *8021*

I   *Shorea alutacea* Ashton *7730*
- I   Malaysia - Sarawak *13845*

V   *Shorea andulensis* Ashton *7730*
- V   Brunei Darussalam *13845*
- V   Malaysia - Sarawak *13845*

I   *Shorea assamica* Dyer ssp. *koordersii* (Brandis) Sym. *7730*
- I   *13845*   Indonesia - Moluccas (Sula, Batjan, Obi) *7730*
- I   *13845*   Indonesia - Sulawesi *7730*
- I   *13845*   Philippines (Luzon) *7730*

I   *Shorea astylosa* Foxw. *7730*
- I   *13845*   Philippines *13845*

I   *Shorea bakoensis* Ashton *7730*
- I   Malaysia - Sarawak (west) *7730*

V   *Shorea bentongensis* Foxw. *7730*
- V   *13926*   Malaysia - Peninsular Malaysia (Selangor; Pahang; Johor) *13845*

R   *Shorea biawak* Ashton *7730*
- R   Brunei Darussalam *13845*
- V   Malaysia - Sarawak *13845*

I   *Shorea blumutensis* Foxw. *7730*
- E   Indonesia - Sumatra (northeast) *13845*
- I   *13926*   Malaysia - Peninsular Malaysia (Johor) *13845*

I   *Shorea bullata* Ashton *7730*
- I   Brunei Darussalam *13845*
- I   Malaysia - Sarawak *13845*

I   *Shorea cara* Kosterm., ined. *6074*
- I   Indonesia - Java (Leuweung Sancang) *6074*

R   *Shorea carapae* Ashton *7730*
- R   Indonesia - Kalimantan
- I   Malaysia - Sarawak

V   *Shorea chaiana* Ashton *7730*
- V   Malaysia - Sarawak (north-east) *13845*

V   *Shorea ciliata* King *7730*
- V   *13926*   Malaysia - Peninsular Malaysia (Penang, Perak, Trengganu) *7609*

V   *Shorea collina* Ridley *7609*
- V   *13926*   Malaysia - Peninsular Malaysia (Terengganu, Pahang, Johor) *7730*
- Ex   *20099*   Singapore *20099*

R   *Shorea congestiflora* (Thwaites) P. Ashton *8021*
- R   *12838*   Sri Lanka *8021*

E   *Shorea conica* (Sloot.) *7730*
- E   Indonesia - Sumatra (east) *13845*

I   *Shorea cordata* Ashton *7730*
- I   Malaysia - Sarawak (central and west) *13845*

R   *Shorea cordifolia* (Thwaites) P. Ashton *8021*
     R   *12838* Sri Lanka *8021*

V   *Shorea dealbata* Foxw. *7730*
     E   Indonesia - Sumatra *13845*
     V   *13926* Malaysia - Peninsular Malaysia *19209*
     V   Malaysia - Sarawak (west) *13845*

I   *Shorea dispar* Ashton *7730*
     I   Malaysia - Sarawak *13845*

R   *Shorea disticha* (Thwaites) P. Ashton *8021*
     R   *12838* Sri Lanka (wet zone) *8021*

E   *Shorea dyeri* Thwaites ex Trimen *8021*
     E   *12838* Sri Lanka *8021*

Ex/E   *Shorea falcata* Vidal
     I   *20985* Vietnam (Kamh Ranh)

V   *Shorea falciferoides* Foxw. *7730*
     V   *13845* Indonesia - Kalimantan *13845*
     E   *13845* Philippines *13845*

I   *Shorea foraminifera* Ashton *7730*
     I   Brunei Darussalam *13845*

I   *Shorea foxworthyi* Sym. *7730*
     E   *13845* Thailand (Peninsular Thailand) *13845*
     I   Indonesia - Kalimantan (south-east) *13845*
     E   Indonesia - Sumatra *13845*
     I   Malaysia - Sabah (east) *13845*
     I   Malaysia - Sarawak (centre & north-east) *13845*

V   *Shorea glauca* King *7730*
     Ex/E   *13845* Thailand (Peninsular Thailand) *13845*
     V   Indonesia - Sumatra *13845*
     V   Malaysia (Peninsular) *13845*

I   *Shorea hemsleyana* (Brandis) Ashton ssp. *grandiflora* (Brandis) Ashton
     I   *13845* Indonesia - Kalimantan (Lower Kapuas) *13845*
     I   *13845* Malaysia - Sarawak *21040*

V   *Shorea hypochra* Hance *7730*
     V   Kampuchea *13845*
     V   *13845* Thailand (S.E. and Peninsular) *13845*
     V   Vietnam *13845*
     V   *13926* Malaysia - Peninsular Malaysia (Selangor, Pahang, north) *13845*

V   *Shorea inaequilateralis* Sym. *7730*
     V   Brunei Darussalam *13845*
     V   Malaysia - Sarawak *13845*

I   *Shorea inappendiculata* Burck *7730*
     I   Indonesia - Kalimantan (east) *13845*
     I   Malaysia - Sabah *13845*
     I   Malaysia - Sarawak *13845*

E   *Shorea induplicata* Sloot. *7730*
     Ex/E   Indonesia - Kalimantan (west) *13845*
     E   Malaysia - Sarawak (west) *13845*

I   *Shorea isoptera* Ashton *7730*
     V   Brunei Darussalam *13845*
     V   Malaysia - Sabah *13845*
     I   Malaysia - Sarawak *13845*

E   *Shorea kuantanensis* Ashton *7730*
     E   *13926* Malaysia - Peninsular Malaysia *13845*

I   *Shorea kudatensis* Wood ex Meijer *7730*
     I   Malaysia - Sabah (north) *13845*

V   *Shorea ladiana* Ashton *7730*
     V   Brunei Darussalam *13845*
     V   Malaysia - Sarawak *13845*

V   *Shorea laxa* Sloot. *7730*

     V   Brunei Darussalam *13845*
     V   Malaysia - Sarawak (northeast) *13845*

E   *Shorea leptoderma* Meijer *7730*
     E   Malaysia - Sabah (east) *13845*

E   *Shorea lissophylla* Thwaites *8021*
     E   *12838* Sri Lanka *8021*

V   *Shorea longiflora* (Brandis) Sym. *7730*
     V   Brunei Darussalam *13845*
     E   Indonesia - Kalimantan (east) *13845*
     V   Malaysia - Sarawak *13845*

V   *Shorea lumutensis* Sym. *7730*
     V   *13926* Malaysia - Peninsular Malaysia (Dindings, Perak) *13845*

V   *Shorea lunduensis* Ashton *7730*
     V   Malaysia - Sarawak *13845*

V   *Shorea macrantha* Brandis *7730*
     E   Indonesia - Sumatra (east) *13845*
     V   Malaysia - Peninsular Malaysia (Pahang, Johor, Perak) *19209*
     V   Malaysia - Sarawak *13845*

R   *Shorea macrobalanos* Ashton *7730*
     R   Malaysia - Sarawak *13845*

I   *Shorea malibato* Foxw. *7730*
     I   *13845* Philippines *13845*

V   *Shorea materialis* Ridley *7730*
     V   Brunei Darussalam *13845*
     E   Indonesia - Sumatra (east) *13845*
     V   *13926* Malaysia - Peninsular Malaysia (east coast region) *19209*
     V   Malaysia - Sarawak (north-east) *13845*

R   *Shorea megistophylla* Ashton *8021*
     R   *12838* Sri Lanka *8021*

I   *Shorea micans* Ashton *7730*
     I   Malaysia - Sabah *13845*

V   *Shorea mujongensis* Ashton *7730*
     V   Malaysia - Sarawak *13845*

V   *Shorea oblongifolia* Thwaites *8021*
     V   *12838* Sri Lanka *8021*

E   *Shorea obovoidea* Sloot. *7730*
     E   Malaysia - Sarawak (west) *13845*

V   *Shorea ochrophloia* Strugn. ex Sym. *7730*
     E   Indonesia - Sumatra (west) *13845*
     V   *13926* Malaysia - Peninsular Malaysia *13845*

E   *Shorea ovalifolia* (Thwaites) P. Ashton *8021*
     E   *12838* Sri Lanka (south-west) *8021*

V   *Shorea pachyphylla* Ridl. ex Sym. *7730*
     V   Brunei Darussalam *13845*
     V   Malaysia - Sarawak *13845*

E   *Shorea pallescens* P. Ashton *8021*
     E   *12838* Sri Lanka *8021*

I   *Shorea pallidifolia* Ashton *7730*
     ?   Indonesia - Kalimantan (west) *21040*
     I   Malaysia - Sarawak *13845*

V   *Shorea polita* Vidal *7730*
     V   *13845* Philippines *13845*

I   *Shorea praestans* Ashton *7730*
     I   Malaysia - Sarawak (central) *13845*

E   *Shorea richetia* Sym. *7730*
     E   Indonesia - Kalimantan (northwest) *13845*
     E   Malaysia - Sarawak (west) *13845*

I   *Shorea rotundifolia* Ashton *7730*

I		Malaysia - Sarawak (central) *13845*

V   *Shorea stipularis* Thwaites *8021*
     V   *12838* Sri Lanka *8021*

V   *Shorea subcylindrica* Sloot. *7730*
     V   Malaysia - Sarawak (west) *13845*

R   *Shorea superba* Sym. *7730*
     R   Brunei Darussalam *13845*
     V   Malaysia - Sabah *13845*
     V   Malaysia - Sarawak *13845*

V   *Shorea symingtonii* G. Wood *7730*
     V   Malaysia - Sabah *13845*

I   *Shorea tenuiramulosa* Ashton *7730*
     I   Malaysia - Sabah (east) *13845*
     E   Malaysia - Sarawak (west) *13845*

R   *Shorea trapezifolia* (Thwaites) P. Ashton *8021*
     R   *12838* Sri Lanka *8021*

E   *Shorea tumbuggaia* Roxb.
     E   India - Andhra Pradesh
     E   India - Tamil Nadu

V   *Shorea waltoni* Wood ex Meijer *7730*
     V   Malaysia - Sabah (east) *13845*

R   *Shorea worthingtonii* Ashton *8021*
     R   *12838* Sri Lanka *8021*

V   *Shorea zeylanica* (Thwaites) P. Ashton *8021*
     V   *12838* Sri Lanka *8021*

V   *Stemonoporus acuminatus* (Thwaites) P. Ashton *8021*
     V   *12838* Sri Lanka *8021*

E   *Stemonoporus affinis* Thwaites *8021*
     E   *16162* Sri Lanka (Knuckles Range) *8021*

V   *Stemonoporus canaliculatus* Thwaites *8021*
     V   *12838* Sri Lanka *8021*

E   *Stemonoporus elegans* Thwaites *8021*
     E   *20013* Sri Lanka (Adam's Peak range) *8021*

I   *Stemonoporus lanceolatus* Thwaites *8021*
     I   *16162* Sri Lanka (Kuruwita Korale) *8021*

E   *Stemonoporus lancifolius* (Thwaites) P. Ashton *8021*
     E   Sri Lanka *8021*

E   *Stemonoporus moonii* Thw. *8021*
     E   *20013* Sri Lanka (Kalutara) *13845*

I   *Stemonoporus nitidus* Thwaites *8021*
     I   *16162* Sri Lanka *8021*

I   *Stemonoporus oblongifolius* Thwaites *8021*
     I   *16162* Sri Lanka *8021*

I   *Stemonoporus petiolaris* Thwaites *8021*
     I   *16162* Sri Lanka (Kitulgala, Gilimale) *8021*

E   *Stemonoporus reticulatus* Thwaites *8021*
     E   *12838* Sri Lanka (Hiniduma, Kanneliya) *8021*

I   *Stemonoporus rigidus* Thwaites *8021*
     I   *16162* Sri Lanka (Ambagamuwa) *8021*

V   *Stemonoporus wightii* (Wight) Alston *21040*
     V   Sri Lanka (Ratnapura District) *8021*

V   *Vateria copallifera* (Retz.) Alston *8021*
     V   *12838* Sri Lanka *8021*

R   *Vateria macrocarpa* B.L. Gupta *11494*
     R   *11494* India - Kerala *11494*

E   *Vateriopsis seychellarum* (Dyer) Yeim *14981*
     E   *14981* Seychelles (Mahé) *14981*

E   *Vatica affinis* Thwaites *8021*
     E   *12838* Sri Lanka (Botaloogodda, Sinharaja) *8021*

E   *Vatica bantamensis* (Hassk.) Benth. & Hook.ex Miq. *7730*
     E   Indonesia - Java (Ujung Kulon) *13845*

I   *Vatica cauliflora* Ashton *7730*
     I   Indonesia - Kalimantan (west) *13845*

I   *Vatica chartacea* Ashton *7730*
     I   Indonesia - Kalimantan (west) *13845*
     V   Malaysia - Sabah (east) *13845*
     V   Malaysia - Sarawak *13845*

I   *Vatica compressa* Ashton *7730*
     I   Malaysia - Sarawak *7730*

V   *Vatica congesta* Ashton *7730*
     V   Malaysia - Sarawak *13845*

I   *Vatica elliptica* Foxw. *7730*
     I   *13845* Philippines (Mindanao) *13845*

I   *Vatica flavida* Foxw. *7609*
     I   *13926* Malaysia - Peninsular Malaysia (south Perak) *7609*

I   *Vatica flavovirens* Sloot. *7730*
     I   Indonesia - Sulawesi *13845*

E   *Vatica guangxiensis* S.L. Mo *17617*
     E   *17617* China - Guangxi (Napu) *11139*

V   *Vatica hullettii* (Ridley) P. Ashton *7730*
     V   Malaysia - Peninsular Malaysia *13845*

E   *Vatica javanica* Sloot. *7730*
     E   Indonesia - Java *13845*
     E   Indonesia - Kalimantan (east) *13845*

V   *Vatica maritima* Sloot. *7730*
     Ex   *13845* Brunei Darussalam *13845*
     E   *13845* Indonesia - Kalimantan (northeast) *13845*
     E   *13845* Malaysia - Sabah *13845*
     V   *13845* Philippines (Palawan) *13845*

I   *Vatica oblongifolia* Hook.f. ssp. *elliptifolia* Ashton *7730*
     I   Brunei Darussalam *7730*
     V   Malaysia - Sarawak *7730*

V   *Vatica oblongifolia* Hook.f. ssp. *multinervosa* Ashton *7730*
     Ex/E   Indonesia - Kalimantan (east, Nunukan Island) *13845*
     V   Malaysia - Sabah *13845*
     V   Malaysia - Sarawak *13845*

V   *Vatica oblongifolia* Hook F. ssp. *selakoensis* Ashton *21040*
     V   *13845* Malaysia - Sarawak (West Kalimantan) *7730*

V   *Vatica obovata* Sloot. *7730*
     V   Indonesia - Sumatra *13845*

I   *Vatica obscura* Trimen *8021*
     I   *16162* Sri Lanka *8021*

I   *Vatica pachyphylla* Merr. *7730*
     I   *13845* Philippines *7730*

R   *Vatica pedicellata* Brandis *7730*
     R   Malaysia - Sarawak (west) *13845*

I   *Vatica rotata* Ashton *7730*
     I   Indonesia - Kalimantan (central) *13845*
     I   Malaysia - Sarawak *13845*

I   *Vatica rynchocarpa* Ashton *7730*
     I   Brunei Darussalam *13845*
     I   Malaysia - Sarawak *13845*

V   *Vatica sarawakensis* Heim *7730*

V		Indonesia - Kalimantan (east) *13845*
V		Malaysia - Sabah *13845*
V		Malaysia - Sarawak *13845*

I   *Vatica scortechinii* (King) Brandis *7730*
     I   *13926* Malaysia - Peninsular Malaysia *13845*

Ex/E   *Vatica soepadmoi* Ashton *7730*
     Ex/E   Indonesia - Sumatra (east) *13845*

V   *Vatica teysmanniana* Burck *7730*
     V   Indonesia - Sumatra (Bengkalis, Bangka) *13845*

V   *Vatica venulosa* Bl. *7730*
     V   Borneo *13845*
     V   Indonesia - Sumatra *13845*
     V   *13926* Malaysia - Peninsular Malaysia *13845*

E   *Vatica xishuangbannaensis* G.D. Tao & J.H. Zhang *17617*
     E   *18038* China - Yunnan (Menla) *11139*

Droseraceae

Number of genera: 4
Number of species: 100
Recorded threatened species: 14   (14%)

Temperate and tropical.

R   II   *Dionaea muscipula* Ellis *20850, 10260*
     R   *20850* U.S. - North Carolina *20850*
     E   *20850* U.S. - South Carolina *20850*

V   *Drosera adelae* F.Muell. *20681*
     V   *20681* Australia - Queensland *20681*

R   *Drosera brevifolia* Pursh. *12224*
     R   *12224* U.S. - Mississippi *12224*

R   *Drosera capillaris* Poir. *12224*
     R   *12224* U.S. - Mississippi *12224*

I   *Drosera colombiana* A. Fernandez *19352*
     I   *19352* Colombia *19352*

V   *Drosera fimbriata* De Buhr *20681, 12732*
     V   *20681* Australia - Western Australia *12732*

R   *Drosera graniticola* N.G.Marchant *20681*
     R   *20681* Australia - Western Australia *20681*

R   *Drosera marchantii* DeBuhr. ssp. *marchantii 20681*
     R   *20681* Australia - Western Australia *12732*

R   *Drosera occidentalis* Morrison ssp. *occidentalis 20681*
     R   *20681* Australia - Western Australia *20681*

E   *Drosera panamensis* Correa & A.S. Taylor *20883, 9006*
     I   *20883* Panama *20883*

V   *Drosera prolifera* C.White *20681*
     V   *20681* Australia - Queensland *20681*

R   *Drosera regia* Stephens *20604, 14874*
     R   *20604* South Africa - Cape Province *20604*

E   *Drosera rotundifolia* L. var. *corsica* Maire ex Briq. *15080*
     E   *15080* France - Corsica *15080*

V   *Drosera schizandra* Diels *20681*
     V   *20681* Australia - Queensland *20681*

Ebenaceae

Number of genera: 5
Number of species: 450
Recorded threatened species: 81   (18%)

Tropical and subtropical.

V   *Diospyros acuminata* (Thwaites) Kosterm. *8021*
     V   *12838* Sri Lanka *8021*

E   *Diospyros acuta* Thwaites *8021*
     E   *12838* Sri Lanka (south-west) *8021*

E   *Diospyros albiflora* Alston *8021*
     E   *12838* Sri Lanka (Morapitiya, Kalutara Dist.) *8021*

E   *Diospyros angulata* Poiret *10082*
     E   *20771* Mauritius *10082*

R   *Diospyros anisandra* Blake *9004*
     R   *9682* Guatemala *9004*
     R   *9682* Mexico *9004*

I   *Diospyros atrata* Alston *8021*
     I   *16162* Sri Lanka (Kandy, Kanneliya) *8021*

I   *Diospyros attenuata* Thwaites *8021*
     I   *16162* Sri Lanka (south-west) *8021*

I   *Diospyros bambuseti* Fletcher *19120*
     I   *19120* Thailand *19120*

V   *Diospyros barteri* Hiern *13102*
     V   *20858* Cameroon
     V   *20858* Ghana *20858*
     V   *20858* Nigeria *18326*

V   *Diospyros blancoi* DC. *10278*
     V   Philippines *10278*

V   *Diospyros boutoniana* DC. *10082*
     V   *20771* Mauritius *10082*

V   *Diospyros campechiana* Lundell *9004*
     V   *9682* Guatemala *9004*
     V   *9682* Mexico *9004*

R   *Diospyros celebica* Bakh. *12983*
     R   Indonesia - Sulawesi *14185*

E   *Diospyros chaetocarpa* Kosterm. *8021*
     E   *12838* Sri Lanka (south-west) *8021*

V   *Diospyros cherrieri* F. White *20893*
     V   *20893* New Caledonia *20893*

R   *Diospyros christophersenii* Fosberg *20671, 7925*
     R   *7925* Western Samoa (Savaii) *20671*

V   *Diospyros chrysophyllos* Poiret *10082*
     V   *20771* Mauritius *10082*

V   *Diospyros conzatii* Standley *9682*
     V   *9682* Mexico *9682*

I   *Diospyros crumenata* Thwaites *8021*
     I   Sri Lanka *8021*

V   *Diospyros diversifolia* Hiern *10082*
     V   *5852* Mauritius - Rodrigues *5852*

V   *Diospyros ebenoides* Kosterm. *8021*
     V   *20013* Sri Lanka (Badulla Dist.; Mirigama) *8021*

E   *Diospyros egrettarum* I. Richardson *10082*
     E   *20771* Mauritius *10936*

I   *Diospyros engleri* Guerke *5926*
     I   *5926* Tanzania (Pugu forest reserve) *5926*

E   *Diospyros erudita* F. White *20893*

E		20893	New Caledonia 20893

V   *Diospyros fastidiosa* F. White 20893
       V   20893   New Caledonia 20893

V   *Diospyros feliciana* Letouzey & F. White
       V   Guinea

R   *Diospyros fengchangensis* Lu
       R   Taiwan

R   *Diospyros glandulifera* De Winter 20604
       R   20604   South Africa - Natal 20604

I   *Diospyros gracilis* Fletcher 19257
       I   19120   Thailand (eastern region) 19257

R   *Diospyros greenwayi* F. White 12948
       R   20057   Kenya 12948
       R   20057   Somalia (southern) 20271
       R   20057   Tanzania 12948

E   *Diospyros hemiteles* I. Richardson 10082
       E   20771   Mauritius 10082

V   *Diospyros hirsuta* L. 8021
       V   12838   Sri Lanka 8021

V   *Diospyros impolita* F.White 20802
       V   20893   New Caledonia 20802

V   *Diospyros johnstoniana* Standley & Steyerm. 9004
       V   9682   Guatemala 9004

V   *Diospyros kabuyeana* F. White 12948
       V   20057   Kenya 12948
       V   20057   Tanzania (Tanga, coast & Mafia Island) 20900

V   *Diospyros kanurii* F. White 20057
       V   20057   Kenya 20057

E   *Diospyros katendei* 20900
       E   20900   Uganda (Kasyoka & Kitomi forest) 20900

I   *Diospyros kerrii* Craib 19120
       I   19120   Thailand 19120

I   *Diospyros koenigii* Kosterm. 8021
       I   16162   Sri Lanka (Gannoruwa, Kandy) 8021

V   *Diospyros kotoensis* Yamaz. 20854
       V   20854   Taiwan (Lan Yu) 20854

V   *Diospyros leucomelas* Poiret 10082
       V   20771   Mauritius 10082

I   *Diospyros longepilosa* Phengklai 19120
       I   19120   Thailand 19120

E   *Diospyros mabacea* (F.Muell.) F.Muell. 20681
       E   20681   Australia - New South Wales 20681

R   *Diospyros macrocarpa* Hiern 20893
       R   20893   New Caledonia 20893

V   *Diospyros magogoana* F. White 12948
       V   20885   Tanzania (Rondo) 20900

V   *Diospyros margaretae* F. White 20893
       V   20893   New Caledonia 20893

V   *Diospyros melanida* Poiret 10082
       V   20771   Mauritius 10082

V   *Diospyros minimifolia* F.White 20802
       V   20893   New Caledonia 20802

I   *Diospyros moonii* Thwaites 8021
       I   16162   Sri Lanka (south-west) 8021

V   *Diospyros mun* Lecomte 6057
       V   20985   Vietnam 6057

R   *Diospyros nebulosa* F.White 20893
       R   20893   New Caledonia 20893

E   *Diospyros neglecta* F. White 20893
       E   20893   New Caledonia 20893

V   *Diospyros neraudii* DC. 10082
       V   20771   Mauritius 10082

V   *Diospyros nodosa* Poiret 10082
       V   20771   Mauritius 10082

V   *Diospyros oaxacana* Standley 9682
       V   9682   Mexico 9682

I   *Diospyros opaca* C.B. Clarke 8021
       I   16162   Sri Lanka 8021

E   *Diospyros oppositifolia* Thwaites 8021
       E   12838   Sri Lanka (Hinidumkanda, Galle) 8021

V   *Diospyros perplexa* F.White 20802
       V   20893   New Caledonia 20802

V   *Diospyros pterocalyx* Bojer ex DC. 10082
       V   20771   Mauritius 10082

R   *Diospyros pubicalix* Bakh. 19120
       R   19120   Thailand 19120

I   *Diospyros pulgarensis* (Elm.) Merr. 13833
       I   13833   Philippines (low altitude) 13833

V   *Diospyros pustulata* F.White 20802
       V   20893   New Caledonia 20802

E   *Diospyros quaesita* Thwaites 8021
       E   12838   Sri Lanka 8021

V   *Diospyros rekoi* Standley 9682
       V   9682   Mexico 9682

V   *Diospyros revaughanii* I. Richardson 10082
       V   20771   Mauritius 10082

V   *Diospyros revolutissima* F. White 20893
       V   20893   New Caledonia 20893

E   *Diospyros rheophytica* Kosterm. 8021
       E   20013   Sri Lanka 8021

E   *Diospyros riojae* Gómez Pompa 9019
       E   11119   Mexico - Veracruz 9019

I   *Diospyros saxosa* Fletcher 19120
       I   19120   Thailand 19120

R   *Diospyros seychellarum* (Hiern) Kosterm. 19181
       R   19182   Seychelles (granitic) 19182

V   *Diospyros sintenisii* (Krug & Urban) Standl. 20883
       R   19002   Puerto Rico 20883

V   *Diospyros tessellaria* Poiret 10082
       V   20771   Mauritius 10082

I   *Diospyros thaiensis* Phengklai 19120
       I   19120   Thailand 19120

V   *Diospyros thwaitesii* Beddome 8021
       V   12838   Sri Lanka 8021

I   *Diospyros trianthos* Phengklai 19120
       I   19120   Thailand 19120

V   *Diospyros trisulca* F. White 20893
       V   20893   New Caledonia 20893

E   *Diospyros veillonii* F.White 20802
       E   20802   New Caledonia (Gadji) 20802

I   *Diospyros vermoesenii* De Wild.
       I   Gabon (Tchibanga)

R   *Diospyros wajirensis* F. White 20057
       R   20057   Kenya 20057
       R   20884   Somalia 20884

V   *Diospyros walkeri* (Wight) Gurke 8021

V   *12838* Sri Lanka *8021*

R   **Diospyros xolocotzii** Madrigal & Rzed. *12071*
    R   *19850* Mexico - Michoacan *12071*

Elaeagnaceae

Number of genera: 3
Number of species: 50
Recorded threatened species: 9 (18%)

Temperate and subtropical Northern Hemisphere, to tropical Asia and northern Australia.

V   **Elaeagnus arakiana** Koidz. *10572*
    V   *20626* Japan (Kyoto) *20626*

E   **Elaeagnus conferta** Roxb. ssp. *dendroidea* Servettaz *14782*
    E   *14782* India - Meghalaya (Khasi hills) *14782*

V   **Elaeagnus mollis** Diels *17617*
    V   *17617* China - Shaanxi (Huxian) *11139*
    V   *17617* China - Shanxi (Xiangning; Hejing; Yicheng) *11139*

R   **Elaeagnus numajiriana** Makino *10572*
    R   *10572* Japan *10572*

R   **Elaeagnus rotundata** Nakai *8622*
    R   *19135* Japan - Kazan Retto *8622*
    R   *19135* Japan - Ogasawara-shoto *8622*

R   **Elaeagnus takeshitae** Makino *10572*
    R   *10572* Japan *10572*

R   **Elaeagnus tricholepis** Momiyama *7731*
    R   Nepal *7731*

V   **Elaeagnus yakushimensis** Masam. *10572*
    V   *20626* Japan (Yakushima Is.) *20626*

R   **Elaeagnus yoshinoi** Makino *10572*
    R   *10572* Japan *10572*

Elaeocarpaceae

Number of genera: 10
Number of species: 400
Recorded threatened species: 44 (11%)

Tropical and subtropical.

R   **Aceratium doggrellii** C.White *20681*
    R   *20681* Australia - Queensland *20681*

R   **Aceratium ferrugineum** C.White *20681*
    R   *20681* Australia - Queensland *20681*

R   **Aceratium sericoleopsis** Balg. *20681*
    R   *20681* Australia - Queensland *20681*

R   **Crinodendron hookeranum** Gay *20883*
    R   *20883* Chile *20883*

R   **Crinodendron tucumanum** Lillo *16336*
    I   *19448* Argentina (Tucumani) *16336*
    R   *20176* Argentina - Catamarca *20176*
    R   *20176* Argentina - Jujuy *20176*
    R   *20176* Argentina - Salta *20176*
    R   *20176* Argentina - Tucuman *20176*

R   **Dubouzetia australiensis** Coode *20681*
    R   *20681* Australia - Northern Territory *20681*

R   **Dubouzetia guillauminii** Virot *20893*
    R   *20893* New Caledonia *20893*

V   **Elaeocarpus biflorus** Tirel *20893*
    V   *20893* New Caledonia *20893*

R   **Elaeocarpus blascoi** Weibel *14782*
    R   *14782* India - Tamil Nadu *14782*

E   **Elaeocarpus bojeri** R.E. Vaughan *10082, 21329*
    E   *20771* Mauritius *10082*

V   **Elaeocarpus calomala** (Blanco) Merr. *13780*
    V   *15960* Philippines *13780*

R   **Elaeocarpus carolinae** B.Hyland & Coode *20681*
    R   *20681* Australia - Queensland *20681*

R   **Elaeocarpus castanaefolius** Guillaumin
    R   New Caledonia

I   **Elaeocarpus ceylanicus** (Arn.) Masters *10252*
    I   *16162* Sri Lanka *10252*

V   **Elaeocarpus colnettianus** Guillaumin *20893*
    V   *20893* New Caledonia *20893*

R   **Elaeocarpus coorangooloo** J.F.Bailey & C.White *20681*
    R   *20681* Australia - Queensland *20681*

I   **Elaeocarpus costatus** M. Taylor
    I   *14226* Australia - NSW - Lord Howe Is. *14226*

R   **Elaeocarpus darlacensis** Gagnepain *6057*
    R   Vietnam *6057*

R   **Elaeocarpus gaussenii** Weibel *14782*
    R   *14782* India (western Ghats) *14782*

V   **Elaeocarpus glandulifer** Masters *10276*
    V   *20013* Sri Lanka *10276*

R   **Elaeocarpus gordonii** Tirel *20893*
    R   *20893* New Caledonia *20893*

R   **Elaeocarpus grahamii** F.Muell. *20681*
    R   *20681* Australia - Queensland *20681*

E   **Elaeocarpus integrifolius** Lam. *10082, 21329*
    E   *20771* Mauritius *10082*

R   **Elaeocarpus johnsonii** F.Muell. ex C.White *20681*
    R   *20681* Australia - Queensland *20681*

E   **Elaeocarpus kaalensis** Daniker *20893*
    E   *20893* New Caledonia *20893*

R   **Elaeocarpus linsmithii** Guymer *20681*
    R   *20681* Australia - Queensland *20681*

V   **Elaeocarpus lucidus** Roxb. *14872*
    V   *14872* Bangladesh *14872*

R   **Elaeocarpus montanus** Thwaites *10252*
    R   *20013* Sri Lanka *10252*

V   **Elaeocarpus moratii** Tirel *20893*
    V   *20893* New Caledonia *20893*

R   **Elaeocarpus munronii** (Wt.) Mast. *14782*
    R   *14782* India - Karnataka *14782*
    R   *14782* India - Maharashtra *14782*
    R   *14782* India - Tamil Nadu *14782*

R   **Elaeocarpus recurvatus** Corner *14782*
    R   *14782* India - Tamil Nadu *14782*

R   **Elaeocarpus sphaericus** (Gaertn.) Schumann var. *hayatae* (Kaneh. & Sasaki) Chang *20511*
    R   *14961* Taiwan (Botel Tobago) *14961*

R   **Elaeocarpus stellaris** L.S.Smith *20681*
    R   *20681* Australia - Queensland *20681*

R   **Elaeocarpus subvillosus** Arn. *10276*
    R   *12838* Sri Lanka *10276*

R   **Elaeocarpus thelmae** B.Hyland & Coode *20681*
    R   *20681* Australia - Queensland *20681*

R   **Elaeocarpus vaccinioides** F. Muell. ex Brongn. & Gris *20893*
    R   *20893* New Caledonia *20893*

V	*Elaeocarpus venustus* Beddome *6987*	
	V	*13883* India - Kerala *6987*
	V	*13883* India - Tamil Nadu *6987*
E	*Elaeocarpus williamsianus* Guymer *20681*	
	E	*20681* Australia - New South Wales *20681*
R	*Peripentadenia mearsii* (C.White) L.S.Smith *20681*	
	R	*20681* Australia - Queensland *20681*
R	*Peripentadenia phelpsii* B.Hyland & Coode *20681*	
	R	*20681* Australia - Queensland *20681*
R	*Sloanea dussii* Urban *19001*	
	R	*19001* Martinique (upper Absalon, Plateau Concorde, morne Sibérie) *19001*
R	*Sloanea koghiensis* Tirel	
	R	New Caledonia
V	*Sloanea lepida* Tirel *20893*	
	V	*20893* New Caledonia *20893*
V	*Sloanea suaveolens* Tirel *20893*	
	V	*20893* New Caledonia *20893*

Elatinaceae

Number of genera:	2	
Number of species:	40	
Recorded threatened species:	5	(12%)

Tropical and subtropical.

R	*Bergia barklyana* G.Leach *20681*	
	R	*20681* Australia - Northern Territory *20681*
R	*Bergia occultipetala* G.Leach *20681*	
	I	*20681* Australia - Northern Territory *20681*
	I	*20681* Australia - South Australia *20681*
R	*Elatine fauquei* Monod *11751*	
	R	Mali (near Bamako) *11751*
R	*Elatine gussonei* (Sommier) Brullo, Lanfranco, Pavone & Ronsisvalle *13351*	
	R	*13351* Malta (confined to the Maltese Islands and Lampedusa) *13351*
V	*Elatine obovata* (Fassett) Mason *20850*	
	I	*20850* U.S. - California *20850*

Epacridaceae

Number of genera:	30	
Number of species:	400	
Recorded threatened species:	60	(15%)

Mostly Australia, New Zealand, and East Indies.

R	*Acrotriche baileyana* (Domin) Powell *20681*	
	R	*20681* Australia - Queensland *20681*
V	*Budawangia gnidioides* (Summerh.) Telford *20681*	
	V	*20681* Australia - New South Wales *20681*
Ex	*Coleanthera virgata* Stschegl. *20681, 14223*	
	Ex	*20681* Australia - Western Australia *20681*
R	*Conostephium minus* Lindley *20681*	
	R	*20681* Australia - Western Australia *20681*
R	*Cyathodes nitida* Jarman *20681*	
	R	*20681* Australia - Tasmania *20681*
V	*Cyathodes robusta* Hook.f.	
	V	New Zealand - Chatham Is.
R	*Cyathodes sulcata* Mihaich *20681*	
	R	*20681* Australia - Tasmania *20681*
E	*Dracophyllum alticola* Daniker *20893*	
	E	*20893* New Caledonia *20893*

R	*Dracophyllum cosmelioides* Pancher ex Oliver	
	R	New Caledonia
R	*Dracophyllum fitzgeraldii* C. Moore & F. Muell.	
	R	*14225* Australia - NSW - Lord Howe Is. *14225*
V	*Dracophyllum ouaiemense* Virot *20893*	
	V	*20893* New Caledonia *20893*
R	*Dracophyllum sayeri* F.Muell. *20681*	
	R	*20681* Australia - Queensland *20681*
V	*Epacris acuminata* Benth. *20681*	
	V	*20681* Australia - Tasmania *20681*
V	*Epacris apsleyensis* R.K.Crowden *20681*	
	V	*20681* Australia - Tasmania *20681*
E	*Epacris barbata* Melville *20681*	
	E	*20681* Australia - Tasmania *20681*
R	*Epacris coriacea* Cunn. ex DC. *20681*	
	R	*20681* Australia - New South Wales *20681*
R	*Epacris curtisiae* Jarman *20681*	
	R	*20681* Australia - Tasmania *20681*
V	*Epacris exserta* R.Br. *20681*	
	V	*20681* Australia - Tasmania *20681*
V	*Epacris glabella* Jarman *20681*	
	V	*20681* Australia - Tasmania *20681*
V	*Epacris grandis* R.K.Crowden *20681*	
	V	*20681* Australia - Tasmania *20681*
E	*Epacris hamiltonii* Maiden & Betche *20681*	
	E	*20681* Australia - New South Wales *20681*
V	*Epacris limbata* K.J.Williams & F.Duncan *20681*	
	V	*20681* Australia - Tasmania *20681*
R	*Epacris marginata* Melville *20681*	
	R	*20681* Australia - Tasmania *20681*
R	*Epacris mucronulata* R.Br. *20681*	
	R	*20681* Australia - Tasmania *20681*
R	*Epacris muelleri* Sonder *20681*	
	R	*20681* Australia - New South Wales *20681*
R	*Epacris myrtifolia* Labill. *20681*	
	R	*20681* Australia - Tasmania *20681*
R	*Epacris navicularis* Jarman *20681*	
	R	*20681* Australia - Tasmania *20681*
V	*Epacris sparsa* R.Br. *20681*	
	V	*20681* Australia - New South Wales *20681*
E	*Epacris stuartii* Stapf *20681*	
	E	*20681* Australia - Western Australia *20681*
R	*Leucopogon cicatricatus* J.Powell *20681*	
	I	*20681* Australia - New South Wales *20681*
	I	*20681* Australia - Queensland *20681*
E	*Leucopogon confertus* Benth. *20681*	
	I	*20681* Australia - New South Wales *20681*
	I	*20681* Australia - Queensland *20681*
Ex	*Leucopogon cryptanthus* Benth. *20681, 14223*	
	Ex	*20681* Australia - Western Australia *20681*
V	*Leucopogon cuspidatus* R.Br. *20681*	
	V	*20681* Australia - Queensland *20681*
V	*Leucopogon exolasius* (F.Muell.) Benth. *20681*	
	V	*20681* Australia - New South Wales *20681*
R	*Leucopogon fletcheri* Maiden & Betche ssp. *fletcheri* *20681*	
	R	*20681* Australia - New South Wales *20681*
R	*Leucopogon grandiflorus* Pedley *20681*	

R   *20681*   Australia - Queensland *20681*

Ex   *Leucopogon marginatus* Fitzg. *20681*
     Ex   *20681*   Australia - Western Australia *20681*

R   *Leucopogon milliganii* (F.Muell.) Rodway *20681*
     R   *20681*   Australia - Tasmania *20681*

R   *Leucopogon neurophyllus* F.Muell. *20681*
     R   *20681*   Australia - Victoria *20681*

V   *Leucopogon obtectus* Benth. *20681*
     V   *20681*   Australia - Western Australia *20681*

R   *Leucopogon riparius* Wakef. *20681*
     R   *20681*   Australia - Victoria *20681*

R   *Leucopogon rupicolus* C.White *20681*
     R   *20681*   Australia - Queensland *20681*

R   *Leucopogon sonderensis* J.H.Willis *20681*
     R   *20681*   Australia - Northern Territory *20681*

R   *Lissanthe sapida* R.Br. *20681*
     R   *20681*   Australia - New South Wales *20681*

E   *Melichrus hirsutus* J.B.Williams ms. *20681*
     E   *20681*   Australia - New South Wales *20681*

R   *Monotoca ledifolia* Cunn. ex Benth. *20681*
     R   *20681*   Australia - New South Wales *20681*

R   *Monotoca linifolia* (Rodway) W.M.Curtis ssp. *algida* Jarman *20681*
     R   *20681*   Australia - Tasmania *20681*

R   *Monotoca linifolia* (Rodway) W.M.Curtis ssp. *linifolia* *20681*
     R   *20681*   Australia - Tasmania *20681*

R   *Monotoca rotundifolia* J.H.Willis *20681*
     I   *20681*   Australia - New South Wales *20681*
     I   *20681*   Australia - Victoria *20681*

R   *Pentachondra ericifolia* Hook.f. *20681*
     R   *20681*   Australia - Tasmania *20681*

R   *Rupicola apiculata* (Cunn.) Telford *20681*
     R   *20681*   Australia - New South Wales *20681*

R   *Rupicola ciliata* Telford *20681*
     R   *20681*   Australia - New South Wales *20681*

R   *Rupicola decumbens* Telford *20681*
     R   *20681*   Australia - New South Wales *20681*

R   *Rupicola sprengelioides* Maiden & Betche *20681*
     R   *20681*   Australia - New South Wales *20681*

R   *Sprengelia distichophylla* (Rodway) W.M.Curtis *20681*
     R   *20681*   Australia - Tasmania *20681*

R   *Sprengelia monticola* (DC.) Druce *20681*
     R   *20681*   Australia - New South Wales *20681*

R   *Styphelia enervia* (Guillaumin) Sleumer
     R   New Caledonia

V   *Styphelia perileuca* J.Powell *20681*
     V   *20681*   Australia - New South Wales *20681*

R   *Styphelia psiloclada* J.Powell *20681*
     R   *20681*   Australia - New South Wales *20681*

I   *Styphelia rapae* Sleumer *20845*
     I   *20845*   French Polynesia - Tubuai Is. (Rapa) *20845*

R   *Styphelia tameiameiae* (Cham. & Schlechtend.) F.H. Mueller var. *marquesensis* F.Brown *20845*
     R   *20845*   French Polynesia - Marquesas Is (Nuku Hiva) *20845*

E   *Styphelia violaceo-spicata* (Guillaumin) McPherson *20893*

     E   *20893*   New Caledonia *20893*

R   *Trochocarpa bellendenkerensis* Domin *20681*
     R   *20681*   Australia - Queensland *20681*

R   *Trochocarpa disticha* (Labill.) Sprengel *20681*
     R   *20681*   Australia - Tasmania *20681*

Eremolepidaceae

Number of genera: 3
Number of species: 12
Recorded threatened species: 1   (8%)

Tropical America.

V   *Eubrachion ambiguum* var. *jamaicense* Krug. & Urb. *20883*
     V   *20883*   Jamaica *20883*

Ericaceae

Number of genera: 125
Number of species: 3,500
Recorded threatened species: 509   (14%)

Cosmopolitan.

I   *Acrostemon xeranthemifolius* (Salisb.) E.G.H.Oliv. *20604*
     I   *20604*   South Africa - Cape Province *20604*

R   *Agapetes meiniana* F.Muell. *20681*
     R   *20681*   Australia - Queensland *20681*

V   *Agapetes neo-caledonica* Guillaumin *20893*
     V   *20893*   New Caledonia *20893*

I   *Agapetes nuttallii* C.B. Clarke *10173*
     I   Bhutan *10173*
     I   India - Arunachal Pradesh *10173*

V   *Agarista angustissima* Taubert *20883*
     V   *20883*   Brazil *20883*

R   *Agarista boliviensis* (Sleumer) Judd *20883*
     V   *20883*   Argentina *20883*
     I   *20883*   Bolivia *20883*

E   *Agarista bracemorensis* (Kunth) G. Don *20883*
     E   *20883*   Peru *20883*

V   *Agarista chapadensis* Kinoshita-Gouvea *20883*
     V   *20883*   Brazil *20883*

V   *Agarista coriifolia* var. *bradei* Judd *20883*
     V   *20883*   Brazil *20883*

E   *Agarista duartei* (Sleumer) Judd *20883*
     E   *20883*   Brazil *20883*

E   *Agarista ericoides* Taubert *20883*
     E   *20883*   Brazil *20883*

R   *Agarista eucalyptoides* (Chamisso & Schlechtendal) Don *20883*
     R   *20883*   Brazil *20883*
     E   *20883*   Uruguay *20883*

V   *Agarista glaberrima* (Sleumer) Judd *20883*
     V   *20883*   Brazil *20883*

R   *Agarista hispidula* (De Candolle) J.D. Hooker ex Niedenzu *20883*
     R   *20883*   Brazil *20883*

R   *Agarista minensis* (Glaziou ex Sleumer) Judd *20883*
     R   *20883*   Brazil *20883*

R   *Agarista niederleinii* (Sleumer) Judd *20883*
     R   *20883*   Brazil *20883*

R   *Agarista niederleinii* (Sleumer) Judd var. *acutifolia*

Judd *20883*
V   *20883* Brazil *20883*

R   *Agarista nummularia* (Chamisso & Schlechtendal)
       G.Don *20883*
      R   *20883* Brazil *20883*

E   *Agarista organensis* (Gardner) J.D.Hooker ex
       Niedenzu *20883*
      E   *20883* Brazil *20883*

V   *Agarista paraguayensis* (Sleumer) Judd *20883*
      V   *20883* Argentina *20883*
      V   *20883* Paraguay *20883*

V   *Agarista pulchra* (Chamisso & Schlechtendal)
       G.Don *20883*
      V   *20883* Brazil *20883*

V   *Agarista revoluta* (Sprengel) J.D.Hooker ex
       Niedenzu *20883*
      V   *20883* Brazil *20883*

E   *Agarista revoluta* (Sprengel) J.D.Hooker ex Niedenzu var.
       velutina (Sprengel) J.D.Hooker ex Niedenzu *20883*
      E   *20883* Brazil *20883*

R   *Agarista sleumeri* Judd *20883*
      R   *20883* Mexico *20883*

E   *Agarista subcordata* (Dunal) Judd *20883*
      E   *20883* Peru *20883*

E   *Agarista subrotunda* (Pohl) G.Don *20883*
      E   *20883* Brazil *20883*

V   *Agarista uleana* (Sleumer) Judd *20883*
      V   *20883* Brazil *20883*

V   *Agarista villarrealana* L.M.Gonzalez V. *20883*
      V   *20883* Brazil *20883*

E   *Agarista virgata* Judd *20883*
      E   *20883* Brazil *20883*

V   *Anthopteropsis insignis* A.C. Sm. *20883, 9006*
      I   *20883* Panama *20883*

R   *Anthopterus cuneatus* A.C. Smith *11135*
      R   Colombia *11135*

R   *Anthopterus oliganthus* A.C. Smith *11135*
      R   Colombia *11135*

R   *Arbutus occidentalis* McVaugh & Rosatti *9683*
      R   *19850* Mexico *9683*

V   *Arbutus pavarii* Pampan.
      V   Libya

V   *Arctostaphylos andersonii* Gray *20850*
      V   *20850* U.S. - California *20850*

V   *Arctostaphylos auriculata* Eastw. *20850*
      V   *20850* U.S. - California *20850*

V   *Arctostaphylos bakeri* Eastw. *20850*
      V   *20850* U.S. - California *20850*

V   *Arctostaphylos bakeri* Eastw. ssp.
       bakeri *20850*
      V   *20850* U.S. - California *20850*

R   *Arctostaphylos canescens* *20850*
      I   *20850* U.S. - California *20850*
      I   *20850* U.S. - Oregon *20850*

R   *Arctostaphylos canescens* Eastw. ssp. *malloryi* W.
       Knight & Gankin *20850*
      R   *20850* U.S. - California *20850*

V   *Arctostaphylos canescens* Eastw. ssp. *sonomensis*
       (Eastw.) P.V. Wells *20850*

V   *20850* U.S. - California *20850*

E   *Arctostaphylos catalinae* P.V. Wells *20850*
      I   *20850* U.S. - California *20850*

V   *Arctostaphylos columbiana* Piper ssp. *nortensis*
       P.V. Wells *20850*
      V   *20850* U.S. - California *20850*

E   *Arctostaphylos confertiflora* Eastw. *20850*
      E   *20850* U.S. - California *20850*

V   *Arctostaphylos cruzensis* J.B. Roof *20850*
      V   *20850* U.S. - California *20850*

E   *Arctostaphylos densiflora* M.S. Baker *20850, 11027*
      E   *20850* U.S. - California (Vine Hill, Sonoma County)
        20850

V   *Arctostaphylos edmundsii* J.T. Howell *20850*
      V   *20850* U.S. - California *20850*

E   *Arctostaphylos glandulosa* Eastw. ssp. *crassifolia*
       (Jepson) P.V. Wells *20850*
      E   *20850* U.S. - California *20850*

V   *Arctostaphylos glutinosa* Schreib. *20850*
      V   *20850* U.S. - California *20850*

R   *Arctostaphylos hispidula* T.J. Howell *20850*
      V   *20850* U.S. - California *20850*
      V   *20850* U.S. - Oregon *20850*

V   *Arctostaphylos hookeri* G. Don *20850*
      I   *20850* U.S. - California *20850*

Ex/E   *Arctostaphylos hookeri* G. Don ssp. *franciscana*
       (Eastw.) Munz *20850*
      Ex   *20850* U.S. - California *20850*

E   *Arctostaphylos hookeri* G. Don ssp. *hearstiorum*
       (Hoover & J.B. Roof) P.V. Wells *20850*
      E   *20850* U.S. - California *20850*

V   *Arctostaphylos hookeri* G. Don ssp.
       hookeri *20850*
      V   *20850* U.S. - California *20850*

V   *Arctostaphylos hookeri* G. Don ssp. *montana*
       (Eastw.) P.V. Wells *20850*
      V   *20850* U.S. - California *20850*

E   *Arctostaphylos hookeri* G. Don ssp. *ravenii* P.
       Wells *20850*
      E   U.S. - California *20850*

E   *Arctostaphylos imbricata* Eastw. *20850*
      E   *20850* U.S. - California *20850*

E   *Arctostaphylos imbricata* Eastw. ssp.
       imbricata *20850*
      I   *20850* U.S. - California *20850*

E   *Arctostaphylos imbricata* Eastw. ssp. *montaraensis*
       (J.B. Roof) P.V. Wells *20850*
      I   *20850* U.S. - California *20850*

V   *Arctostaphylos insularis* Greene ex Parry *20850*
      I   *20850* U.S. - California *20850*

E   *Arctostaphylos klamathensis* S.W. Edwards, Keeler-Wolf &
       W.Knight *20850*
      E   *20850* U.S. - California *20850*

V   *Arctostaphylos luciana* P.V. Wells *20850*
      V   *20850* U.S. - California *20850*

V   *Arctostaphylos manzanita* Parry ssp. *elegans*
       (Eastw.) P.V. Wells *20850*
      V   *20850* U.S. - California *20850*

V   *Arctostaphylos manzanita* Parry ssp. *laevigata*

	(Eastw.) Munz *20850*			
V	20850	U.S. - California *20850*		
E	*Arctostaphylos mendocinoensis* P.V. Wells *20850*			
E	20850	U.S. - California *20850*		
V	*Arctostaphylos montereyensis* Hoover *20850*			
V	20850	U.S. - California *20850*		
V	*Arctostaphylos morroensis* Wies. & Schreib. *20850*			
V	20850	U.S. - California *20850*		
V	*Arctostaphylos myrtifolia* Parry *20850*			
V	20850	U.S. - California *20850*		
V	*Arctostaphylos nisseniana* Merriam *20850*			
V	20850	U.S. - California *20850*		
R	*Arctostaphylos nummularia* Gray *20850*			
I	20850	U.S. - California *20850*		
R	*Arctostaphylos obispoensis* Eastw. *20850*			
I	20850	U.S. - California *20850*		
V	*Arctostaphylos otayensis* Wies. & Schreib. *20850*			
V	20850	U.S. - California *20850*		
V	*Arctostaphylos pajaroensis* (J.E. Adams ex McMinn) J.E. Adams *20850*			
V	20850	U.S. - California *20850*		
E	*Arctostaphylos pallida* Eastw. *20850*			
E	20850	U.S. - California *20850*		
E	*Arctostaphylos pechoensis* (Dudley ex Abrams) Dudley ex Munz *20850*			
E	20850	U.S. - California *20850*		
V	*Arctostaphylos peninsularis* P.V. Wells *20850, 9684*			
V	20850	U.S. - California *20850*		
?		Mexico *9684*		
V	*Arctostaphylos pilosula* Jepson & Wies. ex Jepson *20850*			
V	20850	U.S. - California *20850*		
V	*Arctostaphylos pilosula* Jepson & Wiesl. ssp. *pilosula* *20850*			
V	20850	U.S. - California *20850*		
V	*Arctostaphylos pumila* Nutt. *20850*			
V	20850	U.S. - California *20850*		
V	*Arctostaphylos purissima* P.V. Wells *20850*			
V	20850	U.S. - California *20850*		
V	*Arctostaphylos refugioensis* Gankin *20850*			
I	20850	U.S. - California *20850*		
V	*Arctostaphylos regismontana* Eastw. *20850*			
V	20850	U.S. - California *20850*		
V	*Arctostaphylos rudis* Jepson & Wies. ex Jepson *20850*			
V	20850	U.S. - California *20850*		
V	*Arctostaphylos silvicola* Jepson & Wies. ex Jepson *20850*			
V	20850	U.S. - California *20850*		
R	*Arctostaphylos stanfordiana* Parry *20850*			
I	20850	U.S. - California *20850*		
V	*Arctostaphylos stanfordiana* Parry ssp. *raichei* W.Knight *20850*			
V	20850	U.S. - California *20850*		
E	*Arctostaphylos stanfordiana* Parry ssp. *stanfordiana* *20850*			
E	20850	U.S. - California *20850*		
R	*Arctostaphylos tomentosa* (Pursh) Lindl. *20850*			
I	20850	U.S. - California *20850*		
V	*Arctostaphylos tomentosa* (Pursh) Lindl. ssp.			

	eastwoodiana P.V. Wells *20850*	
V	20850	U.S. - California *20850*
R	*Arctostaphylos truei* W. Knight *20850*	
R	20850	U.S. - California *20850*
V	*Arctostaphylos virgata* Eastw. *20850*	
V	20850	U.S. - California *20850*
V	*Arctostaphylos wellsii* Knight *20850*	
V	20850	U.S. - California *20850*
V	*Bejaria cubensis* Grisebach *20883*	
V	20883	Cuba *20883*
V	*Bejaria imthurnii* N.E.Brown *20883*	
V	20883	Venezuela *20883*
R	*Bejaria infundibula* Clemants *20883*	
R	20883	Peru *20883*
V	*Bejaria ledifolia* Bonpland *20883*	
V	20883	Venezuela *20883*
V	*Bejaria nana* A.C.Smith & Ewan *20883*	
V	20883	Colombia *20883*
V	20883	Venezuela *20883*
E	*Bejaria neblinensis* Maguire, Steyermark & Luteyn *20883*	
E	20883	Venezuela *20883*
V	*Bejaria steyermarkii* A.C.Smith *20883*	
V	20883	Venezuela *20883*
V	*Bejaria subsessilis* Bentham *20883*	
V	20883	Ecuador *20883*
R	*Bejaria tachirensis* A.C.Smith *20883*	
V	20883	Colombia *20883*
R	20883	Venezuela *20883*
V	*Bejaria zamorae* Clemants *20883*	
V	20883	Ecuador *20883*
R	*Cassiope anadyrensis* Jurtz. *20085, 21309*	
R	20085	Russia (E.Europe) - North *20085*
V	*Cassiope lycopodioides* (Pallas) D. Don var. *cristapilosa* (Calder & Taylor) Boivin *20850*	
V	20850	Canada - British Columbia *20850*
I	20850	U.S. - Washington *20850*
V	*Cassiope lycopodioides* (Pallas) D. Don var. *lycopodioides* *20850*	
V	20850	Canada - British Columbia *20850*
I	20850	U.S. - Alaska *20850*
E	*Cavendishia aberrans* Luteyn *20883, 9685*	
I	20883	Panama *20883*
R	*Cavendishia adenophora* Mansfeld *20883, 9685*	
R	19932	Colombia *20883*
E	*Cavendishia albopicata* Luteyn *20883*	
I	20883	Colombia *20883*
R	*Cavendishia allenii* A.C. Sm. *20883, 9006*	
I	20883	Panama *20883*
E	*Cavendishia amoena* A. C. Smith *20883, 9685*	
R	19932	Colombia *20883*
E	*Cavendishia amplexa* Luteyn *20883, 9685*	
R	19932	Colombia *20883*
R	*Cavendishia angustifolia* Mansfeld *9685*	
R	19932	Colombia *9685*
E	*Cavendishia arizonensis* Luteyn *20883, 9685*	
I	20883	Panama *20883*
V	*Cavendishia atroviolacea* Luteyn *20883*	
I	20883	Panama *20883*

V   *Cavendishia atroviolacea* Luteyn var.
       atroviolacea *20883*
    I   *20883* Costa Rica *20883*
    I   *20883* Panama *20883*

E   *Cavendishia atroviolacea* Luteyn var. *folsomii*
       Luteyn *20883, 9685*
    I   *20883* Panama *20883*

E   *Cavendishia aurantiaca* Luteyn *20883*
    I   *20883* Colombia *20883*

E   *Cavendishia barnebyi* Luteyn *20883, 9685*
    V   *19932* Colombia *20883*

V   *Cavendishia bomareoides* A. C. Smith *20883*
    I   *20883* Colombia *20883*

V   *Cavendishia calycina* A.C. Sm. *20883, 9685*
    I   *20883* Panama *20883*

E   *Cavendishia caudata* A. C. Smith *20883*
    I   *20883* Colombia *20883*

V   *Cavendishia chiriquiensis* A.C. Sm. *20883*
    I   *20883* Panama *20883*

E   *Cavendishia chlamydantha* A. C. Smith *20883, 9685*
    R   *19932* Colombia *20883*

E   *Cavendishia chocoensis* A. C. Smith *20883*
    I   *20883* Colombia *20883*

E   *Cavendishia ciliata* Luteyn *20883, 9685*
    I   *20883* Costa Rica *20883*

V   *Cavendishia coccinea* A. C. Smith *20883, 9685*
    V   *19932* Colombia *20883*

V   *Cavendishia colombiana* Luteyn *20883, 9685*
    R   *19932* Colombia *20883*

R   *Cavendishia compacta* A. C. Smith *20883, 9685*
    V   *19932* Colombia *20883*

E   *Cavendishia confertiflora* A. C. Smith *20883, 9037*
    I   *20883* Costa Rica *20883*

E   *Cavendishia copeensis* Luteyn *20883, 9685*
    I   *20883* Panama *20883*

E   *Cavendishia corei* A. C. Smith *20883*
    I   *20883* Colombia *20883*

V   *Cavendishia darienensis* Luteyn *20883*
    I   *20883* Panama *20883*
    I   *20883* Colombia *20883*

E   *Cavendishia dendrophila* A. C. Smith *20883*
    I   *20883* Colombia *20883*

R   *Cavendishia divaricata* A. C. Smith *20883, 9685*
    V   *19932* Colombia *20883*

E   *Cavendishia dulcis* Luteyn *20883, 9685*
    V   *19932* Colombia *20883*

V   *Cavendishia endresii* Hemsley *20883, 9037*
    I   *20883* Costa Rica *20883*

R   *Cavendishia engleriana* Hoerold *20883*
    I   *20883* Colombia *20883*
    I   *20883* Ecuador *20883*

V   *Cavendishia engleriana* Hoerold var. *ecuadorensis*
       Luteyn *20883*
    I   *20883* Ecuador *20883*

E   *Cavendishia erythrostegia* Luteyn *20883, 9685*
    R   *19932* Colombia *20883*

E   *Cavendishia foreroi* Luteyn *20883, 9685*
    V   *19932* Colombia *20883*

E   *Cavendishia fortunensis* Luteyn *20883, 9685*

    I   *20883* Panama *20883*

V   *Cavendishia fusiformis* Luteyn *20883*
    I   *20883* Panama *20883*
    I   *20883* Colombia *20883*

E   *Cavendishia gentryi* Luteyn *20883, 9006*
    I   *20883* Panama *20883*

E   *Cavendishia glandulosa* A. C. Smith *20883*
    I   *20883* Colombia *20883*

E   *Cavendishia grandifolia* Hoerold *20883*
    I   *20883* Ecuador *20883*

E   *Cavendishia grossa* Luteyn *20883*
    I   *20883* Colombia *20883*

R   *Cavendishia isernii* Sleumer *20883*
    I   *20883* Ecuador *20883*
    I   *20883* Peru *20883*

R   *Cavendishia isernii* Sleumer var.
       isernii *20883*
    I   *20883* Ecuador *20883*
    I   *20883* Peru *20883*

V   *Cavendishia isernii* Sleumer var. *pseudospicata*
       (Sleumer) Luteyn *20883*
    I   *20883* Ecuador *20883*

E   *Cavendishia lactiviscida* Luteyn *20883, 9685*
    I   *20883* Costa Rica *20883*

E   *Cavendishia lebroniae* Luteyn *20883*
    I   *20883* Ecuador *20883*

E   *Cavendishia leucantha* Luteyn *20883, 9685*
    V   *19932* Colombia *20883*

R   *Cavendishia lindauiana* Hoerold *20883, 9685*
    I   *20883* Panama *20883*
    I   *20883* Colombia *20883*

V   *Cavendishia longirachis* Luteyn *20883*
    I   *20883* Colombia *20883*

V   *Cavendishia macrocephala* A. C. Smith *20883*
    I   *20883* Colombia *20883*

V   *Cavendishia mariae* Luteyn *20883*
    I   *20883* Ecuador *20883*

V   *Cavendishia megabracteata* Luteyn *20883*
    I   *20883* Panama *20883*
    I   *20883* Colombia *20883*

E   *Cavendishia megabracteata* Luteyn var. *attenuata*
       Luteyn *20883, 9006*
    I   *20883* Panama *20883*

V   *Cavendishia megabracteata* var.
       megabracteata *20883, 9006*
    I   *20883* Panama *20883*

R   *Cavendishia melastomoides* (Kl.) Hemsl. *20883*
    I   *20883* Panama *20883*

V   *Cavendishia melastomoides* Luteyn var. *albiflora*
       Luteyn *20883, 9037*
    I   *20883* Costa Rica *20883*

E   *Cavendishia melastomoides* Luteyn var. *coloradensis*
       Luteyn *20883, 9685*
    I   *20883* Panama *20883*

R   *Cavendishia melastomoides* var.
       melastomoides *20883, 9685*
    I   *20883* Costa Rica *20883*

E   *Cavendishia morii* Luteyn *20883, 9006*
    I   *20883* Panama *20883*

E   *Cavendishia neblinae* Maguire, Steyermark &

Luteyn *20883*

    I   *20883* Venezuela *20883*

V   *Cavendishia nitens* Sleumer *20883, 9685*

    R   *19932* Colombia *20883*

V   *Cavendishia nobilis* var. *capitata* (Bentham)
        Luteyn *20883*

    I   *20883* Ecuador *20883*

R   *Cavendishia nobilis* var. *nobilis* *20883*

    I   *20883* Peru *20883*

V   *Cavendishia oligantha* A. C. Smith *20883*

    I   *20883* Colombia *20883*

V   *Cavendishia orthosepala* A. C. Smith *20883*

    I   *20883* Ecuador *20883*

V   *Cavendishia palustris* A. C. Smith *20883, 9685*

    I   *19353* Colombia *20883*

V   *Cavendishia panamensis* Luteyn *20883, 9006*

    I   *20883* Panama *20883*

E   *Cavendishia pedicellata* Luteyn *20883, 9685*

    I   *19353* Colombia *20883*

E   *Cavendishia pilobracteata* Luteyn *20883, 9685*

    R   *19932* Colombia *20883*

E   *Cavendishia pilosa* Luteyn *20883*

    I   *20883* Colombia *20883*

V   *Cavendishia porphyrea* A. C. Smith *20883, 9685*

    V   *19932* Colombia *20883*

R   *Cavendishia pseudopedunculata* Luteyn *20883, 9685*

    V   *19932* Colombia *20883*

V   *Cavendishia pseudostenophylla* Luteyn *20883, 9685*

    I   *20883* Panama *20883*

R   *Cavendishia punctata* (Ruiz & Pavón ex Jaume Saint-Hilaire)
        Sleumer *20883*

    I   *20883* Peru *20883*

R   *Cavendishia quercina* A.C. Sm. *20883*

    I   *20883* Costa Rica *20883*

    I   *20883* Panama *20883*

E   *Cavendishia revoluta* Luteyn *20883, 9006*

    I   *20883* Panama *20883*

E   *Cavendishia rhynchophylla* A. C. Smith *20883, 9685*

    V   *19932* Colombia *20883*

E   *Cavendishia ruiz-teranii* Luteyn *20883*

    I   *20883* Venezuela *20883*

E   *Cavendishia santafeensis* Luteyn *20883, 9006*

    I   *20883* Panama *20883*

E   *Cavendishia sirensis* Luteyn *20883*

    I   *20883* Peru *20883*

E   *Cavendishia sophoclesioides* A. C. Smith *20883*

    I   *20883* Colombia *20883*

R   *Cavendishia speciosa* A. C. Smith *20883*

    I   *20883* Colombia *20883*

E   *Cavendishia spicata* A. C. Smith *20883, 9685*

    V   *19932* Colombia *20883*

V   *Cavendishia stenophylla* A.C. Sm. *20883, 9006*

    I   *20883* Panama *20883*

E   *Cavendishia subamplexicaulis* A. C. Smith *20883*

    I   *20883* Colombia *20883*

V   *Cavendishia subfasciculata* Luteyn *20883, 9006*

    I   *20883* Panama *20883*

E   *Cavendishia talamancensis* Luteyn *20883, 9685*

    R   *9685*   Costa Rica *20883*

R   *Cavendishia tarapotana* var. *gilgiana* (Hoerold)
        Luteyn *20883*

    I   *20883* Colombia *20883*

    I   *20883* Ecuador *20883*

R   *Cavendishia tenella* A. C. Smith *20883, 9685*

    R   *19932* Colombia *20883*

E   *Cavendishia trujilloensis* Luteyn *20883*

    I   *20883* Venezuela *20883*

V   *Cavendishia tryphera* A. C. Smith *20883, 9685*

    V   *19932* Colombia *20883*

E   *Cavendishia uniflora* Luteyn *20883*

    I   *20883* Colombia *20883*

V   *Cavendishia urophylla* A. C. Smith *20883, 9685*

    V   *19932* Colombia *20883*

E   *Cavendishia vinacea* Luteyn *20883, 9685*

    V   *19932* Colombia *20883*

V   *Cavendishia violacea* Luteyn *20883, 9685*

    V   *19932* Colombia *20883*

V   *Cavendishia wercklei* Hoerold *20883, 9037*

    I   *20883* Costa Rica *20883*

V   *Cavendishia zamorensis* A. C. Smith *20883*

    I   *20883* Ecuador *20883*

R   *Cheilotheca humilis* (Don) Keng var. *glaberrima*
        (Don) Keng *20511*

    R   *20511* Taiwan *20511*

R   *Chimaphila umbellata* (L.) Bart ssp. *domingensis*
        Linnaeus *20883*

    R   *20883* Dominica *20883*

I   *Coilostigma zeyherianum* Klotzch var. *tenufolium*
        (Klotzsch) E.G.H.Oliv. *20604*

    I   *20604* South Africa - Cape Province *20604*

R   *Comarostaphylis arbutoides* ssp. *costaricensis* (Small)
        Diggs *20883*

    R   *20883* Costa Rica *20883*

E   *Comarostaphylis discolor* ssp. *macughii* Diggs,
        Bull. *20883*

    E   *20883* Mexico *20883*

R   *Comarostaphylis discolor* ssp. *manantlanensis* Diggs,
        Bull. *20883*

    R   *20883* Mexico *20883*

R   *Comarostaphylis discolor* ssp. *rupestris* (Hooker)
        Diggs *20883*

    R   *20883* Mexico *20883*

R   *Comarostaphylis diversifolia* (Parry) Greene *20850*

    I   *20850* U.S. - California *20850*

V   *Comarostaphylis diversifolia* (Parry) Greene ssp.
        diversifolia *20850*

    V   *20850* U.S. - California *20850*

V   *Comarostaphylis lanata* Small *20883*

    V   *20883* Mexico *20883*

R   *Comarostaphylis mucronata* Klotzsch *20883*

    R   *20883* Mexico *20883*

R   *Comarostaphylis polifolia* ssp. *coahuilensis* (Kunth)
        Zuccarini ex Klotzsh *20883*

    R   *20883* Mexico *20883*

R   *Comarostaphylis polifolia* ssp. *minor* (Kunth)
        Zuccarini ex Klotzsh *20883*

    R   *20883* Mexico *20883*

V   *Comarostaphylis sharpii* Dorr & Diggs *20883*
   V   *20883* Mexico *20883*

R   *Comarostaphylis spinulosa* (Martens & Galeotti)
   Diggs *20883*
   R   *20883* Mexico *20883*

R   *Comarostaphylis spinulosa* ssp. *glandulifera* (Martens
   & Galeotti) Diggs *20883*
   R   *20883* Mexico *20883*

R   *Daboecia azorica* Tutin & E.F.Warb. *20171*
   R   *19174* Portugal - Azores *19174*

E   *Didonica panamensis* Luteyn & Wilbur *20883, 10747*
   I   *20883* Panama *20883*

E   *Didonica pendula* Luteyn & Wilbur *20883, 9006*
   I   *20883* Panama *20883*

R   *Diplycosia ensifolia* Merr. *7730*
   R   Malaysia - Sabah (Mt Kinabalu) *7730*

I   *Diplycosia epiphytica* Fletcher *19120*
   I   *19120* Thailand *19120*

R   *Diplycosia sphenophylla* Sleumer *7730*
   R   Malaysia - Sabah (Mt Kinabalu) *7730*

V   *Disterigma luteynii* Wilbur *20883, 9006*
   I   *20883* Panama *20883*

E   *Disterigma panamense* Standl. *20883, 9006*
   I   *20883* Panama *20883*

E   *Disterigma trimerum* Wilbur & Luteyn *20883, 9006*
   I   *20883* Panama *20883*

I   *Disterigma ulei* Sleumer *18200*
   I   *9446* Peru *18200*

R   *Disterigma utleyorum* Wilbur & Luteyn *20883, 9688*
   V   *19932* Costa Rica *20883*
   V   *19932* Panama *20883*
   V   *19932* Colombia *9006*
   V   *19932* Ecuador *9006*

V   *Elliottia racemosa* Muhl. ex Ell. *20850*
   I   *20850* U.S. - Florida *20850*
   V   *20850* U.S. - Georgia *20850*
   Ex/E *20850* U.S. - South Carolina *20850*

R   *Empedoclesia stipitata* Luteyn *9686*
   R   *19755* Mexico *9686*

R   *Enkianthus campanulatus* (Miq.) Nichols var.
   longilobus (Nakai) Makino *10573*
   R   *10573* Japan *10573*

R   *Enkianthus perulatus* Schneid. var. *taiwanianus*
   (Ying) Y.C.Liu *20511*
   R   *20511* Taiwan *20511*

R   *Enkianthus ruber* Dop *6057*
   R   Vietnam *6057*

R   *Eremia brevifolia* Benth. *20604*
   R   *20604* South Africa - Cape Province *20604*

R   *Eremiella outeniquae* Compton *20604*
   R   *20604* South Africa - Cape Province *20604*

V   *Erica abbottii* E.G.H.Oliv. *20604*
   V   *20604* South Africa - Cape Province *20604*
   V   *20604* South Africa - Natal *20604*

V   *Erica abelii* E.G.H.Oliv. *20604*
   V   *20604* South Africa - Cape Province *20604*

R   *Erica abietina* L. var. *echiiflora*
   (andrews)dulfer *20604*
   R   *20604* South Africa - Cape Province *20604*

V   *Erica aghillana* Guthrie & Bolus var.

   aghillana *20604*
   V   *20604* South Africa - Cape Province *20604*

Ex *Erica alexandri* Guthrie & Bolus ssp. *acockii*
   (Compton) E.G.H.Oliv. *20604*
   Ex   *20604* South Africa - Cape Province *20604*

E   *Erica alexandri* Guthrie & Bolus ssp.
   alexandri *20604*
   E   *20604* South Africa - Cape Province *20604*

R   *Erica alfredii* Guthrie & Bolus *20604*
   R   *20604* South Africa - Cape Province *20604*

R   *Erica amoena* J.C.Wendl. *20604*
   R   *20604* South Africa - Cape Province *20604*

E   *Erica andevalensis* Cabezudo & Rivera *19818*
   E   *19818* Spain (Andévalo) *19818*

V   *Erica aneimena* Dulfer *20604*
   V   *20604* South Africa - Cape Province *20604*

R   *Erica annectens* Guthrie & Bolus *20604*
   R   *20604* South Africa - Cape Province *20604*

R   *Erica anomala* Hilliard & B.L.Burtt *20604*
   R   *20604* South Africa - Natal *20604*

E   *Erica atrovinosa* E.G.H.Oliv. *20604*
   E   *20604* South Africa - Cape Province *20604*

E   *Erica bakeri* Salter *20604*
   E   *20604* South Africa - Cape Province *20604*

R   *Erica barrydalensis* L.Bolus *20604*
   R   *20604* South Africa - Cape Province *20604*

V   *Erica bauera* Andrews *20604*
   V   *20604* South Africa - Cape Province *20604*

R   *Erica beatricis* Compton *20604*
   R   *20604* South Africa - Cape Province *20604*

R   *Erica blancheana* L.Bolus *20604*
   R   *20604* South Africa - Cape Province *20604*

R   *Erica blesbergensis* H.A.Baker *20604*
   R   *20604* South Africa - Cape Province *20604*

R   *Erica bocquetii* (H. Pesmen) P.F. Stevens *12840*
   R   *20618* Turkey *20618*

E   *Erica bolusiae* Salter *20604, 3774*
   E   *20604* South Africa - Cape Province *20604*

I   *Erica brachycentra* Benth. *20604*
   I   *20604* South Africa - Cape Province *20604*

V   *Erica brachysepala* Guthrie & Bolus *20604*
   V   *20604* South Africa - Cape Province *20604*

R   *Erica caledonica* A.Spreng. *20604*
   R   *20604* South Africa - Cape Province *20604*

R   *Erica capensis* Salter *20604*
   R   *20604* South Africa - Cape Province *20604*

R   *Erica capitata* L. *20604*
   R   *20604* South Africa - Cape Province *20604*

V   *Erica casta* Guthrie & Bolus var. *casta* *20604*
   V   *20604* South Africa - Cape Province *20604*

E   *Erica caterviflora* Salisb. *20604*
   E   *20604* South Africa - Cape Province *20604*

R   *Erica chlorosepala* Benth. *20604*
   R   *20604* South Africa - Cape Province *20604*

E   *Erica chrysocodon* Guthrie & Bolus *20604*
   E   *20604* South Africa - Cape Province *20604*

R   *Erica clavisepala* Guthrie & Bolus *20604*
   R   *20604* South Africa - Cape Province *20604*

R	*Erica comptonii* Salter 20604		
	R	20604	South Africa - Cape Province 20604
R	*Erica cremea* Dulfer 20604		
	R	20604	South Africa - Cape Province 20604
E	*Erica crucistigmatica* Dulfer 20604		
	E	20604	South Africa - Cape Province 20604
V	*Erica cyrillaeflora* Salisb. 20604		
	V	20604	South Africa - Cape Province 20604
R	*Erica diotiflora* Salisb. 20604		
	R	20604	South Africa - Cape Province 20604
I	*Erica dysantha* Benth. 20604		
	I	20604	South Africa - Cape Province 20604
R	*Erica eburnea* Salter 20604		
	R	20604	South Africa - Cape Province 20604
E	*Erica fairii* Bolus 20604		
	E	20604	South Africa - Cape Province 20604
V	*Erica ferrea* P.J.Bergius 20604		
	V	20604	South Africa - Cape Province 20604
I	*Erica flanaganii* Bolus 20604		
	I	20604	South Africa - Natal 20604
R	*Erica fontana* L.Bolus 20604		
	R	20604	South Africa - Cape Province 20604
R	*Erica galgebergensis* H.A.Baker 20604		
	R	20604	South Africa - Cape Province 20604
I	*Erica gossypioides* E.G.H.Oliv. 20604		
	I	20604	South Africa - Cape Province 20604
I	*Erica gracilipes* Guthrie & Bolus 20604		
	I	20604	South Africa - Cape Province 20604
R	*Erica granulatifolia* H.A.Baker 20604		
	R	20604	South Africa - Cape Province 20604
E	*Erica heleogena* Salter 20604		
	E	20604	South Africa - Cape Province 20604
R	*Erica hendricksei* H.A.Baker var. hendricksei 20604		
	R	20604	South Africa - Cape Province 20604
V	*Erica hibbertia* Andrews 20604		
	V	20604	South Africa - Cape Province 20604
R	*Erica hillburttii* (E.G.H.Oliv.) E.G.H.Oliv. 20604		
	R	20604	South Africa - Cape Province 20604
R	*Erica hippurus* Compton 20604		
	R	20604	South Africa - Cape Province 20604
R	*Erica holtii* Schweick. 20604, 5914		
	R	5914	Swaziland 5914
	R	20604	South Africa - Natal 20604
	R	20604	South Africa - Transvaal 20604
R	*Erica inordinata* H.A.Baker 20604		
	R	20604	South Africa - Cape Province 20604
R	*Erica insignis* E.G.H.Oliv. 20604		
	R	20604	South Africa - Cape Province 20604
R	*Erica insolitanthera* H.A.Baker 20604		
	R	20604	South Africa - Cape Province 20604
R	*Erica intricata* H.A.Baker 20604		
	R	20604	South Africa - Cape Province 20604
Ex	*Erica ixanthera* Benth. 20604		
	Ex	20604	South Africa - Cape Province 20604
E	*Erica jasminiflora* Salisb. 20604, 6180		
	E	20604	South Africa - Cape Province 20604
E	*Erica junonia* Bolus var. *junonia* 20604		

	E	20604	South Africa - Cape Province 20604
R	*Erica keeromsbergensis* H.A.Baker 20604		
	R	20604	South Africa - Cape Province 20604
I	*Erica lagenaeformis* Salisb. 20604		
	I	20604	South Africa - Cape Province 20604
R	*Erica lanceolifera* S. Moore 7754		
	R		Zimbabwe (Chimanimani Mts.) 7754
V	*Erica lerouxiae* Bolus 20604		
	V	20604	South Africa - Cape Province 20604
R	*Erica leucosiphon* L.Bolus 20604		
	R	20604	South Africa - Cape Province 20604
V	*Erica limosa* L.Bolus 20604		
	V	20604	South Africa - Cape Province 20604
R	*Erica lowryensis* Bolus var. *lowryensis* 20604		
	R	20604	South Africa - Cape Province 20604
R	*Erica maderensis* (DC.) Bornm.		
	R		Portugal - Madeira
E	*Erica margaritacea* Sol. 20604		
	E	20604	South Africa - Cape Province 20604
R	*Erica marifolia* Sol. 20604		
	R	20604	South Africa - Cape Province 20604
R	*Erica milanjiana* Bolus 7757		
	R		Malawi (Mt. Mulanje) 7757
R	*Erica nana* Salisb. 20604		
	R	20604	South Africa - Cape Province 20604
R	*Erica nematophylla* Guthrie & Bolus 20604		
	R	20604	South Africa - Cape Province 20604
R	*Erica oblongiflora* Benth. 20604		
	R	20604	South Africa - Cape Province 20604
R	*Erica occulta* E.G.H.Oliv. 20604		
	R	20604	South Africa - Cape Province 20604
I	*Erica oligantha* Guthrie & Bolus 20604		
	I	20604	South Africa - Cape Province 20604
R	*Erica oophylla* Benth. 20604		
	R	20604	South Africa - Cape Province 20604
R	*Erica ostiaria* Compton 20604		
	R	20604	South Africa - Cape Province 20604
V	*Erica paludicola* L.Bolus 20604		
	V	20604	South Africa - Cape Province 20604
R	*Erica parvulisepala* H.A.Baker 20604		
	R	20604	South Africa - Cape Province 20604
I	*Erica passerinoides* (Bolus) E.G.H.Oliv. 20604		
	I	20604	South Africa - Cape Province 20604
R	*Erica patersonia* Andrews 20604		
	R	20604	South Africa - Cape Province 20604
R	*Erica pauciovulata* H.A.Baker 20604		
	R	20604	South Africa - Cape Province 20604
E	*Erica physantha* Benth. 20604		
	E	20604	South Africa - Cape Province 20604
V	*Erica pillansii* Bolus 20604		
	V		Southern Africa
	V	20604	South Africa - Cape Province 20604
E	*Erica pilulifera* L. 20604		
	E	20604	South Africa - Cape Province 20604
V	*Erica porteri* Compton 20604		
	V	20604	South Africa - Cape Province 20604
R	*Erica propendens* Andrews 20604		
	R	20604	South Africa - Cape Province 20604

R	*Erica pulvinata* Guthrie & Bolus *20604*	
	R	*20604* South Africa - Cape Province *20604*
V	*Erica purgatoriensis* H.A.Baker *20604*	
	V	*20604* South Africa - Cape Province *20604*
Ex	*Erica pyramidalis* Sol. *20604, 6180*	
	Ex	*20604* South Africa - Cape Province *20604*
V	*Erica quadrisulcata* L.Bolus *20604*	
	V	*20604* South Africa - Cape Province *20604*
V	*Erica regia* Bartl. var. *variegata* Bolus *20604*	
	V	*20604* South Africa - Cape Province *20604*
R	*Erica revoluta* (Bolus) L.E.Davidson *20604, 17458*	
	R	*20604* Swaziland *20604*
	V	*20604* South Africa - Natal *20604*
	R	*20604* South Africa - Transvaal *20604*
E	*Erica rhodopis* Bolus *20604*	
	E	*20604* South Africa - Cape Province *20604*
I	*Erica riparia* H.A.Baker *20604*	
	I	*20604* South Africa - Cape Province *20604*
I	*Erica rivularis* L.E.Davidson *20604, 17458*	
	I	*20604* South Africa - Transvaal *20604*
E	*Erica sacciflora* Salisb. *20604*	
	E	*20604* South Africa - Cape Province *20604*
V	*Erica scoparia* L. ssp. *azorica* (Hochst.) D.A. Webb *8000, 20171*	
	V	Portugal - Azores *8000*
V	*Erica scoparia* L. ssp. *platycodon* A. Hansen & Kunkel	
	V	Spain - Canary Is.
R	*Erica shannonea* Andrews *20604*	
	R	*20604* South Africa - Cape Province *20604*
E	*Erica sociorum* L.Bolus *20604*	
	E	*20604* South Africa - Cape Province *20604*
R	*Erica sonora* Compton *20604*	
	R	*20604* South Africa - Cape Province *20604*
R	*Erica subverticillaris* Diels ex Guthrie & Bolus *20604, 17458*	
	R	*20604* South Africa - Transvaal *20604*
V	*Erica swaziensis* E.G.H.Oliv. *20604, 18023*	
	V	*20604* Swaziland *20604*
R	*Erica toringbergensis* H.A.Baker *20604*	
	R	*20604* South Africa - Cape Province *20604*
R	*Erica trimera* (Engl.) Beentje ssp. *elgonensis* (Mildbr.) Beentje *20057*	
	R	*20057* Kenya *20057*
R	*Erica trimera* (Engl.) Beentje ssp. *keniensis* (S. Moore) Beentje *20057*	
	R	*20057* Kenya *20057*
I	*Erica turbiniflora* Salisb var. *turbiniflora* *20604*	
	I	*20604* South Africa - Cape Province *20604*
Ex	*Erica turgida* Salisb. *20604, 6180*	
	Ex	*20604* South Africa - Cape Province *20604*
R	*Erica urna-viridis* Bolus *20604*	
	R	*20604* South Africa - Cape Province *20604*
I	*Erica ustulescens* Guthrie & Bolus *20604*	
	I	*20604* South Africa - Cape Province *20604*
V	*Erica uysii* H.A.Baker *20604*	
	V	*20604* South Africa - Cape Province *20604*
R	*Erica valida* H.A.Baker *20604*	
	R	*20604* South Africa - Cape Province *20604*
R	*Erica vallis-aranearum* E.G.H.Oliv. *20604*	
	R	*20604* South Africa - Cape Province *20604*
Ex	*Erica velitaris* Salisb. *20604*	
	Ex	*20604* South Africa - Cape Province *20604*
Ex	*Erica verticillata* P.J.Bergius *20604, 6180, 20171*	
	Ex	*20604* South Africa - Cape Province *20604*
R	*Erica vestiflua* Salisb. *20604*	
	R	*20604* South Africa - Cape Province *20604*
I	*Erica vogelpoelii* H.A.Baker *20604*	
	I	*20604* South Africa - Cape Province *20604*
R	*Erica wyliei* Bolus *20604*	
	R	*20604* South Africa - Natal *20604*
R	*Erica zitzikammensis* Dulfer *20604*	
	R	*20604* South Africa - Cape Province *20604*
E	*Gaultheria alnifolia* var. *grata* (A. C. Smith) Luteyn *20883*	
	I	*20883* Colombia *20883*
V	*Gaultheria angustifolia* T.S.Brandegee *20883*	
	V	*20883* Mexico *20883*
V	*Gaultheria bradeana* Sleumer *20883*	
	V	*20883* Brazil *20883*
E	*Gaultheria buxifolia* var. *elassantha* (A. C. Smith) Luteyn *20883*	
	E	*20883* Colombia *20883*
R	*Gaultheria buxifolia* var. *secunda* (E. J. Remy) Luteyn *20883*	
	I	*20883* Bolivia *20883*
	I	*20883* Peru *20883*
E	*Gaultheria chiriquensis* Camp *20883*	
	E	*20883* Panama *20883*
R	*Gaultheria domingensis* Urban *20883*	
	V	*20883* Dominican Republic *20883*
R	*Gaultheria erecta* Ventenat *18200*	
	R	*9446* Peru *18200*
E	*Gaultheria eriophylla* var. *mucronata* (E. J. Remy) Luteyn *20883*	
	I	*20883* Bolivia *20883*
	I	*20883* Peru *20883*
	I	*20883* Venezuela *20883*
R	*Gaultheria glaucifolia* Hemsley *20883*	
	R	*20883* Mexico *20883*
R	*Gaultheria glaucifolia* Hemsley var. *rosei* (Small) Luteyn *20883*	
	R	*20883* Mexico *20883*
V	*Gaultheria howellii* (Sleumer) Middleton *19090*	
	V	*11117* Ecuador - Galapagos (V. Sierra Negra; Santa Cruz) *11117*
R	*Gaultheria itatiaiae* Wawra *20883*	
	R	*20883* Brazil *20883*
R	*Gaultheria lanceolata* Hook.f. *20681, 19090*	
	R	*19090* Australia - Tasmania *19090*
E	*Gaultheria lanigera* var. *rufolanata* (Sleumer) Luteyn *20883*	
	E	*20883* Colombia *20883*
R	*Gaultheria marginata* (N.E. Brown) Middleton *19090*	
	R	*19090* Venezuela *19090*
R	*Gaultheria megalodonta* A.C.Smith *20883*	

V   *20883*   Ecuador   *20883*
V   *20883*   Peru   *20883*

E   *Gaultheria oreogena* A.C.Smith *20883*
    E   *20883*   Colombia   *20883*

R   *Gaultheria purpurascens* HBK *19090*
    R   *19090*   Colombia   *19090*

V   *Gaultheria santanderensis* A.C.Smith *20883*
    V   *20883*   Colombia   *20883*

R   *Gaultheria schultesii* Camp *20883*
    R   *20883*   Mexico   *20883*

V   *Gaultheria sclerophylla* Cuatrecasas *20883*
    I   *20883*   *20883*
    I   *20883*   Ecuador   *20883*

E   *Gaultheria sclerophylla* Cuatrecasas var. *hirsuta*
    Luteyn *20883*
    I   *20883*   Colombia   *20883*
    I   *20883*   Ecuador   *20883*
    I   *20883*   Venezuela   *20883*

R   *Gaultheria serrata* (Vell. Conc.) Sleumer ex
    Kinoshita-Gouvea *20883*
    I   *20883*   Brazil   *20883*

R   *Gaultheria serrata* (Vellozo) Sleumer var. *organensis*
    (Meisner) Luteyn *20883*
    R   *20883*   Brazil   *20883*

V   *Gaultheria setulosa* N.E.Brown *20883*
    V   *20883*   Venezuela   *20883*

V   *Gaultheria sleumeriana* Kinoshita-Gouvea *20883*
    V   *20883*   Brazil   *20883*

R   *Gaultheria strigosa* var. *revoluta* (A. C. Smith)
    Lutèyn *20883*
    I   *20883*   Colombia   *20883*
    R   *20883*   Ecuador   *20883*

I   *Gaultheria swartzii* R.A. Howard *19401*
    I   *19401*   Guadeloupe (La Soufrière)   *19401*

E   *Gaultheria ulei* Sleumer *20883*
    E   *20883*   Brazil   *20883*

V   *Gaultheria viridicarpa* J.B.Williams ms. ssp.
    merinoensis J.B.Williams ms. *20681*
    V   *20681*   Australia - New South Wales   *20681*

V   *Gaultheria viridicarpa* J.B.Williams ms. ssp.
    viridicarpa *20681*
    V   *20681*   Australia - New South Wales   *20681*

R   *Gaylussacia brachycera* (Michx.) Gray *20850*
    E   *20850*   U.S. - Delaware   *20850*
    V   *20850*   U.S. - Kentucky   *20850*
    E   *20850*   U.S. - Maryland   *20850*
    E   *20850*   U.S. - Pennsylvania   *20850*
    V   *20850*   U.S. - Tennessee   *20850*
    V   *20850*   U.S. - Virginia   *20850*
    V   *20850*   U.S. - West Virginia   *20850*

V   *Gonocalyx concolor* Nevl. *20883, 8058*
    I   *20883*   Puerto Rico   *20883*

I   *Grisebachia ciliaris* (L.f.) Klotzsch ssp. *bolusii*
    (N.E.Br.) E.G.H.Oliv. *20604*
    I   *20604*   South Africa - Cape Province   *20604*

I   *Grisebachia ciliaris* (L.f.) Klotzsch ssp. *involuta*
    (Klotzsch) E.G.H.Oliv. *20604*
    I   *20604*   South Africa - Cape Province   *20604*

I   *Grisebachia incana* (Bartl.) Klotzsch *20604*
    I   *20604*   South Africa - Cape Province   *20604*

I   *Grisebachia minutiflora* N.E.Br. ssp. *nodiflora*
    (N.E.Br.) E.G.H.Oliv. *20604*
    I   *20604*   South Africa - Cape Province   *20604*

I   *Grisebachia nivenii* N.E.Br. *20604*
    I   *20604*   South Africa - Cape Province   *20604*

I   *Grisebachia plumosa* Klotzsch ssp. *eciliata*
    E.G.H.Oliv. *20604*
    I   *20604*   South Africa - Cape Province   *20604*

I   *Grisebachia plumosa* Klotzsch ssp. *hirta* (Klotzch)
    E.G.H.Oliv. *20604*
    I   *20604*   South Africa - Cape Province   *20604*

I   *Grisebachia plumosa* Klotzsch ssp. *hispida*
    (Klotzch) E.G.H.Oliv. *20604*
    I   *20604*   South Africa - Cape Province   *20604*

I   *Grisebachia plumosa* Klotzsch ssp. *irrorata*
    (Klotzch) E.G.H.Oliv. *20604*
    I   *20604*   South Africa - Cape Province   *20604*

V   *Grisebachia rigida* N.E.Br. *20604*
    V   *20604*   South Africa - Cape Province   *20604*

I   *Grisebachia secundiflora* E.G.H.Oliv. *20604*
    I   *20604*   South Africa - Cape Province   *20604*

R   II   *Kalmia cuneata* Michx. *20850, 15658*
    V   *20850*   U.S. - North Carolina   *20850*
    E   *20850*   U.S. - South Carolina   *20850*

V   *Kalmia ericoides* Wright ex Grisebach *20883*
    V   *20883*   Cuba   *20883*

V   *Kalmia ericoides* Wright ex Grisebach ssp. *aggregata*
    Wright ex Grisebach *20883*
    V   *20883*   Cuba   *20883*

V   *Kalmiella aggregata* Small
    V   *19105*   Cuba (Juventud Is.)   *5607*

V   *Kalmiella ericoides* C. Wright
    V   *19105*   Cuba (Pinal del Rio; I. Juventud)   *5607*

E   *Kalmiella simulata* Britton & P. Wilson *5607*
    E   *19105*   Cuba (Juventud Is.)   *5607*

E   *Lateropora ovata* A.C. Sm. *20883, 9006*
    R   *21224*   Costa Rica   *21224*
    R   *21224*   Panama   *20883*

E   *Lateropora santafeensis* Wilbur & Luteyn *20883, 9006*
    I   *20883*   Panama   *20883*

E   *Lateropora tubulifera* Wilbur & Luteyn *20883, 10747*
    I   *20883*   Panama   *20883*

R   *Ledodendron vanhoefeni* (Abromeit) Dalgard &
    Fredskild *21309*
    R   *21309*   Denmark - Greenland   *21309*

R   *Ledothamnus atroadenus* Maguire, Steyermark &
    Luteyn *20883*
    R   *20883*   Venezuela   *20883*

R   *Ledothamnus decumbens* Maguire, Steyermark &
    Luteyn *20883*
    R   *20883*   Venezuela   *20883*

E   *Ledothamnus jauaensis* Maguire, Steyermark &
    Luteyn *20883*
    E   *20883*   Venezuela   *20883*

R   *Ledothamnus luteus* Maguire, Steyermark &
    Luteyn *20883*
    R   *20883*   Venezuela   *20883*

E   *Ledothamnus parviflorus* Gleason *20883*
    E   *20883*   Venezuela   *20883*

R   *Ledothamnus sessiliflorus* N.E.Brown *20883*

	R	20883 Venezuela *20883*		
R	**Leucothoe tonkinensis** Dop *6057*			
	R	Vietnam *6057*		
R	**Lyonia affinis** (A. Rich) Urban *5607*			
	R	*19105* Cuba (Santiago de Cuba; Holguin) *5607*		
V	**Lyonia alainii** Judd *20883*			
	V	20883 Dominican Republic *20883*		
E	**Lyonia alpina** Urban & Ekman *20883*			
	E	20883 Haiti *20883*		
R	**Lyonia buchii** Urban *20883*			
	R	20883 Dominican Republic *20883*		
R	**Lyonia chapaensis** (Dop) Merr. *6057*			
	R	Vietnam *6057*		
E	**Lyonia clementis** Acuna & Roig *5607*			
	E	*19105* Cuba (Santiago de Cuba) *5607*		
E	**Lyonia ekmanii** Urban *20883*			
	E	20883 Cuba *20883*		
V	**Lyonia elliptica** (C.Wright ex Small) Alain *20883*			
	V	20883 Cuba *20883*		
R	**Lyonia glandulosa** (A.Richard) *20883*			
	R	20883 Cuba *20883*		
R	**Lyonia glandulosa** (A. Rich.) var. *revolutifolia* Judd *20883*			
	R	20883 Cuba *20883*		
R	**Lyonia glandulosa** (A. Rich.) Griseb. var. *toaensis* (Acuna & Roig) R. Berazain *11840*			
	V	20883 Cuba (Guantanamo) *20883*		
R	**Lyonia heptamera** Urban *20883*			
	R	20883 Dominican Republic *20883*		
R	**Lyonia jamaicensis** (Sw.) D. Don *20883*			
	R	20883 Jamaica *20883*		
V	**Lyonia latifolia** (A.Richard) Grisebach *20883*			
	V	20883 Cuba *20883*		
R	**Lyonia latifolia** (A. Rich.) Griseb. ssp. *calycosa* (Small) Borh. *11840*			
	V	20883 Cuba *11840*		
R	**Lyonia latifolia** (A. Rich.) Griseb. ssp. *latifolia* *11840*			
	R	*19105* Cuba (SC; Gu) *11840*		
E	**Lyonia leonis** Acuna & Roig *5607*			
	E	*19105* Cuba (Santiago de Cuba) *5607*		
E	**Lyonia longipes** Urban *20883*			
	E	20883 Cuba *20883*		
R	**Lyonia macrophylla** (Britton) Ekman ex Urban *20883*			
	R	20883 Cuba *20883*		
E	**Lyonia maestrensis** Acuna & Roig *20883*			
	E	20883 Cuba (Granma) *5607*		
R	**Lyonia microcarpa** Urban & Ekman *20883*			
	R	20883 Dominica *20883*		
R	**Lyonia montecristina** Urban & Ekman *20883*			
	R	20883 Dominican Republic *20883*		
	V	20883 Haiti *20883*		
R	**Lyonia myrtilloides** Grisebach *20883*			
	R	20883 Cuba *20883*		
R	**Lyonia nipensis** Urban *20883*			
	R	20883 Cuba *20883*		
V	**Lyonia nipensis** Urban var. *depressinerva* Judd *20883*			

	V	20883 Cuba *20883*	
R	**Lyonia obtusa** Grisebach *20883*		
	R	20883 Cuba *20883*	
R	**Lyonia octandra** (Sw.) Griseb. *20883*		
	R	20883 Jamaica *20883*	
R	**Lyonia stahlii** Urban *20883*		
	I	20883 Dominican Republic *20883*	
	I	20883 Haiti *20883*	
	I	20883 Puerto Rico *20883*	
R	**Lyonia stahlii** Urban var. *costata* (Persoon) G.Don *20883*		
	R	20883 Dominica *20883*	
	R	20883 Haiti *20883*	
R	**Lyonia tinensis** Urban *20883*		
	R	20883 Dominica *20883*	
V	**Lyonia trinidadensis** Judd *20883*		
	V	20883 Cuba *20883*	
R	**Lyonia truncata** Urban *20883*		
	V	20883 Dominican Republic *20883*	
	V	20883 Haiti *20883*	
	I	20883 Puerto Rico *20883*	
E	**Lyonia truncata** Urban var. *proctorii* Judd *20883*		
	I	20883 Puerto Rico *20883*	
R	**Lyonia tueckheimii** Urban *20883*		
	R	20883 Dominican Republic *20883*	
	E	20883 Haiti *20883*	
V	**Lyonia urbaniana** (Sleumer) Jimenez *20883*		
	V	20883 Dominican Republic *20883*	
E	**Lysiclesia panamensis** Luteyn & Wilbur *20883, 9006*		
	I	20883 Panama *20883*	
V	**Macleania epiphytica** A.C. Sm. *20883, 9006*		
	I	20883 Panama *20883*	
E	**Macleania megabracteolata** Wilbur & Luteyn *20883, 10747*		
	I	20883 Panama *20883*	
V	**Macleania subracemosa** L.O. Williams *9687*		
	V	*11967* Nicaragua *9687*	
E	**Macleania talamancensis** Wilbur & Luteyn *20883, 9688*		
	I	20883 Costa Rica *20883*	
R	**Menziesia goyozanensis** Kikuchi *10573*		
	R	*10573* Japan *10573*	
R	**Menziesia yakushimensis** Tash. & Hatta *10573*		
	R	*10573* Japan *10573*	
R	**Monotropsis odorata** Schwein. ex Ell. *20850*		
	I	20850 U.S. - Alabama *20850*	
	Ex/E	20850 U.S. - Delaware *20850*	
	I	20850 U.S. - Florida *20850*	
	E	20850 U.S. - Georgia *20850*	
	V	20850 U.S. - Kentucky *20850*	
	E	20850 U.S. - Maryland *20850*	
	V	20850 U.S. - North Carolina *20850*	
	E	20850 U.S. - South Carolina *20850*	
	V	20850 U.S. - Tennessee *20850*	
	V	20850 U.S. - Virginia *20850*	
	Ex/E	20850 U.S. - West Virginia *20850*	
R	**Nuihonia sclerantha** Dop *6057*		
	R	Vietnam *6057*	
E	**Orthaea ferreyrae** A.C. Smith *18200*		
	E	*9446* Peru *18200*	
R	**Philippia abietina** (Willd.) Klotzsch *10082*		
	R	*20771* Mauritius *10082*	

R	*Philippia brachyphylla* Benth. *10082*	
	R	*10082* Mauritius *10082*
I	*Philippia mafiensis* Engl. *5926*	
	I	*5926* Tanzania (Mafia Is.) *5926*
R	*Pieris cubensis* (Grisebach) Small *20883*	
	R	*20883* Cuba *20883*
E	*Pieris japonica* (Thunb.) D. Don var. *koidzumiana* (Ohwi) Masam. *10573*	
	E	*10573* Japan *10573*
R	*Pieris phillyreifolia* (Hook.) DC. *20850*	
	V	*20850* U.S. - Alabama *20850*
	I	*20850* U.S. - Florida *20850*
	R	*20850* U.S. - Georgia *20850*
	E	*20850* U.S. - Mississippi *20850*
	I	*20850* U.S. - South Carolina *20850*
	I	*20883* Mexico *20883*
V	*Platycalyx pumila* N.E.Br. *20604*	
	V	*20604* South Africa - Cape Province *20604*
E	*Psammisia darienensis* Luteyn & Wilbur *20883, 9006*	
	I	*20883* Panama *20883*
V	*Psammisia panamensis* A.C. Sm. *20883, 9006*	
	I	*20883* Panama *20883*
R	*Rhododendron abietifolium* Sleumer *7730*	
	R	Malaysia - Sabah (Mt Kinabalu) *7730*
R	*Rhododendron amagianum* Makino *10573*	
	R	*10573* Japan *10573*
R	*Rhododendron baconii* Argent, Lamb & Phillipps *8941*	
	R	Malaysia - Sabah (Mt Tambuyukon, Kinabalu P.) *8941*
E	*Rhododendron boninense* Tuy. *8038*	
	E	*19134* Japan - Ogasawara-shoto (Chichijima) *8038*
R	*Rhododendron breviperulatum* Hayata *20511*	
	R	*20854* Taiwan *20511*
E	*Rhododendron chapmanii* Gray *20850, 17890*	
	E	*20850* U.S. - Florida *20850*
V	*Rhododendron chrysanthum* Pallas *17617*	
	V	*17617* China - Heilongjiang *11139*
	V	*17617* China - Jilin *11139*
	V	*17617* China - Liaoning *11139*
E	*Rhododendron concinnoides* Hutch. & Ward *14732*	
	E	*14732* India - Arunachal Pradesh *14732*
V	*Rhododendron cowanianum* Davidian *7731*	
	V	Nepal (central) *7731*
R	*Rhododendron cumberlandense* E.L. Braun *20850*	
	I	*20850* U.S. - Alabama *20850*
	R	*20850* U.S. - Georgia *20850*
	R	*20850* U.S. - Kentucky *20850*
	E	*20850* U.S. - North Carolina *20850*
	I	*20850* U.S. - South Carolina *20850*
	R	*20850* U.S. - Tennessee *20850*
	R	*20850* U.S. - Virginia *20850*
	I	*20850* U.S. - West Virginia *20850*
V	*Rhododendron cyanocarpum* (Franchet) W. Smith *17617*	
	V	*17617* China - Sichuan (Muli) *11139*
	V	*17617* China - Yunnan (Dalidianchangshan) *11139*
I	*Rhododendron dalhousiae* Hook.f. var. *rhabdotum* (Balf.f. & Cooper) Cullen *3060*	
	I	China *7771*
	I	Bhutan *3060*
	I	India - Arunachal Pradesh *3060*
R	*Rhododendron degronianum* Carr. var. *kyomaruense* (Yamaz.) Hara *10573*	

	R	*10573* Japan *10573*
R	*Rhododendron degronianum* Carr. ssp. *yakushimanum* (Nakai) Hara *10573*	
	R	*10573* Japan *10573*
V	*Rhododendron dilatatum* Miq. var. *satsumaense* Yamaz. *10573*	
	V	*10573* Japan *10573*
I	*Rhododendron elliottii* Watt *10260*	
	I	*14732* India - Manipur *14732*
	I	*14732* India - Nagaland *14732*
R	*Rhododendron eriocarpum* (Hayata) Nakai *10573*	
	R	*10573* Japan *10573*
V	*Rhododendron fictolacteum* Balf.f. *17617*	
	V	*17617* China - Sichuan (Muli) *11139*
	V	*17617* China - Yunnan *11139*
R	*Rhododendron flammeum* (Michx.) Sarg. *20850*	
	R	*20850* U.S. - Georgia *20850*
	V	*20850* U.S. - South Carolina *20850*
R	*Rhododendron fleuryi* Dop *6057*	
	R	Vietnam *6057*
V	*Rhododendron formosum* Wall. *14732*	
	V	*14732* India - Arunachal Pradesh *14732*
	V	*14732* India - Manipur *14732*
	V	*14732* India - Meghalaya *14732*
	V	*14732* India - Nagaland *14732*
R	*Rhododendron haematodes* Franchet *17617*	
	V	*17617* China - Yunnan (Dalidianchangshan) *11139*
	R	*14068* Malaysia - Sabah *14068*
E	*Rhododendron hyperythrum* Hayata	
	E	Taiwan
I	*Rhododendron johnstoneanum* Watt ex Hutch.	
	I	India - Manipur
	I	India - Mizoram
V	*Rhododendron jucundum* Balf.f. & W. Smith *17617*	
	V	*17617* China - Yunnan (Dalidianchangshan) *11139*
E	*Rhododendron kanehirai* E. Wilson *20511*	
	E	*20854* Taiwan *20511*
V	*Rhododendron kawakamii* Hayata	
	V	Taiwan
R	*Rhododendron keiskei* Miq. var. *hypoglaucum* Suto & Suzuki *10573*	
	R	*10573* Japan *10573*
R	*Rhododendron komiyamae* Makino *10573*	
	R	*10573* Japan *10573*
R	*Rhododendron lochiae* F.Muell. *20681, 10260*	
	R	*20681* Australia - Queensland *20681*
R	*Rhododendron longiperulatum* Hayata	
	R	Taiwan (Tatun Range)
R	*Rhododendron lowndesii* Davidian *7731*	
	R	Nepal *7731*
R	*Rhododendron macabeanum* Watt ex Balf. f. *14732*	
	R	*14732* India - Manipur *14732*
	R	*14732* India - Nagaland *14732*
R	*Rhododendron makinoi* Tagg *10573*	
	R	*10573* Japan *10573*
R	*Rhododendron maxwellii* Gibbs *7730*	
	R	Malaysia - Sabah (Mt Kinabalu) *7730*
R	*Rhododendron mayebarae* Nakai & Hara *10573*	
	R	*10573* Japan *10573*

R   *Rhododendron meijeri* Argent, Lamb & Phillipps *8941*
    R   Malaysia - Sabah (Mt Tambuyukon, Kinabalu P.) *8941*

Ex   *Rhododendron mucronulatum* Turcz. var. *albiflora* Nakai
    Ex   Korea, South (Mt Kwanak)

R   *Rhododendron nakaharai* Hayata
    R   *20854* Taiwan (Tatun Range) *20854*

R   *Rhododendron nudipes* Nakai var. *kirishimense* Yamaz. *10573*
    R   *10573* Japan *10573*

R   *Rhododendron osuzuyamense* Yamaz. *10573*
    R   *10573* Japan *10573*

R   *Rhododendron pentaphyllum* Maxim. var. *villosum* Koidz. *10573*
    R   *10573* Japan *10573*

R   *Rhododendron ponticum* L. ssp. *baeticum* (Boiss. & Reuter) Hand.-Mazz. *20171*
    E   *20076* Portugal *20076*
    R   *20660* Spain (Cádiz, Sierra del Algibe) *5403*

E   *Rhododendron protistum* I.B. Balf. & Forrest var. *giganteum* (Forrest & Tagg) Chamberlain *17617*
    E   *17617* China - Yunnan (Tengchong) *11139*

R   *Rhododendron prunifolium* (Small) Millais *20850*
    V   *20850* U.S. - Alabama *20850*
    R   *20850* U.S. - Georgia *20850*

I   *Rhododendron redowskianum* Maxim. *5942*
    I   *5942* Russia (Far East) - Amur *5942*
    I   *5942* Russia (Far East) - Magadan *5942*
    I   *5942* Russia (Far East) - Primorye *5942*
    I   *5942* Russia (Far East) - Sakhalin *5942*
    I   *5942* Russia (Siberia) - Yakutiya *5942*
    V   China - Jilin (Changbaishan) *11139*

R   *Rhododendron sanctum* Nakai var. *lasiogynum* Nakai *10573*
    R   *10573* Japan *10573*

R   *Rhododendron sanctum* Nakai var. *sanctum* *10573*
    R   *10573* Japan *10573*

E   *Rhododendron santapaui* Sastry et al. *14732*
    E   *14732* India - Arunachal Pradesh *14732*

V   *Rhododendron scabrum* G. Don *10573*
    V   *10573* Japan *10573*

I   *Rhododendron sichotense* Pojark. *5942*

R   *Rhododendron sikayotaizanense* Masam.
    R   *20854* Taiwan (Mt Sikayotaizan, C. Ranges) *20854*

E   *Rhododendron subansiriense* Chamberlain *14732*
    E   *14732* India - Arunachal Pradesh *14732*

V   *Rhododendron sulfureum* Franch. *17617*
    V   *17617* China - Yunnan (Diancang & Biluo Mts.) *17617*

R   *Rhododendron taxifolium* *19011*
    R   *19011* Philippines (northern - Mt. Pulog) *19011*

R   *Rhododendron trichocladum* Franchet ssp. *nepalense* Hara *7731*
    R   Nepal (east) *7731*

R   *Rhododendron vaseyi* Gray *20850*
    I   *20850* U.S. - Connecticut *20850*
    R   *20850* U.S. - North Carolina *20850*

R   *Rhododendron viscistylum* Nakai var. *amakusaense*

    Takeda *10573*
    R   *10573* Japan *10573*

R   *Rhododendron viscistylum* Nakai var. *viscistylum* *10573*
    R   *10573* Japan *10573*

E   *Rhododendron wattii* Cowan *14732*
    E   *14732* India - Manipur *14732*

V   *Rhododendron yakuinsulare* Masam. *10573*
    V   *10573* Japan *10573*

R   *Rhododendron yakumontanum* Masam. *10573*
    R   *10573* Japan *10573*

R   *Rhodothamnus sessilifolius* Davis *12840*
    R   *20618* Turkey *12840*

V   *Satyria allenii* A.C. Sm. *20883, 9006*
    I   *20883* Panama *20883*

I   *Scyphogyne calcicola* E.G.H.Oliv. *20604*
    I   *20604* South Africa - Cape Province *20604*

E   *Semiramisia alata* Luteyn *20883*
    I   *20883* Colombia *20883*

E   *Sphyrospermum tuberculatum* Wilbur & Luteyn *20883, 9006*
    I   *20883* Panama *20883*

V   *Syndesmanthus schlechteri* N.E.Br. *20604*
    V   *20604* South Africa - Cape Province *20604*

R   *Tepuia cardonae* A.C.Smith *20883*
    R   *20883* Venezuela *20883*

V   *Tepuia intermedia* Steyermark *20883*
    V   *20883* Venezuela *20883*

V   *Tepuia multiglandulosa* Steyermark & Maguire *20883*
    V   *20883* Venezuela *20883*

R   *Tepuia speciosa* A.C.Smith *20883*
    R   *20883* Venezuela *20883*

R   *Tepuia tatei* Camp *20883*
    R   *20883* Venezuela *20883*

E   *Tepuia vareschii* Steyermark *20883*
    E   *20883* Venezuela *20883*

R   *Tepuia venusta* Camp *20883*
    R   *20883* Venezuela *20883*

E   *Themistoclesia costaricensis* Luteyn & Wilbur *20883*
    I   *20883* Costa Rica *20883*
    I   *20883* Panama *20883*

E   *Themistoclesia revoluta* Wilbur & Luteyn *20883, 10747*
    I   *20883* Panama *20883*

R   *Tsusiophyllum tanakae* Maxim. *10573*
    R   *10573* Japan *10573*

E   *Utleya costaricensis* Wilbur & Luteyn *20883, 9688*
    I   *20883* Costa Rica *20883*

E   *Vaccinium amamianum* Hatus. *10573*
    E   *10573* Japan *10573*

R   *Vaccinium boninense* Nakai *8037*
    R   *19134* Japan - Ogasawara-shoto *8037*

R   *Vaccinium boreale* Hall & Aalders *20850*
    I   *20850* Canada - Labrador *20850*
    I   *20850* Canada - New Brunswick *20850*
    I   *20850* Canada - Newfoundland *20850*
    I   *20850* Canada - Nova Scotia *20850*
    V   *20850* Canada - Quebec *20850*
    E   *20850* U.S. - Maine *20850*
    R   *20850* U.S. - New Hampshire *20850*
    V   *20850* U.S. - New York *20850*

E   *20850*   U.S. - Vermont *20850*

R   *Vaccinium cereum* (L.) J.G.Forster var. *raiateense* (J.Moore) M.Grant *20845*

     R   *20845*   French Polynesia - Society Is. (Raiatea) *20845*

V   *Vaccinium cespitosum* Michx. var. *paludicola* (Camp) Hulten *20850*

     I   *20850*   Canada - British Columbia *20850*
     V   *20850*   U.S. - Alaska *20850*
     I   *20850*   U.S. - California *20850*
     I   *20850*   U.S. - Oregon *20850*
     I   *20850*   U.S. - Washington *20850*

R   *Vaccinium ciliatum* Thunb. *10573*

     R   *10573*   Japan *10573*

V   *Vaccinium costaricense* Wilbur & Luteyn *20883, 9037*

     I   *20883*   Costa Rica *20883*

E   *Vaccinium crassifolium* Andr. ssp. *sempervirens* (Rayner & Henderson) W.B. Kirkman & J.R. Ballington *20850*

     E   *20850*   U.S. - South Carolina *20850*

V   *Vaccinium floccosum* (L. O. Williams) Wilbur & Luteyn *20883, 9006*

     I   *20883*   Panama *20883*

I   *Vaccinium glabrum* Fletcher *19120*

     I   *19120*   Thailand *19120*

R   *Vaccinium hirsutum* Buckl. *20850*

     R   *20850*   U.S. - Georgia *20850*
     V   *20850*   U.S. - North Carolina *20850*
     R   *20850*   U.S. - Tennessee *20850*

V   *Vaccinium jefense* Luteyn & Wilbur *20883*

     I   *20883*   Panama *20883*

R   *Vaccinium koreanum* Nakai *15957*

     R   *15923*   Korea, South *15957*

E   *Vaccinium orosiense* Wilbur & Luteyn *20883, 9006*

     I   *20883*   Costa Rica *20883*

I   *Vaccinium palawanensis* Elm. var. *foxworthii* (Copel.) Sleum. *13833*

     I   *13833*   Philippines (Palawan) *13833*

I   *Vaccinium rapae* Skottsberg *20845*

     I   *20845*   French Polynesia - Tubuai Is. (Rapa) *20845*

E   *Vaccinium santafeensis* Wilbur & Luteyn *20883, 9006*

     I   *20883*   Panama *20883*

R   *Vaccinium shaferi* Acuna & Roig *5607*

     R   *19105*   Cuba (Holguin; Guantanamo) *5607*

E   *Vaccinium sieboldii* Miq. *10573*

     E   *10573*   Japan *10573*

R   *Vaccinium wrightii* Gray var. *formosanum* (Hayata) Li *20511*

     R   *20511*   Taiwan *20511*

R   *Vaccinium yakushimense* Makino *10573*

     R   *10573*   Japan *10573*

V   *Xylococcus bicolor* Nutt. *20850*

     V   *20850*   U.S. - California *20850*

Erythroxylaceae

Number of genera: 4
Number of species: 200
Recorded threatened species: 69   (34%)

Pantropical, especially New World.

V   *Erythroxylum affine* A. St. Hil. *13712*

     V   *13712*   Brazil *13712*

E   *Erythroxylum andrei* Plowman *20883, 13712*

     I   *20883*   Brazil *20883*

V   *Erythroxylum baracoense* Borh. *5607*

     V   *19105*   Cuba (Guantanamo) *5607*

R   *Erythroxylum barbatum* O. Schulz *13712*

     R   *13712*   Brazil *13712*

E   *Erythroxylum bezerrae* Plowman *20883*

     I   *20883*   Peru *20883*

I   *Erythroxylum bicolor* O. Schulz *13712*

     I   *13712*   Brazil *13712*

E   *Erythroxylum bradeanum* O. Schulz *13712*

     E   *13712*   Brazil *13712*

V   *Erythroxylum brennae* D'Arcy & Schanen *20883, 9004*

     E   *19791*   Panama *20883*

I   *Erythroxylum buxus* Peyr. *13712*

     I   *13712*   Brazil *13712*

R   *Erythroxylum campinense* Amaral *13712*

     R   *13712*   Brazil *13712*

V   *Erythroxylum carthagenense* Jacq. *13712*

     V   *19791*   Colombia *19791*
     V   *19791*   Venezuela *13712*

V   *Erythroxylum clarense* Borh. *5607*

     V   *19105*   Cuba *5607*

R   *Erythroxylum coelophlebium* Martius *13712*

     R   *13712*   Brazil *13712*

V   *Erythroxylum columbinum* Martius *13712*

     V   *13712*   Brazil *13712*

R   *Erythroxylum cryptanthum* O. Schulz *13712*

     R   *13712*   Brazil *13712*

E   *Erythroxylum davidii* D'Arcy & Schanen *20883, 9006*

     I   *20883*   Panama *20883*

V   *Erythroxylum dumosum* Alain *5607*

     V   *19105*   Cuba (Holguin) *5607*

Ex   *Erythroxylum echinodendron* Ekman *5607*

     Ex   *19105*   Cuba (VC) *5607*

Ex/E   *Erythroxylum ellipticum* Ramirez *9019*

     Ex/E   *9425*   Mexico *9019*

V   *Erythroxylum foetidum* Plowman *20883*

     I   *20883*   Venezuela *20883*

R   *Erythroxylum gaudichaudii* Peyr. *13712*

     R   *13712*   Brazil *13712*

E   *Erythroxylum glazioui* O. Schulz *13712*

     E   *13712*   Brazil *13712*

V   *Erythroxylum grandiflorum* Peyr. *13712*

     V   *13712*   Brazil *13712*

E   *Erythroxylum guanchezii* Plowman *20883*

     I   *20883*   Venezuela *20883*

E   *Erythroxylum hamigerum* O. Schulz *13712*

     E   *13712*   Brazil *13712*

V   *Erythroxylum horridum* Borh. & Oviedo *5607*

     V   *19105*   Cuba (Holguin) *5607*

R   *Erythroxylum hypericifolium* Lam. *10082*

     R   *14220*   Réunion *10082*
     R   *20771*   Mauritius *10082*

R   *Erythroxylum hypoleucum* Plowman *20883*

     I   *20883*   Venezuela *20883*

R   *Erythroxylum incrassatum* O.E. Schultz *20883, 13336*

R   *13336* Jamaica *20883*

R   *Erythroxylum jamaicense* F. & R. *20883, 13336*

    R   *13336* Jamaica *20883*

E   *Erythroxylum lancifolium* Peyr. *13712*

    E   *13712* Brazil *13712*

E   *Erythroxylum leal-costae* Plowman *20883, 13712*

    I   *20883* Brazil *20883*

V   *Erythroxylum ligustrinum* DC. var. *carajasense*
       Plowman *13712*

    V   *13712* Brazil *13712*

R   *Erythroxylum lindemanii* Plowman *13712*

    R   *13712* Suriname *13712*
    R   *13712* Venezuela *13712*

R   *Erythroxylum lineolatum* DC. *13712*

    R   *19571* Colombia *13712*

V   *Erythroxylum loretense* Plowman *20883*

    I   *20883* Brazil *20883*
    I   *20883* Peru *20883*

I   *Erythroxylum lygoides* O. Schulz *13712*

    I   *13712* Brazil *13712*

I   *Erythroxylum macrocalyx* Martius *13712*

    I   *13712* Brazil *13712*

V   *Erythroxylum mamacoca* Martius *13712*

    V   *13712* Peru *13712*

V   *Erythroxylum maracasense* Plowman *20883, 13712*

    I   *20883* Brazil *20883*

R   *Erythroxylum martii* Peyr. *13712*

    R   *13712* Brazil *13712*

E   *Erythroxylum mattos-silvae* Plowman *20883, 13712*

    I   *20883* Brazil *20883*

E   *Erythroxylum membranaceum* Plowman *20883, 13712*

    I   *20883* Brazil *20883*

I   *Erythroxylum mikanii* Peyr. *13712*

    I   *13712* Brazil *13712*

I   *Erythroxylum nitidum* Spreng. *13712*

    I   *13712* Brazil *13712*

R   *Erythroxylum nobile* O. Schulz *13712*

    R   *13712* Brazil *13712*

V   *Erythroxylum obtusifolium* Hook.f. *10276*

    V   *12838* Sri Lanka *10276*

E   *Erythroxylum occultum* Plowman *20883, 13712*

    I   *20883* Brazil *20883*

R   *Erythroxylum ochranthum* Peyr. *13712*

    R   *13712* Brazil *13712*

V   *Erythroxylum ovalifolium* Peyr. *13712*

    V   *13712* Brazil *13712*

R   *Erythroxylum oxypetalum* O. Schulz *13712*

    R   *13712* Brazil *13712*

E   *Erythroxylum pauferrense* Plowman *20883, 13712*

    I   *20883* Brazil *20883*

E   *Erythroxylum petrae-caballi* Plowman *20883*

    I   *20883* Brazil *20883*

R   *Erythroxylum polygonoides* Martius *13712*

    R   *13712* Brazil *13712*

I   *Erythroxylum reticulatum* Northrop

    I   *4650* Bahamas *4650*

E   *Erythroxylum ruryi* Plowman *20883*

    I   *20883* Bolivia *20883*
    I   *20883* Peru *20883*

E   *Erythroxylum santosii* Plowman *20883, 13712*

    E   *20883* Brazil *20883*

R   *Erythroxylum sechellarum* O. Schulz *14296*

    R   *19181* Seychelles (granitic) *14296*

R   *Erythroxylum shatona* Macbr. *13712*

    R   *13712* Peru *13712*

E   *Erythroxylum simonis* Plowman *20883, 13712*

    I   *20883* Brazil *20883*

E   *Erythroxylum splendidum* Plowman *20883, 13712*

    I   *20883* Brazil *20883*

V   *Erythroxylum steyermarkii* Plowman *20883*

    I   *20883* Venezuela *20883*

E   *Erythroxylum stipulosum* Plowman *20883, 13712*

    I   *20883* Brazil *20883*

R   *Erythroxylum tenue* Plowman *13712*

    R   *13712* Brazil *13712*

E   *Erythroxylum tianguanum* Plowman *20883*

    I   *20883* Brazil *20883*

V   *Erythroxylum tucuruiense* Plowman *13712*

    V   *13712* Brazil *13712*

E   *Erythroxylum undulatum* Plowman *20883*

    I   *20883* Venezuela *20883*

E   *Erythroxylum vasquezii* Plowman *20883*

    I   *20883* Peru *20883*

I   *Erythroxylum virgultosum* Martius *13712*

    I   *13712* Brazil *13712*

R   *Erythroxylum williamsii* Standley ex Plowman *20883*

    I   *20883* Venezuela *20883*

Escalloniaceae

Number of genera: 20
Number of species: 170
Recorded threatened species: 15   (8%)

Southern hemisphere to tropics, esp. South America, Australasia.

R   *Argophyllum cryptophlebum* Zemann *20681*

    R   *20681* Australia - Queensland *20681*

R   *Argophyllum nullumense* R.Baker *20681*

    I   *20681* Australia - New South Wales *20681*
    I   *20681* Australia - Queensland *20681*

I   *Corokia carpodetoides* (F. Muell.) L.S. Smith

    I   *14226* Australia - NSW - Lord Howe Is. *14226*

R   *Corokia macrocarpa* Kirk *19305*

    R   *19305* New Zealand - Chatham Is. *19106*

V   *Corokia whiteana* L.S.Smith *20681*

    V   *20681* Australia - New South Wales *20681*

E   *Escallonia piurensis* Mattf.

    E   *9446* Peru *18200*

V   *Escallonia schreiteri* Sleumer *16336*

    V   *19448* Argentina (Tucumani) *16336*
    V   *20176* Argentina - Salta *20176*
    V   *20176* Argentina - Tucuman *20176*

R   *Platyspermation crassifolium* Guillaumin *20893*

    R   *20893* New Caledonia *20893*

R   *Polyosma annamensis* Gagnepain *6057*

    R   Vietnam *6057*

R   *Polyosma nhatrangensis* Gagnepain *6057*

    R   Vietnam *6057*

I   *Polyosma pulgarensis* Elm *13833*

I   *13833*   Philippines (Palawan) *13833*

R   *Polyosma rigidiuscula* F.Muell. & Bailey *20681*
   R   *20681*   Australia - Queensland *20681*

R   *Quintinia quatrefagesii* F.Muell. *20681*
   R   *20681*   Australia - Queensland *20681*

V   *Roussea simplex* Sm. *10082*
   V   *20771*   Mauritius *10082*

E   *Valdivia gayana* Remy *15088*
   E   *13875*   Chile *13875*

Eucommiaceae

Number of genera: 1
Number of species: 1
Recorded threatened species: 1   (100%)

Montane forests of western China.

R   *Eucommia ulmoides* Oliver *17617*
   R   *17617*   China - Anhui *11139*
   R   *17617*   China - Gansu *11139*
   R   *17617*   China - Guizhou *11139*
   R   *17617*   China - Henan *11139*
   R   *17617*   China - Hubei (west) *11139*
   R   *17617*   China - Hunan *11139*
   R   *17617*   China - Jiangxi *11139*
   R   *17617*   China - Shanxi *11139*
   R   *17617*   China - Sichuan *11139*
   R   *17617*   China - Zhejiang *11139*

Eucryphiaceae

Number of genera: 1
Number of species: 6
Recorded threatened species: 1   (16%)

Eastern Australia; Tasmania; Chile.

R   *Eucryphia glutinosa* (Poepp. et Endl.) Baillon *20883, 13875*
   R   *20883*   Chile *20883*

Euphorbiaceae

Number of genera: 300
Number of species: 7,500
Recorded threatened species: 933   (12%)

Cosmopolitan, especially tropical and subtropical.

R   *Acalypha angustata* Sond. var. *angustata* *20604*
   R   *20604*   South Africa - Natal *20604*

R   *Acalypha balansae* Guillaumin *20893*
   R   *20893*   New Caledonia *20893*

R   *Acalypha elliptica* Sw. *20883*
   R   *20883*   Jamaica *20883*

V   *Acalypha entumenica* Prain *20604*
   V   *20604*   South Africa - Natal *20604*

E   *Acalypha fulva* I.M. Johnston *18200*
   E   *9446*   Peru *18200*

V   *Acalypha hontauyuensis* Keng *14961*
   V   *20854*   Taiwan (Botel Tobago) *14961*

I   *Acalypha hutchinsonii* Britton *5607*
   I   *19105*   Cuba *5607*

E   *Acalypha integrifolia* Willd. var. *longifolia* (Muell.-Arg.) Coode *10082*
   E   *20771*   Mauritius *10082*

E   *Acalypha integrifolia* Willd. var. *marginata* (Poir.) Coode *10082*
   E   *20771*   Mauritius *10082*

R   *Acalypha integrifolia* Willd. ssp. *panduriformis* Coode *10082*
   R   *14220*   Réunion *14220*

E   *Acalypha integrifolia* Willd. var. *parvifolia* (Baill. ex M.-Arg.) Pax & Hoffm. *10082*
   E   *20771*   Mauritius *10082*

V   *Acalypha jamaicensis* Britton *20883, 13336*
   V   *20883*   Jamaica *20883*

R   *Acalypha laevigata* Sw. *20883*
   R   *20883*   Jamaica *20883*

I   *Acalypha lepinei* J.Mueller *20845*
   I   *20845*   French Polynesia - Society Is. *20845*

R   *Acalypha longi-acuminata* Hayata *20511*
   R   *20511*   Taiwan *20511*

V   *Acalypha lyonsii* P.I.Forster *20681*
   V   *20681*   Australia - Queensland *20681*

E   *Acalypha marissima* M. Gilbert *19704*
   E   *19704*   Ethiopia (Welega) *19704*

R   *Acalypha matudai* Hayata *20511*
   R   *20511*   Taiwan *20511*

I   *Acalypha nana* Griseb. *5607*
   I   *19105*   Cuba (Pinar del Rio) *5607*

R   *Acalypha nubicola* McVaugh *9692*
   R   *11182*   Mexico *9692*

R   *Acalypha pruinosa* Urb. *20883, 19890*
   R   *19890*   Jamaica *20883*

E   *Acalypha raivavensis* F.Brown *20845*
   E   *20845*   French Polynesia - Tubuai Is. *20845*

Ex   *Acalypha rubra* Roxb. *18996*
   Ex   *18996*   St Helena *18996*

E   *Acalypha saxicola* Wigg. *9002*
   E   *11182*   Mexico *9002*

V   *Acalypha suirenbiensis* Yamamoto *20511*
   V   *20854*   Taiwan *20511*

R   *Acalypha virgata* L. *20883*
   I   *20883*   Jamaica *20883*

E   *Acalypha virgata* L. var. *pubescens* Fawc. & Rendle *20883, 13336*
   E   *20883*   Jamaica *20883*

V   *Acalypha wigginsii* Webster *11117*
   V   *11117*   Ecuador - Galapagos (Santa Cruz) *11117*

E   *Acalypha wilderi* Merr. *19473*
   E   *19473*   Cook Is.(Southern group) (Rarotonga) *19473*

V   *Acidocroton acunae* Borh. & Muniz *5607*
   V   *19105*   Cuba (Villa Clara) *5607*

V   *Acidocroton ekmanii* Urban *5607*
   V   *19105*   Cuba *5607*

V   *Acidocroton trichophyllus* Urban *5607*
   V   *19105*   Cuba (Holguin) *5607*

R   *Acidocroton verrucosus* Urb. *20883, 13336*
   R   *13336*   Jamaica *20883*

I   *Acidoton microphyllus* Urban *5642*
   I   Dominican Republic (Barahona) *5642*

V   *Actephila foetida* Domin *20681*
   V   *20681*   Australia - Queensland *20681*

Magnoliopsida (dicots): Euphorbiaceae: *Actephila*

R	*Actephila sessilifolia* Benth. *20681*
	R	20681 Australia - Queensland *20681*
R	*Adelia spinosa* (Chordat & Hassler) Pax & Hoffm. *20883*
	I	20883 Argentina *20883*
	R	20883 Paraguay *20883*
V	*Adelia vaseyi* (Coult.) Pax & K. Hoffmann *20850*
	V	20850 U.S. - Texas *20850*
V	*Aerisilvaea sylvestris* A.Radcliffe-smith *20885*
	V	20885 Tanzania (Morogoro District) *20885*
R	*Agrostistachys coriacea* Alston *10276*
	R	12838 Sri Lanka *10276*
V	*Agrostistachys hookeri* (Thwaites) Hook.f. *10252*
	V	12838 Sri Lanka *10252*
V	*Alchornea trewioides* (Benth.) Muell.-Arg. var. *formosae* (Muell.-Arg.) Pax & Hoffm. *20511*
	V	20511 Taiwan *20511*
R	*Alchorneopsis portoricensis* Urban *20883*
	I	20883 Puerto Rico *20883*
E	*Alphandia resinosa* Baillon *20893*
	E	20893 New Caledonia *20893*
V	*Amanoa bracteosa* Planch. *20274*
	V	20858 Côte d'Ivoire *7926*
	V	20858 Ghana *20274*
	V	20858 Liberia *20274*
	V	20858 Sierra Leone *7926*
V	*Amanoa caribaea* Krug and Urb. *20883*
	V	20883 Dominica *20883*
	V	20883 Guadeloupe *20883*
V	*Amanoa strobilacea* Muell.Arg. *20274*
	V	20858 Angola - Cabinda *7926*
	V	20858 Cameroon *7926*
	V	20858 Ghana *20274*
	V	20858 Liberia *7926*
E	*Amperea protensa* Nees *20681, 14223*
	E	20681 Australia - Western Australia *14223*
R	*Amperea spicata* Airy Shaw *20681*
	R	20681 Australia - Northern Territory *20681*
Ex	*Amperea xiphoclada* (Sieber ex Sprengel) Druce var. *pedicellata* R.Henderson *20681*
	Ex	20681 Australia - New South Wales *20681*
V	*Andrachne arida* (Warnock & M.C. Johnston) G.L. Webster *20883, 20850*
	E	20850 U.S. - Texas *20850*
	I	20883 Mexico *20883*
E	*Andrachne brittonii* Urban *5607*
	E	19105 Cuba (Guantánamo) *5607*
R	*Andrachne colchica* (Fischer & C.A. Meyer) Pojark
	R	former USSR *6930*
V	*Andrachne ephemera* M. Gilbert *19704*
	V	19704 Ethiopia (Hararge: Bale; Sidamo) *19704*
R	*Andrachne gruveli* Daveau
	R	Mauritania
R	*Andrachne pusilla* Pojark
	R	former USSR *6930*
E	*Andrachne schweinfurthii* (Balf. f.) A.R. Smith
	E	Yemen - Socotra
I	*Antidesma andamanicum* Hook. F. *7771*
	I	India - Andaman Is. (South) *7771*
R	*Antidesma annamense* Gagnepain *6057*

	R	Vietnam *6057*
I	*Antidesma obliquinervium* Merr. *13833*
	I	13833 Philippines (low altitude) *13833*
I	*Antidesma pachystachys* Hook. f. *19209*
	I	19209 Malaysia - Peninsular Malaysia (Perak, Pahang, Johor) *19209*
R	*Antidesma poilanei* Gagnepain *6057*
	R	Vietnam *6057*
R	*Antidesma pyrifolium* Muell.Arg. *10276*
	R	12838 Sri Lanka *10276*
I	*Antidesma subolivaceum* Elm. *13833*
	I	13833 Philippines (low altitude) *13833*
I	*Antidesma thwaitesianum* Muell. Arg. *10252*
	I	19209 Malaysia - Peninsular Malaysia (Kedah, Pahang) *19209*
	I	16162 Sri Lanka *10252*
R	*Aporusa cardiosperma* (Gaertn.) Merr. *12838*
	R	12838 Sri Lanka *12838*
I	*Aporusa elliptifolia* Merr. *13833*
	I	13833 Philippines (Palawan) *13833*
I	*Aporusa incisa* Airy Shaw *19120*
	I	19120 Thailand *19120*
V	*Aporusa lanceolata* Thwaites *10276*
	V	12838 Sri Lanka *10276*
V	*Argythamnia aphoroides* Muell.-Arg. *20850*
	V	20850 U.S. - Texas *20850*
V	*Argythamnia argyraea* Cory *20850*
	V	20850 U.S. - Texas *20850*
V	*Argythamnia blodgettii* (Torr.) Chapman *20850*
	V	20850 U.S. - Florida *20850*
V	*Argythamnia californica* Brandeg. *20850*
	V	20850 U.S. - California *20850*
E	*Argythamnia macrobotrys* (Pax & Hoffm.) Ingram *20883, 9006*
	I	20883 Panama *20883*
V	*Argythamnia microphylla* Pax *5607*
	V	19105 Cuba (Camaguey) *5607*
V	*Aristogeitonia monophylla* Airy Shaw *19524*
	V	19109 Kenya (Kilifi) *19524*
	V	20057 Tanzania (Tanga, Pangani & coast) *19524*
R	*Ateramnus integer* (F. & R.) Rothm. *20883*
	R	20883 Jamaica *20883*
V	*Austrobuxus cracens* McPherson *20893*
	V	20893 New Caledonia *20893*
R	*Austrobuxus montis-do* Airy Shaw *20893*
	R	20893 New Caledonia *20893*
R	*Austrobuxus swainii* (Beuẓev. & C.White) Airy Shaw *20681*
	I	20681 Australia - New South Wales *20681*
	I	20681 Australia - Queensland *20681*
E	*Avellanita bustillosii* Philippi *15088*
	E	13875 Chile *13875*
I	*Baccaurea glabrifolia* Pax. & Hoffm. *13833*
	I	13833 Philippines (low altitude) *13833*
I	*Baccaurea hookeri* Gage *19209*
	I	19209 Malaysia - Peninsular Malaysia (Perak, Johor) *19209*
	V	20099 Singapore *19209*
I	*Baccaurea odoratissima* Elm. *13833*
	I	13833 Philippines *13833*

R **Baloghia anisomera** Guillaumin
    R   New Caledonia

V **Baloghia marmorata** C.White *20681*
    I   *20681* Australia - New South Wales *20681*
    I   *20681* Australia - Queensland *20681*

E **Baloghia pininsularis** Guillaumin *20893*
    E   *20893* New Caledonia *20893*

E **Bernardia albida** Lundell *9064*
    E   *11182* Mexico - San Luis Potosi *9064*

E **Bernardia venosa** Griseb. *19734*
    E   *19105* Cuba (Guantánamo) *19105*

R **Bertya brownii** S.Moore *20681*
    R   *20681* Australia - New South Wales *20681*

R **Bertya findlayi** F.Muell. *20681*
    I   *20681* Australia - New South Wales *20681*
    I   *20681* Australia - Victoria *20681*

V **Bertya ingramii** T.A.James *20681*
    V   *20681* Australia - New South Wales *20681*

R **Bertya pedicellata** F.Muell. *20681*
    R   *20681* Australia - Queensland *20681*

V **Bertya pinifolia** Planchon *20681*
    V   *20681* Australia - Queensland *20681*

R **Bertya polystigma** Gruning *20681*
    R   *20681* Australia - Queensland *20681*

R **Beyeria gardneri** Airy Shaw *20681*
    R   *20681* Australia - Western Australia *20681*

Ex **Beyeria lepidopetala** F.Muell. *20681, 14223*
    Ex *20681* Australia - Western Australia *20681*

V **Beyeria subtecta** J.Black *20681*
    V   *20681* Australia - South Australia *20681*

I **Blachia reflexa** Benth.
    I   India - Karnataka (Coorg)
    I   India - Kerala (Travancore Hills)
    I   India - Tamil Nadu (Nilgiri Hills)

E **Bocquillonia arborea** Airy Shaw *20893*
    E   *20893* New Caledonia *20893*

E **Bocquillonia castaneifolia** Guillaumin *20893*
    E   *20893* New Caledonia *20893*

V **Bocquillonia longipes** McPherson *20893*
    E   *20893* New Caledonia *20893*

Ex **Bonania myrcifolia** (Griseb.) Benth. & Hook. *5607*
    Ex *19105* Cuba (Guantanamo) *5607*

R **Breynia badouini** Beille *6057*
    R   Vietnam *6057*

R **Breynia diversifolia** Beille *6057*
    R   Vietnam *6057*

R **Breynia grandiflora** Beille *6057*
    R   Vietnam *6057*

V **Bridelia kurzii** Hook. F. *7771*
    V   *14782* India - Andaman Is. *14782*
    V   *14782* India - Nicobar Is. (Kamorta Is.) *7771*

V **Bridelia moonii** Thwaites *10276*
    V   *12838* Sri Lanka *10276*

E **Caperonia neglecta** Webster *20883, 9006*
    R   *9703* Panama *20883*
    R   *9703* Venezuela *11182*

E **Caryodendron angustifolium** Standl. *20883, 9006*
    I   *20883* Panama *20883*

E **Cephalomappa sinensis** (Chun & How) Kosterm. *17617*

    E   *17617* China - Guangxi *11139*

R **Chaetocarpus coriaceus** Thwaites *10276*
    R   *12838* Sri Lanka *10276*

V **Chaetocarpus humilis** (Ekman) Borh. *5607*
    V   *19105* Cuba (Pinar del Rio) *5607*

E **Chaetocarpus pubescens** (Thwaites) Hook.f. *10252*
    E   *12838* Sri Lanka *10252*

R **Chamaesyce abdita** Burch *11117*
    R   Ecuador - Galapagos *11117*

E **Chamaesyce arnottiana** (Endl.) O.& I. Deg. *20850, 14209*
    E   *20850* U.S. - Hawaii (O`ahu - Ko`olau Mts.) *20850*

V **Chamaesyce astyla** (Engelm. ex Boiss.) Millsp. *20883, 20850*
    E   *20850* U.S. - Texas *20850*
    I   *20883* Mexico *20883*

V **Chamaesyce atoto** (J.G.Forster) Croizat *20845*
    V   *20845* French Polynesia - Society Is. (Tahiti) *20845*

V **Chamaesyce atrococca** (Heller) Croizat & Deg. *20850, 14209*
    R   *20850* U.S. - Hawaii (Kaua`i) *20850*

R **Chamaesyce celastroides** (Boiss.) Croizat & Degener var. **celastroides** *20850*
    R   *20850* U.S. - Hawaii *20850*

R **Chamaesyce celastroides** (Boiss.) Croizat & Degener var. **hanapepensis** (Sherff) O.& I. Deg. *20850, 14209*
    R   *20850* U.S. - Hawaii (Kaua`i) *20850*

E **Chamaesyce celastroides** (Boiss.) Croizat & Degener var. **kaenana** (Sherff) O.& I. Deg. *20850, 14209*
    E   *20850* U.S. - Hawaii (O`ahu) *20850*

E **Chamaesyce celastroides** (Boiss.) Croizat & Degener var. **laehiensis** (O.& I. Deg. & Sherff) Koutnik *20850, 14209*
    E   *20850* U.S. - Hawaii (Lana`i, Maui) *20850*

R **Chamaesyce celastroides** (Boiss.) Croizat & Degener var. **lorifolia** (Gray) O.& I. Deg. *20850, 14209*
    R   *20850* U.S. - Hawaii (Lana`i, Maui) *20850*

E **Chamaesyce celastroides** (Boiss.) Croizat & Degener var. **stokesii** (Forbes) O.& I. Deg. *20850, 14209*
    E   *20850* U.S. - Hawaii *20850*

Ex/E **Chamaesyce celastroides** (Boiss.) Croizat & Degener var. **tomentella** (Boiss.) Koutnik *20850, 14209*
    Ex/E *20850* U.S. - Hawaii (O`ahu) *20850*

R **Chamaesyce conferta** Small *20850*
    I   *20850* U.S. - Florida *20850*

V **Chamaesyce cumulicola** Small *20850*
    V   *20850* U.S. - Florida *20850*

R **Chamaesyce degeneri** (Sherff) Croizat & Deg. *20850, 14209*
    R   *20850* U.S. - Hawaii *20850*

V **Chamaesyce deltoidea** (Engelm. ex Chapman) Small *20850*
    I   *20850* U.S. - Florida *20850*

E **Chamaesyce deltoidea** (Engelm. ex Chapman) Small var. **adhaerens** (Small) Burch *20850*
    E   *20850* U.S. - Florida *20850*

E **Chamaesyce deltoidea** (Engelm. ex Chapman) Small ssp. **deltoidea** (Small) Burch *20850*
    E   *20850* U.S. - Florida *20850*

E   *Chamaesyce deltoidea* (Engelm. ex Chapman) Small ssp. *serpyllum* (Small) Burch *20850*
     E   *20850* U.S. - Florida *20850*

E   *Chamaesyce deppeana* (Boiss.) Millsp. *20850, 14209*
     E   *20850* U.S. - Hawaii (O`ahu, Ko`olau Mts.) *20850*

R   *Chamaesyce galapageia* (Robinson & Greenman) Burch *11117*
     R   Ecuador - Galapagos *11117*

E   *Chamaesyce garberi* (Engelm. ex Chapman) Small *20850*
     E   *20850* U.S. - Florida *20850*

V   *Chamaesyce golondrina* (L.C. Wheeler) Shinners *20883, 20850*
     V   *20850* U.S. - Texas *20850*
     I   *20883* Mexico *20883*

R   *Chamaesyce gracillima* (S.Watson) Millsp. *20850*
     I   *20850* U.S. - Arizona *20850*

E   *Chamaesyce halemanui* (Sherff) Croizat & Deg. *20850, 14209*
     E   *20850* U.S. - Hawaii (north-west Kaua`i) *20850*

E   *Chamaesyce herbstii* W.L. Wagner *20850, 14209, 21353*
     E   *20850* U.S. - Hawaii (O`ahu, Wai`anae Mts.) *20850*

V   *Chamaesyce hooveri* (L.C. Wheeler) Koutnik *20850*
     V   *20850* U.S. - California *20850*

V   *Chamaesyce jejuna* (M.C. Johnston & Warnock) Shinners *20850*
     V   *20850* U.S. - Texas *20850*

E   *Chamaesyce kuwaleana* (O. Deg. & Sherff) O.& I. Deg. *20850, 14209*
     E   *20850* U.S. - Hawaii (O`ahu, Wai`anae Mts.) *20850*

I   *Chamaesyce linearifolia* (Roth) Sojak
     I   India - Andhra Pradesh (Kurnool)

R   *Chamaesyce myrtillifolia* (L.) Millsp. *19890*
     R   *19890* Jamaica (St. Andrew) *19890*

R   *Chamaesyce nummularia* (Hook.f.) Burch var. *glabra* (Robinson & Greenman) Burch *11117*
     R   Ecuador - Galapagos (Floreana; Tower) *11117*

R   *Chamaesyce nummularia* (Hook.f.) Burch var. *nummularia* *11117*
     R   Ecuador - Galapagos *11117*

V   *Chamaesyce olowaluana* (Sherff) Croizat & Deg. *20850, 14209*
     V   *20850* U.S. - Hawaii (west Maui, Hawai`i) *20850*

R   *Chamaesyce parishii* (Greene) Millsp. ex Parish *20850*
     I   *20850* U.S. - California *20850*
     I   *20850* U.S. - Nevada *20850*

R   *Chamaesyce perennans* Shinners *20850*
     R   *20850* U.S. - Texas *20850*

E   *Chamaesyce pinetorum* Small *20850*
     E   *20850* U.S. - Florida *20850*

R   *Chamaesyce platysperma* (Engelm. ex S.Watson) Shinners *20883, 20850, 19002*
     E   *20850* U.S. - Arizona *20850*
     E   *20850* U.S. - California *20850*
     I   *20883* Mexico *20883*

R   *Chamaesyce polycarpa* (Benth) Millsp. var. *simulans* (L.C. Wheeler) Shinners *20850*
     R   *20850* U.S. - Texas *20850*

V   *Chamaesyce porteriana* Small *20850*
     I   *20850* U.S. - Florida *20850*

V   *Chamaesyce porteriana* Small var. *porteriana* (Small) Burch *20850*
     V   *20850* U.S. - Florida *20850*

V   *Chamaesyce porteriana* Small var. *scoparia* (Small) Burch *20850*
     V   *20850* U.S. - Florida *20850*

V   *Chamaesyce remyi* (Gray ex Boiss.) Croizat & Deg. *20850, 14209*
     V   *20850* U.S. - Hawaii (Kaua`i) *20850*

Ex/E   *Chamaesyce remyi* (Gray ex Boiss.)Croizat & Deg. var. *hanaleiensis* (Sherff) O.& I. Deg. *20850*
     Ex/E   *20850* U.S. - Hawaii *20850*

E   *Chamaesyce remyi* (Gray ex Boiss.) Croizat & Deg. var. *kauaiensis* (O. Deg. & Sherff) O.& I. Deg. *20850*
     E   *20850* U.S. - Hawaii *20850*

E   *Chamaesyce remyi* (Engelm.) Small var. *remyi* *20850*
     E   *20850* U.S. - Hawaii *20850*

E   *Chamaesyce rockii* (Forbes) Croizat & Deg. *20850, 14209, 21353*
     E   *20850* U.S. - Hawaii (O`ahu - Ko`olau Mts.) *20850*

V   *Chamaesyce skottsbergii* (Sherff) Croizat & Deg. *20850, 14209*
     I   *20850* U.S. - Hawaii (O`ahu, Moloka`i) *20850*

V   *Chamaesyce skottsbergii* (Sherff) Croizat & Degener var. *skottsbergii* *20850*
     V   *20850* U.S. - Hawaii *20850*

E   *Chamaesyce skottsbergii* (Sherff) Croizat & Degener Koutnik var. *vaccinioides* (Sherff) Koutnik *20850, 14209*
     E   *20850* U.S. - Hawaii *20850*

E   *Chamaesyce sparsiflora* (Heller) Koutnik *20850, 14209*
     E   *20850* U.S. - Hawaii (Kaua`i) *20850*

R   *Choriceras majus* Airy Shaw *20681*
     R   *20681* Australia - Queensland *20681*

I   *Chorisandrachne diplosperma* Airy Shaw *19120*
     I   *19120* Thailand *19120*

V   *Claoxylon centenarium* Koidz. *20626*
     V   *20626* Japan - Ogasawara-shoto *20626*

Ex   *Claoxylon grandifolium* (Poiret) Muell. Arg. *10082*
     Ex   *10082* Réunion *10082*
     Ex   *20771* Mauritius *10082*

E   *Claoxylon linostachys* Baillon ssp. *brachyphyllum* (Croizat) Coode *10082*
     E   *20771* Mauritius *10082*

E   *Claoxylon linostachys* Baillon ssp. *linostachys* *10082*
     E   *20771* Mauritius (Macabé Reserve) *10082*

E   *Claoxylon linostachys* Baillon ssp. *pedicellare* Coode *10082*
     E   *20771* Mauritius *10082*

R   *Claoxylon ooumuense* Fosberg & Sachet *20845*
     R   *20845* French Polynesia *20845*

I   *Claoxylon putii* Airy Shaw *19120*
     I   *19120* Thailand *19120*

E   *Claoxylon racemiflorum* A. Juss. *10082*
     E   *14234* Réunion *10082*

V   *Claoxylon setosum* Coode *10082*

I		14234 Réunion *14234*
R	*Claoxylon taitense* J.Mueller *20845*	
I		20845 French Polynesia - Society Is. *20845*
R	*Cleidiocarpon cavaleriei* (Leveille) Airy Shaw *17617*	
R		17617 China - Guangxi *11139*
R		17617 China - Guizhou (Luedian, Chenheng, Xingyi) *11139*
R		17617 China - Yunnan (Wengshanzhou) *11139*
Ex/E	*Cleidion lemurum* *20802*	
Ex/E		20802 New Caledonia *20802*
V	*Cleidion lochmios* McPherson *20893*	
V		20893 New Caledonia *20893*
V	*Cleidion marginatum* McPherson *20893*	
V		20893 New Caledonia *20893*
R	*Cleidion membranaceum* Pax & Hoffm. *11504*	
R		11504 Panama *11504*
R		18200 Peru *10747*
R		11504 Venezuela *11504*
V	*Cleidion veillonii* McPherson *20893*	
V		20893 New Caledonia *20893*
R	*Cleistanthus annamensis* Gagnepain *6057*	
R		Vietnam *6057*
R	*Cleistanthus discolor* Summerh. *20681*	
R		20681 Australia - Queensland *20681*
R	*Cleistanthus evrardii* Leonard *19358*	
R		19358 Zaire (central Forestier) *19358*
R	*Cleistanthus ferrugineus* Muell.Arg. *10276*	
R		12838 Sri Lanka *10276*
R	*Cleistanthus glaucus* Jabl.	
R		Malaysia - Peninsular Malaysia (Perak)
I	*Cleistanthus kingii* Jabl. *19209*	
I		19209 Malaysia - Peninsular Malaysia (Johor) *19209*
I	*Cleistanthus macrophyllus* Hook. f. *7730*	
I		19209 Malaysia - Peninsular Malaysia (Johor) *19209*
R		20099 Singapore *20099*
I	*Cleistanthus parvifolius* Hook.f.	
I		Malaysia - Peninsular Malaysia (Gopeng, Perak)
R	*Cleistanthus robustus* Muell.Arg. *12838*	
R		12838 Sri Lanka *12838*
R	*Clutia brassii* Brenan *7849*	
R		Malawi *7849*
V	*Clutia kamerunica* Pax	
V		Cameroon (Bamenda)
R	*Clutia punctata* Wild *7754*	
R		Zimbabwe (Chimanimani) *7754*
I	*Cnesmone jvanica* Bl. var. *glabriuscula* Balakr. & N. G. Nair *7771*	
I		India - Andaman Is. (South) *7771*
R	*Cnesmone subpeltata* Ridley	
R		Malaysia - Peninsular Malaysia (Perak; Selangor)
Ex	*Cnidoscolus fragrans* (H.B. K.) Pohl *5607*	
Ex		19105 Cuba (Ciud. Habana) *5607*
I	*Cnidoscolus matosii* Leon *5607*	
I		20990 Cuba (Guantanamo) *5607*
E	*Cnidoscolus quinquelobatus* (Mill.) Leon *5607*	
E		19105 Cuba (Prov. Habana, Ciud. Habana) *5607*
I	*Cnidoscolus rangel* (M. Gomez) McVaugh *5607*	
I		20990 Cuba (Pinar del Rio) *5607*

R	*Cocconerion balansae* Baillon	
R		New Caledonia
V	*Cocconerion minus* Baillon *20893*	
V		20893 New Caledonia *20893*
E	*Codiaeum oligogynum* McPherson *20893*	
E		20893 New Caledonia *20893*
R	*Conceveiba hostmannii* Benth. *8679*	
R		8679 Suriname *8679*
E	*Croizatia naiguatensis* Steyerm. *11190*	
E		Venezuela *11190*
E	*Croizatia neotropica* Steyerm. *11190*	
E		Venezuela *11190*
E	*Croizatia panamensis* Webster *20883*	
I		20883 Panama *20883*
I		20883 Colombia *20883*
V	*Croton acunae* Borh. *5607*	
V		19105 Cuba (Holguin) *5607*
R	*Croton alabamensis* E.A. Sm. ex Chapman *20850*	
R		20850 U.S. - Alabama *20850*
Ex/E		20850 U.S. - Tennessee *20850*
I		20850 U.S. - Texas *20850*
I	*Croton alienus* Pax *20057*	
I		19109 Kenya *19109*
R	*Croton alpinus* Gagnepain *6057*	
R		Vietnam *6057*
V	*Croton aubrevillei* J. Leonard *6057*	
V		20858 Côte d'Ivoire *20767*
V		20858 Ghana *20274*
R	*Croton brachypus* Airy Shaw *20681*	
R		20681 Australia - Queensland *20681*
V	*Croton chilensis* Muell.-Arg. *15088*	
V		13875 Chile *13875*
V	*Croton clavuliger* Muell. Arg. *5607*	
V		19105 Cuba *5607*
V	*Croton corallicola* Borh. *5607*	
V		19105 Cuba (Granma) *5607*
E	*Croton cordatulus* Airy Shaw *20893*	
E		20893 New Caledonia *20893*
R	*Croton coryi* Croizat *20850*	
R		20850 U.S. - Texas *20850*
R	*Croton cycloideus* Borh. & Muniz *5607*	
R		19105 Cuba (Santiago de Cuba; Holguin) *5607*
R	*Croton densivestitus* C.White & Francis *20681*	
R		20681 Australia - Queensland *20681*
R	*Croton eberhardtii* Gagnepain *6057*	
R		Vietnam *6057*
V	*Croton elliottii* Chapman *20850*	
E		20850 U.S. - Alabama *20850*
V		20850 U.S. - Florida *20850*
V		20850 U.S. - Georgia *20850*
I		20850 U.S. - South Carolina *20850*
R	*Croton excisus* Urban *5607*	
R		19105 Cuba (Guantanamo) *5607*
R	*Croton floribundus* Spreng. Syst. *20883*	
I		20883 Brazil *20883*
R		20883 Paraguay *20883*
R	*Croton fothergillifolius* Baillon *10082*	
R		20771 Mauritius *10082*
R	*Croton glandulosus* L. var. *floridanus* (Ferguson) R.W. Long *20850*	

R		20850 U.S. - Florida *20850*
R	*Croton glandulosus* L. var. *simpsonii* Ferguson *20850*	
	R	20850 U.S. - Florida *20850*
R	*Croton gracilipes* Baill. *20883*	
	R	20883 Brazil *20883*
	R	20883 Paraguay *20883*
R	*Croton grangerioides* Bojer ex Baillon *10082*	
	R	20771 Mauritius *10082*
R	*Croton grisebachianus* Mull. Arg. *20883*	
	R	20883 Jamaica *20883*
R	*Croton humilis* L. var. *adenophyllus* (Spreng.) Adams, unpublished *20883*	
	I	20883 Jamaica *20883*
V	*Croton impressus* Urban *20883, 15106*	
	?	Hispaniola *8058*
	I	20883 Puerto Rico *20883*
V	*Croton jaucoensis* Borh. *5607*	
	V	19105 Cuba (Guantanamo) *5607*
R	*Croton latsonensis* Gagnepain *6057*	
	R	Vietnam *6057*
V	*Croton laui* Merr. & Metcalf *17617*	
	V	17617 China - Hainan Is. *11139*
R	*Croton laurinus* Sw. *20883*	
	R	20883 Jamaica *20883*
V	*Croton magneticus* Airy Shaw *20681*	
	V	20681 Australia - Queensland *20681*
E	*Croton mauritianus* Lam. *10082*	
	E	14234 Réunion *10082*
E	*Croton moanus* Urban *5607*	
	E	19105 Cuba (Holguin) *5607*
I	*Croton moonii* Thwaites *10252*	
	I	16162 Sri Lanka *10252*
I	*Croton nipensis* Urban *5607*	
	I	19105 Cuba (Holguin) *5607*
E	*Croton nubigenus* Webster *20883*	
	E	20883 Nicaragua *20883*
E	*Croton olivaceus* Muell. Arg. *18200*	
	E	9446 Peru *18200*
R	*Croton pachyrachis* Alain *5607*	
	R	19105 Cuba (Santiago de Cuba; Holguin) *5607*
E	*Croton panduraeformis* Muell. Arg.	
	E	19105 Cuba *19105*
E	*Croton pilgerii* Ule *18200*	
	E	9446 Peru *18200*
E	*Croton poecilanthus* Urban *20883*	
	I	20883 Puerto Rico *20883*
V	*Croton pottsii* (M.C. Johnston) M.C. Johnston var. *thermophilus* (M.C. Johnston) M.C. Johnston *20850*	
	E	20850 U.S. - Texas *20850*
V	*Croton priorianus* Urb. *20883*	
	V	20883 Jamaica *20883*
V	*Croton prostratus* Urban *5607*	
	V	19105 Cuba *5607*
V	*Croton pyriticus* Croiz. *20883*	
	I	20883 Costa Rica *20883*
	E	20883 Panama *20883*
R	*Croton sarcocarpus* Balf. f. *15534*	
	R	15534 Yemen - Socotra *15534*

I	*Croton scabiosus* Beddome	
	I	India - Andhra Pradesh
R	*Croton scouleri* Hook.f. var. *brevifolius* (Andersson) Muell.Arg. *11117*	
	R	Ecuador - Galapagos (Floreana) *11117*
R	*Croton scouleri* Hook.f. var. *darwinii* Webster *11117*	
	R	Ecuador - Galapagos (Darwin; Santa Cruz; Wolf) *11117*
R	*Croton scouleri* Hook.f. var. *grandifolius* Muell.Arg. *11117*	
	R	Ecuador - Galapagos *11117*
I	*Croton sepalinus* Airy Shaw *19120*	
	I	19120 Thailand *19120*
E	*Croton septemnervius* McVaugh *9692*	
	E	11182 Mexico *9692*
R	*Croton stahleianus* Lanj. *8679*	
	R	8679 Suriname *8679*
R	*Croton stockeri* (Airy Shaw) Airy Shaw *20681*	
	R	20681 Australia - Queensland *20681*
V	*Croton suaveolens* Torr. *20850*	
	V	20850 U.S. - Texas *20850*
V	*Croton subdecumbens* Borh. & Muniz *5607*	
	V	19105 Cuba (Cienfuegos) *5607*
R	*Croton sulcifructus* Balf. f. *15534*	
	R	15534 Yemen - Socotra *15534*
V	*Croton suyapensis* A. Molina *9695*	
	V	9730 Honduras *9695*
R	*Croton talaeporos* R.-Sm. *20057*	
	R	20884 Kenya *20057*
	R	20884 Somalia (south) *20556*
R	*Croton tilifolius* Lam. *10082*	
	R	20771 Mauritius *10082*
R	*Croton touranensis* Gagnepain *6057*	
	I	20985 Vietnam *6057*
E	*Croton vaughanii* Croizat *10082*	
	E	20771 Mauritius (Perrier reserve) *10082*
V	*Croton wigginsii* L.C. Wheeler *20883, 20850, 9002*	
	E	20850 U.S. - Arizona *20850*
	E	20850 U.S. - California *20850*
	V	20883 Mexico *20883*
R	*Croton wilburi* McVaugh *9692*	
	R	19850 Mexico - Jalisco *21204*
V	*Croton yunquensis* Griseb. *5607*	
	V	19105 Cuba (Guantanamo) *5607*
V	*Crotonogyne manniana* Muell. Arg. *10260*	
	V	20858 Cameroon *7926*
	V	20858 Equatorial Guinea - Bioko *7926*
	V	20858 Gabon *7926*
	V	20858 Ghana *20858*
	E	20749 Nigeria (Eket) *7926*
I	*Cyclostemon iwahigensis* Elm. *13833*	
	I	13833 Philippines (Palawan) *13833*
I	*Cyclostemon malabaricus* Beddome	
	I	India - Kerala (Travancore Hills)
	I	India - Tamil Nadu (Tirunelveli Hills)
E	*Dalechampia arenalensis* Armbruster *20883*	
	I	20883 Costa Rica *20883*
E	*Dalechampia armbrusteri* Webster *20883*	
	I	20883 Brazil *20883*

E   *Dalechampia attenuistylus* Armbruster *20883*
   I   *20883* Venezuela *20883*

E   *Dalechampia brownsbergensis* Webster &
    Armbruster *20883*
   I   *20883* Suriname *20883*

E   *Dalechampia fernandensii* Webster *20883*
   I   *20883* Brazil *20883*

I   *Dalechampia magnistipula* Webster & Armbruster *11194*
   I   *11182* Mexico *11194*

E   *Dalechampia megacarpa* Armbruster *20883*
   I   *20883* Venezuela *20883*

V   *Dalechampia osana* Armbruster *20883*
   I   *20883* Costa Rica *20883*

E   *Dalechampia papillistigma* Armbruster *20883*
   I   *20883* Venezuela *20883*

R   *Dalechampia stenoloba* Sundar. & Kulk. *11494*
   R   *11494* India - Karnataka (Sukalhatti, Chikmagalur)
          11494

E   *Dalechampia viridissima* Webster *20883*
   I   *20883* Brazil *20883*

E   *Dalechampia websteri* Armbruster *20883*
   I   *20883* Costa Rica *20883*
   I   *20883* Panama *20883*

R   *Discocarpus essequeboensis* Klotzsch *8679*
   R   *8679* Guyana *8679*
   R   *8679* Suriname *8679*

R   *Dodecastigma integrifolium* (Lanj.) Lanj. &
    Sandw. *8679*
   R   Guyana *8679*

V   *Drypetes afzelii* (Pax) Hutch *20274*
   V   *20858* Côte d'Ivoire *7926*
   V   *20858* Ghana *20274*
   V   *20858* Liberia *7926*
   V   *20858* Sierra Leone *7926*

R   *Drypetes andamanica* (Kurz) Pax & Hoffm. *7771*
   R   *14782* India - Andaman Is. (South) *7771*

V   *Drypetes caustica* (Frapp. ex Cordem.) Airy
    Shaw *10082*
   V   *14234* Réunion *14234*
   E   *8764* Mauritius *8764*

Ex/E   *Drypetes dussii* Krug & Urban *19001*
   Ex/E *19001* Martinique *19001*

R   *Drypetes integerrima* (Koidz.) Furusawa *8038*
   R   *19134* Japan - Kazan Retto *8622*
   R   *19134* Japan - Ogasawara-shoto *8038*

I   *Drypetes lanceolata* (Thwaites) Pax & Hoffm. *10252*
   I   *16162* Sri Lanka *10252*

I   *Drypetes leiocarpa* (Kurz) Pax & Hoffm. *7771*
   I   India - Andaman Is. (south) *7771*

I   *Drypetes nervosa* (Hook.f.) Pax & K. Hoffm.
   I   Malaysia - Peninsular Malaysia (Gopeng, Perak)

R   *Drypetes oxyodonta* Airy Shaw
   R   Malaysia - Peninsular Malaysia (Pahang; Kelantan)

I   *Drypetes palawanensis* Pax & Hoffm. *13833*
   I   *13833* Philippines (low and medium altitudes)
          13833

V   *Drypetes pellegrinii* Leandrii *15970*
   V   *20858* Côte d'Ivoire *20274*
   V   *20858* Ghana *15970*

R   *Drypetes poilanei* Gagnepain *6057*
   R   Vietnam *6057*

V   *Drypetes riseleyi* Airy Shaw *14296*
   V   *19181* Seychelles *14296*

V   *Drypetes singroboensis* Aké Assi *11631*
   V   *20887* Côte d'Ivoire *11631*
   V   *20858* Ghana *15970*

E   *Drypetes triplinervia* Muell. Arg. *19105*
   E   *19105* Cuba *19105*

I   *Drypetes usambarica* (Pax) Hutch. var. *mrimae*
    A.Radc.-Sm. *20057*
   I   *19109* Kenya *19109*

V   *Dysopsis hirsuta* (Muell. Arg.) Skottsb. *19116*
   V   *19116* Chile - Juan Fernandez Is. *19116*

R   *Epiprinus balansae* Gagnepain *6057*
   R   Vietnam *6057*

R   *Epiprinus poilanei* Gagnepain *6057*
   R   Vietnam *6057*

R   *Erythrococca pubescens* Radc.-Sm. *20057*
   R   *20057* Kenya *20057*

E   *Erythrococca uniflora* M. Gilbert *19704*
   E   *19704* Ethiopia (Sidamo) *19704*

E   *Euphorbia aaron-rossii* A.& N. Holmgren *20850*
   E   *20850* U.S. - Arizona *20850*

E   II   *Euphorbia abdelkuri* Balf. f. *15534*
   E   *15534* Yemen - Socotra (Abd al Kuri) *15534*

R   II   *Euphorbia actinoclada* S. Carter *17672*
   R   *17672* Ethiopia (South) *17672*
   V   *17672* Kenya (northeast) *17672*
   V   *17672* Somalia (Southwest) *17672*

V   II   *Euphorbia alata* Hook. *20883, 13336*
   V   *13336* Jamaica *20883*

I   II   *Euphorbia albertensis* N.E.Br. *20604, 17672*
   I   *20604* South Africa - Cape Province *20604*

V   II   *Euphorbia albipollinifera* L.C.Leach *20604, 19976*
   V   *20604* South Africa - Cape Province *20604*

     Euphorbia ambacensis N.E. Br. *21391, 17672*
   R   *17672* Angola *17672*

E   I   *Euphorbia ambovombensis* Rauh & Razaf. *15658*
   E   *17672* Madagascar *17672*

V   II   *Euphorbia ampliphylla* Pax *19525*
   V   *17672* Ethiopia *17672*
   V   *17672* Kenya (W.Suk, Elgeyo, Masai) *19525*
   V   *17672* Malawi (Zambia border) *19525*
   V   *17672* Tanzania (Ufipa, Mbeya) *19525*
   V   *17672* Uganda (Karamoja, Mbale) *19525*

R   *Euphorbia anacampseros* Boiss. var. *tmolea* M.S.
    Khan *12840*
   R   *12840* Turkey *12840*

     Euphorbia anachoreta Svent. *21391, 17672*
   E   *14155* Portugal - Salvage Is. *14155*

R   II   *Euphorbia angustiflora* Pax *19525*
   R   *17672* Tanzania (Chunya, Mbeya) *19525*

I   II   *Euphorbia ankarensis* Boit. *17672*
   I   *17672* Madagascar *17672*

V   *Euphorbia apocynoides* Klotzsch *10747*
   V   *16317* Panama *10747*

R   II   *Euphorbia arbuscula* Balf. f. var. *montana* Balf.
    f. *15534*
   R   *15534* Yemen - Socotra *15534*

I   *Euphorbia aristata* Schmalh. *5942*
   I   *5942* Russia - North Caucasus *5942*

R   II   *Euphorbia asthenacantha* S. Carter *19525*
     R   *17672* Tanzania (Kigoma) *19525*

I   II   *Euphorbia atrocarmesina* Leach ssp. *arborea*
     Leach *17672*
     I   *17672* Angola *17672*

I   II   *Euphorbia atrocarmesina* Leach ssp.
     atrocarmesina 17672
     I   Angola

R   II   *Euphorbia atrox* S.Carter *17672*
     R   *17672* Somalia *17672*

R   *Euphorbia austroanatolica* Hub.-Mor. & M.S.
     Khan *12840*
     R   *12840* Turkey *12840*

E   II   *Euphorbia awashensis* M. G. Gilbert *19704*
     E   *19704* Ethiopia (Shewa Upland) *19704*

V   *Euphorbia azorica* Hochst *10260, 20171*
     V   *17672* Portugal - Azores *17672*

R   II   *Euphorbia baioensis* S. Carter *15926*
     R   *17672* Kenya (Northern Frontier Province; Baio
     Mountain) *15926*

E   II   *Euphorbia baleensis* M. Gilbert *19704*
     E   *19704* Ethiopia (Bale) *19704*

R   II   *Euphorbia baliola* N.E.Br. *20604, 17672*
     R   *20604* Namibia *20604*

I   II   *Euphorbia ballyana* Rauh *15926*
     I   *17672* Kenya (Rift valley) *15926*

V   II   *Euphorbia ballyi* S. Carter *17672*
     V   *17672* Somalia *17672*

V   II   *Euphorbia balsamifera* Ait. ssp. *adenensis* (Defl.)
     Bally *17672*
     E   *17672* Yemen, Democratic *17672*
     V   *17672* Somalia *17672*
     V   *17672* Sudan (Red Sea Hills) *17672*

V   II   *Euphorbia barnardii* A.C.White, R.A.Dyer &
     B.Sloane *20604, 15922*
     V   *20604* South Africa - Transvaal *20604*

V   II   *Euphorbia bayeri* L.C.Leach *20604, 20064*
     V   *20604* South Africa - Cape Province *20604*

R   II   *Euphorbia baylissii* Leach *17672*
     R   *17672* Mozambique (Sol do Save) *17672*

R   II   *Euphorbia berotica* N.E.Br. *20604, 17672*
     R   *17672* Angola *17672*
     R   *20604* Namibia *20604*

E   *Euphorbia betulicortex* M. Gilbert *19704*
     E   *19704* Ethiopia (Sidamo) *19704*

E   II   *Euphorbia bitataensis* M. G. Gilbert *19704*
     E   *19704* Ethiopia (Sidamo) *19704*

R   II   *Euphorbia bougheyi* Leach *17672*
     R   *17672* Mozambique *17672*

E   II   *Euphorbia bourgeauana* Gay ex Boiss. *17672*
     E   *20750* Spain - Canary Is. *17672*

R   II   *Euphorbia brakdamensis* N.E.Br. *20604, 17672*
     R   *20604* South Africa - Cape Province *20604*

V   II   *Euphorbia bravoana* Svent. *17672*
     V   *20750* Spain - Canary Is. *17672*

I   II   *Euphorbia brevirama* N.E.Br. *20604, 17672*
     I   *17672* South Africa *17672*
     Ex   *20604* South Africa - Cape Province *20604*

E   II   *Euphorbia brevitorta* Bally *17672*
     E   *17672* Kenya *17672*

R   *Euphorbia briquetii* Emberger & Maire *17672*
     R   *17672* Morocco *17672*

I   *Euphorbia brittonii* Millsp. *17672*
     I   *17672* Bahamas *17672*

R   II   *Euphorbia brunellii* Chiov. *17672*
     R   *17672* Ethiopia *17672*
     R   *17672* Kenya *17672*
     R   *17672* Sudan *17672*
     I   *19007* Uganda *17672*

R   II   *Euphorbia bruynsii* L.C.Leach *20604, 17672*
     R   *17672* South Africa *17672*
     R   *20604* South Africa - Cape Province *20604*

E   II   *Euphorbia burgeri* M. G. Gilbert *19704*
     E   *19704* Ethiopia (Haerege) *19704*

V   II   *Euphorbia buruana* Pax *19525*
     E   *17672* Kenya *17672*
     V   *17672* Tanzania (Masai, Pare, Lushoto) *19525*

R   II   *Euphorbia bwambensis* S. Carter *20556*
     R   *20733* Uganda (Bwamba forest) *7959*

I   II   *Euphorbia cannellii* Leach *17672*
     I   Angola

     Euphorbia capsaintemariensis Rauh var. *tulearensis*
     Rauh *21391, 15926*
     E   *17672* Madagascar (south) *15926*

E   II   *Euphorbia carteriana* Bally *17672*
     E   *17672* Somalia *17672*

R   II   *Euphorbia cibdela* N.E.Br. *20604, 17672*
     R   *20604* Namibia *20604*
     R   *20604* South Africa - Cape Province *20604*

R   II   *Euphorbia classenii* Bally & S. Carter *17672*
     R   *17672* Kenya *17672*

E   II   *Euphorbia clavigera* N.E.Br. *20604, 17672*
     E   *20604* Swaziland *20604*

V   II   *Euphorbia clivicola* R.A.Dyer *20604, 17672*
     V   *20604* South Africa - Transvaal *20604*

I   II   *Euphorbia caerulans* Pax *21391, 17672*
     I   Angola

V   II   *Euphorbia colubrina* Bally & S. Carter *15926*
     V   Ethiopia (Dawa Parma River) *15926*
     V   Kenya (Dawa Parma River) *15926*
     V   *17672* Somalia *17672*

E   II   *Euphorbia columnaris* Bally *17672*
     E   Somalia

I   II   *Euphorbia confinalis* R.A. Dyer ssp. *rhodesiaca*
     Leach *17672*
     I   Zimbabwe

I   II   *Euphorbia congestiflora* Leach *17672*
     I   Angola

V   *Euphorbia corsica* Req. *17672, 20171*
     V   *15080* France - Corsica *15080*

Ex   II   *Euphorbia crassipes* Marloth *20604, 17672*
     Ex   *20604* South Africa - Cape Province *20604*

E   II   *Euphorbia cryptocaulis* M. Gilbert *19704*
     E   *19704* Ethiopia (Sidamo) *19704*

V   *Euphorbia cubensis* Boiss. *5607*
     V   *19105* Cuba (Pinar del Rio) *5607*

I   II   *Euphorbia cuneneana* Leach ssp.
     cuneneana 17672
     I   Angola

I   II   *Euphorbia cuneneana* Leach ssp. *rhizomatosa*

Leach *17672*

I   Angola

E   II   *Euphorbia cussonioides* Bally *17672*

    E   *19109* Kenya *19109*

R   II   *Euphorbia cylindrica* A.C.White, R.A.Dyer &
         B.Sloane *20604, 15937*

    V   *20604* South Africa - Cape Province (north-western; Calvinia District) *20604*

I   I   *Euphorbia cylindrifolia* Marn.-Lap. & Rauh ssp.
         tuberifera Rauh *17672*

    I   Madagascar

E   II   *Euphorbia dalettiensis* M. G. Gilbert *19704*

    E   *19704* Ethiopia (Harerge) *19704*

Ex   *Euphorbia daphnoides* Balf.f. *10082*

    Ex   *5852* Mauritius - Rodrigues *5852*

R   II   *Euphorbia dauana* S. Carter *17672*

    R   *17672* Kenya *17672*

R   *Euphorbia davisii* M.S. Khan *12840*

    R   *12840* Turkey *12840*

I   I   *Euphorbia decaryi* Guillaumin *15658*

    I   Madagascar

I   II   *Euphorbia decepta* N.E.Br. *20604, 15926*

    I   *20604* South Africa - Cape Province (Willowmore) *20604*

R   II   *Euphorbia dekindtii* Pax *17672*

    R   Angola

E   *Euphorbia deltoidea* Engelm. ex Chapman ssp.
         deltoidea *17672*

    E   U.S. - Florida

I   II   *Euphorbia demissa* Leach *17672*

    I   Angola

V   II   *Euphorbia dichroa* S. Carter *15926*

    V   *19007* Uganda (north-eastern) *15926*

I   II   *Euphorbia didiereoides* Denis ex Leandri *17672*

    I   Madagascar

I   II   *Euphorbia dispersa* Leach *17672*

    I   *17672* Angola *17672*

I   II   *Euphorbia dissitispina* Leach *17672*

    I   Zimbabwe

E   *Euphorbia doloensis* M.Gilbert *19704*

    E   *19704* Ethiopia (Sidamo) *19704*

R   II   *Euphorbia dumeticola* P.R.O.Bally & S. Carter *19525*

    R   Tanzania (Ruaha valley) *20921*

R   *Euphorbia duvalii* Lecoq & Lamotte *17672, 20171*

    R   France (south)

V   *Euphorbia dwyeri* Burch *9006*

    V   *16317* Panama *9006*

V   II   *Euphorbia elegantissima* Bally & S. Carter *19525*

    V   Kenya *19525*

    E   Tanzania (Mbulu, Masai) *19525*

R   II   *Euphorbia ellenbeckii* Pax *17672*

    E   *19704* Ethiopia (Sidamo) *19704*

    R   Kenya

    V   Somalia

V   II   *Euphorbia eyassiana* Bally & S. Carter *19525*

    V   Tanzania (Musoma, Masai, Mbulu) *19525*

R   II   *Euphorbia fanshawei* Leach *17672*

    R   *17672* Zambia *17672*

R   II   *Euphorbia fascicaulis* S. Carter *17672*

    R   Somalia

V   II   *Euphorbia fasciculata* Thunb. *20604, 15932*

    V   *20604* South Africa - Cape Province (Knersvlakte) *20604*

R   II   *Euphorbia faucicola* Leach *17672*

    R   Angola

V   *Euphorbia flavicoma* DC. ssp. *costeana* (Rouy) P.
         Fourn. *20528*

    V   *20528* France (Aveyron) *20528*

V   II   *Euphorbia fluminis* S. Carter *15926*

    V   *17435* Kenya (North-eastern; near the Tana River) *15926*

V   *Euphorbia fontquerana* Greuter *17672*

    V   *11496* Spain - Balearic Is. *11496*

R   II   *Euphorbia fortissima* Leach *15926*

    R   *17672* Zambia *15926*

    I   Zimbabwe *15926*

V   II   *Euphorbia fractiflexa* S. Carter & J.R.I. Wood *17672*

    V   *17672* Saudi Arabia *17672*

    V   *17672* Yemen *17672*

I   II   *Euphorbia friedrichiae* Dinter *20604, 15932*

    I   *20604* Namibia *20604*

R   II   *Euphorbia friesiorum* (Hässler) S. Carter *20057*

    R   *19109* Kenya *19109*

V   II   *Euphorbia furcata* N.E. Br. *19525*

    V   Kenya (Kilifi) *19525*

    V   Tanzania (Moshi, Pare) *19525*

E   *Euphorbia gaditana* Coss. *17672, 20171*

    E   *19174* Spain (Cádiz, Sevilla) *20661*

R   *Euphorbia gasparrinii* Boiss. *17672, 20171*

    R   *20804* Italy (Calabria, Abruzzi) *20804*

    R   Italy - Sicily

V   II   *Euphorbia gemmea* Bally & S. Carter *17672*

    V   Kenya

R   *Euphorbia gibelliana* Peola *17672, 20171*

    R   *20804* Italy (Piedmont) *20804*

V   II   *Euphorbia gillettii* Bally & S. Carter ssp.
         gillettii *17672*

    V   *17672* Somalia *17672*

I   II   *Euphorbia gillettii* Bally & S. Carter ssp. *tenuior*
         S. Carter *17672*

    I   *17672* Somalia *17672*

I   II   *Euphorbia giumboensis* Hassler *17672*

    I   Somalia

V   *Euphorbia glauca* Forst.f. *17672*

    V   *19305* New Zealand - Chatham Is. *19106*

    V   *19305* New Zealand - North Is. *19305*

    V   *19305* New Zealand - South Is. *19305*

R   II   *Euphorbia globosa* (Haw.) Sims *20604, 17672*

    R   *20604* South Africa - Cape Province *20604*

R   II   *Euphorbia grandialata* R.A.Dyer *20604, 15922*

    R   *20604* South Africa - Transvaal (Lebowa) *20604*

R   II   *Euphorbia grandicornis* N.E. Br. ssp. *sejuncta*
         Leach *17672*

    R   *17672* Mozambique *17672*

R   II   *Euphorbia graniticola* Leach *17672*

    R   Mozambique

R   II   *Euphorbia greenwayi* Bally & S. Carter *17672*

    R   *17672* Tanzania *15926*

R   *Euphorbia gregersenii* K.Maly ex Beck *17672, 20171*

R   21091   Bosnia & Herzegovina *21091*
R   (former) Yugoslavia

E   II   *Euphorbia groenewaldii* R.A.Dyer *20604, 15922*
    E   20604   South Africa - Transvaal (Pietersburg
                 District) *20604*

R   II   *Euphorbia grosseri* Pax *17672*
    R   Ethiopia

E   II   *Euphorbia gymnocalycioides* M. C. Gilbert & S.
         Carter *19704*
    E   19704   Ethiopia (Sidamo) *19704*

E   *Euphorbia haeleeleana* Herbst *20850, 14209, 21354*
    E   20850   U.S. - Hawaii *20850*

R   *Euphorbia hajirensis* A.R. Smith *15534*
    R   15534   Yemen - Socotra *15534*

R   II   *Euphorbia hallii* R.A.Dyer *20604, 15926*
    R   20604   South Africa - Cape Province (Calvinia)
                 20604

E   II   *Euphorbia handiensis* Burchard *15926*
    E   19174   Spain - Canary Is. (Fuerteventura) *15926*

R   *Euphorbia heleniana* Thell. & Stapf *17672*
    R   18996   St Helena *18996*

V   *Euphorbia hieroglyphica* Coss. & Durieu *10488*
    V   14958   Algeria *10488*

I   *Euphorbia hooveri* Wheeler *17672*
    I   U.S. - California

V   II   *Euphorbia hopetownensis* Nel *20604, 15926*
    V   20604   South Africa - Cape Province (Hopetown)
                 20604

V   II   *Euphorbia horwoodii* S. Carter & Lavranos *15926*
    V   Somalia *15926*

V   II   *Euphorbia hubertii* Pax *19525*
    V   Tanzania (Mwanza, Musoma) *19525*

V   *Euphorbia hyberna* L. ssp. *insularis* (Boiss.)
         Briq. *18264, 20171*
    V   18264   Italy (Liguria, Tuscany) *18264*
    V   18264   Italy - Sardinia *18264*

R   II   *Euphorbia imitata* N.E. Br. *17672*
    R   17672   Angola *17672*

E   II   *Euphorbia immersa* Bally & S. Carter *15926*
    E   17672   Somalia *15926*

I   II   *Euphorbia inaequispina* N.E. Br. *17672*
    I   17672   Ethiopia *17672*
    I   17672   Somalia *17672*

I   II   *Euphorbia inculta* Bally *17672*
    I   17672   Somalia *17672*

R   II   *Euphorbia indurescens* Leach *17672*
    R   17672   Angola *17672*

I   II   *Euphorbia ingenticapsa* Leach *17672*
    I   Angola

R   *Euphorbia innocua* L.C. Wheeler *20850, 17672*
    R   20850   U.S. - Texas *20850*

R   II   *Euphorbia isacantha* Pax *19525*
    R   17672   Malawi *17672*
    R   Tanzania (Songea) *19525*

R   *Euphorbia isaurica* M.S. Khan *12840*
    R   12840   Turkey *12840*

E   II   *Euphorbia jansenvillensis* Nel *20604, 17672*
    E   20604   South Africa - Cape Province *20604*

R   II   *Euphorbia jubata* Leach *15926*
    R   17672   Zambia (central prov. Serenje dist.)

                 15926

R   *Euphorbia katrajensis* Gage *14782*
    R   14782   India - Maharashtra *14782*

R   *Euphorbia kischenensis* Vierh. *15534*
    R   15534   Yemen - Socotra *15534*

R   II   *Euphorbia knuthii* Pax ssp. *johnsonii* (N.E. Br.)
         Leach *17672*
    R   17672   Mozambique *17672*

V   II   *Euphorbia lambii* Svent. *15926*
    V   20750   Spain - Canary Is. (Gomera) *21391*

R   II   *Euphorbia ledienii* Berger var. *dregei* N.E.
         Br. *17672, 20604*
    R   20604   South Africa - Cape Province *20604*

I   *Euphorbia leptoclada* Balf. f. *15534*
    I   15534   Yemen - Socotra *15534*

I   II   *Euphorbia letestui* Raynal *17672*
    I   Cameroon

I   II   *Euphorbia leucochlamys* Chiov. *17672*
    I   17672   Somalia *17672*

V   II   *Euphorbia louwii* L.C.Leach *20604, 15926*
    K   20604   South Africa - Transvaal (north-western)
                 20604

R   II   *Euphorbia lumbricalis* L.C.Leach *20604, 20064*
    R   20604   South Africa - Cape Province *20604*

E   II   *Euphorbia makallensis* S. Carter *15926*
    E   Ethiopia (central Tigrai, Makalle region)
                 15926

R   II   *Euphorbia malevola* Leach ssp. *bechuanica*
         Leach *17672*
    R   17672   Botswana *17672*

R   *Euphorbia malvana* Maire *17672*
    R   Morocco

R   *Euphorbia maresii* Knoche *17672, 20171*
    R   19174   Spain - Balearic Is. *19174*

E   *Euphorbia margalidiana* Kuhbier & Lewejohann *17672*
    E   11496   Spain - Balearic Is. (Ibiza) *17891*

V   II   *Euphorbia marlothiana* N.E.Br. *20604, 17672*
    V   20604   South Africa - Cape Province *20604*

V   II   *Euphorbia marsabitensis* S. Carter *17672*
    V   Kenya

I   II   *Euphorbia masirahensis* Ghazanfar *20146*
    I   20146   Oman (Masirah Island) *20146*

R   *Euphorbia mazicum* Emberger & Maire *17672*
    R   Morocco

         Euphorbia mellifera Aiton *21391, 17672*
    R   Portugal - Madeira
    E   19174   Spain - Canary Is. *19174*

I   II   *Euphorbia meloformis* Aiton *20604, 17672*
    I   20604   South Africa - Cape Province *20604*

V   II   *Euphorbia memoralis* R.A. Dyer *17672*
    V   6088   Zimbabwe *6088*

V   II   *Euphorbia meridionalis* Bally & S. Carter *19525*
    V   Kenya (Nairobi, Machakos) *19525*
    V   Tanzania (Masai) *19525*

I   II   *Euphorbia millotii* Ursch & Leandri *17672*
    I   18294   Madagascar *18294*

R   II   *Euphorbia mitriformis* Bally & S. Carter *17672*
    R   Somalia

R   II   *Euphorbia mlanjeana* Leach *17672*

	R		Malawi
V	II	*Euphorbia monacantha* Pax *17672*	
		V	*19704* Ethiopia (Sidamo; Bale) *19704*
V		*Euphorbia monchiquensis* Franco & P.Silva *17672, 20171*	
		V	*20076* Portugal *20076*
R	I	*Euphorbia moratii* Rauh *15658*	
		R	Madagascar *15926*
I	II	*Euphorbia mosaica* Bally & S. Carter *17672*	
		I	*17672* Somalia *17672*
R	II	*Euphorbia multiclava* Bally & S. Carter *15926*	
		R	*15926* Somalia *15926*
V		*Euphorbia munizii* Borh. *5607*	
		V	*19105* Cuba (Holguin) *5607*
I	II	*Euphorbia mwinilungensis* Leach *17672*	
		I	Angola
		I	*17672* Zambia *17672*
		Euphorbia neohumbertii Rauh var. *aureo-viridiflora* Rauh *21391, 17672*	
		I	Madagascar
V		*Euphorbia nephradenia* Barneby *20850*	
		V	*20850* U.S. - Utah *20850*
I		*Euphorbia nereidum* Jahand. & Maire *17672*	
		I	Morocco
R	II	*Euphorbia nesemannii* R.A.Dyer *20604, 17672*	
		R	*20604* South Africa - Cape Province *20604*
R		*Euphorbia nevadensis* Boiss. & Reut. *17672, 20171*	
		R	*11496* Spain (Sierra Nevada and Levante) *20692*
V	II	*Euphorbia nigrispinioides* M. Gilbert *19704*	
		V	*19704* Ethiopia (Shewa Upland) *19704*
E		*Euphorbia norfolkiana* Boiss. *11649*	
		E	*11649* Australia - Norfolk Is. *11649*
R	II	*Euphorbia noxia* Pax *17672*	
		R	*20884* Somalia (north) *20884*
I	II	*Euphorbia nubigena* Leach var. *nubigena* *15926*	
		I	Angola (north of Quibala) *15926*
I	II	*Euphorbia nyassae* Pax *17672*	
		I	*19035* Tanzania *19035*
I		*Euphorbia obcordata* Balf. f. *15534*	
		I	*15534* Yemen - Socotra *15534*
E	II	*Euphorbia obesa* Hook.f. *20604, 17672*	
		E	*20604* South Africa - Cape Province *20604*
I		*Euphorbia oblanceolata* Balf. f. *15534*	
		I	*15534* Yemen - Socotra *15534*
E		*Euphorbia obovata* Decne. *17672*	
		E	*16168* Egypt (Sinai) *17672*
V	II	*Euphorbia odontophora* S. Carter *15926*	
		V	Kenya (Northern Frontier Province) *15926*
R	II	*Euphorbia ogadenensis* Bally & Carter *19704*	
		R	*19704* Ethiopia (Bale; Harerge) *19704*
R	II	*Euphorbia oligoclada* Leach *17672*	
		R	*17672* Angola *17672*
E		*Euphorbia omariana* M. Gilbert *19704*	
		E	*19704* Ethiopia (Bale) *19704*
R	II	*Euphorbia opuntioides* Welw. *17672*	
		R	*17672* Angola *17672*
I	II	*Euphorbia orbiculifolia* S. Carter *20146*	
		I	*20146* Oman (Dhofar) *20146*

R		*Euphorbia origanoides* L. *3204*	
	R	*3204* Ascension Is. *3204*	
R		*Euphorbia orphanidis* Boiss. *17672, 20171*	
	R	*17672* Greece *17672*	
V	II	*Euphorbia oxystegia* Boiss. *20604, 15937*	
		V	*20604* South Africa - Cape Province (Namaqualand) *20604*
I	II	*Euphorbia pachypodioides* Boit. *17672*	
		I	*17672* Madagascar *17672*
R	II	*Euphorbia panchganiensis* Blatt. & McCann *14782*	
		R	*14782* India - Maharashtra *14782*
V		*Euphorbia papillaris* (Boiss.) Raffaelli & Ricceri *18264*	
		V	*18264* Italy - Sicily *18264*
R	I	*Euphorbia parvicyathophora* Rauh *15658*	
		R	*17672* Madagascar *17672*
R		*Euphorbia parvula* Del. *17672*	
		R	*17672* Egypt *17672*
		R	*17672* Libya *17672*
R	II	*Euphorbia paulianii* Ursch & Léandri *17672*	
		R	*17672* Madagascar *17672*
I	II	*Euphorbia pedemontana* L.C.Leach *20604, 20064*	
		I	*20604* South Africa - Cape Province *20604*
R	II	*Euphorbia pedilanthoides* Denis *15926*	
		R	*17672* Madagascar *15926*
R		*Euphorbia peplidion* Engelm. *20850*	
		R	*20850* U.S. - Texas *20850*
E	II	*Euphorbia perangusta* R.A.Dyer *20604, 15922*	
		E	*20604* South Africa - Transvaal *20604*
I	II	*Euphorbia perarmata* S. Carter *17672*	
		I	*17672* Somalia *17672*
I		*Euphorbia perennans* (Shinn.) Warm. & M. Johnston *17672*	
		I	*17672* U.S. - Texas *17672*
I	II	*Euphorbia perrieri* Drake var. *elongata* Denis *17672*	
		I	*18294* Madagascar *17672*
R	II	*Euphorbia perrieri* Drake var. *perrieri* *17672*	
		R	*17672* Madagascar *17672*
R		*Euphorbia pestalozzae* Boiss. *12840*	
		R	*17672* Turkey *12840*
V	II	*Euphorbia petraea* S. Carter *17672*	
		V	*17672* Uganda *17672*
E	II	*Euphorbia petricola* Bally & S. Carter *15926*	
		E	*17672* Kenya (south-east; 500 to 1000 m elevation) *15926*
R		*Euphorbia petrophila* C.A. Meyer var. *armena* Boiss. *12840*	
		R	*17672* Turkey *12840*
V	II	*Euphorbia phillipsiae* N.E. Br. *17672*	
		V	*17672* Somalia *17672*
V		*Euphorbia pinetorum* (Small) G.L. Webster *20850*	
		V	*20850* U.S. - Florida *20850*
E	II	*Euphorbia piscidermis* Gilbert *17672*	
		E	*17672* Ethiopia *17672*
R		*Euphorbia pisidica* Hub.-Mor. & M.S. Khan *12840*	
		R	*17672* Turkey *12840*
R	II	*Euphorbia platyrrhiza* Leach *17672*	
		R	*17672* Zambia *17672*

I	II	*Euphorbia polycephala* Marloth *20604, 17672*	
		I	*20604* South Africa - Cape Province *20604*
I		*Euphorbia porterana* (Small) R.C.H.M. Oudejans var. *keyensis 17672*	
		I	*17672* U.S. - Florida *17672*
I		*Euphorbia porterana* (Small) R.C.H.M. Oudejans var. *porterana 17672*	
		I	*17672* U.S. - Florida *17672*
I		*Euphorbia porterana* (Small) R.C.H.M. Oudejans var. *scoparia 17672*	
		I	*17672* U.S. - Florida *17672*
I	II	*Euphorbia primulifolia* Baker *15658*	
		I	*17672* Madagascar *15926*
R	II	*Euphorbia proballyana* Leach *19525*	
		R	*17672* Tanzania (Ruaha valley) *20921*
I		*Euphorbia proctorii* (Burch) Correll *17672*	
		I	*17672* Bahamas *17672*
V		*Euphorbia pseudo-apios* Maire & M. Weiller *17672*	
		V	*17672* Libya *17672*
V	II	*Euphorbia pseudoburuana* P.R.O.Bally & S. Carter *19525*	
		V	Kenya (Masai) *15926*
		V	Tanzania (Masai) *19525*
R	II	*Euphorbia pteroclada* Leach *17672*	
		R	*17672* Zaire *17672*
R		*Euphorbia punctata* Del. *17672*	
		R	*17672* Egypt *17672*
R		*Euphorbia purpurea* (Raf.) Fern. *20850, 17672*	
		Ex	*20850* U.S. - Delaware *20850*
		E	*20850* U.S. - Maryland *20850*
		E	*20850* U.S. - New Jersey *20850*
		I	*20850* U.S. - New York *20850*
		V	*20850* U.S. - North Carolina *20850*
		E	*20850* U.S. - Ohio *20850*
		E	*20850* U.S. - Pennsylvania *20850*
		V	*20850* U.S. - Virginia *20850*
		V	*20850* U.S. - West Virginia *20850*
V	II	*Euphorbia quadrangularis* Pax *19525*	
		V	*17672* Tanzania (Maswa, Kilosa, Iringa) *19525*
R	II	*Euphorbia quadrata* Nel *20604, 17672*	
		R	*20604* South Africa - Cape Province *20604*
E	II	*Euphorbia quadrialata* Pax *19525*	
		E	*17672* Tanzania (Pare, Lushoto, Handeni) *19525*
V	II	*Euphorbia quadrilatera* Leach *19525*	
		V	*17672* Tanzania (Chunya, Iringa) *19525*
E	II	*Euphorbia quadrispina* S. Carter *15926*	
		E	*17672* Kenya (near the Dawa Parma River at 400m elevation) *15926*
R	I	*Euphorbia quartziticola* Leandri *15658*	
		R	*17672* Madagascar *15926*
V		*Euphorbia rechingeri* Greuter *17672, 20171*	
		V	*20730* Greece - Crete *17672*
E		*Euphorbia repetita* A. Rich. *19704*	
		E	*19704* Ethiopia (Tigray, Gonder, Wello, Shewa) *19704*
I	II	*Euphorbia reptans* Bally & S. Carter *17672*	
		I	*17672* Somalia *17672*
R	II	*Euphorbia restricta* R.A.Dyer *20604, 15922*	
		R	*20604* South Africa - Transvaal (Drakensberg Mts.) *20604*
R		*Euphorbia rhytidosperma* Boiss. & Bal. *12840*	

		R	*17672* Turkey *12840*
R	II	*Euphorbia richardsiae* Leach ssp. *richardsiae 17672*	
		R	*17672* Malawi *17672*
R	II	*Euphorbia richardsiae* Leach ssp. *robusta* Leach *17672*	
		R	*17672* Malawi *17672*
V	II	*Euphorbia rossii* Rauh & Buchloh *17672*	
		V	*17672* Madagascar *17672*
R	II	*Euphorbia rowlandii* R.A.Dyer *20604, 15922*	
		R	*20604* Zimbabwe *20604*
		R	*20604* South Africa - Transvaal (Kruger N.P. & Venda) *20604*
E	II	*Euphorbia rubella* Pax *21391, 15926*	
		E	*17672* Ethiopia *15926*
R	II	*Euphorbia rubrispinosa* S. Carter *19525*	
		R	*17672* Tanzania (Kigoma) *19525*
E		*Euphorbia ruiziana* (Klotzsch & Garcke) Boiss. *17672*	
		E	*17672* Peru *17672*
I	II	*Euphorbia sacchii* Chiov. *17672*	
		I	*17672* Somalia *17672*
R		*Euphorbia sanasunitensis* Hand.-Mazz. *12840*	
		R	*17672* Turkey *12840*
E	II	*Euphorbia saxorum* Bally & S. Carter *17672*	
		E	*17672* Kenya *17672*
R	II	*Euphorbia schizacantha* Pax *15926*	
		R	*15926* Ethiopia *15926*
		R	*17672* Kenya *17672*
		V	*15926* Somalia *15926*
R	II	*Euphorbia schmitzii* Leach *17672*	
		R	*17672* Zaire *17672*
V	II	*Euphorbia schoenlandii* Pax *20604, 15932*	
		E	*15932* South Africa (Vanrhynsdorp area) *15932*
		V	*20604* South Africa - Cape Province *20604*
I	II	*Euphorbia scitula* Leach *17672*	
		I	*17672* Angola *17672*
R		*Euphorbia sclerocyathium* Korovin & Popov *17672*	
		R	*17672* former USSR *6930*
E	II	*Euphorbia sebsebei* M. G. Gilbert *19704*	
		E	*19704* Ethiopia (Sidamo) *19704*
V		*Euphorbia seguieriana* Necker ssp. *loiseleurii* (Rouy) P. Fourn. *20528*	
		V	*20528* France *20528*
		E	*13892* Netherlands *13892*
R	II	*Euphorbia sekukuniensis* R.A.Dyer *20604, 15922*	
		R	*20604* South Africa - Transvaal (Lebowa) *20604*
I	II	*Euphorbia semperflorens* Leach *15926*	
		I	*17672* Angola (south-western; Mozamedes district) *15926*
V	II	*Euphorbia sepulta* Bally & S. Carter *17672*	
		V	*17672* Somalia *17672*
R	II	*Euphorbia sereti* De Wild. ssp. *sereti 17672*	
		R	*17672* Zaire *17672*
R	II	*Euphorbia socotrana* Balf. f. *15534*	
		R	*15534* Yemen - Socotra *15534*
R	II	*Euphorbia spiralis* Balf. f. *15534*	
		R	*15534* Yemen - Socotra *15534*
I	II	*Euphorbia strangulata* N.E. Br. ssp. *deminuens* Leach *17672*	
		I	*17672* Angola *17672*

I   II   *Euphorbia strangulata* N.E. Br. ssp. strangulata *17672*
     I   *17672* Angola *17672*

R   *Euphorbia strictior* Holz. *20850, 17672*
     R   *20850* U.S. - New Mexico *20850*
     R   *20850* U.S. - Texas *20850*

R   II   *Euphorbia stygiana* H.C.Watson *17672, 20171*
     R   *17672* Portugal - Azores *17672*

R   II   *Euphorbia subscandens* Bally & S. Carter *17672*
     R   *17672* Kenya *17672*

V   *Euphorbia sultan-hassei* Strid *20730*
     V   *20730* Greece - Crete *20730*

E   II   *Euphorbia symmetrica* A.C.White, R.A.Dyer & B.Sloane *20604, 17672*
     E   *17672* South Africa *17672*
     V   *20604* South Africa - Cape Province *20604*

E   *Euphorbia tacnensis* F. Philippi *17672*
     E   *17672* Peru *17672*

E   II   *Euphorbia tanaensis* Bally *17672*
     E   *17672* Kenya (Witu forest) *17435*

E   *Euphorbia telephioides* Chapman *20850, 15914*
     E   *20850* U.S. - Florida (coastal lowlands in Bay, Gulf, & Franklin Cos. (22 sites)) *20850*

R   II   *Euphorbia tenuispinosa* Gilli *17672*
     R   *17672* Kenya *17672*

I   II   *Euphorbia tetracantha* Rendle *17672*
     I   *17672* Ethiopia *17672*

R   *Euphorbia thulinii* S.Carter *20884*
     R   *20884* Somalia (north-east) *20884*

E   II   *Euphorbia torta* Pax & K. Hoffm. *19525*
     E   *17672* Tanzania (Tabora, Iringa) *17672*

V   II   *Euphorbia tortirama* R.A.Dyer *20604, 15922*
     V   *20604* South Africa - Transvaal (Waterberg, Potgieterrust & Zoutpansberg) *20604*

V   *Euphorbia transtagana* Boiss. *17672, 20171*
     V   *20076* Portugal *20076*

   Euphorbia triaculeata Forsk. var. *triacantha* (Ehrenb. ex Boiss.) N.E. Br. *21391, 17672*
     I   *17672* Djibouti *17672*
     V   *17672* Ethiopia *17672*
     I   *17672* Sudan *17672*

V   II   *Euphorbia triaculeata* Forsk. *21391, 17672*
     V   *17672* Saudi Arabia (Arabian Peninsula) *17672*

V   *Euphorbia trichotoma* Kunth *19002*
     I   *20850* U.S. - Florida *20850*

E   II   *Euphorbia turbiniformis* Chiov. *17672*
     E   Somalia

V   II   *Euphorbia turkanensis* S. Carter *17672*
     V   *17672* Kenya *17672*

V   II   *Euphorbia uhligiana* Pax *17672*
     V   *17672* Kenya (Masai) *19525*
     V   *17672* Tanzania (Masai, Lushoto) *19525*

R   II   *Euphorbia umfoloziensis* Peckover *20604, 20064*
     R   *20604* South Africa - Natal *20604*

R   II   *Euphorbia unicornis* R.A. Dyer *17672*
     R   *17672* Mozambique *17672*

E   II   *Euphorbia uniglans* M. Gilbert *19704*
     E   *19704* Ethiopia (Sidamo) *19704*

V   II   *Euphorbia uzmuk* S. Carter & J.R.I. Wood *17672*
     V   *17672* Yemen *17672*

R   II   *Euphorbia vaalputsiana* L.C.Leach *20604, 20064*
     R   *20604* South Africa - Cape Province *20604*

V   II   *Euphorbia valida* N.E.Br. *20604, 17672*
     V   *20604* South Africa - Cape Province *20604*

I   II   *Euphorbia vallaris* Leach *15926*
     I   *15926* Angola (Huila) *15926*

R   *Euphorbia veneris* Khan *14230*
     R   *17672* Cyprus (Troodos) *14230*

I   II   *Euphorbia viduiflora* Leach *17672*
     I   *17672* Angola *17672*

V   II   *Euphorbia vittata* S. Carter *17672*
     V   *17672* Kenya *17672*

E   II   *Euphorbia wakefieldii* N.E. Br. *17672*
     E   *17672* Kenya (Mombasa-Kilifi) *20057*
     E   *20057* Tanzania (South Pare Mnts.) *17435*

V   II   *Euphorbia waterbergensis* R.A.Dyer *20604, 15922*
     V   *20604* South Africa - Transvaal (Waterberg District) *20604*

I   II   *Euphorbia wildii* Leach *7924*
     I   *17672* Zimbabwe *7924*

R   II   *Euphorbia williamsonii* Leach *15926*
     R   *17672* Zambia (Northern Province) *15926*

R   *Euphorbia yaroslavii* Poljakov *17672*
     R   *17672* former USSR *6930*

R   *Euphorbia zhiguliensis* Prokh. *17672, 20171*
     R   *11552* Russian Federation (western) *11552*

R   II   *Euphorbia zoutpansbergensis* R.A.Dyer *20604, 15922*
     R   *20604* South Africa - Transvaal (Zoutpansberg District) *20604*

V   *Excoecaria benthamiana* Hemsley *14296*
     V   *19182* Seychelles (granitic) *14296*

R   *Excoecaria poilanei* Gagnepain *6057*
     R   Vietnam *6057*

I   *Excoecaria rectinervis* (Kurz) Kurz *7771*
     I   India - Nicobar Is. (katchal Is.) *7771*

R   *Excoecaria simii* (Kuntze) Pax *20604*
     R   *20604* South Africa - Cape Province *20604*
     R   *20604* South Africa - Natal *20604*

I   *Fahrenheitia integrifolia* (Airy Shaw) Airy Shaw
     I   India - Kerala
     I   India - Tamil Nadu

E   *Flueggea anatolica* Gemici *20698*
     E   *20698* Turkey *20698*

I   *Flueggea elliptica* (Sprengel) Baillon *11196*
     I   *11196* Ecuador *11196*

E   *Flueggea neowawraea* W. Hayden *20850, 14209*
     E   *20850* U.S. - Hawaii (O`ahu, Hawai`i) *20850*

I   *Flueggea schuechiana* (Muell. Arg.) Webster *11196*
     I   *11182* Brazil *11196*

V   *Fontainea australis* Jessup & Guymer *20681*
     I   *20681* Australia - New South Wales *20681*
     I   *20681* Australia - Queensland *20681*

E   *Fontainea oraria* Jessup & Guymer *20681*
     E   *20681* Australia - New South Wales *20681*

R   *Fontainea picrosperma* C.White *20681*
     R   *20681* Australia - Queensland *20681*

V   *Fontainea rostrata* Jessup & Guymer *20681*
     V   *20681* Australia - Queensland *20681*

V   *Fontainea venosa* Jessup & Guymer *20681*

	V	20681 Australia - Queensland *20681*				

I   *Glochidion andamanicum* **Kurz** *7771*
     I   India - Andaman Is. (South) *7771*

R   *Glochidion balansae* **Beille** *6057*
     R   Vietnam *6057*

I   *Glochidion bourdillonii* **Gamble**
     I   India - Kerala (Travancore Hills)

I   *Glochidion cenabrei* **Merr.** *13833*
     I   *13833* Philippines (low altitude) *13833*

I   *Glochidion dolichostylum* **Merr.** *13833*
     I   *13833* Philippines (low altitude) *13833*

R   *Glochidion kerrii* **Craib** *19120*
     R   *19120* Thailand *19120*

R   *Glochidion manono* **Baillon ex J.Mueller** *20845*
     V   *20845* French Polynesia - Society Is. *20845*

I   *Glochidion nemorale* **Thwaites** *10252*
     I   *16162* Sri Lanka *10252*

I   *Glochidion palawanense* **Elm.** *13833*
     I   *13833* Philippines (Palawan) *13833*

I   *Glochidion pauciflorum* **Gamble**
     I   India - Tamil Nadu

R   *Glochidion pruinosum* **Airy Shaw** *20681*
     R   *20681* Australia - Queensland *20681*

I   *Glochidion pulgarense* **Elm.** *13833*
     I   *13833* Philippines (Mt. Pulgar) *13833*

R   *Glochidion pungens* **Airy Shaw** *20681*
     R   *20681* Australia - Queensland *20681*

E   *Glochidion raivavense* **F.Brown** *8050*
     E   *20845* French Polynesia - Tubuai Is. *20845*

R   *Grimmeodendron jamaicense* **Urb.** *20883, 19890*
     R   *19890* Jamaica *20883*

Ex/E   *Haptanthus hazlettii* **Goldberg & C. Nelson (Family Unresolved)** *20050*
     Ex/E *20050* Honduras *20050*

E   *Hieronima crassistipula* **Urban** *5607*
     E   *19105* Cuba (Juventud Is.) *5607*

V   *Hyeronima clusioides* **(Tul.) Muell.-Arg.** *20883*
     I   *20883* Puerto Rico *20883*

V   *Hyeronima jamaicensis* **Urb.** *20883*
     V   *20883* Jamaica *20883*

E   *Jatropha bullockii* **E. J. Lott** *20883*
     I   *20883* Mexico *20883*

E   *Jatropha chacoana* **Fernández Casas** *20883*
     E   *20883* Paraguay *20883*

E   *Jatropha chamelensis* **Jerez-Jiménez** *11185*
     E   *11182* Mexico - Jalisco *11185*

E   *Jatropha costaricensis* *20883, 11149*
     E   *7961* Costa Rica (nr Playas del Coco) *20883*

R   *Jatropha giffordiana* **Dehgan & Webster** *9002*
     R   *9703* Mexico *9002*

E   *Jatropha horizontalis* **M. Gilbert** *19704*
     E   *19704* Ethiopia (Sidamo) *19704*

R   *Jatropha moranii* **Dehgan & Webster** *9002*
     R   *9703* Mexico *9002*

R   *Jatropha ricinifolia* **Pax in Engl.** *20883*
     R   *20883* Paraguay *20883*

E   *Jatropha stevensii* **Webster** *20883, 11195*
     E   *11182* Nicaragua *20883*

R   *Jatropha vernicosa* **Brandegee** *9002*
     R   *11182* Mexico *9002*

V   *Joannesia princeps* **Vell.** *20883, 10370*
     V   *20883* Brazil *20883*

I   *Koilodepas calycinum* **Beddome** *5375*
     I   India - Tamil Nadu *5375*

I   *Lasiococca comberi* **Haines**
     I   India - Andhra Pradesh

E   *Lasiocroton fawcettii* **Urb.** *20883*
     E   *20883* Jamaica *20883*

E   *Lasiocroton gracilis* **Britton & P. Wilson** *5607*
     E   *19105* Cuba (Santiago de Cuba) *5607*

V   *Lasiocroton harrisii* **Britton** *20883, 13336*
     V   *13336* Jamaica *20883*

R   *Lasiocroton macrophyllus* **(Sw.) Griseb.** *20883*
     R   *20883* Jamaica *20883*

E   *Lasiocroton trelawniensis* **Adams** *20883, 13336*
     E   *13336* Jamaica *20883*

R   *Lautembergia neraudiana* **(Baillon) Coode** *10082*
     R   *20771* Mauritius *10082*
     Ex   *14981* Seychelles *14981*

I   *Leptopus colchicus* **(Fischer & C. Meyer) Pojark.** *5942*
     I   *5942* Georgia *5942*

R   *Leucocroton bracteosus* **Urban** *5607*
     R   *19105* Cuba (Santiago de Cuba) *5607*

R   *Leucocroton brittonii* **Alain** *5607*
     R   *19105* Cuba (Guantanamo) *5607*

R   *Leucocroton discolor* **Urban** *5607*
     R   *19105* Cuba (Santiago de Cuba; Holguin) *5607*

V   *Leucocroton moncadae* **Borh.** *5607*
     V   *19105* Cuba *5607*

V   *Leucocroton pallidus* **Britton** *5607*
     V   *19105* Cuba (Guantanamo) *5607*

R   *Liodendron formosanum* **(Kaneh. & Sas.) H. Keng** *14961*
     R   *20511* Taiwan *20511*

V   *Macaranga beillei* **Prain** *7926*
     V   *20887* Côte d'Ivoire *7926*

V   *Macaranga bicolor* **Muell.-Arg.** *13780*
     V   *15960* Philippines *13780*

V   *Macaranga caudatifolia* **Elm.** *13780*
     V   *15960* Philippines *13780*

I   *Macaranga cogostiflora* **Merr.** *13833*
     I   *13833* Philippines *13833*

R   *Macaranga conglomerata* **Brenan** *20057*
     R   *19109* Kenya (Taita hills) *20057*
     R   *20057* Tanzania (Magamba & Sungwi forest reserves) *17435*

I   *Macaranga flexuosa* **Wight**
     I   India - Tamil Nadu

V   *Macaranga grandifolia* **(Blanco) Merr.** *13780*
     V   *15960* Philippines *13780*

V   *Macaranga mauritiana* **Bojer ex Muell. Arg.** *10082*
     V   *20771* Mauritius *10082*

E   *Macaranga raivavaeensis* **H. Saint John** *20845*
     E   *20845* French Polynesia - Tubuai Is. (Raivavaé) *20845*

R   *Macaranga taitensis* **(J.Mueller) J.Mueller** *20845*
     R   *20845* French Polynesia - Society Is. (Tahiti) *20845*

R *Macaranga trigonostemonoides* Croizat *6057*
    R   Vietnam *6057*

I *Mallotus bracteatus* Hook.f. *17450*
    I   Malaysia - Peninsular Malaysia (Perlis; Perak)

R *Mallotus fuscescens* Muell.Arg. *10276*
    R *12838* Sri Lanka *10276*

I *Mallotus odoratus* Elm. *13833*
    I *13833* Philippines (Camiguin Isand) *13833*

V *Manihot acuminatissima* Mueller von Argau *20883*
    I *20883* Brazil *20883*

E *Manihot affinis* Pax *20883*
    E *20883* Brazil *20883*

E *Manihot alutacea* Rogers & Appan *20883*
    I *20883* Brazil *20883*

E *Manihot anomala* ssp. *cujabensis* (Mueller von Argau) Rogers & Appan *20883*
    E *20883* Brazil *20883*

V *Manihot attenuata* Mueller von Argau *20883*
    I *20883* Brazil *20883*

E *Manihot auriculata* McVaugh *20883, 9702*
    E *20883* Mexico *20883*

E *Manihot brachyandra* Pax & K. Hoffmann *20883*
    E *20883* Brazil *20883*

V *Manihot caerulescens* ssp. *macrantha* (Pax & K. Hoffmann) Rogers & Appan *20883*
    I *20883* Paraguay *20883*

R *Manihot caerulescens* ssp. *paraensis* (Mueller von Argau) Rogers & Appan *20883*
    I *20883* Brazil *20883*

V *Manihot catingae* Ule *20883*
    I *20883* Brazil *20883*

V *Manihot condensata* Rogers & Appan *20883*
    I *20883* Bolivia *20883*

V *Manihot corymbiflora* Pax *20883*
    I *20883* Brazil *20883*

E *Manihot crotalariaeformis* Pohl *20883*
    E *20883* Brazil *20883*

R *Manihot divergens* Pohl *20883*
    R *20883* Brazil *20883*

V *Manihot falcata* Rogers & Appan *20883*
    I *20883* Brazil *20883*

R *Manihot filamentosa* Pittier *20883*
    I *20883* Venezuela *20883*

E *Manihot flemingiana* Rogers & Appan *20883*
    E *20883* Brazil *20883*

V *Manihot fruticulosa* (Pax) Rogers & Appan *20883*
    I *20883* Brazil *20883*

R *Manihot gracilis* ssp. *varians* (Pohl) Rogers & Appan *20883*
    I *20883* Brazil *20883*

R *Manihot guaranitica* ssp. *boliviana* (Pax & K. Hoffmann) Rogers & Appan *20883*
    I *20883* Bolivia *20883*

E *Manihot handroana* N. D. Cruz *20883*
    E *20883* Brazil *20883*

E *Manihot hassleriana* Chodat *20883*
    I *20883* Paraguay *20883*

V *Manihot heptaphylla* Ule *20883*

    I *20883* Brazil *20883*

R *Manihot inflata* Mueller von Argau *20883*
    I *20883* Brazil *20883*

V *Manihot irwinii* Rogers & Appan *20883*
    I *20883* Brazil *20883*

R *Manihot jacobinensis* Mueller von Argau *20883*
    I *20883* Brazil *20883*

V *Manihot janiphoides* Mueller von Argau *20883*
    I *20883* Brazil *20883*

E *Manihot jolyana* N. D. Cruz *20883*
    E *20883* Brazil *20883*

R *Manihot leptopoda* (Mueller von Argau) Rogers & Appan *20883*
    I *20883* Brazil *20883*

R *Manihot longepetiolata* Pohl *20883*
    R *20883* Brazil *20883*

E *Manihot maracasensis* Ule *20883*
    E *20883* Brazil *20883*

R *Manihot marajoara* Chermonte de Miranda apud Huber *20883*
    I *20883* Brazil *20883*

V *Manihot michaelis* McVaugh *20883, 9702*
    V *20883* Mexico *20883*

E *Manihot mirabilis* Pax *20883*
    I *20883* Paraguay *20883*

V *Manihot mossamedensis* Taubert *20883*
    I *20883* Brazil *20883*

V *Manihot nana* Mueller von Argau *20883*
    I *20883* Brazil *20883*

R *Manihot oligantha* Pax *20883*
    R *20883* Brazil *20883*

E *Manihot orbicularis* Pohl *20883*
    E *20883* Brazil *20883*

V *Manihot paviaefolia* Pohl *20883*
    V *20883* Brazil *20883*

V *Manihot peltata* Pohl *20883*
    I *20883* Brazil *20883*

E *Manihot pentaphylla* ssp. *graminifolia* (Chodat & Hassler) Rogers & Appan *20883*
    I *20883* Paraguay *20883*

R *Manihot pentaphylla* ssp. *pentaphylla* *20883*
    I *20883* Brazil *20883*

R *Manihot peruviana* Mueller von Argau *20883*
    I *20883* Peru *20883*

V *Manihot pohlii* Wawra *20883*
    V *20883* Brazil *20883*

V *Manihot populifolia* Pax *20883*
    I *20883* Paraguay *20883*

R *Manihot pseudoglaziovii* Pax & K. Hoffmann *20883*
    R *20883* Brazil *20883*

E *Manihot purpureo-costata* Pohl *20883*
    I *20883* Brazil *20883*

E *Manihot pusilla* Pohl *20883*
    E *20883* Brazil *20883*

E *Manihot quinquefolia* Pohl *20883*
    E *20883* Brazil *20883*

V *Manihot quinqueloba* Pohl *20883*
    I *20883* Brazil *20883*

R	*Manihot reniformis* Pohl *20883*		
	R	*20883* Brazil *20883*	
V	*Manihot reptans* Pax *20883*		
	I	*20883* Brazil *20883*	
R	*Manihot rubricaulis* M. Johnston *20883*		
	I	*20883* Mexico *20883*	
V	*Manihot sagittato-partita* Pohl *20883*		
	I	*20883* Brazil *20883*	
R	*Manihot sparsifolia* Pohl *20883*		
	R	*20883* Brazil *20883*	
R	*Manihot stipularis* Pax *20883*		
	R	*20883* Brazil *20883*	
R	*Manihot surinamensis* Rogers & Appan *20883*		
	I	*20883* Guyana *20883*	
	I	*20883* Suriname *20883*	
	I	*20883* Venezuela *20883*	
V	*Manihot tenella* Mueller von Argau *20883*		
	I	*20883* Brazil *20883*	
	I	*20883* Paraguay *20883*	
R	*Manihot tomentosa* ssp. *araliaefolia* (Pax) Rogers & Appan *20883*		
	R	*20883* Brazil *20883*	
R	*Manihot tripartita* ssp. *humilis* (Mueller von Argau) Rogers & Appan *20883*		
	I	*20883* Brazil *20883*	
V	*Manihot tripartita* ssp. *vestita* (S. Moore) Rogers & Appan *20883*		
	V	*20883* Brazil *20883*	
E	*Manihot tristis* ssp. *surumuensis* (Ule) Rogers & Appan *20883*		
	E	*20883* Brazil *20883*	
R	*Manihot tristis* ssp. *tristis* *20883*		
	I	*20883* Venezuela *20883*	
V	*Manihot variifolia* Pax *20883*		
	I	*20883* Paraguay *20883*	
E	*Manihot walkerae* Croizat *20883, 20850, 9702*		
	E	*20850* U.S. - Texas *20850*	
	I	*20883* Mexico *20883*	
	V	*9702* Mexico - Tamaulipas *9702*	
E	*Manihot warmingii* Mueller von Argau *20883*		
	I	*20883* Brazil *20883*	
E	*Manihot weddelliana* Baillon *20883*		
	E	*20883* Brazil *20883*	
R	*Manihot xavantinensis* Rogers & Appan *20883*		
	I	*20883* Brazil *20883*	
E	*Manihot zehntneri* Ule *20883*		
	E	*20883* Brazil *20883*	
I	*Margaritaria holteana* (Urb. & Ekman) Webster *11198*		
	I	Haiti *11198*	
R	*Meineckia bartlettii* (Standley) Webster *9700*		
	R	*11182* Belize *9700*	
I	*Meineckia filipes* (Balf. f.) Webster *15534*		
	I	*15534* Yemen - Socotra *15534*	
I	*Meineckia longipes* (Wight) Webster		
	I	India - Kerala (Quilon, Malabar)	
	I	India - Tamil Nadu	
R	*Micrantheum serpentinum* Orch. *20681*		
	R	*20681* Australia - Tasmania *20681*	
V	*Micrococca scariosa* Prain *20057*		
	V	*20057* Kenya (Pangani; Gongoni) *20057*	

	V	*20057* Tanzania (Zanzibar, Tanga & coast) *20900*	
I	*Micrococca wightii* (Wallich ex Hook.f.) Prain var. *hirsutum* (Hook.f.) Prain		
	I	India - Tamil Nadu	
I	*Moacroton leonis* Croizat *5607*		
	I	Cuba (Holguin) *5607*	
V	*Moacroton revolutus* Alain *5607*		
	V	*19105* Cuba (Habana, Matanzas) *5607*	
V	*Moacroton tetramerus* Borh. & Muniz *5607*		
	V	*19105* Cuba (Guantanamo) *5607*	
R	*Monadenium arborescens* Bally *19525*		
	R	*19035* Tanzania (Kilosa) *19525*	
R	*Monadenium coccineum* Pax *19525*		
	R	*19035* Tanzania (Masai, Tabora, Dodoma) *19525*	
R	*Monadenium ellenbeckii* N.E. Br. *15926*		
	R	*19035* Ethiopia (southern) *15926*	
	R	*19035* Kenya (northern) *15926*	
	I	*19035* Somalia (northern; isolated colonies) *15926*	
I	*Monadenium erubescens* (Rendle) N.E. Br.		
	I	*19035* Somalia *19035*	
I	*Monadenium guentheri* Pax var. *guentheri* *19035*		
	I	*19035* Kenya *19035*	
I	*Monadenium heteropodum* (Pax) N.E. Br. var. *heteropodum* *19525*		
	I	*19035* Tanzania (Lushoto) *19525*	
I	*Monadenium magnificum* E.A. Bruce *19525*		
	I	*19035* Tanzania (Mpwapwa) *19525*	
R	*Monadenium majus* N.E. Brown *15926*		
	R	*19035* Ethiopia *15926*	
I	*Monadenium montanum* Bally var. *rubellum* Bally *19035*		
	I	*19035* Kenya *19035*	
V	*Monadenium parviflorum* N.E. Br. *7865*		
	V	Malawi (Nyika Plateau) *7865*	
R	*Monadenium reflexum* Chiov. *19035*		
	R	*6087* Ethiopia *6087*	
	I	*19035* Kenya *19035*	
E	*Monadenium shebeliensis* M. Gilbert *19704*		
	E	*19704* Ethiopia (Harerge) *19704*	
R	*Monadenium spinescens* (Pax) Bally *15926*		
	R	*19035* Tanzania (Chunya) *19525*	
I	*Monadenium stellatum* Bally *19035*		
	I	*19035* Somalia *19035*	
E	*Myricanthe discolor* Airy Shaw *20893*		
	E	*20893* New Caledonia *20893*	
V	*Necepsia castaneifolia* (Baill.) Bouchat & J.Leonard ssp. *chirindica* *20909*		
	V	*20909* Zimbabwe *20909*	
V	*Neoroepera buxifolia* Muell. Arg. & F.Muell. *20681*		
	V	*20681* Australia - Queensland *20681*	
R	*Oligoceras eberhardtii* Gagnepain *6057*		
	R	Vietnam *6057*	
R	*Omalanthus stokesii* F.Brown *20845*		
	R	*20845* French Polynesia - Tubuai Is. (Rapa) *20845*	
I	*Omphalea megacarpa* Hemsl. *5932*		
	I	*5932* Trinidad & Tobago *5932*	

R   *Omphalea papuana* Pax & K.Hoffm. *20681*
     R   *20681*   Australia - Queensland *20681*

R   *Omphalea queenslandiae* F.Bailey *20681*
     R   *20681*   Australia - Queensland *20681*

R   *Ophellantha steyermarkii* Standley *9004*
     R   *11182*   Guatemala *9004*

R   *Oreoporanthera petalifera* Orch. & J.B.Davies *20681*
     R   *20681*   Australia - Tasmania *20681*

E   *Ostodes minor* (Thwaites) Muell.arg. *12838*
     E   *12838*   Sri Lanka *12838*

V   *Pedilanthus tithymaloides* ssp. *jamaicensis* (Millsp. & Britton) Dressler *20883*
     V   *20883*   Jamaica *20883*

E   *Pera aperta* Croiz. *20883, 9006*
     I   *20883*   Panama *20883*

R   *Phyllanthus abnormis* G.L. Webster var. *riograndensis* G.L. Webster *20850*
     R   *20850*   U.S. - Texas *20850*

R   *Phyllanthus adiantoides* Klotzsch *8679*
     R   *8679*   Guyana *8679*
     R   *8679*   Suriname *8679*

I   *Phyllanthus affinis* Muell.Arg. *10252*
     I   *16162*   Sri Lanka *10252*

I   *Phyllanthus anabaptizatus* Muell.Arg. *10252*
     I   *16162*   Sri Lanka *10252*

Ex   *Phyllanthus aoraiensis* Nadeaud *20845*
     Ex   *20845*   French Polynesia - Society Is. (Tahiti) *20845*

V   *Phyllanthus aoupinieensis* M. Schmid *20893*
     V   *20893*   New Caledonia *20893*

I   *Phyllanthus apiculatus* Urban *5607*
     I   *5607*   Cuba *5607*

R   *Phyllanthus arbuscula* (Sw.) J.F. Gmel. *20883*
     R   *20883*   Jamaica *20883*

R   *Phyllanthus arenarius* Beille *6057*
     I   *20985*   Vietnam *6057*

V   *Phyllanthus artensis* M. Schmid *20893*
     V   *20893*   New Caledonia *20893*

R   *Phyllanthus austinii* Standley *9004*
     R   *11182*   Guatemala *9004*

V   *Phyllanthus avanguiensis* M. Schmid *20893*
     V   *20893*   New Caledonia *20893*

V   *Phyllanthus axillaris* (Sw.) Mull. *20883, 13336*
     V   *13336*   Jamaica *20883*

R   *Phyllanthus balansae* Beille *6057*
     R   Vietnam *6057*

E   *Phyllanthus baraouaensis* M. Schmid *20893*
     E   *20893*   New Caledonia *20893*

E   *Phyllanthus barbarae* M. C. Johnst. *20883, 12067*
     I   *20883*   Mexico *20883*
     E   *11182*   Mexico - Tamaulipas (south-west) *12067*

E   *Phyllanthus borenensis* M. Gilbert *19704*
     E   *19704*   Ethiopia (Sidamo) *19704*

R   *Phyllanthus brassii* C.White *20681*
     R   *20681*   Australia - Queensland *20681*

V   *Phyllanthus buxoides* Guillaumin *20893*
     V   *20893*   New Caledonia *20893*

I   *Phyllanthus cardiophyllus* Urban *5607*
     I   *5607*   Cuba *5607*

R   *Phyllanthus carinatus* Beille *6057*
     R   Vietnam *6057*

I   *Phyllanthus casearoides* *20802*
     I   *20802*   New Caledonia *20802*

R   *Phyllanthus cauliflorus* (Sw.) Griseb. *20883, 13336*
     R   *13336*   Jamaica *20883*

V   *Phyllanthus cherrieri* M. Schmid *20893*
     V   *20893*   New Caledonia *20893*

V   *Phyllanthus chryseus* Howard *5607*
     V   *19105*   Cuba (Holguin) *5607*

V   *Phyllanthus cladanthus* Mull. *20883*
     V   *20883*   Jamaica *20883*

V   *Phyllanthus comosus* Urban *5607*
     V   *19105*   Cuba (Holguin) *5607*

Ex   *Phyllanthus comptonii* *20893*
     Ex   *20802*   New Caledonia *20802*

R   *Phyllanthus confusus* Brenan *7849*
     R   Malawi *7849*

V   *Phyllanthus conjugatus* M. Schmid *20893*
     V   *20893*   New Caledonia *20893*

R   *Phyllanthus consanguineus* Muell. Arg. *10082*
     R   *14233*   Réunion *10082*

V   *Phyllanthus cristalensis* Urban *5607*
     V   *19105*   Cuba (Santiago de Cuba; Holguin) *5607*

V   *Phyllanthus deciduiramus* Däniker *20893*
     V   *20893*   New Caledonia *20893*

V   *Phyllanthus deplanchei* (Baillon) Muell.Arg. *20802*
     V   *20893*   New Caledonia *20802*

V   *Phyllanthus dewildiorum* M. Gilbert *19704*
     V   *19704*   Ethiopia (Welega, Kefa.) *19704*

V   *Phyllanthus dumbeaensis* M. Schmid *20893*
     V   *20893*   New Caledonia *20893*

R   *Phyllanthus dumetosus* Poiret *10082*
     R   *5852*   Mauritius - Rodrigues *5852*

V   *Phyllanthus dzumacensis* M. Schmid *20893*
     V   *20893*   New Caledonia *20893*

E   *Phyllanthus echinospermus* C. Wright *5607*
     E   *19105*   Cuba (Pinar del Rio) *5607*

V   *Phyllanthus ericoides* Torr. *20883, 20850, 8058*
     E   *20850*   U.S. - Texas *20850*
     I   *20883*   Mexico *20883*

E   *Phyllanthus eximus* Webster & Proctor *20883*
     E   *20883*   Jamaica *20883*

I   *Phyllanthus fadyenii* Urb. *20883, 13336*
     I   *13336*   Jamaica *20883*

V   *Phyllanthus filicifolius* Gage
     V   Malaysia - Peninsular Malaysia (Langkawi, Kedah)

E   *Phyllanthus fractiflexus* M. Schmid *20893*
     E   *20893*   New Caledonia *20893*

I   *Phyllanthus glochidioides* Elm. *13833*
     I   *13833*   Philippines (low altitudes) *13833*

E   *Phyllanthus golonensis* M. Schmid *20893*
     E   *20893*   New Caledonia *20893*

V   *Phyllanthus guillauminii* Däniker *20893*
     V   *20893*   New Caledonia *20893*

E   *Phyllanthus gypsicola* McVaugh *9692*
     E   *11182*   Mexico - Colima *21204*

I   *Phyllanthus hakgalensis* Thwaites ex Trimen *10252*

I   *16162* Sri Lanka *10252*

E *Phyllanthus harrimanii* Webster *11197*
    E   *11182* Mexico *11197*

E *Phyllanthus hexadactylus* McVaugh *9692*
    E   *11182* Mexico *9692*

V *Phyllanthus houailouensis* M. Schmid *20893*
    V   *20893* New Caledonia *20893*

R *Phyllanthus hypospodius* F.Muell. *20681*
    R   *20681* Australia - Queensland *20681*

V *Phyllanthus jaffrei* M. Schmid *20893*
    V   *20893* New Caledonia *20893*

I *Phyllanthus jardinii* J.Mueller *20845*
    I   *20845* French Polynesia - Marquesas Is (Nuku Hiva) *20845*

Ex/E *Phyllanthus jaubertii* *20802*
    Ex/E *20802* New Caledonia *20802*

I *Phyllanthus kerrii* Airy Shaw *19120*
    I   *19120* Thailand *19120*

V *Phyllanthus koghiensis* Guillaumin *20893*
    V   *20893* New Caledonia *20893*

V *Phyllanthus koniamboensis* M. Schmid *20893*
    V   *20893* New Caledonia *20893*

V *Phyllanthus kouaouaensis* M. Schmid *20893*
    V   *20893* New Caledonia *20893*

R *Phyllanthus lanceolatus* Poiret *10082*
    R   *20771* Mauritius *10082*

R *Phyllanthus latifolius* Sw. *20883*
    R   *20883* Jamaica *20883*

V *Phyllanthus leibmannianus* (Small) G.L. Webster ssp. *platylepis* (Small) G.L. Webster *20850*
    V   *20850* U.S. - Florida *20850*

V *Phyllanthus longeramosus* Guillaumin ex M. Schmid *20893*
    V   *20893* New Caledonia *20893*

V *Phyllanthus luciliae* M. Schmid *20893*
    V   *20893* New Caledonia *20893*

V *Phyllanthus mandjeliaensis* M. Schmid *20893*
    V   *20893* New Caledonia *20893*

V *Phyllanthus margaretae* M. Schmid *20893*
    V   *20893* New Caledonia *20893*

E *Phyllanthus mauritianus* H.H. Johnston *10082*
    E   *20771* Mauritius *10082*

E *Phyllanthus mcphersonii* M. Schmid *20893*
    E   *20893* New Caledonia *20893*

R *Phyllanthus megapodus* Webster *10200*
    R   Dominica (only around Diablotins) *10200*
    I   *19001* Martinique *19001*

V *Phyllanthus meuieensis* M. Schmid *20893*
    V   *20893* New Caledonia *20893*

E *Phyllanthus mickelii* McVaugh *9692*
    E   *11182* Mexico *9692*

E *Phyllanthus minarum* Standley & Steyerm. *9004*
    E   *11182* Guatemala *9004*

R *Phyllanthus montanus* (Sw.) Sw. *20883*
    R   *20883* Jamaica *20883*

V *Phyllanthus moratii* M. Schmid *20893*
    V   *20893* New Caledonia *20893*

E *Phyllanthus nanus* Millsp. *5607*

E   *19105* Cuba (Juventud Is.) *5607*

E *Phyllanthus narayanaswamii* Gamble *11494*
    E   *11494* India - Andhra Pradesh (east Ghats) *11494*

E *Phyllanthus natoensis* M. Schmid *20893*
    E   *20893* New Caledonia *20893*

V *Phyllanthus nitens* M. Schmid *20893*
    V   *20893* New Caledonia *20893*

V *Phyllanthus nothisii* M. Schmid *20893*
    V   *20893* New Caledonia *20893*

E *Phyllanthus oppositifolius* Baillon ex Muell. Arg. *10082*
    E   *20771* Mauritius *10082*

R *Phyllanthus orientalis* (Craib) Airy Shaw *19120*
    R   *19120* Thailand *19120*

E *Phyllanthus paucitepalus* M. Schmid *20893*
    E   *20893* New Caledonia *20893*

V *Phyllanthus peltatus* Guillaumin *20893*
    V   *20893* New Caledonia *20893*

V *Phyllanthus pentaphyllus* C. Wright ex Griseb. var. *floridanus* Webster *20850*
    V   *20850* U.S. - Florida *20850*

E *Phyllanthus petchikaraensis* M. Schmid *20893*
    E   *20893* New Caledonia *20893*

R *Phyllanthus phillyreifolius* Poiret var. *commersonii* Muell.-Arg. *10082*
    R   *20771* Mauritius *10082*

E *Phyllanthus phillyreifolius* Poiret var. *gracilipes* Coode *10082*
    E   *20771* Mauritius *10082*

E *Phyllanthus phillyreifolius* Poiret var. *stylifer* Coode *10082*
    E   *20771* Mauritius *10082*

R *Phyllanthus phillyreifolius* Poiret var. *telfairianus* Muell.-Arg. *10082*
    R   *20771* Mauritius *10082*

E *Phyllanthus phillyreifolius* Poiret var. *triangularis* Muell.-Arg. *10082*
    E   *20771* Mauritius *10082*

E *Phyllanthus pileostigma* Coode *10082*
    E   *20771* Mauritius *10082*

E *Phyllanthus pindaiensis* M.Schmid *20802*
    E   *20893* New Caledonia *20802*

E *Phyllanthus pinjenensis* M. Schmid *20893*
    E   *20893* New Caledonia *20893*

E *Phyllanthus pinosius* Urban *5607*
    E   *19105* Cuba (Juventud Is.) *5607*

V *Phyllanthus polygynus* M. Schmid *20893*
    V   *20893* New Caledonia *20893*

V *Phyllanthus poumensis* Guillaumin *20893*
    V   *20893* New Caledonia *20893*

E *Phyllanthus proctoris* Webster *20883*
    E   *20883* Jamaica *20883*

V *Phyllanthus profusus* N.E.Br. *20858*
    V   *20858* Ghana *20858*
    V   *20858* Guinea *7926*
    V   *20858* Liberia *7926*

V *Phyllanthus pterocladus* S. Moore *20893*
    V   *20893* New Caledonia *20893*

E   *Phyllanthus pulverulentus* Urban *5607*
     E   *19105*   Cuba (Santiago de Cuba) *5607*

V   *Phyllanthus quintuplinervis* M. Schmid *20893*
     V   *20893*   New Caledonia *20893*

E   *Phyllanthus revaughanii* Coode *10082*
     E   *20771*   Mauritius *10082*

V   *Phyllanthus rhodocladus* S. Moore *20893*
     V   *20893*   New Caledonia *20893*

E   *Phyllanthus rozennae* M. Schmid *20893*
     E   *20893*   New Caledonia *20893*

R   *Phyllanthus rubescens* Beille *6057*
     R   Vietnam *6057*

R   *Phyllanthus sacleuxii* Radc.-Sm. *20057*
     R   *20057*   Kenya (Shimba, Taita & Salgalla hills) *20057*

R   *Phyllanthus sauropodoides* Airy Shaw *20681*
     R   *20681*   Australia - Queensland *20681*

E   *Phyllanthus standleyi* McVaugh *9692*
     E   *11182*   Mexico *9692*

E   *Phyllanthus stenophyllus* Guillaumin *20893*
     E   *20893*   New Caledonia *20893*

V   *Phyllanthus stipitatus* M. Schmid *20893*
     V   *20893*   New Caledonia *20893*

R   *Phyllanthus talbotii* Sedw. *14782*
     R   *14782*   India - Karnataka *14782*

V   *Phyllanthus tangoensis* M. Schmid *20893*
     V   *20893*   New Caledonia *20893*

V   *Phyllanthus tiebaghiensis* M. Schmid *20893*
     V   *20893*   New Caledonia *20893*

V   *Phyllanthus tireliae* M. Schmid *20893*
     V   *20893*   New Caledonia *20893*

V   *Phyllanthus tixieri* M. Schmid *20893*
     V   *20893*   New Caledonia *20893*

I   *Phyllanthus tuerckheimii* Webster *9704*
     I   *11182*   Guatemala *9704*

E   *Phyllanthus unifoliatus* M.Schmid *20802*
     E   *20893*   New Caledonia *20802*

V   *Phyllanthus unioensis* M. Schmid *20893*
     V   *20893*   New Caledonia *20893*

R   *Phyllanthus urceolatus* Baillon *20845*
     R   *20845*   French Polynesia - Society Is. *20845*

E   *Phyllanthus valerii* Standley *9037*
     E   *11182*   Costa Rica *9037*

E   *Phyllanthus veillonii* M. Schmid *20893*
     E   *20893*   New Caledonia *20893*

V   *Phyllanthus virgultiramus* Däniker *20893*
     V   *20893*   New Caledonia *20893*

R   *Phyllanthus winitii* Airy Shaw *19120*
     R   *19120*   Thailand *19120*

R   *Picrodendron baccatum* (L.) Krug & Urb. *20883*
     R   *20883*   Jamaica *20883*

V   *Platygyne leonis* Alain *5607*
     V   *19105*   Cuba (Guantanamo) *5607*

I   *Podadenia sapida* Thwaites *10252*
     I   *16162*   Sri Lanka *10252*

V   *Podadenia thwaitesii* (Baill.) Muell.arg. *12838*
     V   *12838*   Sri Lanka *12838*

V   *Pseudagrostistachys africana* (Muell. Arg.) Pax & K.

Hoffm. *7926*
     V   *20858*   Cameroon *18326*
     V   *20858*   Equatorial Guinea (Fernando Po) *7926*
     V   *20858*   Equatorial Guinea - Bioko *20274*
     V   *20858*   Ghana *6072*
     V   *20858*   Nigeria *7926*
     V   *20858*   Sao Tome & Principe *7926*

R   *Pseudanthus divaricatissimus* (Muell.Arg.)
Benth. *20681*
     I   *20681*   Australia - New South Wales *20681*
     I   *20681*   Australia - Victoria *20681*

R   *Pseudanthus micranthus* Benth. *20681*
     R   *20681*   Australia - South Australia *20681*

Ex   *Pseudanthus nematophorus* F.Muell. *20681, 14223*
     Ex   *20681*   Australia - Western Australia *20681*

I   *Pseudoglochidion anamalayanum* Gamble *14782*
     I   *14782*   India - Tamil Nadu *14782*

I   *Psilostachys sericea* (Koen. ex Roxb.) Hook.f.
     I   India - Andhra Pradesh (Nellore)
     I   India - Gujarat
     I   India - Kerala

I   *Ptychopyxis plagiocarpa* Airy Shaw *19120*
     I   *19120*   Thailand *19120*

I   *Putranjiva zeylanica* (Thwaites) Muell.Arg. *10252*
     I   *16162*   Sri Lanka *10252*

I   *Reidia beddomei* Gamble
     I   India - Kerala (Travancore Hills)
     I   India - Tamil Nadu (Tirunelveli District)

I   *Reidia gageana* Gamble
     I   India - Kerala (Travancore Hills)
     I   India - Tamil Nadu (Tirunelveli Hills)

I   *Reidia megacarpa* Gamble
     I   India - Tamil Nadu (Devala, south east Wynaad)

I   *Reidia stipulacea* Gamble
     I   India - Tamil Nadu

V   *Reutealis trisperma* (Blanco) Airy Shaw *7730*
     V   *15960*   Philippines *7730*

R   *Richeria grandis* Vahl. *20883*
     I   *20883*   Dominica *20883*
     I   *20883*   Grenada *20883*

V   *Ricinocarpos gloria-medii* J.H.Willis *20681*
     V   *20681*   Australia - Northern Territory *20681*

V   *Ricinocarpos trichophorus* Muell. Arg. *20681*
     V   *20681*   Australia - Western Australia *20681*

R   *Ricinocarpus speciosus* Muell. Arg. *20681*
     I   *20681*   Australia - New South Wales *20681*
     I   *20681*   Australia - Queensland *20681*

R   *Rockinghamia brevipes* Airy Shaw *20681*
     R   *20681*   Australia - Queensland *20681*

V   *Sapium aubrevillei* Leandri *15970*
     V   *20858*   Côte d'Ivoire *20274*
     V   *20858*   Ghana (Atewa) *15970*

R   *Sapium harrisii* Urb. *20883*
     R   *20883*   Jamaica *20883*

R   *Sapium klotzschianum* (Müll. Arg.) Huber *20883*
     I   *20883*   Brazil *20883*
     R   *20883*   Paraguay *20883*

V   *Sapium laurocerasus* Desf. *20883*
     I   *20883*   Puerto Rico *20883*

I   *Sapium luzonicum* Merr. *12983*
     I   *15960*   Philippines *12983*

R   *Sapium paucinervium* Hemsley *8679*
    R   *19954*   French Guiana *18176*
    R   *8679*   Guyana *8679*
    R   *8679*   Suriname *8679*

R   *Sapium solsii* Huft *11505*
    R   *11504*   Ecuador *11505*

I   *Sapium triloculare* Pax & Hoffm. *19524*
    I   *20057*   Kenya (Pangani rocks) *20057*
    I   *5926*   Tanzania (Uzaramo, Masai, Newala) *19524*

I   *Sauropus assimilis* Thwaites *10252*
    I   *16162*   Sri Lanka *10252*

I   *Sauropus calcareus* M.R. Henderson
    I   Malaysia - Peninsular Malaysia

I   *Sauropus retroversus* Wight *10252*
    I   *16162*   Sri Lanka *10252*

R   *Savia bahamensis* Britt. *20850*
    V   *20850*   U.S. - Florida *20850*

E   *Savia fadenii* R.-Sm. *6073*
    E   *20057*   Kenya (Pangani; Cha Simba; Marafa; Chonyi) *17435*

V   *Scagea oligostemon* (Guillaumin) McPherson *20893*
    V   *20893*   New Caledonia *20893*

R   *Sebastiania alpina* (F. & R.) Pax & K. Hoffm. *20883, 13336*
    R   *13336*   Jamaica *20883*

E   *Sebastiania crenulata* Proctor *20883, 13336*
    E   *13336*   Jamaica *20883*

R   *Sebastiania discolor* (Spreng.) Müll. Arg. *20883*
    I   *20883*   Argentina *20883*
    I   *20883*   Brazil *20883*
    R   *20883*   Paraguay *20883*

V   *Sebastiania fasciculata* (Millsp.) Pax & K. Hoffm. *20883, 13336*
    V   *13336*   Jamaica *20883*

E   *Sebastiania howardiana* Proctor *20883, 13336*
    E   *13336*   Jamaica *20883*

V   *Sebastiania lesteri* Proctor *20883*
    V   *20883*   Jamaica *20883*

E   *Sebastiania lesteri* Proctor var. *glabrata* Proctor *20883, 13336*
    E   *13336*   Jamaica *20883*

E   *Sebastiania lesteri* Proctor var. *lesteri* *19890*
    E   *19890*   Jamaica (Clarendon) *19486*

R   *Sebastiania nervosa* (Müll. Arg.) Müll. Arg. *20883*
    I   *20883*   Brazil *20883*
    R   *20883*   Paraguay *20883*

V   *Sebastiania spicata* (Millsp.) Pax & K. Hoffm. *20883, 13336*
    E   *20883*   Jamaica (St. Ann, Clarendon) *20883*

R   *Sebastiania subulata* (Müll. Arg.) Pax in Engl. *20883*
    I   *20883*   Brazil *20883*
    R   *20883*   Paraguay *20883*

I   *Securinega flexuosa* Muell.-Arg. *13780*
    I   *15960*   Philippines *13780*

R   *Stachystemon axillaris* A.S.George *20681*
    R   *20681*   Australia - Western Australia *20681*

V   *Stillingia sylvatica* L. ssp. *tenuis* (Small) D.J. Rogers *20850*
    V   *20850*   U.S. - Florida *20850*

R   *Synadenium compactum* N.E.Br. var. *compactum* *20556, 20057*
    R   *20057*   Kenya (Kamba, Embu) *20057*

R   *Tetracoccus dioicus* Parry *20883, 20850, 8058*
    V   *20850*   U.S. - California *20850*
    I   *20883*   Mexico *20883*

E   *Tetracoccus ilicifolius* Coville & Gilman *20850*
    E   *20850*   U.S. - California *20850*

E   *Thecacoris usumbarensis* Verdc. *19524*
    E   *20057*   Kenya (Kilifi) *19524*
    E   *20057*   Tanzania (Usumbara Mts) *19524*

V   *Tragia abortiva* M. Gilbert *19704*
    V   *19704*   Ethiopia (Gamo Gofa) *19704*

V   *Tragia ashiae* M. Gilbert *19704*
    V   *19704*   Ethiopia (Shewa Upland, Bale.) *19704*

E   *Tragia crenata* M. Gilbert *19704*
    E   *19704*   Ethiopia (Bale) *19704*

V   *Tragia polygonoides* Prain *7926*
    V   Côte d'Ivoire (Bouroukrou) *7926*

V   *Tragia saxicola* Small *20850*
    V   *20850*   U.S. - Florida *20850*

E   *Tragia triumfettoides* M. Gilbert *19704*
    E   *19704*   Ethiopia (Sidamo) *19704*

E   *Tragia uncinata* M. Gilbert *19704*
    E   *19704*   Ethiopia *19704*

I   *Trigonostemon chatterjii* Deb
    I   India - Meghalaya (Khasi hills)

E   *Trigonostemon cherrieri* Veillon *20802*
    E   *20893*   New Caledonia *20802*

I   *Trigonostemon diplopetalus* Thwaites *10252*
    I   *16162*   Sri Lanka *10252*

R   *Trigonostemon fragilis* (Gagnepain) Airy-Shaw *6057*
    V   *20985*   Vietnam *6057*

V   *Trigonostemon inopinatus* Airy Shaw *20681*
    V   *20681*   Australia - Queensland *20681*

I   *Trigonostemon merrillii* Elm. *13833*
    I   *13833*   Philippines (Palawan) *13833*

R   *Trigonostemon pierrei* Gagnepain *6057*
    R   Vietnam *6057*

R   *Victorinia regina* (Leon) Leon *11840*
    R   *19105*   Cuba (Guantanamo) *11840*

V   *Wetria australiensis* P.I.Forster *20681*
    V   *20681*   Australia - Queensland *20681*

R   *Whyanbeelia terrae-reginae* Airy Shaw & B.Hyland *20681*
    R   *20681*   Australia - Queensland *20681*

V   *Zimmermannia ovata* E.A. Bruce *20057*
    V   *20057*   Kenya *20057*

Fagaceae

Number of genera:	6-8	
Number of species:	800	
Recorded threatened species:	96	(12%)

Cosmopolitan, except tropical and South Africa.

R   *Castanea pumila* (L.)Miller var. *ozarkensis* (Ashe) Tucker *20850*
    I   *20850*   U.S. - Alabama *20850*
    R   *20850*   U.S. - Arkansas *20850*
    I   *20850*   U.S. - Louisiana *20850*

I	20850	U.S. - Mississippi	20850
V	20850	U.S. - Missouri	20850
V	20850	U.S. - Oklahoma	20850

E *Castanopsis concinna* Hance *17617*

E	17617	China - Guangdong	11139
E	17617	China - Guangxi (Fangchen)	11139
E	17617	Hong Kong	17617

R *Castanopsis kusanoi* Hayata *20511*

R	20511	Taiwan	20511

R *Castanopsis sempervirens* (Kellogg) Dudley ex Merriam *20850*

I	20850	U.S. - California	20850
I	20850	U.S. - Nevada	20850
I	20850	U.S. - Oregon	20850

R *Castanopsis stellato-spina* Hayata *20511*

R	20511	Taiwan	20511

R *Cyclobalanopsis hypophaea* (Hayata) Kudo *20511*

R		Taiwan (south-east)	

E *Cyclobalanopsis repandifolia* (Liao) Liao *20854*

E	20854	Taiwan (south-east)	20854

E *Fagus hayatae* Palibin ex Hayata *17617*

E	20854	Taiwan (Taoyuan; Yilan)	11139

R *Fagus japonica* Maxim. var. *multinervis* (Nakai) Y.N. Lee

R		Korea, South (Ulnungdo)	17577

I *Lithocarpus craibianus* Barnett *19120*

I	19120	Thailand	19120

I *Lithocarpus echinops* Hjelmquiot *19120*

I	19120	Thailand	19120

V *Lithocarpus ovalis* (Blanco) Rehd. *13780*

V	15960	Philippines	13780

R *Lithocarpus siamensis* A. Camus *19120*

R	19120	Thailand (Khao Luang)	19120

V *Nothofagus alessandrii* Espinosa *20883*

V	20883	Chile	20883

R *Nothofagus baumanniae* (Baum.-Bodenh.) Steenis *20893*

R	20893	New Caledonia	20893

V *Nothofagus discoidea* (Baum.-Bodenh.) Steenis *20893*

V	20893	New Caledonia	20893

V *Nothofagus glauca* (Philippi) Krasser *15088*

V	13875	Chile	13875

V *Nothofagus leonii* Espin. *15088*

V	13875	Chile	13875

I *Nothofagus nuda* *21318*

I	21318	Papua New Guinea	21318

V *Nothofagus obliqua* var. *macrocarpa* (A.DC.) Reiche *20883*

V	20883	Chile	20883

I *Nothofagus womersleyi* *21318*

I	21318	Indonesia - Irian Jaya	21318

E *Pasania dodonaeifolia* Hayata *20854*

E	20854	Taiwan	20854

V *Pasania formosana* (Skan) Schottky *20854*

V	20854	Taiwan (Heng-ch'un)	20854

V *Pasania nantoensis* (Hayata) Schott. *20511*

V	20511	Taiwan	20511

I *Pasania shinsuiensis* (Hayata & Kaneh.) Nakai *20511*

I	20511	Taiwan	20511

E *Quercus acerifolia* (Palmer) Stoynoff & Hess *20850, 20840*

E	20850	U.S. - Arkansas (Logan, Sebastian & Scott Co.)	21003

V *Quercus acuminata* Roxb. *14872*

V	14872	Bangladesh	14872

R *Quercus arkansana* Sarg. *20850*

V	20850	U.S. - Alabama	20850
R	20850	U.S. - Arkansas	20850
E	20850	U.S. - Florida	20850
V	20850	U.S. - Georgia	20850
V	20850	U.S. - Louisiana	20850
I	20850	U.S. - Mississippi	20850
I	20850	U.S. - Texas	20850

I *Quercus basaseachicensis* C.H. Muller *20283*

I	20283	Mexico - Chihuahua	20283
I	21046	Mexico - Durango	21046

R *Quercus benthami* A.DC. *20883*

R	20883	Guatemala	20883
E	20883	Mexico	20883
?		Mexico - Chiapas	21046
?		Mexico - Oaxaca	21046

R *Quercus borucasana* Trel. *20883*

V	20883	Costa Rica	20883
V	20883	Guatemala	20883

Ex/E *Quercus boyntoni* Beadle *20850*

Ex/E	20850	U.S. - Alabama	20850
I	20850	U.S. - Georgia	20850
I	21003	U.S. - Louisiana	21003
I	21003	U.S. - Mississippi	21003
Ex/E	20850	U.S. - Texas	20850

R *Quercus brandegeei* Goldman *21046, 9002*

R	20283	Mexico - Baja California Peninsula (Cape region)	20283

R *Quercus brenesii* Trel. *20883, 17459*

V	20283	Costa Rica	20883

R *Quercus bumelioides* Liebm. *11215*

R	20283	Costa Rica	11215
R	20283	Guatemala	16826
R	20283	Honduras	16826
R	20283	Nicaragua	16826
R	20283	Panama	11215

I *Quercus cedrosensis* C.H. Muller *9002*

I	20840	Mexico (including Cedros Island)	20283
I	20840	Mexico - Baja California Peninsula (del Norte)	20283

I *Quercus chuhuichupensis* C.H. Muller *20283*

I	20283	Mexico - Chihuahua	20283

I *Quercus convallata* Trel. *11503*

I	20283	Mexico - Jalisco	11503
I	20283	Mexico - Nayarit	11503

V *Quercus costaricensis* Liebman *20883, 9037*

V	20883	Costa Rica	20883

R *Quercus crispifolia* Trel. *20883*

I	20883	El Salvador	20883
R	20883	Guatemala	20883
V	20883	Mexico	20883

R *Quercus crispipilis* var. *pannosifolia* Muller *20883*

R	20883	Guatemala	20883
E	20883	Mexico	20883

R *Quercus deliquescens* C.H. Muller *9708*

R	11215	Mexico - Chihuahua	9708

R *Quercus depressa* Humb. & Bonpl. *9707*

R	11215	Mexico	9707
R	20283	Mexico - Hidalgo	20283
R	20283	Mexico - Mexico D.F.	20283

R	20283 Mexico - Oaxaca *20283*	
R	20283 Mexico - Puebla *20283*	
R	20283 Mexico - Veracruz *20283*	
V	***Quercus depressipes*** **Trel.** *20850, 11215*	
E	20850 U.S. - Texas (Davis Mts.) *21003*	
R	*11215* Mexico *11215*	
R	20283 Mexico - Chihuahua *20283*	
R	20283 Mexico - Durango *20283*	
R	20283 Mexico - Jalisco *20283*	
R	20283 Mexico - Zacatecas *20283*	

R ***Quercus devia*** **Goldman** *9002*

    R   *11215* Mexico - Baja California Peninsula (Cape region.) *20283*

V ***Quercus dumosa*** **Nutt.** *20850, 20283*

    E   20850 U.S. - California *20850*

    I   20840 Mexico - Baja California Peninsula (del Norte) *20283*

I ***Quercus durata*** *20916*

    I   20931 U.S. - California (coastal ranges) *20916*

R ***Quercus engelmannii*** **Greene** *20850*

    R   20850 U.S. - California (southern) *20850*

    I   20283 Mexico - Baja California Peninsula (del Norte) *20283*

I ***Quercus excelsa*** **Liebm.** *11503*

    I   20283 Mexico - Jalisco *11503*

    I   20283 Mexico - Veracruz *11503*

R ***Quercus flagellifera*** **Trel.** *20883*

    R   20883 Guatemala *20883*

V ***Quercus fulva*** **Liebm.** *9706*

    V   *11215* Mexico *9706*

    V   20283 Mexico - Chihuahua *20283*

    V   20283 Mexico - Durango *20283*

    V   20283 Mexico - Sinaloa *20283*

I ***Quercus galeanensis*** **C.H. Muller** *20283*

    I   20283 Mexico - Nuevo Leon *20283*

    I   21046 Mexico - Tamaulipas *21046*

R ***Quercus germana*** **Schltr. & Cham.** *11215*

    R   *11215* Mexico (northeastern and eastern) *20283*

E ***Quercus graciliformis*** **C.H. Muller** *20850*

    E   20850 U.S. - Texas (Chisos Mts.) *21003*

I ***Quercus gravesii*** **Sudworth** *20283*

    I   20283 U.S. - Texas *20283*

    I   20283 Mexico - Coahuila *20283*

V ***Quercus gulielmi-treleasei*** **C.H. Mull.** *20883*

    V   20883 Costa Rica *20883*

    E   20883 Panama *20883*

V ***Quercus hinckleyi*** **C.H. Muller** *20850, 17695*

    V   20850 U.S. - Texas (Solitario Peak, Presidio Co.) *21003*

    V   20283 Mexico (northern) *20283*

E ***Quercus hintonii*** **Warb.** *9707*

    E   21046 Mexico - Mexico State *21046*

V ***Quercus hintoniorum*** **Nixon & Müller** *21046*

    V   21046 Mexico - Nuevo Leon (Sierra Lamata) *21046*

V ***Quercus hondai*** **Makino** *20626*

    V   10572 Japan *20626*

R ***Quercus hypoxantha*** **Trel.** *9707*

    R   *11215* Mexico *9707*

    R   20283 Mexico - Coahuila *20283*

    R   20283 Mexico - Nuevo Leon *20283*

I ***Quercus imeretina*** **Stev. ex Woronow** *5942*

    I   5942 Russia - North Caucasus *5942*

    I   5942 Georgia *5942*

I ***Quercus inopina*** *20916*

    I   *20931* U.S. - Florida (central) *20916*

R ***Quercus invaginata*** **Trel.** *11215*

    R   *11215* Mexico *11215*

    R   20283 Mexico - Coahuila *20283*

I ***Quercus liebmannii*** **Oersted et Trel.** *20283*

    I   20283 Mexico - Oaxaca *20283*

I ***Quercus listeoides*** **Dunn** *20283*

    I   20283 Hong Kong (Lantau Is.) *20283*

V ***Quercus macdonaldii*** **Greene** *20850*

    I   20850 U.S. - California (Channel Is. (exc. San Clemente)) *21003*

V ***Quercus macdougallii*** **Martínez** *11215*

    V   20283 Mexico - Oaxaca *20283*

R ***Quercus martinezii*** **C.H. Muller** *9706*

    R   *11215* Mexico *9706*

    R   20283 Mexico - Jalisco *20283*

    R   20283 Mexico - Michoacan *20283*

I ***Quercus miquihuanensis*** **K.C. Nixon & C.H. Muller** *20283*

    I   20283 Mexico - Nuevo Leon *20283*

    I   20283 Mexico - Tamaulipas *20283*

V ***Quercus oglethorpensis*** **Duncan** *20850, 20283*

    V   20850 U.S. - Georgia (northeastern) *20850*

    V   20850 U.S. - Mississippi *20850*

    R   20850 U.S. - South Carolina *20850*

I ***Quercus parvula*** **Greene var.** ***parvula*** *19002*

    I   20915 U.S. - California (Santa Cruz Is. & Santa Barbara Co.) *21003*

R ***Quercus peninsularis*** **Trel.** *9002*

    R   20283 Mexico - Baja California Peninsula (del Norte) *20283*

R ***Quercus planipocula*** **Trel.** *9706*

    R   *11215* Mexico *9706*

    R   20283 Mexico - Guerrero *20283*

    R   20283 Mexico - Michoacan *20283*

    R   20283 Mexico - Nayarit *20283*

    R   20283 Mexico - Sinaloa *20283*

I ***Quercus praeco*** **Trel.** *20283*

    I   20283 Mexico - Jalisco *20283*

    I   20283 Mexico - Nayarit *20283*

R ***Quercus praineana*** **Trel.** *9706*

    V   *11215* Mexico *9706*

    R   20283 Mexico - Jalisco *20283*

    R   20283 Mexico - Sinaloa *20283*

R ***Quercus purulhana*** **Trel.** *9004*

    R   *11215* Belize *9004*

    R   *11215* Guatemala *9004*

    R   *11215* Honduras *9004*

    R   *11215* Nicaragua *9004*

R ***Quercus rapurahuensis*** **Pittier ex Trel.** *9037*

    R   *11215* Costa Rica *9037*

    R   *11215* Panama *9006*

I ***Quercus robur*** **ssp.** ***imeretina*** **(Steven ex Woronow) Menitsky** *20283*

    I   20283 Russian Federation (in Georgia, Caucasus) *20627*

R ***Quercus rysophylla*** **Weath.** *9707*

    R   *11215* Mexico *9707*

    R   20283 Mexico - Nuevo Leon *20283*

    R   20283 Mexico - San Luis Potosi *20283*

    R   20283 Mexico - Tamaulipas *20283*

E ***Quercus sebifera*** **Trel.** *20883, 11215*

    E   20883 Mexico *20883*

	I	20283	Mexico - Chiapas	20283

I		*Quercus sicula* Borzí	20171
	I		Italy - Sicily	8000

R		*Quercus skinneri* Benth.	11215
	R	20283	El Salvador	20283
	R	11215	Guatemala	11215
	R	20283	Honduras	20283
	R	11215	Mexico - Chiapas	21046

R		*Quercus skutchii* Trel.	11215
	R	11215	Guatemala	11215
	R	11215	Mexico	11215
	R	20283	Mexico - Chiapas	20283

I		*Quercus subspathulata* Trel.	11503
	I	20840	Mexico - Durango (southern)	20283
	I	20840	Mexico - Jalisco	20283
	I	20840	Mexico - Nayarit	20283
	I	20840	Mexico - Sinaloa (northern)	20283

E		*Quercus tardifolia* C.H. Muller	21046, 20850
	E	20850	U.S. - Texas (Chisos Mts.)	21003

R		*Quercus tarokoensis* Hayata	20283
	R	20511	Taiwan	20283

R		*Quercus tomentella* Engelm.	20883, 20850, 8058
	V	20283	Mexico - Guadelupe	20283
	R	20850	U.S. - California (Channel Is.)	21003

E		*Quercus tonduzii* Seemen	20883, 9037
	R	20283	Costa Rica	20883

I		*Quercus toumeyi* Sarg.	20283
	I	20283	U.S. - Arizona	20283
	I	20283	U.S. - New Mexico	20283
	I	20283	Mexico - Chihuahua	20283
	I	20283	Mexico - Sonora	20283

I		*Quercus undata* Trel.	20283
	I	20283	Mexico - Durango	20283

R		*Quercus uxoris* McVaugh	9706
	R	11215	Mexico	9706
	R	20283	Mexico - Colima	20283
	R	20283	Mexico - Guerrero	20283
	R	20283	Mexico - Jalisco	20283

E		*Quercus vicentensis* Trelease	20883, 20283
	R	20283	El Salvador	20883
	R	20283	Guatemala	20283
	R	20283	Mexico	20283

E		*Quercus xalapensis* Humb. & Bonpl.	20283
	E	20283	Mexico - Veracruz	20283

E		*Quercus zempoaltepecana* Trel.	20283
	E	20283	Mexico - Oaxaca	20283

V		*Trigonobalanus excelsa* Loz.-Contr.,Hern.Com.&Henao-S.
	V	19353 Colombia 19353

Flacourtiaceae

Number of genera:	85	
Number of species:	800	
Recorded threatened species:	196	(24%)

Tropical.

V		*Abatia canescens* (Gardner) Eichler	20883
	I	20883	Ecuador	20883
	I	20883	Peru	20883

E		*Abatia glabra* Sleumer	20883
	I	20883	Brazil	20883

E		*Abatia microphylla* Taubert	20883
	I	20883	Brazil	20883

R		*Abatia rugosa* Ruiz & Pavon	20883

	I	20883	Peru	20883

R		*Abatia spicata* (Turczaninov) Sleumer	20883
	I	20883	Peru	20883

I		*Asteriastigma macrocarpa* Beddome	
	I		India - Kerala	

R		*Azara salicifolia* Grisebach	20883
	I	20883	Argentina	20883
	I	20883	Bolivia	20883

R		*Azara serrata* var. *fernandeziana* (Gay) Reiche	20883, 19116
	V	19116	Chile - Juan Fernandez Is. (R.Crusoe Is.)	19116
	V	20883	Chile	20883

R		*Baileyoxylon lanceolatum* C.White	20681
	R	20681	Australia - Queensland	20681

R		*Banara acunae* Borh. & Muniz	5607
	R	19105	Cuba (Pinar del Rio)	5607

R		*Banara axilliflora* Sleumer	20883
	I	20883	Brazil	20883
	I	20883	Peru	20883

V		*Banara brasiliensis* (Schott) Bentham	20883
	I	20883	Brazil	20883

V		*Banara brittonii* Roig	20883
	I	20883	Cuba	20883

E		*Banara cordifolia* Urban & Ekman	20883
	I	20883	Dominican Republic	20883
	E	20883	Haiti (Port au Prince to Jacmel)	21008

R		*Banara domingensis* Bentham	20883
	I	20883	Dominican Republic (Sta. Domingo, Samaná peninsula)	21008
	I	20883	Haiti (Rivière Froide, Port au Prince)	21008

E		*Banara excisa* Urban & Ekman	20883
	E	20883	Haiti (Morne La Cldre, St Michel)	21008

R		*Banara ibaguensis* Tulasne	20883
	I	20883	Colombia	20883

V		*Banara kuhlmannii* (Sleumer) Sleumer	20883
	I	20883	Brazil	20883

V		*Banara larensis* Steyermark	20883
	I	20883	Venezuela	20883

E		*Banara leptophylla* Urban & Ekman	20883
	E	20883	Haiti (Morne Brigand Bayeux)	21008

R		*Banara orinocensis* (Cuatrecasas) Sleumer	20883
	I	20883	Colombia	20883
	I	20883	Venezuela	20883

V		*Banara portoricensis* Krug & Urban	20883
	I	20883	Puerto Rico	20883

E		*Banara quinquenervis* Urban & Ekman	20883
	E	20883	Haiti (Morne Palmiste, Port de Paix)	21008

R		*Banara regia* Sandwith	20883
	I	20883	Ecuador	20883

R		*Banara riparia* Sleumer	20883
	I	20883	Ecuador	20883

R		*Banara riscoi* Borh. & Muniz	5607
	R	19105	Cuba (Juventud Is.)	5607

E		*Banara saxicola* Urban & Ekman	20883
	E	20883	Haiti (Rivière Froide, Port au Prince)	21008

E		*Banara selleana* Urban & Ekman	20883
	?		Dominican Republic (Banano, Pedernales)	

21008
I   *20883*   Haiti (Massif de la Selle) *21008*

R   *Banara serrata* (Vellozo) Warburg *20883*
I   *20883*   Brazil *20883*

V   *Banara splendens* Urban *20883*
              Dominican Republic (Isabel de Torres)
              21008
I   *20883*   Haiti (Mirebalais, Grand Bois) *21008*

E   *Banara trinitatis* Sleumer *20883*
E   *20883*   Brazil *20883*

R   *Banara ulmifolia* (H. B. K.) Bentham *20883*
I   *20883*   Colombia *20883*

E   *Banara vanderbiltii* Urban *20883, 7999*
E   *20883*   Puerto Rico (hills west of Bayamon)
              20883

E   *Bartholomaea mollis* Standley & Steyermark *20883,*
     9004
I   *20883*   Guatemala *20883*

R   *Bartholomaea sessiliflora* (Standley) Standley &
     Steyermark *20883*
I   *20883*   Belize *20883*
I   *20883*   Guatemala *20883*
I   *20883*   Mexico *20883*

E   *Berberidopsis corallina* Hook. f. *15088*
E   *14908*   Chile (Regions VII-X) *14908*

I   *Caloncoba lophocarpa* (Oliver) Gilg *7749*
I   Cameroon (Cameroon mt)

E   *Carpotroche froesiana* Sleumer *20883*
I   *20883*   Brazil *20883*

R   *Carpotroche integrifolia* Kuhlmann *20883*
I   *20883*   Brazil *20883*
I   *20883*   Colombia *20883*

R   *Carpotroche pacifica* (Cuatrecasas) Cuatrecasas *20883*
I   *20883*   Colombia *20883*

V   *Carpotroche ramosii* (Cuatrecasas) Cuatrecasas *20883*
I   *20883*   Colombia *20883*

R   *Casearia altiplanensis* Sleumer *20883*
I   *20883*   Brazil *20883*

R   *Casearia annamensis* (Gagnepain) Lescot & Sleum. *6057*
R   Vietnam *6057*

E   *Casearia aquifolia* Wright *20883*
I   *20883*   Cuba *20883*

E   *Casearia atlantica* Sleumer *20883, 9709*
I   *20883*   Panama *20883*

V   *Casearia bahiensis* Sleumer *20883*
I   *20883*   Brazil *20883*

R   *Casearia cajambrensis* Cuatr. *20883*
I   *20883*   Panama *20883*
I   *20883*   Colombia *20883*

V   *Casearia catharinensis* Sleumer *20883*
I   *20883*   Brazil *20883*

R   *Casearia coriifolia* Lescot & Sleumer *20893*
R   *20893*   New Caledonia *20893*

R   *Casearia coronata* Standl. & L.O. Wms. *20883*
I   *20883*   Costa Rica *20883*
I   *20883*   Panama *20883*

R   *Casearia crassinervis* Urban *20883*
I   *20883*   Cuba *20883*

I   *Casearia engleri* Gilg *19526*
I   *5926*   Tanzania (West Usambara mountains) *5926*

R   *Casearia grayi* Jessup *20681*
R   *20681*   Australia - Queensland *20681*

V   *Casearia ilicifolia* Ventenat *20883*
I   *20883*   Dominican Republic (north-west) *21008*
              Haiti *21008*

E   *Casearia kaalaensis* Lescot & Sleumer *20893*
E   *20893*   New Caledonia *20893*

V   *Casearia luetzelburgii* Eichler *20883*
I   *20883*   Brazil *20883*

V   *Casearia manausensis* Sleumer *20883*
I   *20883*   Brazil *20883*

E   *Casearia mauritiana* Bosser *10082*
E   *20771*   Mauritius *10082*

V   *Casearia megacarpa* Cuatrecasas *20883*
I   *20883*   Colombia *20883*

V   *Casearia melliodora* Eichler *20883*
I   *20883*   Brazil *20883*

E   *Casearia mestrensis* Sleumer *20883*
I   *20883*   Brazil *20883*

E   *Casearia mexiae* Sandwith *20883*
I   *20883*   Ecuador *20883*

V   *Casearia moaensis* Marie-Victorin *20883*
I   *20883*   Cuba *20883*

E   *Casearia neblinae* Sleumer *20883*
I   *20883*   Brazil *20883*

R   *Casearia nigricans* Sleumer *20883*
I   *20883*   Peru *20883*

E   *Casearia nigricolor* Sleumer *20883*
I   *20883*   Peru *20883*

R   *Casearia oblongifolia* Cambessèdes *20883, 17462*
I   *20883*   Brazil *20883*
?   Colombia *17462*
?   Ecuador *17462*

V   *Casearia ophiticola* Marie-Victorin *20883*
I   *20883*   Cuba *20883*

E   *Casearia paranaensis* Sleumer *20883*
I   *20883*   Brazil *20883*

R   *Casearia pauciflora* Cambessèdes *20883*
I   *20883*   Brazil *20883*

I   *Casearia pseudoglomerata* Sleum. *19120*
I   *19120*   Thailand *19120*

E   *Casearia quinduensis* Tulasne *20883*
I   *20883*   Colombia *20883*

R   *Casearia rufescens* Cambessèdes *20883*
I   *20883*   Brazil *20883*

R   *Casearia selloana* Eichler *20883*
I   *20883*   Brazil *20883*   .

E   *Casearia sessiliflora* Cambessèdes *20883*
I   *20883*   Brazil *20883*

V   *Casearia standleyana* Sleumer *20883, 9709*
I   *20883*   Costa Rica *20883*

R   *Casearia tachirensis* Steyermark *20883*
I   *20883*   Colombia *20883*
I   *20883*   Venezuela *20883*

R   *Casearia tardieuae* Lescot & Sleumer *6057*
R   Vietnam *6057*

Ex/E   *Casearia tinifolia* Vent. *10082*
Ex/E   *20771*   Mauritius *10082*

V   *Casearia williamsiana* Sleumer *20883, 9709*

I   *20883*   Honduras   *20883*

E   *Casearia zahlbruckneri* Szyszylowicz *20883*
I   *20883*   Peru *20883*

E   *Chiangiodendron mexicanum* T. Wendt *20883*
I   *20883*   Mexico *20883*

I   *Dovyalis spinosissima* Gilg *7749*
I   Malawi *7749*

R   *Erythrospermum monticolum* Thouars var. *amplifolium* (Thouars) Sleumer *10082*
R   *20771*   Mauritius *10082*

R   *Erythrospermum monticolum* Thouars var. *cordifolium* (Clos) Sleumer *10082*
R   *20771*   Mauritius *10082*

E   *Euceraea sleumeriana* Steyermark & Maguire *20883*
I   *20883*   Venezuela *20883*

E   *Homalium betulifolium* Daniker *20893*
E   *20893*   New Caledonia *20893*

E   *Homalium buxifolium* Daniker *20893*
E   *20893*   New Caledonia *20893*

I   *Homalium glabrifolium* Geddes *19120*
I   *19120*   Thailand *19120*

I   *Homalium gracilipes* Sleumer *19526*
I   *5926*   Tanzania (Luwira-Kiteza forest reserve) *5926*

R   *Homalium integrifolium* (Lam.) Baillon *10082*
R   *20771*   Mauritius *10082*

E   *Homalium juxtapositum* Sleumer *20893*
E   *20893*   New Caledonia *20893*

I   *Homalium kunstleri* King *17450*
I   Malaysia - Peninsular Malaysia (Perak)

V   *Homalium lacticum* Gagnepain var. *glabratum* C.Y. Wu *17617*
V   *17617*   China - Yunnan (Jinghong, Mengla, Gengma) *11139*

E   *Homalium mathieuanum* (Vieill.) Briq. *20893*
E   *20893*   New Caledonia *20893*

R   *Homalium mossambicense* Paiva *7749*
R   Mozambique *7749*

I   *Homalium peninsulare* Sleum. *19120*
I   *19120*   Thailand *19120*

E   *Homalium polystachyum* (Vieill.) Briq. *20893*
E   *20893*   New Caledonia *20893*

V   *Homalium rubiginosum* (Vieill.) Warb. *20893*
V   *20893*   New Caledonia *20893*

E   *Homalium rubrocostatum* Sleumer *20893*
E   *20893*   New Caledonia *20893*

V   *Homalium sleumerianum* Lescot *20893*
V   *20893*   New Caledonia *20893*

E   *Hydnocarpus macrocarpa* (Bedd.) ssp. *macrocarpa* *14782, 21025*
E   *14782*   India (southern W. Ghats) *14782*

R   *Hydnocarpus octandra* Thwaites *10252*
R   *12838*   Sri Lanka *10252*

R   *Hydnocarpus saigonensis* Pierre *6057*
R   Vietnam *6057*

R   *Laetia coriacea* Spruce ex Bentham *20883*
I   *20883*   Brazil *20883*
I   *20883*   Venezuela *20883*

V   *Laetia micrantha* A. Robyns *20883, 9006*

I   *20883*   Panama *20883*

V   *Laetia ovalifolia* Macbride *20883*
I   *20883*   Peru *20883*

E   *Laetia ternstroemioides* Grisebach *20883, 5607*
I   *20883*   Cuba (Holguin; Guantanamo) *20883*

E   *Lasiochlamys hurlimannii* (Guillaumin) Sleumer *20893*
E   *20893*   New Caledonia *20893*

V   *Lasiochlamys mandjeliana* Sleumer *20893*
V   *20893*   New Caledonia *20893*

V   *Lasiochlamys pseudocoriacea* Sleumer *20893*
V   *20893*   New Caledonia *20893*

R   *Lasiochlamys trichostemona* (Guillaumin) Sleumer *20893*
R   *20893*   New Caledonia *20893*

E   *Lindackeria ovata* (Bentham) Gilg *20883*
E   *20883*   Brazil *20883*

R   *Lunania cubensis* Turczaninov *20883*
I   *20883*   Cuba *20883*

V   *Lunania dentata* Urban *20883*
I   *20883*   Dominican Republic (Barahona) *21008*

E   *Lunania divaricata* Bentham *20883*
I   *20883*   Cuba *20883*

E   *Lunania dodecandra* Wright *20883, 5607*
R   *19105*   Cuba (Guantanamo) *20883*

R   *Lunania ekmanii* Urban *20883, 19002*
I   *20883*   Dominican Republic *20883*
I   *20883*   Haiti *20883*
I   *20883*   Puerto Rico *20883*

E   *Lunania elongata* Britton & P. Wilson *5607*
E   *19105*   Cuba (Sancti Spiritus) *5607*

R   *Lunania mauritii* Urban *20883*
I   *20883*   Dominican Republic (San Cristóbal) *21008*
I   *20883*   Haiti (Aux Cayes, Pestel) *21008*

V   *Lunania polydactyla* Urban *20883*
V   *20883*   Jamaica *20883*

V   *Lunania racemosa* Hook. *20883*
V   *20883*   Jamaica *20883*

R   *Lunania sauvalii* Grisebach *20883*
I   *20883*   Cuba *20883*

R   *Lunania sauvallii* Griseb. *5607*
R   *19105*   Cuba (Pinar del Rio) *5607*

R   *Lunania scopulorum* Urban & Ekman *20883*
I   *20883*   Dominican Republic (Villa Altagracia, Montes del Bahoruco) *21008*
I   *20883*   Haiti *20883*

V   *Lunania subcoriacea* Britton & Wilson *20883*
I   *20883*   Cuba *20883*

E   *Lunania tenuifolia* Urban & Ekman *20883*
I   *20883*   Haiti (St. Louis du Nord, Morne Baron) *21008*

V   *Mayna hystricina* (Gleason) Sleumer *20883*
I   *20883*   Colombia *20883*

R   *Mayna parviflora* (Macbride) Sleumer *20883*
I   *20883*   Brazil *20883*
I   *20883*   Peru *20883*

E   *Mayna pubescens* (Triana & Karsten) Warburg *20883*
I   *20883*   Colombia *20883*

R   *Mayna suaveolens* (Karsten & Triana) Warburg *20883*
I   *20883*   Colombia *20883*

E	*Neopringlea trinervia* (Standley & Steyerm.) Lemke *20883*		
	I	*20883* Guatemala *20883*	
	I	*20883* Mexico *20883*	
R	*Peterodendron ovatum* (Steumer) Steumer *19526*		
	R	Tanzania (Kondoa, Kilosa, Iringa) *19526*	
R	*Pseudoscolopia polyantha* Gilg. *20604*		
	R	*20604* South Africa - Cape Province *20604*	
	R	*20604* South Africa - Natal *20604*	
R	*Ryania dentata* (H. B. K.) Miquel *20883*		
	I	*20883* Colombia *20883*	
	I	*20883* Venezuela *20883*	
V	*Ryania dentata* (H. B. K.) Miquel var. *dentata 20883*		
	I	*20883* Venezuela *20883*	
V	*Ryania dentata* (H. B. K.) Miquel var. *toxica* Dugand *20883*		
	I	*20883* Colombia *20883*	
E	*Ryania riedeliana* Eichler *20883*		
	I	*20883* Brazil *20883*	
E	*Ryania speciosa* var. *mutisii* Monachino *20883*		
	Ex/E	*20883* Colombia *20883*	
R	*Ryania speciosa* Monachino var. *panamensis* Monachino *20883, 10747*		
	I	*20883* Costa Rica *20883*	
	I	*20883* Nicaragua *20883*	
	I	*20883* Panama *20883*	
I	*Ryparosa inconstans* Craib *19120*		
	I	*19120* Thailand *19120*	
E	*Samyda cubensis* Wilson *20883*		
	I	*20883* Cuba *20883*	
R	*Samyda glabrata* Sw. *20883*		
	R	*20883* Jamaica *20883*	
E	*Samyda lunana* P. Wilson *5607*		
	E	*19105* Cuba (Sancti Spiritus) *5607*	
V	*Samyda mexicana* Rose *20883, 9709*		
	R	*19798* Mexico *20883*	
E	*Samyda microphylla* Urban *20883, 5607*		
	I	*20883* Cuba (Holguin) *20883*	
R	*Samyda spinulosa* Vent. *20883*		
	I	*20883* Dominican Republic *20883*	
	I	*20883* Puerto Rico *20883*	
	I	*20883* USA - Virgin Is. *20883*	
R	*Samyda villosa* Sw. *20883*		
	R	*20883* Jamaica *20883*	
R	*Scolopia heterophylla* (Lam.) Sleumer *10082*		
	V	*14234* Réunion *14234*	
	R	*20771* Mauritius *5852*	
	E	*5852* Mauritius - Rodrigues (Plaine Corail) *5852*	
R	*Scolopia oreophila* (Sleumer) Killick *20604*		
	R	*20604* South Africa - Natal *20604*	
R	*Scolopia steenisiana* Sleumer *17450*		
	R	Malaysia - Peninsular Malaysia (Gua Musang, Kelantan)	
R	*Taraktogenos merrillana* (Li) C.Y. Wu *8482*		
	R	China *8482*	
E	*Trichadenia zeylanica* Thwaites *4705*		
	E	*12838* Sri Lanka *4705*	
E	*Xylosma avilae* Sleumer *20883*		
	I	*20883* Venezuela *20883*	

E	*Xylosma bolivianum* Sleumer *20883*		
	I	*20883* Bolivia *20883*	
V	*Xylosma boulindae* Sleumer *20893*		
	V	*20893* New Caledonia *20893*	
E	*Xylosma capillipes* Guillaumin *20893*		
	E	*20893* New Caledonia *20893*	
V	*Xylosma claraense* Urban *20883*		
	I	*20883* Cuba *20883*	
R	*Xylosma cordatum* (Humboldt, Bonpland & Kunth) Gilg *20883*		
	I	*20883* Ecuador *20883*	
	I	*20883* Peru *20883*	
R	*Xylosma coriaceum* (Poiteau) *20883*		
	I	*20883* Dominican Republic (Puerto Plata, Samaná) *21008*	
	I	*20883* Haiti (Port de Paix, Isla Tortuga) *21008*	
E	*Xylosma crenata* (St. John) St. John *20850*		
	E	*20850* U.S. - Hawaii *20850*	
E	*Xylosma crenatum* (H. St. John) H. St. John *14209, 21349*		
	E	*14209* U.S. - Hawaii (Kaua`i) *14209*	
R	*Xylosma elegans* (Tulasne) Triana & Planchon *20883*		
	I	*20883* Colombia *20883*	
R	*Xylosma fawcettii* Urb. *20883*		
	R	*20883* Jamaica *20883*	
R	*Xylosma gigantifolium* Sleumer		
	R	New Caledonia	
E	*Xylosma glaucescens* Urban *20883*		
	I	*20883* Dominican Republic (Pan de Azúcar, Samaná) *21008*	
	I	*20883* Haiti (Dondon) *21008*	
E	*Xylosma grossecrenatum* (Sleumer) Lescot *20893*		
	E	*20893* New Caledonia *20893*	
R	*Xylosma hispidula* Standl. *20883*		
	I	*20883* Costa Rica *20883*	
	I	*20883* Panama *20883*	
E	*Xylosma inaequinervium* Sleumer *20893*		
	E	*20893* New Caledonia *20893*	
V	*Xylosma kaalense* Sleumer *20893*		
	V	*20893* New Caledonia *20893*	
R	*Xylosma lineolatum* Urban & Ekman *20883*		
	I	*20883* Dominican Republic *20883*	
	I	*20883* Haiti *20883*	
V	*Xylosma longipetiolatum* Legname *20883*		
	I	*20883* Argentina *20883*	
V	*Xylosma lucidum* (Tulasne) Sleumer *20883*		
	I	*20883* Colombia *20883*	
R	*Xylosma maidenii* Sleumer		
	R	*14225* Australia - NSW - Lord Howe Is. *14225*	
V	*Xylosma martinicense* (Krug & Urban) Urban *20883*		
	I	*20883* Guadeloupe *20883*	
	I	*20883* Martinique *20883*	
V	*Xylosma molestum* Sleumer *20893*		
	V	*20893* New Caledonia *20893*	
R	*Xylosma nitida* (Helenius) A. Gray *20883*		
	R	*20883* Jamaica *20883*	
V	*Xylosma obovatum* (Karsten) Triana & Planchon *20883*		
	I	*20883* Colombia *20883*	
R	*Xylosma ovatum* Benth. *20681*		

	R	20681 Australia - Queensland *20681*

E   *Xylosma pachyphyllum* (Krug & Urban) Urban *20883*
    E   20883 Puerto Rico *20883*

I   *Xylosma palawanense* Mend. *13833*
    I   13833 Philippines (low altitude) *13833*

R   *Xylosma paucinervosum* (Steyermark) Sleumer *20883*
    I   20883 Ecuador *20883*
    I   20883 Venezuela *20883*

E   *Xylosma peltatum* (Sleumer) Lescot *20893*
    E   20893 New Caledonia *20893*

E   *Xylosma pininsulare* Guillaumin *20893*
    E   20893 New Caledonia *20893*

V   *Xylosma proctorii* Sleumer *20883, 19890*
    R   19890 Jamaica *20883*

R   *Xylosma pubescens* Grisebach *20883*
    I   20883 Argentina *20883*
    I   20883 Bolivia *20883*

E   *Xylosma raimondii* Sleumer *20883*
    I   20883 Peru *20883*

E   *Xylosma rhombifolium* (Britton & Wilson)
     Sleumer *20883, 5607*
    E   20883 Cuba (Pinar del Rio) *20883*

E   *Xylosma roigiana* Borh. *5607*
    E   19105 Cuba (Las Tunas) *5607*

E   *Xylosma ruizianum* Sleumer *20883*
    I   20883 Peru *20883*

E   *Xylosma sanctae-annae* Sleumer *20883*
    I   20883 Trinidad & Tobago *20883*

V   *Xylosma schroederi* Sleumer ex Herter *20883*
    I   20883 Uruguay *20883*

E   *Xylosma schwaneckeanum* (Krug & Urban) Urban *20883*
    E   20883 Puerto Rico *20883*

V   *Xylosma serpentinum* Sleumer *20893*
    V   20893 New Caledonia *20893*

R   *Xylosma shaferi* (Wilson) Howard & Briggs *20883*
    I   20883 Cuba *20883*

E   *Xylosma sp* see Adams, 1972B *20883*
    E   20883 Jamaica *20883*

V   *Xylosma suaveolens* (J.R. & G. Forster) ssp. *haroldii*
     Sluemer *19187*
    V   19185 Pitcairn (Pitcairn & Henderson Islands)
        19187

V   *Xylosma tuberculatum* Sleumer *20893*
    V   20893 New Caledonia *20893*

I   *Xylotheca tettensis* (Klotzsch) Gilg var. *fissistyla*
     (Warb.) Sleumer *19526*
    I   5926 Tanzania (Bagamoyo & Uzaramo) *19526*

Fouquieriaceae

Number of genera: 1
Number of species: 11
Recorded threatened species: 5   (45%)

Arid parts of Mexico and southwestern United States.

V   ı   *Fouquieria fasciculata* Nash *15658*
    V   19850 Mexico *19850*

R   *Fouquieria leonilae* Miranda *9058*
    R   19850 Mexico *9058*

I   *Fouquieria ochoterenae* Miranda *19850*
    I   19850 Mexico *19850*

I   ı   *Fouquieria purpusii* Brandegee *15658*
    I   19850 Mexico *19850*

R   *Fouquieria shrevei* I.M. Johnston *19850*
    R   19850 Mexico *19850*

Frankeniaceae

Number of genera: 3
Number of species: 80
Recorded threatened species: 6   (7%)

Cosmopolitan, especially Mediterranean region.

Ex   *Frankenia conferta* Diels *20681, 14223*
    Ex   20681 Australia - Western Australia *20681*

Ex   *Frankenia decurrens* Summerh. *20681, 14223*
    Ex   20681 Australia - Western Australia *14223*

R   *Frankenia johnstonii* Correll *20883, 20850, 9114*
    R   20850 U.S. - Texas *20850*
    I   20883 Mexico *20883*
    I   9114 Mexico - Coahuila *9114*
    I   9114 Mexico - Nuevo Leon *9114*
    I   9114 Mexico - Tamaulipas *9114*

V   *Frankenia margaritae* Gonz. Medr. *9710*
    V   19755 Mexico *9710*

Ex   *Frankenia parvula* Turcz. *20681, 14223*
    Ex   20681 Australia - Western Australia *14223*

E   *Frankenia plicata* Melville *20681*
    E   20681 Australia - South Australia *20681*

R   *Frankenia portulacaefolia* Sprengel *18996*
    R   18996 St Helena *18996*

R   *Frankenia pulverulenta* L. *17617, 20171*
    V   5204 Bulgaria (east) *5204*
    V   19949 Romania *20631*
    R   17617 China - Gansu (Mingqing) *11139*
    R   17617 China - Nei Monggol Zizhiqu (Ejinaqi)
        11139
    R   17617 China - Xinjiang Uygur Zizhiqu (Xingyun)
        11139

R   *Frankenia scabra* Lindley *20681*
    R   20681 Australia - Queensland *20681*

Geissolomataceae

Number of genera: 1
Number of species: 1
Recorded threatened species: 1   (100%)

Cape Province (South Africa).

R   *Geissoloma marginatum* (L.) Juss. *20604, 18289*
    R   20604 South Africa - Cape Province (Langeberg Mts.)
        20604

Gentianaceae

Number of genera: 75
Number of species: 1,000
Recorded threatened species: 111   (11%)

Cosmopolitan, especially temperate and subtropical regions and tropical mountains.

V   *Bartonia texana* Correll *20850*
    V   20850 U.S. - Texas *20850*

I   *Canscora hexagona* Kerr. *19120*
    I   19120 Thailand (Tak, Phumipol, Nakhon Ratchasima, Chan Tue
        Kanchanaburi, Si Sawat) *19281*

R   *Centaurium barrelieroides* Pau
    R   Morocco

R   *Centaurium davyi* (Jepson) Abrams *20850*
    I   *20850*   U.S. - California   *20850*

R   *Centaurium enclusense* O.Bolòs, Molin. & P.Monts. *20171*
    R   Spain - Balearic Is.

R   *Centaurium floribundum* (Benth.) B.L. Robins. *20850*
    I   *20850*   U.S. - California   *20850*

R   *Centaurium limoniiforme* Greuter *20171*
    R   Greece

V   *Centaurium malzacianum* Maire
    V   Egypt

V   *Centaurium namophilum* Reveal, Broome & Beatley *20850*
    E   *20850*   U.S. - California   *20850*
    V   *20850*   U.S. - Nevada   *20850*

V   *Centaurium nudicaule* (Engelm.) B.L. Robins. *20850*
    I   *20850*   U.S. - Arizona   *20850*
    I   *20850*   U.S. - New Mexico   *20850*
    I   *20850*   U.S. - Texas   *20850*

R   *Centaurium quadrifolium* (L.) G. Lopez & Jarvis
    R   Spain

E   *Centaurium quadrifolium* (L.) Lopez & Jarvis forma *rigualii* (Esteve) E.Bayer & G.Lopez Gonzalez *20874, 10260*
    E   *20874*   Spain (Murcia)   *20874*

E   *Centaurium rigualii* Esteve *8000, 20171*
    E   *11496*   Spain (Murcia)   *8000*

E   *Centaurium sebaeoides* (Griseb.) Druce *20850, 14209*
    E   *20850*   U.S. - Hawaii   *20850*

R   *Centaurium serpenticola* A. Carltrom *12840*
    R   *12840*   Turkey   *12840*

V   *Centaurium somedanum* Lainz *17781*
    V   *14155*   Spain (Cantabrian Range)   *20874*

R   *Centaurium trichanthum* (Griseb.) B.L. Robins. *20850*
    I   *20850*   U.S. - California   *20850*

R   *Centaurium triphyllum* (W.L.E.Schmidt) Melderis *20171*
    R   Spain

R   *Centaurium venustum* (Gray) B.L. Robins. *20850*
    I   *20850*   U.S. - California   *20850*

R   *Comastoma pulmonarium* (Turcz.) Toyok. ssp. *sectum* (Satake) Toyok. *10573*
    R   *10573*   Japan   *10573*

R   *Djaloniella ypsilostyla* P. Taylor *7926*
    R   Guinea   *7926*

I   *Exacum anamalayanum* Beddome
    I   India - Tamil Nadu

I   *Exacum atropurpureum* Beddome *9330*
    I   India - Tamil Nadu (Upper Kodayar area) *9330*

E   *Exacum caeruleum* Balf. f. *15534*
    E   *15534*   Yemen - Socotra   *15534*

I   *Exacum courtallense* Arn. var. *courtallense*
    I   India - Tamil Nadu

I   *Exacum gracilipes* Balf. f. *15534*
    I   *15534*   Yemen - Socotra   *15534*

I   *Exacum sutaepense* Kerr *19120*
    I   *19120*   Thailand (wide distribution)   *19281*

I   *Faroa richardsiae* Tayl. *5926*
    I   *5926*   Tanzania   *5926*

R   *Frasera albicaulis* (St. John) C.L. Hitchc. var. *idahoensis* (St. John) C.L. Hitchc. *20850*
    R   *20850*   U.S. - Idaho   *20850*
    I   *20850*   U.S. - Oregon   *20850*

V   *Frasera coloradensis* (Rogers) D.M. Post *20850*
    V   *20850*   U.S. - Colorado   *20850*

E   *Frasera gypsicola* (Barneby) D.M. Post *20850*
    E   *20850*   U.S. - Nevada   *20850*
    E   *20850*   U.S. - Utah   *20850*

V   *Frasera neglecta* Hall *20850*
    V   *20850*   U.S. - California   *20850*

R   *Frasera tubulosa* Coville *20850*
    I   *20850*   U.S. - California   *20850*

R   *Gentiana algida* Pallas var. *igarashii* Miyabe & Kudo *10573*
    R   *10573*   Japan   *10573*

R   *Gentiana antipoda* Kirk *19106*
    R   *19305*   New Zealand - Antipodes Is.   *19106*

R   *Gentiana aquatica* L. var. *laeviuscula* (Ohwi) Ohwi *10573*
    R   *10573*   Japan   *10573*

R   *Gentiana austromontana* Pringle & Sharp *20850*
    V   *20850*   U.S. - North Carolina   *20850*
    V   *20850*   U.S. - Tennessee   *20850*
    R   *20850*   U.S. - Virginia   *20850*
    Ex/E   *20850*   U.S. - West Virginia   *20850*

R   *Gentiana autumnalis* L. *20850*
    Ex/E   *20850*   U.S. - Delaware   *20850*
    I   *20850*   U.S. - Georgia   *20850*
    R   *20850*   U.S. - New Jersey   *20850*
    R   *20850*   U.S. - North Carolina   *20850*
    V   *20850*   U.S. - South Carolina   *20850*
    E   *20850*   U.S. - Virginia   *20850*

R   *Gentiana axillariflora* A. Leveille & Vaniot var. *coreana* Kudo *15923*
    R   *15923*   Korea, South (Mt Sorak)   *15923*

E   *Gentiana baeuerlenii* L.G.Adams *20681*
    Ex/E   *20681*   Australia - Capital Territory   *20681*
    E   *20681*   Australia - New South Wales   *20681*

R   *Gentiana boissierii* Scott & Kotschy ex Boiss. *12840*
    R   *12840*   Turkey   *12840*

V   *Gentiana boryi* Boiss. *20171*
    V   Spain

V   *Gentiana bredboensis* L.G.Adams *20681*
    V   *20681*   Australia - New South Wales   *20681*

E   *Gentiana cachemirica* Decne. *14768*
    E   India - Jammu & Kashmir (Kounsarnag) *14768*

R   *Gentiana caliculata* Lex. *9715*
    R   *19850*   Mexico   *9715*

R   *Gentiana chathamica* Cheeseman
    R   New Zealand - Chatham Is.

R   *Gentiana crassuloides* Bureau at Franch. *14722*
    R   *14722*   China   *14722*
    R   *14722*   Bhutan   *14722*
    R   *14722*   India - Arunachal Pradesh   *14722*
    R   *14722*   India - Sikkim   *14722*
    R   *14722*   India - Uttar Pradesh   *14722*
    R   *14722*   Nepal   *14722*

R   *Gentiana cruciata* L. ssp. *phlogifolia* (Schott & Kotschy) Tutin *17823, 20171*
    R   *20631*   Romania   *20631*

R   *Gentiana dschungarica* Regel *10260*

R		former USSR (Turkestan) *6930*	

R   *Gentiana hooperi* Pringle *9715*
    R   *19794*   Mexico *9715*

R   *Gentiana infelix* Clarke in Hook. f. *14722*
    R   *14722*   China *14722*
    R   *14722*   India - Himachal Pradesh *14722*
    R   *14722*   India - Sikkim *14722*
    R   *14722*   India - Uttar Pradesh *14722*

I   *Gentiana laevigata* Martens & Galeotti *9715*
    I   *19794*   Mexico *9715*

R   *Gentiana lagodechiana* (Kusn.) Grossh. *5942*
    I   *5942*   Azerbaijan *5942*

I   *Gentiana leptoclada* Balf. f. et Forr. ssp. *australis* (Craib) Foysk. *19120*
    I   *19120*   Thailand *19120*

R   *Gentiana mirandae* Paray *9715*
    R   *19794*   Mexico *9715*

R   *Gentiana montserratii* Vivant
    R   *11496*   Spain *11496*

R   *Gentiana nipponica* Maxim. var. *robusta* Hara *10573*
    R   *10573*   Japan *10573*

R   *Gentiana ovatiloba* Kusn. *9715*
    R   *19794*   Guatemala *9715*
    R   *19794*   Mexico *9715*

I   *Gentiana paradoxa* Albov *5942*
    I   *5942*   Russia - North Caucasus *5942*
    I   *5942*   Georgia *5942*

R   *Gentiana pennelliana* Fern. *20850*
    R   *20850*   U.S. - Florida *20850*

R   *Gentiana perpusilla* Brandegee *9715*
    R   *19794*   Mexico *9715*

R   *Gentiana plurisetosa* C.T. Mason *20850*
    V   *20850*   U.S. - California *20850*
    E   *20850*   U.S. - Oregon *20850*

R   *Gentiana pumilio* Standley & Steyerm. *9004*
    R   *19794*   Guatemala *9004*
    R   *19794*   Mexico *9004*

R   *Gentiana sagjinoides* Burkill in J. & Proc. *14722*
    R   *14722*   India - Meghalaya (Kumoan) *14722*

V   *Gentiana setigera* Gray *20850*
    E   *20850*   U.S. - California *20850*
    V   *20850*   U.S. - Oregon *20850*

R   *Gentiana shikokiana* Maxim. *10573*
    R   *10573*   Japan *10573*

R   *Gentiana spathacea* Kunth *9715*
    R   *19850*   Mexico *9715*

R   *Gentiana squarrosa* Ledeb. var. *liukiuensis* Hatus. *10573*
    R   *10573*   Japan *10573*

R   *Gentiana tentyoensis* Masamune *20511*
    R   *20511*   Taiwan *20511*

I   *Gentiana timida* Kerr *19120*
    I   *19120*   Thailand (Chiang Mai, Doi Suthep) *19281*

R   *Gentiana tornezyana* Litard. & Maire
    R   Morocco

E   *Gentiana wingecarribiensis* L.G.Adams *20681*
    E   *20681*   Australia - New South Wales *20681*

V   *Gentiana wissmannii* J.B.Williams *20681*
    V   *20681*   Australia - New South Wales *20681*

R   *Gentiana yakumontana* Masam. *10573*
    R   *10573*   Japan *10573*

E   *Gentiana yakusimensis* Makino *10573*
    E   *10573*   Japan *10573*

V   *Gentianella austriaca* (A. et J. Kerner) Holub ssp. *fatrae* (Borb.) Holub *19839*
    V   *19321*   Slovakia *19321*

R   *Gentianella bohemica* Skalicky *15316, 20171*
    R   *2050*   Czech Republic *2050*
    E   *20640*   Germany (Bavarian National Park) *15316*
    I   *17821*   Slovakia *17821*

V   *Gentianella lutescens* (Velen.) Holub ssp. *carpathica* (Wettst.) Holub *19266*
    V   *19321*   Slovakia *19321*

R   *Gentianella lutescens* (Velen.) Holub ssp. *tatrae* (Ronn.) Holub *19321*
    R   *19321*   Slovakia *19321*

R   *Gentianella scarlatinostriata* (Gilg) Zarruchi *18200*
    R   *19965*   Peru *18200*

R   *Gentianella takedae* Satake *10573*
    R   *10573*   Japan *10573*

R   *Gentianella tortuosa* (M.E.Jones) J.Gillett *20850*
    E   *20850*   U.S. - Colorado *20850*
    I   *20850*   U.S. - Nevada *20850*
    E   *20850*   U.S. - Utah *20850*

E   *Gentianella wislizeni* (Engelm.) J.Gillett *20883, 20850*
    E   *20850*   U.S. - Arizona *20850*
    I   *20883*   Mexico *20883*

R   *Gentianella yuparensis* Satake *10573*
    R   *10573*   Japan *10573*

V   *Gentianopsis victorinii* (Fern.) Iltis *20850, 13967*
    V   *20850*   Canada - Quebec *20850*

R   *Gentianopsis yabei* (Takeda & Hara) Ma *10573*
    R   *10573*   Japan *10573*

E   *Halenia euryphylla* Allen *20883, 9006*
    I   *20883*   Panama *20883*

E   *Halenia woodsoniana* Allen *20883, 9006*
    I   *20883*   Panama *20883*

V   *Ixanthus viscosus* Griseb. *17534*
    V   *17534*   Spain - Canary Is. *17534*

V   *Lisianthius adamsii* Weaver *20883*
    V   *20883*   Jamaica *20883*

R   *Lisianthius capitatus* Urb. *20883*
    R   *20883*   Jamaica *20883*

E   *Lisianthius cordifolius* L. *20883*
    E   *20883*   Jamaica *20883*

R   *Lisianthius exsertus* Sw. *20883*
    R   *20883*   Jamaica *20883*

V   *Lisianthius jefensis* A. Robyns & Elias *20883*
    I   *20883*   Panama *20883*

R   *Lisianthius latifolius* Sw. *20883*
    V   *20883*   Jamaica *20883*

V   *Lisianthius peduncularis* L.O. Wms. *20883*
    I   *20883*   Panama *20883*

R   *Lisianthius troyanus* Urb. *20883*
    R   *20883*   Jamaica *20883*

V   *Lisianthius umbellatus* Sw. *20883*
    V   *20883*   Jamaica *20883*

E	*Lisianthus cordifolius* L. *13336*		
	E	*13867* Jamaica (St. Andrew parish) *13336*	
R	*Lisianthus umbellatus* Sw. *13336*		
	R	*13867* Jamaica *13336*	
E	*Macrocarpaea browallioides* (Ewan) A. Robyns & Nilsson *20883, 9006*		
	R	*9429* Panama *20883*	
R	*Macrocarpaea hartii* Krug. & Urb. *20883*		
	R	*20883* Jamaica *20883*	
E	*Prepusa hookeriana* Gardner *17079*		
	E	*17079* Brazil - Rio de Janeiro (Serra dos órgaos, Município de Teresópolis, Nova Friburgo) *17079*	
V	*Sabatia brevifolia* Raf. *20850*		
	E	*20850* U.S. - Alabama *20850*	
	I	*20850* U.S. - Florida *20850*	
	I	*20850* U.S. - Georgia *20850*	
	I	*20850* U.S. - North Carolina *20850*	
	I	*20850* U.S. - South Carolina *20850*	
	I	*20850* U.S. - Virginia *20850*	
V	*Sabatia capitata* (Raf.) Blake *20850*		
	V	*20850* U.S. - Alabama *20850*	
	V	*20850* U.S. - Georgia *20850*	
	I	*20850* U.S. - North Carolina *20850*	
	E	*20850* U.S. - Tennessee *20850*	
R	*Sabatia kennedyana* Fern. *20850, 3064*		
	R	*20850* Canada - Nova Scotia *20850*	
	R	*20850* U.S. - Massachusetts *20850*	
	E	*20850* U.S. - North Carolina *20850*	
	E	*20850* U.S. - Rhode Is. *20850*	
	E	*20850* U.S. - South Carolina *20850*	
	E	*20850* U.S. - Virginia *20850*	
I	*Sebaea fourcadei* Marais *20604*		
	I	*20604* South Africa - Cape Province *20604*	
I	*Swertia beddomei* C.B. Clarke		
	I	India - Karnataka (South Canara, Mysore)	
	I	India - Kerala (Travancore Hills)	
	I	India - Tamil Nadu (Sispara, Nilgiri Hills)	
R	*Swertia noguchiana* Hatus. *10573*		
	R	*10573* Japan *10573*	
R	*Tripterospermum distylum* I. Murata & Yahara *10573*		
	R	*10573* Japan *10573*	
R	*Tripterospermum japonicum* (Sieber & Zucc.) Maxim. var. *albiflorum* Y.N. Lee		
	R	Korea, South (Chejudo) *17577*	
I	*Urogentias ulugurensis* Gilg *5926*		
	I	*5926* Tanzania (Uluguru, Ukaguru) *5926*	
E	*Voyria pulcherrima* (Standl.) L.O. Wms. *20883, 9099*		
	R	*9429* Panama *20883*	

Geraniaceae

Number of genera: 11
Number of species: 700
Recorded threatened species: 85 (12%)

Mainly temperate and subtropical.

Ex/E	*Dirachma socotrana* Schweinf. *15534*		
	Ex/E	*18211* Yemen - Socotra (Muqadrihon Pass) *18211*	
V	*Dirachma somalensis* D.A.Link *20387*		
	V	*20884* Somalia (central) *20387*	
R	*Erodium alpinum* L'Hér. *20171*		
	R	Italy	
R	*Erodium asplenioides* Desf. *20171*		
	R	Algeria	

	R	Tunisia	
R	*Erodium atlanticum* Coss.		
	R	Morocco	
R	*Erodium battandieranum* Rouy *10488*		
	R	*14958* Algeria *10488*	
E	*Erodium beketowii* Schmalh. *20171*		
	E	*20655* Ukraine (south-east) *20649*	
R	*Erodium boissieri* Coss. *20171*		
	R	*11496* Spain *11496*	
E	*Erodium cazorlanum* Heywood *19818, 20171*		
	E	*19818* Spain (Sierras de Cazorla y Segura) *11496*	
R	*Erodium cedrorum* Schott & Kotschy s.l. *12840*		
	R	*12840* Turkey *12840*	
V	*Erodium chrysanthum* L'Hér. ex DC. *17781, 20171*		
	V	Greece	
V	*Erodium daucoides* Boiss. *20171*		
	V	Spain	
R	*Erodium gaussenianum* Monts.		
	R	Spain	
R	*Erodium guicciardii* Heldr. ex Boiss. *20178, 20171*		
	R	*20178* Albania *20178*	
	R	Greece	
I	*Erodium gussonii* Ten. *20171*		
	I	*20804* Italy (south) *20804*	
R	*Erodium hakkiaricum* Davis *12840*		
	R	*12840* Turkey *12840*	
R	*Erodium leucanthum* Boiss. *12840*		
	R	*12840* Turkey *12840*	
R	*Erodium manescavi* Coss. *17919, 20171*		
	R	*20528* France (Pyrénées) *20528*	
R	*Erodium masguindalii* Pau		
	R	Morocco	
R	*Erodium micropetalutum* Boiss. & Hausskn. ex Boiss. *12840*		
	R	*12840* Turkey *12840*	
R	*Erodium microphyllum* Pomel		
	R	Algeria	
	I	Tunisia	
R	*Erodium oreophilum* Quezel		
	R	Chad	
R	*Erodium paui* Sennen *20171*		
	R	*20692* Spain (Iberian Mts.) *20692*	
V	*Erodium paularense* Fernandez-González & Izco *15846*		
	V	*19174* Spain (Sierra de Guadarrama) *15846*	
R	*Erodium pelargoniiflorum* Boiss. & Heldr. *12840*		
	R	*12840* Turkey *12840*	
V	*Erodium petraeum* (Gouan) Willd. ssp. *valentinum* (Lange) D.A.Webb & Chater *20171*		
	V	*20692* Spain (Javalambre, Gúdar & nr Mts.) *20692*	
R	*Erodium recoderii* Auriault & Guitt.		
	R	*20660* Spain (Málaga, Cádiz) *20664*	
R	*Erodium reichardii* (Murray) DC. *20171*		
	R	Spain - Balearic Is.	
V	*Erodium rodiei* (Braun-Blanq.) Poirion *20171*		
	V	*20528* France (Alpes-Maritimes) *20528*	
R	*Erodium rupestre* (Pourr. ex Cav.) Guitt. *11496, 20171*		

R   *11496* Spain *11496*

E   ***Erodium rupicola*** Boiss. *15398, 20171*

     E   *15398* Spain (Sierra Nevada) *15398*

R   ***Erodium sanguis-christi*** Sennen *20171*

     R   Spain

R   ***Erodium sanguis-christi*** Sennen ssp. *sanguis-christi* *20690*

     R   *20692* Spain (Catalonia & Valencian region) *20692*

R   ***Erodium saxatile*** Pau *20690*

     R   *20692* Spain (Valencia, Alicante and Murcia provinces) *20692*

R   ***Erodium sibthorpianum*** Boiss.

     R   Greece

R   ***Erodium sibthorpianum*** Boiss. ssp. *sibthorpianum* *12840*

     R   *12840* Turkey *12840*

V   ***Erodium somanum*** Pesmen *12840*

     V   *12840* Turkey *12840*

R   ***Erodium stevenii*** M. Bieb. *5942*

     R   *11552* Russia - North Caucasus *5942*

V   ***Erodium subintegrifolium*** Eig *8895*

     V   Israel (Sharon & Philistean Plains) *8895*

R   ***Geranium angustipetalum*** Hilliard & B.L.Burtt *20604*

     R   *20604* South Africa - Natal *20604*

E   ***Geranium arboreum*** Gray *20850, 14209*

     E   *20850* U.S. - Hawaii (Maui) *20850*

E   ***Geranium attenuilobum*** G.N. & F.F. Jones *20850*

     I   *20850* U.S. - California *20850*

R   ***Geranium canariense*** Reuter

     R   *20750* Spain - Canary Is. *20750*

E   ***Geranium cazorlense*** Heywood *19818, 20171*

     E   *19818* Spain (Sierra de Cazorla) *19818*

R   ***Geranium cinereum*** Cav var. *elatius* Davis *12840*

     R   *12840* Turkey *12840*

R   ***Geranium cinereum*** Cav var. *palmatipartitum* Hausskn. ex Knuth *12840*

     R   *12840* Turkey *12840*

R   ***Geranium cinereum*** Cav var. *pisidicum* Pesmen & Guner *12840*

     R   *12840* Turkey *12840*

R   ***Geranium cinereum*** Cav var. *ponticum* Davis & Roberts *12840*

     R   *12840* Turkey *12840*

R   ***Geranium davisianum*** Pesmen & Guner *12840*

     R   *12840* Turkey *12840*

R   ***Geranium dolomiticum*** Rothm. *20171*

     R   *19174* Spain *19174*

R   ***Geranium eginense*** Hausskn. & Sint ex Knuth *12840*

     R   *12840* Turkey *12840*

R   ***Geranium glaberrimum*** Boiss. & Heldr. *12840*

     R   *12840* Turkey *12840*

R   ***Geranium graniticola*** Carolin *20681*

     R   *20681* Australia - New South Wales *20681*

E   ***Geranium hanaense*** Medeiros & St. John *20850, 14209*

     E   *20850* U.S. - Hawaii *20850*

E   ***Geranium humile*** Hbd. *20850, 14209*

     E   *20850* U.S. - Hawaii (West Maui) *20850*

E   ***Geranium kauaiense*** (Rock) St. John *20850, 14209*

     E   *20850* U.S. - Hawaii (Kaua`i) *20850*

I   ***Geranium lamberti*** Sweet ssp. *siamense* (Craib) T. Shimizu *19120*

     I   *19120* Thailand *19120*

E   ***Geranium limae*** Knuth *18200*

     E   *9446* Peru *18200*

E   ***Geranium maderense*** Yeo *17781*

     E   Portugal - Madeira *17891*

R   ***Geranium mlanjense*** Laundon *7749*

     R   Malawi *7749*

E   ***Geranium mollendinense*** Knuth *18200*

     E   *9446* Peru *18200*

V   ***Geranium multiflorum*** Gray *20850*

     V   *20850* U.S. - Hawaii *20850*

V   ***Geranium multiflorum*** A.Gray var. *multiflorum* *14209*

     V   *14209* U.S. - Hawaii (east Maui) *14209*

R   ***Geranium placa***

     R   Argentina

R   ***Geranium platipetalum*** Fisch. & Mey. var. *albipetalum* Erik & Demirkus *12840*

     R   *12840* Turkey *12840*

V   ***Geranium purpureum*** Vill. ssp. *forsteri* (Wilmott) H. G. Bak. *5387*

     V   *20587* United Kingdom (Hampshire) *19232*

     Ex/E *5387*   United Kingdom - Channel Is. (Guernsey) *5387*

R   ***Geranium rubescens*** Yeo

     R   *19174* Portugal - Madeira *19174*

R   ***Geranium soboliferum*** Komarov var. *kiusianum* (Koidz.) Hara *10572*

     R   *10572* Japan *10572*

I   ***Geranium tuberaria*** Cambess.

     I   India (W. Himalaya)

R   ***Geranium vagans*** Baker ssp. *whytei* (Baker) Laundon *7749*

     R   Malawi *7749*

I   ***Monsonia lanuginosa*** Knuth *20604, 17458*

     I   *20604* South Africa - Transvaal *20604*

R   ***Pelargonium appendiculatum*** (L.f.) Willd. *20604*

     R   *20604* South Africa - Cape Province *20604*

R   ***Pelargonium boranensis*** Friis & M. Gilbert *6087*

     R   *6087* Ethiopia *6087*

R   ***Pelargonium burgerianum*** J.J.A.van der Walt *20604*

     R   *20604* South Africa - Cape Province *20604*

R   ***Pelargonium caledonicum*** L.Bolus *20604*

     R   *20604* South Africa - Cape Province *20604*

R   ***Pelargonium connivens*** E.M.Marais *20604*

     R   *20604* South Africa - Cape Province *20604*

E   ***Pelargonium cotyledonis*** L'Her. *10260*

     E   *18996* St Helena *18996*

I   ***Pelargonium crassipes*** Harv. *20604*

     I   *20604* South Africa - Cape Province *20604*

R   ***Pelargonium desertorum*** Vorster *20604*

     R   *20604* Namibia *20604*

     R   *20604* South Africa - Cape Province *20604*

I   ***Pelargonium ellaphieae*** E.M.Marais *20604*

     I   *20604* South Africa - Cape Province *20604*

I	**Pelargonium exhibens** Vorster *20604*	
	I	*20604* South Africa - Cape Province *20604*
R	**Pelargonium hystrix** Harv. *20604*	
	R	*20604* South Africa - Cape Province *20604*
I	**Pelargonium lanceolatum** (Cav.) Kern *20604*	
	I	*20604* South Africa - Cape Province *20604*
I	**Pelargonium longicaule** Jacq. var. *angustipetalum* C.Boucher *20604, 17919*	
	I	*20604* South Africa - Cape Province *20604*
R	**Pelargonium mutans** Vorster *20604*	
	R	*20604* South Africa - Natal *20604*
R	**Pelargonium namaquense** Knuth *20604*	
	R	*20604* Namibia *20604*
	R	*20604* South Africa - Cape Province *20604*
R	**Pelargonium nephrophyllum** E.M.Marais *20604*	
	R	*20604* South Africa - Cape Province *20604*
I	**Pelargonium punctatum** (Andrews) Willd. *20604*	
	I	*20604* South Africa - Cape Province *20604*
R	**Pelargonium tongaense** Vorster *20604*	
	R	*20604* South Africa - Natal *20604*
R	**Pelargonium torulosum** E.M.Marais *20604*	
	R	*20604* South Africa - Cape Province *20604*
V	**Rhynchotheca spinosa** Ruiz Lopez & Pavon *19557*	
	V	*19557* Ecuador *19557*

Gesneriaceae

Number of genera: 120
Number of species: 2,500
Recorded threatened species: 265 (10%)

Pantropical, with a few species in temperate regions.

I	**Aeschynanthus ceylanica** Gardner *8021*	
	I	*16162* Sri Lanka *8021*
V	**Alloplectus ambonensis** L. Skog *20883, 9006*	
	I	*20883* Panama *20883*
R	**Alloplectus grisebachianus** (Kuntze) Urb. *20883*	
	R	*20883* Jamaica *20883*
R	**Alloplectus pubescens** (Griseb.) Fawcett *20883, 13336*	
	R	*13336* Jamaica *20883*
E	**Besleria arborescens** Mort. *20883, 9006*	
	I	*9719* Panama *20883*
E	**Besleria calycina** L. Skog *20883, 9006*	
	R	*9719* Panama *20883*
I	**Besleria chiriquensis** Wiehl. *20883, 9718*	
	I	*16317* Panama *20883*
V	**Besleria petiolaris** (Griseb.) Urban *10199*	
	V	Dominica *10199*
E	**Besleria rara** L. Skog *20883, 9006*	
	R	*9719* Panama *20883*
R	**Boea brachycarpa** Ridley	
	R	Malaysia - Peninsular Malaysia
I	**Boea divaricata** Ridley	
	I	Malaysia - Peninsular Malaysia
R	**Boea kinnearii** (F.Muell.) Burtt *20681*	
	R	*20681* Australia - Queensland *20681*
R	**Boea lanata** Ridley	
	R	Malaysia - Peninsular Malaysia
R	**Boea parviflora** Ridley	
	R	Malaysia - Peninsular Malaysia (Perak)

R	**Boea suffruticosa** Ridley	
	R	Malaysia - Peninsular Malaysia (Langkawi, Kedah)
I	**Chirita moonii** Gardner *8021*	
	I	*16162* Sri Lanka *8021*
R	**Chirita sericea** Ridley	
	R	Malaysia - Peninsular Malaysia
I	**Chirita walkeri** Gardner ssp. *parviflora* (C.B. Clarke) Theob. & Grupe *8021*	
	I	*16162* Sri Lanka (Kalutara) *8021*
E	**Codonanthe chiricana** Wiehl. *20883, 9006*	
	V	*9719* Panama *20883*
V	**Codonanthe luteola** Wiehl. *20883, 9006*	
	V	*16317* Panama *20883*
R	**Codonanthe macradenia** J.D. Sm. *20883*	
	R	*20883* Panama *20883*
E	**Columnea allenii** Mort. *20883, 9006*	
	I	*9719* Panama *20883*
I	**Columnea ampliata** (Wiehl.) L. Skog *20883, 9006*	
	I	*16317* Panama *20883*
V	**Columnea argentea** Griseb. *20883, 13336*	
	V	*13336* Jamaica *20883*
V	**Columnea arguta** Mort. *20883, 9006*	
	I	*20883* Panama *20883*
R	**Columnea billbergiana** Beurl. *20883, 9006*	
	I	*20883* Panama *20883*
R	**Columnea brevipila** Urb. *20883*	
	R	*20883* Jamaica *20883*
R	**Columnea canarina** Wiehler *9006*	
	R	*9719* Panama *9006*
E	**Columnea cerropirrana** (Wiehl.) L. Skog *20883, 9006*	
	R	*9719* Panama *20883*
V	**Columnea consanguinea** (Mort.) Morley var. *darienensis* (Morton) B. Morley *20883, 9006*	
	I	*20883* Panama *20883*
R	**Columnea crassa** Mort. *20883, 9006*	
	I	*20883* Panama *20883*
V	**Columnea cruenta** Morley *20883, 10747*	
	I	*20883* Panama *20883*
R	**Columnea dissimilis** Mort. *20883, 9006*	
	I	*20883* Panama *20883*
E	**Columnea dressleri** Wiehl. *20883, 9006*	
	V	*9719* Panama *20883*
E	**Columnea gallicauda** Wiehl. *20883, 9006*	
	R	*9719* Panama *20883*
R	**Columnea harrisii** (Urb.) Britton *20883, 13336*	
	R	*13336* Jamaica *20883*
E	**Columnea hiantiflora** Wiehl. *20883, 9006*	
	V	*9719* Panama *20883*
R	**Columnea hirsutissima** Mort. *20883, 9006*	
	I	*20883* Panama *20883*
V	**Columnea hispida** Sw. *20883, 13336*	
	V	*19890* Jamaica (St. James, Trelawny) *20883*
V	**Columnea illepida** Moore *9006*	
	V	*9719* Panama *9006*
V	**Columnea incarnata** Mort. *20883, 9006*	
	I	*20883* Panama *20883*
R	**Columnea jamaicensis** Urb. *20883, 13336*	
	R	*13336* Jamaica *20883*

V	*Columnea mira* Morley 20883, 9006	
	R	9719 Panama 20883
E	*Columnea moorei* Mort. 20883, 9006	
	R	9719 Panama 20883
V	*Columnea pectinata* Mort. 20883, 9006	
	I	20883 Panama 20883
V	*Columnea perpulchra* Mort. 20883, 9006	
	I	20883 Panama 20883
R	*Columnea proctorii* Stearn 20883, 19890	
	R	20883 Jamaica 20883
E	*Columnea pulchra* (Wiehl.) L. Skog 20883, 9006	
	R	9719 Panama 20883
E	*Columnea rubida* (Mort.) Mort. 20883, 9006	
	V	9719 Panama 20883
V	*Columnea rubra* Mort. 20883, 9006	
	V	9719 Panama 20883
R	*Columnea rutilans* Sw. 20883	
	R	20883 Jamaica 20883
V	*Columnea silvarum* Mort. 20883, 9006	
	R	9719 Panama 20883
R	*Columnea subcordata* Morton 20883, 13336	
	R	13336 Jamaica 20883
R	*Columnea urbanii* Stearn 20883	
	R	20883 Jamaica 20883
V	*Columnea zebranella* Wiehl. 20883, 9718	
	V	16317 Panama 20883
V	*Columnea zebrina* Raymond 20883, 9006	
	I	20883 Panama 20883
V	*Cremosperma maculatum* L. Skog 20883, 9006	
	V	16317 Panama 20883
V	*Cremosperma occidentale* Wiehl. 20883, 9718	
	V	16317 Panama 20883
V	*Cremosperma veraguanum* Wiehl. 20883, 9718	
	I	20883 Panama 20883
I	*Cyrtandra apiculata* C.Clarke 20845	
	I	20845 French Polynesia - Society Is. (Moorea, Tahiti) 20845
E	*Cyrtandra bidwillii* C.Clarke 20845	
	E	20845 French Polynesia - Society Is. (Tahiti) 20845
E	*Cyrtandra biflora* J.R. & J.G.Forster 20845	
	E	20845 French Polynesia - Society Is. (Tahiti) 20845
E	*Cyrtandra biserrata* Hbd. 20850, 14209	
	E	20850 U.S. - Hawaii (east Molokai) 20850
I	*Cyrtandra burttii* Balakr. 7771	
	I	India - Nicobar Is. (Great Nicobar) 7771
R	*Cyrtandra calpidicarpa* (Rock) St. John & Storey 20850, 14209	
	I	20850 U.S. - Hawaii (O`ahu: Ko`olau Mts.) 20850
E	*Cyrtandra connata* Nadeaud 20845	
	E	20845 French Polynesia - Society Is. (Tahiti) 20845
Ex/E	*Cyrtandra crenata* St. John & Storey 20850, 14209	
	Ex/E	20850 U.S. - Hawaii (O`ahu - Ko`olau Mts.) 20850
E	*Cyrtandra cyaneoides* Rock 20850, 14301	
	E	20850 U.S. - Hawaii (Kaua`i) 20850

E	*Cyrtandra dentata* St. John & Storey 20850, 14209	
	E	20850 U.S. - Hawaii (Wai`anae & Ko`olau Mts.) 20850
I	*Cyrtandra elatostemmoides* Elm. 13833	
	I	13833 Philippines (Palawan) 13833
E	*Cyrtandra elizabethae* H. Saint John 20845	
	E	20845 French Polynesia - Tubuai Is. (Raivavaeé, Rurutu) 20845
R	*Cyrtandra feaniana* F. Brown 20845	
	R	20845 French Polynesia - Marquesas Is 20845
Ex/E	*Cyrtandra filipes* Hbd. 20850, 14209	
	Ex/E	20850 U.S. - Hawaii (Molokai, West Maui) 20850
R	*Cyrtandra geminata* Reinecke 7925	
	R	U.S. - American Samoa (Tutuila) 7925
I	*Cyrtandra geminiflora* Nadeaud 20845	
	I	20845 French Polynesia - Society Is. (Tahiti) 20845
E	*Cyrtandra giffardii* Rock 20850, 14209, 21348, 21356	
	E	20850 U.S. - Hawaii 20850
E	*Cyrtandra glabra* Banks ex J. Gaertner 20845	
	E	20845 French Polynesia - Society Is. (Tahiti) 20845
Ex/E	*Cyrtandra gracilis* Hbd. ex C.B. Clarke 20850, 14209	
	Ex/E	20850 U.S. - Hawaii (O`ahu) 20850
R	*Cyrtandra gurkeana* Lauterb.	
	R	Western Samoa
E	*Cyrtandra halawensis* Rock 20850, 14209	
	E	20850 U.S. - Hawaii (east Moloka`i) 20850
E	*Cyrtandra hematos* St. John 20850, 14209	
	E	20850 U.S. - Hawaii (eastern Moloka`i) 20850
I	*Cyrtandra inaequifolia* Kranzle. 13833	
	I	13833 Philippines (Palawan) 13833
R	*Cyrtandra induta* A.Gray 20845	
	R	20845 French Polynesia - Society Is. (Tahiti) 20845
R	*Cyrtandra jonesii* (F.Brown) G.Gillett 20845	
	R	20845 French Polynesia - Marquesas Is 20845
R	*Cyrtandra kalihii* Wawra 20850, 14209	
	I	20850 U.S. - Hawaii (O`ahu - Ko`olau Mts.) 20850
E	*Cyrtandra kaulantha* St. John & Storey 20850, 14209	
	E	20850 U.S. - Hawaii (O`ahu) 20850
E	*Cyrtandra kealiae* Wawra 20850, 14209	
	E	20850 U.S. - Hawaii (Kaua`i) 20850
Ex/E	*Cyrtandra kohalae* Rock 20850, 14209	
	Ex/E	20850 U.S. - Hawaii (Kohala Mts.) 20850
E	*Cyrtandra lillianae* Setchell 19471	
	E	19473 Cook Is.(Southern group) (Rarotonga) 19471
E	*Cyrtandra limahuliensis* St. John 20850, 14209	
	E	20850 U.S. - Hawaii (Kaua`i) 20850
I	*Cyrtandra livida* Kranzl. 13833	
	I	13833 Philippines (Palawan) 13833
I	*Cyrtandra longiflora* J.Moore 20845	
	I	20845 French Polynesia - Society Is. 20845
Ex/E	*Cyrtandra lydgatei* Hbd. 20850, 14209	
	Ex/E	20850 U.S. - Hawaii 20850
V	*Cyrtandra macraei* Gray 20850, 14209	
	I	20850 U.S. - Hawaii (O`ahu) 20850

E   *Cyrtandra macrocalyx* **Hbd.** *20850, 14209*
     E   *20850* U.S. - Hawaii (Moloka`i) *20850*

V   *Cyrtandra madeaudii* **C.Clarke** *20845*
     V   *20845* French Polynesia - Society Is. (Tahiti) *20845*

E   *Cyrtandra mareensis* **Daniker** *20893*
     E   *20893* New Caledonia *20893*

R   *Cyrtandra mooreaensis* **G.Gillett** *20845*
     R   *20845* French Polynesia - Society Is. (Moorea) *20845*

R   *Cyrtandra mucronata* **Nadeaud** *20845*
     R   *20845* French Polynesia - Society Is. (Tahiti) *20845*

E   *Cyrtandra munroi* **Forbes** *20850, 14209*
     E   *20850* U.S. - Hawaii (Lana`i) *20850*

I   *Cyrtandra occidentalis* **Balakr. & Burtt** *7771*
     I   India - Nicobar Is. (Gt. Nicobar Is.) *7771*

E   *Cyrtandra oenobarba* **Mann** *20850*
     E   *20850* U.S. - Hawaii *20850*

R   *Cyrtandra oenobarba* **H. Mann var.** *oenobarba* *14209*
     R   *14209* U.S. - Hawaii *14209*

Ex/E   *Cyrtandra olona* **Forbes** *20850, 14209*
     Ex/E *20850* U.S. - Hawaii (Kaua`i) *20850*

E   *Cyrtandra ootensis* **F. Brown**
     E   French Polynesia - Marquesas Is

E   *Cyrtandra oxybapha* **W.L. Wagner & Herbst** *20850, 14209*
     E   *20850* U.S. - Hawaii (West Maui) *20850*

E   *Cyrtandra pickeringii* **Gray** *20850*
     E   *20850* U.S. - Hawaii *20850*

R   *Cyrtandra pickeringii* **A.Gray var.** *pickeringii* *14209*
     R   *14209* U.S. - Hawaii *14209*

E   *Cyrtandra polyantha* **C.B. Clarke** *20850, 14209*
     E   *20850* U.S. - Hawaii (O`ahu - Wai`anae Mts.) *20850*

R   *Cyrtandra procera* **Hbd.** *20850, 14209*
     I   *20850* U.S. - Hawaii (Moloka`i) *20850*

Ex/E   *Cyrtandra pruinosa* **St. John & Storey** *20850, 14209*
     Ex/E *20850* U.S. - Hawaii (O`ahu - Ko`olau Mts.) *20850*

V   *Cyrtandra raiateensis* **J.Moore** *20845*
     V   *20845* French Polynesia - Society Is. (Raiatea) *20845*

I   *Cyrtandra revoluta* **Fosberg & Sachet** *20845*
     I   *20845* French Polynesia - Marquesas Is (Fatu Hiva) *20845*

Ex/E   *Cyrtandra rivularis* **St. John & Storey** *20850, 14209*
     Ex/E *20850* U.S. - Hawaii (O`ahu - Ko`olau Mts.) *20850*

I   *Cyrtandra rupicola* **Elm.** *13833*
     I   *13833* Philippines (Palawan) *13833*

E   *Cyrtandra sandwicensis* **(Levl.) St. John & Storey** *20850, 14209*
     E   *20850* U.S. - Hawaii (O`ahu - Ko`olau Mts.) *20850*

E   *Cyrtandra sessilis* **St. John & Storey** *20850, 14209*
     E   *20850* U.S. - Hawaii (O`ahu - Ko`olau Mts.) *20850*

E   *Cyrtandra subumbellata* **(Hbd.) St. John &**

Storey *20850, 14209*
     E   *20850* U.S. - Hawaii (O`ahu, Wai`anae Mts.) *20850*

I   *Cyrtandra tahuatensis* **Fosberg & Sachet** *20845*
     I   *20845* French Polynesia - Marquesas Is (Tahuata) *20845*

R   *Cyrtandra taitensis* **W.Rich ex A.Gray** *20845*
     R   *20845* French Polynesia - Society Is. (Tahiti) *20845*

Ex/E   *Cyrtandra tintinnabula* **Rock** *20850, 14209*
     Ex/E *20850* U.S. - Hawaii (Laupahoehoe) *20850*

R   *Cyrtandra tohiveaensis* **G.Gillett** *20845*
     R   *20845* French Polynesia - Society Is. (Moorea) *20845*

E   *Cyrtandra toviana* **F. Brown** *20845*
     E   *20845* French Polynesia - Marquesas Is (Nukua Hiva) *20845*

V   *Cyrtandra vairiae* **Drake** *20845*
     V   *20845* French Polynesia - Society Is. (Tahiti) *20845*

I   *Cyrtandra vescoi* **Drake** *20845*
     I   *20845* French Polynesia - Society Is. (Tahiti) *20845*

E   *Cyrtandra viridiflora* **St. John & Storey** *20850, 14209*
     E   *20850* U.S. - Hawaii (O`ahu - Ko`olau Mts.) *20850*

R   *Cyrtandra waianaeensis* **St. John & Storey** *20850, 14209*
     I   *20850* U.S. - Hawaii (O`ahu,Wai`anae Mts.) *20850*

Ex/E   *Cyrtandra waiolani* **Wawra** *20850*
     Ex/E *20850* U.S. - Hawaii *20850*

Ex   *Cyrtandra waiolani* **Wawra var.** *waiolani* *14209*
     Ex   *14209* U.S. - Hawaii *14209*

V   *Cyrtandra wawrae* **C.B. Clarke** *20850, 14209*
     I   *20850* U.S. - Hawaii (Kaua`i) *20850*

E   *Cyrtandroidea jonesii* **F. Brown**
     E   French Polynesia - Marquesas Is

I   *Dichiloboea acaulis* **Barnett** *19120*
     I   *19120* Thailand *19120*

I   *Dichiloboea glabescens* **Barnett** *19120*
     I   *19120* Thailand *19120*

I   *Dichiloboea glandulifera* **Barnett** *19120*
     I   *19120* Thailand *19120*

I   *Dichiloboea strobilacea* **Barnett** *19102*
     I   *19102* Thailand *19120*

I   *Dichrotrichum biflorum* **Elm.** *13833*
     I   *13833* Philippines (Mt. Pulgar) *13833*

I   *Dichrotrichum pauciflorum* **Merr.** *13833*
     I   *13833* Philippines (Mt. Capoas) *13833*

I   *Didymocarpus fischeri* **Gamble**
     I   India - Tamil Nadu

I   *Didymocarpus floccosus* **Thwaites** *8021*
     I   *16162* Sri Lanka (Dolosbage) *8021*

I   *Didymocarpus meeboldii* **W. Smith**
     I   India - Kerala
     I   India - Tamil Nadu (Madurai hills)

R   *Didymocarpus missionis* **Wallich** *6987*
     R   *14782* India - Tamil Nadu *6987*

I   *Didymocarpus ovalifolia* **Wight** *6987*

	I	India - Tamil Nadu 6987

E *Didymocarpus primulinus* Ridley 7607
  E   7607   Malaysia - Peninsular Malaysia (Klang Gates Ridge) 7607

R *Didymocarpus zeylanicus* R. Br. 8021
  R   20013   Sri Lanka 8021

V *Drymonia aciculata* Wiehl. 20883, 9006
  I   20883   Panama 20883

V *Drymonia flavida* L. Skog 20883, 9006
  V   16317   Panama 20883

E *Drymonia microphylla* Wiehl. 20883, 9718
  I   20883   Panama 20883

V *Drymonia sulphurea* Wiehl. 20883, 9006
  V   16317   Panama 20883

R *Episcia punctata* (Lindley) Hanst. 21204
  R   21204   Mexico - Jalisco 21204

V *Gasteranthus maculatus* Wiehl. 20883, 9718
  V   16317   Panama 20883

R *Gesneria acaulis* L. var. *glabrata*
  Skog 19890
  R   19890   Jamaica 19890

V *Gesneria alpina* (Urb.) Urb. 20883, 19890
  R   19890   Jamaica 20883

R *Gesneria calycina* Sw. 20883, 13336
  R   19890   Jamaica (Portland) 20883

R *Gesneria calycosa* (Hook.) Kuntze 20883
  R   20883   Jamaica 20883

V *Gesneria clandestina* (Griseb.) Urb. 20883, 13336
  V   19890   Jamaica (St. Thomas) 20883

R *Gesneria exserta* Sw. 20883
  R   20883   Jamaica 20883

R *Gesneria fawcettii* Urb. 20883
  R   20883   Jamaica 20883

I *Gesneria glandulosa* (Griseb.) Urban 5607
  I   19105   Cuba (Guantanamo) 5607

V *Gesneria gloxinioides* (Griseb.) Urban 5607
  V   19105   Cuba (Pinar del Rio) 5607

R *Gesneria harrisii* Urb. 20883, 19890
  R   19890   Jamaica 20883

I *Gesneria hypoclada* 15229
  I   15229   Haiti (La Visite & Macaya National Parks) 15229

E *Gesneria jamaicensis* Britton 20883, 13336
  E   19890   Jamaica (St. Elizabeth) 20883

V *Gesneria lindmanii* Urban 5607
  V   19105   Cuba (Guantanamo) 5607

V *Gesneria mimuloides* (Griseb.) Urb. 20883
  V   20883   Jamaica 20883

E *Gesneria neglecta* (Hook.) Kuntze 20883
  E   20883   Jamaica 20883

V *Gesneria onychocalyx* Skog 20883, 19890
  V   19890   Jamaica (Portland) 20883

E *Gesneria pauciflora* Urban 20883, 8058
  I   20883   Puerto Rico 20883

R *Gesneria proctorii* Stearn 20883
  R   20883   Jamaica 20883

R *Gesneria pumila* Sw. 20883
  R   20883   Jamaica 20883

R *Gesneria pumila* Sw. ssp. *mimuloides* (Griseb.)
  Skog. 13336
  R   13336   Jamaica 13336

R *Gesneria pumila* Sw. ssp. *neglecta* (Hook.)
  Skog. 13336
  R   19890   Jamaica 19890

R *Gesneria pumila* Sw. ssp. *proctorii* (Stearn)
  Skog 13336
  R   13336   Jamaica 13336

R *Gesneria scabra* Sw. 20883
  R   20883   Jamaica 20883

I *Gesneria scabra* Sw. var. *fawcettii* (Urb.)
  Skog 19890
  I   19890   Jamaica 19890

R *Gesneria scabra* var. *scabra* 19890
  R   19890   Jamaica 19890

V *Gesneria scabra* var. *sphaerocarpa* (Urb.)
  Skog 19890
  V   19890   Jamaica 19890

R *Gesneria scabra* var. *viridicalyx* Skog 19890
  R   19890   Jamaica 19890

V *Gesneria wrightii* Urban 5607
  V   19105   Cuba (Guantanamo) 5607

R *Gloxinia dodsonii* Wiehler 16958
  R   16958   Ecuador 16958

R *Haberlea rhodopensis* Friv. 5204, 20171
  R   5204   Bulgaria (central & south) 5204

V *Jankaea heldreichii* (Boiss.) Boiss. 17781, 20171
  V   19174   Greece (central (Olimbos)) 8000

R *Kohleria amabilis* (Planchon & Linden) Fritsch 21254
  R   21254   Colombia 21254

R *Lenbrassia australiana* (C.White) G.Gillett 20681
  R   20681   Australia - Queensland 20681

I *Linnaeopsis alba* (E.A. Bruce) B.L. Burtt 5926
  I   5926   Tanzania (Uluguru mountains) 5926

I *Linnaeopsis heckmanniana* Engl. 5926
  I   5926   Tanzania (Uluguru mountains) 5926

I *Linnaeopsis subscandens* B.L. Burtt 5926
  I   5926   Tanzania (Uluguru mountains) 5926

R *Lysionotus ikedae* Hatus. 14961
  R   20854   Taiwan (Botel Tobago) 14961

R *Monophyllaea hirticalyx* Franch.
  R   Malaysia - Peninsular Malaysia

V *Monopyle grandiflora* Wiehl. 20883, 9718
  V   16317   Panama 20883

E *Monopyle panamensis* Mort. 20883, 9006
  E   20883   Panama 20883

V *Moussonia ampla* L. Skog 20883, 9006
  V   16317   Panama 20883

R *Moussonia hirsutissima* (C. Morton) Wiehler 9719
  R   9719   Mexico 9719

V *Moussonia serrulata* (Mort.) Wiehl. 20883, 9006
  R   9719   Panama 20883

R *Moussonia triflora* (Martens & Galeotti) Hanst. 9719
  R   9719   Mexico 9719

R *Nautilocalyx colombianus* Wiehl. 20883
  V   20883   Panama 20883

V *Nautilocalyx colonensis* Wiehl. 20883, 9721

V   *16317*   Panama *20883*

V   *Nautilocalyx dressleri* Wiehl. *20883, 9006*
     V   *16317*   Panama *20883*

R   *Nautilocalyx panamensis* (Seem.) Seem. *20883*
     V   *20883*   Panama *20883*

E   *Nautilocalyx pemphidius* L. Skog *20883*
     I   *20883*   Venezuela *20883*

E   *Nautilocalyx speciosus* Wiehl. *20883, 9721*
     R   *9719*   Panama *20883*

R   *Negria rhabdothamnoides* F. Muell.
     R   *14225*   Australia - NSW - Lord Howe Is. *14225*

V   *Oerstedina cerricola* Wiehl. *20883, 9006*
     I   *20883*   Panama *20883*

E   *Oerstedina suffrutescens* L. Skog *20883, 9006*
     R   *9719*   Panama *20883*

R   *Opithandra primuloides* (Miq.) B.L. Burtt *10573*
     R   *10573*   Japan *10573*

I   *Ornithoboea pseudoflexuosa* Burtt *19120*
     I   *19120*   Thailand *19120*

I   *Paraboea bakeri* M.R. Henderson
     I   Malaysia - Peninsular Malaysia

I   *Paraboea bettiana* M.R. Henderson
     I   Malaysia - Peninsular Malaysia

I   *Paraboea bintangensis* Burtt
     I   Malaysia - Peninsular Malaysia

R   *Paraboea capitata* Ridley
     R   Malaysia - Peninsular Malaysia

R   *Paraboea laxa* Ridley
     R   Malaysia - Peninsular Malaysia (Langkawi, Kedah)

I   *Paraboea vulpina* Ridley
     I   Malaysia - Peninsular Malaysia (Perak)

E   *Paradrymonia alba* Wiehl. *20883, 9721*
     I   *20883*   Panama *20883*

V   *Paradrymonia flava* Wiehl. *20883, 9721*
     R   *9719*   Panama *20883*

V   *Paradrymonia macrophylla* Wiehl. *20883, 9721*
     V   *9719*   Panama *20883*

E   *Paradrymonia ommata* L. Skog *20883, 9006*
     R   *9719*   Panama *20883*

R   *Pearcea bilabiata* Kvist & Skog *21260*
     R   *21260*   Ecuador *21260*

E   *Pheidonocarpa corymbosa* (Sw.) Skog *20883, 19890*
     E   *19890*   Jamaica *20883*

V   *Pheidonocarpa cubensis* (Morton) Borh. *5607*
     V   *19105*   Cuba (Guantanamo) *5607*

V   *Phinaea pulchella* (Griseb.) Morton
     V   *19105*   Cuba (Pinar del Rio) *19105*

R   *Ramonda nathaliae* Pancic & Petrovic *20171*
     R   (former) Yugoslavia

R   *Ramonda serbica* Pancic *8000, 20171*
     R   *20178*   Albania *20178*
     R   *5204*   Bulgaria (north-west) *5204*
     V   Greece
     R   (former) Yugoslavia

V   *Reldia alternifolia* Wiehl. *20883, 9006*
     V   *9719*   Panama *20883*

V   *Reldia veraguensis* Wiehl. *20883, 9006*
     V   *16317*   Panama *20883*

R   *Rhynchoglossum lazulinum* A. Rao & Joseph *14782*
     R   *14782*   India - Arunachal Pradesh *14782*

R   *Rhytidophyllum grande* (Sw.) Mart. *20883*
     R   *20883*   Jamaica *20883*

R   *Rhytidophyllum grande* (Sw.) Mart. var.
     grande *20883*
     R   *20883*   Jamaica *20883*

R   *Rhytidophyllum grande* (Sw.) Mart. ex G. Don var.
     laevigatum C.D. Adams *15911*
     R   *13336*   Jamaica *15911*

V   *Rhytidophyllum minus* Urban *5607*
     V   *19105*   Cuba (Granma) *5607*

I   *Rhytidophyllum rhodocalyx* Urban *5607*
     I   *19105*   Cuba (Granma; Santiago de Cuba) *5607*

V   *Rufodorsia intermedia* Wiehl. *20883, 9006*
     I   *20883*   Panama *20883*

V   *Rufodorsia major* Wiehl. *20883, 9006*
     R   *9719*   Panama *20883*

I   *Saintpaulia confusa* B.L. Burtt *19103*
     I   *8015*   Tanzania (east Usambara Mts.) *19103*

I   *Saintpaulia difficilis* B.L. Burtt *19103*
     I   *19103*   Tanzania (east Usambara Mts.) *19103*

I   *Saintpaulia diplotricha* B.L. Burtt *19103*
     I   *8015*   Tanzania (east Usumbaras & coastal plain) *19103*

I   *Saintpaulia grandifolia* B.L. Burtt *19103*
     I   *8015*   Tanzania (West Usambara mountains) *5926*

I   *Saintpaulia grotei* Engl. *19103*
     I   *19103*   Tanzania (east Usambara Mts.) *19103*

I   *Saintpaulia inconspicua* B.L. Burtt *19103*
     I   *8015*   Tanzania (Uluguru mountains) *19103*

I   *Saintpaulia intermedia* B.L. Burtt *19103*
     I   *8015*   Tanzania (coastal plain, Tanga and E. Usambara mountains) *19103*

E   *Saintpaulia ionantha* H.A. Wendl. *19103*
     E   *19103*   Tanzania (east Usambara Mts.) *5926*

I   *Saintpaulia magungensis* Roberts var. *minima* B.L.
     Burtt *19130*
     I   *19103*   Tanzania (east Usambara Mts.) *5926*

I   *Saintpaulia magungensis* Roberts var. *occidentalis*
     B.L. Burtt *19103*
     I   *8015*   Tanzania (W. Usambara mountains) *19103*

I   *Saintpaulia orbicularis* B.L. Burtt *19103*
     I   *19103*   Tanzania (W. Usambara mountains) *19103*

I   *Saintpaulia orbicularis* Burtt var. *purpurea*
     Burtt *5926*
     I   *8015*   Tanzania *5926*

I   *Saintpaulia pendula* B.J. Burtt *19103*
     I   *19103*   Tanzania (east Usambara Mts.) *5926*

I   *Saintpaulia pendula* Burtt var. *kizarae*
     Burtt *5926*
     I   *8015*   Tanzania (east Usambara Mts.) *5926*

R   *Saintpaulia pusilla* Engl. *19103*
     R   *19103*   Tanzania (Uluguru and Ukaguru mountains) *19103*

E   *Saintpaulia rupicola* B.L. Burtt *6073*
     E   *6073*   Kenya (south, coastal region) *19103*

I   *Saintpaulia shumensis* B.L. Burtt *19103*
     I   *19103*   Tanzania (W. Usambara mountains) *19103*

E   *Saintpaulia teitensis* B.L. Burtt *19103*
     E   *19103*   Kenya (Teita hills) *19103*

I   *Saintpaulia tongwensis* B.L. Burtt *19103*
     I   *19103*   Tanzania (Mt Tongwe) *19103*

I   *Saintpaulia velutina* B.L. Burtt *19103*
     I   *19103*   Tanzania (W. Usamabara mountains) *19103*

R   *Solenophora chiapasensis* D. Gibson *9004*
     R   *9719*   Mexico *9004*

I   *Streptocarpus bambusetii* Burtt *5926*
     I   *5926*   Tanzania (Nguru) *5926*

R   *Streptocarpus brachynema* Hilliard & B.L. Burtt
     R   Mozambique

I   *Streptocarpus bullatus* Mansf. *5926*
     I   *5926*   Tanzania (Uluguru mountains) *5926*

R   *Streptocarpus cyanandrus* B.L. Burtt *7890*
     R   Zimbabwe *7890*

E   *Streptocarpus davyi* S.Moore *20604, 18023*
     E   *20604*   Swaziland *20604*

R   *Streptocarpus decipiens* Hilliard & B.L.Burtt *20604, 17458*
     R   *20604*   South Africa - Transvaal *20604*

I   *Streptocarpus euanthus* Mansf. *5926*
     I   *5926*   Tanzania (N.E. Uluguru mountains) *5926*

V   *Streptocarpus floribundus* Weigend & T.J.Edwards *20604*
     V   *20604*   South Africa - Natal *20604*

R   *Streptocarpus formosus* (Hilliard & B.L.Burtt) Weigend & T.J.Edwards *20604*
     R   *20604*   South Africa - Cape Province *20604*
     R   *20604*   South Africa - Natal *20604*

I   *Streptocarpus gonjaensis* Engl. *5926*
     I   *5926*   Tanzania (east Usambaras Mts.) *5926*

R   *Streptocarpus grandis* C.B. Clarke ssp. *septentrionalis* Hilliard & Burtt
     R   Zimbabwe

I   *Streptocarpus hirsutissimus* E.A. Bruce *5926*
     I   *5926*   Tanzania (Uluguru mountains) *5926*

R   *Streptocarpus hirticapsa* B.L. Burtt *7890*
     R   Zimbabwe *7890*

I   *Streptocarpus holstii* Engl. *5926*
     I   *5926*   Tanzania (east Usambaras Mts.) *5926*

I   *Streptocarpus inflatus* B.L. Burtt *5926*
     I   *5926*   Tanzania (Iringa) *5926*

R   *Streptocarpus kentaniensis* Britten & Story *20604*
     R   *20604*   South Africa - Cape Province *20604*

I   *Streptocarpus kimbozanus* B.L. Burtt *5926*
     I   *5926*   Tanzania (Uluguru mountains) *5926*

I   *Streptocarpus kungwensis* Hill. & Burtt *5926*
     I   *5926*   Tanzania (Mahali) *5926*

R   *Streptocarpus myoporoides* Hilliard & B.L. Burtt
     R   Mozambique

R   *Streptocarpus nimbicola* Hilliard & B.L. Burtt
     R   Malawi

I   *Streptocarpus parensis* Burtt *5926*
     I   *5926*   Tanzania (Pare mountains & possibly W. Usambara mountains) *5926*

R   *Streptocarpus pogonites* Hilliard & B.L.Burtt *20604, 17458*
     R   *20604*   South Africa - Transvaal *20604*

R   *Streptocarpus porphyrostachys* Hilliard *20604*
     I   *20604*   South Africa - Cape Province *20604*
     R   *20604*   South Africa - Natal *20604*

I   *Streptocarpus schliebenii* Mansf. *5926*
     I   *5926*   Tanzania (Nguru and Ukaguru Mts.) *5926*

I   *Streptocarpus stomandrus* Burtt *5926*
     I   *5926*   Tanzania (Nguru mountains) *5926*

I   *Streptocarpus tchenzemae* Gilli *5926*
     I   *5926*   Tanzania (Uluguru mountains) *5926*

I   *Streptocarpus thysanotus* Hilliard & B.L. Burtt *5926*
     I   *5926*   Tanzania (Uluguru mountains) *5926*

R   *Streptocarpus wendlandii* Spreng. *20604*
     R   *20604*   South Africa - Natal *20604*

Globulariaceae

Number of genera: 10
Number of species: 300
Recorded threatened species: 9   (3%)

Africa; Madagascar; Europe; western Asia.

E   *Globularia ascanii* D. Bramwell & Kunkel *17781*
     E   *19174*   Spain - Canary Is. *17891*

R   *Globularia cambessedesii* Willk. *20171*
     R   *11496*   Spain - Balearic Is. (Mallorca) *11496*

R   *Globularia davisiana* O. Schwarz *12840*
     R   *12840*   Turkey *12840*

R   *Globularia dumulosa* O. Schwarz *12840*
     R   *12840*   Turkey *12840*

R   *Globularia incanescens* Viv. *20171*
     R   Italy

V   *Globularia neapolitana* O.Schwarz *18264, 20171*
     V   *18264*   Italy (Campania) *18264*

R   *Globularia repens* Lam. ssp. *borjae* G.López *20692*
     R   *20692*   Spain (central-eastern) *20692*

E   *Globularia sarcophylla* Svent. *17781*
     E   *20750*   Spain - Canary Is. *17891*

E   *Globularia stygia* Orph. ex Boiss. *8000, 20171*
     E   Greece (mountains of N. Peloponnisos) *8000*

Goetzeaceae

Number of genera: 4
Number of species: 7
Recorded threatened species: 1   (14%)

West Indies.

E   *Goetzea elegans* Wydler *20883, 10197*
     I   *20883*   Puerto Rico (Gujataca G. & Quebradillas) *20883*

Gomortegaceae

Number of genera: 1
Number of species: 1
Recorded threatened species: 1   (100%)

Central Chile.

E   *Gomortega keule* (Mol.) Baillon *21089*,
     V   *20883*   Chile *20883*

Goodeniaceae

Number of genera:	14
Number of species:	300
Recorded threatened species:	33 (11%)

Primarily Australia; also New Zealand, Japan, and tropical and subtropical Old and New World.

R   *Anthotium junciforme* (Vriese) D.A.Morrison *20681*
    R   *20681*   Australia - Western Australia *20681*

V   *Coopernookia georgei* Carolin *20681*
    V   *20681*   Australia - Western Australia *20681*

V   *Coopernookia scabridiuscula* Carolin *14223, 20681*
    V   *20681*   Australia - Queensland *20681*

R   *Dampiera diversifolia* Vriese *20681, 10260*
    R   Australia - Western Australia

R   *Dampiera fusca* Rajput & Carolin *20681*
    I   *20681*   Australia - New South Wales *20681*
    I   *20681*   Australia - Victoria *20681*

R   *Goodenia angustifolia* Carolin *20681*
    R   *20681*   Australia - Queensland *20681*

R   *Goodenia chambersii* F.Muell. *20681*
    R   *20681*   Australia - South Australia *20681*

R   *Goodenia faucium* Carolin *20681*
    R   *20681*   Australia - Northern Territory *20681*

R   *Goodenia fordiana* Carolin *20681*
    R   *20681*   Australia - New South Wales *20681*

R   *Goodenia glomerata* Maiden & Betche *20681*
    R   *20681*   Australia - New South Wales *20681*

V   *Goodenia macbarronii* Carolin *20681*
    I   *20681*   Australia - New South Wales *20681*
    I   *20681*   Australia - Queensland *20681*
    I   *20681*   Australia - Victoria *20681*

R   *Goodenia neogoodenia* (C.Gardner & A.S.George) Carolin *20681*
    R   *20681*   Australia - Western Australia *20681*

R   *Goodenia potamica* Carolin *20681*
    R   *20681*   Australia - Northern Territory *20681*

V   *Goodenia quadrifida* (Carolin) Carolin *20681*
    V   *20681*   Australia - Northern Territory *20681*

R   *Goodenia rostrivalvis* Domin *20681*
    R   *20681*   Australia - New South Wales *20681*

R   *Goodenia rupestris* Carolin *20681*
    R   *20681*   Australia - Northern Territory *20681*

R   *Goodenia stenophylla* F.Muell. *20681*
    R   *20681*   Australia - Western Australia *20681*

V   *Goodenia stirlingii* F.M.Bailey *20681*
    V   *20681*   Australia - Queensland *20681*

R   *Goodenia viridula* Carolin *20681*
    R   *20681*   Australia - Queensland *20681*

V   *Lechenaultia chlorantha* F.Muell. *20681*
    V   *20681*   Australia - Western Australia *20681*

V   *Lechenaultia laricina* Lindley *20681*
    V   *20681*   Australia - Western Australia *20681*

R   *Lechenaultia longiloba* F.Muell. *20681*
    R   *20681*   Australia - Western Australia *20681*

V   *Lechenaultia pulvinaris* C.Gardner *20681*
    V   *20681*   Australia - Western Australia *20681*

R   *Lechenaultia superba* F.Muell. *20681*
    R   *20681*   Australia - Western Australia *20681*

V   *Scaevola coccinea* Daniker *20893*
    V   *20893*   New Caledonia *20893*

E   *Scaevola coriacea* Nutt. *20850, 14209*
    E   *20850*   U.S. - Hawaii (Maui - Waiehu) *20850*

R   *Scaevola gaudichaudii* Hook. & Arn. *20850, 14209*
    R   *20850*   U.S. - Hawaii *20850*

E   *Scaevola kilaueae* O. Deg. *20850*
    E   *20850*   U.S. - Hawaii *20850*

Ex   *Scaevola macrophylla* (Vriese) Benth. *20681, 14223*
    Ex   *20681*   Australia - Western Australia *20681*

E   *Scaevola macropyrena* I. Mueller *20893*
    E   *20893*   New Caledonia *20893*

I   *Scaevola tahitensis* Carlquist *20845*
    I   *20845*   French Polynesia - Society Is. (Tahiti) *20845*

R   *Scaevola verticillata* Leenh. *7730*
    R   Malaysia - Sabah (Mt Tambuyukon) *7730*

V   *Velleia perfoliata* R.Br. *20681*
    V   *20681*   Australia - New South Wales *20681*

V   *Verreauxia verreauxii* (Vriese) Carolin *20681*
    V   *20681*   Australia - Western Australia *20681*

Greyiaceae

Number of genera:	1
Number of species:	3
Recorded threatened species:	1 (33%)

South Africa, mainly eastern Transvaal escarpment and the Drakensberg.

R   *Greyia flanaganii* Bolus *20604, 18289*
    R   *20604*   South Africa - Cape Province (Ciskei - rocky slopes) *20604*

Grossulariaceae

Number of genera:	25
Number of species:	180
Recorded threatened species:	17 (9%)

Cosmopolitan.

V   *Ribes amarum* Munz var. *hoffmannii* Munz *20850*
    V   *20850*   U.S. - California *20850*

I   *Ribes armenum* Pojark. *5942*
    I   *5942*   Armenia *5942*

V   *Ribes binominatum* Heller *20850*
    I   *20850*   U.S. - California *20850*
    I   *20850*   U.S. - Oregon *20850*

V   *Ribes canthariforme* Wiggins *20850*
    V   *20850*   U.S. - California *20850*

E   *Ribes divaricatum* (Heller) Jepson var. *parishii* (Heller) Jepson *20850*
    E   *20850*   U.S. - California *20850*

E   *Ribes echinellum* (Coville) Rehd. *20850*
    E   *20850*   U.S. - Florida (shore, Lake Miccosukee) *20850*
    I   *20850*   U.S. - Georgia *20850*
    E   *20850*   U.S. - South Carolina (McCormick Co.) *20850*

V   *Ribes erythrocarpum* Coville & Leib. *20850*
    I   *20850*   U.S. - Oregon *20850*

R   *Ribes integrifolium* Philippi *13875*
    R   *13875*   Chile *13875*

Ex	*Ribes kolymense* (Trautv.) Komarov ex Pojark *6930*	
	Ex *6930* former USSR *6930*	
I	*Ribes malvifolium* Pojark. *5942*	
	I *5942* Tajikistan *5942*	
	I *5942* Uzbekistan *5942*	
E	*Ribes menziesii* Pursh var. *thacherianum* Jepson *20850*	
	I *20850* U.S. - California *20850*	
R	*Ribes niveum* Lindl. *20850*	
	I *20850* U.S. - Idaho *20850*	
	I *20850* U.S. - Nevada *20850*	
	I *20850* U.S. - Oregon *20850*	
	I *20850* U.S. - Washington *20850*	
R	*Ribes oxyacanthoides* L. ssp. *irriguum* (Dougl.) Sinnott *20850*	
	I *20850* Canada - British Columbia *20850*	
	I *20850* U.S. - Idaho *20850*	
	I *20850* U.S. - Montana *20850*	
	R *20850* U.S. - Oregon *20850*	
	V *20850* U.S. - Washington *20850*	
R	*Ribes sandalioticum* (Arrigoni) Arrigoni *18264*	
	R *18264* Italy - Sardinia *18264*	
E	*Ribes sardoum* Martelli *8000, 20171*	
	E *18264* Italy - Sardinia (Monti di Oliena) *19997*	
V	*Ribes sericeum* Eastw. *20850*	
	I *20850* U.S. - California *20850*	
V	*Ribes tularense* (Coville) Fedde *20850, 11051*	
	V *20850* U.S. - California (Tulare County) *20850*	
I	*Ribes ussuriense* Jancz. *5942*	
	I *5942* Russia (Far East) - Primorye (extreme south-east) *5942*	

Grubbiaceae

Number of genera: 1
Number of species: 3
Recorded threatened species: 1 (33%)

Cape Province (South Africa).

R	*Grubbia rourkei* Carlquist *20604*	
	R *20604* South Africa - Cape Province *20604*	

Gunneraceae

Number of genera: 1
Number of species: 50
Recorded threatened species: 5 (10%)

Southern Hemisphere to southern Mexico.

E	*Gunnera hamiltonii* Kirk *86*	
	E *19305* New Zealand - South Is. *19305*	
R	*Gunnera insignis* (Oersted) A. DC. *9037*	
	V *11533* Costa Rica *9037*	
	V *11533* Nicaragua *11533*	
	R *19577* Panama *9037*	
V	*Gunnera kauaiensis* Rock *20850, 14209*	
	I *20850* U.S. - Hawaii *20850*	
I	*Gunnera killipiana* Lundell *10320*	
	I *11533* Guatemala *11533*	
	I *11533* Mexico *10320*	
E	*Gunnera mexicana* Brandegee *11533*	
	E *11533* Mexico *11533*	

Guttiferae

Number of genera: 50
Number of species: 1,200
Recorded threatened species: 152 (12%)

Moist tropical and North temperate.

E	*Ascyrum macrosepalum* S. Brown	
	E Bermuda	
I	*Bonnetia cordifolia* Maguire *21018*	
	I *21018* Venezuela (Bolívar) *21018*	
I	*Bonnetia liesneri* Steyerm. *21018*	
	I *21018* Venezuela (Amazonas) *21018*	
I	*Bonnetia ptariensis* Steyerm. *21018*	
	I *21018* Venezuela (Bolívar) *21018*	
I	*Bonnetia roseiflora* Maguire *21018*	
	I *21018* Venezuela (Bolívar) *21018*	
V	*Calophyllum amblyphyllum* A.C.Sm.& S.Darwin *19630*	
	V *19630* Fiji (Viti Levu south coast) *19630*	
R	*Calophyllum aureo-brunnescens* M.R. Henderson & Wyatt-Smith *17450*	
	R Malaysia - Peninsular Malaysia (Padang Luas, Pahang)	
V	*Calophyllum bracteatum* Thwaites *8021*	
	V *12838* Sri Lanka (south-west) *8021*	
V	*Calophyllum calaba* L. var. *calaba* *10232*	
	V *20013* Sri Lanka *10232*	
V	*Calophyllum calaba* L. var. *worthingtonii* P. Stevens *10232*	
	V *20013* Sri Lanka (south-west) *10232*	
R	*Calophyllum changii* N. Robson *14961*	
	R *14961* Taiwan (Botel Tobago) *14961*	
E	*Calophyllum cordato-oblongum* Thwaites *8021*	
	E *12838* Sri Lanka (Hinidumkanda & Kanneliya) *8021*	
I	*Calophyllum cuneifolium* Thwaites *8021*	
	I *16162* Sri Lanka (Badulla; Madulkelle) *8021*	
R	*Calophyllum eputamen* P. Stevens var. *eputamen* *10082*	
	R *20771* Mauritius *10082*	
R	*Calophyllum eputamen* P. Stevens var. *grandis* P. Stevens *10082*	
	R *20771* Mauritius *10082*	
I	*Calophyllum fraseri* M.R. Henderson & Wyatt-Smith *20224*	
	I Malaysia - Peninsular Malaysia *20224*	
E	*Calophyllum leucocarpum* A.C. Smith *19630*	
	E *19630* Fiji (Vanua Levu) *19630*	
V	*Calophyllum mooni* Wight *12838*	
	V *12838* Sri Lanka *12838*	
E	*Calophyllum nubicola* D'Arcy & Keating *20883, 10747*	
	I *20883* Panama *20883*	
R	*Calophyllum parviflorum* Bojer ex Baker *10082*	
	R *20771* Mauritius *10082*	
R	*Calophyllum poilanei* Gagnepain *6057*	
	R Vietnam *6057*	
I	*Calophyllum pulgarense* Elm. *13833*	
	I *13833* Philippines (Palawan) *13833*	
R	*Calophyllum rotundifolium* Ridley *17450*	
	R Malaysia - Peninsular Malaysia	

V	*Calophyllum subsessile* King *17450*		
	V		Malaysia - Peninsular Malaysia (Perak)
R	*Calophyllum thwaitesii* Planchon & Triana *8021*		
	R	*12838*	Sri Lanka (south-west) *8021*
R	*Calophyllum tomentosum* Wight *8021*		
	R	*20013*	Sri Lanka *8021*
R	*Calophyllum touranense* Gagnepain *6057*		
	R		Vietnam *6057*
I	*Calophyllum vergens* P. Stevens *20013*		
	I	*20013*	Sri Lanka (south-west) *20013*
R	*Clusia alainii* Borh. *5607*		
	R	*19105*	Cuba (Guantanamo) *5607*
R	*Clusia clusioides* (Griseb.) D'Arcy *20883*		
	I	*20883*	Puerto Rico *20883*
E	*Clusia croatii* D'Arcy *20883, 10747*		
	I	*20883*	Panama *20883*
R	*Clusia cuneata* Benth. *8679*		
	R	*8679*	French Guiana *8679*
	R	*8679*	Guyana *8679*
E	*Clusia cupulata* (Maguire) Maguire *20883, 9006*		
	I	*20883*	Panama *20883*
V	*Clusia dukei* Maguire *20883, 9006*		
	I	*20883*	Panama *20883*
V	*Clusia havetioides* var. *havetioides* (Griseb.) Planchon & Triana *20883*		
	V	*20883*	Jamaica *20883*
E	*Clusia havetioides* var. *pauciflora* Proctor *20883, 13336*		
	E	*13336*	Jamaica *20883*
R	*Clusia havetioides* var. *stenocarpa* (Urban) Proctor *20883*		
	R	*20883*	Jamaica *20883*
R	*Clusia jenmani* Engl. *8679*		
	R		Guyana *8679*
E	*Clusia longipetiolata* Schery *20883, 9006*		
	I	*20883*	Panama *20883*
V	*Clusia moaensis* Borh. & Muniz *5607*		
	V	*19105*	Cuba (Holguin) *5607*
E	*Clusia osseocarpa* Maguire *20883, 9006*		
	I	*20883*	Panama *20883*
E	*Clusia plukenetii* Urban *5710*		
	E	*19001*	Barbados (Turners Hall Wd, Bathsteba) *5710*
	Ex/E	*19001*	Martinique (Mont. Pelee; Carbet; Alma) *5710*
	E	*19001*	St Lucia (Demery, Lesser Piton) *5710*
R	*Clusia portlandiana* Howard & Proctor *20883, 13336*		
	R	*13336*	Jamaica *20883*
R	*Clusia robusta* Eyma *8679*		
	R	*8679*	Suriname *8679*
R	*Clusia tabulamontana* Maguire *8679*		
	R	*8679*	Guyana *8679*
	R	*8679*	Suriname *8679*
V	*Garcinia adinantha* A.C. Smith & S. Darwin *19630*		
	V	*19630*	Fiji (Viti Levu, Vanua Levu) *19630*
V	*Garcinia bifasciculata* N. Robson *19527*		
	V	*20885*	Tanzania (Morogoro District) *19527*
R	*Garcinia brassii* C.White *20681*		
	R	*20681*	Australia - Queensland *20681*
I	*Garcinia cadelliana* King *7771*		

	I	*14782*	India - Andaman Is. *7771*
I	*Garcinia calycina* Kurz *7771*		
	I		India - Nicobar Is. *7771*
V	*Garcinia clarensis* Borh. *5607*		
	V	*19105*	Cuba (Matanzas; Villa Clara) *5607*
V	*Garcinia decussata* Adams *20883*		
	V	*20883*	Jamaica *20883*
R	*Garcinia gibbsiae* S.Moore *20681*		
	R	*20681*	Australia - Queensland *20681*
R	*Garcinia hermonii* Kosterm. *8021*		
	R	*12838*	Sri Lanka *8021*
I	*Garcinia imberti* Bourd.		
	I		India - Kerala
I	*Garcinia indica* Choisy		
	I		India - Karnataka
	I		India - Kerala (Wynaad)
I	*Garcinia kingii* Pierre ex Vesque *7771*		
	I	*14782*	India - Andaman Is. *7771*
V	*Garcinia linii* C.E.Chang *20854*		
	V	*20854*	Taiwan *20854*
R	*Garcinia mestonii* Bailey *20681*		
	R	*20681*	Australia - Queensland *20681*
I	*Garcinia opaca* King *19209*		
	I	*19209*	Malaysia - Peninsular Malaysia (Perak, Selangor/Wilayah Persekutuan, Johor, Kelantan, Terengganu) *19209*
R	*Garcinia poilanei* Gagnepain *6057*		
	R		Vietnam *6057*
V	*Garcinia quaesita* Pierre *8021*		
	V	*12838*	Sri Lanka *8021*
I	*Garcinia rubro-echinata* Kosterm.		
	I		India - Kerala
	I		India - Tamil Nadu
I	*Garcinia semseii* B. Verdcourt *10260*		
	I	*5926*	Tanzania (Nguru & Uluguru Mts.) *20921*
I	*Garcinia sulphurea* Elm. *13833*		
	I	*13833*	Philippines (Busuanga) *13833*
I	*Garcinia talbotii* Raiz. ex Santapau		
	I		India - Karnataka
	I		India - Tamil Nadu
I	*Garcinia terpnophylla* (Thwaites) Thwaites var. *acuminata* Thwaites *16162*		
	I	*16162*	Sri Lanka *16162*
E	*Garcinia terpnophylla* (Thwaites) Thwaites var. *terpnophylla* *8021*		
	E	*12838*	Sri Lanka (Kanneliya FoR) *8021*
I	*Garcinia zeylanica* Roxb. *8021*		
	I		Sri Lanka (Godakanda, Hiniduma) *8021*
E	*Hypericum aciferum* (Greuter) N.Robson *8000, 20171*		
	E	*20730*	Greece - Crete (south-west) *8000*
V	*Hypericum adpressum* Raf. ex W. Bart. *20850*		
	Ex/E	*20850*	U.S. - Connecticut *20850*
	V	*20850*	U.S. - Delaware *20850*
	V	*20850*	U.S. - Georgia *20850*
	E	*20850*	U.S. - Illinois *20850*
	E	*20850*	U.S. - Indiana *20850*
	Ex/E	*20850*	U.S. - Kentucky *20850*
	I	*20850*	U.S. - Louisiana *20850*
	E	*20850*	U.S. - Maryland *20850*
	V	*20850*	U.S. - Massachusetts *20850*
	I	*20850*	U.S. - Mississippi *20850*
	I	*20850*	U.S. - Missouri *20850*
	I	*20850*	U.S. - New Hampshire *20850*

V	20850	U.S. - New Jersey *20850*
E	20850	U.S. - New York *20850*
Ex/E	20850	U.S. - North Carolina *20850*
Ex	20850	U.S. - Pennsylvania *20850*
V	20850	U.S. - Rhode Is. *20850*
E	20850	U.S. - South Carolina *20850*
E	20850	U.S. - Tennessee *20850*
I	20850	U.S. - Vermont *20850*
Ex/E	20850	U.S. - Virginia *20850*
I	20850	U.S. - West Virginia *20850*

R *Hypericum amblycalyx* Coustur. & Gand. *20171*
　　R　　20730　Greece - Crete *20730*

R *Hypericum andjerinum* Font Quer & Pau
　　R　　　　Morocco

E *Hypericum aphyllum* Lundell *9004*
　　E　　11981　Belize *9004*

R *Hypericum athoum* Boiss. & Orph. *19174, 20171*
　　R　　19174　Greece *19174*

I *Hypericum atropanatum* Rzazade *5942*
　　I　　5942　Armenia *5942*

R *Hypericum aviculariifolium* Jaub. & Spach ssp. *byzantinum* (Azn.) Robson *12840, 20171*
　　R　　12840　Turkey *12840*

R *Hypericum aviculariifolium* Jaub. & Spach ssp. *byzantium* (Azn.) Robson *12840*
　　R　　12840　Turkey *12840*

R *Hypericum aviculariifolium* Jaub. & Spach ssp. *uniflorum* (Boiss. & Heldr.) Robson *12840*
　　R　　12840　Turkey *12840*

R *Hypericum balfourii* N. Robson *15534*
　　R　　15534　Yemen - Socotra *15534*

R *Hypericum capitatum* Choisy var. *capitatum* *12840*
　　R　　12840　Turkey *12840*

R *Hypericum chapmanii* P. Adams *20850*
　　I　　20850　U.S. - Florida *20850*

R *Hypericum crenulatum* Boiss. *12840*
　　R　　12840　Turkey *12840*

V *Hypericum cumulicola* (Small) P. Adams *20850, 17890*
　　V　　20850　U.S. - Florida (Polk & Highlands Counties) *20850*

R *Hypericum delphicum* Boiss. & Heldr. *20171*
　　R　　19174　Greece *19174*

V *Hypericum edisonianum* (Small) P. Adams & Robson *20850*
　　V　　20850　U.S. - Florida *20850*

V *Hypericum exile* P. Adams *20850*
　　I　　20850　U.S. - Florida *20850*

R *Hypericum fissurale* Woron *12840*
　　R　　12840　Turkey *12840*

R *Hypericum formosanum* Maxim. *20511*
　　R　　20511　Taiwan *20511*

I *Hypericum formosissimum* Takht. *5942*
　　I　　5942　Armenia *5942*

R *Hypericum fragile* Heldr. & Sart. ex Boiss. *20171*
　　R　　　　Greece

R *Hypericum glandulosum* Aiton
　　R　　　　Portugal - Madeira
　　R　　　　Spain - Canary Is.

R *Hypericum graveolens* Buckl. *20850*
　　V　　20850　U.S. - North Carolina *20850*

R	20850	U.S. - Tennessee *20850*

R *Hypericum haplophylloides* Halácsy & Bald. *20178, 20171*
　　R　　20178　Albania *20178*

R *Hypericum hircinum* L. ssp. *cambessedesii* (Mares & Vigineix) Sauvage *10270*
　　R　　　　Spain - Balearic Is.

R *Hypericum huber-morathii* Robson *12840*
　　R　　12840　Turkey *12840*

V *Hypericum imbricatum* Poulter *12840*
　　V　　12840　Turkey *12840*

I *Hypericum japonicum* Thunb. var. *major* Fyson
　　I　　　　India - Tamil Nadu

V *Hypericum jovis* Greuter
　　V　　20730　Greece - Crete *20730*

V *Hypericum kelleri* Bald. *20171*
　　V　　20730　Greece - Crete *20730*

R *Hypericum kotschyanum* Boiss. *12840*
　　R　　12840　Turkey *12840*

V *Hypericum lanuginosum* Lam. var. *pestalozzae* (Boiss.) Robson *12840*
　　V　　12840　Turkey *12840*

V *Hypericum lissophloeus* P. Adams *20850*
　　V　　20850　U.S. - Florida *20850*

R *Hypericum malatyanum* Pesmen *12840*
　　R　　12840　Turkey *12840*

R *Hypericum marginatum* Woron *12840*
　　R　　12840　Turkey *12840*

R *Hypericum metroi* Maire & Sauvage
　　R　　　　Morocco

I *Hypericum millefolium* *15229*
　　I　　15229　Haiti (La Visite & Macaya National Parks) *15229*

R *Hypericum minutum* Davis & Poulter *12840*
　　R　　12840　Turkey *12840*

R *Hypericum mitchellianum* Rydb. *20850*
　　V　　20850　U.S. - North Carolina *20850*
　　R　　20850　U.S. - Tennessee *20850*
　　V　　20850　U.S. - Virginia *20850*
　　Ex　20850　U.S. - West Virginia *20850*

R *Hypericum monodenum* Robson apud Poulter *12840*
　　R　　12840　Turkey *12840*

R *Hypericum nakamurai* (Masamune) Robson *20511*
　　R　　20511　Taiwan *20511*

R *Hypericum neurocalycinum* Boiss. & Heldr. *12840*
　　R　　12840　Turkey *12840*

R *Hypericum nokoense* Ohwi *20511*
　　R　　20511　Taiwan *20511*

R *Hypericum oliganthum* Franchet & Sav. *10572*
　　R　　10572　Japan *10572*

R *Hypericum olympicum* L. ssp. *auriculatum* Robson & Huber-Mor. *12840*
　　R　　12840　Turkey *12840*

R *Hypericum pamphylicum* Robson & Davis *12840*
　　R　　12840　Turkey *12840*

V *Hypericum polyphyllum* Boiss. & Bal. ssp. *lycium* Robson & Hub.-Mor. *12840*
　　V　　12840　Turkey *12840*

R *Hypericum polyphyllum* Boiss. & Bal. ssp.
   polyphyllum *12840*
   R *12840* Turkey *12840*

R *Hypericum pumilio* Bornm. *12840*
   R *12840* Turkey *12840*

E *Hypericum reflexum* L.f. *20750*
   E *20750* Spain - Canary Is. *20750*

R *Hypericum salsolifolius* Hand.-Mazz. *12840*
   R *12840* Turkey *12840*

V *Hypericum salsugineum* Robson & Hub.-Mor *12840*
   V *14197* Turkey *12840*

R *Hypericum saxifragum* Robson & Hub.-Mor *12840*
   R *12840* Turkey *12840*

R *Hypericum scabroides* Robson & Poulter *12840*
   R *12840* Turkey *12840*

R *Hypericum sinaicum* Hochst. *10269*
   R Egypt (Sinai) *10269*

R *Hypericum socotranum* Good *15534*
   R *15534* Yemen - Socotra *15534*

R *Hypericum socotranum* Good ssp. *smithii* N.
   Robson *15534*
   R *15534* Yemen - Socotra *15534*

R *Hypericum sorgerae* Robson *12840*
   R *12840* Turkey *12840*

R *Hypericum strictum* Maleev
   R former European USSR (Caucasus) *6930*

R *Hypericum subalatum* Hayata *20511*
   R *20511* Taiwan *20511*

R *Hypericum taygeteum* Quézel & Contandr. *20171*
   R Greece

R *Hypericum ternatum* Poulter *12840*
   R *20618* Turkey *20618*

R *Hypericum thymbrifolium* Boiss. & Noe *12840*
   R *12840* Turkey *12840*

R *Hypericum thymopsis* Boiss. *12840*
   R *12840* Turkey *12840*

V *Hypericum tortuosum* Balf. f. *15534*
   V *15534* Yemen - Socotra *15534*

R *Hypericum tosaensis* Makino *10572*
   R *10572* Japan *10572*

R *Hypericum uniglandulosum* Hausskn. & Bornm. *12840*
   R *12840* Turkey *12840*

R *Hypericum vacciniifolium* Hayek & Siehe *12840*
   R *20618* Turkey *20618*

R *Hypericum yojiroanum* Tatew. & Kudo *10572*
   R *10572* Japan *10572*

E *Mammea immansueta* D'Arcy *20883, 10747*
   I *20883* Panama *20883*

R *Mammea malayana* Kosterm.
   R Malaysia - Peninsular Malaysia

R *Mammea praetermissa* P.F. Stevens
   R Malaysia - Peninsular Malaysia

R *Mammea shahii* P.F. Stevens
   R Malaysia - Peninsular Malaysia

R *Mammea touriga* (C.White & Francis) L.S.Smith *20681*
   R *20681* Australia - Queensland *20681*

I *Mammea usambarensis* Verdc. *20556, 19527*
   I *5926* Tanzania (West Usambara Mts.) *20921*

R *Mesua daphnifolia* (Ridley) Kosterm. *17450*
   R Malaysia - Peninsular Malaysia

R *Mesua larnachiana* (F.Muell.) Kosterm. *20681*
   R *20681* Australia - Queensland *20681*

I *Mesua manii* (King) Kosterm. *7771*
   I *14782* India - Andaman Is. (South) *7771*

R *Mesua nivenii* Whitm. *17450*
   R Malaysia - Peninsular Malaysia

R *Mesua purseglovei* Whitm. *17450*
   R Malaysia - Peninsular Malaysia

V *Montrouziera cauliflora* Planchon & Triana *20893*
   V *20893* New Caledonia *20893*

I *Poeciloneuron pauciflorum* Beddome *14782*
   I *14782* India - Kerala *14782*
   I *14782* India - Tamil Nadu *14782*

R *Rheedia aristata* Griseb. *11840*
   R *19105* Cuba *11840*

V *Symphonia globulifera* L.f. var. *angustifolia*
   Maguire *10351*
   V *11981* Panama *10351*

E *Thornea matudae* (Lundell) Breedlove & Clintock *9732*
   E *11981* Mexico - Chiapas *9732*

E *Tovomita morii* Maguire *20883, 9006*
   I *20883* Panama *20883*

V *Tovomitopsis angustifolia* Maguire *20883, 9006*
   I *20883* Panama *20883*

E *Tovomitopsis faucis* D'Arcy *20883, 10747*
   I *20883* Panama *20883*

V *Vismia jefensis* N. Robson *20883, 9006*
   R *11981* Panama *20883*

V *Vismia pauciflora* Milne-Redh. *19527*
   V *20885* Tanzania (Lindi) *19527*

R *Vismia torrei* Mendes *7902*
   R Mozambique *7902*

Gyrostemonaceae

Number of genera: 5
Number of species: 17
Recorded threatened species: 1   (5%)

Australia.

V *Codonocarpus pyramidalis* (F.Muell.) Benth. *20681*
   Ex/E *20681* Australia - New South Wales *20681*
   V *20681* Australia - South Australia *20681*

Ex *Gyrostemon reticulatus* A.S.George *20681*
   Ex *20681* Australia - Western Australia *20681*

Halophytaceae

Number of genera: 1
Number of species: 1
Recorded threatened species: 1 (100%)

Argentina.

I *Halophytum ameghinoi* (Speg.) Speg. *16336*
   I *16336* Argentina *16336*
   I *20176* Argentina - Santa Cruz *20176*
   I *20176* Argentina - La Rioja *20176*

Haloragaceae

Number of genera:	8
Number of species:	100
Recorded threatened species:	26 (26%)

Cosmopolitan, especially Southern Hemisphere.

R   *Gonocarpus effusus* Orch. *20681*
    R   *20681*   Australia - Queensland *20681*

E   *Gonocarpus intricatus* (Benth.) Orch. *20681, 14223*
    E   *20681*   Australia - Western Australia *20681*

R   *Gonocarpus longifolius* (Schindler) Orch. *20681*
    I   *20681*   Australia - New South Wales *20681*
    I   *20681*   Australia - Queensland *20681*

R   *Gonocarpus salsoloides* Reichb. ex Sprengel *20681*
    R   *20681*   Australia - New South Wales *20681*

R   *Haloragis eichleri* Orch. *20681*
    R   *20681*   Australia - South Australia *20681*

V   *Haloragis exalata* (F.Muell.) Orch. ssp. exalata *20681*
    I   *20681*   Australia - New South Wales *20681*
    I   *20681*   Australia - Victoria *20681*

V   *Haloragis exalata* (F.Muell.) Orch. ssp. *velutina* Orch. *20681*
    I   *20681*   Australia - New South Wales *20681*
    I   *20681*   Australia - Queensland *20681*

E   *Haloragis eyreana* Orch. *20681*
    E   *20681*   Australia - South Australia *20681*

Ex   *Haloragis platycarpa* Benth. *20681*
    Ex   *20681*   Australia - Western Australia *20681*

I   *Haloragis stokesii* F.Brown *20845*
    I   *20845*   French Polynesia - Tubuai Is. (Rapa) *20845*

V   *Haloragis walkeri* Ohwi *10572*
    V   *10572*   Japan *10572*

R   *Haloragodendron baeuerlenii* (F.Muell.) Orch. *20681*
    I   *20681*   Australia - New South Wales *20681*
    I   *20681*   Australia - Victoria *20681*

R   *Haloragodendron glandulosum* Orch. *20681*
    R   *20681*   Australia - Western Australia *20681*

E   *Haloragodendron lucasii* (Maiden & Betche) Orch. ssp. lucasii *20681*
    E   *20681*   Australia - New South Wales *20681*

R   *Haloragodendron monospermum* (F.Muell.) Orch. *20681*
    R   *20681*   Australia - New South Wales *20681*

I   *Laurembergia indica* (Thwaites) Schindler *10252*
    I   *16162*   Sri Lanka *10252*

I   *Laurembergia zeylanica* (Arn. ex C.B. Clarke) Schindler *10252*
    I   *16162*   Sri Lanka *10252*

E   *Meziella trifida* (Nees) Schindler *20681, 14223*
    E   *20681*   Australia - Western Australia *20681*

R   *Myriophyllum austropygmaeum* Orch. *20681*
    R   *20681*   Australia - Tasmania *20681*

R   *Myriophyllum balladoniense* Orch. *20681*
    R   *20681*   Australia - Western Australia *20681*

V   *Myriophyllum implicatum* Orch. *20681*
    Ex/E   *20681*   Australia - New South Wales *20681*
    V   *20681*   Australia - Queensland *20681*

E   *Myriophyllum lapidicola* Orch. *20681*
    E   *20681*   Australia - Western Australia *20681*

R   *Myriophyllum laxum* Shuttlw. ex Chapman *20850*
    E   *20850*   U.S. - Alabama *20850*
    V   *20850*   U.S. - Florida *20850*
    V   *20850*   U.S. - Georgia *20850*
    I   *20850*   U.S. - Mississippi *20850*
    E   *20850*   U.S. - North Carolina *20850*
    V   *20850*   U.S. - South Carolina *20850*

V   *Myriophyllum petraeum* Orch. *20681*
    V   *20681*   Australia - Western Australia *20681*

V   *Myriophyllum porcatum* Orch.. *20681*
    V   *20681*   Australia - Victoria *20681*

R   *Myriophyllum robustum* Hook.f. *86*
    R   *19305*   New Zealand - North Is. *19305*
    R   *19305*   New Zealand - South Is. *19305*

E   *Myriophyllum sparsiflorum* C. Wright
    E   *19105*   Cuba (Pinar del Rio) *19105*

R   *Myriophyllum ussuriense* (Regel) Maxim. *20850, 14397*
    V   *20850*   Canada - British Columbia *20850*

Hamamelidaceae

Number of genera:	26
Number of species:	100
Recorded threatened species:	22 (22%)

Widespread, especially eastern Asia.

R   *Altingia poilanei* Tard. *6057*
    R   Vietnam *6057*

R   *Chunia bucklandioides* H.T. Chang *17617*
    R   *17617*   China - Hainan Is. *11139*

R   *Corylopsis coreana* Uyeki *15957*
    R   Korea, South (Mt Chiri, Mt Paekwoon, Mt Chogyae) *15957*

R   *Corylopsis glabrescens* Franchet & Sav. *10572*
    R   *10572*   Japan *10572*

R   *Corylopsis gotoana* Makino *10572*
    R   *10572*   Japan *10572*

R   *Corylopsis stenopetala* Hayata *20511*
    R   *20511*   Taiwan *20511*

E   *Disanthus cercidifolius* Maxim. var. *longipes* H.T. Chang *17617*
    E   *17617*   China - Hunan *11139*
    E   *17617*   China - Jiangxi (Nanfeng) *11139*
    E   *17617*   China - Zhejiang (Longquan) *11139*

R   *Distylium gracile* Nakai *20854*
    R   *20854*   Taiwan *20854*

R   *Embolanthera glabrescens* Merr. *6057*
    R   Vietnam *6057*

I   *Embolanthera spicata* Merr. *13833*
    I   *13833*   Philippines (Mt. Victoria) *13833*

R   *Fothergilla major* (Sims) Lodd. *20850*
    V   *20850*   U.S. - Alabama *20850*
    E   *20850*   U.S. - Arkansas *20850*
    E   *20850*   U.S. - Georgia *20850*
    V   *20850*   U.S. - North Carolina *20850*
    E   *20850*   U.S. - South Carolina *20850*
    V   *20850*   U.S. - Tennessee *20850*

R   *Hamamelis japonica* Sieber & Zucc. var. *bitchuensis* Ohwi *10572*
    R   *10572*   Japan *10572*

E   *Liquidambar orientalis* Miller var. *integriloba* Fiori *12840*
    E   *20618*   Turkey *20618*

R *Liquidambar orientalis* Miller var.
    orientalis *20618*
  R   *20731* Greece - East Aegean Is (Rhodes) *20731*
  E   *20618* Turkey *20618*

E *Maingaya malayana* Oliver *10260*
  E   Malaysia - Peninsular Malaysia (Penang, Perak)

R *Matudaea hirsuta* Lundell *10310*
  R   *19755* Mexico - Mexico State *10310*

R *Neostrearia fleckeri* L.S.Smith *20681*
  R   *20681* Australia - Queensland *20681*

R *Noahdendron nicholasii* Endress, B.Hyland &
    Tracey *20681*
  R   *20681* Australia - Queensland *20681*

R *Ostrearia australiana* Baillon *20681*
  R   *20681* Australia - Queensland *20681*

R *Semiliquidambar cathayensis* H.T. Chang *17617*
  R   *17617* China - Fujian *11139*
  R   *17617* China - Guangdong *11139*
  R   *17617* China - Guangxi *11139*
  R   *17617* China - Guizhou *11139*
  R   *17617* China - Hunan (Yizhang) *11139*
  R   *17617* China - Jiangxi *11139*
  R   *17617* China - Zhejiang (Qingyun) *11139*

R *Sinowilsonia henryi* Hemsley *17617*
  R   *17617* China - Gansu *11139*
  R   *17617* China - Henan *11139*
  R   *17617* China - Hubei *11139*
  R   *17617* China - Shaanxi *11139*
  R   *17617* China - Sichuan *11139*

R *Tetrathyrium subcordatum* Benth. *17617*
  R   *17617* China - Guangxi (Longzhou) *11139*
  R   Hong Kong *11139*

I *Trichocladus dentatus* Hutch. *19528*
  I   *5926* Tanzania (Rungwe) *19528*

Hernandiaceae

Number of genera: 4
Number of species: 60
Recorded threatened species: 11 (18%)

Tropical.

R *Hernandia albiflora* (C.T.White) Kubizki *20681*
  R   *20681* Australia - Queensland *20681*

R *Hernandia bivalvis* Benth. *20681*
  R   *20681* Australia - Queensland *20681*

R *Hernandia catalpifolia* Britton & Harris *20883*
  R   *20883* Jamaica *20883*

E *Hernandia cubensis* Griseb. *5607*
  E   *19105* Cuba (Guantanamo) *5607*

Ex *Hernandia drakeana* Nadeaud *20845*
  Ex *20845* French Polynesia - Society Is. (Moorea)
           20845

E *Hernandia hammelii* D'Arcy *20883, 10747*
  I   *20883* Panama *20883*

R *Hernandia jamaicensis* Britton & Harris *20883*
  R   *20883* Jamaica *20883*

E *Hernandia mascarenensis* (Meisn.) Kubitzki *10082*
  E   *14234* Réunion *14234*
  Ex *20771* Mauritius *10082*

I *Hernandia moerenhoutiana* Guillemin ssp. *elliptica*
    H. Saint John *20845*
  I   *20845* French Polynesia - Tubuai Is. *20845*

I *Hernandia tahitensis* J.Moore *20845*
  I   *20845* French Polynesia - Society Is. (Raiatea,
          Tahiti) *20845*
  I   *20845* French Polynesia - Tubuai Is. *20845*

E *Hernandia temarii* Nadeaud *20845*
  E   *20845* French Polynesia - Society Is. (Tahiti)
          20845

R *Sparattanthelium tarapotanum* Meissn. *18200*
  R   *12468* Peru *18200*

Hippocastanaceae

Number of genera: 2
Number of species: 16
Recorded threatened species: 1 (6%)

North America to northern South America; Europe; Southeast
Asia.

V *Aesculus wangii* Hu ex Fang *17617*
  V   *17617* China - Yunnan (Wuenshanzhou; Jingping)
          11139
  V   *21312* Vietnam *21312*

Hoplestigmataceae

Number of genera: 1
Number of species: 2
Recorded threatened species: 1 (50%)

Western tropical Africa.

I *Hoplestigma pierreanum* Gilg
  I   Cameroon (Cameroon mt)

Humiriaceae

Number of genera: 8
Number of species: 50
Recorded threatened species: 4 (8%)

Mainly tropical South America, with one species in Africa.

R *Humiriastrum diguense* (Cuatr.) Cuatr. *20883, 9417*
  V   *20883* Costa Rica *20883*
  I   *20883* Panama *20883*
  I   *20883* Colombia *20883*

R *Vantanea barbourii* Standl. *20883, 9006*
  V   *20883* Costa Rica *20883*
  I   *20883* Nicaragua *20883*
  I   *20883* Panama *20883*

V *Vantanea depleta* McPherson *20883, 12476*
  I   *20883* Panama *20883*

R *Vantanea guianensis* Aublet *8679*
  R   *8679* French Guiana *8679*
  R   *8679* Guyana *8679*
  R   *8679* Suriname *8679*

Hydnoraceae

Number of genera: 2
Number of species: 10
Recorded threatened species: 1 (10%)

Drier parts of Africa, Madagascar.

E *Prosopanche costaricensis* Gómez & Gómez-Laurito *9037*
  E   *9593* Costa Rica *9037*

Hydrangeaceae

Number of genera: 17
Number of species: 170
Recorded threatened species: 18 (10%)

Temperate and subtropical Northern Hemisphere; southeastern Asia and Malesia.

V	*Carpenteria californica* Torr. *20850*	
	V *20850* U.S. - California *20850*	
I	*Deutzia amurensis* Airy Shaw	
	I India (NW Himalaya)	
R	*Deutzia cordatula* Li *20854*	
	R *20854* Taiwan *20854*	
R	*Deutzia coreana* Lev. var. *tozawae* (Nakai) Hatus. *15957*	
	R *15923* Korea, South (Koesan, Haenam) *15957*	
R	*Deutzia coreana* Lev. var. *triradiata* (Nakai) Hatus. *15957*	
	R *15923* Korea, South (Kyongsang-do, Mt Sorak) *15957*	
R	*Deutzia uniflora* Shirai *10572*	
	R *10572* Japan *10572*	
R	*Fendlera rigida* I.M. Johnston *20850*	
	E *20850* U.S. - Texas *20850*	
I	*Hydrangea nebulicola* Nevling & Gómez-Pompa *19850*	
	I *19850* Mexico - Veracruz *9114*	
V	*Jamesia americana* Torr. & Gray var. *macrocalyx* (Small) Engl. *20850*	
	V *20850* U.S. - Utah *20850*	
V	*Jamesia americana* Torr. & Gray var. *zionis* N. & P. Holmgren *20850*	
	V *20850* U.S. - Utah *20850*	
V	*Jamesia tetrapetala* N. & P. Holmgren *20850*	
	V *20850* U.S. - Nevada *20850*	
	E *20850* U.S. - Utah *20850*	
R	*Kirengeshoma palmata* Yatabe *17617*	
	R *17617* China - Anhui (Huanshan, Qinliangfeng) *11139*	
	R *17617* China - Zhejiang (Tianmushan; Longtangshan) *11139*	
	R Japan (Shikoku) *8751*	
R	*Philadelphus cordifolius* Lange *20850*	
	I *20850* U.S. - California *20850*	
V	*Philadelphus crinitus* (C.L. Hitchc.) Hu *20850*	
	I *20850* U.S. - Arizona *20850*	
	E *20850* U.S. - Texas *20850*	
V	*Philadelphus ernestii* Hu *20850*	
	V *20850* U.S. - Texas *20850*	
V	*Philadelphus floridus* Beadle *20850*	
	I *20850* U.S. - Georgia *20850*	
V	*Philadelphus maculatus* (C.L. Hitchc.) Hu *20850*	
	I *20850* U.S. - Arizona *20850*	
V	*Philadelphus pumilus* Rydb. *20850*	
	I *20850* U.S. - California *20850*	
V	*Philadelphus texensis* Hu *20850*	
	V *20850* U.S. - Texas *20850*	
E	*Philadelphus texensis* Hu var. *coryanus* Hu *20850*	
	E *20850* U.S. - Texas *20850*	
V	*Philadelphus texensis* S.Y. Hu var.	

texensis 20850

	V *20850* U.S. - Texas *20850*	
V	*Philadelphus wootonii* Hu *20850*	
	V *20850* U.S. - New Mexico *20850*	

Hydrophyllaceae

Number of genera: 20
Number of species: 250
Recorded threatened species: 82 (32%)

Wide-ranging, especially dry western United States.

R	*Draperia systyla* (Gray) Torr. ex Gray *20850*	
	I *20850* U.S. - California *20850*	
R	*Emmenanthe rosea* (Brand) Constance *20850*	
	I *20850* U.S. - California *20850*	
V	*Eriodictyon altissimum* P.V. Wells *20850*	
	V *20850* U.S. - California *20850*	
V	*Eriodictyon capitatum* Eastw. *20850*	
	V *20850* U.S. - California *20850*	
R	*Eriodictyon crassifolium* Benth. *20850*	
	I *20850* U.S. - California *20850*	
R	*Eriodictyon lanatum* (Brand) Abrams *20850*	
	I *20850* U.S. - California *20850*	
R	*Eriodictyon tomentosum* Benth. *20850*	
	I *20850* U.S. - California *20850*	
R	*Eriodictyon trichocalyx* Heller *20850*	
	I *20850* U.S. - California *20850*	
E	*Hydrolea cubana* (P. Wilson) Alain *5607*	
	E *19105* Cuba (Camaguey) *5607*	
E	*Hydrophyllum brownei* Kral & Bates *20850*	
	E *20850* U.S. - Arkansas *20850*	
R	*Nama retrorsum* J.T. Howell *20850*	
	I *20850* U.S. - Arizona *20850*	
	I *20850* U.S. - New Mexico *20850*	
	V *20850* U.S. - Utah *20850*	
R	*Nama sandwicense* Gray *20850*	
	I *20850* U.S. - Hawaii *20850*	
V	*Nama sandwicensis* A.Gray var. *sandwicensis 14209*	
	V *14209* U.S. - Hawaii *14209*	
R	*Phacelia adenophora* J.T. Howell *20850*	
	I *20850* U.S. - California *20850*	
	I *20850* U.S. - Nevada *20850*	
	I *20850* U.S. - Oregon *20850*	
Ex	*Phacelia amabilis* Constance *20850, 14662*	
	Ex *20850* U.S. - California *20850*	
	I *20850* U.S. - Colorado *20850*	
V	*Phacelia anelsonii* J.F. Macbr. *20850*	
	I *20850* U.S. - California *20850*	
	E *20850* U.S. - Nevada *20850*	
	E *20850* U.S. - Utah *20850*	
V	*Phacelia argentea* A. Nels. & J.F. Macbr. *20850*	
	E *20850* U.S. - California *20850*	
	V *20850* U.S. - Oregon *20850*	
E	*Phacelia argillacea* Atwood *20850*	
	E *20850* U.S. - Utah *20850*	
R	*Phacelia barnebyana* J.T. Howell *20850*	
	I *20850* U.S. - California *20850*	
	I *20850* U.S. - Nevada *20850*	
V	*Phacelia beatleyae* Reveal & Constance *20850*	
	V *20850* U.S. - Nevada *20850*	

R	*Phacelia breweri* Gray *20850*	
	I	*20850* U.S. - California *20850*
R	*Phacelia calthifolia* Brand *20850*	
	I	*20850* U.S. - California *20850*
	I	*20850* U.S. - Nevada *20850*
E	*Phacelia ciliata* Benth. var. *opaca* J.T. Howell *20850*	
	E	*20850* U.S. - California *20850*
Ex	*Phacelia cinerea* Eastw. ex J.F. Macbr. *20850, 14662*	
	Ex	*20850* U.S. - California *20850*
R	*Phacelia congdonii* Greene *20850*	
	I	*20850* U.S. - California *20850*
E	*Phacelia cookei* Constance & Heckard *20850*	
	E	*20850* U.S. - California *20850*
E	*Phacelia cronquistiana* Welsh *20850*	
	I	*20850* U.S. - Arizona *20850*
	E	*20850* U.S. - Utah *20850*
R	*Phacelia dalesiana* J.T. Howell *20850*	
	R	*20850* U.S. - California *20850*
R	*Phacelia demissa* Gray var. *demissa* *20850*	
	I	*20850* U.S. - Arizona *20850*
	I	*20850* U.S. - Colorado *20850*
	I	*20850* U.S. - New Mexico *20850*
		20850 U.S. - Utah *20850*
	I	*20850* U.S. - Wyoming *20850*
R	*Phacelia denticulata* Osterhout *20850*	
	I	*20850* U.S. - Colorado *20850*
	I	*20850* U.S. - New Mexico *20850*
	V	*20850* U.S. - Wyoming *20850*
R	*Phacelia dubia* McVaugh var. *georgiana* Mcvaugh *20850*	
	V	*20850* U.S. - Alabama *20850*
	R	*20850* U.S. - Georgia *20850*
V	*Phacelia exilis* (Gray) G.L. Lee *20850*	
	V	*20850* U.S. - California *20850*
V	*Phacelia floribunda* Greene *20850*	
	E	*20850* U.S. - California *20850*
E	*Phacelia formosula* Osterhout *20850*	
	E	*20850* U.S. - Colorado *20850*
R	*Phacelia geraniifolia* Brand *20850*	
	I	*20850* U.S. - California *20850*
	I	*20850* U.S. - Nevada *20850*
V	*Phacelia glaberrima* (Torr. ex S.Watson) J.T. Howell *20850*	
	V	*20850* U.S. - Nevada *20850*
V	*Phacelia glechomifolia* Gray *20850*	
	I	*20850* U.S. - Arizona *20850*
R	*Phacelia grandiflora* (Benth.) Gray *20850*	
	I	*20850* U.S. - California *20850*
V	*Phacelia greenei* J.T. Howell *20850*	
	V	*20850* U.S. - California *20850*
R	*Phacelia grisea* Gray *20850*	
	I	*20850* U.S. - California *20850*
V	*Phacelia howelliana* Atwood *20850*	
	E	*20850* U.S. - Arizona *20850*
	V	*20850* U.S. - Utah *20850*
V	*Phacelia inconspicua* Greene *20850*	
	V	*20850* U.S. - Idaho *20850*
	E	*20850* U.S. - Nevada *20850*
E	*Phacelia indecora* J.T. Howell *20850*	
	E	*20850* U.S. - Utah *20850*

E	*Phacelia insularis* Munz *20850*	
	I	*20850* U.S. - California *20850*
E	*Phacelia insularis* Munz var. *continentis* J.T. Howell *20850*	
	E	*20850* U.S. - California *20850*
Ex/E	*Phacelia insularis* Munz var. *insularis* *20850*	
	Ex/E	*20850* U.S. - California *20850*
R	*Phacelia inyoensis* (J.F. Macbr.) J.T. Howell *20850*	
	I	*20850* U.S. - California *20850*
V	*Phacelia laxiflora* J.T. Howell *20850*	
	I	*20850* U.S. - Arizona *20850*
	I	*20850* U.S. - Nevada *20850*
	E	*20850* U.S. - Utah *20850*
V	*Phacelia lenta* Piper *20850, 11630*	
	V	*20850* U.S. - Washington *20850*
R	*Phacelia longipes* Torr. ex Gray *20850*	
	I	*20850* U.S. - California *20850*
V	*Phacelia lutea* (Hook. & Arn.) J. T. Howell var. *calva* Cronq. *20850*	
	V	*20850* U.S. - Idaho *20850*
	I	*20850* U.S. - Nevada *20850*
	I	*20850* U.S. - Oregon *20850*
R	*Phacelia lutea* (Hook. & Arn.) J. T. Howell var. *mackenzieorum* J. Grimes & Packard *20850*	
	R	*20850* U.S. - Oregon *20850*
R	*Phacelia lyallii* (Gray) Rydb. *20850, 13153*	
	E	*20850* Canada - Alberta *20850*
	E	*20850* Canada - British Columbia *20850*
	V	*20850* U.S. - Idaho *20850*
	R	*20850* U.S. - Montana *20850*
E	*Phacelia lyonii* (Gray) Rydb. *20850*	
	I	*20850* U.S. - California *20850*
R	*Phacelia mammillarensis* Atwood *20850*	
	R	*20850* U.S. - Utah *20850*
R	*Phacelia marcescens* Eastw. ex J.F. Macbr. *20850*	
	I	*20850* U.S. - California *20850*
E	*Phacelia minutissima* Henderson *20850*	
	E	*20850* U.S. - Idaho *20850*
	E	*20850* U.S. - Nevada *20850*
	Ex/E	*20850* U.S. - Oregon *20850*
	E	*20850* U.S. - Washington *20850*
R	*Phacelia mohavensis* Gray *20850*	
	R	*20850* U.S. - California *20850*
V	*Phacelia mollis* J.F. Macbr. *20850, 1034*	
	E	*20850* Canada - British Columbia *20850*
	E	*20850* Canada - Yukon Territory *20850*
	V	*20850* U.S. - Alaska *20850*
V	*Phacelia monoensis* Halse *20850*	
	V	*20850* U.S. - California *20850*
	V	*20850* U.S. - Nevada *20850*
V	*Phacelia mustelina* Coville *20850*	
	I	*20850* U.S. - California *20850*
	V	*20850* U.S. - Nevada *20850*
R	*Phacelia nashiana* Jepson *20850*	
	R	*20850* U.S. - California *20850*
V	*Phacelia novenmillensis* Munz *20850*	
	V	*20850* U.S. - California *20850*
E	*Phacelia oreopola* Heckard *20850*	
	I	*20850* U.S. - California *20850*
V	*Phacelia pallida* I.M. Johnston *20883, 20850, 8058*	
	E	*20850* U.S. - Texas *20850*
	I	*20883* Mexico *20883*

V   *Phacelia palmeri* Torr. ex S.Watson *20850*
    I   *20850* U.S. - Arizona *20850*
    I   *20850* U.S. - Nevada *20850*
    I   *20850* U.S. - New Mexico *20850*
    V   *20850* U.S. - Utah *20850*

V   *Phacelia parishii* Gray *20850*
    E   *20850* U.S. - California *20850*
    E   *20850* U.S. - Nevada *20850*

R   *Phacelia peirsoniana* J.T. Howell *20850*
    I   *20850* U.S. - California *20850*
    I   *20850* U.S. - Nevada *20850*
    E   *20850* U.S. - Utah *20850*

V   *Phacelia perityloides* Coville *20850*
    I   *20850* U.S. - California *20850*

V   *Phacelia phacelioides* (Benth.) Brand *20850*
    I   *20850* U.S. - California *20850*

R   *Phacelia platyloba* Gray *20850*
    I   *20850* U.S. - California *20850*

R   *Phacelia pringlei* Gray *20850*
    I   *20850* U.S. - California *20850*

V   *Phacelia pulchella* Gray var. *gooddingii* (Brand)
    J.T. Howell *20850*
    I   *20850* U.S. - Arizona *20850*
    V   *20850* U.S. - California *20850*
    I   *20850* U.S. - Nevada *20850*

R   *Phacelia rafaelensis* Atwood *20850*
    V   *20850* U.S. - Arizona *20850*
    R   *20850* U.S. - Utah *20850*

R   *Phacelia salina* (A. Nels.) J.T. Howell *20850*
    I   *20850* U.S. - Nevada *20850*
    I   *20850* U.S. - Utah *20850*
    E   *20850* U.S. - Wyoming *20850*

R   *Phacelia saxicola* Gray *20850*
    I   *20850* U.S. - Arizona *20850*
    I   *20850* U.S. - California *20850*
    I   *20850* U.S. - Nevada *20850*

V   *Phacelia scopulina* (A. Nels.) J. T. Howell var.
    submutica (J.T. Howell) Halse *20850*
    I   *20850* U.S. - Arizona *20850*
    V   *20850* U.S. - Colorado *20850*

V   *Phacelia serrata* J. Voss *20850*
    V   *20850* U.S. - Arizona *20850*

R   *Phacelia stebbinsii* Constance & Heckard *20850*
    R   *20850* U.S. - California *20850*

E   *Phacelia suaveolens* Greene ssp. *keckii* (Munz &
    Johnston) Thorne *20850*
    E   *20850* U.S. - California *20850*

R   *Phacelia umbrosa* Greene *20850*
    I   *20850* U.S. - California *20850*

V   *Phacelia utahensis* J. Voss *20850*
    V   *20850* U.S. - Utah *20850*

R   *Phacelia vallicola* Congd. ex Brand *20850*
    I   *20850* U.S. - California *20850*

R   *Phacelia welshii* Atwood *20850*
    R   *20850* U.S. - Arizona *20850*

E   *Pholistoma auritum* (M.E. Jones) Constance var.
    arizonicum (M.E. Jones) Constance *20850*
    I   *20850* U.S. - Arizona *20850*
    E   *20850* U.S. - California *20850*
    I   *20850* U.S. - Nevada *20850*

R   *Pholistoma racemosum* (Nutt. ex Gray) Constance *20850*
    I   *20850* U.S. - California *20850*

V   *Romanzoffia unalaschensis* Cham. *20850*
    V   *20850* U.S. - Alaska *20850*

Icacinaceae

Number of genera: 50
Number of species: 400
Recorded threatened species: 33   (8%)

Pantropical.

R   *Alsodeiopsis chippii* Hutch. *7926*
    R   Ghana *7926*

I   *Apodytes benthamiana* Wight
    I   India - Meghalaya (Khasi & Jaintia hills)
    I   India - Tamil Nadu

V   *Apodytes geldenhuysii* A.E.van Wyk & Potgieter *20604*
    V   *20604* South Africa - Cape Province *20604*

E   *Calatola columbiana* Sleumer *20883*
    E   *20883* Colombia *20883*

R   *Calatola mollis* Standley *20883*
    R   *20883* Mexico *20883*

R   *Calatola venezuelana* Pittier *20883*
    I   *20883* Colombia *20883*
    I   *20883* Peru *20883*
    I   *20883* Venezuela *20883*

R   *Chlamydocarya anhydathoda* Villiers
    R   Gabon

I   *Chlamydocarya soyauxii* Engl.
    I   Gabon (Libreville & Sibang)

V   *Citronella apogon* (Griseb.) Howard *20883*
    E   *20883* Argentina *20883*
    E   *20883* Bolivia *20883*

E   *Citronella engleriana* (Loesn.) Howard *20883*
    E   *20883* Brazil *20883*

E   *Citronella ilicifolia* (Sleumer) Howard *20883*
    E   *20883* Peru *20883*

R   *Citronella incarum* (Macb.) Howard *20883*
    R   *20883* Peru *20883*

V   *Citronella megaphylla* (Miers) Howard *20883*
    V   *20883* Brazil *20883*

E   *Citronella melliodora* (Sleumer) Howard *20883*
    E   *20883* Peru *20883*

R   *Citronella mucronata* (Ruiz Lopez & Pavon) D.
    Don *13875*
    R   *13875* Chile *13875*

R   *Citronella paniculata* (Mart.) Howard *20883*
    E   *20883* Argentina *20883*
    R   *20883* Brazil *20883*
    V   *20883* Paraguay *20883*

V   *Desmostachys vogelii* Stapf *20858*
    V   *20858* Cameroon *7926*
    V   *20858* Ghana *20858*
    V   *20858* Nigeria *7926*

E   *Discophora montana* Howard *20883*
    E   *20883* Colombia *20883*

R   *Gomphandra comosa* King *7771*
    R   *14782* India - Andaman Is. (south) *7771*
    R   *14782* India - Nicobar Is. *14782*

V   *Grisollea thomassetii* Hemsley *14296*
    V   *19182* Seychelles (granitic) *14296*

I   *Iodes hookeriana* Baill.
    I   Bangladesh

I		India - Meghalaya

E   *Oecopetalum greenmanii* Standley & Steyermark *20883*
    E   *20883* Guatemala *20883*

V   *Oecopetalum guatemalense* Howard *20883*
    E   *20883* Guatemala *20883*
    E   *20883* Mexico *20883*

V   *Ottoschulzia cubensis* (Wright) Urban *20883*
    V   *20883* Cuba *20883*

V   *Ottoschulzia rhodoxylon* (Urban) Urban *20883, 19706*
    V   *20883* Dominican Republic *20883*
    E   *20883* Puerto Rico (western) *20883*

E   *Pennantia baylisiana* (W. Oliver) Baylis *86*
    E   *20625* New Zealand - North Is. (Three King Island) *13378*

R   *Pittosporopsis nervosa* Gagnepain *6057*
    R   Vietnam *6057*

V   *Pleurisanthes flava* Sandwith *20883*
    E   *20883* Brazil *20883*
    E   *20883* Guyana *20883*

E   *Pleurisanthes parviflora* (Ducke) Howard *20883*
    E   *20883* Brazil *20883*

V   *Pleurisanthes simpliciflora* Sleumer *20883*
    V   *20883* Brazil *20883*

I   *Pyrenacantha grandifolia* Engl.
    I   Cameroon (Nkuambe)

I   *Stachyanthus cuneatus* Sleumer
    I   Cameroon

R   *Urandra apicalis* Thwaites *12838*
    R   *12838* Sri Lanka *12838*

Idiospermaceae

Number of genera:	1
Number of species:	1
Recorded threatened species:	1 (100%)

Northern Australia.

R   *Idiospermum australiense* (Diels) S.T.Blake *20681*
    R   *20681* Australia - Queensland *20681*

Illecebraceae

Number of genera:	24
Number of species:	117
Recorded threatened species:	49 (41%)

Widespread.

R   *Dicheranthus plocamoides* Webb *17534*
    R   *15105* Spain - Canary Is. *17534*

V   *Geocarpon minimum* Mackenzie *20850, 19057*
    V   *20850* U.S. - Arkansas *20850*
    E   *20850* U.S. - Louisiana (Winn Parish) *20850*
    V   *20850* U.S. - Missouri *20850*

R   *Gymnocarpos przewalskii* Maxim. *17617*
    R   *17617* China - Gansu *11139*
    R   *17617* China - Nei Monggol Zizhiqu *11139*
    R   *17617* China - Qinghai *11139*
    R   *17617* China - Xinjiang Uygur Zizhiqu *11139*

V   *Herniaria algarvica* Chaudhri *17891, 20171*
    V   Portugal *17891*

R   *Herniaria baetica* Boiss. & Reut. *20171*
    R   Spain

V   *Herniaria berlengiana* (Chaudhri) Franco *17891*
    V   *20076* Portugal *17891*

V   *Herniaria canariensis* Chaudhri
    V   Spain - Canary Is.

I   *Herniaria erckertii* Herm. ssp. *pulvinata* Chaudhri *20604*
    I   *20604* South Africa - Cape Province *20604*
    I   *20604* South Africa - Transvaal *20604*

E   *Herniaria fontanesii* Gay ssp. *empedocleana* (Lojac.) Brullo *18264*
    E   *20738* Italy - Sicily (Porto Empedocle) *20738*

V   *Herniaria latifolia* Lapeyr. ssp. *litardierei* Gamisans *15080*
    V   *15080* France - Corsica *15080*
    E   *18264* Italy - Sardinia *15080*

V   *Herniaria maritima* Link *8000, 20171*
    V   *20076* Portugal *8000*

R   *Herniaria olympica* J.Gay *12840, 20171*
    R   *12840* Turkey *12840*

R   *Herniaria pisidica* Brumm. *12840*
    R   *12840* Turkey *12840*

R   *Herniaria saxatilis* Brumm. *12840*
    R   *12840* Turkey *12840*

I   *Lochia bracteata* Balf. f. *15534*
    I   *15534* Oman (Dhofar) *15534*
    I   *15534* Yemen - Socotra *15534*

R   *Paronychia adalia* Chaudh. *12840*
    R   *12840* Turkey *12840*

V   *Paronychia ahartii* Ertter *20850*
    E   *20850* U.S. - California *20850*

R   *Paronychia americana* (Nutt.) Fenzl ex Walp. *20850*
    I   *20850* U.S. - Alabama *20850*
    I   *20850* U.S. - Florida *20850*
    I   *20850* U.S. - Georgia *20850*
    I   *20850* U.S. - South Carolina *20850*

R   *Paronychia anatolica* Czecz. *12840*
    R   *12840* Turkey *12840*

R   *Paronychia angorensis* Chaudh. *12840*
    R   *12840* Turkey *12840*

R   *Paronychia arabica* (L.) DC. ssp. *euphratica* Choudh. *12840*
    R   *12840* Turkey *12840*

R   *Paronychia argyroloba* Stapf *12840*
    R   *12840* Turkey *12840*

R   *Paronychia beauverdii* Czecz. *12840*
    R   *12840* Turkey *12840*

R   *Paronychia bornmuelleri* Chaudhri *20171*
    R   Greece

R   *Paronychia cataonica* Chaudh. *12840*
    R   *12840* Turkey *12840*

R   *Paronychia chabloziana* Beauverd
    R   Tunisia

R   *Paronychia chartacea* Fern. *20850, 7983*
    V   *20850* U.S. - Florida (south-central peninsula) *20850*

R   *Paronychia chartacea* Fern. ssp. *chartacea* *20850*
    R   *20850* U.S. - Florida *20850*

E   *Paronychia chartacea* Fern. ssp. *minima* L.C. Anders. *20850, 17888*
    E   *20850* U.S. - Florida *20850*

I   *Paronychia chlorolepis* Murb.

I   Tunisia

R   *Paronychia condensata* Chaudh. *12840*
    R   *12840*   Turkey *12840*

E   *Paronychia congesta* Correll *20850*
    E   *20850*   U.S. - Texas *20850*

R   *Paronychia davisii* Chaudh. *12840*
    R   *12840*   Turkey *12840*

R   *Paronychia dudleyi* Chaudh. *12840*
    R   *12840*   Turkey *12840*

R   *Paronychia galatica* Chaudh. *12840*
    R   *12840*   Turkey *12840*

R   *Paronychia gomerensis* (Burchard) Svent. & D. Bramwell *15105*
    R   *15105*   Spain - Canary Is. *15105*

R   *Paronychia jonesii* M.C. Johnston *20850*
    R   *20850*   U.S. - Texas *20850*

R   *Paronychia kayseriana* Chaudh. *12840*
    R   *12840*   Turkey *12840*

V   *Paronychia kurdica* Boiss. var. *fragilis* Chaudhri *12840*
    V   *12840*   Turkey *12840*

R   *Paronychia kurdica* Boiss. ssp. *haussknechtii* Chaudh. *12840*
    R   *12840*   Turkey *12840*

R   *Paronychia kurdica* Boiss. ssp. *montis-munzur* Chaurhri *12840*
    R   *12840*   Turkey *12840*

R   *Paronychia lindheimeri* Englem. ex Gray var. *lindheimeri* *20850*
    I   *20850*   U.S. - New Mexico *20850*
    R   *20850*   U.S. - Texas *20850*

E   *Paronychia lundelliorum* Turner *20850*
    E   *20850*   U.S. - Texas *20850*

R   *Paronychia lycica* Chaudh. *12840*
    R   *12840*   Turkey *12840*

E   *Paronychia maccartii* Correll *20850*
    E   *20850*   U.S. - Texas *20850*

R   *Paronychia paphlagonica* Chaudh. *12840*
    R   *12840*   Turkey *12840*

R   *Paronychia pulvinata* Gray *20850*
    I   *20850*   U.S. - Colorado *20850*
    I   *20850*   U.S. - New Mexico *20850*
    E   *20850*   U.S. - Utah *20850*
    E   *20850*   U.S. - Wyoming *20850*

V   *Paronychia rugelii* (Chapman) Shuttlw. ex Chapman *20850*
    I   *20850*   U.S. - Florida *20850*
    I   *20850*   U.S. - Georgia *20850*

V   *Paronychia rugelii* (Chapman) Shuttlw. ex Chapman var. *interior* (Small) Chaudhri *20850*
    I   *20850*   U.S. - Florida *20850*
    V   *20850*   U.S. - Georgia *20850*

E   *Paronychia rugelii* (Chapman) Shuttlw. ex Chapman var. *rugelii* *20850*
    I   *20850*   U.S. - Florida *20850*
    I   *20850*   U.S. - Georgia *20850*

R   *Paronychia saxatilis* Chaudh. *12840*
    R   *12840*   Turkey *12840*

R   *Paronychia turcica* Chaudh. *12840*
    R   *12840*   Turkey *12840*

V   *Paronychia wilkinsonii* S.Watson *20883, 20850, 8058*
    V   *20850*   U.S. - Texas *20850*
    I   *20883*   Mexico *20883*

R   *Scopulophila parryi* (Hemsley) I.M. Johnston *9661*
    R   *19755*   Mexico *9661*

R   *Scopulophila rixfordii* (Brandeg.) Munz & Johnston *20850*
    I   *20850*   U.S. - California *20850*
    I   *20850*   U.S. - Nevada *20850*

Illiciaceae

Number of genera: 1
Number of species: 40
Recorded threatened species: 3   (7%)

SE Asia, SE US to Hispaniola.

V   *Illicium difengpi* K.I. B. & K.I. M. *17617*
    V   *17617*   China - Guangxi *11139*

E   *Illicium parviflorum* Michx. ex Vent. *20850*
    I   *20850*   U.S. - Alabama *20850*
    E   *20850*   U.S. - Florida *20850*
    Ex/E   *20850*   U.S. - Georgia *20850*

R   *Illicium parvifolium* Merr. *6057*
    R   *20985*   Vietnam *6057*

Ixonanthaceae

Number of genera: 5
Number of species: 30
Recorded threatened species: 1   (3%)

Pantropical.

V   *Ixonanthes khasiana* Hook.f. *11494*
    V   *11494*   India - Assam (Bhutan Hill, Cachar) *11494*
    V   *11494*   India - Meghalaya (Khasi & Jaintia hills) *11494*

Juglandaceae

Number of genera: 7-8
Number of species: 60
Recorded threatened species: 12   (20%)

Widespread in Northern Hemisphere and into South America.

E   *Alfaroa guanacastensis* D. Stone *9037*
    E   *9426*   Costa Rica *9037*

E   *Alfaroa manningii* Leon *9037*
    E   *9426*   Costa Rica *9037*

R   *Alfaroa mexicana* D. Stone *9037*
    R   *19755*   Mexico *9037*

V   *Alfaroa williamsii* A. Molina ssp. *tapantiensis* D. Stone *9037*
    V   *9426*   Costa Rica *9037*

V   *Alfaroa williamsii* A. Molina ssp. *williamsii* *11967*
    V   *11967*   Nicaragua *11967*

R   *Annamocarya sinensis* (Dode) Leroy *17617*
    R   *17617*   China - Guangxi *11139*
    R   *17617*   China - Guizhou (Rongjiang; Snandu) *11139*
    R   *17617*   China - Hunan (Tongdao) *11139*
    R   *17617*   China - Yunnan (Funing; Xichou; Malipe) *11139*
    V   *20985*   Vietnam *6057*

R   *Juglans californica* S.Watson *20850*

I		20850 U.S. - California *20850*

E   *Juglans hindsii* (Jepson) Jepson ex R.E. Sm. *20850*
     E   20850 U.S. - California *20850*
     I   20850 U.S. - Oregon *20850*

I   *Juglans insularis* Griseb. *5607*
     I   20990 Cuba *5607*

R   *Juglans jamaicensis* C. DC. *20883, 17833*
     Ex/E   20883 Jamaica *20883*
     I   20883 Puerto Rico *20883*

V   *Juglans pyriformis* Liebm. *9738*
     V   19850 Mexico *9738*

V   *Oreomunnea mexicana* (Standley) LeRoy ssp.
     costaricensis D. Stone *9037*
     V   9426 Costa Rica *9037*

V   II   *Oreomunnea pterocarpa* Oerst. *20883, 9037*
     V   19943 Costa Rica *20883*

Krameriaceae

Number of genera: 1
Number of species: 15
Recorded threatened species: 3   (20%)

Argentina and Chile, mainly in dry regions.

R   *Krameria bahiana* B. B. Simpson *20883*
     R   20883 Brazil *20883*

V   *Krameria cistoidea* Hook. & Arn. *15088*
     V   13875 Chile *13875*

R   *Krameria paucifolia* (J. Rose) J. Rose *20883*
     R   20883 Mexico *20883*

Labiatae

Number of genera: 200
Number of species: 3,200
Recorded threatened species: 733   (22%)

Cosmopolitan, especially into Mediterranean region and central Asia.

E   *Acanthomintha duttonii* (Abrams) Jokerst *20850*
     E   20850 U.S. - California *20850*

E   *Acanthomintha ilicifolia* (Gray) Gray *20883, 20850,*
     8058
     E   20850 U.S. - California *20850*
     I   20883 Mexico *20883*

E   *Achyrospermum seychellarum* Baker *14296*
     E   14981 Seychelles (Silhouette) *14296*

R   *Acinos corsicus* (Pers.) Getliffe *20171*
     R   15080 France - Corsica *15080*

R   *Acinos exiguus* (Smith) Meikle *14230*
     R   19164 Cyprus (Troodos) *14230*

R   *Acinos troodi* (Post) Leblebici *14230*
     R   19164 Cyprus (Troodos) *14230*

R   *Acinos troodii* (Post) Leblebici ssp. *grandiflora*
     Hartvig & Strid *12840*
     R   12840 Turkey *12840*

R   *Acinos troodii* (Post) Leblebici ssp. *vardaranus* E.
     Leblebici *12840*
     R   12840 Turkey *12840*

I   *Acrocephalus palniensis* Mukerjee *14782*
     I   14782 India - Tamil Nadu (Madurai) *14782*

I   *Acrocephalus sericeus* Benth.
     I   India - Tamil Nadu

I   *Acrocephalus suffruticosus* Wight
     I   India - Tamil Nadu

I   *Acrocephalus wightii* Hook.f.
     I   India - Tamil Nadu

E   *Acrymia ajugiflora* Prain *20739*
     E   20739 Malaysia - Peninsular Malaysia *20739*

E   *Acrymia ajugifolia* Prain *20889*
     E   20889 Malaysia - Peninsular Malaysia (Selangor)
     20889

E   *Ajuga boninsimae* Maxim. *8037*
     E   19134 Japan - Ogasawara-shoto *8037*

R   *Ajuga chamaepitys* (L.) Schreber ssp. *euphratica*
     Davis *12840*
     R   12840 Turkey *12840*

R   *Ajuga incisa* Maxim. *10573*
     R   10573 Japan *10573*

R   *Ajuga piskoi* Degen & Bald. *20171*
     R   20178 Albania (Nemerçe) *8000*

R   *Ajuga postii* Briq. *12840*
     R   12840 Turkey *12840*

R   *Ajuga spectabilis* Nakai *15957*
     R   Korea, South (Mt Baegyang) *15957*

R   *Ajuga tenorii* C.Presl *20171*
     R   Italy
     R   20738 Italy - Sicily (Nebzodi) *20738*

R   *Ajuga vestita* Boiss. *12840*
     R   12840 Turkey *12840*

R   *Ajuga xylorrhiza* Kit Tan *12840*
     R   12840 Turkey *12840*

R   *Amaracus akhdarensis* (Ietsw. & al) Brullo & Furnari
     R   Libya

R   *Amaracus pampaninii* Brullo & Furnari
     R   Libya

V   *Anisochilus argenteus* Gamble *14782*
     V   14782 India (south) *14782*

R   *Anisochilus wightii* Hook.f. *14782*
     R   14782 India - Tamil Nadu *14782*

I   *Arischrada korolkowii* (Regel & Schmalh.) Pobed. *5942*
     I   5942 Kazakhstan *5942*

V   *Ballota andreuzziana* Pampan.
     V   Libya

R   *Ballota cristata* Davis *12840*
     R   12840 Turkey *12840*

R   *Ballota frutescens* (L.) J.Woods *18264, 20171*
     V   20743 France *8000*
     R   18264 Italy (Liguria) *18264*

R   *Ballota inaequidens* Hub.-Mor. & Patzak *12840*
     R   12840 Turkey *12840*

R   *Ballota latibracteolata* Davis & Droszenko *12840*
     R   12840 Turkey *12840*

R   *Ballota macrodonta* Boiss. & Bal. *12840*
     R   12840 Turkey *12840*

R   *Ballota pseudodictamnus* (L.) Benth. *12840, 20171*
     R   12840 Turkey *12840*

R   *Ballota rotundifolia* C. Koch *12840*
     R   12840 Turkey *12840*

R   *Ballota saxatilis* Sieber ex J. &C.Presl. ssp.
     brachyodonta (Boiss.) Davis & Droszenko *12840*
     R   12840 Turkey *12840*

E   *Blephilia hirsuta* Fern. var. *glabrata*
        Fern. *20850*
     I   *20850* Canada - Ontario *20850*
     I   *20850* U.S. - Vermont *20850*

R   *Brazoria arenaria* Lundell *20850*
     R   *20850* U.S. - Texas *20850*

R   *Brazoria pulcherrima* Lundell *20850*
     R   *20850* U.S. - Texas *20850*

R   *Bystropogon canariensis* (L.) L'Herit.
     V   Portugal - Madeira
     R   Spain - Canary Is.

R   *Bystropogon maderensis* Webb
     R   Portugal - Madeira

V   *Bystropogon odoratissimus* Bolle *20750*
     V   *20750* Spain - Canary Is. *20750*

R   *Bystropogon piperitus* Lowe
     R   Portugal - Madeira

V   *Bystropogon plumosus* (L.f.) L'Herit. *20750*
     V   *20750* Spain - Canary Is. *20750*

E   *Bystropogon wildpretii* La Serna *20750*
     E   *20750* Spain - Canary Is. *20750*

R   *Calamintha ashei* (Weatherby) Shinners *20850*
     R   *20850* U.S. - Florida *20850*
     E   *20850* U.S. - Georgia *20850*

R   *Calamintha caroli-henricana* Kit Tan & Sorger *12840*
     R   *12840* Turkey *12840*

E   *Calamintha chandleri* Brandeg. *20883, 20850, 19002*
     E   *20850* U.S. - California *20850*
     I   *20883* Mexico *20883*

R   *Calamintha cretica* (L.) Lam. *20171*
     R   *20730* Greece - Crete *20730*

R   *Calamintha dentata* Chapman *20850*
     R   *20850* U.S. - Florida *20850*

R   *Calamintha glabella* (Michx.) Benth. *20850*
     I   *20850* U.S. - Arkansas *20850*
     I   *20850* U.S. - Kentucky *20850*
     I   *20850* U.S. - Missouri *20850*
     I   *20850* U.S. - Oklahoma *20850*
     R   *20850* U.S. - Tennessee *20850*
     E   *20850* U.S. - Virginia *20850*

R   *Calamintha pamphylica* Boiss. & Heldr. *12840*
     R   *12840* Turkey *12840*

R   *Calamintha rouyana* Rouy *20171*
     R   Spain - Balearic Is.

R   *Calamintha tauricola* Davis *12840*
     R   *12840* Turkey *12840*

I   *Ceratanthus kerrii* Doan *19120*
     I   *19120* Thailand *19120*

R   *Chelonopsis yagiharana* Hisauchi & Matsuno *10573*
     R   *10573* Japan *10573*

R   *Clinopodium multicaule* Kuntze var. *yakushimense*
        (Masam.) Yahara *10573*
     R   *10573* Japan *10573*

I   *Coleus calciola* Murata *19120*
     I   *19120* Thailand *19120*

I   *Coleus elongatus* Trimen *8021*
     I   *16162* Sri Lanka (Ritigala, Anuradhapura) *8021*

V   *Conradina brevifolia* Shinners *20850, 15915*
     V   *20850* U.S. - Florida (L. Wales Ridge) *20850*

E   *Conradina etonia* Kral & McCartney *20850, 15915*

E   *20850* U.S. - Florida (two sites near Etonia Creek)
        20850

E   *Conradina glabra* Shinners *20850, 15915*
     I   *20850* U.S. - Alabama *20850*
     E   *20850* U.S. - Florida (Liberty Co.) *20850*

R   *Conradina grandiflora* Small *20850, 15915*
     R   *20850* U.S. - Florida (scrub vegetation near coast and
        inland) *20850*

V   *Conradina verticillata* Jennison *20850, 14875*
     E   *20850* U.S. - Kentucky *20850*
     E   *20850* U.S. - South Carolina *20850*
     V   *20850* U.S. - Tennessee (north-central) *20850*

E   *Cuminia eriantha* Benth. *19116*
     E   *19116* Chile - Juan Fernandez Is. *19116*

E   *Cuminia fernandezia* Colla *19116*
     E   *19116* Chile - Juan Fernandez Is. *19116*

R   *Cyclotrichium glabrescens* (Bois.& Kot. & Rech. f.)
        Leb. *12840*
     R   *12840* Turkey *12840*

E   *Dicerandra christmanii* R.B. Huck & Judd *20850*
     E   *20850* U.S. - Florida *20850*

E   *Dicerandra cornutissima* R.B. Huck *20850*
     E   *20850* U.S. - Florida (Sumter (Ex) & Marion Co.)
        20850

E   *Dicerandra frutescens* Shinners *20850*
     E   *20850* U.S. - Florida *20850*

E   *Dicerandra immaculata* Lakela *20850*
     E   *20850* U.S. - Florida (Indian R. & St Lucie Co.)
        20850

E   *Dicerandra radfordiana* R.B. Huck *20850*
     E   *20850* U.S. - Georgia *20850*

R   *Dorystaechas hastata* Boiss. et Heldr ex
        Bentham *20618*
     R   *20618* Turkey *19873*

I   *Dracocephalum formosum* Gontsch. *5942*
     I   *5942* Tajikistan *5942*

R   *Dysophylla koehneana* Muschl *19120*
     R   *19120* Thailand *19120*

I   *Dysophylla rugosa* Hook.f.
     I   India - Tamil Nadu (Tirunelveli District)

I   *Elsholtzia densa* Benth.
     I   India - Himachal Pradesh
     I   India - Jammu & Kashmir
     I   India - Uttar Pradesh

R   *Eremostachys pulchra* Popov
     R   former USSR *6930*

R   *Eremostachys zenaidae* Popov *5942*
     R   *5942* Kazakhstan (south-east) *5942*

E   *Eriope trichopes* Epling *5607*
     E   *19105* Cuba (Juventud Is.) *5607*

R   *Euhesperida linearifolia* Brullo & Furnari
     R   Libya

R   *Gomphostemma callicarpoides* (Yamamoto)
        Masamune *20511*
     R   *20511* Taiwan *20511*

R   *Gomphostemma grandiflora* Doan *6057*
     R   Vietnam *6057*

Ex/E   *Haplostachys bryanii* Sherff *20850*
     Ex/E   *20850* U.S. - Hawaii *20850*

Ex   *Haplostachys bryanii* Sherff var.

		bryanii *14209*
	Ex	*14209* U.S. - Hawaii *14209*
E	*Haplostachys haplostachya* (Gray) St. John *20850*	
	E	*20850* U.S. - Hawaii *20850*
E	*Haplostachys haplostachya* (A.Gray) H. St. John var. *haplostachya* *14209*	
	E	*14209* U.S. - Hawaii *14209*
Ex/E	*Haplostachys linearifolia* (Drake) Sherff *20850*	
	Ex/E	*20850* U.S. - Hawaii *20850*
Ex	*Haplostachys linearifolia* (Drake) Sherff var. *linearifolia* *14209*	
	Ex	*14209* U.S. - Hawaii (Moloka`i) *14209*
Ex/E	*Haplostachys munroi* Forbes *20850, 14209*	
	Ex/E	*20850* U.S. - Hawaii (Lana`i) *20850*
Ex/E	*Haplostachys truncata* (Gray) Hbd. *20850, 14209*	
	Ex/E	*20850* U.S. - Hawaii (Maui) *20850*
R	*Hedeoma apiculata* W.S. Stewart *20850*	
	R	*20850* U.S. - New Mexico *20850*
	V	*20850* U.S. - Texas *20850*
V	*Hedeoma costata* Gray *20850*	
	I	*20850* U.S. - Arizona *20850*
	I	*20850* U.S. - New Mexico *20850*
	I	*20850* U.S. - Texas *20850*
V	*Hedeoma dentata* Torr. *20850*	
	I	*20850* U.S. - Arizona *20850*
	I	*20850* U.S. - New Mexico *20850*
V	*Hedeoma mollis* Torr. *20850*	
	I	*20850* U.S. - Texas *20850*
E	*Hedeoma multiflora* Benth. *16336*	
	E	*16336* Argentina *16336*
	E	*20176* Argentina - Buenos Aires *20176*
	E	*20176* Argentina - Cordoba *20176*
	E	*20176* Argentina - Entre Rios *20176*
	E	*20176* Argentina - La Pampa *20176*
	E	*20176* Argentina - Neuquen *20176*
	E	*20176* Argentina - Mendoza *20176*
	E	*20176* Argentina - San Luis *20176*
Ex/E	*Hedeoma pilosa* Irving *20850*	
	Ex/E	*20850* U.S. - Texas *20850*
V	*Hedeoma pulcherrima* Woot. & Standl. *20850*	
	I	*20850* U.S. - New Mexico *20850*
V	*Hedeoma todsenii* Irving *20850*	
	V	*20850* U.S. - New Mexico *20850*
V	*Hemiandra gardneri* O.Sarg. *20681*	
	V	*20681* Australia - Western Australia *20681*
E	*Hemiandra rutilans* O.Sarg. *20681*	
	E	*20681* Australia - Western Australia *20681*
Ex	*Hemigenia clotteniana* Bailey *20681*	
	Ex	*20681* Australia - Queensland *20681*
Ex	*Hemigenia exilis* S.Moore *20681, 14223*	
	Ex	*20681* Australia - Western Australia *20681*
Ex	*Hemigenia obtusa* Benth. *20681, 14223*	
	Ex	*20681* Australia - Western Australia *20681*
R	*Hemigenia platyphylla* (Bartl.) Benth. *20681*	
	R	*20681* Australia - Western Australia *20681*
V	*Hemigenia viscida* S.Moore *20681*	
	V	*20681* Australia - Western Australia *20681*
R	*Hemizygia bolusii* (N.E.Br.) Codd *20604*	
	R	*20604* South Africa - Natal *20604*
R	*Hemizygia cinerea* Codd *20604*	
	R	*20604* Lesotho *20604*

	R	*20604* South Africa - Natal *20604*
	R	*20604* South Africa - Orange Free State *20604*
R	*Hemizygia orithrepes* Wild *7754*	
	R	Zimbabwe (Chimanimani) *7754*
I	*Hemizygia ramosa* Codd *20604*	
	I	*20604* South Africa - Natal *20604*
E	*Hyptis cubensis* Urban *5607*	
	E	*19105* Cuba (Pinar del Rio) *5607*
R	*Hyptis gymnocaulos* Epling *11117*	
	R	Ecuador - Galapagos (Volcan Alcedo, Isabela) *11117*
E	*Hyptis pedalipes* Griseb. *5607*	
	E	*19105* Cuba (Pinar del Rio) *5607*
E	*Hyptis rivularis* Britton *5607*	
	E	*19105* Cuba (Sancti Spiritus) *5607*
E	*Hyptis shafei* Britton *5607*	
	E	*19105* Cuba (Pinar del Rio) *5607*
E	*Hyssopus cretaceus* Dubj. *5942, 20171*	
	E	*20655* Ukraine *5942*
R	*Isodon volkensianus* (Muschl.) Murata *19120*	
	R	*19120* Thailand *19120*
R	*Keiskea macrobracteata* Masamune *20511*	
	R	*20511* Taiwan *20511*
I	*Lagochilus inebrians* Bunge *5942*	
	I	*5942* Tajikistan (west) *5942*
	I	*5942* Uzbekistan *5942*
R	*Lamium armenum* Boiss. ssp. *sintenisii* R. Mill. *12840*	
	R	*12840* Turkey *12840*
R	*Lamium cymbalariifolium* Boiss. *12840*	
	R	*12840* Turkey *12840*
R	*Lamium eriocephalum* Bentham *12840*	
	R	*12840* Turkey *12840*
R	*Lamium garganicum* L. ssp. *nepetifolium* (Boiss.) R. Mill *12840*	
	R	*12840* Turkey *12840*
R	*Lamium garganicum* L. ssp. *pulchrum* R. Mill. *12840*	
	R	*12840* Turkey *12840*
R	*Lamium glaberrimum* (K.Koch) Taliev *20171*	
	E	*20655* Ukraine - Crimea *20654*
	R	former European USSR
R	*Lamium glandulosidens* Hub.-Mor. *12840*	
	R	*12840* Turkey *12840*
R	*Lamium lycium* Boiss. *12840*	
	R	*12840* Turkey *12840*
R	*Lamium microphyllum* Boiss. *12840*	
	R	*12840* Turkey *12840*
R	*Lamium pisidicum* R. Mill *12840*	
	R	*12840* Turkey *12840*
E	*Lamium purpureum* L. var. *aznavourii* Gand. ex Aznav. *12840*	
	E	*12840* Turkey *12840*
R	*Lamium sandrasicum* Davis *12840*	
	R	*12840* Turkey *12840*
R	*Lamium sulphureum* Hausskn. & Sint. ex R. Mill *12840*	
	R	*12840* Turkey *12840*
R	*Lamium tenuiflorum* Fisch. & Mey. *12840*	
	R	*12840* Turkey *12840*

R **Lamium veronicifolium** Bentham *12840*
    R   *12840* Turkey *12840*

R **Lasiocorys hephaestis** Wild *7752*
    R   Zimbabwe *7752*

E **Lasiocorys spiculifolia** Balf. f.
    E   Yemen - Socotra

E **Lavandula buchii** Webb *20750*
    E   *20750* Spain - Canary Is. *20750*

I **Lavandula hasikensis** A.G. Miller *20146*
    I   *20146* Oman *20146*

V **Lepechinia cardiophylla** Epling *20850*
    V   *20850* U.S. - California *20850*

V **Lepechinia fragrans** (Greene) Epling *20850*
    I   *20850* U.S. - California *20850*

V **Lepechinia ganderi** Epling *20850*
    V   *20850* U.S. - California *20850*

R **Leucas angustissima** Sedgw. *11494*
    R   *11494* India - Karnataka (Gersoppa Ghat, north Kanara) *11494*

R **Leucas lamioides** (Muschl.) Murata *19120*
    R   *19120* Thailand *19120*

E **Leucas mukerjiana** Rao & Kumari
    E   *13883* India - Andhra Pradesh *13883*

I **Leucas pubescens** Benth.
    I   India - Tamil Nadu

R **Leucas spiculifera** (Balf. f.) Guerke *15534*
    R   *15534* Yemen - Socotra *15534*

I **Leucas wightiana** Benth.
    I   India - Tamil Nadu (Kanniyakumari)

R **Lycopus cokeri** Ahles *20850*
    R   *20850* U.S. - North Carolina *20850*
    I   *20850* U.S. - South Carolina *20850*

V **Lycopus laurentianus** Rolland Germain *20850*
    V   *20850* Canada - Quebec *20850*

V **Macbridea alba** Chapman *20850, 15914*
    V   *20850* U.S. - Florida *20850*

V **Macbridea caroliniana** (Walt.) Blake *20850*
    E   *20850* U.S. - Alabama *20850*
    I   *20850* U.S. - Florida *20850*
    E   *20850* U.S. - Georgia *20850*
    V   *20850* U.S. - North Carolina *20850*
    I   *20850* U.S. - South Carolina *20850*

R **Marrubium atlanticum** Battand.
    R   Morocco

R **Marrubium bourgaei** Boiss. *12840*
    R   *12840* Turkey *12840*

R **Marrubium fontianum** Maire
    R   Morocco

R **Marrubium globosum** Montbret & Aucher ex Bentham ssp. **micranthum** (Boiss. & Heldr.) Davis *12840*
    R   *12840* Turkey *12840*

R **Marrubium vanense** Hub.-Mor. *12840*
    R   *12840* Turkey *12840*

R **Marrubium vulcanicum** Hub.-Mor. *12840*
    R   *12840* Turkey *12840*

R **Marrubium werneri** Maire
    R   Morocco

R **Meehania montiskoyae** Ohwi *10573*
    R   *10573* Japan *10573*

V **Mentha gattefossei** Maire
    V   Morocco

R **Mentha requienii** Benth. *18264, 20171*
    R   *18264* Italy (Tuscany) *18264*
    R   *18264* Italy - Sardinia *18264*

R **Microcorys elliptica** Conn *20681*
    R   *20681* Australia - Northern Territory *20681*

V **Microcorys eremophiloides** Kenneally *20681*
    V   *20681* Australia - Western Australia *20681*

R **Micromeria acropolitana** Halácsy *20171*
    R   Greece

V **Micromeria bucheri** P. Wilson *5607*
    V   *19105* Cuba (Santiago de Cuba) *5607*

R **Micromeria carica** Davis *12840*
    R   *12840* Turkey *12840*

R **Micromeria cilicica** Hausskn. ex Davis *12840*
    R   *12840* Turkey *12840*

R **Micromeria cremnophila** Boiss. & Heldr. ssp. **amana** (Rech.fil.) Davis *12840*
    R   *12840* Turkey *12840*

R **Micromeria cristata** (Hampe) Griseb. ssp. **carminea** Davis *12840*
    R   *12840* Turkey *12840*

R **Micromeria cristata** (Hampe) Griseb. ssp. **orientalis** Davis *12840*
    R   *12840* Turkey *12840*

R **Micromeria cristata** (Hampe) Griseb. ssp. **phrygia** Davis *12840*
    R   *12840* Turkey *12840*

R **Micromeria cristata** (Hampe) Griseb. ssp. **xylorrhiza** (Boiss. & Heldr.) Davis *12840*
    R   *12840* Turkey *12840*

R **Micromeria cymuligera** Boiss. & Hausskn. *12840*
    R   *12840* Turkey *12840*

R **Micromeria dolichodonta** Davis *12840*
    R   *12840* Turkey *12840*

R **Micromeria elliptica** C. Koch. *12840*
    R   *12840* Turkey *12840*

V **Micromeria fruticosa** (L.) Druce ssp. **giresunica** Davis *12840*
    V   *12840* Turkey *12840*

E **Micromeria glomerata** P. Perez *20750*
    E   *20750* Spain - Canary Is. *20750*

R **Micromeria helianthemifolia** Webb & Berthel. *20750*
    R   *20750* Spain - Canary Is. *20750*

R **Micromeria hispida** Boiss. & Heldr. ex Benth. *20171*
    R   *20731* Greece - Crete *20731*

R **Micromeria kerneri** Murb. *20171*
    V   *21091* Bosnia & Herzegovina *21091*
    R   (former) Yugoslavia

R **Micromeria lasiophylla** Webb & Berthel. ssp. **lasiophylla**
    R   Spain - Canary Is.

R **Micromeria lasiophylla** Webb & Berthel. ssp. **palmensis** (Bolle) Perez de Paz
    R   Spain - Canary Is.

E **Micromeria leucantha** Svent. ex P. Perez *20750*
    E   *20750* Spain - Canary Is. *20750*

R **Micromeria nervosa** (Desf.) Benth. *20171*

R		20731 Greece - Crete *20731*
R	***Micromeria parviflora*** (Vis.) Rchb. *20178, 20171*	
	R	20178 Albania *20178*
	V	21091 Bosnia & Herzegovina *21091*
	R	(former) Yugoslavia
E	***Micromeria pineolens*** Svent. *20750*	
	E	20750 Spain - Canary Is. *20750*
E	***Micromeria rivas-martinezii*** Wildpret *20750*	
	E	20750 Spain - Canary Is. *20750*
R	***Micromeria serbaliana*** Danin & Hedge	
	R	Egypt
R	***Micromeria serpyllifolia*** (M.Bieb.) Boiss. *20171*	
	R	former European USSR (Crimea) *8001*
R	***Micromeria sinaica*** Benth. *16168*	
	R	*16168* Egypt (Gebel Hamata, Isthmic Desert & south Sinai) *16168*
	R	Israel *8895*
	R	Jordan *8937*
V	***Micromeria suborbicularis*** (Alain) Borh. *5607*	
	V	*19105* Cuba (Guantanamo) *5607*
R	***Micromeria tapeinantha*** Rech.f. *20171*	
	R	Greece
E	***Micromeria taygetea*** P.H.Davis *8000, 20171*	
	E	Greece (south - Taïyetos) *8000*
R	***Micromeria varia*** Benth. ssp. ***hierrensis*** Perez de Paz	
	R	Spain - Canary Is.
R	***Micromeria varia*** Benth. ssp. ***rupestris*** (Webb & Berthel.) Perez de Paz	
	R	Spain - Canary Is.
I	***Minthostachys verticillata*** Griseb. *16336*	
	I	*16336* Argentina *16336*
	I	20176 Argentina - Buenos Aires *20176*
	I	20176 Argentina - Catamarca *20176*
	I	20176 Argentina - Jujuy *20176*
	I	20176 Argentina - La Rioja *20176*
	I	20176 Argentina - Mendoza *20176*
	I	20176 Argentina - Salta *20176*
	I	20176 Argentina - Santiago del Estero *20176*
	I	20176 Argentina - San Juan *20176*
	I	20176 Argentina - San Luis *20176*
	I	20176 Argentina - Tucuman *20176*
V	***Monarda citriodora*** Cerv. ex Lag. var. ***parva*** Scora *20850*	
	I	20850 U.S. - Texas *20850*
E	***Monarda fistulosa*** L. ssp. ***brevis*** (Fosberg & Artz) Scora, comb. nov. ined. *20850*	
	I	20850 U.S. - Virginia *20850*
	E	20850 U.S. - West Virginia *20850*
V	***Monarda punctata*** L. var. ***stanfieldii*** (Small) Cory *20850*	
	I	20850 U.S. - Texas *20850*
R	***Monarda punctata*** L. var. ***viridissima*** (Correll) Scora, comb. nov. ined. *20850*	
	R	20850 U.S. - Texas *20850*
V	***Monardella arizonica*** Epling *20850*	
	I	20850 U.S. - Arizona *20850*
E	***Monardella beneolens*** Shevock, Ertter & Jokerst *20850*	
	E	20850 U.S. - California *20850*
V	***Monardella cinerea*** Abrams *20850*	
	I	20850 U.S. - California *20850*
V	***Monardella crispa*** Elmer *20850*	

	V	20850 U.S. - California *20850*
R	***Monardella exilis*** (Gray) Greene *20850*	
	I	20850 U.S. - California *20850*
V	***Monardella exilis*** (Gray) Greene var. ***frutescens*** (Hoover) Jokerst *20850*	
	V	20850 U.S. - California *20850*
V	***Monardella hypoleuca*** A.Gray ssp. ***lanata*** (Abrams) Munz *20850*	
	V	20850 U.S. - California *20850*
Ex/E	***Monardella leucocephala*** Gray *20850, 14662*	
	Ex/E	20850 U.S. - California *20850*
V	***Monardella linoides*** A.Gray ssp. ***oblonga*** (Greene) Abrams *20850*	
	V	20850 U.S. - California *20850*
R	***Monardella linoides*** A.Gray ssp. ***viminea*** (Greene) Abrams *20850*	
	V	20850 U.S. - California *20850*
R	***Monardella macrantha*** A.Gray ssp. ***hallii*** (Abrams) Abrams *20850*	
	R	20850 U.S. - California *20850*
V	***Monardella nana*** A.Gray ssp. ***leptosiphon*** (Torr.) Abrams *20850*	
	V	20850 U.S. - California *20850*
V	***Monardella neglecta*** Greene *20850*	
	I	20850 U.S. - California *20850*
Ex	***Monardella pringlei*** Gray *20850, 14662*	
	Ex	20850 U.S. - California *20850*
V	***Monardella robisonii*** Epling ex Munz *20850*	
	V	20850 U.S. - California *20850*
E	***Monardella stebbinsii*** Hardham & Bartel *20850*	
	E	20850 U.S. - California *20850*
R	***Monardella subglabra*** (Hoover) Hardham *20850*	
	I	20850 U.S. - California *20850*
V	***Monardella viridis*** (I.M. Johnston) Ewan ssp. ***saxicola*** (I.M. Johnston) Ewan *20850*	
	I	20850 U.S. - California *20850*
R	***Mosla bracteata*** Doan *6057*	
	R	Vietnam *6057*
R	***Nepeta aristata*** Boiss. & Kotschy ex Boiss. *12840*	
	R	*12840* Turkey *12840*
R	***Nepeta baytopii*** Hedge & Lamond *12840*	
	R	*12840* Turkey *12840*
V	***Nepeta boissieri*** Willk. *20171*	
	V	Spain *11496*
I	***Nepeta camestris*** Benth.	
	I	India - Himachal Pradesh
	I	India - Jammu & Kashmir
	I	India - Uttar Pradesh
R	***Nepeta camphorata*** Boiss. & Heldr. *20171*	
	R	Greece
R	***Nepeta cantabrica*** Ubera & B. Valdes	
	R	Spain
V	***Nepeta conferta*** Hedge & Lamond *12840*	
	V	*12840* Turkey *12840*
R	***Nepeta crinita*** Montbret & Aucher ex Bentham *12840*	
	R	*12840* Turkey *12840*
V	***Nepeta cyrenaica*** Quezel & Zaffran	
	V	Libya
V	***Nepeta dirphya*** (Boiss.) Heldr. ex Halácsy *8000,*	

20171

V   Greece (east - Evvoia) *8000*

R   *Nepeta foliosa* Moris *18264, 20171*
     R   *18264* Italy - Sardinia *18264*

R   *Nepeta gontscharovii* Kudrj.
     R   former USSR *6930*

R   *Nepeta heldreichii* Halácsy *20171*
     R   Greece

R   *Nepeta ladanolens* Lipsky
     R   former USSR *6930*

R   *Nepeta maussarifi* Lipsky
     R   former USSR *6930*

R   *Nepeta nadinae* Lipsky
     R   former USSR *6930*

V   *Nepeta nuda* L. ssp. *glandulifera* Hub.-Mor. &
       Davis *12840*
     V   *12840* Turkey *12840*

R   *Nepeta nuda* L. ssp. *lydiae* Davis *12840*
     R   *12840* Turkey *12840*

R   *Nepeta numantina* Segura
     R   Spain

R   *Nepeta obtusicrena* Boiss. & Kotschy ex Hedge *12840*
     R   *12840* Turkey *12840*

I   *Nepeta paucifolia* Mukerjee
     I   India - Jammu & Kashmir

R   *Nepeta phyllochlamys* Davis *12840*
     R   *12840* Turkey *12840*

R   *Nepeta plinux* Davis *12840*
     R   *12840* Turkey *12840*

R   *Nepeta scordotis* L. *20171*
     R   Greece

R   *Nepeta septemcrenata* Ehrenb.
     R   Egypt

R   *Nepeta sorgerae* Hedge & Lamond *12840*
     R   *12840* Turkey *12840*

E   *Nepeta sphaciotica* P.H.Davis *8000, 20171*
     E   *20730* Greece - Crete (Levka Ori) *8000*

V   *Nepeta sulfuriflora* Davis *12840*
     V   *12840* Turkey *12840*

R   *Nepeta teydea* Webb & Berthel. *17530*
     R   *19174* Spain - Canary Is. *19174*

R   *Nepeta troodi* Holmboe *14230*
     R   *20710* Cyprus *14230*

V   *Nepeta vivianii* (Coss.) Beguinot & Vaccari
     V   Libya

I   *Ocimum natalense* Ayob. ex A.J.Paton *20604*
     I   *20604* Mozambique *20604*
     I   *20604* South Africa - Natal *20604*

R   *Origanum amanum* Post *12840*
     R   *12840* Turkey *12840*

R   *Origanum bilgeri* Davis *12840*
     R   *12840* Turkey *12840*

R   *Origanum calcaratum* Juss.
     R   *20731* Greece (Cyclades) *20731*

V   *Origanum cordifolium* (Auch.-Eloy & Montbr.)
       Vogel *14230*
     V   *19164* Cyprus *14230*

V   *Origanum dictamnus* L. *8000, 20171*

V   *20731* Greece - Crete *8000*

R   *Origanum floribundum* Munby *10488*
     R   *14958* Algeria *10488*

R   *Origanum haussknechtii* Boiss. *12840*
     R   *12840* Turkey *12840*

R   *Origanum hypericifolium* O. Schwarz & Davis *12840*
     R   *12840* Turkey *12840*

R   *Origanum isthmicum* Danin *17671*
     R   Egypt (Gebal Halal) *17671*

R   *Origanum leptocladum* Boiss. *12840, 20171*
     R   *12840* Turkey *12840*

R   *Origanum micranthum* Vogel *12840*
     R   *12840* Turkey *12840*

R   *Origanum minutiflorum* O. Schwarz & Davis *12840*
     R   *12840* Turkey *12840*

R   *Origanum munzurense* Kit Tan & Sorger *12840*
     R   *12840* Turkey *12840*

I   *Origanum paui* Martinez
     I   Spain

V   *Origanum ramonense* Danin *8895*
     V   Israel (C. Negev) *8895*

R   *Origanum saccatum* Davis *12840*
     R   *12840* Turkey *12840*

V   *Origanum scabrum* Boiss. & Heldr. *17781, 20171*
     V   *17762* Greece *17781*

R   *Origanum solymicum* Davis *12840*
     R   *12840* Turkey *12840*

I   *Origanum syriacum* L. var. *bevanii* (Holmes)
       Ietswaart *14230*
     I   *19164* Cyprus (near Lapithos) *14230*

V   *Origanum vetteri* Briq. & Barbey *20171*
     V   *20731* Greece - Crete (Karpathos) *20731*

I   *Orthosiphon tagawai* Murata *19120*
     I   *19120* Thailand *19120*

V   *Orthosiphon vernalis* Codd *20604, 18023*
     V   *20604* Swaziland *20604*

I   *Otostegia bucharica* B. Fedtsch. *5942*
     I   *5942* Uzbekistan (south-east) *5942*

R   *Phlomis angustissima* Hub.-Mor. *12840*
     R   *12840* Turkey *12840*

R   *Phlomis antiatlantica* Peltier
     R   Morocco

E   *Phlomis aurea* Decne. *16168*
     E   *16168* Egypt (Mountainous Sinai (El Husseiny))
             16168

R   *Phlomis bovei* de Noe *10488*
     R   *14958* Algeria *10488*

V   *Phlomis brevibracteata* Turrill *14230*
     V   *20710* Cyprus *14230*

V   *Phlomis brunneogaleata* Hub.-Mor. *12840*
     V   *12840* Turkey *12840*

R   *Phlomis carica* Rech.fil. *12840*
     R   *12840* Turkey *12840*

R   *Phlomis chimerae* Boissieu *12840*
     R   *20618* Turkey *20618*

R   *Phlomis cypria* Post var. *occidentalis* *14230*
     R   *19164* Cyprus *14230*

V   *Phlomis integrifolia* Hub.-Mor. *12840*

V		*12840* Turkey *12840*
R	*Phlomis leucophracta* Davis & Hub.-Mor. *12840*	
R		*20618* Turkey *20618*
R	*Phlomis longifolia* Boiss. & Bal. var. *bailanica* (Vierh.) Hub.-Mor. *12840*	
R		*20618* Turkey *20618*
E	*Phlomis margaritae* Aparico & Silvestre *20661*	
E		*20661* Spain (Cádiz: Sierra Gratalema) *20661*
R	*Phlomis monocephala* Davis *12840*	
R		*20618* Turkey *20618*
R	*Phlomis physocalyx* Hub.-Mor. *12840*	
R		*12840* Turkey *12840*
R	*Phlomis pichleri* Vierh. *20171*	
R		*20731* Greece - Crete (Kasos, Karpathos, Saria) *20731*
R	*Phlomis sintenisii* Rech.fil. *12840*	
R		*12840* Turkey *12840*
E	*Phyllostegia bracteata* Sherff *20850, 14209*	
E		*20850* U.S. - Hawaii (Maui) *20850*
Ex/E	*Phyllostegia brevidens* Gray *20850*	
Ex/E		*20850* U.S. - Hawaii *20850*
Ex	*Phyllostegia brevidens* A.Gray var. *brevidens* *14209*	
Ex		*14209* U.S. - Hawaii *14209*
E	*Phyllostegia floribunda* Benth. *20850, 14209*	
E		*20850* U.S. - Hawaii (Hawai`i) *20850*
R	*Phyllostegia glabra* (Gaudich.) Benth. *20850, 14209*	
I		*20850* U.S. - Hawaii *20850*
R	*Phyllostegia glabra* (Gaudich.) Benth var. *glabra* *20850*	
I		*20850* U.S. - Hawaii *20850*
Ex/E	*Phyllostegia glabra* (Gaudich.) Benth. var. *lanaiensis* Sherff *20850, 14209*	
Ex/E		*20850* U.S. - Hawaii (Lana`i) *20850*
E	*Phyllostegia helleri* Sherff *20850*	
E		*20850* U.S. - Hawaii *20850*
R	*Phyllostegia helleri* Sherff var. *helleri* *14209*	
R		*14209* U.S. - Hawaii (Kaua`i) *14209*
Ex/E	*Phyllostegia hillebrandii* Mann ex Hbd. *20850, 14209*	
Ex/E		*20850* U.S. - Hawaii (east Maui) *20850*
E	*Phyllostegia hirsuta* Benth. *20850*	
E		*20850* U.S. - Hawaii *20850*
E	*Phyllostegia hispida* Hbd. *20850, 14209*	
I		*20850* U.S. - Hawaii (eastern Moloka`i) *20850*
Ex/E	*Phyllostegia imminuta* (Sherff) St. John *20850*	
Ex/E		*20850* U.S. - Hawaii *20850*
E	*Phyllostegia kaalaensis* St. John *20850*	
E		*20850* U.S. - Hawaii *20850*
Ex/E	*Phyllostegia knudsenii* Hbd. *20850, 14209*	
Ex/E		*20850* U.S. - Hawaii (Kaua`i) *20850*
E	*Phyllostegia mannii* Sherff *20850, 14209*	
E		*20850* U.S. - Hawaii *20850*
E	*Phyllostegia mollis* Benth. *20850, 14209*	
E		*20850* U.S. - Hawaii *20850*
E	*Phyllostegia parviflora* (Gaud.) Benth. *20850*	
E		*20850* U.S. - Hawaii *20850*
Ex/E	*Phyllostegia parviflora* (Gaudich.) Benth. var.	

	glabriuscula Gray *20850, 14209*	
Ex/E		*20850* U.S. - Hawaii (Hawai`i) *20850*
E	*Phyllostegia parviflora* (Gaudich.) Benth. var. *parviflora* *20850, 14209*	
E		*20850* U.S. - Hawaii (West Maui, O`ahu) *20850*
E	*Phyllostegia racemosa* Benth. *20850*	
E		*20850* U.S. - Hawaii *20850*
R	*Phyllostegia racemosa* Benth. var. *racemosa* *14209*	
R		*14209* U.S. - Hawaii *14209*
Ex/E	*Phyllostegia rockii* Sherff *20850, 14209*	
Ex/E		*20850* U.S. - Hawaii (east Maui) *20850*
E	*Phyllostegia stachyoides* Gray *20850*	
E		*20850* U.S. - Hawaii *20850*
Ex	*Phyllostegia tahitensis* Nadeaud *20845*	
Ex		*20845* French Polynesia - Society Is. (Tahiti) *20845*
Ex/E	*Phyllostegia variabilis* Bitter *20850, 14209*	
Ex/E		*20850* U.S. - Hawaii *20850*
E	*Phyllostegia velutina* (Sherff) St. John *20850, 14209*	
E		*20850* U.S. - Hawaii *20850*
V	*Phyllostegia vestita* Benth. *20850, 14209*	
V		*20850* U.S. - Hawaii (Hawai`i & Kohala Mts.) *20850*
Ex/E	*Phyllostegia waimeae* Wawra *20850, 14209*	
Ex/E		*20850* U.S. - Hawaii (Kaua`i) *20850*
E	*Phyllostegia warshaueri* St. John *20850, 14209*	
E		*20850* U.S. - Hawaii *20850*
Ex/E	*Phyllostegia wawrana* Sherff *20850, 14209*	
Ex/E		*20850* U.S. - Hawaii *20850*
V	*Physostegia correllii* (Lundell) Shinners *20883, 20850*	
I		*20850* U.S. - Arizona *20850*
E		*20850* U.S. - Louisiana *20850*
V		*20850* U.S. - Texas *20850*
I		*20883* Mexico *20883*
R	*Physostegia godfreyi* Cantino *20850*	
R		*20850* U.S. - Florida *20850*
R	*Physostegia ledinghamii* (Boivin) Cantino *20850*	
I		*20850* Canada - Alberta *20850*
I		*20850* Canada - Manitoba *20850*
I		*20850* Canada - Mackenzie *20850*
I		*20850* Canada - Saskatchewan *20850*
I		*20850* U.S. - North Dakota *20850*
V	*Physostegia longisepala* Cantino *20850*	
V		*20850* U.S. - Louisiana *20850*
V		*20850* U.S. - Texas *20850*
R	*Pitardia nepetoides* Battand.	
R		Morocco
R	*Plectranthus actites* P.I.Forster *20681*	
R		*20681* Australia - Queensland *20681*
R	*Plectranthus alloplectus* S.T.Blake *20681*	
I		*20681* Australia - New South Wales *20681*
I		*20681* Australia - Queensland *20681*
R	*Plectranthus arenicola* P.Forster *20681*	
R		*20681* Australia - Queensland *20681*
I	*Plectranthus beddomei* Raiz.	
I		India - Tamil Nadu (Tirunelveli Hills)
Ex/E	*Plectranthus bishopianus* Gamble *14782*	
Ex/E		*14782* India - Tamil Nadu (Palani Hills, Madurai Dist) *14782*

R	*Plectranthus blakei* P.Forster *20681*	
	R	20681 Australia - Queensland *20681*
I	*Plectranthus bourneae* Gamble *14782*	
	I	14782 India - Tamil Nadu *14782*
I	*Plectranthus capillipes* Benth. *8021*	
	I	16162 Sri Lanka (Ramboda, Nuwaraeliya Dist.) *8021*
R	*Plectranthus crassus* N.E. Br. *7757*	
	R	Malawi (Mlanje) *7757*
R	*Plectranthus cyanophyllus* P.I.Forster *20681*	
	R	20681 Australia - Queensland *20681*
I	*Plectranthus deccanicus* Briq.	
	I	India - Tamil Nadu
I	*Plectranthus dissitiflorus* (Gurke) J.K. Morton	
	I	Cameroon (Buea, Bimbia)
R	*Plectranthus elegans* Britten *7757*	
	R	Malawi (Mlanje) *7757*
R	*Plectranthus ernstii* Codd *20604*	
	R	20604 South Africa - Cape Province *20604*
	R	20604 South Africa - Natal *20604*
R	*Plectranthus glabriflorus* P.I.Forster *20681*	
	R	20681 Australia - Queensland *20681*
R	*Plectranthus graniticola* P.Forster *20681*	
	R	20681 Australia - Queensland *20681*
V	*Plectranthus gratus* S.T.Blake *20681*	
	V	20681 Australia - Queensland *20681*
V	*Plectranthus habrophyllus* P.I.Forster *20681*	
	V	20681 Australia - Queensland *20681*
E	*Plectranthus hallii* J.K. Morton *7926*	
	E	6072 Ghana (Gambaga scarp) *7926*
R	*Plectranthus hilliardiae* Codd *20604*	
	R	20604 South Africa - Cape Province *20604*
	R	20604 South Africa - Natal *20604*
E	*Plectranthus kunstleri* Prain	
	E	Malaysia - Peninsular Malaysia (K. Dipang, Perak, Langkawi)
V	*Plectranthus leiperi* P.I.Forster *20681*	
	V	20681 Australia - Queensland *20681*
E	*Plectranthus minutus* P.Forster *20681*	
	E	20681 Australia - Queensland *20681*
R	*Plectranthus oertendahlii* T.C.E.Fr. *20604*	
	R	20604 South Africa - Natal *20604*
E	*Plectranthus omissus* P.Forster *20681*	
	E	20681 Australia - Queensland *20681*
R	*Plectranthus oribiensis* Codd *20604*	
	R	20604 South Africa - Natal *20604*
E	*Plectranthus praetermissus* Codd *20604*	
	E	20604 South Africa - Cape Province *20604*
R	*Plectranthus purpuratus* Harv. *20604*	
	R	20604 South Africa - Natal *20604*
E	*Plectranthus socotranus* A.R. Smith *15534*	
	E	15534 Yemen - Socotra *15534*
R	*Plectranthus spectabilis* S.T.Blake *20681*	
	R	20681 Australia - Queensland *20681*
V	*Pogogyne abramsii* J.T. Howell *20850*	
	V	20850 U.S. - California *20850*
E	*Pogogyne clareana* J.T. Howell *20850*	
	E	20850 U.S. - California *20850*
E	*Pogogyne nudiuscula* Gray *20883, 20850, 8058*	

	E	20850 U.S. - California *20850*
	I	20883 Mexico *20883*
R	*Pogostemon atropurpureus* Benth. *14782*	
	R	14782 India - Tamil Nadu (Sispara Ghat, Nilgiri) *14782*
I	*Pogostemon gardneri* Hook.f.	
	I	India - Kerala (Wynaad)
	I	India - Tamil Nadu (Sispara, Nilgiri Hills)
R	*Pogostemon litigiosus* Doan *6057*	
	R	Vietnam *6057*
E	*Pogostemon nilagiricus* Gamble *2268*	
	E	14782 India - Tamil Nadu (Nilgiri Hills) *2268*
E	*Pogostemon paludosus* Benth. *4988*	
	E	14782 India - Tamil Nadu (Nilgiri Hills) *4988*
R	*Pogostemon travancoricus* Beddome *9250*	
	R	14782 India - Kerala (Trivandrum District) *9250*
R	*Prostanthera atroviolacea* Bailey *20681*	
	R	20681 Australia - Queensland *20681*
V	*Prostanthera calycina* Benth. *20681*	
	V	20681 Australia - South Australia *20681*
V	*Prostanthera carrickiana* Conn *20681*	
	V	20681 Australia - Western Australia *20681*
R	*Prostanthera cruciflora* J.H.Willis *20681*	
	R	20681 Australia - New South Wales *20681*
R	*Prostanthera cryptandroides* Benth. *20681*	
	R	20681 Australia - New South Wales *20681*
V	*Prostanthera densa* A.A.Ham. *20681*	
	V	20681 Australia - New South Wales *20681*
V	*Prostanthera discolor* R.Baker *20681*	
	V	20681 Australia - New South Wales *20681*
E	*Prostanthera eurybioides* F.Muell. *20681, 17915*	
	E	20681 Australia - South Australia *20681*
R	*Prostanthera magnifica* C.Gardner *20681*	
	R	20681 Australia - Western Australia *20681*
Ex	*Prostanthera marifolia* R.Br. *20681*	
	Ex	20681 Australia - New South Wales *20681*
R	*Prostanthera monticola* Conn *20681*	
	I	20681 Australia - New South Wales *20681*
	I	20681 Australia - Victoria *20681*
V	*Prostanthera nudula* E.L.Robertson *20681*	
	V	20681 Australia - South Australia *20681*
R	*Prostanthera porcata* Conn *20681*	
	R	20681 Australia - New South Wales *20681*
R	*Prostanthera staurophylla* F.Muell. *20681*	
	R	20681 Australia - New South Wales *20681*
V	*Prostanthera stricta* R.Baker *20681*	
	V	20681 Australia - New South Wales *20681*
R	*Prostanthera walteri* F.Muell. *20681*	
	I	20681 Australia - New South Wales *20681*
	I	20681 Australia - Victoria *20681*
R	*Prunella cretensis* Gand. *20171*	
	R	20731 Greece - Crete *20731*
I	*Pseuderemostachys sewerzowii* (Herder) Popov *5942*	
	I	5942 Kazakhstan (south-east) *5942*
	I	5942 Kyrgyzstan (north) *5942*
R	*Pseudomarrubium eremostachydioides* M.Pop. *5942*	
	R	5942 Kazakhstan *5942*
V	*Pycnanthemum beadlei* (Small) Fern. *20850*	

I		20850	U.S. - Georgia 20850
I		20850	U.S. - North Carolina 20850
I		20850	U.S. - South Carolina 20850
I		20850	U.S. - Tennessee 20850
I		20850	U.S. - Virginia 20850

V   *Pycnanthemum clinopodioides* Torr. & Gray 20850

E	20850	U.S. - Connecticut 20850
Ex/E	20850	U.S. - Delaware 20850
E	20850	U.S. - Maryland 20850
E	20850	U.S. - Massachusetts 20850
E	20850	U.S. - New Jersey 20850
Ex	20850	U.S. - New York 20850
I	20850	U.S. - North Carolina 20850
I	20850	U.S. - Pennsylvania 20850
I	20850	U.S. - South Carolina 20850
E	20850	U.S. - Texas 20850
I	20850	U.S. - Virginia 20850
Ex/E	20850	U.S. - West Virginia 20850

R   *Pycnanthemum curvipes* (Greene) E. Grant & Epling 20850

E	20850	U.S. - Alabama 20850
V	20850	U.S. - Georgia 20850
I	20850	U.S. - North Carolina 20850
V	20850	U.S. - Tennessee 20850

R   *Pycnanthemum floridanum* E. Grant & Epling 20850

R	20850	U.S. - Florida 20850
E	20850	U.S. - Georgia 20850

Ex/E   *Pycnanthemum monotrichum* Fern. 20850, 14662

E	20850	U.S. - Virginia 20850

V   *Pycnanthemum torrei* Benth. 20850

E	20850	U.S. - Connecticut 20850
I	20850	U.S. - Delaware 20850
I	20850	U.S. - District of Columbia 20850
I	20850	U.S. - Georgia 20850
E	20850	U.S. - Illinois 20850
I	20850	U.S. - Kansas 20850
E	20850	U.S. - Maryland 20850
Ex	20850	U.S. - Missouri 20850
Ex/E	20850	U.S. - New Hampshire 20850
E	20850	U.S. - New Jersey 20850
E	20850	U.S. - New York 20850
Ex/E	20850	U.S. - North Carolina 20850
E	20850	U.S. - Pennsylvania 20850
I	20850	U.S. - South Carolina 20850
I	20850	U.S. - Tennessee 20850
V	20850	U.S. - Virginia 20850
E	20850	U.S. - West Virginia 20850

R   *Rhododon ciliatus* (Benth.) Epling 20850

R	20850	U.S. - Texas 20850

V   *Salvia adenocaulon* Davis 12840

V	12840	Turkey 12840

R   *Salvia adenophylla* Hedge & Hub.-Mor. 12840

R	12840	Turkey 12840

R   *Salvia albimaculata* Hedge & Hub.-Mor. 12840

R	12840	Turkey 12840

E   *Salvia amissa* Epling 20850, 9777

I	20850	U.S. - Arizona 20850
?		Mexico 9777

V   *Salvia arizonica* Gray 20850

I	20850	U.S. - Arizona 20850
I	20850	U.S. - Texas 20850

R   *Salvia aucheri* Bentham 12840

R	12840	Turkey 12840

R   *Salvia balansae* de Noe 10488

R	14958	Algeria 10488

Ex/E   *Salvia baldschuanica* Lipsky 5942

Ex/E	5942	Tajikistan 5942

R   *Salvia brachyodon* Vandas 20171

V	21091	Bosnia & Herzegovina 21091
R		(former) Yugoslavia

V   *Salvia brandegei* Munz 20850

E	20850	U.S. - California 20850

E   *Salvia broussonetii* Benth. 20750

E	20750	Spain - Canary Is. 20750

E   *Salvia calcicola* Harley 19563

E	19563	Brazil - Distrito Federal (Brasilia) 19563

R   *Salvia candelabrum* Boiss. 20171

R		Spain

R   *Salvia cedronella* Boiss. 12840

R	12840	Turkey 12840

R   *Salvia chanroenica* Nakai 15957

R	15923	Korea, South (Mt Chongryong, Mt Pukhan, Kangwon-do) 15957

R   *Salvia chionantha* Boiss. 12840

R	12840	Turkey 12840

R   *Salvia cilicica* Boiss. & Kotschy 12840

R	12840	Turkey 12840

E   *Salvia clarendonensis* Britton 20883, 13336

E	20883	Jamaica 20883

R   *Salvia clevelandii* (Gray) Greene 20850

I	20850	U.S. - California 20850

V   *Salvia davidsonii* Greenm. 20850

E	20850	U.S. - Arizona 20850
I	20850	U.S. - New Mexico 20850

R   *Salvia divaricata* Montbret & Aucher ex Bentham 12840

R	12840	Turkey 12840

I   *Salvia dorisiana* Standley 9075

I	9730	Honduras 9075

V   *Salvia dorrii* (Kellogg) Abrams var. *clokeyi* Strachan 20850

V	20850	U.S. - Nevada 20850

V   *Salvia dorrii* (Kellogg) Abrams ssp. *mearnsii* (Britt.) Mcclintock 20850

V	20850	U.S. - Arizona 20850

I   *Salvia eigii* Zoh. 8895

I		Israel (last seen 1950) 8896

R   *Salvia eriocalyx* Bert. 20883, 13336

R	13336	Jamaica 20883

R   *Salvia eriophora* Boiss. & Kotschy 12840

R	12840	Turkey 12840

E   *Salvia ernesti-vargasii* C. Nelson 9649

E	20050	Honduras 9649

R   *Salvia euphratica* Montbret & Aucher ex Bentham 12840

R	12840	Turkey 12840

R   *Salvia garedji* Troitsky

R		former USSR 6930

R   *Salvia gattefossei* Emberger

R		Morocco

Ex   *Salvia gontscharovii* Kudrj. 5942

Ex	5942	Tajikistan 5942

R   *Salvia greatae* Brandeg. 20850

R	20850	U.S. - California 20850

I   *Salvia guarinae* Standley 9075

I	9730	Honduras 9075

V   *Salvia halophila* Hedge 12840

	V	*12840* Turkey *12840*	

E   *Salvia herbanica* Santos & Fernández *20750*
      E   *20750* Spain - Canary Is. *20750*

R   *Salvia huberi* Hedge *12840*
      R   *12840* Turkey *12840*

I   *Salvia insularum* Epling *11117*
      I   Ecuador - Galapagos (V. Alcedo; San Cristobal) *11117*

R   *Salvia interrupta* Schousboe
      R   Morocco

R   *Salvia isensis* Nakai *10573*
      R   *10573* Japan *10573*

E   *Salvia jamaicensis* Fawcett *20883, 13336*
      E   *20883* Jamaica *20883*

R   *Salvia japonica* Thunb. var. *taipingshanensis* (Wu & Huang) Huang & Wu *20511*
      R   *20511* Taiwan *20511*

R   *Salvia jurisicii* Kosanin *20171*
      R   (former) Yugoslavia

V   *Salvia koyamae* Makino *10573*
      V   *10573* Japan *10573*

R   *Salvia kronenburgei* Rech.fil. *12840*
      R   *12840* Turkey *12840*

R   *Salvia leucophylla* Greene *20850*
      I   *20850* U.S. - California *20850*

R   *Salvia manantlanensis* T.P. Ramamoorthy *19850*
      R   *19850* Mexico - Jalisco *21204*

Ex/E   *Salvia micrantha* Vahl var. *blodgettii* (Chapman) Epling *20850*
      Ex/E   *20850* U.S. - Florida *20850*

R   *Salvia munzii* Epling *20850*
      V   *20850* U.S. - California *20850*

R   *Salvia nigrescens* Alain *5607*
      R   *19105* Cuba (SC; Gu) *5607*

R   *Salvia nipponica* Miq. var. *formosana* (Hayata) Kudo *20511*
      R   *20511* Taiwan *20511*

R   *Salvia nydeggeri* Hub.-Mor. *12840*
      R   *12840* Turkey *12840*

R   *Salvia odontochlamys* Hedge *12840*
      R   *12840* Turkey *12840*

R   *Salvia ombrophila* Dusin *19563*
      R   *19563* Brazil *19563*

R   *Salvia omerocalyx* Hayata *10573*
      R   *10573* Japan *10573*

E   *Salvia penstemonoides* Kunth & Bouche *20850*
      E   *20850* U.S. - Texas *20850*

R   *Salvia prostrata* Hook.f. *11117*
      R   Ecuador - Galapagos *11117*

R   *Salvia pseudoserotina* Epling *11117*
      R   Ecuador - Galapagos (Volcan Alcedo; Floreana) *11117*

R   *Salvia quezelii* Hedge & Ajzal-Rafri *12840*
      R   *12840* Turkey *12840*

R   *Salvia reeseana* Hedge & Hub.-Mor. *12840*
      R   *12840* Turkey *12840*

V   *Salvia rhombifolia* Ruiz Lopez & Pavon *18200*
      V   *9446* Peru *18200*

R   *Salvia scabiosifolia* Lam. *8000, 20171*
      R   *5204* Bulgaria (north) *8000*
      I   former European USSR (Crimea) *8001*

V   *Salvia scabrata* Britton & P. Wilson *5607*
      V   *19105* Cuba (Santiago de Cuba; Holguin) *5607*

R   *Salvia sericeo-tomentosa* Rech.fil. *12840*
      R   *12840* Turkey *12840*

R   *Salvia smyrnea* Boiss. *12840*
      R   *12840* Turkey *12840*

E   *Salvia strobilanthiodes* C. Wright *5607*
      E   *19105* Cuba (Guantanamo) *5607*

R   *Salvia summa* A. Nels. *20850*
      R   *20850* U.S. - New Mexico *20850*
      V   *20850* U.S. - Texas *20850*

R   *Salvia tigrina* Hedge & Hub.-Mor. *12840*
      R   *12840* Turkey *12840*

R   *Salvia tobeyi* Hedge *12840*
      R   *12840* Turkey *12840*

R   *Salvia transsilvanica* (Schur ex Griseb.) Schur *17823*
      R   *19949* Romania *19949*

E   *Salvia trichopes* Epling *20883, 9006*
      I   *20883* Panama *20883*

R   *Salvia tubiflora* Smith *13875*
      R   *13875* Chile *13875*
      V   *12468* Peru *18200*

R   *Salvia vaseyi* (Porter) Parish *20850*
      I   *20850* U.S. - California *20850*

R   *Salvia veneris* Hedge *14230*
      R   *19164* Cyprus *14230*

R   *Salvia vermifolia* Hedge & Hub.-Mor. *12840*
      R   *12840* Turkey *12840*

R   *Salvia willeana* (Holmboe) Hedge *14230*
      R   *20710* Cyprus *14230*

R   *Satureja brivesii* (Battand.) Murb.
      R   Morocco

I   *Satureja bzybica* Woronow *5942*
      I   *5942* Russia - North Caucasus *5942*

R   *Satureja candica* Greuter & Burdet *20730*
      R   *20730* Greece - Crete *20730*

R   *Satureja cilicica* Davis *12840*
      R   *12840* Turkey *12840*

R   *Satureja cretica* (L.) Briq. *19121*
      R   *20731* Greece - Crete *20731*

R   *Satureja grandibracteata* Killick *20604*
      R   *20604* South Africa - Natal *20604*

V   *Satureja hispidula* (Boiss. & Reuter) Maire *10488*
      V   *14958* Algeria *10488*

R   *Satureja monantha* Font Quer
      R   Morocco

R   *Satureja multiflora* (Ruiz Lopez & Pavon) Briq. *13875*
      R   *13875* Chile *13875*

R   *Satureja parnassica* Heldr. & Sart. ex Boiss. ssp. *sipylea* Davis *12840*
      R   *12840* Turkey *12840*

R   *Satureja peltieri* Maire
      R   Morocco

R   *Satureja pomelii* Briq. *10488*
      R   *14958* Algeria *10488*

R   *Satureja rumelica* Velen. *5204, 20171*

R	5204	Bulgaria (central) *5204*

E	*Satureja thymbrifolia* Hedge & Feinbrun *8895*	
E		Israel (Judean Desert, Edom) *8895*
R	*Satureja weilleri* Maire	
R		Morocco
V	*Scutellaria alabamensis* Alexander *20850*	
V	20850	U.S. - Alabama *20850*
V	*Scutellaria altamaha* Small *20850*	
I	20850	U.S. - Georgia *20850*
I	20850	U.S. - Massachusetts *20850*
E	20850	U.S. - North Carolina *20850*
I	20850	U.S. - South Carolina *20850*
R	*Scutellaria andamanica* Prain *7771*	
R	14782	India - Andaman Is. (South) *7771*
I	*Scutellaria andrachnoides* Vved. *5942*	
I	5942	Kyrgyzstan *5942*
E	*Scutellaria arenicola* Small *20850*	
I	20850	U.S. - Florida *20850*
V	*Scutellaria arguta* Buckl. *20850*	
I	20850	U.S. - Georgia *20850*
V	20850	U.S. - Kentucky *20850*
Ex/E	20850	U.S. - North Carolina *20850*
I	20850	U.S. - Tennessee *20850*
Ex/E	20850	U.S. - Virginia *20850*
V	*Scutellaria bolanderi* Gray ssp. *austromontana* Epling *20850*	
V	20850	U.S. - California *20850*
V	*Scutellaria bushii* Britt. *20850*	
V	20850	U.S. - Arkansas *20850*
R	20850	U.S. - Missouri *20850*
E	*Scutellaria floridana* Chapman *20850, 15914*	
E	20850	U.S. - Florida *20850*
V	*Scutellaria glabriuscula* Fern. *20850*	
Ex/E	20850	U.S. - Alabama *20850*
I	20850	U.S. - Florida *20850*
I	20850	U.S. - Georgia *20850*
R	*Scutellaria glophyrostachys* Rech.fil. *12840*	
R	12840	Turkey *12840*
R	*Scutellaria heterotricha* Juzepczuk & Vved.	
R		former USSR *6930*
R	*Scutellaria juzepczukii* Gontsch.	
R		former USSR *6930*
V	*Scutellaria kiusiana* Hara var. *kuromidakensis* Yahara *10573*	
V	10573	Japan *10573*
E	*Scutellaria laevis* Shinners *20850*	
E	20850	U.S. - Texas *20850*
E	*Scutellaria lewisiana* Nowicke *20883, 9006*	
I	20883	Panama *20883*
E	*Scutellaria lutilabia* Lane & Nesom *20883*	
I	20883	Mexico *20883*
V	*Scutellaria montana* Chapman *20850*	
V	20850	U.S. - Georgia *20850*
V	20850	U.S. - Tennessee *20850*
R	*Scutellaria naxensis* Bothmer *20171*	
R		Greece
V	*Scutellaria novae-zelandiae* Hook.f. *19305*	
V	19305	New Zealand - South Is. *19305*
E	*Scutellaria ocmulgee* Small *20850*	
E	20850	U.S. - Georgia *20850*
R	*Scutellaria orientalis* L. ssp. *carica*	

	Edmondson *12840*	
R	12840	Turkey *12840*
R	*Scutellaria orientalis* L. ssp. *porphyrostegia* Edmondson *12840*	
R	12840	Turkey *12840*
R	*Scutellaria orientalis* L. ssp. *sintenisii* (Hausskn. ex Bornm.) Edmondson *12840*	
R	12840	Turkey *12840*
R	*Scutellaria orientalis* L. ssp. *tortumensis* Kit Tan & Sorger *12840*	
R	12840	Turkey *12840*
E	*Scutellaria ovata* Hill ssp. *pseudoarguta* Epling *20850, 11630*	
I	20850	U.S. - Indiana *20850*
I	20850	U.S. - Virginia *20850*
Ex/E	20850	U.S. - West Virginia *20850*
R	*Scutellaria pseudoserrata* Epling *20850*	
I	20850	U.S. - Alabama *20850*
I	20850	U.S. - Georgia *20850*
Ex/E	20850	U.S. - North Carolina *20850*
I	20850	U.S. - Tennessee *20850*
I	*Scutellaria robusta* Benth. *8021*	
I	16162	Sri Lanka (Adam's Peak) *8021*
R	*Scutellaria rubicunda* Hornem ssp. *pannosula* (Rech.f.) Edmondson *12840*	
R	12840	Turkey *12840*
R	*Scutellaria rubropunctata* Hayata var. *yakusimensis* (Masam.) Yahara *10573*	
R	10573	Japan *10573*
R	*Scutellaria rupestris* Boiss. & Heldr. *20171*	
R		Greece
V	*Scutellaria thieretii* Shinners *20850*	
I	20850	U.S. - Florida *20850*
V	20850	U.S. - Louisiana *20850*
E	20850	U.S. - Texas *20850*
R	*Scutellaria valdiviana* (D. Clos) Epling *13875*	
R	13875	Chile *13875*
R	*Sideritis albiflora* Huber-Mor. *12840*	
R	12840	Turkey *12840*
R	*Sideritis amasica* Bornm. *12840*	
R	12840	Turkey *12840*
R	*Sideritis argosphacela* (Webb & Berthel.) Clos *19174*	
R	19174	Spain - Canary Is. *19174*
R	*Sideritis argyrea* Davis *12840*	
R	12840	Turkey *12840*
R	*Sideritis armeniaca* Bornm. *12840*	
R	12840	Turkey *12840*
V	*Sideritis barbellata* Mendoza-Heuer	
V		Spain - Canary Is.
R	*Sideritis bilgerana* Davis *12840*	
R	12840	Turkey *12840*
R	*Sideritis brevibracteata* Davis *12840*	
R	12840	Turkey *12840*
V	*Sideritis brevicaulis* Mendoza-Heuer *20750*	
V	20750	Spain - Canary Is. *20750*
R	*Sideritis brevidens* Davis *12840*	
R	12840	Turkey *12840*
V	*Sideritis cabrerae* Ceball. & Ortuno	
V		Spain - Canary Is.
R	*Sideritis canariensis* L.	

R		Spain - Canary Is.
R	***Sideritis candicans*** Aiton	
R		Portugal - Madeira
R	***Sideritis cassia*** Huber-Mor. *12840*	
R	*12840*	Turkey *12840*
V	***Sideritis chamaedrifolia*** Cav. *20699*	
V		Spain
R	***Sideritis cilicica*** Boiss. & Bal. *12840*	
R	*12840*	Turkey *12840*
R	***Sideritis condensata*** (Boiss. & Heldr.) Bentham *12840*	
R	*12840*	Turkey *12840*
R	***Sideritis congesta*** Davis & Huber-Mor. *12840*	
R	*12840*	Turkey *12840*
R	***Sideritis cypria*** Post *14230*	
R		Cyprus *14230*
E	***Sideritis cystosiphon*** Svent. *17891*	
E	*20750*	Spain - Canary Is. *17891*
E	***Sideritis discolor*** (Webb ex de Noe) Bolle *17891*	
E	*20750*	Spain - Canary Is. *17891*
R	***Sideritis eriocephala*** Marrero ex Negrín & Pérez *20750*	
R	*20750*	Spain - Canary Is. *20750*
R	***Sideritis erythrantha*** (Boiss. & Heldr.) Bentham *12840*	
R	*12840*	Turkey *12840*
R	***Sideritis galatica*** Bornm. *12840*	
R	*12840*	Turkey *12840*
R	***Sideritis giennensis*** Pau ex Font Quer *20171*	
R		Spain
R	***Sideritis glauca*** Cav. *11496, 20171*	
R	*20874*	Spain (Alicante, Murcia) *20874*
V	***Sideritis gomeraea*** de Noe ex Bolle *20750*	
V	*20750*	Spain - Canary Is. *20750*
R	***Sideritis hispida*** Davis *12840*	
R	*12840*	Turkey *12840*
R	***Sideritis hololeuca*** (Boiss. & Heldr.) Bentham *12840*	
R	*12840*	Turkey *12840*
R	***Sideritis huber-morathii*** Greuter ex Burdet *12840*	
R	*12840*	Turkey *12840*
R	***Sideritis imbricata*** H. Lindb.	
R		Morocco
R	***Sideritis incana*** L. ssp. *sericea* (Pers.) P.W.Ball ex Heywood *20171*	
R	*20692*	Spain (Muela de Cortes, Valencia province) *20692*
E	***Sideritis infernalis*** Bolle *17891*	
E	*20750*	Spain - Canary Is. *17891*
V	***Sideritis javalambrensis*** Pau *8000, 20171*	
V	*20692*	Spain (Javalambre Mts.) *20692*
V	***Sideritis kuegleriana*** Bornm. *20750*	
V	*20750*	Spain - Canary Is. *20750*
R	***Sideritis laxespicata*** Socorro, I. Tarrega & N.L. Zafra	
R		Spain
R	***Sideritis leptoclada*** O. Schwarz & Davis *12840*	
R	*12840*	Turkey *12840*
R	***Sideritis libanotica*** Labill. ssp. *violescens* (Davis) Davis *12840*	

R	*12840*	Turkey *12840*
V	***Sideritis lycia*** (Boiss. & Heldr.) Bentham *12840*	
V	*12840*	Turkey *12840*
V	***Sideritis macrostachya*** Poiret *20750*	
V	*20750*	Spain - Canary Is. *20750*
R	***Sideritis maireana*** Font Quer & Pau	
R		Morocco
E	***Sideritis marmorea*** Bolle *17891*	
E	*20750*	Spain - Canary Is. *17891*
R	***Sideritis maura*** de Noe *10488*	
R	*14958*	Algeria *10488*
R	***Sideritis mugronensis*** Borja *20692*	
R	*20692*	Spain (Valenica and Albacete provinces) *20692*
E	***Sideritis nervosa*** (Christ) Lid *20750*	
E	*20750*	Spain - Canary Is. *20750*
R	***Sideritis niveotomentosa*** Huber-Mor. *12840*	
R	*12840*	Turkey *12840*
V	***Sideritis nutans*** Svent. *20750*	
V	*20750*	Spain - Canary Is. *20750*
R	***Sideritis osteoxyla*** Pau	
R		Spain (Cabo de Gata)
R	***Sideritis ovata*** Cav. *20171*	
R		Spain
V	***Sideritis penzigii*** (Pitard) Bornm.	
V		Spain - Canary Is.
R	***Sideritis phlomoides*** Boiss. & bal. *12840*	
R	*12840*	Turkey *12840*
R	***Sideritis phrygia*** Bornm. *12840*	
R	*12840*	Turkey *12840*
R	***Sideritis pisidica*** (Boiss. & Heldr.) Bentham *12840*	
R	*12840*	Turkey *12840*
V	***Sideritis pumila*** (Christ) Mendoza-Heuer	
V		Spain - Canary Is.
R	***Sideritis reverchonii*** Willk. *20171*	
R		Spain
R	***Sideritis rubiflora*** Huber-Mor. *12840*	
R	*12840*	Turkey *12840*
R	***Sideritis serrata*** Cav. ex Lag. *8000, 20171*	
R	*20874*	Spain (Albacete) *8000*
R	***Sideritis serratifolia*** Huber-Mor. *12840*	
R	*12840*	Turkey *12840*
R	***Sideritis stachydioides*** Willk. *20171*	
R		Spain
R	***Sideritis stricta*** (Boiss. & Heldr.) Bentham *12840*	
R	*12840*	Turkey *12840*
V	***Sideritis sventenii*** (Kunkel) Mendoza-Heuer *20750*	
V	*20750*	Spain - Canary Is. *19174*
R	***Sideritis tmolea*** Davis *12840*	
R	*12840*	Turkey *12840*
R	***Sideritis trojana*** Bornm. *12840*	
R	*12840*	Turkey *12840*
R	***Sideritis vulcanica*** Huber-Mor. *12840*	
R	*12840*	Turkey *12840*
I	***Solenostemon koualensis*** (Hutch. & Dalz.) J.K. Morton *7926*	
I		Côte d'Ivoire (Mt. Dourou, Sassandra) *7926*

V	*Stachydeoma graveolens* (Chapman ex Gray) Small *20850*		
	V	20850 U.S. - Florida *20850*	
R	*Stachys albanica* Markgr. *20178, 20171*		
	R	20178 Albania *20178*	
R	*Stachys aleurites* (Boiss. & Heldr.) Bentham *12840*		
	R	12840 Turkey *12840*	
R	*Stachys amanica* Davis *12840*		
	R	12840 Turkey *12840*	
R	*Stachys annua* (L.) L. ssp. *cilicica* (Boiss.) Bhattacharjee *12840*		
	R	12840 Turkey *12840*	
R	*Stachys antalyensis* Ayasligil & Davis *12840*		
	R	12840 Turkey *12840*	
R	*Stachys bayburtensis* Bhattacharjee & Huber-Mor. *12840*		
	R	12840 Turkey *12840*	
R	*Stachys beckeana* Dörfl. & Hayek *20178, 20171*		
	R	20178 Albania *20178*	
	R	(former) Yugoslavia *20178*	
R	*Stachys bombycina* Boiss. *12840*		
	R	12840 Turkey *12840*	
R	*Stachys burgsdorffiioides* (Bentham) Boiss. ssp. *ladanoides* Hand.-Mazz. *12840*		
	R	12840 Turkey *12840*	
E	*Stachys buttlerii* R. Mill. *12840*		
	E	12840 Turkey *12840*	
R	*Stachys candida* Bory & Chaub. *20171*		
	R	Greece	
R	*Stachys canescens* Bory & Chaub. *20171*		
	R	Greece	
R	*Stachys cataonica* Bhattacharjee & Huber-Mor. *12840*		
	R	12840 Turkey *12840*	
R	*Stachys chasmosericea* Ayasligil & Davis *12840*		
	R	12840 Turkey *12840*	
R	*Stachys choruhensis* Kit Tan & Sorger *12840*		
	R	12840 Turkey *12840*	
R	*Stachys chrysantha* Boiss. & Heldr. *20171*		
	R	Greece	
R	*Stachys clingmanii* Small *20850*		
	I	20850 U.S. - Alabama *20850*	
	I	20850 U.S. - Indiana *20850*	
	E	20850 U.S. - Maryland *20850*	
	Ex/E	20850 U.S. - North Carolina *20850*	
	E	20850 U.S. - South Carolina *20850*	
	V	20850 U.S. - Tennessee *20850*	
	I	20850 U.S. - Virginia *20850*	
	I	20850 U.S. - West Virginia *20850*	
R	*Stachys cretica* L. ssp. *trapezuntica* Rech.f. *12840*		
	R	12840 Turkey *12840*	
R	*Stachys decumbens* Pers. *20178, 20171*		
	R	20178 Albania *20178*	
	R	Greece *20178*	
R	*Stachys distans* Bentham var. *cilicica* Bhattacharjee & Huber-Mor. *12840*		
	R	12840 Turkey *12840*	
R	*Stachys euadenia* Davis *12840*		
	R	12840 Turkey *12840*	
R	*Stachys euboica* Rech.f. *20171*		
	R	Greece	
I	*Stachys grantii* Battand.		
	I	Morocco	
R	*Stachys guyoniana* de Noe *10488*		
	R	14958 Algeria *10488*	
R	*Stachys huber-morathii* Bhattacharjee *12840*		
	R	12840 Turkey *12840*	
E	*Stachys hyssopifolia* Michaux var. *lythroides* (Small) J. Nelson *20850*		
	E	20850 U.S. - Florida *20850*	
	I	20850 U.S. - Georgia *20850*	
R	*Stachys inanis* Hausskn. & Bornm. *12840*		
	R	12840 Turkey *12840*	
R	*Stachys ionica* Halácsy *20171*		
	R	Greece	
R	*Stachys macrotricha* Rech.f. & Goulimy *20171*		
	R	Greece	
R	*Stachys megalodonta* Hausskn. & Bornm. ex Davis ssp. *mardinensis* Bhattacharjee *12840*		
	R	12840 Turkey *12840*	
R	*Stachys mialhesi* de Noe *10488*		
	R	14958 Algeria *10488*	
R	*Stachys munzurdaghensis* Bhattacharjee *12840*		
	R	12840 Turkey *12840*	
R	*Stachys parolinii* Vis. *20171*		
	R	Greece	
R	*Stachys pinardii* Boiss. *12840*		
	R	12840 Turkey *12840*	
R	*Stachys pseudopinardii* Bhattacharjee & Huber-Mor. *12840*		
	R	12840 Turkey *12840*	
R	*Stachys pumila* Banks & Sol. *12840*		
	R	12840 Turkey *12840*	
R	*Stachys ramosissima* Montbret & Aucher ex Bentham *12840*		
	R	12840 Turkey *12840*	
R	*Stachys rizeensis* Bhattacharjee *12840*		
	R	12840 Turkey *12840*	
R	*Stachys sericantha* Davis *12840*		
	R	12840 Turkey *12840*	
R	*Stachys spreitzenhoferi* Heldr. *20171*		
	R	Greece	
R	*Stachys spruneri* Boiss. ex Benth. *20171*		
	R	Greece	
R	*Stachys subnuda* Montbret & Aucher ex Bentham *12840*		
	R	12840 Turkey *12840*	
R	*Stachys swainsonii* Benth. *20171*		
	R	Greece	
Ex/E	*Stachys talyschensis* Kapeller *5942*		
	Ex/E	5942 Azerbaijan *5942*	
R	*Stachys tetragona* Boiss. & Heldr. *20171*		
	R	Greece	
R	*Stachys tournefortii* Poir. *20171*		
	R	Greece	
	V	Libya	
R	*Stachys tundjeliensis* Kit Tan & Sorger *12840*		
	R	12840 Turkey *12840*	
R	*Stachys virgata* Bory & Chaub. *20171*		
	R	Greece	
I	*Stachys zeyheri* Skan *20604*		

I	20604	South Africa - Cape Province *20604*

Ex/E *Stachys zoharyana* Eig *8895*

    Ex/E   Israel (Sharon Plain; Mt Carmel) *8895*

E *Stenogyne angustifolia* Gray *20850*

    E   20850   U.S. - Hawaii *20850*

E *Stenogyne angustifolia* A. Gray var. *angustifolia* *20850, 14209*

    I   20850   U.S. - Hawaii (Moloka`i, Maui, Hawai`i) *20850*

E *Stenogyne bifida* Hbd. *20850, 14209*

    E   20850   U.S. - Hawaii *20850*

V *Stenogyne calycosa* Sherff *20850, 14209*

    I   20850   U.S. - Hawaii (Maui) *20850*

E *Stenogyne campanulata* Weller & Sakai *20850, 14209*

    E   20850   U.S. - Hawaii (Maui) *20850*

Ex/E *Stenogyne cinerea* Hbd. *20850, 14209*

    Ex/E   20850   U.S. - Hawaii (east Maui) *20850*

Ex/E *Stenogyne cranwelliae* Sherff *20850, 14209*

    Ex/E   20850   U.S. - Hawaii (Kohala Mts.) *20850*

Ex/E *Stenogyne haliakalae* Wawra *20850, 14209*

    Ex/E   20850   U.S. - Hawaii (O`ahu) *20850*

R *Stenogyne kaalae* Wawra *20850*

    I   20850   U.S. - Hawaii *20850*

E *Stenogyne kanehoana* O. Deg. & Sherff *20850, 14209*

    E   20850   U.S. - Hawaii (O`ahu - Wai`anae Mts.) *20850*

V *Stenogyne macrantha* Benth. *20850*

    V   20850   U.S. - Hawaii *20850*

V *Stenogyne microphylla* Benth. *20850, 14209*

    V   20850   U.S. - Hawaii (Maui, Hawai`i) *20850*

Ex/E *Stenogyne oxygona* O. Deg. & Sherff *20850, 14209*

    Ex/E   20850   U.S. - Hawaii (Kohala Mts.) *20850*

V *Stenogyne scrophularioides* Benth. *20850*

    V   20850   U.S. - Hawaii *20850*

Ex/E *Stenogyne viridis* Hbd. *20850, 14209*

    Ex/E   20850   U.S. - Hawaii (West Maui) *20850*

V *Syncolostemon comptonii* Compton *20604, 18023*

    E   20604   Swaziland *20604*

R *Tetradenia barberae* (N.E.Br.) Codd *20604*

    R   20604   South Africa - Cape Province *20604*

V *Teucrium abutiloides* L'Herit. *17891*

    V   Portugal - Madeira *17891*

R *Teucrium alpestre* Sibth. & Sm. ssp. *gracile* (Barbey & Fors.-Major) D.Wood *20171*

    R   20731   Greece - Crete (inc. Karpathos, Saria, Kasos) *20731*

R *Teucrium alyssifolium* Stapf. *12840*

    R   12840   Turkey *12840*

R *Teucrium antitauricum* T. Ekim *12840*

    R   12840   Turkey *12840*

V *Teucrium apollinis* Maire & M. Weiller

    V   Libya

R *Teucrium arduini* L. *20178, 20171*

    R   20178   Albania *20178*

    R   21091   Bosnia & Herzegovina *21091*

    R   (former) Yugoslavia *20178*

R *Teucrium aristatum* Pérez Lara *20171*

    E   20528   France (Bouches-du-Rhône) *20528*

    R   20528   Spain *20528*

R *Teucrium aroanium* Orph. ex Boiss. *20171*

    R   Greece

R *Teucrium atratum* Pomel *10488*

    R   14958   Algeria *10488*

R *Teucrium balfourii* Vierh. *15534*

    R   15534   Yemen - Socotra *15534*

V *Teucrium barbeyanum* Asch. & Taub. ex Dur. & Barr.

    V   Libya

R *Teucrium betonicum* L'Herit. *17891*

    R   Portugal - Madeira *17891*

V *Teucrium brachyandrum* S. Puech *20528*

    V   20528   France (Aude) *20528*

R *Teucrium buxifolium* Schreber ssp. *rivasii* (Rigual ex Greuter & Burdet) M.B. Crespo, Mateo & J. Güemes *20692*

    R   20692   Spain (Alicante) *20692*

R *Teucrium carolipaui* C. Vicioso ex Pau ssp. *fontqueri* (Sennen) Rivas Mart.

    R   Spain

R *Teucrium cavernarum* Davis *12840*

    R   12840   Turkey *12840*

R *Teucrium charidemi* Sandwith *8000, 20171*

    R   Spain (south-east) *11496*

R *Teucrium chrysotrichum* Lange *20171*

    R   Spain

I *Teucrium cinereum* Boiss. *20171*

    I   Spain

R *Teucrium cossonii* D. Wood ssp. *cossonii* *20645*

    R   Spain - Balearic Is.

R *Teucrium cossonii* D. Wood ssp. *fontqueri* Llorens

    R   Spain - Balearic Is.

R *Teucrium cossonii* D.Wood ssp. *punicum* Mayol, Mus & Rosselló *20659*

    R   20645   Spain - Balearic Is. *20645*

R *Teucrium cuneifolium* Sibth. & Sm. *20171*

    R   20731   Greece - Crete *20731*

R *Teucrium dealianum* Emberger & Maire

    R   Morocco

R *Teucrium faurei* Maire

    R   Morocco

V *Teucrium francisci-werneri* Rech.f. *20171*

    V   Greece

R *Teucrium gattefossei* Emberger

    R   Morocco

R *Teucrium gypsophilum* Emberger & Maire

    R   Morocco

R *Teucrium halacsyanum* Heldr. *20171*

    R   Greece

V *Teucrium heterophyllum* L'Herit.

    E   Portugal - Madeira

    V   Spain - Canary Is.

R *Teucrium hifacense* Font Quer *20171*

    R   20692   Spain (north-east of Alicante province) *20692*

R *Teucrium intricatum* Lange *20171*

    R   Spain (Almeria coast)

V *Teucrium kabylicum* Battand. *10488*

    V   14958   Algeria *10488*

R   *Teucrium lanigerum* Lag. *20171*
R   Spain

V   *Teucrium lepicephalum* Pau *17781, 20171*
V   *20692* Spain (Alicante) *20874*

Ex   *Teucrium leucophyllum* Montbret & Aucher ex
      Bentham *12840*
Ex   *12840* Turkey *12840*

R   *Teucrium montbretii* Benth. ssp. *heliotropifolium*
      (Barbay) P.H.Davis *20731*
R   *20731* Greece *20731*

V   *Teucrium montbretii* Bentham ssp. *pamphlicum*
      Davis *12840*
V   *12840* Turkey *12840*

R   *Teucrium odontites* Davis & Bal. *12840*
R   *12840* Turkey *12840*

R   *Teucrium paederotoides* Boiss. & Halkin *12840*
R   *12840* Turkey *12840*

R   *Teucrium pestalozzae* Boiss. *12840*
R   *12840* Turkey *12840*

R   *Teucrium petelotii* Doan *6057*
R   Vietnam *6057*

V   *Teucrium plectranthoides* Gamble *11494*
V   *11494* India - Tamil Nadu (Tirunelveli Hills)
         11494

V   *Teucrium polium* L. ssp. *clapae* S.
      Puech *20528*
V   *20528* France (south) *20528*

R   *Teucrium polium* L. ssp. *purpurascens* (Bentham)
      Puech
V   *20528* France (south) *20528*
R   *20528* Spain - Balearic Is. *20528*

V   *Teucrium salviastrum* Hoffmanns. & Link, non
      Schreb. *8000, 20171*
V   *20076* Portugal (central mountains) *8000*

R   *Teucrium sandrasicum* O. Schwarz *12840*
R   *12840* Turkey *12840*

V   *Teucrium santae* Quezel & Simonneau *10488*
V   *14958* Algeria *10488*

R   *Teucrium serpylloides* Maire & M. Weiller
R   Morocco

I   *Teucrium serranum* Pau
I   Spain

R   *Teucrium tananicum* Maire
R   Morocco

R   *Teucrium teinense* Kudo *10573*
R   *10573* Japan *10573*

R   *Teucrium turredanum* Losa & Rivas Goday *8000, 20171*
R   *20874* Spain (Almeria) *20874*

R   *Teucrium werneri* Rech.f., non Emb. *20171*
R   Morocco

R   *Teucrium zaianum* Emberger & Maire
R   Morocco

V   *Teucrium zanonii* Pampan.
V   Libya

R   *Thymbra calostachya* (Rech.f.) Rech.f. *20171*
R   *20731* Greece - Crete *20731*

R   *Thymbra sintenisii* Bornm. & Azn. ssp. *isaurica*
      Davis *12840*
R   *20618* Turkey *20618*

R   *Thymbra spicata* L. var. *intricata*
      Davis *12840*
R   *20618* Turkey *20618*

R   *Thymus afer* (Pau & F. Quer) Hug.-del-Vill.
R   Morocco

V   *Thymus antoninae* Rouy & Coincy *8000, 20171*
V   *14155* Spain (suth-east) *8000*

R   *Thymus argaeus* Boiss. & bal. *12840*
R   *12840* Turkey *12840*

E   *Thymus aznavourii* Velen. *12840, 20171*
E   *14155* Turkey (Safraköy, near Istanbul) *12840*

R   *Thymus bihoriensis* Jalas *17823, 20171*
R   *19949* Romania *19840*

R   *Thymus binervulatus* Klokov & Roussine *8000, 20171*
R   former European USSR *8000*

R   *Thymus bornmuelleri* Velen *12840*
R   *12840* Turkey *12840*

R   *Thymus borysthenicus* Klokov & Roussine *8001, 20171*
R   former European USSR (Black Sea) *8001*

R   *Thymus canoviridis* Jalas *12840*
R   *12840* Turkey *12840*

V   *Thymus capitellatus* Hoffmanns. & Link *8000, 20171*
V   *20076* Portugal (south) *8000*
E   *14155* Spain *14155*

R   *Thymus cappadocicus* Boiss. var.
      cappadocicus *12840*
R   *12840* Turkey *12840*

R   *Thymus cappadocicus* Boiss. var. *globifer*
      Jalas *12840*
R   *12840* Turkey *12840*

R   *Thymus cariensis* Huber-Mor. *12840*
R   *12840* Turkey *12840*

R   *Thymus carnosus* Boiss. *8000, 20171*
R   *20874* Portugal (south) *8000*
R   *20874* Spain *20874*

R   *Thymus convolutus* Klokov *12840*
R   *19873* Turkey *12840*

E   *Thymus decussatus* Benth. *16168*
E   *16168* Egypt *16168*

V   *Thymus dreatensis* Battand. *10488*
V   *14958* Algeria *10488*

R   *Thymus granatensis* Boiss. *20171*
R   *20660* Spain *20661*

R   *Thymus haussknechtii* Velen. *12840*
R   *12840* Turkey *12840*

R   *Thymus hesperidum* Maire
R   Morocco

V   *Thymus leucostomous* Hausskn. & Velen. var.
      argyllaceus Jalas *12840*
V   *12840* Turkey *12840*

V   *Thymus leucostomus* Hausskn. & Velen var. *gypsaceus*
      Jalas *12840*
V   *12840* Turkey *12840*

R   *Thymus loscosii* Willk. *8000, 20171*
R   *14155* Spain (North-east) *8000*

V   *Thymus lotocephalus* G. Lopez & R. Morales *20686, 20810*
V   *20076* Portugal *20076*

R   *Thymus magnus* Nakai

R		Korea, South

R   *Thymus mastichina* (L.) L. ssp. *donyanae* Morales
     R   Spain

R   *Thymus mentagensis* Battand.
     R   Morocco

R   *Thymus nitens* Lamotte *20171*
     R   France (South)

Ex   *Thymus oehmianus* Ronniger & Soska *20171*
     Ex   (former) Yugoslavia

R   *Thymus origanoides* Webb & Berthel. *20750*
     R   *20750* Spain - Canary Is. *20750*

R   *Thymus pectinatus* Fisch. & Mey. var. *pectinatus* *12840*
     R   *12840* Turkey *12840*

V   *Thymus plasonii* Adamovic *17781*, *20171*
     V   *17781* Greece (Thessaloniki) *17781*

R   *Thymus pubescens* Boiss. & Kotschy var. *cratericola* Jalas *12840*
     R   *12840* Turkey *12840*

R   *Thymus pulvinatus* Celak *12840*
     R   *12840* Turkey *12840*

R   *Thymus revolutus* Celak *12840*
     R   *12840* Turkey *12840*

R   *Thymus richardii* Pers. ssp. *ebusitanus* (Font Quer) Jalas *8000*, *20171*
     R   Spain - Balearic Is. (Ibiza) *8000*

R   *Thymus richardii* Pers. ssp. *nitidus* (Guss.) Jalas *8000*, *20171*
     R   *18264* Italy - Sicily *18264*

I   *Thymus ruiz-latorrei* C. Vicioso
     I   Spain

R   *Thymus sipyleus* Boiss. var. *davisianus* Ronniger *12840*
     R   *12840* Turkey *12840*

R   *Thymus spathulifolius* Hausskn. & Velen *12840*
     R   *12840* Turkey *12840*

V   *Thymus talievii* Klok. & Schost. *8000*
     V   former European USSR *8000*

R   *Thymus villosus* L. ssp. *villosus* *8000*, *20171*
     V   *20076* Portugal (south) *8000*
     R   Spain (south west) *8000*

E   *Trichostema austromontanum* H. Lewis ssp. *compactum* F.H. Lewis *20850*
     E   *20850* U.S. - California *20850*

R   *Trichostema ovatum* Curran *20850*
     I   *20850* U.S. - California *20850*

R   *Trichostema parishii* Vasey *20850*
     I   *20850* U.S. - California *20850*

R   *Trichostema purpusii* Brandegee *9672*
     R   *19755* Mexico *9672*

R   *Trichostema rubisepalum* Elmer *20850*
     I   *20850* U.S. - California *20850*

E   *Trichostema suffrutescens* Kearney *20850*
     I   *20850* U.S. - Florida *20850*

R   *Westringia angustifolia* R.Br. *20681*
     R   *20681* Australia - Tasmania *20681*

R   *Westringia blakeana* B.Boivin *20681*
     I   *20681* Australia - New South Wales *20681*

I	*20681*	Australia - Queensland *20681*

R   *Westringia brevifolia* Benth. var. *raleighii* (Boivin) W.M.Curtis *20681*
     R   *20681* Australia - Tasmania *20681*

E   *Westringia crassifolia* Wakef. *20681*
     E   *20681* Australia - Victoria *20681*

V   *Westringia cremnophila* Wakef. *20681*
     V   *20681* Australia - Victoria *20681*

V   *Westringia davidii* Conn *20681*
     V   *20681* Australia - New South Wales *20681*

R   *Westringia glabra* R.Br. *20681*
     R   *20681* Australia - New South Wales *20681*

R   *Westringia grandifolia* F.Muell. ex Benth. *20681*
     R   *20681* Australia - Queensland *20681*

R   *Westringia lucida* B.Boivin *20681*
     I   *20681* Australia - Capital Territory *20681*
     I   *20681* Australia - New South Wales *20681*
     I   *20681* Australia - Victoria *20681*

V   *Westringia parvifolia* C.White & Francis *20681*
     V   *20681* Australia - Queensland *20681*

V   *Westringia rupicola* S.T.Blake *20681*
     V   *20681* Australia - Queensland *20681*

R   *Westringia saxatilis* Conn *20681*
     R   *20681* Australia - New South Wales *20681*

R   *Westringia sericea* B.Boivin *20681*
     I   *20681* Australia - New South Wales *20681*
     I   *20681* Australia - Queensland *20681*

V   *Wrixonia schultzii* (Tate) Carrick *20681*
     V   *20681* Australia - Northern Territory *20681*

R   *Ziziphora acinoides* L. *20171*
     R   Spain

R   *Ziziphora serpyllacea* M. Bieb. *8001*
     R   Asiatic U.S.S.R. (Caucasus) *8001*

R   *Ziziphora taurica* M. Bieb. ssp. *cleonioides* (Boiss.) Davis *12840*
     R   *12840* Turkey *12840*

Lacistemataceae

Number of genera:	2	
Number of species:	20	
Recorded threatened species:	7	(35%)

Tropical America.

R   *Lacistema krukovii* Sleumer *20883*
     I   *20883* Brazil *20883*
     I   *20883* Colombia *20883*

V   *Lacistema lucidum* Schnizlein *20883*
     I   *20883* Brazil *20883*

V   *Lacistema macbridei* Baehni *20883*
     I   *20883* Peru *20883*

R   *Lacistema nena* Macbride *20883*
     I   *20883* Brazil *20883*
     I   *20883* Peru *20883*

R   *Lacistema robustum* Schnizlein *20883*
     I   *20883* Brazil *20883*

E   *Lacistema serrulatum* Martius *20883*
     I   *20883* Brazil *20883*

R   *Lozania klugii* (Mansfeld) Mansfeld *20883*
     I   *20883* Brazil *20883*
     I   *20883* Colombia *20883*
     I   *20883* Peru *20883*

Lactoridaceae

Number of genera: 1
Number of species: 1
Recorded threatened species: 1 (100%)

San Juan Islands (Chile).

V   *Lactoris fernandeziana* Philippi *19116*
     V   *19125* Chile - Juan Fernandez Is. *19116*

Lardizabalaceae

Number of genera: 8
Number of species: 30
Recorded threatened species: 5 (16%)

Himalayas to Southeast Asia; Chile.

R   *Akebia chingshuiensis* Shimizu *20511*
     R   *20511* Taiwan *20511*

R   *Holboellia chapaensis* Gagnepain *6057*
     R   Vietnam *6057*

I   *Stauntonia formosana* Hayata *20511*
     I   *20511* Taiwan *20511*

I   *Stauntonia keitaoensis* Hayata *20511*
     I   *20511* Taiwan *20511*

R   *Stauntonia purpurea* Y.C.Liu & F.Y.Lu *20511*
     R   *20511* Taiwan *20511*

Lauraceae

Number of genera: 30-50
Number of species: 2,000
Recorded threatened species: 259 (12%)

Tropical and subtropical.

V   *Actinodaphne albifrons* Kosterm. *10252*
     V   *12838* Sri Lanka *10252*

E   *Actinodaphne bourneae* Gamble
     E   *13883* India - Tamil Nadu (Kodaikanal, Palani hills) *13883*

I   *Actinodaphne campanulata* Hook.f. var. *campanulata*
     I   India - Tamil Nadu (Tirunelveli Hills)

I   *Actinodaphne campanulata* Hook.f. var. *obtusa* Gamble
     I   India - Kerala (Travancore) *9315*

E   *Actinodaphne lanata* Meissner
     E   *13883* India - Tamil Nadu (Nilgiri Hills) *13883*

R   *Actinodaphne lawsonii* Gamble *13883*
     R   *13883* India - Kerala (south-east Wynaad) *13883*
     R   *13883* India - Tamil Nadu (Nilgiris) *13883*

I   *Actinodaphne salicina* Meissner
     I   India - Tamil Nadu (Sispara, Nilgiri hills)

R   *Adenodaphne spathulata* Kosterm.
     R   New Caledonia

R   *Aiouea acarodomatifera* Kostermans *20883*
     I   *20883* Brazil *20883*
     ?   Brazil - Minas Gerais *20926*
     ?   Brazil - Rio de Janeiro *20926*
     ?   Brazil - Santa Catarina *20926*

E   *Aiouea angulata* Kostermans *20883*
     E   *20883* Colombia (Boyaca) *20926*

R   *Aiouea benthamiana* Mez *20883*
     I   *20883* Brazil *20883*

     I   *20883* Colombia *20883*
     I   *20883* Venezuela *20883*

V   *Aiouea bracteata* Kostermans *20883*
     V   *20883* Brazil *20883*
     ?   Brazil - Sao Paulo *20926*

R   *Aiouea dubia* (Humboldt, Bonpland & Kunth) Mez *20883*
     I   *20883* Colombia *20883*
     I   *20883* Peru *20883*
     I   *20883* Venezuela (Meridá) *20926*

R   *Aiouea guatemalensis* (Lundell) Renner *20883, 11558*
     I   *20883* Guatemala *20883*

R   *Aiouea impressa* (Meissner) Kostermans *20883*
     I   *20883* Brazil *20883*
     ?   Brazil - Pará *20926*
     I   *20883* French Guiana *20883*

R   *Aiouea inconspicua* van der Werff *20883*
     I   *20883* Mexico *20883*

R   *Aiouea lehmannii* (O. C. Schmidt) Renner *20883*
     I   *20883* Brazil *20883*
     ?   Brazil - Acre *20926*
     I   *20883* Colombia (Chocó & Valle) *20926*

E   *Aiouea macedoana* Vattimo *20883*
     E   *20883* Brazil *20883*
     ?   Brazil - Goias *20926*

R   *Aiouea parvissima* (Lundell) Renner *20883, 10297*
     I   *20883* Guatemala (Petén) *20926*

R   *Aiouea piauhyensis* (Meissner) Mez *20883*
     I   *20883* Brazil *20883*
     ?   Brazil - Goias *20926*
     ?   Brazil - Mato Grosso *20926*
     ?   Brazil - Piaui *20926*

R   *Alseodaphne birmanica* Kosterm *19120*
     R   *19120* Thailand *19120*

E   *Alseodaphne rugosa* Merr. & Chun *11139*
     E   China - Hainan Is. *11139*

I   *Alseodaphne semecarpifolia* Nees var. *angustifolia* Meissner
     I   India - Tamil Nadu

R   *Alseodaphne siamensis* Kosterm. *19120*
     R   *19120* Thailand *19120*

E   *Aniba bracteata* Mez *10199*
     E   Dominica *10199*

R   *Aniba excelsa* Kostermans *20883*
     I   *20883* Guyana *20883*
     I   *20883* Venezuela *20883*

V   *Aniba ferrea* Kubitzki *20883*
     V   *20883* Brazil *20883*

E   *Aniba ferruginea* Kubitzki *20883*
     E   *20883* Venezuela (Amazonas) *20926*

V   *Aniba intermedia* (Meissner) Mez *20883*
     I   *20883* Brazil *20883*
     V   *20883* Brazil - Bahia *20926*

E   *Aniba lancifolia* Kubitzki & Rodrigues *20883*
     E   *20883* Brazil *20883*
     E   *20883* Brazil - Amazonas *20926*

V   *Aniba novo-granatensis* Kubitzki *20883*
     I   *20883* Colombia *20883*

E   *Aniba pedicellata* Kostermans *20883*
     E   *20883* Brazil *20883*
     E   *20883* Brazil - Rio de Janeiro *20926*

E   *Aniba percoriacea* C. K. Allen *20883*
     E   *20883* Suriname *20883*

R   *Aniba permollis* (Nees) Mez *20883*
- **I**   *20883*   Brazil *20883*
- **I**   *20883*   Brazil - Amazonas *20926*
- **I**   *20883*   Guyana *20883*

V   *Aniba ramageana* Mez *20883, 10199*
- **I**   *20883*   Dominica *20883*
- **I**   *19001*   Martinique (La Grande Rivière) *20883*

R   *Aniba robusta* (Klotzsch & Karsten) Mez *20883*
- **I**   *20883*   Venezuela *20883*

E   *Aniba rosaeodora* Ducke *17746*
- **?**   Brazil - Amapa *20926*
- **E**   *17746*   Brazil - Amazonas *17746*
- **E**   *17746*   Brazil - Pará *17746*
- **E**   *10370*   Colombia *10370*
- **E**   *10370*   Ecuador *10370*
- **E**   *10370*   French Guiana *17462*
- **?**   Guyana *20926*
- **E**   *10370*   Peru *10370*
- **E**   *10370*   Suriname *17462*
- **?**   Venezuela (Amazonas) *20926*

V   *Aniba santalodora* Ducke *20883*
- **I**   *20883*   Brazil *20883*
- **?**   Brazil - Amazonas *20926*

E   *Aniba vaupesiana* Kubitzki *20883*
- **E**   *20883*   Colombia (Vaupés) *20926*

R   *Aniba venezuelana* Mez *20883*
- **V**   *20883*   Costa Rica *20883*
- **I**   *20883*   Colombia (Chocó) *20926*
- **I**   *20883*   Venezuela (Carabobo) *20926*

V   *Apollonias ceballosi* Svent. *20750*
- **V**   *20750*   Spain - Canary Is. *20750*

R   *Beilschmiedia ambigua* Robyns & R. Wilczek *19358*
- **R**   *19358*   Zaire (Haut-Katanga) *19358*

V   *Beilschmiedia berteroana* (Gay) Kosterm. *20883, 15088*
- **V**   *20883*   Chile *20883*

I   *Beilschmiedia bourdilloni* Brandis
- **I**   India - Karnataka (South Canara)
- **I**   India - Kerala (Travancore)

R   *Beilschmiedia bracteata* Robyns & R. Wilczek *19358*
- **R**   *19358*   Zaire (central Forestier) *19358*

R   *Beilschmiedia castrisinensis* B.Hyland *20681*
- **R**   *20681*   Australia - Queensland *20681*

R   *Beilschmiedia giorgii* Robyns & R. Wilczek *19358*
- **R**   *19358*   Zaire (central Forestier) *19358*

R   *Beilschmiedia miersii* (Gay) Kosterm. *20883, 15088*
- **R**   *20883*   Chile *20883*

I   *Beilschmiedia nigrifolia* Elm. *13833*
- **I**   *13833*   Philippines (Palawan) *13833*

R   *Beilschmiedia oligandra* S.Smith *20681*
- **R**   *20681*   Australia - Queensland *20681*

R   *Beilschmiedia peninsularis* B.Hyland *20681*
- **R**   *20681*   Australia - Queensland *20681*

V   *Beilschmiedia ugandensis* Rendle *21116*
- **V**   *21116*   Sudan *21116*
- **V**   *21116*   Tanzania *21116*
- **V**   *21116*   Uganda *21116*
- **V**   *21116*   Zaire *21116*

R   *Beilschmiedia vermoesenii* Robyns & R. Wilczek *19358*
- **R**   *19358*   Zaire (Mayumbe) *19358*

R   *Beilschmiedia volckii* B.Hyland *20681*
- **R**   *20681*   Australia - Queensland *20681*

I   *Beilschmiedia wightii* (Nees) Benth. ex Hook.f.
- **I**   India - Kerala (Travancore Hills)

- **I**   India - Tamil Nadu

V   *Beilschmiedia zeylanica* Trimen *10276*
- **V**   *12838*   Sri Lanka *10276*

V   *Caryodaphnopsis burgeri* Zamora & Poveda *20883, 12477*
- **E**   *19943*   Costa Rica *20883*

R   *Caryodaphnopsis fosteri* Henk van der Werff *20883*
- **I**   *20883*   Peru *20883*

V   *Caryodaphnopsis inaequalis* (A.C. Smith) van der Werff & Richter *20883*
- **I**   *20883*   Brazil *20883*
- **I**   *20883*   Ecuador *20883*
- **I**   *20883*   Peru *20883*

Ex   *Cassytha pedicellosa* J.Weber *20681, 14223*
- **Ex**   *20681*   Australia - Tasmania *20681*

R   *Cinnamomum baileyanum* (Bailey) W.D.Francis *20681*
- **R**   *20681*   Australia - Queensland *20681*

R   *Cinnamomum brevipedunculatum* Chang
- **R**   *20854*   Taiwan (Heng-ch'un) *20854*

E   *Cinnamomum capparu-coronde* Blume *11103*
- **E**   *12838*   Sri Lanka (Hinidumkande) *11103*

I   *Cinnamomum citriodorum* Thwaites *10252*
- **I**   *16162*   Sri Lanka *10252*

I   *Cinnamomum glanduliferum* Meisson *7771*
- **I**   *14761*   India - Uttar Pradesh *7771*

R   *Cinnamomum kanahirai* Hay. *20511*
- **R**   *20511*   Taiwan *20511*

E   *Cinnamomum kotoense* Kaneh. & Sas. *14961*
- **E**   *20854*   Taiwan (Botel Tobago) *14961*

R   *Cinnamomum macrocarpum* Hook.f.
- **R**   *18228*   India - Tamil Nadu (Nilgiri Hills) *18228*

E   *Cinnamomum mairei* Leveille *17617*
- **E**   *17617*   China - Sichuan *11139*
- **E**   *17617*   China - Yunnan (Saotong; Daguan; Yiling) *11139*

V   *Cinnamomum mindanaense* Elmer *10278*
- **V**   Philippines *10278*

R   *Cinnamomum osmophloeum* Kaneh. *20511*
- **R**   *20854*   Taiwan *20511*

R   *Cinnamomum perrottetii* Meissner *4988*
- **R**   *18228*   India - Tamil Nadu (Nilgiri Hills) *4988*

R   *Cinnamomum propinquum* Bailey *20681*
- **R**   *20681*   Australia - Queensland *20681*

E   *Cinnamomum pseudomelastoma* *20854*
- **E**   *20854*   Taiwan *20854*

R   *Cinnamomum reticulatum* Hayata *20511*
- **R**   *20511*   Taiwan (Heng-ch'un) *20511*

R   *Cinnamomum riparium* Gamble
- **R**   *18341*   India - Karnataka (Coorg) *18228*
- **R**   *18341*   India - Kerala (Travancore Hills) *18228*
- **R**   *18341*   India - Tamil Nadu *18228*

V   *Cinnamomum travancoricum* Gamble
- **V**   *18228*   India - Kerala *18228*

R   *Cryptocarya bellendenkerana* B.Hyland *20681*
- **R**   *20681*   Australia - Queensland *20681*

E   *Cryptocarya bitriplinerva* Kosterm. *20893*
- **E**   *20893*   New Caledonia *20893*

R   *Cryptocarya claudiana* B.Hyland *20681*
- **R**   *20681*   Australia - Queensland *20681*

R	*Cryptocarya dorrigoensis* B.Hyland & Floyd *20681*	
	R	*20681* Australia - New South Wales *20681*
I	*Cryptocarya ferrarsii* King *14782*	
	I	*14782* India - Andaman Is. (Middle) *7771*
R	*Cryptocarya floydii* Kosterm. *20681*	
	I	*20681* Australia - New South Wales *20681*
	I	*20681* Australia - Queensland *20681*
V	*Cryptocarya foetida* R.Baker *20681*	
	I	*20681* Australia - New South Wales *20681*
	I	*20681* Australia - Queensland *20681*
R	*Cryptocarya glaucocarpa* B.Hyland *20681*	
	R	*20681* Australia - Queensland *20681*
I	*Cryptocarya gregsonii* Maiden	
	I	*14226* Australia - NSW - Lord Howe Is. *14226*
R	*Cryptocarya longifolia* Kosterm.	
	R	New Caledonia
R	*Cryptocarya louvelii* Danguy *6963*	
	R	*6963* Madagascar (centre-east) *10246*
R	*Cryptocarya mannii* Hbd. *20850, 14209*	
	R	*20850* U.S. - Hawaii (Kaua`i, O`ahu) *20850*
E	*Cryptocarya membranacea* Thwaites *10252*	
	E	*12838* Sri Lanka *10252*
R	*Cryptocarya nova-anglica* B.Hyland & Floyd *20681*	
	R	*20681* Australia - New South Wales *20681*
I	*Cryptocarya palawanensis* Merr. *13833*	
	I	*13833* Philippines (Palawan) *13833*
R	*Cryptocarya pleurosperma* C.White & Francis *20681*	
	R	*20681* Australia - Queensland *20681*
I	*Cryptocarya stocksii* Meissner	
	I	India - Karnataka
	I	India - Kerala (Travancore Hills)
	I	India - Tamil Nadu
R	*Cryptocarya wightiana* Thwaites *10276*	
	R	*12838* Sri Lanka *10276*
R	*Cryptocarya williwilliana* B.Hyland & Floyd *20681*	
	R	*20681* Australia - New South Wales *20681*
E	*Dahlgrenodendron natalense* (J.H.Ross) J.J.M.van der Merwe & A.E.van Wyk *20604*	
	E	*20604* South Africa - Cape Province *20604*
	E	*20604* South Africa - Natal *20604*
I	*Dehaasia kerrii* Kosterm. *19120*	
	I	*19120* Thailand *19120*
R	*Dehaasia longipedicellata* (Ridley) Kosterm.	
	R	Malaysia - Peninsular Malaysia
R	*Dehaasia triandra* Merr. *7730*	
	R	Taiwan (Lan Yu)
	I	*15960* Philippines *7730*
V	*Dicypellium caryophyllaceum* (Mart.) Nees *21019, 21020*	
	V	*17746* Brazil - Amazonas (Rio Xingu & Rio Tapajós.) *17079*
	V	*17746* Brazil - Maranhao *17079*
	V	*17746* Brazil - Pará *17079*
R	*Endiandra anthropophagorum* Domin *20681*	
	R	*20681* Australia - Queensland *20681*
R	*Endiandra bellendenkerana* B.Hyland *20681*	
	R	*20681* Australia - Queensland *20681*
R	*Endiandra collinsii* B.Hyland *20681*	
	R	*20681* Australia - Queensland *20681*
E	*Endiandra cooperiana* B.Hyland *20681*	
	E	*20681* Australia - Queensland *20681*
R	*Endiandra dichrophylla* F.Muell. *20681*	
	R	*20681* Australia - Queensland *20681*
V	*Endiandra floydii* B.Hyland *20681*	
	I	*20681* Australia - New South Wales *20681*
	I	*20681* Australia - Queensland *20681*
R	*Endiandra globosa* Maiden & Betche *20681*	
	I	*20681* Australia - New South Wales *20681*
	I	*20681* Australia - Queensland *20681*
R	*Endiandra grayi* B.Hyland *20681*	
	R	*20681* Australia - Queensland *20681*
V	*Endiandra hayesii* Kosterm. *20681*	
	I	*20681* Australia - New South Wales *20681*
	I	*20681* Australia - Queensland *20681*
R	*Endiandra introrsa* C.White *20681*	
	I	*20681* Australia - New South Wales *20681*
	I	*20681* Australia - Queensland *20681*
R	*Endiandra jonesii* B.Hyland *20681*	
	R	*20681* Australia - Queensland *20681*
V	*Endiandra lecardii* Guillaumin *20893*	
	V	*20893* New Caledonia *20893*
R	*Endiandra microneura* C.White *20681*	
	R	*20681* Australia - Queensland *20681*
V	*Endiandra poueboensis* Guillaumin *20893*	
	V	*20893* New Caledonia *20893*
R	*Endiandra sideroxylon* B.Hyland *20681*	
	R	*20681* Australia - Queensland *20681*
R	*Endiandra xanthocarpa* B.Hyland *20681*	
	R	*20681* Australia - Queensland *20681*
E	*Licaria bracteata* van der Werff *20883*	
	I	*20883* Guatemala *20883*
I	*Licaria salicifolia* (Swartz) Kostermans *10199*	
	I	Dominica *10199*
E	*Licaria sericea* (Griseb.) Kosterm. *19001*	
	E	*19001* Dominica *19001*
	E	*19001* Guadeloupe *19001*
	Ex/E	*19001* Martinique *19001*
	E	*19001* St Lucia *19001*
R	*Licaria vernicosa* (Mez) Kosterm. *8679*	
	R	*8679* French Guiana *8679*
	R	*8679* Guyana *8679*
	R	*8679* Suriname *8679*
V	*Lindera melissifolia* (Walt.) Blume *20850, 16005*	
	Ex/E	*20850* U.S. - Alabama (Wilcox Co.) *20850*
	V	*20850* U.S. - Arkansas (Clay Co.) *20850*
	Ex/E	*20850* U.S. - Florida *20850*
	E	*20850* U.S. - Georgia (Wheeler Co.) *20850*
	Ex/E	*20850* U.S. - Louisiana (last seen 1949) *20850*
	E	*20850* U.S. - Mississippi (Sharkey Co.) *20850*
	E	*20850* U.S. - Missouri (Ripley Co.) *20850*
	E	*20850* U.S. - North Carolina *20850*
	E	*20850* U.S. - South Carolina (Berkeley Co.) *20850*
V	*Lindera subcoriacea* B.E. Wofford *20850*	
	E	*20850* U.S. - Alabama *20850*
	E	*20850* U.S. - Florida *20850*
	E	*20850* U.S. - Georgia *20850*
	E	*20850* U.S. - Louisiana *20850*
	E	*20850* U.S. - Mississippi *20850*
	V	*20850* U.S. - North Carolina *20850*
	I	*20850* U.S. - South Carolina *20850*
	V	*20850* U.S. - Virginia *20850*
R	*Litsea aestivalis* (L.) Fern. *20850*	
	V	*20850* U.S. - Florida *20850*

V	20850	U.S. - Georgia *20850*
I	20850	U.S. - Louisiana *20850*
E	20850	U.S. - Maryland *20850*
V	20850	U.S. - North Carolina *20850*
R	20850	U.S. - South Carolina *20850*
I	20850	U.S. - Tennessee *20850*
Ex/E	20850	U.S. - Virginia *20850*

R *Litsea auriculata* **Chien & Cheng** *17617*

    R   *17617* China - Anhui *11139*
    R   *17617* China - Jiangxi (Jiulingshan) *11139*
    R   *17617* China - Zhejiang *11139*

R *Litsea bennettii* **B.Hyland** *20681*

    R   *20681* Australia - Queensland *20681*

I *Litsea cinerea* **(Elm.) Merr.** *13833*

    I   *13833* Philippines (Palawan) *13833*

V *Litsea dilleniifolia* **P.Y. Pai & P.H. Huang** *17617*

    V   *17617* China - Yunnan *11139*

V *Litsea gardneri* **Meissner** *10276*

    V   *12838* Sri Lanka *10276*

R *Litsea granitica* **B.Hyland** *20681*

    R   *20681* Australia - Queensland *20681*

E *Litsea imbricata* **Guillaumin** *20893*

    E   *20893* New Caledonia *20893*

V *Litsea leiantha* **(Kurz) Hook.f.** *7771*

    V   *14782* India - Andaman Is. (South) *7771*

R *Litsea lii* **C.E. Chang** *20511*

    R   *20511* Taiwan *20511*

R *Litsea linii* **C.E. Chang** *20511*

    R   *20511* Taiwan *20511*

V *Litsea longepedunculata* **Kosterm.** *20893*

    V   *20893* New Caledonia *20893*

V *Litsea mackeei* **Kosterm.** *20893*

    E   *20893* New Caledonia *20893*

R *Litsea miana* **Guillaumin**

    R   New Caledonia

I *Litsea mysorensis* **Gamble**

    I   India - Karnataka
    I   India - Kerala (Wynaad)

E *Litsea nemoralis* **(Thwaites) Hook.f.** *10252*

    E   *12838* Sri Lanka *10252*

E *Litsea pierrei* **Lecomte var.** *szemois*
    Liou *17617*

    E   *17617* China - Yunnan (Jinghong, Menhai, Menla)
          11139

R *Litsea sasakii* **Kamikoti** *20511*

    R   *20511* Taiwan *20511*

E *Litsea stenophylla* **Guillaumin** *20893*

    E   *20893* New Caledonia *20893*

I *Litsea travancorica* **Gamble**

    I   India - Kerala (Travancore Hills)

I *Litsea undulata* **Hook.f.** *10252*

    I   *16162* Sri Lanka *10252*

R *Machilus pseudokobu* **Koidz.** *8037*

    R   *19135* Japan - Kazan Retto *8622*
    R   *19134* Japan - Ogasawara-shoto *8037*

E *Mezilaurus caatingae* **van der Werff** *20883*

    I   *20883* Brazil *20883*

E *Mezilaurus duckei* **van der Werff** *20883*

    I   *20883* Brazil *20883*

E *Mezilaurus glaucophylla* **van der Werff** *20883, 10558*

    I   *20883* Costa Rica *20883*

V *Mezilaurus mahuba* **(Samp.) van der Werff** *20883*

    I   *20883* Costa Rica *20883*
    I   *20883* Brazil *20883*

E *Mezilaurus micrantha* **van der Werff** *20883*

    I   *20883* Brazil *20883*

E *Mezilaurus opaca* **Kubitzki & van der Werff** *20883*

    I   *20883* Peru *20883*

E *Mezilaurus palcazuensis* **van der Werff** *20883*

    I   *20883* Peru *20883*

E *Mezilaurus pyriflora* **van der Werff** *20883*

    I   *20883* Brazil *20883*

E *Mezilaurus quadrilocellata* **van der Werff** *20883*

    I   *20883* Colombia *20883*

V *Mezilaurus thoroflora* **van der Werff** *20883*

    I   *20883* Guyana *20883*

R *Nectandra ambigens* **(Blake) C. K. Allen** *20883, 11558*

    I   *20883* Guatemala *20883*
    I   *20883* Honduras *20883*
    I   *20883* Mexico *20883*

R *Nectandra angusta* **Rohwer** *20883*

    R   *20883* Bolivia (Cochabamba; Santa Cruz & Tarija)
          20927

E *Nectandra apiculata* **Rohwer** *20883*

    E   *20883* Bolivia (Cochabamba) *20927*

E *Nectandra astyla* **Rohwer** *20883*

    E   *20883* Peru (San Martín) *20927*

R *Nectandra aurea* **Rohwer** *20883*

    I   *20883* Venezuela (Orinoco river banks) *20927*

V *Nectandra barbellata* **Coe-Teixeira** *20883*

    V   *20883* Brazil *20883*
    ?   Brazil - Espirito Santo *20927*
    ?   Brazil - Sao Paulo *20927*

R *Nectandra bartlettiana* **Lasser** *20883*

    R   *20883* Venezuela (Barinas; Portuguesa & Zulia)
          20927

E *Nectandra bicolor* **Rohwer** *20883*

    I   *20883* Panama (Cerro Jefe) *20926*

R *Nectandra brittonii* **Mez** *20883*

    I   *20883* Bolivia (La Paz) *20927*
    I   *20883* Peru (San Martín & Pasco) *20927*

E *Nectandra brochidodroma* **Rohwer** *20883*

    E   *20883* Peru (Madre de Dios) *20927*

E *Nectandra canaliculata* **Rohwer** *20883*

    E   *20883* Ecuador (Napo) *20927*

E *Nectandra caudatoacuminata* **O. C. Schmidt** *20883*

    E   *20883* Haiti (Massif de la Hotte, Les Roseaux)
          21008

E *Nectandra cerifolia* **Rohwer** *20883*

    E   *20883* Ecuador (Cordillera de Cutucú) *20927*

R *Nectandra citrifolia* **Rusby** *20883*

    I   *20883* Bolivia (La Paz) *20927*
    I   *20883* Peru (San Martín) *20927*

R *Nectandra coeloclada* **Rohwer** *20883*

    I   *20883* Ecuador (Napo & Morona-Santiago) *20927*

E *Nectandra cordata* **Rohwer** *20883*

    E   *20883* Peru (Loreto) *20927*

V *Nectandra crassiloba* **Rohwer** *20883*

    I   *20883* Ecuador (Napo) *20927*

V *Nectandra dasystyla* **Rohwer** *20927, 21306*

    V   *21306* Bolivia (Beni & Pando) *20927*
    V   *21306* Ecuador *20927*

V   *21306* Peru (Loreto) *20927*

E   *Nectandra debilis* Mez *20883*

  E   *20883* Brazil *20883*
  ?   Brazil - Espirito Santo *20927*
  ?   Brazil - Rio de Janeiro *20927*

I   *Nectandra embirensis* Coe-Teixeira *20927, 21306*

  I   *21306* Brazil - Amazonas *20927*
  I   *21306* Ecuador *20927*
  I   *21306* Peru (Loreto) *20927*

E   *Nectandra filiflora* Rohwer *20883*

  E   *20883* Peru (Loreto) *20927*

E   *Nectandra fragrans* Rohwer *20883*

  E   *20883* Ecuador (Cordillera de Cutucu) *20927*

E   *Nectandra fulva* Rohwer *20883*

  E   *20883* Venezuela (Amazonas) *20927*

R   *Nectandra gracilis* Rohwer *20883*

  I   *20883* Ecuador (Napo; Pastaza) *20927*
  I   *20883* Peru (Loreto) *20927*

E   *Nectandra grisea* Rohwer *20883*

  E   *20883* Brazil *20883*
  ?   Brazil - Amazonas *20927*

V   *Nectandra guadaripo* Rohwer *20883*

  I   *20883* Colombia (Nariño) *20927*
  I   *20883* Ecuador (Esmeraldas) *20927*

E   *Nectandra herrerae* O. C. Schmidt *20883*

  E   *20883* Peru (Machu Picchu) *20927*

V   *Nectandra heterotricha* Rohwer *20883*

  I   *20883* Peru (Loreto) *20927*

R   *Nectandra hirtella* Rohwer *20883*

  I   *20883* Peru (Pasco & San Martin) *20927*

E   *Nectandra hypoleuca* Hammel *20883*

  E   *20883* Costa Rica (La Selva Field Station)
     20927

E   *Nectandra impressa* Mez *20883*

  E   *20883* Brazil *20883*

I   *Nectandra japurensis* Nees *20927, 21306*

  I   *21306* Brazil - Amazonas *20927*
  I   *21306* Peru *20927*

R   *Nectandra krugii* Mez *20883, 10199*

  I   *20883* Antigua & Barbuda *20883*
  I   Dominica *20883*
  I   *20883* Dominican Republic (Sierra del Baharuco)
     21008
  I   *20883* Guadeloupe *20883*
  I   *20883* Martinique *20883*
  I   *20883* Netherlands Antilles *20883*
  I   *20883* Puerto Rico *20883*

V   *Nectandra latissima* Rohwer *20883*

  V   *20883* Bolivia (Beni) *20927*

E   *Nectandra leucocome* Rohwer *20883*

  E   *20883* Mexico *20883*
  ?   Mexico - Chiapas *20927*

E   *Nectandra longipetiolata* van der Werff *20883*

  E   *20883* Costa Rica (Limón) *20926*

R   *Nectandra matogrossensis* Coe-Teixeira *20883*

  I   *20883* Brazil *20883*
  ?   Brazil - Bahia *20927*
  ?   Brazil - Mato Grosso *20927*

R   *Nectandra matudai* Lundell *20883*

  R   *20883* Mexico *20883*
  ?   Mexico - Chiapas *20926*
  ?   Mexico - Oaxaca *20926*

V   *Nectandra micranthera* Rohwer *20883*

V   *20883* Brazil *20883*
?   Brazil - Bahia *20927*

R   *Nectandra microcarpa* Meissner *20883, 20137*

  I   *20883* Colombia (Antioquia) *20927*
  I   *20883* Peru (San Martín) *20927*

E   *Nectandra minima* Rohwer *20883*

  E   *20883* Cuba (Isla de la Juventud & the main island)
     20926

R   *Nectandra mirafloris* van der Werff *20883, 11679*

  I   *20883* Nicaragua (Estelí & Matagalpa) *20927*

R   *Nectandra obtusata* Rohwer *20883*

  I   *20883* Colombia (Putumayo) *20927*
  I   *20883* Ecuador (Imbabura; Pichincha &
     Zamora-Chinchipe) *20927*

R   *Nectandra olida* Rohwer *20883*

  I   *20883* Ecuador (Morona-Santiago & Zamora-Chinchipe)
     20927
  I   *20883* Peru (Amazonas & San Martín) *20927*

V   *Nectandra paranaensis* Coe-Teixeira *20883*

  I   *20883* Brazil *20883*
  ?   Brazil - Parana *20927*
  ?   Brazil - Sao Paulo *20927*

V   *Nectandra parviflora* Rohwer *20883*

  I   *20883* Ecuador (Pastaza) *20927*
  ?   Peru (Loreto) *20927*

V   *Nectandra psammophila* Nees *20883*

  V   *20883* Brazil *20883*
  ?   Brazil - Bahia *20927*
  ?   Brazil - Espirito Santo *20927*
  ?   Brazil - Minas Gerais *20927*
  ?   Brazil - Rio de Janeiro *20927*

R   *Nectandra pseudocotea* Allen & Barneby ex
    Rohwer *20883*

  R   *20883* Peru (Loreto & San Martín) *20927*

E   *Nectandra pulchra* O. C. Schmidt *20883*

  E   *20883* Haiti (Morne Rochelois) *21008*

R   *Nectandra ramonensis* Standley *20883*

  V   *20883* Costa Rica (Alajuela & Puntarenas)
     20927
  I   *20883* Panama (Chiriquí; Herrera; Los Santos)
     20927

I   *Nectandra reflexa* Rohwer *20927, 21306*

  I   *21306* Ecuador *20927*
  I   *21306* Peru *20927*

R   *Nectandra rudis* C. K. Allen *20883*

  I   *20883* El Salvador *20883*
  I   *20883* Guatemala *20883*
  I   *20883* Mexico *20883*
  ?   Mexico - Chiapas *20927*

R   *Nectandra ruforamula* Rohwer *20883*

  I   *20883* Venezuela (Amazonas) *20927*

V   *Nectandra smithii* C. K. Allen *20883*

  V   *20883* Costa Rica *20883*
  I   *20883* Panama *20883*

R   *Nectandra sordida* Rohwer *20883*

  R   *20883* Peru (Cajamarca; Junín; Loreto & Pasco)
     20927

E   *Nectandra spicata* Meissner *20883*

  E   *20883* Brazil *20883*
  ?   Brazil - Rio de Janeiro *20927*

E   *Nectandra subbullata* Rohwer *20883*

  E   *20883* Venezuela (Mérida) *20927*

V   *Nectandra utilis* Rohwer *20883*

  I   *20883* Peru (Amazonas & San Martín) *20927*

E	*Nectandra venulosa* Meissner *20883*		
	E	*20883* Brazil *20883*	
	?	Brazil - Minas Gerais *20927*	
E	*Nectandra weddellii* Meissner *20883*		
	E	*20883* Brazil *20883*	
	?	Brazil - Rio de Janeiro *20927*	
E	*Nectandra wurdackii* C. K. Allen & Barneby ex Rohwer *20883, 21306*		
	E	*20883* Peru (Loreto) *20927*	
V	*Nectandra yarinensis* O. C. Schmidt *20883*		
	V	*20883* Peru (Loreto) *20927*	
I	*Neolitsea andamanica* Kosterm. *7771*		
	I	India - Andaman Is. *7771*	
R	*Neolitsea buisanensis* Yamamoto & Kamik.		
	R	Taiwan (Heng-ch'un)	
R	*Neolitsea daibuensis* Kamik.		
	R	Taiwan (southern mountain region)	
R	*Neolitsea gilva* Koidz. *8037*		
	R	*19135* Japan - Ogasawara-shoto *8037*	
R	*Neolitsea hiiranensis* Liu & Liao		
	R	Taiwan (Heng-ch'un)	
I	*Neolitsea incana* Elm. *13833*		
	I	*13833* Philippines (Mt. Pulgar) *13833*	
I	*Neolitsea nicobarica* Kosterm. *7771*		
	I	India - Nicobar Is. *7771*	
I	*Neolitsea vidalii* Merr. *13780*		
	I	*15960* Philippines *13780*	
V	*Ocotea argylei* Robyns & Wilczek *19109*		
	V	*20057* Kenya *19109*	
R	*Ocotea basicordatifolia* Vattimo *17079*		
	R	*17079* Brazil - Sao Paulo (Serra de Paranapiacaba, município de Santo André) *17079*	
V	*Ocotea catharinensis* Mez. *17079*		
	V	*17746* Brazil - Parana *17079*	
	V	*21011* Brazil - Rio de Janeiro *21011*	
	V	*17746* Brazil - Rio Grande do Sul *17079*	
	V	*17746* Brazil - Santa Catarina *17079*	
	V	*17746* Brazil - Sao Paulo *17079*	
I	*Ocotea caundato* (O.C.Schm.) Alain *21008*		
	I	*21008* Haiti (Massif de la Hotte) *21008*	
R	*Ocotea foetens* (Aiton) Benth. & Hook.f. *19174*		
	R	Portugal - Madeira	
	V	*19174* Spain - Canary Is. *19174*	
R	*Ocotea gabonensis* Fouilloy		
	R	Gabon (Lastoursville)	
I	*Ocotea harrisii* Proctor *20883, 13336*		
	I	*13336* Jamaica *20883*	
E	*Ocotea laevigata* (Meisn.) Marais *10082*		
	E	*20771* Mauritius *10082*	
E	*Ocotea lancilimba* Kosterm. *10082*		
	E	*20771* Mauritius *10082*	
V	*Ocotea langsdorffii* Mez *17079*		
	V	*17079* Brazil - Minas Gerais (Serra do Cipó) *21019*	
E	*Ocotea mascarena* (Buchoz) Kosterm. *10082*		
	E	*20771* Mauritius *10082*	
V	*Ocotea moschata* (Pavon ex Meisn.) Mez *20883*		
	I	*20883* Puerto Rico *20883*	
V	*Ocotea porosa* (Nees & Martius) Barroso *10370*		
	?	Argentina - Misiones *21011*	

	V	*17079* Brazil - Parana (Highlands) *10370*	
	V	*21011* Brazil - Rio de Janeiro *21011*	
	V	*17746* Brazil - Rio Grande do Sul *17079*	
	V	*17746* Brazil - Santa Catarina (Northern) *10370*	
	V	*17466* Brazil - Sao Paulo *17079*	
	?	Paraguay *21011*	
V	*Ocotea robertsoniae* Proctor *20883*		
	V	*20883* Jamaica *20883*	
V	*Ocotea staminoides* Proctor *20883, 13336*		
	V	*13336* Jamaica *20883*	
V	*Ocotea uxpanapana* Wendt & van der Werff *20883*		
	I	*20883* Mexico *20883*	
R	*Persea alpigena* var. *harrisii* (Mez) Kopp *20883*		
	R	*20883* Jamaica *20883*	
I	*Persea glabra* Van der Werff *21082*		
	I	*21082* Brazil - Bahia (Pico das Almas) *21082*	
R	*Persea indica* (L.) Spreng. *20171*		
	R	Portugal - Madeira *8000*	
	V	Spain - Canary Is. *8000*	
R	*Persea lingue* (R. et P.) Nees ex Kopp *20883, 11748*		
	E	*16336* Argentina	
	E	*20176* Argentina - Chubut *20176*	
	R	*20883* Chile (Quillota Region - Chiloé Region) *21089*	
V	*Persea meyeniana* Nees *20883, 15088*		
	V	*20883* Chile *20883*	
E	*Persea nummularia* Trel. *5607*		
I	*Persea philippinensis* Elmer. *7730*		
	I	*15960* Philippines *13780*	
I	*Persea shaferi* P. Wilson *5607*		
I	*Persea urbaniana* Mez *10199*		
	I	Dominica *10199*	
	Ex/E	*19001* Martinique (Piton Boucher (700-800m)) *19001*	
V	*Phoebe bournei* (Hemsley) Yang *17617*		
	V	*17617* China - Fujian *11139*	
	V	*17617* China - Guangdong *11139*	
	V	*17617* China - Guangxi *11139*	
	V	*17617* China - Guizhou *11139*	
	V	*17617* China - Hubei *11139*	
	V	*17617* China - Hunan *11139*	
	V	*17617* China - Jiangxi *11139*	
	V	*17617* China - Zhejiang *11139*	
V	*Phoebe chekiangensis* Shang *17617*		
	V	*17617* China - Fujian (Guangzhe; Shaowu) *11139*	
	V	*17617* China - Jiangxi (Qianshan) *11139*	
	V	*17617* China - Zhejiang *11139*	
V	*Phoebe nanmu* (Oliver) Gamble *17617*		
	V	*17617* China - Xizang Zizhiqu (Metue) *11139*	
	V	*17617* China - Yunnan *11139*	
V	*Phoebe zhennan* S. Lee & F.N. Wei *17617*		
	V	*17617* China - Guizhou *11139*	
	V	*17617* China - Hubei *11139*	
	V	*17617* China - Hunan (Longshan) *11139*	
	V	*17617* China - Sichuan *11139*	
R	*Pleurothyrium costanense* van der Werff *20883*		
	I	*20883* Venezuela *20883*	
E	*Pleurothyrium grandiflorum* van der Werff *20883*		
	I	*20883* Colombia *20883*	
E	*Pleurothyrium westphalii* van der Werff *20883*		
	I	*20883* Guatemala *20883*	
R	*Povedadaphne quadriporata* W. Burger *20883, 11999*		

	R	20883	Costa Rica 20883

R   *Sassafras randaiense* (Hayata) Rehder 20511

     R   20511   Taiwan 20511

I   *Temmodaphne thailandica* Kosterm. 19120

     I   19120   Thailand 19120

V   *Umbellularia californica* (Nees) Nutt. var. *fresnensis* Eastw. 20850

     I   20850   U.S. - California 20850

Lecythidaceae

Number of genera:	20
Number of species:	400
Recorded threatened species:	142 (35%)

Tropical, especially rain forests of South America.

R   *Asteranthos brasiliensis* Desfontaines 20883

     I   20883   Brazil 20883
     ?   Brazil - Amazonas 9785
     I   20883   Colombia 20883
     I   20883   Venezuela 20883

E   *Cariniana ianeirensis* R. Knuth 20883, 17079

     E   20883   Brazil 20883
     R   17079   Brazil - Rio de Janeiro 17079

V   *Cariniana integrifolia* Ducke 20883

     V   20883   Brazil 20883
     ?   Brazil - Amazonas 9785

E   *Cariniana kuhlmannii* Ducke 20883, 11980

     E   20883   Brazil 20883
     ?   Brazil - Rondonia 9785

R   *Cariniana multiflora* Ducke 20883

     I   20883   Brazil 20883
     I   20883   Colombia 20883
     I   20883   Peru 20883

E   *Cariniana pachyantha* A. C. Smith 20883, 11980

     E   20883   Brazil 20883
     ?   Brazil - Amazonas 9785

E   *Cariniana pauciramosa* W. Rodrigues 20883

     E   20883   Brazil 20883
     ?   Brazil - Amazonas 9785

E   *Cariniana penduliflora* Prance 20883, 11980

     E   20883   Brazil 20883
     ?   Brazil - Rondonia 9785

E   *Cariniana uaupensis* (Spruce ex Berg) Miers 20883, 11980

     E   20883   Brazil 20883
     ?   Brazil - Amazonas 9785

R   *Corythophora labriculata* (Eyma) S.A.Mori & Prance 20883

     V   20883   Suriname 20883

E   *Couratari asterophora* Rizzini 20883, 11980

     E   20883   Brazil 20883
     ?   Brazil - Bahia 20928

E   *Couratari asterotricha* Prance 20883, 11980

     E   20883   Brazil 20883
     ?   Brazil - Espirito Santo 20928

E   *Couratari atrovinosa* Prance 20883, 11980

     E   20883   Brazil 20883
     ?   Brazil - Amazonas 20928

E   *Couratari calycina* Sandwith 20883, 11980

     E   20883   Guyana 20883

R   *Couratari gloriosa* Sandwith 20883

     I   20883   French Guiana 20883
     I   20883   Guyana 20883

     I   20883   Suriname 20883

V   *Couratari longipedicellata* W. Rodrigues 20883

     E   20883   Brazil 20883
     ?   Brazil - Amazonas 20928

E   *Couratari prancei* W. Rodrigues 20883, 11980

     E   20883   Brazil 20883
     ?   Brazil - Acre 20928
     I   21013   Peru (eastern) 20928

E   *Couratari pyramidata* (Vellozo) Knuth 20883

     E   20883   Brazil 20883
     ?   Brazil - Rio de Janeiro 20928

R   *Couratari riparia* Sandwith 20883

     V   20883   Guyana 20883

R   *Couratari sandwithii* Prance 20883, 8679

     E   20883   Suriname 20883
     E   20883   Venezuela 20883

R   *Couratari scottmorii* Prance 20883, 9783

     E   19943   Costa Rica 20883
     V   11980   Panama 20883

V   *Couratari tauari* Berg 20883

     V   20883   Brazil 20883
     ?   Brazil - Amazonas 20928
     ?   Brazil - Pará 20928

E   *Couroupita cutteri* Mort. & Skutch 20883

     I   20883   Panama 20883

E   *Couroupita darienensis* Pitt. 20883

     I   20883   Panama 20883

V   *Couroupita nicaraguensis* DC. 20883

     I   20883   Costa Rica 20883
     I   20883   El Salvador 20883
     I   20883   Nicaragua 20883
     I   20883   Panama 20883

E   *Couroupita odoratissima* Seem. 20883

     I   20883   Panama 20883

E   *Couroupita parviflora* Standl. 20883

     I   20883   Panama 20883

R   *Eschweilera alata* A. C. Smith 20883, 11980

     R   20883   Guyana 20883
     R   11980   Venezuela 20883

V   *Eschweilera alvimii* S.A.Mori 20883, 11980

     V   20883   Brazil 20883
     ?   Brazil - Alagoas 20928
     ?   Brazil - Bahia 20928
     ?   Brazil - Pernambuco 20928

V   *Eschweilera amplexifolia* S.A.Mori 20883, 11980

     V   11980   Panama 20883

R   *Eschweilera antioquensis* Dugand & Daniel 20883

     I   20883   Panama 20883
     I   20883   Colombia 20883
     I   20883   Venezuela 20883

R   *Eschweilera atropetiolata* S.A.Mori 20883

     V   20883   Brazil 20883
     ?   Brazil - Amazonas 20928

E   *Eschweilera baguensis* S.A.Mori 20883

     E   20883   Peru 20883

E   *Eschweilera beebei* Pittier ex S.A.Mori 20883, 11980

     E   20883   Venezuela 20883

R   *Eschweilera bogotensis* R. Knuth 20883, 11980

     V   20883   Colombia 20883

E   *Eschweilera boltenii* S.A.Mori 20883, 11980

     E   20883   Suriname 20883
     R   11980   Venezuela 11980

V   *Eschweilera cabrerana* Philipson *20883*
    E   *20883* Colombia *20883*

R   *Eschweilera calyculata* Pitt. *20883, 9037*
    V   *9783* Costa Rica *20883*
    V   *9783* Panama *20883*

R   *Eschweilera carinata* S.A.Mori *20883, 11980*
    R   *20883* Brazil *20883*
    ?   Brazil - Amazonas *20928*

R   *Eschweilera chartaceifolia* S.A.Mori *20883*
    I   *20883* Brazil *20883*
    I   *20883* Peru *20883*

E   *Eschweilera collinsii* Pittier *9037*
    E   *9783* Costa Rica *9037*

E   *Eschweilera compressa* (Vellozo) Miers *20883*
    E   *20883* Brazil *20883*
    ?   Brazil - Rio de Janeiro *20928*

R   *Eschweilera congestiflora* (R. Benoist) Eyma *20883, 8679*
    I   *20883* French Guiana *20883*
    I   *20883* Suriname *20883*

R   *Eschweilera costaricensis* S.A.Mori *20883, 13864*
    R   *11980* Costa Rica *20883*
    R   *11980* Nicaragua *20883*

R   *Eschweilera cyathiformis* S.A.Mori *20883*
    E   *20883* Brazil *20883*
    ?   Brazil - Amazonas *20928*

V   *Eschweilera eperuetorum* Sandwith *20883, 8679*
    V   *20883* Guyana *20883*

E   *Eschweilera fanshawei* Sandwith *20883, 11980*
    E   *20883* Guyana *20883*

E   *Eschweilera hondurensis* Standl. *20883*
    E   *20883* Honduras *20883*
    I   *20883* Panama *20883*

R   *Eschweilera integricalyx* S.A.Mori *20883, 11980*
    V   *20883* Colombia *20883*

R   *Eschweilera jacquelyniae* S.A.Mori *20883*
    I   *20883* Panama *20883*

E   *Eschweilera klugii* R. Knuth *20883*
    E   *20883* Peru *20883*

E   *Eschweilera longipedicellata* S.A.Mori *20883, 11980*
    I   *20883* Panama *20883*
    E   *20883* Colombia *20883*

E   *Eschweilera longirachis* S.A.Mori *20883*
    I   *20883* Panama *20883*

E   *Eschweilera macrocarpa* Pittier *20883, 11980*
    E   *20883* Venezuela *20883*

R   *Eschweilera mexicana* Wendt, S.A.Mori & Prance *20883, 12046*
    R   *20883* Mexico *20883*
    V   *11980* Mexico - Oaxaca *12046*
    V   *11980* Mexico - Veracruz *12046*

R   *Eschweilera microcalyx* S.A.Mori *20883, 11980*
    V   *20883* Colombia *20883*

E   *Eschweilera neblinensis* S.A.Mori *20883, 11980*
    E   *20883* Venezuela *20883*

R   *Eschweilera neei* S.A.Mori *20883*
    I   *20883* Panama *20883*
    E   *20883* Colombia *20883*

R   *Eschweilera obversa* (Berg) Miers *20883*
    R   *20883* Brazil *20883*
    ?   Brazil - Amazonas *20928*
    ?   Brazil - Maranhao *20928*

    ?   Brazil - Pará *20928*

V   *Eschweilera pachyderma* Cuatrecasas *20883, 11980*
    R   *11980* Panama *20883*
    E   *20883* Colombia *20883*

V   *Eschweilera panamensis* Pitt. *20883, 9006*
    I   *20883* Panama *20883*
    I   *20883* Colombia *20883*

E   *Eschweilera paniculata* (Berg) Miers *20883*
    E   *20883* Venezuela *20883*

R   *Eschweilera perumbonata* Pittier *20883*
    R   *20883* Venezuela *20883*

E   *Eschweilera piresii* S.A.Mori *20883, 11980*
    E   *20883* Brazil *20883*

E   *Eschweilera piresii* S. A. Mori ssp. *piresii* *20883*
    E   *20883* Brazil *20883*
    ?   Brazil - Pará *20928*

E   *Eschweilera piresii* S. A. Mori ssp. *viridipetala* S. A. Mori *20883, 21344*
    E   *20883* French Guiana *20883*

E   *Eschweilera potaroensis* Sandwith *20883*
    E   *20883* Guyana *20883*

V   *Eschweilera praealta* (Sprague) Sandwith *20883, 11980*
    E   *20883* Colombia *20883*

R   *Eschweilera pseudodecolorans* S.A.Mori *20883*
    I   *20883* Brazil *20883*
    ?   Brazil - Amazonas *20928*

V   *Eschweilera punctata* S.A.Mori *20883, 11980*
    E   *20883* Brazil *20883*
    ?   Brazil - Acre *20928*
    V   *20883* Colombia *20883*

E   *Eschweilera rabeliana* S.A.Mori *20883, 11980*
    E   *20883* Brazil *20883*
    ?   Brazil - Amapa *20928*

E   *Eschweilera reversa* Pitt. *20883*
    I   *20883* Panama *20883*

V   *Eschweilera revoluta* S.A.Mori *20883*
    E   *20883* Venezuela *20883*

V   *Eschweilera rhododendrifolia* (R. Knuth) A. C. Smith *20883, 11980*
    V   *20883* Brazil *20883*
    ?   Brazil - Amazonas *20928*

E   *Eschweilera rimbachii* Standley *20883, 19555*
    E   *20883* Colombia *20883*
    E   *20883* Ecuador *20883*

E   *Eschweilera rionegrense* S.A.Mori *20883, 11980*
    E   *20883* Brazil *20883*
    ?   Brazil - Amazonas *20928*

V   *Eschweilera rodriguesiana* S.A.Mori *20883, 11980*
    V   *20883* Brazil *20883*
    ?   Brazil - Amazonas *20928*

R   *Eschweilera roraimensis* S.A.Mori *20883, 11980*
    I   *20883* Brazil *20883*
    ?   Brazil - Roraima *20928*
    R   *11980* Venezuela *20883*

V   *Eschweilera rufifolia* S.A.Mori *20883*
    V   *20883* Peru *20883*

V   *Eschweilera sclerophylla* Cuatrecasas *20883, 11980*
    V   *20883* Colombia *20883*

V   *Eschweilera squamata* S.A.Mori *20883, 11980*
    V   *20883* French Guiana *20883*

E	*Eschweilera subcordata* S.A.Mori *20883, 11980*		
	E	*20883* Brazil *20883*	
	?		Brazil - Pará (Marajó Is.) *20928*
E	*Eschweilera tetrapetala* S.A.Mori *20883, 11980*		
	E	*20883* Brazil *20883*	
	?		Brazil - Bahia *20928*
V	*Eschweilera venezuelica* S.A.Mori *20883, 11980*		
	E	*20883* Venezuela *20883*	
V	*Eschweilera woodsoniana* Dwyer *9784*		
	V	*9783* Panama *9784*	
V	*Foetidia mauritiana* Lam. *10082*		
	E	*14234* Réunion *10082*	
	V	*20771* Mauritius *10082*	
E	*Foetidia rodriguesiana* F. Friedmann *10082*		
	E	*5852* Mauritius - Rodrigues *5852*	
R	*Grias colombiana* Cuatrecasas *20883, 11980*		
	E	*11980* Colombia *20883*	
V	*Grias haughtii* R. Knuth *20883, 11980*		
	V	*20883* Colombia *20883*	
V	*Grias multinervia* Cuatrecasas *20883, 11980*		
	E	*20883* Colombia *20883*	
	E	*20883* Ecuador *20883*	
R	*Grias peruviana* Miers *20883*		
	I	*20883* Ecuador *20883*	
	I	*20883* Peru *20883*	
E	*Gustavia acuminata* S.A.Mori *20883*		
	E	*20883* Brazil *20883*	
	?		Brazil - Roraima *9785*
	V	*21013* Venezuela *9785*	
V	*Gustavia acuta* S.A.Mori *20883*		
	V	*20883* Venezuela *20883*	
R	*Gustavia angustifolia* Bentham *20883, 19353*		
	I	*20883* Colombia *20883*	
	I	*20883* Ecuador *20883*	
V	*Gustavia brachycarpa* Pitt. *20883, 9785*		
	R	*11980* Costa Rica *20883*	
	R	*11980* Panama *20883*	
E	*Gustavia coriacea* S.A.Mori *20883, 11980*		
	E	*20883* Venezuela *20883*	
V	*Gustavia dodsonii* S.A.Mori *20883, 11980*		
	V	*20883* Ecuador *20883*	
R	*Gustavia dubia* (Kunth) Berg *20883*		
	I	*20883* Panama *20883*	
	I	*20883* Colombia *20883*	
V	*Gustavia erythrocarpa* S.A.Mori *20883*		
	V	*20883* Brazil *20883*	
	?		Brazil - Pará *9785*
V	*Gustavia excelsa* R. Knuth *20883, 14750*		
	V	*20883* Colombia *20883*	
V	*Gustavia flagellata* S.A.Mori *20883, 11980*		
	V	*20883* Venezuela *20883*	
V	*Gustavia flagellata* S. A. Mori var. *costata* S. A. Mori *20883*		
	V	*20883* Venezuela *20883*	
V	*Gustavia flagellata* S.A.Mori var. *flagellata* *20883*		
	V	*20883* Venezuela *20883*	
E	*Gustavia foliosa* Cuatrecasa *20883, 11980*		
	E	*20883* Colombia *20883*	
	E	*20883* Ecuador *20883*	
E	*Gustavia fosteri* S.A.Mori *20883, 9785*		
	V	*11980* Panama *20883*	
E	*Gustavia gentryi* S.A.Mori *20883, 11980*		
	E	*20883* Colombia *20883*	
R	*Gustavia gigantophylla* Sandwith *20883, 11980*		
	R	*11980* Guyana *20883*	
	R	*11980* Venezuela *20883*	
V	*Gustavia gracillima* Miers *20883, 11980*		
	E	*20883* Colombia *20883*	
R	*Gustavia grandibracteata* Croat & S.A.Mori *20883*		
	I	*20883* Panama *20883*	
	I	*20883* Colombia *20883*	
E	*Gustavia inakuama* S.A.Mori *20883*		
	E	*20883* Peru *20883*	
E	*Gustavia latifolia* Miers *20883, 11980*		
	E	*20883* Colombia *20883*	
E	*Gustavia longifuniculata* S.A.Mori *20883, 11980*		
	E	*20883* Colombia *20883*	
E	*Gustavia longipetiolata* Huber *20883*		
	E	*20883* Brazil *20883*	
	?		Brazil - Pará *9785*
R	*Gustavia macarenensis* ssp. *paucisperma* S.A.Mori *20883*		
	V	*20883* Venezuela *20883*	
V	*Gustavia monocaulis* S.A.Mori *20883, 9785*		
	R	*11980* Panama *20883*	
R	*Gustavia nana* Pitt. *20883*		
	I	*20883* Panama *20883*	
V	*Gustavia nana* Pittier ssp. *nana* *20883, 9785*		
	I	*20883* Panama *20883*	
	I	*20883* Colombia *20883*	
R	*Gustavia nana* Pitt ssp. *rhodantha* (Standl.) S.A. Mori *20883*		
	I	*20883* Panama *20883*	
	I	*20883* Colombia *20883*	
V	*Gustavia parviflora* S.A.Mori *20883*		
	V	*20883* Venezuela *20883*	
E	*Gustavia petiolata* S.A.Mori *20883, 11980*		
	E	*20883* Colombia *20883*	
V	*Gustavia pubescens* Ruiz & Pavon ex Berg *20883, 11980*		
	V	*11980* Colombia *11980*	
	V	*20883* Ecuador *20883*	
V	*Gustavia romeroi* S.A.Mori & Garcia-Barriga *20883, 11980*		
	V	*20883* Colombia *20883*	
R	*Gustavia santanderiensis* R. Knuth *20883, 11980*		
	I	*20883* Brazil *20883*	
	?		Brazil - Amazonas *9785*
	R	*11980* Colombia *20883*	
E	*Gustavia serrata* S.A.Mori *20883, 11980*		
	E	*20883* Ecuador *20883*	
E	*Gustavia sessilis* S.A.Mori *20883, 11980*		
	E	*20883* Colombia *20883*	
E	*Gustavia speciosa* (Kunth) de Condolle ssp. *occidentalis* (Cuatrec.) S.A.Mori *9785, 20883, 19353*		
	E	*20883* Colombia *20883*	
R	*Gustavia speciosa* (Kunth) de Candolle ssp. *speciosa* *20883*		
	I	*20883* Colombia *20883*	
	I	*20883* Ecuador *20883*	
E	*Gustavia tejerae* R. Knuth *20883*		

| | | E | 20883 | Venezuela *20883* |

E   *Gustavia terminaliflora* S.A.Mori *20883*
     E   20883   Peru *20883*

R   *Gustavia verticillata* Miers *20883, 9785*
     R   11980   Panama *20883*
     R   11980   Colombia *20883*

R   *Lecythis alutacea* (A. C. Smith) S.A.Mori *20883*
     I   20883   Brazil *20883*
     I   20883   French Guiana *20883*
     I   20883   Guyana *20883*
     I   20883   Suriname *20883*
     I   20883   Venezuela *20883*

R   *Lecythis barnebyi* S.A.Mori *20883, 11980*
     R   20883   Brazil *20883*
     ?   Brazil - Amazonas *20928*

V   *Lecythis brancoensis* (R. Knuth) S.A.Mori *20883*
     I   20883   Brazil *20883*
     I   20883   Guyana *20883*

R   *Lecythis confertiflora* (A.C.Smith) S.A.Mori *18176*
     R   8679   Guyana *8679*

R   *Lecythis lanceolata* Poiret *20883*
     I   20883   Brazil *20883*
     ?   Brazil - Bahia *20928*
     ?   Brazil - Espiritc Santo *20928*
     ?   Brazil - Goias *20928*
     ?   Brazil - Pernambuco *20928*
     ?   Brazil - Rio de Janeiro *20928*

V   *Lecythis mesophylla* S.A.Mori *20883, 9786*
     I   20883   Costa Rica *20883*
     I   20883   Panama *20883*
     I   20883   Colombia *20883*

R   *Lecythis miersiana* S.A.Mori *11980*
     R   11980   Brazil *11980*
     R   11980   Guyana *11980*

R   *Lecythis ollaria* Loefling *20883*
     I   20883   Brazil *20883*
     R   20883   Venezuela *20883*

V   *Lecythis parvifructa* S.A.Mori *20883*
     V   20883   Brazil *20883*
     ?   Brazil - Amazonas *20928*

R   *Lecythis persistens* S.A.Mori ssp. *aurantiaca*
     S.A.Mori *20883, 11980*
     R   11980   French Guiana *20883*

R   *Lecythis pneumatophora* S.A.Mori *20883, 11980*
     R   20883   French Guiana *20883*

R   *Lecythis prancei* S.A.Mori *20883*
     V   20883   Brazil *20883*
     ?   Brazil - Amazonas *20928*

R   *Lecythis retusa* Spruce ex Berg *20883*
     R   20883   Brazil *20883*
     ?   Brazil - Amazonas *20928*

R   *Lecythis schomburgkii* Berg *20883, 11980*
     I   20883   Brazil *20883*
     ?   Brazil - Roraima *20928*
     R   11980   Guyana *20883*

V   *Lecythis schwackei* (R. Knuth) S.A.Mori *20883, 11980*
     V   20883   Brazil *20883*
     ?   Brazil - Minas Gerais *20928*
     ?   Brazil - Rio de Janeiro *20928*

R   *Lecythis serrata* S.A.Mori *20883*
     R   20883   Brazil *20883*
     ?   Brazil - Amazonas *20928*
     ?   Brazil - Pará *20928*
     ?   Brazil - Rondonia *20928*

R   *Lecythis tuyrana* Pitt. *20883, 9006*
     I   20883   Panama *20883*
     I   20883   Colombia *20883*
     I   20883   Ecuador *20883*

E   *Napoleonaea lutea* Baker f. ex Hutch. & Dalz. *7926*
     E   20749   Nigeria (Eket) *7926*

E   *Napoleonaea reptans* Baker f. ex Hutch. & Dalz. *7926*
     E   20749   Nigeria (Eket) *7926*

Leeaceae

Number of genera: 1
Number of species: 70
Recorded threatened species: 5   (7%)

Pantropical.

I   *Leea aquata* L.
     I   India - Orissa (Ganjam forests)

I   *Leea cinera* M. Lawson
     I   India - Kerala (Palghat Cherry, Malabar)

R   *Leea philippinensis* Merr.
     R   Taiwan (Lan Yu & Is. Lutao)
     V   15960   Philippines *13780*

R   *Leea stipulosa* Gagnepain *6057*
     R   Vietnam *6057*

I   *Leea venkobarowii* Gamble
     I   India - Kerala (Travancore)
     I   India - Tamil Nadu

Leguminosae

Number of genera: 590
Number of species: 12,000-14,200
Recorded threatened species: 2206   (16%)

Cosmopolitan, especially tropical and subtropical.

E   *Abarema bigemina* (L.) Kosterm. *8021*
     E   12838   Sri Lanka *8021*

R   *Acacia acrionastes* Pedley *20681*
     I   20681   Australia - New South Wales *20681*
     I   20681   Australia - Queensland *20681*

R   *Acacia aemula* Maslin ms. ssp. *aemula* *20681*
     R   20681   Australia - Western Australia *20681*

R   *Acacia albizioides* Pedley *20681*
     R   20681   Australia - Queensland *20681*

R   *Acacia alcockii* Maslin & Whibley *20681*
     R   20681   Australia - South Australia *20681*

R   *Acacia ammobia* Maconochie *20681*
     R   20681   Australia - Northern Territory *20681*

V   *Acacia ammophila* Pedley *20681*
     V   20681   Australia - Queensland *20681*

E   *Acacia anegadensis* Britt. *20883*
     R   15107   British Virgin Is. (Anegada) *15107*
     I   20883   USA - Virgin Is. *20883*

R   *Acacia ankokib* Chiov. *12346*
     R   20884   Somalia (north-east) *20884*

V   *Acacia anomala* Court *20681*
     V   20681   Australia - Western Australia *20681*

V   *Acacia aphylla* Maslin *20681*
     V   20681   Australia - Western Australia *20681*

V   *Acacia araneosa* Whibley *20681*
     V   20681   Australia - South Australia *20681*

R   *Acacia argutifolia* Maslin *20681*

R   20681   Australia - Western Australia   *20681*

R   *Acacia armitii* F.Muell. ex Maiden   *20681*
   I   20681   Australia - Northern Territory   *20681*
   I   20681   Australia - Queensland   *20681*

R   *Acacia asparagoides* Cunn.   *20681*
   R   20681   Australia - New South Wales   *20681*

V   *Acacia attenuata* Maiden & Blakely   *20681*
   V   20681   Australia - Queensland   *20681*

R   *Acacia ausfeldii* Regel   *20681*
   I   20681   Australia - New South Wales   *20681*
   I   20681   Australia - Victoria   *20681*

V   *Acacia awestoniana* Cowan & Maslin   *20681*
   V   20681   Australia - Western Australia   *20681*

V   *Acacia axillaris* Benth.   *20681*
   V   20681   Australia - Tasmania   *20681*

I   *Acacia barahonensis* Urban   *5642*
   I   Dominican Republic (Barahona)   *5642*

R   *Acacia barringtonensis* Tindale   *20681*
   R   20681   Australia - New South Wales   *20681*

R   *Acacia baueri* Benth. ssp. *aspera* (Maiden & Betche)
     Pedley *20681*
   R   20681   Australia - New South Wales   *20681*

I   *Acacia belairioides* Urban   *11840*
   I   20990   Cuba (Holguin)   *11840*

R   *Acacia blayana* Tindale & Court   *20681*
   R   20681   Australia - New South Wales   *20681*

R   *Acacia brunioides* Cunn. ex G.Don ssp.
     brunioides *20681*
   I   20681   Australia - New South Wales   *20681*
   I   20681   Australia - Queensland   *20681*

R   *Acacia brunioides* Cunn. ex G.Don ssp. *granitica*
     Pedley *20681*
   I   20681   Australia - New South Wales   *20681*
   I   20681   Australia - Queensland   *20681*

R   *Acacia bucheri* Marie-Vict.   *11840*
   R   19105   Cuba   *11840*

R   *Acacia bulgaensis* Tindale & Stuart J.Davies   *20681*
   R   20681   Australia - New South Wales   *20681*

V   *Acacia bynoeana* Benth.   *20681*
   V   20681   Australia - New South Wales   *20681*

V   *Acacia caerulescens* Maslin & Court   *20681*
   V   20681   Australia - Victoria   *20681*

R   *Acacia calantha* Pedley   *20681*
   R   20681   Australia - Queensland   *20681*

R   *Acacia campbellii* Arn.   *14782*
   R   14782   India - Andhra Pradesh   *14782*

R   *Acacia cangaiensis* Tindale & Kodela   *20681*
   R   20681   Australia - New South Wales   *20681*

R   *Acacia caraniana* Chiov.   *12346*
   R   20884   Somalia (north)   *20884*

V   *Acacia carnei* Maiden   *20681*
   I   20681   Australia - New South Wales   *20681*
   I   20681   Australia - South Australia   *20681*

R   *Acacia cernua*   *20884*
   R   20884   Somalia (north)   *20884*

R   *Acacia chalkeri* Maiden   *20681*
   R   20681   Australia - New South Wales   *20681*

R   *Acacia chiapensis* Saff.   *9787*
   R   21281   Mexico   *9787*

V   *Acacia chinchillensis* Tindale   *20681*
   V   20681   Australia - Queensland   *20681*

R   *Acacia chrysotricha* Tindale   *20681*
   R   20681   Australia - New South Wales   *20681*

R   *Acacia clunies-rossiae* Maiden   *20681*
   R   20681   Australia - New South Wales   *20681*

R   *Acacia clydonophora* Maslin ms.   *20681*
   R   20681   Australia - Western Australia   *20681*

R   *Acacia confluens* Maiden & Blakely   *20681*
   R   20681   Australia - South Australia   *20681*

V   *Acacia constablei* Tindale   *20681*
   V   20681   Australia - New South Wales   *20681*

R   *Acacia costiniana* Tindale   *20681*
   R   20681   Australia - New South Wales   *20681*

V   *Acacia courtii* Tindale & Herscovitch   *20681*
   V   20681   Australia - New South Wales   *20681*

R   *Acacia covenyi* Tindale   *20681*
   R   20681   Australia - New South Wales   *20681*

V   *Acacia cowellii* (Britton & Rose) Leon   *5607*
   V   19105   Cuba (Santiago de Cuba)   *5607*

E   *Acacia cretacea* Maslin & Whibley   *20681, 17915*
   E   20681   Australia - South Australia   *17915*

V   *Acacia crombiei* C.White   *20681*
   V   20681   Australia - Queensland   *20681*

E   *Acacia cupeyensis* León   *5607*
   E   19105   Cuba (Las Tunas, Holguin)   *5607*

E   *Acacia curbeloi* Leon   *5607*
   E   19105   Cuba (Las Tunas)   *5607*

V   *Acacia curranii* Maiden   *20681*
   I   20681   Australia - New South Wales   *20681*
   I   20681   Australia - Queensland   *20681*

R   *Acacia daemon* Ekman & Urban   *11840*
   R   19105   Cuba   *11840*

R   *Acacia dallachiana* F.Muell.   *20681*
   I   20681   Australia - New South Wales   *20681*
   I   20681   Australia - Victoria   *20681*

R   *Acacia dangarensis* Tindale & Kodela   *20681*
   R   20681   Australia - New South Wales   *20681*

R   *Acacia densispina* M.Thulin   *20884*
   R   20884   Somalia (central)   *20884*

V   *Acacia denticulosa* F.Muell.   *20681*
   V   20681   Australia - Western Australia   *20681*

V   *Acacia depressa* Maslin   *20681*
   V   20681   Australia - Western Australia   *20681*

V   *Acacia deuteroneura* Pedley   *20681*
   V   20681   Australia - Queensland   *20681*

R   *Acacia dodonaeifolia* Sprengel   *20681*
   R   20681   Australia - South Australia   *20681*

R   *Acacia dolichophylla* Maslin   *20681*
   R   20681   Australia - Northern Territory   *20681*

R   *Acacia empelioclada* Maslin   *20681*
   R   20681   Australia - Western Australia   *20681*

E   *Acacia enterocarpa* R.V.Smith   *20681*
   I   20681   Australia - South Australia   *20681*
   I   20681   Australia - Victoria   *20681*

V   *Acacia eremophiloides* Pedley & P.Forster   *20681*
   V   20681   Australia - Queensland   *20681*

R   *Acacia flagellaris* M.Thulin   *20884*
   R   20884   Somalia (north-east)   *20884*

R *Acacia flagelliformis* Court 20681
  R 20681 Australia - Western Australia 20681

R *Acacia fleckeri* Pedley 20681
  R 20681 Australia - Queensland 20681

V *Acacia flocktoniae* Maiden 20681
  V 20681 Australia - New South Wales 20681

R *Acacia floydii* Tindale 20681
  I 20681 Australia - New South Wales 20681
  I 20681 Australia - Queensland 20681

V *Acacia forrestiana* E.Pritzel 20681
  V 20681 Australia - Western Australia 20681

R *Acacia forsythii* Maiden & Blakely 20681
  R 20681 Australia - New South Wales 20681

R *Acacia fulva* Tindale 20681
  R 20681 Australia - New South Wales 20681

V *Acacia georgensis* Tindale 20681
  V 20681 Australia - New South Wales 20681

R *Acacia gillii* Maiden & Blakely 20681
  R 20681 Australia - South Australia 20681

R *Acacia gittinsii* Pedley 20681
  R 20681 Australia - Queensland 20681

V *Acacia glandulicarpa* Reader 20681
  I 20681 Australia - South Australia 20681
  I 20681 Australia - Victoria 20681

R *Acacia gnidium* Benth. 20681
  R 20681 Australia - Queensland 20681

R *Acacia gracilifolia* Maiden & Blakely 20681
  R 20681 Australia - South Australia 20681

V *Acacia grandifolia* Pedley 20681
  V 20681 Australia - Queensland 20681

R *Acacia grisea* S.Moore 20681
  R 20681 Australia - Western Australia 20681

R *Acacia guinetii* Maslin 20681
  R 20681 Australia - Western Australia 20681

V *Acacia guymeri* Tindale 20681
  V 20681 Australia - Queensland 20681

V *Acacia handonis* Pedley 20681
  V 20681 Australia - Queensland 20681

R *Acacia hebeclada* DC. ssp. *chobiensis* (O.B. Miller) A. Schreiber
  ?   Zambia (south-west) 20932
  ?   Zimbabwe (north-west) 20899
  R   Botswana
  R   Namibia - Caprivi Strip 20932

R *Acacia hexaneura* P.Lang & Cowan 20681
  R 20681 Australia - South Australia 20681

R *Acacia hockingsii* Pedley 20681
  R 20681 Australia - Queensland 20681

I *Acacia hohenackeri* Craib 4988
  I   India - Tamil Nadu 4988

R *Acacia holotricha* Pedley 20681
  R 20681 Australia - Queensland 20681

R *Acacia homaloclada* F.Muell. 20681
  R 20681 Australia - Queensland 20681

R *Acacia howittii* F.Muell. 20681
  R 20681 Australia - Victoria 20681

R *Acacia hylonoma* Pedley 20681
  R 20681 Australia - Queensland 20681

V *Acacia imbricata* F.Muell. 20681

  V 20681 Australia - South Australia 20681

R *Acacia ingramii* Tindale 20681
  R 20681 Australia - New South Wales 20681

R *Acacia islana* Pedley 20681
  R 20681 Australia - Queensland 20681

R *Acacia iteaphylla* Benth. 20681
  R 20681 Australia - South Australia 20681

R *Acacia jackesiana* Pedley 20681
  R 20681 Australia - Queensland 20681

R *Acacia jonesii* F.Muell.& Maiden 20681
  R 20681 Australia - New South Wales 20681

Ex *Acacia kingiana* Maiden & Blakely 20681
  Ex 20681 Australia - Western Australia 20681

V *Acacia koaia* Hbd. 20850, 14209
  V 20850 U.S. - Hawaii 20850

R *Acacia kydrensis* Tindale 20681
  R 20681 Australia - New South Wales 20681

V *Acacia lanuginophylla* R.Cowan & Maslin ms. 20681
  V 20681 Australia - Western Australia 20681

R *Acacia latisepala* Pedley 20681
  I 20681 Australia - New South Wales 20681
  I 20681 Australia - Queensland 20681

V *Acacia latzii* Maslin 20681
  V 20681 Australia - Northern Territory 20681

V *Acacia lauta* Pedley 20681
  V 20681 Australia - Queensland 20681

E *Acacia leptalea* Maslin ms. 20681
  E 20681 Australia - Western Australia 20681

V *Acacia lobulata* Maslin ms. 20681
  V 20681 Australia - Western Australia 20681

R *Acacia longipedunculata* Pedley 20681
  R 20681 Australia - Queensland 20681

R *Acacia lucasii* Blakely 20681
  I 20681 Australia - New South Wales 20681
  I 20681 Australia - Victoria 20681

V *Acacia macnuttiana* Maiden & Blakely 20681
  V 20681 Australia - New South Wales 20681

R *Acacia manubensis* J. Ross 12346
  R 20884 Somalia (north-east) 20884

R *Acacia matthewii* Tindale & Stuart J.Davies 20681
  R 20681 Australia - New South Wales 20681

I *Acacia mbuluensis* Brenan 19533
  I 5926 Tanzania (Kilimanjaro, Mbulu & Moshi) 19533

R *Acacia meiantha* Tindale & Herscovitch 20681
  R 20681 Australia - New South Wales 20681

R *Acacia meiosperma* (Pedley) Pedley 20681
  R 20681 Australia - Queensland 20681

V *Acacia menzelii* J.Black 20681
  V 20681 Australia - South Australia 20681

V *Acacia merrickiae* Maiden & Blakely 20681
  V 20681 Australia - Western Australia 20681

V *Acacia minuta* (L.) Willd. ssp. *minuta* 20850
  V 20850 U.S. - Arizona 20850

R *Acacia moggii* M.Thulin & M.Tardelli 20884
  R 20884 Somalia (central) 20884

R *Acacia montis-usti* Merxm. & A.Schreib. 20604, 12346
  R 20604 Namibia 20604

Magnoliopsida (dicots): Leguminosae: *Acacia*

R	*Acacia ochracea* M.Thulin & A.S.Hassan *20884*	
	R	*20884* Somalia (south-west) *20884*
R	*Acacia olsenii* Tindale *20681*	
	R	*20681* Australia - New South Wales *20681*
R	*Acacia ommatosperma* (Pedley) Pedley *20681*	
	R	*20681* Australia - Queensland *20681*
R	*Acacia orites* Pedley *20681*	
	I	*20681* Australia - New South Wales *20681*
	I	*20681* Australia - Queensland *20681*
V	*Acacia pacensis* Rudd & Carter *20883*	
	I	*20883* Mexico *20883*
R	*Acacia pataczekii* D.Morris *20681*	
	R	*20681* Australia - Tasmania *20681*
R	*Acacia pedleyi* Tindale & Kodela *20681*	
	R	*20681* Australia - Queensland *20681*
V	*Acacia pennivenia* balf.f. *12346*	
	V	*15534* Yemen - Socotra *15534*
V	*Acacia perangusta* (C.White) Pedley *20681*	
	V	*20681* Australia - Queensland *20681*
V	*Acacia peuce* F.Muell. *20681*	
	I	*20681* Australia - Northern Territory *20681*
	I	*20681* Australia - Queensland *20681*
V	*Acacia pharangites* Maslin *20681*	
	V	*20681* Australia - Western Australia *20681*
V	*Acacia phasmoides* J.H.Willis *20681*	
	I	*20681* Australia - New South Wales *20681*
	I	*20681* Australia - Victoria *20681*
R	*Acacia phlebophylla* Williamson *20681*	
	R	*20681* Australia - Victoria *20681*
E	*Acacia pinguifolia* J.Black *20681*	
	E	*20681* Australia - South Australia *20681*
R	*Acacia polyadenia* (Pedley) Pedley *20681*	
	R	*20681* Australia - Queensland *20681*
E	*Acacia polypyrigenes* Greenman *5607*	
	E	*19105* Cuba (Cienfuegos) *5607*
E	*Acacia porcata* P.I.Forster *20681*	
	E	*20681* Australia - Queensland *20681*
R	*Acacia praemorsa* P.Lang & Maslin *20681*	
	R	*20681* Australia - South Australia *20681*
R	*Acacia praetermissa* Tindale *20681*	
	R	*20681* Australia - Northern Territory *20681*
E	*Acacia prasinata* A. Hunde *19704*	
	E	*19704* Ethiopia (Wello Upland) *19704*
Ex	*Acacia prismifolia* E.Pritzel *20681, 14223*	
	Ex	*20681* Australia - Western Australia *20681*
E	*Acacia pseudonigrescens* Brenan & J. Ross *12346*	
	E	*19704* Ethiopia (Kelafo) *20900*
V	*Acacia pubescens* (Vent.) R.Br. *20681*	
	V	*20681* Australia - New South Wales *20681*
R	*Acacia pubicosta* C.White *20681*	
	R	*20681* Australia - Queensland *20681*
V	*Acacia pubifolia* Pedley *20681*	
	I	*20681* Australia - New South Wales *20681*
	I	*20681* Australia - Queensland *20681*
V	*Acacia purpureapetala* Bailey *20681*	
	V	*20681* Australia - Queensland *20681*
V	*Acacia pycnostachya* F.Muell. *20681*	
	V	*20681* Australia - New South Wales *20681*
V	*Acacia pygmaea* Maslin ms. *20681*	

	V	*20681* Australia - Western Australia *20681*
R	*Acacia quornensis* J.Black *20681*	
	R	*20681* Australia - South Australia *20681*
V	*Acacia ramiflora* Domin *20681*	
	V	*20681* Australia - Queensland *20681*
V	*Acacia rhetinocarpa* J.Black *20681*	
	V	*20681* Australia - South Australia *20681*
R	*Acacia rhigiophylla* Benth. *20681*	
	I	*20681* Australia - New South Wales *20681*
	I	*20681* Australia - South Australia *20681*
R	*Acacia robynsiana* Merxm. & A.Schreib. *20604, 12346*	
	R	*20604* Namibia *20604*
E	*Acacia roigii* Leon *5607*	
	E	*19105* Cuba (Las Tunas) *5607*
E	*Acacia ruppii* Maiden & Betche *20681*	
	E	*20681* Australia - Northern Territory *20681*
R	*Acacia sarcophylla* Chiov. *12346*	
	R	*20884* Yemen - Socotra *20884*
	R	*20884* Somalia (north) *20884*
R	*Acacia saxicola* Pedley *20681*	
	R	*20681* Australia - Queensland *20681*
R	*Acacia seifriziana* Leon *5607*	
	R	*19105* Cuba (Guantanamo) *5607*
V	*Acacia semicircinalis* Maiden & Blakely *20681*	
	V	*20681* Australia - Western Australia *20681*
R	*Acacia simulans* Maslin *20681*	
	R	*20681* Australia - Western Australia *20681*
R	*Acacia spania* Pedley *20681*	
	R	*20681* Australia - Queensland *20681*
R	*Acacia spilleriana* J.E.Brown *20681*	
	R	*20681* Australia - South Australia *20681*
R	*Acacia storyi* Tindale *20681*	
	R	*20681* Australia - Queensland *20681*
R	*Acacia subtilinervis* F.Muell. *20681*	
	I	*20681* Australia - New South Wales *20681*
	I	*20681* Australia - Victoria *20681*
R	*Acacia tanganyikensis* Brenan *19533*	
	R	Tanzania (Mwanza, Singida, Dodoma) *19533*
I	*Acacia taylori* Brenan & Exell *12346*	
	I	*5926* Tanzania (Lindi) *19533*
R	*Acacia tayloriana* F.Muell. *20681*	
	R	*20681* Australia - Western Australia *20681*
R	*Acacia tenuinervis* Pedley *20681*	
	R	*20681* Australia - Queensland *20681*
R	*Acacia tessellata* Tindale & Kodela *20681*	
	R	*20681* Australia - New South Wales *20681*
R	*Acacia tolmerensis* G.J.Leach *20681*	
	R	*20681* Australia - Northern Territory *20681*
I	*Acacia torrei* Brenan *7749*	
	I	Mozambique *7749*
R	*Acacia turnbulliana* Brenan	
	R	Kenya *7959*
V	*Acacia undoolyana* G.Leach *20681*	
	V	*20681* Australia - Northern Territory *20681*
V	*Acacia vassalii* Maslin *20681*	
	V	*20681* Australia - Western Australia *20681*
R	*Acacia velutina* var. *monadena* Hassler *20883*	
	I	*20883* Argentina *20883*

	I	20883 Brazil *20883*	
	R	20883 Paraguay *20883*	
E	*Acacia venosa* Hochst. ex Benth. *19704*		
	E	*19704* Ethiopia (West Eritrea, Tigray Upland) *19704*	
R	*Acacia villosa* (Sw.) Willd. *20883,*		
	R	20883 Jamaica *20883*	
Ex	*Acacia volubilis* F.Muell. *20681*		
	Ex	20681 Australia - Western Australia *20681*	
V	*Acacia wardellii* Tindale *20681*		
	V	20681 Australia - Queensland *20681*	
E	*Acacia whibleyana* Cowan & Maslin ms. *20681*		
	E	20681 Australia - South Australia *20681*	
I	*Acacia wightii* Baker		
	I	India - Kerala (Travancore)	
	I	India - Tamil Nadu (Tirunelveli Hills)	
R	*Acacia williamsonii* Court *20681*		
	R	20681 Australia - Victoria *20681*	
V	*Acacia zapatensis* Urban & Ekman *5607*		
	V	*19105* Cuba (Matanzas) *5607*	
E	*Adenanthera bicolor* Moon *8021*		
	E	*12838* Sri Lanka (south-west) *8021*	
I	*Adenanthera intermedia* Merr. *13780*		
	I	*15960* Philippines *13780*	
E	*Adenocarpus faurei* Maire *10488*		
	E	*14958* Algeria *10488*	
E	*Adenocarpus ombriosus* Ceball. & Ortuno *20750*		
	E	20750 Spain - Canary Is. *20750*	
E	*Adenocarpus umbellatus* Coss. *10488*		
	E	*14958* Algeria *10488*	
I	*Adenodolichos acutifoliolatus* Verdc. *19531*		
	I	*5926* Tanzania (Kigoma) *19531*	
R	*Adenodolichos oblongifoliolatus* R. Wilczek *19358*		
	R	*19358* Zaire (Haut-Katanga) *19358*	
R	*Adenodolichos salviifoliolatus* R. Wilczek *19358*		
	R	*19358* Zaire (Haut-Katanga) *19358*	
R	*Adenopodia rotundifolia* (Harms) Brenan *12346*		
	R	20884 Somalia (south) *20884*	
	R	20884 Tanzania (Lushoto and Pare) *12346*	
R	*Adesmia arenicola* (Fries) Burkart *16336*		
	R	*16336* Argentina *16336*	
	R	*20176* Argentina - Jujuy *20176*	
R	*Adesmia balsamica* Bertero ex Colla *13875*		
	R	*13875* Chile *13875*	
R	*Adesmia burkartii* Correa *9417*		
	R	Argentina *9417*	
	R	Chile *9417*	
V	*Adesmia crassicaulis* Philippi *16336*		
	V	*19448* Argentina *19448*	
	V	*20176* Argentina - Catamarca *20176*	
	V	*20176* Argentina - La Rioja *20176*	
	V	*20176* Argentina - Salta *20176*	
R	*Adesmia lihuelensis* Burkart *16336*		
	R	*16336* Argentina *16336*	
R	*Adesmia resinosa* Philippi *13875*		
	R	*13875* Chile *13875*	
V	*Aeschynomene batekensis* Troch. & Koechlin *12346*		
	V	Congo *11793*	
I	*Aeschynomene minutiflora* Taubert ssp. *grandiflora* Verdc. *7918*		

	I	Mozambique *7918*	
I	*Aeschynomene mossambicensis* Verdc. ssp. *mossambicensis* *7918*		
	I	Mozambique *7918*	
I	*Aeschynomene mossoensis* J. Leon. var. *parvifolia* Verdc. *19531*		
	I	*5926* Tanzania (Mpanda) *19531*	
I	*Aeschynomene pleuronervia* DC. *5642*		
	I	Dominican Republic (Santo Domingo) *5642* Haiti *21008*	
E	*Aeschynomene ruspoliana* Taub. & Harms *19704*		
	E	*19704* Ethiopia (Sidamo) *19704*	
I	*Aeschynomene sansibarica* Taub. *19531*		
	I	*5926* Tanzania (Zanzibar) *5926*	
R	*Aeschynomene tenuirama* Baker var. *hebecarpa* Verdc. *7860*		
	R	Malawi *7860*	
R	*Aeschynomene upembensis* J. Léonard *19358*		
	R	*19358* Zaire (Haut-Katanga) *19358*	
V	*Aeschynomene virginica* (L.) B.S.P. *20850, 14474*		
	Ex/E	20850 U.S. - Delaware *20850*	
		U.S. - Georgia	
	E	20850 U.S. - Maryland *20850*	
	E	20850 U.S. - New Jersey *20850*	
	E	20850 U.S. - North Carolina *20850*	
	Ex	20850 U.S. - Pennsylvania *20850*	
	I	20850 U.S. - South Carolina *20850*	
	V	20850 U.S. - Virginia *20850*	
I	*Afgekia sericea* Craib		
	I	Thailand	
R	*Afzelia bella* Harms var. *glabra* Aubrev.		
	R	Congo (Makoua-Owando) *11793*	
I	*Albizia aylmeri* Hutch. *5908*		
	I	*5908* Sudan *5908*	
R	*Albizia coreana* Nakai *15957*		
	R	*15923* Korea, South *15957*	
I	*Albizia euryphylla* Harms *19533*		
	I	*5926* Tanzania (Dodoma) *19533*	
R	*Albizia glabrior* (Koidz.) Ohwi *10572*		
	R	*10572* Japan *10572*	
E	*Albizia guillainii* Guillaumin *20802*		
	E	20893 New Caledonia *20802*	
E	*Albizia lankaensis* Kosterm. *8021*		
	E	Sri Lanka *8021*	
R	*Albizia obbiadensis* (Chiov.) Brenan *12346*		
	R	20884 Somalia (central & south) *20884*	
V	*Albizia plurijuga* (Standley) Britton & Rose *9706*		
	V	*19850* Mexico *9706*	
V	*Albizia suluensis* Gerstner *20604, 15013*		
	V	20604 South Africa - Natal *20604*	
R	*Albizia tanganyicensis* Baker f. ssp. *adamsoniorum* Brenan *20057*		
	R	20057 Kenya (central) *17435*	
R	*Albizia thompsonii* Brandis *14782*		
	R	*14782* India - Andhra Pradesh (Cuddapah) *14782*	
	R	*14782* India - Orissa (Ganjam) *14782*	
	R	*14782* India - Tamil Nadu (Coimbatore) *14782*	
E	*Albizia vaughanii* Brenan *10082, 21329*		
	E	20771 Mauritius *10082*	
V	*Almaleea cambagei* (Maiden & Betche) Crisp & P.H.Weston *20681*		

V		20681	Australia - New South Wales *20681*

R *Almaleea capitata* (J.H.Willis) Crisp & P.Weston *20681*

I		20681	Australia - New South Wales *20681*
I		20681	Australia - Victoria *20681*

R *Almaleea incurvata* (Cunn.) Crisp & P.Weston *20681*

R		20681	Australia - New South Wales *20681*

I *Alysicarpus beddomei* Schindler *2268*

I			India - Tamil Nadu (Nilgiri Hills) *2268*

I *Alysicarpus meeboldii* Schindler

I			India - Jammu & Kashmir

I *Alysicarpus monilifer* (L.) DC. var. *venosus* Blatter & Hallberg

I			India - Rajasthan *7958*

I *Alysicarpus vaginalis* (L.) DC. var. *parviflorus* Verdc. *7918*

I			Mozambique *7918*

I *Amherstia nobilis* Wallich *8321*

I			Myanmar *8321*

R *Ammopiptanthus mongolicus* (Maxim.) Cheng.f. *17617*

R		17617	China - Gansu (Mingqing; Lanzhou) *11139*
R		17617	China - Nei Monggol Zizhiqu *11139*
R		17617	China - Ningxia *11139*

I *Ammopiptanthus nanus* (Popov) Cheng.f. *17617*

I		5942	Kyrgyzstan *5942*
E		17617	China - Xinjiang Uygur Zizhiqu (Wuqia) *11139*

R *Amorpha georgiana* Wilbur *20850*

E		20850	U.S. - Georgia *20850*
R		20850	U.S. - North Carolina *20850*
I		20850	U.S. - South Carolina *20850*

V *Amorpha georgiana* Wilbur var. *confusa* Wilbur *20850*

V		20850	U.S. - North Carolina *20850*
I		20850	U.S. - South Carolina *20850*

V *Amorpha georgiana* Wilbur var. *georgiana* *20850*

E		20850	U.S. - Georgia *20850*
V		20850	U.S. - North Carolina *20850*
I		20850	U.S. - South Carolina *20850*

E *Amorpha herbacea* Walt. var. *crenulata* (Rydb.) Isely *20850*

E		20850	U.S. - Florida *20850*

R *Amorpha laevigata* Nutt. *20850*

I		20850	U.S. - Oklahoma *20850*
E		20850	U.S. - Texas *20850*

R *Amorpha ouachitensis* Wilbur *20850*

R		20850	U.S. - Arkansas *20850*
V		20850	U.S. - Oklahoma *20850*

R *Amorpha schwerinii* Schneid. *20850*

I		20850	U.S. - Alabama *20850*
V		20850	U.S. - Georgia *20850*
I		20850	U.S. - Mississippi *20850*
R		20850	U.S. - North Carolina *20850*
E		20850	U.S. - South Carolina *20850*

I *Amphicarpaea anomalus* Bunge

I			India - Jammu & Kashmir (Ladakh)

I *Amphicarpaea edgeworthii* Benth.

I			India (W. Himalaya)

I *Amphicarpaea flemingii* Ali

I			India - Punjab

R *Amphithalea rostrata* A.L.Schutte & B.-E.van Wyk *20604*

R		20604	South Africa - Cape Province *20604*

E *Anagyris latifolia* Brouss. ex Willd. *17891*

E		20750	Spain - Canary Is. *17891*

R *Anthonotha lebrunii* (J. Léonard) J. Léonard *12346*

R		19358	Zaire *19358*

V *Anthonotha vignei* (Hoyle) J.Leonard *20274*

V		20858	Côte d'Ivoire *7926*
V		20858	Ghana *20274*
V		20858	Liberia *7926*
V		20858	Sierra Leone *7926*

R *Anthyllis aegaea* Turrill *20171*

R			Greece

R *Anthyllis henoniana* Cosson ex Batt. ssp. *valentina* (Esteve) O.Bolòs & Vigo *20699*

R		20692	Spain (Valencia and Albacete provinces) *20692*

V *Anthyllis hystrix* (Willk. ex Barceló) Cardona, Contandr. & E. Sierra *20645*

V		11496	Spain - Balearic Is. (Menorca) *17891*

E *Anthyllis lemanniana* Lowe *17891*

E			Portugal - Madeira *17891*

V *Anthyllis lusitanica* Cullen & Pinto da Silva *20076*

V		20076	Portugal *20076*

R *Anthyllis plumosa* Dominguez

R		20660	Spain (Malaga: Sierra Tejeda, Sierra Almijara) *20661*

R *Anthyllis rupestris* Coss. *20171*

R		20661	Spain (Jaen) *20661*

R *Anthyllis vulneraria* L. ssp. *variegata* (Boiss.) Cullen *12840*

R		12840	Turkey *12840*

R *Aotus carinata* Meisner *20681*

R		20681	Australia - Western Australia *20681*

V *Apios priceana* B.L. Robins. *20850*

E		20850	U.S. - Alabama *20850*
Ex/E		20850	U.S. - Illinois *20850*
E		20850	U.S. - Kentucky *20850*
I		20850	U.S. - Maryland *20850*
E		20850	U.S. - Mississippi *20850*
E		20850	U.S. - South Carolina *20850*
V		20850	U.S. - Tennessee *20850*

R *Apios taiwanianus* Hosok. *20511*

R		20511	Taiwan *20511*

R *Apurimacia dolichocarpa* (Griseb.) Burkart *16336*

R		20176	Argentina - Cordoba *20176*

R *Archidendron hirsutum* Nielsen *20681*

R		20681	Australia - Queensland *20681*

V *Archidendron lovelliae* (Bailey) Nielsen *20681*

V		20681	Australia - Queensland *20681*

R *Archidendron muellerianum* (Maiden & R.Baker) Nielsen *20681*

I		20681	Australia - New South Wales *20681*
I		20681	Australia - Queensland *20681*

R *Archidendron tonkinense* Nielsen *6057*

R			Vietnam *6057*

R *Archidendron whitei* Nielsen *20681*

R		20681	Australia - Queensland *20681*

V *Archidendropsis glandulosa* (Guillaumin) Nielsen *20893*

V		20893	New Caledonia *20893*

V	*Archidendropsis lentiscifolia* (Benth.) Nielsen *20893*	
	V	*20893* New Caledonia *20893*
V	*Archidendropsis paivana* (Fourn.) Nielsen *20893*	
	V	*20893* New Caledonia *20893*
R	*Archidendropsis xanthoxylon* (C.White & Francis) I.Nielsen *20681*	
	R	*20681* Australia - Queensland *20681*
I	*Argyrolobium barbatum* (Meisn.) Walp. *20604*	
	I	*20604* South Africa - Cape Province *20604*
E	*Argyrolobium crinitum* (E.Mey.) Walp. *20604*	
	E	*20604* South Africa - Cape Province *20604*
R	*Argyrolobium harmsianum* Schltr. ex Harms *20604*	
	R	*20604* South Africa - Cape Province *20604*
I	*Argyrolobium pachyphyllum* Schltr. *20604*	
	I	*20604* South Africa - Cape Province *20604*
I	*Argyrolobium parviflorum* T.J.Edwards *20604*	
	I	*20604* South Africa - Cape Province *20604*
I	*Argyrolobium petiolare* (E.Mey.) Walp. *20604*	
	I	*20604* South Africa - Cape Province *20604*
I	*Argyrolobium rarum* Dummer *20604*	
	I	*20604* South Africa - Cape Province *20604*
R	*Argyrolobium schimperianum* A. Rich *19704*	
	R	*19704* Ethiopia *19704*
Ex	*Argyrolobium splendens* (Meisn.) Walp. *20604*	
	Ex	*20604* South Africa - Cape Province *20604*
R	*Arthrocarpum gracile* Balf. f. *15534*	
	R	*15534* Yemen - Socotra *15534*
R	*Aspalathus acanthoclada* R.Dahlgren *20604, 12346*	
	R	*20604* South Africa - Cape Province *20604*
I	*Aspalathus acanthophylla* Eckl. & Zeyh. *20604, 12346*	
	I	*20604* South Africa - Cape Province *20604*
R	*Aspalathus angustifolia* (Lam.) R.Dahlgren ssp. *robusta* (E.Phillips) R. Dahlgren *20604*	
	R	*20604* South Africa - Cape Province *20604*
R	*Aspalathus arenaria* R.Dahlgren *20604*	
	R	*20604* South Africa - Cape Province *20604*
E	*Aspalathus barbigera* R.Dahlgren *20604*	
	E	*20604* South Africa - Cape Province *20604*
V	*Aspalathus bidouwensis* Garab. ex R.Dahlgren *20604*	
	V	*20604* South Africa - Cape Province *20604*
R	*Aspalathus borbonifolia* R. Dahlgren *20803*	
	R	*20803* South Africa - Cape Province *20803*
V	*Aspalathus burchelliana* Benth. *20604*	
	V	*20604* South Africa - Cape Province *20604*
E	*Aspalathus cliffortiifolia* R.Dahlgren *20604*	
	E	*20604* South Africa - Cape Province *20604*
R	*Aspalathus comptonii* R.Dahlgren *20604*	
	R	*20604* South Africa - Cape Province *20604*
R	*Aspalathus desertorum* Bolus *20604*	
	R	*20604* South Africa - Cape Province *20604*
R	*Aspalathus digitifolia* R.Dahlgren *20604*	
	R	*20604* South Africa - Cape Province *20604*
I	*Aspalathus erythrodes* Eckl. & Zeyh. *20604*	
	I	*20604* South Africa - Cape Province *20604*
R	*Aspalathus esterhuyseniae* R.Dahlgren *20604*	
	R	*20604* South Africa - Cape Province *20604*
R	*Aspalathus excelsa* R.Dahlgren *20604*	
	R	*20604* South Africa - Cape Province *20604*

R	*Aspalathus fasciculata* (Thunb.) R.Dahlgren *20604*	
	R	*20604* South Africa - Cape Province *20604*
I	*Aspalathus ferox* Harv. *20604*	
	I	*20604* South Africa - Cape Province *20604*
I	*Aspalathus glabrata* R.Dahlgren *20604*	
	I	*20604* South Africa - Cape Province *20604*
I	*Aspalathus glabrescens* R.Dahlgren *20604*	
	I	*20604* South Africa - Cape Province *20604*
I	*Aspalathus globulosa* E.Mey. *20604*	
	I	*20604* South Africa - Cape Province *20604*
E	*Aspalathus grobleri* R.Dahlgren *20604*	
	E	*20604* South Africa - Cape Province *20604*
R	*Aspalathus humilis* Bolus *20604*	
	R	*20604* South Africa - Cape Province *20604*
I	*Aspalathus incompta* Thunb. *20604*	
	I	*20604* South Africa - Cape Province *20604*
R	*Aspalathus isolata* (R.Dahlgren) R.Dahlgren *20604*	
	R	*20604* South Africa - Cape Province *20604*
R	*Aspalathus karrooensis* R.Dahlgren *20604*	
	R	*20604* South Africa - Cape Province *20604*
I	*Aspalathus lactea* Thunb. ssp. *breviloba* R.Dahlgren *20604*	
	I	*20604* South Africa - Cape Province *20604*
I	*Aspalathus macrantha* Harv. *20604*	
	I	*20604* South Africa - Cape Province *20604*
I	*Aspalathus obliqua* R.Dahlgren *20604*	
	I	*20604* South Africa - Cape Province *20604*
R	*Aspalathus oliveri* R.Dahlgren *20604*	
	R	*20604* South Africa - Cape Province *20604*
E	*Aspalathus prostrata* Eckl. & Zeyh. *20604*	
	E	*20604* South Africa - Cape Province *20604*
V	*Aspalathus repens* R.Dahlgren *20604*	
	V	*20604* South Africa - Cape Province *20604*
R	*Aspalathus rosea* Garab. ex R.Dahlgren *20604*	
	R	*20604* South Africa - Cape Province *20604*
E	*Aspalathus rycroftii* R.Dahlgren *20604*	
	E	*20604* South Africa - Cape Province *20604*
I	*Aspalathus singuliflora* R.Dahlgren *20604*	
	I	*20604* South Africa - Cape Province *20604*
V	*Aspalathus smithii* R.Dahlgren *20604*	
	V	*20604* South Africa - Cape Province *20604*
R	*Aspalathus spectabilis* R.Dahlgren *20604*	
	R	*20604* South Africa - Cape Province *20604*
R	*Aspalathus stokoei* L.Bolus *20604*	
	R	*20604* South Africa - Cape Province *20604*
R	*Aspalathus suaveolens* Eckl. & Zeyh. *20604*	
	R	*20604* South Africa - Cape Province *20604*
Ex	*Aspalathus variegata* Eckl. & Zeyh. *20604, 6180*	
	Ex	*20604* South Africa - Cape Province *20604*
R	*Aspalathus venosa* E.Mey. *20604*	
	R	*20604* South Africa - Cape Province *20604*
R	*Astragalus accidens* S.Watson var. *hendersonii* M.E. Jones *20850*	
	I	*20850* U.S. - California *20850*
	V	*20850* U.S. - Oregon *20850*
R	*Astragalus accumbens* Sheldon *20850*	
	R	*20850* U.S. - New Mexico *20850*
V	*Astragalus ackermanii* Barneby *20850*	

V	20850	U.S. - Nevada 20850

R   *Astragalus acmophyllus* Bunge 12840
   R   12840   Turkey 12840

R   *Astragalus adustus* Bunge 12840
   R   12840   Turkey 12840

V   *Astragalus aequalis* Clokey 20850
   V   20850   U.S. - Nevada 20850

E   *Astragalus agnicidus* Barneby 20850
   E   20850   U.S. - California 20850

R   *Astragalus agraniotii* Orph. ex Boiss. 20171
   R   Greece

R   *Astragalus aintabicus* Bunge 12840
   R   12840   Turkey 12840

R   *Astragalus akscheherensis* Freyn & Bornm. 12840
   R   12840   Turkey 12840

E   *Astragalus albens* Greene 20850
   E   20850   U.S. - California 20850

R   *Astragalus albicalycinus* Huber-Mor. & Mathews 12840
   R   12840   Turkey 12840

R   *Astragalus albifolius* Freyn & Sint. 12840
   R   12840   Turkey 12840

R   *Astragalus alindanus* Boiss. 12840
   R   12840   Turkey 12840

V   *Astragalus alpinus* Fern. var. *brunetianus*
   Fern. 20850
   I   20850   Canada - Labrador 20850
   I   20850   Canada - New Brunswick 20850
   I   20850   Canada - Newfoundland 20850
   I   20850   Canada - Nova Scotia 20850
   I   20850   Canada - Quebec 20850
   V   20850   U.S. - Maine 20850
   Ex/E   20850   U.S. - New Hampshire 20850
   Ex   20850   U.S. - Vermont 20850

R   *Astragalus altanii* Huber-Mor. 12840
   R   12840   Turkey 12840

V   *Astragalus altus* Woot. & Standl. 20850
   V   20850   U.S. - New Mexico 20850

R   *Astragalus amblytropis* Barneby 20850
   R   20850   U.S. - Idaho 20850

R   *Astragalus amnis-amissi* Barneby ex C.L.
   Hitchc. 20850
   R   20850   U.S. - Idaho 20850

V   *Astragalus amphioxys* A.Gray var. *musimonum*
   (Barneby) Barneby 20850
   E   20850   U.S. - Arizona 20850
   V   20850   U.S. - Nevada 20850

V   *Astragalus ampullarius* S.Watson 20850
   E   20850   U.S. - Arizona 20850
   V   20850   U.S. - Utah 20850

R   *Astragalus angustiflorus* C. Koch ssp. *amanus*
   (Boiss.) Chamb. 12840
   R   12840   Turkey 12840

R   *Astragalus anisus* M.E. Jones 20850
   V   20850   U.S. - Colorado 20850

R   *Astragalus anni-novi* Burkart 16336
   R   16336   Argentina 16336
   R   20176   Argentina - Chubut 20176
   R   20176   Argentina - Neuquen 20176
   R   20176   Argentina - Rio Negro 20176

I   *Astragalus anomalus* Bunge
   I   India - Jammu & Kashmir (Ladakh)

V   *Astragalus anserinus* Atwood, Goodrich & Welsh 20850
   E   20850   U.S. - Idaho 20850
   E   20850   U.S. - Nevada 20850
   E   20850   U.S. - Utah 20850

R   *Astragalus antiatlanticus* Emb. & Maire 12346
   R   Morocco 12346

R   *Astragalus antiochianus* Post 12840
   R   12840   Turkey 12840

E   *Astragalus anxius* Meinke & Kaye 20850
   I   20850   U.S. - California 20850
   I   20850   U.S. - Oregon 20850

E   *Astragalus applegatei* M.E. Peck 20850
   I   20850   U.S. - California 20850
   E   20850   U.S. - Oregon 20850

V   *Astragalus aquilanus* Anzalone 17781
   V   19997   Italy (Abruzzo) 19997

R   *Astragalus aquilonius* (Barneby) Barneby 20850
   R   20850   U.S. - Idaho 20850

R   *Astragalus argaeus* Boiss. 12840
   R   12840   Turkey 12840

E   *Astragalus argentinus* Manganaro 16336
   E   20176   Argentina - Buenos Aires 20176

Ex/E   *Astragalus arianus* Gontsch. 5942
   Ex/E   5942   Turkmenistan (Southern valleys) 5942

R   *Astragalus armeniacus* Boiss. 12840
   R   12840   Turkey 12840

R   *Astragalus arnacantha* M.Bieb. 8000, 20171
   R   Bulgaria 8000
   R   11552   Ukraine - Crimea 8000

V   *Astragalus arrectus* A.Gray 20850
   I   20850   U.S. - Idaho 20850
   I   20850   U.S. - Oregon 20850
   E   20850   U.S. - Washington 20850

R   *Astragalus atratus* S.Watson var. *inseptus*
   Barneby 20850
   R   20850   U.S. - Idaho 20850

V   *Astragalus atratus* S.Watson var. *mensanus* M.E.
   Jones 20850
   I   20850   U.S. - California 20850
   I   20850   U.S. - Nevada 20850

R   *Astragalus atratus* S.Watson var. *owyheensis*
   (A.Nels. & J.F.Macbr.) M.E.Jones 20850
   R   20850   U.S. - Idaho 20850
   I   20850   U.S. - Nevada 20850
   R   20850   U.S. - Oregon 20850

R   *Astragalus atrocarpus* Chamb. & Mathews 12840
   R   12840   Turkey 12840

R   *Astragalus austraegaeus* Rech.f. 20171
   R   20731   Greece - East Aegean Is (Rhodes) 20731

R   *Astragalus autranii* Bald. 20178, 20171
   R   20178   Albania 20178

V   *Astragalus aydosensis* Pesmen & Erik 12840
   V   12840   Turkey 12840

I   *Astragalus azraqensis* C. Towns. 8937
   I   Jordan 8937

R   *Astragalus badachschianus* A. Boriss.
   R   former USSR 6930

E   *Astragalus badamensis* Popov
   E   former USSR 6930

I   *Astragalus bakerii* Ali
   I   India - Jammu & Kashmir

I	*Astragalus bakuensis* Bunge *5942*		
	I	*5942*	Azerbaijan *5942*
R	*Astragalus baldaccii* Degen *20178, 20171*		
	Ex/E	*20178*	Albania *20178*
	R		Greece
I	*Astragalus balkisensis* Sirj. & Rech. *12840*		
	I	*12840*	Turkey *12840*
R	*Astragalus barba-jovis* DC *12840*		
	R	*12840*	Turkey *12840*
R	*Astragalus barbarae* Bornm. *12840*		
	R	*12840*	Turkey *12840*
R	*Astragalus barbeyanus* Post *12840*		
	R	*12840*	Turkey *12840*
R	*Astragalus barrii* Barneby *20850*		
	R	*20850*	U.S. - Montana *20850*
	I	*20850*	U.S. - Nebraska *20850*
	R	*20850*	U.S. - South Dakota *20850*
	R	*20850*	U.S. - Wyoming *20850*
R	*Astragalus bashkalensis* Chamb. *12840*		
	R	*12840*	Turkey *12840*
R	*Astragalus baytopianus* Chamb. & Mathews *12840*		
	R	*12840*	Turkey *12840*
V	*Astragalus beathii* C.L. Porter *20850*		
	V	*20850*	U.S. - Arizona *20850*
V	*Astragalus beatleyae* Barneby *20850*		
	R	*20850*	U.S. - Nevada *20850*
R	*Astragalus beckwithii* Barneby var. *sulcatus* Barneby *20850*		
	R	*20850*	U.S. - Idaho *20850*
E	*Astragalus bibullatus* Barneby & Bridges *20850, 14501*		
	E	*20850*	U.S. - Tennessee (Rutherford County) *20850*
I	*Astragalus bobrovii* B. Fedtsch. *5942*		
	I	*5942*	Uzbekistan *5942*
R	*Astragalus bombycalyx* Eig *12840*		
	R	*12840*	Turkey *12840*
R	*Astragalus bonariensis* Gomez-Sosa *16336*		
	R	*16336*	Argentina *16336*
	R	*20176*	Argentina - Buenos Aires *20176*
	R	*20176*	Argentina - Rio Negro *20176*
V	*Astragalus brauntonii* Parish *20850*		
	V	*20850*	U.S. - California *20850*
R	*Astragalus breweri* A.Gray *20850*		
	R	*20850*	U.S. - California *20850*
R	*Astragalus californicus* (Gray) Greene *20850*		
	R	*20850*	U.S. - California *20850*
	R	*20850*	U.S. - Oregon *20850*
R	*Astragalus callithrix* Barneby *20850*		
	R	*20850*	U.S. - Nevada *20850*
	V	*20850*	U.S. - Utah *20850*
V	*Astragalus calycosus* Torr. ex S. Wats. var. *calycosus* *20850*		
	I	*20850*	U.S. - Arizona *20850*
	I	*20850*	U.S. - California *20850*
	I	*20850*	U.S. - Colorado *20850*
	I	*20850*	U.S. - Idaho *20850*
	I	*20850*	U.S. - Nevada *20850*
	V	*20850*	U.S. - Oregon *20850*
	V	*20850*	U.S. - Utah *20850*
	I	*20850*	U.S. - Wyoming *20850*
V	*Astragalus calycosus* Torr. ex S.Watson var. *monophyllidius* (Rydb.) Barneby *20850*		

	V	*20850*	U.S. - Nevada *20850*
	I	*20850*	U.S. - Utah *20850*
R	*Astragalus camelorum* Barbey		
	R		Egypt
R	*Astragalus camptopus* Barneby *20850*		
	R	*20850*	U.S. - Idaho *20850*
	I	*20850*	U.S. - Oregon *20850*
R	*Astragalus canescens* DC. *12840*		
	R	*12840*	Turkey *12840*
V	*Astragalus caprinus* L. ssp. *huetii* (Bunge) Podl. *18264*		
	V	*18264*	Italy - Sicily (central & south-west) *20738*
R	*Astragalus cariensis* Boiss. *12840*		
	R	*12840*	Turkey *12840*
R	*Astragalus castetteri* Barneby *20850*		
	R	*20850*	U.S. - New Mexico *20850*
R	*Astragalus caudiculosus* Boiss. & Huet *12840*		
	R	*12840*	Turkey *12840*
R	*Astragalus celakowskyanus* Freyn & Bornm. *12840*		
	R	*12840*	Turkey *12840*
R	*Astragalus cephalotes* Banks & Bornm. var. *brevicalyx* Eig *12840*		
	R	*12840*	Turkey *12840*
R	*Astragalus cephalotes* Banks & Bornm. var. *sintenianus* (Sirj) Chamb. & Mathews *12840*		
	R	*12840*	Turkey *12840*
R	*Astragalus ceramicus* Sheldon var. *apus* Barneby *20850*		
	R	*20850*	U.S. - Idaho *20850*
	E	*20850*	U.S. - Montana *20850*
R	*Astragalus cerussatus* Sheldon *20850*		
	R	*20850*	U.S. - Colorado *20850*
	I	*20850*	U.S. - New Mexico *20850*
R	*Astragalus chaldiranicus* Kit Tan & Sorger *12840*		
	R	*12840*	Turkey *12840*
V	*Astragalus chamaemeniscus* Barneby *20850*		
	I	*20850*	U.S. - Nevada *20850*
	E	*20850*	U.S. - Utah *20850*
R	*Astragalus chamaephaca* Freyn *12840*		
	R	*12840*	Turkey *12840*
R	*Astragalus chloodes* Barneby *20850*		
	I	*20850*	U.S. - Colorado *20850*
	R	*20850*	U.S. - Utah *20850*
R	*Astragalus chrysochlorus* Boiss. & Kotschy *12840*		
	R	*12840*	Turkey *12840*
R	*Astragalus chthonocephalus* Boiss. & Bal. *12840*		
	R	*12840*	Turkey *12840*
V	*Astragalus chuskanus* Barneby & Spellenberg *20850*		
	E	*20850*	U.S. - Arizona *20850*
	V	*20850*	U.S. - New Mexico *20850*
V	*Astragalus cicerellus* Boiss. & Bal. *12840*		
	V	*12840*	Turkey *12840*
V	*Astragalus cimae* M.E. Jones *20850*		
	I	*20850*	U.S. - California *20850*
	V	*20850*	U.S. - Nevada *20850*
V	*Astragalus cimae* M.E.Jones var. *cimae* *20850*		
	V	*20850*	U.S. - California *20850*
	V	*20850*	U.S. - Nevada *20850*
V	*Astragalus cimae* M.E.Jones var. *sufflatus* Barneby *20850*		

	I	20850 U.S. - California *20850*	

E   *Astragalus clarianus* Jepson *20850*
     E   20850 U.S. - California *20850*

V   *Astragalus clerceanus* Iljin & Krasch. *8000, 20171*
     V   *11552* Russian Federation (Ural Mts) *11552*

R   *Astragalus coadunatus* Huber-Mor. & Chamb. *12840*
     R   *12840* Turkey *12840*

E   *Astragalus cobrensis* A.Gray var. *maguirei*
     Kearney *20850*
     E   20850 U.S. - Arizona *20850*
     E   20850 U.S. - New Mexico *20850*

R   *Astragalus colhuensis* Gomez-Sosa *16336*
     R   *16336* Argentina *16336*
     R   *20176* Argentina - Chubut *20176*

E   *Astragalus collinus* (Hook.)Douglas ex G.Don var.
     laurentii (Rydb.) Barneby *20850*
     E   20850 U.S. - Oregon *20850*

R   *Astragalus coltonii* M. E. Jones var.
     coltonii *20850*
     R   20850 U.S. - Utah *20850*

R   *Astragalus coltonii* M. E. Jones var. *moabensis*
     M.E. Jones *20850*
     I   20850 U.S. - Arizona *20850*
     I   20850 U.S. - Colorado *20850*
     I   20850 U.S. - New Mexico *20850*
     V   20850 U.S. - Utah *20850*
     E   20850 U.S. - Wyoming *20850*

V   *Astragalus columbianus* Barneby *20850*
     V   20850 U.S. - Washington *20850*

R   *Astragalus columnaris* Boiss. *12840*
     R   *12840* Turkey *12840*

R   *Astragalus commagenicus* (Hand.-Mazz.) Sirj. *12840*
     R   *12840* Turkey *12840*

R   *Astragalus comosoides* Cham. & Mathews *12840*
     R   *12840* Turkey *12840*

R   *Astragalus consimilis* Bornm. *12840*
     R   *12840* Turkey *12840*

V   *Astragalus consobrinus* (Barneby) Welsh *20850*
     V   20850 U.S. - Utah *20850*

R   *Astragalus convallarius* E.Green var. *finitimus*
     Barneby *20850*
     R   20850 U.S. - Nevada *20850*
     V   20850 U.S. - Utah *20850*

E   *Astragalus cottonii* M.E. Jones *20850*
     I   20850 U.S. - New Mexico *20850*
     E   20850 U.S. - Washington *20850*

E   *Astragalus cremnophylax* Barneby *20850*
     E   20850 U.S. - Arizona *20850*

E   *Astragalus cremnophylax* Barneby var.
     cremnophylax *20850*
     E   20850 U.S. - Arizona *20850*

E   *Astragalus cremnophylax* Barneby var. *myriorrhaphis*
     Barneby *20850*
     E   20850 U.S. - Arizona *20850*

R   *Astragalus crinitus* Boiss. *12840*
     R   *12840* Turkey *12840*

V   *Astragalus cronquistii* Barneby *20850*
     V   20850 U.S. - Colorado *20850*
     V   20850 U.S. - Utah *20850*

V   *Astragalus curtipes* A.Gray *20850*
     I   20850 U.S. - California *20850*

E   *Astragalus cusickii* Barneby var. *packardiae*
     Barneby *20850*
     E   20850 U.S. - Idaho *20850*

V   *Astragalus cusickii* Barneby var. *sterilis*
     (Barneby) Barneby *20850*
     E   20850 U.S. - Idaho *20850*
     I   20850 U.S. - Oregon *20850*

R   *Astragalus cuspistipulatus* Eig *12840*
     R   *12840* Turkey *12840*

R   *Astragalus cymbibracteatus* Huber-Mor. & Chamb. *12840*
     R   *12840* Turkey *12840*

R   *Astragalus cymboides* M.E. Jones *20850*
     R   20850 U.S. - Utah *20850*

R   *Astragalus cymbostegius* Bunge *12840*
     R   *12840* Turkey *12840*

V   *Astragalus cyrenaicus* Coss.
     V   Libya

R   *Astragalus czorochensis* Charadze *12840*
     R   *12840* Turkey *12840*

R   *Astragalus darwasicus* Basilevsk.
     R   former USSR *6930*

R   *Astragalus dasyanthus* Pall. *8000, 20171*
     R   Bulgaria *8000*
     V   20686 Hungary *17786*
     R   20631 Romania *20631*
     R   (former) Yugoslavia
     I   Russia (E.Europe) - Northwest *8000*

R   *Astragalus dasycarpus* Chamb. *12840*
     R   *12840* Turkey *12840*

V   *Astragalus deanei* (Rydb.) Barneby *20850*
     V   20850 U.S. - California *20850*

V   *Astragalus debequaeus* Welsh *20850*
     V   20850 U.S. - Colorado *20850*

R   *Astragalus decurrens* Boiss. *12840*
     R   *12840* Turkey *12840*

R   *Astragalus delanensis* Sirj. & Rech.f. *12840*
     R   *12840* Turkey *12840*

R   *Astragalus delbesii* Eig *12840*
     R   *12840* Turkey *12840*

R   *Astragalus depressus* L. var. *tasheliensis* Erik &
     Sumbul *12840*
     R   *12840* Turkey *12840*

E   *Astragalus desereticus* Barneby *20850*
     E   20850 U.S. - Utah *20850*

R   *Astragalus desperatus* M. E. Jones var. *conspectus*
     Barneby *20850*
     R   20850 U.S. - Arizona *20850*
     V   20850 U.S. - Utah *20850*

E   *Astragalus desperatus* M. E. Jones var. *neeseae*
     Barneby *20850*
     E   20850 U.S. - Utah *20850*

V   *Astragalus desperatus* M. E. Jones var. *petrophilus*
     M.E. Jones *20850*
     V   20850 U.S. - Utah *20850*

V   *Astragalus deterior* (Barneby) Barneby *20850*
     V   20850 U.S. - Colorado *20850*

R   *Astragalus detritalis* M.E. Jones *20850*
     V   20850 U.S. - Colorado *20850*
     R   20850 U.S. - Utah *20850*

R   *Astragalus diphtherites* Fenzl var. *karatashensis*

(Sirj.) Chamb. *12840*
R   *12840*   Turkey *12840*

R   *Astragalus dirmilensis* Huber-Mor. & Reese *12840*
R   *12840*   Turkey *12840*

R   *Astragalus discessiflorus* Gontsch.
R   former USSR *6930*

R   *Astragalus distinctissimus* Eig *12840*
R   *12840*   Turkey *12840*

R   *Astragalus diversifolius* A.Gray *20850*
V   *20850*   U.S. - Idaho *20850*
I   *20850*   U.S. - Montana *20850*
I   *20850*   U.S. - Nevada *20850*
E   *20850*   U.S. - Utah *20850*
Ex/E   *20850*   U.S. - Wyoming *20850*

V   *Astragalus douglasii* (Torr. & A.Gray) A.Gray var. *perstrictus* (Rydb.) Munz & McBurney ex Munz *20850*
V   *20850*   U.S. - California *20850*

V   *Astragalus drabelliformis* Barneby *20850*
V   *20850*   U.S. - Wyoming *20850*

R   *Astragalus drupaceus* Orph. ex Boiss. *20171*
R   Greece

R   *Astragalus duchesnensis* M.E. Jones *20850*
E   *20850*   U.S. - Colorado *20850*
R   *20850*   U.S. - Utah *20850*

R   *Astragalus edinburghensis* Ponert *12840*
R   *12840*   Turkey *12840*

R   *Astragalus edmodii* (Kuntze) Sheldon *12840*
R   *12840*   Turkey *12840*

R   *Astragalus elatus* Boiss. & Bal. *12840*
R   *12840*   Turkey *12840*

R   *Astragalus elazigensis* Ekim *12840*
R   *12840*   Turkey *12840*

R   *Astragalus elbistanicus* Huber-Mor. & Chamb. *12840*
R   *12840*   Turkey *12840*

R   *Astragalus eliasianus* Kit Tan & Sorger *12840*
R   *12840*   Turkey *12840*

V   *Astragalus endopterus* (Barneby) Barneby *20850*
I   *20850*   U.S. - Arizona *20850*

R   *Astragalus ensiformis* M.E. Jones *20850*
V   *20850*   U.S. - Arizona *20850*
I   *20850*   U.S. - Nevada *20850*
R   *20850*   U.S. - Utah *20850*

E   *Astragalus ensiformis* M. E. Jones var. *gracilior* Barneby *20850*
I   *20850*   U.S. - Nevada *20850*
     20850   U.S. - Utah *20850*

V   *Astragalus episcopus* S.Watson var. *lancearius* (Gray) Isely *20850*
     20850   U.S. - Arizona *20850*
V   *20850*   U.S. - Utah *20850*

R   *Astragalus eriocephalus* Willd. *12840*
R   *12840*   Turkey *12840*

R   *Astragalus ermineus* Matt. *12840*
R   *12840*   Turkey *12840*

E   *Astragalus ertterae* Barneby & Shevock *20850*
E   *20850*   U.S. - California *20850*

V   *Astragalus eurylobus* (Barneby) Barneby *20850*
I   *20850*   U.S. - Arizona *20850*
V   *20850*   U.S. - Nevada *20850*

R   *Astragalus fabrisii* Gomez-Sosa *16336*
R   *16336*   Argentina *16336*

R   *20176*   Argentina - Jujuy *20176*

R   *Astragalus feensis* M.E. Jones *20850*
R   *20850*   U.S. - New Mexico *20850*

R   *Astragalus fissuralis* Alexej. *11552*
R   *11552*   Russian Federation (Caucasus) *11552*

I   *Astragalus flavocreatus* I.M. Johnston *16336*
Ex   *16336*   Argentina *16336*
I   *20176*   Argentina - Catamarca *20176*
I   *20176*   Argentina - La Rioja *20176*
I   *20176*   Argentina - Salta *20176*
I   *20176*   Argentina - Tucuman *20176*
I   *19566*   Bolivia *19566*

R   *Astragalus fodinarum* Boiss. & Noe *12840*
R   *12840*   Turkey *12840*

R   *Astragalus font-queri* Maire & Sennen *12346*
R   Morocco *12346*

R   *Astragalus fresenii* Decne.
R   Egypt

R   *Astragalus froedinii* Murb. *12346*
R   Morocco *12346*

R   *Astragalus fructicosus* Forssk.
R   Egypt
R   Israel

V   *Astragalus funereus* M.E. Jones *20850*
V   *20850*   U.S. - California *20850*
V   *20850*   U.S. - Nevada *20850*

R   *Astragalus gaeobotrys* Boiss. & Bal. *12840*
R   *12840*   Turkey *12840*

E   *Astragalus galilaeus* Freyn & Bornm. *8895*
E   Israel (Upper Galilee) *8895*

R   *Astragalus geniorum* Maire *10488*
R   *14958*   Algeria *10488*

R   *Astragalus gevaschensis* Chamb. & Matt. *12840*
R   *12840*   Turkey *12840*

V   *Astragalus geyeri* A.Gray var. *triquetrus* (Gray) M.E. Jones *20850*
E   *20850*   U.S. - Arizona *20850*
V   *20850*   U.S. - Nevada *20850*

R   *Astragalus giennensis* Heywood *20171*
R   Spain

V   *Astragalus gilviflorus* Dorn var. *purpureus* Dorn *20850*
V   *20850*   U.S. - Wyoming *20850*

R   *Astragalus gilvus* Boiss. *12840*
R   *12840*   Turkey *12840*

R   *Astragalus goeznensis* Eig *12840*
R   *12840*   Turkey *12840*

I   *Astragalus gorodkovii* Jurtz. *21309*
R   *21309*   Russia (E.Europe) - Northwest *21309*

R   *Astragalus grossii* Pau *20171*
R   *20692*   Spain (south-east) *20692*

R   *Astragalus gymnalopecias* Rech.f. *12840*
R   *12840*   Turkey *12840*

R   *Astragalus gypsodes* Barneby *20850*
R   *20850*   U.S. - New Mexico *20850*
V   *20850*   U.S. - Texas *20850*

R   *Astragalus hakkiaricus* Chamb. & Matt. *12840*
R   *12840*   Turkey *12840*

E   *Astragalus hamiltonii* C.L. Porter *20850*
E   *20850*   U.S. - Colorado *20850*

E	20850	U.S. - Utah	20850	

R   *Astragalus hareftae* (Nab.) Sirj *12840*
     R   *12840*   Turkey *12840*

E   *Astragalus harrisonii* Barneby *20850*
     E   *20850*   U.S. - Utah *20850*

R   *Astragalus hartvigii* Kit Tan *12840*
     R   *12840*   Turkey *12840*

I   *Astragalus hegelmairei* Willk. *11496*
     I   *11496*   Spain *11496*

R   *Astragalus helmii* Fischer var. *permiensis* C. Meyer
     ex Rupr.
     R   former USSR

R   *Astragalus henningii* (Steven) Boriss. *20171*
     R   former European USSR

R   *Astragalus hilaris* Bunge *12840*
     R   *12840*   Turkey *12840*

E   *Astragalus holmgreniorum* Barneby *20850*
     E   *20850*   U.S. - Arizona *20850*
     E   *20850*   U.S. - Utah *20850*

R   *Astragalus huber-morathii* Agerer-Kirchhoff *12840*
     R   *12840*   Turkey *12840*

I   *Astragalus huetii* Bunge *20171*
     I   Italy - Sicily

E   *Astragalus humillimus* A.Gray *20850, 12840*
     E   *20850*   U.S. - Colorado *20850*
     E   *20850*   U.S. - New Mexico *20850*

E   *Astragalus hypoxylus* S.Watson *20850*
     E   *20850*   U.S. - Arizona *20850*

Ex/E   *Astragalus idaeus* Bunge *20171*
     Ex/E   *20730*   Greece - Crete *20730*

R   *Astragalus ideae* Sirj. *12840*
     R   *12840*   Turkey *12840*

I   *Astragalus igoshinae* R. Kam. & Jurtz. *21309*
     I   *21309*   Russia (E.Europe) - North *21309*

R   *Astragalus insignis* Gontsch.
     R   former USSR *6930*

R   *Astragalus insularis* Kellogg var. *harwoodii* Munz &
     McBurney ex Munz *20850*
     V   *20850*   U.S. - Arizona *20850*
     I   *20850*   U.S. - California *20850*
     I   *20883*   Mexico *20883*

V   *Astragalus inyoensis* Sheldon *20850*
     I   *20850*   U.S. - California *20850*
     E   *20850*   U.S. - Nevada *20850*

R   *Astragalus isauricus* Huber-Mor. *12840*
     R   *12840*   Turkey *12840*

E   *Astragalus iselyi* Welsh *20850*
     E   *20850*   U.S. - Utah *20850*

R   *Astragalus isparticus* Kit Tan & Sorger *12840*
     R   *12840*   Turkey *12840*

E   *Astragalus jaegerianus* Munz *20850*
     E   *20850*   U.S. - California *20850*

R   *Astragalus jejunus* S.Wats. *20850*
     E   *20850*   U.S. - Colorado *20850*
     R   *20850*   U.S. - Idaho *20850*
     I   *20850*   U.S. - Nevada *20850*
     E   *20850*   U.S. - Utah *20850*
     R   *20850*   U.S. - Wyoming *20850*

E   *Astragalus jejunus* S.Wats. var. *articulatus*
     Dorn *20850*

     E   *20850*   U.S. - Wyoming *20850*

R   *Astragalus jejunus* S.Wats. var.
     jejunus *20850*
     I   *20850*   U.S. - Colorado *20850*
     V   *20850*   U.S. - Idaho *20850*
     I   *20850*   U.S. - Nevada *20850*
     I   *20850*   U.S. - Utah *20850*
     R   *20850*   U.S. - Wyoming *20850*

V   *Astragalus johannis-howellii* Barneby *20850*
     V   *20850*   U.S. - California *20850*
     E   *20850*   U.S. - Nevada *20850*

R   *Astragalus kangalicus* Kit Tan & Sorger *12840*
     R   *12840*   Turkey *12840*

R   *Astragalus karelinianus* Popov *20171*
     R   former European USSR

V   *Astragalus kentrophyta* A.Gray var. *danaus*
     (Barneby) Barneby *20850*
     I   *20850*   U.S. - California *20850*
     I   *20850*   U.S. - Nevada *20850*

Ex   *Astragalus kentrophyta* A.Gray var. *douglasii*
     Barneby *20850*
     Ex   *20850*   U.S. - Oregon *20850*
     Ex   *20850*   U.S. - Washington *20850*

R   *Astragalus kentrophyta* A.Gray var. *neomexicanus*
     (Barneby) Barneby *20850*
     R   *20850*   U.S. - New Mexico *20850*

V   *Astragalus kerrii* Knight & Cully *20850*
     V   *20850*   U.S. - New Mexico *20850*

R   *Astragalus kirshehiricus* Chamb. *12840*
     R   *12840*   Turkey *12840*

R   *Astragalus kitianus* Sorger *12840*
     R   *12840*   Turkey *12840*

V   *Astragalus knightii* Barneby *20850*
     V   *20850*   U.S. - New Mexico *20850*

E   *Astragalus koraiensis* Y.N. Lee
     E   Korea, South

I   *Astragalus kungurensis* Boriss. *11552, 20171*
     I   *5942*   Russia (E.Europe) - East (Urals) *5942*

R   *Astragalus lacteus* Heldr. & Sart. ex Boiss. *20171*
     R   Greece *19121*

R   *Astragalus lagopodioides* Vahl *12840*
     R   *12840*   Turkey *12840*

R   *Astragalus latistipulatus* Chamb. & Matt. *12840*
     R   *12840*   Turkey *12840*

V   *Astragalus lentiformis* Gray ex Brewer &
     S.Watson *20850*
     V   *20850*   U.S. - California *20850*

E   *Astragalus lentiginosus* Douglas ex Hook. var.
     ambiguus Barneby *20850*
     E   *20850*   U.S. - Arizona *20850*

V   *Astragalus lentiginosus* Douglas ex Hook. var.
     antonius Barneby *20850*
     V   *20850*   U.S. - California *20850*

V   *Astragalus lentiginosus* Douglas ex Hook. var.
     coachellae Barneby ex Shreve & Wiggins *20850*
     V   *20850*   U.S. - California *20850*

V   *Astragalus lentiginosus* Douglas ex Hook. var.
     kernensis (Jepson) Barneby *20850*
     I   *20850*   U.S. - California *20850*
     I   *20850*   U.S. - Nevada *20850*

E   *Astragalus lentiginosus* Douglas ex Hook. var. *latus*

(M.E. Jones) M.E. Jones *20850*
- I   *20850*   U.S. - Idaho *20850*
- E   *20850*   U.S. - Nevada *20850*

E   *Astragalus lentiginosus* Douglas ex Hook. var. *micans* Barneby *20850*
- E   *20850*   U.S. - California *20850*
- I   *20850*   U.S. - Nevada *20850*

E   *Astragalus lentiginosus* Douglas ex Hook. var. *piscinensis* Barneby *20850*
- E   *20850*   U.S. - California *20850*

E   *Astragalus lentiginosus* Douglas ex Hook. var. *pohlii* Welsh & Barneby *20850*
- E   *20850*   U.S. - Utah *20850*

E   *Astragalus lentiginosus* Douglas ex Hook. var. *sesquimetralis* (Rydb.) Barneby *20850*
- E   *20850*   U.S. - California *20850*
- E   *20850*   U.S. - Nevada *20850*

E   *Astragalus lentiginosus* Douglas ex Hook. var. *sierrae* M.E. Jones *20850*
- E   *20850*   U.S. - California *20850*

V   *Astragalus lentiginosus* Douglas ex Hook. var. *stramineus* (Rydb.) Barneby *20850*
- I   *20850*   U.S. - Arizona *20850*
- I   *20850*   U.S. - Nevada *20850*
- E   *20850*   U.S. - Utah *20850*

R   *Astragalus leptocaulis* Ledeb.
- R   former USSR *6930*

V   *Astragalus leucolobus* S.Watson ex M.E. Jones *20850*
- V   *20850*   U.S. - California *20850*

V   *Astragalus limnocharis* Barneby *20850*
- V   *20850*   U.S. - Utah *20850*

E   *Astragalus limnocharis* Barneby var. *limnocharis* *20850*
- E   *20850*   U.S. - Utah *20850*

E   *Astragalus limnocharis* Barneby var. *montii* (Welsh) Isely *20850*
- E   *20850*   U.S. - Utah *20850*

V   *Astragalus linifolius* Osterhout *20850*
- V   *20850*   U.S. - Colorado *20850*

R   *Astragalus listoniae* Boiss. *12840*
- R   *12840*   Turkey *12840*

E   *Astragalus loanus* Barneby *20850*
- E   *20850*   U.S. - Utah *20850*

R   *Astragalus longifolius* Lam. *12840*
- R   *12840*   Turkey *12840*

V   *Astragalus longipetalus* Chater *8000, 20171*
- V   Russia (E.Europe) - South (south east) *8000*

E   *Astragalus macrocarpus* DC. ssp. *lefkarensis* Agerer-Kirchoff & Meikle *14230*
- E   *19164*   Cyprus (chalk hill above Pano Lefkara) *14230*

R   *Astragalus macrouroides* Huber-Mor. *12840*
- R   *12840*   Turkey *12840*

V   *Astragalus magdalenae* E.Greene var. *peirsonii* (Munz & McBurney) Barneby *20850*
- V   *20850*   U.S. - California *20850*

R   *Astragalus malacoides* Barneby *20850,*
- R   *20850*   U.S. - Utah *20850*

V   *Astragalus maritimus* Moris *8000, 20171*
- V   *18264*   Italy - Sardinia (Isola di San Pietro)

8000

R   *Astragalus maximus* Willd. var. *dasysemius* Chamb. & Matt. *12840*
- R   *12840*   Turkey *12840*

R   *Astragalus melitensis* Boiss. *12840*
- R   *12840*   Turkey *12840*

V   *Astragalus membranaceus* (Fischer) Bunge var. *mongolicus* (Bunge) Hsiao *11139*
- V   China - Hebei *11139*
- V   China - Nei Monggol Zizhiqu *11139*
- V   China - Shanxi *11139*

R   *Astragalus michauxii* (Kuntze) F.J. Herm. *20850,*
- E   *20850*   U.S. - Alabama *20850*
- I   *20850*   U.S. - Florida *20850*
- V   *20850*   U.S. - Georgia *20850*
- R   *20850*   U.S. - North Carolina *20850*
- I   *20850*   U.S. - South Carolina *20850*

E   *Astragalus microcymbus* Barneby *20850,*
- E   *20850*   U.S. - Colorado *20850*

V   *Astragalus micromerius* Barneby *20850*
- V   *20850*   U.S. - New Mexico *20850*

R   *Astragalus microrchis* Barbey *12840*
- R   *12840*   Turkey *12840*

R   *Astragalus misellus* S.Watson var. *pauper* Barneby *20850*
- I   *20850*   U.S. - Oregon *20850*
- R   *20850*   U.S. - Washington *20850*

R   *Astragalus miser* Dougl. ex Hook. var. *tenuifolius* (Nutt.) Barneby *20850*
- I   *20850*   U.S. - Idaho *20850*
- I   *20850*   U.S. - Nevada *20850*
- E   *20850*   U.S. - Utah *20850*
- V   *20850*   U.S. - Wyoming *20850*

V   *Astragalus missouriensis* Isely var. *humistratus* Isely *20850*
- I   *20850*   U.S. - Colorado *20850*

R   *Astragalus mitchellianus* Boiss. *12840*
- R   *12840*   Turkey *12840*

R   *Astragalus mohavensis* S.Watson *20850*
- I   *20850*   U.S. - California *20850*
- R   *20850*   U.S. - Nevada *20850*

V   *Astragalus mohavensis* S.Watson var. *hemigyrus* (Clokey) Barneby *20850*
- Ex/E   *20850*   U.S. - California *20850*
- V   *20850*   U.S. - Nevada *20850*

R   *Astragalus mokeevae* Popov
- R   former USSR *6930*

V   *Astragalus mokiacensis* A.Gray *20850*
- I   *20850*   U.S. - Arizona *20850*
- E   *20850*   U.S. - Nevada *20850*

R   *Astragalus mollissimus* Torr. var. *coryi* Tidestrom *20850*
- R   *20850*   U.S. - Texas *20850*

V   *Astragalus mollissimus* Torr. var. *marcidus* (Greene ex Rydb.) Barneby *20850*
- V   *20850*   U.S. - Texas *20850*

R   *Astragalus molybdenus* Barneby *20850*
- V   *20850*   U.S. - Colorado *20850*
- V   *20850*   U.S. - Montana *20850*
- I   *20850*   U.S. - Wyoming *20850*

V   *Astragalus monoensis* Barneby *20850*
- V   *20850*   U.S. - California *20850*

R	*Astragalus mordiensis* Nab. *12840*			
	R	*12840*	Turkey *12840*	
R	*Astragalus moyanoi* Speg. *16336*			
	R	*16336*	Argentina *16336*	
	R	*20176*	Argentina - Chubut (Futaleufú) *20176*	
	R	*20176*	Argentina - Neuquen (Huiliches) *20176*	
R	*Astragalus mukisiensis* Rech.f. *12840*			
	R	*12840*	Turkey *12840*	
V	*Astragalus mulfordiae* M.E. Jones *20850*			
	V	*20850*	U.S. - Idaho *20850*	
	E	*20850*	U.S. - Oregon *20850*	
	I	*20850*	U.S. - Washington *20850*	
R	*Astragalus musiniensis* M.E. Jones *20850*			
	I	*20850*	U.S. - Arizona *20850*	
	E	*20850*	U.S. - Colorado *20850*	
	I	*20850*	U.S. - Utah *20850*	
R	*Astragalus nankotaizanensis* Sasaki *20511*			
	R	*20511*	Taiwan *20511*	
V	*Astragalus naturitensis* Payson *20850*			
	V	*20850*	U.S. - Colorado *20850*	
	V	*20850*	U.S. - New Mexico *20850*	
	E	*20850*	U.S. - Utah *20850*	
R	*Astragalus nelsonianus* Barneby *20850*			
	E	*20850*	U.S. - Colorado *20850*	
	E	*20850*	U.S. - Utah *20850*	
	V	*20850*	U.S. - Wyoming *20850*	
R	*Astragalus neomexicanus* Woot. & Standl. *20850*			
	R	*20850*	U.S. - New Mexico *20850*	
R	*Astragalus nervulosus* Eig & Reese emend Huber-Mor. *12840*			
	R	*12840*	Turkey *12840*	
V	*Astragalus nevinii* A.Gray *20850*			
	V	*20850*	U.S. - California *20850*	
V	*Astragalus newberryi* Gray var. *aquarii* Isely *20850*			
	V	*20850*	U.S. - Arizona *20850*	
I	*Astragalus nicharensis* Bunge			
	I		Pakistan	
V	*Astragalus nidularius* Barneby *20850*			
	V	*20850*	U.S. - Utah *20850*	
R	*Astragalus nummularius* Lam. *20171*			
	R	*20730*	Greece - Crete *19121*	
R	*Astragalus nuratensis* Popov			
	R		former USSR *6930*	
E	*Astragalus nutriosensis* Sanderson *20850*			
	E	*20850*	U.S. - Arizona *20850*	
R	*Astragalus nyensis* Barneby *20850*			
	R	*20850*	U.S. - Nevada *20850*	
R	*Astragalus ocakverdii* Kit Tan & Sorger *12840*			
	R	*12840*	Turkey *12840*	
I	*Astragalus olchonensis* Gontsch. *5942*			
	I	*5942*	Russia (Siberia) - Buryatiya (Oz. Baykal) *5942*	
R	*Astragalus oniciformis* Barneby *20850*			
	R	*20850*	U.S. - Idaho *20850*	
V	*Astragalus oocarpus* A.Gray *20850*			
	V	*20850*	U.S. - California *20850*	
E	*Astragalus oophorus* S.Watson var. *clokeyanus* Barneby *20850*			
	E	*20850*	U.S. - Nevada *20850*	
E	*Astragalus oophorus* S.Watson var. *lavinii* Barneby *20850*			
	I	*20850*	U.S. - California *20850*	
	V	*20850*	U.S. - Nevada *20850*	
V	*Astragalus oophorus* S.Watson var. *lonchocalyx* Barneby *20850*			
	V	*20850*	U.S. - Nevada *20850*	
	E	*20850*	U.S. - Utah *20850*	
E	*Astragalus osterhoutii* M.E. Jones *20850, 14845*			
	E	*20850*	U.S. - Colorado (Grand Co.) *20850*	
R	*Astragalus ovalis* Boiss. & Bal. *12840*			
	R	*12840*	Turkey *12840*	
R	*Astragalus ovatus* DC. *12840*			
	R	*12840*	Turkey *12840*	
R	*Astragalus ovinus* Boiss. *12840*			
	R	*12840*	Turkey *12840*	
R	*Astragalus oxypterus* A. Boriss.			
	R		Asiatic U.S.S.R. *6930*	
R	*Astragalus paecilanthus* Boiss. & Heldr. *12840*			
	R	*12840*	Turkey *12840*	
I	*Astragalus pallescens* M.Bieb. *20171*			
	I		former European USSR	
V	*Astragalus panamintensis* Sheldon *20850*			
	I	*20850*	U.S. - California *20850*	
R	*Astragalus panduratus* Bunge *12840*			
	R	*12840*	Turkey *12840*	
E	*Astragalus papasianus* O. Schwarz *12840*			
	E	*12840*	Turkey *12840*	
V	*Astragalus pardalinus* (Rydb.) Barneby *20850*			
	V	*20850*	U.S. - Utah *20850*	
R	*Astragalus patnosicus* Chamb. & Matth. *12840*			
	R	*12840*	Turkey *12840*	
R	*Astragalus paysonii* (Rydb.) Barneby *20850*			
	R	*20850*	U.S. - Idaho *20850*	
	V	*20850*	U.S. - Wyoming *20850*	
R	*Astragalus peckii* Piper *20850*			
	R	*20850*	U.S. - Oregon *20850*	
R	*Astragalus perianus* Barneby *20850*			
	R	*20850*	U.S. - Utah *20850*	
E	*Astragalus peterfii* Jáv. *17823, 20171*			
	E	*19949*	Romania *20631*	
V	*Astragalus phoenix* Barneby *20850*			
	V	*20850*	U.S. - Nevada *20850*	
R	*Astragalus phrygius* Sirj. *12840*			
	R	*12840*	Turkey *12840*	
Ex/E	*Astragalus physocalyx* Fisch. *8000, 20171*			
	Ex/E	*5204*	Bulgaria (Southern - two unconfirmed sites) *5204*	
E	*Astragalus pinonis* M.E. Jones *20850*			
	I	*20850*	U.S. - Arizona *20850*	
	I	*20850*	U.S. - Nevada *20850*	
	E	*20850*	U.S. - Utah *20850*	
E	*Astragalus piscator* Barneby & Welsh *20850*			
	E	*20850*	U.S. - Colorado *20850*	
	E	*20850*	U.S. - Utah *20850*	
R	*Astragalus plumosus* Willd. var. *nitens* (Freyn & Birnm.) Chamb. & Matt *12840*			
	R	*12840*	Turkey *12840*	
R	*Astragalus polemoniacus* Bunge *12840*			
	R	*12840*	Turkey *12840*	
V	*Astragalus porrectus* S.Watson *20850*			

V		20850 U.S. - Nevada 20850	

E *Astragalus preussii* A.Gray var. *cutleri* Barneby 20850

E   20850 U.S. - Utah 20850

V *Astragalus preussii* A.Gray var. *laxiflorus* Gray 20850

I   20850 U.S. - Arizona 20850
E   20850 U.S. - California 20850
I   20850 U.S. - Nevada 20850
Ex/E 20850 U.S. - Utah 20850

E *Astragalus proimanthus* Barneby 20850

E   20850 U.S. - Wyoming 20850

V *Astragalus pseudiodanthus* Barneby 20850

V   20850 U.S. - California 20850
V   20850 U.S. - Nevada 20850

R *Astragalus pseudocaspicus* Fischer 12840

R   12840 Turkey 12840

Ex *Astragalus pseudocylindraceus* Bornm. 12840

Ex   12840 Turkey 12840

V *Astragalus pseudopurpureus* Gusul. 17823, 20171

V   19949 Romania 20631

R *Astragalus pterocarpus* S.Watson 20850

R   20850 U.S. - Nevada 20850

R *Astragalus ptilodes* Boiss.

R   Greece

V *Astragalus pulsiferae* A.Gray var. *pulsiferae* 20850

V   20850 U.S. - California 20850
I   20850 U.S. - Nevada 20850

E *Astragalus pulsiferae* A.Gray var. *suksdorfii* (T.J. Howell) Barneby 20850

E   20850 U.S. - California 20850
I   20850 U.S. - Nevada 20850
E   20850 U.S. - Washington 20850

R *Astragalus punae* I.M. Johnston 16336

R   16336 Argentina 16336
R   20176 Argentina - Jujuy 20176
R   20176 Argentina - Salta 20176

R *Astragalus puniceus* (Greene) Barneby var. *gertrudis* (Greene) Barneby 20850

R   20850 U.S. - New Mexico 20850

R *Astragalus pycnocephalus* Fischer var. *seytunensis* (Bunge) Chamb. 12840

R   12840 Turkey 12840

R *Astragalus pycnostachyus* A.Gray 20850

I   20850 U.S. - California 20850

Ex/E *Astragalus pycnostachyus* A.Gray var. *lanosissimus* (Rydb.) Munz & McBurney ex Munz 20850

Ex/E 20850 U.S. - California 20850

R *Astragalus pycnostachyus* A.Gray var. *pycnostachyus* 20850

I   20850 U.S. - California 20850

R *Astragalus racemosus* Pursh var. *treleasei* C.L. Porter 20850

V   20850 U.S. - Utah 20850
E   20850 U.S. - Wyoming 20850

R *Astragalus rafaelensis* M.E. Jones 20850

E   20850 U.S. - Colorado 20850
R   20850 U.S. - Utah 20850

R *Astragalus ramicaudex* Chamb. 12840

R   12840 Turkey 12840

E *Astragalus raphaelis* Ferro 18264

E   20738 Italy - Sicily 18264

R *Astragalus rarissimus* Popov

R   former USSR 6930

V *Astragalus rattanii* Gray var. *jepsonianus* Barneby 20850

V   20850 U.S. - California 20850

E *Astragalus ravenii* Barneby 20850

E   20850 U.S. - California 20850

R *Astragalus rechingeri* Sirj. 12840

R   12840 Turkey 12840

I *Astragalus reduncus* Pall. 20171

I   former European USSR 8000

R *Astragalus reflexus* Torr. & Gray 20850

R   20850 U.S. - Texas 20850

E *Astragalus remotus* (M.E. Jones) Barneby 20850

E   20850 U.S. - Nevada 20850

R *Astragalus renzii* Huber-Mor. 12840

R   12840 Turkey 12840

V *Astragalus riparius* Barneby 20850

Ex   20850 U.S. - Idaho 20850
V   20850 U.S. - Washington 20850

E *Astragalus robbinsii* (Oakes) A.Gray var. *fernaldii* (Rydb.) Barneby 20850, 15810

E   20850 Canada - Labrador 20850
I   20850 Canada - New Brunswick 20850
E   20850 Canada - Newfoundland 20850
E   20850 Canada - Quebec 20850

V *Astragalus robbinsii* (Oakes) A.Gray var. *harringtonii* (Rydb.) Barneby 20850

V   20850 U.S. - Alaska 20850

E *Astragalus robbinsii* (Oakes) A.Gray var. *jesupii* Egglest. & Sheldon 20850

E   20850 U.S. - New Hampshire 20850
E   20850 U.S. - Vermont (Hartland) 20850

V *Astragalus robbinsii* (Oakes) A.Gray var. *occidentalis* S.Watson 20850

I   20850 Canada - Alberta 20850
I   20850 U.S. - Idaho 20850
V   20850 U.S. - Nevada 20850
I   20850 U.S. - Oregon 20850

Ex *Astragalus robbinsii* (Oakes) A.Gray var. *robbinsii* 20850

Ex   20850 U.S. - Vermont 20850

R *Astragalus robertianus* Kit Tan & Sorger 12840

R   12840 Turkey 12840

V *Astragalus roemeri* Simonk. 17823, 20171

V   19949 Romania 20631

R *Astragalus roseocalycinus* Matt. 12840

R   12840 Turkey 12840

I *Astragalus rubellus* Gontsch. 5942

I   5942 Kyrgyzstan 5942

R *Astragalus rubtzovii* Boriss. 5942

R   5942 Kazakhstan (eastern) 5942

V *Astragalus rusbyi* Greene 20850

I   20850 U.S. - Arizona 20850

E *Astragalus sabulosus* M.E. Jones 20850

E   20850 U.S. - Utah 20850

R *Astragalus sachanevii* Sirj. 12840

R   12840 Turkey 12840

V	*Astragalus saurinus* Barneby 20850	
	I	20850 U.S. - Colorado 20850
	V	20850 U.S. - Utah 20850
R	*Astragalus scabrifolius* Boiss. 12840	
	R	12840 Turkey 12840
R	*Astragalus scaphoides* (M.E. Jones) Rydb. 20850	
	R	20850 U.S. - Idaho 20850
	E	20850 U.S. - Montana 20850
E	*Astragalus schmolliae* C.L. Porter 20850	
	E	20850 U.S. - Colorado 20850
V	*Astragalus sepultipes* (Barneby) Barneby 20850	
	I	20850 U.S. - California 20850
R	*Astragalus serenoi* (Kuntze) Sheldon var. *shockleyi* (M.E. Jones) Barneby 20850	
	I	20850 U.S. - California 20850
	V	20850 U.S. - Nevada 20850
V	*Astragalus serenoi* (Kuntze) Sheldon var. *sordescens* Barneby 20850	
	V	20850 U.S. - Nevada 20850
E	*Astragalus serpens* M.E. Jones 20850	
	E	20850 U.S. - Utah 20850
R	*Astragalus sesquiflorus* S.Watson 20850	
	I	20850 U.S. - Arizona 20850
	E	20850 U.S. - Colorado 20850
	R	20850 U.S. - Utah 20850
E	*Astragalus setosulus* Gontsch. 20171	
	E	20655 Ukraine - Crimea 20653
R	*Astragalus seydishehiricus* Kit Tan & Ocakverdi 12840	
	R	12840 Turkey 12840
V	*Astragalus shevockii* Barneby 20850	
	V	20850 U.S. - California 20850
R	*Astragalus shortianus* Nutt. 20850	
	I	20850 U.S. - Colorado 20850
	E	20850 U.S. - Nebraska 20850
	V	20850 U.S. - New Mexico 20850
	R	20850 U.S. - Wyoming 20850
E	*Astragalus sikokianus* Nakai 10572	
	E	10572 Japan 10572
R	*Astragalus siliceus* Barneby 20850	
	R	20850 U.S. - New Mexico 20850
R	*Astragalus simplicifolius* (Nutt.) Gray 20850	
	R	20850 U.S. - Wyoming 20850
E	*Astragalus sinuatus* Piper 20850	
	I	20850 Canada - British Columbia 20850
	I	20850 U.S. - Idaho 20850
	I	20850 U.S. - Oregon 20850
	E	20850 U.S. - Washington 20850
V	*Astragalus sophoroides* M.E. Jones 20850	
	I	20850 U.S. - Arizona 20850
R	*Astragalus sorgerae* Huber-Mor. & Chamb. 12840	
	R	12840 Turkey 12840
R	*Astragalus soxmaniorum* Lundell 20850	
	V	20850 U.S. - Arkansas 20850
	V	20850 U.S. - Louisiana 20850
	R	20850 U.S. - Texas 20850
R	*Astragalus sparsipilis* Huber-Mor. & Chamb. 12840	
	R	12840 Turkey 12840
R	*Astragalus stenosemioides* Bornm. ex Chamb. & Matt. 12840	
	R	12840 Turkey 12840
V	*Astragalus straturensis* M.E. Jones 20850	

	I	20850 U.S. - Arizona 20850
	I	20850 U.S. - Nevada 20850
	V	20850 U.S. - Utah 20850
R	*Astragalus striatiflorus* M.E. Jones 20850	
	V	20850 U.S. - Arizona 20850
	V	20850 U.S. - Utah 20850
R	*Astragalus stridii* Kit Tan 12840	
	R	12840 Turkey 12840
R	*Astragalus subcinereus* A.Gray 20850	
	I	20850 U.S. - Arizona 20850
	I	20850 U.S. - Nevada 20850
	I	20850 U.S. - Utah 20850
R	*Astragalus suberosus* var. *hartmannii* 18271	
	R	20710 Cyprus (dry fields west of Nicosia) 18271
R	*Astragalus subternatus* Pavlov	
	R	former USSR 6930
R	*Astragalus syringus* Chamb 12840	
	R	12840 Turkey 12840
R	*Astragalus tachdirtensis* Andreanszky 12346	
	R	Morocco 12346
I	*Astragalus taipaishanensis* Y.C. Ho & S.B. Ho 11815	
	I	China - Shaanxi 11815
R	*Astragalus talasseus* Boiss. & Bal. 12840	
	R	12840 Turkey 12840
V	*Astragalus tanaiticus* K.Koch 11552, 20171	
	V	11552 Russian Federation (western) 11552
R	*Astragalus taochius* Woron. 12840	
	R	12840 Turkey 12840
R	*Astragalus tatlii* H. Pesmen 12840	
	R	12840 Turkey 12840
V	*Astragalus taubertianus* E. A. Durand & Barratte 12346	
	V	Libya 12346
R	*Astragalus tegetarioides* M.E. Jones 20850	
	E	20850 U.S. - California 20850
	R	20850 U.S. - Oregon 20850
I	*Astragalus tekutjevii* Gontsch.	
	I	former USSR 6930
E	*Astragalus tener* A.Gray 20850	
	I	20850 U.S. - California 20850
E	*Astragalus tener* A.Gray var. *ferrisiae* A. Liston 20850	
	E	20850 U.S. - California 20850
E	*Astragalus tener* A.Gray var. *tener* 20850	
	E	20850 U.S. - California 20850
E	*Astragalus tener* A.Gray var. *titi* (Eastw.) Barneby 20850	
	E	20850 U.S. - California 20850
R	*Astragalus tennesseensis* A.Gray ex Chapman 20850	
	E	20850 U.S. - Alabama 20850
	E	20850 U.S. - Illinois 20850
	Ex	20850 U.S. - Indiana 20850
	I	20850 U.S. - Missouri 20850
	R	20850 U.S. - Tennessee 20850
R	*Astragalus thiebaetii* Eig 12840	
	R	12840 Turkey 12840
V	*Astragalus tiehmii* Barneby 20850	
	R	20850 U.S. - Nevada 20850
R	*Astragalus tmoleus* Boiss. var. *tmoleus* 12840	
	R	12840 Turkey 12840

R **Astragalus tokachiensis** Yamaz. & Kadota *10572*
   R   *10572* Japan *10572*

R **Astragalus tokatensis** Fischer *12840*
   R   *12840* Turkey *12840*

V **Astragalus toquimanus** Barneby *20850*
   V   *20850* U.S. - Nevada *20850*

R **Astragalus trachytricus** Bunge *12840*
   R   *12840* Turkey *12840*

R **Astragalus transjordanicus** G. Samuelsson ex Rech.f.
   R   Jordan

V **Astragalus traskiae** Eastw. *20850*
   V   *20850* U.S. - California *20850*

R **Astragalus tremolsianus** Pau *8000, 20171*
   R   *20874* Spain (Sierra de Gádor) *11496*

E **Astragalus tricarinatus** A.Gray *20850*
   E   *20850* U.S. - California *20850*

R **Astragalus trichopodus** (Nutt.) Gray *20850*
   I   *20850* U.S. - California *20850*

R **Astragalus trifoliastrum** Huber-Mor. & Matt. *12840*
   R   *12840* Turkey *12840*

R **Astragalus troglodytus** S.Watson *20850*
   R   *20850* U.S. - Arizona *20850*

R **Astragalus tweedyi** Canby *20850*
   R   *20850* U.S. - Oregon *20850*
   V   *20850* U.S. - Washington *20850*

E **Astragalus tyghensis** M.E. Peck *20850*
   E   *20850* U.S. - Oregon *20850*

R **Astragalus uhlwormianus** Freyn & Bornm. *12840*
   R   *12840* Turkey *12840*

R **Astragalus ulashensis** Huber-Mor. & Reese *12840*
   R   *12840* Turkey *12840*

V **Astragalus uncialis** Barneby *20850*
   E   *20850* U.S. - Nevada *20850*
   E   *20850* U.S. - Utah *20850*

R **Astragalus vanulosus** Boiss. *12840*
   R   *12840* Turkey *12840*

R **Astragalus velenowskyi** Nab. *12840*
   R   *12840* Turkey *12840*

V **Astragalus verrucosus** Moris *8000, 20171*
   V   *18264* Italy - Sardinia (western) *17891*

R **Astragalus vesicarius** L. ssp. *vesicarius* (Waldst.
   et Kit.) *8000, 20171*
   R   *19321* Slovakia *19321*

V **Astragalus vexilliflexus** Sheldon var. *nubilus*
   Barneby *20850*
   V   *20850* U.S. - Idaho *20850*

R **Astragalus victoriae** Podlech-Ayerer-Kirchhoff *12840*
   R   *12840* Turkey *12840*

R **Astragalus viridiflorus** A. Boriss.
   R   former USSR *6930*

R **Astragalus voronovianus** (Boriss.) Boriss. *12840*
   R   *12840* Turkey *12840*

V **Astragalus wardii** A.Gray *20850*
   V   *20850* U.S. - Utah *20850*

R **Astragalus wartoensis** Boiss. *12840*
   R   *12840* Turkey *12840*

E **Astragalus webberi** A.Gray ex Brewer & S.Watson *20850*
   E   *20850* U.S. - California *20850*

R **Astragalus weilleri** Emb. et al. *12346*
   R   Morocco *12346*

V **Astragalus welshii** Barneby *20850*
   V   *20850* U.S. - Utah *20850*

R **Astragalus wetherillii** M.E. Jones *20850*
   R   *20850* U.S. - Colorado *20850*
   Ex/E *20850* U.S. - Utah *20850*

R **Astragalus wilmottianus** Stoj. *5204, 20171*
   R   *5204*   Bulgaria (West) *5204*

R **Astragalus wittmannii** Barneby *20850*
   R   *20850* U.S. - New Mexico *20850*

V **Astragalus xiphoides** (Barneby) Barneby *20850*
   V   *20850* U.S. - Arizona *20850*

R **Astragalus yamamotoi** Miyabe & Tatew. *10572*
   R   *10572* Japan *10572*

R **Astragalus yoder-williamsii** Barneby *20850*
   R   *20850* U.S. - Idaho *20850*
   E   *20850* U.S. - Nevada *20850*
   I   *20850* U.S. - Oregon *20850*

R **Astragalus yueksekovae** Matthews *12840*
   R   *12840* Turkey *12840*

R **Astragalus zahlbruckneri** Hand.-Mazz. *12840*
   R   *12840* Turkey *12840*

V **Astragalus zingeri** Korsh. *8000, 20171*
   V   *11552* Russian Federation (western) *11552*

R **Ateleia galzioveana** Baill. *20883*
   I   *20883* Argentina *20883*
   I   *20883* Brazil *20883*
   V   *20883* Paraguay *20883*

I **Ateleia gummifera** D. Dietr. *11840*
   I   *20990* Cuba (Oriente; Matanzas) *11840*

I **Ateleia popenoei** Correll
   I   *4650*   Bahamas *4650*

V **Baikiaea ghesquiereana** J. Léonard *19531*
   V   *20885* Tanzania (Rufiji & Kilwa Districts)
          19531

V **Balsamocarpon brevifolium** D. Clos *11748*
   V   *19534* Chile *11748*

R **Baphia cordifolia** Harms *19531*
   R   Tanzania (Mpwapwa, Iringa) *19531*

I **Baphia keniensis** Brummitt *6073*
   I   *20057* Kenya (Fort Hall) *7959*

V **Baphia pauloi** Brummitt *19531*
   V   *20885* Tanzania (Uluguru mountains) *5926*

V **Baphia puguensis** Brummitt *19531*
   V   *5926*   Tanzania (Pugu & Kazimzumbwi) *5926*

E **Baptisia arachnifera** Duncan *20850*
   E   *20850* U.S. - Georgia *20850*

V **Baptisia calycosa** Canby *20850*
   I   *20850* U.S. - Florida *20850*

E **Baptisia calycosa** Canby var. *calycosa* *20850*
   E   *20850* U.S. - Florida *20850*

E **Baptisia calycosa** Canby var. *villosa*
   Canby *20850*
   E   *20850* U.S. - Florida *20850*

R **Baptisia megacarpa** Chapman ex Torr. & Gray *20850*
   V   *20850* U.S. - Alabama *20850*
   V   *20850* U.S. - Florida *20850*
   E   *20850* U.S. - Georgia *20850*

R **Baptisia simplicifolia** Croom *20850*

	R	20850 U.S. - Florida *20850*
R	*Bauhinia acuruana* Moric. *20883*	
	I	20883 Brazil *20883*
	V	20883 Paraguay *20883*
R	*Bauhinia bowkeri* Harv. *20604*	
	R	20604 South Africa - Cape Province (Transkei) *20604*
R	*Bauhinia clemensiorum* Merr. *6057*	
	R	Vietnam
R	*Bauhinia erythrocalyx* Wunderlin *12055*	
	R	12055 Guatemala *12055*
	R	12055 Mexico *12055*
E	*Bauhinia eucosma* Blake *20883*	
	I	20883 Panama *20883*
R	*Bauhinia fryxellii* Wunderlin *12055*	
	R	12055 Mexico - San Luis Potosi *12055*
V	*Bauhinia guaranitica* Lindm. *20883*	
	V	20883 Paraguay *20883*
R	*Bauhinia heterandra* Benth. *20883*	
	I	20883 Brazil *20883*
	R	20883 Paraguay *20883*
R	*Bauhinia involucrans* Gagnepain *6057*	
	R	Vietnam *6057*
R	*Bauhinia jucunda* Brandegee *12055*	
	R	12055 Mexico - Veracruz *12055*
E	*Bauhinia ligulata* Pitt. *20883*	
	I	20883 Panama *20883*
V	*Bauhinia loeseneriana* Harms *20885*	
	V	20885 Tanzania (south-east) *20885*
V	*Bauhinia lunarioides* Gray ex S.Watson *20883*	
	E	20850 U.S. - Texas *20850*
	V	20883 Mexico *20883*
R	*Bauhinia mollis* (Bong.) Walp. *20883*	
	I	20883 Brazil *20883*
	R	20883 Paraguay *20883*
E	*Bauhinia mombassae* Vatke *20057*	
	E	20057 Kenya *7959*
E	*Bauhinia obovata* Blake *20883*	
	I	20883 Panama *20883*
R	*Bauhinia pansamalana* J.D. Smith *9004*	
	R	12055 Guatemala *9004*
	R	12055 Mexico - Chiapas *9004*
I	*Bauhinia perkinsiae* Merr. *21172, 13833*	
	I	13833 Philippines (low altitude) *13833*
R	*Bauhinia reflexa* Schery *20883*	
	V	20883 Panama *20883*
	I	20883 Colombia *20883*
R	*Bauhinia rufa* (Bong.) Steud. *20883*	
	I	20883 Brazil *20883*
	R	20883 Paraguay *20883*
E	*Bauhinia storkii* (Rose) Schery *20883*	
	I	20883 Panama *20883*
E	*Behaimia roigii* Borh. *5607*	
	E	19105 Cuba (Matanzas) *5607*
I	*Belairia nipensis* Urban *5607*	
	I	19105 Cuba (Santiago de Cuba; Holguin) *5607*
I	*Belairia parvifolia* Britton *5607*	
	I	19105 Cuba (Granma) *5607*
V	*Bembicidium cubense* Rydb. *5607*	
	V	19105 Cuba (Guantanamo) *5607*

I	*Benedictella benoistii* Maire	
	I	Morocco
R	*Bergeronia sericea* Micheli *20883*	
	I	20883 Argentina *20883*
	R	20883 Paraguay *20883*
V	*Berlinia occidentalis* Keay *12346*	
	V	20858 Côte d'Ivoire *20274*
	V	20858 Ghana *20274*
	V	20858 Liberia *20274*
	V	20858 Sierra Leone *20274*
R	*Bossiaea arenicola* J.H.Ross *20681*	
	R	20681 Australia - Queensland *20681*
V	*Bossiaea oligosperma* A.T.Lee *20681*	
	V	20681 Australia - New South Wales *20681*
E	*Bowringia discolor* J.B. Hall *6072*	
	E	6072 Ghana *6072*
V	*Brachysema modestum* Crisp ms. *20681*	
	V	20681 Australia - Western Australia *20681*
E	*Brachysema papilio* Crisp ms. *20681*	
	E	20681 Australia - Western Australia *20681*
R	*Brachysema subcordatum* Benth. *20681*	
	R	20681 Australia - Western Australia *20681*
R	*Brachysema uniflorum* R.Br. ex Benth. *20681*	
	R	20681 Australia - Northern Territory *20681*
R	*Brachystegia bequaertii* De Wild. *12346*	
	R	19358 Zaire (Haut-Katanga) *19358*
R	*Brodriguesia santosii* Cowan *16692*	
	R	16692 Brazil - Bahia *16692*
V	*Brongniartia minutifolia* S.Watson *20883, 20850, 8058*	
	E	20850 U.S. - Texas *20850*
	I	20883 Mexico *20883*
E	*Brongniartia vazquezii* O. Dorado *20883*	
	I	20883 Mexico *20883*
E	*Browneopsis excelsa* Pitt. *20883, 9006*	
	I	20883 Panama *20883*
V	*Bussea eggelingii* Verdc. *19532*	
	V	20885 Tanzania (Lindi) *19532*
V	*Bussea xylocarpa* (Sprague) Sprague & Craib *12346*	
	V	20886 Mozambique (Zambezi river valley) *20886*
I	*Caesalpinia anacantha* Urban *5642*	
	I	Dominican Republic (Isla Beata) *5642* Haiti (Morne à Cabrits) *21008*
I	*Caesalpinia barahonenensis* Urban *5642*	
	I	Dominican Republic (Barahona) *5642* Haiti (Marigot, Miragoane, Port-à-Piment) *21008*
V	*Caesalpinia brachycarpa* (Gray) Fisher *20850*	
	I	20850 U.S. - New Mexico *20850*
	V	20850 U.S. - Texas *20850*
R	*Caesalpinia bracteata* Germish. *20604*	
	R	20604 South Africa - Cape Province *20604*
I	*Caesalpinia buchii* Urban *5642*	
	I	Dominican Republic (Azua) *5642* Haiti (Lago de Fondo to Gonaïves, Hinche, Isla Gonave) *21008*
E	*Caesalpinia caymanensis* Millsp. *19712*	
	E	19434 Cayman Is. (North of George town on Grand Cayman.) *19434*
V	*Caesalpinia culebrae* (Britt. & Wilson) Alain *20883, 8058*	
	I	20883 Puerto Rico (Culebra) *20883*

V　　*Caesalpinia dauensis* Thulin *20057*
　　　V　*20057*　Kenya *20057*

V　　*Caesalpinia echinata* Lam. *17079*
　　　E　*17746*　Brazil - Alagoas *17079*
　　　E　*17746*　Brazil - Bahia *17079*
　　　V　*21011*　Brazil - Espirito Santo *21011*
　　　V　*21011*　Brazil - Minas Gerais *21011*
　　　V　*21011*　Brazil - Paraiba *21011*
　　　E　*17746*　Brazil - Pernambuco *17079*
　　　E　*17079*　Brazil - Rio de Janeiro *17079*
　　　E　*17746*　Brazil - Rio Grande do Norte *17079*
　　　V　*21011*　Brazil - Sergipe *21011*

R　　*Caesalpinia floribunda* Tul. *20883*
　　　I　*20883*　Argentina *20883*
　　　I　*20883*　Bolivia *20883*
　　　I　*20883*　Brazil *20883*
　　　R　*20883*　Paraguay *20883*

E　　*Caesalpinia guanensis* (Britton) Leon *5607*
　　　E　*19105*　Cuba (Pinar del Rio) *5607*

R　　*Caesalpinia hauthalii* Harms in Kuntze *20883*
　　　I　*20883*　Argentina *20883*
　　　R　*20883*　Paraguay *20883*

E　　*Caesalpinia hermeliae* Leon *5607*
　　　E　*19105*　Cuba (Holguin) *5607*

E　　*Caesalpinia hornei* Britton *5607*
　　　E　*19105*　Cuba (Ciego de Avila) *5607*

E　　*Caesalpinia kavaiensis* Mann *20850, 14209*
　　　E　*20850*　U.S. - Hawaii *20850*

E　　*Caesalpinia monensis* Britt. *20883*
　　　I　*20883*　Puerto Rico *20883*

V　　*Caesalpinia phyllanthoides* Standl. *20883, 20850*
　　　E　*20850*　U.S. - Texas *20850*
　　　I　*20883*　Mexico *20883*

E　　*Caesalpinia portoricensis* (Britt. & Wilson)
　　　Alain *20883, 10197*
　　　I　*20883*　Puerto Rico *20883*

V　　*Caesalpinia repens* Eastw. *20850*
　　　I　*20850*　U.S. - Colorado *20850*
　　　V　*20850*　U.S. - Utah *20850*

R　　*Caesalpinia robusta* (C.White) Pedley *20681*
　　　R　*20681*　Australia - Queensland *20681*

E　　*Cajanus mareebensis* (S.Reyn. & Pedley) Maesen *20681*
　　　E　*20681*　Australia - Queensland *20681*

I　　*Cajanus sericus* (Benth.) Maesen
　　　I　　　India - Andhra Pradesh (Vizakapatanam Hills)
　　　I　　　India - Karnataka (Concan)

I　　*Calispepla aegacanthoides* Vved. *5942*
　　　I　*5942*　Uzbekistan *5942*

R　　*Calliandra biflora* Tharp *20883, 20850, 19002*
　　　R　*20850*　U.S. - Texas *20850*
　　　I　*20883*　Mexico *20883*

V　　*Calliandra chilensis* Benth. *5598*
　　　V　*19534*　Chile *5598*

E　　*Calliandra comosa* (Sw.) Benth. *20883*
　　　E　*20883*　Jamaica *20883*

R　　*Calliandra erythrocephala* H. Hern. & M. Sousa *20883*
　　　I　*20883*　Mexico *20883*

R　　*Calliandra gilbertii* Thulin & Hunde *20057*
　　　R　*20057*　Kenya *20057*
　　　R　*20057*　Somalia *20057*

I　　*Calliandra nervosa* (Urban) Urban & Ekman *5642*
　　　I　　　Dominican Republic (Los Haitises) *5642*

　　　　Haiti (south-west peninsula) *21008*

E　　*Calliandra paniculata* Adams *20883, 13336*
　　　E　*20883*　Jamaica *20883*

V　　*Calliandra physocalyx* H. Hern. & M. Sousa *20883*
　　　I　*20883*　Mexico *20883*

R　　*Calliandra pilosa* (Bert. ex DC.) Urb. *20883*
　　　R　*20883*　Jamaica *20883*

R　　*Calliandra prostrata* Benth. *18200*
　　　R　*9446*　Peru *18200*

R　　*Calliandra quetzal* J.D. Smith *9004*
　　　R　*9004*　Guatemala *9004*

R　　*Calophaca sericea* B. Fedtsch. ex A. Boriss.
　　　R　　　former USSR *6930*

I　　*Calopogonium domingense* Urban & Ekman *5642*
　　　I　　　Dominican Republic (Bonao) *5642*

R　　*Calpurnia robinioides* (DC.) E.Mey. nom.
　　　illegit. *20604*
　　　R　*20604*　Lesotho *20604*
　　　I　*20604*　South Africa - Cape Province (Transkei) *20604*
　　　I　*20604*　South Africa - Orange Free State *20604*

V　　*Calpurnia woodii* Schinz *20604, 12346*
　　　V　*20604*　South Africa - Natal *20604*

I　　*Calycotome grosii* Pau & Font Quer
　　　I　　　Morocco

R　　*Campsiandra ferruginea* Stergios *21251*
　　　R　*21251*　Venezuela *21251*

E　　*Canavalia favieri* Nielsen *20802*
　　　E　*20893*　New Caledonia *20802*

R　　*Canavalia kauaiensis* Sauer *20850, 14209*
　　　R　*20850*　U.S. - Hawaii (Kaua`i) *20850*

E　　*Canavalia microsperma* Urban *5607*
　　　E　*19105*　Cuba (Pinar del Rio) *5607*

E　　*Canavalia molokaiensis* O.& I. Deg. & Sauer *20850, 14209*
　　　E　*20850*　U.S. - Hawaii (eastern Molokai) *20850*

E　　*Canavalia napaliensis* St. John *20850, 14209*
　　　E　*20850*　U.S. - Hawaii *20850*

E　　*Canavalia pubescens* Hook. & Arn. *20850, 14209*
　　　E　*20850*　U.S. - Hawaii *20850*

I　　*Canavalia raiateensis* J.Moore *20845*
　　　I　*20845*　French Polynesia - Society Is. (Raiatea) *20845*

R　　*Caragana leiocalycina* (Huber-Mor.) Huber-Mor. *12840*
　　　R　*12840*　Turkey *12840*

I　　*Carmichaelia arenaria* Simpson *19305*
　　　I　*19305*　New Zealand - South Is. *19305*

R　　*Carmichaelia compacta* Petrie *19305*
　　　R　*19305*　New Zealand - South Is. *19305*

R　　*Carmichaelia curta* Petrie *19305*
　　　R　*19305*　New Zealand - South Is. *19305*

R　　*Carmichaelia exsul* F. Muell. *14223*
　　　R　*14223*　Australia - NSW - Lord Howe Is. *14223*

R　　*Carmichaelia hollowayi* Simpson *19305*
　　　R　*19305*　New Zealand - South Is. *19305*

E　　*Carmichaelia kirkii* Hook.f. *86*
　　　E　*19305*　New Zealand - South Is. *19305*

R　　*Carmichaelia lacustris* Simpson
　　　R　　　New Zealand - South Is.

I **Carmichaelia nigrans** Simpson *19305*
   I   *19305* New Zealand - South Is. *19305*

Ex **Carmichaelia prona** Kirk *19305*
   Ex   *19305* New Zealand - South Is. *19305*

R **Carmichaelia williamsii** Kirk *86*
   R   *19305* New Zealand - North Is. *19305*

R **Cassia aculeata** Pohl ex Benth. in Mart. *20883*
   I   *20883* Brazil *20883*
   R   *20883* Paraguay *20883*

I **Cassia acunae** Borh. *5607*
   I   *19105* Cuba (Pinar del Rio) *5607*

I **Cassia angustisiliqua** Lam. *5642*
   I   Dominican Republic (Bayahibe) *5642*
              Haiti *21008*

E **Cassia artensis** (Montr.) Beauv. *20893*
   E   *20893* New Caledonia *20893*

R **Cassia brewsteri** (F.Muell.) F.Muell. ex Benth. var. **marksiana** Bailey *20681*
   I   *20681* Australia - New South Wales *20681*
   I   *20681* Australia - Queensland *20681*

I **Cassia bucherae** (Mold.) Leon *5607*
   I   Cuba (Holguin) *5607*

R **Cassia cernua** Balbis *20883*
   I   *20883* Brazil *20883*
   R   *20883* Paraguay *20883*

I **Cassia diffusissima** (Britton) Leon *5607*
   I   Cuba (Pinar del Rio) *5607*

V **Cassia esmeraldensis** Alain *5607*
   V   *19105* Cuba (Holguin) *5607*

I **Cassia exunguis** Urban *15106*
   I   *15106* Puerto Rico *8058*

E **Cassia fikifiki** Aubrev. & Pellegrin *20887*
   E   *20887* Côte d'Ivoire (south-west) *20887*

R **Cassia garabiensis** Hosok. *20511*
   R   *20511* Taiwan *20511*

V **Cassia guaranitica** Chodat & Hassler *20883*
   V   *20883* Paraguay *20883*

R **Cassia humifusa** Brenan *7959*
   R   Kenya *7959*

V **Cassia mirabilis** Urban *8058*
   V   *19002* Puerto Rico *8058*

I **Cassia niqueroensis** Urban & Ekman *5607*
   I   *5607* Cuba *5607*

R **Cassia queenslandica** C.White *20681*
   R   *20681* Australia - Queensland *20681*

E **Cassia roigii** (Britton) Leon *5607*
   E   *19105* Cuba (Pinar del Rio) *5607*

E **Cassia scleroxyla** Britton *5607*
   E   *19105* Cuba (Santiago de Cuba) *5607*

R **Cassia smaragdina** Macf. *20883*
   R   *20883* Jamaica *20883*

R **Cassia sophora** L. var. **penghuana** Y.C.Liu & F.Y.Lu *20511*
   R   *20511* Taiwan *20511*

E **Cassia spiniflora** Burk. *20883*
   E   *20883* Paraguay *20883*

R **Cassia splendida** Vog. *20883*
   I   *20883* Brazil *20883*
   R   *20883* Paraguay *20883*

V **Cassia turquinae** (Britton) Leon *5607*
   V   *19105* Cuba (Granma; Santiago de Cuba) *5607*

R **Cassia velutina** Vog. *20883*
   I   *20883* Brazil *20883*
   V   *20883* Paraguay *20883*

E **Centrolobium yavizanum** Pitt. *20883, 9006*
   I   *19577* Panama *20883*

V **Centrosema arenicola** (Small) F.J. Herm. *20850*
   V   *20850* U.S. - Florida *20850*

R **Centrosema haitense** Urb. & Ekman *13336*
   R   *13336* Dominica *13336*
   R   *13336* Haiti *13336*
   V   *13336* Jamaica *13336*

Ex/E **Centrosema seymourianum** Fantz *9793*
   Ex/E   *11967* Nicaragua *9793*

I **Ceratonia oreothauma** Hillcoat, Lewis & Verdc. ssp. **oreothauma** *8757*
   I   *20146* Oman (Hajar Mts.) *20146*
   I   *20146* Yemen, Democratic (Hadramaut) *20146*

V **Ceratonia oreothauma** Hillc., G.P. Lewis & Verdc. ssp. **somalensis** Hillc., G.P. Lewis & Verdc. *8757*
   V   *20884* Somalia (north) *8757*

V **Chamaecrista deeringiana** Small & Pennell *20850*
   E   *20850* U.S. - Alabama *20850*
   I   *20850* U.S. - Florida *20850*
   Ex/E   *20850* U.S. - Georgia *20850*

R **Chamaecrista duboisii** (Stey.) Lock *12346*
   R   *19358* Zaire (Haut-Katanga) *19358*

E **Chamaecrista glandulosa** var. **mirabilis** (Pollard) Irwin & Barneby *20883*
   E   *20883* Puerto Rico *20883*

V **Chamaecrista lineata** (Pennell) Irwin & Barneby var. **keyensis** (Pennell) Irwin & Barneby *20850, 19737*
   V   *20850* U.S. - Florida (endemic to Florida Keys pine rocklands) *20850*

R **Chamaecrista oligosperma** (Benth.) Swain & Barneby *16692*
   R   *16692* Brazil - Bahia *16692*

I **Chamaecrista paralias** (Brenan) Lock *12346*
   I   Mozambique *7916*

R **Chamaecrista schmitzii** (Stey.) Lock *12346*
   R   *19358* Zaire (Haut-Katanga) *19358*

R **Chamaecrista swainsonii** (Benth.) Swain & Barneby *16692*
   R   *16692* Brazil - Bahia *16692*

R **Chamaecytisus anatolicus** *20618*
   R   *20618* Turkey *20618*

R **Chamaecytisus blockianus** (Pawl.) Klásk. *8000, 20171*
   R   former European USSR *8000*

R **Chamaecytisus cassius** (Boiss.) Rothm. *12840*
   R   *20618* Turkey *20618*

R **Chamaecytisus kovacevii** (Velen.) Rothm. *5204, 20171*
   R   *5204* Bulgaria (north) *5204*

E **Chamaecytisus nejceffii** (Urum.) Rothm. *8000, 20171*
   E   Bulgaria *19847*

R **Chamaecytisus paczoskii** (V.I.Krecz.) Klásk. *8000, 20171*
   R   former European USSR *8000*

R **Chamaecytisus podolicus** (Blocki) Klásk. *8000, 20171*
   R   former European USSR *8000*

R **Chamaecytisus skrobiszewskii** (Pacz.) Klásk. *8000, 20171*
    R   former European USSR *8000*

R **Chesneya elegans** Fomin *12840*
    R   *12840* Turkey *12840*

R **Chloroleucon chacoënse** (Burk.) Barneby & J.W.Grimes *21094*
    I   *20883* Argentina - Salta *21094*
    I   *20883* Bolivia (west) *21094*
    R   *20883* Paraguay (Chaco central) *21094*

E **Chordospartium muritai** Purdie *8489*
    E   *19305* New Zealand - South Is. (Marlborough) *20625*

V **Chordospartium stevensonii** Cheeseman *86*
    V   *19305* New Zealand - South Is. *19305*

V **Chorizema varium** Benth. *20681, 14223*
    V   *20681* Australia - Western Australia *14223*

R **Chronanthus orientalis** (lois) Heywood et Frodin *19873*
    R   *20618* Turkey *20618*

R **Cicer atlanticum** Maire *12346*
    R   Morocco *12346*

R **Cicer echinospermum** Davis *12840*
    R   *12840* Turkey *12840*

R **Cicer floribundum** Fenzl *12840*
    R   *12840* Turkey *12840*

R **Cicer graecum** Orph. ex Boiss. *20171*
    R   Greece

R **Cicer isauricum** Davis *12840*
    R   *12840* Turkey *12840*

R **Cicer reticulatum** Ladizinsky *12840*
    R   *12840* Turkey *12840*

E **Clianthus puniceus** (Don) Banks Sol. ex Lindley *10260*
    E   *19305* New Zealand - North Is. (Northland to Hawkes Bay) *13378*

R **Clitoria fragrans** Small *20850, 18134*
    R   *20850* U.S. - Florida (L. Wales Ridge) *20850*

R **Coelidium minimum** Granby *20604*
    R   *20604* South Africa - Cape Province *20604*

R **Coelidium obtusilobum** Granby *20604*
    R   *20604* South Africa - Cape Province *20604*

R **Coelidium vlokii** A.L.Schutte & B.-E.van Wyk *20604*
    R   *20604* South Africa - Cape Province *20604*

E **Cojoba chazutense** (Standley) L. Rico *18200*
    E   *9446* Peru *18200*

I **Colutea atabaevii** B. Fedtsch. *5942*
    I   *5942* Turkmenistan (Ashkhabad) *5942*

I **Colutea insularis** Browicz
    I   Greece

I **Colutea komarovii** Takht. *5942*
    I   *5942* Armenia *5942*

R **Colutea melanocalyx** Boiss. & Heldr. ssp. melanocalyx *12840*
    R   *20618* Turkey *20618*

E **Copaifera camibar** Poveda, Zamora & P.E. Sánchez *20883, 19943*
    E   *19943* Costa Rica *20883*

V **Copaifera chodatiana** Hassler *20883*
    V   *20883* Paraguay *20883*

R **Copaifera epunctata** Amshoff *8679*
    R   *8679* Suriname *8679*

V **Copaifera langsdorffii** var. **glabra** Benth. *20883*
    V   *20883* Paraguay *20883*

R **Copaifera langsdorffii** Desf. var. **langsdorffii** *20883*
    I   *20883* Argentina *20883*
    I   *20883* Bolivia *20883*
    I   *20883* Brazil *20883*
    R   *20883* Paraguay *20883*
    I   *20883* Venezuela *20883*

V **Copaifera panamensis** (Britt.) Standl. *20883, 9006*
    V   *19577* Panama *20883*

R **Cordeauxia edulis** Hemsley
    R   *20884* Ethiopia *20884*
    R   *20884* Somalia *20884*

R **Cordyla densiflora** Milne-Redh. *19532*
    R   *19532* Tanzania (Ruaha valley) *20921*

V **Cordyla haraka** Capuron *21038*
    ?   Madagascar (North East) *21038*

R **Cordyla somalensis** J.B.Gillett *12346*
    R   *20884* Somalia *12346*

V **Coursetia apantensis** M. Sousa *20883, 10162*
    I   *20883* Nicaragua *20883*

V **Coursetia elliptica** M. Sousa & Rudd *20883*
    I   *20883* Costa Rica *20883*
    I   *20883* Nicaragua *20883*

V **Coursetia glabella** (Gray) Lavin *20850*
    E   *20850* U.S. - Arizona *20850*
    ?   Mexico *18826*

E **Coursetia insomniifolia** Lavin *20883*
    E   *20883* Mexico *20883*

E **Coursetia oaxacensis** M. Sousa & V. Rudd *20883, 9742*
    I   *20883* Mexico *20883*
    ?   Mexico - Guerrero *9742*
    ?   Mexico - Oaxaca *9742*

E **Coursetia paucifoliolata** M. Sousa *20883, 10162*
    I   *20883* Nicaragua *20883*

E **Coursetia polyphylla** var. **acutifolia** Lavin & M. Sousa *20883, 9742*
    V   *11967* Nicaragua *20883*

E **Coursetia polyphylla** var. **breviloba** M. Sousa & Lavin *20883*
    I   *20883* Guatemala *20883*
    I   *20883* Honduras *20883*
    I   *20883* Nicaragua *20883*

R **Coursetia vicioides** (Nees & Mart.) Benth *16692*
    R   *16692* Brazil - Bahia *16692*

E **Coursetia weberbaueri** Harms *18200*
    E   *9446* Peru *18200*

V **Craibia atlantica** Dunn *20274*
    V   *20858* Cameroon *20274*
    V   *20858* Côte d'Ivoire *20274*
    V   *20858* Ghana *20274*
    V   *20858* Nigeria *7926*

I **Crotalaria adolfi** Harms *19531*
    I   *5926* Tanzania (Njombe & Rungwe) *19531*

E **Crotalaria avonensis** K.R. DeLaney & Wunderlin *20850, 17887*
    E   *20850* U.S. - Florida (L. Wales Ridge) *20850*

E **Crotalaria awasensis** Thulin *19704*

	E	19704	Ethiopia (Shewa Upland; Sidamo) *19704*

R   *Crotalaria ballyi* Polhill *7959*
R   Kenya *7959*

I   *Crotalaria bidiei* Gamble
I   India - Tamil Nadu (Wynaad, Nilgiri Hills)

E   *Crotalaria boudetii* Polhill *12346*
E   19704   Ethiopia (Harerge) *19704*

I   *Crotalaria bourneae* Fyson
I   India - Tamil Nadu

R   *Crotalaria chiayiana* Liu & Lu *20511*
R   20511   Taiwan *20511*

I   *Crotalaria clarkei* Gamble
I   India - Tamil Nadu

E   *Crotalaria clavata* Wight & Arn. *11494*
E   11494   India - Tamil Nadu *11494*

I   *Crotalaria conferta* Fyson
I   India - Tamil Nadu (Palani Hills, Madurai Dist)

I   *Crotalaria dasyclada* Polhill *19531*
I   5926   Tanzania (Ufipa) *19531*

R   *Crotalaria desaegeri* R. Wilczek *19358*
R   19358   Zaire (Bas-Katanga) *19358*

R   *Crotalaria digitata* Hook.
R   13883   India - Karnataka *13883*
R   13883   India - Tamil Nadu *13883*

I   *Crotalaria diminuta* Polhill *19531*
I   5926   Tanzania (Dodoma) *19531*

E   *Crotalaria exaltata* Polhill *19703*
E   19704   Ethiopia (Shewa Upland, Bale, Sidamo, Kefa) *19704*

E   *Crotalaria fallax* Chiov. *19704*
E   19704   Ethiopia (Sidamo) *19704*

I   *Crotalaria filipes* Benth.
I   India - Karnataka (South Canara)

E   *Crotalaria fysonii* Dunn var. *glabra* Gamble
E   13883   India - Tamil Nadu (Palani Hills, Madurai Dist) *13883*

R   *Crotalaria glabripedicellata* R. Wilczek *19358*
R   19358   Zaire (Haut-Katanga) *19358*

R   *Crotalaria globosa* Wight & Arn.
R   13883   India - Karnataka (Mysore) *13883*
R   13883   India - Tamil Nadu *13883*

R   *Crotalaria haumaniana* R. Wilczek *19358*
R   19358   Zaire (Haut-Katanga) *19358*

I   *Crotalaria hemsleyi* Milne-Redh. *19531*
I   5926   Tanzania (Morogoro) *19531*

E   *Crotalaria heterotricha* Polhill *19704*
E   19704   Ethiopia (Harerge) *19704*

E   *Crotalaria hypargyria* Chiov. *19704*
E   19704   Ethiopia (Bale) *19704*

I   *Crotalaria inopinata* (Harms) Polhill *19531*
I   5926   Tanzania (Morogoro Distr.) *19531*

R   *Crotalaria intonsa* Polhill *19704*
R   19704   Ethiopia (Gonder, Shewa Upland, Kefa, Sidamo) *19704*

E   *Crotalaria jijigensis* Thulin *19704*
E   19704   Ethiopia (Harerge) *19704*

R   *Crotalaria kambanguensis* R. Wilczek *19358*
R   19358   Zaire (Kasai) *19358*

E   *Crotalaria kodaiensis* Debberm. & Biswas *11494*
E   11494   India - Tamil Nadu (Kodaikanal hills) *11494*

R   *Crotalaria kundelunguensis* Baker f. *19358*
R   19358   Zaire (Haut-Katanga) *19358*

I   *Crotalaria laxiflora* Bak. *19531*
I   5926   Tanzania (Ufipa) *19531*

E   *Crotalaria longipes* Wight & Arn. *11494*
E   11494   India - Tamil Nadu (Kolli & Nilgiri hills) *11494*

R   *Crotalaria lusamboensis* R. Wilczek *19358*
R   19358   Zaire (Kasai) *19358*

R   *Crotalaria lutescens* Dalz.
R   13883   India - Karnataka (South Canara) *13883*
R   13883   India - Maharashtra *13883*

R   *Crotalaria malaissei* Polhill *12346*
R   19358   Zaire *19358*

I   *Crotalaria melanocalyx* Polhill *19531*
I   5926   Tanzania (Ufipa District) *5926*

R   *Crotalaria meyeriana* Steud. *20604*
R   20604   Namibia *20604*
R   20604   South Africa - Cape Province *20604*

R   *Crotalaria micheliana* R. Wilczek *19358*
R   19358   Zaire (Haut-Katanga) *19358*

R   *Crotalaria milneana* R. Wilczek *19358*
R   19358   Zaire (Bas-Katanga) *19358*

I   *Crotalaria noveoides* Griff. *13883*
I   13883   India - Meghalaya *13883*

I   *Crotalaria ovata* Polhill *19531*
I   5926   Tanzania (Iringa) *5926*

R   *Crotalaria peduncularis* Graham ex Wight & Arn. *11494*
R   11494   India - Kerala (Travancore) *11494*
R   11494   India - Tamil Nadu *11494*

I   *Crotalaria perlaxa* Polhill *19531*
I   5926   Tanzania (Tunduru District) *5926*

E   *Crotalaria polhillii* Thulin *19704*
E   19704   Ethiopia (Shewa Upland, Kefa) *19704*

R   *Crotalaria polyantha* Taubert *12346*
R   19358   Zaire *19358*

R   *Crotalaria priestleyoides* Benth. ex Baker *11494*
R   11494   India - Karnataka *11494*
R   11494   India - Tamil Nadu *11494*

R   *Crotalaria pteropoda* Balf. f. *15534*
R   15534   Yemen - Socotra *15534*

R   *Crotalaria rigida* Heyne ex Roth *11494*
R   11494   India - Andhra Pradesh (Krishna) *11494*
R   11494   India - Karnataka *11494*
R   11494   India - Tamil Nadu *11494*

R   *Crotalaria rupicola* Baker f. *19358*
R   19358   Zaire (Haut-Katanga) *19358*

E   *Crotalaria ruspoliana* Chiov. *19704*
E   19704   Ethiopia (Sidamo) *19704*

R   *Crotalaria rzedowskii* Espinosa *9794*
R   19755   Mexico *9794*

E   *Crotalaria sacculata* Chiov. *19704*
E   19704   Ethiopia (Sidamo) *19704*

E   *Crotalaria sandoorensis* Beddome ex Gamble *11494*
E   11494   India - Karnataka (Sandoor Hills, Bellary Dt) *11494*

R   *Crotalaria scabra* Gamble *13883*

	R	13883	India - Tamil Nadu *13883*

R   *Crotalaria schmitzii* R. Wilczek *19358*
    R   *19358*   Zaire (Haut-Katanga) *19358*

R   *Crotalaria sengensis* Baker f. *19358*
    R   *19358*   Zaire (Haut-Katanga) *19358*

V   *Crotalaria shevaroyensis* Gamble
    V   *18228*   India - Tamil Nadu *18228*

R   *Crotalaria similis* Hemsl. *20511*
    R   *20511*   Taiwan *20511*

R   *Crotalaria stanerana* Baker f. *19358*
    R   *19358*   Zaire (Haut-Katanga) *19358*

R   *Crotalaria strigulosa* Balf. f. *15534*
    R   *15534*   Yemen - Socotra *15534*

R   *Crotalaria tamboensis* R. Wilczek *19358*
    R   *19358*   Zaire (Haut-Katanga) *19358*

E   *Crotalaria trifoliolata* Baker f. *19704*
    E   *19704*   Ethiopia (Bale) *19704*

Ex   *Crotalaria urbaniana* Senn *5607*
    Ex   *19105*   Cuba (Granma) *5607*

E   *Crotalaria vialettei* Battand. *10488*
    E   *14958*   Algeria *10488*

E   *Crudia zeylanica* (Thwaites) Benth. *10252*
    E   *16162*   Sri Lanka *10252*

V   *Cryptosepalum tetraphyllum* (Hook.f.) Benth. *12346*
    V   *20858*   Côte d'Ivoire *20274*
    V   *20858*   Ghana *20274*
    V   *20858*   Guinea *20274*
    V   *20858*   Liberia *20274*
    V   *20858*   Sierra Leone *20274*

E   *Cullen holubii* (Burtt Davy) C.H.Stirt. *20604*
    E   *20604*   South Africa - Transvaal *20604*

I   *Cyclopia bowieana* Harv. *20604*
    I   *20604*   South Africa - Cape Province *20604*

I   *Cyclopia burtonii* Hofmeyer & E.Phillips *20604*
    I   *20604*   South Africa - Cape Province *20604*

V   *Cyclopia latifolia* DC. *20604*
    V   *20604*   South Africa - Cape Province *20604*

E   *Cyclopia longifolia* Vogel *20604*
    E   *20604*   South Africa - Cape Province *20604*

R   *Cyclopia squamosa* A.L.Schutte *20604*
    R   *20604*   South Africa - Cape Province *20604*

V   *Cynometra beddomei* Prain *14782*
    V   *18228*   India - Kerala (Wynaad) *14782*

V   *Cynometra bourdillonii* Gamble *11494*
    V   *11494*   India - Karnataka *11494*

V   *Cynometra brachyrrhachis* Harms *19532*
    V   *20885*   Tanzania (Tanga Region) *20900*

I   *Cynometra cubensis* A. Rich. *5607*
    I   *20990*   Cuba (Pinar del Rio) *5607*

I   *Cynometra engleri* Harms *19532*
    I   *5926*   Tanzania (Tanga Region) *20900*

E   *Cynometra filifera* Harms *19532*
    E   *20885*   Tanzania (Lindi) *19532*

E   *Cynometra gillmanii* Leon *19532*
    E   *20885*   Tanzania (Kilwa) *19532*

I   *Cynometra longipedicellata* Harms *19532*
    I   *5926*   Tanzania (Tanga) *20900*

R   *Cynometra travancorica* Beddome
    R   *13883*   India - Karnataka *13883*

	R	13883	India - Kerala (Travancore Hills) *13883*
	R	13883	India - Tamil Nadu (Tirunelveli Hills) *13883*

V   *Cynometra ulugurensis* Harms *19532*
    V   *20885*   Tanzania (Morogoro) *19532*

R   *Cytisus acutangulus* Jaub & Spach *12840*
    R   *20618*   Turkey *20618*

V   *Cytisus aeolicus* Guss. ex Lindl. *8000, 20171*
    V   *19997*   Italy *19997*

R   *Cytisus ardoini* Fourn. *20528*
    R   *20528*   France (Alpes-Maritimes) *20528*

R   *Cytisus emeriflorus* Rchb. *18264, 20171*
    R   *18264*   Italy *18264*
    E   *18154*   Switzerland *18154*

V   *Cytisus moleroi* Fernandez Casas
    V   *19818*   Spain (Malaga) *19818*

R   *Cytisus sauzeanus* Burnat & Briq. *20171*
    R   *20528*   France (mountains near Grenoble) *20528*

V   *Dalbergia cearensis* Ducke *20883, 17685*
    V   *20883*   Brazil *20883*

E   *Dalbergia darienensis* Rudd *20883, 10747*
    I   *20883*   Panama *20883*

V   *Dalbergia decipularis* Rizz. & Matt. *20883, 17685*
    V   *20883*   Brazil *20883*

R   *Dalbergia eremicola* Polh. *7959*
    R   *20057*   Kenya (Northern Frontier Province) *7959*
    R   *20884*   Somalia *12346*

V   *Dalbergia frutescens* var. *tomentosa* Standl. *20883, 17685*
    V   *20883*   Brazil *20883*
    ?   Brazil - Bahia (Dry forests) *17685*

E   *Dalbergia funera* Standley *9004*
    E   *10359*   El Salvador *9004*
    E   *9443*   Guatemala *9004*

V   *Dalbergia fusca* Pierre var. *enneandra* Zou & Liu *17617*
    V   *17617*   China - Yunnan *11139*

R   I   *Dalbergia nigra* Allem. ex Benth. *20883, 10370*
    R   *20883*   Brazil *20883*
    V   *17746*   Brazil - Bahia (east forests) *13928*
    V   *17746*   Brazil - Espirito Santo *13928*
    I   *10370*   Brazil - Minas Gerais *13928*
    I   *10370*   Brazil - Rio de Janeiro *13928*
    V   *21011*   Brazil - Sao Paulo *21011*

E   *Dalbergia odorifera* T. Chen *17617*
    ?   China *21059*
    E   *17617*   China - Hainan Is. *11139*

E   *Dalbergia setifera* Hutch. & Dalz. *7926*
    E   *20858*   Ghana (Sekondi) *7926*

V   *Dalbergia tonkinensis* Prain *6057*
    ?   China *21310*
    V   *20985*   Vietnam *20065*

V   *Dalea adenopoda* (Rydb.) Isely *20850*
    I   *20850*   U.S. - Florida *20850*

E   *Dalea azurea* (Philippi) Reiche *15088*
    E   *13875*   Chile *13875*

E   *Dalea bartonii* Barneby *20850*
    E   *20850*   U.S. - Texas *20850*

E   *Dalea carthagenensis* Barneby var. *portoricana* R.C. Barneby *20883,*
    V   Puerto Rico *20883*

V	*Dalea foliosa* (Gray) Barneby *20850*			
	E	*20850*	U.S. - Alabama *20850*	
	E	*20850*	U.S. - Illinois *20850*	
	I	*20850*	U.S. - Ohio *20850*	
	V	*20850*	U.S. - Tennessee *20850*	
R	*Dalea hallii* Gray *20850*			
	R	*20850*	U.S. - Texas *20850*	
V	*Dalea reverchonii* (S.Watson) Shinners *20850*			
	V	*20850*	U.S. - Texas *20850*	
E	*Dalea sabinalis* (S.Watson) Shinners *20850*			
	E	*20850*	U.S. - Texas *20850*	
E	*Dalea tentaculoides* H.C. Gentry *20850*			
	E	*20850*	U.S. - Arizona *20850*	
R	*Dalea tenuicaulis* Hook.f. *11117*			
	R		Ecuador - Galapagos *11117*	
E	*Daviesia bursarioides* Crisp ms. *20681*			
	E	*20681*	Australia - Western Australia *20681*	
R	*Daviesia chapmanii* Crisp ms. *20681*			
	R	*20681*	Australia - Western Australia *20681*	
R	*Daviesia crassifolia* Crisp ms. *20681*			
	R	*20681*	Australia - Western Australia *20681*	
V	*Daviesia discolor* Pedley *20681*			
	V	*20681*	Australia - Queensland *20681*	
R	*Daviesia elliptica* Crisp *20681*			
	I	*20681*	Australia - New South Wales *20681*	
	I	*20681*	Australia - Queensland *20681*	
V	*Daviesia euphorbioides* Benth. *20681*			
	V	*20681*	Australia - Western Australia *20681*	
V	*Daviesia laevis* Crisp *20681*			
	V	*20681*	Australia - Victoria *20681*	
V	*Daviesia megacalyx* Crisp ms. *20681*			
	V	*20681*	Australia - Western Australia *20681*	
E	*Daviesia microcarpa* Crisp ms. *20681*			
	E	*20681*	Australia - Western Australia *20681*	
R	*Daviesia microphylla* Benth. *20681*			
	R	*20681*	Australia - Western Australia *20681*	
R	*Daviesia ovata* Benth. *20681*			
	R	*20681*	Australia - Western Australia *20681*	
R	*Daviesia oxylobium* Crisp ms. *20681*			
	R	*20681*	Australia - Western Australia *20681*	
R	*Daviesia pectinata* Lindley *20681*			
	I	*20681*	Australia - South Australia *20681*	
	I	*20681*	Australia - Victoria *20681*	
V	*Daviesia pseudaphylla* Crisp ms. *20681*			
	V	*20681*	Australia - Western Australia *20681*	
E	*Daviesia purpurascens* Crisp *20681*			
	E	*20681*	Australia - Western Australia *20681*	
R	*Daviesia quoquoversus* Crisp *20681*			
	R	*20681*	Australia - Queensland *20681*	
V	*Daviesia speciosa* Crisp ms. *20681*			
	V	*20681*	Australia - Western Australia *20681*	
V	*Daviesia spiralis* Crisp *20681*			
	V	*20681*	Australia - Western Australia *20681*	
R	*Daviesia stricta* Crisp *20681*			
	R	*20681*	Australia - South Australia *20681*	
R	*Daviesia suaveolens* Crisp *20681*			
	R	*20681*	Australia - New South Wales *20681*	
R	*Delonix baccal* (Chiov.) Baker f. *20556*			
	R	*20884*	Ethiopia *7959*	

	R	*20884*	Kenya *6073*	
	R	*20884*	Somalia (south) *20884*	
I	*Delonix regia* (Bojer ex Hook.) Raf. *21039*			
	I	*14010*	Madagascar (West & North) *21039*	
R	*Desmanthus reticulatus* Benth. *20850*			
	R	*20850*	U.S. - Texas *20850*	
V	*Desmodium acanthocladum* F.Muell. *20681*			
	V	*20681*	Australia - New South Wales *20681*	
R	*Desmodium ciliare* (Muhl. ex Willd.) DC. *11560*			
	Ex	*13967*	Canada - Ontario *13967*	
	I	*13967*	U.S. - Kansas *13967*	
	E/V	*13967*	U.S. - New York *13967*	
	E	*13967*	U.S. - Rhode Is. *13967*	
	R	*11560*	Belize *11560*	
	R	*11560*	Honduras *11560*	
E	*Desmodium humifusum* (Muhl. ex Bigelow) Beck *20850*			
	E	*20850*	U.S. - Connecticut *20850*	
	I	*20850*	U.S. - Delaware *20850*	
	E	*20850*	U.S. - Indiana *20850*	
	Ex/E	*20850*	U.S. - Maryland *20850*	
	E	*20850*	U.S. - Massachusetts *20850*	
	Ex/E	*20850*	U.S. - New Jersey *20850*	
	Ex/E	*20850*	U.S. - New York *20850*	
	I	*20850*	U.S. - North Carolina *20850*	
	E	*20850*	U.S. - Pennsylvania *20850*	
	I	*20850*	U.S. - South Carolina *20850*	
R	*Desmodium johnstonii* Standley ex B.G. Schubert *11560*			
	R	*11560*	Guatemala *11560*	
	R	*11560*	Nicaragua *11560*	
I	*Desmodium jucundum* Thwaites *10252*			
	I	*16162*	Sri Lanka *10252*	
E	*Desmodium kaalense* Guillaumin *20893*			
	E	*20893*	New Caledonia *20893*	
R	*Desmodium lindheimeri* Vail *8058*			
	Ex	*11560*	U.S. - Texas *8058*	
	R	*11560*	Mexico *8058*	
R	*Desmodium macrocarpum* Domin *20681*			
	R	*20681*	Australia - Queensland *20681*	
V	*Desmodium ochroleucum* M.A. Curtis ex Canby *20850*			
	I	*20850*	U.S. - Alabama *20850*	
	Ex/E	*20850*	U.S. - Delaware *20850*	
	I	*20850*	U.S. - Florida *20850*	
	Ex/E	*20850*	U.S. - Georgia *20850*	
	E	*20850*	U.S. - Maryland *20850*	
	E	*20850*	U.S. - Mississippi *20850*	
	Ex	*20850*	U.S. - Missouri *20850*	
	Ex	*20850*	U.S. - New Jersey *20850*	
	E	*20850*	U.S. - North Carolina *20850*	
	Ex/E	*20850*	U.S. - Tennessee *20850*	
	E	*20850*	U.S. - Virginia *20850*	
	I	*20850*	U.S. - West Virginia *20850*	
V	*Desmodium saccatum* Schubert *20883, 10747*			
	I	*20883*	Panama *20883*	
E	*Desmodium stenophyllum* Harms *20893*			
	E	*20893*	New Caledonia *20893*	
I	*Desmodium tenuipes* (S.F. Blake) B.G. Schubert *9004*			
	I	*11560*	Guatemala *9004*	
R	*Desmodium wightii* Graham ex Wight & Arn.			
	R	*18228*	India - Tamil Nadu (Nilgiri & Palani Hills) *18228*	
R	*Desmodium wittei* Schubert *19358*			
	R	*19358*	Zaire (Haut-Katanga) *19358*	
R	*Desmodium wynaadense* Beddome ex Gamble			
	R	*18228*	India - Kerala (Travancore Hills) *18228*	
	R	*18228*	India - Tamil Nadu *18228*	

I   *Dialium travancoricum* Bourd. *14782*
    I   *14782* India - Kerala *14782*

I   *Dichrostachys dehiscens* Balf. f. *15534*
    I   *15534* Yemen - Socotra *15534*

R   *Dicraeopetalum stipulare* Harms *6073*
    V   *20057* Ethiopia *7959*
    V   *20057* Kenya *6073*
    R   *20884* Somalia (central & south) *20884*

V   *Didelotia idae* Oldem., De Wit. & Leon. *12346*
    V   *20858* Benin
    V   *20858* Cameroon
    V   *20858* Côte d'Ivoire
    V   *20858* Ghana *20274*
    V   *20858* Liberia
    V   *20858* Nigeria
    V   *20858* Sierra Leone *20274*
    V   *20858* Togo

V   *Didelotia unifoliolata* Leonard *20274*
    V   *20858* Cameroon *16174*
    V   *20858* Côte d'Ivoire *7926*
    V   *20858* Ghana *20274*
    V   *20858* Liberia *7926*
    V   *20858* Sierra Leone *7926*
    V   *20858* Zaire (Forestier Central)

R   *Dillwynia stipulifera* Blakely *20681*
    R   *20681* Australia - New South Wales *20681*

R   *Dillwynia tenuifolia* DC. *20681*
    R   *20681* Australia - New South Wales *20681*

R   *Dimorphandra campinarum* Ducke *20883*
    I   *20883* Brazil *20883*

V   *Dimorphandra coccinea* Ducke *20883*
    I   *20883* Brazil *20883*

R   *Dimorphandra cuprea* ssp. *ferruginea* (Ducke) Freitas
    da Silva *20883*
    I   *20883* Brazil *20883*
    I   *20883* Venezuela *20883*

R   *Dimorphandra davisii* Sprague et Sandwith *20883*
    I   *20883* Guyana *20883*
    I   *20883* Venezuela *20883*

E   *Dimorphandra dissimilis* Cowan *20883*
    I   *20883* Venezuela *20883*

E   *Dimorphandra gigantea* Ducke *20883*
    I   *20883* Brazil *20883*

V   *Dimorphandra ignea* Ducke *20883*
    I   *20883* Brazil *20883*

V   *Dimorphandra jorgei* Freitas da Silva *20883*
    I   *20883* Brazil *20883*

E   *Dimorphandra loretensis* Freitas da Silva *20883*
    I   *20883* Peru *20883*

R   *Dimorphandra macrostachya* ssp. *congestiflora* (Sprague
    et Sandwith) Freitas da Silva *20883*
    I   *20883* Guyana *20883*

E   *Dimorphandra mediocris* Ducke *20883*
    I   *20883* Brazil *20883*

R   *Dimorphandra multiflora* Ducke *20883*
    I   *20883* Brazil *20883*

R   *Dimorphandra unijuga* Tulasne *20883*
    I   *20883* Brazil *20883*
    I   *20883* Venezuela *20883*

V   *Dimorphandra williamii* Freitas da Silva *20883*
    I   *20883* Guyana *20883*

E   *Dimorphandra wilsonii* Rizzini *20883*

    I   *20883* Brazil *20883*

V   *Dioclea reflexa* J.D.Hook. *20681*
    V   *20681* Australia - Queensland *20681*

E   *Dipteryx alata* Vogel *10370*
    E   *10370* Brazil *10370*

R   *Diptychandra aurantiaca* Tul. ssp. *epunctata* (Tul.)
    Lima, Cawalho & Costa *16692*
    R   *16692* Brazil - Bahia *16692*

R   *Dolichos argyros* R. Wilczek *19358*
    R   *19358* Zaire (Haut-Katanga) *19358*

I   *Dolichos cardiophyllus* Harms *19531*
    I   *5926* Tanzania (Iringa) *19531*

I   *Dolichos ciliatus* Klein
    I   India - Tamil Nadu (east coast)

R   *Dolichos complanatus* De Wild. *19358*
    R   *19358* Zaire (Haut-Katanga) *19358*

R   *Dolichos sericophyllus* R. Wilczek *19358*
    R   *19358* Zaire (Haut-Katanga) *19358*

R   *Dolichos trilobus* L. *20511*
    R   *20511* Taiwan *20511*

R   *Dolichos zovuanyi* R. Wilczek *19358*
    R   *19358* Zaire (Haut-Katanga) *19358*

R   *Dorycnium amani* Zohary *12840*
    R   *12840* Turkey *12840*

R   *Dorycnium axilliflorum* Huber-Mor. *12840*
    R   *12840* Turkey *12840*

R   *Dorycnium broussonetii* Webb. & Beth. *10260*
    R   *20750* Spain - Canary Is. *20750*

R   *Dorycnium eriophthalmum* Webb & Berthel. *20750*
    R   *20750* Spain - Canary Is. *20750*

R   *Dorycnium pentaphyllum* Scop. ssp. *fulgurans*
    Cardona, Llorens & E. Sierra *20645*
    R   *20647* Spain - Balearic Is. *20645*

V   *Dorycnium pentaphyllum* Scop. ssp. *transmontana*
    Franco *20076*
    V   *20076* Portugal *20076*

V   *Dorycnium sanguineum* Vural *12840*
    V   *12840* Turkey *12840*

E   *Dorycnium spectabile* Webb & Berthel. *17891*
    E   *20750* Spain - Canary Is. *17891*

R   *Droogmansia chevalieri* (Harms) Hutch. & Dalz. *7926*
    R   Guinea (Bilima) *7926*

R   *Droogmansia elongata* Schubert *19358*
    R   *19358* Zaire (Haut-Katanga) *19358*

R   *Droogmansia lancifolia* Schindler *19358*
    R   *19358* Zaire (Haut-Katanga) *19358*

R   *Droogmansia longirhachis* Schubert *12346*
    R   *19358* Zaire (Haut-Katanga) *19358*

R   *Droogmansia montana* Jacq.-Fel. *7926*
    R   Guinea *7926*

R   *Dumasia miaoliensis* Liu & Lu *20511*
    R   *20511* Taiwan *20511*

R   *Ebenus armitagei* Schweinf. & Taubert *16168*
    E   *16168* Egypt (Ras El Hekma) *16168*
    R   Libya *16168*

R   *Ebenus barbigera* Boiss. *12840*
    R   *12840* Turkey *12840*

R   *Ebenus boissieri* Barber *12840*

	R	*12840* Turkey *12840*	
R	*Ebenus bourgaei* Boiss. *12840*		
	R	*12840* Turkey *12840*	
R	*Ebenus cappadocica* Hausskn. & Siehe ex Bornm. *12840*		
	R	*12840* Turkey *12840*	
R	*Ebenus depressa* Boiss. & Bal. *12840*		
	R	*12840* Turkey *12840*	
R	*Ebenus haussknechtii* Bornm. ex Huber-Mor. *12840*		
	R	*12840* Turkey *12840*	
R	*Ebenus laguroides* Boiss. var. *cilicica* (Boiss.) Bornm. *12840*		
	R	*12840* Turkey *12840*	
R	*Ebenus longipes* Boiss. & Bal. *12840*		
	R	*12840* Turkey *12840*	
R	*Ebenus pisidica* Huber-Mor. & Reese *12840*		
	R	*12840* Turkey *12840*	
R	*Ebenus plumosus* Boiss. & Bal. *12840*		
	R	*12840* Turkey *12840*	
R	*Ebenus reesei* Huber-Mor. *12840*		
	R	*12840* Turkey *12840*	
R	*Ebenus sibthorpii* DC. *20171*		
	R	*20731* Greece - East Aegean Is *20731*	
Ex/E	*Echinospartum algibicum* Talever & Mpauho *20660, 20665*		
	Ex/E	*20665* Spain (Málaga, Sierra Gratalema) *20665*	
R	*Eleiotis trifoliolata* Cooke *14782*		
	R	*14782* India - Karnataka (eastern) *14782*	
R	*Elephantorrhiza obliqua* Burtt Davy *12346*		
	R	*12346* South Africa *12346*	
I	*Elephantorrhiza woodii* E. Phillips *12346*		
	I	*12346* Lesotho *12346*	
	I	*12346* South Africa *12346*	
R	*Entada koshunensis* *20854*		
	R	*20854* Taiwan *20854*	
I	*Entada mossambicensis* Torre *7749*		
	I	Mozambique *7749*	
R	*Entada pursaetha* DC. var. *formosana* (Kaneh.) Ho *20511*		
	R	*20511* Taiwan *20511*	
V	*Eremosparton aphyllum* (Pall.) Fisch. & C.A.Mey. *8000, 20171*		
	V	*11552* Russian Federation (Caucasus, west) *11552*	
I	*Eriosema arachnoideum* Verdc. *19531*		
	I	*5926* Tanzania (Iringa) *19531*	
R	*Eriosema brachybotrys* Harms *19358*		
	R	*19358* Zaire (Haut-Katanga) *19358*	
I	*Eriosema buchananii* Baker f. var. *subprostratum* Verdc. *19531*		
	I	*5926* Tanzania (Mbeya, Rungwe, Njombe) *19531*	
I	*Eriosema chrysadenium* Taub. var. *grandiflorum* Verdc. *19531*		
	I	*5926* Tanzania (Njombe) *19531*	
R	*Eriosema dregei* E.Mey. *20604*		
	R	*20604* South Africa - Cape Province *20604*	
	R	*20604* South Africa - Natal *20604*	
R	*Eriosema humile* Hauman *19358*		
	R	*19358* Zaire (Kasai) *19358*	
R	*Eriosema latifolium* (Benth. ex Harv.)		

		C.H.Stirt. *20604*	
	R	*20604* South Africa - Cape Province *20604*	
	R	*20604* South Africa - Natal *20604*	
R	*Eriosema naviculare* C.H.Stirt. *20604*		
	R	*20604* South Africa - Transvaal *20604*	
I	*Eriosema pseudodistinctum* Verdc. *19531*		
	I	*5926* Tanzania (Iringa) *19531*	
R	*Eriosema tenuicaule* Hauman *19358*		
	R	*19358* Zaire (Kasai) *19358*	
I	*Eriosema transvaalense* C.H.Stirt. *20604, 20039*		
	I	*20039* Southern Africa *20039*	
	K	*20604* Swaziland *20604*	
	I	*20604* South Africa - Transvaal *20604*	
E	*Eriosema tuberosum* A. Rich. *19704*		
	E	*19704* Ethiopia (Tigray Upland, Gonder.) *19704*	
R	*Eriosema umtamvunense* C.H.Stirt. *20604*		
	R	*20604* South Africa - Natal *20604*	
V	*Erythrina acunae* Borh. *5607*		
	V	*19105* Cuba (Holguin) *5607*	
R	*Erythrina boninensis* Tuy. *8038*		
	R	Japan - Ogasawara-shoto *8038*	
V	*Erythrina burana* Chiov. *19704*		
	V	*19704* Ethiopia (Harerge) *19704*	
I	*Erythrina dominguezii* Hassler *16336*		
	I	*16336* Argentina *16336*	
	I	*20176* Argentina - Chaco *20176*	
	I	*20176* Argentina - Formosa *20176*	
	I	*20176* Argentina - Salta *20176*	
E	*Erythrina eggersii* Krukoff & Moldenke *20883, 19002*		
	I	*20883* Puerto Rico *20883*	
	I	*20883* USA - Virgin Is. *20883*	
V	*Erythrina elenae* Howard & Briggs *5607*		
	V	*19105* Cuba (Cienfuegos) *5607*	
E	*Erythrina furcatifolia* M. Gilbert *19704*		
	E	*19704* Ethiopia (Sidamo) *19704*	
I	*Erythrina greenwayi* Verdc. *19531*		
	I	*5926* Tanzania (Ruaha valley) *20921*	
E	*Erythrina sareciana* M. Gilbert *19704*		
	E	*19704* Ethiopia (Bale) *19704*	
Ex	*Erythrina schliebenii* Harms *19531*		
	Ex	*20885* Tanzania (Lindi) *19531*	
E	*Erythrina tahitensis* Nadeaud *20845*		
	E	*20845* French Polynesia - Society Is. (Tahiti) *20845*	
R	*Exostyles venusta* Schott *16692*		
	R	*16692* Brazil - Bahia *16692*	
V	*Eysenhardtia spinosa* Engelm. *20850*		
	V	*20850* U.S. - Texas *20850*	
R	*Flemingia gracilis* (Mukerjee) Ali *14782*		
	R	*14782* India - Karnataka *14782*	
	R	*14782* India - Maharashtra *14782*	
V	*Galactia acunana* Borh. & Muniz *5607*		
	V	*19105* Cuba (Pinar del Rio) *5607*	
V	*Galactia eggersii* Urban *20883, 15106*		
	I	*20883* Puerto Rico *20883*	
	I	*20883* British Virgin Is. (Tortola; Guana) *20883*	
	I	*20883* USA - Virgin Is. (St John; St Thomas) *20883*	
V	*Galactia herradurensis* Urban *5607*		
	V	*19105* Cuba (Pinar del Rio) *5607*	

Magnoliopsida (dicots): Leguminosae: *Galactia*

E	*Galactia isopoda* Urban *5607*			
	E	*19105*	Cuba (Pinar del Rio) *5607*	
E	*Galactia jenningsii* Britton *5607*			
	E	*19105*	Cuba (Pinar del Rio; I. Juventud) *5607*	
I	*Galactia laxiflora* Urb. *20883, 13336*			
	I	*19890*	Dominican Republic *18329*	
	E	*13336*	Jamaica *20883*	
V	*Galactia pinetorum* Small *20850*			
	V	*20850*	U.S. - Florida *20850*	
E	*Galactia sangsterae* Proctor *20883, 13336*			
	E	*19890*	Jamaica *20883*	
E	*Galactia smallii* H.J. Rogers ex Herndon *20850*			
	E	*20850*	U.S. - Florida *20850*	
V	*Galactia uniflora* Urb. *20883*			
	E	*20883*	Jamaica *20883*	
E	*Galega somalensis* (Harms) J.B.Gillett *19704*			
	E	*19704*	Ethiopia (Sidamo) *19704*	
V	*Gastrolobium appressum* C.Gardner *20681*			
	V	*20681*	Australia - Western Australia *20681*	
R	*Gastrolobium callistachys* Meisner *20681*			
	R	*20681*	Australia - Western Australia *20681*	
R	*Gastrolobium glabratum* Crisp ms. *20681*			
	R	*20681*	Australia - Western Australia *20681*	
E	*Gastrolobium glaucum* C.Gardner *20681*			
	E	*20681*	Australia - Western Australia *20681*	
E	*Gastrolobium graniticum* (S.Moore) Crisp *20681*			
	E	*20681*	Australia - Western Australia *20681*	
E	*Gastrolobium hamulosum* Meisner *20681*			
	E	*20681*	Australia - Western Australia *20681*	
R	*Gastrolobium ovalifolium* Henfrey *20681*			
	R	*20681*	Australia - Western Australia *20681*	
V	*Gastrolobium tomentosum* C.Gardner *20681*			
	V	*20681*	Australia - Western Australia *20681*	
R	*Genista acanthoclada* DC. ssp. *fasciculata* (Knoche) O. Bolos & Vigo			
	R		Spain - Balearic Is.	
R	*Genista burdurensis* P. Gibb *12840*			
	R	*20618*	Turkey *20618*	
V	*Genista dorycnifolia* Font Quer *8000, 20171*			
	V	*11496*	Spain - Balearic Is. (Ibiza) *11496*	
R	*Genista dorycnifolia* Font Quer var. *grosii* (Font Quer) Font Quer & Rothm. *20645*			
	R	*20647*	Spain - Balearic Is. *20645*	
R	*Genista halacsyi* Heldr. *20171*			
	R		Greece	
V	*Genista holopetala* (Fleischm. ex W.D.J.Koch) Bald. *8000, 20171*			
	I	*20852*	Croatia *20852*	
	E	*18264*	Italy (Friuli-Venezia Giulia) *19997*	
	V	*13662*	Slovenia (western) *13662*	
R	*Genista lanuginosa* Spach *20171*			
	R	*11496*	Spain (Malaga) *11496*	
Ex/E	*Genista libanotica* Boiss. *20618*			
	Ex/E	*20689*	Turkey *20618*	
R	*Genista lipskyii* Novopokr. & Schischkin			
	R		former USSR *6930*	
R	*Genista lydia* Boiss. var. *antiochia* *20618*			
	R	*20618*	Turkey *20618*	
Ex	*Genista melia* Boiss. *8000, 20171*			
	Ex	*14155*	Greece (Aegean) *8000*	
R	*Genista millii* Heldr. ex Boiss. *20171*			
	R		Greece	
V	*Genista morisii* Colla *18264, 20171*			
	V	*18264*	Italy - Sardinia *18264*	
R	*Genista nissana* Petrovic *20171*			
	R		(former) Yugoslavia	
R	*Genista nociva* Pau & Font Quer			
	R		Morocco	
R	*Genista parnassica* Halácsy *20171*			
	R		Greece	
R	*Genista sakellariadis* Boiss. & Orph. *20171*			
	R		Greece	
R	*Genista sandrasica* Hartvig & Strid *12840*			
	R	*20618*	Turkey *20618*	
E	*Genista spinulosa* Pomel *10488*			
	E	*14958*	Algeria *10488*	
I	*Genista tanaitica* P.A.Smirn. *8001, 20171*			
	I	*5942*	Ukraine *5942*	
R	*Genista tenera* (Jacq. ex Murray) Kuntze			
	R		Portugal - Madeira	
R	*Genista teretifolia* Willk. *20171*			
	R	*11496*	Spain *11496*	
E	*Genista tetragona* Besser *5942, 20171*			
	E	*20655*	Ukraine (southern) *20653*	
V	*Genista tinctoria* L. ssp. *prostrata* Corillion, Figureau, Godeau *20528*			
	V	*20528*	France (Brittany) *20528*	
V	*Genistella sagittalis* ssp. *undulata* Ern *15398*			
	V	*15398*	Spain (Sierra Nevada) *15398*	
E	*Genistidium dumosum* I.M. Johnston *20883, 20850, 8058*			
	E	*20850*	U.S. - Texas *20850*	
	I	*20883*	Mexico *20883*	
E	*Gigasiphon macrosiphon* (Harms) Brenan *19532*			
	E	*20057*	Kenya (Mrima, Gongoni, Muhaka & Marenje forests) *20057*	
	E	*20057*	Tanzania (Usambara Hills & Lindi) *20900*	
V	*Gilbertiodendron bilineatum* (Hutch. & Dalz.) J. Leonard *20274*			
	V	*20858*	Côte d'Ivoire *12346*	
	V	*20858*	Ghana *20274*	
	V	*20858*	Liberia *12346*	
	V	*20858*	Sierra Leone *12346*	
I	*Gilbertiodendron klainei* (Pierre ex Pellegrin) Leonard			
	I		Gabon (Libreville)	
I	*Gilbertiodendron pachyanthum* (Harms) Leonard			
	I		Cameroon	
V	*Gilbertiodendron robynsianum* Aubrev. & Pellegr. *7926*			
	V	*20887*	Côte d'Ivoire (south-west) *20887*	
V	*Gilbertiodendron splendidum* (Hutch. & Diels) J. Leonard *20274*			
	V	*20858*	Côte d'Ivoire *20274*	
	V	*20858*	Ghana *20274*	
	V	*20858*	Sierra Leone *20274*	
V	*Gilletiodendron glandulosum* (Portères) J. Léonard *11751*			
	V		Mali (Kita Massif) *11751*	
I	*Gleditsia assamica* Bor *14782*			

I   *14782* India (northeast) *14782*

R   *Gleditsia pachycarpa* Balansa ex Gagnepain *6057*
   R   Vietnam *6057*

R   *Gleditsia rolfei* L.M. Vidal *15399*
   R   *20854* Taiwan (Heng-ch'un) *20854*

E   *Gleditsia vestita* Chun & How ex B.G. Li *17617*
   E   *17617* China - Hunan (Nanyu) *11139*

R   *Glycine argyrea* Tindale *20681*
   R   *20681* Australia - Queensland *20681*

V   *Glycine latrobeana* (Meisner) Benth. *20681*
   I   *20681* Australia - South Australia *20681*
   I   *20681* Australia - Tasmania *20681*
   I   *20681* Australia - Victoria *20681*

E   *Glycyrrhiza iconica* Hub.-Mor *17781*
   E   *17781* Turkey *17781*

R   *Glycyrrhiza korshinskyi* Grig. *8000, 20171*
   R   *11552* Russian Federation (western, western Siberia) *11552*

V   *Gompholobium virgatum* Sieber ex DC. var. *emarginatum* F.M.Bailey *20681*
   V   *20681* Australia - Queensland *20681*

R   *Gonocytisus dirmilensis* Huber-Mor. *12840*
   R   *20618* Turkey *20618*

R   *Guibourtia chodatiana* (Hassler) J. Léonard *20883*
   I   *20883* Bolivia *20883*
   I   *20883* Brazil *20883*
   R   *20883* Paraguay *20883*

R   *Gymnocladus angustifolius* (Gagnepain) Vidal *6057*
   R   Vietnam *6057*

R   *Hammatolobium lotoides* Fenzl
   R   Greece

V   *Harpalyce acunae* Borh. & Muniz *5607*
   V   *19105* Cuba (Santiago de Cuba; Holguin) *5607*

V   *Harpalyce angustiflora* Leon & Alain *5607*
   V   *19105* Cuba (Holguin) *5607*

V   *Harpalyce baracoensis* Borh. & Muniz *5607*
   V   *19105* Cuba (Guantanamo) *5607*

V   *Harpalyce borhidii* Muniz *5607*
   V   *19105* Cuba (Holguin) *5607*

R   *Harpalyce ekmanii* Urban *5607*
   R   *19105* Cuba (Holguin; Guantanamo) *5607*

V   *Harpalyce flexuosa* Leon & Alain *5607*
   V   *19105* Cuba (Guantanamo) *5607*

V   *Harpalyce foliosa* Borh. & Muniz *5607*
   V   *19105* Cuba (Guantanamo) *5607*

R   *Harpalyce maisiana* Leon & Alain *5607*
   R   *19105* Cuba (Guantanamo) *5607*

R   *Harpalyce mexicana* Rose *9798*
   R   *9706* Mexico *9798*

V   *Harpalyce moana* Borh. & Muniz *5607*
   V   *19105* Cuba (Holguin, Guantanamo) *5607*

R   *Harpalyce toaensis* Borh. & Muniz *5607*
   R   *19105* Cuba (Guantanamo) *5607*

R   *Hedysarum antitauricum* Huber-Mor. & Yurdakulol *12840*
   R   *12840* Turkey *12840*

R   *Hedysarum astragaloides* Benth. ex Baker
   R   *13883* India - Himachal Pradesh *13883*
   R   *13883* India - Jammu & Kashmir *13883*

R   *Hedysarum aucheri* Boiss. *12840*

R   *12840* Turkey *12840*

E   *Hedysarum boreale* Nutt. var. *gremiale* (Rollins) Northstrom & Welsh *20850*
   E   *20850* U.S. - Utah *20850*

R   *Hedysarum boutignyanum* Alleiz. *20171*
   R   France (south-west Alps)

R   *Hedysarum candidissimum* Freyn *12840*
   R   *12840* Turkey *12840*

R   *Hedysarum cretaceum* Fisch. *8000, 20171*
   R   *11552* Russian Federation (south western) *11552*

R   *Hedysarum laxum* Boiss. *12840*
   R   *12840* Turkey *12840*

R   *Hedysarum macedonicum* Bornm. *20171*
   R   (former) Yugoslavia

R   *Hedysarum perrauderianum* Cosson & Durieu *12346*
   R   Algeria *10488*

V   *Hedysarum pycnostachyum* Hedge & Huber-Mor. *12840*
   V   *12840* Turkey *12840*

V   *Hedysarum rotundifolium* Boiss. & Noe *12840*
   V   *12840* Turkey *12840*

R   *Hedysarum ucrainicum* Kaschm. *8000, 20171*
   R   *11552* Russian Federation (western) *11552*

I   *Hedysarum ussuriense* I. Schischkin & Komarov *5942*
   I   *5942* Russia (Far East) - Primorye (south) *5942*

R   *Hedysarum vanense* Hedge & Huber-Mor. *12840*
   R   *12840* Turkey *12840*

R   *Hedysarum zeluanum* Pau
   R   Morocco

I   *Hedysarum zundukii* Pesch. *5942*
   I   *5942* Russia (Siberia) - Irkutsk *5942*

R   *Hippocrepis valentina* Boiss. *20171*
   R   *19174* Spain (North East Alicante Province) *20692*

E   *Hoffmannseggia miranda* Sandw. *18200*
   E   *9446* Peru *18200*

E   *Hoffmannseggia stipulata* Sandw. *18200*
   E   *9446* Peru *18200*

E   *Hoffmannseggia tenella* Tharp & Williams *20850*
   E   *20850* U.S. - Texas (Nueces Co.) *20850*

R   *Hoita strobilina* (Hook. & Arn.) Rydb. *20850*
   I   *20850* U.S. - California *20850*

R   *Hovea corrickiae* J.H.Ross *20681*
   I   *20681* Australia - Tasmania *20681*
   I   *20681* Australia - Victoria *20681*

E   *Humboldtia bourdillonii* Prain *11494*
   E   *11494* India - Kerala (Peermade Ghats) *11494*
   E   *11494* India - Tamil Nadu (Courtallum Ghats) *11494*

R   *Humboldtia decurrens* Beddome ex Oliver *11494*
   R   *11494* India - Kerala (south Western Ghats) *11494*

E   *Humboldtia laurifolia* Vahl
   E   *13883* India - Kerala (Malabar) *13883*
   E   *13883* Sri Lanka *13883*

E   *Humboldtia unijuga* Beddome *9250*
   E   *11494* India - Kerala *11494*
   E   *11494* India - Tamil Nadu (Tirunelveli Hills) *11494*

R	*Humularia descampsii* (De Wild. & T. Durand) Duvign. var. *nyassica* Duvign. *7867*	
	R	Malawi *7867*
R	*Humularia elegantula* Duvign. *19358*	
	R	*19358* Zaire (Kasai) *19358*
I	*Humularia multifoliolata* Verdc. *19531*	
	I	*5926* Tanzania (Mpanda District) *19531*
R	*Humularia upembae* Duvign. *19358*	
	R	*19358* Zaire (Bas-Kasai) *19358*
V	*Hymenaea davisii* Sandw. *20883*	
	V	*20883* Guyana *20883*
R	*Hymenaea palustris* *17462*	
	R	*19961* Peru *17462*
R	*Hymenaea stigonocarpa* var. *pubescens* Benth. *20883*	
	I	*20883* Brazil *20883*
	R	*20883* Paraguay *20883*
V	*Hymenaea torrei* Leon *11840*	
	V	*19105* Cuba (Oriente; Camaguey) *11840*
V	*Hymenostegia aubrevillei* Pellegrin *7926*	
	V	*20858* Côte d'Ivoire *7926*
	V	*20858* Ghana *20274*
	V	*20858* Nigeria *20274*
E	*Hymenostegia gracilipes* Hutch. & Dalz. *7926*	
	E	*20858* Ghana *20274*
R	*Hymenostegia klainei* Pellegrin *12346*	
	R	Gabon *12346*
R	*Hymenostegia normandii* Pellegrin *12346*	
	R	Gabon *12346*
E	*Hymenostegia talbotii* Baker f. *7926*	
	E	*20749* Nigeria (Eket) *7926*
V	*Indigofera ammoxylum* (DC.) Polhill *10082*	
	V	*14234* Réunion *10082*
I	*Indigofera asterocalycina* Gilli *19531*	
	I	*5926* Tanzania (Njombe District) *19531*
R	*Indigofera baileyi* F.Muell. *20681*	
	I	*20681* Australia - New South Wales *20681*
	I	*20681* Australia - Queensland *20681*
R	*Indigofera barberi* Gamble *11494*	
	R	*11494* India - Andhra Pradesh (east Ghats) *11494*
	R	*11494* India - Tamil Nadu (east Ghats) *11494*
R	*Indigofera byobiensis* Hosok. *20854*	
	R	*20854* Taiwan *20854*
R	*Indigofera caerulea* Roxb. var. *monosperma* (Santapau) Santapau	
	R	*13883* India - Gujarat *13883*
	R	*13883* India - Rajasthan *13883*
E	*Indigofera cana* Thulin *19704*	
	E	*19704* Ethiopia (Wello Upland) *19704*
I	*Indigofera cedrorum* Dunn	
	I	India - Himachal Pradesh
	I	India - Jammu & Kashmir
I	*Indigofera coerulea* Roxb. var. *monosperma* Sant. *7771*	
	I	India - Gujarat *7771*
R	*Indigofera constricta* (Thwaites) Trimen	
	R	*13883* India - Karnataka (Nikund Ghat) *13883*
	R	*13883* India - Kerala (Cochin) *13883*
	R	*13883* Sri Lanka *13883*
E	*Indigofera cubensis* Urban *5607*	
	E	*19105* Cuba (Habana, Matanzas) *5607*
E	*Indigofera curvirostrata* Thulin *19704*	
	E	*19704* Ethiopia (Sidamo) *19704*
R	*Indigofera dauensis* J.B.Gillett *7959*	
	R	Kenya (Northern Frontier Province) *7959*
E	*Indigofera dembianensis* (Chiov.) J.B.Gillett *19704*	
	E	*19704* Ethiopia (Tigray Upland, Gonder, Shewa Upland.) *19704*
R	*Indigofera dyeri* Britten var. *parviflora* J.B.Gillett *7917*	
	R	Mozambique *7917*
E	*Indigofera efoliata* F.Muell. *20681*	
	E	*20681* Australia - New South Wales *20681*
E	*Indigofera ellenbeckii* Bak F. *19704*	
	E	*19704* Ethiopia (Harerge) *19704*
R	*Indigofera elwakensis* J.B.Gillett *7959*	
	R	Kenya (Northern Frontier Province) *7959*
R	*Indigofera garissaensis* J.B.Gillett *7959*	
	R	Kenya *7959*
I	*Indigofera hermannioides* J.B.Gillett *19531*	
	I	*5926* Tanzania (Songea District) *19531*
E	*Indigofera kelleri* Baker F. *19704*	
	E	*19704* Ethiopia (Harerge) *19704*
R	*Indigofera leptoclada* Harms *8003*	
	R	Mali *8003*
	R	Senegal *8003*
E	*Indigofera marmorata* Balf. f. *15534*	
	E	*15534* Yemen - Socotra *15534*
R	*Indigofera miniata* (Buckl.) B.L. Turner var. *texana* (Buckl.) B.L. Turner *20850*	
	R	*20850* U.S. - Texas *20850*
R	*Indigofera mooneyi* Thulin *19704*	
	R	*19704* Ethiopia (Welega, Shewa Upland, Kefa, Sidamo) *19704*
I	*Indigofera mwanzae* J.B.Gillett *19531*	
	I	*5926* Tanzania (Kwimba, Mwanza) *19531*
I	*Indigofera nyassica* Gilli var. *viscidior* (J.B.Gillett) J.B.Gillett *19531*	
	I	*5926* Tanzania (Songea District) *19531*
V	*Indigofera panamensis* Rydb. *20883, 10747*	
	I	*20883* Panama *20883*
R	*Indigofera platypoda* E.Mey. *20604*	
	R	*20604* South Africa - Cape Province *20604*
R	*Indigofera pseudoevansii* Hilliard & B.L.Burtt *20604*	
	R	*20604* South Africa - Natal *20604*
V	*Indigofera pseudointricata* J.B.Gillett *15534*	
	V	*15534* Yemen - Socotra *15534*
V	*Indigofera ramulosissima* Hosok. *20854*	
	V	*20854* Taiwan *20854*
V	*Indigofera rothii* Bak. *19704*	
	V	*19704* Ethiopia (Shewa Upland, Harerge) *19704*
R	*Indigofera schultziana* F.Muell. *20681*	
	R	*20681* Australia - Northern Territory *20681*
I	*Indigofera simlensis* Ali	
	I	India - Himachal Pradesh
E	*Indigofera socotrana* Vierh. *15534*	
	E	*15534* Yemen - Socotra *15534*
E	*Indigofera sparsa* Bak. *19704*	
	E	*19704* Ethiopia (Tigray Upland) *19704*

R	*Indigofera superba* C.H.Stirt. *20604*		
	R	20604	South Africa - Cape Province *20604*
I	*Indigofera taylorii* J.B.Gillett *7959*		
	I	5926	Tanzania (Songea) *19531*
R	*Indigofera thesioides* Jarvie & C.H.Stirt. *20604*		
	R	20604	South Africa - Cape Province *20604*
R	*Indigofera triquetra* E.Mey. *20604*		
	R	20604	South Africa - Cape Province *20604*
E	*Indigofera trita* var. *keyensis* (Small) Kartesz & Gandhi *20850*		
	E	20850	U.S. - Florida *20850*
E	*Inga allenii* J. Leon *20883, 10747*		
	I	20883	Panama *20883*
R	*Inga brachystachys* Ducke *8679*		
	R	8679	Guyana *8679*
	R	8679	Suriname *8679*
R	*Inga commewijnensis* Miq. *8679*		
	R	8679	French Guiana *8679*
	R	8679	Suriname *8679*
I	*Inga cynometroides* (Beddome) Baker *14782*		
	I	14782	India - Kerala (south Travancore Hills) *14782*
E	*Inga davidsoniae* Standl. *20883, 9006*		
	I	20883	Panama *20883*
R	*Inga dominicensis* Benth. *10199*		
	R		Dominica *10199*
V	*Inga hayesii* Benth. *20883, 9006*		
	I	20883	Panama *20883*
R	*Inga mucuna* Walp. & Duchass. *20883*		
	R	20883	Panama *20883*
V	*Inga pauciflora* Walp. & Duchass. *20883, 9006*		
	I	20883	Panama *20883*
E	*Inga saffordiana* Pitt. *20883, 9006*		
	I	20883	Panama *20883*
E	*Inga standleyana* Pitt. *20883, 9006*		
	I	20883	Panama *20883*
I	*Intsia acuminata* Merr. *12983*		
	I	15960	Philippines *12983*
E	*Itaobimia magalhaesii* Rizz. *19560*		
	E	19560	Brazil - Minas Gerais *19560*
R	*Jacksonia calycina* Domin *20681*		
	R	20681	Australia - Western Australia *20681*
R	*Jacksonia compressa* Turcz. *20681*		
	R	20681	Australia - Western Australia *20681*
R	*Jacksonia velutina* Benth. *20681*		
	R	20681	Australia - Western Australia *20681*
R	*Julbernardia letouzeyi* J-F.Villiers *12346*		
	R		Cameroon *12346*
E	*Kalappia celebica* Kosterm. *14185*		
	E		Indonesia (Malili) *14185*
V	*Kennedia beckxiana* F.Muell. *20681, 10260*		
	V	20681	Australia - Western Australia *20681*
V	*Kennedia glabrata* (Benth.) Lindley *20681*		
	V	20681	Australia - Western Australia *20681*
V	*Kennedia macrophylla* (Meisner) Benth. *20681, 10260*		
	V	20681	Australia - Western Australia *20681*
V	*Kennedia retrorsa* Hemsley *20681*		
	V	20681	Australia - New South Wales *20681*
R	*Kingiodendron pinnatum* (DC.) Harms *14782, 21025*		

	R	14782	India - Karnataka *14782*
	R	14782	India - Kerala *14782*
	R	14782	India - Tamil Nadu *14782*
I	*Kotschya capitulifera* (Baker) J. Dewit & Duvign. var. *grandiflora* Verdc. *7959*		
	I	5926	Tanzania (Kigoma) *5926*
R	*Kotschya platyphylla* (Brenan) Verdc. *7959*		
	R		Tanzania (Iringa) *7959*
R	*Kotschya recurvifolia* (Taub.) F. White ssp. *longifolia* Verdc. *7959*		
	R		Tanzania *7959*
I	*Kunstleria altroviolacea* (Elm.) Merr. *13833*		
	I	13833	Philippines (low altitude) *13833*
R	*Labichea brassii* C.White & Francis *20681*		
	R	20681	Australia - Queensland *20681*
R	*Labichea buettneriana* F.Muell. *20681*		
	R	20681	Australia - Queensland *20681*
I	*Lasiobema flavum* De Wit		
	I		Malaysia - Peninsular Malaysia
I	*Lasiobema scandens* (Linn.) de Wit. var. *horsefieldii* (Wallich ex Prain) de Wit		
	I		India - Assam
	I		India - Meghalaya
E	*Lathyrus biflorus* T.W. & J.P. Nelson *20850*		
	E	20850	U.S. - California *20850*
R	*Lathyrus bitlisicus* Pesmen *12840*		
	R	12840	Turkey *12840*
R	*Lathyrus cilicicus* Hayek & Siehe *12840*		
	R	12840	Turkey *12840*
R	*Lathyrus cyaneus* (Stev.) Koch var. *pinnatus* Davis *12840*		
	R	12840	Turkey *12840*
Ex	*Lathyrus dominianus* Litv. *6930*		
	Ex	6930	former USSR *6930*
E	*Lathyrus grimesii* Barneby *20850*		
	R	20850	U.S. - Nevada *20850*
V	*Lathyrus hitchcockianus* Barneby & Reveal *20850*		
	I	20850	U.S. - California *20850*
	V	20850	U.S. - Nevada *20850*
V	*Lathyrus jepsonii* E. Greene ssp. *jepsonii* *20850*		
	V	20850	U.S. - California *20850*
R	*Lathyrus kersianus* Davis *12840*		
	R	12840	Turkey *12840*
R	*Lathyrus layardii* J. Ball ex Boiss. *12840*		
	R	12840	Turkey *12840*
E	*Lathyrus lentiformis* Plitm. *8895*		
	E		Israel (Upper Galilee) *8895*
V	*Lathyrus lycius* Boiss. *12840*		
	V	12840	Turkey *12840*
V	*Lathyrus neurolobus* Boiss. & Heldr. *20171*		
	V	20730	Greece - Crete *20730*
I	*Lathyrus nissolia* L. ssp. *futakii* Chriková *19321*		
	I	19321	Slovakia *19321*
R	*Lathyrus pancicii* (Jurisic) Adamovic *8000, 20171*		
	Ex	5204	Bulgaria (west) *5204*
	R		(former) Yugoslavia *8000*
V	*Lathyrus phaselitanus* Huber-Mor. & Davis *12840*		
	V	12840	Turkey *12840*

R **Lathyrus satdaghensis** Davis *12840*
   R   *12840* Turkey *12840*

R **Lathyrus stenolobus** Boiss. *12840*
   R   *12840* Turkey *12840*

R **Lathyrus tauricola** Davis *12840*
   R   *12840* Turkey *12840*

I **Lathyrus trachycarpus** (Boiss.) Boiss. *12840*
   I   *12840* Turkey *12840*

R **Lathyrus tracyi** Bradshaw *20850*
   I   *20850* U.S. - California *20850*

R **Lathyrus undulatus** Boiss. *12840, 20171*
   R   *12840* Turkey *12840*

V **Lathyrus vestitus** Nutt. ex Torr. & Gray ssp. **laetiflorus** (Greene) Broich *20850*
   I   *20850* U.S. - California *20850*

E **Lathyrus vestitus** Nutt. ex Torr. & Gray ssp. **vestitus** *20850*
   I   *20850* U.S. - California *20850*
   I   *20850* U.S. - Oregon *20850*

R **Leptoderris claessensii** De Wild. *19358*
   R   *19358* Zaire (Kasai) *19358*

R **Leptosema chapmanii** Crisp ms. *20681*
   R   *20681* Australia - Queensland *20681*

R **Lespedeza daurica** (Maxim.) Schindl. var. **shimadae** (Masamune) Masamune & Hosok. *20511*
   R   *20511* Taiwan *20511*

V **Lespedeza leptostachya** Engelm. *20850*
   E   *20850* U.S. - Illinois *20850*
   V   *20850* U.S. - Iowa *20850*
   E   *20850* U.S. - Minnesota *20850*
   E   *20850* U.S. - Wisconsin *20850*

R **Lespedeza satsumensis** Nakai *10572*
   R   *10572* Japan *10572*

R **Lessertia dykei** L.Bolus *20604*
   R   *20604* South Africa - Natal *20604*

I **Lessertia globosa** L.Bolus *20604*
   I   *20604* South Africa - Cape Province *20604*

R **Lessertia sneeuwbergensis** Germish. *20604*
   R   *20604* South Africa - Cape Province *20604*

V **Leucaena confertiflora** var. **adenotheloidea** *21316*
   V   *21316* Mexico *21316*

V **Leucaena confertiflora** var. **confertiflora** *21316*
   V   *21316* Mexico *21316*

V **Leucaena cuspidata** *21316*
   V   *21316* Mexico *21316*

V **Leucaena greggii** *21316*
   V   *21316* Mexico *21316*

E **Leucaena involucrata** *21316*
   E   *21316* Mexico - Sonora *21316*

V **Leucaena lempirana** *21316*
   V   *21316* Honduras (northern) *21316*

E **Leucaena magnifica** *21316*
   E   *21316* Guatemala (Chiquimula) *21316*

E **Leucaena matudae** *21316*
   E   *21316* Mexico *21316*

V **Leucaena pueblana** *21316*
   V   *21316* Mexico - Puebla (Tehuacan) *21316*

R **Liparia boucheri** (E.G.H.Oliv. & Fellingham)

   A.L.Schutte *20604*
   R   *20604* South Africa - Cape Province *20604*

I **Loesenera walkeri** (A. Chev.) J. Léonard *12346*
   I   Gabon *12346*

E **Lonchocarpus calcaratus** Hermann *20883, 9006*
   I   *20883* Panama *20883*

E **Lonchocarpus chiricanus** Pitt. *20883, 9006*
   I   *20883* Panama *20883*

R **Lonchocarpus chrysophyllus** Kleinhoonte *8679*
   R   *8679* French Guiana *8679*
   R   *8679* Guyana *8679*
   R   *8679* Suriname *8679*

E **Lonchocarpus ferrugineus** M. Sousa *20883*
   I   *20883* Costa Rica *20883*
   I   *20883* Nicaragua *20883*
   I   *20883* Panama *20883*

E **Lonchocarpus guatemalensis** (Pitt.) Hermann var. **proteranthus** (Pittier) F.J. Herm. *20883, 9006*
   I   *20883* Panama *20883*

R **Lonchocarpus kanurii** Brenan & J.B.Gillett *20057*
   V   *20057* Kenya *20057*
   R   *20884* Somalia (south) *20884*

E **Lonchocarpus monticolus** M. Sousa *20883, 10162*
   V   *11967* Nicaragua *20883*

E **Lonchocarpus morenoi** M. Sousa *20883, 10162*
   V   *11967* Nicaragua *20883*

V **Lonchocarpus patens** Urb. *20883, 19890*
   V   *19890* Jamaica (Trelawny) *20883*

E **Lonchocarpus pilosus** M. Sousa *20883, 10162*
   V   *11967* Nicaragua *20883*

R **Lonchocarpus retiferus** Standley & L.O.Williams *9061*
   R   *11967* Nicaragua *9061*

V **Lonchocarpus verrucosus** M. Sousa *20883*
   I   *20883* Guatemala *20883*
   I   *20883* Mexico *20883*
   I   *20883* Nicaragua *20883*

R **Lotononis acocksii** B.-E.van Wyk *20604*
   R   *20604* South Africa - Cape Province *20604*

R **Lotononis acuminata** Eckl. & Zeyh. *20604*
   R   *20604* South Africa - Cape Province *20604*

R **Lotononis acutiflora** Benth. *20604*
   R   *20604* South Africa - Cape Province *20604*

R **Lotononis anthyllopsis** B.-E.van Wyk *20604*
   R   *20604* South Africa - Cape Province *20604*

R **Lotononis arenicola** Schltr. *20604*
   R   *20604* South Africa - Cape Province *20604*

R **Lotononis argentea** Eckl. & Zeyh. *20604*
   R   *20604* South Africa - Cape Province *20604*

R **Lotononis azureoides** B.-E.van Wyk *20604*
   R   *20604* South Africa - Cape Province *20604*

R **Lotononis carnea** B.-E.van Wyk *20604*
   R   *20604* South Africa - Cape Province *20604*

R **Lotononis complanata** B.-E.van Wyk *20604*
   R   *20604* South Africa - Cape Province *20604*

R **Lotononis comptonii** B.-E.van Wyk *20604*
   R   *20604* South Africa - Cape Province *20604*

R **Lotononis dahlgrenii** B.-E.van Wyk *20604*
   R   *20604* South Africa - Cape Province *20604*

R **Lotononis densa** (Thunb.) Harv. ssp. **congesta** B.-E.Van Wyk *20604*

R		20604 South Africa - Cape Province 20604
R	*Lotononis densa* (Thunb.) Harv. ssp. *densa* 20604	
R		20604 South Africa - Cape Province 20604
R	*Lotononis dissitinodis* B.-E.van Wyk 20604	
R		20604 South Africa - Cape Province 20604
I	*Lotononis esterhuyseniana* B.-E.van Wyk 20604	
I		20604 South Africa - Cape Province 20604
R	*Lotononis exstipulata* L.Bolus 20604	
R		20604 South Africa - Cape Province 20604
R	*Lotononis globulosa* B.-E.van Wyk 20604	
R		20604 South Africa - Cape Province 20604
I	*Lotononis gracilifolia* B.-E.van Wyk 20604	
I		20604 South Africa - Cape Province 20604
I	*Lotononis harveyi* B.-E.van Wyk 20604	
I		20604 South Africa - Cape Province 20604
I	*Lotononis holosericea* (E.Mey.) B.-E.van Wyk 20604	
I		20604 South Africa - Cape Province 20604
R	*Lotononis involucrata* (P.J.Bergius) Benth. ssp. *bracteata* B.-E.Van Wyk 20604	
R		20604 South Africa - Cape Province 20604
R	*Lotononis involucrata* (P.J.Bergius) Benth. ssp. *digitata* B.-E.Van Wyk 20604	
R		20604 South Africa - Cape Province 20604
I	*Lotononis lamprifolia* B.-E.van Wyk 20604	
I		20604 South Africa - Cape Province 20604
R	*Lotononis laticeps* B.-E.van Wyk 20604	
R		20604 South Africa - Cape Province 20604
R	*Lotononis longicephala* B.-E.van Wyk 20604	
R		20604 South Africa - Cape Province 20604
R	*Lotononis macrocarpa* Eckl. & Zeyh. 20604	
R		20604 South Africa - Cape Province 20604
R	*Lotononis magnifica* B.-E.van Wyk 20604	
R		20604 South Africa - Cape Province 20604
R	*Lotononis minima* B.-E.van Wyk 20604	
R		20604 South Africa - Cape Province 20604
R	*Lotononis minor* Dummer & Jenn. 20604	
R		20604 South Africa - Natal 20604
R	*Lotononis mollis* (E.Mey.) Benth. 20604	
R		20604 South Africa - Cape Province 20604
R	*Lotononis newtonii* Dummer 20604	
R		20604 Angola 20604
I	*Lotononis oligocephala* B.-E.van Wyk 20604	
I		20604 South Africa - Cape Province 20604
R	*Lotononis pallens* (Eckl. & Zeyh.) Benth. 20604	
R		20604 South Africa - Cape Province 20604
R	*Lotononis perplexa* (E.Mey.) Eckl. & Zeyh. 20604	
R		20604 South Africa - Cape Province 20604
R	*Lotononis plicata* B.-E.van Wyk 20604	
R		20604 South Africa - Cape Province 20604
I	*Lotononis polycephala* (E.Mey.) Benth. 20604	
I		20604 South Africa - Cape Province 20604
R	*Lotononis purpurescens* B.-E.van Wyk 20604	
R		20604 South Africa - Cape Province 20604
I	*Lotononis racemiflora* B.-E.van Wyk 20604	
I		20604 South Africa - Cape Province 20604
R	*Lotononis sutherlandii* Dummer 20604	
R		20604 South Africa - Natal 20604

I	*Lotononis venosa* B.-E.van Wyk 20604	
I		20604 South Africa - Cape Province 20604
R	*Lotononis viborgioides* Benth. 20604	
R		20604 South Africa - Cape Province 20604
R	*Lotus aduncus* (Griseb.) Nyman 20171	
R		Greece
V	*Lotus argophyllus* (Gray) Greene var. *niveus* (Greene) Munz 20883, 20850	
V		20850 U.S. - California 20850
I		20883 Mexico 20883
V	*Lotus argyraeus* (Greene) Greene var. *multicaulis* (Ottley) Isely 20850	
E		20850 U.S. - California 20850
I		20850 U.S. - Nevada 20850
V	*Lotus argyraeus* (Greene) Greene var. *notitius* Isely 20850	
E		20850 U.S. - California 20850
R	*Lotus armeniacus* Kit Tan & Sorger 12840	
R		12840 Turkey 12840
R	*Lotus azoricus* P.W.Ball 8000, 20171	
R		19174 Portugal - Azores 8000
E	*Lotus berthelotii* Masferrer 14908	
E		14908 Spain - Canary Is. 14908
V	*Lotus callis-viridis* D. Bramwell & D.H. Davis 17781	
V		20750 Spain - Canary Is. 17891
R	*Lotus campylocladus* Webb & Berthel. 10260	
R		19174 Spain - Canary Is. 19174
E	*Lotus crassifolius* Moran ex Isely var. *otayensis* Moran ex Isely 20850	
E		20850 U.S. - California 20850
V	*Lotus dendroideus* (Eastw. ex Noddin) Isely var. *traskiae* (Eastw. ex Noddin) Isely 20850	
V		20850 U.S. - California 20850
R	*Lotus drepanocarpus* Durieu 20171	
R		Algeria
R		Tunisia
V	*Lotus dumetorum* Webb ex R.P. Murray 20750	
V		20750 Spain - Canary Is. 20750
V	*Lotus emeroides* R.P. Murray 20750	
V		20750 Spain - Canary Is. 20750
E	*Lotus eremiticus* Santos 20750	
E		20750 Spain - Canary Is. 20750
E	*Lotus genistoides* Webb 20750	
E		20750 Spain - Canary Is. 20750
R	*Lotus granadensis* Chrtková 20171	
R		Spain
R	*Lotus haydonii* (Orcutt) Greene 20850	
V		20850 U.S. - California 20850
R	*Lotus holosericeus* Webb & Berthel. 20750	
R		20750 Spain - Canary Is. 20750
E	*Lotus kunkelii* (E. Chueca) D. Bramwell & al. 17781	
E		20750 Spain - Canary Is. 17891
E	*Lotus leptophyllus* (Lowe) K. Larsen 20750	
E		20750 Spain - Canary Is. 20750
R	*Lotus macranthus* auct. azor., non Lowe 20171	
R		Portugal - Madeira
R	*Lotus macrotrichus* Boiss.	
R		Greece
E	*Lotus maculatus* Breitfeld 20750	

	E	20750 Spain - Canary Is. *20750*	
V	***Lotus mascaensis*** Burchard *20750*		
	V	20750 Spain - Canary Is. *20750*	
R	***Lotus mlanjeanus*** J.B.Gillett *7861*		
	R	Malawi *7861*	
E	***Lotus nuttallianus*** Greene *20883, 20850, 19002*		
	E	20850 U.S. - California *20850*	
	I	20883 Mexico *20883*	
V	***Lotus oblongifolius*** (Benth.) Greene var. ***cupreus*** (Greene) Ottley *20850*		
	V	20850 U.S. - California *20850*	
R	***Lotus procumbens*** (Greene) Greene *20850*		
	I	20850 U.S. - California *20850*	
E	***Lotus pyranthus*** Pérez *20750*		
	E	20750 Spain - Canary Is. *20750*	
E	***Lotus rubriflorus*** H.K. Sharsmith *20850*		
	E	20850 U.S. - California *20850*	
V	***Lotus salvagensis*** R.P. Murray		
	V	Portugal - Salvage Is.	
V	***Lotus spartioides*** Webb & Berthel. *20750*		
	V	20750 Spain - Canary Is. *20750*	
R	***Lotus unifoliolatus*** (Hook.) Benth. var. ***helleri*** (Britt.) Kartesz & Gandhi *20850*		
	E	20850 U.S. - Georgia *20850*	
	R	20850 U.S. - North Carolina *20850*	
	I	20850 U.S. - South Carolina *20850*	
	E	20850 U.S. - Virginia *20850*	
V	***Lotus yollabolliensis*** Munz *20850*		
	I	20850 U.S. - California *20850*	
V	***Lupinus abramsii*** C.P. Sm. *20850*		
	I	20850 U.S. - California *20850*	
E	***Lupinus antoninus*** Eastw. *20850*		
	E	20850 U.S. - California *20850*	
V	***Lupinus arboreus*** Sims var. ***eximius*** (Burtt-Davy) C.P. Sm. *20850*		
	V	20850 U.S. - California *20850*	
E	***Lupinus arequipensis*** C.P. Smith *18200*		
	E	9446 Peru *18200*	
E	***Lupinus aridus*** Douglas ex Lindley ssp. ***ashlandensis*** Cox *20850*		
	E	20850 U.S. - Oregon *20850*	
V	***Lupinus brevior*** (Jepson) Christian & D. Dunn *20850*		
	I	20850 U.S. - California *20850*	
R	***Lupinus burkei*** D. Dunn & Cox ssp. ***caeruleomontanus*** D. Dunn & Cox *20850*		
	R	20850 U.S. - Oregon *20850*	
V	***Lupinus caudatus*** (Eastw.) Hess & D. Dunn ssp. ***cutleri*** (Eastw.) Hess & D. Dunn *20850*		
	V	20850 U.S. - Arizona *20850*	
	I	20850 U.S. - New Mexico *20850*	
	E	20850 U.S. - Utah *20850*	
R	***Lupinus chamissonis*** Eschsch. *20850*		
	I	20850 U.S. - California *20850*	
V	***Lupinus citrinus*** Kellogg *20850*		
	V	20850 U.S. - California *20850*	
V	***Lupinus citrinus*** Kellogg var. ***citrinus*** *20850*		
	V	20850 U.S. - California *20850*	
E	***Lupinus citrinus*** Kellogg var. ***deflexus*** (Congd.) Jepson *20850*		
	E	20850 U.S. - California *20850*	
R	***Lupinus congdonii*** (C.P. Sm.) D. Dunn *20850*		
	I	20850 U.S. - California *20850*	
E	***Lupinus constancei*** T.W. & J.P. Nelson *20850*		
	E	20850 U.S. - California *20850*	
V	***Lupinus crassus*** Payson *20850*		
	V	20850 U.S. - Colorado *20850*	
R	***Lupinus croceus*** (Eastw.) Munz var. ***pilosellus*** (Eastw.) Munz *20850*		
	I	20850 U.S. - California *20850*	
R	***Lupinus culbertsonii*** Greene *20850*		
	I	20850 U.S. - California *20850*	
R	***Lupinus culbertsonii*** E. Greene ssp. ***culbertsonii*** *20850*		
	E	20850 U.S. - California *20850*	
V	***Lupinus cusickii*** S.Wats. *20850*		
	V	20850 U.S. - Oregon *20850*	
	I	20850 U.S. - Washington *20850*	
Ex/E	***Lupinus cusickii*** S.Wats. ssp. ***abortivus*** (Greene) Cox *20850*		
	I	20850 U.S. - Oregon *20850*	
E	***Lupinus cusickii*** S.Wats. ssp. ***brachypodus*** (Piper) Cox *20850*		
	I	20850 U.S. - Oregon *20850*	
E	***Lupinus cusickii*** S.Wats. ssp. ***cusickii*** *20850*		
	I	20850 U.S. - Oregon *20850*	
	I	20850 U.S. - Washington *20850*	
R	***Lupinus dalesiae*** Eastw. *20850*		
	R	20850 U.S. - California *20850*	
	I	20850 U.S. - Oregon *20850*	
V	***Lupinus duranii*** Eastw. *20850*		
	V	20850 U.S. - California *20850*	
V	***Lupinus elatus*** I.M. Johnston *20850*		
	I	20850 U.S. - California *20850*	
V	***Lupinus elmeri*** Greene *20850*		
	I	20850 U.S. - California *20850*	
V	***Lupinus excubitus*** M.E. Jones var. ***medius*** (Jepson) Munz *20850*		
	V	20850 U.S. - California *20850*	
V	***Lupinus fissicalyx*** Heller *20850*		
	I	20850 U.S. - Oregon *20850*	
R	***Lupinus flavoculatus*** Heller *20850*		
	I	20850 U.S. - California *20850*	
	I	20850 U.S. - Nevada *20850*	
	E	20850 U.S. - Utah *20850*	
R	***Lupinus fulcratus*** Greene *20850*		
	I	20850 U.S. - California *20850*	
	I	20850 U.S. - Nevada *20850*	
V	***Lupinus garfieldensis*** C.P. Sm. *20850*		
	I	20850 U.S. - Washington *20850*	
V	***Lupinus gracilentus*** Greene *20850*		
	I	20850 U.S. - California *20850*	
V	***Lupinus guadalupensis*** Greene *20883, 20850, 8058*		
	V	20850 U.S. - California *20850*	
	I	20883 Mexico *20883*	
V	***Lupinus hillii*** Greene *20850*		
	I	20850 U.S. - Arizona *20850*	
	I	20850 U.S. - New Mexico *20850*	
V	***Lupinus holmgrenianus*** C.P. Sm. *20850*		
	I	20850 U.S. - California *20850*	
	I	20850 U.S. - Nevada *20850*	

R   *Lupinus horizontalis* Heller *20850*
     I   *20850*   U.S. - California   *20850*

V   *Lupinus hyacinthinus* Greene *20850*
     I   *20850*   U.S. - California   *20850*

V   *Lupinus jonesii* Rydb. *20850*
     V   *20850*   U.S. - Utah   *20850*

R   *Lupinus kuschei* Eastw. *20850*
     V   *20850*   Canada - British Columbia   *20850*
     I   *20850*   Canada - Yukon Territory   *20850*
     E   *20850*   U.S. - Alaska   *20850*

V   *Lupinus lapidicola* Heller *20850*
     I   *20850*   U.S. - California   *20850*

E   *Lupinus lemmonii* C.P. Sm. *20850*
     I   *20850*   U.S. - Arizona   *20850*

R   *Lupinus longifolius* (S.Watson) Raven *20850*
     I   *20850*   U.S. - California   *20850*

E   *Lupinus lorenzensis* C.P. Smith *18200*
     E   *9446*   Peru   *18200*

V   *Lupinus ludovicianus* Greene *20850*
     V   *20850*   U.S. - California   *20850*

E   *Lupinus lyallii* Gray ssp. *alcis-temporis* (C.P. Sm.) Cox *20850*
     E   *20850*   U.S. - Idaho   *20850*

V   *Lupinus lyallii* Gray ssp. *minutifolius* (Eastw.) Cox *20850*
     V   *20850*   U.S. - Oregon   *20850*

V   *Lupinus lyallii* Gray ssp. *subpandens* C.P. Sm. ex D. Dunn *20850*
     I   *20850*   U.S. - Colorado   *20850*
     I   *20850*   U.S. - Idaho   *20850*
     I   *20850*   U.S. - Nevada   *20850*
     I   *20850*   U.S. - Oregon   *20850*

Ex/E   *Lupinus magnificus* M.E. Jones var. *magnificus* *20850*
     Ex/E   *20850*   U.S. - California   *20850*

E   *Lupinus magnistipulatus* Planchuelo & Dunn *20883*
     I   *20883*   Brazil   *20883*

V   *Lupinus malacophyllus* Greene *20850*
     V   *20850*   U.S. - Nevada   *20850*

E   *Lupinus mollendoensis* Ulbr. *18200*
     E   *9446*   Peru   *18200*

V   *Lupinus neomexicanus* Greene *20850*
     I   *20850*   U.S. - Arizona   *20850*
     I   *20850*   U.S. - New Mexico   *20850*

R   *Lupinus obtusilobus* Heller *20850*
     I   *20850*   U.S. - California   *20850*
     I   *20850*   U.S. - Nevada   *20850*

R   *Lupinus odoratus* Heller *20850*
     I   *20850*   U.S. - Arizona   *20850*
     I   *20850*   U.S. - California   *20850*
     I   *20850*   U.S. - Nevada   *20850*
     I   *20850*   U.S. - Oregon   *20850*
     I   *20850*   U.S. - Washington   *20850*

V   *Lupinus oreganus* Heller var. *kincaidii* C.P. Sm. *20850*
     Ex/E   *20850*   Canada - British Columbia   *20850*
     V   *20850*   U.S. - Oregon   *20850*
     E   *20850*   U.S. - Washington   *20850*

V   *Lupinus oreganus* Heller var. *oreganus* *20850*
     V   *20850*   U.S. - Oregon   *20850*

R   *Lupinus ornatus* Dougl. ex Lindl. *20850*
     I   *20850*   U.S. - Idaho   *20850*

     I   *20850*   U.S. - Oregon   *20850*
     I   *20850*   U.S. - Washington   *20850*

E   *Lupinus padre-crowleyi* C.P. Sm. *20850*
     E   *20850*   U.S. - California   *20850*

R   *Lupinus pratensis* Heller *20850*
     I   *20850*   U.S. - California   *20850*

E   *Lupinus punto-reyesensis* C.P. Sm. *20850*
     I   *20850*   U.S. - California   *20850*

V   *Lupinus roseolus* Rydb. *20850*
     I   *20850*   U.S. - Wyoming   *20850*

V   *Lupinus sellulus* Kellogg var. *sellulus* *20850*
     I   *20850*   U.S. - California   *20850*
     V   *20850*   U.S. - Idaho   *20850*
     I   *20850*   U.S. - Nevada   *20850*
     I   *20850*   U.S. - Oregon   *20850*
     I   *20850*   U.S. - Washington   *20850*

V   *Lupinus sericatus* Kellogg *20850*
     I   *20850*   U.S. - California   *20850*

R   *Lupinus sericeus* Kellogg ssp. *marianus* (Rydb.) Fleak & D. Dunn *20850*
     R   *20850*   U.S. - Utah   *20850*

E   *Lupinus setifolius* Planchuelo & Dunn *20883*
     I   *20883*   Brazil   *20883*

R   *Lupinus sierrae-blancae* Woot. & Standl. *20850*
     R   *20850*   U.S. - New Mexico   *20850*

R   *Lupinus sierrae-blancae* Woot. & Standl. ssp. *aquilinus* (Woot. & Standl.) Fleak & D. Dunn *20850*
     R   *20850*   U.S. - New Mexico   *20850*

V   *Lupinus sierrae-blancae* Woot. & Standl. ssp. *sierrae-blancae* *20850*
        20850   U.S. - New Mexico   *20850*

V   *Lupinus spectabilis* Hoover *20850*
     V   *20850*   U.S. - California   *20850*

Ex/E   *Lupinus sublanatus* Eastw. *20850, 10260*
     Ex/E   *20850*   U.S. - California   *20850*

V   *Lupinus tidestromii* Greene *20850*
     V   *20850*   U.S. - California   *20850*

E   *Lupinus tidestromii* E. Greene var. *layneae* (Eastw.) Munz *20850*
     E   *20850*   U.S. - California   *20850*

E   *Lupinus tidestromii* E. Greene var. *tidestromii* *20850*
     E   *20850*   U.S. - California   *20850*

I   *Lupinus tucumanensis* C.P. Smith *16336*
     I   *16336*   Argentina   *16336*

V   *Lupinus westianus* Small *20850, 17890*
     V   *20850*   U.S. - Florida   *20850*

E   *Lupinus westianus* Small var. *aridorum* (McFarlin ex Beckner) Isely *20850*
     E   *20850*   U.S. - Florida   *20850*

E   *Machaerium chambersii* Dwyer *20883, 9006*
     I   *20883*   Panama   *20883*

E   *Machaerium glabripes* Pitt. *20883, 9006*
     I   *20883*   Panama   *20883*

R   *Machaerium hirtum* (Vell.) Stellfeld *20883*
     I   *20883*   Brazil   *20883*
     R   *20883*   Paraguay   *20883*

R   *Machaerium scleroxylon* Tul. *20883*
     I   *20883*   Brazil   *20883*
     R   *20883*   Paraguay   *20883*

E *Machaerium villosum* Vogel *10370*
    E   *10370* Brazil *10370*

E *Macrolobium costaricense* W. Burger *9802*
    E   *17459* Costa Rica *9802*

E *Macrolobium pittieri* (Rose) Schery *20883, 9006*
    I   *9426* Panama *20883*

R *Macrosamanea kegelii* (Meisn.) Kleinh. *18176*
    R   *19954* French Guiana *18176*
    R   *8679* Suriname *8679*

R *Macrotyloma coddii* Verdc. *20604*
    R   *20604* South Africa - Natal *20604*

R *Martiodendron meditterraneum* (Mart.ex Benth.) **Koepper** *16692*
    R   *16692* Brazil - Bahia *16692*

V *Medicago cancellata* M.Bieb. *8000, 20171*
    V   *11552* Russian Federation (Caucasus & west) *20628*

R *Medicago citrina* (Font Quer) Greuter *20692*
    E   *20692* Spain (Columbretes Is.) *20692*
    R   *20692* Spain - Balearic Is. *20692*

R *Medicago cyrenaea* Maire & M. Weiller
    R   Libya

R *Medicago pironae* Vis. *20171*
    R   Italy
    R   *13662* Slovenia (western) *13662*

R *Medicago rhodopea* Velen. *5204, 20171*
    R   *5204* Bulgaria (mainly southern and eastern - eight sites) *5204*

R *Medicago shepardii* Post ex Boiss. *12840*
    R   *12840* Turkey *12840*

R *Medicago strasseri* Greuter, Matthäs & Risse *21119*
    R   *20730* Greece - Crete *20730*

V *Melilotus segetalis* (Brot.) Ser. ssp. *fallax* **Franco** *20076*
    V   *20076* Portugal *20076*

V *Microberlinia bisulcata* A. Chev. *7926*
    V   *13924* Cameroon *16174*
    V   *13294* Nigeria (Oban Hills) *20991*

R *Millettia angustistipellata* De Wild. *19358*
    R   *19358* Zaire (Bas-Katanga) *19358*

I *Millettia decipiens* Prain *19209*
    I   *19209* Malaysia - Peninsular Malaysia (Perak) *19209*

I *Millettia elongistyla* J.B.Gillett *7959*
    I   *5926* Tanzania (Morogoro & Ulanga District) *5926*

I *Millettia eriocarpa* Dunn *20556*
    I   *5926* Tanzania (Lindi & Newala) *5926*

I *Millettia foxworthyi* Merr. *13833*
    I   *13833* Philippines (Palawan) *13833*

I *Millettia oblata* Dunn ssp. *stolzii* **J.B.Gillett** *7959*
    I   *5926* Tanzania (Rungwe District) *5926*

V *Millettia oblata* Dunn ssp. *teitensis* **J.B.Gillett** *7959*
    V   *20057* Kenya (Teita district) *7959*

I *Millettia pterocarpa* Dunn *17450*
    I   Malaysia - Peninsular Malaysia

V *Millettia puguensis* J.B.Gillett *7959*
    V   *5926* Tanzania (Uzaramo Distr.) *7959*

R *Millettia pulchra* Kurz var. *microphylla* **Dunn** *20511*
    R   *20511* Taiwan *20511*

I *Millettia sacleuxii* Dunn *7959, 20556*
    I   *5926* Tanzania (Lushoto & Morogoro) *5926*

V *Millettia sericantha* Harms *20556*
    V   *5926* Tanzania (Morogoro Distr.) *7959*

R *Millettia stenopetala* Hauman *19358*
    R   *19358* Zaire (central Forestier) *19358*

V *Millettia tanaensis* J.B.Gillett *20057*
    V   *20057* Kenya (central) *20057*

I *Millettia usaramensis* Taub. var. *parvifolia* **Dunn** *7959*
    I   *5926* Tanzania (Kilwa) *5926*

V *Millettia warneckei* Harms *20274*
    V   *20858* Ghana *20274*
    V   *20858* Guinea *7926*
    V   *20858* Liberia *7926*
    V   *20858* Sierra Leone *7926*
    V   *20858* Togo *7926*

R *Mimosa altoparanensis* Burk. *20883*
    R   *20883* Paraguay *20883*

E *Mimosa apleura* Urban *5607*
    E   *19105* Cuba (Pinar del Rio) *5607*

I *Mimosa azuensis* Britton *5642*
    I   Dominican Republic (Azua, San Cristobal) *21008*

E *Mimosa berlandieri* Leon
    E   *19105* Cuba (Piñar del Rio) *19105*

I *Mimosa farisii* Leonard ex Britton *5642*
    I   Dominican Republic (Najayo, Nigua) *5642*

R *Mimosa fiebrigii* Hassler *20883*
    R   *20883* Paraguay *20883*

R *Mimosa flocculosa* Burk. *20883*
    R   *20883* Paraguay *20883*

V *Mimosa lanuginosa* Glaz. ex Burkart *19565*
    V   *19565* Brazil - Distrito Federal *19565*

I *Mimosa moaensis* Britton & P. Wilson
    I   Cuba (Holguin)

R *Mimosa mossambicensis* Brenan *7749*
    R   Mozambique *7749*

V *Mimosa quadrivalvis* var. *urbaniana* **Barneby** *20883*
    I   *20883* Puerto Rico *20883*

R *Mimosa uliginosa* Chodat & Hassler *20883*
    I   *20883* Argentina *20883*
    V   *20883* Paraguay *20883*

E *Mimosa vellosiella* var. *pubescens* (Benth.) **Burk.** *20883*
    I   *20883* Argentina *20883*
    E   *20883* Paraguay *20883*

E *Mimosa xochipalensis* R. Grether *20883*
    I   *20883* Mexico *20883*

R *Mirbelia confertiflora* Pedley *20681*
    R   *20681* Australia - Queensland *20681*

I *Monopetalanthus durandii* F. Hallé & Normand *12346*
    I   *12346* Gabon (Monts de Cristal) *12346*

I *Monopetalanthus hedinii* (A. Chev.) Pellegrin
    I   Cameroon *16174*

I *Mora abbottii* Rose & Leonard *5642*

I	Dominican Republic (Sierra de Quita Espuela, San Francisco de Macorís) *21008*		

E   *Mucuna fawcettii* Urb. *20883, 13336*
     E   *13336*   Jamaica *20883*

V   *Mucuna killipiana* J. Hernández-C. & C. Barbosa *20883*
     I   *20883*   Colombia *20883*

I   *Mucuna minima* Haines *7771*
     I   *7771*   India - Orissa (Sambalpur) *7771*

R   *Mucuna toyoshimae* Nakai *8038*
     R   *19134*   Japan - Ogasawara-shoto *8038*

Ex   *Nemcia lehmannii* (Meisner) Crisp *20681*
     Ex   *20681*   Australia - Western Australia *20681*

R   *Nemcia stipularis* (Meisner) Crisp *20681*
     R   *20681*   Australia - Western Australia *20681*

I   *Neochevalierodendron stephanii* (A. Chev.) J. Léonard *12346*
     I   Gabon *12346*

R   *Newtonia erlangeri* (Harms) Brenan *17435*
     R   *17435*   Kenya (Boni forest & Tana river) *17435*
     R   *20884*   Somalia *20162*
     R   *17435*   Tanzania *17435*

R   *Nissolia platycalyx* S.Watson *20850*
     E   *20850*   U.S. - Texas *20850*

V   *Nogra dalzellii* (Baker) Merr. *14782*
     V   *14782*   India - Karnataka *14782*
     V   *14782*   India - Maharashtra *14782*

E   *Nogra filicaulis* (Kurz) Merr. *14782*
     E   *14782*   India - Madhaya Pradesh *14782*
     Ex   *14782*   Myanmar *14782*

R   *Notodon cayensis* Britton & Wilson *5607*
     R   *19105*   Cuba (Camaguey) *5607*

R   *Notospartium glabrescens* Petrie
     R   New Zealand - South Is.

R   *Notospartium torulosum* Kirk *86*
     R   *19305*   New Zealand - South Is. *19305*

R   *Oddoniodendron normandii* Aubrév. *12346*
     R   Gabon *12346*

R   *Onobrychis albiflora* Huber-Mor. *12840*
     R   *12840*   Turkey *12840*

Ex   *Onobrychis aliacmonia* Rech.f. *14155*
     Ex   *14155*   Greece *14155*

R   *Onobrychis araxina* Schis. *12840*
     R   *12840*   Turkey *12840*

R   *Onobrychis argaea* Boiss. & Bal. *12840*
     R   *12840*   Turkey *12840*

R   *Onobrychis argyrea* Boiss. ssp. *isaurica* Hedge & Huber-Mor. *12840*
     R   *12840*   Turkey *12840*

R   *Onobrychis beata* Sirj *12840*
     R   *12840*   Turkey *12840*

V   *Onobrychis bornmuelleri* Freyn *12840*
     V   *12840*   Turkey *12840*

V   *Onobrychis cilicica* Kit Tan & Sorger *12840*
     V   *12840*   Turkey *12840*

I   *Onobrychis degenii* auct. bulg., non Dörfl. *20171*
     I   (former) Yugoslavia

R   *Onobrychis densijuga* Hedge ex Huber-Mor. *12840*
     R   *12840*   Turkey *12840*

R   *Onobrychis elata* Boiss. & Bal. *12840*

     R   *12840*   Turkey *12840*

R   *Onobrychis germanicopolitana* Huber-Mor. & Simon *12840*
     R   *12840*   Turkey *12840*

I   *Onobrychis halyensis* Sirj *12840*
     I   *12840*   Turkey *12840*

R   *Onobrychis huetiana* Boiss. *12840*
     R   *12840*   Turkey *12840*

V   *Onobrychis mutensis* Kit Tan & Sorger *12840*
     V   *12840*   Turkey *12840*

R   *Onobrychis nitida* Boiss. *12840*
     R   *12840*   Turkey *12840*

R   *Onobrychis occulta* Hedge & Huber-Mor. *12840*
     R   *12840*   Turkey *12840*

R   *Onobrychis ornata* (Willd.) Desv. *12840*
     R   *12840*   Turkey *12840*

R   *Onobrychis pallasii* (Willd.) M.Bieb. *20171*
     R   former European USSR

R   *Onobrychis paucijuga* Bornm. *12840*
     R   *12840*   Turkey *12840*

R   *Onobrychis pisidica* Boiss. *12840*
     R   *12840*   Turkey *12840*

R   *Onobrychis podperae* Sirj *12840*
     R   *12840*   Turkey *12840*

R   *Onobrychis quadrijuga* Hedge & Huber-Mor. *12840*
     R   *12840*   Turkey *12840*

R   *Onobrychis radiata* (Desf.) Bieb. *20171*
     R   former USSR

Ex/E   *Onobrychis richardii* Bak. *19704*
     Ex/E   *19704*   Ethiopia (Tigray Upland) *19704*

R   *Onobrychis sivasica* Kit Tan & Sorger *12840*
     R   *12840*   Turkey *12840*

V   *Onobrychis sphaciotica* Greuter *20171*
     V   *20731*   Greece - Crete *20731*

R   *Onobrychis stenostachya* Freyn ssp. *krausei* (Sirj.) Hedge *12840*
     R   *12840*   Turkey *12840*

R   *Onobrychis stenostachya* Freyn ssp. *sosnowskyi* (Grossh.) Hedge *12840*
     R   *12840*   Turkey *12840*

I   *Onobrychis tavernierifolia* Stocks ex Boiss. *5942*
     I   *5942*   Uzbekistan *5942*

R   *Ononis adenotricha* Boiss. var. *nuda* Huber-Mor. *12840*
     R   *12840*   Turkey *12840*

V   *Ononis avellana* Pomel *10488*
     V   *14958*   Algeria *10488*

R   *Ononis basiadnata* Huber-Mor. *12840*
     R   *12840*   Turkey *12840*

E   *Ononis christii* Bolle *20750*
     E   *20750*   Spain - Canary Is. *20750*

V   *Ononis crinita* Pomel *10488*
     V   *14958*   Algeria *10488*

V   *Ononis hackelii* Lange *20076, 20171*
     V   *20076*   Portugal *20076*

R   *Ononis hebecarpa* Webb & Berthel. *20750*
     R   *20750*   Spain - Canary Is. *20750*

R   *Ononis jahandiezii* Maire

R   Morocco

R   *Ononis macrosperma* **Huber-Mor.** *12840*
    R   *12840* Turkey *12840*

E   *Ononis megalostachys* **Munby** *10488*
    E   *14958* Algeria *10488*

V   *Ononis natrix* **L. ssp.** *ramosissima* **(Desf.) Batt.** *18223, 20171*
    V   *19052* United Kingdom - Gibraltar *18223*

R   *Ononis rentonarensis* **M.B.Crespo & L.Serra** *20692*
    R   *20692* Spain (Rentonar Mountains, Alicante province) *20692*

I   *Ononis saxicola* **Boiss. & Reut.** *20171*
    I   *20660* Spain (Cádiz, Málaga) *20661*

R   *Ononis sessilifolia* **Bornm.** *12840*
    R   *12840* Turkey *12840*

R   *Ononis verae* **Sirj.** *20171*
    R   *20731* Greece - Crete *20731*

Ex   *Orbexilum stipulatum* **(Torr. & Gray) Rydb.** *20850*
    Ex *20850* U.S. - Kentucky *20850*

V   *Orbexilum virgatum* **(Nutt.) Rydb.** *20850*
    I   *20850* U.S. - Florida *20850*
    I   *20850* U.S. - Georgia *20850*

R   *Ormocarpum caeruleum* **Balf. f.** *15534*
    R   *15534* Yemen - Socotra *15534*

R   *Ormocarpum flavum* **J.B.Gillett** *7959*
    R   Tanzania (Ruaha valley) *20921*

E   *Ormosia cruenta* **Rudd** *20883, 9006*
    R   *19796* Panama *20883*

R   *Ormosia dasycarpa* **Jacks.** *20883*
    R   *20883* Dominica *20883*
    E   *20883* Grenada *20883*
    R   *20883* St Vincent *20883*

V   *Ormosia hosiei* **Hemsley & Wilson** *17617*
    V   *17617* China - Fujian *11139*
    V   *17617* China - Gansu (Wenxian) *11139*
    V   *17617* China - Guizhou (Chishui) *11139*
    V   *17617* China - Hubei *11139*
    V   *17617* China - Jiangsu *11139*
    V   *17617* China - Jiangxi *11139*
    V   *17617* China - Shaanxi *11139*
    V   *17617* China - Sichuan *11139*
    V   *17617* China - Zhejiang *11139*

E   *Ormosia howii* **Merr. & Chen** *17617*
    E   *18038* China - Guangdong (Yangchong; Diaolueshan) *11139*
    E   *18038* China - Hainan Is. *11139*

V   *Ormosia jamaicensis* **Urb.** *20883, 13336*
    V   *13336* Jamaica *20883*

E   *Ormosia panamensis* **Benth.** *20883, 9006*
    R   *19796* Panama *20883*

R   *Ornithopus uncinatus* **Maire & Sam.** *12346*
    R   Morocco *12346*

V   *Otholobium argenteum* **(Thunb.) C.H.Stirt.** *20604*
    V   *20604* South Africa - Cape Province *20604*

V   *Otholobium bolusii* **(H.M.L.Forbes) C.H.Stirt.** *20604*
    V   *20604* South Africa - Cape Province *20604*

R   *Otholobium bowieanum* **(Harv.) C.H.Stirt.** *20604*
    R   *20604* South Africa - Cape Province *20604*

E   *Otholobium carneum* **(E.Mey.) C.H.Stirt.** *20604*
    E   *20604* South Africa - Cape Province *20604*

E   *Otholobium dreweae* **C.H.Stirt. ined.** *20604*
    E   *20604* South Africa - Cape Province *20604*

R   *Otholobium flexuosum* **C.H.Stirt.** *20604*
    R   *20604* South Africa - Cape Province *20604*

V   *Otholobium fruticans* **(L.) C.H.Stirt.** *20604*
    V   *20604* South Africa - Cape Province *20604*

R   *Otholobium hamatum* **(Harv.) C.H.Stirt.** *20604*
    R   *20604* South Africa - Cape Province *20604*

R   *Otholobium heterosepalum* **(Fourc.) C.H.Stirt.** *20604*
    R   *20604* South Africa - Cape Province *20604*

V   *Otholobium incanum* **C.H.Stirt.** *20604*
    V   *20604* South Africa - Cape Province *20604*

E   *Otholobium lanceolatum* **C.H.Stirt. ined.** *20604*
    E   *20604* South Africa - Cape Province *20604*

R   *Otholobium lucens* **C.H.Stirt. ined.** *20604*
    R   *20604* South Africa - Cape Province *20604*

R   *Otholobium macradenium* **(Harv.) C.H.Stirt.** *20604*
    R   *20604* South Africa - Cape Province *20604*

R   *Otholobium nitens* **C.H.Stirt. ined.** *20604*
    R   *20604* South Africa - Cape Province *20604*

R   *Otholobium parviflorum* **(E.Mey.) C.H.Stirt.** *20604*
    R   *20604* South Africa - Cape Province *20604*

R   *Otholobium pictum* **C.H.Stirt.** *20604*
    R   *20604* South Africa - Cape Province *20604*

V   *Otholobium piliferum* **C.H.Stirt. ined.** *20604*
    V   *20604* South Africa - Cape Province *20604*

R   *Otholobium polyphyllum* **(Eckl. & Zeyh.) C.H.Stirt.** *20604, 20039*
    I   *20039* Swaziland *20039*
    R   *20604* South Africa - Cape Province *20604*

E   *Otholobium pungens* **C.H.Stirt.** *20604*
    E   *20604* South Africa - Cape Province *20604*

R   *Otholobium pustulatum* **C.H.Stirt.** *20604*
    R   *20604* South Africa - Cape Province *20604*

R   *Otholobium racemosum* **(Thunb.) C.H.Stirt.** *20604*
    R   *20604* South Africa - Cape Province *20604*

V   *Otholobium rotundifolium* **(L.f.) C.H.Stirt.** *20604*
    V   *20604* South Africa - Cape Province *20604*

V   *Otholobium rubicundum* **C.H.Stirt.** *20604*
    V   *20604* South Africa - Cape Province *20604*

V   *Otholobium sabulosum* **C.H.Stirt. ined.** *20604*
    V   *20604* South Africa - Cape Province *20604*

E   *Otholobium saxosum* **C.H.Stirt. ined.** *20604*
    E   *20604* South Africa - Cape Province *20604*

R   *Otholobium spissum* **C.H.Stirt. ined.** *20604*
    R   *20604* South Africa - Cape Province *20604*

R   *Otholobium swartbergense* **C.H.Stirt.** *20604*
    R   *20604* South Africa - Cape Province *20604*

V   *Otholobium thomii* **(Harv.) C.H.Stirt.** *20604*
    V   *20604* South Africa - Cape Province *20604*

V   *Otholobium venustum* **(Eckl. & Zeyh.) C.H.Stirt.** *20604*
    V   *20604* South Africa - Cape Province *20604*

V   *Otholobium zeyheri* **(Harv.) C.H.Stirt.** *20604*
    V   *20604* South Africa - Cape Province *20604*

V   *Oxystigma msoo* **Harms** *20057*
    V   *20057* Kenya (Pangani, Tana delta) *20057*
    V   *20057* Tanzania (Rau forest, Pangani) *17435*

E   *Oxytropis arctica* **Welsh var.** *barnebyana* **Welsh** *20850, 21309*

E	*20850* U.S. - Alaska *20850*	
I	***Oxytropis argyroleuca*** Bornm. *12840*	
	I	*12840* Turkey *12840*
R	***Oxytropis astragaloides*** A. Boriss	
	R	former USSR *6930*
V	***Oxytropis bellii*** (Britt. ex Macoun) Palibin *20850*	
	I	*20850* Canada - Manitoba *20850*
	I	*20850* Canada - Franklin *20850*
R	***Oxytropis beringensis*** Jurtz. *21309*	
	R	*21309* Russia (E.Europe) - Northwest *21309*
E	***Oxytropis campestris*** (L.) DC. var. ***chartacea*** (Fassett) Barneby *20850*	
	E	*20850* U.S. - Wisconsin *20850*
R	***Oxytropis campestris*** (L.) DC. var. ***columbiana*** (St. John) Barneby *20850*	
	R	*20850* Canada - British Columbia *20850*
	E	*20850* U.S. - Montana *20850*
	E	*20850* U.S. - Washington *20850*
R	***Oxytropis campestris*** (L.) DC. ssp. ***tatrae*** (Borb.) Dost. *19321*	
	R	*19751* Poland *19751*
	V	*19321* Slovakia *19321*
V	***Oxytropis deflexa*** (Pall.) DC. ssp. ***norvegica*** Nordh. *8000, 20171*	
	V	*17832* Norway *8000*
R	***Oxytropis echidna*** Vved. *5942*	
	R	*5942* Kazakhstan *5942*
R	***Oxytropis hidakamontana*** Miyabe & Tatew. *10572*	
	R	*10572* Japan *10572*
R	***Oxytropis hippolyti*** Boriss	
	R	former European USSR
R	***Oxytropis huddelsonii*** Porsild *20850*	
	R	*20850* Canada - British Columbia *20850*
	I	*20850* Canada - Yukon Territory *20850*
	V	*20850* U.S. - Alaska *20850*
R	***Oxytropis jordalii*** ssp. ***davisii*** (Welsh) Elisens & Packer *20850*	
	R	*20850* Canada - British Columbia *20850*
R	***Oxytropis kamtschatica*** Hulten	
	R	Asiatic U.S.S.R. (Far east) *6930*
R	***Oxytropis kateninii*** Jurtz. *21309*	
	R	*21309* Russia (E.Europe) - Northwest *21309*
V	***Oxytropis kobukensis*** Welsh *20850*	
	V	*20850* U.S. - Alaska *20850*
R	***Oxytropis kokrinensis*** Porsild *20850*	
	R	*20850* U.S. - Alaska *20850*
R	***Oxytropis lagopus*** Nutt. var. ***conjugans*** Barneby *20850, 13153*	
	E	*20850* Canada - Alberta *20850*
	R	*20850* U.S. - Montana *20850*
R	***Oxytropis megalantha*** H. Boissieu *10572*	
	R	*10572* Japan *10572*
I	***Oxytropis mumynabadensis*** B. Fedtsch. *5942*	
	I	*5942* Russia (Far East) - Primorye (south) *5942*
R	***Oxytropis nana*** Nutt. var. ***nana*** *20850*	
	R	*20850* U.S. - Wyoming *20850*
R	***Oxytropis nana*** Nutt. var. ***obnapiformis*** (C.L. Porter) Isely *20850*	
	R	*20850* U.S. - Colorado *20850*
	V	*20850* U.S. - Utah *20850*

E	*20850* U.S. - Wyoming *20850*	
R	***Oxytropis nana*** Nutt. var. ***salmonensis*** (Barneby) Isely *20850*	
	R	*20850* U.S. - Idaho *20850*
E	***Oxytropis nigrescens*** (Pallas) Fisch. ex DC. var. ***lonchopoda*** Barneby *20850, 1034*	
	E	*20850* Canada - Yukon Territory *20850*
R	***Oxytropis oreophila*** Gray var. ***jonesii*** (Barneby) Barneby *20850*	
	R	*20850* U.S. - Utah *20850*
R	***Oxytropis prenja*** (Beck) Beck *20178, 20171*	
	R	*20178* Albania *20178*
	V	*21091* Bosnia & Herzegovina *21091*
	R	(former) Yugoslavia
R	***Oxytropis purpurea*** (Baldacci) Markgraf *20178, 20171*	
	R	*20178* Albania *20178*
	R	Greece
R	***Oxytropis putoranica*** M. Ivanova *21309*	
	R	*21309* Russia (E.Europe) - North *21309*
R	***Oxytropis rishiriensis*** Matsum. *10572*	
	R	*10572* Japan *10572*
R	***Oxytropis schmorgunoviae*** Jurtz. *21309*	
	R	*21309* Russia (E.Europe) - North *21309*
R	***Oxytropis shokanbetuensis*** Miyabe & Tatew. *10572*	
	R	*10572* Japan *10572*
R	***Oxytropis sordida*** (Willd.) Pers. ssp. ***arctolenensis*** Jurtz. *21309*	
	R	*21309* Russia (E.Europe) - North *21309*
R	***Oxytropis tichomirovii*** Jurtz. *21309*	
	R	*21309* Russia (E.Europe) - North *21309*
V	***Oxytropis todomoshiriensis*** Miyabe & Miyake *5942*	
	V	*11552* Russia (Far East) - Sakhalin (south) *5942*
R	***Oxytropis uniflora*** Jurtz. *21309*	
	R	*21309* Russia (E.Europe) - Northwest *21309*
R	***Oxytropis uralensis*** (L.) DC. *20171*	
	R	former European USSR
R	***Oxytropis uschakovii*** Jurtz. *21309*	
	R	*21309* Russia (E.Europe) - North *21309*
	R	*21309* Russia (E.Europe) - Northwest *21309*
R	***Oxytropis wrangelii*** Jurtzev *21309*	
	R	*21309* Russia (E.Europe) - North *21309*
	R	*21309* Russia (E.Europe) - Northwest *21309*
	R	former USSR *6930*
R	***Paracalyx balfourii*** (Vierh.) Ali *15534*	
	R	*15534* Yemen - Socotra *15534*
R	***Paracalyx schweinfurthii*** (Wagner & Vierh.) Ali *15534*	
	R	*15534* Yemen - Socotra *15534*
V	***Paramachaerium gruberi*** Brizicky *20883, 9006*	
	E	*20883* Costa Rica *20883*
	I	*20883* Panama *20883*
V	***Parkia bahiae*** H. C. Hopkins *20883*	
	I	*20883* Brazil *20883*
R	***Parkia cachimboensis*** H. C. Hopkins *20883*	
	I	*20883* Brazil *20883*
I	***Parkia harbesonii*** Elm. *13833*	
	I	*13833* Philippines (Palawan) *13833*
R	***Parkia paraensis*** Ducke *20883*	
	I	*20883* Brazil *20883*
R	***Parkia reticulata*** Ducke *20883*	

I	20883	Brazil *20883*
I	20883	French Guiana *20883*

E   *Parkia truncata* Cowan *20883*

I	20883	Venezuela *20883*

R   *Parkinsonia raimondoi* Brenan *12346*

R	20884	Somalia *12346*

R   *Pearsonia mesopontica* Polhill *7884*

R		Zimbabwe *7884*

R   *Pediomelum aromaticum* (Payson) W.A. Weber *20850*

I	20850	U.S. - Arizona *20850*
V	20850	U.S. - Colorado *20850*
V	20850	U.S. - Utah *20850*

R   *Pediomelum castoreum* (S.Watson) Rydb. *20850*

E	20850	U.S. - Arizona *20850*
I	20850	U.S. - California *20850*
I	20850	U.S. - Nevada *20850*

V   *Pediomelum humile* Rydb. *20883, 20850*

V	20850	U.S. - Texas *20850*
E	20883	Mexico *20883*

R   *Pediomelum megalanthum* (Woot. & Standl.) Rydb. *20850*

I	20850	U.S. - Arizona *20850*
R	20850	U.S. - Colorado *20850*
I	20850	U.S. - Nevada *20850*
I	20850	U.S. - New Mexico *20850*
I	20850	U.S. - Utah *20850*

E   *Pediomelum megalanthum* var. *epipsilum* (Barneby) J. Grimes *20850*

E	20850	U.S. - Arizona *20850*
E	20850	U.S. - Utah *20850*

R   *Pediomelum megalanthum* var. *megalanthum* *20850*

I	20850	U.S. - Arizona *20850*
I	20850	U.S. - Colorado *20850*
I	20850	U.S. - New Mexico *20850*
R	20850	U.S. - Utah *20850*

V   *Pediomelum pariense* (Welsh & Atwood) J. Grimes *20850*

V	20850	U.S. - Utah *20850*

Ex/E   *Pediomelum pentaphyllum* (L.) Rydb. *20850*

Ex/E	20850	U.S. - Arizona *20850*
Ex/E	20850	U.S. - New Mexico *20850*
Ex/E	20850	U.S. - Texas *20850*
Ex/E	20883	Mexico *20883*

R   *Pediomelum reverchonii* (S.Watson) Rydb. *20850*

V	20850	U.S. - Oklahoma *20850*
V	20850	U.S. - Texas *20850*

V   *Pellegriniodendron diphyllum* (Harms) J.Leonard *20274*

V	20858	Cameroon *20274*
V	20858	Côte d'Ivoire *20274*
V	20858	Gabon *20274*
V	20858	Ghana *20274*

I   *Peltophorum berteroanum* Urban *5642*

I		Dominican Republic *5642*

I   *Phanera decumbens* (M.R. Henderson) De Wit

I		Malaysia - Peninsular Malaysia

I   *Phanera khasiana* (Baker) Thoth.

I		India - Arunachal Pradesh
I		India - Meghalaya

I   *Phanera nicobarica* Balakr. & Thoth. *7771*

I		India - Nicobar Is. *7771*

I   *Phanera semibifida* (Roxb.) Benth. var. *subglabra* (Merr.) de Wit *13833*

I	13833	Philippines (low altitude) *13833*

I   *Phanera wallichii* (Macbr.) Thoth.

I		India - Assam
I		India - Meghalaya

E   *Phaseolus lignosus* Britton

E		Bermuda

R   *Phaseolus polystachios* (L.) B.S.P. var. *sinuatus* (Nutt.) R. Marechal, J.M. Mascherpa & F. Stainier *20850*

I	20850	U.S. - Alabama *20850*
I	20850	U.S. - Florida *20850*
V	20850	U.S. - Georgia *20850*
E	20850	U.S. - Mississippi *20850*
R	20850	U.S. - North Carolina *20850*
I	20850	U.S. - South Carolina *20850*

R   *Phyllota diffusa* (Hook.f.) F.Muell. *20681*

R	20681	Australia - Tasmania *20681*

V   *Phyllota humifusa* Benth. *20681*

V	20681	Australia - New South Wales *20681*

E   *Piptadenia cebil* Griseb. *20883*

E	20883	Brazil *17750*

V   *Piptadenia hassleriana* Chodat *20883*

V	20883	Paraguay *20883*

R   *Piptadenia paraguaiensis* (Benth.) Lindm. *20883*

I	20883	Argentina *20883*
R	20883	Paraguay *20883*

E   *Piptadenia paraguayensis* (Benth.) Lindm. *16336*

E	16336	Argentina *16336*
E	20176	Argentina - Chaco *20176*
E	20176	Argentina - Formosa *20176*

V   *Piptadeniopsis lomentifera* Burk. *20883*

V	20883	Paraguay *20883*

I   *Pithecellobium abbotti* Rose & Leonard *5642*

I		Dominican Republic (Los Haitises, Loma Quita Espuela, Cordillera Central) *21008*

E   *Pithecellobium barbourianum* Standl. *20883, 9006*

I	20883	Panama *20883*

R   *Pithecellobium campylacanthus* L. Rico & M. Sousa *20883*

I	20883	Honduras *20883*
I	20883	Mexico *20883*

R   *Pithecellobium jupunba* (Willd.) Urb. *20883*

R	20883	Dominica *20883*
R	20883	Grenada *20883*

E   *Pithecellobium micranthum* Benth. *5642*

E		Dominican Republic *5642*
		Haiti *21008*

R   *Pithecellobium pithecolobioides* (Harms ex Kuntze) Hassler *20883*

I	20883	Argentina *20883*
R	20883	Paraguay *20883*

E   *Pithecellobium pseudo-tamarindus* (Britt.) Standl. *20883, 9006*

E	17459	Costa Rica *10539*
I	20883	Panama *20883*

E   *Pithecellobium rufescens* Schery var. *vallense* Schery *20883, 9006*

I	20883	Panama *20883*

R   *Pithecellobium vietnamense* Nielsen *6057*

R		Vietnam *6057*

R   *Plagiosiphon gabonensis* (A. Chev.) Leonard

R		Gabon (Lastoursville)

R   *Platylobium alternifolium* F.Muell. *20681*

R	20681	Australia - Victoria *20681*

I   II   *Platymiscium pleiostachyum* Donn. Sm. *20883, 9037*

E	20883	Costa Rica *20883*
I	10359	El Salvador *10359*

I   *20883* Nicaragua *20883*

R   *Platymiscium trinatis* Benth. var. *durum* Ducke *8679*

     R   *8679* Guyana *8679*
     R   *8679* Suriname *8679*

V   *Podalyria cordata* R.Br. *20604*

     V   *20604* South Africa - Cape Province *20604*

I   *Podalyria microphylla* E.Mey. *20604*

     I   *20604* South Africa - Cape Province *20604*

I   *Podalyria velutina* Burch. ex Benth. *20604*

     I   *20604* South Africa - Cape Province *20604*
     I   *20604* South Africa - Natal *20604*

R   *Poecilanthe ovalifolia* Kleinhoonte *8679*

     R   *8679* Suriname *8679*

E   *Polhillia brevicalyx* (C.H.Stirt.) B.-E.van Wyk & A.L.Schutte *20604*

     E   *20604* South Africa - Cape Province *20604*

R   *Polhillia canescens* C.H.Stirt. *20604*

     R   *20604* South Africa - Cape Province *20604*

R   *Polhillia connata* (Harv.) C.H.Stirt. *20604*

     R   *20604* South Africa - Cape Province *20604*

R   *Polhillia involucrata* (Thunb.) B.-E.van Wyk & A.L.Schutte *20604*

     R   *20604* South Africa - Cape Province *20604*

V   *Polhillia obsoleta* (Harv.) B.-E.van Wyk *20604*

     V   *20604* South Africa - Cape Province *20604*

R   *Polhillia pallens* C.H.Stirt. *20604*

     R   *20604* South Africa - Cape Province *20604*

E   *Priotropis socotrana* Balf. f. *15534*

     E   *15534* Yemen - Socotra *15534*

E   *Prosopis abbreviata* Benth. *16336*

     E   *16336* Argentina *16336*
     E   *20176* Argentina - Cordoba *20176*
     E   *20176* Argentina - Catamarca *20176*
     E   *20176* Argentina - Santiago del Estero *20176*
     E   *20176* Argentina - San Juan *20176*
     E   *20176* Argentina - San Luis *20176*

V   *Prosopis atacamensis* Philippi

     V   *13875* Chile *13875*

V   *Prosopis rojasiana* Burk *20883*

     V   *20883* Paraguay *20883*

E   *Prosopis rubriflora* Hassler *20883*

     E   *20883* Paraguay *20883*

V   *Prosopis tamarugo* Philippi *17681*

     V   *13875* Chile (Northern desert plateau region) *17681*

R   *Psoralea abbottii* C.H.Stirt. ined. *20604*

     R   *20604* South Africa - Cape Province *20604*
     V   *20604* South Africa - Natal *20604*

R   *Psoralea aculeata* L. *20604*

     R   *20604* South Africa - Cape Province *20604*

V   *Psoralea arborea* Sims *20604*

     V   *20604* Swaziland *20604*
     V   *20604* South Africa - Natal *20604*

R   *Psoralea azurea* C.H.Stirt. ined. *20604*

     R   *20604* South Africa - Cape Province *20604*

Ex   *Psoralea cataracta* C.H.Stirt. *20604*

     Ex   *20604* South Africa - Cape Province *20604*

R   *Psoralea crista* C.H.Stirt. ined. *20604*

R   *Psoralea elegans* C.H.Stirt. ined. *20604*

     R   *20604* South Africa - Cape Province *20604*

V   *Psoralea ensifolia* (Houtt.) Merr. *20604*

     V   *20604* South Africa - Cape Province *20604*

E   *Psoralea filifolia* Eckl. & Zeyh. *20604*

     E   *20604* South Africa - Cape Province *20604*

V   *Psoralea fleta* C.H.Stirt. ined. *20604*

     V   *20604* South Africa - Cape Province *20604*

V   *Psoralea glaucescens* Eckl. & Zeyh. *20604*

     V   *20604* South Africa - Cape Province *20604*

E   *Psoralea glaucina* Harv. *20604*

     E   *20604* South Africa - Cape Province *20604*

Ex   *Psoralea gueinzii* Harv. *20604*

     Ex   *20604* South Africa - Cape Province *20604*

R   *Psoralea imbricata* (L.f.) C.H.Stirt. *20604*

     R   *20604* South Africa - Cape Province *20604*

R   *Psoralea imminens* C.H.Stirt. ined. *20604*

     R   *20604* South Africa - Cape Province *20604*

R   *Psoralea implexa* C.H.Stirt. ined. *20604*

     R   *20604* South Africa - Cape Province *20604*

R   *Psoralea intonsa* C.H.Stirt. ined. *20604*

     R   *20604* South Africa - Cape Province *20604*

R   *Psoralea keetii* Schönland ex H.M.L.Forbes *20604*

     R   *20604* South Africa - Cape Province *20604*

R   *Psoralea laevigata* L.f. *20604*

     R   *20604* South Africa - Cape Province *20604*

E   *Psoralea muirii* C.H.Stirt. ined. *20604*

     E   *20604* South Africa - Cape Province *20604*

R   *Psoralea nubicola* C.H.Stirt. ined. *20604*

     R   *20604* South Africa - Cape Province *20604*

R   *Psoralea odoratissima* Jacq. *20604*

     R   *20604* South Africa - Cape Province *20604*

R   *Psoralea oreophila* Schltr. *20604*

     R   *20604* South Africa - Cape Province *20604*

R   *Psoralea oreopola* C.H.Stirt. ined. *20604*

     R   *20604* South Africa - Cape Province *20604*

E   *Psoralea parva* F.Muell. *20681*

     Ex/E   *20681* Australia - New South Wales *20681*
     I   *20681* Australia - South Australia *20681*
     I   *20681* Australia - Victoria *20681*

V   *Psoralea peratica* C.H.Stirt. ined. *20604*

     V   *20604* South Africa - Cape Province *20604*

V   *Psoralea pullata* C.H.Stirt. ined. *20604*

     V   *20604* South Africa - Cape Province *20604*

V   *Psoralea repens* P.J.Bergius *20604*

     V   *20604* South Africa - Cape Province *20604*

R   *Psoralea restioides* Eckl. & Zeyh. *20604*

     R   *20604* South Africa - Cape Province *20604*

V   *Psoralea rigidula* C.H.Stirt. ined. *20604*

     V   *20604* South Africa - Cape Province *20604*

V   *Psoralea rydbergii* Cory *8058*

     V   *19002* U.S. - Texas *8058*
     V   *19002* Mexico *8058*

R   *Psoralea triflora* Thunb. *20604*

     R   *20604* South Africa - Cape Province *20604*

R   *Psoralea trullata* C.H.Stirt *20604*

     R   *20604* South Africa - Cape Province *20604*

R   *Psoralea vlokii* C.H.Stirt. ined. *20604*

     R   *20604* South Africa - Cape Province *20604*

Magnoliopsida (dicots): Leguminosae: *Psoralea*

R	*Psoralidium junceum* (Eastw.) Rydb. *20850*		
	I	20850 U.S. - Arizona *20850*	
	R	20850 U.S. - Utah *20850*	
V	*Psorothamnus arborescens* (Torr. ex Gray) Barneby var. *pubescens* (Parish) Barneby *20850*		
	V	20850 U.S. - Arizona *20850*	
	E	20850 U.S. - Utah *20850*	
R	*Psorothamnus kingii* (S.Watson) Barneby *20850*		
	R	20850 U.S. - Nevada *20850*	
E	*Psorothamnus polydenius* (Torr. ex S. Wats.) Rydb. var. *jonesii* Barneby *20850*		
	E	20850 U.S. - Utah *20850*	
R	*Psorothamnus thompsoniae* (Vail) Welsh & Atwood *20850*		
	V	20850 U.S. - Arizona *20850*	
	I	20850 U.S. - Utah *20850*	
V	*Psorothamnus thompsoniae* (Vail) Welsh & Atwood var. *thompsoniae* *20850*		
	V	20850 U.S. - Utah *20850*	
V	*Psorothamnus thompsoniae* (Vail) Welsh & Atw. var. *whitingii* (Kearney & Peebles) Barneby *20850*		
	E	20850 U.S. - Arizona *20850*	
	E	20850 U.S. - Utah *20850*	
E	II	*Pterocarpus santalinus* Linn.f. *19218, 21025*	
	E	20263 India *20263*	
E	*Ptychosema pusillum* Benth. *20681*		
	E	20681 Australia - Western Australia *20681*	
R	*Pueraria bella* Prain *14782*		
	R	14782 India - Arunachal Pradesh *14782*	
	Ex	14782 Myanmar *14782*	
I	*Pueraria tetragona* Merr. *13833*		
	I	13833 Philippines (low altitude) *13833*	
V	*Pultenaea aristata* DC. *20681*		
	V	20681 Australia - New South Wales *20681*	
V	*Pultenaea baeuerlenii* F.Muell. *20681*		
	V	20681 Australia - New South Wales *20681*	
R	*Pultenaea costata* Williamson *20681*		
	R	20681 Australia - Victoria *20681*	
V	*Pultenaea glabra* Benth. *20681*		
	V	20681 Australia - New South Wales *20681*	
R	*Pultenaea luehmannii* Maiden *20681*		
	R	20681 Australia - Victoria *20681*	
Ex	*Pultenaea maidenii* Reader *20681*		
	Ex	20681 Australia - Victoria *20681*	
E	*Pultenaea parrisiae* J.D.Briggs & Crisp ssp. *elusa* J.D.Briggs & Crisp *20681*		
	E	20681 Australia - New South Wales *20681*	
V	*Pultenaea parrisiae* J.D.Briggs & Crisp ssp. *parrisiae* *20681*		
	I	20681 Australia - New South Wales *20681*	
	I	20681 Australia - Victoria *20681*	
E	*Pultenaea parviflora* DC. *20681*		
	E	20681 Australia - New South Wales *20681*	
R	*Pultenaea patellifolia* Williamson *20681*		
	R	20681 Australia - Victoria *20681*	
E	*Pultenaea pauciflora* M.Scott *20681, 5465*		
	E	20681 Australia - Western Australia *20681*	
R	*Pultenaea pycnocephala* F.Muell. ex Benth. *20681*		
	I	20681 Australia - New South Wales *20681*	
	I	20681 Australia - Queensland *20681*	
V	*Pultenaea selaginoides* Hook.f. *20681*		

	V	20681 Australia - Tasmania *20681*	
V	*Pultenaea setulosa* Benth. *20681*		
	V	20681 Australia - Queensland *20681*	
R	*Pultenaea skinneri* F.Muell. *20681*		
	R	20681 Australia - Western Australia *20681*	
V	*Pultenaea stuartiana* Williamson *20681*		
	I	20681 Australia - New South Wales *20681*	
	I	20681 Australia - Queensland *20681*	
R	*Pultenaea subalpina* (F.Muell.) Druce *20681*		
	R	20681 Australia - Victoria *20681*	
R	*Pultenaea teretifolia* H.Williamson var. *brachyphylla* H.Williamson *20681*		
	R	20681 Australia - South Australia *20681*	
E	*Pultenaea trichophylla* J.Black *20681*		
	E	20681 Australia - South Australia *20681*	
R	*Pultenaea trifida* J.Black *20681*		
	R	20681 Australia - South Australia *20681*	
R	*Pultenaea victoriensis* M.G.Corrick *20681*		
	R	20681 Australia - Victoria *20681*	
V	*Pultenaea villifera* Sieb. ex DC. var. *glabrescens* J.Black *20681*		
	V	20681 Australia - South Australia *20681*	
R	*Pultenaea villifera* Sieb. ex DC. var. *villifera* *20681*		
	R	20681 Australia - New South Wales *20681*	
R	*Pultenaea weindorferi* Reader *20681*		
	R	20681 Australia - Victoria *20681*	
R	*Pultenaea whiteana* S.T.Blake *20681*		
	R	20681 Australia - Queensland *20681*	
R	*Pultenaea williamsoniana* J.H.Willis *20681*		
	R	20681 Australia - Victoria *20681*	
I	*Rafnia crispa* C.H.Stirt. *20604*		
	I	20604 South Africa - Cape Province *20604*	
I	*Rafnia ericifolia* Schltr. *20604*		
	I	20604 South Africa - Cape Province *20604*	
R	*Ramorinoa girolae* Speg. *16336*		
	R	16336 Argentina *16336*	
	R	20176 Argentina - La Rioja *20176*	
	R	20176 Argentina - San Juan *20176*	
	R	20176 Argentina - San Luis *20176*	
V	*Retama raetam* (Forssk.) Webb ssp. *gussonei* (Webb) Greuter *18264*		
	V	18264 Italy - Sicily *18264*	
R	*Rhynchosia albaepauli* Berhaut *8003*		
	R	Senegal *8003*	
I	*Rhynchosia arida* C.H.Stirt. *20604*		
	I	20604 South Africa - Cape Province *20604*	
R	*Rhynchosia axilliflora* Hauman *19358*		
	R	19358 Zaire (Bas-Congo) *19358*	
R	*Rhynchosia beddomei* Baker		
	R	13883 India - Andhra Pradesh (Cuddapah) *13883*	
	R	13883 India - Karnataka (Bellary) *13883*	
I	*Rhynchosia braunii* Harms *7959*		
	I	5926 Tanzania (Rufiji District) *5926*	
I	*Rhynchosia calobotrya* Harms *7959*		
	I	5926 Tanzania (Lindi) *5926*	
R	*Rhynchosia cinerea* Nash *20850*		
	R	20850 U.S. - Florida *20850*	
R	*Rhynchosia clivorum* S. Moore var. *fulvida*		

	Meikle *7849*	
R		Malawi *7849*

I	**Rhynchosia congensis** Baker ssp. *pseudobuettneri* Verdc. *7959*
I	*5926* Tanzania (Lushoto & Tanga) *5926*

I	**Rhynchosia connata** Baker f. *20604*
I	*20604* South Africa - Natal *20604*

R	**Rhynchosia emarginata** Germish. *20604*
R	*20604* South Africa - Cape Province *20604*

E	**Rhynchosia erlangeri** Harms *19704*
E	*19704* Ethiopia (Harerge) *19704*

E	**Rhynchosia erythraea** Schweinf. *19704*
E	*19704* Ethiopia (West Eritrea, Shewa Upland) *19704*

I	**Rhynchosia foliosa** Markötter *20604*
I	*20604* South Africa - Natal *20604*

V	**Rhynchosia holtzii** Harms *7959*
V	*5926* Tanzania (Pugu forest reserve) *5926*

R	**Rhynchosia longissima** Hauman *19358*
R	*19358* Zaire (Haut-Katanga) *19358*

R	**Rhynchosia lukafuensis** Baker f. *19358*
R	*19358* Zaire (Haut-Katanga) *19358*

V	**Rhynchosia malacotricha** Harms. *19704*
V	*19704* Ethiopia (Shewa Upland, Harerge, Bale) *19704*

R	**Rhynchosia oblongifoliolata** Hauman *19358*
R	*19358* Zaire (Haut-Katanga) *19358*

E	**Rhynchosia ramosa** Verdc. *19704*
E	*19704* Ethiopia (Harerge) *19704*

R	**Rhynchosia salicifolia** Hauman *19358*
R	*19358* Zaire (Kasai) *19358*

Ex/E	**Rhynchosia splendens** Schweinf. *19704*
Ex/E	*19704* Ethiopia (Gonder) *19704*

R	**Rhynchosia stipulosa** A. Rich *19704*
R	*19704* Ethiopia (Tigray Upland, Welega, Gamo Gofa) *19704*

V	**Rhynchosia swartzii** (Vail) Urban *20850*
I	*20850* U.S. - Florida *20850*

V	**Rhynchosia velutina** Wight & Arn.
V	*13883* India - Tamil Nadu *13883*

E	**Rivasgodaya nervosa** F. Esteve *17534*
E	*17534* Spain - Canary Is. *17534*

V	**Robinia hispida** L. var. *fertilis* (Ashe) Clausen *20850*
I	*20850* U.S. - Connecticut *20850*
I	*20850* U.S. - Georgia *20850*
I	*20850* U.S. - Iowa *20850*
I	*20850* U.S. - Kentucky *20850*
I	*20850* U.S. - Maryland *20850*
E	*20850* U.S. - North Carolina *20850*
I	*20850* U.S. - Ohio *20850*
I	*20850* U.S. - Tennessee *20850*
I	*20850* U.S. - Virginia *20850*

R	**Robinia hispida** L. var. *rosea* Pursh *20850*
I	*20850* U.S. - Alabama *20850*
I	*20850* U.S. - Georgia *20850*
V	*20850* U.S. - Kentucky *20850*
V	*20850* U.S. - North Carolina *20850*
I	*20850* U.S. - South Carolina *20850*
I	*20850* U.S. - Tennessee *20850*

R	**Robinia viscosa** Vent. *20850, 20171*
I	*20850* U.S. - Delaware *20850*
I	*20850* U.S. - Georgia *20850*
I	*20850* U.S. - Kentucky *20850*
I	*20850* U.S. - Maryland *20850*
I	*20850* U.S. - Michigan *20850*
R	*20850* U.S. - North Carolina *20850*
V	*20850* U.S. - Tennessee *20850*
I	*20850* U.S. - Wisconsin *20850*

E	**Robinia viscosa** Vent. var. *hartwegii* (Koehne) Ashe *20850*
I	*20850* U.S. - Georgia *20850*
E	*20850* U.S. - North Carolina *20850*
I	*20850* U.S. - South Carolina *20850*

R	**Robinia viscosa** Vent. var. *viscosa* *20850*
I	*20850* Canada - New Brunswick *20850*
I	*20850* Canada - Nova Scotia *20850*
I	*20850* Canada - Ontario *20850*
I	*20850* Canada - Prince Edward Is. *20850*
I	*20850* U.S. - Connecticut *20850*
I	*20850* U.S. - Delaware *20850*
I	*20850* U.S. - Georgia *20850*
I	*20850* U.S. - Illinois *20850*
I	*20850* U.S. - Kentucky *20850*
I	*20850* U.S. - Maryland *20850*
I	*20850* U.S. - Michigan *20850*
I	*20850* U.S. - New Hampshire *20850*
I	*20850* U.S. - New Jersey *20850*
I	*20850* U.S. - New York *20850*
R	*20850* U.S. - North Carolina *20850*
I	*20850* U.S. - Ohio *20850*
I	*20850* U.S. - Pennsylvania *20850*
I	*20850* U.S. - South Carolina *20850*
V	*20850* U.S. - Tennessee *20850*
I	*20850* U.S. - Virginia *20850*
I	*20850* U.S. - West Virginia *20850*
I	*20850* U.S. - Wisconsin *20850*

E	**Rupertia hallii** (Rydb.) J. Grimes *20850*
E	*20850* U.S. - California *20850*

R	**Rupertia rigida** (Parish) J. Grimes *20850*
V	*20850* U.S. - California *20850*

I	**Sabinea carinalis** Griseb. *10199*
I	Dominica *10199*

R	**Sauvallella immarginata** (C. Wright) Rydb. *5607*
R	*19105* Cuba (Pinar del Rio) *5607*

I	**Schrankia portoricensis** Urban *10197*
I	*15106* Puerto Rico *8058*

R	**Sclerolobium aureum** Mart. var. *aureum* *20883*
I	*20883* Brazil *20883*
R	*20883* Paraguay *20883*

V	**Sclerolobium costaricense** Poveda & Zamora *20883*
V	*20883* Costa Rica *20883*

R	**Senna acclinis** (F.Muell.) Randell *20681*
I	*20681* Australia - New South Wales *20681*
I	*20681* Australia - Queensland *20681*

E	**Senna caudata** (Standl.) Irwin & Barneby *20883, 10747*
I	*20883* Panama. *20883*

R	**Senna cushina** (J.F. Macbr.) H. Irwin & Barneby *18200*
R	*12468* Peru *18200*

V	**Senna orcuttii** (Britt. & Rose) Irwin & Barneby *20850*
I	*20850* U.S. - New Mexico *20850*
V	*20850* U.S. - Texas *20850*

R	**Senna procumbens** Randell *20681*
R	*20681* Australia - Northern Territory *20681*

V	**Senna ripleyana** (Irwin & Barneby) Irwin & Barneby *20883, 20850, 19002*
Ex/E	*20850* U.S. - Texas *20850*

V   20883   Mexico   *20883*

V   *Serialbizzia acle* (Blanco) Kosterm.
     V   *15960*   Philippines   *15960*

V   *Serianthes calycina* Benth. *20893*
     V   *20893*   New Caledonia   *20802*

R   *Serianthes ebudarum* *21021*
     R   *21021*   Vanuatu   *21021*

E   *Serianthes germainii* Guillaumin *20893*
     E   *20893*   New Caledonia   *20802*

V   *Serianthes margaretae* Nielsen *20893*
     V   *20893*   New Caledonia   *20893*

R   *Serianthes myriadenia* J.Planchon ex Bentham *20845*
     I   *20845*   French Polynesia - Marquesas Is (Nuku Hiva) *20845*
     R   *20845*   French Polynesia - Society Is. (Moorea, Raiatea, Tahiti) *20845*

E   *Serianthes nelsonii* Merr. *8840*
     E   *20825*   North Mariana Is. (Rota) *20825*
     E   *20825*   U.S. - Guam *20825*

R   *Serianthes petitiana* Guillaumin *20893*
     R   *20893*   New Caledonia *20893*

R   *Serianthes rurutensis* (F.Brown) I.Nielsen *20845*
     R   *20845*   French Polynesia - Tubuai Is. *20845*

I   *Sesbania goetzei* Harms ssp. *multiflora* J.B.Gillett *7959*
     I   *5926*   Tanzania (Pare Distr.) *7959*

R   *Sesbania macroptera* Micheli *20883*
     I   *20883*   Argentina *20883*
     R   *20883*   Paraguay *20883*

R   *Sesbania marchionica* F. Brown
     R   French Polynesia - Marquesas Is

R   *Sesbania molokaiensis* (Deg. & Sherff) Deg. & I. Deg. *14107*
     R   *14107*   U.S. - Hawaii (Molokai) *14107*

I   *Sesbania paludosa* (Roxb.) Prain
     I   India - Kerala (Travancore)

V   *Sesbania tomentosa* Hook. & Arn. *20883, 20850, 14209*
     V   *20850*   U.S. - Hawaii (Oahu) *20850*
     I   *20883*   Puerto Rico *20883*

V   *Sindora tonkinensis* A. Chev *15100*
     V   *20985*   Vietnam *15100*

R   *Smithia agharkarii* Hemadri *13883*
     R   *13883*   India - Maharashtra *13883*

I   *Smithia venkobarowii* Gamble
     I   India - Kerala (Peermade, Travancore Hills)

V   *Sophora arizonica* S.Watson *20850*
     V   *20850*   U.S. - Arizona *20850*

V   *Sophora fernandeziana* (Phil.) Skottsb. *20883, 19116*
     V   *19125*   Chile - Juan Fernandez Is. *19116*
     V   *20883*   Chile *20883*

V   *Sophora fraseri* Benth. *20681*
     I   *20681*   Australia - New South Wales *20681*
     I   *20681*   Australia - Queensland *20681*

V   *Sophora gypsophila* B.L. Turner & Powell *20850*
     R   *20850*   U.S. - New Mexico *20850*
     E   *20850*   U.S. - Texas *20850*

V   *Sophora gypsophila* B.L. Turner & A.M. Powell var. *guadalupensis* B.L. Turner & Powell *20850, 11630*
     V   *20850*   U.S. - New Mexico *20850*
     E   *20850*   U.S. - Texas *20850*

R   *Sophora howinsula* (W. Oliver) P. Green *10260*
     R   *14225*   Australia - NSW - Lord Howe Is. *14225*

V   *Sophora leachiana* M.E. Peck *20850*
     V   *20850*   U.S. - Oregon *20850*

R   *Sophora linearifolia* Griseb. *16336*
     R   *16336*   Argentina *16336*
     R   *20176*   Argentina - Cordoba *20176*
     R   *20176*   Argentina - San Luis *20176*

E   *Sophora mangarevaensis* H. Saint John *20845*
     E   *20845*   French Polynesia - Tuamotu Is. (Gambier, Mangaréva) *20845*

V   *Sophora masafuerana* (Phil.) Skottsb. *20883, 19116*
     V   *19125*   Chile - Juan Fernandez Is. *19116*
     V   *20883*   Chile *20883*

V   *Sophora polyphylla* Urban *5607*
     V   *19105*   Cuba (Holguin) *5607*

E   *Sophora raivavaeensis* H. Saint John *20845*
     E   *20845*   French Polynesia - Tubuai Is. (Raiavavaé) *20845*

I   *Sophora rapaensis* H. Saint John *20845*
     I   *20845*   French Polynesia - Tubuai Is. (Rapa) *20845*

V   *Sophora rhynchocarpa* Griseb. *21056*
     V   *19448*   Argentina *16336*
     R   *20176*   Argentina - Salta *20176*
     R   *20176*   Argentina - Tucuman *20176*

E   *Sophora saxicola* Proctor *20883, 19890*
     E   *19890*   Jamaica (Trelawny) *20883*

V   *Sophora toromiro* (Phil.) Skottsb. *20883, 10260*
     Ex   *14777*   Chile - Easter Is. *14777*
     V   *20883*   Chile *20883*

I   *Sophora violacea* Thwaites *8021*
     I   *16162*   Sri Lanka *8021*

I   *Sophora zeylanica* Trimen *8021*
     I   *16162*   Sri Lanka *8021*

R   *Spatholobus balansae* Gagnepain *6057*
     R   Vietnam *6057*

V   *Spatholobus listeri* Prain *14872*
     V   *14872*   Bangladesh *14872*

R   *Sphaerolobium acanthos* Crisp *20681*
     R   *20681*   Australia - Victoria *20681*

E   *Sphaerophysa kotschyana* Boiss. *12840*
     E   *14155*   Turkey *12840*

R   *Stahlia monosperma* (Tul.) Urban *20883, 10197*
     I   *20883*   Dominican Republic (east near Macao) *20883*
     I   *20883*   Puerto Rico (south western and south eastern) *20883*
     I   *20883*   USA - Virgin Is. *20883*

R   *Stenodrepanum bergii* Harms *16336*
     R   *16336*   Argentina *16336*
     R   *20176*   Argentina - Cordoba *20176*

V   *Stirtonanthus tayloriana* (L.Bolus) B.-E.van Wyk & A.L.Schutte *20604*
     V   *20604*   South Africa - Cape Province *20604*

R   *Storckiella australiensis* J.Ross & B.Hyland *20681*
     R   *20681*   Australia - Queensland *20681*

Ex   *Streblorrhiza speciosa* Endl. *19108*
     Ex   *14226*   Australia - Norfolk Is. (Philip Is.) *8177*

V   *Strongylodon macrobotrys* A.Gray *10278*
     V   Philippines *10278*

R   *Stryphnodendron flammatum* Kleinhoonte *8679*
     R   *8679*   Suriname *8679*

I   *Stryphnodendron obovatum* Benth. *20883, 12346*
     I   *20883*   Brazil *20883*
     R   *20883*   Paraguay *20883*

V   *Stryphnodendron porcatum* Neill & Occhioni *20883*
     I   *20883*   Ecuador *20883*

V   *Stuhlmannia moavi* Taub. *10370*
     V   *20057*   Madagascar *17435*
     V   *20057*   Kenya *17435*
     V   *20885*   Tanzania (Handeni & Lindi) *7959*

E   *Stylosanthes cayennensis* Mohlenbrock *20883*
     E   *20883*   French Guiana *20883*

E   *Stylosanthes figueroae* Mohlenbrock *20883*
     E   *20883*   Colombia *20883*

R   *Stylosanthes hippocampoides* Mohlenbrock *20883, 20137*
     R   *20883*   Argentina *20883*
     E   *20137*   Argentina - Buenos Aires *20137*
     E   *20883*   Uruguay *20883*

E   *Stylosanthes macrocarpa* Blake *20883*
     E   *20883*   Mexico *20883*

E   *Stylosanthes macrosoma* Blake *20883*
     E   *20883*   Paraguay *20883*

R   *Stylosanthes nervosa* Macbr. *20883*
     E   *20883*   Argentina *20883*
     E   *20883*   Bolivia *20883*
     E   *20883*   Peru *20883*
     E   *20883*   Venezuela *20883*

E   *Stylosanthes sericeiceps* Blake *20883*
     E   *20883*   Venezuela *20883*

R   *Stylosanthes subsericea* Blake *20883*
     R   *20883*   Honduras *20883*
     E   *20883*   Mexico *20883*

V   *Swainsona murrayana* Wawra *20681*
     I   *20681*   Australia - New South Wales *20681*
     I   *20681*   Australia - Queensland *20681*
     I   *20681*   Australia - South Australia *20681*
     I   *20681*   Australia - Victoria *20681*

R   *Swainsona pyrophila* J.Thompson *20681*
     I   *20681*   Australia - New South Wales *20681*
     I   *20681*   Australia - South Australia *20681*
     I   *20681*   Australia - Victoria *20681*

R   *Swainsona sejuncta* J.Thompson *20681*
     R   *20681*   Australia - Queensland *20681*

R   *Swainsona tephrotricha* F.Muell. *20681*
     R   *20681*   Australia - South Australia *20681*

R   *Swartzia acutifolia* var. *acutifolia* *20883*
     I   *20883*   Brazil *20883*

E   *Swartzia acutifolia* var. *leiogyna*
     Bentham *20883*
     I   *20883*   Brazil *20883*

V   *Swartzia acutifolia* var. *parvipetala*
     Cowan *20883*
     I   *20883*   Brazil *20883*

E   *Swartzia acutifolia* var. *submarginata*
     Bentham *20883*
     I   *20883*   Brazil *20883*

E   *Swartzia acutifolia* var. *ynesiana*
     Cowan *20883*
     I   *20883*   Brazil *20883*

V   *Swartzia amazonica* Moore *20883*
     I   *20883*   Brazil *20883*

E   *Swartzia amazonica* Moore var.
     amazonica *20883*
     I   *20883*   Brazil *20883*

E   *Swartzia amazonica* Moore var. *cinerea* (Ducke)
     Cowan *20883*
     I   *20883*   Brazil *20883*

R   *Swartzia amplifolia* var. *colombiana*
     Cowan *20883*
     I   *20883*   Colombia *20883*
     I   *20883*   Ecuador *20883*

E   *Swartzia amplifolia* var. *rigida* Cowan *20883*
     I   *20883*   Colombia *20883*

E   *Swartzia amshoffiana* Cowan *20883*
     I   *20883*   Suriname *20883*

E   *Swartzia angustifoliola* Schery *20883*
     I   *20883*   Venezuela *20883*

E   *Swartzia anomala* Cowan *20883*
     I   *20883*   Guyana *20883*

V   *Swartzia apetala* var. *blanchetii* (Bentham)
     Cowan *20883*
     I   *20883*   Brazil *20883*

R   *Swartzia apetala* var. *glabra* (Vogel)
     Cowan *20883*
     I   *20883*   Brazil *20883*

R   *Swartzia apetala* var. *subcordata*
     Cowan *20883*
     I   *20883*   Brazil *20883*

E   *Swartzia apiculata* Cowan *20883*
     I   *20883*   Guyana *20883*

V   *Swartzia aptera* A. De Candolle *20883*
     I   *20883*   Brazil *20883*
     I   *20883*   French Guiana *20883*

E   *Swartzia benthamiana* var. *yatuensis*
     Cowan *20883*
     E   *20883*   Venezuela *20883*

V   *Swartzia brachyrachis* var. *colombiana*
     Cowan *20883*
     I   *20883*   Colombia *20883*

E   *Swartzia brachyrachis* var. *peruviana*
     Cowan *20883*
     I   *20883*   Peru *20883*

R   *Swartzia brachyrachis* var. *snethlageae* (Ducke)
     Ducke *20883*
     I   *20883*   Brazil *20883*

V   *Swartzia buntingii* Cowan *20883*
     I   *20883*   Venezuela *20883*

E   *Swartzia cabrerae* Cowan *20883*
     I   *20883*   Colombia *20883*

R   *Swartzia caribaea* Grisebach *20883, 10199*
     I   *20883*   Dominica *20883*
     I   *20883*   Guadeloupe *20883*

E   *Swartzia caudata* Cowan *20883*
     I   *20883*   Venezuela *20883*

R   *Swartzia conferta* var. *vaupesiana*
     Cowan *20883*
     I   *20883*   Brazil *20883*
     I   *20883*   Colombia *20883*

E   *Swartzia costata* (Rusby) Cowan *20883*
     I   *20883*   Bolivia *20883*

E   *Swartzia cubensis* (Britton & Rose) Cowan var.

nicaraguensis (Britton & Rose) Cowan *20883, 9808*
I   *20883* Nicaragua *20883*

E   **Swartzia cupavenensis** Cowan *20883*
I   *20883* Venezuela *20883*

E   **Swartzia curranii** Cowan *20883*
I   *20883* Brazil *20883*

E   **Swartzia davisii** Sandwith *20883*
I   *20883* Guyana *20883*

R   **Swartzia discocarpa** Ducke *20883*
I   *20883* Brazil *20883*

E   **Swartzia dolichopoda** Cowan *20883*
I   *20883* Venezuela *20883*

V   **Swartzia duckei** Huber *20883*
I   *20883* Brazil *20883*

R   **Swartzia eriocarpa** Bentham *20883*
I   *20883* Guyana *20883*

E   **Swartzia fanshawei** Cowan *20883*
I   *20883* Guyana *20883*

E   **Swartzia fimbriata** Ducke *20883*
I   *20883* Brazil *20883*

V   **Swartzia floribunda** Spruce ex Bentham *20883*
I   *20883* Venezuela *20883*

E   **Swartzia foliolosa** Cowan *20883*
I   *20883* Colombia *20883*

E   **Swartzia fraterna** Cowan *20883*
I   *20883* Brazil *20883*

E   **Swartzia froesii** Cowan *20883*
I   *20883* Brazil *20883*

E   **Swartzia gigantea** Cowan *20883*
I   *20883* Brazil *20883*

E   **Swartzia glazioviana** (Taubert) Glaziou *20883, 17079*
I   *20883* Brazil *20883*
E   *17079* Brazil - Rio de Janeiro (Cabo Frio, Sao Pedro, Aideia) *17079*

E   **Swartzia grazielana** Rizz. *20883*
I   *20883* Brazil *20883*

R   **Swartzia guatemalensis** (Donnell Smith) Pittier *20883, 9004*
I   *20883* Guatemala *20883*

V   **Swartzia haughtii** Cowan *20883*
I   *20883* Ecuador *20883*

V   **Swartzia hostmannii** Bentham *20883*
I   *20883* French Guiana *20883*
I   *20883* Suriname *20883*

R   **Swartzia ingifolia** Ducke *20883*
I   *20883* Brazil *20883*

V   **Swartzia iniridensis** Cowan *20883*
I   *20883* Colombia *20883*

E   **Swartzia jenmanii** Sandwith *20883*
I   *20883* Guyana *20883*

R   **Swartzia jorori** Harms *20883*
I   *20883* Bolivia *20883*

E   **Swartzia katawa** Cowan *20883*
I   *20883* Guyana *20883*

R   **Swartzia krukovii** Cowan *20883*
I   *20883* Brazil *20883*

R   **Swartzia lamellata** Ducke *20883*
E   *20883* Brazil *20883*
E   *20883* Guyana *20883*

E   **Swartzia lamellata** Ducke var. **kaieteurensis** Cowan *20883*
E   *20883* Guyana *20883*

V   **Swartzia lamellata** Ducke var. **lamellata** *20883*
I   *20883* Brazil *20883*

R   **Swartzia langsdorffii** Raddi *20883*
I   *20883* Brazil *20883*

E   **Swartzia latifolia** var. **latifolia** *20883*
I   *20883* Guyana *20883*

V   **Swartzia leblondii** Cowan *20883*
I   *20883* French Guiana *20883*

V   **Swartzia leiogyne** (Sandwith) Cowan *20883*
I   *20883* Guyana *20883*

V   **Swartzia littlei** Cowan *20883*
I   *20883* Ecuador *20883*

V   **Swartzia longicarpa** Amshoff *20883*
I   *20883* Suriname *20883*

E   **Swartzia longipedicellata** Sandwith *20883*
I   *20883* Guyana *20883*

V   **Swartzia longistipitata** Ducke *20883*
I   *20883* Brazil *20883*

E   **Swartzia lucida** Cowan *20883*
I   *20883* Brazil *20883*

E   **Swartzia macrophylla** Willdenow ex Vogel *20883, 9808*
I   *19353* Colombia *20883*

R   **Swartzia macrosema** Harms *20883*
I   *20883* Colombia *20883*
I   *20883* Peru *20883*

E   **Swartzia macrostachya** var. **glabrifolia** Cowan *20883*
I   *20883* Brazil *20883*

E   **Swartzia macrostachya** var. **kuhlmannii** (Hoehne) Cowan *20883*
I   *20883* Brazil *20883*

V   **Swartzia macrostachya** var. **macrostachya** *20883*
I   *20883* Brazil *20883*

V   **Swartzia macrostachya** var. **riedelii** Cowan *20883*
I   *20883* Brazil *20883*

E   **Swartzia magdalenae** Britton & Killip *20883, 9808*
I   *19353* Colombia *20883*

V   **Swartzia maguirei** Cowan *20883*
I   *20883* Venezuela *20883*

E   **Swartzia mangabalensis** Cowan *20883*
I   *20883* Brazil *20883*

R   **Swartzia martii** Eichler ex Bentham *20883*
I   *20883* Brazil *20883*

R   **Swartzia microcarpa** Spruce ex Bentham *20883*
I   *20883* Brazil *20883*
I   *20883* Colombia *20883*

E   **Swartzia monachiana** Cowan *20883*
I   *20883* Colombia *20883*

E   **Swartzia mucronifera** Cowan *20883*
I   *20883* Colombia *20883*

R   **Swartzia myrtifolia** var. **peruviana** Cowan *20883*
I   *20883* Peru *20883*

R   **Swartzia myrtifolia** var. **standleyi** (Britton & Rose)

Cowan *20883*
I	*20883*	Guatemala	*20883*
I	*20883*	Honduras	*20883*

E *Swartzia nuda* Schery *20883, 9808*
I	*20883*	Panama	*20883*

E *Swartzia oblonga* Bentham *20883*
I	*20883*	Venezuela	*20883*

E *Swartzia oraria* Cowan *20883*
I	*20883*	Colombia	*20883*

E *Swartzia pachyphylla* Harms *20883*
I	*20883*	Venezuela	*20883*

E *Swartzia panacoco* Cowan var. *altsonii* (Sandwith)
Cowan *20883*
I	*20883*	Guyana	*20883*

E *Swartzia panacoco* Cowan var. *kamarangensis*
Cowan *20883*
I	*20883*	Guyana	*20883*

V *Swartzia panacoco* Cowan var. *panacoco* *20883*
I	*20883*	French Guiana	*20883*

V *Swartzia panacoco* Cowan var. *sagotii* (Sandwith)
Cowan *20883*
I	*20883*	French Guiana	*20883*

E *Swartzia panacoco* Cowan var. *sandwithiana* (Cowan)
Cowan *20883*
I	*20883*	Guyana	*20883*

V *Swartzia panacoco* Cowan var. *tepuiensis* (Schery)
Cowan *20883*
I	*20883*	Venezuela	*20883*

V *Swartzia parvifolia* Schery *20883*
I	*20883*	Venezuela	*20883*

E *Swartzia pernitida* Cowan *20883*
I	*20883*	Brazil	*20883*

V *Swartzia phaneroptera* Standley *20883*
I	*20883*	Guatemala	*20883*
V	*20883*	Honduras	*20883*

V *Swartzia piarensis* Cowan *20883*
I	*20883*	Venezuela	*20883*

V *Swartzia pickelii* Killip ex Ducke *20883*
I	*20883*	Brazil	*20883*

R *Swartzia picta* var. *bolivarensis*
Cowan *20883*
I	*20883*	Brazil	*20883*
I	*20883*	Venezuela	*20883*

V *Swartzia pittieri* Schery *20883*
I	*20883*	Venezuela	*20883*

E *Swartzia prolata* Cowan *20883*
I	*20883*	Brazil	*20883*

V *Swartzia racemosa* var. *klugii* Cowan *20883*
I	*20883*	Peru	*20883*

V *Swartzia racemosa* var. *major* Cowan *20883*
I	*20883*	Brazil	*20883*
I	*20883*	Colombia	*20883*

R *Swartzia remiger* Amshoff *20883*
R	*20883*	Suriname	*20883*

E *Swartzia riedelii* Cowan *20883*
I	*20883*	Brazil	*20883*

E *Swartzia roraimae* Sandwith *20883*
I	*20883*	Venezuela	*20883*

V *Swartzia santanderensis* Cowan *20883*

I	*20883*	Colombia	*20883*

R *Swartzia schomburgkii* var. *guayanensis*
Cowan *20883*
I	*20883*	Venezuela	*20883*

R *Swartzia schomburgkii* var. *rigida*
Cowan *20883*
I	*20883*	Brazil	*20883*
I	*20883*	Colombia	*20883*

R *Swartzia schultesii* Cowan *20883*
I	*20883*	Colombia	*20883*

E *Swartzia schunkei* R. S. Cowan *20883*
I	*20883*	Peru	*20883*

E *Swartzia sericea* var. *emarginata*
Ducke *20883*
I	*20883*	Brazil	*20883*

E *Swartzia sprucei* var. *sprucei* *20883*
I	*20883*	Venezuela	*20883*

R *Swartzia sprucei* var. *tessellata*
Cowan *20883*
I	*20883*	Guyana	*20883*
I	*20883*	Venezuela	*20883*

R *Swartzia steyermarkii* Cowan *20883*
I	*20883*	Venezuela	*20883*

R *Swartzia stipellata* Cowan *20883*
I	*20883*	Brazil	*20883*

E *Swartzia sumorum* Molina *20883, 9808*
I	*20883*	Nicaragua	*20883*

R *Swartzia tomentifera* (Ducke) Ducke *20883*
I	*20883*	Brazil	*20883*

E *Swartzia trinitensis* Urban *20883*
E	*20883*	Trinidad & Tobago	*20883*
E	*20883*	Venezuela	*20883*

V *Swartzia ulei* Harms *20883*
I	*20883*	Brazil	*20883*

R *Swartzia vaupesiana* Cowan *20883*
I	*20883*	Colombia	*20883*
I	*20883*	Venezuela	*20883*

V *Swartzia vaupesiana* var. *glauca* Cowan *20883*
I	*20883*	Venezuela	*20883*

E *Swartzia vaupesiana* var. *vaupesiana* *20883*
I	*20883*	Colombia	*20883*

E *Swartzia velutina* Spruce ex Bentham *20883*
I	*20883*	Brazil	*20883*

E *Swartzia wurdackii* Cowan *20883*
I	*20883*	Venezuela	*20883*

E *Swartzia xanthopetala* Sandwith *20883*
I	*20883*	Guyana	*20883*

R *Tachigali micrantha* (L.O.Williams) Zanucchi &
Herendeen *18200*
R	*18200*	Peru	*17462*

R *Tachigali setifera* (Ducke) Zannucchi &
Herendeen *18200*
R	*18200*	Peru	*18200*

Ex/E *Talbotiella gentii* Hutch. & Greenway *7926*
Ex/E	*20858*	Ghana	*6072*

V *Taverniera schimperi* Jaub. & Spach *19704*
V	*19704*	Ethiopia (West Eritrea, Tigray Upland, Shewa Upland)	*19704*

E *Taverniera sericophylla* Balf. f. *15534*
E	*19011*	Yemen - Socotra (western coast)	*15534*

E	*Teline benehoavensis* (Bolle ex Svent.) Santos	
	E	Spain - Canary Is.
V	*Teline gomerae* (Gibbs & Dingw.) Kunkel	
	V	Spain - Canary Is.
V	*Teline linifolia* (L.) Webb & Berthel. ssp. *gomerae* P.E. Gibbs & Dingwall	
	V	Spain - Canary Is.
V	*Teline linifolia* (L.) Webb & Berthel. ssp. *pallida* (Poiret) P.E. Gibbs & Dingwall	
	V	Spain - Canary Is.
R	*Teline linifolia* (L.) Webb & Berthel. ssp. *rosmarinifolia* (Webb & Berth.) Gibbs & Dingw.	
	R	Spain - Canary Is.
E	*Teline linifolia* (L.) Webb & Berthel. ssp. *teneriffae* P.E. Gibbs & Dingwall	
	E	Spain - Canary Is.
E	*Teline nervosa* A. Hansen & Sunding 20750	
	E	20750 Spain - Canary Is. 20750
R	*Teline osyroides* (Svent.) P.E. Gibbs & Dingwall 20750	
	R	20750 Spain - Canary Is. 20750
E	*Teline osyroides* (Svent.) Gibbs & Dingw. ssp. *osyroides*	
	E	Spain - Canary Is.
R	*Teline osyroides* (Svent.) Gibbs & Ding. ssp. *sericea* (O. Kuntze) Arco, et al.	
	R	Spain - Canary Is.
R	*Teline paivae* (Lowe) P.E. Gibbs & Dingwall	
	R	Portugal - Madeira
E	*Teline rosmarinifolia* Webb & Berthel. ssp. *eurifolia* Arco	
	E	Spain - Canary Is.
R	*Teline rosmarinifolia* Webb & Berthel. ssp. *rosmarinifolia* 17781	
	R	Spain - Canary Is. 17891
E	*Teline salsoloides* Arco & Acebes 17891	
	E	20750 Spain - Canary Is. 17891
V	*Teline splendens* (Webb & Berthel.) Arco 20750	
	V	20750 Spain - Canary Is. 20750
R	*Templetonia drummondii* Benth. 20681	
	R	20681 Australia - Western Australia 20681
V	*Tephrosia abbottiae* C.E.Wood 20914	
	V	20914 Mexico - Guerrero 20914
	V	20914 Mexico - Mexico State 20914
E	*Tephrosia angustissima* Shuttlw. ex Chapman 20850	
	E	20850 U.S. - Florida 20850
Ex/E	*Tephrosia angustissima* Shuttlw. ex Chapman var. *angustissima* 20850	
	Ex/E	20850 U.S. - Florida 20850
E	*Tephrosia angustissima* Shuttlw. ex Chapman var. *corallicola* (Small) Isely 20850	
	E	20850 U.S. - Florida 20850
E	*Tephrosia angustissima* Shuttlw. ex Chapman var. *curtissii* (Small ex Rydb.) Isely 20850	
	E	20850 U.S. - Florida 20850
I	*Tephrosia bachmannii* Harms 20604	
	I	20604 South Africa - Natal 20604
R	*Tephrosia barberi* Drumm. 14782	
	R	14782 India - Tamil Nadu 14782

R	*Tephrosia calophylla* Beddome 14782	
	R	14782 India - Tamil Nadu 14782
R	*Tephrosia cana* Brandegee 20914	
	R	20914 Mexico - Baja California Sur 20914
R	*Tephrosia carrollii* O. Téllez 20914	
	R	20914 Mexico - Nayarit 20914
	R	20914 Mexico - Oaxaca 20914
I	*Tephrosia collina* V. Sharma var. *lanuginocarpa* V. Sharma	
	I	India - Gujarat (Kutch)
	I	India - Rajasthan
R	*Tephrosia conzattii* (Rydb.) Standley 20914	
	R	20914 Mexico - Jalisco 20914
	R	20914 Mexico - Michoacan 20914
	R	20914 Mexico - Nayarit 20914
	R	20914 Mexico - Oaxaca 20914
R	*Tephrosia cuernavacana* (Rose) MacBride 20914	
	R	20914 Mexico - Morelos 20914
V	*Tephrosia dichroocarpa* Steud. ex A. Rich 19704	
	V	19704 Ethiopia (Tigray, Gonder, Gojam) 19704
V	*Tephrosia diversifolia* (Rose) MacBride 20914	
	V	20914 Mexico - Michoacan 20914
R	*Tephrosia foliolosa* (Rydb.) Riley 20914	
	R	20914 Mexico 20914
R	*Tephrosia fulvinervis* Hochst. ex A. Rich 19704	
	R	19704 Ethiopia (West Eritrea, Tigray Upland, Gonder, Shewa Upland.) 19704
R	*Tephrosia gobensis* Brummitt 18023	
	R	Mozambique
	I	18023 Swaziland 18023
V	*Tephrosia guayameoensis* O.Téllez 20914	
	V	20914 Mexico - Guerrero 20914
V	*Tephrosia hochstetteri* Chiov. 19704	
	V	19704 Ethiopia (West Eritrea, Tigray Upland) 19704
V	*Tephrosia hypoleuca* Riley 20914	
	V	20914 Mexico - Sinaloa 20914
V	*Tephrosia inandensis* H.M.L.Forbes 20604	
	V	20604 South Africa - Natal 20604
R	*Tephrosia jamnagerensis* Santapau	
	R	13883 India - Gujarat 13883
I	*Tephrosia kalamboensis* Brummitt & J.B.Gillett 7959	
	I	5926 Tanzania (Ufipa District) 5926
Ex	*Tephrosia kassasi* Boulos 12346	
	Ex	12346 Egypt 12346
R	*Tephrosia kazibensis* Cronq. 19358	
	R	19358 Zaire (Haut-Katanga) 19358
E	*Tephrosia leratiana* Harms 20893	
	E	20893 New Caledonia 20893
V	*Tephrosia leveillei* Domin 20681	
	V	20681 Australia - Queensland 20681
R	*Tephrosia lindheimeri* A.Gray 20914	
	R	20914 U.S. - Texas (south-east) 20914
	R	20914 Mexico (north-east) 20914
R	*Tephrosia linearibracteolata* O. Téllez (ined.) 20914	
	R	20914 Mexico - Oaxaca 20914
R	*Tephrosia madrensis* Seem. 20914	
	R	20914 Mexico - Durango 20914
	R	20914 Mexico - Nayarit 20914
R	*Tephrosia major* Micheli 20914	

R	20914	Mexico - Jalisco	20914
R	20914	Mexico - Michoacan	20914

V   *Tephrosia mexicana* C.E.Wood 20914
V	20914	Mexico - Mexico State	20914

V   *Tephrosia microcarpa* O.Téllez 20914
V	20914	Mexico - Nayarit	20914

I   *Tephrosia natalensis* H.M. Forbes ssp. natalensis 18023
I	18023	Swaziland	18023

E   *Tephrosia odorata* Balf. f. 15534
E	15534	Yemen - Socotra	15534

R   *Tephrosia pachypoda* Riley 20914
R	20914	Mexico - Nayarit	20914
R	20914	Mexico - Sinaloa	20914

V   *Tephrosia palmeri* S.Watson 20914
V	20914	Mexico - Baja California Sur	20914

I   *Tephrosia pentaphylla* (Roxb.) Sweet
I		India - Karnataka (Bellary)

V   *Tephrosia platyphylla* (Rose) Standl. 20914
V	20914	Mexico	20914

V   *Tephrosia pogonocalyx* C.E.Wood 20914
V	20914	Mexico - Mexico State	20914

R   *Tephrosia pondoensis* (Codd) Schrire 20604
R	20604	South Africa - Cape Province	20604
R	20604	South Africa - Natal	20604

R   *Tephrosia potosina* Brandeg. 20914
R	20914	Mexico - Nuevo Leon	20914
R	20914	Mexico - San Luis Potosi	20914

V   *Tephrosia pringlei* (Rose) Maebr. 20914
V	20914	Mexico - Oaxaca	20914

V   *Tephrosia quercetorum* C.E.Wood 20914
V	20914	Mexico - Guerrero	20914

V   *Tephrosia rugelii* Shuttlw. ex B.L. Robins. 20850
I	20850	U.S. - Florida	20850

R   *Tephrosia saxicola* C.E.Wood 20914
R	20914	Mexico - Jalisco	20914
R	20914	Mexico - Sinaloa	20914

V   *Tephrosia seemannii* (Britten et Bak. f.) K. Schum. 20914
V	20914	Mexico - Durango	20914

R   *Tephrosia simulans* C.E.Wood 20914
R	20914	Mexico - Jalisco	20914

V   *Tephrosia sousae* O.Téllez 20914
V	20914	Mexico - Nayarit	20914

R   *Tephrosia tenella* A.Gray 20914
R	20914	Mexico	20914

R   *Tephrosia tepicana* Standley 20914
R	20914	Mexico - Jalisco	20914
R	20914	Mexico - Nayarit	20914

R   *Tephrosia thurberi* (Rydb.) C.E. Wood 20883, 20850
R	20850	U.S. - Arizona	20850
V	20914	Mexico - Chihuahua	20914

R   *Tephrosia tuitoensis* A. Téllez 20914
R	20914	Mexico - Jalisco	20914

V   *Tephrosia vernicosa* C.E.Wood 20914
V	20914	Mexico - Jalisco	20914

R   *Tephrosia viridiflora* O. Tellez 10153
R	20914	Mexico - Jalisco	10153
R	20914	Mexico - Nayarit	20914

R   *Tephrosia wynaadensis* Drumm. 14782

R	14782	India - Kerala	14782

V   *Tessmannia densiflora* Harms 7959
V	20885	Tanzania (Rufiji & Kilwa Districts) 20885	

V   *Tessmannia martiniana* Harms var. martiniana 7959
V	20885	Tanzania (coast)	20885

V   *Tessmannia martiniana* Harms var. *pauloi* J.Leonard 20556
V	20885	Tanzania (coast)	20885

R   *Tetraberlinia moreliana* Aubrév. 12346
R		Gabon 12346

Ex   *Tetragonolobus wiedemannii* Boiss. 8000, 20171
Ex	14155	Greece (Paros)	8000

I   *Thermopsis inflata* Cambess.
I		India - Himachal Pradesh
I		India - Jammu & Kashmir

V   *Thermopsis macrophylla* Hook. & Arn. var. *semota* Jepson 20850
E	20850	U.S. - California	20850

E   *Thermopsis turcica* Kit Tan, Vural & Kucukoduk 12840
E	12840	Turkey	12840

Ex   *Trifolium acutiflorum* Murb. 12346
Ex	12346	Morocco	12346

E   *Trifolium amoenum* Greene 20850, 14662
E	20850	U.S. - California	20850

R   *Trifolium andersonii* Gray ssp. *monoense* (Greene) J. Gillett 20850
I	20850	U.S. - California	20850
R	20850	U.S. - Nevada	20850

R   *Trifolium andinum* Nutt. 20850
I	20850	U.S. - Arizona	20850
E	20850	U.S. - Colorado	20850
E	20850	U.S. - Nevada	20850
V	20850	U.S. - Utah	20850
V	20850	U.S. - Wyoming	20850

E   *Trifolium andinum* Nutt. var. *podocephalum* Barneby 20850
E	20850	U.S. - Nevada	20850

R   *Trifolium apertum* Bobrov var. *kilaeum* Zoh. & lenr. 12840
R	12840	Turkey	12840

V   *Trifolium barbeyi* Gibelli & Belli 20171
V	20731	Greece - Crete (Karpathos)	20731

V   *Trifolium batmanicum* Katznelson 12840
V	12840	Turkey	12840

R   *Trifolium bivonae* Guss. 20171
R		Italy - Sicily

E   *Trifolium calcaricum* Collins and Wieboldt 20850
E	20850	U.S. - Tennessee	20850
E	20850	U.S. - Virginia	20850

E   *Trifolium chilaloense* Thulin 19704
E	19704	Ethiopia (Arsi)	19704

R   *Trifolium davisii* Hossain 12840
R	12840	Turkey	12840

V   *Trifolium dedeckerae* J. Gillett 20850
V	20850	U.S. - California	20850

R   *Trifolium dolopium* Heldr. & Hausskn. ex Gibelli & Belli 20171
R		Greece

R **Trifolium eriocephalum** Nutt. ssp. *arcuatum* (Piper)
J. Gillett *20850*

- I *20850* U.S. - Idaho *20850*
- E *20850* U.S. - Montana *20850*
- I *20850* U.S. - Oregon *20850*
- I *20850* U.S. - Washington *20850*

V **Trifolium euxinum** Zoh. *12840*

- V *12840* Turkey *12840*

V **Trifolium gracilentum** Torr. & Gray var. *palmeri*
(S.Watson) McDermott *20850*

- V *20850* U.S. - California *20850*

E **Trifolium haydenii** Porter var. *barnebyi*
Isely *20850*

   20850 U.S. - Wyoming *20850*

V **Trifolium kingii** (Greene) J. Gillett ssp. *macilentum*
(Greene) J. Gillett *20850*

- E *20850* U.S. - Arizona *20850*
- I *20850* U.S. - Colorado *20850*
- I *20850* U.S. - Idaho *20850*
- I *20850* U.S. - Nevada *20850*
- I *20850* U.S. - Utah *20850*

E **Trifolium leibergii** A. Nels. & J.F. Macbr. *20850*

- E *20850* U.S. - Nevada *20850*
- E *20850* U.S. - Oregon *20850*

R **Trifolium longidentatum** Nab. *12840*

- R *12840* Turkey *12840*

V **Trifolium neurophyllum** Greene *20850*

- V *20850* U.S. - Arizona *20850*
- E *20850* U.S. - New Mexico *20850*

V **Trifolium owyheense** Gilkey *20850*

- E *20850* U.S. - Idaho *20850*
- V *20850* U.S. - Oregon *20850*

E **Trifolium pachycalyx** Zoh. *12840*

- E *12840* Turkey *12840*

V **Trifolium pichisermollii** J.B.Gillett *19704*

- V *19704* Ethiopia (Gojam, Shewa Upland) *19704*

V **Trifolium plumosum** (J.S. Martin) J. Gillett ssp.
amplifolium (J.S. Martin) J. Gillett *20850*

- V *20850* U.S. - Idaho *20850*

E **Trifolium polyodon** Greene *20850*

- E *20850* U.S. - California *20850*

R **Trifolium praetermissum** Greuter, Pleger & Raus *20731*

- R *20731* Greece - Crete (inc. Karpathos) *20731*

E **Trifolium rollinsii** J.Gillett *20850*

- E *20850* U.S. - Nevada *20850*

R **Trifolium roussaenanum** Boiss. *12840*

- R *12840* Turkey *12840*

R **Trifolium saxatile** All. *8000, 20171*

- V   Austria *8000*
- R *20528* France (Alps) *20528*
- R *18264* Italy *19997*
- R *18154* Switzerland *18154*

E **Trifolium somalense** Taub. *19704*

- E *19704* Ethiopia (Sidamo) *19704*

R **Trifolium spananthum** Thulin *19704*

- R *19704* Ethiopia (Wello Upland, Arsi, Bale, Kefa) *19704*

R **Trifolium stoloniferum** Muhl. ex Eat. *20850*

- Ex/E *20850* U.S. - Arkansas *20850*
- E *20850* U.S. - Indiana *20850*
- Ex *20850* U.S. - Kansas *20850*
- V *20850* U.S. - Kentucky *20850*
- E *20850* U.S. - Missouri *20850*

- V *20850* U.S. - Ohio *20850*
- I *20850* U.S. - Virginia *20850*
- V *20850* U.S. - West Virginia *20850*

V **Trifolium thompsonii** Morton *20850*

- V *20850* U.S. - Washington *20850*

E **Trifolium trichocalyx** Heller *20850*

- E *20850* U.S. - California *20850*

I **Trifolium ukingense** Harms *7959*

- I *5926* Tanzania (Njombe District) *5926*

R **Trifolium velebiticum** Degen *20171*

- R   (former) Yugoslavia

I **Trifolium wentzelianum** Harms var.
wentzelianum *7959*

- I *5926* Tanzania (Njombe District) *5926*

E **Trigonella arenicola** Huber-Mor. *12840*

- E *12840* Turkey *12840*

E **Trigonella balachowskyi** Leredde *10488*

- E *14958* Algeria *10488*

R **Trigonella cephalotes** Boiss. & Bal. *12840*

- R *12840* Turkey *12840*

R **Trigonella cilicica** Huber-Mor. *12840*

- R *12840* Turkey *12840*

V **Trigonella halophila** Boiss. *12840*

- V *12840* Turkey *12840*

R **Trigonella lycica** Huber-Mor. *12840*

- R *12840* Turkey *12840*

V **Trigonella moabitica** Zohary

- V   Jordan

R **Trigonella pamphylica** Huber-Mor. & Sirj. *12840*

- R *12840* Turkey *12840*

V **Trigonella polycarpa** Boiss. & Heldr. *12840*

- V *12840* Turkey *12840*

R **Trigonella pseudocapitata** Coutandi. ex Quezel *12840*

- R *12840* Turkey *12840*

R **Trigonella rechingeri** Sirj. *20171*

- R   Greece

R **Trigonella rhytidocarpa** Boiss. & Bal. *12840*

- R *12840* Turkey *12840*

R **Trigonella rigida** Boiss. & Bal. *12840*

- R *12840* Turkey *12840*

R **Trigonella sirjaevii** Huber-Mor. *12840*

- R *12840* Turkey *12840*

V **Ulex densus** Welw. ex Webb *8000, 20171*

- V *20076* Portugal (west-central) *8000*

R **Umtiza listeriana** Sim *20604*

- R *20604* South Africa - Cape Province *20604*

I **Vavilova formosa** (Steven) Fed. *5942*

- I *5942* Russia - North Caucasus *5942*
- I *5942* Armenia *5942*
- I *5942* Azerbaijan *5942*

R **Vicia aphylla** C. Smith ex Link

- R   Spain - Canary Is.

I **Vicia benthamiana** Ali

- I   India - Jammu & Kashmir

E **Vicia bifoliolata** Rodr. *8000, 20171*

- E *20874* Spain - Balearic Is. (Menorca) *8000*

R **Vicia canescens** Lab. ssp. *leucomalla* (Bornm.)
Davis *12840*

- R *12840* Turkey *12840*

V   *Vicia capreolata* Lowe
     V   Portugal - Madeira

R   *Vicia cirhosa* Chr. Sm.
     R   Spain - Canary Is.

I   *Vicia davisii* Greuter
     I   Greece

Ex   *Vicia dennesiana* H.C.Watson *8000, 20171*
     Ex   *20216* Portugal - Azores (Sao Miguel) *8000*

R   *Vicia filicaulis* Webb & Berthel. *20750*
     R   *20750* Spain - Canary Is. *20750*

I   *Vicia fulgens* Battand. *10488*
     I   *14958* Algeria *10488*

R   *Vicia garbiensis* Font Quer & Pau
     R   Morocco

V   *Vicia giacominiana* Segelberg *18264*
     V   *18264* Italy (Puglia) *18264*

R   *Vicia glareosa* Davis *12840*
     R   *12840* Turkey *12840*

R   *Vicia hololasia* Woronow *11552*
     R   *11552* Russian Federation (Caucasus) *11552*

V   *Vicia lomensis* J.F. Macbr. *18200*
     V   *9446* Peru *18200*

E   *Vicia menziesii* Spreng. *20850, 14209*
     E   *20850* U.S. - Hawaii *20850*

R   *Vicia montenegrina* Rohlena *20171*
     V   *21091* Bosnia & Herzegovina *21091*
     I   Bulgaria
     R   (former) Yugoslavia

E   *Vicia ocalensis* Godfrey & Kral *20850*
     E   *20850* U.S. - Florida *20850*

V   *Vicia portosanctana* Menezes
     V   Portugal - Madeira

R   *Vicia quadrijuga* Davis *12840*
     R   *12840* Turkey *12840*

V   *Vicia scandens* R.P. Murray *20750*
     V   *20750* Spain - Canary Is. *20750*

R   *Vicia sinaica* Boulos
     R   Egypt

R   *Vicia splendens* Davis *12840*
     R   *12840* Turkey *12840*

V   *Vigna debanensis* Martelli *19704*
     V   *19704* Ethiopia (West Eritrea, Tigray Upland.) *19704*

R   *Vigna dolomitica* R. Wilczek *19358*
     R   *19358* Zaire (Haut-Katanga) *19358*

R   *Vigna khandalensis* (Sant.) Raghavan & Wadhwa *14782*
     R   *14782* India - Maharashtra *14782*

E   *Vigna owahuensis* Vogel *20850*
     E   *20850* U.S. - Hawaii *20850*

Ex/E   *Weberbauerella brongniartioides* Ulbr. *18200*
     Ex/E *12468* Peru *18200*

Ex/E   *Weberbauerella raimondiana* Ferreyra *18200*
     Ex/E *12468* Peru *18200*

R   *Wiborgia humilis* (Thunb.) R.Dahlgren *20604*
     R   *20604* South Africa - Cape Province *20604*

I   *Xanthocercis rabiensis* Maesen *21002*
     I   *21002* Gabon *21002*

I   *Xiphotheca elliptica* (DC.) A.L.Schutte & B.-E.van Wyk *20604*
     I   *20604* South Africa - Cape Province *20604*

I   *Xiphotheca lanceolata* (E.Mey.) Eckl. & Zeyh. *20604*
     I   *20604* South Africa - Cape Province *20604*

V   *Xiphotheca phylicoides* A.L.Schutte & B.-E.van Wyk *20604*
     V   *20604* South Africa - Cape Province *20604*

R   *Xiphotheca tecta* (Thunb.) A.L.Schutte & B.-E.van Wyk *20604*
     R   *20604* South Africa - Cape Province *20604*

R   *Zenkerella capparidacea* (Taubert) J. Léonard *12346*
     R   *5926* Tanzania (Uluguru mountains) *5926*

R   *Zenkerella capparidacea* (Taubert) J. Léonard ssp. *capparidacea 20911*
     R   *5926* Tanzania (Uluguru mountains) *5926*

R   *Zenkerella capparidacea* (Taubert) J. Léonard ssp. *grotei* (Harms) Temu *20911*
     R   *5926* Tanzania (Usambara mountains) *5926*

I   *Zenkerella egregia* J. Léonard *20556*
     I   *5926* Tanzania (East Usambara, Uluguru & Nguru Mts.) *20921*

R   *Zornia acuta* S.Reyn. & Holland *20681*
     R   *20681* Australia - Northern Territory *20681*

I   *Zornia punctatissima* Milne-Redh. *7959*
     I   *5926* Tanzania (Chunya) *5926*

E   *Zornia vaughaniana* Mohlenbr. *10082*
     E   *20771* Mauritius *10082*

Leitneriaceae

Number of genera:	1	
Number of species:	1	
Recorded threatened species:	1	(100%)

Southeastern United States.

R   *Leitneria floridana* Chapman *20850*
     R   *20850* U.S. - Arkansas *20850*
     R   *20850* U.S. - Florida *20850*
     E   *20850* U.S. - Georgia *20850*
     V   *20850* U.S. - Missouri *20850*
     E   *20850* U.S. - Texas *20850*

Lennoaceae

Number of genera:	3	
Number of species:	4 - 5	
Recorded threatened species:	2	(40%)

New World from southwestern United States to Colombia and Venezuela.

R   *Pholisma arenarium* Nutt. ex Hook. *20883, 20850, 8058*
     E   *20850* U.S. - Arizona *20850*
     I   *20850* U.S. - California *20850*
     I   *20883* Mexico *20883*
     ?   Mexico - Baja California Peninsula *8058*

R   *Pholisma sonorae* (Torr. ex Gray) Yatskievych *20883, 20850*
     E   *20850* U.S. - Arizona *20850*
     E   *20850* U.S. - California *20850*
     I   *20883* Mexico *20883*

Lentibulariaceae

Number of genera:	5
Number of species:	200
Recorded threatened species:	24 (12%)

Cosmopolitan.

I **Pinguicula bohemica** Krajina *2050*
    E   *2050* Czech Republic (Elbe River basin) *2050*
    I   *17821* Slovakia *17821*

R **Pinguicula fiorii** Tammaro & Pace *18264*
    R   *18264* Italy (Abruzzi) *18264*

V **Pinguicula grandiflora** Lam. ssp. *coenocantabrica*
    Rivas Mart. T.E. Diaz, et al.
    V   Spain

V **Pinguicula grandiflora** Lam. ssp. *dertosensis*
    (Cañigueral) O.Bolòs & Vigo *20692*
    V   *20692* Spain (Puertos de Tortosa y Beceite) *20692*

V **Pinguicula ionantha** Godfrey *20850, 15917*
    V   *20850* U.S. - Florida *20850*

R **Pinguicula longifolia** Ramond ex DC. ssp.
    reichenbachiana (J.Schindl.) Casper *20171*
    E   *20528* France (south-east) *20528*
    R   *20804* Italy *20528*

R **Pinguicula lutea** Walt. *12224*
    R   *12224* U.S. - Mississippi *12224*

V **Pinguicula nevadensis** (H.Lindb.) Casper *15398, 20171*
    V   *20874* Spain *15398*

R **Pinguicula primulifolia** Wood & Godfrey *12224*
    R   *12224* U.S. - Mississippi *12224*

V **Pinguicula racemosa** Miyoshi *10573*
    V   *10573* Japan *10573*

E **Pinguicula vallisneriifolia** Webb *19174, 20171*
    E   *19174* Spain *19174*

E **Pinguicula vulgaris** L. ssp. *bicolor* (Wol.) A.D.
    Löve *19306*
    E   *18216* Poland *18216*

I **Utricularia biovularioides** (Kulhm.) P. Taylor *20103*
    I   Brazil - Goias *20103*

I **Utricularia cecilii** P. Taylor *20103*
    I   *20103* India - Karnataka *20103*

I **Utricularia corynephora** P. Taylor *20103*
    I   *20103* Myanmar (Tavoy District, Paungdaw) *20103*
    I   *20103* Thailand (Oom, near Renong.) *20103*

I **Utricularia determannii** P. Taylor *20103*
    I   *20103* Suriname (Wilhelmina Mts.) *20103*

V **Utricularia dimorphantha** Makino *10573*
    V   *10573* Japan *10573*

I **Utricularia garrettii** P. Taylor *20103*
    I   *20103* Thailand (Doi Angka, Pa Ngem, north rock.) *20103*

R **Utricularia hamiltonii** F.Lloyd *20681, 20103*
    R   *20681* Australia - Northern Territory *20681*

R **Utricularia holtzei** F.Muell. *20681, 20103*
    R   *20681* Australia - Northern Territory *20681*

I **Utricularia letestui** P. Taylor *20103*
    I   *20103* Central African Republic (Boukoko) *20103*

I **Utricularia mirabilis** P. Taylor *20103*
    I   *20103* Venezuela *20103*

I **Utricularia panamensis** Steyerm. ex P. Taylor *20103*
    I   *20103* Panama (Coclé prov.) *20103*

I **Utricularia peranomala** P. Taylor *20103*
    I   *20103* China - Guangxi (Tzu Yuen district) *20103*

R **Utricularia rhododactylos** P.Taylor *20681, 20103*
    R   *20681* Australia - Northern Territory *20681*

Limnanthaceae

Number of genera:	2
Number of species:	11
Recorded threatened species:	8 (72%)

Temperate North America.

E **Limnanthes bakeri** J.T. Howell *20850*
    E   *20850* U.S. - California *20850*

E **Limnanthes douglasii** R. Br. ssp. *sulphurea* (C.T.
    Mason) C.T. Mason *20850*
    E   *20850* U.S. - California *20850*

V **Limnanthes floccosa** J.Howell ssp. *bellingeriana*
    (M.E. Peck) Arroyo *20850*
    E   *20850* U.S. - California *20850*
    V   *20850* U.S. - Oregon *20850*

E **Limnanthes floccosa** J. Howell ssp. *californica*
    Arroyo *20850*
    E   *20850* U.S. - California *20850*

E **Limnanthes floccosa** J. Howell ssp. *grandiflora*
    Arroyo *20850*
    E   *20850* U.S. - Oregon *20850*

E **Limnanthes floccosa** J. Howell ssp. *pumila* (T.J.
    Howell) Arroyo *20850*
    E   *20850* U.S. - Oregon *20850*

R **Limnanthes gracilis** T.J. Howell *20850*
    I   *20850* U.S. - California *20850*
    I   *20850* U.S. - Oregon *20850*

V **Limnanthes gracilis** T. J. Howell ssp.
    gracilis *20850*
    I   *20850* U.S. - California *20850*
    V   *20850* U.S. - Oregon *20850*

V **Limnanthes gracilis** T.Howell ssp. *parishii*
    (Jepson) Beauchamp *20850*
    V   *20850* U.S. - California *20850*
    I   *20850* U.S. - Oregon *20850*

V **Limnanthes macounii** Trel. *20850, 10701*
    V   *20850* Canada - British Columbia *20850*

R **Limnanthes montana** Jepson *20850*
    I   *20850* U.S. - California *20850*

R **Limnanthes striata** Jepson *20850*
    I   *20850* U.S. - California *20850*

V **Limnanthes vinculans** Ornduff *20850*
    V   *20850* U.S. - California *20850*

Linaceae

Number of genera:	6
Number of species:	220
Recorded threatened species:	48 (21%)

Widespread, especially temperate and subtropical.

V **Hesperolinon adenophyllum** (Gray) Small *20850*
    V   *20850* U.S. - California *20850*

V **Hesperolinon bicarpellatum** (H.K. Sharsmith) H.K.
    Sharsmith *20850*

	V	20850 U.S. - California *20850*

V   *Hesperolinon breweri* (Gray) Small *20850*
    V   20850 U.S. - California *20850*

R   *Hesperolinon californicum* (Benth.) Small *20850*
    I   20850 U.S. - California *20850*

R   *Hesperolinon clevelandii* (Greene) Small *20850*
    I   20850 U.S. - California *20850*

V   *Hesperolinon congestum* (Gray) Small *20850*
    V   20850 U.S. - California *20850*

E   *Hesperolinon didymocarpum* H.K. Sharsmith *20850*
    E   20850 U.S. - California *20850*

R   *Hesperolinon disjunctum* H.K. Sharsmith *20850*
    I   20850 U.S. - California *20850*

E   *Hesperolinon drymarioides* (Curran) Small *20850*
    E   20850 U.S. - California *20850*

R   *Hesperolinon spergulinum* (Gray) Small *20850*
    I   20850 U.S. - California *20850*

E   *Hesperolinon tehamense* H.K. Sharsmith *20850*
    E   20850 U.S. - California *20850*

R   *Hugonia belli* Sedgwick *10505*
    R   14782 India - Karnataka *10505*
    R   14782 India - Kerala (Cannanore) *10505*

R   *Hugonia elliptica* N. Robson *7749*
    R   Mozambique *7749*

I   *Hugonia grandiflora* N. Robson *5926*
    I   5926 Tanzania (Lindi) *5926*

R   *Hugonia serrata* Lam. *10082*
    V   14234 Réunion *10082*
    R   20771 Mauritius (Maurice) *10082*

R   *Hugonia tomentosa* Cav. *10082*
    R   20771 Mauritius *10082*

R   *Linum anisocalyx* Davis *12840*
    R   12840 Turkey *12840*

E   *Linum arenicola* (Small) Winkl. *20850*
    E   20850 U.S. - Florida *20850*

R   *Linum aretioides* Boiss *12840*
    R   12840 Turkey *12840*

R   *Linum boissieri* Asch. & Sint. ex Boiss. *12840, 20171*
    R   12840 Turkey *12840*

R   *Linum caespitosum* Sibth. & Sm. *20171*
    R   20730 Greece - Crete *20730*

V   *Linum carteri* Small *20850*
    E   20850 U.S. - Florida *20850*

E   *Linum carteri* Small var. *carteri* *20850*
    E   20850 U.S. - Florida *20850*

V   *Linum carteri* Small var. *smallii*
    Rogers *20850*
    V   20850 U.S. - Florida *20850*

R   *Linum ciliatum* Hayek *12840*
    R   12840 Turkey *12840*

E   *Linum cratericola* Eliasson *11117*
    E   Ecuador - Galapagos (NE of Floreana) *9389*

R   *Linum doerfleri* Rech.f. *20171*
    R   20730 Greece - Crete *20730*

E   *Linum dolomiticum* Borbas *8000, 20171*
    E   19576 Hungary (dolomite hills near Budapest) *8000*

R   *Linum elegans* Spruner ex Boiss. *5204, 20171*

R   5204 Bulgaria (south-west three sites) *5204*

R   *Linum empetrifolium* (Boiss.) Davis *12840*
    R   12840 Turkey *12840*

R   *Linum goulimyi* Rech.f. *20171*
    R   Greece

R   *Linum gyaricum* Vierh. *20171*
    R   20731 Greece - East Aegean Is *20731*

E   *Linum gypsogenium* Nesom *20883*
    I   20883 Mexico *20883*

R   *Linum harlingii* Eliasson *11117*
    R   Ecuador - Galapagos (V. Wolf & Darwin, Isabela) *11117*

R   *Linum hirsutum* L. ssp. *oreocaricum* Davis *12840*
    R   12840 Turkey *12840*

V   *Linum hirsutum* L. var. *platyphyllum* Davis *12840*
    V   12840 Turkey *12840*

V   *Linum leonii* F.W.Schultz *20171*
    V   France
    V   20640 Germany *20644*

V   *Linum lewisii* Pursh var. *lepagei* (Boivin) Rogers *20850*
    I   20850 Canada - Manitoba *20850*
    E   20850 Canada - Keewatin *20850*
    V   20850 Canada - Ontario *20850*

V   *Linum lundellii* Rogers *20850, 9812*
    I   20850 U.S. - Texas *20850*
    ?   Mexico *9812*

V   *Linum macrocarpum* Rogers *20850*
    E   20850 U.S. - Alabama *20850*
    V   20850 U.S. - Mississippi *20850*

R   *Linum monogynum* var. *chathamicum* *19305*
    R   19305 New Zealand - Chatham Is. *19305*

R   *Linum mucronatum* Bertol var. *gypsiocola* *12840*
    R   12840 Turkey *12840*

R   *Linum mucronatum* Bertol var. *papilliferum* (Huber-Mor. & Reese) Davis *12840*
    R   12840 Turkey *12840*

R   *Linum pamphylicum* (Boiss.) Podp. *12840*
    R   12840 Turkey *12840*

E   *Linum prostratum* Dombey ex Lam. var. *parvum* (I.M. Johnston) Mildner *18200*
    E   9446 Peru *18200*

R   *Linum pycnophullum* Boiss. & Heldr. ssp. *kurdicum* Davis *12840*
    R   12840 Turkey *12840*

R   *Linum subasperifolium* Humbert & Maire
    R   Morocco

E   *Linum tauricum* Willd. ssp. *bosphori* Davis *12840*
    E   12840 Turkey *12840*

R   *Linum triflorum* Davis *12840*
    R   12840 Turkey *12840*

R   *Linum villarianum* Pau
    R   Morocco

V   *Linum westii* Rogers *20850*
    V   20850 U.S. - Florida *20850*
    I   20850 U.S. - Mississippi *20850*

I   *Philbornea palawanica* Hallier. F. *13833*
    I   *13833* Philippines (Palawan) *13833*

Loasaceae

Number of genera: 14
Number of species: 200
Recorded threatened species: 25   (12%)

American tropics and subtropics, Arabia and SW Africa.

R   *Eucnide rupestris* (Baill.) H.J. Thompson & Ernst *20850*
    E   *20850* U.S. - Arizona *20850*
    V   *20850* U.S. - California *20850*

V   *Loasa fulva* Urb. & Gilg *18200*
    V   *9446* Peru *18200*

V   *Loasa nitida* Desr. *18200*
    V   *9446* Peru *18200*

V   *Mentzelia argillosa* J. Darl. *20850*
    V   *20850* U.S. - Colorado *20850*
    E   *20850* U.S. - Utah *20850*

V   *Mentzelia candelaria* H.J. Thompson & Prigge *20850*
    V   *20850* U.S. - Nevada *20850*

E   *Mentzelia chrysantha* Engelm. ex Brandeg. *20850*
    E   *20850* U.S. - Colorado *20850*
    I   *20850* U.S. - Nebraska *20850*
    I   *20850* U.S. - Wyoming *20850*

V   *Mentzelia densa* Greene *20850*
    V   *20850* U.S. - Colorado *20850*

V   *Mentzelia desertorum* (A. Davids.) H.J. Thompson & Roberts *20850*
    I   *20850* U.S. - Arizona *20850*
    I   *20850* U.S. - California *20850*

V   *Mentzelia eremophila* (Jepson) H.J. Thompson & Roberts *20850*
    I   *20850* U.S. - California *20850*

R   *Mentzelia gracilenta* (Nutt.) Torr. & Gray *20850*
    I   *20850* U.S. - California *20850*
    I   *20850* U.S. - Nevada *20850*

E   *Mentzelia leucophylla* Brandeg. *20850*
    E   *20850* U.S. - Nevada (Ash Meadows, Nye Co.) *20850*

E   *Mentzelia marginata* (Osterhout) H.J. Thompson & Prigge *20850*
    I   *20850* U.S. - Colorado *20850*
    E   *20850* U.S. - Utah *20850*

V   *Mentzelia mollis* M.E. Peck *20850*
    V   *20850* U.S. - Idaho *20850*
    E   *20850* U.S. - Nevada *20850*
    V   *20850* U.S. - Oregon *20850*

V   *Mentzelia multicaulis* (Osterhout) A. Nels. ex J.Darl. *20850*
    I   *20850* U.S. - Colorado *20850*
    V   *20850* U.S. - Utah *20850*

E   *Mentzelia multicaulis* (Osterhout) A. Nels. ex J.Darl. var. *librina* Thorne & F.G. Sm. *20850*
    E   *20850* U.S. - Utah *20850*

V   *Mentzelia multicaulis* (Osterhout) A. Nels. ex J.Darl. var. *multicaulis* *20850*
    I   *20850* U.S. - Colorado *20850*
    I   *20850* U.S. - Utah *20850*

Ex   *Mentzelia nitens* Greene var. *leptocaulis* J. Darl. *20850*
    Ex   *20850* U.S. - Arizona *20850*

R   *Mentzelia obscura* H.J. Thompson & Roberts *20850*
    I   *20850* U.S. - Arizona *20850*
    I   *20850* U.S. - California *20850*
    I   *20850* U.S. - Nevada *20850*
    E   *20850* U.S. - Utah *20850*

R   *Mentzelia oreophila* J. Darl. *20850*
    I   *20850* U.S. - Arizona *20850*
    I   *20850* U.S. - California *20850*
    I   *20850* U.S. - Nevada *20850*

E   *Mentzelia packardiae* Glad. *20850*
    E   *20850* U.S. - Nevada *20850*
    E   *20850* U.S. - Oregon *20850*

V   *Mentzelia polita* A. Nels. *20850*
    I   *20850* U.S. - California *20850*
    I   *20850* U.S. - Nevada *20850*
    I   *20850* U.S. - Utah *20850*

V   *Mentzelia pumila* (Nutt.) Torr. & Gray var. *lagarosa* Thorne *20850*
    I   *20850* U.S. - Nevada *20850*
    V   *20850* U.S. - Utah *20850*

R   *Mentzelia reflexa* Coville *20850*
    I   *20850* U.S. - California *20850*
    I   *20850* U.S. - Nevada *20850*

E   *Mentzelia shultziorum* Prigge *20850*
    E   *20850* U.S. - Utah *20850*

R   *Mentzelia torreyi* Gray var. *acerosa* (M.E. Jones) Barneby *20850*
    R   *20850* U.S. - Idaho *20850*

V   *Mentzelia tridentata* (A. Davids.) H.J. Thompson & Roberts *20850*
    I   *20850* U.S. - California *20850*

V   *Petalonyx thurberi* A. Gray ssp. *gilmanii* (Munz) W. Davis & H.J. Thompson *20850*
    V   *20850* U.S. - California *20850*
    I   *20850* U.S. - Nevada *20850*

R   *Plakothira frutescens* Florence *20845*
    R   *20845* French Polynesia - Marquesas Is (Nuku Hiva) *20845*

Loganiaceae

Number of genera: 20
Number of species: 500
Recorded threatened species: 37   (7%)

Tropical and subtropical; relatively few species in temperate regions.

I   *Fagraea calcarea* M.R. Henderson
    I   Malaysia - Peninsular Malaysia (Pahang)

R   *Geniostoma astylum* A.Gray *20845*
    R   *20845* French Polynesia - Society Is. (Moorea, Tahiti) *20845*

E   *Geniostoma calcicola* A.C. Smith *19630*
    E   *19630* Fiji (Fulanga) *19630*

R   *Geniostoma clavatum* J.Moore *20845*
    R   *20845* French Polynesia - Society Is. (Raiatea) *20845*

V   *Geniostoma clavigerum* A.C. Smith & Stone *19630*
    V   *19630* Fiji (north western Viti Levu) *19630*

I   *Geniostoma gagneae* Fosberg & Sachet *20845*
    I   *20845* French Polynesia - Marquesas Is (Faut Hiva) *20845*

I   *Geniostoma hallei* Sachet & Fosb.
    I   French Polynesia - Marquesas Is

I   *Geniostoma hallei* Fosberg & Sachet var. *fatuivense* Fosberg & Sachet *20845*
- I   *20845* French Polynesia - Marquesas Is (Faut Hiva) *20845*

I   *Geniostoma hallei* Fosberg & Sachet var. *hallei* *20845*, *20845*
- I   *20845* French Polynesia - Marquesas Is (Tahuata) *20845*

I   *Geniostoma hallei* Fosberg & Sachet var. *hivaoense* Fosberg & Sachet *20845*
- I   *20845* French Polynesia - Marquesas Is (Hiva Oa) *20845*

V   *Geniostoma hendersonense* H. St. John *8050*
- V   *19185* Pitcairn (Henderson Is.) *8050*

R   *Geniostoma pedunculatum* Bojer ex DC. *10082*
- R   *14220* Réunion *14220*
- R   *20771* Mauritius *10936*

R   *Geniostoma petiolosum* C. Moore & F. Muell.
- R   *14225* Australia - NSW - Lord Howe Is. *14225*

R   *Geniostoma stipulare* A.C. Smith & Stone *19630*
- R   *19630* Fiji (Viti Levu, Vanua Levu) *19630*

E   *Labordia cyrtandrae* (Baill.) St. John *20850*
- E   *20850* U.S. - Hawaii *20850*

R   *Labordia fagraeoidea* Gaud. *20850*
- R   *20850* U.S. - Hawaii *20850*

E   *Labordia helleri* Sherff *20850*
- E   *20850* U.S. - Hawaii *20850*

R   *Labordia helleri* Sherff var. *helleri* *14209*
- R   *14209* U.S. - Hawaii (Kaua`i) *14209*

R   *Labordia hirtella* Mann *20850*, *14209*
- I   *20850* U.S. - Hawaii *20850*

V   *Labordia hosakana* (Sherff) W.L. Wagner, Herbst & Sohmer *20850*, *14209*
- I   *20850* U.S. - Hawaii (O`ahu - Ko`olau Mts.) *20850*

E   *Labordia kaalae* Forbes *20850*
- E   *20850* U.S. - Hawaii *20850*

E   *Labordia lydgatei* Forbes *20850*, *14209*
- E   *20850* U.S. - Hawaii (Kaua`i) *20850*

E   *Labordia pumila* (Hbd.) Skottsberg *20850*, *14209*
- E   *20850* U.S. - Hawaii (Kaua`i) *20850*

V   *Labordia sessilis* Gray *20850*, *14209*
- I   *20850* U.S. - Hawaii (O`ahu - Ko`olau Mts.) *20850*

E   *Labordia tinifolia* A.Gray var. *lanaiensis* Sherff *20850*, *14209*
- E   *20850* U.S. - Hawaii (Lana`i, Moloka`i) *20850*

E   *Labordia tinifolia* A. Gray var. *wahiawaensis* St. John *20850*, *21352*
- E   *20850* U.S. - Hawaii *20850*

R   *Logania cordifolia* Hook. *20681*
- R   *20681* Australia - Queensland *20681*

Ex   *Logania depressa* *19305*
- Ex   *19305* New Zealand - North Is. *19305*

V   *Logania diffusa* R.Henderson *20681*
- V   *20681* Australia - Queensland *20681*

E   *Logania imbricata* (Guillaumin) Steenis & Leenh. *20893*
- E   *20893* New Caledonia *20893*

V   *Logania insularis* J.Black *20681*

V   *20681* Australia - South Australia *20681*

V   *Neuburgia macroloba* (A.C.Sm.) A.C.Smith *19630*
- V   *19630* Fiji (Taveuni) *19630*

E   *Spigelia ambigua* C. Wright *5607*
- E   *19105* Cuba (Pinar del Rio; I. Juventud) *5607*

V   *Spigelia gentianoides* Chapman ex A. DC. *20850*, *17890*
- V   *20850* U.S. - Alabama *20850*
- E   *20850* U.S. - Florida *20850*

E   *Spigelia loganioides* (Torr. & Gray ex Endl. & Fenzl) A. DC. *20850*, *17890*
- E   *20850* U.S. - Florida *20850*

R   *Spigelia texana* (Torr. & Gray) A. DC. *20850*
- R   *20850* U.S. - Texas *20850*

I   *Strychnos colubrina* L.
- I   India - Andhra Pradesh (Veligonda hills)
- I   India - Karnataka (South Canara)
- I   India - Kerala (Travancore)

V   *Strychnos henryii* Merr. & Yamamoto ex Yamamoto *20854*
- V   *20854* Taiwan *20854*

V   *Strychnos millepunctata* Leeuwenb. *20887*
- V   *20887* Côte d'Ivoire *20887*

I   *Strychnos narcondamensis* A.W. Hill *7771*
- I   India - Nicobar Is. (Narcondam) *7771*

I   *Strychnos odorata* A. Chev. *7926*
- I   Côte d'Ivoire

I   *Strychnos oleifolia* Hill *13833*
- I   *13833* Philippines (low altitude) *13833*

V   *Strychnos tetragona* A.W. Hill *10276*
- V   *12838* Sri Lanka *10276*

Loranthaceae

Number of genera:	60-70	
Number of species:	700	
Recorded threatened species:	40	(5%)

Mainly tropical, extending into temperate areas.

V   *Alepis flavida* Teigh. *19305*
- V   *19305* New Zealand - North Is. *19305*
- V   *19305* New Zealand - South Is. *19305*

R   *Amyema tridactylum* Barlow *20681*
- R   *20681* Australia - Northern Territory *20681*

R   *Atkinsonia ligustrina* F.Muell. *20681*
- R   *20681* Australia - New South Wales *20681*

Ex/E   *Bakerella clavata* (Desr.) Balle var. *aldabrensis* (Turrill) S. Balle *14981*
- Ex/E   *14981* Seychelles *14981*

Ex/E   *Bakerella clavata* (Desr.) S. Balle ssp. *sechellensis* (Baker) S. Balle *14296*
- Ex/E   *14981* Seychelles (granitic) *14296*

V   *Bakerella hoyifolia* (Baker) S. Balle *10082*
- Ex   *14220* Réunion *14220*
- V   *20771* Mauritius *10936*

R   *Berhautia senegalensis* Balle *7926*
- R   *19919* Gambia *19919*
- R   Senegal *7926*

E   *Cladocolea dimorpha* Kuijt *9815*
- E   *9815* Mexico - Puebla *9815*

E   *Cladocolea hintonii* Kuijt *9815*
- E   *9815* Mexico - Guerrero *9815*

E   *Cladocolea hondurensis* Kuijt *9815*

E   9815   Honduras 9815

E   *Cladocolea pedicellata* Kuijt 9815
E   9815   Mexico 9815

E   *Cladocolea tehuacanensis* (Oliver) Tieghem 9815
E   9815   Mexico 9815

R   *Dendropemon acutifolius* Urban 5607
R   19105   Cuba (Santiago de Cuba) 5607

Ex/E   *Dendropemon brevipes* Britton 4650
Ex/E 4650   Bahamas 4650

E   *Dendropemon caymanensis* Proctor 19712
E   19434   Cayman Is. (little Cayman) 19712

R   *Dendropemon pauciflorus* (Sw.) van Teigh. 20883
R   20883   Jamaica 20883

V   *Dendropemon sintenisii* Krug & Urban 20883
I   20883   Puerto Rico 20883

I   *Elytranthe elmeri* (Merr.) Merr. 13833
I   13833   Philippines (Palawan) 13833

I   *Helixanthera pulchra* (DC.) Danser 19120
I   19120   Thailand 19120

I   *Loranthus palawanensis* Merr. 13833
I   13833   Philippines (Palawan) 13833

R   *Lysiana filifolia* Barlow 20681
R   20681   Australia - Queensland 20681

R   *Muellerina myrtifolia* (Cunn. ex Benth.) Barlow 20681
I   20681   Australia - New South Wales 20681
I   20681   Australia - Queensland 20681

E   *Notanthera berteroi* 19125
E   19125   Chile - Juan Fernandez Is. 19116

V   *Panamanthus panamensis* (Rizz.) Kuijt 16389
V   16317   Panama 16389

V   *Peraxilla colensoi* 19305
V   19305   New Zealand - North Is. 19305
V   19305   New Zealand - South Is. 19305

V   *Peraxilla tetrapetala* 19305
V   19305   New Zealand - North Is. 19305
V   19305   New Zealand - South Is. 19305

R   *Phragmanthera erythraea* (Sprague) M.Gilbert 19704
R   19704   Ethiopia (West Eritrea; Tigray Upland; Shewa Upland) 19704

R   *Phragmanthera nigritana* (Benth.) Balle var. *obovata* Balle
R   Côte d'Ivoire

R   *Phragmanthera sarertaensisi* (Hutch. & E.A.Bruce) M. Gilbert 19704
R   19704   Ethiopia (Harerge, Arsi, Sidamo.) 19704

I   *Phthirusa jamaicensis* Krug & Urb. 20883, 13336
I   13336   Jamaica 20883

R   *Phthirusa lepidobotrys* (Griseb.) Eichl. 20883
R   20883   Jamaica 20883

E   *Phthirusa pittieri* Krause 20883, 10747
I   20883   Panama 20883

E   *Plicosepalus ogadenensis* M. Gilbert 19704
E   19704   Ethiopia (Harerge) 19704

E   *Plicosepalus robustus* Wiens & Polhill 19704
E   19704   Ethiopia (Sidamo) 19704

I   *Psittacanthus americanus* (L.) Mart. 10199
I   Dominica 10199

V   *Psittacanthus hamulifer* Kuijt 9816
V   16317   Panama 9816

Ex   *Psittacanthus nudus* (A. Molina) Kuijt & Feuer 9815
Ex   9815   Honduras 9815

E   *Psittacanthus pusillus* Kuijt 20883, 9816
E   9815   Panama 20883

R   *Scurrula pseudochinensis* (Yam.) Liu & Chen 20511
R   20511   Taiwan 20511

R   *Scurrula ritozanensis* (Hayata) Danser 20511
R   20511   Taiwan 20511

E   *Struthanthus johnstonii* Standley & Steyerm. 9004
E   9815   Guatemala 9004

Ex   *Trilepidea adamsii* (Cheeseman) Tieghem 86
Ex   15135   New Zealand - North Is. 15135

R   *Tupeia antarctica* 19305
R   19305   New Zealand - North Is. 19305
R   19305   New Zealand - South Is. 19305

Lythraceae

Number of genera: 24
Number of species: 500
Recorded threatened species: 57   (11%)

Mainly tropical; also temperate.

V   *Cuphea aspera* Chapman 20850
V   20850   U.S. - Florida 20850
I   20850   U.S. - Georgia 20850

R   *Cuphea baillonis* Koehne 11373
?   Mexico - Jalisco 21240

R   *Cuphea caeciliae* Koehne 11373
?   Mexico - Chiapas 21240

R   *Cuphea caesariata* S.A. Graham 11373
R   11373   Mexico 11373

R   *Cuphea crassiflora* S.A. Graham 9817
R   11373   Mexico 9817

R   *Cuphea delicatula* Brandegee 11373
R   11373   Mexico 11373

R   *Cuphea dibrachiata* S.A. Graham 9818
R   11373   Mexico 9818

R   *Cuphea flavovirens* S.A. Graham 9818
?   Mexico - Guerrero 21240

R   *Cuphea gaumeri* Koehne 11373
R   11373   Mexico 11373

R   *Cuphea heteropetala* Koehne 11373
?   Mexico - Oaxaca 21240

I   *Cuphea heydei* Koehne ex J.D. Smith 9004
I   11373   Guatemala 9004

R   *Cuphea inflata* S.A. Graham 11373
R   11373   Mexico 11373

R   *Cuphea karwinskii* Koehne 11373
R   11373   Mexico 11373

R   *Cuphea megalophylla* S.F. Blake 11373
R   11373   Mexico 11373

R   *Cuphea mexiae* Bacigal. 11373
?   Mexico - Jalisco 21240

R   *Cuphea michoacana* R. Foster 11372
R   11373   Mexico 11372

R   *Cuphea ornithoides* R. Foster 11372
R   11373   Mexico 11372

R   *Cuphea ownbeyi* S.A. Graham 9818
R   11373   Mexico 9818

Magnoliopsida (dicots): Lythraceae: *Cuphea*

R   *Cuphea painteri* Rose *11373*
     R   *11373* Mexico *11373*

R   *Cuphea palustris* Koehne *11373*
     R   *11373* Mexico *11373*

R   *Cuphea pertenuis* R. Foster *11372*
     R   *11373* Mexico *11372*

R   *Cuphea purpurascens* Bacigal. *11373*
     R   *11373* Mexico *11373*

R   *Cuphea quaternata* Bacigal. *11373*
     R   *21240* Mexico - Durango *21240*
     R   *21240* Mexico - Nayarit *21240*
     R   *21240* Mexico - Zacatecas *21240*

R   *Cuphea rasilis* S.A. Graham *9817*
     ?   Mexico - Nayarit *21240*

R   *Cuphea retroscabra* S.Watson *11373*
     R   *21240* Mexico - Jalisco *21240*
     R   *21240* Mexico - Nayarit *21240*

R   *Cuphea roseana* Koehne *11373*
     R   *11373* Mexico *11373*

R   *Cuphea salicifolia* Cham. & Schldl. *11373*
     R   *11373* Mexico *11373*

R   *Cuphea spectabilis* S.A. Graham *9817*
     R   *11373* Mexico *9817*

R   *Cuphea trichochila* R. Foster *11372*
     ?   Mexico - Guerrero *21240*

R   *Cuphea viscosa* Rose *11373*
     R   *11373* Mexico *11373*

I   *Ginoria davisii* M. Johnston *11123*
     I   *11373* Mexico - Veracruz *11123*

V   *Ginoria koehneana* Urban *5607*
     V   *19105* Cuba (Las Tunas, Holguin) *5607*

I   *Ginoria nudiflora* (Hemsley) Koehne *11373*
     I   *11373* Mexico - Oaxaca *11373*

E   *Ginoria thomasiana* Alain *5607*
     E   *19105* Cuba (Pinar del Rio) *5607*

R   *Lafoensia pacari* St.-Hil. *20883*
     I   *20883* Brazil *20883*
     R   *20883* Paraguay *20883*

R   *Lagerstroemia fauriei* Koehne *10572*
     R   *10572* Japan *10572*

R   *Lagerstroemia minuticarpa* Debberm. ex P.C. Kanjilal *14782*
     R   *14782* India - Assam *14782*
     R   *14782* India - Sikkim *14782*

I   *Lagerstroemia rottleri* C.B. Clarke
     I   India

I   *Lagerstroemia thomsonii* Koehne
     I   India - Karnataka
     I   India - Tamil Nadu

E   *Lourtella resinosa* S. A. Graham *20883*
     I   *20883* Peru *20883*

R   *Lythrum castellanum* Gonz.Albo ex Borja *20171*
     R   *20660* Spain (Cidad Real, Albacete) *11496*

E   *Lythrum curtissii* Fern. *20850*
     E   *20850* U.S. - Florida *20850*
     E   *20850* U.S. - Georgia *20850*

V   *Lythrum flagellare* Shuttlw. ex Chapman *20850*
     V   *20850* U.S. - Florida *20850*

V   *Lythrum flexuosum* auct., non Lag. *8000, 20171*
     V   *20874* Spain (centre & east) *20690*

R   *Nesaea longipes* Gray *20850*
     I   *20850* U.S. - New Mexico *20850*
     R   *20850* U.S. - Texas *20850*

R   *Nesaea pygmaea* Fernandes & A. Diniz *7749*
     R   Mozambique *7749*

R   *Nesaea wardii* Immelman *20604*
     R   *20604* South Africa - Natal *20604*

E   *Punica protopunica* Balf. f. *15534*
     E   *15534* Yemen - Socotra *15534*

I   *Rotala floribunda* (Wt.) Koehne
     I   India - Maharashtra (Mahabaleshwar hills)

R   *Rotala juniperina* Fernandes *7749*
     R   Malawi *7749*

I   *Rotala malampuzhensis* R.V. Nair
     I   India - Kerala

I   *Rotala occultiflora* Koehne *9228*
     I   India - Kerala (Malabar coast)
     I   India - Madhaya Pradesh *9228*

V   *Rotala ritchiei* (C.B. Clarke) Koehne *11494*
     Ex/E   *11494* India - Karnataka (Belgaum) *11494*
     V   *11494* India - Maharashtra (Pune District) *11494*

I   *Rotala rubra* (Buch.-Ham. ex D. Don) Hara
     I   Nepal

V   *Rotala simpliciuscula* (Kz.) Koehne *14872*
     V   *14872* Bangladesh (Chittagong) *14872*

E   *Sonneratia hainanensis* Ko, E.Y. Chen & S.Y. Chen *17617*
     E   *18038* China - Hainan Is. *11139*

E   *Tetrataxis salicifolia* (Thouars ex Tul.) Baker *10082*
     E   *20771* Mauritius *10082*

Magnoliaceae

Number of genera: 12
Number of species: 220
Recorded threatened species: 43   (19%)

Widespread, especially Northern Hemisphere.

R   *Liriodendron chinense* (Hemsley) Sarg. *20709, 17617*
     R   *17617* China - Anhui *11139*
     R   *17617* China - Fujian *11139*
     R   *17617* China - Guangxi *11139*
     R   *17617* China - Guizhou *11139*
     R   *17617* China - Hubei (Fang Xian, Badong Xian) *11139*
     R   *17617* China - Hunan *11139*
     R   *17617* China - Jiangxi (Kuling) *11139*
     R   *17617* China - Shaanxi *11139*
     R   *17617* China - Sichuan *11139*
     R   *17617* China - Yunnan *11139*
     R   *17617* China - Zhejiang *11139*
     I   *20985* Vietnam *6057*

V   *Magnolia amoena* Cheng *20709, 17617*
     V   *17617* China - Anhui *11139*
     V   *17617* China - Jiangsu (Yixing; Liyang) *11139*
     V   *17617* China - Jiangxi (Qianshan) *11139*
     V   *17617* China - Zhejiang *11139*

R   *Magnolia ashei* Weatherby *20850*
     R   *20850* U.S. - Florida *20850*

R   *Magnolia blaoensis* (Gagnepain) Dandy *6057*
     R   Vietnam *6057*

R   *Magnolia cacuminicola* Bisse *11840*
     R   *19105* Cuba (Guantanamo) *11840*

R **Magnolia champacifolia** Dandy *6057*
  R   Vietnam *6057*

R **Magnolia clemensiorum** Dandy *6057*
  R   Vietnam *6057*

I **Magnolia cubensis** Urban ssp. *acunae* Imkhanitskaya *11840*
  I   20990   Cuba (Las Villas) *11840*

V **Magnolia cylindrica** Wilson *20709, 17617*
  V   *17617*   China - Anhui *11139*
  V   *17617*   China - Fujian *11139*
  V   *17617*   China - Jiangxi *11139*
  V   *17617*   China - Zhejiang *11139*

E **Magnolia dealbata** Zucc. *9019*
  E   *9114*   Mexico - Veracruz *9019*

I **Magnolia griffithii** Hook.f. & Thomson
  I   India - Assam

I **Magnolia gustavi** King
  I   India - Assam

V **Magnolia iltisiana** Vásquez *21204*
  E   21229   Mexico - Guerrero *21229*
  E   21229   Mexico - Jalisco *21229*
  E   21229   Mexico - Michoacan *21229*

E **Magnolia kachirachirai** (Kaneh. & Yamamoto) Dandy *20689*
  E   20854   Taiwan *20689*

R **Magnolia nana** Dandy *6057*
  R   Vietnam *6057*

V **Magnolia officinalis** Rehder & Wilson *20709*
  V   *11139*   China - Anhui *11139*
  V   *11139*   China - Fujian *11139*
  V   *17617*   China - Gansu *11139*
  V   *11139*   China - Guangdong *11139*
  V   *17617*   China - Guangxi *11139*
  V   *17617*   China - Guizhou *11139*
  V   *17617*   China - Hubei *11139*
  V   *11139*   China - Hunan *11139*
  V   *11139*   China - Jiangxi *11139*
  V   *17617*   China - Shaanxi *11139*
  V   *17617*   China - Sichuan *11139*
  V   *11139*   China - Zhejiang *11139*

R **Magnolia pacifica** A. Vázquez ssp. *pacifica* *20883*
  R   20883   Mexico *20883*

R **Magnolia pacifica** ssp. *pugana* H.H. Iltis & A. Vázquez *20883*
  R   20883   Mexico *20883*

R **Magnolia pacifica** ssp. *tarahumara* A. Vázquez *20883*
  R   20883   Mexico *20883*

E **Magnolia palescens** Urban & Ekman *5642*
  E   19547   Dominican Republic (Constanza region) *21008*

E **Magnolia panamensis** A. Vázquez and H.H. Iltis *20883*
  E   20883   Panama *20883*

E **Magnolia portoricensis** Bello *20883*
  I   20883   Puerto Rico *20883*

Ex **Magnolia pseudokobus** Abe & Akasawa *10572*
  Ex   20626   Japan (Aioi-machi) *20626*

V **Magnolia sinensis** (Rehder & Wilson) Stapf *20709, 17617*
  V   *17617*   China - Sichuan (Tianquan; Lushan; Wenchuan) *11139*

V **Magnolia sororum** Sieb. ssp. *lutea* A.

      Vázquez *20883*
  V   20883   Costa Rica *20883*

V **Magnolia sororum** Seib. ssp. *sororum* Siebert *20883*
  V   20883   Panama *20883*

E **Magnolia splendens** Urban *20883*
  I   20883   Puerto Rico *20883*

V **Magnolia tamaulipana** A. Vázquez *20883*
  V   20883   Mexico *20883*

V **Magnolia wilsonii** (Finet & Gagnepain) Rehder *20709, 17617*
  V   *17617*   China - Guizhou (Panxian; Anshong) *11139*
  V   *17617*   China - Sichuan *11139*
  V   China - Yunnan *11139*

E **Magnolia zenii** Cheng *20709, 17617*
  E   *17617*   China - Jiangsu (Jurong, Baohuashan) *11139*

E **Manglietia aromatica** Dandy *20709, 17617*
  E   *17617*   China - Guangxi (Longzhou, Nape) *11139*
  E   *17617*   China - Yunnan (Xixi; Maguan; Guangnan) *11139*

E **Manglietia grandis** Hu & Cheng *20709, 17617*
  E   *17617*   China - Guangxi (Jingxi, Nape) *11139*
  E   *17617*   China - Yunnan (Malipe, Jingping, Maguan) *11139*

E **Manglietia megaphylla** Hu & Cheng *20709, 17617*
  E   *17617*   China - Guangxi (Jingxi, Nape) *11139*
  E   *17617*   China - Yunnan (Xixi; Malipe) *11139*

R **Manglietia rufibarbata** Dandy *6057*
  R   Vietnam *6057*

R **Michelia chapaensis** Dandy *20709, 6057*
  R   China *6057*
  R   Vietnam *6057*

R **Michelia punduana** Hook.f. & Thomson *11494*
  R   *11494*   India - Meghalaya (Khasi hills) *11494*
  R   *11494*   India - Nagaland *11494*

R **Michelia salicifolia** Agnostini *20689, 14182*
  R   *14182*   Indonesia - Sumatra *14182*

R **Michelia subulifera** Dandy *6057*
  R   Vietnam *6057*

E **Michelia wilsonii** Finet & Gagnepain *20709, 17617*
  E   *17617*   China - Sichuan *11139*
  E   *17617*   China - Yunnan *8482*

I **Pachylarnax pleiocarpa** Dandy *20689*
  I   India - Assam (Lakhimpur) *20689*

E **Talauma caricifragrans** Loz.-Contr. *16890*
  E   19352   Colombia *16890*

R **Talauma dodecapetala** (Lam) Urb. *20883, 10199*
  I   20883   Dominica *20883*
  I   20883   Grenada *20883*
  I   20883   Martinique *20883*

V **Talauma gilbertoi** Loz.-Contr. *16890*
  V   19352   Colombia *16890*

V **Talauma hernandezii** Loz.-Contr. *16890*
  V   19352   Colombia *16890*

R **Talauma orbiculata** Britton & P. Wilson *11840*
  R   19105   Cuba (Oriente) *11840*

I **Talauma pulgarensis** Elm. *13833*
  I   13833   Philippines (Palawan) *13833*

E **Talauma sambuensis** Pitt. *20883, 9006*
  I   20883   Panama *20883*

Malesherbiaceae

Number of genera:	1-2	
Number of species:	25	
Recorded threatened species:	4	(16%)

Andes from Chile to Peru.

R   *Malesherbia angustisecta* Harms. *13875*
     R   *13875* Chile *13875*

R   *Malesherbia auristipulata* Ric. Sal. *13875*
     R   *13875* Chile *13875*

R   *Malesherbia tocopillana* Ric. Sal. *13875*
     R   *13875* Chile *13875*

E   *Malesherbia weberbaueri* Gilg *18200*
     E   *19965* Peru *19965*

Malpighiaceae

Number of genera:	60	
Number of species:	1,200	
Recorded threatened species:	109	(9%)

Tropical and subtropical, especially South America.

V   *Acridocarpus alopecurus* Sprague var. *machaeropterus* Niedenzu *7959*
     V   *5926* Tanzania (Uzaramo Distr.) *7959*

R   *Acridocarpus congestus* Lannert *7959*
     R   Tanzania (Morogoro Distr.) *7959*

R   *Acridocarpus monodii* Arenes & P. Jaeger *11751*
     R   Mali *11751*

I   *Acridocarpus pauciglandulosus* Launert *5926*
     I   *5926* Tanzania (Lindi & Newala) *5926*

V   *Acridocarpus scheffleri* Engl. *5926*
     V   *5926* Tanzania *5926*

V   *Acridocarpus taxon a* *20057*
     V   *20057* Kenya (Ngangao forest, Taita hills) *20057*

R   *Aspidopterys canarensis* Dalz. *11494*
     R   *11494* India - Karnataka *11494*
     R   *11494* India - Kerala *11494*
     R   *11494* India - Maharashtra (Bombay) *11494*

I   *Aspidopterys hutchinsonii* Haines *7771*
     I   *7771* India - Orissa (Mayurbhanj) *7771*

R   *Aspidopterys tomentosa* Haines var. *hutchinsonii* (Haines) Srivastava *11494*
     R   *11494* India - Orissa (Mayurbhanj Hills) *11494*

R   *Banisteriopsis acapulcensis* var. *llanensis* B. Gates *20883*
     I   *20883* Venezuela *20883*

V   *Banisteriopsis alternifolia* (Steyermark) B. Gates *20883*
     I   *20883* Trinidad & Tobago *20883*
     I   *20883* Venezuela *20883*

V   *Banisteriopsis amplectens* B. Gates *20883*
     I   *20883* Brazil *20883*

R   *Banisteriopsis andersonii* B. Gates *20883*
     I   *20883* Brazil *20883*

R   *Banisteriopsis arborea* B. Gates *20883*
     I   *20883* Brazil *20883*

V   *Banisteriopsis basifixa* B. Gates *20883*
     I   *20883* Brazil *20883*

R   *Banisteriopsis brevipedicellata* B. Gates *20883*
     I   *20883* Brazil *20883*

V   *Banisteriopsis byssacea* B. Gates *20883*
     I   *20883* Brazil *20883*

V   *Banisteriopsis cachimbensis* B. Gates *20883*
     I   *20883* Brazil *20883*

R   *Banisteriopsis caduciflora* (Niedenzu) B. Gates *20883*
     I   *20883* Brazil *20883*
     I   *20883* Peru *20883*

R   *Banisteriopsis calcicola* B. Gates *20883*
     I   *20883* Brazil *20883*

V   *Banisteriopsis cipoensis* B. Gates *20883*
     I   *20883* Brazil *20883*

R   *Banisteriopsis cornifolia* var. *cornifolia* *20883*
     I   *20883* Colombia *20883*
     I   *20883* Venezuela *20883*

E   *Banisteriopsis cornifolia* var. *standleyi* B. Gates *20883*
     I   *20883* Guatemala *20883*

V   *Banisteriopsis goiana* B. Gates *20883*
     I   *20883* Brazil *20883*

V   *Banisteriopsis grandifolia* (Niedenzu) B. Gates *20883*
     I   *20883* Venezuela *20883*

V   *Banisteriopsis harleyi* B. Gates *20883*
     I   *20883* Brazil *20883*

E   *Banisteriopsis hatschbachii* B. Gates *20883*
     I   *20883* Brazil *20883*

E   *Banisteriopsis hirsuta* B. Gates *20883*
     I   *20883* Brazil *20883*

R   *Banisteriopsis hypericifolia* (Jussieu) Anderson & Gates *20883*
     I   *20883* Brazil *20883*

V   *Banisteriopsis irwinii* B. Gates *20883*
     I   *20883* Brazil *20883*

R   *Banisteriopsis krukoffii* B. Gates *20883*
     I   *20883* Brazil *20883*
     I   *20883* Venezuela *20883*

R   *Banisteriopsis latifolia* (Adr. Jussieu) B. Gates *20883*
     I   *20883* Brazil *20883*

E   *Banisteriopsis leiocarpa* (Jussieu) B. Gates *20883*
     I   *20883* Peru *20883*

E   *Banisteriopsis longipilifera* B. Gates *20883*
     I   *20883* Brazil *20883*

E   *Banisteriopsis magdalenensis* B. Gates *20883*
     E   *20883* Brazil *20883*

E   *Banisteriopsis multifoliolata* (Adr. Jussieu) B. Gates *20883*
     I   *20883* Brazil *20883*

V   *Banisteriopsis nigrescens* (Jussieu) B. Gates *20883*
     I   *20883* Brazil *20883*

R   *Banisteriopsis paraguariensis* B. Gates *20883*
     I   *20883* Brazil *20883*
     I   *20883* Paraguay *20883*

R   *Banisteriopsis parviflora* (Jussieu) B. Gates *20883*
     I   *20883* Brazil *20883*

V   *Banisteriopsis parvifolia* (Niedenzu) B. Gates *20883*
     I   *20883* Peru *20883*

V   *Banisteriopsis parviglandula* B. Gates *20883*
     I   *20883* Brazil *20883*

R **Banisteriopsis patula** B. Gates *20883*
  I   *20883* Brazil *20883*

E **Banisteriopsis peruviana** (Niedenzu) B. Gates *20883*
  I   *20883* Peru *20883*

R **Banisteriopsis platyptera** (Griseb.) Cuatr. *20883*
  I   *20883* Panama *20883*
  I   *20883* Brazil *20883*
  I   *20883* Venezuela *20883*

V **Banisteriopsis populifolia** (Niedenzu) B. Gates *20883*
  I   *20883* Peru *20883*

V **Banisteriopsis pseudojaunsia** (Niedenzu) B. Gates *20883*
  I   *20883* Brazil *20883*

V **Banisteriopsis pubescens** (Niedenzu) Cuatrecasas *20883*
  I   *20883* Colombia *20883*
  I   *20883* Ecuador *20883*

E **Banisteriopsis pulchra** var. *glabrata* B. Gates *20883*
  I   *20883* Bolivia *20883*

V **Banisteriopsis quadriglandula** B. Gates *20883*
  I   *20883* Brazil *20883*

V **Banisteriopsis rondoniensis** B. Gates *20883*
  I   *20883* Brazil *20883*

E **Banisteriopsis salicifolia** (de Candolle) B. Gates *20883*
  E   *20883* Brazil *20883*

E **Banisteriopsis schunkei** B. Gates *20883*
  I   *20883* Peru *20883*

V **Banisteriopsis scutellata** (Grisebach) B. Gates *20883*
  I   *20883* Brazil *20883*

E **Banisteriopsis sellowiana** (Jussieu) B. Gates *20883*
  E   *20883* Brazil *20883*

R **Banisteriopsis sepium** (Jussieu) B. Gates *20883*
  I   *20883* Brazil *20883*

R **Banisteriopsis valvata** Anderson & Gates *20883*
  I   *20883* Brazil *20883*

V **Banisteriopsis velutinissima** B. Gates *20883*
  I   *20883* Peru *20883*

R **Banisteriopsis virgultosa** (Jussieu) Anderson & Gates *20883*
  I   *20883* Brazil *20883*

V **Banisteriopsis woytkowskii** B. Gates *20883*
  I   *20883* Peru *20883*

I **Brachylophon anastomosans** Craib *19120*
  I   *19120* Thailand *19120*

E **Bunchosia acuminata** Dobson *20883*
  I   *20883* Brazil *20883*

E **Bunchosia articulata** Dobson *20883*
  I   *20883* Cuba *20883*

V **Bunchosia diphylla** (Dobson) Cuatr. & Croat ssp. *brevisurcularis* (Dobson) Cuatrec. & Croat *20883, 10747*
  I   *20883* Panama *20883*

V **Bunchosia jamaicensis** Urb. & Ndz. *20883*
  V   *20883* Jamaica *20883*

R **Bunchosia linearifolia** P. Wilson *5607*
  R   *19105* Cuba (Guantanamo) *5607*

E **Bunchosia macilenta** Dobson *20883*
  I   *20883* Brazil *20883*

E **Bunchosia pauciflora** Dobson *20883*
  I   *20883* Haiti *20883*

E **Bunchosia quaesitor** Dobson *20883*
  I   *20883* Haiti *20883*

E **Bunchosia systyla** (Niedenzu) Dobson *20883*
  I   *20883* Brazil *20883*

E **Bunchosia tutensis** Dobson *20883, 10747*
  I   *20883* Panama *20883*

V **Byrsonima horneana** Britton & Small *8058*
  V   *19002* Puerto Rico *8058*

R **Byrsonima incarnata** Sandw. *8679*
  R   Guyana *8679*

R **Byrsonima lucida** (P. Mill.) DC. *20883, 20850, 19002*
  V   *20850* U.S. - Florida *20850*
  I   *20883* Puerto Rico *20883*
  I   *20883* USA - Virgin Is. *20883*

V **Byrsonima moensis** Acuna & Roig *5607*
  V   *19105* Cuba (Holguin) *5607*

E **Byrsonima nemoralis** var. *dressleri* (Lewis) Cuatr. & Croat *20883*
  I   *20883* Panama *20883*

I **Byrsonima ophiticola** Small ex Britton
  I   *19002* Puerto Rico *8058*

E **Callaeum chiapense** (Lundell) D. M. Johnson *20883*
  I   *20883* Mexico *20883*

R **Callaeum macropterum** (DC.) D.M. Johnson *20883, 20850, 19002*
  I   *20850* U.S. - Arizona *20850*
  I   *20883* Mexico *20883*

E **Callaeum reticulatum** D. M. Johnson *20883*
  I   *20883* Ecuador *20883*
  I   *20883* Peru *20883*

E **Diplopterys cururuensis** B. Gates *20883*
  I   *20883* Brazil *20883*

E **Diplopterys mexicana** B. Gates *20883*
  E   *20883* Mexico *20883*

E **Heteropteris buricana** Cuatr. & Croat *20883*
  I   *20883* Panama *20883*

E **Heteropteris laurifolia** (L.) A. Juss. var. *brevibracteolata* Cuatr. & Croat *20883*
  I   *20883* Panama *20883*

E **Heteropteris panamensis** Cuatr. & Croat *20883*
  I   *20883* Panama *20883*

V **Hiptage calcicola** Sirirugosa *19120*
  V   *19120* Thailand *19120*

I **Hiptage condita** Craib *19120*
  I   *19120* Thailand *19120*

I **Hiptage detergens** Craib *19120*
  I   *19120* Thailand *19120*

I **Hiptage glabrifolia** Craib *19120*
  I   *19120* Thailand *19120*

E **Hiraea grandifolia** Cuatr. & Croat var. *parvifructa* Cuatrec. & Croat *20883, 10747*
  I   *20883* Panama *20883*

V **Malpighia acunana** Borh. & Muniz *5607*
  V   *19105* Cuba (Santiago de Cuba) *5607*

E **Malpighia cauliflora** Proctor & Vivaldi *20883, 13336*
  E   *20883* Jamaica *20883*

V **Malpighia harrisii** Small *20883, 13336*

V	13336 Jamaica 20883	

V   *Malpighia infestissima* L.C. Rich. ex Niedenzu 20883, 8058
     I   20883   Puerto Rico (Maguey; Vieques; Culebra) 20883
     I   19826   British Virgin Is. (Virgin Gorda; Anegada; Norman Island) 19826
     I   20883   USA - Virgin Is. (St. Thomas; St. John) 20883

E   *Malpighia obtusifolia* Proctor 20883, 19890
     R   19890   Jamaica 20883

E   *Malpighia proctorii* Vivaldi 20883, 13336
     E   13336   Jamaica 20883

V   *Malpighia wrightiana* Acuna & Roig 5607
     V   19105   Cuba (Pinar del Rio) 5607

R   *Mascagnia hirea* (Gaertn.) F. & R. 20883
     R   20883   Jamaica 20883

E   *Pterandra isthmica* Cuatr. & Croat 20883, 10747
     I   20883   Panama 20883

E   *Spachea correae* Cuatr. & Croat 20883, 10747
     I   20883   Panama 20883

V   *Stigmaphyllon bahiense* C. Anderson 20883
     I   20883   Brazil 20883

R   *Stigmaphyllon blanchetii* C. Anderson 20883
     I   20883   Brazil 20883

E   *Stigmaphyllon cavernulosum* C. Anderson 20883
     I   20883   Brazil 20883

E   *Tetrapteris hirsutula* Cuatr. & Croat 20883, 10747
     I   20883   Panama 20883

E   *Tetrapteris tysonii* Cuatr. & Croat 20883, 10747
     I   20883   Panama 20883

R   *Triaspis dumeticula* Launert 7749
     R   Zimbabwe 7749

I   *Triaspis letestuana* Launert
     I   Gabon

R   *Triaspis nelsonii* Oliver ssp. *canescens* (Engl.) Launert 7749
     R   Mozambique 7749

I   *Triaspis schliebenii* Ernst 7959
     I   5926   Tanzania (Lindi) 5926

R   *Triaspis suffulta* Launert 7749
     R   Mozambique 7749

E   *Triopteris brittonii* Small 20883
     E   20883   Jamaica 20883

I   *Triopterys brittonii* Small 13336
     I   13336   Jamaica 13336

Malvaceae

Number of genera: 75
Number of species: 1,000-1,500
Recorded threatened species: 233   (18%)

Cosmopolitan, but centered in S America.

I   *Abutilon bidentatum* Hochst. var. *major* (Blatter & Hallberg) Bhandari 7771
     I   India - Rajasthan (west) 7771

E   *Abutilon eremitopetalum* Caum 20850, 14209
     E   20850   U.S. - Hawaii (east Lanai) 20850

V   *Abutilon exstipulare* (Cav.) G. Don 10082
     V   14234   Réunion 10082

I   *Abutilon fruticosum* Guillemin & Perrottet var. *chrysocarpa* Blatter & Hallberg 7771
     I   India - Rajasthan (Jaisalmer) 7771

E   *Abutilon julianae* Endl. 11649
     E   11649   Australia - Norfolk Is. 11649

R   *Abutilon listeri* Baker f. 881
     R   14224   Australia - Christmas Is. 881

R   *Abutilon macropodum* Guillemin & Perrottet 8003
     R   Senegal 8003

I   *Abutilon mangarevicum* Fosberg 20845
     I   20845   French Polynesia - Tuamotu Is. 20845

E   *Abutilon menziesii* Seem. 20850, 14209
     E   20850   U.S. - Hawaii 20850

V   *Abutilon parishii* S.Watson 20883, 20850, 19002
     V   20850   U.S. - Arizona 20850
        20883   Mexico 20883

V   *Abutilon pitcairnense* Fosb. 8615
     V   19185   Pitcairn (Pitcairn Is.) 8615

E   *Abutilon procerum* Fryx. 20883, 11577
     I   20883   Mexico 20883
     R   11598   Mexico - Tamaulipas 11577

I   *Abutilon ramosum* Guillemin & Perrottet
     I   India - Karnataka
     I   India - Kerala

Ex/E   *Abutilon ranadei* Woodrow 11494
     Ex/E   11494   India - Maharashtra 11494

R   *Abutilon sachetianum* Fosberg 20845
     R   20845   French Polynesia - Marquesas Is 20845

E   *Abutilon sandwicense* (O. Deg.) Christoph. 20850, 14209
     E   20850   U.S. - Hawaii (Waianae Mts, Oahu) 20850

R   *Abutilon straminicarpum* Fryx. 9821
     R   9821   Mexico 9821

R   *Abutilon tehuantepecense* Fryx. 9822
     R   9821   Mexico 9822

V   *Abutilon thurberi* Gray 20883, 20850, 19002
     E   20850   U.S. - Arizona 20850
     I   20883   Mexico 20883

E   *Abutilothamnus yaracuyensis* Fryx. 20883
     I   20883   Venezuela 20883

V   *Acaulimalva alismatifolia* (Schum. & Hieron.) Krapov. 18200
     V   12468   Peru 18200

R   *Acaulimalva engleriana* (Ulbr.) Krapov. 18200
     R   12468   Peru 18200

V   *Acaulimalva sulphurea* Krapov. 18200
     V   12468   Peru 18200

R   *Alcea freyniana* Iljin
     R   former USSR 6930

R   *Alcea galilaea* Zoh. 8895
     R   Israel 8895

R   *Allowissadula chiangii* M. Johnston 9821
     R   9821   Mexico 9821

R   *Allowissadula glandulosa* (Rose) D. Bates 9821
     R   9821   Mexico 9821

R   *Althaea longiflora* Boiss. & Reut. 8000, 20171
     V   20076   Portugal 8000
     R   Spain 8000

V   *Anisodontea alexandri* (Baker f.) Bates 20604, 6180

V *20604* South Africa - Cape Province *20604*

V *Anisodontea dissecta* (Harv.) Bates *20604*

   V *20604* South Africa - Cape Province *20604*

R *Anisodontea malvastroides* (Baker f.) Bates *20604*

   R *20604* South Africa - Cape Province *20604*

I *Anisodontea pseudocapensis* Bates *20604*

   I *20604* South Africa - Cape Province *20604*

R *Anisodontea racemosa* (Harv.) Bates *20604*

   R *20604* South Africa - Cape Province *20604*

I *Anisodontea theronii* Bates *20604*

   I *20604* South Africa - Cape Province *20604*

R *Anoda henricksonii* M. Johnston *11581*

   R *11598* Mexico *11581*

R *Anoda pristina* Fryx. *13865*

   R *9821* Mexico *9821*

R *Bakeridesia nelsonii* (Rose) D. Bates *9821*

   R *9821* Guatemala *9821*

   R *9821* Mexico *9821*

R *Batesimalva killipii* Krapov. ex Fryx. *20883*

   I *20883* Venezuela *20883*

R *Batesimalva pulchella* Fryx. *9822*

   R *9821* Mexico *9822*

V *Batesimalva violacea* (Rose) Fryxell *20883, 20850, 8058*

   E *20850* U.S. - Texas *20850*

   I *20883* Mexico *20883*

R *Briquetia inermis* Fryx. *9822*

   R *9821* Mexico *9822*

R *Briquetia sonorae* Fryx. *9822*

   R *9821* Mexico *9822*

R *Callirhoe bushii* Fern. *20850*

   R *20850* U.S. - Arkansas *20850*

   I *20850* U.S. - Iowa *20850*

   E *20850* U.S. - Kansas *20850*

   V *20850* U.S. - Missouri *20850*

   R *20850* U.S. - Oklahoma *20850*

V *Callirhoe scabriuscula* B.L. Robins. *20850*

   V *20850* U.S. - Texas *20850*

R *Corynabutilon ochsenii* (Philippi) Kearney *13875*

   R *13875* Chile *13875*

R *Cristaria multifida* Cav. *18200*

   R *9446* Peru *18200*

R *Decaschistia byrnesii* Fryxell ssp. *byrnesii* *20681*

   R *20681* Australia - Northern Territory *20681*

E *Decaschistia rufa* Craib *11494*

   E *11494* India - Tamil Nadu *11494*

I *Decaschistia triloba* Wight

   I India - Karnataka

V *Dendrosida batesii* Fryx. *9821*

   V *16360* Mexico *9821*

V *Dendrosida breedlovei* Fryx. *9826*

   V *19850* Mexico *9826*

V *Dendrosida oxypetala* (Triana & Planchon) Fryx. *20883*

   I *20883* Colombia *20883*

I *Dendrosida parviflora* Fryx. *9823*

   I *11598* Mexico *9823*

V *Dendrosida wingfieldii* Fryx. *20883*

   I *20883* Venezuela *20883*

E *Dicellostyles axillaris* (Thwaites) Thwaites *10252*

   E *16162* Sri Lanka *10252*

E *Dirhamphis mexicana* Fryxell *20883, 11578*

   I *20883* Mexico *20883*

   ? Mexico - Colima *11578*

   ? Mexico - Guerrero

R *Eremalche parryi* (Greene) Greene *20850*

   I *20850* U.S. - California *20850*

E *Eremalche parryi* (Greene) Greene ssp. *kernensis* (C.B. Wolf) Bates *20850*

   E *20850* U.S. - California *20850*

R *Eremalche parryi* (Greene) Greene ssp. *parryi* *20850*

   I *20850* U.S. - California *20850*

E *Fryxellia pygmaea* (Correll) Bates *20883, 20850, 11572*

   Ex/E *20850* U.S. - Texas *20850*

   I *20883* Mexico *20883*

E *Goethea alnifolia* Garke. *5532*

   E *5532* Brazil - Rio de Janeiro *5532*

R *Gossypium cunninghamii* Todaro *20681*

   R *20681* Australia - Northern Territory *20681*

R *Gossypium hirsutum* L. var. *taitense* (Parlatore) Roberty *20845*

   I *20845* French Polynesia - Marquesas Is *20845*

   R *20845* French Polynesia - Society Is. *20845*

R *Gossypium klotzschianum* Andersson *11117*

   R Ecuador - Galapagos (Isabela, Marchena, south Cruz) *11117*

R *Gossypium nelsonii* Fryxell *20681*

   R *20681* Australia - Northern Territory *20681*

V *Gossypium raimondii* Ulbr. *9821*

   V *9446* Peru *9821*

R *Gossypium tomentosum* Nutt. ex Seem. *20850, 14209*

   R *20850* U.S. - Hawaii *20850*

R *Gossypium trilobum* (DC.) Skovsted *9821*

   R *9821* Mexico *9821*

V *Gossypium turneri* Fryx. *9825*

   V *9821* Mexico - Sonora *9825*

V *Hampea appendiculata* Fryx. var. *longicalyx* Fryx. *20883, 9090*

   I *20883* Panama *20883*

R *Hampea breedlovei* Fryx. *9063*

   R *9821* Mexico *9063*

E *Hampea dukei* A. Robyns *20883, 10747*

   I *20883* Panama *20883*

R *Hampea latifolia* Standley *9821*

   R *9821* Guatemala *9821*

   R *9821* Mexico *9821*

E *Hampea micrantha* A. Robyns *20883, 9090*

   I *20883* Panama *20883*

V *Hampea montebellensis* Fryx. *9063*

   V *19850* Mexico *19850*

V *Hampea reynae* Fryx. *9821*

   V *11218* El Salvador *9821*

R *Herissantia dressleri* Fryx. *9821*

   R *9821* Mexico *9821*

Ex/E *Hibiscadelphus bombycinus* Forbes *20850, 14209*

   Ex/E *20850* U.S. - Hawaii (Kawaihae) *20850*

Ex/E *Hibiscadelphus crucibracteatus* Hobdy *20850, 14209*

Ex   *20850* U.S. - Hawaii (Lana`i) *20850*

E   *Hibiscadelphus distans* Bishop & Herbst *20850, 14209*

    E   *20850* U.S. - Hawaii (Kaua`i) *20850*

Ex/E *Hibiscadelphus giffardianus* Rock *20850, 14209, 21355*

    Ex/E *20850* U.S. - Hawaii (Mauna Loa) *20850*

Ex/E *Hibiscadelphus hualalaiensis* Rock *20850, 14209, 21355*

    Ex   *20850* U.S. - Hawaii (north Kona) *20850*

Ex/E *Hibiscadelphus wilderianus* Rock *20850, 14209*

    Ex/E *20850* U.S. - Hawaii (east Maui) *20850*

E   *Hibiscadelphus woodii* Lorence & W.L. Wagner *20850, 21352*

    E   *20850* U.S. - Hawaii *20850*

R   *Hibiscus acapulcensis* Fryx. *9821*

    R   *9821* Mexico *9821*

E   *Hibiscus arnottianus* Gray ssp. *immaculata* (Roe) D. Bates *20850*

    E   *20850* U.S. - Hawaii *20850*

E   *Hibiscus arnottianus* A.Gray ssp. *immaculatus* (M. Roe) D. Bates *14209, 21358*

    E   *14209* U.S. - Hawaii (Moloka`i) *14209*

R   *Hibiscus australensis* Fosberg *20845*

    I   *20845* French Polynesia - Tubuai Is. *20845*

R   *Hibiscus barnardii* Exell *20604*

    R   *20604* South Africa - Transvaal *20604*

V   *Hibiscus boryanus* DC. *10082*

    V   *14234* Réunion *14234*

    E   *20771* Mauritius *10082*

E   *Hibiscus brackenridgei* Gray *20850*

    I   *20850* U.S. - Hawaii *20850*

E   *Hibiscus brackenridgei* A.Gray ssp. *brackenridgei* *20850, 14209*

    E   *20850* U.S. - Hawaii *20850*

E   *Hibiscus brackenridgei* A.Gray ssp. *mokuleianus* (Roe) D. Bates *20850, 14209*

    E   *20850* U.S. - Hawaii (Kaua`i, O`ahu) *20850*

E   *Hibiscus clayi* O.& I. Deg. *20850, 14209, 21349*

    E   *20850* U.S. - Hawaii (Kauai) *20850*

V   *Hibiscus columnaris* Cav. *10082*

    V   *14234* Réunion *10082*

    E   *20771* Mauritius *10082*

E   *Hibiscus dasycalyx* Blake & Shiller *20850*

    E   *20850* U.S. - Texas *20850*

E   *Hibiscus eggersii* Urban *5607*

    E   *19105* Cuba (Pinar del Rio) *5607*

E   *Hibiscus fragilis* DC. *10082*

    E   *20771* Mauritius *10082*

E   *Hibiscus genevii* Bojer ex Hook. *10082*

    E   *20771* Mauritius *10082*

R   *Hibiscus guandensis* Exell *7749*

    R   Zimbabwe *7749*

E   *Hibiscus insularis* Endl. *11649*

    E   *11649* Australia - Norfolk Is. *11649*

V   *Hibiscus kokio* Hbd. ex Wawra *20850*

    I   *20850* U.S. - Hawaii *20850*

V   *Hibiscus kokio* Hbd. ex Wawra ssp. *kokio* *20850*

    V   *20850* U.S. - Hawaii *20850*

E   *Hibiscus kokio* Hbd. ex Wawra ssp. *saintjohnianus*

    (Roe) D.Bates *20850, 14209*

    E   *20850* U.S. - Hawaii (north-west Kaua`i) *20850*

E   *Hibiscus liliiflorus* Cav. *10082*

    Ex *10082* Réunion *10082*

    E   *5852* Mauritius - Rodrigues *5852*

R   *Hibiscus lobatus* (J.A.Murray) Kuntze *20681*

    R   *20681* Australia - Northern Territory *20681*

I   *Hibiscus lonchosepalus* Hochr. *7926*

    I   Benin (Agouagon) *7926*

R   *Hibiscus longifilus* Fryx. *9821*

    R   *9821* Mexico *9821*

E   *Hibiscus malacophyllus* Balf. f. *15534*

    E   *15534* Yemen - Socotra *15534*

R   *Hibiscus menzeliae* Wilson & Byrnes *20681*

    R   *20681* Australia - Northern Territory *20681*

Ex   *Hibiscus nelsonii* Rose & Standley *9821*

    Ex *9821* Mexico *9821*

R   *Hibiscus pseudohirtus* Hochr. *11751*

    R   Mali (Macina) *11751*

R   *Hibiscus rupicola* Exell *7749*

    R   Mozambique *7749*

E   *Hibiscus socotranus* Lucas *15534*

    E   *15534* Yemen - Socotra *15534*

V   *Hibiscus spiralis* Cav. *9821*

    V   *16360* Mexico *9821*

E   *Hibiscus stenanthus* Balf. f. *15534*

    E   *15534* Yemen - Socotra *15534*

Ex/E *Hibiscus storckii* Seemann *19630*

    Ex/E *19630* Fiji (Taveuni) *19630*

R   *Hibiscus torrei* Baker f. *7749*

    R   Mozambique *7749*

E   *Hibiscus urbanii* Helwig *5607*

    E   *19105* Cuba (Pinar del Rio) *5607*

E   *Hibiscus waimeae* A. Heller ssp. *hannerae* (O.& I. Deg.) D. Bates *20850, 14209, 21352*

    E   *20850* U.S. - Hawaii (Kaua`i) *20850*

R   *Hibiscus waimeae* A.A. Heller ssp. *waimeae* *14209*

    R   *14209* U.S. - Hawaii (Kaua`i) *14209*

R   *Iliamna bakeri* (Jepson) Wiggins *20850*

    I   *20850* U.S. - California *20850*

    I   *20850* U.S. - Oregon *20850*

E   *Iliamna corei* Sherff *20850*

    E   *20850* U.S. - Virginia (Giles Co.) *20850*

V   *Iliamna longisepala* (Torr.) Wiggins *20850*

    I   *20850* U.S. - Oregon *20850*

    V   *20850* U.S. - Washington *20850*

E   *Julostylis angustifolia* (Arn.) Thwaites *10252*

    E   *16162* Sri Lanka *10252*

R   *Kitaibelia balansae* Boiss. *12840*

    R   *12840* Turkey *12840*

Ex/E *Kokia cookei* O. Deg. *20850, 14209*

    Ex *20850* U.S. - Hawaii (Molokai) *20850*

I   *Kokia distans* *18799*

    I   *18799* U.S. - Hawaii *18799*

E   *Kokia drynarioides* (Seem.) Lewt. *20850, 14209*

    E   *20850* U.S. - Hawaii (north Kona) *20850*

E   *Kokia kauaiensis* (Rock) O. Deg. & Duvel *20850, 14209, 21352*

	E 20850	U.S. - Hawaii (west Kaua`i) *20850*
Ex/E	*Kokia lanceolata* Lewt. *20850, 14209*	
	Ex/E 20850	U.S. - Hawaii (O`ahu) *20850*
R	*Kosteletzkya ramosa* Fryx. *9826*	
	R 9821	Mexico *9826*
I	*Kosteletzkya reclinata* Fryx. *9826*	
	I 9821	Mexico *9826*
R	*Kosteletzkya thurberi* A.Gray *9821*	
	R 9821	Mexico *9821*
R	*Lavatera acerifolia* Cav.	
	R 19174	Spain - Canary Is. *19174*
E	*Lavatera assurgentiflora* Philbrick ssp. *assurgentiflora 20850*	
	E 20850	U.S. - California *20850*
V	*Lavatera assurgentiflora* R. Philbrick ssp. *glabra* R. Philbrick *20850*	
	V 20850	U.S. - California *20850*
R	*Lavatera lindsayi* Moran *9821*	
	R 9821	Mexico *9821*
I	*Lavatera maroccana* (Battand. & Trabut) Maire	
	I	Morocco
R	*Lavatera mauritanica* Durieu ssp. *davaei* (Cout.) Cout. *8000, 20171*	
	V 14155	Portugal *8322*
	R 20692	Spain (Valencia, Murcia & Andalusia) *20692*
R	*Lavatera microphylla* Baker f.	
	R	Morocco
R	*Lavatera occidentalis* Watson *9821*	
	R 9821	Mexico *9821*
E	*Lavatera phoenicea* Vent. *20750*	
	E 19174	Spain - Canary Is. *19174*
R	*Lavatera venosa* Watson *9821*	
	R 9821	Mexico *9821*
R	*Lavatera vidali* Pau	
	R	Morocco
V	*Lawrencia buchananensis* Lander *20681*	
	V 20681	Australia - Queensland *20681*
E	*Lebronnecia kokioides* Fosb & Sachet. *10260*	
	E 20845	French Polynesia - Marquesas Is *20845*
R	*Macrostelia grandifolia* Fryxell *20681*	
	R 20681	Australia - Queensland *20681*
E	*Malacothamnus abbottii* (Eastw.) Kearney *20850, 14662*	
	E 20850	U.S. - California *20850*
V	*Malacothamnus aboriginum* (B.L. Robins.) Greene *20850*	
	V 20850	U.S. - California *20850*
E	*Malacothamnus clementinus* (Munz & Johnston) Kearney *20850*	
	E 20850	U.S. - California *20850*
Ex/E	*Malacothamnus davidsonii* (B.L. Robins.) Greene *20850*	
	Ex/E 20850	U.S. - California *20850*
R	*Malacothamnus densiflorus* (S.Watson) Greene *20850*	
	I 20850	U.S. - California *20850*
E	*Malacothamnus fasciculatus* (Nutt.) E. Greene var. *nesioticus* (B.L. Robins.) Kearney *20850*	
	E 20850	U.S. - California *20850*
V	*Malacothamnus jonesii* (Munz) Kearney *20850*	
	I 20850	U.S. - California *20850*
R	*Malacothamnus marrubioides* (Dur. & Hilg.)	

	Greene *20850*	
	I 20850	U.S. - California *20850*
R	*Malope anatolica* Huber-Mor. *12840*	
	R 12840	Turkey *12840*
E	*Malvaviscus arboreus* Cav. var. *lobatus* A. Robyns *20883*	
	I 20883	Panama *20883*
R	*Meximalva venusta* (Schldl.) Fryx. *9822*	
	R 9821	Mexico *9822*
V	*Modiolastrum sandemannii* (Sandw.) S.R. Hill & Fryxell *18200*	
	V 9446	Peru *18200*
R	*Nototriche caesia* A.W. Hill *16336*	
	R 19448	Argentina *16336*
	R 20176	Argentina - Catamarca *20176*
	R 20176	Argentina - Jujuy *20176*
	R 20176	Argentina - La Rioja *20176*
	R 20176	Argentina - Mendoza *20176*
	R 20176	Argentina - Salta *20176*
	R 20176	Argentina - San Juan *20176*
	R 20176	Argentina - Tucuman *20176*
R	*Nototriche calchaquensis* Krapov. *16336*	
	R 19558	Argentina *16336*
	R 20176	Argentina - Catamarca *20176*
	R 20176	Argentina - Tucuman *20176*
R	*Nototriche cupuliforme* Krapov. *18200*	
	R 12468	Peru *18200*
R	*Nototriche digitulifolia* Hill *18200*	
	R 12468	Peru *18200*
R	*Nototriche ellipticifolia* Hochr. *18200*	
	R 12468	Peru *18200*
R	*Nototriche epileuca* Hill *18200*	
	R 12468	Peru *18200*
R	*Nototriche foetida* Ulbr. *18200*	
	R 12468	Peru *18200*
R	*Nototriche longituba* Burtt & Hill *18200*	
	R 12468	Peru *18200*
R	*Nototriche lopezii* Krapov. *18200*	
	R 12468	Peru *18200*
R	*Nototriche nigrescens* Hill *18200*	
	R 12468	Peru *18200*
R	*Nototriche pellicea* Hill *18200*	
	R 12468	Peru *18200*
R	*Nototriche pseudopichinchensis* Hochr. *18200*	
	R 12468	Peru *18200*
R	*Nototriche rohmederi* Krapov. *16336*	
	R 19448	Argentina *16336*
	R 20176	Argentina - Catamarca *20176*
	R 20176	Argentina - Tucuman *20176*
R	*Nototriche salina* Burtt & Hill *18200*	
	R 12468	Peru *18200*
R	*Nototriche tovari* Krapov. *18200*	
	R 12468	Peru *18200*
R	*Nototriche tucumana* Krapov. *16336*	
	R 19448	Argentina *16336*
	R 20176	Argentina - Catamarca *20176*
	R 20176	Argentina - Tucuman *20176*
R	*Nototriche turritella* Hill *18200*	
	R 12468	Peru *18200*
R	*Nototriche vargasii* Krapov. *18200*	
	R 12468	Peru *18200*

V **Palaua guentheri** Bruns *18200*
   V *9446* Peru *18200*

V **Palaua rhombifolia** Graham *18200*
   V *9446* Peru *18200*

V **Palaua tomentosa** Hochr. *18200*
   V *9446* Peru *18200*

V **Palaua trisepala** Hochr. *18200*
   V *9446* Peru *18200*

V **Palaua velutina** Ulbr. & Hill *18200*
   V *9446* Peru *18200*

V **Pavonia alnifolia** St. Hil. *17079*
   V *17746* Brazil - Espirito Santo (Itapemirim) *17079*
   V *17746* Brazil - Rio de Janeiro *17079*

I **Pavonia arabica** Hochst. ex Steudel var. *glutinosa* Blatter & Hallberg *7771*
   I   India - Rajasthan (Jaiselmer, Barmer, Jodhpur) *7771*

V **Pavonia calcicola** (Britton) Ekman *5607*
   V *19105* Cuba *5607*

E **Pavonia discolor** Fryxell *20883*
   I *20883* Mexico *20883*

R **Pavonia durangensis** Fryx. *14294*
   R *14294* Mexico - Durango *14294*

I **Pavonia elegans** Garcke *20604*
   I *20604* South Africa - Transvaal *20604*

I **Pavonia hirtiflora** Benth. *9827*
   I *9821* Mexico *9827*

R **Pavonia integrifolia** Schery *9827*
   R *9821* Mexico *9827*

I **Pavonia langlassei** Hochr. *9827*
   I *9821* Mexico *9827*

Ex **Pavonia lourteigae** Fosberg & Sachet *20845*
   Ex *20845* French Polynesia - Society Is. (Bora Bora) *20845*

R **Pavonia macdougallii** Fryx. *9826*
   R *9821* Mexico *9826*

Ex **Pavonia papilionacea** Cavanilles *20845*
   Ex *20845* French Polynesia - Society Is. (Tahiti) *20845*

V **Pavonia pulidoae** Fryx. *9823*
   V *9821* Mexico *9823*

R **Pavonia rogersii** N.E. Br. *7749*
   R   Zimbabwe *7749*

R **Pavonia spicata** Cav. var. *troyana* (Urb.) F. & R. *20883*
   R *20883* Jamaica *20883*

V **Peltaea krapovickasiorum** Fryx. *20883*
   I *20883* Venezuela *20883*

E **Periptera ctenotricha** Fryxell *20883, 11578*
   I *20883* Mexico *20883*
   R *11598* Mexico - Jalisco *11578*

R **Periptera macrostelis** Rose *9828*
   R *9821* Mexico *9828*

R **Periptera trichostemon** Bullock *9828*
   R *9821* Mexico - Sinaloa *9828*

I **Phymosia anomala** Fryx. *9829*
   I *9821* Mexico *9829*

I **Phymosia crenulata** (Brandegee) Fryx. *9829*
   I *9821* Mexico *9829*

I **Phymosia floribunda** (Schldl.) Fryx. *9829*
   I *9821* Mexico *9829*

R **Phymosia rzedowskii** Fryx. *9829*
   R *16360* Mexico *9829*

R **Plagianthus regius** var. *chathamicus* *19305*
   R *19305* New Zealand - Chatham Is. *19305*

E **Robinsonella erasmi-sosae** C. Nelson *11582*
   E *11582* Honduras *11582*

R **Robinsonella hintonii** Fryx. *9836*
   R *9821* Mexico *9836*

R **Robinsonella macvaughii** Fryx. *9836*
   R *9821* Mexico *9836*

I **Sida eggersii** E.G. Baker *15106*
   E *15106* Puerto Rico (Culebra) *19934*
   I *15106* British Virgin Is. *19934*

V **Sida hermaphrodita** (L.) Rusby *20850*
   I *20850* U.S. - District of Columbia *20850*
   E *20850* U.S. - Indiana *20850*
   V *20850* U.S. - Kentucky *20850*
   E *20850* U.S. - Maryland *20850*
   E *20850* U.S. - Michigan *20850*
   R *20850* U.S. - Ohio *20850*
   E *20850* U.S. - Pennsylvania *20850*
   Ex/E *20850* U.S. - Tennessee *20850*
   E *20850* U.S. - Virginia *20850*
   R *20850* U.S. - West Virginia *20850*

R **Sida hyalina** Fryx. *9821*
   R *9821* Mexico *9821*

Ex/E **Sida inflexa** Fern. *20850, 14662*
   I *20850* U.S. - North Carolina *20850*
   Ex/E *20850* U.S. - Virginia *20850*

R **Sida potosina** Brandegee *9821*
   R *9821* Mexico *9821*

E **Sidalcea calycosa** M. E. Jones ssp. *rhizomata* (Jepson) Munz *20850*
   E *20850* U.S. - California *20850*

V **Sidalcea covillei** Greene *20850*
   V *20850* U.S. - California *20850*

R **Sidalcea hickmanii** Greene *20850*
   I *20850* U.S. - California *20850*

E **Sidalcea hickmanii** E. Greene ssp. *anomala* C.L. Hitchc. *20850*
   E *20850* U.S. - California *20850*

V **Sidalcea hickmanii** E. Greene ssp. *hickmanii* *20850*
   I *20850* U.S. - California *20850*

V **Sidalcea hickmanii** E. Greene ssp. *parishii* (B.L. Robins.) C.L. Hitchc. *20850*
   V *20850* U.S. - California *20850*

V **Sidalcea hickmanii** E. Greene ssp. *viridis* C.L. Hitchc. *20850*
   I *20850* U.S. - California *20850*

V **Sidalcea hirtipes** C.L. Hitchc. *20850*
   V *20850* U.S. - Oregon *20850*
   E *20850* U.S. - Washington *20850*

E **Sidalcea keckii** Wiggins *20850, 14662*
   E *20850* U.S. - California *20850*

E **Sidalcea malviflora** C.L. Hitchc. ssp. *patula* C.L. Hitchc. *20850*
   E *20850* U.S. - California *20850*
   E *20850* U.S. - Oregon *20850*

R **Sidalcea multifida** Greene *20850*

I   *20850*   U.S. - California *20850*

I   *20850*   U.S. - Oregon *20850*

V   *Sidalcea nelsoniana* **Piper** *20850, 14774*

     V   *20850*   U.S. - Oregon (Willamette Valley & adjacent Coast Range) *20850*

     E   *20850*   U.S. - Washington *20850*

E   *Sidalcea oregana* **(Nutt. ex Torr. & Gray) Gray var. *calva* C.L. Hitchc.** *20850*

     E   *20850*   U.S. - Washington *20850*

E   *Sidalcea oregana* **(Nutt. ex Torr. & Gray) Gray ssp. *eximia* (Greene) C.L. Hitchc.** *20850*

     E   *20850*   U.S. - California *20850*

E   *Sidalcea oregana* **(Nutt. ex Torr. & Gray) Gray ssp. *hydrophila* (Heller) C.L. Hitchc.** *20850*

     E   *20850*   U.S. - California *20850*

E   *Sidalcea oregana* **(Nutt. ex Torr. & Gray) Gray ssp. *valida* (Greene) C.L. Hitchc.** *20850*

     E   *20850*   U.S. - California *20850*

     I   *20850*   U.S. - Oregon *20850*

E   *Sidalcea pedata* **Gray** *20850*

     E   *20850*   U.S. - California (San Bernardino Co.) *20850*

R   *Sidalcea ranunculacea* **Greene** *20850*

     I   *20850*   U.S. - California *20850*

V   *Sidalcea robusta* **Heller ex Roush** *20850*

     V   *20850*   U.S. - California *20850*

Ex/E   *Sidalcea setosa* **C.L. Hitchc. ssp. *querceta* C.L. Hitchc.** *20850*

     Ex/E   *20850*   U.S. - Oregon *20850*

E   *Sidalcea stipularis* **J.T. Howell & True** *20850*

     E   *20850*   U.S. - California *20850*

R   *Sidastrum tehuacanum* **(Brandegee) Fryx.** *9821*

     R   *9821*   Mexico *9821*

R   *Sphaeralcea caespitosa* **M.E. Jones** *20850*

     V   *20850*   U.S. - Nevada *20850*

     V   *20850*   U.S. - Utah *20850*

E   *Sphaeralcea janeae* **(Welsh) Welsh** *20850*

     E   *20850*   U.S. - Utah *20850*

R   *Sphaeralcea palmeri* **Rose** *9821*

     R   *9821*   Mexico *9821*

Ex/E   *Sphaeralcea procera* **C.L. Porter** *20850, 14662*

     Ex/E   *20850*   U.S. - New Mexico *20850*

V   *Sphaeralcea psoraloides* **Welsh** *20850*

     V   *20850*   U.S. - Utah *20850*

E   *Sphaeralcea rusbyi* **A. Gray ssp. *eremicola* (Jepson) Kearney** *20850*

     E   *20850*   U.S. - California *20850*

R   *Sphaeralcea sulphurea* **Watson** *9821*

     R   *9821*   Mexico *9821*

R   *Symphyochlamys erlangeri* **Guerke** *20884*

     R   *20884*   Somalia (south) *20884*

R   *Thespesia grandiflora* **DC.** *20883*

     I   *20883*   Puerto Rico *20883*

I   *Ulbrichia beatensis* **Urban** *5642*

     I   Dominican Republic (Isla Beata) *5642*

R   *Urena lobata* **L. var. *multifida* (Cav.) Hochr.** *10082*

     Ex   *10082*   Réunion *10082*

     Ex   *10082*   Mauritius *10082*

     R   *20771*   Mauritius - Rodrigues *5852*

Ex   *Urena lobata* **L. var. *tricuspis* (Cav.) Guerke** *10082*

     Ex   *10082*   Réunion *10082*

R   *Urocarpidium insulare* **(Kearney) Krapov.** *11117*

     R   Ecuador - Galapagos (Fernandina, Isabela, Wolf) *11117*

V   *Wercklea cocleana* **(A. Robyns) Fryx.** *20883, 9821*

     R   *9821*   Panama *20883*

E   *Wercklea flavovirens* **Proctor** *20883, 13336*

     E   *20883*   Jamaica *20883*

E   *Wercklea grandiflora* **Fryx.** *20883, 9821*

     I   *20883*   Panama *20883*

Marcgraviaceae

Number of genera: 5
Number of species: 100
Recorded threatened species: 5   (5%)

Tropical America.

E   *Marcgravia atropuncta* **de Roon** *20883*

     I   *20883*   Panama *20883*

R   *Marcgravia brachysepala* **Urb.** *20883*

     R   *20883*   Jamaica *20883*

R   *Ruyschia jimenezii* **Standley** *9037*

     R   *9426*   Costa Rica *9037*

R   *Ruyschia valerii* **Standley** *9037*

     R   *9426*   Costa Rica *9037*

V   *Souroubea venosa* **Schery** *20883, 9006*

     I   *20883*   Panama *20883*

Medusagynaceae

Number of genera: 1
Number of species: 1
Recorded threatened species: 1   (100%)

Seychelles.

E   *Medusagyne oppositifolia* **Baker** *14296*

     E   *14981*   Seychelles (Mahé) *14296*

Medusandraceae

Number of genera: 1
Number of species: 1
Recorded threatened species: 1   (100%)

Rainforests of tropical western Africa.

I   *Medusandra richardsiana* **Brenan**

     I   Cameroon

Melastomataceae

Number of genera: 200
Number of species: 4,000
Recorded threatened species: 487   (12%)

Tropical and subtropical, especially South America.

R   *Aciotis aristellata* **Markgraf** *11351*

     R   *19558*   Ecuador *11351*

R   *Aciotis asplundii* **Wurdack** *11351*

     R   *19558*   Ecuador *11351*

V   *Adamea stenocarpa* **(Jacq.-Fel.) Jacq.-Fel.** *7926*

     V   Guinea (Mt. Konosso) *7926*

E   *Adelobotrys jefensis* **Almeda** *20883, 9835*

     E   *9835*   Panama *20883*

E	*Adelobotrys panamensis* Almeda *20883, 10747*	
	I	*20883* Panama *20883*
R	*Amphiblemma letouzeyi* Jacq.-Fel.	
	R	Cameroon
R	*Astronidium degeneri* A.C. Smith *19630*	
	R	*19630* Fiji (Viti Levu) *19630*
Ex/E	*Astronidium floribundum* (Gillespie) A.C. Smith *19630*	
	Ex/E	*19630* Fiji (Mt. Korombamba) *19630*
E	*Astronidium inflatum* (A.C.Sm.) A.C. Smith *19630*	
	E	*19630* Fiji (Vanua Levu) *19630*
Ex/E	*Astronidium kasiense* A.C. Smith *19630*	
	Ex/E	*19630* Fiji (Mt. Kasi) *19630*
E	*Astronidium lepidotum* A.C. Smith *19453*	
	E	*19630* Fiji (Viti Levu) *19453*
I	*Astronidium ovalifolium* (Decne. ex Triana) J.Maxwell *20845*	
	I	*20845* French Polynesia - Society Is. (Raiatea) *20845*
E	*Astronidium pallidiflorum* A.C. Smith *19630*	
	E	*19630* Fiji (Viti Levu) *19630*
E	*Astronidium saulae* A.C. Smith *19452*	
	E	*19630* Fiji (Viti Levu) *19452*
E	*Astronidium sessile* (A.C. Sm.) A.C. Smith *19630*	
	E	*19630* Fiji (Vanua Levu) *19630*
R	*Axinaea pauciflora* Cogn. *11351*	
	R	*19558* Ecuador *11351*
R	*Axinaea sclerophylla* Triana *11351*	
	R	*19558* Ecuador *11351*
R	*Axinaea sessilifolia* Triana *11351*	
	R	*19558* Ecuador *11351*
E	*Axinaea sodiroi* Wurdack *11351*	
	E	*19558* Ecuador *11351*
E	*Blakea acostae* Wurdack *11351*	
	E	*19558* Ecuador *11351*
V	*Blakea austin-smithii* Standley *9037*	
	V	*9835* Costa Rica *9037*
E	*Blakea brunnea* Woods. & Schery *20883, 9006*	
	R	*9835* Panama *20883*
R	*Blakea campii* Wurdack *11351*	
	R	*19558* Ecuador *11351*
R	*Blakea chlorantha* Almeda *9836*	
	R	*9836* Costa Rica *9836*
E	*Blakea crinita* Gleason *20883, 9006*	
	R	*9835* Panama *20883*
E	*Blakea elliptica* (Gleason) Almeda *20883, 10747*	
	E	*9835* Panama *20883*
E	*Blakea eriocalyx* Wurdack *11351*	
	E	*19558* Ecuador *11351*
R	*Blakea florida* L.O. Williams *9529*	
	R	*9835* Costa Rica *9529*
R	*Blakea formicaria* Wurdack *11351*	
	R	*19558* Ecuador *11351*
E	*Blakea fuchsioides* Almadea *20883*	
	I	*20883* Panama *20883*
R	*Blakea glandulosa* Gleason *11351*	
	R	*19558* Ecuador *11351*
R	*Blakea guatemalensis* J.D. Smith *9004*	
	R	*9835* Guatemala *9004*

R	*Blakea hispida* Markgraf ssp. *hispida* *11351*	
	R	*19558* Ecuador *11351*
R	*Blakea hispida* Markgraf ssp. *stenopetala* Wurdack *11351*	
	R	*19558* Ecuador *11351*
V	*Blakea incompta* Markgraf *11351*	
	V	*19558* Ecuador *11351*
R	*Blakea involvens* Markgraf *11351*	
	R	*19558* Ecuador *11351*
R	*Blakea jativae* Wurdack *11351*	
	R	*19558* Ecuador *11351*
V	*Blakea lanuginesa* Wurdack *11351*	
	V	*19558* Ecuador *11351*
R	*Blakea littoralis* L.O. Williams *9529*	
	R	*9836* Costa Rica *9529*
R	*Blakea madisonii* Wurdack *11351*	
	R	*19558* Ecuador *11351*
E	*Blakea micrantha* Almeda *20883, 10747*	
	I	*20883* Panama *20883*
R	*Blakea oldemanii* Wurdack *11351*	
	R	*19558* Ecuador *11351*
E	*Blakea parvifolia* Gleason *20883*	
	I	*20883* Panama *20883*
V	*Blakea penduliflora* Almeda *9835*	
	V	*9835* Costa Rica *9835*
V	*Blakea pichinchensis* Wurdack *11351*	
	V	*19558* Ecuador *11351*
R	*Blakea quadriflora* Gleason *11351*	
	R	*19558* Ecuador *11351*
V	*Blakea rotundifolia* D.Don. *11351*	
	V	*19558* Ecuador *11351*
R	*Blakea subpeltata* Cogn. *9037*	
	R	*9835* Costa Rica *9037*
R	*Blakea subvaginata* Wurdack *11351*	
	R	*19558* Ecuador *11351*
R	*Blakea urbaniana* Cogn. *20883, 13336*	
	R	*13336* Jamaica *20883*
E	*Blakea wilburiana* Almeda *20883, 9837*	
	V	*9835* Panama *20883*
R	*Brachyotum andreanum* Cogn. *11351*	
	R	*19558* Ecuador *11351*
R	*Brachyotum azuayense* Wurdack *11351*	
	R	*19558* Ecuador *11351*
R	*Brachyotum benthamianum* Triana *11351*	
	R	*19558* Ecuador *11351*
R	*Brachyotum campanulare* (Bonpl.) Triana *11351*	
	R	*19558* Ecuador *11351*
R	*Brachyotum campii* Wurdack *11351*	
	R	*19558* Ecuador *11351*
V	*Brachyotum ecuadorense* Wurdack *11351*	
	V	*19558* Ecuador *11351*
R	*Brachyotum fictum* Wurdack *11351*	
	R	*19558* Ecuador *11351*
R	*Brachyotum fraternum* Wurdack *11351*	
	R	*19558* Ecuador *11351*
V	*Brachyotum gleasonii* Wurdack *11351*	
	V	*19558* Ecuador *11351*
R	*Brachyotum gracilescens* Triana *11351*	

R   *19558* Ecuador *11351*

R   **Brachyotum harlingii** Wurdack *11351*
    R   *19558* Ecuador *11351*

R   **Brachyotum jamesonii** Triana *11351*
    R   *19558* Ecuador *11351*

R   **Brachyotum rotundifolium** Cogn. *11351*
    R   *19558* Ecuador *11351*

R   **Brachyotum rugosum** Wurdack *11351*
    R   *19558* Ecuador *11351*

I   **Brachyotum trichocalyx** Triana *11351*
    I   *19558* Ecuador *11351*

R   **Bredia rotundifolia** *20854*
    R   *20854* Taiwan *20854*

R   **Cailliella praerupticola** Jacq.-Fel. *7926*
    R   Guinea (Benna massif) *7926*

R   **Calvoa calliantha** Jacq.-Fel.
    R   Cameroon

I   **Calvoa stenophylla** Jacq.-Fel.
    I   *7927* Cameroon *7927*

E   **Calycogonium acunanum** Borh. & Muniz *5607*
    E   *19105* Cuba (Holguin) *5607*

E   **Calycogonium ellipticum** C. Wright
    E   *19105* Cuba *19105*

R   **Calycogonium glabratum** (Sw.) DC. *20883*
    V   *20883* Jamaica *20883*

V   **Calycogonium microphyllum** C. Wright *5607*
    V   *19105* Cuba (Pinar del Rio) *5607*

V   **Calycogonium plicatum** Griseb. *5607*
    V   *19105* Cuba (Guantanamo) *5607*

V   **Calycogonium rubens** Borh. *5607*
    V   *19105* Cuba (Santiago de Cuba; Holguin) *5607*

V   **Calycogonium saxicola** Britton & P. Wilson *5607*
    V   *19105* Cuba (Pinar del Rio) *5607*

V   **Calycogonium susannae** Borh. *5607*
    V   *19105* Cuba (Holguin; Guantanamo) *5607*

I   **Calycogonium torbecianum** Urb. & Ekman *15229*
    I   *15229* Haiti (La Visite & Macaya National Parks) *15229*

E   **Centronia grandiflora** Standl. *20883, 9006*
    R   *9835* Panama *20883*

R   **Chaetolepis cufodontisii** Standley *9037*
    R   *9835* Costa Rica *9037*

V   **Charianthus nodosus** (Desv.) Triana *5710*
    V   *19001* Martinique (Montagne Pelée; Pitons du Carbet; Morne Jacob) *5710*

R   **Charianthus purpureus** D. Don. var. *rugosus* Hodge *10199*
    R   Dominica *10199*

R   **Cincinnobotrys letouzeyi** Jacq.-Fel.
    R   Cameroon

R   **Clidemia acostae** Wurdack *11351*
    R   *19558* Ecuador *11351*

I   **Clidemia asplundii** Wurdack *11351*
    I   *19558* Ecuador *11351*

R   **Clidemia campii** Wurdack *11351*
    R   *19558* Ecuador *11351*

R   **Clidemia caudata** Wurdack *11351*
    R   *19558* Ecuador *11351*

E   **Clidemia collina** Gleason *20883, 9006*
    V   *9836* Panama *20883*

R   **Clidemia crossosepala** Griseb. *20883*
    I   *20883* Jamaica *20883*

V   **Clidemia crossosepala** Griseb. var. *adamsii* Proctor *20883, 13336*
    V   *13336* Jamaica *20883*

R   **Clidemia crossosepala** Griseb. var. *crossosepala* Griseb. *20883*
    R   *20883* Jamaica *20883*

R   **Clidemia cutucuensis** Wurdack *11351*
    R   *19558* Ecuador *11351*

R   **Clidemia cymifera** J.D. Smith *9004*
    R   *9835* Guatemala *9004*

R   **Clidemia diffusa** J.D. Smith *9004*
    R   *9836* Guatemala *9004*

R   **Clidemia donnell-smithii** Cogn. *9004*
    R   *9836* Guatemala *9004*

R   **Clidemia ecuadorensis** Gleason *11351*
    R   *19558* Ecuador *11351*

R   **Clidemia fraterna** Gleason *9037*
    R   *9835* Costa Rica *9037*
    R   *9835* Panama *9006*

V   **Clidemia fulva** Gleason *9004*
    V   *9836* Guatemala *9004*
    V   *9836* Honduras *9004*

R   **Clidemia garciabarrigae** Wurdack *19558*
    R   *19558* Ecuador *19558*

R   **Clidemia globuliflora** (Cogn.) L.O. Williams *9835*
    R   *9836* Costa Rica *9835*

V   **Clidemia grisebachii** Cogn. *20883*
    V   *20883* Jamaica *20883*

I   **Clidemia imparilis** Wurdack *11351*
    I   *19558* Ecuador *11351*

V   **Clidemia lundellii** Wurdack *9838*
    V   *9836* Guatemala *9838*

E   **Clidemia macrandra** (C. Wright) Cogn. *5607*
    E   *19105* Cuba (Juventud Is.) *5607*

R   **Clidemia matudae** L.O. Williams *9004*
    R   *9835* Guatemala *9004*
    V   *9835* Mexico *9004*

V   **Clidemia mortoniana** Standley *9037*
    V   *9836* Costa Rica *9037*

E   **Clidemia oblonga** Gleason *20883, 9006*
    R   *9836* Panama *20883*

E   **Clidemia pittieri** Gleason *20883, 9006*
    V   *9836* Panama *20883*

R   **Clidemia pubescens** Gleason *9037*
    R   *9836* Costa Rica *9037*

R   **Clidemia swartzii** Griseb. *20883, 13336*
    R   *13336* Jamaica *20883*

E   **Clidemia taurina** Gleason *20883, 9006*
    R   *9836* Panama *20883*

E   **Clidemia tetrapetala** Almeda *20883, 10747*
    I   *20883* Panama *20883*

V   **Clidemia trichosantha** Almeda *20883, 10747*
    V   *9835* Panama *20883*

R   **Clidemia tuerckheimii** (J.D. Smith) Gleason *9004*
    R   *9836* Guatemala *9004*

R	*Clidemia utleyana* Almeda 9839		
	R	9835	Costa Rica 9839
	V	9835	Panama 10747
R	*Conostegia brenesii* Standley 9037		
	R	9835	Costa Rica 9037
V	*Conostegia chiriquensis* Woods. & Schery 20883, 9006		
	V	16317	Panama 20883
V	*Conostegia grisebachii* Cogn. 20883, 13336		
	V	13336	Jamaica 20883
E	*Conostegia hirsuta* Gleason 20883, 9006		
	E	20883	Panama 20883
R	*Conostegia oerstediana* O. Berg ex Triana var. bigibbosa (Cogn.) Schnell 9836		
	R	9836	Costa Rica 9836
R	*Conostegia pyxidata* Proctor 20883, 13336		
	R	13336	Jamaica 20883
R	*Conostegia setifera* Standley 9037		
	R	9835	Costa Rica 9037
	R	11967	Nicaragua 9426
V	*Conostegia subprocera* Proctor 20883, 13336		
	V	13336	Jamaica 20883
V	*Conostegia superba* Naud. 20883		
	V	20883	Jamaica 20883
R	*Conostegia vulcanicola* J.D. Smith 9037		
	R	9836	Costa Rica 9037
R	*Dionychastrum schliebenii* A. & R. Fernandes 7959		
	R	5926	Tanzania (Morogoro Distr.) 7959
I	*Dissotis alata* A. & R. Fernandes 7959		
	I	5926	Tanzania (Buha) 5926
R	*Dissotis angustifolia* A. & R. Fernades 7749		
	R		Mozambique 7749
I	*Dissotis aprica* Engl. 20556		
	I	5926	Tanzania 7959
I	*Dissotis arborescens* A. & R. Fernandes 20556, 7959		
	I	5926	Tanzania (Iringa) 5926
I	*Dissotis bussei* Engl. 20556, 7959		
	I	5926	Tanzania (Iringa & Kondoa) 5926
R	*Dissotis dichaetantheroides* Wick. 7959		
	R	5926	Tanzania (Morogoro Distr.) 7959
I	*Dissotis formosa* A. & R. Fernandes 7959		
	I	5926	Tanzania (Songea District) 5926
I	*Dissotis glandulicalyx* Wickens 20556, 7959		
	I	5926	Tanzania (Mpanda District) 5926
R	*Dissotis humilis* A. Chev. & Jacq.-Fel. 7926		
	R		Guinea 7926
R	*Dissotis johnstoniana* Baker. f. var. *strigosa* Brenan 7749		
	R		Malawi 7749
R	*Dissotis lanata* A. & R. Fernandes 7749		
	R		Malawi 7749
R	*Dissotis linearis* Jacq.-Fel. 7926		
	R		Guinea 7926
I	*Dissotis pachytricha* R.E. Fries var. *grandisquamulosa* Wickens 7959		
	I	5926	Tanzania (Buha & Kigoma) 5926
R	*Dissotis polyantha* Gilg 7959		
	R		Tanzania 7959
I	*Dissotis pterocaulos* Wickens 5926		
	I	5926	Tanzania 5926

R	*Dissotis pygmaea* A. Chev. & Jacq.-Fel. 7926		
	R		Guinea 7926
I	*Dissotis sessili-cordata* Wickens 7959		
	I	5926	Tanzania (Mpanda District) 5926
R	*Dissotis sessilis* Hutch. ex Brenan 7926		
	R		Sierra Leone (Loma Mts.) 7926
R	*Dissotis splendens* A. Chev. & Jacq.-Fel. 7926		
	R		Guinea 7926
R	*Dissotis sylvestris* Jacq.-Fel. 7926		
	R		Guinea 7926
E	*Graffenrieda bella* Almeda 20883, 10747		
	R	9835	Panama 20883
R	*Graffenrieda harlingii* Wurdack 11351		
	R	19558	Ecuador 11351
I	*Gravesia gabonensis* Jacq.-Fel.		
	I	7927	Gabon 7927
I	*Gravesia hylophila* (Gilg) A. & R. Fernandes 7959		
	I	5926	Tanzania (Uluguru mts) 5926
R	*Gravesia pulchra* (Gilg) Wick. var. *glandulosa* (A. & R. Fernandes) Wick. 7959		
	R	5926	Tanzania (Morogoro Distr.) 7959
R	*Gravesia pulchra* (Gilg) Wick. var. *pulchra* 7959		
	R	5926	Tanzania (Morogoro Distr.) 7959
R	*Gravesia riparia* A. & R. Fernandes 7959		
	R	5926	Tanzania (Uluguru Mts.) 7959
R	*Guyonia tenella* Naudin 7926		
	R		Guinea (Fouta Djalon) 7926
R	*Henriettea granularis* (Urban) Alain 11840		
	R	19105	Cuba (Pinar del Rio) 11840
E	*Henriettea membranifolia* (Cogn.) Alain 20883		
	V	19002	Puerto Rico 20883
V	*Henriettea punctata* (Griseb.) M. Gomez 5607		
	V	19105	Cuba (Guantanamo) 5607
V	*Henriettea squamata* (Alain) Alain 5607		
	V	19105	Cuba (Holguin) 5607
V	*Henriettea squamulosum* (Cogn.) Judd 20883		
	I	20883	Puerto Rico 20883
V	*Henriettella hondurensis* Wurdack 9840		
	V	9836	Honduras 9840
E	*Henriettella lateriflora* (Vahl) Triana 10199		
	E		Dominica 10199
V	*Henriettella lundellii* Wurdack 9840		
	V	9836	Guatemala 9840
R	*Henriettella odorata* Markgraf 11351		
	R	19558	Ecuador 11351
R	*Heterocentron elegans* (Schltr.) Kuntze 9004		
	R	9835	Guatemala 9004
	R	9835	Mexico 9004
R	*Heterocentron hirtellum* (Cogn.) L.O. Williams 9004		
	R	9835	Guatemala 9004
V	*Heterocentron suffruticosum* Brandegee 9004		
	V	9836	Guatemala 9004
	V	9836	Mexico 9004
V	*Heterotrichum cymosum* (Wendl. ex Spreng.) Urban 20883, 20513		
	I	20883	Puerto Rico 20883
E	*Kendrickia walkeri* Hook.f. 14782		
	E	14782	India - Tamil Nadu 14782

E   *14782*   Sri Lanka (doubtful occurrence) *14782*

R   *Lavoisiera itambana* DC. *17079*

    R   *17079*   Brazil - Minas Gerais (Pico de Itambé, município de Diamantina) *17079*

R   *Leandra pastazana* Wurdack *11351*

    R   *19558*   Ecuador *11351*

R   *Leandra subulata* Gleason *9006*

    R   *9835*   Costa Rica *10747*
    R   *9836*   Panama *9006*

I   *Mecranium ovatum* Cogn. *19408*

    I   *19408*   Dominican Republic *19408*

R   *Medinilla balls-headleyi* F.Muell. *20681*

    R   *20681*   Australia - Queensland *20681*

E   *Medinilla decora* A.C. Smith *19630*

    E   *19630*   Fiji (Viti Levu) *19630*

R   *Medinilla hayataiana* H. Keng *14961*

    R   *20854*   Taiwan (Lan Yu) *20854*

R   *Medinilla kambikambi* A.C. Smith *19630*

    R   *19630*   Fiji (Vanua Levu) *19630*

Ex/E   *Medinilla kandavuensis* A.C. Smith *19630*

    Ex/E   *19630*   Fiji (Kanavu) *19630*

V   *Medinilla loranthoides* Naudin *10082*

    V   *14234*   Réunion *10082*

I   *Medinilla maculata* Gardner *10252*

    I   *16162*   Sri Lanka *10252*

V   *Medinilla magnifica* Lindley *10278*

    V   Philippines *10278*

E   *Medinilla spectabilis* A.C. Smith *19630*

    E   *19630*   Fiji (Taveuni) *19630*

V   *Medinilla waterhousei* Seem. *19454*

    V   *19630*   Fiji (Taveuni, Vanua Levu) *19454*

R   *Melastoma pentapetarum* (Toyota) Toyota *8037*

    R   *19134*   Japan - Ogasawara-shoto *8037*

E   *Melastoma tetramerum* Hayata *8038*

    E   *19134*   Japan - Ogasawara-shoto (Chichijima; Hahajima) *8038*

R   *Melastomastrum theifolium* (G. Don) A. & R. Fernandes var. *controversum* (A. Chev. & Jacq.-Fel.) Jacq.-F

    R   Guinea

R   *Memecylon arnottianum* Wight ex Thwaites *10276*

    R   *12838*   Sri Lanka *10276*

R   *Memecylon brenanii* A. & R. Fernandes *20556*

    R   *5926*   Tanzania (Usambara mountains) *5926*

Ex/E   *Memecylon buxoides* Wick. *7959*

    Ex/E   *19109*   Kenya (Kitni) *7959*

V   *Memecylon clarkeanum* Cogn. *12838*

    V   *12838*   Sri Lanka *12838*

E   *Memecylon cordatum* Lam. *10082*

    E   *20771*   Réunion *10082*
    E   *20771*   Mauritius *10082*

I   *Memecylon deccanense* C.B. Clarke *9315*

    I   India - Kerala *9315*

I   *Memecylon deminutum* Brenan *7959*

    I   *5926*   Tanzania (Usambara and Pare mountains) *5926*

R   *Memecylon eleagni* Blume *14296*

    R   *19182*   Seychelles (granitic) *14296*

E   *Memecylon elegantulum* Thwaites *10276*

    E   *12838*   Sri Lanka *10276*

E   *Memecylon ellipticum* Thwaites *10252*

    E   *12838*   Sri Lanka *10252*

R   *Memecylon erubescens* Gilg *7959*

    R   *5926*   Tanzania (east Usambara Mts.) *5926*

E   *Memecylon flavescens* Gamble *4988*

    E   *14782*   India - Tamil Nadu (Nilgiri Hills) *4988*

V   *Memecylon fragrans* A. & R. Fernandes *7959*

    V   *19109*   Kenya *7959*

R   *Memecylon gardneri* Thwaites *10276*

    R   *12838*   Sri Lanka *10276*

I   *Memecylon gracillimum* Alston *10252*

    I   *16162*   Sri Lanka *10252*

E   *Memecylon grande* Retz. *12838*

    E   *12838*   Sri Lanka *12838*

V   *Memecylon greenwayii* Brenan *7959*

    V   *5926*   Tanzania (Usambara Mts.) *5926*

I   *Memecylon lawsonii* Gamble *6295*

    I   India - Tamil Nadu *6295*

I   *Memecylon leucanthum* Thwaites *10252*

    I   *16162*   Sri Lanka *10252*

I   *Memecylon macrocarpum* Thwaites *10252*

    I   *16162*   Sri Lanka *10252*

I   *Memecylon madgolense* Gamble

    I   India - Andhra Pradesh

R   *Memecylon microphyllum* Gilg *7959*

    R   *5926*   Tanzania (east Usambara Mts.) *5926*

I   *Memecylon mouririifolium* Brenan *5926*

    I   *5926*   Tanzania *5926*

V   *Memecylon myrtiforme* Naudin *10082*

    V   *20771*   Mauritius *10082*

I   *Memecylon odoratum* Elm. *13833*

    I   *13833*   Philippines (Palawan) *13833*

I   *Memecylon orbiculare* Thwaites *10252*

    I   *16162*   Sri Lanka *10252*

R   *Memecylon ovatifolium* (Poiret) Wickens *10082*

    R   *20771*   Mauritius *10082*

I   *Memecylon ovoideum* Thwaites *10252*

    I   *16162*   Sri Lanka *10252*

I   *Memecylon phyllanthifolium* Thwaites ex C.B. Clarke *10252*

    I   *16162*   Sri Lanka *10252*

R   *Memecylon procteri* A. & R. Fernandes *7959*

    R   *5926*   Tanzania (Usambara mountains) *5926*

I   *Memecylon revolutum* Thwaites *10252*

    I   *16162*   Sri Lanka *10252*

E   *Memecylon rhinophyllum* Thwaites *12838*

    E   *12838*   Sri Lanka *12838*

R   *Memecylon rostratum* Thwaites *10276*

    R   *12838*   Sri Lanka *10276*

I   *Memecylon rotundatum* (Thwaites) Cogn. & Bremer *10252*

    I   *16162*   Sri Lanka *10252*

I   *Memecylon schliebenii* Markgr. *5926*

    I   *5926*   Tanzania *5926*

R   *Memecylon semseii* A. & R. Fernandes *7959*

    R   *5926*   Tanzania (Lushoto) *7959*

I   *Memecylon sisparense* Gamble *14782*

    I   *14782*   India - Tamil Nadu (Nilgiri Hills) *14782*

R   *Memecylon sylvaticum* Thwaites *12838*
   R   *12838*   Sri Lanka *12838*

V   *Memecylon teitense* Wick. *7959*
   V   *20057*   Kenya (Taita hills) *6073*

V   *Memecylon varians* Thwaites *12838*
   V   *12838*   Sri Lanka *12838*

I   *Memecylon wightiana* Triana
   I   India - Kerala (Malabar, Travancore coast)

I   *Meriania acostae* Wurdack *11351*
   I   *19558*   Ecuador *11351*

I   *Meriania almedae* Wurdack *11351*
   I   *19558*   Ecuador *11351*

R   *Meriania ampla* Wurdack *11351*
   R   *19558*   Ecuador *11351*

I   *Meriania amplexicaulis* Wurdack *11351*
   I   *19558*   Ecuador *11351*

R   *Meriania anderssonii* Wurdack *19558*
   R   *19558*   Ecuador *19558*

E   *Meriania brevipedunculata* Judd & Skean *20883*
   I   *20883*   Haiti *20883*

R   *Meriania campii* Wurdack *11351*
   R   *19558*   Ecuador *11351*

R   *Meriania costata* Wurdack *11351*
   R   *19558*   Ecuador *11351*

R   *Meriania cuneifolia* Gleason ssp.
     cuneifolia 11351
   R   *19558*   Ecuador *11351*

I   *Meriania cuneifolia* Gleason ssp. *subandina*
     Wurdack *11351*
   I   *19558*   Ecuador *11351*

R   *Meriania denticulata* (Gleason) Wurdack *11351*
   R   *19558*   Ecuador *11351*

I   *Meriania drakei* (Cogn) Wurdack ssp. *chontalensis*
     Wurdack *11351*
   I   *19558*   Ecuador *11351*

R   *Meriania drakei* (Cogn.) Wurdack ssp.
     drakei 11351
   R   *19558*   Ecuador *11351*

R   *Meriania finicola* Wurdack *19558*
   R   *19558*   Ecuador *19558*

R   *Meriania furvanthera* Wurdack *11351*
   R   *19558*   Ecuador *11351*

I   *Meriania kirkbridei* Wurdack *11351*
   I   *19558*   Ecuador *11351*

R   *Meriania leucantha* (Sw.) Sw. *20883*
   R   *20883*   Jamaica *20883*

I   *Meriania loxensis* Gleason *11351*
   I   *19558*   Ecuador *11351*

I   *Meriania maguirei* Wurdack *11351*
   I   *19558*   Ecuador *11351*

E   *Meriania panamensis* Woods. & Schery *20883, 9006*
   E   *9835*   Panama *20883*

E   *Meriania parvifolia* Judd & Skean *20883*
   I   *20883*   Haiti *20883*

R   *Meriania pastazana* Wurdack *11351*
   R   *19558*   Ecuador *11351*

V   *Meriania pichinchensis* Wurdack *19558*
   V   *19558*   Ecuador *19558*

R   *Meriania rigida* (Benth.) Triana *11351*
   R   *19558*   Ecuador *11351*

I   *Meriania stellata* Wurdack *11351*
   I   *19558*   Ecuador *11351*

E   *Miconia acunae* Borh. *5607*
   E   *19105*   Cuba (Granma; Santiago de Cuba) *5607*

E   *Miconia adrieni* J.F. Macbr. *18200*
   E   *9446*   Peru *18200*

R   *Miconia aequatorialis* Wurdack *11351*
   R   *19558*   Ecuador *11351*

R   *Miconia attenuata* DC. *20883*
   R   *20883*   Jamaica *20883*

R   *Miconia barbipilis* Gleason *11351*
   R   *19558*   Ecuador *11351*

R   *Miconia barclayana* Wurdack *11351*
   R   *19558*   Ecuador *11351*

R   *Miconia beneolens* Wurdack *11351*
   R   *19558*   Ecuador *11351*

R   *Miconia benoistii* Wurdack *11351*
   R   *19558*   Ecuador *11351*

R   *Miconia bipatrialis* Wurdack *11351*
   R   *19558*   Ecuador *11351*

R   *Miconia bolivarensis* Wurdack *11351*
   R   *19558*   Ecuador *11351*

R   *Miconia brevitheca* Gleason *11351*
   R   *19558*   Ecuador *11351*

R   *Miconia caelata* (Bonpl.) DC. *11351*
   R   *19558*   Ecuador *11351*

R   *Miconia caesariata* Wurdack *11351*
   R   *19558*   Ecuador *11351*

R   *Miconia cajanumana* Wurdack *11351*
   R   *19558*   Ecuador *11351*

R   *Miconia campii* Wurdack *11351*
   R   *19558*   Ecuador *11351*

R   *Miconia capitellata* (DC.) Cogn *11351*
   R   *19558*   Ecuador *11351*

R   *Miconia castillensis* Wurdack *11351*
   R   *19558*   Ecuador *11351*

E   *Miconia centrosperma* Almeda *20883, 12041*
   I   *20883*   Panama *20883*

R   *Miconia cercophora* Wurdack ssp. *canelosana*
     Wurdack *11351*
   R   *19558*   Ecuador *11351*

R   *Miconia cercophora* Wurdack ssp. *esetulosa*
     Wurdack *11351*
   R   *19558*   Ecuador *11351*

V   *Miconia chiriquiensis* Almeda *9835*
   E   *9835*   Costa Rica *10747*
   V   *16826*   Panama *9835*

E   *Miconia coloradensis* Almeda *20883, 10747*
   I   *20883*   Panama *20883*

E   *Miconia concinna* Almeda *20883, 10747*
   I   *20883*   Panama *20883*

E   *Miconia confertiflora* Almeda *9835*
   E   *9835*   Costa Rica *9835*

V   *Miconia contrerasii* Wurdack *9838*
   V   *9836*   Guatemala *9838*

R   *Miconia corazonica* Wurdack *11351*

R   *19558* Ecuador *11351*

V   *Miconia cordifolia* (Alain) Borh. *5607*
     V   *19105* Cuba (Holguin) *5607*

R   *Miconia coriacea* (Swartz) DC. *10199*
     R   Dominica *10199*

R   *Miconia cosangensis* Wurdack *11351*
     R   *19558* Ecuador *11351*

R   *Miconia crocea* (Desr.) Naud. var. *setosa*
     Markgraf *11351*
     R   *19558* Ecuador *11351*

V   *Miconia dapsiliflora* Wurdack *11351*
     V   *19558* Ecuador *11351*

R   *Miconia dielsii* Markgraf *11351*
     R   *19558* Ecuador *11351*

R   *Miconia dissimulans* Wurdack *11351*
     R   *19558* Ecuador *11351*

R   *Miconia dodsonii* Wurdack *11351*
     R   *19558* Ecuador *11351*

R   *Miconia echinoidea* Standley & Steyerm. *9004*
     R   *9836* Guatemala *9004*
     R   *9836* Mexico *9004*

V   *Miconia explicita* Wurdack *11351*
     V   *19558* Ecuador *11351*

E   *Miconia ferreyrae* Wurdack *18200*
     E   *9446* Peru *18200*

E   *Miconia foveolata* Cogn. *20883*
     I   *20883* Puerto Rico *20883*

I   *Miconia fuertesii* Cogn. *5642*
     I   Dominican Republic *5642*

V   *Miconia fulvostellata* L.O. Williams *9004*
     V   *9836* Belize *9004*
     V   *9836* Guatemala *9004*

R   *Miconia gibba* Markgraf *11351*
     R   *19558* Ecuador *11351*

R   *Miconia glandulistyla* Wurdack *11351*
     R   *19558* Ecuador *11351*

R   *Miconia gonioclada* Triana *11351*
     R   *19558* Ecuador *11351*

R   *Miconia guayaquilensis* (Bonpl.) D.Don *11351*
     R   *19558* Ecuador *11351*

R   *Miconia heterochaeta* Wurdack *19558*
     R   *19558* Ecuador *11351*

R   *Miconia hirsutivena* Gleason *11351*
     R   *19558* Ecuador *11351*

R   *Miconia huigrensis* Wurdack *11351*
     R   *19558* Ecuador *11351*

R   *Miconia imitans* Wurdack *11351*
     R   *19558* Ecuador *11351*

R   *Miconia inanis* Cogn.& Gleason Ex.Gleason *11351*
     R   *19558* Ecuador *11351*

R   *Miconia innata* Gleason *11351*
     R   *19558* Ecuador *11351*

V   *Miconia lenticellata* Alain *5607*
     V   *19105* Cuba (Holguin; Guantanamo) *5607*

R   *Miconia littlei* Wurdack *11351*
     R   *19558* Ecuador *11351*

I   *Miconia longisetosa* Wurdack *11351*
     I   *19558* Ecuador *11351*

R   *Miconia macbrydeana* Wurdack *11351*
     R   *19558* Ecuador *11351*

R   *Miconia media* (D.Don) Naud ssp. *ecuadorensis*
     Wurdack *11351*
     R   *19558* Ecuador *11351*

R   *Miconia mediocris* Wurdack *11351*
     R   *19558* Ecuador *11351*

E   *Miconia melanotricha* Gleason var. *panamensis*
     Gleason *20883, 9006*
     R   *9836* Panama *20883*

R   *Miconia namandensis* Wurdack *11351*
     R   *19558* Ecuador *11351*

R   *Miconia nasella* Wurdack *11351*
     R   *19558* Ecuador *11351*

V   *Miconia nubicola* Proctor *20883, 13336*
     V   *13336* Jamaica *20883*

R   *Miconia ochracea* Triana *19352*
     R   *9836* Colombia *19352*
     R   *9836* Ecuador *11351*

V   *Miconia ottoschulzii* Urban & Ekman *20883, 19002*
     I   *20883* Puerto Rico *20883*

E   *Miconia panamensis* Gleason *20883, 9006*
     I   *20883* Panama *20883*

V   *Miconia perelegans* Urban *5607*
     V   *19105* Cuba (Juventud Is.) *5607*

R   *Miconia pernettifolia* Triana *11351*
     R   *19558* Ecuador *11351*

R   *Miconia petersonii* Urban *5607*
     R   *19105* Cuba (Santiago de Cuba; Holguin) *5607*

R   *Miconia phaeochaeta* Wurdack *19558*
     R   *19558* Ecuador *19558*

R   *Miconia poortmannii* (Cogn.) Wurdack *11351*
     R   *19558* Ecuador *11351*

R   *Miconia porphyrotricha* (Markgraf) Wurdack *11351*
     R   *19558* Ecuador *11351*

R   *Miconia prietoi* Wurdack *11351*
     R   *19558* Ecuador *11351*

V   *Miconia pseudorigida* Proctor *20883, 13336*
     V   *13336* Jamaica *20883*

V   *Miconia purulensis* J.D. Smith *9004*
     V   *9836* Guatemala *9004*

E   *Miconia pycnoneura* Urban *20883*
     I   *20883* Puerto Rico *20883*

V   *Miconia quadrangularis* Proctor var. *glandulosa*
     Proctor *20883, 13336*
     V   *13336* Jamaica *20883*

R   *Miconia remotiflora* Urban *5607*
     R   *19105* Cuba (Granma) *5607*

I   *Miconia reticulata* Triana *19352*
     I   *19352* Colombia *19352*

I   *Miconia rigidissima* *15229*
     I   *15229* Haiti (La Visite & Macaya National Parks) *15229*

R   *Miconia rimbachii* Wurdack *11351*
     R   *19558* Ecuador *11351*

R   *Miconia rivetii* Danguy & Chermezon *11351*
     R   *19558* Ecuador *11351*

V   *Miconia robinsoniana* Cogn. *11117*
     V   *14980* Ecuador - Galapagos (Santa Cruz; San

Cristobal) *11117*

E   *Miconia rufostellulata* Pitt. *20883, 9006*
    R   *9836*   Panama *20883*

V   *Miconia santaritensis* Almeda *20883, 12041*
    I   *20883*   Panama *20883*

R   *Miconia santata* Gleason *11351*
    R   *19558*   Ecuador *11351*

I   *Miconia sodiroi* Wurdack *11351*
    I   *19558*   Ecuador *11351*

R   *Miconia stenophylla* Wurdack *11351*
    R   *19558*   Ecuador *11351*

R   *Miconia suborbicularis* Cogn. *11351*
    R   *19558*   Ecuador *11351*

V   *Miconia tixixensis* Standley & Steyerm. *9004*
    V   *9836*   Guatemala *9004*

V   *Miconia uninervis* Alain *5607*
    V   *19105*   Cuba (Holguin, Guantanamo) *5607*

R   *Miconia villonacensis* Wurdack *11351*
    R   *19558*   Ecuador *11351*

R   *Monochaetum alpestre* Naudin *9841*
    R   *9835*   Mexico *9841*

E   *Monochaetum candollei* Cogn. *9841*
    E   *9835*   Mexico *9841*

E   *Monochaetum compactum* Almeda *20883, 9841*
    V   *9835*   Panama *20883*

V   *Monochaetum exaltatum* Almeda *20883, 9841*
    V   *9835*   Panama *20883*

R   *Monochaetum linearifolium* Almeda *9841*
    R   *9835*   Costa Rica *9841*

R   *Monochaetum macrantherum* Gleason *9841*
    R   *9835*   Costa Rica *9841*

E   *Monochaetum rubescens* Gleason *9841*
    E   *9835*   Mexico *9841*

V   *Monochaetum talamancense* Almeda *9841*
    V   *9835*   Costa Rica *9841*

R   *Monochaetum trichophyllum* Almeda *9841*
    R   *9835*   Panama *9841*

V   *Monolena guatemalensis* J.D. Smith *9004*
    V   *9836*   Guatemala *9004*

E   *Mouriri ambiconvexa* Morley *20883*
    I   *20883*   Colombia *20883*

V   *Mouriri angustifolia* Spruce ex Triana *20883*
    I   *20883*   Colombia *20883*
    I   *20883*   Venezuela *20883*

E   *Mouriri arborea* Gardner *20883*
    I   *20883*   Brazil *20883*

E   *Mouriri bahiensis* Morley *20883*
    I   *20883*   Brazil *20883*

R   *Mouriri cearensis* Huber *20883*
    I   *20883*   Brazil *20883*

E   *Mouriri cearensis* Huber ssp. *carajasica*
    Morley *20883*
    I   *20883*   Brazil *20883*

R   *Mouriri cearensis* Huber ssp. *cearensis* *20883*
    I   *20883*   Brazil *20883*

R   *Mouriri chamissoana* Cogniaux *20883, 20310*
    I   *20883*   Brazil *20883*
    ?   Brazil - Santa Catarina *20310*

E   *Mouriri coibensis* Morley *20883, 9842*
    R   *9836*   Panama *20883*

R   *Mouriri completens* (Pitt.) Burret *20883*
    I   *20883*   Panama *20883*
    I   *20883*   Colombia *20883*

R   *Mouriri crassifolia* Sagot *20883*
    I   *20883*   Brazil *20883*
    I   *20883*   French Guiana *20883*
    I   *20883*   Suriname *20883*

R   *Mouriri cyphocarpa* Standl. *20883*
    I   *20883*   Guatemala *20883*
    I   *20883*   Nicaragua *20883*
    I   *20883*   Panama *20883*

V   *Mouriri doriana* Saldanha ex Cogniaux *20883*
    I   *20883*   Brazil *20883*

R   *Mouriri dumetosa* Cogniaux *20883*
    I   *20883*   Brazil *20883*
    I   *20883*   French Guiana *20883*

R   *Mouriri emarginata* var. *rostrata* (Urban)
    Morley *20883*
    I   *20883*   Cuba *20883*

R   *Mouriri eugeniaefolia* Spruce ex Triana *20883*
    I   *20883*   Brazil *20883*

E   *Mouriri exadenia* Morley *20883, 18200*
    E   *12468*   Peru *20883*

V   *Mouriri floribunda* Markgraf *20883, 18200*
    E   *12468*   Peru *20883*

V   *Mouriri francavillana* Cogniaux *20883*
    I   *20883*   Brazil *20883*
    ?   Brazil - Amapa (Oiapock) *21028*
    ?   Brazil - Amazonas (east) *21028*
    I   *20883*   French Guiana (south-east) *21028*

E   *Mouriri froesii* Morley *20883*
    I   *20883*   Brazil *20883*

R   *Mouriri gardneri* Triana *20883*
    I   *20883*   Brazil *20883*

V   *Mouriri gonavensis* Urban & Ekman *20883*
    I   *20883*   Haiti *20883*

E   *Mouriri gonavensis* Urban & Ekman var.
    gonavensis *20883*
    I   *20883*   Haiti *20883*

V   *Mouriri gonavensis* Urban & Ekman var. *hottensis*
    (Urban & Ekman) Morley *20883*
    I   *20883*   Haiti *20883*

R   *Mouriri helleri* Britt. var. *helleri* *20883*
    I   *20883*   Puerto Rico *20883*

R   *Mouriri helleri* Britt. var. *samanensis* (Urban)
    Morley *20883*
    I   *20883*   Dominican Republic *20883*

E   *Mouriri lancifolia* Urban & Ekman *20883*
    I   *20883*   Haiti *20883*

R   *Mouriri longifolia* (H. B. K.) Morley *20883*
    I   *20883*   Venezuela *20883*

R   *Mouriri maestralis* Urban *5607*
    R   *19105*   Cuba (Granma; Santiago de Cuba) *5607*

E   *Mouriri megasperma* Morley *20883*
    I   *20883*   Brazil *20883*

E   *Mouriri micradenia* Ducke *20883*
    I   *20883*   Brazil *20883*

E   *Mouriri micranthera* Morley *20883*

I	20883	Colombia	20883

E   *Mouriri monopora* Morley 20883
   I   20883   Brazil   20883

R   *Mouriri muelleri* Cogniaux 20883, 9842
   I   20883   Mexico   20883

R   *Mouriri myrtilloides* **ssp.** *myrtilloides* 20883
   I   20883   Haiti   20883
   I   20883   Jamaica   20883

V   *Mouriri myrtilloides* **ssp.** *orinocensis*
    Morley 20883
   I   20883   Colombia   20883
   I   20883   Venezuela   20883

E   *Mouriri obtusiloba* Morley 20883
   I   20883   Brazil   20883

E   *Mouriri pachyphylla* Burret 20883
   I   20883   Colombia   20883

E   *Mouriri panamensis* Morley 20883, 9842
   V   16360   Panama   20883

R   *Mouriri peruviana* Morley 20883
   I   20883   Peru   20883

R   *Mouriri pranceana* Morley 20883
   I   20883   Brazil   20883

E   *Mouriri regeliana* Cogniaux 20883
   I   20883   Brazil   20883

R   *Mouriri spathulata* **var.** *brachypoda* (Urban & Ekman)
    Morley 20883
   I   20883   Dominican Republic   20883
   I   20883   Haiti   20883

R   *Mouriri spathulata* **var.** *spathulata* 20883
   I   20883   Cuba   20883

V   *Mouriri steyermarkii* Standley ex Standley &
    Steyermark 20883, 9004
   V   9836   Guatemala   20883

E   *Mouriri tessmannii* Markgraf 20883, 18200
   E   12468   Peru   20883

R   *Mouriri torquata* Morley 20883
   I   20883   Brazil   20883

R   *Mouriri uncitheca* Morley & Wurdack 20883
   I   20883   Venezuela   20883

R   *Mouriri valenzuelana* A. Richard 20883
   I   20883   Cuba   20883

E   *Mouriri viridicosta* Morley 20883
   I   20883   French Guiana   20883

I   *Osbeckia aspera* (L.) Blume
   I   India - Kerala (Travancore coast)

I   *Osbeckia lawsoni* Gamble
   I   India - Kerala

I   *Osbeckia porteresii* Jacq.-Fel. 7926
   I   Guinea 7926

I   *Osbeckia stellata* Buch. Ham. ex Ker-Gawler var.
    hispidissima (Wight) Hansen
   I   India - Andhra Pradesh (Vizakapatanam District)
   I   India - Karnataka (Wostara)
   I   India - Orissa (Ganjam Hills)

I   *Osbeckia travancorica* Beddome ex Gamble
   I   India - Kerala (lower hills, Travancore)

R   *Ossaea asplundii* Wurdack 11351
   R   19558   Ecuador   11351

V   *Ossaea baracoensis* Borh. & Muniz 5607

   V   19105   Cuba (Holguin; Guantanamo)   5607

R   *Ossaea boekei* Wurdack 11351
   R   19558   Ecuador   11351

E   *Ossaea costata* Urban 5607
   E   19105   Cuba (Guantanamo)   5607

V   *Ossaea elliptica* Alain 5607
   V   19105   Cuba (Guantanamo)   5607

E   *Ossaea filisepala* Urban 5607
   E   19105   Cuba (Guantanamo)   5607

V   *Ossaea heterotricha* (Griseb.) C. Wright 5607
   V   19105   Cuba (Guantanamo)   5607

I   *Ossaea hirtella* (Sw.) Triana 20883, 13336
   I   13336   Jamaica   20883

E   *Ossaea hypoglauca* (C. Wright) M. Gomez
   E   19105   Cuba   19105

E   *Ossaea krugiana* Cogn. 20883
   I   20883   Puerto Rico   20883

R   *Ossaea micarensis* Urban 5607
   R   19105   Cuba (Santiago de Cuba)   5607

E   *Ossaea neurotricha* C. Wright 5607
   E   19105   Cuba (Guantanamo)   5607

V   *Ossaea palenquinsis* Wurdack 11351
   V   19558   Ecuador   11351

R   *Ossaea pulchra* Alain 5607
   R   19105   Cuba (Guantanamo)   5607

R   *Ossaea rubescens* (Triana) Cogn. 19558
   R   19558   Ecuador   19558

R   *Ossaea sparrei* Wurdack 11351
   R   19558   Ecuador   11351

R   *Ossaea wilsoni* Alain 5607
   R   19105   Cuba (Guantanamo)   5607

E   *Pachyanthus clementis* P. Wilson 5607
   E   19105   Cuba (Sancti Spiritus)   5607

E   *Pachyanthus lunanus* Britton & P. Wilson 5607
   E   19105   Cuba   5607

E   *Pachyanthus oleifolius* Griseb. 5607
   E   19105   Cuba (SC; Ho; Gu)   5607

E   *Pachyanthus tetramerus* Urban & Ekman 5607
   E   19105   Cuba (Pinar del Rio)   5607

E   *Phyllagathis magnifica* A. Weber 11926
   E   Malaysia - Peninsular Malaysia (Genting
    Highlands) 11926

E   *Phyllagathis stonei* A. Weber 11925
   E   Malaysia - Peninsular Malaysia (Genting Highlands;
    Gombak) 11925

R   *Pilocosta campanensis* (Almeda & Whiffin)
    Almeda 21289
   R   21300   Panama   21289

R   *Pilocosta erythrophylla* (Gleason) Almeda &
    Whiffin 9835
   R   9836   Costa Rica   9835

R   *Plethiandra sessiliflora* Ridley
   R   Malaysia - Peninsular Malaysia (Selangor)
   Ex   20099   Singapore   20099

I   *Primularia pulchella* Brenan 5926
   I   5926   Tanzania   5926

R   *Rhexia aristosa* Britt. 20850
   E   20850   U.S. - Alabama   20850
   V   20850   U.S. - Delaware   20850

V	20850	U.S. - Georgia	20850
I	20850	U.S. - Maryland	20850
E	20850	U.S. - New Jersey	20850
R	20850	U.S. - North Carolina	20850
V	20850	U.S. - South Carolina	20850
I	20850	U.S. - Virginia	20850

V *Rhexia parviflora* Chapman *20850*

E	20850	U.S. - Alabama	20850
V	20850	U.S. - Florida	20850
I	20850	U.S. - Georgia	20850

V *Rhexia salicifolia* Kral & Bostick *20850*

E	20850	U.S. - Alabama	20850
V	20850	U.S. - Florida	20850

R *Rhynchanthera medialis* Standley & Steyerm. *9004*

R	9835	Guatemala	9004

I *Sonerila barnesii* C. Fischer

I		India - Tamil Nadu (Nadugani, Tirunelveli Hills)

I *Sonerila cordifolia* Cogn. *10252*

I	16162	Sri Lanka	10252

I *Sonerila elegans* Wight

I		India - Tamil Nadu

I *Sonerila firma* (Thwaites) Lundm. *10252*

I	16162	Sri Lanka	10252

I *Sonerila gardneri* Thwaites *10252*

I	16162	Sri Lanka	10252

I *Sonerila lanceolata* Thwaites *10252*

I	16162	Sri Lanka	10252

I *Sonerila nemakadensis* C. Fischer

I		India - Kerala (Travancore)

I *Sonerila pilosula* Thwaites *10252*

I	16162	Sri Lanka	10252

I *Sonerila pulneyensis* Gamble *6295*

I		India - Tamil Nadu *6295*

I *Sonerila robusta* Arn. *10252*

I	16162	Sri Lanka	10252

I *Sonerila siamensis* Nayar *19120*

I	19120	Thailand	19120

I *Sonerila spectabilis* Nayar *19120*

I	19120	Thailand	19120

I *Sonerila tomentella* Thwaites *10252*

I	16162	Sri Lanka	10252

I *Sonerila wightiana* Arn. *10252*

I	16162	Sri Lanka	10252

V *Spathandra barteri* Hook.f. *20274*

V	20858	Tropical Africa (Guinea-wide)	20858
V	20858	Ghana	20274

E *Tessmannianthus carinatus* Almeda *20883*

I	20883	Panama	20883

E *Tessmannianthus gordonii* Almeda *20883*

I	20883	Panama	20883

V *Tessmannianthus panamensis* Almeda *14292*

V	16317	Panama	14292

V *Tetrazygia albicans* (D. Don ex Naud.) Triana *20883, 13336*

V	13336	Jamaica	20883

E *Tetrazygia aurea* Howard & Briggs *5607*

E	19105	Cuba (Sancti Spiritus)	5607

V *Tetrazygia elegans* Urban *5607*

V	19105	Cuba (SC; Gu)	5607

V *Tetrazygiopsis ekmanii* (Urban) Borh. *5607*

V	19105	Cuba (Granma)	5607

R *Tibouchina andersonii* Wurdack *11351*

R	19558	Ecuador	11351

R *Tibouchina campii* Wurdack *11351*

R	19558	Ecuador	11351

V *Tibouchina chamaecistus* (Naudin) Cogn. *5710*

V	5710	Martinique	5710

R *Tibouchina gleasoniana* Wurdack *11351*

R	19558	Ecuador	11351

R *Tibouchina inopinata* Wurdack *9836*

R	9836	Costa Rica	9836
R	9835	Panama	10747

R *Tibouchina oroensis* Gleason *11351*

R	19558	Ecuador	11351

I *Tococa broadwayi* Urb. *5932*

I	5932	Trinidad & Tobago (Tobago)	5932

E *Tococa croatii* Almeda *20883*

I	20883	Panama	20883

R *Topobea acuminata* Wurdack *19558*

R	19558	Ecuador	19558

R *Topobea aeruginosa* (Standley) L.O. Williams *9529*

R	9835	Honduras	9529
V	11967	Nicaragua	9529

R *Topobea brenesii* Standley *9037*

R	9836	Costa Rica	9037

R *Topobea brevibractea* Gleason *11351*

R	19558	Ecuador	11351

R *Topobea calophylla* Almeda *10747*

R	9835	Panama	10747

R *Topobea caudata* Wurdack *19558*

R	19558	Ecuador	19558

E *Topobea cooperi* Gleason *20883, 9006*

E	9835	Panama	20883

E *Topobea cordata* Gleason *20883, 9006*

V	9835	Panama	20883

R *Topobea cutucuensis* Wurdack *11351*

R	19558	Ecuador	11351

R *Topobea eplingii* Wurdack *11351*

R	19558	Ecuador	11351

R *Topobea induta* Markgraf *11351*

R	19558	Ecuador	11351

R *Topobea macbrydei* Wurdack *11351*

R	19558	Ecuador	11351

R *Topobea maguirei* Wurdack *11351*

R	19558	Ecuador	11351

E *Topobea pluvialis* Standl. *20883, 9006*

V	9835	Panama	20883

E *Topobea regeliana* Cogn. *20883, 9006*

I	20883	Panama	20883

R *Topobea standleyi* L.O. Williams *9004*

R	9835	Guatemala	9004

R *Topobea toachiensis* Wurdack *11351*

R	19558	Ecuador	11351

R *Topobea verrucosa* Wurdack *11351*

R	19558	Ecuador	11351

R *Triolena asplundii* Wurdack *11351*

R	19558	Ecuador	11351

V *Triolena calciphila* (Standley & Steyerm.) Standley & L.O.

Williams *9004*

    V   *9836* Guatemala *9004*

V *Triolena izabalensis* Standley & Steyerm. *9004*

    V   *9836* Guatemala *9004*

R *Triolena pedomontana* Wurdack *11351*

    R   *19558* Ecuador *11351*

R *Triolena pustulata* Triana *11351*

    R   *19558* Ecuador *11351*

V *Triolena roseiflora* (Standley & Steyerm.) Standley & L.O. Williams *9004*

    V   *9836* Guatemala *9004*

V *Triolena stenophylla* (Standley & Steyerm.) Standley & L.O. Williams *9004*

    V   *9836* Guatemala *9004*

V *Tristemma schliebenii* Markgraf *7959*

    V   *5926* Tanzania (Rufyi Distr.) *7959*

R *Votomita guianensis* Aublet *20883*

    I   *20883* French Guiana *20883*

    ?   Guyana (Pakaraima Mts.) *21028*

    I   *20883* Suriname (east) *21028*

E *Votomita monadelpha* (Ducke) Morley *20883*

    I   *20883* Brazil *20883*

R *Votomita monantha* (Urban) Morley *20883*

    I   *20883* Cuba *20883*

E *Votomita orbinaxia* Morley *20883*

    I   *20883* Brazil *20883*

E *Votomita orinocensis* Morley *20883*

    I   *20883* Venezuela *20883*

E *Votomita plerocarpa* (Morley) Morley *20883*

    I   *20883* Brazil *20883*

E *Votomita pubescens* Morley *20883*

    I   *20883* Peru *20883*

I *Warneckea memecyloides* (Benth.) H.Jacques-Felix *10260*

    V   *20858* Cameroon *18326*

    V   *20858* Côte d'Ivoire *18326*

    I   *7927* Gabon *7927*

    V   *20858* Ghana *20274*

    V   *20858* Nigeria *18326*

Meliaceae

Number of genera: 51
Number of species: 550
Recorded threatened species: 109 (19%)

Tropical and subtropical; some in temperate regions.

V *Aglaia iloilo* (Blanco) Merr. *13780*

    V   *15960* Philippines *13780*

V *Amoora dasyclada* (How & T. Chen) C.Y. Wu *17617*

    V   *17617* China - Hainan Is. *11139*

    V   *17617* China - Yunnan (Xishuangbanna) *11139*

V *Aphanamixis cumingiana* (C. DC.) Harms. *13780*

    V   *15960* Philippines *13780*

R *Cabralea canjerana* ssp. *polytricha* Adr. Jussieu *20883*

    I   *20883* Brazil *20883*

    ?   Brazil - Goias *9843*

    ?   Brazil - Minas Gerais *9843*

R *Cedrela montana* Moritz ex Turcz. *20883*

    I   *20883* Colombia *20883*

    I   *20883* Ecuador *20883*

    I   *20883* Peru *20883*

    I   *20883* Venezuela *20883*

V *Cedrela oaxacensis* C. de Candolle & Rose *20883, 9004*

    V   *20883* Mexico *20883*

    R   *19801* Mexico - Oaxaca *9004*

E *Cedrela weberbaueri* Harms *19965*

    E   *20041* Peru *19965*

I *Dysoxylum angustifolium* Merr. *13833*

    I   *13833* Philippines (Palawan) *13833*

I *Dysoxylum beddomei* Hiern

    I   India - Kerala (Peermade & Cardomom Hills)

I *Dysoxylum ficiforme* (Wight) Gamble

    I   India - Kerala (Koni & Ranni valleys)

R *Dysoxylum kuskusense* (Hayata) Kaneh. & Hatus.

    R   Taiwan (Heng-ch'un Pen., Lan Yu)

R *Dysoxylum pachyphyllum* Hemsley

    R   *14225* Australia - NSW - Lord Howe Is. *14225*

E *Dysoxylum pachypodum* (Baillon) C.DC. *20893*

    E   *20893* New Caledonia *20893*

I *Dysoxylum palawanensis* Merr. *13833*

    I   *13833* Philippines (low altitude) *13833*

V *Dysoxylum patersonianum* (Endl.) Maiden

    V   *14225* Australia - Norfolk Is. *14288*

E *Dysoxylum peerisi* Kosterm. *12838*

    E   *12838* Sri Lanka *12838*

V *Dysoxylum turczaninowii* C. DC. *13780*

    V   *15960* Philippines *13780*

E *Guarea carapoides* Harms *20883*

    E   *20883* Peru *20883*

E *Guarea cartaguenya* Cuatrecasas *20883*

    I   *20883* Colombia *20883*

    I   *20883* Ecuador *20883*

E *Guarea casimiriana* Harms *20883*

    E   *20883* Peru *20883*

E *Guarea caulobotrys* Cuatrecasas *20883*

    I   *20883* Colombia *20883*

V *Guarea convergens* Pennington *20883*

    V   *20883* Brazil *20883*

    ?   Brazil - Amazonas *9843*

E *Guarea corrugata* Cuatrecasas *20883*

    E   *20883* Colombia *20883*

E *Guarea costata* Adr. Jussieu *20883*

    E   *20883* French Guiana *20883*

    E   *20883* Suriname *20883*

E *Guarea crispa* Pennington *20883*

    E   *20883* Brazil *20883*

    ?   Brazil - Amazonas *9843*

V *Guarea cristata* Pennington *20883*

    I   *20883* Brazil *20883*

    I   *20883* Peru *20883*

R *Guarea guentheri* Harms *20883*

    I   *20883* Brazil *20883*

    I   *20883* Peru *20883*

R *Guarea humaitensis* Pennington *20883*

    R   *20883* Brazil *20883*

V *Guarea jamaicensis* Proctor *20883, 13336*

    V   *13336* Jamaica *20883*

R *Guarea juglandiformis* Pennington *20883*

    I   *20883* Brazil *20883*

    ?   Brazil - Acre *9843*

    I   *20883* Peru *20883*

V   *Guarea macropetala* Penning. *20883, 10747*
     I   *20883* Panama *20883*

R   *Guarea macrophylla* Vahl ssp.
       macrophylla 20883
     I   *20883 20883*
     I   *20883* Antigua & Barbuda *20883*
     I   *20883* Dominica *20883*
     I   *20883* Guadeloupe *20883*
     I   *20883* Grenada *20883*
     I   *20883* Martinique *20883*
     I   *20883* Montserrat *20883*
     I   *20883* St Vincent *20883*
     I   *20883* USA - Virgin Is. *20883*

V   *Guarea polymera* Little *20883*
     I   *20883* Colombia *20883*
     I   *20883* Ecuador *20883*

E   *Guarea pyriformis* Pennington *20883, 9843*
     E   *20883* Costa Rica *20883*

E   *Guarea sphenophylla* Urban *20883*
     E   *20883* Dominican Republic (La Ho, Nalga de Maco)
         21008
     E   *20883* Haiti (Grand Bois, Morne Formon) *21008*

E   *Guarea sprucei* C. de Candolle *20883*
     E   *20883* Brazil *20883*
     ?   Brazil - Amazonas *9843*

R   *Guarea trunciflora* C. de Candolle *20883*
     I   *20883* Brazil *20883*
     ?   Brazil - Amazonas *9843*
     ?   Brazil - Pará *9843*
     I   *20883* Peru *20883*

R   *Guarea velutina* Adr. Jussieu *20883*
     V   *20883* Brazil *20883*
     ?   Brazil - Amazonas *9843*
     ?   Brazil - Pará *9843*
     ?   Brazil - Roraima *9843*

R   *Guarea venenata* Pennington *20883*
     I   *20883* Brazil *20883*
     ?   Brazil - Amazonas *9843*
     I   *20883* Colombia *20883*

I   *Munronia palawanensis* (Merr.) Harms *13833*
     I   *13833* Philippines (Palawan) *13833*

V   *Owenia cepiodora* F.Muell. *20681*
     I   *20681* Australia - New South Wales *20681*
     I   *20681* Australia - Queensland *20681*

V   *Pseudocarapa championii* Hemsley *10276*
     V   *12838* Sri Lanka *10276*

R   *Ruagea hirsuta* (C. DC) Harms *20883*
     I   *20883* Bolivia *20883*
     I   *20883* Colombia *20883*
     I   *20883* Ecuador *20883*
     I   *20883* Peru *20883*

E   *Ruagea ovalis* (Rusby) Harms *20883*
     E   *20883* Bolivia *20883*

V   *Sandoricum vidalii* Merr. *13780*
     V   *15960* Philippines *13780*

V   *Schmardaea microphylla* (Hooker) Karsten ex C.
       Mueller *20883*
     I   *20883* Colombia *20883*
     I   *20883* Ecuador *20883*
     I   *20883* Peru *20883*
     I   *20883* Venezuela *20883*

V   *Trichilia acuminata* (Humb. & Bonpl. ex Roemer & Schultes) C.
       de Candolle *20883*
     I   *20883* Panama *20883*
     I   *20883* Colombia *20883*

I   *Trichilia adolfi* Harms *20883, 9843*
     I   *20883* Costa Rica *20883*

R   *Trichilia appendiculata* C. de Candolle *20883*
     I   *20883* Colombia *20883*

R   *Trichilia aquifolia* P. Wilson *20883*
     I   *20883* Dominican Republic (Baní to Barahona, Isla
         Beata) *21008*
     I   *20883* Haiti (central, Isla Tortuga) *21008*

V   *Trichilia areolata* Pennington *20883*
     V   *20883* Brazil *20883*
     ?   Brazil - Amazonas *9843*
     ?   Brazil - Pará *9843*

E   *Trichilia blanchetii* C. DC. *20883*
     E   *20883* Brazil *20883*
     ?   Brazil - Bahia *9843*

V   *Trichilia breviflora* Blake & Standley *20883*
     I   *20883* Belize *20883*
     I   *20883* Guatemala *20883*
     I   *20883* Honduras *20883*

R   *Trichilia bullata* Pennington *20883*
     R   *20883* Brazil *20883*
     ?   Brazil - Amazonas *9843*

R   *Trichilia casaretti* C. de Candolle *20883*
     I   *20883* Brazil *20883*
     ?   Brazil - Bahia *9843*
     ?   Brazil - Minas Gerais *9843*
     ?   Brazil - Rio de Janeiro *9843*
     ?   Brazil - Santa Catarina *9843*
     ?   Brazil - Sao Paulo *9843*

E   *Trichilia chirriactensis* (Standley & Steyermark)
       Pennington *20883, 9843*
     R   *19801* Guatemala *20883*

E   *Trichilia discolor* Adr. Jussieu *20883*
     E   *20883* Brazil *20883*
     ?   Brazil - Pará *9843*

V   *Trichilia elsae* Harms *20883*
     V   *20883* Brazil *20883*
     ?   Brazil - Acre *9843*

R   *Trichilia emarginata* (Turczaninov) C. DC. *20883*
     V   *20883* Brazil *20883*
     ?   Brazil - Acre *9843*
     ?   Brazil - Bahia *9843*
     ?   Brazil - Minas Gerais *9843*
     ?   Brazil - Pará *9843*
     ?   Brazil - Rio de Janeiro *9843*
     ?   Brazil - Roraima *9843*
     ?   Brazil - Sao Paulo *9843*

R   *Trichilia erythrocarpa* Lundell *20883*
     I   *20883* Belize *20883*
     I   *20883* Guatemala *20883*
     I   *20883* Mexico *20883*
     I   *20883* Peru *20883*

R   *Trichilia fasciculata* Pennington *20883*
     V   *20883* Brazil *20883*

E   *Trichilia florbranca* Pennington *20883*
     E   *20883* Brazil *20883*
     ?   Brazil - Bahia *9843*

E   *Trichilia gamopetala* Pennington *20883*
     E   *20883* Venezuela *20883*

V   *Trichilia hispida* Pennington *20883*
     I   *20883* Brazil *20883*
     ?   Brazil - Amazonas *9843*
     I   *20883* Peru *20883*

E   *Trichilia laxipaniculata* Cuatrecasas *20883*
     I   *20883* Colombia *20883*

	I	*20883*	Ecuador *20883*
R	*Trichilia lecointei* ducke *20883*		
	I	*20883*	Brazil *20883*
	?		Brazil - Pará *9843*
	I	*20883*	Guyana *20883*
R	*Trichilia lepidota* Martius *20883*		
	I	*20883*	Brazil *20883*
	I	*20883*	Suriname *20883*
	I	*20883*	Venezuela *20883*
V	*Trichilia lepidota* Martius ssp. *lepidota* *20883*		
	V	*20883*	Brazil *20883*
	?		Brazil - Bahia *9843*
R	*Trichilia lepidota* Martius ssp. *leucastera* (Sandwith) Pennington *20883*		
	I	*20883*	Guyana *20883*
	I	*20883*	Suriname *20883*
	I	*20883*	Venezuela *20883*
R	*Trichilia lepidota* Martius ssp. *schumanniana* (Harms) Pennington *20883*		
	R	*20883*	Brazil *20883*
	?		Brazil - Minas Gerais *9843*
	?		Brazil - Parana *9843*
	?		Brazil - Rio de Janeiro *9843*
	?		Brazil - Rio Grande do Sul *9843*
	?		Brazil - Santa Catarina *9843*
	?		Brazil - Sao Paulo *9843*
R	*Trichilia magnifoliola* Pennington *20883*		
	R	*20883*	Brazil *20883*
	?		Brazil - Bahia *9843*
	?		Brazil - Espirito Santo *9843*
	?		Brazil - Minas Gerais *9843*
R	*Trichilia maynasiana* ssp. *lanceolata* (C. DC.) Pennington *20883*		
	I	*20883*	Colombia *20883*
	I	*20883*	Peru *20883*
R	*Trichilia micropetala* Pennington *20883*		
	I	*20883*	Brazil *20883*
	?		Brazil - Amapa *9843*
	?		Brazil - Pará *9843*
R	*Trichilia minutiflora* Standley *20883, 10397*		
	I	*20883*	Belize *20883*
	I	*20883*	Guatemala *20883*
	I	*20883*	Mexico *20883*
	?		Mexico - Quintana Roo *10397*
E	*Trichilia monacantha* Urban *20883*		
	E	*20883*	Dominican Republic (Santiago) *21008*
R	*Trichilia moschata* ssp. *matudai* (Lundell) Pennington *20883*		
	I	*20883*	Guatemala *20883*
	I	*20883*	Mexico *20883*
V	*Trichilia ornithothera* J.J.De Wilde *20274*		
	V	*20858*	Côte d'Ivoire *20274*
	V	*20858*	Ghana *20274*
V	*Trichilia pachypoda* (Rusby) C. de Candolle ex Harms *20883, 19961*		
	I	*20883*	Bolivia *20883*
	V	*19961*	Peru *20883*
R	*Trichilia pallens* C. de Candolle *20883*		
	R	*20883*	Brazil *20883*
	?		Brazil - Minas Gerais *9843*
	?		Brazil - Parana *9843*
	?		Brazil - Rio de Janeiro *9843*
	?		Brazil - Rio Grande do Sul *9843*
	?		Brazil - Santa Catarina *9843*
	?		Brazil - Sao Paulo *9843*
	R	*20883*	Paraguay *20883*
R	*Trichilia pallida* Sw. *19890*		
	V	*19890*	Jamaica *19890*
	R	*19890*	Puerto Rico *19890*
V	*Trichilia pittieri* C. DC. *20883, 9843*		
	V	*20883*	Costa Rica *20883*
R	*Trichilia pseudostipularis* (A. Juss.) C. de Candolle *20883*		
	R	*20883*	Brazil *20883*
	?		Brazil - Bahia *9843*
	?		Brazil - Espirito Santo *9843*
	?		Brazil - Rio de Janeiro *9843*
	?		Brazil - Santa Catarina *9843*
V	*Trichilia pungens* Urban *20883, 5607*		
	E	*20883*	Cuba (Camaguey, Las Tunas, Holguin) *20883*
R	*Trichilia ramalhoi* Rizzini, Leandra *20883*		
	R	*20883*	Brazil *20883*
	?		Brazil - Bahia *9843*
	?		Brazil - Ceara *9843*
	?		Brazil - Espirito Santo *9843*
R	*Trichilia reticulata* P. Wilson *20883*		
	R	*20883*	Jamaica *20883*
R	*Trichilia schomburgkii* ssp. *javariensis* *20883*		
	I	*20883*	Brazil *20883*
	?		Brazil - Amazonas *9843*
	?		Brazil - Pará *9843*
	I	*20883*	Colombia *20883*
R	*Trichilia silvatica* C. DC. *20883*		
	R	*20883*	Brazil *20883*
	?		Brazil - Bahia *9843*
	?		Brazil - Espirito Santo *9843*
	?		Brazil - Rio de Janeiro *9843*
	?		Brazil - Santa Catarina *9843*
	?		Brazil - Sao Paulo *9843*
R	*Trichilia solitudinis* Harms *20883*		
	I	*20883*	Brazil *20883*
	?		Brazil - Pará *9843*
	?		Brazil - Roraima *9843*
	I	*20883*	Peru *20883*
R	*Trichilia stellato-tomentosa* Kuntze *20883*		
	I	*20883*	Argentina *20883*
	I	*20883*	Bolivia *20883*
	I	*20883*	Brazil *20883*
	?		Brazil - Mato Grosso do Sul *9843*
	R	*20883*	Paraguay *20883*
E	*Trichilia stenophylla* Urban & Ekman *20883*		
	E	*20883*	Haiti (Môle St. Nicolas to Bombarde (NW)) *21008*
V	*Trichilia stipitata* Pennington *20883*		
	I	*20883*	Colombia *20883*
	I	*20883*	Peru *20883*
V	*Trichilia surumuensis* C. de Candolle *20883*		
	V	*20883*	Brazil *20883*
	?		Brazil - Roraima *9843*
	I	*20883*	Guyana *20883*
V	*Trichilia tetrapetala* C. DC. *20883*		
	V	*20883*	Brazil *20883*
	?		Brazil - Espirito Santo *9843*
	?		Brazil - Rio de Janeiro *9843*
R	*Trichilia tomentosa* H.B.K. *20883*		
	I	*20883*	Mexico *20883*
	I	*20883*	Panama *20883*
	I	*20883*	Bolivia *20883*
	I	*20883*	Peru *20883*
V	*Trichilia trachyantha* C. de Candolle *20883, 11840*		

V   *20883* Cuba (Oriente; Las Villas) *20883*

E   ***Trichilia triacantha*** Urban *20883, 10197*

    E   *20883* Puerto Rico *20883*

V   ***Trichilia trifolia*** ssp. ***palmeri*** (C. de Candolle)
    Pennington *20883*

    V   *20883* Mexico *20883*

E   ***Trichilia trifolia*** ssp. ***pteleaefolia*** (Adr. Jussieu)
    Pennington *20883*

    E   *20883* Brazil *20883*
    ?   Brazil - Minas Gerais *9843*
    ?   Brazil - Rio de Janeiro *9843*

E   ***Trichilia ulei*** C. de Candolle *20883*

    I   *20883* Peru *20883*

V   ***Turraea adjanohounii*** Aké Assi *20887*

    V   *20887* Côte d'Ivoire (south-west) *20887*

R   ***Turraea casimiriana*** Harms *19421*

    R   *10082* Réunion *10082*
    R   *20771* Mauritius (Ile aux Aigrettes) *10082*

R   ***Turraea cornucopia*** White & Styles *20057*

    R   *20057* Kenya *20057*

E   ***Turraea decandra*** (Cav.) Harms *10082*

    Ex   *14220* Réunion *14220*
    E   *20771* Mauritius *10082*

V   ***Turraea fischeri*** Gurke ssp. ***eylesii*** (Baker f.)
    Styles & White *7749*

    V   *20909* Zimbabwe (Matopos Hills) *20909*

E   ***Turraea ghanensis*** J.B. Hall *6072*

    E   *6072* Ghana *6072*

V   ***Turraea kimbozensis*** Cheek *20556*

    V   *20885* Tanzania (Morogoro District) *20556*

E   ***Turraea laciniata*** (Balf.f.) Harms *10082*

    E   *5852* Mauritius - Rodrigues *5852*

R   ***Turraea oppositifolia*** (Cav.) Harms *10082*

    E   *14220* Réunion *14220*
    R   *20771* Mauritius *10082*

I   ***Turraea pulchella*** (Harms) T.D.Penn. *20604*

    I   *20604* South Africa - Cape Province *20604*
    V   *20604* South Africa - Natal *20604*

E   ***Turraea rigida*** Vent. *10082*

    E   *20771* Mauritius *10082*

V   ***Turraea streyi*** F.White & Styles *20604*

    V   *20604* South Africa - Natal *20604*

E   ***Turraea trichopoda*** (Baillon) Harms *10082*

    E   *20771* Mauritius *10082*

V   ***Walsura gardneri*** Thwaites *12838*

    V   *12838* Sri Lanka *12838*

Melianthaceae

Number of genera: 2
Number of species: 8-36
Recorded threatened species: 2 (9%)

Africa.

I   ***Bersama rosea*** Hoyle *5926*

    I   *5926* Tanzania *5926*

V   ***Bersama swynnertonii*** Baker f. *7749*

    V   *20909* Zimbabwe *7749*

Meliosmaceae

Number of genera: 2
Number of species: 27
Recorded threatened species: 16 (59%)

Tropical and East Asia, tropical America.

I   ***Meliosma abbreviata*** *15229*

    I   *15229* Haiti (La Visite & Macaya National Parks) *15229*

R   ***Meliosma caudata*** Merr. *6057*

    R   Vietnam *6057*

R   ***Meliosma cinerea*** Vidal *6057*

    R   Vietnam *6057*

R   ***Meliosma clemensiorum*** Merr. *6057*

    R   Vietnam *6057*

E   ***Meliosma cordata*** A. Gentry *20883, 10747*

    I   *20883* Panama *20883*

E   ***Meliosma corymbosa*** A. Gentry *20883, 10161*

    V   *11967* Nicaragua *20883*

R   ***Meliosma donnaiensis*** Gagnepain *6057*

    R   Vietnam *6057*

V   ***Meliosma hachijoensis*** Nakai *10572*

    V   *10572* Japan (Isls. Izu) *20626*

E   ***Meliosma hartshornii*** A. Gentry *20883, 10161*

    I   *20883* Costa Rica *20883*

R   ***Meliosma kontumensis*** Vidal *6057*

    R   Vietnam *6057*

E   ***Meliosma linearifolia*** A. Gentry *20883, 10747*

    I   *20883* Panama *20883*

R   ***Meliosma longipes*** Merr. *6057*

    R   Vietnam *6057*

V   ***Meliosma nanarum*** A. Gentry *20883, 10161*

    V   *11967* Nicaragua *20883*

V   ***Meliosma peytonii*** A. Gentry *20883*

    I   *20883* Peru *20883*

E   ***Meliosma solomonii*** A. Gentry *20883*

    I   *20883* Bolivia *20883*

E   ***Meliosma vasquezii*** A. Gentry *20883*

    I   *20883* Peru *20883*

Menispermaceae

Number of genera: 70
Number of species: 400
Recorded threatened species: 38 (9%)

Tropical and subtropical.

I   ***Albertisia mecistophylla*** (Miers) Forman *14782*

    I   *14782* India - Assam *14782*
    I   *14782* India - Meghalaya *14782*

I   ***Albertisia puberula*** Forman *19120*

    I   *19120* Thailand *19120*

E   ***Carronia pedicellata*** Forman *20681*

    E   *20681* Australia - Queensland *20681*

I   ***Cissampelos hispida*** Forman *19120*

    I   *19120* Thailand (Chiang Mai) *19120*

I   ***Cissampelos nigrescens*** Diels var. ***cardiophylla***
    Troupin *5926*

    I   *5926* Tanzania *5926*

E   ***Cissampelos reticulata*** Borh. *5607*

E   *19105*   Cuba (Guantanamo) *5607*

I   **Cissampelos rigidifolia (Engl.) Diels var. lanuginosa** Troupin *5926*
    I   *5926*   Tanzania *5926*

R   **Coscinium fenestratum (Gaertn) Coleb.** *16162*
    E   *20263*   India *20263*
    V   *20985*   Vietnam *20985*
    R   *20099*   Singapore *20099*
    I   *16162*   Sri Lanka *16162*

R   **Cyclea aphylla** Gagnepain *6057*
    R   Vietnam *6057*

I   **Cyclea debiliflora** Miers *14782*
    I   *14782*   India - Meghalaya *14782*

E   **Cyclea fissicalyx** Dunn *14782*
    E   *20263*   India - Kerala (Wynnad, Malabar) *14782*

I   **Cyclea watti** Diels *14782*
    I   *14782*   India - Nagaland *14782*

R   **Elephantomene eburnea** Barneby & Krukoff *8679*
    R   French Guiana *8679*

E   **Eleutharrhena macrocarpa** (Diels) Forman *17617*
    E   *17617*   China - Yunnan (Jinghong, Xishuangbanna) *17617*

I   **Epinetrum apiculatum** Troupin *7959*
    I   *5926*   Tanzania (Usambara Mts.) *7959*

V   **Epinetrum cordifolium** Mangenot & Miege *7926*
    V   Côte d'Ivoire *7926*

V   **Epinetrum mangenotii** Guillaumet & Debray
    V   Côte d'Ivoire (Bas-Cavally)

E   **Hyperbaena acutifolia** Britton *5607*
    E   *19105*   Cuba (Sancti Spiritus) *5607*

E   **Hyperbaena allenii** Standl. *20883, 9006*
    I   *20883*   Panama *20883*

I   **Hyperbaena macrophylla** Ekman *5607*
    I   *19105*   Cuba (Santiago de Cuba) *5607*

Ex   **Hyperbaena obovata** Urban *5607*
    Ex   *19105*   Cuba (Holguin; Guantanamo) *5607*

E   **Hyperbaena ovata** Urban *5607*
    E   *19105*   Cuba (Sancti Spiritus) *5607*

E   **Hyperbaena paucinervis** Urban *5607*
    E   *19105*   Cuba (Santiago de Cuba) *5607*

R   **Hyperbaena prioriana** Miers *20883*
    R   *20883*   Jamaica *20883*

E   **Hyperbaena valida** Miers *20883*
    E   *20883*   Jamaica *20883*

R   **Hypserpa smilacifolia** Diels *20681*
    R   *20681*   Australia - Queensland *20681*

R   **Pericampylus trinervatus** Yamoto *20511*
    R   *20511*   Taiwan *20511*

I   **Pycnarrhena elliptica** Diels. *13833*
    I   *13833*   Philippines (low altitude) *13833*

I   **Rhigiocarya peltata** Miege *7926*
    I   *19264*   Côte d'Ivoire *7926*

I   **Stephania andamanica** Diels *7771*
    I   *14782*   India - Andaman Is. (South Andaman Island) *7771*

I   **Stephania creba** Forman *19120*
    I   *19120*   Thailand *19120*

I   **Stephania papillosa** Craib *19120*
    I   *19120*   Thailand *19120*

I   **Stephania suberosa** Forman
    I   *19120*   Thailand *19120*

I   **Stephania tomentella** Forman *19120*
    I   *19120*   Thailand *19120*

R   **Tiliacora australiana** Forman *20681*
    I   *20681*   Australia - Northern Territory *20681*
    I   *20681*   Australia - Queensland *20681*

I   **Tinospora andamanica** Diels *7771*
    I   India - Andaman Is. *7771*

R   **Tinospora dentata** Diels *20511*
    R   *20511*   Taiwan *20511*

I   **Tinospora siamensis** Forman *19120*
    I   *19120*   Thailand *19120*

R   **Tinospora tinosporoides** (F.Muell.) Forman *20681*
    I   *20681*   Australia - New South Wales *20681*
    I   *20681*   Australia - Queensland *20681*

Menyanthaceae

Number of genera: 5
Number of species: 30-35
Recorded threatened species: 6   (18%)

Cosmopolitan.

E   **Nymphoides ekmanii** (Urban) Alain *5607*
    E   *19105*   Cuba (Juventud Is.) *5607*

I   **Nymphoides hastata** (Pierre) Kerr *19120*
    I   *19120*   Thailand *19120*

R   **Nymphoides planosperma** H.I.Aston *20681*
    R   *20681*   Australia - Northern Territory *20681*

V   **Villarsia calthifolia** F.Muell. *20681*
    V   *20681*   Australia - Western Australia *20681*

R   **Villarsia marchantii** Ornduff *20681*
    R   *20681*   Australia - Western Australia *20681*

R   **Villarsia submersa** Aston *20681*
    R   *20681*   Australia - Western Australia *20681*

Molluginaceae

Number of genera: 13
Number of species: 100
Recorded threatened species: 12   (12%)

Tropical and subtropical, especially Africa.

I   **Glinus runkewitzii** Tackh. & Boulos
    I   Egypt

V   **Hypertelis acida** (Hook.f.) K. Muller *18996*
    V   *18996*   St Helena *18996*

R   **Macarthuria complanata** E.Ross *20681*
    R   *20681*   Australia - Queensland *20681*

R   **Macarthuria ephedroides** C.White *20681*
    R   *20681*   Australia - Queensland *20681*

V   **Mollugo brevipes** Urban *5607*
    V   *19105*   Cuba (Pinar del Rio) *5607*

V   **Mollugo crockeri** J. Howell *11117*
    V   Ecuador - Galapagos (Santiago) *11117*

V   **Mollugo cubensis** Urban *5607*
    V   *19105*   Cuba (Pinar del Rio) *5607*

E   **Mollugo deltoidea** Leon *5607*
    E   *19105*   Cuba (Holguin) *5607*

E   **Mollugo enneandra** C. Wright *5607*
    E   *19105*   Cuba (Pinar del Rio) *5607*

R   *Mollugo flavescens* Andersson ssp. *insularis* (J.
     Howell) Eliasson *11117*
     R   Ecuador - Galapagos (Floreana; San Cristobal)
        11117

I   *Mollugo flavescens* Andersson ssp. *striata* (J.
     Howell) Eliasson *11117*
     I   Ecuador - Galapagos (Tower; Wolf) *11117*

R   *Mollugo floriana* (Robinson) J. Howell ssp.
     floriana *11117*
     R   Ecuador - Galapagos (Fernadina, Onslow,
        SantaFe) *5670*

R   *Mollugo floriana* (Robinson) J. Howell ssp.
     gypsophiloides J. Howell *11117*
     R   Ecuador - Galapagos (Pinzon) *11117*

I   *Mollugo floriana* (Robinson) J. Howell ssp.
     santacruziana (Christoph.) Eliasson *11117*
     I   Ecuador - Galapagos *11117*

E   *Mollugo pinosia* Urban *5607*
     E   *19105* Cuba (Juventud Is.) *5607*

Monimiaceae

Number of genera: 30-35
Number of species: 450
Recorded threatened species: 23   (5%)

Tropical and subtropical, especially Southern Hemisphere.

V   *Hedycarya aragoensis* Jeremie *20893*
     V   *20893* New Caledonia *20893*

R   *Hedycarya perbracteolata* Jérémie *20893*
     R   *20893* New Caledonia *20893*

V   *Hortonia angustifolia* Trimen *10276*
     V   *12838* Sri Lanka *10276*

E   *Mollinedia darienensis* Standl. *20883, 10747*
     I   *20883* Panama *20883*

R   *Mollinedia gilgiana* Perkins *17079*
     R   *17079* Brazil - Rio de Janeiro (município de Nova
       Friburgo) *17079*

V   *Mollinedia glabra* (Sprengel) Perkins *17079*
     V   *17079* Brazil - Rio de Janeiro (município do Rio de Janeiro,
       município de Macaé) *17079*

E   *Mollinedia lamprophylla* Perkins. *17079*
     E   *17079* Brazil - Rio de Janeiro (Município do Rio de
       Janeiro) *17079*

R   *Mollinedia pallida* Lundell *10299*
     R   *9989* Mexico - Chiapas *10299*

R   *Palmeria hypotephra* (F.Muell.) Domin *20681*
     R   *20681* Australia - Queensland *20681*

R   *Siparuna glabrescens* (Presl) DC. *10199*
     R   *19001* Dominica *10199*
     R   *19001* Martinique (Trace des Jésuites; crétes du
       Cournan) *19001*
     R   *19001* St Vincent *10199*

R   *Siparuna palenquensis* Renner & Hausner *21273*
     R   *21273* Ecuador *21273*

R   *Steganthera australiana* C.White *20681*
     R   *20681* Australia - Queensland *20681*

R   *Tambourissa amplifolia* (Boj. ex Tul.)A. DC. *10082*
     R   *20771* Mauritius *10082*

E   *Tambourissa cocottensis* D. Lorence *10082*
     E   *20771* Mauritius *10082*

R   *Tambourissa cordifolia* D. Lorence *10082*

R   *20771* Mauritius *10082*

R   *Tambourissa crassa* D. Lorence *10082*
     R   *14220* Réunion *10082*

R   *Tambourissa ficus* (Tul.) A. DC. *10082*
     R   *20771* Mauritius *10082*

E   *Tambourissa pedicellata* Baker *10082*
     E   *20771* Mauritius *10082*

V   *Tambourissa quadrifida* Sonn. *10082*
     V   *20771* Mauritius *10082*

V   *Tambourissa sieberi* A. DC. *10082*
     V   *20771* Mauritius *10082*

R   *Tambourissa tau* D. Lorence *10082*
     R   *20771* Mauritius *10082*

E   *Tambourissa tetragona* A. DC. *10082*
     E   *20771* Mauritius *10082*

R   *Wilkiea wardellii* (F.Muell.) Perkins *20681*
     R   *20681* Australia - Queensland *20681*

Montiniaceae

Number of genera: 2
Number of species: 3
Recorded threatened species: 1   (33%)

South Africa, East Africa, Madagascar.

E   *Grevea madagascariensis* Baillon ssp. *keniensis*
     Verdc. *6073*
     E   *6073* Kenya (Kwale) *7959*

Moraceae

Number of genera: 40
Number of species: 1,000
Recorded threatened species: 110   (11%)

Tropical and subtropical.

V   *Artocarpus blancoi* Merrill *12983*
     V   *15960* Philippines *12983*

V   *Artocarpus hypargyreus* Hance ex Benth. *11139*
     V   China - Fujian *11139*
     V   China - Guangdong *11139*
     V   China - Hunan *11139*
     V   China - Jiangxi *11139*
     V   China - Yunnan *11139*

R   *Artocarpus nobilis* Thwaites *8021*
     R   *12838* Sri Lanka *8021*

V   *Artocarpus rubrovenus* Warb. *12983*
     V   *15960* Philippines (Luzon) *20676*

V   *Artocarpus treculianus* Elmer *12983*
     V   *15960* Philippines *12983*

R   *Brosimum acutifolium* ssp. *acutifolium* *20883*
     I   *20883* Brazil *20883*
     ?   Brazil - Amazonas *21022*
     I   *20883* French Guiana *20883*
     I   *20883* Suriname *20883*

R   *Brosimum acutifolium* ssp. *interjectum*
     Berg *20883*
     R   *20883* Brazil *20883*

E   *Brosimum glaucum* Taubert *20883, 17079*
     E   *20883* Brazil *20883*
     R   *17079* Brazil - Minas Gerais *17079*

R   *Brosimum glaziovii* Taubert *17079*
     ?   Brazil *20883*
     I   *21011* Brazil - Parana *21011*

R   *17746*   Brazil - Rio de Janeiro *17079*

R   *17746*   Brazil - Santa Catarina *17079*

I   *21011*   Brazil - Sao Paulo *21011*

R   *Brosimum utile* ssp. *allenii* (Woodson) C.C. Berg *20883*

   I   *20883*   Costa Rica *20883*

V   *Brosimum utile* ssp. *darienense* C.C. Berg *20883, 9990*

   V   *20883*   Panama *20883*

V   *Brosimum utile* ssp. *magdalenense* C.C. Berg *20883*

   V   *20883*   Colombia *20883*

I   *Broussonetia zeylanica* (Thwaites) Corner *8021*

   I   *16162*   Sri Lanka *8021*

R   *Castilla elastica* ssp. *gummifera* (Miquel) Berg *20883*

   I   *20883*   Colombia *20883*

   I   *20883*   Ecuador *20883*

R   *Diplothorax tonkinensis* Gagnepain *6057*

   R   Vietnam *6057*

E   *Dorstenia alberti* Carauta, Valente & Sucre *2383*

   E   *11120*   Brazil - Bahia *2383*

   E   *11120*   Brazil - Espirito Santo *2383*

E   *Dorstenia albertorum* Carauta, Valente & Sucre *16473*

   E   *16473*   Brazil - Bahia *16473*

   E   *16473*   Brazil - Espirito Santo *16473*

   E   *16473*   Brazil - Rio de Janeiro *16473*

V   *Dorstenia amazonica* Carauta & Valente *2383*

   V   *2383*   Brazil - Pará *2383*

E   *Dorstenia appendiculata* Miq. *11120*

   E   *11120*   Brazil (east) *11120*

V   *Dorstenia arifolia* Lam. *17079*

   V   *17746*   Brazil - Espirito Santo *17079*

   V   *17746*   Brazil - Minas Gerais (Manhuaçu) *17079*

   V   *17746*   Brazil - Rio de Janeiro *17079*

   V   *17746*   Brazil - Sao Paulo *17079*

V   *Dorstenia aristeguieta* Cuatuc. *11120*

   V   *11120*   Venezuela *11120*

I   *Dorstenia astyanactis* Ake Assi

   I   Côte d'Ivoire

E   *Dorstenia bahiensis* Klotzsch ex Fisch. & Mey *2383*

   E   *2383*   Brazil - Rio de Janeiro *2383*

R   *Dorstenia belizensis* C.C. Berg *9991*

   R   *11120*   Belize *9991*

E   *Dorstenia boliviana* C.C. Berg *11120*

   E   *11120*   Bolivia *11120*

E   *Dorstenia bonijesu* Carauta & Valente *11120*

   E   *11120*   Brazil (east) *11120*

E   *Dorstenia bowmaniana* Baker *2383*

   E   *11120*   Brazil - Guanabara *16473*

   E   *11120*   Brazil - Rio de Janeiro *16473*

Ex/E   *Dorstenia brevipetiolata* C.C.Berg *11120*

   Ex/E *11120*   Brazil (east) *11120*

E   *Dorstenia carautae* C.C.Berg *11120*

   E   *11120*   Brazil (east) *11120*

E   *Dorstenia cayapia* Vell. *17079*

   E   *17746*   Brazil - Bahia (Porto Seguro) *17079*

   E   *17746*   Brazil - Espirito Santo *17079*

   E   *17746*   Brazil - Minas Gerais *17079*

   E   *17746*   Brazil - Rio de Janeiro *17079*

   E   *17746*   Brazil - Sao Paulo (Aparecida) *17079*

Ex/E   *Dorstenia colombiana* Cuatrec. *11120*

Ex/E *11120*   Colombia *11120*

Ex/E   *Dorstenia conceptionis* Caruata *11120*

   Ex/E *11120*   Brazil (east) *11120*

E   *Dorstenia contensis* Carauta & C.C.Berg *11120*

   E   *11120*   Brazil (east) *11120*

I   *Dorstenia crenulata* C. Wright *5607*

   I   *19105*   Cuba (Guantanamo) *5607*

E   *Dorstenia ekmanii* Urban *5607*

   E   *19105*   Cuba (Cienfuegos; Villa Clara) *5607*

R   *Dorstenia elata* Hook. *17079*

   R   *17746*   Brazil - Espirito Santo *17079*

   R   *17746*   Brazil - Minas Gerais (Mariana) *17079*

   R   *17746*   Brazil - Rio de Janeiro *17079*

I   *Dorstenia erythrandra* C. Wright *5607*

   I   *19105*   Cuba (Guantanamo) *5607*

V   *Dorstenia excentrica* Moric. *11120*

   V   *11120*   Mexico *11120*

R   *Dorstenia ficus* Vell. *17079*

   R   *17079*   Brazil - Rio de Janeiro (Rio de Janeiro - Maciço do Gericinó) *17079*

E   *Dorstenia fischeri* Bureau *17079*

   E   *17079*   Brazil - Rio de Janeiro (Serra de Macaé) *17079*

V   *Dorstenia gigas* Schweinf. *15534*

   V   *15534*   Yemen - Socotra *15534*

R   *Dorstenia gracilis* Carauta, Valente & Sucre *16473*

   R   *16473*   Brazil - Espirito Santo *16473*

E   *Dorstenia heringeri* Carauta & Valente *2383*

   E   *2383*   Brazil (central) *2383*

E   *Dorstenia hildegardis* Carauta, Valente & Benth. *11120*

   E   *11120*   Brazil (east) *11120*

R   *Dorstenia jamaicensis* Britton *20883, 13336*

   R   *13336*   Jamaica (Manchester) *20883*

V   *Dorstenia milaneziana* Carauta, Valente & Sucre *2383*

   V   *11120*   Brazil - Espirito Santo *2383*

I   *Dorstenia nipensis* Urban & Ekman *5607*

   I   *19105*   Cuba (Santiago de Cuba; Holguin) *5607*

E   *Dorstenia nummularia* Urban & Ekman *5607*

   E   *19105*   Cuba (Cienfuegos; Villa Clara) *5607*

E   *Dorstenia panamensis* C.C. Berg *9992*

   E   *11120*   Panama *9992*

I   *Dorstenia peruviana* C.C. Berg *11120*

   I   *11120*   Peru *11120*

I   *Dorstenia poinsettiifolia* Engl. var. *angularis* Hijman & C. Berg

   I   Cameroon

V   *Dorstenia ramosa* (Desv.) Car. et al. *17079*

   V   *17079*   Brazil - Rio de Janeiro *17079*

E   *Dorstenia rocana* Britton *5607*

   E   *19105*   Cuba (Sancti Spiritus) *5607*

I   *Dorstenia roigii* Britton *5607*

   I   *19105*   Cuba (Pinar del Rio) *5607*

E   *Dorstenia setosa* Moric. *11120*

   E   *11120*   Brazil (east) *11120*

V   *Dorstenia soerensenii* Friis *19704*

   V   *19704*   Ethiopia (Ilubabor, Kefa) *19704*

I   *Dorstenia tuberosa* C. Wright *5607*

   I   *19105*   Cuba (Guantanamo) *5607*

V   *Dorstenia turnraefolia* Fisch.& Mey *2383*
     V   *2383*   Brazil (sorras da Mar & da Mantiqueria) *2383*

E   *Dorstenia umbricola* A.C. Smith *11120*
     E   *11120*   Peru *11120*

R   *Dorstenia urceolata* Schott *19567*
     R   *19567*   Brazil - Rio de Janeiro *19567*

E   *Dorstenia uxpanapana* C.C. Berg & T. Wendt *11120*
     E   *11120*   Mexico *11120*

R   *Ficus andamanica* Corner *7771*
     R   *14782*   India - Andaman Is. (South Andaman Islands) *7771*

E   *Ficus aripuanensis* C.C. Berg & F. Kooy ex Vaxquez Avila Et. al. *20081*
     E   *20081*   Brazil - Mato Grosso *20081*
     E   *20081*   Brazil - Pará *20081*

R   *Ficus bizanae* Hutch. & Burtt Davy *20604*
     R   *20604*   South Africa - Cape Province *20604*
     R   *20604*   South Africa - Natal *20604*

V   *Ficus bojeri* Baker *14296*
     V   *19182*   Seychelles (granitic) *14296*

R   *Ficus brevibracteata* W. Burger *9037*
     R   *19754*   Costa Rica *9037*

R   *Ficus bullenei* I.M. Johnston *9037*
     R   *19754*   Costa Rica *9037*
     R   *19754*   Panama *9037*

R   *Ficus caldasiana* Dugand *9037*
     R   *19754*   Costa Rica *9037*
     R   *19754*   Colombia *9037*

R   *Ficus cataractarum* Vieill.
     R   New Caledonia

R   *Ficus caudato-longifolia* Sata *20854*
     R   *20854*   Taiwan *20854*

I   *Ficus costata* Ait. *14736*
     I   *14736*   India - Nicobar Is. *14736*
     I   *16162*   Sri Lanka *7771*

R   *Ficus densifolia* Miq. *10082*
     R   *14220*   Réunion *14220*
     Ex   *20771*   Mauritius *10082*

I   *Ficus ekmanii* Rossb. *5607*
     I   *19105*   Cuba (Santiago de Cuba) *5607*

V   *Ficus iidaiana* Rehder & Wilson *8037*
     V   *19134*   Japan - Ogasawara-shoto *20626*

R   *Ficus laterisyce* W. Burger *9037*
     R   *19754*   Costa Rica *9037*

R   *Ficus macrophylla* Desf. ex Pers. ssp. *columnaris* (C. Moore) P. Green *10604*
     R   *14225*   Australia - NSW - Lord Howe Is. *10604*

I   *Ficus meizonochlamys* Rossb. *5607*
     I   *19105*   Cuba (Santiago de Cuba; Holguin) *5607*

R   *Ficus mexiae* Standley *20081*
     R   *20081*   Brazil - Bahia *20081*
     R   *20081*   Brazil - Minas Gerais *20081*

I   *Ficus muelleriana* C.C.Berg *21079*
     I   *21079*   Mozambique *21079*

V   *Ficus mutabilis* Bureau *20893*
     V   *20893*   New Caledonia *20893*

I   *Ficus nishimurae* Koidz. *8037*
     I   *19134*   Japan - Kazan Retto *8622*
     V   *19134*   Japan - Ogasawara-shoto *8037*

I   *Ficus oreslia* C. Berg
     I   Cameroon

V   *Ficus pseudopalma* Blanco *13780*
     V   *15960*   Philippines *13780*

R   *Ficus reflexa* Thunb. ssp. *aldabrensis* (Baker) Berg *19181*
     R   *19182*   Seychelles - Coralline Is. *14296*

R   *Ficus reflexa* Thunb. ssp. *seychellensis* (Baker) Berg *19182*
     R   *19182*   Seychelles (granitic) *14296*

R   *Ficus tannoensis* Hayata *20854*
     R   *20854*   Taiwan *20854*

V   *Ficus ulmifolia* Lam. *13780*
     V   *15960*   Philippines *13780*

E   *Ficus ursina* Standley *20081*
     E   *20081*   Brazil - Acre *20081*

R   *Helicostylis heterotricha* Ducke *20883*
     I   *20883*   Brazil *20883*
     I   *21022*   Brazil - Amazonas *21022*

R   *Helicostylis turbinata* Berg *20883*
     I   *20883*   Brazil *20883*

I   *Maclura braziliensis* (Martius) Endl. *11120*
     I   *11120*   Honduras *11120*
     V   *16826*   Nicaragua *16826*
     I   *11120*   Brazil (south-east) *21022*
     Ex   *20042*   Peru *20042*
     I   *11120*   Venezuela *11120*

R   *Malaisia scandens* (Lour.) Planchon ssp. *megacarpa* P. Green *10604*
     R   *10604*   Australia - NSW - Lord Howe Is. *10604*

E   *Morus boninensis* Koidz. *8038*
     E   *18128*   Japan - Ogasawara-shoto *20626*

E   *Naucleopsis chiguila* Benoist *20883, 11120*
     Ex/E   *11120*   Ecuador *20883*

R   *Naucleopsis imitans* (Ducke) Berg *20883*
     I   *20883*   Brazil *20883*
     I   *20883*   Peru *20883*

R   *Naucleopsis inaequalis* (Ducke) Berg *20883*
     I   *20883*   Brazil *20883*

E   *Naucleopsis jamariensis* Berg *20883, 11120*
     E   *20883*   Brazil *20883*

R   *Naucleopsis macrophylla* Miquel *20883, 20513*
     I   *20883*   Brazil *20883*

R   *Naucleopsis naga* Pittier *20883, 9037*
     V   *20883*   Costa Rica *20883*
     V   *11120*   Honduras *20883*

E   *Naucleopsis pseudo-naga* (Mildbraed) Berg *20883*
     E   *20883*   Brazil *20883*

E   *Naucleopsis riparia* Berg *20883, 11120*
     E   *20883*   Brazil *20883*

R   *Paratrophis smithii* Cheeseman
     R   New Zealand - North Is.

E   *Perebea glabrifolia* (Ducke) Berg *20883*
     E   *20883*   Brazil *20883*
     E   *21022*   Brazil - Amazonas *21022*

E   *Perebea guianensis* ssp. *hirsuta* Berg *20883*
     E   *20883*   Brazil *20883*

E   *Perebea guianensis* ssp. *pseudopeltata* (Mildbraed) Berg *20883*
     I   *20883*   Peru *20883*

V	*Perebea humilis* Berg *20883*	
	I	*20883* Peru *20883*
V	*Perebea longepedunculata* Berg *20883*	
	I	*20883* Peru *20883*
R	*Perebea tessmannii* Mildbraed *20883*	
	I	*20883* Brazil *20883*
	I	*20883* Peru *20883*
R	*Pseudolmedia guaranitica* Hassler *20883*	
	I	*20883* Paraguay *20883*
R	*Pseudolmedia hirtula* Kuhlmann *20883*	
	I	*20883* Brazil (south-east & south) *21022*
R	*Pseudolmedia rigida* ssp. *araguensis* Berg *20883*	
	I	*20883* Venezuela *20883*
R	*Pseudolmedia rigida* ssp. *eggersii* (Standley) Berg *20883*	
	I	*20883* Ecuador *20883*
V	*Streblus sclerophyllus* Corner *20893*	
	V	*20893* New Caledonia *20893*
V	*Trophis cuspidata* Lundell *9004*	
	V	*11120* Guatemala *9004*
	V	*11120* Mexico *9004*
V	*Trophis involucrata* W. Burger *9037*	
	V	*19754* Costa Rica *9037*
R	*Trymatococcus paraensis* Ducke *20883*	
	I	*20883* Brazil *20883*
	I	*20883* Guyana *20883*
	I	*20883* Suriname *20883*

Morinaceae

Number of genera:
Number of species: 13
Recorded threatened species: 2 (15%)

Balkans to Himalaya and China.

R	*Morina persica* L. ssp. *decussatifolia* Erik & Demirkus *12840*	
	R	*12840* Turkey *12840*
I	*Morina subinervis* Boiss. *12840*	
	I	*12840* Turkey *12840*

Moringaceae

Number of genera: 1
Number of species: 10
Recorded threatened species: 2 (20%)

Xeric Africa; Madagascar; India.

I	*Moringa arborea* Verdc. *7959*	
	I	*19109* Kenya (Ramu) *7959*
R	*Moringa drouhardii* Jum. *10368*	
	R	*10368* Madagascar *10368*

Myoporaceae

Number of genera: 3-4
Number of species: 125
Recorded threatened species: 32 (25%)

Australia; Asia; Pacific islands; West Indies; northern South America.

R	*Eremophila alatisepala* Chinnock *20681*	
	R	*20681* Australia - Queensland *20681*
R	*Eremophila barbata* Chinnock *20681*	

	R	*20681* Australia - South Australia *20681*
R	*Eremophila biserrata* Chinnock *20681*	
	R	*20681* Australia - Western Australia *20681*
E	*Eremophila caerulea* (S.Moore) Diels ssp. *merrallii* Chinnock ms. *20681*	
	E	*20681* Australia - Western Australia *20681*
V	*Eremophila denticulata* F.Muell. ssp. *denticulata* *20681*	
	V	*20681* Australia - Western Australia *20681*
V	*Eremophila denticulata* F.Muell. ssp. *trisulcata* Chinnock ms. *20681*	
	V	*20681* Australia - Western Australia *20681*
R	*Eremophila hillii* E.A.Shaw *20681*	
	I	*20681* Australia - South Australia *20681*
	I	*20681* Australia - Western Australia *20681*
V	*Eremophila inflata* C.Gardner *20681*	
	V	*20681* Australia - Western Australia *20681*
V	*Eremophila microtheca* F.Muell. ex Benth. *20681*	
	V	*20681* Australia - Western Australia *20681*
E	*Eremophila nivea* Chinnock *20681*	
	E	*20681* Australia - Western Australia *20681*
R	*Eremophila pentaptera* J.Black *20681*	
	R	*20681* Australia - South Australia *20681*
V	*Eremophila prostrata* Chinnock ms. *20681*	
	V	*20681* Australia - Northern Territory *20681*
V	*Eremophila racemosa* Endl. *20681*	
	V	*20681* Australia - Western Australia *20681*
V	*Eremophila resinosa* (Endl.) F.Muell. *20681*	
	V	*20681* Australia - Western Australia *20681*
R	*Eremophila serpens* Chinnock *20681*	
	R	*20681* Australia - Western Australia *20681*
V	*Eremophila subteretifolia* Chinnock ms. *20681*	
	V	*20681* Australia - Western Australia *20681*
V	*Eremophila ternifolia* Chinnock *20681*	
	V	*20681* Australia - Western Australia *20681*
V	*Eremophila tetraptera* C.White *20681*	
	V	*20681* Australia - Queensland *20681*
E	*Eremophila veneta* Chinnock ms. *20681*	
	E	*20681* Australia - Western Australia *20681*
Ex	*Eremophila vernicosa* Chinnock ms. *20681*	
	Ex	*20681* Australia - Western Australia *20681*
E	*Eremophila verticillata* Chinnock *20681*	
	E	*20681* Australia - Western Australia *20681*
V	*Eremophila virens* C.Gardner *20681*	
	V	*20681* Australia - Western Australia *20681*
V	*Eremophila viscida* Endl. *20681*	
	V	*20681* Australia - Western Australia *20681*
R	*Eremophila youngii* Chinnock ms. ssp. *lepidota* Chinnock ms. *20681*	
	R	*20681* Australia - Western Australia *20681*
R	*Myoporum bateae* F.Muell. *20681*	
	R	*20681* Australia - New South Wales *20681*
R	*Myoporum boninense* Koidz. *19134*	
	R	*18338* North Mariana Is. *18338*
	R	*19134* Japan - Ogasawara-shoto *19134*
	R	*18338* U.S. - Guam *18338*
V	*Myoporum cordifolium* (F.Muell.) Druce *20681*	
	V	*20681* Australia - Western Australia *20681*
R	*Myoporum floribundum* Cunn. ex Benth. *20681*	

I	*20681*	Australia - New South Wales *20681*	
I	*20681*	Australia - Victoria *20681*	

R **Myoporum laetum** Forst.f. var. *decumbens* Simpson

R		New Zealand - North Is.

E **Myoporum mauritianum** A. DC. *10082*

Ex	*20771*	Mauritius *5852*
E	*5852*	Mauritius - Rodrigues *5852*

R **Myoporum obscurum** Endl. *11649*

R	*19108*	Australia - Norfolk Is. *11649*

I **Myoporum rimatarense** F.Brown *20845*

I	*20845*	French Polynesia - Tubuai Is. (Rimatara) *20845*

E **Myoporum stokesii** F.Brown *20845*

E	*20845*	French Polynesia - Tubuai Is. (Rimatara) *20845*

E **Myoporum turbinatum** Chinnock *20681*

E	*20681*	Australia - Western Australia *20681*

Myricaceae

Number of genera:	3	
Number of species:	50	
Recorded threatened species:	5	(10%)

Mostly temperate and subtropical.

R **Myrica adenophora** Hance var. *kusanoi* Hayata

R	*20854*	Taiwan (south) *20854*

R **Myrica calcicola** Proctor *19890*

R	*19890*	Jamaica (Portland) *19486*

E **Myrica holdridgeana** Lundell *20883*

I	*20883*	Puerto Rico *20883*

V **Myrica phanerodonta** Standley *9037*

V	*19754*	Costa Rica *9037*

R **Myrica rivas-martinezii** A. Santos *17891*

R	*20750*	Spain - Canary Is. *17891*

Myristicaceae

Number of genera:	15	
Number of species:	300	
Recorded threatened species:	19	(6%)

Tropical.

I **Gymnacranthera canarica** (King) Warb. *21141, 10150*

I		India - Karnataka *10150*
I		India - Kerala *10150*

V **Horsfieldia hainanensis** Merr. *11139*

V		China - Hainan Is. *11139*
V		China - Guangxi (Longzhou) *11139*

V **Horsfieldia iryaghedi** (Gaertn.) Warb. *12838*

V	*12838*	Sri Lanka *12838*

I **Horsfieldia macrocarpa** var. *canarioides* (King) Sinclair *7771*

I		India - Andaman Is. *7771*

R **Horsfieldia megacarpa** Merr. *13780*

R	*15960*	Philippines *13780*

V **Horsfieldia pandurifolia** Hu *17617*

V	*17617*	China - Yunnan *11139*

E **Horsfieldia tetratepala** C.Y. Wu & W.T. Wang *17617*

E	*17617*	China - Yunnan (Menla; Jinghong; Changyu) *11139*

E **Iryanthera megistocarpa** A. Gentry *20883, 9993*

I	*20883*	Panama *20883*

V **Knema bengalensis** de Wilde *21143, 14872*

V	*14872*	Bangladesh *14872*

I **Knema lateritica** Elm. *13833*

I	*13833*	Philippines (low altitude) *13833*

E **Myristica ceylanica** A. DC. *10276*

E	*12838*	Sri Lanka *10276*

V **Myristica dactyloides** Gaertn. *12838*

V	*20013*	Sri Lanka *12838*

E **Myristica malabarica** Lam. *21163, 20263, 21025*

E	*20263*	India - Kerala *21163*

E **Myristica yunnanensis** Y.H. Li *17617*

E	*17617*	China - Yunnan (Menla) *11139*

E **Otoba acuminata** (Standl.) A. Gentry *20883, 10747*

I	*20883*	Panama *20883*

V **Otoba parvifolia** (Mangraf) A. Gentry *18200*

V	*19977*	Peru *18200*

E **Virola megacarpa** A. Gentry *20883, 9993*

I	*20883*	Panama *20883*

R **Virola urbaniana** Warb. *19564*

R	*19564*	Brazil - Goias *19564*

R **Virola weberbaueri** Markgraf *18200*

R	*12468*	Peru *18200*

Myrsinaceae

Number of genera:	30	
Number of species:	1,000	
Recorded threatened species:	191	(19%)

Tropical and subtropical New and Old World; also temperate Old World.

R **Antistrophe serratifolia** (Beddome) Hook.f. *11494*

R	*11494*	India - Kerala (Silent Valley; Nilgiris) *11494*
R	*11494*	India - Tamil Nadu *11494*

I **Ardisia alata** Fletch. *19120*

I	*19120*	Thailand *19120*

V **Ardisia alstonii** Lund. *20883, 9006*

I	*20883*	Panama *20883*

I **Ardisia amplexicaulis** Beddome

I		India - Kerala

V **Ardisia antonensis** Lund. *20883, 9006*

V	*16317*	Panama *20883*

R **Ardisia bakeri** C.White *20681*

I	*20681*	Australia - New South Wales *20681*
I	*20681*	Australia - Queensland *20681*

V **Ardisia bartlettii** Lund. *20883, 9006*

?		Costa Rica *10747*
I	*20883*	Panama *20883*

R **Ardisia bifaria** C.White & Francis *20681*

R	*20681*	Australia - Queensland *20681*

I **Ardisia biflora** King & Gamble

I		Malaysia - Peninsular Malaysia (Perak)

V **Ardisia breedlovei** Lundell *20883*

I	*20883*	Mexico *20883*

V **Ardisia brenesii** Standley *9037*

V	*11212*	Costa Rica *9037*
V	*11212*	Nicaragua *11212*

R **Ardisia brevicaulis** Diels var. *violacea* (Suzuki)

Walker *20511*
R   *20511*   Taiwan *20511*

V   *Ardisia brittonii* Stearn *20883, 13336*
    V   *13336*   Jamaica *20883*

E   *Ardisia byrsonimae* Stearn *20883, 13336*
    E   *13336*   Jamaica *20883*

I   *Ardisia confusa* K. Lars. et C.M. Hu *19120*
    I   *19120*   Thailand *19120*

V   *Ardisia crassipes* Lund. *20883, 9006*
    V   *16317*   Panama *20883*

I   *Ardisia curvistylis* Yang *19120*
    I   *19120*   Thailand *19120*

V   *Ardisia darienensis* Lund. *20883, 9006*
    V   *16317*   Panama *20883*

E   *Ardisia dukei* Lundell *20883*
    I   *20883*   Panama *20883*

E   *Ardisia dwyeri* Lund. *20883*
    I   *20883*   Panama *20883*

E   *Ardisia fendleri* Lund. *20883*
    I   *20883*   Panama *20883*

I   *Ardisia ficifolia* L. Lars. et C.M. Hu *19120*
    I   *19120*   Thailand *19120*

I   *Ardisia fimbriata* Fletch. *19120*
    I   *19120*   Thailand *19120*

I   *Ardisia fletcherii* R. Lars. et C.M. Hu *19120*
    I   *19120*   Thailand *19120*

I   *Ardisia foliosa* Furt. *19209*
    I   *19209*   Malaysia - Peninsular Malaysia *19209*

V   *Ardisia furfuracella* Standl. *20883, 9006*
    V   *16317*   Panama *20883*

V   *Ardisia geniculata* Lund. *20883, 9006*
    V   *16317*   Panama *20883*

V   *Ardisia glomerata* Lund. *20883, 9006*
    V   *16317*   Panama *20883*

I   *Ardisia gracillima* K. Lars. et C.M. Hu *19120*
    I   *19120*   Thailand *19120*

V   *Ardisia hagenii* Lund. *20883, 9006*
    V   *16317*   Panama *20883*

V   *Ardisia ionantha* K. Lars. et C.M. Hu *19120*
    V   *19120*   Thailand *19120*

I   *Ardisia iwahigensis* Elm. *13833*
    I   *13833*   Philippines (Palawan) *13833*

R   *Ardisia jamaicensis* Lundell *20883*
    R   *20883*   Jamaica *20883*

R   *Ardisia kusukusensis* Hay. *20854*
    R   *20854*   Taiwan *20854*

I   *Ardisia lankawiensis* King & Gamble
    I   Malaysia - Peninsular Malaysia

V   *Ardisia lewisii* Lund. *20883, 9006*
    V   *16317*   Panama *20883*

E   *Ardisia luquillensis* (Britt.) Alain *20883*
    I   *20883*   Puerto Rico *20883*

I   *Ardisia maehongsonia* K. Lars. et C.M. Hu *19120*
    I   *19120*   Thailand *19120*

E   *Ardisia magdalenae* Stehlé *19001*
    E   *19001*   Martinique (Montagne du Vauclin) *19001*

V   *Ardisia maxonii* Standl. *20883, 9006*
    I   *20883*   Panama *20883*

R   *Ardisia melastomoides* Pitard *6057*
    R   Vietnam *6057*

I   *Ardisia meziana* King & Gamble
    I   Malaysia - Peninsular Malaysia (Perak)

R   *Ardisia miaoliensis* *20854*
    R   *20854*   Taiwan *20854*

V   *Ardisia microcalyx* Lund. *20883, 9006*
    V   *16317*   Panama *20883*

V   *Ardisia nervosissima* Lund. *20883, 9006*
    V   *16317*   Panama *20883*

E   *Ardisia nigrita* Lund. *20883*
    I   *20883*   Panama *20883*

V   *Ardisia opaca* Lund. *20883, 9006*
    V   *16317*   Panama *20883*

I   *Ardisia pachyphylla* Merr. *13833*
    I   *13833*   Philippines (low altitude) *13833*

I   *Ardisia palawanensis* Merr. *13833*
    I   *13833*   Philippines (low altitude) *13833*

E   *Ardisia panamensis* Lund. *20883, 9006*
    V   *11212*   Panama *20883*

I   *Ardisia paralleloneura* K. Lars et C.M. Hu *19120*
    I   *19120*   Thailand *19120*

I   *Ardisia patula* K. Lars et C.M. Hu *19120*
    I   *19120*   Thailand *19120*

V   *Ardisia philippinensis* A. DC. *10278*
    V   Philippines *10278*

I   *Ardisia puberula* Fletch. *19120*
    I   *19120*   Thailand *19120*

R   *Ardisia pulchra* Ridley *881*
    R   *14224*   Australia - Christmas Is. *881*

E   *Ardisia pulverulenta* Mez *20883*
    I   *20883*   Panama *20883*

I   *Ardisia quinquangularis* A. DC.
    I   India - Meghalaya

R   *Ardisia recliniflora* Pitard *6057*
    R   Vietnam *6057*

V   *Ardisia reflexiflora* Lund. *20883, 9006*
    V   *16317*   Panama *20883*

I   *Ardisia rhynchophylla* C.B. Clarke
    I   India - Meghalaya (Cherrapunji, Khasi Hills)

R   *Ardisia roseiflora* Pitard *6057*
    R   Vietnam *6057*

I   *Ardisia rubro-glandulosa* Fletch. *19120*
    I   *19120*   Thailand *19120*

I   *Ardisia salvadorensis* Lundell *9065*
    I   *11218*   El Salvador *9065*

V   *Ardisia scheryi* Lund. *20883, 9006*
    V   *16317*   Panama *20883*

V   *Ardisia solomonii* (Lundell) Pipoly *9426*
    V   *11212*   Costa Rica *9426*

R   *Ardisia splendens* Pitard *6057*
    R   Vietnam *6057*

V   *Ardisia squamulosa* Presl. *13780*
    V   *15960*   Philippines *13780*

R   *Ardisia stenosepala* *20854*
    R   *20854*   Taiwan *20854*

V   *Ardisia subsessilifolia* Lund. *20883, 9006*
    V   *16317*   Panama *20883*

I   *Ardisia tetramera* **K. Lars. et C.M. Hu** *19120*
     I   *19120*   Thailand *19120*

I   *Ardisia tumida* **Furt.** *19209*
     I   *19209*   Malaysia - Peninsular Malaysia *19209*

V   *Ardisia tysonii* **Lund.** *20883, 9006*
     V   *16317*   Panama *20883*

I   *Ardisia undulato-dentata* **Fletch.** *19120*
     I   *19120*   Thailand *19120*

I   *Ardisia urbanii* **Stearn** *20883, 13336*
     I   *19890*   Jamaica (Trelawny) *20883*

V   *Ardisia wedelii* **Lundell** *9006*
     V   *11212*   Costa Rica *11212*
     V   *11212*   Nicaragua *9006*
     V   *11212*   Panama *9006*

V   *Ardisia whitei* **Lund.** *20883, 9006*
     V   *16317*   Panama *20883*

E   *Badula balfouriana* **(O. Kuntze) Mez** *10082*
     E   *5852*   Mauritius - Rodrigues *5852*

V   *Badula borbonica* **A. DC. var. *borbonica*** *10082*
     V   *10082*   Réunion *10082*

E   *Badula borbonica* **A. DC. var. *macrophylla* (Cordem.) Coode** *10082*
     E   *10082*   Réunion *10082*

E   *Badula crassa* **A.DC.** *10082, 21329*
     Ex   *10082*   Réunion *10082*
     E   *20771*   Mauritius *10082*

E   *Badula decumbens* **(Cordem.) Coode** *10082*
     E   *14233*   Réunion *10082*

E   *Badula fragilis* **Bosser & Coode** *10082*
     E   *10082*   Réunion *10082*

V   *Badula multiflora* **A. DC.** *10082*
     V   *20771*   Mauritius *10082*

E   *Badula nitida* **(Coode) Coode** *10082*
     E   *14220*   Réunion *10082*

Ex   *Badula ovalifolia* **A. DC.** *10082*
     Ex   *14233*   Réunion *10082*

Ex/E   *Badula platyphylla* **(A. DC.) Coode** *10082, 21329*
     Ex/E   *20771*   Mauritius *10082*

E   *Badula reticulata* **A. DC.** *10082, 21329*
     E   *20771*   Mauritius *10082*

R   *Badula sieberi* **A. DC.** *10082*
     R   *20771*   Mauritius *10082*

I   *Cybianthus colombianus* **Pipoly** *11589*
     I   *11589*   Colombia *11589*

E   *Cybianthus magnus* **(Mez) Pipoly ssp. *asymmetricus* (Mez) Pipoly** *10323*
     E   *11589*   Panama *10323*
     E   *11589*   Colombia *10323*
     E   *11589*   Ecuador *10323*
     E   *10323*   Peru *10323*

R   *Cybianthus poeppigii* **Mez** *11212*
     I   *11212*   Costa Rica *10323*
     I   *11212*   Panama *10323*
     I   *11212*   Colombia *10323*
     R   *18200*   Peru *11212*

R   *Cybianthus rostratus* **(Hassk.) Agostini** *19001*
     R   *19001*   Martinique *19001*

I   *Discocalyx palawanensis* **Elm. ex Merr.** *13833*
     I   *13833*   Philippines (low altitude) *13833*

R   *Elingamita johnsonii* **Baylis** *86*

     R   *19305*   New Zealand - North Is. (Three Kings Island) *19305*

I   *Embelia calcarea* **Fletcher**
     I   Malaysia - Peninsular Malaysia (Langkawi, Kedah)

R   *Embelia demissa* **Cordem.** *10082*
     R   *14233*   Réunion *10082*

I   *Embelia disticha* **Fletcher** *19120*
     I   *19120*   Thailand *19120*

I   *Embelia gardneriana* **Wight**
     I   India - Tamil Nadu (Sispara Ghat, Nilgiri)

I   *Embelia grandiflora* **Fletcher** *19120*
     I   *19120*   Thailand *19120*

R   *Embelia grayi* **S.T.Reynolds** *20681*
     R   *20681*   Australia - Queensland *20681*

V   *Embelia keniensis* **R.E. Fries** *20057*
     V   *20057*   Kenya (Mt. Kenya, Tigoni) *20057*

I   *Embelia kerrii* **Fletcher** *19120*
     I   *19120*   Thailand (Khao Yai) *19120*

I   *Embelia micrantha* **(A. DC) A. DC.** *10082*
     I   *10082*   Réunion *10082*
     E   *20771*   Mauritius *10082*

I   *Embelia microcalyx* **Kurz** *7771*
     I   India - Nicobar Is. (Katchal Is.) *7771*

I   *Embelia sootepensis* **Craib** *19120*
     I   *19120*   Thailand *19120*

R   *Geissanthus betancurii* **Pipoly** *21278*
     R   *21278*   Colombia (Chocó) *21278*

V   *Heberdenia bahamensis* **(Gaertn.) Sprague** *17534*
     V   *17534*   Spain - Canary Is. *17534*

V   *Heberdenia excelsa* **(Aiton) Banks ex DC.**
     V   Portugal - Madeira
     V   *19174*   Spain - Canary Is. *19174*

R   *Maesa calophylla* **Pitard** *6057*
     R   Vietnam *6057*

I   *Maesa crenata* **Fletch.** *19120*
     I   *19120*   Thailand *19120*

I   *Maesa glomerata* **K. Lars. et C.M. Hu** *19120*
     I   *19120*   Thailand *19120*

I   *Maesa integrifolia* **Ridl.** *19120*
     I   *19120*   Thailand *19120*

I   *Maesa linealata* **Fletch** *19120*
     I   *19120*   Thailand *19120*

I   *Maesa megalobotrys* **Merr.** *13833*
     I   *13833*   Philippines (low altitude) *13833*

R   *Maesa nuda* **Hutch. & Dalz.** *7926*
     R   Guinea *7926*
     R   Senegal *8003*

I   *Maesa pahangiana* **K. & G.** *19209*
     I   *19209*   Malaysia - Peninsular Malaysia (Pahang) *19209*

V   *Maesa sublanceolata* **Fletch.** *19120*
     V   *19120*   Thailand *19120*

R   *Maesa vestita* **Jacq.-Fel.**
     R   Guinea

I   *Myrsine adamsonii* **Fosberg & Sachet** *20845*
     I   *20845*   French Polynesia - Marquesas Is (Nuku Hiva) *20845*

I   *Myrsine andersonii* **Fosberg & Sachet** *20845*
     I   *20845*   French Polynesia - Tubuai Is. (Tubuai, Raivavae,

Rapa) *20845*

I   *Myrsine brownii* **Fosberg & Sachet** *20845*
     I   *20845*   French Polynesia - Tubuai Is. (Tubuai, Raivavae) *20845*

V   *Myrsine canariensis* **(Willd.) Spreng.**
     V   Spain - Canary Is.

E   *Myrsine coclensis* **Lund.** *20883, 10747*
     I   *20883*   Panama *20883*

V   *Myrsine degeneri* **Hosaka** *14209, 20850*
     I   *20850*   U.S. - Hawaii *20850*

R   *Myrsine fernseei* **(Mez) Hosaka** *20850, 14209*
     R   *20850*   U.S. - Hawaii (Kaua`i) *20850*

V   *Myrsine fosbergii* **Hosaka** *20850, 14209*
     V   *20850*   U.S. - Hawaii (O`ahu) *20850*

I   *Myrsine gracilissima* **Fosberg & Sachet** *20845*
     I   *20845*   French Polynesia - Marquesas Is (Hiva Oa) *20845*

R   *Myrsine grantii* **Fosberg & Sachet var.** *tobiiensis* **Fosberg & Sachet** *20845*
     R   *20845*   French Polynesia - Marquesas Is (Nuku Hiva) *20845*

E   *Myrsine hartii* **(M.Grant) Fosberg & Sachet** *20845*
     E   *20845*   French Polynesia - Society Is. (Tahiti) *20845*

R   *Myrsine helleri* **(O.& I. Deg.) St. John** *20850, 14209*
     R   *20850*   U.S. - Hawaii (Kaua`i) *20850*

V   *Myrsine hosakae* **H. St. John** *8050*
     V   *19185*   Pitcairn (Henderson Is.) *8050*

E   *Myrsine juddii* **Hosaka** *20850, 14209*
     E   *20850*   U.S. - Hawaii (Oahu - Ko`olau Mts.) *20850*

E   *Myrsine knudsenii* **(Rock) Hosaka** *20850, 14209*
     E   *20850*   U.S. - Hawaii (Kaua`i) *20850*

E   *Myrsine linearifolia* **Hosaka** *20850*
     E   *20850*   U.S. - Hawaii *20850*

E   *Myrsine longifolia* **Nadeaud** *20845*
     E   *20845*   French Polynesia - Society Is. (Tahiti) *20845*

I   *Myrsine magnoliifolia*   *15229*
     I   *15229*   Haiti (La Visite & Macaya National Parks) *15229*

E   *Myrsine mezii* **Hosaka** *20850, 14209*
     E   *20850*   U.S. - Hawaii *20850*

I   *Myrsine obovata* **(J.Moore) Fosberg & Sachet** *20845*
     I   *20845*   French Polynesia - Society Is. (Raiatea) *20845*

V   *Myrsine okabeana* **(Tuy.) Walker** *8038*
     V   *19134*   Japan - Ogasawara-shoto (Chichijima) *8038*

R   *Myrsine oliveri* **Allan** *86*
     R   *19305*   New Zealand - North Is. (Three Kings Island) *19305*

I   *Myrsine orohenensis* **(J.Moore) Fosberg & Sachet** *20845*
     I   *20845*   French Polynesia - Society Is. (Tahiti) *20845*

R   *Myrsine ovalis* **Nadeaud var.** *ovalis* *20845*
     R   *20845*   French Polynesia - Society Is. *20845*

E   *Myrsine petiolata* **Hosaka** *20850, 14209*
     E   *20850*   U.S. - Hawaii (Kaua`i) *20850*

R   *Myrsine pillansii* **Adamson** *20604*
     R   *20604*   South Africa - Cape Province *20604*

     V   *20604*   South Africa - Natal *20604*
     R   *20604*   South Africa - Transvaal *20604*

I   *Myrsine raiateensis* **(J.Moore) Fosberg & Sachet** *20845*
     I   *20845*   French Polynesia - Society Is. (Raiatea) *20845*

R   *Myrsine resinosa* **(A.C. Smith) Pipoly** *21280*
     R   *21280*   Guyana *21280*

E   *Myrsine ronuiensis* **(M.Grant) Fosberg & Sachet** *20845*
     E   *20845*   French Polynesia - Society Is. (Tahiti) *20845*

E   *Myrsine sytsmae* **Lund.** *20883, 10747*
     I   *20883*   Panama *20883*

I   *Myrsine tahuatensis* **Fosberg & Sachet** *20845*
     I   *20845*   French Polynesia - Marquesas Is (Tahuata) *20845*

E   *Myrsine vaccinioides* **W.L. Wagner, Herbst & Sohmer** *20850*
     E   *20850*   U.S. - Hawaii *20850*

I   *Myrsine vescoi* **Drake** *20845*
     I   *20845*   French Polynesia - Society Is. (Tahiti) *20845*

V   *Parathesis amplifolia* **Lund.** *20883, 9006*
     V   *16317*   Panama *20883*

R   *Parathesis aurantiaca* **Lundell** *9004*
     R   *10359*   El Salvador *9004*

V   *Parathesis congesta* **Lundell** *11218*
     V   *10359*   El Salvador *11218*

V   *Parathesis panamensis* **Lund.** *20883, 9006*
     V   *16317*   Panama *20883*

R   *Parathesis rothschuhiana* **Mez** *11212*
     R   *11121*   Nicaragua *11212*

V   *Parathesis seibertii* **Lund.** *20883, 9006*
     I   *20883*   Panama *20883*

V   *Pleiomeris canariensis* **(Willd.) A. DC.** *20750*
     V   *17534*   Spain - Canary Is. *17534*

E   *Rapanea allenii* **Lund.** *20883*
     I   *20883*   Panama *20883*

E   *Rapanea gilliana* **(Sond.) Mez** *20604*
     E   *20604*   South Africa - Cape Province *20604*

R   *Rapanea grandifolia* **S. Moore**
     R   New Caledonia

R   *Rapanea mccomishii* **Sprague** *14223*
     R   *14223*   Australia - NSW - Lord Howe Is. *14223*

R   *Rapanea myrtillina* **Mez**
     R   *14226*   Australia - NSW - Lord Howe Is. *14226*

V   *Rapanea perforata* **Mez** *20883*
     V   *20883*   Paraguay *20883*

R   *Rapanea platystigma* **(F. Muell.) Mez**
     R   *14225*   Australia - NSW - Lord Howe Is. *14225*

R   *Rapanea ralstoniae* **P. Green** *10604*
     R   *19108*   Australia - Norfolk Is. *10604*

E   *Rapanea seychellarum* **Mez** *14296*
     E   *14981*   Seychelles (Mahé & Silhouette) *14296*

I   *Rapanea striata* **Mez**
     I   India - Karnataka (Mysore)

I   *Rapanea subpedicellata* **Fletch.** *19120*
     I   *19120*   Thailand *19120*

I   *Rapanea thwaitesii* **Mez**
     I   India - Tamil Nadu (Palani Hills, Madurai Dist)

R   *Rapanea umbellata* (Mart.) Mez. *20883, 15247*
     I   *20883* Brazil *20883*
     ?   Brazil - Rio Grande do Sul (floresta do Alto Uruguai, floresta Pluvial Atlântica) *20311*
     ?   Brazil - Santa Catarina *20310*
     R   *20883* Paraguay *20883*

I   *Stylogyne glomeruliflora* Cuatrec. *11589*
     I   *11589* Colombia *11589*

V   *Stylogyne hayesii* Mez *20883, 9006*
     V   *16317* Panama *20883*

I   *Stylogyne minutiflora* Cuatrec. *11589*
     I   *11589* Colombia *11589*

R   *Tapeinosperma amplexicaule* Mez
     R   New Caledonia

R   *Tapeinosperma aragoense* Guillaumin
     R   New Caledonia

V   *Tapeinosperma campanula* Mez *20893*
     V   *20893* New Caledonia *20893*

I   *Wallenia apiculata* Urban *5642*
     I   Dominican Republic (El Tetero, Azua) *5642*

R   *Wallenia calyptrata* Urb. *20883*
     R   *20883* Jamaica *20883*

R   *Wallenia clusioides* (Griseb.) Mez *20883*
     R   *20883* Jamaica *20883*

R   *Wallenia corymbosa* Urb. *20883*
     R   *20883* Jamaica *20883*

R   *Wallenia crassifolia* Mez *20883*
     R   *20883* Jamaica *20883*

I   *Wallenia discolor* Urb. *20883, 13336*
     I   *13336* Jamaica *20883*

R   *Wallenia elliptica* Urb. *20883, 13336*
     R   *13336* Jamaica (St. Ann) *20883*

R   *Wallenia erythrocarpa* Urb. *20883, 13336*
     R   *13336* Jamaica *20883*

V   *Wallenia fawcettii* Mez *20883, 19890*
     R   *19890* Jamaica *20883*

R   *Wallenia grisebachii* Mez *20883*
     R   *20883* Jamaica *20883*

I   *Wallenia punctulata* Urb. *20883, 13336*
     I   *13336* Jamaica *20883*

R   *Wallenia purdieana* Mez *20883*
     R   *20883* Jamaica *20883*

R   *Wallenia sylvestris* Urb. *20883, 13336*
     R   *13336* Jamaica (Port., St. Thomas) *20883*

I   *Wallenia urbaniana* Mez *5642*
     I   Dominican Republic (Belladere) *5642*

R   *Wallenia venosa* Griseb. *20883*
     R   *20883* Jamaica *20883*

V   *Wallenia xylosteoides* (Griseb.) Mez *20883, 13336*
     V   *13336* Jamaica (St. Ann) *20883*

Myrtaceae

Number of genera: 140
Number of species: 3,000
Recorded threatened species: 747   (24%)

Tropical and subtropical; temperate Australia.

V   *Acca lanuginosa* (Ruiz & Pavon ex G. Don) McVaugh *20883*
     I   *20883* Peru *20883*

V   *Acca macrostema* (Ruiz & Pavon ex G. Don) McVaugh *20883*
     I   *20883* Peru *20883*

R   *Acmena divaricata* Merr. & Perry *20681*
     R   *20681* Australia - Queensland *20681*

R   *Acmena mackinnoniana* B.Hyland *20681*
     R   *20681* Australia - Queensland *20681*

R   *Acmenosperma pringlei* B.Hyland *20681*
     R   *20681* Australia - Queensland *20681*

E   *Amomyrtus luma* (Mol.) Legr. et Kausel *20176*
     E   *20176* Argentina - Chubut *20176*
     E   *20176* Argentina - Neuquen *20176*
     E   *20176* Argentina - Rio Negro *20176*

R   *Angophora crassifolia* (G.Leach) L.A.S.Johnson & K.Hill *20681*
     R   *20681* Australia - New South Wales *20681*

R   *Angophora robur* L.A.S.Johnson & K.Hill *20681*
     R   *20681* Australia - New South Wales *20681*

R   *Astartea intratropica* F.Muell. *20681*
     R   *20681* Australia - Northern Territory *20681*

R   *Asteromyrtus arnhemica* ? *20681*
     R   *20681* Australia - Northern Territory *20681*

E   *Aulomyrcia tomentosa* Almeda *20883, 10747*
     I   *20883* Panama *20883*

E   *Aulomyrcia zetekiana* (Standl.) Amshoff *20883, 9006*
     I   *20883* Panama *20883*

E   *Austromyrtus fragrantissima* (Benth.) Burret *20681*
     I   *20681* Australia - New South Wales *20681*
     I   *20681* Australia - Queensland *20681*

E   *Austromyrtus gonoclada* (F.Muell.) Burret *20681*
     E   *20681* Australia - Queensland *20681*

V   *Austromyrtus horizontalis* (Pancher ex Brongn. & Gris) Burret *20802*
     V   *20893* New Caledonia *20802*

R   *Austromyrtus inophloia* (J.F.Bailey & C.White) Burret *20681*
     R   *20681* Australia - Queensland *20681*

R   *Austromyrtus lasioclada* (F.Muell.) L.S.Smith *20681*
     R   *20681* Australia - Queensland *20681*

V   *Austromyrtus lotoides* (Vieill. ex Guillaumin) Burret *20802*
     V   *20893* New Caledonia *20802*

R   *Austromyrtus lucida* (Gaertner) L.S.Smith *20681*
     R   *20681* Australia - Queensland *20681*

R   *Austromyrtus pubiflora* (C.White) L.S.Smith *20681*
     R   *20681* Australia - Queensland *20681*

R   *Backhousia anisata* Vickery *20681*
     R   *20681* Australia - New South Wales *20681*

R   *Backhousia bancroftii* F.Muell. & Bailey *20681*
     R   *20681* Australia - Queensland *20681*

V   *Baeckea arbuscula* Benth. *20681*
     V   *20681* Australia - Western Australia *20681*

E   *Baeckea camphorata* Sims *20681*
     E   *20681* Australia - New South Wales *20681*

R   *Baeckea crenatifolia* F.Muell. *20681*
     R   *20681* Australia - Victoria *20681*

R   *Baeckea denticulata* Maiden & Betche *20681*
     R   *20681* Australia - New South Wales *20681*

R *Barongia lophandra* Peter G.Wilson & B.Hyland *20681*
    R   *20681* Australia - Queensland *20681*

R *Callistemon acuminatus* Cheel *20681*
    R   *20681* Australia - New South Wales *20681*

V *Callistemon brevisepalus* J.Wyndham Dawson *20893*
    V   *20893* New Caledonia *20893*

R *Callistemon chisholmii* Cheel *20681*
    R   *20681* Australia - Queensland *20681*

R *Callistemon flavovirens* (Cheel) Cheel *20681*
    I   *20681* Australia - New South Wales *20681*
    I   *20681* Australia - Queensland *20681*

R *Callistemon formosus* S.T.Blake *20681*
    R   *20681* Australia - Queensland *20681*

R *Callistemon linearifolius* (Link.) DC. *20681*
    R   *20681* Australia - New South Wales *20681*

R *Callistemon pauciflorus* Spencer & Lumley *20681*
    R   *20681* Australia - Northern Territory *20681*

R *Callistemon pearsonii* Spencer & Lumley *20681*
    R   *20681* Australia - Queensland *20681*

R *Callistemon pungens* P.F.Lumley & R.D.Spencer *20681*
    I   *20681* Australia - New South Wales *20681*
    I   *20681* Australia - Queensland *20681*

R *Callistemon shiressii* Blakely *20681*
    R   *20681* Australia - New South Wales *20681*

Ex *Calothamnus accedens* T.J.Hawkeswood *20681*
    Ex *20681* Australia - Western Australia *20681*

R *Calothamnus graniticus* T.J.Hawkeswood ssp. *graniticus* *20681*
    R   *20681* Australia - Western Australia *20681*

R *Calothamnus pachystachyus* Benth. *20681*
    R   *20681* Australia - Western Australia *20681*

R *Calothamnus rupestris* Schauer *20681*
    R   *20681* Australia - Western Australia *20681*

I *Calycolpus excisus* (Urban) Bisse *11840*
    I   *19105* Cuba (Santiago de Cuba; Holguin) *11840*

V *Calycorectes moana* Borh. & Muniz *5607*
    V   *19105* Cuba (Holguin) *5607*

V *Calyptranthes acunae* Borh. & Muniz *5607*
    V   *19105* Cuba (Holguin) *5607*

E *Calyptranthes acutissima* Urb. *20883, 13336*
    E   *19890* Jamaica (Hanover) *20883*

V *Calyptranthes albicans* Borh. *5607*
    V   *19105* Cuba (Holguin) *5607*

R *Calyptranthes anacletoi* Borh. & Muniz *5607*
    R   *19105* Cuba (Guantanamo) *5607*

E *Calyptranthes arenicola* Urban *5607*
    E   *19105* Cuba (Pinar del Rio) *5607*

V *Calyptranthes baracoensis* Borh. *5607*
    V   *19105* Cuba (Guantanamo) *5607*

R *Calyptranthes capitata* Proctor *20883, 13336*
    R   *19890* Jamaica (St. Ann, Clarendon) *20883*

E *Calyptranthes clementis* Britton & Wilson *5607*
    E   *19105* Cuba *5607*

V *Calyptranthes cristalensis* Borh. *5607*
    V   *19105* Cuba (Holguin) *5607*

E *Calyptranthes discolor* Urb. *20883, 13336*
    E   *20883* Jamaica (Hanover, Dolphin Head) *20883*

R *Calyptranthes ekmanii* Urb. *20883, 13336*
    R   *19890* Haiti (southwest) *18329*
    R   *13336* Jamaica (Port.) *20883*

E *Calyptranthes elegans* Krug & Urban *19001*
    Ex/E *19001* Martinique *19001*
    E   *19001* St Lucia *10199*
    E   *19001* St Vincent *10199*

V *Calyptranthes ermitensis* Borh. *5607*
    V   *19105* Cuba (Guantanamo) *5607*

V *Calyptranthes exasperata* Borh. *5607*
    V   *19105* Cuba (Holguin) *5607*

R *Calyptranthes flavo-viridis* Urban *5607*
    R   *19105* Cuba (Pinar del Rio) *5607*

R *Calyptranthes kiaerskovii* Krug & Urban *15107*
    R   *15107* British Virgin Is. (Tortola) *15107*

V *Calyptranthes krugii* Kiaersk. *20883*
    I   *20883* Puerto Rico *20883*

R *Calyptranthes leonis* Borh. & Muniz *5607*
    R   *19105* Cuba (Guantanamo) *5607*

V *Calyptranthes linearis* Alain *5607*
    V   *19105* Cuba (Holguin) *5607*

E *Calyptranthes luquillensis* Alain *20883, 8058*
    I   *20883* Puerto Rico (Luquillo Mts.) *18551*

V *Calyptranthes mayarensis* Borh. *5607*
    V   *19105* Cuba (Holguin) *5607*

V *Calyptranthes minutiflora* Borh. *5607*
    V   *19105* Cuba (Holguin) *5607*

V *Calyptranthes munizii* Borh. *5607*
    V   *19105* Cuba (Holguin) *5607*

R *Calyptranthes nodosa* Urb. *20883, 13336*
    R   *19890* Jamaica *20883*

E *Calyptranthes peduncularis* Alain *20883, 8058*
    I   *20883* Puerto Rico *20883*

R *Calyptranthes pocsiana* Borh. *5607*
    R   *19105* Cuba (Holguin) *5607*

I *Calyptranthes polyneura* Urban *5607*
    I   *19105* Cuba (Santiago de Cuba, Holguin) *5607*

E *Calyptranthes portoricensis* Britt. *20883*
    I   *20883* Puerto Rico *20883*

E *Calyptranthes pozasiana* Urban *5607*
    E   *19105* Cuba (Pinar del Rio) *5607*

V *Calyptranthes pseudomoaensis* Borh. & Muniz *5607*
    V   *19105* Cuba (Guantanamo) *5607*

E *Calyptranthes rostrata* Griseb. *5607*
    E   *19105* Cuba (Guantanamo) *5607*

E *Calyptranthes thomasiana* Berg *20883, 8058*
    I   *20883* Puerto Rico (DS 2790: Vieques) *20883*
    I   *20883* USA - Virgin Is. (DS 2790: St Thomas) *20883*

I *Calyptranthes toaensis* Borh. *5607*
    I   *19105* Cuba (Guantanamo) *5607*

E *Calyptranthes triflora* Alain *20883*
    V   *19002* Puerto Rico *20883*

E *Calyptranthes tumidonodia* Schery *20883, 9006*
    I   *20883* Panama *20883*

R *Calyptranthes umbelliformis* Krug. & Urb. *20883*
    R   *20883* Jamaica *20883*

E *Calyptranthes uniflora* Proctor *20883, 13336*
    E   *13336* Jamaica *20883*

R *Calyptranthes wilsonii* Griseb. *20883*

	R	20883	Jamaica	20883
V	*Calyptranthes woodburyi* Alain 20883, 19002			
	I	20883	Puerto Rico	20883
E	*Calytrix breviseta* Lindley ssp. breviseta 20681			
	E	20681	Australia - Western Australia	20681
R	*Calytrix faucicola* Craven 20681			
	R	20681	Australia - Northern Territory	20681
V	*Calytrix gurulmundensis* Craven 20681			
	V	20681	Australia - Queensland	20681
R	*Calytrix inopinata* Craven 20681			
	R	20681	Australia - Northern Territory	20681
R	*Calytrix islensis* Craven 20681			
	R	20681	Australia - Queensland	20681
R	*Calytrix micrairoides* Craven 20681			
	R	20681	Australia - Northern Territory	20681
R	*Calytrix mimiana* Craven 20681			
	R	20681	Australia - Northern Territory	20681
R	*Calytrix rupestris* Craven 20681			
	R	20681	Australia - Northern Territory	20681
R	*Calytrix smeatoniana* (F.Muell.) Craven 20681			
	R	20681	Australia - South Australia	20681
R	*Calytrix surdiviperana* Craven 20681			
	R	20681	Australia - Northern Territory	20681
R	*Calytrix sylvana* Craven 20681			
	R	20681	Australia - Western Australia	20681
R	*Calytrix verticillata* Craven 20681			
	R	20681	Australia - Northern Territory	20681
R	*Campomanesia aurea* var. *hatschbachii* (Mattos) Legrand 20883			
	I	20883	Brazil	20883
	I	20883	Uruguay	20883
E	*Campomanesia hirsuta* Gardner 20883			
	E	20883	Brazil	20883
	?		Brazil - Rio de Janeiro	11731
E	*Campomanesia laurifolia* Gardner 20883			
	I	20883	Brazil	20883
	?		Brazil - Rio de Janeiro	11731
E	*Campomanesia lundiana* (Kiaerskou) Mattos 20883			
	E	20883	Brazil	20883
	Ex	11731	Brazil - Rio de Janeiro	11731
V	*Campomanesia neriiflora* (Berg) Niedenzu 20883			
	I	20883	Brazil	20883
	?		Brazil - Parana	11731
	?		Brazil - Sao Paulo	11731
E	*Campomanesia pabstiana* Mattos & Legrand 20883			
	E	20883	Brazil	20883
	?		Brazil - Distrito Federal	11731
R	*Campomanesia phaea* (Berg) Landrum 20883			
	I	20883	Brazil	20883
	?		Brazil - Rio de Janeiro	11731
	?		Brazil - Sao Paulo	11731
E	*Campomanesia prosthecesepala* Kiaerskou 20883			
	E	20883	Brazil	20883
	?		Brazil - Minas Gerais	11731
R	*Campomanesia reitziana* Legrand 20883, 20310			
	I	20883	Brazil	20883
	?		Brazil - Santa Catarina	20310
V	*Campomanesia rufa* (Berg) Niedenzu 20883			
	I	20883	Brazil	20883
	?		Brazil - Minas Gerais	11731

V	*Campomanesia schlechtendaliana* (Berg) Niedenzu 20883			
	I	20883	Brazil	20883
E	*Campomanesia schlechtendaliana* (Berg) Neidenzu var. *rugosa* (Berg) Landrum 20883			
	E	20883	Brazil	20883
	?		Brazil - Rio de Janeiro (Cabo Frio)	11731
V	*Campomanesia schlechtendaliana* (Berg) Niedenzu var. *schlechtendaliana* 20883			
	I	20883	Brazil	20883
	?		Brazil - Parana	11731
	?		Brazil - Rio de Janeiro	11731
E	*Campomanesia sessiliflora* var. *sessiliflora* 20883			
	E	20883	Brazil	20883
	?		Brazil - Sao Paulo	11731
E	*Campomanesia viatoris* Landrum 20883			
	E	20883	Brazil	20883
	?		Brazil - Alagoas	11731
R	*Campomanesia xanthocarpa* var. *littoralis* (Legrand) Landrum 20883			
	I	20883	Brazil	20883
	?		Brazil - Rio Grande do Sul	11731
	?		Brazil - Santa Catarina	11731
V	*Chamelaucium erythrochlorum* N.G.Marchant & Keighery ms. 20681			
	V	20681	Australia - Western Australia	20681
E	*Chamelaucium griffinii* N.G.Marchant & Keighery ms. 20681			
	E	20681	Australia - Western Australia	20681
V	*Chamelaucium roycei* N.G.Marchant & Keighery 20681			
	V	20681	Australia - Western Australia	20681
R	*Choricarpia subargentea* (C.White) L.A.S.Johnson 20681			
	I	20681	Australia - New South Wales	20681
	I	20681	Australia - Queensland	20681
I	*Cleistocalyx nicobaricus* (King) Merr. & Perry 7771			
	I		India - Nicobar Is. (Katchal Is.)	7771
E	*Cloezia aquarum* (Guillaumin) J.Wyndam Dawson 20893			
	E	20893	New Caledonia	20893
R	*Cloezia deplanchei* Brongn. & Gris			
	R		New Caledonia	
V	*Cupheanthus microphyllus* Guillaumin 20893			
	V	20893	New Caledonia	20893
V	*Darwinia acerosa* Fitzg. 20681			
	V	20681	Australia - Western Australia	20681
E	*Darwinia apiculata* N.G.Marchant 20681			
	E	20681	Australia - Western Australia	20681
V	*Darwinia biflora* (Cheel) B.G.Briggs 20681			
	V	20681	Australia - New South Wales	20681
R	*Darwinia briggsiae* Craven & S.R.Jones 20681			
	R	20681	Australia - New South Wales	20681
E	*Darwinia carnea* C.Gardner 20681			
	E	20681	Australia - Western Australia	20681
V	*Darwinia collina* C.Gardner 20681			
	V	20681	Australia - Western Australia	20681
R	*Darwinia diminuta* B.G.Briggs 20681			
	R	20681	Australia - New South Wales	20681
E	*Darwinia ferricola* N.G.Marchant & Keighery ms. 20681			
	E	20681	Australia - Western Australia	20681
R	*Darwinia glaucophylla* B.G.Briggs 20681			

R   *20681*   Australia - New South Wales *20681*

R   *Darwinia grandiflora* (Benth.) R.Baker & H.G.Smith *20681*

   R   *20681*   Australia - New South Wales *20681*

R   *Darwinia hypericifolia* (Turcz.) Domin *20681*

   R   *20681*   Australia - Western Australia *20681*

R   *Darwinia lejostyla* (Turcz.) Domin *20681*

   R   *20681*   Australia - Western Australia *20681*

V   *Darwinia macrostegia* (Turcz.) Benth. *20681*

   V   *20681*   Australia - Western Australia *20681*

V   *Darwinia masonii* C.Gardner *20681*

   V   *20681*   Australia - Western Australia *20681*

V   *Darwinia meeboldii* C.Gardner *20681*

   V   *20681*   Australia - Western Australia *20681*

V   *Darwinia oxylepis* (Turcz.) N.G.Marchant & Keighery *20681*

   V   *20681*   Australia - Western Australia *20681*

R   *Darwinia peduncularis* B.G.Briggs *20681*

   R   *20681*   Australia - New South Wales *20681*

R   *Darwinia polycephala* C.Gardner *20681*

   R   *20681*   Australia - Western Australia *20681*

R   *Darwinia procera* B.G.Briggs *20681*

   R   *20681*   Australia - New South Wales *20681*

R   *Darwinia sanguinea* (Meisner) Benth. *20681*

   R   *20681*   Australia - Western Australia *20681*

V   *Darwinia squarrosa* (Turcz.) Domin *20681*

   V   *20681*   Australia - Western Australia *20681*

V   *Darwinia wittwerorum* N.G.Marchant & Keighery *20681*

   V   *20681*   Australia - Western Australia *20681*

E   *Eucalyptus absita* Grayling & Brooker *20681*

   E   *20681*   Australia - Western Australia *20681*

R   *Eucalyptus alligatrix* L.A.S.Johnson & K.Hill ssp. *alligatrix* *20681*

   R   *20681*   Australia - Victoria *20681*

V   *Eucalyptus alligatrix* L.A.S.Johnson & K.Hill ssp. *limaensis* Brooker, Slee & J.D.Briggs ms. *20681*

   V   *20681*   Australia - Victoria *20681*

V   *Eucalyptus alligatrix* L.A.S.Johnson & K.Hill ssp. *miscella* Brooker, Slee & J.D.Briggs ms. *20681*

   V   *20681*   Australia - New South Wales *20681*

R   *Eucalyptus apiculata* R.Baker & H.G.Smith *20681*

   R   *20681*   Australia - New South Wales *20681*

R   *Eucalyptus approximans* Maiden *20681*

   R   *20681*   Australia - New South Wales *20681*

V   *Eucalyptus aquatica* (Blakely) L.A.S.Johnson & K.Hill *20681*

   V   *20681*   Australia - New South Wales *20681*

R   *Eucalyptus aquilina* Brooker *20681*

   R   *20681*   Australia - Western Australia *20681*

R   *Eucalyptus archeri* Maiden & Blakely *20681*

   R   *20681*   Australia - Tasmania *20681*

V   *Eucalyptus argophloia* Blakely *20681*

   V   *20681*   Australia - Queensland *20681*

V   *Eucalyptus argutifolia* Grayling & Brooker *20681*

   V   *20681*   Australia - Western Australia *20681*

V   *Eucalyptus articulata* Brooker & Hopper *20681*

   V   *20681*   Australia - Western Australia *20681*

R   *Eucalyptus aspersa* Brooker & Hopper *20681*

R   *20681*   Australia - Western Australia *20681*

R   *Eucalyptus badjensis* Beuzev. & Welch *20681*

   R   *20681*   Australia - New South Wales *20681*

R   *Eucalyptus baeuerlenii* F.Muell. *20681*

   R   *20681*   Australia - New South Wales *20681*

V   *Eucalyptus balanites* Grayling & Brooker *20681*

   V   *20681*   Australia - Western Australia *20681*

R   *Eucalyptus barberi* L.A.S.Johnson & Blaxell *20681*

   R   *20681*   Australia - Tasmania *20681*

V   *Eucalyptus beaniana* L.A.S.Johnson & K.Hill *20681*

   V   *20681*   Australia - Queensland *20681*

V   *Eucalyptus beardiana* Brooker & Blaxell *20681*

   V   *20681*   Australia - Western Australia *20681*

V   *Eucalyptus bennettiae* D.Carr & S.Carr *20681*

   V   *20681*   Australia - Western Australia *20681*

R   *Eucalyptus bensonii* L.A.S.Johnson & K.Hill *20681*

   R   *20681*   Australia - New South Wales *20681*

V   *Eucalyptus benthamii* Maiden & Cambage *20681*

   V   *20681*   Australia - New South Wales *20681*

V   *Eucalyptus blaxellii* L.A.S.Johnson & K.Hill *20681*

   V   *20681*   Australia - Western Australia *20681*

R   *Eucalyptus brachyphylla* C.Gardner *20681*

   R   *20681*   Australia - Western Australia *20681*

V   *Eucalyptus brevipes* Brooker *20681*

   V   *20681*   Australia - Western Australia *20681*

V   *Eucalyptus burdettiana* Blakely & Steedman *20681*

   V   *20681*   Australia - Western Australia *20681*

R   *Eucalyptus burgessiana* L.A.S.Johnson & Blaxell *20681, 16162*

   R   *20681*   Australia - New South Wales *20681*

V   *Eucalyptus cadens* J.D.Briggs & Crisp *20681*

   V   *20681*   Australia - Victoria *20681*

R   *Eucalyptus caesia* Benth. ssp. *caesia* *20681*

   R   *20681*   Australia - Western Australia *20681*

R   *Eucalyptus caesia* Benth. ssp. *magna* Brooker & Hopper *20681*

   R   *20681*   Australia - Western Australia *20681*

R   *Eucalyptus calcicola* Brooker *20681*

   R   *20681*   Australia - Western Australia *20681*

V   *Eucalyptus caleyi* Maiden ssp. *ovendenii* L.A.S.Johnson & K.Hill *20681*

   V   *20681*   Australia - New South Wales *20681*

V   *Eucalyptus camfieldii* Maiden *20681*

   V   *20681*   Australia - New South Wales *20681*

V   *Eucalyptus camphora* R.Baker ssp. *relicta* L.A.S.Johnson & K.Hill *20681*

   I   *20681*   Australia - New South Wales *20681*
   I   *20681*   Australia - Queensland *20681*

V   *Eucalyptus cannonii* R.T.Baker *20681*

   V   *20681*   Australia - New South Wales *20681*

R   *Eucalyptus carnabyi* Blakely & Steedman *20681*

   R   *20681*   Australia - Western Australia *20681*

V   *Eucalyptus ceracea* Brooker & Done *20681*

   V   *20681*   Australia - Western Australia *20681*

V   *Eucalyptus cerasiformis* Brooker & Blaxell *20681*

   V   *20681*   Australia - Western Australia *20681*

R   *Eucalyptus cinerea* F.Muell. ex Benth. ssp. *triplex* (L.Johnson & K.Hill) Brooker, Slee & J.D.Briggs ms. *20681*

	I	*20681*	Australia - Capital Territory *20681*
	I	*20681*	Australia - New South Wales *20681*
V	*Eucalyptus clandestina* A.R.Bean *20681*		
	V	*20681*	Australia - Queensland *20681*
R	*Eucalyptus codonocarpa* Blakely & McKie *20681*		
	I	*20681*	Australia - New South Wales *20681*
	I	*20681*	Australia - Queensland *20681*
V	*Eucalyptus conglomerata* Maiden & Blakely *20681*		
	V	*20681*	Australia - Queensland *20681*
E	*Eucalyptus copulans* L.A.S.Johnson & K.Hill *20681*		
	E	*20681*	Australia - New South Wales *20681*
R	*Eucalyptus cordata* Labill. *20681*		
	R	*20681*	Australia - Tasmania *20681*
V	*Eucalyptus coronata* C.Gardner *20681*		
	V	*20681*	Australia - Western Australia *20681*
R	*Eucalyptus corynodes* A.R.Bean & Brooker *20681*		
	R	*20681*	Australia - Queensland *20681*
E	*Eucalyptus crenulata* Blakely & Beuzev. *20681*		
	E	*20681*	Australia - Victoria *20681*
R	*Eucalyptus cretata* P.Lang & Brooker *20681*		
	R	*20681*	Australia - South Australia *20681*
V	*Eucalyptus crispata* Brooker & Hopper *20681*		
	V	*20681*	Australia - Western Australia *20681*
V	*Eucalyptus crucis* Maiden ssp. *crucis* *20681*		
	V	*20681*	Australia - Western Australia *20681*
E	*Eucalyptus crucis* Maiden ssp. *praecipua* Brooker & Hopper *20681*		
	E	*20681*	Australia - Western Australia *20681*
R	*Eucalyptus cunninghamii* G.Don *20681*		
	R	*20681*	Australia - New South Wales *20681*
E	*Eucalyptus cuprea* Brooker & Hopper *20681*		
	E	*20681*	Australia - Western Australia *20681*
R	*Eucalyptus curtisii* Blakely & J.W.White *20681*		
	R	*20681*	Australia - Queensland *20681*
R	*Eucalyptus deflexa* Brooker *20681*		
	R	*20681*	Australia - Western Australia *20681*
R	*Eucalyptus desmondensis* Maiden & Blakely *20681*		
	R	*20681*	Australia - Western Australia *20681*
R	*Eucalyptus deuaensis* Boland & Gilmour *20681*		
	R	*20681*	Australia - New South Wales *20681*
R	*Eucalyptus disclusa* L.A.S.Johnson & Blaxell *20681*		
	R	*20681*	Australia - Queensland *20681*
E	*Eucalyptus dolerosa* Brooker & Hopper *20681*		
	E	*20681*	Australia - Western Australia *20681*
R	*Eucalyptus dolichorhyncha* (Brooker) Brooker & Hopper *20681*		
	R	*20681*	Australia - Western Australia *20681*
R	*Eucalyptus dunnii* Maiden *20681*		
	I	*20681*	Australia - New South Wales *20681*
	I	*20681*	Australia - Queensland *20681*
R	*Eucalyptus ebbanoensis* Maiden ssp. *photina* Brooker & Hopper *20681*		
	R	*20681*	Australia - Western Australia *20681*
R	*Eucalyptus elaeophloia* Chappill, Crisp & Prober *20681*		
	R	*20681*	Australia - Victoria *20681*
R	*Eucalyptus erectifolia* Brooker & Hopper *20681*		
	R	*20681*	Australia - Western Australia *20681*
R	*Eucalyptus exilipes* Brooker & Bean *20681*		

	R	*20681*	Australia - Queensland *20681*
R	*Eucalyptus exilis* Brooker *20681*		
	R	*20681*	Australia - Western Australia *20681*
R	*Eucalyptus fergusonii* R.Baker ssp. *dorsiventralis* *20681*		
	R	*20681*	Australia - New South Wales *20681*
R	*Eucalyptus formanii* C.Gardner *20681*		
	R	*20681*	Australia - Western Australia *20681*
R	*Eucalyptus froggattii* Blakely *20681*		
	R	*20681*	Australia - Victoria *20681*
R	*Eucalyptus fusiformis* Boland & Kleinig *20681*		
	I	*20681*	Australia - New South Wales *20681*
	I	*20681*	Australia - Queensland *20681*
R	*Eucalyptus georgei* Brooker & Blaxell ssp. *fulgida* Brooker & Hopper *20681*		
	R	*20681*	Australia - Western Australia *20681*
R	*Eucalyptus georgei* Brooker & Blaxell ssp. *georgei* *20681*		
	R	*20681*	Australia - Western Australia *20681*
R	*Eucalyptus gilbertensis* (Maiden & Blakely) S.T.Blake *20681*		
	R	*20681*	Australia - Queensland *20681*
V	*Eucalyptus glaucina* (Blakely) L.A.S.Johnson *20681*		
	V	*20681*	Australia - New South Wales *20681*
V	*Eucalyptus goniantha* Turcz. ssp. *goniantha* *20681*		
	V	*20681*	Australia - Western Australia *20681*
R	*Eucalyptus gregsoniana* L.A.S.Johnson & Blaxell *20681*		
	R	*20681*	Australia - New South Wales *20681*
V	*Eucalyptus hallii* Brooker *20681*		
	V	*20681*	Australia - Queensland *20681*
R	*Eucalyptus howittiana* F.Muell. *20681*		
	R	*20681*	Australia - Queensland *20681*
R	*Eucalyptus hypostomatica* L.A.S.Johnson & K.Hill *20681*		
	R	*20681*	Australia - New South Wales *20681*
V	*Eucalyptus imlayensis* Crisp & Brooker *20681*		
	V	*20681*	Australia - New South Wales *20681*
E	*Eucalyptus impensa* Brooker & Hopper *20681*		
	E	*20681*	Australia - Western Australia *20681*
V	*Eucalyptus infera* A.R.Bean *20681*		
	V	*20681*	Australia - Queensland *20681*
V	*Eucalyptus insularis* Brooker *20681*		
	V	*20681*	Australia - Western Australia *20681*
V	*Eucalyptus johnsoniana* Brooker & Blaxell *20681*		
	V	*20681*	Australia - Western Australia *20681*
V	*Eucalyptus kabiana* L.A.S.Johnson & K.Hill *20681*		
	V	*20681*	Australia - Queensland *20681*
V	*Eucalyptus kartzoffiana* L.A.S.Johnson & Blaxell *20681*		
	V	*20681*	Australia - New South Wales *20681*
R	*Eucalyptus kitsoniana* Maiden *20681*		
	R	*20681*	Australia - Victoria *20681*
R	*Eucalyptus koolpinensis* Brooker & Dunlop *20681*		
	R	*20681*	Australia - Northern Territory *20681*
R	*Eucalyptus kruseana* F.Muell. *20681*		
	R	*20681*	Australia - Western Australia *20681*
V	*Eucalyptus langleyi* L.A.S.Johnson & Blaxell *20681*		
	V	*20681*	Australia - New South Wales *20681*

R	*Eucalyptus lansdowneana* F.Muell. & J.E.Brown ssp. *lansdowneana* 20681		
	R	20681	Australia - South Australia 20681
R	*Eucalyptus largeana* Blakely & Beuzev. 20681		
	R	20681	Australia - New South Wales 20681
R	*Eucalyptus latens* Brooker 20681		
	R	20681	Australia - Western Australia 20681
V	*Eucalyptus lateritica* Brooker & Hopper 20681		
	V	20681	Australia - Western Australia 20681
R	*Eucalyptus latiuscula* (Blakely) L.A.S.Johnson & K.Hill 20681		
	R	20681	Australia - New South Wales 20681
V	*Eucalyptus leprophloia* Brooker & Hopper 20681		
	V	20681	Australia - Western Australia 20681
V	*Eucalyptus leptoloma* Brooker & A.R.Bean 20681		
	V	20681	Australia - Queensland 20681
R	*Eucalyptus ligulata* Brooker 20681		
	R	20681	Australia - Western Australia 20681
R	*Eucalyptus lockyeri* Blaxell & K. Hill 20681		
	R	20681	Australia - Queensland 20681
R	*Eucalyptus lucens* Brooker & Dunlop 20681		
	R	20681	Australia - Northern Territory 20681
R	*Eucalyptus luehmanniana* F.Muell. 20681		
	R	20681	Australia - New South Wales 20681
R	*Eucalyptus macarthurii* Deane & Maiden 20681		
	R	20681	Australia - New South Wales 20681
R	*Eucalyptus macrocarpa* Hook. ssp. *elachantha* Brooker & Hopper 20681		
	R	20681	Australia - Western Australia 20681
R	*Eucalyptus malacoxylon* Blakely 20681		
	R	20681	Australia - New South Wales 20681
V	*Eucalyptus mckieana* Blakely 20681		
	V	20681	Australia - New South Wales 20681
R	*Eucalyptus melanoleuca* S.T.Blake 20681		
	R	20681	Australia - Queensland 20681
R	*Eucalyptus melanophitra* Brooker & Hopper 20681		
	R	20681	Australia - Western Australia 20681
V	*Eucalyptus merrickiae* Maiden & Blakely 20681		
	V	20681	Australia - Western Australia 20681
R	*Eucalyptus michaeliana* Blakely 20681		
	I	20681	Australia - New South Wales 20681
	I	20681	Australia - Queensland 20681
R	*Eucalyptus microcodon* L.A.S.Johnson & K.Hill 20681		
	I	20681	Australia - New South Wales 20681
	I	20681	Australia - Queensland 20681
R	*Eucalyptus mitchelliana* Cambage 20681		
	R	20681	Australia - Victoria 20681
V	*Eucalyptus mooreana* (Fitzg.) Maiden 20681		
	V	20681	Australia - Western Australia 20681
E	*Eucalyptus morrisbyi* R.G.Brett 20681		
	E	20681	Australia - Tasmania 20681
R	*Eucalyptus nandewarica* L.A.S.Johnson & K.Hill 20681		
	R	20681	Australia - New South Wales 20681
R	*Eucalyptus neglecta* Maiden 20681		
	R	20681	Australia - Victoria 20681
V	*Eucalyptus nicholii* Maiden & Blakely 20681		
	V	20681	Australia - New South Wales 20681
R	*Eucalyptus nigrifunda* Brooker & Hopper 20681		
	R	20681	Australia - Western Australia 20681
R	*Eucalyptus olida* L.A.S.Johnson & K.Hill 20681		
	R	20681	Australia - New South Wales 20681
V	*Eucalyptus olivacea* Brooker & Hopper ms. 20681		
	V	20681	Australia - Western Australia 20681
R	*Eucalyptus olsenii* L.A.S.Johnson & Blaxell 20681		
	R	20681	Australia - New South Wales 20681
R	*Eucalyptus pachycalyx* Maiden & Blakely ssp. *pachycalyx* 20681		
	R	20681	Australia - Queensland 20681
R	*Eucalyptus pachycalyx* Maiden & Blakely ssp. *waajensis* L.A.S.Johnson & K.Hill 20681		
	R	20681	Australia - Queensland 20681
V	*Eucalyptus paedoglauca* L.A.S.Johnson & Blaxell 20681		
	V	20681	Australia - Queensland 20681
R	*Eucalyptus paliformis* L.A.S.Johnson & Blaxell 20681		
	R	20681	Australia - New South Wales 20681
V	*Eucalyptus parramattensis* C.Hall ssp. *decadens* L.A.S.Johnson & Blaxell 20681		
	V	20681	Australia - New South Wales 20681
V	*Eucalyptus parvula* L.A.S.Johnson & K.Hill 20681		
	V	20681	Australia - New South Wales 20681
R	*Eucalyptus pendens* Brooker 20681		
	R	20681	Australia - Western Australia 20681
R	*Eucalyptus percostata* Brooker & P.Lang 20681		
	R	20681	Australia - South Australia 20681
R	*Eucalyptus petalophylla* Brooker & A.R. Bean 20681		
	R	20681	Australia - Queensland 20681
E	*Eucalyptus phylacis* L.A.S.Johnson & K.Hill 20681		
	E	20681	Australia - Western Australia 20681
R	*Eucalyptus pilbarensis* Brooker & Edgcombe 20681		
	R	20681	Australia - Western Australia 20681
V	*Eucalyptus platydisca* L.A.S.Johnson & K.Hill ms. 20681		
	V	20681	Australia - Western Australia 20681
V	*Eucalyptus pruiniramis* L.A.S.Johnson & K.Hill 20681		
	V	20681	Australia - Western Australia 20681
V	*Eucalyptus pulverulenta* Sims 20681		
	V	20681	Australia - New South Wales 20681
V	*Eucalyptus pumila* Cambage 20681		
	V	20681	Australia - New South Wales 20681
R	*Eucalyptus quadricostata* Brooker 20681		
	R	20681	Australia - Queensland 20681
R	*Eucalyptus rameliana* F.Muell. 20681		
	R	20681	Australia - Western Australia 20681
V	*Eucalyptus raveretiana* F.Muell. 20681		
	V	20681	Australia - Queensland 20681
E	*Eucalyptus recurva* Crisp 20681		
	E	20681	Australia - New South Wales 20681
E	*Eucalyptus rhodantha* Blakely & Steedman 20681		
	E	20681	Australia - Western Australia 20681
E	*Eucalyptus rhodantha* Blakely & Steedman var. *petiolaris* Blakely & Steedman 20681		
	E	20681	Australia - Western Australia 20681
V	*Eucalyptus rhodops* D.J.Carr & S.M.Carr 20681		
	V	20681	Australia - Queensland 20681
R	*Eucalyptus rhombica* A.R.Bean & Brooker 20681		
	R	20681	Australia - Queensland 20681
R	*Eucalyptus risdonii* Hook.f. 20681		

	R	20681 Australia - Tasmania 20681
V	*Eucalyptus robertsonii* Blakely ssp. *hemisphaerica* 20681	
	V	20681 Australia - New South Wales 20681
V	*Eucalyptus rubida* Deane & Maiden ssp. *barbigerorum* L.A.S.Johnson & K.Hill 20681	
	V	20681 Australia - New South Wales 20681
V	*Eucalyptus rubida* Deane & Maiden ssp. *canobolensis* L.A.S.Johnson & K.Hill 20681	
	V	20681 Australia - New South Wales 20681
V	*Eucalyptus rubida* Deane & Maiden ssp. *septemflora* L.A.S.Johnson & K.Hill 20681	
	V	20681 Australia - Victoria 20681
R	*Eucalyptus rubiginosa* Brooker 20681	
	R	20681 Australia - Queensland 20681
R	*Eucalyptus rudderi* Maiden 20681	
	R	20681 Australia - New South Wales 20681
R	*Eucalyptus rudis* Endl. ssp. *cratyantha* Brooker & Hopper 20681	
	R	20681 Australia - Western Australia 20681
R	*Eucalyptus rummeryi* Maiden 20681	
	R	20681 Australia - New South Wales 20681
R	*Eucalyptus saxatilis* Kirkpatr. & Brooker 20681	
	I	20681 Australia - New South Wales 20681
	I	20681 Australia - Victoria 20681
R	*Eucalyptus scabrida* Brooker & A.R. Bean 20681	
	R	20681 Australia - Queensland 20681
V	*Eucalyptus scoparia* Maiden 20681	
	V	20681 Australia - Queensland 20681
R	*Eucalyptus serpentinicola* L.A.S.Johnson & Blaxell 20681	
	R	20681 Australia - New South Wales 20681
R	*Eucalyptus sicilifolia* L.A.S.Johnson & K.Hill 20681	
	R	20681 Australia - Queensland 20681
R	*Eucalyptus spectatrix* L.A.S.Johnson & K.Hill 20681	
	R	20681 Australia - New South Wales 20681
R	*Eucalyptus sphaerocarpa* L.A.S.Johnson & Blaxell 20681	
	R	20681 Australia - Queensland 20681
V	*Eucalyptus steedmanii* C.Gardner 20681	
	V	20681 Australia - Western Australia 20681
R	*Eucalyptus stoatei* C.Gardner 20681	
	R	20681 Australia - Western Australia 20681
V	*Eucalyptus strzeleckii* K.Rule 20681	
	V	20681 Australia - Victoria 20681
R	*Eucalyptus sturgissiana* L.A.S.Johnson & Blaxell 20681	
	R	20681 Australia - New South Wales 20681
V	*Eucalyptus suberea* Brooker & Hopper 20681	
	V	20681 Australia - Western Australia 20681
V	*Eucalyptus synandra* Crisp 20681	
	V	20681 Australia - Western Australia 20681
R	*Eucalyptus taurina* A.R.Bean & Brooker 20681	
	R	20681 Australia - Queensland 20681
V	*Eucalyptus terrica* A.R.Bean 20681	
	V	20681 Australia - Queensland 20681
V	*Eucalyptus tetrapleura* L.A.S.Johnson 20681	
	V	20681 Australia - New South Wales 20681
R	*Eucalyptus triflora* (Maiden) Blakely 20681	

	R	20681 Australia - New South Wales 20681
V	*Eucalyptus virens* Brooker & Bean 20681	
	V	20681 Australia - Queensland 20681
R	*Eucalyptus wilcoxii* Boland & Kleinig 20681	
	R	20681 Australia - New South Wales 20681
V	*Eucalyptus xanthope* Bean & Brooker 20681	
	V	20681 Australia - Queensland 20681
R	*Eucalyptus yarraensis* Maiden & Cambage 20681	
	R	20681 Australia - Victoria 20681
R	*Eucalyptus youmanii* Blakely & McKie 20681	
	R	20681 Australia - New South Wales 20681
R	*Eucalyptus zopherophloia* Brooker & Hopper 20681	
	R	20681 Australia - Western Australia 20681
E	*Eugenia abbreviata* Urb. 20883, 13336	
	E	19890 Jamaica 20883
E	*Eugenia aboukirensis* Proctor 20883, 13336	
	E	19890 Jamaica (St. Ann) 20883
E	*Eugenia aceitillo* Urban 5607	
	E	19105 Cuba (Granma) 5607
E	*Eugenia acunai* Alain 5607	
	E	19105 Cuba (Santiago de Cuba) 5607
V	*Eugenia acutisepala* Proctor 20883, 13336	
	V	19890 Jamaica (St. Catherine) 20883
V	*Eugenia acutissima* Urban & Ekman 5607	
	V	19105 Cuba (Pinar del Rio) 5607
V	*Eugenia alexandri* Krug & Urb. 20883	
	V	20883 Jamaica 20883
E	*Eugenia amblyophylla* Urban 5607	
	E	19105 Cuba (Santiago de Cuba) 5607
E	*Eugenia amoena* Thwaites 8021	
	E	12838 Sri Lanka (Galle & Ratnapura) 8021
R	*Eugenia amplifolia* Urb. 20883	
	R	20883 Jamaica 20883
E	*Eugenia anafensis* Britton & P. Wilson 5607	
	E	19105 Cuba (Prov. Habana) 5607
Ex/E	*Eugenia argentea* Beddome 11494	
	Ex/E	11494 India - Kerala (Wynad forests) 11494
E	*Eugenia atricha* Urban 5607	
	E	19105 Cuba (Prov. Habana; Ciud. Habana) 5607
E	*Eugenia bayatensis* Urban 5607	
	E	19105 Cuba (Santiago de Cuba; Holguin) 5607
E	*Eugenia bellonis* Krug & Urban ex Urban 20883	
	I	20883 Puerto Rico 20883
E	*Eugenia bojeri* Baker 10082, 21329	
	E	20771 Mauritius 10082
R	*Eugenia brachythrix* Urb. 20883, 13336	
	R	19890 Jamaica (Portland) 20883
V	*Eugenia brownei* Urb. 20883, 13336	
	V	19890 Jamaica (St. Elizabeth) 20883
I	*Eugenia bryanii* (Kaneh.) Hosok.	
	I	18338 U.S. - Guam 18338
I	*Eugenia castanea* Merr. 19209	
	I	19209 Malaysia - Peninsular Malaysia (Perak, Johor) 19209
E	*Eugenia ceibana* Urban 5607	
	E	19105 Cuba (Juventud Is.) 5607
R	*Eugenia chrootrichoides* Proctor 20883	
	R	20883 Jamaica 20883

E   *Eugenia chrysobalanoides* Dc. *19001*
- E   *19001*   Barbados *10199*
- E   *19001*   Guadeloupe *10199*
- E   *19001*   Martinique (l'Anse Couleuvre) *10199*
- E   *19001*   St Kitts - Nevis (Nevis) *10199*

R   *Eugenia clarendonensis* Urb. *20883*
- R   *20883*   Jamaica *20883*

V   *Eugenia copacabanensis* Kiaerskou *19560*
- V   *19560*   Brazil - Rio de Janeiro *19560*

I   *Eugenia cordata* (Swartz) DC. var. *sintensii* (Kiaerskou) Krug & Urban *10199*
- I   Dominica *10199*

I   *Eugenia cotinifolia* Jacq. ssp. *codyensis* (Munro ex Wight) Ashton
- I   India - Karnataka (Coorg, south Canara)
- I   India - Kerala (Travancore)
- I   India - Tamil Nadu (Nilgiri Hills)

E   *Eugenia cotinifolia* Jacq. ssp. *phyllraeoides* (Trimen) P. Ashton *8021*
- E   *20013*   Sri Lanka (Laggala, Matale) *8021*

V   *Eugenia crassicaulis* Proctor *20883, 13336*
- V   *19890*   Jamaica (Portland) *20883*

E   *Eugenia crassipetala* Guého & A.J. Scott *10082*
- E   *20771*   Mauritius *10082*

V   *Eugenia crenata* O. Berg *20883*
- V   *20883*   Jamaica *20883*

E   *Eugenia daenikeri* Guillaumin *20893*
- E   *20893*   New Caledonia *20893*

E   *Eugenia discifera* Gamble *1172*
- E   *11494*   India - Kerala *11494*
- E   *11494*   India - Tamil Nadu (Sethur Hills, Kamarajar Dt) *11494*

R   *Eugenia disticha* (Sw.) DC. *20883*
- R   *20883*   Jamaica *20883*

E   *Eugenia duplicata* Britton & P. Wilson *5607*
- E   *19105*   Cuba (Prov. Habana) *5607*

E   *Eugenia eggersii* Kiaersk. *20883*
- I   *20883*   Puerto Rico *20883*

R   *Eugenia elliptica* Lam. *10082*
- R   *20771*   Mauritius *10082*

V   *Eugenia eperforata* Urb. *13336*
- V   *19890*   Jamaica (St. Ann) *19890*

V   *Eugenia eriantha* Urban *5607*
- V   *19105*   Cuba (Granma) *5607*

V   *Eugenia ericoides* Guillaumin *20893*
- V   *20893*   New Caledonia *20893*

R   *Eugenia erythrophylla* Strey *20604*
- R   *20604*   South Africa - Cape Province *20604*
- R   *20604*   South Africa - Natal *20604*

R   *Eugenia eurycheila* Berg *8679*
- R   Guyana *8679*

R   *Eugenia fasciculata* Guého & A.J. Scott *10082*
- R   *20771*   Mauritius *10082*

I   *Eugenia floccosa* Beddome *6987*
- I   India - Tamil Nadu *6987*

I   *Eugenia fulva* Thwaites *8021*
- I   *16162*   Sri Lanka *8021*

V   *Eugenia gatopensis* Guillaumin *20893*
- V   *20893*   New Caledonia *20893*

R   *Eugenia gigantea* Ridley *881*

- R   *14224*   Australia - Christmas Is. *881*

I   *Eugenia glabra* Alston *8021*
- I   *16162*   Sri Lanka (Galle) *8021*

E   *Eugenia grifensis* Urban *5607*
- E   *19105*   Cuba (Pinar del Rio) *5607*

V   *Eugenia gryposperma* Krug & Urban *8767*
- V   *19001*   Martinique (Montagne du Vauclin) *19001*

E   *Eugenia guanensis* Urban *5607*
- E   *19105*   Cuba (Pinar del Rio) *5607*

V   *Eugenia haematocarpa* Alain *20883, 10197*
- V   *20883*   Puerto Rico *20883*

E   *Eugenia hanoverensis* Proctor *20883, 13336*
- E   *13336*   Jamaica *20883*

R   *Eugenia harrisii* Krug & Urb. *20883*
- R   *20883*   Jamaica *20883*

I   *Eugenia harrisii* Krug & Urb. var. *grandifolia* Krug & Urb. *20883, 13336*
- I   *19890*   Jamaica *20883*

R   *Eugenia harrisii* Krug & Urb. var. *harrisii* *20883*
- R   *20883*   Jamaica *20883*

R   *Eugenia hastilis* (Blume) Guého & A.J. Scott *10082*
- R   *20771*   Mauritius *10082*

V   *Eugenia heterochroa* Urb. *20883, 13336*
- V   *19890*   Jamaica (Clarendon) *20883*

R   *Eugenia hodgei* McVaugh *10199*
- R   *19001*   Dominica *10199*
- R   *19001*   Martinique *19001*

R   *Eugenia howardiana* Proctor *13336*
- R   *19890*   Jamaica (Manchester, St. Ann) *19890*

E   *Eugenia ignota* Britton & P. Wilson *5607*
- E   *19105*   Cuba (Juventud Is.) *5607*

R   *Eugenia ilhensis* Berg. *20883*
- I   *20883*   Brazil *20883*
- R   *20883*   Paraguay *20883*

E   *Eugenia insignis* Thwaites *12838*
- E   *12838*   Sri Lanka *12838*

V   *Eugenia isosticta* Urb. *20883*
- V   *20883*   Jamaica *20883*

E   *Eugenia iteophylla* Krug & Urban *5607*
- E   *19105*   Cuba (Santiago de Cuba) *5607*

R   *Eugenia jamaicensis* O. Berg *20883*
- R   *20883*   Jamaica *20883*

I   *Eugenia jeremiensis* Urb. & Ekman *20883, 13336*
- I   *19890*   Haiti (southwest) *18329*
- V   *13336*   Jamaica *20883*

I   *Eugenia jossinia* Duthie
- I   India - Tamil Nadu

V   *Eugenia kaalensis* Guillaumin *20893*
- V   *20893*   New Caledonia *20893*

E   *Eugenia kellyana* Proctor *20883, 13336*
- E   *13336*   Jamaica *20883*

E   *Eugenia koolauensis* O. Deg. *20850, 14209, 21357*
- E   *20850*   U.S. - Hawaii (Oahu - Ko`olau Mts.) *20850*

R   *Eugenia lamprophylla* Urb. *20883, 13336*
- R   *19890*   Jamaica (central) *20883*

V   *Eugenia laurae* Proctor *20883, 13336*
- V   *13336*   Jamaica *20883*

V	*Eugenia libanensis* Urban *5607*	
	V	*19105* Cuba (Guantanamo) *5607*
R	*Eugenia mabaeoides* Wight ssp. *mabaeoides* *8021*	
	R	*20013* Sri Lanka *8021*
I	*Eugenia mabaeoides* Wight ssp. *pedunculata* (Trimen) P. Ashton *8021*	
	I	*16162* Sri Lanka (Rangala, Kandy District) *8021*
V	*Eugenia mackeeana* Guillaumin *20893*	
	V	*20893* New Caledonia *20893*
V	*Eugenia mandevillensis* Urb. *20883*	
	I	*20883* Jamaica *20883*
R	*Eugenia mandevillensis* Urb. var. *mandevillensis* Urb. *20883, 13336*	
	R	*19890* Jamaica (Manchester) *20883*
V	*Eugenia mandevillensis* Urb. var. *perratonii* (Proctor) Proctor *20883*	
	V	*20883* Jamaica *20883*
R	*Eugenia marchiana* Griseb. *20883*	
	R	*20883* Jamaica *20883*
I	*Eugenia margarettae* Alain *8058*	
	I	*19002* Puerto Rico *8058*
V	*Eugenia moensis* Britton & P. Wilson *5607*	
	V	*19105* Cuba (Holguin; Guantanamo) *5607*
E	*Eugenia mollifolia* Urban *5607*	
	E	*19105* Cuba (Ciud. Habana) *5607*
V	*Eugenia naguana* Urban *5607*	
	V	*19105* Cuba (Granma) *5607*
I	*Eugenia nemestrina* Hend. *19209*	
	I	*19209* Malaysia - Peninsular Malaysia (Terengganu, Pahang) *19209*
	V	*20099* Singapore
E	*Eugenia nesiotica* Standl. *20883, 9006*	
	E	*20883* Panama *20883*
V	*Eugenia nicholsii* F. & R. *20883, 13336*	
	V	*19890* Jamaica (St. Andrew, Portland) *20883*
V	*Eugenia noumeensis* Guillaumin *20802*	
	V	*20893* New Caledonia *20802*
I	*Eugenia octopleura* Krug & Urban *10199*	
	I	Dominica *10199*
	E	*19001* Martinique (hauteur de socomor) *19001*
R	*Eugenia ogoouensis* Amshoff	
	R	Gabon
E	*Eugenia oligadenia* Urban *5607*	
	E	Cuba (Granma) *5607*
I	*Eugenia palumbis* Merr.	
	I	*18338* U.S. - Guam *18338*
V	*Eugenia peninsularis* Urban *5607*	
	V	*19105* Cuba (Granma) *5607*
V	*Eugenia perforata* Urb. *20883*	
	V	*20883* Jamaica *20883*
V	*Eugenia phyllocardia* Urban *5607*	
	V	*19105* Cuba (Pinar del Rio) *5607*
E	*Eugenia pinariensis* Urban *5607*	
	E	*19105* Cuba (Pinar del Rio) *5607*
R	*Eugenia pollicina* Guého & A.J. Scott *10082*	
	R	*20771* Mauritius *10082*
E	*Eugenia polypora* Urb. *20883, 13336*	
	E	*19890* Jamaica (Hanover) *20883*
E	*Eugenia pozasia* Urban & Ekman *5607*	
	E	*19105* Cuba (Pinar del Rio) *5607*
R	*Eugenia pseudomato* Legr. *20176*	
	R	*20176* Argentina - Tucuman *20176*
E	*Eugenia psiloclada* Urban *5607*	
	E	*19105* Cuba (Holguin) *5607*
I	*Eugenia pusilla* N.E.Br. *20604*	
	I	*20604* South Africa - Transvaal *20604*
V	*Eugenia pycnoneura* Urb. *20883, 13336*	
	V	*19890* Jamaica (Portland) *20883*
I	*Eugenia quadrata* King *19209*	
	I	*19209* Malaysia - Peninsular Malaysia (Perak) *19209*
E	*Eugenia rendlei* Urb. *20883, 13336*	
	E	*19890* Jamaica (St. Thomas) *20883*
I	*Eugenia rivulorum* Thwaites *8021*	
	I	*16162* Sri Lanka *8021*
V	*Eugenia rocana* Britton & P. Wilson *5607*	
	V	*19105* Cuba (Pinar del Rio; Prov.Habana) *5607*
E	*Eugenia rodriguesensis* Guého & A.J. Scott *10082*	
	E	*5852* Mauritius - Rodrigues *5852*
E	*Eugenia roigii* Urban *5607*	
	E	*19105* Cuba (Pinar del Rio) *5607*
R	*Eugenia rotundata* Trimen *8021*	
	R	*20013* Sri Lanka *8021*
I	*Eugenia rufo-fulva* Thwaites *8021*	
	I	*16162* Sri Lanka *8021*
E	*Eugenia sachetae* Proctor *20883, 13336*	
	E	*19890* Jamaica (Trelawny) *20883*
E	*Eugenia salamancana* Standl. *20883, 9006*	
	I	*20883* Panama *20883*
V	*Eugenia schultziana* Urb. *20883*	
	V	*20883* Jamaica *20883*
E	*Eugenia sebastiani* Urban *5607*	
	E	*19105* Cuba (Pinar del Rio) *5607*
E	*Eugenia serrei* Urban *5607*	
	E	*19105* Cuba (Habana) *5607*
V	*Eugenia shaferi* Urban *5607*	
	V	*19105* Cuba (Camaguey) *5607*
R	*Eugenia sieberi* Guého & A.J. Scott *10082*	
	R	*20771* Mauritius *10082*
V	*Eugenia simii* Dummer *20604*	
	V	*20604* South Africa - Cape Province *20604*
	V	*20604* South Africa - Natal *20604*
	?	South Africa - Transvaal *20604*
Ex/E	*Eugenia singampattiana* Beddome *11494*	
	Ex/E	*11494* India - Tamil Nadu (Papanasam & Singampatti) *11494*
V	*Eugenia sloanei* Urb. *20883*	
	V	*20883* Jamaica *20883*
V	*Eugenia stahlii* (Kiaersk.) Krug & Urban ex Urban *20883*	
	I	*20883* Puerto Rico *20883*
V	*Eugenia stenoptera* Urban *5607*	
	V	*19105* Cuba (Guantanamo) *5607*
E	*Eugenia stewardsonii* Britt. *20883*	
	I	*20883* Puerto Rico *20883*
V	*Eugenia sulcivenia* Krug & Urb. *20883, 13336*	
	V	*19890* Jamaica (St. Andrew) *20883*

V	*Eugenia tabouensis* Aubrev. 7926		
	V	20887 Côte d'Ivoire (Bas-Cavally) 7926	
E	*Eugenia terpnophylla* Thwaites 8021		
	E	12838 Sri Lanka 8021	
R	*Eugenia tholloni* Amshoff		
	R	Gabon	
R	*Eugenia tinifolia* Lam. 10082		
	R	20771 Mauritius 10082	
R	*Eugenia umtamvunensis* A.E.van Wyk 20604		
	R	20604 South Africa - Cape Province 20604	
	R	20604 South Africa - Natal 20604	
E	*Eugenia underwoodii* Britt. 20883		
	I	20883 Puerto Rico 20883	
	Ex/E	19934 British Virgin Is. (Guana) 19934	
V	*Eugenia vaughanii* Guého & A.J. Scott 10082		
	V	20771 Mauritius 10082	
R	*Eugenia verdoorniae* A.E.van Wyk 20604		
	R	20604 South Africa - Cape Province 20604	
	R	20604 South Africa - Natal 20604	
V	*Eugenia victorini* Alain 5607		
	V	19105 Cuba (Juventud Is.) 5607	
R	*Eugenia virgultosa* (Sw.) DC. 20883		
	I	20883 Jamaica 20883	
V	*Eugenia virotii* Guillaumin 20893		
	V	20893 New Caledonia 20893	
R	*Eugenia websteri* Proctor 20883		
	R	20883 Jamaica 20883	
R	*Eugenia wilsonella* F. & R. 20883		
	R	20883 Jamaica 20883	
E	*Eugenia woodburyana* Alain 20883, 19002		
	I	20883 Puerto Rico 20883	
V	*Eugenia woodfrediana* Urban 5607		
	V	19105 Cuba (Holguin) 5607	
R	*Eugenia zeyheri* Harv. 20604		
	R	20604 South Africa - Cape Province 20604	
R	*Homoranthus biflorus* Craven & S.R.Jones 20681		
	R	20681 Australia - New South Wales 20681	
R	*Homoranthus cernuus* (R.Baker) Craven & S.R.Jones 20681		
	R	20681 Australia - New South Wales 20681	
V	*Homoranthus darwinioides* (Maiden & Betche) Cheel 20681		
	V	20681 Australia - New South Wales 20681	
R	*Homoranthus decasetus* Byrnes 20681		
	R	20681 Australia - Queensland 20681	
V	*Homoranthus decumbens* (Byrnes) Craven & S.R.Jones 20681		
	V	20681 Australia - Queensland 20681	
R	*Homoranthus floydii* Craven & S.R.Jones 20681		
	R	20681 Australia - New South Wales 20681	
V	*Homoranthus lunatus* Craven & S.R.Jones 20681		
	V	20681 Australia - New South Wales 20681	
R	*Homoranthus melanostictus* Craven & S.R.Jones 20681		
	R	20681 Australia - Queensland 20681	
V	*Homoranthus montanus* Craven & S.R.Jones 20681		
	V	20681 Australia - Queensland 20681	
R	*Homoranthus papillatus* Byrnes 20681		
	R	20681 Australia - Queensland 20681	
V	*Homoranthus porteri* (C.White) Craven &		

	S.R.Jones 20681		
	V	20681 Australia - Queensland 20681	
V	*Homoranthus prolixus* Craven & S.R.Jones 20681		
	V	20681 Australia - New South Wales 20681	
R	*Homoranthus thomasii* (Benth.) Craven & S.R.Jones 20681		
	R	20681 Australia - Queensland 20681	
R	*Homoranthus tropicus* Byrnes 20681		
	R	20681 Australia - Queensland 20681	
R	*Homoranthus zeteticorum* Craven & S.R.Jones 20681		
	R	20681 Australia - Queensland 20681	
E	*Hypocalymma longifolium* F.Muell. 20681, 14223		
	E	20681 Australia - Western Australia 20681	
I	*Jambosa beddomei* (Duthie) Gamble		
	I	India - Tamil Nadu	
I	*Jambosa bourdillonii* Gamble		
	I	India - Kerala (Travancore Hills)	
I	*Jambosa courtallensis* Gamble		
	I	India - Tamil Nadu (Tirunelveli District)	
V	*Jambosa longifolia* Brongn. & Gris.		
	V	New Caledonia	
I	*Jambosa rama-varma* (Bourd.) Gamble		
	I	India - Kerala (Travancore Hills)	
	I	India - Tamil Nadu (Tirunelveli Hills)	
I	*Krokia leonis* Borh. & Muniz 5607		
	I	5607 Cuba 5607	
I	*Krokia pilotoana* (Urban) Borh. 5607		
	I	5607 Cuba 5607	
R	*Kunzea bracteolata* Maiden & Betche 20681		
	I	20681 Australia - New South Wales 20681	
	I	20681 Australia - Queensland 20681	
V	*Kunzea cambagei* Maiden & Betche 20681		
	V	20681 Australia - New South Wales 20681	
R	*Kunzea flavescens* C.White & Francis 20681		
	R	20681 Australia - Queensland 20681	
R	*Kunzea graniticola* Byrnes 20681		
	R	20681 Australia - Queensland 20681	
V	*Kunzea pauciflora* Schauer 20681		
	V	20681 Australia - Western Australia 20681	
V	*Kunzea rupestris* Blakely 20681		
	V	20681 Australia - New South Wales 20681	
R	*Legrandia concinna* (R. A. Philippi) Kausel 20883, 15088		
	R	20883 Chile 20883	
R	*Leptospermum argenteum* J.Thompson 20681		
	R	20681 Australia - New South Wales 20681	
R	*Leptospermum blakelyi* J.Thompson 20681		
	R	20681 Australia - New South Wales 20681	
R	*Leptospermum crassifolium* J.Thompson 20681		
	R	20681 Australia - New South Wales 20681	
V	*Leptospermum deanei* J.Thompson 20681		
	V	20681 Australia - New South Wales 20681	
R	*Leptospermum deuense* J.Thompson 20681		
	R	20681 Australia - New South Wales 20681	
R	*Leptospermum epacridoideum* Cheel 20681		
	R	20681 Australia - New South Wales 20681	
R	*Leptospermum luehmannii* Bailey 20681		
	R	20681 Australia - Queensland 20681	

R	*Leptospermum namadgiensis* Lyne 20681	
	I	20681 Australia - Capital Territory 20681
	I	20681 Australia - New South Wales 20681

| R | *Leptospermum oreophilum* J.Thompson 20681 | |
| | R | 20681 Australia - Queensland 20681 |

| R | *Leptospermum pallidum* A.R.Bean 20681 | |
| | R | 20681 Australia - Queensland 20681 |

| R | *Leptospermum petraeum* J.Thompson 20681 | |
| | R | 20681 Australia - New South Wales 20681 |

| R | *Leptospermum purpurascens* J.Thompson 20681 | |
| | R | 20681 Australia - Queensland 20681 |

| R | *Leptospermum rupicola* J.Thompson 20681 | |
| | R | 20681 Australia - New South Wales 20681 |

| R | *Leptospermum spectabile* J.Thompson 20681 | |
| | R | 20681 Australia - New South Wales 20681 |

| R | *Leptospermum subglabratum* J.Thompson 20681 | |
| | R | 20681 Australia - New South Wales 20681 |

| V | *Leptospermum thompsonii* J.Thompson 20681 | |
| | V | 20681 Australia - New South Wales 20681 |

| R | *Leptospermum venustum* A.R.Bean 20681 | |
| | R | 20681 Australia - Queensland 20681 |

| R | *Leptospermum wooroonooran* Bailey 20681 | |
| | R | 20681 Australia - Queensland 20681 |

| E | *Marlierea sintenisii* Kiaersk. 20883, 10197 | |
| | V | 19002 Puerto Rico 20883 |

| R | *Melaleuca basicephala* Benth. 20681 | |
| | R | 20681 Australia - Western Australia 20681 |

| R | *Melaleuca cheelii* C.White 20681 | |
| | R | 20681 Australia - Queensland 20681 |

| R | *Melaleuca cliffortioides* Diels 20681 | |
| | R | 20681 Australia - Western Australia 20681 |

R	*Melaleuca corrugata* Eardley 20681	
	I	20681 Australia - Northern Territory 20681
	I	20681 Australia - South Australia 20681

| R | *Melaleuca deanei* F.Muell. 20681 | |
| | R | 20681 Australia - New South Wales 20681 |

| R | *Melaleuca fissurata* Barlow 20681 | |
| | R | 20681 Australia - Western Australia 20681 |

| V | *Melaleuca gnidioides* Brongn. & Gris 20893 | |
| | V | 20893 New Caledonia 20893 |

R	*Melaleuca groveana* Cheel & C.White 20681	
	I	20681 Australia - New South Wales 20681
	I	20681 Australia - Queensland 20681

| R | *Melaleuca howeana* Cheel | |
| | R | 14225 Australia - NSW - Lord Howe Is. 14225 |

| V | *Melaleuca kunzeoides* Byrnes 20681 | |
| | V | 20681 Australia - Queensland 20681 |

| R | *Melaleuca pustulata* Hook.f. 20681 | |
| | R | 20681 Australia - Tasmania 20681 |

| V | *Melaleuca sciotostyla* Barlow 20681 | |
| | V | 20681 Australia - Western Australia 20681 |

| R | *Melaleuca tortifolia* Byrnes 20681 | |
| | R | 20681 Australia - New South Wales 20681 |

| E | *Meteoromyrtus wynaadensis* (Beddome) Gamble 14782 | |
| | E | 14782 India - Tamil Nadu 14782 |

| E | *Metrosideros bartlettii* 19305 | |
| | E | 19305 New Zealand - North Is. (Northland) 20625 |

| E | *Metrosideros boninensis* (Hayata ex Koidz.) | |

Tuyama 8038
| | E | 19134 Japan - Ogasawara-shoto 20626 |

| E | *Metrosideros carminea* W. Oliver 86 | |
| | E | New Zealand - North Is. |

| V | *Metrosideros cherrieri* J. Wyndham Dawson 20893 | |
| | V | 20893 New Caledonia 20893 |

| R | *Metrosideros dolichandra* Schlechter | |
| | R | New Caledonia |

| R | *Metrosideros gregoryi* Christoph. 7925 | |
| | R | Western Samoa (Savaii) 7925 |

| R | *Metrosideros humboldtiana* Guillaumin 20893 | |
| | R | 20893 New Caledonia 20893 |

| V | *Metrosideros longipetiolata* J. Wyndham Dawson 20893 | |
| | V | 20893 New Caledonia 20893 |

| R | *Metrosideros nervulosa* C. Moore & F. Muell. | |
| | R | 14225 Australia - NSW - Lord Howe Is. 14225 |

R	*Metrosideros polymorpha* Gaud. var. *newellii* (Rock)	
	St. John 20850, 14209	
	R	20850 U.S. - Hawaii (Hawai`i) 20850

| V | *Metrosideros punctata* J. Wyndham Dawson 20893 | |
| | V | 20893 New Caledonia 20893 |

| E | *Metrosideros tetrasticha* Guillaumin 20893 | |
| | E | 20893 New Caledonia 20893 |

| V | *Micromyrtus blakelyi* J.W.Green 20681 | |
| | V | 20681 Australia - New South Wales 20681 |

| V | *Micromyrtus minutiflora* Benth. 20681 | |
| | V | 20681 Australia - New South Wales 20681 |

| V | *Mitranthes clarendonensis* (Proctor) Proctor 20883, 13336 | |
| | V | 13336 Jamaica 20883 |

| V | *Mitranthes glabra* Proctor 20883 | |
| | V | 20883 Jamaica 20883 |

| E | *Mitranthes macrophylla* Proctor 20883, 13336 | |
| | E | 13336 Jamaica 20883 |

| I | *Mitranthes maxonii* (Britton & Urban) Proctor 20883, 13336 | |
| | I | 13336 Jamaica 20883 |

| V | *Mitranthes nivea* Proctor 20883, 13336 | |
| | V | 13336 Jamaica 20883 |

| V | *Mitrantia bilocularis* Peter G.Wilson & B.Hyland 20681 | |
| | V | 20681 Australia - Queensland 20681 |

| R | *Monimiastrum acutisepalum* Guého & A.J. Scott 10082 | |
| | R | 20771 Mauritius 10082 |

| Ex | *Monimiastrum fasciculatum* Guého & A.J. Scott 10082 | |
| | Ex | 20771 Mauritius 10082 |

| R | *Monimiastrum pixidatum* Guého & A.J. Scott 10082 | |
| | R | 20771 Mauritius 10082 |

| R | *Monimiastrum psidioideum* Guého & A.J. Scott 10082 | |
| | R | 20771 Mauritius 10082 |

| E | *Mosiera flavicans* (Urban & Ekman) Bisse ssp. *pastelillensis* (Urban) Bisse 11840 | |
| | E | 19105 Cuba 19105 |

| E | *Mozartia emarginata* Mold. 5607 | |
| | E | 19105 Cuba (Holguin) 5607 |

| I | *Mozartia maestrensis* Urban 11840 | |
| | I | 20990 Cuba (Oriente) 11840 |

| E | *Mozartia oligostemon* Urban 5607 | |

E   *19105*   Cuba (Cienfuegos; Villa Clara) *5607*

V   ***Myrceugenia acutiflora*** (Kiaerskou) Legrand & Kausel *20883*

    I   *20883*   Brazil *20883*

R   ***Myrceugenia alpigena*** (D.C.) Landrum var. *alpigena* *20883*

    R   *20883*   Brazil *20883*

E   ***Myrceugenia alpigena*** (D.C.) Landrum var. *longifolia* (Burret) Landrum *20883*

    E   *20883*   Brazil *20883*

R   ***Myrceugenia bracteosa*** (A. P. de Candolle) Legrand & Kausel *20883*

    R   *20883*   Brazil *20883*

E   ***Myrceugenia brevipedicellata*** (Burret) Legrand & Kausel *20883*

    E   *20883*   Brazil *20883*

E   ***Myrceugenia colchaguensis*** (R. A. Philippi) Navas *20883, 13875*

    E   *20883*   Chile *20883*

V   ***Myrceugenia correifolia*** (Hooker & Arnott) Berg *20883*

    V   *20883*   Chile *20883*

E   ***Myrceugenia franciscensis*** (Berg) Landrum *20883*

    E   *20883*   Brazil *20883*

R   ***Myrceugenia glaucescens*** var. *latior* (Burret) Landrum *20883*

    I   *20883*   Brazil *20883*

E   ***Myrceugenia hatschbachii*** Landrum *20883*

    E   *20883*   Brazil *20883*

E   ***Myrceugenia hoehnei*** (Burret) Legrand & Kausel *20883*

    E   *20883*   Brazil *20883*

E   ***Myrceugenia kleinii*** Legrand & Kausel *20883*

    E   *20883*   Brazil *20883*

E   ***Myrceugenia leptocalyx*** Legrand *20883*

    E   *20883*   Brazil *20883*

V   ***Myrceugenia leptospermoides*** (A. P. de Candolle) Kausel *20883, 13875*

    V   *20883*   Chile *20883*

R   ***Myrceugenia oxysepala*** (Burret) Legrand & Kausel *20883*

    R   *20883*   Brazil *20883*

V   ***Myrceugenia pilotantha*** var. *pilotantha* *20883*

    I   *20883*   Brazil *20883*

V   ***Myrceugenia pinifolia*** (F. Philippi) Kausel *20883, 13875*

    V   *20883*   Chile *20883*

R   ***Myrceugenia reitzii*** Legrand & Kausel *20883*

    R   *20883*   Brazil *20883*

V   ***Myrceugenia rufa*** (Colla) Skottsberg ex Kausel *20883, 13875*

    R   *13875*   Chile *20883*

R   ***Myrceugenia rufescens*** (A. P. de Candolle) Legrand & Kausel *20883*

    I   *20883*   Brazil *20883*

V   ***Myrceugenia schultzei*** Johow *20883*

    V   *20883*   Chile *20883*

V   ***Myrceugenia scutellata*** Legrand *20883*

    I   *20883*   Brazil *20883*

V   ***Myrceugenia seriatoramosa*** (Kiaerskou) Legrand & Kausel *20883*

V   *20883*   Brazil *20883*

E   ***Myrceugenia smithii*** Landrum *20883*

    E   *20883*   Brazil *20883*

R   ***Myrceugenia venosa*** Legrand *20883*

    R   *20883*   Brazil *20883*

V   ***Myrcia borhidii*** Muniz *5607*

    V   *19105*   Cuba (Holguin) *5607*

E   ***Myrcia calcicola*** Proctor *20883, 13336*

    E   *20883*   Jamaica *20883*

R   ***Myrcia dasyblasta*** Berg in Mart. *20883*

    I   *20883*   Brazil *20883*

    R   *20883*   Paraguay *20883*

I   ***Myrcia edulis*** Krug & Urban var. *dominicana* Krug & Urban *10200*

    I   Dominica *10200*

V   ***Myrcia fosteri*** Croat *20883*

    V   *20883*   Panama *20883*

V   ***Myrcia gatunensis*** Standl. *20883, 9006*

    V   *20883*   Panama *20883*

R   ***Myrcia martinicensis*** Krug & Urban *19001*

    R   *19001*   Martinique (above Pitons & Mt. Pelée) *19001*

E   ***Myrcia paganii*** Krug & Urban *20883, 10197*

    V   *19002*   Puerto Rico *20883*

R   ***Myrcia pistrinalis*** McVaugh *8679*

    R   *8679*   Suriname *8679*

I   ***Myrcia skeldingii*** Proctor *20883, 13336*

    I   *19890*   Jamaica (Mason River Savannah) *20883*

E   ***Myrcianthes callicoma*** McVaugh

    E   *19558*   Argentina *16336*

    E   *20176*   Argentina - Tucuman *20176*

E   ***Myrcianthes ferreyrae*** (McVaugh) McVaugh *18200*

    E   *9446*   Peru *18200*

R   ***Myrcianthes minimifolia*** (McVaugh) Mcvaugh *18200*

    R   *9446*   Peru *18200*

R   ***Myrcianthes pseudo-mato*** (Legrand) McVaugh *19448*

    R   *16336*   Argentina *16336*

R   ***Myrcianthes quinqueloba*** (McVaugh) McVaugh *18200*

    R   *9446*   Peru *18200*

R   ***Myrciaria cuspidata*** Berg in Mart. *20883*

    I   *20883*   Brazil *20883*

    R   *20883*   Paraguay *20883*

V   ***Myrrhinium atropurpureum*** var. *atropurpureum* *20883*

    V   *20883*   Brazil *20883*

E   ***Myrteola leucomyrtillus*** (Griseb.) Reiche *20176*

    E   *20176*   Argentina - Neuquen *20176*

    E   *20176*   Argentina - Rio Negro *20176*

E   ***Myrteola nummualria*** (Poir.) O.Berg. var. *barneoudii* (O.Berg.) Kausel *20176*

    E   *20176*   Argentina - Neuquen *20176*

    E   *20176*   Argentina - Rio Negro *20176*

E   ***Myrtus claraensis*** (Urban) Bisse *5607*

    E   *19105*   Cuba (Sancti Spiritus) *5607*

E   ***Myrtus crenulata*** (Urban & Ekman) Bisse *5607*

    E   *19105*   Cuba *5607*

V   ***Myrtus del-riscoi*** Borh. & Muniz *5607*

    V   *19105*   Cuba (Santiago de Cuba) *5607*

E   ***Myrtus muniziana*** (Borh.) Borh. *5607*

    E   *19105*   Cuba (Prov. Habana) *5607*

Magnoliopsida (dicots): Myrtaceae: *Myrtus*

E   *Myrtus nummularioides* (Britton & P. Wilson)
     Urban *5607*
     E   *19105*   Cuba (Guantanamo) *5607*

R   *Pimenta adenoclada* (Urban) Burret *20883*
     I   *20883*   Cuba *20883*

V   *Pimenta cainitoides* (Urban) Burret *20883, 5607*
     V   *19105*   Cuba (Granma; Santiago de Cuba) *20883*

E   *Pimenta ferruginea* (Grisebach) Burret *20883*
     E   *20883*   Cuba *20883*

V   *Pimenta haitiensis* (Urban) Landrum *20883, 19408*
     V   *20883*   Dominican Republic *20883*

R   *Pimenta jamaicensis* (Britton & Harris) Proctor *20883*
     R   *20883*   Jamaica *20883*

R   *Pimenta obscura* Proctor *20883, 13336*
     R   *13336*   Jamaica *20883*

E   *Pimenta odiolens* (Urban) Burret *20883*
     E   *20883*   Cuba *20883*

E   *Pimenta oligantha* (Urban) Burret *20883*
     E   *20883*   Cuba *20883*

E   *Pimenta podocarpoides* (Areces) Landrum *20883*
     E   *20883*   Cuba *20883*

V   *Pimenta pseudocaryophyllus* var. *hoehnei* (Burret)
     Landrum *20883*
     I   *20883*   Brazil *20883*

V   *Pimenta racemosa* (Mill.) J. W. Moore var.
     hispaniolensis (Urban) Landrum *20883*
     I   *20883*   Dominican Republic *20883*
     I   *20883*   Haiti *20883*

V   *Pimenta racemosa* (Mill) J. W. Moore var. *ozua*
     (Urban & Ekman) Landrum *20883*
     I   *20883*   Dominican Republic *20883*
     I   *20883*   Haiti *20883*

E   *Pimenta racemosa* (Mill.) J. W. Moore var.
     terebinthina (Burret) Landrum *20883*
     E   *20883*   Dominican Republic *20883*

V   *Pimenta richardii* Proctor *11731, 20883, 13336*
     V   *13336*   Jamaica *20883*

V   *Plinia acunae* Borh. & Muniz *5607*
     V   *19105*   Cuba (Holguin; Guantanamo) *5607*

R   *Plinia costata* Amshoff *8679*
     R   *8679*   Suriname *8679*

V   *Plinia dermatodes* Urban *5607*
     V   *19105*   Cuba (Pinar del Rio) *5607*

R   *Plinia formosa* Urban *5607*
     R   *19105*   Cuba (Guantanamo) *5607*

E   *Plinia moaensis* Borh. *5607*
     E   *19105*   Cuba (Holguin) *5607*

V   *Plinia orthoclada* Urban *5607*
     V   *19105*   Cuba (Pinar del Rio) *5607*

V   *Plinia ramosissima* (Urban) Urban *5607*
     V   *19105*   Cuba (Santiago de Cuba; Holguin) *5607*

V   *Plinia rubrinervis* Urban *5607*
     V   *19105*   Cuba (Pinar del Rio) *5607*

E   *Plinia rupestris* Ekman & Urban *5607*
     E   *19105*   Cuba (Pinar del Rio) *5607*

V   *Plinia stenophylla* Urban *5607*
     V   *19105*   Cuba (Holguin) *5607*

E   *Plinia toscanosia* Urban *5607*
     E   *19105*   Cuba (Pinar del Rio) *5607*

I   *Pseudoeugenia perakensis* Scort. *19209*
     I   *19209*   Malaysia - Peninsular Malaysia (Pulau Pinang/Penang &
         Prai, Perak, Pahang, Kelantan) *19209*

V   *Psidium albescens* Urb. *20883*
     V   *20883*   Jamaica *20883*

I   *Psidium androsianum* (Urban) Correll
     I   *4650*   Bahamas *4650*

E   *Psidium celastroides* Urban *5607*
     E   *19105*   Cuba (Cienfuegos; Villa Clara) *5607*

I   *Psidium dumetorum* Proctor *20883, 13336*
     I   *13336*   Jamaica (Clarendon) *20883*

R   *Psidium galapageium* Hook.f. var. *howellii* D.
     Porter *11117*
     R   Ecuador - Galapagos (San Cristobal; Santa
         Cruz) *11117*

V   *Psidium harrisianum* Urb. *20883, 13336*
     V   *20883*   Jamaica (Clarendon, Peckham woods)
         20883

E   *Psidium havanense* Urban *5607*
     E   *19105*   Cuba (Prov. Habana; Ciud. Habana) *5607*

R   *Psidium nutans* Berg. *20883*
     I   *20883*   Argentina *20883*
     I   *20883*   Brazil *20883*
     R   *20883*   Paraguay *20883*

R   *Psidium ooideum* Berg in Mart. *20883*
     I   *20883*   Brazil *20883*
     R   *20883*   Paraguay *20883*

E   *Psidium sintenisii* (Kiaersk.) Alain *20883, 10197*
     I   *20883*   Puerto Rico *20883*

R   *Regelia cymbifolia* (Schauer) C.Gardner *20681*
     R   *20681*   Australia - Western Australia *20681*

R   *Regelia megacephala* C.Gardner *20681*
     R   *20681*   Australia - Western Australia *20681*

E   *Reicheia coquimbensis* (Barneoud) Kausel *15088*
     E   *13875*   Chile *13875*

R   *Rhodamnia glabrescens* Guymer & Jessup *20681*
     R   *20681*   Australia - Queensland *20681*

R   *Rhodamnia maideniana* C.White *20681*
     I   *20681*   Australia - New South Wales *20681*
     I   *20681*   Australia - Queensland *20681*

R   *Rhodamnia pauciovulata* Guymer *20681*
     R   *20681*   Australia - Queensland *20681*

R   *Rhodomyrtus effusa* Guymer *20681*
     R   *20681*   Australia - Queensland *20681*

R   *Rinzia crassifolia* Turcz. *20681*
     R   *20681*   Australia - Western Australia *20681*

V   *Ristantia gouldii* Peter G.Wilson & B.Hyland *20681*
     V   *20681*   Australia - Queensland *20681*

R   *Ristantia pachysperma* (F.Muell. & Bailey) Wilson &
     Waterh. *20681*
     R   *20681*   Australia - Queensland *20681*

R   *Ristantia waterhousei* Peter G.Wilson &
     B.Hyland *20681*
     R   *20681*   Australia - Queensland *20681*

R   *Sphaerantia chartacea* Peter G.Wilson &
     B.Hyland *20681*
     R   *20681*   Australia - Queensland *20681*

R   *Sphaerantia discolor* Peter G.Wilson & B.Hyland *20681*
     R   *20681*   Australia - Queensland *20681*

R   *Syncarpia hillii* Bailey *20681*

R		20681	Australia - Queensland *20681*
R	*Syzygium alatoramulum* B.Hyland *20681*		
R		20681	Australia - Queensland *20681*
R	*Syzygium alliiligneum* B.Hyland *20681*		
R		20681	Australia - Queensland *20681*
I	*Syzygium andamanicum* (King) Balakr. *10499*		
I		14782	India - Andaman Is. *10499*
R	*Syzygium argyropedicum* B.Hyland *20681*		
R		20681	Australia - Queensland *20681*
R	*Syzygium assimile* Thwaites var. *acuminata* P. Ashton *8021*		
R		20013	Sri Lanka *8021*
Ex	*Syzygium balfourii* (Baker) Guého & A.J. Scott *10082*		
Ex		5852	Mauritius - Rodrigues *5852*
I	*Syzygium benthamianum* (Wight ex Duthie) Gamble		
I			India - Tamil Nadu (Sispara, Nilgiri Hills)
E	*Syzygium bijouxii* Guého & A.J. Scott *10082*		
E		20771	Mauritius *10082*
R	*Syzygium boonjee* B.Hyland *20681*		
R		20681	Australia - Queensland *20681*
R	*Syzygium borbonicum* Guého & A.J. Scott *10082*		
R		14220	Réunion *10082*
Ex/E	*Syzygium bourdillonii* (Gamble) Rathakr. & Nair *11494*		
Ex/E		11494	India - Kerala (Merchiston; Colatoorpolay) *11494*
I	*Syzygium calvinii* (Elm.) Merr. *13833*		
I		13833	Philippines (Palawan) *13833*
I	*Syzygium capoasensis* (Merr.) Merr. *13833*		
I		13833	Philippines (Palawan) *13833*
I	*Syzygium chavaran* (Bourd.) Gamble		
I			India - Kerala (north Travancore)
R	*Syzygium commersonii* Guého & A.J. Scott *10082*		
R		20771	Mauritius *10082*
R	*Syzygium contractum* Guého & A.J. Scott *10082*		
R		20771	Mauritius *10082*
V	*Syzygium cordifolium* Walp. ssp. *cordifolium* *8021*		
V		12838	Sri Lanka *8021*
R	*Syzygium cordifolium* Walp. ssp. *spissum* (Alston) P. Ashton *8021*		
R		20013	Sri Lanka *8021*
E	*Syzygium courtallense* (Gamble) Alston *11494*		
E		11494	India - Tamil Nadu (Courtallum Hills) *11494*
V	*Syzygium cylindricum* (Wight) Alston *8021*		
V		12838	Sri Lanka *8021*
R	*Syzygium dansiei* B.Hyland *20681*		
R		20681	Australia - Queensland *20681*
R	*Syzygium densinervium* Merr. var. *insulare* Chang *20854*		
R		20854	Taiwan *20854*
I	*Syzygium ecostulatum* (Elm.) Merr. *13833*		
I		13833	Philippines (low altitude) *13833*
R	*Syzygium euphlebium* (Hayata) S.A.Mori *20511*		
R		20854	Taiwan (Heng-ch'un Peninsula) *20511*
R	*Syzygium firmum* Thwaites *8021*		
R		12838	Sri Lanka *8021*
E	*Syzygium gambleanum* Rathakr. & Chitra *11494*		
E		11494	India - Tamil Nadu (Kannyakumari) *11494*
I	*Syzygium iwahigensis* (Elm.) Merr. *13833*		
I		13833	Philippines (low altitude) *13833*
I	*Syzygium ixoides* (Elm.) Merr. *13833*		
I		13833	Philippines (Palawan) *13833*
I	*Syzygium kurzii* (Duthie) Balakr. var. *andamanica* King *10499*		
I			India - Andaman Is. *10499*
R	*Syzygium kusukusense* (Hayata) S.A.Mori		
R			Taiwan (Heng-ch'un)
R	*Syzygium lanyunense* Chang *20854*		
R		20854	Taiwan *20854*
R	*Syzygium latifolium* (Poiret) DC. *10082*		
R		20771	Mauritius *10082*
I	*Syzygium lewisii* Alston *8021*		
I		16162	Sri Lanka (Ratnapura Dist.) *8021*
R	*Syzygium macilwraithianum* B.Hyland *20681*		
R		20681	Australia - Queensland *20681*
V	*Syzygium makul* Gaertner *8021*		
V		12838	Sri Lanka *8021*
R	*Syzygium mamillatum* Bosser & Guého *10082*		
R		20771	Mauritius *11082*
R	*Syzygium manii* (King) Balakr. *10499*		
R		14782	India - Andaman Is. *14782*
R	*Syzygium mauritianum* Guého & A.J. Scott *10082*		
R		20771	Mauritius *10082*
R	*Syzygium micranthum* Thwaites *8021*		
R		12838	Sri Lanka *8021*
I	*Syzygium myhendrae* (Beddome ex Brandis) Gamble		
I			India - Kerala (Travancore Hills)
I			India - Tamil Nadu (Tirunelveli Hills)
R	*Syzygium neesianum* Arn. *8021*		
R		12838	Sri Lanka *8021*
I	*Syzygium occidentalis* (Bourd.) Ghandhi		
I			India - Kerala
Ex/E	*Syzygium palghatense* Gamble *11494*		
Ex/E		11494	India - Kerala (Palghat Hills) *11494*
V	*Syzygium paniculatum* Gaertner *20681*		
V		20681	Australia - New South Wales *20681*
R	*Syzygium petrinense* Bosser & Guého *10082*		
R		20771	Mauritius *10082*
E	*Syzygium phyllyraeoides* (Trimen) Santapau *12838*		
E		12838	Sri Lanka *12838*
V	*Syzygium pondoense* Engl. *20604*		
V		20604	South Africa - Cape Province *20604*
V		20604	South Africa - Natal *20604*
E	*Syzygium populifolium* (Baker) Guého & A.J. Scott *10082*		
E		20771	Mauritius *10082*
R	*Syzygium pseudofastigiatum* B.Hyland *20681*		
R		20681	Australia - Queensland *20681*
I	*Syzygium pulgarensis* (C.B. Rob.) Merr. *13833*		
I		13833	Philippines (Palawan) *13833*
I	*Syzygium purpuricarpum* (Elm.) Merr. *13833*		
I		13833	Philippines (Palawan) *13833*
R	*Syzygium rampans* (Baker) Guého & A.J. Scott *10082*		
R		20771	Mauritius *10082*
R	*Syzygium revolutum* Walp. ssp. *cyclophyllum* (Alston) P. Ashton *8021*		
R		20013	Sri Lanka *8021*

R	*Syzygium rubrimolle* B.Hyland *20681*	
	R *20681* Australia - Queensland *20681*	
R	*Syzygium sharonae* B.Hyland *20681*	
	R *20681* Australia - Queensland *20681*	
E	*Syzygium spathulatum* Thwaites *8021*	
	E *20013* Sri Lanka *8021*	
I	*Syzygium stocksii* (Duthie) Gamble	
	I India - Karnataka (South Canara)	
	I India - Kerala (Wynaad Hills)	
R	*Syzygium sylvestre* Thwaites *12838*	
	R *12838* Sri Lanka *12838*	
E	*Syzygium travancoricum* Gamble *11494, 21304, 21025*	
	E *11494* India - Kerala (south) *11494*	
V	*Syzygium vaughanii* Guého & A.J. Scott *10082*	
	V *20771* Mauritius *10082*	
V	*Syzygium velorum* B.Hyland *20681*	
	V *20681* Australia - Queensland *20681*	
R	*Syzygium venosum* (Lam.) Guého & A.J. Scott *10082*	
	R *20771* Mauritius *10082*	
I	*Syzygium wrightii* (Baker) A.J. Scott *19181*	
	I *19182* Seychelles (granitic) *14296*	
R	*Syzygium xerampelinum* B.Hyland *20681*	
	R *20681* Australia - Queensland *20681*	
E	*Temu divaricatum* (Berg.) Berg. *16336*	
	E *16336* Argentina *16336*	
	E *20176* Argentina - Neuquen *20176*	
	E *20176* Argentina - Rio Negro *20176*	
	E *20176* Chile *20176*	
R	*Thaleropia queenslandica* (L.S.Smith) Peter G.Wilson *20681*	
	R *20681* Australia - Queensland *20681*	
R	*Thryptomene hexandra* C.White *20681*	
	I *20681* Australia - New South Wales *20681*	
	I *20681* Australia - Queensland *20681*	
V	*Thryptomene wittweri* J.W.Green *20681*	
	I *20681* Australia - Northern Territory *20681*	
	I *20681* Australia - Western Australia *20681*	
V	*Tristania decorticata* Merr. *13780*	
	V *15960* Philippines *13780*	
V	*Tristania littoralis* Merr. *13780*	
	V *15960* Philippines *13780*	
V	*Tristaniopsis jaffrei* J.Wyndham Dawson *20893*	
	V *20893* New Caledonia *20893*	
R	*Tristaniopsis lucida* J.Wyndham Dawson *20893*	
	R *20893* New Caledonia *20893*	
V	*Tristaniopsis macphersonii* J.Wyndham Dawson *20893*	
	V *20893* New Caledonia *20893*	
V	*Tristaniopsis minutiflora* J.Wyndham Dawson *20893*	
	V *20893* New Caledonia *20893*	
V	*Tristaniopsis ninndoensis* J.Wyndham Dawson *20893*	
	V *20893* New Caledonia *20893*	
E	*Tristaniopsis polyandra* Guillaumin *20893*	
	E *20893* New Caledonia *20893*	
V	*Tristaniopsis reticulata* J.Wyndham Dawson *20893*	
	V *20893* New Caledonia *20893*	
V	*Tristaniopsis vieillardii* Brongn. & Gris *20893*	
	V *20893* New Caledonia *20893*	
E	*Tristaniopsis yateensis* J.Wyndham Dawson *20893*	
	E *20893* New Caledonia *20893*	

V	*Ugni selkirkii* (Hook. & Arn.) O. Berg *19116*	
	V *19125* Chile - Juan Fernandez Is. *19116*	
E	*Ugni warscewiczii* Berg *20883*	
	I *20883* Panama *20883*	
E	*Uromyrtus australis* A.J.Scott *20681*	
	E *20681* Australia - New South Wales *20681*	
R	*Uromyrtus metrosideros* (Bailey) A.J.Scott *20681*	
	R *20681* Australia - Queensland *20681*	
E	*Verticordia albida* A.S.George *20681*	
	E *20681* Australia - Western Australia *20681*	
R	*Verticordia aurea* A.S.George *20681*	
	R *20681* Australia - Western Australia *20681*	
R	*Verticordia capillaris* A.S.George *20681*	
	R *20681* Australia - Western Australia *20681*	
V	*Verticordia carinata* Turcz. *20681, 14223*	
	V *20681* Australia - Western Australia *20681*	
V	*Verticordia crebra* A.S.George *20681*	
	V *20681* Australia - Western Australia *20681*	
V	*Verticordia fimbrilepis* Turcz. ssp. *australis* A.S.George *20681*	
	V *20681* Australia - Western Australia *20681*	
E	*Verticordia fimbrilepis* Turcz. ssp. *fimbrilepis* *20681*	
	E *20681* Australia - Western Australia *20681*	
E	*Verticordia harveyi* Benth. *20681*	
	E *20681* Australia - Western Australia *20681*	
V	*Verticordia helichrysantha* Benth. *20681*	
	V *20681* Australia - Western Australia *20681*	
E	*Verticordia hughanii* F.Muell. *20681*	
	E *20681* Australia - Western Australia *20681*	
R	*Verticordia integra* A.S.George *20681*	
	R *20681* Australia - Western Australia *20681*	
R	*Verticordia lehmannii* Schauer *20681*	
	R *20681* Australia - Western Australia *20681*	
R	*Verticordia lindleyi* Schauer ssp. *lindleyi* *20681*	
	R *20681* Australia - Western Australia *20681*	
R	*Verticordia multiflora* Turcz. ssp. *multiflora* *20681*	
	R *20681* Australia - Western Australia *20681*	
R	*Verticordia paludosa* A.S.George *20681*	
	R *20681* Australia - Western Australia *20681*	
R	*Verticordia penicillaris* F.Muell. *20681*	
	R *20681* Australia - Western Australia *20681*	
E	*Verticordia pityrhops* A.S.George *20681*	
	E *20681* Australia - Western Australia *20681*	
E	*Verticordia plumosa* (Desf.) Druce var. *ananeotes* A.S.George *20681*	
	E *20681* Australia - Western Australia *20681*	
R	*Verticordia polytricha* Benth. *20681*	
	R *20681* Australia - Western Australia *20681*	
V	*Verticordia staminosa* C.Gardner & A.S.George ssp. *cylindracea* A.S.George *20681*	
	V *20681* Australia - Western Australia *20681*	
E	*Verticordia staminosa* C.Gardner & A.S.George ssp. *staminosa* *20681*	
	E *20681* Australia - Western Australia *20681*	
R	*Verticordia vicinella* A.S.George *20681*	
	R *20681* Australia - Western Australia *20681*	

R	*Waterhousea hedraiophylla* (F.Muell.) B.Hyland *20681*	
	R	*20681* Australia - Queensland *20681*
R	*Waterhousea mulgraveana* B.Hyland *20681*	
	R	*20681* Australia - Queensland *20681*
R	*Xanthostemon arenarius* Peter G.Wilson *20681*	
	R	*20681* Australia - Queensland *20681*
R	*Xanthostemon bracteatus* Merr. *13780*	
	R	*15960* Philippines *13780*
V	*Xanthostemon carlii* J.Wyndham Dawson *20893*	
	V	*20893* New Caledonia *20893*
R	*Xanthostemon formosus* Peter G.Wilson *20681*	
	R	*20681* Australia - Queensland *20681*
E	*Xanthostemon francii* Guillaumin *20893*	
	E	*20893* New Caledonia *20893*
I	*Xanthostemon glaucum* Pampan.	
	I	New Caledonia
Ex/E	*Xanthostemon glaucus* Pampan. *20893*	
	Ex/E	*20802* New Caledonia *20802*
R	*Xanthostemon graniticus* Peter G.Wilson *20681*	
	R	*20681* Australia - Queensland *20681*
R	*Xanthostemon grisei* Guillaumin	
	R	New Caledonia
R	*Xanthostemon gugerlii* Merr.	
	R	New Caledonia
E	*Xanthostemon lateriflorus* Guillaumin *20893*	
	E	*20893* New Caledonia *20893*
E	*Xanthostemon longipes* Guillaumin *20893*	
	E	*20893* New Caledonia *20893*
V	*Xanthostemon oppositifolius* Bailey *20681*	
	V	*20681* Australia - Queensland *20681*
Ex	*Xanthostemon sebertii* Guillaumin *20802*	
	Ex	*20802* New Caledonia (Prony Bay) *20802*
R	*Xanthostemon sulfureus* Guillaumin *20893*	
	R	New Caledonia
V	*Xanthostemon verdugonianus* Naves *13780*	
	V	*15960* Philippines *13780*
R	*Xanthostemon vieillardii* Brongn. & Gris *20893*	
	V	*20893* New Caledonia *20893*
R	*Xanthostemon whitei* Gugerli *20681*	
	R	*20681* Australia - Queensland *20681*
R	*Xanthostemon xerophilus* Peter G.Wilson *20681*	
	R	*20681* Australia - Queensland *20681*
V	*Xanthostemon youngii* C.White & Francis *20681*	
	V	*20681* Australia - Queensland *20681*

Nepenthaceae

Number of genera: 1
Number of species: 75
Recorded threatened species: 19 (25%)

East Indies to Madagascar.

I	*II*	*Nepenthes burbidgeae* Hook. f. ex Burb.	
		I	Malaysia - Sabah (Mt Kinabalu, Mt Tambuyukon)
R	*II*	*Nepenthes burkei* Masters var. *burkei*	
		R	Philippines
I	*II*	*Nepenthes deaniana* Macfarlane *13833*	
		I	*13833* Philippines (Mt. Pulgar) *13833*
R	*II*	*Nepenthes destillatoria* Brion *20013*	
		R	*20013* Sri Lanka *20013*

V	*II*	*Nepenthes edwardsiana* Hook. f.	
		V	Malaysia - Sabah
E	*II*	*Nepenthes gracillima* Ridley *13873*	
		E	Malaysia - Peninsular Malaysia *13873*
I	*I*	*Nepenthes khasiana* Hook. f. *15658*	
		I	India - Assam (Khasi hills)
		I	India - Meghalaya (Jaintia hills)
R	*II*	*Nepenthes lowii* Hook. f.	
		R	Brunei Darussalam *13868*
		V	Malaysia - Sabah
		R	*14965* Malaysia - Sarawak (incl. G. Mulu) *14965*
V	*II*	*Nepenthes madagascariensis* Poir. *8316*	
		V	Madagascar *8316*
R	*II*	*Nepenthes masaolensis* R. Schmid-Hollinger *8316*	
		R	Madagascar *8316*
E	*II*	*Nepenthes muluensis* M. Hotta	
		E	Malaysia - Sarawak *13868*
Ex/E	*II*	*Nepenthes neglecta* Macfarlane *13868*	
		Ex/E	*12225* Malaysia - Sabah (Labuan) *13868*
E	*II*	*Nepenthes northiana* Hook. f. *14965*	
		E	*14965* Malaysia - Sarawak (Tai Ton (limestone)) *14965*
R	*II*	*Nepenthes paniculata* Danser *19588*	
		R	*19588* Indonesia - Irian Jaya (Doorman Top) *8316*
V	*II*	*Nepenthes pervillei* Blume *14296*	
		V	Seychelles (granitic) *14296*
I	*II*	*Nepenthes philippinensis* Macfarlane *13833*	
		I	*13833* Philippines (Palawan) *13833*
V	*I*	*Nepenthes rajah* Hook. f. *15658*	
		V	*20889* Malaysia - Sabah (Mt Kinabalu; Mt Tambuyukon) *20889*
R	*II*	*Nepenthes veitchii* Hook. f.	
		R	Brunei Darussalam *13868*
		I	Malaysia - Sabah
		I	Malaysia - Sarawak
V	*II*	*Nepenthes villosa* Hook.	
		V	Malaysia - Sabah (Mt Kinabalu)

Nesogenaceae

Number of genera: 1
Number of species: 7
Recorded threatened species: 3 (42%)

East Africa, Madagascar, Indian Ocean, South Pacific.

Ex/E	*Nesogenes decumbens* Balf.f. *10082*	
	Ex/E	Mauritius - Rodrigues *5852*
I	*Nesogenes euphrasioides* (W.J.Hooker & Arnott) A.L.DC. *19473, 20845*	
	E	*19473* Cook Is.(Southern group) (Mauke and Mitiaro) *19473*
	I	*20845* French Polynesia - Society Is. (Tupai) *20845*
	I	*20845* French Polynesia - Tuamotu Is. *20845*
Ex	*Nesogenes orerensis* (Cordem.) Marais *10082*	
	Ex	*10082* Réunion *10082*
E	*Nesogenes rotensis* *20818*	
	E	*20819* North Mariana Is. (Rota) *20819*

Nyctaginaceae

Number of genera:		30
Number of species:		300
Recorded threatened species:		49 (16%)

Pantropical, particularly America.

V   *Abronia alba* Eastw. *20850*
  I   *20850* U.S. - California *20850*

E   *Abronia alpina* Brandeg. *20850*
  E   *20850* U.S. - California *20850*

R   *Abronia ameliae* Lundell *20850*
  R   *20850* U.S. - Texas *20850*

E   *Abronia ammophila* Greene *20850*
  E   *20850* U.S. - Wyoming *20850*

R   *Abronia bigelovii* Heimerl *20850*
  R   *20850* U.S. - New Mexico *20850*

V   *Abronia latifolia* Eschsch. *13154*
  V   *10701* Canada - British Columbia *10701*

E   *Abronia macrocarpa* L.A. Gal. *20850, 17694*
  E   *20850* U.S. - Texas *20850*

R   *Abronia minor* Standl. *20850*
  I   *20850* U.S. - California *20850*

V   *Abronia neurophylla* Standl. *20850*
  I   *20850* U.S. - California *20850*

Ex   *Abronia umbellata* Lam. ssp. *acutalata* (Standl.)
    Tillett *20850, 13154*
  Ex   *20850* Canada - British Columbia *20850*
  Ex   *13154* U.S. - Oregon *13154*
  Ex   *20850* U.S. - Washington *20850*

V   *Abronia umbellata* Lam. ssp. *breviflora* (Standl.)
    Munz *20850*
  V   *20850* U.S. - California *20850*
  E   *20850* U.S. - Oregon *20850*

V   *Acleisanthes crassifolia* Gray *20883, 20850, 8058*
  V   *20850* U.S. - Texas *20850*
  I   *20883* Mexico *20883*

V   *Acleisanthes wrightii* (Gray) Benth. & Hook. f. ex
    Hemsl. *20850*
  V   *20850* U.S. - Texas *20850*

R   *Anulocaulis annulatus* (Coville) Standl. *20850*
  I   *20850* U.S. - California *20850*

R   *Anulocaulis leiosolenus* I.M. Johnston var.
    lasianthus I.M. Johnston *20850*
  R   *20850* U.S. - Texas *20850*

V   *Anulocaulis reflexus* I.M. Johnston *20883, 20850*
  E   *20850* U.S. - Texas *20850*
  I   *20883* Mexico *20883*

E   *Boerhavia diffusa* L. var. *leiocarpa* (Heimerl)
    Adams *20883*
  E   *20883* Jamaica *20883*

V   *Boerhavia mathisiana* F.B. Jones *20850, 11630*
  E   *20850* U.S. - Texas *20850*

V   *Boerhavia megaptera* Standl. *20850*
  I   *20850* U.S. - Arizona *20850*

R   *Caribea littoralis* Alain *11840*
  R   *19105* Cuba (Guantanamo) *11840*

R   *Commicarpus heimerlii* (Vierh.) Meikle *10778*
  R   *15534* Yemen - Socotra *10778*

R   *Commicarpus simonyi* (Heimerl & Vierh.) Meikle *15534*
  R   *15534* Yemen - Socotra *15534*

R   *Guapira clarensis* Borh. *11840*
  R   *19105* Cuba (Las Villas) *11840*

E   *Guapira leonis* (Standley) Lundell
  E   *19105* Cuba (Prov. Habana) *19105*

R   *Guapira rotundifolia* (Heimerl) Lundell *20883*
  R   *20883* Jamaica *20883*

E   *Guapira standleyana* Woods. *20883, 9006*
  I   *20883* Panama *20883*

I   *Guapira suborbiculata* (Duss) Lundell *10200*
  I   Dominica *10200*
  I   Martinique *10200*

R   *Guapira witsbergeri* Lundell *9444*
  R   *10359* El Salvador *9444*

V   *Mirabilis collina* Shinners *20850*
  V   *20850* U.S. - Texas *20850*

V   *Mirabilis macfarlanei* Constance & Rollins *20850*
  V   *20850* U.S. - Idaho *20850*
  E   *20850* U.S. - Oregon *20850*

V   *Mirabilis pauciflora* (Buckl.) Standl. *20850*
  I   *20850* U.S. - Oklahoma *20850*
  V   *20850* U.S. - Texas *20850*

R   *Mirabilis pudica* Barneby *20850*
  R   *20850* U.S. - Nevada *20850*

E   *Mirabilis rotundifolia* (Greene) Standl. *20883, 20850*
  E   *20850* U.S. - Colorado *20850*
  I   *20883* Puerto Rico *20883*

E   *Neea amplexicaulis* Dwyer & Hayden *20883, 10001*
  I   *20883* Panama *20883*

E   *Neea darienensis* Dwyer & Hayden *20883, 10001*
  I   *20883* Panama *20883*

E   *Neea ekmanii* Heimerl *5607*
  E   *19105* Cuba (Cienfuegos, Villa Clara) *5607*

E   *Neea elegans* Dwyer & Hayden *20883, 10001*
  I   *20883* Panama *20883*

R   *Okenia hypogaea* Schlecht. & Cham. *20850*
  V   *20850* U.S. - Florida *20850*

R   *Pisonia albida* (Heimerl) Britt. ex Standl. *20883*
  I   *20883* Puerto Rico *20883*

V   *Pisonia costata* (Bojer ex Bouton) Choisy *10082*
  V   *20771* Mauritius *10082*

R   *Pisonia donnell-smithii* Heimerl ex Standley *9004*
  I   *10359* El Salvador *10359*
  R   *9004* Guatemala *9004*

R   *Pisonia ekmani* Heimerl *5607*
  R   *19105* Cuba (Las Tunas, Holguin) *5607*

E   *Pisonia floridana* Britt. ex Small *20850, 14662*
  E   *20850* U.S. - Florida *20850*

E   *Pisonia graciliscens* (Heimerl) Stenmerik *20845*
  E   *20845* French Polynesia - Society Is. (Tahiti)
            20845

R   *Pisonia lanceolata* (Poiret) Choisy *10082*
  E   *14234* Réunion *14234*
  R   *20771* Mauritius *10082*

E   *Pisonia sechellarum* F. Friedmann *14296*
  E   *14981* Seychelles (Silhouette, possibly formerly on
            Mahé) *14296*

I   *Pisonia siphonocarpa* (Heimerl) Stenmerik *20845*
  I   *20845* French Polynesia - Society Is. (Moorea)
            20845

Ex/E **Pisonia suborbiculata** Hemsley ex Duss *19001*

    Ex/E *19001* Martinique (Pointe du Vauclin; Cap Salomon) *19001*

V **Pisonia sylvatica** Standley *9037*

    V *9426* Costa Rica *9037*

E **Pisonia wagneriana** Fosberg *20850, 14209*

    E *20850* U.S. - Hawaii (Kaua`i) *20850*

R **Pisoniella arborescens** (Lagasca & Rodriguez) Standley *9015*

    R *19755* Mexico *9015*

Nymphaeaceae

Number of genera:	5
Number of species:	50
Recorded threatened species:	4 (8%)

Cosmopolitan, in fresh water habitats.

V **Nuphar lutea** ssp. *sagittifolia* (Walt.) E.O. Beal *20850*

    I *20850* U.S. - Indiana *20850*
    V *20850* U.S. - North Carolina *20850*
    I *20850* U.S. - South Carolina *20850*
    E *20850* U.S. - Virginia *20850*

V **Nuphar lutea** ssp. *ulvacea* (Mill. & Standl.) E.O. Beal *20850*

    V *20850* U.S. - Florida *20850*

R **Nuphar pumilum** DC. var. *ozense* (Miki) Hara *10572*

    R *10572* Japan *10572*

V **Nuphar shimadai** Hayata *20511*

    V *20511* Taiwan *20511*

V **Nuphar subintegerrimum** (Casp.) Makino *10572*

    V *10572* Japan *10572*

Ochnaceae

Number of genera:	30
Number of species:	400
Recorded threatened species:	15 (3%)

Tropical, especially Brazil.

I **Brackenridgea palustris** Bartell. ssp. *foxworthyi* (Elm.) Kanis *13833*

    I *13833* Philippines (low altitude) *13833*

R **Fleurydora felicis** A. Chev. *7926*

    R Guinea *7926*

R **Indosinia involucrata** (Gagnepain) Vidal *6057*

    I *20985* Vietnam *6057*

E **Ochna rufescens** Thwaites *12838*

    E *12838* Sri Lanka *12838*

Ex **Ouratea alaternifolia** (A. Rich.) M. Gomez *5607*

    Ex *15112* Cuba (Habana) *5607*

V **Ouratea amplectens** (Stapf) Engl. *20274*

    V *20858* Ghana *20274*
    V *20858* Liberia *7926*

E **Ouratea cocleensis** Dwyer *20883, 9006*

    I *20883* Panama *20883*

E **Ouratea elegans** Urb. *20883, 13336*

    E *20883* Jamaica *20883*

E **Ouratea flexipedicellata** Dwyer *20883, 9006*

    I *20883* Panama *20883*

R **Ouratea gillyana** (Dwyer) Sandw. & Maguire *8679*

    R Guyana *8679*

R **Ouratea jamaicensis** (Planch.) Urb. *20883*

    R *20883* Jamaica *20883*

E **Ouratea patelliformis** Dwyer *20883, 9006*

    I *20883* Panama *20883*

R **Ouratea sacleuxii** (van Tiegh.) Beentje *20057*

    R *20057* Kenya (Shimba hills) *20057*
    R *20057* Tanzania *17435*

V **Ouratea schusteri** Engler *20057*

    V *20057* Kenya (Taita hills & Kasigau) *20057*
    V *20057* Tanzania (western Usambaras; Uluguru Mnts.) *17435*

V **Sauvagesia paucielata** Sastre *20883, 10747*

    V *16317* Panama *20883*

R **Sinia rhodoleuca** Diels *17617*

    R *17617* China - Guangdong (Fengkai, Huaiji, Lianshan) *11139*
    R *17617* China - Guangxi *11139*

Olacaceae

Number of genera:	24-30
Number of species:	250
Recorded threatened species:	59 (23%)

Tropical and subtropical.

I **Anacolosa densiflora** Beddome

    I India - Kerala (Travancore Hills)
    I India - Tamil Nadu

R **Brachynema ramiflorum** Bentham *20883*

    I *20883* Brazil *20883*

V **Cathedra bahiensis** Sleumer *20883*

    I *20883* Brazil *20883*

E **Cathedra grandiflora** Loesener *20883*

    E *20883* Brazil *20883*

R **Cathedra paraensis** Sleumer *20883*

    I *20883* Brazil *20883*

R **Cathedra rubricaulis** Miers *20883*

    I *20883* Brazil *20883*

R **Curupira tefeensis** Black *20883*

    I *20883* Brazil *20883*

E **Douradoa consimilis** Sleumer *20883*

    I *20883* Brazil *20883*

E **Dulacia crassa** (Monachino) Sleumer *20883*

    I *20883* Guyana *20883*

R **Dulacia cyanocarpa** Sleumer *20883*

    I *20883* Venezuela *20883*

V **Dulacia egleri** (Rangel) Sleumer *20883*

    I *20883* Brazil *20883*

R **Dulacia gardneriana** (Bentham) O. Kuntze *20883*

    I *20883* Brazil *20883*

E **Dulacia papillosa** (Rangel) Sleumer *20883*

    I *20883* Brazil *20883*

V **Dulacia pauciflora** (Bentham) O. Kuntze *20883*

    I *20883* Brazil *20883*

E **Dulacia singularis** Vellozo *20883*

    I *20883* Brazil *20883*

V **Dulacia tepuiensis** (Steyermark) Sleumer & Steyermark *20883*

    I *20883* Venezuela *20883*

E **Heisteria amazonica** Sleumer *20883*

	I		20883 Brazil 20883
E	*Heisteria amphoricarpa* (Ducke) Sleumer 20883		
	I		20883 Brazil 20883
V	*Heisteria asplundii* Sleumer 20883		
	I		20883 Ecuador 20883
E	*Heisteria blanchetiana* (Engler) Sleumer 20883		
	I		20883 Brazil 20883
R	*Heisteria citrifolia* Engler 20883		
	I		20883 Brazil 20883
R	*Heisteria concinna* Standl. 20883		
	I		20883 Costa Rica 20883
	I		20883 Panama 20883
R	*Heisteria costaricensis* J.D. Sm. 20883		
	I		20883 Costa Rica 20883
	I		20883 Panama 20883
R	*Heisteria huberiana* Sleumer 20883		
	I		20883 Brazil 20883
R	*Heisteria maguirei* Sleumer 20883		
	I		20883 Brazil 20883
	I		20883 Guyana 20883
	I		20883 Venezuela 20883
V	*Heisteria maytenoides* Spruce ex Engler 20883		
	I		20883 Venezuela 20883
R	*Heisteria petandra* (Bentham ex Reisseck) Engler 20883		
	I		20883 Brazil 20883
	I		20883 Venezuela 20883
E	*Heisteria salicifolia* Engler 20883		
	E		20883 Brazil 20883
E	*Heisteria skutchii* Sleumer 20883		
	I		20883 Costa Rica 20883
R	*Malania oleifera* Chun & Lee 17617		
	R		17617 China - Guangxi 11139
	R		17617 China - Yunnan (Funing; Guangnan; Wengshan) 11139
I	*Octoknema orientalis* Mildbr. 20556		
	I		5926 Tanzania (Udzungwa & Mahenge Mts.) 20921
V	*Olax angulata* A.S.George 20681		
	V		20681 Australia - New South Wales 20681
R	*Olax evrardii* Gagnepain 6057		
	R		Vietnam 6057
I	*Olax imbricata* Roxb. var. *membranifolia* Kurz 7771		
	I		India - Nicobar Is. (Katchal Is.) 7771
I	*Olax kilimandscharica* Knobl. 5926		
	I		5926 Tanzania (Kilimanjaro) 5926
I	*Olax pentandra* Sleumer 5926		
	I		5926 Tanzania 5926
V	*Olax psittacorum* (Lam.) Vahl 10082		
	V		14234 Réunion 14234
	E		20771 Mauritius 10082
R	*Olax schliebenii* Knobl. 5926		
	R		5926 Tanzania 5926
E	*Schoepfia arenaria* Britt. 20883		
	E		20883 Puerto Rico 20883
R	*Schoepfia californica* Brandegee 20883		
	I		20883 Mexico 20883
E	*Schoepfia cubensis* Britton & Wilson 20883, 5607		
	R		19105 Cuba (Holguin) 20883
E	*Schoepfia didyma* Wright ex Grisebach 20883		

	I		20883 Cuba 20883
R	*Schoepfia haitiensis* Urban & Britton 20883		
	I		20883 Dominican Republic 20883
	I		20883 Haiti 20883
R	*Schoepfia harrisii* Urb. 20883, 13336		
	R		13336 Jamaica (Clarendon, Trelawny) 20883
R	*Schoepfia multiflora* Urb. 20883		
	R		20883 Jamaica 20883
R	*Schoepfia pringlei* Robinson 20883		
	I		20883 Mexico 20883
E	*Schoepfia scopulorum* Alain 20883		
	I		20883 Cuba 20883
E	*Schoepfia shreveana* Wiggins 20883		
	I		20883 Mexico 20883
E	*Schoepfia stenophylla* Urban 20883, 5607		
	E		20883 Cuba (Granma; Santiago de Cuba) 20883
V	*Schoepfia tepuiensis* Steyermark 20883		
	I		20883 Venezuela 20883
R	*Schoepfia tetramera* Herzog 20883		
	I		20883 Bolivia 20883
E	*Schoepfia velutina* Sandwith 20883		
	I		20883 Brazil 20883
R	*Strombosia nana* Kosterm. 12838		
	R		12838 Sri Lanka 12838
V	*Tetrastylidium peruvianum* Sleumer 20883		
	I		20883 Brazil 20883
	I		20883 Peru 20883
R	*Ximenia coriacea* Engler 20883		
	I		20883 Brazil 20883
R	*Ximenia horrida* Urban & Ekman 20883		
	I		20883 Dominican Republic (Pedernales, Azua) 21008
	I		20883 Haiti 20883
R	*Ximenia parviflora* var. *glauca* DeFilipps 20883		
	I		20883 Mexico 20883
E	*Ximenia pubescens* Standley 20883		
	E		20883 Mexico 20883
V	*Ximenia roigii* León 20883, 5607		
	E		19105 Cuba (Las Tunas) 20883

Oleaceae

Number of genera:	30	
Number of species:	600	
Recorded threatened species:	70	(11%)

Nearly cosmopolitan, especially Asia and Malesia.

E	*Abeliophyllum distichum* Nakai 15957		
	E		15957 Korea, South (Mt. Kunja) 15957
E	*Chionanthus acunae* (Borh. & Muniz) Borh. 5607		
	E		19105 Cuba (Camaguey) 5607
V	*Chionanthus adamsii* Stearn 20883, 13336		
	V		13336 Jamaica 20883
E	*Chionanthus ayresii* A.J. Scott 10082		
	E		20771 Mauritius 10082
E	*Chionanthus boutonii* A.J. Scott 10082		
	E		20771 Mauritius 10082
E	*Chionanthus broomeana* (Horne ex Oliver) A.J. Scott var. *broomeana* 10082		
	E		20771 Mauritius 10082

R *Chionanthus jamaicensis* (Urb.) Stearn 20883, 13336
    R 13336 Jamaica 20883

V *Chionanthus moncadae* (Borh. & Muniz) Borh. 5607
    V 19105 Cuba (Holguin) 5607

E *Chionanthus proctorii* Stearn 20883, 13336
    E 13336 Jamaica 20883

R *Chionanthus pygmaeus* Small 20850
    R 20850 U.S. - Florida 20850

R *Forestiera eggersiana* Krug & Urban 19934
    I 19934 Puerto Rico 19934
    I 19934 St Martin & St Barthelemy 19934
    R 19934 British Virgin Is. 19934
    I 19934 USA - Virgin Is. 19934

V *Forestiera ekmanii* Borh. 5607
    V 19105 Cuba (Pinar del Rio) 5607

R *Forestiera godfreyi* L.C. Anders. 20850
    V 20850 U.S. - Florida 20850
    E 20850 U.S. - Georgia 20850
    I 20850 U.S. - South Carolina 20850

V *Forestiera segregata* (Jacq.) Krug & Urban var.
    pinetorum (Small) M.C. Johnston 20850
    V 20850 U.S. - Florida 20850

V *Forsythia japonica* Makino var.
    japonica 10573
    V 10573 Japan 10573

V *Forsythia japonica* Makino var. *subintegra*
    Hara 10573
    V 10573 Japan 10573

E *Forsythia saxatilis* Nakai 15957
    E 15923 Korea, South (Mt Kwanak, Mt Pukhan)
              15957

R *Fraxinus gooddingii* Little 20883, 20850, 8058
    R 20850 U.S. - Arizona 20850
    V 20883 Mexico 20883

V *Fraxinus papillosa* Lingelsh. 20850
    I 20850 U.S. - Arizona 20850
    I 20850 U.S. - New Mexico 20850
    I 20850 U.S. - Texas 20850

R *Haenianthus grandifolius* Urban 5607
    R 19105 Cuba 5607

I *Henslowia erythrocarpa* Kurz 7771
    I India - Nicobar Is. (Kamorta Is.) 7771

I *Hesperelaea palmeri* A.Gray 12015
    I 19850 Mexico (Guadalupe I.) 12015

I *Jasminum andamanicam* Balakr. & N.G. Nair 7771
    I India - Andaman Is. (South and Middle
        Andamans) 7771

I *Jasminum angustitubum* Knobl. 5926
    I 5926 Tanzania 5926

V *Jasminum azoricum* L. 17891
    V Portugal - Madeira 17891

R *Jasminum barrelierii* Webb & Berthel.
    R Spain - Canary Is.

E *Jasminum carissoides* Kerr 19120
    E 19120 Thailand 19120

R *Jasminum cordatum* Ridley
    R Malaysia - Peninsular Malaysia (Perak; Selangor)

I *Jasminum curtisii* King & Gamble
    I Malaysia - Peninsular Malaysia (Perlis; Ipoh, Perak)

I *Jasminum ellipticum* Knobl. 5926
    I 5926 Tanzania (Lindi) 5926

I *Jasminum fluminense* Vell. ssp. *socotranum* P.S.
    Green 15534
    I 15534 Yemen - Socotra 15534

I *Jasminum insularum* Kerr 19120
    I 19120 Thailand 19120

V *Jasminum kriegeri* Guillaumin 20893
    V 20893 New Caledonia 20893

V *Jasminum linearifolium* Guillaumin 20893
    V 20893 New Caledonia 20893

E *Jasminum noumeense* Schltr. 20802
    E 20893 New Caledonia 20802

V *Jasminum promonturianum* Däniker 20893
    V 20893 New Caledonia 20893

I *Jasminum putii* Kerr 19120
    I 19120 Thailand 19120

I *Jasminum rarum* Kerr 19120
    I 19120 Thailand 19120

E *Jasminum sempervirens* Kerr 19120
    E 19120 Thailand 19120

E *Jasminum stellipilum* Kerr 19120
    E 19120 Thailand 19120

E *Jasminum tangense* Kerr 19120
    E 19120 Thailand 19120

R *Jasminum unifoliolatum* Balakr. & Nair 10177
    R 14782 India - Andaman Is. (Saddle Peak, N.
        Andamans) 10177

E *Jasminum virgatum* Kerr. 19120
    E 19120 Thailand 19120

I *Jasminum wightii* C.B. Clarke
    I India - Tamil Nadu (Coimbatore)

R *Jasminum wrayi* King & Gamble
    R Malaysia - Peninsular Malaysia (Perak; Kelantan)

I *Ligustrum decaisnei* C.B. Clarke var. *beddomei*
    Gamble
    I India - Karnataka (Kiggatnad, Coorg)

V *Ligustrum matudae* Kaneh.
    V Taiwan (Heng-ch'un)

E *Ligustrum microcarpum* Kanehira & Sasaki 20854
    E 20854 Taiwan 20854

R *Ligustrum morrisonense* Kanehira & Sasaki 20511
    R 20511 Taiwan 20511

R *Ligustrum pricei* Hayata 20854
    R 20854 Taiwan 20854

R *Ligustrum seisuiense* Shimizu & Kao 20511
    R Taiwan (Mt Chingshui)

V *Ligustrum tamakii* Hatus. 20626
    V 20626 Japan (Ryukyu) 20626

V *Linociera albidiflora* (Thwaites) C.B. Clarke 12838
    V 12838 Sri Lanka 12838

I *Linociera calcicola* Kerr 19120
    I 19120 Thailand 19120

I *Linociera eriorachis* Kerr 19120
    I 19120 Thailand 19120

I *Linociera procera* Kerr 19120
    I 19120 Thailand 19120

E *Linociera sutepensis* Kerr 19120
    E 19120 Thailand 19120

I *Linociera velutina* Kerr 19120

I   *19120*   Thailand *19120*

I   *Myxopyrum confertum* **Kerr** *19120*
    I   *19120*   Thailand *19120*

V   *Notelaea lloydii* **Guymer** *20681*
    V   *20681*   Australia - Queensland *20681*

R   *Notelaea pungens* **Guymer** *20681*
    R   *20681*   Australia - Queensland *20681*

R   *Olea europaea* **L. ssp.** *cerasiformis* **(Webb & Berth.) Kunkel & Sund.**
    R   Portugal - Madeira
    R   Spain - Canary Is.

R   *Olea schliebenii* **Knobl.** *7959*
    R   Tanzania (Uluguru Mts.) *7959*

V   *Osmanthus okinawensis* **Hatus.** *20626*
    V   *20626*   Japan (Ryukyu Islands) *20626*

V   *Osmanthus rigidus* **Nakai** *10573*
    V   *10573*   Japan (Isls. Tokara) *20626*

R   *Osmanthus scortechinii* **King & Gamble**
    R   Malaysia - Peninsular Malaysia

I   *Picconia azorica* **(Tutin) Knobl.** *8000, 20171*
    I   *19174*   Portugal - Azores *8000*

V   *Picconia excelsa* **(Aiton) DC.** *17534*
    V   Portugal - Madeira
    V   *17534*   Spain - Canary Is. *17534*

I   *Schrebera greenwayi* **Turrill** *5926*
    I   *5926*   Tanzania *5926*

R   *Syringa josikaea* **J.Jacq. ex Rchb.** *5942, 20171*
    R   *19949*   Romania *17823*
    I   *5942*   Ukraine *5942*

E   *Syringa pinnatifolia* **Hemsley var.** *alashanica* **Ma & S.Q. Zhou** *11139*
    E   China - Ningxia (Helanshan) *11139*

E   *Syringa pinnatifolia* **Hemsley var.** *pinnatifolia* *17617*
    E   *17617*   China - Qinghai (Xunhua) *11139*
    E   *17617*   China - Shaanxi (Huxian, Taibaoshan, Zhouzi) *11139*
    E   *17617*   China - Sichuan (J'chuan, Baoxing, Kangding) *11139*

Oliniaceae

Number of genera:	1	
Number of species:	8	
Recorded threatened species:	2	(25%)

Southern and eastern Africa; ?St. Helena.

I   *Plectronia ficiformis* **(Hook.f.) Gamble**
    I   India - Karnataka (Mysore)
    I   India - Tamil Nadu (Palani & Sivagiri Hills)

I   *Plectronia pergracilis* **(Bourd.) Gamble**
    I   India - Kerala (Colatoorpolay, Travancore)

Onagraceae

Number of genera:	17	
Number of species:	675	
Recorded threatened species:	119	(17%)

Temperate and subtropical, especially New World.

V   *Boisduvalia cleistogama* **Curran** *20850*
    I   *20850*   U.S. - California *20850*

R   *Boisduvalia macrantha* **Heller** *20850*
    I   *20850*   U.S. - California *20850*

I   *20850*   U.S. - Idaho *20850*
I   *20850*   U.S. - Oregon *20850*

R   *Camissonia arenaria* **(A. Nels.) Raven** *20850*
    I   *20850*   U.S. - Arizona *20850*
    I   *20850*   U.S. - California *20850*

V   *Camissonia atwoodii* **Cronq.** *20850*
    E   *20850*   U.S. - Utah *20850*

E   *Camissonia benitensis* **Raven** *20850*
    E   *20850*   U.S. - California (San Benito Co.) *20850*

V   *Camissonia bistorta* **(Nutt. ex Torr. & Gray) Raven** *20850*
    I   *20850*   Canada - British Columbia *20850*
    I   *20850*   U.S. - California *20850*

R   *Camissonia boothii* **(Dougl. ex Lehm.) Raven ssp.** *alyssoides* **(Hook. & Arn.) Raven** *20850*
    I   *20850*   U.S. - California *20850*
    I   *20850*   U.S. - Idaho *20850*
    R   *20850*   U.S. - Nevada *20850*
    I   *20850*   U.S. - Oregon *20850*
    I   *20850*   U.S. - Utah *20850*

R   *Camissonia campestris* **(Greene) Raven** *20850*
    I   *20850*   U.S. - California *20850*
    I   *20850*   U.S. - Nevada *20850*

R   *Camissonia cardiophylla* **(Torr.) Raven** *20850*
    I   *20850*   U.S. - Arizona *20850*
    I   *20850*   U.S. - California *20850*
    I   *20850*   U.S. - Nevada *20850*

E   *Camissonia confertiflora* **(Raven) Raven** *20850*
    E   *20850*   U.S. - Arizona *20850*

V   *Camissonia confusa* **Raven** *20850*
    I   *20850*   U.S. - Arizona *20850*
    I   *20850*   U.S. - California *20850*

E   *Camissonia exilis* **(Raven) Raven** *20850*
    E   *20850*   U.S. - Arizona *20850*
    E   *20850*   U.S. - Utah *20850*

E   *Camissonia gouldii* **Raven** *20850*
    E   *20850*   U.S. - Arizona *20850*
    E   *20850*   U.S. - Utah *20850*

V   *Camissonia guadalupensis* **(S.Watson) Raven** *20850*
    I   *20850*   U.S. - California *20850*

E   *Camissonia guadalupensis* **(S.Watson)Raven ssp.** *clementina* **(Raven) Raven** *20850*
    E   *20850*   U.S. - California *20850*

E   *Camissonia hardhamiae* **Raven** *20850*
    E   *20850*   U.S. - California *20850*

V   *Camissonia heterochroma* **(S.Watson) Raven** *20850*
    I   *20850*   U.S. - California *20850*
    I   *20850*   U.S. - Nevada *20850*

R   *Camissonia hirtella* **(Greene) Raven** *20850*
    I   *20850*   U.S. - California *20850*

R   *Camissonia ignota* **(Jepson) Raven** *20850*
    I   *20850*   U.S. - California *20850*

E   *Camissonia integrifolia* **Raven** *20850*
    I   *20850*   U.S. - California *20850*

V   *Camissonia lacustris* **Raven** *20850*
    I   *20850*   U.S. - California *20850*

E   *Camissonia lewisii* **Raven** *20850*
    I   *20850*   U.S. - California *20850*

V   *Camissonia luciae* **Raven** *20850*
    I   *20850*   U.S. - California *20850*

V   *Camissonia megalantha* **(Munz) Raven** *20850*

V   *20850* U.S. - Nevada *20850*

R   *Camissonia micrantha* (Hornem. ex Spreng.) Raven *20850*
I   *20850* Canada - British Columbia *20850*
I   *20850* U.S. - California *20850*

R   *Camissonia nevadensis* (Kellogg) Raven *20850*
R   *20850* U.S. - Nevada *20850*

R   *Camissonia ovata* (Nutt. ex Torr. & Gray) Raven *20850*
I   *20850* U.S. - California *20850*
I   *20850* U.S. - Oregon *20850*

R   *Camissonia pallida* (Abrams) Raven *20850*
I   *20850* U.S. - Arizona *20850*
I   *20850* U.S. - California *20850*
I   *20850* U.S. - Nevada *20850*

R   *Camissonia palmeri* (S.Watson) Raven *20850*
I   *20850* U.S. - Arizona *20850*
I   *20850* U.S. - California *20850*
E   *20850* U.S. - Idaho *20850*
I   *20850* U.S. - Nevada *20850*
I   *20850* U.S. - Oregon *20850*

V   *Camissonia parryi* (S.Watson) Raven *20850*
I   *20850* U.S. - Arizona *20850*
I   *20850* U.S. - Nevada *20850*
V   *20850* U.S. - Utah *20850*

R   *Camissonia pygmaea* (Dougl. ex Lehm.) Raven *20850*
I   *20850* U.S. - Idaho *20850*
Ex/E *20850* U.S. - Oregon *20850*
E   *20850* U.S. - Washington *20850*

V   *Camissonia sierrae* Raven *20850*
I   *20850* U.S. - California *20850*

E   *Camissonia sierrae* Raven ssp. *alticola* Raven *20850*
E   *20850* U.S. - California *20850*

V   *Camissonia specuicola* (Raven) Raven *20850*
V   *20850* U.S. - Arizona *20850*

E   *Camissonia specuicola* (Raven) Raven ssp. *hesperia* (Raven) Raven *20850*
E   *20850* U.S. - Arizona *20850*

V   *Camissonia specuicola* (Raven) Raven ssp. *specuicola* *20850*
V   *20850* U.S. - Arizona *20850*

R   *Camissonia strigulosa* (Fisch. & C.A. Mey.) Raven *20850*
I   *20850* U.S. - Arizona *20850*
I   *20850* U.S. - California *20850*

R   *Camissonia tanacetifolia* (Torr. & A.Gray) Raven ssp. *quadriperforata* Raven *20850*
R   *20850* U.S. - California *20850*

R   *Clarkia affinis* H.F. & M.E. Lewis *20850*
I   *20850* U.S. - California *20850*

R   *Clarkia arcuata* (Kellogg) A. Nels. & J.F. Macbr. *20850*
I   *20850* U.S. - California *20850*

R   *Clarkia australis* E. Small *20850*
R   *20850* U.S. - California *20850*

V   *Clarkia biloba* (Durand) Nelson & J.F. Macbr. ssp. *australis* H.F. & M.E. Lewis *20850*
V   *20850* U.S. - California *20850*

V   *Clarkia borealis* E. Small *20850*
I   *20850* U.S. - California *20850*

E   *Clarkia borealis* E. Small ssp. *arida* E. Small *20850*

E   *20850* U.S. - California *20850*

V   *Clarkia borealis* E. Small ssp. *borealis* *20850*
I   *20850* U.S. - California *20850*

V   *Clarkia bottae* (Spach) H.F. & M.E. Lewis *20850*
I   *20850* U.S. - California *20850*

R   *Clarkia breweri* (Gray) Greene *20850*
R   *20850* U.S. - California *20850*

V   *Clarkia concinna* (Fisch & Mey.) Greene ssp. *automixa* R.N. Bowman *20850*
V   *20850* U.S. - California *20850*

E   *Clarkia concinna* (Fisch & Mey.) Greene ssp. *raichei* G. Allen, V. Ford & L. Gottlieb *20850*
E   *20850* U.S. - California *20850*

R   *Clarkia cylindrica* (Jepson) H.F. & M.E. Lewis *20850*
I   *20850* U.S. - California *20850*

R   *Clarkia davyi* (Jepson) H.F. & M.E. Lewis *20850*
I   *20850* U.S. - California *20850*

V   *Clarkia delicata* (Abrams) A. Nels. & J.F. Macbr. *20850*
I   *20850* U.S. - California *20850*

R   *Clarkia dudleyana* (Abrams) J.F. Macbr. *20850*
I   *20850* U.S. - California *20850*

E   *Clarkia franciscana* Lewis & Raven *20850*
E   *20850* U.S. - California *20850*

V   *Clarkia gracilis* (Piper) A. Nels. & J. F. Macbr. ssp. *albicaulis* (Jepson) H.F. & M.E. Lewis *20850*
V   *20850* U.S. - California *20850*

E   *Clarkia imbricata* H.F. & M.E. Lewis *20850*
E   *20850* U.S. - California *20850*

V   *Clarkia jolonensis* Parnell *20850*
I   *20850* U.S. - California *20850*

R   *Clarkia lassenensis* (Eastw.) H.F. & M.E. Lewis *20850*
I   *20850* U.S. - California *20850*
I   *20850* U.S. - Nevada *20850*
I   *20850* U.S. - Oregon *20850*

V   *Clarkia lewisii* Raven & Parnell *20850*
I   *20850* U.S. - California *20850*

E   *Clarkia lingulata* H.F. & M.E. Lewis *20850*
E   *20850* U.S. - California *20850*

R   *Clarkia modesta* Jepson *20850*
I   *20850* U.S. - California *20850*

E   *Clarkia mosquinii* E. Small *20850*
I   *20850* U.S. - California *20850*

E   *Clarkia mosquinii* E. Small ssp. *mosquinii* *20850, 14662*
E   *20850* U.S. - California *20850*

E   *Clarkia mosquinii* E. Small ssp. *xerophila* E. Small *20850*
E   *20850* U.S. - California *20850*

R   *Clarkia nitens* H.F. & M.E. Lewis *20850*
I   *20850* U.S. - California *20850*

R   *Clarkia prostrata* H.F. & M.E. Lewis *20850*
I   *20850* U.S. - California *20850*

R   *Clarkia purpurea* (W. Curtis) A. Nels. & J.F. Macbr. *20850*
I   *20850* Canada - British Columbia *20850*
I   *20850* U.S. - Arizona *20850*
I   *20850* U.S. - California *20850*
I   *20850* U.S. - Oregon *20850*

I	20850	U.S. - Pennsylvania	20850
I	20850	U.S. - Washington	20850

V *Clarkia rostrata* W.S. Davis 20850
    V   20850 U.S. - California 20850

R *Clarkia rubicunda* (Lindl.) H.F. & M.E. Lewis 20850
    I   20850 U.S. - California 20850

R *Clarkia similis* Lewis & Ernst 20850
    I   20850 U.S. - California 20850

R *Clarkia speciosa* H.F. & M.E. Lewis 20850
    I   20850 U.S. - California 20850

E *Clarkia speciosa* H.F. & M.E. Lewis ssp. *immaculata*
    H.F. & M.E. Lewis 20850
    E   20850 U.S. - California 20850

E *Clarkia springvillensis* Vasek 20850
    E   20850 U.S. - California 20850

V *Clarkia stellata* Mosquin 20850
    I   20850 U.S. - California 20850

R *Clarkia tembloriensis* Vasek 20850
    I   20850 U.S. - California 20850

E *Clarkia tembloriensis* Vasek ssp. *calientensis*
    (Vasek) Holsinger 20850
    E   20850 U.S. - California 20850

R *Clarkia williamsonii* (Dur. & Hilg.) H.F. & M.E.
    Lewis 20850
    I   20850 U.S. - California 20850

I *Epilobium glaciale* Raven
    I   India - Jammu & Kashmir

R *Epilobium nankotaizanense* Yamamoto 17617
    R   17617 Taiwan (Nanhudashan) 11139

V *Epilobium nevadense* Munz 20850
    V   20850 U.S. - Nevada 20850
    E   20850 U.S. - Utah 20850

V *Epilobium nivium* Brandeg. 20850
    I   20850 U.S. - California 20850

E *Epilobium numidicum* Battand. 10488
    E   14958 Algeria 10488

V *Epilobium oreganum* Greene 20850
    I   20850 Canada - Alberta 20850
    I   20850 Canada - British Columbia 20850
    E   20850 U.S. - California 20850
    E   20850 U.S. - Oregon 20850

R *Epilobium perpusillum* Hausskn. 20681
    R   20681 Australia - Tasmania 20681

R *Epilobium psilotum* Maire & G. Samuelsson
    R   Morocco

R *Epilobium purpuratum* Hook.f. 19305
    R   19305 New Zealand - South Is. 19305

R *Epilobium rigidum* Hausskn. 20850
    I   20850 U.S. - California 20850
    V   20850 U.S. - Oregon 20850

V *Epilobium septentrionale* (Keck) R.N. Bowman &
    Hoch 20850
    V   20850 U.S. - California 20850

R *Epilobium shiroumense* Matsum. & Nakai 10572
    R   10572 Japan 10572

R *Epilobium siskiyouense* (Munz) Hoch & Raven 20850
    V   20850 U.S. - California 20850
    V   20850 U.S. - Oregon 20850

R *Epilobium tomlinsonianum* Adams 20883
    R   20883 Jamaica 20883

R *Epilobium tundrarum* Sam. 20171
    R   former European USSR (Arctic)

R *Epilobium willisii* Raven & Engelhorn 20681
    R   20681 Australia - Tasmania 20681
    Ex/E 20681 Australia - Victoria 20681

R *Fuchsia cyrtandroides* J.Moore 20845
    R   20845 French Polynesia - Society Is. (Tahiti)
             20845

R *Fuchsia decidua* Standley 10003
    R   10003 Mexico 10003

E *Fuchsia huanucoensis* P. Berry 20883
    I   20883 Peru 20883

E *Fuchsia nana* P. Berry 20883
    I   20883 Bolivia 20883

E *Fuchsia pachyrrhiza* P.Berry & B.A.Stein 20883
    I   20883 Peru 20883

E *Fuchsia pilaloensis* P. Berry 20883
    I   20883 Ecuador 20883

V *Gaura boquillensis* Raven & Gregory 20850
    V   20850 U.S. - Texas 20850

V *Gaura macrocarpa* Rothrock 20850
    V   20850 U.S. - Texas 20850

V *Gaura neomexicana* Wooton ssp. *coloradensis* (Rydb.)
    Raven & Gregory 20850
    E   20850 U.S. - Colorado 20850
    E   20850 U.S. - Nebraska 20850
    V   20850 U.S. - Wyoming 20850

R *Gaura villosa* (Munz) Raven & Gregory ssp. *parksii*
    (Munz) Raven & Gregory 20850
    R   20850 U.S. - Texas 20850

R *Gayophytum oligospermum* Lewis & Szweykowski 20850
    I   20850 U.S. - California 20850

Ex *Lopezia conjugens* Brandegee 10003
    Ex   10003 Mexico 10003

R *Lopezia grandiflora* Zucc. var.
    grandiflora 10004
    R   10003 Mexico 10004

R *Lopezia lopezioides* (Hook. & Arn.) Plitm.,
    Raven 10004
    R   10003 Mexico 10004

R *Lopezia miniata* Lagasca ex DC. ssp. *hintonii*
    (Foster) Plitm., Raven & Breed. 10004
    R   10003 Mexico - Guerrero 10004

R *Lopezia nuevo-leonis* Plitm. Raven & Breedlove 10004
    R   10003 Mexico 10004

Ex *Lopezia sinaloensis* Munz 10006
    Ex   10003 Mexico 10006

R *Lopezia smithii* Rose 10006
    R   10003 Mexico 10006

R *Lopezia suffrutescens* Munz 10006
    R   10003 Mexico 10006

R *Ludwigia anastomosans* (DC.) Hara 11375
    R   11375 Brazil 11375

R *Ludwigia brachyphylla* (Micheli) Hara 11375
    R   11375 Brazil 11375

R *Ludwigia bullata* (Hassler) Hara 11375
    R   11375 Bolivia 11375
    R   11375 Brazil 11375
    R   11375 Paraguay 11375

Ex/E *Ludwigia burchellii* (Micheli) Hara 11375

Ex/E *11375* Brazil *11375*

R   *Ludwigia densiflora* (Micheli) Hara *11375*
- R   Bolivia *11375*
- R   Brazil *11375*
- R   Colombia *11375*
- R   *18200* Peru *11375*
- R   Venezuela *11375*

R   *Ludwigia lanceolata* Ell. *20850*
- I   *20850* U.S. - Florida *20850*
- I   *20850* U.S. - Georgia *20850*
- E   *20850* U.S. - North Carolina *20850*
- I   *20850* U.S. - South Carolina *20850*

V   *Ludwigia ravenii* Peng *20850*
- I   *20850* U.S. - Florida *20850*
- V   *20850* U.S. - North Carolina *20850*
- I   *20850* U.S. - South Carolina *20850*
- E   *20850* U.S. - Virginia *20850*

V   *Ludwigia spathulata* Torr. & Gray *20850*
- V   *20850* U.S. - Alabama *20850*
- I   *20850* U.S. - Florida *20850*
- I   *20850* U.S. - South Carolina *20850*

E   *Ludwigia stricta* (C. Wright) C. Wright
- E   *19105* Cuba (Pinar del Rio) *19105*

V   *Oenothera acutissima* W.L. Wagner *20850*
- V   *20850* U.S. - Colorado *20850*
- E   *20850* U.S. - Utah *20850*

E   *Oenothera californica* (S. Wats.) S. Wats. ssp. *eurekensis* (Munz & Roos) W. Klein *20850*
- E   *20850* U.S. - California *20850*

R   *Oenothera cavernae* Munz *20850*
- I   *20850* U.S. - Arizona *20850*
- I   *20850* U.S. - Colorado *20850*
- I   *20850* U.S. - Nevada *20850*
- E   *20850* U.S. - Utah *20850*

E   *Oenothera deltoides* Torr. & Fremont ssp. *howellii* (Munz) W. Klein *20850*
- E   *20850* U.S. - California *20850*

V   *Oenothera harringtonii* W.L. Wagner *20850*
- V   *20850* U.S. - Colorado *20850*

V   *Oenothera organensis* Munz *20850*
- V   *20850* U.S. - New Mexico *20850*

V   *Oenothera pilosella* Raf. ssp. *sessilis* (Pennell) Straley *20850*
- V   *20850* U.S. - Arkansas *20850*
- I   *20850* U.S. - Louisiana *20850*
- Ex/E *20850* U.S. - Texas *20850*

R   *Oenothera psammophila* (A.Nels. & J.F.Macbr.) W.L.Wagner, Stockhouse & Klein *20850*
- I   *20850* Canada - Alberta *20850*
- R   *20850* U.S. - Idaho *20850*

R   *Oenothera tamrae* W. Dietr. & W.L. Wagner *10557*
- R   *10557* Mexico - Nayarit *10557*

V   *Oenothera wolfii* (Munz) Raven, W. Dietr. & Stubbe *20850*
- E   *20850* U.S. - California *20850*
- E   *20850* U.S. - Oregon *20850*

R   *Oenothera xylocarpa* Coville *20850*
- I   *20850* U.S. - California *20850*
- I   *20850* U.S. - Nevada *20850*

Opiliaceae
Number of genera: 9
Number of species: 50
Recorded threatened species: 1 (2%)

Tropical and subtropical.

R   *Rhopalopilia hallei* Villiers
- R   Gabon (Lebama)

Oxalidaceae
Number of genera: 7-8
Number of species: 900
Recorded threatened species: 31 (3%)

Centeres in tropics and subtropics, widespread in temperate regions.

V   *Biophytum falcifolium* Lourt. *20883, 10747*
- V   *16317* Panama *20883*

V   *Biophytum mucronatum* Lourt. *20883, 10747*
- V   *16317* Panama *20883*

V   *Biophytum panamense* Lourt. *20883, 10747*
- V   *16317* Panama *20883*

R   *Biophytum soukupii* Lourt. *10747*
- V   *16317* Panama *10747*
- R   *18200* Peru *10747*

I   *Biophytum turianense* Kabuye *5926*
- I   *5926* Tanzania *5926*

V   *Oxalis balansae* Guillaumin *20893*
- V   *20893* New Caledonia *20893*

R   *Oxalis bradei* Knuth *9037*
- R   *9426* Costa Rica *9037*

V   *Oxalis bulbigera* Knuth *18200*
- V   *9446* Peru *18200*

I   *Oxalis burtoniae* Salter *20604*
- I   *20604* South Africa - Cape Province *20604*

V   *Oxalis cajalbanensis* Urban *5607*
- V   *19105* Cuba (Pinar del Rio) *5607*

R   *Oxalis calvinensis* Knuth *20604*
- R   *20604* South Africa - Cape Province *20604*

R   *Oxalis cathara* Salter *20604*
- R   *20604* South Africa - Cape Province *20604*

R   *Oxalis deserticola* Salter *20604*
- R   *20604* South Africa - Cape Province *20604*

I   *Oxalis fragilis* Salter var. *fragilis* *20604*
- I   *20604* South Africa - Cape Province *20604*

I   *Oxalis fragilis* Salter var. *pellucida* Salter *20604*
- I   South Africa - Cape Province

R   *Oxalis gagneorum* Fosberg & Sachet *20845*
- V   *20845* French Polynesia - Marquesas Is *20845*

V   *Oxalis illinoensis* Schwegm. *20850*
- E   *20850* U.S. - Illinois *20850*
- V   *20850* U.S. - Indiana *20850*
- I   *20850* U.S. - Kentucky *20850*

R   *Oxalis involuta* Salter *20604*
- R   *20604* South Africa - Cape Province *20604*

V   *Oxalis levis* Salter *20604*
- V   *20604* South Africa - Cape Province *20604*

I   *Oxalis lindaviana* Schltr. *20604*
- I   *20604* South Africa - Cape Province *20604*

Magnoliopsida (dicots): Oxalidaceae: *Oxalis*

V	*Oxalis lomana* Diels *18200*	
	V	9446 Peru *18200*
R	*Oxalis melanosticta* Sond. var. *latifolia* Salter *20604*	
	R	20604 South Africa - Cape Province *20604*
I	*Oxalis microdonta* Salter *20604*	
	I	20604 South Africa - Cape Province *20604*
E	*Oxalis natans* L.f. *20604*	
	E	20604 South Africa - Cape Province *20604*
R	*Oxalis occulifera* E.G.H.Olive. *20604*	
	R	20604 South Africa - Cape Province *20604*
V	*Oxalis perineson* Salter & Exell *20604*	
	V	20604 South Africa - Cape Province *20604*
R	*Oxalis senecta* Salter *20604*	
	R	20604 South Africa - Cape Province *20604*
V	*Oxalis sepalosa* Diels *18200*	
	V	9446 Peru *18200*
I	*Oxalis simplex* Salter *20604*	
	I	20604 South Africa - Cape Province *20604*
I	*Oxalis subsessilis* L.Bolus *20604*	
	I	20604 South Africa - Cape Province *20604*
R	*Oxalis taimoni* Yamamoto *20511*	
	R	20511 Taiwan *20511*
R	*Oxalis virginea* Jacq. *20604*	
	R	20604 South Africa - Cape Province *20604*

Paeoniaceae

Number of genera: 1
Number of species: 30
Recorded threatened species: 11 (36%)

Eurasia, especially temperate eastern Asia.

R	*Paeonia cambessedesii* (Willk.) Willk. *8000, 20171*	
	R	20645 Spain - Balearic Is. *17891*
V	*Paeonia clusii* Stern *20171*	
	V	20731 Greece - Crete *20731*
V	*Paeonia delavayi* Franchet var. *lutea* (Franchet) Fin. & Gagnepain *17617*	
	V	17617 China - Sichuan (Muli) *11139*
	V	17617 China - Xizang Zizhiqu *11139*
	V	17617 China - Yunnan *11139*
R	*Paeonia kavachensis* Aznav. *6930*	
	R	11552 Russian Federation (Caucasus) *11552*
I	*Paeonia macrophylla* (Albov) N. Lom. *5942*	
	I	5942 Georgia *5942*
R	*Paeonia mascula* (L.) Mill. ssp. *hellenica* Tzanoudakis *20171*	
	R	20731 Greece (Peloponnisos, West Aegean, Cyclades) *20731*
V	*Paeonia mascula* (L.) Miller ssp. *russoi* (Biv.) Cullen & Heywood var. *corsica* (Sieber ex Tausch) Gürke *15080*	
	V	15080 France - Corsica *15080*
	V	20805 Italy - Sardinia *15080*
I	*Paeonia mlokosewitschii* N. Lom. *5942*	
	I	5942 Russia - North Caucasus *5942*
V	*Paeonia parnassica* Tzanoudakis *17781, 20171*	
	V	20731 Greece (Sterea Ellas) *20731*
I	*Paeonia steveniana* Kem.-Nat. *5942*	
	I	5942 Russia - North Caucasus *5942*

	I	5942 Georgia *5942*
V	*Paeonia suffruticosa* Andr. var. *papaveracea* (Andr.) Kerner *17617*	
	V	17617 China - Gansu *11139*
	V	17617 China - Henan *11139*
	V	17617 China - Shaanxi *11139*
E	*Paeonia suffruticosa* Andr. var. *spontanea* Rehder *11139*	
	E	China - Shaanxi *11139*
	E	China - Shanxi (Keshan) *11139*
E	*Paeonia szechuanica* Fang *17617*	
	E	17617 China - Sichuan (Markang, Jingchuan) *11139*

Papaveraceae

Number of genera: 25
Number of species: 200
Recorded threatened species: 84 (42%)

Temperate & tropical Northern Hemisphere.

V	*Arctomecon californica* Torr. & Frem. *20850*	
	V	20850 U.S. - Arizona *20850*
	R	20850 U.S. - Nevada *20850*
E	*Arctomecon humilis* Coville *20850*	
	E	20850 U.S. - Utah *20850*
R	*Arctomecon merriamii* Coville *20850*	
	R	20850 U.S. - California *20850*
	V	20850 U.S. - Nevada *20850*
E	*Argemone arizonica* G.B. Ownbey *20850*	
	E	20850 U.S. - Arizona *20850*
R	*Argemone burkartii* Soraru *19574*	
	R	19574 Argentina *19574*
R	*Argemone corymbosa* Greene *20850*	
	I	20850 U.S. - Arizona *20850*
	I	20850 U.S. - California *20850*
	I	20850 U.S. - Nevada *20850*
	V	20850 U.S. - Utah *20850*
V	*Argemone munita* Durand & Hilg. ssp. *robusta* G.B. Ownbey *20850*	
	V	20850 U.S. - California *20850*
V	*Argemone pleiacantha* E.Greene ssp. *pinnatisecta* G.B. Ownbey *20850*	
	V	20850 U.S. - New Mexico *20850*
V	*Canbya candida* Parry ex Gray *20850*	
	V	20850 U.S. - California *20850*
R	*Corydalis acaulis* (Wulfen) Pers. *20171*	
	R	(former) Yugoslavia
R	*Corydalis aquae-gelidae* M.E. Peck & Wilson *20850*	
	V	20850 U.S. - Oregon *20850*
	V	20850 U.S. - Washington *20850*
V	*Corydalis caseana* (Rydb.) G.B. Ownbey ssp. *brachycarpa* (Rydb.) G.B. Ownbey *20850*	
	V	20850 U.S. - Utah *20850*
V	*Corydalis caseana* (Rydb.) G.B. Ownbey ssp. *brandegei* (S.Watson) G.B. Ownbey *20850*	
	V	20850 U.S. - Colorado *20850*
	I	20850 U.S. - New Mexico *20850*
R	*Corydalis caseana* (S.Watson) G.B. Ownbey ssp. *hastata* (Rydb.) G.B. Ownbey *20850*	
	R	20850 U.S. - Idaho *20850*
E	*Corydalis cashmeriana* Royle *14768*	
	E	India - Jammu & Kashmir (Mahdev) *14768*

R   *Corydalis curvicalcarata* Miyabe & Kudo *10572*
     R   *10572*   Japan *10572*

V   *Corydalis gotlandica* Lidén *18216, 20171*
     V   *20083*   Sweden *18216*

R   *Corydalis integra* Barbey & Fors.-Major *20171*
     R   Greece

R   *Corydalis pallida* (Thunb.) Pers. var. *sparsimamma*
     (Thunb.) Pers. *20511*
     R   *20511*   Taiwan *20511*

R   *Corydalis rutifolia* (Sm.) DC. *20171*
     R   Greece

R   *Corydalis rutifolia* (Sibth. & Sm.) DC. ssp. *kurdica*
     Cullen & Davis *12840*
     R   *12840*   Turkey *12840*

V   *Corydalis sewerzowii* Regel
     V   former USSR *6930*

R   *Corydalis solida* (L.) Swartz ssp. *tauricola* Cullen
     & Davis *12840*
     R   *12840*   Turkey *12840*

R   *Corydalis thasia* (Stoy. & Kit.) Stoy. & Kit.
     R   Greece

R   *Corydalis uniflora* (Sieber) Nyman *20171*
     R   *20730*   Greece - Crete *20730*

E   *Dendromecon rigida* Benth. ssp. *rhamnoides* (Greene)
     Thorne *20850*
     E   *20850*   U.S. - California *20850*

R   *Dicentra chrysantha* (Hook. & Arn.) Walp. *20850*
     I   *20850*   U.S. - California *20850*

V   *Dicentra nevadensis* Eastw. *20850*
     V   *20850*   U.S. - California *20850*

R   *Dicentra ochroleuca* Engelm. *20850*
     I   *20850*   U.S. - California *20850*

I   *Dicentra spectabilis* (L.) Lem. *11815, 20171*
     I   China - Gansu *11815*

E   *Eschscholzia lemmonii* Greene ssp. *kernensis* (Munz)
     C. Clark *20850*
     E   *20850*   U.S. - California *20850*

V   *Eschscholzia minutiflora* S.Watson ssp. *twisselmannii*
     C. Clark *20850*
     V   *20850*   U.S. - California *20850*

E   *Eschscholzia procera* Greene *20850*
     E   *20850*   U.S. - California *20850*

E   *Eschscholzia rhombipetala* Greene *20850, 14662*
     E   *20850*   U.S. - California *20850*

E   *Fumaria caroliana* Pugsley *20171*
     E   *20528*   France (Arras) *20528*

R   *Fumaria coccinea* Lowe ex Pugsley *15104*
     R   Spain - Canary Is.

I   *Fumaria jankae* Hausskn. *17823, 20171*
     I   *19949*   Romania *20631*

R   *Fumaria mairei* Pugsley *10487*
     R   *14958*   Algeria *10487*

R   *Fumaria occidentalis* Pugsley *8000, 20171*
     R   *19701*   United Kingdom *5387*

I   *Fumariola turkestanica* Korsh. *5942*
     I   *5942*   Tajikistan *5942*

R   *Glaucium acutidentatum* Hausskn. & Bornm. *12840*
     R   *12840*   Turkey *12840*

R   *Glaucium cappadocicum* Boiss. *12840*
     R   *12840*   Turkey *12840*

V   *Glaucium grandiflorum* Boiss. & Huet var. *turquatum*
     Cullen *12840*
     V   *12840*   Turkey *12840*

R   *Hylomecon hylomeconoides* T. Lee *15957*
     R   *15923*   Korea, South (Mt Chiri) *15957*

R   *Hypecoum aequilobum* Viv. *20171*
     R   Egypt
     V   Libya

R   *Hypecoum dimidiatum* Del.
     R   Egypt

R   *Meconella denticulata* Greene *20850*
     I   *20850*   U.S. - California *20850*

V   *Meconella oregana* Nutt. *20850, 10701*
     V   *20850*   Canada - British Columbia *20850*
     I   *20850*   U.S. - California *20850*
     E   *20850*   U.S. - Oregon *20850*
     E   *20850*   U.S. - Washington *20850*

E   *Meconopsis aculeata* Royle *14768*
     E   India - Jammu & Kashmir *14768*

V   *Meconopsis latifolia* Prain *11494*
     V   *11494*   India - Jammu & Kashmir (Kashmir Himalaya)
       11494

R   *Papaver alboroseum* Hulten *20850, 10701*
     E   *20850*   Canada - British Columbia *20850*
     E   *13967*   Canada - Northwest Territories (Franklin)
       13967
     I   *20850*   U.S. - Alaska *20850*

R   *Papaver argemone* L. ssp. *davisii*
     Kaderit *12840*
     R   *12840*   Turkey *12840*

R   *Papaver atrovirens* Petrovsky *21309*
     R   *21309*   Russia (E.Europe) - Northwest *21309*

I   *Papaver bracteatum* Lindl. *5942, 20171*
     I   *5942*   Russia - North Caucasus *5942*

R   *Papaver calvareum* Petrovsky *21309*
     R   *21309*   Russia (E.Europe) - North *21309*
     R   *21309*   Russia (E.Europe) - Northwest *21309*

R   *Papaver chionophilum* Petrovsky *21309*
     R   *21309*   Russia (E.Europe) - North *21309*

R   *Papaver decaisnei* Hochst. & Steudel
     R   Egypt

I   *Papaver divergens* Fedde & Bornm.
     I   Egypt

V   *Papaver fauriei* Fedde *10572*
     V   *10572*   Japan *10572*

V   *Papaver guerlekense* Stapf *12840, 20171*
     V   *12840*   Turkey *12840*

I   *Papaver himalaicum* Cretz.
     I   India - Jammu & Kashmir

V   *Papaver laestadianum* (Nordh.) Nordh. *17832, 20171,*
     21309
     V   *17832*   Norway *17832*
     V   *20083*   Sweden *18216*

R   *Papaver leucotrichum* Tolm. *21309*
     R   *21309*   Russia (E.Europe) - North *21309*

R   *Papaver maeoticum* Klokov *20171*
     R   former European USSR

E   *Papaver mcconnellii* Hulten *20850, 6796*
     E   *20850*   Canada - Mackenzie *20850*

E	*20850*	Canada - Yukon Territory	*20850*
E	*13967*	U.S. - Alaska	*13967*

R   *Papaver multiradiatum* Petrovsky *21309*

     R   *21309*   Russia (E.Europe) - North *21309*

R   *Papaver nigrotinctum* Fedde *20171*

     R   Greece

R   *Papaver nudicaule* L. ssp. *insulare*
         Petrovsky *21309*

     R   *21309*   Russia (E.Europe) - North *21309*

R   *Papaver pilosum* Sibth. & Sm. *12840*

     R   *12840*   Turkey *12840*

R   *Papaver pygmaeum* Rydb. *20850, 13153*

     V   *20850*   Canada - Alberta *20850*
     V   *20850*   Canada - British Columbia *20850*
     R   *20850*   U.S. - Montana *20850*
     E   *20850*   U.S. - Utah *20850*

R   *Papaver spicatum* Boiss. & Bal. *12840*

     V   *17832*   Norway *17832*
     R   *12840*   Turkey *12840*

I   *Papaver stipitatum* Fedde *20171*

     I   Greece

R   *Papaver strictum* Boiss. & Bal. *12840*

     R   *12840*   Turkey *12840*

I   *Papaver tatricum* (Nyár) Ehrendorfer *19839*

     I   *17821*   Czech Republic *17821*
     V   *19321*   Slovakia *19321*

R   *Papaver tenellum* Tolmatchew

     R   former USSR *6930*

R   *Papaver uschakovii* Tolm. & Petrovsky *21309*

     R   *21309*   Russia (E.Europe) - North *21309*

R   *Papaver walpolei* Porsild *20850, 5942*

     I   *5942*   Russia (Far East) - Magadan (north) *5942*
     E   *20850*   Canada - Yukon Territory *20850*
     V   *20850*   U.S. - Alaska *20850*
     ?   U.S. - Arkansas

R   *Roemeria carica* A. Baytop *12840*

     R   *12840*   Turkey *12840*

R   *Roemeria procumbens* Aarons. & Oppenh. *8895*

     I   Israel *8895*
     R   Jordan *8899*

R   *Romneya coulteri* Harvey *20850*

     I   *20850*   Canada - British Columbia *20850*
     R   *20850*   U.S. - California *20850*

R   *Romneya trichocalyx* Eastw. *20850*

     I   *20850*   U.S. - California *20850*

R   *Rupicapnos muricaria* Pomel *10487*

     R   *14958*   Algeria *10487*

V   *Sarcocapnos baetica* (Boiss. & Reut.) Nyman ssp. *baetica* *19818, 20171*

     V   *19818*   Spain (South) *8000*

V   *Sarcocapnos crassifolia* (Desf.) DC. ssp. *speciosa* (Boiss.) Rouy *19818, 20171*

     V   *19818*   Spain (Almeria & Granada) *19818*

R   *Sarcocapnos integrifolia* (Boiss.) Cuatrec. *20171*

     R   Spain

R   *Sarcocapnos saetabensis* Mateo & Figuerola *20171*

     R   *20692*   Spain (Valencia and Alicante provinces) *20692*

V   *Sarcocapnos speciosa* Boiss. *15398, 20171*

     V   *15398*   Spain (Sierra Nevada) *15398*

Parnassiaceae

Number of genera:	2
Number of species:	16
Recorded threatened species:	3 (18%)

North temperate region to Mexico, Chile, Uruguay.

R   *Parnassia caroliniana* Michx. *20850*

     E   *20850*   U.S. - Florida *20850*
     V   *20850*   U.S. - North Carolina *20850*
     E   *20850*   U.S. - South Carolina *20850*
     I   *20850*   U.S. - Wisconsin *20850*

R   *Parnassia cirrata* Piper *20850*

     I   *20850*   U.S. - California *20850*

I   *Parnassia siamensis* Fletcher *19120*

     I   *19120*   Thailand *19120*

Passifloraceae

Number of genera:	16
Number of species:	650
Recorded threatened species:	48 (7%)

Tropical and warm temperate, especially tropical America and Africa.

I   *Adenia aculeata* (Hook.f.) Engl. *6087*

     I   *6087*   Ethiopia *6087*

I   *Adenia ellenbecki* Harms *6087*

     I   *6087*   Ethiopia *6087*

R   *Adenia fruticosa* Burtt Davy ssp. *simplicifolia* W.J.De Wilde *6088, 20604*

     R   *6088*   Zimbabwe *6088*
     I   *20604*   South Africa - Transvaal *20604*

V   *Adenia globosa* Engl. ssp. *pseudoglobosa* (Verdc.) De Wilde *7959*

     V   *6073*   Kenya *7959*

V   *Adenia karibaensis* de Wilde *7749*

     V   *6088*   Zimbabwe (Zambezi valley) *20574*

R   *Adenia metriosiphon* De Wilde *20057*

     R   *19109*   Kenya *19109*

Ex   *Adenia natalensis* W.J.de Wilde *20604*

     Ex   *20604*   South Africa - Natal *20604*

R   *Basananthe parvifolia* (Baker f.) de Wilde *7749*

     R   Zimbabwe *7749*

R   *Passiflora brevipes* Killip *9004*

     R   *11911*   Belize *9004*
     R   *11911*   Guatemala *9004*

V   *Passiflora calcicola* Proctor *20883, 13336*

     V   *13336*   Jamaica *20883*

R   *Passiflora citrina* MacDougal *20883*

     I   *20883*   Guatemala *20883*
     I   *20883*   Honduras *20883*

I   *Passiflora clypeophylla* Masters *9004*

     I   *10166*   Guatemala *9004*

R   *Passiflora colinvauxii* Wiggins *11117*

     R   Ecuador - Galapagos (Santa Cruz) *11117*

E   *Passiflora colombiana* L. Escobar *20883*

     I   *20883*   Colombia *20883*

V   *Passiflora cumbalensis* var. *caucana* L. Escobar *20883*

     I   *20883*   Colombia *20883*

E   *Passiflora cumbalensis* var. *macrochlamys* (Harms.) L. Escobar *20883*

	I	20883	Peru	20883

E *Passiflora cumbalensis* var. *mesadenia* (Killip) L. Escobar 20883

	I	20883	Peru	20883

V *Passiflora cumbalensis* var. *peruana* L. Escobar 20883

	I	20883	Peru	20883

E *Passiflora cumbalensis* var. *pilosa* L. Escobar 20883

	I	20883	Ecuador	20883

E *Passiflora dasyadenia* Urban 11840

E *Passiflora deltoifolia* Holm-Nielsen & Lawesson 20883

	I	20883	Ecuador	20883

R *Passiflora eggersii* Harms 11351

	R	11351	Ecuador	11351

R *Passiflora emarginata* Humb. & Bonpl. 19352

	R	19352	Colombia	19352

E *Passiflora eueidipabulum* Knapp & Mallet 20883, 10747

	R	17824	Costa Rica	17824
	I	20883	Panama (Colón)	20883

E *Passiflora fernandezii* L. Escobar 20883

	I	20883	Bolivia	20883

I *Passiflora flexipes* Triana & Planchon 19552

	I	19552	Colombia	19552

E *Passiflora herbertiana* Ker-Gawler ssp. *insulaehowei* P. Green

	E	23	Australia - NSW - Lord Howe Is.	23

E *Passiflora huamachucoensis* L. Escobar 20883, 18200

	V	18200	Peru	20883

I *Passiflora insignis* (Mast.) Hook 19552

	I	19552	Bolivia	19552

R *Passiflora lancetillensis* J.Macdougal 21323

	R	21326	Belize	21323

R *Passiflora lancifolia* Desv. 20883

	R	20883	Jamaica	20883

I *Passiflora leptomischa* Harms 19552

	I	19552	Colombia	19552

E *Passiflora macdougaliana* Knapp & Mallet 20883, 10747

	I	20883	Panama (Colón)	20883

R *Passiflora macfadyenii* Adams 20883, 13336

	R	13336	Jamaica	20883

V *Passiflora montana* Holm-Nielsen & Lawesson 20883

	I	20883	Ecuador	20883

R *Passiflora oblongata* Sw. 20883

	R	20883	Jamaica	20883

R *Passiflora obovata* Killip 9004

	R	21323	Belize	9004
	R	21323	Costa Rica	17824
	R	21323	Guatemala	17824

R *Passiflora palenquensis* Holm-Nielsen & Lawesson 20883

	I	20883	Colombia	20883
	I	20883	Ecuador	20883

E *Passiflora parritae* (Masters) Bailey 19552

	E	19552	Colombia	19552

R *Passiflora pendens* J. MacDougal 17824

	R	17824	Mexico - Chiapas	17824

E *Passiflora pergrandis* Holm-Nielsen & Lawesson 20883

	I	20883	Ecuador	20883

I *Passiflora pterocarpa* J. MacDougal 17824

	I	10166	Guatemala	17824

E *Passiflora rugosa* var. *venezolana* L. Escobar 20883

	I	20883	Colombia	20883
	I	20883	Venezuela	20883

E *Passiflora runa* L. Escobar 20883, 18200

	R	19552	Peru	20883

I *Passiflora semiciliosa* Planchon & Linden 19552

	I	19552	Colombia	19552

R *Passiflora tica* Gómez-Laurito & L. D. Gómez 10166

	R	10166	Costa Rica	10166

I *Passiflora triflora* Macf. 20883, 13336

	I	13336	Jamaica	20883

V *Passiflora trifoliata* var. *tarmensis* L. Escobar 20883

	I	20883	Peru	20883

I *Passiflora uncinata* J. MacDougal 17824

	I	17824	Mexico	17824

E *Passiflora viridescens* L. Escobar 20883

	I	20883	Peru	20883

E *Passiflora williamsii* Killip 20883, 10747

	I	20883	Panama (Canal Area, Coclé, Darién, Los Santos, Panamá)	20883

R *Passiflora yucatanensis* Killip 9681

	R	21323	Mexico - Yucatan	9681

R *Passiflora zamorana* Killip 11351

	R	11351	Ecuador	11351

Pedaliaceae

Number of genera:	20	
Number of species:	80	
Recorded threatened species:	3	(3%)

Mostly tropical, especially along seacoast or in arid regions, with only a few species in temperate climates.

R *Proboscidea altheifolia* (Benth.) Decne 18200

	R	12468	Peru	18200

R *Proboscidea sabulosa* Correll 20850

	R	20850	U.S. - New Mexico	20850
	V	20850	U.S. - Texas	20850

E *Proboscidea spicata* Correll 20850

	E	20850	U.S. - Texas	20850

Pellicieraceae

Number of genera:	1	
Number of species:	1	
Recorded threatened species:	1	(100%)

Costa Rica, Panama, Columbia.

I *Pelliciera rhizophorae* Triana & Planchon 9006

	I	17459	Costa Rica	9006
	V	16826	Nicaragua	16826
	V	19577	Panama	9006
	V	23	Colombia	9006
	V	23	Ecuador	9006

Penaeaceae

Number of genera:		7
Number of species:		20
Recorded threatened species:		14 (70%)

Cape Province (South Africa), especially in the southwest.

R	*Brachysiphon microphyllus* Rourke 20604
	R 20604 South Africa - Cape Province 20604

R	*Brachysiphon mundii* Sond. 20604
	R 20604 South Africa - Cape Province 20604

R	*Brachysiphon rupestris* Sond. 20604
	R 20604 South Africa - Cape Province 20604

R	*Endonema lateriflora* (L.f.) Gilg 20604
	R 20604 South Africa - Cape Province 20604

V	*Endonema retzioides* Sond. 20604
	V 20604 South Africa - Cape Province 20604

V	*Glischrocolla formosa* (Thunb.) R.Dahlgren 20604
	V 20604 South Africa - Cape Province 20604

R	*Sonderothamnus petraeus* (W.F.Barker) R.Dahlgren 20604
	R 20604 South Africa - Cape Province 20604

R	*Sonderothamnus speciosus* (Sond.) R.Dahlgren 20604
	R 20604 South Africa - Cape Province 20604

R	*Stylapterus barbatus* Juss. 20604
	R 20604 South Africa - Cape Province 20604

R	*Stylapterus dubius* (Steph.) R.Dahlgren 20604
	R 20604 South Africa - Cape Province 20604

R	*Stylapterus ericifolius* (Juss.) R.Dahlgren 20604
	R 20604 South Africa - Cape Province 20604

V	*Stylapterus ericoides* Adr. Juss. ssp. *ericoides* 20604
	V 20604 South Africa - Cape Province 20604

R	*Stylapterus ericoides* Adr. Juss. ssp. *pallidus* R. Dahlgren 20604
	R 20604 South Africa - Cape Province 20604

E	*Stylapterus micranthus* R.Dahlgren 20604, 3374
	E 20604 South Africa - Cape Province 20604

R	*Stylapterus sulcatus* R.Dahlgren 20604
	R 20604 South Africa - Cape Province 20604

Pentaphragmataceae

Number of genera:		1
Number of species:		30
Recorded threatened species:		2 (6%)

Southeast Asia and nearby Pacific islands.

R	*Pentaphragma honbaensis* Gagnepain 6057
	R Vietnam 6057

I	*Pentaphragma winitii* Craib 19120
	I 19120 Thailand 19120

Phytolaccaceae

Number of genera:		18
Number of species:		125
Recorded threatened species:		5 (4%)

Tropical and subtropical.

R	*Nowickea glabra* J. Martinez & McDonald 14245
	R 14245 Mexico - Morelos 14245

R	*Nowickea xolocotzii* J. Martinez & McDonald 14245
	R 14245 Mexico - Jalisco 14245

E	*Phytolacca icosandra* var. *anomala* Proctor 20883
	E 20883 Jamaica 20883

V	*Phytolacca sandwicensis* Endl. 20850, 14209
	I 20850 U.S. - Hawaii 20850

V	*Phytolacca tetramera* Hauman 16336
	V 20176 Argentina - Buenos Aires 20176

Piperaceae

Number of genera:		10
Number of species:		1,400-2,000
Recorded threatened species:		162 (9%)

Tropical.

R	*Macropiper melchior* 19305
	R 19305 New Zealand - North Is. (Three Kings Island) 19305

E	*Peperomia abdita* Proctor 20883
	E 20883 Jamaica 20883

R	*Peperomia acaulis* Alain 5607
	R 19105 Cuba 5607

I	*Peperomia adamsonia* (F.Brown) Yuncker 20845
	I 20845 French Polynesia - Marquesas Is (Hiva Oa) 20845

E	*Peperomia albescens* Trel. 20883, 9006
	I 20883 Panama 20883

R	*Peperomia alpina* (Sw.) A. Dietr. 20883
	R 20883 Jamaica 20883

I	*Peperomia andrei* C. DC. 16929
	I 16929 Colombia 16929

R	*Peperomia austin-smithii* W. Burger 9037
	R 19754 Costa Rica 9037

R	*Peperomia barbata* C.DC. 20883
	R 20883 Jamaica 20883

R	*Peperomia barbata* C. DC. var. *barbata* C. D.C. 20883
	R 20883 Jamaica 20883

R	*Peperomia barbata* C. D.C. var. *puberula* Yuncker 20883
	R 20883 Jamaica 20883

R	*Peperomia barbinodis* Trel. 9037
	R 19754 Costa Rica 9037
	R 19754 Panama 9037

E	*Peperomia bifrons* Trel. 20883, 9006
	I 20883 Panama 20883

R	*Peperomia boninsimensis* Makino 8622
	R 19134 Japan - Kazan Retto (Minami-Iwojima) 8622
	R 19134 Japan - Ogasawara-shoto (Hahajima) 8622

E	*Peperomia brevipeduncula* Trel. 20883, 9006
	I 20883 Panama 20883

R	*Peperomia caliginigaudens* Trel. & Yuncker 16929
	R 11589 Colombia 16929

Ex/E	*Peperomia carpinterana* C. DC. 9037
	Ex/E 19754 Costa Rica 9037
	Ex/E 19754 Guatemala 9037

E	*Peperomia caudulilimba* C. DC. 20883, 9006
	I 20883 Panama 20883

E	*Peperomia caudulilimba* (C. DC.) Yuncker var.

cylindribacca (C. DC.) Yuncker *20883, 10747*
I *20883* Panama *20883*

E *Peperomia chiriquiensis* Yuncker *20883, 9006*
I *20883* Panama *20883*

E *Peperomia chrysleri* Yuncker *20883, 9006*
I *20883* Panama *20883*

E *Peperomia ciliolibractea* C. DC. *20883, 9006*
I *20883* Panama *20883*

E *Peperomia cocleana* Trel. *20883, 9006*
I *20883* Panama *20883*

E *Peperomia cordulata* C. DC. *20883, 9006*
I *20883* Panama *20883*

E *Peperomia cordulatiformis* Trel. *20883, 9006*
I *20883* Panama *20883*

R *Peperomia crassicaulis* F. & R. *20883*
R *20883* Jamaica *20883*

E *Peperomia crystallina* Ruiz Lopez & Pavon *18200*
E *9446* Peru *18200*

E *Peperomia davidsonii* Yuncker *20883, 9006*
I *20883* Panama *20883*

Ex/E *Peperomia degeneri* Yuncker *20850, 14209*
Ex/E *20850* U.S. - Hawaii (Moloka`i - Kalua`aha) *20850*

E *Peperomia delascioi* Steyermark *20883*
I *20883* Venezuela *20883*

E *Peperomia digitinervia* Trel. *20883, 9006*
I *20883* Panama *20883*

V *Peperomia discolor* C. DC. *20883, 13336*
V *13336* Jamaica (St. Thomas) *20883*

R *Peperomia esperanzana* Trel. *9037*
R *19754* Costa Rica *9037*

R *Peperomia expallescens* C. DC. *20850, 14209*
R *20850* U.S. - Hawaii (Moloka`i & Maui) *20850*

R *Peperomia fawcettii* C.DC. *20883, 19890*
R *19890* Jamaica *20883*

E *Peperomia flexinervia* Yuncker *20883, 9006*
I *20883* Panama *20883*

I *Peperomia glandulosa* C. DC. *16929*
I *11589* Colombia *16929*

V *Peperomia guanensis* Trel. *5607*
V *19105* Cuba (Pinar del Rio) *5607*

R *Peperomia harrisii* C.DC. *20883, 13336*
R *13336* Jamaica (St. Andrew, Hanover) *20883*

V *Peperomia hendersonensis* Yuncker *8050*
V *19185* Pitcairn (Henderson Is.) *8050*

Ex *Peperomia hirta* Balf.f. *5852*
Ex *5852* Mauritius - Rodrigues (Mt Limon) *5852*

E *Peperomia hygrophiloides* C. DC. *20883, 9006*
I *20883* Panama *20883*

E *Peperomia insueta* Trel. *20883, 9006*
I *20883* Panama *20883*

V *Peperomia jamaicana* Yuncker *20883, 13336*
V *13336* Jamaica (Portland) *20883*

V *Peperomia killipii* Trel. *20883, 9006, 21227*
I *20883* Panama *20883*

R *Peperomia kotana* C. DC.
R Malaysia - Peninsular Malaysia (Kedah, Kelantan, Pahang)

R *Peperomia lewisii* Proctor *20883, 13336*

R *13336* Jamaica (Portland) *20883*

E *Peperomia limaensis* Trel.
E *9446* Peru *18200*

E *Peperomia machaerodonta* Trel. *20883, 10747*
I *20883* Panama *20883*

E *Peperomia margaritifera* Bertero ex Hook. *19116*
E *19125* Chile - Juan Fernandez Is. *19116*

E *Peperomia maxwellana* C. DC. *20889, 10260*
E *20889* Malaysia - Peninsular Malaysia *20889*

E *Peperomia megalopoda* Trel. *20883*
I *20883* Puerto Rico *20883*

R *Peperomia montecristana* Trel. *9037*
R *19754* Costa Rica *9037*
R *19754* Nicaragua *9037*

E *Peperomia mutilata* Trel. *5607*
E *19105* Cuba (Guantanamo) *5607*

R *Peperomia nakaharai* Hayata *20511*
R *20511* Taiwan *20511*

E *Peperomia nievecitana* Trel. *20883*
I *20883* Panama *20883*

E *Peperomia nonhispidula* Trel. *18200*
E *9446* Peru *18200*

R *Peperomia obscurifolia* C. DC. *20883, 9006*
R *20883* Panama *20883*

R *Peperomia obtusilimba* C. DC. *11117*
R Ecuador - Galapagos *11117*

E *Peperomia perglandulosa* Yuncker *20883, 9006*
I *20883* Panama *20883*

R *Peperomia petiolata* Hook.f. *11117*
R Ecuador - Galapagos *11117*

V *Peperomia pitcairnensis* (Lauterbach) C.DC *19185*
V *19185* Pitcairn *19185*

E *Peperomia portobellensis* Beurl. *20883, 9006*
I *20883* Panama *20883*

V *Peperomia proctorii* Yuncker *20883, 19890*
R *19890* Jamaica *20883*

E *Peperomia pseudogalapagensis* Trel. *18200*
E *9446* Peru *18200*

V *Peperomia reticulata* Balf.f. *5852*
V *5852* Mauritius - Rodrigues *5852*

E *Peperomia rockii* C. DC. *20850, 14209*
E *20850* U.S. - Hawaii (east Moloka`i) *20850*

Ex *Peperomia rodriguezi* Balf.f. *5852*
Ex *5852* Mauritius - Rodrigues (Mont Piton) *5852*

E *Peperomia rossii* Rendle *881*
E *14224* Australia - Christmas Is. *881*

I *Peperomia rubramenta* Trel. & Yuncker *16929*
I *11589* Colombia *16929*

I *Peperomia santanderana* Trel. & Yuncker *16929*
I *11589* Colombia *16929*

R *Peperomia septentrionalis* S. Brown
R Bermuda

R *Peperomia simplex* Desv. ex Buch.-Ham. *20883*
R *20883* Jamaica *20883*

V *Peperomia skottsbergii* C. DC. *19116*
V *19125* Chile - Juan Fernandez Is. *19116*

E *Peperomia subpetiolata* Yuncker *20850, 14209*
E *20850* U.S. - Hawaii (east Maui) *20850*

R   *Peperomia tenellaeformis* Trel. *9037*
  R *19754* Costa Rica *9037*
  R *19754* Panama *10747*

E   *Peperomia umbelliformis* C. DC. *18200*
  E *9446* Peru *18200*

E   *Peperomia umbrigaudens* Yuncker *20883, 9006*
  I *20883* Panama *20883*

E   *Peperomia urocarpoides* C. DC. *20883, 9006*
  I *20883* Panama *20883*

E   *Peperomia valliculae* Trel. *20883, 9006*
  I *20883* Panama *20883*

R   *Peperomia vinasiana* C. DC. *9037*
  R *19754* Costa Rica *19754*

E   *Peperomia wedelii* Yuncker *20883, 9006*
  I *20883* Panama *20883*

E   *Peperomia wheeleri* Britt. *20883, 19738*
  I *20883* Puerto Rico (N. coast of Culebra I.)
     20883
  I *20883* USA - Virgin Is. *20883*

E   *Piper aequale* (Trel.) Yuncker var. *laurifolium*
  (Trel.) Yuncker *20883, 9006*
  I *20883* Panama *20883*

R   *Piper aereum* Trel. *9037*
  R *19754* Costa Rica *9037*

E   *Piper albopunctulatissimum* Trel. *20883, 9006*
  I *20883* Panama *20883*

R   *Piper albozonatum* C. DC. *16929*
  R *11589* Colombia *16929*

I   *Piper amalago* (Griseb.) F. & R. var. *variifolium*
  (Griseb.) Fawc. & Rendle *20883, 13336*
  I *13336* Jamaica (Manchester) *20883*

E   *Piper arboreum* Aublet ssp. *tuberculatum* (Jacq.)
  Tebbs *18200*
  E *9446* Peru *18200*

E   *Piper aristolochiaefolium* (Trel.) Yuncker *20883,*
  9006
   20883 Panama *20883*

V   *Piper artanthopse* C. DC. *9037*
  V *19754* Costa Rica *9037*

E   *Piper augustum* var. *cocleanum* (Trel.)
  Yuncker *20883*
  I *20883* Panama *20883*

R   *Piper barberi* Gamble *20263*
  R *13883* India - Tamil Nadu (southern W. Ghats)
     13883

E   *Piper brittonorum* Trel. *5607*
  E *19105* Cuba (Juventud Is.) *5607*

E   *Piper campanum* Yuncker *20883, 9006*
  I *20883* Panama *20883*

E   *Piper cativalense* Trel. *20883, 9006*
  I *20883* Panama *20883*

E   *Piper cojimaranum* Trel. *5607*
  E *19105* Cuba (Ciud. Habana) *5607*

Ex   *Piper collinum* C. DC. *20742*
  Ex *20742* Malaysia - Peninsular Malaysia *20742*

E   *Piper colon-insulae* Trel. *20883, 9006*
  I *20883* Panama *20883*

E   *Piper cooperi* Yuncker *20883, 10747*
  I *20883* Panama *20883*

V   *Piper cordulatum* C. DC. *20883, 9006*
  V *20883* Panama *20883*

R   *Piper corei* (Yuncker) Callejas *16929*
  R *11589* Colombia *16929*

E   *Piper crassispicatum* Opiz *20883, 9006*
  I *20883* Panama *20883*

R   *Piper crenatifolium* Trel. & Yuncker *16929*
  R *11589* Colombia *16929*

R   *Piper curtirachis* W. Burger *9037*
  R *19754* Costa Rica *9037*

R   *Piper cuspidispicum* Trel. *9037*
  R *19754* Costa Rica *9037*

E   *Piper davidsonii* Yuncker *20883, 9006*
  I *20883* Panama *20883*

R   *Piper deductum* Trel. *9037*
  R *19754* Costa Rica *9037*

E   *Piper distigmatum* Yuncker *20883, 9006*
  I *20883* Panama *20883*

E   *Piper erubescentispicum* Trel. *20883, 9006*
  I *20883* Panama *20883*

R   *Piper fadyenii* C. DC. *20883*
  R *20883* Jamaica *20883*

R   *Piper gesnerioides* Callejas *16929*
  R *11589* Colombia *16929*

E   *Piper gonocarpum* Trel. *20883, 9006*
  I *20883* Panama *20883*

V   *Piper guanacostense* C. DC. *9037*
  V *19754* Costa Rica *9037*

V   *Piper guanahacabibense* Borh.
  V *19105* Cuba (Pinar del Rio) *19105*

I   *Piper haprium* Buch.-Ham. ex Hook.f.
  I India - Kerala (Travancore Hills)
  I India - Tamil Nadu (Tirunelveli Hills)

V   *Piper hirtellipetiolum* var. *harveyanum* (Trel.)
  Yuncker *20883*
  I *20883* Panama *20883*

E   *Piper hirtellipetiolum* var. *tapianum* (Trel.)
  Yuncker *20883*
  I *20883* Panama *20883*

E   *Piper hispidum* Yuncker var. *ellipticifolium*
  Yuncker *20883, 9006*
  I *20883* Panama *20883*

E   *Piper humorigaudens* Trel. *20883, 9006*
  I *20883* Panama *20883*

E   *Piper infraluteum* Trel. *20883, 9006*
  I *20883* Panama *20883*

R   *Piper kawakamii* Hayata *20511*
  R *20511* Taiwan *20511*

R   *Piper kwashoense* Hayata *20511*
  R *20511* Taiwan *20511*

E   *Piper lucigaudens* C. DC. *20883, 9006*
  I *20883* Panama *20883*

E   *Piper lucigaudens* (Trel.) Yuncker var. *alleni*
  (Trel.) Yuncker *20883, 9006*
  I *20883* Panama *20883*

E   *Piper magnantherum* C. DC. *20883, 9006*
  I *20883* Panama *20883*

R   *Piper maxonii* C. DC. *9037*

R   *19754* Costa Rica *9037*
I   *19754* Panama *9037*

E   ***Piper maxonii*** (Trel.) Yuncker var. *varium* (Trel.)
Yuncker *20883, 10747*
I   *20883* Panama *20883*

R   ***Piper mestonii*** Bailey *20681*
R   *20681* Australia - Queensland *20681*

E   ***Piper minute-scabiosum*** Trel. *20883, 9037*
I   *20883* Panama *20883*

E   ***Piper monzonense*** C. DC. *18200*
E   *9446* Peru *18200*

I   ***Piper moscopanense*** Yuncker *16929*
I   *11589* Colombia *16929*

R   ***Piper mucronatum*** C. DC.
R   Malaysia - Peninsular Malaysia

I   ***Piper palawanum*** C. DC. *13833*
I   *13833* Philippines (Palawan) *13833*

E   ***Piper parmatum*** Dressler *20883, 9006*
I   *20883* Panama *20883*

E   ***Piper perbrevicaule*** Yuncker var. *subglabrilimbum*
Yuncker *20883, 9006*
I   *20883* Panama *20883*

R   ***Piper perditum*** Trel.
R   *19105* Cuba (Pinar del Rio) *19105*

E   ***Piper perlasense*** Yuncker *20883, 9006*
I   *20883* Panama *20883*

R   ***Piper permolle*** Trel. & Yuncker *16929*
R   *11589* Colombia *16929*

I   ***Piper perpunctatum*** D. DC. *13833*
I   *13833* Philippines (low altitude) *13833*

E   ***Piper persubulatum*** C. DC. *20883, 9006*
I   *20883* Panama *20883*

E   ***Piper peruligerum*** Trel. *20883, 9006*
I   *20883* Panama *20883*

E   ***Piper pinoganense*** Trel. *20883, 9006*
I   *20883* Panama *20883*

V   ***Piper pittieri*** C. DC. *9037*
V   *19754* Costa Rica *9037*
V   *19754* Panama *9037*

R   ***Piper poasanum*** C. DC. *9037*
R   *19754* Costa Rica *9037*
R   *19754* Panama *9037*

E   ***Piper postelsianum*** Maxim. *8037*
E   *19134* Japan - Ogasawara-shoto *8037*

E   ***Piper pseudo-cativalense*** Trel. *20883, 9006*
I   *20883* Panama *20883*

E   ***Piper pseudo-garagaranum*** Trel. *20883, 9006*
I   *20883* Panama *20883*

E   ***Piper pubistipulum*** C. DC. *20883, 9006*
I   *20883* Panama *20883*

I   ***Piper pykarahense*** C. DC. *2268*
I   India - Tamil Nadu (Nilgiri Hills) *2268*

R   ***Piper reptabundum*** C. DC. *9037*
R   *19754* Costa Rica *9037*
R   *19754* Panama *9006*

E   ***Piper sambuanum*** C. DC. *20883, 9006*
I   *20883* Panama *20883*

R   ***Piper scortechinii*** C. DC.
R   Malaysia - Peninsular Malaysia

I   ***Piper scutilimbum*** C. DC. *16929*
I   *11589* Colombia *16929*

R   ***Piper spoliatum*** Trel. & Yuncker *16929*
R   *11589* Colombia *16929*

E   ***Piper stevensi*** Trel. *20883, 9006*
I   *20883* Panama *20883*

E   ***Piper storkii*** Trel. *20883, 9006*
I   *20883* Panama *20883*

E   ***Piper subcaudatum*** Trel. *20883, 9006*
I   *20883* Panama *20883*

E   ***Piper subquinquenerve*** Trel. *20883, 9006*
I   *20883* Panama *20883*

E   ***Piper subrepens*** Trel. *20883, 9006*
I   *20883* Panama *20883*

R   ***Piper sumideranum*** Trel. *5607*
R   *19105* Cuba (Pinar del Rio) *5607*

E   ***Piper tecumense*** Trel. *20883, 9006*
I   *20883* Panama *20883*

E   ***Piper tocacheanum*** C. DC. *18200*
E   *9446* Peru *18200*

E   ***Piper variitrichum*** Yuncker *20883, 9006*
I   *20883* Panama *20883*

R   ***Piper verrucosum*** Sw. *20883*
R   *20883* Jamaica *20883*

E   ***Piper via-chicoense*** Yuncker *20883, 9006*
I   *20883* Panama *20883*

E   ***Piper viridicaule*** Trel. *20883, 9006*
I   *20883* Panama *20883*

E   ***Piper wagneri*** C. DC. *20883, 9006*
I   *20883* Panama *20883*

R   ***Piper yanaconense*** Trel. & Yuncker *16929*
R   *11589* Colombia *16929*

R   ***Piper zacatense*** C. DC. *9037*
R   *19754* Costa Rica *9037*
R   *11967* Nicaragua *9426*

R   ***Trianaeopiper cuatrecasasii*** Trel. & Yuncker *16929*
R   *11589* Colombia *16929*

Pittosporaceae

Number of genera:	9
Number of species:	200
Recorded threatened species:	36 (18%)

Tropical and warm temperate Old World, especially Australia.

E   ***Bentleya spinescens*** E.M.Bennett *20681*
E   *20681* Australia - Western Australia *20681*

R   ***Billardiera granulata*** (Turcz.) E.Bennett *20681*
R   *20681* Australia - Western Australia *20681*

V   ***Billardiera mollis*** E.M.Bennett *20681*
V   *20681* Australia - Western Australia *20681*

V   ***Cheiranthera volubilis*** Benth. *20681*
V   *20681* Australia - South Australia *20681*

E   ***Pittosporum aliferum*** Veillon & Tirel *20893*
E   *20893* New Caledonia *20893*

V   ***Pittosporum artense*** Guillaumin *20893*
V   *20893* New Caledonia *20893*

E   ***Pittosporum balfourii*** Cuf. *10082*
E   *5852* Mauritius - Rodrigues (Grande Mt) *5852*

V   ***Pittosporum beecheyi*** Tuyama *20626*

V		*19134* Japan - Ogasawara-shoto *20626*
V	*Pittosporum bracteolatum* Endl. *19108*	
	V	Australia - Norfolk Is.
E	*Pittosporum brevispinum* Veillon & Tirel *20893*	
	E	*20893* New Caledonia *20893*
V	*Pittosporum chichijimense* Nakai *8038*	
	V	*20626* Japan - Ogasawara-shoto *20626*
V	*Pittosporum collinum* Guillaumin *20893*	
	V	*20893* New Caledonia *20893*
V	*Pittosporum dallii* Cheeseman *86*	
	V	*19305* New Zealand - South Is. (Nelson) *20625*
I	*Pittosporum eriocarpum* Royle *11494*	
	I	*11494* India - Himachal Pradesh *11494*
	I	*11494* India - Uttar Pradesh (Kumaun) *11494*
R	*Pittosporum erioloma* C. Moore & F. Muell.	
	R	*14225* Australia - NSW - Lord Howe Is. *14225*
E	*Pittosporum gatopense* Guillaumin *20893*	
	E	*20893* New Caledonia *20893*
I	*Pittosporum goetzei* Engl. *20556, 5926*	
	I	*5926* Tanzania *5926*
E	*Pittosporum gomonenense* Guillaumin *20893*	
	E	*20893* New Caledonia *20893*
R	*Pittosporum illicioides* Makino var. *angustifolium* Lu *20854*	
	R	*20854* Taiwan *20854*
I	*Pittosporum lutchuense* Koidz. *10572*	
	I	*10572* Japan *10572*
E	*Pittosporum muricatum* Veillon & Tirel *20893*	
	E	*20893* New Caledonia *20893*
E	*Pittosporum napaliense* Sherff *20850, 14209*	
	E	*20850* U.S. - Hawaii *20850*
R	*Pittosporum obcordatum* Raoul *86*	
	R	*20625* New Zealand - North Is. *19305*
	R	*20625* New Zealand - South Is. *19305*
R	*Pittosporum oreillyanum* C.White *20681*	
	I	*20681* Australia - New South Wales *20681*
	I	*20681* Australia - Queensland *20681*
E	*Pittosporum ornatum* Veillon & Tirel *20893*	
	E	*20893* New Caledonia *20893*
V	*Pittosporum orohenense* J.Moore *20845*	
	V	*20845* French Polynesia - Society Is. (Tahiti) *20845*
V	*Pittosporum paniense* Guillaumin *20893*	
	V	*20893* New Caledonia *20893*
E	*Pittosporum parvifolium* Hayata *8038*	
	E	*19134* Japan - Ogasawara-shoto *20626*
R	*Pittosporum pimeleoides* ssp. *pimeleoides* *19305*	
	R	*19305* New Zealand - North Is. *19305*
E	*Pittosporum raivavaeense* H. Saint John *20845*	
	E	*20845* French Polynesia - Tubuai Is. (Raivavae) *20845*
R	*Pittosporum samoense* Christoph. *7925*	
	R	Western Samoa (Savaii) *7925*
V	*Pittosporum senacia* Putt. ssp. *wrightii* (Hemsley) Cuf. *14296*	
	V	*19182* Seychelles (granitic) *14296*
E	*Pittosporum stenophyllum* Guillaumin *20893*	
	E	*20893* New Caledonia *20893*
Ex	*Pittosporum tanianum* Veillon & Tirel *20802*	

	Ex	*20802* New Caledonia *20802*
R	*Pittosporum terminalioides* Planch. ex Gray *20850, 14209*	
	I	*20850* U.S. - Hawaii *20850*
V	*Pittosporum turneri* Petrie *20625*	
	V	*20625* New Zealand - North Is. *20625*
R	*Pittosporum turnerii* *19305*	
	R	*19305* New Zealand - North Is. *19305*

Plantaginaceae

Number of genera:	3
Number of species:	254
Recorded threatened species:	33 (12%)

Cosmopolitan.

V	*Plantago algarbiensis* *17891*	
	V	*20076* Portugal *17891*
V	*Plantago almogravensis* *17891*	
	V	*20076* Portugal *17891*
R	*Plantago anatolica* B. Tutel & R. Mill *12840*	
	R	*12840* Turkey *12840*
R	*Plantago asiatica* L. var. *yakusimensis* (Masam.) Ohwi *10573*	
	R	*10573* Japan *10573*
R	*Plantago asphodeloides* Svent.	
	R	Spain - Canary Is.
V	*Plantago atrata* Hoppe ssp. *carpatica* (Pilger) Soó *19839*	
	V	*19321* Slovakia *19321*
E	*Plantago atrata* Hoppe ssp. *sudetica* (Pilger) Holub *2050*	
	E	*19449* Czech Republic (Velká Kotlina cirque) *2050*
R	*Plantago bismarckii* Niederl. *16336*	
	R	*16336* Argentina *16336*
	E	*20137* Argentina - Buenos Aires *20137*
R	*Plantago canescens* Adams ssp. *jurtzevii* Tzvelev *21309*	
	R	*21309* Russia (E.Europe) - North *21309*
	E	former USSR *6930*
I	*Plantago chamaepsyllium* Zoh. *8895*	
	I	Egypt
	I	Israel *8895*
R	*Plantago cladarophylla* B.G.Briggs, Carolin & Pulley *20681*	
	R	*20681* Australia - New South Wales *20681*
R	*Plantago euphratica* Decne ex Barneoud *12840*	
	R	*12840* Turkey '*12840*
V	*Plantago famarae* Svent. *20750*	
	V	*20750* Spain - Canary Is. *20750*
E	*Plantago fernandezia* Bertero *19116*	
	E	*19125* Chile - Juan Fernandez Is. *19116*
R	*Plantago galapagensis* Rahn *11117*	
	R	Ecuador - Galapagos *11117*
E	*Plantago hawaiensis* (Gray) Pilger *20850, 14209*	
	E	*20850* U.S. - Hawaii *20850*
R	*Plantago hedleyi* Maiden	
	R	*14226* Australia - NSW - Lord Howe Is. *14226*
V	*Plantago holosteum* Scop. var. *littoralis* (Rouy) Kérguélen *20528*	

V   20528   France (west)   20528

V   *Plantago leiopetala* Lowe
    V   Portugal - Madeira

E   *Plantago libyca* Beguinot & Vaccari
    E   Libya

V   *Plantago maderensis* Decaisne
    V   Portugal - Madeira

E   *Plantago malato-belizii* Lawalree   17891
    E   Portugal - Madeira   17891

R   *Plantago obconica*   19305
    R   19305   New Zealand - South Is.   19305

R   *Plantago palustris* L.Fraser & Vick.   20681
    R   20681   Australia - New South Wales   20681

E   *Plantago picta* Colenso   86
    E   New Zealand - North Is.

V   *Plantago princeps* Cham. & Schldl.   20850, 14209
    I   14209   U.S. - Hawaii (O`ahu)   20850

E   *Plantago princeps* Cham. & Schldl. var. *anomala*
    Rock   20850
    E   20850   U.S. - Hawaii   20850

E   *Plantago princeps* Cham. & Schldl. var. *laxiflora*
    Gray   20850, 14209
    E   20850   U.S. - Hawaii   20850

R   *Plantago princeps* Cham. & Schldl. var. *laxifolia*
    A.Gray   14209
    R   14209   U.S. - Hawaii   14209

E   *Plantago princeps* Cham. & Schldl. var.
    longibracteata Mann   20850, 14209
    E   20850   U.S. - Hawaii (Kaua`i & O`ahu)   20850

E   *Plantago princeps* Cham. & Schldl. var.
    princeps   20850
    E   20850   U.S. - Hawaii   20850

R   *Plantago reniformis* Beck   20178, 20171
    R   20178   Albania   20178
    V   21091   Bosnia & Herzegovina   21091
    R   (former) Yugoslavia   20178

E   *Plantago robusta* Roxb.   18996
    E   18996   St Helena   18996

I   *Plantago rupicola* Pilger   20845
    I   20845   French Polynesia - Tubuai Is. (Rapa)
          20845

R   *Plantago schwarzenbergiana* Schur   17786, 20171
    R   20686   Hungary   20686
    R   19949   Romania   20631
    I   former European USSR

V   *Plantago sparsiflora* Michx.   20850
    I   20850   U.S. - Florida   20850
    V   20850   U.S. - Georgia   20850
    E   20850   U.S. - North Carolina   20850
    I   20850   U.S. - South Carolina   20850

E   *Plantago spathulata* ssp. *picta*   19305
    E   19305   New Zealand - North Is.   19305

R   *Plantago subspathulata* Pilger
    R   Portugal - Madeira

I   *Plantago tunetana* Murb.
    V   Algeria
    I   Tunisia

Plumbaginaceae

Number of genera: 12
Number of species: 400
Recorded threatened species: 180   (45%)

Widespread, especially Mediterranean.

R   *Acantholimon acerosum* Willd. var. *parvifolium*
    Bokhari   12840
    R   12840   Turkey   12840

R   *Acantholimon caryophyllaceum* Boiss. ssp. *parviflorum*
    Bokhari   12840
    R   12840   Turkey   12840

R   *Acantholimon confertiflorum* Bokhari   12840
    R   12840   Turkey   12840

R   *Acantholimon damassanum* Mobayen var. *lancibracteatum*
    Bokhari   12840
    R   12840   Turkey   12840

V   *Acantholimon halophilum* Bokhari   12840
    V   12840   Turkey   12840

R   *Acantholimon knorringianum* Lincz.
    R   former USSR   6930

R   *Acantholimon langaricum* O. & B. Fedtsch.
    R   former USSR   6930

R   *Acantholimon puberulum* Boiss. & Bal. var.
    longiscapum Bokhari   12840
    R   12840   Turkey   12840

R   *Acantholimon reflexifolium* Bokhari   12840
    R   12840   Turkey   12840

R   *Acantholimon ruprechtii* Bunge
    R   former USSR   6930

R   *Acantholimon saxifragiforme* (Hausskn. & Sint.) ex
    Bokhari   12840
    R   12840   Turkey   12840

R   *Acantholimon spirizianum* Mobayen   12840
    R   12840   Turkey   12840

R   *Acantholimon strigillosum* Bokhari   12840
    R   12840   Turkey   12840

R   *Acantholimon ulicinum* (Will. ex Schultes) Boiss. var.
    purpurascens (Bokhari) Bokhari ex Edmondson   12840
    R   12840   Turkey   12840

R   *Armeria alpinifolia* Pau & Font Quer
    R   Morocco

Ex   *Armeria arcuata* Welw. ex Boiss. & Reut.   20171
    Ex   8000   Portugal   8000

V   *Armeria berlengensis* Daveau   8000, 20171
    V   20076   Portugal (Ilha Berlenga)   8000

V   *Armeria colorata* Pau   11496
    V   11496   Spain   11496

E   *Armeria euscadiensis* Vivant
    E   Spain

E   *Armeria helodes* F. Martini & Poldini   17891
    E   18264   Italy (Friuli-Venezia Giulia)   17891

R   *Armeria hispalensis* Pau   11496
    R   11496   Spain (Sevilla)   11496

E   *Armeria humilis* (Link) Schult.   8000, 20171
    E   20076   Portugal   8000

R   *Armeria maderensis* Lowe
    R   Portugal - Madeira

V	*Armeria malinvaudii* Coste & Soulié *20528*	
	V	20528 France (Languedoc) *20528*
E	*Armeria maritima* (Mill.) Willd. ssp. *barcensis* Siminkai *8000, 20171*	
	E	19949 Romania *8000*
E	*Armeria maritima* (Miller)Willd. ssp. *interior* (Raup) Pors. *20850, 2063*	
	E	20850 Canada - Saskatchewan (L. Athabasca) *20850*
I	*Armeria maritima* (Mill.) Willd. ssp. *purpurea* (W.D.J.Koch) A.Löve & D.Löve *20171*	
	I	Germany
	Ex	18154 Switzerland *18154*
Ex/E	*Armeria pocutica* Pawl. *20171*	
	Ex/E	20655 Ukraine (Carpathian Mts) *20655*
E	*Armeria pseudarmeria* (Murray) Mansf. *8000, 20171*	
	E	20076 Portugal (west-central - Cabo da Roca) *8000*
V	*Armeria rouyana* Daveau *8000, 20171*	
	V	20076 Portugal (south west) *8000*
V	*Armeria sampaioi* (Bernis) Nieto Feliner *20076*	
	V	20076 Portugal *17891*
R	*Armeria sancta* Janka *20171*	
	R	Greece
R	*Armeria soleirolii* (Duby) Godr. *8000, 20171*	
	R	20528 France - Corsica *19174*
V	*Armeria sulcitana* Arrigoni	
	V	20805 Italy - Sardinia *20805*
R	*Armeria trojana* Bokhari & Quezel *12840*	
	R	12840 Turkey *12840*
R	*Armeria vandasii* Hayek *20171*	
	R	(former) Yugoslavia
V	*Armeria velutina* Welw. ex Boiss. & Reut. *17891, 20171*	
	E	20076 Portugal (south) *17891*
	V	Spain (south west) *17891*
I	*Armeria vestita* Willk. *11496*	
	I	11496 Spain *11496*
V	*Armeria welwitschii* Boiss. *20171*	
	V	8322 Portugal *8322*
I	*Ceratostigma stapfianum* Hoss. *19120*	
	I	19120 Thailand *19120*
R	*Dyerophytum pendulum* (Balf. f.) Kuntze *15534*	
	R	15534 Yemen - Socotra *15534*
R	*Dyerophytum socotrana* J.R. Edmondson *15534*	
	R	15534 Yemen - Socotra *15534*
V	*Goniolimon graminifolium* (Aiton) Boiss. *20171*	
	V	former European USSR
R	*Goniolimon heldreichii* Halácsy *20171*	
	R	Greece
V	*Goniolimon italicum* Tammaro, Pignatti & Frizzi *18264*	
	V	18264 Italy (Abruzzi) *18264*
R	*Goniolimon sartorii* Boiss. *20171*	
	R	Greece
I	*Ikonnikovia kaufmanniana* (Regel) Lincz. *5942*	
	I	5942 Kazakhstan (south-east) *5942*
R	*Limoniopsis davisii* BKokhari *12840*	
	R	12840 Turkey *12840*
V	*Limonium acuminatum* L.Bolus *20604*	

	V	20604 South Africa - Cape Province *20604*
R	*Limonium album* (Coincy) Sennen *11496, 20171*	
	R	11496 Spain (Murcia) *11496*
V	*Limonium algusae* (Brullo) Greuter *20744*	
	V	20744 Italy - Sicily (Isola di Linosa) *20744*
V	*Limonium ampuriense* Arrigoni & Diana *18264*	
	V	18264 Italy - Sardinia *18264*
V	*Limonium anatolicum* Hedge *12840*	
	V	12840 Turkey *12840*
R	*Limonium angustebracteatum* Erben *20648*	
	R	20692 Spain (Levante) *20692*
V	*Limonium antonii-llorensii* Llorens	
	V	Spain - Balearic Is.
I	*Limonium aragonense* (Debeaux) Pignatti *20171*	
	I	11496 Spain *11496*
E	*Limonium arborescens* (Brouss.) Kuntze *17891*	
	E	19174 Spain - Canary Is. *17891*
R	*Limonium arenosum* Erben	
	R	11496 Spain (Murcia) *11496*
V	*Limonium asterotrichum* (C.E.Salmon) C.E.Salmon *8000, 20171*	
	V	5204 Bulgaria (central) *5204*
R	*Limonium bosanum* Arrigoni & Diana *18264*	
	R	18264 Italy - Sardinia *18264*
V	*Limonium bourgeaui* (Webb) Kuntze *20750*	
	V	20750 Spain - Canary Is. *20750*
E	*Limonium brassicifolium* (Webb & Berthel.) Kuntze *20171*	
	E	20750 Spain - Canary Is. *20750*
R	*Limonium caesium* (Girard) Kuntze *20171*	
	R	20692 Spain (south-eastern provinces) *20692*
V	*Limonium calcarae* (Tod. ex Janka) Pignatti *18264, 20171*	
	V	20738 Italy - Sicily *18264*
I	*Limonium capense* (L.Bolus) L.Bolus *20604*	
	I	20604 South Africa - Cape Province *20604*
V	*Limonium capitis-marci* Arrigoni & Diana *18264*	
	V	18264 Italy - Sardinia *18264*
R	*Limonium carpathum* (Rech.f.) Rech.f. *20171*	
	R	20730 Greece - Crete (inc. Karpathos) *20730*
V	*Limonium carthaginense* (Rouyh) Hubbart & Sand. *11496*	
	V	11496 Spain *11496*
I	*Limonium castellonense* Erben & Podl.	
	I	19174 Spain *19174*
Ex	*Limonium catanense* (Tineo ex Lojac.) Brullo *20744*	
	Ex	20744 Italy - Sicily (Catania) *20744*
E	*Limonium cavanillesii* Erben *19174*	
	E	20692 Spain (near Peñiscola) *19174*
R	*Limonium cofrentanum* Erben *20648*	
	R	20692 Spain (near Cofrentes, Valencia province) *20692*
R	*Limonium coincyi* Sennen *20171*	
	R	11496 Spain (Murcia) *11496*
E	*Limonium companyonis* (Gren. & Billot) Kuntze	
	E	France
R	*Limonium cordatum* (L.) Mill. *20171*	
	R	20813 France *20813*
	V	Italy

R   *Limonium cosyrense* (Guss.) Kuntze *20171*
      R   Italy - Sicily

I   *Limonium cudayense* Sauvage & Vindt
      I   Morocco

I   *Limonium decumbens* (Boiss.) Kuntze *20604*
      I   *20604* South Africa - Cape Province *20604*

E   *Limonium dendroides* Svent. *17891*
      E   *19174* Spain - Canary Is. *17891*

R   *Limonium densiflorum* (Guss.) Kuntze *20171, 20744*
      R   *20744* Italy - Sicily (west coast) *20744*

R   *Limonium divaricatum* (Rouy) Brullo *20744*
      R   *20744* Italy - Sicily (west coast) *20744*

V   *Limonium dodartii* ssp. *lusitanicum* *17891*
      V   *20076* Portugal *17891*

Ex   *Limonium dubyi* (Gren. & Godr.) Kuntze *20171*
      Ex   *20528* France (south-west) *20528*

V   *Limonium duforei* (Girard) Kuntze *19174*
      V   *19174* Spain *19174*

E   *Limonium dufourei* (Girard) Kuntze *20171*
      E   *20692* Spain (Castellón & Valencia provinces) *20692*

V   *Limonium effusum* (Boiss.) O. Kuntz *12840*
      V   *12840* Turkey *12840*

V   *Limonium emarginatum* (Willd.) Kuntze *18223, 20171*
      V   *19052* United Kingdom - Gibraltar *19052*

V   *Limonium emporitanum* Fernandez Casas & Molero
      V   *11496* Spain *11496*

V   *Limonium erectum* Erben
      V   Spain

E   *Limonium estevei* Fernandez Casas *19174*
      E   *19818* Spain *19174*

V   *Limonium etruscum* Arrigoni & Rizzotto *18264*
      V   *18264* Italy (Tuscany) *18264*

R   *Limonium eugeniae* Sennen *20171*
      R   *11496* Spain *11496*

R   *Limonium formenterae* Llorens
      R   Spain - Balearic Is.

R   *Limonium frederici* (Barbey) Rech.f. *20171*
      R   Greece

E   *Limonium fruticans* (Webb) Kuntze *19174*
      E   *19174* Spain - Canary Is. *19174*

R   *Limonium furfuraceum* (Lag.) Kuntze *20171*
      R   *20692* Spain (Alicante) *20692*

R   *Limonium furnarii* Brullo *20744*
      R   *20744* Italy - Sicily *20744*

R   *Limonium gibertii* (Sennen) Sennen *19174, 20171*
      R   *19174* Spain *19174*
      R   Spain - Balearic Is.

V   *Limonium glomeratum* (Tausch) Erben *20744*
      V   *20738* Italy - Sicily (Mazara del Vallo) *20744*

R   *Limonium grosii* Llorens
      R   Spain - Balearic Is.

R   *Limonium halophilum* Pignatti *20744*
      R   *20744* Italy - Sicily (Mazara del Vallo) *20744*

R   *Limonium hermaeum* (Pignatti) Pignatti *20171*
      R   Italy - Sardinia

V   *Limonium hierapetrae* Rech. fil. *20730*
      V   *20730* Greece - Crete *20730*

V   *Limonium iconicum* (Boiss. & Heldr.) O. Kuntze *12840*
      V   *12840* Turkey *12840*

E   *Limonium imbricatum* (Webb & Berthel.) Hubbard. *19174*
      E   *19174* Spain - Canary Is. *19174*

V   *Limonium inarimense* (Guss.) Pignatti ssp. *inarimense* *20171*
      V   Italy (Campania) *20804*
      V   Italy - Sicily

V   *Limonium insulare* (Beg. & Landi) Arrigoni & Diana *18264*
      V   *20805* Italy - Sardinia *18264*

R   *Limonium intermedium* (Guss.) Brullo *18264*
      R   *18264* Italy - Sicily *18264*

V   *Limonium ionicum* Brullo *20744*
      V   *20744* Italy - Sicily (Isola Bella) *20744*

V   *Limonium japygicum* (H.Groves) Pignatti *20171*
      V   Italy (Puglia) *20804*

V   *Limonium johannis* Pignatti *20171*
      V   Italy
      V   Italy - Sicily

R   *Limonium kraussianum* (Buchinger ex Boiss.) Kuntze *20604*
      R   *20604* South Africa - Cape Province *20604*

E   *Limonium laetum* (Nyman) Pignatti *18264, 20171*
      E   *20805* Italy - Sardinia *18264*

V   *Limonium lanceolatum* (Hoffmanns. & Link) Franco *20076*
      V   *20076* Portugal *17891*

E   *Limonium lausianum* Pignatti *20171*
      E   *20805* Italy - Sardinia *20805*

R   *Limonium letourneuxii* (Coss.) Pons & Quezel *10488*
      R   *14958* Algeria *10488*

V   *Limonium lilacinum* (Boiss. & Bal.) Wagenitz *12840*
      V   *12840* Turkey *12840*

R   *Limonium lilybaeum* Brullo *18264*
      R   *18264* Italy - Sicily *18264*

R   *Limonium lingua* (Pomel) Pons & Quezel *10488*
      R   *14958* Algeria *10488*

R   *Limonium lojaconoi* Brullo *20744*
      R   *20744* Italy - Sicily (Trápani & Favignana Is.) *20744*

R   *Limonium lopadusanum* Brullo *20744*
      R   *20744* Italy - Sicily (Isole Pelagie) *20744*

R   *Limonium lucentinum* Pignatti & Freitag *20171*
      R   Spain

E   *Limonium macrophyllum* (Brouss.) Kuntze *20750*
      E   *20750* Spain - Canary Is. *20750*

E   *Limonium macropterum* (Webb & Berthel.) Kuntze *20750*
      E   *20750* Spain - Canary Is. *20750*

E   *Limonium magallufianum* Llorens
      E   Spain - Balearic Is.

E   *Limonium majoricum* Pignatti *20171*
      E   Spain - Balearic Is.

R   *Limonium majus* (Boiss.) Erben
      R   Spain

E   *Limonium malacitanum* B. Diez
      E   *19818* Spain (Malaga) *19818*

R   *Limonium marisolii* Llorens
      R   Spain - Balearic Is.

V	*Limonium merxmuelleri* Erben *18264*	
	V	*18264* Italy - Sardinia *18264*
V	*Limonium multiflorum* Erben *17891*	
	V	*20076* Portugal *17891*
E	*Limonium neo-castellonense* Socorro & Tarrega	
	E	Spain
E	*Limonium optimae* Raimondo *20744*	
	E	*20738* Italy - Sicily *20744*
V	*Limonium opulentum* (Lojac.) Greuter *20744*	
	V	*20744* Italy - Sicily (Porto Empedocle) *20744*
R	*Limonium ovalifolium* (Poiret) Kuntze ssp. *canariense* Pignatti	
	R	Spain - Canary Is.
R	*Limonium ovalifolium* (Poiret) Kuntze ssp. *pyramidata* (Lowe) A. Hansen & Sunding	
	R	Portugal - Madeira
R	*Limonium pachynense* Brullo *18264*	
	R	*18264* Italy - Sicily *18264*
V	*Limonium panormitanum* (Tod.) Pignatti *20171*	
	V	Italy - Sicily
R	*Limonium parvibracteatum* Pignatti *20171*	
	R	*20692* Spain (Alicante) *20692*
V	*Limonium parvifolium* (Tineo) Pignatti *8000, 20171*	
	V	Italy
	V	*20744* Italy - Sicily (Pantelleria) *20744*
E	*Limonium pavonianum* Brullo *20744*	
	E	*20738* Italy - Sicily (Cava d'Aliga, Sampieri) *20744*
V	*Limonium perezii* (Stapf) Hubbard *20750*	
	V	*20750* Spain - Canary Is. *20750*
R	*Limonium ponzoi* (Fiori & Beg.) Brullo *20744*	
	R	*20744* Italy - Sicily (west coast) *20744*
V	*Limonium preauxii* (Webb & Berthel.) Kuntze *20750*	
	V	*20750* Spain - Canary Is. *20750*
E	*Limonium pseudodictyocladon* (Pign.) Llorens *11496*	
	E	*11496* Spain - Balearic Is. (Mallorca) *11496*
E	*Limonium pseudolaetum* Arrigoni & Diana *18264*	
	E	*18264* Italy - Sardinia *18264*
V	*Limonium puberulum* (Webb & Berthel.) Kuntze *20750*	
	V	*20750* Spain - Canary Is. *20750*
R	*Limonium pujosii* Sauvage & Vindt	
	R	Morocco
E	*Limonium pulviniforme* Arrigoni & Diana *18264*	
	E	*18264* Italy - Sardinia *18264*
I	*Limonium purpuratum* (L.) F.T.Hubb. ex L.H.Bailey *20604*	
	I	*20604* South Africa - Cape Province *20604*
I	*Limonium pycnanthum* (C. Koch) O. Kuntze *12840*	
	I	*12840* Turkey *12840*
R	*Limonium recurvum* C.E. Salmon *8000, 20171*	
	R	*20587* United Kingdom (maritime cliffs, southern England) *19232*
E	*Limonium redivivum* (Svent.) Kunkel & Sunding *19174*	
	E	*20750* Spain - Canary Is. *19174*
V	*Limonium remotispiculum* (Lacaita) Pignatti *18264, 20171*	
	V	*18264* Italy (Campania, Basilicata, Calabria) *18264*
R	*Limonium retusum* Llorens	

	R	Spain - Balearic Is.
R	*Limonium revolutum* Erben	
	R	Spain
E	*Limonium rigualii* M.B.Crespo & Erben *20648*	
	E	*20692* Spain (north-east of Alicante province) *20692*
V	*Limonium ruizii* (Font Quer) Fernandez Casas	
	V	Spain
R	*Limonium rumicifolium* (Svent.) Kunkel & Sunding *19174*	
	R	*19174* Spain - Canary Is. *19174*
R	*Limonium rungsii* Sauvage & Vindt	
	R	Morocco
R	*Limonium salsuginosum* (Boiss.) O. Kuntze	
	R	Spain
V	*Limonium santapolense* Erben *20648*	
	V	*20692* Spain (near Santa Pola, Alicante Province) *20692*
R	*Limonium scopulorum* M.B.Crespo & Erben *20701*	
	R	*20690* Spain (La Marina Alta, Alicante) *20690*
R	*Limonium selinuntinum* Brullo *20744*	
	R	*20744* Italy - Sicily *20744*
E	*Limonium spectabile* (Svent.) Kunkel & Sunding *17891*	
	E	*19174* Spain - Canary Is. *17891*
V	*Limonium strictissimum* *17891*	
	V	*20726* France - Corsica *18264*
	V	*20805* Italy - Sardinia *17891*
V	*Limonium subglabrum* Erben	
	V	Spain
R	*Limonium subrotundifolium* (Beguinot & Vaccari) Brullo	
	R	Libya
R	*Limonium sucronicum* Erben *20648*	
	R	*20692* Spain (Albacete & Valencia) *20692*
E	*Limonium sventenii* Santos & Fernandez Galvan *17891*	
	E	*20750* Spain - Canary Is. *17891*
R	*Limonium syracusanum* Brullo *20744*	
	R	*20744* Italy - Sicily (east coast) *20744*
V	*Limonium tabernense* Erben	
	V	Spain (gypsum soils)
V	*Limonium tamaricoides* Bokhari *12840*	
	V	*12840* Turkey *12840*
E	*Limonium tauromenitanum* Brullo *20744*	
	E	*20738* Italy - Sicily *20744*
V	*Limonium tenoreanum* (Guss.) Pignatti *20171*	
	V	Italy
R	*Limonium tenuifolium* (Bertol. & Moris) *18264*	
	R	*18264* Italy - Sardinia *18264*
R	*Limonium teretifolium* L.Bolus *20604*	
	R	*20604* South Africa - Cape Province *20604*
R	*Limonium teuchirae* Brullo	
	R	Libya
R	*Limonium tharrosianum* Arrigoni & Diana *18264*	
	R	*18264* Italy - Sardinia *18264*
V	*Limonium thiniense* Erben *20648*	
	V	Spain
E	*Limonium todaroanum* Raimonda & Pignatti *18264*	
	E	*18264* Italy - Sicily *18264*
R	*Limonium vanense* Kit Tan & Sorger *12840*	
	R	*12840* Turkey *12840*

R   *Limonium vestitum* (C.E.Salmon) C.E.Salmon *20171*
   R   (former) Yugoslavia

R   *Limonium zeraphae* Brullo *13351*
   R   *13351* Malta *13351*

E   *Neogontscharovia mira* (Lincz.) Lincz.
   E   Asiatic U.S.S.R. *6930*

R   *Neogontscharovia miranda* (Lincz.) Lincz.
   R   Asiatic U.S.S.R. *6930*

Podostemaceae

Number of genera: 40
Number of species: 200
Recorded threatened species: 20   (10%)

Mostly tropical, especially Asia and America.

V   *Cladopus austrosatsumensis* (Koidz.) Ohwi *10572*
   V   *10572* Japan *10572*

V   *Cladopus doianus* Koriba *10572*
   V   *10572* Japan *10572*

E   *Dicraeanthus taylori* De Wilde & Guillaumet
   E   Côte d'Ivoire

R   *Diplobryum minutale* Cusson *6057*
   R   Vietnam *6057*

I   *Hydrobryopsis sessilis* (Willis) Engl.
   I   India - Karnataka

V   *Hydrobryum floribundum* Koidz. *10572*
   V   *10572* Japan *10572*

E   *Hydrobryum japonicum* Imamura *10572*
   E   *10572* Japan *10572*

V   *Hydrobryum puncticulatum* Koidz. *10572*
   V   *10572* Japan *10572*

I   *Indotristicha tirunelveliana* Sharma, Karthi. &
   Shetty *13883*
   I   *13883* India - Tamil Nadu (Tirunelveli Hills)
       13883

E   *Inversodicraea bowlingii* J.B. Hall *6072*
   E   *6072* Ghana *6072*

I   *Inversodicraea musciformis* G. Taylor
   I   Cameroon (Kokeka Mts, Mba)

E   *Ledermaniella bowlingii* (J. Hall) C. Cusset
   E   Ghana (Kwahu-Nteso, River Asuboni)

E   *Marathrum allenii* Woods. *20883, 10747*
   I   *20883* Panama *20883*

E   *Marathrum cubanum* C. Wright *5607*
   E   *19105* Cuba (Pinar del Rio) *5607*

E   *Marathrum leptophyllum* Royen *20883*
   I   *20883* Panama *20883*

E   *Marathrum pusillum* Royen *20883*
   I   *20883* Panama *20883*

R   *Marathrum rubrum* *19850*
   R   *19850* Mexico *19850*

I   *Polypleurella micrantha* V. Royen *19120*
   I   *19120* Thailand *19120*

R   *Willisia selagonoides* (Bedd.) Warm. ex Willis *13883*
   R   *13883* India - Kerala *13883*

I   *Zeylanidium johnsonii* (Wight) Engl.
   I   India - Kerala (Malabar)

Polemoniaceae

Number of genera: 18
Number of species: 300
Recorded threatened species: 102   (34%)

North temperate (Eurasia, Alaska to western South America), especially temperate North America.

R   *Collomia debilis* Payson var. *camporum*
   Payson *20850*
   V   *20850* U.S. - Idaho *20850*
   I   *20850* U.S. - Montana *20850*

R   *Collomia macrocalyx* Leib. ex Brand *20850*
   I   *20850* U.S. - Idaho *20850*
   R   *20850* U.S. - Oregon *20850*

R   *Collomia mazama* Coville *20850*
   R   *20850* U.S. - Oregon *20850*

V   *Collomia rawsoniana* Greene *20850*
   V   *20850* U.S. - California *20850*
   I   *20850* U.S. - Oregon *20850*

E   *Collomia renacta* E. Joyal *20850*
   E   *20850* U.S. - Nevada *20850*
   E   *20850* U.S. - Oregon *20850*

R   *Eriastrum abramsii* (Elmer) Mason *20850*
   I   *20850* U.S. - California *20850*

R   *Eriastrum brandegeae* Mason *20850*
   R   *20850* U.S. - California *20850*

E   *Eriastrum densifolium* (Benth.) H. Mason ssp.
   sanctorum (Milliken) H. Mason *20850*
   E   *20850* U.S. - California (Santa Ana River drainage)
       20850

V   *Eriastrum hooveri* (Jepson) Mason *20850*
   V   *20850* U.S. - California *20850*

R   *Eriastrum tracyi* Mason *20850*
   I   *20850* U.S. - California *20850*

V   *Gilia austrooccidentalis* (A.& V. Grant) A.& V.
   Grant *20850*
   I   *20850* U.S. - California *20850*

V   *Gilia brecciarum* M. E. Jones ssp. *jacens* (A.& V.
   Grant) Day *20850*
   I   *20850* U.S. - California *20850*

E   *Gilia caespitosa* Gray *20850*
   E   *20850* U.S. - Utah *20850*

R   *Gilia cana* (M.E. Jones) Heller *20850*
   I   *20850* U.S. - California *20850*
   I   *20850* U.S. - Nevada *20850*

V   *Gilia caruifolia* Abrams *20850*
   I   *20850* U.S. - California *20850*

R   *Gilia diegensis* (Munz) A.& V. Grant *20850*
   I   *20850* U.S. - California *20850*

R   *Gilia formosa* Greene ex Brand *20883, 20850*
   R   *20850* U.S. - New Mexico *20850*
       20883 Mexico *20883*

V   *Gilia haydenii* Gray *20850*
   I   *20850* U.S. - Colorado *20850*
   I   *20850* U.S. - New Mexico *20850*
   E   *20850* U.S. - Utah *20850*

R   *Gilia inyoensis* I.M. Johnston *20850*
   I   *20850* U.S. - California *20850*
   I   *20850* U.S. - Nevada *20850*

R   *Gilia ludens* Shinners *20850*
   R   *20850* U.S. - Texas *20850*

E	*Gilia maculata* Parish *20850*		
	E	*20850* U.S. - California *20850*	
R	*Gilia mcvickerae* M.E. Jones *20850*		
		20850 U.S. - Utah *20850*	
	I	*20850* U.S. - Wyoming *20850*	
R	*Gilia minor* A.& V. Grant *20850*		
	I	*20850* U.S. - Arizona *20850*	
	I	*20850* U.S. - California *20850*	
	I	*20850* U.S. - Nevada *20850*	
V	*Gilia nyensis* Reveal *20850*		
	V	*20850* U.S. - Nevada *20850*	
R	*Gilia penstemonoides* M.E. Jones *20850*		
	V	*20850* U.S. - Colorado *20850*	
V	*Gilia ripleyi* Barneby *20850*		
	I	*20850* U.S. - California *20850*	
	V	*20850* U.S. - Nevada *20850*	
R	*Gilia scopulorum* M.E. Jones *20850*		
	I	*20850* U.S. - Arizona *20850*	
	I	*20850* U.S. - California *20850*	
	I	*20850* U.S. - Nevada *20850*	
	E	*20850* U.S. - Utah *20850*	
R	*Gilia splendens* Dougl. ex Mason & A. Grant *20850*		
	I	*20850* U.S. - California *20850*	
R	*Gilia stenothyrsa* Gray *20850*		
	E	*20850* U.S. - Colorado *20850*	
	V	*20850* U.S. - Utah *20850*	
R	*Gilia tenuiflora* Benth. *20850*		
	I	*20850* U.S. - California *20850*	
V	*Gilia tenuiflora* Benth. ssp. *arenaria* (Benth.) A.& V. Grant *20850*		
	V	*20850* U.S. - California *20850*	
E	*Gilia tenuiflora* Benth. ssp. *hoffmannii* (Eastw.) A.& V. Grant *20850*		
	E	*20850* U.S. - California *20850*	
E	*Gilia tenuis* F.G. Sm. & Neese *20850*		
	E	*20850* U.S. - Utah *20850*	
V	*Ipomopsis aggregata* Grant & Wilken ssp. *weberi* Grant & Wilken *20850*		
	E	*20850* U.S. - Colorado *20850*	
	I	*20850* U.S. - Idaho *20850*	
	E	*20850* U.S. - Wyoming *20850*	
R	*Ipomopsis congesta* (Hook.) V. Grant ssp. *crebrifolia* (Nutt.) Day *20850*		
	E	*20850* U.S. - Colorado *20850*	
	V	*20850* U.S. - Montana *20850*	
	I	*20850* U.S. - Nevada *20850*	
	I	*20850* U.S. - New Mexico *20850*	
	I	*20850* U.S. - Utah *20850*	
	V	*20850* U.S. - Wyoming *20850*	
V	*Ipomopsis globularis* (Brand) W.A. Weber *20850*		
	I	*20850* U.S. - Colorado *20850*	
R	*Ipomopsis longiflora* (Torr.) V.Grant ssp. *australis* Fletcher & W.L.Wagner *20883, 20850, 19002*		
	I	*20850* U.S. - Arizona *20850*	
	I	*20850* U.S. - Nebraska *20850*	
	I	*20850* U.S. - New Mexico *20850*	
	I	*20850* U.S. - Oklahoma *20850*	
	I	*20850* U.S. - South Dakota *20850*	
	I	*20850* U.S. - Texas *20850*	
	I	*20850* U.S. - Utah *20850*	
		20883 Mexico *20883*	
V	*Ipomopsis minutiflora* (Benth.) V. Grant *20850, 10701*		
	V	*20850* Canada - British Columbia *20850*	
	I	*20850* U.S. - Idaho *20850*	

	I	*20850* U.S. - Oregon *20850*	
	I	*20850* U.S. - Washington *20850*	
E	*Ipomopsis polyantha* (Rydb.) V. Grant *20850*		
	E	*20850* U.S. - Colorado *20850*	
	I	*20850* U.S. - New Mexico *20850*	
E	*Ipomopsis sancti-spiritus* Wilken & Fletcher *20850*		
	E	*20850* U.S. - New Mexico *20850*	
V	*Ipomopsis spicata* (Nutt.) V. Grant. ssp. *capitata* (Gray) V.Grant *20850*		
	V	*20850* U.S. - Colorado *20850*	
V	*Ipomopsis spicata* (Nutt.) V. Grant ssp. *robruthii* Wilken & Hartman *20850, 10260*		
	V	*20850* U.S. - Wyoming *20850*	
V	*Ipomopsis spicata* (Nutt.) V. Grant. ssp. *tridactyla* (Rydb.) Wilken & Hartman *20850*		
	V	*20850* U.S. - Utah *20850*	
V	*Ipomopsis tenuifolia* (Gray) V. Grant *20850*		
	I	*20850* U.S. - Arizona *20850*	
	I	*20850* U.S. - California *20850*	
	I	*20850* U.S. - Wyoming *20850*	
V	*Leptodactylon californicum* Hook. & Arn. ssp. *tomentosum* Gordon *20850*		
	V	*20850* U.S. - California *20850*	
E	*Leptodactylon glabrum* Patterson & Yoder-Williams *20850*		
	V	*20850* U.S. - Idaho *20850*	
	E	*20850* U.S. - Nevada *20850*	
V	*Leptodactylon jaegeri* (Munz) Wherry *20850*		
	V	*20850* U.S. - California *20850*	
R	*Leptodactylon watsonii* (Gray) Rydb. *20850*		
	I	*20850* U.S. - Colorado *20850*	
	I	*20850* U.S. - Idaho *20850*	
	I	*20850* U.S. - Nevada *20850*	
	R	*20850* U.S. - Utah *20850*	
	E	*20850* U.S. - Wyoming *20850*	
V	*Linanthus acicularis* Greene *20850*		
	V	*20850* U.S. - California *20850*	
R	*Linanthus ambiguus* (Rattan) Greene *20850*		
	R	*20850* U.S. - California *20850*	
V	*Linanthus bellus* (Gray) Greene *20883, 20850, 19002*		
	I	*20850* U.S. - California *20850*	
	I	*20883* Mexico *20883*	
V	*Linanthus breviculus* (Gray) Greene *20850*		
	I	*20850* U.S. - California *20850*	
V	*Linanthus concinnus* Milliken *20850*		
	V	*20850* U.S. - California *20850*	
R	*Linanthus dichotomus* Benth. *20850*		
	I	*20850* U.S. - Arizona *20850*	
	I	*20850* U.S. - California *20850*	
	I	*20850* U.S. - Nevada *20850*	
	E	*20850* U.S. - Utah *20850*	
R	*Linanthus floribundus* (Gray) Greene & Milliken ssp. *hallii* (Jepson) Mason *20850*		
	V	*20850* U.S. - California *20850*	
R	*Linanthus grandiflorus* (Benth.) Greene *20850*		
	R	*20850* U.S. - California *20850*	
Ex/E	*Linanthus harknessii* (Curran) E. Greene ssp. *condensatus* Mason *20850*		
	Ex/E	*20850* U.S. - California *20850*	
V	*Linanthus killipii* Mason *20850*		
	V	*20850* U.S. - California *20850*	
R	*Linanthus liniflorus* (Benth.) Greene *20850*		

I	20850	U.S. - California *20850*
I	20850	U.S. - Idaho *20850*
I	20850	U.S. - Oregon *20850*
I	20850	U.S. - Washington *20850*

R   *Linanthus nudatus* Greene *20850*

I	20850	U.S. - California *20850*

V   *Linanthus nuttallii* T.W. Nelson & Patterson ssp. *howellii* T.W. Nelson & Patterson *20850*

V	20850	U.S. - California *20850*

V   *Linanthus pachyphyllus* Patterson *20850*

I	20850	U.S. - California *20850*
I	20850	U.S. - Nevada *20850*

V   *Linanthus pygmaeus* (Brand) J. T. Howell ssp. *pygmaeus* *20850*

V	20850	U.S. - California *20850*

V   *Linanthus serrulatus* Greene *20850*

I	20850	U.S. - California *20850*

R   *Navarretia cotulifolia* (Benth.) Hook. & Arn. *20850*

I	20850	U.S. - California *20850*

R   *Navarretia filicaulis* (Torr. ex Gray) Greene *20850*

I	20850	U.S. - California *20850*

V   *Navarretia fossalis* Moran *20883, 20850, 8058*

V	20850	U.S. - California *20850*
I	20883	Mexico *20883*
?		Mexico - Baja California Peninsula *8058*

R   *Navarretia heterodoxa* (Greene) Greene *20850*

I	20850	U.S. - California *20850*

R   *Navarretia jepsonii* V. Bailey ex Jepson *20850*

I	20850	U.S. - California *20850*

V   *Navarretia leucocephala* Benth. ssp. *bakeri* (Mason) Day *20850*

V	20850	U.S. - California *20850*

E   *Navarretia leucocephala* Benth. ssp. *pauciflora* (Mason) Day *20850*

E	20850	U.S. - California *20850*

E   *Navarretia leucocephala* Benth. ssp. *plieantha* (Mason) Day *20850*

E	20850	U.S. - California *20850*

E   *Navarretia myersii* Allen & Day *20850*

E	20850	U.S. - California *20850*

V   *Navarretia nigelliformis* Greene ssp. *radians* (J.T. Howell) Day *20850*

V	20850	U.S. - California *20850*

R   *Navarretia prolifera* E. Greene ssp. *lutea* (Brand) Mason *20850*

R	20850	U.S. - California *20850*

V   *Navarretia prostrata* (Gray) Greene *20850*

I	20850	U.S. - California *20850*

V   *Navarretia rosulata* Brand *20850*

V	20850	U.S. - California *20850*

E   *Navarretia setiloba* Coville *20850*

E	20850	U.S. - California *20850*

V   *Phlox amabilis* Brand *20850*

I	20850	U.S. - Arizona *20850*

R   *Phlox bifida* Beck ssp. *stellaria* (Gray) Wherry *20850*

V	20850	U.S. - Arkansas *20850*
Ex/E	20850	U.S. - Illinois *20850*
E	20850	U.S. - Indiana *20850*
V	20850	U.S. - Kentucky *20850*
V	20850	U.S. - Missouri *20850*

R	20850	U.S. - Tennessee *20850*

V   *Phlox buckleyi* Wherry *20850*

V	20850	U.S. - Virginia *20850*
E	20850	U.S. - West Virginia *20850*

V   *Phlox cluteana* A. Nels. *20850*

V	20850	U.S. - Arizona *20850*
I	20850	U.S. - New Mexico *20850*
V	20850	U.S. - Utah *20850*

R   *Phlox dispersa* C.W. Sharsmith *20850*

R	20850	U.S. - California *20850*

V   *Phlox dolichantha* Gray *20850*

V	20850	U.S. - California *20850*

R   *Phlox drummondii* (Wherry) Wherry ssp. *johnstonii* (Wherry) Wherry *20850*

R	20850	U.S. - Texas *20850*

V   *Phlox floridana* Benth. *20850*

I	20850	U.S. - Alabama *20850*
I	20850	U.S. - Florida *20850*
I	20850	U.S. - Georgia *20850*

V   *Phlox gladiformis* (M.E. Jones) E. Nels. *20850*

V	20850	U.S. - Nevada *20850*
V	20850	U.S. - Utah *20850*

R   *Phlox griseola* Wherry *20850*

I	20850	U.S. - Arizona *20850*
I	20850	U.S. - Nevada *20850*
E	20850	U.S. - Utah *20850*

E   *Phlox hirsuta* E. Nels. *20850*

E	20850	U.S. - California *20850*

E   *Phlox idahonis* Wherry *20850*

E	20850	U.S. - Idaho *20850*

V   *Phlox jonesii* Wherry *20850*

I	20850	U.S. - Utah *20850*

R   *Phlox kelseyi* Britt. ssp. *salina* (M.E. Jones) Wherry *20850*

I	20850	U.S. - Colorado *20850*
I	20850	U.S. - Idaho *20850*
I	20850	U.S. - Nevada *20850*

V   *Phlox longipilosa* Waterfall *20850*

V	20850	U.S. - Oklahoma *20850*

V   *Phlox missoulensis* Wherry *20850*

V	20850	U.S. - Montana *20850*

V   *Phlox nivalis* Lodd. ssp. *texensis* Lundell *20850, 14871*

V	20850	U.S. - Texas (east Texas) *20850*

V   *Phlox oklahomensis* Wherry *20850*

I	20850	U.S. - Arkansas *20850*
V	20850	U.S. - Kansas *20850*
I	20850	U.S. - Nebraska *20850*
E	20850	U.S. - Oklahoma *20850*
E	20850	U.S. - Texas *20850*

V   *Phlox pungens* Dorn *20850*

V	20850	U.S. - Wyoming *20850*

V   *Phlox richardsonii* Benth. ssp. *richardsonii* *20850*

I	20850	Canada - Franklin *20850*
I	20850	Canada - Yukon Territory *20850*
E	20850	U.S. - Alaska *20850*

R   *Phlox sibirica* L. *20850*

I	20850	Canada - Franklin *20850*
I	20850	Canada - Yukon Territory *20850*

R   *Polemonium caeruleum* L. var. *nipponicum* K. Ito *10573*

R		10573	Japan *10573*

E   *Polemonium chartaceum* Mason *20850*
- E   *20850*   U.S. - California *20850*
- E   *20850*   U.S. - Nevada *20850*

R   *Polemonium eximium* Greene *20850*
- I   *20850*   U.S. - California *20850*

E   *Polemonium kiushianum* Kitam. *10573*
- E   *10573*   Japan *10573*

E   *Polemonium nevadense* Wherry *20850*
- E   *20850*   U.S. - Nevada *20850*

E   *Polemonium occidentale* Greene ex Brand ssp. *lacustre* Wherry *20850*
- I   *20850*   U.S. - Minnesota *20850*
- E   *20850*   U.S. - Wisconsin *20850*

R   *Polemonium pauciflorum* S.Watson *20883, 20850, 19002*
- I   *20850*   U.S. - Arizona *20850*
- E   *20850*   U.S. - Texas *20850*
-   *20883*   Mexico *20883*

E   *Polemonium pauciflorum* S.Watson ssp. *hinckleyi* (Standl.) Wherry *20850*
- E   *20850*   U.S. - Arizona *20850*
- E   *20850*   U.S. - Texas *20850*

E   *Polemonium pectinatum* Greene *20850*
- E   *20850*   U.S. - Washington *20850*

R   *Polemonium vanbruntiae* Britt. *20850*
- E   *20850*   Canada - New Brunswick *20850*
- E   *20850*   Canada - Quebec *20850*
- E   *20850*   U.S. - Maine *20850*
- V   *20850*   U.S. - Maryland *20850*
- Ex   *20850*   U.S. - New Jersey *20850*
- R   *20850*   U.S. - New York *20850*
- E   *20850*   U.S. - Pennsylvania *20850*
- V   *20850*   U.S. - Vermont *20850*
- V   *20850*   U.S. - West Virginia *20850*

Polygalaceae

Number of genera:	12
Number of species:	750
Recorded threatened species:	92 (12%)

Nearly cosmopolitan.

R   *Comesperma breviflorum* Pedley *20681*
- R   *20681*   Australia - Queensland *20681*

V   *Comesperma oblongatum* (R.Br.ex Benth.) Pedley *20681*
- V   *20681*   Australia - Queensland *20681*

R   *Comesperma praecelsum* F.Muell. *20681*
- R   *20681*   Australia - Queensland *20681*

V   *Monnina amplibracteata* Ferreyra *18200*
- V   *12468*   Peru *18200*

V   *Monnina confusa* Ferreyra *18200*
- V   *12468*   Peru *18200*

V   *Monnina ebracteata* Ferreyra *18200*
- V   *12468*   Peru *18200*

V   *Monnina gaudroniana* Ferreyra *18200*
- V   *12468*   Peru *18200*

E   *Monnina huallagensis* Chodat *18200*
- E   *9446*   Peru *18200*

I   *Monnina idroboana* Ferreyra *19352*
- I   *19352*   Colombia *19352*

R   *Monnina macrostachya* Ruiz Lopez & Pavon *18200*
- R   *9446*   Peru *18200*

V   *Monnina membranifolia* Ferreyra *18200*
- V   *12468*   Peru *18200*

E   *Monnina polystachya* Ruiz Lopez & Pavon *18200*
- E   *9446*   Peru *18200*

E   *Monnina ruiziana* Chodat *18200*
- E   *9446*   Peru *18200*

V   *Monnina sanmarcosana* Ferreyra *18200*
- V   *12468*   Peru *18200*

V   *Monnina soukupiana* Ferreyra *18200*
- V   *12468*   Peru *18200*

V   *Monnina valcarceliana* Ferreyra *18200*
- V   *12468*   Peru *18200*

E   *Monnina woytkowskii* Ferreyra *18200*
- E   *20046*   Peru *18200*

V   *Monnina wurdackii* Ferreyra *18200*
- V   *12468*   Peru *18200*

I   *Muraltia aciphylla* Levyns *20604*
- I   *20604*   South Africa - Cape Province *20604*

R   *Muraltia alba* Levyns *20604*
- R   *20604*   South Africa - Cape Province *20604*

I   *Muraltia angustiflora* Levyns *20604*
- I   *20604*   South Africa - Cape Province *20604*

V   *Muraltia barkerae* Levyns *20604*
- V   *20604*   South Africa - Cape Province *20604*

R   *Muraltia bondii* Vlok *20604*
- R   *20604*   South Africa - Cape Province *20604*

V   *Muraltia calycina* Harv. *20604*
- V   *20604*   South Africa - Cape Province *20604*

R   *Muraltia chamaepitys* Chodat *20604*
- R   *20604*   South Africa - Cape Province *20604*

R   *Muraltia comptonii* Levyns *20604*
- R   *20604*   South Africa - Cape Province *20604*

I   *Muraltia concava* Levyns *20604*
- I   *20604*   South Africa - Cape Province *20604*

I   *Muraltia cuspifolia* Chodat *20604*
- I   *20604*   South Africa - Cape Province *20604*

I   *Muraltia elsieae* Paiva *20604*
- I   *20604*   South Africa - Cape Province *20604*

I   *Muraltia ferox* Levyns *20604*
- I   *20604*   South Africa - Cape Province *20604*

R   *Muraltia guthriei* Levyns *20604*
- R   *20604*   South Africa - Cape Province *20604*

I   *Muraltia harveyana* Levyns *20604*
- I   *20604*   South Africa - Cape Province *20604*

I   *Muraltia hirsuta* Levyns *20604*
- I   *20604*   South Africa - Cape Province *20604*

I   *Muraltia karroica* Levyns *20604*
- I   *20604*   South Africa - Cape Province *20604*

R   *Muraltia pottebergensis* Levyns *20604*
- R   *20604*   South Africa - Cape Province *20604*

E   *Muraltia satureioides* DC. var. *salteri* Levyns *20604*
- E   *20604*   South Africa - Cape Province *20604*

R   *Polygala anderssonii* Robinson *11117*
- R   Ecuador - Galapagos (Isabela, Santiago, south Cruz) *11117*

Ex/E   *Polygala antillensis* Chodat *5710*
- Ex/E   *5710*   Martinique (heights of Saint-Pierre) *5710*

R	*Polygala arcuata* Hayata *17617*	
	R	20854 Taiwan *11139*
V	*Polygala aschersoniana* Chodat	
	V	Libya
V	*Polygala balduinii* Nutt. var. *carteri* (Small) R.R.Sm. & Ward *20883*	
	R	20883 Cuba *20883*
R	*Polygala bennae* Jacq.-Fel. *7926*	
	R	Guinea *7926*
V	*Polygala boykinii* Nutt. var. *sparsifolia* Wheelock *20850*	
	V	20850 U.S. - Florida *20850*
I	*Polygala brachyptera* Griseb. *5607*	
	I	19105 Cuba *5607*
R	*Polygala carueliana* (A.W.Benn.) Burnat ex Caruel *20171*	
	R	Italy
R	*Polygala cowellii* (Britt.) Blake *20883, 10197*	
	R	20883 Puerto Rico *20883*
R	*Polygala cristata* P. Taylor *7926*	
	R	Sierra Leone *7926*
I	*Polygala dasyphylla* Levyns *20604*	
	I	20604 South Africa - Cape Province *20604*
I	*Polygala dispar* Ghazanfar *20146*	
	I	20146 Oman (western Hajar) *20146*
R	*Polygala doerfleri* Hayek *20178, 20171*	
	R	20178 Albania *20178*
E	*Polygala dukei* Barringer *20883, 10073*	
	I	20883 Panama *20883*
E	*Polygala esterae* Chod. *20604*	
	E	20604 South Africa - Cape Province *20604*
E	*Polygala fendleri* Blake var. *heterothrix* Blake *20883, 9006*	
	I	20883 Panama *20883*
R	*Polygala fransisci* Exell *7749*	
	R	Mozambique *7749*
R	*Polygala galapageia* Hook.f. var. *galapageia* *11117*	
	R	Ecuador - Galapagos *11117*
R	*Polygala galapageia* Hook.f. var. *insularis* (A.W. Bennett) Robinson *11117*	
	R	Ecuador - Galapagos *11117*
V	*Polygala helenae* Greuter	
	V	Greece
R	*Polygala heterorhyncha* (Barneby) T. Wendt *20850*	
	E	20850 U.S. - California *20850*
	V	20850 U.S. - Nevada *20850*
R	*Polygala hispida* (Burch.) DC. *20039*	
	R	20039 Southern Africa *20039*
	I	20039 Swaziland *20039*
R	*Polygala hookeri* Torr. & Gray *20850*	
	E	20850 U.S. - Alabama *20850*
	I	20850 U.S. - Florida *20850*
	E	20850 U.S. - Louisiana *20850*
	E	20850 U.S. - Mississippi *20850*
	V	20850 U.S. - North Carolina *20850*
	I	20850 U.S. - South Carolina *20850*
	V	20850 U.S. - Texas *20850*
V	*Polygala inespectata* Pesman & Erik *12840*	
	V	12840 Turkey *12840*

E	*Polygala jefensis* W.H. Lewis *20883, 9006*	
	I	20883 Panama *20883*
I	*Polygala langebergensis* Levyns *20604*	
	I	20604 South Africa - Cape Province *20604*
V	*Polygala leptostachys* Shuttlw. *20850*	
	R	20883 U.S. - Florida *20883*
	E	20883 U.S. - Georgia *20883*
	?	20883 U.S. - Mississippi *20883*
V	*Polygala lewtonii* Small *20850, 18134*	
	V	20850 U.S. - Florida *20850*
R	*Polygala luteo-alba* Gagnepain *6057*	
	R	Vietnam *6057*
V	*Polygala maravillasensis* Correll *20850*	
	E	20850 U.S. - Texas *20850*
I	*Polygala messambuziensis* Paiva	
	I	Mozambique
R	*Polygala minutifolia* Rose *10059*	
	R	10059 Mexico *10059*
R	*Polygala murati* J. Felix ssp. *murati*	
	R	Chad
R	*Polygala murati* J. Felix ssp. *purpurea* Carv.Vasc. & Gillet	
	R	Chad
V	*Polygala panamensis* Chod. *20883, 9006*	
	I	20883 Panama *20883*
R	*Polygala pisaurensis* Caldesi *18264, 20171*	
	R	18264 Italy (Marches) *18264*
I	*Polygala pottebergensis* Levyns *20604*	
	I	20604 South Africa - Cape Province *20604*
R	*Polygala praticola* Chodat *20604*	
	R	20604 South Africa - Natal *20604*
R	*Polygala pruinosa* Boiss. ssp. *megaptera* Cullen *12840*	
	R	12840 Turkey *12840*
R	*Polygala rhynchosperma* Blake *5607*	
	E	20883 Cuba *20883*
V	*Polygala rimulicola* Steyermark *20850*	
	V	20850 U.S. - New Mexico *20850*
	V	20850 U.S. - Texas *20850*
E	*Polygala rimulicola* Steyermark var. *mescalerorum* T. Wendt & T.K. Todsen *20850*	
	E	20850 U.S. - New Mexico *20850*
V	*Polygala rimulicola* Steyermark var. *rimulicola* *20850*	
	V	20850 U.S. - New Mexico (Carlsbad Cavern NP) *20850*
	V	20850 U.S. - Texas *20850*
R	*Polygala rusbyi* Greene *20850*	
	R	20850 U.S. - Arizona *20850*
R	*Polygala sardoa* Chodat *20171*	
	R	Italy - Sardinia
E	*Polygala sinisca* Arrigoni *18264*	
	E	18264 Italy - Sardinia *18264*
E	*Polygala smallii* R.R. Sm. & Ward *20850*	
	E	20850 U.S. - Florida (Broward & Dade Counties) *20850*
E	*Polygala supina* Schreb. ssp. *hospita* (A. Kerner) Mcneill *17823, 20171*	
	E	19949 Romania *17823*
I	*Polygala tenuicaulis* Hook.f.	

I		Cameroon (Cameroon mt)
R	*Polygala torrei* Exell *7749*	
R		Mozambique *7749*
I	*Polygala tricholopha* Chodat	
I		India - Assam
I		India - Meghalaya
R	*Polygala vayredae* Costa *20171*	
R		Spain
I	*Polygala wilsonii* Small ex Britton & Millsp.	
I	*4650*	Bahamas *4650*
E	*Polygala wurdackiana* W.H. Lewis *20883, 9006*	
I	*20883*	Panama *20883*
I	*Securidaca atro-violacea* Elm. *13833*	
I	*13833*	Philippines (Palawan) *13833*
I	*Securidaca lophosoma* (Blake) Cheesman *5932*	
I	*5932*	Trinidad & Tobago (Trinidad) *5932*
R	*Securidaca macrophylla* (Benth.) Wurd. *8679*	
R		French Guiana *8679*
R	*Securidaca pyramidalis* Sprague *8679*	
R		Guyana *8679*
R	*Xanthophyllum annamense* Gagnepain *6057*	
R		Vietnam *6057*

Polygonaceae

Number of genera:		30
Number of species:		1,000
Recorded threatened species:		228 (22%)

Mainly temperate Northern Hemisphere.

R	*Aristocapsa insignis* (Curran) Reveal & Hardham *20850*	
R	*20850*	U.S. - California *20850*
I	*Atraphaxis muschketowii* Krasn. *5942*	
I	*5942*	Kazakhstan *5942*
I	*Atraphaxis teretifolia* (Popov) Komarov *5942*	
I	*5942*	Kazakhstan *5942*
R	*Bistorta hayachinensis* (Makino) Gross *10572*	
R	*10572*	Japan *10572*
I	*Calligonum bakuense* Litv.	
I	*5942*	Azerbaijan (Baku) *5942*
E	*Calligonum calvescens* Maire *10487*	
E	*14958*	Algeria *10487*
V	*Calligonum polygonoides* L. ssp. *polygonoides* Soskov *16168*	
V	*16168*	Egypt *16168*
I	*Calligonum triste* Litv. *5942*	
I	*5942*	Kazakhstan *5942*
V	*Chorizanthe angustifolia* Nutt. *20850*	
I	*20850*	U.S. - California *20850*
R	*Chorizanthe biloba* Goodman *20850*	
I	*20850*	U.S. - California *20850*
E	*Chorizanthe biloba* Goodman var. *immemora* Reveal & Hardham *20850*	
E	*20850*	U.S. - California *20850*
V	*Chorizanthe breweri* S.Watson *20850*	
V	*20850*	U.S. - California *20850*
R	*Chorizanthe clevelandii* Parry *20850*	
I	*20850*	U.S. - California *20850*
R	*Chorizanthe cuspidata* S.Watson *20850*	
I	*20850*	U.S. - California *20850*

V	*Chorizanthe cuspidata* S.Watson var. *cuspidata* *20850*	
V	*20850*	U.S. - California *20850*
E	*Chorizanthe cuspidata* S.Watson var. *villosa* (Eastw.) Munz *20850*	
E	*20850*	U.S. - California *20850*
R	*Chorizanthe diffusa* Benth. *20850*	
I	*20850*	U.S. - California *20850*
R	*Chorizanthe fimbriata* Nutt. *20850*	
I	*20850*	U.S. - California *20850*
E	*Chorizanthe howellii* Goodman *20850*	
E	*20850*	U.S. - California *20850*
R	*Chorizanthe membranacea* Benth. *20850*	
I	*20850*	U.S. - California *20850*
I	*20850*	U.S. - Oregon *20850*
R	*Chorizanthe obovata* Goodman *20850*	
I	*20850*	U.S. - California *20850*
E	*Chorizanthe orcuttiana* Parry *20850*	
E	*20850*	U.S. - California *20850*
R	*Chorizanthe palmeri* S.Watson *20850*	
I	*20850*	U.S. - California *20850*
Ex/E	*Chorizanthe parryi* S.Watson var. *fernandina* (S. Watson) Jepson *20850*	
Ex/E	*20850*	U.S. - California *20850*
E	*Chorizanthe pungens* Benth. *20850*	
I	*20850*	U.S. - California *20850*
E	*Chorizanthe pungens* Benth. var. *hartwegiana* Reveal & Hardham *20850*	
E	*20850*	U.S. - California *20850*
V	*Chorizanthe pungens* Benth. var. *pungens* *20850*	
V	*20850*	U.S. - California *20850*
V	*Chorizanthe rectispina* Goodman *20850*	
E	*20850*	U.S. - California *20850*
V	*Chorizanthe robusta* Parry *20850, 19002*	
I	*20850*	U.S. - California *20850*
E	*Chorizanthe robusta* Parry var. *hartwegii* (Benth.) Reveal & Morgan *20850*	
E	*20850*	U.S. - California *20850*
E	*Chorizanthe robusta* Parry var. *robusta* *20850*	
E	*20850*	U.S. - California *20850*
V	*Chorizanthe spinosa* S.Watson *20850*	
V	*20850*	U.S. - California *20850*
R	*Chorizanthe stellulata* Benth. *20850*	
I	*20850*	U.S. - California *20850*
R	*Chorizanthe uniaristata* Torr. & Gray *20850*	
I	*20850*	U.S. - California *20850*
E	*Chorizanthe valida* S.Watson *20850*	
E	*20850*	U.S. - California *20850*
R	*Chorizanthe ventricosa* Goodman *20850*	
I	*20850*	U.S. - California *20850*
V	*Chorizanthe xantii* S.Watson var. *leucotheca* Goodman *20850*	
V	*20850*	U.S. - California *20850*
E	*Coccoloba acuna* Howard *5607*	
E	*19105*	Cuba (Holguin) *5607*
V	*Coccoloba caravellae* Sastre & Fiard *19001*	
V	*19001*	Martinique (Domaine de la Caravelle) *5710*

E   *Coccoloba clementis* Howard *5607*
     E   *19105*   Cuba (Holguin) *5607*

R   *Coccoloba conduplicata* Maguire *8679*
     R   *8679*   Suriname *8679*

V   *Coccoloba coriacea* A. Rich. *5607*
     V   *19105*   Cuba (Pinar del Rio) *5607*

I   *Coccoloba fawcettii* Schmidt *21008*
     I   *21008*   Dominican Republic (Barahona) *21008*

E   *Coccoloba lasseri* Lund. *20883, 9006*
     I   *20883*   Panama *20883*

V   *Coccoloba manzanillensis* Beurl. *20883, 9006*
     V   *20883*   Panama *20883*

V   *Coccoloba munizii* Borh. *5607*
     V   *19105*   Cuba (Guantanamo) *5607*

E   *Coccoloba pallida* C. Wright *20883*
     I   *20883*   Puerto Rico *20883*

R   *Coccoloba plumieri* Griseb. *20883*
     R   *20883*   Jamaica *20883*

V   *Coccoloba priorii* Fawcett & Rendle *20883*
     V   *20883*   Jamaica *20883*

E   *Coccoloba proctorii* Howard *20883, 13336*
     E   *13336*   Jamaica *20883*

E   *Coccoloba retirensis* Howard *5607*
     E   *19105*   Cuba (Pinar del Rio) *5607*

V   *Coccoloba rugosa* Desf. *20883*
     I   *20883*   Puerto Rico *20883*
     I   *20883*   USA - Virgin Is. *20883*

R   *Coccoloba toaensis* Alain *5607*
     R   *19105*   Cuba (Guantanamo) *5607*

R   *Coccoloba troyana* Urb. *20883*
     R   *20883*   Jamaica *20883*

I   *Coccoloba zebra* Griseb. *20883, 13336*
     I   *13336*   Jamaica *20883*

V   *Dedeckera eurekensis* Reveal & J.T. Howell *20850*
     V   *20850*   U.S. - California *20850*

E   *Dodecahema leptoceras* (Gray ex Benth.) Reveal & Hardham *20850*
     E   *20850*   U.S. - California *20850*

R   *Eriogonum acaule* Nutt. *20850*
     E   *20850*   U.S. - Colorado *20850*
     I   *20850*   U.S. - Idaho *20850*
     R   *20850*   U.S. - Wyoming *20850*

V   *Eriogonum aliquantum* Reveal *20850*
     V   *20850*   U.S. - New Mexico *20850*

V   *Eriogonum alpinum* Engelm. *20850*
     V   *20850*   U.S. - California *20850*

V   *Eriogonum ammophilum* Reveal *20850*
     I   *20850*   U.S. - Utah *20850*

R   *Eriogonum ampullaceum* J.T. Howell *20850*
     R   *20850*   U.S. - California *20850*
     E   *20850*   U.S. - Nevada *20850*

V   *Eriogonum anemophilum* Greene *20850*
     V   *20850*   U.S. - Nevada *20850*

E   *Eriogonum apachense* Reveal *20850*
     E   *20850*   U.S. - Arizona *20850*

R   *Eriogonum apiculatum* S.Watson *20850*
     I   *20850*   U.S. - California *20850*

V   *Eriogonum apricum* J.T. Howell *20850*
     I   *20850*   U.S. - California *20850*

V   *Eriogonum apricum* J. Howell var. *apricum* *20850*
     V   *20850*   U.S. - California *20850*

E   *Eriogonum apricum* J. Howell var. *prostratum* Myatt *20850*
     E   *20850*   U.S. - California *20850*

E   *Eriogonum arborescens* Greene *20850*
     I   *20850*   U.S. - California *20850*

V   *Eriogonum aretioides* Barneby *20850*
     V   *20850*   U.S. - Utah *20850*

E   *Eriogonum argophyllum* Reveal *20850*
     E   *20850*   U.S. - Nevada *20850*

V   *Eriogonum beatleyae* Reveal *20850*
     E   *20850*   U.S. - California *20850*
     V   *20850*   U.S. - Nevada *20850*

V   *Eriogonum bifurcatum* Reveal *20850*
     E   *20850*   U.S. - California *20850*
     E   *20850*   U.S. - Nevada *20850*

V   *Eriogonum brandegei* Rydb. *20850*
     V   *20850*   U.S. - Colorado *20850*

R   *Eriogonum breedlovei* (J.T. Howell) Reveal *20850*
     I   *20850*   U.S. - California *20850*

V   *Eriogonum breedlovei* (J.T. Howell) Reveal var. *breedlovei* *20850*
     V   *20850*   U.S. - California *20850*

V   *Eriogonum breedlovei* (J.T. Howell) Reveal var. *shevockii* J.T. Howell *20850*
     V   *20850*   U.S. - California *20850*

E   *Eriogonum butterworthianum* J.T. Howell *20850*
     E   *20850*   U.S. - California *20850*

R   *Eriogonum capillare* Small *20850*
     V   *20850*   U.S. - Arizona *20850*
     E   *20850*   U.S. - New Mexico *20850*

V   *Eriogonum capistratum* Reveal var. *welshii* Reveal *20850*
     V   *20850*   U.S. - Idaho *20850*

E   *Eriogonum chrysops* Rydb. *20850*
     E   *20850*   U.S. - Oregon *20850*

V   *Eriogonum cinereum* Benth. *20850*
     I   *20850*   U.S. - California *20850*

R   *Eriogonum cithariforme* S.Watson *20850*
     I   *20850*   U.S. - California *20850*

R   *Eriogonum clavellatum* Small *20850*
     E   *20850*   U.S. - Colorado *20850*
     E   *20850*   U.S. - Utah *20850*

R   *Eriogonum coloradense* Small *20850*
     V   *20850*   U.S. - Colorado *20850*

V   *Eriogonum concinnum* Reveal *20850*
     V   *20850*   U.S. - Nevada *20850*

V   *Eriogonum contiguum* (Reveal) Reveal *20850*
     I   *20850*   U.S. - California *20850*
     E   *20850*   U.S. - Nevada *20850*

R   *Eriogonum contortum* Small *20850*
     V   *20850*   U.S. - Colorado *20850*
     V   *20850*   U.S. - Utah *20850*

R   *Eriogonum correllii* Reveal *20850*
     I   *20850*   U.S. - Oklahoma *20850*
     R   *20850*   U.S. - Texas *20850*

R   *Eriogonum corymbosum* (Welsh) Reveal var. *revealianum* (Welsh) Reveal *20850*

R		20850 U.S. - Utah *20850*		
R	***Eriogonum covilleanum*** Eastw. *20850*			
	I	20850 U.S. - California *20850*		
V	***Eriogonum crocatum*** A. Davids. *20850*			
	V	20850 U.S. - California *20850*		
E	***Eriogonum cronquistii*** Reveal *20850*			
	I	20850 U.S. - Utah *20850*		
V	***Eriogonum crosbyae*** Reveal *20850*			
	R	20850 U.S. - Nevada *20850*		
	V	20850 U.S. - Oregon *20850*		
V	***Eriogonum cusickii*** M.E. Jones *20850*			
	V	20850 U.S. - Oregon *20850*		
V	***Eriogonum darrovii*** Kearney *20850*			
	E	20850 U.S. - Arizona *20850*		
	E	20850 U.S. - Nevada *20850*		
	E	20850 U.S. - Utah *20850*		
R	***Eriogonum dasyanthemum*** Torr. & Gray *20850*			
	I	20850 U.S. - California *20850*		
R	***Eriogonum deserticola*** S.Watson *20883, 20850, 19002*			
	E	20850 U.S. - Arizona *20850*		
	I	20850 U.S. - California *20850*		
	I	20883 Mexico *20883*		
R	***Eriogonum diclinum*** Reveal *20850*			
	I	20850 U.S. - California *20850*		
	V	20850 U.S. - Oregon *20850*		
R	***Eriogonum elegans*** Greene *20850*			
	I	20850 U.S. - California *20850*		
R	***Eriogonum ephedroides*** Reveal *20850*			
	E	20850 U.S. - Colorado *20850*		
		20850 U.S. - Utah *20850*		
E	***Eriogonum eremicola*** J.T. Howell & Reveal *20850*			
	E	20850 U.S. - California *20850*		
V	***Eriogonum eremicum*** Reveal *20850*			
	V	20850 U.S. - Utah *20850*		
E	***Eriogonum ericifolium*** Torr. & A. Gray var. ***thornei*** Reveal & Henrickson *20850*			
	E	20850 U.S. - California *20850*		
E	***Eriogonum esmeraldense*** S.Watson var. ***toiyabense*** J.T. Howell *20850*			
	V	20850 U.S. - Nevada *20850*		
V	***Eriogonum exilifolium*** Reveal *20850*			
	I	20850 U.S. - Colorado *20850*		
	V	20850 U.S. - Wyoming *20850*		
R	***Eriogonum fasciculatum*** Benth. *20850*			
	I	20850 U.S. - Arizona *20850*		
	I	20850 U.S. - California *20850*		
	I	20850 U.S. - Nevada *20850*		
	V	20850 U.S. - Utah *20850*		
V	***Eriogonum flavum*** Nutt. var. ***aquilinum*** Reveal *20850*			
	V	20850 U.S. - Alaska *20850*		
R	***Eriogonum foliosum*** S.Watson *20850, 9002*			
	V	20850 U.S. - California *20850*		
	?	Mexico *9002*		
V	***Eriogonum giganteum*** S.Watson *20850*			
	I	20850 U.S. - California *20850*		
V	***Eriogonum giganteum*** S.Watson var. ***compactum*** Dunkle *20850*			
	V	20850 U.S. - California *20850*		
V	***Eriogonum giganteum*** S.Watson var. ***formosum*** Brandeg. *20850*			
	V	20850 U.S. - California *20850*		
E	***Eriogonum glandulosum*** (Nutt.) Nutt. ex Benth. *20850*			
	I	20850 U.S. - California *20850*		
	I	20850 U.S. - Nevada *20850*		
R	***Eriogonum gracillimum*** S.Watson *20850*			
	I	20850 U.S. - California *20850*		
R	***Eriogonum grande*** Greene *20850*			
	I	20850 U.S. - California *20850*		
E	***Eriogonum grande*** Greene var. ***rubescens*** (Greene) Munz *20850*			
	E	20850 U.S. - California *20850*		
V	***Eriogonum grande*** Greene var. ***timorum*** Reveal *20850*			
	E	20850 U.S. - California *20850*		
V	***Eriogonum greggii*** Torr. & Gray *20883, 19002*			
	E	20850 U.S. - Texas *20850*		
	I	20883 Mexico *20883*		
E	***Eriogonum gypsophilum*** Woot. & Standl. *20850*			
	E	20850 U.S. - New Mexico *20850*		
V	***Eriogonum heermannii*** Munz var. ***clokeyi*** Reveal *20850*			
	V	20850 U.S. - Nevada *20850*		
V	***Eriogonum heermannii*** Munz var. ***floccosum*** Munz *20850*			
	I	20850 U.S. - California *20850*		
	E	20850 U.S. - Nevada *20850*		
R	***Eriogonum hemipterum*** (Torr.) S. Stokes *20850*			
	V	20850 U.S. - Texas *20850*		
V	***Eriogonum hirtellum*** J.T. Howell & Bacig. *20850*			
	V	20850 U.S. - California *20850*		
	I	20850 U.S. - Oregon *20850*		
R	***Eriogonum hirtiflorum*** Gray ex S.Watson *20850*			
	I	20850 U.S. - California *20850*		
R	***Eriogonum hoffmannii*** S. Stokes *20850*			
	I	20850 U.S. - California *20850*		
V	***Eriogonum hoffmannii*** S. Stokes var. ***hoffmannii*** *20850*			
	I	20850 U.S. - California *20850*		
V	***Eriogonum hoffmannii*** S. Stokes var. ***robustius*** S. Stokes *20850*			
	I	20850 U.S. - California *20850*		
E	***Eriogonum holmgrenii*** Reveal *20850*			
	E	20850 U.S. - Nevada *20850*		
E	***Eriogonum hylophilum*** Reveal & Brotherson *20850*			
	I	20850 U.S. - Utah *20850*		
R	***Eriogonum inerme*** (S.Watson) Jepson *20850*			
	I	20850 U.S. - California *20850*		
V	***Eriogonum jamesii*** Benth. var. ***rupicola*** Reveal *20850*			
	V	20850 U.S. - Utah *20850*		
V	***Eriogonum jonesii*** S.Watson *20850*			
	I	20850 U.S. - Arizona *20850*		
E	***Eriogonum kelloggii*** Gray *20850, 2457*			
	E	20850 U.S. - California *20850*		
R	***Eriogonum kennedyi*** C.L.Porter ex S.Watson var. ***alpigenum*** Munz & Johnston *20850*			
	R	20850 U.S. - California *20850*		
V	***Eriogonum kennedyi*** C.L. Porter ex S.Watson var. ***austromontanum*** Munz & Johnston *20850*			
	V	20850 U.S. - California *20850*		

E   *Eriogonum kennedyi* C.L. Porter ex S.Watson var. *pinicola* Reveal 20850
   E   20850   U.S. - California 20850

V   *Eriogonum kingii* Torr. & Gray 20850
   I   20850   U.S. - Idaho 20850
   I   20850   U.S. - Nevada 20850
   I   20850   U.S. - Oregon 20850

R   *Eriogonum lagopus* Rydb. 20850
   R   20850   U.S. - Montana 20850
   E   20850   U.S. - Wyoming 20850

V   *Eriogonum lancifolium* Reveal & Brotherson 20850
   20850   U.S. - Utah 20850

R   *Eriogonum latens* Jepson 20850
   I   20850   U.S. - California 20850
   I   20850   U.S. - Nevada 20850

V   *Eriogonum lemmonii* S.Watson 20850
   V   20850   U.S. - Nevada 20850

E   *Eriogonum lewisii* Reveal 20850
   V   20850   U.S. - Nevada 20850

V   *Eriogonum lobbii* Torr. & A.Gray var. *robustum* (E. Greene) M.E. Jones 20850
   V   20850   U.S. - Nevada 20850

V   *Eriogonum loganum* A. Nels. 20850
   V   20850   U.S. - Utah 20850

E   *Eriogonum lonchophyllum* Torr. & Gray var. *lonchophyllum* 20850
   I   20850   U.S. - Colorado 20850
   I   20850   U.S. - New Mexico 20850
   E   20850   U.S. - Utah 20850

R   *Eriogonum lonchophyllum* Torr. & Gray var. *saurinum* (Reveal) Welsh 20850
   E   20850   U.S. - Colorado 20850
   R   20850   U.S. - Utah 20850

R   *Eriogonum longifolium* Nutt. var. *gnaphalifolium* Gandog. 20850, 18134
   R   20850   U.S. - Florida 20850

E   *Eriogonum longifolium* Nutt. var. *harperi* (Goodman) Reveal 20850
   V   20850   U.S. - Alabama 20850
   I   20850   U.S. - Florida 20850
   I   20850   U.S. - Kentucky 20850
   E   20850   U.S. - Tennessee 20850

R   *Eriogonum luteolum* Greene var. *caninum* (Greene) Reveal 20850
   R   20850   U.S. - California 20850

V   *Eriogonum meledonum* Reveal 20850
   V   20850   U.S. - Idaho 20850

V   *Eriogonum microthecum* Nutt. var. *corymbosoides* Reveal 20850
   V   20850   U.S. - California 20850

E   *Eriogonum microthecum* Nutt. var. *johnstonii* Reveal 20850
   E   20850   U.S. - California 20850

V   *Eriogonum microthecum* Nutt. var. *panamintense* S. Stokes 20850
   V   20850   U.S. - California 20850

V   *Eriogonum mohavense* S.Watson 20850
   I   20850   U.S. - California 20850

V   *Eriogonum molestum* S.Watson 20850
   I   20850   U.S. - California 20850

E   *Eriogonum mortonianum* Reveal 20850

   E   20850   U.S. - Arizona 20850

V   *Eriogonum natum* Reveal 20850
   I   20850   U.S. - Utah 20850

V   *Eriogonum nealleyi* Coult. 20850
   V   20850   U.S. - Texas 20850

V   *Eriogonum nervulosum* (S. Stokes) Reveal 20850
   V   20850   U.S. - California 20850

V   *Eriogonum nortonii* Greene 20850
   V   20850   U.S. - California 20850

V   *Eriogonum nudum* Douglas ex Benth. var. *decurrens* (S. Stokes) M.L. Bowerman 20850
   V   20850   U.S. - California 20850

V   *Eriogonum nudum* Douglas ex Benth. var. *indictum* (Jepson) Reveal 20850
   V   20850   U.S. - California 20850

V   *Eriogonum nudum* Douglas ex Benth. var. *murinum* Reveal 20850
   V   20850   U.S. - California 20850

V   *Eriogonum nudum* Douglas ex Benth. var. *regirivum* Reveal & J. Stebbins 20850
   V   20850   U.S. - California 20850

V   *Eriogonum nutans* S.Watson var. *glabratum* Reveal 20850
   I   20850   U.S. - California 20850
   I   20850   U.S. - Nevada 20850

V   *Eriogonum nutans* S.Watson var. *nutans* 20850
   I   20850   U.S. - California 20850
   R   20850   U.S. - Nevada 20850
   I   20850   U.S. - Oregon 20850
   E   20850   U.S. - Utah 20850

R   *Eriogonum ochrocephalum* Reveal var. *alexanderae* Reveal 20850
   V   20850   U.S. - California 20850
   I   20850   U.S. - Nevada 20850

R   *Eriogonum ochrocephalum* Reveal var. *calcareum* (S. Stokes) M.E. Peck 20850
   Ex/E   20850   U.S. - Idaho 20850
   R   20850   U.S. - Oregon 20850

R   *Eriogonum ostlundii* M.E. Jones 20850
   20850   U.S. - Utah 20850

V   *Eriogonum ovalifolium* Nutt. var. *caelestinum* Reveal 20850
   V   20850   U.S. - Nevada 20850

V   *Eriogonum ovalifolium* Nutt. var. *eximium* (Tidestrom) J.T. Howell 20850
   V   20850   U.S. - California 20850
   I   20850   U.S. - Nevada 20850

E   *Eriogonum ovalifolium* Nutt. var. *vineum* (Small) Jepson 20850
   E   20850   U.S. - California 20850

E   *Eriogonum ovalifolium* Nutt. var. *williamsiae* Reveal 20850
   E   20850   U.S. - Nevada (Steamboat Hot Springs) 20850

R   *Eriogonum panamintense* Morton 20850
   I   20850   U.S. - California 20850
   I   20850   U.S. - Nevada 20850

R   *Eriogonum panguicense* (M.E. Jones) Reveal 20850
   R   20850   U.S. - Utah 20850

V   *Eriogonum panguicense* (M.E. Jones) Rev. var. *alpestre* (S. Stokes) Reveal 20850

I	20850 U.S. - Utah *20850*	

V   *Eriogonum pelinophilum* Reveal *20850*
     V   20850 U.S. - Colorado *20850*

V   *Eriogonum pharnaceoides* Reveal var. *cervinum*
     Reveal *20850*
     I   20850 U.S. - Arizona *20850*
     I   20850 U.S. - Nevada *20850*
     E   20850 U.S. - Utah *20850*

V   *Eriogonum polypodum* Small *20850*
     I   20850 U.S. - California *20850*

E   *Eriogonum prattenianum* Reveal & Shevock var. *avium*
     Reveal & Shevock *20850*
     E   20850 U.S. - California *20850*

V   *Eriogonum prociduum* Reveal *20850*
     V   20850 U.S. - California *20850*
     E   20850 U.S. - Nevada *20850*
     V   20850 U.S. - Oregon *20850*

V   *Eriogonum ripleyi* J.T. Howell *20850*
     V   20850 U.S. - Arizona *20850*

V   *Eriogonum rixfordii* S. Stokes *20850*
     I   20850 U.S. - California *20850*
     I   20850 U.S. - Nevada *20850*

R   *Eriogonum rubricaule* Tidestrom *20850*
     R   20850 U.S. - Nevada *20850*

R   *Eriogonum salicornioides* Gandog. *20850*
     R   20850 U.S. - Idaho *20850*
     I   20850 U.S. - Nevada *20850*
     R   20850 U.S. - Oregon *20850*

R   *Eriogonum saxatile* S.Watson *20850*
     I   20850 U.S. - California *20850*
     I   20850 U.S. - Nevada *20850*

R   *Eriogonum scabrellum* Reveal *20850*
     I   20850 U.S. - Colorado *20850*
     R   20850 U.S. - New Mexico *20850*
     E   20850 U.S. - Utah *20850*

R   *Eriogonum scopulorum* Reveal *20850*
     R   20850 U.S. - Oregon *20850*

E   *Eriogonum shockleyi* Reveal var. *packardiae*
     Reveal *20850*
     V   20850 U.S. - Idaho *20850*

E   *Eriogonum smithii* Reveal *20850*
     E   20850 U.S. - Utah *20850*

E   *Eriogonum soredium* Reveal *20850*
     E   20850 U.S. - Utah *20850*

R   *Eriogonum spathulatum* Gray *20850*
     R   20850 U.S. - Utah *20850*

V   *Eriogonum suffruticosum* S.Watson *20850*
     V   20850 U.S. - Texas *20850*

R   *Eriogonum tenellum* Benth. var. *ramosissimum*
     Benth. *20850*
     R   20850 U.S. - Texas *20850*

V   *Eriogonum thompsoniae* S.Watson var. *albiflorum*
     Reveal *20850*
     I   20850 U.S. - Arizona *20850*
     V   20850 U.S. - Utah *20850*

V   *Eriogonum thompsoniae* S.Watson var. *atwoodii*
     Reveal *20850*
     V   20850 U.S. - Arizona *20850*

E   *Eriogonum tiehmii* Reveal *20850*
     E   20850 U.S. - Nevada *20850*

R   *Eriogonum tripodum* Greene *20850*

     V   20850 U.S. - California *20850*

Ex/E   *Eriogonum truncatum* Torr. & Gray *20850, 14662*
     Ex/E   20850 U.S. - California *20850*

R   *Eriogonum tumulosum* (Barneby) Reveal *20850*
     V   20850 U.S. - Colorado *20850*
     V   20850 U.S. - Utah *20850*

V   *Eriogonum twisselmannii* (J.T. Howell) Reveal *20850*
     V   20850 U.S. - California *20850*

V   *Eriogonum umbellatum* Torr. var. *humistratum*
     Reveal *20850*
     V   20850 U.S. - California *20850*

V   *Eriogonum umbellatum* Torr. var. *torreyanum*
     (A.Gray) M.E. Jones *20850*
     V   20850 U.S. - California *20850*
     I   20850 U.S. - Oregon *20850*

R   *Eriogonum ursinum* S.Watson *20850*
     I   20850 U.S. - California *20850*
     I   20850 U.S. - Oregon *20850*

R   *Eriogonum viridescens* Heller *20850*
     I   20850 U.S. - California *20850*

V   *Eriogonum viscidulum* J.T. Howell *20850*
     V   20850 U.S. - Nevada *20850*

R   *Eriogonum visheri* A. Nels. *20850*
     V   20850 U.S. - North Dakota *20850*
     R   20850 U.S. - South Dakota *20850*

E   *Eriogonum wrightii* Torr. ex Benth. var. *olanchense*
     (J.T. Howell) Reveal *20850*
     E   20850 U.S. - California *20850*

R   *Eriogonum zionis* J.T.Howell var. *coccineum*
     J.T.Howell *20850*
     R   20850 U.S. - Arizona *20850*

V   *Eriogonum zionis* J.T.Howell var.
     zionis *20850*
     E   20850 U.S. - Arizona *20850*
     V   20850 U.S. - Utah *20850*

E   *Gilmania luteola* (Coville) Coville *20850*
     E   20850 U.S. - California *20850*

V   *Goodmania luteola* (Parry) Reveal & Ertter *20850*
     R   20850 U.S. - California *20850*
     E   20850 U.S. - Nevada *20850*

R   *Hollisteria lanata* S.Watson *20850*
     I   20850 U.S. - California *20850*

R   *Mucronea perfoliata* (Gray) Heller *20850*
     I   20850 U.S. - California *20850*

E   *Muehlenbeckia astonii* *19305*
     E   19305 New Zealand - North Is. *19305*
     E   19305 New Zealand - South Is. *19305*

I   *Oxygonum ellipticum* R. Graham *5926*
     I   5926 Tanzania *5926*

I   *Oxygonum leptopus* Mildbr. *5926*
     I   5926 Tanzania *5926*

I   *Oxygonum lobatum* R. Graham *5926*
     I   5926 Tanzania *5926*

R   *Oxygonum schliebenii* Mildbr. *7959*
     R   Tanzania *7959*

I   *Oxygonum subfastigiatum* R. Graham *5926*
     I   5926 Tanzania *5926*

V   *Oxytheca emarginata* Hall *20850*
     I   20850 U.S. - California *20850*

V   *Oxytheca parishii* Parry var. *abramsii* (McGregor)

	Munz *20850*			
V	*20850*	U.S. - California	*20850*	

E   *Oxytheca parishii* **Parry var.** *goodmaniana* **Ertter** *20850*

| E | *20850* | U.S. - California | *20850* |

V   *Oxytheca watsonii* **Torr. & Gray** *20850*

| E | *20850* | U.S. - California | *20850* |
| V | *20850* | U.S. - Nevada | *20850* |

V   *Persicaria elatior* **(R.Br.) Sojak** *20681*

| I | *20681* | Australia - New South Wales | *20681* |
| I | *20681* | Australia - Queensland | *20681* |

R   *Polygonella basiramia* **(Small) Nesom & Bates** *20850, 7983*

| R | *20850* | U.S. - Florida (Polk & Highlands Counties) *20850* |

V   *Polygonella macrophylla* **Small** *20850*

| E | *20850* | U.S. - Alabama | *20850* |
| V | *20850* | U.S. - Florida | *20850* |

R   *Polygonella myriophylla* **(Small) Horton** *20850, 17890*

| R | *20850* | U.S. - Florida (L. Wales Ridge) | *20850* |

V   *Polygonella parksii* **Cory** *20850*

| V | *20850* | U.S. - Texas | *20850* |

R   *Polygonum afyonicum* **E. Leblebici & Y. Gemici** *12840*

| R | *12840* | Turkey | *12840* |

E   *Polygonum albanicum* **Jáv.** *20178, 20171*

| E | *20178* | Albania | *20178* |

I   *Polygonum amgense* **V. Michaleva & V. Perfiljeva** *11552*

| I | *5942* | Russia (Far East) - Khabarovsk | *5942* |

I   *Polygonum arianum* **Grigor.** *5942*

| I | *5942* | Turkmenistan | *5942* |

R   *Polygonum aschersonianum* **H.Gross** *20171*

| R | | former European USSR |

R   *Polygonum galapagense* **Caruel** *11117*

| R | | Ecuador - Galapagos | *11117* |

R   *Polygonum glaucum* **Nutt.** *20883, 20850, 19002*

I	*20883*	France - St Pierre & Miquelon	*20883*
I	*20850*	U.S. - Alabama	*20850*
Ex/E	*20850*	U.S. - Connecticut	*20850*
Ex/E	*20850*	U.S. - Delaware	*20850*
I	*20850*	U.S. - Florida	*20850*
E	*20850*	U.S. - Georgia	*20850*
I	*20850*	U.S. - Maine	*20850*
E	*20850*	U.S. - Maryland	*20850*
R	*20850*	U.S. - Massachusetts	*20850*
I	*20850*	U.S. - Mississippi	*20850*
E	*20850*	U.S. - New Jersey	*20850*
R	*20850*	U.S. - New York	*20850*
E	*20850*	U.S. - North Carolina	*20850*
E	*20850*	U.S. - Rhode Is.	*20850*
I	*20850*	U.S. - South Carolina	*20850*
E	*20850*	U.S. - Virginia	*20850*

R   *Polygonum icaricum* **Rech.f.** *20171*

| R | | Greece |

R   *Polygonum idaeum* **Hayek** *20171*

| R | *20731* | Greece - Crete | *20731* |

E   *Polygonum marinense* **Mert. & Raven** *20850*

| E | *20850* | U.S. - California | *20850* |

R   *Polygonum obtusifolium* **Tackh. & Boulos**

| R | | Egypt |

I   *Polygonum ovczinnikovii* **Czukav.** *5942*

| I | *5942* | Tajikistan | *5942* |

V   *Polygonum paralongum* **Coode & Cullen** *12840*

| V | *12840* | Turkey | *12840* |

E   *Polygonum polygaloides* **(L.C. Wheeler) Hickman ssp.** *esotericum* **(L.C. Wheeler) Hickman** *20850*

| E | *20850* | U.S. - California | *20850* |
| I | *20850* | U.S. - Oregon | *20850* |

R   *Polygonum salebrosum* **Coode & Cullen** *12840*

| R | *12840* | Turkey | *12840* |

R   *Polygonum striatulum* **B.L. Robins.** *20850*

I	*20850*	U.S. - Louisiana	*20850*
I	*20850*	U.S. - Oklahoma	*20850*
R	*20850*	U.S. - Texas	*20850*

R   *Rheum rhaponticum* **L.** *5204, 20171*

| R | *5204* | Bulgaria | *5204* |
| R | | Norway |

R   *Rumex amanus* **Rech.** *12840*

| R | *12840* | Turkey | *12840* |

R   *Rumex azoricus* **Rech.f.** *8000, 20171*

| R | | Portugal - Azores | *8000* |

V   *Rumex beringensis* **Jurtzev & Petrovsky** *20850*

| E | *20850* | U.S. - Alaska | *20850* |

V   *Rumex bithynicus* **Rech. f.** *12840*

| V | *12840* | Turkey | *12840* |

E   *Rumex costaricensis* **Rech.f.** *9037*

| E | *19754* | Costa Rica | *9037* |

R   *Rumex drummondii* **Meisner** *20681*

| R | *20681* | Australia - Western Australia | *20681* |

R   *Rumex gracilescens* **Rech.** *12840*

| R | *12840* | Turkey | *12840* |

V   *Rumex krausei* **Jurtzev & Petrovsky** *20850, 21309*

| R | *21309* | Russia (E.Europe) - North | *21309* |
| E | *20850* | U.S. - Alaska | *20850* |

I   *Rumex limoniastrum* **Jaub. & Spach.** *20146*

| I | *20146* | Oman (north) | *20146* |

V   *Rumex nepalensis* **Sprengel var.** *andreanus* **(Makino) Kitam.** *10572*

| V | *10572* | Japan | *10572* |

R   *Rumex olympicus* **Boiss.** *12840*

| R | *12840* | Turkey | *12840* |

V   *Rumex orthoneurus* **Rech. f.** *20850*

| V | *20850* | U.S. - Arizona | *20850* |
| V | *20850* | U.S. - New Mexico | *20850* |

R   *Rumex peruanus* **Reichb.f.** *18200*

| R | *12468* | Peru | *18200* |

E   *Rumex rothschildianus* **Aarons. ex Evenari** *8895*

| E | | Israel (Sharon & Philistean Plains) *8895* |

V   *Rumex rupestris* **Le Gall** *8000, 20171*

V	*20528*	France (coastal)	*8000*
V	*17781*	Spain (north-west)	*8000*
V	*5387*	United Kingdom	*19232*
V	*17781*	United Kingdom - Channel Is.	*17781*

R   *Rumex tmoleus* **Boiss.** *12840*

| R | *12840* | Turkey | *12840* |

Ex/E   *Rumex tomentella* **Rech. f.** *20850*

| Ex/E | *20850* | U.S. - New Mexico | *20850* |

E   *Rumex tunetanus* **G. Barratte & Murb.**

| E | | Tunisia |

R   *Ruprechtia jamesonii* **Meisn.** *18200*

| R | *16943* | Ecuador | *16943* |
| R | *19962* | Peru | *18200* |

V   *Systenotheca vortriedei* **(Brandeg.) Reveal & Hardham** *20850*

I   *20850* U.S. - California *20850*

Portulacaceae

Number of genera:	20
Number of species:	500
Recorded threatened species:	52 (10%)

Cosmopolitan, especially western North America and Andes.

R   *II*   *Anacampseros comptonii* **Pillans** *20604, 20306*
     R   *20604* South Africa - Cape Province *20604*

R   *II*   *Anacampseros filamentosa* (Haw.) Sims ssp.
     filamentosa *20306, 20604*
     R   *20604* South Africa - Cape Province *20306*
     R   *20604* South Africa - Orange Free State (Griqualand
          west) *20306*

R   *II*   *Anacampseros filamentosa* (Haw.) Sims ssp. *tomentosa*
     (A. Berger) Gerbaulet *20306*
     R   *20604* Namibia *20306*

R   *II*   *Anacampseros lanceolata* (Haw.) Sweet ssp.
     lanceolata *20306*
     R   *20803* Botswana *20803*
     R   *20604* South Africa - Cape Province *20604*

R   *II*   *Anacampseros lanceolata* (Haw.) Sweet ssp. *nebrownii*
     (Poelln.) Gerbaulet *20306*
     R   *20604* South Africa - Cape Province *20306*

R   *II*   *Anacampseros papyracea* E. Meyer ex Fenzl ssp.
     papyracea *20306, 20604*
     R   *20604* South Africa - Cape Province *20306*

R   *II*   *Anacampseros scopata* G.Will. *20604, 20308*
     R   *20604* South Africa - Cape Province *20604*

R   *Avonia mallei* G.Will. *20604*
     R   *20604* South Africa - Cape Province *20604*

E   *Calandrinia alba* (Ruiz Lopez & Pavon) DC. *18200*
     E   *9446* Peru *18200*

E   *Calandrinia feltonii* Skottsb. *19744*
     E   *20272* Falkland Is. (West Point Island) *19744*

E   *Calandrinia galapagosa* H. St. John *11117*
     E   *14980* Ecuador - Galapagos (San Cristobal)
          11117

E   *Cistanthe pulchella* (Eastw.) Hershkovitz *20850*
     E   *20850* U.S. - California *20850*

E   *Cistanthe pygmaea* (Parish ex Rydb.)
     Hershkovitz *20850*
     I   *20850* U.S. - California *20850*

V   *Cistanthe tweedyi* (Gray) Hershkovitz *20850*
     E   *20850* Canada - British Columbia *20850*
     I   *20850* U.S. - Washington *20850*

R   *Claytonia arctica* M.F. Adams *20850, 1034*
     E   *20850* Canada - Yukon Territory *20850*
     E   *20850* U.S. - Alaska *20850*

R   *Claytonia gypsophiloides* Fisch. & C.A. Mey. *20850*
     I   *20850* U.S. - California *20850*

R   *Claytonia lanceolata* Pursh var. *pacifica*
     McNeill *20850*
     I   *20850* Canada - British Columbia *20850*
     E   *20850* U.S. - Washington *20850*

E   *Claytonia lanceolata* Pursh var. *peirsonii* Munz &
     Johnston *20850*
     E   *20850* U.S. - California *20850*

R   *Claytonia megarhiza* (A.Gray) Parry ex S.Watson var.
     nivalis (English) C.L. Hitchc. *20850*

I   *20850* U.S. - Washington *20850*

E   *Claytonia ogilviensis* McNeill *20850, 1034*
     E   *20850* Canada - Yukon Territory *20850*

R   *Claytonia palustris* Swanson & Kelley *20850*
     R   *20850* U.S. - California *20850*

V   *Claytonia saxosa* Brandeg. *20850, 10701*
     I   *20850* U.S. - California *20850*

R   *Claytonia vassilievii* ssp. *petrovskyi* Jurtz. et M.
     Griczuk *20085, 21309*
     R   *20085* Russia (E.Europe) - North *20085*

R   *Claytoniella vassilievii* (Kusen.) Jurtzev *8001*
     R   Arctic CIS (Arctic Anadyr) *6930*

R   *Claytoniella vassilievii* (Kuzen.) Jurtz. ssp.
     vassilievii *20085, 21309*
     R   *20085* Russia (E.Europe) - North *20085*

V   *Lewisia cantelovii* J.T. Howell *20850*
     V   *20850* U.S. - California *20850*

V   *Lewisia congdonii* (Rydb.) S. Clay *20850*
     V   *20850* U.S. - California *20850*

R   *Lewisia cotyledon* (S. Wats.) B. L. Robins. var.
     cotyledon *20850*
     I   *20850* U.S. - California *20850*
     R   *20850* U.S. - Oregon *20850*

V   *II*   *Lewisia cotyledon* (S.Watson) Robinson var. *heckneri*
     (Morton) Munz *20850*
     V   *20850* U.S. - California *20850*

V   *Lewisia disepala* Rydb. *20850*
     I   *20850* U.S. - California *20850*

V   *Lewisia longipetala* (Piper) S. Clay *20850*
     V   *20850* U.S. - California *20850*

E   *II*   *Lewisia maguirei* A. Holmgren *20850, 15658*
     E   *20850* U.S. - Nevada *20850*

V   *II*   *Lewisia serrata* Heckard & Stebbins *20850, 15658*
     V   *20850* U.S. - California *20850*

R   *Lewisia sierrae* Ferris *20850*
     I   *20850* U.S. - California *20850*
     I   *20850* U.S. - Nevada *20850*

E   *Lewisia stebbinsii* Gankin & Hildreth *20850*
     E   *20850* U.S. - California *20850*

R   *Montia bostockii* (Porsild) Welsh *20850, 1034*
     E   *20850* Canada - British Columbia *20850*
     V   *20850* Canada - Yukon Territory *20850*
     V   *20850* U.S. - Alaska *20850*

R   *Montia fontana* L. ssp. *variabilis* S.M.
     Walters *20850, 20171*
     I   *20850* Canada - British Columbia *20850*
     I   *20850* U.S. - California *20850*
     I   *20850* U.S. - Nevada *20850*

R   *Montia howellii* S.Watson *20850, 10701*
     V   *20850* Canada - British Columbia *20850*
     Ex/E *20850* U.S. - California *20850*
     V   *20850* U.S. - Oregon *20850*
     V   *20850* U.S. - Washington *20850*

E   *Portulaca aurantiaca* Proctor *20883*
     E   *20883* Jamaica *20883*

E   *Portulaca biloba* Urban *20850*
     E   *20850* U.S. - Georgia *20850*
     I   *20850* U.S. - Virginia *20850*

R   *Portulaca boninensis* Tuy. *8622*
     R   *19134* Japan - Kazan Retto *8622*
     R   *19134* Japan - Ogasawara-shoto *8622*

E	*Portulaca caulerpoides* Britt. & Wilson ex Britt. 20883, 20850, 8058	
	I	20850 U.S. - Florida 20850
	I	20883 Puerto Rico 20883
R	*Portulaca insularis* Hosok. 20511	
	R	20511 Taiwan 20511
E	*Portulaca molokiniensis* Hobdy 20850, 14209	
	E	20850 U.S. - Hawaii (Kaho`olawe) 20850
E	*Portulaca sclerocarpa* Gray 20850, 14209	
	E	20850 U.S. - Hawaii 20850
R	*Portulaca smallii* P. Wilson 20850	
	R	20850 U.S. - Georgia 20850
	I	20850 U.S. - Louisiana 20850
	V	20850 U.S. - North Carolina 20850
	I	20850 U.S. - South Carolina 20850
	E	20850 U.S. - Virginia 20850
V	*Portulaca trianthemoides* Bremek. 20604	
	V	20604 South Africa - Transvaal 20604
R	*Portulaca tuberculata* Leon 5607	
	R	19105 Cuba (Granma) 5607
E	*Portulaca villosa* Cham. 20850, 14209	
	E	20850 U.S. - Hawaii 20850
R	*Sedopsis filsonii* (J.H.Willis) J.H.Willis 20681	
	R	20681 Australia - Northern Territory 20681
R	*Talinum calcaricum* Ware 20850	
	V	20850 U.S. - Alabama 20850
	E	20850 U.S. - Kentucky 20850
	R	20850 U.S. - Tennessee 20850
V	*Talinum confertiflorum* Greene 20850	
	I	20850 U.S. - New Mexico 20850
R	*Talinum longipes* Woot. & Standl. 20850	
	R	20850 U.S. - New Mexico 20850
	I	20850 U.S. - Texas 20850
V	*Talinum marginatum* Greene 20883, 20850, 8058	
	E	20850 U.S. - Arizona 20850
	I	20883 Mexico 20883
R	*Talinum mengesii* W. Wolf 20850	
	V	20850 U.S. - Alabama 20850
	R	20850 U.S. - Georgia 20850
	E	20850 U.S. - North Carolina 20850
	I	20850 U.S. - South Carolina 20850
	E	20850 U.S. - Tennessee 20850
	E	20850 U.S. - Virginia 20850
V	*Talinum sediforme* Poelln. 20850, 10701	
	V	20850 Canada - British Columbia 20850
	V	20850 U.S. - Washington 20850
E	*Talinum thompsonii* Atwood & Welsh 20850	
	E	20850 U.S. - Utah 20850
V	*Talinum validulum* Greene 20850	
	V	20850 U.S. - Arizona 20850

Primulaceae

Number of genera:	30
Number of species:	1,000
Recorded threatened species:	112 (11%)

Mostly temperate and cold Northern Hemisphere; montane tropical.

R	*Anagallis brevipes* P. Taylor 7959	
	R	5926 Tanzania (Rungwe) 7959
R	*Anagallis kingaensis* Engl. 7959	
	R	5926 Tanzania 7959
R	*Anagallis oligantha* P. Taylor 7862	

	R	Malawi 7862
I	*Androsace aizoon* Duby	
	I	India - Jammu & Kashmir
V	*Androsace alaskana* Coville & Standl. ex Hulten 20850, 1034	
	I	20850 Canada - British Columbia 20850
	E	20850 Canada - Yukon Territory 20850
	V	20850 U.S. - Alaska 20850
R	*Androsace brevis* (Hegetschw.) Ces. 18264, 20171	
	R	18264 Italy (Lombardy) 18264
	E	18154 Switzerland 18154
I	*Androsace bryomorpha* Lipsky 5942	
	I	5942 Tajikistan 5942
R	*Androsace chaixii* Gren. & Godr. 20171	
	R	France (mountains in south-east)
R	*Androsace cylindrica* DC. 8000, 20171	
	V	France (central Pyrenees) 8000
	R	Spain (central Pyrenees) 8000
I	*Androsace cylindrica* DC. ssp. *cylindrica* 20528	
	V	20528 France (Pyrenees) 20528
	I	20528 Spain (Aragon) 20528
I	*Androsace cylindrica* DC. ssp. *hirtella* (Dufour) Greuter & Burdet 20528,	
	I	20528 France (Pyrenees) 20528
	I	20528 Spain 20528
V	*Androsace elongata* L. ssp. *acuta* (Greene) G.T. Robbins 20850	
	V	20850 U.S. - California 20850
	I	20850 U.S. - Nevada 20850
	Ex/E	20850 U.S. - Oregon 20850
I	*Androsace koso-poljanskii* Ovcz. 5942, 20171	
	I	5942 Ukraine 5942
I	*Androsace mucronifolia* Watt	
	I	India - Jammu & Kashmir
V	*Androsace rioxana* Segura	
	V	Spain
R	*Androsace semiperennis* Jurtz. 20085, 21309	
	R	20085 Russia (E.Europe) - North 20085
I	*Ardisiandra primuloides* Knuth 5926	
	I	5926 Tanzania 5926
V	*Coris hispanica* Lange 20171	
	V	Spain
V	II *Cyclamen cilicicum* Boiss. & Heldr. 12840	
	V	12840 Turkey (S. Anatolia) 12840
	Cyclamen fatrense Halda and Soják 21389, 19839	
	I	17821 Czech Republic 17821
	V	19321 Slovakia (Vel'ká Fatra & Tatry Mts.) 6951
V	II *Cyclamen intaminatum* (Meikle) Grey-Wilson 15934	
	V	19873 Turkey (WC & WS) 15934
	Cyclamen kuznetzovii Kotov & Czernova 21389	
	E	20655 Ukraine - Crimea 5942
I	II *Cyclamen libanoticum* Hildebr. 15934	
	I	15934 Lebanon (scattered mountain localities north-east of Beirut) 15934
V	II *Cyclamen mirabile* Hildebr. 15934	
	V	14071 Turkey (south-west Anatolia) 8619
I	II *Cyclamen pseudibericum* Hildebr. 12840	
	I	15934 Turkey (South, Amanus and Anti-Taurus) 12840

V	*II*	*Cyclamen rohlfsianum* Aschers. *15934*
	V	Libya (Cyrenaica, Benghazi to Derna) *15934*
V	*II*	*Cyclamen trochopteranthum* Schwarz *12840*
	V	Turkey (SW Anatolia) *15934*
I		*Dionysia hissarica* Lipsky *5942*
	I	*5942* Tajikistan *5942*
I		*Dionysia involucrata* Zaprj. *5942*
	I	*5942* Tajikistan *5942*
I		*Dionysia mira* Wendelbo *20146*
	I	*20146* Oman (Hajar Mts.) *20146*
R		*Dionysia teucroides* Davis & Wendelbo *12840*
	R	*12840* Turkey *12840*
V		*Dodecatheon austrofrigidum* sp. nov. ined. *20850*
	V	*20850* U.S. - Oregon *20850*
	E	*20850* U.S. - Washington *20850*
V		*Dodecatheon clevelandii* Greene *20850*
	I	*20850* U.S. - California *20850*
R		*Dodecatheon frenchii* (Vasey) Rydb. *20850*
	V	*20850* U.S. - Arkansas *20850*
	R	*20850* U.S. - Illinois *20850*
	V	*20850* U.S. - Indiana *20850*
	R	*20850* U.S. - Kentucky *20850*
	E	*20850* U.S. - Missouri *20850*
	I	*20850* U.S. - Wisconsin *20850*
R		*Dodecatheon hansenii* (Greene) H.J. Thompson *20850*
	I	*20850* U.S. - California *20850*
R		*Dodecatheon poeticum* Henderson *20850*
	R	*20850* U.S. - Oregon *20850*
	V	*20850* U.S. - Washington *20850*
V		*Dodecatheon pulchellum* (Raf.) Merr. ssp. *macrocarpum* (Gray) Taylor & MacBryde *20850*
	I	*20850* Canada - British Columbia *20850*
	V	*20850* U.S. - Alaska *20850*
	I	*20850* U.S. - Oregon *20850*
	I	*20850* U.S. - Washington *20850*
R		*Dodecatheon subalpinum* Eastw. *20850*
	I	*20850* U.S. - California *20850*
V		*Douglasia alaskana* (Coville & Standl. ex Hulten) S. Kelso *20850*
	E	*20850* Canada - British Columbia *20850*
	I	*20850* Canada - Yukon Territory *20850*
	I	*20850* U.S. - Alaska *20850*
R		*Douglasia arctica* Hook. *20850*
	I	*20850* Canada - Mackenzie *20850*
	I	*20850* Canada - Yukon Territory *20850*
	V	*20850* U.S. - Alaska *20850*
R		*Douglasia beringensis* Kelso, Yurtsev & Murray *20085, 21309*
R		*Douglasia gormanii* Constance *20850*
	E	*20850* Canada - British Columbia *20850*
	I	*20850* Canada - Yukon Territory *20850*
	V	*20850* U.S. - Alaska *20850*
R		*Douglasia idahoensis* D. Henderson *20850*
	V	*20850* U.S. - Idaho *20850*
V		*Douglasia nivalis* Lindl. *20850*
	I	*20850* Canada - Alberta *20850*
	E	*20850* Canada - British Columbia *20850*
	I	*20850* U.S. - Washington *20850*
V		*Douglasia nivalis* Lindl. var. *nivalis* *20850*
	I	*20850* Canada - Alberta *20850*
	I	*20850* Canada - British Columbia *20850*
	I	*20850* U.S. - Washington *20850*

R		*Lysimachia asperulifolia* Poir. *20850*
	R	*20850* U.S. - North Carolina *20850*
	E	*20850* U.S. - South Carolina *20850*
R		*Lysimachia cousiniana* Coss. & Durieu *10488*
	R	*14958* Algeria *10488*
E		*Lysimachia daphnoides* (Gray) Hbd. *20850, 14209*
	E	*20850* U.S. - Hawaii (Kaua`i) *20850*
E		*Lysimachia filifolia* Forbes *20850, 14209*
	E	*20850* U.S. - Hawaii (Kaua`i & O`ahu) *20850*
Ex/E		*Lysimachia forbesii* Rock *20850, 14209*
	Ex/E	*20850* U.S. - Hawaii (O`ahu) *20850*
R		*Lysimachia fraseri* Duby *20850*
	E	*20850* U.S. - Alabama *20850*
	E	*20850* U.S. - Georgia *20850*
	E	*20850* U.S. - Illinois *20850*
	E	*20850* U.S. - Kentucky *20850*
	V	*20850* U.S. - North Carolina *20850*
	E	*20850* U.S. - South Carolina *20850*
	E	*20850* U.S. - Tennessee *20850*
I		*Lysimachia garrettii* Franchet *19120*
	I	*19120* Thailand *19120*
E		*Lysimachia glutinosa* Rock *20850, 14209*
	E	*20850* U.S. - Hawaii (Kaua`i - Koke`e) *20850*
V		*Lysimachia graminea* (Greene) Hand.-Maz. *20850*
	V	*20850* U.S. - Alabama *20850*
E		*Lysimachia kalalauensis* Skottsberg *20850, 14209*
	E	*20850* U.S. - Hawaii (Kaua`i) *20850*
V		*Lysimachia liukiuensis* Hatus. *10573*
	V	*10573* Japan *10573*
R		*Lysimachia loomisii* Torr. *20850*
	I	*20850* U.S. - Georgia *20850*
	R	*20850* U.S. - North Carolina *20850*
	I	*20850* U.S. - South Carolina *20850*
E		*Lysimachia lydgatei* Hbd. *20850, 14209*
	E	*20850* U.S. - Hawaii (West Maui) *20850*
E		*Lysimachia maxima* (R. Knuth) St. John *20850, 14209*
	E	*20850* U.S. - Hawaii (east Moloka`i) *20850*
E		*Lysimachia minoricensis* Rodr. *15316, 20171*
	E	*20645* Spain - Balearic Is. (Minorca) *15316*
V		*Lysimachia ohsumiensis* Hara *10573*
	V	*10573* Japan *10573*
I		*Lysimachia rapensis* F.Brown *20845*
	I	*20845* French Polynesia - Tubuai Is. (Rapa) *20845*
V		*Lysimachia remyi* Hillebrand *14209*
	V	*14209* U.S. - Hawaii (Moloka`i & Maui) *14209*
V		*Lysimachia tashiroi* Makino *10573*
	V	*10573* Japan *10573*
E		*Lysimachia venosa* (Wawra) St. John *20850, 14209*
	E	*20850* U.S. - Hawaii (Mt Wai`ale`ale) *20850*
E		*Primula alcalina* Cholewa & D. Henderson *20850*
	E	*20850* U.S. - Idaho *20850*
R		*Primula allionii* Loisel. *18264, 20171*
	R	*20528* France (Alpes-Maritimes) *19174*
	R	*18264* Italy (Piedmont, Liguria) *20804*
V		*Primula angustifolia* Torr. *20850*
	I	*20850* U.S. - Colorado *20850*
	I	*20850* U.S. - New Mexico *20850*
V		*Primula apennina* Widmer *8000, 20171*
	V	*18264* Italy (N. Apenninies of Toscana & Emilia-Romagna) *19997*

I	***Primula beringensis*** (A. Pors.) Jurtzev *5942*
	I *5942* Russia (Far East) - Magadan (south) *5942*
R	***Primula boveana*** Decne. *10269*
	R Egypt (Sinai) *10269*
E	***Primula capillaris*** N.& A. Holmgren *20850*
	E *20850* U.S. - Nevada *20850*
I	***Primula clarkei*** Watt
	I India - Jammu & Kashmir
R	***Primula cuneifolia*** Ledeb. var. ***heterodonta*** (Franchet) Makino *10573*
	R *10573* Japan *10573*
R	***Primula daonensis*** (Leyb.) Leyb. *18154, 20171*
	I Austria *8000*
	I Italy *8000*
	R *18154* Switzerland *18154*
I	***Primula darialica*** Rupr. *5942*
	I *5942* Russia - North Caucasus *5942*
R	***Primula davisii*** W.W. Sm. *12840*
	R *12840* Turkey *12840*
R	***Primula deorum*** Velen. *5204, 20171*
	R *5204* Bulgaria (Rila Mt.) *5204*
E	***Primula domensis*** Kass & Welsh *20850*
	E *20850* U.S. - Utah *20850*
I	***Primula drumondiana*** Craib.
	I India - Himachal Pradesh
I	***Primula elatior*** (L.) Hill ssp. ***tatrensis*** (Domin) Soó *19321*
	I *19321* Slovakia *19321*
I	***Primula eugeniae*** Feodorov *5942*
	I *5942* Kyrgyzstan *5942*
Ex/E	***Primula flexuosa*** Turkev. *5942*
	Ex/E *5942* Tajikistan *5942*
R	***Primula frondosa*** Janka *5204, 20171*
	R *5204* Bulgaria (central) *5204*
R	***Primula glaucescens*** Moretti *8000, 20171*
	R *18264* Italy *19997*
I	***Primula halleri*** J.F. Gmelin ssp. ***platyphylla*** O. Schwarz *19321*
	I *19321* Slovakia *19321*
R	***Primula hidakana*** Miyabe & Kubo var. ***hidakana*** *10573*
	R *10573* Japan *10573*
R	***Primula hidakana*** Miyabe var. ***kamuiana*** Hara *10573*
	R *10573* Japan *10573*
I	***Primula juliae*** Kusnezov *5942*
	I *5942* Azerbaijan *5942*
R	***Primula kisoana*** Miq. var. ***shikokiana*** Makino *10573*
	R *10573* Japan *10573*
R	***Primula kitaibeliana*** Schott *20171*
	R *21091* Bosnia & Herzegovina *21091*
	R (former) Yugoslavia
R	***Primula komarovii*** Losinsk. *20171*
	R former European USSR *6930*
I	***Primula larsenii*** C. H. Hu *19120*
	I *19120* Thailand *19120*
R	***Primula longipes*** Freyn & Sint. *12840*
	R *12840* Turkey *12840*

R	***Primula macrocarpa*** Maxim. *10573*
	R *10573* Japan *10573*
E	***Primula maguirei*** L.O. Williams *20850*
	E *20850* U.S. - Utah (Logan Canyon, Cache County) *20850*
I	***Primula megaseifolia*** Boiss. & Bal. ex Boiss. *5942*
	I *5942* Georgia *5942*
R	***Primula minkwitziae*** W.W. Smith
	R former USSR *6930*
E	***Primula minutissima*** Jack ex Duby *14768*
	E India - Jammu & Kashmir (Apharwat Mts) *14768*
R	***Primula modesta*** Bisset & S. Moore var. ***matsumurae*** (Pititm.) Takeda *10573*
	R *10573* Japan *10573*
E	***Primula nevadensis*** N. Holmgren *20850*
	E *20850* U.S. - Nevada *20850*
V	***Primula palinuri*** Petagna *8000, 20171*
	V *18264* Italy (Campania, Basilicata, Calabria) *19997*
R	***Primula reinii*** Franchet & Sav. var. ***kitadakensis*** (Hara) Ohwi *10573*
	R *10573* Japan *10573*
R	***Primula reinii*** Franchet & Sav. var. ***myogiensis*** Hara *10573*
	R *10573* Japan *10573*
R	***Primula reinii*** Franchet & Sav. var. ***reinii*** *10573*
	R *10573* Japan *10573*
E	***Primula reinii*** Franchet & Sav. var. ***rhodotricha*** Ohwi *10573*
	E *10573* Japan *10573*
I	***Primula siamensis*** Craib *19120*
	I Thailand (Doi Chiengdao)
R	***Primula sorachiana*** Miyabe & Tatew. *10573*
	R *10573* Japan *10573*
R	***Primula suffrutescens*** Gray *20850*
	I *20850* U.S. - California *20850*
R	***Primula takedana*** Tatew. *10573*
	R *10573* Japan *10573*
V	***Primula tschuktschorum*** Kjellm. *20850, 21309*
	I *20850* Canada - Yukon Territory *20850*
	V *20850* U.S. - Alaska (Bering Straits) *20850*
R	***Primula vulgaris*** Huds. ssp. ***balearica*** (Willk.) W.W. Smith & Forrest *20171*
	R Spain - Balearic Is.
E	***Primula wulfeniana*** Schott ssp. ***baumganteniana*** (Degen & Moesz) Ludi *19266, 20171*
	E *19949* Romania (south Carpathians) *19266*
R	***Primula yuparensis*** Takeda *10573*
	R *10573* Japan *10573*
V	***Samolus vagans*** Greene *20850*
	I *20850* U.S. - Arizona *20850*
R	***Soldanella calabrella*** Kress *18264*
	R *18264* Italy (Calabria) *18264*
R	***Soldanella minima*** Hoppe ssp. ***samnitica*** Cristofolini & Pignatti *18264, 20171*
	R *18264* Italy (Abruzzi) *18264*
R	***Soldanella pindicola*** Hausskn. *20171*
	R Greece

V   *Soldanella villosa* Darracq *8000, 20171*
      V   *20528* France (west Pyrenees) *8000*
      V   *20874* Spain (Pyrenees) *8000*

Proteaceae

Number of genera:	75
Number of species:	1,000
Recorded threatened species:	353 (35%)

Tropical and subtropical, especially warmer Southern Hemisphere.

V   *Adenanthos cunninghamii* Meisner *20681*
      V   *20681* Australia - Western Australia *20681*

R   *Adenanthos detmoldii* F.Muell. *20681*
      R   *20681* Australia - Western Australia *20681*

V   *Adenanthos dobagii* E.C.Nelson *20681*
      V   *20681* Australia - Western Australia *20681*

V   *Adenanthos ellipticus* A.S.George *20681*
      V   *20681* Australia - Western Australia *20681*

V   *Adenanthos eyrei* E.C.Nelson *20681*
      V   *20681* Australia - Western Australia *20681*

V   *Adenanthos ileticos* E.C.Nelson *20681*
      V   *20681* Australia - Western Australia *20681*

R   *Adenanthos labillardierei* E.C.Nelson *20681*
      R   *20681* Australia - Western Australia *20681*

V   *Adenanthos pungens* Meisner ssp. *effusus*
      E.C.Nelson *20681*
      V   *20681* Australia - Western Australia *20681*

V   *Adenanthos pungens* Meisner ssp.
      pungens *20681*
      V   *20681* Australia - Western Australia *20681*

V   *Alloxylon flammeum* P.Weston & Crisp *20681*
      V   *20681* Australia - Queensland *20681*

R   *Alloxylon pinnatum* (Maiden & Betche) P.Weston &
      Crisp *20681*
      I   *20681* Australia - New South Wales *20681*
      I   *20681* Australia - Queensland *20681*

R   *Austromuellera trinervia* C.White *20681*
      R   *20681* Australia - Queensland *20681*

R   *Banksia benthamiana* C.Gardner *20681*
      R   *20681* Australia - Western Australia *20681*

E   *Banksia brownii* R.Br. *20681*
      E   *20681* Australia - Western Australia *20681*

R   *Banksia chamaephyton* A.S.George *20681*
      R   *20681* Australia - Western Australia *20681*

R   *Banksia conferta* A.S.George *20681*
      I   *20681* Australia - New South Wales *20681*
      I   *20681* Australia - Queensland *20681*

V   *Banksia cuneata* A.S.George *20681*
      V   *20681* Australia - Western Australia *20681*

R   *Banksia elegans* Meisner *20681*
      R   *20681* Australia - Western Australia *20681*

V   *Banksia goodii* R.Br. *20681*
      V   *20681* Australia - Western Australia *20681*

R   *Banksia laevigata* Meisner ssp.
      laevigata *20681*
      R   *20681* Australia - Western Australia *20681*

R   *Banksia meisneri* Lehm. var. *ascendens*
      A.S.George *20681*
      R   *20681* Australia - Western Australia *20681*

V   *Banksia oligantha* A.S.George *20681*
      V   *20681* Australia - Western Australia *20681*

R   *Banksia plagiocarpa* A.S.George *20681*
      R   *20681* Australia - Queensland *20681*

R   *Banksia solandri* R.Br. *20681*
      R   *20681* Australia - Western Australia *20681*

V   *Banksia sphaerocarpa* R.Br. var. *dolichostyla*
      A.S.George *20681*
      V   *20681* Australia - Western Australia *20681*

V   *Banksia tricuspis* Meisner *20681*
      V   *20681* Australia - Western Australia *20681*

V   *Banksia verticillata* R.Br. *20681*
      V   *20681* Australia - Western Australia *20681*

E   *Beauprea congesta* Virot *20893*
      E   *20893* New Caledonia *20893*

V   *Beauprea crassifolia* Virot *20893*
      V   *20893* New Caledonia *20893*

I   *Beauprea penariensis* Guillaumin *20802*
      I   *20802* New Caledonia *20802*

R   *Buckinghamia ferruginiflora* D.Foreman &
      B.Hyland *20681*
      R   *20681* Australia - Queensland *20681*

R   *Conospermum burgessiorum* L.A.S.Johnson &
      McGillivray *20681*
      I   *20681* Australia - New South Wales *20681*
      I   *20681* Australia - Queensland *20681*

V   *Conospermum toddii* F.Muell. *20681*
      V   *20681* Australia - Western Australia *20681*

R   *Conospermum undulatum* Lindley *20681*
      R   *20681* Australia - Western Australia *20681*

R   *Darlingia ferruginea* Bailey *20681*
      R   *20681* Australia - Queensland *20681*

E   *Diastella buekii* (Gand.) Rourke *20604*
      E   *20604* South Africa - Cape Province *20604*

R   *Diastella fraterna* Rourke *20604*
      R   *20604* South Africa - Cape Province *20604*

R   *Diastella myrtifolia* (Thunb.) Salisb. ex
      Knight *20604*
      R   *20604* South Africa - Cape Province *20604*

V   *Diastella parilis* Salisb. ex Knight *20604*
      V   *20604* South Africa - Cape Province *20604*

V   *Diastella proteoides* (L.) Druce *20604*
      V   *20604* South Africa - Cape Province *20604*

R   *Diastella thymelaeoides* (P.J.Bergius) Rourke ssp.
      meridiana Rourke *20604*
      R   *20604* South Africa - Cape Province *18023*

R   *Diastella thymelaeoides* (P.J.Bergius) Rourke ssp.
      thymelaeoides *20604*
      R   *20604* South Africa - Cape Province *18023*

R   *Dryandra comosa* Meisner *20681*
      R   *20681* Australia - Western Australia *20681*

R   *Dryandra concinna* R.Br. *20681*
      R   *20681* Australia - Western Australia *20681*

R   *Dryandra foliolata* R.Br. *20681*
      R   *20681* Australia - Western Australia *20681*

E   *Dryandra mimica* A.S.George *20681*
      E   *20681* Australia - Western Australia *20681*

E   *Dryandra montana* (A.S.George) *20681*
      E   *20681* Australia - Western Australia *20681*

R   *Dryandra polycephala* Benth. *20681*
     R   *20681*   Australia - Western Australia *20681*

R   *Dryandra preissii* Meisner *20681*
     R   *20681*   Australia - Western Australia *20681*

R   *Dryandra pulchella* Meisner *20681*
     R   *20681*   Australia - Western Australia *20681*

R   *Dryandra sclerophylla* Meisner *20681*
     R   *20681*   Australia - Western Australia *20681*

R   *Dryandra serra* R.Br. *20681*
     R   *20681*   Australia - Western Australia *20681*

V   *Dryandra serratuloides* Meisner ssp. *perissa* A.S.George *20681*
     V   *20681*   Australia - Western Australia *20681*

V   *Dryandra serratuloides* Meisner ssp. *serratuloides* *20681*
     V   *20681*   Australia - Western Australia *20681*

R   *Dryandra shanklandiorum* R.P.Randall *20681*
     R   *20681*   Australia - Western Australia *20681*

V   *Floydia praealta* (F.Muell.) L.A.S.Johnson & B.G.Briggs *20681*
     I   *20681*   Australia - New South Wales *20681*
     I   *20681*   Australia - Queensland *20681*

R   *Franklandia triaristata* Benth. *20681*
     R   *20681*   Australia - Western Australia *20681*

E   *Grevillea acanthifolia* A.Cunn. ssp. *paludosa* *20681*
     E   *20681*   Australia - New South Wales *20681*

R   *Grevillea acanthifolia* Cunn. ssp. *stenomera* (F.Muell. ex Benth.) McGillivray *20681*
     R   *20681*   Australia - New South Wales *20681*

R   *Grevillea acerata* McGillivray *20681*
     R   *20681*   Australia - New South Wales *20681*

R   *Grevillea adenotricha* McGillivray *20681*
     R   *20681*   Australia - Western Australia *20681*

R   *Grevillea asteriscosa* Diels *20681*
     R   *20681*   Australia - Western Australia *20681*

V   *Grevillea banyabba* P.Olde & N.Marriott *20681*
     V   *20681*   Australia - New South Wales *20681*

R   *Grevillea barklyana* Benth. ssp. *barklyana* *20681*
     R   *20681*   Australia - Victoria *20681*

R   *Grevillea barklyana* F.Muell. ex Benth. ssp. *macleayana* McGillivray *20681*
     R   *20681*   Australia - New South Wales *20681*

E   *Grevillea batrachioides* McGillivray *20681, 14223*
     E   *20681*   Australia - Western Australia *20681*

R   *Grevillea baxteri* R.Br. *20681*
     R   *20681*   Australia - Western Australia *20681*

E   *Grevillea beadleana* McGillivray *20681*
     E   *20681*   Australia - New South Wales *20681*

R   *Grevillea bedggoodiana* McGillivray *20681*
     R   *20681*   Australia - Victoria *20681*

R   *Grevillea benthamiana* McGillivray *20681*
     R   *20681*   Australia - Northern Territory *20681*

R   *Grevillea brevis* P.Olde & N.Marriott *20681*
     R   *20681*   Australia - Northern Territory *20681*

E   *Grevillea caleyi* R.Br. *20681*
     E   *20681*   Australia - New South Wales *20681*

E   *Grevillea calliantha* R.Makinson & P.Olde *20681*
     E   *20681*   Australia - Western Australia *20681*

E   *Grevillea christiniae* McGillivray *20681*
     E   *20681*   Australia - Western Australia *20681*

R   *Grevillea cirsiifolia* Meisner *20681*
     R   *20681*   Australia - Western Australia *20681*

R   *Grevillea confertifolia* F.Muell. *20681*
     R   *20681*   Australia - Victoria *20681*

R   *Grevillea cyranostigma* McGillivray *20681*
     R   *20681*   Australia - Queensland *20681*

R   *Grevillea diminuta* L.A.S.Johnson *20681*
     I   *20681*   Australia - Capital Territory *20681*
     I   *20681*   Australia - New South Wales *20681*

R   *Grevillea dissecta* (McGillivray) P.Olde & N.Marriott *20681*
     R   *20681*   Australia - Western Australia *20681*

R   *Grevillea drummondii* Meisner *20681*
     R   *20681*   Australia - Western Australia *20681*

E   *Grevillea dryandroides* C.Gardner ssp. *dryandroides* *20681*
     E   *20681*   Australia - Western Australia *20681*

V   *Grevillea dryandroides* C.Gardner ssp. *hirsuta* P.Olde & N.Marriott *20681*
     V   *20681*   Australia - Western Australia *20681*

R   *Grevillea erectiloba* F.Muell. *20681*
     R   *20681*   Australia - Western Australia *20681*

V   *Grevillea evansiana* McKee *20681*
     V   *20681*   Australia - New South Wales *20681*

E   *Grevillea flexuosa* (Lindley) Meisner *20681, 14223*
     E   *20681*   Australia - Western Australia *20681*

R   *Grevillea floripendula* R.V.Smith *20681*
     R   *20681*   Australia - Victoria *20681*

R   *Grevillea glabrescens* P.Olde & N.Marriott *20681*
     R   *20681*   Australia - Northern Territory *20681*

V   *Grevillea glossadenia* McGillivray *20681*
     V   *20681*   Australia - Queensland *20681*

V   *Grevillea guthrieana* P.Olde & N.Marriott *20681*
     V   *20681*   Australia - New South Wales *20681*

E   *Grevillea iaspicula* McGillivray *20681*
     E   *20681*   Australia - New South Wales *20681*

V   *Grevillea inconspicua* Diels *20681*
     V   *20681*   Australia - Western Australia *20681*

V   *Grevillea infecunda* McGillivray *20681*
     V   *20681*   Australia - Victoria *20681*

V   *Grevillea infundibularis* A.S.George *20681*
     V   *20681*   Australia - Western Australia *20681*

V   *Grevillea involucrata* A.S.George *20681*
     V   *20681*   Australia - Western Australia *20681*

R   *Grevillea jephcottii* J.H.Willis *20681*
     R   *20681*   Australia - Victoria *20681*

R   *Grevillea johnsonii* McGillivray *20681*
     R   *20681*   Australia - New South Wales *20681*

V   *Grevillea kennedyana* F.Muell. *20681*
     I   *20681*   Australia - New South Wales *20681*
     I   *20681*   Australia - Queensland *20681*

R   *Grevillea linsmithii* McGillivray *20681*
     I   *20681*   Australia - New South Wales *20681*
     I   *20681*   Australia - Queensland *20681*

R   *Grevillea longicuspis* McGillivray *20681*
     R   *20681*   Australia - Northern Territory *20681*

R	*Grevillea longifolia* R.Br. *20681*	
	R	*20681* Australia - New South Wales *20681*
E	*Grevillea masonii* P.Olde & N.Marriott *20681*	
	E	*20681* Australia - New South Wales *20681*
E	*Grevillea maxwellii* McGillivray *20681*	
	E	*20681* Australia - Western Australia *20681*
E	*Grevillea mccutcheonii* Keighery & Cranfield ms. *20681*	
	E	*20681* Australia - Western Australia *20681*
R	*Grevillea microstegia* Molyneux *20681*	
	R	*20681* Australia - Victoria *20681*
R	*Grevillea miniata* Fitzg. *20681*	
	R	*20681* Australia - Western Australia *20681*
V	*Grevillea mollis* P.Olde & Molyneux *20681*	
	V	*20681* Australia - New South Wales *20681*
R	*Grevillea montis-cole* R.V.Smith ssp. *brevistyla* R.V.Smith *20681*	
	R	*20681* Australia - Victoria *20681*
R	*Grevillea montis-cole* R.V.Smith ssp. *montis-cole* *20681*	
	R	*20681* Australia - Victoria *20681*
R	*Grevillea muricata* J.Black *20681*	
	R	*20681* Australia - South Australia *20681*
R	*Grevillea obtecta* Molyneux *20681*	
	R	*20681* Australia - Victoria *20681*
E	*Grevillea obtusiflora* R.Br. *20681*	
	E	*20681* Australia - New South Wales *20681*
R	*Grevillea oldei* McGillivray *20681*	
	R	*20681* Australia - New South Wales *20681*
R	*Grevillea olivacea* A.S.George *20681*	
	R	*20681* Australia - Western Australia *20681*
R	*Grevillea pimeleoides* Fitzg. *20681*	
	R	*20681* Australia - Western Australia *20681*
R	*Grevillea prostrata* C.Gardner & A.S.George *20681*	
	R	*20681* Australia - Western Australia *20681*
E	*Grevillea pythara* P.Olde & N.Marriott *20681*	
	E	*20681* Australia - Western Australia *20681*
V	*Grevillea quadricauda* P.Olde & N.Marriott *20681*	
	I	*20681* Australia - New South Wales *20681*
	I	*20681* Australia - Queensland *20681*
R	*Grevillea renwickiana* F.Muell. *20681*	
	R	*20681* Australia - New South Wales *20681*
R	*Grevillea repens* Meisner *20681*	
	R	*20681* Australia - Victoria *20681*
V	*Grevillea rhizomatosa* P.Olde & N.Marriott *20681*	
	V	*20681* Australia - New South Wales *20681*
R	*Grevillea ripicola* A.S.George *20681*	
	R	*20681* Australia - Western Australia *20681*
V	*Grevillea rivularis* L.A.S.Johnson & McGillivray *20681*	
	V	*20681* Australia - New South Wales *20681*
R	*Grevillea rogersii* Maiden *20681*	
	R	*20681* Australia - South Australia *20681*
R	*Grevillea rudis* Meisner *20681*	
	R	*20681* Australia - Western Australia *20681*
R	*Grevillea saccata* Benth. *20681*	
	R	*20681* Australia - Western Australia *20681*
E	*Grevillea scapigera* A.S.George *20681*	

	E	*20681* Australia - Western Australia *20681*
V	*Grevillea scortechinii* (F.Muell. ex Scortech.) F.Muell. ssp. *sarmentosa* (Blakely & McKie) McGillivray *20681*	
	V	*20681* Australia - New South Wales *20681*
E	*Grevillea scortechinii* (F.Muell. ex Scortech.) F.Muell. ssp. *scortechinii* *20681*	
	E	*20681* Australia - Queensland *20681*
V	*Grevillea shiressii* Blakely *20681*	
	V	*20681* Australia - New South Wales *20681*
R	*Grevillea singuliflora* F.Muell. *20681*	
	R	*20681* Australia - Queensland *20681*
R	*Grevillea steiglitziana* Wakef. *20681*	
	R	*20681* Australia - Victoria *20681*
R	*Grevillea tetrapleura* McGillivray *20681*	
	R	*20681* Australia - Western Australia *20681*
R	*Grevillea thelemanniana* Huegel ssp. *thelemanniana* *20681*	
	R	*20681* Australia - Western Australia *20681*
V	*Grevillea treueriana* F.Muell. *20681*	
	V	*20681* Australia - South Australia *20681*
V	*Grevillea venusta* R.Br. *20681*	
	V	*20681* Australia - Queensland *20681*
R	*Grevillea versicolor* McGillivray *20681*	
	R	*20681* Australia - Northern Territory *20681*
E	*Grevillea wilkinsonii* R.Makinson *20681*	
	E	*20681* Australia - New South Wales *20681*
E	*Grevillea williamsonii* F.Muell. *20681*	
	E	*20681* Australia - Victoria *20681*
R	*Grevillea willisii* R.V.Smith & McGillivray *20681*	
	R	*20681* Australia - Victoria *20681*
E	*Hakea aculeata* A.S.George *20681*	
	E	*20681* Australia - Western Australia *20681*
R	*Hakea aenigma* W.R.Barker & Haegi *20681*	
	R	*20681* Australia - South Australia *20681*
R	*Hakea constablei* L.A.S.Johnson *20681*	
	R	*20681* Australia - New South Wales *20681*
V	*Hakea fraseri* R.Br. *20681*	
	V	*20681* Australia - New South Wales *20681*
R	*Hakea grammatophylla* (F.Muell.) F.Muell. *20681*	
	R	*20681* Australia - Northern Territory *20681*
V	*Hakea megalosperma* Meisner *20681*	
	V	*20681* Australia - Western Australia *20681*
R	*Hakea neurophylla* Meisner *20681*	
	R	*20681* Australia - Western Australia *20681*
E	*Hakea pulvinifera* L.A.S.Johnson *20681, 5465*	
	E	*20681* Australia - New South Wales *20681*
R	*Hakea standleyensis* Maconochie *20681*	
	R	*20681* Australia - Northern Territory *20681*
V	*Hakea trineura* F.Muell. *20681*	
	V	*20681* Australia - Queensland *20681*
R	*Helicia blakei* D.Foreman *20681*	
	R	*20681* Australia - Queensland *20681*
E	*Helicia ceylanica* Gardner *8021*	
	E	*20013* Sri Lanka *8021*
R	*Helicia grayi* D.Foreman *20681*	
	R	*20681* Australia - Queensland *20681*
R	*Helicia lamingtoniana* (F.Bailey) C.White & L.S.Smith *20681*	

R   *20681*   Australia - Queensland *20681*

R   *Helicia lewisensis* D.Foreman *20681*
     R   *20681*   Australia - Queensland *20681*

I   *Helicia nilagirica* Beddome
     I   India - Kerala (Walaghat)
     I   India - Tamil Nadu

R   *Helicia recurva* D.Foreman *20681*
     R   *20681*   Australia - Queensland *20681*

E   *Helicia shweliensis* W. Smith *17617*
     E   *17617*   China - Yunnan *11139*

I   *Helicia travancorica* Beddome ex Hook.f.
     I   India - Kerala (Travancore Hills)
     I   India - Tamil Nadu (Tirunelveli Hills)

I   *Heliciopsis velutina* (Prain) Sleum. *19209*
     I   *19209*   Malaysia - Peninsular Malaysia (Terengganu, Pahang, Selangor/Wilayah Persekutuan, Johor) *19209*

R   *Hicksbeachia pinnatifolia* F.Muell. *20681*
     I   *20681*   Australia - New South Wales *20681*
     I   *20681*   Australia - Queensland *20681*

R   *Hollandaea sayeriana* (F.Muell.) L.S.Smith *20681*
     R   *20681*   Australia - Queensland *20681*

V   *Isopogon fletcheri* F.Muell. *20681*
     V   *20681*   Australia - New South Wales *20681*

E   *Isopogon uncinatus* R.Br. *20681*
     E   *20681*   Australia - Western Australia *20681*

V   *Kermadecia pronyensis* (Guillaumin) Guillaumin *20893*
     V   *20893*   New Caledonia *20893*

E   *Lambertia echinata* R.Br. ssp. *echinata* *20681*
     E   *20681*   Australia - Western Australia *20681*

E   *Lambertia fairallii* Keighery *20681*
     E   *20681*   Australia - Western Australia *20681*

E   *Lambertia orbifolia* C.Gardner *20681*
     E   *20681*   Australia - Western Australia *20681*

R   *Lambertia rariflora* Meisner *20681*
     R   *20681*   Australia - Western Australia *20681*

R   *Leucadendron argenteum* (L.) R.Br. *20604*
     R   *20604*   South Africa - Cape Province *20604*

E   *Leucadendron bonum* I.Williams *20604*
     E   *20604*   South Africa - Cape Province *20604*

R   *Leucadendron brunioides* Meissner var. *flumenlupinum* I. Williams *20604*
     R   *20604*   South Africa - Cape Province *20604*

R   *Leucadendron cadens* I.Williams *20604*
     R   *20604*   South Africa - Cape Province *20604*

E   *Leucadendron chamelaea* (Lam.) I.Williams *20604*
     E   *20604*   South Africa - Cape Province *20604*

R   *Leucadendron concavum* I.Williams *20604*
     R   *20604*   South Africa - Cape Province *20604*

E   *Leucadendron coriaceum* E.Phillips & Hutch. *20604*
     E   *20604*   South Africa - Cape Province *20604*

V   *Leucadendron corymbosum* P.J.Bergius *20604*
     V   *20604*   South Africa - Cape Province *20604*

E   *Leucadendron cryptocephalum* L.Guthrie *20604*
     E   *20604*   South Africa - Cape Province *20604*

V   *Leucadendron daphnoides* (Thunb.) Meisn. *20604*
     V   *20604*   South Africa - Cape Province *20604*

R   *Leucadendron diemontianum* I.Williams *20604*
     R   *20604*   South Africa - Cape Province *20604*

R   *Leucadendron discolor* E.Phillips & Hutch. *20604*

R   *20604*   South Africa - Cape Province *20604*

R   *Leucadendron dregei* E.Mey. ex Meisn. *20604*
     R   *20604*   South Africa - Cape Province *20604*

V   *Leucadendron elimense* E.Phillips ssp. *elimense* *20604*
     V   *20604*   South Africa - Cape Province *20604*

E   *Leucadendron elimense* E.Phillips ssp. *salteri* I. Williams *20604*
     E   *20604*   South Africa - Cape Province *20604*

E   *Leucadendron elimense* E.Phillips ssp. *vyeboomense* I. Williams *20604*
     E   *20604*   South Africa - Cape Province *20604*

E   *Leucadendron flexuosum* I.Williams *20604*
     E   *20604*   South Africa - Cape Province *20604*

E   *Leucadendron floridum* R.Br. *20604*
     E   *20604*   South Africa - Cape Province *20604*

V   *Leucadendron galpinii* E.Phillips & Hutch. *20604*
     V   *20604*   South Africa - Cape Province *20604*

E   *Leucadendron globosum* (Kenn. ex Andrews) I.Williams *20604*
     E   *20604*   South Africa - Cape Province *20604*

E   *Leucadendron laxum* I.Williams *20604*
     E   *20604*   South Africa - Cape Province *20604*

E   *Leucadendron levisanus* (L.) P.J.Bergius *20604*
     E   *20604*   South Africa - Cape Province *20604*

R   *Leucadendron loeriense* I.Williams *20604*
     R   *20604*   South Africa - Cape Province *20604*

E   *Leucadendron macowanii* E.Phillips *20604*
     E   *20604*   South Africa - Cape Province *20604*

R   *Leucadendron nervosum* E.Phillips & Hutch. *20604*
     R   *20604*   South Africa - Cape Province *20604*

R   *Leucadendron nobile* I.Williams *20604*
     R   *20604*   South Africa - Cape Province *20604*

V   *Leucadendron olens* I.Williams *20604*
     V   *20604*   South Africa - Cape Province *20604*

V   *Leucadendron orientale* I.Williams *20604*
     V   *20604*   South Africa - Cape Province *20604*

V   *Leucadendron platyspermum* R.Br. *20604*
     V   *20604*   South Africa - Cape Province *20604*

R   *Leucadendron pondoense* A.E.van Wyk *20604*
     R   *20604*   South Africa - Cape Province *20604*

R   *Leucadendron radiatum* E.Phillips & Hutch. *20604*
     R   *20604*   South Africa - Cape Province *20604*

R   *Leucadendron remotum* I.Williams *20604*
     R   *20604*   South Africa - Cape Province *20604*

R   *Leucadendron roodii* E.Phillips *20604*
     R   *20604*   South Africa - Cape Province *20604*

R   *Leucadendron rourkei* I.Williams *20604*
     R   *20604*   South Africa - Cape Province *20604*

E   *Leucadendron sericeum* (Thunb.) R.Br. *20604*
     E   *20604*   South Africa - Cape Province *20604*

R   *Leucadendron singulare* I.Williams *20604*
     R   *20604*   South Africa - Cape Province *20604*

V   *Leucadendron sorocephalodes* E.Phillips & Hutch. *20604*
     V   *20604*   South Africa - Cape Province *20604*

Ex   *Leucadendron spirale* (Salisb. ex Knight) I.Williams *20604, 6180*

| | Ex | 20604 | South Africa - Cape Province 20604 |

E   *Leucadendron stelligerum* I.Williams 20604
     E   20604   South Africa - Cape Province 20604

R   *Leucadendron strobilinum* (L.) Druce 20604
     R   20604   South Africa - Cape Province 20604

E   *Leucadendron thymifolium* (Salisb. ex Knight) I.Williams 20604
     E   20604   South Africa - Cape Province 20604

V   *Leucadendron tradouwense* I.Williams 20604
     V   20604   South Africa - Cape Province 20604

E   *Leucadendron verticillatum* (Thunb.) Meisn. 20604
     E   20604   South Africa - Cape Province 20604

E   *Leucospermum arenarium* Rycroft 20604
     E   20604   South Africa - Cape Province 20604

R   *Leucospermum cordatum* E.Phillips 20604
     R   20604   South Africa - Cape Province 20604

V   *Leucospermum formosum* (Andrews) Sweet 20604
     V   20604   South Africa - Cape Province 20604

V   *Leucospermum fulgens* Rourke 20604
     V   20604   South Africa - Cape Province 20604

V   *Leucospermum grandiflorum* (Salisb.) R.Br. 20604
     V   20604   South Africa - Cape Province 20604

R   *Leucospermum gueinzii* Meisn. 20604
     R   20604   South Africa - Cape Province 20604

R   *Leucospermum hamatum* Rourke 20604
     R   20604   South Africa - Cape Province 20604

E   *Leucospermum harpagonatum* Rourke 20604
     E   20604   South Africa - Cape Province 20604

V   *Leucospermum heterophyllum* (Thunb.) Rourke 20604
     V   20604   South Africa - Cape Province 20604

V   *Leucospermum innovans* Rourke 20604
     V   20604   South Africa - Cape Province 20604
     V   20604   South Africa - Natal 20604

R   *Leucospermum muirii* E.Phillips 20604
     R   20604   South Africa - Cape Province 20604

V   *Leucospermum parile* (Salisb. ex Knight) Sweet 20604
     V   20604   South Africa - Cape Province 20604

R   *Leucospermum pedunculatum* Klotzsch 20604
     R   20604   South Africa - Cape Province 20604

R   *Leucospermum pluridens* Rourke 20604
     V   20604   South Africa - Cape Province 20604

R   *Leucospermum profugum* Rourke 20604
     R   20604   South Africa - Cape Province 20604

R   *Leucospermum saxosum* S.Moore 20604
     R   20604   South Africa - Transvaal 20604

R   *Leucospermum secundifolium* Rourke 20604
     R   20604   South Africa - Cape Province 20604

V   *Leucospermum tomentosum* (Thunb.) R.Br. 20604
     V   20604   South Africa - Cape Province 20604

E   *Lomatia tasmanica* W.M.Curtis 20681
     E   20681   Australia - Tasmania 20681

E   *Macadamia angustifolia* Virot 20893
     E   20893   New Caledonia 20893

V   *Macadamia claudiensis* C.L.Gross & B.Hyland 20681
     V   20681   Australia - Queensland 20681

R   *Macadamia grandis* C.L.Gross & B.Hyland 20681
     R   20681   Australia - Queensland 20681

R   *Macadamia heyana* (F.Bailey) Sleumer 20681
     R   20681   Australia - Queensland 20681

V   *Macadamia integrifolia* Maiden & Betche 20681, 19911
     V   20681   Australia - Queensland 20681

E   *Macadamia jansenii* C.L.Gross & P.Weston 20681
     E   20681   Australia - Queensland 20681

V   *Macadamia neurophylla* (Guillaumin) Virot 20893
     V   20893   New Caledonia 20893

V   *Macadamia ternifolia* F.Muell. 20681
     V   20681   Australia - Queensland 20681

V   *Macadamia tetraphylla* L.A.S.Johnson 20681
     I   20681   Australia - New South Wales 20681
     I   20681   Australia - Queensland 20681

R   *Macadamia vieillardii* (Brongn. & Gris) Sleumer
     R   New Caledonia

E   *Malagasia alticola* (Capuron) L. Johnson & B. Briggs 19140
     E   19140   Madagascar 19140

R   *Mimetes arboreus* Rourke 20604
     R   20604   South Africa - Cape Province 20604

R   *Mimetes argenteus* Salisb. ex Knight 20604
     R   20604   South Africa - Cape Province 20604

R   *Mimetes capitulatus* (L.) R.Br. 20604
     R   20604   South Africa - Cape Province 20604

R   *Mimetes chrysanthus* Rourke 20604
     R   20604   South Africa - Cape Province 20604

V   *Mimetes hirtus* (L.) Salisb. ex Knight 20604
     V   20604   South Africa - Cape Province 20604

R   *Mimetes hottentoticus* E.Phillips & Hutch. 20604
     R   20604   South Africa - Cape Province 20604

R   *Mimetes palustris* Salisb. ex Knight 20604
     R   20604   South Africa - Cape Province 20604

R   *Mimetes pauciflorus* R.Br. 20604
     R   20604   South Africa - Cape Province 20604

R   *Mimetes splendidus* Salisb. ex Knight 20604
     R   20604   South Africa - Cape Province 20604

Ex   *Mimetes stokoei* E.Phillips & Hutch. 20604, 6180
     Ex   20604   South Africa - Cape Province 20604

R   *Orites milliganii* Meisner 20681
     R   20681   Australia - Tasmania 20681

R   *Orites myrtoidea* (Poepp. & Endl.) Benth. ex Hook. 13875
     R   13875   Chile 13875

R   I   *Orothamnus zeyheri* Pappe ex Hook.f. 20604, 14908
     R   20604   South Africa - Cape Province 20604

V   *Paranomus abrotanifolius* Salisb. ex Knight 20604
     V   20604   South Africa - Cape Province 20604

R   *Paranomus adiantifolius* Salisb. ex Knight 20604
     R   20604   South Africa - Cape Province 20604

R   *Paranomus capitatus* (R.Br.) Kuntze 20604
     R   20604   South Africa - Cape Province 20604

R   *Paranomus centaureoides* Levyns 20604
     R   20604   South Africa - Cape Province 20604

R   *Paranomus diversifolius* Phillips 20803, 20803
     R   South Africa - Cape Province

R   *Paranomus esterhuyseniae* Levyns 20604
     R   20604   South Africa - Cape Province 20604

V   *Paranomus longicaulis* Salisb ex Knight 20604
     V   20604   South Africa - Cape Province 20604

V	*Paranomus reflexus* (E.Phillips & Hutch.) N.E.Br. *20604*		
	V	*20604*	South Africa - Cape Province *20604*
R	*Paranomus roodebergensis* (Compton) Levyns *20604*		
	R	*20604*	South Africa - Cape Province *20604*
R	*Paranomus spicatus* (P.J.Bergius) Kuntze *20604*		
	R	*20604*	South Africa - Cape Province *20604*
V	*Persoonia acerosa* Sieber ex Schultes & Schultes f. *20681*		
	V	*20681*	Australia - New South Wales *20681*
V	*Persoonia bargoensis* P.Weston & L.A.S.Johnson *20681*		
	V	*20681*	Australia - New South Wales *20681*
R	*Persoonia brevifolia* (Benth.) L.A.S.Johnson & P.Weston *20681*		
	I	*20681*	Australia - New South Wales *20681*
	I	*20681*	Australia - Victoria *20681*
R	*Persoonia daphnoides* Cunn. ex R.Br. *20681*		
	I	*20681*	Australia - New South Wales *20681*
	I	*20681*	Australia - Queensland *20681*
V	*Persoonia glaucescens* Sieber ex Schultes & Schultes f. *20681*		
	V	*20681*	Australia - New South Wales *20681*
Ex	*Persoonia laxa* L.A.S.Johnson & P.Weston *20681*		
	Ex	*20681*	Australia - New South Wales *20681*
V	*Persoonia marginata* R.Br. *20681*		
	V	*20681*	Australia - New South Wales *20681*
E	*Persoonia mollis* R.Br. ssp. *maxima* S.Krauss & L.A.S.Johnson *20681*		
	E	*20681*	Australia - New South Wales *20681*
R	*Persoonia mollis* R.Br. ssp. *revoluta* (Schultes) S.Krauss & L.A.S.Johnson *20681*		
	R	*20681*	Australia - New South Wales *20681*
R	*Persoonia moscalii* Orch. *20681*		
	R	*20681*	Australia - Tasmania *20681*
R	*Persoonia muelleri* (P.Parm.) Orch. var. *angustifolia* (Benth.) Orch. *20681*		
	R	*20681*	Australia - Tasmania *20681*
R	*Persoonia muelleri* (P.Parm.) Orch. var. *densifolia* Orch. *20681*		
	R	*20681*	Australia - Tasmania *20681*
E	*Persoonia nutans* R.Br. *20681*		
	E	*20681*	Australia - New South Wales *20681*
R	*Persoonia oxycoccoides* Sieber ex Sprengel *20681*		
	R	*20681*	Australia - New South Wales *20681*
R	*Persoonia procumbens* L.A.S.Johnson & P.Weston *20681*		
	R	*20681*	Australia - New South Wales *20681*
Ex	*Persoonia prostrata* R.Br. *20681*		
	Ex	*20681*	Australia - Queensland *20681*
R	*Persoonia recedens* Gandoger *20681*		
	R	*20681*	Australia - New South Wales *20681*
R	*Persoonia rufa* L.A.S.Johnson & P.Weston *20681*		
	R	*20681*	Australia - New South Wales *20681*
R	*Persoonia terminalis* L.A.S.Johnson & P.Weston ssp. *recurva* L.A.S.Johnson & P.Weston *20681*		
	I	*20681*	Australia - New South Wales *20681*
	I	*20681*	Australia - Queensland *20681*
R	*Persoonia terminalis* L.A.S.Johnson & P.Weston ssp. *terminalis* L.A.S.Johnson & P.Weston *20681*		
	R	*20681*	Australia - New South Wales *20681*

R	*Persoonia volcanica* P.Weston & L.A.S.Johnson *20681*		
	I	*20681*	Australia - New South Wales *20681*
	I	*20681*	Australia - Queensland *20681*
E	*Petrophile latericola* Keighery ms. *20681*		
	E	*20681*	Australia - Western Australia *20681*
V	*Protea angustata* R.Br. *20604*		
	V	*20604*	South Africa - Cape Province *20604*
R	*Protea aristata* E.Phillips *20604*		
	R	*20604*	South Africa - Cape Province *20604*
I	*Protea asymmetrica* Beard *7765*		
	I		Zimbabwe *7765*
R	*Protea aurea* (Burm.f.) Rourke ssp. *potbergensis* Rourke *20604*		
	R	*20604*	South Africa - Cape Province *20604*
R	*Protea comptonii* Beard *20604, 20039*		
	R	*20039*	Southern Africa *20039*
	E	*20604*	Swaziland *20604*
	V	*20604*	South Africa - Natal *20604*
	V	*20604*	South Africa - Transvaal *20604*
R	*Protea convexa* E.Phillips *20604*		
	R	*20604*	South Africa - Cape Province *20604*
R	*Protea cryophila* Bolus *20604*		
	R	*20604*	South Africa - Cape Province *20604*
V	*Protea curvata* N.E.Br. *20604*		
	V	*20604*	South Africa - Transvaal *20604*
V	*Protea decurrens* E.Phillips *20604*		
	V	*20604*	South Africa - Cape Province *20604*
V	*Protea dracomontana* Beard		
	V		Zimbabwe
R	*Protea holosericea* (Salisb. ex Knight) Rourke *20604*		
	R	*20604*	South Africa - Cape Province *20604*
R	*Protea inopina* Rourke *20604*		
	R	*20604*	South Africa - Cape Province *20604*
V	*Protea laetans* L.E.Davidson *20604, 17458*		
	V	*20604*	South Africa - Transvaal *20604*
V	*Protea lanceolata* E.Mey. ex Meisn. *20604*		
	V	*20604*	South Africa - Cape Province *20604*
V	*Protea mucronifolia* Salisb. *20604*		
	V	*20604*	South Africa - Cape Province *20604*
E	*Protea namaquana* Rourke *20604*		
	E	*20604*	South Africa - Cape Province *20604*
E	*Protea nubigena* Rourke *20604*		
	E	*20604*	South Africa - Natal *20604*
R	*Protea nyasae* Rendle *7757*		
	R		Malawi (Mt. Mlanje) *7757*
E I	*Protea odorata* Thunb. *20604*		
	E	*20604*	South Africa - Cape Province *20604*
R	*Protea pruinosa* Rourke *20604*		
	R	*20604*	South Africa - Cape Province *20604*
E	*Protea pudens* Rourke *20604*		
	E	*20604*	South Africa - Cape Province *20604*
V	*Protea restionifolia* (Salisb. ex Knight) Rycroft *20604*		
	V	*20604*	South Africa - Cape Province *20604*
E	*Protea roupelliae* Meissner var. *hamiltonii* Beard ex Rourke *20604*		
	E	*20604*	South Africa - Transvaal *20604*
V	*Protea scorzonerifolia* (Salisb. ex Knight) Rycroft *20604*		

V		20604 South Africa - Cape Province 20604	
R	*Protea venusta* Compton 20604		
	R	20604 South Africa - Cape Province 20604	
E	*Roupala percoriacea* A. Gentry 20883, 10060		
	I	20883 Panama 20883	
R	*Roupala schultzii* Mennega 8679		
	R	8679 Suriname 8679	
E	*Serruria aemula* Salisb. ex Knight 20604		
	E	20604 South Africa - Cape Province 20604	
V	*Serruria altiscapa* Rourke 20604		
	V	20604 South Africa - Cape Province 20604	
R	*Serruria balanocephala* Rourke 20604		
	R	20604 South Africa - Cape Province 20604	
V	*Serruria brownii* Meisn. 20604		
	V	20604 South Africa - Cape Province 20604	
R	*Serruria candicans* R.Br. 20604		
	R	20604 South Africa - Cape Province 20604	
V	*Serruria collina* Salisb. ex Knight 20604		
	V	20604 South Africa - Cape Province 20604	
R	*Serruria confragosa* Rourke 20604		
	R	20604 South Africa - Cape Province 20604	
V	*Serruria cyanoides* (L.) R.Br. 20604		
	V	20604 South Africa - Cape Province 20604	
R	*Serruria decumbens* (Thunb.) R.Br. 20604		
	R	20604 South Africa - Cape Province 20604	
V	*Serruria deluvialis* Rourke 20604		
	V	20604 South Africa - Cape Province 20604	
R	*Serruria flagellifolia* Salisb. ex Knight 20604		
	R	20604 South Africa - Cape Province 20604	
R	*Serruria flava* Meisn. 20604		
	R	20604 South Africa - Cape Province 20604	
V	*Serruria florida* (Thunb.) Salisb. ex Knight 20604, 10260		
	V	20604 South Africa - Cape Province 20604	
E	*Serruria foeniculacea* R.Br. 20604		
	E	20604 South Africa - Cape Province 20604	
E	*Serruria furcellata* R.Br. 20604		
	E	20604 South Africa - Cape Province 20604	
R	*Serruria hirsuta* R.Br. 20604		
	R	20604 South Africa - Cape Province 20604	
V	*Serruria incrassata* Meisn. 20604		
	V	20604 South Africa - Cape Province 20604	
R	*Serruria kraussii* Meisn. 20604		
	R	20604 South Africa - Cape Province 20604	
R	*Serruria leipoldtii* E.Phillips & Hutch. 20604		
	R	20604 South Africa - Cape Province 20604	
E	*Serruria linearis* Salisb. ex Knight 20604		
	E	20604 South Africa - Cape Province 20604	
R	*Serruria meisneriana* Schltr. 20604		
	R	20604 South Africa - Cape Province 20604	
V	*Serruria millefolia* Salisb. ex Knight 20604		
	V	20604 South Africa - Cape Province 20604	
R	*Serruria pinnata* R.Br. 20604		
	R	20604 South Africa - Cape Province 20604	
E	*Serruria roxburghii* R.Br. 20604		
	E	20604 South Africa - Cape Province 20604	
E	*Serruria trilopha* Salisb. ex Knight 20604		
	E	20604 South Africa - Cape Province 20604	

R	*Serruria triternata* (Thunb.) R.Br. 20604		
	R	20604 South Africa - Cape Province 20604	
R	*Serruria viridifolia* Rourke 20604		
	R	20604 South Africa - Cape Province 20604	
R	*Serruria williamsii* Rourke 20604		
	R	20604 South Africa - Cape Province 20604	
R	*Sorocephalus alopecurus* Rourke 20604		
	R	20604 South Africa - Cape Province 20604	
R	*Sorocephalus capitatus* Rourke 20604		
	R	20604 South Africa - Cape Province 20604	
V	*Sorocephalus crassifolius* Hutch. 20604		
	V	20604 South Africa - Cape Province 20604	
E	*Sorocephalus imbricatus* (Thunb.) R.Br. 20604		
	E	20604 South Africa - Cape Province 20604	
E	*Sorocephalus palustris* Rourke 20604		
	E	20604 South Africa - Cape Province 20604	
E	*Sorocephalus pinifolius* (Salisb. ex Knight) Rourke 20604		
	E	20604 South Africa - Cape Province 20604	
V	*Sorocephalus scabridus* Meisn. 20604		
	V	20604 South Africa - Cape Province 20604	
E	*Sorocephalus tenuifolius* R.Br. 20604, 6180		
	E	20604 South Africa - Cape Province 20604	
R	*Sorocephalus teretifolius* (Meisn.) E.Phillips 20604		
	R	20604 South Africa - Cape Province 20604	
R	*Spatalla argentea* Rourke 20604		
	R	20604 South Africa - Cape Province 20604	
R	*Spatalla barbigera* Salisb. ex Knight 20604		
	R	20604 South Africa - Cape Province 20604	
R	*Spatalla colorata* Meisn. 20604		
	R	20604 South Africa - Cape Province 20604	
V	*Spatalla ericoides* E.Phillips 20604		
	V	20604 South Africa - Cape Province 20604	
R	*Spatalla nubicola* Rourke 20604		
	R	20604 South Africa - Cape Province 20604	
E	*Spatalla prolifera* (Thunb.) Salisb. ex Knight 20604		
	E	20604 South Africa - Cape Province 20604	
R	*Spatalla propinqua* R.Br. 20604		
	R	20604 South Africa - Cape Province 20604	
R	*Spatalla salsoloides* (R.Br.) Rourke 20604		
	R	20604 South Africa - Cape Province 20604	
E	*Spatalla tulbaghensis* (E.Phillips) Rourke 20604		
	E	20604 South Africa - Cape Province 20604	
R	*Sphalmium racemosum* (C.White) B.G.Briggs, Hyland & L.A.S.Johnson 20681		
	R	20681 Australia - Queensland 20681	
R	*Stenocarpus cryptocarpus* D.Foreman & B.Hyland 20681		
	R	20681 Australia - Queensland 20681	
R	*Stenocarpus davallioides* D.Foreman & B.Hyland 20681		
	R	20681 Australia - Queensland 20681	
Ex	*Stenocarpus dumbeensis* Guillaumin 20802		
	Ex	20802 New Caledonia 20802	
E	*Stenocarpus heterophyllus* Brong. & Gris 20893		
	E	20893 New Caledonia 20893	
Ex/E	*Stenocarpus villosus* Brongn. & Gris 20802		
	Ex/E	20802 New Caledonia 20802	
R	*Synaphea pinnata* Lindley 20681		
	R	20681 Australia - Western Australia 20681	

R   *Telopea aspera* Crisp & P.H.Weston ms. *20681*
    R   *20681* Australia - New South Wales *20681*

R   *Triunia montana* (C.White) D.Foreman *20681*
    R   *20681* Australia - Queensland *20681*

E   *Triunia robusta* (C.White) D.Foreman *20681, 14223*
    E   *20681* Australia - Queensland *20681*

V   *Vexatorella alpina* (Salisb. ex Knight) Rourke *20604*
    V   *20604* South Africa - Cape Province *20604*

R   *Vexatorella latebrosa* Rourke *20604*
    R   *20604* South Africa - Cape Province *20604*

Quiinaceae

Number of genera:	4
Number of species:	40
Recorded threatened species:	6 (15%)

Tropical America, especially Amazon basin.

E   *Froesia venezuelensis* Steyermark & Bunting *20883*
    I   *20883* Venezuela *20883*

V   *Lacunaria panamensis* (Standl.) Standl. *20883, 9006*
    E   *20883* Costa Rica *20883*
    E   *21313* Honduras *21313*
    V   *16317* Panama *20883*

E   *Quiina colonensis* (D'Arcy) D'Arcy *20883, 10747*
    I   *20883* Panama *20883*

R   *Quiina indigofera* Sandw. *8679*
    R   Guyana *8679*

V   *Quiina jamaicensis* Griseb. *20883*
    V   *20883* Jamaica *20883*

R   *Quiina sessilis* Choisy *8679*
    R   French Guiana *8679*

Rafflesiaceae

Number of genera:	7
Number of species:	50
Recorded threatened species:	9 (18%)

Tropical and subtropical.

R   *Mitrastemon yamamotoi* Makino var. *kanehirai* Makino *20511*
    R   *20511* Taiwan *20511*

R   *Mitrastemon yamamotoi* Makino var. *kawasasakii* Makino *20511*
    R   *20511* Taiwan *20511*

R   *Pilostyles collina* Dell *20681*
    R   *20681* Australia - Western Australia *20681*

R   *Rafflesia cantleyi* Solms-Laub. *19773*
    R   *19956* Malaysia - Peninsular Malaysia *19773*

I   *Rafflesia hasseltii* Sur. *19773*
    I   *19956* Indonesia - Sumatra (west coast)
    I   *19956* Malaysia - Peninsular Malaysia *19956*

V   *Rafflesia keithii* Meijer
    V   Malaysia - Sabah (Mt Kinabalu; near Ranau)

R   *Rafflesia kerrii* Meijer *19773*
    R   *19956* Thailand (south) *19956*
    R   *19956* Malaysia - Peninsular Malaysia (Kedah & Gunong Chamah) *19956*

E   *Rafflesia manillana* Teschemacher *10278*
    E   Philippines (Luzon) *11305*

V   *Rafflesia pricei* Meijer *19773*
    V   Malaysia - Sabah *19773*

R   *Rafflesia zollingeriana* *15206*
    R   *15206* Indonesia - Java (Meru Bitiri reserve) *15206*

Ranunculaceae

Number of genera:	50
Number of species:	2,000
Recorded threatened species:	294 (14%)

Widespread, especially North temperate and boreal.

I   *Aconitum apoiense* Nakai *10572*
    I   *10572* Japan *10572*

I   *Aconitum balfourii* Stapf var. *rhombilobum* Stapf
    I   India - Uttar Pradesh (Garhwal Himalaya; Kumaun)

R   *Aconitum bartletii* Yamamoto var. *formosanum* (Tamura) Liu & Hsieh *20511*
    R   *20511* Taiwan *20511*

R   *Aconitum bartletii* Yamamoto var. *fukutomei* (Hayata) Liu & Hsieh *20511*
    R   *20511* Taiwan *20511*

V   *Aconitum brachypodum* Diels *17617*
    V   *17617* China - Sichuan (Muli) *11139*
    V   *17617* China - Yunnan *11139*

R   *Aconitum callibotryon* Rchb. *2050, 20171*
    R   *2050* Czech Republic *2050*

V   *Aconitum chrysopilum* Nakai *10572*
    V   *10572* Japan *10572*

I   *Aconitum falconeri* Stapf var. *falconeri* *14761*
    I   *14761* India - Uttar Pradesh (Garhwal; Kumaun) *14761*

V   *Aconitum falconeri* Stapf var. *latilobum* Stapf *13883*
    V   *13883* India - Himachal Pradesh (Bashahr) *13883*

I   *Aconitum ferox* Wallich ex Seringe *11494*
    I   *19160* Bhutan *19160*
    V   *11494* India - Himachal Pradesh *11494*
    V   *11494* India - Sikkim *11494*
    V   India - Uttar Pradesh *9998*
    V   Nepal *9998*

R   *Aconitum firmum* (Reichenb.) Gayer ssp. *moravicum* Skalicky *2050*
    R   *2050* Czech Republic *2050*
    V   *19321* Slovakia *19321*

V   *Aconitum infectum* Greene *20850*
    I   *20850* U.S. - Arizona *20850*

V   *Aconitum itoseyanum* Miyabe & Tatew. *10572*
    V   *10572* Japan *10572*

V   *Aconitum jaluense* Komarov ssp. *iwatekense* (Nakai) Kadota *10572*
    V   *10572* Japan *10572*

E   *Aconitum kashmiricum* Stapf ex Coventry
    E   *14768* India - Jammu & Kashmir *14768*

I   *Aconitum kishidae* Nakai *10572*
    I   *10572* Japan *10572*

I   *Aconitum kitadakense* Nakai *10572*
    I   *10572* Japan *10572*

I   *Aconitum lasiocarpum* Reichenb. *7897*
    V   *18216* Poland (east Carpathians) *7897*
    I   *19321* Slovakia *19321*

V   *Aconitum metajaponicum* Nakai *10572*
    V   *10572* Japan *10572*

I   *Aconitum moschatum* (Bruhl) Stapf
    I   India - Jammu & Kashmir

E   *Aconitum nagarum* Stapf var. *heterotrichum* Fletcher & Lauener *11139*
    E   China - Yunnan *11139*

V   *Aconitum napellus* L. ssp. *corsicum* (Grayer) Seitz. *14166, 20171*
    V   *20528* France - Corsica (Coscione Plateau, Zicavo) *20528*

V   *Aconitum napellus* L. ssp. *firmum* (Reichenb.) Gáyer *19266, 20171*
    V   *19321* Slovakia *19321*

R   *Aconitum nevadense* Uechtr. *20171*
    R   Spain

R   *Aconitum noveboracense* Gray ex Coville *20850*
    V   *20850* U.S. - Iowa *20850*
    V   *20850* U.S. - New York *20850*
    E   *20850* U.S. - Ohio *20850*
    E   *20850* U.S. - Wisconsin *20850*

R   *Aconitum sanyoense* Nakai *10572*
    R   *10572* Japan *10572*

R   *Aconitum senanens* Nakai var. *isidzukae* (Nakai) Kadota *10572*
    R   *10572* Japan *10572*

I   *Aconitum septemcarpum* Nakai *10572*
    I   *10572* Japan *10572*

V   *Aconitum talassicum* Popov
    V   former USSR *6930*

V   *Aconitum variegatum* L. ssp. *pyrenaicum* Vivant ex Delay *20171*
    V   *20528* France (west Pyrenees) *20528*
    V   *20528* Spain (west Pyrenees) *20528*

R   *Aconitum zigzag* Lev. & Van. *10572*
    R   *10572* Japan *10572*

E   *Adonis cyllenea* Boiss., Heldr. & Orph. *8000, 20171*
    E   *19174* Greece (Mt Parnias) *19174*

R   *Adonis distorta* Ten. *8000, 20171*
    R   *18264* Italy (Appennines) *8000*

R   *Anemone edwardsiana* Tharp *20850*
    I   *20850* U.S. - New Mexico *20850*
    R   *20850* U.S. - Texas *20850*

R   *Anemone edwardsiana* Tharp var. *edwardsiana* Correll *20850*
    R   *20850* U.S. - Texas *20850*

E   *Anemone edwardsiana* Tharp var. *petraea* Correll *20850*
    E   *20850* U.S. - Texas *20850*

R   *Anemone koraiensis* Nakai *15957*
    R   *15923* Korea, South (Sepo, Kangwon-do) *15957*

I   *Anemone kusnetzowii* Woronow ex Grossh. *5942*
    I   *5942* Armenia *5942*

R   *Anemone minima* DC. *20850*
    I   *20850* U.S. - Maryland *20850*
    V   *20850* U.S. - North Carolina *20850*
    I   *20850* U.S. - Tennessee *20850*
    R   *20850* U.S. - Virginia *20850*
    I   *20850* U.S. - West Virginia *20850*

V   *Anemone oregana* A.Gray var. *felix* (M.E. Peck) C.L. Hitchc. *20850*

    E   *20850* U.S. - Oregon *20850*
    I   *20850* U.S. - Washington *20850*

V   *Anemone sikokiana* Makino *10572*
    V   *10572* Japan *10572*

V   *Anemone stylosa* A. Nels. *20850*
    I   *20850* U.S. - Arizona *20850*
    I   *20850* U.S. - Utah *20850*

E   *Anemone uralensis* Fisch. ex DC. *11552, 20171*
    E   *11552* Russian Federation (Ural Mts.) *11552*

R   *Aquilegia aragonensis* Willk. *11496*
    R   *11496* Spain (Huesca) *11496*

E   *Aquilegia barbaricina* Arrigoni & E.Nardi *18264, 20171*
    E   *18264* Italy - Sardinia *18264*

V   *Aquilegia cazorlensis* Heywood *8000, 20171*
    V   *20874* Spain (Cerro Cabañas, Jaén) *8000*

R   *Aquilegia champagnatii* Moraldo, E.Nardi & la Valva *18264, 20171*
    R   *18264* Italy (Campania) *18264*

V   *Aquilegia chrysantha* Gray var. *chaplinei* (Standl. ex Payson) Lott *20850*
    V   *20850* U.S. - New Mexico *20850*
    V   *20850* U.S. - Texas *20850*

E   *Aquilegia chrysantha* Gray var. *hinckleyana* (Munz) Lott *20850*
    E   *20850* U.S. - Texas *20850*

R   *Aquilegia chrysantha* Gray var. *rydbergii* Munz *20850*
    Ex/E   *20850* U.S. - Colorado *20850*

V   *Aquilegia coerulea* Eastw. var. *daileyae* Eastw. *20850*
    I   *20850* U.S. - Colorado *20850*

R   *Aquilegia colchica* Kemul.-Nath. *6930*
    R   Asiatic U.S.S.R. (Caucasus) *6930*

R   *Aquilegia dinarica* G. Beck *20171*
    R   *20178* Albania *20178*
    V   *21091* Bosnia & Herzegovina *21091*
    R   (former) Yugoslavia

V   *Aquilegia discolor* Levier & Leresche *20171*
    V   Spain

R   *Aquilegia eximia* Van Houtte ex Planch. *20850*
    I   *20850* U.S. - California *20850*

E   *Aquilegia flavescens* S.Watson var. *rubicunda* (Tidestrom) Welsh *20850*
    E   *20850* U.S. - Utah *20850*

E   *Aquilegia formosa* Fisch. var. *fosteri* Welsh *20850*
    E   *20850* U.S. - Utah *20850*

R   *Aquilegia grata* Zimmeter *20171*
    V   *21091* Bosnia & Herzegovina *21091*
    R   (former) Yugoslavia

V   *Aquilegia laramiensis* A. Nels. *20850*
    V   *20850* U.S. - Wyoming *20850*

E   *Aquilegia litardierei* Briq. *20171*
    E   *20726* France - Corsica *12844*

R   *Aquilegia longissima* Gray *20883, 20850, 19002*
    I   *20850* U.S. - Arizona *20850*
    V   *20850* U.S. - Texas *20850*
    I   *20883* Mexico *20883*

R   *Aquilegia magellensis* Huter, Porta & Rigo *18264*
    R   *18264* Italy (Abruzzi) *18264*

Ex/E   *Aquilegia micrantha* Eastw. var. *mancosana*
     Eastw. *20850*
     Ex/E *20850* U.S. - Colorado *20850*

I   *Aquilegia nakaoi* Tamura
     I   India - Jammu & Kashmir

R   *Aquilegia nigricans* Baumg. ssp. *subscaposa*
     (Borbás) Soó *17823, 20171*
     R   *19949* Romania *20631*

E   *Aquilegia nivalis* Falc. ex Jackson *14768*
     E   India - Jammu & Kashmir (Apharwat) *14768*

V   *Aquilegia nugorensis* Arrigoni & E.Nardi *18264, 20171*
     V   *18264* Italy - Sardinia *18264*

R   *Aquilegia ottonis* Orph. ex Boiss. *20171*
     R   Greece
     E   Italy

V   *Aquilegia ottonis* Orph. ex Boiss. ssp. *taygetea*
     (Orph.) Strid *14166, 20171*
     V   *20171* Greece *20171*

R   *Aquilegia paui* Font Quer *20171*
     R   Spain

R   *Aquilegia pubescens* Coville *20850*
     I   *20850* U.S. - California *20850*

R   *Aquilegia saximontana* Rydb. *20850*
     R   *20850* U.S. - Colorado *20850*

R   *Aquilegia thalictrifolia* Schott & Kotschy *20171*
     R   Italy

I   *Beckwithia glacialis* (L.) Löve & D. Löve ssp.
     alakensis Jurtz., Kelso & Murray ined. *21309*
     I   *21309* U.S. - Alaska *21309*

V   *Callianthemum insigne* Nakai var. *hondoense*
     Ohwi *10572*
     V   *10572* Japan *10572*

V   *Callianthemum kerneranum* Freyn ex A.Kern. *20171*
     V   Italy

V   *Callianthemum kernerianum* Freyn ex A.Kern. *18264,*
     20171
     V   *18264* Italy (Trentino-Alto Adige, Veneto)
       18264

V   *Callianthemum miyabenum* Tatew. *10572*
     V   *10572* Japan *10572*

R   *Caltha phylloptera* A.W.Hill *20681*
     R   *20681* Australia - Tasmania *20681*

V   *Cimicifuga arizonica* S.Watson *20850*
     V   *20850* U.S. - Arizona *20850*

V   *Cimicifuga elata* Nutt. *20850, 10701*
     E   *20850* Canada - British Columbia *20850*
     V   *20850* U.S. - Oregon *20850*
     V   *20850* U.S. - Washington *20850*

R   *Cimicifuga rubifolia* Kearney *20850*
     E   *20850* U.S. - Alabama *20850*
     V   *20850* U.S. - Illinois *20850*
     E   *20850* U.S. - Indiana *20850*
     V   *20850* U.S. - Kentucky *20850*
     R   *20850* U.S. - Tennessee *20850*
     E   *20850* U.S. - Virginia *20850*

V   *Clematis addisonii* Britt. *20850*
     V   *20850* U.S. - Virginia *20850*

E   *Clematis apiculata* Hook.f. & Thomson *11494*
     E   *11494* India - Meghalaya (Khasi hills) *11494*

V   *Clematis bourdillonii* Dunn *14782*
     V   *14782* India - Kerala *14782*

R   *Clematis chiisanensis* Nakai *15957*
     R   *15923* Korea, South (north to Mt Chiri) *15957*

R   *Clematis coactilis* (Fern.) Keener *20850*
     V   *20850* U.S. - Virginia *20850*

E   *Clematis dubia* (Endl.) P.S. Green *19108*
     E   *19108* Australia - Norfolk Is. *19108*

E   *Clematis elisabethae-carolae* Greuter *20730*
     E   *20730* Greece - Crete *20730*

V   *Clematis fawcettii* F.Muell. *20681*
     I   *20681* Australia - New South Wales *20681*
     I   *20681* Australia - Queensland *20681*

V   *Clematis hirsutissima* Pursh var. *arizonica*
     (Heller) Erickson *20850*
     E   *20850* U.S. - Arizona *20850*
     V   *20850* U.S. - New Mexico *20850*

R   *Clematis kakoulimensis* Schnell *7926*
     R   Guinea (Mt. Kakoulima) *7926*

R   *Clematis marmoraria* Sneddon *19305*
     R   *19305* New Zealand - South Is. *19305*

E   *Clematis morefieldii* Kral *20850, 14512*
     E   *20850* U.S. - Alabama (Madison Co.) *20850*

R   *Clematis palmeri* Rose *20850, 19002*
     E   *20850* U.S. - Arizona *20850*
     I   *20850* U.S. - New Mexico *20850*

V   *Clematis sigensis* Engl. *20057*
     V   *19109* Kenya *19109*

E   *Clematis socialis* Kral *20850*
     E   *20850* U.S. - Alabama (St Clair & Cherokee Co.)
       20850

R   *Clematis terniflora* DC. var. *boninensis* (Hayata)
     Tuy. *8037*
     R   *19134* Japan - Ogasawara-shoto *8037*

R   *Clematis theobromina* Dunn *14782*
     R   *14782* India - Tamil Nadu *14782*

R   *Clematis trichotoma* Nakai *15957*
     R   *15923* Korea, South (north to Chollanam-do)
       15957

V   *Clematis viticaulis* Steele *20850*
     V   *20850* U.S. - Virginia *20850*

R   *Consolida armeniaca* (Stapf ex Huth) Schrod. *12840*
     R   *12840* Turkey *12840*

R   *Consolida cornuta* (Davis & Hossain) Davis *12840*
     R   *12840* Turkey *12840*

I   *Consolida cruciata* (Davis & Hossain) Davis *12840*
     I   *12840* Turkey *12840*

R   *Consolida lineolata* Huber-Mor. & Simon *12840*
     R   *12840* Turkey *12840*

R   *Consolida olopetala* (Boiss.) Hayek *12840, 20171*
     R   *12840* Turkey *12840*

E   *Consolida samia* P.H. Davis *8000*
     E   *20731* Greece - East Aegean Is *20731*

R   *Consolida staminosa* Davis & Sorger *12840*
     R   *12840* Turkey *12840*

R   *Consolida stapfiana* Davis & sorger *12840*
     R   *12840* Turkey *12840*

I   *Consolida tuntasiana* (Halacsy) Soo *20171*
     I   Greece

V   *Coptis chinensis* Franchet *11139*
     V   China - Hubei *11139*
     V   China - Shaanxi *11139*

V		China - Sichuan *11139*	
E	20985	Vietnam *6057*	

V *Coptis chinensis* Franchet var. *brevisepala* W.T. Wang & Hsiao *17617*

V	17617	China - Anhui *11139*
V	17617	China - Fujian *11139*
V	17617	China - Guangdong *11139*
V	17617	China - Guangxi *11139*
V	17617	China - Jiangxi *11139*
V	17617	China - Zhejiang *11139*
E		Vietnam *6057*

V *Coptis lutescens* Tamura *10572*

V	10572	Japan *10572*

E *Coptis omeiensis* (Chen) C.Y. Young *17617*

E	17617	China - Sichuan (Emei, Ebian, Hongya) *11139*

R *Coptis ramosa* (Makino) Tamura *10572*

R	10572	Japan *10572*

V *Coptis teeta* Wallich *17617*

V	17617	China - Xizang Zizhiqu (Metue; Chayu) *11139*
V	17617	China - Yunnan *11139*
E	14782	India - Arunachal Pradesh *9248*
V	8318	Myanmar *8318*

V *Delphinium alabamicum* Kral *20850*

V	20850	U.S. - Alabama *20850*

V *Delphinium alpestre* Rydb. *20850*

R	20850	U.S. - Colorado *20850*
V	20850	U.S. - New Mexico *20850*

I *Delphinium altissimum* Wall. var. *siamensis* (Craib) T. Shimizu *19120*

I	19120	Thailand *19120*

R *Delphinium anatolicum* Misirdali et al. *12840*

R	12840	Turkey *12840*

E *Delphinium bakeri* Ewan *20850*

E	20850	U.S. - California *20850*

E *Delphinium bicornutum* Warnock ssp. *oaxacanum* Warnock *20883, 9751*

I	20883	Mexico *20883*
?		Mexico - Oaxaca *9751*

R *Delphinium bithynicum* Davis *12840*

R	12840	Turkey *12840*

E *Delphinium calcar-equitis* Hemsley *9751*

E	9751	Mexico - Chihuahua *9751*

E *Delphinium californicum* Torr. & A.Gray ssp. *interius* (Eastw.) Ewan *20850*

I	20850	U.S. - California *20850*

R *Delphinium cardinale* Hook. *20850*

I	20850	U.S. - California *20850*

E *Delphinium caseyi* B.L. Burtt *14230*

E	19164	Cyprus (limestone mountain summits) *14230*

R *Delphinium cilicicum* Davis & Kit Tan *12840*

R	12840	Turkey *12840*

R *Delphinium cinereum* Boiss. *12840*

R	12840	Turkey *12840*

V *Delphinium cossonianum* Battand.

V		Morocco

R *Delphinium cyphoplectrum* Boiss. var. *vanense* (Rech.) Davis *12840*

R	12840	Turkey *12840*

R *Delphinium decorum* Fisch. & C.A. Mey. *20850*

I	20850	U.S. - California *20850*
I	20850	U.S. - Oregon *20850*

V *Delphinium decorum* Fisch. & C.A. Mey. ssp. *decorum* *20850*

I	20850	U.S. - California *20850*

V *Delphinium decorum* Fisch. & C.A. Mey. ssp. *tracyi* Ewan *20850*

I	20850	U.S. - California *20850*
I	20850	U.S. - Oregon *20850*

R *Delphinium dolichostachyum* Chowdhuri & Davis *12840*

R	12840	Turkey *12840*

R *Delphinium exaltatum* Ait. *20850*

E	20850	U.S. - Alabama *20850*
I	20850	U.S. - Maine *20850*
E	20850	U.S. - Maryland *20850*
V	20850	U.S. - Missouri *20850*
E	20850	U.S. - North Carolina *20850*
R	20850	U.S. - Ohio *20850*
E	20850	U.S. - Pennsylvania *20850*
E	20850	U.S. - Tennessee *20850*
R	20850	U.S. - Virginia *20850*
E	20850	U.S. - West Virginia *20850*

I *Delphinium fissum* Waldst. & Kit. *5942, 20171*

V	21091	Bosnia & Herzegovina *21091*
I	5942	Georgia *5942*
I	5942	Moldova *5942*
I	5942	Ukraine - Crimea *5942*

R *Delphinium gauthieri* Rouy

R		Spain

R *Delphinium glaucescens* Rydb. *20850*

I	20850	U.S. - Idaho *20850*
I	20850	U.S. - Montana *20850*

R *Delphinium gracilentum* Greene *20850*

I	20850	U.S. - California *20850*

R *Delphinium gypsophilum* Ewan *20850*

I	20850	U.S. - California *20850*

R *Delphinium gypsophilum* Ewan ssp. *gypsophilum* *20850*

I	20850	U.S. - California *20850*

V *Delphinium gypsophilum* Ewan ssp. *parviflorum* Lewis & Epling *20850*

I	20850	U.S. - California *20850*

V *Delphinium hansenii* (Greene) Greene ssp. *ewanianum* Warnock *20850*

V	20850	U.S. - California *20850*

V *Delphinium hesperium* A.Gray ssp. *cuyamacae* (Abrams) Lewis & Epling *20850*

V	20850	U.S. - California *20850*

I *Delphinium hirschfeldianum* Heldr. & Holzm. *20171*

I		Greece

V *Delphinium hutchinsoniae* Ewan *20850*

V	20850	U.S. - California *20850*

R *Delphinium ilgazense* Davis *12840*

R	12840	Turkey *12840*

R *Delphinium inopinum* (Jepson) Lewis & Epling *20850*

R	20850	U.S. - California *20850*

I *Delphinium koelzii* Munz

I		India - Himachal Pradesh (Kulu)

V *Delphinium leucophaeum* Greene *20850*

V	20850	U.S. - Oregon *20850*
E	20850	U.S. - Washington *20850*

E *Delphinium luteum* Heller *20850*

E   20850 U.S. - California *20850*

R   *Delphinium multiplex* (Ewan) C.L. Hitchc. *20850*
    I   *20850* U.S. - Washington *20850*

R   *Delphinium munzianum* Davis & Kit Tan *12840*
    R   *12840* Turkey *12840*

R   *Delphinium nevadense* Kunze *20171*
    R   Spain

R   *Delphinium newtonianum* D.M. Moore *20850*
    R   *20850* U.S. - Arkansas *20850*

V   *Delphinium nuttallianum* (Ewan) C.L. Hitchc. var. *lineapetalum* (Ewan) C.L. Hitchc. *20850*
    I   *20850* U.S. - Oregon *20850*
    I   *20850* U.S. - Washington *20850*

R   *Delphinium nydeggeri* Huber-Mor. *12840*
    R   *12840* Turkey *12840*

I   *Delphinium ovczinnikovii* Kamelin & Pissjauk. *5942*
    I   *5942* Uzbekistan *5942*

V   *Delphinium oxysepalum* Borbás & Pax *8000, 20171*
    V   *19751* Poland (Tatry Mts.) *19751*
    V   *19321* Slovakia (central part of west Carpathians) *6951*

E   *Delphinium parryi* Gray ssp. *blochmaniae* (Greene) Lewis & Epling *20850*
    E   *20850* U.S. - California *20850*

V   *Delphinium parryi* Gray ssp. *eastwoodiae* Ewan *20850*
    I   *20850* U.S. - California *20850*

V   *Delphinium parryi* Gray ssp. *purpureum* (Lewis & Epling) Warnock *20850*
    V   *20850* U.S. - California *20850*

E   *Delphinium pavonaceum* Ewan *20850*
    E   *20850* U.S. - Oregon *20850*

R   *Delphinium polycladon* Eastw. *20850*
    I   *20850* U.S. - California *20850*
    I   *20850* U.S. - Nevada *20850*

R   *Delphinium pratense* Eastw. *20850*
    I   *20850* U.S. - California *20850*

V   *Delphinium puniceum* Pall. *20171*
    V   *11552* Russian Federation (Caucasus, west) *11552*

V   *Delphinium purpusii* Brandeg. *20850*
    I   *20850* U.S. - California *20850*

R   *Delphinium queneri* Davis *12840*
    R   *12840* Turkey *12840*

V   *Delphinium recurvatum* Greene *20850*
    V   *20850* U.S. - California *20850*

V   *Delphinium robustum* Rydb. *20850*
    I   *20850* U.S. - Colorado *20850*
    I   *20850* U.S. - New Mexico *20850*

I   *Delphinium roylei* Munz
    I   India - Himachal Pradesh
    I   India - Jammu & Kashmir

R   *Delphinium scopulorum* Gray *20850*
    I   *20850* U.S. - Arizona *20850*
    I   *20850* U.S. - New Mexico *20850*

V   *Delphinium simonkaianum* Pawl. *17823, 20171*
    V   *19949* Romania *20631*

V   *Delphinium sordidum* Cuatrec. *20171*
    V   Spain

R   *Delphinium treleasei* Bush ex K.C. Davis *20850*

    R   *20850* U.S. - Arkansas *20850*
    R   *20850* U.S. - Missouri *20850*

R   *Delphinium uliginosum* Curran *20850*
    I   *20850* U.S. - California *20850*
    I   *20850* U.S. - Oregon *20850*

E   *Delphinium variegatum* Torr. & A.Gray ssp. *kinkiense* (Munz) Warnock *20850*
    E   *20850* U.S. - California *20850*

E   *Delphinium variegatum* Torr. & A.Gray ssp. *thornei* Munz *20850*
    E   *20850* U.S. - California *20850*

V   *Delphinium viridescens* Leib. *20850*
    V   *20850* U.S. - Washington *20850*

V   *Delphinium xantholeucum* Piper *20850*
    I   *20850* U.S. - Washington *20850*

V   *Enemion hallii* (Gray) Drumm. & Hutchinson *20850*
    I   *20850* U.S. - Oregon *20850*
    I   *20850* U.S. - Washington *20850*

R   *Enemion savilei* (Calder & Taylor) Keener *20850, 10701*
    R   *20850* Canada - British Columbia *20850*

R   *Hamadryas argentea* Hook.f.
    R   Falkland Is.

R   *Helleborus lividus* Aiton *20171*
    R   Spain - Balearic Is.

R   *Helleborus orientalis* Lam. *20171*
    R   Greece

R   *Helleborus vesicarius* Auch. *12840*
    R   *12840* Turkey *12840*

R   *Isopyrum arisanense* (Hayata) Ohwi *20511*
    R   *20511* Taiwan *20511*

R   *Isopyrum hakonense* F. Maek. & Tuy. *10572*
    R   *10572* Japan *10572*

I   *Isopyrum ludlowii* Tamura & Lawner
    I   India - Jammu & Kashmir (Lidar Valley, nr Pahlgam)

R   *Isopyrum numajirianum* Makino *10572*
    R   *10572* Japan *10572*

R   *Isopyrum ohwianum* (Koidz.) Tamura & Lauener *10572*
    R   *10572* Japan *10572*

V   *Isopyrum pterogiocaudatum* Koidz. *10572*
    V   *10572* Japan *10572*

R   *Kingdonia uniflora* Balf.f. & W. Smith *17617*
    R   *17617* China - Gansu *11139*
    R   *17617* China - Shaanxi (Taibe; Meixian) *11139*
    R   *17617* China - Sichuan *11139*
    R   *17617* China - Yunnan (Deging) *11139*

V   *Laccopetalum giganteum* (Wedd.) Ulbr. *18200*
    V   *12468* Peru *18200*

R   *Megaleranthis saniculifolia* Ohwi *15923*
    R   *15923* Korea, South (Mt Chiri, Mt Kaya, Mt Tokyu) *15923*

V   *Myosurus minimus* L. ssp. *apus* (Greene) Campbell *20850*
    V   *2050* Czech Republic *2050*
    V   *20850* U.S. - California *20850*
    I   *20850* U.S. - Oregon *20850*

V   *Myosurus minimus* (Huth) Campbell var. *sessiliflorus* (Huth) Campbell *20850*
    I   *20850* U.S. - California *20850*
    E   *20850* U.S. - Oregon *20850*

V   *Nigella arvensis* L. var. *oblanceolata*

Davis *12840*

V   *12840* Turkey *12840*

R   *Nigella carpatha* Strid *20171*

    R   *20730* Greece - Crete (Karpathos, Kasos) *20730*

R   *Nigella doerfleri* Vierh. *20171*

    R   *20731* Greece - Crete *20731*

R   *Nigella fumariifolia* Kotschy *20171*

    R   Greece

R   *Nigella icarica* Strid

    R   Greece

R   *Nigella lancifolia* Huber-Mor. *12840*

    R   *12840* Turkey *12840*

R   *Nigella stricta* Strid *20171*

    R   Greece

R   *Oreithales integrifolia* (Kunth) Schlecht. *18200*

    R   *12468* Peru *18200*

R   *Pulsatilla halleri* (All.) Willd. ssp. *slavica* (G.
      Reuss) Zamels *8000, 20171*

    V   *18216* Poland (west Tatra Mts.) *20798*

    R   *19947* Romania *19840*

    V   *19321* Slovakia *6951*

I   *Pulsatilla hungarica* Soó *19841*

    V   Hungary

    I   *19321* Slovakia *19321*

R   *Pulsatilla kostyczewii* (Korsch.) Juzepczuk

    R   former USSR *6930*

V   *Pulsatilla pratensis* (L.) Mill. ssp. *hungarica*
      (soó) Soó *17762, 20171*

    V   *20686* Hungary *20686*

    V   *19949* Romania *17762*

R   *Pulsatilla pratensis* (L.) Miller ssp. *zimmermannii*
      Soó *20686*

    R   *20686* Hungary *20686*

V   *Pulsatilla subslavica* Futak ex Goliásová *19321*

    V   *19321* Slovakia *19321*

R   *Pulsatilla vulgaris* Mill. ssp.
      gotlandica *18216, 20171*

    R   *20083* Sweden *18216*

I   *Pulsatilla wallichiana* (Royle) Ulbr.

    I   India - Himachal Pradesh

    I   India - Jammu & Kashmir

R   *Ranunculus abnormis* Cutanda & Willk. *20171*

    V   *20076* Portugal *20076*

    R   Spain (west & central) *8000*

V   *Ranunculus acetosellifolius* Boiss. *15398, 20171*

    V   *14155* Spain (Sierra Nevada) *15398*

E   *Ranunculus acriformis* A. Gray var. *aestivalis* L.
      Benson *20850*

    E   *20850* U.S. - Utah *20850*

V   *Ranunculus anemoneus* F.Muell. *20681*

    V   *20681* Australia - New South Wales *20681*

V   *Ranunculus austrooreganus* L. Benson *20850*

    V   *20850* U.S. - Oregon *20850*

R   *Ranunculus barceloi* Grau *20171*

    R   *20728* Spain - Balearic Is. *20728*

R   *Ranunculus bilobus* Bertol. *20171*

    R   Italy

R   *Ranunculus bingoeldaghensis* A. Engin *12840*

    R   *12840* Turkey *12840*

R   *Ranunculus bonariensis* Poir. var. *trisepalus*

     (Gillies ex Hook. & Arn.) Lourteig *20850*

    I   *20850* U.S. - California *20850*

Ex   *Ranunculus bulbosus* L. ssp. *adscendens* (Brotero)
      Neves forma *macranthus* (Sommier & Caruana Gatto)
      Lanfranco *13351*

    Ex   *13351* Malta *13351*

E   *Ranunculus cabrerensis* Rothm.

    E   Spain

V   *Ranunculus cacuminis* Strid & Papan. *20171*

    V   Greece

    V   (former) Yugoslavia

E   *Ranunculus caprarum* Skottsb. *19116*

    E   *19125* Chile - Juan Fernandez Is. *19116*

R   *Ranunculus carolii* Christoph.

    R   Tristan da Cunha

R   *Ranunculus clivicola* B.G.Briggs *20681*

    R   *20681* Australia - New South Wales *20681*

R   *Ranunculus collicolus* Y.Menadue *20681*

    R   *20681* Australia - Tasmania *20681*

R   *Ranunculus crateris* Davis *12840*

    R   *12840* Turkey *12840*

R   *Ranunculus cupreus* Boiss. & Heldr. *20171*

    R   *20731* Greece - Crete (and Karpathos) *20731*

V   *Ranunculus cyclocarpus* Pampan.

    V   Libya

R   *Ranunculus cymbalarifolius* Balb. ex Moris *20171*

    R   Italy - Sardinia

Ex/E   *Ranunculus degenii* Kummerle & Jav. *20178, 20171*

    Ex/E   *20178* Albania *20178*

R   *Ranunculus dissectifolius* Benth. *20681*

    R   *20681* Australia - New South Wales *20681*

R   *Ranunculus dissectus* Bieb. ssp. *ermenekensis* Kit
      Tan & M. Vural *12840*

    R   *12840* Turkey *12840*

R   *Ranunculus dissectus* Bieb. ssp. *rigidulus* (Boiss.)
      Davis *12840*

    R   *12840* Turkey *12840*

R   *Ranunculus eichlerianus* B.G.Briggs *20681*

    R   *20681* Australia - Victoria *20681*

R   *Ranunculus formosa-montanus* Ohwi *20511*

    R   *20511* Taiwan *20511*

V   *Ranunculus glaberrimus* (A. Nels. & J.F. Macbr.) L. Benson
      var. *reconditus* (A. Nels. & J.F. Macbr.) L.
      Benson *20850*

    I   *20850* U.S. - Nevada *20850*

    E   *20850* U.S. - Oregon *20850*

    E   *20850* U.S. - Washington *20850*

R   *Ranunculus godleyanus* Hook.f. *86*

    R   *19305* New Zealand - South Is. *19305*

R   *Ranunculus grahamii* Petrie

    R   New Zealand - South Is.

R   *Ranunculus guenerii* Y. Ayasligil & Davis *12840*

    R   *12840* Turkey *12840*

R   *Ranunculus haastii* Hook.f. ssp. *piliferus* F.
      Fisher

    R   New Zealand - South Is.

E   *Ranunculus hawaiensis* Gray *20850, 14209*

    E   *20850* U.S. - Hawaii (east Maui & Hawai`i)
         20850

Ex   *Ranunculus hayekii* Dörfl. *20178, 20171*
- Ex   *20178*   Albania *20178*
- R   *21091*   Bosnia & Herzegovina *21091*

V   *Ranunculus hexasepalus* (L. Benson) L. Benson *20850*
- I   *20850*   Canada - British Columbia *20850*

R   *Ranunculus hillii* Lourt. *16336*
- I   *16336*   Argentina *16336*
- R   *20176*   Argentina - Catamarca *20176*
- R   *20176*   Argentina - Tucuman *20176*

V   *Ranunculus inamoenus* (Gray) L. Benson var. *subaffinis* (Gray) L. Benson *20850*
- V   *20850*   U.S. - Arizona *20850*

R   *Ranunculus isthmicus* Boiss. ssp. *tenuifolous* (Stev.) Davis *12840*
- R   *12840*   Turkey *12840*

R   *Ranunculus jugosus* Y.Menadue *20681*
- R   *20681*   Australia - Tasmania *20681*

V   *Ranunculus kitadakeanus* Ohwi *10572*
- V   *10572*   Japan *10572*

E   *Ranunculus kykkoensis* Meikle *14230*
- E   *19164*   Cyprus *14230*

R   *Ranunculus macauleyi* Gray *20850*
- I   *20850*   U.S. - Colorado *20850*
- I   *20850*   U.S. - New Mexico *20850*

E   *Ranunculus macropetalus* DC. *18200*
- E   *19965*   Peru *19965*

R   *Ranunculus macropus* *19305*
- R   *19305*   New Zealand - South Is. *19305*

I   *Ranunculus maculatus* Cockayne & Allan
- I   New Zealand - South Is.

V   *Ranunculus mauiensis* Gray *20850, 14209*
- V   *20850*   U.S. - Hawaii *20850*

R   *Ranunculus miliarakesii* Halácsy *20171*
- R   Greece

R   *Ranunculus millii* Boiss. & Heldr. *20171*
- R   Greece

R   *Ranunculus munzurensis* S. Erik & S. Yildirimli *12840*
- R   *12840*   Turkey *12840*

R   *Ranunculus nankotaizanus* Ohwi *20511*
- R   *20511*   Taiwan *20511*

R   *Ranunculus niphophilus* B.G.Briggs *20681*
- R   *20681*   Australia - New South Wales *20681*

R   *Ranunculus pacificus* (Hulten) L. Benson *20850*
- R   *20850*   U.S. - Alaska *20850*

R   *Ranunculus poluninii* Davis *12840*
- R   *12840*   Turkey *12840*

E   *Ranunculus prasinus* Y.Menadue *20681*
- E   *20681*   Australia - Tasmania *20681*

R   *Ranunculus productus* B.G.Briggs *20681*
- R   *20681*   Australia - New South Wales *20681*

R   *Ranunculus punctatus* Jurtz. *21309*
- R   *21309*   Russia (E.Europe) - North *21309*

E   *Ranunculus radinotrichus* Greuter & Strid *20731, 20171*
- E   *20731*   Greece - Crete *20731*

V   *Ranunculus revelieri* Boreau ssp. *revelieri* *20171*
- V   *20528*   France - Corsica *20528*
- E   *20743*   Italy - Sardinia *20743*

V   *Ranunculus revelieri* Boreau ssp. *rodiei* (Litard.) Tutin *20171*
- V   *20528*   France (Var) *20528*

I   *Ranunculus sajanensis* Popov *5942*
- I   *5942*   Kyrgyzstan *5942*

R   *Ranunculus setaceus* Rodway *20681*
- R   *20681*   Australia - Tasmania *20681*

R   *Ranunculus sintenisii* Freyn *12840*
- R   *19873*   Turkey *12840*

R   *Ranunculus subhomophyllus* (Halácsy) Vierh. *20171*
- R   Greece

I   *Ranunculus taisanensis* Hayata var. *tripartitus* Ohwi *20511*
- I   *20511*   Taiwan *20511*

R   *Ranunculus tempskyanus* Freyn & Sint. *12840*
- R   *12840*   Turkey *12840*

R   *Ranunculus ternatifolius* *19305*
- R   *19305*   New Zealand - North Is. *19305*
- R   *19305*   New Zealand - South Is. *19305*

R   *Ranunculus thasius* Halácsy *20171*
- R   Greece

V   *Ranunculus turneri* Greene *20850, 6796*
- E   *20850*   Canada - Mackenzie *20850*
- E   *20850*   Canada - Yukon Territory *20850*
- E   *20850*   U.S. - Alaska *20850*

R   *Ranunculus vanensis* Davis *12840*
- R   *12840*   Turkey *12840*

R   *Ranunculus viridis* *19305*
- R   *19305*   New Zealand - South Is. *19305*

I   *Ranunculus wettsteinii* Dörfl. *20178, 20171*
- Ex/E   *20178*   Albania *20178*
- I   (former) Yugoslavia

E   *Ranunculus weyleri* Marès *8000, 20171*
- E   *20874*   Spain - Balearic Is. (north Mallorca) *20874*

V   *Ranunculus yaegatakensis* Masam. *10572*
- V   *10572*   Japan *10572*

R   *Ranunculus yakusimensis* Masam. *10572*
- R   *10572*   Japan *10572*

V   *Ranunculus yatsugatakensis* Honda & Kumaz. *10572*
- V   *10572*   Japan *10572*

V   *Shibateranthis pinnatifida* (Maxim.) Satake & Okuy. *10572*
- V   *10572*   Japan *10572*

V   *Thalictrum arkansanum* Boivin *20850*
- V   *20850*   U.S. - Arkansas *20850*
- E   *20850*   U.S. - Oklahoma *20850*
- E   *20850*   U.S. - Texas *20850*

R   *Thalictrum calabricum* Spreng. *20171*
- R   Italy
- R   Italy - Sicily

I   *Thalictrum calicolum* T. Shimizu *19120*
- I   *19120*   Thailand *19120*

E   *Thalictrum cooleyi* Ahles *20850, 15925*
- E   *20850*   U.S. - Florida (Walton Co.) *20850*
- E   *20850*   U.S. - North Carolina (South East) *20850*

R   *Thalictrum coreanum* Leveille *15957*
- R   *15923*   Korea, South (north to Mt Sorak and Mt Chuwang) *15957*

I   *Thalictrum dalzellii* Hook. *14782*

I	14782	India - Karnataka *14782*
I	14782	India - Maharashtra *14782*

V   *Thalictrum debile* Buckl. *20850*

V	20850	U.S. - Alabama *20850*
E	20850	U.S. - Georgia *20850*
E	20850	U.S. - Mississippi *20850*

R   *Thalictrum filamentosum* Maxim. var. *yakushimae* Tamura *10572*

R	10572	Japan *10572*

R   *Thalictrum foetidum* L. var. *apoiense* Shimizu *10572*

R	10572	Japan *10572*

V   *Thalictrum foetidum* L. var. *iwatense* Shimizu *10572*

V	10572	Japan *10572*

R   *Thalictrum heliophilum* Wilken & DeMott *20850*

R	20850	U.S. - Colorado *20850*

V   *Thalictrum henricksonii* M. Johnston *10061*

V	19800	Mexico - Zacatecas *10061*

V   *Thalictrum hultenii* Boivin *20850*

I	20850	Canada - Ontario *20850*
I	20850	U.S. - Alaska *20850*

R   *Thalictrum integrifolium* Maxim. *10572*

R	10572	Japan *10572*

V   *Thalictrum maritimum* Dufour *20171*

V	20692	Spain (Castellón & Valencia provinces) *20692*

V   *Thalictrum minus* L. var. *sekimotoanum* Kitam. *10572*

V	10572	Japan *10572*

V   *Thalictrum mirabile* Small *20850*

E	20850	U.S. - Alabama *20850*
I	20850	U.S. - Kentucky *20850*
V	20850	U.S. - Tennessee *20850*

V   *Thalictrum nigromontanum* Boivin *20850*

I	20850	U.S. - South Dakota *20850*

R   *Thalictrum rubescens* Ohwi *20511*

R	20511	Taiwan *20511*

E   *Thalictrum subrotundum* Boivin *20850*

E	20850	U.S. - Alabama *20850*
E	20850	U.S. - Florida *20850*
I	20850	U.S. - Georgia *20850*
I	20850	U.S. - North Carolina *20850*
I	20850	U.S. - South Carolina *20850*

V   *Thalictrum texanum* (Gray) Small *20850*

V	20850	U.S. - Texas *20850*

V   *Thalictrum toyamae* Ohwi *10572*

V	10572	Japan *10572*

R   *Thalictrum uncinatum* Rehmann *20171*

R		former European USSR

E   *Thalictrum viridulum* Boivin *20883, 9006*

I	20883	Panama *20883*

E   *Trollius acaulis* Lindley *14768*

E		India - Jammu & Kashmir (Mahdev, Gumri) *14768*

R   *Trollius akiyamae* Toyok. *10572*

R	10572	Japan *10572*

R   *Trollius laxus* Salisb. ssp. *laxus* *20850*

E	20850	U.S. - Connecticut *20850*
I	20850	U.S. - Maine *20850*
I	20850	U.S. - Michigan *20850*
E	20850	U.S. - New Jersey *20850*

R	20850	U.S. - New York *20850*
E	20850	U.S. - Ohio *20850*
E	20850	U.S. - Pennsylvania *20850*

R   *Trollius pulcher* Makino *10572*

R	10572	Japan *10572*

Resedaceae

Number of genera:	6	
Number of species:	70	
Recorded threatened species:	15	(21%)

Northern Hemisphere, mostly Old World, especially Mediterranean.

R   *Reseda armena* Boiss. *12840*

R	12840	Turkey *12840*

R   *Reseda balansae* Muller *12840*

R	12840	Turkey *12840*

R   *Reseda battandieri* Pitard

R		Morocco

R   *Reseda complicata* Bory *20171*

R		Spain

R   *Reseda coodei* Huber-Mor. *12840*

R	12840	Turkey *12840*

R   *Reseda crystallina* Webb & Berthel. *20171*

R		Spain - Canary Is.

I   *Reseda germanicopolitana* Huber-Mor. *12840*

I	12840	Turkey *12840*

R   *Reseda jacquinii* Rchb. *20171*

R		France (Cevennes, south-east Pyrenees)

R   *Reseda scoparia* Brouss. ex Willd.

R		Spain - Canary Is.

R   *Reseda tomentosa* Boiss. var. *tomentosa* *12840*

R	12840	Turkey *12840*

R   *Reseda tymphaea* Hausskn. *20171*

R		Greece

R   *Reseda viridis* Balf. f. *15534*

R	14209	Yemen - Socotra *14209*

R   *Reseda vivantii* Monts.

R		Spain

R   *Sesamoides minus* (Lange) Kuntze

R		Spain

R   *Sesamoides spathulifolium* (Revel ex Bory) Rothm.

R		Spain

Rhabdodendraceae

Number of genera:	1	
Number of species:	3	
Recorded threatened species:	1	(33%)

Tropical South America.

E   *Rhabdodendron gardneranum* (Bentham) Sandwith *20883*

I	20883	Brazil *20883*

Rhamnaceae

Number of genera:	55	
Number of species:	900	
Recorded threatened species:	171	(19%)

Cosmopolitan, especially tropical and subtropical.

R   *Adolphia californica* S.Watson *20850*

V	20850	U.S. - California *20850*

V	*Alphitonia erubescens* Baillon 20893	
	V	20893 New Caledonia 20893

R	*Alphitonia ponderosa* Hbd. 20850, 14209	
	R	20850 U.S. - Hawaii 20850

V	*Auerodendron acunae* Borh. & Muniz 5607	
	V	19105 Cuba (Holguin) 5607

E	*Auerodendron glaucescens* Urban 5607	
	E	19105 Cuba (Guantanamo) 5607

V	*Auerodendron jamaicense* (Urb.) Urb. 20883	
	V	20883 Jamaica 20883

R	*Auerodendron martii* Alain 5607	
	R	19105 Cuba (Pinar del Rio) 5607

E	*Auerodendron pauciflorum* Alain 20883, 19002	
	E	20883 Puerto Rico 20883

E	*Berchemiella wilsonii* Nakai 17617	
	E	17617 China - Anhui (Hueshan, Yuxian) 11139
	E	17617 China - Hubei (Xingshan) 11139

R	*Ceanothus arboreus* Greene 20850	
	I	20850 U.S. - California 20850

V	*Ceanothus connivens* Greene 20850	
	I	20850 U.S. - California 20850

R	*Ceanothus crassifolius* Torr. 20850	
	I	20850 U.S. - California 20850

V	*Ceanothus cuneatus* (Hook.) Nutt. ex Torr. & Gray ssp. *sonomensis* (J.T. Howell) C. Schmidt 20850	
	I	20850 U.S. - California 20850

V	*Ceanothus cyaneus* Eastw. 20850	
	V	20850 U.S. - California 20850

V	*Ceanothus dentatus* Torr. & Gray 20850	
	I	20850 U.S. - California 20850

R	*Ceanothus diversifolius* Kellogg 20850	
	I	20850 U.S. - California 20850

E	*Ceanothus ferrisiae* McMinn 20850	
	E	20850 U.S. - California 20850

R	*Ceanothus foliosus* Parry 20850	
	I	20850 U.S. - California 20850

E	*Ceanothus foliosus* Parry ssp. *vineatus* (McMinn) C. Schmidt 20850	
	E	20850 U.S. - California 20850

R	*Ceanothus gloriosus* J.T. Howell 20850	
	I	20850 U.S. - California 20850

E	*Ceanothus gloriosus* J.T. Howell ssp. *masonii* (McMinn) C. Schmidt 20850	
	I	20850 U.S. - California 20850

V	*Ceanothus gloriosus* J.T. Howell ssp. *porrectus* (J.T. Howell) C. Schmidt 20850	
	V	20850 U.S. - California 20850

R	*Ceanothus griseus* (Trel. ex B.L. Robins.) McMinn 20850	
	I	20850 U.S. - California 20850

E	*Ceanothus hearstiorum* Hoover & J.B. Roof 20850	
	E	20850 U.S. - California 20850

V	*Ceanothus impressus* Trel. 20850	
	I	20850 U.S. - California 20850

R	*Ceanothus incanus* Torr. & Gray 20850	
	I	20850 U.S. - California 20850

R	*Ceanothus jepsonii* Greene 20850	
	I	20850 U.S. - California 20850

R	*Ceanothus lemmonii* Parry 20850	
	I	20850 U.S. - California 20850

R	*Ceanothus leucodermis* Greene 20850	
	I	20850 U.S. - California 20850

V	*Ceanothus maritimus* Hoover 20850	
	V	20850 U.S. - California 20850

V	*Ceanothus megacarpus* Nutt. ssp. *insularis* (Eastw.) Raven 20850	
	V	20850 U.S. - California 20850

V	*Ceanothus oliganthus* Nutt. 20850	
	I	20850 U.S. - California 20850

R	*Ceanothus oliganthus* Nutt. ssp. *sorediatus* (Hook. & Arn.) C. Schmidt 20850	
	I	20850 U.S. - California 20850

E	*Ceanothus ophiochilus* Boyd, Ross & Arnseth 20850	
	E	20850 U.S. - California 20850

V	*Ceanothus palmeri* Trel. 20850	
	I	20850 U.S. - California 20850

R	*Ceanothus papillosus* Torr. & Gray 20850	
	I	20850 U.S. - California 20850

R	*Ceanothus parryi* Trel. 20850	
	I	20850 U.S. - California 20850

R	*Ceanothus parvifolius* (S.Watson) Trel. 20850	
	I	20850 U.S. - California 20850

R	*Ceanothus pinetorum* Coville 20850	
	I	20850 U.S. - California 20850

V	*Ceanothus prostratus* Benth. ssp. *confusus* (J.T. Howell) C. Schmidt 20850	
	V	20850 U.S. - California 20850

R	*Ceanothus prostratus* Benth. ssp. *pumilus* (Greene) C. Schmidt 20850	
	I	20850 U.S. - California 20850
	I	20850 U.S. - Oregon 20850

V	*Ceanothus purpureus* Jepson 20850	
	V	20850 U.S. - California 20850

V	*Ceanothus purpureus* Jepson ssp. *divergens* (Parry) C. Schmidt 20850	
	I	20850 U.S. - California 20850

V	*Ceanothus roderickii* Knight 20850	
	V	20850 U.S. - California 20850

V	*Ceanothus spinosus* Nutt. 20850	
	I	20850 U.S. - California 20850

R	*Ceanothus tomentosus* Parry 20850	
	I	20850 U.S. - California 20850

V	*Ceanothus verrucosus* Nutt. 20850	
	V	20850 U.S. - California 20850

E	*Colletia spartioides* Bertero ex Colla 19116	
	E	19125 Chile - Juan Fernandez Is. 19116

V	*Colubrina cubensis* (Jacq.) Brongn. 20850	
	E	20850 U.S. - Florida 20850

E	*Colubrina cubensis* (Jacq.) Brongn. var. *floridana* M.C. Johnston 20850	
	E	20850 U.S. - Florida 20850

I	*Colubrina johnstonii* Wendt 10081	
	I	19800 Mexico - Veracruz 10081

R	*Colubrina nicholsonii* A.E.van Wyk & Schrire 20604	
	R	20604 South Africa - Cape Province 20604

V	*Colubrina obscura* (Schrank) M.C. Johnston 20883, 19890	

R   *19890* Jamaica *20883*

E *Colubrina oppositifolia* Brongn. ex Mann *20850, 14209, 21348, 21356*
    E   *20850* U.S. - Hawaii (O`ahu & Hawai`i) *20850*

R *Colubrina pedunculata* Baker f. *881*
    R   *14224* Australia - Christmas Is. *881*

V *Colubrina stricta* Engelm. ex M.C. Johnston *20883, 20850, 8058*
    E   *20850* U.S. - Texas *20850*
    I   *20883* Mexico *20883*

E *Condalia hookeri* M.C. Johnston var. *edwardsiana* (Cory) M.C. Johnston *20850*
    E   *20850* U.S. - Texas *20850*

R *Cryptandra exilis* D.Morris *20681*
    R   *20681* Australia - Tasmania *20681*

R *Cryptandra intratropica* Fitzg. ssp. *brevis* K.Thiele ms. *20681*
    R   *20681* Australia - Northern Territory *20681*

R *Cryptandra lanosiflora* F.Muell. *20681*
    I   *20681* Australia - New South Wales *20681*
    I   *20681* Australia - Queensland *20681*

R *Cryptandra polyclada* Diels *20681*
    R   *20681* Australia - Western Australia *20681*

R *Discaria nitida* Tortosa *20681*
    I   *20681* Australia - New South Wales *20681*
    I   *20681* Australia - Victoria *20681*

R *Discaria pubescens* (Brongn.) Druce *20681*
    I   *20681* Australia - Capital Territory *20681*
    I   *20681* Australia - New South Wales *20681*
    I   *20681* Australia - Queensland *20681*
    I   *20681* Australia - Tasmania *20681*
    I   *20681* Australia - Victoria *20681*

E *Doerpfeldia cubensis* (Britton) Urban *11840*
    E   *19105* Cuba (Oriente; Las Villas) *11840*

V *Emmenosperma pancherianum* Baillon *20802*
    V   *20893* New Caledonia *20802*

R *Gouania australiana* F.Muell. *20681*
    R   *20681* Australia - Queensland *20681*

E *Gouania axilliflora* M. C. Johnst *20883*
    I   *20883* Peru *20883*

V *Gouania ekmanii* Alain *5607*
    V   *19105* Cuba (Pinar del Rio) *5607*

E *Gouania hillebrandii* Oliver ex Hbd. *20850, 14209*
    E   *20850* U.S. - Hawaii (Maui & Moloka`i) *20850*

E *Gouania leguatii* Guého *10082*
    E   *5852* Mauritius - Rodrigues (Cascade Mourouk) *5852*

E *Gouania mangarevica* Fosberg *20845*
    E   *20845* French Polynesia - Tuamotu Is. *20845*

E *Gouania mauritiana* Lam. ssp. *mauritiana* *10082*
    E   *14234* Réunion *14234*
    Ex   *20771* Mauritius *10936*

E *Gouania meyenii* Steud. *20850, 14209*
    E   *20850* U.S. - Hawaii (O`ahu) *20850*

V *Gouania tiliifolia* Lam. *19420*
    Ex   *14220* Réunion *14220*
    V   *20771* Mauritius *19420*

E *Gouania vitifolia* Gray *20850, 14209*
    E   *20850* U.S. - Hawaii *20850*

V *Lasiodiscus mildbraedii* Engl. ssp. *ferrugineus* (Verdc.) Faden *20057*
    V   *20057* Kenya (coastal) *17435*

Ex/E *Lasiodiscus rozeirae* Exell *20799*
    Ex/E   *20799* Sao Tome & Principe (D. Eugenia) *20799*

E *Nesiota elliptica* Hook.f. *18996*
    E   *18996* St Helena *18996*

R *Phylica affinis* Sond. *20604*
    R   *20604* South Africa - Cape Province *20604*

R *Phylica agathosmoides* Pillans *20604*
    R   *20604* South Africa - Cape Province *20604*

E *Phylica ampliata* Pillans *20604*
    E   *20604* South Africa - Cape Province *20604*

R *Phylica brevifolia* Eckl. & Zeyh. *20604*
    R   *20604* South Africa - Cape Province *20604*

R *Phylica fruticosa* Schltr. *20604*
    R   *20604* South Africa - Cape Province *20604*

I *Phylica greyi* Pillans *20604*
    I   *20604* South Africa - Cape Province *20604*

V *Phylica natalensis* Pillans *20604*
    V   *20604* South Africa - Natal *20604*

V *Phylica parvula* Pillans *20604*
    V   *20604* South Africa - Cape Province *20604*

R *Phylica pearsonii* Pillans *20604*
    R   *20604* South Africa - Cape Province *20604*

R *Phylica plumigera* Pillans *20604*
    R   *20604* South Africa - Cape Province *20604*

E *Phylica polifolia* (Vahl) Pillans *18996*
    E   *18996* St Helena *18996*

R *Phylica retorta* Pillans *20604*
    R   *20604* South Africa - Cape Province *20604*

R *Phylica retrorsa* E.Mey. ex Sond. *20604*
    R   *20604* South Africa - Cape Province *20604*

I *Phylica schlechteri* Pillans *20604*
    I   *20604* South Africa - Cape Province *20604*

I *Phylica simii* Pillans *20604*
    I   *20604* South Africa - Cape Province *20604*

I *Phylica stenopetala* Schltr. var. *stenopetala* *20604*
    I   *20604* South Africa - Cape Province *20604*

R *Pomaderris bilocularis* A.S.George *20681*
    R   *20681* Australia - Western Australia *20681*

R *Pomaderris brogoensis* N.G.Walsh *20681*
    R   *20681* Australia - New South Wales *20681*

V *Pomaderris brunnea* Wakef. *20681*
    V   *20681* Australia - New South Wales *20681*

V *Pomaderris clivicola* E.Ross *20681*
    V   *20681* Australia - Queensland *20681*

R *Pomaderris cocoparrana* N.G.Walsh *20681*
    R   *20681* Australia - New South Wales *20681*

R *Pomaderris costata* Wakef. *20681*
    I   *20681* Australia - New South Wales *20681*
    I   *20681* Australia - Victoria *20681*

E *Pomaderris cotoneaster* Wakef. *20681*
    I   *20681* Australia - New South Wales *20681*
    I   *20681* Australia - Victoria *20681*

V *Pomaderris gilmourii* N.G.Walsh var. *cana* N.G.Walsh *20681*
    V   *20681* Australia - New South Wales *20681*

R **Pomaderris gilmourii** N.G.Walsh var. *gilmourii* N.G.Walsh *20681*
   R   *20681* Australia - New South Wales *20681*

R **Pomaderris grandis** F.Muell. *20681*
   R   *20681* Australia - Western Australia *20681*

R **Pomaderris halmaturina** N.G.Walsh ssp. continentis *20681*
   I   *20681* Australia - South Australia *20681*
   I   *20681* Australia - Victoria *20681*

V **Pomaderris halmaturina** J.Black ssp. halmaturina *20681*
   V   *20681* Australia - South Australia *20681*

R **Pomaderris hamiltonii** *19305*
   R   *19305* New Zealand - North Is. *19305*

R **Pomaderris humilis** N.G.Walsh *20681*
   R   *20681* Australia - Victoria *20681*

R **Pomaderris notata** S.T.Blake *20681*
   I   *20681* Australia - New South Wales *20681*
   I   *20681* Australia - Queensland *20681*

R **Pomaderris oblongifolia** N.G.Walsh *20681*
   R   *20681* Australia - Victoria *20681*

R **Pomaderris oraria** F.Muell. ex Reisseck ssp. calcicola N.G.Walsh *20681*
   R   *20681* Australia - Victoria *20681*

R **Pomaderris oraria** F.Muell. ex Reisseck ssp. oraria *20681*
   I   *20681* Australia - Tasmania *20681*
   I   *20681* Australia - Victoria *20681*

V **Pomaderris pallida** Wakef. *20681*
   I   *20681* Australia - Capital Territory *20681*
   I   *20681* Australia - New South Wales *20681*

V **Pomaderris parrisiae** N.G.Walsh *20681*
   V   *20681* Australia - New South Wales *20681*

R **Pomaderris pauciflora** Wakef. *20681*
   I   *20681* Australia - New South Wales *20681*
   I   *20681* Australia - Victoria *20681*

V **Pomaderris rugosa** Cheeseman
   V   New Zealand - North Is.

V **Pomaderris sericea** Wakef. *20681*
   Ex/E *20681* Australia - New South Wales *20681*
   V   *20681* Australia - Victoria *20681*

V **Pomaderris subplicata** N.G.Walsh *20681*
   V   *20681* Australia - Victoria *20681*

R **Pomaderris tropica** Wakef. *20681*
   R   *20681* Australia - Queensland *20681*

R **Pomaderris virgata** N.G.Walsh *20681*
   R   *20681* Australia - New South Wales *20681*

R **Reynosia guama** Urban *15107*
   R   *15107* Puerto Rico *15107*
   R   *15107* British Virgin Is. (Jost Van Dyke, Virgin Gorda) *15107*
   R   *15107* USA - Virgin Is. *15107*

E **Reynosia jamaicensis** M.C. Johnston *20883, 13336*
   E   *13336* Jamaica *20883*

R **Reynosia microphylla** Urban *11840*
   R   *19105* Cuba (La Habana) *11840*

V **Reynosia moaensis** Borh. & Muniz *5607*
   V   *19105* Cuba (Holguin) *19105*

R **Rhamnidium brevifolium** Borh. *5607*
   R   *19105* Cuba (Guantanamo) *19105*

E **Rhamnidium caloneurum** Standl. *20883, 9006*
   I   *20883* Panama *20883*

V **Rhamnidium dictyophyllum** Urb. *20883, 13336*
   V   *13336* Jamaica *20883*

R **Rhamnidium potrerilloanum** Borh. & Muniz *5607*
   R   *19105* Cuba (Sancti Spiritus) *5607*

R **Rhamnus breedlovei** L.A. & M.C. Johnston *20883*
   R   *20883* Guatemala *20883*
   R   *20883* Mexico *20883*

R **Rhamnus capraeifolia** var. *grandifolia* M.C. & L.A. Johnston *20883*
   V   *20883* Costa Rica *20883*
   V   *20883* El Salvador *20883*
   V   *20883* Guatemala *20883*
   R   *20883* Mexico *20883*

V **Rhamnus glandulosa** Aiton *19174*
   V   Portugal - Madeira
   V   *19174* Spain - Canary Is. *19174*

V **Rhamnus glaucophylla** Sommier *18264*
   V   *18264* Italy (Tuscany) *18264*

R **Rhamnus goudotiana** Triana & Planchon *20883*
   R   *20883* Colombia *20883*
   V   *20883* Venezuela *20883*

R **Rhamnus granulosa** (Ruiz & Pavon) Weberbauer *20883*
   R   *20883* Colombia *20883*
   E   *20883* Ecuador *20883*
   E   *20883* Peru *20883*

R **Rhamnus hintonii** M.C. & L.A. Johnston *20883, 10062*
   R   *20883* Mexico *20883*

R **Rhamnus hirtellus** Boiss. *12840*
   R   *20618* Turkey *20618*

R **Rhamnus integrifolia** DC.
   R   Spain - Canary Is.

R **Rhamnus intermedius** Steud. & Hochst. *20178, 20171*
   R   *20178* Albania *20178*
   R   *21091* Bosnia & Herzegovina *21091*
   R   (former) Yugoslavia

R **Rhamnus ishidae** Miyabe & Kudo *10572*
   R   *10572* Japan *10572*

R **Rhamnus kayacikii** Davis & F. Yaltirik *12840*
   R   *20618* Turkey *20618*

E **Rhamnus lindeniana** Triana & Planchon *20883*
   E   *20883* Venezuela *20883*

V **Rhamnus lojaconoi** Raimondo *18264*
   V   *18264* Italy - Sicily *18264*

V **Rhamnus longistyla** C.B. Wolf *20883, 9004*
   V   *20883* Mexico *20883*

E **Rhamnus macrocarpa** Standley *20883, 10062*
   E   *20883* Mexico *20883*

R **Rhamnus mcvaughii** L.A. & M.C. Johnston *20883, 10062*
   R   *20883* Mexico *20883*

R **Rhamnus nitidus** Davis *12840*
   R   *20618* Turkey *20618*

R **Rhamnus oreodendron** L.O. Wms. *20883*
   R   *20883* Costa Rica *20883*
   I   *20883* Panama *20883*

V **Rhamnus palmeri** S.Watson *20883, 10062*
   V   *20883* Mexico *20883*

V **Rhamnus persicifolius** Moris *18264, 20171*
   Ex *15080* France - Corsica *12844*
   V   *18264* Italy - Sardinia *18264*

R	*Rhamnus pichleri* Schneider & Bornm. ex Bornm. *12840*	
	R	20618 Turkey *20618*
E	*Rhamnus pirifolia* Greene 20850	
	I	20850 U.S. - California *20850*
V	*Rhamnus pompana* M.C. & L.A. Johnston 20883, 10062	
	V	20883 Mexico *20883*
V	*Rhamnus rosei* M.C. & L.A. Johnston 20883, 10062	
	I	20883 Mexico *20883*
R	*Rhamnus scopulorum* (M. E. Jones) Wolf 20883, 10062	
	V	20883 Mexico *20883*
Ex/E	*Rhamnus seravschanica* (Komarov) Kamelin *5942*	
	Ex/E 5942 Uzbekistan *5942*	
V	*Rhamnus serrata* L. A. Johnston var. *guatemalensis* L.A. Johnston 20883, 10062	
	I	20883 Guatemala *20883*
R	*Rhamnus sphaerosperma* Sw. var. *longipes* M.C. & L.A. Johnston 20883	
	R	20883 Dominican Republic *20883*
	V	20883 Haiti *20883*
	V	20883 Puerto Rico *20883*
R	*Rhamnus sphaerosperma* Sw. var. *mesoamericana* M.C. & L.A. Johnston 20883	
	R	20883 El Salvador *20883*
	R	20883 Guatemala *20883*
	R	20883 Honduras *20883*
	R	20883 Mexico *20883*
R	*Rhamnus sphaerosperma* Sw. var. *sphaerosperma* Swartz 20883	
	E	20883 Cuba *20883*
	R	20883 Jamaica *20883*
R	*Rhamnus ulei* Pilger 20883	
	V	20883 Guyana *20883*
	R	20883 Venezuela *20883*
R	*Sarcomphalus havanensis* (Kunth) Griseb. *11840*	
	R	19105 Cuba *11840*
R	*Spyridium burragorang* K.Thiele ms. 20681	
	R	20681 Australia - New South Wales *20681*
R	*Spyridium cinereum* Wakef. 20681	
	I	20681 Australia - New South Wales *20681*
	I	20681 Australia - Victoria *20681*
V	*Spyridium coactilifolium* Reisseck 20681	
	V	20681 Australia - South Australia *20681*
V	*Spyridium eriocephalum* Fenzl var. *glabrisepalum* J.Black 20681	
	V	20681 Australia - South Australia *20681*
R	*Spyridium gunnii* (Hook.f.) Benth. 20681	
	R	20681 Australia - Tasmania *20681*
V	*Spyridium microphyllum* (Reisseck) Druce 20681	
	V	20681 Australia - Tasmania *20681*
V	*Spyridium obcordatum* (Hook.f.) W.M.Curtis 20681	
	V	20681 Australia - Tasmania *20681*
R	*Spyridium spathulatum* (F.Muell.) Benth. 20681	
	I	20681 Australia - South Australia *20681*
	I	20681 Australia - Victoria *20681*
V	*Stenanthemum pimeleoides* (Hook.f.) Benth. 20681	
	V	20681 Australia - Tasmania *20681*
V	*Trymalium minutiflorum* E.Ross 20681	
	V	20681 Australia - Queensland *20681*
R	*Trymalium ramosissimum* Audas 20681	
	R	20681 Australia - Victoria *20681*

I	*Ventilago palawanensis* Elm. *13833*	
	I	13833 Philippines (Palawan) *13833*
V	*Ziziphus bidens* (Urban) M.C. Johnston *5607*	
	V	19105 Cuba (Guantanamo) *5607*
E	*Ziziphus celata* Judd & Hall 20850	
	E	20850 U.S. - Florida *20850*
E	*Ziziphus guaranitica* Malme *16336*	
	E	16336 Argentina *16336*
	E	20176 Argentina - Formosa *20176*
I	*Ziziphus horrida* Roth	
	I	India - Andhra Pradesh (Kurnool)
	I	India - Karnataka (Mysore)
V	*Ziziphus hutchinsonii* Merr. *13780*	
	V	15960 Philippines *13780*
R	*Ziziphus mistol* Griseb. 20883	
	I	20883 Argentina *20883*
		Bolivia *21056*
	R	20883 Paraguay *20883*
I	*Ziziphus palawanensis* Elm. *13833*	
	I	13833 Philippines (Palawan) *13833*
R	*Ziziphus robertsoniana* Beentje Sp. Nov. Ined. 20057	
	R	20057 Kenya *20057*
V	*Ziziphus talanai* (Blanco) Merr. *13780*	
	V	15960 Philippines *13780*
I	*Ziziphus truncata* Blatter & Hallberg *7771*	
	I	India - Rajasthan (west) *7771*

Rhizophoraceae

Number of genera:		14
Number of species:		100
Recorded threatened species:		12 (12%)

Tropical and subtropical.

E	*Carallia diplopetala* Hand.-Mazz. *17617*	
	E	17617 China - Guangxi (Shiwandashan) *11139*
V	*Cassipourea adami* Jacq.-Fel. *7926*	
	V	Guinea *7926*
V	*Cassipourea brittoniana* F. & R. 20883, 13336	
	V	19890 Jamaica (Trelawny) *20883*
E	*Cassipourea eketensis* Baker f. *7926*	
	E	20749 Nigeria (Eket) *7926*
I	*Cassipourea firestoneana* Cooper & Record *16029*	
	I	16029 Liberia *16029*
R	*Cassipourea flanaganii* (Schinz) Alston 20604	
	R	20604 South Africa - Cape Province *20604*
	I	15013 South Africa - Natal *15013*
V	*Cassipourea hiotou* Aubrev. & Pellegrin 20274	
	V	20887 Côte d'Ivoire (south-west) *20887*
	V	20858 Ghana *20274*
E	*Cassipourea subcordata* Britton 20883, 13336	
	E	13336 Jamaica *20883*
E	*Cassipourea subsessilis* Britton 20883, 13336	
	E	13336 Jamaica *20883*
E	*Cassipourea swaziensis* Compton 20604, 18023	
	E	20604 Swaziland *20604*
Ex/E	*Cassipourea thomassetii* Alston *5437*	
	Ex/E 5437 Seychelles - Coralline Is. (Aldabra) *5437*	
R	*Pellacalyx yunnanensis* Hu *17617*	
	R	17617 China - Yunnan (Mengla) *11139*

Rhoipteleaceae

Number of genera:	1
Number of species:	1
Recorded threatened species:	1 (100%)

Southwestern China and North Vietnam.

R   *Rhoiptelea chiliantha* Diels & Hand.-Mazz. *17617*
- **R**   *17617*   China - Guangxi *11139*
- **R**   *17617*   China - Guizhou *11139*
- **R**   *17617*   China - Yunnan (Xichou; Bingbian) *11139*
- **I**   *20985*   Vietnam *6057*

Rhynchocalycaceae

Number of genera:	1
Number of species:	1
Recorded threatened species:	1 (100%)

South Africa.

V   *Rhynchocalyx lawsonioides* Oliv. *20604, 18289*
- **V**   *20604*   South Africa - Cape Province *20604*
- **V**   *20604*   South Africa - Natal (southern (sandstone region)) *20604*

Roridulaceae

Number of genera:	1
Number of species:	2
Recorded threatened species:	1 (50%)

Cape Province (South Africa).

R   *Roridula gorgonias* Planch. *20604, 18289*
- **V**   *14874*   South Africa (southern mountainous regions) *14874*
- **R**   *20604*   South Africa - Cape Province *20604*

Rosaceae

Number of genera:	100
Number of species:	3,000
Recorded threatened species:	419 (13%)

Cosmopolitan, especially temperate and subtropical Northern Hemisphere.

R   *Acaena californica* Bitter *20850*
- **I**   *20850*   U.S. - California *20850*

Ex/E   *Acaena exigua* Gray *20850, 14209*
- **Ex/E**   *20850*   U.S. - Hawaii (Maui & Lana`i) *20850*

R   *Acaena novae-zelandiae* Kirk *19106*
- **R**   *19106*   New Zealand - Antipodes Is. (Campbell Is.) *19106*

E   *Acaena rorida* B.H. Macmill. *19305*
- **E**   *19305*   New Zealand - North Is. *19305*

R   *Agrimonia incisa* Torr. & Gray *20850*
- **V**   *20850*   U.S. - Alabama *20850*
- **V**   *20850*   U.S. - Florida *20850*
- **R**   *20850*   U.S. - Georgia *20850*
- **E**   *20850*   U.S. - Mississippi *20850*
- **I**   *20850*   U.S. - North Carolina *20850*
- **E**   *20850*   U.S. - South Carolina *20850*
- **E**   *20850*   U.S. - Texas *20850*

R   *Alchemilla achtarovii* Pawl. *5204*
- **R**   *5204*   Bulgaria (central) *5204*

R   *Alchemilla amoena* (Czeczott.) Rothm. *12840*
- **R**   *12840*   Turkey *12840*

R   *Alchemilla asteroantha* Rothm. *5204, 20171*
- **R**   *5204*   Bulgaria (central) *5204*

V   *Alchemilla bandericensis* Pawl. *5204, 20171*
- **V**   *5204*   Bulgaria (south-west) *5204*

R   *Alchemilla bornmuelleri* Rothm. *12840*
- **R**   *12840*   Turkey *12840*

R   *Alchemilla bursensis* B. Pawl *12840*
- **R**   *12840*   Turkey *12840*

R   *Alchemilla buseriana* Rothm. *12840*
- **R**   *12840*   Turkey *12840*

I   *Alchemilla cashmiriana* Rothm.
- **I**   India (West Himalaya)

R   *Alchemilla ciminensis* B. Pawl. *12840*
- **R**   *12840*   Turkey *12840*

R   *Alchemilla erzincanensis* B. Pawl. *12840*
- **R**   *12840*   Turkey *12840*

V   *Alchemilla filicaulis* Buser ssp. *vestita* (Buser) M.E. Bradshaw *20883, 20850, 19002, 20171*
- **I**   *20850*   Canada - Labrador *20850*
- **I**   *20850*   Canada - Newfoundland *20850*
- **I**   *20850*   Canada - Nova Scotia *20850*
- **I**   *20850*   Canada - Ontario *20850*
- **I**   *20850*   Canada - Quebec *20850*
- **I**   *20883*   France - St Pierre & Miquelon *20883*
- **I**   *20850*   U.S. - Massachusetts *20850*
- **I**   *20850*   U.S. - New Mexico *20850*

V   *Alchemilla haumanii* Rothm. *19704*
- **V**   *19704*   Ethiopia *19704*

R   *Alchemilla hirsutiflora* (Buser) Rothm. *12840*
- **R**   *12840*   Turkey *12840*

I   *Alchemilla indica* Gardner var. *sibthorpioides* Hook.f. *8021*
- **I**   *16162*   Sri Lanka (Horton Plains) *8021*

R   *Alchemilla jumrukczalica* Pawl. *5204, 20171*
- **R**   *5204*   Bulgaria (central) *5204*

R   *Alchemilla orduensis* B. Pawl. *12840*
- **R**   *12840*   Turkey *12840*

R   *Alchemilla orturcica* B. Pawl. *12840*
- **R**   *12840*   Turkey *12840*

R   *Alchemilla pirinica* Pawl. *5204, 20171*
- **R**   *5204*   Bulgaria (south-west) *5204*

R   *Alchemilla procerrima* Frohner *12840*
- **R**   *12840*   Turkey *12840*

R   *Alchemilla sciadiophylla* Bothm. *12840*
- **R**   *12840*   Turkey *12840*

R   *Alchemilla sintenisii* Rothm. *12840*
- **R**   *12840*   Turkey *12840*

R   *Alchemilla tiryalensis* B. Pawl. *12840*
- **R**   *12840*   Turkey *12840*

I   *Amelanchier chelmea* (halácsy) Browicz *21119*
- **I**   *21119*   Greece *21119*

V   *Amelanchier fernaldii* Wieg. *20850*
- **I**   *20850*   Canada - New Brunswick *20850*
- **I**   *20850*   Canada - Nova Scotia *20850*
- **I**   *20850*   Canada - Prince Edward Is. *20850*
- **I**   *20850*   Canada - Quebec *20850*

R   *Amelanchier nantucketensis* Bickn. *20850*
- **E**   *20850*   Canada - Nova Scotia *20850*
- **I**   *20850*   U.S. - Maine *20850*
- **I**   *20850*   U.S. - Maryland *20850*
- **R**   *20850*   U.S. - Massachusetts *20850*
- **E**   *20850*   U.S. - New York *20850*

R   *Amelanchier parviflora* Boiss. var. *dentata* Browicz *12840*

	R	20618	Turkey 20618
E	**Amelanchier utahensis** Koehne ssp. *covillei* (Standl.) Clokey 20850		
	I	20850	U.S. - Arizona 20850
	I	20850	U.S. - California 20850
	I	20850	U.S. - Nevada 20850
E	**Amygdalus balansae** 20618		
	E	20618	Turkey 20618
R	**Amygdalus carduchorum** ssp. *serrata* 20618		
	R	20618	Turkey 20618
V	**Amygdalus korshinskyi** (Hand.-Mazz.) Bornm. 20618		
	V	20618	Turkey 20618
R	**Amygdalus nairica** Feodorov & Takht.		
	R		former USSR 6930
I	**Amygdalus susakensis** Vassilcz. 5942		
	I	5942	Kyrgyzstan 5942
R	**Amygdalus trichamygdalus** var. *elongata* 20618		
	R	20618	Turkey 20618
I	**Amygdalus vavilovii** M. Pop. 5942		
	I	5942	Tajikistan 5942
E	**Aphanes bachiti** (Haum. & Balle) 19704		
	E	19704	Ethiopia (Gonder) 19704
R	**Aruncus astilboides** Maxim. 10572		
	R	10572	Japan 10572
R	**Aruncus dioicus** Fern. var. *subrotundus* Hara 10572		
	R	10572	Japan 10572
E	**Bencomia brachystachya** Svent. 17534		
	E	17534	Spain - Canary Is. 17534
I	**Bencomia caudata** (Aiton) Webb & Berthel. 17534		
	I		Portugal - Madeira
	V	17534	Spain - Canary Is. 17534
E	**Bencomia exstipulata** Svent. 17530		
	E	17534	Spain - Canary Is. 17534
E	**Bencomia sphaerocarpa** Svent. 17534		
	E	17781	Spain - Canary Is. (El Hierro) 17534
I	**Cerasus blinovskii** Totschilina 5942		
	I	5942	Turkmenistan (near Ashkhabad) 5942
R	**Cerasus erzincanica** Yildirimli 20618		
	R	20618	Turkey 20618
R	**Cerasus hippophaeoides** 20618		
	R	20618	Turkey 20618
E	**Cercocarpus mexicanus** Henrickson 20883, 10184		
	I	20883	Mexico 20883
	?		Mexico - Nuevo Leon 10184
V	**Cercocarpus montanus** Raf. var. *blancheae* (Schneid.) F.L. Martin 20850		
	V	20850	U.S. - California 20850
V	**Cercocarpus rzedowskii** Henrickson 20883		
	I	20883	Mexico 20883
E	**Cercocarpus traskiae** Eastw. 20850		
	E	20850	U.S. - California 20850
R	**Chamaebatia foliolosa** Benth. 20850		
	I	20850	U.S. - California 20850
E	**Chamaemeles coriacea** Lindl. 17781		
	E		Portugal - Madeira
V	**Cliffortia acockii** Weim. 20604		
	V	20604	South Africa - Cape Province 20604
R	**Cliffortia aculeata** Weim. 20604		

	R	20604	South Africa - Cape Province 20604
I	**Cliffortia acutifolia** Weim. 20604		
	I	20604	South Africa - Cape Province 20604
R	**Cliffortia alata** N.E.Br. 20604		
	R	20604	South Africa - Cape Province 20604
R	**Cliffortia arborea** Marloth 20604		
	R	20604	South Africa - Cape Province 20604
R	**Cliffortia burgersii** E.G.H.Oliv. & Fellingham 20604		
	R	20604	South Africa - Cape Province 20604
R	**Cliffortia conifera** E.G.H.Oliv. & Fellingham 20604		
	R	20604	South Africa - Cape Province 20604
E	**Cliffortia ericifolia** L.f. 20604		
	E	20604	South Africa - Cape Province 20604
I	**Cliffortia geniculata** Weim. 20604		
	I	20604	South Africa - Cape Province 20604
R	**Cliffortia hantamensis** Diels 20604		
	R	20604	South Africa - Cape Province 20604
R	**Cliffortia nivenioides** Fellingham 20604		
	R	20604	South Africa - Cape Province 20604
I	**Cliffortia strigosa** Weim. 20604		
	I	20604	South Africa - Cape Province 20604
V	**Cotoneaster buxifolius** Wallich ex Lindley 11494		
	V	11494	India - Tamil Nadu 11494
I	**Cotoneaster cashmirensis** Klotz		
	I		India - Jammu & Kashmir
R	**Cotoneaster cinnabarinus** Juz. 11552, 20171		
	R	20085	Russia (E.Europe) - North 20085
	R	11552	Russian Federation (extreme north west) 11552
V	**Cotoneaster delphinensis** Châtenier 20528		
	V	20528	France (south-east) 20528
I	**Cotoneaster karatavicus** Pojark. 5942		
	I	5942	Kazakhstan 5942
I	**Cotoneaster lucidus** Schlecht. 5942, 20628		
	I	5942	Russia (Siberia) - Buryatiya 5942
	I	5942	Russia (Siberia) - Irkutsk 5942
I	**Cotoneaster simonsii** Baker 11494, 20171		
	I	11494	India - Sikkim 11494
R	**Cotoneaster tauricus** Pojark. 20171		
	R		former European USSR
E	**Cotoneaster wilsonii** Nakai		
	E	15923	Korea, South (Ulnung Island) 15923
R	**Crataegus aegeica** Pojark. 20171		
	R		Greece
R	**Crataegus anamesa** Sarg. 20850		
	R	20850	U.S. - Texas 20850
V	**Crataegus aronia** (L.) Bosc. var. *dentata* Browicz 12840		
	V	20618	Turkey 20618
R	**Crataegus aronia** (L.) Bosc. var. *minuta* Browicz 12840		
	R	20618	Turkey 20618
R	**Crataegus brazoria** Sarg. 20850		
	R	20850	U.S. - Texas 20850
V	**Crataegus canadensis** Sarg. 20850		
	I	20850	Canada - Quebec 20850
R	**Crataegus davisii** Browicz 12840		
	R	20618	Turkey 20618
I	**Crataegus dikmensis** Pojark 12840		

I	20618	Turkey	20618

V   *Crataegus douglasii* Welsh var. *duchesnensis* Welsh 20850

     V   20850   U.S. - Utah   20850

Ex/E   *Crataegus harbisonii* Beadle 20850, 14662

     Ex/E 20850   U.S. - Alabama   20850
     I   20850   U.S. - Georgia   20850
     Ex/E 20850   U.S. - Tennessee   20850

V   *Crataegus harveyana* Sarg. 20850

     I   20850   U.S. - Arkansas   20850
     I   20850   U.S. - Missouri   20850

R   *Crataegus karadaghensis* Pojark. 20171

     R   former European USSR

V   *Crataegus lacrimata* Small 20850

     I   20850   U.S. - Florida   20850

V   *Crataegus latebrosa* Sarg. 20850

     I   20850   U.S. - Arkansas   20850
     I   20850   U.S. - Missouri   20850

V   *Crataegus lumaria* Ashe 20850, 14352

     I   20850   Canada - Ontario   20850
     I   20850   U.S. - Connecticut   20850
     I   20850   U.S. - Michigan   20850
     I   20850   U.S. - New York   20850
     I   20850   U.S. - Wisconsin   20850

V   *Crataegus membranacea* Sarg. 20850

     I   20850   U.S. - Connecticut   20850
     I   20850   U.S. - Vermont   20850

V   *Crataegus mendosa* Beadle 20850

     I   20850   U.S. - Alabama   20850

E   *Crataegus monogyna* Jacq. ssp. *maritima* Corillion 20528

     E   20528   France (west)   20528

E   *Crataegus nitidula* Sarg. 20850, 14662

     Ex/E 20850   Canada - Ontario   20850
     I   20850   U.S. - Michigan   20850
     I   20850   U.S. - Pennsylvania   20850
     I   20850   U.S. - Wisconsin   20850

E   *Crataegus perjuncunda* Sarg. 20850

     E   20850   Canada - Ontario   20850
     I   20850   U.S. - New York   20850

I   *Crataegus pojarkovae* Kossych 5942, 20171

     I   5942   Ukraine - Crimea   5942

R   *Crataegus poliophylla* Sarg. 20850

     R   20850   U.S. - Texas   20850

V   *Crataegus pulcherrima* Ashe 20850

     I   20850   U.S. - Alabama   20850
     I   20850   U.S. - Florida   20850
     E   20850   U.S. - Georgia   20850
     I   20850   U.S. - Mississippi   20850

E   *Crataegus saligna* Greene 20850

     I   20850   U.S. - Colorado   20850

R   *Crataegus stenosepala* Sarg. 20850

     R   20850   U.S. - Texas   20850

R   *Crataegus sutherlandensis* Sarg. 20850

     R   20850   U.S. - Texas   20850

R   *Crataegus taurica* Pojark. 20171

     R   Ukraine - Crimea   8000
     R   former European USSR (Crimea)   8000

R   *Crataegus texana* Buckl. 20850

     R   20850   U.S. - Texas   20850

V   *Crataegus triflora* Chapman 20850

     V   20850   U.S. - Alabama   20850

     E   20850   U.S. - Georgia   20850
     E   20850   U.S. - Louisiana   20850
     E   20850   U.S. - Mississippi   20850
     I   20850   U.S. - Tennessee   20850

R   *Crataegus ucrainica* Pojark. 20171

     R   former European USSR

R   *Crataegus viburnifolia* Sarg. 20850

     R   20850   U.S. - Texas   20850

V   *Crataegus warneri* Sarg. 20850

     V   20850   U.S. - Texas   20850

V   *Dendriopoterium menendezii* Svent. 17534

     V   20750   Spain - Canary Is.   17534

E   *Dendriopoterium pulidoi* Svent 17534

     E   20750   Spain - Canary Is. (Gran Canaria)   17534

R   *Filipendula formosa* Nakai 15923

     R   15923   Korea, South (Mt Chiri)   15957

V   *Filipendula occidentalis* (S.Watson) T.J. Howell 20850

     V   20850   U.S. - Oregon   20850
     V   20850   U.S. - Washington   20850

R   *Filipendula tsuguwoi* Ohwi 10572

     R   10572   Japan   10572

I   *Fragaria bucharica* Los.-Losinsk. 5942

     I   5942   Tajikistan   5942

V   *Geum geniculatum* Michx. 20850

     V   20850   U.S. - North Carolina   20850
     E   20850   U.S. - Tennessee   20850

V   *Geum peckii* Pursh 20850, 3064

     V   20850   Canada - Nova Scotia   20850
     I   20850   U.S. - Maine   20850
     V   20850   U.S. - New Hampshire   20850

R   *Geum pusillum* Petrie 19305

     R   19305   New Zealand - South Is.   19305

E   *Geum radiatum* Michx. 20850

     E   20850   U.S. - North Carolina   20850
     E   20850   U.S. - Tennessee   20850

E   *Geum rossii* (R. Br.) Ser. var. *depressum* (Greene) C.L. Hitchc. 20850

     E   20850   U.S. - Washington   20850

R   *Geum talbotianum* W.M.Curtis 20681

     R   20681   Australia - Tasmania   20681

E   *Horkelia bolanderi* Gray 20850

     E   20850   U.S. - California   20850

V   *Horkelia congesta* Keck ssp. *congesta* 20850

     V   20850   U.S. - Oregon   20850

E   *Horkelia cuneata* (Gray) Keck ssp. *sericea* (Gray) Keck 20850

     E   20850   U.S. - California   20850

R   *Horkelia frondosa* (Greene) Rydb. 20850

     I   20850   U.S. - California   20850

E   *Horkelia hendersonii* T.J. Howell 20850

     E   20850   U.S. - California   20850
     V   20850   U.S. - Oregon   20850

V   *Horkelia hispidula* Rydb. 20850

     V   20850   U.S. - California   20850

V   *Horkelia marinensis* (Elmer) Crum ex Keck 20850

     V   20850   U.S. - California   20850

V   *Horkelia parryi* Greene 20850

     V   20850   U.S. - California   20850

R   *Horkelia tenuiloba* (Torr.) Gray 20850

I	20850	U.S. - California	20850

R   *Horkelia truncata* Rydb. 20850
V	20850	U.S. - California	20850

E   *Horkelia tularensis* (J.T. Howell) Munz 20850
E	20850	U.S. - California	20850

E   *Horkelia wilderae* Parish 20850
E	20850	U.S. - California	20850

E   *Hulthemosa guzarica* Juzepczuk
E	former USSR	6930

V   *Ivesia aperta* (J.T. Howell) Munz 20850
V	20850	U.S. - California	20850
I	20850	U.S. - Nevada	20850

V   *Ivesia aperta* (J.T. Howell) Munz var. *aperta* 20850
V	20850	U.S. - California	20850
I	20850	U.S. - Nevada	20850

E   *Ivesia aperta* (J. T. Howell) Munz var. *canina* Ertter 20850
E	20850	U.S. - California	20850

V   *Ivesia argyrocoma* (Rydb.) Rydb. 20850, 17788
V	20850	U.S. - California (San Bernardino mountains) 20850

V   *Ivesia arizonica* (Eastw. ex J.T. Howell) Ertter 20850
I	20850	U.S. - Arizona	20850
I	20850	U.S. - California	20850
I	20850	U.S. - Nevada	20850

V   *Ivesia baileyi* S.Watson var. *beneolens* (A. Nels. & J.F. Macbr.) Ertter 20850
E	20850	U.S. - California	20850
I	20850	U.S. - Idaho	20850
I	20850	U.S. - Nevada	20850
I	20850	U.S. - Oregon	20850

E   *Ivesia callida* (Hall) Rydb. 20850
E	20850	U.S. - California	20850

E   *Ivesia cryptocaulis* (Clokey) Keck 20850, 19002
E	20850	U.S. - Nevada	20850

V   *Ivesia jaegeri* Munz & Johnston 20850
E	20850	U.S. - California	20850
V	20850	U.S. - Nevada	20850

R   *Ivesia kingii* S.Watson 20850
I	20850	U.S. - California	20850
R	20850	U.S. - Nevada	20850
E	20850	U.S. - Utah	20850

E   *Ivesia kingii* S.Watson var. *eremica* (Coville) Ertter 20850
E	20850	U.S. - Nevada	20850

E   *Ivesia longibracteata* Ertter 20850
E	20850	U.S. - California	20850

R   *Ivesia lycopodioides* Gray 20850
I	20850	U.S. - California	20850
I	20850	U.S. - Nevada	20850

R   *Ivesia muirii* Gray 20850
I	20850	U.S. - California	20850

R   *Ivesia multifoliolata* (Torr.) Keck 20850
R	20850	U.S. - Arizona	20850

V   *Ivesia paniculata* T.W. & J.P. Nelson 20850
V	20850	U.S. - California	20850

E   *Ivesia patellifera* (J.T. Howell) Ertter 20850
E	20850	U.S. - California	20850

V   *Ivesia pickeringii* Torr. ex Gray 20850

V	20850	U.S. - California	20850

E   *Ivesia pityocharis* Ertter 20850
V	20850	U.S. - Nevada	20850

V   *Ivesia purpurascens* (S.Watson) Keck 20850
I	20850	U.S. - California	20850

R   *Ivesia pygmaea* Gray 20850
I	20850	U.S. - California	20850
I	20850	U.S. - Nevada	20850

E   *Ivesia rhypara* Ertter & Reveal 20850
E	20850	U.S. - Nevada	20850
E	20850	U.S. - Oregon	20850

E   *Ivesia rhypara* Ertter & Reveal var. *rhypara* 20850
E	20850	U.S. - Nevada	20850
E	20850	U.S. - Oregon	20850

E   *Ivesia rhypara* Ertter & Reveal var. *shellyi* Ertter 20850
E	20850	U.S. - Oregon	20850

V   *Ivesia sericoleuca* (Rydb.) Rydb. 20850
V	20850	U.S. - California	20850
I	20850	U.S. - Nevada	20850

R   *Ivesia shockleyi* S.Watson 20850
I	20850	U.S. - California	20850
I	20850	U.S. - Nevada	20850
E	20850	U.S. - Oregon	20850
E	20850	U.S. - Utah	20850

E   *Ivesia shockleyi* S.Watson var. *ostleri* Ertter 20850
E	20850	U.S. - Utah	20850

V   *Ivesia unguiculata* Gray 20850
V	20850	U.S. - California	20850

V   *Ivesia utahensis* S.Watson 20850
V	20850	U.S. - Utah	20850

V   *Ivesia webberi* Gray 20850
V	20850	U.S. - California	20850
V	20850	U.S. - Nevada	20850

V   *Lyonothamnus floribundus* Gray 20850
I	20850	U.S. - California	20850

V   *Lyonothamnus floribundus* A.Gray ssp. *aspleniifolius* (Greene) Raven 20850
V	20850	U.S. - California	20850

E   *Lyonothamnus floribundus* A.Gray ssp. *floribundus* 20850
E	20850	U.S. - California	20850

R   *Malus florentina* (Zuccagni) C.K.Schneid. 20178, 20171
R	20178	Albania	20178
R		Greece	
R		Italy	
R		(former) Yugoslavia	
R	20618	Turkey (Anatolia)	20618

E   *Malus hupehensis* (Pamp.) Rehd. 20626
E	20626	Japan (Oita; Kumamoto) 20626

V   *Malus spontanea* (Makino) Makino 10572
V	20626	Japan (Miyazaki; Kagoshima) 20626

V   *Malus sylvestris* Mill. var. *microphylla* Browicz 12840
V	12840	Turkey 12840

R   *Malus trilobata* (Labill.) C.K.Schneid. 20171
R		Greece (north-east) 8000
?		Israel 8000
?		Lebanon 8000

	?		Syria *8000*
E	*Marcetella maderensis* (Bornm.) Svent.		
	E		Portugal - Madeira
R	*Marcetella moquiniana* (Webb & Berthel.) Svent. *17534*		
	R	*17534*	Spain - Canary Is. *17534*
E	*Margyracaena skottsbergii* *19125*		
	E	*19125*	Chile - Juan Fernandez Is. *19116*
E	*Margyricarpus digynus* (Bitter) Skottsb. *19116*		
	E	*19125*	Chile - Juan Fernandez Is. *19116*
E	*Mespilus canescens* Phipps *20850*		
	E	*20850*	U.S. - Arkansas *20850*
V	*Neviusia alabamensis* Gray *20850, 14010*		
	V	*20850*	U.S. - Alabama *20850*
	E	*20850*	U.S. - Arkansas *20850*
	E	*20850*	U.S. - Georgia *20850*
	E	*20850*	U.S. - Mississippi *20850*
	Ex	*20850*	U.S. - Missouri *20850*
	E	*20850*	U.S. - South Carolina *20850*
	E	*20850*	U.S. - Tennessee *20850*
E	*Neviusia cliftonii* Shevock, Ertter & Taylor *20850, 17908*		
	E	*20850*	U.S. - California (Lake Shasta) *20850*
R	*Petrophyton acuminatum* Rydb. *20850*		
	I	*20850*	U.S. - California *20850*
E	*Petrophyton cinerascens* (Piper) Rydb. *20850*		
	E	*20850*	U.S. - Washington *20850*
R	*Petrophyton hendersonii* (Canby) Rydb. *20850*		
	I	*20850*	U.S. - Washington *20850*
R	*Photinia ardisifolia* Hayata *20854*		
	R	*20854*	Taiwan *20854*
I	*Photinia lasiopetala* Hayata		
	I		Taiwan
I	*Polylepis australis* Bitter *13766*		
	V	*19572*	Argentina *13766*
	I	*20176*	Argentina - Cordoba *20176*
	I	*20176*	Argentina - Catamarca *20176*
	I	*20176*	Argentina - Jujuy *20176*
	I	*20176*	Argentina - La Rioja *20176*
	I	*20176*	Argentina - San Juan *20176*
	I	*20176*	Argentina - San Luis *20176*
	I	*20176*	Argentina - Tucuman *20176*
E	*Polylepis hieronymi* Pilger *13766*		
	E	*13766*	Argentina *13766*
	E	*13766*	Bolivia *13766*
V	*Polylepis lanuginosa* Kunth *13766*		
	V	*19572*	Ecuador *13766*
E	*Polylepis multijuga* Pilger *13766*		
	E	*20046*	Peru *13766*
E	*Polylepis pepei* B. Simpson *13766*		
	E	*13766*	Bolivia *13766*
	E	*20046*	Peru *13766*
V	*Polylepis racemosa* Ruiz Lopez & Pavon *13766*		
	V	*12468*	Peru *13766*
V	*Polylepis subsericans* J.F. Macbr. *13766*		
	V	*12468*	Peru *13766*
R	*Polylepis tarapacana* Phil. *20883, 13766*		
	E		Argentina *13766*
	I	*20883*	Bolivia *20883*
	V	*20883*	Chile (Regions I,II) *20883*
	I	*20883*	Peru *20883*
I	*Polylepis tomentella* Wedd. *13766*		
	I	*16336*	Argentina *13766*
	I	*20176*	Argentina - Jujuy *20176*

	V	*19448*	Bolivia *13766*
	V	*19535*	Chile *13766*
	V	*12468*	Peru *13766*
R	*Potentilla aladagensis* E. Leblebici *12840*		
	R	*12840*	Turkey *12840*
V	*Potentilla albiflora* L.O. Williams *20850*		
	I	*20850*	U.S. - Arizona *20850*
R	*Potentilla ambigens* Greene *20850*		
	E	*20850*	U.S. - Colorado *20850*
	I	*20850*	U.S. - New Mexico *20850*
	Ex/E	*20850*	U.S. - Wyoming *20850*
R	*Potentilla anadyrensis* Juzepczuk		
	R		former USSR *6930*
E	*Potentilla angelliae* N. Holmgren *20850*		
	E	*20850*	U.S. - Utah *20850*
R	*Potentilla anjuica* Petrovsky *21309*		
	R	*21309*	Russia (E.Europe) - North *21309*
R	*Potentilla arctoalaskensis* Jurtz. *21309*		
	R	*21309*	Russia (E.Europe) - Northwest *21309*
R	*Potentilla armeniaca* Siegfr. ex Th.Wolf *12840*		
	R	*12840*	Turkey *12840*
R	*Potentilla asinaria* Maire		
	R		Morocco
E	*Potentilla basaltica* Tiehm & Ertter *20850*		
	E	*20850*	U.S. - California *20850*
	E	*20850*	U.S. - Nevada *20850*
R	*Potentilla beringensis* Jurtz. *11552, 21309*		
	R	*21309*	Russia (E.Europe) - North *21309*
	E	*11552*	Russian Federation (extreme north east) *11552*
R	*Potentilla brooksensis* Jurtz. *21309*		
	R	*21309*	Russia (E.Europe) - North *21309*
R	*Potentilla buccoana* Clem. *12840*		
	R	*12840*	Turkey *12840*
R	*Potentilla buchneri* Kit Tan & Sorger *12840*		
	R	*12840*	Turkey *12840*
R	*Potentilla cappadocica* Boiss. *12840*		
	R	*12840*	Turkey *12840*
R	*Potentilla carniolica* A.Kern. *20171*		
	K	*21091*	Bosnia & Herzegovina *21091*
	R		(former) Yugoslavia
	Potentilla chrysantha Trev. ssp. *pastorum* Sojak *19607*		
	R	*19947*	Romania *19947*
E	*Potentilla cottamii* N. Holmgren *20850*		
	E	*20850*	U.S. - Nevada *20850*
	E	*20850*	U.S. - Utah *20850*
V	*Potentilla cristae* Ferlatte & Strother *20850*		
	V	*20850*	U.S. - California *20850*
R	*Potentilla czegitunica* Jurtz. *21309*		
	R	*21309*	Russia (E.Europe) - North *21309*
V	*Potentilla delphinensis* Gren. & Godr. *8000, 20171*		
	V	*20528*	France (alps) *17891*
R	*Potentilla dezhnevii* Jurtz. *21309*		
	R	*21309*	Russia (E.Europe) - North *21309*
R	*Potentilla discipulorum* Davis. *12840*		
	R	*12840*	Turkey *12840*
R	*Potentilla diversifolia* Lehm. var. *ranunculus* (Lange) Boivin *20850*		
	I	*20850*	Denmark - Greenland *20850*

I *20850* Canada - Labrador *20850*

R *Potentilla doddsii* Davis *12840*
  R *12840* Turkey *12840*

R *Potentilla doerfleri* Wettst. *20171*
  R   (former) Yugoslavia

V *Potentilla effusa* Douglas ex Lehm. var. *rupincola*
   (Osterhout) T. Wolf *20850, 11630*
  V *20850* U.S. - Colorado *20850*

R *Potentilla emilii-popii* Nyár. *5204, 20171*
  R *5204* Bulgaria (North-eastern - two sites and one
     area) *5204*
  V *19949* Romania *20631*

V *Potentilla eversmanniana* Fisch. ex Ledeb. *11552,
  20171*
  V *11552* Russian Federation (Ural Mts.) *11552*

E *Potentilla glandulosa* Lindl. ssp. *ewanii*
  Keck *20850*
  E *20850* U.S. - California *20850*

R *Potentilla goulandrii* Rech.f.
  R   Greece

R *Potentilla grammopetala* Moretti *20171*
  I   Italy *8000*
  R *18154* Switzerland *18154*

V *Potentilla grayi* S.Watson *20850*
  I *20850* U.S. - California *20850*

R *Potentilla guarensis* Monts.
  R   Spain

R *Potentilla guilliermondii* Emberger & Maire
  R   Morocco

E *Potentilla hickmanii* Eastw. *20850*
  E *20850* U.S. - California *20850*

R *Potentilla isaurica* (Davis) B. Pawl. *12840*
  R *12840* Turkey *12840*

I *Potentilla kashmirica* Hook.f.
  I   India - Jammu & Kashmir

V *Potentilla macounii* Rydb. *20850*
  I *20850* Canada - Alberta *20850*
  I *20850* U.S. - Montana *20850*

V *Potentilla mascuinii* Monts.
  V   Spain

R *Potentilla matsumurae* Th.Wolf var. *yuparensis*
  Kudo *10572*
  R *10572* Japan *10572*

Ex *Potentilla multijuga* Lehm. *20850, 14662*
  Ex *20850* U.S. - California *20850*

R *Potentilla murrayi* Jurtz. *21309*
  R *21309* U.S. - Alaska *21309*

E *Potentilla pensylvanica* (Rydb.) Welsh & Johnston var.
  paucijuga (Rydb.) Welsh & Johnston *20850*
  I *20850* U.S. - Colorado *20850*
  E *20850* U.S. - Utah *20850*

R *Potentilla pulvinaris* Fenzl *12840*
  R *12840* Turkey *12840*

R *Potentilla reuteri* Boiss. *20171*
  R   Spain

R *Potentilla riparia* Murata *10572*
  R *10572* Japan *10572*

E *Potentilla robbinsiana* Oakes ex Rydb. *20850*
  E *20850* U.S. - New Hampshire *20850*

V *Potentilla sierrae-blancae* Woot. & Rydb. *20850*
  V *20850* U.S. - New Mexico *20850*

R *Potentilla subpalmata* Ledeb. *12840*
  R *12840* Turkey *12840*

R *Potentilla tauricola* H. Pesmen *12840*
  R *12840* Turkey *12840*

R *Potentilla tollii* Trautv.
  R   former USSR *6930*

R *Potentilla tschaunensis* Juz. ex Jurtz. *21309*
  R *21309* Russia (E.Europe) - North *21309*

R *Potentilla uschakovii* Jurtz. *21309*
  R *21309* Russia (E.Europe) - North *21309*

R *Potentilla visianii* Pancic *20178, 20171*
  R *20178* Albania *20178*
  V *21091* Bosnia & Herzegovina *21091*
  R   (former) Yugoslavia *20178*

Ex *Potentilla volgarica* Juz. *11552*
  Ex *11552* Russian Federation (western) *11552*

R *Potentilla wheeleri* S.Watson *20850*
  I *20850* U.S. - Arizona *20850*
  I *20850* U.S. - California *20850*

R *Potentilla wrangelii* Petrovsky *21309*
  R *21309* Russia (E.Europe) - North *21309*
  R   former USSR *6930*

R *Prunus alleghaniensis* (W. Wight) Sarg. var. *davisii*
  (W. Wight) Sarg. *20850*
  R *20850* U.S. - Michigan *20850*

R *Prunus cocomilia* Ten var. *puberula* (Schneider)
  Browicz *12840*
  R *20618* Turkey *20618*

I *Prunus darvasica* Temb. *5942*
  I *5942* Tajikistan *5942*

V *Prunus geniculata* Harper *20850, 17890*
  V *20850* U.S. - Florida (Lake, Polk & Highland Co.)
     20850

I *Prunus grisen* (C. Muell.) Kalkm. var. *tomentosa*
  (K. & V.) Kalkm. *13833*
  I *13833* Philippines (low and medium altitudes)
     13833

R *Prunus himalaica* Kitam. *7738*
  R   Nepal *7738*

V *Prunus incisa* Thunb. var. *bukosanensis* (Honda)
  Hara *20626*
  V *20626* Japan (Saitama; Tokyo) *20626*

R *Prunus kurdica* Fenzl *12840*
  R *20618* Turkey *20618*

R *Prunus lusitanica* L. ssp. *azorica* (Mouillef.)
  Franco *8000, 20171*
  R   Portugal - Azores *17891*

V *Prunus lyonii* (Eastw.) Sarg. *20850*
  I *20850* U.S. - California *20850*

E *Prunus maritima* Walter var. *gravesii* (Small) G.J.
  Anderson *20850*
  E *20850* U.S. - Connecticut *20850*

R *Prunus matuurai* Sas.
  R   Taiwan (Taipingshan)

V *Prunus murrayana* Palmer *20850*
  V *20850* U.S. - Texas *20850*

E *Prunus pleuradenia* Griseb. *19001*
  E *19001* Dominica *19001*

E	*19001*	Guadeloupe *19001*
E	*19001*	Grenada *19001*
E	*19001*	Martinique (Morne Bois la Roche; summit of Montagne du Vauclin) *19001*
E	*19001*	St Kitts - Nevis *19001*
E	*19001*	St Vincent *19001*

V   *Prunus pruninosa* Schrenk *19909*
    V   *19909*   China - Xinjiang Uygur Zizhiqu *19909*

I   *Prunus pulgarensis* (Elm.) Kalkm. *13833*
    I   *13833*   Philippines (Palawan) *13833*

R   *Prunus ramburii* Boiss. *20171*
    R   Spain (Sierra Nevada & Sierra de Gádor) *8000*

R   *Prunus taiwaniana* Hayata *20511*
    R   *20511*   Taiwan (central) *20511*

R   *Prunus takasagomontana* Sas.
    R   Taiwan (Mt Lala)

R   *Prunus transarisanensis* Hayata *20511*
    R   *20511*   Taiwan (Mt Alishan) *20511*

V   *Prunus walkeri* (Wight) Kalkman *8021*
    V   *12838*   Sri Lanka *8021*

E   *Purshia subintegra* (Kearney) Henrickson (pro hyb.) *20850*
    E   *20850*   U.S. - Arizona *20850*

R   *Pyrus anatolica* Browicz *12840*
    R   *20618*   Turkey *20618*

I   *Pyrus asiae-mediae* (Popov) Maleev *5942*
    I   *5942*   Kazakhstan (south) *5942*

I   *Pyrus cajon* V. Zapr. *5942*
    I   *5942*   Tajikistan *5942*

R   *Pyrus hakkiarica* Browicz *12840*
    R   *20618*   Turkey *20618*

E   *Pyrus kawakamii* Hayata *20511*
    E   *20511*   Taiwan (northern & central) *20511*

I   *Pyrus raddeana* Woronow *5942*
    I   *5942*   Armenia *5942*
    I   *5942*   Azerbaijan *5942*

R   *Pyrus salicifolia* Pallas var. *serrulata* Browicz *12840*
    R   *20618*   Turkey *20618*

V   *Pyrus serikensis* *20618*
    V   *20618*   Turkey *20618*

R   *Pyrus syriaca* Boiss. var. *microphylla* Zoh. ex Browicz *20618*
    R   *20618*   Turkey *20618*

R   *Pyrus yaltirikii* Browicz *12840*
    R   *20618*   Turkey *20618*

E   *Rosa arabica* Crepin *16168*
    E   *16168*   Egypt (mountains of S. Sinai) *16168*

R   *Rosa blanda* Ait. var. *glabra* Crepin *20850*
    I   *20850*   Canada - New Brunswick *20850*
    I   *20850*   Canada - Nova Scotia *20850*
    I   *20850*   Canada - Ontario *20850*
    I   *20850*   Canada - Quebec *20850*
    V   *20850*   U.S. - Maine *20850*
    I   *20850*   U.S. - Minnesota *20850*
    I   *20850*   U.S. - New York *20850*

R   *Rosa dumalis* Bechat. var. *anatalyensis* (Menden) O. Nilson *12840*
    R   *12840*   Turkey *12840*

R   *Rosa dumalis* ssp. *boissieri* var. *antalyensis* *20618*
    R   *20618*   Turkey *20618*

R   *Rosa hirtula* Nakai *10572*
    R   *10572*   Japan *10572*

V   *Rosa mandonii* Desegl.
    V   Portugal - Madeira

R   *Rosa minutifolia* Engelm. *20850*
    E   *20850*   U.S. - California *20850*

E   *Rosa stellata* W.H. Lewis var. *erlansoniae* W.H. Lewis *20850*
    I   *20850*   U.S. - New Mexico *20850*
    E   *20850*   U.S. - Texas *20850*

I   *Rosa tsinlingensis* Pax & Hoffm. *11815*
    I   China - Shaanxi (Taibeishan; Baoji) *11815*

V   *Rosa villosa* L. var. *sancti-andreae* (Deg. et Trtm.) Soó *17786*
    V   *20686*   Hungary *17786*

V   *Rubus aculiferus* Bailey *20850*
    I   *20850*   U.S. - New Hampshire *20850*

E   *Rubus adenocaulis* Fern. *20850*
    I   *20850*   Canada - Nova Scotia *20850*

E   *Rubus aethiopicus* A. Grah. *19704*
    E   *19704*   Ethiopia (Shwea Upland, Sidamo) *19704*

Ex/E   *Rubus aliceae* Bailey *20850*
    Ex/E   *20850*   U.S. - New Mexico *20850*

I   *Rubus almorensis* Dunn
    I   India - Uttar Pradesh

V   *Rubus alter* Bailey *20850*
    I   *20850*   U.S. - Maine *20850*
    I   *20850*   U.S. - New Hampshire *20850*

V   *Rubus amamianus* Hatus. & Ohwi *10572*
    V   *10572*   Japan *10572*

E   *Rubus amnicola* Blanch. *20850*
    I   *20850*   Canada - Nova Scotia *20850*
    I   *20850*   U.S. - Maine *20850*
    I   *20850*   U.S. - New Hampshire *20850*
    I   *20850*   U.S. - New Jersey *20850*

V   *Rubus bartonianus* M.E. Peck *20850*
    V   *20850*   U.S. - Idaho *20850*
    V   *20850*   U.S. - Oregon *20850*

Ex/E   *Rubus beatus* Bailey *20850*
    I   *20850*   U.S. - New York *20850*

V   *Rubus bicknellii* Bailey *20850*
    I   *20850*   U.S. - Massachusetts *20850*

Ex/E   *Rubus blanchardianus* Bailey *20850*
    I   *20850*   U.S. - Vermont *20850*

R   *Rubus bollei* Focke
    R   Spain - Canary Is.

V   *Rubus burnhamii* Bailey *20850*
    I   *20850*   U.S. - New York *20850*

V   *Rubus centralis* Bailey *20850*
    E   *20850*   U.S. - Indiana *20850*
    I   *20850*   U.S. - Maryland *20850*
    I   *20850*   U.S. - Michigan *20850*
    I   *20850*   U.S. - Pennsylvania *20850*

V   *Rubus clarus* Bailey *20850*
    I   *20850*   U.S. - Virginia *20850*

Ex/E   *Rubus conabilis* Bailey *20850*
    I   *20850*   U.S. - Michigan *20850*

Ex/E	*Rubus conanictuensis* Bailey *20850*		
	I	*20850* U.S. - Rhode Is. *20850*	
V	*Rubus cubitans* Blanch. *20850*		
	I	*20850* U.S. - Vermont *20850*	
V	*Rubus curtipes* Bailey *20850*		
	I	*20850* U.S. - Massachusetts *20850*	
	I	*20850* U.S. - Virginia *20850*	
Ex/E	*Rubus darlingtonii* Bailey *20850*		
	I	*20850* U.S. - Michigan *20850*	
E	*Rubus defectionis* Fern. *20850*		
	I	*20850* U.S. - Virginia *20850*	
E	*Rubus emeritus* Bailey *20850*		
	I	*20850* Canada - New Brunswick *20850*	
E	*Rubus erlangeri* Engl. *19704*		
	E	*19704* Ethiopia (Sidamo, Bale) *19704*	
V	*Rubus flavinanus* Blanch. *20850*		
	I	*20850* U.S. - Maryland *20850*	
	I	*20850* U.S. - Vermont *20850*	
	I	*20850* U.S. - West Virginia *20850*	
I	*Rubus fockei* Gandhi		
	I	India - Karnataka	
	I	India - Kerala (Attapadi Hills)	
	I	India - Tamil Nadu	
E	*Rubus fryei* H.A. & T. Davis *20850*		
	I	*20850* U.S. - West Virginia *20850*	
V	*Rubus furtivus* Bailey *20850*		
	I	*20850* U.S. - New York *20850*	
V	*Rubus genevierii* Boreau ssp. *herminii* (Samp.) P. Cout. *20076, 20686*		
	V	*20076* Portugal *20076*	
Ex/E	*Rubus glaucifolius* Kellogg var. *ganderi* (Bailey) Munz *20850*		
	Ex/E	*20850* U.S. - California *20850*	
V	*Rubus gulosus* Bailey *20850*		
	I	*20850* Canada - New Brunswick *20850*	
	I	*20850* U.S. - Maine *20850*	
E	*Rubus hancinianus* Bailey *20850*		
	I	*20850* U.S. - Kansas *20850*	
	I	*20850* U.S. - Missouri *20850*	
E	*Rubus hanesii* Bailey *20850*		
	I	*20850* U.S. - Michigan *20850*	
V	*Rubus harmonicus* Bailey *20850*		
	I	*20850* U.S. - Maine *20850*	
	I	*20850* U.S. - West Virginia *20850*	
V	*Rubus hispidoides* Bailey *20850*		
	I	*20850* U.S. - Massachusetts *20850*	
R	*Rubus hochstetterorum* Seub. *20171*		
	R	Portugal - Azores	
V	*Rubus huttonii* Bailey *20850*		
	I	*20850* U.S. - West Virginia *20850*	
E	*Rubus hypolasius* Fern. *20850*		
	I	*20850* U.S. - New Jersey *20850*	
	I	*20850* U.S. - Virginia *20850*	
Ex/E	*Rubus impar* Bailey *20850*		
	I	*20850* U.S. - Illinois *20850*	
	Ex	*20850* U.S. - Indiana *20850*	
	I	*20850* U.S. - Missouri *20850*	
E	*Rubus inclinis* Bailey *20850*		
	I	*20850* U.S. - New York *20850*	
V	*Rubus indianensis* Bailey *20850*		
	I	*20850* U.S. - Indiana *20850*	

	I	*20850* U.S. - Kentucky *20850*	
V	*Rubus inferior* Bailey *20850*		
	I	*20850* U.S. - Florida *20850*	
V	*Rubus iniens* Bailey *20850*		
	I	*20850* U.S. - Delaware *20850*	
	I	*20850* U.S. - Virginia *20850*	
V	*Rubus injunctus* Bailey *20850*		
	I	*20850* U.S. - Pennsylvania *20850*	
	I	*20850* U.S. - Virginia *20850*	
	I	*20850* U.S. - West Virginia *20850*	
V	*Rubus insulanus* Bailey *20850*		
	I	*20850* U.S. - Connecticut *20850*	
	I	*20850* U.S. - New York *20850*	
	I	*20850* U.S. - Rhode Is. *20850*	
R	*Rubus intermitten* Bolle *6057*		
	R	Vietnam *6057*	
I	*Rubus iringanus* C.E. Gust *5926*		
	I	*5926* Tanzania *5926*	
E	*Rubus kelloggii* Blanch. *20850*		
	I	*20850* U.S. - Missouri *20850*	
R	*Rubus keniensis* Standley *20057*		
	R	*20057* Kenya (Mt Kenya; Nyandarua) *20057*	
V	*Rubus largus* Bailey *20850*		
	I	*20850* U.S. - Texas *20850*	
E	*Rubus leucodermis* Dougl. ex Torr. & Gray var. *bernardinus* (Greene) Jepson *20850*		
	I	*20850* U.S. - California *20850*	
Ex/E	*Rubus leucodermis* Dougl. ex Torr. & Gray var. *trinitatis* Berger *20850*		
	I	*20850* U.S. - California *20850*	
V	*Rubus libratus* Bailey *20850*		
	I	*20850* U.S. - Delaware *20850*	
	I	*20850* U.S. - Maryland *20850*	
V	*Rubus macraei* Gray *20850, 14209*		
	V	*20850* U.S. - Hawaii (Maui & Hawai`i) *20850*	
Ex/E	*Rubus macvaughii* Bailey *20850*		
	I	*20850* U.S. - Texas *20850*	
V	*Rubus mananensis* Bailey *20850*		
	I	*20850* Canada - New Brunswick *20850*	
Ex/E	*Rubus maniseesensis* Bailey *20850*		
	I	*20850* U.S. - Rhode Is. *20850*	
Ex/E	*Rubus multilicius* Bailey *20850*		
	I	*20850* U.S. - Maine *20850*	
V	*Rubus nakaii* Tuy. *8037*		
	V	*19134* Japan - Ogasawara-shoto *8037*	
E	*Rubus nefrens* Bailey *20850*		
	I	*20850* U.S. - Kentucky *20850*	
	I	*20850* U.S. - Minnesota *20850*	
	I	*20850* U.S. - Missouri *20850*	
	I	*20850* U.S. - New York *20850*	
	I	*20850* U.S. - Ohio *20850*	
	I	*20850* U.S. - Oklahoma *20850*	
	I	*20850* U.S. - Tennessee *20850*	
	I	*20850* U.S. - Virginia *20850*	
E	*Rubus nigerrimus* (Greene) Rydb. *20850*		
	I	*20850* U.S. - Oregon *20850*	
	E	*20850* U.S. - Washington *20850*	
V	*Rubus nishimuranus* Koidz. *8037*		
	V	*19134* Japan - Ogasawara-shoto *8037*	
E	*Rubus notatus* Bailey var. *ortus* Bailey *20850*		
	E	*20850* U.S. - Connecticut *20850*	

V	***Rubus novanglicus*** Bailey *20850*	
	I	*20850* U.S. - Connecticut *20850*
E	***Rubus novocaesarius*** Bailey *20850*	
	I	*20850* U.S. - New Jersey *20850*
R	***Rubus ochraceus*** Card. *6057*	
	R	Vietnam *6057*
E	***Rubus onustus*** Bailey *20850*	
	I	*20850* U.S. - New York *20850*
V	***Rubus originalis*** Bailey *20850*	
	I	*20850* U.S. - Maryland *20850*
	I	*20850* U.S. - New Jersey *20850*
	I	*20850* U.S. - West Virginia *20850*
R	***Rubus ovatus*** Thuan *6057*	
	R	Vietnam *6057*
R	***Rubus palmatifolius*** Thuan *6057*	
	R	Vietnam *6057*
E	***Rubus paludivagus*** Fern. *20850*	
	I	*20850* U.S. - Massachusetts *20850*
E	***Rubus panamanus*** Bailey *20883, 9004*	
	I	*20883* Panama *20883*
V	***Rubus parlinii*** Bailey *20850*	
	I	*20850* U.S. - Connecticut *20850*
	I	*20850* U.S. - Maine *20850*
	I	*20850* U.S. - Vermont *20850*
Ex/E	***Rubus particularis*** Bailey *20850*	
	I	*20850* U.S. - West Virginia *20850*
V	***Rubus pascuus*** Bailey *20850*	
	I	*20850* U.S. - Alabama *20850*
	I	*20850* U.S. - Delaware *20850*
	I	*20850* U.S. - Maryland *20850*
	I	*20850* U.S. - North Carolina *20850*
	I	*20850* U.S. - Oklahoma *20850*
	I	*20850* U.S. - South Carolina *20850*
	I	*20850* U.S. - Texas *20850*
	I	*20850* U.S. - Virginia *20850*
	I	*20850* U.S. - West Virginia *20850*
Ex/E	***Rubus pernagaeus*** Fern. *20850*	
	I	*20850* U.S. - Virginia *20850*
Ex/E	***Rubus plexus*** Fern. *20850*	
	I	*20850* U.S. - Virginia *20850*
I	***Rubus porotoensis*** R. Graham *5926*	
	I	*5926* Tanzania *5926*
V	***Rubus porteri*** Bailey *20850*	
	I	*20850* U.S. - Pennsylvania *20850*
Ex/E	***Rubus positivus*** Bailey *20850*	
	I	*20850* U.S. - Connecticut *20850*
E	***Rubus praecipuus*** Bailey *20883, 10747*	
	I	*20883* Panama *20883*
E	***Rubus prosper*** Bailey *20850*	
	I	*20850* U.S. - Rhode Is. *20850*
V	***Rubus pubescens*** Raf. var. *scius* Bailey *20850*	
	I	*20850* Canada - Labrador *20850*
	I	*20850* Canada - New Brunswick *20850*
	I	*20850* Canada - Newfoundland *20850*
	I	*20850* Canada - Nova Scotia *20850*
	I	*20850* Canada - Prince Edward Is. *20850*
	I	*20850* Canada - Quebec *20850*
	I	*20883* France - St Pierre & Miquelon *20883*
V	***Rubus quebecensis*** Bailey *20850*	
	I	*20850* Canada - Quebec *20850*
V	***Rubus racemiger*** Bailey *20850*	

	I	*20850* U.S. - Maryland *20850*
	I	*20850* U.S. - Pennsylvania *20850*
	I	*20850* U.S. - West Virginia *20850*
E	***Rubus saltuensis*** Bailey *20850*	
	I	*20850* U.S. - Connecticut *20850*
V	***Rubus scambens*** Bailey *20850*	
	I	*20850* U.S. - District of Columbia *20850*
	I	*20850* U.S. - Maryland *20850*
	I	*20850* U.S. - Virginia *20850*
Ex/E	***Rubus sceleratus*** Brainerd *20850*	
	I	*20850* U.S. - New Hampshire *20850*
V	***Rubus sewardianus*** Fern. *20850*	
	I	*20850* U.S. - New Jersey *20850*
	I	*20850* U.S. - Virginia *20850*
V	***Rubus suppar*** Bailey *20850*	
	I	*20850* Canada - New Brunswick *20850*
	I	*20850* Canada - Nova Scotia *20850*
E	***Rubus tantus*** Bailey *20883, 9006*	
	I	*20883* Panama *20883*
V	***Rubus tardatus*** Blanch. *20850*	
	I	*20850* Canada - Nova Scotia *20850*
	I	*20850* Canada - Ontario *20850*
	I	*20850* Canada - Prince Edward Is. *20850*
	I	*20850* Canada - Quebec *20850*
	I	*20850* U.S. - Delaware *20850*
	I	*20850* U.S. - Maine *20850*
	I	*20850* U.S. - Michigan *20850*
	I	*20850* U.S. - Pennsylvania *20850*
	I	*20850* U.S. - Vermont *20850*
V	***Rubus terraltanus*** Bailey *20850*	
	I	*20850* U.S. - West Virginia *20850*
R	***Rubus tonkinensis*** Bolle *6057*	
	R	Vietnam *6057*
I	***Rubus transvaaliensis*** C.E. Gust var. *kyimbilensis* C.E. Gust *5926*	
	I	*5926* Tanzania *5926*
R	***Rubus tuyamae*** Hatus. *8622*	
	R	*19134* Japan - Kazan Retto *8622*
Ex/E	***Rubus tygartensis*** H.A. & T. Davis *20850*	
	I	*20850* U.S. - West Virginia *20850*
Ex/E	***Rubus ucetanus*** Bailey *20850*	
	I	*20850* U.S. - Florida *20850*
V	***Rubus vagus*** Bailey *20850*	
	I	*20850* U.S. - Michigan *20850*
	I	*20850* U.S. - Ohio *20850*
E	***Rubus variispinus*** Bailey *20850*	
	I	*20850* U.S. - Michigan *20850*
V	***Rubus velox*** Bailey *20850*	
	I	*20850* U.S. - Texas *20850*
V	***Rubus vigoratus*** Bailey *20850*	
	I	*20850* Canada - Nova Scotia *20850*
	I	*20850* U.S. - Massachusetts *20850*
V	***Rubus virilis*** Bailey *20850*	
	I	*20850* U.S. - Missouri *20850*
Ex/E	***Rubus vitifolius*** Cham. & Schlecht. var. *eastwoodianus* (Rydb.) Munz *20850*	
	I	*20850* U.S. - California *20850*
Ex/E	***Rubus vitifolius*** Cham. & Schlecht. var. *titanus* (Bailey) Bailey *20850*	
	I	*20850* U.S. - California *20850*
V	***Rubus weatherbyi*** Bailey *20850*	
	I	*20850* Canada - New Brunswick *20850*

I	20850	Canada - Nova Scotia	20850

V *Rubus whartoniae* Bailey *20850*

V	20850	U.S. - Kentucky	20850
E	20850	U.S. - Tennessee	20850

I *Rubus wightii* Gamble

I		India - Tamil Nadu (Sivagiri Hills, Tirunelveli)

R *Sanguisorba albanica* András. & Jáv. *20178, 20171*

R	20178	Albania	20178

R *Sanguisorba cretica* Hayek *20171*

R	20731	Greece - Crete	20731

R *Sanguisorba dodecandra* Moretti *18264, 20171*

R	18264	Italy (Lombardy)	18264

R *Sanguisorba hakusanensis* Makino var. *japonensis* Ohwi *10572*

R	10572	Japan	10572

I *Sanguisorba indicum* (Gardner) Tirv. *8021*

I	16162	Sri Lanka	8021

I *Sanguisorba magnifica* I. Schischkin & Komarov *5942*

I	5942	Russia (Far East) - Primorye (south)	5942

R *Sanguisorba obtusa* Maxim. *10572*

R	10572	Japan	10572

E *Sibbaldia omeiensis* Yu & Li *17617*

E	17617	China - Sichuan (Emishan)	11139

Ex/E *Sorbaria olgae* I. Zinserl. *5942*

Ex/E	5942	Uzbekistan	5942

R *Sorbaria rhoifolia* Kom. *11552*

R	11552	Russian Federation (extreme south east)	11552

V *Sorbus amabilis* Cheng ex Yu *17617*

V	17617	China - Anhui (Huangshan)	11139
V	17617	China - Fujian	11139
V	17617	China - Zhejiang	11139

R *Sorbus arranensis* Hedl. *20171*

R	20587	United Kingdom	20587

V *Sorbus austriaca* (Beck) Hedl. ssp. *hazslinszkyana* Soó *17786, 20171*

V	20686	Hungary	17786

I *Sorbus bohemica* Kovanda *2050, 20171*

I	2050	Czech Republic	2050

R *Sorbus borbasii* Jáv. *17823, 20171*

R	19949	Romania	20631

R *Sorbus dacica* Borbás *17823, 20171*

R	19949	Romania	17823

R *Sorbus lancifolia* Hedl. *17832, 20171*

R	17832	Norway	17832

E *Sorbus maderensis* Dode *17891*

E		Portugal - Madeira	17891

R *Sorbus neglecta* Hedl. *17832, 20171*

R	17832	Norway	17832

I *Sorbus sudetica* (Tausch) Fritsch *8000, 20171*

E	2050	Czech Republic (Karkonosze Mts.)	2050
?		Germany	8000
I	7897	Poland	7897

R *Sorbus teodorii* Liljef. *20171*

R	20673	Finland	20673
R	20083	Sweden	20083

I *Spiraea diversifolia* Dunn

I		India - Uttar Pradesh

R *Spiraea faurieana* Schneider *10572*

R	10572	Japan	10572

R *Spiraea miyabei* Koidz. *10572*

R	10572	Japan	10572

R *Spiraea tarokoensis* Hayata *20854*

R	20854	Taiwan	20854

V *Spiraea virginiana* Britt. *20850*

I	20850	U.S. - Alabama	20850
E	20850	U.S. - Georgia	20850
V	20850	U.S. - Kentucky	20850
E	20850	U.S. - North Carolina	20850
E	20850	U.S. - Ohio	20850
Ex	20850	U.S. - Pennsylvania	20850
E	20850	U.S. - Tennessee	20850
E	20850	U.S. - Virginia	20850
E	20850	U.S. - West Virginia	20850

I *Spiraeanthus schrenkianus* (Fischer & C. Meyer) Maxim. *5942*

I	5942	Kazakhstan	5942
I	5942	Uzbekistan	5942

E *Stephanandra incisa* var. *quadrifissa* T. Lee *15923*

E	15923	Korea, South	15923

R *Stephanandra tanakae* Franchet & Sav. *10572*

R	10572	Japan	10572

R *Taihangia rupestris* Yu & Li var. *ciliata* Yu & Li *11139*

R		China - Hebei (Wuan)	11139

R *Taihangia rupestris* Yu & Li var. *rupestris* *17617*

R	17617	China - Henan	11139

V *Vauquelinia californica* (Standl.) Hess & Henrickson ssp. *pauciflora* (Standl.) Hess & Henrickson *20883, 19002*

E	20850	U.S. - Arizona	20850
E	20850	U.S. - New Mexico	20850
I	20883	Mexico	20883

R *Waldsteinia idahoensis* Piper *20850*

R	20850	U.S. - Idaho	20850
E	20850	U.S. - Montana	20850

V *Waldsteinia lobata* (Baldw.) Torr. & Gray *20850*

V	20850	U.S. - Georgia	20850
Ex/E	20850	U.S. - North Carolina	20850
V	20850	U.S. - South Carolina	20850

Rubiaceae

Number of genera:	450	
Number of species:	6,500	
Recorded threatened species:	1120	(17%)

Mainly tropics and subtropics.

E *Acranthera grandiflora* Beddome *11494*

E	11494	India - Tamil Nadu (Tirunelveli)	11494

V *Acranthera tomentosa* R. Br. ex Hook. f. *13883*

V	13883	India - Assam	13883
V	13883	India - Meghalaya	13883
V	13883	India - Nagaland	13883

V *Acrosynanthus jamaicensis* Howard & Proctor *20883, 13336*

V	13336	Jamaica	20883

I *Agathisanthemum chlorophyllum* (Hochst.) Bremek var. *chlorophyllum* *20604*

I	20604	South Africa - Natal	20604

I *Agathisanthemum chlorophyllum* (Hochst.) Bremek var. *pubescens* Bremek. *20604*

I   20604 South Africa - Natal 20604

R   *Alberta magna* E.Mey. 20604
- R   20604 South Africa - Cape Province 20604
- R   20604 South Africa - Natal 20604

R   *Alleizettella rubra* Pitard 6057
- R   20985 Vietnam 6057

R   *Alseis blackiana* Hemsl. 20883
- V   20883 Panama 20883
- I   20883 Colombia 20883

I   *Alseis dariensis* Dwyer 20883, 9006
- I   16317 Panama 20883

V   *Alseis peruviana* Standley 17462
- V   19962 Peru 18200

V   *Amaioua magnicarpa* Dwyer 20883, 9006
- V   16317 Panama 20883

E   *Amaioua pedicellata* Dwyer 20883, 9006
- I   20883 Panama 20883

R   *Amaracarpus saxicola* Ridley
- R   Malaysia - Peninsular Malaysia (Kelantan, Pahang)

E   *Amphidasya spathulata* Dwyer 20883, 9006
- I   20883 Panama 20883

R   *Anisomeris brachypoda* (J.D. Smith) Standley 9004
- R   19802 Guatemala 9004

V   *Anthospermum cameroonense* Hutch. & Dalziel
- V   Cameroon (Cameroon mt)

V   *Anthospermum streyi* Puff 20604
- V   20604 South Africa - Natal 20604

E   *Antirhea aromatica* Castillo-Campos & Lorence 20883, 12069
- I   20883 Mexico 20883
- ?   Mexico - Veracruz 12069

R   *Antirhea bifurcata* (Desr.) Hook.f. 10082
- R   20771 Mauritius (lowland forest) 5852
- E   5852 Mauritius - Rodrigues 5852

R   *Antirhea jamaicensis* Urb. 20883
- R   20883 Jamaica 20883

R   *Antirhea nipensis* Borh. & Muniz 5607
- R   19105 Cuba (Santiago de Cuba; Holguin) 5607

V   *Antirhea obtusifolia* Urban 20883
- I   20883 Puerto Rico 20883

V   *Antirhea orbicularis* Alain 5607
- V   19105 Cuba (Holguin) 5607

R   *Antirhea pedicellaris* Borh. & Bisse 5607
- R   19105 Cuba (Holguin) 5607

E   *Antirhea portoricensis* (Britt. & Wilson) Standl. 20883
- I   20883 Puerto Rico 20883

E   *Antirhea sintenisii* Urban 20883
- I   20883 Puerto Rico 20883

E   *Antirhea tomentosa* (Sw.) Fawcett 20883, 13336
- E   13336 Jamaica (Trelawny) 20883

V   *Antirhea trichantha* (Griseb.) Hemsl. 20883, 9006
- V   20883 Panama 20883

I   *Antirhoea livida* Elm. 13833
- I   13833 Philippines (low altitude) 13833

R   *Appunia seibertii* Standl. 20883
- V   20883 Panama 20883

R   *Argostemma bariensis* Pierre ex Pitard 6057
- R   Vietnam 6057

I   *Argostemma condensatum* Craib 19120
- I   19120 Thailand 19120

R   *Argostemma inaequilaterum* Bennett
- R   Malaysia - Peninsular Malaysia

I   *Argostemma khasianum* Clarke 14782
- I   14782 India - Meghalaya 14782

E   *Argostemma lobulatum* Craib 19120
- E   19120 Thailand 19120

E   *Argostemma saxicolum* Geddes 19120
- E   19120 Thailand 19120

R   *Asperula abbreviata* (Halácsy) Rech.f. 20171
- R   Greece

R   *Asperula antalyensis* Ehrend. 12840
- R   12840 Turkey 12840

V   *Asperula asthenes* Airy Shaw & Turrill 20681
- V   20681 Australia - New South Wales 20681

R   *Asperula baenitzii* Heldr. ex Boiss. 20171
- R   Greece

R   *Asperula baldaccii* (Halácsy) Ehrend. 20171
- R   (former) Yugoslavia

R   *Asperula beckiana* Degen 20171
- R   (former) Yugoslavia

R   *Asperula calabra* (Fiori) Ehrend. & Krendl 20171
- R   Italy

R   *Asperula capitellata* Houuskn. ex Bornm. & Bornm. 12840
- R   12840 Turkey 12840

R   *Asperula charophyton* Airy Shaw & Turrill 20681
- I   20681 Australia - New South Wales 20681
- I   20681 Australia - Queensland 20681

R   *Asperula cilicica* Hausskn. & Ehrend. 12840
- R   12840 Turkey 12840

I   *Asperula coa* Rech.f.
- I   Greece

V   *Asperula crassula* Greuter & Zaffan 19121
- V   20730 Greece - Crete 19121

R   *Asperula garganica* Huter, Porta & Rigo ex Ehrend. & Krendl 20171
- R   Italy

R   *Asperula gussonii* Boiss. 20171
- R   20738 Italy - Sicily (Rocca Busambia) 20738

R   *Asperula hercegovina* Degen 20171
- R   21091 Bosnia & Herzegovina 21091
- R   (former) Yugoslavia

R   *Asperula hexaphylla* All. 20171
- R   France
- R   Italy

R   *Asperula lasiantha* Nakai 15957
- R   15923 Korea, South (Mt Chiri) 15957

R   *Asperula lilaciflora* Boiss. ssp. *lilaciflora* 12840
- R   12840 Turkey 12840

R   *Asperula lilaciflora* Boiss. ssp. *mutensis* Schonb.-Tem. 12840
- R   12840 Turkey 12840

R   *Asperula litardierei* Humbert
- R   Morocco

V   *Asperula littoralis* Sibth. & Sm. 12840, 20171
- V   12840 Turkey 12840

R   ***Asperula lycia*** Stapf *12840*
     R   *12840*   Turkey *12840*

R   ***Asperula muscosa*** Boiss. & Heldr. *20171*
     R   Greece

R   ***Asperula neglecta*** Moris, non Guss. *20171*
     R   Italy

R   ***Asperula nitida*** Sm. ssp. ***hirtella*** (Boiss.)
       Ehrend. *12840*
     R   *12840*   Turkey *12840*

R   ***Asperula nitida*** Sm. ssp. ***subcapitellata***
       Ehrend. *12840*
     R   *12840*   Turkey *12840*

R   ***Asperula oetaea*** (Boiss.) Heldr. ex Halácsy *20171*
     R   Greece

I   ***Asperula ophiolithica*** Ehrend. *20171*
     I   Greece

R   ***Asperula paui*** Font Quer *8000, 20171*
     V   *20692*   Spain (north-east of Alicante) *20692*
     R   Spain - Balearic Is.

R   ***Asperula pseudochlorantha*** Ehrend. *12840*
     R   *12840*   Turkey *12840*

V   ***Asperula purpurea*** ssp. ***spadicum*** Boyce *19121*
     V   *19121*   Greece - Crete *19121*

V   ***Asperula rupestris*** (Vis.) Rchb., non Tineo *18264,*
       20171
     V   *18264*   Italy - Sicily (northwestern & southwestern
          parts) *20738*

R   ***Asperula saxicola*** Ehrend. *20171*
     R   Greece

R   ***Asperula sintenisii*** Acherson ex Bornm. *12840*
     R   *12840*   Turkey *12840*

R   ***Asperula staliana*** Vis. *20171*
     R   (former) Yugoslavia

R   ***Asperula stricta*** Boiss. ssp. ***elmaliensis***
       Schonb.-Tem. *12840*
     R   *12840*   Turkey *12840*

R   ***Asperula stricta*** Boiss. ssp. ***grandiflora***
       Schonb.-Tem. *12840*
     R   *12840*   Turkey *12840*

R   ***Asperula suberosa*** Sibth. & Sm. *5204, 20171*
     R   *5204*   Bulgaria (south-west) *5204*
     R   Greece *8000*

I   ***Asperula suffruticosa*** Boiss. & Heldr. *20171*
     I   Greece

R   ***Asperula syrticola*** (Miq.) Toelken *20681*
     Ex/E *20681*   Australia - New South Wales *20681*
     R   *20681*   Australia - South Australia *20681*

R   ***Asperula taygetea*** Boiss. & Heldr. *20171*
     R   Greece

R   ***Asperula tephrocarpa*** Czern. ex Popov &
       Chrshan. *20171*
     R   former European USSR

R   ***Asperula tournefortii*** Sieber ex Spreng. *20171*
     R   *20731*   Greece - East Aegean Is *20731*

R   ***Asperula virgata*** Hub.-Mor. ex Ehre.&
       Scho.-Tem. *12840*
     R   *12840*   Turkey *12840*

R   ***Asperula wettsteinii*** Adamovic *20171*
     R   *21091*   Bosnia & Herzegovina *21091*
     R   (former) Yugoslavia

R   ***Asperula woronowii*** Krecz. *12840*
     R   *12840*   Turkey *12840*

I   ***Badusa palawanensis*** Ridsd. *13833*
     I   *13833*   Philippines (Palawan) *13833*

E   ***Bathysa veraguensis*** Dwyer *20883, 9006*
     I   *20883*   Panama *20883*

Ex   ***Bertiera bistipulata*** Bojer ex Wernh. *10082*
     Ex   *20771*   Mauritius *10082*

E   ***Bikkia kaalaensis*** Halle & Jeremie *20893*
     E   *20893*   New Caledonia *20893*

E   ***Bikkia lenormandii*** Halle & Jeremie *20893*
     E   *20893*   New Caledonia *20893*

R   ***Bikkia pachyphylla*** Guillaumin *20893*
     R   *20893*   New Caledonia *20893*

R   ***Bobea myrtoides*** (F.Muell.) Valeton *20681*
     R   *20681*   Australia - Queensland *20681*

V   ***Bobea sandwicensis*** (Gray) Hbd. *20850, 14209*
     V   *20850*   U.S. - Hawaii *20850*

V   ***Bobea timonioides*** (Hook. f.) Hbd. *20850, 14209*
     V   *20850*   U.S. - Hawaii *20850*

V   ***Borojoa atlantica*** Dwyer *20883, 9006*
     V   *16317*   Panama *20883*

I   ***Borreria felis-insulae*** Correll
     I   *4650*   Bahamas *4650*

I   ***Borreria inaguensis*** Britton
     I   *4650*   Bahamas *4650*

I   ***Borreria linearifolia*** Hook.f. *11117*
     I   Ecuador - Galapagos *11117*

R   ***Borreria perpusilla*** Hook.f. *11117*
     R   Ecuador - Galapagos *11117*

V   ***Borreria pumilio*** Standl. *20883, 9006*
     V   *16317*   Panama *20883*

I   ***Borreria rotundifolia*** Andersson *11117*
     I   Ecuador - Galapagos (Santa Cruz) *11117*

R   ***Borreria suaveolens*** G. Meyer *20883*
     V   *20883*   Panama *20883*

I   ***Borreria suberecta*** Hook.f. *11117*
     I   Ecuador - Galapagos *11117*

R   ***Bouvardia langlassei*** Standley *9989*
     R   *9989*   Mexico *9989*

R   ***Bouvardia rosea*** Schldl. *10063*
     R   *19850*   Mexico *10063*

R   ***Bouvardia xestosperma*** (Robinson & Greenman) Terrell & S.D
       Koch *21287*
     R   *21287*   Mexico *21287*

R   ***Bouvardia xylosteoides*** Hooker & Arn. *10063*
     R   *16360*   Mexico *10063*

V   ***Byrsophyllum ellipticum*** (Thwaites) Beddome *10252*
     V   *12838*   Sri Lanka *10252*

I   ***Byrsophyllum tetrandrum*** (Beddome) Hook.f. *6987*
     I   India - Kerala *6987*
     I   India - Tamil Nadu *6987*

R   ***Canthium aciculatum*** Ridley
     R   Malaysia - Peninsular Malaysia (Perak; Kedah; Kelantan)

V   ***Canthium carinatum*** Summerh. *14296*
     V   *19182*   Seychelles *14296*

R   ***Canthium cochinchinensis*** Pierre ex Pitard *6057*
     R   Vietnam *6057*

V **Canthium costatum** C.White *20681*
   V   *20681* Australia - Queensland *20681*

R **Canthium dicoccum** Merr. *10276*
   R   *12838* Sri Lanka *10276*

V **Canthium fadenii** Bridson *20057*
   V   *20057* Kenya (Thika) *20057*

V **Canthium glaucum** Hiern ssp. *frangula* *20057*
   V   *20057* Kenya *20057*

V **Canthium glaucum** Hiern ssp. *glaucum* *20057*
   V   *20057* Kenya *20057*
   V   *20057* Somalia *17435*

R **Canthium keniense** Bullock *20057*
   R   *20057* Kenya *20057*

V **Canthium kilifiensis** Bridson ined. *20057*
   V   *20057* Kenya *20057*

I **Canthium macrocarpum** Thwaites *10252*
   I   *16162* Sri Lanka *10252*

I **Canthium odoratum** (Forster f.) Seemann var. *tinianense* (Kaneh.) Fosb. *20818*
   I   *18338* North Mariana Is. *18338*
   I   *18338* U.S. - Guam *18338*

I **Canthium robynsianum** Bullock *20057*
   I   *20057* Kenya *20057*
   I   *20057* Tanzania *17435*

V **Canthium rondoense** Bridson *20885*
   V   *20885* Tanzania (Rondo Plateau) *20885*

V **Canthium sechellense** Summerh. *14296*
   V   *19182* Seychelles *14296*

E **Captaincookia margaretae** Hallé *20802*
   E   *20893* New Caledonia *14010*

R **Carpacoce gigantea** Puff *20604*
   R   *20604* South Africa - Cape Province *20604*

E **Casasia acunae** Borh. & Fernandez *5607*
   E   *19105* Cuba (Holguin) *5607*

R **Casasia longipes** Urb. *20883*
   R   *20883* Jamaica *20883*

E **Catesbaea gamboana** Urban *5607*
   E   *19105* Cuba (Las Tunas, Granma) *5607*

E **Catesbaea macracantha** C. Wright *5607*
   E   *19105* Cuba (Sancti Spiritus) *5607*

V **Catesbaea parviflora** Sw. *20883, 19002*
   E   *20850* U.S. - Florida *20850*
   V   *20883* Jamaica *20883*
   I   *20883* Puerto Rico *20883*

I **Cephaelis abouabouensis** Schnell *7926*
   I   Côte d'Ivoire *7926*

I **Cephaelis baillehachei** Ake Assi
   I   Côte d'Ivoire

V **Cephaelis camponutans** Dwyer & Hayden *20883, 9006, 21221*
   I   *20883* Panama *20883*

V **Cephaelis correae** Dwyer & Hayden *20883, 9006*
   V   *16317* Panama *20883*

V **Cephaelis croatii** Dwyer *20883, 9006*
   V   *16317* Panama *20883*

I **Cephaelis dichroa** (Standl.) Standl. *20883, 9006*
   I   *16317* Panama *20883*

V **Cephaelis dimorphandrioides** Dwyer *20883, 9006*
   V   *16317* Panama *20883*

E **Cephaelis gaugeri** Dwyer *20883, 9006*
   I   *20883* Panama *20883*

R **Cephaelis glomerulata** J.D. Sm. *20883*
   R   *20883* Panama *20883*

V **Cephaelis insueta** Dwyer *20883, 9006*
   V   *16317* Panama *20883*

V **Cephaelis kennedyi** Dwyer *20883, 9006*
   V   *16317* Panama *20883*

V **Cephaelis nana** (Standl.) Standl. *20883*
   E   *20883* Panama *20883*

E **Cephaelis panamensis** Dwyer *20883, 9006*
   I   *20883* Panama *20883*

I **Cephaelis schnellii** Ake Assi *7926*
   I   Côte d'Ivoire *7926*

E **Cephaelis vultusmimi** Dwyer *20883, 9006*
   I   *20883* Panama *20883*

I **Chamaepentas greenwayi** Bremek. var. *greenwayi* *7959*
   I   *5926* Tanzania (Pare Distr.) *7959*

E **Chassalia boryana** DC. *10082*
   E   *20771* Mauritius *10082*

E **Chassalia bosseri** Verdc. *10082*
   E   *14220* Réunion *10082*

E **Chassalia capitata** DC. *10082*
   E   *20771* Mauritius *10082*

V **Chassalia coriacea** Verdc. var. *coriacea* *10082*
   V   *20771* Mauritius *10082*

E **Chassalia coriacea** Verdc. var. *johnstonii* Verdc. *10082*
   E   *20771* Mauritius *10082*

R **Chassalia discolor** Schumann ssp. *taitensis* Verdc. *7959*
   R   *20057* Kenya (Teita Hills) *7959*

E **Chassalia grandifolia** DC. *10082*
   E   *20771* Mauritius *10082*

E **Chassalia lanceolata** (Poiret) A. Chev. ssp. *lanceolata* *10082*
   E   *20771* Mauritius *10082*

E **Chassalia lanceolata** (Poiret) A. Chev. ssp. *latifolia* Verdc. *10082*
   E   *20771* Mauritius *10082*

V **Chassalia petrinensis** Verdc. *10082*
   V   *20771* Mauritius *10082*

I **Chazaliella abrupta** (Hiern) Petit & Verdc. var. *parvifolia* Verdc. *7959*
   I   Kenya *7959*

R **Chimarrhis cymosa** ssp. *jamaicensis* Urb. *20883*
   R   *20883* Jamaica *20883*

I **Chimarrhis microcarpa** Standley *5932*
   I   *5932* Trinidad & Tobago (Trinidad) *5932*

R **Chiococca bermudiana** S. Brown
   R   Bermuda

E **Chiococca jefensis** Dwyer *20883, 9006*
   I   *20883* Panama *20883*

R **Chiococca steyermarkii** Standley *9004*
   R   *19802* Guatemala *9004*

I **Chiococca stricta** Correll

I	4650	Bahamas	4650

E *Chione buxifolia* Dwyer & Hayden 20883, 9006
> I   20883   Panama 20883

E *Chione campanensis* Dwyer 20883, 9006
> I   20883   Panama 20883

V *Chione darienensis* Dwyer 20883, 9006
> V   16317   Panama 20883

I *Chione panamensis* Steyerm. 20883, 9006
> I   16317   Panama 20883

E *Chomelia atlantica* Dwyer 20883, 9006
> I   20883   Panama 20883

I *Chomelia coclensis* Dwyer 20883, 9006
> I   16317   Panama 20883

E *Chomelia grandicarpa* Dwyer 20883, 9006
> I   20883   Panama 20883

E *Chomelia leucophylla* Dwyer 20883, 9006
> I   20883   Panama 20883

V *Chomelia peninsularis* Dwyer 20883, 9006
> V   16317   Panama 20883

E *Chomelia psilocarpa* Dwyer & Hayden 20883, 9006
> I   20883   Panama 20883

V *Cinchona carabayensis* Wedd. 20883
> V   20883   Peru 20883

V *Cinchona delessertiana* Standley 20883
> V   20883   Peru 20883

R *Cinchona glandulifera* Ruiz et. Pav. 20883
> R   20883   Peru 20883

R *Cinchona humboldtiana* Lamb. 20883
> V   20883   Peru 20883

V *Cinchona nitida* Ruiz et Pav. 20883
> V   20883   Peru 20883

V *Cinchona rufinervis* Wedd. 20883
> I   20883   Bolivia 20883
> E   20883   Peru 20883

R *Clarkella nana* (Edgw.) Hook.f. 14782
> R   14782   India - Uttar Pradesh (western Himalayas)
>   14782

I *Clarkella nana* (Edgw.) Hook.f. var. *siamensis*
  (Craib) Fukuoka & Kurosaki 19120
> I   19120   Thailand 19120

V *Coccocypselum guianense* Proctor var. *glabratum*
  Proctor 20883, 13336
> V   13336   Jamaica 20883

R *Coccocypselum pseudotontanea* Griseb. 20883, 13336
> R   13336   Jamaica (St. Andrew, Portland) 20883

I *Coffea costatifructa* Bridson 21072
> I   21072   Tanzania (Mafia Is. & Selous Game Reserve)
>   21072

I *Coffea crassifolia* Gamble
> I   India - Kerala (Travancore Hills)
> I   India - Tamil Nadu

V *Coffea fadenii* Bridson 20057
> V   20057   Kenya (Mbololo forest, Taita hills)
>   20057

Ex *Coffea lemblinii* (A. Chev.) Keay 7926
> Ex   20887   Côte d'Ivoire 7926

R *Coffea macrocarpa* A. Rich. 10082
> R   20771   Mauritius 10082

E *Coffea myrtifolia* (A.Rich. ex DC.) Leroy 10082

E	20771	Mauritius	10082

I *Coffea pocsii* Bridson 21072
> I   21072   Tanzania (Kitulanghalo Forest Reserve)
>   21072

V *Coffea rhamniphylla* (Chiov.) Bridson 20057
> V   20057   Kenya 20057

V *Coffea togoensis* A. Chev. 20274
> V   20858   Ghana 20274
> V   20858   Togo 7926

I *Coleactina papalis* Halle
> I   Gabon (Moughimba)

R *Commitheca letestuana* Halle
> R   Gabon (Haute Ngounye)

V *Condaminea petiolata* Dwyer 20883, 9006
> V   16317   Panama 20883

R *Coprosma bauerii* Endl. 11649
> R   19108   Australia - Norfolk Is. (Norfolk & Philip
>   Islands.) 11649

I *Coprosma cookei* Fosberg 20845
> I   20845   French Polynesia - Tubuai Is. (Rapa)
>   20845

I *Coprosma esulcata* (F.Brown) Fosberg 20845
> I   20845   French Polynesia - Marquesas Is 20845

R *Coprosma intertexta* Simpson
> R   New Zealand - South Is.

R *Coprosma lanceolaris* F. Muell.
> R   14225   Australia - NSW - Lord Howe Is. 14225

R *Coprosma niphophila* Orchard 20681
> R   20681   Australia - New South Wales 20681

R *Coprosma obconica* Kirk var. *obconica* 20625
> R   19305   New Zealand - North Is. (Taihape) 20625
> R   19305   New Zealand - South Is. (Nelson; Marlborough)
>   20625

R *Coprosma oliveri* Fosberg 20883, 19116
> V   19125   Chile - Juan Fernandez Is. 19116
> R   20883   Chile 20883

R *Coprosma pilosa* Endl. 19108
> R   19108   Australia - Norfolk Is. 14288

R *Coprosma prisca* W. Oliver
> R   14225   Australia - NSW - Lord Howe Is. 14225

R *Coprosma putida* C. Moore & F. Muell.
> R   14225   Australia - NSW - Lord Howe Is. 14225

V *Coprosma rapensis* F. Brown var. *benefica* (Oliver)
  Fosb. 8617
> V   19185   Pitcairn (Pitcairn Island) 8617

I *Coprosma rapensis* F.Brown var. *mangarevica*
  Fosberg 20845
> I   20845   French Polynesia - Tuamotu Is. 20845

V *Coprosma setosa* J.Moore 20845
> V   20845   French Polynesia - Society Is. (Raiatea)
>   20845

I *Coprosma taitensis* A.Gray var. *glabrata* (J.Moore)
  Fosberg 20845
> I   20845   French Polynesia - Society Is. (Raiatea)
>   20845

I *Coprosma taitensis* A.Gray var. *oliveri*
  Fosberg 20845
> I   20845   French Polynesia - Society Is. (Moorea,
>   Tahiti) 20845

I *Coprosma taitensis* A.Gray var. *raiateensis*
  (J.Moore) Fosberg 20845

I		20845	French Polynesia 20845

E ***Coprosma velutina*** Fosberg *20845*
    E   20845 French Polynesia *20845*

E ***Coprosma violacea*** *20625*
    E   20625 New Zealand - North Is. *20625*
    E   20625 New Zealand - South Is. *20625*

V ***Coprosma waima*** Druce *19305*
    V   19305 New Zealand - North Is. *19305*

R ***Coussarea austin-smithii*** Standley *9037*
    R   19803 Costa Rica *9037*

V ***Coussarea cerroazulensis*** Dwyer & Hayden *20883, 9006*
    I   20883 Panama *20883*

R ***Coussarea curvigemmia*** Dwyer *20883*
    V   20883 Panama *20883*

E ***Coussarea durifolia*** Dwyer *20883, 9006*
    R   12468 Panama *20883*

V ***Coussarea enneantha*** Standl. *20883, 9006*
    I   20883 Panama *20883*

E ***Coussarea jefensis*** Dwyer *20883, 9006*
    I   20883 Panama *20883*

V ***Coussarea loftonii*** (Dwyer & Hayden) Dwyer *20883, 9006*
    I   20883 Panama *20883*

V ***Coussarea mediocris*** Standley & Steyerm. *9004*
    V   19802 Guatemala *9004*

V ***Coussarea morii*** Dwyer *20883, 9006*
    V   16317 Panama *20883*

V ***Coussarea neei*** Dwyer *20883, 9006*
    V   16317 Panama *20883*

V ***Coussarea veraguensis*** Dwyer *20883, 9006*
    V   16317 Panama *20883*

E ***Coussarea villosula*** Dwyer *20883, 9006*
    I   20883 Panama *20883*

R ***Coutaportla guatemalensis*** (Standley) Lorence *20883*
    V   20883 Guatemala *20883*
    R   20883 Mexico *20883*

I ***Craterispermum longipedunculatum*** Verdc. *5926*
    I   5926 Tanzania *5926*

R ***Craterispermum microdon*** Baker *14296*
    R   19182 Seychelles (granitic) *14296*

R ***Crucianella sorgerae*** Ehrend. *12840*
    R   12840 Turkey *12840*

R ***Cruciata mixta*** Ehrend. ex Schonb.-Tem. *12840*
    R   12840 Turkey *12840*

R ***Crusea coronata*** Robinson & Greenman *10064*
    R   9989 Mexico *10064*

R ***Crusea hispida*** (Miller) Robinson var. ***grandiflora*** (P.G. Wilson) W. Anderson *10064*
    R   9989 Mexico *10064*

R ***Crusea lucida*** Benth. *10064*
    R   9989 Mexico *10064*

I ***Cuviera latior*** Wernham var. ***evorombila*** Halle
    I   Gabon

R ***Cuviera pierrei*** Halle
    R   Gabon

R ***Cuviera uncinula*** Halle
    R   Gabon

V ***Cyclophyllum tenuipes*** Guillaumin *20893*
    V   20893 New Caledonia *20893*

R ***Damnacanthus macrophyllus*** Siebold *10573*
    R   10573 Japan *10573*

Ex ***Danais corymbosa*** Balf.f. *10082*
    Ex   5852 Mauritius - Rodrigues *5852*

Ex ***Danais sulcata*** Pers. *10082*
    Ex   20771 Mauritius *10082*

I ***Deppea amaranthina*** Standley & Steyerm. *9004*
    I   19802 Guatemala *9004*

R ***Deppea flava*** (Brandegee) L.O. Williams *9004*
    R   19802 Guatemala *9004*
    R   9989 Mexico *9004*

E ***Deppea panamensis*** Dwyer *20883, 9006*
    I   20883 Panama *20883*

V ***Dichilanthe zeylanica*** Thwaites *10252*
    V   12838 Sri Lanka *10252*

V ***Didymaea hispidula*** L.O. Williams *9004*
    V   19802 Guatemala *9004*

V ***Didymaea microphylla*** L.O. Williams *9004*
    V   19802 Guatemala *9004*

R ***Diodia denudata*** Standl. *20883*
    V   20883 Panama *20883*

I ***Diplospora andamanica*** Balakr. & Nair *10177*
    I   India - Andaman Is. (Saddle Peak, N. Andamans) *10177*

I ***Dolichometra leucantha*** Schumann *7959*
    I   5926 Tanzania (Lushoto) *7959*

R ***Doricera trilocularis*** (Balf.f.) Verdc. *10082*
    R   5852 Mauritius - Rodrigues *5852*

E ***Dunnia sinensis*** Tutcher *17617*
    E   17617 China - Guangdong *11139*

R ***Duroia costaricensis*** Standley *9037*
    R   19803 Costa Rica *9037*

Ex/E ***Duroia genipifolia*** Standley & Steyerm. *9004*
    Ex/E   19802 Guatemala *9004*

V ***Eizia mexicana*** Standley *9004*
    V   9989 Mexico *9004*

E ***Elaeagia nitidifolia*** Dwyer *20883, 9006*
    I   20883 Panama *20883*

R ***Emmenopterys henryi*** Oliver *17617*
    R   17617 China - Anhui *11139*
    R   17617 China - Fujian *11139*
    R   17617 China - Guizhou *17617*
    R   17617 China - Hubei *11139*
    R   17617 China - Hunan *11139*
    R   17617 China - Jiangsu (Yixing) *11139*
    R   17617 China - Jiangxi *11139*
    R   17617 China - Zhejiang *11139*

R ***Eriosemopsis subanisophylla*** Robyns *20604*
    R   20604 South Africa - Cape Province *20604*
    R   20604 South Africa - Natal *20604*

R ***Erithalis harrisii*** Urb. *20883*
    R   20883 Jamaica *20883*

R ***Erithalis quadrangularis*** Krug & Urb. *20883*
    R   20883 Jamaica *20883*

V ***Erithalis revoluta*** Urban *20883, 8058*
    I   19002 Puerto Rico *20883*

I ***Erithalis salmeoides*** Correll
    I   4650 Bahamas *4650*

Magnoliopsida (dicots): Rubiaceae: *Erithalis*

I   *Ernodea gigantea* Correll
    I   Bahamas

R   *Exostema brachycarpum* (Sw.) Schult. *20883*
    R   *20883*   Jamaica *20883*

V   *Exostema lancifolium* Borh. & Acuna *5607*
    V   *19105*   Cuba (Holguin) *5607*

E   *Exostema orbiculatum* Proctor *20883, 13336*
    E   *13336*   Jamaica *20883*

R   *Exostema triflorum* (W. Wright) G. Don *20883, 13336*
    R   *13336*   Jamaica (St. Ann, Portland) *20883*

E   *Faramea altipetens* Dwyer *20883, 9006*
    I   *20883*   Panama *20883*

R   *Faramea belizensis* Standley *9004*
    R   *9004*   Belize *9004*
    R   *9004*   Guatemala *9004*

V   *Faramea bocataurensis* Dwyer *20883, 9006*
    V   *16317*   Panama *20883*

E   *Faramea caput-anguis* Dwyer & Hayden *20883, 9006*
    I   *20883*   Panama *20883*

R   *Faramea cobana* J.D. Smith *9004*
    R   *19802*   Guatemala *9004*

R   *Faramea cyanea* Muell.-Arg. *20883*
    I   *20883*   Brazil *20883*
    R   *20883*   Paraguay *20883*

R   *Faramea hondurae* Standley *9037*
    R   *19803*   Costa Rica *9037*

E   *Faramea jefensis* Dwyer & Hayden *20883, 9006*
    I   *20883*   Panama *20883*

I   *Faramea liesneri* Dwyer *20883, 9006*
    I   *16317*   Panama *20883*

I   *Faramea ovalis* Standl. *20883, 9006*
    I   *19803*   Costa Rica *9037*
    V   *16317*   Panama *20883*

E   *Faramea papulata* Dwyer & Hayden *20883, 9006*
    I   *20883*   Panama *20883*

V   *Faramea pauciflora* Dwyer *20883, 9006*
    V   *16317*   Panama *20883*

R   *Faramea porophylla* (Vell.) Muell.-Arg. in
      Mart. *20883*
    I   *20883*   Brazil *20883*
    R   *20883*   Paraguay *20883*

E   *Faramea scalaris* Standl. *20883, 9006*
    I   *20883*   Panama *20883*

E   *Faramea standleyana* L.O. Williams *9004*
    E   *19802*   Guatemala *9004*

V   *Faramea terreyeae* Standl. *20883, 9006*
    V   *16317*   Panama *20883*

V   *Faramea woodsonii* Standl. *20883, 9006*
    V   *16317*   Panama *20883*

R   *Fernelia obovata* Lam. *10082*
    R   *20771*   Mauritius *10082*

E   *Fernelia pedunculata* Gaertn.f. *10082*
    E   *14220*   Réunion *10082*

Ex   *Gaertnera boivini* Drake *20775*
    Ex   *20771*   Mauritius *20775*

Ex   *Gaertnera calycina* Bojer *10082*
    Ex   *20771*   Mauritius *10082*

Ex   *Gaertnera crassiflora* Bojer *10082*
    Ex   *20771*   Mauritius *10082*

R   *Gaertnera cuneifolia* Bojer *10082*
    R   *20771*   Mauritius *10082*

R   *Gaertnera edentata* Bojer *10082*
    R   *20771*   Mauritius *10082*

E   *Gaertnera hirtiflora* Verdc. *10082*
    E   *20771*   Mauritius *10082*

E   *Gaertnera longifolia* Bojer var.
      longifolia *10082*
    E   *20771*   Mauritius *10082*

Ex   *Gaertnera longifolia* Bojer var. *pubescens*
      Verdc. *10082*
    Ex   *20771*   Mauritius *10082*

Ex   *Gaertnera noddosa* Drake *20775*
    Ex   *20771*   Mauritius *20775*

Ex   *Gaertnera oxycarpa* Drake *20775*
    Ex   *20771*   Mauritius *20775*

E   *Gaertnera pendula* Bojer *10082*
    E   *20771*   Mauritius *10082*

R   *Gaertnera petrinensis* Verdc. *10082*
    R   *20771*   Mauritius *10082*

Ex   *Gaertnera quadriseta* A. DC. *10082*
    Ex   *20771*   Mauritius *10082*

R   *Gaertnera rosea* Thwaites ex Benth. *10276*
    R   *12838*   Sri Lanka *10276*

E   *Gaertnera truncata* A. DC. *10082*
    E   *20771*   Mauritius *10082*

R   *Galium amorginum* Halácsy *20171*
    R   Greece

R   *Galium andrewsii* (Dempster) Dempster & Stebbins ssp.
      gatense (Dempster) Dempster & Stebbins *20850*
    R   *20850*   U.S. - California *20850*

V   *Galium angustifolium* Nutt. ex A.Gray ssp.
      borregoense Dempster & Stebbins *20850*
    V   *20850*   U.S. - California *20850*

V   *Galium angustifolium* Nutt. ex A.Gray ssp. *jacinticum*
      Dempster & Stebbins *20850*
    V   *20850*   U.S. - California *20850*

V   *Galium angustifolium* Nutt. ex A.Gray ssp. *onycense*
      (Dempster) Dempster & Stebbins *20850*
    I   *20850*   U.S. - California *20850*

R   *Galium angustissimum* (Hausskn. & Bornm.)
      Ehrend. *12840*
    R   *12840*   Turkey *12840*

R   *Galium antitaurica* Ehrend. *12840*
    R   *12840*   Turkey *12840*

E   *Galium antuneziae* Dempster *20883*
    I   *20883*   Peru *20883*

R   *Galium aretioides* Boiss. *12840*
    R   *12840*   Turkey *12840*

E   *Galium argense* Dempster & Ehrend. *20850*
    I   *20850*   U.S. - California *20850*

R   *Galium baillonii* D.Brândza *17823, 20171*
    R   *19949*   Romania *20631*

R   *Galium balearicum* Briq. *20171*
    R   Spain - Balearic Is.

R   *Galium basalticum* Ehrend. & Schonb.-Tem. *12840*
    R   *12840*   Turkey *12840*

R   *Galium baytopianum* Ehrend. & Schonb.-Tem. *12840*
    R   *12840*   Turkey *12840*

R **Galium boreo-aethiopicum** Puff *19704*
    R   *19704* Ethiopia (Gonder, Wello Upland) *19704*

R **Galium bornmuelleri** Hausskn. ex Bornm. *12840*
    R   *12840* Turkey *12840*

R **Galium bredasdorpense** Puff *20604*
    R   *20604* South Africa - Cape Province *20604*

V **Galium buxifolium** Greene *20850*
    V   *20850* U.S. - California *20850*

E **Galium cajamarcense** Dempster *20883*
    I   *20883* Peru *20883*

V **Galium californicum** Hook. & Arn. ssp. *luciense*
    Dempster & Stebbins *20850*
    V   *20850* U.S. - California *20850*

E **Galium californicum** Hook. & Arn. ssp. *primum*
    Dempster & Stebbins *20850*
    E   *20850* U.S. - California *20850*

E **Galium californicum** Hook. & Arn. ssp. *sierrae*
    Dempster & Stebbins *20850*
    E   *20850* U.S. - California *20850*

R **Galium campanelliferum** Ehrend. & Schonb.-Tem. *12840*
    R   *12840* Turkey *12840*

R **Galium canum** Reg. ex DC. ssp. *antalyense*
    Ehrend. *12840*
    R   *12840* Turkey *12840*

R **Galium carmenicola** Dempster *10066*
    R   *19797* Mexico *10066*

R **Galium carterae** Dempster *10065*
    R   *19797* Mexico *10065*

R **Galium catalinense** Gray *20850*
    I   *20850* U.S. - California *20850*

V **Galium catalinense** A. Gray ssp. *acrispum*
    Dempster *20850*
    V   *20850* U.S. - California *20850*

R **Galium catalinense** Gray ssp.
    catalinense *20850*
    I   *20850* U.S. - California *20850*

R **Galium ceratocarpon** Boiss. *12840*
    R   *12840* Turkey *12840*

R **Galium collomiae** J.T. Howell *20850*
    R   *20850* U.S. - Arizona *20850*

I **Galium confertum** Royle
    I   India - Himachal Pradesh

R **Galium cornigerum** Boiss. & Hausskn. *12840*
    R   *12840* Turkey *12840*

V **Galium correllii** Dempster *20883, 19002*
    E   *20850* U.S. - Texas *20850*
    I   *20883* Mexico *20883*

V **Galium cracoviense** Ehrend. *7897, 20171*
    V   *19306* Poland (south, near Czçstochowa) *8000*

R **Galium cyllenium** Boiss. & Heldr. *20171*
    R   Greece

E **Galium dempsterae** B. L. Turner *20883, 10077*
    I   *20883* Mexico *20883*
    ?   Mexico - Nuevo Leon *10077*

R **Galium diechii** Bornm. *12840*
    R   *12840* Turkey *12840*

R **Galium exsurgens** Ehrend. & Schonb.-Tem. *12840*
    R   *12840* Turkey *12840*

E **Galium fosbergii** Dempster *20883*

    I   *20883* Peru *20883*

R **Galium fukuyamai** Masamune *20511*
    R   *20511* Taiwan *20511*

R **Galium galiopsis** (Hand.-Mazz.) Ehrend *12840*
    R   *12840* Turkey *12840*

V **Galium glabrescens** (Ehrend.) Dempster & Ehrend. ssp.
    modocense Dempster & Ehrend. *20850*
    V   *20850* U.S. - California *20850*

R **Galium glaucophyllum** Em.Schmid *20171*
    R   Italy - Sardinia

V **Galium globuliferum** Huber-Mor. & Reese *12840*
    V   *12840* Turkey *12840*

E **Galium grande** McClatchie *20850*
    E   *20850* U.S. - California *20850*

V **Galium hallii** Munz & Johnston *20850*
    I   *20850* U.S. - California *20850*

V **Galium hardhamiae** Dempster *20850*
    V   *20850* U.S. - California *20850*

V **Galium hierochuntinum** Bornm. *8895*
    V   Israel *8895*

R **Galium hilendiae** Dempster & Ehrend. *20850*
    I   *20850* U.S. - California *20850*
    R   *20850* U.S. - Nevada *20850*

V **Galium hilendiae** Dempster & Ehrend. ssp. *carneum*
    (Hilend & Howell) Dempster & Ehrend. *20850*
    I   *20850* U.S. - California *20850*
    I   *20850* U.S. - Nevada *20850*

V **Galium hilendiae** Dempster & Ehrend. ssp.
    kingstonense (Dempster) Dempster & Ehrend. *20850*
    E   *20850* U.S. - California *20850*
    E   *20850* U.S. - Nevada *20850*

R **Galium huber-morathii** Ehrend. & Schonb.-Tem. *12840*
    R   *12840* Turkey *12840*

E **Galium hypotrichium** Ehrend. ssp. *tomentellum*
    Ehrend. *20850*
    E   *20850* U.S. - California *20850*

R **Galium hypoxylon** Ehrend. & Schonb.-Tem *12840*
    R   *12840* Turkey *12840*

R **Galium incanum** Sibth. & Sm. ssp. *creticum*
    Ehrend. *20171*
    R   *20730* Greece - Crete *20730*

R **Galium incrassatum** Halácsy *20171*
    R   *20730* Greece - Crete *20730*

R **Galium isauricum** Ehrend. & Schonb.-Tem. *12840*
    R   *12840* Turkey *12840*

V **Galium jepsonii** Hilend & Howell *20850*
    I   *20850* U.S. - California *20850*

E **Galium johnstonii** Dempster & Stebbins *20850*
    I   *20850* U.S. - California *20850*

R **Galium kamtschaticum** Steller var. *yakusimense*
    (Masam.) Yamaz. *10573*
    R   *10573* Japan *10573*

R **Galium koreanum** Nakai *15957*
    R   *15923* Korea, South (south to Chungchong-do)
           15957

I **Galium lacrimiforme** Dempster *10075*
    I   *19797* Mexico *10075*

R **Galium lasiocarpum** Boiss. *12840*
    R   *12840* Turkey *12840*

V	*Galium litorale* Guss. *8000, 20171*	
	V	*18264* Italy - Sicily *19997*
I	*Galium maborasense* Masamune *20511*	
	I	*20511* Taiwan *20511*
R	*Galium matthewsii* Gray *20850*	
	I	*20850* U.S. - California *20850*
	I	*20850* U.S. - Nevada *20850*
R	*Galium membranaceum* Ehrend. *12840*	
	R	*12840* Turkey *12840*
R	*Galium moldavicum* (Dobrescu) Franco *17762, 20171*	
	V	*19949* Romania *20631*
	R	former European USSR *8001*
R	*Galium monticolum* Sond. *20604*	
	R	*20604* South Africa - Cape Province *20604*
R	*Galium montis-arerae* Merxm. & Ehrend. *18264, 20171*	
	R	*18264* Italy (Lombardy) *18264*
R	*Galium moranii* Dempster *10065*	
	R	*19797* Mexico *10065*
V	*Galium muricatum* W. Wight *20850*	
	I	*20850* U.S. - California *20850*
I	*Galium nankotaizanum* Ohwi *20511*	
	I	*20511* Taiwan *20511*
E	*Galium niewerthii* Franchet & Sav. *10573*	
	E	*10573* Japan *10573*
E	*Galium numidicum* Pomel *10488*	
	E	*14958* Algeria *10488*
R	*Galium olympicum* auct. ital., non Boiss. *12840, 20171*	
	R	*12840* Turkey *12840*
R	*Galium palaeoitalicum* Ehrend. *20171*	
	R	Italy
R	*Galium pamphylicum* Boiss. & Heldr. *12840*	
	R	*12840* Turkey *12840*
R	*Galium papilliferum* Ehrend. & Schonb.-Tem. *12840*	
	R	*12840* Turkey *12840*
R	*Galium parishii* Hilend & Howell *20850*	
	I	*20850* U.S. - California *20850*
	I	*20850* U.S. - Nevada *20850*
R	*Galium parvulum* Hub.-Mor. ex Ehre. & Scho.-Tem *12840*	
	R	*12840* Turkey *12840*
E	*Galium philistaeum* Boiss. *8895*	
	E	Israel *8895*
R	*Galium productum* Lowe	
	R	Portugal - Madeira
R	*Galium pseudocapitatum* Hub.-Mor. ex Ehrend. & Schonb. *12840*	
	R	*12840* Turkey *12840*
R	*Galium pterocarpum* Ehrend. *12840*	
	R	*12840* Turkey *12840*
R	*Galium pulvinatum* Boiss. *20171*	
	R	*11496* Spain *11496*
I	*Galium quichense* Dempster *9004*	
	I	*19797* Guatemala *9004*
R	*Galium reiseri* Halácsy *20171*	
	R	Greece
R	*Galium roddii* Ehrend. & McGillivray *20681*	
	R	*20681* Australia - New South Wales *20681*
R	*Galium runcinatum* Ehrend. & Schonb.-Tem. *12840*	
	R	*12840* Turkey *12840*

R	*Galium saxosum* (Chaix) Breistr. *20171*	
	R	*20528* France (Alps) *20528*
R	*Galium scopulorum* Schonb.-Tem. *12840*	
	R	*12840* Turkey *12840*
V	*Galium serpenticum* Dempster ssp. *scotticum* Dempster & Ehrend. *20850*	
	V	*20850* U.S. - California *20850*
E	*Galium serpenticum* Dempster ssp. *warnerense* Dempster & Ehrend. *20850*	
	E	*20850* U.S. - California *20850*
	R	*20850* U.S. - Oregon *20850*
R	*Galium setuliferum* Ehrend. & Schonb.-Tem. *12840*	
	R	*12840* Turkey *12840*
R	*Galium siehanum* Ehrand. *12840*	
	R	*12840* Turkey *12840*
R	*Galium sinaicum* (Del. ex Decne.) Boiss. *10269*	
	R	Egypt (Sinai) *10269*
R	*Galium sorgerae* Ehrend. & Schonb.-Tem *12840*	
	R	*12840* Turkey *12840*
V	*Galium stojanovii* Degen *8000, 20171*	
	V	*5204* Bulgaria (south-west) *5204*
R	*Galium sudeticum* Tausch *7897, 20171*	
	E	*2050* Czech Republic *2050*
	R	*18216* Poland *7897*
I	*Galium taiwanense* Masamune *20511*	
	I	*20511* Taiwan *20511*
R	*Galium tanganyikense* Ehrendorfer & Verdc. *7959*	
	R	*5926* Tanzania (Njombe/Mbeya Distr.) *7959*
I	*Galium tarokoense* Hayata *20511*	
	I	*20511* Taiwan *20511*
R	*Galium thasium* Stoy. & Kit.	
	R	Greece
R	*Galium tmoleum* Boiss. *12840*	
	R	*12840* Turkey *12840*
R	*Galium tolosianum* Boiss. & Kotschy *12840*	
	R	*12840* Turkey *12840*
R	*Galium tortumense* Ehrend. & Schonb.-Tem. *12840*	
	R	*12840* Turkey *12840*
R	*Galium tubiflorumq* Ehrend. *12840*	
	R	*12840* Turkey *12840*
R	*Galium viridiflorum* Boiss. & Reut. *8000, 20171*	
	R	*20874* Spain (Málaga Hills) *20874*
R	*Galium xylorrhizum* Boiss. & Huet *12840*	
	R	*12840* Turkey *12840*
R	*Galium zabense* Ehrend. *12840*	
	R	*12840* Turkey *12840*
E	*Gardenia actinocarpa* Puttock *20681*	
	E	*20681* Australia - Queensland *20681*
E	*Gardenia anapetes* A.C. Smith *19630*	
	E	*19630* Fiji (Vanua Levu) *19630*
R	*Gardenia annamensis* Pitard *6057*	
	R	Vietnam *6057*
E	*Gardenia brighamii* Mann *20850, 14209*	
	E	*20850* U.S. - Hawaii *20850*
E	*Gardenia candida* A.C. Smith *19630*	
	E	*19630* Fiji (Vanua Levu) *19630*
R	*Gardenia chevalieri* Pitard *6057*	
	R	Vietnam *6057*

V	*Gardenia grievei* Horne ex Baker *19630*	
	V	*19630* Fiji (Vanua Levu) *19630*
R	*Gardenia hillii* Horne ex Baker *19630*	
	R	*19630* Fiji (Vanua Levu, Kanavu, Rabi) *19630*
E	*Gardenia mannii* St. John & Kuykend. *20850, 14209, 21353*	
	E	*20850* U.S. - Hawaii (O`ahu) *20850*
V	*Gardenia remyi* Mann *20850, 14209*	
	V	*20850* U.S. - Hawaii *20850*
E	*Gardenia vitiensis* Seemann *19630*	
	E	*19630* Fiji (Vanua Levu) *19630*
V	*Genipa curviflora* Dwyer *20883, 9006*	
	V	*16317* Panama *20883*
E	*Geophila croatii* Steyerm. *20883, 9006*	
	E	*20883* Panama *20883*
E	*Gleasonia cururuensis* Egler *20883*	
	E	*20883* Brazil *20883*
R	*Gleasonia duidana* Standley *20883*	
	R	*20883* Venezuela *20883*
R	*Gleasonia duidana* Standley var. *duidana* *20883*	
	R	*20883* Venezuela *20883*
V	*Gleasonia duidana* Standley var. *latifolia* Steyermark *20883*	
	V	*20883* Venezuela *20883*
E	*Gleasonia macrocalyx* Ducke *20883*	
	E	*20883* Brazil *20883*
V	*Glionnetia sericea* (Baker) Tirv. *14296*	
	V	*19182* Seychelles (granitic) *14296*
I	*Gonzalagunia brenesii* Standley *9037*	
	I	*19802* Costa Rica *9037*
V	*Gonzalagunia kallunkii* Dwyer *20883, 9006*	
	V	*16317* Panama *20883*
R	*Gonzalagunia rojasii* Standley *9004*	
	R	*19803* Guatemala *9004*
R	*Gonzalagunia rudis* (Standl.) Standl. *20883*	
	R	*20883* Panama *20883*
R	*Gonzalagunia thrysoidea* (J.D. Smith) Robinson *9004*	
	R	*19802* Guatemala *9004*
V	*Gonzalagunia veraguensis* Dwyer *20883, 9006*	
	V	*16317* Panama *20883*
V	*Guettarda amblyophylla* Urban *5607*	
	V	*19105* Cuba (Pinar del Rio) *5607*
I	*Guettarda brenesii* Standley *9037*	
	I	*19803* Costa Rica *9037*
I	*Guettarda cobanensis* J.D. Smith *9004*	
	I	*19802* Guatemala *9004*
E	*Guettarda cobrensis* Standl. *5607*	
	E	*19105* Cuba (Santiago de Cuba) *5607*
R	*Guettarda foliacea* Standl. *20883*	
	V	*20883* Panama *20883*
V	*Guettarda frangulifolia* Urb. *20883*	
	V	*20883* Jamaica *20883*
I	*Guettarda longiflora* Griseb. *13336*	
	I	*13336* Jamaica (St. Ann, St. Thomas) *13336*
R	*Guettarda macrosperma* J.D. Sm. *20883*	
	V	*20883* Panama *20883*
E	*Guettarda nervosa* Urban & Ekman *5607*	

	E	*19105* Cuba *5607*
V	*Guettarda noumeana* Baillon *20802*	
	V	*20893* New Caledonia *20802*
R	*Guettarda odorata* (Jacq.) Lam. *20883*	
	I	*20883* Puerto Rico *20883*
	I	*20883* USA - Virgin Is. *20883*
	R	*20883* Panama *20883*
E	*Guettarda organosia* Urban *5607*	
	E	*19105* Cuba (Pinar del Rio) *5607*
I	*Guettarda petenensis* Lundell *9004*	
	I	*19802* Guatemala *9004*
R	*Guettarda poasana* Standley *9037*	
	R	*19802* Costa Rica *9037*
	V	*16317* Nicaragua *16826*
E	*Guettarda ramuliflora* Beurl. *20883, 9006*	
	I	*20883* Panama *20883*
E	*Guettarda retusa* C. Wright *5607*	
	E	*19105* Cuba (Pinar del Rio) *5607*
E	*Guettarda roigiana* Borh. & Muniz *5607*	
	E	*19105* Cuba (Villa Clara) *5607*
V	*Guettarda sanblasensis* Dwyer *20883, 9006*	
	V	*16317* Panama *20883*
E	*Guettarda turrialbana* Zamora & Poveda *20883, 12478*	
	E	*20883* Costa Rica *20883*
R	*Guettarda viburnoides* Cham. & Schlecht. *20883*	
	I	*20883* Brazil *20883*
	R	*20883* Paraguay *20883*
R	*Hamelia papillosa* Urb. *20883, 19890*	
	R	*19890* Jamaica (central, western) *20883*
V	*Hamelia sanguinea* Elias *20883, 9006*	
	I	*20883* Panama *20883*
E	*Hedyotis albonervia* Beddome *11494*	
	E	*11494* India - Tamil Nadu *11494*
I	*Hedyotis anamalayana* (Gamble) R. Rao & Hemadri	
	I	India - Tamil Nadu
I	*Hedyotis andamanica* Kurz *7771*	
	I	India - Andaman Is. *7771*
	I	India - Nicobar Is. (Nicobar) *7771*
R	*Hedyotis angulata* Fosberg ex Shinners *20850*	
	R	*20850* U.S. - New Mexico *20850*
	I	*20850* U.S. - Texas *20850*
I	*Hedyotis bambusetorum* Merr. *13833*	
	I	*13833* Philippines (Palawan) *13833*
V	*Hedyotis barberi* (Gamble) A.N. Henry & Subram.	
	V	*13883* India - Tamil Nadu (Tirunelveli Hills) *13883*
E	*Hedyotis beddomei* Hook.f. *11494*	
	E	*11494* India - Kerala (Palghat Hills) *11494*
V	*Hedyotis bourdillonii* (Gamble) R. Rao & Hemadri *10508*	
	V	*13883* India - Kerala (Travancore; Silent Valley) *10508*
R	*Hedyotis brunonis* Merr. *13883*	
	R	*13883* Bangladesh *13883*
	R	*13883* India - Assam *13883*
	R	*13883* Myanmar *13883*
E	*Hedyotis butterwickiae* (Terrell) Nesom *20850*	
	E	*20850* U.S. - Texas *20850*
R	*Hedyotis buxifolia* Bedd. *13883*	
	R	*13883* India - Kerala *13883*
	R	*13883* India - Tamil Nadu *13883*

I   *Hedyotis congesta* Wall. var. *nicobarica*
     King *7771*
     R   *20099* Singapore *20099*
     I   India - Nicobar Is. *7771*

E   *Hedyotis cookiana* (Cham. & Schlecht.) Steud. *20850, 14209*
     E   *20850* U.S. - Hawaii (Hawai`i & Kaua`i) *20850*

E   *Hedyotis coriacea* Sm. *20850, 14209*
     E   *20850* U.S. - Hawaii *20850*

I   *Hedyotis cymosa* Thwaites *10252*
     I   *16162* Sri Lanka *10252*

E   *Hedyotis cystisoides* Craib *19120*
     E   *19120* Thailand *19120*

E   *Hedyotis degeneri* Fosberg *20850, 14209*
     I   *20850* U.S. - Hawaii (O`ahu - Wai`anae Mts) *20850*

E   *Hedyotis degeneri* Fosberg var. *coprosmifolia* Fosb. *20850*
     E   *20850* U.S. - Hawaii *20850*

E   *Hedyotis degeneri* Fosberg var. *degeneri* *20850*
     E   *20850* U.S. - Hawaii *20850*

E   *Hedyotis elatior* (Mann) Fosberg *20850, 14209*
     E   *20850* U.S. - Hawaii *20850*

R   *Hedyotis eualata* (bedd. ex Gamble) Henry et Subramanyam *13883*
     R   *13883* India - Kerala *13883*
     R   *13883* India - Tamil Nadu *13883*

I   *Hedyotis evenia* Thwaites *10252*
     I   *16162* Sri Lanka *10252*

E   *Hedyotis fluviatilis* (Forbes) Fosberg *20850, 14209*
     E   *20850* U.S. - Hawaii (Oahu, Ko`olau Mts) *20850*

Ex/E   *Hedyotis foliosa* (Hbd.) Fosberg *20850, 14209*
     Ex/E *20850* U.S. - Hawaii (east Maui) *20850*

E   *Hedyotis formosa* (Hbd.) Fosberg *20850, 14209*
     E   *20850* U.S. - Hawaii (West Maui) *20850*

I   *Hedyotis gardneri* Thwaites *10252*
     I   *16162* Sri Lanka *10252*

E   *Hedyotis geddesiana* Craib *19120*
     E   *19120* Thailand *19120*

Ex/E   *Hedyotis hirsutissima* Beddome *11494*
     Ex/E *11494* India - Tamil Nadu *11494*

I   *Hedyotis inamoena* Thwaites *10252*
     I   *16162* Sri Lanka *10252*

I   *Hedyotis kingiana* Elm. *13833*
     I   *13833* Philippines (low altitude) *13833*

V   *Hedyotis knudsenii* (Hbd.) Fosberg *20883*
     I   *20850* U.S. - Hawaii (Kaua`i - Koke`e area) *20850*

E   *Hedyotis littoralis* (Hbd.) Fosberg *20850, 14209*
     E   *20850* U.S. - Hawaii *20850*

E   *Hedyotis lychnidifolia* Craib *19120*
     E   *19120* Thailand *19120*

E   *Hedyotis mannii* Fosberg *20850, 14209*
     E   *20850* U.S. - Hawaii *20850*

R   *Hedyotis megalantha* Merr.
     R   *18338* U.S. - Guam *18338*

R   *Hedyotis mexicana* (Hook. & Arn.) Hatus. *8037*
     R   *19134* Japan - Ogasawara-shoto *8037*

V   *Hedyotis mullerae* Fosberg *20850*
     E   *20850* U.S. - Texas *20850*

E   *Hedyotis nigricans* (Lam.) Fern. var. *pulvinata* (Small) Fosberg *20850*
     E   *20850* U.S. - Florida *20850*

E   *Hedyotis parvula* (Gray) Fosberg *20850, 14209*
     E   *20850* U.S. - Hawaii (O`ahu - Wai`anae Mts) *20850*

I   *Hedyotis perhispida* Elm. *13833*
     I   *13833* Philippines (low altitude) *13833*

R   *Hedyotis philippensis* (Willd. ex Sprengel) Merr. ex C.Robinson *20681*
     R   *20681* Australia - Queensland *20681*

E   *Hedyotis punicea* Craib *19120*
     E   *19120* Thailand *19120*

I   *Hedyotis quinquenervia* Thwaites *10252*
     I   *16162* Sri Lanka *10252*

V   *Hedyotis ramarowii* (Gamble) R. Rao & Hemadri *11494*
     V   *11494* India - Kerala (Travancore) *11494*
     V   *11494* India - Tamil Nadu *11494*

I   *Hedyotis rhinophylla* Thwaites ex Trimen *10252*
     I   *16162* Sri Lanka *10252*

E   *Hedyotis schlechtendahliana* Steudel var. *remyi* (Hbd.) Fosberg *20850, 14209*
     E   *20850* U.S. - Hawaii *20850*

I   *Hedyotis shuteri* (Hook.f.) R. Rao & Hemadri
     I   India - Tamil Nadu (east coast near Madras)

I   *Hedyotis sisaparensis* Gage *2268*
     I   India - Tamil Nadu (Nilgiri Hills) *2268*

E   *Hedyotis spellenbergii* Nesom & Vorobik *20883*
     I   *20883* Mexico *20883*

E   *Hedyotis st.-johnii* B.C. Stone & M.A. Lane *20850, 14209*
     E   *20850* U.S. - Hawaii (Kaua`i) *20850*

I   *Hedyotis stocksii* (Hk.f. & Th.) R. Rao & Hemadri
     I   India - Karnataka (Mysore)

R   *Hedyotis swersioides* Hook.f. *13883*
     R   *13883* India - Kerala *13883*
     R   *13883* India - Tamil Nadu *13883*

I   *Hedyotis travancorica* Beddome
     I   India - Kerala (Travancore Hills)
     I   India - Tamil Nadu (Tirunelveli Hills)

E   *Hedyotis tryblium* Herbst & W.L. Wagner *20850, 14209*
     E   *20850* U.S. - Hawaii (Kaua`i) *20850*

I   *Hedyotis villosastripulata* (Gamble) R. Rao & Hemadri *5379*
     I   India - Kerala (Travancore Hills)
     I   India - Tamil Nadu (Muthukuzhivayal) *5379*

I   *Hedyotis wynaadensis* (Gamble) R. Rao & Hemadri
     I   India - Kerala (Wynaad)

V   *Henriquezia jenmanii* Schumann *20883*
     V   *20883* Guyana *20883*

E   *Henriquezia nitida* var. *longisepala* (Bremekamp) Rogers *20883*
     E   *20883* Brazil *20883*

R   *Henriquezia nitida* var. *macrophylla* (Ducke) Steyermark *20883*
     R   *20883* Brazil *20883*

E   *Hillia chiapensis* Dwyer ssp. *grandifolia*

Dwyer *20883, 9006*
I   *20883* Panama *20883*

E   *Hillia ligulifolia* Dwyer *20883, 9006*
I   *20883* Panama *20883*

I   *Hillia macrocarpa* Standley & Steyerm. *9004*
I   *19802* Guatemala *9004*

V   *Hodgkinsonia frutescens* C.White *20681*
V   *20681* Australia - Queensland *20681*

E   *Hoffmannia araneopedaria* Dwyer *20883, 9006*
I   *20883* Panama *20883*

E   *Hoffmannia areolata* Standl. *20883, 9006*
I   *20883* Panama *20883*

I   *Hoffmannia calycosa* J.D. Smith *9004*
I   *19802* Guatemala *9004*

E   *Hoffmannia capillacea* Dwyer *20883, 9006*
I   *20883* Panama *20883*

I   *Hoffmannia cauliflora* Hemsley *9004*
I   *19802* Guatemala *9004*

E   *Hoffmannia cercidifolia* Dwyer *20883, 9006*
I   *20883* Panama *20883*

R   *Hoffmannia chiapensis* Standley *9004*
R   *19802* Guatemala *9004*
R   *9989* Mexico *9004*

I   *Hoffmannia confertiflora* Standley *9004*
I   *19802* Guatemala *9004*

V   *Hoffmannia davidsoniae* Standl. *20883, 9006*
I   *20883* Panama *20883*

V   *Hoffmannia fimbrianthera* Dwyer *20883, 9006*
V   *16317* Panama *20883*

V   *Hoffmannia haydenii* Dwyer *20883, 9006*
V   *16317* Panama *20883*

V   *Hoffmannia kirkbridei* Dwyer *20883, 9006*
V   *16317* Panama *20883*

V   *Hoffmannia lancistigma* Dwyer *20883, 9006*
V   *16317* Panama *20883*

E   *Hoffmannia lewisiana* Dwyer *20883, 9006*
I   *20883* Panama *20883*

E   *Hoffmannia longicalycina* Dwyer *20883, 9006*
R   *19803* Panama *20883*

I   *Hoffmannia macrosiphon* Standley *9004*
I   *19802* Guatemala *9004*

V   *Hoffmannia manussatani* Dwyer *20883, 9006*
V   *16317* Panama *20883*

V   *Hoffmannia morii* Dwyer *20883, 9006*
V   *16317* Panama *20883*

V   *Hoffmannia ostaurea* Dwyer *20883, 9006*
V   *16317* Panama *20883*

V   *Hoffmannia pedunculata* Sw. *20883, 13336*
V   *13336* Jamaica (St. Andrew, Portland) *20883*

I   *Hoffmannia phoenicopoda* Schum. *9004*
I   *19802* Guatemala *9004*

R   *Hoffmannia pittieri* Standl. *20883, 9006*
I   *20883* Panama *20883*

E   *Hoffmannia pustulata* Dwyer *20883, 9006*
I   *20883* Panama *20883*

Ex/E   *Hoffmannia racemifera* Standley & Steyerm. *9004*
Ex/E *19802* Guatemala *9004*

V   *Hoffmannia rexmontis* Dwyer *20883, 9006*

V   *16317* Panama *20883*

V   *Hoffmannia rubripigmenta* Dwyer *20883, 9006*
V   *16317* Panama *20883*

I   *Hoffmannia sessilifolia* L.O. Williams *9004*
I   *19802* Guatemala *9004*

I   *Hoffmannia teruae* L.O. Williams & A. Molina *9004*
I   *19802* Guatemala *9004*

I   *Hoffmannia tetrastigma* J.D. Smith *9004*
I   *19802* Guatemala *9004*

I   *Hoffmannia tuerckheimii* J.D. Smith *9004*
I   *19802* Guatemala *9004*

I   *Hoffmannia tuerckheimii* J.D. Smith var. *glabra*
Standley & Steyerm. *9004*
I   *19802* Guatemala *9004*

I   *Hoffmannia uniflora* Standley *9004*
I   *19802* Guatemala *9004*

I   *Hoffmannia vulcanicola* Standley & Steyerm. *9004*
I   *19802* Guatemala *9004*

I   *Hoffmannia wilsonii* Standley *9004*
I   *19802* Guatemala *9004*

V   *Hoffmannia witheringioides* Dwyer *20883, 9006*
V   *16317* Panama *20883*

E   *Holstianthus barbigularis* Steyermark *20883*
I   *20883* Venezuela *20883*

E   *Houstonia correllii* (W.H. Lewis) Terrell *20850*
E   *20850* U.S. - Texas *20850*

E   *Houstonia croftiae* Britt. & Rusby *20850*
E   *20850* U.S. - Texas *20850*

R   *Houstonia ouachitana* (E.B. Sm.) Terrell *20850*
R   *20850* U.S. - Arkansas *20850*
E   *20850* U.S. - Oklahoma *20850*

V   *Houstonia purpurea* (Small) Terrell var. *montana*
(Small) Terrell *20850*
V   *20850* U.S. - North Carolina *20850*
E   *20850* U.S. - Tennessee *20850*

R   *Indopolysolenia wallichii* (Hook. F.) Bennet *14782*
R   *14782* India - Meghalaya *14782*

R   *Isidorea elliptica* Alain *5607*
R   *19105* Cuba (Guantanamo) *5607*

R   *Isidorea leonis* Alain *5607*
R   *19105* Cuba (Guantanamo) *5607*

R   *Isidorea microphylla* Borh. *5607*
R   *19105* Cuba (Guantanamo) *5607*

V   *Isidorea polyneura* (Urban) Aiello *5607*
V   *19105* Cuba (Santiago de Cuba) *5607*

V   *Isidorea rheedioides* Borh. *5607*
V   *19105* Cuba (Guantanamo) *5607*

I   *Ixora andamanica* Bremek. *7771*
I   India - Andaman Is. *7771*

R   *Ixora baileyana* Bailey *20681*
R   *20681* Australia - Queensland *20681*

I   *Ixora capitulifera* Elm. *13833*
I   *13833* Philippines (Palawan) *13833*

I   *Ixora capituliflora* Bremek. *7771*
I   India - Andaman Is. *7771*

R   *Ixora clerodendron* Ridley
R   Malaysia - Peninsular Malaysia (Pahang)

I   *Ixora cuneifolia* Roxb. var. *macrocarpa*

	Kurz *7771*	
I		India - Nicobar Is. (Pulu Milo Is.) *7771*
R	*Ixora delpyana* Pierre ex Pitard *6057*	
R		Vietnam *6057*
R	*Ixora floribunda* (A. Rich.) Griseb. *20883*	
E		*20883* Panama *20883*
I	*Ixora hymenophylla* Bremek. *7771*	
I		India - Andaman Is. *7771*
I	*Ixora intermedia* Elm. *13833*	
I		*13833* Philippines (low altitude) *13833*
I	*Ixora johnsonii* Hook.f.	
I		India - Kerala (Travancore)
V	*Ixora jucunda* Thwaites *10276*	
V		*12838* Sri Lanka *10276*
I	*Ixora lawsoni* Gamble	
I		India - Karnataka (Coorg)
I		India - Kerala (Mannanthody)
I	*Ixora longibracteata* Bremek. *7771*	
I		India - Nicobar Is. *7771*
E	*Ixora marquesensis* F. Brown	
E		French Polynesia - Marquesas Is
I	*Ixora palawanensis* Elm. *13833*	
I		*13833* Philippines (low altitude) *13833*
V	*Ixora pudica* Baker *14296*	
V		*19182* Seychelles (granitic) *14296*
I	*Ixora saulierei* Gamble	
I		India - Tamil Nadu (Palani Hills)
Ex/E	*Ixora scheffleri* K. Schum. & K. Krause ssp. *keniensis* Bridson *20057*	
Ex/E		*20057* Kenya (Mt. Kenya) *20057*
I	*Ixora spathoidea* F. Brown	
I		French Polynesia - Marquesas Is
I	*Ixora tenuifolia* Bremek. *7771*	
I		India - Nicobar Is. *7771*
V	*Joosia panamensis* Dwyer *20883, 9006*	
I		*20883* Panama *20883*
R	*Kailarsenia jardinei* (F.Muell. ex Benth.) Puttock *20681*	
R		*20681* Australia - Queensland *20681*
R	*Keenania microcephala* Pitard *6057*	
R		Vietnam *6057*
R	*Knoxia linearis* Gamble	
R		*7771* India - Orissa (Mahendragiri, Ganjam) *7771*
I		India - Tamil Nadu (Mahendragiri hills)
V	*Ladenbergia laurifolia* Dwyer *20883, 9006*	
V		*16317* Panama *20883*
R	*Lasianthus appressihirtus* Simizu var. *maximus* Simizu *20511*	
R		*20511* Taiwan *20511*
R	*Lasianthus baviensis* (Drake) Pitard *6057*	
R		Vietnam *6057*
I	*Lasianthus blumeanus* Wight	
I		India - Tamil Nadu (Tirunelveli District)
R	*Lasianthus caeruleus* Pitard *6057*	
R		Vietnam *6057*
I	*Lasianthus capitulatus* Wight	
I		India - Karnataka (Bruhmagiri Hills)
I		India - Tamil Nadu (Nilgiri & Palani Hills)

I	*Lasianthus ciliatus* Wight	
I		India - Tamil Nadu (Nilagiri Hills)
I	*Lasianthus dichotomus* Wight *9327*	
I		India - Tamil Nadu *9327*
R	*Lasianthus obliquinervis* Merr. var. *simizui* Merr. *20511*	
R		*20511* Taiwan *20511*
R	*Lasianthus obliquinervis* Merr. var. *taitoensis* Merr. *20511*	
R		*20511* Taiwan *20511*
I	*Lasianthus oblongifolius* Beddome	
I		India - Tamil Nadu (Papanasam Hills)
I	*Lasianthus obovatus* Beddome	
I		India - Kerala (Athramalai Hills)
R	*Lasianthus oliganthus* Thwaites *10276*	
R		*12838* Sri Lanka *10276*
R	*Lasianthus pierrei* Pitard *6057*	
R		Vietnam *6057*
I	*Lasianthus rhinophyllus* (Thwaites) Thwaites *10252*	
I		*16162* Sri Lanka *10252*
R	*Lasianthus saprosmoides* Pitard *6057*	
R		Vietnam *6057*
I	*Lasianthus thwaitesii* Hook. f. *16162*	
I		*16162* Sri Lanka *16162*
I	*Lasianthus truncatus* Beddome	
I		India - Andhra Pradesh (Vizakapatanam)
I		*7771* India - Orissa (Mahendragiri hills, Ganjam) *7771*
V	*Leptactina papyrophloea* Verdc. *20556*	
V		*20885* Tanzania (Rondo Plateau) *20885*
I	*Leptodermis griffithii* Hook.f.	
I		India - Meghalaya
R	*Leptodermis pulchella* Yatabe *10573*	
R		*10573* Japan *10573*
I	*Leptodermis scabrida* Hook.f.	
I		India - Arunachal Pradesh (Mishmee Hills)
R	*Lindenia rivalis* Benth. *20883*	
V		*20883* Panama *20883*
E	*Machaonia acunae* Borh. & Fernandez *5607*	
E		*19105* Cuba (Juventud Is.) *5607*
V	*Machaonia cymosa* (Sw.) Griseb. *20883*	
V		*20883* Jamaica *20883*
V	*Machaonia dumosa* Borh. & Fernandez *5607*	
V		*19105* Cuba (Pinar del Rio) *5607*
R	*Machaonia pubescens* Borh. & Fernandez *5607*	
R		*19105* Cuba (Cienfuegos) *5607*
R	*Machaonia rotundata* Griseb. *20883*	
R		*20883* Jamaica *20883*
E	*Machaonia tiffina* Urban & Ekman *5607*	
E		*19105* Cuba (SS; CA; C) *5607*
R	*Machaonia urbaniana* Standl. *5607*	
R		*19105* Cuba (Santiago de Cuba) *5607*
V	*Machaonia urbinoi* Borh. & Muniz *5607*	
V		*19105* Cuba (Holguin) *5607*
R	*Macrocnemum jamaicense* L. *20883*	
R		*20883* Jamaica *20883*
V	*Manettia bocataurensis* Dwyer *20883, 9006*	
V		*16317* Panama *20883*

E	*Manettia hydrophila* Dwyer *20883, 9006*	
	I	*20883* Panama *20883*
V	*Mitracarpus acunae* Alain *5607*	
	V	*19105* Cuba (Santiago de Cuba) *5607*
E	*Mitracarpus depauperatus* Britton & P. Wilson *5607*	
	E	*19105* Cuba (Juventud Is.) *5607*
E	*Mitracarpus maxwelliac* Britt. & Wilson *20883*	
	I	*20883* Puerto Rico *20883*
E	*Mitracarpus polycladus* Urban *20883, 8058*	
	I	*20883* Netherlands Antilles *20883*
	I	*20883* Puerto Rico *20883*
V	*Mitracarpus scaberulus* Urban *5607*	
	V	*19105* Cuba (Pinar del Rio) *5607*
E	*Mitrostigma greenwayi* Bridson	
	E	Kenya
V	*Montamans panamensis* Dwyer *20883, 9006*	
	V	*16317* Panama *20883*
I	*Morinda reticulata* Gamble	
	I	India - Kerala (Travancore Hills)
R	*Morinda trimera* Hbd. *20850, 14209*	
	R	*20850* U.S. - Hawaii (Oahu, Lanai & Maui) *20850*
R	*Mouretia tonkinensis* Pitard *6057*	
	R	Vietnam *6057*
E	*Mussaenda anomala* Li *17617*	
	E	*17617* China - Guangxi (Dayaoshan) *11139*
R	*Mussaenda chevalieri* Pitard *6057*	
	I	*20985* Vietnam *6057*
R	*Mussaenda dinhensis* Pierre ex Pitard *6057*	
	R	Vietnam *6057*
I	*Mussaenda grandifolia* Elm. *13833*	
	I	*13833* Philippines (low altitude) *13833*
Ex/E	*Mussaenda landia* Poiret var. *holosericea* (J.E. Smith) Verdc. *10082*	
	Ex/E	*10082* Réunion *10082*
	Ex	*20771* Mauritius *10082*
R	*Mussaenda landia* Poiret var. *stadmanii* (DC.) Verdc. *10082*	
	R	*20771* Mauritius *10082*
I	*Mussaenda longisepala* Geddes *19120*	
	I	*19120* Thailand *19120*
I	*Mussaenda mollis* Geddes *19120*	
	I	*19120* Thailand *19120*
I	*Mussaenda monticola* Krause var. *glabrescens* Bridson *5926*	
	I	*5926* Tanzania *5926*
I	*Mussaenda palawanensis* Merr. *13833*	
	I	*13833* Philippines (low altitude) *13833*
I	*Mussaenda setosa* Merr. *13833*	
	I	*13833* Philippines (Palawan) *13833*
R	*Mussaenda taiwaniana* Kanehira *20854*	
	R	*20854* Taiwan *20854*
I	*Mycetia mukerjiana* Deb & R. Dutta	
	I	India - Assam (Makum hills)
R	*Myonima nitens* (Poiret) Verdc. *10082*	
	R	*20771* Mauritius *10082*
E	*Myonima vaughanii* Verdc. *10082*	
	E	*20771* Mauritius *10082*
R	*Myonima violacea* (Lam.) Verdc. var. *ovata* (Poiret) Verdc. *10082*	

	R	*20771* Mauritius *10082*
R	*Nargedia macrocarpa* (Thwaites) Beddome *10252*	
	R	*12838* Sri Lanka *10252*
I	*Nauclea gageana* King *7771*	
	I	*14782* India - Andaman Is. *7771*
I	*Neanotis carnosa* (Dalz.) W. Lewis *14782*	
	I	*14782* India - Karnataka *14782*
I	*Neanotis monosperma* (Wight & Arn.) W. Lewis	
	I	India - Karnataka (Mysore)
	I	India - Tamil Nadu (Nilgiri & Palani Hills)
I	*Neanotis montholonii* (Hook.f.) W. Lewis	
	I	India - Karnataka (Mysore and Concan)
	I	India - Kerala
R	*Neanotis oxyphylla* (G. Don) Lewis *14782*	
	R	*14782* India - Meghalaya *14782*
V	*Neanotis prainiana* (Talbot) Lewis *14782*	
	V	*14782* India - Karnataka *14782*
I	*Neanotis rheedii* (Wight & Arn.) W. Lewis *14782*	
	I	India - Karnataka
	I	India - Kerala (Cochin)
	I	India - Tamil Nadu
V	*Neofranciella pterocarpon* Guillaumin	
	V	New Caledonia
R	*Nertera assurgens* Thouars *19938*	
	R	Tristan da Cunha (Inaccessible & Tristan Is.) *19938*
R	*Nertera holmboei* Christoph. *19938*	
	R	Tristan da Cunha (Inaccessible, Nightingale Is.) *19938*
E	*Nesohedyotis arborea* (Roxb.) Bremekamp *18996*	
	E	*18996* St Helena *18996*
I	*Neurocalyx gardneri* Thwaites *10252*	
	I	*16162* Sri Lanka *10252*
E	*Nodocarpaea radicans* A.Gray *5607*	
	E	*19105* Cuba (Pinar del Rio; I. Juventud) *5607*
R	*Notodontia balansae* Pitard *6057*	
	R	Vietnam *6057*
R	*Notodontia micrantha* (Drake) Pitard *6057*	
	R	Vietnam *6057*
V	*Ochreinauclea missionis* (Wall. ex G. Don) Ridsd. *14782, 21025*	
	V	*14782* India (central and southern W. Ghats) *14782*
Ex	*Oldenlandia adscensionis* (DC.) Cronk *3204*	
	Ex	*3204* Ascension Is. *3204*
I	*Oldenlandia aegialoides* Bremek. *5926*	
	I	*5926* Tanzania *5926*
I	*Oldenlandia albonervia* (Beddome) Gamble	
	I	India - Kerala (Travancore Hills)
	I	India - Tamil Nadu (Tirunelveli Hills)
R	*Oldenlandia cana* Bremek. *7883*	
	R	Zimbabwe *7883*
E	*Oldenlandia cornata* Craib *19120*	
	E	*19120* Thailand *19120*
I	*Oldenlandia forcipistipula* Verdc. *5926*	
	I	*5926* Tanzania *5926*
I	*Oldenlandia glauca* Blatter	
	I	India - Rajasthan (Mt Abu)
E	*Oldenlandia lanceolata* Craib *19120*	
	E	*19120* Thailand *19120*

V   *Oldenlandia lancifolia* (Schumacher) DC. *20883*
    I   *20883*   Puerto Rico *20883*
    E   *20883*   Panama *20883*

I   *Oldenlandia marcanii* Craib *19120*
    I   *19120*   Thailand *19120*

R   *Oldenlandia microtheca* (D.F. K. Schldl. & Cham.)
        DC. *9004*
    I   *19802*   Guatemala *9004*
    R   *9989*   Mexico *9004*

I   *Oldenlandia oxycoccoides* Bremek. *5926*
    I   *5926*   Tanzania *5926*

I   *Oldenlandia patula* Bremek. *5926*
    I   *5926*   Tanzania *5926*

R   *Oldenlandia polyclada* (F.Muell.) F.Muell. *20681*
    R   *20681*   Australia - Queensland *20681*

R   *Oldenlandia sieberi* Baker var. *congesta*
        Balf.f. *10082*
    R   *5852*   Mauritius - Rodrigues *5852*

Ex   *Oldenlandia sieberi* Baker var. *sieberi* *10082*
    Ex   *20771*   Mauritius *10082*

R   *Oldenlandia thysanota* (Halford) Halford *20681*
    R   *20681*   Australia - Northern Territory *20681*

I   *Oldenlandia uvinsae* Verdc. *5926*
    I   *5926*   Tanzania *5926*

R   *Omiltemia filisepala* (Standley) Morton *19850*
    R   *19850*   Mexico *19850*

R   *Omiltemia longipes* Standley *19850*
    R   *19850*   Mexico *19850*

Ex   *Opercularia acolytantha* Diels *20681*
    Ex   *20681*   Australia - Western Australia *20681*

I   *Ophiorrhiza alata* Craib *19120*
    I   *19120*   Thailand *19120*

I   *Ophiorrhiza angkae* Craib *19120*
    I   *19120*   Thailand *19120*

I   *Ophiorrhiza approximata* Craib *19120*
    I   *19120*   Thailand *19120*

Ex/E   *Ophiorrhiza barnesii* C. Fischer *11494*
    Ex/E   *11494*   India - Kerala (Travancore) *11494*

I   *Ophiorrhiza bicolor* Craib *19120*
    I   *19120*   Thailand *19120*

Ex   *Ophiorrhiza brunonis* Wight & Arn. *11494*
    Ex   *11494*   India - Karnataka *11494*
    Ex   *11494*   India - Kerala *11494*
    Ex   *11494*   India - Tamil Nadu *11494*

I   *Ophiorrhiza calcarea* Craib *19120*
    I   *19120*   Thailand *19120*

Ex   *Ophiorrhiza caudata* C. Fischer *11494*
    Ex   *11494*   India - Kerala (Idikki) *11494*

I   *Ophiorrhiza codyensis* Gamble
    I   India - Karnataka (Coorg, Sampaji Ghat)

I   *Ophiorrhiza condensa* Craib *19120*
    I   *19120*   Thailand *19120*

R   *Ophiorrhiza fruticosa* Ridley
    R   Malaysia - Peninsular Malaysia

I   *Ophiorrhiza gracilis* Kurz *13883*
    I   *13883*   India - Nagaland (Kohima) *13883*
    I   *13883*   Myanmar (Tenasserim) *13883*

I   *Ophiorrhiza griffithii* Hook.f. *13883*
    I   *13883*   India - Nagaland *13883*
    I   *13883*   Myanmar *13883*

E   *Ophiorrhiza hispida* Hook.f. *13883*
    E   *13883*   India - Assam *13883*
    E   *13883*   India - Meghalaya *13883*
    E   *13883*   Myanmar *13883*

E   *Ophiorrhiza incarnata* C. Fischer *11494*
    E   *11494*   India - Kerala *11494*

I   *Ophiorrhiza kratensis* Craib *19120*
    I   *19120*   Thailand *19120*

R   *Ophiorrhiza longerepens* Ridley
    R   Malaysia - Peninsular Malaysia (Gua Musang)

E   *Ophiorrhiza longipes* Craib *19120*
    E   *19120*   Thailand *19120*

I   *Ophiorrhiza membranacea* Craib *19120*
    I   *19120*   Thailand *19120*

I   *Ophiorrhiza munnarensis* C. Fischer
    I   India - Kerala (Idikki)

I   *Ophiorrhiza nicobarica* Balakr. *7771*
    I   India - Nicobar Is. (Gt. Nicobar Is.)
         7771

I   *Ophiorrhiza pallida* Thwaites *10252*
    I   *16162*   Sri Lanka *10252*

I   *Ophiorrhiza patula* Craib *19120*
    I   *19120*   Thailand *19120*

I   *Ophiorrhiza pulgarense* Elm. *13833*
    I   *13833*   Philippines (Palawan) *13833*

Ex/E   *Ophiorrhiza pykarensis* Gamble *11494*
    Ex/E   India - Tamil Nadu (Pykara Falls, Nilgiris)
         4988

Ex   *Ophiorrhiza radicans* Gardn. *13883*
    Ex   *13883*   India - Kerala *13883*
    Ex   *13883*   Sri Lanka *13883*

I   *Ophiorrhiza ridleyana* Craib *19120*
    I   *19120*   Thailand *19120*

I   *Ophiorrhiza ripicola* Craib *19120*
    I   *19120*   Thailand *19120*

I   *Ophiorrhiza roxburghiana* Wight
    I   India - Tamil Nadu (Palani Hills; Periya shola)

E   *Ophiorrhiza subcapitata* Wall. ex Hook.f. *13883*
    E   *13883*   India - Meghalaya (Khasi & Jaintea hills)
         13883

I   *Ophiorrhiza subpunicea* Craib *19120*
    I   *19120*   Thailand *19120*

V   *Ophiorrhiza tingens* Clarke ex Fischer *13883*
    V   *13883*   India - Assam *13883*
    V   *13883*   India - Meghalaya *13883*
    V   *13883*   India - Nagaland *13883*
    V   *13883*   India - Tripura *13883*
    V   *13883*   Myanmar *13883*

V   *Ophiorrhiza villosa* Roxb. *14872*
    V   *14872*   Bangladesh *14872*

E   *Ophiorrhiza wattii* C. Fischer *11494*
    E   *11494*   India - Manipur *11494*
    E   *11494*   India - Meghalaya *11494*
    E   *11494*   India - Nagaland *11494*

I   *Otiophora pycnoclada* K. Schum. *5926*
    I   *5926*   Tanzania *5926*

V   *Oxyanthus pyriformis* (Hochst.) Skeels ssp.
        brevitubus Bridson *20057*
    V   *20057*   Kenya *20057*
    V   *20057*   Tanzania (Mt. Meru) *17435*

R   *Oxyanthus pyriformis* (Hochst.) Skeels ssp.

		longitubus Bridson *20057*	
R		20057 Kenya *20057*	
R	*Pachystigma gillettii* (Tennant) Verdc. *20057*		
R		20057 Kenya *20057*	
V	*Palicourea bella* (Standl.) Dwyer *20883, 9006*		
V		*16317* Panama *20883*	
V	*Palicourea chiriquina* Standl. *20883, 9006*		
V		*16317* Panama *20883*	
R	*Palicourea fastigiata* Benth. *20883*		
E		20883 Panama *20883*	
E	*Palicourea gibbosa* Dwyer *20883, 9006*		
I		20883 Panama *20883*	
E	*Palicourea grandibracteata* Dwyer *20883*		
I		20883 Panama *20883*	
V	*Palicourea montensis* Dwyer *20883, 9006*		
V		*16317* Panama *20883*	
V	*Palicourea ochnoides* Dwyer *20883, 9006*		
V		*16317* Panama *20883*	
V	*Palicourea panamensis* Standl. *20883*		
I		20883 Panama *20883*	
V	*Palicourea pauciflora* Standl. *20883, 9006*		
V		*16317* Panama *20883*	
V	*Palicourea pulchra* Proctor var. *hispidula*		
	Proctor *20883, 13336*		
V		*13336* Jamaica (Trelawny) *20883*	
E	*Palicourea rigidifolia* (Dwyer & Hayden) Dwyer *20883*		
I		20883 Panama *20883*	
V	*Palicourea spathacea* C. M. Taylor *20883, 12018*		
I		20883 Costa Rica *20883*	
I		20883 Panama *20883*	
R	*Palicourea triphylla* (Muell.-Arg.) DC. *20883*		
R		20883 Panama *20883*	
E	*Palicourea tumidonodosa* Dwyer *20883, 9006*		
I		20883 Panama *20883*	
E	*Palicourea veraguensis* Dwyer *20883*		
I		20883 Panama *20883*	
R	*Palicourea wilesii* Adams *20883, 15911*		
R		20883 Jamaica *20883*	
I	*Pausinystalia brachythyrsum* (K.Schum.)		
	W.Brandt *21006*		
I		21006 Cameroon (Bipinde) *21006*	
V	*Pausinystalia lane-poolei* (Hutch.) Hutch ex Lane-Poole		
	ssp. *lane-poolei* *21006, 20274*		
V		20858 Ghana *20274*	
V		20858 Liberia *7926*	
V		20858 Sierra Leone *7926*	
I	*Pavetta axillipara* Bremek. *7959*		
I		Tanzania (Morogoro Distr.) *7959*	
I	*Pavetta bagshawei* S. Moore *5926*		
I		5926 Tanzania (Usambara mountains) *5926*	
R	*Pavetta bruceana* Bremek. *5926*		
R		5926 Tanzania (Uluguru mountains) *5926*	
R	*Pavetta cinereifolia* Berhaut *7926*		
R		Mali *7926*	
R		Senegal *7926*	
R	*Pavetta coelophlebia* Bremek. *5926*		
R		5926 Tanzania (south Nguru mountains) *5926*	
I	*Pavetta concinna* Bremek.		
I		India - Tamil Nadu (Tirunelveli District)	

R	*Pavetta crebrifolia* Hiern var. *kimbozensis*		
	(Bremak.) Bridson *7959*		
R		5926 Tanzania (Uluguru mnts.) *5926*	
V	*Pavetta hohenackeri* Bremek. *14782*		
V		*14782* India - Tamil Nadu (Sispara & Nilgiri Hills)	
		4988	
I	*Pavetta hymenophylla* Brem. *20057*		
I		20057 Kenya (Mt. Kenya) *20057*	
R	*Pavetta linearifolia* Brem. *20057*		
R		20057 Kenya *20057*	
R		20057 Tanzania (coastal) *17435*	
R	*Pavetta madrassica* Bremek.		
R		*18228* India - Andhra Pradesh *18228*	
R		*18228* India - Tamil Nadu *18228*	
V	*Pavetta mollissima* Hutchinson & Dalziel *20858*		
V		20858 Côte d'Ivoire *20858*	
V		20858 Ghana *20858*	
I	*Pavetta nemoralis* Bremek.		
I		India - Kerala (Kavalai, Cochin)	
I	*Pavetta oblanceolata* Brem. *14782*		
I		*14782* India - Kerala *14782*	
I	*Pavetta olivaceo-nigra* K.schum. *5926*		
I		5926 Tanzania (Usambara mountains) *5926*	
I	*Pavetta pauciflora* Ridley		
I		Malaysia - Peninsular Malaysia (Gua Batu, Selangor)	
I	*Pavetta phanerophlebia* Merr. *13833*		
I		*13833* Philippines (low and medium altitudes)	
		13833	
I	*Pavetta sansibarica* K.Schum var. *rufipila*		
	(Bremak.) Bridson *7959*		
I		5926 Tanzania (Uluguru mnts.) *5926*	
R	*Pavetta sparsipila* Bremek. *5926*		
R		5926 Tanzania (Uluguru mountains) *5926*	
V	*Pavetta sphaerobotrys* K. Schum. ssp. *tanaica*		
	(Brem.) Bridson *20057*		
V		20057 Kenya *20057*	
I	*Pavetta subferruginea* Merr. *13833*		
I		*13833* Philippines (low altitude) *13833*	
I	*Pavetta tarennoides* S. Moore *20057*		
I		20057 Kenya (Shimba hills) *20057*	
R	*Pavetta teitana* K. Schum. *20057*		
R		20057 Kenya *20057*	
Ex/E	*Pavetta wightii* Hook. F. *14782*		
	Ex/E *14782* India - Tamil Nadu *14782*		
E	*Pentagonia alba* Dwyer *20883, 9006*		
I		20883 Panama *20883*	
V	*Pentagonia bocataurensis* Dwyer *20883, 9006*		
V		*16317* Panama *20883*	
V	*Pentagonia brachyotis* (Standl.) Standl. *20883, 9006*		
I		20883 Panama *20883*	
V	*Pentagonia tinajita* Seem. *20883, 9006*		
V		*16317* Panama *20883*	
V	*Pentagonia veraguensis* Dwyer *20883, 9006*		
V		*16317* Panama *20883*	
R	*Pentaloncha humilis* Hook.f.		
R		Gabon (Monts de Cristal)	
I	*Pentas coiolaena* K. Schum. *5926*		
I		5926 Tanzania (Uluguru mountains) *5926*	
E	*Pentas concinna* K. Schum. *19704*		

E	19704	Ethiopia (Harerge) *19704*
R	*Pentas longituba* Schumann *7959*	
	R	Tanzania (Morogoro Distr.) *7959*
R	*Pentas tenuis* Verdc. *19704*	
	R	19704 Ethiopia (Welega, Bale, Kefa, Sidamo.) *19704*
I	*Pentas ulugurica* (Verdc.) Hepper *5926*	
	I	5926 Tanzania (Uluguru mountains) *5926*
E	*Phialanthus jamaicensis* Urb. *20883, 13336*	
	E	13336 Jamaica *20883*
E	*Phialanthus linearis* Alain *5607*	
	E	19105 Cuba (Holguin) *5607*
V	*Phialanthus revolutus* Urb. *20883, 13336*	
	V	13336 Jamaica *20883*
Ex	*Phyllacanthus grisebachianus* Hook. f. *5607*	
	Ex	19105 Cuba (Pinar del Rio) *5607*
R	*Pinarophyllon flavum* Brandegee *9004*	
	R	19850 Mexico *9004*
E	*Platycarpum acreanum* Rogers *20883*	
	E	20883 Brazil *20883*
R	*Platycarpum decipiens* Woodson & Steyermark *20883*	
	R	20883 Venezuela *20883*
E	*Platycarpum duckei* Steyermark *20883*	
	E	20883 Brazil *20883*
E	*Platycarpum eglandulosum* Steyermark *20883*	
	E	20883 Guyana *20883*
E	*Platycarpum egleri* Rogers *20883*	
	E	20883 Brazil *20883*
E	*Platycarpum froesii* Bremekamp *20883*	
	E	20883 Brazil *20883*
E	*Platycarpum maguirei* Steyermark *20883*	
	E	20883 Venezuela *20883*
R	*Platycarpum negrense* Ducke *20883*	
	V	20883 Brazil *20883*
	E	20883 Venezuela *20883*
E	*Platycarpum negrense* Ducke var. *glaucum* Rogers *20883*	
	E	20883 Venezuela *20883*
V	*Platycarpum negrense* Ducke var. *negrense* *20883*	
	V	20883 Brazil *20883*
V	*Platycarpum orinocense* var. *grandiflorum* Steyermark *20883*	
	V	20883 Venezuela *20883*
R	*Platycarpum rhododactylum* Woodson & Steyermark *20883*	
	R	20883 Venezuela *20883*
R	*Platycarpum rugosum* Steyermark *20883*	
	R	20883 Venezuela *20883*
V	*Platycarpum schultesii* var. *schultesii* *20883*	
	V	20883 Colombia *20883*
R	*Platycarpum schultesii* var. *zarucchii* Rogers *20883*	
	I	20883 Colombia *20883*
	R	20883 Venezuela *20883*
V	*Polysphaeria aethiopica* Verdc. *19704*	
	V	19704 Ethiopia (Bale, Sidamo) *19704*
V	*Portlandia albiflora* Britton & Harris *20883*	
	V	20883 Jamaica *20883*
V	*Portlandia coccinea* Sw. *20883, 19890*	

	R	19890 Jamaica *20883*
R	*Portlandia grandiflora* L. *20883*	
	R	20883 Jamaica *20883*
E	*Portlandia harrisii* Britton *20883, 13336*	
	E	13336 Jamaica (Clarendon, St. Ann) *20883*
R	*Portlandia latifolia* Britton & Harris *20883*	
	R	20883 Jamaica *20883*
E	*Portlandia microsepala* Urb. *20883, 13336*	
	E	13336 Jamaica (St. Ann, Clarendon) *20883*
I	*Prismatomeris andamanica* Ridley *14782*	
	I	14782 India - Andaman Is. (S. Andaman Is.) *7771*
R	*Psathura borbonica* J. Gmelin var. *grandiflora* Baker *10082*	
	R	20771 Mauritius *10082*
R	*Psathura myrtifolia* A. Rich. ex DC. *10082*	
	R	20771 Mauritius *10082*
E	*Psathura sechellarum* Baker *19181*	
	E	14981 Seychelles (granitic) *14296*
R	*Psathura terniflora* A. Rich. ex DC. *10082*	
	R	20771 Mauritius *10082*
R	*Pseudomussaenda capsulifera* (Balf. f.) Wernham *15534*	
	R	15534 Yemen - Socotra *15534*
R	*Pseudopyxis heterophylla* (Miq.) Maxim. *10573*	
	R	10573 Japan *10573*
I	*Pseudosabicea sanguinosa* Halle	
	I	Gabon
E	*Psychotria aborensis* Dunn *11494*	
	E	11494 India - Arunachal Pradesh *11494*
V	*Psychotria adamsonii* Fosb.	
	V	French Polynesia - Marquesas Is
V	*Psychotria aggregata* Standl. *20883, 9006*	
	I	20883 Panama *20883*
R	*Psychotria albidocalyx* K. Schumann var. *mosambicensis* Petit	
	R	Mozambique
V	*Psychotria allenii* Standl. *20883, 9006*	
	I	20883 Panama *20883*
R	*Psychotria andamanica* Kurz. *14782*	
	R	14782 India - Andaman Is. *7771*
	R	14782 India - Nicobar Is. *14782*
E	*Psychotria angustata* Andersson *11117*	
	E	14980 Ecuador - Galapagos *9389*
E	*Psychotria bakeri* Dwyer *20883, 9006*	
	I	20883 Panama *20883*
I	*Psychotria balabacensis* Merr. *13833*	
	I	13833 Philippines (Balabac Island) *13833*
Ex	*Psychotria balfouriana* Verdc. *10082*	
	Ex	5852 Mauritius - Rodrigues *10936*
Ex	*Psychotria banaona* Urban *5607*	
	Ex	19105 Cuba (Sancti Spiritus) *5607*
I	*Psychotria barberi* Gamble	
	I	India - Kerala (Travancore Hills)
	I	India - Tamil Nadu
R	*Psychotria baviensis* (Drake) Pitard *6057*	
	R	15734 Vietnam *6057*
V	*Psychotria boquetensis* Dwyer *20883, 9006*	
	V	16317 Panama *20883*
V	*Psychotria bowermanae* Fosb.	

V		French Polynesia - Marquesas Is

E   *Psychotria bryonicola* Proctor *20883, 13336*
- E   *13336*   Jamaica *20883*

V   *Psychotria calophylla* Standl. *20883*
- V   *20883*   Panama *20883*

I   *Psychotria calopogon* L.O. Williams *9004*
- I   *19802*   Guatemala *9004*

R   *Psychotria cantleyi* Ridley
- R   Malaysia - Peninsular Malaysia
- R   *20099*   Singapore *20099*

R   *Psychotria capillacea* (Muell.-Arg.) Standl. *20883*
- I   *20883*   Brazil *20883*
- V   *20883*   Paraguay *20883*

R   *Psychotria capitata* R. & P. *20883*
- I   *20883*   Panama *20883*

R   *Psychotria capitata* R. & P. ssp. *capitata* *20883*
- R   *20883*   Panama *20883*

E   *Psychotria capitata* Dwyer ssp. *fissistipularis* Dwyer *20883, 9006*
- I   *20883*   Panama *20883*

V   *Psychotria carnosocarpa* Dwyer & Hayden *20883, 9006*
- V   *16317*   Panama *20883*

R   *Psychotria carronis* C. Moore & F. Muell.
- R   *14225*   Australia - NSW - Lord Howe Is. *14225*

R   *Psychotria castaneifolia* Petit *7959*
- R   Tanzania (Morogoro Distr.) *7959*

E   *Psychotria cathetoneura* Urban *5607*
- E   *19105*   Cuba (Guantanamo) *5607*

V   *Psychotria catillicalyx* Dwyer *20883, 9006*
- V   *16317*   Panama *20883*

I   *Psychotria chrysocalymma* L.O. Williams *9004*
- I   *19802*   Guatemala *9004*

V   *Psychotria clarendonensis* Urb. *20883, 13336*
- V   *13336*   Jamaica (Clarendon) *20883*

V   *Psychotria clusioides* PROCTOR *20883, 13336*
- V   *13336*   Jamaica (Portland) *20883*

V   *Psychotria coeloneura* Urb. *20883*
- V   *20883*   Jamaica *20883*

R   *Psychotria condorensis* Pierre ex Pitard *6057*
- R   Vietnam *6057*

I   *Psychotria congesta* Spreng. ex DC. *13336*
- I   *13336*   Jamaica *13336*

V   *Psychotria crassipetala* Petit *6073*
- V   *20057*   Kenya (Teita district) *7959*

V   *Psychotria croceovenosa* Dwyer *20883, 9006*
- V   *16317*   Panama *20883*

Ex/E   *Psychotria cyrilli-nelsonii* A. Molina *20050*
- Ex/E   *20050*   Honduras *20050*

E   *Psychotria danceri* Urb. *19890*
- E   *19890*   Jamaica (Holland Mtn.) *19890*

R   *Psychotria dasyophthalma* Griseb. *20883, 13336*
- R   *13336*   Jamaica *20883*

E   *Psychotria deverdiana* Guillaumin *20893*
- E   *20893*   New Caledonia *20893*

R   *Psychotria discolor* (Griseb.) Rolfe *20883*
- R   *20883*   Jamaica *20883*

R   *Psychotria dolichantha* Urb. *20883*

R	*20883*	Jamaica *20883*

R   *Psychotria dolphiniana* Urb. *20883*
- R   *20883*   Jamaica *20883*

V   *Psychotria domatiata* Adams *20883, 15911*
- R   *13336*   Jamaica (Portland) *20883*

V   *Psychotria dosbocensis* Dwyer *20883, 9006*
- V   *16317*   Panama *20883*

E   *Psychotria durilancifolia* Dwyer *20883, 9006*
- I   *20883*   Panama *20883*

E   *Psychotria ekmanii* Urban *5607*
- E   *19105*   Cuba (Granma) *5607*

V   *Psychotria esulcata* F. Brown
- V   French Polynesia - Marquesas Is

V   *Psychotria fendleri* Standl. *20883, 9006*
- I   *20883*   Panama *20883*

R   *Psychotria foetens* Sw. *20883, 13336*
- R   *13336*   Jamaica *20883*

V   *Psychotria foetida* Griseb. *20883*
- V   *20883*   Jamaica *20883*

E   *Psychotria geronensis* Urban *5607*
- E   *19105*   Cuba (Juventud Is.) *5607*

I   *Psychotria glandulifera* Thwaites ex Hook.f. *10252*
- I   *16162*   Sri Lanka *10252*

E   *Psychotria globicephala* Gamble
- E   *13883*   India - Tamil Nadu (Tirunelveli District) *13883*

R   *Psychotria graciliflora* Benth. *20883*
- R   *20883*   Panama *20883*

R   *Psychotria granadensis* Benth. *20883*
- E   *20883*   Panama *20883*

E   *Psychotria grandiflora* Mann *20850, 14209*
- E   *20850*   U.S. - Hawaii *20850*

V   *Psychotria greeneana* Urban
- V   *19105*   Cuba (Pinar del Rio) *19105*

V   *Psychotria greenwelliae* Fosberg *20850, 14209*
- I   *20850*   U.S. - Hawaii (Kaua`i - Koke`e) *20850*

V   *Psychotria hammelii* Dwyer *20883, 9006*
- V   *16317*   Panama *20883*

E   *Psychotria hanoverensis* Proctor *20883, 13336*
- E   *13336*   Jamaica *20883*

V   *Psychotria hassleriana* (Chodat) Standl. *20883*
- V   *20883*   Paraguay *20883*

I   *Psychotria helferi* Kurz. var. *angustifolia* King *7771*
- I   India - Andaman Is. (S. Andaman Is.) *7771*

Ex/E   *Psychotria hexandra* H. Mann var. *hosakana* Fosberg *20850*
- Ex/E   *20850*   U.S. - Hawaii *20850*

E   *Psychotria hexandra* H.Mann var. *oahuensis* O. Deg. & Fosberg *20850*
- E   *20850*   U.S. - Hawaii *20850*

Ex/E   *Psychotria hexandra* H. Mann var. *rockii* Fosberg *20850*
- Ex/E   *20850*   U.S. - Hawaii *20850*

I   *Psychotria heydei* Standley *9004*
- I   *19802*   Guatemala *9004*

V   *Psychotria hirsuta* Sw. *20883*
- V   *20883*   Jamaica *20883*

V   *Psychotria hivaoana* Fosb.
   V   French Polynesia - Marquesas Is

E   *Psychotria hobdyi* Sohmer *20850, 14209*
   E   *20850* U.S. - Hawaii (Kaua`i) *20850*

E   *Psychotria impatiens* Dwyer *20883, 9006*
   I   *20883* Panama *20883*

V   *Psychotria insignis* Standl. *20883, 9006*
   V   *16317* Panama *20883*

R   *Psychotria iringensis* Verdc. *7959*
   R   Tanzania (Iringa) *7959*

I   *Psychotria iwahigensis* Elm. *13833*
   I   *13833* Philippines (low altitude) *13833*

V   *Psychotria izabalensis* L.O. Williams *9004*
   V   *19802* Guatemala *9004*

V   *Psychotria le-bronnecii* Fosb.
   V   French Polynesia - Marquesas Is

E   *Psychotria liesneri* Dwyer *20883, 9006*
   I   *20883* Panama *20883*

I   *Psychotria lilacina* Standley & Steyerm. *9004*
   I   *19802* Guatemala *9004*

R   *Psychotria limonensis* Krause *20883*
   V   *20883* Panama *20883*

V   *Psychotria longipedunculata* Dwyer *20883, 9006*
   V   *16317* Panama *20883*

I   *Psychotria longipetiolata* Thwaites *10252*
   I   *16162* Sri Lanka *10252*

V   *Psychotria lunanii* Urb. *20883, 13336*
   V   *13336* Jamaica (St. Catherine) *20883*

R   *Psychotria manna* Urb. *20883*
   R   *20883* Jamaica *20883*

E   *Psychotria marchionica* (Drake) F. Brown
   E   French Polynesia - Marquesas Is

V   *Psychotria martii* Acuna & Roig *5607*
   V   *19105* Cuba (Sancti Spiritus) *5607*

I   *Psychotria moonii* (Thwaites) Hook.f. *10252*
   I   *16162* Sri Lanka *10252*

V   *Psychotria morii* Dwyer *20883, 9006*
   V   *16317* Panama *20883*

V   *Psychotria mumfordiana* F. Brown
   V   French Polynesia - Marquesas Is

R   *Psychotria myrstiphyllum* Sw. *20883*
   R   *20883* Jamaica *20883*

V   *Psychotria nebulosa* (Dwyer) C.M. Taylor *21286*
   V   *16317* Panama *21286*

I   *Psychotria nicobarica* Kurz *7771*
   I   India - Nicobar Is. (Katchal Is.) *7771*

V   *Psychotria nubiphila* Dwyer *20883, 9006*
   V   *16317* Panama *20883*

R   *Psychotria officinalis* Sandw. *20883*
   R   *20883* Panama *20883*

E   *Psychotria olgae* Dwyer & Hayden *20883, 9006*
   I   *20883* Panama *20883*

R   *Psychotria orchidearum* Standl. *20883*
   I   *20883* Panama *20883*

R   *Psychotria orchidearum* Standl. ssp.
      orchidearum *20883*
   V   *20883* Panama *20883*

R   *Psychotria orchidearum* Dwyer ssp. *persedens*

      Dwyer *20883, 9006*
   I   *20883* Panama *20883*

I   *Psychotria oreodoxa* L.O. Williams *9004*
   I   *19802* Guatemala *9004*

E   *Psychotria oresbia* Dwyer *20883, 9006*
   I   *20883* Panama *20883*

I   *Psychotria orogenes* L.O. Williams *9004*
   I   *19802* Guatemala *9004*

V   *Psychotria ostaurea* Dwyer & Hayden *20883, 9006, 21221*
   V   *16317* Panama *20883*

R   *Psychotria pachecoana* Standley & Steyerm. *9004*
   R   *19802* Guatemala *9004*

V   *Psychotria panamensis* Standl. *20883*
   I   *20883* Panama *20883*

I   *Psychotria pandurata* Verdc. *5926*
   I   *5926* Tanzania (Usambara and Uluguru mountains) *5926*

R   *Psychotria pedunculata* var. *caudata*
      Adams *20883*
   R   *20883* Jamaica *20883*

I   *Psychotria pendula* Hook. F. *14782*
   I   *14782* India - Andaman Is. (S. Andaman Is.) *7771*

R   *Psychotria pervillei* Baker *14296*
   R   *19182* Seychelles (Mahé, Praslin, Silhouette) *14296*
   Ex/E *19182* Seychelles - Coralline Is. (Aldabra) *14296*

V   *Psychotria petitii* Verdc. *6073*
   V   *20057* Kenya (Teita district) *7959*

R   *Psychotria pittieri* Standl. *20883*
   I   *20883* Panama *20883*

E   *Psychotria pittieri* Dwyer ssp. *oinochrophylla*
      Dwyer *20883, 9006*
   I   *20883* Panama *20883*

R   *Psychotria pittieri* Standl. ssp.
      pittieri *20883*
   R   *20883* Panama *20883*

E   *Psychotria pleeana* Urban *19001*
   E   *19001* Martinique *19001*
   E   *19001* St Lucia *19001*

R   *Psychotria plicata* Urb. *20883, 13336*
   R   *13336* Jamaica *20883*

I   *Psychotria plurivenia* Thwaites *10252*
   I   *16162* Sri Lanka *10252*

R   *Psychotria poilanei* Pitard *6057*
   R   Vietnam *6057*

I   *Psychotria polyneura* Kurz var. *longipetiolate*
      King *7771*
   I   India - Andaman Is. *7771*

R   *Psychotria pseudoplatyphylla* Petit *20057*
   R   *20057* Kenya (Taita hills) *20057*
   R   *20057* Tanzania (Mt. Meru; Mt. Kilimanjaro) *17435*

V   *Psychotria pumiliocarpa* Dwyer *20883, 9006*
   V   *16317* Panama *20883*

V   *Psychotria purdiaei* Urb. *20883*
   V   *20883* Jamaica *20883*

I   *Psychotria pyramidata* Elm. *13833*

I	*13833* Philippines *13833*	
V	*Psychotria quadrangulata* Dwyer 20883, 9006	
	V *16317* Panama *20883*	
R	*Psychotria racemosa* (Aubl.) Raeusch. *20883*	
	R *20883* Panama *20883*	
I	*Psychotria repens* Elm. *13833*	
	I *13833* Philippines *13833*	
E	*Psychotria rivularis* Urban *5607*	
	E *19105* Cuba (Pinar del Rio) *5607*	
V	*Psychotria roseocrema* (Dwyer) C.M. Taylor *21286*	
	V *16317* Panama *21286*	
E	*Psychotria rosulatifolia* Dwyer 20883, 9006	
	I *20883* Panama *20883*	
V	*Psychotria sanfelicensis* Dwyer 20883, 9006	
	V *16317* Panama *20883*	
V	*Psychotria santaritensis* Dwyer 20883, 9006	
	V *16317* Panama *20883*	
I	*Psychotria sclerocarpa* Whistler *9147*	
	I Western Samoa (Savaii; ? Upolu) *9147*	
V	*Psychotria siccorubra* Dwyer 20883, 9006	
	V *16317* Panama *20883*	
E	*Psychotria silhouettae* F. Friedmann *14981*	
	E *14981* Seychelles (Silhouette) *14981*	
I	*Psychotria siphonophora* Urb. 20883, 13336	
	I *19890* Jamaica (Trelawny) *20883*	
I	*Psychotria stenophylla* (Thwaites) Hook.f. *10252*	
	I *16162* Sri Lanka *10252*	
I	*Psychotria steyermarkii* Standley *9004*	
	I *19802* Guatemala *9004*	
R	*Psychotria subcordata* Britton 20883, 13336	
	R *13336* Jamaica (St. Thomas) *20883*	
R	*Psychotria submontana* Domin *20681*	
	R *20681* Australia - Queensland *20681*	
V	*Psychotria subvelutina* Ekman & Urban *5607*	
	V *19105* Cuba (Pinar del Rio) *5607*	
V	*Psychotria taitensis* Verdc. *6073*	
	V *20057* Kenya (Teita district) *7959*	
E	*Psychotria taupotinii* F. Brown *9006*	
	E French Polynesia - Marquesas Is *9006*	
V	*Psychotria taurina* Dwyer 20883, 9006	
	V *16317* Panama *20883*	
V	*Psychotria torrei* Acuna & Roig *5607*	
	V *19105* Cuba (Guantanamo) *5607*	
E	*Psychotria toviana* F. Brown	
	E French Polynesia - Marquesas Is	
V	*Psychotria tutensis* Dwyer 20883, 9006	
	V *16317* Panama *20883*	
Ex/E	*Psychotria tylophora* Kurz *11494*	
	Ex/E *11494* India - Nicobar Is. *11494*	
V	*Psychotria umbelliformis* Dwyer & Hayden 20883, 9006	
	I *20883* Panama *20883*	
V	*Psychotria vallensis* Dwyer 20883, 9006	
	I *20883* Panama *20883*	
V	*Psychotria veraguensis* Dwyer 20883, 9006	
	V *16317* Panama *20883*	
V	*Psychotria wilburiana* Dwyer 20883, 9006	
	V *16317* Panama *20883*	
I	*Psychotria wullschlaegelii* Urb. 20883, 13336	

I	*13336* Jamaica *20883*
E	*Psychotria xerococcoides* Dwyer 20883, 9006
	I *20883* Panama *20883*
V	*Psydrax paradoxa* (Virot) Comb. Ined. *20893*
	V *20893* New Caledonia *20893*
I	*Pubistylus andamanensis* Thoth. *7771*
	I India - Andaman Is. *7771*
R	*Pyrostria commersonii* J.F. Gmelin *10082*
	R *14220* Réunion *10082*
V	*Pyrostria cordifolia* A. Rich. ex DC. var. *cordifolia* *10082*
	V *20771* Mauritius *10082*
V	*Pyrostria cordifolia* A. Rich. ex DC. var. *polymorpha* (A. Rich. ex DC.) Verdc. *10082*
	V *20771* Mauritius *10082*
V	*Pyrostria fasciculata* Bojer ex Baker *10082*
	V Mauritius *10082*
Ex	*Pyrostria ferruginea* Verdc. *10082*
	Ex *20771* Mauritius *10082*
E	*Pyrostria macrophylla* A. Rich. ex DC. var. *grandistipula* Verdc. *10082*
	E *20771* Mauritius *10082*
R	*Pyrostria macrophylla* A. Rich. ex DC. var. *macrophylla* *10082*
	R *20771* Mauritius *10082*
R	*Pyrostria viburnoides* (Baker) Verdc. *10082*
	R *20771* Mauritius *10082*
Ex	*Ramosmania heterophylla* (Balf.f.) Tirvengadum & Verdc. *10082*
	Ex *15079* Mauritius - Rodrigues *5852*
E	*Ramosmania rodriguesii* Tirvengadum *15079*
	E *15079* Mauritius - Rodrigues *15079*
V	*Randia aculeata* (Spreng.) Adams var. *jamaicensis* (Spreng.) C.D. Adams 20883, 15911
	V *20883* Jamaica (St. Andrew, Clarendon) *20883*
E	*Randia acunae* Borh. *5607*
	E *19105* Cuba (Camaguey) *5607*
V	*Randia armata* var. *ferox* (Schum.) Bernardi *20883*
	V *20883* Paraguay *20883*
R	*Randia armata* var. *pubescens* (H.B.K.) R. Knuth. *20883*
	I *20883* Brazil *20883*
	R *20883* Paraguay *20883*
R	*Randia audasii* C.White *20681*
	R *20681* Australia - Queensland *20681*
V	*Randia megalocarpa* Dwyer 20883, 9006
	V *16317* Panama *20883*
E	*Randia moorei* F.Muell. ex Benth. *20681*
	I *20681* Australia - New South Wales *20681*
	I *20681* Australia - Queensland *20681*
V	*Randia portoricensis* (Urban) Britt. & Standl. 20883, 10197
	I *20883* Puerto Rico *20883*
I	*Randia standleyana* L.O. Williams *9004*
	I *19802* Guatemala *9004*
R	*Randia stipulosa* C. Moore & F. Muell.
	R *14225* Australia - NSW - Lord Howe Is. *14225*
E	*Raritebe blumii* (Dwyer) Dwyer 20883, 9006

	I	20883 Panama *20883*	

V   *Raritebe darienensis* (Dwyer) Dwyer *20883, 9006*
     V   *16317* Panama *20883*

E   *Raritebe euryphyllum* (Standl.) Dwyer *20883, 9006*
     I   20883 Panama *20883*

R   *Raritebe panamensis* (Dwyer) Dwyer *20883, 9006*
     I   20883 Panama *20883*

V   *Raritebe trifoliatum* (Dwyer & Hayden) Dwyer *20883, 9006*
     I   20883 Panama *20883*

E   *Raritebe victoriae* (Dwyer) Dwyer *20883, 9006*
     I   20883 Panama *20883*

E   *Remijia chelomaphylla* G.A. Sullivan *18200*
     E   *19542* Peru *18200*

I   *Rhipidantha chlorantha* (K. Schum.) Bremek. *5926*
     I   *5926* Tanzania *5926*

E   *Richardia arenicola* (B. & W.) W. Lewis & R. Oliver *5607*
     E   *19105* Cuba (Pinar del Rio; I. Juventud) *5607*

E   *Richardia ciliata* (B. & W.) W. Lewis & R. Oliver *5607*
     E   *19105* Cuba (Juventud Is.) *5607*

V   *Richardia lomensis* (Krause) Standley *18200*
     V   *9446* Peru *18200*

V   *Robynsia glabrata* Hutch. *20274*
     V   *20858* Côte d'Ivoire *7926*
     V   *20858* Ghana *20274*
     V   *20858* Nigeria (south) *7926*

R   *Rondeletia adamsii* Proctor *20883, 13336*
     R   *13336* Jamaica (Clarendon, Trelawny) *20883*

I   *Rondeletia aetheocalymna* J.D. Smith *9004*
     I   *19802* Guatemala *9004*

V   *Rondeletia amplexicaulis* Urb. *20883, 13336*
     V   *13336* Jamaica (Trelawny) *20883*

E   *Rondeletia apiculata* Urban *5607*
     E   *19105* Cuba (Santiago de Cuba) *5607*

R   *Rondeletia aspera* Standley *9037*
     R   *19803* Costa Rica *9037*

V   *Rondeletia bertieroides* Standl. *20883, 10747*
     I   20883 Panama *20883*

E   *Rondeletia bicolor* Britton *5607*
     E   *19105* Cuba (Sancti Spiritus) *5607*

V   *Rondeletia brachyphylla* Proctor *20883, 15911*
     V   *13336* Jamaica *20883*

R   *Rondeletia brachystantha* Standley & Steyerm. *9004*
     I   *19802* Guatemala *9004*
     R   *9989* Mexico *9004*

Ex   *Rondeletia brandegeeana* Lorence *21277*
     Ex   *21277* Mexico - Chiapas *21277*

E   *Rondeletia buddleioides* Benth var. *aspera* Kirkbride *20883, 9006*
     R   *19803* Panama *20883*

R   *Rondeletia buddleioides* Benth. var. *buddleioides* *20883*
     V   20883 Panama *20883*

R   *Rondeletia calycosa* J.D. Smith *9037*
     R   *19803* Costa Rica *9037*

V   *Rondeletia chinajensis* Standley & Steyerm. *9004*
     V   *19802* Guatemala *9004*

E   *Rondeletia cincta* Griseb. *20883, 13336*
     E   20883 Jamaica (Hanover, Dolphin Head) *20883*

E   *Rondeletia clarendonensis* Britton *20883, 13336*
     E   20883 Jamaica *20883*

V   *Rondeletia cooperi* Standl. *20883, 9006*
     I   20883 Costa Rica *20883*
     V   *16317* Panama *20883*

V   *Rondeletia cordovana* Standley & Steyerm. *9004*
     V   *19802* Guatemala *9004*

V   *Rondeletia cymulosa* Proctor *20883, 13336*
     V   *13336* Jamaica (Trelawny) *20883*

I   *Rondeletia daphnoides* Griseb. *20883, 13336*
     I   *13336* Jamaica (St. Ann) *20883*

E   *Rondeletia darcyi* Dwyer *20883, 9006*
     I   *19803* Panama *20883*

V   *Rondeletia darienensis* Standl. *20883, 9006*
     V   *16317* Panama *20883*

V   *Rondeletia diplocalyx* Urban *5607*
     V   *19105* Cuba (Santiago de Cuba; Holguin) *5607*

E   *Rondeletia dolphinensis* Proctor *20883, 13336*
     E   *13336* Jamaica *20883*

I   *Rondeletia domatiata* *15229*
     I   *15229* Haiti (La Visite & Macaya National Parks) *15229*

V   *Rondeletia ekmanii* Britton & Standl. *5607*
     V   *19105* Cuba (Granma; Santiago de Cuba) *5607*

V   *Rondeletia elegans* Britton *20883*
     V   20883 Jamaica *20883*

E   *Rondeletia gamboana* Urban *5607*
     E   *19105* Cuba (Las Tunas, Granma) *5607*

R   *Rondeletia glauca* Griseb. *20883*
     R   20883 Jamaica *20883*

V   *Rondeletia hamelifolia* Dwyer & Hayden *20883, 9006*
     R   *19803* Panama *20883*

R   *Rondeletia harrisii* Urb. *20883*
     R   20883 Jamaica *20883*

R   *Rondeletia hirsuta* Sw. *20883*
     R   20883 Jamaica *20883*

R   *Rondeletia hirta* Sw. *20883*
     R   20883 Jamaica *20883*

R   *Rondeletia impressa* Krug & Urb. *20883, 13336*
     R   *13336* Jamaica *20883*

E   *Rondeletia incana* Sw. *20883, 13336*
     E   *13336* Jamaica (Manchester) *20883*

I   *Rondeletia izabalensis* Standley & Steyerm. *9004*
     I   *19802* Guatemala *9004*

E   *Rondeletia jamaicensis* Proctor *20883, 13336*
     E   *13336* Jamaica (St. Ann) *20883*

V   *Rondeletia kirkbridei* Dwyer *20883, 9006*
     V   *16317* Panama *20883*

E   *Rondeletia leonis* Britton *5607*
     E   *19105* Cuba *5607*

R   *Rondeletia ligulata* Urb. *20883, 13336*
     R   *13336* Jamaica *20883*

V   *Rondeletia linguiformis* Hemsley *9004*
     V   *19802* Guatemala *9004*

V   *Rondeletia macrocalyx* Standley & Steyerm. *9004*
     V   *19802* Guatemala *9004*

R   *Rondeletia martinicensis* Krug & Urban *19001*
     R   *19001*   Martinique *19001*

V   *Rondeletia micarensis* Urban *5607*
     V   *19105*   Cuba (Santiago de Cuba) *5607*

E   *Rondeletia monantha* Urban & Ekman *5607*
     E   *19105*   Cuba (Sancti Spiritus) *5607*

I   *Rondeletia myriantha* Standley & Steyerm. var. *armentalis* L.O. Williams *9004*
     I   *19802*   Guatemala *9004*

E   *Rondeletia nemoralis* Proctor *20883, 13336*
     E   *13336*   Jamaica *20883*

E   *Rondeletia odorata* Hook. var. *breviflora* Hooker *20883, 9006*
     E   *20883*   Panama *20883*

R   *Rondeletia pallida* Britton *20883*
     R   *20883*   Jamaica *20883*

V   *Rondeletia panamensis* DC. *20883*
     V   *20883*   Panama *20883*

V   *Rondeletia pansamalana* Standley *9004*
     V   *19802*   Guatemala *9004*

R   *Rondeletia parviflora* Poiret *19001*
     R   *19001*   Dominica *19001*
     R   *19001*   Guadeloupe *19001*
     R   *19001*   Martinique *19001*

V   *Rondeletia paucinervis* Urban & Ekman *5607*
     V   *19105*   Cuba (Santiago de Cuba; Holguin) *5607*

I   *Rondeletia petiolata* Proctor *20883, 13336*
     I   *13336*   Jamaica *20883*

V   *Rondeletia platysepala* Standl. *20883, 9006*
     V   *16317*   Panama *20883*

R   *Rondeletia portlandensis* Proctor *20883, 13336*
     R   *13336*   Jamaica (Portland) *20883*

R   *Rondeletia portoricensis* Krug & Urban *20883*
     I   *20883*   Puerto Rico *20883*

V   *Rondeletia pycnophylla* Urban *5607*
     V   *19105*   Cuba (Santiago de Cuba; Holguin) *5607*

R   *Rondeletia racemosa* Sw. *20883*
     R   *20883*   Jamaica *20883*

I   *Rondeletia rubens* L.O. Williams *9004*
     I   *19802*   Guatemala *9004*

E   *Rondeletia rugelii* Urban *5607*
     E   *19105*   Cuba (Matanzas) *5607*

E   *Rondeletia salicifolia* Dwyer & Hayden ssp. *brevicolla* Kirkbride *20883, 9006*
     R   *19803*   Panama *20883*

V   *Rondeletia salicifolia* Dwyer & Hayden var. *salicifolia* *20883*
     I   *20883*   Panama *20883*

E   *Rondeletia saxicola* Britton *20883, 13336*
     E   *13336*   Jamaica (Clarendon, Manchester) *20883*

V   *Rondeletia secunda* Standl. *20883, 9006*
     R   *19803*   Panama *20883*

I   *Rondeletia secundiflora* Robinson *9004*
     I   *19802*   Guatemala *9004*

R   *Rondeletia seleriana* Loes. *9004*
     R   *19802*   Guatemala *9004*

R   *Rondeletia skutchii* Standley & Steyerm. *9004*
     R   *19802*   Guatemala *9004*

V   *Rondeletia subsessilifolia* Proctor *20883, 13336*

     V   *13336*   Jamaica (Portland) *20883*

R   *Rondeletia sylvestris* S. Moore *20883*
     R   *20883*   Jamaica *20883*

V   *Rondeletia umbellulata* Sw. *20883, 13336*
     V   *13336*   Jamaica (Westmoreland, St. James) *20883*

R   *Rondeletia zolleriana* Standley & Steyerm. *9004*
     R   *19802*   Guatemala *9004*

E   *Rothmannia annae* (E. Wright) Keay *14296*
     E   *14981*   Seychelles (Aride Is.) *10678*

I   *Rubia cretacea* Pojark. *5942*
     I   *5942*   Kazakhstan (north-east of Caspian Sea) *5942*

R   *Rubia davisiana* Ehrend. *12840*
     R   *12840*   Turkey *12840*

V   *Rubia edgeworthii* Hook.f. *13883*
     V   *13883*   India (Western Himalayas) *13883*

V   *Rubia himalayensis* Klotzsch *13883*
     V   *13883*   Afghanistan *13883*
     V   *13883*   India - Jammu & Kashmir *13883*
     V   *13883*   Pakistan *13883*

I   *Rubia laevissima* Tscherneva *5942*
     I   *5942*   Kazakhstan (south) *5942*
     I   *5942*   Kyrgyzstan (north-west) *5942*
     I   *5942*   Uzbekistan (east - border with Kyrgystan) *5942*

Ex/E   *Rubia rezniczenkoana* Litv. *5942*
     Ex/E   *5942*   Kazakhstan (east) *5942*

V   *Rudgea amplexicaulis* Dwyer *20883, 9006*
     V   *16317*   Panama *20883*

V   *Rudgea chiriquiensis* Dwyer *20883, 9006*
     V   *16317*   Panama *20883*

V   *Rudgea coronicarpa* Dwyer *9006*
     V   *16317*   Panama *9006*

R   *Rudgea discolor* Benth. *20883*
     I   *20883*   Brazil *20883*
     R   *20883*   Paraguay *20883*

E   *Rudgea isthmensis* Standl. *20883, 9006*
     I   *20883*   Panama *20883*

R   *Rudgea parquioides* (Cham.) Muell.-Arg. *20883*
     I   *20883*   Argentina *20883*
     I   *20883*   Brazil *20883*
     R   *20883*   Paraguay *20883*

R   *Rudgea pittieri* Standl. *20883*
     V   *20883*   Panama *20883*

V   *Rudgea simiarum* Standley & Steyerm. *9004*
     V   *19802*   Guatemala *9004*

R   *Rustia occidentalis* (Benth.) Hemsl. *20883*
     V   *20883*   Panama *20883*

V   *Rustia panamensis* Dwyer *20883, 9006*
     I   *20883*   Panama *20883*

V   *Rytigynia induta* (Bullock) Verdc. & Bridson *20057*
     V   *20057*   Kenya *20057*
     V   *20057*   Tanzania (Loliondo, Kondo, Mt. Ufiomi) *17435*

V   *Rytigynia longipedicellata* Verdcourt *20885*
     V   *20885*   Tanzania *20885*

V   *Rytigynia mrimaensis* Verdc. *20057*
     V   *20057*   Kenya (Mrima hill, Watamu & Gedi forest) *20057*

R   *Rytigynia parvifolia* Verdc. *20057*
     R   *20057*   Kenya *20057*

Magnoliopsida (dicots): Rubiaceae: *Rytigynia*

I   *Sabicea caminata* Halle
     I   Gabon (Belinga & Makokou)

R   *Sabicea hirta* Sw. *20883*
     R   *20883* Jamaica *20883*

E   *Sabicea stellaris* Dwyer *20883, 9006*
     I   *20883* Panama *20883*

R   *Sabicea villosa* var. *adpressa* (Wernh.)
     Standl. *20883*
     V   *20883* Panama *20883*

R   *Saprosma cochinchinensis* Pitard *6057*
     R   Vietnam *6057*

I   *Saprosma fragrans* Beddome
     I   India - Kerala (Malabar)
     I   India - Tamil Nadu

I   *Saprosma scabridum* (Thwaites) Beddome *10252*
     I   *16162* Sri Lanka *10252*

V   *Schmidtottia cucullata* Borh. *5607*
     V   *19105* Cuba (Holguin) *5607*

E   *Schmidtottia marmorata* Urban *5607*
     E   *19105* Cuba (Guantanamo) *5607*

V   *Schmidtottia monticola* Borh. *5607*
     V   *19105* Cuba (Holguin) *5607*

V   *Schmidtottia parvifolia* Alain *5607*
     V   *19105* Cuba (Guantanamo) *5607*

V   *Schmidtottia scabra* Borh. & Acuna *5607*
     V   *19105* Cuba (Holguin) *5607*

V   *Schmidtottia sessilifolia* (Britton) Urban *5607*
     V   *19105* Cuba (Holguin) *5607*

V   *Schumanniophyton problematicum* (A.Chev.)
     Aubrev. *20274*
     ?   Côte d'Ivoire *7926*
     V   *20858* Ghana *20274*
     ?   Sierra Leone *7926*

V   *Scolosanthus acunae* Borh. & Muniz *5607*
     V   *19105* Cuba (Pinar del Rio) *5607*

E   *Scolosanthus granulatus* Urban *5607*
     E   *19105* Cuba (Guantanamo) *5607*

V   *Scolosanthus hirsutus* Borh. *5607*
     V   *19105* Cuba (Guantanamo) *5607*

R   *Scolosanthus hispidus* Borh. & Muniz *5607*
     R   *19105* Cuba (Guantanamo) *5607*

E   *Scolosanthus howardii* Borhidi *13336*
     E   *13336* Jamaica *13336*

E   *Scolosanthus moanus* Borh. & Muniz *5607*
     E   *19105* Cuba (Holguin) *5607*

V   *Scolosanthus reticulatus* Borh. *5607*
     V   *19105* Cuba (Holguin) *5607*

V   *Scolosanthus strictus* Urban *5607*
     V   *19105* Cuba (Guantanamo) *5607*

E   *Scolosanthus wrightianus* (Griseb.) C. Wright
     E   *19105* Cuba *19105*

E   *Scyphochlamys revoluta* Balf.f. *10082*
     E   *5852* Mauritius - Rodrigues *5852*

E   *Scyphostachys pedunculatus* Thwaites *10252*
     E   *12838* Sri Lanka *10252*

R   *Sericanthe pellegrini* (Halle) Robbrecht
     R   Gabon

R   *Sericanthe testui* (Halle) Robbrecht var.
     pseudosalacia (Halle) Robbrecht

     R   Gabon

E   *Sericanthe toupetou* (aubrev. & Pellegrin) E.
     Robbrecht *10260*
     E   *20858* Côte d'Ivoire *20858*
     E   *20858* Ghana *15970*

V   *Shaferocharis cubensis* Urban *5607*
     V   *19105* Cuba (Holguin) *5607*

V   *Shaferocharis multiflora* Bohr. & Muniz *5607*
     V   *19105* Cuba (Holguin; Guantanamo) *5607*

V   *Shaferocharis villosa* Bohr. & Bisse *5607*
     V   *19105* Cuba (Guantanamo) *5607*

I   *Sherbournea kiliotricha* Halle
     I   Gabon (Belinga)

I   *Sherbournea myosura* Halle
     I   Gabon (Lastoursville)

V   *Simira darienensis* Dwyer *20883, 9006*
     V   *16317* Panama *20883*

V   *Simira maxonii* (Standl.) Steyerm. *20883*
     V   *20883* Costa Rica *20883*
     V   *20883* Panama *20883*

I   *Sommera guatemalensis* Standley *9004*
     I   *19802* Guatemala *9004*

I   *Spermacoce azurea* Verdc. *5926*
     I   *5926* Tanzania *5926*

E   *Spermacoce exasperata* Urban *5607*
     E   *19105* Cuba (Guantanamo) *5607*

I   *Spermacoce milnei* Verdc. *5926*
     I   *5926* Tanzania *5926*

I   *Spermacoce oligantha* Urban *5607*
     I   *19105* Cuba (Santiago de Cuba) *5607*

I   *Spermacoce taylorii* Verdc. *5926*
     I   *5926* Tanzania *5926*

R   *Sphinctanthus hasslerianus* Chodat *20883*
     R   *20883* Paraguay *20883*

E   *Stachyarrhena dichroa* Standl. *20883, 9006*
     I   *20883* Panama *20883*

E   *Steyermarkia guatemalensis* Standley *9004*
     E   *19803* Guatemala *9004*

I   *Tapiphyllum cinerascens* (Hiern) Robyns *7959*
     I   *5926* Tanzania *5926*

I   *Tapiphyllum obtusifolium* (K. Schum.) Robyns *5926*
     I   *5926* Tanzania *5926*

V   *Tapiphyllum schliebenii* Verdc. *20556*
     V   *20885* Tanzania (Lindi region) *20556*

V   *Tarenna agumbensis* Sundararaghaven *13883*
     V   *13883* India - Karnataka *13883*

R   *Tarenna annamensis* Pitard *6057*
     R   Vietnam *6057*

R   *Tarenna baviensis* (Drake) Pitard *6057*
     R   Vietnam *6057*

I   *Tarenna calcarea* Ridley
     I   Malaysia - Peninsular Malaysia (Perak)

R   *Tarenna cymosa* (Willd. ex Roem. & Schultes)
     Verdc. *10082*
     R   *20771* Mauritius *10082*

R   *Tarenna kibuwae* Bridson *20057*
     R   *20057* Kenya (Garissa) *20057*

R   *Tarenna pulchra* (Ridl.) Ridl. *19209*

	R	Malaysia - Peninsular Malaysia (Pahang, Selangor/Wilayah Persekutuan) *19209*
E	*Tarenna vignei* Hutch. & Dalz. var. *vignei* *7926*	
	E	*6072* Ghana (Amentia) *7926*
V	*Temnopteryx sericea* Hook.f.	
	V	Gabon
I	*Timonius ferrugineus* Merr. *13833*	
	I	*13833* Philippines (Palawan) *13833*
R	*Timonius jambosella* (Gaertn.) Thwaites *12838*	
	R	*12838* Sri Lanka *12838*
I	*Timonius palawanensis* Elm. *13833*	
	I	*13833* Philippines (low altitude) *13833*
V	*Timonius sechellensis* Summerh. *14296*	
	V	*19182* Seychelles (granitic) *14296*
E	*Tocoyena formosa* (Cham. & Schlecht.) K. Schum. *20883*	
	E	*20883* Paraguay *20883*
E	*Tricalysia africana* (Sim) Robbr. *20604*	
	E	*20604* South Africa - Cape Province *20604*
R	*Tricalysia bridsoniana* Robyns var. *bridsoniana* *20057*	
	R	*20057* Kenya *20057*
R	*Tricalysia concolor* Halle	
	R	Gabon (Belinga)
I	*Tricalysia coriacea* (Benth.) Hiern ssp. *angustifolia* (Garcia) Robbrecht *20932*	
	I	*20932* Malawi (Mt. Mulanje) *20932*
	I	*20932* Mozambique (Zimbabwe border) *20932*
	I	*20932* Zimbabwe *20932*
V	*Tricalysia erythrospora* (Thwaites) Alston *10252*	
	V	*12838* Sri Lanka *10252*
I	*Tricalysia obstetrix* Halle	
	I	Gabon (Belinga)
I	*Tricalysia pangolina* Halle *7927*	
	I	Gabon (Nzoumou) *7927*
I	*Tricalysia potamogala* Halle *7927*	
	I	*7927* Gabon (Minvoul) *7927*
I	*Tricalysia sessilis* (Elm.) Merr. *13833*	
	I	*13833* Philippines (Iwahig River) *13833*
I	*Tricalysia soyauxii* Schumann var. *pedunculosa* Halle	
	I	Gabon
I	*Tricalysia soyauxii* Schumann var. *pilosula* Halle	
	I	Gabon
R	*Uncaria donisii* E. Petit	
	R	Gabon
I	*Uncaria glavcascens* Craib *19120*	
	I	*19120* Thailand *19120*
I	*Uncaria quadrangularis* Geddes *19120*	
	I	*19120* Thailand *19120*
R	*Uncaria thwaitesii* (Hook.f.) Alston *12838*	
	R	*12838* Sri Lanka *12838*
I	*Urophyllum aequale* Craib *19120*	
	I	*19120* Thailand *19120*
I	*Urophyllum andamanicum* King & Gamble *7771*	
	I	India - Andaman Is. (S. Andamans) *7771*
R	*Urophyllum argenteum* Pitard *6057*	
	R	Vietnam *6057*

I	*Urophyllum crassum* Craib *19120*	
	I	*19120* Thailand *19120*
R	*Urophyllum ellipticum* (Wight) Thwaites *12838*	
	R	*12838* Sri Lanka *12838*
I	*Urophyllum elliptifolium* Merr. *13833*	
	I	*13833* Philippines (Mt. Pulgar) *13833*
E	*Urophyllum longipes* Craib *19120*	
	E	*19120* Thailand *19120*
I	*Urophyllum talangense* Craib *19120*	
	E	*19120* Thailand *19120*
R	*Urophyllum tonkinense* Pitard *6057*	
	R	Vietnam *6057*
R	*Valantia calva* Brullo *18264*	
	R	*18264* Italy - Sicily *18264*
R	*Valantia deltoidea* Brullo *18264*	
	R	*18264* Italy - Sicily *18264*
I	*Virectaria salicoides* (C.H. Wright) Brem. *7927*	
	I	Gabon (Monts de Cristal) *7927*
E	*Virectaria tenella* J. Hall *6072*	
	E	*6072* Ghana (Amedzofe) *6072*
E	*Wendlandia andamanica* Cowan *11494*	
	E	*11494* India - Andaman Is. (Port Blair, Andaman I.) *11494*
Ex	*Wendlandia angustifolia* Wight *11494*	
	Ex	*11494* India - Tamil Nadu (Courtallum & Tirunelveli) *11494*
R	*Wendlandia basistaminea* F.Muell. *20681*	
	R	*20681* Australia - Queensland *20681*
R	*Wendlandia connata* C.White *20681*	
	R	*20681* Australia - Queensland *20681*
I	*Wendlandia lawii* Hook.f.	
	I	India - Karnataka (Mysore)
R	*Xanthophytopsis balansae* Pitard *6057*	
	R	Vietnam *6057*
R	*Xantonneopsis robinsonii* Pitard *6057*	
	I	*20985* Vietnam *6057*

Rutaceae

Number of genera:	150
Number of species:	1,500
Recorded threatened species:	382 (25%)

Nearly cosmopolitan, especially South Africa and Australia.

R	*Acmadenia alternifolia* Cham. *20604*	
	R	*20604* South Africa - Cape Province *20604*
R	*Acmadenia argillophila* I.Williams *20604*	
	R	*20604* South Africa - Cape Province *20604*
Ex	*Acmadenia baileyensis* I.Williams *20604*	
	Ex	*20604* South Africa - Cape Province *20604*
Ex	*Acmadenia candida* I.Williams *20604, 10260*	
	Ex	*20604* South Africa - Cape Province *20604*
V	*Acmadenia gracilis* Dummer *20604*	
	V	*20604* South Africa - Cape Province *20604*
V	*Acmadenia laxa* I.Williams *20604*	
	V	*20604* South Africa - Cape Province *20604*
R	*Acmadenia macradenia* (Sond.) Dummer *20604*	
	R	*20604* South Africa - Cape Province *20604*
I	*Acmadenia macropetala* (P.E.Glover) Compton *20604*	
	I	*20604* South Africa - Cape Province *20604*

V	*Acmadenia maculata* I.Williams 20604	
	V	20604 South Africa - Cape Province 20604
R	*Acmadenia matroosbergensis* E.Phillips 20604	
	R	20604 South Africa - Cape Province 20604
V	*Acmadenia nivea* I.Williams 20604	
	V	20604 South Africa - Cape Province 20604
R	*Acmadenia niveni* Sond. 20803	
	R	20803 South Africa - Cape Province 20803
V	*Acmadenia rupicola* I.Williams 20604	
	V	20604 South Africa - Cape Province 20604
R	*Acmadenia tenax* I.Williams 20604	
	R	20604 South Africa - Cape Province 20604
R	*Acmadenia tetragona* (L.f.) Bartl. & H.L.Wendl. 20604	
	R	20604 South Africa - Cape Province 20604
R	*Acradenia frankliniae* Kippist 20681	
	R	20681 Australia - Tasmania 20681
R	*Acronychia aberrans* T.Hartley 20681, 7896	
	R	20681 Australia - Queensland 20681
R	*Acronychia acuminata* T.Hartley 20681, 7896	
	R	20681 Australia - Queensland 7896
R	*Acronychia baeuerlenii* T.Hartley 20681, 7896	
	I	20681 Australia - New South Wales 7896
	I	20681 Australia - Queensland 7896
R	*Acronychia chooreechillum* (Bailey) C.White 20681, 7896	
	R	20681 Australia - Queensland 20681
R	*Acronychia crassipetala* T.Hartley 20681, 7896	
	R	20681 Australia - Queensland 7896
R	*Acronychia eungellensis* T.Hartley & B.Hyland 20681	
	R	20681 Australia - Queensland 7896
R	*Acronychia heterophylla* A.Gray 7925	
	R	U.S. - American Samoa (Tutuila) 7925
E	*Acronychia littoralis* T.Hartley & J.Williams 20681	
	I	20681 Australia - New South Wales 20681
	I	20681 Australia - Queensland 20681
R	*Adenandra dahlgrenii* Strid 20604	
	R	20604 South Africa - Cape Province 20604
I	*Adenandra gracilis* Eckl. & Zeyh. 20604	
	I	20604 South Africa - Cape Province 20604
R	*Adenandra marginata* (L.f.) Roem. & Schult. ssp. *mucronata* Strid 20604	
	R	20604 South Africa - Cape Province 20604
I	*Adenandra multiflora* Strid 20604	
	I	20604 South Africa - Cape Province 20604
R	*Adenandra odoratissima* Strid ssp. *odoratissima* 20604	
	R	20604 South Africa - Cape Province 20604
R	*Adenandra odoratissima* Strid ssp. *tenuis* Strid 20604	
	R	20604 South Africa - Cape Province 20604
I	*Adenandra schlechteri* Dummer 20604	
	I	20604 South Africa - Cape Province 20604
R	*Adenandra villosa* (P.J.Bergius) Licht. ex Roem. & Schult. ssp. *apiculata* Strid 20604	
	R	20604 South Africa - Cape Province 20604
R	*Adenandra villosa* (P.J.Bergius) Licht. ex Roem. & Schult. ssp. *imbricata* Strid 20604	
	R	20604 South Africa - Cape Province 20604
I	*Adenandra villosa* (P.J.Bergius) Licht. ex Roem. & Schult.	

	ssp. *pedicellata* Strid 20604	
	I	20604 South Africa - Cape Province 20604
R	*Adenandra villosa* (P.J.Bergius) Licht. ex Roem. & Schult. ssp. *robusta* Strid 20604	
	R	20604 South Africa - Cape Province 20604
V	*Agathosma abrupta* Pillans 20604	
	V	20604 South Africa - Cape Province 20604
R	*Agathosma adnata* Pillans 20604	
	R	20604 South Africa - Cape Province 20604
R	*Agathosma affinis* Sond. 20604	
	R	20604 South Africa - Cape Province 20604
R	*Agathosma bicolor* Dummer 20604	
	R	20604 South Africa - Cape Province 20604
R	*Agathosma capitata* Sond. 20604	
	R	20604 South Africa - Cape Province 20604
E	*Agathosma cephalodes* E.Mey. ex Sond. 20604	
	E	20604 South Africa - Cape Province 20604
R	*Agathosma concava* Pillans 20604	
	R	20604 South Africa - Cape Province 20604
R	*Agathosma conferta* Pillans 20604	
	R	20604 South Africa - Cape Province 20604
R	*Agathosma cordifolia* Pillans 20604	
	R	20604 South Africa - Cape Province 20604
E	*Agathosma corymbosa* (Montin) G.Don 20604	
	E	20604 South Africa - Cape Province 20604
R	*Agathosma dentata* Pillans 20604	
	R	20604 South Africa - Cape Province 20604
R	*Agathosma distans* Pillans 20604	
	R	20604 South Africa - Cape Province 20604
R	*Agathosma dregeana* Sond. 20604	
	R	20604 South Africa - Cape Province 20604
I	*Agathosma elata* Sond. 20604	
	I	20604 South Africa - Cape Province 20604
V	*Agathosma eriantha* (Steud.) Steud. 20604	
	V	20604 South Africa - Cape Province 20604
R	*Agathosma florida* Sond. 20604	
	R	20604 South Africa - Cape Province 20604
R	*Agathosma foleyana* Dummer 20604	
	R	20604 South Africa - Cape Province 20604
I	*Agathosma glabrata* Bartl. & H.L.Wendl. 20604	
	I	20604 South Africa - Cape Province 20604
V	*Agathosma glandulosa* (Thunb.) Sond. 20604	
	V	20604 South Africa - Cape Province 20604
I	*Agathosma gnidiiflora* Dummer 20604	
	I	20604 South Africa - Cape Province 20604
E	*Agathosma involucrata* Eckl. & Zeyh. 20604	
	E	20604 South Africa - Cape Province 20604
V	*Agathosma marifolia* Eckl. & Zeyh. 20604	
	V	20604 South Africa - Cape Province 20604
E	*Agathosma minuta* Schltdl. 20604	
	E	20604 South Africa - Cape Province 20604
R	*Agathosma namaquensis* Pillans 20604	
	R	20604 South Africa - Cape Province 20604
E	*Agathosma orbicularis* (Thunb.) Bartl. & H.L.Wendl. 20604, 10260	
	E	20604 South Africa - Cape Province 20604
I	*Agathosma pallens* Pillans 20604	
	I	20604 South Africa - Cape Province 20604

R	*Agathosma phillipsii* Dummer *20604*		
	R	*20604* South Africa - Cape Province *20604*	
R	*Agathosma pulchella* (L.) Link *20604*		
	R	*20604* South Africa - Cape Province *20604*	
R	*Agathosma salina* Eckl. & Zeyh. *20604*		
	R	*20604* South Africa - Cape Province *20604*	
R	*Agathosma sedifolia* Schltdl. *20604*		
	R	*20604* South Africa - Cape Province *20604*	
V	*Agathosma spinosa* Sond. *20604*		
	V	*20604* South Africa - Cape Province *20604*	
R	*Agathosma stenosepala* Pillans *20604*		
	R	*20604* South Africa - Cape Province *20604*	
R	*Agathosma stokoei* Pillans *20604*		
	R	*20604* South Africa - Cape Province *20604*	
V	*Agathosma subteretifolia* Pillans *20604*		
	V	*20604* South Africa - Cape Province *20604*	
R	*Agathosma thymifolia* Schltdl. *20604*		
	R	*20604* South Africa - Cape Province *20604*	
R	*Agathosma umbonata* Pillans *20604*		
	R	*20604* South Africa - Cape Province *20604*	
R	*Agathosma unicarpellata* (Fourc.) Pillans *20604*		
	R	*20604* South Africa - Cape Province *20604*	
R	*Agathosma zwartbergense* Pillans *20604*		
	R	*20604* South Africa - Cape Province *20604*	
V	*Amyris polymorpha* Urban *5607*		
	V	*19105* Cuba (Granma) *5607*	
V	*Asterolasia drummondii* Paul G.Wilson *20681*		
	V	*20681* Australia - Western Australia *20681*	
E	*Asterolasia elegans* L.McDougall & M.F.Porteners *20681*		
	E	*20681* Australia - New South Wales *20681*	
V	*Asterolasia grandiflora* (Hook.) Benth. *20681*		
	V	*20681* Australia - Western Australia *20681*	
R	*Asterolasia hexapetala* (Juss.f.) Druce *20681*		
	R	*20681* Australia - New South Wales *20681*	
R	*Asterolasia muricata* J.Black *20681*		
	R	*20681* Australia - South Australia *20681*	
V	*Asterolasia nivea* (Paul G.Wilson) Paul G.Wilson *20681*		
	V	*20681* Australia - Western Australia *20681*	
V	*Asterolasia phebalioides* F.Muell. *20681*		
	I	*20681* Australia - South Australia *20681*	
	I	*20681* Australia - Victoria *20681*	
I	*Atalantia missionis* (Wight) Oliver		
	I		India - Andhra Pradesh (Cuddapah)
	I		India - Kerala (Quilon)
	I		India - Tamil Nadu
E	*Balfourodendron riedelianum* Engl. *10370*		
	E	*10370* Argentina (Selva Misionera) *13928*	
	E	*10370* Brazil - Parana *10370*	
	E	*10370* Brazil - Rio Grande do Sul *10370*	
	E	*10370* Brazil - Santa Catarina *10370*	
	E	*10370* Brazil - Sao Paulo *13928*	
	E	*10370* Paraguay (north & central) *13928*	
R	*Balsamocitrus camerunensis* Letouzey		
	R		Cameroon
V	*Boninia crassifolia* Nakai *8037*		
	V	*19134* Japan - Ogasawara-shoto (Chichijima) *8037*	
R	*Boninia glabra* Planchon *8037*		

	R	*19134* Japan - Ogasawara-shoto *8037*	
V	*Boronella koniamboensis* (Däniker) T.G.Hartley *20893*		
	V	*20893* New Caledonia *20893*	
V	*Boronia adamsiana* F.Muell. *20681, 320*		
	V	*20681* Australia - Western Australia *20681*	
R	*Boronia amabilis* S.T.Blake *20681*		
	R	*20681* Australia - Queensland *20681*	
R	*Boronia chartaceae* P.Weston *20681*		
	R	*20681* Australia - New South Wales *20681*	
R	*Boronia citrata* N.G.Walsh *20681*		
	R	*20681* Australia - Victoria *20681*	
V	*Boronia deanei* Maiden & Betche *20681*		
	V	*20681* Australia - New South Wales *20681*	
R	*Boronia eriantha* Lindley *20681*		
	R	*20681* Australia - Queensland *20681*	
R	*Boronia fraseri* Hook. *20681*		
	R	*20681* Australia - New South Wales *20681*	
R	*Boronia galbraithiae* D.E.Albrecht *20681*		
	R	*20681* Australia - Victoria *20681*	
V	*Boronia granitica* Maiden & Betche *20681*		
	I	*20681* Australia - New South Wales *20681*	
	I	*20681* Australia - Queensland *20681*	
V	*Boronia keysii* Domin *20681*		
	V	*20681* Australia - Queensland *20681*	
R	*Boronia latipinna* J.H.Willis *20681*		
	R	*20681* Australia - Victoria *20681*	
E	*Boronia repanda* (Maiden & Betche) Maiden & Betche *20681*		
	I	*20681* Australia - New South Wales *20681*	
	I	*20681* Australia - Queensland *20681*	
V	*Boronia revoluta* Paul G.Wilson *20681*		
	V	*20681* Australia - Western Australia *20681*	
R	*Boronia rivularis* C.White *20681*		
	R	*20681* Australia - Queensland *20681*	
R	*Boronia rubiginosa* Endl. *20681*		
	R	*20681* Australia - New South Wales *20681*	
R	*Boronia serrulata* Smith *20681*		
	R	*20681* Australia - New South Wales *20681*	
R	*Boronia subulifolia* Cheel *20681*		
	R	*20681* Australia - New South Wales *20681*	
R	*Boronia tenuis* (Lindley) Benth. *20681*		
	R	*20681* Australia - Western Australia *20681*	
V	*Boronia umbellata* P.Weston *20681*		
	V	*20681* Australia - New South Wales *20681*	
R	*Bosistoa floydii* T.Hartley *20681*		
	R	*20681* Australia - New South Wales *20681*	
E	*Burkillanthus malaccensis* (Ridley) Swingle *19006*		
	K	*19006* Indonesia - Sumatra (Asahan) *19006*	
	Ex	*19006* Malaysia - Peninsular Malaysia (Malacca) *19006*	
	I	*19006* Malaysia - Sarawak (Bintulu) *19006*	
V	*Choisya dumosa* (Torr.) Gray var. *mollis* (Standl.) L. Benson *20850*		
	V	*20850* U.S. - Arizona *20850*	
V	*Citropsis gabunensis* Swingle & Kellerman *10260*		
	V	*20858* Tropical Africa (Guinea-wide) *20858*	
	V	*20858* Ghana *15970*	
V	*Citrus neo-caledonica* Guillaumin		
	V		New Caledonia

E   *Citrus oxanthera* Beauv.
     E   New Caledonia

R   *Citrus taiwanica* Tamaka & Limada *20854*
     R   *20854*   Taiwan *20854*

I   *Clausena grandifolia* Merr. *13833*
     I   *13833*   Philippines (Palawan) *13833*

V   *Cneoridium dumosum* (Nutt.) Hook. f. ex Baill. *20850*
     I   *20850*   U.S. - California *20850*

R   *Coleonema virgatum* (Schltdl.) Eckl. & Zeyh. *20604*
     R   *20604*   South Africa - Cape Province *20604*

V   *Correa baeuerlenii* F.Muell. *20681*
     V   *20681*   Australia - New South Wales *20681*

V   *Correa calycina* J.Black *20681*
     V   *20681*   Australia - South Australia *20681*

R   *Dictamnus hispanicus* Webb ex Willk. *20171*
     R   *20692*   Spain (central, south and east) *20692*

E   *Diosma aristata* I.Williams *20604*
     E   *20604*   South Africa - Cape Province *20604*

V   *Diosma aspalathoides* Lam. *20604*
     V   *20604*   South Africa - Cape Province *20604*

R   *Diosma awilana* I.Williams *20604*
     R   *20604*   South Africa - Cape Province *20604*

V   *Diosma dichotoma* P.J.Bergius *20604*
     V   *20604*   South Africa - Cape Province *20604*

Ex   *Diosma fallax* I.Williams *20604*
     Ex   *20604*   South Africa - Cape Province *20604*

R   *Diosma haelkraalensis* I.Williams *20604*
     R   *20604*   South Africa - Cape Province *20604*

E   *Diosma parvula* I.Williams *20604*
     E   *20604*   South Africa - Cape Province *20604*

R   *Diosma passerinoides* Steud. *20604*
     R   *20604*   South Africa - Cape Province *20604*

I   *Diosma strumosa* I.Williams *20604*
     I   *20604*   South Africa - Cape Province *20604*

R   *Diosma tenella* I.Williams *20604*
     R   *20604*   South Africa - Cape Province *20604*

R   *Diphasiopsis fadenii* Kokwaro *7959*
     R   *20057*   Kenya *7959*

V   *Drummondita ericoides* Harv. *20681*
     V   *20681*   Australia - Western Australia *20681*

V   *Drummondita hassellii* (F.Muell.) Paul G.Wilson var. *longifolia* Paul G.Wilson *20681*
     V   *20681*   Australia - Western Australia *20681*

V   *Dutaillyea amosensis* (Guillaumin) T.Hartley *20893*
     V   *20893*   New Caledonia *20893*

R   *Empleurum fragrans* P.E.Glover *20604*
     R   *20604*   South Africa - Cape Province *20604*

R   *Eriostemon ericifolius* Benth. *20681*
     R   *20681*   Australia - New South Wales *20681*

Ex   *Eriostemon falcatus* Paul G.Wilson *20681, 14223*
     Ex   *20681*   Australia - Western Australia *20681*

R   *Eriostemon myoporoides* DC. ssp. *epilosus* Paul G.Wilson *20681*
     I   *20681*   Australia - New South Wales *20681*
     I   *20681*   Australia - Queensland *20681*

R   *Eriostemon obovalis* Cunn. *20681*
     R   *20681*   Australia - New South Wales *20681*

V   *Eriostemon wonganensis* Paul G.Wilson *20681*

     V   *20681*   Australia - Western Australia *20681*

E   *Erythrochiton incomparabilis* Riley *20883*
     I   *20883*   Panama *20883*

R   *Esenbeckia berlandieri* Baill. ssp. *acapulcensis* (Rose) Kaastra *20883*
     R   *20883*   Mexico *20883*

V   *Esenbeckia collina* Brandegee *20883*
     E   *20883*   Mexico *20883*

E   *Esenbeckia collina* Brandegee ssp. *collina* Brandegee *20883*
     E   *20883*   Mexico *20883*

E   *Esenbeckia collina* Brandegee ssp. *conspecta* Kaastra *20883*
     E   *20883*   Mexico *20883*

E   *Esenbeckia cornuta* Engler *20883*
     I   *20883*   Peru *20883*

E   *Esenbeckia cowanii* Kaastra *20883, 8679*
     E   *20883*   French Guiana *20883*

V   *Esenbeckia echinoidea* Standley & Steyermark *20883, 9004*
     I   *20883*   Guatemala *20883*

E   *Esenbeckia feddemae* Kaastra *20883*
     E   *20883*   Mexico *20883*

V   *Esenbeckia grandiflora* ssp. *brevipetiolata* Kaastra *20883*
     I   *20883*   Brazil *20883*

R   *Esenbeckia hieronymi* Engler *20883*
     I   *20883*   Brazil *20883*

R   *Esenbeckia irwiniana* Kaastra *20883*
     I   *20883*   Brazil *20883*

V   *Esenbeckia macrantha* Rose *20883*
     I   *20883*   Mexico *20883*

V   *Esenbeckia nesiotica* Standley *20883*
     I   *20883*   Mexico *20883*

V   *Esenbeckia oligantha* Kaastra *20883*
     I   *20883*   Brazil *20883*

R   *Esenbeckia pentaphylla* ssp. *australensis* Kaastra *20883*
     I   *20883*   Panama *20883*
     I   *20883*   Colombia *20883*

R   *Esenbeckia pentaphylla* ssp. *pentaphylla* *20883*
     I   *20883*   Jamaica *20883*

R   *Esenbeckia pilocarpoides* ssp. *maurioides* (Martius) Kaastra *20883*
     I   *20883*   Brazil *20883*

E   *Esenbeckia scrotiformis* Kaastra *20883*
     E   *20883*   Brazil *20883*

R   *Euchaetis avisylvana* I.Williams *20604*
     R   *20604*   South Africa - Cape Province *20604*

R   *Euchaetis esterhuyseniae* I.Williams *20604*
     R   *20604*   South Africa - Cape Province *20604*

R   *Euchaetis intonsa* I.Williams *20604*
     R   *20604*   South Africa - Cape Province *20604*

E   *Euchaetis longicornis* I.Williams *20604*
     E   *20604*   South Africa - Cape Province *20604*

I   *Euchaetis pungens* (Bartl. & H.L.Wendl.) I.Williams *20604*
     I   *20604*   South Africa - Cape Province *20604*

E   *Euchaetis schlechteri* Schinz *20604*

R   20604   South Africa - Cape Province   *20604*

R   *Euchaetis tricarpellata* **I.Williams** *20604*

    R   20604   South Africa - Cape Province   *20604*

R   *Euodia chapelieri* **Baillon var.** *chapelieri* *10082*

    R   20771   Mauritius   *10082*

E   *Euodia chapelieri* **Baillon var.** *sessilis* **Coode** *10082*

    E   20771   Mauritius   *10082*

R   *Euodia irifica* **Coode** *10082*

    R   14233   Réunion   *10082*

V   *Euodia littoralis* **Endl.** *11649*

    V   11649   Australia - Norfolk Is. (Mostly in Mount Pitt National Park.) *11649*

V   *Euodia nishimurae* **Koidz.** *18128*

    V   19134   Japan - Ogasawara-shoto   *18128*

E   *Euodia obtusifolia* **DC. var.** *brachypoda* **Coode** *10082*

    E   20771   Mauritius   *10082*

R   *Euodia obtusifolia* **DC. var.** *cuneifolia* **Coode** *10082*

    R   20771   Mauritius   *10082*

R   *Euodia obtusifolia* **DC. var.** *gigas* **Vaughan ex Coode** *10082*

    R   20771   Mauritius   *10082*

R   *Euodia obtusifolia* **DC. var.** *inaequalis* **Coode** *10082*

    R   14220   Réunion   *10082*

R   *Euodia obtusifolia* **DC. var.** *obtusifolia* *10082*

    R   20771   Mauritius   *10082*

R   *Euodia pasteuriana* **Chev. ex Guillaumin** *6057*

    R   Vietnam   *6057*

R   *Euodia polybotrya* **C. Moore & F. Muell.**

    R   14225   Australia - NSW - Lord Howe Is.   *14225*

E   *Euodia segregis* **Cordem.** *10082*

    E   14233   Réunion   *10082*

R   *Euodia simplicifolia* **Ridley** *19006*

    R   19006   Malaysia - Peninsular Malaysia   *19006*

R   *Euodia wagapensis* **Guillaumin**

    R   New Caledonia

I   *Evodia arborea* **Elm.** *13833*

    I   13833   Philippines (Palawan)   *13833*

V   *Evodia nishimurae* **Koidz.** *20626*

    V   20626   Japan - Ogasawara-shoto   *20626*

I   *Evodia pulgarensis* **Elm.** *13833*

    I   13833   Philippines (Mt. Pulgar)   *13833*

I   *Fagara curbeloi* **(Alain) Kereszty** *5607*

    I   Cuba (Las Tunas)   *5607*

I   *Fagara duplicipunctata* **(C. Wright) Krug & Urban** *5607*

    I   Cuba (Pinar del Rio)   *5607*

V   *Fagara externa* **Skottsb.** *19116*

    V   19125   Chile - Juan Fernandez Is.   *19116*

R   *Fagara jamaicensis* **(P. Wilson) Engl.** *20883*

    R   20883   Jamaica   *20883*

E   *Fagara mezoneurospinosa* **Ake Assi** *20887*

    E   20887   Côte d'Ivoire   *11631*

R   *Fagara rhodoxylon* **Urb.** *20883*

    R   20883   Jamaica   *20883*

R   *Flindersia brassii* **T.Hartley & B.Hyland** *20681*

    R   20681   Australia - Queensland   *20681*

R   *Flindersia oppositifolia* **(F.Muell.) T.Hartley & Jessup** *20681*

    R   20681   Australia - Queensland   *20681*

R   *Fortunella polyandra* **(Ridley) Tanaka** *19006*

    R   19006   Malaysia - Peninsular Malaysia   *19006*

Ex   *Galipea ossana* **DC.** *5607*

    Ex   19105   Cuba (Pinar del Rio; Prov.Habana)   *5607*

E   *Galipea panamensis* **Elias** *20883, 9006*

    I   20883   Panama   *20883*

R   *Geijera salicifolia* **Schott**

    R   New Caledonia

R   *Glycosmis collina* **Stone** *19006*

    R   Malaysia - Peninsular Malaysia

R   *Glycosmis crassifolia* **Ridley** *19006*

    R   19006   Malaysia - Peninsular Malaysia   *19006*

R   *Glycosmis macrocarpa* **Wight.** *14782*

    R   14782   India - Kerala   *14782*

    R   14782   India - Tamil Nadu   *14782*

V   *Glycosmis perakensis* **Naray.** *19006*

    V   19006   Malaysia - Peninsular Malaysia (Perak & Taman Negara)   *19006*

R   *Glycosmis touranensis* **Guillaumin** *6057*

    R   Vietnam   *6057*

R   *Haplophyllum balcanicum* **Vandas** *5204, 20171*

    R   5204   Bulgaria (south)   *5204*

    R   Greece

R   *Haplophyllum boissieranum* **Vis. & Pancic** *20178, 20171*

    R   20178   Albania   *20178*

    E   21091   Bosnia & Herzegovina   *21091*

    R   (former) Yugoslavia

R   *Haplophyllum cappadocicum* **Spach** *12840*

    R   12840   Turkey   *12840*

R   *Haplophyllum megalanthum* **Bornm.** *12840*

    R   12840   Turkey   *12840*

R   *Haplophyllum pumiliforme* **Huber-Mor. & Reese** *12840*

    R   12840   Turkey   *12840*

R   *Haplophyllum suaveolens* **(DC.) G. Don var.** *cilicicum* **(Boiss.) C.C. Townsend** *12840*

    R   12840   Turkey   *12840*

R   *Haplophyllum vulcanicum* **Boiss. & Heldr.** *12840*

    R   12840   Turkey   *12840*

E   *Helietta glaucescens* **Urban** *5607*

    E   19105   Cuba (Santiago de Cuba)   *5607*

R   *Helietta mollis* **(Miq.) Kastra** *20883*

    R   20883   Brazil   *20883*

    R   20883   Paraguay   *20883*

Ex   *Kodalyodendron cubensis* **Borh. & Acuna** *5607*

    Ex   19105   Cuba (Holguin)   *5607*

R   *Maclurodendron magnificum* **T. Hartley** *7895*

    E   19006   Malaysia - Peninsular Malaysia (G. Ulu Kali, Pahang)   *7895*

R   *Macrostylis barbigera* **(L.f.) Bartl. & H.L.Wendl.** *20604*

    R   20604   South Africa - Cape Province   *20604*

R   *Macrostylis cassiopoides* **(Turcz.) I.Williams ssp.** *cassiopoides* *20604*

    R   20604   South Africa - Cape Province   *20604*

R   *Macrostylis cassiopoides* **(Turcz.) I.Williams ssp.**

	dregeana (Sond.) I.Williams *20604*
R	20604 South Africa - Cape Province *20604*

V	*Macrostylis cauliflora* I.Williams *20604*
V	20604 South Africa - Cape Province *20604*

R	*Macrostylis hirta* E.Mey. ex Sond. *20604*
R	20604 South Africa - Cape Province *20604*

R	*Macrostylis ramulosa* I.Williams *20604*
R	20604 South Africa - Cape Province *20604*

E	*Macrostylis villosa* (Thunb.) Sond. ssp. *minor* I.Williams *20604*
E	20604 South Africa - Cape Province *20604*

I	*Macrostylis villosa* (Thunb.) Sond. ssp. *villosa 20604*
I	20604 South Africa - Cape Province *20604*

E	*Medicosma articulata* T.Hartley *20893*
E	20893 New Caledonia *20893*

E	*Medicosma diversifolia* T.Hartley *20893*
E	20893 New Caledonia *20893*

V	*Medicosma elliptica* T.Hartley *20681*
V	20681 Australia - Queensland *20681*

E	*Medicosma exigua* T.Hartley *20893*
E	20893 New Caledonia *20893*

R	*Medicosma glandulosa* T.Hartley *20681*
R	20681 Australia - Queensland *20681*

E	*Medicosma gracilis* T.Hartley *20893*
E	20893 New Caledonia *20893*

E	*Medicosma latifolia* T.Hartley *20893*
E	20893 New Caledonia *20893*

E	*Medicosma leratii* (Guillaumin) T.Hartley *20893*
E	20893 New Caledonia *20893*

V	*Medicosma obovata* T.Hartley *20681*
V	20681 Australia - Queensland *20681*

E	*Medicosma parvifolia* T.Hartley *20893*
E	20893 New Caledonia *20893*

E	*Medicosma petiolaris* T.Hartley *20893*
E	20893 New Caledonia *20893*

R	*Medicosma sessiliflora* (C.White) T.Hartley *20681*
R	20681 Australia - Queensland *20681*

E	*Medicosma suberosa* T.Hartley *20893*
E	20893 New Caledonia *20893*

E	*Medicosma subsessilis* T.Hartley *20893*
E	20893 New Caledonia *20893*

E	*Medicosma tahafeana* T.Hartley *20893*
E	20893 New Caledonia *20893*

E	*Melicope adscendens* (St. John & Hume) T.G. Hartley & B.C. Stone *20850, 14301*
E	20850 U.S. - Hawaii (east Maui) *20850*

E	*Melicope ballⁱⁱoui* (Rock) T.G. Hartley & B.C. Stone *20850, 14209*
E	20850 U.S. - Hawaii (Maui, Haleakala) *20850*

E	*Melicope christophersenii* (St. John) T.G. Hartley & B.C. Stone *20850, 14209*
E	20850 U.S. - Hawaii (O`ahu, Wai`anae Mts.) *20850*

E	*Melicope cinerea* Gray *20850, 14209*
E	20850 U.S. - Hawaii (Maui, O`ahu) *20850*

R	*Melicope contermina* C. Moore & F. Muell. *14223*
R	14223 Australia - NSW - Lord Howe Is. *14223*

Ex/E	*Melicope cruciata* (Heller) T.G. Hartley & B.C. Stone *20850, 14209*
Ex/E	20850 U.S. - Hawaii *20850*

Ex/E	*Melicope degeneri* (B.C. Stone) T.G. Hartley & B.C. Stone *20850, 14209*
Ex/E	20850 U.S. - Hawaii (Kaua`i) *20850*

Ex/E	*Melicope haleakalae* (B.C. Stone) T.G. Hartley & B.C. Stone *20850, 14209*
Ex/E	20850 U.S. - Hawaii (Maui) *20850*

E	*Melicope haupuensis* (St. John) T.G. Hartley & B.C. Stone *20850, 14209, 21349*
E	20850 U.S.·- Hawaii (Kaua`i) *20850*

V	*Melicope hawaiensis* (Wawra) T.G. Hartley & B.C. Stone *20850, 14209*
V	20850 U.S. - Hawaii *20850*

V	*Melicope indica* Wight *14782*
V	14782 India - Tamil Nadu *14782*

R	*Melicope kaalaensis* (St. John) T.G. Hartley & B.C. Stone *20850, 14209*
I	20850 U.S. - Hawaii (O`ahu, Wai`anae Mts) *20850*

E	*Melicope knudsenii* (Hbd.) T.G. Hartley & B.C. Stone *20850, 14209, 21349*
E	20850 U.S. - Hawaii (Maui & Kaua`i) *20850*

R	*Melicope littoralis* (Endl.) T.G. Hartley *19108*
R	19108 Australia - Norfolk Is. (Mostly in Mount Pitt National Park) *19108*

R	*Melicope lucida* (A.Gray) A.C. Smith
R	U.S. - American Samoa (Tutuila)

E	*Melicope lydgatei* (Hbd.) T.G. Hartley & B.C. Stone *20850, 14209*
E	20850 U.S. - Hawaii (O`ahu) *20850*

E	*Melicope macropus* (Hbd.) T.G. Hartley & B.C. Stone *20850, 14209*
E	20850 U.S. - Hawaii (Kaua`i) *20850*

E	*Melicope makahae* (B.C. Stone) T.G. Hartley & B.C. Stone *20850, 14209*
E	20850 U.S. - Hawaii (O`ahu) *20850*

E	*Melicope mucronulata* (St. John) T.G. Hartley & B.C. Stone *20850, 14209*
E	20850 U.S. - Hawaii (Moloka`i) *20850*

Ex/E	*Melicope munroi* (St. John) T.G. Hartley & B.C. Stone *20850, 14209*
Ex/E	20850 U.S. - Hawaii (Lana`i) *20850*

Ex	*Melicope nealae* (St. John) T. Hartley & B. Stone *14209*
Ex	19002 U.S. - Hawaii (Kaua`i) *14209*

Ex/E	*Melicope nealiae* (B.C. Stone) T.G. Hartley & B.C. Stone *20850*
Ex/E	20850 U.S. - Hawaii *20850*

Ex/E	*Melicope obovata* (St. John) T.G. Hartley & B.C. Stone *20850, 14209*
Ex/E	20850 U.S. - Hawaii *20850*

E	*Melicope orbicularis* (Hbd.) T.G. Hartley & B.C. Stone *20850, 14209*
E	20850 U.S. - Hawaii (Maui) *20850*

E	*Melicope ovalis* (St. John) T.G. Hartley & B.C. Stone *20850, 14209*
E	20850 U.S. - Hawaii (east Maui) *20850*

E	*Melicope pallida* (Hbd.) T.G. Hartley & B.C.

Stone *20850, 14301, 21349*
  E   *20850* U.S. - Hawaii *20850*

Ex/E *Melicope paniculata* (St. John) T.G. Hartley & B.C.
    Stone *20850, 14209*
    Ex/E *20850* U.S. - Hawaii (Kaua`i) *20850*

E *Melicope puberula* (St. John) T.G. Hartley & B.C.
    Stone *20850, 14209*
    E   *20850* U.S. - Hawaii (Kaua`i) *20850*

E *Melicope quadrangularis* (St.John & Hume) T.G.Hartley &
    B.C.Stone *20850, 14301, 21349*
    E   *20850* U.S. - Hawaii (Kaua`i) *20850*

E *Melicope reflexa* (St. John) T.G. Hartley & B.C.
    Stone *20850, 14301*
    E   *20850* U.S. - Hawaii (east Moloka`i) *20850*

R *Melicope rotundifolia* (Gray) T.G. Hartley & B.C.
    Stone *20850, 14209*
    I   *20850* U.S. - Hawaii (O`ahu) *20850*

E *Melicope saint-johnii* (Hume) T.G. Hartley & B.C.
    Stone *20850, 14209, 21353*
    E   *20850* U.S. - Hawaii (O`ahu) *20850*

E *Melicope sandwicensis* (Hook. & Arn.) T.G. Hartley & B.C.
    Stone *20850, 14209*
    E   *20850* U.S. - Hawaii (O`ahu) *20850*

E *Melicope suberosa* Stone *19006*
    E   *19006* Malaysia - Peninsular Malaysia (G. Ulu Kali, Pahang) *19006*

E *Melicope waialealae* (Wawra) T.G. Hartley & B.C.
    Stone *20850, 14209*
    E   *20850* U.S. - Hawaii (Moloka`i) *20850*

Ex/E *Melicope wailauensis* (St. John) T.G. Hartley & B.C.
    Stone *20850, 14301*
    Ex/E *20850* U.S. - Hawaii (Moloka`i) *20850*

R *Melicope wawraeana* (Rock) T.G. Hartley & B.C.
    Stone *20850, 14209*
    I   *20850* U.S. - Hawaii (O`ahu, Kaua`i) *20850*

E *Melicope zahlbruckneri* (Rock) T.G. Hartley & B.C.
    Stone *20850, 14209, 21355*
    E   *20850* U.S. - Hawaii *20850*

E *Metrodorea maracasana* Kaastra *20883*
    E   *20883* Brazil *20883*

R *Microcitrus garrawayae* (Bailey) Swingle *20681*
    R   *20681* Australia - Queensland *20681*

R *Microcitrus inodora* (Bailey) Swingle *20681*
    R   *20681* Australia - Queensland *20681*

R *Murraya paniculata* (L.) Jack var. *omphalocarpa*
    (L.) Jack *20511*
    R   *20511* Taiwan *20511*

R *Neobyrnesia suberosa* J.A.Armstrong *20681*
    R   *20681* Australia - Northern Territory *20681*

V *Oricia suaveolens* (Engl.) Verdoorn *20274*
    V   *20858* Côte d'Ivoire *7926*
    V   *20858* Ghana *20274*
    V   *20858* Guinea *18326*
    V   *20858* Nigeria *18326*
    V   *20858* Sierra Leone *7926*
    V   *20858* Zaire *18326*

I *Oricia trifoliolata* (Engl.) I. Verd.
    I   Cameroon (Limbe)

R *Oriciopsis glaberrima* Engl.
    R   Cameroon (Bertona)

V *Oxanthera aurantium* Tanaka *20893*
    V   *20893* New Caledonia *20893*

V *Oxanthera brevipes* Stone *20893*
    V   *20893* New Caledonia *20893*

E *Oxanthera fragrans* Montr. *20893*
    E   *20893* New Caledonia *20893*

E *Oxanthera neocaledonica* (Guillaumin) Tanaka *20893*
    E   *20893* New Caledonia *20893*

Ex/E *Oxanthera undulata* (Guillaumin) Swingle *20802*
    Ex/E *20802* New Caledonia *20802*

Ex *Pelea fatuhivensis* F. Brown
    Ex   French Polynesia - Marquesas Is

I *Pelea nukuhivensis* F. Brown
    I   French Polynesia - Marquesas Is

Ex *Pelea obovata* H. St. John *14209*
    Ex   *14209* U.S. - Hawaii *14209*

R *Phebalium ambiens* (F.Muell.) Maiden & Betch *20681*
    I   *20681* Australia - New South Wales *20681*
    I   *20681* Australia - Queensland *20681*

R *Phebalium brachyphyllum* Benth. *20681*
    R   *20681* Australia - South Australia *20681*
    Ex/E *20681* Australia - Victoria *20681*

R *Phebalium carruthersii* (F.Muell.) Maiden & Betche *20681*
    R   *20681* Australia - New South Wales *20681*

E *Phebalium daviesii* Hook.f. *20681, 14223*
    E   *20681* Australia - Tasmania *20681*

E *Phebalium elatius* (F.Muell.) Benth. ssp. *beckleri*
    (F.Muell.) Paul G.Wilson *20681*
    E   *20681* Australia - Queensland *20681*

R *Phebalium ellipticum* Paul G.Wilson *20681*
    R   *20681* Australia - New South Wales *20681*

E *Phebalium equestre* D.A.Cooke *20681*
    E   *20681* Australia - South Australia *20681*

R *Phebalium frondosum* N.G.Walsh & D.Albrecht *20681*
    R   *20681* Australia - Victoria *20681*

V *Phebalium glandulosum* Hook. ssp. *eglandulosum*
    (Blakely) Paul G.Wilson *20681*
    I   *20681* Australia - New South Wales *20681*
    I   *20681* Australia - Queensland *20681*

R *Phebalium gracile* C.White *20681*
    R   *20681* Australia - Queensland *20681*

R *Phebalium hillebrandii* J.H.Willis *20681*
    R   *20681* Australia - South Australia *20681*

E *Phebalium lachnaeoides* Cunn. *20681, 14223*
    E   *20681* Australia - New South Wales *20681*

V *Phebalium lowanense* J.H.Willis *20681*
    I   *20681* Australia - South Australia *20681*
    I   *20681* Australia - Victoria *20681*

R *Phebalium montanum* Hook. *20681*
    R   *20681* Australia - Tasmania *20681*

R *Phebalium obcordatum* Benth. *20681*
    I   *20681* Australia - New South Wales *20681*
    I   *20681* Australia - Victoria *20681*

V *Phebalium obtusifolium* Paul G.Wilson *20681*
    V   *20681* Australia - Queensland *20681*

R *Phebalium oldfieldii* (F.Muell.) F.Muell. ex Benth. *20681*
    R   *20681* Australia - Tasmania *20681*

V *Phebalium ralstonii* (F.Muell.) Benth. *20681*
    V   *20681* Australia - New South Wales *20681*

V *Phebalium rhytidophyllum* D.Albrecht & N.Walsh *20681*
    V   *20681* Australia - New South Wales *20681*

R *Phebalium rotundifolium* (Cunn. ex Endl.)
    Benth. *20681*
    I   *20681* Australia - New South Wales *20681*
    I   *20681* Australia - Queensland *20681*

R *Phebalium squamulosum* Vent. ssp. *verrucosum* Paul
    G.Wilson *20681*
    R   *20681* Australia - New South Wales *20681*

V *Phebalium sympetalum* Paul G.Wilson *20681*
    V   *20681* Australia - New South Wales *20681*

R *Phebalium viridiflorum* Paul G.Wilson *20681*
    R   *20681* Australia - New South Wales *20681*

V *Phebalium whitei* Paul G.Wilson *20681*
    V   *20681* Australia - Queensland *20681*

R *Phebalium wilsonii* N.G.Walsh & D.Albrecht *20681*
    R   *20681* Australia - Victoria *20681*

E *Phellodendron amurense* Rupr. var. *wilsonii* (Hayata
    & Kaneh.) C.E. Chang *20854*
    E   *20854* Taiwan (north & central) *20854*

V *Pilocarpus cubensis* (Borh. & Muniz) Lippold *5607*
    V   *19105* Cuba (Santiago de Cuba) *5607*

V *Pilocarpus demerarae* Sandwith *20883*
    I   *20883* Guyana *20883*

E *Pilocarpus goudotianus* ssp. *heterochromus*
    Kaastra *20883*
    E   *20883* Colombia *20883*

E *Pilocarpus grandiflorus* Engler *20883*
    E   *20883* Brazil *20883*

E *Pilocarpus jaborandi* Holmes *20883, 17079*
    E   *20883* Brazil *20883*
    E   *17079* Brazil - Ceara *17079*
    E   *17746* Brazil - Pernambuco *17746*

R *Pilocarpus microphyllus* Stapf ex Wardleworth *20883,*
    17079
    I   *20883* Brazil *20883*
    E   *17746* Brazil - Maranhao *17746*
    E   *17079* Brazil - Pará (município de Marabá, serra Norte, Sao Luis,
            Maranhao, município de Parnaíba) *17079*
    E   *17746* Brazil - Piaui *17079*
    I   *20883* Suriname *20883*

R *Pilocarpus pennatifolius* var. *pilosus*
    Kaastra *20883*
    I   *20883* Brazil *20883*

R *Pilocarpus racemosus* ssp. *viridulus*
    Kaastra *20883*
    I   *20883* Costa Rica *20883*
    I   *20883* El Salvador *20883*

R *Pilocarpus spicatus* ssp. *aracatensis*
    Kaastra *20883*
    R   *20883* Brazil *20883*

R *Pilocarpus spicatus* ssp. *longeracemosus* (Martius ex
    Engler) Kaastra *20883*
    R   *20883* Brazil *20883*

R *Pitavia punctata* (R. et P.) Mol. *20883, 15088*
    R   *20883* Chile *20883*

V *Platydesma cornuta* Hbd. *20850, 14209*
    I   *20850* U.S. - Hawaii (O`ahu - Ko`olau Mts)
             20850

E *Platydesma cornuta* Hillebr. var.
    cornuta *20850*
    E   *20850* U.S. - Hawaii *20850*

V *Platydesma cornuta* Hillebrand var. *decurrens* B.C.
    Stone *20850, 14209*
    V   *20850* U.S. - Hawaii (O`ahu - Wai`anae Mts)
             20850

E *Platydesma remyi* (Sherff) O.& I. Deg., Sherff & B.C.
    Stone *20850, 14209*
    E   *20850* U.S. - Hawaii (Hamakua-Kohala) *20850*

E *Platydesma rostrata* Hbd. *20850, 14209*
    E   *20850* U.S. - Hawaii (Kaua`i) *20850*

R *Pleiospermium annamense* Guillaumin *6057*
    R   Vietnam *6057*

E *Raulinoa echinata* Cowan *20883*
    E   *20883* Brazil *20883*

V *Ravenia baracoensis* Borh. & Muniz *5607*
    V   *19105* Cuba (Guantanamo) *5607*

V *Ravenia carabiai* Kirouac *5607*
    V   *19105* Cuba (Holguin) *5607*

I *Ravenia swartziana* (Miers) F. & R. *20883, 13336*
    I   *13336* Jamaica *20883*

V *Ravenia urbanii* Engl. ex Urban *20883, 15106*
    I   *20883* Puerto Rico *20883*

R *Ruta chalepensis* L. ssp. *fumariifolia* (Boiss. &
    Heldr.) Nyman *20731*
    R   *20731* Greece - Crete *20731*

E *Ruta microcarpa* Svent. *17781*
    E   *20750* Spain - Canary Is. *20750*

R *Ruta oreojasme* Webb *20750*
    R   *20750* Spain - Canary Is. *20750*

V *Ruta pinnata* L.f. *20750*
    V   *20750* Spain - Canary Is. *20750*

E *Sarcomelicope glauca* T.Hartley *20893*
    E   *20893* New Caledonia *20893*

E *Sarcomelicope sarcococca* Engl.
    E   New Caledonia

R *Skimmia arisanensis* Hayata *20511*
    R   *20511* Taiwan *20511*

E *Spathelia coccinea* Proctor *20883, 13336*
    E   *13336* Jamaica *20883*

V *Spathelia glabrescens* Planch. *20883*
    V   *20883* Jamaica *20883*

R *Spathelia lobulata* Urban *5607*
    R   *19105* Cuba (Santiago de Cuba; Holguin) *5607*

V *Spathelia splendens* Urban *5607*
    V   *19105* Cuba (Holguin; Guantanamo) *5607*

V *Teclea carpopunctifera* A. Chev. *7926*
    V   *20887* Côte d'Ivoire (Fresco) *7926*

I *Teclea ferruginea* A. Chev. *7926*
    I   Mali (Sangali) *7926*

R *Teclea hanangensis* Kokwaro var.
    hanangensis *20057*
    R   *20057* Kenya (Moyale; Matakweni; Kilibasi; possibly
            Marsabit) *20057*
    R   *20057* Tanzania *17435*

R *Teclea hanangensis* Kokwaro var.
    unifoliolata *7959*
    R   *20057* Kenya *7959*

R	*Teclea macedoi* Exell & Mendonca *7906*		
	R	Mozambique *7906*	
I	*Thamnosma socotrana* Balf. f. *15534*		
	I	*15534* Yemen - Socotra *15534*	
R	*Thoreldora cochinchinensis* Pierre *6057*		
	R	Vietnam *6057*	
R	*Vepris carringtoniana* Mendonca *7749*		
	R	Mozambique *7749*	
R	*Vepris drummondii* Mendonca *7749*		
	V	*20909* Zimbabwe *7749*	
E	*Vepris glandulosa* (Hoyle & Leakey) Kokwaro *20057*		
	E	*20057* Kenya (Muguga; Ragati; Limuru) *20057*	
I	*Vepris hanangensis* (Kokwaro) W. Mziray var. unifoliata *21065*		
	I	*21065* Kenya (Karura Forest) *21065*	
E	*Vepris heterophylla* (Engl.) Letouzey *20274*		
	E	*20858* Cameroon *20274*	
	E	*20858* Ghana *6072*	
	E	*20858* Mali *20274*	
R	*Vepris mandangoa* Lisowski *19358*		
	R	*19358* Zaire *19358*	
R	*Vepris samburuensis* Kokwaro *7959*		
	R	*20057* Kenya (Northern Frontier Provence) *7959*	
R	*Zanthoxylum arnottianum* Maxim. *8038*		
	R	*19134* Japan - Ogasawara-shoto *8038*	
V	*Zanthoxylum atchoum* (Aké Assi) Waterman *20887*		
	V	*20887* Côte d'Ivoire *20887*	
V	*Zanthoxylum brieyi* *21117*		
	V	*21117* Zaire *21117*	
I	*Zanthoxylum caudatum* Alston *8021*		
	I	*16162* Sri Lanka (Dotalugala Kanda, Eratne) *8021*	
V	*Zanthoxylum chevalieri* Waterman *20274*		
	V	*20858* Tropical Africa (Upper Guinea) *20274*	
	V	*20858* Ghana *20274*	
R	*Zanthoxylum dipetalum* Mann *20850, 14209*		
	I	*20850* U.S. - Hawaii *20850*	
R	*Zanthoxylum dipetalum* Mann var. dipetalum *20850*		
	R	*20850* U.S. - Hawaii *20850*	
E	*Zanthoxylum dipetalum* H. Mann var. *tomentosum* Rock *20850, 14209, 21355*		
	E	*20850* U.S. - Hawaii (North Kona) *20850*	
E	*Zanthoxylum eliasii* D.M. Porter *20883, 9006*		
	I	*20883* Panama *20883*	
R	*Zanthoxylum ferrugineum* J.D. Smith *9037*		
	?		Belize *21313*
	R	*19793*	Costa Rica *9037*
	?		El Salvador *21313*
	?		Guatemala *21313*
	?		Honduras *21313*
	?		Nicaragua *21313*
	?		Panama *21313*
V	*Zanthoxylum harrisii* P.Wilson ex Britton *19435*		
	V	*13336* Jamaica (Portland) *13336*	
R	*Zanthoxylum hartii* (Krug & Urb.) P.Wilson *19435*		
	R	*13867* Jamaica *13336*	
E	*Zanthoxylum hawaiiense* Hbd. *20850, 21348, 21356*		
	E	*20850* U.S. - Hawaii *20850*	
V	*Zanthoxylum hawaiiense* Hillebrand var. hawaiiense *14209*		

	V	*14209* U.S. - Hawaii *14209*	
V	*Zanthoxylum heterophyllum* (Lam.) Smith *10082*		
	V	*14234* Réunion *14234*	
	E	*20771* Mauritius *5852*	
	Ex	*5852* Mauritius - Rodrigues *10936*	
E	*Zanthoxylum jaimei* D.M. Porter *20883, 9006*		
	I	*20883* Panama *20883*	
R	*Zanthoxylum kauaense* Gray *20850, 14209*		
	R	*20850* U.S. - Hawaii *20850*	
Ex	*Zanthoxylum leonis* Alain *15112*		
	Ex	*15112* Cuba *15112*	
E	*Zanthoxylum negrilense* Fawc. & Rendle *19435*		
	E	*13336* Jamaica (Westmoreland) *13336*	
V	*Zanthoxylum oahuense* Hbd. *20850, 14209*		
	V	*20850* U.S. - Hawaii *20850*	
E	*Zanthoxylum paniculatum* Balf.f. *10082*		
	E	*5852* Mauritius - Rodrigues (Anse Quitor) *5852*	
E	*Zanthoxylum parvum* Shinners *20850*		
	E	*20850* U.S. - Texas *20850*	
I	*Zanthoxylum pistaciiflorum* Hayata *20511*		
	I	*20511* Taiwan *20511*	
E	*Zanthoxylum psammophilum* (Aké Assi) Waterman *20887*		
	E	*20887* Côte d'Ivoire *20887*	
E	*Zanthoxylum pucro* D.M. Porter *20883, 9006*		
	I	*20883* Panama *20883*	
E	*Zanthoxylum thomasianum* (Krug & Urban) Krug & Urban e Wilson *20883, 7967*		
	I	*20883* Puerto Rico *20883*	
	I	*20883* USA - Virgin Is. (St Thomas & St John) *20883*	
E	*Zanthoxylum tripetalum* (Standl.) D.M. Porter *20883, 10747*		
	I	*20883* Panama *20883*	
R	*Zanthoxylum wutaiense* Chen *20511*		
	R	*20511* Taiwan *20511*	
E	*Zieria adenophora* Blakely *20681, 14223*		
	E	*20681* Australia - New South Wales *20681*	
E	*Zieria baeuerlenii* J.A.Armstrong ms. *20681*		
	E	*20681* Australia - New South Wales *20681*	
E	*Zieria buxijugum* J.D.Briggs & J.A.Armstrong ms. *20681*		
	E	*20681* Australia - New South Wales *20681*	
V	*Zieria chevalieri* Virot *20893*		
	V	*20893* New Caledonia *20893*	
V	*Zieria citriodora* J.A.Armstrong ms. *20681*		
	I	*20681* Australia - New South Wales *20681*	
	I	*20681* Australia - Victoria *20681*	
V	*Zieria collina* C.White *20681*		
	V	*20681* Australia - Queensland *20681*	
V	*Zieria covenyi* J.A.Armstrong ms. *20681*		
	V	*20681* Australia - New South Wales *20681*	
R	*Zieria floydii* J.A.Armstrong ms. *20681*		
	R	*20681* Australia - New South Wales *20681*	
E	*Zieria formosa* J.D.Briggs & J.A.Armstrong ms. *20681*		
	E	*20681* Australia - New South Wales *20681*	
V	*Zieria granulata* (F.Muell.) Benth. *20681*		
	V	*20681* Australia - New South Wales *20681*	
R	*Zieria hindii* J.A.Armstrong ms. *20681*		
	R	*20681* Australia - New South Wales *20681*	

The 1997 IUCN Red List of Threatened Plants

Magnoliopsida (dicots): Rutaceae: *Zieria*

V	*Zieria ingramii* J.A.Armstrong ms. *20681*	
	V	*20681* Australia - New South Wales *20681*
V	*Zieria involucrata* Benth. *20681*	
	V	*20681* Australia - New South Wales *20681*
V	*Zieria lasiocaulis* J.A.Armstrong ms. *20681*	
	V	*20681* Australia - New South Wales *20681*
R	*Zieria montana* J.A.Armstrong ms. *20681*	
	R	*20681* Australia - Queensland *20681*
V	*Zieria murphyi* Blakely *20681*	
	V	*20681* Australia - New South Wales *20681*
E	*Zieria obcordata* Cunn. *20681*	
	E	*20681* Australia - New South Wales *20681*
V	*Zieria obovata* (C.T.White) J.A.Armstrong ms *20681*	
	V	*20681* Australia - Queensland *20681*
R	*Zieria odorifera* J.A.Armstrong ms. *20681*	
	R	*20681* Australia - New South Wales *20681*
E	*Zieria parrisiae* J.D.Briggs & J.A.Armstrong ms. *20681*	
	E	*20681* Australia - New South Wales *20681*
E	*Zieria prostrata* J.A.Armstrong ms. *20681, 17916*	
	E	*20681* Australia - New South Wales *20681*
V	*Zieria rimulosa* C.White *20681*	
	V	*20681* Australia - Queensland *20681*
V	*Zieria tuberculata* J.A.Armstrong ms. *20681*	
	V	*20681* Australia - New South Wales *20681*
V	*Zieria verrucosa* J.A.Armstrong ms. *20681*	
	V	*20681* Australia - Queensland *20681*

Sabiaceae

Number of genera:	3
Number of species:	30
Recorded threatened species:	3 (10%)

Southeast Asia; tropical America.

R	*Sabia kontumensis* Gagnepain *6057*	
	R	Vietnam *6057*
I	*Sabia malabarica* Beddome	
	I	India - Kerala (Palghat)
	I	India - Tamil Nadu
R	*Sabia transarisanensis* Hayata *20511*	
	R	*20511* Taiwan *20511*

Salicaceae

Number of genera:	2
Number of species:	340
Recorded threatened species:	41 (12%)

Mostly North temperate; also Australia and Malay Archipelago.

I	*Populus berkarensis* Polj. *5942*	
	I	*5942* Kazakhstan (south) *5942*
I	*Populus cataracti* Komarov *5942*	
	I	*5942* Tajikistan (western border) *5942*
V	*Populus guzmanantlensis* Vázquez & Cuevas *21204*	
	V	*21204* Mexico - Jalisco *21204*
R	*Populus ilicifolia* (Engl.) Rouleau *20556, 10370*	
	R	*20057* Kenya *20057*
	E	Tanzania
R	*Populus simaroa* Rzed. *10071*	
	R	*19755* Mexico *10071*

R	*Salix antiatlantica* Maire & Wilczek	
	R	Morocco
V	*Salix arizonica* Dorn *20850*	
	V	*20850* U.S. - Arizona *20850*
	E	*20850* U.S. - Utah *20850*
V	*Salix brachycarpa* Nutt. var. *fullertonensis* (Schneid.) Argus *20883, 20850, 14352*	
	V	*13967* Canada - Franklin *13967*
	I	*20850* Canada - Ontario *20850*
	I	*20883* Puerto Rico *20883*
E	*Salix brachycarpa* Nutt. var. *psammophila* Raup *20850, 2063*	
	I	*20850* Canada - Manitoba *20850*
	E	*20850* Canada - Saskatchewan *20850*
R	*Salix breweri* Bebb *20850*	
	I	*20850* U.S. - California *20850*
	I	*20850* U.S. - Oregon *20850*
E	*Salix chlorolepis* Fern. *20850, 5567*	
	E	*20850* Canada - Quebec *20850*
V	*Salix floridana* Chapman *20850*	
	V	*20850* U.S. - Florida *20850*
	Ex/E	*20850* U.S. - Georgia *20850*
R	*Salix hegetschweileri* Heer *18264, 20171*	
	I	Austria *8000*
	I	France *8000*
	E	*18264* Italy (Trentino-Alto Adige) *18264*
	R	*18154* Switzerland *18154*
R	*Salix hidakamontana* Hara *10572*	
	R	Japan (Hidaka, Sorachi)
V	*Salix hukuokana* Kimura *10572*	
	V	*10572* Japan (Miyagi; Gunma) *20626*
R	*Salix hulteni* Floderus *15957*	
	R	*15923* Korea, South (Mt Sorak) *15957*
V	*Salix jejuna* Fern. *20850, 14366*	
	V	*20850* Canada - Newfoundland (Island) *20850*
V	*Salix kenoensis* Koidz. *10572*	
	V	*10572* Japan *10572*
R	*Salix kusanoi* (Hayata) Schneider *20511*	
	R	*20854* Taiwan *20511*
V	*Salix magnifica* Hemsl. *17617*	
	V	*17617* China - Sichuan *11139*
R	*Salix morii* Hayata *20854*	
	R	*20854* Taiwan *20854*
R	*Salix morrisonicola* Kimura *20511*	
	R	*20511* Taiwan *20511*
V	*Salix okamotoana* Koidz. *20854*	
	V	*20854* Taiwan *20854*
V	*Salix paludicola* Koidz. *10572*	
	V	*20626* Japan (Mt. Daisetsu) *20626*
R	*Salix pauciflora* Koidz. *10572*	
	R	*10572* Japan *10572*
E	*Salix pedunculata* Fern. *20850, 14366*	
	I	*20850* Canada - Labrador *20850*
	E	*20850* Canada - Newfoundland *20850*
	I	*20850* Canada - Ontario *20850*
V	*Salix planifolia* Pursh ssp. *tyrrellii* (Raup) Argus *20850, 14354*	
	I	*20850* Canada - Alberta *20850*
	E	*13967* Canada - British Columbia *13967*
	E	*13967* Canada - Mackenzie *13967*
	V	*20850* Canada - Saskatchewan *20850*
V	*Salix raupii* Argus *20850, 14346*	

E	20850	Canada - Alberta	*20850*
E	20850	Canada - British Columbia	*20850*
E	20850	Canada - Mackenzie	*20850*

V   *Salix reticulata* L. ssp. *glabellicarpa*
Argus *20850, 14352*

E	20850	Canada - British Columbia	*20850*
E	20850	U.S. - Alaska	*20850*

R   *Salix rizeensis* *20618*

R	20618	Turkey	*20618*

R   *Salix rorida* Lacksch. var. *roridaeformis*
Ohwi *10572*

R		Japan (Nagano)	

V   *Salix rupifraga* Koidz. *10572*

V	20626	Japan (Gunma; Nagano; Yamanashi)	*20626*

V   *Salix salvifolia* Brot. ssp. *australis*
Franco *20076*

V	20076	Portugal	*17891*

V   *Salix silicicola* Raup *20850, 2063*

E	20850	Canada - Keewatin	*20850*
V	20850	Canada - Saskatchewan	*20850*

R   *Salix stolonifera* Cov. ssp. *carbonicola*
Petrovsky *21309*

R	21309	Russia (E.Europe) - North	*21309*

R   *Salix tagawana* Koidz. *20854*

R	20854	Taiwan	*20854*

R   *Salix taiwanalpina* Kimura *20511*

R	20511	Taiwan	*20511*

R   *Salix takasagoalpina* Koidz. *20854*

R	20854	Taiwan	*20854*

V   *Salix tarraconensis* Pau *19174, 20171*

V	20692	Spain (Macizos de Cardó & Els Ports) *20692*	

R   *Salix trabzonica* A. Skv. *12840*

R	20618	Turkey	*20618*

V   *Salix turnorii* Raup *20850, 2063*

V	20850	Canada - Saskatchewan	*20850*

R   *Salix tweedyi* (Bebb ex Rose) Ball *20850, 13967*

E	20850	Canada - British Columbia	*20850*
I	20850	U.S. - Idaho	*20850*
I	20850	U.S. - Montana	*20850*
E	20850	U.S. - Washington	*20850*
V	20850	U.S. - Wyoming	*20850*

Santalaceae

Number of genera:	35	
Number of species:	400	
Recorded threatened species:	35	(8%)

Nearly cosmopolitan, especially arid climates.

V   *Amphorogyne staufferi* Markgraf *20893*

V	20893	New Caledonia	*20893*

V   *Buckleya distichophylla* (Nutt.) Torr. *20850*

V	20850	U.S. - North Carolina	*20850*
V	20850	U.S. - Tennessee	*20850*
V	20850	U.S. - Virginia	*20850*

V   *Elaphanthera baumannii* (Stauffer) Hallé *20893*

V	20893	New Caledonia	*20893*

R   *Exocarpos baumannii* Stauffer

R		New Caledonia	

V   *Exocarpos clavatus* Stauffer *20893*

V	20893	New Caledonia	*20893*

E   *Exocarpos gaudichaudii* A. DC. *20850, 14209*

E	20850	U.S. - Hawaii	*20850*

R   *Exocarpos homalocladus* C. Moore & F. Muell.

R	14225	Australia - NSW - Lord Howe Is.	*14225*

E   *Exocarpos luteolus* Forbes *20850, 14209*

E	20850	U.S. - Hawaii (Kaua`i)	*20850*

R   *Exocarpos menziesii* Stauffer *20850, 14209*

I	20850	U.S. - Hawaii	*20850*

I   *Exocarpos rolfeanus* (O. Kuntze) Merr. *13833*

I	13833	Philippines (Palawan)	*13833*

V   *Exocarpos spathulatus* Schltr. *20893*

V	20893	New Caledonia	*20893*

V   *Kunkeliella canariensis* Stearn *17534*

V	20750	Spain - Canary Is.	*17534*

E   *Kunkeliella psilotoclada* (Svent.) Stearn *17534*

E	20750	Spain - Canary Is.	*17534*

V   *Kunkeliella subsucculenta* Kammer *17534*

V	20750	Spain - Canary Is.	*17534*

Ex   *Leptomeria dielsiana* Pilger *20681, 14223*

Ex	20681	Australia - Western Australia	*20681*

Ex   *Leptomeria laxa* Miq. *20681*

Ex	20681	Australia - Western Australia	*20681*

E   *Quinchamalium brevistaminatum* Pilger *18200*

E	9446	Peru	*18200*

E   *Quinchamalium lomae* Pilger *18200*

E	9446	Peru	*18200*

E   *Santalum boninense* (Nakai) Tuy. *8038*

E	19134	Japan - Ogasawara-shoto	*8038*

Ex   *Santalum fernandezianum* F. Philippi *19116*

Ex	19116	Chile - Juan Fernandez Is.	*19116*

R   *Santalum freycinetianum* Gaud. *20850, 14209*

I	20850	U.S. - Hawaii	*20850*

V   *Santalum freycinetianum* Gaudich. var. *lanaiense*
Rock *20850, 14209*

V	20850	U.S. - Hawaii (Lana`i & Maui)	*20850*

V   *Santalum haleakalae* Hbd. *20850, 14209*

I	14209	U.S. - Hawaii (East Maui)	*20850*

V   *Santalum insulare* Bertero ex DC. var. *hendersonensis*
(F.Brown) Fosberg & Sachet *19185*

V	19185	Pitcairn (Henderson Is.)	*19187*

I   *Santalum marchionense* Skottsb.

I		French Polynesia - Marquesas Is	

V   *Spirogardnera rubescens* Stauffer *20681*

V	20681	Australia - Western Australia	*20681*

R   *Thesium aureum* Jaub. & Spach *12840*

R	12840	Turkey	*12840*

R   *Thesium auriculatum* Vandas *20178, 20171*

R	20178	Albania	*20178*
R	21091	Bosnia & Herzegovina	*21091*
R		(former) Yugoslavia	*20178*

R   *Thesium bertramii* Aznav. *12840*

R	12840	Turkey	*12840*

R   *Thesium chimanimanense* Brenan *7758*

R		Zimbabwe (Chimanimani)	*7758*

R   *Thesium cilicicum* Bornm. *12840*

R	12840	Turkey	*12840*

R   *Thesium coarctiflorum* Hendrych

R		Greece	

R   *Thesium dolichomeres* Brenan *7758*

	R		Zimbabwe (Chimanimani) *7758*
R	*Thesium kernerianum* Simonk. *17823, 20171*		
	R	*19949*	Romania (S. & E. Carpathians) *19266*
R	*Thesium litoreum* Brenan *20604*		
	R	*20604*	South Africa - Cape Province *20604*
R	*Thesium matteii* Chiov. *19704*		
	R	*19704*	Ethiopia (Gojam, Shewa Upland, Arsi.) *19704*
R	*Thesium minkwitzianum* B. Fedtsch.		
	R		former USSR *6930*
R	*Thesium oreogetum* hendrych *12840*		
	R	*12840*	Turkey *12840*
Ex	*Thesium polygaloides* A.W.Hill *20604*		
	Ex	*20604*	South Africa - Natal *20604*
V	*Thesium scabriflorum* Davis *12840*		
	V	*12840*	Turkey *12840*
R	*Thesium stelleroides* Jaub. & Spach *12840*		
	R	*12840*	Turkey *12840*

Sapindaceae

Number of genera:	140
Number of species:	1,500
Recorded threatened species:	144 (9%)

Tropical and subtropical; some in temperate regions.

V	*Alectryon macrococcus* Radlk. *20850, 14209*		
	I	*14209*	U.S. - Hawaii *20850*
E	*Alectryon macrococcus* Radlk. var. *auwahiensis* G. Linney *20850, 14209*		
	E	*20850*	U.S. - Hawaii (east Maui) *20850*
V	*Alectryon macrococcus* Radlk. var. *macrococcus* *20850*		
	V	*20850*	U.S. - Hawaii *20850*
E	*Alectryon ramiflorus* S.Reynolds *20681, 21304*		
	E	*20681*	Australia - Queensland *20681*
R	*Alectryon samoensis* Christoph. *7925*		
	R		Western Samoa (Savaii) *7925*
R	*Alectryon tropicus* S.T.Reynolds *20681*		
	R	*20681*	Australia - Queensland *20681*
R	*Allophylus agbala* Hauman *19358*		
	R	*19358*	Zaire (Ubangi-Uele) *19358*
R	*Allophylus amplissimus* Hauman *19358*		
	R	*19358*	Zaire (Haut-Katanga) *19358*
V	*Allophylus chirindensis* Baker f. *20572*		
	V	*20932*	Mozambique (Espungabera) *20932*
	V	*20909*	Zimbabwe (east) *20575*
R	*Allophylus concanicus* Radlk. *13883*		
	R	*13883*	India - Maharashtra *13883*
E	*Allophylus gentryi* Croat *20883, 9006*		
	I	*20883*	Panama *20883*
V	*Allophylus hispidus* (Thwaites) Trimen *10276*		
	V	*12838*	Sri Lanka *10276*
R	*Allophylus letestui* Pellegrin *7927*		
	R		Gabon (Ayem & Koulamotou) *7927*
V	*Allophylus marquesensis* F. Brown		
	V		French Polynesia - Marquesas Is
R	*Allophylus pachyphyllus* Radlk. *20883, 13336*		
	R	*13336*	Jamaica *20883*
V	*Allophylus sechellensis* Summerh. *14296*		

	V	*19181*	Seychelles *14296*
V	*Allophylus zeylanicus* L. *10276*		
	V	*12838*	Sri Lanka *10276*
V	*Allophylus zimmermannianus* F.G. Davies Ined. *20057*		
	E/V	*20057*	Kenya *20057*
	V	*20900*	Tanzania (coast) *20900*
V	*Amesiodendron tienlinensis* H.S. Lo *17617*		
	V	*17617*	China - Guangxi *11139*
	V	*17617*	China - Guizhou *11139*
R	*Arytera dictyoneura* S.T.Reynolds *20681*		
	R	*20681*	Australia - Queensland *20681*
V	*Arytera nekorensis* H.Turner *20893*		
	V	*20893*	New Caledonia *20893*
R	*Atalaya calcicola* S.T.Reynolds *20681*		
	R	*20681*	Australia - Queensland *20681*
R	*Atalaya capensis* R.A.Dyer *20604*		
	R	*20604*	South Africa - Cape Province *20604*
E	*Atalaya collina* S.Reynolds *20681*		
	E	*20681*	Australia - Queensland *20681*
R	*Atalaya natalensis* R.A.Dyer *20604*		
	R	*20604*	South Africa - Natal *20604*
R	*Atalaya rigida* S.T.Reynolds *20681*		
	R	*20681*	Australia - Queensland *20681*
R	*Bottegoa insignis* Chiov. *20057*		
	R	*20884*	Ethiopia *20884*
	R	*20884*	Kenya *20057*
	R	*20884*	Somalia (central & south) *20884*
R	*Camptolepis ramiflora* (Taub.) Radjk. *7959*		
	?		Madagascar *20271*
	R	*20884*	Kenya (east) *20884*
	R	*20884*	Somalia (south) *20271*
	R	*20884*	Tanzania (east) *7959*
V	*Cardiospermum dissectum* (S.Watson) Radlk. *20850*		
	V	*20850*	U.S. - Texas *20850*
R	*Cardiospermum galapageium* Robinson & Greenman *11117*		
	R		Ecuador - Galapagos (Isabela, Santiago, south Cruz) *11117*
R	*Chytranthus obliquinervis* Radlk. *17435*		
	R	*17435*	Kenya *17435*
	R	*17435*	Tanzania (east Usambaras) *17435*
R	*Chytranthus verecundus* Halle & Ake Assi		
	R		Côte d'Ivoire
E	*Cossinia australiana* S.T.Reynolds *20681*		
	E	*20681*	Australia - Queensland *20681*
V	*Cossinia trifoliata* (Baillon) Radlk. *20893*		
	V	*20893*	New Caledonia *20893*
E	*Cupania dukei* Croat *20883, 9006*		
	I	*20883*	Panama *20883*
E	*Cupania sylvatica* Croat var. *fosteri* Croat *20883, 9006*		
	I	*20883*	Panama *20883*
Ex	*Cupaniopsis crassivalvis* Radlk. *20802*		
	Ex	*20802*	New Caledonia *20802*
E	*Cupaniopsis glabra* Adema *20893*		
	E	*20893*	New Caledonia *20893*
V	*Cupaniopsis globosa* Adèma *20802*		
	V	*20893*	New Caledonia *20802*
E	*Cupaniopsis mouana* Guillaumin *20893*		
	E	*20893*	New Caledonia *20893*
R	*Cupaniopsis newmanii* S.T.Reynolds *20681*		

	I	20681	Australia - New South Wales *20681*
	I	20681	Australia - Queensland *20681*
E	*Cupaniopsis rosea* Adema *20893*		
	E	20893	New Caledonia *20893*
E	*Cupaniopsis rotundifolia* Adema *20893*		
	E	20893	New Caledonia *20893*
V	*Cupaniopsis shirleyana* (Bailey) Radlk. *20681*		
	V	20681	Australia - Queensland *20681*
E	*Cupaniopsis squamosa* Adema *20893*		
	E	20893	New Caledonia *20893*
E	*Cupaniopsis subfalcata* Adema *20893*		
	E	20893	New Caledonia *20893*
V	*Cupaniopsis tomentella* (F.Muell. ex Benth.) S.Reyn. *20681*		
	V	20681	Australia - Queensland *20681*
E	*Cupaniopsis tontoutensis* Guillaumin *20893*		
	E	20893	New Caledonia *20893*
R	*Deinbollia longiacuminata* Hauman *19358*		
	R	19358	Zaire (central Forestier) *19358*
V	*Deinbollia molliuscula* Radlk. *20858*		
	V	20858	Côte d'Ivoire *20858*
	V	20858	Ghana *20858*
E	*Deinbollia nyasica* Exell *7749*		
	E		Malawi *7749*
R	*Deinbollia rambaensis* Pellegrin *7927*		
	R		Gabon (Ramba) *7927*
I	*Deinbollia saligna* Keay *20274*		
	I	20274	Cameroon *20749*
	I	20274	Ghana *20274*
	I	20274	Nigeria *20274*
E	*Deinbollia voltensis* Hutch. ex Burtt, Davy & Hoyle *7926*		
	E	6072	Ghana (Yeji, River Volta) *7926*
V	*Dimocarpus longan* Lour. *17617*		
	?		China *21059*
	V	17617	China - Hainan Is. *11139*
R	*Diploglottis bracteata* Leenh. *20681*		
	R	20681	Australia - Queensland *20681*
R	*Diploglottis harpullioides* S.T.Reynolds *20681*		
	R	20681	Australia - Queensland *20681*
R	*Diploglottis pedleyi* S.T.Reynolds *20681*		
	R	20681	Australia - Queensland *20681*
R	*Distichostemon arnhemicus* S.T.Reynolds *20681*		
	R	20681	Australia - Northern Territory *20681*
R	*Dodonaea biloba* J.West *20681*		
	R	20681	Australia - Queensland *20681*
R	*Dodonaea hackettiana* Fitzg. *20681*		
	R	20681	Australia - Western Australia *20681*
R	*Dodonaea hirsuta* Maiden & Betche *20681*		
	I	20681	Australia - New South Wales *20681*
	I	20681	Australia - Queensland *20681*
R	*Dodonaea macrossanii* F.Muell. & Scortechini *20681*		
	I	20681	Australia - New South Wales *20681*
	I	20681	Australia - Queensland *20681*
V	*Dodonaea procumbens* F.Muell. *20681*		
	I	20681	Australia - New South Wales *20681*
	I	20681	Australia - South Australia *20681*
	I	20681	Australia - Victoria *20681*
R	*Dodonaea rhombifolia* Wakef. *20681*		
	I	20681	Australia - New South Wales *20681*

	I	20681	Australia - Victoria *20681*
V	*Dodonaea rupicola* C.White *20681*		
	V	20681	Australia - Queensland *20681*
R	*Dodonaea serratifolia* McGillivray *20681*		
	R	20681	Australia - New South Wales *20681*
E	*Dodonaea subglandulifera* J.West *20681*		
	E	20681	Australia - South Australia *20681*
R	*Dodonaea uncinata* J.West *20681*		
	R	20681	Australia - Queensland *20681*
R	*Dodonaea viscosa* Jacq. var. *galapagensis* (Sherff) D. Porter *11117*		
	R		Ecuador - Galapagos (V. Darwin & Alcedo; Pinta) *11117*
V	*Elattostachys dzumacensis* Adéma *20893*		
	V	20893	New Caledonia *20893*
E	*Erythrophysa septentrionalis* Verdc. *19704*		
	E	19704	Ethiopia (Harerge) *19704*
R	*Erythrophysa transvaalensis* I.Verd. *20604*		
	R	20604	South Africa - Transvaal *20604*
Ex	*Euchorium cubense* Ekman & Radlk. *5607*		
	Ex	19105	Cuba (Pinar del Rio) *5607*
R	*Eurycorymbus cavaleriei* (A. Leve.) Rehder & Hand.-Mazz. *17617*		
	R	17617	China - Fujian *11139*
	R	17617	China - Guangdong *11139*
	R	17617	China - Guangxi *11139*
	R	17617	China - Guizhou *11139*
	R	17617	China - Hubei *11139*
	R	17617	China - Hunan *11139*
	R	17617	China - Jiangxi *11139*
	R	17617	China - Yunnan *11139*
	R	17617	Taiwan *17617*
V	*Glenniea unijuga* (Thwaites) Radlk. *10276*		
	V	12838	Sri Lanka *10276*
R	*Guioa coriacea* (Radlk.) Radlk.		
	R	14225	Australia - NSW - Lord Howe Is. *14225*
R	*Guioa krempfii* Gagnepain *6057*		
	R		Vietnam *6057*
R	*Haplocoelopsis africana* F.G. Davies *20057*		
	?		Angola *20900*
	R	20057	Kenya *20057*
	R	20057	Tanzania *17435*
R	*Haplocoelum mombasense* Bullock *20057*		
	R	20057	Kenya *20057*
	R	20057	Tanzania *17435*
I	*Haplocoelum trigonocarpum* Radlk. *20057*		
	I	20057	Kenya *20057*
	I	20057	Mozambique *17435*
	R	20884	Somalia *20884*
	I	20057	Tanzania *17435*
V	*Hedyachras philippinensis* Radlk.		
	V		Philippines
R	*Hornea mauritiana* Baker *10082*		
	R	20771	Mauritius *10082*
V	*Houssayanthus incanus* (Radlk.) Ferruci *20883*		
	I	20883	Paraguay *20883*
E	*Lecaniodiscus punctatus* J.B. Hall *10260*		
	E	20858	Cameroon *10260*
	E	20858	Ghana (Baku & Supong Frs.) *20274*
R	*Lepiderema hirsuta* S.T.Reynolds *20681*		
	R	20681	Australia - Queensland *20681*
R	*Lepiderema largiflorens* S.T.Reynolds *20681*		

R   20681   Australia - Queensland *20681*

R   *Lepiderema pulchella* Radlk. *20681*
    I   20681   Australia - New South Wales *20681*
    I   20681   Australia - Queensland *20681*

R   *Lepisanthes banaensis* Gagnepain *6057*
    R   Vietnam *6057*

I   *Lepisanthes palawanica* Radlk. *13833*
    I   13833   Philippines *13833*

V   *Litchi chinensis* Sonn. var. *euspontanea*
       Hsue *17617*
    V   17617   China - Guangdong (Xuweng) *11139*
    V   17617   China - Hainan Is. *11139*

E   *Matayba kennedyi* Croat *20883, 9006*
    I   20883   Panama *20883*

R   *Matayba miquelii* Uittien *8679*
    R   8679   Suriname *8679*

R   *Mischocarpus albescens* S.T.Reynolds *20681*
    R   20681   Australia - Queensland *20681*

I   *Mischocarpus endotrichus* Radlk. *13833*
    I   13833   Philippines (Palawan) *13833*

R   *Molinaea macrantha* Radlk. *10082*
    R   20771   Mauritius *10082*

R   *Otophora poilanei* Gagnepain *6057*
    R   Vietnam *6057*

Ex/E   *Otophora unilocularis* (Leenh.) Lo *17617, 21304*
    Ex/E   17617   China - Hainan Is. (Ledong) *11139*

E   *Paranephelium hainanensis* H.S. Lo *17617*
    E   17617   China - Hainan Is. (Yaxian) *11139*

E   *Paullinia allenii* Standl. *20883, 9006*
    I   20883   Panama *20883*

V   *Paullinia baileyi* Standl. *20883, 9006*
    I   20883   Panama *20883*

R   *Paullinia bernhardi* Uittien *8679*
    R   8679   Suriname *8679*

E   *Paullinia bristanii* Croat *20883, 9006*
    I   20883   Panama *20883*

E   *Paullinia buricana* Croat *20883, 9006*
    I   20883   Panama *20883*

E   *Paullinia correae* Croat *20883, 9006*
    I   20883   Panama *20883*

E   *Paullinia dukei* Croat *20883, 9006*
    I   20883   Panama *20883*

V   *Paullinia eliasii* Croat *20883, 9006*
    I   20883   Panama *20883*

I   *Paullinia excisa* Radlk. *5932*
    I   5932   Trinidad & Tobago (Tobago) *5932*

E   *Paullinia funicularis* Radlk. *20883, 9006*
    I   20883   Panama *20883*

E   *Paullinia kallunkii* Croat *20883, 9006*
    I   20883   Panama *20883*

E   *Paullinia morii* Croat *20883, 9006*
    I   20883   Panama *20883*

R   *Paullinia novemalata* Uittien *8679*
    R   8679   Suriname *8679*

E   *Paullinia panamensis* Croat *20883, 9006*
    I   20883   Panama *20883*

E   *Paullinia pilonensis* Croat *20883, 9006*
    I   20883   Panama *20883*

V   *Paullinia sessiliflora* Croat var. *angustirachis*
       Croat *20883, 9006*
    I   20883   Panama *20883*

E   *Paullinia sternii* Croat *20883, 9006*
    I   20883   Panama *20883*

E   *Placodiscus attenuatus* J.B. Hall *20274, 10260*
    E   20858   Côte d'Ivoire *10260*
    E   20858   Ghana *20858*

V   *Placodiscus bancoensis* Aubrev. & Pellegr. *20274*
    V   20858   Côte d'Ivoire *20274*
    V   20858   Ghana *20274*

V   *Placodiscus boya* Aubrev. & Pellegr. *15970*
    V   20858   Côte d'Ivoire *20858*
    V   20858   Ghana *15970*

V   *Placodiscus bracteosus* J.B.Hall *20274*
    V   20858   Côte d'Ivoire *20274*
    V   20858   Ghana *20274*

V   *Placodiscus oblongifolius* J.B.Hall *20274*
    V   20858   Tropical Africa (Upper Guinea) *20274*
    V   20858   Ghana *20274*

R   *Placodiscus paniculatus* Hauman *19358*
    R   19358   Zaire (central Forestier) *19358*

E   *Placodiscus pseudostipularis* Radlk. *20274*
    V   20858   Côte d'Ivoire *7926*
    E   20858   Ghana *20274*
    V   20858   Liberia *7926*
    V   20858   Sierra Leone *7926*

R   *Podonephelium parvifolium* Radlk.
    R   New Caledonia

R   *Pseudima costaricensis* L.O. Williams & P.
       Allen *11990*
    R   11992   Costa Rica *11990*

R   *Sapindus boninensis* Nakai *8622*
    R   19134   Japan - Kazan Retto *8622*
    R   19134   Japan - Ogasawara-shoto *8622*

V   *Sapindus grandifolius* Lippold *5607*
    V   19105   Cuba (Guantanamo) *5607*

V   *Sapindus oahuensis* Hillebrand *20850*
    I   20850   U.S. - Hawaii (Kaua`i and O`ahu) *20850*

R   *Sarcopteryx acuminata* S.T.Reynolds *20681*
    R   20681   Australia - Queensland *20681*

R   *Sarcopteryx montana* S.T.Reynolds *20681*
    R   20681   Australia - Queensland *20681*

R   *Sarcotoechia heterophylla* S.T.Reynolds *20681*
    R   20681   Australia - Queensland *20681*

R   *Sarcotoechia serrata* S.T.Reynolds *20681*
    R   20681   Australia - Queensland *20681*

R   *Sarcotoechia villosa* S.T.Reynolds *20681*
    R   20681   Australia - Queensland *20681*

V   *Serjania allenii* Croat *20883*
    I   20883   Panama *20883*

E   *Serjania darcyi* Croat *20883, 9006*
    I   20883   Panama *20883*

V   *Serjania equestris* Macf. *20883*
    V   20883   Jamaica *20883*

R   *Serjania laevigata* Radlk. *20883*
    R   20883   Jamaica *20883*

V   *Serjania linearifolia* Lippold *5607*
    V   19105   Cuba (Granma) *5607*

E   *Serjania pluvialiflorens* Croat *20883*

	I	20883	Panama *20883*
R	***Storthocalyx sordidus*** Radlk.		
	R		New Caledonia
E	***Talisia dwyeri*** Croat *20883, 9006*		
	I	20883	Panama *20883*
R	***Talisia eximia*** Kramer *8679*		
	R	8679	Suriname *8679*
R	***Talisia microphylla*** Uittien *8679*		
	R	8679	Suriname *8679*
E	***Thouinia acunae*** Borh. & Muniz *5607*		
	E	19105	Cuba (Santiago de Cuba) *5607*
R	***Thouinia striata*** Radlk. *20883*		
	I	20883	Puerto Rico *20883*
I	***Thraulococcus simplicifolius*** (Thwaites) Radlk. *10252*		
	I	16162	Sri Lanka *16162*
R	***Toechima monticola*** S.T.Blake *20681*		
	R	20681	Australia - Queensland *20681*
E	***Toechima pterocarpum*** S.T.Reynolds *20681*		
	E	20681	Australia - Queensland *20681*

Sapotaceae

Number of genera: 70
Number of species: 800
Recorded threatened species: 361 (45%)

Tropical.

	Aesandra dongnaiensis Pierre *6057*		
	R		Vietnam *6057*
R	***Amorphospermum whitei*** Aubrev. *20681*		
	I	20681	Australia - New South Wales *20681*
	I	20681	Australia - Queensland *20681*
E	***Aubregrinia taiensis*** Aubrev. & Pellegrin *7926*		
	E	20887	Côte d'Ivoire *7926*
	E	20858	Ghana *6072*
E	***Beccariella brevipedicellata*** (Royen) Aubrev. *20893*		
	E	20893	New Caledonia *20893*
I	***Breviea sericea*** Aubrev. & Pellegr. *20274*		
	V	20887	Côte d'Ivoire *20274*
	I	6072	Ghana *20274*
	?		Zaire *20274*
	Bumelia acunae Borh. *5607*		
	E	19105	Cuba (Holguin; Guantanamo) *5607*
	Bumelia harmandii Lecomte *6057*		
	R		Vietnam *6057*
	Bumelia nigra Sw. *20883*		
	R	20883	Jamaica *20883*
	Bumelia octosepala (Urb.) Stearn *20883, 19890*		
	R	19890	Jamaica (Cockpit) *20883*
	Bumelia revoluta Urban *5607*		
	V	19105	Cuba (Holguin; Guantanamo) *5607*
R	***Chromolucuma baehniana*** Monachino *20883*		
	I	20883	Brazil *20883*
	I	20883	Guyana *20883*
R	***Chromolucuma rubriflora*** Ducke *20883*		
	I	20883	Brazil *20883*
	I	20883	Venezuela *20883*
R	***Chrysophyllum acreanum*** A. C. Smith *20883*		
	I	20883	Brazil *20883*
	I	20883	Brazil - Acre *20883*
E	***Chrysophyllum albipilum*** Cronq. *20883*		

	I	20883	Peru *20883*
R	***Chrysophyllum arenarium*** F. Allemao *20883*		
	I	20883	Brazil *20883*
	R	20992	Brazil - Ceara *16326*
	R	20992	Brazil - Maranhao *16326*
	R	20992	Brazil - Pernambuco *16326*
E	***Chrysophyllum azaguieanum*** Miege *20274*		
	E	20858	Côte d'Ivoire *20858*
	E	20858	Ghana *20274*
R	***Chrysophyllum bombycinum*** Pennington *20883*		
	I	20883	Brazil *20883*
	I	20883	Peru *20883*
R	***Chrysophyllum brenesii*** Cronq. *20883, 16326*		
	I	20883	Costa Rica (Pacific drainage) *20883*
	I	20883	Panama (Pacific drainage) *20883*
E	***Chrysophyllum durifructum*** (Rodrigues) Pennington *20883*		
	E	20883	Brazil *20883*
	E	20992	Brazil - Amazonas *16326*
E	***Chrysophyllum eggersii*** Pierre *20883*		
	I	20883	Puerto Rico *20883*
	I	20883	USA - Virgin Is. *20883*
E	***Chrysophyllum euryphyllum*** Pennington *20883*		
	E	20883	Colombia *20883*
R	***Chrysophyllum flexuosum*** Martius *20883*		
	I	20883	Brazil *20883*
	R	20992	Brazil - Bahia *16326*
	R	20992	Brazil - Minas Gerais *16326*
	R	20992	Brazil - Rio de Janeiro *16326*
	R	20992	Brazil - Sao Paulo *16326*
R	***Chrysophyllum hirsutum*** Cronq. *20883, 16326*		
	I	20883	Costa Rica *20883*
	I	20883	Panama (central) *20883*
E	***Chrysophyllum imperiale*** (Linden ex Koch) Bentham & Hooker *20883*		
	E	20883	Brazil *20883*
	E	20992	Brazil - Minas Gerais *16326*
	E	20992	Brazil - Rio de Janeiro *16326*
R	***Chrysophyllum inornatum*** Martius *20883*		
	R	20883	Brazil *20883*
	R	20992	Brazil - Parana *16326*
	R	20992	Brazil - Rio Grande do Sul *16326*
	R	20992	Brazil - Santa Catarina *16326*
E	***Chrysophyllum januariense*** Eichler *20883*		
	E	20883	Brazil *20883*
	Ex	20992	Brazil - Rio de Janeiro *16326*
V	***Chrysophyllum lanatum*** Pennington *20883*		
	I	20883	Colombia *20883*
R	***Chrysophyllum lucentifolium*** Cronquist ssp. *lucentifolium* *20883*		
	R	20883	Brazil *20883*
	R	20992	Brazil - Bahia *16326*
	R	20992	Brazil - Espirito Santo *16326*
	R	20992	Brazil - Rio de Janeiro *16326*
R	***Chrysophyllum oliviforme*** L. ssp. *angustifolium* (Lamarck) Pennington *20883*		
	I	20883	Dominican Republic *20883*
	I	20883	Haiti *20883*
R	***Chrysophyllum ovale*** Rusby *20883*		
	I	20883	Bolivia *20883*
	I	20883	Brazil *20883*
	I	20883	Peru *20883*
V	***Chrysophyllum paranaense*** Pennington *20883*		
	V	20883	Brazil *20883*
	V	20992	Brazil - Parana *16326*

V		20992	Brazil - Sao Paulo *16326*

R   *Chrysophyllum parvulum* Pittier *20883*
- I   20883   Colombia *20883*
- I   20883   Venezuela *20883*

R   *Chrysophyllum pauciflorum* Lam. *20883*
- I   20883   Puerto Rico *20883*
- I   20883   USA - Virgin Is. *20883*

E   *Chrysophyllum revolutum* Martius & Eichler *20883*
- I   20883   Peru *20883*

R   *Chrysophyllum scalare* Pennington *20883*
- I   20883   Peru *20883*
- I   20883   Venezuela *20883*

R   *Chrysophyllum splendens* Sprengel *20883*
- R   20883   Brazil *20883*
- V   20992   Brazil - Bahia *16326*
- V   20992   Brazil - Espirito Santo *16326*
- V   20992   Brazil - Pernambuco *16326*

E   *Chrysophyllum striatum* Pennington *20883, 16326*
- I   20883   Panama (Los Santos) *20883*

E   *Chrysophyllum subspinosum* Monachino *20883*
- E   20883   Brazil *20883*
- E   20992   Brazil - Bahia *16326*

E   *Chrysophyllum superbum* Pennington *20883*
- E   20883   Brazil *20883*

R   *Chrysophyllum viride* Martius & Eichler *20883, 20311*
- I   20883   Brazil *20883*
- ?   Brazil - Rio Grande do Sul *20311*
- ?   Brazil - Santa Catarina *20310*

I   *Delpydora macrophylla* Pierre
- I   Gabon (Libreville)

I   *Diploknema siamensis* Fletcher *19120*
- I   19120   Thailand *19120*

R   *Ecclinusa bullata* Pennington *20883*
- I   20883   Brazil *20883*
- I   20883   Venezuela *20883*

E   *Ecclinusa dumetorum* (Baehni) Pennington *20883*
- E   20883   Suriname *20883*

R   *Ecclinusa lancifolia* (Martius & Eichler) Eyma *20883*
- I   20883   Brazil *20883*
- V   20992   Brazil - Amazonas *16326*

V   *Ecclinusa orinocoensis* Aubréville *20883*
- I   20883   Venezuela *20883*

E   *Ecclinusa parviflora* Pennington *20883*
- I   20883   Venezuela *20883*

R   *Ecclinusa psilophylla* Sandwith *20883*
- I   20883   Guyana *20883*
- I   20883   Suriname *20883*

R   *Ecclinusa ulei* Gilly ex Cronquist *20883*
- I   20883   Venezuela *20883*

V   *Elaeoluma crispa* Pennington *20883*
- I   20883   Venezuela *20883*

V   *Gluema ivorensis* Aubrev. & Pellegrin *7926*
- V   20858   Cameroon *9772*
- V   20858   Côte d'Ivoire
- V   20858   Gabon
- V   20858   Ghana *20274*

R   *Handeliodendron bodinieri* (Leveille) Rehder *17617*
- R   China - Guangxi *11139*
- R   17617   China - Guizhou *11139*

I   *Isonandra montana* (Thwaites) Gamble
- I   India - Kerala (Travancore Hills)

R   *Isonandra perakensis* King & Gamble

R		Malaysia - Peninsular Malaysia (Pahang; Kelantan)

V   *Isonandra stocksii* Clarke *14782*
- V   14782   India (western peninsular India) *14782*

I   *Isonandra villosa* Wight *14782*
- I   14782   India - Kerala *14782*
- I   14782   India - Tamil Nadu *14782*

E   *Iteiluma leptostylidifolium* (Guillaumin) Aubrev. *20893*
- E   20893   New Caledonia *20893*

E   *Iteiluma pinifolium* (Baillon) Aubrev. *20893*
- E   20893   New Caledonia *20893*

E   *Iteiluma rheophytopsis* (Royen) Aubrev. *20893*
- E   20893   New Caledonia *20893*

V   *Labourdonnaisia glauca* Bojer *10082*
- V   20771   Mauritius *10082*

V   *Labourdonnaisia revoluta* Bojer *10082*
- V   20771   Mauritius *10082*

I   *Lecomtedoxa heitzana* (A. Chev.) Aubrev.
- I   Gabon

I   *Lecomtedoxa nogo* (A. Chev.) Aubrev. *7927*
- I   Gabon (Fernan Vaz) *7927*

E   *Leptostylis gatopensis* Guillaumin *20893*
- E   20893   New Caledonia *20893*

E   *Leptostylis goroensis* Aubrev. *20893*
- E   20893   New Caledonia *20893*

V   *Leptostylis multiflora* Vink *20893*
- V   20893   New Caledonia *20893*

V   *Leptostylis petiolata* Vink *20893*
- E   20893   New Caledonia *20893*

R   *Madhuca alpina* (Chev.) Chev. *6057*
- R   Vietnam *6057*

Ex/E   *Madhuca bourdillonii* (Gamble) Raiz. *14782*
- Ex/E   14782   India - Kerala (Travancore) *14782*

I   *Madhuca calcicola* P. van Royen
- I   Malaysia - Peninsular Malaysia (Langkawi, Kedah)

E   *Madhuca diplostemon* (Clarke) van Royen *14782*
- E   20263   India *14782*

R   *Madhuca elliptica* (Pierre & Dub.) H.J. Lam *6057*
- R   Vietnam *6057*

R   *Madhuca floribunda* (Pierre) H.J. Lam *6057*
- R   Vietnam *6057*

V   *Madhuca fulva* Macbr. *10276*
- V   12838   Sri Lanka *10276*

V   *Madhuca hainanensis* Chun & How *17617*
- V   17617   China - Hainan Is. *11139*

Ex/E   *Madhuca insignis* (Radlk.) H.J. Lam *14782*
- Ex/E   14782   India - Karnataka *14782*

I   *Madhuca kerrii* Fletcher *12983*
- I   19120   Thailand *12983*

I   *Madhuca longistyla* (K. & G.) Lam *19209*
- I   19209   Malaysia - Peninsular Malaysia (Perak) *19209*

E   *Madhuca moonii* (Thwaites) H.J. Lam *10252*
- E   12838   Sri Lanka *10252*

R   *Madhuca pasquieri* (Dubard) Lam. *17617*
- R   17617   China - Guangdong *11139*
- R   17617   China - Guangxi *11139*
- R   17617   China - Yunnan (Malipe, Bingbian) *11139*
- K   20985   Vietnam *6057*

I   *Madhuca punctata* Fletcher *19120*
   I   *19120*   Thailand *19120*

I   *Madhuca tokinsis* Aubreville *19120*
   I   *19120*   Thailand *19120*

E   *Manilkara bella* Monachino *20883*
   E   *20883*   Brazil *20883*
   E   *20992*   Brazil - Espirito Santo *16326*
   E   *20992*   Brazil - Rio de Janeiro *16326*

E   *Manilkara bolivarensis* Pennington *20883*
   I   *20883*   Venezuela *20883*

R   *Manilkara cavalcantei* Pires & Rodrigues ex
   Pennington *20883*
   R   *20883*   Brazil *20883*
   E   *20992*   Brazil - Amazonas *16326*
   E   *20992*   Brazil - Pará *16326*

E   *Manilkara dardanoi* Ducke *20883*
   E   *20883*   Brazil *20883*
   E   *20992*   Brazil - Pernambuco *16326*

E   *Manilkara decrescens* Pennington *20883*
   E   *20883*   Brazil *20883*
   E   *20992*   Brazil - Bahia *16326*

E   *Manilkara elata* (F. Allemao ex Miquel)
   Monachino *20883*
   E   *20883*   Brazil *20883*
   E   *20992*   Brazil - Bahia *16326*
   E   *20992*   Brazil - Espirito Santo *16326*

V   *Manilkara excelsa* (Ducke) Standley *20883*
   V   *20883*   Brazil *20883*
   V   *20992*   Brazil - Amazonas *16326*
   V   *20992*   Brazil - Mato Grosso *16326*
   V   *20992*   Brazil - Pará *16326*

V   *Manilkara excisa* (Urb.) Gilly *20883, 13336*
   V   *13336*   Jamaica (St. James, Trelawny) *20883*

E   *Manilkara gonavensis* (Urban & Ekman) Gilly ex
   Cronquist *20883*
   E   *20883*   Haiti *20883*

R   *Manilkara jaimiqui* (C. Wright ex Griseb.) Dubard ssp.
   haitensis (Cronquist) Cronquist *20883*
   I   *20883*   Dominican Republic *20883*
   I   *20883*   Haiti *20883*
   I   *20883*   Puerto Rico *20883*

R   *Manilkara jaimiqui* (C. Wright ex Griseb.) Dubard ssp.
   jaimiqui (C. Wright) Dubard *20883*
   R   *20883*   Cuba *20883*
   R   *20883*   Jamaica *20883*

R   *Manilkara jaimiqui* (C. Wright ex Griseb.) Dubard ssp.
   wrightiana (Pierre) Cronquist *20883*
   R   *20883*   Cuba *20883*

E   *Manilkara longifolia* (A. de Candolle) Dubard *20883*
   E   *20883*   Brazil *20883*
   E   *20992*   Brazil - Bahia *16326*
   E   *20992*   Brazil - Espirito Santo *16326*

V   *Manilkara maxima* Pennington *20883*
   V   *20883*   Brazil *20883*
   V   *20992*   Brazil - Bahia *16326*

E   *Manilkara mayarensis* (Ekman ex Urban)
   Cronquist *20883*
   E   *20883*   Cuba *20883*

E   *Manilkara multifida* Pennington *20883*
   E   *20883*   Brazil *20883*
   E   *20992*   Brazil - Bahia *16326*

E   *Manilkara nicholsonii* A.E.van Wyk *20604*
   E   *20604*   South Africa - Cape Province *20604*

   E   *20604*   South Africa - Natal *20604*

R   *Manilkara paraensis* (Huber) Standley *20883*
   R   *20883*   Brazil *20883*
   R   *20992*   Brazil - Maranhao *16326*
   R   *20992*   Brazil - Mato Grosso *16326*
   R   *20992*   Brazil - Pará *16326*

V   *Manilkara pleeana* (Pierre ex Baill.) Cronq. *20883,*
   15107
   R   *15107*   Puerto Rico (incl. Vieques) *20883*
   R   *15107*   British Virgin Is. (Tortola) *15107*
   I   *20883*   USA - Virgin Is. (St. John) *20883*

E   *Manilkara pubicarpa* Monachino *20883*
   E   *20883*   Guyana *20883*

R   *Manilkara rufula* (Miquel) Lam *20883*
   R   *20883*   Brazil *20883*
   R   *20992*   Brazil - Bahia *16326*
   R   *20992*   Brazil - Ceara *16326*
   R   *20992*   Brazil - Paraiba *16326*
   R   *20992*   Brazil - Pernambuco *16326*
   R   *20992*   Brazil - Piaui *16326*
   R   *20992*   Brazil - Sergipe *16326*

E   *Manilkara spectabilis* (Pittier) Standley *20883,*
   16326
   E   *20883*   Costa Rica *20883*

R   *Manilkara subsericea* (Martius) Dubard *20883, 20310*
   R   *20883*   Brazil *20883*
   R   *20992*   Brazil - Parana *16326*
   R   *20992*   Brazil - Rio de Janeiro *16326*
   R   *20992*   Brazil - Santa Catarina *20310*
   R   *20992*   Brazil - Sao Paulo *16326*

V   *Manilkara valenzuelana* (A. Rich.) T.D.
   Pennington *20883*
   I   *20883*   Cuba *20883*
   I   *20883*   Dominican Republic *20883*
   I   *20883*   Haiti *20883*
   I   *20883*   Puerto Rico *20883*

   Mastichodendron floribundum (Griseb.) Cronq. *20883,*
   13336
   V   *13336*   Jamaica *20883*

V   *Micropholis brochidodroma* Pennington *20883*
   I   *20883*   Peru *20883*

R   *Micropholis casiquiarensis* Aubréville *20883*
   I   *20883*   Brazil *20883*
   I   *20883*   Venezuela *20883*

E   *Micropholis caudata* Pennington *20883*
   I   *20883*   Brazil *20883*
   E   *20992*   Brazil - Amazonas *16326*

R   *Micropholis cayennesis* Pennington *20883*
   I   *20883*   Brazil *20883*
   I   *20883*   French Guiana *20883*

V   *Micropholis compta* Pierre *20883*
   I   *20883*   Brazil *20883*
   V   *20992*   Brazil - Bahia *16326*
   V   *20992*   Brazil - Rio de Janeiro *16326*

R   *Micropholis crassipedicellata* (Martius & Eichler)
   Pierre *20883*
   I   *20883*   Brazil *20883*
   R   *20992*   Brazil - Bahia *16326*
   R   *20992*   Brazil - Espirito Santo *16326*
   R   *20992*   Brazil - Rio de Janeiro *16326*
   R   *20992*   Brazil - Sao Paulo *16326*

R   *Micropholis cylindrocarpa* (Poeppig) Pierre *20883*
   I   *20883*   Brazil *20883*
   I   *20883*   Peru *20883*

E   *Micropholis emarginata* Pennington *20883*

	I	20883 Brazil *20883*	
	E	20992 Brazil - Bahia *16326*	
R	*Micropholis garciniifolia* Pierre *20883*		
	I	20883 Puerto Rico *20883*	
R	*Micropholis gnaphaloclados* (Martius) Pierre *20883*		
	I	20883 Brazil *20883*	
	R	20992 Brazil - Bahia *16326*	
	R	20992 Brazil - Espirito Santo *16326*	
	R	20992 Brazil - Mato Grosso *16326*	
	R	20992 Brazil - Pernambuco *16326*	
E	*Micropholis grandiflora* Aubréville *20883*		
	I	20883 Brazil *20883*	
R	*Micropholis humboldtiana* (Roemer & Schultes) Pennington *20883*		
	I	20883 Brazil *20883*	
	I	20883 Venezuela *20883*	
E	*Micropholis macrophylla* (Krause) Pennington *20883*		
	I	20883 Peru *20883*	
R	*Micropholis madeirensis* (Baehni) Aubréville *20883*		
	I	20883 Brazil *20883*	
	I	20883 Peru *20883*	
R	*Micropholis maguirei* Aubréville *20883*		
	I	20883 Brazil *20883*	
	I	20883 Venezuela *20883*	
E	*Micropholis polita* (Grisebach) Pierre *20883*		
	I	20883 Cuba *20883*	
V	*Micropholis resinifera* (Ducke) Eyma *20883*		
	V	20883 Brazil *20883*	
	V	20992 Brazil - Amazonas *16326*	
E	*Micropholis retusa* (Spruce ex Miquel) Eyma *20883*		
	E	20883 Brazil *20883*	
R	*Micropholis rugosa* (Sw.) Pierre *20883*		
	R	20883 Jamaica *20883*	
R	*Micropholis sanctae-rosae* (Baehni) Pennington *20883*		
	I	20883 Brazil *20883*	
	I	20883 French Guiana *20883*	
	I	20883 Peru *20883*	
E	*Micropholis spectabilis* (Steyermark) Pennington *20883*		
	I	20883 Venezuela *20883*	
R	*Micropholis splendens* Gilly ex Aubréville *20883*		
	I	20883 Brazil *20883*	
	I	20883 Venezuela *20883*	
E	*Micropholis submarginalis* Pires & Pennington *20883*		
	I	20883 Brazil *20883*	
R	*Micropholis suborbicularis* Aubréville *20883*		
	I	20883 Venezuela *20883*	
E	*Micropholis venamoensis* (Steyermark) Pennington *20883*		
	I	20883 Venezuela *20883*	
R	*Micropholis williamii* Aubréville & Pellegrin *17462*		
	?	Brazil *17462*	
	R	20992 Brazil - Amazonas *16326*	
	R	20992 Brazil - Pará *16326*	
I	*Mimusops acutifolia* Mildbr. *5926*		
	I	5926 Tanzania (Lindi) *5926*	
I	*Mimusops andamanensis* King & Gamble *7771*		
	I	India - Andaman Is. *7771*	
R	*Mimusops angel* Chiov. *20271*		
	R	20884 Somalia (north-east) *20884*	
V	*Mimusops erythroxylon* Bojer ex DC. *10082*		
	V	20771 Mauritius *10082*	

V	*Mimusops petiolaris* (DC.) Dubard *10082*	
	V	20771 Mauritius *10082*
V	*Mimusops sechellarum* (Oliver) Hemsley *14296*	
	V	19181 Seychelles (granitic) *14296*
I	*Mimusops zeylanica* Kosterm.	
	I	Sri Lanka
E	*Neolemonniera clitandrifolia* (A.Chev.) Heine *20274*	
	E	20858 Ghana *20274*
	E	20858 Liberia *20274*
	E	20858 Nigeria (southeast) *20274*
	E	20858 Sierra Leone *20274*
V	*Nesoluma polynesicum* (Hbd.) Baill. *20850, 14209*	
	E	19473 Cook Is.(Southern group) (Mauke) *19473*
	?	French Polynesia - Tubuai Is.
	V	20850 U.S. - Hawaii (Hawai`i, Lana`i, Maui, O`ahu, Moloka`i, Kaua`i) *20850*
V	*Nesoluma st.-johnianum* H.J. Lam & B.J.D. Meeuse *8050*	
	V	19185 Pitcairn (Henderson Is.) *8050*
R	*Northea hornei* (Hartog) Pierre *19181*	
	R	19181 Seychelles (granitic) *19182*
E	*Ochrothallus blanchonii* Aubrev. *20893*	
	E	20893 New Caledonia *20893*
V	*Ochrothallus francii* (Guillaum.& Dubard) Guillaumin *20893*	
	V	20893 New Caledonia *20893*
V	*Pachystela subverticillata* E.A. Bruce *7959*	
	V	20057 Kenya *7959*
V	*Pachystela taxon a* *20057*	
	V	20057 Kenya (Shimba hills) *20057*
V	*Palaquium canaliculatum* (Thwaites) Engl. *12838*	
	V	12838 Sri Lanka *12838*
I	*Palaquium garrettii* Fletcher *19120*	
	I	19120 Thailand *19120*
R	*Palaquium grande* (Thwaites) Engl. *12838*	
	R	12838 Sri Lanka *12838*
R	*Palaquium laevifolium* (Thwaites) Engl. *12838*	
	R	12838 Sri Lanka *12838*
V	*Palaquium luzoniense* Vidal *15960*	
	V	15960 Philippines *15960*
V	*Palaquium mindanaense* Merr. *15960*	
	V	15960 Philippines *15960*
I	*Palaquium neo-ebudicum* *21021*	
	I	21021 Vanuatu *21021*
V	*Palaquium pauciflorum* (Thwaites) Engl. *12838*	
	V	12838 Sri Lanka *12838*
R	*Palaquium petiolare* (Thwaites) Engl. *12838*	
	R	12838 Sri Lanka *12838*
V	*Palaquium philippense* (Perr.) C.B. Rob. *13780*	
	V	15960 Philippines *20224*
I	*Palaquium punctatum* Fletcher *19120*	
	I	19120 Thailand *19120*
V	*Palaquium rubiginosum* (Thwaites) Engl. *12838*	
	V	12838 Sri Lanka *12838*
R	*Palaquium thwaitesii* Trimen *10252*	
	R	12838 Sri Lanka *10252*
E	*Payena thorelii* Pierre ex Dabard *19120*	
	E	19120 Thailand *19120*
E	*Planchonella contermina* Pierre ex Dubard *20893*	
	E	20893 New Caledonia *20893*

V   *Planchonella daenikeri* Aubrev. *20893*
     V   *20893*   New Caledonia *20893*

E   *Planchonella eerwah* (Bailey) P.Royen *20681*
     E   *20681*   Australia - Queensland *20681*

E   *Planchonella kaalaensis* Aubrev. *20893*
     E   *20893*   New Caledonia *20893*

I   *Planchonella kerrii* Fletcher *19120*
     I   *19120*   Thailand *19120*

R   *Planchonella koumaciensis* Aubrev.
     R   New Caledonia

R   *Planchonella macrocarpa* P.Royen *20681*
     R   *20681*   Australia - Queensland *20681*

R   *Planchonella pronyensis* Guillaumin
     R   New Caledonia

E   *Planchonella punctata* Fletcher *19120*
     E   *19120*   Thailand *19120*

I   *Planchonella sericea* Fletcher *19120*
     I   *19120*   Thailand *19120*

I   *Planchonella siamensis* Fletcher *19120*
     I   *19120*   Thailand *19120*

R   *Planchonella singuliflora* (C.White & Francis)
     P.Royen *20681*
     R   *20681*   Australia - Queensland *20681*

R   *Planchonella vieillardii* (Baillon) Dubard *20802*
     R   New Caledonia

V   *Pouteria alnifolia* (Bak.) Pierre var. *sacleuxii*
     (Lecomte) J.H.Hemsl. *20911*
     V   *20911*   Tanzania (Zanzibar Is.) *20911*

E   *Pouteria amapaensis* Pires & Pennington *20883*
     E   *20883*   Brazil *20883*
     E   *20992*   Brazil - Amapa *16326*

R   *Pouteria amygdalina* (Standley) Baehni *20883, 16326*
     I   *20883*   Belize *20883*
     I   *20883*   Guatemala (Petén) *20883*

E   *Pouteria andarahiensis* Pennington *20883*
     I   *20883*   Brazil *20883*
     E   *20992*   Brazil - Bahia *16326*

R   *Pouteria anteridata* Pennington *20883*
     I   *20883*   Venezuela *20883*

E   *Pouteria arcuata* Pennington *20883*
     E   *20883*   Venezuela *20883*

E   *Pouteria areolatifolia* Lundell *20883, 16326*
     I   *20883*   Guatemala (Petén) *20883*

V   *Pouteria arguacoensium* (Karsten) Baehni *20883*
     I   *20883*   Colombia *20883*

R   *Pouteria aristata* (Britton & Wilson) Baehni *20883*
     I   *20883*   Cuba *20883*

R   *Pouteria atabapoensis* (Aubréville) Pennington *20883*
     I   *20883*   Brazil *20883*
     I   *20883*   Venezuela *20883*

R   *Pouteria austin-smithii* (Standley) Cronquist *20883, 16326*
     I   *20883*   Costa Rica *20883*

V   *Pouteria bapeba* Pennington *20883*
     I   *20883*   Brazil *20883*
     V   *20992*   Brazil - Bahia *16326*

R   *Pouteria beaurepairei* (Glaziou & Raunkiaer)
     Baehni *20883*
     R   *20883*   Brazil *20883*
     R   *20992*   Brazil - Parana *16326*

R   *20992*   Brazil - Rio de Janeiro *16326*
R   *20992*   Brazil - Santa Catarina *16326*
R   *20992*   Brazil - Sao Paulo *16326*

R   *Pouteria belizensis* (Standley) Cronquist *20883, 16326*
     I   *20883*   Belize *20883*
     I   *20883*   Guatemala *20883*
     I   *20883*   Mexico (southeast) *20883*

E   *Pouteria benai* (Aubréville & Pellegrin)
     Pennington *20883*
     E   *20883*   French Guiana *20883*

V   *Pouteria boninensis* Baehni *8038*
     V   *19134*   Japan - Ogasawara-shoto *20626*

E   *Pouteria bonneriana* Bernardi *20883*
     I   *20883*   Peru *20883*

V   *Pouteria brachyandra* (Aubréville & Pellegrin)
     Pennington *20883*
     I   *20883*   Brazil *20883*
     I   *20883*   French Guiana *20883*
     I   *20883*   Guyana *20883*
     I   *20883*   Suriname *20883*

E   *Pouteria bracteata* Pennington *20883*
     I   *20883*   Colombia *20883*

E   *Pouteria brevensis* Pires *20883*
     E   *20883*   Brazil *20883*
     E   *20992*   Brazil - Pará *16326*

E   *Pouteria brevipetiolata* Pennington *20883*
     I   *20883*   Ecuador *20883*

V   *Pouteria briocheoides* Lundell *20883, 16326*
     I   *20883*   Guatemala (Petén) *20883*

R   *Pouteria buenaventurensis* (Aubrev.) Pilz *20883, 16326*
     I   *20883*   Panama (Colón, Panamá) *20883*
     I   *20883*   Colombia (Pacific) *20883*

V   *Pouteria bullata* (S. Moore) Baehni *20883*
     I   *20883*   Brazil *20883*
     V   *20992*   Brazil - Parana *16326*
     V   *20992*   Brazil - Rio de Janeiro *16326*
     V   *20992*   Brazil - Sao Paulo *16326*

E   *Pouteria butyrocarpa* (Kuhlmann) Pennington *20883*
     E   *20883*   Brazil *20883*
     E   *20992*   Brazil - Bahia *16326*
     E   *20992*   Brazil - Espirito Santo *16326*

R   *Pouteria calistophylla* (Standl.) Baehni *20883, 16326*
     I   *20883*   Costa Rica *20883*
     I   *20883*   Panama (Bocas del Toro) *20883*

V   *Pouteria canaimaensis* Pennington *20883*
     I   *20883*   Venezuela *20883*

R   *Pouteria capacifolia* Pilz *20883*
     I   *20883*   Ecuador *20883*

R   *Pouteria cayennensis* (A. de Candolle) Eyma *20883*
     I   *20883*   French Guiana *20883*
     I   *20883*   Guyana *20883*
     I   *20883*   Venezuela *20883*

E   *Pouteria chocoensis* (Aubréville) Pennington *20883*
     E   *20883*   Colombia *20883*

R   *Pouteria cicatricata* Pennington *20883*
     I   *20883*   Brazil *20883*
     R   *20992*   Brazil - Amazonas *16326*
     R   *20992*   Brazil - Rondonia *16326*

E   *Pouteria cinnamomea* Baehni *20883*
     I   *20883*   Peru *20883*

E   *Pouteria coelomatica* Rizzini *20883*

E		20883	Brazil *20883*
E		20992	Brazil - Bahia *16326*

V *Pouteria collina* (Little) Pennington *20883*
| I | 20883 | Colombia *20883* |
| I | 20883 | Ecuador *20883* |

R *Pouteria congestifolia* Pilz *20883, 16326*
| V | 20883 | Costa Rica *20883* |
| I | 20883 | Panama (Coclé, Chiriquí) *20883* |

R *Pouteria crassiflora* Pires & Pennington *20883*
| I | 20883 | Brazil *20883* |
| V | 20992 | Brazil - Amapa *16326* |

E *Pouteria cubensis* Baehni *20883*
| E | 20883 | Cuba *20883* |

E *Pouteria decussata* (Ducke) Baehni *20883*
| I | 20883 | Brazil *20883* |
| E | 20992 | Brazil - Amapa *16326* |

R *Pouteria dictyoneura* (Griseb.) Radlk. ssp. *dictyoneura 20883*
| I | 20883 | Cuba *20883* |

R *Pouteria dominigensis* (Gaertn. f.) Baehni ssp. *cuprea* (Urban & Ekman) Pennington *20883*
| I | 20883 | Dominican Republic *20883* |
| I | 20883 | Haiti *20883* |

R *Pouteria ephedrantha* (A. C. Smith) Pennington *20883*
| I | 20883 | Brazil *20883* |
| I | 20883 | Peru *20883* |

E *Pouteria espinae* (Standley) Baehni *20883*
| I | 20883 | Colombia *20883* |

E *Pouteria euryphylla* (Standl.) Baehni *20883, 16326*
| I | 20883 | Panama (Chiriquí) *20883* |

V *Pouteria exfoliata* Pennington *20883, 16326*
| I | 20883 | Costa Rica *20883* |

E *Pouteria exstaminodia* Pires & Pennington *20883*
| E | 20883 | Brazil *20883* |
| E | 20992 | Brazil - Amapa *16326* |

E *Pouteria filiformis* Pennington *20883, 16326*
| I | 20883 | Costa Rica (Limón) *20883* |

R *Pouteria fossicola* Cronq. *20883, 10747*
| I | 20883 | Costa Rica (Central) *20883* |
| I | 20883 | Panama (Canal Area, Coclé, Colón, Darién) *20883* |

V *Pouteria foveolata* Pennington *20883, 16326*
| I | 20883 | Costa Rica *20883* |
| I | 20883 | Nicaragua *20883* |

R *Pouteria fragrans* (Pierre) Dubard *20883*
| I | 20883 | Paraguay *20883* |

E *Pouteria fulva* Pennington *20883*
| I | 20883 | Brazil *20883* |

R *Pouteria furcata* Pennington *20883*
I	20883	Brazil *20883*
V	20992	Brazil - Maranhao *16326*
V	20992	Brazil - Piaui *16326*

R *Pouteria gabrielensis* (Gilly ex Aubréville) Pennington *20883*
I	20883	Brazil *20883*
I	20883	Colombia *20883*
I	20883	Venezuela *20883*

E *Pouteria gigantea* (Diels) Pilz *20883*
| I | 20883 | Ecuador *20883* |

V *Pouteria glauca* Pennington *20883*
| I | 20883 | Peru *20883* |

E *Pouteria gracilis* Pennington *20883*

I		20883	Peru *20883*

R *Pouteria grandiflora* (A. de Candolle) Baehni *20883*
I	20883	Brazil *20883*
R	20992	Brazil - Bahia *16326*
R	20992	Brazil - Pernambuco *16326*
R	20992	Brazil - Rio de Janeiro *16326*

R *Pouteria grandis* Eyma *20883*
I	20883	French Guiana *20883*
I	20883	Guyana *20883*
I	20883	Suriname *20883*

V *Pouteria hotteana* (Urban & Ekman) Baehni *20883, 19002*
| I | 20883 | Haiti *20883* |
| I | 20883 | Puerto Rico *20883* |

R *Pouteria izabalensis* (Standley) Baehni *20883, 16326*
I	20883	Belize *20883*
I	20883	Guatemala (Atlantic forest) *20883*
I	20883	Honduras (Atlantic forest) *20883*
I	20883	Nicaragua (Atlantic forest) *20883*

E *Pouteria juruana* Krause *20883*
| E | 20883 | Brazil (western Amazonia) *20883* |
| E | 20883 | Colombia (Putamayo) *16326* |

E *Pouteria kaieteurensis* Pennington *20883*
| E | 20883 | Guyana *20883* |

E *Pouteria krukovii* (A. C. Smith) Baehni *20883*
| I | 20883 | Brazil *20883* |
| I | 20883 | Peru *20883* |

E *Pouteria latianthera* Pennington *20883*
| I | 20883 | Brazil *20883* |
| E | 20992 | Brazil - Amapa *16326* |

R *Pouteria leptopedicellata* Pilz *20883, 16326*
| I | 20883 | Costa Rica *20883* |
| I | 20883 | Panama (Colón) *20883* |

R *Pouteria longifolia* (Martius & Eichler) Pennington *20883*
| I | 20883 | Bolivia *20883* |
| I | 20883 | Peru *20883* |

R *Pouteria lucens* (Martius & Miquel) Radlkofer *20883*
| I | 20883 | Brazil *20883* |
| V | 20992 | Brazil - Amazonas *16326* |

V *Pouteria macahensis* Pennington *20883*
I	20883	Brazil *20883*
E	20992	Brazil - Bahia *16326*
E	20992	Brazil - Rio de Janeiro *16326*

R *Pouteria macrocarpa* (Martius) Dietrich *16326*
R	16326	Costa Rica *16326*
R	16326	Brazil - Amazonas *16326*
V	20992	Brazil - Mato Grosso *16326*
V	20992	Brazil - Pará *16326*
R	16326	Colombia *16326*

R *Pouteria maguirei* (Aubréville) Pennington *20883*
| I | 20883 | Brazil *20883* |
| I | 20883 | Venezuela *20883* |

V *Pouteria melanopoda* Eyma *20883*
| I | 20883 | French Guiana *20883* |
| I | 20883 | Suriname *20883* |

E *Pouteria micrantha* (Urban) Baehni *20883*
| E | 20883 | Cuba *20883* |

V *Pouteria microstrigosa* Pennington *20883*
I	20883	Brazil *20883*
V	20992	Brazil - Bahia *16326*
V	20992	Brazil - Espirito Santo *16326*
V	20992	Brazil - Mato Grosso *16326*

E *Pouteria minima* Pennington *20883*

I   20883 Brazil *20883*
E   20992 Brazil - Amazonas *16326*

E   *Pouteria moaensis* Alain *20883*

    E   20883 Cuba *20883*

E   *Pouteria nemorosa* Baehni *20883*

    I   20883 Bolivia *20883*

V   *Pouteria nudipetala* Pennington *20883*

    I   20883 Brazil *20883*
    I   20883 Peru *20883*

R   *Pouteria oppositifolia* (Ducke) Baehni *20883*

    I   20883 Brazil *20883*
    V   20992 Brazil - Amapa *16326*
    V   20992 Brazil - Pará *16326*

R   *Pouteria orinocoensis* (Aubréville) Pennington *20883*

    I   20883 Venezuela *20883*

E   *Pouteria oxypetala* Pennington *20883*

    E   20883 Brazil *20883*
    E   20992 Brazil - Sao Paulo *16326*

E   *Pouteria pachycalyx* Pennington *20883*

    E   20883 Brazil *20883*
    E   20992 Brazil - Espirito Santo *16326*

R   *Pouteria pachyphylla* Pennington *20883*

    R   20883 Brazil *20883*
    V   20992 Brazil - Amazonas *16326*
    V   20992 Brazil - Rondonia *16326*

E   *Pouteria pallens* Pennington *20883*

    I   20883 Brazil *20883*
    E   20992 Brazil - Rondonia *16326*

R   *Pouteria pallida* (C. F. Gaertner) Baehni *20883, 19001*

    I   20883   *20883*
    I   20883 Dominica *20883*
    I   20883 Guadeloupe *20883*
    I   20883 Martinique *20883*

E   *Pouteria peduncularis* (Martius & Eichler) Baehni *20883*

    E   20883 Brazil *20883*
    E   20992 Brazil - Bahia *16326*

E   *Pouteria penicillata* Baehni *20883*

    E   20883 Guyana *20883*

E   *Pouteria pentasperma* (Standl.) Baehni *20883, 10747*

    I   20883 Panama (Bocas del Toro, Darién) *20883*

E   *Pouteria peruviensis* Rizzini *20883*

    I   20883 Peru *20883*

V   *Pouteria petiolata* Pennington *20883*

    I   20883 Brazil *20883*
    V   20992 Brazil - Amazonas *16326*
    V   20992 Brazil - Pará *16326*

R   *Pouteria pimichinensis* Pennington *20883*

    I   20883 Venezuela *20883*

E   *Pouteria pisquiensis* Baehni *20883*

    I   20883 Peru *20883*

R   *Pouteria platyphylla* (A. C. Smith) Baehni *20883*

    I   20883 Brazil *20883*
    I   20883 Peru *20883*

E   *Pouteria polysepala* Pennington *20883*

    E   20883 Brazil *20883*
    E   20992 Brazil - Amazonas *16326*

E   *Pouteria psammophila* (Martius) Radlkofer *20883*

    I   20883 Brazil *20883*
    E   20992 Brazil - Rio de Janeiro *16326*
    E   20992 Brazil - Sao Paulo *16326*

E   *Pouteria puberula* Pennington *20883*

    I   20883 Venezuela *20883*

V   *Pouteria pubescens* (Aubréville & Pellegrin) Pennington *20883*

    I   20883 Brazil *20883*
    I   20883 Peru *20883*

R   *Pouteria putamen-ovi* Pennington *20883*

    I   20883 Brazil *20883*
    I   20883 Peru *20883*

R   *Pouteria reticulata* ssp. *surinamensis* Pennington *20883*

    I   20883 Brazil *20883*
    I   20883 Guyana *20883*
    I   20883 Suriname *20883*

V   *Pouteria retinervis* Pennington *20883*

    I   20883 Brazil *20883*
    I   20883 French Guiana *20883*

E   *Pouteria rhynchocarpa* Pennington *20883, 16326*

    E   20883 Mexico *20883*

R   *Pouteria rigida* (Martius & Eichler) Radlkofer ssp. *rigida* *20883*

    I   20883 Brazil *20883*
    I   20883 Guyana *20883*
    I   20883 Venezuela *20883*

R   *Pouteria rigida* (Martius & Eichler) Radlkofer ssp. *tomentosa* (Aubréville) Pennington *20883*

    I   20883 Venezuela *20883*

R   *Pouteria rigidopsis* Monachino ex Pennington *20883*

    I   20883 Venezuela *20883*

R   *Pouteria rodriguesiana* Pires & Pennington *20883*

    I   20883 Brazil *20883*
    I   20883 French Guiana *20883*
    I   20883 Suriname *20883*

V   *Pouteria rufotomentosa* (Lundell) Pennington *20883, 16326*

    I   20883 Guatemala (Baja Verapaz) *20883*

R   *Pouteria sagotiana* (Baillon) Eyma *20883*

    I   20883 Brazil *20883*
    I   20883 French Guiana *20883*
    I   20883 Guyana *20883*
    I   20883 Suriname *20883*

E   *Pouteria sambuensis* (Pitt.) Baehni *20883, 10747*

    I   20883 Panama (Darién) *20883*

V   *Pouteria sclerocarpa* (Pitt.) Cronq. *20883, 16326*

    I   20883 Panama (San Blas) *20883*
    I   20883 Colombia *20883*
    I   20883 Ecuador (Amazonian) *20883*

R   *Pouteria scrobiculata* Monachino ex Pennington *20883*

    I   20883 Brazil *20883*
    I   20883 Venezuela *20883*

R   *Pouteria semecarpifolia* (Pierre) Pierre *20883, 19001*

    R   19001 Dominica *20883*
    I   20883 Guadeloupe *20883*
    R   19001 Martinique *20883*
    R   19001 St Lucia *19001*
    R   19001 St Vincent *19001*

E   *Pouteria sessilis* Pennington *20883*

    I   20883 Peru *20883*

E   *Pouteria silvestris* Pennington *20883, 16326*

    I   20883 Costa Rica (Heredia) *20883*

R   *Pouteria singularis* Pennington *20883*

    I   20883 Brazil *20883*
    I   20883 French Guiana *20883*

E   *Pouteria sipapoensis* Pennington *20883*

I   *20883* Venezuela *20883*

R   *Pouteria splendens* (A. de Candolle) Kuntze *20883, 15088*

    R   *20883* Chile *20883*

E   *Pouteria stenophylla* Baehni *20883*

    E   *20883* Brazil *20883*
    Ex *20992* Brazil - Rio de Janeiro *16326*

V   *Pouteria subsessilifolia* Cronquist *20883*

    I   *20883* Brazil *20883*
    E   *20992* Brazil - Bahia *16326*

V   *Pouteria tarumanensis* Pires *20883*

    I   *20883* Brazil *20883*
    E   *20992* Brazil - Amazonas *16326*

R   *Pouteria tenuisepala* Pires & Pennington *20883*

    I   *20883* Brazil *20883*
    I   *20883* French Guiana *20883*

R   *Pouteria trigonosperma* Eyma *20883*

    I   *20883* Guyana *20883*
    I   *20883* Suriname *20883*

E   *Pouteria triplarifolia* Standley & Williams ex Allen ex Pennington *20883, 16326*

    I   *20883* Costa Rica (Puntarenas) *20883*

R   *Pouteria vernicosa* Pennington *20883*

    I   *20883* Brazil *20883*
    I   *20883* Peru *20883*

V   *Pouteria villamilii* (Merr.) Baehni *20224*

    V   *15960* Philippines (Luzon, Siargao) *20224*

R   *Pouteria virescens* Baehni *20883*

    I   *20883* Brazil *20883*
    I   *20883* French Guiana *20883*
    I   *20883* Guyana *20883*

R   *Pouteria williamii* (Aubréville & Pellegrin) Pennington *20883*

    I   *20883* Brazil *20883*
    I   *20883* French Guiana *20883*

E   *Pradosia argentea* (Kunth) Pennington *20883*

    I   *20883* Peru *20883*

R   *Pradosia atroviolacea* Ducke *20883*

    I   *20883* Brazil *20883*
    I   *20883* Colombia *20883*
    I   *20883* Peru *20883*

R   *Pradosia cochlearia* ssp. *cochlearia* *20883*

    I   *20883* Brazil *20883*
    I   *20883* French Guiana *20883*

E   *Pradosia cuatrecasasii* (Aubréville) Pennington *20883*

    E   *20883* Colombia *20883*

E   *Pradosia decipiens* Ducke *20883*

    E   *20883* Brazil *20883*

E   *Pradosia glaziovii* (Pierre) Pennington *20883*

    E   *20883* Brazil *20883*
    Ex *20992* Brazil - Rio de Janeiro *16326*

R   *Pradosia granulosa* Pires & Pennington *20883*

    R   *20883* Brazil *20883*
    V   *20992* Brazil - Maranhao *16326*
    V   *20992* Brazil - Pará *16326*

R   *Pradosia grisebachii* (Pierre) Pennington *20883*

    I   *20883* Trinidad & Tobago *20883*
    I   *20883* Venezuela *20883*

V   *Pradosia huberi* (Ducke) Ducke *20883*

    I   *20883* Brazil *20883*
    I   *20883* French Guiana *20883*

E   *Pradosia kuhlmannii* Toledo *20883*

I   *20883* Brazil *20883*
E   *20992* Brazil - Rio de Janeiro *16326*

R   *Pradosia montana* Pennington *20883*

    I   *20883* Ecuador *20883*

E   *Pradosia mutisii* Cronq. *20883*

    I   *20883* Colombia *20883*

R   *Pradosia subverticillata* Ducke *20883*

    I   *20883* Brazil *20883*
    V   *20992* Brazil - Amazonas *16326*
    V   *20992* Brazil - Pará *16326*

E   *Pradosia verrucosa* Ducke *20883*

    E   *20883* Brazil *20883*
    E   *20992* Brazil - Pernambuco *16326*

R   *Pradosia verticillata* Ducke *20883*

    I   *20883* Brazil *20883*
    I   *20883* French Guiana *20883*

V   *Pycnandra paniensis* Aubrev. *20893*

    V   *20893* New Caledonia *20893*

V   *Sarcaulus inflexus* (A. C. Smith) Pennington *20883*

    I   *20883* Brazil *20883*
    V   *20992* Brazil - Amazonas *16326*
    V   *20992* Brazil - Mato Grosso *16326*

V   *Sarcaulus oblatus* Pennington *20883*

    I   *20883* Ecuador *20883*

R   *Sarcaulus vestitus* (Baehni) Pennington *20883*

    I   *20883* Brazil *20883*
    V   *20992* Brazil - Acre *16326*
    V   *20992* Brazil - Amazonas *16326*

E   *Sarcaulus wurdackii* Aubréville *20883*

    I   *20883* Peru *20883*

R   *Sarcosperma angustifolium* Gagnepain *6057*

    R   Vietnam *6057*

R   *Sarcosperma kontumense* Gagnepain ex Aubrev. *6057*

    R   Vietnam *6057*

I   *Sarcosperma siamensis* Fletcher *19120*

    I   *19120* Thailand *19120*

E   *Sideroxylon acunae* (Borhidi) Pennington *20883*

    I   *20883* Cuba *20883*

V   *Sideroxylon altamiranoi* (Rose and Standley) Pennington *20883*

    I   *20883* Mexico *20883*

E   *Sideroxylon angustum* Pennington *20883*

    I   *20883* Cuba *20883*

E   *Sideroxylon anomalum* (Urban) Pennington *20883*

    E   *20883* Dominican Republic *20883*

E   *Sideroxylon boutonianum* A. DC. *10082*

    E   *20771* Mauritius (Mainland & Ile aux Aigrettes) *10082*

E   *Sideroxylon bullatum* (Howard & Proctor) Pennington *20883, 19435*

    R   *13336* Jamaica (Portland) *20883*

R   *Sideroxylon capiri* (A. de Candolle) Pittier ssp. *capiri* *20883*

    I   *20883* Mexico *20883*

R   *Sideroxylon cartilagineum* (Cronquist) Pennington *20883*

    I   *20883* Mexico *20883*

R   *Sideroxylon confertum* C. Wright *20883*

    R   *20883* Cuba *20883*

R   *Sideroxylon contrerasii* (Lundell) Pennington *20883*

    I   *20883* Costa Rica *20883*

I   *20883*   Guatemala *20883*
I   *20883*   Mexico *20883*
I   *20883*   Panama *20883*

E   *Sideroxylon dominicanum* (Whetstone & Atkinson) Pennington *20883*
   E   *20883*   Dominican Republic *20883*

E   *Sideroxylon durifolium* (Standley) Pennington *20883*
   E   *20883*   Belize *20883*

E   *Sideroxylon eriocarpum* (Greenman & Conzatti) Pennington *20883*
   E   *20883*   Mexico *20883*

V   *Sideroxylon eucoriaceum* (Lundell) Pennington *20883*
   I   *20883*   Guatemala *20883*
   I   *20883*   Mexico *20883*

E   *Sideroxylon excavatum* Pennington *20883*
   I   *20883*   Mexico *20883*

R   *Sideroxylon floribundum* Grisebach *20883*
   I   *20883*   Jamaica *20883*

R   *Sideroxylon floribundum* Grisebach ssp. *belizense* (Lundell) Pennington *20883*
   I   *20883*   Belize *20883*
   I   *20883*   Guatemala *20883*

V   *Sideroxylon floribundum* Grisebach ssp. *floribundum* *20883*
   I   *20883*   Jamaica *20883*

E   *Sideroxylon galeatum* (A.W. Hill) Baehni *10082*
   E   *5852*   Mauritius - Rodrigues *5852*

E   *Sideroxylon grandiflorum* A. DC. *10082*
   E   *20771*   Mauritius *10082*

E   *Sideroxylon hirtiantherum* Pennington *20883*
   I   *20883*   Guatemala *20883*

E   *Sideroxylon ibarrae* (Lundell) Pennington *20883*
   I   *20883*   Guatemala *20883*

V   *Sideroxylon jubilla* (Ekman ex Urban) Pennington *20883*
   I   *20883*   Cuba *20883*

V   *Sideroxylon majus* (Gaertner f.) Baehni *10082*
   V   *14234*   Réunion *10082*

R   *Sideroxylon montanum* (Swartz) Pennington *20883*
   I   *20883*   Jamaica *20883*

E   *Sideroxylon octosepalum* (Urban) Pennington *20883*
   I   *20883*   Jamaica *20883*

E   *Sideroxylon peninsulare* (Brandegee) Pennington *20883*
   I   *20883*   Mexico *20883*

R   *Sideroxylon persimile* ssp. *subsessiliflorum* (Hemsley) Pennington *20883*
   R   *20883*   Mexico *20883*

R   *Sideroxylon picardae* (Urban) Pennington *20883*
   I   *20883*   Dominican Republic *20883*
   I   *20883*   Haiti *20883*

R   *Sideroxylon repens* (Urban & Ekman) Pennington *20883*
   I   *20883*   Dominican Republic *20883*
   I   *20883*   Haiti *20883*

V   *Sideroxylon retinerve* Pennington *20883*
   I   *20883*   Honduras *20883*

R   *Sideroxylon rotundifolium* (Swartz) Pennington *20883*
   I   *20883*   Jamaica *20883*

E   *Sideroxylon rubiginosum* Pennington *20883*
   E   *20883*   Dominican Republic *20883*

V   *Sideroxylon sessiliflorum* (Poiret) Capuron ex Aubréville *10082*
   V   *20771*   Mauritius *10082*

E   *Sideroxylon socorrense* (Brandegee) Pennington *20883*
   E   *20883*   Mexico *20883*

E   *Sideroxylon thornei* (Cronq.) T.D. Pennington *20850*
   E   *20850*   U.S. - Alabama *20850*
   E   *20850*   U.S. - Florida *20850*
   E   *20850*   U.S. - Georgia *20850*

R   *Sideroxylon verruculosum* (Cronquist) Pennington *20883*
   R   *20883*   Mexico *20883*

V   *Synsepalum aubrevillei* (Pellegrin) Aubrev. & Pellegr. *7926*
   V   *20858*   Côte d'Ivoire *7926*
   V   *20858*   Ghana *20274*

E   *Synsepalum tsounkpe* Aubrev. & Pellegrin *7926*
   E   *20887*   Côte d'Ivoire *7926*

V   *Vitellaria paradoxa* C.E.Gaertner *20833, 21116*
   V   *21116*   Sudan *21116*
   V   *21116*   Uganda *21116*
   V   *21116*   Zaire *21116*

V   *Vitellariopsis ferruginea* Kupicha *7749*
   ?   Mozambique (Beira) *20843*
   V   *20909*   Zimbabwe *7749*

I   *Vitellariopsis kirkii* (Baker) Dubard *20057*
   I   *20057*   Kenya *20057*
   I   *20057*   Tanzania (Pangani; Kisarawe) *17435*

R   *Xantolis balansae* (Lecomte) Royen *6057*
   R   Vietnam *6057*

R   *Xantolis baranense* (Lecomte) Royen *6057*
   R   Vietnam *6057*

Sarraceniaceae

Number of genera: 3
Number of species: 15
Recorded threatened species: 5   (33%)

Easter and northwestern United States; northern South America.

R   II   *Sarracenia alata* (A.W. Wood) Wood *12224*
   R   *19629*   U.S. - Alabama *19629*
   R   *19629*   U.S. - Florida *19629*
   R   *19629*   U.S. - Louisiana *19629*
   R   *12224*   U.S. - Mississippi *12224*
   R   *19629*   U.S. - Texas *19629*

R   II   *Sarracenia flava* L. *19629*
   R   *19629*   U.S. - Alabama *19629*
   I   *19629*   U.S. - Florida *19629*
   R   *19629*   U.S. - Georgia *19629*
   I   *19629*   U.S. - Mississippi *19629*
   R   *19629*   U.S. - North Carolina *19629*
   I   *19629*   U.S. - Pennsylvania *19629*
   I   *19629*   U.S. - South Carolina *19629*
   E   *19629*   U.S. - Virginia *19629*

R   II   *Sarracenia leucophylla* Raf. *20850, 19629*
   R   *20850*   U.S. - Alabama *20850*
   R   *20850*   U.S. - Florida *20850*
   Ex/E   *20850*   U.S. - Georgia *20850*
   V   *20850*   U.S. - Mississippi *20850*

V   I   *Sarracenia oreophila* (Kearney) Wherry *.20850, 15658*
   V   *20850*   U.S. - Alabama *20850*
   E   *20850*   U.S. - Georgia *20850*
   E   *20850*   U.S. - North Carolina *20850*
   Ex/E   *20850*   U.S. - Tennessee *20850*

R   II   *Sarracenia rubra* Walt. *20850*

	I	20850	U.S. - Alabama	20850
	V	20850	U.S. - Florida	20850
	V	20850	U.S. - Georgia	20850
	E	20850	U.S. - Mississippi	20850
	R	20850	U.S. - North Carolina	20850
	E	20850	U.S. - South Carolina	20850

V I *Sarracenia rubra* Walter ssp. *alabamensis* (F.W. & R.B. Case) Schnell 20850, 19629

    V 20850 U.S. - Alabama 20850

V II *Sarracenia rubra* Walter ssp. *gulfensis* Schnell 20850, 19629

    I 20850 U.S. - Florida 20850
    I 20850 U.S. - Georgia 20850

E I *Sarracenia rubra* Walter ssp. *jonesii* (Wherry) Wherry 20850, 19629

    E 20850 U.S. - North Carolina 20850
    I 20850 U.S. - South Carolina 20850

R II *Sarracenia rubra* Walter ssp. *rubra* 20850, 19629

    I 20850 U.S. - Alabama 20850
    I 20850 U.S. - Florida 20850
    V 20850 U.S. - Georgia 20850
    R 20850 U.S. - North Carolina 20850
    I 20850 U.S. - South Carolina 20850

R II *Sarracenia rubra* Walter ssp. *wherryi* (F.W. & R.B. Case) Schnell 20850, 19629

    R 20850 U.S. - Alabama 20850
    E 20850 U.S. - Mississippi 20850

Saxifragaceae

Number of genera:	40
Number of species:	475-700
Recorded threatened species:	102 (17%)

Cosmopolitan, especially temperate and cold Northern Hemisphere.

Ex/E *Astilbe crenatiloba* (Britt.) Small 20850, 14662

    Ex/E 20850 U.S. - North Carolina 20850
    Ex/E 20850 U.S. - Tennessee 20850

V *Bensoniella oregana* (Abrams & Bacig.) Morton 20850

    V 20850 U.S. - California 20850
    V 20850 U.S. - Oregon 20850

I *Bergenia hissarica* Boriss. 5942

    I 5942 Uzbekistan (south-east) 5942

I *Bergenia ugamica* Pavlov 5942

    I 5942 Kyrgyzstan 5942

R *Bolandra oregana* S.Watson 20850

    I 20850 U.S. - Idaho 20850
    R 20850 U.S. - Oregon 20850
    V 20850 U.S. - Washington 20850

R *Chrysoplenium album* Maxim. var. *flavum* Hara 10572

    R 10572 Japan 10572

R *Chrysoplenium maximowiczii* Franchet & Sav. 10572

    R 10572 Japan 10572

R *Chrysosplenium hebetatum* Ohwi 20511

    R 20511 Taiwan 20511

V *Chrysosplenium iowense* Rydb. 20850

    I 20850 Canada - Alberta 20850
    Ex/E 20850 Canada - British Columbia 20850
    I 20850 Canada - Manitoba 20850
    I 20850 Canada - Franklin 20850
    E 20850 Canada - Saskatchewan 20850
    R 20850 U.S. - Iowa 20850
    E 20850 U.S. - Minnesota 20850

R *Chrysosplenium rimosum* Komarov ssp. *dezhnevii* Jurtzev 5942, 21309

    I 5942 Russia (Far East) - Magadan (eastern peninsula) 5942
    R 20085 Russia (E.Europe) - North 20085

V *Chrysosplenium rosendahlii* Packer 20850

    R 20085 Russia (E.Europe) - North 20085
    I 20850 Canada - Franklin 20850

R *Conimitella williamsii* (D.C. Eat.) Rydb. 20850, 15882

    V 20850 Canada - Alberta 20850
    E 20850 U.S. - Colorado 20850
    I 20850 U.S. - Idaho 20850
    I 20850 U.S. - Montana 20850
    E 20850 U.S. - Wyoming 20850

V *Heuchera abramsii* Rydb. 20850

    I 20850 U.S. - California 20850

V *Heuchera alba* Rydb. 20850

    V 20850 U.S. - Virginia 20850
    V 20850 U.S. - West Virginia 20850

E *Heuchera alpestris* Rosendahl, Butters & Lakela 20850

    I 20850 U.S. - California 20850

V *Heuchera brevistaminea* Wiggins 20850

    V 20850 U.S. - California 20850

V *Heuchera cespitosa* Eastw. 20850

    I 20850 U.S. - California 20850

V *Heuchera duranii* Bacig. 20850

    I 20850 U.S. - California 20850
    V 20850 U.S. - Nevada 20850

R *Heuchera eastwoodiae* Rosendahl, Butters & Lakela 20850

    R 20850 U.S. - Arizona 20850

R *Heuchera glomerulata* Rosendahl, Butters & Lakela 20850

    R 20850 U.S. - Arizona 20850
    E 20850 U.S. - New Mexico 20850

R *Heuchera grossulariifolia* Rydb. var. *tenuifolia* (Wheelock) C.L. Hitchc. 20850

    I 20850 Canada - British Columbia 20850
    I 20850 U.S. - Idaho 20850
    I 20850 U.S. - Oregon 20850
    R 20850 U.S. - Washington 20850

R *Heuchera hallii* Gray 20850

    I 20850 U.S. - Colorado 20850

V *Heuchera hirsutissima* Rosendahl, Butters & Lakela 20850

    V 20850 U.S. - California 20850

V *Heuchera maxima* Greene 20850

    V 20850 U.S. - California 20850

V *Heuchera merriamii* Eastw. 20850

    I 20850 U.S. - California 20850
    I 20850 U.S. - Oregon 20850

V *Heuchera parishii* Rydb. 20850

    V 20850 U.S. - California 20850

R *Heuchera pilosissima* Fisch. & C.A. Mey. 20850

    I 20850 U.S. - California 20850
    I 20850 U.S. - Oregon 20850

V *Heuchera pulchella* Woot. & Standl. 20850

    V 20850 U.S. - New Mexico 20850

V *Heuchera rubescens* (Greene) M.G. Stewart var. *versicolor* (Greene) M.G. Stewart 20850

    I 20850 U.S. - Arizona 20850
    I 20850 U.S. - California 20850

I	20850	U.S. - Colorado 20850
I	20850	U.S. - New Mexico 20850
I	20850	U.S. - Texas 20850
V	20850	U.S. - Utah 20850

R *Heuchera villosa* Michaux var. *arkansana* (Rydb.) E.B. Sm. 20850

    R   20850 U.S. - Arkansas 20850

R *Heuchera wootonii* Rydb. 20850

    R   20850 U.S. - New Mexico 20850

R *Jepsonia heterandra* Eastw. 20850

    R   20850 U.S. - California 20850

R *Lithophragma cymbalaria* Torr. & Gray 20850

    I   20850 U.S. - California 20850

E *Lithophragma maximum* Bacig. 20850

    E   20850 U.S. - California 20850

R *Lithophragma parviflorum* (Hook.) Nutt. ex Torr. & Gray var. *trifoliatum* (Eastw.) Jepson 20850

    I   20850 U.S. - California 20850

R *Mitella doiana* Ohwi 10572

    R   10572 Japan 10572

R *Mitella koshiensis* Ohwi var. *furusei* (Ohwi) Ohwi 10572

    R   10572 Japan 10572

R *Mitella leiopetala* Ohwi & Okuy. 10572

    R   10572 Japan 10572

R *Peltoboykinia tellimoides* (Maxim.) Hara 10572

    R   10572 Japan 10572

R *Peltoboykinia watanabei* (Yatabe) Hara 10572

    R   10572 Japan 10572

R *Saxifraga acerifolia* Wakab. & Satomi 10572

    R   10572 Japan 10572

V *Saxifraga aleutica* Hulten 20850, 21309

    V   20850 U.S. - Alaska 20850

Ex *Saxifraga amphibia* Sünd. 18154

    Ex   Austria
    Ex   Germany
    Ex   18154 Switzerland 18154

R *Saxifraga apetala* Piper 20850

    V   20850 U.S. - Montana 20850
    R   20850 U.S. - Washington 20850

R *Saxifraga arachnoidea* Sternb. 18264, 20171

    R   18264 Italy (Lombardy, Trentino-Alto Adige) 18264

R *Saxifraga artvinensis* Matthews 12840

    R   12840 Turkey 12840

R *Saxifraga babiana* T.E.Díaz & Fern.Prieto 20171

    R   Spain

V *Saxifraga berica* (Bég.) D.A.Webb 8000, 20171

    V   18264 Italy (Colli Berici) 19997

R *Saxifraga biternata* Boiss. 20171

    R   Spain

R *Saxifraga blepharophylla* A.Kern. ex Hayek 20171

    R   Austria

R *Saxifraga boissieri* Engl. 20171

    R   20661 Spain (Cádiz, Málaga) 20661

V *Saxifraga bryophora* Grimes & Packard var. *tobiasiae* J. Grimes & Packard 20850

    V   20850 U.S. - Idaho 20850

R *Saxifraga caballeroi* N. Camara & Sennen

    R   Spain

R *Saxifraga careyana* Gray 20850

    E   20850 U.S. - Alabama 20850
    I   20850 U.S. - Georgia 20850
    R   20850 U.S. - North Carolina 20850
    E   20850 U.S. - South Carolina 20850
    R   20850 U.S. - Tennessee 20850
    V   20850 U.S. - Virginia 20850

V *Saxifraga caroliniana* Gray 20850

    V   20850 U.S. - North Carolina 20850
    E   20850 U.S. - Tennessee 20850
    V   20850 U.S. - Virginia 20850
    E   20850 U.S. - West Virginia 20850

R *Saxifraga cebennensis* Rouy & E.G.Camus 20171

    R   France (Cevennes)

E *Saxifraga cintrana* Kuzinsky ex Willk. 8000, 20171

    E   20076 Portugal 14155

I *Saxifraga columnaris* Schmalh. 5942

    I   5942 Russia - North Caucasus 5942

R *Saxifraga corsica* (Ser.) Gren. & Godr. ssp. *cossoniana* (Boiss.) D. Webb 20171

    R   20692 Spain 20692
    R   20692 Spain - Balearic Is. (Pytiusic islands) 20692

R *Saxifraga diapensioides* Bellardi 20171

    R   France
    R   8623 Italy 8623
    R   18154 Switzerland 18154

I *Saxifraga dinnikii* Schmalh. 5942

    I   5942 Russia - North Caucasus 5942

R *Saxifraga embergeri* Maire

    R   Morocco

R *Saxifraga erioblasta* Boiss. & Reut. 20171

    R   Spain

V *Saxifraga exarata* Vill ssp. *delphinensis* (Ravaud) Kerguélen 20528

    V   20528 France 20528

V *Saxifraga exarata* Vill. ssp. *lamottei* (Luizet) D.A.Webb 20171

    V   20528 France (Massif central) 20528

R *Saxifraga facchinii* W.D.J.Koch 20171

    R   20804 Italy (Dolomites) 20804

R *Saxifraga florulenta* Moretti 8000, 20171

    R   20528 France (central Maritime Alps) 8000
    R   18264 Italy (Piemonte) 19997

I *Saxifraga gemmipara* Franch. var. *siamensis* T. Shimizu 19120

    I   19120 Thailand 19120

R *Saxifraga gemmulosa* Boiss. 20171

    R   Spain

V *Saxifraga globulifera* Desf. ssp. *gibraltarica* Ser. 18223

    V   19052 United Kingdom - Gibraltar 18223

V *Saxifraga hederifolia* A. Rich 19704

    V   19704 Ethiopia (Tigray Upland, Gonder, Gojam, Arsi.) 19704

E *Saxifraga hitchcockiana* Elvander 20850

    E   20850 U.S. - Oregon 20850

R *Saxifraga italica* D.A.Webb 20171

    R   Italy

E *Saxifraga jacquemontiana* Decne. 14768

    E   India - Jammu & Kashmir (Damamsar) 14768

R	*Saxifraga lactea* Turcz. *11552*	
	R	*11552* Russian Federation (extreme south east) *11552*
V	*Saxifraga losae* Sennen *20171*	
	V	Spain
R	*Saxifraga luizetiana* Emberger & Maire	
	R	Morocco
R	*Saxifraga maireana* Luizet	
	R	Morocco
R	*Saxifraga maweana* Baker	
	R	Morocco
V	*Saxifraga moncayensis* D.A.Webb *2017!*	
	V	Spain
V	*Saxifraga moschata* Wulf. ssp. *basaltica* Br.-Bl. *7897*	
	V	*20798* Poland (Karkonosze Mts.) *7897*
V	*Saxifraga moschata* Wulf. in Jacq. ssp. *dominii* Soó em S.Pawl *19839*	
	V	*19321* Slovakia *19321*
V	*Saxifraga moschata* Wulf. in Jacq. ssp. *kotulae* S. Pawl *19839*	
	V	*19751* Poland *19751*
	V	*19321* Slovakia *19321*
R	*Saxifraga mutata* L. ssp. *demissa* (Schott & Kotschy) D.A. Webb *17823, 20171*	
	R	*19949* Romania *20631*
V	*Saxifraga nelsoniana* D. Don ssp. *carlottae* (Calder & Savile) Hulten *20850*	
	V	*20850* Canada - British Columbia *20850*
	I	*20850* U.S. - Alaska *20850*
R	*Saxifraga nevadensis* Boiss. *20171*	
	R	Spain
R	*Saxifraga nishidae* Miyabe & Kudo *10572*	
	R	*10572* Japan *10572*
R	*Saxifraga numidica* Maire *10488*	
	R	*14958* Algeria *10488*
R	*Saxifraga oblongifolia* Nakai *15957*	
	R	*15923* Korea, South (Mt Sorak) *15923*
R	*Saxifraga palmeri* Bush *20850*	
	I	*20850* U.S. - Arkansas *20850*
	I	*20850* U.S. - Oklahoma *20850*
R	*Saxifraga pickeringii* C. Simon	
	R	Portugal - Madeira
R	*Saxifraga portosanctana* Boiss. *17891*	
	R	*14155* Portugal - Madeira *14155*
R	*Saxifraga presolanensis* Engl. *8000, 20171*	
	R	*19997* Italy (Lombardia) *19997*
R	*Saxifraga reuterana* Boiss. *20171*	
	R	Spain
I	*Saxifraga rigoi* Porta *20171*	
	I	Spain (mountains in south east)
V	*Saxifraga subapetala* E.Nels. *20850*	
	E	*20850* Canada - Alberta *20850*
	I	*20850* U.S. - Idaho *20850*
	I	*20850* U.S. - Montana *20850*
	V	*20850* U.S. - Wyoming *20850*
R	*Saxifraga taylorii* Calder & Savile *20850, 10701*	
	R	*20850* Canada - British Columbia *20850*
V	*Saxifraga tempestiva* Elvander & Denton *20850*	
	V	*20850* U.S. - Montana *20850*

E	*Saxifraga tischii* Skelly *20850*	
	I	*20850* Canada - British Columbia *20850*
	I	*20850* U.S. - Washington *20850*
V	*Saxifraga tombeanensis* Boiss. ex Engl. *8000, 20171*	
	V	*18264* Italy (Lombardia, Trentino-Alto Adige & Veneto) *19997*
R	*Saxifraga valdensis* DC. *8000, 20171*	
	R	*20528* France (south-west Alps) *8000*
	I	*20528* Italy (S.W. Alps) *19997*
R	*Saxifraga vandellii* Sternb. *20171*	
	R	Italy
R	*Saxifraga vayredana* Luizet *8000, 20171*	
	R	Spain (Near Montseny, N.N.E. of Barcelona) *8000*
R	*Saxifraga werneri* Font Quer & Pau	
	R	Morocco
R	*Sullivantia hapemanii* (Coult. & Fisher) Coult. *20850*	
	R	*20850* U.S. - Colorado *20850*
	I	*20850* U.S. - Idaho *20850*
	E	*20850* U.S. - Montana *20850*
	V	*20850* U.S. - Wyoming *20850*
R	*Sullivantia hapemanii* (Coult. & Fisher) Coult. var. *hapemanii* *20850*	
	V	*20850* U.S. - Idaho *20850*
	I	*20850* U.S. - Montana *20850*
	R	*20850* U.S. - Wyoming *20850*
R	*Sullivantia hapemanii* (Coult. & Fisher) Coult. var. *purpusii* (Brand) Soltis *20850*	
	R	*20850* U.S. - Colorado *20850*
V	*Sullivantia oregana* S.Watson *20850*	
	V	*20850* U.S. - Oregon *20850*
	E	*20850* U.S. - Washington *20850*

Schisandraceae

Number of genera:	2
Number of species:	50
Recorded threatened species:	3 (6%)

Tropical and temperate eastern Asia; southeastern United States.

I	*Schisandra grandiflora* (Wallich) Hook.f. & Thomson	
	I	India - Himachal Pradesh (Simla)
	I	India - Meghalaya
	I	India - Sikkim
	I	India - Uttar Pradesh (Garhwal; Kumaun)
R	*Schisandra nigra* Max. *15923*	
	R	*15923* Korea, South (Huksando) *15923*
I	*Schisandra propinqua* (Wallich) Baillon	
	I	India - Sikkim
	I	India - Uttar Pradesh (Garhwal; Kumaun)

Scrophulariaceae

Number of genera:	190
Number of species:	4,000
Recorded threatened species:	969 (24%)

Cosmopolitan, especially temperate regions and tropical mountains.

V	*Acanthorrhinum rivas-martinezii* (Schez-Mata) Fdez-Casas & Schez-Mata *19174*	
	V	*19174* Spain *19174*
I	*Adenosma malabaricum* Hook.f.	
	I	India - Kerala (Malabar coast)
I	*Adenosma subrepens* (Thwaites) Benth. ex Hook.f. *8021*	

	I	*16162*	Sri Lanka (Hewessa, Ratnapura) *8021*
R			***Aeginetia mpomii*** Letouzey
	R		Cameroon
E			***Agalinis acuta*** Pennell *20850*
	E	*20850*	U.S. - Connecticut *20850*
	E	*20850*	U.S. - Maryland *20850*
	E	*20850*	U.S. - Massachusetts *20850*
	E	*20850*	U.S. - New York *20850*
	E	*20850*	U.S. - Rhode Is. *20850*
R			***Agalinis auriculata*** (Michx.) Blake *20850*
	Ex/E	*20850*	U.S. - Alabama *20850*
	E	*20850*	U.S. - Arkansas *20850*
	I	*20850*	U.S. - District of Columbia *20850*
	V	*20850*	U.S. - Illinois *20850*
	E	*20850*	U.S. - Indiana *20850*
	V	*20850*	U.S. - Iowa *20850*
	V	*20850*	U.S. - Kansas *20850*
	E	*20850*	U.S. - Maryland *20850*
	Ex	*20850*	U.S. - Michigan *20850*
	E	*20850*	U.S. - Minnesota *20850*
	E	*20850*	U.S. - Mississippi *20850*
	V	*20850*	U.S. - Missouri *20850*
	Ex	*20850*	U.S. - New Jersey *20850*
	E	*20850*	U.S. - Ohio *20850*
	E	*20850*	U.S. - Oklahoma *20850*
	E	*20850*	U.S. - Pennsylvania *20850*
	E	*20850*	U.S. - South Carolina *20850*
	E	*20850*	U.S. - Tennessee *20850*
	Ex	*20850*	U.S. - Texas *20850*
	E	*20850*	U.S. - Virginia *20850*
	Ex/E	*20850*	U.S. - West Virginia *20850*
	Ex	*20850*	U.S. - Wisconsin *20850*
Ex/E			***Agalinis caddoensis*** Pennell *20850, 14662*
	Ex/E	*20850*	U.S. - Louisiana *20850*
Ex/E			***Agalinis calycina*** Pennell *20850*
	Ex/E	*20850*	U.S. - Texas *20850*
R			***Agalinis divaricata*** (Chapman) Pennell *20850*
	Ex/E	*20850*	U.S. - Alabama *20850*
	I	*20850*	U.S. - Florida *20850*
	E	*20850*	U.S. - Georgia *20850*
	I	*20850*	U.S. - Mississippi *20850*
I			***Agalinis kingsii*** Proctor *19712*
	I		Cayman Is. (Grand Cayman) *19434*
V			***Agalinis neoscotica*** (Greene) Fern. *20850*
	I	*20850*	Canada - Nova Scotia *20850*
	E	*20850*	U.S. - Maine *20850*
Ex/E			***Agalinis nuttallii*** Shinners *20850*
	Ex/E	*20850*	U.S. - Arkansas *20850*
R			***Agalinis pennellii*** K. Barringer *10260*
	R	*12468*	Peru *18200*
R			***Agalinis skinneriana*** (Wood) Britt. *20850, 14352*
	V	*20850*	Canada - Ontario *20850*
	I	*20850*	U.S. - Alabama *20850*
	I	*20850*	U.S. - Arkansas *20850*
	V	*20850*	U.S. - Illinois *20850*
	E	*20850*	U.S. - Indiana *20850*
	V	*20850*	U.S. - Iowa *20850*
	E	*20850*	U.S. - Kansas *20850*
	E	*20850*	U.S. - Kentucky *20850*
	I	*20850*	U.S. - Louisiana *20850*
	E	*20850*	U.S. - Maryland *20850*
	E	*20850*	U.S. - Michigan *20850*
	R	*20850*	U.S. - Missouri *20850*
	E	*20850*	U.S. - Nebraska *20850*
	V	*20850*	U.S. - Ohio *20850*
	I	*20850*	U.S. - Oklahoma *20850*
	E	*20850*	U.S. - Tennessee *20850*
	E	*20850*	U.S. - Wisconsin *20850*
I			***Alonsoa peduncularis*** (Kunze) Wettst. *20604*

	I	*20604*	South Africa - Cape Province *20604*
V			***Amphianthus pusillus*** Torr. *20850*
	E	*20850*	U.S. - Alabama *20850*
	V	*20850*	U.S. - Georgia *20850*
	E	*20850*	U.S. - South Carolina *20850*
E			***Amphiolanthus longipes*** Urban *5607*
	E	*19105*	Cuba *5607*
V			***Anarrhinum longipedicellatum*** R.Fern. *8000, 20171*
	V	*20076*	Portugal *8000*
E			***Anarrhinum pubescens*** Fresen. *16168*
	E	*16168*	Egypt (Sinai) *16168*
R			***Angelonia verticellata*** Philcox *11530*
	R	*11530*	Brazil *11530*
I			***Anticharis glandulosa*** Asch. var. ***caerulea*** Blatter & Hallberg *7772*
	I		India - Rajasthan (Jaisalmer) *7771*
R			***Antirrhinum charidemi*** Lange *8000, 20171*
	R	*20874*	Spain (Cabo de Gata) *8000*
R			***Antirrhinum chrysothales*** Font Quer
	R		Morocco
R			***Antirrhinum costatum*** Wiggins *12495*
	R	*12495*	Mexico *12495*
R			***Antirrhinum gebelicum*** Brullo & Furnari
	R		Libya
R			***Antirrhinum grosii*** Font Quer *20171*
	R	*11496*	Spain (Prov. Avila & Salamanca: Sierra de Gredos) *11496*
E			***Antirrhinum lopesianum*** Rothm. *8000, 20171*
	E	*20076*	Portugal *8000*
V			***Antirrhinum microphyllum*** Rothm. *11496, 20171*
	V	*11496*	Spain (Prov. Cuenca & Guadalajara: Sierras south of Saedon) *11496*
V			***Antirrhinum pertegasii*** Rothm. *20171*
	V	*11496*	Spain (Puertos de Tortosa-Beceite) *20692*
R			***Antirrhinum pulverulentum*** Lázaro Ibiza *20171*
	R		Spain
R			***Antirrhinum rupestre*** Boiss. & Reut. *20171*
	R		Spain
R			***Antirrhinum saccharatum*** Fernandez Casas
	R		Spain
R			***Antirrhinum valentinum*** Font Quer *20171*
	R	*20692*	Spain (Valencia) *11496*
V			***Aureolaria patula*** (Chapman) Pennell *20850*
	E	*20850*	U.S. - Alabama *20850*
	E	*20850*	U.S. - Georgia *20850*
	V	*20850*	U.S. - Kentucky *20850*
	V	*20850*	U.S. - Tennessee *20850*
R			***Bacopa eisenii*** (Kellogg) Pennell *20850*
	I	*20850*	U.S. - California *20850*
	I	*20850*	U.S. - Nevada *20850*
E			***Bacopa longipes*** (Pennell) Standl. *5607*
	E	*19105*	Cuba (Pinar del Rio; I. Juventud) *5607*
E			***Bacopa minuta*** Borh. & Muniz *5607*
	E	*19105*	Cuba (Holguin) *5607*
R			***Bartsia patriciae*** N.Holmgren *11351*
	R	*12777*	Ecuador *11351*
R			***Bartsia pumila*** Benth. *11351*
	R	*12777*	Ecuador *11351*
R			***Bartsia spicata*** Ramond *20171*

R		France
I		Spain
R	***Besseya bullii*** (Eat.) Rydb. *20850*	
	R	*20850* U.S. - Illinois *20850*
	E	*20850* U.S. - Indiana *20850*
	R	*20850* U.S. - Iowa *20850*
	E	*20850* U.S. - Michigan *20850*
	E	*20850* U.S. - Minnesota *20850*
	Ex/E	*20850* U.S. - Ohio *20850*
	R	*20850* U.S. - Wisconsin *20850*
V	***Besseya oblongifolia*** Pennell *20850*	
	V	*20850* U.S. - New Mexico *20850*
V	***Besseya ritteriana*** (Eastw.) Rydb. *20850*	
	I	*20850* U.S. - Colorado *20850*
I	***Bonnaya bracteoides*** Blatter & Hallberg *7771*	
	I	India - Rajasthan (Mt Abu) *7771*
R	***Bowkeria citrina*** Thode *20604*	
	R	*20604* South Africa - Natal *20604*
E	***Buchnera flexuosa*** Philcox *11532*	
	E	*11532* Brazil *11532*
R	***Buchnera rubriflora*** Philcox *11531*	
	R	*11531* Colombia *11531*
V	***Calceolaria adenanthera*** ssp. *adenanthera* *20883, 11351*	
	V	*20883* Ecuador *20883*
E	***Calceolaria adenanthera*** ssp. *bracteata* Molau *20883, 11351*	
	E	*20883* Ecuador *20883*
E	***Calceolaria adenocalyx*** Molau *20883, 17279*	
	E	*20883* Colombia *20883*
E	***Calceolaria ajugoides*** Kränzlin *20883, 18200*	
	E	*20883* Peru *20883*
E	***Calceolaria amoena*** Molau *20883, 12777*	
	E	*20883* Bolivia (La Paz) *20883*
R	***Calceolaria angustiflora*** Ruiz & Pavón *20883, 12777*	
	R	*20883* Peru *20883*
V	***Calceolaria anisanthera*** Pennell *20883*	
	I	*20883* Ecuador *20883*
	V	*20883* Peru *20883*
V	***Calceolaria annua*** Edwin *20883*	
	V	*20883* Peru *20883*
V	***Calceolaria aperta*** Edwin *20883, 18200*	
	V	*20883* Peru *20883*
E	***Calceolaria aperta*** Edwin ssp. *aperta* *20883*	
	E	*20883* Peru *20883*
E	***Calceolaria aperta*** Edwin ssp. *incana* (Molau) Molau *20883*	
	E	*20883* Peru *20883*
R	***Calceolaria aquatica*** Braun & Bouché *20883*	
	V	*20883* Bolivia *20883*
V	***Calceolaria arbuscula*** Molau *20883, 18200*	
	V	*20883* Peru *20883*
E	***Calceolaria argentea*** H.B.K. *20883*	
	E	*20883* Peru *20883*
V	***Calceolaria atahualpae*** ssp. *witasekiana* (Kränzlin)Molau *20883*	
	V	*20883* Peru *20883*
V	***Calceolaria aurea*** Pennell *20883*	
	V	*20883* Peru *20883*
E	***Calceolaria australis*** (Molau) Molau *20883, 11351*	

	E	*20883* Ecuador *20883*
E	***Calceolaria barbata*** Molau *20883, 12777*	
	E	*20883* Peru *20883*
R	***Calceolaria bartsiifolia*** Weddell *20883*	
	R	*20883* Bolivia *20883*
V	***Calceolaria bicolor*** Ruiz & Pavón *20883*	
	V	*20883* Peru *20883*
E	***Calceolaria bogotensis*** (Pennell) Pennell *20883, 12777*	
	E	*12777* Bolivia *12777*
	E	*20883* Colombia *20883*
V	***Calceolaria brachiata*** Kränzlin *20883, 11351*	
	V	*20883* Ecuador *20883*
E	***Calceolaria bullata*** Molau *20883, 18200*	
	E	*20883* Peru *20883*
E	***Calceolaria caespitosa*** Moalu *20883, 18200*	
	E	*20883* Peru *20883*
V	***Calceolaria cataractarum*** Molau *20883*	
	V	*20883* Colombia *20883*
	V	*20883* Ecuador *20883*
V	***Calceolaria chaetostemon*** Pennell *20883*	
	V	*20883* Peru *20883*
V	***Calceolaria chrysosphaera*** Pennell *20883*	
	V	*20883* Peru *20883*
R	***Calceolaria colombiana*** Pennell *20883*	
	R	*20883* Colombia *20883*
V	***Calceolaria commutata*** Molau *20883, 12777*	
	V	*20883* Ecuador *20883*
E	***Calceolaria concava*** Molau *20883, 18200*	
	E	*20883* Peru *20883*
E	***Calceolaria connatifolia*** Pennell *20883, 18200*	
	E	*20883* Peru *20883*
E	***Calceolaria cordifolia*** Molau *20883, 18200*	
	E	*20883* Peru *20883*
V	***Calceolaria cordiformis*** Edwin *20883, 18200*	
	V	*20883* Peru *20883*
E	***Calceolaria crassa*** Molau *20883, 12777*	
	E	*20883* Bolivia *20883*
V	***Calceolaria cromosa*** Pennell ssp. *cromosa* *20883*	
	V	*20883* Ecuador *20883*
	V	*20883* Peru *20883*
V	***Calceolaria cromosa*** ssp. *elegans* Molau *20883*	
	V	*20883* Peru *20883*
E	***Calceolaria cumbemayensis*** Molau *20883, 18200*	
	E	*20883* Peru *20883*
V	***Calceolaria cuneiformis*** ssp. *xerophila* Molau *20883*	
	V	*20883* Peru *20883*
E	***Calceolaria cypripediiflora*** Kränzlin *20883*	
	E	*20883* Peru *20883*
V	***Calceolaria cyripediiflora*** Kranzlin *18200*	
	V	*12777* Peru *18200*
E	***Calceolaria deflexa*** ssp. *cuneata* Molau *20883*	
	E	*20883* Peru *20883*
E	***Calceolaria densiflora*** Molau *20883, 18200*	
	E	*20883* Peru *20883*

E	*Calceolaria dentifolia* Edwin *20883*		
	E	*20883* Peru	*20883*
V	*Calceolaria dilatata* Benth. *20883*		
	V	*20883* Ecuador	*20883*
E	*Calceolaria discotheca* Molau *20883, 18200*		
	E	*20883* Peru	*20883*
E	*Calceolaria divaricata* H.B.K. *20883, 18200*		
	E	*20883* Peru	*20883*
V	*Calceolaria engleriana* ssp. *lutea* Molau *20883*		
	V	*20883* Peru	*20883*
E	*Calceolaria ericoides* ssp. *peruviana* Molau *20883*		
	E	*20883* Peru	*20883*
E	*Calceolaria extensa* Benth. *20883, 18200*		
	E	*20883* Peru (Amazonas)	*20883*
V	*Calceolaria ferruginea* Cavanilles *20883, 11351*		
	V	*20883* Ecuador	*20883*
E	*Calceolaria frondosa* Molau *20883, 12777*		
	E	*20883* Ecuador	*20883*
V	*Calceolaria fusca* Pennell *20883*		
	E	*20883* Colombia	*20883*
	V	*20883* Ecuador	*20883*
	E	*20883* Peru	*20883*
E	*Calceolaria gaultherioides* Molau *20883, 18200*		
	E	*20883* Peru	*20883*
R	*Calceolaria glacialis* Weddell *20883*		
	V	*20883* Argentina	*20883*
	E	*20883* Bolivia	*20883*
V	*Calceolaria glauca* Ruiz & Pavón *20883*		
	V	*20883* Peru	*20883*
E	*Calceolaria gossypina* Benth. *20883, 11351*		
	E	*20883* Ecuador	*20883*
E	*Calceolaria grandiflora* Pennell *20883, 11351*		
	E	*20883* Ecuador	*20883*
E	*Calceolaria helianthemoides* H.B.K. *20883*		
	E	*20883* Ecuador	*20883*
E	*Calceolaria heterophylla* Ruiz & Pavón *20883, 17208*		
	E	*20883* Peru	*20883*
E	*Calceolaria hirsuta* Molau *20883, 18200*		
	E	*20883* Peru	*20883*
V	*Calceolaria hirtifolia* Pennell *20883*		
	E	*20883* Colombia	*20883*
V	*Calceolaria hispida* ssp. *acaulis* Molau *20883*		
	V	*20883* Peru	*20883*
V	*Calceolaria inamoena* ssp. *mellefoliata* (Kranzlin) Molau *20883*		
	V	*20883* Peru	*20883*
E	*Calceolaria inaudita* Kränzlin *20883, 18200*		
	E	*20883* Peru	*20883*
E	*Calceolaria incachacensis* Kränzlin *20883, 12777*		
	E	*20883* Bolivia (Cochabamba)	*20883*
V	*Calceolaria incarum* ssp. *incarum* *20883*		
	V	*20883* Peru	*20883*
V	*Calceolaria incarum* ssp. *sanchezii* Molau *20883*		
	V	*20883* Peru	*20883*
V	*Calceolaria inflexa* Ruiz & Pavón *20883, 18200*		

	V	*20883* Peru	*20883*
V	*Calceolaria jujuyensis* Botta *20883, 17279*		
	E	*20883* Argentina	*20883*
	V	*20883* Bolivia	*20883*
V	*Calceolaria laevis* Molau *20883*		
	V	*20883* Peru	*20883*
V	*Calceolaria lanata* H.B.K. *20883*		
	V	*20883* Ecuador	*20883*
E	*Calceolaria lasiocalyx* Pennell *20883, 12777*		
	E	*20883* Peru	*20883*
E	*Calceolaria lavandulifolia* H.B.K. *20883*		
	E	*20883* Ecuador	*20883*
V	*Calceolaria leptantha* Pennell *20883, 18200*		
	V	*20883* Peru	*20883*
R	*Calceolaria leucanthera* Pennell *20883, 17279*		
	V	*20883* Colombia	*20883*
	E	*20883* Venezuela	*20883*
E	*Calceolaria llamaensis* (Edwin) Molau *20883, 18200*		
	E	*20883* Peru	*20883*
R	*Calceolaria lojensis* Pennell *20883*		
	R	*20883* Ecuador	*20883*
	E	*20883* Peru	*20883*
E	*Calceolaria ludens* Kränzlin *20883, 18200*		
	E	*20883* Peru	*20883*
E	*Calceolaria luteocalyx* Edwin *20883, 18200*		
	E	*20883* Peru	*20883*
V	*Calceolaria maculata* Edwin *20883, 18200*		
	V	*20883* Peru	*20883*
R	*Calceolaria mandoniana* Kranzlin *20883*		
	V	*20883* Bolivia	*20883*
	E	*20883* Peru	*20883*
E	*Calceolaria martinezii* Kränzlin *20883, 11351*		
	E	*20883* Ecuador	*20883*
E	*Calceolaria melissifolia* ssp. *pseudoscabra* (Edwin) Molau *20883*		
	E	*20883* Peru	*20883*
E	*Calceolaria mexicana* ssp. *perijensis* (Pennell) Molau *20883*		
	E	*20883* Colombia	*20883*
E	*Calceolaria mexicana* ssp. *prostrata* Benth. *20883*		
	E	*20883* Venezuela	*20883*
V	*Calceolaria micans* Molau *20883*		
	V	*20883* Peru	*20883*
R	*Calceolaria microbefaria* ssp. *microbefaria* *20883, 12777*		
	E	*20883* Costa Rica	*20883*
	R	*20883* Colombia	*20883*
	R	*20883* Venezuela	*20883*
E	*Calceolaria microbefaria* ssp. *tatamana* (Pennell) Molau *20883*		
	E	*20883* Colombia	*20883*
V	*Calceolaria monantha* Kränzlin *20883, 12777*		
	V	*20883* Bolivia	*20883*
V	*Calceolaria moyobambae* Kranzlin *20883, 18200*		
	V	*20883* Peru	*20883*
V	*Calceolaria myriophylla* Kränzlin *20883*		
	V	*20883* Peru	*20883*
E	*Calceolaria neglecta* Molau *20883*		
	E	*20883* Peru	*20883*

V *Calceolaria nevadensis* ssp. *meridensis* (Pennell) Molau *20883*
   V   *20883* Venezuela *20883*

V *Calceolaria nevadensis* ssp. *nevadensis* *20883*
   V   *20883* Colombia *20883*
   E   *20883* Venezuela *20883*

E *Calceolaria obliqua* Molau *20883, 12777*
   E   *20883* Peru *20883*

E *Calceolaria oblonga* Ruiz & Pavón *20883, 18200*
   E   *20883* Peru *20883*

E *Calceolaria obtusa* Molau *20883, 11351*
   E   *20883* Ecuador *20883*

E *Calceolaria odontophylla* Molau *20883, 11351*
   E   *20883* Ecuador *20883*

E *Calceolaria olivaceae* Molau *20883*
   E   *20883* Peru *20883*

E *Calceolaria oreophila* Molau *20883, 18200*
   E   *20883* Peru *20883*

V *Calceolaria oxyphylla* Molau *20883, 11351*
   V   *20883* Ecuador *20883*

R *Calceolaria parvifolia* ssp. *guentheri* (Kränzlin) Molau *20883*
   R   *20883* Bolivia *20883*

E *Calceolaria pedunculata* Molau *20883*
   E   *20883* Ecuador *20883*

E *Calceolaria pedunculata* Molau ssp. *pedunculata* *20883*
   E   *20883* Ecuador *20883*

E *Calceolaria pedunculata* Molau ssp. *sumacensis* Molau *20883, 11351*
   E   *20883* Ecuador *20883*

V *Calceolaria penlandii* ssp. *penlandii* *20883*
   E   *20883* Colombia *20883*
   V   *20883* Ecuador *20883*

V *Calceolaria penlandii* ssp. *puraceensis* (Pennell) Molau *20883*
   V   *20883* Colombia *20883*

E *Calceolaria percaespitosa* Wooden *20883, 18200*
   E   *20883* Peru *20883*

V *Calceolaria phaeotricha* Molau *20883*
   V   *20883* Ecuador *20883*

E *Calceolaria pilosa* Molau *20883, 18200*
   E   *20883* Peru *20883*

E *Calceolaria pinnata* ssp. *delicatula* (Kranzlin) Molau *20883*
   E   *20883* Peru *20883*

V *Calceolaria pisacomensis* Meyen ex Walpers *20883*
   V   *20883* Peru *20883*

E *Calceolaria platyzyga* Diels *20883, 11351*
   E   *20883* Ecuador *20883*

V *Calceolaria procera* Pennell *20883, 18200*
   V   *20883* Peru *20883*

V *Calceolaria pulverulenta* Ruiz & Pavón *20883, 18200*
   V   *20883* Peru *20883*

E *Calceolaria pumila* Edwin *20883, 18200*
   E   *20883* Peru *20883*

E *Calceolaria punicea* Ruiz & Pavón *20883, 18200*
   E   *20883* Peru *20883*

R *Calceolaria purpurascens* (Kränzlin) Molau *20883*
   R   *20883* Ecuador *20883*

V *Calceolaria ramosa* Molau *20883, 18200*
   V   *20883* Peru *20883*

E *Calceolaria rariflora* Molau *20883*
   E   *20883* Peru *20883*

V *Calceolaria reichlinii* Edwin *20883*
   V   *20883* Peru *20883*

V *Calceolaria revoluta* Pennell *20883*
   V   *20883* Peru *20883*

E *Calceolaria rhacodes* Kränzlin *20883*
   E   *20883* Peru *20883*

E *Calceolaria rhododendroides* Kränzlin *20883, 18200*
   E   *20883* Peru *20883*

V *Calceolaria rosmarinifolia* Lam. *20883*
   V   *20883* Ecuador *20883*

V *Calceolaria rotundifolia* (H.B.K.) Kuntze *20883, 18200*
   V   *20883* Peru *20883*

R *Calceolaria rupestris* Molau *20883*
   R   *20883* Peru *20883*

E *Calceolaria salicifolia* ssp. *nigricans* *20883*
   E   *20883* Peru *20883*

E *Calceolaria salicifolia* ssp. *salicifolia* *20883*
   E   *20883* Peru *20883*

E *Calceolaria sclerophylla* Molau *20883*
   E   *20883* Peru *20883*

E *Calceolaria semiconnata* Pennell *20883, 11351*
   E   *20883* Ecuador *20883*

V *Calceolaria sericea* Pennell *20883*
   V   *20883* Ecuador *20883*

E *Calceolaria serrata* Lam. *20883*
   E   *20883* Ecuador *20883*

E *Calceolaria sibthorpioides* H.B.K. *20883, 18200*
   E   *20883* Peru *20883*

E *Calceolaria sonchensis* Edwin *20883, 18200*
   E   *20883* Peru *20883*

V *Calceolaria soratensis* Kränzlin *20883, 12777*
   V   *20883* Bolivia *20883*

E *Calceolaria sotarensis* Pennell *20883, 17279*
   E   *20883* Colombia *20883*

V *Calceolaria speciosa* Pennell *20883, 18200*
   V   *20883* Peru *20883*

R *Calceolaria spruceana* Kranzlin *20883*
   R   *20883* Ecuador *20883*

V *Calceolaria stricta* H.B.K. *20883, 11351*
   V   *20883* Ecuador *20883*

E *Calceolaria ternata* Molau *20883*
   E   *20883* Ecuador *20883*
   E   *20883* Peru *20883*

R *Calceolaria tetragona* ssp. *endopogon* (Kränzlin) Molau *20883*
   R   *20883* Peru *20883*

R *Calceolaria tetragona* Benth ssp. *tetragona* *20883*
   R   *20883* Peru *20883*

E *Calceolaria trichanthera* Molau *20883, 17279*
   E   *20883* Colombia *20883*

V *Calceolaria trilobata* ssp. *aequilateralis* (Edwin)

Molau *20883*
V   *20883* Peru *20883*

E   *Calceolaria tucumana* Descole *20883*
    E   *20883* Argentina *20883*
    E   *20883* Bolivia *20883*

R   *Calceolaria vaccinioides* Kränzlin *20883*
    V   *20883* Bolivia *20883*
    V   *20883* Peru *20883*

V   *Calceolaria vaccinoides* Kranzlin *18200*
    V   *17279* Bolivia *17279*
    V   *17279* Peru *18200*

E   *Calceolaria variifolia* Edwin *20883*
    E   *20883* Ecuador *20883*
    V   *12468* Peru *11351*

E   *Calceolaria velutinoides* Edwin *20883*
    E   *20883* Peru *20883*

V   *Calceolaria viscosa* Ruiz y Pavón *20883*
    V   *20883* Peru *20883*

V   *Calceolaria vulpina* Kränzlin *20883*
    V   *20883* Peru *20883*

E   *Calceolaria weberbaueriana* Kränzlin *20883*
    E   *20883* Peru *20883*

E   *Calceolaria zamorana* Molau *20883, 11351*
    E   *20883* Ecuador *20883*

I   *Campbellia aurantiaca* Wight *10252*
    I   *16162* Sri Lanka *10252*

R   *Camptoloma canariense* (Webb) & Berth.) Hilliard *20750*
    R   *20750* Spain - Canary Is. *20750*

V   *Campylanthus mirandae* A.G. Miller *20146*
    V   *20146* Oman *20146*

R   *Campylanthus ramosissimus* Wight
    R   *13883* India - Gujarat (Kutch) *13883*
    R   *13883* Pakistan *13883*

V   *Campylanthus salsoloides* (L.f.) Roth
    V   Spain - Canary Is.

R   *Castilleja affinis* Hook. & Arn. *20850*
    I   *20850* U.S. - California *20850*

V   *Castilleja aquariensis* N. Holmgren *20850*
    V   *20850* U.S. - Utah *20850*

R   *Castilleja arachnoidea* Greenm. *20850*
    I   *20850* U.S. - California *20850*
    I   *20850* U.S. - Nevada *20850*
    I   *20850* U.S. - Oregon *20850*

R   *Castilleja arctica* Kyrl. et Serg. ssp. *vorkutensis* Rebr. *20085, 21309*
    R   *20085* Russia (E.Europe) - North *20085*

V   *Castilleja brevistyla* (Hoover) Chuang & Heckard *20850*
    I   *20850* U.S. - California *20850*

V   *Castilleja campestris* ssp. *succulenta* (Hoover) Chuang & Heckard *20850*
    V   *20850* U.S. - California *20850*

R   *Castilleja chlorotica* Piper *20850*
    R   *20850* U.S. - Oregon *20850*

E   *Castilleja christii* N. Holmgren *20850*
    E   *20850* U.S. - Idaho *20850*

E   *Castilleja ciliata* Pennell *20850*
    E   *20850* U.S. - Texas *20850*

V   *Castilleja cinerea* Gray *20850, 17788*

    V   *20850* U.S. - California (San Bernadino mountains) *20850*

R   *Castilleja crista-galli* Rydb. *20850*
    I   *20850* U.S. - Idaho *20850*
    I   *20850* U.S. - Montana *20850*
    V   *20850* U.S. - Wyoming *20850*

Ex   *Castilleja cruenta* Standl. *20850, 14662*
    Ex   *20850* U.S. - Arizona *20850*

V   *Castilleja cryptantha* Pennell & G.N. Jones *20850*
    V   *20850* U.S. - Washington *20850*

R   *Castilleja dissitiflora* N. Holmgren *20850*
    R   *20850* U.S. - Nevada *20850*

R   *Castilleja disticha* Eastw. *20850*
    I   *20850* U.S. - California *20850*

V   *Castilleja elongata* Pennell *20850*
    V   *20850* U.S. - Texas *20850*

V   *Castilleja franciscana* Pennell *20850*
    I   *20850* U.S. - California *20850*

V   *Castilleja fraterna* Greenm. *20850*
    V   *20850* U.S. - Oregon *20850*

E   *Castilleja fulva* Pennell *20850*
    Ex/E   *20850* Canada - British Columbia *20850*

V   *Castilleja gleasonii* Elmer *20850*
    V   *20850* U.S. - California *20850*

V   *Castilleja grisea* Dunkle *20850*
    V   *20850* U.S. - California *20850*

R   *Castilleja hololeuca* Greene *20850*
    I   *20850* U.S. - California *20850*

R   *Castilleja jepsonii* Bacig. & Heckard *20850*
    I   *20850* U.S. - California *20850*

V   *Castilleja kaibabensis* N. Holmgren *20850*
    V   *20850* U.S. - Arizona *20850*

R   *Castilleja lemmonii* Gray *20850*
    I   *20850* U.S. - California *20850*
    I   *20850* U.S. - Nevada *20850*

E   *Castilleja levisecta* Greenm. *20850, 10701*
    E   *20850* Canada - British Columbia *20850*
    Ex   *20850* U.S. - Oregon *20850*
    E   *20850* U.S. - Washington *20850*

Ex/E   *Castilleja ludoviciana* Pennell *20850, 14662*
    I   *20850* U.S. - Louisiana *20850*

R   *Castilleja martinii* Abrams *20850*
    I   *20850* U.S. - California *20850*
    V   *20850* U.S. - Nevada *20850*
    I   *20850* U.S. - Oregon *20850*

R   *Castilleja martinii* (Pennell) N. Holmgren var. *clokeyi* (Pennell)N.Holmgren *20850*
    I   *20850* U.S. - California *20850*
    V   *20850* U.S. - Nevada *20850*

R   *Castilleja mcvaughii* N. Holmgren *10089*
    R   *19850* Mexico - Jalisco *21204*

V   *Castilleja mendocinensis* (Eastw.) Pennell *20850*
    V   *20850* U.S. - California *20850*

E   *Castilleja mollis* Pennell *20850*
    E   *20850* U.S. - California *20850*

V   *Castilleja montigena* Heckard *20850*
    I   *20850* U.S. - California *20850*

R   *Castilleja nana* Eastw. *20850*
    I   *20850* U.S. - California *20850*
    I   *20850* U.S. - Nevada *20850*
    E   *20850* U.S. - Utah *20850*

Magnoliopsida (dicots): Scrophulariaceae: *Castilleja*

E	*Castilleja neglecta* Zeile *20850*	
	E	20850 U.S. - California *20850*
V	*Castilleja nervata* Eastw. *20850*	
	I	20850 U.S. - Arizona *20850*
	R	20883 Mexico *20883*
R	*Castilleja nivea* Pennell & Ownbey *20850*	
	I	20850 U.S. - Montana *20850*
	V	20850 U.S. - Wyoming *20850*
V	*Castilleja parviflora* (G.N. Jones) Ownbey var. *olympica* (G.N. Jones) Ownbey *20850*	
	I	20850 U.S. - Washington *20850*
E	*Castilleja parviflora* Bong. var. *oreopola* (Greenm.) Ownbey *20850*	
	I	20850 U.S. - Alaska *20850*
	I	20850 U.S. - Oregon *20850*
	I	20850 U.S. - Washington *20850*
V	*Castilleja parvula* Rydb. *20850*	
	V	20850 U.S. - Utah *20850*
V	*Castilleja peckiana* Pennell *20850*	
	I	20850 U.S. - Nevada *20850*
	I	20850 U.S. - Oregon *20850'*
V	*Castilleja peirsonii* Eastw. *20850*	
	I	20850 U.S. - California *20850*
R	*Castilleja pilosa* (Pennell) N. Holmgren var. *steenensis* (Pennell) N. Holmgren *20850*	
	R	20850 U.S. - Oregon *20850*
V	*Castilleja praeterita* Heckard & Bacig. *20850*	
	I	20850 U.S. - California *20850*
V	*Castilleja puberula* Rydb. *20850*	
	I	20850 U.S. - Colorado *20850*
R	*Castilleja pulchella* Rydb. *20850*	
	E	20850 U.S. - Idaho *20850*
	I	20850 U.S. - Montana *20850*
	V	20850 U.S. - Utah *20850*
	R	20850 U.S. - Wyoming *20850*
V	*Castilleja revealii* N. Holmgren *20850, 19002*	
	V	20850 U.S. - Utah *20850*
V	*Castilleja rubida* Piper *20850*	
	V	20850 U.S. - Oregon *20850*
V	*Castilleja rupicola* Piper ex Fern. *20850, 10701*	
	E	20850 Canada - British Columbia *20850*
	I	20850 U.S. - Oregon *20850*
	I	20850 U.S. - Washington *20850*
E	*Castilleja salsuginosa* N. Holmgren *20850*	
	E	20850 U.S. - Nevada *20850*
V	*Castilleja schizotricha* Greenm. *20850*	
	I	20850 U.S. - California *20850*
	V	20850 U.S. - Oregon *20850*
R	*Castilleja schrenkii* Rebrist. *20171*	
	R	former European USSR
R	*Castilleja subinclusa* Greene *20850*	
	I	20850 U.S. - California *20850*
Ex/E	*Castilleja uliginosa* Eastw. *20850*	
	Ex	20850 U.S. - California *20850*
R	*Castilleja venusta* Rzed. *10071*	
	R	19755 Mexico *10071*
V	*Castilleja wightii* Elmer *20850*	
	I	20850 U.S. - California *20850*
R	*Castilleja yukonis* Pennell *20850*	
	I	20850 Canada - Mackenzie *20850*
	I	20850 Canada - Yukon Territory *20850*

	I	20850 U.S. - Alaska *20850*
R	*Celsia mairei* Murb.	
	R	Morocco
R	*Celsia pinnatisecta* Battand. *10488*	
	R	14958 Algeria *10488*
R	*Celsia valentina* Font Quer *20171*	
	R	Spain
R	*Chaenorhinum glareosum* (Boiss.) Willk. *20171*	
	R	11496 Spain (Sierra Nevada) *11496*
R	*Chaenorhinum idaeum* Rech.f. *20171*	
	R	20730 Greece - Crete *20730*
R	*Chaenorhinum rubrifolium* (Robill. & Castagne ex DC.) Fourr. ssp. *formenterae* (Gandoger) R. Fernandes *20171*	
	R	Spain - Balearic Is.
V	*Chaenorhinum serpyllifolium* (Lange) Lange ssp. *lusitanicum* R. Fernandes *17891, 20171*	
	V	20076 Portugal *17891*
E	*Chaenorhinum tenellum* (Cav.) Lange *20171*	
	E	20692 Spain (Valencia) *20692*
E	*Chaenorrhinum minus* (L.) Lange ssp. *pseudorubrifolium* Gamisans *20528*	
	E	20528 France - Corsica *20528*
V	*Charadrophila capensis* Marloth *20604*	
	V	20604 South Africa - Cape Province *20604*
E	*Cheilophyllum dentatum* Urban *5607*	
	E	19105 Cuba (Matanzas; Villa Clara) *5607*
V	*Cheilophyllum jamaicense* Pennell *13336*	
	V	13336 Jamaica (Clarendon, St. Elizabeth) *19486*
E	*Cheilophyllum micranthum* Urban *5607*	
	E	19105 Cuba (Ciego de Avila; Camaguey) *5607*
E	*Cheilophyllum microphyllum* Pennell *5607*	
	E	19105 Cuba (Pinar del Rio) *5607*
V	*Cheilophyllum sphaerocarpum* Urban *5607*	
	V	19105 Cuba (Villa Clara) *5607*
R	*Chelone cuthbertii* Small *20850*	
	E	20850 U.S. - Georgia *20850*
	R	20850 U.S. - North Carolina *20850*
	I	20850 U.S. - South Carolina *20850*
	V	20850 U.S. - Virginia *20850*
R	*Chelone obliqua* L. var. *speciosa* Pennell & Wherry *20850*	
	Ex/E	20850 U.S. - Arkansas *20850*
	R	20850 U.S. - Illinois *20850*
	R	20850 U.S. - Indiana *20850*
	Ex/E	20850 U.S. - Iowa *20850*
	R	20850 U.S. - Kentucky *20850*
	E	20850 U.S. - Michigan *20850*
	I	20850 U.S. - Minnesota *20850*
	E	20850 U.S. - Missouri *20850*
I	*Chionohebe glabra* (Cheesem.) M.J. Heads *19305*	
	I	19305 New Zealand *19305*
I	*Christisonia saulieri* Dunn	
	I	India - Tamil Nadu
I	*Christisonia subacaulis* (Benth.) Gardner	
	I	India - Tamil Nadu (Tirunelveli Hills)
I	*Christisonia thwaitesii* Trimen *10252*	
	I	16162 Sri Lanka *10252*
E	*Cistanche tubulosa* (Shrenk) Wight *11139*	
	E	China - Xinjiang Uygur Zizhiqu *11139*

V	*Collinsia antonina* Hardham *20850*	
	E *20850* U.S. - California *20850*	
V	*Collinsia callosa* Parish *20850*	
	I *20850* U.S. - California *20850*	
	I *20850* U.S. - Nevada *20850*	
R	*Collinsia childii* Parry ex Gray *20850*	
	I *20850* U.S. - California *20850*	
R	*Collinsia concolor* Greene *20850*	
	I *20850* U.S. - California *20850*	
V	*Collinsia corymbosa* Herder *20850*	
	V *20850* U.S. - California *20850*	
V	*Collinsia multicolor* Lindl. & Paxton *20850*	
	V *20850* U.S. - California *20850*	
V	*Collinsia parryi* Gray *20850*	
	I *20850* U.S. - California *20850*	
R	*Collinsia tinctoria* Hartw. ex Benth. *20850*	
	I *20850* U.S. - California *20850*	
R	*Collinsia torreyi* Gray *20850*	
	I *20850* U.S. - California *20850*	
	I *20850* U.S. - Nevada *20850*	
	I *20850* U.S. - Oregon *20850*	
R	*Cordylanthus eremicus* (Coville & Morton) Munz *20850*	
	I *20850* U.S. - California *20850*	
R	*Cordylanthus eremicus* (Coville & Morton) Munz ssp. *eremicus* *20850*	
	I *20850* U.S. - California *20850*	
E	*Cordylanthus eremicus* (Coville & Morton) Munz ssp. *kernensis* Chuang & Heckard *20850*	
	I *20850* U.S. - California *20850*	
R	*Cordylanthus kingii* S.Watson ssp. *kingii* *20850*	
	I *20850* U.S. - Nevada *20850*	
	V *20850* U.S. - Utah *20850*	
R	*Cordylanthus laxiflorus* Gray *20850*	
	I *20850* U.S. - Arizona *20850*	
	I *20850* U.S. - New Mexico *20850*	
R	*Cordylanthus maritimus* Nutt. ex Benth. *20850*	
	I *20850* U.S. - Arizona *20850*	
	I *20850* U.S. - California *20850*	
	I *20850* U.S. - Nevada *20850*	
	I *20850* U.S. - Oregon *20850*	
	V *20850* U.S. - Utah *20850*	
V	*Cordylanthus maritimus* Nutt. ex Benth. ssp. *maritimus* *20883, 20850, 8058*	
	V *20850* U.S. - California *20850*	
	I *20883* Mexico *20883*	
	? Mexico - Baja California Peninsula *8058*	
V	*Cordylanthus maritimus* Nutt. ex Benth. ssp. *palustris* (Behr) Chuang & Heckard *20850*	
	V *20850* U.S. - California *20850*	
	E *20850* U.S. - Oregon *20850*	
V	*Cordylanthus mollis* S.Gray *20850*	
	I *20850* U.S. - California *20850*	
V	*Cordylanthus mollis* A.Gray ssp. *hispidus* (Pennell) Chuang & Heckard *20850*	
	V *20850* U.S. - California *20850*	
E	*Cordylanthus mollis* A.Gray ssp. *mollis* *20850*	
	E *20850* U.S. - California *20850*	
V	*Cordylanthus nevinii* Gray *20850*	
	E *20850* U.S. - Arizona *20850*	
	I *20850* U.S. - California *20850*	
E	*Cordylanthus nidularius* J.T. Howell *20850*	

	E *20850* U.S. - California *20850*	
V	*Cordylanthus orcuttianus* Gray *20850*	
	E *20850* U.S. - California *20850*	
E	*Cordylanthus palmatus* (Ferris) J.F. Macbr. *20850, 17796*	
	E *20850* U.S. - California *20850*	
R	*Cordylanthus pilosus* Gray *20850*	
	I *20850* U.S. - California *20850*	
R	*Cordylanthus pilosus* Gray ssp. *hansenii* (Ferris) Chuang & Heckard *20850*	
	I *20850* U.S. - California *20850*	
V	*Cordylanthus pringlei* Gray *20850*	
	I *20850* U.S. - California *20850*	
E	*Cordylanthus rigidus* (Benth.) Jepson ssp. *littoralis* (Ferris) Chuang & Heckard *20850*	
	E *20850* U.S. - California *20850*	
V	*Cordylanthus tecopensis* Munz & Roos *20850*	
	E *20850* U.S. - California *20850*	
	V *20850* U.S. - Nevada *20850*	
E	*Cordylanthus tenuis* A.Gray ssp. *barbatus* Chuang & Heckard *20850*	
	E *20850* U.S. - California *20850*	
E	*Cordylanthus tenuis* A.Gray ssp. *brunneus* (Jepson) Munz *20850*	
	I *20850* U.S. - California *20850*	
E	*Cordylanthus tenuis* A.Gray ssp. *capillaris* (Pennell) Chuang & Heckard *20850, 10260*	
	E *20850* U.S. - California *20850*	
E	*Cordylanthus tenuis* A.Gray ssp. *pallescens* (Pennell) Chuang & Heckard *20850, 10260*	
	E *20850* U.S. - California *20850*	
R	*Cordylanthus tenuis* A.Gray ssp. *viscidus* (T.J. Howell) Chuang & Heckard *20850*	
	I *20850* U.S. - California *20850*	
	I *20850* U.S. - Oregon *20850*	
R	*Cymbalaria muelleri* (Moris) A. Chev. *20171*	
	R Italy - Sardinia	
R	*Derwentia arenaria* (Benth.) B.G.Briggs & Ehrend. *20681*	
	I *20681* Australia - New South Wales *20681*	
	I *20681* Australia - Queensland *20681*	
R	*Derwentia decorosa* (F.Muell.) B.G.Briggs & Ehrend. *20681*	
	R *20681* Australia - South Australia *20681*	
R	*Derwentia nivea* (Lindley) B.G.Briggs & Ehrend. *20681*	
	I *20681* Australia - New South Wales *20681*	
	I *20681* Australia - Tasmania *20681*	
	I *20681* Australia - Victoria *20681*	
I	*Diascia austromontana* K.E.Steiner *20604*	
	I *20604* Lesotho *20604*	
	I *20604* South Africa - Natal *20604*	
I	*Diascia heterandra* Benth. *20604*	
	I *20604* South Africa - Cape Province *20604*	
R	*Diascia insignis* K.E.Steiner *20604*	
	R *20604* South Africa - Cape Province *20604*	
V	*Diascia lewisiae* K.E.Steiner *20604*	
	V *20604* South Africa - Cape Province *20604*	
R	*Diascia patens* (Thunb.) Fourc. *20604*	
	R *20604* South Africa - Cape Province *20604*	
I	*Diascia tugelensis* Hilliard & B.L.Burtt *20604*	

I		20604 South Africa - Natal 20604
I		20604 South Africa - Orange Free State 20604

I *Diascia vigilis* Hilliard & B.L.Burtt 20604
  I 20604 Lesotho 20604
  I 20604 South Africa - Natal 20604
  I 20604 South Africa - Orange Free State 20604

I *Diclis stellarioides* Hiern 20604
  I 20604 South Africa - Cape Province 20604

E *Digitalis atlantica* Pomel 10488
  E 14958 Algeria 10488

R *Digitalis dubia* Rodriguez ssp. *palaui* Garc. Font.
  & Marcos
  R   Spain - Balearic Is.

R *Digitalis leucophaea* Smith ssp. *leucophaea*
  R   Greece

V *Diplacus aridus* Abrams 20850, 8058
  I 20850 U.S. - California 20850

V *Diplacus aurantiacus* W. Curtis ssp. *australis*
  (McMinn) R.M. Beeks 20850
  I 20850 U.S. - California 20850

V *Diplacus calycinus* Eastw. 20850
  I 20850 U.S. - California 20850

V *Diplacus clevelandii* (Brandeg.) Greene 20850
  I 20850 U.S. - California 20850

V *Diplacus fasciculatus* (Pennell) McMinn 20850
  I 20850 U.S. - California 20850

V *Diplacus linearis* (Benth.) Greene 20850
  I 20850 U.S. - California 20850

V *Diplacus lompocensis* McMinn 20850
  I 20850 U.S. - California 20850

V *Diplacus parviflorus* Greene 20850
  I 20850 U.S. - California 20850

R *Diplacus puniceus* Nutt. 20850
  I 20850 U.S. - California 20850

R *Diplacus rutilus* (A.L. Grant) McMinn 20850
  I 20850 U.S. - California 20850

R *Euphrasia alsa* F.Muell. 20681
  R 20681 Australia - New South Wales 20681

V *Euphrasia amphisysepala* W.R.Barker 20681
  V 20681 Australia - Tasmania 20681

R *Euphrasia arctica* Lange ex Rostr. ssp. *minor*
  Yeo 20171
  R 18216 Denmark 18216

Ex *Euphrasia arguta* R.Br. 20681, 14223
  Ex 20681 Australia - New South Wales 14223

I *Euphrasia azorica* H.C.Watson 8000, 20171
  I   Portugal - Azores 8000

V *Euphrasia bella* S.T.Blake 20681
  I 20681 Australia - New South Wales 20681
  I 20681 Australia - Queensland 20681

V *Euphrasia bowdeniae* W.R.Barker 20681
  V 20681 Australia - New South Wales 20681

R *Euphrasia calida* Yeo 20085, 20171
  R 20085 Iceland 20085

R *Euphrasia cambrica* Pugsley 8000, 20171
  R 5387 United Kingdom (Caernarvonshire) 19232

R *Euphrasia campbelliae* Pugsley 20171
  R 5387 United Kingdom (Scotland - Isle of Lewis)
    8000

R *Euphrasia christii* Favrat 18154, 20171
  I   Italy 8000
  R 18154 Switzerland 18154

E *Euphrasia collina* R.Br. ssp. *muelleri* (Wettst.)
  W.R.Barker 20681
  Ex/E 20681 Australia - New South Wales 20681
  Ex/E 20681 Australia - South Australia 20681
  E 20681 Australia - Victoria 20681

E *Euphrasia collina* R.Br. ssp. *osbornii*
  W.R.Barker 20681
  E 20681 Australia - South Australia 20681

R *Euphrasia collina* R.Br. ssp. *trichocalycina*
  (Gand.) W.R.Barker 20681
  I 20681 Australia - South Australia 20681
  I 20681 Australia - Victoria 20681

R *Euphrasia dunensis* Wünst. 18216, 20171
  R 18216 Denmark 18216

V *Euphrasia eichleri* Barker 20681
  V 20681 Australia - Victoria 20681

I *Euphrasia exaristata* Smejkal 6951, 20171
  I 19321 Slovakia (Vysoké Tatry mountains) 6951

E *Euphrasia formosissima* Skottsb. 19116
  E 19125 Chile - Juan Fernandez Is. 19116

V *Euphrasia genargentea* (Feoli) Diana Corrias 17891
  V 18264 Italy - Sardinia 18264

R *Euphrasia gibbsiae* Du Rietz ssp. *comberi* (Du
  Rietz) W.R.Barker 20681
  R 20681 Australia - Tasmania 20681

R *Euphrasia gibbsiae* Du Rietz ssp. *discolor*
  W.R.Barker 20681
  R 20681 Australia - Tasmania 20681

R *Euphrasia gibbsiae* Du Rietz ssp. *microdonta*
  W.R.Barker 20681
  R 20681 Australia - Tasmania 20681

R *Euphrasia gibbsiae* Du Rietz ssp. *pulvinestris*
  W.R.Barker 20681
  R 20681 Australia - Tasmania 20681

I *Euphrasia grandiflora* Hochst. 8000, 20171
  I   Portugal - Azores 8000

R *Euphrasia hachijoensis* Nakai 10573
  R 10573 Japan 10573

R *Euphrasia heslop-harrisonii* Pugsley 8000, 20171
  R 5387 United Kingdom (North Scotland) 19232

V *Euphrasia insignis* Wettst. var. *idzuensis* (Takeda)
  Yamaz. 10573
  V 10573 Japan 10573

R *Euphrasia insignis* Wettst. var. *iinumai* (Takeda)
  Yamaz. 10573
  R 10573 Japan 10573

R *Euphrasia insignis* Wettst. var. *pubigera* (Koidz.)
  Murata 10573
  R 10573 Japan 10573

R *Euphrasia marchesettii* Wettst. 8000, 20171
  V 18264 Italy 19997
  R   Slovenia 19997

R *Euphrasia maximowiczii* Wettst. var. *calcarea*
  Yamaz. 10573
  R 10573 Japan 10573

V *Euphrasia mendoncae* Samp. 8000, 20171
  V 20076 Portugal (north east) 8000

R	*Euphrasia microphylla* Koidz. *10573*		
	R	*10573* Japan *10573*	
Ex/E	*Euphrasia omiensis* Y. Kimura *10573*		
	Ex/E	*10573* Japan *10573*	
R	*Euphrasia orthocheila* W.R.Barker *20681*		
	I	*20681* Australia - New South Wales *20681*	
	I	*20681* Australia - Queensland *20681*	
V	*Euphrasia phragmostoma* W.R.Barker *20681*		
	V	*20681* Australia - Tasmania *20681*	
R	*Euphrasia ramulosa* W.R.Barker *20681*		
	R	*20681* Australia - New South Wales *20681*	
R	*Euphrasia rivularis* Pugsley *20171*		
	R	*5387* United Kingdom (Wales and N.W. England) *8000*	
R	*Euphrasia rotundifolia* Pugsley *20171*		
	R	*5387* United Kingdom (N. Scotland) *8000*	
R	*Euphrasia salisburgensis* Funck var. *schoenicola* Yeo. *18216*		
	R	*20083* Sweden *18216*	
V	*Euphrasia semipicta* W.R.Barker *20681*		
	V	*20681* Australia - Tasmania *20681*	
I	*Euphrasia slovaca* (P.F. Yeo) Holub *2050*		
	I	*2050* Czech Republic *2050*	
	V	*19321* Slovakia *19321*	
I	*Euphrasia stipitata* Smejkal		
	I	Czech Republic	
	I	Slovakia	
R	*Euphrasia tarokoana* Ohwi *20511*		
	R	*20511* Taiwan *20511*	
R	*Euphrasia vigursii* Davey *20171*		
	R	*5387* United Kingdom (S.W. England) *8000*	
V	*Euphrasia willkommii* Freyn *20171*		
	V	Spain	
R	*Freylinia crispa* Van Jaarsv. *20604*		
	R	*20604* South Africa - Cape Province *20604*	
I	*Freylinia decurrens* Levyns ex Van Jaarsv. *20604*		
	I	*20604* South Africa - Cape Province *20604*	
E	*Freylinia longiflora* Benth. *20604*		
	E	*20604* South Africa - Cape Province *20604*	
E	*Freylinia visseri* Van Jaarsv. *20604*		
	E	*20604* South Africa - Cape Province *20604*	
R	*Freylinia vlokii* Van Jaarsv. *20604*		
	R	*20604* South Africa - Cape Province *20604*	
R	*Galvezia leucantha* Wiggins ssp. *leucantha* *11117*		
	R	Ecuador - Galapagos *11117*	
E	*Galvezia leucantha* Wiggins ssp. *pubescens* Wiggins *11117*		
	E	*14980* Ecuador - Galapagos (Rabida) *11117*	
V	*Gambelia speciosa* Nutt. *20850*		
	I	*20850* U.S. - California *20850*	
V	*Gibsoniothamnus cornutus* (A. Gentry) D'Arcy var. *latidentatus* (A. Gentry) D'Arcy *20883, 9006*		
	I	*20883* Panama *20883*	
V	*Gibsoniothamnus mirificus* A. Gentry *20883, 9006*		
	I	*20883* Panama *20883*	
E	*Graderia fruticosa* Balf. f. *15534*		
	E	*15534* Yemen - Socotra *15534*	
V	*Gratiola heterosepala* Mason & Bacig. *20850*		

	V	*20850* U.S. - California *20850*	
	E	*20850* U.S. - Oregon *20850*	
V	*Hebe acutiflora* Cockayne *86*		
	V	*19305* New Zealand - North Is. *19305*	
R	*Hebe adamsii* *19305*		
	R	*19305* New Zealand - North Is. *19305*	
V	*Hebe armstrongii* (J. Armstr.) Cockayne & Allan *86*		
	V	*19305* New Zealand - South Is. *19305*	
V	*Hebe barkeri* (Cockayne) Cockayne *86*		
	V	*19305* New Zealand - Chatham Is. *19106*	
R	*Hebe biggarii* Cockayne		
	R	New Zealand - South Is.	
E	*Hebe breviracemosa* (W. Oliver) Cockayne & Allan *86*		
	E	*19305* New Zealand - Kermadec Is. (Raoul I.) *8177*	
V	*Hebe cupressoides* (Hook.f.) Cockayne & Allan *86*		
	V	*19305* New Zealand - South Is. *19305*	
R	*Hebe dieffenbachii* *19305*		
	R	*19305* New Zealand - Chatham Is. *19305*	
R	*Hebe macrocarpa* (Vahl) Cockayne & Allan var. *brevifolia* (Cheeseman) L. Moore		
	R	New Zealand - North Is.	
R	*Hebe poppelwellii* (Cockayne) Cockayne & Allan		
	R	New Zealand - South Is.	
I	*Hebe ramosissima* Simpson & J. Thomson		
	I	New Zealand - South Is.	
V	*Hebe speciosa* (R.Cunn. ex A.Cunn.) Andersen *19305, 20171*		
	V	*19305* New Zealand - North Is. *19305*	
E	*Hemianthus reflexus* C. Wright *19105*		
	E	*19105* Cuba (Pinar del Rio) *19105*	
E	*Holmgrenanthe pterophila* (Coville & Morton) Elisens *20850*		
	E	*20850* U.S. - California *20850*	
V	*Howelliella ovata* (Eastw.) Rothm. *20850*		
	V	*20850* U.S. - California *20850*	
R	*Ilysanthes congesta* A. Raynal		
	R	Senegal	
R	*Isoplexis canariensis* (L.) Loud. *17534*		
	R	*17534* Spain - Canary Is. *17534*	
E	*Isoplexis chalcantha* Svent. & O'Shanahan *17534*		
	E	*17534* Spain - Canary Is. *17534*	
E	*Isoplexis isabelliana* (Webb & Berthel.) Morris *10260*		
	E	*20750* Spain - Canary Is. *17534*	
R	*Isoplexis sceptrum* (L.f.) Loudon		
	R	Portugal - Madeira	
V	*Jamesbrittenia incisa* (Thunb.) Hilliard *20604*		
	V	*20604* South Africa - Cape Province *20604*	
R	*Jamesbrittenia megaphylla* Hilliard *20604*		
	R	*20604* Namibia *20604*	
	R	*20604* South Africa - Cape Province *20604*	
R	*Kickxia aegyptiaca* (L.) Nab. ssp. *tibestica* Wick.		
	R	Chad	
E	*Kickxia aegyptiaca* (L.) Nab. ssp. *virgata* Wick.		
	E	Sudan	
R	*Kickxia judaica* Danin *8895*		
	R	Israel *8895*	

E	***Kickxia macilenta*** (Decne.) Danin *16168*	
	E	*16168* Egypt (S. Sinai) *16168*
V	***Kickxia pendula*** (Kunkel) Kunkel	
	V	*20750* Spain - Canary Is. *20750*
I	***Kickxia scariosepala*** Tackh. & Boulos	
	I	Egypt
R	***Kickxia scoparia*** (Spreng.) Kunkel & Sunding	
	R	Spain - Canary Is.
V	***Kickxia urbanii*** (Pitard) K. Larsen	
	V	Spain - Canary Is.
R	***Lafuentea jeanpertiana*** Maire	
	R	Morocco
R	***Lafuentea rotundifolia*** Lag. *20171*	
	R	*20692* Spain (Betic Mountains) *20692*
R	***Lagotis takedana*** Miyabe & Tatew. *10573*	
	R	*10573* Japan *10573*
R	***Lagotis uralensis*** Schischk. *20171*	
	R	former European USSR
R	***Lagotis yezoensis*** Tatew. *10573*	
	R	*10573* Japan *10573*
R	***Lathraea rhodopea*** Dingler *5204, 20171*	
	R	*5204* Bulgaria *5204*
	R	Greece
E	***Lendneria ageratifolia*** (C. Wright) Pennell *5607*	
	E	*19105* Cuba (Pinar del Rio) *5607*
V	***Limnophila cana*** Griff. *14872*	
	V	*14872* Bangladesh *14872*
I	***Limnophila parviflora*** Yamaz. *19120*	
	I	*19120* Thailand *19120*
I	***Limnophila siamensis*** Yamaz. *19120*	
	I	*19120* Thailand *19120*
I	***Limnophila verticillata*** Yamaz. *19120*	
	I	*19120* Thailand *19120*
V	***Limosella granitica*** W.R.Barker *20681*	
	V	*20681* Australia - South Australia *20681*
E	***Limosella pubiflora*** Pennell *20850, 14662*	
	Ex/E	*20850* U.S. - Arizona *20850*
	E	*20850* U.S. - New Mexico *20850*
R	***Linaria aeruginea*** (Gouan) Cav. ssp. ***pruinosa*** Chater & B. Valdes *20171*	
	R	*20727* Spain - Balearic Is. *20727*
V	***Linaria algarviana*** Chav. *8000, 20171*	
	V	*14155* Portugal (W. Algarve) *14155*
R	***Linaria alpina*** Miller ssp. ***petraea*** (Jord.) Rouy *18154*	
	I	France
	R	*18154* Switzerland *18154*
R	***Linaria amoi*** Campo ex Amo *20171*	
	R	*20660* Spain (Málaga, Sierra Tejeda, Sierra Almijara) *11496*
R	***Linaria arabiniana*** M.B.Crespo, De la Torre & J.L Solanas *20692*	
	R	*20692* Spain (near Benidorm, Alicante province) *20692*
R	***Linaria arcusangeli*** Atzei & Camarda *18264*	
	R	*18264* Italy - Sardinia *18264*
R	***Linaria arenicola*** Pau & Font Quer	
	R	Morocco
R	***Linaria benitori*** Fernandez Casas	

	R	Spain (Cabo de Gata)
I	***Linaria biebersteinii*** Besser *20171*	
	I	former European USSR
E	***Linaria burceziana*** Maire *10488*	
	E	*14958* Algeria *10488*
R	***Linaria cavanillesii*** Chav. *20171*	
	R	*20692* Spain (east) *20692*
R	***Linaria chalapensis*** (L.) Miller var. ***brevicalyx*** Davis *12840*	
	R	*12840* Turkey *12840*
R	***Linaria clementei*** Haens. ex Boiss. *20171*	
	R	*20660* Spain (Málaga, Sierra Mujas, Sierra Blanca) *11496*
V	***Linaria coutinhoi*** Valdés *8000, 20171*	
	V	*20076* Portugal (northern) *8000*
V	***Linaria cretacea*** Fisch. ex Spreng. *20171*	
	V	former European USSR
R	***Linaria decipiens*** Battand. *10488*	
	R	*14958* Algeria *10488*
R	***Linaria depauperata*** Leresche ex Lange ssp. ***hegelmaierii*** (Lange) De la Torre, Alcaraz & M.B.Crespo *20692*	
	R	*20692* Spain (north of Alicante province) *20692*
R	***Linaria faucicola*** Leresche & Levier *20171*	
	R	Spain
V	***Linaria flava*** (Poiret) Desf. var. ***corsica*** (Sommier) Fiori *15080*	
	V	*15080* France - Corsica *15080*
R	***Linaria gattefossei*** Maire & M. Weiller	
	R	Morocco
R	***Linaria genistifolia*** (L.) Miller ssp. ***polyclada*** (Fenzl) Davis *12840*	
	R	*12840* Turkey *12840*
R	***Linaria glacialis*** Boiss. *20171*	
	R	Spain
E	***Linaria hellenica*** Turrill *17891, 20171*	
	E	Greece *17891*
R	***Linaria huteri*** Lange *20171*	
	R	Spain
R	***Linaria kurdica*** Boiss. & Hohen ssp. ***eriocalyx*** (Boiss.) Davis *12840*	
	R	*12840* Turkey *12840*
R	***Linaria lamarckii*** Rouy *20076, 20171*	
	V	*20076* Portugal *20076*
	R	*20660* Spain (Huelva) *5403*
R	***Linaria microsepala*** A.Kern. *20171*	
	R	*21091* Bosnia & Herzegovina *21091*
	R	(former) Yugoslavia
R	***Linaria nevadensis*** (Boiss.) Boiss. & Reut. *20171*	
	R	Spain
R	***Linaria nigricans*** Lange *20171*	
	R	Spain
V	***Linaria orbensis*** Carretero & Boira *20692*	
	V	*20692* Spain (near Orba, Alicante province) *20692*
R	***Linaria platycalyx*** Boiss. *20171*	
	R	*20664* Spain (Cádiz, Málaga) *20664*
V	***Linaria ricardoi*** Cout. *8000, 20171*	
	V	*20076* Portugal (south) *8000*

R   *Linaria thymifolia* (Vahl) DC. *20171*
     R   *20528*   France (west coast) *20528*

R   *Linaria tonzigii* Lona *8000, 20171*
     R   *14155*   Italy *8000*

R   *Linaria tursica* B. Valdes & Cabezudo *17891*
     R   *20874*   Spain (Huelva, Doñana, Cádiz) *19818*

R   *Linaria weilleri* Emberger & Maire
     R   Morocco

V   *Lindenbergia arabica* (S. Moore) Hartl. *20146*
     V   *20146*   Oman (western Hajar) *20146*

E   *Lindernia alterniflora* (C. Wright) Alain *5607*
     E   *19105*   Cuba (Pinar del Rio; I. Juventud) *5607*

I   *Lindernia cephalantha* Yamaz. *19120*
     I   *19120*   Thailand *19120*

I   *Lindernia khaoyaiensis* Yamaz. *19120*
     I   *19120*   Thailand *19120*

I   *Lindernia maxwellii* Yamaz. *19120*
     I   *19120*   Thailand *19120*

I   *Lindernia minima* (Benth.) Mukherjee
     I   India - Tamil Nadu

V   *Lindernia multicaulis* (Urban) Alain *5607*
     V   *19105*   Cuba (Matanzas; Cienfuegos) *5607*

I   *Lindernia rivularis* Kerr ex Barnett *19120*
     I   *19120*   Thailand *19120*

R   *Lindernia rupestris* W.R.Barker ms. *20681*
     R   *20681*   Australia - Northern Territory *20681*

I   *Lindernia satakei* Yamaz. *19120*
     I   *19120*   Thailand *19120*

R   *Lindernia setulosa* (Maxim.) Tuy. *10573*
     R   *10573*   Japan *10573*

R   *Lophospermum chiapense* Elisens *16387*
     R   *16387*   Mexico - Chiapas *16387*

R   *Mabrya coccinea* (I.M. Johnston) Elisens *16387*
     R   *16387*   Mexico - Coahuila *16387*

R   *Mabrya flaviflora* (I.M. Johnston) D. Sutton *16387*
     R   *16387*   Mexico - Baja California Peninsula *16387*

R   *Mabrya geniculata* (H. Robinson & Fern.) Elisens var. *lanata* Elisens *16387*
     R   *16387*   Mexico - Sonora *16387*

R   *Macranthera flammea* (Bartr.) Pennell *20850*
     V   *20850*   U.S. - Alabama *20850*
     V   *20850*   U.S. - Florida *20850*
     V   *20850*   U.S. - Georgia *20850*
     E   *20850*   U.S. - Louisiana *20850*
     R   *20850*   U.S. - Mississippi *20850*

I   *Manulea cinerea* Hilliard *20604*
     I   *20604*   South Africa - Cape Province *20604*

R   *Manulea florifera* Hilliard & B.L.Burtt *20604*
     R   *20604*   South Africa - Cape Province *20604*
     R   *20604*   South Africa - Natal *20604*

I   *Manulea incana* Thunb. *20604*
     I   *20604*   South Africa - Cape Province *20604*

R   *Manulea ovatifolia* Hilliard *20604*
     R   *20604*   South Africa - Cape Province *20604*

I   *Manulea ramulosa* Hilliard *20604*
     I   *20604*   South Africa - Cape Province *20604*

V   *Mazus novaezeelandiae* *19305*
     V   *19305*   New Zealand - North Is. *19305*
     V   *19305*   New Zealand - South Is. *19305*

R   *Melampyrum arvense* L. var. *elatius* Boiss. *12840*
     R   *12840*   Turkey *12840*

V   *Melampyrum ciliatum* Boiss. & Heldr. *20171*
     V   Greece

R   *Melampyrum doerfleri* Ronniger *20178, 20171*
     R   *20178*   Albania *20178*
     V   *21091*   Bosnia & Herzegovina *21091*
     R   (former) Yugoslavia

R   *Melampyrum heracleoticum* Boiss. & Orph. *20178, 20171*
     R   *20178*   Albania *20178*
     R   Greece
     R   (former) Yugoslavia *20178*

R   *Melampyrum laxum* Miq. var. *yakusimense* Tuy. *10573*
     R   *10573*   Japan *10573*

R   *Melampyrum trichocalycinum* Vandas *20171*
     V   *21091*   Bosnia & Herzegovina *21091*
     R   (former) Yugoslavia

R   *Melanospermum rudolfii* Hilliard *20604*
     R   *20604*   South Africa - Transvaal *20604*

Ex/E   *Micranthemum micranthemoides* (Nutt.) Wettst. *20850, 14662*
     Ex   *20850*   U.S. - Delaware *20850*
     Ex   *20850*   U.S. - District of Columbia *20850*
     Ex/E   *20850*   U.S. - Maryland *20850*
     Ex/E   *20850*   U.S. - New Jersey *20850*
     Ex   *20850*   U.S. - New York *20850*
     Ex   *20850*   U.S. - Pennsylvania *20850*
     Ex/E   *20850*   U.S. - Virginia *20850*

E   *Micranthemum rotundatum* C. Wright *5607*
     E   *19105*   Cuba (Pinar del Rio; I. Juventud) *5607*

V   *Mimulus acutidens* Greene *20850*
     I   *20850*   U.S. - California *20850*

R   *Mimulus androsaceus* Curran ex Greene *20850*
     I   *20850*   U.S. - California *20850*

E   *Mimulus angustifolius* (Greene) A.L. Grant *20850*
     E   *20850*   U.S. - Nevada *20850*

R   *Mimulus arenarius* A.L. Grant *20850*
     I   *20850*   U.S. - California *20850*

R   *Mimulus barbatus* Greene *20850*
     I   *20850*   U.S. - California *20850*

V   *Mimulus biolettii* Eastw. *20850*
     I   *20850*   U.S. - California *20850*

V   *Mimulus brachiatus* Pennell *20850*
     V   *20850*   U.S. - California *20850*

Ex   *Mimulus brandegei* Pennell *20850, 14662*
     Ex   *20850*   U.S. - California *20850*

R   *Mimulus cleistogamus* J.T. Howell *20850*
     I   *20850*   U.S. - California *20850*

V   *Mimulus dentilobus* B.L. Robins. & Fern. *20850*
     I   *20850*   U.S. - Arizona *20850*
     I   *20850*   U.S. - New Mexico *20850*
     E   *20850*   U.S. - Texas *20850*

R   *Mimulus dudleyi* A.L. Grant *20850*
     I   *20850*   U.S. - California *20850*

R   *Mimulus eastwoodiae* Rydb. *20850*
     I   *20850*   U.S. - Arizona *20850*
     E   *20850*   U.S. - Colorado *20850*
     I   *20850*   U.S. - Nevada *20850*
     R   *20850*   U.S. - Utah *20850*

V   *Mimulus exiguus* Gray *20850*

V		20850 U.S. - California 20850	
V	*Mimulus filicaulis* S.Watson 20850		
	V	20850 U.S. - California 20850	
V	*Mimulus gemmiparus* W.A. Weber 20850		
	V	20850 U.S. - Colorado 20850	
E	*Mimulus glabratus* H.B. K. var. *michiganensis* (Pennell) Fassett 20850		
	E	20850 U.S. - Michigan 20850	
V	*Mimulus glaucescens* Greene 20850		
	V	20850 U.S. - California 20850	
V	*Mimulus gracilipes* B.L. Robins. 20850		
	I	20850 U.S. - California 20850	
E	*Mimulus hymenophyllus* Meinke 20850		
	E	20850 U.S. - Idaho 20850	
	E	20850 U.S. - Oregon 20850	
R	*Mimulus johnstonii* A.L. Grant 20850		
	I	20850 U.S. - California 20850	
V	*Mimulus jungermannioides* Suksdorf 20850		
	V	20850 U.S. - Oregon 20850	
	Ex	20850 U.S. - Washington 20850	
E	*Mimulus latifolius* Gray 20850		
	I	20850 U.S. - California 20850	
V	*Mimulus mohavensis* J.G. Lemmon 20850		
	V	20850 U.S. - California 20850	
R	*Mimulus montioides* Gray 20850		
	I	20850 U.S. - California 20850	
	I	20850 U.S. - Nevada 20850	
V	*Mimulus norrisii* Heckard & Shevock 20850		
	V	20850 U.S. - California 20850	
V	*Mimulus nudatus* Curran ex Greene 20850		
	I	20850 U.S. - California 20850	
V	*Mimulus ovatus* (Gray) N. Holmgren 20850		
	V	20850 U.S. - Nevada 20850	
R	*Mimulus parishii* Greene 20850		
	I	20850 U.S. - California 20850	
	I	20850 U.S. - Nevada 20850	
R	*Mimulus pictus* (Curran ex Greene) Gray 20850		
	R	20850 U.S. - California 20850	
R	*Mimulus platycalyx* Pennell 20850		
	I	20850 U.S. - California 20850	
R	*Mimulus platylaemus* Pennell 20850		
	I	20850 U.S. - California 20850	
V	*Mimulus purpureus* A.L. Grant var. *purpureus* 20850		
	V	20850 U.S. - California 20850	
R	*Mimulus rattanii* Gray 20850		
	I	20850 U.S. - California 20850	
R	*Mimulus rattanii* Gray var. *decurtatus* (A.L. Grant) Pennell 20850		
	R	20850 U.S. - California 20850	
V	*Mimulus ringens* L. var. *colpophilus* Fern. 20850		
	I	20850 Canada - Quebec 20850	
	V	20850 U.S. - Maine 20850	
	I	20850 U.S. - Vermont 20850	
R	*Mimulus rupicola* Coville & A.L. Grant 20850		
	R	20850 U.S. - California 20850	
E	*Mimulus shevockii* Heckard & Bacig. 20850		
	E	20850 U.S. - California 20850	
R	*Mimulus spissus* A.L. Grant 20850		

	I	20850 U.S. - Arizona 20850	
	I	20850 U.S. - California 20850	
	R	20850 U.S. - Nevada 20850	
	E	20850 U.S. - Utah 20850	
V	*Mimulus subsecundus* Gray 20850		
	V	20850 U.S. - California 20850	
Ex	*Mimulus traskiae* A.L. Grant 20850, 14662		
	Ex	20850 U.S. - California 20850	
V	*Mimulus verbenaceus* Greene 20850		
	I	20850 U.S. - Arizona 20850	
	I	20850 U.S. - Utah 20850	
R	*Mimulus washingtonensis* Gandog. 20850		
	I	20850 U.S. - Idaho 20850	
	R	20850 U.S. - Oregon 20850	
	V	20850 U.S. - Washington 20850	
	I	20850 U.S. - Wyoming 20850	
Ex	*Mimulus whipplei* A.L. Grant 20850, 14662		
	Ex	20850 U.S. - California 20850	
V	*Mimulus whitneyi* Gray 20850		
	I	20850 U.S. - California 20850	
R	*Misopates rivas-martinezii* 15846		
	R	15846 Spain 15846	
V	*Monttea chilensis* Gay 15088		
	V	13875 Chile 13875	
I	*Nathaliella alaica* B. Fedtsch. 5942		
	I	5942 Kyrgyzstan (south) 5942	
	I	5942 Tajikistan 5942	
R	*Necranthus orobanchioides* Gilli 12840		
	R	12840 Turkey 12840	
R	*Nemesia chrysolopha* Diels 20604		
	R	20604 South Africa - Cape Province 20604	
E	*Nemesia micrantha* Hiern 20604		
	E	20604 South Africa - Cape Province 20604	
R	*Nemesia picta* Schltr. 20604		
	R	20604 South Africa - Cape Province 20604	
R	*Nemesia saccata* E.Mey. ex Benth. 20604		
	R	20604 South Africa - Cape Province 20604	
R	*Nemesia strumosa* Benth. 20604		
	R	20604 South Africa - Cape Province 20604	
E	*Neopicrorhiza scrophulariiflora* (Pennell) Hong 17617		
	E	17617 China - Xizang Zizhiqu 11139	
	E	17617 China - Yunnan 11139	
R	*Odontites asturicus* (Lainz) Lainz		
	R	Spain	
E	*Odontites discolor* Pomel 10488		
	E	14958 Algeria 10488	
R	*Odontites fradini* Pomel 10488		
	R	14958 Algeria 10488	
E	*Odontites granatensis* Boiss. 15398, 20171		
	E	15398 Spain 15398	
V	*Odontites holliana* (Lowe) Benth. 17891		
	V	Portugal - Madeira 17891	
I	*Odontites jaubertiana* (Boreau) D.Dietr. ex Walp. 20171		
	I	France (west, central & south)	
R	*Orobanche armena* Tzvelev 12840		
	R	12840 Turkey 12840	
Ex/E	*Orobanche berthelotii* Webb & Berthel. 20216		
	Ex/E	20216 Spain - Canary Is. (Tenerife) 20216	
R	*Orobanche boninsimae* (Maxim.) Tuy. 8037		

R   *19134* Japan - Ogasawara-shoto *8037*

R   **Orobanche densiflora** Salzmann forma *melitensis*
Beck *13351*

   R   *17933* Malta (Mellieha Bay and Ramla tat-Torri) *17933*

R   **Orobanche ducellieri** Maire *10488*

   R   *14958* Algeria *10488*

R   **Orobanche fuscovinosa** Maire

   R   Morocco

R   **Orobanche hadroantha** Beck *12840*

   R   *12840* Turkey *12840*

R   **Orobanche haenseleri** Reut. *20171*

   R   Spain

R   **Orobanche hookeriana** Ball

   R   Morocco

R   **Orobanche humbertii** Maire

   R   Morocco

R   **Orobanche leptantha** Pomel *10488*

   R   *14958* Algeria *10488*

V   **Orobanche parishii** (Jepson) Heckard ssp. *brachyloba*
Heckard *20850*

   V   *20850* U.S. - California *20850*

R   **Orobanche schweinfurthii** G. Beck

   R   Egypt

V   **Orobanche sideana** Gilli *12840*

   V   *12840* Turkey *12840*

E   **Orobanche solenanthi** Novopokr. & Pissjauka

   E   former USSR *6930*

R   **Orobanche trichocalyx** (Webb & Berthel.) Beck *20171*

   V   *20076* Portugal *20076*
   R   Spain

E   **Orobanche valida** Jepson ssp. *valida* *20850*

   E   *20850* U.S. - California *20850*

V   **Orobanche vallicola** (Jepson) Heckard *20850*

   I   *20850* U.S. - California *20850*

E   **Orthocarpus bachystachyus** Gray *20850*

   E   *20850* U.S. - California *20850*

R   **Orthocarpus bracteosus** Benth. *20850, 10701*

   V   *20850* Canada - British Columbia *20850*
   I   *20850* U.S. - California *20850*
   I   *20850* U.S. - Maryland *20850*
   I   *20850* U.S. - New York *20850*
   I   *20850* U.S. - Oregon *20850*
   E   *20850* U.S. - Washington *20850*

Ex   **Orthocarpus pachystachyus** Gray *20850, 14662*

   Ex   *20850* U.S. - California *20850*

R   **Otacanthus villosus** Philcox *11530*

   R   *11530* Brazil *11530*

R   **Parahebe lithophila** B.G.Briggs & Ehrend. *20681*

   R   *20681* Australia - New South Wales *20681*

R   **Parahebe trifida** W. Oliver

   R   New Zealand - South Is.

R   **Parentucellia floribunda** Viv.

   R   Libya

R   **Paulownia taiwaniana** Hu & Cheng *20511*

   R   *20511* Taiwan *20511*

V   **Pedicularis angustifolia** Benth. *20850*

   V   *20850* U.S. - New Mexico *20850*

R   **Pedicularis asparagoides** Lapeyr. *20171*

   V   *20528* France (Pyrenees) *20528*

R   Spain (east Pyrenees) *20171*

R   **Pedicularis baumgartenii** Simonk. *17823, 20171*

   R   *19949* Romania *20631*

V   **Pedicularis bracteosa** Benth. ex Hook. var. *flavida*
(Pennell) Cronq. *20850*

   V   *20850* U.S. - California *20850*
   I   *20850* U.S. - Oregon *20850*
   I   *20850* U.S. - Washington *20850*

V   **Pedicularis contorta** N. Reese var. *rubicunda* N.
Reese *20850*

   I   *20850* U.S. - Idaho *20850*
   V   *20850* U.S. - Montana *20850*

V   **Pedicularis dudleyi** Elmer *20850*

   V   *20850* U.S. - California *20850*

R   **Pedicularis ferdinandi** Bornm. *20171*

   R   (former) Yugoslavia

V   **Pedicularis furbishiae** S.Watson *20850, 4321*

   E   *20850* Canada - New Brunswick *20850*
   V   *20850* U.S. - Maine *20850*

R   **Pedicularis glabra** McVaugh & Mellichamp *10096*

   R   *19850* Mexico *10096*

R   **Pedicularis heterodonta** Pancic *20171*

   V   *21091* Bosnia & Herzegovina *21091*
   R   (former) Yugoslavia

R   **Pedicularis howellii** Gray *20850*

   I   *20850* U.S. - California *20850*
   V   *20850* U.S. - Oregon *20850*

R   **Pedicularis limnogena** A.Kern. *20171*

   R   Greece
   R   *19949* Romania *19417*
   R   (former) Yugoslavia

R   **Pedicularis nanfutashanensis** Yamazaki *20511*

   R   *20511* Taiwan *20511*

E   **Pedicularis numidica** Pomel *10488*

   E   *14958* Algeria *10488*.

R   **Pedicularis ochiaiana** Makino *10573*

   R   *10573* Japan *10573*

R   **Pedicularis olympica** Boiss. *12840*

   R   *12840* Turkey *12840*

V   **Pedicularis parryi** (Greene) G.D. Carr ssp.
mogollonica (Greene) G.D. Carr *20850*

   I   *20850* U.S. - Arizona *20850*
   I   *20850* U.S. - Colorado *20850*
   V   *20850* U.S. - New Mexico *20850*
   I   *20850* U.S. - Utah *20850*
   E   *20850* U.S. - Wyoming *20850*

R   **Pedicularis pulchella** Pennell *20850*

   I   *20850* U.S. - Montana *20850*
   V   *20850* U.S. - Wyoming *20850*

V   **Pedicularis rainierensis** Pennell & Warren *20850*

   V   *20850* U.S. - Washington *20850*

R   **Pedicularis refracta** Maxim. *10573*

   R   *10573* Japan *10573*

R   **Pedicularis resupinata** L. var. *microphylla*
Honda *10573*

   R   *10573* Japan *10573*

V   **Pedicularis semibarbata** Gray var. *charlestonensis*
Pennell & Clokey *20850*

   V   *20850* U.S. - Nevada *20850*

I   **Pedicularis siamensis** Tsoong

   I   Thailand (Doi Chiengdao)

Magnoliopsida (dicots): Scrophulariaceae: *Pedicularis*

V *Pedicularis sudetica* Willd. ssp.
   sudetica 20800
     V 20800 Poland 20800

R *Pedicularis tripinnata* Martens & Galeotti 10096
     R 19755 Mexico 10096

V *Penstemon absarokensis* Evert 20850
     V 20850 U.S. - Wyoming 20850

R *Penstemon acaulis* L.O. Williams 20850
     E 20850 U.S. - Utah 20850
     E 20850 U.S. - Wyoming 20850

V *Penstemon alamosensis* Pennell & Nisbet 20850
     V 20850 U.S. - New Mexico 20850
     E 20850 U.S. - Texas 20850

V *Penstemon albomarginatus* M.E. Jones 20850
     V 20850 U.S. - Arizona 20850
     E 20850 U.S. - California 20850
     E 20850 U.S. - Nevada 20850

V *Penstemon ammophilus* N. Holmgren & L. Shultz 20850
     V 20850 U.S. - Utah 20850

V *Penstemon angustifolius* Nutt. ex Pursh var. *dulcis*
   Neese 20850
     V 20850 U.S. - Utah 20850

R *Penstemon angustifolius* Nutt. ex Pursh var.
   vernalensis H. Holmgren 20850
     I 20850 U.S. - Colorado 20850
     R 20850 U.S. - Utah 20850

V *Penstemon arenarius* Greene 20850
     V 20850 U.S. - Nevada 20850

V *Penstemon atwoodii* Welsh 20850
     V 20850 U.S. - Utah 20850

R *Penstemon barbatus* (Cav.) Roth ssp. *trichander*
   (Gray) Keck 20850
     I 20850 U.S. - Arizona 20850
     I 20850 U.S. - Colorado 20850
     I 20850 U.S. - New Mexico 20850
     E 20850 U.S. - Utah 20850

R *Penstemon barnebyi* N. Holmgren 20850
     E 20850 U.S. - California 20850
     R 20850 U.S. - Nevada 20850

V *Penstemon barrettiae* Gray 20850
     V 20850 U.S. - Oregon 20850
     V 20850 U.S. - Washington 20850

V *Penstemon bicolor* (Brandeg.) Clokey & Keck 20850
     E 20850 U.S. - Arizona 20850
     I 20850 U.S. - California 20850
     I 20850 U.S. - Nevada 20850

V *Penstemon bicolor* (Brandegee) Clokey & Keck ssp.
   bicolor 20850
     V 20850 U.S. - Nevada 20850

V *Penstemon bicolor* (Brandegee) Clokey & Keck ssp.
   roseus Clokey & Keck 20850
     E 20850 U.S. - Arizona 20850
     I 20850 U.S. - Nevada 20850

V *Penstemon bracteatus* Keck 20850
     V 20850 U.S. - Utah 20850

R *Penstemon breviculus* (Keck) Nisbet & R.C.
   Jackson 20850
     I 20850 U.S. - Arizona 20850
     V 20850 U.S. - Colorado 20850
     V 20850 U.S. - New Mexico 20850
     E 20850 U.S. - Utah 20850

R *Penstemon caesius* Gray 20850
     I 20850 U.S. - California 20850

V *Penstemon calcareus* Brandeg. 20850
     I 20850 U.S. - California 20850

Ex/E *Penstemon campanulatus* (Cav.) Willd. 20850
     Ex/E 20850 U.S. - New Mexico 20850

R *Penstemon cardinalis* Woot. & Standl. 20850
     R 20850 U.S. - New Mexico 20850
     V 20850 U.S. - Texas 20850

V *Penstemon cardinalis* Woot. & Standl. ssp.
   cardinalis 20850
     V 20850 U.S. - New Mexico 20850

V *Penstemon cardinalis* Woot. & Standl. ssp. *regalis*
   (A. Nels.) Nisbet & R.C. Jackson 20850
     V 20850 U.S. - New Mexico 20850
     V 20850 U.S. - Texas 20850

R *Penstemon caryi* Pennell 20850
     R 20850 U.S. - Montana 20850
     V 20850 U.S. - Wyoming 20850

R *Penstemon clevelandii* Gray ssp.
   clevelandii 20850
     I 20850 U.S. - California 20850

R *Penstemon clevelandii* Gray ssp. *mohavensis*
   Keck 20850
     I 20850 U.S. - California 20850

V *Penstemon clutei* A. Nels. 20850
     V 20850 U.S. - Arizona 20850

V *Penstemon compactus* (Keck) Crosswhite 20850
     V 20850 U.S. - Idaho 20850
     V 20850 U.S. - Utah 20850

R *Penstemon concinnus* Keck 20850
     V 20850 U.S. - Nevada 20850
     R 20850 U.S. - Utah 20850

R *Penstemon confusus* M.E. Jones 20850
     I 20850 U.S. - Nevada 20850
     R 20850 U.S. - Utah 20850

E *Penstemon crandallii* A. Nels. ssp. *atratus*
   Keck 20850
     I 20850 U.S. - Colorado 20850
     E 20850 U.S. - Utah 20850

V *Penstemon crandallii* A. Nels. ssp. *procumbens*
   (Greene) Keck 20850
     I 20850 U.S. - Colorado 20850

E *Penstemon deamii* Pennell 20850
     I 20850 U.S. - Illinois 20850
     E 20850 U.S. - Indiana 20850
     I 20850 U.S. - Kentucky 20850

E *Penstemon debilis* O'Kane & J. Anderson 20850
     E 20850 U.S. - Colorado 20850

V *Penstemon degeneri* Crosswhite 20850
     V 20850 U.S. - Colorado 20850

R *Penstemon deustus* Dougl. ex Lindl. var. *pedicellatus*
   M.E. Jones 20850
     I 20850 U.S. - California 20850
     I 20850 U.S. - Nevada 20850
     I 20850 U.S. - Oregon 20850
     E 20850 U.S. - Utah 20850

V *Penstemon deustus* (Suksdorf) Pennell & Keck var.
   variabilis (Suksdorf) Cronq. 20850
     I 20850 U.S. - Oregon 20850
     E 20850 U.S. - Washington 20850

E *Penstemon discolor* Keck 20850
     E 20850 U.S. - Arizona 20850

V *Penstemon dissectus* Ell. 20850

V   *20850*   U.S. - Georgia   *20850*

V   *Penstemon distans* N. Holmgren *20850*
    V   *20850*   U.S. - Arizona   *20850*

E   *Penstemon dolius* M. E. Jones ex Pennell var. *duchesnensis* N. Holmgren *20850*
    E   *20850*   U.S. - Utah   *20850*

V   *Penstemon eriantherus* (Piper) A. Nels. var. *whitedii* (Piper) A. Nels. *20850*
    I   *20850*   U.S. - Washington   *20850*

V   *Penstemon filiformis* (Keck) Keck *20850*
    V   *20850*   U.S. - California   *20850*

R   *Penstemon flavescens* Pennell *20850*
    I   *20850*   U.S. - Idaho   *20850*
    R   *20850*   U.S. - Montana   *20850*

V   *Penstemon floribundus* D. Danley *20850*
    V   *20850*   U.S. - Nevada   *20850*

R   *Penstemon floridus* Brandeg. *20850*
    I   *20850*   U.S. - California   *20850*
    I   *20850*   U.S. - Nevada   *20850*

V   *Penstemon floridus* Brandeg. var. *austinii* (Eastw.) N. Holmgren *20850*
    I   *20850*   U.S. - California   *20850*
    I   *20850*   U.S. - Nevada   *20850*

R   *Penstemon floridus* Brandeg. var. *floridus* *20850*
    I   *20850*   U.S. - California   *20850*
    I   *20850*   U.S. - Nevada   *20850*

V   *Penstemon flowersii* Neese & Welsh *20850, 11630*
    V   *20850*   U.S. - Utah   *20850*

R   *Penstemon fruticiformis* Coville *20850*
    I   *20850*   U.S. - California   *20850*
    V   *20850*   U.S. - Nevada   *20850*

V   *Penstemon fruticiformis* Coville ssp. *amargosae* Keck *20850*
    I   *20850*   U.S. - California   *20850*
    V   *20850*   U.S. - Nevada   *20850*

V   *Penstemon fruticiformis* Coville ssp. *fruticiformis* *20850*
    I   *20850*   U.S. - California   *20850*
    I   *20850*   U.S. - Nevada   *20850*

E   *Penstemon gibbensii* Dorn *20850*
    E   *20850*   U.S. - Colorado   *20850*
    E   *20850*   U.S. - Utah   *20850*
    E   *20850*   U.S. - Wyoming   *20850*

R   *Penstemon glaucinus* Pennell *20850*
    R   *20850*   U.S. - Oregon   *20850*

V   *Penstemon goodrichii* N. Holmgren *20850*
    V   *20850*   U.S. - Utah   *20850*

V   *Penstemon grahamii* Keck *20850*
    V   *20850*   U.S. - Colorado   *20850*
    V   *20850*   U.S. - Utah   *20850*

R   *Penstemon grinnellii* Eastw. *20850*
    I   *20850*   U.S. - California   *20850*

R   *Penstemon grinnellii* Eastw. ssp. *grinnellii* *20850*
    I   *20850*   U.S. - California   *20850*

R   *Penstemon grinnellii* Eastw. ssp. *scrophularioides* (M.E. Jones) Munz *20850*
    I   *20850*   U.S. - California   *20850*

R   *Penstemon guadalupensis* Heller *20850*
    R   *20850*   U.S. - Texas   *20850*

R   *Penstemon harringtonii* Penl. *20850*
    R   *20850*   U.S. - Colorado   *20850*

E   *Penstemon haydenii* S.Watson *20850*
    E   *20850*   U.S. - Nebraska (Cherry; Hooker; Garden Co.) *20850*

R   *Penstemon heterodoxus* Gray ssp. *cephalophorus* (Greene) Keck *20850*
    I   *20850*   U.S. - California   *20850*

V   *Penstemon humilis* (Pennell) Keck ssp. *obtusifolius* (Pennell) Keck *20850*
    V   *20850*   U.S. - Utah   *20850*

E   *Penstemon idahoensis* Atwood & Welsh *20850*
    E   *20850*   U.S. - Idaho   *20850*
    E   *20850*   U.S. - Utah   *20850*

R   *Penstemon incertus* Brandeg. *20850*
    I   *20850*   U.S. - California   *20850*

R   *Penstemon kingii* S.Watson *20850*
    R   *20850*   U.S. - Nevada   *20850*
    I   *20850*   U.S. - Oregon   *20850*

R   *Penstemon laevis* Pennell *20850*
    I   *20850*   U.S. - Arizona   *20850*
    E   *20850*   U.S. - Utah   *20850*

R   *Penstemon laricifolius* Hook & Arn. ssp. *exilifolius* (A. Nels.) Keck *20850*
    E   *20850*   U.S. - Colorado   *20850*
    E   *20850*   U.S. - Wyoming   *20850*

R   *Penstemon leiophyllus* Pennell *20850*
    R   *20850*   U.S. - Nevada   *20850*
    V   *20850*   U.S. - Utah   *20850*

E   *Penstemon leiophyllus* Pennell var. *francisci-pennellii* (Crosswhite) N. Holmgren *20850*
    E   *20850*   U.S. - Nevada   *20850*

V   *Penstemon leiophyllus* Pennell var. *keckii* (Clokey) N. Holmgren *20850*
    V   *20850*   U.S. - Nevada   *20850*

R   *Penstemon lemhiensis* (Keck) Keck & Cronq. *20850*
    R   *20850*   U.S. - Idaho   *20850*
    V   *20850*   U.S. - Montana   *20850*

V   *Penstemon leonardii* (N. Holmgren) Neese var. *patricus* (N. Holmgren) Neese *20850*
    I   *20850*   U.S. - Nevada   *20850*
    V   *20850*   U.S. - Utah   *20850*

Ex/E   *Penstemon leptanthus* Pennell *20850, 14662*
    Ex/E   *20850*   U.S. - Utah   *20850*

E   *Penstemon linarioides* Gray ssp. *maguirei* Keck *20850*
    E   *20850*   U.S. - Arizona   *20850*
    Ex/E   *20850*   U.S. - New Mexico   *20850*

E   *Penstemon marcusii* (Keck) N. Holmgren *20850*
    E   *20850*   U.S. - Utah   *20850*

R   *Penstemon mensarum* Pennell *20850*
    R   *20850*   U.S. - Colorado   *20850*

R   *Penstemon monoensis* Heller *20850*
    I   *20850*   U.S. - California   *20850*

E   *Penstemon moriahensis* N. Holmgren *20850*
    E   *20850*   U.S. - Nevada   *20850*

R   *Penstemon nanus* Keck *20850*
    R   *20850*   U.S. - Utah   *20850*

E   *Penstemon navajoa* N. Holmgren *20850*
    E   *20850*   U.S. - Utah   *20850*

V   *Penstemon nudiflorus* Gray *20850*

I   *20850* U.S. - Arizona *20850*

R   *Penstemon oklahomensis* Pennell *20850*
    R   *20850* U.S. - Oklahoma *20850*

V   *Penstemon osterhoutii* Pennell *20850*
    V   *20850* U.S. - Colorado *20850*

V   *Penstemon pahutensis* N. Holmgren *20850*
    I   *20850* U.S. - California *20850*
    V   *20850* U.S. - Nevada *20850*

Ex/E   *Penstemon parviflorus* Pennell *20850, 14662*
    Ex/E *20850* U.S. - Colorado *20850*
    Ex   *20850* U.S. - New Mexico *20850*

V   *Penstemon parvus* Pennell *20850*
    V   *20850* U.S. - Utah *20850*

E   *Penstemon patens* (M.E. Jones) N. Holmgren *20850*
    I   *20850* U.S. - California *20850*
    I   *20850* U.S. - Nevada *20850*

R   *Penstemon paysoniorum* Keck *20850*
    R   *20850* U.S. - Wyoming *20850*

R   *Penstemon peckii* Pennell *20850*
    R   *20850* U.S. - Oregon *20850*

E   *Penstemon penlandii* W.A. Weber *20850, 14845*
    E   *20850* U.S. - Colorado (Grand Co.) *20850*

V   *Penstemon perpulcher* A. Nels. *20850*
    I   *20850* U.S. - Idaho *20850*
    I   *20850* U.S. - Oregon *20850*

V   *Penstemon personatus* Keck *20850*
    V   *20850* U.S. - California *20850*

V   *Penstemon petiolatus* Brandeg. *20850*
    E   *20850* U.S. - Arizona *20850*
    I   *20850* U.S. - Nevada *20850*
    E   *20850* U.S. - Utah *20850*

E   *Penstemon pinorum* L.& J. Shultz *20850*
    E   *20850* U.S. - Utah *20850*

V   *Penstemon platyphyllus* Rydb. *20850*
    I   *20850* U.S. - Nevada *20850*
    V   *20850* U.S. - Utah *20850*

V   *Penstemon procerus* Douglas ex Graham var. *modestus*
    (Greene) N. Holmgren *20850*
    V   *20850* U.S. - Nevada *20850*

R   *Penstemon pseudospectabilis* M.E. Jones *20850*
    I   *20850* U.S. - Arizona *20850*
    I   *20850* U.S. - California *20850*
    I   *20850* U.S. - New Mexico *20850*
    I   *20850* U.S. - Utah *20850*

E   *Penstemon pudicus* Reveal & Beatley *20850*
    E   *20850* U.S. - Nevada *20850*

V   *Penstemon rattanii* Gray ssp. *kleei* (Greene)
    Keck *20850*
    V   *20850* U.S. - California *20850*

R   *Penstemon retrorsus* Payson ex Pennell *20850*
    R   *20850* U.S. - Colorado *20850*

V   *Penstemon rubicundus* Keck *20850*
    V   *20850* U.S. - Nevada *20850*

V   *Penstemon scapoides* Keck *20850*
    I   *20850* U.S. - California *20850*

E   *Penstemon scariosus* Pennell var. *albifluvis*
    (England) N. Holmgren *20850*
    E   *20850* U.S. - Colorado *20850*
    E   *20850* U.S. - Utah *20850*

R   *Penstemon scariosus* Pennell var. *garrettii*
    (Pennell) N. Holmgren *20850*

I   *20850* U.S. - Utah *20850*

V   *Penstemon shastensis* Keck *20850*
    I   *20850* U.S. - California *20850*

V   *Penstemon spectabilis* Keck ssp. *subviscosus*
    Keck *20850*
    I   *20850* U.S. - California *20850*

V   *Penstemon stephensii* Brandeg. *20850*
    V   *20850* U.S. - California *20850*

R   *Penstemon strictiformis* Rydb. *20850*
    I   *20850* U.S. - Arizona *20850*
    I   *20850* U.S. - Colorado *20850*
    I   *20850* U.S. - New Mexico *20850*
    E   *20850* U.S. - Utah *20850*

V   *Penstemon subulatus* M.E. Jones *20850*
    I   *20850* U.S. - Arizona *20850*

V   *Penstemon sudans* M.E. Jones *20850*
    I   *20850* U.S. - California *20850*
    I   *20850* U.S. - Nevada *20850*

V   *Penstemon teucrioides* Greene *20850*
    I   *20850* U.S. - Colorado *20850*

V   *Penstemon thompsoniae* (A. Gray) Rydb. ssp. *jaegeri*
    Keck *20850*
    V   *20850* U.S. - Nevada *20850*

V   *Penstemon tidestromii* Pennell *20850*
    V   *20850* U.S. - Utah *20850*

E   *Penstemon tracyi* Keck *20850*
    E   *20850* U.S. - California *20850*

R   *Penstemon triflorus* Heller *20850*
    I   *20850* U.S. - Texas *20850*

R   *Penstemon triflorus* Heller ssp. *integrifolius*
    Pennell *20850*
    R   *20850* U.S. - Texas *20850*

R   *Penstemon triflorus* Heller ssp.
    triflorus *20850*
    I   *20850* U.S. - Texas *20850*

R   *Penstemon uintahensis* Pennell *20850*
    R   *20850* U.S. - Utah *20850*

V   *Penstemon wardii* Gray *20850*
    V   *20850* U.S. - Utah *20850*

R   *Penstemon washingtonensis* Keck *20850*
    I   *20850* U.S. - Washington *20850*

R   *Penstemon wrightii* Hook. *20850*
    R   *20850* U.S. - Texas *20850*

R   *Penstemon yampaensis* Penl. *20850*
    R   *20850* U.S. - Colorado *20850*
    I   *20850* U.S. - Utah *20850*

R   *Phyllopodium dolomiticum* Hilliard *20604*
    R   *20604* South Africa - Cape Province *20604*

I   *Phyllopodium lupuliforme* (Thell.) Hilliard *20604*
    I   *20604* South Africa - Cape Province *20604*

R   *Phyllopodium tweedense* Hilliard *20604*
    R   *20604* South Africa - Cape Province *20604*

R   *Physocalyx scaberrimus* Philcox *11530*
    R   *11530* Brazil *11530*

R   *Polycarena comptonii* Hilliard *20604*
    R   *20604* South Africa - Cape Province *20604*

R   *Porodittia triandra* (Cavanilles) G. Don *20883*
    R   *20883* Peru *20883*

R   *Pseudolysimachion kiusiana* (Furumi) Yamaz. var.

kitadakemontana Yamaz. *10573*
R   *10573*   Japan *10573*

R   *Pseudolysimachion ogurae* Yamaz. *10573*
R   *10573*   Japan *10573*

R   *Pseudolysimachion ornatum* (Monjus) Yamaz. *10573*
R   *10573*   Japan *10573*

R   *Pseudolysimachion sieboldianum* (Miq.) Yamaz. *10573*
R   *10573*   Japan *10573*

R   *Pseudolysimachion subsessilis* (Miq.) Yamaz. *10573*
R   *10573*   Japan *10573*

R   *Reyemia chasmanthiflora* Hilliard *20604*
R   *20604*   South Africa - Cape Province *20604*

I   *Rhamphicarpa medwedewii* Albov *5942*
I   *5942*   Georgia *5942*

R   *Rhinanthus dinaricus* Murb. *20171*
R   (former) Yugoslavia

E   *Rhinanthus halophilus* U.Schneid. *20171*
E   Germany

E   *Rhinanthus osiliensis* (Ronn. & Saarson) Vassilcz. *5942, 20620*
E   *18216*   Estonia (Saaremaa) *5942*

R   *Rhinanthus pindicus* (Sterneck) Soó *20171*
R   Greece

Ex   *Rhinanthus serotinus* ssp. *arenarius* *18216*
Ex   *18216*   Germany (Mecklenburg-Vorpommern state) *18216*

R   *Rhinanthus serotinus* (Schönh.) Oborny ssp. *halophilus* (U. Schneid.) Hartl *18216*
R   *18216*   Denmark *18216*
E   *18216*   Germany (Mecklenbury-Vorpommern state) *18216*

R   *Rhynchocorys odontophylla* Burbridge & Richard *12840*
R   *12840*   Turkey *12840*

V   *Sairocarpus subcordatus* (Gray) D.A. Sutton *20850*
V   *20850*   U.S. - California *20850*

R   *Sairocarpus vexillocalyculatus* (Kellogg) D.A. Sutton *20850*
I   *20850*   U.S. - California *20850*

V   *Schwalbea americana* L. *20850*
Ex/E *20850*   U.S. - Alabama *20850*
Ex/E *20850*   U.S. - Connecticut *20850*
Ex/E *20850*   U.S. - Delaware *20850*
E   *20850*   U.S. - Florida *20850*
E   *20850*   U.S. - Georgia *20850*
Ex/E *20850*   U.S. - Kentucky *20850*
I   *20850*   U.S. - Louisiana *20850*
Ex   *20850*   U.S. - Maryland *20850*
Ex   *20850*   U.S. - Massachusetts *20850*
E   *20850*   U.S. - Mississippi *20850*
E   *20850*   U.S. - New Jersey *20850*
Ex   *20850*   U.S. - New York *20850*
E   *20850*   U.S. - North Carolina *20850*
V   *20850*   U.S. - South Carolina *20850*
Ex/E *20850*   U.S. - Tennessee *20850*
I   *20850*   U.S. - Texas *20850*
Ex/E *20850*   U.S. - Virginia *20850*

R   *Scrophularia amana* Lall *12840*
R   *12840*   Turkey *12840*

V   *Scrophularia anagae* Bolle
V   Spain - Canary Is.

V   *Scrophularia atrata* Pennell *20850*
V   *20850*   U.S. - California *20850*

R   *Scrophularia bitlisica* Lall *12840*

R   *12840*   Turkey *12840*

R   *Scrophularia bosniaca* Beck *20178, 20171*
R   *20178*   Albania *20178*
R   *21091*   Bosnia & Herzegovina *21091*
R   (former) Yugoslavia *20178*

V   *Scrophularia calliantha* Webb & Berthel. *20750*
V   *20750*   Spain - Canary Is. *20750*

R   *Scrophularia candelabrum* Heywood *12840*
R   *12840*   Turkey *12840*

R   *Scrophularia capillaris* Boiss. & Bal. *12840*
R   *12840*   Turkey *12840*

R   *Scrophularia carduchorum* R. Mill. *12840*
R   *12840*   Turkey *12840*

I   *Scrophularia cretacea* Fisch. ex Spreng. *5942, 20171*
I   *5942*   Russia (E.Europe) - South *5942*
I   *5942*   Ukraine *5942*

V   *Scrophularia grandiflora* DC. ssp. *grandiflora* *8000, 20171*
V   *20076*   Portugal *8000*

R   *Scrophularia gypsicola* Huber-Mor. & lall *12840*
R   *12840*   Turkey *12840*

R   *Scrophularia hirta* Lowe
R   Portugal - Madeira

R   *Scrophularia koraiensis* Nakai *15957*
R   *15923*   Korea, South (Mt Chiri) *15957*

V   *Scrophularia laevis* Woot. & Standl. *20850*
V   *20850*   U.S. - New Mexico *20850*

R   *Scrophularia langeana* Bolle
R   Spain - Canary Is.

R   *Scrophularia lepidota* Boiss. *12840*
R   *12840*   Turkey *12840*

R   *Scrophularia libanotica* Boiss. var. *antalyensis* Y. Ayasligil & R. Mill. *12840*
R   *12840*   Turkey *12840*

R   *Scrophularia libanotica* Boiss. var. *nevshehirensis* R. Mill. *12840*
R   *12840*   Turkey *12840*

R   *Scrophularia libanotica* Boiss. var. *oligantha* Heywood *12840*
R   *12840*   Turkey *12840*

R   *Scrophularia lowei* Dalgaard
R   Portugal - Madeira

V   *Scrophularia macrantha* Greene ex Stiefelhagen *20850*
V   *20850*   U.S. - New Mexico *20850*

R   *Scrophularia mersinensis* Lall *12840*
R   *12840*   Turkey *12840*

R   *Scrophularia morisii* Valsecchi *18264*
R   *18264*   Italy - Sardinia *18264*

R   *Scrophularia oblongifolia* Loisel. *20171*
R   Spain

R   *Scrophularia oxyrhyncha* Coincy
R   Spain

R   *Scrophularia pumilio* Lall *12840*
R   *12840*   Turkey *12840*

R   *Scrophularia racemosa* Lowe
R   Portugal - Madeira

I   *Scrophularia schousboei* Lange *20171*
I   Spain

R   *Scrophularia scoplii* Hoppe ex Pers. var. *parryi* R.

Mill. *12840*
R   *12840* Turkey *12840*

R   *Scrophularia scopolii* Hoppe ex Pers. var. ***burdurensis*** (H. Pesmen) R. Mill. *12840*
R   *12840* Turkey *12840*

R   *Scrophularia scopolii* Hoppe ex Pers. var. ***longirostrata*** Heywood *12840*
R   *12840* Turkey *12840*

R   *Scrophularia serratifolia* Huber-Mor ex Lall *12840*
R   *12840* Turkey *12840*

E   *Scrophularia smithii* Hornem. ssp. ***hierrensis*** Dalgaard
E   Spain - Canary Is.

R   *Scrophularia smithii* Horem. ssp. ***smithii***
R   Spain - Canary Is.

I   *Scrophularia spinulescens* Degen & Hausskn. *20171*
I   Greece

R   *Scrophularia subsequiloba* Lall *12840*
R   *12840* Turkey *12840*

R   *Scrophularia taygetea* Boiss. *20171*
R   Greece

R   *Scrophularia tenuipes* Coss. & Durieu *10488*
R   *14958* Algeria *10488*

R   *Scrophularia trisecta* Pau
R   *21091* Bosnia & Herzegovina *21091*
R   Morocco

R   *Scrophularia versicolor* Boiss. *12840*
R   *12840* Turkey *12840*

V   *Scrophularia villosa* Pennell *20850*
V   *20850* U.S. - California *20850*

I   *Selago longicalyx* Hilliard *20604*
I   *20604* South Africa - Natal *20604*
I   *20604* South Africa - Transvaal *20604*

V   *Selago longiflora* Rolfe *20604*
V   *20604* South Africa - Natal *20604*

I   *Selago monticola* J.M.Wood & M.S.Evans *20604*
I   *20604* South Africa - Natal *20604*

E   *Selago swaziensis* Rolfe *20604, 18023*
E   *20604* Swaziland *20604*

V   *Sibthorpia peregrina* L. *8000, 20171*
V   Portugal - Madeira *8000*

I   *Spirostegia bucharica* (B. Fedtsch.) Ivanina *5942*
I   *5942* Uzbekistan (south) *5942*

E   *Stemodia haegii* W.R.Barker ms. *20681*
E   *20681* Australia - South Australia *20681*

R   *Striga bilabiata* (Thunb.) Kuntze ssp. ***jaegeri*** Hepper *7926*
R   Mali (Kita Massif) *7926*
R   Senegal *7926*

R   *Sutera canariensis* (Webb & Berth.) Sund. & Kunkel
R   Spain - Canary Is.

R   *Sutera fodina* Wild *7752*
R   Zimbabwe *7752*

R   *Sutera placida* Hilliard *20604*
R   *20604* South Africa - Cape Province *20604*

I   *Sutera racemosa* (Benth.) Kuntze *20604*
I   *20604* South Africa - Cape Province *20604*

R   *Sutera titanophila* Hilliard *20604*
R   *20604* South Africa - Cape Province *20604*

R   *Synthyris canbyi* Pennell *20850*
R   *20850* U.S. - Montana *20850*

R   *Synthyris laciniata* (Gray) Rydb. *20850*
I   *20850* U.S. - Utah *20850*

Ex/E   *Synthyris missurica* (Raf.) Pennell ssp. ***hirsuta*** Pennell *20850*
I   *20850* U.S. - Oregon *20850*

V   *Synthyris pinnatifida* S.Watson var. ***lanuginosa*** (Piper) Cronq. *20850*
V   *20850* U.S. - Washington *20850*

R   *Synthyris platycarpa* Gail & Pennell *20850*
R   *20850* U.S. - Idaho *20850*

E   *Synthyris ranunculina* Pennell *20850*
E   *20850* U.S. - Nevada *20850*

V   *Torenia ranongensis* Yamaz. *19120*
V   *19120* Thailand *19120*

I   *Torenia thailandica* Yamaz. *19120*
I   *19120* Thailand *19120*

R   *Tozzia alpina* L. ssp. ***carpathica*** *8000, 20171*
R   *18216* Poland (Carpathians) *18216*
V   *19321* Slovakia (Carpathians) *19321*

V   *Triphysaria floribunda* (Benth.) Chuang & Heckard *20850*
V   *20850* U.S. - California *20850*

R   *Verbascum acaule* (Bory & Chaub.) Kuntze *20171*
R   Greece

R   *Verbascum adeliae* Heldr. *20171*
R   Greece

R   *Verbascum adenocarpum* Huber-Mor. *12840*
R   *12840* Turkey *12840*

R   *Verbascum adenophorum* Boiss. *12840*
R   *12840* Turkey *12840*

R   *Verbascum afyonense* Huber-Mor. *12840*
R   *12840* Turkey *12840*

R   *Verbascum agastachyum* Huber-Mor. *12840*
R   *12840* Turkey *12840*

R   *Verbascum amanum* Boiss. *12840*
R   *12840* Turkey *12840*

R   *Verbascum anastasii* Nab. *12840*
R   *12840* Turkey *12840*

R   *Verbascum ancyritanum* Bornm. *12840*
R   *12840* Turkey *12840*

V   *Verbascum anisophyllum* Murb. *8000, 20171*
V   *5204* Bulgaria (west) *8000*

R   *Verbascum antitauricum* Huber-Mor. *12840*
R   *12840* Turkey *12840*

R   *Verbascum apiculatum* Huber-Mor. *12840*
R   *12840* Turkey *12840*

R   *Verbascum argenteum* Ten. *20171*
R   Italy

R   *Verbascum ballsianum* Murb. *12840*
R   *12840* Turkey *12840*

V   *Verbascum basivelatum* Huber-Mor. *12840*
V   *12840* Turkey *12840*

R   *Verbascum bellum* Huber-Mor. *12840*
R   *12840* Turkey *12840*

R   *Verbascum biledschikianum* Bornm. *12840*
R   *12840* Turkey *12840*

R	*Verbascum biscutellifolium* Bentham *12840*	
	R	*12840* Turkey *12840*
R	*Verbascum bombyciferum* Boiss. *12840*	
	R	*12840* Turkey *12840*
R	*Verbascum botuliforme* Murb. *20171*	
	R	Greece
R	*Verbascum bourgeauanum* Huber-Mor. *12840*	
	R	*12840* Turkey *12840*
R	*Verbascum brandianum* Huber-Mor. *12840*	
	R	*12840* Turkey *12840*
Ex	*Verbascum calycosum* Hausskn. & Murb. *12840*	
	Ex	*12840* Turkey *12840*
R	*Verbascum campestre* Boiss. & Heldre. *12840*	
	R	*12840* Turkey *12840*
R	*Verbascum cariense* Huber-Mor. *12840*	
	R	*12840* Turkey *12840*
R	*Verbascum cerinum* Boiss. & Heldr. *12840*	
	R	*12840* Turkey *12840*
R	*Verbascum charputense* Murb. var. *adenophorum* Huber-Mor. *12840*	
	R	*12840* Turkey *12840*
V	*Verbascum chazaliei* Boiss. *12840*	
	V	*12840* Turkey *12840*
R	*Verbascum cheiranthifolium* Boiss. var. *heldrechii* Boiss. *12840*	
	R	*12840* Turkey *12840*
R	*Verbascum cheiranthifolium* Boiss. var. *obtusiusculum* Huber-Mor. *12840*	
	R	*12840* Turkey *12840*
R	*Verbascum chionophyllum* Huber et Mor. *12840*	
	R	*12840* Turkey *12840*
R	*Verbascum cholorostegium* Bornm. et Murb. *12840*	
	R	*12840* Turkey *12840*
R	*Verbascum chrysorrhacos* Boiss. *12840*	
	R	*12840* Turkey *12840*
R	*Verbascum cilicicum* Boiss. *12840*	
	R	*12840* Turkey *12840*
R	*Verbascum cilicium* (Boiss. et Heldr.) O. Kuntze *12840*	
	R	*12840* Turkey *12840*
R	*Verbascum conocarpum* Moris ssp. *conradiae* Jeanmonod *15080*	
	R	*20726* France - Corsica *15080*
R	*Verbascum coronopifolium* (Boiss. et Bal.) O. Kuntz *12840*	
	R	*12840* Turkey *12840*
R	*Verbascum cucullatibracteatum* Huber et Mor. *12840*	
	R	*12840* Turkey *12840*
I	*Verbascum cylindrocarpum* Griseb. *20171*	
	I	Greece
E	*Verbascum cylleneum* (Boiss. & Heldr.) Kuntze *20171*	
	E	Greece
R	*Verbascum cymigerum* Huber et Mor. *12840*	
	R	*12840* Turkey *12840*
V	*Verbascum dalamanicum* Huber et Mor. *12840*	
	V	*12840* Turkey *12840*
V	*Verbascum davidoffii* Murb. *8000, 20171*	
	V	*5204* Bulgaria (south) *5204*

R	*Verbascum davisianum* Huber et Mor. *12840*	
	R	*12840* Turkey *12840*
R	*Verbascum decursivum* Huber et Mor. *12840*	
	R	*12840* Turkey *12840*
V	*Verbascum degenii* Halácsy *12840, 20171*	
	V	*19873* Turkey *12840*
R	*Verbascum delphicum* Boiss. & Heldr. *20171*	
	R	Greece
R	*Verbascum demirizianum* Huber et Mor. *12840*	
	R	*12840* Turkey *12840*
R	*Verbascum detersile* Boiss. et Heldr. *12840*	
	R	*12840* Turkey *12840*
R	*Verbascum discolor* Murb. *12840*	
	R	*12840* Turkey *12840*
R	*Verbascum diversifolium* Hochst. *12840*	
	R	*12840* Turkey *12840*
R	*Verbascum drymophilum* Huber et Mor. *12840*	
	R	*12840* Turkey *12840*
R	*Verbascum dudleyanum* (Huber et Mor.) Huber et Mor. *12840*	
	R	*12840* Turkey *12840*
R	*Verbascum dumulosum* Davis et Huber et Mor. *12840*	
	R	*12840* Turkey *12840*
R	*Verbascum durmitoreum* Rohlena *20171*	
	R	(former) Yugoslavia
R	*Verbascum eleonarae* Huber et Mor. *12840*	
	R	*12840* Turkey *12840*
R	*Verbascum eriocarpum* (Freyn & Sint.) Bornm. *12840*	
	R	*12840* Turkey *12840*
R	*Verbascum euboicum* Murb. & Rech.f. *20171*	
	R	Greece
R	*Verbascum euphraticum* Bentham *12840*	
	R	*12840* Turkey *12840*
I	*Verbascum exuberans* Huber-Mor. *12840*	
	I	*12840* Turkey *12840*
R	*Verbascum flabellifolium* (Huber-Mor.) Huber-Mor. *12840*	
	R	*12840* Turkey *12840*
R	*Verbascum flavipannosum* Huber-Mor. *12840*	
	R	*12840* Turkey *12840*
V	*Verbascum fontqueri* Benedí & J.M. Monts. *11496*	
	V	*11496* Spain (Valencia province) *20692*
R	*Verbascum freynii* (Sint.) Murb. *12840*	
	R	*12840* Turkey *12840*
R	*Verbascum germaniciae* Hausskn. *12840*	
	R	*12840* Turkey *12840*
R	*Verbascum globiferum* Huber-Mor. *12840*	
	R	*12840* Turkey *12840*
R	*Verbascum gracilescens* Huber-Mor. *12840*	
	R	*12840* Turkey *12840*
R	*Verbascum hadschinense* Freyn *12840*	
	R	*12840* Turkey *12840*
R	*Verbascum hajastanicum* Bordz. *8001*	
	R	former USSR *6930*
V	*Verbascum helianthomoides* Huber-Mor. *12840*	
	V	*12840* Turkey *12840*
R	*Verbascum hervieri* Degen *20171*	
	R	Spain

R	*Verbascum herzogii* Bornm. *20171*	
	R	(former) Yugoslavia
R	*Verbascum heterobarbatum* Huber-Mor. *12840*	
	R	*12840* Turkey *12840*
R	*Verbascum heterodontum* Huber-Mor. *12840*	
	R	*12840* Turkey *12840*
R	*Verbascum iconicum* Huber-Mor. *12840*	
	R	*12840* Turkey *12840*
R	*Verbascum ikaricum* Murb.	
	R	Greece
R	*Verbascum inaequale* Freyn & Sint. *12840*	
	R	*12840* Turkey *12840*
R	*Verbascum infidelium* Boiss. & Hausskn. *12840*	
	R	*12840* Turkey *12840*
R	*Verbascum inulifolium* Huber-Mor. *12840*	
	R	*12840* Turkey *12840*
R	*Verbascum isauricum* Boiss. & Heldr. *12840*	
	R	*12840* Turkey *12840*
V	*Verbascum jankaeanum* Pancic *8000, 20171*	
	V	*5204* Bulgaria (west) *5204*
R	*Verbascum lachnopus* Huber-Mor. *12840*	
	R	*12840* Turkey *12840*
R	*Verbascum laciniatum* (Poir.) Kuntze *20171*	
	R	Spain
R	*Verbascum latisepalum* Huber-Mor. *12840*	
	R	*12840* Turkey *12840*
R	*Verbascum leiocarpum* Murb. *12840*	
	R	*12840* Turkey *12840*
R	*Verbascum leiranthoides* Murb. *12840*	
	R	*12840* Turkey *12840*
R	*Verbascum leptocladum* Boiss. & Heldr. *12840*	
	R	*12840* Turkey *12840*
R	*Verbascum leuconeurum* Boiss. & Heldr. *12840*	
	R	*12840* Turkey *12840*
R	*Verbascum linearilobum* (Boiss.) Huber-Mor. *12840*	
	R	*12840* Turkey *12840*
R	*Verbascum linguifolium* Huber-Mor. *12840*	
	R	*12840* Turkey *12840*
V	*Verbascum litigiosum* Samp. *8000, 20171*	
	V	*20076* Portugal *8000*
V	*Verbascum lobatum* Huber-Mor. *12840*	
	V	*12840* Turkey *12840*
R	*Verbascum longipedicellatum* Huber-Mor. *12840*	
	R	*12840* Turkey *12840*
R	*Verbascum luciliae* (Boiss.) O. Kuntz *12840*	
	R	*12840* Turkey *12840*
R	*Verbascum luridifolium* Huber-Mor. *12840*	
	R	*12840* Turkey *12840*
R	*Verbascum lyratifolium* Kochel *12840*	
	R	*12840* Turkey *12840*
R	*Verbascum macedonicum* Kosanin & Murb. *20171*	
	R	(former) Yugoslavia
V	*Verbascum maendri* Bornm. *12480*	
	V	Turkey *12480*
R	*Verbascum meincheanum* Murb. *12480*	
	R	Turkey *12480*
R	*Verbascum melitense* Huber-Mor. *12480*	
	R	Turkey *12480*

R	*Verbascum microsepalum* Huber-Mor. *12840*		
	R	*12840* Turkey *12840*	
R	*Verbascum murbeckianum* Huber-Mor. *12480*		
	R	Turkey *12480*	
R	*Verbascum myrianthum* Boiss. *12480*		
	R	Turkey *12480*	
R	*Verbascum napifolium* Boiss. *12480*		
	R	Turkey *12480*	
R	*Verbascum nevadense* Boiss. *20171*		
	R	Spain	
R	*Verbascum nicolai* Rohlena *20178, 20171*		
	R	*20178* Albania *20178*	
	R	*21091* Bosnia & Herzegovina *21091*	
	R	(former) Yugoslavia *20178*	
R	*Verbascum nudatum* Murb. *12480*		
	R	Turkey *12480*	
R	*Verbascum nudiusculum* Huber-Mor. *12480*		
	R	Turkey *12480*	
R	*Verbascum obtusifolium* Huber-Mor. *12840*		
	R	*12840* Turkey *12840*	
R	*Verbascum olympicum* Boiss. *12840*		
	R	*12840* Turkey *12840*	
R	*Verbascum oocarpum* Murb. *12840*		
	I	*2050* Czech Republic *2050*	
	R	*12840* Turkey *12840*	
R	*Verbascum orbicularifolium* Huber-Mor. *12840*		
	R	*12840* Turkey *12840*	
R	*Verbascum pallidiflorum* Huber-Mor. *12840*		
	R	*12840* Turkey *12840*	
R	*Verbascum pelium* Halácsy *20171*		
	R	Greece	
R	*Verbascum pellitum* Huber-Mor. *12840*		
	R	*12840* Turkey *12840*	
R	*Verbascum pentelicum* Murb. *20171*		
	R	Greece	
R	*Verbascum pestalozzae* Boiss. *12840*		
	R	*12840* Turkey *12840*	
R	*Verbascum petiolare* Boiss. & Kotschy *12840*		
	R	*12840* Turkey *12840*	
R	*Verbascum phrygium* Bornm. *12840*		
	R	*12840* Turkey *12840*	
R	*Verbascum pinardii* Boiss. *12840*		
	R	*12840* Turkey *12840*	
R	*Verbascum pinetorum* (Boiss.) O. Kuntze *12840*		
	R	*12840* Turkey *12840*	
R	*Verbascum prusianum* auct., non Boiss. *12840, 20171*		
	R	*12840* Turkey *12840*	
R	*Verbascum pseudoholotrichum* Huber-Mor. *12840*		
	R	*12840* Turkey *12840*	
R	*Verbascum pseudovarians* Huber-Mor. *12840*		
	R	*12840* Turkey *12840*	
R	*Verbascum pterocalycinum* Huber-Mor. *12840*		
	R	*12840* Turkey *12840*	
R	*Verbascum pterocladum* Huber-Mor. *12840*		
	R	*12840* Turkey *12840*	
R	*Verbascum pumiliforme* Huber-Mor. *12840*		
	R	*12840* Turkey *12840*	
V	*Verbascum pumilum* Boiss. & Heldr. *12840*		
	V	*12840* Turkey *12840*	

R   *Verbascum purpureum* (Janka) Hub.-Mor. *8000, 20171*
     R   *5204*   Bulgaria (east) *5204*
     E   *19949*   Romania (south Dobrogea) *19840*
     R   Turkey *8000*

V   *Verbascum pyroliforme* (Boiss. & Heldr.) O.
     Kuntze *12840*
     V   *12840*   Turkey *12840*

R   *Verbascum reeseanum* Huber-Mor. *12840*
     R   *12840*   Turkey *12840*

R   *Verbascum reiseri* Halácsy *20171*
     R   Greece

R   *Verbascum renzii* Huber-Mor. *12840*
     R   *12840*   Turkey *12840*

R   *Verbascum rubricaule* Boiss. & Heldr. *12840*
     R   *12840*   Turkey *12840*

R   *Verbascum serpenticola* Huber-Mor. *12840*
     R   *12840*   Turkey *12840*

R   *Verbascum siculum* Tod. ex Lojac. *20171*
     R   Italy
     R   Italy - Sicily

R   *Verbascum simavicum* Huber-Mor. *12840*
     R   *12840*   Turkey *12840*

V   *Verbascum smyrnaeum* Boiss. *12840*
     V   *12840*   Turkey *12840*

R   *Verbascum songaricum* Schrenk ex Fisch. & Mey. ssp.
     subdecurrens Huber-Mor. *12840*
     R   *12840*   Turkey *12840*

R   *Verbascum sorgerae* (Huber-Mor.) Huber-Mor. *12840*
     R   *12840*   Turkey *12840*

I   *Verbascum spathulisepalum* Greuter & Rech.f.
     I   Greece

R   *Verbascum spectabile* Bieb. var. *isandrum*
     Huber-Mor. *12840*
     R   *12840*   Turkey *12840*

R   *Verbascum sphenandroides* C. Koch. *12840*
     R   *12840*   Turkey *12840*

R   *Verbascum spodiotrichum* (Huber-Mor.)
     Huber-Mor. *12840*
     R   *12840*   Turkey *12840*

R   *Verbascum stachydifolium* Boiss. & Heldr. *12840*
     R   *12840*   Turkey *12840*

R   *Verbascum stenocarpum* Boiss. & Heldr. *12840*
     R   *12840*   Turkey *12840*

R   *Verbascum stenostachyum* Huber-Mor. *12840*
     R   *12840*   Turkey *12840*

V   *Verbascum stepporum* Huber-Mor. *12840*
     V   *12840*   Turkey *12840*

R   *Verbascum subnivale* Boiss. & Hausskn. *12840*
     R   *12840*   Turkey *12840*

R   *Verbascum subserratum* Huber-Mor. *12840*
     R   *12840*   Turkey *12840*

V   *Verbascum syriacum* Schrader
     V   Greece

R   *Verbascum tauri* Boiss. & Kotschy *12840*
     R   *12840*   Turkey *12840*

R   *Verbascum tenue* Murb. *12840*
     R   *12840*   Turkey *12840*

R   *Verbascum tetrandrum* G. Barratte & Murb.
     R   Morocco

R   *Verbascum transolympicum* Huber-Mor. *12840*
     R   *12840*   Turkey *12840*

R   *Verbascum trapifolium* (Stapf.) Huber-Mor. *12840*
     R   *12840*   Turkey *12840*

R   *Verbascum trichostylum* Huber-Mor. *12840*
     R   *12840*   Turkey *12840*

R   *Verbascum urceolatum* Huber-Mor. *12840*
     R   *12840*   Turkey *12840*

R   *Verbascum urobracteatum* Huber-Mor. *12840*
     R   *12840*   Turkey *12840*

R   *Verbascum vanense* Huber-Mor. *12840*
     R   *12840*   Turkey *12840*

R   *Verbascum varians* Freyn & Sint. var. *stepporum*
     Huber-Mor. *12840*
     R   *12840*   Turkey *12840*

R   *Verbascum varians* Freyn & Sint. var. *trapezunticum*
     Murb. *12840*
     R   *12840*   Turkey *12840*

R   *Verbascum vulcanicum* Boiss. & Heldr. var. *viridans*
     Huber-Mor. *12840*
     R   *12840*   Turkey *12840*

E   *Veronica allahuekberensis* Ozturk *12840*
     E   *12840*   Turkey *12840*

I   *Veronica anagallis* L. var. *bracteosa* Blatter &
     Hallberg *7771*
     I   India - Rajasthan (Mt Abu, Sirohu District)
        7771

I   *Veronica anagallis-aquetica* L. var. *bracteata*
     Blatter & Hallberg
     I   India - Rajasthan

R   *Veronica antalyensis* Fischer, Erik & Sumbul *12840*
     R   *12840*   Turkey *12840*

I   *Veronica beccabunga* L. var. *attenuata* Blatter &
     Hallberg
     I   India - Rajasthan

R   *Veronica bombycina* Boiss. et Kotschy ssp.
     bolkardaghensis Fischer *12840*
     R   *12840*   Turkey *12840*

R   *Veronica bombycina* Boiss. & Kotschy ssp. *froediniana*
     Rech.f. *12840*
     R   *12840*   Turkey *12840*

R   *Veronica cetikii* Ozturk *12840*
     R   *12840*   Turkey *12840*

R   *Veronica cuneifolia* D. Don ssp. *massicytica*
     Fischer *12840*
     R   *12840*   Turkey *12840*

I   *Veronica dabneyi* Hochst. *20171*
     I   Portugal - Azores

R   *Veronica donii* Rommpp *12840*
     R   *12840*   Turkey *12840*

I   *Veronica filifolia* Lipsky *5942*
     I   *5942*   Russia - North Caucasus *5942*

R   *Veronica fredericae* Fischer *12840*
     R   *12840*   Turkey *12840*

R   *Veronica fuhsii* Freyn & Sint. *12840*
     R   *12840*   Turkey *12840*

R   *Veronica gentianoides* Vahl. ssp. *kopgecidiensis* A.
     Ozturk *12840*
     R   *12840*   Turkey *12840*

R   *Veronica hispidula* Boiss. & Huet ssp. *ixodes*
     (Boiss. & Bal.) Fischer *12840*
     R   *12840* Turkey *12840*

R   *Veronica jabalambrensis* Pau
     R   Spain

E   *Veronica kaiseri* Tackh.
     E   Egypt

R   *Veronica kavusica* Rech.f. *19121, 20171*
     R   *20808* Greece (Kefallinia) *20808*

R   *Veronica kotschyana* Bentham *12840*
     R   *12840* Turkey *12840*

R   *Veronica lycica* E. Lehm. *12840*
     R   *12840* Turkey *12840*

R   *Veronica macrostachya* Vahl ssp. *sorgerae*
     Fischer *12840*
     R   *12840* Turkey *12840*

I   *Veronica micrantha* Hoffmanns. & Link *8000, 20171*
     I   *20874* Portugal *8000*

E   *Veronica micromeria* Woot. & Standl. *20850*
     I   *20850* U.S. - New Mexico *20850*

R   *Veronica montbretti* Fischer *12840*
     R   *12840* Turkey *12840*

E   *Veronica musa* Tackh. & Hadidi
     E   Egypt

E   *Veronica oetaea* L.-A. Gustavsson *17891*
     E   Greece *17891*

R   *Veronica oltensis* Woronow *12840*
     R   *12840* Turkey *12840*

R   *Veronica orientalis* Miller ssp. *carduchorum*
     Davis *12840*
     R   *12840* Turkey *12840*

R   *Veronica polium* Davis *12840*
     R   *12840* Turkey *12840*

R   *Veronica pusilla* Kotschy var. *erciyasdagi*
     (Fischer) Fischer *12840*
     R   *12840* Turkey *12840*

R   *Veronica quezelii* Fischer *12840*
     R   *12840* Turkey *12840*

R   *Veronica surculosa* Bioss. & Bal. *12840*
     R   *12840* Turkey *12840*

R   *Veronica tauricola* Bornm. *12840*
     R   *12840* Turkey *12840*

R   *Veronica thymoides* Davis ssp.
     thymoides *12840*
     R   *12840* Turkey *12840*

R   *Veronica turrilliana* Stoj. & Stef. *5204, 20171*
     R   *5204* Bulgaria (east) *5204*
     R   Turkey (European) *2203*

E   *Veronicastrum liukiuense* (Ohwi) Yamaz. *10573*
     E   *10573* Japan *10573*

E   *Veronicastrum tagawae* (Ohwi) Yamaz. *10573*
     E   *10573* Japan *10573*

E   *Veronicastrum villosum* Yamaz. *10573*
     E   *10573* Japan *10573*

Ex/E   *Wulfenia baldaccii* Degen *20178, 20171*
     Ex/E *20178* Albania *20178*

E   *Xylocalyx aculeolatus* S. Carter *15534*
     E   *15534* Yemen - Socotra *15534*

E   *Xylocalyx asper* Balf. f. *15534*
     E   *15534* Yemen - Socotra *15534*

Scytopetalaceae

Number of genera: 5
Number of species: 20
Recorded threatened species: 3   (15%)

Tropical western Africa.

V   *Rhaptopetalum beguei* Mangenot *20274, 11631*
     V   *20858* Cameroon *18326*
     V   *20858* Côte d'Ivoire *11631*
     V   *20858* Equatorial Guinea - Bioko *18326*
     V   *20858* Gabon *18326*
     V   *20858* Ghana *20274*
     V   *20858* Nigeria (Ogoja & Calabar forests) *18326*

R   *Rhaptopetalum belingense* Letouzey
     R   Gabon (Belinga)

R   *Rhaptopetalum sindarense* Pellegrin
     R   Gabon *20920*

Simaroubaceae

Number of genera: 25
Number of species: 150
Recorded threatened species: 21   (14%)

Pantropical, some in warm temperate regions.

R   *Ailanthus altissima* (Miller) Swingle var. *tanakai*
     (Hayata) Kaneh. & Sas. *20511*
     R   *20854* Taiwan (central) *20511*

R   *Ailanthus fordii* Nooteb.
     R   Hong Kong

V   *Alvaradoa jamaicensis* Benth. *20883*
     V   *20883* Jamaica *20883*

E   *Alvaradoa lewisii* Howard & Proctor *20883, 13336*
     E   *13336* Jamaica (Trelawny) *20883*

V   *Brucea macrocarpa* Stannard *20057*
     V   *20057* Kenya *20057*

R   *Castela macrophylla* Urb. *20883*
     R   *20883* Jamaica *20883*

V   *Castela victorinii* Acuna & Roig *5607*
     V   *19105* Cuba (Guantanamo) *5607*

V   *Gymnostemon zaizou* Aubrev. & Pellegrin *7926*
     V   *20887* Côte d'Ivoire (Sassandra & Cavally forest)
        7926

R   *Hannoa kitombetombe* Gilbert *19358*
     R   *19358* Zaire (Haut-Katanga) *19358*

R   *Kirkia burgeri* B.Stannard ssp. *somalensis*
     B.Stannard *20884*
     R   *20884* Somalia (north) *20884*

R   *Kirkia dewinteri* Merxm. & Heine *20604*
     R   *20604* Namibia *20604*

V   *Nothospondias staudtii* Engl. *11631*
     V   *20858* Cameroon *7926*
     V   *20858* Côte d'Ivoire *11631*
     V   *20858* Gabon *7926*
     V   *20858* Ghana *20274*
     V   *20858* Nigeria *7926*

V   *Picramnia dwyeri* D.M. Porter *20883*
     I   *20883* Panama *20883*

V   *Picrasma cubensis* Radlk. & Urban *5607*
     V   *19105* Cuba (Pinar del Rio) *5607*

V   *Pierreodendron kerstingii* (Engl.) Little *7926*
     V   *20858* Benin (Bassila Peninsula) *7954*
     V   *20858* Côte d'Ivoire *7926*
     V   *20858* Ghana *20274*
     V   *20858* Togo *7926*

R   *Quassia baileyana* (Oliver) Nooteb. *20681*
     R   *20681* Australia - Queensland *20681*

V   *Quassia bidwillii* (Hook.f.) Nooteb. *20681*
     V   *20681* Australia - Queensland *20681*

V   *Simaba praecox* Hassler *20883*
     V   *20883* Paraguay *20883*

R   *Simaba trichilioides* A.St.Hil. *20883*
     R   *20883* Brazil *20883*
     R   *20883* Paraguay *20883*

V   *Soulamea cardioptera* Baillon *20893*
     V   *20893* New Caledonia *20893*

I   *Soulamea terminalioides* Baker *14296*
     I   *19181* Seychelles (granitic) *14296*

Solanaceae

Number of genera: 85
Number of species: 2,800
Recorded threatened species: 218   (7%)

Nearly cosmopolitan, especially tropical South America.

R   *Anthocercis angustifolia* F.Muell. *20681*
     R   *20681* Australia - South Australia *20681*

E   *Anthocercis gracilis* Benth. *20681*
     E   *20681* Australia - Western Australia *20681*

I   *Atropa komarovii* Blin. & Shalyt *5942*
     I   *5942* Turkmenistan *5942*

R   *Brunfelsia acunae* Hadac *5607*
     R   *19105* Cuba (Holguin) *5607*

E   *Brunfelsia clarensis* Britton & P. Wilson *5607*
     E   *19105* Cuba (Villa Clara) *5607*

E   *Brunfelsia densifolia* Krug & Urban *20883*
     I   *20883* Puerto Rico *20883*

V   *Brunfelsia dwyeri* D'Arcy *20883, 9006*
     E   *19577* Panama *20883*

R   *Brunfelsia jamaicensis* (Benth.) Griseb. *20883*
     R   *20883* Jamaica *20883*

E   *Brunfelsia lactea* Krug & Urban *20883*
     I   *20883* Puerto Rico *20883*

V   *Brunfelsia linearis* Ekman *5607*
     V   *19105* Cuba (SC; Ho; Gu) *5607*

R   *Brunfelsia membranacea* Urb. *20883, 13336*
     R   *13336* Jamaica (St. Andrew, St. Catherine) *20883*

I   *Brunfelsia picardae* Krug & Urb. *15229*
     I   *15229* Haiti (La Visite & Macaya Parks) *15229*

R   *Brunfelsia plicata* Urb. *20883*
     R   *20883* Jamaica *20883*

R   *Brunfelsia pluriflora* Urban *5607*
     R   *19105* Cuba (Holguin) *5607*

E   *Brunfelsia portoricensis* Krug & Urban *20883*
     I   *20883* Puerto Rico *20883*

R   *Brunfelsia splendida* Urb. *20883*
     R   *20883* Jamaica *20883*

R   *Brunfelsia undulata* Sw. *20883*
     R   *20883* Jamaica *20883*

     I   *20883* Puerto Rico *20883*
     I   *20883* Panama *20883*

R   *Capsicum galapagoense* Hieser & P.G. Smith *11117*
     R   Ecuador - Galapagos (Isabela, Santa Cruz) *11117*

E   *Capsicum tovarii* Eshbaugh, Smith & Nickrent *18200*
     E   *19965* Peru *18200*

R   *Cestrum ekmanii* Urban & Schulz *5607*
     R   *19105* Cuba (Guantanamo) *5607*

E   *Cestrum gracile* Francey *20883, 9006*
     I   *20883* Panama *20883*

V   *Cestrum jacaltenaginum* Loes. var. *tomentosum* Francey *9006*
     V   *16317* Panama *9006*

E   *Cestrum jacaltenanginum* var. *tomentosum* Francey *20883*
     I   *20883* Panama *20883*

E   *Cestrum jimenezii* Alain *20883*
     I   *20883* Dominican Republic *20883*

V   *Cestrum johnniegentrianum* D'Arcy *20883, 9006*
     V   *16317* Panama *20883*

V   *Cestrum langeanum* D'Arcy *20883, 9006*
     V   *16317* Panama *20883*

V   *Cestrum moaense* Borh. & Muniz *5607*
     V   *19105* Cuba (Holguin) *5607*

R   *Cyphanthera anthocercidea* (F.Muell.) Haegi *20681*
     R   *20681* Australia - Victoria *20681*

R   *Cyphanthera scabrella* (Benth.) Miers *20681*
     R   *20681* Australia - New South Wales *20681*

R   *Cyphanthera tasmanica* Miers *20681*
     R   *20681* Australia - Tasmania *20681*

R   *Grabowskia glauca* (Phil.) Johnst. *13875*
     R   *19536* Chile - Juan Fernandez Is. *19536*
     R   *13875* Chile *13875*

R   *Grammosolen truncatus* (Ising) Haegi *20681*
     R   *20681* Australia - South Australia *20681*

V   *Lycianthes acidochondra* (Bitt.) Bitt. *20883, 9006*
     I   *20883* Panama *20883*

V   *Lycianthes beckneriana* D'Arcy *20883, 9006*
     V   *16317* Panama *20883*

V   *Lycianthes hawkesiana* D'Arcy *20883, 9006*
     I   *20883* Panama *20883*

I   *Lycianthes hortulana* Standley & L.O. Williams *9061*
     I   *9730* Honduras *9061*

V   *Lycianthes howardiana* D'Arcy *20883, 9006*
     V   *16317* Panama *20883*

V   *Lycianthes hygrophila* Bitt. *20883, 9006*
     V   *16317* Panama *20883*

V   *Lycianthes luteynii* D'Arcy *20883, 9006*
     V   *16317* Panama *20883*

V   *Lycianthes maxonii* D'Arcy var. *grandidentata* D'Arcy *20883, 9006*
     V   *16317* Panama *20883*

V   *Lycianthes porteriana* D'Arcy *20883, 9006*
     V   *16317* Panama *20883*

V   *Lycianthes tysoniana* D'Arcy *20883, 9006*
     V   *16317* Panama *20883*

I   *Lycium acnistoides* Griseb. *5607*
     I   *19105* Cuba *5607*

E   *Lycium hassei* Greene *20850, 14662*
     E   20850   U.S. - California   *20850*

R   *Lycium minimum* C. Hitchc. *11117*
     R   Ecuador - Galapagos   *11117*

R   *Lycium puberulum* (Correll) Chiang var. *berberioides*
     (Correll) Chiang *20850*
     R   20850   U.S. - Texas   *20850*

E   *Lycium richii* Gray *20850*
     I   20850   U.S. - California   *20850*

V   *Lycium texanum* Correll *20850*
     V   20850   U.S. - Texas   *20850*

Ex   *Lycium verrucosum* Eastw. *20850, 8058*
     Ex   20850   U.S. - California   *20850*
     Ex   14662   Mexico   *8058*

Ex   *Mandragora autumnalis* Bertol. *20171*
     Ex   20736   Spain - Balearic Is.   *20736*

R   *Mandragora officinarum* L. *8000, 20171*
     V   21091   Bosnia & Herzegovina   *21091*
     V   18264   Italy (Veneto)   *19997*
     R   (former) Yugoslavia   *8000*

V   *Markea crosbiana* D'Arcy *20883, 9006*
     V   16317   Panama   *20883*

Ex   *Mellissia begonifolia* (Roxb.) Hook.f. *18996*
     Ex   18996   St Helena   *18996*

R   *Nicotiana africana* Merxm. *20604*
     R   20604   Namibia   *20604*

R   *Nicotiana burbidgeae* Symon *20681*
     R   20681   Australia - South Australia   *20681*

E   *Nicotiana cordifolia* Philippi *19116*
     E   19125   Chile - Juan Fernandez Is.   *19116*

V   *Nicotiana fatuhivensis* F. Brown
     V   French Polynesia - Marquesas Is

R   *Nierembergia angustifolia* Kunth *10104*
     R   19755   Mexico   *10104*

V   *Nolana adansoni* (F. ex R. &S.) I.M. Johnston *18200*
     V   9446   Peru   *18200*

R   *Nolana balsamifera* (Gaudich.) Mesa *13875*
     R   13875   Chile   *13875*

R   *Nolana confinis* I.M. Johnston *18200*
     R   9446   Peru   *18200*

R   *Nolana galapagensis* (Christoph.) I.M. Johnston *11117*
     R   Ecuador - Galapagos   *11117*

R   *Nolana inflata* Ruiz Lopez & Pavon *18200*
     R   12468   Peru   *18200*

R   *Nolana laxa* (Miers) I.M. Johnston *18200*
     R   18200   Peru   *18200*

V   *Nolana minor* Ferreyra *17208*
     V   17208   Peru   *18200*

E   *Nolana scaposa* Ferreyra *18200*
     E   12468   Peru   *18200*

E   *Nolana spathulata* Ruiz Lopez & Pavon *18200*
     E   9446   Peru   *18200*

E   *Nolana thinophila* I.M. Johnston *18200*
     E   9446   Peru   *18200*

V   *Nolana tomentella* Ferreyra *12468*
     V   12468   Peru   *12468*

E   *Normania nava* (Webb & Berthel.) Franc.-Ort. & R.M.
     Lister *20216*
     E   20216   Spain - Canary Is. (Tenerife, Gran Canaria)

     20216

E   *Normania triphylla* (Lowe) Lowe *20216*
     E   20216   Portugal - Madeira   *20216*

E   *Nothocestrum breviflorum* Gray *20850, 14209, 21348,*
     21356
     E   20850   U.S. - Hawaii   *20850*

E   *Nothocestrum latifolium* Gray *20850, 14209*
     E   20850   U.S. - Hawaii   *20850*

R   *Nothocestrum longifolium* Gray *20850, 14209*
     R   20850   U.S. - Hawaii   *20850*

E   *Nothocestrum peltatum* Skottsberg *20850, 14209, 21349*
     E   20850   U.S. - Hawaii (Kaua`i)   *20850*

V   *Oryctes nevadensis* S.Watson *20850*
     E   20850   U.S. - California   *20850*
     V   20850   U.S. - Nevada   *20850*

R   *Pauia belladonna* Deb & R. Dutta
     R   13883   India - Arunachal Pradesh (Tirap)   *13883*

R   *Physaliastrum savatieri* (Makino) Makino *10573*
     R   10573   Japan   *10573*

R   *Physalis arenicola* Kearney *20850*
     I   20850   U.S. - Alabama   *20850*
     I   20850   U.S. - Florida   *20850*
     I   20850   U.S. - Georgia   *20850*
     I   20850   U.S. - Mississippi   *20850*

I   *Physalis carnosa* Standley & Steyerm. *9004*
     I   19904   Guatemala (San Marcos)   *19904*

R   *Physalis carpenteri* Riddell ex Rydb. *20850*
     Ex/E   20850   U.S. - Alabama   *20850*
     I   20850   U.S. - Florida   *20850*
     E   20850   U.S. - Louisiana   *20850*

R   *Physalis chamaesarachoides* Makino *10573*
     R   10573   Japan   *10573*

V   *Physalis crassifolia* Benth. var.
     crassifolia 20850
     I   20850   U.S. - Arizona   *20850*
     I   20850   U.S. - California   *20850*
     I   20850   U.S. - Nevada   *20850*

R   *Physalis glutinosa* Schldl. *10102*
     R   19755   Mexico   *10102*

V   *Physalis latiphysa* Waterfall *20850*
     I   20850   U.S. - Arizona   *20850*

R   *Physalis linii* Liu & Ou *20511*
     R   20511   Taiwan   *20511*

R   *Physalis parvianthera* Waterf. *10102*
     R   19755   Mexico   *10102*

V   *Physochlaina infundibularis* Kuang *11815*
     V   20756   China - Hunan   *20756*
     V   20756   China - Shaanxi (Huashan; Shalueping;)
       11815
     V   20756   China - Shanxi (south)   *11815*

V   *Rahowardiana wardiana* D'Arcy *20883, 9006*
     V   16317   Panama   *20883*

R   *Salpichroa microloba* Keel *20883*
     E   20883   Ecuador   *20883*
     R   20883   Peru   *20883*

V   *Salpichroa microphylla* (Dunal) Keel *18200*
     V   12468   Peru   *18200*

V   *Salpichroa proboscidea* Benoist *18200*
     V   12468   Peru   *18200*

R   *Scopolia parviflora* (Dunn) Nakai
     R   Korea, South

R **Solandra hirsuta** Dunal *20883*
   R   *20883* Jamaica *20883*

R **Solanum acropterum** Griseb. *20883*
   R   *20883* Jamaica *20883*

V **Solanum acroscopicum** Ochoa *18200*
   V   *12468* Peru *18200*

I **Solanum agrimonifolium** Rydberg. *19866*
   I   *19915* Guatemala *19866*
   I   *19915* Honduras (Morozán) *19866*
   I   *19915* Mexico - Chiapas *19866*
   I   *19915* Mexico - Oaxaca *19866*

R **Solanum amnicola** S. Knapp *18200*
   R   *12468* Peru *18200*

V **Solanum amotapense** Svenson *18200*
   V   *9446* Peru *18200*

E **Solanum anamatophilum** Ochoa *18200*
   E   *12468* Peru *18200*

V **Solanum antacochense** C. Ochoa *18200*
   V   *12468* Peru *18200*

R **Solanum aviculare** Forst.f. var. *latifolium* Baylis
   R   New Zealand - North Is.

E **Solanum ayacuchense** Ochoa *18200*
   E   *12468* Peru *18200*

Ex/E **Solanum bahamense** L. var. *rugelii* D'Arcy *20850*
   Ex/E *20850* U.S. - Florida *20850*

Ex **Solanum bauerianum** Endl. *15112*
   Ex   *14223* Australia - NSW - Lord Howe Is. *14223*
   Ex   *19108* Australia - Norfolk Is. *15112*

R **Solanum biflorum** Lour. var. *kotoensis* Liu & Ou *20511*
   R   *20511* Taiwan *20511*

E **Solanum bill-hookeri** Ochoa *13828*
   E   Brazil *13828*

V **Solanum buesii** Vargas *18200*
   V   *12468* Peru *18200*

V **Solanum bukasovii** Rybin var. *bukasovii* *18200*
   V   Peru

I **Solanum bulbocastanum** Dun. ssp. *partitum* (Corr.) Hawkes *19866*
   I   *19915* Guatemala *19866*
   I   *19915* Mexico - Chiapas *19866*

Ex **Solanum cajamarquense** Ochoa *18200*
   Ex   *12468* Peru *18200*

R **Solanum cajanumense** Kunth *21107*
   V   *20883* Colombia *20883*
   R   *20883* Ecuador *20883*
   E   *20883* Peru (northern) *21037*

R **Solanum cardiophyllum** Lindl. ssp. *lanceolatum* (Berth.) Bitt. *19866*
   R   *19915* Mexico - Hidalgo *19866*
   R   *19915* Mexico - Oaxaca *19866*
   R   *19915* Mexico - Puebla *19866*
   R   *19915* Mexico - Tlaxcala *19866*

V **Solanum carduiforme** F.Muell. *20681*
   V   *20681* Australia - Queensland *20681*

E **Solanum carolinense** L. var. *hirsutum* (Nutt.) Gray *20850*
   E   *20850* U.S. - Alabama *20850*
   Ex/E *20850* U.S. - Georgia *20850*

R **Solanum cerasiferum** Dunal ssp. *crepinii* (Van Heurck) Bitter *7926*
   R   Senegal *7926*

R **Solanum circinatum** Bohs ssp. *ramosa* *21107*
   R   *20883* Colombia (Magdalena, Cauca & Patía valleys) *21037*

I **Solanum clarum** Correll *19866*
   I   *19915* Guatemala *19866*
   I   *19915* Mexico - Chiapas *19866*

E **Solanum clerodendroides** Hutch. & Dalz. *7926*
   E   *20749* Nigeria (Eket) *7926*

Ex/E **Solanum conocarpum** Dunal *20883, 14662*
   I   *20883* Puerto Rico *20883*
   I   *20883* USA - Virgin Is. (St John) *20883*

V **Solanum contumazaense** Ochoa *18200*
   V   *12468* Peru *18200*

I **Solanum crassifolium** Lam. *20604*
   I   *20604* South Africa - Cape Province *20604*

E **Solanum darienense** S. Knapp *20883, 10160*
   I   *20883* Panama *20883*

I **Solanum davisense** M.D. Whalen *20883, 20850*
   I   *20850* U.S. - Texas *20850*
   I   *20883* Mexico *20883*

R **Solanum dimorphispinum** C.White *20681*
   R   *20681* Australia - Queensland *20681*

R **Solanum diversifolium** Dunal ssp. *chloranthum* (Rusby) Bohs *21107*
   V   *20883* Costa Rica (Alajuela & Limón) *21037*
   R   *20883* Panama (Chiriquí & San Blas) *21037*
   R   *20883* Colombia *20883*
   R   *20883* Venezuela *20883*

V **Solanum diversifolium** Dunal ssp. *diversifolium* *21107*
   V   *20883* Venezuela (coastal) *21037*

E **Solanum dolosum** Morton ex S. Knapp *20883*
   I   *20883* Colombia *20883*

E **Solanum drymophilum** O.E. Schulz *20883, 10197*
   I   *20883* Puerto Rico *20883*

R **Solanum endopogon** (Bitter) Bohs ssp. *guianensis* *21107*
   V   *20883* Brazil *20883*
   ?   Brazil - Amapa *21037*
   ?   Brazil - Pará *21037*
   R   *20883* French Guiana *20883*

V **Solanum exiguum** Bohs *21107*
   V   *20883* Bolivia (Beni & Cochabamba) *21037*

R **Solanum fallax** Bohs *21107*
   E   *20883* Colombia *20883*
   R   *20883* Ecuador (western) *21037*

V **Solanum fernandezianum** Philippi *19116*
   V   *19125* Chile - Juan Fernandez Is. *19116*

V **Solanum fortunense** Bohs *21107*
   E   *20883* Costa Rica *20883*
   V   *20883* Panama (Chiriquí & Coclé) *21037*

V **Solanum fosbergianum** D'Arcy *20883, 10747*
   I   *20883* Panama *20883*

V **Solanum gracilifrons** Bitter ex Engl. *18200*
   V   *12468* Peru *18200*

V **Solanum granelianum** D'Arcy *20883, 10747*
   V   *16317* Panama (Darién) *20883*

I **Solanum guamense** Merr. *20818*

I	20818	North Mariana Is. *18035*	
E	20818	U.S. - Guam *18035*	

R   *Solanum guerreroense* Correll *19866*
     R   *19915*   Mexico - Guerrero *19866*
     R   *19915*   Mexico - Jalisco *19866*

V   *Solanum guzmanguense* Whalen & Sagast. *18200*
     V   *12468*   Peru *18200*

R   *Solanum hamulosum* C.White *20681*
     R   *20681*   Australia - Queensland *20681*

V   *Solanum hastiformum* Corr. *18200*
     V   *12468*   Peru *18200*

R   *Solanum hidetaroi* Masamune *20511*
     R   *20511*   Taiwan *20511*

R   *Solanum hintonii* Correll *10108*
     R   *19866*   Mexico - Mexico State (near Temascáltepec) *19866*

R   *Solanum hjertingii* Hawkes *19866*
     R   *19915*   Mexico - Coahuila *19866*
     R   *19915*   Mexico - Nuevo Leon *19866*

R   *Solanum hjertingii* Hawkes var. *physaloides* (Correll) Hawkes *19866*
     R   *19915*   Mexico - Tamaulipas *19866*

R   *Solanum hougasii* Correll *19866*
     R   *19866*   Mexico - Jalisco *19866*
     R   *19866*   Mexico - Michoacan *19866*

E   *Solanum hugonis* Heine *20802*
     E   *20893*   New Caledonia *20802*

I   *Solanum humectophilum* Ochoa *18200*
     I   *12468*   Peru *18200*

V   *Solanum inaeguale* Vell. *20883*
     V   *20883*   Brazil *20883*

Ex/E   *Solanum incompletum* Dunal *20850, 14209*
     Ex/E   *20850*   U.S. - Hawaii *20850*

V   *Solanum ingaefolium* Ochoa *18200*
     V   *12468*   Peru *18200*

E   *Solanum insulae-pinorum* Heine *20893*
     E   *20893*   New Caledonia *20893*

R   *Solanum iopetalum* (Bitt.) Hawkes *19866*
     R   *19915*   Mexico - Hidalgo *19866*
     R   *19915*   Mexico - Puebla *19866*
     R   *19915*   Mexico - Veracruz *19866*

V   *Solanum jalcae* Ochoa *18200*
     V   *12468*   Peru *18200*

V   *Solanum karsensis* Symon *20681*
     V   *20681*   Australia - New South Wales *20681*

I   *Solanum kurzii* Bruce ex Prain
     I   India - Tamil Nadu (Coimbatore Hills)

R   *Solanum latiflorum* Bohs *21107*
     R   *20883*   Brazil *20883*
     ?   Brazil - Minas Gerais *21037*
     ?   Brazil - Rio de Janeiro *21037*
     ?   Brazil - Sao Paulo *21037*

V   *Solanum leptosepalum* Correll *20850, 19866*
     E   *20850*   U.S. - Texas *20850*
     I   *19915*   Mexico (north-east) *19866*

I   *Solanum lesteri* Hawkes & Hjerting *19866*
     I   *19915*   Mexico - Oaxaca *19866*

V   *Solanum lidii* Sunding *17891*
     V   *20750*   Spain - Canary Is. *17891*

V   *Solanum longiconicum* Bitter *9037*
     V   *19915*   Costa Rica (Cortago, San José) *19866*

     V   *19915*   Panama (Chiriquí) *19866*

R   *Solanum lumholtzianum* Bartlett *20883, 20850, 19002*
     R   *20850*   U.S. - Arizona *20850*
     20883   Mexico *20883*

R   *Solanum lycopersicoides* Dunal *18200*
     R   *12468*   Peru (Tacna) *19866*

I   *Solanum macropilosum* Correll *10108*
     I   *19915*   Mexico - Nuevo Leon *19866*

E   *Solanum malacothrix* S. Knapp *12036*
     E   *12036*   Mexico *12036*

E   *Solanum masafueranum* Bitter & Skottsb. *19116*
     E   *19125*   Chile - Juan Fernandez Is. *19116*

V   *Solanum microleprodes* D'Arcy var. *felicis* D'Arcy *20883, 10747*
     V   *16317*   Panama (Chiriquí) *20883*

V   *Solanum microleprodes* Bitt. var. *microleprodes* *20883, 10747*
     I   *20883*   Panama (Bocas del Toro; Chiriquí; Darién; Veraguas) *20883*

V   *Solanum mucronatum* O.E. Schulz *20883, 15106*
     I   *20883*   Puerto Rico *20883*
     I   *20883*   USA - Virgin Is. *20883*

I   *Solanum multiflorum* Vargas *18200*
     I   *12468*   Peru *18200*

R   *Solanum multiglochidiatum* Domin *20681*
     R   *20681*   Australia - Queensland *20681*

I   *Solanum nayaritense* (Bitter) Rydb. *19866*
     I   *19915*   Mexico - Nayarit *19866*
     I   *19915*   Mexico - Zacatecas *19866*

V   *Solanum nelsonii* Dunal *20850, 14209*
     V   *20850*   U.S. - Hawaii *20850*

I   *Solanum nemorosum* Ochoa *18200*
     I   *12468*   Peru *18200*

I   *Solanum neovargasii* Ochoa *18200*
     I   *12468*   Peru *18200*

V   *Solanum ovum-fringillae* (Dunal) Bohs *21107*
     V   *20883*   Brazil *20883*
     ?   Brazil - Pernambuco *21037*

I   *Solanum palustre* Poepp. ex Schlechtd. *19866*
     I   *19866*   Chile (near Valparaiso) *19866*

V   *Solanum pancheri* Guillaumin *20893*
     V   *20893*   New Caledonia *20893*

V   *Solanum paralum* Bohs *21107*
     V   *20883*   Brazil *20883*
     ?   Brazil - Bahia *21037*
     ?   Brazil - Rio de Janeiro *21037*
     ?   Brazil - Sao Paulo *21037*

I   *Solanum pascoense* Ochoa *18200*
     I   *12468*   Peru *18200*

V   *Solanum perattenuatum* I.M. Johnst. *20883, 10747*
     V   *16317*   Panama (Panamá) *20883*

V   *Solanum pillahuatense* Vargas *18200*
     V   *12468*   Peru *18200*

R   *Solanum pinetorum* (L.B.Sm.& Downs) Bohs *21107*
     R   *20883*   Brazil *20883*
     ?   Brazil - Minas Gerais *21037*
     ?   Brazil - Parana *21037*
     ?   Brazil - Rio de Janeiro *21037*
     ?   Brazil - Santa Catarina *21037*
     ?   Brazil - Sao Paulo *21037*

V   *Solanum piurae* Bitter *18200*

V   12468 Peru *18200*

V   *Solanum plowmanii* S. Knapp *21252*
V   21252 Peru *21252*

R   *Solanum polygamum* Vahl *20883, 19002*
I   20883 Puerto Rico *20883*
I   20883 USA - Virgin Is. *20883*

R   *Solanum premnifolium* (Miers) Bohs *21107*
R   20883 Brazil *20883*
?   Brazil - Bahia *21037*
?   Brazil - Parana *21037*
?   Brazil - Rio de Janeiro *21037*
?   Brazil - Sao Paulo *21037*

I   *Solanum proetermissum* Kerr ex Barnett *19120*
I   19120 Thailand *19120*

I   *Solanum pseuderanthemoides* Schltr. *20802*
I   20802 New Caledonia *20802*

R   *Solanum punctulatum* Dunal *20883*
R   20883 Jamaica *20883*

E   *Solanum puttii* Kerr ex Barnett *19120*
E   19120 Thailand *19120*

V   *Solanum raquialatum* Ochoa *18200*
V   12468 Peru *18200*

V   *Solanum rhomboideilanceolatum* Ochoa *18200*
V   12468 Peru *18200*

E   *Solanum robinsonianum* Bitter *19116*
E   19125 Chile - Juan Fernandez Is. *19116*

R   *Solanum rojasianum* (Standl.& Steyerm.) Bohs *21107*
E   20883 Belize *20883*
R   20883 Guatemala *20883*
E   20883 Mexico *20883*

E   *Solanum roseum* Bohs *21107*
E   20883 Bolivia (La Paz) *21037*

I   *Solanum sagraeanum* A. Rich. *5607*
I   19105 Cuba *5607*

I   *Solanum sanctae-rosae* Hawkes *16336*
I   19448 Argentina *16336*
I   20176 Argentina - Catamarca *20176*
I   20176 Argentina - Jujuy *20176*
I   20176 Argentina - Salta *20176*
I   20176 Argentina - Tucuman *20176*

E   *Solanum sandwicense* Hook. & Arn. *20850, 14209*
E   20850 U.S. - Hawaii (Kaua`i and O`ahu) *20850*

R   *Solanum santosii* S. Knapp *21252*
R   21252 Brazil *21252*

I   *Solanum sawyeri* Ochoa *18200*
I   12468 Peru *18200*

I   *Solanum scabrifolium* Ochoa *18200*
I   12468 Peru *18200*

I   *Solanum scopulorum* Kerr ex Barnett *19120*
I   19120 Thailand *19120*

V   *Solanum sibundoyense* (Bohs) Bohs *21107*
V   20883 Colombia (Sibundoy) *21037*

R   *Solanum sporadotrichum* F.Muell. *20681*
R   20681 Australia - Queensland *20681*

I   *Solanum stenophyllidium* Bitter *19866*
I   19866 Mexico - Jalisco *19866*

R   *Solanum stoloniferum* Schelchtd. & Bché ssp. *moreliae* Hawkes *19866*
R   19915 Mexico - Michoacan (Morelia) *19866*

V   *Solanum styraciflorum* Schltr. *20893*
V   20893 New Caledonia *20893*

R   *Solanum sycocarpum* Mart.& Sendtn. *21107*
R   20883 Brazil *20883*
?   Brazil - Bahia *21037*
?   Brazil - Espirito Santo *21037*
?   Brazil - Rio de Janeiro *21037*

R   *Solanum tabanoense* *11975*
R   19975 Colombia (southern Colombia) *19975*
R   19975 Ecuador *19975*
R   19975 Peru *19975*

V   *Solanum tenuilobatum* Parish *20883, 20850, 8058*
E   20850 U.S. - California *20850*
I   20883 Mexico *20883*

V   *Solanum trinitense* Ochoa *18200*
V   12468 Peru *18200*

R   *Solanum troyanum* Urb. *20883, 19890*
R   19890 Jamaica *20883*

E   *Solanum unifoliatum* S. Knapp *20883*
I   20883 Colombia *20883*

E   *Solanum vaccinioides* Schltr. *20893*
E   20893 New Caledonia *20893*

V   *Solanum vespertilio* Aiton *20216*
V   20750 Spain - Canary Is. *20750*

I   *Solanum villuspetalum* Vargas *18200*
I   12468 Peru *18200*

V   *Solanum wallacei* (Gray) Parish var. *clokeyi* (Munz) McMinn *20850*
I   20850 U.S. - California *20850*

E   *Solanum woodburyi* Howard *20883*
I   20883 Puerto Rico *20883*

E   *Solanum xantii* Gray var. *montanum* Munz *20850*
I   20850 U.S. - California *20850*
I   20850 U.S. - Nevada *20850*

V   *Solanum xantii* Gray var. *obispoense* (Eastw.) Wiggins *20850*
I   20850 U.S. - California *20850*

V   *Solanum yanamonense* S. Knapp *18200*
V   12468 Peru *18200*

I   *Tubocapsicum boninense* Koidz. *8048*
I   19134 Japan - Kazan Retto *8622*
Ex   19134 Japan - Ogasawara-shoto (Hahajima) *8048*

V   *Witheringia bristaniana* D'Arcy *20883, 9006*
V   16317 Panama *20883*

E   *Witheringia filipes* Alain *20883*
I   20883 Dominican Republic *20883*

V   *Witheringia hunzikeri* D'Arcy *20883, 9006*
I   20883 Panama *20883*

Sphenostemonaceae

Number of genera: 1
Number of species: 7
Recorded threatened species: 1   (14%)

Malesia to Australia and New Caledonia.

I   *Sphenostemon oppositifolium* Hurl.
I   New Caledonia

Stachyuraceae

Number of genera: 1
Number of species: 5-6
Recorded threatened species: 1   (16%)

Himalayan region to Japan.

V   *Stachyurus macrocarpus* Koidz. *20626, 18128*
    V   *20626* Japan - Ogasawara-shoto *20626*

V   *Stachyurus macrocarpus* Koidz. var. *purnifolius*
    Tuyama *20626*
    V   *20626* Japan - Ogasawara-shoto *20626*

Stackhousiaceae

Number of genera: 3
Number of species: 20-25
Recorded threatened species: 2   (8%)

Australia and New Zealand; southwestern Pacific.

R   *Stackhousia tryonii* F.Bailey *20681*
    R   *20681* Australia - Queensland *20681*

R   *Tripterococcus brachylobus* W.R.Barker ms. *20681*
    R   *20681* Australia - Western Australia *20681*

Staphyleaceae

Number of genera: 5
Number of species: 50
Recorded threatened species: 3   (6%)

Americas, Eurasia, Malay Archipelago.

I   *Staphylea colchica* Steven *5942*
    I   *5942* Georgia *5942*

R   *Tapiscia sinensis* Oliver *17617*
    R   *17617* China - Anhui *11139*
    R   *17617* China - Fujian *11139*
    R   *17617* China - Guangxi *11139*
    R   *17617* China - Guizhou *11139*
    R   *17617* China - Hubei *11139*
    R   *17617* China - Hunan *11139*
    R   *17617* China - Jiangxi *11139*
    R   *17617* China - Sichuan *11139*
    R   *17617* China - Zhejiang *11139*

R   *Turpinia indochinensis* Merr. *6057*
    R   Vietnam *6057*

Sterculiaceae

Number of genera: 65
Number of species: 1,000
Recorded threatened species: 106   (10%)

Tropical and subtropical.

V   *Acropogon aoupiniensis* Morat *20893*
    V   *20893* New Caledonia *20893*

V   *Acropogon bullatus* (Pancher & Serbert) Morat *20893*
    V   *20893* New Caledonia *20893*

V   *Acropogon domatifer* Morat *20893*
    V   *20893* New Caledonia *20893*

V   *Acropogon fatsioides* Schltr. *20893*
    V   *20893* New Caledonia *20893*

V   *Acropogon megaphyllus* (Bureau & Poisson ex Guillaumin)
    Morat *20893*
    V   *20893* New Caledonia *20893*

E   *Acropogon veillonii* Morat *20893*
    E   *20893* New Caledonia *20893*

Ex   *Astiria rosea* Lindl. *10082*
    Ex   *20771* Mauritius *10082*

E   *Ayenia cajalbanensis* Alain *5607*

E   *Ayenia laevigata* Sw. *20883*
    I   *20883* Jamaica *20883*

E   *Ayenia laevigata* Sw. var. *acuminata*
    Adams *20883, 13336*
    E   *13336* Jamaica (Trelawny) *20883*

V   *Ayenia laevigata* Sw. var. *laevigata* *20883,*
    13336
    V   *13336* Jamaica *20883*

V   *Ayenia limitaris* Cristobal *20883, 20850, 8058*
    E   *20850* U.S. - Texas *20850*
    I   *20883* Mexico *20883*

R   *Brachychiton acuminatus* Guymer *20681*
    R   *20681* Australia - Western Australia *20681*

R   *Brachychiton albidus* Guymer *20681*
    R   *20681* Australia - Queensland *20681*

R   *Brachychiton collinus* Guymer *20681*
    R   *20681* Australia - Queensland *20681*

R   *Brachychiton compactus* Guymer *20681*
    R   *20681* Australia - Queensland *20681*

R   *Brachychiton grandiflorus* Guymer *20681*
    R   *20681* Australia - Queensland *20681*

R   *Brachychiton obtusilobus* Guymer *20681*
    R   *20681* Australia - Western Australia *20681*

R   *Brachychiton vitifolius* (Bailey) Guymer *20681*
    R   *20681* Australia - Queensland *20681*

R   *Brachychiton xanthophyllus* Guymer *20681*
    R   *20681* Australia - Western Australia *20681*

Ex   *Byttneria ivorensis* Hallé *20887*
    Ex   *20887* Côte d'Ivoire *20887*

I   *Byttneria microphylla* Jacq. *11840*
    E   *19105* Cuba (Oriente; Pinar del Rio) *11840*
    I   *19408* Dominican Republic (Montecristi, Azua,
        Barahona) *21008*
        Haiti *21008*

I   *Byttneria scopiura* C. Wright *5607*

E   *Cola attiensis* Aubrev. & Pellegrin *7926*
    E   *20887* Côte d'Ivoire *7926*

E   *Cola boxiana* Brenan & Keay *15970*
    E   *20858* Ghana *20274*

I   *Cola crispiflora* Schumann *7927*
    I   Gabon (Haut Ogooue) *7927*

I   *Cola duparquetiana* Baillon
    I   Gabon (Lastoursville)

R   *Cola letestui* Pellegrin *7927*
    R   Gabon (Lastoursville) *7927*

E   *Cola octoloboides* Brenan *20057*
    E   *20057* Kenya *19109*

V   *Cola porphyrantha* Brenan *20057*
    V   *20057* Kenya *19109*

V   *Cola reticulata* A. Chev. *20274*
    V   *20858* Côte d'Ivoire *7926*
    V   *20858* Ghana *20274*
    V   *20858* Guinea (Mt. Nzo) *7926*

V   *Cola uloloma* Brenan *20057*
    V   *20057* Kenya *19109*
    V   *20057* Tanzania (Pangani & coast) *17435*

V   *Cola umbratilis* Brenan & Keay *7926*

V	20858	Côte d'Ivoire	20274
V	20858	Ghana	7926

I   *Dombeya acutangula* Cav. ssp. *acutangula* 10082

I	5852	Réunion	5852
E	5852	Mauritius - Rodrigues	5852

V   *Dombeya acutangula* Cav. var. *palmata* (Cav.) Arènes 10082

V	14234	Réunion	10082

E   *Dombeya acutangula* Cav. ssp. *rosea* F.Friedmann 20771

E	12249	Mauritius	12249

V   *Dombeya blattiolens* Frappier ex Cordem. 10082

V		Réunion	10082

V   *Dombeya delislei* Arènes 10082

V	14220	Réunion	10082

V   *Dombeya elegans* Cordem. var. *virescens* Cordem. 10082

V	14220	Réunion	10082

I   *Dombeya ferruginea* Cav. ssp. *borbonica* Friedm. 10082

I	14220	Réunion	10082

R   *Dombeya ferruginea* Cav. ssp. *ferruginea* 10082

R	20771	Mauritius	10082

R   *Dombeya lastii* K. Schumann 7749

R		Mozambique	7749

R   *Dombeya leachii* Wild 7749

R		Mozambique	7749

I   *Dombeya longebracteolata* Seyani 20924

I	20924	Ethiopia (Kefa, Gamo Gofa, Sidamo)	20924

E   *Dombeya mauritiana* Friedmann 10082

E	20771	Mauritius	10082

E   *Dombeya populnea* (Cav.) Baker 10082

E	14234	Réunion	10082
E	20771	Mauritius	10082

R   *Dombeya punctata* Cav. 10082

R	14220	Réunion	10082

E   *Dombeya rodriguesiana* F. Friedmann 10082

E	5852	Mauritius - Rodrigues	10936

R   *Dombeya rotundifolia* (Hochst.) Planchon var. *velutina* Verdoorn

R	20604	Namibia	20604

V   *Dombeya umbellata* Cav. 10082

V	14220	Réunion	10082

V   *Eriolaena lushingtonii* Dunn 14782

V	14782	India - Andhra Pradesh	14782
V	14782	India - Tamil Nadu	14782

E   *Firmiana hainanensis* Kosterm. 17617

E	17617	China - Hainan Is.	11139

R   *Firmiana major* (W. Smith) Hand.-Mazz. 17617

R	17617	China - Yunnan	11139

E   *Fremontodendron decumbens* R. Lloyd 20850

E	20850	U.S. - California	20850

R   *Fremontodendron mexicanum* A. Davids. 20883, 20850, 8058

V	20850	U.S. - California	20850
I	20883	Mexico	20883

E   *Helicteres calcicola* Alain 11840

E	19105	Cuba (Pinar del Rio)	11840

R   *Helicteres linifolia* Cowie ms. 20681

R	20681	Australia - Northern Territory	20681

V   *Heritiera longipetiolata* Kaneh. 20825

V	20825	North Mariana Is.	18035
V	20825	Micronesia - Caroline Is. (Pohnpei)	20825
V	20818	U.S. - Guam	18338

V   *Heritiera parvifolia* Merr. 17617

V	17617	China - Hainan Is.	11139

I   *Hermannia cordifolia* Harv. 20604

I	20604	South Africa - Cape Province	20604

R   *Hermannia disticha* Schrad. 20604

R	20604	South Africa - Cape Province	20604

I   *Hermannia helicoidea* I.Verd. 20604

	20604	South Africa - Cape Province	20604

I   *Hermannia micrantha* Adamson 20604

I	20604	South Africa - Cape Province	20604

I   *Hermannia pillansii* Compton 20604

I	20604	South Africa - Cape Province	20604

E   *Hermannia procumbens* Cav. ssp. *procumbens* (Thunb.)De Winter 20604

E	20604	South Africa - Cape Province	20604

I   *Hermannia rudis* N.E.Br. 20604

I	20604	South Africa - Cape Province	20604

V   *Hermannia rugosa* Adamson 20604

V	20604	South Africa - Cape Province	20604

I   *Hermannia sandersonii* Harv. 20604

I	20604	South Africa - Natal	20604

I   *Hermannia torrei* Wild 7749

I		Mozambique	7749

E   *Herrania balaensis* Pruess 11658

E	11658	Ecuador	11658

R   *Hildegardia australiensis* G.Leach & Cheek 20681

R	20681	Australia - Northern Territory	20681

V   *Hildegardia gillettii* L.J.Dorr & L.C.Barnett 20884

V	20884	Somalia (south)	20884

E   *Hildegardia populifolia* (Roxb.) Schott & Endl. 14782

E	14782	India - Andhra Pradesh	14782
E	14782	India - Tamil Nadu	14782

R   *Keraudrenia corollata* (Steetz) Druce var. *denticulata* C.White 20681

I	20681	Australia - New South Wales	20681
I	20681	Australia - Queensland	20681

R   *Lasiopetalum bracteatum* (Endl.) Benth. 20681

R	20681	Australia - Western Australia	20681

R   *Lasiopetalum joyceae* Blakely 20681

R	20681	Australia - New South Wales	20681

V   *Lasiopetalum longistamineum* Maiden & Betche 20681

V	20681	Australia - New South Wales	20681

V   *Lasiopetalum micranthum* Hook.f. 20681

V	20681	Australia - Tasmania	20681

Ex   *Lasiopetalum rotundifolium* Paust 20681

Ex	20681	Australia - Western Australia	20681

I   *Melhania futteyporensis* Munro ex Masters var. *major* (Blatter & Hallberg) Santapau 7771

I		India - Rajasthan (western)	7771

I   *Melhania magnifolia* Blatter & Hallberg 7771

I		India - Rajasthan (western)	7771

I   *Melhania polygama* I.Verd. 20604

	I	20604 South Africa - Natal 20604	

E   *Melochia manducata* **C. Wright** *5607*
     E   *19105* Cuba (Pinar del Rio) *5607*

Ex/E   *Nephropetalum pringlei* **Robinson & Greenman** *8058*
     Ex/E *14662* U.S. - Texas *8058*
     Ex/E *14662* Mexico *8058*

E   *Pterospermum kingtungense* **C.Y. Wu ex Hsue** *17617*
     E   *17617* China - Yunnan (Jingdong) *11139*

R   *Pterospermum menglunense* **Hsue** *17617*
     R   *17617* China - Yunnan (Mengla) *11139*

R   *Pterospermum reticulatum* **Wight & Arn.** *14782*
     R   *14782* India - Karnataka *14782*
     R   *14782* India - Kerala *14782*
     R   *14782* India - Tamil Nadu *14782*

R   *Pterospermum yunnanense* **Hsue** *17617*
     R   *17617* China - Yunnan (Mengla; Jinghong) *11139*

R   *Pterygota amazonica* **L.O. Williams** *18200*
     R   *12468* Peru *18200*

I   *Pterygota thwaitesii* **(Masters) Alston** *10252*
     I   *16162* Sri Lanka *10252*

R   *Reevesia formosana* **Sprague** *20511*
     R   *20511* Taiwan (south) *20511*

E   *Reevesia rotundifolia* **Chun** *17617*
     E   *17617* China - Guangxi (Shiwandashan) *11139*

R   *Reevesia yersinii* **Chev.** *6057*
     R   Vietnam *6057*

E   *Ruizia cordata* **Cav.** *10082*
     E   *14234* Réunion *10082*

R   *Rulingia hermanniifolia* **(DC.) Steetz** *20681*
     I   *20681* Australia - New South Wales *20681*
     I   *20681* Australia - Queensland *20681*

V   *Rulingia procumbens* **Maiden & Betche** *20681*
     V   *20681* Australia - New South Wales *20681*

E   *Rulingia prostrata* **Maiden & Betche** *20681*
     Ex/E *20681* Australia - New South Wales *20681*
     E   *20681* Australia - Victoria *20681*

R   *Rulingia salviifolia* **Benth.** *20681*
     I   *20681* Australia - New South Wales *20681*
     I   *20681* Australia - Queensland *20681*

R   *Sterculia alexandri* **Harv.** *20604*
     R   *20604* South Africa - Cape Province *20604*

I   *Sterculia bicolor* **Mast.** *19209*
     I   *19209* Malaysia - Peninsular Malaysia (Perak &
             Terengganu.) *19209*
     V   *20099* Singapore *20099*

Ex   *Sterculia khasiana* **Deb.** *11494*
     Ex   *11494* India - Meghalaya (Khasi hills) *11494*

I   *Sterculia populnifolia* **Roxb.**
     I   India

V   *Sterculia schliebenii* **Mildbr.** *20057*
     V   *20885* Kenya *20057*
     V   *20885* Mozambique *20885*
     V   *20885* Tanzania *20885*

I   *Sterculia zeylanica* **Kosterm.**
     I   Sri Lanka

I   *Theobroma cirmolinae* **Cuatrec.** *19352*
     I   *19352* Colombia (Pacific region) *19764*

Ex   *Thomasia gardneri* **Paust** *20681*
     Ex   *20681* Australia - Western Australia *20681*

V   *Thomasia glabripetala* **S.J.Patrick** *20681*
     V   *20681* Australia - Western Australia *20681*

V   *Thomasia montana* **Steudel** *20681*
     V   *20681* Australia - Western Australia *20681*

R   *Trochetia blackburniana* **Bojer ex Baher** *10082*
     R   *20771* Mauritius *10082*

E   *Trochetia boutoniana* **Friedmann** *10082*
     E   *20771* Mauritius *10082*

V   *Trochetia granulata* **Cordem.** *10082*
     V   *14234* Réunion *10082*

Ex   *Trochetia parviflora* **Bojer ex Baker** *10082*
     Ex   *20771* Mauritius *10082*

V   *Trochetia triflora* **DC.** *10082*
     V   *20771* Mauritius *10082*

E   *Trochetia uniflora* **DC.** *10082*
     E   *20771* Mauritius *10082*

Ex   *Trochetiopsis erythroxylon* **(Forster f.) Marais** *18996*
     Ex   *18996* St Helena *18996*

E   *Trochetiopsis melanoxylon* **(R. Br. ex Aiton f.)**
     Marais *18996*
     E   *18996* St Helena *18996*

R   *Ungeria floribunda* **Schott & Endl.** *11649*
     R   *19108* Australia - Norfolk Is. *11649*

E   *Waltheria nipensis* **(Britton) Alain** *5607*
     E   *19105* Cuba (Holguin) *5607*

Stilbaceae

Number of genera:	5
Number of species:	12
Recorded threatened species:	1 (8%)

Winter rainfall regions of Cape Province (South Africa).

R   *Thesmophora scopulosa* **Rourke** *20604*
     R   *20604* South Africa - Cape Province *20604*

Stylidiaceae

Number of genera:	5
Number of species:	155
Recorded threatened species:	9 (5%)

Centered in Australia.

E   *Stylidium coroniforme* **R.Erickson & J.H.Willis** *20681*
     E   *20681* Australia - Western Australia *20681*

R   *Stylidium expeditionis* **S.Carlquist** *20681*
     R   *20681* Australia - Western Australia *20681*

V   *Stylidium galioides* **C.Gardner** *20681*
     V   *20681* Australia - Western Australia *20681*

R   *Stylidium inversiflorum* **S.Carlquist** *20681*
     R   *20681* Australia - Western Australia *20681*

V   *Stylidium merrallii* **(F.Muell.) E.Pritzel** *20681,*
14223
     V   *20681* Australia - Western Australia *20681*

R   *Stylidium plantagineum* **Sonder** *20681*
     R   *20681* Australia - Western Australia *20681*

E   *Stylidium scabridum* **Lindley** *20681*
     E   *20681* Australia - Western Australia *20681*

R   *Stylidium tenuicarpum* **S.Carlquist** *20681*
     R   *20681* Australia - Western Australia *20681*

R   *Stylidium tepperianum* **(F.Muell.) Mildbr.** *20681*
     R   *20681* Australia - South Australia *20681*

Styracaceae

Number of genera:	10	
Number of species:	150	
Recorded threatened species:	14	(9%)

Widely disjunct in both hemispheres.

R   *Halesia macgregorii* Chun *17617*
- **R**   *17617* China - Fujian *11139*
- **R**   *17617* China - Guangdong *11139*
- **R**   *17617* China - Guangxi *11139*
- **R**   *17617* China - Hunan *11139*
- **R**   *17617* China - Jiangxi *11139*
- **R**   *17617* China - Zhejiang *11139*

I   *Huodendron siamicum* Fletcher *19120*
- **I**   *19120* Thailand *19120*

V   *Pterostyrax psilophylla* Diels ex Perkins *17617*
- **V**   *17617* China - Guangxi *11139*
- **V**   *17617* China - Guizhou *11139*
- **V**   *17617* China - Hubei *11139*
- **V**   *17617* China - Hunan *11139*
- **V**   *17617* China - Sichuan *11139*
- **V**   *17617* China - Yunnan (Zhengxun) *11139*

V   *Rehderodendron macrocarpum* Hu *17617*
- **V**   *17617* China - Guangxi (Lingyun) *11139*
- **V**   *17617* China - Guizhou *11139*
- **V**   *17617* China - Sichuan *11139*
- **V**   *17617* China - Yunnan (Wenshan; Jingping) *11139*

E   *Sinojackia dolichocarpa* C.J. Qi *17617*
- **E**   *17617* China - Hunan (Shimeng; Shangzhi) *11139*

E   *Sinojackia xylocarpa* Hu *17617*
- **E**   *17617* China - Jiangsu (Nanjing; Jiangpu; Jurong) *11139*

E   *Styrax betongensis* Fletcher *19120*
- **E**   *19120* Thailand *19120*

R   *Styrax formosana* Matsum. var. *hayataiana* (Perkins) Li *20511*
- **R**   *20511* Taiwan *20511*

R   *Styrax matsumurei* Perkins *20854*
- **R**   *20854* Taiwan *20854*

R   *Styrax platanifolius* Engelm. ex Torr. *20850*
- **R**   *20850* U.S. - Texas *20850*

V   *Styrax portoricensis* Krug & Urban *20883, 10197*
- **V**   *20883* Puerto Rico *20883*

R   *Styrax tafelbergensis* Maguire *8679*
- **R**   *8679* Suriname *8679*

E   *Styrax texanus* Cory *20850*
- **E**   *20850* U.S. - Texas *20850*

I   *Styrax youngiae* Cory *20883, 20850*
- **Ex/E**   *20850* U.S. - Texas *20850*
- **I**   *20883* Mexico *20883*

Surianaceae

Number of genera:	4	
Number of species:	6	
Recorded threatened species:	1	(16%)

Australia and tropical maritime.

R   *Cadellia pentastylis* F.Muell. *20681*
- **I**   *20681* Australia - New South Wales *20681*
- **I**   *20681* Australia - Queensland *20681*

Symplocaceae

Number of genera:	1	
Number of species:	300-400	
Recorded threatened species:	43	(12%)

Tropical and subtropical America; southern and eastern Asia; Australia; East Indies.

I   *Symplocos abietorum* Standley & Steyerm. *9004*
- **I**   *9835* Guatemala *9004*

R   *Symplocos ampulliformis* C.White *20681*
- **R**   *20681* Australia - Queensland *20681*

R   *Symplocos anamallayana* Beddome
- **R**   *18228* India - Tamil Nadu *18228*

R   *Symplocos austromexicana* Almeda *10114*
- **R**   *16360* Mexico - Oaxaca *10114*

V   *Symplocos baeuerlenii* R.T.Baker *20681*
- **I**   *20681* Australia - New South Wales *20681*
- **I**   *20681* Australia - Queensland *20681*

I   *Symplocos barberi* Gamble
- **I**   India - Tamil Nadu (Tirunelveli Hills)

V   *Symplocos boninensis* Rehder & Wilson *8037*
- **V**   *19134* Japan - Ogasawara-shoto *20626*

V   *Symplocos breedlovei* Lundell *10294*
- **V**   *9835* Mexico *10294*

R   *Symplocos candelabrum* Brand
- **R**   *14225* Australia - NSW - Lord Howe Is. *14225*

E   *Symplocos ciponimoides* Griseb. *5607*
- **E**   *19105* Cuba (Holguin) *5607*

R   *Symplocos coccinea* Humb. *9019*
- **R**   *9114* Mexico - Veracruz *9019*

R   *Symplocos cordifolia* Thwaites *8021*
- **R**   *20013* Sri Lanka *8021*

V   *Symplocos coronata* Thwaites var. *coronata* *8021*
- **V**   *12838* Sri Lanka *8021*

V   *Symplocos coronata* Thwaites var. *glabrifolia* (Thwaites) Nooteb. *8021*
- **V**   *12838* Sri Lanka *8021*

R   *Symplocos crassiramifera* Nooteb. *20681*
- **R**   *20681* Australia - Queensland *20681*

R   *Symplocos disepala* Guillaumin *6057*
- **R**   Vietnam *6057*

E   *Symplocos diversifolia* Brand var. *appressa* Nooteb. *8021*
- **E**   Sri Lanka (Kurulugala, Bulutota) *8021*

R   *Symplocos elegans* Thw. *16162*
- **R**   *20013* Sri Lanka *16162*

R   *Symplocos excelsa* L.O. Williams *9084*
- **R**   *16360* Mexico *9084*

R   *Symplocos graniticola* Jessup *20681*
- **R**   *20681* Australia - Queensland *20681*

R   *Symplocos harroldii* Jessup *20681*
- **R**   *20681* Australia - Queensland *20681*

R   *Symplocos hayesii* C.White & Francis *20681*
- **R**   *20681* Australia - Queensland *20681*

V   *Symplocos hintonii* Lundell *10294*
- **V**   *9835* Mexico *10294*

V   *Symplocos hispidula* Thwaites *12838*

	V	12838 Sri Lanka *12838*
R	*Symplocos hylandii* Nooteb. *20681*	
	R	20681 Australia - Queensland *20681*
E	*Symplocos incahuasensis* Sagástegui & Dillon *20883*	
	I	20883 Peru *20883*
R	*Symplocos johnsonii* Standley *9004*	
	R	9835 Guatemala *9004*
E	*Symplocos kawakamii* Hayata *8038*	
	E	18128 Japan - Ogasawara-shoto (Chichijima) *8038*
E	*Symplocos lanata* Krug & Urban *20883*	
	I	20883 Puerto Rico *20883*
V	*Symplocos longipes* Lundell *10294*	
	V	9835 Mexico *10294*
V	*Symplocos moaensis* Borh. *5607*	
	V	19105 Cuba (Guantanamo) *5607*
R	*Symplocos nokoensis* (Hayata) Kanehira *20854*	
	R	20854 Taiwan *20854*
I	*Symplocos octopetala* Sw. *20883, 13336*	
	R	20883 Jamaica *20883*
R	*Symplocos olivacea* Merr. *6057*	
	R	Vietnam *6057*
R	*Symplocos ovalis* C. Wright *5607*	
	R	19105 Cuba (Pinar del Rio) *5607*
V	*Symplocos pergracilis* (Nakai) Yamaz. *8038*	
	V	19134 Japan - Ogasawara-shoto *8038*
R	*Symplocos shilanensis* Liu & Lu *20854*	
	R	20854 Taiwan *20854*
R	*Symplocos singuliflora* Guillaumin *6057*	
	R	Vietnam *6057*
E	*Symplocos sousae* Almeda *20883, 10130*	
	I	20883 Costa Rica *20883*
	I	19850 Mexico - Jalisco *10130*
	I	19850 Mexico - Oaxaca *10130*
R	*Symplocos stawellii* F.Muell. var. *montana* C.T.White *20681*	
	R	20681 Australia - Queensland *20681*
R	*Symplocos tubulifera* Krug. & Urb. *20883, 13336*	
	R	13336 Jamaica (St. Catherine, St. Ann) *20883*
R	*Symplocos vatteri* Standley & Steyerm. *9004*	
	R	9835 Guatemala *9004*
V	*Symplocos versicolor* C.B. Clarke *12838*	
	V	12838 Sri Lanka *12838*
I	*Symplocos villosa* Brand	
	I	India - Kerala (Peermade Hills, Travancore)

Tamaricaceae

Number of genera:	4-5
Number of species:	100
Recorded threatened species:	4 (4%)

Eurasia and Africa, especially Mediterranean region.

R	*Reaumuria badhysi* Korovin	
	R	former USSR *6930*
R	*Reaumuria zakirovii* Gorschk.	
	R	former USSR *6930*
R	*Tamarix negevensis* Zoh. *8895*	
	R	Egypt
	I	Israel *8895*
V	*Tamarix taklamakanensis* M.T. Liu *17617*	

	V	17617 China - Xinjiang Uygur Zizhiqu (Talimupendi) *11139*

Theaceae

Number of genera:	40
Number of species:	600
Recorded threatened species:	73 (12%)

Tropical and subtropical.

R	*Adinandra formosana* Hayata var. *hypochlora* (Hayata) Yamamoto ex Keng *20511*	
	R	20511 Taiwan *20511*
R	*Adinandra formosana* Hayata var. *obtussisima* (Hayata) Keng *20511*	
	R	20511 Taiwan *20511*
E	*Adinandra griffithii* Dyer *11494*	
	E	11494 India - Meghalaya (Khasi hills) *11494*
R	*Adinandra microcarpa* Gagnepain *6057*	
	R	Vietnam *6057*
R	*Anneslea fragrans* Wallich var. *lanceolata* Hayata *20854*	
	R	20854 Taiwan (southern-most part) *20854*
R	*Anneslea ternstroemioides* Gagnepain *6057*	
	R	Vietnam *6057*
R	*Apterosperma oblata* H.T. Chang *17617*	
	R	17617 China - Guangdong (Yangchong; Xingyi) *11139*
	R	17617 China - Guangxi (Guiping) *11139*
V	*Camellia crapnelliana* Tutcher *17617*	
	V	17617 China - Fujian *11139*
	V	17617 China - Guangxi *11139*
	V	17617 China - Zhejiang (Qingyuan) *11139*
	E	Hong Kong (Jiulong) *11139*
R	*Camellia euphlebia* Merr. ex Sealy *11139*	
	R	China - Guangxi (Fuangchen) *11139*
R	*Camellia fleuryi* (Chev.) Sealy *6057*	
	I	20985 Vietnam *6057*
R	*Camellia gilbertii* (Chev.) Sealy *6057*	
	I	20985 Vietnam *6057*
E	*Camellia granthamiana* Sealy *17617*	
	E	17617 China - Guangdong (Lufeng, Dapu) *11139*
	E	Hong Kong (Jiouleung) *11139*
V	*Camellia grijsii* Hance *17617*	
	V	17617 China - Fujian *11139*
	V	17617 China - Guangxi *11139*
	V	17617 China - Hubei (Yichang) *11139*
	V	17617 China - Hunan (Yiuxian; Yongshong) *11139*
	V	17617 China - Jiangxi (Lichuan) *11139*
V	*Camellia hengchunensis* Chang *20854*	
	V	20854 Taiwan *20854*
R	*Camellia indochinensis* Merr. *6057*	
	R	Vietnam *6057*
R	*Camellia japonica* L. var. *hozanensis* L. *20511*	
	R	20511 Taiwan *20511*
R	*Camellia krempfii* (Gagnepain) Sealy *6057*	
	R	Vietnam *6057*
I	*Camellia megacarpa* (Elm.) Cohen-Stuartt *13833*	
	I	13833 Philippines (Palawan) *13833*
R	*Camellia pingguoensis* D. Fang *11139*	
	R	China - Guangxi (Pinggue; Tiandong)

11139

R	*Camellia pubipetala* Y. Wan & S.Z. Huang *11139*	
	R	China - Guangxi (Longan, Daxing) *11139*
V	*Camellia reticulata* Lindley *17617*	
	V	*17617* China - Yunnan *11139*
R	*Camellia sinensis* (L.) O.Ktze ssp. *buisanensis* (L.) O.Ktze *20511*	
	R	*20511* Taiwan *20511*
R	*Camellia transnokoenis* Hayata *20511*	
	R	*20511* Taiwan *20511*
R	*Camellia tunghinensis* H.T. Chang *11139*	
	R	China - Guangxi (Fuangcheng) *11139*
R	*Cleyera japonica* Thunb. var. *grandiflora* (Wall. ex Choisy) Kobuski *14782*	
	R	*14782* India - Meghalaya *14782*
R	*Cleyera japonica* Thunb. var. *hayatai* Thunb. *20511*	
	R	*20511* Taiwan *20511*
R	*Cleyera japonica* Thunb. var. *taipehensis* Thunb. *20511*	
	R	*20511* Taiwan *20511*
I	*Eurya acuminata* DC. var. *arisanensis* DC. *20511*	
	I	*20511* Taiwan *20511*
E	*Eurya boninensis* Koidz. *8037*	
	E	*19134* Japan - Ogasawara-shoto *20626*
R	*Eurya rengechiensis* Yamamoto *20854*	
	R	*20854* Taiwan *20854*
V	*Eurya sandwicensis* Gray *20850, 14209*	
	V	*20850* U.S. - Hawaii *20850*
R	*Eurya yakusimensis* Masam. *10572*	
	R	*10572* Japan *10572*
V	*Eurya zigzag* Masam. *20626*	
	V	*20626* Japan (Ryukyu) *20626*
E	*Euryodendron excelsum* H.T. Chang *17617*	
	E	*17617* China - Guangdong (Yangchong) *11139*
	E	*17617* China - Guangxi (Pinnan) *11139*
Ex/E	*Franklinia alatamaha* Bartr. ex Marsh. *20850, 14662*	
	Ex	*20850* U.S. - Georgia *20850*
I	*Freziera biserrata* A.L. Weitzman *21018*	
	I	*21018* Costa Rica (Limón) *21018*
I	*Freziera cordata* Tulasne *10200*	
	E	*19001* Dominica *10200*
	I	Guadeloupe (only on two peaks) *10200*
	E	*19001* Martinique (Mt. Pelée between 900-1300m; Pitons du Carbet) *10200*
I	*Freziera cyanocantha* A.L. Weitzman *21018*	
	?	Peru (Huánuco) *21018*
I	*Freziera echinata* A.L.Weitzman *21018*	
	I	*21018* Colombia (Cauca) *21018*
E	*Freziera forerorum* A. Gentry *9006, 21304*	
	E	*23* Panama *9006*
I	*Freziera jaramilloi* A.H.Gentry *21018*	
	I	*21018* Colombia (Chocó) *21018*
R	*Freziera ordata* Tul. *5710*	
	R	Dominica (Trois Pitons; Morne Anglais) *5710*
	R	*5710* Guadeloupe (La Soufriere, Citerne) *5710*
	Ex/E	*5710* Martinique (Montagne Pelée) *5710*
I	*Freziera retinveria* Kobuski *21018*	

	I	*21018* Colombia (Norte de Santander) *21018*
V	*Freziera sericea* Humb. & Bonpl. *19352*	
	V	*19352* Colombia *19352*
I	*Freziera smithiana* Kobuski *21018*	
	I	*21018* Colombia (Santander) *21018*
I	*Freziera spathulifolia* (Melch.) Kobuski *21018*	
	I	*21018* Peru (Huánuco) *21018*
I	*Freziera stuebelii* (Hieron.) A.L.Weitzman *21018*	
	I	*21018* Colombia (Putumayo) *21018*
I	*Freziera uniauriculata* A.L.Weitzman *21018*	
	I	*21018* Bolivia (La Paz) *21018*
I	*Freziera varibracteata* A.L.Weitzman *21018*	
	I	*21018* Bolivia (La Paz) *21018*
I	*Freziera velutina* A.L.Weitzman *21018*	
	I	*21018* Colombia (Chocó) *21018*
E	*Gordonia speciosa* (Gardner) Choisy *10252*	
	E	*20013* Sri Lanka *10252*
E	*Gordonia zeylanica* Wight *10276*	
	E	*20013* Sri Lanka *10276*
R	*Hartia tonkinensis* Merr. *6057*	
	R	Vietnam *6057*
E	*Laplacea brenesii* Standley *9037*	
	E	*17459* Costa Rica *9037*
E	*Laplacea curtyana* A. Rich. *11840*	
	E	*19105* Cuba *11840*
V	*Laplacea glabrata* Proctor *20883, 13336*	
	V	*13336* Jamaica *20883*
V	*Laplacea portoricensis* (Krug & Urban) Dyer *20883, 10197*	
	?	Hispaniola *8058*
	V	*20883* Puerto Rico *20883*
	?	*19002* Mexico *19002*
	?	*19002* Country Unknown *19002*
E	*Laplacea villosa* (Macf.) Griseb. *20883, 19890*	
	E	*19890* Jamaica *20883*
I	*Pyrenaria khasiana* R.N. Paul *14782*	
	I	*14782* India - Meghalaya *14782*
R	*Schima superba* Gardn. & Champ. var. *kankoensis* (Hayata) Keng *20511*	
	R	*20511* Taiwan *20511*
I	*Schima wallichi* (DC.) Korth. ssp. *crenata* (Korth.) Bloembergen var. *pulgarensis* (Elm.) Bloembergen *13833*	
	I	*13833* Philippines (Palawan) *13833*
V	*Stuartia sinensis* Rehder & Wilson *17617*	
	V	*17617* China - Anhui *11139*
	V	*17617* China - Fujian *11139*
	V	*17617* China - Guangxi *11139*
	V	*17617* China - Guizhou *11139*
	V	*17617* China - Henan *11139*
	V	*17617* China - Hubei *11139*
	V	*17617* China - Hunan *11139*
	V	*17617* China - Jiangxi *11139*
	V	*17617* China - Sichuan *11139*
	V	*17617* China - Yunnan *11139*
	V	*17617* China - Zhejiang *11139*
E	*Ternstroemia bullata* Proctor *20883, 13336*	
	E	*13336* Jamaica *20883*
E	*Ternstroemia calycina* F. & R. *20883, 13336*	
	E	*20883* Jamaica *20883*
R	*Ternstroemia chapaensis* Gagnepain *6057*	

R		Vietnam *6057*	
E	*Ternstroemia elliptica* Sw. *8767*		
	E	*19001*	Antigua & Barbuda *19001*
	E	*19001*	Dominica *19001*
	E	*19001*	Guadeloupe *19001*
	E	*19001*	Martinique *19001*
	E	*19001*	Montserrat *19001*
	E	*19001*	St Kitts - Nevis *19001*
	E	*19001*	St Vincent *19001*
E	*Ternstroemia glomerata* Proctor *20883, 13336*		
	E	*13336*	Jamaica *20883*
I	*Ternstroemia granulata* Krug & Urb. *20883, 13336*		
	I	*13336*	Jamaica *20883*
R	*Ternstroemia hartii* Krug & Urb. *20883*		
	R	*20883*	Jamaica *20883*
E	*Ternstroemia heptasepala* Krug & Urban *20883*		
	I	*20883*	Puerto Rico *20883*
R	*Ternstroemia howardiana* Kobuski *20883, 13336*		
	R	*13336*	Jamaica (Portland) *20883*
V	*Ternstroemia luquillensis* Krug & Urban *20883, 10197*		
	V	*20883*	Puerto Rico (Luquilio Mts.) *20883*
R	*Ternstroemia oligostemon* Krug & Urban *19001*		
	R	*19001*	Guadeloupe *19001*
	Ex/E	*19001*	Martinique *19001*
	R	*19001*	Trinidad & Tobago *19001*
V	*Ternstroemia rostrata* Krug & Urb. *20883*		
	V	*20883*	Jamaica *20883*
E	*Ternstroemia subsessilis* (Britt.) Kobuski *20883*		
	I	*20883*	Puerto Rico *20883*
R	*Visnea mocanera* L. fil. *17534*		
	R		Portugal - Madeira
	V	*17534*	Spain - Canary Is. *17534*

Theligonaceae

Number of genera:	1
Number of species:	3
Recorded threatened species:	1 (33%)

Temperate eastern Asia to Mediterranean region and Canary Islands.

R	*Theligonum formosanum* (Ohwi) Ohwi & Liu *20511*		
	R	*20511*	Taiwan *20511*

Theophrastaceae

Number of genera:	4
Number of species:	100
Recorded threatened species:	21 (21%)

Mostly New World tropical.

E	*Clavija pubens* D'Arcy *20883, 10747*		
	I	*20883*	Panama *20883*
V	*Clavija repanda* Stahl *11213*		
	V	*11213*	Ecuador *11213*
R	*Deherainia matudae* Lundell *11213*		
	R	*11213*	Guatemala *11213*
	R	*11213*	Mexico *11213*
V	*Jacquinia aciphylla* L. Lepper *11840*		
	V	*19105*	Cuba (Camaguey) *11840*
R	*Jacquinia acunana* Borh. & Muniz *5607*		
	R		Cuba (Holguin, Guantanamo) *5607*
V	*Jacquinia bissei* L. Lepper *11840*		
	V	*19105*	Cuba (Santiago de Cuba) *11840*

I	*Jacquinia comosa* Urban *5642*		
	I		Dominican Republic (Trujin; Barahona) *5642*
R	*Jacquinia cristalensis* L. Lepper *11840*		
	R	*19105*	Cuba (Holguin) *11840*
E	*Jacquinia curtissii* Britton *5607*		
	E	*19105*	Cuba (Juventud Is.) *5607*
R	*Jacquinia eggersii* Urban *5642*		
	R		Dominican Republic (Santiago) *5642*
V	*Jacquinia juniperifolia* L. Lepper *11840*		
	V	*19105*	Cuba (Camaguey) *11840*
V	*Jacquinia lippoldii* L. Lepper *11840*		
	V	*19105*	Cuba (Guantanamo) *11840*
I	*Jacquinia longifolia* Standley *9004*		
	I	*11213*	Belize *9004*
	I	*11213*	Honduras *11213*
	I	*11213*	Nicaragua *11213*
V	*Jacquinia macrantha* Urb. *20883*		
	V	*20883*	Jamaica *20883*
V	*Jacquinia macrantha* Urb. var. *clarendonensis* Stearn *20883, 19890*		
	E	*19890*	Jamaica *20883*
V	*Jacquinia macrantha* Urb. var. *macrantha* *20883, 13336*		
	V	*13336*	Jamaica *20883*
V	*Jacquinia montana* Stahl *16402*		
	V	*11213*	Nicaragua *11213*
E	*Jacquinia oligantha* Borh. *5607*		
	E	*19105*	Cuba (Santiago de Cuba, Holguin) *5607*
E	*Jacquinia proctorii* Stearn *20883, 19890*		
	V	*19890*	Jamaica (St. Elizabeth) *20883*
V	*Jacquinia seleriana* Urb. & Loes. *11213*		
	V	*11213*	Mexico *11213*
R	*Jacquinia sessiliflora* Alain *5607*		
	R	*19105*	Cuba (Santiago de Cuba; Holguin) *5607*
I	*Jacquinia umbellata* A. DC. *10197*		
	I	*15106*	Puerto Rico *8058*
E	*Jacquinia verticillaris* Urban *5607*		
	E	*19105*	Cuba (Santiago de Cuba) *5607*

Thymelaeaceae

Number of genera:	50
Number of species:	500
Recorded threatened species:	72 (14%)

Cosmopolitan.

V	*Aquilaria sinensis* (Lour.) Gilg *17617*		
	V	*17617*	China - Guangdong *11139*
	V	*17617*	China - Guangxi *17617*
	V	*17617*	China - Yunnan (Jinghong) *11139*
I	*Craterosiphon schmitzii* Robyns		
	I	*6086*	Zaire (Haut-Katanga) *6086*
R	*Cryptadenia laxa* C.H.Wright *20604*		
	R	*20604*	South Africa - Cape Province *20604*
V	*Daphne arbuscula* Celak *8000, 20171*		
	V	*17821*	Czech Republic *17821*
	V	*19615*	Slovakia (Muránka vysocina Mts.) *6951*
E	*Daphne baksanica* Pobed. *5942*		
	E	*11552*	Russia - North Caucasus *11552*
R	*Daphne jasminea* Sibth. & Sm. *20171*		

R		Greece (Gulf of Korinthos) *21119*	
R		Libya *21119*	

V   *Daphne malyana* Blecic *20171*

| R | *21091* | Bosnia & Herzegovina *21091* |
| V | | (former) Yugoslavia |

R   *Daphne petraea* Leyb. *8000, 20171*

| R | *18264* | Italy (Lombardia & Trentino-Alto Adige) *19997* |

R   *Daphne reichsteinii* Landholt & Hauser *18264*

| R | *18264* | Italy (Lombardy) *18264* |

E   *Daphne rodriguezii* Texidor *8000, 20171*

| E | *20874* | Spain - Balearic Is. (Menorca) *8000* |

I   *Daphne sophia* Kalen. *5942, 20171*

| I | *5942* | Ukraine *5942* |

V   *Daphnopsis angustifolia* C. Wright *5607*

| V | *19105* | Cuba (Holguin) *5607* |

V   *Daphnopsis calcicola* Ekman *5607*

| V | *19105* | Cuba (Pinar del Rio) *5607* |

E   *Daphnopsis grandis* Nevling & Barringer *11680*

| E | *11680* | Ecuador *11680* |

I   *Daphnopsis hellerana* Urban

| I | | Puerto Rico *8058* |

E   *Daphnopsis helleriana* Urban *20883, 19738*

| E | *20883* | Puerto Rico (northern) *20883* |

V   *Daphnopsis philippiana* Krug & Urban *20883, 20513*

| I | *20883* | Puerto Rico *20883* |

E   *Deltaria brachyblastophora* Steenis *20893*

| E | *20893* | New Caledonia *20893* |

I   *Dicranolepis soyauxii* Engl.

| I | | Gabon |

R   *Dicranolepis usambarica* Gilg. *20057*

| R | *19109* | Kenya *19109* |
| R | *20057* | Tanzania *17435* |

V   *Dirca occidentalis* Gray *20850*

| V | *20850* | U.S. - California *20850* |

V   *Jedda multicaulis* Clarkson *20681*

| V | *20681* | Australia - Queensland *20681* |

R   *Lachnaea eriocephala* L. *20604*

| R | *20604* | South Africa - Cape Province *20604* |

I   *Lachnaea glomerata* Fourc. *20604*

| I | *20604* | South Africa - Cape Province *20604* |

R   *Lachnaea purpurea* Andrews *20604*

| R | *20604* | South Africa - Cape Province *20604* |

V   *Oreodendron biflorum* C.White *20681*

| V | *20681* | Australia - Queensland *20681* |

R   *Passerina burchellii* Thoday *20604*

| R | *20604* | South Africa - Cape Province *20604* |

E   *Passerina paludosa* Thoday *20604*

| E | *20604* | South Africa - Cape Province *20604* |

R   *Peddiea kivuensis* Robyns *19358*

| R | *19358* | Zaire (central Forestier) *19358* |

R   *Pimelea arenaria* Cunn. *86*

R	*19305*	New Zealand - Chatham Is. *19106*
R	*19305*	New Zealand - North Is. *19305*
R	*19305*	New Zealand - South Is. *19305*

R   *Pimelea ciliolaris* (Threlfall) Rye *20681*

| R | *20681* | Australia - New South Wales *20681* |

R   *Pimelea congesta* C. Moore & F. Muell.

| R | *14225* | Australia - NSW - Lord Howe Is. *14225* |

R   *Pimelea crosby-smithiana* Petrie

| R | | New Zealand - South Is. |

R   *Pimelea filiformis* J.D.Hook *20681*

| R | *20681* | Australia - Tasmania *20681* |

R   *Pimelea interioris* Rye *20681*

| R | *20681* | Australia - Northern Territory *20681* |

V   *Pimelea leptospermoides* F.Muell. *20681*

| V | *20681* | Australia - Queensland *20681* |

R   *Pimelea milliganii* Meisner *20681*

| R | *20681* | Australia - Tasmania *20681* |

R   *Pimelea pagophila* Rye *20681*

| R | *20681* | Australia - Victoria *20681* |

R   *Pimelea physodes* Hook. *20681*

| R | *20681* | Australia - Western Australia *20681* |

R   *Pimelea pygmaea* F.Muell. *20681*

| R | *20681* | Australia - Tasmania *20681* |

E   *Pimelea rara* Rye *20681*

| E | *20681* | Australia - Western Australia *20681* |

E   *Pimelea spicata* R.Br. *20681*

| E | *20681* | Australia - New South Wales *20681* |

Ex   *Pimelea spinescens* Rye ssp. *pubiflora* Rye *20681*

| Ex | *20681* | Australia - Victoria *20681* |

V   *Pimelea spinescens* Rye ssp. *spinescens* *20681*

| V | *20681* | Australia - Victoria *20681* |

R   *Pimelea umbratica* Cunn. ex Meisner *20681*

| I | *20681* | Australia - New South Wales *20681* |
| I | *20681* | Australia - Queensland *20681* |

V   *Pimelea venosa* Threlfall *20681*

| V | *20681* | Australia - New South Wales *20681* |

R   *Pimelea williamsonii* J.Black *20681*

| I | *20681* | Australia - South Australia *20681* |
| I | *20681* | Australia - Victoria *20681* |

E   *Schoenobiblus panamensis* Standl. & L.O. Wms. *20883, 9006*

| I | *20883* | Panama *20883* |

R   *Stellera formosana* (Hayata) Li *20511*

| R | *20511* | Taiwan *20511* |

E   *Stelleropsis caucasica* Pobed. *5942*

| E | *11552* | Transcaucasus (Georgia) *11552* |

I   *Stelleropsis magakjanii* (Sosn.) Pobed. *5942*

| I | *5942* | Armenia *5942* |

R   *Struthiola anomala* Hilliard *20604*

| R | *20604* | South Africa - Natal *20604* |

I   *Struthiola montana* Peterson *7759*

| I | | Zimbabwe (Chimanimani) *7759* |

R   *Struthiola pondoensis* Gilg ex C.H.Wright *20604*

| R | *20604* | South Africa - Cape Province *20604* |
| R | *20604* | South Africa - Natal *20604* |

R   *Struthiola rhodesiana* Peterson *7876*

| R | | Zimbabwe *7876* |

E   *Thymelaea broterana* Cout. *8000, 20171*

| E | *20076* | Portugal (north) *8000* |

R   *Thymelaea cilcicica* Meissner *12840*

| R | *12840* | Turkey *12840* |

V   *Thymelaea dendryobryum* Rothm. *20171*

| V | | Spain |

R   *Thymelaea granatensis* Pau ex Lacaita *11496, 20171*

| R | *11496* | Spain *11496* |

R   ***Thymelaea putorioides*** Emberger & Maire
    R   Morocco

I   ***Thymelaea sempervirens*** Murb.
    I   Tunisia

R   ***Thymelaea tartonraira*** (L.) All. *20171*
    R   *20727* Spain - Balearic Is. *20727*

E   ***Thymelaea tartonraira*** (L.) All. ssp. ***thomasii***
    (Duby) Briq. *20171*
    E   *20726* France - Corsica *15080*

E   ***Thymelaea thomasii*** Duby
    E   *20726* France - Corsica *20726*

R   ***Wikstroemia australis*** Endl. *11649*
    R   *19108* Australia - Norfolk Is. (Ridges and upper valley sides, Mt. Pitt N.P.) *11649*

E   ***Wikstroemia bicornuta*** Hbd. *20850, 14209*
    E   *20850* U.S. - Hawaii *20850*

V   ***Wikstroemia capitellata*** Hara *10572*
    V   *10572* Japan *10572*

Ex/E   ***Wikstroemia hanalei*** Wawra *20850, 14209*
    Ex/E *20850* U.S. - Hawaii (North Kaua`i) *20850*

V   ***Wikstroemia kudoi*** Makino *10572*
    V   *10572* Japan *10572*

R   ***Wikstroemia mononectaria*** Hayata *20854*
    R   *20854* Taiwan *20854*

V   ***Wikstroemia oahuensis*** (A. Gray) Rock var. ***palustris***
    (Hochr.) Peterson *20850, 14209*
    I   *20850* U.S. - Hawaii (Kaua`i) *20850*

Ex/E   ***Wikstroemia skottsbergiana*** Sparre *20850, 14209*
    Ex/E *20850* U.S. - Hawaii (Kaua`i) *20850*

R   ***Wikstroemia taiwanensis*** C.E.Chang *20511*
    R   *20511* Taiwan *20511*

V   ***Wikstroemia uva-ursi*** A.Gray *20850, 14209*
    I   *20850* U.S. - Hawaii *20850*

V   ***Wikstroemia uva-ursi*** A. Gray var. ***kauaiensis***
    Skottsberg *20850, 14209*
    I   *20850* U.S. - Hawaii *20850*

V   ***Wikstroemia uva-ursi*** A.Gray var.
    uva-ursi *20850*
    I   *20850* U.S. - Hawaii *20850*

Ex/E   ***Wikstroemia villosa*** Hbd. *20850, 14209*
    Ex/E *20850* U.S. - Hawaii (Maui) *20850*

Tiliaceae

Number of genera:	50
Number of species:	450
Recorded threatened species:	27 (6%)

Tropical and subtropical.

R   ***Apeiba intermedia*** Uittien *8679*
    R   *8679* Suriname *8679*

V   ***Burretiodendron hsienmu*** Chun & How *17617*
    V   *17617* China - Guangxi (south-west) *10642*
    V   *17617* China - Yunnan (southeastern limestone) *17617*
    V   *15734* Vietnam *6057*

R   ***Corchorus aestuans*** L. var. ***brevicaulis***
    L. *20511*
    R   *20511* Taiwan *20511*

E   ***Corchorus cunninghamii*** F.Muell. *20681*
    I   *20681* Australia - New South Wales *20681*

    I   *20681* Australia - Queensland *20681*

R   ***Corchorus macropterus*** G.Leach & Cheek *20681*
    R   *20681* Australia - Northern Territory *20681*

E   ***Craigia kwangsiensis*** Hsue *17617*
    E   *18038* China - Guangxi (Tianling) *11139*

V   ***Diplodiscus paniculatus*** Turcz. *13780*
    V   *15960* Philippines *13780*

R   ***Erinocarpus nimmonii*** Graham *14782*
    R   *14782* India - Karnataka *14782*
    R   *14782* India - Maharashtra *14782*

I   ***Grewia insularis*** Ridley *881*
    I   *14224* Australia - Christmas Is. *881*

R   ***Grewia limae*** Wild *7749*
    R   Mozambique *7749*

I   ***Grewia palawanensis*** Merr. *13833*
    I   *13833* Philippines (low altitude) *13833*

R   ***Grewia pondoensis*** Burret *20604*
    R   *20604* South Africa - Cape Province *20604*
    R   *20604* South Africa - Natal *20604*

R   ***Grewia rogersii*** Burtt Davy & Greenway *14695*
    R   *14695* Southern Africa *14695*

R   ***Hasseltia lateriflora*** Rusby *20883, 19553*
    R   *19553* Colombia *20883*

R   ***Hasseltiopsis dioica*** (Bentham) Sleumer *20883, 20513*
    I   *20883* Belize *20883*
    I   *20883* Costa Rica *20883*
    I   *20883* Guatemala *20883*
    I   *20883* Honduras *20883*
    I   *20883* Mexico *20883*

R   ***Macrohasseltia macroterantha*** (Standl. & L.O. Wms.) L.O.
    Wms. *20883, 9678*
    I   *20883* Costa Rica *20883*
    I   *20883* Honduras *20883*
    I   *20883* Nicaragua *20883*
    I   *20883* Panama *20883*

E   ***Mortoniodendron hirsutum*** Standl. *20883, 9006*
    I   *20883* Panama *20883*

R   ***Neosprucea montana*** Cuatrecasas *20883*
    I   *20883* Colombia *20883*
    I   *20883* Peru *20883*

R   ***Neosprucea pedicellata*** Little *20883*
    I   *20883* Colombia *20883*
    I   *20883* Ecuador *20883*

R   ***Neosprucea sararensis*** Cuatrecasas *20883*
    I   *20883* Colombia *20883*

V   ***Neosprucea sucumbiensis*** Cuatrecasas *20883*
    I   *20883* Colombia *20883*
    I   *20883* Ecuador *20883*

Ex/E   ***Pentaplaris doroteae*** L.O. Williams & Standley *12053*
    Ex/E *11992* Costa Rica *12053*

R   ***Prockia flava*** Karsten *20883*
    I   *20883* Venezuela *20883*

E   ***Tilia chyugokuensis*** Hatus. *10572*
    E   *20626* Japan (Hiroshima) *20626*

R   ***Tilia taquetii*** C.K. Schneider *15957*
    R   *17577* Korea, South (Mt Chiri, Pyonganpuk-do and south to Kangwon-do) *15957*

I   ***Triumfetta glabra*** Rottler ex Sprengel *10252*
    I   *16162* Sri Lanka *10252*

I   ***Triumfetta sloanei*** F. & R. *20883, 13336*
    I   *13336* Jamaica *20883*

Tovariaceae

Number of genera: 1
Number of species: 2
Recorded threatened species: 1 (50%)

Tropical America.

V   ***Tovaria diffusa*** (Macf.) F. & R. *20883, 13336*
     V   *13336* Jamaica (Portland) *20883*

Trapaceae

Number of genera: 1
Number of species: 15
Recorded threatened species: 1 (6%)

Tropical and subtropical Africa and Eurasia.

V   ***Trapa taiwanensis*** Nakai *20511*
     V   *20511* Taiwan *20511*

Tremandraceae

Number of genera: 3
Number of species: 28
Recorded threatened species: 9 (32%)

Australia and Tasmania.

V   ***Tetratheca aphylla*** F.Muell. *20681*
     V   *20681* Australia - Western Australia *20681*

E   ***Tetratheca deltoidea*** J.Thompson *20681, 14223*
     E   *20681* Australia - Western Australia *20681*

Ex   ***Tetratheca elliptica*** J.Thompson *20681, 14223*
     Ex   *20681* Australia - Western Australia *20681*

Ex   ***Tetratheca fasciculata*** J.Thompson *20681, 14223*
     Ex   *20681* Australia - Western Australia *20681*

V   ***Tetratheca glandulosa*** Smith *20681*
     V   *20681* Australia - New South Wales *20681*

E   ***Tetratheca gunnii*** Hook.f. *20681*
     E   *20681* Australia - Tasmania *20681*

V   ***Tetratheca harperi*** F.Muell. *20681*
     V   *20681* Australia - Western Australia *20681*

V   ***Tetratheca juncea*** Smith *20681*
     V   *20681* Australia - New South Wales *20681*

R   ***Tetratheca neglecta*** J.Thompson *20681*
     R   *20681* Australia - New South Wales *20681*

E   ***Tetratheca paynterae*** J.Alford ms. *20681*
     E   *20681* Australia - Western Australia *20681*

R   ***Tetratheca stenocarpa*** J.H.Willis *20681*
     R   *20681* Australia - Victoria *20681*

Trigoniaceae

Number of genera: 3
Number of species: 26
Recorded threatened species: 17 (65%)

Subtropical in moist lowland forests.

R   ***Trigonia boliviana*** Warming *20883*
     I   *20883* Bolivia *20883*
     I   *20883* Paraguay *20883*

E   ***Trigonia bracteata*** Lleras *20883*
     E   *20883* Venezuela *20883*

R   ***Trigonia candelabra*** Lleras *20883*
     I   *20883* Brazil *20883*
     E   *20883* Suriname *20883*

E   ***Trigonia coppenamensis*** Stafleu *20883*
     E   *20883* Suriname *20883*

V   ***Trigonia costanensis*** Steyermark & Badillo *20883*
     V   *20883* Venezuela *20883*

V   ***Trigonia echiteifolia*** Rusby *20883*
     I   *20883* Bolivia *20883*
     I   *20883* Brazil *20883*

E   ***Trigonia eriosperma*** ssp. ***simplex*** (Warming) Lleras *20883*
     E   *20883* Brazil *20883*

V   ***Trigonia floccosa*** Rusby *20883*
     V   *20883* Bolivia *20883*

R   ***Trigonia laevis*** var. ***laevis*** *20883*
     I   *20883* French Guiana *20883*
     I   *20883* Guyana *20883*

E   ***Trigonia macrantha*** Warming *20883*
     E   *20883* Peru *20883*

R   ***Trigonia nivea*** var. ***fasciculata*** (Grisebach) Lleras *20883*
     I   *20883* Brazil *20883*

R   ***Trigonia paniculata*** Warming *20883*
     I   *20883* Brazil *20883*

E   ***Trigonia prancei*** Lleras *20883*
     E   *20883* Peru *20883*

V   ***Trigonia reticulata*** Lleras *20883*
     I   *20883* Guyana *20883*
     I   *20883* Venezuela *20883*

E   ***Trigonia rotundifolia*** Lleras *20883*
     E   *20883* Brazil *20883*

V   ***Trigonia rytidocarpa*** Casaretto *20883*
     V   *20883* Brazil *20883*

E   ***Trigonia subcymosa*** Bentham *20883*
     E   *20883* Guyana *20883*

Trimeniaceae

Number of genera: 2
Number of species: 5
Recorded threatened species: 1 (20%)

New Guinea; New Caledonia; Fiji; southeastern Australia.

E   ***Trimenia marquesensis*** F. Brown
     E   French Polynesia - Marquesas Is

Tropaeolaceae

Number of genera: 3
Number of species: 92
Recorded threatened species: 4 (4%)

Mexico to Chile (in mountains), Patagonia.

R   ***Tropaeolum capillare*** Buchenau *19575*
     R   *19575* Argentina *19575*

R   ***Tropaeolum crenatiflorum*** Hook.f. *18200*
     R   *12468* Peru *18200*

R   ***Tropaeolum looseri*** Sparre *5598*
     R   *19536* Chile *5598*

E   ***Tropaeolum meyeri*** Sparre *19575*
     E   *19575* Argentina *19575*

Turneraceae

Number of genera:	8
Number of species:	120
Recorded threatened species:	8 (6%)

Tropical and subtropical America and Africa; Madagascar.

R   *Loewia thomasii* (Urban) J. Lewis *7959*
   R   *17435* Kenya (Limuru, Mt. Kenya) *17435*

R   *Mathurina penduliflora* Balf.f. *10082*
   R   *5852* Mauritius - Rodrigues *5852*

I   *Streptopetalum graminifolium* Urb. *5926*
   I   *5926* Tanzania *5926*

V   *Turnera concinna* Arbo *20883*
   I   *20883* Bolivia *20883*
   I   *20883* Brazil *20883*
   I   *20883* Paraguay *20883*

R   *Turnera glaziovii* Urb. *8679*
   R   *19954* French Guiana *18176*
   R   *8679* Suriname *8679*

E   *Turnera rupestris* Aublet var.
   rupestris *19578*
   E   *19578* French Guiana (rapids of the lower Sinnamary
               river) *19578*

R   *Turnera thomasii* (Urban) J. Lewis *6073*
   R   *6073* Kenya *6073*

E   *Turnera zeasperma* Adams & Been *20883, 13336*
   E   *13336* Jamaica (St. Andrew) *20883*

Ulmaceae

Number of genera:	18
Number of species:	150
Recorded threatened species:	18 (12%)

Widespread, especially Northern Hemisphere.

E   *Ampelocera glabra* Kuhlm. *19567*
   E   *19567* Brazil - Rio de Janeiro *19567*

V   *Celtis balansae* Planchon *20893*
   V   *20893* New Caledonia *20893*

R   *Celtis conferta* Planchon ssp. *amblyphylla* (F.
   Muell.) P. Green *10604*
   R   *14225* Australia - NSW - Lord Howe Is. *10604*

R   *Celtis edulis* Nakai *15957*
   R   *15923* Korea, South (Mt Taegi (Kangwon-do), Myongchon
          (Hamkyongpuk-do)) *15957*

E   *Celtis hypoleuca* Planchon *20893*
   E   *20893* New Caledonia *20893*

V   *Celtis jamaicensis* Planch. *20883*
   R   *20883* Jamaica *20883*

V   *Celtis lindheimeri* Engelm. ex K. Koch *20883, 20850,
   19002*
   I   *20850* U.S. - Texas *20850*
   I   *20883* Mexico *20883*

V   *Celtis luzonica* Warb. *12983*
   V   *15960* Philippines *12983*

V   *Celtis nervosa* Hemsl. *20511*
   V   *20511* Taiwan *20511*

R   *Gironniera mollissima* Gagnepain *6057*
   R   Vietnam *6057*

E   *Gironniera scabrida* (Thwaites) Alston *12838*
   E   *12838* Sri Lanka *12838*

R   *Pteroceltis tatarinowii* Maxim. *17617*
   R   *17617* China - Anhui *11139*
   R   *17617* China - Fujian *11139*
   R   *17617* China - Gansu *11139*
   R   *17617* China - Guangdong *11139*
   R   *17617* China - Guangxi *11139*
   R   *17617* China - Guizhou *11139*
   R   *17617* China - Hebei *11139*
   R   *17617* China - Henan *11139*
   R   *17617* China - Hubei *11139*
   R   *17617* China - Hunan *11139*
   R   *17617* China - Jiangsu *11139*
   R   *17617* China - Jiangxi *11139*
   R   *17617* China - Liaoning *11139*
   R   *17617* China - Qinghai *11139*
   R   *17617* China - Shaanxi *11139*
   R   *17617* China - Shandong *11139*
   R   *17617* China - Shanxi *11139*
   R   *17617* China - Sichuan *11139*
   R   *17617* China - Zhejiang *11139*

E   *Ulmus chenmoui* Cheng *17617*
   E   *17617* China - Anhui (Langyashan) *11139*
   E   *17617* China - Jiangsu *11139*

E   *Ulmus elongata* L.K. Fu & C.S. Ding *17617*
   E   *17617* China - Anhui (Qimeng; Jixi) *11139*
   E   *17617* China - Fujian (Laizhou) *11139*
   E   *17617* China - Jiangxi (Zhixi; Quanshan) *11139*
   E   *17617* China - Zhejiang *11139*

V   *Ulmus gaussenii* Cheng *17617*
   V   *17617* China - Anhui (Langyashan) *11139*

E   *Ulmus wallichiana* Planchon *9159*
   E   Afghanistan (north-east) *9159*
   E   India - Jammu & Kashmir *9159*
   E   Nepal (west) *9159*
   E   Pakistan *9159*

V   *Zelkova abelicea* (Lam.) Boiss. *17891, 20171*
   V   *20731* Greece - Crete *8000*

E   *Zelkova sicula* Di Pasquale, Garfi & Quézel *21105*
   E   *21105* Italy - Sicily *21105*

Umbelliferae

Number of genera:	300-428
Number of species:	3,000
Recorded threatened species:	470 (15%)

Nearly cosmopolitan, especially North temperate regions and
tropical mountains.

V   *Aciphylla dieffenbachii* Kirk *19305*
   V   *19305* New Zealand - Chatham Is. *19106*

V   *Aciphylla traversii* (F. Muell.) Hook.f. *86*
   V   *19305* New Zealand - Chatham Is. *19106*

R   *Aciphylla trifoliolata* Petrie *19305*
   R   *19305* New Zealand - South Is. *19305*

I   *Acronema pseudotenera* Mukh. *13883*
   I   *13883* India - Sikkim (Momay Samdong) *13883*

I   *Actinolema macrolema* Boiss. *5942*
   I   *5942* Armenia *5942*

V   *Actinotus schwarzii* F.Muell. *20681*
   V   *20681* Australia - Northern Territory *20681*

I   *Alepidea parva* Compton *20604, 20039*
   R   *20604* Swaziland *20604*

R   *Alepidea stellata* Weim. *20604*
   R   *20604* South Africa - Natal *20604*

R   *Alepidea wyliei* Dummer *20604*
   R   *20604* South Africa - Natal *20604*

V   *Aletes anisatus* (Gray) Theobald & Tseng *20850*
     I   *20850*   U.S. - Colorado *20850*

V   *Aletes humilis* Coult. & Rose *20850*
     V   *20850*   U.S. - Colorado *20850*
     Ex/E *20850*   U.S. - Wyoming *20850*

R   *Ammi huntii* H.C.Watson *20171*
     R   *19174*   Portugal - Azores *19174*

V   *Ammi procerum* Lowe
     V   Portugal - Madeira

R   *Ammi trifoliatum* (H.C.Watson) Trel. *8000, 20171*
     R   Portugal - Azores *8000*

R   *Ammiopsis aristidis* Coss. *10488*
     R   *14958*   Algeria *10488*

I   *Ammiopsis daucoides* Boiss.
     I   Morocco

R   *Ammoselinum giganteum* Coult. & Rose *20850*
     E   *20850*   U.S. - Arizona *20850*
     Ex/E *20850*   U.S. - California *20850*

R   *Angelica acutiloba* Kitag. ssp. *lineariloba*
     Kitam. *10572*
     R   *10572*   Japan *10572*

R   *Angelica angelicastrum* (Hoffmanns. & Link)
     Cout. *20171*
     R   Portugal (Serra de Estrêla) *8000*

E   *Angelica dentata* (Chapman) Coult. & Rose *20850*
     I   *20850*   U.S. - Florida *20850*
     V   *20850*   U.S. - Georgia *20850*

R   *Angelica hakonensis* Maxim. var.
     hakonensis *10572*
     R   *10572*   Japan *10572*

R   *Angelica hakonensis* Maxim. var. *nikoensis* (Yabe)
     Hara *10572*
     R   *10572*   Japan *10572*

V   *Angelica heterocarpa* J.Lloyd *8000, 20171*
     V   *20528*   France (southwestern) *20528*

E   *Angelica laurentiana* Fern. *20850, 14366*
     E   *20850*   Canada - Labrador *20850*
     E   *20850*   Canada - Newfoundland *20850*
     I   *20850*   Canada - Quebec *20850*

I   *Angelica nubigena* (Clarke) Mukh. *13883*
     I   *13883*   India - Sikkim (N.E at Chola and Yakla passes)
         13883

R   *Angelica pachycarpa* Lange *20171*
     E   *20076*   Portugal *20076*
     R   Spain

R   *Angelica pseudoshikokiana* Kitag. *10572*
     R   *10572*   Japan *10572*

I   *Angelica saxicola* Makino var. *yoshinagae* Murata &
     Yaman. *10572*
     I   *10572*   Japan *10572*

V   *Angelica scabrida* Clokey & Mathias ex Clokey *20850*
     V   *20850*   U.S. - Nevada *20850*

R   *Angelica ubatakensis* Kitag. var.
     ubatakensis *10572*
     R   *10572*   Japan *10572*

R   *Angelica ubatakensis* Kitag. var. *valida*
     Kitag. *10572*
     R   *10572*   Japan *10572*

V   *Angelica wheeleri* S.Watson *20850*
     V   *20850*   U.S. - Utah *20850*

R   *Angelica yakusimensis* Hara *10572*
     R   *10572*   Japan *10572*

R   *Anginon jaarsveldii* B.L.Burtt *20604*
     R   *20604*   South Africa - Cape Province *20604*

E   *Anisotome acutifolia* (Kirk) Cockayne *86*
     E   New Zealand - South Is.

I   *Annesorhiza marlothii* H.Wolff *20604*
     I   *20604*   South Africa - Cape Province *20604*

E   *Apium bermejoi* Llorens *17891*
     E   *11496*   Spain - Balearic Is. (north-east Menorca)
         20821

E   *Apium fernandezianum* Johow *19116*
     E   *19125*   Chile - Juan Fernandez Is. *19116*

R   *Apium insulare* P.S. Short *14223*
     R   *14223*   Australia - NSW - Lord Howe Is. *14223*

V   *Apium prostratum* Labill. ssp. *phillipii* Keighery
     ms. *20681*
     V   *20681*   Australia - Western Australia *20681*

E   *Apodicarpum ikeoi* Makino *10572*
     E   *10572*   Japan *10572*

E   *Asciadium coronopifolium* Griseb. *5607*
     E   *19105*   Cuba (Pinar del Rio) *5607*

R   *Asteriscium vidalii* Philippi *13875*
     R   *13875*   Chile *13875*

R   *Astrantia pauciflora* Bertol. *20171*
     R   Italy

V   *Athamanta cortiana* Ferrarini *8000, 20171*
     V   *18264*   Italy (Apuan Alps - Toscana) *8000*

R   *Athamanta densa* Boiss. & Orph. *20178, 20171*
     R   *20178*   Albania *20178*
     R   Greece

R   *Athamanta macedonica* (L.) Spreng. ssp. *albanica*
     Alston & Sandwith *20178, 20171*
     R   *20178*   Albania *20178*

R   *Athamanta turbith* (L.) Brot. ssp. *hungarica*
     (Borbas) Tutin *17823, 20171*
     R   *19949*   Romania *20631*

R   *Aulacospermum popovii* (Korovin) Kljuyk., Pim. &
     Tik. *5942*
     R   *5942*   Kazakhstan (on the border with Kirgizstan)
         5942
     R   *5942*   Kyrgyzstan (northern border with Kazakhstan)
         5942

I   *Azorella ecuadorensis* Domin *11351*
     I   *19573*   Ecuador *11351*

E   *Bunium brevifolium* Lowe *17781*
     E   Portugal - Madeira *17891*

R   *Bunium chaberti* Battand. *10488*
     R   *14958*   Algeria *10488*

V   *Bunium crassifolium* Battand. *10488*
     V   *14958*   Algeria *10488*

V   *Bunium elatum* Battand. *10488*
     V   *14958*   Algeria *10488*

R   *Bunium microcarpum* (Boiss.) Freyn ssp. *longiradiatum*
     Hedge & Lamond *12840*
     R   *12840*   Turkey *12840*

R   *Bupleurum acutifolium* Boiss. *20171*
     E   *20076*   Portugal *20076*
     R   Spain

R   *Bupleurum aira* Snogerup *20171*

R		Greece

| R | *Bupleurum anatolicum* Huber-Mor. & Reese *12840* | . |
| | R | *12840* Turkey *12840* |

| R | *Bupleurum antonii* Maire | |
| | R | Morocco |

| V | *Bupleurum bourgaei* Boiss. & Reut. *11496* | |
| | V | *11496* Spain *11496* |

| E | *Bupleurum capillare* Boiss. & Heldr. *8000, 20171* | |
| | E | Greece (Delphi-Levadhia) *8000* |

| R | *Bupleurum davisii* Snogerup *12840* | |
| | R | *12840* Turkey *12840* |

| R | *Bupleurum dianthifolium* Guss. *18264, 20171* | |
| | R | *18264* Italy - Sicily (Isola di Marettimo) *18264* |

| R | *Bupleurum eginense* (Wolff) Snogerup *12840* | |
| | R | *12840* Turkey *12840* |

| V | *Bupleurum elatum* Guss. *18264, 20171* | |
| | V | *18264* Italy - Sicily (Madonie Mts.) *20738* |

| R | *Bupleurum eruberescens* Boiss. *12840* | |
| | R | *12840* Turkey *12840* |

V	*Bupleurum falcatum* L. ssp. *dilatatum* Schur *8000, 20171*	
	V	*19751* Poland *19751*
	V	*19321* Slovakia *19321*

R	*Bupleurum foliosum* Salzm. ex DC. *19052, 20171*	
	R	Spain *19052*
	Ex	*19052* United Kingdom - Gibraltar *19052*

| V | *Bupleurum gaudianum* Snogerup *20730* | |
| | V | *20730* Greece - Crete *20730* |

| V | *Bupleurum handiense* (Bolle) Kunkel *17891* | |
| | V | *20750* Spain - Canary Is. *17891* |

| E | *Bupleurum kakiskalae* Greuter *10260* | |
| | E | *20730* Greece - Crete *10260* |

| R | *Bupleurum koechelii* Fenzl *12840* | |
| | R | *12840* Turkey *12840* |

| E | *Bupleurum latissimum* Nakai *15957* | |
| | E | *17577* Korea, South (Dagelet & Ulnung Is.) *15957* |

| R | *Bupleurum nipponicum* Kozo-Polj. var. *yesoense* Hara *10572* | |
| | R | *10572* Japan *10572* |

| R | *Bupleurum pauciradiatum* Fenzl *12840, 20171* | |
| | R | *12840* Turkey *12840* |

| I | *Bupleurum pendikum* Snogerup *12840* | |
| | I | *12840* Turkey *12840* |

| R | *Bupleurum plantagineum* Desf. *10488* | |
| | R | *14958* Algeria *10488* |

| R | *Bupleurum polyactis* Post ex Snogerup *12840* | |
| | R | *12840* Turkey *12840* |

| R | *Bupleurum pulchellum* Boiss. & Heldr. *12840* | |
| | R | *12840* Turkey *12840* |

| R | *Bupleurum salicifolium* R. Br. ssp. *aciphyllum* Sunding & Kunkel | |
| | R | Spain - Canary Is. |

| I | *Bupleurum sintenisii* Aschers. & Urban ex Huter *14230* | |
| | I | *5409* Cyprus *14230* |

| R | *Bupleurum subspinosum* Maire | |
| | R | Morocco |

| R | *Bupleurum subuniflorum* Boiss. & Heldr. *12840* | |

R		*12840* Turkey *12840*

| R | *Bupleurum zoharii* Snogerup *12840* | |
| | R | *12840* Turkey *12840* |

| V | *Cachrys ferulacea* (L.) Calest. *17823, 20171* | |
| | V | *19949* Romania *20631* |

| R | *Carum asinorum* Litard. & Maire | |
| | R | Morocco |

| I | *Carum calcicolum* Balf. f. *15534* | |
| | I | *15534* Yemen - Socotra *15534* |

| R | *Carum lacuum* Emberger | |
| | R | Morocco |

| R | *Carum montanum* (Coss. & Dur.) Benth. & Hook. *10488* | |
| | R | *14958* Algeria *10488* |

| R | *Carum proliferum* Maire | |
| | R | Morocco |

| R | *Carum rupicola* Hardvig & Strid *12840* | |
| | R | *12840* Turkey *12840* |

| Ex/E | *Carum villosum* Haines *11494* | |
| | Ex/E | *11494* India - Bihar (Ramnagar, North Champaran) *11494* |

| I | *Centella hermannifolia* (Echl. Zeyh.) Domin var. *hermanniifolia* *20604* | |
| | I | *20604* South Africa - Cape Province *20604* |

| R | *Centella obtriangularis* Cannon *7749* | |
| | R | Mozambique *7749* |

| I | *Cephalopodum badachschanicum* Korovin *5942* | |
| | I | *5942* Tajikistan *5942* |

| I | *Chaerophyllum azoricum* Trel. *8000, 20171* | |
| | I | *19174* Portugal - Azores *8000* |

R	*Chaerophyllum coloratum* L. *20178, 20171*	
	R	*20178* Albania *20178*
	R	*21091* Bosnia & Herzegovina *21091*
	R	(former) Yugoslavia

| V | *Chaerophyllum creticum* Boiss. & Heldr. *20171* | |
| | V | *20730* Greece - Crete *20730* |

| R | *Chaerophyllum hakkiaricum* Hedge & Lamond *12840* | |
| | R | *12840* Turkey *12840* |

R	*Chaerophyllum heldreichii* Orph. ex Boiss. *20178, 20171*	
	R	*20178* Albania *20178*
	R	Greece

| R | *Chaerophyllum karsianum* Kit Tan ex Ocakverdi *12840* | |
| | R | *12840* Turkey *12840* |

| I | *Chaerophyllum orientalis* (Clarke) Mukh. *13883* | |
| | I | *13883* India - Arunachal Pradesh (Naga hills) *13883* |

| R | *Chamarea longipedicellata* B.L.Burtt *20604* | |
| | R | *20604* South Africa - Cape Province *20604* |

| R | *Chamarea snijmaniae* B.L.Burtt *20604* | |
| | R | *20604* South Africa - Cape Province *20604* |

E	*Changium smyrnioides* Wolff *17617*	
	E	*17617* China - Anhui *11139*
	E	*17617* China - Jiangsu *11139*
	E	*17617* China - Jiangxi *11139*
	E	*17617* China - Zhejiang *11139*

| V | *Cicuta maculata* L. var. *victorinii* (Fern.) Boivin *20850, 13967* | |
| | V | *20850* Canada - Quebec *20850* |

| R | *Coelopleurum trichocarpum* (Hara) Kitag. *10572* | |
| | R | *10572* Japan *10572* |

R   *Conioselinum boreale* Schischk. *20171*
      R   former USSR *6930*

V   *Conioselinum mexicanum* Coult. & Rose *20883, 19002*
      E   20850   U.S. - Arizona *20850*
      I   20883   Mexico *20883*

R   *Conioselinum victoris* Schischkin
      R   former USSR *6930*

I   *Cotopaxia asplundii* Mathias & Constance *11351*
      I   19573   Ecuador *11351*

R   *Cymbocarpum amanum* Rech. f. *12840*
      R   12840   Turkey *12840*

V   *Cymopterus acaulis* (Pursh) Raf. var. *greeleyorum*
      J. Grimes & Packard *20850*
      V   20850   U.S. - Idaho *20850*
      E   20850   U.S. - Oregon *20850*

E   *Cymopterus acaulis* (Pursh) Raf. var. *higginsii*
      (Welsh) Goodrich *20850*
      E   20850   U.S. - Utah *20850*

V   *Cymopterus basalticus* M.E. Jones *20850*
      E   20850   U.S. - Nevada *20850*
      V   20850   U.S. - Utah *20850*

E   *Cymopterus beckii* Welsh & Goodrich *20850*
      E   20850   U.S. - Utah *20850*

V   *Cymopterus cinerarius* Gray *20850*
      I   20850   U.S. - California *20850*
      I   20850   U.S. - Nevada *20850*

R   *Cymopterus coulteri* (M.E. Jones) Mathias *20850*
      R   20850   U.S. - Utah *20850*

V   *Cymopterus davisii* Hartman *20850*
      V   20850   U.S. - Idaho *20850*

V   *Cymopterus deserticola* Brandeg. *20850*
      V   20850   U.S. - California *20850*

V   *Cymopterus douglassii* Hartman & Constance *20850*
      V   20850   U.S. - Idaho *20850*

R   *Cymopterus duchesnensis* M.E. Jones *20850*
      E   20850   U.S. - Colorado *20850*
      V   20850   U.S. - Utah *20850*

V   *Cymopterus evertii* Hartman & Kirkpatrick *20850*
      E   20850   U.S. - Utah *20850*
      V   20850   U.S. - Wyoming *20850*

E   *Cymopterus goodrichii* Welsh & Neese *20850*
      E   20850   U.S. - Nevada *20850*

R   *Cymopterus jonesii* Coult. & Rose *20850*
      I   20850   U.S. - Nevada *20850*
      I   20850   U.S. - Utah *20850*

R   *Cymopterus lapidosus* (M.E. Jones) M.E. Jones *20850*
      E   20850   U.S. - Utah *20850*
      R   20850   U.S. - Wyoming *20850*

V   *Cymopterus megacephalus* M.E. Jones *20850*
      V   20850   U.S. - Arizona *20850*

V   *Cymopterus minimus* (Mathias) Mathias *20850*
      V   20850   U.S. - Utah *20850*

E   *Cymopterus panamintensis* Coult. & Rose *20850*
      I   20850   U.S. - California *20850*

V   *Cymopterus planosus* (Osterhout) Mathias *20850*
      I   20850   U.S. - Colorado *20850*

V   *Cymopterus ripleyi* Barneby *20850*
      E   20850   U.S. - California *20850*
      V   20850   U.S. - Nevada *20850*

R   *Cymopterus rosei* (M.E. Jones) M.E. Jones *20850*

      R   20850   U.S. - Utah *20850*

R   *Cymopterus williamsii* Hartman & Constance *20850*
      R   20850   U.S. - Wyoming *20850*

R   *Daucus carota* L. ssp. *gadecaei* (Rouy & Camus)
      Heywood *20171*
      R   France

R   *Daucus conchitae* Greuter
      R   Greece

I   *Daucus lopadusanus* Tineo *13351*
      I   13351   Malta (Marfa & Comino.) *13351*

R   *Diposis bulbocastanum* DC. *19536*
      R   19536   Chile *19536*

E   *Domeykoa amplexicaulis* (Wolff) Mathias &
      Constance *18200*
      E   9446   Peru *18200*

E   *Domeykoa saniculifolia* Mathias & Constance *18200*
      E   9446   Peru *18200*

R   *Donnellsmithia silvicola* Constance & Bye *10117*
      R   19850   Mexico *10117*

I   *Dorema glabrum* Fischer & C. Meyer *5942*
      I   5942   Armenia *5942*

I   *Dorema karataviense* Korovin *5942*
      I   5942   Kazakhstan *5942*

I   *Dorema microcarpum* Korovin *5942*
      I   5942   Kyrgyzstan *5942*
      I   5942   Uzbekistan *5942*

V   *Dracosciadium italae* Hilliard & B.L.Burtt *20604*
      V   20604   South Africa - Natal *20604*

R   *Dracosciadium saniculifolium* Hilliard &
      B.L.Burtt *20604*
      R   20604   South Africa - Natal *20604*

R   *Echinophora carvifolia* Boiss. & Bal. *12840*
      R   12840   Turkey *12840*

R   *Echinophora chrysantha* Freyn & Sint. *12840*
      R   12840   Turkey *12840*

R   *Echinophora tirchophylla* J.E. Smith *12840*
      R   12840   Turkey *12840*

R   *Elaeoselinum exinvolucratum* Coss. & Balansa
      R   Morocco

R   *Elaeoselinum humile* Ball
      R   Morocco

E   *Eremocharis ferreyrae* Mathias & Constance *18200*
      E   9446   Peru *18200*

V   *Eremocharis longiramea* (Wolff) I.M. Johnston *11546*
      V   9446   Peru *18200*

E   *Eremocharis piscoensis* Mathias & Constance *18200*
      E   9446   Peru *18200*

V   *Eriosynaphe longifolia* (Fisch. ex Spreng.)
      DC. *11552, 20171*
      V   11552   Russian Federation (western) *11552*

R   *Eryngium alpinum* L. *14229, 20171*
      V   14155   Austria *14155*
      V   21091   Bosnia & Herzegovina *21091*
      V   20528   France (Alps) *20528*
      V   18264   Italy *19997*
      R   14229   Liechtenstein *14229*
      R   13662   Slovenia (north eastern) *13662*
      V   18154   Switzerland *18154*
      I   (former) Yugoslavia *8000*

R   *Eryngium amorginum* Rech.f. *20171*

R		20731 Greece (Cyclades) *20731*		
V	***Eryngium aristulatum*** Jepson var. *parishii* (Coult. & Rose) Mathias & Constance *20850*			
	V	20850 U.S. - California *20850*		
V	***Eryngium atlanticum*** Battand. & Pitard			
	V	Morocco		
R	***Eryngium bornmuelleri*** Nab. *12840*			
	R	12840 Turkey *12840*		
E	***Eryngium bupleuroides*** Hook. & Arn. *19116*			
	E	19125 Chile - Juan Fernandez Is. *19116*		
R	***Eryngium caespitiferum*** Font Quer & Pau			
	R	Morocco		
E	***Eryngium castrense*** Jepson *20850*			
	I	20850 U.S. - California *20850*		
E	***Eryngium constancei*** Sheikh *20850*			
	E	20850 U.S. - California (Loch Lomond) *20850*		
E	***Eryngium cuneifolium*** Small *20850, 17890*			
	E	20850 U.S. - Florida *20850*		
	I	20850 U.S. - Georgia *20850*		
E	***Eryngium fernandeziana*** Skottsb. *19125*			
	E	19116 Chile - Juan Fernandez Is. *19116*		
V	***Eryngium fontanum*** A.E.Holland & E.J.Thompson *20681*			
	V	20681 Australia - Queensland *20681*		
I	***Eryngium grossii*** Font Quer			
	I	11496 Spain (Malaga) *11496*		
R	***Eryngium ilex*** Davis *12840*			
	R	12840 Turkey *12840*		
E	***Eryngium inaccessum*** Skottsb. *19116*			
	E	19125 Chile - Juan Fernandez Is. *19116*		
R	***Eryngium isauricum*** Contandr. ex Quezel *12840*			
	R	12840 Turkey *12840*		
R	***Eryngium juresianum*** (M. Lainz) M. Lainz			
	R	Spain		
V	***Eryngium mathiasiae*** Sheikh *20850*			
	V	20850 U.S. - California *20850*		
V	***Eryngium phyteumae*** Delar. f. *20883, 20850*			
	I	20850 U.S. - Arizona *20850*		
	I	20883 Mexico *20883*		
R	***Eryngium pinnatisectum*** Jepson *20850*			
	R	20850 U.S. - California *20850*		
V	***Eryngium pseudothoriifolium*** Contandr. ex Quezel *12840*			
	V	12840 Turkey *12840*		
V	***Eryngium racemosum*** Jepson *20850*			
	V	20850 U.S. - California *20850*		
E	***Eryngium sarcophyllum*** Hook. & Arn. *19116*			
	E	19125 Chile - Juan Fernandez Is. *19116*		
R	***Eryngium serbicum*** Pancic *20171*			
	R	(former) Yugoslavia		
V	***Eryngium spinosepalum*** Mathias *20850*			
	V	20850 U.S. - California *20850*		
R	***Eryngium ternatum*** Poir. *20171*			
	R	20730 Greece - Crete *20730*		
R	***Eryngium thorifolium*** Boiss. *12840*			
	R	12840 Turkey *12840*		
V	***Eryngium viviparum*** J.Gay *8000, 20171*			
	E	20528 France (Brittany) *20528*		
	Ex	20705 Portugal (north) *8000*		
	V	20874 Spain (north west) *8000*		

I	***Eryngium wanaturii*** Woronow *5942*		
	I	5942 Armenia *5942*	
R	***Eurytaenia hinckleyi*** Mathias & Constance *20850*		
	R	20850 U.S. - Texas *20850*	
R	***Ferula amanicola*** Huber-Mor. & Pesmen *12840*		
	R	12840 Turkey *12840*	
R	***Ferula bolivari*** Pau		
	R	Morocco	
R	***Ferula cypria*** Post *14230*		
	R	19164 Cyprus *14230*	
V	***Ferula daninii*** Zoh. *8895*		
	V	Israel (Negev) *8895*	
R	***Ferula drudeana*** Korovin *12840*		
	R	12840 Turkey *12840*	
I	***Ferula eugenii*** Kamelin *5942*		
	I	5942 Tajikistan *5942*	
I	***Ferula gigantea*** B. Fedtsch. *5942*		
	I	5942 Tajikistan *5942*	
R	***Ferula glaberrima*** Korovin		
	R	former USSR *6930*	
V	***Ferula halophila*** H. Pesmen *12840*		
	V	12840 Turkey *12840*	
V	***Ferula huber-morathii*** H. Pesmen *12840*		
	V	12840 Turkey *12840*	
V	***Ferula lancerottensis*** Parl. *20750*		
	V	20750 Spain - Canary Is. *20750*	
E	***Ferula latipinna*** Santos *17891*		
	E	20750 Spain - Canary Is. *17891*	
I	***Ferula lithophila*** Pim. *5942*		
	I	5942 Uzbekistan *5942*	
V	***Ferula longipedunculata*** H. Pesmen *12840*		
	V	12840 Turkey *12840*	
V	***Ferula loscosii*** (Lange) Willk. *20171*		
	V	11496 Spain *11496*	
R	***Ferula lycia*** Boiss. *12840*		
	R	12840 Turkey *12840*	
I	***Ferula moschata*** (Reinsch) Koso-Polj.		
	I	Asiatic U.S.S.R. (Tien Shan) *6930*	
V	***Ferula sinkiangensis*** K.M. Shen *17617*		
	V	17617 China - Xinjiang Uygur Zizhiqu (Yining) *11139*	
I	***Ferula sumbul*** (Kauffm.) Hook.f. *5942*		
	I	5942 Tajikistan *5942*	
	I	5942 Uzbekistan *5942*	
R	***Ferula tenuissima*** Huber-Mor. & Pesmen *12840*		
	R	12840 Turkey *12840*	
I	***Ferula turcomanica*** (Schischkin) Pim. *5942*		
	I	5942 Turkmenistan *5942*	
R	***Ferulago antiochia*** Saya & Miski *12840*		
	R	12840 Turkey *12840*	
R	***Ferulago balancheana*** Post *12840*		
	R	19873 Turkey *12840*	
E	***Ferulago bracteata*** Boiss. & Hausskn. *12840*		
	E	12840 Turkey *12840*	
R	***Ferulago cypria*** H. Wolff *14230*		
	R	19164 Cyprus *14230*	
R	***Ferulago isaurica*** H. Pesman *12840*		
	R	12840 Turkey *12840*	

E	***Ferulago kurdica*** Post *12840*	
	E	*12840* Turkey *12840*
R	***Ferulago latiloba*** Schischkin *12840*	
	R	*12840* Turkey *12840*
V	***Ferulago longistylis*** Boiss. *12840*	
	V	*12840* Turkey *12840*
R	***Ferulago muglae*** H. Pesmen *12840*	
	R	*12840* Turkey *12840*
R	***Ferulago pachyloba*** (Fenzl) Boiss. *12840*	
	R	*12840* Turkey *12840*
R	***Ferulago sandrasica*** H. Pesmen & Quezel *12840*	
	R	*12840* Turkey *12840*
R	***Ferulago sartorii*** Boiss. *20171*	
	R	Greece
R	***Ferulago serpentinica*** Rech.f. *20171*	
	R	Greece
R	***Ferulago silaifolia*** (Boiss.) Boiss. *12840*	
	R	*12840* Turkey *12840*
R	***Ferulago thyrsiflora*** (Sibth. & Sm.) W.D.J.Koch *20171*	
	R	*20730* Greece - Crete *20730*
R	***Froriepia gracillima*** Leute *12840*	
	R	*12840* Turkey *12840*
Ex	***Geocaryum bornmuelleri*** (Wolff) Engstr.	
	Ex	Greece
R	***Geocaryum creticum*** (Boiss. & Heldr.) P.W.Ball *20730*	
	R	*20730* Greece - Crete *20730*
Ex	***Geocaryum divaricatum*** (Boiss. & Orph.) Engstr.	
	Ex	Greece
R	***Geocaryum euboicum*** (Rech.f.) Engstr.	
	R	Greece
R	***Gingidia algens*** (F.Muell.) Dawson *20681*	
	I	*20681* Australia - Capital Territory *20681*
	I	*20681* Australia - New South Wales *20681*
R	***Grammosciadium confertum*** Huber-Mor. & Lamond *12840*	
	R	*12840* Turkey *12840*
I	***Halosciastrum melanotilingia*** (Boiss.) Pim.& Tikhom.	
	I	*5942* Russia (Far East) - Primorye *5942*
R	***Heptaptera angustifolia*** (Bertol.) Tutin *20171*	
	R	Italy (Puglia, Basilicata)
R	***Heptaptera cilicica*** (Boiss. & Bal.) Tutin *12840*	
	R	*12840* Turkey *12840*
I	***Heptaptera macedonica*** (Bornm.) Tutin *20171*	
	I	(former) Yugoslavia
I	***Heracleum aquilegifolium*** C.B. Clarke	
	I	India - Karnataka (Concan)
	I	India - Tamil Nadu
R	***Heracleum argaeum*** Boiss. & Bal. *12840*	
	R	*12840* Turkey *12840*
R	***Heracleum carpaticum*** Porcius *17823, 20171*	
	V	*19949* Romania *20631*
	R	former European USSR
I	***Heracleum jacquemontii*** C.B. Clarke *11494*	
	I	*11494* India (NW Himalaya) *11494*
R	***Heracleum ligusticifolium*** M.Bieb. *20171*	
	R	former European USSR
V	***Heracleum minimum*** Lam. *20171*	
	V	France (mountains in south-east)
R	***Heracleum paphlagonicum*** Czecz. *12840*	
	R	*12840* Turkey *12840*

R	***Heracleum pastinaca*** Fenzl *12840*	
	R	*12840* Turkey *12840*
R	***Heracleum pesmenianum*** Ekim *12840*	
	R	*12840* Turkey *12840*
I	***Heracleum pubescens*** (Hoffm.) M.Bieb. *20171*	
	I	former European USSR
R	***Heracleum pumilum*** Vill. *20528*	
	R	*20528* France (Alps) *20528*
R	***Heracleum sphondylium*** L. ssp. ***artvinense*** (Manden.) Davis *12840*	
	R	*12840* Turkey *12840*
R	***Hladnikia pastinacifolia*** Rchb. *8000, 20171*	
	R	*13662* Slovenia (west) *13662*
V	***Horstrissea dolinicola*** W.Greuter, Gerstb. & Egli *20730*	
	V	*20730* Greece - Crete *20730*
I	***Hydrocotyle brittonii*** Mathias *20883, 13336*	
	I	*13336* Jamaica (St. Andrew) *20883*
R	***Hydrocotyle comocarpa*** F.Muell. *20681*	
	I	*20681* Australia - South Australia *20681*
	I	*20681* Australia - Tasmania *20681*
R	***Hydrocotyle conferta*** Wt. *13883*	
	R	*13883* India - Tamil Nadu (Nilgiri and Pulney mountains) *13883*
I	***Hydrocotyle feaniana*** F. Brown *20845*	
	I	*20845* French Polynesia - Marquesas Is *20845*
I	***Hydrocotyle grossulariaefolia*** Rusby var. ***jamesonii*** Mathias *11351*	
	I	*19573* Ecuador *11351*
I	***Hydrocotyle hexagona*** Mathias *11351*	
	I	*19573* Ecuador *11351*
R	***Hydrocotyle keelungensis*** Liu Chao & Chuang *20511*	
	R	*20511* Taiwan *20511*
V	***Hydrocotyle lemnoides*** Benth. *20681*	
	V	*20681* Australia - Western Australia *20681*
V	***Hydrocotyle oligantha*** Urban *5607*	
	V	*19105* Cuba (Santiago de Cuba) *5607*
I	***Hydrocotyle palmata*** Mathias *18200*	
	I	Ecuador *11351*
	V	*18200* Peru *18200*
I	***Hydrocotyle pennellii*** Rose ex Mathias *11351*	
	I	Colombia *11351*
	I	Ecuador *11351*
E	***Hydrocotyle pygmaea*** C. Wright *5607*	
	E	*19105* Cuba (Pinar del Rio) *5607*
V	***Imperatoria lowei*** Coss.	
	V	Portugal - Madeira
V	***Johrenia polyscias*** Bornm. *12840*	
	V	*12840* Turkey *12840*
R	***Johrenia silenoides*** Boiss. & Bal. *12840*	
	R	*12840* Turkey *12840*
I	***Komarovia anisosperma*** Korovin *5942*	
	I	*5942* Tajikistan *5942*
	I	*5942* Uzbekistan *5942*
R	***Kosopoljanskia turkestanica*** Korovin *5942*	
	R	*5942* Kazakhstan (south east border) *5942*
	R	*5942* Kyrgyzstan *5942*
	R	*5942* Turkmenistan (eastern) *5942*
R	***Kundmannia anatolica*** Huber-Mor. *12840*	
	R	*12840* Turkey *12840*

R **Kundmannia syriaca** Boiss. *12840*
   R   *12840* Turkey *12840*

R **Laserpitium affine** Ledeb. *5942*
   R   Turkey (Pontus range) *8001*
   I   *5942* Georgia *5942*

R **Laserpitium carduchorum** Hedge & Lamond *12840*
   R   *12840* Turkey *12840*

E **Laserpitium longiradium** Boiss. *15398, 20171*
   E   *15398* Spain (Sierra Nevada) *15398*

I **Ledebouriella seseloides** (Hoffmann) H. Wolff
   I   former USSR *6930*

R **Lereschia thomasii** (Ten.) Boiss. *18264, 20171*
   R   *18264* Italy (Basilicata, Calabria) *18264*

Ex/E **Ligusticum albanicum** Jáv. *20178, 20171*
   Ex/E *20178* Albania *20178*

Ex/E **Ligusticum albo-alatum** Haines *11494*
   Ex/E *11494* India - Bihar (Samripat; Ranchi District) *11494*
   Ex/E *11494* India - Orissa (Sarguja, Raigarh District) *11494*

R **Ligusticum calderi** Mathias & Constance *20850, 10701*
   R   *20850* Canada - British Columbia *20850*
   E   *20850* U.S. - Alaska *20850*

R **Ligusticum californicum** Coult. & Rose *20850*
   I   *20850* U.S. - California *20850*

R **Ligusticum corsicum** J.Gay *19174, 20171*
   R   *19174* France - Corsica *15080*

E **Ligusticum lucidum** Mill. ssp. *huteri* (P. Porta & G. Rigo) O. Bolos *20171*
   E   *20651* Spain - Balearic Is. *20645*

R **Ligusticum olympicum** Novak
   R   Greece

R **Ligusticum porteri** (Rydb.) Mathias & Constance var. *brevilobum* (Rydb.) Mathias & Constance *20850*
   I   *20850* U.S. - Nevada *20850*
         20850 U.S. - Utah *20850*

R **Ligusticum rhizomaticum** Hartvig
   R   Greece (Gramos range)

R **Lilaeopsis carolinensis** Coult. & Rose *20850*
   E   *20850* U.S. - Alabama *20850*
   Ex/E *20850* U.S. - Arkansas *20850*
   V   *20850* U.S. - Florida *20850*
   Ex/E *20850* U.S. - Georgia *20850*
   I   *20850* U.S. - Louisiana *20850*
   V   *20850* U.S. - Mississippi *20850*
   R   *20850* U.S. - North Carolina *20850*
   E   *20850* U.S. - South Carolina *20850*
   E   *20850* U.S. - Virginia *20850*

R **Lilaeopsis masonii** Mathias & Constance *20850*
   R   *20850* U.S. - California *20850*

V **Lilaeopsis schaffneriana** Coult. & Rose var. *recurva* (A.W. Hill) Affolter *20883, 20850*
   V   *20850* U.S. - Arizona *20850*
   I   *20883* Mexico *20883*

V **Lomatium attenuatum** Evert *20850*
   V   *20850* U.S. - Montana *20850*
   V   *20850* U.S. - Wyoming *20850*

R **Lomatium bicolor** (S. Wats.) Coult. & Rose var. *bicolor* *20850*
   I   *20850* U.S. - Idaho *20850*
   R   *20850* U.S. - Montana *20850*
   I   *20850* U.S. - Utah *20850*
   I   *20850* U.S. - Wyoming *20850*

V **Lomatium bradshawii** (Rose ex Mathias) Mathias & Constance *20850*
   V   *20850* U.S. - Oregon *20850*

R **Lomatium ciliolatum** Jepson *20850*
   I   *20850* U.S. - California *20850*

R **Lomatium ciliolatum** Jepson var. *ciliolatum* *20850, 10260*
   I   *20850* U.S. - California *20850*

R **Lomatium ciliolatum** Jepson var. *hooveri* Mathias & Constance *20850*
   I   *20850* U.S. - California *20850*

V **Lomatium concinnum** (Osterhout) Mathias *20850*
   V   *20850* U.S. - Colorado *20850*

V **Lomatium congdonii** Coult. & Rose *20850*
   V   *20850* U.S. - California *20850*

E **Lomatium cookii** J.S. Kagan *20850*
   E   *20850* U.S. - Oregon *20850*

V **Lomatium cuspidatum** Mathias & Constance *20850*
   I   *20850* U.S. - Washington *20850*

E **Lomatium erythrocarpum** Meinke & Constance *20850*
   E   *20850* U.S. - Oregon *20850*

E **Lomatium greenmanii** Mathias *20850*
   E   *20850* U.S. - Oregon *20850*

V **Lomatium insulare** (Eastw.) Munz *20850*
   V   *20850* U.S. - California *20850*

V **Lomatium junceum** Barneby & N. Holmgren *20850*
   V   *20850* U.S. - Utah *20850*

R **Lomatium laevigatum** (Nutt.) Coult. & Rose *20850*
   R   *20850* U.S. - Oregon *20850*
   R   *20850* U.S. - Washington *20850*

E **Lomatium latilobum** (Rydb.) Mathias *20850*
   E   *20850* U.S. - Colorado *20850*
   E   *20850* U.S. - Utah *20850*

V **Lomatium lucidum** (Nutt. ex Torr. & Gray) Jepson *20850*
   I   *20850* U.S. - California *20850*

V **Lomatium minimum** (Mathias) Mathias *20850*
   V   *20850* U.S. - Utah *20850*

R **Lomatium mohavense** (Coult. & Rose) Coult. & Rose ssp. *mohavense* *20850*
   I   *20850* U.S. - California *20850*

R **Lomatium nuttallii** (Gray) J.F. Macbr. *20850*
   E   *20850* U.S. - Colorado *20850*
   I   *20850* U.S. - Idaho *20850*
   E   *20850* U.S. - Montana *20850*
   E   *20850* U.S. - Nebraska *20850*
   I   *20850* U.S. - Nevada *20850*
   I   *20850* U.S. - New Mexico *20850*
   Ex/E *20850* U.S. - South Dakota *20850*
   I   *20850* U.S. - Utah *20850*
   R   *20850* U.S. - Wyoming *20850*

R **Lomatium plummerae** (Coult. & Rose) Coult. & Rose *20850*
   I   *20850* U.S. - California *20850*
   I   *20850* U.S. - Nevada *20850*

V **Lomatium repostum** (Jepson) Mathias *20850*
   V   *20850* U.S. - California *20850*

R **Lomatium rollinsii** Mathias & Constance *20850*
   R   *20850* U.S. - Idaho *20850*
   R   *20850* U.S. - Oregon *20850*
   V   *20850* U.S. - Washington *20850*

R **Lomatium salmoniflorum** (Coult. & Rose) Mathias &

Constance *20850*

V		*20850* U.S. - Idaho *20850*	
Ex/E		*20850* U.S. - Oregon *20850*	
I		*20850* U.S. - Washington *20850*	
R	*Lomatium scabrum* (Coult. & Rose) Mathias *20850*		
I		*20850* U.S. - Arizona *20850*	
I		*20850* U.S. - Nevada *20850*	
I		*20850* U.S. - Utah *20850*	
E	*Lomatium shevockii* Hartman & Constance *20850*		
E		*20850* U.S. - California *20850*	
V	*Lomatium stebbinsii* Schlessman & Constance *20850*		
V		*20850* U.S. - California *20850*	
R	*Lomatium suksdorfii* (S.Watson) Coult. & Rose *20850*		
V		*20850* U.S. - Oregon *20850*	
R		*20850* U.S. - Washington *20850*	
V	*Lomatium thompsonii* (Mathias) Cronq. *20850*		
I		*20850* U.S. - Washington *20850*	
R	*Lomatium torreyi* (Coult. & Rose) Coult. & Rose *20850*		
I		*20850* U.S. - California *20850*	
V	*Lomatium tuberosum* Hoover *20850*		
V		*20850* U.S. - Washington *20850*	
R	*Melanoselinum decipiens* (Schrad. & J.C.Wendl.) Hoffm. *8000, 20171*		
R		*19174* Portugal - Azores *8000*	
R		*19174* Portugal - Madeira *8000*	
I	*Mogoltavia sewertzowii* (Regel) Korovin *5942*		
I		*5942* Kyrgyzstan *5942*	
I		*5942* Uzbekistan *5942*	
E	*Monizia edulis* Lowe *17891*		
E		Portugal - Madeira *17891*	
E		Portugal - Salvage Is. *17891*	
R	*Muretia aurea* Boiss. *12840*		
R		*12840* Turkey *12840*	
V	*Musineon lineare* (Rydb.) Mathias *20850*		
E		*20850* U.S. - Idaho *20850*	
V		*20850* U.S. - Utah *20850*	
R	*Musineon vaginatum* Rydb. *20850*		
R		*20850* U.S. - Montana *20850*	
I		*20850* U.S. - Wyoming *20850*	
V	*Myrrhidendron maxonii* Coult. & Rose *20883, 9006*		
R		*19577* Panama *20883*	
E	*Naufraga balearica* Constance & Cannon *8000, 20171*		
Ex		*15080* France - Corsica *12844*	
E		*20874* Spain - Balearic Is. (Mallorca) *8000*	
V	*Neoparrya lithophila* Mathias *20850*		
V		*20850* U.S. - Colorado *20850*	
I		*20850* U.S. - New Mexico *20850*	
I	*Niphogeton azorelloides* Mathias & Constance *18200*		
I		Ecuador *11351*	
V		*18200* Peru *18200*	
E	*Nirarathamnos asarifolius* Balf. f. *15534*		
E		*15534* Yemen - Socotra *18211*	
E	*Oenanthe conioides* Lange *17781, 20171*		
E		*20640* Germany *17891*	
V	*Oenanthe foucaudii* Tess. *20171*		
V		*20528* France (west) *20528*	
V	*Oenanthe pteridifolia* Lowe		
V		Portugal - Madeira	
V	*Olymposciadium caespitosum* (Sm.) Wolff *12840*		
V		*12840* Turkey *12840*	
R	*Oreomyrrhis brevipes* Mathias & Constance *20681*		

I		*20681* Australia - New South Wales *20681*	
I		*20681* Australia - Victoria *20681*	
R	*Oreomyrrhis gunnii* Mathias & Constance *20681*		
R		*20681* Australia - Tasmania *20681*	
R	*Oreomyrrhis sessiliflora* Hook.f. *20681*		
R		*20681* Australia - Tasmania *20681*	
R	*Oreonana clementis* (M.E. Jones) Jepson *20850*		
I		*20850* U.S. - California *20850*	
R	*Oreonana purpurascens* Shevock & Constance *20850*		
R		*20850* U.S. - California *20850*	
E	*Oreoxis humilis* Raf. *20850*		
E		*20850* U.S. - Colorado *20850*	
E	*Oreoxis trotteri* Welsh & Goodrich *20850*		
E		*20850* U.S. - Utah *20850*	
R	*Oschatzia cuneifolia* (F.Muell.) Drude *20681*		
I		*20681* Australia - New South Wales *20681*	
I		*20681* Australia - Victoria *20681*	
R	*Osmorhiza brachypoda* Torr. *20850*		
E		*20850* U.S. - Arizona *20850*	
I		*20850* U.S. - California *20850*	
E	*Osmorhiza mexicana* Griseb. ssp. *bipatriata* (Constance & Shan) Lowry & A.G. Jones(Con. & Shan) *20883, 20850, 8058*		
E		*20850* U.S. - Texas *20850*	
I		*20883* Mexico *20883*	
V	*Oxypolis canbyi* (Coult. & Rose) Fern. *20850*		
Ex/E		*20850* U.S. - Delaware (Ellendale, Sussex Co.) *20850*	
V		*20850* U.S. - Georgia (Burke & Lee & Sumter Co.) *20850*	
E		*20850* U.S. - Maryland (Chester River watershed) *20850*	
E		*20850* U.S. - North Carolina (Caroline Bay, Scotland Co.) *20850*	
E		*20850* U.S. - South Carolina *20850*	
R	*Oxypolis greenmanii* Mathias & Constance *20850*		
R		*20850* U.S. - Florida *20850*	
R	*Oxypolis ternata* (Nutt.) Heller *20850*		
V		*20850* U.S. - Florida *20850*	
V		*20850* U.S. - Georgia *20850*	
R		*20850* U.S. - North Carolina *20850*	
I		*20850* U.S. - South Carolina *20850*	
E		*20850* U.S. - Texas *20850*	
Ex/E		*20850* U.S. - Virginia *20850*	
V	*Pachyctenium mirabile* Maire & Pampan.		
V		Libya	
I	*Parasilaus asiaticus* (Korovin) Pim. *5942*		
I		*5942* Tajikistan *5942*	
R	*Pastinaca armena* Fisch. & Mey. ssp. *dentata* (Freyn & Sint) Chamb. *12840*		
R		*12840* Turkey *12840*	
R	*Pastinacopsis glacialis* Golosk. *5942*		
R		*5942* Kazakhstan (south-east border with Kyrgyzstan) *5942*	
R		*5942* Kyrgyzstan (Os Issyk-Kul) *5942*	
R	*Pentapeltis silvatica* (Diels)Domin *20681*		
R		*20681* Australia - Western Australia *20681*	
R	*Perideridia californica* (Torr.) A. Nels. & J.F. Macbr. *20850*		
I		*20850* U.S. - California *20850*	
E	*Perideridia erythrorhiza* (Piper) Chuang & Constance *20850*		
E		*20850* U.S. - Oregon *20850*	

V	*Perideridia gairdneri* (Hook & Arn.) Mathias ssp. *gairdneri* 20850		
	I	20850 U.S. - California 20850	
R	*Perideridia pringlei* (Coult. & Rose) A. Nels. & J.F. Macbr. 20850		
	R	20850 U.S. - California 20850	
V	*Petagnia saniculifolia* Guss. 8000, 20171		
	V	19997 Italy - Sicily (Northern) 19997	
R	*Peucedanum achaicum* Halácsy 20171		
	R	Greece	
R	*Peucedanum anamallayense* C.B. Clarke 13883		
	R	13883 India - Tamil Nadu (Coimbatore) 13883	
R	*Peucedanum arenarium* Waldst. & Kit ssp. *urbanii* (Freyn & Sint. ex Wolff) Chamb 12840		
	R	12840 Turkey 12840	
I	*Peucedanum beluchistanicum* Wolff		
	I	Pakistan	
R	*Peucedanum boninense* Tuy. 8038		
	R	19134 Japan - Ogasawara-shoto 8038	
I	*Peucedanum camerunensis* Jacq.-Fel.		
	I	Cameroon (Foumban)	
I	*Peucedanum ceylanicum* Gardner 8021		
	I	16162 Sri Lanka (Galagama, Belihul-oya) 8021	
R	*Peucedanum cordatum* Balf. f. 15534		
	R	15534 Yemen - Socotra 15534	
I	*Peucedanum hissaricum* Korovin 5942		
	I	5942 Tajikistan 5942	
R	*Peucedanum khamiesbergense* B.L.Burtt 20604		
	R	20604 South Africa - Cape Province 20604	
R	*Peucedanum mogoltavicum* Korovin		
	R	former USSR 6930	
R	*Peucedanum multivittatum* Maxim. var. *linearilobum* Tatew. 10572		
	R	10572 Japan 10572	
R	*Peucedanum pearsonii* Adamson 20604		
	R	20604 South Africa - Cape Province 20604	
V	*Peucedanum sandwicense* Hbd. 20850		
	V	20850 U.S. - Hawaii 20850	
E	*Peucedanum sandwicense* Hillebrand var. *sandwicense* 14209		
	E	14209 U.S. - Hawaii 14209	
I	*Peucedanum zedelmeyerianum* Manden. 5942		
	I	5942 Armenia 5942	
R	*Pilopleura goloskokovii* (Korovin) Pim. 5942		
	R	4952 Kazakhstan (south-east) 5942	
V	*Pimpinella anagodendron* Bolle 19174		
	V	19174 Spain - Canary Is. 19174	
R	*Pimpinella anisetum* Boiss. & Bal. 12840		
	R	12840 Turkey 12840	
R	*Pimpinella battandieri* Chabert 10488		
	R	14958 Algeria 10488	
R	*Pimpinella bicknellii* Briq. 20171		
	R	20645 Spain - Balearic Is. 20645	
R	*Pimpinella cypria* Boiss. 14230		
	R	19164 Cyprus 14230	
Ex/E	*Pimpinella evoluta* (C.B. Clarke) Mukherjee 11494		
	Ex/E	11494 India - Nagaland (Jakpho, Naga hills) 11494	

R	*Pimpinella flabellifolia* (Boiss.) Bent & Hook ex Drude 12840		
	R	12840 Turkey 12840	
I	*Pimpinella flaccida* Clarke 13883		
	I	13883 India - Nagaland (Kohima) 13883	
I	*Pimpinella hazarensis* Wolff		
	I	Pakistan	
R	*Pimpinella isaurica* Matthews 12840		
	R	12840 Turkey 12840	
R	*Pimpinella junoniae* Ceball. & Ortuno		
	R	Spain - Canary Is.	
R	*Pimpinella katrajensis* Rao et Hemadri 13883		
	R	13883 India - Maharashtra 13883	
R	*Pimpinella krookii* H.Wolff 20604		
	R	20604 South Africa - Natal 20604	
R	*Pimpinella pretenderis* (Heldr.) Orph. ex Halácsy 20171		
	R	Greece	
R	*Pimpinella procumbens* (Boiss.) H.Wolff 20171		
	R	Spain	
Ex/E	*Pimpinella pulneyensis* Gamble 11494		
	Ex/E	11494 India - Tamil Nadu (Palani Hills, Madurai Dist) 11494	
E	*Pimpinella rupicola* Svent. 20750		
	E	20750 Spain - Canary Is. 20750	
R	*Pimpinella siifolia* Leresche 20171		
	R	20528 France (Pyrénées-Atlantique) 20528	
	R	20528 Spain 20528	
E	*Pimpinella tirupatiensis* Balakr. & Subram.		
	E	13883 India - Andhra Pradesh 13883	
Ex/E	*Pimpinella tongloensis* Mukherjee 11494		
	Ex/E	11494 India - Assam (Singaleela Range) 11494	
	Ex/E	11494 India - Sikkim (Singaleela Range) 11494	
R	*Platysace cirrosa* Bunge 20681		
	R	20681 Australia - Western Australia 20681	
R	*Platysace clelandii* Maiden & Betche 20681		
	R	20681 Australia - New South Wales 20681	
Ex	*Platysace dissecta* (Benth.) Norman 20681, 14223		
	Ex	20681 Australia - Western Australia 20681	
R	*Platysace heterophylla* (Benth.) Norman var. *tepperi* (J.Black) H.Eichler 20681		
	R	20681 Australia - South Australia 20681	
R	*Platysace stephensonii* (Turcz.) Norman 20681		
	R	20681 Australia - New South Wales 20681	
E	*Podistera yukonensis* Mathias & Constance 20850, 1034		
	E	20850 Canada - Yukon Territory 20850	
	E	20850 U.S. - Alaska 20850	
I	*Polylophium panjutinii* Manden. & Schischkin 5942		
	I	5942 Georgia 5942	
R	*Polyzygus tuberosus* Dalz. 14782		
	R	14782 India - Karnataka 14782	
	R	14782 India - Maharashtra 14782	
R	*Prangos denticulata* Fisch. & Mey. 12840		
	R	12840 Turkey 12840	
R	*Prangos herderi* (Regel) Herrnst. & Heyn 5942		
	R	5942 Kazakhstan 5942	
I	*Prangos scrabifolia* Post ex Beauv. 12840		
	I	12840 Turkey 12840	
I	*Prangos trifida* (Miller) Herrnst. & Heyn 5942		

	I	*5942*	Russia (E.Europe) - Northwest *5942*

I   *Pternopetalum radiatum* (W. Smith) Mukherjee *11494*
- I   *11494*   India - Sikkim *11494*

V   *Ptilimnium nodosum* (Rose) Mathias *20850*
- E   *20850*   U.S. - Alabama (seasonally flooded rocky streams) *20850*
- V   *20850*   U.S. - Arkansas (seasonally flooded rocky streams) *20850*
- E   *20850*   U.S. - Georgia (granite outcrop) *20850*
- E   *20850*   U.S. - Maryland (seasonally flooded rocky streams) *20850*
- E   *20850*   U.S. - North Carolina (seasonally flooded rocky streams) *20850*
- E   *20850*   U.S. - South Carolina (coastal plain ponds) *20850*
- I   *20850*   U.S. - Virginia *20850*
- E   *20850*   U.S. - West Virginia (seasonally flooded rocky streams) *20850*

R   *Rhabdosciadium microcalycinum* Hand.-mazz. *12840*
- R   *12840*   Turkey *12840*

V   *Rutheopsis herbanica* (Bolle) Hansen & Kunkel *20750*
- V   *20750*   Spain - Canary Is. *17534*

R   *Sanicula azorica* Guthnick ex Seub. *8000, 20171*
- R   Portugal - Azores *8000*

R   *Sanicula hoffmannii* (Munz) Shan & Constance (pro hyb.) *20850*
- R   *20850*   U.S. - California *20850*

R   *Sanicula kaiensis* Makino & Hisauchi *10572*
- R   *10572*   Japan *10572*

Ex/E   *Sanicula kauaiensis* St. John *20850, 14209*
- Ex/E   *20850*   U.S. - Hawaii *20850*

R   *Sanicula lamelligera* Hance var. *wakayamensis* Murata *10572*
- R   *10572*   Japan *10572*

V   *Sanicula maritima* Kellogg ex S.Watson *20850*
- V   *20850*   U.S. - California *20850*

E   *Sanicula mariversa* Nagata & Gon *20850, 14209*
- E   *20850*   U.S. - Hawaii (O`ahu - Wai`anae Mts.) *20850*

E   *Sanicula purpurea* St. John & Hosaka *20850, 14209*
- E   *20850*   U.S. - Hawaii (O`ahu, Maui) *20850*

V   *Sanicula sandwicensis* Gray *20850, 14209*
- V   *20850*   U.S. - Hawaii *20850*

V   *Sanicula saxatilis* Greene *20850*
- V   *20850*   U.S. - California *20850*

I   *Scaligera chitralica* Hiroe
- I   Pakistan

R   *Scaligeria capillifolia* Post *12840*
- R   *12840*   Turkey *12840*

R   *Scaligeria halophila* (Rech.f.) Rech.f.
- R   Greece

R   *Scaligeria moreana* Engstrand
- R   Greece

R   *Scandix balansae* Reuter ex Boiss. *12840*
- R   *12840*   Turkey *12840*

R   *Schrenkia kultiassovii* Korovin *5942*
- R   *5942*   Kazakhstan (east) *5942*

R   *Schtschurowskia margaritae* Korovin *5942*
- R   *5942*   Kazakhstan (south-east) *5942*

I   *Schultzia benthami* C.B. Clarke
- I   India - Karnataka (Canara coast)

Ex/E   *Sclerotiaria pentaceros* (Korovin) Korovin *5942*
- Ex/E   *5942*   Kazakhstan *5942*

I   *Semenovia rubtzovii* (Schischkin) Manden. *5942*
- I   *5942*   Kazakhstan *5942*

R   *Seseli aroanicum* Hartvig
- R   Greece (Mt Chelmos)

R   *Seseli degenii* Urum. *5204, 20171*
- R   *5204*   Bulgaria (north) *5204*

V   *Seseli djianeae* Gamisans *15080*
- V   *20528*   France - Corsica *20528*

I   *Seseli elatum* L. ssp. *heterophyllum* (Janka) Holub *19321*
- I   *19321*   Slovakia *19321*

I   *Seseli eryngioides* (Korovin) Pim. & V. Tikhom. *5942*
- I   *5942*   Kyrgyzstan *5942*

V   *Seseli farrenyi* Molero & Pujadas *19174*
- V   *19174*   Spain *19174*

E   *Seseli intricatum* Boiss. *8000, 20171*
- E   *19818*   Spain (Sierra de Gádor) *8000*

R   *Seseli lehmannii* Degen *20171*
- R   former European USSR

R   *Seseli leucospermum* Waldst. & Kit. *8000, 20171*
- R   *20686*   Hungary *8000*

R   *Seseli malyi* A.Kern. *13662, 20171*
- R   *13662*   Slovenia (southern) *13662*

R   *Seseli parnassicum* Boiss. & Heldr. *20171*
- R   Greece

V   *Seseli peixoteanum* Samp. *8000, 20171*
- V   *20076*   Portugal *20076*

R   *Seseli ramosissimum* (Port.) Ces. *12840, 20171*
- R   *12840*   Turkey *12840*

R   *Seseli resinosum* Freyn & Sint. *12840*
- R   *12840*   Turkey *12840*

I   *Seseli saxicolum* (Albov) Pim. *5042*
- I   *5942*   Georgia *5942*

R   *Seseli tomentosum* Vis. *20171*
- R   *21091*   Bosnia & Herzegovina *21091*
- R   (former) Yugoslavia

R   *Seseli webbii* Coss.
- R   Spain - Canary Is.

V   *Shoshonea pulvinata* Evert & Constance *20850*
- E   *20850*   U.S. - Montana *20850*
- V   *20850*   U.S. - Wyoming *20850*

E   *Sium burchellii* Hemsley *10260*
- E   *18996*   St Helena *18996*

E   *Sium helenianum* Hook.f. *18996*
- E   *18996*   St Helena *18996*

I   *Smyrniopsis aucheri* Boiss. *5942*
- I   *5942*   Armenia *5942*
- I   *5942*   Azerbaijan *5942*

R   *Smyrnium gelaticum* Czecz. *12840*
- R   *12840*   Turkey *12840*

E   *Spananthe paniculata* Jacq. var. *peruviana* Wolff *18200*
- E   *9446*   Peru *18200*

E   *Spermolepis hawaiiensis* H. Wolff *20850, 14209*
- E   *20850*   U.S. - Hawaii (O`ahu, West Maui) *20850*

I   *Sphaerosciadium denaense* (Schischkin) Pim. & Kljuykov *5942*

I	5942	Tajikistan *5942*
I	5942	Uzbekistan *5942*

R   *Stefanoffia insoluta* **Kijuykov** *12840*
    R   *12840*   Turkey *12840*

R   *Steganotaenia commiphoroides* **M.Thulin** *20884*
    E   *20884*   Ethiopia *20884*
    R   *20884*   Somalia (south) *20884*

I   *Stenotaenia macrocarpa* **Freyn & Sint. ssp.**
    daralaghezica **(Takht.) Takht.** *5942*
    I   *5942*   Armenia *5942*

I   *Tauschia allioides* **Bye & Constance** *10120*
    I   *19850*   Mexico *10120*

R   *Tauschia bicolor* **Constance & Bye** *10117*
    R   *19850*   Mexico *10117*

I   *Tauschia hintoniorum* **Constance & Affolter** *20883,*
    10188
    I   *20883*   Mexico *20883*

V   *Tauschia hooveri* **Mathias & Constance** *20850*
    V   *20850*   U.S. - Washington *20850*

E   *Tauschia howellii* **(Coult. & Rose) J.F. Macbr.** *20850*
    E   *20850*   U.S. - California *20850*
    E   *20850*   U.S. - Oregon *20850*

I   *Tauschia infernicola* **Constance & Affolter** *20883,*
    10188
    I   *20883*   Mexico *20883*

I   *Tauschia moorei* **Constance & Affolter** *20883, 10188*
    I   *20883*   Mexico *20883*

R   *Tauschia tarahumara* **Constance & Bye** *10117*
    R   *19850*   Mexico *10117*

R   *Tauschia tenuissima* **(Geyer ex Hook.) Mathias &**
    Constance *20850*
    R   *20850*   U.S. - Idaho *20850*
    Ex   *20850*   U.S. - Washington *20850*

V   *Thorella verticillatinundata* **(Thore) Briq.** *17891,*
    20171
    V   France (south-west and west-central)
           8000
    V   *20076*   Portugal (west) *8000*

V   *Tilingia tsusimensis* **Kitag.** *10572*
    V   *10572*   Japan *10572*

R   *Tinguarra cervariaefolia* **Parl.** *17534*
    R   *17534*   Spain - Canary Is. *17534*

R   *Tinguarra montana* **Webb ex Christ** *17534*
    R   *17534*   Spain - Canary Is. *17534*

R   *Todaroa aurea* **Parl.** *17534*
    R   *17534*   Spain - Canary Is. *17534*

R   *Tordylium elegans* **Alava & Huber-Mor.** *12840*
    R   *12840*   Turkey *12840*

R   *Tordylium lanatum* **(Boiss.) Boiss.** *12840*
    R   *12840*   Turkey *12840*

R   *Tordylium macropetalum* **Boiss.** *12840*
    R   *12840*   Turkey *12840*

R   *Tordylium pestalozzae* **Boiss.** *20171*
    R   Greece

V   *Tordylium pustulosum* **Boiss.** *12840*
    V   *12840*   Turkey *12840*

R   *Torilis triradiata* **Boiss. & Heldr.** *12840*
    R   *12840*   Turkey *12840*

R   *Trachymene geraniifolia* **Bailey** *20681*
    R   *20681*   Australia - Queensland *20681*

R   *Trachymene inflata* **Maconochie** *20681*
    R   *20681*   Australia - Northern Territory *20681*

R   *Trigonosciadium intermedium* **Freyn & Sint.** *12840*
    R   *12840*   Turkey *12840*

R   *Trinia crithmifolia* **(Willd.) H.Wolff** *20171*
    R   former European USSR

R   *Trinia kitaibelii* **auct., non M.Bieb.** *20171*
    R   former European USSR

I   *Vvedenskya pinnatifolia* **Korovin** *5942*
    I   *5942*   Uzbekistan *5942*

R   *Xanthosia tomentosa* **A.S.George** *20681*
    R   *20681*   Australia - Western Australia *20681*

I   *Zeravschania regeliana* **Korovin** *5942*
    I   *5942*   Tajikistan *5942*
    I   *5942*   Uzbekistan *5942*

Urticaceae

Number of genera:	45	
Number of species:	700	
Recorded threatened species:	117	(16%)

Tropical and subtropical.

E   *Boehmeria australis* **Endl. var.**
    australis *11649*
    E   *11649*   Australia - Norfolk Is. *11649*

V   *Boehmeria australis* **Endl. var. *dealbata***
    (Cheeseman) Sykes *20625, 11649*
    V   *19106*   New Zealand - Kermadec Is. (Raoul Island)
            20625

R   *Boehmeria calophleba* **C. Moore & F. Muell.**
    R   *14225*   Australia - NSW - Lord Howe Is. *14225*

R   *Boehmeria excelsa* **(Bert. ex Steud.) Wedd.** *20883,*
    19116
    V   *19125*   Chile - Juan Fernandez Is. *19116*
    V   *20883*   Chile *20883*

R   *Boehmeria hwaliensis* **Liu & Lu** *20511*
    R   *20511*   Taiwan *20511*

R   *Boehmeria jamaicensis* **Urb.** *20883*
    R   *20883*   Jamaica *20883*

R   *Boehmeria pilushanensis* **Liu & Lu** *20511*
    R   *20511*   Taiwan *20511*

I   *Boehmeria tirapensis* **Deb & R. Dutta**
    I   India - Arunachal Pradesh (Tirap District)

V   *Debregeasia dentata* **Hook.f.** *14872*
    V   *14872*   Bangladesh *14872*

I   *Droguetia gaudichaudiana* **Marais**
    I   *14220*   Réunion *14220*

R   *Elatostema curtisii* **(Ridley) H. Schroter**
    R   Malaysia - Peninsular Malaysia

E   *Elatostema montanum* **Endl.** *19108*
    E   *14225*   Australia - Norfolk Is. *14288*

I   *Elatostema palawanensis* **C.B. Rob.** *13833*
    I   *13833*   Philippines (Palawan) *13833*

I   *Elatostema ranongensis* **Yahara** *19120*
    I   *19120*   Thailand *19120*

E   *Elatostema stenophyllum* **Merr.**
    E   U.S. - Guam

R   *Elatostema tutuilense* **Whistler** *8006*
    R   U.S. - American Samoa (Tutuila) *8006*

I   *Elatostema walkerae* **Hook.f.** *10252*

I	*16162* Sri Lanka *10252*	
R	*Elatostema yakushimensis* Hatus. *10572*	
	R	*10572* Japan *10572*
V	*Gesnouinia arborea* (L.f.) Gaudich. *17534*	
	V	*19174* Spain - Canary Is. *17534*
R	*Gyrotaenia microcarpa* (Wedd.) F. & R. *20883*	
	R	*20883* Jamaica *20883*
R	*Gyrotaenia spicata* (Wedd.) Wedd. *20883*	
	R	*20883* Jamaica *20883*
E	*Hesperocnide sandwicensis* (Weddell) Weddell *20850, 14209*	
	E	*20850* U.S. - Hawaii *20850*
R	*Meniscogyne petelotii* Gagnepain *6057*	
	R	Vietnam *6057*
E	*Neraudia angulata* Cowan *20850*	
	I	*20850* U.S. - Hawaii *20850*
E	*Neraudia angulata* R. Cowan var. angulata *20850*	
	E	*20850* U.S. - Hawaii *20850*
E	*Neraudia angulata* Cowan var. *dentata* O. Deg. & Cowan *20850, 14209*	
	E	*20850* U.S. - Hawaii *20850*
E	*Neraudia kauaiensis* (Hbd.) Cowan *20850, 14209*	
	E	*20850* U.S. - Hawaii (Kaua`i) *20850*
V	*Neraudia melastomifolia* Gaud. *20850, 14209*	
	V	*20850* U.S. - Hawaii *20850*
E	*Neraudia ovata* Gaud. *20850, 14209, 21355*	
	E	*20850* U.S. - Hawaii (Hawai`i) *20850*
E	*Neraudia sericea* Gaud. *20850, 14209*	
	E	*20850* U.S. - Hawaii *20850*
E	*Obetia aldabrensis* Frits *14981*	
	E	*14981* Seychelles *14981*
V	*Obetia ficifolia* (Poiret) Gaudich. *10082*	
	V	*14234* Réunion *14234*
	Ex	*20771* Mauritius *5852*
	E	*5852* Mauritius - Rodrigues (Grande Mt) *5852*
I	*Parietaria fernandeziana* *19116*	
	I	*19125* Chile - Juan Fernandez Is. *19116*
R	*Parietaria filamentosa* Webb & Berthel.	
	R	Spain - Canary Is.
R	*Pellionia arisanensis* Hayata var. *pygmaea* Yamamoto *20511*	
	R	*20511* Taiwan *20511*
R	*Pellionia yosiei* Hara *10572*	
	R	*10572* Japan *10572*
R	*Petelotiella tonkinensis* (Gagnepain) Gagnepain *6057*	
	R	Vietnam *6057*
I	*Phenax microphyllus* Urban *5607*	
	I	*19105* Cuba *5607*
V	*Pilea ambecarpa* Urban *5607*	
	V	*19105* Cuba (Guantanamo) *5607*
V	*Pilea andersonii* Adams *20883, 13336*	
	V	*13336* Jamaica (St. Thomas) *20883*
R	*Pilea angustifolia* Killip *9037*	
	R	*19754* Costa Rica *9037*
R	*Pilea appendicilata* F. & R. *20883, 13336*	
	R	*13336* Jamaica (Clarendon, Manchester) *20883*
E	*Pilea articulata* Wedd. *10082*	
	E	*20771* Mauritius *10082*

E	*Pilea balfourii* Baker *10082*		
	E	*5852* Mauritius - Rodrigues (Cascade Victoire) *5852*	
R	*Pilea beguinotti* Cuf. *9037*		
	R	*19754* Costa Rica *9037*	
E	*Pilea bisepal* *19473*		
	E	*19473* Cook Is.(Southern group) (Rarotonga) *19473*	
Ex/E	*Pilea boehmerioides* Wedd. *10082*		
	Ex/E	*20771* Mauritius *10082*	
V	*Pilea borbonica* Marais *10082*		
	V	*14220* Réunion *10082*	
R	*Pilea brevistipula* Urb. *20883*		
	R	*20883* Jamaica *20883*	
E	*Pilea cadetii* Marais *10082*		
	E	*14220* Réunion *10082*	
R	*Pilea carnosa* Britton *5607*		
	R	*19105* Cuba (Granma; Guantanamo) *5607*	
E	*Pilea cataractae* Marais *10082*		
	E	*20771* Mauritius *10082*	
E	*Pilea chiriquina* Killip *20883, 9006*		
	I	*20883* Panama *20883*	
V	*Pilea ciliata* (Sw.) Blume *20883*		
	V	*20883* Jamaica *20883*	
I	*Pilea clandestina* Wedd. *20883, 13336*		
	I	*19890* Jamaica (west) *20883*	
E	*Pilea cocottei* Marais *10082*		
	E	*20771* Mauritius *10082*	
R	*Pilea crassifolia* (Willd.) Blume *20883*		
	R	*20883* Jamaica *20883*	
E	*Pilea crenulata* (Sw.) Urb. *20883*		
	E	*20883* Jamaica *20883*	
R	*Pilea cuneiformis* Wedd. *10082*		
	R	*20771* Mauritius *10082*	
R	*Pilea elizabethae* F. & R. *20883*		
	R	*20883* Jamaica *20883*	
V	*Pilea filipes* (Griseb.) Urban *5607*		
	V	*19105* Cuba (Guantanamo) *5607*	
V	*Pilea flavicaulis* Urb. & Britton *20883*		
	V	*20883* Jamaica *20883*	
V	*Pilea harrisii* Urb. *20883*		
	V	*20883* Jamaica *20883*	
V	*Pilea impressa* Urb. *20883*		
	V	*20883* Jamaica *20883*	
E	*Pilea impressa* Urb. var. *barbata* Adams *20883, 13336*		
	E	*20883* Jamaica (Clarendon) *20883*	
R	*Pilea impressa* Urb. var. *impressa* *20883, 13336*		
	R	*13336* Jamaica (Hanover, Trelawny) *20883*	
V	*Pilea kiotensis* Ohwi *10572*		
	V	*10572* Japan *10572*	
E	*Pilea laciniata* Urban *5607*		
	E	*19105* Cuba (Guantanamo) *5607*	
E	*Pilea laevicaulis* Wedd. *10082*		
	E	*20771* Mauritius *10082*	
R	*Pilea lamiifolia* F. & R. *20883*		
	R	*20883* Jamaica *20883*	

R	*Pilea lamiifolia* F. & R. var. *lamiifolia* 20883	
	R	20883 Jamaica 20883
R	*Pilea lamiifolia* F. & R. var. *puberula* F. & R. 20883	
	R	20883 Jamaica 20883
E	*Pilea lamioides* Wedd. 18200	
	E	9446 Peru 18200
V	*Pilea laurae* Adams 20883, 13336	
	V	13336 Jamaica (Trelawny) 20883
E	*Pilea leptophylla* Urban 20883	
	I	20883 Puerto Rico 20883
E	*Pilea libanensis* Urban 5607	
	E	19105 Cuba (Guantanamo) 5607
V	*Pilea loeseneri* Urban & Ekman 5607	
	V	19105 Cuba (Guantanamo) 5607
R	*Pilea lucens* (Poiret) Wedd. ssp. *lucens* 10082	
	R	20771 Mauritius 10082
R	*Pilea lucida* (Sw.) Blume 20883	
	R	20883 Jamaica 20883
R	*Pilea maxonii* Britton 20883	
	R	20883 Jamaica 20883
R	*Pilea oblanceolata* F. & R. 20883, 13336	
	R	13336 Jamaica (Clarendon) 20883
R	*Pilea obtusangula* Urban 5607	
	R	19105 Cuba (SC; Gu) 5607
V	*Pilea ordinata* Adams 20883, 13336	
	V	13336 Jamaica (Hanover) 20883
V	*Pilea phaeocarpa* Urban 5607	
	V	19105 Cuba (Guantanamo) 5607
E	*Pilea pollicaris* Marais 10082	
	E	20771 Mauritius 10082
R	*Pilea portlandiana* Adams 20883, 13336	
	R	13336 Jamaica (Portland) 20883
V	*Pilea proctorii* Adams 20883, 13336	
	V	13336 Jamaica (west) 20883
E	*Pilea radicans* (Sw.) Wedd. 20883	
	E	20883 Jamaica 20883
R	*Pilea reticulata* (Sw.) Wedd. 20883	
	R	20883 Jamaica 20883
V	*Pilea richardii* Urban 20883, 15106 20883 Puerto Rico 20883	
	I	20883 USA - Virgin Is. (DS 2790: St Thomas) 20883
V	*Pilea rotundata* Griseb. 20883	
	V	20883 Jamaica 20883
V	*Pilea rufa* (Sw.) Wedd. 20883	
	V	20883 Jamaica 20883
V	*Pilea rufa* (Sw.) Wedd. var. *microstipula* Adams 20883, 13336	
	V	13336 Jamaica (Hanover) 20883
V	*Pilea rufa* (Sw.) Wedd. var. *rufa* 20883	
	V	20883 Jamaica 20883
V	*Pilea rufescens* F. & R. 20883, 13336	
	V	13336 Jamaica (Trelawny) 20883
E	*Pilea rugosissima* Killip 20883, 9006	
	I	19577 Panama 20883
V	*Pilea saxicola* Urb. 20883, 13336	

	V	13336 Jamaica (Trelawny) 20883
E	*Pilea serrulata* (Sw.) Wedd. 20883	
	E	20883 Jamaica 20883
I	*Pilea serrulata* (Sw.) Wedd. var. *serrulata* 13336	
	I	13336 Jamaica 13336
V	*Pilea sessiliflora* (Sw.) Wedd. 20883, 13336	
	V	13336 Jamaica (Manchester) 20883
R	*Pilea shaferi* Britton & P. Wilson 5607	
	R	19105 Cuba (Guantanamo) 5607
V	*Pilea silvicola* F. & R. 20883, 13336	
	V	13336 Jamaica (Clarendon) 20883
V	*Pilea sohayakiensis* Kitam. 10572	
	V	10572 Japan 10572
V	*Pilea sumideroensis* Britton 5607	
	V	19105 Cuba (Pinar del Rio) 5607
V	*Pilea suta* Adams 20883, 13336	
	V	13336 Jamaica (Manchester) 20883
Ex	*Pilea thouarsiana* Wedd. 10082	
	Ex	20771 Mauritius 10082
V	*Pilea tilarana* W. Burger 9037	
	V	19754 Costa Rica 9037
Ex	*Pilea trilobata* (Poiret) Wedd. 10082	
	Ex	20771 Mauritius 10082
R	*Pilea verbascifolia* (Poiret) Wedd.	
	R	20771 Mauritius 10082
V	*Pilea virgata* Wedd. 20883	
	V	20883 Jamaica 20883
R	*Pilea weddellii* F. & R. 20883	
	I	20883 Jamaica 20883
V	*Pilea wilsonii* Urb. 20883, 13336	
	V	13336 Jamaica (Portland) 20883
V	*Pilea wullschlaegelii* Urb. 20883, 13336	
	V	19890 Jamaica (Manchester) 20883
V	*Pilea yunckeri* Adams 20883, 13336	
	V	13336 Jamaica (Portland) 20883
V	*Pilea yunquensis* (Urban) Britt. & Wilson 20883, 8058	
	I	20883 Puerto Rico 20883
E	*Pipturus henryanus* F. Brown	
	E	French Polynesia - Marquesas Is
R	*Pouzolzia laevigata* (Poiret) Gaudich. 10082	
	R	14220 Réunion 14220
	R	20771 Mauritius 10082
E	*Procris boninensis* Tuy. 8038	
	E	18128 Japan - Ogasawara-shoto (Hahajima) 8038
V	*Procris insularis* H. Schroter 14296	
	V	19181 Seychelles (granitic) 14296
Ex/E	*Rousselia erratica* Standley & Steyerm. 9061	
	Ex/E	11967 Nicaragua 9061
R	*Urera acuminata* (Poiret) Decne. 10082	
	R	20771 Mauritius 10082
E	*Urera chlorocarpa* Urban 20883, 19002	
	I	20883 Puerto Rico 20883
R	*Urera expansa* (Sw.) Griseb. 20883	
	R	20883 Jamaica 20883
E	*Urera kaalae* Wawra 20850, 14209	
	E	20850 U.S. - Hawaii (O`ahu) 20850
R	*Urtica atrovirens* Req ex Loisel. ssp. *bianorii*	

	(Knoche) Font quer & Garc. *20727*	
R		Spain - Balearic Is.
E	*Urtica fernandeziana* (Rich.) H. Ross *19116*	
E	*19125* Chile - Juan Fernandez Is. *19116*	
E	*Urtica masafuerana* Philippi *19116*	
E	*19125* Chile - Juan Fernandez Is. *19116*	
R	*Urtica rupestris* Guss. *18264, 20171*	
R	*18264* Italy - Sicily *18264*	
R	*Urtica stachyoides* Webb & Berthel.	
R		Spain - Canary Is.

Vahliaceae

Number of genera:	1	
Number of species:	5	
Recorded threatened species:	1	(20%)

Africa to north-west India, Indochina.

R	*Vahlia capensis* (L. f.) Thunb. ssp. *machrantha*	
	(Klotzsch) Bridson *7749*	
R		Mozambique *7749*

Valerianaceae

Number of genera:	13	
Number of species:	300	
Recorded threatened species:	31	(10%)

Nearly cosmopolitan, especially North temperate regions and Andes.

R	*Centranthus kellereri* (Stoj. Stef. et Georg.) Stoj. et Stef. *19709*	
R	*19709* Bulgaria *19709*	
R	*Centranthus nevadensis* Boiss. *20171*	
R	*20664* Spain (Granada, Málaga, Cádiz) *20664*	
E	*Centranthus trinervis* (Viv.) Bég. *8000, 20171*	
E	*15080* France - Corsica *20528*	
E	*19174* Italy - Sardinia *19174*	
R	*Patrinia saniculaefolia* Hemsley ex Nakai *15957*	
R	*15923* Korea, South *15957*	
R	*Patrinia triloba* Miq. var. *kozushimensis* Honda *10573*	
R	*10573* Japan *10573*	
V	*Patrinia triloba* Miq. var. *takeuchiana* Ohwi *10573*	
V	*10573* Japan *10573*	
R	*Stangea henrici* Graebner *18200*	
R	*12468* Peru *18200*	
R	*Stangea rhizantha* (A.Gray) Killip *18200*	
R	*12468* Peru *18200*	
I	*Valeriana ajanensis* (Regel & Tiling) Komarov *5942*	
I	*5942* Russia (Far East) - Khabarovsk *5942*	
I	*Valeriana beddomei* C.B. Clarke	
I		India - Tamil Nadu
R	*Valeriana bertiscea* Pancic *20178, 20171*	
R	*20178* Albania *20178*	
R	*21091* Bosnia & Herzegovina *21091*	
R		Greece
R		(former) Yugoslavia
R	*Valeriana bolkarica* Contandr. ex Quezel *12840*	
R	*12840* Turkey *12840*	
R	*Valeriana celtica* L. ssp. *celtica* *20171*	
R		France

R		Italy
R	*18154* Switzerland *18154*	
R	*Valeriana celtica* ssp. *pennina* Vierh. *18154*	
R	*18154* Switzerland *18154*	
I	*Valeriana coleophylla* Diels *11351*	
I	*11351* Ecuador *11351*	
R	*Valeriana crinii* Orph. ex Boiss. *20178, 20171*	
R	*20178* Albania *20178*	
R		Greece *20178*
R	*Valeriana longiflora* Willk. *20171*	
R		Spain
R	*Valeriana olenaea* Boiss. & Heldr. *20171*	
R		Greece
R	*Valeriana oliganthe* Boiss. & Heldr. *12840*	
R	*12840* Turkey *12840*	
R	*Valeriana phitosiana* Quézel & Contandr. *20171*	
R		Greece
R	*Valeriana pinnatifida* Ruiz Lopez & Pavon *18200*	
R	*9446* Peru *18200*	
R	*Valeriana pratensis* Dierb. ex E.Walther, [non (Benth.) Benth. ex Steud.] *11986, 20171*	
R	*16360* Mexico *11986*	
R	*Valeriana speluncaria* Boiss. ssp. *glabriuscula* Contandr. ex Quezel *12840*	
R	*12840* Turkey *12840*	
R	*Valeriana texana* Steyermark *20850*	
V	*20850* U.S. - New Mexico *20850*	
V	*20850* U.S. - Texas *20850*	
I	*Valerianella affinis* Balf. f. *15534*	
I	*15534* Yemen - Socotra *15534*	
R	*Valerianella divaricata* Lange *20171*	
R		Spain
V	*Valerianella fusiformis* Pau *20171*	
V		Spain
R	*Valerianella leptocarpa* Pomel *10488*	
R	*14958* Algeria *10488*	
R	*Valerianella martinii* Loscos *20171*	
R	*20692* Spain (central and eastern) *20692*	
V	*Valerianella multidentata* Loscos & J.Pardo *20171*	
V		Spain
R	*Valerianella ozarkana* Dyal *20850*	
R	*20850* U.S. - Arkansas *20850*	
V	*20850* U.S. - Missouri *20850*	
I	*20850* U.S. - Oklahoma *20850*	
R	*Valerianella palmeri* Dyal *20850*	
R	*20850* U.S. - Arkansas *20850*	
E	*20850* U.S. - Oklahoma *20850*	
V	*Valerianella texana* Dyal *20850*	
V	*20850* U.S. - Texas *20850*	

Verbenaceae

Number of genera:	100	
Number of species:	2,600	
Recorded threatened species:	122	(4%)

Pantropical, with only a few species in temperate regions.

Ex/E	*Aegiphila caymanensis* Moldenke *19712*	
	Ex/E *19434* Cayman Is. (Grand Cayman) *19712*	
V	*Aegiphila foetida* Sw. *20883*	
V	*20883* Jamaica *20883*	

Magnoliopsida (dicots): Verbenaceae: *Aegiphila*

R **Aegiphila obtusa** Urb. *20883, 13336*
　　R　*13336* Jamaica (St. Catherine, Manchester) *20883*

R **Aegiphila oligoneura** Urb. *20883, 13336*
　　R　*13336* Jamaica (St. Elizabeth, Manchester) *20883*

I **Aegiphila plicata** Urb. *20883, 13336*
　　I　*13336* Jamaica *20883*

I **Aegiphila swartziana** Urb. *13336*
　　I　*19890* Jamaica *19890*

R **Aegiphila trifida** Sw. *20883*
　　R　*20883* Jamaica *20883*

V **Aegiphila uniflora** Urb. *20883, 13336*
　　V　*13336* Jamaica (Portland) *20883*

V **Callicarpa ampla** Schauer *20883, 10197*
　　V　*20883* Puerto Rico *20883*
　　I　*20883* USA - Virgin Is. *20883*

R **Callicarpa bracteata** Dop *6057*
　　I　*20985* Vietnam *6057*

E **Callicarpa crassinervis** Urban *5607*
　　E　*19105* Cuba (Guantanamo) *5607*

V **Callicarpa floccosa** Urban *5607*
　　V　*19105* Cuba (Santiago de Cuba) *5607*

R **Callicarpa glabra** H.J. Lam *19136*
　　R　*19136* Japan - Ogasawara-shoto *19136*

I **Callicarpa glandulosa** Fletcher *19120*
　　I　*19120* Thailand *19120*

R **Callicarpa hypoleucophylla** Lin & Wang *20854*
　　R　*20854* Taiwan *20854*

V **Callicarpa leonis** Mold. *5607*
　　V　*19105* Cuba (Holguin, Guantanamo) *5607*

E **Callicarpa nishimurae** Koidz. *8038*
　　E　*19134* Japan - Ogasawara-shoto (Chichijima; Anijima) *8038*

R **Callicarpa petelotii** Dop *6057*
　　R　　Vietnam *6057*

R **Callicarpa remotiflora** Lin & Wang *20511*
　　R　*20511* Taiwan *20511*

R **Callicarpa remotiserrulata** Hayata *20854*
　　R　*20854* Taiwan (Heng-ch'un) *20511*

I **Callicarpa reticulata** Sw. *20883, 13336*
　　I　*13336* Jamaica *20883*

I **Callicarpa rivularis** Merr. *13833*
　　I　*13833* Philippines (Palawan) *13833*

R **Callicarpa thozetii** Munir *20681*
　　R　*20681* Australia - Queensland *20681*

R **Callicarpa yakushimensis** Koidz. *10573*
　　R　*10573* Japan *10573*

I **Caryopteris mongholica** Bunge *5942*
　　I　*5942* Russia (Siberia) - Buryatiya (south of Lake Baikal) *5942*
　　V　*20756* China - Gansu (south-east) *20756*
　　V　*20756* China - Hubei (north) *20756*
　　V　*20756* China - Ningxia *20756*
　　V　*20756* China - Shaanxi (south) *20756*
　　V　*20756* China - Shanxi (east) *20756*

R **Caryopteris nepalensis** Moldenke *7731*
　　R　　Nepal (central & east) *7731*

E **Citharexylum ekmanii** Mold. *5607*
　　E　*19105* Cuba (Cienfuegos; Villa Clara) *5607*

V **Citharexylum sulcatum** Mold. var. *hirtellum* Mold. *19352*
　　V　*19352* Colombia *19352*

V **Citharexylum ternatum** Mold. *5607*
　　V　*19105* Cuba (Granma) *5607*

I **Clerodendrum chlorisepalum** Merr. ex Moldenke *19120*
　　I　*19120* Thailand *19120*

I **Clerodendrum galeatum** Balf. f. *15534*
　　I　*15534* Yemen - Socotra *15534*

R **Clerodendrum grayi** Munir *20681*
　　R　*20681* Australia - Queensland *20681*

R **Clerodendrum harmandianum** Dop *6057*
　　R　　Vietnam *6057*

R **Clerodendrum laciniatum** Balf.f. *10082*
　　R　*5852* Mauritius - Rodrigues *5852*

I **Clerodendrum lankawiense** King & Gamble var. *andamanense* Moldenke *7771*
　　I　　India - Andaman Is. (S. Andaman Is.) *7771*

I **Clerodendrum leucophloeum** Balf. f. *15534*
　　I　*15534* Yemen - Socotra *15534*

R **Clerodendrum molle** Kunth var. *glabrescens* Svenson *11117*
　　R　　Ecuador - Galapagos (Santa Cruz) *11117*

R **Clerodendrum nhatrangense** Dop *6057*
　　R　　Vietnam *6057*

I **Clerodendrum ridleyi** King & Gamble
　　I　*19209* Malaysia - Peninsular Malaysia (Perak, Selangor/Wilayah Persekutuan) *19209*

I **Clerodendrum sansibarense** Gürke *5926*
　　I　*5926* Tanzania (Zanzibar) *5926*

V **Coelocarpum haggierensis** Miller & Nyberg *15534*
　　V　*15534* Yemen - Socotra *15534*

R **Coelocarpum socotranum** Balf. f. *15534*
　　R　*15534* Yemen - Socotra *15534*

I **Congea hansenii** Moldenke *19120*
　　I　*19120* Thailand *19120*

E **Cornutia obovata** Urban *20883, 19706*
　　I　*20883* Puerto Rico *20883*

R **Cornutia thyrsoidea** Moldenke *20883*
　　R　*20883* Jamaica *20883*

Ex **Dicrastylis morrisonii** Munir *20681, 14223*
　　Ex　*20681* Australia - Western Australia *20681*

I **Duranta arida** Britton & P. Wilson *5607*
　　I　　Cuba (Guantanamo) *5607*

E **Duranta parviflora** Turcz. *5607*
　　E　*19105* Cuba (Santiago de Cuba) *5607*

R **Duranta stenostachya** Todaro *19001*
　　R　*19001* Dominica *19001*
　　R　*19001* Martinique (Massif de la Montagne Pelée above 600m) *19001*

I **Garrettia siamensis** Fletcher *19120*
　　I　*19120* Thailand (Doi Chiengdao) *19120*

V **Glandularia maritima** (Small) Small *20850*
　　V　*20850* U.S. - Florida *20850*

E **Glandularia tampensis** (Nash) Small *20850*
　　E　*20850* U.S. - Florida *20850*

R **Glossocarya crenata** Fletcher *19120*
　　R　*19120* Thailand *19120*

I	*Glossocarya longiflora* Fletcher *19120*		
	I	*19120* Thailand *19120*	
I	*Glossocarya siamensis* Craib *19120*		
	I	*19120* Thailand *19120*	
R	*Gmelina hainanensis* Oliver *17617*		
	V	*17617* China - Hainan Is. *11139*	
	R	Vietnam *6057*	
E	*Gmelina lignum-vitreum* Guillaumin *20893*		
	E	*20893* New Caledonia *20893*	
I	*Gmelina paniculata* Fletcher *19120*		
	I	*19120* Thailand *19120*	
I	*Gmelina tomentosa* Fletcher *19120*		
	I	*19120* Thailand *19120*	
E	*Holmskioldia gigas* Faden *20885*		
	Ex/E	*20057* Kenya (Mwarakaya) *20057*	
	E	*20885* Tanzania (Kilwa) *20900*	
I	*Hymenopyramis acuminata* Fletcher *19120*		
	I	*19120* Thailand *19120*	
R	*Lantana angustifolia* Mill. *20883*		
	R	*20883* Jamaica *20883*	
V	*Lantana depressa* Small *20850*		
	I	*20850* U.S. - Alabama *20850*	
	V	*20850* U.S. - Florida *20850*	
	I	*20850* U.S. - Georgia *20850*	
	I	*20850* U.S. - South Carolina *20850*	
E	*Lantana depressa* Small var. *depressa* *20850, 10260*		
	E	*20850* U.S. - Florida *20850*	
V	*Lantana depressa* Small var. *floridana* (Moldenke) R.W. Sanders *20850*		
	I	*20850* U.S. - Alabama *20850*	
	V	*20850* U.S. - Florida *20850*	
	I	*20850* U.S. - Georgia *20850*	
	I	*20850* U.S. - South Carolina *20850*	
E	*Lantana depressa* Small var. *sanibelensis* R.W. Sanders *20850*		
	E	*20850* U.S. - Florida *20850*	
	I	*20850* U.S. - Georgia *20850*	
E	*Lantana dwyeriana* Mold. *20883*		
	I	*20883* Mexico *20883*	
E	*Lantana glandulosissima* Mold. var. *grandis* Mold. *20883, 10747*		
	I	*20883* Panama *20883*	
R	*Lantana jamaicensis* Britton *20883*		
	R	*20883* Jamaica *20883*	
E	*Lippia acuminata* C. Wright *5607*		
	E	*19105* Cuba *5607*	
R	*Lippia herrerae* Mold. *18200*		
	R	*12468* Peru *12468*	
R	*Lippia rosmarinifolia* Andersson *11117*		
	R	Ecuador - Galapagos *11117*	
E	*Lippia salicifolia* Andersson *11117*		
	E	*14980* Ecuador - Galapagos *9389*	
V	*Nashia armata* (Urban) Mold. *5607*		
	V	*19105* Cuba (Santiago de Cuba) *5607*	
E	*Nashia cayensis* Britton *5607*		
	E	*19105* Cuba (Camaguey) *5607*	
I	*Nashia inaguensis* Millsp.		
	I	*4650* Bahamas *4650*	
E	*Nashia myrtifolia* (Griseb.) Mold.		

	E	*19105* Cuba *19105*	
V	*Nashia nipensis* (Urban) Mold. *5607*		
	V	*19105* Cuba (Holguin) *5607*	
R	*Nashia variifolia* (Urban) Mold. *5607*		
	R	*19105* Cuba *5607*	
V	*Newcastelia velutina* Munir *20681*		
	V	*20681* Australia - Queensland *20681*	
V	*Oxera cauliflora* Deplanche ex Dubard *20893*		
	V	*20893* New Caledonia *20893*	
R	*Oxera crassifolia* Guillaumin *20893*		
	R	New Caledonia *20893*	
V	*Oxera macrocalyx* Dubard *20893*		
	V	*20893* New Caledonia *20893*	
V	*Oxera nuda* Virot *20893*		
	V	*20893* New Caledonia *20893*	
V	*Paravitex siamica* Fletcher *19120*		
	V	*19120* Thailand *19120*	
E	*Parodianthus ilicifolius* (Moldenke) Tronc. *16336*		
	E	*16336* Argentina *16336*	
E	*Petrea morii* Mold. *20883, 10747*		
	I	*20883* Panama *20883*	
V	*Pityrodia augustensis* Munir *20681*		
	V	*20681* Australia - Western Australia *20681*	
R	*Pityrodia byrnesii* Munir *20681*		
	R	*20681* Australia - Northern Territory *20681*	
R	*Pityrodia gilruthiana* Munir *20681*		
	R	*20681* Australia - Northern Territory *20681*	
R	*Pityrodia lanceolata* Munir *20681*		
	R	*20681* Australia - Northern Territory *20681*	
R	*Pityrodia megalophylla* Munir *20681*		
	R	*20681* Australia - Northern Territory *20681*	
R	*Pityrodia puberula* Munir *20681*		
	R	*20681* Australia - Northern Territory *20681*	
E	*Pityrodia scabra* A.S.George *20681*		
	E	*20681* Australia - Western Australia *20681*	
R	*Pityrodia serrata* Munir *20681*		
	R	*20681* Australia - Northern Territory *20681*	
R	*Pityrodia spenceri* Munir *20681*		
	R	*20681* Australia - Northern Territory *20681*	
I	*Premna annulata* Fletcher *19120*		
	I	*19120* Thailand *19120*	
I	*Premna collinsae* Craib *19120*		
	I	*19120* Thailand *19120*	
V	*Premna grandifolia* A.D.J. Meeuse *7926*		
	V	*20887* Côte d'Ivoire *7926*	
I	*Premna maxima* T.C.E. Fr. *20556, 20057*		
	I	*20057* Kenya *20057*	
I	*Premna paucinervis* (C.B. Clarke) Gamble		
	I	India - Tamil Nadu (Coimbatore)	
I	*Premna purpurascens* Thwaites *8021*		
	I	*16162* Sri Lanka (Doluwakanda, Ambagamuwa) *8021*	
V	*Premna szemaoensis* Pei *17617*		
	V	*17617* China - Yunnan *11139*	
I	*Premna thwaitesii* Clarke *8021*		
	I	*16162* Sri Lanka (Madugoda, Kandy) *8021*	
Ex/E	*Priva portoricensis* Urban *20883, 14662*		
	I	*20883* Puerto Rico *20883*	

R **Pseudocarpidium shaferi** Britton *5607*
   R   *19105* Cuba (Guantanamo) *5607*

R **Rhaphithamnus venustus** (Phil.) Rob. *20883, 19116*
   V   *19125* Chile - Juan Fernandez Is. *19116*
   R   *20883* Chile *20883*

I **Sphenodesme odorata** Fletcher *19120*
   I   *19120* Thailand *19120*

I **Sphenodesme orbicularis** Fletcher *19120*
   I   *19120* Thailand *19120*

E **Stachytarpheta subincisa** Turcz. *5607*
   E   *19105* Cuba *5607*

E **Tectona philippinensis** Benth. & Hook.f. *10278*
   E   *15960* Philippines (Luzon) *20224*

V **Verbena californica** Moldenke *20850*
   V   *20850* U.S. - California *20850*

E **Verbena clavata** Ruiz Lopez & Pavon var. **casmensis** Mold. *18200*
   E   *9446* Peru *18200*

E **Verbena clemensiorum** Moldenke *20850*
   I   *20850* U.S. - California *20850*

V **Verbena grisea** Robinson & Greenman *11117*
   V   Ecuador - Galapagos (Pinzon) *11117*

R **Verbena plicata** Moldenke var. **degeneri** Moldenke *20850*
   R   *20850* U.S. - Texas *20850*

Ex/E **Verbena riparia** Raf. ex Small & Heller *20850*
   I   *20850* U.S. - Louisiana *20850*
   Ex/E *20850* U.S. - North Carolina *20850*
   I   *20850* U.S. - Virginia *20850*

R **Verbena sedula** Mold. var. **sedula** *11117*
   R   Ecuador - Galapagos (Santa Cruz) *11117*

V **Vitex acunae** Borh. & Muniz *5607*
   V   *19105* Cuba (Pinar del Rio) *5607*

V **Vitex clementis** Britton & P. Wilson *5607*
   V   *19105* Cuba (Granma; Santiago de Cuba) *5607*

E **Vitex evoluta** Däniker *20893*
   E   *20893* New Caledonia *20893*

V **Vitex floridula** Duchass. & Walp. *20883, 9006*
   I   *20883* Panama *20883*

V **Vitex keniensis** Turrill *20556, 20057*
   V   Kenya *20057*

V **Vitex praetervisa** Borh. *5607*
   V   *19105* Cuba (Granma) *5607*

I **Vitex wimberleyii** Kurz *7771*
   I   India - Andaman Is. (S. Andaman Is.) *7771*

R **Vitex zanzibarensis** Vatke *20057*
   R   *20057* Kenya (Gongoni; Kinondo) *20057*
   R   *20057* Tanzania *17435*

Violaceae

Number of genera: 16
Number of species: 800
Recorded threatened species: 110 (13%)

Cosmopolitan.

V **Allexis cauliflora** (Oliver) Pierre *6072*
   V   *20858* Tropical Africa (Guinea-wide) *20858*
   V   *20858* Ghana *6072*
   V   *20858* Nigeria *7848*

I **Anchietea frangulifolia** (Kunth) Melchior *19352*

   I   *19352* Colombia *19352*

E **Gloeospermum ferrugineostictum** A. Robyns *20883, 10747*
   I   *20883* Panama *20883*

E **Gloeospermum portobelense** A. Robyns *20883, 9006*
   I   *20883* Panama *20883*

I **Gloeospermum sclerophyllum** Cuatrec. *19352*
   I   *19352* Colombia *19352*

E **Hybanthus humilis** (Rose & Dowell) Standley *11121*
   E   *19804* Mexico *11121*

E **Hybanthus jefensis** Todzia *20883*
   I   *20883* Panama *20883*

E **Hybanthus longipes** (Dowell) Standley *11121*
   E   *19804* Mexico *11121*

I **Hybanthus ramosissimus** (Thwaites) Melchior *10252*
   I   *16162* Sri Lanka *10252*

I **Hybanthus travancoricus** (Beddome) Melchior
   I   India - Kerala
   I   India - Tamil Nadu

E **Hybanthus verticillatus** (Gray) Cory & Parks var. **platyphyllus** (Gray) Cory & Parks *20850*
   20850 U.S. - Texas *20850*

E **Isodendrion hosakae** St. John *20850, 14209*
   E   *20850* U.S. - Hawaii *20850*

E **Isodendrion laurifolium** Gray *20850, 14209*
   E   *20850* U.S. - Hawaii (O`ahu) *20850*

V **Isodendrion longifolium** Gray *20850, 14209*
   V   *20850* U.S. - Hawaii (Kaua`i & O`ahu) *20850*

E **Isodendrion pyrifolium** Gray *20850, 14209*
   E   *20850* U.S. - Hawaii *20850*

I **Leonia occidentalis** Cuatrec. *19352*
   I   *19352* Colombia *19352*

E **Melicytus latifolius** (Endl.) P. Green *11649*
   E   *11649* Australia - Norfolk Is. *11649*

V **Melicytus novae-zelandiae** (A. Cunn) P. Green ssp. **centurionis** P. Green
   V   *14225* Australia - NSW - Lord Howe Is. *14225*

R **Melicytus ramiflorus** J. & G. Forster ssp. **oblongifolius** (A. Cunn) P. Green *19108*
   R   *19108* Australia - Norfolk Is. *14288*

E **Rinorea antioquiensis** Smith & Fernández *20883*
   I   *20883* Colombia (Antioquía) *11995*

E **Rinorea bicornuta** Hekking *20883*
   I   *20883* Brazil *20883*
   ?   Brazil - Amazonas *11995*

E **Rinorea blakeana** Standl. *20883*
   I   *20883* Panama *20883*

E **Rinorea brachythrix** Blake *20883, 9006*
   I   *20883* Panama (Darién & San Blás) *11995*

R **Rinorea convallarioides** (Bakh.f.) Eyles var. **marsabitensis** Grey-Wilson *7959*
   R   *20057* Kenya *7959*

E **Rinorea cordata** Smith & Fernández *20883*
   I   *20883* Colombia (Santander) *11995*

R **Rinorea crenata** Blake *20883, 9037*
   I   *20883* Costa Rica *20883*
   I   *20883* Panama *20883*

E **Rinorea deflexa** (Bentham) Blake *20883*
   E   *20883* Ecuador (Esmeralda) *11995*

V   *Rinorea djalonensis* A. Chev. ex Hutch. & Dalz. *7926*
     V   Guinea *7926*

R   *Rinorea endotricha* Sandwith *20883*
     I   *20883* Guyana *20883*
     R   *20883* Venezuela (Bolívar) *11995*

R   *Rinorea haughtii* Smith & Fernández *20883*
     I   *20883* Colombia (Santander) *11995*

V   *Rinorea hirsuta* Hekking *20883*
     I   *20883* Panama (Dariéb) *11995*
     I   *20883* Colombia (Chocó) *11995*

V   *Rinorea hymenosepala* Blake *20883*
     V   *20883* Colombia (Antioquía & César) *11995*

E   *Rinorea laurifolia* Smith & Fernández *20883*
     I   *20883* Colombia (Santander) *11995*

E   *Rinorea longistipulata* Hekking *20883*
     I   *20883* Brazil *20883*
     ?   Brazil - Acre *11995*

E   *Rinorea marginata* (Triana & Planchon) Rusby ex
       Johnston *20883*
     E   *20883* Colombia (Tolimá) *11995*

E   *Rinorea maximiliani* (Eichler in Martius)
       Kuntze *20883*
     I   *20883* Brazil *20883*
     ?   Brazil - Espirito Santo *11995*

E   *Rinorea oraria* Steyermark & Fernández *20883*
     I   *20883* Venezuela (Distrito Federal) *11995*

E   *Rinorea pectino-squamata* Hekking *20883*
     E   *20883* French Guiana (north) *11995*

R   *Rinorea quangtriensis* Gagnep. *6057*
     R   Vietnam *6057*

V   *Rinorea ramiziana* Glaziou ex Hekking *20883*
     I   *20883* Brazil *20883*
     ?   Brazil - Espirito Santo *11995*
     ?   Brazil - Rio de Janeiro *11995*

R   *Rinorea ulmifolia* (Kunth in Humboldt, Bonpland & Kunth)
       Kuntze *20883*
     R   *20883* Colombia (Río Magdalena valley) *11995*

E   *Rinorea uxpanapana* Wendt *20883, 10131*
     I   *20883* Mexico *20883*
     I   *21017* Mexico - Veracruz *11995*

E   *Rinorea villosiflora* Hekking *20883*
     E   *20883* Brazil *20883*
     ?   Brazil - Maranhao *11995*

R   *Viola alliariaefolia* Nakai *10572*
     R   *10572* Japan *10572*

V   *Viola anagae* Gilli *20750*
     V   *20750* Spain - Canary Is. *20750*

V   *Viola athois* W.Becker *8000, 20171*
     V   Greece (northern - Athos) *8000*

R   *Viola beckiana* Fiala *20178, 20171*
     R   *20178* Albania *20178*
     V   *21091* Bosnia & Herzegovina *21091*
     R   (former) Yugoslavia *20178*

R   *Viola biflora* L. ssp. *carlottae* Calder &
       Taylor *20850, 10701*
     R   *20850* Canada - British Columbia *20850*
     I   *20850* U.S. - Alaska *20850*

R   *Viola brachyphylla* W. Becker *20171*
     R   (former) Yugoslavia

R   *Viola brevistipulata* W. Becker var. *hidakana*
       Nakai *10572*

R   *10572* Japan *10572*

R   *Viola brittoniana* Pollard var. *pectinata* (Bickn.)
       Alexander *20850*
     I   *20850* U.S. - Connecticut *20850*
     I   *20850* U.S. - Maryland *20850*
     E   *20850* U.S. - Massachusetts *20850*
     I   *20850* U.S. - New Jersey *20850*
     I   *20850* U.S. - New York *20850*
     I   *20850* U.S. - North Carolina *20850*
     I   *20850* U.S. - Virginia *20850*

V   *Viola californica* M.S. Baker *20850*
     I   *20850* U.S. - California *20850*

R   *Viola cazorlensis* Gand. *8000, 20171*
     R   Spain (south-east) *8000*

R   *Viola chamissoniana* Gingins *20850, 14209*
     I   *14209* U.S. - Hawaii (O`ahu) *20850*

E   *Viola chamissoniana* Gingens ssp.
       chamissoniana *20850*
     E   *20850* U.S. - Hawaii *20850*

V   *Viola charlestonensis* M.S. Baker & J.C. Clausen ex
       Clokey *20850*
     I   *20850* U.S. - Arizona *20850*
     V   *20850* U.S. - Nevada *20850*
     V   *20850* U.S. - Utah *20850*

E   *Viola cheiranthifolia* Humb. & Bonpl. *19174*
     E   *20750* Spain - Canary Is. *19174*

R   *Viola cilicica* Contandr. ex Quezel *12840*
     R   *12840* Turkey *12840*

I   *Viola collina* Besser ssp. *porphyrea* (Uechtritz) W.
       Becker *19616*
     I   *19616* Poland (south) *19616*

R   *Viola comollia* Massara *18264, 20171*
     R   *18264* Italy (Lombardy) *18264*

R   *Viola cornuta* ssp. *montcaunica* *15846*
     R   *15846* Spain *15846*

R   *Viola crassifolia* Fenzl *12840*
     R   *12840* Turkey *12840*

R   *Viola cretica* Boiss. & Heldr. *20171*
     R   *20731* Greece - Crete *20731*

Ex   *Viola cryana* Gillot *17781, 20171*
     Ex   *20528* France (Yonne) *20528*

I   *Viola cuatrecasasii* Smith & Fernandez *19352*
     I   *19352* Colombia *19352*

I   *Viola dacica* Borbás *8000, 20171*
     I   *19321* Slovakia *19321*

R   *Viola delphinantha* Boiss. *5204, 20171*
     R   *5204* Bulgaria (south-west) *5204*
     V   Greece (northern) *8000*

R   *Viola dichroa* Boiss. & Huet *12840*
     R   *12840* Turkey *12840*

R   *Viola dubyana* Burnat ex Gremli *20171*
     R   Italy

R   *Viola elegantula* Schott *20178, 20171*
     R   *20178* Albania *20178*
     V   *21091* Bosnia & Herzegovina *21091*
     R   (former) Yugoslavia *20178*

R   *Viola eximia* Formánek *20171*
     R   Greece
     R   (former) Yugoslavia

V   *Viola flettii* Piper *20850*
     I   *20850* U.S. - Washington *20850*

E	*Viola guadalupensis* A. Powell & B. Wauer *20850*	
	E	*20850* U.S. - Texas *20850*
R	*Viola hederacea* Labill. ssp. *curtisiae* L.G.Adams *20681*	
	R	*20681* Australia - Tasmania *20681*
R	*Viola heldreichiana* Boiss. *20171*	
	R	Greece
E	*Viola helenae* Forbes & Lydgate *20850*	
	E	*20850* U.S. - Hawaii *20850*
E	*Viola helenae* C. Forbes & Lydgate var. *helena 14209*	
	E	*14209* U.S. - Hawaii (Kaua`i) *14209*
I	*Viola himalayensis* W. Becker	
	I	India - Jammu & Kashmir
V	*Viola hispida* Lam. *8000, 20171*	
	V	*20528* France (north-west, near Rouen) *8000*
I	*Viola hissarica* Juz. *5942*	
	I	*5942* Tajikistan *5942*
R	*Viola improcera* L.G.Adams *20681*	
	I	*20681* Australia - Capital Territory *20681*
	I	*20681* Australia - New South Wales *20681*
	I	*20681* Australia - Victoria *20681*
I	*Viola incisa* Turcz. *5942*	
	I	*5942* Russia (Siberia) - Altai (south) *5942*
	I	*5942* Russia (Siberia) - Irkutsk (L. Baikal) *5942*
	I	*5942* Russia (Siberia) - Krasnoyarsk *5942*
R	*Viola isaurica* Contandr. ex Quezel *12840*	
	R	*12840* Turkey *12840*
R	*Viola jaubertiana* Marès & Vigin. *8000, 20171*	
	R	*20874* Spain - Balearic Is. (Mallorca) *8000*
R	*Viola jooi* Janka *17823, 20171*	
	R	*19949* Romania *19840*
	E	*20655* Ukraine (Carpathian Mts.) *20649*
R	*Viola kauaensis* Gray *20850, 14209*	
	I	*20850* U.S. - Hawaii (O`ahu) *20850*
R	*Viola kitamiana* Nakai *10572*	
	R	*10572* Japan *10572*
R	*Viola kosaninii* (Degen) Hayek *20178, 20171*	
	Ex	*20178* Albania *20178*
	R	(former) Yugoslavia
I	*Viola kunawarensis* Royle	
	I	India (NW Himalaya)
E	*Viola lanaiensis* Becker *20850, 14209*	
	E	*20850* U.S. - Hawaii (Lana`i) *20850*
V	*Viola lanceolata* L. ssp. *occidentalis* (Gray) Russell *20850*	
	V	*20850* U.S. - California *20850*
	V	*20850* U.S. - Oregon *20850*
I	*Viola lutea* Huds. ssp. *sudetica* (Willd.) W. Becker *8000, 20171*	
	I	*19321* Slovakia *19321*
V	*Viola maccabeana* M.S. Baker *20850, 10701*	
	V	*20850* Canada - British Columbia *20850*
R	*Viola magellensis* Porta & Rigo ex Strobl *18264, 20171*	
	R	*18264* Italy (Abruzzi) *18264*
E	*Viola oahuensis* Forbes *20850, 14209*	
	E	*20850* U.S. - Hawaii (Kaua`i) *20850*
V	*Viola oreades* M.Bieb. *8000, 20171*	

	V	*20655* Ukraine - Crimea *8000*
V	*Viola palmensis* Webb & Berthel. *20750*	
	V	*20750* Spain - Canary Is. *20750*
V	*Viola paradoxa* Lowe *17891*	
	V	Portugal - Madeira *17891*
R	*Viola perinensis* W. Becker *5204, 20171*	
	R	*5204* Bulgaria (south-west) *5204*
	R	Greece
E	*Viola pinetorum* Greene ssp. *grisea* (Jepson) R.J. Little *20850*	
	E	*20850* U.S. - California *20850*
Ex/E	*Viola plantaginea* Webb ex Christ *20216*	
	Ex/E	*20216* Spain - Canary Is. (Gomera) *20216*
V	*Viola praemorsa* Dougl. ex Lindl. ssp. *flavovirens* (Pollard) Fabijan *20850*	
	I	*20850* U.S. - Idaho *20850*
	I	*20850* U.S. - Montana *20850*
	I	*20850* U.S. - Oregon *20850*
	I	*20850* U.S. - Utah *20850*
	I	*20850* U.S. - Washington *20850*
	I	*20850* U.S. - Wyoming *20850*
R	*Viola praemorsa* Dougl. ex Lindl. ssp. *praemorsa 20850, 14414*	
	V	*20850* Canada - British Columbia *20850*
	I	*20850* U.S. - California *20850*
	I	*20850* U.S. - Oregon *20850*
	I	*20850* U.S. - Washington *20850*
R	*Viola sachalinensis* H. Boissieu var. *alpina* Hara *10572*	
	R	*10572* Japan *10572*
R	*Viola sandrasea* Melchior *12840*	
	R	*12840* Turkey *12840*
R	*Viola speciosa* Pant. *5204, 20171*	
	R	*20178* Albania *20178*
	R	*5204* Bulgaria (south-west) *5204*
	R	(former) Yugoslavia
R	*Viola stojanowii* W.Becker *5204, 20171*	
	R	*5204* Bulgaria (south-west) *5204*
	R	Greece
E	*Viola stolonifera* Rodr. *20171*	
	E	Spain - Balearic Is.
R	*Viola stris-notata* (J. Wagner) Merxm. & Lippert	
	R	Greece
V	*Viola tomentosa* M.S. Baker & J.C. Clausen *20850*	
	V	*20850* U.S. - California *20850*
R	*Viola verecunda* A.Gray var. *yakusimana* (Nakai) Ohwi *10572*	
	R	*10572* Japan *10572*
I	*Viola wailenalenae* (Rock) Skottsb. *14209*	
	I	U.S. - Hawaii
R	*Viola yazawana* Makino *10572*	
	R	*10572* Japan *10572*
R	*Viola yubariana* Nakai *10572*	
	R	*10572* Japan *10572*

Viscaceae

Number of genera:	7-8
Number of species:	350
Recorded threatened species:	39 (11%)

Cosmopolitan, especially tropical.

V	*Arceuthobium microcarpum* (Engelm.) Hawksworth &

Wiens *20850*
- I   *20850*   U.S. - Arizona *20850*
- I   *20850*   U.S. - New Mexico *20850*

E   *Dendrophthora amoebandra* C. Wright *5607*
- E   *19105*   Cuba (Pinar del Rio) *5607*

R   *Dendrophthora densifrons* (Ule) Kuijt *21271*
- R   *21270*   Venezuela *21270*

E   *Dendrophthora guatemalensis* Standley *9004*
- E   *9815*   Guatemala *9004*

I   *Dendrophthora lanceifolia* Urban *5607*
- I   *19105*   Cuba (Santiago de Cuba) *5607*

V   *Dendrophthora mancinellae* (C. Wright) Eichl. *5607*
- V   *19105*   Cuba (Pinar del Rio) *5607*

E   *Dendrophthora mexicana* Kuijt *9815*
- E   *9815*   Mexico *9815*

E   *Dendrophthora nuda* Proctor *20883, 13336*
- E   *19890*   Jamaica (St. Elizabeth) *20883*

V   *Dendrophthora panamensis* Kuijt *20883, 9816*
- V   *16317*   Panama *20883*

E   *Dendrophthora picotensis* Urban *5607*
- E   *19105*   Cuba (Santiago de Cuba) *5607*

E   *Dendrophthora sessilifolia* (Griseb.) Krug & Urban *5607*
- E   *19105*   Cuba (Pinar del Rio) *5607*

Ex   *Dendrophthora terminalis* Kuijt *9037*
- Ex   *9815*   Costa Rica *9037*

E   *Ginalloa andamanica* Kurz *14782*
- E   *14782*   India - Andaman Is. (South) *7771*

I   *Ginalloa spathulifolia* (Thwaites) Oliver ex Hook.f. *10252*
- I   *16162*   Sri Lanka *10252*

E   *Korthalsella degeneri* Danser *20850, 14209*
- E   *20850*   U.S. - Hawaii (O`ahu) *20850*

R   *Korthalsella mumfordii* F. Brown
- R   French Polynesia - Marquesas Is

E   *Korthalsella opuntia* (Thunb.) Merrill var. *bojeri* (Van Tieghem) Danser *10082*
- E   *14220*   Réunion *5852*
- E   *20771*   Mauritius *5852*
- Ex   *5852*   Mauritius - Rodrigues (Riviere Baleine) *10936*

I   *Notothixos floccosus* (Thwaites) Oliver *10252*
- I   *16162*   Sri Lanka *10252*

I   *Phoradendron aguilarii* Standley & Steyerm. *9004*
- I   *9815*   Guatemala *9004*

V   *Phoradendron albovaginatum* Urb. *20883, 13336*
- V   *13336*   Jamaica (St. Catherine) *20883*

R   *Phoradendron anceps* (Spreng.) Krug & Urb. *13336*
- R   *19890*   Dominican Republic *19890*
- R   *19890*   Haiti *19890*
- V   *13336*   Jamaica (St. Thomas) *13336*

I   *Phoradendron aurantiacum* Trel. *9004*
- I   *9815*   Guatemala *9004*

E   *Phoradendron campbellii* Krug. & Urb. *20883*
- E   *20883*   Jamaica *20883*

R   *Phoradendron crenulatum* Urb. *20883*
- R   *20883*   Jamaica *20883*

R   *Phoradendron galeottii* Trel. *9661*
- R   *19755*   Mexico *9661*

V   *Phoradendron hawksworthii* (Wiens) Wiens *20850*

I   *20850*   U.S. - Texas *20850*

I   *Phoradendron herminieri* Trel. *10199*
- I   Dominica *10199*

I   *Phoradendron hexastichum* (DC.) Griseb. *10199*
- I   Dominica *10199*

I   *Phoradendron heydeanum* Trel. *9004*
- I   *9815*   Guatemala *9004*

I   *Phoradendron huehuetecum* Standley & Steyerm. *9004*
- I   *9815*   Guatemala *9004*

I   *Phoradendron lapatanum* Trel. *5607*
- I   *19105*   Cuba (Matanzas) *5607*

I   *Phoradendron libertadanum* Trel. *9004*
- I   *9815*   Guatemala *9004*

I   *Phoradendron rondeletiae* Trel. *9004*
- I   *9815*   Guatemala *9004*

V   *Phoradendron solandrae* Proctor *20883, 13336*
- V   *13336*   Jamaica (Clarendon, Manchester) *20883*

I   *Phoradendron treleaseanum* Standley & Steyerm. *9004*
- I   *9815*   Guatemala *9004*

I   *Phoradendron uspantanum* Trel. *9004*
- I   *9815*   Guatemala *9004*

I   *Phoradendron vulcanicum* Trel. *9004*
- I   *9815*   Guatemala *9004*

E   *Phoradendron woodsonii* Trel. *20883, 9006*
- V   *9815*   Panama *20883*

R   *Viscum congolense* De Wild. & T. Durand var. *chevalieri* Balle
- R   Côte d'Ivoire

I   *Viscum mysorense* Gamble *14782*
- I   *14782*   India - Karnataka *14782*

Vitaceae

Number of genera:	11
Number of species:	700
Recorded threatened species:	36 (5%)

Tropical and subtropical; a few in temperate regions.

I   *Ampelocissus alexandri* Urb. *20883, 13336*
- I   *13336*   Jamaica (St. Ann) *20883*

I   *Ampelocissus arnottiana* Planchon *10178*
- I   India - Karnataka (South Canara)
- E   India - Kerala (Quilon District) *10178*
- I   India - Tamil Nadu (Tirunelveli)

I   *Ampelocissus eriocladus* (Wight & Arn.) Planchon
- I   India - Tamil Nadu (Tirunelveli Hills)

E   *Ampelocissus floccosa* (Ridley) Galet *12921*
- E   Malaysia - Peninsular Malaysia (G. Pulai & Jeram Toi) *12921*

R   *Cayratia pedata* (Lam.) Juss. ex Gagnepain var. *glabra* Gamble *13883*
- R   *13883*   India - Tamil Nadu (Nilgiris) *13883*

V   *Cayratia roxburghii* (Wight & Arn.) Gagnepain *11494*
- V   *11494*   India - Kerala (Trivandrum & Quilon Dist.) *11494*
- V   *11494*   India - Tamil Nadu (Tirunelveli District) *11494*

V   *Cissus corallicola* Urban *5607*
- V   *19105*   Cuba (Santiago de Cuba) *5607*

I   *Cissus dinklagei* Gilg & Brandt var. *pilosa* Descoings

I		Gabon
R	*Cissus gambiana* Descoings *8003*	
R		Senegal (Kedougou) *8003*
R	*Cissus hamaderohensis* A.R. Smith *15534*	
R		*15534* Yemen - Socotra *15534*
R	*Cissus kouandeensis* A. Chev. *7926*	
R		Benin (Kouande) *7926*
R	*Cissus kouilouensis* Desc.	
R		Congo *11793*
R	*Cissus lanyuensis* (Chang) F.Y.Lu *20511*	
R		*20511* Taiwan *20511*
E	*Cissus neei* Croat *20883, 10123*	
I		*20883* Panama *20883*
R	*Cissus paniculata* (Balf. f.) Planchon *15534*	
R		*15534* Yemen - Socotra *15534*
R	*Cissus prunifera* Descoings	
R		Gabon
V	*Cissus rupicola* Urban *5607*	
V		*19105* Cuba (Pinar del Rio) *5607*
E	*Cissus spectabilis* (Kurz) Planchon *14782*	
E		*14782* India - Sikkim *14782*
E		*14782* India - West Bengal *14782*
I	*Cissus touraensis* A. Chev. *7926*	
I		Côte d'Ivoire *7926*
I	*Cyphostemma allophylloides* (Gilg & Brandt) Desc. *5926*	
I		*5926* Tanzania (Usambara mountains) *5926*
R	*Cyphostemma amplexum* (Baker) Descoings *7749*	
R		Mozambique *7749*
I	*Cyphostemma braunii* (Gilg & Brandt) Desc. *5926*	
I		*5926* Tanzania (Usambara mountains) *5926*
E	*Cyphostemma burgeri* Vollesen *19704*	
E		*19704* Ethiopia (Harerge) *19704*
R	*Cyphostemma jiguu* Verdc. *20057*	
R		*20057* Kenya *20057*
I	*Cyphostemma laza* Descoings var. *laza* *10368*	
I		Madagascar
I	*Cyphostemma laza* Descoings var. *parviflora* Descoings *10368*	
I		Madagascar
R	*Cyphostemma mappia* (Lam.) Descoings *10082*	
R		*20771* Mauritius *10082*
I	*Cyphostemma milleri* Wild & Drummond *7749*	
I		Zimbabwe *7749*
I	*Cyphostemma njegerre* (Gilg & Strauss) Desc. *5926*	
I		*5926* Tanzania (Usambara mountains) *5926*
R	*Cyphostemma pannosum* Vollesen *19704*	
R		*19704* Ethiopia (Welega, Ilubabor, Gamo Gofa.) *19704*
I	*Cyphostemma ukerewense* (Gilg) Descoings var. *gabonicum* Descoings	
I		Gabon
E	*Pterisanthes grandis* Ridley *12544*	
E		Malaysia - Sabah (Trus Madi) *12544*
E	*Pterisanthes pulchra* Ridley *11232*	
E		Malaysia - Peninsular Malaysia *11232*
R	*Tetrastigma alatum* Li *20511*	
R		*20511* Taiwan *20511*

I	*Tetrastigma andamanicum* (King) Susseng. *7771*	
I		India - Andaman Is. *7771*
R	*Tetrastigma touranense* Gagnepain *6057*	
R		Vietnam *6057*
V	*Vitis shuttleworthii* House *20850*	
I		*20850* U.S. - Florida *20850*

Vochysiaceae

Number of genera: 7
Number of species: 200
Recorded threatened species: 3 (1%)

Mostly tropical America, one species in Africa.

V	*Callisthene hassleri* Briq. *20999, 20883*	
E		*20883* Paraguay *20883*
I	*Vochysia duquei* Pilger *19352*	
I		*19352* Colombia *19352*
E	*Vochysia oppugnata* (Vell.) Warm. *2359*	
E		*2359* Brazil - Rio de Janeiro *2359*

Winteraceae

Number of genera: 9
Number of species: 100
Recorded threatened species: 11 (11%)

Primarily islands of southwestern Pacific.

R	*Bubbia howeana* (F. Muell.) Tieghem	
R		*14225* Australia - NSW - Lord Howe Is. *14225*
E	*Drimys brasiliensis* Miers *16336*	
E		*16336* Argentina *16336*
E		*20176* Argentina - Misiones *20176*
V	*Tasmannia glaucifolia* J.B.Williams *20681*	
V		*20681* Australia - Northern Territory *20681*
V	*Tasmannia purpurascens* (Vick.) A.C.Smith *20681*	
V		*20681* Australia - New South Wales *20681*
R	*Tasmannia vickeriana* (A.C.Smith) A.C.Smith *20681*	
R		*20681* Australia - Victoria *20681*
R	*Tasmannia xerophila* (P.Parm.) M.Gray ssp. *robusta* Raleigh *20681*	
R		*20681* Australia - Victoria *20681*
V	*Zygogynum cristatum* Vink *20893*	
V		*20893* New Caledonia *20893*
E	*Zygogynum oligostigma* Vink *20893*	
V		*20893* New Caledonia *20893*
R	*Zygogynum queenslandianum* (Vink) Vink ssp. *australe* (Vink) Vink *20681*	
R		*20681* Australia - Queensland *20681*
R	*Zygogynum queenslandianum* (Vink) Vink ssp. *queenslandianum* *20681*	
R		*20681* Australia - Queensland *20681*
R	*Zygogynum semecarpoides* (F.Muell.) Vink var. *whiteanum* (A.C.Smith) Vink *20681*	
R		*20681* Australia - Queensland *20681*
V	*Zygogynum tanyostigma* Vink *20893*	
V		*20893* New Caledonia *20893*

Zygophyllaceae

Number of genera:	30	
Number of species:	250	
Recorded threatened species:	13	(5%)

Mostly arid tropical and subtropical, sometimes in saline habitats.

R   *Bulnesia arborea* Engl. *20883, 13928*
     I   *20883* Colombia *20883*
     I   *20883* Venezuela *20883*

R   *Fagonia kassasii* Hadidi
     R   Egypt

R   *Fagonia malvana* Maire & Weiller
     R   Morocco

Ex   *Fagonia taeckholmiana* Hadidi *16168*
     Ex   *16168* Egypt (Heliopolis desert, nr Cairo)
              16168

R   *Fagonia thebaica* Boiss.
     R   Egypt
     R   Libya

I   *Guaiacum coulteri* Gray *9019*
     I   *19848* Mexico *19848*
     V   *16360* Mexico - Jalisco *9019*

E   *Kallstroemia perennans* B.L. Turner *20850*
     E   *20850* U.S. - Texas *20850*

E   *Metharme lanata* Philippi *15088*
     E   *13875* Chile *13875*

R   *Pintoa chilensis* Gay *13875*
     R   *13875* Chile *13875*

V   *Porlieria chilensis* I.M. Johnston *15088*
     V   *13875* Chile *13875*

R   *Tetraena mongolica* Maxim. *17617*
     R   *17617* China - Nei Monggol Zizhiqu *11139*

R   *Zygophyllum darvasicum* A. Boriss.
     R   former USSR *6930*

R   *Zygophyllum hybridum* Tate *20681*
     R   *20681* Australia - South Australia *20681*

R   *Zygophyllum kaschgaricum* A. Boriss.
     R   former USSR *6930*

R   *Zygophyllum teretifolium* Schltr. *20604*
     R   *20604* South Africa - Cape Province *20604*

Liliopsida (monocots)

Agavaceae

Number of genera:	18	
Number of species:	350-410	
Recorded threatened species:	68	(17%)

Warm, mostly arid regions of New and Old Worlds; a few in distinctly temperate climates.

E   *Agave acicularis* Trel. *11840*
     E   *19105* Cuba (Cienfuegos) *11840*

I   *Agave acklinicola* Trel.
     I   *4650* Bahamas *19889*

R   *Agave angustifolia* Haw. var. *nivea* (Trel.)
        Gentry *19889*
     R   *19753* Guatemala *19889*

E   I   *Agave arizonica* Gentry & J.H. Weber *20850, 11055*
     E   *20850* U.S. - Arizona (Tonto National Forest)
              20850

V   *Agave bracteosa* Watson *19848*
     V   *19848* Mexico - Nuevo Leon *19889*

I   *Agave cacozela* Trel.
     I   *4650* Bahamas *19889*

V   *Agave chrysantha* Peebles *20850*
     I   *20850* U.S. - Arizona *20850*

R   *Agave congesta* H.S. Gentry *19788*
     R   *19850* Mexico - Chiapas *19788*

V   *Agave dasylirioides* Jacobi & Bouche *19850*
     V   *19850* Mexico - Morelos *19889*

V   *Agave eggersiana* Trel. *20883, 15106*
     I   *20883* USA - Virgin Is. (St Croix, St Thomas)
              20883

V   *Agave glomeruliflora* (Engelm.) Berger *20883, 20850, 19889*
     V   *20850* U.S. - Texas *20850*
     E   *20883* Mexico *20883*
     ?   Mexico - Coahuila *19889*

E   *Agave grisea* Trel. *11840*
     E   *19105* Cuba (Cienfuegos) *11840*

V   *Agave guiengola* H.S. Gentry *9079*
     V   *19848* Mexico - Oaxaca *19889*

R   *Agave harrisii* Trelease *20883*
     R   *20883* Jamaica *20883*

V   *Agave impressa* H.S. Gentry *19850*
     V   *19848* Mexico - Sinaloa *19889*

I   *Agave indagatorum* Trel.
     I   *4650* Bahamas *19889*

E   *Agave intermixta* Trel. *5642*
     E   Dominican Republic (Santiago) *19889*

R   *Agave kewensis* Jacobi *19788*
     R   *19850* Mexico - Chiapas *19788*

R   *Agave lagunae* Trel. *9004*
     R   *19753* Guatemala *9004*

R   *Agave longipes* Trelease *20883, 13336*
     R   *13336* Jamaica *20883*

E   *Agave lurida* Ait. *19850*
     E   *19848* Mexico - Oaxaca *19889*

I   *Agave millspaughii* Trel.
     I   *4650* Bahamas *19889*

V   *Agave murpheyi* F. Gibson *20883, 20850, 19889*
     V   *20850* U.S. - Arizona *20850*
     E   *20883* Mexico *20883*

I   *Agave nashii* Trel.
     I   *4650* Bahamas *19889*

V   *Agave neglecta* Small *20850, 19889*
     I   *20850* U.S. - Florida *20850*

E   *Agave nizandensis* Cutak *19850*
     E   *19848* Mexico - Oaxaca *19889*

E   *Agave papyrocarpa* Trel. *11840*
     E   *19105* Cuba (Isla de la Juventud) *11840*

R   *Agave parrasana* Berger *19889*
     R   *19848* Mexico - Coahuila *19889*

R   *Agave parviflora* Torr. *20883, 20850*
     V   *20850* U.S. - Arizona *20850*
     I   *20883* Mexico *20883*

V   I   *Agave parviflora* Torr. ssp. *flexiflora* H.S.
        Gentry *19889*
     V   *19850* Mexico - Sonora *19889*

R   *Agave peacockii* Croucher *19850*
     R   *19848* Mexico - Puebla (Tehuacán) *19889*

E   *Agave schottii* Engelm. var. *treleasei* (Toumey)
     Kearney & Peebles *20850, 19889*
     E   *20850* U.S. - Arizona *20850*

R   *Agave shawii* Engelm. *20850*
     E   *20850* U.S. - California *20850*

R   *Agave tecta* Trel. *9004*
     R   *19753* Guatemala *9004*

R   *Agave thomasae* Trel. *9004*
     R   *19753* Guatemala *9004*

R   *Agave titanota* H.S. Gentry *19850*
     R   *19850* Mexico - Oaxaca *19889*

R   *Agave utahensis* Engelm. *20850*
     R   *20850* U.S. - Arizona *20850*
     V   *20850* U.S. - California *20850*
     R   *20850* U.S. - Nevada *20850*
     V   *20850* U.S. - Utah *20850*

V   *Agave utahensis* Engelm. var. *eborispina* (Hester)
     Breitung *20850*
     V   *20850* U.S. - California *20850*
     V   *20850* U.S. - Nevada *20850*

R   *Agave utahensis* Engelm. var. *nevadensis* Engelm. ex
     Greenman & Roush *20850*
     R   *20850* U.S. - California *20850*
     R   *20850* U.S. - Nevada *20850*

E   II   *Agave victoriae-reginae* T. Moore *9019*
     E   *19848* Mexico - Coahuila *19889*
     E   *19848* Mexico - Nuevo Leon *19889*

R   *Agave vizcainoensis* H.S. Gentry *19889*
     R   *19848* Mexico - Baja California Sur *19889*

E   *Agave wercklei* Weber ex Werckle *19788*
     E   *9426* Costa Rica *9037*

R   *Beschorneria albiflora* Matuda *9054*
     R   *19850* Mexico *9054*

R   *Beschorneria calcicola* A. Garcia-Mendoza *19850*
     R   *19850* Mexico *19850*

R   *Beschorneria wrightii* Hook. f. *19850*
     R   *19850* Mexico *19850*

R   *Cordyline congesta* (Sweet) Steudel *20681*
     I   *20681* Australia - New South Wales *20681*
     I   *20681* Australia - Queensland *20681*

R   *Cordyline obtecta* Baker *19108*
     R   *19108* Australia - Norfolk Is. *14288*

V   *Furcraea bedinghausii* K. Koch *9055*
     V   *19850* Mexico *9055*

I   *Furcraea macdougallii* Matuda *19850*
     I   *19850* Mexico *19850*

R   *Furcraea stratiotes* Boye Petersen *19788*
     R   *16826* Nicaragua *19788*

R   *Hesperaloe funifera* (K. Koch) Trel. *20850*
     E   *20850* U.S. - Texas *20850*

R   *Manfreda guerrerensis* Matuda *19850*
     R   *19850* Mexico *19850*

V   *Manfreda longiflora* (Rose) Verhoek-Williams *20850*
     V   *20850* U.S. - Texas *20850*
     V   *19850* Mexico *19850*

V   *Manfreda nanchititlensis* Matuda *9054*
     V   *19850* Mexico *9054*

R   *Manfreda planifolia* (Watson) Rose *19850*
     R   *19850* Mexico *19850*

R   *Manfreda potosina* (Rob. & Greenman) Rose *19850*
     R   *19850* Mexico *19850*

R   *Polianthes densiflora* (B.L. Robinson & Fern.)
     Shiners *19850*
     R   *19850* Mexico *19850*

R   *Polianthes howardii* S. Verhoek *19850*
     R   *19850* Mexico *19850*

R   *Polianthes longiflora* Rose *19850*
     R   *19850* Mexico *19850*

R   *Polianthes palustris* Rose *19850*
     R   *19850* Mexico *19850*

R   *Polianthes platyphylla* Rose *19850*
     R   *19850* Mexico *19850*

E   *Yucca angustissima* (Welsh) Reveal var. *toftiae*
     (Welsh) Reveal *20850*
     E   *20850* U.S. - Utah *20850*

R   *Yucca endlichiana* Trel. *9055*
     R   *19850* Mexico *9055*

R   *Yucca grandiflora* Gentry *19850*
     R   *19850* Mexico *19850*

V   *Yucca jaliscensis* Trel. *9055*
     V   *21204* Mexico - Jalisco *21204*
     V   *21204* Mexico - Nayarit *21204*

V   *Yucca lacandonica* Gómez Pompa & Valdes *9057*
     V   *9425* Mexico *9057*

R   *Yucca madrensis* H. Gentry *9055*
     R   *21222* Mexico - Sonora *21222*

E   *Yucca necopina* Shinners *20850*
     E   *20850* U.S. - Texas *20850*

R   *Yucca pallida* McKelvey *20850*
     R   *20850* U.S. - Texas *20850*

R   *Yucca reverchonii* Trel. *20850*
     R   *20850* U.S. - Texas *20850*

E   *Yucca tenuistyla* Trel. *20850*
     E   *20850* U.S. - Texas *20850*

Alismataceae

Number of genera:	12	
Number of species:	75	
Recorded threatened species:	10	(13%)

Cosmopolitan, especially Northen Hemisphere.

R   *Alisma wahlenbergii* (Holmb.) Juz. *5942, 20171*
     R   *20673* Finland (Oulu) *8000*
     E   *20083* Sweden *8000*
     E   *11552* Russia (E.Europe) - Northwest *20627*

R   *Echinodorus eglandulosus* Holm-Nielsen & R.
     Haynes *11244*
     R   *11351* Ecuador *11244*

R   *Echinodorus parvulus* Engelm. *20883, 19002*
     I   *20850* Canada - Ontario *20850*
     E   *20850* U.S. - Alabama *20850*
     E   *20850* U.S. - Connecticut *20850*
     Ex/E   *20850* U.S. - Delaware *20850*
     I   *20850* U.S. - Florida *20850*
     E   *20850* U.S. - Georgia *20850*
     E   *20850* U.S. - Illinois *20850*
     E   *20850* U.S. - Indiana *20850*
     E   *20850* U.S. - Kansas *20850*
     E   *20850* U.S. - Kentucky *20850*
     Ex/E   *20850* U.S. - Louisiana *20850*

Ex	*20850*	U.S. - Massachusetts	*20850*
E	*20850*	U.S. - Michigan	*20850*
E	*20850*	U.S. - Mississippi	*20850*
E	*20850*	U.S. - Missouri	*20850*
Ex	*20850*	U.S. - New Jersey	*20850*
Ex	*20850*	U.S. - New York	*20850*
E	*20850*	U.S. - North Carolina	*20850*
I	*20850*	U.S. - Oklahoma	*20850*
V	*20850*	U.S. - South Carolina	*20850*
R	*20850*	U.S. - Texas	*20850*
I	*20883*	Puerto Rico	*20883*
I	*20883*	USA - Virgin Is.	*20883*

V   *Sagittaria ambigua* J.G. Sm. *20850*

E	*20850*	U.S. - Arkansas	*20850*
E	*20850*	U.S. - Kansas	*20850*
E	*20850*	U.S. - Missouri	*20850*
I	*20850*	U.S. - Oklahoma	*20850*

E   *Sagittaria fasciculata* E.O. Beal *20850*

E	*20850*	U.S. - North Carolina	*20850*
E	*20850*	U.S. - South Carolina	*20850*

R   *Sagittaria graminea* Michx. var. *chapmanii* J.G. Sm. *20850*

I	*20850*	U.S. - Alabama	*20850*
I	*20850*	U.S. - Florida	*20850*
I	*20850*	U.S. - Georgia	*20850*
I	*20850*	U.S. - Louisiana	*20850*
I	*20850*	U.S. - Mississippi	*20850*
E	*20850*	U.S. - North Carolina	*20850*

V   *Sagittaria sanfordii* Greene *20850*

V	*20850*	U.S. - California	*20850*

E   *Sagittaria secundifolia* Kral *20850*

E	*20850*	U.S. - Alabama	*20850*
E	*20850*	U.S. - Georgia	*20850*

R   *Sagittaria teres* S.Watson *20850*

Ex/E	*20850*	U.S. - Delaware	*20850*
I	*20850*	U.S. - Georgia	*20850*
Ex/E	*20850*	U.S. - Maryland	*20850*
R	*20850*	U.S. - Massachusetts	*20850*
E	*20850*	U.S. - New Jersey	*20850*
E	*20850*	U.S. - New York	*20850*
E	*20850*	U.S. - Rhode Is.	*20850*
I	*20850*	U.S. - South Carolina	*20850*

R   *Wiesneria triandra* (Dalz.) Mich. *14782*

R	*14782*	India - Goa, Daman & Diu	*14782*
I		India - Karnataka (Concan)	*4988*
E		India - Kerala (nr Parappanangadi; Kottur) *5727*	
R	*14782*	India - Maharashtra (Sindhudurg district) *14782*	

Alliaceae

Number of genera: 31
Number of species: 832
Recorded threatened species: 164   (19%)

Widespread.

R   *Agapanthus walshii* L.Bolus *20604*

R	*20604*	South Africa - Cape Province	*20604*

R   *Allium aaseae* Ownbey *20850*

R	*20850*	U.S. - Idaho	*20850*

V   *Allium aethusanum* Garbari *18264*

V	*18264*	Italy - Sicily	*20738*

R   *Allium alpinarii* Ozhatay & Kollmann *12840*

R	*12840*	Turkey	*12840*

R   *Allium atrorubens* S.Watson *20850*

I	*20850*	U.S. - Arizona	*20850*
V	*20850*	U.S. - California	*20850*

I	*20850*	U.S. - Nevada	*20850*
V	*20850*	U.S. - Utah	*20850*

E   *Allium auriculatum* Kunth

E		India - Himachal Pradesh
E		India - Jammu & Kashmir

I   *Allium autumnale* P.H. Davis *14230*

I	*19164*	Cyprus	*14230*

R   *Allium balansae* Boiss. *12840*

R	*12840*	Turkey	*12840*

V   *Allium baytopiorum* Kollmann & Ozhatay *12840*

V	*19873*	Turkey	*12840*

R   *Allium brevicaule* Boiss. & Bal. *12840*

R	*12840*	Turkey	*12840*

R   *Allium burlewii* A. Davids. *20850*

R	*20850*	U.S. - California	*20850*

R   *Allium canadense* L. var. *ecristatum* (M.E. Jones) Ownbey *20850*

R	*20850*	U.S. - Texas	*20850*

R   *Allium chrysonemum* Stearn *20171*

R	*11496*	Spain (Jaen, Cordoba, & Granada)	*11496*

R   *Allium circinnatum* Sieber *20171*

R	*20730*	Greece - Crete	*19121*

R   *Allium columbianum* (Ownbey & Mingrone) P. Peterson, Anna Rieseberg *20850*

I	*20850*	U.S. - Idaho	*20850*
E	*20850*	U.S. - Montana	*20850*
I	*20850*	U.S. - Washington	*20850*

V   *Allium constrictum* (Ownbey & Mingrone) P. Peterson, Annable Rieseberg *20850*

V	*20850*	U.S. - Washington	*20850*

E   *Allium crameri* Asch. & Boiss.

E		Egypt

I   *Allium czelghauricum* Bordz. *12840*

I	*19873*	Turkey	*12840*

R   *Allium decidum* Ozhatay & Kollmann *12840*

R	*12840*	Turkey	*12840*

E   *Allium dictuon* St. John *20850*

E	*20850*	U.S. - Washington	*20850*

R   *Allium dilatatum* Zahar. *20171*

R	*20730*	Greece - Crete	*19121*

R   *Allium djimilense* Boiss. & Regel *12840*

R	*12840*	Turkey	*12840*

R   *Allium eldivanense* Ozhatay *12840*

R	*12840*	Turkey	*12840*

V   *Allium elmendorfii* M.E. Jones ex Ownbey *20850*

V	*20850*	U.S. - Texas	*20850*

I   *Allium eugenii* Vved. *5942*

I	*5942*	Turkmenistan	*5942*

V   *Allium fimbriatum* S.Wats. var. *sharsmithiae* Ownbey & Aase *20850*

V	*20850*	U.S. - California	*20850*

R   *Allium flavum* L. var. *pilosum* Kollmann & Koyuncu *12840*

R	*12840*	Turkey	*12840*

R   *Allium frigidum* Boiss. & Heldr. *20171*

R		Greece

R   *Allium gayi* Boiss. *12840*

R	*12840*	Turkey	*12840*

R   *Allium glumaceum* Boiss. & Hausskn. *12840*

R		12840 Turkey *12840*

R   *Allium gooddingii* Ownbey *20850*
- R   20850   U.S. - Arizona *20850*
- V   20850   U.S. - New Mexico *20850*

I   *Allium gorumsense* Boiss. *12840*
- I   19873   Turkey *12840*

V   *Allium grande* Lipsky *5942*
- V   11552   Russia - North Caucasus (near coast) *5942*

R   *Allium grosii* Font Quer *8000, 20171*
- R   20821   Spain - Balearic Is. (Ibiza) *8000*

R   *Allium heldreichii* Boiss. *20171*
- R   Greece

V   *Allium hickmanii* Eastw. *20850*
- V   20850   U.S. - California *20850*

R   *Allium hoffmanii* Ownbey ex Traub *20850*
- I   20850   U.S. - California *20850*

R   *Allium howellii* Eastw. *20850*
- I   20850   U.S. - California *20850*

R   *Allium ilgazense* Ozhatay *12840*
- R   12840   Turkey *12840*

I   *Allium incisum* Fomin *12840*
- I   19873   Turkey *12840*

R   *Allium insubricum* Boiss. & Reuter *18264, 20171*
- R   18264   Italy (Lombardy) *18264*

R   *Allium isauricum* Huber-Mor. & Wendelbo *12840*
- R   12840   Turkey *12840*

E   *Allium jepsonii* (Ownbey & Aase ex Traub) S. Denison & McNeal *20850*
- E   20850   U.S. - California *20850*

V   *Allium jubatum* MacBride *19426*
- V   19426   Bulgaria *19426*

V   *Allium junceum* Sm. ssp. *tridentatum* Kollmann, Ozhatay & Koyuncu *12840*
- V   12840   Turkey *12840*

E   *Allium karamanglui* Koyuncu & Kollmann *12840*
- E   12840   Turkey *12840*

R   *Allium kastambulense* Kollmann *12840*
- R   12840   Turkey *12840*

I   *Allium koenigianum* Grossh. *12840*
- I   19873   Turkey *12840*

I   *Allium kurtzianum* (Acherson & Sint.) ex Kollmann *12840*
- I   19873   Turkey *12840*

R   *Allium lacunosum* S.Watson var. *davisiae* (M.E. Jones) McNeal & Ownbey *20850*
- I   20850   U.S. - California *20850*

R   *Allium lojaconoi* Brullo, Lanfranco & Pavone *13351*
- R   Malta *13351*

R   *Allium longanum* Pamp. *8000, 20171*
- R   Greece (Cyclades) *20731*
- V   Egypt *8000*
- V   Libya

R   *Allium lopadosanum* Bartolo, Brullo & Pavone *18264*
- R   18264   Italy - Sicily *18264*

E   *Allium loratum* Baker
- E   India - Jammu & Kashmir

R   *Allium luteolum* Halácsy *20171*
- R   20731   Greece (Cyclades) *20731*

R   *Allium macedonicum* Zahar. *20171*
- R   20731   Greece (north-east) *20731*

R   *Allium macrochaetum* Boiss. & Hausskn. ssp. *tuncelianum* Kollmann *12840*
- R   12840   Turkey *12840*

R   *Allium madidum* S.Watson *20850*
- R   20850   U.S. - Idaho *20850*
- R   20850   U.S. - Oregon *20850*

R   *Allium mareoticum* Bornm. & Gauba
- R   Egypt

R   *Allium mariae* Bordz.
- R   former USSR *6930*

R   *Allium melananthum* Coincy *20171*
- R   11496   Spain (Alicante & Murcia) *11496*

Ex/E   *Allium microbulbum* Prokh. *5942*
- Ex/E   5942   Russia (Siberia) - Chita *5942*

V   *Allium microspathum* Ekberg0 *12840*
- V   19873   Turkey *12840*

R   *Allium monticola* A. Davids. *20850*
- I   20850   U.S. - California *20850*

R   *Allium monticola* A.Davids. var. *keckii* (Munz) Ownbey & Aase *20850*
- I   20850   U.S. - California *20850*

E   *Allium munzii* (Ownbey & Aase ex Traub) McNeal *20850*
- E   20850   U.S. - California *20850*

R   *Allium narcissiflorum* Vill. *18264, 20171*
- R   18264   Italy (Piedmont, Liguria) *18264*

V   *Allium nemrutaghense* Kit Tan & Sorger *12840*
- V   19873   Turkey *12840*

R   *Allium obtusiflorum* DC. *8000, 20171*
- R   20738   Italy - Sicily (north-west & south-west) *8000*

V   *Allium oltense* Grossh. *12840*
- V   19873   Turkey *12840*

R   *Allium oxyphilum* Wherry *20850*
- R   20850   U.S. - West Virginia *20850*

R   *Allium parishii* S.Watson *20850*
- E   20850   U.S. - Arizona *20850*
- I   20850   U.S. - California *20850*

R   *Allium parnassicum* (Boiss.) Halácsy *20171*
- R   20731   Greece (Sterea Ellas, Southern Pindos) *20731*

E   *Allium passeyi* N.& A. Holmgren *20850*
- E   20850   U.S. - Utah *20850*

Ex/E   *Allium paulii* Vved. *5942*
- Ex/E   5942   Tajikistan *5942*

V   *Allium peninsulare* Lemmon ex Greene var. *franciscanum* McNeal & Owenbey *20850*
- V   20850   U.S. - California *20850*

R   *Allium peroninianum* Aznav. *12840*
- R   12840   Turkey *12840*

R   *Allium pervestitum* Klokov *20171*
- R   former European USSR

R   *Allium phanerantherum* Boiss. & Hausskn. ssp. *deciduum* Kollmann & Koyuncu *12840*
- R   12840   Turkey *12840*

R   *Allium phrygium* Boiss. *12840*
- R   19873   Turkey *12840*

R   *Allium pilosum* Sibth. & Smith *20171*

	R	20731	Greece (Cyclades) 20731
R	*Allium pleianthum* S.Watson 20850		
	R	20850	U.S. - Oregon 20850
R	*Allium proponticum* Stearn & Özhatay 12840, 20171		
	R	19873	Turkey 12840
I	*Allium pskemense* B. Fedtsch. 5942		
	I	5942	Kazakhstan (border with Kyrgyzstan) 5942
	I	5942	Kyrgyzstan (border with Kazakhstan) 5942
R	*Allium pumilum* Vved. 11552		
	R	11552	Russian Federation (Siberia) 20627
V	*Allium punctum* Henderson 20850		
	I	20850	U.S. - California 20850
	I	20850	U.S. - Nevada 20850
	I	20850	U.S. - Oregon 20850
R	*Allium pyrenaicum* Costa & Vayr. 20171		
	R	11496	Spain (Pyrenees) 11496
R	*Allium regelianum* A.K.Becker 5942, 20171		
	E	11552	Russia (E.Europe) - South 11552
	R	20655	Ukraine (south) 20649
R	*Allium regnieri* Maire		
	R		Morocco
I	*Allium rhetoreanum* Nab. 12840		
	I	19873	Turkey 12840
R	*Allium robertianum* Kollmann 12840		
	R	12840	Turkey 12840
R	*Allium robinsonii* Henderson 20850		
	Ex	20850	U.S. - Oregon 20850
	I	20850	U.S. - Washington 20850
E	*Allium rouyi* Gaut. 20171		
	E	20660	Spain 11496
E	*Allium roylei* Stearn		
	E		India - Jammu & Kashmir
R	*Allium sanbornii* Wood 20850		
	I	20850	U.S. - California 20850
	I	20850	U.S. - Oregon 20850
R	*Allium sanbornii* Wood var. *congdonii* Jepson 20850		
	R	20850	U.S. - California 20850
R	*Allium sanbornii* Wood var. *sanbornii* 20850		
	R	20850	U.S. - California 20850
	I	20850	U.S. - Oregon 20850
R	*Allium sandrasicum* Kollmann, Ozhatay & Bothmer 12840		
	R	12840	Turkey 12840
R	*Allium scabriflorum* Boiss. 12840		
	R	19873	Turkey 12840
V	*Allium schoenoprasum* L. var. *idzuense* (Hara) Hara 11164		
	V	11164	Japan 11164
R	*Allium schoenoprasum* L. var. *shibutuense* Kitam. 11164		
	R	11164	Japan 11164
R	*Allium schoenoprasum* L. var. *yezomonticola* Hara 11164		
	R	11164	Japan 11164
V	*Allium scilloides* Douglas ex S.Watson 20850		
	?	20850	U.S. - Washington 20850
E	*Allium seirotrichum* Ducell. & Maire 10487		
	E	14958	Algeria 10487
Ex/E	*Allium sergii* Vved. 5942		
	Ex/E	5942	Kazakhstan (Tien Shan) 5942

R	*Allium serra* McNeal & Ownbey 20850		
	I	20850	U.S. - California 20850
V	*Allium shatakiense* Rech. f. 12840		
	V	19873	Turkey 12840
E	*Allium shevockii* McNeal 20850		
	E	20850	U.S. - California 20850
I	*Allium sieheanum* (Hausskn. ex) Kollmann 12840		
	I	19873	Turkey 12840
R	*Allium sinaiticum* Boiss.		
	R		Egypt
V	*Allium sintenisii* Freyn 12840		
	V	19873	Turkey 12840
R	*Allium sivasicum* Ozhatay & Kollmann 12840		
	R	19873	Turkey 12840
V	*Allium sosnowskyanum* Miscz. 12840		
	V	19873	Turkey 12840
V	*Allium speculae* Ownbey & Aase 20850		
	E	20850	U.S. - Alabama 20850
	V	20850	U.S. - Georgia 20850
R	*Allium stearnianum* Koyuncu, Ozhatay & Kollmann 12840		
	R	19873	Turkey 12840
I	*Allium stenopetalum* Boiss. & Kotschy 12840		
	I	19873	Turkey 12840
V	*Allium stipitatum* Regel		
	V		former USSR 6930
R	*Allium stojanovii* Kov. 5204, 20171		
	R	5204	Bulgaria (east) 5204
V	*Allium stracheyi* Baker 14782		
	V	14782	India - Jammu & Kashmir 14782
	V	14782	India - Uttar Pradesh 14782
R	*Allium stylosum* O. Schwarz 12840		
	R	19873	Turkey 12840
R	*Allium tauricola* Boiss. 12840		
	R	19873	Turkey 12840
R	*Allium tchihatschewii* Boiss. 12840		
	R	12840	Turkey 12840
V	*Allium togashii* Hara 11164		
	V	11164	Japan 11164
R	*Allium tolmiei* (Hook.) Baker ex S.Watson var. *persimile* Ownbey 20850		
	R	20850	U.S. - Idaho 20850
R	*Allium tolmiei* (Hook.) Baker ex S.Watson var. *platyphyllum* (Tidestrom) Ownbey 20850		
	R	20850	U.S. - Idaho 20850
	R	20850	U.S. - Oregon 20850
R	*Allium transvestiens* Vved.		
	R		former USSR 6930
I	*Allium trautvetteranum* Regel 5942		
	I	5942	Tajikistan 5942
V	*Allium tribracteatum* Torr. 20850		
	V	20850	U.S. - California 20850
E	*Allium trichocnemis* Gay 10487		
	E	14958	Algeria 10487
V	*Allium tuolumnense* (Ownbey & Aase ex Traub) S. Denison & McNeal 20850		
	V	20850	U.S. - California 20850
R	*Allium valdecallosum* Maire & M. Weiller		
	R		Morocco
V	*Allium virguncule* F. Maek. & Kitam. var. *kiiense*		

Murata *11164*

V   *11164* Japan *11164*

V   *Allium virguncule* F. Maekawa & Kitamura var.
        virguncule *11164*

V   *11164* Japan *11164*

V   *Allium vuralii* Kit Tan *12840*

V   *12840* Turkey *12840*

R   *Allium wiedemannianum* Regel *12840*

R   *12840* Turkey *12840*

I   *Allium willeanum* Holmboe *14230*

I   *19164* Cyprus *14230*

V   *Allium yosemitense* Eastw. *20850*

V   *20850* U.S. - California *20850*

R   *Ancrumia cuspidata* Harvey ex Baker *11748*

R   *19534* Chile *11748*

E   *Bloomeria humilis* Hoover *20850*

E   *20850* U.S. - California *20850*

R   *Brodiaea californica* Lindl. *20850*

I   *20850* U.S. - California *20850*
I   *20850* U.S. - Oregon *20850*

E   *Brodiaea coronaria* (Salisb.)Engl. ssp. *rosea*
        (Greene) Niehaus *20850*

E   *20850* U.S. - California *20850*

V   *Brodiaea filifolia* S.Watson *20850*

V   *20850* U.S. - California *20850*

V   *Brodiaea insignis* (Jepson) Niehaus *20850*

V   *20850* U.S. - California *20850*

V   *Brodiaea kinkiensis* Niehaus *20850*

V   *20850* U.S. - California *20850*

V   *Brodiaea leptandra* (Greene) Baker *20850*

I   *20850* U.S. - California *20850*

V   *Brodiaea orcuttii* (Greene) Baker *20883, 20850, 8058*

V   *20850* U.S. - California *20850*
I   *20883* Mexico *20883*

E   *Brodiaea pallida* Hoover *20850*

E   *20850* U.S. - California *20850*

R   *Brodiaea stellaris* S.Watson *20850*

I   *20850* U.S. - California *20850*

R   *Caloscordum inutile* (Makino) Okuy. & Kitagawa *11164*

R   *11164* Japan *11164*

R   *Dichelostemma lacuna-vernalis* Lenz *20850*

I   *20850* U.S. - California *20850*

V   *Dichelostemma venustum* (Greene) Hoover *20850*

I   *20850* U.S. - California *20850*

R   *Erinna gilliesioides* Philippi *11748*

R   *19534* Chile *11748*

R   *Gethyum antropurpureum* Philippi *11748*

R   *19534* Chile *11748*

E   *Gilliesia monophylla* Reiche *19534*

E   *19534* Chile *19534*

R   *Gilliesia montana* Poeppig & Endl. *19534*

R   *19534* Chile *19534*

Ex   *Ipheion tweedianum* (Griseb.) Traub *16336*

Ex   *16336* Argentina *16336*
Ex   *20137* Argentina - Buenos Aires *20137*
Ex   *20176* Argentina - Entre Rios *20176*

V   *Leucocoryne purpurea* Gay *5598*

V   *19534* Chile *5598*

V   *Muilla clevelandii* (S.Watson) Hoover *20883, 20850,*

8058

V   *20850* U.S. - California *20850*
I   *20883* Mexico *20883*
?   Mexico - Baja California Peninsula *8058*

I   *Nectaroscordum dioscoridis* (Sibth. & Sm.)
        Zahar. *5942, 20171*

I   *5942* Azerbaijan *5942*
I   *5942* Ukraine *5942*

R   *Nectaroscordum meliophillum* (Juz.) Stank.

R   former European USSR

I   *Nectaroscordum tripedale* (Trautv.) Grossh. *11552*

I   *5942* Russia - North Caucasus *5942*
V   *11552* Armenia *11552*
V   *11552* Azerbaijan *11552*

E   *Petronymphe decora* H.E. Moore *19850*

E   *19848* Mexico *19850*

R   *Speea humilis* (Philippi) Loes. *6164*

R   *19534* Chile *6164*

R   *Steinmannia graminifolia* (Philippi f. ex Philippi)
        Loese *19534*

R   *19536* Chile *19534*

E   *Triteleia clementina* Hoover *20850*

E   *20850* U.S. - California *20850*

V   *Triteleia crocea* (Wood) Greene var. *modesta* (Hall)
        Hoover *20850*

V   *20850* U.S. - California *20850*

V   *Triteleia dudleyi* Hoover *20850*

I   *20850* U.S. - California *20850*

V   *Triteleia hendersonii* (M.E. Peck) Hoover var.
        leachiae (M.E. Peck) Hoover *20850*

V   *20850* U.S. - Oregon *20850*

R   *Triteleia lemmoniae* (S.Watson) Greene *20850*

R   *20850* U.S. - Arizona *20850*

V   *Triteleia lugens* Greene *20850*

I   *20850* U.S. - California *20850*

R   *Triteleia peduncularis* Lindl. *20850*

I   *20850* U.S. - California *20850*

Ex/E   *Triteleia versicolor* Hoover *20850*

I   *20850* U.S. - California *20850*

Aloaceae

Number of genera:	5
Number of species:	700
Recorded threatened species:	206 (29%)

Arabia, Africa, Madagascar.

R   *II   Aloe acutissima* H. Perrier var. *antanimorensis* G.
        Reyn. *10368*

R   *20578* Madagascar (Toliara) *20578*

E   *I   Aloe albiflora* Guillaumin *10368*

E   *20578* Madagascar (Toliara) *20578*

V   *II   Aloe albovestita* S. Carter & Brandham

V   Somalia

R   *II   Aloe ambigens* Chiov. *17668*

R   *17668* Somalia *17668*

V   *II   Aloe amudatensis* G. Reyn. *20264*

V   Kenya
V   *19007* Uganda *19007*

R   *II   Aloe andringitrensis* H. Perrier *10368*

R   *20578* Madagascar (Fianarantsoa) *20578*

V   *II   Aloe archeri* Lavranos *20264*

V		Kenya *20264*	

R *II* ***Aloe arenicola*** Reynolds *20604, 18295*
    R *18295* Namibia *18295*
    V *20604* South Africa - Cape Province *20604*

R *II* ***Aloe asperifolia*** A. Berger *18295*
    R *18295* Namibia *18295*

I *II* ***Aloe babatiensis*** Christian & Verdoorn *20264*
    I *5926* Tanzania *20264*

R *I* ***Aloe bakeri*** Scott Elliot *10368*
    R *20578* Madagascar (Toliara) *20578*

E *II* ***Aloe ballii*** *20932*
    E *20932* Mozambique (Zimbabwe border) *20932*
    E *20932* Zimbabwe (Rusitu Valley) *20932*

I *II* ***Aloe ballyi*** G. Reyn. *20057*
    I *20057* Kenya *20057*
    E *20057* Tanzania *17435*

V *II* ***Aloe bargalensis*** Lavranos
    V Somalia

V *II* ***Aloe bella*** G. Rowley
    V Somalia

E *I* ***Aloe bellatula*** G. Reynolds *10368*
    E *20578* Madagascar (Fianarantsoa) *20578*

R *II* ***Aloe betsiliensis*** H. Perrier *20578*
    R *18295* Madagascar (Toliara) *20578*

I *II* ***Aloe boscawenii*** Christian *20264*
    I *5926* Tanzania (Tanga) *20264*

E *II* ***Aloe bowiea*** Schult. & Schult.f. *20604*
    E *20604* South Africa - Cape Province *20604*

V *II* ***Aloe breviscapa*** G. Reyn. & Bally
    V Somalia

R *II* ***Aloe buchlohii*** Rauh *20578*
    R *20578* Madagascar (Toliara) *20578*

R *II* ***Aloe buhrii*** Lavranos *20604*
    R *20604* South Africa - Cape Province *20604*

I *II* ***Aloe bullockii*** G. Reyn. *5926*
    I *5926* Tanzania (Buha, Kahama) *20264*

I *II* ***Aloe bussei*** A. Berger *20264*
    I *5926* Tanzania *20264*

E *I* ***Aloe calcairophila*** G. Reyn. *18294*
    E *20578* Madagascar (Fianarantsoa) *20578*

R *II* ***Aloe calidophila*** G. Reyn. *20264*
    R Ethiopia
    R Kenya

V *II* ***Aloe cameronii*** Hemsl. var. ***bondana*** G. Reyn.
    V Zimbabwe

I *II* ***Aloe canarina*** S. Carter *20264*
    I *19007* Uganda (Karamoja) *20264*

R *II* ***Aloe cannellii*** Leach
    R *17668* Mozambique *17668*

R *II* ***Aloe capitata*** Baker var. ***cipolinicola*** H. Perrier *20578*
    R *20578* Madagascar (Fianarantsoa) *20578*

R *II* ***Aloe capitata*** Baker var. ***silvicola*** H. Perrier *20578*
    R *20578* Madagascar (Mahajunga) *20578*

V *II* ***Aloe cheranganiensis*** S. Carter & Brandham *20057*
    V *20057* Kenya *20057*
    V *20057* Uganda *20264*

E *II* ***Aloe chlorantha*** Lavranos *20604*
    E *20604* South Africa - Cape Province *20604*

R *II* ***Aloe chortolirioides*** A. Berger var. ***boastii*** (Letty) G. Reyn.
    R Swaziland

V *II* ***Aloe chrysostachys*** Lavranos & Newton *20264*
    V Kenya

V *II* ***Aloe classenii*** G. Reyn. *20264*
    V Kenya

R *II* ***Aloe comosa*** Marloth & A.Berger *20604*
    R *20604* South Africa - Cape Province *20604*

E *I* ***Aloe compressa*** H. Perrier var. ***compressa*** *18294*
    E *20578* Madagascar (Antananarivo) *20578*

E *I* ***Aloe compressa*** H. Perrier var. ***rugosquamosa*** H. Perrier *18294*
    E *20578* Madagascar (Antananarivo) *20578*

E *I* ***Aloe compressa*** H. Perrier var. ***schistophila*** H. Perrier *18294*
    E *20578* Madagascar (Antananarivo) *20578*

R *II* ***Aloe confusa*** Engl. *20264*
    R *17668* Kenya *17668*
    V *5926* Tanzania *5926*

R *II* ***Aloe conifera*** H. Perrier *20578*
    R *20578* Madagascar (Fianarantsoa) *20578*

E *II* ***Aloe cremersii*** Lavranos *20578*
    E *20578* Madagascar (Fianarantsoa) *20578*

R *II* ***Aloe cremnophila*** G. Reyn. & Bally
    R Somalia

R *II* ***Aloe cryptoflora*** G. Reyn. *20578*
    R *20578* Madagascar (Fianarantsoa) *20578*

R *II* ***Aloe dabenorisana*** Van Jaarsv. *20604*
    R *20604* South Africa - Cape Province *20604*

V *II* ***Aloe decurva*** G. Reyn.
    V Mozambique

E *I* ***Aloe descoingsii*** G. Reyn. *18294*
    E *20578* Madagascar (Toliara) *20578*

V *II* ***Aloe deserti*** Engl. *20264*
    V Kenya
    V Tanzania

V *II* ***Aloe dhufarensis*** Lavranos *20146*
    V *17668* Oman *17668*

R *II* ***Aloe dinteri*** A.Berger *20604, 18295*
    R *20604* Namibia *20604*

R *II* ***Aloe distans*** Haw. *20604*
    R *20604* South Africa - Cape Province *20604*

R *II* ***Aloe doei*** Lavranos *18295*
    R Yemen, Democratic

I *II* ***Aloe dorothea*** A. Berger *20264*
    I *5926* Tanzania *5926*

V *II* ***Aloe elgonica*** Bullock *20264*
    V Kenya

R *II* ***Aloe eminens*** G. Reyn. & Bally *20884*
    R *20884* Somalia (north) *20884*

R *II* ***Aloe erythrophylla*** Bosser *20578*
    R *20578* Madagascar (Fianarantsoa) *20578*

V *II* ***Aloe fibrosa*** Lavranos & Newton *20264*
    V Kenya
    V *17668* Tanzania *17668*

R	*II*	*Aloe fievetii* G. Reyn. *20578*	
	R	20578 Madagascar (Fianarantsoa) *20578*	
I	*II*	*Aloe flexilifolia* Christian *20264*	
	I	5926 Tanzania *5926*	
R	*II*	*Aloe forbesii* Balf. f. *15534*	
	R	15534 Yemen - Socotra (Hajh) *15534*	
R	*II*	*Aloe fulleri* Lavranos	
	R	17668 Yemen, Democratic *17668*	
R	*II*	*Aloe gerstneri* Reynolds *20604*	
	R	20604 South Africa - Natal *20604*	
R	*II*	*Aloe gracilis* Haw. var. *decumbens* G. Reyn. *20803*	
	R	20803 South Africa - Cape Province *20803*	
V	*II*	*Aloe grisea* S. Carter & Brandham	
	V	Somalia	
R	*II*	*Aloe haemanthifolia* A.Berger & Marloth *20604*	
	R	20604 South Africa - Cape Province *20604*	
V	*II*	*Aloe harlana* G. Reyn.	
	V	Ethiopia	
R	*I*	*Aloe haworthioides* Baker var. *aurantiaca* H. Perrier *18294*	
	R	20578 Madagascar (Fianarantsoa) *20578*	
R	*I*	*Aloe haworthioides* Baker var. *haworthioides* *18294*	
	R	20578 Madagascar (Fianarantsoa) *20578*	
E	*I*	*Aloe helenae* Danguy *18294*	
	E	18294 Madagascar (Toliara) *20578*	
V	*II*	*Aloe heliderana* Lavranos	
	V	Somalia	
I	*II*	*Aloe howmanii* G. Reynolds *7763*	
	I	Zimbabwe *7763*	
R	*II*	*Aloe ibitiensis* H. Perrier *20578*	
	R	18294 Madagascar (Antananarivo) *20578*	
R	*II*	*Aloe inamara* Leach	
	R	17668 Angola *17668*	
R	*II*	*Aloe inconspicua* Plowes *20604, 19976*	
	R	20604 South Africa - Natal *20604*	
V	*II*	*Aloe inermis* Forsk.	
	V	17668 Saudi Arabia *17668*	
	V	17668 Yemen *17668*	
	V	Somalia	
R	*II*	*Aloe itremensis* G. Reyn. *20578*	
	R	20578 Madagascar (Fianarantsoa) *20578*	
I	*II*	*Aloe jacksonii* G. Reyn.	
	I	Ethiopia	
E	*II*	*Aloe jucunda* G. Reyn.	
	E	Somalia	
R	*II*	*Aloe juvenna* Brandham & S. Carter *20264*	
	R	17668 Kenya *17668*	
V	*II*	*Aloe keithii* Reynolds *20604, 18023*	
	R	20604 Swaziland *20604*	
E	*II*	*Aloe kilifiensis* Christian *20264*	
	E	Kenya	
V	*II*	*Aloe krapohliana* Marloth *20604*	
	V	20604 South Africa - Cape Province *20604*	
R	*II*	*Aloe kulalensis* Newton & Beentje *20057*	
	R	20057 Kenya (Mt. Kulal) *20057*	
R	*I*	*Aloe laeta* A. Berger var. *laeta* *20578*	
	R	20578 Madagascar (Antananarivo) *20578*	

R	*I*	*Aloe laeta* A. Berger var. *maniaensis* H. Perrier *20578*	
	R	20578 Madagascar (Fianarantsoa) *20578*	
I	*II*	*Aloe leachii* Reynolds *20264*	
	I	5926 Tanzania *5926*	
V	*II*	*Aloe lensayuensis* Lavranos & Newton *20264*	
	V	Kenya	
I	*II*	*Aloe leptosiphon* A. Berger *20264*	
	I	5926 Tanzania *20264*	
V	*II*	*Aloe longistyla* Baker *20604*	
	V	20604 South Africa - Cape Province *20604*	
R	*II*	*Aloe mcloughlinii* Christian	
	R	Ethiopia	
V	*II*	*Aloe medishiana* G. Reyn. & Bally	
	V	Somalia	
V	*II*	*Aloe menachensis* (Schweinf.) Blatter	
	V	17668 Yemen *17668*	
V	*II*	*Aloe mendesii* G. Reyn. *6968*	
	V	6968 Angola *6968*	
V	*II*	*Aloe meruana* Lavranos *20264*	
	V	Kenya	
R	*II*	*Aloe meyeri* Van Jaarsv. *20604*	
	R	20604 Namibia *20604*	
	R	20604 South Africa - Cape Province *20604*	
R	*II*	*Aloe microcantha* Haw. *20604*	
	R	20604 South Africa - Cape Province *20604*	
R	*II*	*Aloe millotii* G. Reynolds *18294*	
	R	20578 Madagascar (Toliara) *20578*	
R	*II*	*Aloe monotropa* I.Verd. *20604, 17458*	
	R	20604 South Africa - Transvaal *20604*	
R	*II*	*Aloe monticola* G. Reyn.	
	R	Ethiopia	
E	*II*	*Aloe morijensis* S. Carter & Brandham *20264*	
	E	Kenya (Masai) *20264*	
	E	Tanzania (Masai) *20264*	
I	*II*	*Aloe musapana* G. Reyn.	
	I	Zimbabwe	
V	*II*	*Aloe nyeriensis* Christian *20057*	
	V	20057 Kenya *20057*	
E	*II*	*Aloe ortholopha* Christian & Milne-Redh. *6088*	
	E	6088 Zimbabwe *6088*	
E	*I*	*Aloe parallelifolia* H. Perrier *18294*	
	E	20578 Madagascar (Antananarivo) *20578*	
E	*I*	*Aloe parvula* A. Berger *18294*	
	E	20578 Madagascar (Fianarantsoa) *20578*	
R	*II*	*Aloe patersonii* B. Mathew	
	R	17668 Zaire *17668*	
V	*II*	*Aloe pearsonii* Schönland *20604*	
	V	20604 Namibia *20604*	
	V	20604 South Africa - Cape Province *20604*	
V	*II*	*Aloe peckii* Bally & Verdoorn	
	V	Somalia	
R	*II*	*Aloe peglerae* Schönland *20604*	
	R	20604 South Africa - Transvaal *20604*	
I	*II*	*Aloe penduliflora* Baker *20264*	
	V	17668 Kenya *17668*	
	I	5926 Tanzania *5926*	
R	*II*	*Aloe perrieri* G. Reynolds *18294*	
	R	20578 Madagascar (Fianarantsoa) *20578*	

R	*II*	***Aloe petrophila*** Pillans *20604*		
	R	*20604*	South Africa - Transvaal *20604*	
R	*II*	***Aloe pictifolia*** D.S.Hardy *20604*		
	R	*20604*	South Africa - Cape Province *20604*	
E	*I*	***Aloe pillansii*** L.Guthrie *20604*		
	E	*20604*	Namibia *20604*	
	E	*20604*	South Africa - Cape Province *20604*	
E	*I*	***Aloe polyphylla*** Schönland ex Pillans *20604, 6966*		
	E	*20604*	Lesotho *20604*	
	Ex	*20604*	South Africa - Orange Free State *20604*	
R	*II*	***Aloe powysiorum*** Newton & Beentje *20057*		
	R	*20057*	Kenya *20057*	
R	*II*	***Aloe prinslooi*** I.Verd. & D.S.Hardy *20604*		
	R	*20604*	South Africa - Natal *20604*	
R	*II*	***Aloe pruinosa*** Reynolds *20604*		
	R	*20604*	South Africa - Natal *20604*	
R	*II*	***Aloe pubescens*** G. Reyn.		
	R		Ethiopia	
V	*II*	***Aloe ramosissima*** Pillans *20604*		
	V	*20604*	Namibia *20604*	
	V	*20604*	South Africa - Cape Province *20604*	
R	*I*	***Aloe rauhii*** G. Reynolds *18294*		
	R	*20578*	Madagascar (Toliara) *20578*	
I	*II*	***Aloe reitzii*** G. Reyn. var. *reitzii* *20604*		
	I	*20604*	South Africa - Transvaal *20604*	
R	*II*	***Aloe reitzii*** G. Reyn. var. *vernalis* Hardy *20604*		
	R	*20604*	South Africa - Natal *20604*	
R	*II*	***Aloe retrospiciens*** G. Reyn. & Bally		
	R		Ethiopia	
	R		Somalia	
V	*II*	***Aloe reynoldsii*** Letty *20604*		
	V	*20604*	South Africa - Cape Province (Transkei) *20604*	
I	*II*	***Aloe richardsiae*** Reynolds *5926*		
	I	*5926*	Tanzania *20264*	
R	*II*	***Aloe rigens*** G. Reyn. & Bally var. *mortimeri* Lavranos		
	R	*17668*	Yemen, Democratic *17668*	
V	*II*	***Aloe rivae*** Baker *20264*		
	V		Ethiopia (south) *20264*	
	V		Kenya (Northern Frontier Province) *20264*	
V	*II*	***Aloe rubroviolacea*** Schweinf.		
	V	*17668*	Saudi Arabia *17668*	
	V	*17668*	Yemen, Democratic *17668*	
V	*II*	***Aloe rugosifolia*** M.G. Gilbert & Sebsebe Demissew *20264*		
	V		Ethiopia (south) *20264*	
	V		Kenya (Northern Frontier Province) *20264*	
V	*II*	***Aloe saundersiae*** (Reynolds) Reynolds *20604*		
	V	*20604*	South Africa - Natal *20604*	
R	*II*	***Aloe schelpei*** G. Reyn.		
	R		Ethiopia	
V	*II*	***Aloe scobinifolia*** G. Reyn. & Bally		
	V		Somalia	
V	*II*	***Aloe simii*** Pole Evans *20604*		
	V	*20604*	South Africa - Transvaal *20604*	
V	*II*	***Aloe sinana*** G. Reyn.		
	V		Ethiopia	
V	*II*	***Aloe somaliensis*** W. Watson		

	V		Somalia	
R	*II*	***Aloe soutpansbergensis*** I.Verd. *20604*		
	R	*20604*	South Africa - Transvaal *20604*	
E	*II*	***Aloe squarrosa*** Baker *15534*		
	E	*15534*	Yemen - Socotra (western cliffs) *15534*	
R	*II*	***Aloe striata*** Haw. ssp. *komaggasensis* (Kritzinger & Van Jaarsv.) Glen & D.S.Hardy *20604*		
	R	*20604*	South Africa - Cape Province *20604*	
E	*I*	***Aloe suzannae*** Decary *18294*		
	E	*18294*	Madagascar (Toliara) *20578*	
I	*II*	***Aloe tauri*** Leach		
	I		Zimbabwe	
I	*II*	***Aloe thompsoniae*** Groenew. *20604, 17458*		
	I	*20604*	South Africa - Transvaal *20604*	
V	*I*	***Aloe thorncroftii*** Pole Evans *20604, 15658*		
	V	*20604*	South Africa - Transvaal *20604*	
V	*II*	***Aloe tororoana*** G. Reyn. *20264*		
	V	*19007*	Uganda *19007*	
R	*II*	***Aloe trachyticola*** (H. Perrier) G. Reyn. *20578*		
	R	*20578*	Madagascar *20578*	
V	*II*	***Aloe trigonantha*** Leach		
	V		Ethiopia	
E	*II*	***Aloe ukambensis*** G. Reyn. *20264*		
	E		Kenya	
V	*II*	***Aloe vacillans*** Forssk.		
	V	*17668*	Saudi Arabia *17668*	
	V	*17668*	Yemen *17668*	
	V	*17668*	Yemen, Democratic *17668*	
R	*II*	***Aloe vandermerwei*** Reynolds *20604*		
	R	*20604*	South Africa - Transvaal *20604*	
R	*I*	***Aloe versicolor*** Guillaumin *18294*		
	R	*20578*	Madagascar (Toliara) *20578*	
R	*II*	***Aloe veseyi*** G. Reyn. *20264*		
	R	*17668*	Tanzania *17668*	
	R	*17668*	Zambia *17668*	
R	*II*	***Aloe viguieri*** H. Perrier *20578*		
	R	*20578*	Madagascar (Toliara) *20578*	
V	*II*	***Aloe vituensis*** Baker *20264*		
	V		Kenya	
R	*II*	***Aloe vogtsii*** Reynolds *20604*		
	R	*20604*	South Africa - Transvaal *20604*	
R	*I*	***Aloe vossii*** Reynolds *20604, 15658*		
	R	*20604*	South Africa - Transvaal *20604*	
E	*II*	***Aloe whitcombii*** Lavaranos *20146*		
	E	*20146*	Oman (Dhofar) *20146*	
I	*II*	***Aloe wildii*** (G. Reyn.) G. Reyn.		
	I		Zimbabwe	
R		***Astroloba herrei*** Uitewaal *20604*		
	R	*20604*	South Africa - Cape Province *20604*	
E		***Gasteria baylissiana*** Rauh *20604, 19170*		
	E	*19170*	South Africa (four plants at one site) *19170*	
	E	*20604*	South Africa - Cape Province *20604*	
R		***Gasteria bicolor*** Haw. var. *liliputana* (Poelln.) *20604*		
	R	*20604*	South Africa - Cape Province *20604*	
V		***Gasteria croucheri*** (Hook.f.) Baker *20604*		
	V	*20604*	South Africa - Cape Province *20604*	
	V	*20604*	South Africa - Natal *20604*	

R   *Gasteria ellaphieae* Van Jaarsv. *20604*
     R   *20604*   South Africa - Cape Province *20604*

R   *Gasteria glomerata* Van Jaarsv. *20604*
     R   *20604*   South Africa - Cape Province *20604*

R   *Gasteria rawlinsonii* Oberm. *20604*
     R   *20604*   South Africa - Cape Province *20604*

R   *Gasteria vlokii* Van Jaarsv. *20604*
     R   *20604*   South Africa - Cape Province *20604*

V   *Haworthia archeri* W.F.Barker ex M.B.Bayer var. *archeri* *20604*
     V   *20604*   South Africa - Cape Province *20604*

E   *Haworthia archeri* W.F.Barker ex M.B.Bayer var. *dimorpha* M.B.Bayer *20604*
     E   *20604*   South Africa - Cape Province *20604*

R   *Haworthia blackburniae* W.F.Barker *20604*
     R   *20604*   South Africa - Cape Province *20604*

V   *Haworthia bruynsii* M.B.Bayer *20604*
     V   *20604*   South Africa - Cape Province *20604*

E   *Haworthia comptoniana* G.G.Sm. *20604*
     E   *20604*   South Africa - Cape Province *20604*

V   *Haworthia emelyae* Poelln. var. *emelyae* *20604*
     V   *20604*   South Africa - Cape Province *20604*

E   *Haworthia emelyae* Poelln. var. *multifolia* M.B.Bayer *20604*
     E   *20604*   South Africa - Cape Province *20604*

R   *Haworthia fasciata* (Willd.) Haw. *20604*
     R   *20604*   South Africa - Cape Province *20604*

V   *Haworthia floribunda* Poelln. *20604*
     V   *20604*   South Africa - Cape Province *20604*

R   *Haworthia graminifolia* G.G.Sm. *20604*
     R   *20604*   South Africa - Cape Province *20604*

V   *Haworthia heidelbergensis* G.G.Sm. *20604*
     V   *20604*   South Africa - Cape Province *20604*

V   *Haworthia kingiana* Poelln. *20604*
     V   *20604*   South Africa - Cape Province *20604*

V   *Haworthia koelmaniorum* Oberm. & D.S.Hardy *20604*
     V   *20604*   South Africa - Transvaal *20604*

V   *Haworthia limifolia* Marloth var. *gigantea* M.B.Bayer *20604*
     V   *20604*   South Africa - Natal *20604*

I   *Haworthia limifolia* Marloth var. *ubomboensis* (Verdoorn) G.G. Sm. *20039*
     I   *20039*   Swaziland *20039*

V   *Haworthia lockwoodii* Archibald *20604*
     V   *20604*   South Africa - Cape Province *20604*

I   *Haworthia macmurtryi* C.L.Scott *20604*
     I   *20604*   South Africa - Transvaal *20604*

E   *Haworthia magnifica* Poelln. var. *major* (G.G.Sm.) M.B.Bayer *20604*
     E   *20604*   South Africa - Cape Province *20604*

E   *Haworthia magnifica* Poelln. var. *ubomboensis* (I.Verd.) G.G.Sm. *20604*
     E   *20604*   South Africa - Cape Province *20604*

E   *Haworthia marginata* (Lam.) Stearn *20604*
     E   *20604*   South Africa - Cape Province *20604*

V   *Haworthia maughanii* Poelln. *20604*
     V   *20604*   South Africa - Cape Province *20604*

E   *Haworthia mirabilis* (Haw.) Haw. ssp. *badia* (Poelln.) M.B.Bayer *20604*
     E   *20604*   South Africa - Cape Province *20604*

E   *Haworthia mirabilis* (Haw.) Haw. ssp. *mundula* (G.G.Sm.) M.B.Bayer *20604*
     E   *20604*   South Africa - Cape Province *20604*

V   *Haworthia mutica* Haw. *20604*
     V   *20604*   South Africa - Cape Province *20604*

V   *Haworthia nortieri* G.G.Sm. var. *globosiflora* (G.G.Sm.) M.B.Bayer *20604*
     V   *20604*   South Africa - Cape Province *20604*

E   *Haworthia parksiana* Poelln. *20604*
     E   *20604*   South Africa - Cape Province *20604*

E   *Haworthia pehlemanniae* C.L.Scott *20604*
     E   *20604*   South Africa - Cape Province *20604*

E   *Haworthia poellnitziana* Uitewaal *20604*
     E   *20604*   South Africa - Cape Province *20604*

V   *Haworthia pubescens* M.B.Bayer *20604*
     V   *20604*   South Africa - Cape Province *20604*

E   *Haworthia pygmaea* Poelln. *20604*
     E   *20601*   South Africa - Cape Province *20604*

E   *Haworthia retusa* (L.) Duval var. *dekanahii* (G.G.Sm.) M.B.Bayer *20604*
     E   *20604*   South Africa - Cape Province *20604*

I   *Haworthia rubriflora* (L. Bolus) C.A.E. Parr
     I   Southern Africa

E   *Haworthia serrata* M.B.Bayer *20604*
     E   *20604*   South Africa - Cape Province *20604*

V   *Haworthia sordida* Haw. *20604*
     V   *20604*   South Africa - Cape Province *20604*

V   *Haworthia springbokvlakensis* C.L.Scott *20604*
     V   *20604*   South Africa - Cape Province *20604*

E   *Haworthia starkiana* Poelln. var. *lateganiae* (Poelln.) M.B.Bayer *20604, 20604*
     E   *20604*   South Africa - Cape Province *20604*

V   *Haworthia truncata* Schönland *20604*
     V   *20604*   South Africa - Cape Province *20604*

R   *Haworthia wittebergensis* W.F.Barker *20604*
     R   *20604*   South Africa - Cape Province *20604*

V   *Haworthia woolleyi* Poelln. *20604*
     V   *20604*   South Africa - Cape Province *20604*

R   *Lomatophyllum antsingyense* Leandri *10368*
     R   *20578*   Madagascar (Mahajunga) *20578*

E   *Lomatophyllum lomatophylloides* (Balf.f.) Marais *10082*
     E   *5852*   Mauritius - Rodrigues (Grande Mt) *5852*

V   *Lomatophyllum macrum* (Haw.) Salm-Dyck *14234*
     V   *14234*   Réunion *14234*

R   *Lomatophyllum occidentale* H. Perrier *10368*
     R   *20578*   Madagascar (Mahajunga) *20578*

R   *Lomatophyllum orientale* H. Perrier *10368*
     R   *20578*   Madagascar (Fianarantsoa) *20578*

R   *Lomatophyllum prostratum* H. Perrier *10368*
     R   *20578*   Madagascar (Mahajunga) *20578*

V   *Lomatophyllum purpureum* (Lam.) T. Durand & Schinz *10082*
     V   *20771*   Mauritius *10082*

R   *Lomatophyllum roseum* H. Perrier *10368*
     R   *20578*   Madagascar (Mahajunga) *20578*

R   *Lomatophyllum sociale* H. Perrier *10368*

R	20578	Madagascar (Mahajunga) *20578*

E   *Lomatophyllum tormentorii* **Marais** *10082*

E	20771	Mauritius (Round I & Gunner's Quoin) *10936*

R   *Lomatophyllum viviparum* **H. Perrier** *10368*

R	20578	Madagascar (Antsiranana) *20578*

R   *Poellnitzia rubriflora* **(L.Bolus) Uitewaal** *20604*

R	20604	South Africa - Cape Province *20604*

Alstroemeriaceae

Number of genera:	4	
Number of species:	152	
Recorded threatened species:	5	(3%)

Mexico to South America.

R   *Bomarea brevis* **(Herbert) Baker** *12379*

V	19354	Bolivia *12379*
R	18200	Peru *18200*

E   *Bomarea engleriana* **Kranzlin**

E	9446	Peru *18200*

E   *Bomarea filicaulis* **Kranzlin**

E	9446	Peru *18200*

E   *Leontochir ovallei* **Philippi** *11748*

E	19534	Chile *11748*

I   *Schickendantzia hieronymi* **Pax** *16336*

I	19448	Argentina *16336*

Amaryllidaceae

Number of genera:	65	
Number of species:	700	
Recorded threatened species:	176	(25%)

Widespread.

E   *Amaryllis arboricola* **Ravenna** *16336*

E	16336	Argentina *16336*

V   *Amaryllis santacatarina* **Traub** *6164*

V		Brazil - Rio Grande do Sul
V		Brazil - Santa Catarina

V   *Amaryllis scopulorum* **(Baker) Traub.& Uphof.** *6164*

V	6164	Bolivia (Sorata) *6164*

E   *Amaryllis traubii* **Mold.** *18200*

E	9446	Peru *18200*

R   *Apodolirion bolusii* **Baker** *20604*

R	20604	South Africa - Cape Province *20604*

R   *Apodolirion lanceolatum* **(Thunb.) Baker** *20604*

R	20604	South Africa - Cape Province *20604*

E   *Brunsvigia gydobergensis* **D. & U.Müll.-Doblies** *20604*

E	20604	South Africa - Cape Province *20604*

R   *Brunsvigia herrei* **Leight. ex W.F.Barker** *20604*

R	20604	South Africa - Cape Province *20604*

V   *Brunsvigia litoralis* **R.A.Dyer** *20604*

V	20604	South Africa - Cape Province *20604*

R   *Brunsvigia pulchra* **(W.F.Barker) D. & U.Müll.-Doblies** *20604*

R	20604	South Africa - Cape Province *20604*

E   *Caliphruria hartwegiana* **Herbert** *11202*

E	11202	Colombia *11202*

R   *Caliphruria korsakoffii* **(Traub) Meerow** *11202*

R	19926	Peru *11202*

E   *Caliphruria subedentata* **Baker** *11202*

E	11202	Colombia *11202*

Ex   *Caliphruria tenera* **Baker** *11202*

Ex		Colombia *11202*

V   *Cooperia jonesii* **Cory** *20850*

I	20850	U.S. - Texas *20850*

E   *Cooperia smallii* **Alexander** *20850*

I	20850	U.S. - Texas *20850*

R   *Cooperia traubii* **Hayward** *20850*

R	20850	U.S. - Texas *20850*

I   *Crinum balfourii* **Baker** *15534*

I	15534	Yemen - Socotra *15534*

R   *Crinum baumii* **Harms**

R		Namibia

R   *Crinum campanulatum* **Herb.** *20604*

R	20604	South Africa - Cape Province *20604*

E   *Crinum darienensis* **Woods.** *20883, 9006*

I	20883	Panama *20883*

R   *Crinum eleonorae* **Blatter & McCann** *11494*

R	11494	India - Maharashtra (Lingmala, Mahabaleshwar) *11494*

R   *Crinum lineare* **L.f.** *20604*

R	20604	South Africa - Cape Province *20604*

E   *Crinum mauritianum* **Lodd.** *10082*

E	20771	Mauritius *10082*

I   *Crinum piliferum* **Nordal**

I		Kenya

I   *Crinum pusillum* **Herb.** *7771*

I	7771	India - Nicobar Is. *7771*

R   *Crinum rautanenianum* **Schinz**

R		Namibia

R   *Crinum strictum* **Herbert** *20850*

R	20850	U.S. - Texas *20850*

V   *Crinum thaianum* **J. Schulze** *19120*

V	19120	Thailand *19120*

V   *Cyrtanthus brachysiphon* **Hilliard & B.L.Burtt** *20604*

V	20604	South Africa - Natal *20604*

V   *Cyrtanthus carneus* **Lindl.** *20604*

V	20604	South Africa - Cape Province *20604*

R   *Cyrtanthus clavatus* **(L'Hér.) R.A.Dyer** *20604*

R	20604	South Africa - Cape Province *20604*

R   *Cyrtanthus erubescens* **Killick** *20604*

R	20604	South Africa - Natal *20604*

R   *Cyrtanthus eucallus* **R.A.Dyer** *20604*

R	20604	South Africa - Transvaal *20604*

R   *Cyrtanthus flammosus* **Snijman & Van Jaarsv.** *20604*

R	20604	South Africa - Cape Province *20604*

V   *Cyrtanthus guthrieae* **L.Bolus** *20604*

V	20604	South Africa - Cape Province *20604*

R   *Cyrtanthus helictus* **Lehm.** *20604*

R	20604	South Africa - Cape Province *20604*

R   *Cyrtanthus herrei* **(Leight.) R.A.Dyer** *20604*

R	20604	Namibia *20604*
R	20604	South Africa - Cape Province *20604*

R   *Cyrtanthus huttonii* **Baker** *20604, 17458*

R	20604	South Africa - Cape Province *20604*
R	20604	South Africa - Transvaal *20604*

R   *Cyrtanthus leucanthus* **Schltr.** *20604*

R	20604	South Africa - Cape Province *20604*

V   *Cyrtanthus odorus* Ker Gawl. *20604*
     V   *20604*   South Africa - Cape Province *20604*

I   *Cyrtanthus sanguineus* (Lindley) Walp. ssp. *ballyi*
     Nordal
     I   Kenya

I   *Cyrtanthus sanguineus* (Lindley) Walp. ssp. *minor*
     Nordal
     I   Kenya

R   *Cyrtanthus sanguineus* (Lindley) Walp. ssp.
     salmonoides (Bally & Carter) Nordal
     R   Kenya *7954*

R   *Cyrtanthus smithiae* Watt ex Harv. *20604*
     R   *20604*   South Africa - Cape Province *20604*

V   *Cyrtanthus spiralis* Burch. ex Ker Gawl. *20604*
     V   *20604*   South Africa - Cape Province *20604*

V   *Cyrtanthus staadensis* Schönland *20604*
     V   *20604*   South Africa - Cape Province *20604*

R   *Cyrtanthus thorncroftii* C.H.Wright *20604*
     R   *20604*   South Africa - Transvaal *20604*

V   *Eucharis amazonica* Linden ex Planchon *18200*
     V   *18200*   Peru *11202*

V   *Eucharis astrophiala* (Ravenna) Ravenna *11202*
     V   *11202*   Ecuador *11202*

E   *Eucharis bonplandii* (Kunth) Traub *11203*
     E   *11202*   Colombia *11203*

E   *Eucharis bouchei* Woods. & Allen *20883*
     I   *20883*   Panama *20883*

R   *Eucharis bouchei* Woodson & Allen var.
     bouchei *12783*
     R   *12783*   Costa Rica *11203*
     R   *11203*   Guatemala *11203*
     R   *12783*   Panama *11203*

R   *Eucharis bouchei* Woodson & Allen var. *darienensis*
     Meerow *12783*
     R   *12783*   Guatemala *12783*
     R   *12783*   Panama *12783*

R   *Eucharis bouchei* Woodson & Allen var. *dressleri*
     Meerow *12783*
     R   *12783*   Panama *12783*

R   *Eucharis candida* Planchon & Lindley *11202*
     R   *11202*   Colombia *11202*
     V   *11202*   Ecuador *11202*
     R   *11202*   Peru *11202*

E   *Eucharis caucana* Meerow *11202*
     E   *11202*   Colombia *11202*

E   *Eucharis corynandra* (Ravenna) Ravenna *11202*
     E   Peru *11202*

V   *Eucharis cyaneosperma* Meerow *10186*
     V   Bolivia *10186*
     V   Brazil *10186*
     V   Peru *10186*

R   *Eucharis formosa* Meerow *10186*
     R   *19353*   Colombia *10186*
     V   Ecuador *10186*
     V   Peru *10186*

Ex   *Eucharis lehmannii* Regel *11202*
     Ex   *11202*   Colombia *11202*

R   *Eucharis moorei* (Baker) Meerow *10186*
     V   Ecuador *10186*
     R   *11351*   Peru *10186*

E   *Eucharis oxyandra* (Ravenna) Meerow *11202*

     E   Peru *11202*

E   *Eucharis plicata* Meerow ssp. *brevidentata*
     Meerow *11202*
     E   *19926*   Bolivia *11202*
     E   *19926*   Peru *11202*

E   *Eucharis plicata* Meerow ssp. *plicata* *11202*
     E   *19926*   Peru *11202*

R   *Eucharis sanderi* Baker *11202*
     R   *19926*   Colombia *11202*

V   *Eucharis ulei* Kranzlin *11202*
     V   *11202*   Bolivia *11202*
     V   *11203*   Brazil *11202*
     V   Colombia *11202*
     V   Peru *11202*

E   *Eucrosia aurantiaca* (Baker) Pax *11205*
     E   *11202*   Ecuador *11205*

E   *Eucrosia bicolor* var. *plowmanii*
     Meerow *20883*
     I   *20883*   Peru *20883*

R   *Eucrosia dodsonii* Meerow & Dehgan *11205*
     R   *19926*   Ecuador *11205*

R   *Eucrosia eucrosioides* (Herbert) Pax *11205*
     V   *11202*   Ecuador *11205*
     R   *11202*   Peru *11205*

Ex   *Eucrosia mirabilis* (Baker) Pax *11205*
     Ex   *19926*   Peru *11205*

R   *Eucrosia tubiflora* Meerow *11205*
     R   Peru *11205*

I   II   *Galanthus alpinus* Sosn. *5942*
     I   *5942*   Armenia *5942*
     I   *5942*   Georgia *5942*

I   II   *Galanthus elwesii* Hook.f. *20171*
     I   *5942*   Ukraine *5942*

R   II   *Galanthus lagodechianus* Kem.-Nat. *5942*
     R   *11552*   Russia - North Caucasus *11552*
     R   *11552*   Transcaucasus *11552*

     Galanthus nivalis L. ssp. *cilicicus* (Baker)
     Gottl.-Tann. *21389, 17665*
     I   *17664*   Turkey (South west) *17665*

V   II   *Galanthus plicatus* M. Bieb. ssp. *byzantinus*
     (Baker) D.A. Webb *12840*
     V   *12840*   Turkey *12840*

Ex   *Gethyllis latifolia* Masson ex Baker *20604, 10260*
     Ex   *20604*   South Africa - Cape Province *20604*

V   *Gethyllis multifolia* L.Bolus *20604*
     V   *20604*   South Africa - Cape Province *20604*

V   *Griffinia hyacinthina* Ker-gawl. *6164*
     V   Brazil - Sao Paulo

Ex   *Griffinia liboniana* Lem. *6164*
     Ex   *6164*   Brazil - Minas Gerais *6164*

Ex   *Habranthus caerulens* (Griseb.) Traub *10540*
     Ex   *10540*   Argentina *10540*
     Ex   *20176*   Argentina - Entre Rios *20176*

V   *Haemanthus amarylloides* Jacq. ssp.
     amarylloides *20604*
     V   *20604*   South Africa - Cape Province *20604*

V   *Haemanthus amarylloides* Jacq. ssp. *toximontanus*
     Snijman *20604*
     V   *20604*   South Africa - Cape Province *20604*

V   *Haemanthus canaliculatus* Levyns *20604*

	V	20604 South Africa - Cape Province *20604*	
R	*Haemanthus dasyphyllus* Snijman *20604*		
	R	20604 South Africa - Cape Province *20604*	
R	*Haemanthus grandifolius* Balf. f. *15534*		
	R	15534 Yemen - Socotra *15534*	
R	*Haemanthus graniticus* Snijman *20604*		
	R	20604 South Africa - Cape Province *20604*	
R	*Haemanthus lanceifolius* Jacq. *20604*		
	R	20604 South Africa - Cape Province *20604*	
R	*Haemanthus namaquensis* R.A.Dyer *20604*		
	R	20604 Namibia *20604*	
	R	20604 South Africa - Cape Province *20604*	
R	*Haemanthus nortieri* Isaac *20604*		
	R	20604 South Africa - Cape Province *20604*	
I	*Haemanthus pole-evansii* Oberm. *7753*		
	I	Zimbabwe *7753*	
R	*Haemanthus pubescens* L.f. ssp. *arenicola* Snijman *20604*		
	R	20604 South Africa - Cape Province *20604*	
R	*Haemanthus pubescens* L.f. ssp. *leipoldtii* Snijman *20604*		
	R	20604 South Africa - Cape Province *20604*	
E	*Haemanthus pumilio* Jacq. *20604*		
	E	20604 South Africa - Cape Province *20604*	
R	*Haemanthus tristis* Snijman *20604*		
	R	20604 South Africa - Cape Province *20604*	
V	*Hessea bruce-bayeri* (D. & U.Müll.-Doblies) Snijman *20604*		
	V	20604 Namibia *20604*	
	V	20604 South Africa - Cape Province *20604*	
R	*Hessea cinnamomea* (L'Hér.) T.Durand & Schinz. *20604*		
	R	20604 South Africa - Cape Province *20604*	
V	*Hessea incana* Snijman *20604*		
	V	20604 South Africa - Cape Province *20604*	
E	*Hessea mathewsii* W.F.Barker *20604*		
	E	20604 South Africa - Cape Province *20604*	
R	*Hessea pilosula* D. & U.Müll.-Doblies *20604*		
	R	20604 South Africa - Cape Province *20604*	
I	*Hessea pulcherrima* (D. & U.Müll.-Doblies) Snijman *20604*		
	I	20604 South Africa - Cape Province *20604*	
R	*Hessea pusilla* Snijman *20604*		
	R	20604 South Africa - Cape Province *20604*	
R	*Hessea stenosiphon* (Snijman) D. & U.Müll.-Doblies *20604*		
	R	20604 South Africa - Cape Province *20604*	
R	*Hessea undosa* Snijman *20604*		
	R	20604 South Africa - Cape Province *20604*	
E	*Hippeastrum arboricolum* Ravenna *10540*		
	E	10540 Argentina *10540*	
E	*Hippeastrum aviflorum* Ravenna *10540*		
	E	10540 Argentina *10540*	
E	*Hippeastrum canterai* Arechav. *10540*		
	E	10540 Uruguay (Tranqueras) *10540*	
E	*Hippeastrum ferreyrae* (Traub) Gereau & Brako *18200*		
	E	9446 Peru *18200*	
V	*Hippeastrum petiolatum* Pax *10540*		
	E	10540 Argentina *10540*	
	V	19926 Brazil *19926*	

E	*Hymenocallis concinna* Baker *19850*		
	E	19848 Mexico *19850*	
E	*Hymenocallis durangoensis* T.M. Howard *19850*		
	E	19848 Mexico *19850*	
E	*Hymenocallis duvalensis* Traub *20850*		
	I	20850 U.S. - Florida *20850*	
V	*Hymenocallis guerreroensis* T.M. Howard *19850*		
	V	19850 Mexico *19850*	
E	*Hymenocallis henryae* Traub *20850*		
	E	20850 U.S. - Florida *20850*	
V	*Hymenocallis leavenworthii* (Standl.& Steyerm) J.A. Bauml *19850*		
	V	19850 Mexico *19850*	
E	*Ismene amancaes* (Ruiz Lopez & Pavon) Herbert *18200*		
	E	19926 Peru *18200*	
R	*Ismene longipetala* (Lindley) Meerow *11351*		
	E	19926 Ecuador *11184*	
	R	18200 Peru *18200*	
R	*Ismene morrisonii* (Vargas) Gereau & Meerow *18200*		
	R	11184 Peru *18200*	
R	*Ismene narcissiflora* (Jacq.) M. Roemer *18200*		
	R	12468 Peru *18200*	
V	*Ismene vargasii* (Velarde) Gereau & Meerow *18200*		
	V	12468 Peru *18200*	
R	*Leptochiton helianthus* (Ravenna) Gereau & Meerow *18200*		
	R	11206 Peru *18200*	
I	*Leucojum aestivum* L. ssp. *pulchellum* (Salisb.) Briq. *8000, 20171*		
	V	20528 France (south east) *20528*	
	E	20726 France - Corsica *12844*	
	I	20528 Italy - Sardinia *20528*	
	I	20528 Italy - Sicily *20528*	
	I	20528 Spain - Balearic Is. *20528*	
E	*Leucojum fabrei* Quézel & B. Girerd *20528*		
	E	20528 France (Vaucluse) *20528*	
R	*Leucojum fontianum* Maire		
	R	Morocco	
V	*Leucojum nicaeense* Ardoino *8000, 20171*		
	V	19174 France (south-east to Italian frontier) *8000*	
V	*Leucojum valentinum* Pau *20171*		
	V	20692 Spain (Castellón & Valencia provinces) *20692*	
R	*Leucojum valentinum* Pau. ssp. *vlorense* Pap. et Qosja *20178*		
	R	20178 Albania *20178*	
V	*Leucojum vernum* L. ssp. *carpaticum* (Spring.) O. Schwartz *19839*		
	V	19751 Poland *19751*	
	V	19321 Slovakia *19321*	
Ex	*Mathieua galanthoides* Klotzsch *11207*		
	Ex	Peru *11207*	
I	*Narcissus broussonetii* Lag.		
	I	Morocco	
V	*Narcissus bujei* (Fern.Casas) Fern. *19970*		
	V	19818 Spain (Málaga, & Cádiz) *19970*	
R	*Narcissus calcicarpetanus* Fernandez Casas		
	R	19970 Spain (Duratón) *19970*	
I	*Narcissus calcicola* Mendonça *8000, 20171*		

I		20874 Portugal (west central) *19970*	
I		20874 Spain (south) *20704*	

R *Narcissus conspicuus* (Haw.) Sweet *19970*
    R   *19970* Spain (south-central) *19970*

R *Narcissus gaditanus* Boiss. & Reut. *8000, 20171*
    R   *19970* Portugal (Monchique to Lagos) *8000*
    R   *19970* Spain (Huelva) *8000*

R *Narcissus genesii-lopezii* Fernández Casas *19970*
    R   *19970* Spain *19970*

R *Narcissus longispathus* Pugsley *8000, 20171*
    R   *19174* Spain (South east: Sierra de Cazorla) *8000*

V *Narcissus munozii-garmendiae* Fernandez Casas
    V   *19970* Spain (Ciudad Royal) *19970*

V *Narcissus perez-chiscanoi* Fernández Casas *19970*
    V   *19970* Spain (south-central) *19970*

E *Narcissus pseudonarcissus* L. ssp. *nevadensis* (Pugsley) A. Fernandes *8000, 20171*
    E   *15398* Spain (Sierra Nevada) *15398*

R *Narcissus pseudonarcissus* L. ssp. *primigenius* (Fernández Suárez ex Laínz) Fernández Casas & Laínz *19970*
    R   *19970* Spain (Léon: Asturias) *19970*

V *Narcissus radinganorum* Fern. Casas *20692*
    V   *20692* Spain (Valencia, Cuenca and Albacete provinces) *20692*

E *Narcissus scaberulus* Henriq. *8000, 20171*
    E   *20076* Portugal (Beira Alta) *8000*

E *Narcissus tortifolius* Fernandez Casas *19818*
    E   *19818* Spain (Sierra Cabrera) *17778*

V *Narcissus triandrus* L. ssp. *capax* (Salisb.) D.A. Webb *8000, 20171*
    V   *20528* France (north-west) *8000*

R *Nerine gibsonii* Douglas *20604*
    R   *20604* South Africa - Cape Province (Transkei) *20604*

R *Nerine gracilis* R.A.Dyer *20604*
    R   *20604* South Africa - Transvaal *20604*

R *Nerine marincowitzii* Snijman *20604*
    R   *20604* South Africa - Cape Province *20604*

R *Nerine masonorum* L.Bolus *20604*
    R   *20604* South Africa - Cape Province *20604*

R *Nerine pudica* Hook.f. *20604*
    R   *20604* South Africa - Cape Province *20604*

E *Pamianthe parviflora* Meerow *11208*
    E   *11202* Ecuador *11208*

R *Pancratium canariense* Ker-Gawl. *15105*
    R   *15105* Spain - Canary Is. *15105*

I *Pancratium parvum* Dalz.
    I   India - Karnataka

R *Paramongaia weberbaueri* Velarde Nunez
    R   *19926* Bolivia *19926*
    V   *12468* Peru *18200*

R *Phaedranassa tunguraguae* Ravenna *11351*
    R   *6164* Ecuador *11351*

V *Phycella ignea* Lindley *19534*
    V   *19534* Chile *19534*

R *Placea amoena* Philippi *19535*
    R   *19535* Chile *19535*

R *Placea arzae* Philippi *5598*
    R   *5598* Chile *5598*

E *Plagiolirion horsmannii* Baker *11207, 20751*
    E   *19926* Colombia *11207*

R *Rauhia decora* Ravenna *11209*
    R   *18200* Peru *11209*

R *Rauhia multiflora* (Kunth) Ravenna *11184*
    R   *18200* Peru *11184*

R *Rauhia staminosa* Ravenna *11184*
    R   *18200* Peru *11184*

E *Rhodophiala araucana* (Philippi) Traub *5462*
    E   *5462* Argentina *5462*
    E   *20176* Argentina - Neuquen (Ñorquín) *20176*

V *Rhodophiala bagnoldii* (Herbert) Traub *19534*
    V   *19534* Chile *19534*

R *Stenomesson coccineum* (Ruiz Lopez & Pavon) Herbert
    R   *12468* Peru *18200*

R *Stenomesson mirabilis* Ravenna *11210*
    R   *18200* Peru *11210*

R *Stenomesson variegatum* (Ruiz Lopez & Pavon) J.F. Macbr. *18200*
    R   *12468* Peru *18200*

E *II* *Sternbergia candida* B. Mathew & T. Baytop *17663*
    E   *17662* Turkey (Nr Fethiye in Mugla Province) *12840*

I *II* *Sternbergia schubertii* Schenk *17663*
    I   *12840* Turkey *12840*

R *Strumaria aestivalis* Snijman *20604*
    R   *20604* South Africa - Cape Province *20604*

R *Strumaria barbarae* Oberm. *20604*
    R   *20604* Namibia *20604*
    R   *20604* South Africa - Cape Province *20604*

I *Strumaria bidentata* Schinz *20604*
    I   *20604* Namibia *20604*
    I   *20604* South Africa - Cape Province *20604*

R *Strumaria discifera* Marloth ex Snijman ssp. *bulbifera* Snijman *20604*
    R   *20604* South Africa - Cape Province *20604*

R *Strumaria karoopoortensis* (D. & U.Müll.-Doblies) Snijman *20604*
    R   *20604* South Africa - Cape Province *20604*

E *Strumaria leipoldtii* (L.Bolus) Snijman *20604*
    E   *20604* South Africa - Cape Province *20604*

R *Strumaria massoniella* (D. & U.Müll.-Doblies) Snijman *20604*
    R   *20604* South Africa - Cape Province *20604*

V *Strumaria merxmuelleriana* (D. & U.Müll.-Doblies) Snijman *20604*
    V   *20604* South Africa - Cape Province *20604*

R *Strumaria perryae* Snijman *20604*
    R   *20604* South Africa - Cape Province *20604*

V *Strumaria picta* W.F.Barker *20604*
    V   *20604* South Africa - Cape Province *20604*

R *Strumaria pubescens* W.F.Barker *20604*
    R   *20604* South Africa - Cape Province *20604*

R *Strumaria pygmaea* Snijman *20604*
    R   *20604* South Africa - Cape Province *20604*

V *Strumaria unguiculata* (W.F.Barker) Snijman *20604*
    V   *20604* South Africa - Cape Province *20604*

R *Strumaria villosa* Snijman *20604*
    R   *20604* South Africa - Cape Province *20604*

R *Strumaria watermeyeri* L.Bolus ssp. *botterkloofensis*
(D. & U.Müll.-Doblies) Snijman *20604*
  R *20604* South Africa - Cape Province *20604*

I *Ungernia spiralis* Proskor. *5942*
  I *5942* Turkmenistan *5942*

I *Ungernia victoris* Vved. ex Artjush. *5942*
  I *5942* Tajikistan *5942*
  I *5942* Uzbekistan *5942*

E *Urceolina ayacucensis* Ravenna *11110*
  E *19926* Peru *11184*

E *Worsleya rayneri* (J.D. Hooker) Traub. &
Moldenke *17079*
  E *17079* Brazil - Rio de Janeiro (Município de
Petrópolis) *17079*

V *Zephyranthes conzatti* Greenm. *19850*
  V *19850* Mexico *19850*

V *Zephyranthes refugiensis* F.B. Jones *20850*
  I *20850* U.S. - Texas *20850*

V *Zephyranthes simpsonii* Chapman *20850*
  V *20850* U.S. - Florida *20850*
  Ex/E *20850* U.S. - Georgia *20850*
  I *20850* U.S. - South Carolina *20850*

Anthericaceae

Number of genera: 29
Number of species: 481
Recorded threatened species: 22   (4%)

Old World, especially Australasia & 5 genera in New World.

R *Anthericum milanjianum* Rendle *7757*
  R   Malawi (Mlanje) *7757*

R *Anthericum nyasae* Rendle *7757*
  R   Malawi (Mlanje) *7757*

E *Borya mirabilis* D.M.Churchill *20681*
  E *20681* Australia - Victoria *20681*

R *Chlorophytum borivilianum* Santapau & R.R. Fernandes
  R *13883* India - Gujarat *13883*
  R *13883* India - Maharashtra *13883*

I *Chlorophytum glaucum* Dalz.
  I   India - Karnataka (Concan)

R *Chlorophytum lewisiae* Oberm. *20604*
  R *20604* South Africa - Cape Province *20604*

I *Chlorophytum malabaricum* Dalz.
  I   India (south Western Ghats)

R *Chlorophytum namaquense* Schltr. ex Poelln. *20604*
  R *20604* South Africa - Cape Province *20604*

I *Chlorophytum nzii* A. Chev ex Hepper *7926*
  I   Côte d'Ivoire *7926*

E *Diamena stenantha* (Ravenna) Ravenna *11136*
  E   Peru *11136*

E *Echeandia bolivarensis* Cruden *20883*
  I *20883* Bolivia *20883*

R *Echeandia chandleri* (Greenm. & C.H. Thompson) M.C.
Johnston *20883, 20850*
  R *20850* U.S. - Texas *20850*
  I *20883* Mexico *20883*

E *Echeandia venusta* Woods. *20883, 9006*
  I *20883* Panama *20883*

R *Eremocrinum albomarginatum* (M.E. Jones) M.E.
Jones *20850*
  V *20850* U.S. - Arizona *20850*

R *20850* U.S. - Utah *20850*

V *Hensmania chapmanii* Keighery *20681*
  V *20681* Australia - Western Australia *20681*

V *Laxmannia jamesii* Keighery *20681*
  V *20681* Australia - Western Australia *20681*

R *Sowerbaea multicaulis* E.Pritzel *20681*
  R *20681* Australia - Western Australia *20681*

V *Sowerbaea subtilis* D.A.Stewart *20681*
  V *20681* Australia - Queensland *20681*

V *Stawellia dimorphantha* F.Muell. *20681*
  V *20681* Australia - Western Australia *20681*

R *Thysanotus glaucus* Endl. *20681*
  R *20681* Australia - Western Australia *20681*

R *Thysanotus virgatus* Brittan *20681*
  R *20681* Australia - New South Wales *20681*

R *Thysanotus wangariensis* Brittan *20681*
  R *20681* Australia - South Australia *20681*

Aponogetonaceae

Number of genera: 1
Number of species: 40
Recorded threatened species: 7   (17%)

Warmer and tropical regions of the old world.

I *Aponogeton appendiulatus* van Bruggen *13883*
  I *13883* India - Kerala *13883*
  I *13883* India - Tamil Nadu *13883*

E *Aponogeton bullosus* H.Bruggen *20681*
  E *20681* Australia - Queensland *20681*

R *Aponogeton fotianus* Rayn.
  R   Chad

V *Aponogeton hexatepalus* H.Bruggen *20681*
  V *20681* Australia - Western Australia *20681*

R *Aponogeton queenslandicus* H.Bruggen *20681*
  R *20681* Australia - Queensland *20681*

R *Aponogeton ranunculiflorus* Jacot Guill. &
Marais *20604, 6966*
  R *20604* Lesotho *20604*
  R *20604* South Africa - Natal (Near Sehlabethebe -
Lesoto) *20604*

V *Aponogeton satarensis* Sund., A.R. Kulk. &
Yadav *11494*
  V *11494* India - Maharashtra (Satara District)
11494

Araceae

Number of genera: 110
Number of species: 1,800
Recorded threatened species: 223   (12%)

Mostly tropical and subtropical.

V *Aglaonema clarkei* Hook.f. *14872*
  V *14872* Bangladesh *14872*

R *Aglaonema decurrens* Buchet *6057*
  R   Vietnam *6057*

I *Aglaonema nicobaricum* Hook. F *7771*
  I   India - Nicobar Is. *7771*

R *Alloschemone occidentalis* (Poeppig) Engler &
Krause *7201*
  R *7201* Brazil - Amazonas (Tefe) *7201*

I *Alocasia montana* (Roxb.) Schott

	I		India - Andhra Pradesh (north Circars)
V	*Alocasia sanderiana* Bulliard *10278*		
	V		Philippines (Misamis, Agusan R, Pautar) *12756*
I	*Alocasia sinuata* N.E. Br. *13833*		
	I	*13833*	Philippines (Palawan) *13833*
V	*Alocasia zebrina* C. Koch & Veitch *10278*		
	V		Philippines (Luzon) *12755*
I	*Amorphophallus carnosus* Engl. *7771*		
	I		India - Andaman Is. *7771*
I	*Amorphophallus dubius* Blume *20013*		
	I		India - Kerala (Malabar)
	I	*20013*	Sri Lanka *20013*
R	*Amorphophallus hirtus* N.E. Br. var. *kiushianus* (Makino) M. Hotta *11164*		
	R	*11164*	Japan *11164*
I	*Amorphophallus hohenackeri* Engl. *14727*		
	I		India - Karnataka (nr Mangalore, South Canara) *14727*
R	*Amorphophallus longistylus* Kurz ex Hook. F. *7771*		
	R	*14782*	India - Andaman Is. *14782*
R	*Amorphophallus oncophyllus* Prain ex Hook. F. *7771*		
	R	*14782*	India - Andaman Is. *7771*
I	*Amorphophallus preussii* (Engl.) N.E. Br.		
	I		Cameroon (Buea)
I	*Amorphophallus staudtii* (Engl.) N.E. Br.		
	I		Cameroon
V	*Amorphophallus titanum* Becc.		
	V		Indonesia - Sumatra
R	*Anaphyllum beddomei* Engler *14727*		
	R	*14727*	India - Tamil Nadu *14727*
I	*Anaphyllum weightii* Schott *14727*		
	I	*14727*	India - Kerala *14727*
	I	*14727*	India - Tamil Nadu *14727*
R	*Anthurium acutangulum* Engl. *20883*		
	V	*20883*	Panama *20883*
I	*Anthurium amnicola* Dressler *20883, 9070*		
	I	*16317*	Panama *20883*
V	*Anthurium angustilobum* Croat *20883, 10747*		
	V	*16317*	Panama *20883*
V	*Anthurium antonianum* Croat *10747*		
	V	*16317*	Panama *10747*
E	*Anthurium antonioanum* Croat *20883, 10766*		
	I	*20883*	Panama *20883*
	?		Colombia *10766*
I	*Anthurium barryi* Croat *20883, 10766*		
	I	*16317*	Panama *20883*
V	*Anthurium beltianum* Standley & L.O. Williams *9078*		
	V	*11967*	Nicaragua *9078*
V	*Anthurium bicollectivum* Croat *20883, 10766*		
	I	*20883*	Panama *20883*
	?		Colombia *10766*
V	*Anthurium brevispadix* Croat *20883, 10766*		
	V	*16317*	Panama *20883*
V	*Anthurium caloveboranum* Croat *20883, 10766*		
	I	*20883*	Panama *20883*
I	*Anthurium cartiense* Croat *20883, 10766*		
	I	*16317*	Panama *20883*
V	*Anthurium cerrocampanense* Croat *20883, 10766*		

	I	*20883*	Panama *20883*
V	*Anthurium cerropirrense* Croat *20883, 10766*		
	V	*16317*	Panama *20883*
V	*Anthurium chiriquense* Standl. *20883, 9006*		
	V	*16317*	Panama *20883*
I	*Anthurium chorranum* Croat *10766*		
	I	*16317*	Panama *10766*
E	*Anthurium chorrense* Croat *20883*		
	I	*20883*	Panama *20883*
V	*Anthurium chromostachyum* Croat *20883, 10766*		
	V	*16317*	Panama *20883*
E	*Anthurium cinereopetiolatum* Croat *20883, 10766*		
	I	*20883*	Panama *20883*
	?		Colombia *10766*
V	*Anthurium circinatum* Croat *20883, 10766*		
	I	*20883*	Panama *20883*
V	*Anthurium coclense* Croat *20883, 10766*		
	I	*20883*	Panama *20883*
I	*Anthurium collinsii* Croat *20883, 10766*		
	I	*16317*	Panama *20883*
V	*Anthurium colonense* Croat *20883, 10766*		
	I	*20883*	Panama *20883*
V	*Anthurium colonicum* K. Krause *20883, 9006*		
	I	*20883*	Panama *20883*
I	*Anthurium coloradense* Croat *20883, 10766*		
	I	*16317*	Panama *20883*
R	*Anthurium concolor* K. Krause *20883*		
	V	*20883*	Panama *20883*
V	*Anthurium correae* Croat *20883, 10766*		
	I	*20883*	Panama *20883*
I	*Anthurium crassilaminum* Croat *20883, 10766*		
	I	*16317*	Panama *20883*
V	*Anthurium crassiradix* Croat var. *crassiradix* *20883, 10766*		
	I	*20883*	Panama *20883*
I	*Anthurium crassiradix* Croat var. *purpureospadix* Croat *20883, 10766*		
	I	*16317*	Panama *20883*
I	*Anthurium crassitepalum* Croat *20883, 10766*		
	I	*16317*	Panama *20883*
V	*Anthurium cuasicanum* Croat *20883, 10766*		
	V	*16317*	Panama *20883*
V	*Anthurium cubense* Engler *5607*		
	V	*19105*	Cuba (SC; Gu) *5607*
V	*Anthurium cucullispathum* Croat *20883, 10766*		
	I	*20883*	Panama *20883*
I	*Anthurium curvilaminum* Croat *20883, 10766*		
	I	*16317*	Panama *20883*
V	*Anthurium curvispadix* Croat *20883, 10766*		
	I	*20883*	Panama *20883*
I	*Anthurium dichrophyllum* Croat *20883, 10766*		
	I	*16317*	Panama *20883*
R	*Anthurium dressleri* Croat *20883*		
	V	*20883*	Panama *20883*
V	*Anthurium dukei* Croat *20883, 10766*		
	V	*16317*	Panama *20883*
V	*Anthurium folsomianum* Croat *20883, 10766*		
	V	*16317*	Panama *20883*

Liliopsida (monocots): Araceae: *Anthurium*

E   *Anthurium foreroanum* Croat *20883, 10766*
    I   *20883* Panama *20883*
    ?   Colombia *10766*

I   *Anthurium fusiforme* Croat *20883, 10766*
    I   *16317* Panama *20883*

V   *Anthurium gentryi* Croat *20883, 10766*
    V   *16317* Panama *20883*

V   *Anthurium globosum* Croat *20883, 10766*
    I   *20883* Panama *20883*

I   *Anthurium gracililaminum* Croat *20883, 10766*
    I   *16317* Panama *20883*

V   *Anthurium gracilispadix* Croat *20883, 10766*
    I   *20883* Panama *20883*

R   *Anthurium gymnopus* Griseb. *11840*
    R   *19105* Cuba (Pinar del Rio) *11840*

R   *Anthurium hacumense* Engl. *20883*
    R   *20883* Panama *20883*

I   *Anthurium hammelii* Croat *20883, 10766*
    I   *16317* Panama *20883*

V   *Anthurium hebetatum* Croat *20883*
    I   *20883* Panama *20883*

I   *Anthurium hornitense* Croat *20883, 10766*
    I   *16317* Panama *20883*

V   *Anthurium impolitum* Croat *20883, 10766*
    I   *20883* Panama *20883*

E   *Anthurium inconspicuum* N.E. Br. *2409*
    E   *2409* Brazil - Rio de Janeiro (Sao Cristovao, Taquara de Tijuca) *2409*

V   *Anthurium jefense* Croat *20883, 10766*
    V   *16317* Panama *20883*

I   *Anthurium kallunkiae* Croat *20883, 10766*
    I   *16317* Panama *20883*

I   *Anthurium kamemotoanum* Croat *20883, 10766*
    I   *16317* Panama *20883*

I   *Anthurium lactifructum* Croat *20883, 10766*
    I   *16317* Panama *20883*

I   *Anthurium lancifolium* Croat var. *albifructum* Croat *20883, 10766*
    I   *16317* Panama *20883*

I   *Anthurium leptocaule* Croat *20883, 10766*
    I   *16317* Panama *20883*

Ex   *Anthurium leuconeurum* Lemaire *9078*
    Ex   *9078* Mexico *9078*

E   *Anthurium llanense* Croat *20883*
    I   *20883* Panama *20883*

I   *Anthurium llanense* Croat ssp. *llanense* *10766*
    I   *16317* Panama *10766*

R   *Anthurium longipetiolatum* Engler *2409*
    R   *2409* Brazil - Rio de Janeiro (Organ Mtns.) *2409*

V   *Anthurium longistipitatum* Croat *20883, 10766*
    I   *20883* Panama *20883*

V   *Anthurium luteynii* Croat *20883, 10766*
    I   *20883* Panama *20883*

V   *Anthurium madisonianum* Croat *20883, 10766*
    I   *20883* Panama *20883*

R   *Anthurium mancuniense* Adams *20883, 13336*
    R   *19890* Jamaica *20883*

R   *Anthurium maximiliani* Schott *2409*

    R   *2409* Brazil - Rio de Janeiro *2409*

V   *Anthurium melastomatis* Croat *20883, 10766*
    V   *16317* Panama *20883*

V   *Anthurium myosuroides* (H.B.K.) Endl. *20883*
    E   *20883* Panama *20883*

R   *Anthurium nanospadix* Engler *2409*
    R   *2409* Brazil - Rio de Janeiro (Organ Mtns.) *2409*

V   *Anthurium nervatum* Croat *20883, 10766*
    I   *20883* Panama *20883*

E   *Anthurium niqueanum* Croat *20883, 10766*
    I   *20883* Panama *20883*
    ?   Colombia *10766*

E   *Anthurium nobile* Engler *2409*
    E   *2409* Brazil - Rio de Janeiro (Petropolis) *2409*

V   *Anthurium oxystachyum* Croat *20883, 10766*
    V   *16317* Panama *20883*

V   *Anthurium pageanum* Croat *20883, 10766*
    I   *20883* Panama *20883*

R   *Anthurium paludosum* Engl. *20883*
    V   *20883* Panama *20883*

V   *Anthurium panamense* Croat *20883, 10766*
    I   *20883* Panama *20883*

I   *Anthurium papillilaminum* Croat *20883, 10766*
    I   *16317* Panama *20883*

R   *Anthurium parvum* N.E. Br. *2409*
    R   *2409* Brazil - Rio de Janeiro (Teresopolis, Organ Mtns.) *2409*

I   *Anthurium pauciflorum* Croat *20883, 10766*
    I   *16317* Panama *20883*

V   *Anthurium pirrense* Croat *20883, 10766*
    V   *16317* Panama *20883*

V   *Anthurium pittieri* Engl. var. *morii* Croat *20883, 10766*
    I   *20883* Panama *20883*

I   *Anthurium platyrhizum* Croat *20883, 10766*
    I   *16317* Panama *20883*

V   *Anthurium podophyllum* (Cham. & Schldl.) Kunth *9071*
    V   *19850* Mexico *9071*

I   *Anthurium pseudospectabile* Croat *20883, 10766*
    I   *16317* Panama *20883*

V   *Anthurium purpureospathum* Croat *20883, 9078*
    I   *20883* Panama *20883*

R   *Anthurium ramonense* K. Krause *20883*
    R   *20883* Panama *20883*

I   *Anthurium redolens* Croat *20883, 10766*
    I   *16317* Panama *20883*

I   *Anthurium roseospadix* Croat *20883, 10766*
    I   *16317* Panama *20883*

V   *Anthurium rotundistigmatum* Croat *20883, 10766*
    I   *20883* Panama *20883*

E   *Anthurium rubrifructum* Croat *20883, 10766*
    I   *20883* Panama *20883*
    ?   Colombia *10766*

V   *Anthurium rupicola* Croat *20883, 10766*
    I   *20883* Panama *20883*

V   *Anthurium sagawae* Croat *20883, 10766*
    V   *16317* Panama *20883*

V   *Anthurium sanctifidense* Croat *20883, 10766*
    I   *20883* Panama *20883*
    ?   Colombia *10766*

V   *Anthurium sapense* Croat *20883, 10766*
    V   *16317* Panama *20883*

V   *Anthurium subrotundum* Croat *20883, 10766*
    V   *16317* Panama *20883*

I   *Anthurium supraglandulum* Croat *20883, 10766*
    I   *16317* Panama *20883*

I   *Anthurium sytsmae* Croat *20883, 10766*
    I   *16317* Panama *20883*

E   *Anthurium tacarcunense* Croat *20883, 10766*
    I   *20883* Panama *20883*
    ?   Colombia *10766*

I   *Anthurium teribense* Croat *20883, 10766*
    I   *16317* Panama *20883*

V   *Anthurium terryae* Standl. & L.O. Wms. *20883, 10766*
    V   *16317* Panama *20883*

R   *Anthurium theresiopolitanum* Engler *2409*
    R   *2409* Brazil - Rio de Janeiro (Teresopolis, Organ
            Mtns.) *2409*

V   *Anthurium tutense* Croat *20883, 10766*
    V   *16317* Panama *20883*

V   *Anthurium tysonii* Croat *20883, 10766*
    V   *16317* Panama *20883*

V   *Anthurium venosum* Griseb. *20883, 19890*
    R   *19890* Cuba *20883*
    V   *19890* Jamaica *20883*

I   *Anthurium wedelianum* Croat ssp. *viridispadix*
    Croat *20883, 10766*
    I   *16317* Panama *20883*

V   *Anthurium wedelianum* Croat ssp.
    wedelianum *20883, 10766*
    I   *20883* Panama *20883*

R   *Arisaema abei* Serizawa *11164*
    R   *11164* Japan *11164*

R   *Arisaema aprile* J. Murata *11164*
    R   *11164* Japan *11164*

I   *Arisaema attenuatum* Barnes et Fischer *14727*
    I   *14727* India *14727*

I   *Arisaema auriculata* Barnes *14727*
    I   *14727* India - Tamil Nadu (Nilambur Ghats)
            18341

I   *Arisaema barnesii* C. Fischer
    I   India - Karnataka
    I   India - Tamil Nadu

I   *Arisaema constrictum* Barnes *10252*
    I   *16162* Sri Lanka *10252*

R   *Arisaema cucullatum* H. Hotta *11164*
    R   *11164* Japan *11164*

R   *Arisaema heterocephalum* Koidz. ssp.
    heterocephalum *11164*
    R   *11164* Japan *11164*

E   *Arisaema heterocephalum* Koidz. ssp. *majus* (Seriz.)
    J. Murata *11164*
    E   *11164* Japan *11164*

R   *Arisaema ishizuchiense* Murata var. *alpicola*
    Seriz. *11164*
    R   *11164* Japan *11164*

R   *Arisaema ishizuchiense* Murata ssp. *brevicollum*
    Ohashi & J. Murata *11164*
    R   *11164* Japan *11164*

R   *Arisaema ishizuchiense* Murata ssp.
    ishizuchiense *11164*
    R   *11164* Japan *11164*

R   *Arisaema iyoanum* Makino ssp. *iyoanum* *11164*
    R   *11164* Japan *11164*

R   *Arisaema iyoanum* Makino ssp. *nakaianum* (Ohba)
    Ohashi & J. Murata *11164*
    R   *11164* Japan *11164*

E   *Arisaema kawashimae* Serizawa *11164*
    E   *11164* Japan *11164*

E   *Arisaema kuratae* Seriz. *11164*
    E   *11164* Japan *11164*

R   *Arisaema longipedunculatum* M. Hotta var.
    longipedunculatum *11164*
    R   *11164* Japan *11164*

E   *Arisaema longipedunculatum* M. Hotta var.
    yakumontanum Seriz. *11164*
    E   *11164* Japan *11164*

E   *Arisaema minamitanii* Seriz. *11164*
    E   *11164* Japan *11164*

E   *Arisaema minus* (Serizawa) J. Murata *11164*
    E   *11164* Japan *11164*

I   *Arisaema murrayi* Hook.f.
    I   India - Karnataka (Concan)
    I   India - Tamil Nadu (Nilgiri Hills)

R   *Arisaema nikoense* Nakai ssp. *australe* (M. Hotta)
    Seriz. *11164*
    R   *11164* Japan *11164*

R   *Arisaema nikoense* Nakai var. *kaimontanum*
    Seriz. *11164*
    R   *11164* Japan *11164*

E   *Arisaema ogatae* Koidz. *11164*
    E   *11164* Japan *11164*

E   *Arisaema ovale* Nakai var. *inaense* (Serizawa) J.
    Murata *11164*
    E   *11164* Japan *11164*

I   *Arisaema psittacus* Barnes
    I   India - Kerala (Travancore Hills)

I   *Arisaema pulcherum* N.E. Br.
    I   India - Tamil Nadu (Sispara, Nilgiri Hills)

I   *Arisaema sarracenioides* Barnes et Fischer *14727*
    I   *14727* India (Naimakad gap and Munnar-Devicolam)
            14727

E   *Arisaema seppikoense* Kitamura *11164*
    E   *11164* Japan *11164*

R   *Arisaema sikokianum* Fr. & Sar. *11164*
    R   *11164* Japan *11164*

I   *Arisaema translucens* C. Fischer *14727*
    I   India - Tamil Nadu (Nilgiri Hills)
            14727

I   *Arisaema tuberculatum* C. Fischer *4988*
    I   India - Tamil Nadu (Nilgiri Hills) *4988*

I   *Arisaema tylophorum* C. Fischer *14727*
    I   India - Tamil Nadu (Nilgiri Hills) *4988*

E   *Arisaema undulatifolium* Nakai ssp. *nambae* (Kitam.)
    Ohashi & J. Murata *11164*
    E   *11164* Japan *11164*

I	*Arisaema wightii* Schott	
	I	India - Tamil Nadu (Nilgiri Hills)
R	*Arum balansanum* R. Mill *12840*	
	R	*12840* Turkey *12840*
R	*Arum conophalloides* Kotschy ex Schott var. *caudatum* Engler *12840*	
	R	*19873* Turkey *12840*
R	*Arum dioscoridis* Sm. var. *luschanii* R. Mill. *12840*	
	R	*12840* Turkey *12840*
R	*Arum euxinum* R. Mill *12840*	
	R	*19873* Turkey *12840*
V	*Arum pupureospadiceum* Boyce *19121*	
	V	*19121* Greece *19121*
V	*Arum purpureospathum* P. Boyce *14166*	
	V	*20730* Greece - Crete (south-west) *14166*
E	*Asterostigma fabrisii* Crisci *16336*	
	E	*20176* Argentina - Misiones (Eldorado) *20176*
R	*Asterostigma vermicida* Hauman & Vanderveken *19575*	
	R	*19575* Argentina *19575*
V	*Biarum davisii* Turrill *8000, 20171*	
	V	*19121* Greece (Simi) *19121*
	V	*19121* Turkey (south-west Anatolia) *19121*
R	*Biarum davisii* Turrill ssp. *davisii* *19121*	
	R	*20730* Greece - Crete *19121*
R	*Biarum dispar* (Schott) Talavera *14958, 20171*	
	R	*14958* Algeria *14958*
R	*Biarum eximium* (Schott & Kotschy) Engler *12840*	
	R	*19873* Turkey *12840*
R	*Biarum galiani* Talavera *20171*	
	R	*20076* Portugal *20076*
	R	Spain
R	*Biarum spruneri* Boiss. *20171*	
	R	*20730* Greece - Crete *19121*
R	*Biarum tenuifolium* (L.) Schott. ssp. *idaeum* *20731*	
	R	*20730* Greece - Crete *19121*
R	*Biarum tenuifolium* (L.) Schott ssp. *idomenaeum* P.C.Boyce & Athanasiou *20731*	
	R	*19121* Greece - Crete *19121*
R	*Caladium paradoxum* Bogner & Mayo *20883*	
	I	*20883* Colombia *20883*
I	*Callopsis hallaei* Bogner	
	I	Gabon
R	*Chlorospatha croatiana* Grayum *20883*	
	I	*20883* Costa Rica *20883*
	I	*20883* Panama *20883*
	I	*20883* Colombia *20883*
E	*Chlorospatha croatiana* Grayum ssp. *enneaphylla* Grayum *20883*	
	I	*20883* Costa Rica *20883*
	I	*20883* Panama *20883*
E	*Chlorospatha gentryi* Grayum *20883*	
	I	*20883* Colombia *20883*
Ex	*Chlorospatha kressii* Grayum *21274*	
	Ex	*21274* Colombia (Chocó) *21274*
I	*Cryptocoryne cognata* Schott *14727*	
	I	*14782* India - Karnataka (Concan) *14782*
V	*Cryptocoryne cognatoides* Blatter & McCann *11494*	
	V	*11494* India - Karnataka (North Kanara) *11494*

	V	*11494* India - Maharashtra *11494*
I	*Cryptocoryne consobrina* Schott *14727*	
	I	India (Western Ghats)
E	*Cryptocoryne elliptica* N.E. Br. *20740, 10260*	
	E	*20740* Malaysia *20740*
I	*Cryptocoryne thwaitesii* Schott *10252*	
	I	*16162* Sri Lanka *10252*
E	*Cryptocoryne tortuosa* Blatter & McCann *11494*	
	E	*11494* India - Maharashtra (Mahabaleshwar, Satara) *11494*
I	*Cryptocoryne wightii* Schott	
	I	India - Karnataka (Mysore)
	I	India - Kerala (Calicut)
V	*Culcasia panduriformis* Engl. & K. Krause	
	V	Cameroon
R	*Culcasia rotundifolia* Bogner	
	R	Gabon
V	*Dieffenbachia pittieri* Engl. & K.Krause *20883*	
	V	*20833* Panama *20883*
V	*Dracunculus canariensis* Kunth *15105*	
	V	*15105* Spain - Canary Is. *15105*
I	*Hapaline appendiculata* Ridley *9402*	
	I	Malaysia - Sarawak *9402*
R	*Hapaline colaniae* Gagnepain *6057*	
	R	Vietnam *6057*
I	*Homalomena elmeri* Engl. *13833*	
	I	*13833* Philippines (low and medium altitudes) *13833*
I	*Homalomena palawanensis* Engl. *13833*	
	I	*13833* Philippines (low altitude) *13833*
I	*Lagenandra meeboldii* (Engl.) C. Fischer	
	I	India - Karnataka (Agalhatti, Mysore)
	I	India - Kerala (Tuppanad, south Malabar)
I	*Lagenandra undulata* Sastry *14727*	
	I	India - Arunachal Pradesh (Subansiri) *14727*
R	*Lazarum mirabile* A.Hay *20681*	
	R	*20681* Australia - Northern Territory *20681*
R	*Monstera costaricensis* (Engl. & Krause) Croat & Grayum *11992*	
	R	*11992* Costa Rica *11992*
R	*Monstera gracilis* Engl. *8485*	
	R	*8485* Colombia *8485*
E	*Nephthytis swainei* J. Bogner *10260*	
	E	*6072* Ghana *6072*
Ex	*Philodendron clementis* C. Wright ex Griseb. *11840*	
	Ex	*19105* Cuba (PR; LV; LH) *11840*
I	*Philodendron fendleri* Krause *5932*	
	I	*5932* Trinidad & Tobago (Trinidad) *5932*
E	*Philodendron scaberulum* C. Wright *5607*	
	E	*19105* Cuba (Pinar del Rio) *5607*
I	*Philodendron scandens* C. Koch & H. Sello *19712*	
	I	*19712* Cayman Is. (Grand Cayman) *19712*
V	*Philodendron schottii* C. Koch *20883*	
	V	*20883* Jamaica *20883*
I	*Pothos armatus* C. Fischer *14727*	
	I	India - Karnataka (Tambracheri Ghat, Malabar)
R	*Pothos brassii* Burtt *20681*	
	R	*20681* Australia - Queensland *20681*

R	*Pothos brownii* Domin *20681*	
	R	20681 Australia - Queensland 20681
R	*Pothos penicilliger* Gagnepain *6057*	
	R	Vietnam 6057
I	*Pothos thomsonianus* Schott *14727*	
	I	India - Karnataka (Carnatic)
	I	India - Kerala (Travancore Hills) 14727
R	*Pothos touranensis* Gagnepain *6057*	
	R	Vietnam 6057
I	*Protarum sechellarum* Engl. *14296*	
	I	19182 Seychelles (granitic) 14296
I	*Pycnospatha soerensii* S.Y. Hu *19120*	
	I	19120 Thailand 19120
R	*Raphidophora laichauensis* Gagnepain *6057*	
	R	Vietnam 6057
R	*Remusatia vivipara* (Roxb.) Schott *20681*	
	I	20681 Australia - Northern Territory 20681
	I	20681 Australia - Queensland 20681
R	*Rhaphidophora pachyphylla* Krause *20681*	
	R	20681 Australia - Queensland 20681
I	*Rhaphidophora palawanensis* Merr. *13833*	
	I	13833 Philippines 13833
R	*Scindapsus annamicus* Gagnepain *6057*	
	R	Vietnam 6057
R	*Spathiphyllum atrovirens* Schott *9037*	
	R	9111 Costa Rica 9037
R	*Theriophonum dalzellii* Schott *14727*	
	R	14727 India - Karnataka 14727
	R	14727 India - Maharashtra 14727
I	*Theriophonum fischeri* Sivadasan *14727*	
	I	India - Kerala (central)
	I	India - Tamil Nadu (south-west) 14727
V	*Theriophonum sivaganganum* (Ramam. et Seb.) Bogner *14727*	
	V	14727 India - Tamil Nadu 14727
I	*Thomsonia larsenii* S.Y. Hu *19120*	
	I	19120 Thailand 19120
I	*Typhonium cordifolium* S.Y. Hu *19120*	
	I	19120 Thailand 19120
R	*Typhonium eliosurum* (Benth.) O.Evans *20681*	
	R	20681 Australia - New South Wales 20681
E	*Typhonium incurvatum* Blatter & McCann *11494*	
	E	11494 India - Maharashtra (Bombay-Sion) 11494
R	*Typhonium jonesii* A.Hay *20681*	
	R	20681 Australia - Northern Territory 20681
I	*Typhonium larsenii* *19120*	
	I	19120 Thailand 19120
V	*Typhonium listeri* Prain *14872*	
	V	14872 Bangladesh 14872
E	*Urospathella wurdackii* (Bunting) Bunting *20883*	
	I	20883 Venezuela 20883
E	*Xanthosoma caladioides* Grayum *20883, 9482*	
	I	20883 Panama 20883
I	*Zantedeschia jucunda* Letty *20604*	
	I	20604 South Africa - Transvaal 20604
R	*Zantedeschia odorata* P.L.Perry *20604*	
	R	20604 South Africa - Cape Province 20604
R	*Zantedeschia pentlandii* (Watson) Wittm. *20604*	
	R	20604 South Africa - Transvaal 20604

Asparagaceae

Number of genera: 1
Number of species: 50-60
Recorded threatened species: 13 (23%)

Widespread in Old World.

R	*Asparagus arborescens* Willd. ex J.A. & J.H. Schultes	
	R	Spain - Canary Is.
I	*Asparagus asiaticus* L.	
	I	India - Karnataka (Bellary)
R	*Asparagus coodei* Davis *12840*	
	R	12840 Turkey 12840
E	*Asparagus fallax* Svent. *20750*	
	E	20750 Spain - Canary Is. 20750
I	*Asparagus fysoni* Macbr.	
	I	India - Tamil Nadu (Nilgiri Hills)
I	*Asparagus jacquemonti* Baker *14782*	
	I	14782 India - Maharashtra 14782
R	*Asparagus litoralis* Steven *20171*	
	R	former European USSR
E	*Asparagus lycaonicus* Davis *12840*	
	E	12840 Turkey 12840
V	*Asparagus nesiotes* Svent.	
	E	Portugal - Salvage Is.
	V	Spain - Canary Is.
R	*Asparagus pastorianus* Webb & Berthel.	
	R	Spain - Canary Is.
R	*Asparagus plocamoides* Webb ex Svent.	
	R	Spain - Canary Is.
I	*Asparagus rottleri* Baker *14782*	
	I	14782 India (Deccan Peninsula) 14782
R	*Asparagus umbellatus* Link ssp. *lowei* (Kunth) Valdes	
	R	Portugal - Madeira

Asphodelaceae

Number of genera: 11
Number of species: 319
Recorded threatened species: 48 (15%)

Europe, Africa, Asia, New Zealand and Mexico.

R	*Asphodeline anatolica* E. Tuzlaci *12840*	
	R	12840 Turkey 12840
R	*Asphodeline cilicica* E. Tuzlaci *12840*	
	R	12840 Turkey 12840
V	*Asphodeline damascena* (Boiss.) Baker ssp. *ovoidea* E. Tuzlaci *12840*	
	V	12840 Turkey 12840
R	*Asphodeline damascena* (Boiss.) Baker ssp. *rugosa* E. Tuzlaci *12840*	
	R	12840 Turkey 12840
R	*Asphodeline peshmeniana* E. Tuzlaci *12840*	
	R	12840 Turkey 12840
R	*Asphodeline prismatocarpa* J. Gay ex Baker *12840*	
	R	12840 Turkey 12840
I	*Asphodeline tenuior* (Bieb.) Ledeb. *5942*	
	I	5942 Russia - North Caucasus 5942
R	*Asphodeline tenuior* (Fischer) Ledeb. var. *puberulenta* E. Tuzlaci *12840*	

R   12840   Turkey *12840*

E   *Asphodelus bento-rainhae* P.Silva *8000, 20171*
     E   20076   Portugal (central - Serra da Gardunha) *8000*

R   *Bulbine brunsvigiifolia* Baker *20604*
     R   20604   South Africa - Cape Province *20604*

R   *Bulbine diphylla* Schltr. ex Poelln. *20604*
     R   20604   South Africa - Cape Province *20604*

R   *Bulbine fallax* Poelln. *20604*
     R   20604   South Africa - Cape Province *20604*

V   *Bulbine haworthioides* B.Nord. *20604*
     V   20604   South Africa - Cape Province *20604*

R   *Bulbine louwii* L.I.Hall *20604*
     R   20604   South Africa - Cape Province *20604*

E   *Bulbine margarethae* L.I.Hall *20604*
     E   20604   South Africa - Cape Province *20604*

R   *Bulbine orchioides* Drège ex Poelln. *20604*
     R   20604   South Africa - Cape Province *20604*

R   *Bulbine striata* Baijnath & Van Jaarsv. *20604*
     R   20604   South Africa - Cape Province *20604*

V   *Bulbine wiesei* L.I.Hall *20604*
     V   20604   South Africa - Cape Province *20604*

R   *Bulbinella nana* P.L.Perry *20604*
     R   20604   South Africa - Cape Province *20604*

I   *Eremurus candidus* Vved. *5942*
     I   5942   Tajikistan *5942*

Ex/E   *Eremurus chloranthus* Popov *5942*
     Ex/E *5942*   Uzbekistan *5942*

R   *Eremurus hilariae* Popov & Vved. *5942*
     R   5942   Kazakhstan *5942*

I   *Eremurus kopetdaghensis* Popov ex B. Fedtsch. *5942*
     I   5942   Turkmenistan (west) *5942*

Ex/E   *Eremurus korovinii* B. Fedtsch. *5942*
     Ex/E *5942*   Kazakhstan (south) *5942*

I   *Eremurus lachnostegius* Vved. *5942*
     I   5942   Tajikistan (west) *5942*

I   *Eremurus roseolus* Vved. *5942*
     I   5942   Tajikistan *5942*

R   *Kniphofia acraea* Codd *20604*
     R   20604   South Africa - Cape Province *20604*

R   *Kniphofia bruceae* (Codd) Codd *20604*
     R   20604   South Africa - Cape Province *20604*

I   *Kniphofia citrina* Baker *20604*
     I   20604   South Africa - Cape Province *20604*

R   *Kniphofia coddiana* Cufod. *20604*
     R   20604   South Africa - Cape Province (Transkei) *20604*
     R   20604   South Africa - Natal *20604*

R   *Kniphofia coralligemma* E.A.Bruce *20604*
     R   20604   South Africa - Transvaal *20604*

I   *Kniphofia crassifolia* Baker *20604, 17458*
     I   20604   South Africa - Transvaal *20604*

R   *Kniphofia ensifolia* Baker ssp. *autumnalis* Codd *20604*
     R   20604   South Africa - Orange Free State *20604*

R   *Kniphofia evansii* Baker *20604*
     R   20604   South Africa - Natal *20604*

V   *Kniphofia flammula* Codd *20604*
     V   20604   South Africa - Natal *20604*

V   *Kniphofia hirsuta* Codd *20604*
     V   20604   Lesotho *20604*
     V   20604   South Africa - Cape Province *20604*

R   *Kniphofia kirkii* Baker *5926*
     R   5926   Tanzania *5926*

E   *Kniphofia latifolia* Codd *20604*
     E   20604   South Africa - Natal *20604*

E   *Kniphofia leucocephala* Baijnath *20604*
     E   20604   South Africa - Natal *20604*

R   *Kniphofia mulanjeana* Blackmoore *7866*
     R   Malawi *7866*

Ex   *Kniphofia pauciflora* Baker *20604*
     Ex   20604   South Africa - Natal *20604*

V   *Kniphofia reflexum* Hutch. ex Codd
     V   Cameroon (Lakom & Bamenda)

R   *Kniphofia rigidifolia* E.A.Bruce *20604*
     R   20604   South Africa - Transvaal *20604*

R   *Kniphofia sarmentosa* (Andrews) Kunth *20604*
     R   20604   South Africa - Cape Province *20604*

R   *Kniphofia triangularis* Kunth ssp. *obtusiloba* (Berger) Codd *20604*
     R   20604   South Africa - Natal *20604*
     R   20604   South Africa - Transvaal *20604*

E   *Kniphofia umbrina* Codd *20604, 18023*
     E   20604   Swaziland *20604*

I   *Trachyandra adamsonii* (Compton) Oberm. *20604*
     I   20604   South Africa - Cape Province *20604*

R   *Trachyandra aridimontana* J.C.Manning *20604*
     R   20604   South Africa - Cape Province *20604*

R   *Trachyandra prolifera* P.L.Perry *20604*
     R   20604   South Africa - Cape Province *20604*

R   *Trachyandra thyrsoidea* (Baker) Oberm. *20604*
     R   20604   South Africa - Cape Province *20604*

R   *Trachyandra zebrina* (Schltr. ex Poelln.) Oberm. *20604*
     R   20604   South Africa - Cape Province *20604*

Asteliaceae

Number of genera: 4
Number of species: 34
Recorded threatened species: 9   (26%)

Mascarenes, New Guinea, Australasia, Pacific, Chile.

V   *Astelia australiana* (J.H.Willis) L.Moore *20681*
     V   20681   Australia - Victoria *20681*

E   *Astelia chathamica* (Skottsb.) L. Moore *86*
     E   19305   New Zealand - Chatham Is. *19106*

E   *Astelia tovii* F. Brown
     E   French Polynesia - Marquesas Is

E   *Astelia waialealae* Wawra *20850, 14209*
     I   20850   U.S. - Hawaii *20850*

R   *Milligania johnstonii* F.Muell. ex Benth. *20681*
     R   20681   Australia - Tasmania *20681*

R   *Milligania lindoniana* Rodway ex W.M.Curtis *20681*
     R   20681   Australia - Tasmania *20681*

R   *Milligania longifolia* Hook.f. *20681*
     R   20681   Australia - Tasmania *20681*

R   *Milligania stylosa* (F.Muell. ex Hook.f.) F.Muell. ex Benth. *20681*
     R   20681   Australia - Tasmania *20681*

V   *Neoastelia spectabilis* J.B.Williams *20681*
    V   *20681*   Australia - New South Wales *20681*

Blandfordiaceae

Number of genera:	1
Number of species:	4
Recorded threatened species:	1 (25%)

Eastern Australia.

R   *Blandfordia cunninghamii* Lindley *20681*
    R   *20681*   Australia - New South Wales *20681*

Bromeliaceae

Number of genera:	45
Number of species:	2,000
Recorded threatened species:	480 (24%)

New World, except one species in western tropical Africa.

R   *Abromeitiella brevifolia* (Gridebach)
      Castellanos *20883, 9097*
    R   *19575*   Argentina *20883*
    V   *20883*   Bolivia *20883*

R   *Abromeitiella lorentziana* (Mez) Castellanos *20883,*
      9097
    R   *1975*   Argentina *20883*

V   *Aechmea allenii* L.B. Sm. *20883, 9097*
    V   *16317*   Panama *20883*

R   *Aechmea apocalyptica* Reitz *17746*
    R   *17079*   Brazil *17079*
    R   *17746*   Brazil - Parana *17746*
    R   *17746*   Brazil - Santa Catarina *17746*
    R   *17746*   Brazil - Sao Paulo *17746*

R   *Aechmea blumenavii* Reitz *17746*
    R   *17746*   Brazil - Santa Catarina (Itajaf, Tubarao)
        17746

V   *Aechmea decurva* Proctor *20883, 13336*
    V   *13336*   Jamaica *20883*

I   *Aechmea dichlamydea* Baker *9097*
    V   Trinidad & Tobago
    I   Venezuela

R   *Aechmea dichlamydea* Baker var. *pariaensis*
      Pittendre. *16228*
    R   *23*   Venezuela (Sucre) *16228*

R   *Aechmea kertesziae* Reitz *9097*
    R   Brazil - Santa Catarina *9097*

R   *Aechmea kleinii* Reitz *17746*
    R   *17746*   Brazil - Santa Catarina *17746*

I   *Aechmea orlandiana* Lyman B. Smith var.
      orlandiana 11245
    I   *11245*   Brazil *11245*

R   *Aechmea pimenti-velosi* Reitz *17746*
    R   *17746*   Brazil - Santa Catarina *17746*

V   *Bromelia superba* Mez *20883, 13336*
    V   *13336*   Jamaica *20883*

V   *Catopsis werckleana* Mez *9097*
    V   *9426*   Costa Rica *9097*

V   *Comnellia caricifolia* L.B. Smith *20883*
    E   *20883*   Guyana *20883*
    E   *20883*   Venezuela *20883*

E   *Comnellia quelchii* N.E. Brown *20883*
    E   *20883*   Venezuela *20883*

R   *Connellia augustae* (Richard Schomburgk) N.E.

      Brown *20883*
    E   *20883*   Guyana *20883*
    R   *20883*   Venezuela *20883*

E   *Connellia nutans* L.B. Smith *20883*
    E   *20883*   Venezuela *20883*

V   *Cottendorfia argentea* (L.B.Smith) L.B. Smith *20883*
    V   *20883*   Venezuela *20883*

E   *Cottendorfia brachyphylla* (L.B. Smith) L.B.
      Smith *20883*
    E   *20883*   Venezuela *20883*

E   *Cottendorfia cylindrostachya* (L.B. Smith) L.B.
      Smith *20883*
    E   *20883*   Venezuela *20883*

E   *Cottendorfia dendritica* L.B. Smith *20883*
    E   *20883*   Brazil *20883*

E   *Cottendorfia dyckioides* L.B. Smith *20883*
    E   *20883*   Venezuela *20883*

R   *Cottendorfia florida* Schultes filius *20883*
    R   *20883*   Brazil *20883*

R   *Cottendorfia geniculata* (L.B. Smith) L.B.
      Smith *20883*
    E   *20883*   Guyana *20883*
    R   *20883*   Venezuela *20883*

E   *Cottendorfia glacillima* L.B. Smith *20883*
    E   *20883*   Venezuela *20883*

R   *Cottendorfia guianensis* var. *guinansis 20883*
    V   *20883*   Guyana *20883*
    V   *20883*   Venezuela *20883*

E   *Cottendorfia guianensis* var. *vestita* L.B.
      Smith *20883*
    E   *20883*   Venezuela *20883*

E   *Cottendorfia longipes* L.B. Smith *20883*
    E   *20883*   Venezuela *20883*

E   *Cottendorfia maguirei* L.B. Smith *20883*
    E   *20883*   Brazil *20883*

V   *Cottendorfia minor* (L.B. Smith) L.B. Smith *20883*
    V   *20883*   Venezuela *20883*

V   *Cottendorfia navioides* (L.B. Smith) L.B. Smith *20883*
    V   *20883*   Venezuela *20883*

E   *Cottendorfia nubigena* L.B. Smith *20883*
    E   *20883*   Venezuela *20883*

V   *Cottendorfia paludosa* (L.B. Smith) L.B. Smith *20883*
    E   *20883*   Guyana *20883*
    E   *20883*   Venezuela *20883*

E   *Cottendorfia phelpsiae* (L.B.Smith) L.B. Smith *20883*
    E   *20883*   Venezuela *20883*

E   *Cottendorfia savannensis* L.B. Smith *20883*
    E   *20883*   Venezuela *20883*

V   *Cottendorfia serrulata* var. *reductata* (L.B. Smith)
      L.B. Smith *20883*
    E   *20883*   Guyana *20883*
    E   *20883*   Venezuela *20883*

E   *Cottendorfia serrulata* var. *serrulata 20883*
    E   *20883*   Venezuela *20883*

E   *Cottendorfia stenophylla* (L.B. Smith) L.B.
      Smith *20883*
    E   *20883*   Venezuela *20883*

E   *Cottendorfia steyermarkii* (L.B. Smith) L.B.
      Smith *20883*
    E   *20883*   Venezuela *20883*

E *Cottendorfia subsimplex* (L.B. Smith) L.B. Smith *20883*
    E   *20883* Venezuela *20883*

E *Cottendorfia thyrsoidea* (L.B. Smith) L.B. Smith *20883*
    E   *20883* Venezuela *20883*

V *Cottendorfia wurdackii* (L.B. Smith) L.B. Smith *20883*
    E   *20883* Guyana *20883*
    E   *20883* Venezuela *20883*

V *Deuterocohnia chrysantha* (Philippi) Mez *15088*
    V   *13875* Chile *13875*

V *Deuterocohnia chysantha* (Philippi) Mez *20883*
    V   *20883* Argentina *20883*

V *Deuterocohnia digitata* L.B. Smith *20883*
    E   *20883* Argentina *20883*
    E   *20883* Bolivia *20883*

R *Deuterocohnia haumanii* Castellanos *20883*
    R   *20883* Argentina *20883*

R *Deuterocohnia meziana* O. Kuntze ex Mez *20883*
    E   *20883* Bolivia *20883*
    E   *20883* Brazil *20883*
    V   *20883* Paraguay *20883*

V *Deuterocohnia strobilifera* var. *inermis* L.B. Smith *20883*
    E   *20883* Argentina *20883*
    V   *20883* Bolivia *20883*

E *Deuterocohnia strobilifera* var. *strobilifera* *20883*
    E   *20883* Bolivia *20883*

E *Dyckia cabrerae* L.B. Smith & Reitz *17079*
    E   *17079* Brazil - Santa Catarina *17079*

E *Dyckia hatschbachii* L.B. Smith *17079*
    E   *17746* Brazil - Parana *17746*
    E   *17079* Brazil - Santa Catarina (northeast) *17079*

E *Dyckia ibiramensis* Reitz *17079*
    E   *17079* Brazil - Santa Catarina (Rio Itajaí do Norte) *17079*

E *Dyckia macedoi* L.B. Smith *17928*
    E   *17928* Brazil - Minas Gerais (Serra do Cipó) *17928*

E *Dyckia sanmartiniensis* *5462*
    E   *5462* Argentina *5462*

E *Encholirium bradeanum* L.B. Smith *20883*
    E   *20883* Brazil *20883*

E *Encholirium densiflorum* Ule *20883*
    E   *20883* Brazil *20883*

E *Encholirium glaziovii* Mez *20883*
    E   *20883* Brazil *20883*

E *Encholirium gracile* L.B. Smith *20883*
    E   *20883* Brazil *20883*

E *Encholirium hoehneanum* L.B. Smith *20883*
    E   *20883* Brazil *20883*

E *Encholirium horridum* L.B. Smith *20883*
    E   *20883* Brazil *20883*

E *Encholirium irwinii* L.B. Smith *20883*
    E   *20883* Brazil *20883*

E *Encholirium lutzii* L.B. Smith *20883*
    E   *20883* Brazil *20883*

E *Encholirium magalhaesii* L.B. Smith *20883*

E   *20883* Brazil *20883*

E *Encholirium rupestre* Ule *20883*
    E   *20883* Brazil *20883*

R *Encholirium spectabile* Martius ex Schultes filius *20883*
    R   *20883* Brazil *20883*

E *Encholirium subsecundum* (Baker) Mez *20883*
    E   *20883* Brazil *20883*

R *Fernseea itataiae* (Wawra) Baker *17079*
    R   *17079* Brazil - Minas Gerais (Parque Nacional de Itataia) *17079*
    R   *17746* Brazil - Rio de Janeiro (Parque Nacional de Itataia) *17746*

R *Fosterella albicans* (Grisebach) L.B. Smith *20883*
    V   *20883* Argentina *20883*
    E   *20883* Bolivia *20883*

E *Fosterella aletroides* (L.B. Smith) L.B. Smith *20883*
    E   *20883* Peru *20883*

E *Fosterella gracilis* (Rusby) L.B. Smith *20883*
    E   *20883* Bolivia *20883*

E *Fosterella graminea* (L.B. Smith) L.B. Smith *20883*
    E   *20883* Bolivia *20883*

E *Fosterella pearcei* (Beker) L.B. Smith *20883*
    E   *20883* Bolivia *20883*

R *Fosterella penduliflora* (C.H. Wright) L.B. Smith *20883*
    V   *20883* Argentina *20883*
    E   *20883* Bolivia *20883*
    E   *20883* Peru *20883*

E *Fosterella petiolata* (Mez) L.B. Smith *20883*
    E   *20883* Peru *20883*

E *Fosterella rojasii* (L.B. Smith) L.B. Smith *20883*
    E   *20883* Paraguay *20883*

V *Fosterella rusbyi* (Mez) L.B. Smith *20883*
    E   *20883* Bolivia *20883*
    E   *20883* Peru *20883*

R *Fosterella schidosperma* (Baker) L.B. Smith *20883*
    E   *20883* Bolivia *20883*
    V   *20883* Peru *20883*

E *Fosterella villosula* (Harms) L.B. Smith *20883*
    E   *20883* Bolivia *20883*

E *Fosterella weddelliana* (Brongniart ex Baker) L.B. Smith *20883*
    E   *20883* Bolivia *20883*

I *Glomeropitcairnia erectiflora* Mez *9097*
    V   Trinidad & Tobago
    I   Venezuela

E *Greigia berteroi* *19116*
    E   *19125* Chile - Juan Fernandez Is. *19116*

I *Greigia rohwederi* Lyman B. Smith *9097*
    I   *21291* El Salvador *9097*

V *Greigia sylvicola* Standley *9097*
    V   *9426* Costa Rica *9097*

R *Guzmania andreana* (E. Morren) Mez *9097*
    R   *19352* Colombia *9097*

V *Guzmania condensata* Mez & Werckle *9097*
    V   *9426* Costa Rica *9097*

I *Guzmania ecuadoriensis* Gilmartin *9097*
    I   *19550* Ecuador *9097*

R *Guzmania erythrolepis* Brongn. ex Planch. *20883*

V		20883 Jamaica 20883
I		20883 Puerto Rico 20883
V	*Guzmania fawcettii* Mez 20883	
V		20883 Jamaica 20883
I	*Guzmania filiorum* L.B. Sm. 20883, 9097	
I		16317 Panama 20883
V	*Guzmania kennedyae* Lyman B. Smith & Read 10747	
V		16317 Panama 10747
R	*Guzmania lehmanniana* (Wittm.) Mez	
R		Colombia
I	*Guzmania macropoda* L.B. Sm. 20883, 9097	
I		16317 Panama 20883
R	*Guzmania palustris* (Wittm.) Mez 9097	
R		19352 Colombia 9097
R	*Guzmania rauhiana* H.E. Luther 10260	
R		11245 Ecuador 11245
E	*Guzmania virescens* L.B. Sm. var. *laxior* Lyman B. Smith 20883, 9097	
I		20883 Panama 20883
V		19788 Venezuela 19788
E	*Hechtia conzattiana* Lyman B. Smith 9097	
E		19790 Mexico - Oaxaca 9097
E	*Hechtia fragilis* Burt-Utley & Utley 10155	
E		19790 Mexico - Oaxaca 10155
V	*Hechtia pedicellata* S.Watson 9097	
V		19761 Mexico - Jalisco 9097
E	*Hechtia reticulata* Lyman B. Smith 9097	
E		19790 Mexico - Colima 9097
V	*Hechtia zacatecae* Lyman B. Smith 9097	
V		19761 Mexico - Zacatecas 9097
R	*Hohenbergia abbreviata* L.B. Sm. & Proctor 20883, 13336	
R		13336 Jamaica 20883
R	*Hohenbergia belemii* Lyman B. Smith 16686	
R		16686 Brazil (Belem) 16686
I	*Hohenbergia brittoniana* L.B. Sm. 20883, 13336	
I		13336 Jamaica 20883
E	*Hohenbergia caymanensis* Britton 19712	
E		19434 Cayman Is. (Grand Cayman) 19434
V	*Hohenbergia distans* (Griseb.) Bak. 20883, 13336	
V		13336 Jamaica 20883
V	*Hohenbergia fawcettii* Mez 20883, 19890	
R		19890 Jamaica 20883
I	*Hohenbergia gnetacea* Mez 20883, 13336	
I		13336 Jamaica 20883
R	*Hohenbergia inermis* Mez 20883	
R		20883 Jamaica 20883
R	*Hohenbergia jamaicana* L.B. Sm. & Proctor 20883, 13336	
R		13336 Jamaica 20883
V	*Hohenbergia laesslei* L.B. Sm. 20883, 13336	
V		13336 Jamaica 20883
V	*Hohenbergia negrilensis* Britton ex L.B. Sm. 20883, 13336	
V		13336 Jamaica 20883
V	*Hohenbergia proctorii* L.B.Sm. 20883	
V		20883 Jamaica 20883
R	*Hohenbergia spinulosa* Mez 20883	
R		20883 Jamaica 20883

R	*Hohenbergia urbaniana* Mez 20883	
R		20883 Jamaica 20883
E	*Hohenbergiopsis guatemalensis* (Lyman B. Smith) Lyman B. & R. Read 19170	
E		19170 Guatemala (montane forest, 30 plants remain) 19170
E	*Lindmania aurea* L.B. Smith, Steyermark & Robinson 20883	
I		20883 Venezuela 20883
E	*Lindmania imitans* L.B. Smith, Steyermark & Robinson 20883	
I		20883 Venezuela 20883
E	*Lindmania piresii* L.B. Smith, Steyermark & Robinson 20883	
I		20883 Brazil 20883
E	*Lindmania riparia* L.B. Smith, Steyermark & Robinson 20883	
I		20883 Venezuela 20883
E	*Lindmania saxicola* L.B. Smith, Steyermark & Robinson 20883	
I		20883 Venezuela 20883
E	*Lindmania sessilis* L. B. Smith, Steyermark & Robinson 20883	
I		20883 Venezuela 20883
R	*Lymania corallina* (Brong. ex Beer) Read 13830	
R		13830 Brazil 13830
E	*Navia berryana* L.B. Smith, Steyermark & Robinson 20883	
I		20883 Venezuela 20883
E	*Navia crassicaulis* L.B. Smith, Steyermark & Robinson 20883	
I		20883 Venezuela 20883
E	*Navia culcitaria* L.B. smith, Steyermark & Robinson 20883	
I		20883 Venezuela 20883
E	*Navia delascionis* L.B. Smith, Steyermark & Robinson 20883	
I		20883 Venezuela 20883
E	*Navia filifera* L.B. smith, Steyermark & Robinson 20883	
I		20883 Venezuela 20883
E	*Navia huberiana* L. B. Smith, Steyermark & Robinson 20883	
I		20883 Venezuela 20883
E	*Navia liesneri* L.B. Smith, Steyermark & Robinson 20883	
I		20883 Venezuela 20883
E	*Navia linearis* L.B. Smith, Steyermark & Robinson 20883	
I		20883 Venezuela 20883
E	*Navia pedemontana* L.B. Smith, Steyermark & Robinson 20883	
I		20883 Venezuela 20883
E	*Navia piresii* L.B. Smith, Steyermark & Robinson 20883	
I		20883 Brazil 20883
E	*Navia plowmanii* L.B. Smith, Steyermark & Robinson 20883	
I		20883 Venezuela 20883
E	*Navia polyglomerata* L.B. Smith, Steyermark &	

Robinson *20883*

I *20883* Venezuela *20883*

I *Neoregelia gavionensis* Martinelli & Leme *17014*

I *12014* Brazil - Rio de Janeiro *17014*

E *Pitcairnia agavifolia* L.B. Smith *20883*

E *20883* Venezuela *20883*

E *Pitcairnia alborubra* Baker *20883*

E *20883* Colombia *20883*

V *Pitcairnia amblyosperma* L.B. Smith *20883*

V *20883* Mexico *20883*

R *Pitcairnia andreana* Linden *9097*

R *19352* Colombia *9097*

E *Pitcairnia anomala* Hoehne *20883*

E *20883* Brazil *20883*

R *Pitcairnia aphelandriflora* Lem. *20883*

E *20883* Panama *20883*

E *20883* Ecuador *20883*

E *20883* Peru *20883*

V *Pitcairnia armata* Maury *20883*

V *20883* Venezuela *20883*

R *Pitcairnia billbergioides* Lyman B. Smith *13831*

R *13831* Peru *13831*

R *Pitcairnia bradei* Markgraf *20883*

R *20883* Brazil *20883*

E *Pitcairnia breweri* L.B. Smith *20883*

E *20883* Venezuela *20883*

R *Pitcairnia bromeliifolia* var. *wynteri*
      Read *20883*

R *20883* Jamaica *20883*

R *Pitcairnia bulbosa* L.B. Smith *20883*

I *20883* Colombia *20883*

V *20883* Venezuela *20883*

R *Pitcairnia caricifolia* var. *caricifolia* *20883*

V *20883* Brazil *20883*

V *20883* Colombia *20883*

V *20883* Guyana *20883*

E *20883* Suriname *20883*

E *20883* Venezuela *20883*

E *Pitcairnia caricifolia* var. *macrantha* L.B.
      Smith *20883*

E *20883* Venezuela *20883*

E *Pitcairnia cassapensis* Mez *18200*

E *9446* Peru *18200*

V *Pitcairnia chiriquensis* L.B. Sm. *20883, 9097*

V *16317* Panama *20883*

V *Pitcairnia costata* L.B. Smith *20883*

I *20883* Colombia *20883*

E *20883* Ecuador *20883*

E *Pitcairnia ctenophylla* L.B. Smith *20883*

E *20883* Venezuela *20883*

E *Pitcairnia cyanopetala* Ule *18200*

E *9446* Peru *18200*

I *Pitcairnia feliciana* (A. Chev.) Harms & Mildbr. *7926*

I Guinea *7926*

E *Pitcairnia ferreyrae* Lyman B. Smith *18200*

E *9446* Peru *18200*

E *Pitcairnia filispina* L.B. Smith *20883*

E *20883* Venezuela *20883*

E *Pitcairnia geyskesii* L.B. Smith *20883*

E *20883* Suriname *20883*

V *Pitcairnia halophila* Lyman B. Smith *9097*

V *9426* Costa Rica *9097*

E *Pitcairnia harlingii* L.B. Smith *20883, 9097*

E *20883* Ecuador *20883*

E *Pitcairnia heliophila* L.B. Smith *20883*

E *20883* Colombia *20883*

V *Pitcairnia incarnata* Baker *20883*

I *20883* French Guiana *20883*

I *20883* Guyana *20883*

R *Pitcairnia juncoides* L.B. Smith *20883*

R *20883* Venezuela *20883*

E *Pitcairnia killipiana* Lyman B. Smith *20883*

E *20883* Colombia *20883*

E *Pitcairnia killipiana* Lyman B. Smith var. *viridis*
      Varadarajan & Forero *20883*

I *20883* Colombia *20883*

R *Pitcairnia kressii* Luther *11245*

R *11245* Panama *11245*

E *Pitcairnia kunhardtiana* L.B. Smith *20883*

E *20883* Venezuela *20883*

R *Pitcairnia laxissima* Baker *9097*

R *19352* Colombia *9097*

E *Pitcairnia limae* L.B. Smith *20883*

E *20883* Brazil *20883*

E *Pitcairnia maguirei* L.B. Smith *20883*

E *20883* Venezuela *20883*

V *Pitcairnia membranifolia* Baker *9097*

V *9426* Costa Rica *9097*

E *Pitcairnia mituensis* L.B. Smith *20883*

E *20883* Colombia *20883*

V *Pitcairnia nuda* Baker *20883*

E *20883* Guyana *20883*

E *20883* Suriname *20883*

E *20883* Venezuela *20883*

E *Pitcairnia occidentalis* var. *alversonii* (Lyman B.
      Smith & Read) *20883*

I *20883* Colombia *20883*

E *Pitcairnia patentiflora* var. *armata* L.B.
      Smith *20883*

E *20883* Venezuela *20883*

E *Pitcairnia patentiflora* var. *macrantha* L.B.
      Smith *20883*

E *20883* Colombia *20883*

R *Pitcairnia patentiflora* var. *subintegra* L.B.
      Smith *20883*

E *20883* Brazil *20883*

V *20883* Colombia *20883*

E *Pitcairnia platypetala* Mez *20883*

E *20883* Brazil *20883*

V *Pitcairnia pruinosa* Humboldt, Bonpland & Kunth *20883*

V *20883* Venezuela *20883*

R *Pitcairnia punicea* Scheidweiler *20883*

V *20883* Guatemala *20883*

V *20883* Mexico *20883*

E *Pitcairnia quesnelioides* L.B. Smith *20883*

E *20883* Colombia *20883*

R *Pitcairnia rubiginosa* var. *amazonica* (Baker) L.B.
      Smith *20883*

V *20883* Brazil *20883*

E *20883* Colombia *20883*

	I	20883	Venezuela *20883*

R   *Pitcairnia rubiginosa* **var.** *rubiginosa* *20883*

	V	20883	Brazil *20883*
	E	20883	Colombia *20883*
	E	20883	French Guiana *20883*

R   *Pitcairnia sordida* **Lyman B. Smith** *9097*

	R	19761	Mexico - Guerrero *9097*

V   *Pitcairnia spicata* **(Lamarck) Mez** *5710*

	V	5710	Martinique (Mont. Pelee; Carbet etc.) *5710*

E   *Pitcairnia tarapotensis* **Baker** *18200*

	E	9446	Peru *18200*

R   *Pitcairnia tillandsioides* **Lyman B. Smith** *9097*

	R	19761	Mexico - Guerrero *9097*

R   *Pitcairnia tuerckheimii* **J.D. Smith var.** *tuerckheimii* *9097*

	R	19761	Guatemala *9097*
	R	19761	Mexico *9097*

V   *Pitcairnia turbinella* **L.B. Smith** *20883*

	E	20883	Venezuela *20883*

Ex   *Pitcairnia undulata* **Scheidw.** *9097*

	Ex	9097	Brazil *9097*

E   *Pitcairnia wardackii* **L.B. Smith** *20883*

	E	20883	Venezuela *20883*

R   *Pitcairnia xanthocalyx* **Martius** *9097*

	R	19761	Mexico *9097*

E   *Puya adscendens* **L.B. Smith** *20883*

	E	20883	Peru *20883*

E   *Puya aequatorialis* **var.** *aequatorialis* *20883*

	E	20883	Ecuador *20883*

E   *Puya aequatorialis* **var.** *albiflora* **André** *20883*

	E	20883	Ecuador *20883*

E   *Puya alata* **L.B. Smith** *20883*

	E	20883	Bolivia *20883*

E   *Puya alba* **L.B. Smith** *20883*

	E	20883	Bolivia *20883*

E   *Puya alpicola* **L.B. Smith** *20883*

	E	20883	Colombia *20883*

V   *Puya angulonis* **L.B. Smith** *20883*

	V	20883	Peru *20883*

E   *Puya angusta* **L.B. Smith** *20883*

	E	20883	Peru *20883*

E   *Puya araneosa* **L.B. Smith** *20883*

	E	20883	Peru *20883*

E   *Puya argentea* **L.B. Smith** *20883*

	E	20883	Peru *20883*

V   *Puya aristeguietae* **L.B. Smith** *20883*

	V	20883	Venezuela *20883*

E   *Puya atra* **L.B. Smith** *20883, 12379*

	E	20883	Bolivia (Yungas, Cochabamba) *20883*

E   *Puya barkleyana* **L.B. Smith** *20883*

	E	20883	Colombia *20883*

E   *Puya bicolor* **L.B. Smith** *20883*

	E	20883	Colombia *20883*

E   *Puya boyacana* **Cuatrecasas** *20883*

	E	20883	Colombia *20883*

E   *Puya brachystachya* **(Baker) Mez** *20883*

	E	20883	Colombia *20883*

E   *Puya brittoniana* **Baker** *20883*

	E	20883	Bolivia *20883*

E   *Puya cardenasasii* **L.B. Smith** *20883*

	E	20883	Bolivia *20883*

E   *Puya cardonae* **L.B. Smith** *20883*

	E	20883	Venezuela *20883*

E   *Puya castellanosii* **L.B. Snith** *20883*

	E	20883	Argentina *20883*

E   *Puya cerrateana* **L.B. Smith** *20883*

	E	20883	Peru *20883*

E   *Puya chasmichensis* **L.B. Smith** *20883*

	E	20883	Peru *20883*

V   *Puya clava-herculis* **Mez & Sodiro** *20883*

	E	20883	Colombia *20883*
	E	20883	Ecuador *20883*

E   *Puya commixta* **L.B. Smith** *20883*

	E	20883	Peru *20883*

E   *Puya compacta* **L.B. Smith** *20883*

	E	20883	Ecuador *20883*

V   *Puya coquimbensis* **Mez** *15088*

	V	13875	Chile *13875*

E   *Puya coriacea* **L.B. Smith** *20883*

	E	20883	Peru *20883*

E   *Puya cristata* **L.B. Smith** *20883*

	E	20883	Bolivia *20883*

E   *Puya cryptantha* **Cuatrecasas** *20883*

	E	20883	Colombia *20883*

E   *Puya ctenorhyncha* **L.B. Smith** *20883*

	E	20883	Bolivia *20883*

E   *Puya cuatrecasasii* **L.B. Smith** *20883*

	E	20883	Colombia *20883*

E   *Puya cylindrica* **Mez** *20883*

	E	20883	Peru *20883*

V   *Puya dasylirioides* **Standley** *20883, 9097*

	V	20883	Costa Rica *20883*

R   *Puya densiflora* **Harms** *20883*

	R	20883	Peru *20883*

E   *Puya depauperata* **L.B. Smith** *20883*

	E	20883	Peru *20883*

E   *Puya dolichostrobila* **Harms** *20883*

	E	20883	Peru *20883*

R   *Puya dyckioides* **(Baker) Mez** *20883*

	R	20883	Argentina *20883*
	E	20883	Bolivia *20883*

V   *Puya eryngioides* **André** *20883*

	V	20883	Ecuador *20883*

E   *Puya exigua* **Mez** *20883*

	E	20883	Ecuador *20883*

V   *Puya fastuosa* **Mez** *20883*

	V	20883	Ecuador *20883*
	I	20883	Peru *20883*

E   *Puya ferox* **Mez** *20883*

	E	20883	Peru *20883*

E   *Puya ferreyrae* **L.B. Smith** *20883*

	E	20883	Peru *20883*

E   *Puya fiebrigii* **Mez** *20883*

	E	20883	Bolivia *20883*

E   *Puya floccosa* **var.** *compacta* **L.B. Smith** *20883*

E   20883 Venezuela 20883

E   ***Puya fosteriana*** L.B. Smith 20883
    E   20883 Bolivia 20883

E   ***Puya fulgens*** L.B. Smith 20883
    E   20883 Peru 20883

E   ***Puya furfuracea*** (Wildenow) L.B. Smith 20883
    E   20883 Colombia 20883

E   ***Puya gargantae*** L.B. Smith 20883
    E   20883 Colombia 20883

E   ***Puya gigas*** André 20883
    E   20883 Colombia 20883

E   ***Puya glabrescens*** L.B. Smith 20883
    E   20883 Bolivia 20883

E   ***Puya glandulosa*** L.B. Smith 20883
    E   20883 Peru 20883

E   ***Puya glareosa*** L.B. Smith 20883
    E   20883 Bolivia 20883

E   ***Puya glaucovirens*** Mez 20883
    E   20883 Peru 20883

R   ***Puya glomerifera*** L.B. Smith 20883
    R   20883 Ecuador 20883

R   ***Puya goudotiana*** Mez 20883
    R   20883 Colombia 20883

E   ***Puya gracilis*** L.B. Smith 20883
    E   20883 Peru 20883

E   ***Puya grandidens*** Mez 20883
    E   20883 Peru 20883

E   ***Puya grantii*** L.B. Smith 20883
    E   20883 Colombia 20883

E   ***Puya grubbii*** L.B. Smith 20883
    E   20883 Colombia 20883

R   ***Puya hamata*** L.B. Smith 20883
    V   20883 Colombia 20883
    V   20883 Ecuador 20883
    E   20883 Peru 20883

E   ***Puya harmsii*** (Castellanos) Castellanos 20883
    E   20883 Argentina 20883

E   ***Puya herrerae*** Hanrms 20883
    E   20883 Peru 20883

V   ***Puya herzogii*** Wittmack 20883
    V   20883 Bolivia 20883

V   ***Puya hofstenii*** Mez 20883
    I   20883 Argentina 20883
    I   20883 Bolivia 20883

E   ***Puya huancavelicae*** L.B. Smith 20883
    E   20883 Peru 20883

V   ***Puya humilis*** Mez 20883
    V   20883 Bolivia 20883

E   ***Puya hutchisonii*** L.B. Smith 20883
    E   20883 Peru 20883

E   ***Puya iltisiana*** L.B. Smith 20883
    E   20883 Peru 20883

E   ***Puya isabellina*** Mez 20883
    E   20883 Peru 20883

R   ***Puya killipii*** Cuatrecasas 20883
    V   20883 Colombia 20883
    V   20883 Venezuela 20883

E   ***Puya kuntzeana*** Mez 20883
    E   20883 Bolivia 20883

E   ***Puya laccata*** Mez 20883
    E   20883 Peru 20883

V   ***Puya lanata*** (Humboldt, Bonpland & Kunth) Schultes filius 20883
    V   20883 Ecuador 20883
    E   20883 Peru 20883

E   ***Puya lanuginosa*** (Ruiz & Pavón) Schules filius 20883
    E   20883 Peru 20883

R   ***Puya lasiopoda*** L.B. Smith 20883
    E   20883 Peru 20883

E   ***Puya laxa*** L.B. Smith 20883
    E   20883 Bolivia 20883

E   ***Puya lehmanniana*** L.B. Smith 20883
    E   20883 Colombia 20883

V   ***Puya leptostachya*** L.B. Smith 20883
    I   20883 Bolivia 20883
    E   20883 Peru 20883

V   ***Puya lilloi*** Castellanos 20883
    E   20883 Argentina 20883

V   ***Puya lineata*** Mez 20883
    V   20883 Colombia 20883

E   ***Puya llatensis*** L.B. Smith 20883
    E   20883 Peru 20883

E   ***Puya longisepala*** Mez 20883
    E   20883 Peru 20883

V   ***Puya longistyla*** Mez 20883
    V   20883 Peru 20883

E   ***Puya lopezii*** L.B. Smith 20883
    E   20883 Peru 20883

E   ***Puya macbridei*** L.B. Smith 20883
    E   20883 Peru 20883

E   ***Puya macropoda*** L.B. Smith 20883
    E   20883 Peru 20883

E   ***Puya macrura*** Mez 20883
    E   20883 Peru 20883

E   ***Puya maculata*** L.B. Smith 20883
    E   20883 Ecuador 20883

E   ***Puya mariae*** L.B. Smith 20883
    E   20883 Peru 20883

E   ***Puya medica*** L.B. Smith 20883
    E   20883 Peru 20883

E   ***Puya membranacea*** L.B. Smith 20883
    E   20883 Peru 20883

E   ***Puya meziana*** Wittmack 20883
    E   20883 Bolivia 20883

E   ***Puya micrantha*** Mez 20883
    E   20883 Argentina 20883

E   ***Puya minima*** L.B. Smith 20883
    E   20883 Bolivia 20883

E   ***Puya mitis*** Mez 20883
    E   20883 Peru 20883

E   ***Puya mollis*** Baker ex Mez 20883
    E   20883 Bolivia 20883

E   ***Puya nana*** Wittmarck 20883
    E   20883 Bolivia 20883

E   ***Puya nigrescens*** L.B. Smith 20883
    E   20883 Peru 20883

R   ***Puya nitida*** Mez 20883

	R	20883 Colombia 20883	

E *Puya nivalis* Baker 20883
    E   20883 Colombia 20883

E *Puya nutans* L.B. Smith 20883
    E   20883 Ecuador 20883

E *Puya obconica* L.B. Smith 20883
    E   20883 Ecuador 20883

E *Puya occidentalis* L.B. Smith 20883
    E   20883 Colombia 20883

E *Puya olivacea* Wittmack 20883
    E   20883 Bolivia 20883

E *Puya oxyantha* Mez 20883
    E   20883 Peru 20883

E *Puya parviflora* L.B. Smith 20883
    E   20883 Ecuador 20883

E *Puya paupera* Mez 20883
    E   20883 Bolivia 20883

E *Puya pearcei* (Beker) Mez 20883
    E   20883 Bolivia 20883

E *Puya penduliflora* L.B. Smith 20883
    E   20883 Bolivia 20883

E *Puya phelpsiae* L.B. Smith 20883
    E   20883 Venezuela 20883

E *Puya pichinchae* Mez & Sodiro 20883
    E   20883 Ecuador 20883

E *Puya pitcairnioides* L.B. Smith 20883
    E   20883 Peru 20883

E *Puya ponderosa* L.B. Smith 20883
    E   20883 Peru 20883

E *Puya potosina* L.B. Smith 20883
    E   20883 Bolivia 20883

E *Puya pratensis* L.B. Smith 20883
    E   20883 Peru 20883

E *Puya pygmaea* L.B. Smith 20883, 9097
    E   20883 Ecuador 20883

E *Puya pyramidata* (Ruiz & Pavón) Schultes filius 20883
    E   20883 Peru 20883

V *Puya raimondii* Harms. 20883, 12379
    E   20883 Bolivia 20883
    E   20883 Peru 20883

E *Puya ramosa* L.B. Smith 20883
    E   20883 Peru 20883

E *Puya rauhii* L.B. Smith 20883
    E   20883 Peru 20883

E *Puya reducta* L.B. Smith 20883
    E   20883 Bolivia 20883

E *Puya reflexiflora* Mez 20883
    E   20883 Peru 20883

E *Puya riparia* L.B. Smith 20883
    E   20883 Bolivia 20883

E *Puya roezlii* E. Morren 20883
    E   20883 Peru 20883

E *Puya roseana* L.B. Smith 20883
    E   20883 Ecuador 20883

E *Puya rusbyi* (Baker) Mez 20883
    E   20883 Bolivia 20883

E *Puya sagasteguii* L.B. Smith 20883
    E   20883 Peru 20883

E *Puya sanctae-crucis* (Baker) L.B. Smith 20883
    E   20883 Bolivia 20883

E *Puya sanctae-martae* L.B. Smith 20883
    E   20883 Colombia 20883

E *Puya santenderensis* Cuatercasas 20883
    E   20883 Colombia 20883

V *Puya santosii* var. *santosii* 20883
    V   20883 Colombia 20883

V *Puya santosii* var. *verdensis* Cuatrecasas 20883
    V   20883 Colombia 20883

E *Puya secunda* L.B. Smith 20883
    E   20883 Bolivia 20883

E *Puya simulans* L.B. Smith 20883
    E   20883 Peru 20883

V *Puya smithii* Castellanos 20883
    V   20883 Argentina 20883

E *Puya sodiroana* Mez 20883
    E   20883 Ecuador 20883

V *Puya solomonii* G. S. Varadarajan 20883
    I   20883 Bolivia 20883

R *Puya spathacea* (Grisebach) Mez 20883
    R   20883 Argentina 20883

E *Puya stenothyrsa* (Baker) Mez 20883
    E   20883 Bolivia 20883

E *Puya stipitata* L.B. Smith 20883
    E   20883 Peru 20883

E *Puya strobilantha* Mez 20883
    E   20883 Peru 20883

R *Puya thomasiana* André 20883, 9097
    I   20883 Colombia 20883
    E   20883 Ecuador 20883

E *Puya tovariana* L.B. Smith 20883
    E   20883 Peru 20883

V *Puya trianae* Beker 20883
    V   20883 Colombia 20883

E *Puya tristis* L.B. Smith 20883
    E   20883 Bolivia 20883

E *Puya trollii* L.B. Smith 20883
    E   20883 Bolivia 20883

E *Puya tuberosa* Mez 20883
    E   20883 Bolivia 20883

E *Puya tunarensis* Mez 20883
    E   20883 Bolivia 20883

E *Puya ugentiana* L.B. Smith 20883
    E   20883 Peru 20883

E *Puya ultima* L.B. Smith 20883
    E   20883 Bolivia 20883

E *Puya valida* L.B. Smith 20883
    E   20883 Bolivia 20883

E *Puya vargasiana* L.B. Smith 20883
    E   20883 Peru 20883

E *Puya venezuelana* L.B. Smith 20883
    E   20883 Venezuela 20883

V *Puya venusta* Philippi 15088
    V   13875 Chile 13875

V *Puya vestita* André 20883
    V   20883 Colombia 20883

E   *20883*   Ecuador *20883*

E   ***Puya volcanensis*** Castilon *20883*

    E   *20883*   Argentina *20883*

V   ***Puya weberbaueri*** Mez *20883, 18200*

    V   *19448*   Argentina *19448*

    E   *20883*   Bolivia *20883*

    V   *20883*   Peru *20883*

R   ***Puya weberiana*** E. Monrren ex Mez *20883*

    R   *20883*   Argentina *20883*

E   ***Puya weddelliana*** (Baker) Mez *20883*

    E   *20883*   Bolivia *20883*

E   ***Puya westii*** L.B. Smith *20883*

    E   *20883*   Peru *20883*

E   ***Puya wrightii*** L.B. Smith *20883*

    E   *20883*   Peru *20883*

E   ***Puya wurdackii*** L.B. Smith *20883*

    E   *20883*   Peru *20883*

E   ***Puya yakespala*** Castellanos *20883*

    E   *20883*   Argentina *20883*

R   ***Quesnelia imbricata*** Lyman B. Smith *9097*

    R   Brazil - Santa Catarina *9097*

E   ***Steyerbromelia diffusa*** L.B. Smith, Steyermark & robinson *20883*

    I   *20883*   Venezuela *20883*

E   ***Tillandsia acuminata*** L. B. Smith *20883*

    E   *20883*   Colombia *20883*

R   ***Tillandsia adamsii*** R.W. Read *20883, 13336*

    R   *13336*   Jamaica *20883*

E   ***Tillandsia aequatorialis*** L. B. Smith *20883*

    E   *20883*   Ecuador *20883*

V   ***Tillandsia aizoides*** Gardner *14821*

    V   *14821*   Argentina *14821*

R   ***Tillandsia albertiana*** Veuvorst *16228*

    R   *19549*   Argentina *16228*

V   ***Tillandsia antillana*** L.B. Sm. *20883*

    V   *20883*   Guadeloupe *20883*

    V   *20883*   Jamaica *20883*

E   ***Tillandsia argenta*** C.H. Wright *14821*

    E   *16336*   Argentina *9097*

    E   *20176*   Argentina - Cordoba *20176*

    E   *20176*   Argentina - Catamarca *20176*

    E   *20176*   Argentina - Jujuy *20176*

    E   *20176*   Argentina - La Rioja *20176*

    E   *20176*   Argentina - Salta *20176*

    E   *20176*   Argentina - Santiago del Estero *20176*

E   ***Tillandsia atroviridipetala*** Matuda *14821*

    E   *14821*   Mexico *14821*

V   ***Tillandsia baileyi*** Rose ex Small *20883, 19002*

    V   *20850*   U.S. - Texas *20850*

    V   *20883*   Mexico *20883*

E   ***Tillandsia balsasensis*** Rauh *14821*

    E   *14821*   Peru *14821*

E   ***Tillandsia boliviana*** Mez *20883*

    E   *20883*   Bolivia *20883*

E   ***Tillandsia bongarana*** L. B. Smith *20883*

    E   *20883*   Peru *20883*

E   ***Tillandsia brachyphylla*** Baker *14821*

    E   *14821*   Brazil (Serra de Orgaos) *14821*

V   ***Tillandsia brevicapsula*** Gilmartin *20883*

    E   *20883*   Ecuador *20883*

    E   *20883*   Peru *20883*

E   ***Tillandsia brevilingua*** Mez ex Harms in Engler & Prantl *20883, 18200*

    E   *20883*   Peru *20883*

V   ***Tillandsia butzii*** Mez *14821*

    V   *14821*   Costa Rica *9097*

    V   *14821*   El Salvador *9097*

    V   *14821*   Guatemala *9097*

    V   *14821*   Honduras *9097*

    V   *14821*   Mexico *9097*

    V   *14821*   Nicaragua *9097*

    V   *14821*   Panama *9097*

E   ***Tillandsia cacticola*** Lyman B. Smith *14821*

    E   *14821*   Peru *14821*

V   ***Tillandsia calcicola*** L.B. Sm. & Proctor *20883, 13336*

    V   *13336*   Jamaica *20883*

E   ***Tillandsia califanii*** Rauh *9097*

    E   *14821*   Mexico - Puebla *9097*

V   ***Tillandsia caput-medusae*** E. Morren *14821*

    V   *14821*   Costa Rica *9097*

    V   *14821*   El Salvador *9097*

    V   *14821*   Guatemala *9097*

    V   *14821*   Honduras *9097*

    V   *14821*   Mexico *9097*

    V   *14821*   Nicaragua *9097*

    V   *14821*   Panama *19788*

V   ***Tillandsia carlos-hankii*** Matuda *9097*

    V   *16360*   Mexico - Oaxaca *9097*

E   ***Tillandsia carminea*** Till *14821*

    E   *14821*   Brazil (Serra de Orgaos) *14821*

V   ***Tillandsia chiapensis*** Gardner *14821*

    V   *14821*   Mexico *14821*

E   ***Tillandsia confinis*** var. ***caudata*** L. B. Smith *20883*

    E   *20883*   Colombia *20883*

R   ***Tillandsia copanensis*** Rauh & Rutschmann *14821*

    R   *14821*   Honduras *14821*

V   ***Tillandsia deppeana*** Steudel *20883*

    R   *20883*   Mexico *20883*

E   ***Tillandsia dexteri*** Luther *14821*

    E   *14821*   Costa Rica *14821*

V   ***Tillandsia dudleyi*** L. B. Smith *20883*

    V   *20883*   Peru *20883*

R   ***Tillandsia duidae*** L. B. Smith *20883*

    R   *20883*   Venezuela *20883*

R   ***Tillandsia dyeriana*** Andre *9097*

    R   *11245*   Ecuador *9097*

E   ***Tillandsia edithae*** Rauh *14821*

    E   *14821*   Bolivia *14821*

E   ***Tillandsia fassettii*** L. B. Smith *20883*

    E   *20883*   Colombia *20883*

I   ***Tillandsia fawcettii*** Mez *20883, 13336*

    I   *13336*   Jamaica *20883*

R   ***Tillandsia fendleri*** var. ***reducta*** (L. B. Smith) L. B. Smith *20883*

    E   *20883*   Colombia *20883*

    I   *20883*   Ecuador *20883*

    V   *20883*   Venezuela *20883*

E   ***Tillandsia filifolia*** Schltdl. & Cham. *14821*

    E   *14821*   Belize *9097*

    E   *14821*   Costa Rica *9097*

    E   *14821*   Guatemala *9097*

    E   *14821*   Honduras *9097*

    E   *14821*   Mexico *9097*

E		*14821*	Nicaragua	*19788*

E   *Tillandsia fuchsii* W. Till *14821*
- E   *14821*   Guatemala *14821*
- E   *14821*   Mexico *14821*

E   *Tillandsia fusiformis* L. B. Smith *20883*
- E   *20883*   Colombia *20883*

E   *Tillandsia glauca* L.B. Smith *20883*
- E   *20883*   Peru *20883*

E   *Tillandsia grazielae* Sucre & Braga *14821*
- E   *14821*   Brazil (Serra de Orgaos) *14821*

R   *Tillandsia heteromorpha* Rauh *18200*
- R   *12468*   Peru *18200*

V   *Tillandsia heterophylla* E. Morren *20883, 9097*
- V   *20883*   Mexico *20883*

E   *Tillandsia hildae* Rauh *14821*
- E   *14821*   Peru *14821*

E   *Tillandsia hondurensis* Rauh *14821*
- E   *14821*   Honduras *14821*

E   *Tillandsia ignesiae* Mez *9097*
- E   *14821*   Mexico (oak forests, southern Mexico) *9097*

V   *Tillandsia ionantha* Planchon *14821*
- V   *14821*   Costa Rica *21207*
- V   *14821*   El Salvador *9097*
- V   *14821*   Guatemala *9097*
- V   *14821*   Honduras *9097*
- V   *14821*   Mexico *9097*
- E   *14821*   Mexico - Chiapas *9097*
- V   *14821*   Nicaragua *9097*

E   *Tillandsia ixioides* Grisebach *14821*
- E   *14821*   Argentina *14821*
- E   *14821*   Bolivia *14821*
- E   *14821*   Paraguay *14821*
- E   *14821*   Uruguay *14821*

E   II   *Tillandsia kammii* Rauh *14821*
- E   *14821*   Honduras *14821*

E   II   *Tillandsia kautskyi* Pereira *14821*
- E   *14821*   Brazil *14821*

E   *Tillandsia klausii* Ehlers *14821*
- E   *14821*   Mexico - Chiapas *16396*

V   *Tillandsia krukofiana* L. B. Smith *20883*
- V   *20883*   Bolivia *20883*

E   *Tillandsia kuntzeana* Mez *20883*
- E   *20883*   Bolivia *20883*

E   *Tillandsia lajensis* André *20883, 9097*
- R   *19352*   Colombia *9097*
- E   *20883*   Peru *20883*

E   *Tillandsia lindenii* Regel var. *lindenii* *9097*
- E   *18200*   Peru *18200*

E   *Tillandsia lineatispica* Mez *20883, 5851*
- I   *20883*   Puerto Rico (Culebra, Viques) *20883*
- I   *20883*   USA - Virgin Is. (St John) *20883*

E   *Tillandsia lopezii* L. B. Smith *20883*
- E   *20883*   Peru *20883*

V   *Tillandsia macrodactylon* Mez *20883*
- V   *20883*   Peru *20883*

E   *Tillandsia magnusiana* Wittmack *14821*
- E   *14821*   El Salvador *9097*
- E   *14821*   Guatemala *9097*
- E   *14821*   Honduras *9097*
- E   *14821*   Mexico *9097*
- E   *14821*   Nicaragua *9097*

E   *Tillandsia matudae* Lyman B. Smith *9097*
- E   *14821*   Guatemala *14821*
- E   *14821*   Mexico - Chiapas *9097*

V   II   *Tillandsia mauryana* Lyman B. Smith *9097*
- V   *14821*   Mexico *9097*

R   *Tillandsia mexicana* Lyman B. Smith *9097*
- R   *19761*   Mexico *9097*

V   *Tillandsia muhriae* Rauh *21204*
- V   *14821*   Argentina *14821*

V   *Tillandsia myosura* Grisebach ex Baker *14821*
- V   *14821*   Argentina *14821*
- V   *14821*   Bolivia *14821*
- V   *14821*   Peru *14821*
- V   *14821*   Uruguay *14821*

E   *Tillandsia nervisepala* (Gilmartin) L. B. Smith *20883, 16228*
- E   *20883*   Ecuador (Loja) *20883*

E   *Tillandsia nuptialis* Braga & Sucre *14821*
- E   *14821*   Brazil *14821*

E   *Tillandsia oropezana* L. Hromadnik *14821*
- E   *14821*   Bolivia *14821*

V   *Tillandsia ortgesiana* E. Morren ex Mez *9097*
- V   *19850*   Mexico *9097*

E   *Tillandsia plagiotropica* Rohw. *9097*
- E   *14821*   El Salvador *9097*
- E   *14821*   Guatemala *11245*

E   *Tillandsia plumosa* Baker *9097*
- E   *14821*   Mexico (north of Oaxaca) *9097*

E   *Tillandsia pomacochae* Rauh *20883*
- E   *20883*   Peru *20883*

I   *Tillandsia pretiosa* Mez. *16228*
- I   *19550*   Ecuador *16228*

V   *Tillandsia pueblensis* Lyman B. Smith var. *pueblensis* *9097*
- V   *19850*   Mexico *9097*

E   *Tillandsia pyramidata* var. *vivpara* Rauh *20883*
- E   *20883*   Peru *20883*

R   *Tillandsia rariflora* Andre *9097*
- R   *19352*   Colombia *9097*

E   *Tillandsia reclinata* Pereira & Martinelli *14821*
- E   *14821*   Brazil (Serra de Orgaos) *14821*

E   *Tillandsia reuteri* Rauh *20883*
- I   *20883*   Colombia *20883*
- E   *20883*   Peru *20883*

E   *Tillandsia reversa* L.B. Smith *20883*
- E   *20883*   Peru *20883*

E   *Tillandsia rhodosticta* L. B. Smith *20883*
- E   *20883*   Ecuador *20883*

R   *Tillandsia rhomboidea* Andre *9097*
- R   *19352*   Colombia *9097*

E   *Tillandsia roezlii* E. Morren *20883*
- E   *20883*   Peru *20883*

V   *Tillandsia roland-gosselinii* Mez *9097*
- V   *19848*   Mexico *19848*
- V   *19850*   Mexico - Colima *9097*
- V   *19850*   Mexico - Jalisco *9706*

V   *Tillandsia seideliana* Pereira *14821*
- V   *14821*   Brazil (Santa Catarina) *14821*

V   *Tillandsia selleana* Harms *20883*

V		20883	Dominican Republic *20883*
E		20883	Haiti *20883*
V		20883	Jamaica *20883*

V *Tillandsia sigmoidea* L. B. Smith *20883*

V	20883	Colombia *20883*

V *Tillandsia socialis* Lyman B. Smith *9097*

V	19850	Mexico - Chiapas *9097*

E *Tillandsia somnians* L. B. Smith *20883*

E	20883	Peru *20883*

E II *Tillandsia sprengeliana* Klotzsch ex Mez *14821*

E	14821	Brazil *14821*

V *Tillandsia stenoura* var. *mauroi*
Gilmartin *20883*

E	20883	Ecuador *20883*
E	20883	Peru *20883*

V *Tillandsia stenoura* var. *tripinnata* (L. B. Smith) L.
B. Smith *20883*

I	20883	Ecuador *20883*
V	20883	Peru *20883*

V *Tillandsia streptophylla* Scheidw. ex Morren *14821*

V	14821	Belize *9097*
V	14821	Guatemala *9097*
V	14821	Honduras *9097*
V	14821	Mexico *9097*
V	14821	Nicaragua *19788*

E *Tillandsia subconcolor* L. B. Smith *20883*

E	20883	Peru *20883*

R *Tillandsia subteres* H. Luther *20050*

R	20050	Honduras *20050*

E II *Tillandsia sucrei* Lyman B. Smith *14821*

E	14821	Brazil *14821*

V *Tillandsia superba* Mez & Sodiro *20883*

V	20883	Ecuador *20883*

E *Tillandsia tectorum* E. Morren *14821*

E	14821	Ecuador *14821*
E	14821	Peru *14821*

R *Tillandsia trapeziformis* Mez *9097*

R	19352	Colombia *9097*

E *Tillandsia trelawniensis* Proctor *20883, 13336*

E	13336	Jamaica *20883*

I *Tillandsia truncata* Lyman B.Smith *16228*

I	19550	Ecuador *16228*

E *Tillandsia undulatobracteata* Rauh *20883*

E	20883	Peru *20883*

R *Tillandsia walteri* Mez *20883*

E	20883	Bolivia *20883*
E	20883	Ecuador *20883*
R	20883	Peru *20883*

E *Tillandsia werdermannii* Harms *18200*

E	14821	Chile *14821*
E	9446	Peru *18200*

V *Tillandsia wurdackii* L. B. Smith *20883*

V	20883	Peru *20883*

E II *Tillandsia xerographica* Rohw. *9097*

E	14821	El Salvador *9097*
E	14821	Guatemala *9097*
E	14821	Mexico *9097*

E *Tillandsia xiphioides* Ker Gawler *11127*

E	14821	Argentina *14821*
E	14821	Bolivia *14821*
E	14821	Brazil *11127*
E	14821	Paraguay *14821*

E		Uruguay *11127*

E *Tillandsia zecheri* Till *14821*

E	14821	Argentina *14821*

V *Vriesea ampla* Lyman B. Smith *9097*

V	9426	Costa Rica *9097*

V *Vriesea apiculata* Lyman B. Smith *9097*

V	9426	Costa Rica *9097*

V *Vriesea balanophora* (Mez) Lyman B. Smith &
Pittendr. *9097*

V	9426	Costa Rica *9097*

V *Vriesea bicolor* Lyman B. Smith *9097*

V	9426	Costa Rica *9097*

I *Vriesea biguassuensis* Reitz *17079*

I	17079	Brazil - Santa Catarina (Vale do Rio Biguaçu) *17079*

V *Vriesea bracteosa* (Mez & Werckle) Lyman B. Smith &
Pittendr. *9097*

V	9426	Costa Rica *9097*

V *Vriesea brunei* Mez & Werckle *9097*

V	9426	Costa Rica *9097*

V *Vriesea camptoclada* Mez & Werckle *9097*

V	9426	Costa Rica *9097*

V *Vriesea discolor* (Mez & Werckle) Lyman B. Smith &
Pittendr. *9097*

V	9426	Costa Rica *9097*

V *Vriesea dodsonii* Lyman B. Smith *9097*

V	9426	Costa Rica *9097*

R *Vriesea gibba* L.B. Sm. *20883*

R	20883	Jamaica *20883*

V *Vriesea hainesiorum* Lyman B. Smith *9097*

V	9426	Costa Rica *9097*

E *Vriesea harmsiana* (Lyman B. Smith) Lyman B.
Smith *18200*

E	9446	Peru *18200*

E *Vriesea lancifolia* Lyman B. Smith *17008*

E	17008	Brazil - Bahia *17008*

V *Vriesea macrantha* Mez & Werckle *9097*

V	9426	Costa Rica *9097*

V *Vriesea macrochlamys* Mez & Werckle *9097*

V	9426	Costa Rica *9097*

V *Vriesea malzinei* E. Morren var. *disticha* Lyman B.
Smith *9097*

V	19850	Mexico - Chiapas *9097*

R *Vriesea muelleri* Mez *9097*

R		Brazil *9097*

V *Vriesea notata* Lyman B. Smith & Pittendr. *9097*

V	9426	Costa Rica *9097*

V *Vriesea nutans* Lyman B. Smith *9097*

V	9426	Costa Rica *9097*

E *Vriesea pinottii* Reitz *17079*

E	17746	Brazil - Parana *17079*
E	17746	Brazil - Santa Catarina *17079*

V *Vriesea rugosa* Mez & Werckle *9097*

V	9426	Costa Rica *9097*

V *Vriesea singuliflora* (Mez & Werckle) Lyman B. Smith &
Pittendr. *9097*

V	9426	Costa Rica *9097*

R *Vriesea swartzii* Mez *20883*

R	20883	Jamaica *20883*

V   *Vriesea tonduziana* Lyman B. Smith *9097*
     V   *9426*   Costa Rica *9097*

I   *Vriesea triangularis* Reitz *17079*
     I   *17079*   Brazil - Santa Catarina (Município de Sao Martinho) *17079*

V   *Vriesea triflora* Lyman B. Smith & Pittendr. *9097*
     V   *9426*   Costa Rica *9097*

R   *Vriesea triligulata* Mez *7200*
     R   *7200*   Brazil - Rio de Janeiro (Organ Mtns.) *7200*

R   *Vriesea vanhyningii* Lyman B. Smith *9097*
     R   *19755*   Mexico - Oaxaca *9097*

V   *Vriesea viridis* (Mez & Werckle) Lyman B. Smith & Pittendr. *9097*
     V   *9426*   Costa Rica *9097*

V   *Vriesea woodsoniana* L.B. Sm. *20883, 10747*
     V   *16317* Panama *20883*

Burmanniaceae

Number of genera: 20
Number of species: 130
Recorded threatened species: 14   (10%)

Pantropical, with a few species in temperate regions.

I   *Afrothismia pachyantha* Schltr.
     I   Cameroon (Moliwe)

V   *Glaziocharis abei* Akasawa *11164*
     V   *11164*   Japan *11164*

Ex/E   *Glaziocharis machensis* Taubert ex Warm. *11306*
     Ex/E *11306*   Brazil - Rio de Janeiro *11306*

R   *Gymnosiphon fawcettii* Urb. *20883, 13336*
     R   *13336*   Jamaica *20883*

R   *Gymnosiphon nivens* (Griseb.) Urban *10199*
     R   Dominica *10199*

R   *Gymnosiphon sphaerocarpus* Urban *10199*
     R   Dominica *10199*

I   *Haplothismia exanulata* Airy Shaw
     I   India - Kerala (Travancore; Cochin)

I   *Oxygyne triandra* Schltr.
     I   Cameroon (Moliwe)

Ex/E   *Thismia americana* N.E. Pfeiffer *20850, 14662*
     Ex   *20850*   U.S. - Illinois *20850*

Ex/E   *Thismia caudata* P. Maas & Maas *10118*
     Ex/E *10118*   Brazil - Rio de Janeiro *10118*

I   *Thismia gardneriana* Hook.f. ex Thwaites *8021*
     I   *16162*   Sri Lanka (Kuruwita, Ratnapura) *8021*

Ex/E   *Thismia macahensis* (Miers) F. Muell. *10118*
     Ex/E *11306*   Brazil - Rio de Janeiro (Organ Mtns.) *10118*

I   *Thismia mirabilis* K. Larsen *19120*
     I   *19120*   Thailand (Khao Yai) *19120*

Ex/E   *Triscyphus fungiformis* Taubert ex Warm. *11306*
     Ex/E *11306*   Brazil (Ato Mache, Organ Mtns.) *11306*

Calectasiaceae

Number of genera: 1
Number of species: 1
Recorded threatened species: 1   (100%)

Australia.

V   *Calectasia arnoldii* K.Dixon ms. *20681*
     V   *20681*   Australia - Western Australia *20681*

Cannaceae

Number of genera: 1
Number of species: 50
Recorded threatened species: 1   (2%)

Tropical and subtropical New World.

V   *Canna pertusa* Urban *20883, 20850, 10197*
     I   *20850*   U.S. - Florida *20850*
     I   *20883*   Puerto Rico *20883*

Centrolepidaceae

Number of genera: 4
Number of species: 35
Recorded threatened species: 6   (17%)

Australia; Southeast Asia; Pacific Islands; southernmost South America; mostly in nutrient-poor soils.

V   *Centrolepis caespitosus* D.Cooke *20681, 14223*
     V   *20681*   Australia - Western Australia *14223*

R   *Centrolepis muscoides* (Hook.f.) Hieron. *20681*
     R   *20681*   Australia - Tasmania *20681*

V   *Centrolepis paludicola* W.M.Curtis *20681*
     V   *20681*   Australia - Tasmania *20681*

E   *Centrolepis pedderensis* W.M.Curtis *20681*
     E   *20681*   Australia - Tasmania *20681*

R   *Centrolepis pulvinata* (R.Br.) Roemer & Schultes *20681*
     R   *20681*   Australia - Tasmania *20681*

R   *Gaimardia amblyphylla* W.M.Curtis *20681*
     R   *20681*   Australia - Tasmania *20681*

Colchicaceae

Number of genera: 16
Number of species: 106
Recorded threatened species: 34   (32%)

Widespread in Old World.

R   *Androcymbium cruciatum* U. & D.Müll.-Doblies *20604*
     R   *20604*   South Africa - Cape Province *20604*

E   *Androcymbium europaeum* (Lange) K.Richt. *8000, 20171*
     E   *19818*   Spain (Almeria) *8000*

R   *Androcymbium henssenianum* U. & D.Müll.-Doblies *20604*
     R   *20604*   South Africa - Cape Province *20604*

V   *Androcymbium hierrensis* Santos *20750*
     V   *20750*   Spain - Canary Is. *20750*

R   *Androcymbium poeltianum* U. & D.Müll.-Doblies *20604*
     R   *20604*   South Africa - Cape Province *20604*

V   *Androcymbium psammophilum* Svent. *20750*
     V   *20750*   Spain - Canary Is. *17891*

E   *Androcymbium rechingeri* Greuter *8000, 20171*
     E   *20730*   Greece - Crete (island of Elaphonisos) *8000*
     E   *19121*   Libya *19121*

R   *Androcymbium villosum* U. & D.Müll.-Doblies *20604*
     R   *20604*   South Africa - Cape Province *20604*

R   *Colchicum baytopiorum* C.D. Brickel *12840*
     R   *12840*   Turkey *12840*

V   *Colchicum borisii* Stef. *8000, 20171*
     V   *5204*   Bulgaria (South Bulgaria - one site only.)

5204

R *Colchicum bornmuelleri* Freyn *12840*
   R   *12840* Turkey *12840*

R *Colchicum cornigerum* (Schweinf.) Tackh. & Drar *10269*
   R   Egypt *10269*

V *Colchicum corsicum* Baker *15080, 20171*
   E   *20528* France - Corsica *20528*
   V   *19174* Italy - Sardinia *15080*

V *Colchicum cousturieri* Greuter *8000, 20171*
   V   *20730* Greece - Crete *8000*

V *Colchicum davidovii* Stef. *8000, 20171*
   V   *5204* Bulgaria (east) *5204*

R *Colchicum diampolis* Delip. et Ceschm. *5204, 20171*
   R   *5204* Bulgaria (east) *5204*

I *Colchicum fominii* Bordz. *8000, 20171*
   V   *19949* Romania *8000*
   I   *5942* Moldova *5942*
   I   *5942* Ukraine *5942*

R *Colchicum macedonicum* Kosanin *20171*
   R   (former) Yugoslavia

V *Colchicum micranthum* Boiss. *12840, 20171*
   V   *19873* Turkey (Istanbul) *12840*

R *Colchicum pieperanum* Markgr. *20178, 20171*
   R   *20178* Albania *20178*

R *Colchicum rhodopaeum* Kov. *5204, 20171*
   R   *5204* Bulgaria (Southern Bulgaria - one site only .) *5204*

V *Iphigenia magnifica* Ansari & R. Rao *11494*
   V   *11494* India - Karnataka *11494*
   V   *11494* India - Maharashtra *11494*

R *Iphigenia novae-zelandiae* (Hook.f.) Baker *19305*
   R   *19305* New Zealand - North Is. *19305*
   R   *19305* New Zealand - South Is. *19305*

E *Iphigenia sahyadrica* Ansari & R. Rao *11494*
   E   *11494* India - Karnataka (Halial, Hulical) *11494*

V *Iphigenia stellata* Blatter *11494*
   V   *11494* India - Maharashtra (Satara & Kolhapur District) *11494*

R *Merendera androcymbioides* Valdés *20171*
   R   *20660* Spain (Cádiz, Málaga, Còrdoba) *11496*

R *Merendera rhodopaea* Velen. *5204, 20171*
   R   *5204* Bulgaria (Southern Bulgaria - two sites.) *5204*

R *Ornithoglossum gracile* B.Nord. *20604*
   R   *20604* South Africa - Cape Province *20604*

R *Ornithoglossum parviflorum* B.Nord. var. *namaquense* B.Nord. *20604*
   R   *20604* South Africa - Cape Province *20604*

V *Wurmbea calcicola* T.D.Macfarlane *20681*
   V   *20681* Australia - Western Australia *20681*

R *Wurmbea compacta* B.Nord. *20604*
   R   *20604* South Africa - Cape Province *20604*

R *Wurmbea drummondii* Benth. *20681*
   R   *20681* Australia - Western Australia *20681*

R *Wurmbea murchisoniana* T.D.Macfarlane *20681*
   R   *20681* Australia - Western Australia *20681*

V *Wurmbea tubulosa* Benth. *20681*
   V   *20681* Australia - Western Australia *20681*

Commelinaceae

Number of genera: 50
Number of species: 700
Recorded threatened species: 29   (4%)

Tropical, subtropical and warmer temperate.

I *Aetheolirion stenolobium* Forman
   I   Thailand

I *Aneilema ochraceum* Dalz.
   I   India - Karnataka
   I   India - Kerala (Quilon)

E *Belosynapsis kewensis* Hassk. *11494*
   E   *11494* India - Tamil Nadu (Tinnevelly & Kanyakumari) *11494*

V *Belosynapsis vivipara* (Dalz.) Sprague & Fischer *11494*
   V   *11494* India - Karnataka *11494*
   V   *11494* India - Maharashtra *11494*
   V   India - Tamil Nadu *9998*

R *Callisia micrantha* (Torr.) D.R. Hunt *20850*
   R   *20850* U.S. - Texas *20850*

R *Cartonema brachyantherum* Benth. *20681*
   R   *20681* Australia - Queensland *20681*

R *Commelina hirsuta* (Wight) C.B. Clarke *11494*
   R   *11494* India - Tamil Nadu (Nilgiri & Pulney Hills) *11494*

R *Commelina indehiscens* Barnes *14782*
   R   *14782* India - Karnataka *14782*
   R   *14782* India - Kerala *14782*
   R   *14782* India - Tamil Nadu *14782*

R *Commelina mina* Y.N. Lee & Oh.Y.
   R   Korea, South

E *Commelina rupicola* Font Quer *5399*
   E   *5399* Morocco (Southwest of the city of Ifni.) *5399*

I *Commelina subulata* Roth
   I   India (Deccan hills)

V *Commelina tricolor* Barnes *11494*
   V   *11494* India - Tamil Nadu (Karadimalais) *11494*

V *Commelina wightii* R. Rao *11494*
   V   *11494* India - Tamil Nadu (Nilgiri & Pulney Hills) *11494*

R *Cyanotis burmanniana* Wight *13883*
   R   *13883* India - Kerala (Malabar) *13883*

I *Cyanotis cerifolia* Rolla Rao et Kammathy *13883*
   I   *13883* India - Tamil Nadu *13883*

I *Cyanotis obtusa* (Trimen) Trimen *10252*
   I   *16162* Sri Lanka *10252*

I *Cyanotis vaginata* Wight
   I   India - Kerala (Malabar)

R *Dictyospermum ovalifolium* Wight *11494*
   R   India - Karnataka *9998*
   R   *11494* India - Kerala (Thenmalai) *11494*
   R   *11494* India - Maharashtra (Koncan) *11494*

V *Murdannia lanceolata* (Wight) Kammathy *11494*
   V   *11494* India - Kerala *11494*
   V   *11494* India - Tamil Nadu *11494*

R *Murdannia lanuginosa* (wall. ex Clarke) Bruckn. *13883*
   R   *13883* India *13883*

I *Murdannia versicolor* (Dalz.) Bruckner
   I   India - Karnataka (Concan)

I	*Palisota orientalis* Schumann *5926*	
	I	*5926* Tanzania (Usumbaras & Nguru mts) *5926*
E	*Pollia americana* Faden *20883, 10747*	
	I	*20883* Panama *20883*
I	*Pollia pentasperma* C.B. Clarke *11494*	
	I	*11494* India - Assam (Lushai hills) *11494*
	I	*11494* India - Meghalaya (Shillong) *11494*
	I	*11494* India - Nagaland (Kohima, Naga hills) *11494*
Ex	*Sauvallea blainii* C. Wright *5607*	
	Ex	*19105* Cuba (Pinar del Rio) *5607*
R	*Streptolirion elegans* Cherf. *6057*	
	R	Vietnam *6057*
V	*Tradescantia ozarkana* E.S. Anderson & Woods. *20850*	
	R	*20850* U.S. - Arkansas *20850*
	V	*20850* U.S. - Missouri *20850*
	E	*20850* U.S. - Oklahoma *20850*
R	*Tradescantia pedicellata* Celarier *20850*	
	R	*20850* U.S. - Texas *20850*
I	*Triceratella drummondii* Brenan *7755*	
	I	Zimbabwe *7755*
V	*Tripogandra elata* D.R. Hunt *19561*	
	V	*19561* Brazil - Distrito Federal *19561*
	V	*19561* Brazil - Goias *19561*

Convallariaceae

Number of genera:	25
Number of species:	172
Recorded threatened species:	25 (14%)

Predominantly North temperate.

R	*Disporum parvifolium* (S.Watson) Britt. *20850*	
	I	*20850* U.S. - California *20850*
	I	*20850* U.S. - Oregon *20850*
R	*Kuntheria pedunculata* (F.Muell.) Conran & Cliff. *20681*	
	R	*20681* Australia - Queensland *20681*
R	*Maianthemum gigas* (Woodson) LaFrankie var. *crassipes* (Standley & Steyerm.) LaFrankie *9775*	
	R	*9775* Guatemala *9775*
	R	*9775* Mexico - Chiapas *9775*
R	*Maianthemum macrophyllum* (Martens & Galeotti) LaFrankie *9775*	
	R	*9775* Mexico - Veracruz *9775*
E	*Maianthemum paludicola* LaFrankie *9775*	
	E	Costa Rica *9775*
Ex/E	*Maianthemum salvinii* (Baker) LaFrankie *9775*	
	Ex/E	*9775* Guatemala *9775*
I	*Ophiopogon intermedius* Don var. *gracilipes* Hook.f.	
	I	India - Tamil Nadu (Nilgiri Hills)
R	*Ophiopogon tonkinensis* Rodriguez *6057*	
	R	*20985* Vietnam *6057*
I	*Peliosanthes courtallensis* Wight	
	I	India - Tamil Nadu
R	*Polygonatum cryptanthum* Lev. & Van. *11164*	
	R	*11164* Japan *11164*
V	*Polygonatum desoulavyi* Komar. var. *azegamii* Ohwi *11164*	
	V	*11164* Japan *11164*
V	*Polygonatum domonense* Satake *11164*	

	V	*11164* Japan *11164*
I	*Polygonatum graminifolium* Hook.	
	I	India (W. Himalaya)
V	*Polygonatum miserum* Satake *11164*	
	V	*11164* Japan *11164*
I	*Smilacina fusca* Wallich	
	I	India - Meghalaya
R	*Smilacina japonica* A.Gray var. *robusta* (Makino & Honda) Ohwi *11164*	
	R	*11164* Japan *11164*
V	*Streptopus roseus* var. *roseus* *20850*	
	I	*20850* Canada - Ontario *20850*
	E	*20850* U.S. - North Carolina *20850*
	I	*20850* U.S. - Pennsylvania *20850*
	R	*20850* U.S. - Tennessee *20850*
	I	*20850* U.S. - Virginia *20850*
	I	*20850* U.S. - West Virginia *20850*
R	*Tricyrtis dilatata* Nakai *15957*	
	R	*15923* Korea, South (Mt Paekyang, Mt Halla, Mt Chiri, Kwangn Anmyon Isl.) *15957*
R	*Tricyrtis flava* Maxim. *11164*	
	R	Japan (Osuzu Mts) *11169*
V	*Tricyrtis ishiiana* (Kitag. & T. Koy.) Ohwi & Okuy. var. *ishiiana* *11169*	
	V	Japan (Tanzawa Mts, Sagami Prov.) *11169*
V	*Tricyrtis ishiiana* (Kitag. & T. Koy.) Ohwi & Okuy. var. *surugensis* Yamaz. *11169*	
	V	Japan (Mt Tenjingadake, Suruga) *11169*
V	*Tricyrtis macranthopsis* Masam. *11164*	
	V	Japan (Kii) *11169*
R	*Tricyrtis ohsumensis* Masam. *11164*	
	R	*11164* Japan *11164*
R	*Tricyrtis ovatifolia* Ying *20511*	
	R	*20511* Taiwan (Laiyi Hsiang, Pingtung) *20511*
V	*Tricyrtis perfoliata* Masam. *11164*	
	V	Japan (Osuzu Mts) *11169*
R	*Tupistra grandia* Ridley	
	R	Malaysia - Peninsular Malaysia

Costaceae

Number of genera:	4
Number of species:	150
Recorded threatened species:	17 (11%)

Pantropical, especially New World.

V	*Costus cordatus* Maas *9660*	
	V	*11306* Colombia *9660*
V	*Costus cupreifolius* Maas *9660*	
	V	*11306* Colombia *9660*
R	*Costus curcumoides* Maas *18176*	
	R	*11306* French Guiana *18176*
R	*Costus cuspidatus* (Nees & Martius) Maas *17079*	
	R	*17746* Brazil - Bahia *17079*
	R	*17746* Brazil - Espirito Santo *17746*
	R	*17746* Brazil - Rio de Janeiro *17079*
R	*Costus fragilis* Maas *17079*	
	R	*17079* Brazil - Pará *17079*
R	*Costus fusiformis* Maas *17079*	
	R	*17079* Brazil - Pará *17079*
R	*Costus geothyrsus* Schumann *11306*	
	R	*11306* Ecuador *11306*

R   *Costus leucanthus* Maas *19352*
    R   *11306* Colombia *11306*
    R   *11306* Ecuador *11306*

R   *Costus montanus* Maas *9660*
    R   *11306* Costa Rica *9660*

V   *Costus plowmanii* Maas *19352*
    V   *11306* Colombia *9660*

R   *Costus productus* Gleason ex Maas var. *productus 18200*
    R   *11306* Peru *18200*

V   *Costus productus* Gleason ex Maas var. *strigosus* (Maas) Maas *19352*
    V   *11306* Colombia *9660*

V   *Costus quasi-appendiculatus* Woodrow ex. Maas *10125*
    V   *11306* Bolivia *11306*

V   *Costus stenophyllus* Standley & L.O. Williams *9660*
    V   *11306* Costa Rica *9660*

E   *Costus vinosus* Maas *20883, 9660*
    R   *9429* Panama *20883*

V   *Costus zamoranus* Steyerm. *10125*
    V   *11306* Ecuador *10125*

V   *Costus zingiberoides* J.F. Macbr. *18200*
    V   *11306* Peru *18200*

V   *Monocostus uniflorus* (Poepping ex O.G. Petersen) Maas *18200*
    V   *11306* Peru *18200*

Cyanastraceae

Number of genera: 1
Number of species: 4-7
Recorded threatened species: 1 (16%)

Forests of tropical Africa.

I   *Cyanastrum johnstonii* Bak. var. *cuneifolium* Carter *5926*
    I   *5926* Tanzania *5926*

Cyclanthaceae

Number of genera: 11
Number of species: 180
Recorded threatened species: 6 (3%)

Tropical America.

E   *Asplundia ferruginea* Grayum & Hammel *20883*
    I   *20883* Costa Rica *20883*

I   *Asplundia insignis* (Duchass) Harl. ex Griseb. *10199*
    I   Dominica *10199*

R   *Dianthoveus cremnophilus* Hammel & Wilder *20883*
    I   *20883* Colombia *20883*
    I   *20883* Ecuador *20883*

I   *Dicranopygium insulare* (Gleason) Harling *5932*
    I   *5932* Trinidad & Tobago (Tobago) *5932*

E   *Sphaeradenia carrilloana* Grayum & Hammel *20883*
    I   *20883* Costa Rica *20883*

R   *Sphaeradenia irazuensis* (Cuf.) Harling *10545*
    R   *10545* Costa Rica *10545*

Cyperaceae

Number of genera: 70
Number of species: 4,000
Recorded threatened species: 280 (7%)

Cosmopolitan, most abundant in temperate regions.

R   *Afrotrilepis jaegeri* Raynal *7926*
    R   Sierra Leone *7926*

V   *Baumea complanata* (Benggren) Blake *86*
    V   *19305* New Zealand - North Is. (Ngawha, Northland) *10794*

R   *Baumea veillonis* Raynal *20893*
    R   *20893* New Caledonia *20893*

R   *Bulbostylis lichtensteiniana* (Kunth) C.B. Clarke *18996*
    R   *18996* St Helena *18996*

I   *Bulbostylis mozambica* Raym.
    I   Mozambique

Ex   *Bulbostylis neglecta* (Hemsley) C.B. Clarke *18996*
    Ex   *18996* St Helena *18996*

E   *Calyptrocarya delascioi* Davidse & Kral *20883*
    I   *20883* Venezuela *20883*

E   *Calyptrocarya montesii* Davidse & Kral *20883*
    I   *20883* Venezuela *20883*

Ex   *Carex aboriginum* M.E. Jones *20850, 14662*
    I   *20850* Canada - British Columbia *20850*
    Ex   *20850* U.S. - Idaho *20850*

E   *Carex albida* Bailey *20850*
    E   *20850* U.S. - California *20850*

V   *Carex amplectens* Mackenzie *20850*
    I   *20850* U.S. - California *20850*

R   *Carex amplisquama* F.J. Herm. *20850*
    R   *20850* U.S. - Georgia *20850*
    I   *20850* U.S. - South Carolina *20850*

R   *Carex annulata* Kuk.
    R   *7771* China - Xizang Zizhiqu (Karakorum) *7771*
    I   India - Jammu & Kashmir *7771*

V   *Carex arapahoensis* Clokey *20850*
    I   *20850* U.S. - Colorado *20850*
    E   *20850* U.S. - Utah *20850*

V   *Carex atroviridis* Ohwi *11164*
    V   *11164* Japan *11164*

E   *Carex austromexicana* Reznicek *20883, 11379*
    I   *20883* Mexico *20883*

V   *Carex baltzellii* Chapman ex Dewey *20850*
    E   *20850* U.S. - Alabama *20850*
    V   *20850* U.S. - Florida *20850*
    E   *20850* U.S. - Georgia *20850*
    E   *20850* U.S. - Mississippi *20850*

R   *Carex bermudiana* Hemsley *2897*
    R   *2897* Bermuda *2897*

V   *Carex berteroniana* Steudel *19116*
    V   *19125* Chile - Juan Fernandez Is. *19116*

V   *Carex bicknellii* F.J. Herm. var. *opaca* F.J. Herm. *20850*
    V   *20850* U.S. - Arkansas *20850*
    I   *20850* U.S. - Mississippi *20850*
    V   *20850* U.S. - Missouri *20850*

R   *Carex biltmoreana* Mackenzie *20850*
    E   *20850* U.S. - Georgia *20850*
    R   *20850* U.S. - North Carolina *20850*

E	20850	U.S. - South Carolina	*20850*
I	20850	U.S. - Virginia	*20850*

I *Carex borii* Nelmes
I		India - Himachal Pradesh
I		India - Jammu & Kashmir

R *Carex brassii* Nelmes *7849*
R		Malawi *7849*

R *Carex bromoides* Willd. var. *montana*
Naczi *20850*
I	20850	U.S. - North Carolina	*20850*
I	20850	U.S. - South Carolina	*20850*
I	20850	U.S. - Virginia	*20850*

E *Carex brunnipes* Rezniceck *20883, 11383*
I	20883	Guatemala	*20883*
I	20883	Mexico	*20883*

V *Carex calderae* A. Hansen *17530*
V	19174	Spain - Canary Is.	*19174*

V *Carex camposii* Boiss. & Reut. *17781, 20171*
V	8322	Portugal	*11496*
V	11496	Spain (Sierra Nevada)	*11496*

V *Carex canariensis* Kukenthal
V		Spain - Canary Is.

I *Carex cataphyllodes* Nelmes *19120*
I	19120	Thailand	*19120*

R *Carex chapmanii* Steud. *20850*
V	20850	U.S. - Florida	*20850*
R	20850	U.S. - North Carolina	*20850*
E	20850	U.S. - South Carolina	*20850*
E	20850	U.S. - Tennessee	*20850*
I	20850	U.S. - Virginia	*20850*

V *Carex chihuahuensis* Mackenzie *20850*
I	20850	U.S. - Arizona	*20850*

V *Carex chinoi* Ohwi & T. Koyama *11164*
V	11164	Japan	*11164*

I *Carex christii* Arn. ex Boeckeler
I		India - Tamil Nadu (Nilgiri Hills)

R *Carex cilicica* Boiss. ssp. *muglaica* O.
Nilson *12840*
R	12840	Turkey	*12840*

R *Carex cilicica* Boiss. ssp. *muratica* O.
Nilson *12840*
R	12840	Turkey	*12840*

R *Carex cochinchinensis* Raym. *6057*
R		Vietnam *6057*

R *Carex congdonii* Bailey *20850*
I	20850	U.S. - California	*20850*

V *Carex cretica* Gradst. & J.Kern *8000, 20171*
V	20808	Greece - East Aegean Is	*20808*

R *Carex cubensis* Kuk. *5607*
R	19105	Cuba (Santiago de Cuba)	*5607*

R *Carex curatorum* Stacey *20850*
E	20850	U.S. - Arizona	*20850*
E	20850	U.S. - Utah	*20850*

V *Carex davyi* Mackenzie *20850*
I	20850	U.S. - California	*20850*

E *Carex dianae* Steudel *18996*
E	18996	St Helena	*18996*

R *Carex doenitzii* Bocklr. var. *okuboi* (Franch.)
Kukenth *11164*
R	11164	Japan	*11164*

V *Carex durieui* Steud. *20171*

V	20076	Portugal (north-west)	*8000*
V	14155	Spain (north-west)	*8000*

I *Carex enysii* Petrie
I		New Zealand - South Is.

R *Carex eriocarpa* Hausskn. Kuk. *12840*
R	12840	Turkey	*12840*

E *Carex feanii* F. Brown
E		French Polynesia - Marquesas Is

R *Carex fimbriata* Schkuhr *20171*
V	20528	France (Alps)	*20528*
R	20528	Italy	*20528*
R	18154	Switzerland	*18154*

V *Carex fissa* Mackenzie *20850*
I	20850	U.S. - Arkansas	*20850*
I	20850	U.S. - Florida	*20850*
E	20850	U.S. - Georgia	*20850*
E	20850	U.S. - Kansas	*20850*
I	20850	U.S. - Louisiana	*20850*
I	20850	U.S. - Mississippi	*20850*
I	20850	U.S. - Missouri	*20850*
V	20850	U.S. - Oklahoma	*20850*

E *Carex flexirostris* Reznicek *20883, 11383*
I	20883	Mexico	*20883*
?		Mexico - Oaxaca	*11383*

R *Carex fusanensis* Ohwi *15957*
R	15923	Korea, South (Pusan, Masan)	*15957*

I *Carex fuscifructus* C.B. Clarke *11494*
I	11494	India - Assam (Makum forests, Lakhimpur) *11494*	

R *Carex gifuendis* Franch. *11164*
R	11164	Japan	*11164*

R *Carex hachijoensis* Akiy. *11164*
R	11164	Japan	*11164*

R *Carex hashimotoi* Ohwi *11164*
R	11164	Japan	*11164*

V *Carex hirtissima* W. Boott *20850*
I	20850	U.S. - California	*20850*

E *Carex humahuacaensis* Wheeler *20883*
I	20883	Argentina	*20883*

V *Carex idaea* Greuter Matthäs & Risse *20730*
V	20730	Greece - Crete	*20730*

V *Carex idahoa* Bailey *20850*
Ex/E	20850	U.S. - Idaho	*20850*
V	20850	U.S. - Montana	*20850*

E *Carex impressinervia* Bryson, Kral & Manhart *20850*
E	20850	U.S. - Alabama	*20850*
I	20850	U.S. - Georgia	*20850*
E	20850	U.S. - Mississippi	*20850*
E	20850	U.S. - North Carolina	*20850*

V *Carex impura* Ohwi *11164*
V	11164	Japan	*11164*

R *Carex incurviformis* Mackenzie var. *danaensis*
(Stacey) F.J. Herm. *20850*
V	20850	U.S. - California	*20850*
I	20850	U.S. - Colorado	*20850*
E	20850	U.S. - Montana	*20850*
V	20850	U.S. - Wyoming	*20850*

E *Carex inopinata* V. Cook *86*
E	19305	New Zealand - South Is.	*19305*

E *Carex ixtapalucensis* Reznicek *20883, 11383*
I	20883	Mexico	*20883*
E	11383	Mexico - Mexico State	*11383*

V *Carex juniperorum* Catling, Reznicek, and Crins *20850*

E	20850	Canada - Ontario *20850*
E	20850	U.S. - Kentucky *20850*
E	20850	U.S. - Ohio *20850*

I *Carex kingiana* Clarke *13883*

I	13883	India - Sikkim *13883*

I *Carex kirkii* Petrie

I		New Zealand - South Is.

R *Carex kirkii* Petrie ssp. *elatior* *19305*

R	19305	New Zealand - South Is. *19305*

R *Carex kucyniakii* Raym. *6057*

R		Vietnam *6057*

R *Carex latebracteata* Waterfall *20850*

R	20850	U.S. - Arkansas *20850*
V	20850	U.S. - Oklahoma *20850*

V *Carex lenticularis* Michaux var. *dolia* (M.E. Jones) L.A. Standley *20850*

I	20850	Canada - Alberta *20850*
I	20850	Canada - British Columbia *20850*
I	20850	Canada - Yukon Territory *20850*
V	20850	U.S. - Alaska *20850*
E	20850	U.S. - Montana *20850*

R *Carex luzulina* Olney var. *atropurpurea* Dorn *20850*

I	20850	U.S. - Montana *20850*
V	20850	U.S. - Wyoming *20850*

R *Carex malaccensis* C.B. Clarke

R		Malaysia - Peninsular Malaysia (Langkawi, Kedah)

V *Carex malato-belizii* Raymond *17891*

V		Portugal - Madeira *17891*

V *Carex manhartii* Bryson *20850*

V	20850	U.S. - Georgia *20850*
V	20850	U.S. - North Carolina *20850*
I	20850	U.S. - South Carolina *20850*
V	20850	U.S. - Tennessee *20850*

R *Carex markgrafii* Kük. *20178, 20171*

R	20178	Albania *20178*

R *Carex mayebarana* Ohwi *11164*

R	11164	Japan *11164*

E *Carex mcvaughii* Reznicek *20883, 11379*

I	20883	Mexico *20883*

V *Carex misandroides* Fern. *20850*

E	20850	Canada - Newfoundland *20850*
E	20850	Canada - Quebec *20850*

R *Carex misera* Buckl. *20850*

E	20850	U.S. - Georgia *20850*
R	20850	U.S. - North Carolina *20850*
V	20850	U.S. - Tennessee *20850*

E *Carex moorei* Wheeler *20883*

I	20883	Argentina *20883*
I	20883	Chile *20883*

V *Carex morrowii* Boott var. *laxa* Ohwi *11164*

V	11164	Japan *11164*

R *Carex munroi* Boott ex C.B. Clarke *11494*

R	7771	India - Himachal Pradesh (Kinnaur) *11494*

E *Carex myosurus* Nees. var. *oraestans* (C.B. Clarke) Kuk.

E		India - Uttar Pradesh

R *Carex neesiana* Endl. *19108*

R	19108	Australia - Norfolk Is. *14288*

R *Carex nelsonii* Mackenzie *20850*

I	20850	U.S. - Colorado *20850*

I	20850	U.S. - Montana *20850*
V	20850	U.S. - Utah *20850*
V	20850	U.S. - Wyoming *20850*

R *Carex neo-petelotii* Raym. *6057*

R		Vietnam *6057*

I *Carex niigatensis* Ohwi *11164*

I	11164	Japan *11164*

V *Carex obispoensis* Stacey *20850*

V	20850	U.S. - California *20850*

R *Carex okamotoi* Ohwi *15957*

R	15923	Korea, South (Mt Chiri, Mt Choryong) *15957*

R *Carex omurae* T. Koyama *11164*

R	11164	Japan *11164*

R *Carex oreocharis* Holm *20850, 19002*

I	20850	U.S. - Arizona *20850*
E	20850	U.S. - Colorado *20850*
I	20850	U.S. - New Mexico *20850*
E	20850	U.S. - Wyoming *20850*

V *Carex oronensis* Fern. *20850*

V	20850	U.S. - Maine *20850*

R *Carex oshimensis* Nakai *11164*

R	11164	Japan *11164*

E *Carex oxylepis* J.K. Underwood var. *pubescens* J.K. Underwood *20850, 19002*

I	20850	U.S. - Arkansas *20850*
I	20850	U.S. - Kentucky *20850*
E	20850	U.S. - Tennessee *20850*

E *Carex paucifructus* Mackenzie *20850, 10260*

E	20850	U.S. - California *20850*

R *Carex paupera* Nelmes *20681*

R	20681	Australia - Victoria *20681*

V *Carex perglobosa* Mackenzie *20850*

I	20850	U.S. - Colorado *20850*
E	20850	U.S. - Utah *20850*

E *Carex perraudieriana* Gay ex Bornm. *20750*

E	20750	Spain - Canary Is. *20750*

R *Carex phaeodon* T. Koyama *11164*

R	11164	Japan *11164*

V *Carex polymorpha* Muhl. *20850*

E	20850	U.S. - Connecticut *20850*
Ex/E	20850	U.S. - Delaware *20850*
E	20850	U.S. - Maine *20850*
Ex/E	20850	U.S. - Maryland *20850*
E	20850	U.S. - Massachusetts *20850*
E	20850	U.S. - New Hampshire *20850*
E	20850	U.S. - New Jersey *20850*
Ex	20850	U.S. - New York *20850*
E	20850	U.S. - Pennsylvania *20850*
E	20850	U.S. - Rhode Is. *20850*
V	20850	U.S. - Virginia *20850*
E	20850	U.S. - West Virginia *20850*

R *Carex porrecta* Reznicek & Camelbeke *21250*

R	21250	Costa Rica *21250*
R	21250	Colombia *21250*
R	21250	Ecuador *21250*
R	21250	Venezuela *21250*

I *Carex pseudoaperta* Kuk. *11494*

I	11494	India - Tamil Nadu (Nilgiri Hills) *11494*

R *Carex raleighii* Nelmes *20681*

I	20681	Australia - New South Wales *20681*
I	20681	Australia - Tasmania *20681*
I	20681	Australia - Victoria *20681*

I	***Carex rara*** Boott	
	I	India - Assam
	I	India - Meghalaya
E	***Carex rariflora*** (Wahl.)Sm. var. *androgyna* Porsild *20850, 6796*	
	E	*20850* Canada - Mackenzie *20850*
Ex	***Carex repanda*** C.B. Clarke *11494*	
	Ex	*11494* India - Meghalaya (Cherrapunji; Shillong) *11494*
E	***Carex roanensis*** F.J. Herm. *20850*	
	E	*20850* U.S. - Georgia *20850*
	E	*20850* U.S. - North Carolina *20850*
	E	*20850* U.S. - Tennessee *20850*
R	***Carex rufina*** Drej. *20850, 14360, 20171*	
	I	*20850* Canada - Manitoba *20850*
	E	*20850* Canada - Keewatin *20850*
	V	*20850* Canada - Quebec *20850*
R	***Carex ruthii*** Mackenzie *20850*	
	V	*20850* U.S. - Georgia *20850*
	R	*20850* U.S. - North Carolina *20850*
	I	*20850* U.S. - South Carolina *20850*
	E	*20850* U.S. - Tennessee *20850*
	R	*20850* U.S. - Virginia *20850*
R	***Carex scabriuscula*** Mackenzie *20850*	
	R	*20850* U.S. - Oregon *20850*
R	***Carex schweinitzii*** Dewey ex Schwein. *20850*	
	R	*20850* Canada - Ontario *20850*
	E	*20850* U.S. - Connecticut *20850*
	I	*20850* U.S. - Maryland *20850*
	E	*20850* U.S. - Massachusetts *20850*
	R	*20850* U.S. - Michigan *20850*
	I	*20850* U.S. - New Jersey *20850*
	V	*20850* U.S. - New York *20850*
	E	*20850* U.S. - North Carolina *20850*
	V	*20850* U.S. - Pennsylvania *20850*
	I	*20850* U.S. - Tennessee *20850*
	E	*20850* U.S. - Vermont *20850*
	E	*20850* U.S. - Virginia *20850*
	E	*20850* U.S. - Wisconsin *20850*
R	***Carex scitaeformis*** Kuk. *11164*	
	R	*11164* Japan *11164*
R	***Carex siroumensis*** Koidz. *11164*	
	R	*11164* Japan *11164*
R	***Carex socialis*** Mohlenbrock & Schwegm. *20850*	
	I	*20850* U.S. - Alabama *20850*
	I	*20850* U.S. - Arkansas *20850*
	I	*20850* U.S. - Georgia *20850*
	R	*20850* U.S. - Illinois *20850*
	V	*20850* U.S. - Indiana *20850*
	R	*20850* U.S. - Kentucky *20850*
	E	*20850* U.S. - Mississippi *20850*
	I	*20850* U.S. - Missouri *20850*
	E	*20850* U.S. - North Carolina *20850*
	I	*20850* U.S. - Oklahoma *20850*
	I	*20850* U.S. - South Carolina *20850*
	V	*20850* U.S. - Tennessee *20850*
V	***Carex specuicola*** J.T. Howell *20850, 14581*	
	V	*20850* U.S. - Arizona (Navajo Indian Reservation) *20850*
	E	*20850* U.S. - Utah *20850*
R	***Carex subcernua*** Ohwi *11164*	
	R	*11164* Japan *11164*
I	***Carex taprobanensis*** T. Koyama *8021*	
	I	*16162* Sri Lanka (Bible Rock, Kegalle Dist.) *8021*
R	***Carex tashiroana*** Ohwi *11164*	
	R	*11164* Japan *11164*

R	***Carex tenuior*** T. Koyama & Chuang *11164*	
	R	*11164* Japan *11164*
V	***Carex tompkinsii*** J.T. Howell *20850*	
	V	*20850* U.S. - California *20850*
E	***Carex toroensis*** G. Wheeler *20883*	
	I	*20883* Chile *20883*
R	***Carex tsushimensis*** (Ohwi) Ohwi *11164*	
	R	*11164* Japan *11164*
R	***Carex tuberculata*** Liebm. *9674*	
	R	*11383* Mexico - Mexico State *9674*
	R	*11383* Mexico - Puebla *9674*
V	***Carex tumidula*** Ohwi *11164*	
	V	*11164* Japan *11164*
R	***Carex vallis-pulchrae*** Philippi *20883*	
	I	*20883* Argentina *20883*
	I	*20883* Chile *20883*
V	***Carex vallis-pulchrae*** var. *barrosiana* G. Wheeler *20883*	
	I	*20883* Argentina *20883*
	I	*20883* Chile *20883*
I	***Carex vicinalis*** Boott *11494*	
	I	*11494* India - Tamil Nadu (Nilgiri Hills) *11494*
E	***Carex viridula*** Michx. var. *saxilittoralis* (A. Robertson) Crins *20850, 14366*	
	E	*20850* Canada - Newfoundland (Island) *20850*
	E	*20850* Canada - Nova Scotia *20850*
Ex/E	***Carex wahuensis*** C.A.Mey ssp. *herbstii* T. Koyama *20850, 14209*	
	Ex/E	*20850* U.S. - Hawaii *20850*
R	***Carex whitneyi*** Olney *20850*	
	I	*20850* U.S. - California *20850*
	I	*20850* U.S. - Nevada *20850*
	I	*20850* U.S. - Oregon *20850*
R	***Carex wiegandii*** Mackenzie *20883, 20850, 19002*	
	I	*20850* Canada - Labrador *20850*
	I	*20850* Canada - New Brunswick *20850*
	I	*20850* Canada - Newfoundland *20850*
	I	*20850* Canada - Nova Scotia *20850*
	E	*20850* Canada - Ontario *20850*
	I	*20850* Canada - Prince Edward Is. *20850*
	V	*20850* Canada - Quebec *20850*
	I	*20883* France - St Pierre & Miquelon *20883*
	V	*20850* U.S. - Maine *20850*
	E	*20850* U.S. - Massachusetts *20850*
	E	*20850* U.S. - Michigan *20850*
	E	*20850* U.S. - New Hampshire *20850*
	I	*20850* U.S. - New Jersey *20850*
	E	*20850* U.S. - New York *20850*
	V	*20850* U.S. - Pennsylvania *20850*
	Ex/E	*20850* U.S. - Vermont *20850*
I	***Carex wightiana*** Nees	
	I	India - Kerala (Travancore)
	I	India - Tamil Nadu (Courtallum Hills)
V	***Carex yakusimensis*** Masam. *11164*	
	V	*11164* Japan *11164*
E	***Chorizandra gigantea*** Raynal	
	E	New Caledonia
R	***Cyperus appendiculatus*** (Brongn.) Kunth var. *appendiculatus* *14222*	
	R	*19213* Ascension Is. *14222*
Ex/E	***Cyperus auriculatus*** Nees & Meyen *20883, 20850*	
	Ex/E	*20850* U.S. - Hawaii *20850*
	I	*20883* Puerto Rico *20883*

E	*Cyperus cephalanthus* Torr. & Hook. *20850*		
	E	20850 U.S. - Louisiana *20850*	
	Ex/E	20850 U.S. - Texas *20850*	
R	*Cyperus feanii* F. Brown		
	R	French Polynesia - Marquesas Is	
R	*Cyperus grandifolius* Andersson *11117*		
	R	Ecuador - Galapagos *11117*	
R	*Cyperus granitophilus* McVaugh *20850*		
	V	20850 U.S. - Alabama *20850*	
	R	20850 U.S. - Georgia *20850*	
	E	20850 U.S. - North Carolina *20850*	
	I	20850 U.S. - South Carolina *20850*	
	E	20850 U.S. - Tennessee *20850*	
	E	20850 U.S. - Virginia *20850*	
R	*Cyperus grayioides* Mohlenbrock *20850*		
	I	20850 U.S. - Arkansas *20850*	
	V	20850 U.S. - Illinois *20850*	
	E	20850 U.S. - Louisiana *20850*	
	E	20850 U.S. - Missouri *20850*	
	R	20850 U.S. - Texas *20850*	
R	*Cyperus harrisii* Kuk. *20883, 13336*		
	R	13336 Jamaica (St. Andrew) *20883*	
E	*Cyperus herndoniae* Tucker *20883*		
	I	20883 Costa Rica *20883*	
	I	20883 Mexico *20883*	
Ex/E	*Cyperus kunthianus* (Gaud.) Hbd. *20850*		
	Ex/E	20850 U.S. - Hawaii *20850*	
I	*Cyperus kurzii* Clarke *7771*		
	I	India - Andaman Is. *7771*	
R	*Cyperus lateriticus* Raynal *7926*		
	R	Senegal *7926*	
V	*Cyperus louisianensis* Thieret *20850*		
	E	20850 U.S. - Louisiana *20850*	
	R	20850 U.S. - Mississippi *20850*	
R	*Cyperus melanorrhyncha* Nelmes *12840*		
	R	12840 Turkey *12840*	
I	*Cyperus noeanus* Boiss. *12840*		
	I	12840 Turkey *12840*	
V	*Cyperus onerosus* M.C. Johnston *20850*		
	V	20850 U.S. - Texas *20850*	
E	*Cyperus papyrus* L. ssp. *hadidii* Chrtek & Slavikova		
	E	Egypt	
E	*Cyperus pennatiformis* Kukenth. *20850*		
	I	20850 U.S. - Hawaii *20850*	
R	*Cyperus pennellii* O'Neill & Benedict *14294*		
	R	14294 Mexico - Durango *14294*	
R	*Cyperus peruvianus* (Lam.) F.N.Williams var. *foliatus* (Kük.) Kük. *13336*		
	R	13336 Jamaica (St. Ann, St. Mary) *19890*	
V	*Cyperus pinetorum* Britton *5607*		
	V	19105 Cuba (Pinar del Rio; I. Juventud) *5607*	
R	*Cyperus rupicolus* S.T. Blake *20681*		
	I	20681 Australia - New South Wales *20681*	
	I	20681 Australia - Queensland *20681*	
V	*Cyperus semifertilis* S.T.Blake *20681*		
	V	20681 Australia - Queensland *20681*	
R	*Cyperus teneriffae* Poiret		
	R	Spain - Canary Is.	
E	*Cyperus trachysanthos* Hook. & Arn. *20850, 14209*		
	E	20850 U.S. - Hawaii *20850*	

R	*Cyperus trichodes* Griseb. *20883, 13336*		
	R	13336 Jamaica (Manchester, St. Elizabeth) *20883*	
E	*Cyperus urbanii* Boeckl. *20883*		
	V	19002 Puerto Rico *20883*	
	I	20883 USA - Virgin Is. *20883*	
R	*Eleocharis austrotexana* M.C. Johnston *20850*		
	R	20850 U.S. - Texas *20850*	
Ex	*Eleocharis bermudiana* Britton		
	Ex	Bermuda	
R	*Eleocharis blakeana* L.A.S.Johnson & O.Evans *20681*		
	I	20681 Australia - New South Wales *20681*	
	I	20681 Australia - Queensland *20681*	
E	*Eleocharis brachycarpa* Svens. *20883, 20850, 8058*		
	Ex/E	20850 U.S. - Texas *20850*	
	I	20883 Mexico *20883*	
R	*Eleocharis calocarpa* Chermezon		
	R	Côte d'Ivoire	
E	*Eleocharis cylindrica* Buckl. *20883, 20850, 8058*		
	I	20850 U.S. - New Mexico *20850*	
	E	20850 U.S. - Texas *20850*	
	I	20883 Mexico *20883*	
R	*Eleocharis decumbens* C.B. Clarke *20850*		
	I	20850 U.S. - California *20850*	
V	*Eleocharis flavescens* (Poir.) Urban var. *thermalis* (Rydb.) Cronq. *20850*		
	I	20850 U.S. - Montana *20850*	
	V	20850 U.S. - Wyoming *20850*	
I	*Eleocharis lankana* T. Koyama *8021*		
	I	16162 Sri Lanka (Yakkala, Colombo District) *8021*	
V	*Eleocharis neozelandica* C.B. Clarke ex Kirk *19305*		
	V	19305 New Zealand - North Is. *19305*	
	V	19305 New Zealand - South Is. *19305*	
V	*Eleocharis obicis* L.A.S.Johnson & O.Evans *20681*		
	V	20681 Australia - New South Wales *20681*	
V	*Eleocharis parvinux* Ohwi *11164*		
	V	11164 Japan *11164*	
V	*Eleocharis rzedowskii* S. Gonzalez *11380*		
	V	14294 Mexico - Nuevo Leon *11380*	
R	*Eleocharis uniflora* Seberg *19536*		
	R	19536 Chile *19536*	
R	*Ficinia gydomontana* Arnold *20604*		
	R	20604 South Africa - Cape Province *20604*	
I	*Ficinia micrantha* C.B.Clarke *20604*		
	I	20604 South Africa - Cape Province *20604*	
E	*Fimbristylis adjuncta* S.T.Blake *20681*		
	E	20681 Australia - Queensland *20681*	
I	*Fimbristylis aggregata* C. Fischer		
	I	India - Tamil Nadu	
I	*Fimbristylis arnottiana* Boeckeler		
	I	India - Kerala (Cannanore)	
I	*Fimbristylis brunneoides* Kerr *19120*		
	I	19120 Thailand (Phu Kradeung) *19120*	
I	*Fimbristylis contorta* C. Fischer		
	I	India - Tamil Nadu (Courtallum Hills)	
R	*Fimbristylis dipsacea* (Rottb.) C.B.Clarke *20681*		
	R	20681 Australia - Northern Territory *20681*	
R	*Fimbristylis harrisii* (Britton) C.D. Adams *15911*		
	I	19890 Haiti (southeast) *18329*	

R	*15911* Jamaica (Portland, St. Thomas) *19890*	

E *Fimbristylis hawaiiensis* **Hbd.** *20850, 14209*
    E   20850 U.S. - Hawaii *20850*

V *Fimbristylis ophiticola* **Britton** *5607*
    V   *19105* Cuba *5607*

V *Fimbristylis perpusilla* **Harper ex Small & Britt.** *20850*
    E   20850 U.S. - Delaware *20850*
    E   20850 U.S. - Georgia *20850*
    V   20850 U.S. - Maryland *20850*
    E   20850 U.S. - North Carolina *20850*
    V   20850 U.S. - South Carolina *20850*
    E   20850 U.S. - Tennessee *20850*
    E   20850 U.S. - Virginia *20850*

I *Fimbristylis psammophila* **Kerr** *19120*
    I   *19120* Thailand *19120*

I *Fimbristylis savanicola* **Kerr** *19120*
    I   *19120* Thailand *19120*

I *Fimbristylis smitinandii* **T. Koyama** *19120*
    I   *19120* Thailand *19120*

I *Fimbristylis spicigera* **Kerr** *19120*
    I   *19120* Thailand *19120*

R *Fimbristylis stolonifera* **C.B. Clarke** *11494*
    I   *11494* India - Manipur *11494*
    R   *11494* India - Meghalaya (Khasi hills, Mawphlong) *11494*

R *Fimbristylis vagans* **S.T.Blake** *20681*
    R   20681 Australia - Queensland *20681*

I *Fimbristylis zeylanica* **T. Koyama** *8021*
    I   *16162* Sri Lanka (Wilpattu NP) *8021*

R *Fuirena nyasensis* **Nelmes** *7849*
    R   Malawi *7849*

R *Gahnia hystrix* **J.Black** *20681*
    R   20681 Australia - South Australia *20681*

R *Gahnia insignis* **S.T.Blake** *20681*
    I   20681 Australia - New South Wales *20681*
    I   20681 Australia - Queensland *20681*

E *Gahnia lanaiensis* **O.& I. Deg. & J. Kern** *20850, 14209*
    E   20850 U.S. - Hawaii (Lana`ihale, Lana`i) *20850*

R *Gahnia marquisensis* **F. Brown**
    R   French Polynesia - Marquesas Is
    I   French Polynesia - Society Is.

R *Gahnia rodwayi* **F.Muell. ex Rodway** *20681*
    R   20681 Australia - Tasmania *20681*

I *Hypolytrum balakrishnanii* **Nooteboom** *7771*
    I   India - Andaman Is. (South) *7771*

I *Hypolytrum longirostre* **Thwaites** *8021*
    I   Sri Lanka (Hiniduma, Bambarabotuwa) *8021*

R *Hypolytrum mauritianum* **Nees ex Kunth** *10082*
    R   *10082* Mauritius *10082*

I *Isolepis inconspicua* **(Levyns) J.Raynal** *20604*
    I   20604 South Africa - Cape Province *20604*

R *Isolepis limbata* **W.M.Curtis** *20681*
    R   20681 Australia - Tasmania *20681*

R *Isolepis tasmanica* **(S.T.Blake) K.L.Wilson** *20681*
    R   20681 Australia - Tasmania *20681*

I *Kobresia duthiei* **C.B. Clarke**
    I   India - Himachal Pradesh
    I   India - Uttar Pradesh

I *Kobresia trinervis* **(Nees) Boeck. var.** *foliosa*
    (C.B. Clarke) Kuk.

    I   India - Uttar Pradesh

E *Koyamaea neblinensis* **W. Thomas & Davidse** *20883*
    I   *20883* Brazil *20883*
    I   *20883* Venezuela *20883*

R *Kyllinga nudiceps* **Clarke ex Standley** *9037*
    R   *19792* Costa Rica *9037*

E *Kyllinga urbanii* **Kuk.** *5607*
    E   *19105* Cuba (Pinar del Rio) *5607*

R *Lepidosperma rupestre* **Benth.** *20681*
    R   *20681* Australia - Western Australia *20681*

R *Lipocarpha prieuriana* **Steudel var.** *crassicuspis*
    Raynal *7926*
    R   Senegal *7926*

I *Lophoschoenus hornei* **(C.B. Clarke) Stapf** *14296*
    I   *19182* Seychelles (granitic) *14296*

R *Machaerina insularis* **(Benth.) T. Koyama**
    R   *14225* Australia - NSW - Lord Howe Is. *14225*

I *Machaerina restioides* **(Swartz) Vahl** *10199*
    I   Dominica *10199*

I *Mapania immersa* **(Thwaites) Benth. ex Clarke** *8021*
    I   *16162* Sri Lanka (Sinharaja; Pasdun Korale) *8021*

E *Mariscus fauriei* **(Kukenth.) T. koyama** *14209*
    E   *14209* U.S. - Hawaii *14209*

R *Mariscus kunthianus* **Gaud.** *14209*
    R   *14209* U.S. - Hawaii (West Maui) *14209*

E *Mariscus pennatiformis* **(Kukenth.) T. koyama** *14209*
    E   *14209* U.S. - Hawaii *14209*

E *Mariscus pennatiformis* **(Kukenth.) T. koyama ssp.** *bryanii* **(Kukenth.) T. Koyama** *14209*
    E   *14209* U.S. - Hawaii (north-east Laysan) *14209*

Ex/E *Mariscus rockii* **(Kukenth.) T. Koyama** *14209*
    Ex/E *14209* U.S. - Hawaii (Kaua`i - Wao`alae Valley) *14209*

V *Mariscus urbanii* **C.B. Clarke** *8058*
    V   *19002* Puerto Rico *8058*

R *Pycreus acaulis* **Nelmes** *7858*
    R   Malawi *7858*

V *Pycreus felicis* **Raynal** *7926*
    V   Guinea (Fouta Djalon) *7926*

R *Pycreus pagotii* **Rayn.**
    R   Chad

R *Pycreus spissiflorus* **C.B. Clarke** *7757*
    R   Malawi (Mlanje) *7757*

R *Reedia spathacea* **F.Muell.** *20681*
    R   *20681* Australia - Western Australia *20681*

E *Rhynchospora argentea* **Standl.** *20883, 9006*
    I   *20883* Panama *20883*

E *Rhynchospora bucherorum* **Leon** *5607*
    E   *19105* Cuba (Holguin) *5607*

E *Rhynchospora californica* **Gale** *20850*
    E   20850 U.S. - California *20850*

E *Rhynchospora crinipes* **Gale** *20850*
    E   20850 U.S. - Alabama *20850*
    E   20850 U.S. - Florida *20850*
    E   20850 U.S. - Georgia *20850*
    E   20850 U.S. - Mississippi *20850*
    E   20850 U.S. - North Carolina *20850*

E *Rhynchospora culixa* **Gale** *20850*
    E   20850 U.S. - Florida *20850*

Ex/E *20850* U.S. - Georgia *20850*

R   *Rhynchospora decurrens* **Chapman** *20850*
- I   *20850* U.S. - Alabama *20850*
- V   *20850* U.S. - Florida *20850*
- E   *20850* U.S. - Georgia *20850*
- I   *20850* U.S. - Louisiana *20850*
- E   *20850* U.S. - North Carolina *20850*

R   *Rhynchospora floridensis* **(Britt.) H. Pfeiffer** *20850*
- R   *20850* U.S. - Florida *20850*
- I   *20883* Bahamas *20883*

V   *Rhynchospora grisebachii* **Boeckl.** *5607*
- V   *19105* Cuba (Pinar del Rio) *5607*

R   *Rhynchospora harperi* **Small** *20850*
- I   *20850* U.S. - Alabama *20850*
- E   *20850* U.S. - Delaware *20850*
- I   *20850* U.S. - Florida *20850*
- E   *20850* U.S. - Georgia *20850*
- E   *20850* U.S. - North Carolina *20850*
- I   *20850* U.S. - South Carolina *20850*

R   *Rhynchospora indianolensis* **Small** *20850*
- R   *20850* U.S. - Texas *20850*

V   *Rhynchospora intermedia* **(Chapman) Britt.** *20850*
- I   *20850* U.S. - Alabama *20850*
- I   *20850* U.S. - Florida *20850*

E   *Rhynchospora joveroensis* **Britton** *5607*
- E   *19105* Cuba (Pinar del Rio) *5607*

E   *Rhynchospora knieskernii* **Carey** *20850, 14775*
- Ex/E   *20850* U.S. - Delaware *20850*
- E   *20850* U.S. - New Jersey (pine barrens) *20850*
- I   *20850* U.S. - South Carolina *20850*

E   *Rhynchospora nuda* **Gale** *5607*
- E   *19105* Cuba (Juventud Is.) *5607*

R   *Rhynchospora pallida* **M.A. Curtis** *20850*
- I   *20850* U.S. - Alabama *20850*
- Ex/E   *20850* U.S. - Delaware *20850*
- Ex/E   *20850* U.S. - Maryland *20850*
- R   *20850* U.S. - New Jersey *20850*
- Ex   *20850* U.S. - New York *20850*
- R   *20850* U.S. - North Carolina *20850*
- I   *20850* U.S. - South Carolina *20850*
- Ex/E   *20850* U.S. - Virginia *20850*

R   *Rhynchospora pleiantha* **(Kukenth.) Gale** *20850*
- E   *20850* U.S. - Alabama *20850*
- I   *20850* U.S. - Florida *20850*
- Ex/E   *20850* U.S. - Georgia *20850*
- I   *20850* U.S. - Louisiana *20850*
- E   *20850* U.S. - North Carolina *20850*

E   *Rhynchospora punctata* **Ell.** *20850*
- I   *20850* U.S. - Florida *20850*
- E   *20850* U.S. - Georgia *20850*

E   *Rhynchospora siguaneana* **Britton** *5607*
- E   *19105* Cuba (Juventud Is.) *5607*

E   *Rhynchospora solitaria* **Harper** *20850*
- E   *20850* U.S. - Georgia *20850*

E   *Rhynchospora squamulosa* **Kuk.** *5607*
- E   *19105* Cuba (Pinar del Rio) *5607*

E   *Rhynchospora subimberbis* **Griseb.** *5607*
- E   *19105* Cuba (Pinar del Rio) *5607*

I   *Rhynchospora submarginata* **Keukenth.** *14782*
- I   *14782* India - Kerala *14782*

V   *Rhynchospora sulcata* **Gale** *20850*
- I   *20850* U.S. - Florida *20850*
- I   *20850* U.S. - Georgia *20850*
- I   *20850* U.S. - South Carolina *20850*

E   *Rhynchospora thornei* **Kral** *20850*
- E   *20850* U.S. - Alabama *20850*
- I   *20850* U.S. - Florida *20850*
- E   *20850* U.S. - Georgia *20850*
- E   *20850* U.S. - North Carolina *20850*
- I   *20850* U.S. - Tennessee *20850*

R   *Schoenoxiphium strictum* **Kukkonen** *20604*
- R   *20604* South Africa - Natal *20604*

R   *Schoenus absconditus* **Kuk.** *20681*
- R   *20681* Australia - Tasmania *20681*

R   *Schoenus andrewsii* **Fitzg.** *20681*
- R   *20681* Australia - Western Australia *20681*

R   *Schoenus biglumis* **Kuk.** *20681*
- R   *20681* Australia - Tasmania *20681*

R   *Schoenus discifer* **Tate** *20681*
- R   *20681* Australia - South Australia *20681*

V   *Schoenus natans* **(F.Muell.) Benth.** *20681, 14223*
- V   *20681* Australia - Western Australia *20681*

R   *Schoenus pygmaeus* **S.T.Blake** *20681*
- R   *20681* Australia - Tasmania *20681*

R   *Scirpus ancistrochaetus* **Schuyler** *20850, 14711*
- E   *20850* U.S. - Maryland *20850*
- E   *20850* U.S. - Massachusetts *20850*
- E   *20850* U.S. - New Hampshire *20850*
- Ex   *20850* U.S. - New York *20850*
- V   *20850* U.S. - Pennsylvania *20850*
- E   *20850* U.S. - Vermont *20850*
- V   *20850* U.S. - Virginia *20850*
- E   *20850* U.S. - West Virginia *20850*

I   *Scirpus delicatulus* **(Nees) Levyns** *20604*
- I   *20604* South Africa - Cape Province *20604*

V   *Scirpus flaccidifolius* **(Fern.) Schuyler** *20850*
- E   *20850* U.S. - North Carolina *20850*
- E   *20850* U.S. - Virginia *20850*

R   *Scirpus grandicuspis* **(Steudel) R. Berhaut** *7926*
- R   Senegal *7926*

V   *Scirpus hallii* **Gray** *20850*
- I   *20850* U.S. - Alabama *20850*
- E   *20850* U.S. - Georgia *20850*
- E   *20850* U.S. - Illinois *20850*
- E   *20850* U.S. - Indiana *20850*
- Ex/E   *20850* U.S. - Iowa *20850*
- E   *20850* U.S. - Kansas *20850*
- E   *20850* U.S. - Kentucky *20850*
- Ex   *20850* U.S. - Massachusetts *20850*
- E   *20850* U.S. - Michigan *20850*
- E   *20850* U.S. - Missouri *20850*
- E   *20850* U.S. - Nebraska *20850*
- I   *20850* U.S. - Ohio *20850*
- E   *20850* U.S. - Oklahoma *20850*
- Ex/E   *20850* U.S. - Wisconsin *20850*

V   *Scirpus longii* **Fern.** *20850, 3064*
- E   *20850* Canada - Nova Scotia *20850*
- Ex/E   *20850* U.S. - Connecticut *20850*
- E   *20850* U.S. - Maine *20850*
- E   *20850* U.S. - Massachusetts *20850*
- E   *20850* U.S. - New Hampshire *20850*
- V   *20850* U.S. - New Jersey *20850*
- Ex   *20850* U.S. - New York *20850*
- E   *20850* U.S. - Rhode Is. *20850*

V   *Scirpus rollandii* **Fern.** *20850*
- V   *20850* Canada - Alberta *20850*
- V   *20850* Canada - British Columbia *20850*
- I   *20850* Canada - Labrador *20850*
- E   *20850* Canada - Quebec *20850*
- E   *20850* Canada - Saskatchewan *20850*
- E   *20850* Canada - Yukon Territory *20850*

I		20850	U.S. - Alaska	20850
I		20850	U.S. - California	20850
E		20850	U.S. - Colorado	20850
E		20850	U.S. - Montana	20850
E		20850	U.S. - Wyoming	20850

I   *Scleria alta* Boeck. *14721*

E		14721	India - Assam	14721
I		14782	India - Meghalaya	14782
E		14721	India - West Bengal	14721

Ex   *Scleria anomala* (Steud.) J.Raynal *10082*

Ex	20771	Mauritius	10082

E   *Scleria bracteata* Cav. var. *assamic* C.B. Clarke *14721*

E		14721	India - Assam	14721

R   *Scleria chevalieri* Raynal *7926*

R		Senegal *7926*

V   *Scleria doradoensis* Britton *8058*

V	19002	Puerto Rico	8058

R   *Scleria glabra* Boeck. var. *pallidior* Rayn.

R		Chad

V   *Scleria guineensis* Raynal *7926*

V		Guinea *7926*

I   *Scleria mikawana* Makino *11164*

I	11164	Japan	11164

R   *Scleria monticola* Napper *7926*

R		Sierra Leone *7926*

E   *Scleria motemboensis* Britton *5607*

E	19105	Cuba (Matanzas; Villa Clara)	5607

I   *Scleria pilosa* Boeckeler *8021*

I	16162	Sri Lanka (Kalutara)	8021

V   *Scleria sheilae* Raynal

V		Cameroon

V   *Tetraria australiensis* C.B.Clarke *20681, 14223*

V	20681	Australia - Western Australia	20681

I   *Tetraria paludosa* Levyns *20604*

I	20604	South Africa - Cape Province	20604

V   *Thoracostachyum angustifolium* C.B. Clarke *14296*

V	19182	Seychelles (granitic)	14296

I   *Thoracostachyum floribundum* (Ness) C.B. Clarke *14296*

I	19182	Seychelles (granitic)	14296

I   *Torulinium correllii* Koyama

I	4650	Bahamas *4650*

I   *Trianoptiles solitaria* (C.B.Clarke) Levyns *20604*

I	20604	South Africa - Cape Province	20604

I   *Trianoptiles stipitata* Levyns *20604*

I	20604	South Africa - Cape Province	20604

V   *Tricostularia guillauminii* (Kük.) Raynal *20893*

V	20893	New Caledonia	20893

V   *Uncinia costata* Kuk. *19116*

V	19125	Chile - Juan Fernandez Is.	19116

R   *Uncinia debilior* F. Muell.

R	14225	Australia - NSW - Lord Howe Is.	14225

Dioscoreaceae

Number of genera:	6
Number of species:	630
Recorded threatened species:	72 (11%)

Tropical and subtropical, with a few species in North temperate region.

E   *Borderea chouardii* (Gaussen) Heslot *8000, 20171*

E	11496	Spain	8000

E   *Dioscorea aguilarii* Standley & Steyerm. *19788*

E	19788	Guatemala (Izabal)	9004

R   *Dioscorea asclepiadea* Prain & Burkill *11164*

R	11164	Japan	11164

R   *Dioscorea bartlettii* C. Morton *19788*

R	20765	Belize	19788
R	20765	Guatemala	19788
R	20765	Honduras	19788
R	20765	Mexico - Campeche	19788
R	20765	Mexico - Chiapas	19788
R	20765	Mexico - Oaxaca	19788
R	20765	Mexico - Quintana Roo	19788
R	20765	Mexico - Tabasco	19788
R	20765	Mexico - Veracruz	19788
R	20765	Mexico - Yucatan	19788

I   *Dioscorea belophylla* Voight

I		India (Western Ghats)

E   *Dioscorea bernoulliana* Prain et Burkill *19788*

E	20765	Guatemala	19788

R   *Dioscorea brownii* Schinz *20604*

R	20604	South Africa - Cape Province	20604
R	20604	South Africa - Natal	20604

V   *Dioscorea carpomaculata* Téllez & B.G. Schubert var. *cinerea* (Uline ex Knuth) Téllez & B.G. Schubert *19788*

V	20765	Mexico - Chiapas	19788

I   *Dioscorea caucasica* Lipsky *5942*

I	5942	Georgia	5942

V   *Dioscorea chaponensis* Knuth *19788*

V	20765	Panama (east)	19788
V	20765	Colombia (north)	19788

E   *Dioscorea chiapasensis* Matuda *19788*

E	20765	Guatemala	19788
E	20765	Mexico - Chiapas	19788

V   *Dioscorea conzattii* Knuth *19907*

V	20765	Mexico - Oaxaca	20765

E   *Dioscorea cruzensis* Knuth *9706*

E	20765	Mexico - Veracruz	9706

E   *Dioscorea cyphocarpa* Robinson *19907*

E	20765	Mexico - Guerrero	20765
E	20765	Mexico - Oaxaca	20765

E   *Dioscorea dicranandra* J.D. Smith *19788*

E	20765	Guatemala (Chiquimulas)	20765

R   *Dioscorea dissimulans* Prain & Burkill *6057*

R		Vietnam *6057*

E   *Dioscorea ekmanii* Knuth *5607*

V   *Dioscorea elephantipes* (L'Hér.) Engl. *20604*

V	20604	South Africa - Cape Province	20604

E   *Dioscorea escuintlensis* Matuda *19788*

E	20756	Guatemala	9679

V   *Dioscorea gallegosii* E. Matuda *19907*

V	20765	Mexico - Guerrero	20765

E   *Dioscorea guerrerensis* Knuth *19907*

E	20765	Mexico - Guerrero	20765

E   *Dioscorea herradurensis* (Knuth) P. Wilson *5607*

E   *Dioscorea hintoni* Knuth *19907*

E	20765	Mexico	19907

E   *Dioscorea igualamontana* Matuda *19907*

E	20765	Mexico - Guerrero	20765

R   *Dioscorea izuensis* Akahori *11164*

R   *11164*   Japan *11164*

R   *Dioscorea jaliscana* S.Watson *9681*

    R   *20765*   Mexico - Colima *20765*
    R   *20765*   Mexico - Jalisco *20765*
    R   *20765*   Mexico - Nayarit *20765*
    R   *20765*   Mexico - Sinaloa *20765*
    R   *20765*   Mexico - Tamaulipas *20765*

I   *Dioscorea kalkapershadii* Prain & Burkill

    I   India - Tamil Nadu (Shevaroy Hills, Salem Dist)

E   *Dioscorea koepperi* Standley *19788*

    E   *20765*   Honduras *19788*

R   *Dioscorea lepida* C. Morton *19788*

    V   *9426*   Costa Rica *19788*
    R   *20765*   El Salvador *20765*
    R   *20765*   Guatemala *19788*
    R   *20765*   Honduras *19788*
    R   *20765*   Mexico - Chiapas *19788*
    R   *20765*   Panama (Coclé; Chiriquí; Panamá; Veraguas) *10747*

E   *Dioscorea lobata* Uline *19907*

    E   *20765*   Mexico - Mexico D.F. *20765*
    E   *20765*   Mexico - Oaxaca *20765*

V   *Dioscorea longituba* Uline *19907*

    V   *20765*   Mexico *19907*
    V   *20765*   Mexico - Guerrero *20765*

R   *Dioscorea matagalpensis* Uline *19788*

    R   *20765*   Belize *19788*
    R   *20765*   Costa Rica *20765*
    R   *20765*   El Salvador *20765*
    R   *20765*   Guatemala *19788*
    R   *20765*   Honduras *19788*
    R   *20765*   Mexico - Campeche *19788*
    R   *20765*   Mexico - Chiapas *19788*
    R   *20765*   Mexico - Quintana Roo *19788*
    R   *20765*   Mexico - Tabasco *19788*
    R   *20765*   Mexico - Yucatan *19788*
    R   *20765*   Nicaragua *19788*
    R   *20765*   Panama *19788*

E   *Dioscorea matudae* O. Téllez-Valdés & B.G. Schubert *19907*

    E   *20765*   Mexico - Queretaro *20765*

E   *Dioscorea mcvaughii* B.G. Schubert *19907*

    E   *20765*   Mexico - Nayarit *20765*

E   *Dioscorea mesoamericana* O.Téllez-Valdés & A.I. Martínez-Rodríguez *20753, 19788*

    E   *20765*   Mexico - Chiapas *19788*
    E   *20765*   Mexico - Oaxaca *19788*

R   *Dioscorea minima* Robinson & Seaton *19907*

    R   *20765*   Mexico - Jalisco *20765*
    R   *20765*   Mexico - Michoacan *20765*
    R   *20765*   Mexico - Nayarit *20765*
    R   *20765*   Mexico - Sinaloa *20765*

V   *Dioscorea mitis* C. Morton *9681*

    V   *20765*   Mexico - Jalisco *20765*
    V   *20765*   Mexico - Michoacan *20765*

V   *Dioscorea morelosana* (Uline) Matuda *19907*

    V   *20765*   Mexico - Morelos *20765*

R   *Dioscorea multinervis* Benth. *19907*

    R   *20765*   Mexico - Chihuahua *20765*
    R   *20765*   Mexico - Jalisco *20765*
    R   *20765*   Mexico - Michoacan *20765*
    R   *20765*   Mexico - Nayarit *20765*

E   *Dioscorea nematodes* Uline ex Knuth *19907*

    E   *20765*   Mexico - Guanajuato *20765*

V   *Dioscorea oaxacensis* Uline *19907*

    V   *20765*   Mexico - Oaxaca *20765*

I   *Dioscorea oppositifolia* L. var. *dukhunensis* Prain & Burkill

    I   India

E   *Dioscorea oreodoxa* B.G. Schubert *19907*

    E   *20765*   Mexico - Colima *20765*

I   *Dioscorea palawana* Prain & Burk. *13833*

    I   *13833*   Philippines (Palawan) *13833*

E   *Dioscorea panamensis* Knuth *20883, 19788*

    V   *20765*   Panama (Canal area; Panamá) *20883*
    V   *20765*   Colombia *20765*
    V   *20765*   Venezuela *20765*

V   *Dioscorea pantojensis* Knuth *19907*

    V   *20765*   Mexico *19907*

R   *Dioscorea petelotii* Prain & Burkill *6057*

    R   Vietnam *6057*

V   *Dioscorea platycolpota* Uline *19907*

    V   *20765*   Mexico *19907*

R   *Dioscorea plumifera* Robinson *19907*

    R   *20765*   Mexico *19907*

V   *Dioscorea pringlei* Robinson *9681*

    V   *20765*   Mexico *9681*

E   *Dioscorea pumicicola* Uline *19907*

    E   *20765*   Mexico - Morelos *20765*

V   *Dioscorea reversiflora* Uline *19907*

    V   *20765*   Mexico - Nayarit *20765*
    V   *20765*   Mexico - Sinaloa *20765*

I   *Dioscorea rogersii* Prain & Burk. *7771*

    I   *14782*   India - Andaman Is. *7771*

V   *Dioscorea salvadorensis* Standley *19788*

    V   *20765*   El Salvador *9681*

E   *Dioscorea sanchez-colinii* E. Matuda *19907*

    E   *20765*   Mexico *19907*

E   *Dioscorea sandwithii* B.G. Schubert *19788*

    E   *20765*   Belize *19788*

V   *Dioscorea sessiliflora* McVaugh *19907*

    V   *20765*   Mexico - Nayarit *20765*

R   *Dioscorea sparsiflora* var. *maculata* Uline *19907*

    R   *20765*   Mexico *19907*

E   *Dioscorea spiculiflora* Hemsley var. *fasciculocongesta* Sosa & B.G. Schubert *9706*

    E   *20765*   Mexico - Puebla *20765*
    E   *20765*   Mexico - Veracruz *9706*

R   *Dioscorea standleyi* C. Morton *19788*

    R   *20765*   Costa Rica *19788*
    R   *20765*   Panama (Bocas Del Toro; Chiriquí; Colón; Panamá) *19788*

V   *Dioscorea sumiderensis* B.G. Schubert & Téllez *19788*

    V   *20765*   Guatemala *20765*
    V   *20765*   Mexico - Chiapas *19788*

E   *Dioscorea tacanensis* Lundell *19788*

    E   *20765*   Mexico - Chiapas *19788*

E   *Dioscorea tancitarensis* Matuda *19907*

    E   *20765*   Mexico - Michoacan *20765*

V   *Dioscorea temascaltepensis* Knuth *19907*

    V   *20765*   Mexico *19907*

V   *Dioscorea tublperianthia* Matuda *19907*

    V   *20765*   Mexico *19907*

R   *Dioscorea ulinei* Greenman ex Knuth *19907*

    R   *20765*   Mexico *19907*

V   ***Dioscorea urceolata*** Uline *19907*
     V   *20765* Mexico *19907*

I   ***Dioscorea vexans*** Prain & Burk. *7771*
     I   India - Andaman Is. *7771*

I   ***Dioscorea wightii*** Hook.f.
     I   India - Kerala (Travancore Hills)
     I   India - Tamil Nadu (Courtallum, Tirunelveli H.)

V   ***Rajania cyclophylla*** (Urb.) R. Kunth *20883, 13336*
     V   *13336* Jamaica *20883*

E   ***Rajania hermannii*** Knuth *5607*
     E   *19105* Cuba (Pinar del Rio) *5607*

Ex   ***Rajania prestoniensis*** Knuth *5607*
     Ex   *19105* Cuba (Holguin) *19105*

I   ***Rajania theresensis*** Uline *5607*
     I   *5607* Cuba *5607*

Dracaenaceae

Number of genera: 6
Number of species: 156
Recorded threatened species: 20   (12%)

Tropics and subtropics, to south-west USA.

V   ***Beaucarnea goldmanii*** Rose *19850*
     V   *19850* Mexico *19850*

V   ***Beaucarnea gracilis*** Lem. *19850*
     V   *19850* Mexico *19850*

V   ***Beaucarnea hiriartiae*** L. Hernandez Sandoval *19850*
     V   *19850* Mexico *19850*

V   ***Beaucarnea pliabilis*** (Baker) Rose *19850*
     V   *19850* Mexico *19850*

V   ***Beaucarnea purpusii*** Rose *19848*
     V   *19848* Mexico *19848*

V   ***Beaucarnea stricta*** Lem. *19850*
     V   *19850* Mexico *19850*

R   ***Dasylirion palaciosii*** Rzed. *19850*
     R   *19850* Mexico *19850*

E   ***Dracaena concinna*** Kunth *10082*
     E   *20771* Mauritius (Ile aux Aigrettes) *10082*

V   ***Dracaena draco*** (L.) L. *18124, 7389*
     E   Portugal - Madeira
     V   Spain - Canary Is.
     V   Cape Verde Is.

V   ***Dracaena floribunda*** Baker *10082*
     V   *20771* Mauritius *10082*

E   ***Dracaena goldieana*** W. Bull *7926*
     E   Nigeria *7926*

Ex   ***Dracaena umbraculifera*** Jacq. *10082*
     Ex   *20771* Mauritius *10082*

V   ***Nolina arenicola*** Correll *20850*
     V   *20850* U.S. - Texas *20850*

R   ***Nolina atopocarpa*** Bartlett *20850*
     R   *20850* U.S. - Florida *20850*

V   ***Nolina brittoniana*** Nash *20850, 18134*
     V   *20850* U.S. - Florida (L. Wales Ridge) *20850*

V   I   ***Nolina interrata*** Gentry *20883, 20850, 8058*
     E   *20850* U.S. - California *20850*
     E   *20883* Mexico *20883*

V   ***Pleomele auwahiensis*** St. John *14209, 20850*
     I   *20850* U.S. - Hawaii *20850*

V   ***Pleomele fernaldii*** St. John *20850, 14209*

     I   *20850* U.S. - Hawaii (Lanai) *20850*

E   ***Pleomele forbesii*** O. Deg. *20850, 14209*
     E   *20850* U.S. - Hawaii (O`ahu) *20850*

V   ***Pleomele halapepe*** St. John *14209, 20850*
     I   *20850* U.S. - Hawaii (O`ahu) *20850*

E   ***Pleomele hawaiiensis*** O.& I. Deg. *20850, 14209, 21355*
     E   *20850* U.S. - Hawaii *20850*

Eriocaulaceae

Number of genera: 13
Number of species: 1,200
Recorded threatened species: 63   (5%)

Tropical and subtropical, with a few species in temperate regions.

V   ***Eriocaulon amanoanum*** T. Koyama *11164*
     V   *11164* Japan *11164*

E   ***Eriocaulon arenicola*** Britton & Small *5607*
     E   *19105* Cuba (Juventud Is.) *5607*

R   ***Eriocaulon atroides*** Satake *11164*
     R   *11164* Japan *11164*

V   ***Eriocaulon australasicum*** (F.Muell.) Korn *20681*
     I   *20681* Australia - New South Wales *20681*
     I   *20681* Australia - Victoria *20681*

Ex/E   ***Eriocaulon barba-caprae*** Fyson *14720*
     Ex/E *14720* India - Karnataka *14720*
     Ex/E *14720* India - Meghalaya *14720*

Ex/E   ***Eriocaulon barbeyanum*** Ruhl. *14720*
     Ex/E *14720* India - Karnataka *14720*

E   ***Eriocaulon carsonii*** F.Muell. *20681*
     I   *20681* Australia - New South Wales *20681*
     I   *20681* Australia - Queensland *20681*
     I   *20681* Australia - South Australia *20681*

I   ***Eriocaulon cauliferum*** Makino *11164*
     I   *11164* Japan *11164*

E   ***Eriocaulon cubense*** Ruhl. *5607*
     E   *19105* Cuba (Juventud Is.) *5607*

I   ***Eriocaulon dalzellii*** Koern.
     I   India - Karnataka (south Concan)

R   ***Eriocaulon dimorphoelytrum*** T. Koyama *11164*
     R   *11164* Japan *11164*

Ex   ***Eriocaulon echinospermoideum*** Ruhl. *5607*
     Ex   *19105* Cuba (Villa Clara) *5607*

E   ***Eriocaulon ekmanii*** Ruhl. *5607*
     E   *19105* Cuba (Pinar del Rio) *5607*

E   ***Eriocaulon europeplon*** Koern *14720*
     E   *14720* India - Gujarat *14720*
     E   *14720* India - Maharashtra *14720*

I   ***Eriocaulon fluviatile*** Trimen *10252*
     I   *16162* Sri Lanka *10252*

I   ***Eriocaulon fusiforme*** Britton & Small *5607*
     I   *19105* Cuba (Juventud Is.) *5607*

R   ***Eriocaulon gamblei*** C. Fischer *14720*
     R   *14720* India - Tamil Nadu (Naduvattam, Nilgiri) *14720*

R   ***Eriocaulon geoffreyi*** Fyson *14720*
     R   *14720* India - Tamil Nadu *14720*

V   ***Eriocaulon glaberrimum*** Satake *11164*
     V   *11164* Japan *11164*

R   ***Eriocaulon gregatum*** Koern *14720*

R	14720	India - Meghalaya	14720

I *Eriocaulon heleocharioides* Satake 11164
I	11164	Japan	11164

V *Eriocaulon humile* Moldenke 14782
V	14782	India - Maharashtra (western Ghats) 14782	

R *Eriocaulon inundatum* Mold. 7926
R		Senegal (Fremaria)	7926

I *Eriocaulon japonicum* Koern. 11164
I	11164	Japan	11164

Ex *Eriocaulon johnstonii* Ruhl. 10082
Ex	20771	Mauritius	10082

V *Eriocaulon koernickianum* Van Heurck & Muell.-Arg. 20850
V	20850	U.S. - Arkansas	20850
E	20850	U.S. - Georgia	20850
E	20850	U.S. - Oklahoma	20850
E	20850	U.S. - Texas	20850

V *Eriocaulon kusiroense* Satake 11164
V	11164	Japan	11164

I *Eriocaulon longicuspis* Hook.f. 10252
I	16162	Sri Lanka	10252

V *Eriocaulon longipedunculatum* Lecomte
V	New Caledonia

I *Eriocaulon margaretae* Fyson
I	India - Karnataka (Rudrasiri, Mysore)

V *Eriocaulon mikawanum* Satake & T. Koyama 11164
V	11164	Japan	11164

Ex *Eriocaulon minutissimum* Ruhl. 5607
Ex	19105	Cuba (Pinar del Rio)	5607

E *Eriocaulon miserrimum* Ruhl. 5607
E	19105	Cuba (Juventud Is.)	5607

R *Eriocaulon mysorense* Fyson 14720
R	14720	India - Karnataka	14720

V *Eriocaulon nakasimanum* Satake 11164
V	11164	Japan	11164

R *Eriocaulon nanellum* Ohwi var. *nanellum* 11164
R	11164	Japan	11164

R *Eriocaulon nanellum* Ohwi var. *nosoriense* Ohwi 11164
R	11164	Japan	11164

R *Eriocaulon nanellum* Ohwi var. *piliferum* Satake 11164
R	11164	Japan	11164

R *Eriocaulon nasuense* Satake 11164
R	11164	Japan	11164

E *Eriocaulon olivaceum* Mold. 5607
E	19105	Cuba (Juventud Is.)	5607

I *Eriocaulon ovoideum* Britton & Small 5607
I	19105	Cuba (Juventud Is.)	5607

R *Eriocaulon ozense* T. Koyama 11164
R	11164	Japan	11164

V *Eriocaulon pallescens* (Nakai) Satake 11164
V	11164	Japan	11164

E *Eriocaulon panamense* Mold. 20883, 9006
I	20883	Panama	20883

R *Eriocaulon parkeri* B.L. Robins. 20850, 4380
E	20850	Canada - New Brunswick	20850
V	20850	Canada - Quebec	20850
E	20850	U.S. - Connecticut	20850

V	20850	U.S. - Delaware	20850
Ex	20850	U.S. - District of Columbia	20850
R	20850	U.S. - Maine	20850
V	20850	U.S. - Maryland	20850
E	20850	U.S. - Massachusetts	20850
V	20850	U.S. - New Jersey	20850
Ex	20850	U.S. - New York	20850
E	20850	U.S. - North Carolina	20850
Ex	20850	U.S. - Pennsylvania	20850
V	20850	U.S. - Virginia	20850

E *Eriocaulon pectinatum* Ruhl. 14720
E	14720	India - Tamil Nadu (Nilgiri Hills)	2268

R *Eriocaulon perplexum* Satake & Hara 11164
R	11164	Japan	11164

R *Eriocaulon plumale* N.E. Br. ssp. *kindiae* (Lecomte) Meikle 7926
R		Guinea	7926

I *Eriocaulon pumilo* Hook.f.
I	India - Uttar Pradesh

V *Eriocaulon ravenelii* Chapman 20850
I	20850	U.S. - Florida	20850
?	20850	U.S. - Georgia	20850
R	20850	U.S. - Mississippi	20850
I	20850	U.S. - South Carolina	20850

R *Eriocaulon satakeanum* Tatew. & Ku.Ito 11164
R	11164	Japan	11164

E *Eriocaulon seemannii* Mold. 20883, 9006
I	20883	Panama	20883

R *Eriocaulon sekimotoi* Honda 11164
R	11164	Japan	11164

I *Eriocaulon seticuspe* Ohwi 11164
I	11164	Japan	11164

R *Eriocaulon takae* Koidz. 11164
R	11164	Japan	11164

R *Eriocaulon thomasi* Fyson 14720
R	14720	India - Karnataka	14720
R	14720	India - Maharashtra	14720

R *Eriocaulon tutidae* Satake 11164
R	11164	Japan	11164

I *Eriocaulon walkeri* Hook.f. 10252
I	16162	Sri Lanka	10252

R *Eriocaulon zyotanii* Satake 11164
R	11164	Japan	11164

V *Lachnocaulon beyrichianum* Sporleder ex Koern. 20850
I	20850	U.S. - Alabama	20850
V	20850	U.S. - Florida	20850
E	20850	U.S. - Georgia	20850
V	20850	U.S. - North Carolina	20850
I	20850	U.S. - South Carolina	20850

Ex *Lachnocaulon cubense* Ruhl. 5607
Ex	19105	Cuba (Villa Clara)	5607

R *Lachnocaulon digynum* Koern. 20850
V	20850	U.S. - Alabama	20850
V	20850	U.S. - Florida	20850
V	20850	U.S. - Louisiana	20850
V	20850	U.S. - Mississippi	20850
E	20850	U.S. - Texas	20850

V *Lachnocaulon engleri* Ruhl. 20850
E	20850	U.S. - Alabama	20850
E	20850	U.S. - Florida	20850

R *Mesanthemum benneae* Jacq.-Fel. 7926
R		Guinea (Kindia)	7926

R *Paepalanthus nipensis* L. Gonzalez Geigel 11840

	R	Cuba (Holguin) *11840*
V	*Paepalanthus pungens* Griseb. *11840*	
	V	Cuba (Holguin) *11840*
I	*Syngonanthus davidsei* Hauft *20883, 12068*	
	I	*20883* Mexico *20883*
V	*Syngonanthus insularis* Mold. *5607*	
	V	*19105* Cuba (Juventud Is.) *5607*
E	*Syngonanthus pittieri* Mold. *20883, 9006*	
	I	*20883* Panama *20883*

Eriospermaceae

Number of genera:	1
Number of species:	80-100
Recorded threatened species:	36 (40%)

Africa south of the Sahara, especially southwestern Cape Province (South Africa).

R	*Eriospermum aequilibre* Poelln. *20604*	
	R	*20604* South Africa - Cape Province *20604*
R	*Eriospermum algiferum* Marloth ex A.V.Duthie *20604*	
	R	*20604* South Africa - Cape Province *20604*
R	*Eriospermum arachnoideum* P.L.Perry *20604*	
	R	*20604* South Africa - Cape Province *20604*
R	*Eriospermum arenosum* P.L.Perry *20604*	
	R	*20604* South Africa - Cape Province *20604*
R	*Eriospermum aribesense* P.L.Perry *20604*	
	R	*20604* South Africa - Cape Province *20604*
R	*Eriospermum armianum* P.L.Perry *20604*	
	R	*20604* South Africa - Cape Province *20604*
R	*Eriospermum attenuatum* Marloth ex P.L.Perry *20604*	
	R	*20604* South Africa - Cape Province *20604*
R	*Eriospermum bracteatum* Archibald *20604*	
	R	*20604* South Africa - Cape Province *20604*
R	*Eriospermum bruynsii* P.L.Perry *20604*	
	R	*20604* South Africa - Cape Province *20604*
R	*Eriospermum calcareum* P.L.Perry *20604*	
	R	*20604* South Africa - Cape Province *20604*
R	*Eriospermum ciliatum* P.L.Perry *20604*	
	R	*20604* South Africa - Cape Province *20604*
R	*Eriospermum coactum* P.L.Perry *20604*	
	R	*20604* South Africa - Cape Province *20604*
R	*Eriospermum crispum* P.L.Perry *20604*	
	R	*20604* South Africa - Cape Province *20604*
R	*Eriospermum erinum* P.L.Perry *20604*	
	R	*20604* South Africa - Cape Province *20604*
R	*Eriospermum eriophorum* Marloth ex P.L.Perry *20604*	
	R	*20604* South Africa - Cape Province *20604*
R	*Eriospermum ernstii* P.L.Perry *20604*	
	R	*20604* South Africa - Cape Province *20604*
R	*Eriospermum exigium* P.L.Perry *20604*	
	R	*20604* South Africa - Cape Province *20604*
R	*Eriospermum filicaule* Marloth ex P.L.Perry *20604*	
	R	*20604* South Africa - Cape Province *20604*
R	*Eriospermum fragile* P.L.Perry *20604*	
	R	*20604* South Africa - Cape Province *20604*
R	*Eriospermum glaciale* P.L.Perry *20604*	
	R	*20604* South Africa - Cape Province *20604*
R	*Eriospermum inconspicuum* P.L.Perry *20604*	
	R	*20604* South Africa - Cape Province *20604*

R	*Eriospermum minutipustulatum* P.L.Perry *20604*	
	R	*20604* South Africa - Cape Province *20604*
R	*Eriospermum occultum* Archibald *20604*	
	R	*20604* South Africa - Cape Province *20604*
R	*Eriospermum papilliferum* A.V.Duthie *20604*	
	R	*20604* South Africa - Cape Province *20604*
R	*Eriospermum parvulum* P.L.Perry *20604*	
	R	*20604* South Africa - Cape Province *20604*
I	*Eriospermum phippsii* Wild *7754*	
	I	Zimbabwe (Chimanimani) *7754*
R	*Eriospermum pusillum* P.L.Perry *20604*	
	R	*20604* South Africa - Cape Province *20604*
R	*Eriospermum ramosum* P.L.Perry *20604*	
	R	*20604* South Africa - Cape Province *20604*
R	*Eriospermum ratelpoortianum* P.L.Perry *20604*	
	R	*20604* South Africa - Cape Province *20604*
R	*Eriospermum rhizomatum* P.L.Perry *20604*	
	R	*20604* South Africa - Cape Province *20604*
R	*Eriospermum sabulosum* P.L.Perry *20604*	
	R	*20604* South Africa - Cape Province *20604*
R	*Eriospermum subtile* P.L.Perry *20604*	
	R	*20604* South Africa - Cape Province *20604*
R	*Eriospermum titanopsoides* P.L.Perry *20604*	
	R	*20604* South Africa - Cape Province *20604*
R	*Eriospermum tuberculatum* P.L.Perry *20604*	
	R	*20604* South Africa - Cape Province *20604*
R	*Eriospermum vermiforme* Marloth ex P.L.Perry *20604*	
	R	*20604* South Africa - Cape Province *20604*
R	*Eriospermum viscosum* Marloth ex P.L.Perry *20604*	
	R	*20604* South Africa - Cape Province *20604*

Gramineae

Number of genera:	500
Number of species:	8,000
Recorded threatened species:	776 (9%)

Cosmopolitan, especially tropical and North temperate semi-arid regions with seasonal rainfall.

R	*Agropyron brandzae* Pantu & Solacolu *17823, 20171*	
	R	*19949* Romania *20631*
I	*Agropyron cimmericum* Nevski *20171*	
	I	former European USSR
R	*Agropyron dasyanthum* Ledeb. *20171*	
	R	former European USSR
R	*Agropyron deweyi* A. Love *12840*	
	R	*12840* Turkey *12840*
I	*Agropyron duthiei* Meld.	
	I	India - Himachal Pradesh
	I	India - Uttar Pradesh
R	*Agropyron embergeri* Maire	
	R	Morocco
R	*Agropyron tanaiticum* Nevski *20171*	
	R	former European USSR
I	*Agropyron tsukushiense* Ohwi *11164*	
	I	*11164* Japan *11164*
R	*Agropyropsis lolium* (Balansa) A. Camus *10487*	
	R	*14958* Algeria *10487*
E	*Agrostis adamsonii* Vickery *20681, 14223*	
	E	*20681* Australia - Victoria *14223*

E   *Agrostis aristiglumis* Swallen *20850*
     E   *20850*   U.S. - California *20850*

R   *Agrostis billardieri* R.Br. var. *tenuiseta*
       D.Morris *20681*
     R   *20681*   Australia - Tasmania *14223*

V   *Agrostis blasdalei* A.S. Hitchc. *20850*
     V   *20850*   U.S. - California *20850*

V   *Agrostis blasdalei* A. Hitchc. var.
       blasdalei *20850*
     V   *20850*   U.S. - California *20850*

E   *Agrostis blasdalei* A. Hitchc. var. *marinensis*
       Crampton *20850*
     E   *20850*   U.S. - California *20850*

V   *Agrostis clivicola* Crampton var. *punta-reyesensis*
       Crampton *20850*
     E   *20850*   U.S. - California *20850*

I   *Agrostis cypricola* Lindb.f. *14230*
     I   *14230*   Cyprus (Boghazi) *14230*

I   *Agrostis dimorpholemma* Ohwi *11164*
     I   *11164*   Japan *11164*

R   *Agrostis eriantha* Hack. var. *planifolia* Gooss. &
       Papendorf *20604*
     R   *20604*   South Africa - Transvaal *20604*

I   *Agrostis goughensis* C.E.Hubb. *19938*
     I   *19938* Tristan da Cunha *19938*

E   *Agrostis hendersonii* A.S. Hitchc. *20850*
     E   *20850*   U.S. - California *20850*
     Ex/E *20850* U.S. - Oregon *20850*

I   *Agrostis hideoi* Ohwi *11164*
     I   *11164*   Japan *11164*

I   *Agrostis holdgateana* C.E. Hubb.
     I   Tristan da Cunha

V   *Agrostis hooveri* Swallen *20850*
     I   *20850*   U.S. - California *20850*

V   *Agrostis howellii* Scribn. *20850*
     V   *20850*   U.S. - Oregon *20850*

R   *Agrostis lepida* A.S. Hitchc. *20850*
     I   *20850*   U.S. - California *20850*
     I   *20850*   U.S. - Oregon *20850*

E   *Agrostis limitanea* J.Black *20681, 14223*
     E   *20681*   Australia - South Australia *14223*

I   *Agrostis masafuerana* Pilger *19116*
     I   *19125*   Chile - Juan Fernandez Is. *19116*

R   *Agrostis meionectes* Vickery *20681*
     I   *20681*   Australia - New South Wales *20681*
     I   *20681*   Australia - Victoria *20681*

R   *Agrostis moldavica* Dobrescu & Beldie *17823, 20171*
     R   *19949* Romania *20631*

R   *Agrostis novogaliciana* McVaugh *9706*
     R   *19850* Mexico - Jalisco *21204*

V   *Agrostis pittieri* Hackel *9037*
     V   *9727*   Costa Rica *9037*

E   *Agrostis rossiae* Vasey *20850*
     E   *20850*   U.S. - Wyoming *20850*

R   *Agrostis sandwicensis* Hbd. *20850, 14209*
     R   *20850*   U.S. - Hawaii *20850*

I   *Agrostis schmidii* (Hook.f.) Bor
     I   India - Tamil Nadu

R   *Agrostis trachychlaena* C.E. Hubb. *19938*

R   Tristan da Cunha *19938*

I   *Agrostis wacei* C.E. Hubb. *19938*
     I   Tristan da Cunha *19938*

R   *Alloeochaete geniculata* Kabuye *7859*
     R   Malawi *7859*

R   *Alloeochaete oreogena* Launert *7869*
     R   Malawi *7869*

V   *Allolepis texana* (Vasey) Soderstrom & Decker *20883,*
     20850
     E   *20850*   U.S. - Texas *20850*
     I   *20883*   Mexico *20883*

E   *Alopecurus aequalis* Sobol. var. *sonomensis*
       Rubtzoff *20850*
     E   *20850*   U.S. - California *20850*

R   *Alopecurus laguroides* Bal. *12840*
     R   *12840*   Turkey *12840*

V   *Alopecurus thracicus* Penev & Kozuharov *8000, 20171*
     V   *5204*   Bulgaria (south) *5204*

Ex   *Amphibromus whitei* C.E.Hubb. *20681*
     Ex   *20681*   Australia - Queensland *20681*

E   *Ancistrachne numaeensis* (Bal.) S.T. Blake *20893*
     E   *20893*   New Caledonia *20893*

R   *Andropogon arctatus* Chapman *20850*
     E   *20850*   U.S. - Alabama *20850*
     R   *20850*   U.S. - Florida *20850*

R   *Andropogon flavescens* J.S. Presl *18200*
     R   *19966* Peru *19966*

I   *Andropogon longipes* Hackel
     I   India - Tamil Nadu (Nilgiri Hills)

R   *Andropogon pringlei* Scribner & Merr. *9722*
     R   *19755* Mexico *9722*

E   *Andropogon pteropholis* W.D. Clayton *7926*
     E   *6072*   Ghana *7926*

R   *Andropogon spadiceus* Swallen *20850, 9722*
     E   *20850*   U.S. - Texas *20850*
     ?   Mexico *9722*

E   *Anomochloa marantoidea* Brongn. *13825*
     E   *13825*   Brazil - Bahia *13825*

R   *Antonella nicorae* (Antón) Caro *20176*
     R   *20176*   Argentina - San Luis *20176*

R   *Apera baytopiana* M. Dogan *12840*
     R   *12840*   Turkey *12840*

R   *Apera triaristata* M. Dogan *12840*
     R   *12840*   Turkey *12840*

E   *Arberella lancifolia* Soders. & Zuloaga *20883, 9722*
     I   *20883*   Panama *20883*

V   *Aristida annua* B.Simon *20681*
     V   *20681*   Australia - Queensland *20681*

R   *Aristida brachyathera* Coss. & Balansa *10487*
     R   *14958*   Algeria *10487*

R   *Aristida brainii* Melderis *7749*
     R   Zimbabwe *7749*

E   *Aristida brittonorum* Hitchc. *5607*
     E   *19105*   Cuba (Pinar del Rio; I. Juventud) *5607*

E   *Aristida chaseae* A.S. Hitchc. *20883, 19002*
     I   *20883*   Puerto Rico *20883*

R   *Aristida chiclayense* Tovar *9722*
     R   *19966* Peru *9722*

R   *Aristida divulsa* Andersson *11117*

	R		Ecuador - Galapagos *11117*
E	*Aristida granitica* B.Simon *20681*		
	E	*20681*	Australia - Queensland *20681*
R	*Aristida kunthiana* Trin. & Rupr. *7926*		
	R		Mali *7926*
	R		Senegal *7926*
R	*Aristida patula* Chapman ex Nash *20850*		
	I	*20850*	U.S. - Florida *20850*
R	*Aristida peruviana* Beetle *9722*		
	R	*19966*	Peru *9722*
E	*Aristida portoricensis* Pilger *20883*		
	I	*20883*	Puerto Rico *20883*
V	*Aristida rhizomophora* Swallen *20850*		
	V	*20850*	U.S. - Florida *20850*
V	*Aristida simpliciflora* Chapman *20850*		
	E	*20850*	U.S. - Alabama *20850*
	V	*20850*	U.S. - Florida *20850*
	Ex/E	*20850*	U.S. - Georgia *20850*
	E	*20850*	U.S. - Mississippi *20850*
	E	*20850*	U.S. - South Carolina *20850*
R	*Aristida tarapotana* Mez *19966*		
	R	*19966*	Peru *19966*
R	*Aristida villosa* Robinson & Greenman *11117*		
	R		Ecuador - Galapagos *11117*
R	*Arrhenatherum calderae* A. Hansen		
	R		Spain - Canary Is.
I	*Arthraxon depressus* Stapf ex C. Fischer		
	I		India - Karnataka (Agalatti, Mysore)
V	*Arthraxon hispidus* (Thunb.) Makino *20681*		
	I	*20681*	Australia - New South Wales *20681*
	I	*20681*	Australia - Queensland *20681*
V	*Arthraxon mauritianus* Stapf ex C.E.Hubb. *20773*		
	V	*20771*	Mauritius *20773*
I	*Arthraxon meeboldii* Stapf		
	I		India - Karnataka (Mangalore)
R	*Arundinaria baviensis* Balansa *6057*		
	R	*19120*	Vietnam *6057*
I	*Arundinaria densiflora* Munro *20892*		
	I		India - Kerala
R	*Arundinaria vicinia* King *6057*		
	R		Vietnam *6057*
R	*Arundinella grevillensis* B.Simon *20681*		
	R	*20681*	Australia - Queensland *20681*
R	*Arundinella montana* S.T.Blake *20681*		
	R	*20681*	Australia - Queensland *20681*
E	*Australopyrum calcis* ssp. *calcis 19305*		
	E	*19305*	New Zealand - South Is. *19305*
V	*Australopyrum calcis* ssp. *optatum 19305*		
	V	*19305*	New Zealand - North Is. *19305*
I	*Avena breviaristata* G. Barratte *10487*		
	I	*14958*	Algeria *10487*
R	*Avena canariensis* Baum & al.		
	R		Spain - Canary Is.
R	*Avena saxatilis* (Lojac.) Rocha Afonso *20171*		
	R	*20738*	Italy - Sicily (Lipari, Marettinio, Limosa) *20738*
R	*Avenula crassifolia* (Font Quer) Holub *20171*		
	R		Spain - Balearic Is.
R	*Avenula delicatula* Franco *20171*		

	V	*20076*	Portugal (north-east) *20076*
	R		Spain
V	*Avenula hackelii* (Henriq.) Holub *8000, 20171*		
	V	*20076*	Portugal (south-west) *8000*
R	*Axonopus casiquiarensis* Davidse *20883*		
	I	*20883*	Venezuela *20883*
V	*Axonopus chimantensis* Davidse *20883*		
	I	*20883*	Venezuela *20883*
E	*Axonopus jeanyae* Davidse *20883*		
	I	*20883*	Panama *20883*
E	*Axonopus rupestris* Davidse *20883*		
	I	*20883*	Brazil *20883*
V	*Axonopus volcanicus* Pohl *9037*		
	V	*9727*	Costa Rica *9037*
R	*Bellardiochloa argaea* (Boiss. & Bal.) R. Mill *12840*		
	R	*12840*	Turkey *12840*
R	*Bellardiochloa carica* R. Mill *12840*		
	R	*12840*	Turkey *12840*
R	*Bhidea burnsiana* Bor *11494*		
	R	*11494*	India - Karnataka *11494*
	R	*11494*	India - Maharashtra *11494*
V	*Bothriochloa biloba* S.T.Blake *20681*		
	I	*20681*	Australia - New South Wales *20681*
	I	*20681*	Australia - Queensland *20681*
V	*Bothriochloa bunyensis* B.Simon *20681*		
	V	*20681*	Australia - Queensland *20681*
R	*Bothriochloa wrightii* (Hack.) Henr. *20850*		
	I	*20850*	U.S. - Arizona *20850*
	I	*20850*	U.S. - New Mexico *20850*
	E	*20850*	U.S. - Texas *20850*
R	*Bouteloua eludens* Griffiths *20850*		
	I	*20850*	U.S. - Arizona *20850*
	I	*20850*	U.S. - New Mexico *20850*
E	*Bouteloua kayi* Warnock *20850*		
	E	*20850*	U.S. - Texas *20850*
R	*Bouteloua parryi* (Fourn.) Griffiths *20850*		
	I	*20850*	U.S. - Arizona *20850*
	I	*20850*	U.S. - New Mexico *20850*
	I	*20850*	U.S. - Texas *20850*
R	*Bouteloua rothrockii* Vasey *20850*		
	I	*20850*	U.S. - Arizona *20850*
	I	*20850*	U.S. - New Mexico *20850*
	I	*20850*	U.S. - Utah *20850*
R	*Brachiaria dura* Stapf var. *pilosa* J.G.Anderson *20604*		
	R	*20604*	South Africa - Cape Province *20604*
I	*Brachiaria longiflora* W. Clayton		
	I		Kenya
R	*Brachypodium arbuscula* Knoche		
	R		Spain - Canary Is.
R	*Brachypodium kotschy* Boiss. *12840*		
	R	*12840*	Turkey *12840*
R	*Brachypodium sanctum* (Janka) Janka *5204, 20171*		
	R	*5204*	Bulgaria (Southern Bulgaria - three areas.) *5204*
R	*Brachypodium sylvaticum* Beau. ssp. *creticum* H.Scholz & Greuter *20730*		
	R	*20730*	Greece - Crete *20730*
R	*Brachystachyum densiflorum* (Reudle) Keng *17617*		
	R	*17617*	China - Anhui *11139*
	R	*17617*	China - Jiangsu *11139*

R   *17617*   China - Zhejiang   *11139*

R   ***Bromus armenus*** Boiss. *12840*
R   *12840*   Turkey   *12840*

Ex   ***Bromus brachystachys*** Hornung *20171*
Ex   *20644*   Germany   *20644*

E   ***Bromus catharticus*** M. Vahl var. *striatus* (A. Hitchc.) Pinto *18200*
E   *9446*   Peru   *18200*

R   ***Bromus garamas*** Maire *10487*
R   *14958*   Algeria   *10487*

E   ***Bromus grossus*** Desf. ex DC. *8000, 20171*
E   *20593*   Belgium   *20593*
Ex   *20609*   Luxembourg   *20609*
E   *18154*   Switzerland   *18154*

Ex   ***Bromus interruptus*** (Hack.) Druce *17781, 20171*
Ex   *5387*   United Kingdom (south and east England)   *8000*

I   ***Bromus macrocladus*** Boiss. *12840*
I   *12840*   Turkey   *12840*

R   ***Bromus mango*** Desv. *19448*
E   *16336*   Argentina   *19448*
R   *20176*   Argentina - Chubut   *20176*
R   *20176*   Argentina - Neuquen   *20176*
R   *20176*   Argentina - Rio Negro   *20176*
Ex   *19534*   Chile   *19534*

R   ***Bromus maroccanus*** Pau & Font Quer
R   Morocco

R   ***Bromus moesiacus*** Velen. *8000, 20171*
R   *19709*   Bulgaria   *8000*

E   ***Bromus psammophilus*** P.M. Smith *12840*
E   *12840*   Turkey   *12840*

R   ***Bromus sinaicus*** (Hackel) Tackh.
R   Egypt

R   ***Bromus villosissimus*** A. Hitchc. *18200*
R   *19966*   Peru   *19966*

R   ***Buchlomimus nervatus*** (Swallen) Reeder, Reeder & Rzed. *9722*
R   *19755*   Mexico   *9722*

E   ***Buergersiochloa bambusoides*** Pilger *13825*
E   *13825*   Indonesia - Irian Jaya   *13825*
E   *13825*   Papua New Guinea   *13825*

R   ***Calamagrostis ampliflora*** Tovar *18200*
R   *19966*   Peru   *19966*

R   ***Calamagrostis bolanderi*** Thurb. *20850, 19002*
I   *20850*   U.S. - California   *20850*

E   ***Calamagrostis cainii*** A.S. Hitchc. *20850*
E   *20850*   U.S. - North Carolina   *20850*
E   *20850*   U.S. - Tennessee   *20850*

E   ***Calamagrostis cleefii*** Escalona *20883*
I   *20883*   Colombia   *20883*

R   ***Calamagrostis coronalis*** Tovar *18200*
R   *19966*   Peru   *19966*

R   ***Calamagrostis crassiglumis*** Thurb. *20850, 13967*
V   *20850*   Canada - British Columbia   *20850*
E   *20850*   U.S. - Alaska   *20850*
E   *20850*   U.S. - California   *20850*
E   *20850*   U.S. - Washington   *20850*

I   ***Calamagrostis decora*** Hook.f.
I   India - Jammu & Kashmir

R   ***Calamagrostis densa*** Vasey *20883, 20850, 8058*
R   *20850*   U.S. - California   *20850*

I   *20883*   Mexico   *20883*

I   ***Calamagrostis deschampsiiformis*** C.E. Hubb. *19938*
I   Tristan da Cunha (Inaccessible, Gough, Tristan Is.)   *19938*

V   ***Calamagrostis expansa*** (Munro ex Hbd.) A.S. Hitchc. *20850, 14209*
V   *20850*   U.S. - Hawaii (Maui)   *20850*

R   ***Calamagrostis foliosa*** Kearney *20850*
R   *20850*   U.S. - California   *20850*

E   ***Calamagrostis guamanensis*** Escalona *20883*
I   *20883*   Ecuador   *20883*

E   ***Calamagrostis hillebrandii*** (Munro ex Hbd.) A.S. Hitchc. *20850, 14209*
E   *20850*   U.S. - Hawaii   *20850*

V   ***Calamagrostis ophitidis*** (J.T. Howell) Nygren *20850*
I   *20850*   U.S. - California   *20850*

E   ***Calamagrostis perplexa*** Scribn. *20850*
I   *20850*   Canada - Ontario   *20850*
I   *20850*   U.S. - Maine   *20850*
I   *20850*   U.S. - Minnesota   *20850*
I   *20850*   U.S. - New Hampshire   *20850*
E   *20850*   U.S. - New York   *20850*

V   ***Calamagrostis pittieri*** Hackel *9037*
V   *9727*   Costa Rica   *9037*

V   ***Calamagrostis porteri*** A.Grey ssp. *insperata* (Swallen) C.W. Greene *20850*
Ex/E   *20850*   U.S. - Arkansas   *20850*
E   *20850*   U.S. - Illinois   *20850*
E   *20850*   U.S. - Indiana   *20850*
E   *20850*   U.S. - Kentucky   *20850*
V   *20850*   U.S. - Missouri   *20850*
E   *20850*   U.S. - Ohio   *20850*

E   ***Calamagrostis ramonae*** Escalona *20883*
I   *20883*   Venezuela   *20883*

E   ***Calamagrostis rauhii*** Tovar *18200*
E   *19966*   Peru   *19966*

E   ***Calamagrostis robertii*** Porsild *20850, 1034*
E   *20850*   Canada - Yukon Territory   *20850*

V   ***Calamagrostis scotica*** (Druce) Druce *17781, 20171*
V   *5387*   United Kingdom (N.E. Scotland)   *8000*

E   ***Calamagrostis swallenii*** Tovar *18200*
E   *19966*   Peru   *19966*

R   ***Calamagrostis tashiroi*** Ohwi *11164*
R   *11164*   Japan   *11164*

R   ***Calamagrostis tweedyi*** (Scribn.) Scribn. ex Vasey *20850*
E   *20850*   U.S. - Idaho   *20850*
V   *20850*   U.S. - Montana   *20850*
V   *20850*   U.S. - Washington   *20850*

V   ***Calamovilfa arcuata*** K.E. Rogers *20850*
E   *20850*   U.S. - Arkansas   *20850*
I   *20850*   U.S. - North Dakota   *20850*
V   *20850*   U.S. - Oklahoma   *20850*
I   *20850*   U.S. - Oregon   *20850*
I   *20850*   U.S. - South Dakota   *20850*
V   *20850*   U.S. - Tennessee   *20850*
I   *20850*   U.S. - Washington   *20850*
I   *20850*   U.S. - Wyoming   *20850*

V   ***Calamovilfa curtissii*** (Vasey) Scribn. *20850*
V   *20850*   U.S. - Florida   *20850*

I   ***Catabrosa aquatica*** (L.) P. Beauv. var. *angusta* Stapf *7771*
I   India - Jammu & Kashmir (Ladakh)   *7771*

R	*Catapodium mamoraeum* (Maire) Maire & M. Weiller		
	R		Morocco

E	*Cenchrus agrimonioides* Trin. 20850, 14209		
	E	20850	U.S. - Hawaii 20850

E	*Cenchrus agrimonioides* Trin. var. *agrimonioides* 20850		
	E	20850	U.S. - Hawaii 20850

Ex/E	*Cenchrus agrimonioides* Trin. var. *laysanensis* F.Br. 20850, 14209		
	Ex/E	20850	U.S. - Hawaii 20850

I	*Cenchrus prieurii* (Kunth) Maire var. *scabra* Bhandari		
	I		India - Rajasthan (west) 7771

I	*Cenchrus rajasthanensis* Kanodia & Nanda 7771		
	I		India - Rajasthan (Jaisalmer & Jodhpur) 7771

R	*Cephalostachyum capitatum* Munro var. *decomposita* Gamble 14723		
	R	14723	India - Sikkim 14723

R	*Chaboissaea ligulata* Fourn. 9722		
	R	19755	Mexico 9722

I	*Chaetotropis imberbis* (Philippi) Bjorkman 19116		
	I	19125	Chile - Juan Fernandez Is. 19116

V	*Chimonobambusa quadrangularis* (Fenji) Makino 15100		
	V	20756	China - Anhui 20756
	V	20756	China - Fujian 20756
	V	20756	China - Guangdong 20756
	V	20756	China - Guangxi 20756
	V	20756	China - Hubei 20756
	V	20756	China - Jiangxi 20756
	V	20756	China - Zhejiang 20756
	R	20985	Vietnam 15100

R	*Chionochloa conspicua* (G. Forst.) Zotov 14223		
	R	14223	Australia - NSW - Lord Howe Is. 14223

R	*Chionochloa frigida* (Vick.) Conert 20681		
	R	20681	Australia - New South Wales 20681

V	*Chionochloa spiralis* Zotov 86		
	V	19305	New Zealand - South Is. 19305

E	*Chloris arenaria* Hitchc. & Ekman 5607		
	E	19105	Cuba (Pinar del Rio; Cienfuegos) 5607

E	*Chloris cheesemani* Hack ex Cheesem. 19473		
	E	19473	Cook Is.(Southern group) (Rarotonga) 19473

R	*Chloris ferruginea* Renvoize		
	R		Kenya (Northern Frontier Province) 7959

V	*Chloris filiformis* (Vahl) Poiret 10082, 20773		
	V	20771	Mauritius 20773

V	*Chloris texensis* Nash 20850		
	V	20850	U.S. - Texas 20850

I	*Chlorocalymma cryptacanthum* Clayton 5926		
	I	5926	Tanzania 5926

R	*Chondrosum elata* (Reeder & C. Reeder) W. Clayton 19788		
	R	19755	Mexico 9722

V	*Chrysopogon macleishii* Cope 20146		
	V	20146	Oman (Dhofar) 20146

I	*Chrysopogon perlaxus* Bor 19120		
	I	19120	Thailand 19120

I	*Chrysopogon velutinus* (Hook.f.) Bor		
	I		India - Andhra Pradesh (Cuddapah)

V	*Chusquea aperta* G. Clark 20883, 11973		
	I	20883	Mexico 20883
	?		Mexico - Oaxaca 11973

V	*Chusquea bilimekii* Fourn. 9722		
	V	14344	Mexico - Veracruz 9722

V	*Chusquea fernandeziana* Philippi 19116		
	V	19125	Chile - Juan Fernandez Is. 19116

E	*Chusquea latifolia* Clark 20883		
	I	20883	Colombia 20883

V	*Chusquea longiligulata* (Soderstrom & C. Calderón) L. Clark 14344		
	V	9727	Costa Rica 14344

V	*Chusquea pohlii* Clark 20883, 11974		
	I	20883	Costa Rica 20883

I	*Cinna valdiviana* Philippi		
	I		Chile

R	*Clausospicula extensa* Lazarides 20681		
	R	20681	Australia - Northern Territory 20681

I	*Coelachne japonica* Hackel 11164		
	I	11164	Japan 11164

R	*Coelachne minuta* Bor 11494		
	R	11494	India - Maharashtra 11494

I	*Coelachne soerensenii* Bor 19120		
	I	19120	Thailand 19120

R	*Coelorachis tuberculosa* (Nash) Nash 20850		
	E	20850	U.S. - Alabama 20850
	R	20850	U.S. - Florida 20850

R	*Coleanthus subtilis* (Tratt.) Seidl. 8000, 20171		
	Ex		Austria
	R	2050	Czech Republic 2050
	V	20528	France 8000
	I	20640	Germany 8000
	Ex	8000	Italy 8000
	Ex	8000	Norway 8000
	V	14155	Slovakia 8000
	I	5942	Russia (Far East) - Khabarovsk 5942
	I	5942	Russia (E.Europe) - Northwest 5942
	I	5942	Russia (Far East) - Primorye 5942

R	*Colpodium drakensbergense* Hedberg & I.Hedberg 20604		
	R	20604	Lesotho 20604
	R	20604	South Africa - Natal 20604

E	*Cortaderia turbaria* H.E. Conner 19305		
	E	19305	New Zealand - Chatham Is. 19305

R	*Crithopsis delileana* (Schult.) Roshev. 20171		
	R		Greece

V	*Crypsis minuartioides* Mez 14952		
	V	14952	Israel (coastal plain) 14952

V	*Cryptochloa decumbens* Soders. & Zuloaga 20883, 12044		
	I	20883	Panama 20883

V	*Cryptochloa dressleri* Soders. 20883, 10747		
	I	20883	Panama 20883

V	*Ctenium floridanum* (A.S. Hitchc.) A.S. Hitchc. 20850		
	V	20850	U.S. - Florida 20850
	E	20850	U.S. - Georgia 20850

R	*Ctenium newtonii* Hackel var. *annuum* Lebrun		
	R		Chad

R	*Ctenium plumosum* (A. Hitchc.) Swallen 9722		
	R	19755	Mexico 9722

I	*Cymbopogon calciphilus* Bor 19120		
	I	19120	Thailand 19120

R   *Cymbopogon dependens* **B.Simon** *20681*
     R   *20681*   Australia - Northern Territory *20681*

R   *Cymbopogon flexuosus* (Nees ex Steudel) Watson var. *microstachys* (Hook.f.) Bor
     E   India - Uttar Pradesh
     R   *20099*   Singapore *20099*

V   *Cymbopogon osmastonii* **R. Parker** *14872*
     V   *14872*   Bangladesh *14872*
     I   India - Uttar Pradesh

I   *Cymbopogon ramnagarensis* **B.K. Gupta**
     I   India - Jammu & Kashmir

I   *Cymbopogon siamensis* **Bor** *19120*
     I   *19120*   Thailand *19120*

R   *Dactylis smithii* **Link**
     R   Portugal - Madeira
     R   Spain - Canary Is.

R   *Danthonia nitens* **D.Morris** *20681*
     R   *20681*   Australia - Tasmania *20681*

V   *Danthonia paschalis* **Pilger** *14777*
     V   *17912*   Chile - Easter Is. (Rano Kao) *14777*

E   *Danthonia popinensis* **D.Morris** *20681*
     E   *20681*   Australia - Tasmania *20681*

R   *Danthonia remota* **D.Morris** *20681*
     R   *20681*   Australia - Tasmania *20681*

R   *Danthonia unarede* **Raoul** *14223*
     R   *14223*   Australia - NSW - Lord Howe Is. *14223*

R   *Danthoniopsis scopulorum* (J.B.Phipps) **J.B.Phipps** *20604*
     R   *20604*   South Africa - Natal *20604*

V   *Deschampsia argentea* (Lowe) **Lowe**
     V   Portugal - Madeira

E   *Deschampsia cespitosa* (L.) **P.Beauv. ssp.** *alpina* (L.) **Tzvelev** *20850, 15886, 20171*
     E   *20850*   Canada - Labrador *20850*
     E   *20850*   Canada - Franklin *20850*
     E   *20850*   Canada - Quebec *20850*

I   *Deschampsia christophersenii* **C.E. Hubb.** *19938*
     I   Tristan da Cunha (Inaccessible & Tristan Is.) *19938*

V   *Deschampsia congestiformis* **Booth** *20850*
     I   *20850*   U.S. - Montana *20850*

I   *Deschampsia litoralis* (Gaudin) **Reuter** *18154*
     Ex   *20528*   France *20528*
     I   Germany *20528*
     E   *18154*   Switzerland *18154*

V   *Deschampsia mackenzieana* **Raup** *20850, 2063*
     V   *20850*   Canada - Saskatchewan *20850*

E   *Deschampsia maderensis* (Hackel & Bornm.) **Buschm.** *17891*
     E   Portugal - Madeira *17891*

I   *Deschampsia mejlandii* **C.E. Hubb.** *19938*
     I   Tristan da Cunha *19938*

I   *Deschampsia rhenana* **Gremli** *18154*
     I   Germany
     E   *18154*   Switzerland *18154*

I   *Deschampsia robusta* **C.E. Hubb.**
     I   Tristan da Cunha

I   *Deschampsia turczaninowii* **Litv.** *5942*
     I   *5942*   Russia (Siberia) - Irkutsk (L. Baikal) *5942*

I   *Deschampsia wacei* **C.E. Hubb.**
     I   Tristan da Cunha

R   *Deyeuxia affinis* **M.Gray** *20681*
     I   *20681*   Australia - New South Wales *20681*
     I   *20681*   Australia - Victoria *20681*

E   *Deyeuxia appressa* **Vickery** *20681*
     E   *20681*   Australia - New South Wales *20681*

R   *Deyeuxia apsleyensis* **D.Morris** *20681*
     R   *20681*   Australia - Tasmania *20681*

R   *Deyeuxia curta* **Wedd. var.** *longearistata* **Turpe** *19448*
     R   *16336*   Argentina *16336*
     R   *20176*   Argentina - Tucuman *20176*

Ex   *Deyeuxia drummondii* (Steudel) **Vick.** *20681, 14223*
     Ex   *20681*   Australia - Western Australia *20681*

I   *Deyeuxia kashmeriana* **Bor**
     I   India - Jammu & Kashmir

Ex   *Deyeuxia lawrencei* **Vickery** *20681, 14223*
     Ex   *20681*   Australia - Tasmania *20681*

Ex/E   *Deyeuxia simlensis* **Bor** *11494*
     Ex/E *11494*   India - Himachal Pradesh (Simla) *11494*

R   *Deyeuxia talariata* **N.G.Walsh** *20681*
     I   *20681*   Australia - New South Wales *20681*
     I   *20681*   Australia - Victoria *20681*

R   *Dichanthelium isachnoides* (Munro ex Hbd.) **C.A. Clark & Gould** *20850, 14209*
     I   *20850*   U.S. - Hawaii *20850*

V   *Dichanthelium koolauense* (St. John & Hosaka) **C.A. Clark & Gould** *20850, 14209*
     I   *20850*   U.S. - Hawaii (O`ahu) *20850*

R   *Dichanthium armatum* (Hook.f.) **Blatter & McCann** *11494*
     R   *11494*   India - Maharashtra *11494*

R   *Dichanthium compressum* (Hook.f.) **Jain & Deshpande** *11494*
     R   *11494*   India - Maharashtra (Pune District) *11494*

V   *Dichanthium maccannii* **Blatter** *11494*
     V   *11494*   India - Maharashtra (Panchagani, Satara Dist.) *11494*

R   *Dichanthium mucronulatum* **Jansen**
     R   Malaysia - Peninsular Malaysia

I   *Dichanthium pallidum* (Hook.f.) **Stapf ex C. Fischer**
     I   India - Tamil Nadu (Nilgiri Hills)

R   *Dichanthium panchaganiense* **Blatt. et McCann** *13883*
     R   *13883*   India - Maharashtra *13883*

V   *Dichanthium queenslandicum* **B.Simon** *20681*
     V   *20681*   Australia - Queensland *20681*

V   *Dichanthium woodrowii* (Hook.f.) **Jain & Deshpande** *11494*
     V   *11494*   India - Maharashtra (Paud, Mawal taluka, Pune) *11494*

R   *Digitaria aristulata* (Steudel) **Stapf** *7926*
     R   Mali *7926*
     R   Senegal *7926*

V   *Digitaria costaricensis* **Pohl** *9037*
     V   *9727*   Costa Rica *9037*

E   *Digitaria floridana* **A.S. Hitchc.** *20850*
     E   *20850*   U.S. - Florida *20850*
     I   *20850*   U.S. - Georgia *20850*

R   *Digitaria gentilis* **Henrard** *7926*
     R   Senegal (Hana) *7926*

I   Tristan da Cunha

E	*Digitaria gracillima* (Scribn.) Fern. *20850*	
	E	*20850* U.S. - Florida *20850*
E	*Digitaria hirsuta* Swallen *20883, 9006*	
	I	*20883* Panama *20883*
I	*Digitaria monobotrys* (Veken) Clayton, ined. *5926*	
	I	*5926* Tanzania *5926*
I	*Digitaria monopholis* Clayton *5926*	
	I	*5926* Tanzania *5926*
I	*Digitaria myurus* Stapf *5926*	
	I	*5926* Tanzania *5926*
R	*Digitaria paniculata* Soderstrom & McVaugh *9706*	
	R	*19850* Mexico - Jalisco *21204*
E	*Digitaria pauciflora* A.S. Hitchc. *20850*	
	E	*20850* U.S. - Florida *20850*
I	*Digitaria petelotii* Bor *19120*	
	I	*19120* Thailand *19120*
R	*Digitaria phaeotricha* (Chiov.) Robyns var. *patens* W. Clayton *7926*	
	R	Sierra Leone (Mt. Loma) *7926*
E	*Digitaria pinetorum* Hitchc. *5607*	
	E	*19105* Cuba (Pinar del Rio; I. Juventud) *5607*
R	*Digitaria platycarpha* (Trin.) Stapf *8037*	
	R	*19134* Japan - Ogasawara-shoto *8037*
E	*Digitaria porrecta* S.T.Blake *20681*	
	I	*20681* Australia - New South Wales *20681*
	I	*20681* Australia - Queensland *20681*
V	*Digitaria simpsonii* (Vasey) Fern. *20850*	
	I	*20850* U.S. - Florida *20850*
R	*Dimeria blatterii* Bor *13883*	
	R	*13883* India - Maharashtra (Western Ghats in Pune and Ratnagiri districts) *13883*
I	*Dimeria ciliata* Merr. *13833*	
	I	*13833* Philippines (Palawan) *13833*
R	*Dimeria woodrowii* Stapf *11494*	
	R	*11494* India - Goa, Daman & Diu *11494*
	R	*11494* India - Karnataka *11494*
	R	*11494* India - Maharashtra *11494*
I	*Dinochloa dielsiana* Pilg. *20891*	
	I	*13833* Philippines *20891*
I	*Dinochloa palawanense* (Gamble) S. Dransf., comb. nov. *20891*	
	I	*13833* Philippines (Palawan) *20891*
V	*Dissanthelium amplivaginatum* Tovar *18200*	
	V	*19966* Peru *18200*
Ex/E	*Dissanthelium californicum* (Nutt.) Benth. *20883, 20850, 8058*	
	Ex/E	*20850* U.S. - California *20850*
	Ex/E	*20883* Mexico *20883*
V	*Dissanthelium densum* Swallen & Tovar *18200*	
	V	*19966* Peru *18200*
V	*Dissanthelium giganteum* Tovar *18200*	
	V	*19966* Peru *18200*
V	*Dissochondrus biflorus* (Hbd.) Kuntze ex Hack. *20850, 14209*	
	V	*20850* U.S. - Hawaii *20850*
R	*Dolichochaete rehmannii* (Hackel) Phipps ssp. *mosambicensis* Phipps *7921*	
	R	Mozambique *7921*
R	*Dregeochloa calviniensis* Conert *20604*	
	R	*20604* South Africa - Cape Province *20604*
V	*Dregeochloa pumila* (Nees) Conert *20604*	
	V	*20604* Namibia *20604*
	V	*20604* South Africa - Cape Province *20604*
R	*Echinochloa paludigena* Wieg. *20850*	
	I	*20850* U.S. - Florida *20850*
	I	*20850* U.S. - Texas *20850*
E	*Echinolaena oplismenoides* (Munro ex Doell) Stieber *20883*	
	I	*20883* Brazil *20883*
	I	*20883* Ecuador *20883*
V	*Echinolaena standleyi* (A. S. Hitchc.) Stieber *20883*	
	I	*20883* Belize *20883*
	I	*20883* Guatemala *20883*
	I	*20883* Honduras *20883*
	I	*20883* Mexico *20883*
V	*Ectrosia blakei* C.E.Hubb. *20681*	
	V	*20681* Australia - Queensland *20681*
R	*Ehrharta eburnea* Gibbs Russ. *20604*	
	R	*20604* South Africa - Cape Province *20604*
I	*Ekmanochloa aristata* Ekman *13825*	
	I	*13825* Cuba (Oriente) *13825*
R	*Ekmanochloa subaphylla* Hitchcock *13825*	
	R	*13825* Cuba (Oriente) *13825*
R	*Elionurus tripsacioides* Humb. & Bonpl. var. *sericeus* Hackel *10831*	
	R	*10831* Mexico - Veracruz *10831*
R	*Elymus clivorum* Melderis *12840*	
	R	*12840* Turkey *12840*
R	*Elymus erosiglumis* Melderis *12840*	
	R	*12840* Turkey *12840*
R	*Elymus lazicus* (Boiss.) Melderis ssp. *lazicus* *12840*	
	R	*12840* Turkey *12840*
R	*Elymus longearistatus* (Boiss.) Tzvelev ssp. *sintenisii* Melderis *12840*	
	R	*12840* Turkey *12840*
R	*Elymus nodosus* (Nevski) Melderis ssp. *gypsecolus* Melderis *12840*	
	R	*12840* Turkey *12840*
R	*Elymus nodosus* (Nevski) Melderis ssp. *platyphyllus* Melderis *12840*	
	R	*12840* Turkey *12840*
R	*Elymus sosnowskyi* (Hackel) Melderis *12840*	
	R	*12840* Turkey *12840*
R	*Elymus stebbinsii* Gould *20850*	
	I	*20850* U.S. - California *20850*
	I	*20850* U.S. - Nevada *20850*
V	*Elymus svensonii* Church *20850*	
	R	*20850* U.S. - Kentucky *20850*
	E	*20850* U.S. - Tennessee *20850*
E	*Elymus vulpinus* Rydb. *20850*	
	I	*20850* Canada - Alberta *20850*
	I	*20850* Canada - British Columbia *20850*
	I	*20850* Canada - Saskatchewan *20850*
	I	*20850* U.S. - Montana *20850*
	I	*20850* U.S. - Nebraska *20850*
I	*Elymus yubaridakensis* (Honda) Ohwi *11164*	
	I	*11164* Japan *11164*
R	*Elytrigia corsica* (Hackel) J. Holub *15080*	
	R	*15080* France - Corsica *15080*
I	*Elytrigia stipifolia* (Czern. ex Nevski) *5942, 20171*	

I	5942	Russia - North Caucasus	*5942*
I	5942	Russia (E.Europe) - South	*5942*
I	5942	Ukraine	*5942*

E   *Elytrigia tilcarense* (Hunziker) Covas *20176*

    E   *20176*   Argentina - Jujuy *20176*

I   *Eragrostis aristiglumis* Kabuye *5926*

    I   *5926*   Tanzania (Iringa) *5926*

V   *Eragrostis attenuata* A. Hitchc. *18200*

    V   *19966*   Peru *18200*

Ex/E   *Eragrostis deflexa* A.S. Hitchc. *20850, 14209*

    Ex/E   *20850*   U.S. - Hawaii (Lana`i, Hawai`i) *20850*

R   *Eragrostis desolata* Launert *7768*

    R   Zimbabwe *7768*

R   *Eragrostis diarrhena* (Schult. & Schult.f.) Steud. *20171*

    R   former European USSR

E   *Eragrostis ekmanii* Hitchc. *5607*

    E   *19105*   Cuba (Juventud Is.) *5607*

E   *Eragrostis fosbergii* Whitney *20850, 14209*

    E   *20850*   U.S. - Hawaii (O`ahu) *20850*

R   *Eragrostis glischra* Launert *7768*

    R   Zimbabwe *7768*

V   *Eragrostis glutinosa* (Sw.) Trin. *20883*

    V   *20883*   Cuba *20883*
    Ex/E   *20883*   Jamaica *20883*
    I   *20883*   Puerto Rico *20883*
    I   *20883*   USA - Virgin Is. *20883*

Ex/E   *Eragrostis hosakai* O. Deg. *20850, 14209*

    Ex/E   *20850*   U.S. - Hawaii (Moloka`i, Mauna Loa) *20850*

R   *Eragrostis kneuckeri* Hackel & Bornm.

    R   Egypt

R   *Eragrostis marquisensis* F. Brown

    R   French Polynesia - Marquesas Is

Ex/E   *Eragrostis mauiensis* A.S. Hitchc. *20850, 14209*

    Ex/E   *20850*   U.S. - Hawaii (Lana`i, Maui) *20850*

I   *Eragrostis pseudopoa* C.E. Hubb. *5926*

    I   *5926*   Tanzania (Iringa) *5926*

V   *Eragrostis raynaliana* Lebrun

    V   Cameroon

R   *Eragrostis rigidiuscula* Domin *20681*

    R   *20681*   Australia - Northern Territory *20681*

Ex   *Eragrostis rottleri* Stapf *11494*

    Ex   *11494*   India - Tamil Nadu (Tranquebar) *11494*

R   *Eragrostis saxatilis* Hemsley *18996*

    R   *18996*   St Helena *18996*

V   *Eragrostis tracyi* A.S. Hitchc. *20850*

    V   *20850*   U.S. - Florida *20850*

V   *Eragrostis xerophila* F. Brown

    V   French Polynesia - Marquesas Is

R   *Eremopoa attalica* H. Scholz *12840*

    R   *12840*   Turkey *12840*

V   *Eremopoa mardinensis* R. Mill *12840*

    V   *12840*   Turkey *12840*

R   *Eriochloa lemmonii* Vasey & Scribner *10181*

    R   *10181*   U.S. - Arkansas *10181*
    R   *10181*   Mexico - Chihuahua *10181*
    R   *10181*   Mexico - Sonora *10181*

V   *Eriochloa michauxii* (Poir.) A.S. Hitchc. *20850*

    I   *20850*   U.S. - Alabama *20850*

I	20850	U.S. - Florida	*20850*
V	20850	U.S. - Georgia	*20850*
I	20850	U.S. - Louisiana	*20850*
I	20850	U.S. - South Carolina	*20850*

V   *Eriochloa michauxii* (Poiret) A. Hitchc. var. *simpsonii* A. Hitchc. *20850*

    E   *20850*   U.S. - Florida *20850*

Ex   *Eriochrysis rangacharii* Fischer *11494*

    Ex   *11494*   India - Tamil Nadu (Paikara, Nilgiri District) *11494*

R   *Erioneuron nealleyi* (Vasey) Tateoka *20850*

    I   *20850*   U.S. - New Mexico *20850*
    I   *20850*   U.S. - Texas *20850*

V   *Eustachys floridana* Chapman *20850*

    E   *20850*   U.S. - Alabama *20850*
    I   *20850*   U.S. - Florida *20850*
    I   *20850*   U.S. - Georgia *20850*

V   *Eustachys neglecta* (Nash) Nash *20850*

    I   *20850*   U.S. - Florida *20850*

I   *Farrago racemosa* W. Clayton *5926*

    I   *5926*   Tanzania (Lindi) *5926*

R   *Festuca agustini* Lindinger

    R   Spain - Canary Is.

R   *Festuca albida* Lowe

    R   Portugal - Madeira

R   *Festuca anatolica* Markgr.-Dannenb. ssp. *borealis* Markgr.-Dannenb. *12840*

    R   *12840*   Turkey *12840*

I   *Festuca bargusinensis* Malysch. *11552, 5942*

    I   *5942*   Russia (Siberia) - Buryatiya *5942*

Ex   *Festuca benthamiana* Vickery *20681, 14223*

    R   *20681*   Australia - South Australia *14223*

V   *Festuca breistrofferi* Chas, Kerguélen & Plonka *20528*

    V   *20528*   France (Alps) *20528*

R   *Festuca brevissima* Jurtzev *20850, 4480*

    E   *20850*   Canada - Yukon Territory *20850*
    R   *20850*   U.S. - Alaska *20850*

E   *Festuca brigantina* (Markgr.-Dann.) Markgr.-Dann. *8000, 20171*

    E   *20076*   Portugal (north east) *8000*

R   *Festuca cappadocica* (Hackel) Markgr.-Dannenb. *12840*

    R   *12840*   Turkey *12840*

R   *Festuca cataonica* (Hackel ex Boiss.) Markgr.-Dan. *12840*

    R   *12840*   Turkey *12840*

R   *Festuca clementei* Boiss. *20171*

    R   *11496*   Spain (Betic Mountains) *20690*

R   *Festuca cratericola* Markgr.-Dannenb. *12840*

    R   *12840*   Turkey *12840*

R   *Festuca cyllenica* Boiss. & Heldr. ssp. *uluana* Markgr.-Dannenb. *12840*

    R   *12840*   Turkey *12840*

R   *Festuca dasyclada* Hack. ex Beal *20850*

    R   *20850*   U.S. - Colorado *20850*
    E   *20850*   U.S. - Utah *20850*

R   *Festuca decolorata* Markgr.-Dannenb. *12840*

    R   *12840*   Turkey *12840*

E   *Festuca densiflora* Tovar *12468*

    E   *19966*   Peru *12468*

R   *Festuca dissitiflora* Steudel *16336*

Liliopsida (monocots): Gramineae: *Festuca*

I	*16336*	Argentina *16336*
R	*20176*	Argentina - Catamarca *20176*
R	*20176*	Argentina - Jujuy *20176*
R	*20176*	Argentina - La Rioja *20176*
R	*20176*	Argentina - Salta *20176*

R ***Festuca divergens*** Tovar *12468*
R	*19966*	Peru *12468*

V ***Festuca donax*** Lowe
V		Portugal - Madeira

R ***Festuca durandoi*** Clauson ssp. ***capillifolia*** (Pau ex Willk.) Rivas Ponce, Cebolla & M.B.Crespo *20692*
R	*20692*	Spain (east) *20692*

V ***Festuca duriotagana*** Franco & R. Afonso *20076*
V	*20076*	Portugal *20076*

R ***Festuca frigida*** (Hack.) K.Richt. *20171*
R	*11496*	Spain *11496*

R ***Festuca grandiaristata*** Markgr.-Dann. *20171*
R		Greece

V ***Festuca hawaiiensis*** A.S. Hitchc. *20850, 14209*
V	*20850*	U.S. - Hawaii (Hawai`i & Maui) *20850*

E ***Festuca henriquesii*** Hack. *8000, 20171*
E	*20076*	Portugal (north central) *8000*

R ***Festuca humbertii*** Litard. & Maire
R		Morocco

R ***Festuca ilgazensis*** Markgr.-Dannenb. *12840*
R	*12840*	Turkey *12840*

E ***Festuca lahonderei*** Kerguélen & Plonka *20528*
E	*20528*	France (west) *20528*

R ***Festuca lazistanica*** Alexeev *12840*
R	*12840*	Turkey *12840*

E ***Festuca levingei*** Stapf
E		India - Jammu & Kashmir

E ***Festuca ligulata*** Swallen *20883, 20850*
E	*20850*	U.S. - Texas *20850*
E	*20883*	Mexico *20883*

R ***Festuca livida*** Willd. *9722*
R	*19755*	Mexico *9722*

I ***Festuca lucida*** Stapf
I		India - Himachal Pradesh
I		India - Jammu & Kashmir
I		India - Uttar Pradesh

R ***Festuca macedonica*** J.Vetter *20171*
R		Greece

V ***Festuca morisiana*** Parl. *8000, 20171*
V		Italy - Sardinia (Mt Gennargentu) *8000*

R ***Festuca olympica*** J.Vetter *20171*
R		Greece

R ***Festuca oviniformis*** J.Vetter *20171*
R		Greece

R ***Festuca paphlagonica*** (St.-Yves) Markgr.-Dannenb. ssp. ***paphlagonica*** *12840*
R	*12840*	Turkey *12840*

R ***Festuca pirinica*** Horvat ex Markgr.-Dann. *5204, 20171*
R	*5204*	Bulgaria (south) *5204*

R ***Festuca plebeia*** R.Br. *20681*
R	*20681*	Australia - Tasmania *20681*

R ***Festuca pontica*** (E. Alekseev) Markgr.-Dannenb. *12840*
R	*12840*	Turkey *12840*

R ***Festuca pseudoeskia*** Boiss. *11496*
R	*11496*	Spain *11496*

R ***Festuca pseudosupina*** Vetter
R		Greece

R ***Festuca puctoria*** Sm. *12840*
R	*12840*	Turkey *12840*

R ***Festuca querana*** Litard. *20171*
R		Spain

R ***Festuca reverchonii*** Hack. *20171*
R		Spain

R ***Festuca rosei*** Piper *9722*
R	*19755*	Mexico *9722*

R ***Festuca rubra*** L. ssp. ***pseudorivularis*** Markgr.-Dannenb. *12840*
R	*12840*	Turkey *12840*

R ***Festuca takedana*** Ohwi *11164*
R	*11164*	Japan *11164*

R ***Festuca ventanicola*** Speg. *16336*
R	*16336*	Argentina *16336*
R	*20176*	Argentina - Buenos Aires *20176*

R ***Festuca wagneri*** (Degen, Thaisz & Flatt) Krajina *17786, 20171*
R	*20686*	Hungary *20686*
R	*19949*	Romania *20631*

R ***Festuca woronowii*** Hackel ssp. ***argaea*** Markgr.-Dannenb. *12840*
R	*12840*	Turkey *12840*

R ***Festuca xenophontis*** Markgr.-Dannenb. *12840*
R	*12840*	Turkey *12840*

R ***Festuca ziganensis*** Markgr.-Dannenb. *12840*
R	*12840*	Turkey *12840*

E ***Froesiochloa boutelouoides*** G.A. Black *13825*
E	*13825*	Brazil - Maranhao *13825*
E	*13825*	French Guiana *13825*
E	*13825*	Suriname *13825*

E ***Garnotia cheesemani*** Hack. ex Cheesem. *19473*
E	*19473*	Cook Is.(Southern group) (Rarotonga) *19473*

I ***Garnotia schmidii*** Hook.f.
I		India - Tamil Nadu (Nilgiri Hills)

E ***Garnotia sechellensis*** C.E. Hubb. & Summerh. *14296*
E	*14981*	Seychelles (Mahé & Silhouette) *14296*

I ***Gaudinia hispanica*** Stace & Tutin *8000, 20171*
I		Spain (Andalusia) *11496*

Ex ***Glyceria drummondii*** (Steudel) C.E.Hubb. *20681*
Ex	*20681*	Australia - Western Australia *20681*

I ***Glyceria insularis*** C.E. Hubb.
I		Tristan da Cunha *19938*

R ***Glyceria leptostachya*** Buckl. *20850, 10701*
V	*20850*	Canada - British Columbia *20850*
E	*20850*	U.S. - Alaska *20850*
I	*20850*	U.S. - California *20850*
I	*20850*	U.S. - Oregon *20850*
I	*20850*	U.S. - Washington *20850*

V ***Glyceria nubigena*** W.A. Anderson *20850*
V	*20850*	U.S. - North Carolina *20850*
V	*20850*	U.S. - Tennessee *20850*

E ***Glyceria otisii*** A.S. Hitchc. *20850*
I	*20850*	U.S. - Oregon *20850*
I	*20850*	U.S. - Washington *20850*

R ***Glyphochloa divergens*** (Hook.) Clayton *11494*
R	*11494*	India - Karnataka *11494*

V ***Glyphochloa talbotii*** (Hook.f.) Clayton *11494*

V   *11494* India - Goa, Daman & Diu *11494*

R   ***Glyphochola santapaui*** (Jain & Deshpande) Clayton *13883*
     R   *13883* India - Maharashtra (Ratnagiri District) *13883*

I   ***Greenia oblonga*** Craib *19120*
     I   *19120* Thailand *19120*

I   ***Greenia siamensis*** Craib *19120*
     I   *19120* Thailand *19120*

E   ***Guadua calderoniana*** Londoño & Judziewicz *21275*
     E   *21275* Brazil - Bahia *21275*

V   ***Gymnopogon chapmanianus*** A.S. Hitchc. *20850*
     V   *20850* U.S. - Florida *20850*
     I   *20850* U.S. - Georgia *20850*

R   ***Helictotrichon barbatum*** (Nees) Schweick. *20604*
     R   *20604* South Africa - Cape Province *20604*

R   ***Helictotrichon hideoi*** Ohwi *11164*
     R   *11164* Japan *11164*

R   ***Helictotrichon murcicum*** Holub *20171*
     R   Spain

I   ***Helictotrichon namaquense*** Schweick. *20604*
     I   *20604* South Africa - Cape Province *20604*

R   ***Helictotrichon petzense*** H.Melzer *20171*
     R   Austria
     R   (former) Yugoslavia

R   ***Helictotrichon pubescens*** (Hudson) Besser ex Schult. & Sch.f ssp. *longifolia* (Boiss.) M. Dogan *12840*
     R   *12840* Turkey *12840*

R   ***Helictotrichon sarracenorum*** (Gand.) Holub *20171*
     R   Spain

I   ***Hemarthria debilis*** Bor *19120*
     I   *19120* Thailand *19120*

I   ***Hemarthria stolonifera*** Bor *19120*
     I   *19120* Thailand (thailand) *19120*

I   ***Heteropogon bellariensis*** (Hackel) C. Fischer
     I   India - Andhra Pradesh

I   ***Heteropogon polystachyos*** (Roxb.) Schult.
     I   India (Peninsular India)

R   ***Hierochloe alpina*** (Sorensen) G. Weim. ssp. *orthantha* (Sorensen) G. Weim. *20850*
     I   *20850* Canada - Labrador *20850*
     I   *20850* Canada - Newfoundland *20850*
     E   *20850* Canada - Ontario *20850*
     I   *20850* Canada - Quebec *20850*
     I   *20850* U.S. - Kentucky *20850*
     I   *20850* U.S. - North Carolina *20850*

R   ***Hierochloe submutica*** F.Muell. *20681*
     I   *20681* Australia - New South Wales *20681*
     I   *20681* Australia - Victoria *20681*

E   ***Hilaria annua*** J. & C. Reeder *20883*
     I   *20883* Mexico *20883*

E   ***Hilaria davidsei*** Pohl *9037*
     E   *9727* Costa Rica *9037*

V   ***Holcus caespitosus*** Boiss. *19818, 20171*
     V   *19818* Spain (Andalucía) *19818*

R   ***Holcus grandiflorus*** Boiss. & Reut. *20171*
     R   *11496* Spain *11496*

I   ***Holcus setiglumis*** Boiss. & Reut. ssp. *duriensis* Pinto da Silva *8000, 20171*
     I   *20874* Portugal (north-east) *8000*
     I   *20874* Spain *20874*

R   ***Homopholis belsonii*** C.E.Hubb. *20681*
     R   *20681* Australia - New South Wales *20681*
     Ex/E   *20681* Australia - Queensland *20681*

R   ***Hordeum mustersii*** Nicora *16336*
     R   *16336* Argentina *16336*
     R   *20176* Argentina - Santa Cruz (Güer Aike) *20176*

R   ***Hordeum parodii*** Covas *19574*
     R   *19574* Argentina *19574*

Ex   ***Hubbardia heptaneuron*** Bor *11494*
     Ex   *11494* India - Karnataka (Gersoppa Falls, north Canara) *11494*

V   ***Humbertochloa greenwayi*** C.E. Hubbard *7959*
     V   *5926* Tanzania (Uzaramo Distr.) *7959*

I   ***Hypseochloa cameroonensis*** C.E. Hubb.
     I   Cameroon (Cameroon Mt)

V   ***Ichnanthus drepanophyllus*** Mez *20883*
     I   *20883* Brazil *20883*

E   ***Ichnanthus lancifolius*** var. *weberbaueri* (Mez) Stieber *20883*
     I   *20883* Peru *20883*
     I   *20883* Venezuela *20883*

E   ***Ichnanthus longiglumis*** Mez *20883*
     I   *20883* Brazil *20883*

I   ***Isachne angladei*** C. Fischer *14724*
     I   India - Tamil Nadu (endemic to Anaimalai and Palni Hills.) *14724*

I   ***Isachne deccanensis*** Bor *14724*
     I   India - Tamil Nadu (Nilgiri Hills) *14724*

R   ***Isachne dimyloides*** Bor *14724*
     R   *14724* India - Sikkim *14724*

R   ***Isachne fischeri*** Bor *11494*
     R   *11494* India - Kerala *11494*

V   ***Isachne guineensis*** Stapf & C.E. Hubbard *7926*
     V   Guinea *7926*

R   ***Isachne langkawiensis*** Jansen
     R   Malaysia - Peninsular Malaysia (Langkawi, Kedah)

I   ***Isachne lisboae*** Hook.f. *11494*
     I   *11494* India - Karnataka *11494*
     I   *11494* India - Maharashtra (Panchgani; Mahabaleshwar) *11494*

R   ***Isachne oreades*** (Domin) Bor *14724*
     R   *14724* India - Tamil Nadu (Nilgri Hills) *14724*

I   ***Isachne puberula*** Bor *19120*
     I   *19120* Thailand *19120*

R   ***Isachne pygmaea*** Griseb. *20883*
     R   *20883* Jamaica *20883*

R   ***Isachne setosa*** Hook. f. *14724*
     R   *14724* India - Karnataka *14724*
     R   *14724* India - Kerala *14724*
     R   *14724* India - Tamil Nadu *14724*

V   ***Ischaemum byrone*** (Trin.) A.S. Hitchc. *20850, 14209*
     ?   Fiji *8006*
     ?   French Polynesia - Society Is. (Magaia) *8006*
     ?   Niue *8006*
     ?   Tonga *8006*
     R   U.S. - American Samoa (Pioa Mt, Tutuila) *8006*
     V   *20850* U.S. - Hawaii (Moloka`i, Maui, and Hawai`i) *20850*

I   ***Ischaemum glaucescens*** Merr. *13833*

	I	*13833* Philippines (L. Manguao) *13833*
I	*Ischaemum hansenii* Bor *19120*	
	I	*19120* Thailand *19120*
I	*Ischaemum kingii* Hook.f.	
	I	India - Rajasthan (Mt Abu)
E	*Ischaemum polystachyum* Presl var. *polystachyum*	
	E	U.S. - Guam (Mariana Is.)
R	*Ischaemum raizadae* Haemadri & Billore *13883*	
	R	*13883* India - Maharashtra (three districts) *13883*
I	*Ischaemum santapaui* Bor	
	I	India - Gujarat (Dangs)
	I	India - Maharashtra (Karjat)
I	*Ischnochloa falconeri* Hook.f.	
	I	India - Uttar Pradesh
R	*Koeleria embergeri* Quezel	
	R	Morocco
I	*Koeleria majorifolia* Borb. *17786*	
	I	*17786* Hungary *17786*
I	*Koeleria sclerophylla* P.A.Smirn. *5942, 20171*	
	I	*5942* Russia (E.Europe) - South *5942*
	I	*5942* Kazakhstan *5942*
E	*Leersia stipitata* Bor *19120*	
	E	*19120* Thailand *19120*
R	*Leptochloa ginae* Maire	
	R	Morocco
E	*Lepturidium insulare* Hitchc. & Ekman *5607*	
	E	*19105* Cuba (Juventud Is.) *5607*
R	*Lepturus geminatus* C.E.Hubb. *20681*	
	R	*20681* Australia - Queensland *20681*
R	*Lepturus xerophilus* Domin *20681*	
	R	*20681* Australia - Queensland *20681*
V	*Leymus pacificus* (Gould) Dewey *20850*	
	I	*20850* U.S. - California *20850*
I	*Libyella cyrenaica* (E. Dur. & G. Barratte) Pampan.	
	I	Libya
R	*Limnopoa meeboldii* (C. Fischer) C.E. Hubb. *11494*	
	R	*14724* India - Kerala *11494*
V	*Lithachne humilis* Soderstrom & C. Calderón *12013*	
	V	*9727* Honduras *12013*
V	*Lolium lowei* Menezes	
	V	Portugal - Madeira
	V	Spain - Canary Is.
E	*Lophochlaena oregona* (Chase) P.H. But *20850*	
	E	*20850* U.S. - Oregon *20850*
E	*Lophochlaena refracta* var. *hooverianus* (L. Benson) A.& D. Love *20850*	
	E	*20850* U.S. - California *20850*
I	*Lophochloa clarkeana* (Domin) Bor	
	I	India - Jammu & Kashmir
R	*Loudetia jaegerana* A. Camus *7926*	
	R	Sierra Leone *7926*
R	*Loxodera strigosa* (Gledhill) W. Clayton *7926*	
	R	Sierra Leone (Loma Mts.) *7926*
I	*Maclurolyra tecta* C. Calderón & Soderstrom *13825*	
	I	*13825* Panama *13825*
	I	*13825* Colombia *13825*
I	*Maltebrunia schliebenii* (Pilger) C.E. Hubbard *7959*	

	I	*5926* Tanzania (Ulanga Distr.) *7959*
V	*Megalachne berteroniana* Steud. *19116*	
	V	*19125* Chile - Juan Fernandez Is. *19116*
V	*Megalachne masafuerana* *19116*	
	V	*19125* Chile - Juan Fernandez Is. *19116*
R	*Melica lilloi* Bech. *16336*	
	R	*16336* Argentina *16336*
	R	*20176* Argentina - Catamarca *20176*
	R	*20176* Argentina - Tucuman *20176*
R	*Melica parodiana* Torres *16336*	
	R	*16336* Argentina *16336*
	R	*20176* Argentina - Buenos Aires *20176*
R	*Melica teneriffae* Hackel ex Christ	
	R	Spain - Canary Is.
I	*Melinis drakensbergensis* (C.E.Hubb. & Schweick.) Clayton *20604*	
	I	*20604* South Africa - Transvaal *20604*
R	*Merxmuellera setacea* N.P.Barker *20604*	
	R	*20604* South Africa - Cape Province *20604*
R	*Micraira compacta* Lazarides *20681*	
	R	*20681* Australia - Northern Territory *20681*
R	*Micraira dentata* Lazarides *20681*	
	R	*20681* Australia - Northern Territory *20681*
R	*Micraira inserta* Lazarides *20681*	
	R	*20681* Australia - Northern Territory *20681*
R	*Micraira multinervia* Lazarides *20681*	
	R	*20681* Australia - Northern Territory *20681*
R	*Micraira pungens* Lazarides *20681*	
	R	*20681* Australia - Northern Territory *20681*
R	*Micraira spinifera* Lazarides *20681*	
	R	*20681* Australia - Northern Territory *20681*
R	*Micraira subspicata* Lazarides *20681*	
	R	*20681* Australia - Northern Territory *20681*
R	*Micraira viscidula* Lazarides *20681*	
	R	*20681* Australia - Northern Territory *20681*
V	*Micropyropsis tuberosa* Romero-Zarco & Cabezudo *17781*	
	V	*20874* Spain (Huelva) *11496*
R	*Miscanthus changii* Y.N. Lee *15923*	
	R	*15923* Korea, South (Mt Sorak) *15923*
R	*Miscanthus chejuensis* Y.N. Lee *15923*	
	R	*15923* Korea, South (Mt Sorak) *15923*
E	*Muhlenbergia bradegei* C.G.Reeder *20883*	
	I	*20883* Mexico *20883*
V	*Muhlenbergia californica* Vasey *20850*	
	V	*20850* U.S. - California *20850*
V	*Muhlenbergia curtifolia* Scribn. *20850*	
	I	*20850* U.S. - Arizona *20850*
	I	*20850* U.S. - Nevada *20850*
	I	*20850* U.S. - Utah *20850*
V	*Muhlenbergia dubioides* C.O. Goodding *20850*	
	V	*20850* U.S. - Arizona *20850*
R	*Muhlenbergia jaliscana* Swallen *9722*	
	R	*19850* Mexico - Jalisco *21204*
E	*Muhlenbergia majalcensis* P. Peterson *20883*	
	I	*20883* Mexico *20883*
R	*Muhlenbergia purpusii* Mez *9722*	
	R	*19755* Mexico *9722*
R	*Muhlenbergia texana* Buckl. *20850*	
	I	*20850* U.S. - Arizona *20850*

I	20850	U.S. - New Mexico *20850*
I	20850	U.S. - Texas *20850*

R   *Muhlenbergia torreyana* (J.A. Schultes) A.S. Hitchc. *20850*

Ex/E	20850	U.S. - Delaware *20850*
Ex/E	20850	U.S. - Georgia *20850*
E	20850	U.S. - Maryland *20850*
R	20850	U.S. - New Jersey *20850*
Ex	20850	U.S. - New York *20850*
E	20850	U.S. - North Carolina *20850*
E	20850	U.S. - Tennessee *20850*

V   *Muhlenbergia villosa* Swallen *20850*

	20850	U.S. - New Mexico *20850*
V	20850	U.S. - Texas *20850*

R   *Muhlenbergia xerophila* C.O. Goodding *20883, 20850*

V	20850	U.S. - Arizona *20850*
I	20883	Mexico *20883*

R   *Nematopoa longipes* (Stapf & Hubbard) Hubbard *7874*

R		Zimbabwe *7874*

V   *Neostapfia colusana* (Burtt-Davy) Burtt-Davy *20850*

V	20850	U.S. - California *20850*

R   *Neurachne tenuifolia* S.T.Blake *20681*

R	20681	Australia - Northern Territory *20681*

R   *Notochloe microdon* (Benth.) Domin *20681*

R	20681	Australia - New South Wales *20681*

R   *Ochlandra ebracteata* Raizada and Chatterjee *14723*

R	14723	India - Kerala *14723*

R   *Ochlandra setigera* Gamble *14723*

R	14723	India - Tamil Nadu *14723*

R   *Ochlandra sivagiriana* Camus *14723*

R	14723	India - Tamil Nadu (Sivagiri and Pulney Hills) *14723*

I   *Olmeca recta* Soderstrom *10831*

I	19850	Mexico *10831*

I   *Olmeca reflexa* Soderstrom *10831*

I	19850	Mexico *10831*

E   *Olyra filiformis* Trinius *13826*

E	13825	Brazil - Bahia *13826*

E   *Olyra latispicula* Soderstrom & Zuloaga *13826*

E	13825	Brazil - Bahia *13826*

V   *Orcuttia californica* Vasey *20883, 20850, 8058*

V	20850	U.S. - California *20850*
I	20883	Mexico *20883*

V   *Orcuttia inaequalis* Hoover *20850*

V	20850	U.S. - California *20850*

V   *Orcuttia pilosa* Hoover *20850*

V	20850	U.S. - California *20850*

V   *Orcuttia tenuis* A.S. Hitchc. *20850*

V	20850	U.S. - California *20850*

E   *Orcuttia viscida* (Hoover) J. Reeder *20850*

E	20850	U.S. - California *20850*

R   *Oropetium hesperidum* Maire

R		Morocco

I   *Oryza jeyporensis* Govindasw. & Krishnam.

I	7771	India - Orissa (Jeypore Tract) *7771*

E   *Oryza neocaledonica* Morat *20893*

E	20893	New Caledonia *20084*

R   *Oryza rehderiana* Chun *8482*

R		China *8482*

R   *Oryzopsis contracta* (B.L. Johnson) Schlechter *20850*

I	20850	U.S. - Colorado *20850*

I	20850	U.S. - Montana *20850*
R	20850	U.S. - Wyoming *20850*

I   *Oryzopsis humilis* Bor

I		India - Uttar Pradesh

I   *Oryzopsis stewartiana* Bor

I		India - Himachal Pradesh

V   *Panicum abscissum* Swallen *20850*

V	20850	U.S. - Florida *20850*

E   *Panicum beecheyi* Hook. & Arn. *20850, 14209*

E	20850	U.S. - Hawaii *20850*

I   *Panicum beyeri* Hitchc. & Ekman *5607*

I	19105	Cuba *5607*

R   *Panicum calocarpum* R. Berhaut *7926*

R		Senegal (Badi) *7926*

E   *Panicum fauriei* Hitchc. var. *carteri* (Hosaka) Davidse *20850, 14209*

E	20850	U.S. - Hawaii *20850*

E   *Panicum hirstii* Swallen *20850*

E	20850	U.S. - Delaware *20850*
Ex/E	20850	U.S. - Georgia *20850*
E	20850	U.S. - New Jersey *20850*
E	20850	U.S. - North Carolina *20850*

E   *Panicum lacustre* Hitchc. & Ekman *5607*

E	19105	Cuba (Pinar del Rio) *5607*

E   *Panicum lineale* St. John *20850, 14209*

E	20850	U.S. - Hawaii *20850*

V   *Panicum lithophilum* Swallen *20850*

E	20850	U.S. - Alabama *20850*
V	20850	U.S. - Georgia *20850*
E	20850	U.S. - North Carolina *20850*
I	20850	U.S. - South Carolina *20850*

E   *Panicum mohavense* J. Reeder *20850*

I	20850	U.S. - Arizona *20850*
I	20850	U.S. - New Mexico *20850*

E   *Panicum niihauense* St. John *20850, 14209*

E	20850	U.S. - Hawaii (Ni`iahu) *20850*

V   *Panicum ramosius* A.S. Hitchc. *20850, 14209*

I	20850	U.S. - Hawaii *20850*
I	20850	U.S. - Kentucky *20850*

E   *Panicum stevensianum* A.S. Hitchc. & Chase *20883*

I	20883	Cuba *20883*
I	20883	Puerto Rico *20883*

R   *Panicum stramineum* A.S. Hitchc. & Chase *20850*

I	20850	U.S. - Arizona *20850*
I	20850	U.S. - New Mexico *20850*

E   *Panicum sublaeve* Swallen *20883, 9726*

I	20883	Panama *20883*

R   *Panicum tamaulipense* Waller & Morden *20883*

I	20883	Mexico *20883*

I   *Parahyparrhenia siamensis* W.D. Clayton *19120*

I	19120	Thailand *19120*

V   *Pariana parvispica* Pohl *9727*

V	9727	Costa Rica *9727*

E   *Pariana strigosa* Swallen *20883, 9006*

I	20883	Panama *20883*

V   *Paspalidium grandispiculatum* B.Simon *20681*

V	20681	Australia - Queensland *20681*

R   *Paspalidium scabrifolium* S.T.Blake *20681*

R	20681	Australia - Queensland *20681*

R   *Paspalidium udum* S.T.Blake *20681*

I	20681	Australia - Northern Territory *20681*

	I	20681	Australia - Queensland *20681*
I	*Paspalum acutifolium* Leon *5607*		
	I	19105	Cuba *5607*
Ex	*Paspalum amphicarpum* Ekman *5607*		
	Ex	19105	Cuba (Prov. Habana) *5607*
E	*Paspalum edmondi* Leon *5607*		
	E	19105	Cuba (Matanzas; Villa Clara) *5607*
I	*Paspalum galapageium* Chase var. *minoratum* Chase *11117*		
	I		Ecuador - Galapagos *11117*
E	*Paspalum insulare* Ekman *5607*		
	E	19105	Cuba *5607*
Ex	*Paspalum jimenezii* Chase *9037*		
	Ex	9727	Costa Rica *9037*
R	*Paspalum reptatum* Hitchc. & Chase *13336*		
	R	13336	Cuba *13336*
	E	13336	Jamaica (Clarendon) *19890*
E	*Paspalum uyucensis* Pohl *20883, 9490*		
	I	20883	IIonduras *20883*
E	*Paspalum wrightii* Hitchc. & Chase *5607*		
	E	19105	Cuba (Pinar del Rio) *5607*
R	*Pennisetum marquisense* F. Brown		
	R		French Polynesia - Marquesas Is
I	*Pennisetum schliebenii* Pilg. *5926*		
	I	5926	Tanzania *5926*
I	*Pennisetum stolzii* Mez *5926*		
	I	5926	Tanzania *5926*
E	*Pennisetum tempisquense* Pohl *9037*		
	E	9727	Costa Rica *9037*
I	*Pennisetum validum* Mez *5926*		
	I	5926	Tanzania *5926*
R	*Pentameris longiglumis* (Nees) Stapf ssp. *gymnocolea* N.P.Barker *20604*		
	R	20604	South Africa - Cape Province *20604*
V	*Pentameris longiglumis* (Nees) Stapf ssp. *longiglumis* *20604*		
	V	20604	South Africa - Cape Province *20604*
I	*Pentaschistis barbata* (Nees) H.P.Linder ssp. *orientalis* H.P.Linder *20604*		
	I	20604	South Africa - Cape Province *20604*
R	*Pentaschistis calcicola* H.P.Linder var. *hirsuta* H.P.Linder *20604*		
	R	20604	South Africa - Cape Province *20604*
I	*Pentaschistis ecklonii* (Nees) McClean *20604*		
	I	20604	South Africa - Cape Province *20604*
R	*Pentaschistis elegans* (Nees) Stapf *20604*		
	R	20604	South Africa - Cape Province *20604*
R	*Pentaschistis lima* (Nees) Stapf *20604*		
	R	20604	South Africa - Cape Province *20604*
E	*Phalaris maderensis* (Menezes) Menezes *17891*		
	E		Portugal - Madeira *17891*
R	*Phippsia wilczekii* Hackel *16336*		
	R	16336	Argentina *16336*
E	*Phleum crypsoides* (d'Urv.) Hack. ssp. *sardoum* (Hack.) Horn *20171*		
	E	18264	Italy - Sardinia *18264*
I	*Phyllostachys assamica* Gamble ex Brandis *14723*		
	I	14723	India - Arunachal Pradesh *14723*

R	*Piptochaetinum calvenscens* Parodi *16336*		
	R	16336	Argentina *16336*
R	*Piptochaetium calvescens* Parodi *20178*		
	R	20176	Argentina - Buenos Aires (curamalal) *20176*
V	*Plectrachne bromoides* (F.Muell.) C.E.Hubb. *20681, 14223*		
	V	20681	Australia - Western Australia *20681*
R	*Plectrachne contorta* Lazarides *20681*		
	R	20681	Australia - Northern Territory *20681*
V	*Plinthanthesis rodwayi* (C.E.Hubb.) S.T.Blake *20681*		
	V	20681	Australia - New South Wales *20681*
R	*Poa aitosensis* Koz. et Stoeva *5204*		
	R	5204	Bulgaria (east) *5204*
E	*Poa alopecurus* (Gaudich.) Kunth *16336*		
	E	16336	Argentina *16336*
	E		Chile
I	*Poa angustata* Parodi *16336*		
	I	16336	Argentina *16336*
V	*Poa atropurpurea* Scribn. *20850*		
	V	20850	U.S. - California *20850*
R	*Poa aucklandica* ssp. *rakiura* *19305*		
	R	19305	New Zealand - South Is. *19305*
R	*Poa breviglumis* var. *moarii* *19106*		
	R	19106	New Zealand - Antipodes Is. *19106*
R	*Poa calchaquiensis* Hackel *16336*		
	R	16336	Argentina *16336*
	R	20176	Argentina - Catamarca *20176*
	R	20176	Argentina - Jujuy *20176*
	R	20176	Argentina - La Rioja *20176*
	R	20176	Argentina - Salta *20176*
	R	20176	Argentina - Tucuman *20176*
R	*Poa chirripoensis* Pohl *9037*		
	R	9727	Costa Rica *9037*
R	*Poa davisii* Bor *12840*		
	R	12840	Turkey *12840*
R	*Poa erinacea* Speg. *16336*		
	R	16336	Argentina *16336*
	R	20176	Argentina - Chubut *20176*
E	*Poa eyerdamii* Hulten *20850*		
	I	20850	U.S. - Alaska *20850*
V	*Poa fernaldiana* Nannf. *20850, 14366*		
	I	20850	Canada - Labrador *20850*
	E	20850	Canada - Newfoundland (Island) *20850*
	V	20850	Canada - Quebec *20850*
	E	20850	U.S. - Maine *20850*
	V	20850	U.S. - New Hampshire *20850*
	E	20850	U.S. - New York *20850*
	E	20850	U.S. - Vermont *20850*
E	*Poa fibrata* Swallen *20850*		
	E	20850	U.S. - California *20850*
R	*Poa glauca* Vahl var. *kitadakensis* (Ohwi) Ohwi *11164*		
	R	11164	Japan *11164*
I	*Poa granitica* Braun-Blanq. *6951, 20171*		
	I	19321	Slovakia (Only from the Tatras) *6951*
R	*Poa halmaturina* J.Black *20681*		
	I	20681	Australia - South Australia *20681*
	I	20681	Australia - Tasmania *20681*
E	*Poa hartzii* Landog. ssp. *alaskana* Soreng *20850, 21309*		
	E	20850	U.S. - Alaska *20850*

R **Poa hayachinensis** Koidz. *11164*
   R   *11164*   Japan *11164*

R **Poa hothamensis** Vickery var. *parviflora*
   N.G.Walsh *20681*
   R   *20681*   Australia - Victoria *20681*

R **Poa humillima** Pilger *16336*
   R   *16336*   Argentina *16336*
   R   *20176*   Argentina - Catamarca *20176*
   R   *20176*   Argentina - Tucuman *20176*

R **Poa incrassata** Petrie
   R   *19106*   New Zealand - Antipodes Is. *19106*

R **Poa iridifolia** Hauman *16336*
   R   *16336*   Argentina *16336*
   R   *20176*   Argentina - Buenos Aires *20176*

E **Poa laxa** Haenke ssp. *banffiana*
   Soreng *20850*
   I   *20850*   Canada - Alberta *20850*
   Ex/E   *20850*   Canada - British Columbia *20850*
   I   *20850*   U.S. - Montana *20850*

R **Poa laxa** Haenke ssp. *pruinosa* E.J.
   Nyárády *17823*
   R   *19949*   Romania *19840*

R **Poa laxiflora** Buckl. *20850*
   R   *20850*   Canada - British Columbia *20850*
   V   *20850*   U.S. - Alaska *20850*
   R   *20850*   U.S. - Oregon *20850*
   E   *20850*   U.S. - Washington *20850*

R **Poa legionensis** Fernandez Casas & Lainz
   R   Spain

R **Poa lowanensis** N.G.Walsh *20681*
   R   *20681*   Australia - Victoria *20681*

R **Poa macroclada** Rydb. *20850*
   I   *20850*   U.S. - Colorado *20850*
   I   *20850*   U.S. - Idaho *20850*
   I   *20850*   U.S. - Montana *20850*

E **Poa mannii** Munro ex Hbd. *20850, 14209*
   E   *20850*   U.S. - Hawaii *20850*

R **Poa molineri** Balbis ssp. *glacialis*
   Beldie *17823*
   R   *19949*   Romania *19840*

E **Poa napensis** Beetle *20850*
   E   *20850*   U.S. - California *20850*

E **Poa nascopieana** Polunin *20850, 15886*
   E   *20850*   Canada - Franklin *20850*

R **Poa ogamontana** R. Mochizuki *11164*
   R   *11164*   Japan *11164*

R **Poa paludigena** Fern. & Wieg. *20850*
   Ex   *20850*   U.S. - Illinois *20850*
   R   *20850*   U.S. - Indiana *20850*
   V   *20850*   U.S. - Iowa *20850*
   V   *20850*   U.S. - Michigan *20850*
   E   *20850*   U.S. - Minnesota *20850*
   E   *20850*   U.S. - New York *20850*
   E   *20850*   U.S. - North Carolina *20850*
   V   *20850*   U.S. - Ohio *20850*
   V   *20850*   U.S. - Pennsylvania *20850*
   V   *20850*   U.S. - Virginia *20850*
   E   *20850*   U.S. - Wisconsin *20850*

R **Poa pannonica** A.Kern. ssp. *scabra* (Asch. &
   Graebn.) Soó *20171*
   R   *20686*   Hungary *20686*

R **Poa pentapolitana** H. Scholz
   R   Libya

R **Poa pirinica** Stoj. & Acht. *5204, 20171*
   R   *5204*   Bulgaria (south) *5204*
   R   Greece

V **Poa porsildii** Gjaerevoll *20850, 6796*
   E   *20850*   Canada - Mackenzie *20850*
   E   *20850*   Canada - Yukon Territory *20850*
   E   *20850*   U.S. - Alaska *20850*

R **Poa pringlei** Scribn. *20850*
   I   *20850*   U.S. - California *20850*
   I   *20850*   U.S. - Idaho *20850*
   I   *20850*   U.S. - Montana *20850*
   I   *20850*   U.S. - Nevada *20850*
   I   *20850*   U.S. - Oregon *20850*
   I   *20850*   U.S. - Washington *20850*

I **Poa pseudamoena** Bor
   I   India - Uttar Pradesh (Kumaun, Garhwal)

R **Poa pseudobulbosa** Bor *12840*
   R   *12840*   Turkey *12840*

R **Poa rehmannii** (Asch. & Graebn.) Wol *8000, 20171*
   R   *19949*   Romania *8000*
   I   former European USSR *8000*

E **Poa rhadina** Bor
   E   India - Uttar Pradesh (Tehri Garhwal)

I **Poa riphaea** (Asch. & Graebn.) Fritsch *2050, 20171*
   Ex/E   *2050*   Czech Republic (Hruby Jeseník Mts.)
       6951
   I   *17821*   Slovakia *17821*

R **Poa sachalinensis** (Koidz.) Honda var.
   yatsugatakensis (Honda) Ohwi *11164*
   R   *11164*   Japan *11164*

V **Poa sallacustris** N.G.Walsh *20681*
   V   *20681*   Australia - Victoria *20681*

E **Poa sandvicensis** (Reichart) A.S. Hitchc. *20850,*
   14209
   E   *20850*   U.S. - Hawaii (Kaua`i) *20850*

R **Poa schizantha** Parodi *16336*
   R   *16336*   Argentina *16336*
   R   *20176*   Argentina - Buenos Aires *20176*

R **Poa senex** *19305*
   R   *19305*   New Zealand - South Is. *19305*

V **Poa sierrae** J.T. Howell *20850*
   I   *20850*   U.S. - California *20850*

E **Poa siphonoglossa** Hack. *20850, 14209*
   E   *20850*   U.S. - Hawaii (Kaua`i) *20850*

R **Poa speluncarum** Edmondson *12840*
   R   *12840*   Turkey *12840*

R **Poa strictiramea** A.S. Hitchc. *20850, 9722*
   R   *20850*   U.S. - Texas *20850*
   ?   Mexico *9722*

R **Poa sudicola** *19305*
   R   *19305*   New Zealand - South Is. *19305*

R **Poa talamancae** Pohl *9037*
   R   *9727*   Costa Rica *9037*

R **Poa trichophylla** Heldr. & Sart. ex Boiss. *20171*
   R   Greece

R **Poa umbricola** Vickery *20681*
   R   *20681*   Australia - South Australia *20681*

R **Poa unilateralis** Scribn. *20850*
   I   *20850*   U.S. - California *20850*
   I   *20850*   U.S. - Oregon *20850*
   E   *20850*   U.S. - Washington *20850*

R **Poa vaseyochloa** Scribn. *20850*

I		20850 U.S. - Oregon *20850*
I		20850 U.S. - Washington *20850*
I	*Podophorus bromoides* **Philippi** *19116*	
	I	*19125* Chile - Juan Fernandez Is. *19116*
E	*Pohlidium petiolatum* **Davidse, Soderstrom &**	
	Ellis *20883, 12066*	
	R	*19874* Panama *20883*
I	*Polyneura squarrosa* **Peter** *5926*	
	I	*5926* Tanzania *5926*
I	*Polypogon mollis* **(Th.) C.E. Hubb. & E.W.**	
	Groves *11938*	
	I	Tristan da Cunha (Inaccessible & Tristan Is.) *19938*
V	*Prionanthium dentatum* **(L.f.) Henrard** *20604*	
	V	*20604* South Africa - Cape Province *20604*
E	*Prionanthium ecklonii* **(Nees) Stapf** *20604*	
	E	*20604* South Africa - Cape Province *20604*
V	*Prionanthium pholiuroides* **Stapf** *20604*	
	V	*20604* South Africa - Cape Province *20604*
I	*Psathyrostachys huashanica* **Keng** *11815*	
	I	China - Shaanxi (Huashan) *11815*
V	*Pseudarrhenatherum pallens* **(Link) Holub** *8000, 20171*	
	V	*20076* Portugal *8000*
I	*Pseudodanthonia himalaica* **(Hook.f.) Bor & C.E. Hubb.**	
	I	India - Uttar Pradesh
R	*Pseudophleum gibbum* **(Boiss.) M. Dogan** *12840*	
	R	*12840* Turkey *12840*
V	*Ptilagrostis mongholica* **(Turcz. ex Trin.) Griseb. ssp.**	
	porteri **(Rydb.) Barkworth** *20850*	
	V	*20850* U.S. - Colorado *20850*
R	*Puccinellia agrostidea* **Sorensen** *20850*	
	V	*20850* Canada - Mackenzie *20850*
	E	*20850* Canada - Yukon Territory *20850*
	E	*20850* U.S. - Alaska *20850*
V	*Puccinellia anisoclada* **(V. Kreez.) V. Kreez. ssp.**	
	melderisiana **Kit Tan** *12840*	
	V	*12840* Turkey *12840*
V	*Puccinellia arctica* **(Hook.) Fern. & Weatherby** *20850,* *13967*	
	I	*20850* Canada - British Columbia *20850*
	E	*20850* Canada - Franklin *20850*
	I	*20850* Canada - Saskatchewan *20850*
	E	*20850* Canada - Yukon Territory *20850*
	E	*20850* U.S. - Alaska *20850*
V	*Puccinellia bruggemannii* **Sorensen** *20850, 21309*	
	?	Denmark - Greenland (Extreme North and East) *21309*
	I	*20850* Canada - Franklin *20850*
R	*Puccinellia byrrangensis* **Tzvel.** *21309*	
	R	*21309* Russia (E.Europe) - North *21309*
R	*Puccinellia deschampsioides* **Sorensen** *20850, 6796*	
	I	*20850* Canada - Manitoba *20850*
	I	*20850* Canada - Keewatin *20850*
	E	*20850* Canada - Quebec *20850*
	E	*20850* Canada - Yukon Territory *20850*
V	*Puccinellia fasciculata* **(Torr.) E.P.Bicknell ssp.**	
	pungens **(Pau) W.E. Hughes** *8000, 20171*	
	V	*20874* Spain (east) *8000*
V	*Puccinellia foucaudii* **(Hackel) Coste** *20528*	
	V	*20528* France (west coasts) *20528*
R	*Puccinellia gorodkovii* **Tzvel.** *21309*	
	R	*21309* Russia (E.Europe) - North *21309*

E	*Puccinellia howellii* **J.I. Davis** *20850*	
	E	*20850* U.S. - California *20850*
V	*Puccinellia hultenii* **Swallen** *20850*	
		20850 U.S. - Alaska *20850*
R	*Puccinellia jenissejensis* **(Roshev.) Tzvel.** *21309*	
	R	*21309* Russia (E.Europe) - North *21309*
V	*Puccinellia kamtschatica* **Holmb.** *20850*	
	V	*20850* U.S. - Alaska *20850*
R	*Puccinellia kashmiriana* **Bor**	
	R	*13883* India - Himachal Pradesh *13883*
	R	*13883* India - Jammu & Kashmir *13883*
E	*Puccinellia parishii* **A.S. Hitchc.** *20850*	
	E	*20850* U.S. - Arizona *20850*
	E	*20850* U.S. - California *20850*
	E	*20850* U.S. - New Mexico *20850*
E	*Puccinellia poacea* **Sorensen** *20850, 15886, 21309*	
	E	*20850* Canada - Franklin *20850*
E	*Puccinellia sublaevis* **(Holmb.) Tzvelev** *20850*	
	I	*20850* U.S. - Alaska *20850*
R	*Puccinellia svalbardensis* **Rönning** *20171, 21309*	
	R	*21309* Norway *21309*
I	*Puccinellia thomsonii* **J. Stewart**	
	I	India - Jammu & Kashmir
V	*Puccinellia wrightii* **(Scribn. & Merr.) Tzvelev** *20850*	
	I	*20850* U.S. - Alaska *20850*
R	*Pucciphippsia czukzorum* **Tzvel.** *21309*	
	R	*21309* Russia (E.Europe) - North *21309*
R	*Qiongzhuea tumidinoda* **Hsueh & Yi** *17617*	
	R	*17617* China - Sichuan *11139*
	R	*17617* China - Yunnan *11139*
E	*Rehia nervata* *13825*	
	E	*13825* French Guiana *13825*
	E	*13825* Suriname *13825*
E	*Rhipidocladum clarkiae* **Pohl** *20883, 12070*	
	I	*20883* Costa Rica *20883*
V	*Rhipidocladum maxonii* **(A. Hitchc.) McClure** *9037*	
	V	*9727* Costa Rica *9037*
E	*Rhipidocladum pacuarense* **Pohl** *20883, 12069*	
	I	*20883* Costa Rica *20883*
R	*Roegneria nepliana* **V. Vassil.** *21309*	
	R	*21309* Russia (E.Europe) - North *21309*
R	*Roegneria villosa* **V. Vassil. ssp.** ***coerulea***	
	Jurtz. *21309*	
	R	*21309* Russia (E.Europe) - North *21309*
R	*Rytidosperma petrosum* **Connor & Edgar** *19305*	
	R	*19305* New Zealand - North Is. *19305*
	R	*19305* New Zealand - South Is. *19305*
R	*Rytidosperma tenue* **(Petrie) Connor & Edgar** *19305*	
	R	*19305* New Zealand - South Is. *19305*
I	*Sacciolepis fenestrata* **Bor** *19120*	
	I	*19120* Thailand *19120*
R	*Sasa borealis* **var.** ***chiisanensis*** **(Nakai) T.**	
	Lee *15957*	
	R	*15923* Korea, South (Mt Chiri) *15957*
E	*Saugetia pleiostachya* **Hitchc. & Ekman** *5607*	
	E	*19105* Cuba (Pinar del Rio) *5607*
R	*Schaffnerella gracilis* **(Benth.) Nash** *9722*	
	R	*19755* Mexico *9722*
E	*Schizachyrium impressum* **(Hackel) A. Camus**	
	E	India - Jammu & Kashmir

R	*Schizachyrium lomaense* **A. Camus** *7926*	
	R	Sierra Leone *7926*
E	*Schizachyrium niveum* **(Swallen) Gould** *20850*	
	E	*20850* U.S. - Florida *20850*
R	*Schizachyrium paranjpyeanum* **(Bhide) Raizada et Jain** *13883*	
	R	*13883* India - Karnataka *13883*
	R	*13883* India - Maharashtra *13883*
E	*Schizachyrium parvifolium* **(Hitchc.) Borh. & Catasus** *5607*	
	E	*19105* Cuba (Pinar del Rio) *5607*
I	*Schizostachyum palawanense* **Gamble** *13833*	
	I	*13833* Philippines (low and medium altitudes) *13833*
R	*Schmidtia quinqueseta* **Benth. ex Ficalho & Hiern**	
	R	Egypt
V	*Secale africanum* **Stapf** *20604*	
	V	*20604* South Africa - Cape Province *20604*
R	*Secale cereale* **L. var. *ancestrale* (Zhuk.) Kit Tan** *12840*	
	R	*12840* Turkey *12840*
I	*Secale kuprijanovii* **Grossh.** *5942*	
	I	*5942* Russia - North Caucasus *5942*
	I	*5942* Georgia *5942*
R	*Secale rhodopaecum* **Delip.** *5204*	
	R	*5204* Bulgaria (South Bulgaria - one site only.) *5204*
I	*Secale vavilovii* **Grossh.** *5942*	
	I	*5942* Armenia *5942*
	I	*5942* Azerbaijan *5942*
R	*Semiarundinaria pantlingii* **Gamble** *14723*	
	R	*14723* Bhutan *14723*
	R	*14723* India - Arunachal Pradesh *14723*
	R	*14723* India - Sikkim *14723*
R	*Sesleria araratica* **Kit Tan** *12840*	
	R	*12840* Turkey *12840*
R	*Sesleria doerfleri* **Hayek** *20171*	
	R	*20731* Greece - Crete *20731*
R	*Sesleria heuflerana* **Schur ssp. *hungarica* (Ujhelyi) Deyl** *19321, 20171*	
	R	*20686* Hungary *20686*
	I	*19751* Poland *19751*
	V	*19321* Slovakia *19321*
R	*Sesleria klasterskii* **Deyl**	
	R	Bulgaria
R	*Sesleria taygetea* **Hayek** *20171*	
	R	Greece
V	*Setaria jaffrei* **Morat** *20893*	
	V	*20893* New Caledonia *20893*
E	*Setaria paraguayensis* **Pensiero** *20883*	
	E	*20883* Paraguay *20883*
R	*Simplicia buchananii* **Zotov**	
	R	New Zealand - South Is.
E	*Simplicia laxa* **Kirk** *86*	
	E	*19305* New Zealand - South Is. *19305*
V	*Sorghastrum apalachicolense* **D.W. Hall** *20850*	
	I	*20850* U.S. - Florida *20850*
	E	*20850* U.S. - Mississippi *20850*
R	*Sorghum annuum* **Trabut** *10487*	
	R	*14958* Algeria *10487*
R	*Sorghum macrospermum* **Garber** *20681*	

	R	*20681* Australia - Northern Territory *20681*
R	*Sphenopus ehrenbergii* **Hausskn.**	
	R	Egypt
	R	Libya
	R	Tunisia
E	*Sporobolus caespitosus* **Kunth** *3204*	
	E	*3204* Ascension Is. *3204*
Ex/E	*Sporobolus durus* **Brongn.** *3204*	
	Ex/E	*3204* Ascension Is. *3204*
V	*Sporobolus interruptus* **Vasey** *20850*	
	I	*20850* U.S. - Arizona *20850*
R	*Sporobolus lanuginellus* **Maire**	
	R	Morocco
Ex	*Sporobolus linearus* **Mez** *20773*	
	Ex	*20771* Mauritius *20773*
Ex	*Sporobolus mauritianus* **(Steud.) Durand & Schinz** *20773*	
	Ex	*20771* Mauritius *20773*
V	*Sporobolus minimus* **Cope** *20146*	
	V	*20146* Oman (Dhofar) *20146*
	V	*20146* Somalia (Dhofar) *20146*
V	*Sporobolus temomairemensis* **Judziewicz & Peterson** *20883*	
	I	*20883* Brazil *20883*
	I	*20883* Suriname *20883*
E	*Sporobolus teretifolius* **Harper** *20850*	
	V	*20850* U.S. - Georgia *20850*
	E	*20850* U.S. - North Carolina *20850*
	I	*20850* U.S. - South Carolina *20850*
R	*Sporobolus tharpii* **A.S. Hitchc.** *20850*	
	R	*20850* U.S. - Texas *20850*
R	*Stipa aktauensis* **Roshev.**	
	R	former USSR *6930*
I	*Stipa anomala* **P.A.Smirn.** *5942, 20171*	
	I	*5942* Russia (E.Europe) - South *5942*
	I	*5942* Ukraine *5942*
R	*Stipa apertifolia* **Martinovsky** *20171*	
	R	Spain
R	*Stipa aquarii* **Vickery, S.W.L.Jacobs & Everett** *20681*	
	R	*20681* Australia - Northern Territory *20681*
E	*Stipa austroitalica* **Martinovsky** *8000, 20171*	
	E	Italy *8000*
	E	Italy - Sicily *8000*
V	*Stipa bavarica* **Martinovsky & H.Scholz** *8000, 20171*	
	V	*20640* Germany (near Neuburg, Danube River) *20644*
R	*Stipa breviglumis* **J.Black** *20681*	
	I	*20681* Australia - South Australia *20681*
	I	*20681* Australia - Victoria *20681*
R	*Stipa centralis* **Vickery, S.W.L.Jacobs & Everett** *20681*	
	R	*20681* Australia - Northern Territory *20681*
I	*Stipa chitralensis* **Bor**	
	I	India - Jammu & Kashmir
V	*Stipa crassiculmis* **Smirnow ssp. *heterotricha* Dihoru & Roman** *17823*	
	V	*19949* Romania *19840*
R	*Stipa cretacea* **P.A.Smirn.** *8000, 20171*	
	R	former European USSR *8000*
V	*Stipa danubialis* **Dihoru & Roman** *8000, 20171*	
	V	*19949* Romania *8000*

R	*Stipa dasyphylla* (Lindem.) Trautv. *8000, 20171*		
	R	2050	Czech Republic *2050*
	E	20640	Germany *20640*
	V	20686	Hungary *17786*
	R	19947	Romania *19840*
	V	19321	Slovakia *19321*
	V	11552	Russian Federation (west, Ural Mts., south-west Siberia) *11552*

R **Stipa diegoensis** Swallen *20850*
    R 20850 U.S. - California *20850*

R **Stipa echinata** Vickery, S.W.L.Jacobs & Everett *20681*
    R 20681 Australia - South Australia *20681*

R **Stipa feresetacea** Vickery, S.W.L.Jacobs & Everett *20681*
    R 20681 Australia - Northern Territory *20681*

R **Stipa hendersonii** (Vasey) Muhl. *20850*
    V 20850 U.S. - Oregon *20850*
    V 20850 U.S. - Washington *20850*

V **Stipa hirticulmis** Hatch, Valdés & Morden *20883, 12065*
    I 20883 Mexico *20883*

Ex/E **Stipa horridula** Pilger in Skottsberg *19117*
    Ex/E 19117 Chile - Easter Is. (slopes of Mt. Katiki.) *19117*

I **Stipa karataviensis** Rosch. *5942*
    I 5942 Kazakhstan *5942*

R **Stipa lithophila** P.A.Smirn. *5942, 20171*
    R 5942 Ukraine - Crimea *5942*

R **Stipa longiplumosa** Roshev.
    R   former USSR *6930*

R **Stipa magnifica** Junge
    R   former USSR *6930*

R **Stipa mayeri** Martinovsky *20171*
    R   (former) Yugoslavia

V **Stipa metatoris** Everett & S.W.L.Jacobs *20681*
    I 20681 Australia - New South Wales *20681*
    I 20681 Australia - South Australia *20681*

R **Stipa multispiculis** J.Black *20681*
    R 20681 Australia - South Australia *20681*

R **Stipa novakii** Martinovsky *20171*
    R   (former) Yugoslavia

V **Stipa nullanulla** Everett & S.W.L.Jacobs *20681*
    I 20681 Australia - New South Wales *20681*
    I 20681 Australia - South Australia *20681*
    I 20681 Australia - Victoria *20681*

I **Stipa pellita** (Trin. & Rupr.) Tzvelev *5942*
    I 5942 Azerbaijan (Baku) *5942*

R **Stipa petriei** Buchan. *19305*
    R 19305 New Zealand - South Is. *19305*

R **Stipa rechingeri** Martinovsky *20171*
    R   Greece

V **Stipa sicula** Moraldo, La Valva, Ricciardi & Caputo *18264*
    V 18264 Italy - Sicily *18264*

R **Stipa stillmanii** Boland. *20850*
    I 20850 U.S. - California *20850*

V **Stipa styriaca** Martinovsky *20171*
    V   Austria

I **Stipa syreistschikowii** P. Smirn. *20654*
    I 5942 Russia - North Caucasus *5942*
    E 20655 Ukraine - Crimea *20655*

R **Stipa trichoides** P. Smirnow
    R   former USSR *6930*

E **Stipa veneta** Moraldo *17891*
    E 18264 Italy (Veneto) *18264*

R **Stipa ventanicola** Cabrera & Torres *16336*
    R 20176 Argentina - Buenos Aires *20176*

E **Stipa wakoolica** Vickery, S.W.L.Jacobs & Everett *20681*
    E 20681 Australia - New South Wales *20681*

R **Stipa zalesskii** Wilensky *8000*
    R   Czech Republic
    R   Slovakia
    V 11552 Russian Federation (Caucasus, west, south-west & east Siberia) *11552*

I **Stipagrostis dhofariensis** Cope *20146*
    I 20146 Oman (Dhofar) *20146*

E **Stipagrostis drarii** (Tackh.) de Winter
    E   Egypt

I **Stipagrostis masirahensis** H. Scholz *20146*
    I 20146 Oman (Masirah Island) *20146*

R **Stipagrostis proxima** (Steud) De Winter *20604*
    R 20604 South Africa - Cape Province *20604*
    R 20604 South Africa - Orange Free State *20604*

R **Stipagrostis rigidifolia** H. Scholz
    R   Chad

R **Stipagrostis zittelii** (Asch.) de Winter
    R   Egypt
    R   Libya

Ex **Streptochaeta angustifolia** Soderstrom *13827*
    Ex 13827 Brazil *13827*

E **Sucrea monophylla** Soderstrom *13825*
    E 13825 Brazil - Bahia *13825*

Ex **Sucrea sampaiana** (A. Hitch.) Soderstrom *13825*
    Ex 13825 Brazil - Espirito Santo *13825*

E **Swallenia alexandrae** (Swallen) Soderstrom & Decker *20850*
    E 20850 U.S. - California *20850*

I **Teinostachyum beddomei** C. Fischer
    I   India - Kerala (Travancore Hills)
    I   India - Tamil Nadu (Nilgiri Hills)

R **Thamnocalamus tessellatus** (Nees) Soderstr. & R.P.Ellis *20604*
    I 20039 Swaziland *20604*
    V 20604 South Africa - Cape Province *20604*
    R 20604 South Africa - Natal *20604*
    V 20604 South Africa - Orange Free State *20604*

E **Thrasya ciliatifolia** Swallen *20883, 9006*
    I 20883 Panama *20883*

E **Thrasya gracilis** Swallen *20883, 10747*
    I 20883 Panama *20883*

V **Torreyochloa californica** (Beetle) Church *20850*
    I 20850 U.S. - California *20850*

E **Tovarochloa peruviana** J. MacFarlane & But *12468*
    E 19966 Peru *12468*

I **Triniochloa micrantha** (Scribner) A. Hitchc. *9722*
    I 19850 Mexico *9722*

R **Triodia lanata** J.Black *20681*
    R 20681 Australia - South Australia *20681*

I **Tripogon larsenii** Bor *19120*
    I 19120 Thailand *19120*

R **Tripogon longearistatus** Honda var. *japonicus* Honda *11164*

    R   *11164*   Japan *11164*

V **Tripsacum floridanum** Porter ex Vasey *20850*

    V   *20850*   U.S. - Florida *20850*

I **Triscenia ovina** Griseb. *5607*

    I   *19105*   Cuba *5607*

V **Trisetaria dufourei** (Boiss.) Paunero *8000, 20171*

    V   *14155*   Portugal (south) *8000*

    V   *14155*   Spain (south west) *8000*

R **Trisetaria nitida** (Desf.) Maire *10487*

    R   *14958*   Algeria *10487*

Ex/E **Trisetum burnoufii** Req. ex Parl. *20171*

    Ex/E *20726*   France - Corsica *15080*

V **Trisetum conradiae** Gamisans *15080, 20171*

    V   *20528*   France - Corsica *15080*

V **Trisetum gracile** (Moris) Boiss. *20171*

    V   *20528*   France - Corsica *20528*

    V   *20528*   Italy - Sardinia *20528*

R **Trisetum howellii** A. Hitchc. *11117*

    R   Ecuador - Galapagos *11117*

E **Trisetum inaequale** Whitney *20850, 14209*

    E   *20850*   U.S. - Hawaii (Lana`i and Maui) *20850*

R **Trisetum longiglume** Hackel var. *glabrata* Nicora *16336*

    R   *16336*   Argentina *16336*

R **Trisetum longiglume** Hackel var. *longiglume 16336*

    R   *16336*   Argentina *16336*

    R   *16337*   Chile *16337*

I **Trisetum micans** (Hook.f.) Bor

    I   India - Jammu & Kashmir

    I   India - Uttar Pradesh (Tehri Garhwal)

R **Trisetum thospiticum** Chrtek *12840*

    R   *12840*   Turkey *12840*

R **Trisetum wrangelense** (Petrovsky) Probat. *21309*

    R   *21309*   Russia (E.Europe) - North *21309*

I **Triticum araraticum** Jakubz. *5942*

    I   *5942*   Armenia *5942*

    I   *5942*   Azerbaijan *5942*

I **Triticum timopheevii** (Zhuk.) Zhuk. *5942*

    I   *5942*   Georgia *5942*

I **Triticum urartu** Thumanjan ex Gandilyan *5942*

    I   *5942*   Armenia *5942*

V **Tuctoria greenei** (Vasey) J. Reeder *20850*

    V   *20850*   U.S. - California *20850*

E **Tuctoria mucronata** (Crampton) J. Reeder *20850, 11059*

    E   *20850*   U.S. - California (central Solano County) *20850*

E **Urelytrum pallidum** C.E. Hubbard *7926*

    E   *6072*   Ghana *7926*

E **Urelytrum semispirale** W. Clayton *7926*

    E   *6072*   Ghana *7926*

R **Vaseyochloa multinervosa** (Vasey) A.S. Hitchc. *20850*

    R   *20850*   U.S. - Texas *20850*

R **Ventenata eigiana** (H. Scholz & Raus) M. Dogan *12840*

    R   *12840*   Turkey *12840*

R **Vetiveria arguta** (Steud.) C.E. Hubb. *5852*

    R   *20771*   Mauritius (incl. Round Is.) *20773*

    V   *5852*   Mauritius - Rodrigues (Grande Mt & Mont

Malartic) *5852*

V **Vulpia fontquerana** Melderis & Stace *19818, 20171*

    V   *19818*   Spain (Cádiz & Huelva) *19818*

E **Vulpia obtusa** Trabut *10487*

    E   *14958*   Algeria *10487*

R **Whiteochloa multiciliata** Lazarides *20681*

    R   *20681*   Australia - Northern Territory *20681*

R **Willbleibia stolonifera** (Parodi) Herter *16336*

    R   *16336*   Argentina *16336*

R **Willkommia texana** A.S. Hitchc. *20850*

    R   *20850*   U.S. - Texas *20850*

V **Zea diploperennis** Iltis, Doebley & Guzmán *20883, 9019*

    V   *9114*   Mexico - Jalisco *9114*

Ex **Zea mexicana** (Schrader) Reeves & Mangelsd. *10260*

    Ex   *9114*   Mexico *9114*

E **Zea perennis** (A. Hitchc.) Mangelsd. & Reeves *9019*

    E   *9114*   Mexico - Jalisco *9114*

E **Zeugites panamensis** Swallen *20883, 9006*

    I   *20883*   Panama *20883*

I **Zingeria biebersteiniana** (Claus) P. Smirn. *11552, 20171*

    I   *5942*   Russia (E.Europe) - South *5942*

    I   *5942*   Georgia *5942*

    I   *5942*   Kazakhstan *5942*

    I   *5942*   Ukraine - Crimea *5942*

R **Zingeria verticillata** (Boiss. & Bal.) Chrtek *12840*

    R   *12840*   Turkey *12840*

E **Zizania texana** A.S. Hitchc. *20850*

    E   *20850*   U.S. - Texas *20850*

Haemodoraceae

Number of genera:	16
Number of species:	100
Recorded threatened species:	15 (15%)

Mostly Southern Hemisphere, but reaching northern United States.

V **Anigozanthos bicolor** Endl. ssp. *minor* (Benth.) Hopper *20681*

    V   *20681*   Australia - Western Australia *20681*

V **Anigozanthos humilis** Lindley ssp. *chrysanthus* Hopper *20681*

    V   *20681*   Australia - Western Australia *20681*

V **Anigozanthos viridis** Endl. ssp. *terraspectans* Hopper *20681*

    V   *20681*   Australia - Western Australia *20681*

V **Conostylis drummondii** Benth. *20681*

    V   *20681*   Australia - Western Australia *20681*

V **Conostylis lepidospermoides** Hopper *20681*

    V   *20681*   Australia - Western Australia *20681*

V **Conostylis micrantha** Hopper *20681*

    V   *20681*   Australia - Western Australia *20681*

V **Conostylis misera** Endl. *20681*

    V   *20681*   Australia - Western Australia *20681*

R **Conostylis pauciflora** Hopper ssp. *pauciflora 20681*

    R   *20681*   Australia - Western Australia *20681*

V **Conostylis rogeri** Hopper *20681*

    V   *20681*   Australia - Western Australia *20681*

V	*Conostylis seorsiflora* F.Muell. ssp. *trichophylla* Hopper *20681*		
	V	*20681*	Australia - Western Australia *20681*
E	*Conostylis setigera* R.Br. ssp. *dasys* Hopper *20681*		
	E	*20681*	Australia - Western Australia *20681*
V	*Conostylis wonganensis* Hopper *20681*		
	V	*20681*	Australia - Western Australia *20681*
R	*Haemodorum distichophyllum* Hook. *20681*		
	R	*20681*	Australia - Tasmania *20681*
V	*Tribonanthes purpurea* Hopper *20681*		
	V	*20681*	Australia - Western Australia *20681*
R	*Xiphidium xanthorrhizon* Wrigth *20883*		
	R	*20883*	Cuba *20883*

Heliconiaceae

Number of genera: 1
Number of species: 100
Recorded threatened species: 43 (43%)

Tropical and subtropical South and Central America; one species widespread in southwestern Pacific islands.

V	*Heliconia angusta* Vell. *17079*		
	V	*17746*	Brazil - Espirito Santo *17079*
	V	*17079*	Brazil - Rio de Janeiro (município do Rio de Janeiro, Magé, Petrópolis & Teresópolis) *17079*
R	*Heliconia atropurpurea* Daniels & Stiles *10760*		
	R	*11125*	Costa Rica *10760*
	V	*11125*	Panama *10760*
E	*Heliconia barryana* Kress *9484*		
	E	*9992*	Panama *9484*
E	*Heliconia beckneri* R.R. Smith *10760*		
	E	*11548*	Costa Rica *10760*
E	*Heliconia bella* Kress *9484*		
	E	*9992*	Panama *9484*
E	*Heliconia calatheaphylla* Daniels & Stiles *10760*		
	E	*9992*	Costa Rica *10760*
E	*Heliconia citrina* L. Emygdio & E. Santos *17079*		
	E	*17079*	Brazil - Rio de Janeiro (Município de Rio Bonito, Braçana Fazenda das Cachoeiras) *17079*
V	*Heliconia clinophila* R.R. Smith *10760*		
	V	*9992*	Costa Rica *10760*
R	*Heliconia colgantea* R.R. Smith ex Daniels & Stiles *10759*		
	E	*11125*	Costa Rica *10759*
	R	*11125*	Panama *10759*
R	*Heliconia collinsiana* Griggs var. *velutina* Kress *10759*		
	R	*11125*	El Salvador *10759*
	R	*11125*	Guatemala *10759*
E	*Heliconia crassa* Griggs *9992*		
	E	*9992*	Guatemala *9992*
V	*Heliconia danielsiana* Kress *10759*		
	V	*9992*	Costa Rica *10759*
R	*Heliconia dasyantha* Koch & Bouche *9987*		
	R	*8679*	French Guiana *9987*
	R	*8679*	Suriname *9987*
V	*Heliconia farinosa* Raddi. *17079*		
	V	*17079*	Brazil - Rio de Janeiro *17079*
V	*Heliconia fluminensis* L. Emygdio & E. Santos. *17079*		
	V	*17079*	Brazil - Rio de Janeiro *17079*
V	*Heliconia golfodulcensis* Daniels & Stiles *10760*		
	V	*9992*	Costa Rica *10760*
R	*Heliconia ignescens* Daniels & Stiles *10760*		
	R	*11125*	Costa Rica *10760*
	R	*11125*	Panama *10760*
V	*Heliconia lacletteana* L. Emygdio & Santos *17079*		
	V	*17079*	Brazil - Espirito Santo *17079*
	V	*17079*	Brazil - Rio de Janeiro (Município de Rio Bonito, Braçana, Fazenda das Cachoeiras) *17079*
R	*Heliconia lankesteri* Standley var. *rubra* Daniels & Stiles *10760*		
	R	*11125*	Costa Rica *10760*
	R	*11125*	Panama *10760*
R	*Heliconia lennartiana* Kress *9484*		
	R	*9992*	Panama *9484*
V	*Heliconia lindsayana* Kress *9484*		
	V	*9992*	Panama *9484*
R	*Heliconia lophocarpa* Daniels & Stiles *10760*		
	R	*11125*	Costa Rica *10760*
	R	*11125*	Panama *10760*
V	*Heliconia lutea* Kress *9484*		
	V	*9992*	Panama *9484*
E	*Heliconia maculata* Kress *20883, 10759*		
	R	*9992*	Panama *20883*
E	*Heliconia magnifica* Kress *20883, 10759*		
	V	*9992*	Panama *20883*
E	*Heliconia necrobracteata* Kress *20883, 10759*		
	V	*9992*	Panama *20883*
R	*Heliconia nutans* Woodson *10759*		
	R	*11125*	Costa Rica *10759*
	R	*11125*	Panama *10759*
R	*Heliconia osaensis* Cuf. *10760*		
	R	*11125*	Costa Rica *10760*
	R	*11125*	Panama *10760*
R	*Heliconia pogonantha* Cuf. var. *pubescens* Daniels & Stiles *10759*		
	R	*9992*	Costa Rica *10759*
V	*Heliconia pogonantha* Kress var. *veraguasensis* Kress *20883, 10759*		
	V	*9992*	Panama *20883*
E	*Heliconia ramonensis* Kress var. *glabra* Kress *20883, 10759*		
	V	*9992*	Panama *20883*
E	*Heliconia ramonensis* Kress var. *lanuginosa* Kress *20883, 10759*		
	V	*9992*	Panama *20883*
R	*Heliconia ramonensis* Daniels & Stiles var. *ramonensis* *10759*		
	R	*9992*	Costa Rica *10759*
V	*Heliconia ramonensis* Kress var. *xanthotricha* Kress *20883, 10759*		
	V	*9992*	Panama *20883*
V	*Heliconia rodriguezii* Stiles *11125*		
	V	*9992*	Costa Rica *11125*
V	*Heliconia sampaioana* L. Emygdio *17079*		
	V	*17079*	Brazil - Rio de Janeiro (Tijuca & Teresópolis) *17079*
V	*Heliconia secunda* R.R. Smith var. *viridiflora* Daniels & Stiles *10759*		
	V	*11125*	Costa Rica *10759*
	V	*11125*	Nicaragua *10759*

E	*Heliconia sessilis* Kress 20883			
	I	20883	Panama	20883
R	*Heliconia stilesii* Kress 10747			
	V	11125	Costa Rica	10747
	R	11125	Panama	10747
V	*Heliconia swartziana* Roem. & Schult. 20883			
	V	20883	Jamaica	20883
E	*Heliconia tacarcuna* L. Andersson 20883			
	I	20883	Panama	20883
R	*Heliconia talamanacana* Daniels & Stiles 10759			
	R	11125	Costa Rica	10759
	R	11125	Panama	10759
V	*Heliconia thomasiana* Kress 9484			
	V	9992	Panama	9484
E	*Heliconia umbrophila* Daniels & Stiles 10760			
	E	9992	Costa Rica	10760
R	*Heliconia vulcanicola* Stiles 11547			
	R	9992	Costa Rica	11547
E	*Heliconia xanthovillosa* Kress 20883, 10759			
	R	9992	Panama	20883
R	*Heliconia zebrina* Plowman, Kress & Kennedy 11124			
	R	18200	Peru	11124

Hostaceae

Number of genera: 1
Number of species: 40
Recorded threatened species: 4 (10%)

China to Japan.

R	*Hosta alismifolia* Fujita 11164			
	R	11164	Japan	11164
E	*Hosta hypoleuca* Murata 11164			
	E	11164	Japan	11164
R	*Hosta pulchella* Fujita 11164			
	R	11164	Japan	11164
V	*Hosta tibai* F. Maek. 11164			
	V	11164	Japan	11164

Hyacinthaceae

Number of genera: 46
Number of species: 654
Recorded threatened species: 134 (20%)

Eurasia, Africa, North America.

R	*Albuca crinifolia* Baker 20604			
	R	20604	South Africa - Natal	20604
I	*Albuca scabra* U. & D.Müll.-Doblies ined. 20604			
	I	20604	South Africa - Cape Province	20604
E	*Amphisiphon stylosa* W.F.Barker 20604			
	E	20604	South Africa - Cape Province	20604
R	*Androsiphon capensis* Schlechter 20803			
	R	20803	South Africa - Cape Province	20803
V	*Bellevalia brevipedicellata* Turrill 20171			
	V	20730	Greece - Crete	20730
R	*Bellevalia cyrenaica* Maire & M. Weiller			
	R		Libya	
R	*Bellevalia forniculata* (Fomin) Deloney 12840			
	R	12840	Turkey	12840
E	*Bellevalia hackelii* Freyn 8000, 20171			
	E	20076	Portugal (south)	8000

R	*Bellevalia lipskyi* (Miscz.) E.Wulff 20171			
	R		former European USSR	
V	*Bellevalia modesta* Wendelbo 12840			
	V	12840	Turkey	12840
V	*Bellevalia pomelii* Maire 10487			
	V	14958	Algeria	10487
R	*Bellevalia rixii* Wendelbo 12840			
	R	12840	Turkey	12840
E	*Bellevalia salah-eidii* Tackh. & Boulos			
	E		Egypt	
	E		Libya	
R	*Bowiea gariepensis* Van Jaarsv. 20604			
	R	20604	Namibia	20604
	R	20604	South Africa - Cape Province	20604
V	*Camassia howellii* S.Watson 20850			
	V	20850	U.S. - Oregon	20850
V	*Camassia leichtlinii* (Baker) S.Wats. ssp. *suksdorfii* (Greenm.) Gould 20850, 10701			
	I	20850	Canada - British Columbia	20850
	I	20850	U.S. - California	20850
	I	20850	U.S. - Oregon	20850
	I	20850	U.S. - Washington	20850
R	*Chionodoxa forbesii* Baker 12840			
	R	19873	Turkey	12840
E	*Chionodoxa lochiae* Meikle 14230			
	E	19164	Cyprus	14230
V	*Chionodoxa luciliae* Boiss. 12840			
	V	12840	Turkey	12840
V	*Chionodoxa sardensis* Whittall ex Barr & Sugden 12840			
	V	12840	Turkey	12840
V	*Chlorogalum grandiflorum* Hoover 20850			
	V	20850	U.S. - California	20850
E	*Chlorogalum pomeridianum* Hoover var. *minus* Hoover 20850			
	E	20850	U.S. - California	20850
E	*Chlorogalum purpureum* Brandeg. 20850			
	I	20850	U.S. - California	20850
E	*Chlorogalum purpureum* Brandegee var. *purpureum* 20850			
	E	20850	U.S. - California	20850
E	*Chlorogalum purpureum* Brandegee var. *reductum* Hoover 20850			
	E	20850	U.S. - California	20850
V	*Daubenya aurea* Lindl. 20604			
	V	20604	South Africa - Cape Province	20604
Ex	*Dipcadi concanense* (Dalz.) Baker 11494			
	Ex	11494	India (south)	11494
E	*Dipcadi maharashtrensis* Deb & Dasgupta 11494			
	E	11494	India - Maharashtra (Panchgani plateau) 11494		
I	*Dipcadi minor* Hook.f. 11494			
	I	11494	India - Maharashtra (Deccan Plateau) 11494		
I	*Dipcadi montanum* (Dalz.) Baker var. *madrasicum* (Barnes) Deb & Das Gupta			
	I		India - Tamil Nadu	
Ex	*Dipcadi reidii* Deb & Dasgupta 11494			
	Ex	11494	India (W. Himalaya)	11494
V	*Dipcadi saxorum* Blatter 11494			
	V	11494	India - Maharashtra (Boriveli NP)	11494

I *Dipcadi turkestanicum* Vved. *5942*
  I *5942* Tajikistan (border with Uzbekistan) *5942*
  I *5942* Uzbekistan (border with Tajikistan) *5942*

R *Drimia minor* (A.V.Duthie) Jessop *20604*
  R *20604* South Africa - Cape Province *20604*

R *Drimia razii* Ansari *13883*
  R *13883* India - Maharashtra *13883*

R *Eucomis vandermerwei* I.Verd. *20604*
  R *20604* South Africa - Orange Free State *20604*
  R *20604* South Africa - Transvaal *20604*

E *Hastingsia atropurpurea* Becking *20850*
  E *20850* U.S. - Oregon *20850*

V *Hastingsia bracteosa* S.Watson *20850*
  V *20850* U.S. - Oregon *20850*

R *Hesperocallis undulata* Gray *20850*
  I *20850* U.S. - Arizona *20850*
  I *20850* U.S. - California *20850*
  I *20850* U.S. - Nevada *20850*

R *Hyacinthella acutiloba* K. Pearson & Wendolbo *12840*
  R *12840* Turkey *12840*

R *Hyacinthella atchleyi* (A.K.Jacks. & Turrill)
    Feinbrun *8000, 20171*
  R *14155* Greece *8000*

R *Hyacinthella campanulata* K. Persson & Wendolbo *12840*
  R *12840* Turkey *12840*

R *Hyacinthella dalmatica* (Baker) Chouard *20171*
  V *21091* Bosnia & Herzegovina *21091*
  R   (former) Yugoslavia

R *Hyacinthella glabrescens* (Boiss.) K. Persson & Wendolbo *12840*
  R *12840* Turkey *12840*

R *Hyacinthella hispida* (J. Gay) Chouard *12840*
  R *12840* Turkey *12840*

R *Hyacinthella micrantha* (Boiss.) Chouard *12840*
  R *12840* Turkey *12840*

I *Hyacinthella pallasiana* (Steven) Losinsk. *8000, 20171*
  I   former European USSR *8000*

R *Hyacinthella siirtensis* Matthew *12840*
  R *12840* Turkey *12840*

I *Hyacinthella transcaspica* (Litv.) Chouard *5942*
  I *5942* Turkmenistan *5942*

V *Hyacinthoides vicentina* (Hoffmanns. & Link) Rothm. *8000, 20171*
  V *20076* Portugal (south west) *8000*

V *Hyacinthus orientalis* L. ssp. *chionophilus* Wendelbo *12840*
  V *12840* Turkey *12840*

R *Lachenalia ameliae* W.F.Barker *20604*
  R *20604* South Africa - Cape Province *20604*

R *Lachenalia angelica* W.F.Barker *20604*
  R *20604* South Africa - Cape Province *20604*

R *Lachenalia barkeriana* U.Müll.-Doblies, B.Nord. & D.Müll.-Doblies *20604*
  R *20604* South Africa - Cape Province *20604*

R *Lachenalia buchubergensis* Dinter *20604*
  R *20604* Namibia *20604*
  R *20604* South Africa - Cape Province *20604*

I *Lachenalia campanulata* Baker *20604*
  I *20604* South Africa - Cape Province *20604*

R *Lachenalia concordiana* Schltr. ex W.F.Barker *20604*
  R *20604* South Africa - Cape Province *20604*

I *Lachenalia convallarioides* Baker *20604*
  I *20604* South Africa - Cape Province *20604*

R *Lachenalia dasybotrya* Diels *20604*
  R *20604* South Africa - Cape Province *20604*

R *Lachenalia dehoopensis* W.F.Barker *20604*
  R *20604* South Africa - Cape Province *20604*

V *Lachenalia duncanii* W.F.Barker *20604*
  V *20604* South Africa - Cape Province *20604*

R *Lachenalia glaucophylla* W.F.Barker *20604*
  R *20604* South Africa - Cape Province *20604*

I *Lachenalia haarlemensis* Fourc. *20604*
  I *20604* South Africa - Cape Province *20604*

R *Lachenalia kliprandensis* W.F.Barker *20604*
  R *20604* South Africa - Cape Province *20604*

R *Lachenalia macgregoriorum* W.F.Barker *20604*
  R *20604* South Africa - Cape Province *20604*

R *Lachenalia martinae* W.F.Barker *20604*
  R *20604* South Africa - Cape Province *20604*

E *Lachenalia mathewsii* W.F.Barker *20604, 3774*
  E *20604* South Africa - Cape Province *20604*

R *Lachenalia maximiliani* Schltr. ex W.F.Barker *20604*
  R *20604* South Africa - Cape Province *20604*

E *Lachenalia minima* W.F.Barker *20604*
  E *20604* South Africa - Cape Province *20604*

E *Lachenalia moniliformis* W.F.Barker *20604*
  E *20604* South Africa - Cape Province *20604*

R *Lachenalia nordenstamii* W.F.Barker *20604*
  R *20604* Namibia *20604*
  R *20604* South Africa - Cape Province *20604*

I *Lachenalia physocaulos* W.F.Barker *20604*
  I *20604* South Africa - Cape Province *20604*

E *Lachenalia polyphylla* Baker *20604, 17789*
  E *20604* South Africa - Cape Province (Tulbagh district) *20604*

R *Lachenalia polypodantha* Schltr. ex W.F.Barker *20604*
  R *20604* South Africa - Cape Province *20604*

E *Lachenalia purpureo-caerulea* Jacq. *20604*
  E *20604* South Africa - Cape Province *20604*

I *Lachenalia rhodantha* Baker *20604*
  I *20604* South Africa - Cape Province *20604*

R *Lachenalia schelpei* W.F.Barker *20604*
  R *20604* South Africa - Cape Province *20604*

R *Lachenalia thomasiae* W.F.Barker & G.D.Duncan *20604*
  R *20604* South Africa - Cape Province *20604*

R *Lachenalia verticillata* W.F.Barker *20604*
  R *20604* South Africa - Cape Province *20604*

E *Lachenalia viridiflora* W.F.Barker *20604*
  E *20604* South Africa - Cape Province *20604*

R *Ledebouria cremnophila* S.Venter ined. *20604*
  R *20604* South Africa - Transvaal *20604*

E *Leopoldia albiflora* Tackh. & Boulos
  E   Egypt

R *Leopoldia bicolor* (Boiss.) Eig & Feinbrun
  R   Egypt

V *Leopoldia gussonei* Parl. *19997*
  V *19997* Italy - Sicily (southern) *19997*

E **Leopoldia longistyla** Tackh. & Boulos
    E   Egypt

R **Leopoldia salah-eidii** Tackh. & Boulos
    R   Egypt

R **Muscari dionysicum** Rech.f. *20171*
    R   Greece

V **Muscari discolor** Boiss. & Hausskn. *12840*
    V   *12840* Turkey *12840*

R **Muscari latifolium** Kirk *12840*
    R   *12840* Turkey *12840*

R **Muscari microstomum** Davis & Stuart *12840*
    R   *12840* Turkey *12840*

V **Muscari muscarimi** Medik. *12840, 20171*
    V   *12840* Turkey *12840*

R **Muscari sandrasicum** Karlen *12840*
    R   *12840* Turkey *12840*

R **Neopatersonia namaquensis** G.J.Lewis *20604*
    R   *20604* South Africa - Cape Province *20604*

R **Ornithogalum amphibolum** Zahar. *5942, 20171*
    R   Bulgaria *8000*
    V   *19949* Romania *8000*
    I   *5942* Moldova *5942*

I **Ornithogalum arcuatum** Velen. *5942, 20171*
    I   *5942* Azerbaijan *5942*

R **Ornithogalum atticum** Boiss. & Heldr. *20171*
    R   Greece

R **Ornithogalum costatum** Zahar. *20171*
    R   Greece

R **Ornithogalum deltoideum** Baker *20604*
    R   *20604* Namibia *20604*
    R   *20604* South Africa - Cape Province *20604*

R **Ornithogalum diluculum** Oberm. *20604*
    R   *20604* South Africa - Cape Province *20604*

R **Ornithogalum esterhuyseniae** Oberm. *20604*
    R   *20604* South Africa - Cape Province *20604*

R **Ornithogalum exaratum** Zahar. *20171*
    R   Greece

R **Ornithogalum geniculatum** Oberm. *20604*
    R   *20604* Namibia *20604*
    R   *20604* South Africa - Cape Province *20604*

R **Ornithogalum glandulosum** Oberm. *20604*
    R   *20604* Namibia *20604*
    R   *20604* South Africa - Cape Province *20604*

V **Ornithogalum hallii** Oberm. *20604*
    V   *20604* South Africa - Cape Province *20604*

I **Ornithogalum hyrcanum** Grossh. *5942*
    I   *5942* Azerbaijan *5942*

R **Ornithogalum inclusum** Leight. *20604*
    R   *20604* South Africa - Cape Province *20604*

R **Ornithogalum naviculum** W.F.Barker *20604*
    R   *20604* South Africa - Cape Province *20604*

R **Ornithogalum nivale** Boiss. *12840*
    R   *12840* Turkey *12840*

R **Ornithogalum oreoides** Zahar. *8000, 20171*
    R   Bulgaria *8000*
    I   *19417* Romania *8000*
    I   *5942* Moldova *5942*

R **Ornithogalum orthophyllum** Ten. ssp. *acuminatum* (Schur) Zahar. *17823, 20171*
    R   *19949* Romania *20635*

V **Ornithogalum orthophyllum** Ten. ssp. *psammophilum* (Zahar.) Zahar. *8000, 20171*
    V   *19949* Romania (eastern) *8000*

R **Ornithogalum pilosum** L.f. ssp. *pullatum* (Leight.) Oberm. *20604*
    R   *20604* South Africa - Cape Province *20604*

E **Ornithogalum rupestre** L.f. *20604*
    E   *20604* South Africa - Cape Province *20604*

R **Ornithogalum sardienii** Van Jaarsv. *20604*
    R   *20604* South Africa - Cape Province *20604*

I **Ornithogalum secundum** Jacq.
    I   Southern Africa

R **Ornithogalum sorgerae** H. Wittmann *12840*
    R   *12840* Turkey *12840*

I **Ornithogalum thermophilum** Leight. *20604*
    I   *20604* South Africa - Cape Province *20604*

R **Ornithogalum unifoliatum** (G.D.Rowley) Oberm. *20604*
    R   *20604* South Africa - Cape Province *20604*

R **Ornithogalum zebrinum** (Baker) Oberm. *20604*
    R   *20604* South Africa - Cape Province *20604*

I **Rhadamanthus urantherus** R.A.Dyer *20604*
    I   *20604* South Africa - Cape Province *20604*

R **Schoenolirion wrightii** Sherman *20850*
    I   *20850* U.S. - Alabama *20850*
    V   *20850* U.S. - Arkansas *20850*
    V   *20850* U.S. - Texas *20850*

R **Scilla atropatana** Grossh.
    R   former USSR *6930*

V **Scilla beirana** Samp. *8000, 20171*
    V   *20076* Portugal (Beira Alta) *8000*

V **Scilla corsica** Boullu *20528*
    V   *20528* France - Corsica *20528*
    V   *20528* Italy - Sardinia *20528*

R **Scilla cupanii** Guss. *18264, 20171*
    R   *18264* Italy - Sicily *18264*

R **Scilla hughii** Tineo ex Guss. *18264, 20171*
    R   *18264* Italy (Campania) *18264*
    R   *18264* Italy - Sicily *18264*

R **Scilla latifolia** Willd.
    I   Morocco
    R   Spain - Canary Is.

R **Scilla lazulina** Wild *7754*
    R   Zimbabwe *7754*

R **Scilla leepii** Speta *12840*
    R   *12840* Turkey *12840*

R **Scilla litardierei** Breistr. *20171*
    V   *21091* Bosnia & Herzegovina *21091*
    V   *13662* Slovenia (central) *13662*

V **Scilla maderensis** Menezes *17891*
    E   Portugal - Madeira *17891*
    V   Portugal - Salvage Is.

R **Scilla messeniaca** Boiss. *20171*
    R   *20731* Greece (Peloponnisos) *20731*

E **Scilla morrisii** Meikle *14230*
    E   *19164* Cyprus *14230*

R **Scilla odorata** Link *8000, 20171*
    V   *20076* Portugal (south) *8000*
    R   Spain (south) *8000*

R **Scilla paui** Lacaita *11496*
    R   *11496* Spain *11496*

R   *Scilla plumbea* Lindl. *20604*
     R   *20604*   South Africa - Cape Province *20604*

R   *Scilla reverchonii* Degen & Hervier *20171*
     R   Spain

E   *Scilla viridis* Blatter & Hallberg *11494*
     E   *11494*   India - Maharashtra *11494*

I   *Urginea minor* A.V.Duthie *20604*
     I   *20604*   South Africa - Cape Province *20604*

Ex   *Urginea polyphylla* Hook.f. *11494*
     Ex   *11494*   India (Deccan Plateau) *11494*

Hydatellaceae

Number of genera: 2
Number of species: 7
Recorded threatened species: 2   (28%)

Australia, New Zealand, Tasmania.

R   *Hydatella filamentosa* (Rodway) W.M.Curtis *20681*
     R   *20681*   Australia - Tasmania *20681*

V   *Hydatella inconspicua* (Cheeseman) Cheeseman *86*
     V   *19305*   New Zealand - North Is. *19305*

Ex   *Hydatella leptogyne* Diels *20681, 14223*
     Ex   *20681*   Australia - Western Australia *20681*

Hydrocharitaceae

Number of genera: 15
Number of species: 100
Recorded threatened species: 14   (14%)

Cosmopolitan.

Ex/E   *Elodea schweinitzii* (Planch.) Caspary *20850, 14662*
     Ex/E   *20850*   U.S. - New York *20850*
     Ex   *20850*   U.S. - Pennsylvania *20850*

V   *Halophila johnsonii* Eiseman *20850*
     V   *20850*   U.S. - Florida *20850*

I   *Hydrilla polysperma* Blatter
     I   India - Rajasthan (Mt Abu)

V   *Hydrocharis dubia* (Blume) Backer *20681*
     V   *20681*   Australia - Queensland *20681*

R   *Najas affinis* Rendle *7926*
     R   Senegal *7926*

R   *Najas ancistocarpa* A. Br. *11164*
     R   *11164*   Japan *11164*

E   *Najas filifolia* Haynes *20850*
     E   *20850*   U.S. - Florida *20850*
     E   *20850*   U.S. - Georgia *20850*
     I   *20850*   U.S. - Mississippi *20850*

R   *Najas japonica* Nakai *11164*
     R   *11164*   Japan *11164*

R   *Najas tenuicaulis* Miki *11164*
     R   *11164*   Japan *11164*

I   *Najas tenuissima* (A.Braun) Magnus *20673, 20171*
     V   *20673*   Finland *20673*
     I   *5942*   Russia (E.Europe) - Central *5942*
     I   *5942*   Russia (E.Europe) - Northwest *5942*
     I   *5942*   Estonia *5942*

V   *Najas yezoensis* Miyabe *11164*
     V   *11164*   Japan *11164*

V   *Ottelia acuminata* (Gagnepain) Dandy *17617*
     V   *17617*   China - Guangdong (Wengchang) *11139*
     V   *17617*   China - Hainan Is. *11139*
     V   *17617*   China - Guangxi (Jingxi) *11139*

     V   *17617*   China - Guizhou *11139*
     V   *17617*   China - Sichuan (Bushi) *11139*
     V   *17617*   China - Yunnan *11139*

R   *Vallisneria gracilis* F.M.Bailey *20681*
     R   *20681*   Australia - Queensland *20681*

R   *Vallisneria higoensis* (Miki) Ohwi *11164*
     R   *11164*   Japan *11164*

Hypoxidaceae

Number of genera: 9
Number of species: 142
Recorded threatened species: 6   (4%)

New World, Old World tropics and South Africa.

R   *Curculigo sechellensis* Bojer *14296*
     R   *19182*   Seychelles *14296*

E   *Hypoxidia maheensis* F. Friedmann *14296*
     E   *14981*   Seychelles (granitic) *14296*

V   *Hypoxidia rhizophylla* (Baker) F. Friedmann *14296*
     V   *19182*   Seychelles (granitic) *14296*

I   *Pauridia longituba* M.F.Thomps. *20604*
     I   *20604*   South Africa - Cape Province *20604*

R   *Spiloxene maximilianii* (Schltr.) Garside *20604*
     R   *20604*   South Africa - Cape Province *20604*

I   *Spiloxene minuta* (L.) Fourc. *20604*
     I   *20604*   South Africa - Cape Province *20604*

Iridaceae

Number of genera: 80
Number of species: 1,500
Recorded threatened species: 484   (32%)

Cosmopolitan, especially South Africa.

V   *Ainea conzattii* (R. Foster) Ravenna *10540*
     V   *19850*   Mexico *10540*

E   *Aristea biflora* Weim. *20604*
     E   *20604*   South Africa - Cape Province *20604*

E   *Aristea lugens* (L.f.) Horton ex Steud. *20604, 10260*
     E   *20604*   South Africa - Cape Province *20604*

V   *Aristea palustris* Schltr. *20604*
     V   *20604*   South Africa - Cape Province *20604*

V   *Aristea platycaulis* Baker *20604*
     V   *20604*   South Africa - Cape Province *20604*

R   *Aristea singularis* Weim. *20604*
     R   *20604*   South Africa - Cape Province *20604*

R   *Babiana auriculata* G.J.Lewis *20604*
     R   *20604*   South Africa - Cape Province *20604*

R   *Babiana cedarbergensis* G.J.Lewis *20604*
     R   *20604*   South Africa - Cape Province *20604*

R   *Babiana geniculata* G.J.Lewis *20604*
     R   *20604*   South Africa - Cape Province *20604*

I   *Babiana hypogea* Burch. var. *longituba* G.J.Lewis *20604*
     I   *20604*   South Africa - Transvaal *20604*

I   *Babiana klaverensis* G.J.Lewis *20604*
     I   *20604*   South Africa - Cape Province *20604*

R   *Babiana leipoldtii* G.J.Lewis *20604*
     R   *20604*   South Africa - Cape Province *20604*

R   *Babiana lewisiana* B.Nord. *20604*
     R   *20604*   South Africa - Cape Province *20604*

R **Babiana lobata** G.J.Lewis *20604*
    R   *20604* South Africa - Cape Province *20604*

V **Babiana pygmaea** (Burm.f.) N.E.Br. *20604*
    V   *20604* South Africa - Cape Province *20604*

R **Babiana salteri** G.J.Lewis *20604*
    R   *20604* South Africa - Cape Province *20604*

R **Babiana socotrana** Hook. f. *15534*
    R   *15534* Yemen - Socotra *15534*

R **Babiana stenomera** Schltr. *20604*
    R   *20604* South Africa - Cape Province *20604*

R **Babiana striata** (Jacq.) G.J.Lewis var. *planifolia* G.J.Lewis *20604*
    R   *20604* South Africa - Cape Province *20604*

R **Babiana virginea** Goldblatt *20604*
    R   *20604* South Africa - Cape Province *20604*

R **Bobartia gladiata** (L.f.) Ker ssp. *major* (Lewis) Strid *20604*
    R   *20604* South Africa - Cape Province *20604*

R **Bobartia lilacina** G.J.Lewis *20604*
    R   *20604* South Africa - Cape Province *20604*

R **Bobartia macrospatha** Baker ssp. *anceps* (Baker) Strid *20604*
    R   *20604* South Africa - Cape Province *20604*

R **Bobartia orientalis** J.B.Gillett ssp. *occidentalis* Strid *20604*
    R   *20604* South Africa - Cape Province *20604*

R **Bobartia paniculata** G.J.Lewis *20604*
    R   *20604* South Africa - Cape Province *20604*

E **Bobartia parva** J.B.Gillett *20604*
    E   *20604* South Africa - Cape Province *20604*

R **Bobartia robusta** Baker *20604*
    R   *20604* South Africa - Cape Province *20604*

E **Calydorea azurea** Klatt *10540*
    E   *10540* Argentina *10540*

V **Calydorea coelestina** (Bartr.) Goldblatt & Henrich *20850, 19766*
    V   *20850* U.S. - Florida *20850*

E **Calydorea pallens** Griseb. *16336*
    E   *16336* Argentina *16336*
    E   *20176* Argentina - Jujuy *20176*
    E   *20176* Argentina - Tucuman *20176*

E **Calydorea xiphioides** (Poeppig) Espin. *11748*
    E   *10540* Chile *11748*

E **Cardenanthus venturii** R. Foster *16336*
    E   *16336* Argentina *16336*
    E   *20176* Argentina - Jujuy *20176*
    E   *20176* Argentina - Tucuman *20176*

E **Catila amabilis** Ravenna *10540*
    E   *10540* Argentina *10540*
    E   *10540* Uruguay *10540*

I **Chasmanthe bicolor** (Gasp. ex Ten.) N.E.Br. *20604*
    I   *20604* South Africa - Cape Province *20604*

R **Chasmanthe floribunda** (Salisb.) N.E.Br. var. *duckittii* G.J.Lewis ex L.Bolus *20604*
    R   *20604* South Africa - Cape Province *20604*

E **Cipura rupicola** Goldblatt & Henrich *20883*
    I   *20883* Venezuela *20883*

R **Crocosmia fucata** (Herb.) M.P.de Vos *20604*
    R   *20604* South Africa - Cape Province *20604*

I **Crocosmia masonorum** (L.Bolus) N.E.Br. *20604*
    I   *20604* South Africa - Cape Province *20604*

R **Crocosmia pearsei** Oberm. *20604*
    R   *20604* South Africa - Natal *20604*

V **Crocus abatensis** T. Baytop & Mathew *12840*
    V   *14155* Turkey (L. Abant in Bolu) *12840*

R **Crocus adanensis** T. Baytop & Mathew *12840*
    R   *12840* Turkey *12840*

R **Crocus aerius** Herbert *12840*
    R   *12840* Turkey *12840*

I **Crocus angustifolius** Weston *5942, 20171*
    I   *5942* Moldova *5942*
    I   *5942* Ukraine *5942*

R **Crocus asumaniae** Mathew *12840*
    R   *12840* Turkey *12840*

R **Crocus baytopiorum** Mathew *12840*
    R   *12840* Turkey *12840*

R **Crocus biflorus** Miller ssp. *artvinensis* (J. Phill.) Mathew *12840*
    R   *12840* Turkey *12840*

V **Crocus boulosii** Greuter
    V   Libya

R **Crocus cancellatus** Herbert ssp. *cancellatus* *12840*
    R   *12840* Turkey *12840*

R **Crocus cancellatus** Herbert ssp. *lycius* Mathew *12840*
    R   *12840* Turkey *12840*

R **Crocus cancellatus** Herbert ssp. *pamphylicus* Mathew *12840*
    R   *12840* Turkey *12840*

E **Crocus cyprius** Boiss. & Kotschy *14230*
    E   *19164* Cyprus *14230*

I **Crocus discolor** G.Reuss *8000, 20171*
    I   *19321* Slovakia *19321*

R **Crocus etruscus** Parl. *8000, 20171*
    R   *19174* Italy (Toscana & Emilia-Romagna) *19997*

R **Crocus flavus** Meston ssp. *dissectus* T. Baytop & Mathew *12840*
    R   *12840* Turkey *12840*

R **Crocus gargaricus** Herbert *12840*
    R   *12840* Turkey *12840*

R **Crocus goulimyi** Turrill *20171*
    R   Greece

E **Crocus hartmannianus** Holmboe *14230*
    E   *19164* Cyprus *14230*

I **Crocus imperati** Ten. *20171*
    I   Italy

R **Crocus karduchorum** Kotschy ex Maw *12840*
    R   *12840* Turkey *12840*

R **Crocus kotschyanus** C. Koch. ssp. *cappadocicus* Mathew *12840*
    R   *12840* Turkey *12840*

R **Crocus kotschyanus** C. Koch. ssp. *hakkariensis* Mathew *12840*
    R   *12840* Turkey *12840*

R **Crocus leichtlinii** (D. Dewar) Bowles *12840*
    R   *12840* Turkey *12840*

R **Crocus olivieri** Gay ssp. *balansae* (Gay ex Baker) Mathew

R		Greece

V *Crocus olivieri* Gay ssp. *istanbulensis* Mathew *12840*
  V *12840* Turkey *12840*

R *Crocus oreocreticus* B.L.Burtt *20171*
  R *20730* Greece - Crete *20730*

V *Crocus pestalozzae* Boiss. *12840, 20171*
  V *19873* Turkey *12840*

R *Crocus reticulatus* Steven ex Adams ssp. *hittiticus* (T. Baytop & Mathew) Mathew *12840*
  R *12840* Turkey *12840*

V *Crocus robertianus* C.D.Brickell *17781, 20171*
  V *17781* Greece (north - Pindhos Mountains) *17781*

R *Crocus sieheanus* Barr ex Burtt *12840*
  R *12840* Turkey *12840*

R *Crocus speciosus* Bieb. ssp. *ilgazensis* Mathew *12840*
  R *12840* Turkey *12840*

R *Crocus speciosus* Bieb. ssp. *xantholaimos* Mathew *12840*
  R *12840* Turkey *12840*

E *Cypella aquatilis* Ravenna *10540*
  E *10540* Brazil - Parana *10540*

E *Cypella armosa* Ravenna *10540*
  E *10540* Argentina *10540*
  E *10540* Paraguay *10540*

E *Cypella craterantha* Ravenna *18200*
  E *10540* Peru *18200*

E *Cypella crenata* Ravenna *10540*
  E *10540* Brazil - Minas Gerais *10540*

E *Cypella curuzupensis* Ravenna *10540*
  E *10540* Paraguay *10540*

E *Cypella discolor* Ravenna *10540*
  E *10540* Brazil - Rio Grande do Sul *10540*

E *Cypella fucata* Ravenna *10540*
  E *10540* Brazil - Rio Grande do Sul *10540*
  E *10540* Brazil - Santa Catarina *10540*
  E *10540* Uruguay (Depto. Cerro Largo) *10540*

E *Cypella hauthali* (Kuntze) R. Foster *10540*
  E *10540* Argentina *10540*

E *Cypella hauthali* (Kuntze) R. Foster ssp. *opalina* Ravenna *10540*
  E *10540* Argentina *10540*

E *Cypella herberti* (Lindley) Herbert *10540*
  E *10540* Argentina *10540*
  E *10540* Brazil *10540*
  E *10540* Uruguay *10540*

E *Cypella herberti* (Lindley) Herbert ssp. *brevicristata* Ravenna *10540*
  E *10540* Argentina *10540*
  E *10540* Uruguay *10540*

E *Cypella herberti* (Lindley) Herbert ssp. *wolffhuegelii* (Hauman) Ravenna *10540*
  E *10540* Argentina *10540*

E *Cypella laeta* Ravenna *10540*
  E *10540* Argentina *10540*

E *Cypella lapidosa* Ravenna *10540*
  E *10540* Argentina *10540*

E *Cypella laxa* Ravenna *10540*
  E *10540* Brazil - Parana *10540*

  E *10540* Brazil - Santa Catarina *10540*

E *Cypella oreophila* Speg. *10540*
  E *10540* Argentina *10540*

E *Cypella osteniana* Beauv. *10540*
  E *10540* Peru (Lavalleja) *10540*

E *Cypella pabstiana* Ravenna *10540*
  E *10540* Brazil - Parana *10540*

E *Cypella pusilla* (Link, Klotzsch & Otto) Bentham & Hook.f. *10540*
  E *10540* Brazil - Rio Grande do Sul (Porto Alegre) *10540*

R *Dierama dubium* N.E.Br. *20604*
  R *20604* South Africa - Natal *20604*

Ex/E *Dierama elatum* N.E.Br. *20604, 18023*
  Ex *20604* Swaziland *20604*

E *Dierama erectum* Hilliard *20604*
  E *20604* South Africa - Natal *20604*

R *Dierama luteoalbidum* I.Verd. *20604*
  R *20604* South Africa - Natal *20604*

R *Dierama nixonianum* Hilliard *20604*
  R *20604* South Africa - Natal *20604*

V *Dierama pallidum* Hilliard *20604*
  V *20604* South Africa - Natal *20604*

V *Dierama pulcherrimum* (Hook.f.) Baker *20604*
  V *20604* South Africa - Cape Province *20604*

R *Dierama pumilum* N.E.Br. *20604*
  R *20604* South Africa - Natal *20604*

R *Dierama tysonii* N.E.Br. *20604*
  R *20604* South Africa - Natal *20604*

R *Dietes bicolor* (Steud.) Sweet ex Klatt *20604*
  R *20604* South Africa - Cape Province *20604*

R *Dietes robinsoniana* (C. Moore & F. Muell.) Klatt
  R *14225* Australia - NSW - Lord Howe Is. *14225*

E *Ennealophus fimbriatus* Ravenna *11130*
  E *10540* Argentina *11130*

R *Ferraria brevifolia* G.J.Lewis *20604*
  R *20604* South Africa - Cape Province *20604*

R *Ferraria crispa* Burm. ssp. *nortieri* M.P.De Vos *20604*
  R *20604* South Africa - Cape Province *20604*

R *Ferraria densepunctulata* M.P.de Vos *20604*
  R *20604* South Africa - Cape Province *20604*

I *Ferraria divaricata* Sweet ssp. *arenosa* De Vos
  I   Southern Africa

R *Ferraria foliosa* G.J.Lewis *20604*
  R *20604* South Africa - Cape Province *20604*

R *Ferraria kamiesbergensis* M.P.de Vos *20604*
  R *20604* South Africa - Cape Province *20604*

V *Fosteria oaxacana* Molseed *9733*
  V *19850* Mexico *9733*

R *Freesia elimensis* L.Bolus *20604*
  R *20604* South Africa - Cape Province *20604*

R *Freesia sparrmannii* (Thunb.) N.E.Br. *20604*
  R *20604* South Africa - Cape Province *20604*

V *Freesia speciosa* L.Bolus *20604*
  V *20604* South Africa - Cape Province *20604*

V *Freesia verrucosa* (Vogel) Goldblatt &

J.C.Manning *20604*
V   *20604* South Africa - Cape Province *20604*

E   *Galaxia alata* Goldblatt *20604*
E   *20604* South Africa - Cape Province *20604*

R   *Galaxia barnardii* Goldblatt *20604*
R   *20604* South Africa - Cape Province *20604*

R   *Galaxia fenestralis* Goldblatt & E.G.H.Oliv. *20604*
R   *20604* South Africa - Cape Province *20604*

E   *Galaxia grandiflora* Andrews *20604*
E   *20604* South Africa - Cape Province *20604*

R   *Galaxia kamiesmontana* Goldblatt *20604*
R   *20604* South Africa - Cape Province *20604*

R   *Galaxia variabilis* G.J.Lewis *20604*
R   *20604* South Africa - Cape Province *20604*

R   *Geissorhiza arenicola* Goldblatt *20604*
R   *20604* South Africa - Cape Province *20604*

R   *Geissorhiza brevituba* (G.J.Lewis) Goldblatt *20604*
R   *20604* South Africa - Cape Province *20604*

R   *Geissorhiza callista* Goldblatt *20604*
R   *20604* South Africa - Cape Province *20604*

R   *Geissorhiza corrugata* Klatt *20604*
R   *20604* South Africa - Cape Province *20604*

I   *Geissorhiza darlingensis* Goldblatt *20604*
I   *20604* South Africa - Cape Province *20604*

R   *Geissorhiza elsiae* Goldblatt *20604*
R   *20604* South Africa - Cape Province *20604*

V   *Geissorhiza eurystigma* L.Bolus *20604*
V   *20604* South Africa - Cape Province *20604*

R   *Geissorhiza furva* Ker Gawl. ex Baker *20604*
R   *20604* South Africa - Cape Province *20604*

V   *Geissorhiza geminata* E.Mey. ex Baker *20604*
V   *20604* South Africa - Cape Province *20604*

R   *Geissorhiza inaequalis* L.Bolus *20604*
R   *20604* South Africa - Cape Province *20604*

R   *Geissorhiza kamiesmontana* Goldblatt *20604*
R   *20604* South Africa - Cape Province *20604*

R   *Geissorhiza karooica* Goldblatt *20604*
R   *20604* South Africa - Cape Province *20604*

R   *Geissorhiza lithicola* Goldblatt *20604*
R   *20604* South Africa - Cape Province *20604*

E   *Geissorhiza louisabolusiae* R.C.Foster *20604*
E   *20604* South Africa - Cape Province *20604*

E   *Geissorhiza malmesburiensis* R.C.Foster *20604*
E   *20604* South Africa - Cape Province *20604*

V   *Geissorhiza mathewsii* L.Bolus *20604*
V   *20604* South Africa - Cape Province *20604*

I   *Geissorhiza monanthos* Eckl. *20604*
I   *20604* South Africa - Cape Province *20604*

R   *Geissorhiza namaquensis* W.F.Barker *20604*
R   *20604* South Africa - Cape Province *20604*

R   *Geissorhiza nigromontana* Goldblatt *20604*
R   *20604* South Africa - Cape Province *20604*

R   *Geissorhiza outeniquensis* Goldblatt *20604*
R   *20604* South Africa - Cape Province *20604*

R   *Geissorhiza pappei* Baker *20604*
R   *20604* South Africa - Cape Province *20604*

V   *Geissorhiza purpurascens* Goldblatt *20604*
V   *20604* South Africa - Cape Province *20604*

R   *Geissorhiza rupicola* Goldblatt & J.C.Manning *20604*
R   *20604* South Africa - Cape Province *20604*

R   *Geissorhiza silenoides* Goldblatt & J.C.Manning *20604*
R   *20604* South Africa - Cape Province *20604*

R   *Geissorhiza spiralis* (Burch.) M.P.de Vos ex Goldblatt *20604*
R   *20604* South Africa - Cape Province *20604*

V   *Geissorhiza splendidissima* Diels *20604*
V   *20604* South Africa - Cape Province *20604*

R   *Geissorhiza subrigida* L.Bolus *20604*
R   *20604* South Africa - Cape Province *20604*

R   *Geissorhiza uliginosa* Goldblatt & J.C.Manning *20604*
R   *20604* South Africa - Cape Province *20604*

E   *Gelasine azurea* Herbert *10540*
Ex   *10540* Argentina *10540*
E   *10540* Brazil *10540*
E   *10540* Uruguay *10540*

E   *Gelasine uruguaiensis* Ravenna ssp. *orientalis* Ravenna *10540*
E   *10540* Uruguay (Trienta & Tres) *10540*

E   *Gelasine uruguaiensis* Ravenna ssp. *uruguaiensis* *10540*
E   *10540* Uruguay (Durazno) *10540*

R   *Gladiolus acuminatus* F.Bolus *20604*
R   *20604* South Africa - Cape Province *20604*

E   *Gladiolus alatus* L. var. *algoensis* Herb. *6180, 20604*
E   *20604* South Africa - Cape Province *20604*

R   *Gladiolus appendiculatus* Lewis var. *appendiculatus* *20604*
R   *20604* South Africa - Transvaal *20604*

E   *Gladiolus appendiculatus* Lewis var. *longifolius* Lewis
E   *20039* Swaziland *20039*

E   *Gladiolus aureus* Baker *20604*
E   *20604* South Africa - Cape Province *20604*

R   *Gladiolus bellus* C.H. Wright *7757*
R   Malawi (Mlanje) *7757*

R   *Gladiolus bilineatus* G.J.Lewis *20604*
R   *20604* South Africa - Cape Province *20604*

R   *Gladiolus bonaespei* Goldblatt & M.P.de Vos *20604*
R   *20604* South Africa - Cape Province *20604*

R   *Gladiolus brevitubus* G.J.Lewis *20604*
R   *20604* South Africa - Cape Province *20604*

R   *Gladiolus buckerveldii* (L.Bolus) Goldblatt *20604*
R   *20604* South Africa - Cape Province *20604*

R   *Gladiolus calcaratus* G.J.Lewis *20604, 17458*
R   *20604* South Africa - Transvaal *20604*

R   *Gladiolus carinatus* Aiton ssp. *parviflorus* Lewis *20604*
R   *20604* South Africa - Cape Province *20604*

R   *Gladiolus carmineus* C.H.Wright *20604*
R   *20604* South Africa - Cape Province *20604*

R   *Gladiolus cataractarum* Oberm. *20604*
R   *20604* South Africa - Transvaal *20604*

E   *Gladiolus citrinus* Klatt *20604*
E   *20604* South Africa - Cape Province *20604*

R   *Gladiolus comptonii* G.J.Lewis *20604*
R   *20604* South Africa - Cape Province *20604*

R   *Gladiolus cruentus* T.Moore *20604*
    R   *20803*   South Africa - Natal *20604*

R   *Gladiolus debilis* Ker Gawl. var. *variegatus* G.J.Lewis *20604*
    R   *20604*   South Africa - Cape Province *20604*

R   *Gladiolus delpierrei* Goldblatt *20604*
    R   *20604*   South Africa - Cape Province *20604*

R   *Gladiolus deserticola* Goldblatt *20604*
    R   *20604*   South Africa - Cape Province *20604*

R   *Gladiolus dolomiticus* Oberm. *20604*
    R   *20604*   South Africa - Transvaal *20604*

R   *Gladiolus emiliae* L.Bolus *20604*
    R   *20604*   South Africa - Cape Province *20604*

R   *Gladiolus engysiphon* G.J.Lewis *20604*
    R   *20604*   South Africa - Cape Province *20604*

R   *Gladiolus exiguus* G.J.Lewis *20604, 17458*
    R   *20604*   South Africa - Transvaal *20604*

R   *Gladiolus exilis* G.J.Lewis *20604*
    R   *20604*   South Africa - Cape Province *20604*

Ex   *Gladiolus felicis* Mirek *17809*
    Ex   *20800*   Czech Republic *20800*
    Ex   *18216*   Poland (Carpathians) *17809*
    Ex   *20800*   Lithuania *20800*

R   *Gladiolus floribundus* Jacq. ssp. *miniatus* (Eckl.) Oberm. *20604*
    R   *20604*   South Africa - Cape Province *20604*

V   *Gladiolus fourcadei* (L.Bolus) Goldblatt & M.P.de Vos *20604*
    V   *20604*   South Africa - Cape Province *20604*

R   *Gladiolus gracilis* Jacq. var. *latifolius* Lewis *20604*
    R   *20604*   South Africa - Cape Province *20604*

R   *Gladiolus humilis* Stapf *12840*
    R   *12840*   Turkey *12840*

I   *Gladiolus huttonii* (N.E.Br.) Goldblatt & M.P.de Vos *20604*
    I   *20604*   South Africa - Cape Province *20604*

R   *Gladiolus jonquilliodorus* Eckl. ex Bolus & Wolley-Dod *20604*
    R   *20604*   South Africa - Cape Province *20604*

R   *Gladiolus kamiesbergensis* G.J.Lewis *20604*
    R   *20604*   South Africa - Cape Province *20604*

E   *Gladiolus lapeirousioides* Goldblatt *20604*
    E   *20604*   South Africa - Cape Province *20604*

R   *Gladiolus leptosiphon* F.Bolus *20604*
    R   *20604*   South Africa - Cape Province *20604*

R   *Gladiolus loteniensis* Hilliard & B.L.Burtt *20604*
    R   *20604*   South Africa - Natal *20604*

V   *Gladiolus macneilii* Oberm. *20604, 17458*
    V   *20604*   South Africa - Transvaal *20604*

R   *Gladiolus micranthus* Stapf *12840*
    R   *12840*   Turkey *12840*

R   *Gladiolus microcarpus* G.J.Lewis ssp. *italaensis* Oberm. *20604*
    V   *20604*   South Africa - Natal *20604*
    R   *20604*   South Africa - Transvaal *20604*

R   *Gladiolus monticola* G.J.Lewis *20604*
    R   *20604*   South Africa - Cape Province *20604*

V   *Gladiolus mostertiae* L.Bolus *20604*

    V   *20604*   South Africa - Cape Province *20604*

R   *Gladiolus nerineoides* G.J.Lewis *20604*
    R   *20604*   South Africa - Cape Province *20604*

V   *Gladiolus nigromontanus* Goldblatt *20604*
    V   *20604*   South Africa - Cape Province *20604*

R   *Gladiolus oppositiflorus* Herbert ssp. *oppositiflorus* *20604*
    R   *20604*   South Africa - Cape Province *20604*

R   *Gladiolus oreocharis* Schltr. *20604*
    R   *20604*   South Africa - Cape Province *20604*

R   *Gladiolus ornatus* Klatt *20604*
    R   *20604*   South Africa - Cape Province *20604*

V   *Gladiolus overbergensis* Goldblatt & M.P.de Vos *20604*
    V   *20604*   South Africa - Cape Province *20604*

I   *Gladiolus palustris* Gaudin *8000, 20171*
    I   Albania *8000*
    E   *19710*   Austria *8000*
    I   Bulgaria *8000*
    E   *2050*   Czech Republic (Bohemia) *19710*
    V   *20528*   France (east) *20528*
    E   *19710*   Germany *8000*
    E   *19710*   Hungary *8000*
    I   Italy *8000*
    E   *14229*   Liechtenstein *14229*
    E   *18216*   Poland *8000*
    I   Romania *8000*
    E   *19710*   Slovakia *19321*
    E   *18154*   Switzerland *8000*
    I   (former) Yugoslavia *8000*
    I   *5942*   Byelarus *5942*
    Ex   *18216*   Lithuania *17779*
    I   *5942*   Ukraine *5942*

R   *Gladiolus pole-evansii* I.Verd. *20604*
    R   *20604*   South Africa - Transvaal *20604*

R   *Gladiolus pritzelli* Diels var. *sufflavus* G.J.Lewis *20604*
    R   *20604*   South Africa - Cape Province *20604*

R   *Gladiolus punctulatus* Schrank var. *punctulatus* *20803*
    R   *20803*   South Africa - Cape Province *20803*

E   *Gladiolus quadrangulus* (D.Delaroche) Barnard *20604*
    E   *20604*   South Africa - Cape Province *20604*

I   *Gladiolus recurvus* L. *20604*
    I   *20604*   South Africa - Cape Province *20604*

R   *Gladiolus reuteri* Boiss. *20171*
    R   Spain

R   *Gladiolus robertsoniae* F.Bolus *20604*
    R   *20604*   South Africa - Orange Free State *20604*
    R   *20604*   South Africa - Transvaal *20604*

R   *Gladiolus robustus* Goldblatt *20604*
    R   *20604*   South Africa - Cape Province *20604*

R   *Gladiolus rogersii* Baker var. *vlokii* Goldblatt *20604*
    R   *20604*   South Africa - Cape Province *20604*

R   *Gladiolus salteri* G.J.Lewis *20604*
    R   *20604*   South Africa - Cape Province *20604*

R   *Gladiolus sempervirens* G.J.Lewis *20604*
    R   *20604*   South Africa - Cape Province *20604*

R   *Gladiolus stefaniae* Oberm. *20604*
    R   *20604*   South Africa - Cape Province *20604*

R   *Gladiolus stokoei* G.J.Lewis *20604*
    R   *20604*   South Africa - Cape Province *20604*

R   *Gladiolus symonsii* F.Bolus *20604*
     R   *20604*   South Africa - Natal *20604*

E   *Gladiolus vandermerwei* (L.Bolus) Goldblatt & M.P.de Vos *20604*
     E   *20604*   South Africa - Cape Province *20604*

R   *Gladiolus varius* Bolus f. var. *varius* *20604*
     I   *20039*   Swaziland *20039*
     R   *20604*   South Africa - Transvaal *20604*

R   *Gladiolus vigilans* Barnard *20604*
     R   *20604*   South Africa - Cape Province *20604*

R   *Gynandriris anomala* Goldblatt *20604*
     R   *20604*   South Africa - Cape Province *20604*

R   *Gynandriris hesperantha* Goldblatt *20604*
     R   *20604*   South Africa - Cape Province *20604*

E   *Herbertia amatorum* C.H. Wright *10540*
     E   *10540*   Brazil - Rio Grande do Sul *10540*

E   *Herbertia lahue* (Molina) Goldbl. *10540*
     E   *10540*   Chile *10540*

E   *Herbertia pulchella* Sweet *10540*
     E   *10540*   Brazil *10540*
     E   *10540*   Uruguay *10540*

R   *Hesperantha alborosea* Hilliard & B.L.Burtt *20604*
     R   *20604*   South Africa - Natal *20604*

I   *Hesperantha alpina* (Hook.f.) Pax ex Engl.
     I   Cameroon (Cameroon mt)

R   *Hesperantha ballii* Wild *7754*
     R   Zimbabwe (Chimanimani) *7754*

R   *Hesperantha ciliolata* Goldblatt *20604*
     R   *20604*   South Africa - Cape Province *20604*

R   *Hesperantha elsiae* Goldblatt *20604*
     R   *20604*   South Africa - Cape Province *20604*

R   *Hesperantha flava* G.J.Lewis *20604*
     R   *20604*   South Africa - Cape Province *20604*

V   *Hesperantha gracilis* Baker *20604*
     V   *20604*   South Africa - Natal *20604*

R   *Hesperantha hantamensis* Schltr. ex R.C.Foster *20604*
     R   *20604*   South Africa - Cape Province *20604*

E   *Hesperantha juncifolia* Goldblatt *20604*
     E   *20604*   South Africa - Cape Province *20604*

R   *Hesperantha karooica* Goldblatt *20604*
     R   *20604*   South Africa - Cape Province *20604*

R   *Hesperantha minima* (Baker) R.C.Foster *20604*
     R   *20604*   South Africa - Cape Province *20604*

R   *Hesperantha namaquana* Goldblatt *20604*
     R   *20604*   South Africa - Cape Province *20604*

R   *Hesperantha oligantha* (Diels) Goldblatt *20604*
     R   *20604*   South Africa - Cape Province *20604*

E   *Hesperantha pallescens* Goldblatt *20604*
     E   *20604*   South Africa - Cape Province *20604*

I   *Hesperantha pubinervia* Hilliard & B.L.Burtt *20604*
     I   *20604*   South Africa - Natal *20604*

R   *Hesperantha purpurea* Goldblatt *20604*
     R   *20604*   South Africa - Cape Province *20604*

R   *Hesperantha quadrangula* Goldblatt *20604*
     R   *20604*   South Africa - Cape Province *20604*

R   *Hesperantha rivulicola* Goldblatt *20604*
     R   *20604*   South Africa - Cape Province *20604*

Ex   *Hesperantha saldanhae* Goldblatt *20604, 10260*

     Ex   *20604*   South Africa - Cape Province *20604*

R   *Hesperantha teretifolia* Goldblatt *20604*
     R   *20604*   South Africa - Cape Province *20604*

R   *Hesperantha truncatula* Goldblatt *20604*
     R   *20604*   South Africa - Cape Province *20604*

E   *Hesperantha umbricola* Goldblatt *20604, 20039*
     E   *20604*   Swaziland *20604*

R   *Hesperantha vaginata* (Sweet) Goldblatt *20604*
     R   *20604*   South Africa - Cape Province *20604*

R   *Hesperoxiphion niveum* Ravenna *18200*
     R   *10540*   Peru *18200*

R   *Hexaglottis namaquana* Goldblatt *20604*
     R   *20604*   South Africa - Cape Province *20604*

R   *Hexaglottis virgata* (Jacq.) Sweet ssp. *karooica* Goldblatt *20604*
     R   *20604*   South Africa - Cape Province *20604*

R   *Homeria autumnalis* Goldblatt *20604*
     R   *20604*   South Africa - Cape Province *20604*

R   *Homeria bolusiae* Goldblatt *20604*
     R   *20604*   South Africa - Cape Province *20604*

R   *Homeria cedarmontana* Goldblatt *20604*
     R   *20604*   South Africa - Cape Province *20604*

R   *Homeria comptonii* L.Bolus *20604*
     R   *20604*   South Africa - Cape Province *20604*

E   *Homeria elegans* (Jacq.) Sweet *20604*
     E   *20604*   South Africa - Cape Province *20604*

R   *Homeria fenestrata* Goldblatt *20604*
     R   *20604*   South Africa - Cape Province *20604*

R   *Homeria fuscomontana* Goldblatt *20604*
     R   *20604*   South Africa - Cape Province *20604*

R   *Homeria odorata* L.Bolus *20604*
     R   *20604*   South Africa - Cape Province *20604*

R   *Homeria patens* Goldblatt *20604*
     R   *20604*   South Africa - Cape Province *20604*

R   *Homeria pendula* Goldblatt *20604*
     R   *20604*   South Africa - Cape Province *20604*

V   *Homeria radians* (Goldblatt) Goldblatt *20604*
     V   *20604*   South Africa - Cape Province *20604*

R   *Homeria ramosissima* Schltr. *20604*
     R   *20604*   South Africa - Cape Province *20604*

R   *Homeria spiralis* L.Bolus *20604*
     R   *20604*   South Africa - Cape Province *20604*

I   *Iridodictyum winkleri* (Regel) Rodionenko *5942*
     I   *5942*   Kazakhstan *5942*
     I   *5942*   Kyrgyzstan *5942*
     I   *5942*   Tajikistan *5942*

I   *Iridodictyum winogradowii* (Fomin) Rodionenko *5942*
     I   *5942*   Armenia *5942*

E   *Iris acutiloba* C. Meyer *5942*
     E   *5942*   Russia - North Caucasus *5942*
     E   *5942*   Azerbaijan (Caucasus) *5942*

Ex   *Iris antilibanotica* Dinsm. *8934*
     Ex   *8934*   Syria (heights above Bludan) *8934*

R   *Iris auranitica* Dinsm. *8897*
     R   Syria *8897*

E   *Iris basaltica* Dinsm. *8897*
     E   Syria (Tell Kalakh-Hadidia region) *8897*

R   *Iris bostrensis* Mout. *8897*
     R   Syria *8897*

E	*Iris calcarea* Dinsm. *8897*	
	E	Syria *8897*
I	*Iris camillae* Grossh. *5942*	
	I	*5942* Azerbaijan *5942*
E	*Iris cedreti* Dinsm. *8934*	
	E	Lebanon *8934*
Ex	*Iris damascena* Mont. *8897*	
	Ex	*8934* Syria (Jabl Qassoun) *8897*
I	*Iris darwasica* Regel *5942*	
	I	*5942* Tajikistan *5942*
I	*Iris duthiei* Foster	
	I	India - Uttar Pradesh (Kumaun)
I	*Iris ewbankiana* Foster *5942*	
	I	*5942* Turkmenistan *5942*
R	*Iris fernaldii* R.C. Foster *20850*	
	I	*20850* U.S. - California *20850*
I	*Iris grossheimii* Woronow ex Grossh. *5942*	
	I	*5942* Armenia *5942*
R	*Iris helenae* Barbey	
	R	Egypt
R	*Iris histrioides* (Wilson) Arnott *12840*	
	R	*12840* Turkey *12840*
R	*Iris hyeruchamensis* Avishai *8934*	
	R	Israel *8934*
I	*Iris iberica* Hoffm. *5942*	
	I	*5942* Azerbaijan *5942*
R	*Iris jordana* Dinsm. *8937*	
	R	Israel *8934*
	E	Jordan *8937*
V	*Iris junonia* Schott & Kotschy ex Schott *12840*	
	V	*12840* Turkey *12840*
E	*Iris kirkwoodii* Chaudhri *8934*	
	E	Syria *8934*
R	*Iris kolpakowskiana* Regel	
	R	former USSR *6930*
R	*Iris lacustris* Nutt. *20850, 14352*	
	R	*20850* Canada - Ontario *20850*
	R	*20850* U.S. - Michigan *20850*
	V	*20850* U.S. - Wisconsin *20850*
I	*Iris lortetii* Barbey *14908*	
	E	Israel
	I	Lebanon
I	*Iris lycotis* Woronow *5942*	
	I	*5942* Armenia *5942*
R	*Iris marsica* Ricci & Colasante *8000, 20171*	
	R	*18264* Italy *19997*
I	*Iris milesii* Foster	
	I	India - Himachal Pradesh
	I	India - Jammu & Kashmir
E	*Iris munzii* R.C. Foster *20850*	
	I	*20850* U.S. - California *20850*
R	*Iris nectarifera* A. Guner *12840*	
	R	*12840* Turkey *12840*
R	*Iris odaesanensis* Y.N. Lee *15957*	
	R	*15923* Korea, South (Mt Odae, Mt Sorak, Mt Kyebang) *15957*
R	*Iris pamphylica* Hedge *12840*	
	R	*19174* Turkey *12840*
V	*Iris paradoxa* Steven	
	V	former USSR (Caucasus) *6930*
E	*Iris petrana* Dinsm. *8937*	
	E	Jordan *8937*
R	*Iris purdyi* Eastw. *20850*	
	I	*20850* U.S. - California *20850*
	I	*20850* U.S. - Oregon *20850*
R	*Iris purpureobractea* B. Mathew & T. Baytop *12840*	
	R	*12840* Turkey *12840*
R	*Iris revoluta* Colasante *18264*	
	R	*18264* Italy (Puglia) *18264*
E	*Iris rossii* Baker var. *album* Y.N. Lee	
	E	Korea, South
E	*Iris samaria* Dinsm. *8934*	
	E	Israel *8934*
I	*Iris schelkownikwii* (Fomin) Fomin	
	I	former USSR *6930*
R	*Iris serotina* Willk. *20171*	
	R	Spain
I	*Iris sicula* Tod. *13351, 20171*	
	I	*7072* Italy - Sicily *7072*
	V	*13351* Malta (Gozo.) *13351*
E	*Iris sofarana* Foster *8897*	
	E	Lebanon *8897*
V	*Iris sprengeri* Siehe *8619*	
	V	*19873* Turkey *8619*
V	*Iris stenophylla* Hausskn. & Siehe ex Baker ssp. *allisonii* B. Mathew *12840*	
	V	*19873* Turkey *12840*
E	*Iris susiana* L. *8934*	
	E	Turkey *8934*
E	*Iris swensoniana* Chaudhri *8934*	
	E	Syria *8934*
R	*Iris taochia* Woronow ex Grossh. *12840*	
	R	*12840* Turkey *12840*
R	*Iris tenax* Lenz ssp. *klamathensis* Lenz *20850*	
	I	*20850* U.S. - California *20850*
V	*Iris thompsonii* R.C.Foster *20850*	
	I	*20850* U.S. - California *20850*
	I	*20850* U.S. - Oregon *20850*
V	*Iris timofejewii* Woronow *11552*	
	V	*11552* Russian Federation (Caucasus) *11552*
Ex	*Iris westii* Dinsm. *8934*	
	Ex	*8934* Lebanon (Mashghara-Jezzine area) *8934*
V	*Iris xanthospuria* B. Mathew & T. Baytop *12840*	
	V	*12840* Turkey *12840*
E	*Iris yebrudii* Chaudhri *8934*	
	E	Syria *8934*
R	*Ixia acaulis* Goldblatt & J.C.Manning *20604*	
	R	*20604* South Africa - Cape Province *20604*
R	*Ixia bellendenii* R.C.Foster *20604*	
	R	*20604* South Africa - Cape Province *20604*
R	*Ixia brevituba* G.J.Lewis *20604*	
	R	*20604* South Africa - Cape Province *20604*
R	*Ixia brunneobracteata* G.J.Lewis *20604*	
	R	*20604* South Africa - Cape Province *20604*
E	*Ixia campanulata* Houtt. *20604*	
	E	*20604* South Africa - Cape Province *20604*
V	*Ixia collina* Goldblatt & Snijman *20604*	

	V	20604	South Africa - Cape Province	20604
V	***Ixia curta*** Andrews 20604			
	V	20604	South Africa - Cape Province	20604
R	***Ixia esterhuyseniae*** M.P.de Vos 20604			
	R	20604	South Africa - Cape Province	20604
E	***Ixia frederickii*** M.P.de Vos 20604			
	E	20604	South Africa - Cape Province	20604
R	***Ixia gloriosa*** G.J.Lewis 20604			
	R	20604	South Africa - Cape Province	20604
E	***Ixia leipoldtii*** G.J.Lewis 20604			
	E	20604	South Africa - Cape Province	20604
V	***Ixia maculata*** L. var. *maculata* 20604			
	V	20604	South Africa - Cape Province	20604
R	***Ixia mostertii*** M.P.de Vos 20604			
	R	20604	South Africa - Cape Province	20604
I	***Ixia patens*** Aiton var. *linearifolia* G.J.Lewis 20604, 20604			
	I	20604	South Africa - Cape Province	20604
R	***Ixia pumilio*** Goldblatt & Snijman 20604			
	R	20604	South Africa - Cape Province	20604
R	***Ixia purpureorosea*** G.J.Lewis 20604			
	R	20604	South Africa - Cape Province	20604
R	***Ixia splendida*** G.J.Lewis 20604			
	R	20604	South Africa - Cape Province	20604
I	***Ixia stolonifera*** G.J.Lewis 20604			
	I	20604	South Africa - Cape Province	20604
E	***Ixia tenuifolia*** Vahl 20604			
	E	20604	South Africa - Cape Province	20604
R	***Ixia thomasiae*** Goldblatt 20604			
	R	20604	South Africa - Cape Province	20604
V	***Ixia versicolor*** G.J.Lewis 20604			
	V	20604	South Africa - Cape Province	20604
I	***Ixia vinacea*** G.J.Lewis 20604			
	I	20604	South Africa - Cape Province	20604
V	***Ixia viridiflora*** Lam. var. *viridiflora* 20604			
	V	20604	South Africa - Cape Province	20604
I	***Juno magnifica*** (Vved.) Vved. 5942			
	I	5942	Uzbekistan	5942
R	***Klattia flava*** (G.J.Lewis) Goldblatt 20604			
	R	20604	South Africa - Cape Province	20604
R	***Klattia partita*** Ker Gawl. ex Baker 20604			
	R	20604	South Africa - Cape Province	20604
V	***Lapeirousia azurea*** (Eckl. ex Baker) Goldblatt 20604			
	V	20604	South Africa - Cape Province	20604
R	***Lapeirousia exilis*** Goldblatt 20604			
	R	20604	South Africa - Cape Province	20604
R	***Lapeirousia montana*** Klatt 20604			
	R	20604	South Africa - Cape Province	20604
R	***Lapeirousia oreogena*** Schltr. ex Goldblatt 20604			
	R	20604	South Africa - Cape Province	20604
V	***Lapeirousia simulans*** Goldblatt & J.C.Manning 20604			
	V	20604	South Africa - Cape Province	20604
R	***Lapeirousia tenuis*** (Goldblatt) Goldblatt & J.C.Manning 20604			
	R	20604	South Africa - Cape Province	20604
R	***Lapeirousia verecunda*** Goldblatt 20604			
	R	20604	South Africa - Cape Province	20604
R	***Libertia pulchella*** (R.Br.) Sprengel var. *pygmaea*			

	D.Morris 20681			
	R	20681	Australia - Tasmania	20681
E	***Libertia tricocca*** Philippi 6164			
	E	6164	Chile	6164
I	***Mastigostyla brevicaulis*** (Baker) Fost. 6164			
	I	6164	Bolivia (La Paz & Sorata)	6164
V	***Mastigostyla mirabilis*** Ravenna 16336			
	V	16336	Argentina	16336
	V	20176	Argentina - Tucuman	20176
E	***Moraea amissa*** Goldblatt 20604			
	E	20604	South Africa - Cape Province	20604
E	***Moraea aristata*** (D.Delaroche) Asch. & Graebn. 20604, 7389			
	E	20604	South Africa - Cape Province	20604
E	***Moraea atropunctata*** Goldblatt 20604			
	E	20604	South Africa - Cape Province	20604
R	***Moraea barkerae*** Goldblatt 20604			
	R	20604	South Africa - Cape Province	20604
V	***Moraea barnardii*** L.Bolus 20604			
	V	20604	South Africa - Cape Province	20604
E	***Moraea calcicola*** Goldblatt 20604			
	E	20604	South Africa - Cape Province	20604
V	***Moraea cooperi*** Baker 20604			
	V	20604	South Africa - Cape Province	20604
V	***Moraea debilis*** Goldblatt 20604			
	V	20604	South Africa - Cape Province	20604
R	***Moraea deserticola*** Goldblatt 20604			
	R	20604	South Africa - Cape Province	20604
R	***Moraea elsiae*** Goldblatt 20604			
	R	20604	South Africa - Cape Province	20604
E	***Moraea flexuosa*** Goldblatt 20604			
	E	20604	South Africa - Cape Province	20604
E	***Moraea gigandra*** L.Bolus 20604			
	E	20604	South Africa - Cape Province	20604
I	***Moraea hiemalis*** Goldblatt 20604			
	I	20604	South Africa - Natal	20604
E	***Moraea incurva*** G.J.Lewis 20604, 3774			
	E	20604	South Africa - Cape Province (Tulbagh district)	20604
R	***Moraea indecora*** Goldblatt 20604			
	R	20604	South Africa - Cape Province	20604
E	***Moraea insolens*** Goldblatt 20604			
	E	20604	South Africa - Cape Province	20604
E	***Moraea linderi*** Goldblatt 20604			
	E	20604	South Africa - Cape Province	20604
V	***Moraea longiaristata*** Goldblatt 20604			
	V	20604	South Africa - Cape Province	20604
V	***Moraea longiflora*** Ker Gawl. 20604			
	V	20604	South Africa - Cape Province	20604
E	***Moraea loubseri*** Goldblatt 20604, 3774			
	E	20604	South Africa - Cape Province	20604
R	***Moraea macgregorii*** Goldblatt 20604			
	R	20604	South Africa - Cape Province	20604
R	***Moraea namaquamontana*** Goldblatt 20604			
	R	20604	South Africa - Cape Province	20604
V	***Moraea neopavonia*** R.C.Foster 20604			
	V	20604	South Africa - Cape Province	20604
R	***Moraea nubigena*** Goldblatt 20604			

R   *20604* South Africa - Cape Province *20604*

V   *Moraea tulbaghensis* L.Bolus *20604*

    V   *20604* South Africa - Cape Province *20604*

I   *Moraea unibracteata* Goldblatt *20604*

    I   *20604* South Africa - Natal *20604*

R   *Moraea vallisavium* Goldblatt *20604*

    R   *20604* South Africa - Cape Province *20604*

R   *Moraea verecunda* Goldblatt *20604*

    R   *20604* South Africa - Cape Province *20604*

R   *Moraea villosa* (Ker Gawl.) Ker Gawl. ssp. *elandsmontana* Goldblatt *20604*

    R   *20604* South Africa - Cape Province *20604*

R   *Moraea vlokii* Goldblatt *20604*

    R   *20604* South Africa - Cape Province *20604*

E   *Moraea worcesterensis* Goldblatt *20604*

    E   *20604* South Africa - Cape Province *20604*

V   *Nemastylis floridana* Small *20850*

    V   *20850* U.S. - Florida *20850*

R   *Nivenia concinna* N.E.Br. *20604*

    R   *20604* South Africa - Cape Province *20604*

R   *Nivenia dispar* N.E.Br. *20604*

    R   *20604* South Africa - Cape Province *20604*

R   *Nivenia fruticosa* (L.f.) Baker *20604*

    R   *20604* South Africa - Cape Province *20604*

R   *Nivenia stenosiphon* Goldblatt *20604*

    R   *20604* South Africa - Cape Province *20604*

R   *Nivenia stokoei* (L.Guthrie) N.E.Br. *20604*

    R   *20604* South Africa - Cape Province *20604*

R   *Roggeveldia fistulosa* Goldblatt *20604*

    R   *20604* South Africa - Cape Province *20604*

R   *Roggeveldia montana* Goldblatt *20604*

    R   *20604* South Africa - Cape Province *20604*

R   *Romulea albomarginata* M.P.de Vos *20604*

    R   *20604* South Africa - Cape Province *20604*

V   *Romulea amoena* Schltr. ex Bég. *20604*

    V   *20604* South Africa - Cape Province *20604*

R   *Romulea antiatlantica* Maire

    R   Morocco

V   *Romulea aquatica* G.J.Lewis *20604*

    V   *20604* South Africa - Cape Province *20604*

R   *Romulea barkerae* M.P.de Vos *20604*

    R   *20604* South Africa - Cape Province *20604*

R   *Romulea battandieri* Beguinot *10487*

    R   *14958* Algeria *10487*

R   *Romulea biflora* (Bég.) M.P.de Vos *20604*

    R   *20604* South Africa - Cape Province *20604*

R   *Romulea columnae* Sebast. & Mauri ssp. *hartungii* (Parl.) Kunkel

    R   Spain - Canary Is.

V   *Romulea elliptica* M.P.de Vos *20604*

    V   *20604* South Africa - Cape Province *20604*

V   *Romulea eximia* M.P.de Vos *20604*

    V   *20604* South Africa - Cape Province *20604*

R   *Romulea hallii* M.P.de Vos *20604*

    R   *20604* South Africa - Cape Province *20604*

R   *Romulea hantamensis* (Diels) Goldblatt *20604*

    R   *20604* South Africa - Cape Province *20604*

V   *Romulea jugicola* M.P.de Vos *20604*

    V   *20604* South Africa - Cape Province *20604*

R   *Romulea kamisensis* M.P.de Vos *20604*

    R   *20604* South Africa - Cape Province *20604*

R   *Romulea linaresii* Parl. ssp. *linaresii* *18264, 20171*

    R   *18264* Italy - Sicily *18264*

V   *Romulea luteoflora* (M.P.De Vos) M.P de Vos var. *sanisensis* M.P. de Vos *20604*

    V   *20604* Lesotho *20604*

    V   *20604* South Africa - Natal *20604*

I   *Romulea malaniae* M.P.de Vos *20604*

    I   *20604* South Africa - Cape Province *20604*

I   *Romulea melitensis* Bég. *13351, 20171*

    I   *13351* Malta *13351*

V   *Romulea membranacea* M.P.de Vos *20604*

    V   *20604* South Africa - Cape Province *20604*

I   *Romulea monadelpha* (Sweet) Baker *20604*

    I   *20604* South Africa - Cape Province *20604*

R   *Romulea monticola* M.P.de Vos *20604*

    R   *20604* South Africa - Cape Province *20604*

R   *Romulea multifida* M.P.de Vos *20604*

    R   *20604* South Africa - Cape Province *20604*

I   *Romulea multisulcata* M.P.de Vos *20604*

    I   *20604* South Africa - Cape Province *20604*

I   *Romulea namaquensis* M.P.de Vos *20604*

    I   *20604* South Africa - Cape Province *20604*

V   *Romulea neglecta* (Schult.) M.P.de Vos *20604, 20171*

    V   *20604* South Africa - Cape Province *20604*

Ex   *Romulea papyracea* Wolley-Dod *20604, 6180*

    Ex   *20604* South Africa - Cape Province *20604*

R   *Romulea pearsonii* M.P.de Vos *20604*

    R   *20604* South Africa - Cape Province *20604*

R   *Romulea penzigii* Beguinot *10487*

    R   *14958* Algeria *10487*

V   *Romulea revelierei* Jord. & Fourr. *15080, 20171*

    V   *20726* France - Corsica *15080*

V   *Romulea saldanhensis* M.P.de Vos *20604*

    V   *20604* South Africa - Cape Province *20604*

R   *Romulea sanguinalis* M.P.de Vos *20604*

    R   *20604* South Africa - Cape Province *20604*

I   *Romulea sinispinosensis* M.P.de Vos *20604*

    I   *20604* South Africa - Cape Province *20604*

R   *Romulea sladenii* M.P.de Vos *20604*

    R   *20604* South Africa - Cape Province *20604*

I   *Romulea sphaerocarpa* M.P.de Vos *20604*

    I   *20604* South Africa - Cape Province *20604*

R   *Romulea subfistulosa* M.P.de Vos *20604*

    R   *20604* South Africa - Cape Province *20604*

Ex   *Romulea sulphurea* Bég. *20604, 6180*

    Ex   *20604* South Africa - Cape Province *20604*

R   *Romulea syringodeoflora* M.P.de Vos *20604*

    R   *20604* South Africa - Cape Province *20604*

R   *Romulea tortilis* Baker var. *dissecta* De Vos *20604*

    R   *20604* South Africa - Cape Province *20604*

R   *Romulea tortilis* Baker var. *tortilis* *20604*

    R   *20604* South Africa - Cape Province *20604*

R   *Romulea toximontana* M.P.de Vos *20604*

V		20604	South Africa - Cape Province *20604*

V   *Romulea unifolia* M.P.de Vos *20604*

| V | 20604 | South Africa - Cape Province *20604* |

R   *Romulea vaillantii* Quezel *10487*

| R | 14958 | Algeria *10487* |

R   *Romulea vanzyliae* M.P.de Vos *20604*

| R | 20604 | South Africa - Cape Province *20604* |

R   *Romulea vinacea* M.P.de Vos *20604*

| R | 20604 | South Africa - Cape Province *20604* |

R   *Romulea vlokii* M.P.de Vos *20604*

| R | 20604 | South Africa - Cape Province *20604* |

R   *Sessilanthera heliantha* (Ravenna) Cruden *12780*

| R | 19850 | Mexico - Chiapas *12780* |
| R | 19850 | Mexico - Guerrero *12780* |

V   *Sisyrinchium acre* Mann *20850, 14209*

| I | 20850 | U.S. - Hawaii *20850* |
| I | 20850 | U.S. - Maine *20850* |

R   *Sisyrinchium cernuum* (Bickn.) Kearney *20850*

| V | 20850 | U.S. - Arizona *20850* |
| E | 20850 | U.S. - Texas *20850* |

R   *Sisyrinchium conzatii* Calderón & Rzedowski *20883*

| I | 20883 | Mexico *20883* |

V   *Sisyrinchium dichotomum* Bickn. *20850*

| V | 20850 | U.S. - North Carolina *20850* |
| I | 20850 | U.S. - South Carolina *20850* |

Ex/E   *Sisyrinchium farwellii* Bickn. *20850, 14662*

| Ex | 20850 | U.S. - Michigan *20850* |
| I | 20850 | U.S. - Wisconsin *20850* |

V   *Sisyrinchium funereum* Bickn. *20850*

| I | 20850 | U.S. - California *20850* |

R   *Sisyrinchium galapagense* Ravenna *11117*

| R | | Ecuador - Galapagos *11117* |

R   *Sisyrinchium groenlandicum* Bocher *19002, 21309*

| R | 21309 | Denmark - Greenland *19002* |

Ex/E   *Sisyrinchium macrocarpon* Bickn. *20850*

| I | 20850 | U.S. - Arizona *20850* |

V   *Sisyrinchium pallidum* Cholewa & D. Henderson *20850*

| V | 20850 | U.S. - Colorado *20850* |
| V | 20850 | U.S. - Wyoming *20850* |

V   *Sisyrinchium sarmentosum* Suksdorf ex Greene *20850*

I	20850	Canada - British Columbia *20850*
I	20850	Canada - Manitoba *20850*
I	20850	U.S. - North Dakota *20850*
E	20850	U.S. - Oregon *20850*
V	20850	U.S. - Washington *20850*

V   *Sisyrinchium xerophyllum* Greene *20850*

I	20850	U.S. - Florida *20850*
I	20850	U.S. - Georgia *20850*
I	20850	U.S. - North Carolina *20850*

R   *Sparaxis caryophyllacea* Goldblatt *20604*

| R | 20604 | South Africa - Cape Province *20604* |

V   *Sparaxis elegans* (Sweet) Goldblatt *20604*

| V | 20604 | South Africa - Cape Province *20604* |

R   *Sparaxis fragrans* (Jacq.) Ker Gawl. *20604*

| R | 20604 | South Africa - Cape Province *20604* |

R   *Sparaxis galeata* Ker Gawl. *20604*

| R | 20604 | South Africa - Cape Province *20604* |

R   *Sparaxis grandiflora* (D.Delaroche) Ker Gawl ssp. *grandiflora* *20604*

| R | 20604 | South Africa - Cape Province *20604* |

E   *Sparaxis maculosa* Goldblatt *20604*

E		20604	South Africa - Cape Province *20604*

R   *Sparaxis pillansii* L.Bolus *20604*

| R | 20604 | South Africa - Cape Province *20604* |

Ex   *Sparaxis roxburghii* (Baker) Goldblatt *20604*

| Ex | 20604 | South Africa - Cape Province *20604* |

V   *Sparaxis tricolor* (Schneev.) Ker Gawl. *20604*

| V | 20604 | South Africa - Cape Province *20604* |

V   *Syringodea derustensis* M.P.de Vos *20604*

| V | 20604 | South Africa - Cape Province *20604* |

R   *Thereianthus racemosus* (Klatt) G.J.Lewis *20604*

| R | 20604 | South Africa - Cape Province *20604* |

R   *Tigridia bicolor* Molseed *11131*

| R | 19850 | Mexico - Oaxaca *11131* |

E   *Tigridia bracteolata* (Klatt) Macbr. *10540*

| E | 10540 | Bolivia *10540* |

R   *Tigridia hintonii* Molseed *11131*

| R | 19850 | Mexico - Guerrero *11131* |

R   *Tigridia huajuapanensis* Molseed ex Cruden *9736*

| R | 19850 | Mexico *9736* |

E   *Tigridia minuta* Ravenna *18200*

| E | 12468 | Peru *18200* |

R   *Tigridia philippiana* I.M. Johnston *6164*

| R | 19534 | Chile *6164* |

E   *Trimezia caerulea* (Ker-Gawl.) Ravenna *6164*

| E | 6164 | Brazil - Rio de Janeiro *6164* |
| E | 6164 | Brazil - Rio Grande do Sul *6164* |

E   *Trimezia glauca* (Bak.) Ravenna *6164*

E	6164	Brazil - Minas Gerais *6164*
E	6164	Brazil - Rio de Janeiro *6164*
E	6164	Brazil - Sao Paulo *6164*

R   *Trimezia lutea* (Klatt) Fost. *10540*

| R | 10540 | Brazil *10540* |
| E | 10540 | Colombia *10540* |

E   *Trimezia martii* (Baker) R. Foster *10540*

| E | 10540 | Argentina *10540* |
| E | 10540 | Paraguay *10540* |

E   *Trimezia northiana* (Schneev.) Ravenna *6164*

| E | 6164 | Brazil - Rio de Janeiro *6164* |

E   *Trimezia silvestris* (Vell.) Ravenna *6164*

| E | 6164 | Brazil - Rio de Janeiro *6164* |
| E | 6164 | Brazil - Sao Paulo *6164* |

E   *Trimezia spectabilis* Ravenna *6164*

| E | 6164 | Brazil *6164* |
| E | 6164 | Colombia *6164* |

R   *Tritonia delpierrei* M.P.de Vos *20604*

| R | 20604 | South Africa - Cape Province *20604* |

R   *Tritonia flabellifolia* (D.Delaroche) G.J.Lewis var. *thomasiae* M.P de Vos *20604*

| R | 20604 | South Africa - Cape Province *20604* |

R   *Tritonia florentiae* (Marloth) Goldblatt *20604*

| R | 20604 | South Africa - Cape Province *20604* |

R   *Tritonia kamisbergensis* Klatt *20604*

| R | 20604 | South Africa - Cape Province *20604* |

R   *Tritonia marlothii* M.P.de Vos *20604*

| R | 20604 | South Africa - Cape Province *20604* |

R   *Tritonia tugwelliae* L.Bolus *20604*

| R | 20604 | South Africa - Cape Province *20604* |

R   *Tritonia watermeyeri* L.Bolus *20604*

| R | 20604 | South Africa - Cape Province *20604* |

I	*Tritoniopsis elongata* (L.Bolus) G.J.Lewis *20604*		
	I	*20604* South Africa - Cape Province *20604*	
V	*Tritoniopsis flexuosa* (L.f.) G.J.Lewis *20604*		
	V	*20604* South Africa - Cape Province *20604*	
R	*Tritoniopsis latifolia* G.J.Lewis *20604*		
	R	*20604* South Africa - Cape Province *20604*	
E	*Tucma simplex* Ravenna *10540*		
	E	*10540* Argentina *10540*	
E	*Tucma venustula* Ravenna *16336*		
	E	*16336* Argentina *16336*	
R	*Watsonia bachmannii* L.Bolus *20604*		
	R	*20604* South Africa - Cape Province *20604*	
	R	*20604* South Africa - Natal *20604*	
I	*Watsonia canaliculata* Goldblatt *20604*		
	I	*20604* South Africa - Natal *20604*	
Ex	*Watsonia distans* L.Bolus *20604*		
	Ex	*20604* South Africa - Cape Province *20604*	
E	*Watsonia dubia* Eckl. ex Klatt *20604*		
	E	*20604* South Africa Cape Province *20604*	
R	*Watsonia emiliae* L.Bolus *20604*		
	R	*20604* South Africa - Cape Province *20604*	
E	*Watsonia humilis* Mill. *20604*		
	E	*20604* South Africa - Cape Province *20604*	
R	*Watsonia hysterantha* J.W.Mathews & L.Bolus *20604*		
	R	*20604* South Africa - Cape Province *20604*	
R	*Watsonia inclinata* Goldblatt *20604*		
	R	*20604* South Africa - Cape Province *20604*	
	R	*20604* South Africa - Natal *20604*	
R	*Watsonia latifolia* N.E.Br. ex Oberm. *20604, 18023*		
	R	*20604* Swaziland *20604*	
	R	*20604* South Africa - Natal *20604*	
	R	*20604* South Africa - Transvaal *20604*	
R	*Watsonia mtamvunae* Goldblatt *20604*		
	R	*20604* South Africa - Cape Province *20604*	
	R	*20604* South Africa - Natal *20604*	
R	*Watsonia occulta* L.Bolus *20604, 17458*		
	R	*20604* South Africa - Transvaal *20604*	
R	*Watsonia pondoensis* Goldblatt *20604*		
	R	*20604* South Africa - Cape Province *20604*	
	R	*20604* South Africa - Natal *20604*	
R	*Watsonia rogersii* L.Bolus *20604*		
	R	*20604* South Africa - Cape Province *20604*	
R	*Watsonia rourkei* Goldblatt *20604*		
	R	*20604* South Africa - Cape Province *20604*	
I	*Watsonia strictiflora* Ker Gawl. *20604*		
	I	*20604* South Africa - Cape Province *20604*	
R	*Watsonia transvaalensis* Baker *20604*		
	R	*20604* South Africa - Transvaal *20604*	
R	*Watsonia versfeldii* J.W.Mathews & L.Bolus *20604*		
	R	*20604* South Africa - Cape Province *20604*	
R	*Watsonia wilmsii* L.Bolus *20604, 17458*		
	R	*20604* South Africa - Orange Free State *20604*	
	R	*20604* South Africa - Transvaal *20604*	
R	*Witsenia maura* (L.) Thunb. *20604, 11102*		
	R	*20604* South Africa - Cape Province (south-west, 12 populations) *20604*	
R	*Xenoscapa uliginosa* Goldblatt & J.C.Manning *20604*		
	R	*20604* South Africa - Cape Province *20604*	

Juncaceae

Number of genera:	8	
Number of species:	300	
Recorded threatened species:	22	(7%)

Temperate or cold regions, or montane tropical.

I	*Juncus arianus* Krecz.		
	I	former USSR *6930*	
V	*Juncus caesariensis* Coville *20850*		
	E	*20850* U.S. - Maryland *20850*	
	V	*20850* U.S. - New Jersey *20850*	
	E	*20850* U.S. - North Carolina *20850*	
	V	*20850* U.S. - Virginia *20850*	
R	*Juncus chlorocephalus* Engelm. *20850*		
	I	*20850* U.S. - California *20850*	
	I	*20850* U.S. - Nevada *20850*	
E	*Juncus guadeloupensis* Buchenau & Urban *5710*		
	E	*5710* Guadeloupe (La Soufrière massif) *5710*	
I	*Juncus hizenensis* Satake *11164*		
	I	*11164* Japan *11164*	
V	*Juncus leiospermus* F.J. Herm. *20850*		
	V	*20850* U.S. - California *20850*	
E	*Juncus leiospermus* F.J. Herm. var. *ahartii* Ertter *20850, 10260*		
	E	*20850* U.S. - California *20850*	
V	*Juncus leiospermus* F.J. Herm. var. *leiospermus* *20850*		
	V	*20850* U.S. - California *20850*	
V	*Juncus megaspermus* F.J. Herm. *20850*		
	I	*20850* U.S. - California *20850*	
R	*Juncus sikkimensis* Hook.f. *14782*		
	R	*14782* India - Sikkim *14782*	
V	*Juncus triformis* Engelm. *20850*		
	I	*20850* U.S. - California *20850*	
R	*Juncus tweedyi* Rydb. *20850*		
	E	*20850* U.S. - Colorado *20850*	
	E	*20850* U.S. - Idaho *20850*	
	I	*20850* U.S. - Montana *20850*	
	E	*20850* U.S. - Utah *20850*	
	V	*20850* U.S. - Wyoming *20850*	
R	*Juncus valvatus* Link *8000, 20171*		
	V	*20076* Portugal (central and south) *8000*	
	R	Algeria	
	R	Tunisia	
I	*Juncus yakeisidakensis* Satake *11164*		
	I	*11164* Japan *11164*	
V	*Luzula canariensis* Poiret *20750*		
	V	*20750* Spain - Canary Is. *20750*	
R	*Luzula castellansii* Barros *16336*		
	R	*16336* Argentina *16336*	
	R	*20176* Argentina - Salta *20176*	
R	*Luzula crenulata* Buchenau *19305*		
	R	*19305* New Zealand - South Is. *19305*	
R	*Luzula deflexa* Kozuharov *5204, 20171*		
	R	*5204* Bulgaria (central & west) *5204*	
R	*Luzula elegans* Lowe *8000, 20171*		
	E	*20076* Portugal *20076*	
	R	Portugal - Madeira *8000*	
	V	Spain - Canary Is. *8000*	
R	*Luzula hieronymi* Buchenau & Griseb. var. *pusilla* Castillon *16336*		

R	*16336*	Argentina	*16336*
R	*20176*	Argentina - Tucuman	*20176*

R   *Luzula longiflora* Benth.

R	*14225*	Australia - NSW - Lord Howe Is.	*14225*

E   *Luzula masafuerana* Skottsb. *19116*

E	*19125*	Chile - Juan Fernandez Is.	*19116*

R   *Luzula seubertii* Lowe

R		Portugal - Madeira	

I   *Microschoenus duthiei* C.B. Clarke *11494*

I	*11494*	India - Uttar Pradesh	*11494*

Juncaginaceae

Number of genera:	5	
Number of species:	20	
Recorded threatened species:	1	(5%)

Temperate and cold Northern and Southern Hemisphere.

V   *Triglochin gaspense* Lieth & D. Love *20850, 14419*

E	*20850*	Canada - New Brunswick	*20850*
E	*20850*	Canada - Newfoundland	*20850*
E	*20850*	Canada - Prince Edward Is.	*20850*
V	*20850*	Canada - Quebec	*20850*
Ex/E	*20850*	U.S. - Maine	*20850*

Lemnaceae

Number of genera:	6	
Number of species:	31	
Recorded threatened species:	3	(9%)

Cosmopolitan.

I   *Lemna maxima* Blatter & Hallberg

I		India - Rajasthan (Mt Abu)	

I   *Lemna minima* Blatter & Hallberg

I		India - Rajasthan (Mt Abu)	

R   *Wolffiella monodii* Jovet-Ast

R		Chad	

Liliaceae

Number of genera:	11	
Number of species:	460	
Recorded threatened species:	149	(32%)

Cosmopolitan.

V   *Amana latifolia* (Makino) Honda *11164*

V	*11164*	Japan	*11164*

V   *Calochortus amabilis* Purdy *20850*

I	*20850*	U.S. - California	*20850*

V   *Calochortus amoenus* Greene *20850*

I	*20850*	U.S. - California	*20850*

R   *Calochortus catalinae* S.Watson *20850*

R	*20850*	U.S. - California	*20850*

V   *Calochortus clavatus* S.Watson var. *avius* Jepson *20850*

V	*20850*	U.S. - California	*20850*

E   *Calochortus clavatus* S.Watson var. *gracilis* Ownbey *20850*

E	*20850*	U.S. - California	*20850*

E   *Calochortus clavatus* S.Watson var. *recurvifolius* Hoover *20850*

E	*20850*	U.S. - California	*20850*

V   *Calochortus coeruleus* (Kellogg) S.Watson *20850*

I	*20850*	U.S. - California	*20850*

I	*20850*	U.S. - Oregon	*20850*

V   *Calochortus concolor* (Baker) Purdy *20850*

I	*20850*	U.S. - California	*20850*

E   *Calochortus coxii* M. Godfrey & F. Callahan *20850*

E	*20850*	U.S. - Oregon	*20850*

V   *Calochortus dunnii* Purdy *20883, 20850, 8058*

V	*20850*	U.S. - California	*20850*
I	*20883*	Mexico	*20883*

V   *Calochortus excavatus* Greene *20850*

V	*20850*	U.S. - California	*20850*

R   *Calochortus foliosus* Ownbey *19850*

R	*19850*	Mexico	*19850*

V   *Calochortus greenei* S.Watson *20850*

V	*20850*	U.S. - California	*20850*
V	*20850*	U.S. - Oregon	*20850*

R   *Calochortus howellii* S.Watson *20850*

R	*20850*	U.S. - Oregon	*20850*

Ex   *Calochortus indecorus* Ownbey & M.E. Peck *20850, 14662*

Ex	*20850*	U.S. - Oregon	*20850*

R   *Calochortus longebarbatus* S.Watson *20850*

R	*20850*	U.S. - California	*20850*
I	*20850*	U.S. - Oregon	*20850*
I	*20850*	U.S. - Washington	*20850*

R   *Calochortus longebarbatus* S.Watson var. *longebarbatus* *20850*

R	*20850*	U.S. - California	*20850*
R	*20850*	U.S. - Oregon	*20850*
V	*20850*	U.S. - Washington	*20850*

V   *Calochortus longebarbatus* S.Watson var. *peckii* Ownbey *20850*

V	*20850*	U.S. - Oregon	*20850*

R   *Calochortus lyallii* Baker *20850, 10701*

E	*20850*	Canada - British Columbia	*20850*
I	*20850*	U.S. - Washington	*20850*

V   *Calochortus macrocarpus* Dougl. var. *maculosus* (A.Nels. & J.F.Macbr.) A.Nels. & J.F.Macbr. *20850*

V	*20850*	U.S. - Idaho	*20850*
I	*20850*	U.S. - Oregon	*20850*
I	*20850*	U.S. - Washington	*20850*

R   *Calochortus marcellae* Nesom *20883*

I	*20883*	Mexico	*20883*

R   *Calochortus minimus* Ownbey *20850*

I	*20850*	U.S. - California	*20850*

Ex/E   *Calochortus monanthus* Ownbey *20850, 14662*

Ex/E	*20850*	U.S. - California	*20850*

R   *Calochortus nitidus* Dougl. *20850*

R	*20850*	U.S. - Idaho	*20850*
I	*20850*	U.S. - Nevada	*20850*
I	*20850*	U.S. - Oregon	*20850*
Ex	*20850*	U.S. - Washington	*20850*

V   *Calochortus obispoensis* J.G. Lemmon *20850*

V	*20850*	U.S. - California	*20850*

V   *Calochortus palmeri* S.Watson *20850*

I	*20850*	U.S. - California	*20850*

E   *Calochortus palmeri* S.Watson var. *munzii* Ownbey *20850*

E	*20850*	U.S. - California	*20850*

V   *Calochortus palmeri* S.Watson var. *palmeri* *20850*

V	*20850*	U.S. - California	*20850*

V	*Calochortus panamintensis* (Ownbey) Reveal *20850*	
	V	*20850* U.S. - California *20850*
	I	*20850* U.S. - Nevada *20850*
E	*Calochortus persistens* Ownbey *20850*	
	E	*20850* U.S. - California *20850*
V	*Calochortus plummerae* Greene *20850*	
	V	*20850* U.S. - California *20850*
V	*Calochortus pulchellus* Dougl. ex Benth. *20850*	
	V	*20850* U.S. - California *20850*
E	*Calochortus raichei* Farwig & Girard *20850*	
	E	*20850* U.S. - California *20850*
V	*Calochortus striatus* Parish *20850*	
	V	*20850* U.S. - California *20850*
	E	*20850* U.S. - Nevada *20850*
E	*Calochortus tiburonensis* A.J. Hill *20850*	
	E	*20850* U.S. - California *20850*
E	*Calochortus umpquaensis* N.A. Fredricks *20850*	
	E	*20850* U.S. - Oregon *20850*
R	*Calochortus vestae* Purdy *20850*	
	I	*20850* U.S. - California *20850*
R	*Calochortus weedii* Wood *20850*	
	I	*20850* U.S. - California *20850*
R	*Calochortus weedii* Wood var. *intermedius* Ownbey *20850*	
	R	*20850* U.S. - California *20850*
V	*Calochortus weedii* Wood var. *vestus* Purdy *20850*	
	V	*20850* U.S. - California *20850*
E	*Calochortus westonii* Eastw. *20850*	
	E	*20850* U.S. - California *20850*
I	*Erythronium caucasicum* Woronow *5942*	
	I	*5942* Russia - North Caucasus *5942*
	I	*5942* Georgia *5942*
R	*Erythronium dens-canis* L. ssp. *niveum* (Baumg.) Buia & Paun *17823*	
	R	*19949* Romania *20631*
E	*Erythronium elegans* Hammond & Chambers *20850*	
	E	*20850* U.S. - Oregon *20850*
R	*Erythronium grandiflorum* Pursh ssp. *candidum* Piper *20850*	
	I	*20850* U.S. - Idaho *20850*
	R	*20850* U.S. - Montana *20850*
	I	*20850* U.S. - Washington *20850*
R	*Erythronium grandiflorum* Pursh ssp. *nudipetalum* Applegate *20850*	
	R	*20850* U.S. - Idaho *20850*
R	*Erythronium helenae* Applegate *20850*	
	R	*20850* U.S. - California *20850*
E	*Erythronium pluriflorum* Shevock, Bartel & Allen *20850*	
	E	*20850* U.S. - California *20850*
E	*Erythronium propullans* Gray *20850*	
	I	*20850* Canada - Ontario *20850*
	E	*20850* U.S. - Minnesota (Rice and Goodhue Counties) *20850*
V	*Erythronium pusaterii* (Munz & J.T. Howell) Shevock, Bartel & Allen *20850*	
	V	*20850* U.S. - California *20850*
V	*Erythronium tuolumnense* Applegate *20850*	
	V	*20850* U.S. - California *20850*

R	*Erythronium umbilicatum* Parks & Hardin ssp. *monostolum* Parks & Hardin *20850*	
	R	*20850* U.S. - North Carolina *20850*
	I	*20850* U.S. - Tennessee *20850*
R	*Evrardiella dodecandra* Gagnepain *6057*	
	R	Vietnam *6057*
R	*Fritillaria acmopetala* Boiss. ssp. *wendelboi* Rix *12840*	
	R	*12840* Turkey *12840*
R	*Fritillaria alburyana* Rix *12840*	
	R	*12840* Turkey *12840*
R	*Fritillaria alfredae* Post ssp. *glaucoviridis* (Turrill) Rix *12840*	
	R	*12840* Turkey *12840*
R	*Fritillaria amabilis* Koidz. *11164*	
	R	*11164* Japan *11164*
R	*Fritillaria assyriaca* Baker ssp. *melananthera* Rix *12840*	
	R	*12840* Turkey *12840*
R	*Fritillaria aurea* Schott *12840*	
	R	*12840* Turkey *12840*
V	*Fritillaria ayakoana* Naruh. *11164*	
	V	*11164* Japan *11164*
V	*Fritillaria brandegei* Eastw. *20850*	
	I	*20850* U.S. - California *20850*
R	*Fritillaria carica* Rix ssp. *serpenticola* Rix *12840*	
	R	*12840* Turkey *12840*
V	*Fritillaria conica* Boiss. *8000, 20171*	
	V	*19174* Greece (south: west Peloponnisos) *8000*
R	*Fritillaria davisii* Turrill *20171*	
	R	Greece
R	*Fritillaria drenovskii* Degen & Stoj. *8000, 20171*	
	V	*19426* Bulgaria (south west) *8000*
	R	Greece (north east) *8000*
V	*Fritillaria eastwoodiae* Macfarlane *20850*	
	V	*20850* U.S. - California *20850*
R	*Fritillaria epirotica* Turrill ex Rix *17781, 20171*	
	R	*17781* Greece (Epirus Mts.) *17781*
E	*Fritillaria euboeica* Rix *17781, 20171*	
	E	*17781* Greece (south Evvoia) *17781*
V	*Fritillaria falcata* (Jepson) D.E. Beetle *20850*	
	V	*20850* U.S. - California *20850*
	I	*20850* U.S. - Oregon *20850*
R	*Fritillaria fleischeriana* Steud. & Hoch. ex Sch.& Sch.f. *12840*	
	R	*12840* Turkey *12840*
R	*Fritillaria forbesii* Baker *12840*	
	R	*12840* Turkey *12840*
E	*Fritillaria gentneri* Gilkey *20850*	
	E	*20850* U.S. - Oregon *20850*
I	*Fritillaria grandiflora* Grossh. *5942*	
	I	*5942* Azerbaijan *5942*
R	*Fritillaria gussichiae* (Degen & Dörfl.) Rix *8000, 20171*	
	R	Bulgaria *8000*
	R	Greece *8000*
	R	(former) Yugoslavia *8000*
R	*Fritillaria involucrata* All. *17781, 20171*	
	R	*17781* France (south-east) *17781*

V   *19997*   Italy (Piemonte & Liguria) *19997*

R   *Fritillaria japonica* Miq. *11164*
     R   *11164*   Japan *11164*

V   *Fritillaria kaiensis* Naruh. *11164*
     V   *11164*   Japan *11164*

V   *Fritillaria liliacea* Lindl. *20850, 14908*
     V   *20850*   U.S. - California *20850*

R   *Fritillaria macedonica* Bornm. *20178, 20171*
     R   *20178*   Albania *20178*
     R   (former) Yugoslavia

V   *Fritillaria michailovskyi* Fomin *12840*
     V   *12840*   Turkey *12840*

R   *Fritillaria minima* Rix *12840*
     R   *12840*   Turkey *12840*

V   *Fritillaria muraiana* Ohwi *11164*
     V   *11164*   Japan *11164*

R   *Fritillaria obliqua* Ker Gawl. *8000, 20171*
     R   Greece (south (Attiki)) *8000*

E   *Fritillaria ojaiensis* A. Davids. *20850*
     E   *20850*   U.S. - California *20850*

V   *Fritillaria pallidiflora* Schrenk *11139*
     V   China - Xinjiang Uygur Zizhiqu *11139*

R   *Fritillaria pluriflora* Torr. ex Benth. *20850*
     R   *20850*   U.S. - California *20850*

R   *Fritillaria pontica* Wahlenb. *5204, 20171*
     R   *5204*   Bulgaria *5204*

I   *Fritillaria raddeana* Regel *5942*
     I   *5942*   Uzbekistan *5942*

R   *Fritillaria rhodia* Hansen
     R   Greece

R   *Fritillaria rhodocanakis* Orph. ex Baker *8000, 20171*
     R   Greece (south - island of Idhra) *8000*

V   *Fritillaria shikokiana* Naruh. *11164*
     V   *11164*   Japan *11164*

R   *Fritillaria sibthorpiana* auct. balcan., non (Sibth. & Sm.)
     Baker *12840, 20171*
     R   *12840*   Turkey *12840*

V   *Fritillaria striata* Eastw. *20850*
     V   *20850*   U.S. - California *20850*

R   *Fritillaria tubaeformis* Gren. & Godron *18264*
     R   *18264*   Italy *18264*

R   *Fritillaria tuntasia* Heldr. ex Halácsy *17781, 20171*
     R   *17781*   Greece (Kythnos) *17781*

R   *Fritillaria viridea* Kellogg *20850*
     R   *20850*   U.S. - California *20850*

I   *Fritillaria viridiflora* Post *12840*
     I   *12840*   Turkey *12840*

R   *Fritillaria whittallii* Baker *12840*
     R   *12840*   Turkey *12840*

R   *Gagea mauritanica* Durieu *10487*
     R   *14958*   Algeria *10487*

V   *Gagea tenuissima* Miscz. *12840*
     V   *12840*   Turkey *12840*

R   *Lilium carniolicum* Bernh. ex W. Koch var. *artvinense*
     (Miscz.) Davis & Henderson *12840*
     R   *12840*   Turkey *12840*

I   *Lilium caucasicum* (Miscz. ex Grossh.) Grossh. *5942*
     I   *5942*   Russia - North Caucasus *5942*

I   *Lilium cernuum* Kom. *11552*
     I   *5942*   Russia (Far East) - Primorye (south) *5942*

V   *Lilium ciliatum* Davis *12840*
     V   *12840*   Turkey *12840*

R   *Lilium grayi* S.Watson *20850*
     R   *20850*   U.S. - North Carolina *20850*
     E   *20850*   U.S. - Tennessee *20850*
     V   *20850*   U.S. - Virginia *20850*

R   *Lilium humboldtii* Roezl & Leichtl. ex Duchartre ssp.
     humboldtii *20850*
     R   *20850*   U.S. - California *20850*

R   *Lilium humboldtii* Roezl & Leichtl. ex Duchartre ssp.
     ocellatum (Kellogg) Thorne *20850*
     R   *20850*   U.S. - California *20850*

E   *Lilium iridollae* Henry *20850*
     E   *20850*   U.S. - Alabama *20850*
     E   *20850*   U.S. - Florida *20850*
     E   *20850*   U.S. - North Carolina *20850*
     I   *20850*   U.S. - South Carolina *20850*
     E   *20850*   U.S. - Virginia *20850*

I   *Lilium ledebourii* (Baker) Boiss. *5942*
     I   *5942*   Azerbaijan *5942*

E   *Lilium mackliniae* Sealy *11494*
     E   *11494*   India - Manipur (Shirhoy Hill) *11494*

V   *Lilium maculatum* Thunb. var. *bukosanense* (Honda)
     Hara *11164*
     V   *11164*   Japan *11164*

R   *Lilium maculatum* Thunb. var. *monticola*
     Hara *11164*
     R   *11164*   Japan *11164*

V   *Lilium maritimum* Kellogg *20850*
     V   *20850*   U.S. - California *20850*

I   *Lilium neilgherrense* Wight
     I   India - Karnataka
     I   India - Tamil Nadu *2268*

E   *Lilium occidentale* Purdy *20850*
     E   *20850*   U.S. - California *20850*
     E   *20850*   U.S. - Oregon *20850*

E   *Lilium pardalinum* Kellogg ssp. *pitkinense* (Beane &
     Vollmer) M. Skinner *20850*
     E   *20850*   U.S. - California *20850*

R   *Lilium parryi* S.Watson *20850, 14908*
     V   *20850*   U.S. - Arizona *20850*
     V   *20850*   U.S. - California *20850*

V   *Lilium pomponium* L. *17781, 20171*
     V   *17781*   France (Provence) *17781*
     E   *18264*   Italy (Liguria) *19997*

R   *Lilium rhodopaeum* Delip. *5204, 20171*
     V   *19426*   Bulgaria (south - one area and one site.) *5204*
     R   *14000*   Greece *14000*

R   *Lilium rubellum* Baker *11164*
     R   *11164*   Japan *11164*

I   *Lilium wallichianum* Schultes f. *7771*
     I   India - Uttar Pradesh (Chamoli Dist. Kumaun) *7771*
     V   Nepal *7771*

R   *Lloydia himalensis* Royle *13883*
     R   *13883*   Bhutan (Mela and Thang Chu-Ritang) *13883*
     R   *13883*   India - Himachal Pradesh (Simla) *13883*
     R   *13883*   India - Jammu & Kashmir *13883*

R		13883 India - Sikkim (tsomgo) *13883*
R		13883 Nepal (Arun Valley, Kumgrang La.) *13883*

R **Lloydia serotina** (L.) Salisb. ex Reichenb. ssp. *flava* Calder & Taylor *20850*
   R   20850 Canada - British Columbia *20850*

R **Tenicroa multifolia** (G.J.Lewis) Oberm. *20604*
   R   20604 South Africa - Cape Province *20604*

R **Tenicroa nana** Snijman *20604*
   R   20604 South Africa - Cape Province *20604*

I **Tenicroa planifolia** D. & U.Müll.-Doblies ined. *20604*
   I   20604 South Africa - Cape Province *20604*

I **Tulipa albertii** Regel *5942*
   I   5942 Kazakhstan *5942*
   I   5942 Kyrgyzstan *5942*

Ex **Tulipa aximensis** E.P.Perrier & Songeon *20171*
   Ex 20528 France (Savoie) *20528*

Ex **Tulipa billietiana** Jord. *20171*
   Ex 20528 France (Savoie & Alpes-Maritimes) *20528*

R **Tulipa carinata** Vved.
   R   former USSR *6930*

E **Tulipa cypria** Stapf *14230*
   E   20710 Cyprus *14230*

E **Tulipa didieri** Jord. *18154, 20171*
   E   20528 France (Savoie) *20528*

V **Tulipa doerfleri** Gand. *20171*
   V   20731 Greece - Crete *20731*

E **Tulipa fosteriana** Irving
   E   former USSR *6930*

V **Tulipa goulimyi** Sealy & Turrill *17781, 20171*
   V   19174 Greece *19174*

I **Tulipa greigii** Regel *5942*
   I   5942 Kazakhstan (southern) *5942*
   I   5942 Kyrgyzstan *5942*

E **Tulipa grengiolensis** Thommen *18154, 20677*
   E   18154 Switzerland *18154*

R **Tulipa heteropetala** Ledeb.
   R   former USSR *6930*

E **Tulipa hoogiana** B. Fedtsch.
   E   former USSR *6930*

I **Tulipa ingens** Hoog. *5942*
   I   5942 Tajikistan *5942*
   I   5942 Uzbekistan *5942*

I **Tulipa kaufmanniana** Regel *5942*
   I   5942 Kazakhstan (southeastern) *5942*
   I   5942 Kyrgyzstan *5942*

V **Tulipa korolkowii** Regel
   V   former USSR *6930*

E **Tulipa kuschkensis** B. Fedtsch.
   E   former USSR *6930*

I **Tulipa lanata** Regel *5942*
   I   5942 Tajikistan (south-east) *5942*
   I   5942 Uzbekistan (south-east) *5942*

R **Tulipa linifolia** Regel
   R   former USSR *6930*

E **Tulipa lortetii** Jord. *20171*
   E   20528 France (south-east) *20528*

Ex **Tulipa marjoletii** Perr. & Song. *20528*
   Ex 20528 France (Savoie) *20528*

E **Tulipa mauriana** Jord. & Fourr. *20171*

   E   20528 France (Savoie) *20528*

R **Tulipa maximowiczii** Regel
   R   former USSR *6930*

I **Tulipa mogoltavica** Popov & Vved. *5942*
   I   5942 Kyrgyzstan *5942*
   I   5942 Uzbekistan *5942*

E **Tulipa montisandrei** J.Prudhomme *20528*
   E   20528 France (Savoie: Hermillon) *20528*

I **Tulipa ostrowskiana** Regel *5942*
   I   5942 Kazakhstan *5942*
   I   5942 Kyrgyzstan *5942*

Ex **Tulipa planifolia** Jord. *20171*
   Ex 20528 France (Savoie) *20528*

E **Tulipa platystigma** Jord. *20171*
   E   20528 France (Hautes-Alpes) *20528*

V **Tulipa praestans** Hoog
   V   former USSR *6930*

R **Tulipa regelii** Krasnov *5942*
   R   5942 Kazakhstan (south-east) *5942*

V **Tulipa rhodopaea** Vel. *5204*
   V   5204 Bulgaria (Southern Bulgaria - one site only.) *5204*

R **Tulipa rosea** Vved.
   R   former USSR *6930*

R **Tulipa schmidtii** Fomin
   R   former USSR *6930*

Ex **Tulipa sprengeri** Baker *12840*
   Ex 12840 Turkey *12840*

E **Tulipa subpraestans** Vved.
   E   former USSR *6930*

R **Tulipa tarda** Stapf
   R   former USSR *6930*

V **Tulipa urumoffii** Hayek *5204, 20171*
   V   5204 Bulgaria (Rodopi) *8000*

V **Tulipa wilsoniana** Hoog
   V   former USSR *6930*

R **Tulipa zenaidae** Vved.
   R   former USSR *6930*

Limnocharitaceae

Number of genera:	3	
Number of species:	7-12	
Recorded threatened species:	3	(30%)

Tropics and subtropics.

R **Hydrocleys mattogrossensis** (Kuntze) Holm-Nielsen & Haynes *20883*
   I   20883 Bolivia *20883*
   I   20883 Brazil *20883*

R **Hydrocleys modesta** Pedersen *20883*
   V   20883 Argentina *20883*
   V   20883 Brazil *20883*
   E   20883 Paraguay *20883*

R **Hydrocleys parviflora** Seubert *20883*
   E   20883 El Salvador *20883*
   V   20883 Honduras *20883*
   V   20883 Mexico *20883*
   V   20883 Nicaragua *20883*
   V   20883 Bolivia *20883*
   V   20883 Brazil *20883*
   E   20883 Colombia *20883*
   V   20883 Venezuela *20883*

Lomandraceae

Number of genera: 6
Number of species: 42
Recorded threatened species: 6 (14%)

New Guinea, Australia, New Caledonia.

R   *Lomandra brevis* A.T.Lee *20681*
   R   *20681* Australia - New South Wales *20681*

R   *Lomandra fluviatilis* (R.Br.) A.Lee *20681*
   R   *20681* Australia - New South Wales *20681*

R   *Lomandra patens* A.T.Lee *20681*
   I   *20681* Australia - New South Wales *20681*
   I   *20681* Australia - Northern Territory *20681*

R   *Lomandra teres* T.D.Macfarlane *20681*
   R   *20681* Australia - Queensland *20681*

R   *Romnalda grallata* R.Henderson *20681*
   R   *20681* Australia - Queensland *20681*

V   *Romnalda strobilacea* R.Henderson *20681*
   V   *20681* Australia - Queensland *20681*

Lowiaceae

Number of genera: 1
Number of species: 6
Recorded threatened species: 1 (16%)

Southern China; Malay Peninsula; Pacific islands.

R   *Orchidantha chinensis* T.L. Wu *17617*
   R   *17617* China - Guangdong (Xingyi) *11139*
   R   *17617* China - Guangxi (Shangshi) *11139*

Marantaceae

Number of genera: 30
Number of species: 400
Recorded threatened species: 11 (2%)

Pantropical, especially New World.

E   *Calathea allenii* Woods. *20883, 9006*
   I   *20883* Panama *20883*

E   *Calathea coriacea* H. Kennedy *20883, 9832*
   I   *20883* Costa Rica *20883*
   I   *20883* Panama *20883*

E   *Calathea dressleri* H. Kennedy *20883, 9833*
   I   *20883* Panama *20883*

R   *Calathea misantlensis* Lascurain *21248*
   R   *21248* Mexico - Veracruz *21248*

E   *Calathea verecunda* H. Kennedy *20883, 10747*
   I   *20883* Panama *20883*

I   *Marantochloa congensis* (Schumann) Leonard & Mull. var. *microphylla* Koechlin
   I   Gabon

I   *Phrynium cadellianum* Baker *7771*
   I   India - Andaman Is. *7771*

V   *Phrynium imbricatum* Roxb. *14872*
   V   *14872* Bangladesh *14872*

I   *Phrynium paniculatum* Balakr. *7771*
   I   India - Nicobar Is. (Gt. Nicobar Is.) *7771*

I   *Stachyphrynium spicatum* (Roxb.) Schumann *4988*
   I   India - Karnataka *4988*
   I   India - Kerala *9336*

E   *Thalia angustifolia* C. Wright *5607*

E   *19105* Cuba (Pinar del Rio) *5607*

Melanthiaceae

Number of genera: 24
Number of species: 146
Recorded threatened species: 17 (11%)

Widespread except Africa, mostly north temperate.

E   *Aletris bracteata* Northrop *20850*
   I   *20850* U.S. - Florida *20850*

V   *Aletris makiyataroi* Naruh. *11164*
   V   *11164* Japan *11164*

E   *Chionographis japonica* Maxim. var. *hisauchiana* Okuyama *11164*
   E   *11164* Japan *11164*

E   *Chionographis japonica* Maxim. var. *minoensis* Hara *11164*
   E   *11164* Japan *11164*

E   *Harperocallis flava* McDaniel *20850*
   E   *20850* U.S. - Florida (Franklin & Liberty Co.) *20850*

R   *Helonias bullata* L. *20850, 14594*
   R   *20850* U.S. - Delaware (Coastal Plain) *20850*
   E   *20850* U.S. - Georgia (Rabun County) *20850*
   V   *20850* U.S. - Maryland (Anne Arundel, Cecil, & Dorchester Counties) *20850*
   R   *20850* U.S. - New Jersey *20850*
   Ex *20850* U.S. - New York *20850*
   V   *20850* U.S. - North Carolina (Jackson, Henderson, & Transylva Counties) *20850*
   I   *20850* U.S. - Pennsylvania *20850*
   E   *20850* U.S. - South Carolina (Greenville County) *20850*
   V   *20850* U.S. - Virginia *20850*

R   *Japonolirion osense* Nakai *11164*
   R   *11164* Japan *11164*

V   *Narthecium americanum* Ker-Gawl. *20850*
   Ex *20850* U.S. - Delaware *20850*
   I   *20850* U.S. - Maryland *20850*
   V   *20850* U.S. - New Jersey *20850*
   Ex *20850* U.S. - North Carolina *20850*
   Ex/E *20850* U.S. - South Carolina *20850*

R   *Narthecium scardicum* Kosanin *20178, 20171*
   R   *20178* Albania *20178*
   V   Greece
   R   (former) Yugoslavia

R   *Schoenocaulon pringlei* Greenman *9114*
   R   *9019* Mexico *9114*

R   *Tofieldia coccinea* Richards. var. *akkana* T. Shimizu *11164*
   R   *11164* Japan *11164*

V   *Tofieldia coccinea* Richards. var. *geibiensis* (Kikuchi) Hara *11164*
   V   *11164* Japan *11164*

V   *Tofieldia coccinea* Richards. var. *kiusiana* (Okuy.) Hara *11164*
   V   *11164* Japan *11164*

R   *Tofieldia fauriei* Leveilie & Vaniot *15957*
   R   *15923* Korea, South (Mt Halla) *15957*

R   *Tofieldia glabra* Nutt. *20850*
   I   *20850* U.S. - Connecticut *20850*
   I   *20850* U.S. - Georgia *20850*
   R   *20850* U.S. - North Carolina *20850*
   I   *20850* U.S. - South Carolina *20850*

E **Tofieldia glutinosa** C.L. Hitchc. ssp. *absona* C.L.
Hitchc. *20850*
  I *20850* U.S. - Idaho *20850*

I **Veratrum chiengdaoense** K. Larsen
  I Thailand (Doi Chiengdao)

V **Veratrum tenuipetalum** Heller *20850*
  I *20850* U.S. - Colorado *20850*
  E *20850* U.S. - Wyoming *20850*

R **Zigadenus brevibracteatus** (M.E. Jones) Hall *20850*
  I *20850* U.S. - California *20850*

V **Zigadenus vaginatus** (Rydb.) J.F. Macbr. *20850*
  V *20850* U.S. - Colorado *20850*
  V *20850* U.S. - Utah *20850*

Musaceae

Number of genera: 2
Number of species: 42
Recorded threatened species: 2   (4%)

Tropical and subtropical Old World.

Ex **Musa fitzalanii** F.Muell. *20681*
  Ex *20681* Australia - Queensland *20681*

V **Musa gracilis** Holttum *8260*
  V Malaysia - Peninsular Malaysia (Johor) *19209*

R **Musa jackeyi** W.Hill *20681*
  R *20681* Australia - Queensland *20681*

Orchidaceae

Number of genera: 800
Number of species: 25,000-35,000
Recorded threatened species: 1779   (5%)

Cosmopolitan.

R II **Aa nervosa** (Kranzlin) Schltr. *5595*
  R *19534* Chile *5595*

R II **Acianthus amplexicaulis** (Bailey) Rolfe *20681*
  I *20681* Australia - New South Wales *20681*
  I *20681* Australia - Queensland *20681*

R II **Acianthus apprimus** D.L.Jones *20681*
  R *20681* Australia - New South Wales *20681*

R II **Acianthus exiguus** D.L.Jones *20681*
  R *20681* Australia - New South Wales *20681*

Ex II **Acianthus ledwardii** Rupp *20681*
  Ex *20681* Australia - New South Wales *20681*

R II **Acianthus sublestus** Dockr. *20681*
  R *20681* Australia - Queensland *20681*

R II **Acianthus vulcanicus** Schodde *14794*
  R *14793* PNG - Bougainville (N.Solomon Is.) *14794*
  R *14793* Solomon Is. - South *14794*

V II **Acineta barkeri** (Bateman) Lindley *9019*
  V *18110* Guatemala *18110*
  V *9019* Mexico - Chiapas *9019*
  V *18110* Mexico - Guerrero *18110*
  V *9019* Mexico - Oaxaca *9019*
  V *18110* Mexico - Puebla *11933*
  V *9019* Mexico - Veracruz *9019*

R II **Acineta erythroxantha** Reichb.f. *9037*
  E *9426* Costa Rica *9037*
  R *10007* Mexico *9037*

E II **Acineta gymnostele** Schltr. *9037*
  E *9426* Costa Rica *9037*

V II **Acostaea costaricensis** Schltr. ssp. *bicornis* (Luer) Luer *12470*
  V *16317* Panama *12470*

V II **Acostaea costaricensis** Schltr. ssp. *unicornis* (Luer) Luer *12470*
  V *16317* Panama *12470*

V II **Acostaea trilobata** Luer *12470*
  V *19045* Ecuador *19045*

V II **Acriopsis densiflora** Lindl. var. *borneensis* (Ridley) M.E. Minderh. & Vogel *19218*
  V *19218* Malaysia - Sabah *19218*

R II **Acrolophia barbata** (Thunb.) H.P.Linder *20604*
  R *20604* South Africa - Cape Province *20604*

V II **Acrolophia bolusii** Rolfe *20604*
  V *20604* South Africa - Cape Province *20604*

R II **Acrolophia micrantha** (Lindl.) Schltr. & Bolus *20604*
  R *20604* South Africa - Cape Province *20604*

V II **Acrolophia ustulata** (Bolus) Schltr. & Bolus *20604, 3774*
  V *20604* South Africa - Cape Province *20604*

E II **Aeranthes arachnites** Lindley var. *balfourii* S. Moore *5852*
  E *5852* Mauritius - Rodrigues (Grande Mt & Mont Cimetiere) *5852*

I II **Aerides fieldingii** Williams *4300*
  I India - Assam *4300*
  I India - Meghalaya (Khasi hills) *4300*
  I India - Sikkim *4300*

I II **Aerides vandara** Reichb. *4300*
  V *19161* Bhutan *4300*
  I India - Assam *4300*
  I India - Meghalaya (Khasi hills) *4300*
  I India - Nagaland *4300*

V II **Agrostophyllum occidentale** Schltr. *14296*
  Ex/E *19182* Madagascar *10246*
  V *19182* Seychelles *14296*

I II **Agrostophyllum zeylanicum** Hook.f. *8021*
  I *16162* Sri Lanka *8021*

V II **Alamania punicea** Llave & Lex. *9423*
  V *16360* Mexico *9423*

R II **Allochilus eberhardtii** Gagnepain *6057*
  R Vietnam *6057*

V II **Amparoa beloglossa** (Reichb.f.) Schltr. *10047*
  V *19850* Mexico *10047*

R II **Anacamptis urvilleana** Sommier & Caruana *17934, 20171*
  R *17934* Malta *17934*

R II **Androcorys japonensis** F. Maek. *11164*
  R *11164* Japan *11164*

Ex II **Angraecum carpophorum** *10082*
  Ex *10082* Réunion *10082*
  Ex *20771* Mauritius *10082*

V II **Angraecum liliodorum** Frapp ex Cordem. *10082*
  V *10082* Réunion *10082*
  V *20771* Mauritius *10082*

Ex II **Angraecum obversifolium** Frapp. *10082*
  Ex *10082* Réunion *10082*
  Ex *20771* Mauritius *10082*

V II **Angraecum ramosum** Thouars *10082*
  V *10082* Réunion *10082*
  V *20771* Mauritius *10082*

R II **Anoectochilus chapaensis** Gagnepain *6057*

R		20985 Vietnam *6057*	

E II *Anoectochilus nicobaricus* Balakr. & Chakrab. *5231*
    E   *11494* India - Nicobar Is. (Great Nicobar) *11494*

Ex/E II *Anoectochilus rotundifolius* (Blatter) Balakr. *11494*
    Ex/E *11494* India - Tamil Nadu (High Wavy Mts, Madura) *11494*

R II *Anoectochilus sandvicensis* Lindl. *20850, 14209*
    I   *20850* U.S. - Hawaii *20850*

I II *Anoectochilus sikkimensis* King & Pantl. *4300*
    I   India - Sikkim *4300*

V II *Anoectochilus tetrapterus* Hook.f. *11494*
    V   *11494* India - Manipur *11494*

R II *Anoectochilus yungianus* S. Y. Hu *19924*
    R   *19924* Hong Kong (New Territories) *19924*

V II *Apatostelis atrorubens* (L.O. Williams) Garay *11502*
    V   *16317* Panama *11502*

R II *Aphyllorchis anomala* Dockr. *20681*
    R   *20681* Australia - Queensland *20681*

Ex/E II *Aphyllorchis gollani* Duthie *11494*
    Ex/E *11494* India - Uttar Pradesh (Tehri-Garwhal) *11494*

I II *Aphyllorchis vaginata* Hook.f.
    I   India - Meghalaya (Khasi hills)

R II *Appendicula australiensis* (Bailey) M.A.Clements & D.L.Jones *20681*
    R   *20681* Australia - Queensland *20681*

V II *Appendicula congener* Blume *8309*
    V   *19047* Indonesia - Java (West Java) *8309*

V II *Appendicula densiflora* Ridley *19047*
    V   *19047* Malaysia - Peninsular Malaysia *19047*

R II *Arachnis beccarii* Reichb. f. var. *imthurnii* (Rolfe) Tan *14794*
    R   *14794* PNG - Bougainville (N.Solomon Is.) *14794*
    R   *14793* Solomon Is. - South *14794*

R II *Arachnis clarkei* (Reichb. f.) J.J. Smith *4300*
    R   *19161* Bhutan *4300*
    I   India - Arunachal Pradesh
    I   India - Meghalaya
    I   India - Sikkim *4300*

I II *Arachnis limax* Seidenf. *19120*
    I   *19120* Thailand *19120*

V II *Arachnis lowii* Reichb.f. *19047*
    V   *19047* Indonesia - Kalimantan *19047*
    E   *14965* Malaysia - Sarawak *14965*

E II *Archineottia gaudissartii* (Hand.-Mazz.) S.C. Chen *17617*
    E   *17617* China - Henan (Shongshan) *11139*
    E   *17617* China - Shanxi (Taiyushan) *11139*

R II *Archineottia microglottis* (Duthie) S.C. Chen *11494*
    R   *11494* India - Uttar Pradesh *11494*

I II *Armodorum siamensis* Schlts. *19120*
    I   *19120* Thailand *19120*

V II *Arnottia mauritiana* A. Rich. *10082*
    V   *10082* Réunion *10082*
    V   *20771* Mauritius *10082*

V II *Arpophyllum jamaicense* Schltr. *20883, 19890*
    V   *19890* Jamaica *20883*

V II *Artorima erubescens* (Lindley) Dressler & Pollard *10007*
    V   *18110* Mexico - Guerrero *18110*

V		*18110* Mexico - Oaxaca *18110*	

I II *Ascocentrum semiteretifolium* Seidenf. *19120*
    I   *19120* Thailand *19120*

I II *Ascochilus nitidus* Seidenf. *19120*
    I   *19120* Thailand *1920*

V II *Barbosella circinata* Luer *10009*
    ?   Costa Rica *21258*
    V   *10020* Panama *10009*

V II *Barbosella geminata* Luer *10009*
    V   *9426* Costa Rica *10009*

V II *Barkeria dorotheae* Halbinger *11938*
    V   *19850* Mexico *11938*

R II *Barkeria halbingeri* Thien *11344*
    R   *11933* Mexico *11344*

E II *Barkeria lindleyana* Bateman ex Lindley ssp. lindleyana *9422*
    E   *9426* Costa Rica *9422*

V II *Barkeria melanocaulon* A. Rich. & Galeotti *9422*
    V   *19850* Mexico - Oaxaca *9422*

V II *Barkeria scandens* (Llave & Lex.) Dressler & Halbinger *11938*
    V   *16360* Mexico *11938*

R II *Barkeria shoemakeri* F. Halbinger *9422*
    R   *11119* Mexico - Michoacan *9422*

V II *Barkeria strophinx* (Reichb.f.) Halbinger *19850*
    V   *19850* Mexico *19850*

R II *Barkeria uniflora* (Llave & Lex.) Dressler & Halbinger *9422*
    R   *10007* Guatemala *9422*
    V   *10007* Mexico *9422*

E II *Barlia metlesicsiana* Teschner *20750*
    E   *20750* Spain - Canary Is. *20750*

E II *Basiphyllaea angustifolia* Schlechter *20883, 19408*
    I   *20883* Cuba *20883*
    E   *19408* Dominican Republic *19408*
    ?   Hispaniola *8058*
    I   *20883* Puerto Rico *20883*

V II *Basiphyllaea corallicola* (Small) Ames *20883, 20850, 19002*
    E   *20850* U.S. - Florida *20850*
    ?   Cuba *19002*
    I   *20883* Puerto Rico *20883*

R II *Baskervillea pastasae* Garay *19045*
    R   *19045* Ecuador *19045*

I II *Biermannia jainiana* S.N. Hegde & A. Nageswara Rao *10260*
    I   India - Arunachal Pradesh *9416*

E II *Bipinnula taltalensis* Johnston. *20580*
    E   *20580* Chile - Antofagasta (Paposo National Park) *20580*

R II *Bletia florida* (Salisb.) R.Br. *20883*
    R   *20883* Jamaica *20883*

R II *Bletia greenmaniana* L.O. Williams *9423*
    R   *16360* Mexico *9423*

V II *Bletia macristhmochila* Greenman *9423*
    V   *10007* Mexico *9423*

R II *Bletia nelsonii* Ames *9423*
    R   *11933* Mexico *9423*

V II *Bletia urbana* Dressler *11938*
    V   *19850* Mexico *11938*

Liliopsida (monocots): Orchidaceae: *Bletia*

R	II	*Bolusiella maudiae* (Bolus) Schltr. *20604*	
	R	20604	South Africa - Natal *20604*
R	II	*Bonatea eminii* (Kraenzlin) Rolfe *7959*	
	R	5926	Tanzania (Dodoma) *7959*
R	II	*Bonatea lamprophylla* J.L.Stewart *20604*	
	R	20604	South Africa - Natal *20604*
R	II	*Bonatea rabaiensis* (Rendle) Rolfe *6073*	
	R	6073	Kenya *6073*
	I	5926	Tanzania *7959*
I	II	*Bonatea saundersiae* (Harv.) T.Durand & Schinz *20604*	
	I	20604	South Africa - Natal *20604*
R	II	*Bonatea stereophylla* (Kraenzlin) Summerh. *7959*	
	R	5926	Tanzania (Njombe Distr.) *7959*
E	II	*Bonatea tentaculifera* Summerh. *6073*	
	E	6073	Kenya (Nairobi City Park) *7959*
E	II	*Brachionidium ballatrix* Luer & Hirtz *19045*	
	E	19045	Ecuador *19045*
V	II	*Brachionidium ciliolatum* Garay *20883, 15106*	
	I	20883	Puerto Rico *20883*
R	II	*Brachionidium dussii* Cogn. *19400*	
	R	19400	Guadeloupe *19400*
E	II	*Brachionidium operosum* Luer & Hirtz *19045*	
	E	19045	Ecuador *19045*
E	II	*Brachionidium parvifolium* (Lindl.) Lindl. *19045*	
	E	19045	Ecuador *19045*
E	II	*Brachionidium pteroglossum* Luer *19045*	
	E	19045	Ecuador *19045*
E	II	*Brachionidium simplex* Garay *19045*	
	E	19045	Ecuador *19045*
V	II	*Brachionidium uxorium* Luer & Vásquez *21301*	
	V	21301	Puerto Rico *21301*
E	II	*Brachionidium zunagense* Luer & Hirtz *19045*	
	E	19045	Ecuador *19045*
R	II	*Brachycorythis macowaniana* Rchb.f. *20604*	
	R	20604	South Africa - Cape Province *20604*
R	II	*Brachycorythis tanganyikensis* Summerh. *7959*	
	R	5926	Tanzania (Morogoro Distr.) *7959*
R	II	*Brachypeza archytas* (Ridley) Garay *881*	
	R	14224	Australia - Christmas Is. *881*
V	II	*Broughtonia negrilensis* Fowlie *19890*	
	V	19890	Jamaica *19221*
R	II	*Broughtonia sanguinea* (Sw.) R. Br. *20883, 19890*	
	V	19890	Jamaica *20883*
R	II	*Bulbophyllum acutiflorum* A. Rich. *11494*	
	R	11494	India - Tamil Nadu *11494*
I	II	*Bulbophyllum adangensis* Seidenf. *19120*	
	I	19120	Thailand *19120*
I	II	*Bulbophyllum albibracteatum* Seidenf. *19120*	
	I	19120	Thailand *19120*
R	II	*Bulbophyllum albidum* (Wight) Hook.f. *11494*	
	R	11494	India - Tamil Nadu *11494*
I	II	*Bulbophyllum angusteovatum* Seidenf. *19120*	
	I	19120	Thailand *19120*
I	II	*Bulbophyllum annandale* Ridl. *19120*	
	I	19120	Thailand *19120*
I	II	*Bulbophyllum ardjunense* J.J. Smith *8309*	
	I		Indonesia - Java (east) *8309*
R	II	*Bulbophyllum aureum* (Hook.f.) J.J. Smith *11494*	

	R	11494	India - Kerala (Muthukuzhivayal, Wynaad) *11494*
V	II	*Bulbophyllum bibundiense* Schltr.	
	V		Cameroon (Moliwe)
I	II	*Bulbophyllum bisetoides* Seidenf. *19120*	
	I	19120	Thailand *19120*
I	II	*Bulbophyllum brevistelidium* Seidenf. *19120*	
	I	19120	Thailand *19120*
V	II	*Bulbophyllum caespitosum* Thouars *10082*	
	V	20771	Mauritius *10082*
V	II	*Bulbophyllum capilligerum* J.J. Smith *8309*	
	V	19047	Indonesia - Java (east) *8309*
V	II	*Bulbophyllum carunculaelabrum* Carr *19047*	
	V	19047	Malaysia - Peninsular Malaysia (Johor, Bt Kajang, Kemaman) *19047*
R	II	*Bulbophyllum crassifolium* Thwaites ex Trimen *8021*	
	R	20013	Sri Lanka (Ritigala, Kukul Korale) *8021*
R	II	*Bulbophyllum dennisii* J.J. Wood *14794*	
	R	14793	PNG - Bougainville (N.Solomon Is.) *14794*
	R	14793	Solomon Is. - South *14794*
I	II	*Bulbophyllum dhaninivatii* Seidenf. *19120*	
	I	19120	Thailand *19120*
I	II	*Bulbophyllum didymotropis* Seidenf. *19120*	
	I	19120	Thailand *19120*
I	II	*Bulbophyllum echinulus* Seidenf. *19120*	
	I	19120	Thailand *19120*
R	II	*Bulbophyllum elegans* Gardner ex Thwaites *8021*	
	R	20013	Sri Lanka *8021*
V	II	*Bulbophyllum elegantulum* (Rolfe) J.J. Smith *11494*	
	V	11494	India - Karnataka (Coorg) *11494*
	V	11494	India - Tamil Nadu (Kudini, Nilgiri hills) *11494*
R	II	*Bulbophyllum elliae* Reichb.f. *8021*	
	R	20013	Sri Lanka *8021*
R	II	*Bulbophyllum evrardii* Gagnepain *6057*	
	R	20985	Vietnam *6057*
I	II	*Bulbophyllum filiforme* Kranzlin	
	I		Cameroon
R	II	*Bulbophyllum fractiflexum* J.J. Smith ssp. *solomonense* J. Vermeulen & B. Lewis *14794*	
	R	14793	PNG - Bougainville (N.Solomon Is.) *14794*
	R	14793	Solomon Is. - South *14794*
I	II	*Bulbophyllum fusco-purpureum* Wight	
	I		India - Tamil Nadu (Nilagiri Hills) *4988*
I	II	*Bulbophyllum gibbolabium* Seidenf. *19120*	
	I	19120	Thailand *19120*
V	II	*Bulbophyllum globosum* *19047*	
	V	19047	Malaysia - Peninsular Malaysia *19047*
V	II	*Bulbophyllum globuliforme* Nicholls *20681*	
	I	20681	Australia - New South Wales *20681*
	I	20681	Australia - Queensland *20681*
R	II	*Bulbophyllum grandimesense* B.Gray & D.L.Jones *20681*	
	R	20681	Australia - Queensland *20681*
R	II	*Bulbophyllum inaequale* (Blume) Lindley *8309*	
	R		Indonesia - Java (West & East Java) *8309*
E	II	*Bulbophyllum jamaicense* Cogn. *20883, 19890*	
	E	19890	Jamaica (St. Andrew, St. Thomas) *20883*

V   II   *Bulbophyllum javanicum* Miq. *19047*
     V   *19047* Indonesia - Java *19047*

V   II   *Bulbophyllum kaitiense* (Wight) Reichb. F. *13883*
     V   *13883* India - Tamil Nadu (Nilgiris) *13883*

V   II   *Bulbophyllum longibulbus* Schltr.
     V   Cameroon (Nyassosso)

V   II   *Bulbophyllum lophoglottis* (Guillaumin) Halle *20893*
     V   *20893* New Caledonia *20893*

E   II   *Bulbophyllum macraei* (Lindley) Reichb.f. var. *tanegashimense* F. Maek. *11164*
     E   *11164* Japan *11164*

R   II   *Bulbophyllum makakense* J. Hansen
     R   Cameroon

R   II   *Bulbophyllum maskeliyense* Liv. *8021*
     R   *20013* Sri Lanka *8021*

I   II   *Bulbophyllum melanoxanthum* J. Vermeulen & B. Lewis *14794*
     I   *14793* PNG - Bougainville (N.Solomon Is.) *14794*
     I   *14793* Solomon Is. - South (New Georgia) *14794*

V   II   *Bulbophyllum modicum* Summerh.
     V   Cameroon (Buea)

I   II   *Bulbophyllum mysorense* J.J. Smith
     I   India - Karnataka (Mysore Hills) *4988*

V   II   *Bulbophyllum obscurum* J.J. Smith *8309*
     V   *19047* Indonesia - Java (West Java) *8309*

V   II   *Bulbophyllum perakense* Ridley *19047*
     V   *19047* Malaysia - Peninsular Malaysia (Perak) *19047*

V   II   *Bulbophyllum petiolatum* J.J. Smith *8309*
     V   *19047* Indonesia - Java (West Java) *8309*

V   II   *Bulbophyllum pulchellum* Ridley *19047*
     V   *19047* Malaysia - Peninsular Malaysia *19047*

R   II   *Bulbophyllum puntjakense* J.J. Smith *8309*
     R   Indonesia - Java (West Java) *8309*

I   II   *Bulbophyllum purpureum* Thwaites *8021*
     I   *16162* Sri Lanka (Kandy) *8021*

Ex   II   *Bulbophyllum pusillum* Thouars *10082*
     Ex   *20771* Mauritius *10082*

I   II   *Bulbophyllum putii* Seidenf. *19120*
     I   *19120* Thailand *19120*

I   II   *Bulbophyllum raui* Arora
     I   India - Uttar Pradesh (Kumaun)

E   II   *Bulbophyllum rothschildianum* (O'Brien) J.J. Smith *16294*
     E   *16294* India (hills in northeastern India) *16294*

I   II   *Bulbophyllum sanitii* Seidenf. *19120*
     I   *19120* Thailand *19120*

R   II   *Bulbophyllum scotiifolium* J.J. Smith *8309*
     R   Indonesia - Java (West Java) *8309*

R   II   *Bulbophyllum semiteratifolium* Gagnepain *6057*
     R   Vietnam *6057*

I   II   *Bulbophyllum stramineum* Ames *13833*
     I   *13833* Philippines (Palawan) *13833*

I   II   *Bulbophyllum subtenellum* Seidenf. *19120*
     I   *19120* Thailand *19120*

V   II   *Bulbophyllum teretifolium* Schltr.
     V   Cameroon (Bibundi)

I   II   *Bulbophyllum tricarinatum* Petch *8021*
     I   *16162* Sri Lanka (Maturata, Nuwara Eliya) *8021*

I   II   *Bulbophyllum tricornoides* Seidenfaden *19120*
     I   *19120* Thailand *19120*

I   II   *Bulbophyllum tripaleum* Seidenf. *19120*
     I   *19120* Thailand *19120*

I   II   *Bulbophyllum triviale* Seidenf. *19120*
     I   *19120* Thailand *19120*

R   II   *Bulbophyllum truncatum* J.J. Smith *8309*
     R   Indonesia - Java (central) *8309*

I   II   *Bulbophyllum unciniferum* Seidenf. *19120*
     I   *19120* Thailand *19120*

R   II   *Bulbophyllum undecifilum* J.J. Smith *8309*
     R   Indonesia - Java (West Java) *8309*

R   II   *Bulbophyllum vutimenaense* B. Lewis *17690*
     R   *17690* Vanuatu (Espiritu Santo, Cumberland Peninsula) *17690*

E   II   *Bulbophyllum wagneri* Schltr. *20883, 10012*
     I   *20883* Panama *20883*

I   II   *Bulbophyllum wangkaense* Seidenf. *19120*
     I   *19120* Thailand *19120*

R   II   *Bulbophyllum weinthalii* R.Rogers *20681*
     I   *20681* Australia - New South Wales *20681*
     I   *20681* Australia - Queensland *20681*

R   II   *Bulbophyllum windsorense* B.Gray & D.L.Jones *20681*
     R   *20681* Australia - Queensland *20681*

R   II   *Bulbophyllum wolfei* B.Gray & D.L.Jones *20681*
     R   *20681* Australia - Queensland *20681*

V   II   *Bulbophyllum wrightii* Summerh.
     V   Cameroon (M'bonge)

V   II   *Bulbophyllum xanthum* Ridley *19047*
     V   *19047* Malaysia - Peninsular Malaysia *19047*

I   II   *Bulbophyllum xylocarpi* J.J. Smith *8309*
     I   Indonesia - Java (central) *8309*

I   II   *Bulleyia yunnanensis* Schltr. *20756*
     V   *20756* China - Yunnan *20756*
     I   India - Arunachal Pradesh
     I   India - West Bengal (Darjeeling)

R   II   *Burnettia cuneata* Lindley *20681*
     I   *20681* Australia - New South Wales *20681*
     I   *20681* Australia - Tasmania *20681*
     I   *20681* Australia - Victoria *20681*

R   II   *Cadetia collinsii* Lavarack *20681*
     R   *20681* Australia - Queensland *20681*

R   II   *Cadetia quadrangularis* Cribb & B. Lewis *14795*
     R   *14795* Vanuatu (Efate) *14795*

R   II   *Cadetia wariana* Schltr. *20681*
     R   *20681* Australia - Queensland *20681*

E   II   *Caladenia amoena* D.L.Jones *20681*
     E   *20681* Australia - Victoria *20681*

E   II   *Caladenia argocalla* D.L.Jones *20681*
     E   *20681* Australia - South Australia *20681*

R   II   *Caladenia arrecta* Hopper & A.P.Brown ms. *20681*
     R   *20681* Australia - Western Australia *20681*

Ex   II   *Caladenia atkinsonii* Rodway *20681, 14223*
     Ex   *20681* Australia - Tasmania *20681*

E   II   *Caladenia atroclavia* D.L.Jones & M.A.Clements *20681*
     E   *20681* Australia - Queensland *20681*

E   II   *Caladenia audasii* R.Rogers *20681*
     Ex/E   *20681* Australia - South Australia *20681*

	E	20681	Australia - Victoria	20681

E   II   *Caladenia behrii* Schldl. 20681
     E   20681   Australia - South Australia   20681

R   II   *Caladenia bicalliata* R.Rogers 20681
     R   20681   Australia - South Australia   20681

Ex   II   *Caladenia brachyscapa* G.W.Carr 20681
     Ex   20681   Australia - Victoria   20681

V   II   *Caladenia brumalis* D.L.Jones 20681
     V   20681   Australia - South Australia   20681

E   II   *Caladenia bryceana* R.S.Rogers ssp.
         bryceana 20681
     E   20681   Australia - Western Australia   20681

V   II   *Caladenia bryceana* R.Rogers ssp. *cracens* Hopper &
         A.P.Brown ms. 20681
     V   20681   Australia - Western Australia   20681

E   II   *Caladenia busselliana* Hopper & A.P.Brown ms. 20681
     E   20681   Australia - Western Australia   20681

V   II   *Caladenia caesarea* (Domin) M.A.Clements & Hopper ssp.
         maritima Hopper & A.P.Brown 20681
     V   20681   Australia - Western Australia   20681

V   II   *Caladenia calcicola* G.W.Carr 20681
     I   20681   Australia - South Australia   20681
     I   20681   Australia - Victoria   20681

V   II   *Caladenia caudata* Nicholls 20681
     V   20681   Australia - Tasmania   20681

V   II   *Caladenia christineae* Hopper & A.P.Brown ms. 20681
     V   20681   Australia - Western Australia   20681

E   II   *Caladenia colorata* D.L.Jones 20681
     I   20681   Australia - South Australia   20681
     I   20681   Australia - Victoria   20681

V   II   *Caladenia concolor* Fitzg. 20681
     I   20681   Australia - New South Wales   20681
     I   20681   Australia - Victoria   20681

R   II   *Caladenia cristata* R.Rogers 20681
     R   20681   Australia - Western Australia   20681

V   II   *Caladenia dorrienii* Domin 20681
     V   20681   Australia - Western Australia   20681

E   II   *Caladenia elegans* Hopper & A.P.Brown ms. 20681
     E   20681   Australia - Western Australia   20681

V   II   *Caladenia excelsa* Hopper & A.P.Brown ms. 20681
     V   20681   Australia - Western Australia   20681

V   II   *Caladenia exstans* Hopper & A.P.Brown ms. 20681
     V   20681   Australia - Western Australia   20681

V   II   *Caladenia formosa* G.W.Carr 20681
     I   20681   Australia - South Australia   20681
     I   20681   Australia - Victoria   20681

R   II   *Caladenia fragrantissima* D.L.Jones & G.Carr ssp.
         fragrantissima 20681
     I   20681   Australia - South Australia   20681
     I   20681   Australia - Victoria   20681

E   II   *Caladenia fragrantissima* D.L.Jones & G.W.Carr ssp.
         orientalis G.W.Carr 20681
     E   20681   Australia - Victoria   20681

E   II   *Caladenia fulva* G.W.Carr 20681
     E   20681   Australia - Victoria   20681

E   II   *Caladenia gladiolata* R.Rogers 20681
     E   20681   Australia - South Australia   20681

V   II   *Caladenia harringtoniae* Hopper & A.P.Brown ms. 20681
     V   20681   Australia - Western Australia   20681

E   II   *Caladenia hastata* (Nicholls) Rupp 20681
     E   20681   Australia - Victoria   20681

V   II   *Caladenia hoffmanii* Hopper & A.P.Brown ms. 20681
     V   20681   Australia - Western Australia   20681

V   II   *Caladenia huegelii* Hopper & A.P.Brown ms. 20681
     V   20681   Australia - Western Australia   20681

V   II   *Caladenia insularis* G.W.Carr 20681
     V   20681   Australia - Victoria   20681

R   II   *Caladenia integra* E.Coleman 20681
     R   20681   Australia - Western Australia   20681

R   II   *Caladenia interjacens* Hopper & A.P.Brown ms. 20681
     R   20681   Australia - Western Australia   20681

E   II   *Caladenia lowanensis* G.W.Carr 20681
     E   20681   Australia - Victoria   20681

E   II   *Caladenia macroclavia* D.L.Jones 20681
     E   20681   Australia - South Australia   20681

R   II   *Caladenia necrophylla* D.L.Jones 20681
     R   20681   Australia - South Australia   20681

V   II   *Caladenia ovata* R.Rogers 20681
     V   20681   Australia - South Australia   20681

R   II   *Caladenia plicata* Fitzg. 20681
     R   20681   Australia - Western Australia   20681

Ex   II   *Caladenia pumila* R.Rogers 20681
     Ex   20681   Australia - Victoria   20681

E   II   *Caladenia richardsiorum* D.L.Jones 20681
     E   20681   Australia - South Australia   20681

E   II   *Caladenia rigida* R.Rogers 20681
     E   20681   Australia - South Australia   20681

E   II   *Caladenia robinsonii* G.W.Carr 20681
     E   20681   Australia - Victoria   20681

E   II   *Caladenia rosella* G.W.Carr 20681
     E   20681   Australia - New South Wales   20681
     Ex/E   20681   Australia - Victoria   20681

R   II   *Caladenia speciosa* Hopper & A.P.Brown ms. 20681
     R   20681   Australia - Western Australia   20681

E   II   *Caladenia tensa* G.W.Carr 20681
     E   20681   Australia - Victoria   20681

V   II   *Caladenia tessellata* Fitzg. 20681
     V   20681   Australia - New South Wales   20681

E   II   *Caladenia thysanochila* G.W.Carr 20681
     E   20681   Australia - Victoria   20681

R   II   *Caladenia valida* (Nicholls) M.A.Clements &
         D.L.Jones 20681
     I   20681   Australia - South Australia   20681
     I   20681   Australia - Victoria   20681

R   II   *Caladenia venusta* G.W.Carr 20681
     I   20681   Australia - South Australia   20681
     I   20681   Australia - Victoria   20681

V   II   *Caladenia versicolor* G.W.Carr 20681
     I   20681   Australia - South Australia   20681
     I   20681   Australia - Victoria   20681

E   II   *Caladenia viridescens* Hopper & A.P.Brown ms. 20681
     E   20681   Australia - Western Australia   20681

V   II   *Caladenia voigtii* Hopper & A.P.Brown ms. 20681
     V   20681   Australia - Western Australia   20681

R   II   *Caladenia vulgaris* D.L.Jones 20681
     R   20681   Australia - South Australia   20681

V   II   *Caladenia wanosa* A.S.George 20681
     V   20681   Australia - Western Australia   20681

V	II	*Caladenia williamsonii* D.L.Jones ms. *20681*	
	V	20681	Australia - Tasmania *20681*
E	II	*Caladenia winfieldii* Hopper & A.P.Brown ms. *20681*	
	E	20681	Australia - Western Australia *20681*
V	II	*Caladenia woolcockiorum* D.L.Jones *20681*	
	V	20681	Australia - South Australia *20681*
E	II	*Caladenia xanthochila* D. & C.Beardsell *20681*	
	Ex/E	20681	Australia - South Australia *20681*
	E	20681	Australia - Victoria *20681*
E	II	*Caladenia xantholeuca* D.L.Jones *20681*	
	E	20681	Australia - South Australia *20681*
I	II	*Calanthe alismaefolia* Lindley	
	I		India - Arunachal Pradesh
	I		India - Meghalaya (Khasi hills)
	I		India - Uttar Pradesh (Mussoorie)
R	II	*Calanthe alpina* Hook.f.	
	R	13883	Bhutan *13883*
	R	13883	India - Sikkim *13883*
	R	13883	India - Uttar Pradesh (Garhwal; Kumaun) *13883*
	R	13883	Nepal *13883*
I	II	*Calanthe antropophora* Ridl. *19120*	
	I	19120	Thailand *19120*
R	II	*Calanthe apostasioides* Schltr. *14794*	
	R	14793	Solomon Is. - South *14794*
V	II	*Calanthe aristulifera* Reichb.f. *11164*	
	V	11164	Japan *11164*
I	II	*Calanthe breviflos* Ridley *8309*	
	I		Indonesia - Java (West Java) *8309*
V	II	*Calanthe bungoana* Ohwi *11164*	
	V	11164	Japan *11164*
V	II	*Calanthe candida* Bosser *10082*	
	V	10082	Réunion *10082*
	V	20771	Mauritius *10082*
R	II	*Calanthe discolor* Lindley *8751*	
	R	15923	Korea, South *7588*
	V		Japan *8751*
R	II	*Calanthe ecallosa* J.J. Smith *8309*	
	R		Indonesia - Java (West Java) *8309*
V	II	*Calanthe fauriei* Schltr. *11164*	
	V	11164	Japan *11164*
E	II	*Calanthe hattorii* Schltr. *8038*	
	E	18128	Japan - Ogasawara-shoto (Hahajima) *8038*
I	II	*Calanthe herbacea* Lindley	
	I		India - Sikkim
I	II	*Calanthe hirsuta* Seidenf. *19120*	
	I	19120	Thailand *19120*
V	II	*Calanthe izuinsularis* (Satomi) Ohwi & Satomi *11164*	
	V	11164	Japan *11164*
V	II	*Calanthe nipponica* Makino *11164*	
	V	11164	Japan *11164*
V	II	*Calanthe oblanceolata* Ohwi & T. Koyama *11164*	
	V	11164	Japan *11164*
R	II	*Calanthe petelotiana* Gagnepain *6057*	
	R		Vietnam *6057*
V	II	*Calanthe rubens* Ridley *19047*	
	V	19047	Malaysia - Peninsular Malaysia *19047*
V	II	*Calanthe schlechteri* Hara *11164*	
	V	11164	Japan *11164*
I	II	*Calanthe simplex* Seidenfaden *19120*	

	I	19120	Thailand *19120*
Ex	II	*Calanthe whiteana* King & Pantl.	
	Ex		India - Sikkim (Choongthang)
E	II	*Calochilus psednus* D.L.Jones *20681*	
	E	20681	Australia - Queensland *20681*
E	II	*Calochilus richiae* Nicholls *20681*	
	E	20681	Australia - Victoria *20681*
E	II	*Campylocentrum filiforme* (Sw.)Cogn. *20883, 19890*	
	Ex/E	20883	Jamaica *20883*
E	II	*Campylocentrum hirtzii* Dodson *19045*	
	E	19045	Ecuador *19045*
R	II	*Campylocentrum hondurense* Ames *10028*	
	R	10028	Belize *10028*
	R	10028	Honduras *10028*
V	II	*Campylocentrum madisonii* Dodson *19045*	
	V	19045	Ecuador *19045*
R	II	*Campylocentrum microphyllum* Ames & Correll *9004*	
	R	9004	Guatemala *9004*
	R	9004	Mexico *9004*
E	II	*Campylocentrum minus* F. & R. *20883, 19890*	
	E	19890	Jamaica (Portland) *20883*
E	II	*Campylocentrum tenellum* Todzia *20883*	
	I	20883	Panama *20883*
R	II	*Catasetum laminatum* Lindley *9423*	
	R		Mexico *11938*
	I		Mexico - Guerrero *9423*
	I		Mexico - Michoacan *9423*
	I		Mexico - Oaxaca *9423*
R	II	*Cattleya bowringiana* Veitch *9004*	
	R	10048	Belize *9004*
	R	10048	Guatemala *9004*
R	II	*Cattleya granulosa* Lindley *9004*	
	R	9004	Guatemala *9004*
	R	9004	Brazil *9004*
V	II	*Cattleya iricolor* Reichb.f. *12482*	
	V		Ecuador
	E	12468	Peru *12482*
V	II	*Cattleya jenmanii* Rolfe *6154*	
	V	21264	Guyana *21264*
	V	21264	Venezuela *6154*
R	II	*Cattleya lawrenceana* Reichb.f. *6154*	
	R	21264	Guyana *9987*
	R	21264	Venezuela *6154*
V	II	*Cattleya maxima* Lindley *18200*	
	V		Ecuador
	E	12482	Peru *18200*
E	II	*Cattleya mooreana* Withner, Allison & Grenard *18200*	
	E	16388	Peru *16388*
R	II	*Cattleya porphyroglossa* Linden & Reichb.f. *10260*	
	R	16388	Brazil *16388*
E	II	*Cattleya rex* O'Brien *18200*	
	E	12482	Peru *18200*
E	II	*Cattleya schilleriana* Reichb.f. *17079*	
	E	17079	Brazil - Espirito Santo (region Domingos Martins) *17079*
I	I	*Cattleya trianae* Linden & Reichb.f.	
	I	20922	Colombia
V	II	*Cephalanthera cucullata* Boiss. & Heldr. *8000, 20171*	
	V	20730	Greece - Crete *8000*
R	II	*Cephalanthera kotschyana* Renz & Taub. *12840*	
	R	19873	Turkey *12840*

E   II   *Ceratandra venosa* (Lindl.) Schltr. *20604*
     E   *20604*   South Africa - Cape Province *20604*

R   II   *Ceratostylis backeri* J.J. Smith *8309*
     R   Indonesia - Java (central) *8309*

R   II   *Ceratostylis brevibrachiata* J.J. Smith *8309*
     R   Indonesia - Java (east) *8309*

R   II   *Ceratostylis evrardii* Gagnepain *6057*
     R   *20985* Vietnam *6057*

R   II   *Ceratostylis pygmaea* Evrard *6057*
     R   Vietnam *6057*

I   II   *Ceratostylis thailandica* Seidenf. *19120*
     I   *19120* Thailand (Khao Luang) *19120*

R   II   *Changnienia amoena* Chien *17617*
     R   *17617* China - Anhui *11139*
     R   *17617* China - Hubei *11139*
     R   *17617* China - Hunan *11139*
     R   *17617* China - Jiangsu *11139*
     R   *17617* China - Jiangxi *11139*
     R   *17617* China - Shaanxi *11139*
     R   *17617* China - Sichuan *11139*
     R   *17617* China - Zhejiang *11139*

I   II   *Chaseella pseudohydra* Summerh. *7764*
     I   Zimbabwe *7764*

E   II   *Chaubardiella dalassandroi* Dodson & Dalstroem *19045*
     E   *19045* Ecuador *19045*

I   II   *Cheirostylis didfymacantha* Seidenf. *19120*
     I   *19120* Thailand *19120*

R   II   *Cheirostylis javanica* J.J. Smith *8309*
     R   Indonesia - Java (east) *8309*

I   II   *Cheirostylis thailandica* Seidenf. *19120*
     I   *19120* Thailand *19120*

R   II   *Chiloglottis longiclavata* D.L.Jones *20681*
     R   *20681* Australia - Queensland *20681*

R   II   *Chiloglottis palachila* D.L.Jones *20681*
     R   *20681* Australia - New South Wales *20681*

I   II   *Chiloschista extinctoriformis* Seidenf. *19120*
     I   *19120* Thailand *19120*

I   II   *Chiloschista ramifora* Seidenf. *19120*
     I   *19120* Thailand *19120*

I   II   *Chiloschista trudelii* Seidenf. *19120*
     I   *19120* Thailand *19120*

I   II   *Chiloschista viridiflora* Seidenf. *19120*
     I   *19120* Thailand *19120*

R   II   *Chloraea subpandurata* Hauman *16336*
     R   *16336* Argentina *16336*
     R   *20176* Argentina - Buenos Aires *20176*
     R   *20176* Argentina - Jujuy *20176*
     R   *20176* Argentina - Salta *20176*

Ex/E II   *Chloraea venosa* Griseb. *18200*
     Ex/E   *12482* Peru *18200*

V   II   *Chondrorhyncha ecuadorensis* Dodson *19045*
     V   *19045* Ecuador *19045*

E   II   *Chondrorhyncha endresii* Schltr. *9037*
     E   *9426* Costa Rica *9037*

E   II   *Chondrorhyncha hirtzii* Dodson *19045*
     E   *19045* Ecuador *19045*

E   II   *Chondrorhyncha suarezii* Dodson *19045*
     E   *19045* Ecuador *19045*

V   II   *Chondrorhyncha velastiguii* Dodson *19045*
     V   *19045* Ecuador *19045*

E   II   *Chondrorhyncha wercklei* (Schltr.) C. Schweinf. *10012*
     E   *9426* Costa Rica *10012*

V   II   *Chrysocycnis ecuadorense* Dodson & Garay *19045*
     V   *19045* Ecuador *19045*

R   II   *Chrysoglossum chapaensis* (Gagnepain) Tang & Wang *6057*
     R   Vietnam *6057*

I   II   *Chrysoglossum hallbergii* Blatter *11494*
     I   *11494* India - Tamil Nadu (High Wavy Mts, Madura) *11494*

V   II   *Chysis limminghei* Linden & Reichb.f. *11933*
     V   *10007* Mexico *11933*

I   II   *Cirrhopetalum acutiflorum* Hook.f. *4988*
     I   India - Tamil Nadu (Nilgiri Hills) *4988*

E   II   *Cirrhopetalum boninense* Schltr. *8038*
     E   *18128* Japan - Ogasawara-shoto (Chichijima; Hahajima) *8038*

R   II   *Cirrhopetalum miniatum* Rolfe *6057*
     R   Vietnam *6057*

V   II   *Cischweinfia pusilla* (C. Schweinf.) Dressler & N.H. Williams *9006*
     E   *9426* Costa Rica *9006*
     V   *19577* Panama *9006*

V   II   *Cischweinfia rostrata* Dressler & N. Williams *19045*
     V   *19045* Ecuador *19045*

R   II   *Cleisostoma montanum* (J.J. Smith) Garay *8309*
     R   Indonesia - Java (central & east Java) *8309*

R   II   *Cleistes unifoliata* (C. Schweinf.) Carnevali & I. Ramírez *21285*
     R   *21285* Suriname *21285*
     R   *21285* Venezuela *21285*

V   II   *Clowesia dodsoniana* Aguirre *10044*
     V   Mexico - Chiapas *10044*
     V   Mexico - Colima *10044*
     V   Mexico - Guerrero *10044*
     V   Mexico - Jalisco *10044*
     V   Mexico - Michoacan *10044*
     V   Mexico - Nayarit *10044*
     V   Mexico - Oaxaca *10044*
     ?   Nicaragua *21233*

V   II   *Clowesia glaucoglossa* (Reichb.f.) Dodson *9424*
     V   *16360* Mexico *9424*

V   II   *Clowesia rosea* Lindley *19850*
     V   *19850* Mexico *19850*

V   II   *Clowesia thylaciochila* (Lemaire) Dodson *9424*
     V   *10007* Mexico *9424*
     ?   Mexico Central *21233*

E   II   *Cochleanthes anatona* Dressler *20883, 10747*
     I   *20883* Panama *20883*

V   II   *Cochleanthes picta* (Reichb.f.) Garay *10020*
     E   *9426* Costa Rica *10020*
     V   *19577* Panama *10020*

R   II   *Coelia guatemalensis* Reichb.f. *11364*
     V   *10359* El Salvador *11364*
     R   *9004* Guatemala *11364*
     R   *11938* Mexico *11938*
     I   *11938* Mexico - Chiapas *11364*

E   II   *Coelogyne anceps* Hook.f. *19047*
     E   *19047* Malaysia - Peninsular Malaysia (Perak) *19047*

I   II   *Coelogyne angustifolia* Wight
     I   India - Tamil Nadu (Nilagiri Hills)

4988

I	II	*Coelogyne barbata* Griff. *4300*	
	I		India - Meghalaya (Khasi hills) *4300*
	I		India - Sikkim *4300*
R	II	*Coelogyne cristata* Lindley *4300*	
	R	*19161*	Bhutan *4300*
	I		India - Assam *4300*
	I		India - Meghalaya (Khasi hills) *4300*
	I		India - Sikkim *4300*
I	II	*Coelogyne flaccida* Lindley *4300*	
	I		India - Meghalaya (Khasi & Jaintia hills) *4300*
R	II	*Coelogyne lawrenceana* Rolfe *6057*	
	R		Vietnam *6057*
E	II	*Coelogyne membranifolia* Carr *19047*	
	E	*19047*	Malaysia - Peninsular Malaysia (Johor, Pahang) *19047*
V	II	*Coelogyne mossiae* Rolfe *11494*	
	V	*11494*	India - Kerala (Idukki) *11494*
	V	*11494*	India - Tamil Nadu *11494*
R	II	*Coelogyne nitida* (Wallich ex Don) Lindley *4300*	
	R	*19161*	Bhutan *4300*
	I		India - Assam *4300*
	I		India - Meghalaya (Khasi hills) *4300*
	I		India - Sikkim *4300*
I	II	*Coelogyne palawanense* Ames *13833*	
	I	*13833*	Philippines (Mt. Capoas) *13833*
I	II	*Coelogyne prolifera* Lindley *4300*	
	I		India - Assam *4300*
	I		India - Meghalaya (Khasi Hills) *4300*
	I		India - Nagaland *4300*
R	II	*Coelogyne susanae* Cribb & B. Lewis *14794*	
	R	*14793*	PNG - Bougainville (N.Solomon Is.) *14794*
	R	*14793*	Solomon Is. - South *14794*
V	II	*Coelogyne tiomanensis* M.R. Henderson *19047*	
	V	*19047*	Malaysia - Peninsular Malaysia (Pulau Tioman) *19047*
Ex/E	II	*Coelogyne treutleri* Hook.f. *11494*	
	Ex/E	*11494*	India - Sikkim (Sikkim Himalaya) *11494*
I	II	*Coelogyne zeylanica* Hook.f. *8021*	
	I	*16162*	Sri Lanka *8021*
V	II	*Comparettia speciosa* Reichb. f. *12482*	
	V	*19045*	Ecuador *19045*
	E	*12482*	Peru *12482*
I	II	*Constantia cipoensis* C. Porto & Brade	
	I	*14664*	Brazil - Minas Gerais (Serra do Cipo) *14664*
I	II	*Corallorrhiza ehrenbergii* Reichb.f. *9432*	
	I		Mexico *9423*
	I		Mexico - Nuevo Leon *9423*
	I		Mexico - Puebla *9423*
	I		Mexico - Veracruz *9423*
I	II	*Corallorrhiza williamsii* Correll *9114*	
	I	*10359*	El Salvador *10359*
	I	*9114*	Mexico *9114*
R	II	*Corybas abellianus* Dockr. *20681*	
	R	*20681*	Australia - Queensland *20681*
R	II	*Corybas acutus* Dransf. & Comber *8309*	
	R		Indonesia - Java (Dieng Plateau, central Java) *8309*
E	II	*Corybas bancanus* (J.J. Smith) Schltr. *10141*	
	E	*19047*	Indonesia - Sumatra (Bangka) *10141*
V	II	*Corybas dentatus* D.L.Jones *20681*	

	V	*20681*	Australia - South Australia *20681*
R	II	*Corybas gemmatus* Cribb & B. Lewis *14794*	
	R	*14793*	Solomon Is. - South (Kolombangara & Rendova) *14794*
R	II	*Corybas kinabaluensis* Carr *10141*	
	R	*14068*	Malaysia - Sabah (Mt Kinabalu) *10141*
V	II	*Corybas limpidus* D.L.Jones *20681*	
	V	*20681*	Australia - Western Australia *20681*
R	II	*Corybas longipedunculatus* Van Royen *14794*	
	R	*14793*	PNG - Bougainville (N.Solomon Is.) *14794*
	R	*14793*	Solomon Is. - South *14794*
V	II	*Corybas montanus* D.L.Jones *20681*	
	V	*20681*	Australia - Queensland *20681*
R	II	*Corybas piliferus* Dransf. *10141*	
	R	*14068*	Malaysia - Sabah *10141*
R	II	*Corybas praetermissus* Dransf. & Comber *8309*	
	R		Indonesia - Java (West Java) *8309*
R	II	*Corybas serpentinus* Dransf. *10141*	
	R	*14068*	Malaysia - Sabah (Bukit Silam) *10141*
I	II	*Corybas solomonensis* Van Royen *14794*	
	I	*14793*	PNG - Bougainville (N.Solomon Is.) *14794*
R	II	*Corybas taiwanensis* T.P. Lin & S.Y. Lu *10141*	
	R	*20511*	Taiwan *10141*
E	II	*Corybas unguiculatus* (R. Br.) Reichb.f.	
	E		New Zealand - North Is.
I	II	*Corybas vinosus* (J.J. Smith) Schltr. *8309*	
	I		Indonesia - Java (West Java) *8309*
I	II	*Corycium bifidum* Sond. *20604*	
	I	*20604*	South Africa - Cape Province *20604*
V	II	*Corycium ingeanum* E.G.H.Oliv. *20604*	
	V	*20604*	South Africa - Cape Province *20604*
V	II	*Corycium microglossum* Lindl. *20604*	
	V	*20604*	South Africa - Cape Province *20604*
Ex	II	*Corycium vestitum* Sweet *20604, 3774*	
	Ex	*20604*	South Africa - Cape Province *20604*
I	II	*Corymborkis brevistylis* (Hook.f.) Holttum	
	I		Malaysia - Peninsular Malaysia (Perak)
E	II	*Corymborkis subdensa* (Schltr.) Masam. *8038*	
	E	*19134*	Japan - Ogasawara-shoto *8038*
R	II	*Cranichis galatea* Dod *15638*	
	R	*15638*	Haiti (massif de la Hotte) *15638*
V	II	*Cranichis lichenophila* D. Weber *11117*	
	V	*11117*	Ecuador - Galapagos (V. Alcedo & Cerro Azul) *11117*
E	II	*Cranichis ricartii* Ackerman *20883, 19002*	
	I	*20883*	Puerto Rico *20883*
R	II	*Cryptocentrum calcaratum* Schltr. *9037*	
	R	*9426*	Costa Rica *9037*
	R	*19577*	Panama *10012*
R	II	*Cryptochilus petelotii* Gagnepain *6057*	
	R		Vietnam *6057*
R	II	*Cryptostylis alismifolia* F. Muell. *8006*	
	R		U.S. - American Samoa *8006*
	R		Western Samoa *8006*
V	II	*Cryptostylis hunteriana* Nicholls *20681*	
	I	*20681*	Australia - New South Wales *20681*
	I	*20681*	Australia - Victoria *20681*
R	II	*Cryptostylis javanica* J.J. Smith *8309*	

R		Indonesia - Java (West Java; East Java) *8309*		
V	II	*Cuitlauzina pendula* Llave & Lex. *9706*		
		V	*16360*	Mexico *9706*
R	II	*Cyanicula ixoides* (Lindley) Hopper & A.P.Brown ms. ssp. *candida* Hopper & A.P.Brown ms. *20681*		
		R	*20681*	Australia - Western Australia *20681*
R	II	*Cyanicula ixoides* (Lindley) Hopper & A.P.Brown ms. ssp. *ixoides* *20681*		
		R	*20681*	Australia - Western Australia *20681*
E	II	*Cycnoches suarezii* Dodson *19045*		
		E	*19045*	Ecuador *19045*
R	II	*Cymbidium banaense* Gagnepain		
		R		Vietnam
R	II	*Cymbidium erythrostylum* Rolfe *15919*		
		R		Vietnam
R	II	*Cymbidium evrardii* Guillaumin		
		R		Vietnam
E	II	*Cymbidium hartinahianum* Comber & Nasution *15919*		
		E		Indonesia - Sumatra *15919*
V	II	*Cymbidium rectum* Ridley *14068*		
		V	*19215*	Malaysia - Sabah *14068*
R	II	*Cymbidium schroederi* Rolfe *15919*		
		R		Vietnam
E	II	*Cymbidium whiteae* King & Pantl. *11494*		
		E	*11494*	India - Sikkim *11494*
R	II	*Cynorkis anisoloba* Summerh. *7875*		
		R		Zimbabwe *7875*
I	II	*Cynorkis compacta* (Rchb.f.) Rolfe *20604*		
		I	*20604*	South Africa - Natal *20604*
R	II	*Cynorkis usambarae* Rolfe *7959*		
		R	*5926*	Tanzania (Usambara Mts.) *7959*
R	II	*Cypripedium arietinum* Ait. f. *20850*		
		I	*20850*	Canada - Manitoba *20850*
		I	*20850*	Canada - Nova Scotia *20850*
		R	*20850*	Canada - Ontario *20850*
		V	*20850*	Canada - Quebec *20850*
		E	*20850*	Canada - Saskatchewan *20850*
		Ex/E	*20850*	U.S. - Connecticut *20850*
		E	*20850*	U.S. - Maine *20850*
		E	*20850*	U.S. - Massachusetts *20850*
		R	*20850*	U.S. - Michigan *20850*
		E	*20850*	U.S. - Minnesota *20850*
		E	*20850*	U.S. - New Hampshire *20850*
		V	*20850*	U.S. - New York *20850*
		V	*20850*	U.S. - Vermont *20850*
		E	*20850*	U.S. - Wisconsin *20850*
R	II	*Cypripedium dicksonianum* Hágsater *11315*		
		R	*19850*	Mexico - Chiapas *11315*
V	II	*Cypripedium guttatum* Sw. var. *yatabeanum* (Makino) Pfitzer *11164*		
		V	*11164*	Japan *11164*
I	II	*Cypripedium irapeanum* Llave & Lex. *9004*		
		E	*9443*	Guatemala *9004*
		I	*19824*	Honduras *19824*
		V	*11119*	Mexico *9004*
		I	*11119*	Mexico - Chiapas *9004*
		I	*19824*	Mexico - Durango *19824*
		I	*11119*	Mexico - Guerrero *9004*
		I	*11119*	Mexico - Jalisco *9004*
		I	*19824*	Mexico - Michoacan *19824*
		I	*19824*	Mexico - Morelos *19824*
		I	*19824*	Mexico - Nayarit *19824*
		I	*19824*	Mexico - Oaxaca *19824*
		I	*11119*	Mexico - Puebla *9004*
		I	*19824*	Mexico - Queretaro *19824*
		I	*11119*	Mexico - Sinaloa *9004*
		I	*11119*	Mexico - Tabasco *9004*
		I	*11119*	Mexico - Veracruz *9004*
R	II	*Cypripedium kentuckiense* C.F. Reed *20850, 11630*		
		E	*20850*	U.S. - Alabama *20850*
		R	*20850*	U.S. - Arkansas *20850*
		R	*20850*	U.S. - Kentucky *20850*
		E	*20850*	U.S. - Louisiana *20850*
		I	*20850*	U.S. - Mississippi *20850*
		E	*20850*	U.S. - Oklahoma *20850*
		E	*20850*	U.S. - Tennessee *20850*
		E	*20850*	U.S. - Texas *20850*
V	II	*Cypripedium macranthum* Sw. var. *hoteiatsumorianum* Sadovsky *11164*		
		V	*11164*	Japan *11164*
E	II	*Cypripedium macranthum* Sw. var. *rebunense* (Kudo) Miyabe & Kudo *11164*		
		E	*11164*	Japan *11164*
V	II	*Cypripedium planipetalum* (Fern.) Morris & Eames *20850*		
		I	*20850*	Canada - Newfoundland *20850*
		V	*20850*	Canada - Quebec *20850*
		I	*20850*	U.S. - Michigan *20850*
		I	*20850*	U.S. - North Dakota *20850*
R	II	*Cyrtorchis arcuata* (Lindley) Schltr. ssp. *leonensis* Summerh. *7926*		
		R		Sierra Leone *7926*
E	II	*Dactylorhiza chuhensis* Renz & Taub. *12840*		
		E	*12840*	Turkey *12840*
V	II	*Dactylorhiza fuchsii* (Druce) Soó ssp. *sooana* (Borsos) Borsos *8000, 20171*		
		V	*19751*	Poland *19751*
		V	*19321*	Slovakia *19321*
R	II	*Dactylorhiza kalopissii* Erich Nelson		
		I	*19425*	Bulgaria *19425*
		R		Greece
R	II	*Dactylorhiza nieschalkiorum* H. Bauumann & Kunk. *12840*		
		R	*19873*	Turkey *12840*
R	II	*Dactylorhiza osmanica* (KI.) Soo var. *anatolica* (Nelson) Renz & Taub. *12840*		
		R	*12840*	Turkey *12840*
R	II	*Deiregyne ramentacea* (Lindley) Schltr. *11338*		
		R	*11933*	Mexico *11338*
R	II	*Dendrobium aegle* Ridley *19047*		
		V	*19047*	Malaysia - Peninsular Malaysia (Taiping Hills; Batu Pahat) *19047*
		R	*14068*	Malaysia - Sarawak *14068*
R	II	*Dendrobium alexandrae* Schltr. *9326*		
		R		Papua New Guinea (Morobe) *9326*
V	II	*Dendrobium angulatum* Lindl. *19047*		
		V	*19047*	Indonesia - Java *19047*
V	II	*Dendrobium angustifolium* Lindl. *19047*		
		V	*19047*	Indonesia - Java *19047*
R	II	*Dendrobium arachnites* Reichb.f.		
		R	*13883*	India *13883*
		V	*13883*	Myanmar *13883*
Ex/E	II	*Dendrobium aurantiacum* Reichb. f. *13883*		
		Ex/E	*13883*	Bangladesh (Sylhet) *13883*
		Ex/E	*13883*	Bhutan *13883*
V	II	*Dendrobium aureilobum* J.J. Smith *19047*		

V 19047 Indonesia - Java *19047*

V II *Dendrobium bigibbum* Lindley *20681, 8745*

    V 20681 Australia - Queensland *8745*

I II *Dendrobium brachypus* (Endl.) Reichb.f. *11649*

    I 11649 Australia - Norfolk Is. *11649*

I II *Dendrobium brevimentum* Seidenf. *19120*

    I 19120 Vietnam *19120*

I II *Dendrobium campbellii* Cribb & B. Lewis *14794*

    I 14793 Solomon Is. - South (Rendova and Makira) *14794*

V II *Dendrobium capra* J.J. Smith *8309*

    V 19047 Indonesia - Java (east) *8309*

V II *Dendrobium carronii* Lavarack & Cribb *20681*

    V 20681 Australia - Queensland *20681*

R II *Dendrobium ciliatilabellum* Seidenf. *19120*

    R 19120 Thailand *19120*

V II *Dendrobium clavator* Ridley *19047*

    V 19047 Malaysia - Peninsular Malaysia (Johore, Perak) *19047*

I I *Dendrobium cruentum* Reichb.f.

    I 20922 Thailand (Setul)

R II *Dendrobium dalatense* Gagnepain *6057*

    R Vietnam *6057*

I II *Dendrobium deltatum* Seidenf. *19120*

    I 19120 Thailand *19120*

I II *Dendrobium erostelle* Seidenf. *19120*

    I 19120 Thailand *19120*

I II *Dendrobium eserre* Seidenf. *19120*

    I 19120 Thailand *19120*

R II *Dendrobium evaginatum* Gagnepain *6057*

    R Vietnam *6057*

V II *Dendrobium fellowsii* F.Muell. *20681*

    V 20681 Australia - Queensland *20681*

E II *Dendrobium flavidulum* Ridley ex Hook.f. *19470*

    E Malaysia - Peninsular Malaysia (Penang; Kelantan; S. Johor)

    E Singapore

E II *Dendrobium flexile* Ridley *19470*

    E Malaysia - Peninsular Malaysia (Johor)

    Ex 20099 Singapore *20099*

I II *Dendrobium gamblei* King & Pantl.

    I India - Uttar Pradesh (Dehra Dun)

I II *Dendrobium garrettii* Seidenf. *19120*

    I 19120 Thailand *19120*

R II *Dendrobium gnomus* Ames *14794*

    R 14793 Solomon Is. - South *14794*

R II *Dendrobium greenianum* Cribb & B. Lewis *14795*

    R 14795 Vanuatu (Pentecost) *14795*

R II *Dendrobium jacobsonii* J.J. Smith *8309*

    R Indonesia - Java (east) *8309*

V II *Dendrobium johannis* H.G.Reichb. *20681, 8745*

    V 20681 Australia - Queensland *20681*

R II *Dendrobium kuhlii* (Blume) Lindley *8309*

    R Indonesia - Java (West Java) *8309*

I II *Dendrobium lagarum* Seidenf. *19120*

    I 19120 Thailand *19120*

R II *Dendrobium langbianense* Gagnepain *6057*

    R Vietnam *6057*

V II *Dendrobium lithocola* D.L.Jones & M.A.Clements *20681*

V 20681 Australia - Queensland *20681*

R II *Dendrobium lowii* Lindley

    R 14068 Malaysia - Sarawak *14068*

I II *Dendrobium lumatum* Lindle *13833*

    I 13833 Philippines (Palawan) *13833*

I II *Dendrobium maccarthiae* Thwaites *8021*

    I 16162 Sri Lanka (Kuruwita Kanda, Ratnapura) *8021*

R II *Dendrobium macropus* (Endl.) Reichb.f. ex Lindley var. **howeanum** (Maiden) P. Green *10604*

    R 10604 Australia - NSW - Lord Howe Is. *10604*

R II *Dendrobium macropus* (Endl.) Reichb.f. ex Lindley ssp. **macropus** *10604*

    R 19108 Australia - Norfolk Is. *10604*

R II *Dendrobium malbrownii* Dockr. *20681, 8745*

    R 20681 Australia - Queensland *8745*

I II *Dendrobium microbulbon* A. Rich.

    I India - Gujarat

    I India - Maharashtra

    I India - Tamil Nadu

R II *Dendrobium mooreanum* Lindley *14795*

    R Vanuatu *14795*

V II *Dendrobium moorei* F. Muell.

    V 14226 Australia - NSW - Lord Howe Is. *14226*

I II *Dendrobium mucronatum* Seidenf. *19120*

    I 19120 Thailand *19120*

E II *Dendrobium munificum* (Finet) Halle *20893*

    E 20893 New Caledonia *20893*

V II *Dendrobium muricatum* Finet *20893*

    V 20893 New Caledonia *20893*

I II *Dendrobium normale* Falc.

    I India - Uttar Pradesh

R II *Dendrobium paniferum* J.J. Smith *8309*

    R Indonesia - Java (West & East Java) *8309*

E II *Dendrobium pauciflorum* King & Pantl.

    E India - Sikkim

    E India - West Bengal

I II *Dendrobium pensile* Ridley *9272*

    E Malaysia - Peninsular Malaysia (Johor, Pahang) *9272*

    Ex 20099 Singapore *20099*

    I 14736 India - Nicobar Is. (Great Nicobar) *5231*

V II *Dendrobium phalaenopsis* Fitzg. *20681*

    V 20681 Australia - Queensland *20681*

I II *Dendrobium rechingerorum* Schltr. *14794*

    I 14793 PNG - Bougainville (N.Solomon Is.) *14794*

    I 14793 Solomon Is. - South *14794*

V II *Dendrobium rennellii* Cribb *14794*

    V 14793 Solomon Is. - South (Rennell and Bellona) *14794*

R II *Dendrobium ruginosum* Ames *14794*

    R 14793 PNG - Bougainville (N.Solomon Is.) *14794*

    R 14793 Solomon Is. - South *14794*

R II *Dendrobium salomonense* Schltr. *14794*

    R 14793 PNG - Bougainville (N.Solomon Is.) *14794*

    R 14793 Solomon Is. - South *14794*

I II *Dendrobium sancristobalense* Cribb *14794*

	I		*14793* Solomon Is. - South (San Cristobal) *14794*	

R II *Dendrobium schneiderae* Bailey *20681, 8745*
    I   *20681* Australia - New South Wales *8745*
    I   *20681* Australia - Queensland *8745*

V II *Dendrobium spectatissimum* Reichb.f. *10260*
    V   *14068* Malaysia - Sabah (Mt Kinabalu) *10379*

E II *Dendrobium tenuicaule* Hk. f. *7771*
    E   *14782* India - Andaman Is. (middle Andamans) *7771*

R II *Dendrobium toressae* (Bailey) Dockr. *20681, 8745*
    R   *20681* Australia - Queensland *8745*

V II *Dendrobium tozerensis* Lavarack *20681, 8745*
    V   *20681* Australia - Queensland *8745*

I II *Dendrobium umbonatum* Seidenf. *19120*
    I   *19120* Thailand *19120*

R II *Dendrobium vagans* Schltr. *7925*
    R   Western Samoa (Savaii) *7925*

R II *Dendrobium vanikorense* Ames *14794*
    R   *14793* PNG - Bougainville (N.Solomon Is.) *14794*
    R   *14793* Solomon Is. - South *14794*

R II *Dendrobium wassellii* S.T.Blake *20681, 8745*
    R   *20681* Australia - Queensland *8745*

I II *Dendrobium ypsilon* Seidenf. *19120*
    I   *19120* Thailand *19120*

R II *Dendrochilum abbreviatum* J.J. Smith *8309*
    R   Indonesia - Java *8309*

E II *Dendrochilum crassum* Ridley *19047*
    E   *19047* Malaysia - Peninsular Malaysia *19047*

R II *Dendrochilum edentulum* Blume *8309*
    R   Indonesia - Java (West Java; Central Java) *8309*

I II *Dendrochilum palawanense* Ames *13833*
    I   *13833* Philippines (Palawan) *13833*

I II *Dendrochilum viride* Seidenf. *19120*
    I   *19120* Thailand *19120*

E II *Dendrophylax barrettiae* F. & R. *20883, 19890*
    V   *19890* Jamaica (Clarendon, St. Ann) *20883*

V II *Dendrophylax fawcettii* Rolfe *19712*
    V   *19434* Cayman Is. (Grand Cayman) *19434*

R II *Dendrophylax funalis* (Sw.) Benth. *20883*
    R   *20883* Jamaica *20883*

V II *Diaphananthe bueae* (Schltr.) Schltr.
    V   Cameroon (Buea)

R II *Diaphananthe millarii* (Bolus) H.P.Linder *20604*
    R   *20604* South Africa - Cape Province *20604*
    R   *20604* South Africa - Natal *20604*

R II *Diaphananthe suborbicularis* Summerh. *7926*
    R   Ghana (Kpandu/Wurobong) *7926*

E II *Dichaea riopalenquensis* Dodson *19045*
    E   *19045* Ecuador *19045*

E II *Didiciea cunninghamii* King & Prain ex King & Pantl. *11494*
    E   *11494* India - Sikkim (Lachen Valley) *11494*
    E   *11494* India - Uttar Pradesh (Garhwal Himalaya) *11494*

V II *Didymoplexis verrucosa* J.L.Stewart & Hennessy *20604*
    V   *20604* South Africa - Natal *20604*

I II *Diglyphosa macrophylla* King & Pantl.
    I   India - Sikkim

R II *Dignathe pygmaeus* Lindley *10047*
    R   *11933* Mexico - Hidalgo *10047*

V II *Dilomilis bissei* H. Dietrich *11840*
    V   *19105* Cuba (Guantanamo) *11840*

E II *Diplandrorchis sinica* S.C. Chen *17617*
    E   *17617* China - Liaoning (Hengreng) *11139*

R II *Diplocaulobium magnilabre* Cribb & B. Lewis *14794*
    R   *14793* PNG - Bougainville (N.Solomon Is.) *14794*
    R   *14793* Solomon Is. - South *14794*

I II *Diplomeris pulchella* D. Don *11494*
    V   *11494* India - Arunachal Pradesh (Namdapha FoR, Tirap Dist.) *11494*
    I   *11494* India - Meghalaya (Khasi & Garo hills) *11494*

R II *Dipodium ensifolium* F.Muell. *20681*
    R   *20681* Australia - Queensland *20681*

R II *Dipodium pulchellum* D.L.Jones & M.A.Clements *20681*
    R   *20681* Australia - Queensland *20681*

V II *Dipteranthus estradae* Dodson *19045, 16963*
    V   *19045* Ecuador *19045*

V II *Disa arida* Vlok *20604*
    V   *20604* South Africa - Cape Province *20604*

R II *Disa bodkinii* Bolus *20604, 2327*
    R   *20604* South Africa - Cape Province *20604*

R II *Disa brevipetala* H.P.Linder *20604*
    R   *20604* South Africa - Cape Province *20604*

R II *Disa galpinii* Rolfe *20604*
    R   *20604* South Africa - Cape Province (Transkei) *20604*
    R   *20604* South Africa - Natal *20604*

E II *Disa hallackii* Rolfe *20803*
    E   *20604* South Africa - Cape Province *20604*

I II *Disa intermedia* H.P.Linder *20604, 18023*
    R   *20604* Swaziland *20604*

R II *Disa longifolia* Lindl. *20604*
    R   *20604* South Africa - Cape Province *20604*

I II *Disa longilabris* Schltr. *5926*
    I   *5926* Tanzania *5926*

R II *Disa marlothii* Bolus *20604*
    R   *20604* South Africa - Cape Province *20604*

R II *Disa minor* (Sond.) Rchb.f. *20604*
    R   *20604* South Africa - Cape Province *20604*

I II *Disa montana* Sond. *20604*
    I   *20604* South Africa - Cape Province *20604*

R II *Disa neglecta* Sond. *20604*
    R   *20604* South Africa - Cape Province *20604*

R II *Disa oreophila* Bolus ssp. *erecta* H.P.Linder *20604*
    R   *20604* Lesotho *20604*
    R   *20604* South Africa - Cape Province *20604*
    R   *20604* South Africa - Natal *20604*

R II *Disa ovalifolia* Sond. *20604*
    R   *20604* South Africa - Cape Province *20604*

I II *Disa rungweensis* Schltr. ssp. *rungweensis* *5926*
    I   *5926* Tanzania *5926*

R II *Disa salteri* G.J.Lewis *20604*
    R   *20604* South Africa - Cape Province *20604*

E II *Disa scullyi* Bolus *20604*

		E	20604	South Africa - Cape Province *20604*
		E	20604	South Africa - Natal *20604*

R II *Disa subtenuicornis* H.P.Linder *20604*
     R   20604   South Africa - Cape Province *20604*

R II *Disa tenella* (L.f.) Sw. ssp. *tenella* *20604*
     R   20604   South Africa - Cape Province *20604*

R II *Disa tenuis* Lindl. *20803*
     R   20604   South Africa - Cape Province *20604*

R II *Disa walteri* Schltr. *7959*
     R   5926   Tanzania (Mbeya Mt.) *7959*

I II *Disperis anthoceros* Rchb. f. var. *grandiflora* Verdc. *5926*
     I   5926   Tanzania *5926*

R II *Disperis aphylla* Kraenzlin ssp. *bifolia* Verdc. *7959*
     R   5926   Tanzania (Lushoto) *7959*

R II *Disperis bodkinii* Bolus *20604*
     R   20604   South Africa - Cape Province *20604*

R II *Disperis bolusiana* Schltr. ex Bolus ssp. *macrocorys* (Rolfe) J.C.Manning *20604*
     R   20604   South Africa - Cape Province *20604*

R II *Disperis decipiens* Verdc. *5926*
     R   5926   Tanzania *5926*

R II *Disperis egregia* Summerh. *7959*
     R   5926   Tanzania (Usambara Mts.) *7959*

R II *Disperis javanica* J.J. Smith *8309*
     R   Indonesia - Java (central & east Java) *8309*

V II *Disperis kamerunensis* Schltr.
     V   Cameroon (Cameroon mt & Musake)

I II *Disperis monophylla* Blatter ex C. Fischer
     I   India - Tamil Nadu (High Wavy Mtns, Madurai) *4988*

I II *Disperis parvifolia* Schltr. *5926*
     I   5926   Tanzania *5926*

R II *Disperis purpurata* Rchb.f. ssp. *pallescens* Bruyns *20604*
     R   20604   South Africa - Cape Province *20604*

V II *Diuris aequalis* H.G.Reichb. *20681*
     V   20681   Australia - New South Wales *20681*

Ex II *Diuris bracteata* Fitzg. *20681*
     Ex   20681   Australia - New South Wales *20681*

R II *Diuris brevifolia* R.Rogers *20681*
     R   20681   Australia - South Australia *20681*

V II *Diuris drummondii* Lindley *20681*
     V   20681   Australia - Western Australia *20681*

E II *Diuris fragrantissima* D.L.Jones & M.A.Clements *20681*
     E   20681   Australia - Victoria *20681*

E II *Diuris micrantha* D.L.Jones *20681*
     E   20681   Australia - Western Australia *20681*

V II *Diuris ochroma* D.L.Jones *20681*
     V   20681   Australia - Victoria *20681*

R II *Diuris oporina* D.L.Jones *20681*
     R   20681   Australia - Queensland *20681*

E II *Diuris pedunculata* R.Br. *20681*
     E   20681   Australia - New South Wales *20681*

V II *Diuris praecox* D.L.Jones *20681*
     V   20681   Australia - New South Wales *20681*

V II *Diuris purdiei* Diels *20681*

     V   20681   Australia - Western Australia *20681*

R II *Diuris recurva* D.L.Jones *20681*
     R   20681   Australia - Western Australia *20681*

V II *Diuris venosa* Rupp *20681*
     V   20681   Australia - New South Wales *20681*

R II *Domingoa kienastii* (Reichb.f.) Dressler *10007*
     R   10007   Mexico *10007*

E II *Dracula dalessandroi* Luer *21294*
     E   19045   Ecuador *19045*

R II *Dracula decussata* Luer & Escobar *21294*
     R   21294   Colombia *21294*

E II *Dracula deltoidea* (Luer) Luer *21294*
     E   19045   Ecuador *19045*

E II *Dracula dodsonii* (Luer) Luer *21294*
     E   19045   Ecuador *19045*

E II *Dracula fuligifera* Luer *21294*
     E   19045   Ecuador *19045*

R II *Dracula gorgonella* Luer & Escobar *21294*
     R   21294   Colombia *21294*

R II *Dracula hawleyi* Luer *21294*
     R   21294   Ecuador *21294*

E II *Dracula marsupialis* Luer & Escobar *21294*
     E   19045   Ecuador *19045*

R II *Dracula minas* Luer & Escobar *21294*
     R   21294   Colombia *21294*

R II *Dracula nycterina* (Reichb.f.) Luer *21294*
     R   21294   Colombia *21294*

R II *Dracula octavioi* Luer & Escobar *21294*
     R   21294   Colombia *21294*

R II *Dracula ortiziana* Luer & Escobar *21294*
     R   21294   Colombia *21294*

E II *Dracula polyphemus* (Luer) Luer *19045, 21294*
     E   19045   Ecuador *19045*

E II *Dracula portilloae* Luer & Andreetta *19045, 21294*
     E   19045   Ecuador *19045*

V II *Dracula rezekiana* Luer & Hawley *19045*
     V   19045   Ecuador *19045*

R II *Dracula ubangina* Luer & Andreetta *21294*
     R   21294   Ecuador *21294*

V II *Dracula vampira* (Luer) Luer *19045, 21294*
     V   19045   Ecuador *19045*

V II *Dracula venosa* (Rolfe) Luer *19045, 21294*
     V   19045   Ecuador *19045*

V II *Dracula wallisii* (Rchb.f.) Luer *19045, 21294*
     V   21294   Colombia *21294*

V II *Dracula woolwardiae* (Kränzl.) Luer *19045, 21294*
     V   19045   Ecuador *19045*

V II *Drakaea concolor* Hopper & A.P.Brown ms. *20681*
     V   20681   Australia - Western Australia *20681*

V II *Drakaea confluens* Hopper & A.P.Brown ms. *20681*
     V   20681   Australia - Western Australia *20681*

V II *Drakaea elastica* Lindley *20681*
     V   20681   Australia - Western Australia *20681*

E II *Drakaea isolata* Hopper & A.P.Brown ms. *20681*
     E   20681   Australia - Western Australia *20681*

V II *Drakaea micrantha* Hopper & A.P.Brown ms. *20681*
     V   20681   Australia - Western Australia *20681*

V II *Drakonorchis barbarella* Hopper & A.P.Brown ms. *20681*

V		20681	Australia - Western Australia	20681

E II *Drakonorchis drakeoides* Hopper & A.P.Brown ms. *20681*
    E   *20681*   Australia - Western Australia *20681*

V II *Dryadella hirtzii* Luer *19045*
    V   *19045*   Ecuador *19045*

V II *Eleorchis japonica* (A.Gray) F. Maek. var. *conformis*
    (F. Maek.) F. Maek. *11164*
    V   *11164*   Japan *11164*

R II *Elleanthus alberti* Schltr. *9037*
    R   *9426*   Costa Rica *9037*
    E/V   *11967*   Nicaragua *9426*

V II *Elleanthus ecuadorensis* Garay *19045*
    V   *19045*   Ecuador *19045*

E II *Elleanthus hirsutis* Barringer *20883*
    I   *20883*   Peru *20883*

V II *Elleanthus isochiloides* Lojtnant *19045, 16963*
    V   *19045*   Ecuador *19045*

E II *Elleanthus steyermarkii* Barringer *20883*
    I   *20883*   Ecuador *20883*

V II *Elleanthus ventricosus* Schltr. *19045*
    V   *19045*   Ecuador *19045*

I II *Embreea rodigasiana* (Claes. ex Cogn.) Dodson *16963*
    I   Colombia *16963*
    V   Ecuador *16963*

V II *Encyclia adenocaula* (Llave & Lex.) Schltr. *10007*
    V   *16360*   Mexico *10007*

I II *Encyclia citrina* (Llave & Lex.) Dressler *9019*
    I   *19848*   Mexico *9019*
    V   *9114*   Mexico - Oaxaca *9019*
    V   *9114*   Mexico - Veracruz *9019*

V II *Encyclia cochleata* (Ames) Dressler var. *triandra*
    (Ames) Dressler *20850*
    V   *20850*   U.S. - Florida *20850*

R II *Encyclia cretacea* Dressler & Pollard *11348*
    R   *11933*   Mexico - Oaxaca *11348*

R II *Encyclia favoris* (Reichb.f.) Soto Arenas *11933*
    R   *11933*   Mexico *11933*

V II *Encyclia flabellata* (Lindley) Thurston &
    Thurston *18110*
    V   *18110*   Mexico - Veracruz *18110*

R II *Encyclia ghiesbreghtiana* (A. Rich. & Galeotti)
    Dressler *10011*
    R   *10011*   Mexico *10011*

R II *Encyclia hastata* (Lindley) Dressler & Pollard *11938*
    R   *11938*   Mexico *11938*

R II *Encyclia inaguensis* Nash ex Britton & Millsp. *3119*
    R   *3119*   Bahamas (Great & Little Inagua) *8766*
    R   *3119*   Turks & Caicos Is. *8766*

R II *Encyclia kienastii* (Reichb.f.) Dressler &
    Pollard *9019*
    R   *9114*   Mexico - Oaxaca *9019*

R II *Encyclia lorata* Dressler & Pollard *11938*
    R   *11938*   Mexico *11938*

R II *Encyclia magnispatha* (Ames, Hubb., & Schweinf.)
    Dressler *10007*
    R   *10007*   Mexico *10007*

V II *Encyclia mariae* (Ames) Hoehne *10007*
    V   *16360*   Mexico *10007*

R II *Encyclia oestlundii* (Ames, Hubb., Schweinf.) Hágsater &
    Sterm. *11332*

R		*11938*	Mexico *9423*	
I		*11938*	Mexico - Guerrero *11332*	
I		*11938*	Mexico - Mexico State *11332*	

V II *Encyclia pastoris* (Llave & Lex.) Schltr. *11345*
    V   *11345*   Mexico *11345*

R II *Encyclia pollardiana* (Withner) Dressler &
    Pollard *11362*
    R   *11933*   Mexico *11362*
    I   *11933*   Mexico - Jalisco *11362*
    I   *11933*   Mexico - Michoacan *11362*

V II *Encyclia pringlei* (Rolfe) Schltr. *10007*
    V   *10007*   Mexico *10007*

V II *Encyclia sima* Dressler *21264*
    V   *21264*   Panama *21264*

V II *Encyclia sintenisii* (Reichenb. f.) Britt. *20883*
    I   *20883*   Cuba *20883*
    ?   Hispaniola *8058*
    I   *20883*   Jamaica *20883*
    I   *20883*   Puerto Rico *20883*
    ?   *19002*   Mexico *19002*
    ?   *19002*   Country Unknown *19002*

V II *Encyclia subulatifolia* (A. Rich. & Galeotti)
    Dressler *10007*
    V   *10007*   Mexico *10007*

V II *Encyclia tenuissima* (Ames, Hubb., & Schweinf.)
    Dressler *10007*
    V   *10007*   Mexico *10007*

R II *Ephippianthus sawadanus* (F. Maek.) Ohwi *11164*
    R   *11164*   Japan *11164*

E II *Epiblema grandiflorum* R.Br. var. *cyanea* K.Dixon
    ms. *20681*
    E   *20681*   Australia - Western Australia *20681*

V II *Epidendrum allenii* L.O. Wms. *20883, 9006*
    V   *20883*   Panama *20883*
    V   *19045*   Ecuador *19045*

V II *Epidendrum alticola* Ames & Correll *9004*
    E   *9443*   Guatemala *9004*
    V   *19850*   Mexico *11279*

E II *Epidendrum angustilobum* F. & R. *20883*
    E   *20883*   Jamaica *20883*

V II *Epidendrum atacazoicum* Schltr. *19045*
    V   *19045*   Ecuador *19045*

I II *Epidendrum augustilobum* F. & R. *19890*
    I   *19890*   Jamaica (St. Andrew) *19890*

V II *Epidendrum batesii* Dodson *19045*
    V   *19045*   Ecuador *19045*

E II *Epidendrum bisulcatum* Ames *20883, 9006*
    I   *20883*   Panama *20883*

V II *Epidendrum cirrhochilum* Lehm & Krzl. *19045*
    V   *19045*   Ecuador *19045*

R II *Epidendrum dentilobum* Ames, Hubb., & C.
    Schweinf. *9006*
    R   *10020*   Panama *9006*

V II *Epidendrum diothonaeoides* Schltr. *19045*
    V   *19045*   Ecuador *19045*

I II *Epidendrum discoidale* Lindl. *10199*
    I   Dominica *10199*

R II *Epidendrum dorsocarinatum* Hágsater *11319*
    R   *11933*   Mexico - Mexico State *11319*

R II *Epidendrum dressleri* Hágsater *11279*
    R   *19850*   Mexico - Veracruz *11279*

V   II   *Epidendrum echinatum* Lojnant *19045*
     V   *19045*   Ecuador *19045*

V   II   *Epidendrum ellipsophyllum* L.O. Wms. *20883, 9006*
     V   *16317*   Panama *20883*

R   II   *Epidendrum examinis* Rosillo *9706*
     R   *11933*   Mexico - Jalisco *21204*

R   II   *Epidendrum fimbriatum* Kunth *19045*
     V   *12379*   Bolivia *12379*
     V   *19045*   Ecuador *19045*
     R   *18200*   Peru *18200*

R   II   *Epidendrum gasteriferum* Scheeren *10016*
     R   *10007*   Mexico - Oaxaca *10016*

V   II   *Epidendrum gentryi* Dodson vel aff. *19045*
     V   *19045*   Ecuador *19045*

V   II   *Epidendrum gonzalez-tamayoi* Hágsater *20025*
     V   *20025*   Mexico - Guerrero *20025*
     V   *20025*   Mexico - Jalisco *20025*
     V   *20025*   Mexico - Nayarit *20025*
     V   *20025*   Mexico - Oaxaca *20025*

Ex   II   *Epidendrum ilense* Dodson *19045*
     Ex   *19045*   Ecuador *19045*

V   II   *Epidendrum insulanum* Schltr. *9037*
     V   *9426*   Costa Rica *9037*

E   II   *Epidendrum kingsii* C.D. Adams *19712*
     E   *19434*   Cayman Is. *19434*

R   II   *Epidendrum lacertinum* Lindley *9114*
     R   *9004*   Guatemala *9004*
     R   *11938*   Mexico *9114*

V   II   *Epidendrum lacerum* Lindl. *20883, 15106*
     I   *20883*   Cuba *20883*
        20883   Puerto Rico *20883*

R   II   *Epidendrum litense* Dodson & Hágsater *20025*
     R   *19045*   Ecuador *19045*

V   II   *Epidendrum lueri* Dodson & Hagsater *19045*
     V   *19045*   Ecuador *19045*

R   II   *Epidendrum marmoratum* A. Rich. & Galeotti *9423*
     R   *10007*   Mexico *9423*

R   II   *Epidendrum matudae* L.O. Williams *9099*
     R   *9114*   Mexico - Guerrero *9099*
     R   *9114*   Mexico - Morelos *9099*

E   II   *Epidendrum medusae* (Rchb. f.) Seib. *19045*
     E   *19045*   Ecuador *19045*

R   II   *Epidendrum miserum* Lindley *9423*
     R   *9423*   Mexico *9423*

V   II   *Epidendrum morganii* Dodson & Garay *19045*
     V   *19045*   Ecuador *19045*

V   II   *Epidendrum mutelianum* Cogn. *5710*
     V   *5710*   Guadeloupe *5710*

V   II   *Epidendrum nanopsis* Dodson & Hagsater *19045*
     V   *19045*   Ecuador *19045*

R   II   *Epidendrum nutans* Sw. *20883*
     R   *20883*   Jamaica *20883*

V   II   *Epidendrum parvilabre* Lindl. *19045, 21296*
     V   *19045*   Ecuador *19045*

E   II   *Epidendrum parvilobum* F. & R. *20883, 19890*
     E   *19890*   Jamaica (Hanover, Dolphin Head) *20883*

V   II   *Epidendrum pichinchae* Schltr. *19045*
     V   *19045*   Ecuador *19045*

V   II   *Epidendrum platychilum* Schltr. *19045*
     V   *19045*   Ecuador *19045*

R   II   *Epidendrum pollardii* Hágsater *20025*
     R   *20025*   Mexico - Guerrero *20025*
     R   *20025*   Mexico - Oaxaca *20025*

E   II   *Epidendrum probiflorum* Schltr. *20883, 9006*
     I   *20883*   Panama *20883*

I   II   *Epidendrum pseudonocturnum* Hágsater & Dodson *20025*
     I   *20025*   Ecuador *20025*

V   II   *Epidendrum quisayanum* Schtr. *19045*
     V   *19045*   Ecuador *19045*

R   II   *Epidendrum radioferens* (Ames, Hubb., & Schweinf.)
       Hágsater *11933*
     R   *9004*   Guatemala *11933*
     V   *11933*   Mexico *11933*

V   II   *Epidendrum renilabium* Schltr. *19045*
     V   *19045*   Ecuador *19045*

E   II   *Epidendrum rigidum* L.O. Wms. var. *angustisegmentum*
       L.O. Williams *20883, 9006*
     I   *20883*   Panama *20883*

V   II   *Epidendrum rousseauae* Schltr. *20883*
     V   *20883*   Panama *20883*

R   II   *Epidendrum rowleyi* Withner & Pollard *11320*
     R   *11938*   Mexico *11320*
     I   *11938*   Mexico - Guerrero *11320*
     I   *11938*   Mexico - Oaxaca *11320*

I   II   *Epidendrum scalpelligerum* Reichb. f. *19890*
     I   *19890*   Cuba *19890*
     E   *19890*   Jamaica (St. Ann) *19890*

R   II   *Epidendrum tungurahuae* Schltr. *19045*
     R   *19045*   Ecuador *19045*

R   II   *Epidendrum verrucosum* Sw. var. *hansenii*
       Adams *19890*
     R   *19890*   Jamaica (St. Andrew, Manchester) *19890*

V   II   *Epidendrum verucosum* var. *hansenii*
       Adams *20883*
     V   *20883*   Jamaica *20883*

V   II   *Epidendrum vulcanicola* A.H. Heller *10018*
     V   *11967*   Nicaragua *10018*

V   II   *Epidendrum werffii* Dodson & Hagsater *19045*
     V   *19045*   Ecuador *19045*

V   II   *Epidendrum williamsii* Dodson *19045*
     V   *19045*   Ecuador *19045*

R   II   *Epigeneium chapaense* Gagnepain *6057*
     R   Vietnam *6057*

V   II   *Epilyna hirtzii* Dodson *19045*
     V   *19045*   Ecuador *19045*

V   II   *Epipactis albensis* Nováková et Rydlo *2050*
     E   *17786*   Czech Republic *2050*
     V   *19321*   Slovakia *19321*

V   II   *Epipactis cretica* J. Kalopissis & K. Robatsch *10260*
     V   *20730*   Greece - Crete *10260*

R   II   *Epipactis pontica* Taub. *12840*
     I   *19321*   Slovakia *19321*
     R   *19873*   Turkey *12840*

V   II   *Epipactis troodi* Lindb.f. *14230*
     V   *19164*   Cyprus *14230*
     V   *19873*   Turkey (Amanus mts.) *14230*

R   II   *Epipogium japonicum* Makino *11164*
     R   *11164*   Japan *11164*

I   II   *Epipogium sessanum* Hegde & Rao *9416*
     I   India - Arunachal Pradesh *9416*

R	II	*Eria albiflora* Rolfe	
	R	13883 India - Tamil Nadu (Western Ghats) 13883	
R	II	*Eria articulata* Lindley 8021	
	R	20013 Sri Lanka 8021	
I	II	*Eria curranii* Leavitt 13833	
	I	13833 Philippines (Palawan) 13833	
R	II	*Eria dacrydium* Gagnepain 6057	
	R	Vietnam 6057	
R	II	*Eria irukandjiana* St.Cloud 20681	
	R	20681 Australia - Queensland 20681	
R	II	*Eria junghuhnii* J.J. Smith 8309	
	R	Indonesia - Java 8309	
R	II	*Eria lindleyi* Thwaites 8021	
	R	20013 Sri Lanka 8021	
R	II	*Eria occidentalis* Seidenf. 11494	
	R	11494 India - Uttar Pradesh (Kumaun) 11494	
I	II	*Eria palawanensis* Ames 13833	
	I	13833 Philippines (Mt. Pulgar) 13833	
E	II	*Eria pudica* Ridl. 19209	
	E	Malaysia - Peninsular Malaysia (Johor, Negeri Sembilan) 19209	
	Ex	20099 Singapore 20099	
R	II	*Eria rhynchostyloides* O'Brien 8309	
	R	Indonesia - Java (West Java; East Java) 8309	
R	II	*Eria subaliena* Gagnepain 6057	
	R	Vietnam 6057	
R	II	*Eria thwaitesii* Trimen 8021	
	R	20013 Sri Lanka 8021	
R	II	*Eria tonkinensis* Gagnepain 6057	
	R	Vietnam 6057	
V	II	*Erycina echinata* (Kunth) Lindley 9423	
	V	10042 Mexico 9423	
I	II	*Erythrodes hirtella* (Swartz) Fawcett & Rendle 10199	
	I	Dominica 10199	
	I	19408 Dominican Republic 19408	
E	II	*Erythrodes jamaicensis* (F. & R.) F. & R. 20883, 19890	
	E	20883 Jamaica 20883	
I	II	*Eulophia candida* (Lindley) Reichb.f.	
	I	India - Assam	
	I	India - Sikkim	
I	II	*Eulophia coddii* A.V.Hall 20604	
	I	20604 South Africa - Transvaal 20604	
R	II	*Eulophia cooperi* Rchb.f. 20604	
	R	20604 South Africa - Orange Free State 20604	
	R	20604 South Africa - Transvaal 20604	
I	II	*Eulophia cullenii* (Wight) Blume 9216	
	I	India - Kerala (Travancore Hills) 9216	
	I	India - Tamil Nadu 4988	
V	II	*Eulophia exaltata* Reichb.f. 8309	
	V	19047 Indonesia - Java (east) 8309	
I	II	*Eulophia holubii* Rolfe 20604	
	I	20604 Botswana 20604	
	I	20604 Namibia 20604	
V	II	*Eulophia javanica* J.J. Smith 8309	
	V	19047 Indonesia - Java (West Java; Central Java) 8309	
I	II	*Eulophia leachii* Greatrex ex A.V.Hall 20604	
	I	20604 Zimbabwe 20604	

	I	20604 Namibia 20604	
	I	20604 South Africa - Natal 20604	
	V	20604 South Africa - Transvaal 20604	
I	II	*Eulophia leucantha* (Kraenzlin) Solch	
	I	Namibia	
I	II	*Eulophia litoralis* Schltr. 20604	
	I	20604 South Africa - Cape Province 20604	
R	II	*Eulophia mackinnonii* Duthie 11494	
	R	11494 India - Madhaya Pradesh 11494	
	R	11494 India - Uttar Pradesh 11494	
E	II	*Eulophia nicobarica* Balakr. & N.G. Nair 7771	
	E	13883 India - Nicobar Is. 7771	
I	II	*Eulophia obtusa* (Lindley) Hook.f.	
	I	India - Uttar Pradesh	
V	II	*Eulophia platypetala* Lindl. 20604	
	V	20604 South Africa - Cape Province 20604	
I	II	*Eulophia ramentacea* Lindley ex Wight	
	I	India (Western Ghats; ? Deccan P.)	
	I	India - Gujarat	
	I	India - Karnataka	
Ex/E	II	*Eulophia seychellarum* Rolfe ex Summerhayes 19446	
	Ex/E	19446 Seychelles (incl.Cousin Is.) 19446	
V	II	*Eulophia toyoshimae* Nakai 8038	
	V	19134 Japan - Ogasawara-shoto (Hahajima) 8038	
R	II	*Eurystyles ananassocomos* (Reichenb. f.) Schlechter 20883, 19002	
		20883 Cuba 20883	
	E	19408 Dominican Republic 19408	
	V	20883 Jamaica 20883	
	I	20883 Puerto Rico 20883	
R	II	*Evotella rubiginosa* (Sond. ex Bolus) Kurzweil & H.P.Linder 20604	
	R	20604 South Africa - Cape Province 20604	
V	II	*Fernandezia maculata* Garay & Dunsterv. 16958	
	V	10010 Ecuador 16958	
E	II	*Flickingeria hesperis* Seidenf. 11494	
	E	11494 India - Uttar Pradesh (Askot; Kumaun) 11494	
R	II	*Flickingeria nativitatis* (Ridley) J.J. Wood 14224	
	R	14224 Australia - Christmas Is. 14224	
R	II	*Flickingeria punctilosa* (J.J. Smith) Hawkes 8309	
	R	Indonesia - Java (West Java; East Java) 8309	
R	II	*Galeola affinis* J.J. Smith 8309	
	R	Indonesia - Java (West Java; East Java) 8309	
I	II	*Galeola cathcartii* Hook.f.	
	I	India - Sikkim	
I	II	*Galeola falconeri* Hook.f.	
	I	India - Arunachal Pradesh (Kameng)	
	I	India - Sikkim	
	I	India - Uttar Pradesh (Garhwal)	
I	II	*Galeola lindleyana* Reichb.f. 4300	
	I	India - Meghalaya 4300	
	I	India - Nagaland 4300	
	I	India - Sikkim 4300	
R	II	*Galeottiella sarcoglossa* (A. Rich. & Galeotti) Schltr. 11933	
	R	9004 Guatemala 11933	
	R	19850 Mexico - Guerrero 11933	
	I	19850 Mexico - Hidalgo 11933	
	I	19850 Mexico - Jalisco 9706	
	I	19850 Mexico - Michoacan 11933	

		I	19850	Mexico - Morelos *11933*
		I	19850	Mexico - Oaxaca *11933*
E	II	*Gastrochilus ciliaris* F. Maek. *11164*		
		E	11164	Japan *11164*
V	II	*Gastrochilus japonicus* (Makino) Schltr. *11164*		
		V	11164	Japan *11164*
I	II	*Gastrochilus minor* Seidenf *19120*		
		I	19120	Thailand *19120*
I	II	*Gastrochilus rutilans* Seidenf. *19120*		
		I	19120	Thailand *19120*
I	II	*Gastrochilus suavis* Seidenf. *19120*		
		I	19120	Thailand *19120*
V	II	*Gastrodia africana* Kranzlin		
		V		Cameroon
E	II	*Gastrodia boninensis* Tuy. *8038*		
		E	19134	Japan - Ogasawara-shoto *8038*
R	II	*Gastrodia crispa* J.J. Smith *8309*		
		R		Indonesia - Java (West Java) *8309*
I	II	*Gastrodia dyeriana* King & Pantl.		
		I		India - Sikkim
I	II	*Gastrodia exilis* Hook.f. *9249*		
		I		India - Meghalaya (Jaintia hills) *9249*
R	II	*Gastrodia gracilis* Blume *11164*		
		R	11164	Japan *11164*
R	II	*Gastrodia queenslandica* Dockr. *20681*		
		R	20681	Australia - Queensland *20681*
I	II	*Gastrodia zeylanica* Schltr. *8021*		
		I	16162	Sri Lanka *8021*
I	II	*Gavilea insularis* *19125*		
		I	19125	Chile - Juan Fernandez Is. *19125*
R	II	*Genoplesium alticolum* D.Jones & B.Gray *20681*		
		R	20681	Australia - Queensland *20681*
R	II	*Genoplesium arrectum* D.L.Jones *20681*		
		R	20681	Australia - Victoria *20681*
R	II	*Genoplesium baueri* R.Br. *20681*		
		R	20681	Australia - New South Wales *20681*
R	II	*Genoplesium brachystachyum* (Lindley) D.L.Jones & M.A.Clements *20681, 10260*		
		R	20681	Australia - Tasmania *20681*
R	II	*Genoplesium pedersonii* D.L.Jones *20681*		
		R	20681	Australia - Queensland *20681*
E	II	*Genoplesium rhyoliticum* D.L.Jones & M.A.Clements *20681*		
		E	20681	Australia - New South Wales *20681*
R	II	*Genoplesium sigmoideum* D.L.Jones *20681*		
		R	20681	Australia - Queensland *20681*
R	II	*Genoplesium superbum* D.L.Jones *20681*		
		R	20681	Australia - New South Wales *20681*
E	II	*Genoplesium tectum* D.L.Jones *20681*		
		E	20681	Australia - Queensland *20681*
R	II	*Genoplesium validum* D.L.Jones *20681*		
		R	20681	Australia - Queensland *20681*
V	II	*Genyorchis macrantha* Summerh.		
		V		Cameroon (Cameroon mt)
V	II	*Genyorchis platybulbon* Schltr.		
		V		Cameroon (Moliwe & Limbe)
V	II	*Gongora amparoana* Schltr. *9037*		
		V	9426	Costa Rica *9037*

V	II	*Gongora gibba* Dressler *20883, 10747*		
		V	16317	Panama *20883*
R	II	*Goodyera boninensis* Nakai *8038*		
		R	19134	Japan - Ogasawara-shoto *8038*
R	II	*Goodyera glauca* J.J. Smith *8309*		
		R		Indonesia - Java (east) *8309*
E	II	*Goodyera macrophylla* Lowe *17781*		
		E		Portugal - Madeira *17891*
I	II	*Goodyera recurva* Lindley		
		I		India - Meghalaya (Khasi hills)
R	II	*Goodyera viridiflora* (Blume) Blume *20681, 8309*		
		R		Indonesia - Java (West Java; East Java) *8309*
		R	20681	Australia - Queensland *20681*
V	II	*Govenia bella* Greenwood *11278*		
		V	11278	Mexico - Oaxaca *11278*
V	II	*Govenia purpusii* Schltr. *10007*		
		V	10007	Mexico *10007*
R	II	*Govenia tequilana* Dressler & Hágsater *9706*		
		R	11933	Mexico *9706*
I	II	*Grosourdya callifera* Seidenf. *19120*		
		I	19120	Thailand *19120*
R	II	*Gunnarella nambana* B. Lewis *17617*		
		R	17690	Vanuatu (Malekula) *17690*
V	II	*Gymnadenia fujisanensis* Sugim. *11164*		
		V	11164	Japan *11164*
R	II	*Gymnigritella runei* Teppner & Klein *18216, 21309*		
		R	20083	Sweden *18216*
E	II	*Habenaria amplifolia* *19473*		
		E	19473	Cook Is.(Southern group) (Rarotonga) *19473*
R	II	*Habenaria andamanica* Hook. F. *7771*		
		R	14782	India - Andaman Is. (South Andaman Is.) *7771*
R	II	*Habenaria angustissima* Summerh. *7926*		
		R		Guinea *7926*
R	II	*Habenaria apiculata* Summerh. *7959*		
		R	5926	Tanzania (Arusha Distr.) *7959*
E	II	*Habenaria avicula* Schltr. *20883, 9006*		
		I	20883	Panama *20883*
V	II	*Habenaria bantamensis* J.J. Smith *8309*		
		V	19047	Indonesia - Java (West & East Java) *8309*
R	II	*Habenaria barnesii* Summerh. ex C. Fischer *11494*		
		R	11494	India - Kerala (Idukki) *11494*
		R	11494	India - Tamil Nadu (Nilagiri Hills) *11494*
I	II	*Habenaria bougainvilleae* Renz *14794*		
		I	14793	PNG - Bougainville (N.Solomon Is.) *14794*
		I	14793	Solomon Is. - South (Guadalcanal) *14794*
R	II	*Habenaria brevilabiata* A. Rich. & Galeotti *9423*		
		R	11933	Mexico *9423*
R	II	*Habenaria burtii* Summerh. *7959*		
		R	5926	Tanzania (Dodoma) *7959*
R	II	*Habenaria busseana* Kraenzlin *7959*		
		R	5926	Tanzania (Songea Distr.) *7959*
R	II	*Habenaria chapaensis* Gagnepain *6057*		
		R		Vietnam *6057*
R	II	*Habenaria cordifolia* Summerh. *7959*		

	R		5926	Tanzania (Songea Distr.) 7959	
R	II	*Habenaria corydophora* Reich.f. *18200*			
	I				Colombia
	R		18200	Peru *18200*	
V	II	*Habenaria curvicalcar* J.J. Smith *8309*			
	V		19047	Indonesia - Java (West Java) *8309*	
I	II	*Habenaria denticulata* Reichb.f.			
	I				India - Tamil Nadu *4988*
E	II	*Habenaria divaricata* Rogers & White *20681*			
	E		20681	Australia - Queensland *20681*	
R	II	*Habenaria dussii* Cogn. *19400*			
	R		19400	Guadeloupe *19400*	
R	II	*Habenaria evrardii* Gagnepain *6057*			
	R				Vietnam *6057*
I	II	*Habenaria fimbriata* Wight			
	I				India - Tamil Nadu (Nilagiri Hills) *4988*

R II *Habenaria flagellifera* Makino var. *yosiei*
      Hara *11164*
      R   *11164* Japan *11164*

V II *Habenaria giriensis* J.J. Smith *8309*
      V   *19047* Indonesia - Java (east) *8309*

I II *Habenaria haareri* Summerh. *5926*
      I   *5926* Tanzania (Kilimanjaro) *5926*

Ex/E II *Habenaria horsfieldiana* Kranzlin *8309*
      Ex/E *19047* Indonesia - Java *8309*

V II *Habenaria insularis* Schltr. *20893*
      V   *20893* New Caledonia *20893*

V II *Habenaria iyoensis* Ohwi *11164*
      V   *11164* Japan *11164*

V II *Habenaria keniensis* Summerh. *6073*
      V   *6073* Kenya (Mt. Elgon, Naivasha distr.) *7959*

R II *Habenaria kingii* Hook.f.
      R   Malaysia - Peninsular Malaysia (Perak)

V II *Habenaria lacertifera* (Lindley) Benth. var.
      triangularis (F. Maek.) Satomi *11164*
      V   *11164* Japan *11164*

Ex II *Habenaria lancifolia* A.Rich. *10082*
      Ex *20771* Mauritius *10082*

E II *Habenaria macraithii* Lavarack *20681*
      E   *20681* Australia - Queensland *20681*

I II *Habenaria maitlandii* Summerh.
      I   Cameroon (Nchan and Bamenda)

V II *Habenaria marquisensis* F. Brown
      V   French Polynesia - Marquesas Is

V II *Habenaria medusa* *19047*
      V   *19047* Indonesia - Java *19047*

R II *Habenaria multipartita* Blume ex Kranzlin *8309*
      R   Indonesia - Java *8309*

I II *Habenaria nyikana* Rchb. f. ssp. *pubipetala*
      Summerh. *5926*
      I   *5926* Tanzania *5926*

R II *Habenaria occlusa* Summerh. *7959*
      R   *5926* Tanzania (Mbeya Peak) *7959*

R II *Habenaria odorata* Schltr. *7959*
      R   *5926* Tanzania (Rungwe Distr.) *7959*

R II *Habenaria panchganiensis* Sant. & Kapad. *14782*
      R   *14782* India - Maharashtra (]) *14782*

I II *Habenaria polyodon* Hook.f. *2268*

	I				India - Tamil Nadu (Nilgiri Hills) 2268

E II *Habenaria purdiei* F. & R. *20883, 19890*
      V   *19890* Jamaica *20883*

V II *Habenaria reflex* *19047*
      V   *19047* Indonesia - Java *19047*

I II *Habenaria richardiana* Wight
      I   India - Kerala (Travancore) *4988*
      I   India - Tamil Nadu *4988*

R II *Habenaria richardsiae* Summerh. *7959*
      R   *5926* Tanzania (Njombe Distr.) *7959*

Ex II *Habenaria rosellata* (Thouars) Schltr. *10082*
      Ex *10082* Réunion *10082*
      Ex *20771* Mauritius *10082*

I II *Habenaria singularis* Summerh. *7881*
      I   Zimbabwe *7881*

E II *Habenaria socialis* F. & R. *20883, 19890*
      I   *19890* Jamaica *20883*

R II *Habenaria subauriculata* Robinson & Greenman *11933*
      R   *10007* Mexico - Oaxaca *11933*
      R   *10007* Mexico - Puebla *11933*

E II *Habenaria thomsonii* Reichb.f. *6073*
      E   *6073* Kenya (Londiani) *7959*

V II *Habenaria undulata* (J.J. Smith) J.J. Smith *8309*
      V   *19047* Indonesia - Java *8309*

R II *Habenaria vaupelii* Schltr. *8006*
      R   U.S. - American Samoa (Tau) *8006*
      R   Western Samoa (Savaii; Upolu) *8006*

Ex II *Habenaria vesiculosa* A.Rich. *10082*
      Ex *20771* Mauritius *10082*

V II *Habenaria woodii* Schltr. *20604*
      V   *20604* South Africa - Natal *20604*

R II *Habenaria xanthantha* F.Muell. *20681*
      R   *20681* Australia - Queensland *20681*

R II *Hagsatera brachycolumna* (L.O. Williams) Gonz.
      Tam. *10021*
      R   *11933* Mexico *10021*

R II *Hagsatera rosilloi* Gonz.Tam. *9706*
      R   *11933* Mexico - Jalisco *21204*

E II *Hancockia japonica* (Hatus.) F. Maek. *11164*
      E   *11164* Japan *11164*

V II *Harrisella uniflora* H. Dietrich *11840*
      V   Cuba (Santiago de Cuba) *11840*

V II *Hederorkis scandens* Thouars *10082*
      V   *20771* Mauritius *10082*

V II *Helcia sanguinolenta* Lindley *12482*
      V   *19045* Ecuador *18105*
      E   *18200* Peru *18200*

E II *Herschelianthe barbata* (L.f.) N.C.Anthony *20604*
      E   *20604* South Africa - Cape Province *20604*

E II *Herschelianthe excelsa* (Thunb.) Rolfe nom.
      illegit. *20604*
      E   *20604* South Africa - Cape Province *20604*

I II *Herschelianthe forcipata* (Schltr.) Rauschert *20604*
      I   *20604* South Africa - Cape Province *20604*

R II *Herschelianthe forficaria* (Bolus) N.C.Anthony *20604*
      R   *20604* South Africa - Cape Province *20604*

V II *Herschelianthe lugens* (Bolus) Rauschert var.
      lugens *20604*
      V   *20604* South Africa - Cape Province *20604*

I   II   *Herschelianthe lugens* (Bolus) Rauschert var.
     nigrescens (H.P.Linder) N.C.Anthony *20604*
     I   *20604*   South Africa - Cape Province *20604*

V   II   *Herschelianthe schlechteriana* (Bolus)
     N.C.Anthony *20803*
     V   *20604*   South Africa - Cape Province *20604*

V   II   *Herschelianthe spathulata* (L.f.) Rauschert ssp.
     tripartita (Lindl.) N.C.Anthony *20604*
     V   *20604*   South Africa - Cape Province *20604*

R   II   *Hetaeria lamellata* Blume *8309*
     R   Indonesia - Java (West Java; East Java) *8309*

I   II   *Hetaeria ovalifolia* (Wight) Benth. *4988*
     I   India - Kerala *11153*
     I   India - Tamil Nadu (Courtallum, Tirunelveli Hills) *4988*

R   II   *Hexalectris brevicaulis* L.O. Williams *9423*
     R   *11119*   Mexico *9423*

R   II   *Hexalectris nitida* L.O. Williams *20850*
     E   *20850*   U.S. - New Mexico *20850*
     R   *20850*   U.S. - Texas *20850*

E   II   *Hexalectris revoluta* Correll *20883, 20850, 9423*
     E   *20850*   U.S. - Texas *20850*
     I   *20883*   Mexico *20883*

V   II   *Hexalectris warnockii* Ames & Correll *20850*
     E   *20850*   U.S. - Arizona *20850*
     I   *20850*   U.S. - New Mexico *20850*
     V   *20850*   U.S. - Texas *20850*

I   II   *Himantoglossum formosum* (Stev.) C. Koch *5942*
     I   *5942*   Azerbaijan *5942*

V   II   *Hirtzia benzingii* Dodson *19045, 11274*
     V   *19045*   Ecuador *19045*

I   II   *Holothrix majubensis* C. & R.H.Archer ined. *20604*
     I   *20604*   South Africa - Natal *20604*

E   II   *Holothrix pentadactyla* (Summerh.) Summerh. *6073*
     E   *6073*   Kenya *7959*

I   II   *Holothrix pilosa* (Burch. ex Lindl.) Rchb.f. *20604*
     I   *20604*   South Africa - Cape Province *20604*

I   II   *Holothrix pleistodactyla* Krzl. *5926*
     I   *5926*   Tanzania *5926*

I   II   *Holothrix socotrana* Rolfe *15534*
     I   *15534*   Yemen - Socotra *15534*

I   II   *Holothrix triloba* (Rolfe) Krzl. *5926*
     I   *5926*   Tanzania *5926*

R   II   *Homalopetalum costaricense* Schltr. *9037*
     R   *9426*   Costa Rica *9037*

R   II   *Hymenorchis javanicus* (Teijsm. & Binnend.)
     Schltr. *8309*
     R   Indonesia - Java (West Java) *8309*

E   II   *Ipsea malabarica* (Reichb.f.) Hook.f. *11494*
     E   *11494*   India - Kerala (Silent Valley, Palghat Dt) *11494*

E   II   *Ipsea speciosa* Lindley *8021*
     E   *20013*   Sri Lanka *8021*

V   II   *Isotria medeoloides* (Pursh) Raf. *20850, 14352*
     E   *20850*   Canada - Ontario *20850*
     E   *20850*   U.S. - Connecticut *20850*
     E   *20850*   U.S. - Delaware *20850*
     Ex   *20850*   U.S. - District of Columbia *20850*
     V   *20850*   U.S. - Georgia *20850*
     E   *20850*   U.S. - Illinois *20850*
     V   *20850*   U.S. - Maine *20850*

     Ex/E *20850*   U.S. - Maryland *20850*
     E   *20850*   U.S. - Massachusetts *20850*
     E   *20850*   U.S. - Michigan *20850*
     Ex   *20850*   U.S. - Missouri *20850*
     V   *20850*   U.S. - New Hampshire *20850*
     E   *20850*   U.S. - New Jersey *20850*
     Ex/E *20850*   U.S. - New York *20850*
     E   *20850*   U.S. - North Carolina *20850*
     E   *20850*   U.S. - Ohio *20850*
     E   *20850*   U.S. - Pennsylvania *20850*
     E   *20850*   U.S. - Rhode Is. *20850*
     E   *20850*   U.S. - South Carolina *20850*
     E   *20850*   U.S. - Tennessee *20850*
     Ex/E *20850*   U.S. - Vermont *20850*
     V   *20850*   U.S. - Virginia *20850*

V   II   *Jumellea fragrans* (Thouars) Schltr. *10082*
     V   *20771*   Mauritius *10082*
     V   *10082*   Mauritius - Rodrigues *10082*

V   II   *Jumellea recta* (Thouars) Schltr. *10082*
     V   *10082*   Réunion *10082*
     V   *20771*   Mauritius *10082*
     E   *5852*   Mauritius - Rodrigues (Mont Cimetiere) *10082*

R   II   *Kefersteinia hirtzii* Dodson *19045*
     R   *19045*   Ecuador *19045*

V   II   *Kefersteinia lindneri* Dodson *19045*
     V   *19045*   Ecuador *19045*

E   II   *Kefersteinia subquadrata* Schltr. *9426*
     E   *9593*   Costa Rica *9426*

R   II   *Kionophyton sawyeri* (Standley & L.O. Williams)
     Garay *11933*
     R   *11933*   Mexico - Morelos *11933*

R   II   *Koellensteinia eburnea* (Barb.& Rodr.) Sealtr. *16585*
     R   *16585*   Brazil - Minas Gerais *16585*

R   II   *Lacaena bicolor* Lindley *9114*
     R   *21290*   Belize *12779*
     R   *21290*   Costa Rica *12497*
     V   *10359*   El Salvador *10359*
     R   *9004*   Guatemala *9004*
     R   *9004*   Honduras *9004*
     V   *16360*   Mexico - Oaxaca *9114*
     V   *11967*   Nicaragua *10360*

E   II   *Laelia anceps* Lindley forma *blanca* *9019*
     E   *9019*   Mexico - Puebla *9019*
     E   *9019*   Mexico - Veracruz *9019*

E   II   *Laelia anceps* Lindley var. *dawsonii* *19850*
     E   *21196*   Mexico - Chiapas *21196*

R   II   *Laelia esalqueana* Blumensch. ex Pabst *16585*
     R   *16585*   Brazil *16585*

I   II   *Laelia fidelensis* Pabst *17079*
     I   *17746*   Brazil - Rio de Janeiro *17079*

V   II   *Laelia furfuracea* Lindley *9423*
     V   *10007*   Mexico *9423*

E   II   *Laelia gouldiana* Reichb.f. *9423*
     E   *11933*   Mexico *9423*

E   II   *Laelia grandis* Lindley & Paxton *17079*
     E   *17079*   Brazil - Bahia (Sul da Bahia, a Rio do Meio.) *17079*

V   I   *Laelia jongheana* Reichb.f. *17079*
     V   *17079*   Brazil - Minas Gerais *17079*

E   I   *Laelia lobata* (Lindl.) Veitch *15658*
     E   *17079*   Brazil - Rio de Janeiro (Pedra da Gávea, Tijuca, escarpa da Vista Chinesa) *17079*

V   II   *Laelia speciosa* (Kunth) Schltr. *9019*
     V   *11119*   Mexico *9019*

E   II   *Laelia tenebrosa* Rolfe *17079*
     E   *17079*   Brazil - Espirito Santo (município de Mimoso do Sul.) *17079*

R   II   *Laelia virens* Lindley *17079*
     R   *17746*   Brazil - Espirito Santo *17079*
     R   *17746*   Brazil - Minas Gerais *17079*
     R   *17746*   Brazil - Rio de Janeiro (Nova Friburgo, Alto Macaé, Teresópolis) *17079*

E   II   *Laelia xanthina* Lindley *17079*
     E   *17079*   Brazil - Espirito Santo (Domingos Martins) *17079*

R   II   *Lecanorchis hojurikuensis* Masamunea *11164*
     R   *11164*   Japan *11164*

R   II   *Lecanorchis kiiensis* Murata *11164*
     R   *11164*   Japan *11164*

R   II   *Lecanorchis kiusiana* Tuy. *11164*
     R   *11164*   Japan *11164*

R   II   *Lecanorchis trachycaula* Ohwi *11164*
     R   *11164*   Japan *11164*

V   II   *Lemboglossum apterum* (Llave & Lex.) Halbinger *11335*
     V   *16360*   Mexico *11335*

V   II   *Lemboglossum candidulum* (Reichb.f.) Halbinger *11335*
     V   *16360*   Mexico *11335*

V   II   *Lemboglossum cervantesii* (Llave & Lex.) Halbinger *11335*
     V   *16360*   Mexico *11335*

V   II   *Lemboglossum ehrenbergii* (Link, Klotz. & Otto) Halbinger *11335*
     V   *16360*   Mexico *11335*

R   II   *Lemboglossum galeottianum* (A. Rich.) Halbinger *11335*
     R   *19850*   Mexico *11335*

V   II   *Lemboglossum madrense* (Reichb. f) Halbinger *19850*
     V   *19850*   Mexico *19850*

E   II   *Leochilus hagsateri* M. W. Chase *20883, 10049*
     I   *20883*   Mexico *20883*

V   II   *Leochilus hyalinobulbon* (Llave & Lex.) Schltr. *10041*
     V   Mexico - Guerrero *10041*
     V   Mexico - Jalisco *10041*
     V   Mexico - Michoacan *10041*
     V   Mexico - Morelos *10041*
     V   Mexico - Nayarit *10041*
     V   Mexico - Oaxaca *10041*

I   II   *Leochilus labiatus* (Swartz) Kuntze *10199*
     I   Dominica *10199*
     E   *19408*   Dominican Republic *19408*

R   II   *Leochilus leiboldii* Reichb.f. *11566*
     R   *11119*   Mexico - Oaxaca *9423*

E   II   *Leochilus puertoricensis* Chase *20883, 19002*
     I   *20883*   Puerto Rico *20883*

V   II   *Lepanthes acoridilabia* Ames & C. Schweinf. *9037*
     V   *9426*   Costa Rica *9037*

V   II   *Lepanthes acostaei* Schltr. *9037*
     V   *9426*   Costa Rica *9037*

V   II   *Lepanthes acuminata* Schltr. ssp. *ernestii* Salazar & Soto Arenas *21265*
     V   *21265*   Mexico - Chiapas *21265*

E   II   *Lepanthes adamsii* Hespenheide *20883, 19890*
     V   *19890*   Jamaica (Portland) *20883*

R   II   *Lepanthes aries* Luer *19045*
     R   *19045*   Ecuador *19045*

V   II   *Lepanthes attenuata* Salazar, Soto Arenas & O. Suárez *21265*
     V   *21265*   Mexico - Oaxaca *21265*
     V   *21265*   Mexico - Veracruz *21265*

R   II   *Lepanthes aurita* Luer & Escobar *19045*
     R   *19045*   Ecuador *19045*

V   II   *Lepanthes ballatrix* Luer *19045*
     V   *19045*   Ecuador *19045*

V   II   *Lepanthes barbae* Schltr. *9037*
     V   *9426*   Costa Rica *9037*

R   II   *Lepanthes benzingii* Luer *19045*
     R   *19045*   Ecuador *19045*

V   II   *Lepanthes bifalcis* Luer *19045*
     V   *19045*   Ecuador *19045*

V   II   *Lepanthes bifaria* Luer *19045*
     V   *19045*   Ecuador *19045*

V   II   *Lepanthes blepharistes* Reichb.f. *9006*
     V   *9426*   Costa Rica *9006*
     E/V   *11967*   Nicaragua *10034*

V   II   *Lepanthes brachypogon* Luer *19045*
     V   *19045*   Ecuador *19045*

V   II   *Lepanthes bradei* Schltr. *9037*
     V   *9426*   Costa Rica *9037*

E   II   *Lepanthes brownii* Hespenheide *20883, 19890*
     V   *19890*   Jamaica (St. James) *20883*

V   II   *Lepanthes calodictyon* Hook. *19045*
     V   *19045*   Ecuador *19045*

V   II   *Lepanthes camposii* Salazar & Soto Arenas *21265*
     V   *21265*   Mexico - Guerrero *21265*
     V   *21265*   Mexico - Oaxaca *21265*

V   II   *Lepanthes cascajalensis* Ames *9037*
     V   *9426*   Costa Rica *9037*

V   II   *Lepanthes chameleon* Ames *9037*
     V   *9426*   Costa Rica *9037*

R   II   *Lepanthes ciliaris* Luer & Hirtz *19045, 21295*
     R   *19045*   Ecuador *19045*

V   II   *Lepanthes ciliisepala* Schltr. *9037*
     V   *9426*   Costa Rica *9037*

V   II   *Lepanthes cochlearifolia* (Sw.) Sw. *20883, 19890*
     R   *19890*   Jamaica (Portland) *20883*

V   II   *Lepanthes columbar* Luer *19045*
     V   *19045*   Ecuador *19045*

V   II   *Lepanthes confusa* Ames & C. Schweinf. *9037*
     V   *9426*   Costa Rica *9037*

V   II   *Lepanthes convexa* Hespenheide *20883, 19890*
     V   *19890*   Jamaica (Trelawny) *20883*

V   II   *Lepanthes cotyledon* Luer *19045*
     V   *19045*   Ecuador *19045*

R   II   *Lepanthes craticia* Luer *19045*
     R   *19045*   Ecuador *19045*

R   II   *Lepanthes dalessandroi* Luer *19045*
     R   *19045*   Ecuador *19045*

V   II   *Lepanthes deleastes* Luer *19045*
     V   *19045*   Ecuador *19045*

R   II   *Lepanthes deliqua* Luer *19045*
     R   *19045*   Ecuador *19045*

R   II   *Lepanthes delphax* Luer *19045*
     R   *19045*   Ecuador *19045*

R   II   *Lepanthes divaricata* F. & R. *20883*
     R   *20883*   Jamaica *20883*

E	II	*Lepanthes dodiana* Stimson 20883	
	I	20883 Puerto Rico 20883	
R	II	*Lepanthes dodsonii* Luer 19045	
	R	19045 Ecuador 19045	
R	II	*Lepanthes electilis* Luer 19045	
	R	19045 Ecuador 19045	
V	II	*Lepanthes elliptica* F. & R. 20883	
	V	20883 Jamaica 20883	
E	II	*Lepanthes eltoroensis* Stimson 20883, 8058	
	I	20883 Puerto Rico 20883	
R	II	*Lepanthes erepsis* Luer & Hirtz 19045, 21295	
	R	19045 Ecuador 19045	
V	II	*Lepanthes estrellensis* Ames 9037	
	V	9426 Costa Rica 9037	
V	II	*Lepanthes exasperata* Ames & C. Schweinf. 9037	
	V	9426 Costa Rica 9037	
R	II	*Lepanthes excedens* Ames & Correll 9004	
	R	19752 Guatemala 9004	
R	II	*Lepanthes flexuosa* Luer 19045	
	R	19045 Ecuador 19045	
R	II	*Lepanthes focalis* Luer 19045	
	R	19045 Ecuador 19045	
R	II	*Lepanthes furcatipetala* Garay 19408	
	E	19408 Dominican Republic 19408	
	R	15638 Haiti (massif de la Hotte) 15638	
R	II	*Lepanthes fusiformis* Luer 19045	
	R	19045 Ecuador 19045	
R	II	*Lepanthes gabriellae* Salazar & Soto Arenas 21265	
	R	21265 Mexico - Oaxaca 21265	
R	II	*Lepanthes grypha* Luer 19045	
	R	19045 Ecuador 19045	
V	II	*Lepanthes guanacastensis* Ames & C. Schweinf. 9006	
	V	9426 Costa Rica 9006	
	E/V	11967 Nicaragua 10034	
V	II	*Lepanthes homotaxis* Luer & Escobar 19045	
	V	19045 Ecuador 19045	
R	II	*Lepanthes ictalurus* Luer 19045	
	R	19045 Ecuador 19045	
E	II	*Lepanthes ilense* Dodson 19045	
	E	19045 Ecuador 19045	
R	II	*Lepanthes illex* Luer 19045	
	R	19045 Ecuador 19045	
R	II	*Lepanthes imoena* Luer 19045	
	R	19045 Ecuador 19045	
V	II	*Lepanthes inornata* Schltr. 9037	
	V	9426 Costa Rica 9037	
E	II	*Lepanthes insectiflora* C. Schweinf. 20883, 9006	
	I	20883 Panama 20883	
R	II	*Lepanthes intermedia* Hespenheide 20883	
	R	20883 Jamaica 20883	
R	II	*Lepanthes intonsa* Luer 19045	
	R	19045 Ecuador 19045	
R	II	*Lepanthes intricata* Luer 19045	
	R	19045 Ecuador 19045	
V	II	*Lepanthes jimenezii* Schltr. 9037	
	V	9426 Costa Rica 9037	
V	II	*Lepanthes jubata* Luer 19045	
	V	19045 Ecuador 19045	

E	II	*Lepanthes lanceolata* Hespenheide 20883, 19890	
	V	19890 Jamaica (St. James) 20883	
V	II	*Lepanthes latisepala* Ames & C. Schweinf. 9037	
	V	9426 Costa Rica 9037	
V	II	*Lepanthes lindleyana* Oersted & Reichb.f. var. *angustifolia* Ames, Hubb. & C. Schweinf. 9037	
	V	9426 Costa Rica 9037	
R	II	*Lepanthes loddigesiana* Reichb. 20883	
	R	20883 Jamaica 20883	
R	II	*Lepanthes lophius* Luer & Escobar 19045	
	R	19045 Ecuador 19045	
R	II	*Lepanthes machorroi* Salazar & Soto Arenas 21265	
	R	21265 Mexico - Oaxaca 21265	
R	II	*Lepanthes magnifica* Luer 19045	
	R	19045 Ecuador 19045	
R	II	*Lepanthes mariae* Salazar, Soto Arenas & O. Suárez 21265	
	R	21265 Mexico - Oaxaca 21265	
E	II	*Lepanthes maxonii* Schltr. 20883, 9006	
	I	20883 Panama 20883	
R	II	*Lepanthes megalostele* Luer 19045	
	R	19045 Ecuador 19045	
V	II	*Lepanthes menatoi* Luer & Vásquez 19045	
	V	19045 Ecuador 19045	
V	II	*Lepanthes microglottis* Schltr. 9037	
	V	9426 Costa Rica 9037	
R	II	*Lepanthes micropogon* Luer 19045	
	R	19045 Ecuador 19045	
V	II	*Lepanthes minutilabia* Ames & C. Schweinf. 9037	
	V	9426 Costa Rica 9037	
R	II	*Lepanthes mixe* Salazar & Soto Arenas 21265	
	R	21265 Mexico - Oaxaca 21265	
V	II	*Lepanthes multiflora* Adams & Hespenheide 20883, 19890	
	R	19890 Jamaica (St. James, Trelawny) 20883	
R	II	*Lepanthes muscula* Luer & Escobar 19045	
	R	19045 Ecuador 19045	
R	II	*Lepanthes nigriscapa* R.E. Schultes & G.W. Dillon 21265	
	R	21265 Mexico - Oaxaca 21265	
R	II	*Lepanthes nivea* Luer 19045	
	R	19045 Ecuador 19045	
R	II	*Lepanthes nontecta* Luer 19045	
	R	19045 Ecuador 19045	
I	II	*Lepanthes nubicula* Reichb.f. 19352	
	I	19352 Colombia 19352	
R	II	*Lepanthes oaxacana* Salazar, Soto Arenas & O. Suárez 21265	
	R	21265 Mexico - Oaxaca 21265	
R	II	*Lepanthes obtusa* F. & R. 20883	
	R	20883 Jamaica 20883	
V	II	*Lepanthes obtusipetala* (F. & R.) F. & R. 20883	
	V	20883 Jamaica 20883	
R	II	*Lepanthes orchestris* Luer & Vasquez 19045	
	R	19045 Ecuador 19045	
R	II	*Lepanthes otara* Luer 19045	
	R	19045 Ecuador 19045	
R	II	*Lepanthes ovalis* (Sw.) F. & R. 20883	

	R	20883 Jamaica 20883	

R II *Lepanthes papilionacea* Salazar, Soto Arenas & O. Suárez 21265

    R   21265 Mexico - Oaxaca 21265

E II *Lepanthes paradoxa* Luer 19045

    R   19045 Ecuador 19045

R II *Lepanthes peniculus* Luer 19045

    R   19045 Ecuador 19045

R II *Lepanthes pentoxys* Luer 19045

    R   19045 Ecuador 19045

V II *Lepanthes pleurorachis* Luer 19045

    V   19045 Ecuador 19045

R II *Lepanthes pollex* Luer 19045

    R   19045 Ecuador 19045

R II *Lepanthes polytricha* Luer 19045

    R   19045 Ecuador 19045

E II *Lepanthes proctorii* Garay & Hespenheide 20883, 19890

    V   19890 Jamaica (Portland) 20883

R II *Lepanthes pseudocaulescens* Lyman B. Smith & Harris 19045, 21295

    ?   Colombia 21295

    R   19045 Ecuador 19045

R II *Lepanthes pubes* Luer & Escobar 19045

    R   19045 Ecuador 19045

R II *Lepanthes pubescens* Luer 19045

    R   19045 Ecuador 19045

R II *Lepanthes pulchella* (Sw.) Sw. 20883

    R   20883 Jamaica 20883

R II *Lepanthes quadrata* F. & R. 20883

    R   20883 Jamaica 20883

R II *Lepanthes quaternaria* Luer 19045

    R   19045 Ecuador 19045

V II *Lepanthes ramonensis* Schltr. 9037

    V   9426 Costa Rica 9037

R II *Lepanthes rhombipetala* Schltr. 19045

    I   19352 Colombia 19352

    R   19045 Ecuador 19045

R II *Lepanthes rotundata* Griseb. 20883

    R   20883 Jamaica 20883

R II *Lepanthes saltator* Luer 19045

    R   19045 Ecuador 19045

V II *Lepanthes schizix* Luer 19045

    V   19045 Ecuador 19045

E II *Lepanthes simplex* Hespenheide 20883, 19890

    V   19890 Jamaica (Trelawny) 20883

R II *Lepanthes sousae* Salazar & Soto Arenas 21265

    R   21265 Mexico - Oaxaca 21265

V II *Lepanthes standleyi* Ames 9037

    V   9426 Costa Rica 9037

R II *Lepanthes stupenda* Luer 19045

    R   19045 Ecuador 19045

V II *Lepanthes subdimidiata* Ames & C. Schweinf. 9037

    V   9426 Costa Rica 9037

R II *Lepanthes teres* Luer 19045

    R   19045 Ecuador 19045

V II *Lepanthes tipulifera* Reichb.f. 9037

    V   9426 Costa Rica 9037

E II *Lepanthes trichodactyla* Lindley 5607

    E   19105 Cuba (Santiago de Cuba) 5607

V II *Lepanthes tridens* Ames 9037

    V   9426 Costa Rica 9037

V II *Lepanthes tridentata* (Sw.) Sw. 20883, 19890

    R   19890 Jamaica 20883

E II *Lepanthes tubuliflora* Hespenheide 20883, 19890

    I   19890 Jamaica 20883

E II *Lepanthes unguicularis* Hespenheide 20883, 19890

    V   19890 Jamaica (St. James) 20883

V II *Lepanthes villosa* Lojtnant 19045, 21295

    V   19045 Ecuador 19045

E II *Lepanthes vinacea* Hespenheide 20883, 19890

    V   19890 Jamaica (St. Andrew, St. Thomas) 20883

V II *Lepanthes wendlandii* Reichb.f. 9037

    V   9426 Costa Rica 9037

V II *Lepanthes wercklei* Schltr. 9037

    V   9426 Costa Rica 9037

V II *Lepanthes woodiana* F. & R. 20883

    V   20883 Jamaica 20883

R II *Lepanthes wullschlaegelii* F. & R. 20883

    R   20883 Jamaica 20883

V II *Lepanthes ximenae* Luer 19045

    V   19045 Ecuador 19045

R II *Lepanthes yuvilensis* Catling 21269

    R   21269 Mexico - Oaxaca 21269

E II *Lepanthopsis microlepanthes* (Griseb.) Ames 20883, 5607

    E   20883 Cuba (Santiago de Cuba) 20883

    E   19408 Dominican Republic 19408

    E   19890 Jamaica (Clarendon, Portland) 20883

I II *Lesliea miralilies* Seidenf. 19120

    I   19120 Thailand 19120

R II *Ligeophila clavigera* (Reichb.f.) Garay 11933

    R   19850 Mexico 11933

    R   21266 Panama 21266

R II *Liparis aaronii* Cribb & B. Lewis 14795

    R   14795 Vanuatu 14795

E II *Liparis adamsii* Proctor 20883, 19890

    E   19890 Jamaica 20883

I II *Liparis barbata* Lindley 8021

    I   16162 Sri Lanka 8021

I II *Liparis beddomei* Ridley

    I   India - Tamil Nadu (Palani Hills) 4988

V II *Liparis biloba* Wight 11494

    V   11494 India - Tamil Nadu (Kollimund, Nilagiri hills) 11494

I II *Liparis brachyglottis* Reichb.f. ex Trimen. 8021

    I   16162 Sri Lanka 8021

R II *Liparis chapaensis* Gagnepain 6057

    R   Vietnam 6057

E II *Liparis clypeolum* Lindley var. *marquesensis* F. Brown

    E   French Polynesia - Marquesas Is

R II *Liparis decurrens* (Blume) Reichb.f. 8309

    R   Indonesia - Java 8309

I II *Liparis duthiei* Hook.f.

    I   India - Tamil Nadu (Nilagiri Hills) 4988

V II *Liparis elegantula* Krzl. 19045

V   *19045* Ecuador *19045*

V   II   *Liparis ferruginea* Lindl. *19209*
    V   *19047* Malaysia - Peninsular Malaysia (Melaka, Perak) *19209*
    Ex   *20099* Singapore *20099*

V   II   *Liparis furcata* (Hook.f.) Ridley *19047*
    V   *19047* Malaysia - Peninsular Malaysia (Taiping Hills) *19047*

E   II   *Liparis guamensis* Ames
    E   *18338* U.S. - Guam *18338*

E   II   *Liparis harrisii* Fawcett & Rendle *20883, 19890*
    R   *19890* Jamaica *20883*
    I   *20883* Puerto Rico *20883*

V   II   *Liparis hirtzii* Dodson *19045*
    V   *19045* Ecuador *19045*

I   II   *Liparis hostaefolia* (Koidz.) Koidz. ex Tuy. *8622*
    I   *19134* Japan - Kazan Retto (Minami-Iwojima) *8622*
    Ex   *19134* Japan - Ogasawara-shoto *8622*

Ex/E   II   *Liparis lauterbachii* Schltr. *8309*
    Ex/E   *19047* Indonesia - Java (east) *8309*

V   II   *Liparis lueri* Dodson *19045*
    V   *19045* Ecuador *19045*

V   II   *Liparis nigrescens* Schltr. *19045*
    V   *19045* Ecuador *19045*

I   II   *Liparis palawanensis* Ames *13833*
    I   *13833* Philippines (Palawan) *13833*

I   II   *Liparis platybolba* Hayata *11164*
    I   *11164* Japan *11164*

I   II   *Liparis platyphylla* Ridley
    I   India - Tamil Nadu *4988*

R   II   *Liparis prianganensis* J.J. Smith *8309*
    R   Indonesia - Java (West Java) *8309*

I   II   *Liparis pulchella* Hook.f.
    I   India - Meghalaya
    I   India - Nagaland

V   II   *Liparis saundersiana* Reichenb. f. *20883, 19890*
    V   *19890* Jamaica (St Andrews) *20883*
    I   *20883* Puerto Rico *20883*

R   II   *Liparis tonkinensis* Gagnepain *6057*
    R   Vietnam *6057*

R   II   *Liparis tradescantifolia* (Blume) Lindley *8309*
    R   Indonesia - Java (West Java) *8309*

R   II   *Listera auriculata* Wieg. *20850*
    I   *20850* Canada - Labrador *20850*
    I   *20850* Canada - New Brunswick *20850*
    I   *20850* Canada - Newfoundland *20850*
    R   *20850* Canada - Ontario *20850*
    R   *20850* Canada - Quebec *20850*
    E   *20850* U.S. - Maine *20850*
    V   *20850* U.S. - Michigan *20850*
    E   *20850* U.S. - Minnesota *20850*
    E   *20850* U.S. - New Hampshire *20850*
    E   *20850* U.S. - New York *20850*
    E   *20850* U.S. - Vermont *20850*
    E   *20850* U.S. - Wisconsin *20850*

V   II   *Lockhartia amoena* Endres & Reichb.f. var. *triangulabia* C. Schweinf. & P. Allen *9006*
    V   *19577* Panama *9006*

R   II   *Lockhartia dipleura* Schltr. *9037*
    R   *9426* Costa Rica *9037*

V   II   *Lockhartia obtusata* L.O. Wms. *20883, 9006*
    V   *16317* Panama *20883*

V   II   *Luisia boninensis* Schltr. *8038*
    V   *19134* Japan - Ogasawara-shoto *8038*

R   II   *Luisia taurina* J.J. Smith *8309*
    R   Indonesia - Java (West Java; East Java) *8309*

V   II   *Lycaste crinita* Lindley *9423*
    V   *10007* Mexico *9423*

E   II   *Lycaste hirtzii* Dodson *19045*
    E   *19045* Ecuador *19045*

R   II   *Lycaste macrophylla* Cogn. var. *desboisiana* Cogn. *10034*
    R   *10034* Costa Rica *10034*
    E/V   *11967* Nicaragua *10034*

E   II   *Lycaste powellii* Schltr. *20883, 10012*
    R   *10010* Panama *20883*

E   II   *Lycaste skinneri* (Bateman ex Lindley) Lindley *2790*
    E   *10359* El Salvador *10359*
    E   *11938* Guatemala *2790*
    E   *11938* Honduras *2790*
    E   *11938* Mexico - Chiapas *9114*

V   II   *Lycaste suaveolens* Summerh. *10013*
    V   *10359* El Salvador *10013*
    E   *9443* Guatemala *9443*
    E/V   *11967* Nicaragua *10034*

V   II   *Lycaste sulfurea* Reichb.f. *10013*
    V   *10359* El Salvador *10013*

V   II   *Lycomormium ecuadorense* Sweet *19045*
    V   *19045* Ecuador *19045*

R   II   *Macodes cominsii* (Rolfe) Rolfe *14794*
    R   *14793* Solomon Is. - South *14794*

R   II   *Macroclinium borjaense* Dodson *19045*
    R   *19045* Ecuador *19045*

V   II   *Macroclinium cordesii* (L.O. Williams) Dodson *11274*
    V   *9426* Costa Rica *9037*
    V   *19577* Panama *9037*

R   II   *Macroclinium dalstroemii* Dodson *19045, 11274*
    R   *19045* Ecuador *19045*

R   II   *Macroclinium hirtzii* Dodson *19045*
    R   *19045* Ecuador *19045*

R   II   *Macroclinium paniculatum* (Ames & Schweinf.) Dodson *10034*
    R   *10034* Costa Rica *10034*
    E/V   *11967* Nicaragua *10034*

R   II   *Malaxis acianthoides* (Schltr.) Ames *9004*
    R   *9004* Guatemala *9004*

V   II   *Malaxis bayardii* Fern. *20850*
    I   *20850* U.S. - Connecticut *20850*
    E   *20850* U.S. - Massachusetts *20850*
    I   *20850* U.S. - New Jersey *20850*
    E   *20850* U.S. - New York *20850*
    Ex/E   *20850* U.S. - North Carolina *20850*
    V   *20850* U.S. - Pennsylvania *20850*
    I   *20850* U.S. - Rhode Is. *20850*
    I   *20850* U.S. - Virginia *20850*

I   II   *Malaxis boninensis* (Koidz.) Nackej. *8622*
    I   *19134* Japan - Kazan Retto *8622*
    Ex   *19134* Japan - Ogasawara-shoto *8622*

R   II   *Malaxis cuprea* (J.J. Smith) Bakh.f. *8309*
    R   Indonesia - Java (West Java) *8309*

R   II   *Malaxis ehrenbergii* (Reichb.f.) Kuntze *11933*
    R   *21204* Mexico - Jalisco *21204*
    R   *21204* Mexico - Nayarit *21204*

R II *Malaxis fimbriata* Lavarack *20681*
    R *20681* Australia - Queensland *20681*

R II *Malaxis greenwoodiana* Salazar & M.A. Sota
    Arenas *19850*
    R *19850* Mexico *19850*

R II *Malaxis hagsateri* Salazar *19850*
    R *19850* Mexico *19850*

E II *Malaxis hahajimensis* S. Kobayashi *8037*
    E *19134* Japan - Ogasawara-shoto *8037*

V II *Malaxis integra* (F. & R.) F. & R. *20883, 19890*
    V *19890* Jamaica *20883*

I II *Malaxis lancifolia* (Thwaites) Kuntze *8021*
    I *16162* Sri Lanka (Ratnapura Dist.; Kitulgala)
    8021

E II *Malaxis lawleri* Lavarack & B.Gray *20681*
    E *20681* Australia - Queensland *20681*

V II *Malaxis lloensis* (Schltr.) Dodson *19045*
    V *19045* Ecuador *19045*

I II *Malaxis massonii* (Ridl.) Kuntze *10199*
    I Dominica *10199*

R II *Malaxis obovata* (J.J. Smith) Ames & C.
    Schweinf. *8309*
    R Indonesia - Java (West Java) *8309*

R II *Malaxis padilliana* L.O. Williams *19575*
    R *19575* Argentina *19575*

E II *Malaxis pittieri* (Schltr.) Ames *20883, 9006*
    I *20883* Panama *20883*

R II *Malaxis pollardii* L.O. Williams *11363*
    ? Mexico - Jalisco *21204*
    R *11933* Mexico - Oaxaca *11363*

R II *Malaxis sagittata* (J.J. Smith) Ames *8309*
    R Indonesia - Java (West Java) *8309*

V II *Malaxis seychellarum* (Kraenzlin) Summerh. *14296*
    V *19182* Seychelles (granitic) *14296*

R II *Malaxis streptopetala* (H. Robinson & Greenman)
    Ames *9423*
    R *11933* Mexico *9423*

R II *Malaxis tenggerensis* (J.J. Smith) Bakh.f. *8309*
    R Indonesia - Java (east) *8309*

E II *Malaxis woodsonii* L.O. Wms. *20883, 9006*
    I *20883* Panama *20883*

E II *Malleola andamanica* Balakr. & Bhargava *11494*
    E *11494* India - Andaman Is. (Little & south Andamans)
    11494

I II *Malleola kawakamii* (J.J. Smith) J.J. Sm. &
    Schltr. *8309*
    I Indonesia - Java (east) *8309*

I II *Malleola undulata* (Ridley) J.J. Smith & Schltr.
    I Malaysia - Peninsular Malaysia (Perak)

E II *Masdevallia agaster* Luer *19045*
    E *19045* Ecuador *19045*

E II *Masdevallia amaluzae* Luer *19045*
    E *19045* Ecuador *19045*

V II *Masdevallia ampullacea* Luer & Andretta *19045*
    V *19045* Ecuador *19045*

V II *Masdevallia andreettana* Luer *19045*
    V *19045* Ecuador *19045*

V II *Masdevallia attenuata* Reichb.f. *9037*
    E *9426* Costa Rica *9037*

    V *16317* Panama *9037*

R II *Masdevallia buccinator* Reichb.f & Warsc. *18089*
    R *18089* Colombia *18089*

V II *Masdevallia calura* Reichb.f. *10012*
    V *9426* Costa Rica *10012*

E II *Masdevallia carmenensis* Luer & Malo *19045*
    E *19045* Ecuador *19045*

R II *Masdevallia cerastes* Luer & R.Escobar *18089*
    R *18089* Colombia *18089*

V II *Masdevallia chaetostoma* Luer *19045*
    V *19045* Ecuador *19045*

V II *Masdevallia collina* L.O. Wms. *20883, 9037*
    V *16317* Panama *20883*

E II *Masdevallia concinna* Koeniger *18200*
    E *12468* Peru *18200*

V II *Masdevallia cupularis* Reichb.f. *9037*
    V *9426* Costa Rica *9037*

V II *Masdevallia delphina* Luer *19045*
    V *19045* Ecuador *19045*

V II *Masdevallia don-quijote* Luer & Andreetta *19045*
    V *19045* Ecuador *19045*

V II *Masdevallia dynastes* Luer *19045*
    V *19045* Ecuador *19045*

R II *Masdevallia empusa* Luer *19045*
    R *19045* Ecuador *19045*

V II *Masdevallia flaveola* Reichb.f. *9037*
    V *9426* Costa Rica *9037*

E II *Masdevallia fuchsii* Luer *18089*
    E *20046* Peru *18089*

R II *Masdevallia fugueroae* Luer *19045*
    R *19045* Ecuador *19045*

R II *Masdevallia gilbertoi* Luer & R.Escobar *18089*
    R *18089* Colombia *18089*

R II *Masdevallia graminea* Luer *19045*
    R *19045* Ecuador *19045*

V II *Masdevallia instar* Luer & Andreetta *19045*
    V *19045* Ecuador *19045*

E II *Masdevallia iris* Luer & R.Escobar *18089*
    E *18089* Venezuela *18089*

E II *Masdevallia lamprotyria* Koniger *18089*
    E *20046* Peru *18089*

Ex/E II *Masdevallia lynchiphora* Koeniger *18200*
    Ex/E *12468* Peru *18200*

R II *Masdevallia marthae* Luer & R.Escobar *18089*
    R *18089* Colombia *18089*

Ex II *Masdevallia menatoi* Luer & Vasq *18089*
    Ex *18089* Bolivia *18089*

R II *Masdevallia mendozae* Luer *19045*
    R *19045* Ecuador *19045*

V II *Masdevallia norops* Luer & Andreettae *19045*
    V *19045* Ecuador *19045*

V II *Masdevallia ova-avis* Luer *19045*
    V *19045* Ecuador *19045*

E II *Masdevallia panguiensis* Luer & Andreetta *19045*
    E *19045* Ecuador *19045*

E II *Masdevallia patula* Luer & Malo *19045*
    E *19045* Ecuador *19045*

E II *Masdevallia pernix* Koniger *18089*

E   18200 Peru *18200*

E II *Masdevallia pinocchio* Luer & Andreetta *19045*
E   *19045* Ecuador *19045*

V II *Masdevallia pleurothalloides* Luer *10015*
V   *10020* Panama *10015*

E II *Masdevallia prosartema* Koeniger *18200*
E   *18200* Peru *18200*

R II *Masdevallia purpurella* Luer & R.Escobar *18089*
R   *18089* Colombia *18089*

V II *Masdevallia rafaeliana* Luer *17000*
V   *18089* Costa Rica *17000*

V II *Masdevallia reichenbachiana* Endres ex Reichb.f. *9037*
V   *9426* Costa Rica *9037*

V II *Masdevallia rolfeana* Kranzlin *9037*
V   *9426* Costa Rica *9037*

R II *Masdevallia sanctae-inesae* Luer & Malo *19045*
R   *19045* Ecuador *19045*

R II *Masdevallia scobina* Luer & R.Escobar *18089*
R   *18089* Colombia *18089*

R II *Masdevallia segurae* Luer & R.Escobar *18089*
R   *18089* Colombia *18089*

R II *Masdevallia stenorhynchos* Kranzlin *18089*
R   *18089* Colombia *18089*

V II *Masdevallia strobelii* Sweet & Garay *10010*
V   *10010* Ecuador *10010*

I II *Masdevallia tovarensis* Reichb.f. *6154*
I   *6154* Venezuela *6154*

R II *Masdevallia urosalpinx* Luer *19045*
R   *19045* Ecuador *19045*

E II *Masdevallia veitchiana* Reichb.f *18089*
E   *18089* Peru (Machu Picchu) *18089*

Ex/E II *Masdevallia walteri* Luer *17000*
Ex/E *17000* Costa Rica *17000*

R II *Maxillaria chacoensis* Dodson *19045*
R   *19045* Ecuador *19045*

R II *Maxillaria gentryi* Dodson *19045, 11274*
R   *19045* Ecuador *19045*

V II *Maxillaria grandis* Reichb.f. *18200*
V   Ecuador *19437*
E   *12482* Peru *18200*

R II *Maxillaria histrionica* (Reichb.f.) L.O. Williams *9423*
R   *11933* Mexico *9423*

I II *Maxillaria inflexa* (Lindl.) Griseb. *10199*
I   Dominica *10199*
E   *19408* Dominican Republic *19408*

V II *Maxillaria jucunda* Lehm. & Krzl. *19045*
V   *19045* Ecuador *19045*

V II *Maxillaria lehmannii* Reichb. f. *19045*
V   *19045* Ecuador *19045*

V II *Maxillaria marmoliana* Dodson *19045*
V   *19045* Ecuador *19045*

V II *Maxillaria molitor* Rchb.f. *19045, 16956*
V   *19045* Ecuador *19045*

V II *Maxillaria mombachoensis* A.H. Heller ex Atwood *10034*
V   *11967* Nicaragua *10034*

V II *Maxillaria oestlundiana* L.O. Williams *9423*
V   *19850* Mexico *9423*

R II *Maxillaria perryae* Dodson *19045*
R   *19045* Ecuador *19045*

E II *Maxillaria powellii* Schltr. *20883, 9006*
I   *20883* Panama *20883*

V II *Maxillaria pseudoreichenheimiana* Dodson *19045*
V   *19045* Ecuador *19045*

E II *Maxillaria swartziana* Adams *20883, 19890*
V   *19890* Jamaica (St. Andrew, Portland) *20883*

E II *Megastylis latissima* (Schltr.) Schltr. *20893*
E   *20893* New Caledonia *20893*

E II *Megastylis paradoxa* (Kranzlin) Halle *20893*
E   *20893* New Caledonia *20893*

I II *Mesadenus portoricensis* Schlechter
I   *19002* Puerto Rico *8058*

V II *Mesoglossum londesboroughianum* (Reichb.f.) Halbinger *10047*
V   *19850* Mexico *10047*

V II *Mexicoa ghiesbrechtiana* (Rich. & Galeotti) Garay *10011*
V   *16360* Mexico *10011*

R II *Mexipedium xerophyticum* (Soto, Salazar & Hágsater) V.A.Al & M.W.Chase *21268*
R   *21268* Mexico *21268*

V II *Microtis globula* R.Bates *20681*
V   *20681* Australia - Western Australia *20681*

R II *Microtis pulchella* R.Br. *20681*
R   *20681* Australia - Western Australia *20681*

V II *Miltoniopsis warscewiczii* (Reichb.f.) Garay & Dunsterv. *9037*
E   *9426* Costa Rica *9037*
V   *19577* Panama *9037*

Ex II *Monadenia ecalcarata* G.J.Lewis *20604*
Ex   *20604* South Africa - Cape Province *20604*

V II *Monadenia macrostachya* Lindl. *20604*
V   *20604* South Africa - Cape Province *20604*

E II *Monadenia physodes* (Sw.) Rchb.f. *20604*
E   *20604* South Africa - Cape Province *20604*

R II *Monadenia sabulosa* (Bolus) Kraenzl. *20604*
R   *20604* South Africa - Cape Province *20604*

V II *Mormodes andreettae* Dodson *19045*
V   *19045* Ecuador *19045*

R II *Mormodes dayanum* Reichb.f. *9423*
R   *16360* Mexico *9423*

V II *Mormodes hookeri* Lemaire *9037*
V   *9426* Costa Rica *9037*
E   *19577* Panama *9037*

V II *Mormodes lancilabris* Pabst *20883, 10035*
V   *16317* Panama *20883*

R II *Mormodes luxata* Lindley *9423*
R   *11933* Mexico *9423*

R II *Mormodes maculata* (Klotzsch) L.O. Williams *9423*
R   *11933* Mexico *9423*

V II *Mormodes maculata* (Klotzsch) L.O. Williams var. unicolor (Hook.) L.O. Williams *9423*
V   *16360* Mexico - Jalisco *9423*

R II *Mormodes nagelii* L.O. Williams *9423*
R   *11336* Mexico *9423*

I II *Mormodes oceloteoides* Rosillo *11322*
I   *11933* Mexico - Jalisco *11322*

I		I	11933	Mexico - Nayarit *11322*

I II *Mormodes pabstiana* Cardenas, Ramirez & Rosillo *11324*
  I 11933 Mexico - Jalisco *11324*

I II *Mormodes pardalinata* Rosillo *9423*
  I 11933 Mexico - Jalisco *9423*

V II *Mormodes porphyrophlebia* Salazar *19848*
  V 21185 Mexico - Oaxaca *21185*

I II *Mormodes ramirezii* Rosillo *11938*
  I 11938 Mexico - Jalisco *21204*

I II *Mormodes saccata* Rosillo *11325*
  I 11933 Mexico - Jalisco *11325*

I II *Mormodes sanguineoclaustra* Fowlie *19850*
  I 19850 Mexico *19850*

R II *Mormodes sotoana* Salazar *19850*
  R 21190 Guatemala *21190*
  R 21190 Mexico - Chiapas *21190*

R II *Mormodes tezontle* Rosillo *11938*
  R 16360 Mexico - Jalisco *11938*

R II *Mormodes tuxtlensis* Salazar *12781*
  R 12781 Mexico - Veracruz *12781*

E II *Mormodes uncia* Reichb.f. *19848*
  E 19848 Mexico *19848*

R II *Mormodes vernixoidea* *17203*
  R 17203 Suriname *17203*

R II *Neobolusia stolzii* Schltr. var. *glabripetala*
      Summerh. *7879*
  R   Zimbabwe *7879*

E II *Neocogniauxia monophylla* (Griseb.) Schltr. *20883, 19890*
  R 19890 Jamaica (St. Andrew, Portland) *20883*

V II *Neofinetia falcata* (Thunb.) Hu *8751*
  E 15923 Korea, South *7588*
  V   Japan *8751*

R II *Neomoorea irrorata* Rolfe *9006*
  R 10020 Panama *9006*
  R 9006 Colombia *9006*

I II *Neottia kashmiriana* (Duthie) P. Beauv.
  I   India - Jammu & Kashmir

Ex/E II *Neottia ussuriensis* (Komarov & Nevski) Soo *5942*
  Ex/E 5942 Russia (Far East) - Primorye (south) *5942*

I II *Nervilia biflora* (Roxb.) Schltr.
  I   India - Kerala (Malabar, Wynaad) *4988*

E II *Nervilia jacksoniae* Rinehart & Fosberg *20819*
  E 20819 North Mariana Is. (Rota) *20819*
  E 20819 U.S. - Guam *20819*

I II *Nervilia mackinnonii* (Duthie) Schltr.
  I   India - Uttar Pradesh (Mussoorie; Kumaun)

R II *Nervilia nipponica* Makino *11164*
  R 11164 Japan *11164*

R II *Neuwiedia annamensis* Gagnepain *6057*
  R   Vietnam *6057*

R II *Neuwiedia balansae* Baillon & Gagnepain *6057*
  R   Vietnam *6057*

R II *Neuwiedia javanica* J.J. Smith *8309*
  R   Indonesia - Java (West Java) *8309*

R II *Nigritella lithopolitanica* Ravnik *13662*
  R 20757 Austria (Kärnten) *20757*
  R 13662 Slovenia *13662*

V II *Notylia lankesteri* Ames *9037*
  V 9426 Costa Rica *9037*
  V 19577 Panama *10012*

E II *Notylia latilabia* A. & S. *20883, 9006*
  I 20883 Panama *20883*

R II *Oberonia acarus* Evrard & Gagnepain *6057*
  R   Vietnam *6057*

Ex II *Oberonia attenuata* Dockr. *20681*
  Ex 20681 Australia - Queensland *20681*

I II *Oberonia calcicola* Holttum
  I   Malaysia - Peninsular Malaysia (Langkawi, Kedah)

R II *Oberonia carnosa* Lavarack *20681*
  R 20681 Australia - Queensland *20681*

R II *Oberonia caudata* King & Prantl
  R   Malaysia - Peninsular Malaysia (Perak)

I II *Oberonia claviloba* Jayaw. *8021*
  I 16162 Sri Lanka *8021*

I II *Oberonia dolabrata* Jayaw. *8021*
  I 16162 Sri Lanka (Corbet's Gap, Kandy) *8021*

E II *Oberonia flabellata* Holtt. *19209*
  E   Malaysia - Peninsular Malaysia (Johor) *19209*
  E   Singapore

R II *Oberonia flava* Ridley
  R   Malaysia - Peninsular Malaysia

I II *Oberonia forcipata* Lindley *8021*
  I 16162 Sri Lanka *8021*

I II *Oberonia fornicata* Jayaw. *8021*
  I 16162 Sri Lanka (Rangala, Kandy District) *8021*

R II *Oberonia langbianensis* Gagnepain *6057*
  R   Vietnam *6057*

R II *Oberonia microphylla* (Blume) Lindley *8309*
  R   Indonesia - Java *8309*

I II *Oberonia quadrilatera* Jayaw. *8021*
  I 16162 Sri Lanka (Hunnasgiriya, Doluwa Kanda) *8021*

I II *Oberonia scyllae* Lindley *8021*
  I 16162 Sri Lanka *8021*

E II *Oberonia titania* Lindley *10604*
  E 19108 Australia - Norfolk Is. *10604*

R II *Oberonia transversiloba* Holttum
  R   Malaysia - Peninsular Malaysia (Pahang)

I II *Oberonia variabilis* Kerr *11164*
  I 11164 Japan *11164*

I II *Oberonia wallie-silvae* Jayaw. *8021*
  I 16162 Sri Lanka (Rangala, Kandy District) *8021*

I II *Oberonia weragamaensis* Jayaw. *8021*
  I 16162 Sri Lanka (Weragama, Ratnapura Dist.) *8021*

V II *Odontochilus hatusimanus* Ohwi & T. Koyama *11164*
  V 11164 Japan *11164*

R II *Odontoglossum epidendroides* Kunth *18200*
  R   Ecuador
  R 18200 Peru *18200*

V II *Odontoglossum funis* (Lehm. & Krzl.) Garay *19045*
  V 19045 Ecuador *19045*

V II *Odontoglossum hallii* Lindl. *19045*
  V 19045 Ecuador *19045*

V II *Odontoglossum longipes* Rchb.f. & Warsc. *19045*
    V   *19045* Ecuador *19045*

Ex/E II *Oeceoclades seychellarum* (Summerh.) Garay & P.
    Taylor *14296*
    Ex/E   Seychelles (Mahé) *14296*

E II *Oeoniella aphrodite* (Balf. f. & S. Moore)
    Schltr. *5852*
    E   20771 Réunion *5852*
    E   20771 Mauritius (mainland & Aigrettes Is.)
                   5852
    E   5852   Mauritius - Rodrigues (Grande Mt., Mt.
                   Ciemtière) *5852*
    E   Seychelles *14296*

V II *Oliveriana ecuadorensis* Dodson *19045*
    V   *19045* Ecuador *19045*

E II *Oncidium angustisepalum* Kranzlin *9037*
    E   9426   Costa Rica *9037*

R II *Oncidium calochilum* Cogn. *19712*
    I   19712 Cayman Is. (Grand Cayman) *19434*
    R   19712 Cuba *19434*
    E   19408 Dominican Republic *19408*
    I   19712 Haiti *19434*

E II *Oncidium caymanense* Moir *19712*
    E   19434 Cayman Is. (Grand Cayman) *19434*

V II *Oncidium chelidonizon* Kranzlin *9037*
    V   9426   Costa Rica *9037*

V II *Oncidium costaricense* Schltr. *9037*
    V   9426   Costa Rica *9037*

V II *Oncidium dichromaticum* Reichb.f. *9037*
    V   9426   Costa Rica *9037*

R II *Oncidium flavovirens* L.O. Williams *9423*
    R   11933 Mexico *9423*

V II *Oncidium floridanum* Ames *20883, 20850, 19002*
    E   20850 U.S. - Florida *20850*
    I   20883 Bahamas *20883*

E II *Oncidium gauntlettii* Withner & Jesup *20883, 19890*
    E   19890 Jamaica (Westmoreland, Hanover) *20883*

R II *Oncidium karwinskii* (Lindley) Dressler & L.O.
    Williams *10011*
    R   11933 Mexico *10011*

E II *Oncidium loxense* Lindley *19045*
    E   19045 Ecuador *19045*

V II *Oncidium margalefii* Hágsater *18110*
    V   18110 Mexico - Guerrero *18110*
    V   18110 Mexico - Oaxaca *18110*

V II *Oncidium monachicum* Rchb.f. *19045*
    V   19045 Ecuador *19045*

I II *Oncidium oestlundianum* L.O. Williams *9423*
    I   11119 Mexico - Jalisco *9423*
    I   11119 Mexico - Morelos *9423*
    I   11119 Mexico - Nayarit *9423*

R II *Oncidium panduriforme* Ames & C. Schweinf. *9037*
    V   9426   Costa Rica *9037*
    R   19577 Panama *9006*

I II *Oncidium papilio* Lindley *6154*
    I   6154   Venezuela *6154*

V II *Oncidium pastasae* Rchb.f. *19045*
    V   19045 Ecuador *19045*

V II *Oncidium phalaenopsis* Lindley *19045*
    V   19045 Ecuador *19045*

R II *Oncidium pollardii* Dodson & Hágsater *11354*

    R   19850 Mexico - Oaxaca *11354*

V II *Oncidium reichenheimii* (Linden & Reichb.f.) Garay &
    Stacy *10012*
    E   9426   Costa Rica *10012*
    V   10007 Mexico *10012*

V II *Oncidium sclerophyllum* Kranzlin *9037*
    V   9426   Costa Rica *9037*

R II *Oncidium stelligerum* Reichb.f. *9114*
    R   9004   Guatemala *9004*
    R   19850 Mexico *9114*

V II *Oncidium storkii* Ames & C. Schweinf. *9037*
    V   9426   Costa Rica *9037*

V II *Oncidium stramineum* Bateman ex Lindley *9423*
    V   16360 Mexico - Veracruz *9423*

V II *Oncidium tetrapetalum* (Jacq.) Willd. *19890*
    V   19890 Jamaica *19221*

V II *Oncidium tetraskelidion* Kranzlin *9037*
    V   9426   Costa Rica *9037*

V II *Oncidium tigrinum* Llave & Lex. *9423*
    V   10007 Mexico *9423*

R II *Oncidium toachicum* Dodson *19045*
    R   19045 Ecuador *19045*

E II *Oncidium triquetrum* (Sw.) R. Br. *20883, 19890*
    E   19890 Jamaica (west & central) *20883*

V II *Oncidium turialbae* Schltr. *9037*
    V   9426   Costa Rica *9037*

V II *Oncidium umbonatum* Rchb.f. *19045*
    V   19045 Ecuador *19045*

V II *Oncidium unguiculatum* Lindley *11933*
    V   16360 Mexico *11933*

E II *Oncidium usneoides* Lindley *5607*
    E   19105 Cuba (Guantanamo) *5607*

V II *Oncidium variegatum* (Sw.) Willd. *20883, 20850, 19002*
    I   20850 U.S. - Florida *20850*
    ?   Islands of the Caribbean (Greater Antilles)
                   19434
    I   20883 Puerto Rico *20883*
    I   20883 USA - Virgin Is. *20883*

R II *Ophrys aesculapii* Renz *20171*
    R   Greece

V II *Ophrys argolica* Fleischm. ssp. *elegans* (Renz)
    Erich Nelson *14230*
    V   19164 Cyprus *14230*
    E   19873 Turkey *14230*

V II *Ophrys aveyronensis* (J.J. Wood) Delforge *20528*
    V   20528 France (south) *20528*

E II *Ophrys bornmuelleri* M. Schulze ex Bornm. ssp.
    carduchorum Renz & Taub. *12840*
    E   12840 Turkey *12840*

I II *Ophrys caucasica* Woronow ex Grossh. *5942, 20627*
    I   5942   Russia - North Caucasus *5942*
    I   5942   Armenia *5942*
    I   5942   Azerbaijan *5942*

R II *Ophrys gottfriediana* Renz *20171*
    R   Greece

E II *Ophrys holoserica* (Burnm. f.) Greuter ssp.
    heterochila Renz & Taub. *12840*
    E   12840 Turkey *12840*

I II *Ophrys holosericea* Greut. ssp. *holubyana*
    (Andrasovszky) Dostál *8000*

	I		19321	Slovakia	*19321*

E   II   *Ophrys isaura* **Renz & Taub.** *12840*

     E   *12840*   Turkey *12840*

V   II   *Ophrys kotschyi* **Fleischm. & Soo** *14230*

     V   *19164*   Cyprus *14230*

V   II   *Ophrys lunulata* **Parl.** *8000, 20171*

     Ex   Italy - Sardinia *17781*
     V   *18264*   Italy - Sicily *17781*
     Ex   *17781*   Malta *17781*

E   II   *Ophrys lycia* **Renz & Taub.** *12840*

     E   *12840*   Turkey *12840*

I   II   *Ophrys oestrifera* **M.Bieb.** *5942, 20171*

     I   *5942*   Russia - North Caucasus *5942*
     I   *5942*   Armenia *5942*
     I   *5942*   Azerbaijan *5942*
     I   *5942*   Georgia *5942*
     I   *5942*   Ukraine - Crimea (south) *5942*

E   II   *Ophrys phrygia* **Fleishm. & Bornm.** *12840*

     E   *19873*   Turkey *12840*

E   II   *Ophrys reinholdii* **Spruner ex Fleischm. ssp.
       leucotaenia Renz & Taub.** *12840*

     E   *12840*   Turkey *12840*

R   II   *Ophrys sphegodes* **Mill. ssp. *helenae* (Renz) D.M.
       Moore** *20171*

     R   Greece

V   II   *Ophrys splendida* **Golz & Reinhard** *17457, 20528*

     V   *20528*   France (south) *20528*

R   II   *Ophrys transhyrcana* **Czernjak. ssp. *amanensis*
       (Nelson) Renz & Taub.** *12840*

     R   *12840*   Turkey *12840*

R   II   *Orchis albanica* **Goelz et Reinhard** *20178*

     R   *20178*   Albania *20178*

V   II   *Orchis canariensis* **Lindl.**

     V   Spain - Canary Is.

V   II   *Orchis chidori* **(Makino) Schltr. var. *curtipes*
       (Ohwi) Ohwi** *11164*

     V   *11164*   Japan *11164*

V   II   *Orchis cyrenaica* **E. Dur. & G. Barratte**

     V   Libya

I   II   *Orchis fedtschenkoi* **Czerniak.** *5942*

     I   *5942*   Turkmenistan *5942*

E   II   *Orchis graminifolia* **(Reichb.f.) Tang & Wang var.
       kurokamiana (Ohwi & Hatus.) Ohwi** *11164*

     E   *11164*   Japan *11164*

E   II   *Orchis graminifolia* **(Reichb.f.) Tang & Wang var.
       suzukiana Ohwi** *11164*

     E   *11164*   Japan *11164*

E   II   *Orchis scopulorum* **Summerh.** *17781*

     E   Portugal - Madeira *17891*

V   II   *Orchis spitzelii* **Saut. ex W.D.J.Koch ssp.
       nitidifolia (Teschner) Soo** *20171*

     V   *20731*   Greece - Crete *20731*

I   II   *Oreorchis indica* **(Lindley) Hook.f.**

     I   India - Himachal Pradesh (Simla)
     I   India - Uttar Pradesh (Garhwal; Kumaun)

I   II   *Oreorchis rolfei* **Duthie** *11494*

     I   India - Uttar Pradesh

V   II   *Ornithocephalus bryostachyus* **Schltr.** *19045*

     V   *19045*   Ecuador *19045*

V   II   *Ornithocephalus cochleariformis* **C. Schweinf.** *20883,*

    9006
     V   *16317*   Panama *20883*

V   II   *Ornithocephalus falcatus* **Foche** *19045*

     V   *19045*   Ecuador *19045*

R   II   *Ornithocephalus iridifolius* **Reichb.f.** *9004*

     R   *9004*   Guatemala *9004*
     V   *10007*   Mexico *9004*

I   II   *Pachites appressa* **Lindl.** *20604*

     I   *20604*   South Africa - Cape Province *20604*

R   II   *Pachites bodkini* **Bolus** *10260, 20604*

     R   *20604*   South Africa - Cape Province *20604*

R   II   *Pachyphyllum costaricense* **(Ames & Schweinf.) L.O.
       Williams** *10012*

     R   *9426*   Costa Rica *10012*

R   II   *Pachyphyllum mexacanum* **Dressler & Hagsater** *19850*

     R   *19850*   Mexico *19850*

E   II   *Palmorchis powellii* **(Ames) Schweinf. & Corr.** *20883,*
       9006

     R   *18265*   Costa Rica (La Selva) *11571*
     R   *10020*   Panama *20883*
     R   *18265*   Colombia (Bahia Solano) *18265*

V   II   *Palmorchis trilobulata* **L.O. Wms.** *20883, 9006*

     R   *9426*   Costa Rica *10012*
     V   *20883*   Panama *20883*

V   II   *Paphinia herrerae* **Dodson** *19045*

     V   *19045*   Ecuador *19045*

E   I   *Paphiopedilum armeniacum* **S.C. Chen & F.Y. Liu** *15918*

     E   China - Yunnan (south) *15918*

V   I   *Paphiopedilum barbigerum* **Tang & Wang** *15918*

     V   *20756*   China - Guangxi *20756*
     V   *20756*   China - Guizhou *20756*

V   I   *Paphiopedilum bougainvilleanum* **Fowlie** *14794*

     V   *14793*   Papua New Guinea (wet montane forest, 1100-1850
        m.) *14794*

R   I   *Paphiopedilum charlesworthii* **(Rolfe) Pfitz.** *15918*

     R   Myanmar (Shan States only) *15918*

E   I   *Paphiopedilum dayanum* **(Lindl.) Stein** *15918*

     E   Malaysia - Sabah (Mt Kinabalu)

Ex/E   I   *Paphiopedilum delenatii* **Guillaumin** *6057*

     Ex/E   *19695*   Vietnam *6057*

E   I   *Paphiopedilum druryi* **(Beddome) Stein** *11494*

     E   *4988*   India - Kerala (Travancore & Kalakkad Hills)
        11494

R   I   *Paphiopedilum emersonii* **Koopowitz & Cribb** *15918*

     R   *15918*   China - Guizhou *15918*

E   I   *Paphiopedilum exul* **(Ridley) Rolfe** *15918*

     E   Thailand (peninsular Thailand) *15918*

E   I   *Paphiopedilum fairrieanum* **(Lindley) Stein** *11494*

     E   *11494*   Bhutan (Chumbi) *11494*
     E   *11494*   India - Arunachal Pradesh *11494*
     E   *11494*   India - Sikkim *11494*

E   I   *Paphiopedilum glaucophyllum* **J.J. Smith** *15918*

     E   *15918*   Indonesia - Java (east) *15918*

R   I   *Paphiopedilum godefroyae* **(Godef.-Leb.) Stein** *15918*

     I   Thailand *15918*
     R   Vietnam

R   I   *Paphiopedilum hirsutissimum* **(Lindley & Hook.)
       Stein** *4300*

     R   *14782*   India *14782*
     I   India - Manipur *4300*
     I   *20985*   Vietnam *20985*

E I *Paphiopedilum javanicum* Pfitz. var.
      virens *14908*
    E *14908* Malaysia - Sabah (Mt Kinabalu and the Crocker
      Range) *14908*

I I *Paphiopedilum kalopakingii* Fowlie *15918*
    I Indonesia - Kalimantan

V I *Paphiopedilum liemianum* (Fowlie) Karasawa &
      Saito *15918*
    V Indonesia - Sumatra (northern) *15198*

E I *Paphiopedilum malipoense* S.C. Chen & Tsi *9157*
    E *20756* China - Yunnan *9157*

R I *Paphiopedilum mastersianum* (Reichb. f.) Stein *15918*
    R Indonesia - Moluccas

E I *Paphiopedilum micranthum* Tang & Wang *15918*
    E *20756* China - Yunnan (south) *20756*

I I *Paphiopedilum niveum* (Reichb. f.) Stein *15918*
    I Thailand (south) *15918*
    I Indonesia - Kalimantan
    I *15961* Malaysia - Peninsular Malaysia *15961*

I I *Paphiopedilum philippinense* (Reichb. f.) Stein *15918*
    E *14068* Malaysia - Sabah *8941*
    I Philippines

R I *Paphiopedilum philippinense* (Reichb. f.) Stein var.
      roebelenii (Veitch) Cribb *15918*
    R *15918* Philippines (Luzon) *15918*

I I *Paphiopedilum primulinum* M. Wood & Taylor *15918*
    I Indonesia - Sumatra (north) *15918*

I I *Paphiopedilum randsii* Fowlie *15918*
    I *15918* Philippines (Mindanao) *15918*

E I *Paphiopedilum rothschildianum* (Reichb. f.)
      Stein *15918*
    E *14068* Malaysia - Sabah (Mt Kinabalu) *14068*

E I *Paphiopedilum sanderianum* (Reichb. f.) Stein *15918*
    E *14068* Malaysia - Sarawak *14068*

E I *Paphiopedilum stonei* (Hook. f.) Stein *15918*
    E *14068* Malaysia - Sarawak *14068*

I I *Paphiopedilum sukhakulii* Schoser & Senghas *15918*
    I Thailand (Phu Luang)

I I *Paphiopedilum superbiens* (Reichb. f.) Stein *15918*
    I Indonesia - Sumatra (north and central)
    15918

E I *Paphiopedilum tonsum* (Reichb. f.) Stein *15918*
    E Indonesia - Sumatra *15918*

V I *Paphiopedilum victoria-regina* (Sander) M. Wood *15918*
    V Indonesia - Sumatra

R I *Paphiopedilum wardii* Summerh. *11494*
    E *11494* India - Arunachal Pradesh *11494*
    R Myanmar

V I *Paphiopedilum wentworthianum* Schoser & Fowlie *14794*
    V *14793* PNG - Bougainville (N.Solomon Is.) *14794*
    V *14793* Solomon Is. - South (central Guadalcanal)
    14794

R II *Papperitzia leiboldii* Reichb.f. *11938*
    R *19850* Mexico - Oaxaca *11938*

E II *Paracaleana dixonii* Hopper & A.P.Brown ms. *20681*
    E *20681* Australia - Western Australia *20681*

E II *Paraphalaenopsis labukensis* Shim, Lamb & Chan *19215*
    E *14068* Malaysia - Sabah *14068*

E II *Paraphalaenopsis laycocki* (M.R. Henderson) A.
      Hawkes *19215*

E *19215* Indonesia - Kalimantan *19215*

V II *Paraphalaenopsis serpentilingua* (J.J. Smith) A.
      Hawkes *19047*
    V *19047* Indonesia - Kalimantan *19047*

R II *Pedilochilus hermonii* Cribb & B. Lewis *14795*
    R *14795* Vanuatu (Anatom & Espiritu Santo) *14795*

I I *Peristeria elata* Hooker *9037*
    V *9426* Costa Rica *9037*
    I *10359* El Salvador *10747*
    I *10020* Panama *9037*
    I *2790* Colombia *9037*
    I *2790* Venezuela *9037*

R II *Peristylus banfieldii* (Bailey) Lavarack *20681*
    R *20681* Australia - Queensland *20681*

I II *Peristylus brachyphyllus* A. Rich.
    I India - Karnataka *4988*
    I India - Tamil Nadu (Nilagiri Hills)
    4988

R II *Peristylus langbianensis* (Gagnepain) Tang &
      Wang *6057*
    R Vietnam *6057*

V II *Peristylus minimiflorus* (Kranzlin) Halle *20893*
    V *20893* New Caledonia *20893*

I II *Peristylus secundus* (Lindley) Rathakr.
    I India - Karnataka *4988*
    I India - Kerala *4988*
    I India - Tamil Nadu *4988*

R II *Peristylus stenodontus* (Reichb. f.) Renz &
      Vodonaivalu *14795*
    R *14795* Vanuatu (Anatom & Vanua Lava) *14795*

R II *Peristylus wheatleyi* Cribb & B. Lewis *14795*
    R *14795* Vanuatu *14795*

E II *Pescatoria costaricensis* Schltr. *9037*
    E *9426* Costa Rica *9037*

V II *Phaius australis* F.Muell. *20681*
    I *20681* Australia - New South Wales *20681*
    I *20681* Australia - Queensland *20681*

E II *Phaius bernaysii* Rowland ex H.G.Reichb. *20681*
    E *20681* Australia - Queensland *20681*

I II *Phaius epiphyticus* Seidenf. *19120*
    I *19120* Thailand *19120*

V II *Phaius longibracteatus* Frapp. *10082*
    V *10082* Réunion *10082*
    V *20771* Mauritius *10082*

I II *Phaius mishmensis* Reichb.f. *4300*
    I India - Assam (Upper Assam) *4300*
    I India - Meghalaya *4300*
    I India - Sikkim *4300*

E II *Phaius villosus* Rchb.f. *10082*
    E *20771* Mauritius *10082*

R II *Phalaenopsis amboinensis* J.J. Smith
    R Indonesia - Moluccas
    R Indonesia - Sulawesi
    V *19047* Malaysia *19047*

V II *Phalaenopsis appendiculata* Carr *19047*
    V *19047* Malaysia - Peninsular Malaysia *19047*

E II *Phalaenopsis cochlearis* Holttum
    E *14068* Malaysia - Sarawak *14068*

V II *Phalaenopsis deliciosa* *19047*
    V *19047* Indonesia - Java *19047*

E II *Phalaenopsis fimbriata* J.J. Smith *19047*
    E *19047* Indonesia - Java *19047*

	I	Indonesia - Sumatra
V	II	*Phalaenopsis javanica* J.J. Smith *19047*
	V	*19047* Indonesia - Java *19047*
V	II	*Phalaenopsis laycockii* *19047*
	V	*19047* Indonesia - Kalimantan *19047*
V	II	*Phalaenopsis modesta* J.J. Smith *19215*
	V	*14068* Malaysia - Sabah *14068*
V	II	*Phalaenopsis schilleriana* Reichb.f. *19047*
	V	*19047* Philippines *19047*
E	II	*Phalaenopsis speciosa* Reichb.f. var. *speciosa* *5231*
	E	India - Andaman Is. *5231*
	E	India - Nicobar Is. *5231*
V	II	*Phalaenopsis stuartiana* Reichb.f. *19047*
	V	*19047* Philippines *19047*
I	II	*Phalaenopsis thalebanii* Seidenf. *19120*
	I	*19120* Thailand *19120*
I	II	*Pholidota aidiolepis* Seidenf. et de Vogel *19120*
	I	*19120* Thailand *19120*
I	II	*Pholidota calceata* Reichb.f.
	I	India - Meghalaya (Khasi hills)
R	II	*Pholidota cantonensis* Rolfe *19924*
	R	*19924* Hong Kong *19924*
I	II	*Pholidota grandiflora* Seidenf. *19120*
	I	*19120* Thailand *19120*
I	II	*Pholidota scaposa* Seidenf. *19120*
	I	*19120* Thailand *19120*
R	II	*Pholidota wattii* King & Pantl. *11494*
	R	*11494* India - Arunachal Pradesh (Subansiri) *11494*
	R	*11494* India - Assam (North Cachar) *11494*
V	I	*Phragmipedium besseae* Dodson & Kuhn. *18200*
	V	*19045* Ecuador *19045*
	Ex/E	*18200* Peru *18200*
V	I	*Phragmipedium czerwiakowianum* (Reichb.f.) Rolfe *18200*
	V	*12468* Peru *18200*
E	I	*Phragmipedium exstaminodium* Castaño, Hágsater, & Aguirre *12788*
	E	*11336* Mexico - Chiapas *12788*
R	I	*Phragmipedium lindleyanum* (Schomb. ex Lindley) Rolfe *18176*
	R	*21264* Brazil *21264*
	R	*19954* French Guiana *18176*
	R	*21264* Guyana *18176*
	?	Surinam *18176*
	R	*21264* Venezuela *21264*
R	II	*Phreatia evrardii* Gagnepain *6057*
	R	Vietnam *6057*
E	II	*Phreatia limenophylax* (Endl.) Benth. *19108*
	E	*19108* Australia - Norfolk Is. *14288*
R	II	*Phreatia listeri* Rolfe *881*
	R	*14224* Australia - Christmas Is. *881*
V	II	*Phreatia thompsonii* Ames
	V	*18338* U.S. - Guam (Lamlam) *18338*
E	II	*Physinga polygonata* (Lindl.) H. Dietrich *11840*
	E	Cuba (Guantanamo) *11840*
R	II	*Physoceras boryanum* (A.Rich.)Posser *10082*
	R	*10082* Réunion *10082*
	Ex	*20771* Mauritius *10082*
R	II	*Physogyne gonzalezii* (L.O. Williams) Burns-Balogh *21198*
	R	*11338* Mexico *11338*
E	II	*Piperia yadonii* Morgan & Ackerman *20850*
	E	*20850* U.S. - California *20850*
R	II	*Platanthera amabilis* Koidz. *11164*
	R	*11164* Japan *11164*
R	II	*Platanthera boninensis* Koidz. *8038*
	R	*19134* Japan - Ogasawara-shoto *8038*
R	II	*Platanthera brevicalcarata* Hayata ssp. *yakumontana* (Masam.) Masam. *11164*
	R	*11164* Japan *11164*
E	II	*Platanthera holochila* (Hbd.) Kraenzlin *20850, 14209*
	E	*20850* U.S. - Hawaii *20850*
V	II	*Platanthera integrilabia* (Correll) Luer *20850*
	V	*20850* U.S. - Alabama *20850*
	E	*20850* U.S. - Georgia *20850*
	E	*20850* U.S. - Kentucky *20850*
	I	*20850* U.S. - Louisiana *20850*
	E	*20850* U.S. - Mississippi *20850*
	Ex	*20850* U.S. - North Carolina *20850*
	E	*20850* U.S. - South Carolina *20850*
	V	*20850* U.S. - Tennessee *20850*
	I	*20850* U.S. - Virginia *20850*
V	II	*Platanthera leucophaea* (Nutt.) Lindl. *20850, 14352*
	V	*20850* Canada - Ontario *20850*
	E	*20850* U.S. - Illinois *20850*
	Ex	*20850* U.S. - Indiana *20850*
	E	*20850* U.S. - Iowa *20850*
	I	*20850* U.S. - Louisiana *20850*
	E	*20850* U.S. - Maine *20850*
	E	*20850* U.S. - Michigan *20850*
	Ex	*20850* U.S. - Missouri *20850*
	Ex/E	*20850* U.S. - Nebraska *20850*
	Ex	*20850* U.S. - New Jersey *20850*
	Ex/E	*20850* U.S. - New York *20850*
	V	*20850* U.S. - Ohio *20850*
	Ex	*20850* U.S. - Oklahoma *20850*
	Ex	*20850* U.S. - Pennsylvania *20850*
	E	*20850* U.S. - Virginia *20850*
	E	*20850* U.S. - Wisconsin *20850*
R	II	*Platanthera mandarinorum* Reich.f. var. *hachijoensis* (Honda) Murata *11164*
	R	*11164* Japan *11164*
R	II	*Platanthera mandarinorum* Reichb.f. var. *masamunei* (Honda) K. Inoue *11164*
	R	*11164* Japan *11164*
V	II	*Platanthera micrantha* (Hochst.) Schltr. *20171*
	V	Portugal - Azores
R	II	*Platanthera okubou* Makino *11164*
	R	*11164* Japan *11164*
V	II	*Platanthera praeclara* Sheviak & Bowles *20850, 13967*
	I	*20850* Canada - Manitoba *20850*
	V	*20850* U.S. - Iowa *20850*
	E	*20850* U.S. - Kansas *20850*
	E	*20850* U.S. - Minnesota *20850*
	E	*20850* U.S. - Missouri *20850*
	E	*20850* U.S. - Nebraska *20850*
	V	*20850* U.S. - North Dakota *20850*
	E	*20850* U.S. - Oklahoma *20850*
	Ex/E	*20850* U.S. - South Dakota *20850*
R	II	*Platanthera sparsiflora* (S. Wats.) Schlechter var. *ensifolia* (Rydb.) Luer *20850*
	I	*20850* U.S. - Arizona *20850*
	V	*20850* U.S. - Colorado *20850*
	I	*20850* U.S. - Nevada *20850*

R	II	*Platanthera uzenensis* (Ohwi) F. Maek. *11164*	
	R	*11164* Japan *11164*	
V	II	*Platanthera zothecina* (Higgins & Welsh) Kartesz & Gandhi *20850*	
	I	*20850* U.S. - Arizona *20850*	
	E	*20850* U.S. - Colorado *20850*	
	V	*20850* U.S. - Utah *20850*	
I	II	*Platycoryne affinis* Summerh. *7877*	
	I	Zimbabwe *7877*	
V	II	*Platyglottis coriacea* L.O. Wms. *20883, 9006*	
	V	*16317* Panama *20883*	
E	II	*Platylepis sechellarum* S. Moore *14296*	
	E	*14981* Seychelles (Mahé, Silhouette) *14296*	
R	II	*Platystele acicularis* Luer & Hirtz *14291*	
	R	*19045* Ecuador *19045*	
R	II	*Platystele crinita* Luer & Hirtz *21293*	
	R	*19045* Ecuador *19045*	
R	II	*Platystele enervis* Luer *21293*	
	R	*19045* Ecuador *19045*	
R	II	*Platystele hirtzii* Luer *21293*	
	R	*19045* Ecuador *19045*	
R	II	*Platystele jesupiorum* Luer *21293*	
	R	*19045* Ecuador *19045*	
R	II	*Platystele napintzae* Luer & Hirtz *19045*	
	R	*19045* Ecuador *19045*	
R	II	*Platystele perpusilla* (Reichb.f.) Garay *14291*	
	R	*14291* Costa Rica *14291*	
	R	*14291* Panama *14291*	
R	II	*Platystele psix* Luer & Hirtz *19045*	
	R	*19045* Ecuador *19045*	
V	II	*Platystele pubescens* Luer *21293*	
	V	*19045* Ecuador *19045*	
R	II	*Platystele sulcata* Luer & Hirtz *19045*	
	R	*19045* Ecuador *19045*	
R	II	*Platystele vetulus* Luer & Hirtz *21293*	
	R	*19045* Ecuador *19045*	
R	II	*Plectorrhiza erecta* (Fitzg.) Dockr. *14223*	
	R	*14223* Australia - NSW - Lord Howe Is. *14223*	
R	II	*Pleione formosana* Hayata *20511*	
	R	*20511* Taiwan *20511*	
Ex	II	*Pleione lagenaria* Lindley *11494*	
	Ex	*11494* India - Meghalaya (Khasi hills) *11494*	
V	II	*Pleurothallis acanthodes* Luer *19045*	
	V	*19054* Ecuador *19045*	
R	II	*Pleurothallis alpestris* (Sw.) Lindl. *20883, 19890*	
	V	*19890* Jamaica *20883*	
V	II	*Pleurothallis annectens* Luer *10008*	
	V	*16317* Panama *10008*	
E	II	*Pleurothallis antonensis* L.O. Wms. *20883, 9006*	
	V	*18110* Mexico - Chiapas *18110*	
	V	*18110* Mexico - Veracruz *18110*	
	I	*20883* Panama *20883*	
E	II	*Pleurothallis archicolonae* Luer *20883, 10008*	
	I	*20883* Panama *20883*	
R	II	*Pleurothallis aspergillum* Luer & Hirtz *21293*	
	R	*19045* Ecuador *19045*	
R	II	*Pleurothallis atacasana* Luer *19045*	
	R	*19045* Ecuador *19045*	
I	II	*Pleurothallis brachyglottis* Reichb. f. *5607*	
	I	*19105* Cuba (Guantanamo) *5607*	
E	II	*Pleurothallis cactantha* Luer *20883, 10008*	
	I	*20883* Panama *20883*	
E	II	*Pleurothallis campicola* Luer *20883, 10747*	
	I	*20883* Panama *20883*	
I	II	*Pleurothallis cardiophyllax* Reichb. f. *19352*	
	I	*19352* Colombia *19352*	
E	II	*Pleurothallis caymanensis* C.D. Adams *19712*	
	E	*19434* Cayman Is. (Grand Cayman) *19434*	
V	II	*Pleurothallis cernua* Luer *19045*	
	V	*19045* Ecuador *19045*	
V	II	*Pleurothallis chontalensis* A.H. Heller & A. Hawkes *10017*	
	V	*11967* Nicaragua *10017*	
V	II	*Pleurothallis citrophila* Luer *20883, 10008*	
	V	*16317* Panama *20883*	
V	II	*Pleurothallis cobraeformis* L.O. Wms. *20883, 9006*	
	V	*16317* Panama *20883*	
R	II	*Pleurothallis condorensis* Luer & Hirtz *21293*	
	R	*19045* Ecuador *19045*	
V	II	*Pleurothallis cypripedioides* Luer *19045*	
	V	*19045* Ecuador *19045*	
R	II	*Pleurothallis delicatula* Lindl. *20883, 19890*	
	V	*19890* Jamaica *20883*	
R	II	*Pleurothallis dibolia* Luer *19045*	
	R	*19045* Ecuador *19045*	
V	II	*Pleurothallis dodsonii* Luer *19045*	
	V	*19045* Ecuador *19045*	
E	II	*Pleurothallis dressleri* Luer *20883, 10008*	
	I	*20883* Panama *20883*	
R	II	*Pleurothallis echinocarpa* C. Schweinf. *21294*	
	R	*21294* Ecuador *21294*	
E	II	*Pleurothallis ellipsophylla* L.O. Wms. *20883, 9006*	
	R	*11994* Costa Rica *11994*	
	I	*20883* Panama *20883*	
R	II	*Pleurothallis ensata* Luer *19045*	
	R	*19045* Ecuador *19045*	
V	II	*Pleurothallis eximia* L.O. Williams *9423*	
	V	*19850* Mexico *9423*	
E	II	*Pleurothallis guttata* Luer *20883, 10008*	
	I	*20883* Panama *20883*	
E	II	*Pleurothallis harpago* Luer *20883, 10747*	
	I	*20883* Panama *20883*	
I	II	*Pleurothallis helenae* F. & R. *19890*	
	I	*19408* Dominican Republic *19408*	
	V	*19890* Haiti (north west) *19890*	
	V	*19890* Jamaica *19221*	
R	II	*Pleurothallis hintonii* L.O. Williams *9423*	
	R	*19850* Mexico *9423*	
V	II	*Pleurothallis hirsutula* F. & R. *20883, 19890*	
	V	*19890* Jamaica (central) *20883*	
E	II	*Pleurothallis hymenantha* Lindley *5607*	
	E	*19105* Cuba (Santiago de Cuba) *5607*	
E	II	*Pleurothallis imago* Luer *20883, 10008*	
	I	*20883* Panama *20883*	
E	II	*Pleurothallis isthmica* Luer *20883*	
	I	*20883* Panama *20883*	
R	II	*Pleurothallis jalapensis* (Kranzlin) Luer *21267*	
	R	Guatemala	

	R		Mexico - Chiapas	

E	II	*Pleurothallis jamaicensis* Rolfe *20883, 19890*
	I	*19890* Jamaica *20883*
R	II	*Pleurothallis lacera* Luer *19045*
	R	*19045* Ecuador *19045*
E	II	*Pleurothallis laxa* (Sw.) Lindl. *20883, 19408*
	E	*19408* Dominican Republic *19408*
	E	*20883* Jamaica *20883*
E	II	*Pleurothallis macrantha* L.O. Wms. *20883, 9006*
	I	*20883* Panama *20883*
E	II	*Pleurothallis mammillata* Luer *20883, 10008*
	I	*20883* Panama *20883*
R	II	*Pleurothallis mazei* Urb. *19400*
	R	*19400* Islands of the Caribbean (Greater Antilles) *19400*
	E	*19408* Dominican Republic *19408*
R	II	*Pleurothallis miranda* Luer *19045*
	R	*19045* Ecuador *19045*
E	II	*Pleurothallis monophylla* (Hook.) F. & R. *20883, 19890*
	I	*19890* Jamaica *20883*
E	II	*Pleurothallis mucronata* Lindley *5607*
	E	*19105* Cuba (Guantanamo) *5607*
E	II	*Pleurothallis mystax* Luer *20883, 10008*
	I	*20883* Panama *20883*
R	II	*Pleurothallis nelsonii* Ames *9423*
	R	*19850* Mexico *9423*
R	II	*Pleurothallis nigriflora* L.O. Williams *9423*
	R	*19850* Mexico *9423*
V	II	*Pleurothallis oblanceolata* L. O. Williams *19850*
	V	*19850* Mexico *19850*
E	II	*Pleurothallis operculata* Luer *20883, 10747*
	I	*20883* Panama *20883*
I	II	*Pleurothallis ophioglossoides* (Jacq.) Garay & Sweet *10199*
	I	Dominica *10199*
V	II	*Pleurothallis pallida* Luer *20883, 10008*
	V	*16317* Panama *20883*
E	II	*Pleurothallis pan* Luer *20883*
	I	*20883* Panama *20883*
R	II	*Pleurothallis parviflora* Luer *19045*
	R	*19045* Ecuador *19045*
E	II	*Pleurothallis peculiaris* Luer *20883, 10008*
	I	*20883* Panama *20883*
R	II	*Pleurothallis perryi* Luer *19045*
	R	*19045* Ecuador *19045*
E	II	*Pleurothallis phyllocardia* Rchb. f. *20883*
	I	*20883* Panama *20883*
R	II	*Pleurothallis pidax* Luer *19045*
	R	*19045* Ecuador *19045*
V	II	*Pleurothallis pilifera* Lindl. *19045*
	V	*19045* Ecuador *19045*
E	II	*Pleurothallis polysticha* Luer *20883, 10747*
	I	*20883* Panama *20883*
E	II	*Pleurothallis praegrandis* Ames *20883*
	I	*20883* Panama *20883*
R	II	*Pleurothallis prolaticollaris* Luer *19045*
	R	*19045* Ecuador *19045*
R	II	*Pleurothallis punicea* Luer *19045*

	R	*19045* Ecuador *19045*
E	II	*Pleurothallis rhodoglossa* Schltr. *20883*
	I	*20883* Panama *20883*
E	II	*Pleurothallis rhomboglossa* Reichb. f. *5607*
	E	*19105* Cuba (Guantanamo) *5607*
E	II	*Pleurothallis rotundifolia* Rolfe *20883, 19890*
	I	*19890* Jamaica *20883*
V	II	*Pleurothallis rubella* Luer *10008*
	V	*16317* Panama *10008*
E	II	*Pleurothallis rubellia* Luer *20883*
	I	*20883* Panama *20883*
V	II	*Pleurothallis scitula* Luer *20883, 10008*
	?	Costa Rica *21258*
	V	*16317* Panama *20883*
V	II	*Pleurothallis scoparum* Rchb.f. *21293*
	V	*19045* Ecuador *19045*
E	II	*Pleurothallis sempergemmata* Luer *20883*
	I	*20883* Panama *20883*
V	II	*Pleurothallis simulans* L.O. Wms. *20883, 9006*
	V	*16317* Panama *20883*
R	II	*Pleurothallis sphaerantha* Luer *19045*
	R	*19045* Ecuador *19045*
R	II	*Pleurothallis stevensonii* Luer *19045*
	R	*19045* Ecuador *19045*
E	II	*Pleurothallis tantilla* Luer *20883, 10747*
	I	*20883* Panama *20883*
E	II	*Pleurothallis telamon* Luer *20883, 10747*
	I	*20883* Panama *20883*
V	II	*Pleurothallis thymochila* Luer *10008*
	V	*16317* Panama *10008*
E	II	*Pleurothallis thymochils* Luer *20883*
	I	*20883* Panama *20883*
V	II	*Pleurothallis titan* Luer *20883, 10008*
	V	*16317* Panama *20883*
E	II	*Pleurothallis trilobata* F. & R. *20883, 19890*
	V	*19890* Jamaica (St. Andrews, Portland) *20883*
V	II	*Pleurothallis tropida* Luer *20883, 10747*
	V	*16317* Panama *20883*
R	II	*Pleurothallis tryssa* Luer *19045*
	R	*19045* Ecuador *19045*
R	II	*Pleurothallis unguicallosa* Ames & C. Schweinf. *9423*
	R	*11933* Mexico *9423*
E	II	*Pleurothallis veraguacensis* Luer *20883, 10008*
	I	*20883* Panama *20883*
V	II	*Pleurothallis volcanica* Luer *20883, 10008*
	V	*16317* Panama *20883*
V	II	*Pleurothallis vorator* Luer & Vasquez *21293*
	V	*21293* Bolivia *21293*
	V	*19045* Ecuador *19045*
R	II	*Pleurothallis xanthella* Luer *19045*
	R	*19045* Ecuador *19045*
V	II	*Polystachya albescens* Ridley ssp. *angustifolia* (Summerh.) Summerh.
	V	Cameroon (Buea)
I	II	*Polystachya greatrexii* Summerh. *7881*
	I	Zimbabwe *7881*
R	II	*Polystachya testuana* Summerh.
	R	Gabon

I   II   *Pomatocalpa linearifolia*   *19120*
    I   *19120*   Thailand   *19120*

R   II   *Ponera dressleriana*   Soto Arenas   *19850*
       Mexico
    R   *21184*   Mexico - Morelos   *21184*

R   II   *Ponera exilis*   Dressler   *10015*
    R   *10007*   Mexico   *10015*

V   II   *Ponthieva angustipetala*   Greenwood   *10042*
    V   *10042*   Mexico - Oaxaca   *10042*

V   II   *Ponthieva brittoniae*   Ames   *20850*
    E   *20850*   U.S. - Florida   *20850*
    I   *20850*   U.S. - Georgia   *20850*
    I   *20883*   Puerto Rico   *20883*
    I   *20883*   USA - Virgin Is.   *20883*

R   II   *Ponthieva cuyujana*   Dodson & Hirtz   *19045*
    R   *19045*   Ecuador   *19045*

R   II   *Ponthieva harrisii*   Cogn.   *19890*
    E   *19408*   Dominican Republic   *19408*
    E   *19890*   Haiti (south west)   *19890*
    R   *19890*   Jamaica   *19221*

R   II   *Ponthieva parviflora*   Ames & C. Schweinf.   *9423*
    R   *19850*   Mexico   *9423*

V   II   *Porroglossum amethystinum*   (Reichb.f.) Garay   *12470*
    V   *19045*   Ecuador   *19045*

R   II   *Porroglossum andreettae*   Luer   *12470*
    R   *12470*   Ecuador   *12470*

V   II   *Porroglossum cindylosepalum*   Sweet   *19045, 21297*
    V   *19045*   Ecuador   *19045*

R   II   *Porroglossum dalstroemii*   Luer   *12470*
    R   *19045*   Ecuador   *19045*

R   II   *Porroglossum dreisei*   Luer & Andreetta   *19045*
    R   *19045*   Ecuador   *19045*

R   II   *Porroglossum hirtzii*   Luer   *12470*
    R   *19045*   Ecuador   *19045*

V   II   *Porroglossum meridionale*   P. Ortiz   *12470*
    V   *19045*   Ecuador   *19045*

R   II   *Porroglossum schramii*   Luer   *12470*
    R   *12470*   Ecuador   *12470*

R   II   *Porroglossum taylorianum*   Luer   *12470*
    R   *12470*   Ecuador   *12470*

R   II   *Porroglossum teaguei*   Luer   *12470*
    R   *12470*   Ecuador   *12470*

E   II   *Prasophyllum affine*   Lindley   *20681*
    E   *20681*   Australia - New South Wales   *20681*

R   II   *Prasophyllum campestre*   R.Bates & D.L.Jones   *20681*
    I   *20681*   Australia - New South Wales   *20681*
    I   *20681*   Australia - Queensland   *20681*

R   II   *Prasophyllum carnosum*   R.Bates & D.L.Jones ms.   *20681*
    R   *20681*   Australia - South Australia   *20681*

V   II   *Prasophyllum concinnum*   Nicholls   *20681, 14223*
    V   *20681*   Australia - Tasmania   *20681*

E   II   *Prasophyllum correctum*   D.L.Jones   *20681*
    E   *20681*   Australia - Victoria   *20681*

E   II   *Prasophyllum diversiflorum*   Nicholls   *20681, 14223*
    E   *20681*   Australia - Victoria   *20681*

R   II   *Prasophyllum dossenum*   R.Bates & D.L.Jones   *20681*
    R   *20681*   Australia - New South Wales   *20681*

R   II   *Prasophyllum exilis*   D.L.Jones & R.Bates   *20681*
    I   *20681*   Australia - New South Wales   *20681*
    I   *20681*   Australia - Queensland   *20681*

R   II   *Prasophyllum firthii*   Cady = Genoplesium
       brachystachyum   *20681*
    R   *20681*   Australia - Tasmania   *20681*

V   II   *Prasophyllum frenchii*   F.Muell.   *20681*
    I   *20681*   Australia - South Australia   *20681*
    I   *20681*   Australia - Victoria   *20681*

V   II   *Prasophyllum fuscum*   R.Br.   *20681*
    V   *20681*   Australia - New South Wales   *20681*

R   II   *Prasophyllum montanum*   R.Bates & D.L.Jones   *20681*
    I   *20681*   Australia - Capital Territory   *20681*
    I   *20681*   Australia - New South Wales   *20681*
    I   *20681*   Australia - Victoria   *20681*

V   II   *Prasophyllum morganii*   Nicholls   *20681, 14223*
    V   *20681*   Australia - New South Wales   *20681*
    Ex/E   *20681*   Australia - Victoria   *20681*

V   II   *Prasophyllum pallidum*   Nicholls   *20681*
    V   *20681*   Australia - South Australia   *20681*

E   II   *Prasophyllum petilum*   D.L.Jones & R.Bates   *20681*
    E   *20681*   Australia - Capital Territory   *20681*

Ex   II   *Prasophyllum robustum*   (Nicholls) M.A.Clements &
       D.L.Jones   *20681*
    Ex   *20681*   Australia - Tasmania   *20681*

E   II   *Prasophyllum subbisectum*   Nicholls   *20681, 14223*
    E   *20681*   Australia - Victoria   *20681*

R   II   *Prasophyllum triangulare*   Fitzg.   *20681*
    R   *20681*   Australia - Western Australia   *20681*

V   II   *Prasophyllum validum*   R.Rogers   *20681*
    V   *20681*   Australia - South Australia   *20681*

V   II   *Prasophyllum wallum*   R.Bates & D.L.Jones   *20681*
    V   *20681*   Australia - Queensland   *20681*

R   II   *Pseudocentrum guadeloupense*   Cogn.   *19400*
    R   *19400*   Guadeloupe   *19400*

E   II   *Pseudocentrum minus*   Benth.   *20883, 19408*
    E   *19408*   Dominican Republic   *19408*
    E   *20883*   Jamaica   *20883*

I   II   *Pseudocentrum sylvicola*   Reichb.f.   *19352*
    I   *19352*   Colombia   *19352*

R   II   *Pseudocranichis thysanochila*   (Robinson & Greenman)
       Garay   *11933*
    R   *19850*   Mexico   *11933*

E   II   *Psychilis krugii*   (Bello) Sauleda   *20883*
    I   *20883*   Puerto Rico   *20883*

R   II   *Psygmorchis zamorensis*   Dodson   *16956*
    R   *10010*   Ecuador   *16956*

E   II   *Pterichis leo*   L.D. Gómez   *9426*
    E   *9593*   Costa Rica   *9426*

E   II   *Pterichis proctorii*   Garay   *20883, 19890*
    E   *19890*   Jamaica   *20883*

I   II   *Pteroceras javanicum*   (J.J. Smith) Bakh.f.   *8309*
    I   Indonesia - Java (east)   *8309*

V   II   *Pteroglossaspis ecristata*   (Fern.) Rolfe   *20883,*
       20850, 11630
    I   *20850*   U.S. - Alabama   *20850*
    V   *20850*   U.S. - Florida   *20850*
    E   *20850*   U.S. - Georgia   *20850*
    V   *20850*   U.S. - Louisiana   *20850*
    E   *20850*   U.S. - Mississippi   *20850*
    E   *20850*   U.S. - North Carolina   *20850*
    V   *20850*   U.S. - South Carolina   *20850*
    E   *20883*   Cuba (Pinar del Rio)   *20883*

R   II   *Pterostylis arenicola*   M.A.Clements & J.Stewart   *20681*

	R	20681 Australia - South Australia 20681
E	II	*Pterostylis basaltica* D.L.Jones & M.A.Clements 20681
	E	20681 Australia - Victoria 20681
V	II	*Pterostylis bicornis* D.L.Jones & M.A.Clements 20681
	V	20681 Australia - Queensland 20681
R	II	*Pterostylis cheraphila* D.L.Jones & M.A.Clements 20681
	R	20681 Australia - Victoria 20681
V	II	*Pterostylis chlorogramma* D.L.Jones & M.A.Clements 20681
	V	20681 Australia - New South Wales 20681
V	II	*Pterostylis cobarensis* M.A.Clements 20681
	V	20681 Australia - New South Wales 20681
V	II	*Pterostylis commutata* D.L.Jones 20681
	V	20681 Australia - Tasmania 20681
V	II	*Pterostylis cucullata* R.Br. 20681
	I	20681 Australia - New South Wales 20681
	I	20681 Australia - South Australia 20681
	I	20681 Australia - Tasmania 20681
	I	20681 Australia - Victoria 20681
E	II	*Pterostylis despectans* (Nicholls) M.A.Clements & D.L.Jones 20681
	I	20681 Australia - South Australia 20681
	I	20681 Australia - Victoria 20681
E	II	*Pterostylis gibbosa* R.Br. 20681
	E	20681 Australia - New South Wales 20681
E	II	*Pterostylis micromega* 19305
	E	19305 New Zealand - North Is. 19305
	E	19305 New Zealand - South Is. 19305
E	II	*Pterostylis nana* 19305
	E	19305 New Zealand - North Is. 19305
V	II	*Pterostylis nigricans* D.L.Jones & M.A.Clements 20681
	I	20681 Australia - New South Wales 20681
	I	20681 Australia - Queensland 20681
R	II	*Pterostylis plumosa* 19305
	R	19305 New Zealand - North Is. 19305
V	II	*Pterostylis pulchella* Messmer 20681
	V	20681 Australia - New South Wales 20681
R	II	*Pterostylis smaragdyna* D.L.Jones & M.A.Clements 20681
	R	20681 Australia - Victoria 20681
V	II	*Pterostylis tenuissima* Nicholls 20681, 8552
	I	20681 Australia - South Australia 20681
	I	20681 Australia - Victoria 8552
Ex	II	*Pterostylis valida* (Nicholls) D.L.Jones 20681
	Ex	20681 Australia - Victoria 20681
R	II	*Pterostylis woollsii* Fitzg. 20681
	I	20681 Australia - New South Wales 20681
	I	20681 Australia - Queensland 20681
	I	20681 Australia - Victoria 20681
V	II	*Pterostylis xerophila* M.A.Clements 20681
	V	20681 Australia - South Australia 20681
E	II	*Pterygodium cruciferum* Sond. 20604
	E	20604 South Africa - Cape Province 20604
R	II	*Pterygodium newdigateae* Bolus var. *cleistogamum* Bolus 20604
	R	20604 South Africa - Cape Province 20604
I	II	*Pterygodium newdigateae* Bolus var. *newdigateae* 20604
	I	20604 South Africa - Cape Province 20604

I	II	*Pterygodium pentherianum* Schltr. 20604
	I	20604 South Africa - Cape Province 20604
R	II	*Pterygodium ukingense* Schltr. 7959
	R	5926 Tanzania (Rungwe Distr.) 7959
I	I	*Renanthera imschootiana* Rolfe
	E	11494 India - Manipur 11494
	E	11494 India - Mizoram 11494
	E	11494 India - Nagaland 11494
	I	20922 Myanmar 11494
	I	20922 SE Asia to Papua New Guinea 11494
V	II	*Restrepia angustilabia* Schltr. 9037
	V	9426 Costa Rica 9037
V	II	*Restrepia aspasicensium* Reichb.f. 9426
	V	9593 Costa Rica 9426
R	II	*Restrepia chrysoglossa* Luer & R. Escobar 21259
	R	21259 Colombia 21259
R	II	*Restrepia escobariana* Luer 21298
	R	21298 Colombia 21298
R	II	*Restrepia teaguei* Luer 19045
	R	19045 Ecuador 19045
R	II	*Restrepiopsis pandurata* Luer & Hirtz 19045
	R	19045 Ecuador 19045
V	II	*Rhinerrhiza moorei* (H.G.Reichb.) M.A.Clements, B.Wallace & D.L.Jones 20681
	V	20681 Australia - Queensland 20681
V	II	*Rhizanthella gardneri* R.Rogers 20681
	V	20681 Australia - Western Australia 20681
E	II	*Rhynchostele hortensiae* (Rodriguez) Soto Arenas & Salazar 19823
	E	9426 Costa Rica 11335
R	II	*Rhynchostele uroskinneri* (Lindley) Soto Arenas & Salazar 19823
	R	10086 Guatemala 10086
	R	10086 Mexico - Chiapas 10086
I	II	*Rhynchostylis coelestis* Reichb.f.
	I	Thailand
I	II	*Rhynchostylis latifolia* C. Fischer 4988
	I	India - Karnataka (Cadamany, Mysore) 4988
I	II	*Risleya atropurpurea* King & Pantl.
	I	India - Sikkim
R	II	*Robiquetia wassellii* Dockr. 20681
	R	20681 Australia - Queensland 20681
R	II	*Robiquetia woodfordii* (Rolfe) Garay 14794
	R	14793 Solomon Is. - South 14794
R	II	*Rodriguezia dressleriana* Gonz.Tam. 9706
	R	11933 Mexico 9706
V	II	*Rossioglossum insleayi* (Baker ex Lindl.) Garay & Kenn 10011
	V	10007 Mexico 10011
I	II	*Rossioglossum schlieperianum* (Reichb.f.) Garay & Kennedy 9037
	E	9426 Costa Rica 9037
	I	16317 Panama 9006
V	II	*Rossioglossum splendens* (Reichb.f.) Garay & Kennedy 9706
	V	19850 Mexico 9706
R	II	*Saccolabiopsis rectifolia* (Dockr.) Garay 20681
	R	20681 Australia - Queensland 20681
R	II	*Saccolabium pusillum* Blume 8309

	R		Indonesia - Java (West Java; Central Java) *8309*
R	II	*Saccolabium sigmoideum* J.J. Smith *8309*	
	R		Indonesia - Java (central) *8309*
V	II	*Sarcanthus flaccidus* *19047*	
	V	*19047*	Indonesia - Java *19047*
V	II	*Sarcanthus inflexilobus* Holttum *19047*	
	V	*19047*	Malaysia - Peninsular Malaysia (Gua Musang, Kelantan) *19047*
V	II	*Sarcanthus kunstleri* King & Prantl *19047*	
	V	*19047*	Malaysia - Peninsular Malaysia (Perak) *19047*
I	II	*Sarcanthus malleifer* J.J. Sm. *13833*	
	I	*13833*	Philippines (Palawan) *13833*
V	II	*Sarcanthus muticus* *19047*	
	V	*19047*	Indonesia - Java *19047*
V	II	*Sarcanthus pensilis* Ridley *19047*	
	V	*19047*	Malaysia - Peninsular Malaysia (Pahang; Johore) *19047*
V	II	*Sarcanthus rugoius* *19047*	
	V	*19047*	Malaysia - Peninsular Malaysia *19047*
R	II	*Sarcanthus rugulosus* (Ridley) Holttum	
	R		Malaysia - Peninsular Malaysia
V	II	*Sarcanthus suaveolens* *19047*	
	V	*19047*	Indonesia - Java *19047*
R	II	*Sarcochilus aequalis* D.L.Jones & M.A.Clements *20681*	
	R	*20681*	Australia - New South Wales *20681*
R	II	*Sarcochilus dilatatus* F.Muell. *20681*	
	Ex/E	*20681*	Australia - New South Wales *20681*
	R	*20681*	Australia - Queensland *20681*
V	II	*Sarcochilus fitzgeraldii* F.Muell. *20681*	
	I	*20681*	Australia - New South Wales *20681*
	I	*20681*	Australia - Queensland *20681*
V	II	*Sarcochilus hartmannii* F.Muell. *20681*	
	I	*20681*	Australia - New South Wales *20681*
	I	*20681*	Australia - Queensland *20681*
V	II	*Sarcochilus hirticalcar* (Dockr.) M.A.Clements & B.Wallace *20681*	
	V	*20681*	Australia - Queensland *20681*
R	II	*Sarcochilus serrulatus* D.L.Jones *20681*	
	R	*20681*	Australia - Queensland *20681*
R	II	*Sarcochilus uniflorus* Gagnepain *6057*	
	R		Vietnam *6057*
V	II	*Sarcochilus weinthalii* Bailey *20681*	
	I	*20681*	Australia - New South Wales *20681*
	I	*20681*	Australia - Queensland *20681*
I	II	*Sarcoglyphis thailandica* Seidenf. *19120*	
	I	*19120*	Thailand *19120*
R	II	*Satyridium rostratum* Lindl. *20604*	
	R	*20604*	South Africa - Cape Province *20604*
R	II	*Satyrium aberrans* Summerh. *5926*	
	R	*5926*	Tanzania (Mbeya Mt.) *5926*
I	II	*Satyrium carneum* (Dryand.) Sims *20604*	
	I	*20604*	South Africa - Cape Province *20604*
R	II	*Satyrium comptum* Summerh. *7959*	
	R	*5926*	Tanzania *7959*
R	II	*Satyrium foliosum* Sw. *20604*	
	R	*20604*	South Africa - Cape Province *20604*
E	II	*Satyrium hallackii* Bolus ssp. *hallackii* *20604*	

	E	*20604*	South Africa - Cape Province *20604*
I	II	*Satyrium kermesinum* Krzl. *5926*	
	I	*5926*	Tanzania *5926*
I	II	*Satyrium mirum* Summerh. *7881*	
	I		Zimbabwe *7881*
I	II	*Satyrium monophyllum* Krzl. *5926*	
	I	*5926*	Tanzania *5926*
E	II	*Satyrium muticum* Lindl. *20604*	
	E	*20604*	South Africa - Cape Province *20604*
I	II	*Satyrium princeps* Bolus *20604*	
	I	*20604*	South Africa - Cape Province *20604*
R	II	*Scaphosepalum andreettae* Luer *21292*	
	R	*19045*	Ecuador *19045*
R	II	*Scaphosepalum beluosum* Luer *21292*	
	R	*19045*	Ecuador *19045*
R	II	*Scaphosepalum dodsonii* Luer *21292*	
	R	*19045*	Ecuador *19045*
E	II	*Scaphosepalum elasmotopus* Schltr. *20883, 9006*	
	E	*20883*	Panama *20883*
V	II	*Scaphosepalum fimbriatum* Luer & Hirtz *21292*	
	V	*19045*	Ecuador *19045*
E	II	*Scaphosepalum hirtzii* Luer *21292*	
	E	*19045*	Ecuador *19045*
R	II	*Scaphosepalum microdactylum* Rolfe *10034*	
	R	*11570*	Costa Rica *10034*
	R	*11570*	Guatemala *10034*
	R	*11570*	Honduras *10034*
	R	*11570*	Mexico *10034*
	R	*11570*	Nicaragua *10034*
	R	*11570*	Panama *10034*
	R	*11570*	Colombia *10034*
V	II	*Scaphosepalum ovulare* Luer *21292*	
	V	*19045*	Ecuador *19045*
R	II	*Scaphosepalum pleurothallodes* Luer & Hirtz *19045*	
	R	*19045*	Ecuador *19045*
R	II	*Scelochilus aureus* Schltr. *9037*	
	R	*9426*	Costa Rica *9037*
R	II	*Scelochilus chiribogae* Dodson *19045*	
	R	*19045*	Ecuador *19045*
V	II	*Scelochilus heterophylla* Rchb.f *19045*	
	V	*19045*	Ecuador *19045*
V	II	*Scelochilus hirtzii* Dodson *19045*	
	V	*19045*	Ecuador *19045*
V	II	*Scelochilus jamesonii* Lindl. *19045*	
	V	*19045*	Ecuador *19045*
R	II	*Scelochilus luerae* Dodson *19045*	
	R	*19045*	Ecuador *19045*
R	II	*Schiedeella nagelii* (L.O. Williams) Garay *11337*	
	R	*19850*	Mexico *11337*
E	II	*Schiedeella stolonifera* (Ames & C. Schweinf.) Balogh *11337*	
	E	*10359*	Guatemala *11337*
R	II	*Schistotylus purpuratus* (Rupp) Dockr. *20681*	
	R	*20681*	Australia - New South Wales *20681*
R	II	*Schizochilus gerrardii* (Rchb.f.) Bolus *20604*	
	R	*20604*	South Africa - Natal *20604*
V	II	*Schizochilus obliquum* Lindl. ssp. *obliquum* *20604*	
	V	*20604*	South Africa - Cape Province *20604*

V   II   *Schizodium longipetalum* Lindl. *20604*
       V   20604   South Africa - Cape Province *20604*

R   II   *Schlimia jasminodora* Planch. & Linden ex Lindley &
         Paxton *21264*
       R   21264   Costa Rica *21264*

R   II   *Schlimmia condorana* Dodson *19045*
       R   19045   Ecuador *19045*

I   II   *Schoenorchis spathulata* Seidenf. *19120*
       I   19120   Thailand *19120*

I   II   *Selenipedium chica* Rchb. f. *20883, 9006*
       I   20883   Panama *20883*

R   II   *Serapias nurrica* Corrias *15080*
       V   15080   France - Corsica *15080*
       R   20805   Italy - Sardinia *15080*

R   II   *Serapias orientalis* Nelson ssp.
         apulica *18264*
       R   18264   Italy (Puglia) *18264*

E   II   *Sievekingia butcheri* Dressler *20883, 10030*
       E.   10020   Panama *20883*

R   II   *Sievekingia hirtzii* Waldvogel *19045, 16956*
       R   19045   Ecuador *19045*

R   II   *Sievekingia marsupialis* Dodson *19045*
       R   19045   Ecuador *19045*

E   II   *Sigmatostalix abortiva* L.O. Wms. *20883, 9006*
       I   20883   Panama *20883*

V   II   *Sigmatostalix adamsii* Dodson *19045*
       V   19045   Ecuador *19045*

R   II   *Sigmatostalix mexicana* L.O. Williams *9423*
       R   11933   Mexico *9423*

R   II   *Sigmatostalix morganii* Dodson *19045*
       R   19045   Ecuador *19045*

R   II   *Sigmatostalix unguiculata* C. Schweinf. *10012*
       R   9426   Costa Rica *10012*

E   II   *Sobralia allenii* L.O. Wms. *20883, 9006*
       V   16358   Panama *20883*

V   II   *Sobralia bletiae* Reichb.f. *9037*
       V   9426   Costa Rica *9037*
       V   19577   Panama *9037*

R   II   *Sobralia callosa* L.O. Williams *9006*
       R   19577   Panama *9006*

R   II   *Sobralia chatoensis* A.H. Heller & A. Hawkes *10017*
       R   11967   Nicaragua *10017*

V   II   *Sobralia labiata* Warsc. & Reichb.f. *9037*
       V   9426   Costa Rica *9037*
       V   19577   Panama *9037*

V   II   *Sobralia macrantha* Lindley var. *kienastiana*
         Reichb.f. *10013*
       V   9426   Costa Rica *10013*
       E   10359   El Salvador *10013*

V   II   *Sobralia neglecta* Schltr. *9037*
       V   9426   Costa Rica *9037*

V   II   *Sobralia pfavii* Schltr. *9037*
       V   9426   Costa Rica *9037*

V   II   *Sobralia triandra* A.H. Heller & A. Hawkes *10017*
       V   11967   Nicaragua *10017*

E   II   *Sophronitis mantiqueirae* Fowlie var. *varonica*
         Hort. *9745*
       E   9745   Brazil *9745*

R   II   *Spathoglottis confusa* Schltr.
       R   14068   Indonesia - Kalimantan *14068*

R   II   *Spathoglottis kimballiana* Hort. Sander
       R   14068   Indonesia - Kalimantan *14068*

R   II   *Sphyrastylis cryptantha* (C. Schweinf. & P. Allen)
         Garay *10020*
       R   19577   Panama *10020*

E   II   *Spiranthes delitescens* Sheviak *20850*
       E   20850   U.S. - Arizona *20850*

V   II   *Spiranthes diluvialis* Sheviak *20850, 15044*
       I   20850   U.S. - Arizona *20850*
       V   20850   U.S. - Colorado *20850*
       E   20850   U.S. - Montana *20850*
       Ex/E 20850   U.S. - Nevada *20850*
       I   20850   U.S. - South Dakota *20850*
       E   20850   U.S. - Utah *20850*
       E   20850   U.S. - Wyoming *20850*

E   II   *Spiranthes infernalis* Sheviak *20850*
       E   20850   U.S. - Nevada *20850*

E   II   *Spiranthes lanceolata* (Aublet) Leon var. *paludicola*
         Luer *20850*
       E   20850   U.S. - Florida *20850*

R   II   *Spiranthes longilabris* Lindl. *20883, 20850, 19002*
       E   20850   U.S. - Alabama *20850*
       I   20850   U.S. - Florida *20850*
       E   20850   U.S. - Georgia *20850*
       I   20850   U.S. - Louisiana *20850*
       V   20850   U.S. - Mississippi *20850*
       E   20850   U.S. - North Carolina *20850*
       I   20850   U.S. - South Carolina *20850*
       E   20850   U.S. - Texas *20850*
       I   20850   U.S. - Virginia *20850*
       I   20883   USA - Virgin Is. *20883*

R   II   *Spiranthes obliqua* J.J. Smith *8309*
       R   Indonesia - Java (West & East Java)
                   8309

R   II   *Spiranthes parksii* Correll *20850*
       R   20850   U.S. - Texas (nr College Station, Brazos)
                   20850

R   II   *Spiranthes prasophylla* Reichb.f. var. *cleistogama*
         Ames & Correll *9004*
       V   9426   Costa Rica *9004*
       R   9004   Guatemala *9004*

V   II   *Stanhopea embreei* Dodson *19045*
       V   19045   Ecuador *19045*

V   II   *Stanhopea frymirei* Dodson *19045*
       V   19045   Ecuador *19045*

V   II   *Stanhopea hernandezii* (Kunth) Schltr. *10010*
       V   16360   Mexico *10010*

R   II   *Stanhopea lewisae* Ames & Correll *9004*
       R   10020   Guatemala *9004*

V   II   *Stanhopea martiana* Bateman ex Lindley *9423*
       V   16360   Mexico *9423*

V   II   *Stanhopea napoensis* Dodson *16956*
       V   10010   Ecuador *16956*

V   II   *Stanhopea tigrina* Bateman ex Lindley *10037*
       V   10007   Mexico *10037*

E   II   *Stelis allenii* L.O. Wms. *20883, 10747*
       I   20883   Panama *20883*

E   II   *Stelis atrorubens* L.O. Wms. *20883*
       I   20883   Panama *20883*

E   II   *Stelis collina* Schltr. *20883*
       I   20883   Panama *20883*

V   II   *Stelis hirtzii* Luer *19045*
    V   *19045*   Ecuador *19045*

E   II   *Stelis loculifera* Luer *20883, 10747*
    I   *20883*   Panama *20883*

E   II   *Stelis longipetiolata* Ames *20883, 9006*
    I   *20883*   Panama *20883*

R   II   *Stelis micrantha* (Sw.) Sw. *20883*
    R   *20883*   Jamaica *20883*

E   II   *Stelis striolata* Lindley *18200*
    E   *9446*   Peru *18200*

R   II   *Stellilabium distantiflorum* Ames & C. Schweinf. *9037*
    R   *9426*   Costa Rica *9037*

V   II   *Stellilabium microglossum* (Schltr) Dodson *19045*
    V   *19045*   Ecuador *19045*

R   II   *Stenia palorae* Dodson & Hirtz *19045*
    R   *19045*   Ecuador *19045*

V   II   *Stenorrhynchos bracteosus* Ames & C. Schweinf. *9037*
    V   *9426*   Costa Rica *9037*

R   II   *Stigmatodactylus javanicus* Schltr. & J.J. Smith *8309*
    R   Indonesia - Java (east west) *8309*
    I   Indonesia - Sumatra

V   II   *Stigmatodactylus sikokianus* Maxim. *11164*
    V   *11164*   Japan *11164*

R   II   *Suarezia ecuadorana* Dodson *19045*
    R   *19045*   Ecuador *19045*

I   II   *Sunipia angustipetala* Seidenf. *19120*
    I   *19120*   Thailand *19120*

I   II   *Sunipia australis* (Seidenf.) Hunt *19120*
    I   *19120*   Thailand *19120*

I   II   *Sunipia thailandica* (seidenf. & Smitin.) Hunt *19120*
    I   *19120*   Thailand *19120*

R   II   *Systeloglossum acuminatum* Ames & C. Schweinf. *9037*
    R   *9426*   Costa Rica *9037*

R   II   *Systeloglossum costaricense* Schltr. *9037*
    R   *9426*   Costa Rica *9037*

E   II   *Taeniophyllum andamanicum* Balakr. & Bhargava *11494*
    E   *11494*   India - Andaman Is. *11494*

I   II   *Taeniophyllum gilimalense* Jayaw. *8021*
    I   *16162*   Sri Lanka (Gilimale, Ratnapura) *8021*

I   II   *Taeniophyllum insulare* Seidenf. *19120*
    I   *19120*   Thailand *19120*

I   II   *Taeniophyllum quadrilobium* Seidenf. *19120*
    I   *19120*   Thailand *19120*

R   II   *Tangtsinia nanchuanica* S.C. Chen *17617*
    R   *17617*   China - Sichuan (Nanchuanjingfeshan) *11139*

E   II   *Teagueia teaguei* Luer *19045*
    E   *19054*   Ecuador *19045*

R   II   *Teagueia tentaculata* Luer & Hirtz *19045*
    R   *19045*   Ecuador *19045*

V   II   *Telipogon ampliflorus* C. Schweinf. *10012*
    E   *9426*   Costa Rica *10012*
    V   *19577*   Panama *10012*

V   II   *Telipogon aureus* Lindl. *19045*
    V   *19045*   Ecuador *19045*

V   II   *Telipogon biolleyi* Schltr. *19869*
    E   *9426*   Costa Rica *9037*
    V   *16317*   Panama *9006*

E   II   *Telipogon bruckmuelleri* Reichb.f. *9426*

    E   *9593*   Costa Rica *9426*

E   II   *Telipogon buenavistae* Kranzlin *9037*
    E   *9426*   Costa Rica *9037*

E   II   *Telipogon christobalensis* Kranzlin *9037*
    E   *9426*   Costa Rica *9037*

R   II   *Telipogon cnyujensis* Dodson & Escobar *19045*
    R   *19045*   Ecuador *19045*

E   II   *Telipogon costaricensis* Schltr. *9037*
    E   *9426*   Costa Rica *9037*

V   II   *Telipogon ecuadorensis* Schltr. *19045*
    V   *19045*   Ecuador *19045*

E   II   *Telipogon gracilipes* Schltr. *9037*
    E   *9426*   Costa Rica *9037*

R   II   *Telipogon guacamayoensis* Dodson & Escobar *19045*
    R   *19045*   Ecuador *19045*

R   II   *Telipogon hirtzii* Dodson & Escobar *19045*
    R   *19045*   Ecuador *19045*

R   II   *Telipogon penningtonii* Dodson & Escobar *19045*
    R   *19045*   Ecuador *19045*

E   II   *Telipogon pfavii* Schltr. *9037*
    E   *9426*   Costa Rica *9037*

E   II   *Telipogon setosus* Ames *9037*
    E   *9426*   Costa Rica *9037*

E   II   *Telipogon storkii* Ames & C. Schweinf. *9037*
    E   *9426*   Costa Rica *9037*

E   II   *Tetramicra bulbosa* Mansf. *19890*
    E   *19408*   Dominican Republic *19408*
    E   *19890*   Haiti (southeast) *18329*
    E   *19890*   Jamaica (Trelawny) *19221*

R   II   *Thelasis succosa* Carr
    R   Malaysia - Peninsular Malaysia (Kota Glanggi, Pahang)

R   II   *Thelymitra apiculata* (A.S.George) M.A.Clements & D.L.Jones *20681*
    R   *20681*   Australia - Western Australia *20681*

E   II   *Thelymitra dedmaniae* R.Rogers *20681*
    E   *20681*   Australia - Western Australia *20681*

E   II   *Thelymitra epipactoides* F.Muell. *20681, 19805*
    Ex/E   *20681*   Australia - New South Wales *19805*
    E   *20681*   Australia - South Australia *19805*
    E   *20681*   Australia - Victoria *19805*

V   II   *Thelymitra mackibbinii* F.Muell. *20681*
    V   *20681*   Australia - Victoria *20681*

V   II   *Thelymitra psammophila* C.R.P.Andrews *20681*
    V   *20681*   Australia - Western Australia *20681*

V   II   *Thelymitra stellata* Lindley *20681*
    V   *20681*   Australia - Western Australia *20681*

R   II   *Thelymitra tholiformis* *19305*
    R   *19305*   New Zealand - North Is. *19305*

R   II   *Thrixspermum obtusum* (Blume) Reichb.f. *8309*
    R   Indonesia - Java *8309*

E   II   *Tipularia japonica* Matsum. var. *harae* F. Maek. *11164*
    E   *11164*   Japan *11164*

R   II   *Tolumnia bahamensis* (Nash ex Britt. & Millsp.) G.J. Braem *20850*
    E   *20850*   U.S. - Florida *20850*

R   II   *Trevoria ecuadorensis* Rolfe *16963*
    R   *10010*   Ecuador *16963*

V   II   *Triaristella trichaete* (Reichb.f.) Luer *10009*

		V 9426 Costa Rica *10009*
I	II	*Trias mollis* Seidenf. *19120*
		I *19120* Thailand *19120*
I	II	*Trias rosea* (Ridl.) Seidenf. *19120*
		I *19120* Thailand *19120*
R	II	*Trichocentrum albiflorum* Rolfe *9423, 21219*
		R *11933* Mexico *9423*
V	II	*Trichocentrum brenesii* Schltr. *9037*
		E *9426* Costa Rica *9037*
		V *19577* Panama *10020*
R	II	*Trichocentrum hoegii* Reichb.f. *11938*
		R *11933* Mexico *9423*
R	II	*Trichocentrum pfavii* Reichb.f. *9037*
		E *9426* Costa Rica *9037*
		R *19577* Panama *9037*
V	II	*Trichocentrum tigrinum* Linden & Reichb. f. *12482*
		V Ecuador
		E *18200* Peru *12482*
V	II	*Trichoglottis australiensis* Dockr. *20681*
		V *20681* Australia - Queensland *20681*
R	II	*Trichoglottis javanica* J.J. Smith *8309*
		R Indonesia - Java (West Java; East Java) *8309*
E	II	*Trichopilia punctata* Rolfe *9037*
		E *9426* Costa Rica *9037*
V	II	*Trichopilia rostrata* Rchb.f. *19045*
		V *19045* Ecuador *19045*
V	II	*Trigonidium grande* Garay *19045, 16956*
		V *19045* Ecuador *19045*
E	II	*Triphora craigheadii* Luer *20850*
		E *20850* U.S. - Florida *20850*
Ex/E	II	*Triphora latifolia* Luer f. *20850, 14662*
		Ex/E *20850* U.S. - Florida *20850*
R	II	*Triphora nitida* Schltr. *9037*
		R *9426* Costa Rica *9037*
R	II	*Triphora ravenii* L.O. Williams *9426*
		R *9426* Costa Rica *9426*
		R *18265* Panama (Chiriquí) *18265*
V	II	*Triphora wagneri* Schltr. *20883, 9006*
		V *20883* Panama *20883*
R	II	*Trisetella abbreviata* Luer *21293*
		R *19045* Ecuador *19045*
R	II	*Trisetella andreettae* Luer *21293*
		R *19045* Ecuador *19045*
R	II	*Trisetella fissidens* Luer & Hirtz *21293*
		R *19045* Ecuador *19045*
R	II	*Trisetella gemmata* (Richb.f.) Luer *18089*
		R *18089* Colombia *18089*
R	II	*Trisetella hirtzii* Luer *21293*
		R *19045* Ecuador *19045*
R	II	*Trisetella pantex* (Luer) Luer *21293*
		R *19045* Ecuador *19045*
R	II	*Tropidia nipponica* Masam. var. *hachijoensis* F. Maek. *11164*
		R *11164* Japan *11164*
I	II	*Tuberolabium carnosum* Seidenf. *19120*
		I *19120* Thailand *19120*
I	II	*Vanda arcuata* J.J. Smith
		I Indonesia - Sulawesi

R	I	*Vanda coerulea* Griffith ex Lindley *4300*
		R *14782* India - Arunachal Pradesh *10868*
		R *14782* India - Assam *10868*
		R *14782* India - Manipur *14782*
		R *14782* India - Meghalaya *4300*
		R *14782* India - Mizoram *10868*
		R *14782* India - Nagaland *14782*
		I Myanmar
		I Thailand
V	II	*Vanda devoogtii* J.J. Smith
		V Indonesia - Sulawesi
I	II	*Vanda drakei* Reichb.f.
		I Indonesia - Lesser Sunda Is.
I	II	*Vanda foetida* J.J. Smith
		I Indonesia - Sumatra
I	II	*Vanda furva* Lindley
		I Indonesia - Moluccas
E	II	*Vanda hastifera* Reichb.f. *14068*
		E *14068* Indonesia - Kalimantan *14068*
I	II	*Vanda leucostele* Schltr.
		I Indonesia - Sumatra
I	II	*Vanda lombokensis* J.J. Smith
		I Indonesia - Lesser Sunda Is. (Lombok)
I	II	*Vanda punctata* Ridley
		I Indonesia - Lesser Sunda Is.
V	II	*Vanda sanderiana* Reichb.f. *10278*
		V Philippines *10278*
V	II	*Vanda sumatrana* Schltr.
		V Indonesia - Sumatra
E	II	*Vanda thwaitesii* Hook.f. *8021*
		E *16162* Sri Lanka (Hunnasgiriya, Kandy) *8021*
I	II	*Vanda tricuspidata* J.J. Smith
		I Indonesia - Lesser Sunda Is.
Ex/E	II	*Vanda wightii* Reichb.f. *11494*
		Ex/E *11494* India - Tamil Nadu *11494*
V	II	*Vanilla argentina* Hicken *16336*
		V *16336* Argentina *16336*
		V *20176* Argentina - Formosa *20176*
V	II	*Vanilla calopogon* Reichb.f. *10278*
		V Philippines *10278*
I	II	*Vanilla correllii* Sauleda & R.M. Adams
		I *4650* Bahamas *4650*
V	II	*Vanilla helleri* A. Hawkes *10017*
		V *11967* Nicaragua *10017*
R	II	*Vanilla hostmanni* Rolfe *17203*
		R *17203* Suriname *17203*
R	II	*Vanilla marowijnensis* Pulle *17203*
		R *17203* Suriname *17203*
R	II	*Vanilla phaeantha* Reichenb. f. *20883, 20850, 19890*
		V *20850* U.S. - Florida *20850*
		R *20883* Cuba *20883*
		E *19408* Dominican Republic *19408*
		E *20883* Jamaica *20883*
		? St Vincent *19890*
		R *20883* Trinidad & Tobago *20883*
		R *20883* Suriname *20883*
I	II	*Vanilla phalaenopsis* Reichenb. f. *14296*
		I *19182* Seychelles (granitic) *14296*
I	II	*Vanilla walkeriae* Wight
		I India - Karnataka (Jerganhalli, Mysore) *9139*
		I India - Kerala (Travancore Hills) *4988*

		I	India - Tamil Nadu (Coimbatore hills) *4988*	

V   II   *Vanilla wightiana* Lindley ex Hook.f. *11494*
- **V**   *11494*   India - Kerala (Tinnevelly; Kanyakumari) *11494*

E   II   *Vrydagzynea paludosa* J.J.Smith *20681*
- **E**   *20681*   Australia - Queensland *20681*

R   II   *Warrea costaricensis* Schltr. *11938*
- **R**   *11570*   Costa Rica *10034*
- **R**   *11570*   Guatemala *10034*
- **V**   *19850*   Mexico *11938*
- **R**   *11570*   Nicaragua *10034*
- **R**   *11570*   Panama *10034*

E   II   *Wullschlaegelia aphylla* (Swartz) Rchb. f. *10199*
- **E**   Dominica *10199*
- **E**   *19408*   Dominican Republic *19408*

R   II   *Xylobium brachypus* (Reichb.f.) Hemsley *9004*
- **R**   *9004*   Guatemala *9004*

V   II   *Xylobium powelii* Schltr. *9037*
- **V**   *9426*   Costa Rica *9037*
- **E/V**   *11967*   Nicaragua *10747*
- **V**   *19577*   Panama *9037*

R   II   *Xylobium sulfurinum* (Lemaire) Schltr. *9004*
- **R**   *9004*   Guatemala *9004*

V   II   *Yoania australis* Hatch *86*
- **V**   *86*   New Zealand - North Is. *86*

R   II   *Zetagyne albiflora* Ridley *6057*
- **R**   Vietnam *6057*

I   II   *Zeuxine andamanica* King & Pantl. *7771*
- **I**   India - Andaman Is. (South Andaman Is.) *7771*

Ex   II   *Zeuxine boninensis* Tuy. *8038*
- **Ex**   *15112*   Japan - Ogasawara-shoto *8038*

R   II   *Zeuxine elatior* Schltr. var. *angustata* Cribb & B. Lewis *14794*
- **R**   *14793*   Solomon Is. - South *14794*

V   II   *Zeuxine exilis* Ridley *881*
- **V**   *14224*   Australia - Christmas Is. *881*

E   II   *Zeuxine palustris* Ridley *19047*
- **E**   *19047*   Malaysia - Peninsular Malaysia (Ulu Temango, Perak) *19047*

E   II   *Zeuxine peniformis* *19047*
- **E**   *19047*   Malaysia - Peninsular Malaysia *19047*

Ex/E   II   *Zeuxine pulchra* King & Pantl. *11494*
- **Ex/E**   *11494*   India - Meghalaya (Khasi hills) *11494*
- **Ex/E**   *11494*   India - Sikkim (Lachung Valley) *11494*

I   II   *Zeuxine rolfiana* King & Pantl. *7771*
- **I**   India - Andaman Is. (south Andaman Is.) *7771*

V   II   *Zeuxine rupestris* Ridley *19047*
- **V**   *19047*   Malaysia - Peninsular Malaysia (Penang Hill) *19047*

R   II   *Zeuxine sphaerochila* Fleischm. & Rech. *8006*
- **R**   U.S. - American Samoa *8006*
- **I**   Western Samoa *8006*

E   II   *Zeuxine tjiampeana* J.J. Smith *8309*
- **E**   *19047*   Indonesia - Java (West Java) *8309*

R   II   *Zeuxine tonkinensis* Gagnepain *6057*
- **R**   Vietnam *6057*

V   II   *Zeuxine viridiflora* J.J. Smith *8309*
- **V**   *19047*   Indonesia - Java (West Java; East Java) *8309*

Palmae

Number of genera: 200
Number of species: 3,000
Recorded threatened species: 869   (28%)

Tropical and warm temperate.

V   *Acanthophoenix rubra* (Bory) H.A. Wendl. *10082*
- **V**   *6165*   Réunion *10082*
- **E**   *20771*   Mauritius *10082*

V   *Acrocomia media* O.F. Cook *20883, 8020*
- **I**   *20883*   Puerto Rico *20883*
- **I**   *20883*   USA - Virgin Is. *20883*

R   *Actinokentia divaricata* (Brongn.) Dammer *10238*
- **R**   *15184*   New Caledonia *10238*

R   *Actinokentia huerlimannii* H.E. Moore *10237*
- **R**   *20893*   New Caledonia *10237*

R   *Aiphanes acaulis* Galeano & R. Bernal *10741*
- **R**   *16853*   Colombia (Choco) *10741*

R   *Aiphanes chiribogensis* Borchsenius & Balslev *17946*
- **R**   *17946*   Ecuador *17954*

I   *Aiphanes deltoidea* Burret *20883, 8020*
- **E**   *20883*   Brazil *20883*
- **I**   *20826*   Colombia *20883*
- **V**   *20883*   Peru *20883*

I   *Aiphanes duquei* Burret *8020*
- **I**   *16853*   Colombia *8020*

R   *Aiphanes gracilis* Burret *8020*
- **R**   *18200*   Peru *17955*

I   *Aiphanes hirsuta* Burret ssp. *fosteriorum* (H.E.Moore) Borchsenius & R.Bernal *20826*
- **I**   *16853*   Colombia (south-west) *20826*
- **I**   Ecuador (north-west) *20826*

I   *Aiphanes hirsuta* Burret ssp. *intermedia* Borchsenius & R.Bernal *20826*
- **I**   *16853*   Colombia (west) *20826*

I   *Aiphanes hirsuta* Burret ssp. *kalbreyeri* (Burret) Borchsenius & R.Bernal *20826*
- **I**   *16853*   Colombia (west) *20826*

E   *Aiphanes leiostachys* Burret *8020*
- **E**   *6197*   Colombia *8020*

V   *Aiphanes lindeniana* (H. Wendl.) H. Wendl. *8020*
- **V**   *16853*   Colombia *8020*

V   *Aiphanes linearis* Burret *8020*
- **V**   *16853*   Colombia *8020*

E   *Aiphanes parvifolia* Burret *8020*
- **E**   *16853*   Colombia *8020*

V   *Aiphanes simplex* Burret *8020*
- **V**   *16853*   Colombia *8020*

V   *Aiphanes spicata* Borchsenius & Bernal *19698*
- **V**   *19698*   Peru *19698*

V   *Aiphanes truncata* (Brongniart ex C. Martius) H. A. Wendl. *20883, 8020*
- **I**   *20883*   Bolivia (Beni, Cochabamba, La Paz, S. Cruz) *20883*
- **I**   *20883*   Paraguay *20883*

R   *Aiphanes ulei* (Dammer) Burret *8020*
- **I**   Brazil *20826*
- **I**   Colombia *20826*
- **I**   Ecuador *20826*
- **R**   *19698*   Peru *17955*

R   *Aiphanes verrucosa* Borchsenius & Balslev *17946*

R	17946	Ecuador *17946*

R *Aiphanes weberbaueri* Burret *8020*
    R   20826 Ecuador (south) *20826*
    R   18200 Peru *17955*

V *Allagoptera arenaria* (Gomes) Kuntze *8020*
    V   8743 Brazil (Atlantic forest) *8743*

V *Allagoptera brevicalyx* M. Moraes *17954*
    V   17954 Brazil *17954*

V *Alloschmidia glabrata* (Becc.) H.E. Moore *9996*
    V   20893 New Caledonia *15184*

V *Alsmithia longipes* H.E. Moore *10532*
    V   15184 Fiji (Taveuni & Viti Levu) *10532*

V *Ammandra dasyneura* (Burret) Barfod *20883, 15728*
    I   20826 Colombia *20883*
    I   20826 Ecuador (north) *20883*

R *Aphandra natalia* (Balslev and Hendersson)
    Barfod *20883, 15728*
    I   20883 Brazil *20883*
    R   20883 Ecuador (Andes eastern foothills) *20883*
    R   20883 Peru *20883*

E *Archontophoenix myolensis* Dowe *20681*
    E   20681 Australia - Queensland *20681*

E *Areca abdulrahmanii* Dransf. *4066*
    E   14703 Malaysia - Sarawak (G. Mulu NP) *4066*

E *Areca ahmadii* Dransf. *10630*
    E   14703 Malaysia - Sarawak *10630*

E *Areca andersonii* Dransf. *10630*
    E   14703 Malaysia - Sarawak *10630*

V *Areca arundinacea* Becc. *10630*
    V   14703 Malaysia - Sarawak *10630*

E *Areca brachypoda* Dransf. *10630*
    E   14703 Malaysia - Sarawak *10630*

R *Areca camariensis* Becc.
    R   14726 Philippines *14726*

I *Areca catechu* L. var. *batanensis*
    Becc. *14726*
    I   14726 Philippines (Batan Is.) *14726*

I *Areca catechu* L. var. *silvatica*
    Becc. *14726*
    I   14726 Philippines (near Lake Manguao) *13833*

E *Areca chaiana* Dransf. *10630*
    E   14703 Malaysia - Sarawak *10630*

E *Areca concinna* Thwaites *11813*
    E   19614 Sri Lanka *16162*

I *Areca costulata* Becc. *14726*
    I   14726 Philippines (Dinagat) *14726*

E *Areca dayung* Dransf. *4066*
    E   14703 Malaysia - Sarawak *4066*

V *Areca glandiformis* Lam. *14828*
    V   14828 Indonesia - Moluccas *14828*

R *Areca guppyana* Becc. *15138*
    R   15138 Solomon Is. - South *15138*

I *Areca hutchinsoniana* Becc. *14726*
    I   14726 Philippines (Basilan, Siassi) *14726*

V *Areca ipot* Becc. *14726*
    V   14726 Philippines (Luzon) *14726*

E *Areca jugahpunya* Dransf. *10630*
    E   14703 Malaysia - Sarawak *10630*

E *Areca klingkangensis* Dransf. *10630*

E	14703	Malaysia - Sarawak *10630*

I *Areca macrocarpa* Becc. *14726*
    I   14726 Philippines (Mindanao) *14726*

I *Areca mammillata* Becc. *13833*
    I   13833 Philippines (low altitude) *13833*

V *Areca parens* Becc. *14726*
    V   14726 Philippines (Camarines Sur) *14726*

V *Areca ridleyana* Becc ex Furtado *10260*
    V   Malaysia - Peninsular Malaysia *10249*

E *Areca subacaulis* (Becc.) Dransf. *11813*
    E   14703 Malaysia - Sarawak *10570*

I *Areca whitfordii* Becc. var. *luzonensis*
    Becc. *14726*
    I   14726 Philippines (Luzon) *14726*

I *Areca whitfordii* Becc. var. *whitfordii* *14726*
    I   14726 Philippines (Mindoro) *14726*

R *Arenga listeri* Becc. *5170*
    R   17945 Australia - Christmas Is. *5170*

V *Arenga longipes* Mogea *14828*
    V   14828 Indonesia - Sumatra *14828*

R *Arenga retroflorescens* H.E. Moore & Meijer *14712*
    E   14712 Malaysia - Sabah *14712*
    R   14828 Malaysia - Sarawak *14828*

V *Arenga wightii* Griff. *14827*
    V   14827 India - Karnataka *14827*
    V   14827 India - Kerala *14827*
    V   14827 India - Tamil Nadu *14827*

R *Asterogyne guianense* Granville & Henderson *19618*
    R   19614 French Guiana *19618*

E *Asterogyne guianensis* Granv. & Henderson *20883*
    E   20883 French Guiana *20883*

R *Asterogyne ramosa* (H.E. Moore) J.G.W. Boer *8020*
    R   Venezuela *8020*

R *Asterogyne spicata* (H.E. Moore) J.G.W. Boer *8020*
    R   Venezuela *8020*

V *Asterogyne yaracuyense* Henderson & Steyermark *19619*
    V   19614 Venezuela *19619*

V *Astrocaryum aculeatissimum* (Schott) Burret *8020*
    V   19614 Brazil (Atlantic forest) *8020*

I *Astrocaryum alatum* H.F. Loomis *8020*
    V   Costa Rica *8020*
    I   20826 Nicaragua *20826*
    V   Panama *8020*

R *Astrocaryum huaimi* C. Martius *20883, 8020*
    R   20883 Bolivia *20883*
    R   20883 Brazil *20883*
    V   20883 Peru *20883*

V *Astrocaryum malybo* Karsten *8020*
    V   16853 Colombia *8020*

V *Astrocaryum murumuru* Mart. var. *ciliatum* (Kahn &
    Millán) Henderson *20883*
    V   20883 Colombia *20883*

V *Astrocaryum murumuru* Mart. var. *ferrugineum* (Kahn
    & Millán) Henderson *20883, 20826*
    V   20883 Brazil *20883*

R *Astrocaryum murumuru* Mart. var. *huicungo* (Dammer)
    Henderson *20883*
    R   20883 Peru *20883*

R *Astrocaryum murumuru* Mart. var. *huincungo* (Kahn &
    Millán) Henderson *20826*

R   *19614* Peru *17955*

R   *Astrocaryum murumuru* Mart. var. *javarense* (Trail) Henderson *20883*

   V   *20883* Brazil *20883*
   V   *20883* Peru *20883*

R   *Astrocaryum murumuru* Mart. var. *macrocalyx* (Burret) Henderson *20883*

   R   *20883* Colombia *20883*
   V   *20883* Peru *20883*

E   *Astrocaryum murumuru* Mart. var. *perangustatum* (Kahn & Millán) Henderson *20883, 20826*

   E   *20883* Peru *20883*

V   *Astrocaryum murumuru* Mart. var. *urostachys* (Burret) Henderson *20883*

   V   *20883* Ecuador *20883*
   E   *20883* Peru *20883*

E   *Astrocaryum triandrum* Galeano, Bernal & Kahn *20883, 16853*

   V   *16853* Colombia *20883*

I   *Attalea amygdalina* Knuth. *8020*

   I   *16853* Colombia *8020*

R   *Attalea attaleoides* (Barb. Rodr.) Wess. Boer *20883, 8020*

   V   *20883* Brazil *20883*
   R   *20883* French Guiana *20883*
   E   *20883* Suriname *20883*

R   *Attalea colenda* (Cook) Balslev & Henderson *20883, 14868*

   V   *20883* Colombia (Narino) *20883*
   R   *20883* Ecuador (western Andean slopes) *20883*
   I   *20883* Peru *20883*

E   *Attalea crassispatha* (Mart.) Burret *14799*

   E   *14799* Haiti (southwestern peninsula) *8743*

R   *Attalea cuatrecasana* (Dugand) R.Bernal, Galeano & Henderson *20826*

   I   *20826* Bolivia *20826*
   V   *19614* Brazil *8020*
   R   *16853* Colombia *20826*
   I   *20826* Ecuador *20826*

V   *Attalea dubia* (Mart.) Burret *8020*

   V   *19614* Brazil (Atlantic forest) *8743*

R   *Attalea eichleri* (Drude) Henderson *20883, 20826*

   E   *20883* Bolivia *20883*
   R   *20883* Brazil *20883*

I   *Attalea geraensis* Barb. Rodr. *8020*

   V   *19614* Brazil (Atlantic forest) *8743*
   I   Brazil - Bahia *20826*
   I   Brazil - Goias *20826*
   I   Brazil - Minas Gerais *20826*
   I   Brazil - Rio de Janeiro *20826*
   I   Brazil - Sao Paulo *20826*
   I   Paraguay *20826*

V   *Attalea humilis* Mart. ex Sprengel *8020*

   V   *19614* Brazil (Atlantic forest) *8743*

V   *Attalea iguadummat* de Nerves *20883*

   I   *20883* Panama *20883*

R   *Attalea luetzelburgii* (Burret) Wess. Boer. *20883*

   E   *20883* Brazil *20883*
   E   *20883* Colombia *20883*
   E   *20883* Venezuela *20883*

I   *Attalea oleifera* Barb. Rodr. *8020*

   I   Brazil - Alagoas *20826*
   V   *19614* Brazil - Bahia (Reconcavo) *8743*
   I   Brazil - Espirito Santo *20826*

   I   Brazil - Paraiba *20826*
   I   Brazil - Pernambuco *20826*
   I   Brazil - Sergipe *20826*

E   *Attalea septuagenata* Dugand *20883, 11813*

   E   *20883* Colombia (Amazon) *20883*

V   *Attalea spectabilis* Mart. *20883*

   V   *20883* Brazil *20883*

R   *Attalea tessmannii* Burret *20883, 11813*

   E   *20883* Brazil *20883*
   V   *20883* Peru (Amazon) *20883*

R   *Bactris acanthocarpa* var. *intermedia* Henderson *20883*

   E   *20883* Brazil *20883*
   R   *20883* French Guiana *20883*

R   *Bactris aubletiana* Trail *20883, 8020*

   I   *20883* French Guiana *20883*
   E   *20883* Suriname *20883*

V   *Bactris caryotifolia* Mart. *8020*

   V   *19614* Brazil (Atlantic forest) *8020*

I   *Bactris charnleyae* Nevers & Grayum *20826*

   I   *20826* Panama *20826*

R   *Bactris coloniata* L.H. Bailey *20883, 8020*

   R   *20883* Panama *20883*
   E   *20883* Colombia *20883*
   I   *20826* Peru *20883*

R   *Bactris concinna* var. *sigmoidea* Henderson *20883*

   V   *20883* Bolivia *20883*
   E   *20883* Brazil *20883*
   R   *20883* Peru *20883*

R   *Bactris constanciae* Barb. Rodr. *20883, 8020*

   V   *20883* Brazil *20883*
   R   *20883* French Guiana *20883*
   E   *20883* Guyana *20883*
   E   *20883* Suriname *20883*

E   *Bactris faucium* C. Martius *20883, 8020*

   E   *20883* Bolivia *20883*

R   *Bactris fissifrons* Mart. *20883, 8020*

   V   *20883* Brazil *20883*
   V   *20883* Colombia *20883*
   V   *20883* Peru *20883*

V   *Bactris hirta* var. *mollis* (Dammer) Henderson *20883*

   E   *20883* Brazil *20883*
   E   *20883* Colombia *20883*
   V   *20883* Peru *20883*

V   *Bactris jamaicana* L.H. Bailey *20883, 8020*

   V   *20883* Jamaica *20883*

V   *Bactris longiseta* H. Wendl. ex Burret *8020*

   V   Costa Rica *8020*

R   *Bactris major* Jacq.f. var. *megalocarpa* (Trail) Henderson *20883*

   E   *20883* Brazil *20883*
   V   *20883* Colombia *20883*
   V   *20883* Guyana *20883*
   V   *20883* Venezuela *20883*

R   *Bactris major* Jacq.f. var. *socialis* Drude in Mart. *20883*

   R   *20883* Bolivia *20883*

R   *Bactris maraja* Mart. var. *chaetospatha* (Mart.) Henderson *20883*

   V   *20883* Brazil *20883*
   V   *20883* Peru *20883*

V	**Bactris oraria** L.H. Bailey *20883*	
	V	*20883* Panama *20883*
V	**Bactris pickelii** Burret *8020*	
	V	*19614* Brazil (Atlantic forest) *8743*
R	**Bactris ptariana** Steyerm. *20883, 8020*	
	R	*20883* Guyana *20883*
	E	*20883* Venezuela *20883*
R	**Bactris rhapidacantha** Wess. Boer. *20883*	
	R	*20883* French Guiana *20883*
	V	*20883* Suriname *20883*
I	**Bactris setulosa** Karsten *8020*	
	I	Trinidad & Tobago *20826*
	I	*16853* Colombia *20826*
	I	Ecuador *20826*
	V	Venezuela *20826*
R	**Bactris socialis** C. Martius *20883, 8020*	
	R	*20883* Bolivia *20883*
	I	*20883* Brazil *20883*
V	**Bactris syagroides** Barb. Rodr. & Trail *20883, 8020*	
	V	*20883* Brazil *20883*
V	**Bactris tefensis** Henderson *20883*	
	V	*20883* Brazil *20883*
V	**Bactris turbinocarpa** Barb. Rodr. *20883, 8020*	
	E	*20883* Brazil *20883*
	V	*20883* Suriname *20883*
R	**Balaka brachyclamys** Burr. *15308*	
	R	*15308* Western Samoa (Savai'i and Upolu) *15308*
R	**Balaka longirostris** Becc. *10253*	
	R	*17945* Fiji (Viti Levu) *10253*
V	**Balaka macrocarpa** Burret *10253*	
	V	*17945* Fiji (Viti Levu & Vanua Levu) *10253*
R	**Balaka microcarpa** Burret *10253*	
	R	*17945* Fiji (SE Viti Levu) *10253*
R	**Balaka samoensis** Becc. *15308*	
	R	*15308* Western Samoa (Savai'i) *15308*
V	**Balaka seemannii** (H.A. Wendl.) Becc. *10253*	
	V	*15184* Fiji (Vanua Levu & Taveuni) *10253*
R	**Balaka taitensis** (Wendl.) Becc. *15308*	
	R	*17945* Western Samoa (Upolu) *15308*
R	**Balaka tuasivica** Christophersen *17945*	
	R	*17945* Western Samoa (Savai'i) *17945*
V	**Barcella odora** (Trail) Drude in Mart. *20883, 9996*	
	V	*20883* Brazil *20883*
R	**Basselinia deplanchei** (Brong. & Gris.) Vieill. *10238*	
	R	*15184* New Caledonia *10238*
V	**Basselinia favieri** H.E. Moore *10523*	
	V	*20893* New Caledonia (Mont Panié) *10523*
I	**Basselinia gracilis** (Brongn. & Gris) Vieill. *10238*	
	I	*15184* New Caledonia *10238*
R	**Basselinia humboldtiana** (Brongn.) H.E. Moore *10523*	
	R	*20893* New Caledonia (southeast) *10523*
V	**Basselinia iterata** H.E. Moore *10523*	
	V	*20893* New Caledonia (northeast) *10523*
R	**Basselinia pancheri** (Brongn. & Gris) Vieill. *10238*	
	R	*15184* New Caledonia *10238*
R	**Basselinia porphyrea** H.E. Moore *10523*	
	R	*20893* New Caledonia (serpentine, southwest) *10523*
R	**Basselinia sordida** H.E. Moore *10523*	
	R	*10523* New Caledonia (serpentine, west) *10523*
V	**Basselinia tomentosa** Becc. *10238*	
	V	*20893* New Caledonia *10238*
R	**Basselinia velutina** Becc. *10238*	
	R	*15184* New Caledonia *10238*
V	**Basselinia vestita** H.E. Moore *10523*	
	V	*20893* New Caledonia (serpentine) *10523*
E	**Beccariophoenix madagascariensis** Jum. & H. Perrier *11813*	
	E	*20071* Madagascar (Analamazaotra) *20071*
R	**Bentinckia condapanna** Berry *13883*	
	R	*14827* India - Kerala *14827*
	R	*13883* India - Tamil Nadu (S Travancore & Tirunelveli Hills) *13883*
V	**Bentinckia nicobarica** (Kurz) Becc. *14827*	
	V	*14827* India - Nicobar Is. *14827*
I	**Borassodendron machadonis** Becc. *10260*	
	I	Thailand *10238*
	V	Malaysia - Peninsular Malaysia *10249*
V	**Borassus madagascariensis** Bojer ex Jum. & H. Perrier *10246*	
	V	*20071* Madagascar (west) *20071*
E	**Borassus sambiranensis** Jum. & H. Perrier *10246*	
	E	*17951* Madagascar (north-west) *20071*
V	**Brahea aculeata** (T.S. Brandegee) H.E. Moore *10260*	
	V	*19850* Mexico *8020*
V	**Brahea decumbens** Rzed. *8020*	
	V	Mexico *8020*
E	**Brahea edulis** S.Watson *11813*	
	E	*11813* Mexico - Guadelupe (island slopes) *8743*
R	**Brahea moorei** L.H. Bailey ex H.E. Moore *8020*	
	R	*19850* Mexico *8020*
I	**Brahea nitida** Andre *8778*	
	I	*20827* Guatemala *20826*
	V	Mexico *8778*
V	**Brahea pimo** Becc. *10260*	
	V	Mexico *8020*
R	**Brongniartikentia lanuginosa** H.E. Moore *20893*	
	R	*20893* New Caledonia *15184*
R	**Brongniartikentia vaginata** (Brongn.) Becc.	
	R	*15184* New Caledonia *15184*
V	**Burretiokentia hapala** H.E. Moore	
	V	*2014* New Caledonia *2014*
R	**Burretiokentia vieillardii** (Brongn. & Gris) Pichi-Serm. *10238*	
	R	*15184* New Caledonia *10238*
E	**Butia campicola** Barb. Rodr. *20826*	
	E	Paraguay *20826*
I	**Butia eriospatha** (Mart. ex Drude) Becc. *20310*	
	V	*19614* Brazil (Atlantic forest) *8743*
	I	*19614* Brazil - Rio Grande do Sul *20311*
	I	*19614* Brazil - Santa Catarina *20310*
R	**Butia microspadix** Burret *8904*	
	R	*19614* Brazil *8904*
V	**Butia purpurascens** Glassman *8904*	
	V	*19614* Brazil (Cerrados in Goias) *8904*
V	**Calamus adspersus** Blume *10238*	
	V	Indonesia - Java *10238*
	V	Indonesia - Sumatra *10238*
V	**Calamus andamanicus** Kurz *14827*	
	V	*14827* India - Andaman Is. *14827*

V	*Calamus asperrimus* Blume *10238*	
	V	Indonesia - Java *10238*
I	*Calamus bicolor* Becc. *14726*	
	I	*14726* Philippines (Mindanao) *14726*
I	*Calamus brandisii* Becc. ex Becc. & Hook.f. *4988*	
	I	India - Karnataka (Canara) *4988*
	I	India - Kerala (Courtallum Hills) *10235*
	I	India - Tamil Nadu (Courtallum Hills) *4988*
R	*Calamus ceratophorus* Conrard. *13955*	
	R	*15313* Vietnam (Phu Khanh) *13955*
V	*Calamus ciliaris* Blume *10260*	
	V	Indonesia - Java *10238*
	V	Indonesia - Sumatra (west, one small area) *10238*
	V	*14703* Malaysia - Sarawak *14703*
V	*Calamus cockburnii* Dransf. *10259*	
	V	Malaysia - Peninsular Malaysia (Pahang) *10259*
E	*Calamus conjugatus* Furt. *10260*	
	E	*14703* Malaysia - Sarawak *14703*
V	*Calamus corneri* Furt. *10259*	
	V	Malaysia - Peninsular Malaysia *10259*
R	*Calamus crassifolius* J. Dransf. *15142*	
	R	*15142* Malaysia - Sarawak (kerangas forest) *15142*
I	*Calamus cumingianaus* Becc. *14726*	
	I	*14726* Philippines (Luzon) *14726*
E	*Calamus delicatulus* Thwaites *7956*	
	E	*17945* Sri Lanka *7956*
V	*Calamus digitatus* Becc. *7956*	
	V	*17945* Sri Lanka *7956*
R	*Calamus dilaceratus* Becc. *14782*	
	R	*14782* India - Andaman Is. *14782*
I	*Calamus dimorphacanthus* Becc. var. *montalbanicus* Becc. *16098*	
	I	*14726* Philippines (Luzon) *14726*
I	*Calamus dimorphacanthus* Becc. var. *zambalensis* Becc. *16098*	
	I	*14726* Philippines (Luzon) *14726*
R	*Calamus dioicus* Lour. *10260*	
	R	Vietnam *8794*
I	*Calamus discolor* Mart. var. *discolor* *14726*	
	I	*14726* Philippines (Luzon) *14726*
I	*Calamus discolor* Mart. var. *negrosensis* Becc. *14726*	
	I	*14726* Philippines (Siargao) *14726*
R	*Calamus dongnaiensis* Pierre ex Becc. *10260*	
	R	Vietnam (south) *8794*
E	*Calamus endauensis* Dransf. *10259*	
	E	*14701* Malaysia - Peninsular Malaysia (Johor) *10259*
V	*Calamus erectus* Roxb. var. *birmanicus* Becc. *16073*	
	V	*20756* China - Yunnan *16073*
V	*Calamus filipendulus* Becc. *10259*	
	V	Malaysia - Peninsular Malaysia *10259*
I	*Calamus foxworthyi* Becc. *14726*	
	I	*14726* Philippines (Palawan) *14726*
R	*Calamus godefroyi* Becc. *10260*	

	R	Vietnam *10260*
I	*Calamus grandifolius* Becc. *14726*	
	I	*14726* Philippines (Luzon) *14726*
R	*Calamus harmandii* Pierre ex Becc. *10667*	
	R	*15313* Laos *10667*
E	*Calamus hepburnii* Dransf. *10258*	
	E	*17950* Malaysia - Sabah *10258*
V	*Calamus holttumii* Furt. *10259*	
	V	*14701* Malaysia - Peninsular Malaysia (Johor, Trengganu) *10259*
R	*Calamus huegelianus* Mart. *10235*	
	R	India - Tamil Nadu (Nilgiri Hills) *18341*
V	*Calamus hypertrichosus* Becc. *14703*	
	V	*14703* Malaysia - Sarawak *14703*
R	*Calamus impar* Becc. *14828*	
	R	*14828* Indonesia - Kalimantan *14828*
	R	*14828* Malaysia - Sabah *14828*
	R	*14828* Malaysia - Sarawak *14828*
V	*Calamus inermis* T. Anders. *14827*	
	V	*19161* Bhutan *14665*
	V	*14827* India - Sikkim *14827*
	V	*14827* India - West Bengal *14827*
I	*Calamus jenningsianus* Becc. *14726*	
	I	*14726* Philippines (Mindoro) *14726*
R	*Calamus koordersianus* Becc. *14828*	
	R	*14828* Indonesia - Sulawesi *14828*
R	*Calamus laevigatus* Mart. var. *serpentinus* Dransf. *10258*	
	R	*14712* Malaysia - Sabah (ultrabasic rock, lowlands) *10258*
V	*Calamus laxissimus* Ridley *10259*	
	V	*14701* Malaysia - Peninsular Malaysia *10259*
V	*Calamus longispathus* Ridley *10259*	
	V	Malaysia - Peninsular Malaysia *10259*
I	*Calamus megaphyllus* Becc. *14726*	
	I	*14726* Philippines (Leyte) *14726*
V	*Calamus melanoloma* Mart. *10238*	
	V	Indonesia - Java *10238*
I	*Calamus melanorhynchus* Becc. *14726*	
	I	*14726* Philippines (Mindanao) *14726*
V	*Calamus merrillii* Becc. var. *merrillii* *14726*	
	V	Philippines
I	*Calamus meyenianus* Schauer *14726*	
	I	*14726* Philippines (Pangasi, Nueva Vizcaya) *14726*
E	*Calamus minutus* Dransf. *10259*	
	E	*14701* Malaysia - Peninsular Malaysia (Trengganu) *10259*
I	*Calamus mitis* Becc. *14726*	
	I	*14726* Philippines (Batanes, Babuyan) *14726*
E	*Calamus moorhousei* Furt. *10259*	
	E	*14701* Malaysia - Peninsular Malaysia (Negri Sembilan) *10259*
I	*Calamus moseleyanus* Becc. *14726*	
	I	*14726* Philippines (Basilan, Malanipa) *14726*
I	*Calamus multinervis* Becc. *14726*	
	I	*14726* Philippines (Mindanao) *14726*
V	*Calamus multirameus* Ridley *10259*	
	V	Malaysia - Peninsular Malaysia (Perak) *10259*

V	***Calamus nagbettai*** R.R. Fernandez & Dey *14827*	
	V	*14827* India - Karnataka (Coorg & south Kanara) *14827*
R	***Calamus nicobaricus*** Becc. *10235*	
	R	India - Nicobar Is. (Great Nicobar) *10235*
R	***Calamus nielsenii*** Dransf. *14703*	
	R	*14703* Malaysia - Sarawak *14703*
E	***Calamus ovoideus*** Thwaites ex Trimen *7956*	
	E	*17945* Sri Lanka *7956*
E	***Calamus pachystemonus*** Thwaites *7956*	
	E	*19614* Sri Lanka *7956*
E	***Calamus padangensis*** Furt. *10259*	
	E	*14701* Malaysia - Peninsular Malaysia (G. Padang) *10259*
R	***Calamus penicillatus*** Roxb. *10259*	
	R	Malaysia - Peninsular Malaysia (Penang Hill) *10259*
V	***Calamus poensis*** Becc. *14703*	
	V	*14703* Malaysia - Sarawak *14703*
V	***Calamus poilanei*** Conrard. *13955*	
	K	*20985* Vietnam (Lam Dong, Phu Khanh) *13955*
E	***Calamus pulaiensis*** Becc. *10249*	
	E	*14701* Malaysia - Peninsular Malaysia *10249*
R	***Calamus pycnocarpus*** (Furt.) Dransf. *10259*	
	R	Malaysia - Peninsular Malaysia (Trengganu) *10259*
V	***Calamus quinquenervius*** Roxb. *7956*	
	V	*14872* Bangladesh *7956*
E	***Calamus radiatus*** Thwaites *7956*	
	E	*17945* Sri Lanka *7956*
E	***Calamus radulosus*** Becc. *10259*	
	E	*14701* Malaysia - Peninsular Malaysia (Perak) *10259*
V	***Calamus ridleyanus*** Becc. *10259*	
	V	*14701* Malaysia - Peninsular Malaysia (Trengganu; Johor) *10259*
	V	*20099* Singapore *20099*
V	***Calamus rivalis*** Thwaites ex Trimen *7956*	
	V	*19614* Sri Lanka *7956*
V	***Calamus robinsonianus*** Becc. *14828*	
	V	*14828* Indonesia - Moluccas *14828*
R	***Calamus scutellaris*** Becc. *13955*	
	R	*15313* Vietnam (Thanh Hoa.) *13955*
V	***Calamus sedens*** Dransf. *10259*	
	V	Malaysia - Peninsular Malaysia *10259*
V	***Calamus semoi*** Becc. *14703*	
	V	*14703* Malaysia - Sarawak *14703*
E	***Calamus senalingensis*** Dransf. *10259*	
	E	*14701* Malaysia - Peninsular Malaysia (Negeri Sembilan) *10259*
E	***Calamus setulosus*** Dransf. *10259*	
	E	*14701* Malaysia - Peninsular Malaysia (Perak) *10259*
V	***Calamus simplex*** Becc. *10259*	
	V	Malaysia - Peninsular Malaysia *10259*
R	***Calamus spectabilis*** Blume *10238*	
	Ex/E	Indonesia - Java *10238*
	R	Indonesia - Sumatra *10238*
I	***Calamus spectatissimus*** Furt. *10259*	
	I	Thailand *8794*

	I	Indonesia - Kalimantan *10259*
	I	Indonesia - Sumatra *10259*
	E/V	Malaysia - Peninsular Malaysia (Perak, 1 coll.) *10259*
V	***Calamus tanakadatei*** Furt. *10259*	
	V	Malaysia - Peninsular Malaysia *10259*
R	***Calamus tonkinensis*** Becc. *10260*	
	R	Vietnam *8794*
I	***Calamus trispermus*** Becc. *14726*	
	I	*14726* Philippines (Luzon) *14726*
V	***Calamus vanuatuensis*** J. Dowe *15184*	
	V	*19614* Vanuatu *15184*
I	***Calamus vidalianus*** Becc. *14726*	
	I	*14726* Philippines (Luzon) *14726*
I	***Calamus vinosus*** Becc. *14726*	
	I	*14726* Philippines (Mindanao) *14726*
R	***Calamus vitiensis*** Warb. ex Becc. *10253*	
	R	*15184* Fiji (Viti Levu & Taveuni) *10253*
V	***Calamus whitmorei*** Dransf. *10259*	
	V	Malaysia - Peninsular Malaysia *10259*
E	***Calamus zeylanicus*** Becc. *7956*	
	E	*17945* Sri Lanka *7956*
V	***Calospatha scortechinii*** Becc. *10259*	
	V	Malaysia - Peninsular Malaysia *10259*
V	***Calyptrogyne anomala*** de Nevers & Henderson *20883*	
	I	*20883* Panama *20883*
I	***Calyptrogyne condensata*** (L.H. Bailey) J.G. W. Boer *8020*	
	I	Costa Rica *8020*
	I	Panama *8020*
I	***Calyptrogyne kunaria*** Nevers *20826*	
	I	*20826* Panama *20826*
I	***Calyptrogyne pubescens*** Nevers *20826*	
	I	*20826* Panama *20826*
I	***Calyptrogyne trichostachys*** Burret *8020*	
	V	Costa Rica *8020*
	I	*20827* Panama *20826*
R	***Calyptronoma occidentalis*** (Sw.) H.E. Moore *20883, 9996*	
	I	*20990* Cuba *20990*
	R	*20883* Jamaica *20883*
E	***Calyptronoma rivalis*** (O.F. Cook) Bailey *20883, 14799*	
	E	*8743* Dominican Republic *8743*
	V	*14799* Haiti *14799*
	I	*20883* Puerto Rico (north-west) *20883*
R	***Campecarpus fulcitus*** (Brongn.) Becc. *13954*	
	R	*15184* New Caledonia (Southern end of Grande Terre, at altitude (100- 800m)) *15184*
E	***Carpoxylon macrospermum*** H.A. Wendland & Drude *15139*	
	E	*15139* Vanuatu *15139*
I	***Caryota no*** Becc. *23*	
	I	Indonesia - Kalimantan
	I	*14712* Malaysia - Sabah *14712*
	I	Malaysia - Sarawak
I	***Caryota rumphiana*** Mart. var. *oxyodonta* Becc. *14726*	
	I	*14726* Philippines (Luzon) *14726*
E	***Ceratolobus glaucescens*** Blume *11813*	
	E	*14828* Indonesia - Java *14828*
E	***Ceratolobus pseudoconcolor*** Dransf. *10571*	
	E	Indonesia - Java (west, 600-900 m, 2 locs)

10571

E		Indonesia - Sumatra (south)	*10571*

E **Ceroxylon alpinum** Bonpl. ex D.C. ssp. *alpinum* 20826

E	8743	Colombia (Cordillera Occidental)	*8743*
E	20826	Venezuela	*20826*

E **Ceroxylon alpinum** Bonpl. ex D.C. ssp. *ecuadorense* Galeano 20826

E	20826	Ecuador	*20826*

I **Ceroxylon quindiuense** (Karsten) H. Wendl. 8020

I	19436	Colombia (central Andes)	*8020*

E **Ceroxylon sasaimae** Galeano 20826

E	20826	Colombia	*20826*

V **Chamaedorea adscendens** (Dammer) Burret 8020

V	17615	Belize	*8020*
V	17615	Guatemala	*8020*

R **Chamaedorea allenii** L.H. Bailey 20883, 17615

I	14236	Costa Rica	*20826*
R	20883	Panama	*20883*
K	17615	Colombia	*14242*

E **Chamaedorea amabilis** H. Wendl. ex Dammer 11813

E	8743	Costa Rica	*8743*
E	15202	Panama	*14813*
E	15202	Colombia	*14813*

R **Chamaedorea angustisecta** Burret 20883, 17615

R	20883	Bolivia	*20883*
V	20883	Brazil	*20883*
R	20883	Peru	*20883*

E **Chamaedorea brachyclada** H. Wendl. 8020

E	14236	Costa Rica	*11997*
E	14236	Panama	*8020*

E **Chamaedorea brachypoda** Standley & Steyerm. 8020

E	15202	Guatemala	*8020*
E	20826	Honduras	*20826*

I **Chamaedorea carchensis** Standley & Steyerm. 8020

I	17615	Guatemala	*8020*
V	19850	Mexico - Chiapas	*20826*

R **Chamaedorea castillo-montii** D.R. Hodel 15202

R	15202	Guatemala	*15202*

E **Chamaedorea correae** D.R. Hodel & N.W. Uhl 14797

E	17615	Panama (Veragues, Cocle, Colon)	*14797*

R **Chamaedorea deckeriana** (Klotzsch) Hemsley 8020

V	15202	Costa Rica	*8020*
V	14236	Panama	*15202*
R	16853	Colombia	*16853*

I **Chamaedorea deneversiana** M.H. Grayum & D.R. Hodel 15202

I	15202	Panama	*15202*
I	20826	Ecuador	*20826*

I **Chamaedorea donnell-smithii** Dammer 8020

I	15202	Honduras	*8020*

V **Chamaedorea fractiflexa** D.R. Hodel & J.J. Castillo 15202

V	19848	Guatemala	*15202*
V	19848	Mexico - Chiapas	*15202*

R **Chamaedorea fragans** (R. & P.) C. Martius 20883

I	20883	Bolivia	*20883*
R	20883	Peru	*20883*

I **Chamaedorea geonomiformis** H. Wendl. 17615

V	15202	Belize	*8020*
I	20826	Costa Rica	*20826*
V	15202	Guatemala	*8020*
V	15202	Honduras	*8020*

V	19850	Mexico - Chiapas	*20826*
V	19850	Mexico - Oaxaca	*20826*
V	19850	Mexico - Veracruz	*20826*

E **Chamaedorea glaucifolia** H. Wendl. 8020

E	19850	Mexico - Chiapas	*8020*

V **Chamaedorea graminifolia** H. Wendl. 17615

V	17615	Belize	*15202*
V	17615	Costa Rica	*17615*
V	17615	Guatemala	*15202*
V	17615	Mexico	*15202*

R **Chamaedorea guntheriana** D.R. Hodel & N.W. Uhl 14797

R	15202	Panama	*14797*

V **Chamaedorea hooperiana** Hodel 17615

V	17615	Mexico - Veracruz	*20826*

R **Chamaedorea klotzschiana** H. Wendl. 8020

R	19850	Mexico - Veracruz	*20826*

I **Chamaedorea lehmannii** Burret 8020

I	15202	Guatemala	*8020*

R **Chamaedorea lucidifrons** L.H. Bailey 20883, 17615

R	20883	Panama	*20883*

E **Chamaedorea macrospadix** Oersted 8020

E	20826	Costa Rica	*8020*

V **Chamaedorea microphylla** Wendl. 20883, 17615

V	20883	Panama	*20883*

V **Chamaedorea microspadix** Burret 8020

V	19850	Mexico	*8020*

R **Chamaedorea murriensis** Galeano 9997

I	20826	Panama	*20826*
R	15202	Colombia	*20826*

R **Chamaedorea nationsiana** D.R. Hodel & J.J. Castillo 15202

R	15202	Guatemala	*15202*

V **Chamaedorea oreophila** C. Martius 8020

V	15202	Mexico - Oaxaca	*20826*
V	15202	Mexico - Veracruz	*20826*

V **Chamaedorea pachecoana** Standley & Steyerm. 8020

V	15202	Guatemala	*8020*

I **Chamaedorea palmeriana** D.R. Hodel & N.W. Uhl 15202

I	15202	Costa Rica	*15202*
I	15202	Panama	*15202*

I **Chamaedorea parvifolia** Burret 17615

I	17615	Costa Rica	*8020*

V **Chamaedorea pittieri** L.H. Bailey 20883, 17615

I	17615	Costa Rica	*16283*
V	20883	Panama	*20883*

V **Chamaedorea pochutlensis** Liebm. ex C. Martius 8020

V	19850	Mexico	*8020*

E **Chamaedorea pumila** H. Wendl. ex Dammer 17615

E	15202	Costa Rica	*8020*

I **Chamaedorea pygmaea** H. Wendl. 17615

V	17615	Costa Rica	*15202*
I	20826	Guatemala	*20826*
V	17615	Panama	*8020*
V	17615	Colombia	*8020*

V **Chamaedorea queroana** D.R. Hodel 15202

V	19850	Mexico - Oaxaca	*15202*

V **Chamaedorea radicalis** C. Martius 8020

V	15202	Mexico	*8020*

V **Chamaedorea rhizomatosa** D.R. Hodel 15202

V	19850	Mexico - Oaxaca	*15202*

V **Chamaedorea rigida** H. Wendl. ex Dammer 17615

	V	*19850* Mexico - Oaxaca *8020*	

I   *Chamaedorea robertii* D.R. Hodel & N.W. Uhl *15202*

    I   *15202* Costa Rica *15202*
    I   *15202* Panama *15202*

I   *Chamaedorea rojasiana* Standley & Steyerm. *8020*

    I   *15202* Guatemala *8020*
    V   *19850* Mexico - Chiapas *8020*

I   *Chamaedorea sartorii* Liebm. *8020*

    I   *15202* Honduras *8020*
    V   *19850* Mexico - Oaxaca *20826*
    V   *19850* Mexico - Puebla *20826*
    V   *19850* Mexico - Veracruz *20826*

E   *Chamaedorea scheryi* L.H. Bailey *20883, 8020*

    I   *15202* Costa Rica *15202*
    E   *20883* Panama *20883*

V   *Chamaedorea schiedeana* C. Martius *8020*

    V   *19850* Mexico - Oaxaca *20826*
    V   *19850* Mexico - Puebla *20826*
    V   *19850* Mexico - Veracruz *9114*

V   *Chamaedorea seifrizii* Burret *8020*

    V   *15202* Belize *15202*
    V   *15202* Guatemala *15202*
    V   *15202* Honduras *15202*
    V   *20826* Mexico - Campeche *20826*
    V   *20826* Mexico - Quintana Roo *20826*
    V   *15202* Mexico - Tabasco *9114*
    V   *15202* Mexico - Yucatan *9114*

V   *Chamaedorea selvae* Hodel *17615*

    V   *17615* Costa Rica *17615*
    V   *17615* Nicaragua *17615*

V   *Chamaedorea simplex* Burret *8020*

    E   *15202* Guatemala *8020*
    V   *20826* Mexico - Chiapas *20826*

V   *Chamaedorea smithii* A. Gentry *20883, 8801*

    I   *20883* Peru (Rondayacu Podocarp forests) *20883*

V   *Chamaedorea stolonifera* H. Wendl. ex Hook. *8020*

    V   *20826* Mexico - Chiapas *20826*

V   *Chamaedorea stricta* Standley & Steyerm. *8020*

    E   *15202* Costa Rica *15202*
    E   *15202* Guatemala *8020*
    V   *20826* Mexico - Chiapas *20826*
    V   *20826* Panama *20826*

E   *Chamaedorea sullivaniorum* D.R. Hodel & N.W. Uhl *14797*

    E   *15202* Costa Rica *15202*
    E   *15202* Panama *15202*
    E   *15202* Colombia *15202*

E   *Chamaedorea tenerrima* Burret *8020*

    E   *15202* Guatemala *8020*

E   *Chamaedorea tuerckheimii* (Dammer) Burret *8020*

    E   *15202* Guatemala *8020*
    E   *20826* Mexico - Oaxaca *20826*
    E   *15202* Mexico - Veracruz *9114*

E   *Chamaedorea undulatifolia* D.R. Hodel & N.W. Uhl *14798*

    E   *15202* Costa Rica (Puntarenas, Alajuela, Heredia, San Jose) *14798*

E   *Chamaedorea verecunda* Grayum & D.R. Hodel *14805*

    E   *14805* Panama (Chiriqui province) *14805*

I   *Chamaedorea volcanensis* D.R. Hodel & J.J. Castillo *15202*

    I   *15202* Guatemala *15202*

V   *Chamaedorea whitelockiana* D.R. Hodel & N.W. Uhl *14811*

	V	*20826* Mexico - Chiapas *20826*	
	V	*19850* Mexico - Oaxaca *14811*	

R   *Chambeyronia lepidota* H.E. Moore *10237*

    R   *20893* New Caledonia *10237*

R   *Chambeyronia macrocarpa* Vieill. ex Becc. *10238*

    R   *15184* New Caledonia *10238*

R   *Chelyocarpus chuco* (C. Martius) H. Moore *20883, 9996*

    R   *20883* Bolivia *20883*
    I   *20883* Brazil *20883*

R   *Chelyocarpus dianeurus* (Burret) H.E. Moore *11813*

    R   *16853* Colombia (west) *8743*

E   *Chelyocarpus repens* F. Kahn & K. Mejia *20883, 15155*

    I   *20883* Peru *20883*

E   *Chuniophoenix hainanensis* Burret *17617*

    E   *17617* China - Hainan Is. *11139*

E   *Chuniophoenix humilis* C.Z. Tang & T.L. Wu *11139*

    E   China - Hainan Is. *11139*

R   *Clinosperma bracteale* (Brongn.) Becc.

    R   *15184* New Caledonia *15184*

R   *Clinostigma exorrhizum* (H.A. Wendl.) Becc. *10253*

    R   *15184* Fiji (Viti Levu, Vanua Levu, Taveuni, Gau) *10253*

V   *Clinostigma haerestigma* H.E. Moore *15138*

    V   *15138* Solomon Is. - South (ultrabasic soils, southeast Ysabel) *15138*

R   *Clinostigma harlandii* Becc. *13954*

    R   *13954* Vanuatu (Vanua Lava, Espiritu Santo, Pentecost, Efate, Erromango, Aneityum (?)) *13954*

R   *Clinostigma samoense* Wendl. *15308*

    R   *17945* Western Samoa (Upolu) *15308*

R   *Clinostigma savoryana* (Rehder & Wils.) Moore & Fosb. *10237*

    R   *19134* Japan - Ogasawara-shoto *18128*

E   *Coccothrinax borhidiana* Muniz *5607*

    E   *19105* Cuba (Matanzas) *5607*

R   *Coccothrinax crinita* Becc. ssp. *brevicrinis* Borhidi & Muniz *9774*

    R   *19105* Cuba (Cienfuegos; S. Spiritus) *9774*

E   *Coccothrinax crinita* Becc. ssp. *crinita* *11813*

    E   *19105* Cuba (Pinar del Rio) *9774*

I   *Coccothrinax ekmanii* Burret *14799*

    I   *20826* Cuba *20826*
    I   Dominican Republic *8020*
    E/V *15199* Haiti *8020*

R   *Coccothrinax inaguensis* R.W. Read *8020*

    R   Bahamas *8766*
    E   *19105* Cuba *20826*
    R   Turks & Caicos Is. *8766*

I   *Coccothrinax miraguama* (Kunth) Leon *20826*

    I   *20990* Cuba *20826*
    I   *20826* Dominican Republic *20826*
    I   *20826* Haiti *20826*

R   *Coccothrinax pauciramosa* Burret *11813*

    R   *20826* Cuba *20826*

V   *Colpothrinax wrightii* Griseb. & H. Wendl. ex Siebert & Voss *9244*

    V   *19105* Cuba (Pinar del Rio; I. de Pines) *9774*

R   *Copernicia baileyana* León *9244*

    R   *20826* Cuba *9774*

R   *Copernicia brittonorum* León *9244*

R		*19105* Cuba (PR; M; Ci) *5607*

E   *Copernicia ekmanii* **Burret** *11813*

    E   *14799* Haiti (north-west) *8743*

R   *Copernicia gigas* **E.L. Ekman ex Burret** *9244*

    R   *19105* Cuba *5607*

R   *Copernicia hospita* **Mart.** *9244*

    R   *20826* Cuba *9774*

R   *Copernicia rigida* **Britton & Wilson** *9244*

    R   *20826* Cuba *9774*

R   *Corypha macropoda* **Kurz** *14782*

    R   *14782* India - Andaman Is. (south) *14782*

I   *Corypha microclada* **Becc.** *14726*

    I   *14726* Philippines (Biliran Is.) *14726*

Ex   *Corypha taliera* **Roxb.** *14827*

    Ex   *14827* India (Bengal) *14827*

R   *Corypha umbraculifera* **L.** *17661*

    R   *17661* India - Kerala (Malabar coast) *4988*
    R   *19614* Sri Lanka *17661*

E   *Cryosophila cookii* **Bartlett** *11813*

    E   *8743* Costa Rica *8743*

I   *Cryosophila grayumii* **R.Evans** *20826*

    I   *20826* Costa Rica *20826*

V   *Cryosophila guagara* **Allen** *8020*

    V   Costa Rica *8020*
    V   *21205* Panama *20826*

I   *Cryosophila kalbreyeri* **(Dammer ex Burret) Dahlgren** *11813*

    I   *20826* Panama *20826*
    I   *20826* Colombia (north-west) *8743*

V   *Cryosophila nana* **(Kunth) Blume ex Salomon** *8020*

    V   *19850* Mexico *8020*

V   *Cryosophila williamsii* **P.H. Allen** *8020*

    V   *19614* Honduras *8020*

R   *Cyphokentia macrostachya* **Brongn.** *10238*

    R   *15184* New Caledonia *10238*

V   *Cyphophoenix elegans* **(Brongn. & Gris) H. Wendl.** *10238*

    V   *20893* New Caledonia *10238*

E   *Cyphophoenix nucele* **H.E. Moore** *20893*

    E   *20893* New Caledonia (Loyalty Is.) *15184*

R   *Cyphosperma balansae* **(Brongn.) H. Wendl. ex Salomon** *10238*

    R   *15184* New Caledonia *10238*

V   *Cyphosperma tanga* **(H.E. Moore) H.E. Moore** *10253*

    V   *15184* Fiji (Viti Levu) *10253*

R   *Cyphosperma trichospadix* **(Burret) H.E. Moore** *10253*

    R   *15184* Fiji (Vanua Levu & Taveuni) *10253*

R   *Cyphosperma voutmelensis* **J. Dowe** *15184*

    R   *19614* Vanuatu *15184*

R   *Cyrtostachys kisu* **Beccari** *15138*

    R   *17945* Solomon Is. - South *15138*

I   *Daemonorops affinis* **Becc.** *14726*

    I   *14726* Philippines (Mindanao) *14726*

I   *Daemonorops clemensiana* **Becc.** *14726*

    I   *14726* Philippines (Mindanao) *14726*

I   *Daemonorops curranii* **Becc.** *14726*

    I   *14726* Philippines (low altitude) *13833*

I   *Daemonorops gracilis* **Becc.** *14726*

    I   *14726* Philippines (low altitude) *13833*

R   *Daemonorops leptopus* **(Griff.) Mart.** *10259*

    V   Malaysia - Peninsular Malaysia (Terengganu, Pahang, Melaka, Negeri Sembilan, Johor) *10259*
    R   *20099* Singapore *20099*

I   *Daemonorops loheriana* **Becc.** *14726*

    I   *14726* Philippines (Luzon) *14726*

R   *Daemonorops longispathus* **Becc.** *15313*

    R   *15313* Vietnam *15313*

V   *Daemonorops macrophylla* **Becc.** *10259*

    V   Malaysia - Peninsular Malaysia *10259*

R   *Daemonorops manii* **Becc.** *10235*

    R   India - Andaman Is. *10235*

I   *Daemonorops margaritae* **(Hance) Becc. var. palawanicus** **Becc.** *13833*

    I   *13833* Philippines *13833*

E   *Daemonorops oligophylla* **Becc.** *10259*

    E   *14701* Malaysia - Peninsular Malaysia (Perak, type loc. only) *10259*

I   *Daemonorops pannosa* **Becc.** *14726*

    I   *14726* Philippines (Leyte) *14726*

V   *Daemonorops sepal* **Becc.** *10259*

    V   Malaysia - Peninsular Malaysia *10259*

E   *Daemonorops unijuga* **Dransf.** *14703*

    E   *14703* Malaysia - Sarawak *14703*

I   *Daemonorops urdanetana* **Becc.** *14726*

    I   *14726* Philippines (Mindanao) *14726*

V   *Deckenia nobilis* **H.A. Wendl.** *14296*

    V   Seychelles (granitic) *14296*

R   *Desmoncus cirrhiperus* **Gentry & Zardini** *16853*

    R   *16853* Colombia *16853*

E   *Desmoncus latisectus* **Burret** *20883, 8020*

    E   *20883* Bolivia *20883*

R   *Desmoncus mitis* var. *leptoclonos* **Henderson** *20883*

    V   *20883* Bolivia *20883*
    R   *20883* Brazil *20883*

R   *Desmoncus mitis* var. *leptospadix* **(Mart.) Henderson** *20883*

    I   *20883* Bolivia *20883*
    I   *20883* Brazil *20883*
    E   *20883* Colombia *20883*
    R   *20883* Peru *20883*

R   *Desmoncus mitis* var. *rurrenabaquensis* **Henderson** *20883*

    R   *20883* Bolivia *20883*
    R   *20883* Peru *20883*

R   *Desmoncus polyacanthos* var. *prunifer* **(Mart.) Henderson** *20883*

    V   *20883* Colombia *20883*
    V   *20883* Ecuador *20883*
    R   *20883* Peru *20883*

R   *Desmoncus stans* **Grayum & de Nevers** *11992*

    R   *11992* Costa Rica *11992*

R   *Dictyocaryum fuscum* **(Karsten) H. A. Wendland** *20883, 8020*

    I   *20883* Venezuela *20883*

E   *Dictyosperma album* **(Bory) H.Wendl. & Drude ex Scheffer var. album** *10082*

    E   *10082* Réunion *10082*
    E   *20771* Mauritius *10082*

E   *Dictyosperma album* **(Bory) H.Wendl. & Drude ex Scheffer**

	var. *aureum* Balf.f. *10082*
E	5852 Mauritius - Rodrigues *5852*

E	*Dictyosperma album* (Bory) Wendl. & Drude ex Scheff. var. *conjugatum* Moore & Guého *10082*
E	20771 Mauritius (Round Is.) *10598*

R	*Drymophloeus lepidotus* H.E. Moore *15138*
R	17945 Solomon Is. - South *15138*

E	*Drymophloeus oliviformis* (Giseke) Miq. *14828*
E	14828 Indonesia - Moluccas *14828*

R	*Drymophloeus pachycladus* (Burret) H.E. Moore *15138*
R	17945 Solomon Is. - South (Makira) *15138*

R	*Drymophloeus samoensis* *17945*
R	17945 Western Samoa *17945*

R	*Drymophloeus subdistichus* (H.E. Moore) H.E. Moore *15138*
R	15138 Solomon Is. - South *15138*

Ex/E	*Dypsis acaulis* J. Dransf. *20071*
Ex/E	20071 Madagascar (Masoala Peninsula) *20071*

Ex/E	*Dypsis ambanjae* Beentje *20071*
Ex/E	20071 Madagascar (Sambirano River) *20071*

E	*Dypsis ambilaensis* J. Dransf. *20071*
E	20071 Madagascar *20071*

E	*Dypsis ambositrae* Beentje *20071*
E	20071 Madagascar (near Ambositra) *20071*

E	*Dypsis ampasindavae* Beentje *20071*
E	20071 Madagascar (Nosy Be; Manongarivo Mts) *20071*

R	*Dypsis andapae* Beentje *20071*
R	20071 Madagascar *20071*

R	*Dypsis andrianatonga* Beentje *20071*
R	20071 Madagascar *20071*

E	*Dypsis angusta* Jum. *10246*
E	20071 Madagascar *20071*

E	*Dypsis angustifolia* (H. Perrier) Beentje & J. Dransf. *10246*
E	20071 Madagascar (Betampona) *20071*

Ex/E	*Dypsis anovensis* J. Dransf. *20071*
Ex/E	20071 Madagascar (Anove River) *20071*

E	*Dypsis antanambensis* Beentje *20071*
E	20071 Madagascar (Mananara Avaratra) *20071*

I	*Dypsis aquatilis* Beentje *20071*
I	20071 Madagascar (Manantenina) *20071*

E	*Dypsis arenarum* (Jum.) Beentje & J. Dransf. *20071*
E	20071 Madagascar *20071*

E	*Dypsis basilonga* (Jum. & H. Perrier) Beentje & J. Dransf. *20071*
E	20071 Madagascar (Vatovavy) *20071*

E	*Dypsis beentjei* J. Dransf. *20071*
E	20071 Madagascar (east coast) *20071*

E	*Dypsis bejofo* Beentje *20071*
E	20071 Madagascar *20071*

V	*Dypsis bernierana* (Baill.) Beentje & J. Dransf. *20071*
V	20071 Madagascar *20071*

Ex/E	*Dypsis betamponensis* (Jum.) Beentje & J. Dransf. *20071*
Ex/E	20071 Madagascar (Betampona) *20071*

E	*Dypsis boiviniana* Baill. *10246*
E	20071 Madagascar *20071*

V	*Dypsis bonsai* Beentje *20071*
V	20071 Madagascar *20071*

Ex/E	*Dypsis bosseri* J. Dransf. *20071*
Ex/E	20071 Madagascar *20071*

E	*Dypsis brevicaulis* (Guillaumet) Beentje & J. Dransf. *20071*
E	20071 Madagascar (east coast) *20071*

Ex/E	*Dypsis canaliculata* (Jum.) Beentje & Dransf. *20071*
Ex/E	20071 Madagascar *20071*

Ex/E	*Dypsis canescens* (Jum. & Perrier) Beentje & J. Dransf. *20071*
Ex/E	20071 Madagascar (north west) *20071*

E	*Dypsis caudata* Beentje *20071*
E	20071 Madagascar (Masoala Peninsula) *20071*

Ex/E	*Dypsis ceracea* (Jum.) Beentje & J. Dransf. *20071*
Ex/E	20071 Madagascar (Marojejy, Betampona) *20071*

E	*Dypsis commersoniana* (Baill.) Beentje & J. Dransf. *20071*
E	20071 Madagascar (south east) *20071*

V	*Dypsis concinna* Baker *20071*
V	20071 Madagascar *20071*

V	*Dypsis confusa* Beentje *20071*
V	20071 Madagascar *20071*

E	*Dypsis cookei* J. Dransf. *20071*
E	20071 Madagascar (Marojejy) *20071*

V	*Dypsis coriacea* Beentje *20071*
V	20071 Madagascar *20071*

V	*Dypsis corniculata* (Becc.) Beentje & J. Dransf. *20071*
V	20071 Madagascar *20071*

V	*Dypsis coursii* Beentje *20071*
V	20071 Madagascar (Marojejy area) *20071*

R	*Dypsis crinita* (Jum. & H. Perrier) Beentje & J. Dransf. *20071*
R	20071 Madagascar *20071*

I	*Dypsis curtisii* Baker *20071*
I	20071 Madagascar *20071*

V	II *Dypsis decaryi* (Jum.) Beentje & J. Dransf. *20071*
V	20071 Madagascar (south) *20071*

E	II *Dypsis decipiens* (Becc.) Beentje & J. Dransf. *20071*
E	20071 Madagascar *20071*

E	*Dypsis digitata* (Becc.) Beentje & J.dransf. *20071*
E	20071 Madagascar *20071*

E	*Dypsis dransfieldii* Beentje *20071*
E	20071 Madagascar (Masoala Peninsula) *20071*

E	*Dypsis elegans* Beentje *20071*
E	20071 Madagascar (Manombo forest) *20071*

E	*Dypsis eriostachys* J. Dransf. *20071*
E	20071 Madagascar (Vatovavy) *20071*

E	*Dypsis faneva* Beentje *20071*
E	20071 Madagascar *20071*

E	*Dypsis fanjana* Beentje *20071*
E	20071 Madagascar (Mananara) *20071*

V	*Dypsis fasciculata* Jum. *10246*
V	20071 Madagascar *20071*

Ex/E	*Dypsis furcata* J. Dransf. *20071*
Ex/E	20071 Madagascar (central east coast) *20071*

E	*Dypsis glabrescens* (Becc.) Becc. *10246*

E   *2007I*   Madagascar *2007I*

I   *Dypsis heteromorpha* (Jum.) Beentje & J. Dransf. *2007I*

   I   *2007I*   Madagascar *2007I*

R   *Dypsis heterophylla* Baker *2007I*

   R   *2007I*   Madagascar *2007I*

V   *Dypsis hiarakae* Beentje *2007I*

   V   *2007I*   Madagascar *2007I*

V   *Dypsis hildebrandtii* Becc. *10246*

   V   *2007I*   Madagascar (central) *2007I*

E   *Dypsis hovomantsina* Beentje *2007I*

   E   *2007I*   Madagascar (Marojejy, Betampona) *2007I*

I   *Dypsis humbertii* (Jum.) Beentje & J. Dransf. *2007I*

   I   *2007I*   Madagascar (south east) *2007I*

E   *Dypsis ifanadianae* Beentje *2007I*

   E   *2007I*   Madagascar (Ifanadiana) *2007I*

E   *Dypsis integra* (Jum.) Beentje & J. Dransf. *2007I*

   E   *2007I*   Madagascar *2007I*

E   *Dypsis intermedia* Beentje *2007I*

   E   *2007I*   Madagascar (Manombo) *2007I*

E   *Dypsis interrupta* J. Dransf. *2007I*

   E   *2007I*   Madagascar *2007I*

V   *Dypsis jumelleana* Beentje & J. Dransf. *2007I*

   V   *2007I*   Madagascar *2007I*

E   *Dypsis laevis* J. Dransf. *2007I*

   E   *2007I*   Madagascar *2007I*

I   *Dypsis lanceolata* (Becc.) Beentje & J. Dransf. *2007I*

   I   *2007I*   Comoros (Grand Comore, Moheli) *2007I*

V   *Dypsis lantzeana* Baill. *10246*

   V   *2007I*   Madagascar (north-east) *2007I*

Ex/E   *Dypsis lanuginosa* J. Dransf. *2007I*

   Ex/E   *2007I*   Madagascar (Lower Mangoro) *2007I*

Ex/E   *Dypsis ligulata* (Jum.) Beentje & J. Dransf. *2007I*

   Ex/E   *2007I*   Madagascar (north west) *2007I*

V   *Dypsis lokohoensis* J. Dransf. *2007I*

   V   *2007I*   Madagascar (Marojejy) *2007I*

V   *Dypsis louvelii* Jum. & H. Perrier *11813*

   V   *2007I*   Madagascar (Analamazoatra) *2007I*

Ex/E   *Dypsis lucens* (Jum.) Beentje & J. Dransf. *2007I*

   Ex/E   *2007I*   Madagascar (Antongil Bay) *2007I*

E   *Dypsis lutea* (Jum.) Beentje & J. Dransf. *2007I*

   E   *2007I*   Madagascar (Masoala and Moramanga) *2007I*

R   *Dypsis madagascariensis* (Becc.) Beentje & J. Dransf. *2007I*

   R   *2007I*   Madagascar (north-west and west) *2007I*

E   *Dypsis mahia* Beentje *2007I*

   E   *2007I*   Madagascar (Manombo) *2007I*

V   *Dypsis malcomberi* Beentje *2007I*

   V   *2007I*   Madagascar (Andohahela) *2007I*

V   *Dypsis mananjarensis* (Jum. & H. Perrier) Beentje & J. Dransf. *2007I*

   V   *2007I*   Madagascar *2007I*

E   *Dypsis mangorensis* (Jum.) Beentje & J. Dransf. *2007I*

   E   *2007I*   Madagascar (Mananara) *2007I*

V   *Dypsis marojejyi* Beentje *2007I*

   V   *2007I*   Madagascar (Marojejy massif) *2007I*

V   *Dypsis mcdonaldiana* Beentje *2007I*

   V   *2007I*   Madagascar (south-east) *2007I*

V   *Dypsis minuta* Beentje *2007I*

   V   *2007I*   Madagascar (Masoala & Maroantsetra) *2007I*

E   *Dypsis mirabilis* J. Dransf. *2007I*

   E   *2007I*   Madagascar (Marojejy) *2007I*

V   *Dypsis mocquerysiana* Becc. *11813*

   V   *17951*   Madagascar *2007I*

Ex/E   *Dypsis monostachya* Jum. *10246*

   Ex/E   *2007I*   Madagascar *2007I*

E   *Dypsis moorei* Beentje *2007I*

   E   *2007I*   Madagascar (Masoala peninsula) *2007I*

E   *Dypsis nauseosa* (Jum. & H. Perrier) Beentje & J. Dransf. *2007I*

   E   *2007I*   Madagascar (coast of Fianarantsoa) *2007I*

E   *Dypsis nossibensis* (Becc.) Beentje & J. Dransf. *2007I*

   E   *2007I*   Madagascar (Lokobe forest) *2007I*

V   *Dypsis onilahensis* (Jum. & H. Perrier) Beentje & J. Dransf. *2007I*

   V   *2007I*   Madagascar *2007I*

V   *Dypsis oreophila* Beentje *2007I*

   V   *2007I*   Madagascar *2007I*

E   *Dypsis oropedionis* Beentje *2007I*

   E   *2007I*   Madagascar *2007I*

E   *Dypsis ovobontsira* Beentje *2007I*

   E   *2007I*   Madagascar (Mananara) *2007I*

V   *Dypsis pachyramea* J. Dransf. *2007I*

   V   *2007I*   Madagascar (Masoala Peninsula) *2007I*

V   *Dypsis paludosa* J. Dransf. *2007I*

   V   *2007I*   Madagascar (east coast) *2007I*

V   *Dypsis pembana* (Moore) Beentje & J. Dransf. *2007I*

   V   *2007I*   Tanzania (Pemba) *2007I*

V   *Dypsis perrieri* (Jum.) Beentje & J. Dransf. *2007I*

   V   *2007I*   Madagascar *2007I*

Ex/E   *Dypsis pervillei* (Jum.) Beentje & J. Dransf. *2007I*

   Ex/E   *2007I*   Madagascar (Betampona) *2007I*

V   *Dypsis pilulifera* (Becc.) Beentje & J. Dransf. *2007I*

   V   *2007I*   Madagascar *2007I*

Ex/E   *Dypsis plurisecta* Jum. *10246*

   Ex/E   *2007I*   Madagascar *2007I*

E   *Dypsis poivreana* (Baill.) Beentje & J. Dransf. *2007I*

   E   *2007I*   Madagascar (coastal Fenoarivo) *2007I*

V   *Dypsis prestoniana* Beentje *2007I*

   V   *2007I*   Madagascar (Midongy; Mahanoro) *2007I*

V   *Dypsis procera* Jum. *10246*

   V   *17951*   Madagascar (Antongil) *2007I*

E   *Dypsis psammophila* Beentje *2007I*

   E   *2007I*   Madagascar *2007I*

Ex/E   *Dypsis pulchella* J. Dransf. *2007I*

   Ex/E   *2007I*   Madagascar *2007I*

V   *Dypsis pumila* Beentje *2007I*

   V   *2007I*   Madagascar (Marojejy Mts) *2007I*

V   *Dypsis pusilla* Beentje *2007I*

   V   *2007I*   Madagascar *2007I*

E   *Dypsis ramentacea* J. Dransf. *2007I*

   E   *2007I*   Madagascar (Mananara, Antanambe) *2007I*

Ex/E   *Dypsis remotiflora* J. Dransf. *2007I*

   Ex/E   *2007I*   Madagascar (east) *2007I*

V	*Dypsis rivularis* (Jum. & H. Perrier) Beentje & J. Dransf. *20071*		
	V	*20071*	Madagascar *20071*
E	*Dypsis sahanofensis* (Jum. & H. Perrier) Beentje & J. Dransf. *20071*		
	E	*20071*	Madagascar *20071*
E	*Dypsis saintelucei* Beentje *20071*		
	E	*20071*	Madagascar (Sainte-Luce forest) *20071*
E	*Dypsis sanctaemariae* J. Dransf. *20071*		
	E	*20071*	Madagascar (Sainte-Marie Is.) *20071*
E	*Dypsis scandens* J. Dransf. *20071*		
	E	*20071*	Madagascar (Ifanadiana) *20071*
V	*Dypsis schatzii* Beentje *20071*		
	V	*20071*	Madagascar (Betampona) *20071*
V	*Dypsis scottiana* (Jum.) Beentje & J. Dransf. *20071*		
	V	*20071*	Madagascar (south-east) *20071*
V	*Dypsis serpentina* Beentje *20071*		
	V	*20071*	Madagascar (Mananara) *20071*
E	*Dypsis simianensis* (Jum.) Beentje & J. Dransf. *20071*		
	E	*20071*	Madagascar *20071*
E	*Dypsis singularis* Beentje *20071*		
	E	*20071*	Madagascar (Manombo forest) *20071*
Ex/E	*Dypsis soanieranae* Beentje *20071*		
	Ex/E	*20071*	Madagascar (Soanierana-Ivongo) *20071*
R	*Dypsis spicata* J. Dransf. *20071*		
	R	*20071*	Madagascar (Marojejy) *20071*
Ex/E	*Dypsis tanalensis* (Jum. & H. Perrier) Beentje & J. Dransf. *20071*		
	Ex/E	*20071*	Madagascar (Vohipeno) *20071*
E	*Dypsis tenuissima* Beentje *20071*		
	E	*20071*	Madagascar (Andohahela) *20071*
R	*Dypsis thermarum* J. Dransf. *20071*		
	R	*20071*	Madagascar (Ranomafana) *20071*
R	*Dypsis thiryana* (Jum.) Beentje & J. Dransf. *20071*		
	R	*20071*	Madagascar *20071*
E	*Dypsis tokoravina* Beentje *20071*		
	E	*20071*	Madagascar *20071*
E	*Dypsis trapezoidea* J. Dransf. *20071*		
	E	*20071*	Madagascar (Vatovavy, Ifanadiana) *20071*
I	*Dypsis tsaratananensis* (Jum.) Beentje & J. Dransf. *20071*		
	I	*20071*	Madagascar (Mt Tsaratanana) *20071*
E	*Dypsis tsaravotsira* Beentje *20071*		
	E	*20071*	Madagascar *20071*
V	*Dypsis utilis* (Jum.) Beentje & J. Dransf. *20071*		
	V	*20071*	Madagascar (east) *20071*
V	*Dypsis viridis* Jum. *10246*		
	V	*20071*	Madagascar *20071*
V	*Dypsis zahamenae* J. Dransf. *20071*		
	V	*20071*	Madagascar (Zahamena Reserve) *20071*
R	*Eugeissona brachystachys* Ridley *17749*		
	R		Malaysia - Peninsular Malaysia *10249*
E	*Euterpe andicola* Brongn. ex C. Martius *20883, 8020*		
	E	20883	Bolivia *20883*
R	*Euterpe catinga* A.R. Wallace *8020*		
	R	*19614*	Brazil *8020*
	I	*16853*	Colombia *8020*
	R	*19614*	Peru *17955*
R	*Euterpe edulis* Mart. *20883, 14840*		

	R	*20883*	Argentina (Iguazu NP) *20883*
	E	*20176*	Argentina - Misiones *20176*
	I	*20883*	Brazil *20883*
	V	*15148*	Brazil - Espirito Santo *15148*
	?		Brazil - Rio Grande do Sul *20311*
	?		Brazil - Santa Catarina *20310*
	R	*20883*	Paraguay *20883*
E	*Euterpe haenkeana* Brongn. ex C. Martius *20883, 8020*		
	E	*20883*	Bolivia *20883*
E	*Euterpe longevaginata* C. Martius *20883, 8020*		
	E	*20883*	Bolivia *20883*
V	*Euterpe luminosa* Henderson, Galeano & Meza *19698*		
	V	*19698*	Peru *19698*
E	*Gaussia attenuata* (O.F. Cook) Becc. *20883, 9148*		
	I	*20883*	Puerto Rico *20883*
E	*Gaussia gomez-pompae* (Quero) Quero *20883, 10260*		
	I	*20883*	Mexico *20883*
	V	*19850*	Mexico - Oaxaca *9148*
	V	*19850*	Mexico - Tabasco *9148*
	V	*19850*	Mexico - Veracruz *9148*
V	*Gaussia maya* (Cook) Quero & R. W. Read *20883, 17616*		
	I	*20883*	Belize *20883*
	E	*20883*	Guatemala *20883*
	I	*20883*	Mexico *20883*
	I	*17616*	Mexico - Oaxaca *17616*
	I	*17616*	Mexico - Quintana Roo *17616*
	I	*17616*	Mexico - Veracruz *17616*
R	*Gaussia spirituana* Moya & Leiva *19625*		
	R	*19625*	Cuba *19625*
V	*Geonoma andicola* Dammer ex Burret *19698*		
	V	*19698*	Peru *19698*
R	*Geonoma arundinacea* Mart. *20883, 8020*		
	V	*20883*	Brazil *20883*
	V	*20883*	Colombia *20883*
	V	*20883*	Ecuador *20883*
	R	*20883*	Peru *20883*
R	*Geonoma brevispatha* var. *occidentale* Henderson *20883*		
	V	*20883*	Bolivia *20883*
	V	*20883*	Brazil *20883*
	V	*20883*	Peru *20883*
E	*Geonoma chlamydostachys* Galeano *10740*		
	E	*16853*	Colombia (S.E. Antioquia, 300-1000 m) *10740*
R	*Geonoma congesta* H. Wendl. ex Spruce *8020*		
	V		Costa Rica *8020*
	I	*20826*	Honduras *20826*
	R		Nicaragua *8020*
	V		Panama *8020*
	I	*16853*	Colombia *20826*
R	*Geonoma divisa* H.E. Moore *9149*		
	R	*20826*	Panama *20826*
	R	*16853*	Colombia (Choco) *9149*
V	*Geonoma gamiova* Barb. Rodr. *8020*		
	V	*19614*	Brazil (Atlantic forest) *8743*
R	*Geonoma longepedunculata* Burret *20883*		
	R	*20883*	Colombia *20883*
	R	*20883*	Ecuador *20883*
	R	*20883*	Peru *20883*
R	*Geonoma megalospatha* Burret *20883, 8020*		
	V	*20883*	Bolivia *20883*
	I	*20883*	Ecuador *20883*
	I	*20883*	Peru *20883*
V	*Geonoma membranacea* H. Wendl. ex Spruce *8020*		
	V		Guatemala *8020*

V   *19850* Mexico *19850*

V   *Geonoma myriantha* Dammer *20883*
- V   *20883* Brazil *20883*

R   *Geonoma oldemannii* Granv. *8793*
- I   *20826* Brazil (East Amazonia) *20826*
- R   French Guiana *8777*

E   *Geonoma orbignyana* C. Martius *20883, 8020*
- E   *20883* Bolivia *20883*

R   *Geonoma pachydicrana* Burret *20883, 8020*
- E   *20883* Bolivia *20883*
- I   *20883* Colombia *20883*

I   *Geonoma paradoxa* Burret *8020*
- I   *16853* Colombia *8020*

R   *Geonoma paraguanensis* H.Karst. *8020*
- R   Venezuela *8020*

V   *Geonoma pauciflora* Mart. *8020*
- V   *19614* Brazil *8020*

V   *Geonoma pohliana* Mart. *8020*
- V   *19614* Brazil *8020*

V   *Geonoma polyandra* Skov *20883*
- E   *20883* Colombia *20883*
- V   *20883* Ecuador *20883*

I   *Geonoma pulchra* F. Engel *8020*
- I   *16853* Colombia *8020*

R   *Geonoma rubescens* H. Wendl. ex Drude *8020*
- R   *20826* Brazil (Atlantic forest) *8743*

R   *Geonoma scoparia* Grayum & de Nevers *11992*
- R   *11992* Costa Rica *11992*

I   *Geonoma tenuissima* H.E. Moore *10739*
- I   *20826* Ecuador (Los Rios Province) *10739*

E   *Geonoma trigona* (Ruíz & Pavón) A. Gentry *20883, 8801*
- V   *19698* Peru (Pasco, 2800-3000 m) *20883*

R   *Geonoma umbraculiformis* Wess. Boer *20883, 8777*
- V   *20883* Brazil *20883*
- R   *20883* French Guiana (3 locs, montane forest) *20883*
- E   *20883* Guyana *20883*
- E   *20883* Suriname *20883*

V   *Guihaia argyrata* (Lee & Wei) Lee, Wei & J. Dransf. *15144*
- V   *19614* China *15144*

V   *Guihaia grossefibrosa* (Gagnep) J. Dransf., S.K. Lee & F. n Wei *13955*
- I   *20985* Vietnam *13955*

R   *Gulubia hombronii* Becc. *11179*
- R   *17945* Solomon Is. - South *11179*

R   *Gulubia microcarpa* Essig *11179*
- R   *15184* Fiji (near Ngaloa, Viti Levu) *11179*

V   *Hedyscepe canterburyana* (C. Moore & F. Muell.) H. Wendl. *15166*
- V   *15166* Australia - NSW - Lord Howe Is. *15166*

I   *Heterospathe elmeri* Becc. *16067*
- I   *14726* Philippines (Camiguin) *14726*

R   *Heterospathe minor* Burret *15138*
- R   *17945* Solomon Is. - South *15138*

R   *Heterospathe woodfordiana* Beccari *15138*
- R   *17945* Solomon Is. - South *15138*

R   *Howea belmoreana* (C. Moore & F. Muell.) Becc. *15166*
- R   *15166* Australia - NSW - Lord Howe Is. *15166*

R   *Howea forsteriana* (C. Moore & F. Muell.) Becc. *15166*

R   *15166* Australia - NSW - Lord Howe Is. *15166*

E   *Hyophorbe amaricaulis* Martius *10082*
- E   *20771* Mauritius *10082*

V   *Hyophorbe indica* Gaertner *10082*
- V   *2014* Réunion *6165*

E   *Hyophorbe lagenicaulis* (L. Bailey) H.E. Moore *10082*
- E   *20771* Mauritius (Round Is.) *6165*

E   *Hyophorbe vaughanii* L. Bailey *10082*
- E   *20771* Mauritius *6165*

E   *Hyophorbe verschaffeltii* H.A. Wendl. *10082*
- E   *5852* Mauritius - Rodrigues *5852*

V   *Hyospathe concinna* H. Moore *20883, 16853*
- V   *20883* Panama *20883*
- I   *16853* Colombia *16853*

V   *Hyphaene dichotoma* (White) Furt. *17661*
- V   *17661* India - Gujarat *4988*
- V   *17661* India - Maharashtra *4988*

R   *Hyphaene obovata* Furt. *10288*
- R   Mozambique *10288*

V   *Iguanura ambigua* Becc. *10291*
- V   *14703* Malaysia - Sarawak (G. Mattang) *10291*

R   *Iguanura bicornis* Becc. *10291*
- R   Thailand *10291*
- E/V   Malaysia - Peninsular Malaysia *10291*

E   *Iguanura chaiana* Kiew *10292*
- E   *14703* Malaysia - Sarawak *10292*

E   *Iguanura corniculata* Becc. *10291*
- E   *14701* Malaysia - Peninsular Malaysia *10291*

R   *Iguanura curvata* Kiew *10292*
- R   *14703* Malaysia - Sarawak *10292*

V   *Iguanura elegans* Becc. *10291*
- V   *14703* Malaysia - Sarawak *10291*

E   *Iguanura leucocarpa* Blume *10291*
- E   *14828* Indonesia - Sumatra (Padang and Palembang) *10291*

V   *Iguanura melinauensis* Kiew *10291*
- V   *14703* Malaysia - Sarawak *10291*

V   *Iguanura minor* Kiew *10291*
- V   *14703* Malaysia - Sarawak *10291*

V   *Iguanura myochodoides* Kiew *10291*
- V   *14703* Malaysia - Sarawak *10291*

V   *Iguanura palmuncula* Becc. var. *magna* Kiew *14703*
- V   *14703* Malaysia - Sarawak *14703*

V   *Iguanura palmuncula* Becc. var. *palmuncula* *10291*
- V   *14703* Malaysia - Sarawak *10291*

R   *Iguanura polymorpha* Becc. *10291*
- R   Thailand (south) *10292*
- V   Malaysia - Peninsular Malaysia (Johor, Perak, Terengganu) *19209*
- V   *14703* Malaysia - Sarawak *10291*

V   *Iguanura remotiflora* H. Wendl. *10291*
- V   *14703* Malaysia - Sarawak *10291*

V   *Iguanura sanderiana* Ridley *10291*
- V   *14703* Malaysia - Sarawak *10291*

R   *Itaya amicorum* H.E. Moore *2014, 20883*
- R   *19614* Brazil (Rio Javari) *8743*
- E   *20883* Colombia *20883*
- R   *19614* Peru (Loreto) *8743*

V   *Johannesteijsmannia altifrons* (Reichb. f. & Zoll.) H.E.
Moore *10293*
   V   Thailand *8794*
   V   *14828* Indonesia - Sumatra *23*
   V   Malaysia - Peninsular Malaysia (Johor) *19209*
   V   *14703* Malaysia - Sarawak *23*

E   *Johannesteijsmannia lanceolata* Dransf. *10293*
   E   *14701* Malaysia - Peninsular Malaysia *10293*

E   *Johannesteijsmannia magnifica* Dransf. *10293*
   E   *14701* Malaysia - Peninsular Malaysia *10293*

V   *Johannesteijsmannia perakensis* Dransf. *10293*
   V   Malaysia - Peninsular Malaysia *10293*

R   *Juania australis* (Mart.) Drude ex Hook. f. *20883, 14807*
   V   *19125* Chile - Juan Fernandez Is. *19116*
   R   *20883* Chile *20883*

V   *Jubaea chilensis* (Mol.) Baillon *20883, 11813, 20171*
   V   *20883* Chile *20883*

V   *Jubaeopsis caffra* Becc. *20604, 14801*
   V   *20604* South Africa - Cape Province (Mkambati reserve) *20604*

E   *Kentiopsis oliviformis* (Brongn. & Gris)
Brongn. *11813*
   E   *20893* New Caledonia *10238*

R   *Kerriodoxa elegans* Dransf. *11388*
   R   *19037* Thailand (Thalang, Phuket; Khao Sok) *11388*

V   *Korthalsia junghuhnii* Miq. *10670*
   V   Indonesia - Java *10670*

V   *Korthalsia lanceolata* Dransf. *10259*
   V   *14701* Malaysia - Peninsular Malaysia *10259*

I   *Korthalsia merrillii* Becc. *10670*
   I   *13833* Philippines *10670*

R   *Korthalsia rogersii* Becc. *10670*
   R   *14782* India - Andaman Is. (type coll. only, 1904) *10670*

I   *Korthalsia squamosa* Becc. *13833*
   I   *13833* Philippines (low altitude) *13833*

V   *Korthalsia tenuissima* Becc. *10259*
   V   *14701* Malaysia - Peninsular Malaysia *10259*

E   *Latania loddigesii* Martius *10082*
   E   *20771* Mauritius *6165*

E   *Latania lontaroides* (Gaertner) H.E. Moore *10082*
   E   *2014* Réunion *6165*

V   *Latania verschaffeltii* Lemaire *10082*
   V   *5825* Mauritius - Rodrigues *5852*

E   *Lavoixia macrocarpa* H.E. Moore *11813*
   E   *15184* New Caledonia *15184*

E   *Lemurophoenix halleuxii* J. Dransf. *14788*
   E   *17951* Madagascar (Sahavary, Masoala) *20071*

R   *Leopoldinia major* Wallace *20883, 8020*
   V   *20883* Brazil *20883*
   E   *20883* Colombia *20883*
   R   *20883* Venezuela (south (Amazonas)) *20883*

R   *Leopoldinia piassaba* Wallace *20883, 8020*
   E   *20883* Brazil *20883*
   E   *20883* Colombia *20883*
   V   *20883* Venezuela *20883*

R   *Lepidocaryum tenue* var. *casiquiarense* (Spruce)
Henderson *20883*

   V   *20883* Brazil *20883*
   V   *20883* Colombia *20883*
   V   *20883* Venezuela *20883*

R   *Lepidocaryum tenue* var. *gracile* (Mart.)
Henderson *20883*
   R   *20883* Brazil *20883*
   E   *20883* Guyana *20883*

V   *Lepidorrhachis mooreana* (F. Muell.) Cook *14223*
   V   *19614* Australia - NSW - Lord Howe Is. *14223*

R   *Licuala acutifida* Mart. *10249*
   R   Malaysia - Peninsular Malaysia (Penang) *10249*
   I   Singapore *7956*

R   *Licuala cabalionii* J. Dowe *15184*
   R   *15184* Vanuatu *15184*

V   *Licuala calciphila* Becc. *13955*
   V   *15313* Vietnam *13955*

V   *Licuala confusa* Furtado *10249*
   V   Malaysia - Peninsular Malaysia *10249*

E   *Licuala corneri* Furt. *10249*
   E   *14701* Malaysia - Peninsular Malaysia *10249*

R   *Licuala dransfieldii* R. Kiew *10260*
   R   *14701* Malaysia - Peninsular Malaysia (Ulu Endau area in Johore) *14701*

R   *Licuala fatua* Becc. *13955*
   R   *15313* Vietnam *13955*

R   *Licuala glaberrima* Gagnepain *10260*
   R   Vietnam *6057*

R   *Licuala gracilis* Blume *10238*
   R   Indonesia - Java *10238*

E   *Licuala hallieriana* Becc. *14703*
   E   *14703* Malaysia - Sarawak *14703*

V   *Licuala hexasepala* Gagnep *13955*
   V   *15313* Vietnam (Quang Nam-Da Nang, Khanh Hoa) *13955*

E   *Licuala kemamanensis* Furt. *10249*
   E   *14701* Malaysia - Peninsular Malaysia *10249*

V   *Licuala kiahii* Furt. *10249*
   V   *14701* Malaysia - Peninsular Malaysia *10249*

V   *Licuala lanata* Dransf. *14703*
   V   *14703* Malaysia - Sarawak (G. Mulu NP) *14703*

V   *Licuala lanuginosa* Ridley *10249*
   V   Malaysia - Peninsular Malaysia *10249*

V   *Licuala longicalycata* Furt. *10249*
   V   Malaysia - Peninsular Malaysia *10249*

V   *Licuala malajana* Becc. *10249*
   V   Malaysia - Peninsular Malaysia *10249*

V   *Licuala mirabilis* Furt. *10249*
   V   Malaysia - Peninsular Malaysia *10249*

V   *Licuala modesta* Becc. *10249*
   V   Malaysia - Peninsular Malaysia *10249*

E   *Licuala moyseyi* Furtado *10249*
   E   *14701* Malaysia - Peninsular Malaysia *10249*

V   *Licuala pahangensis* Furt. *10249*
   V   Malaysia - Peninsular Malaysia *10249*

R   *Licuala pumila* Blume *10238*
   R   Indonesia - Java *10238*
   R   Indonesia - Sumatra *10238*

V   *Licuala pusilla* Becc. *10249*
   V   Malaysia - Peninsular Malaysia *10249*

E	*Licuala ridleyana* Becc. *10249*	
	E	Malaysia - Peninsular Malaysia *10249*
R	*Licuala robinsoniana* Becc. *10260*	
	R	Vietnam *6057*
R	*Licuala scortechinii* Becc. *10249*	
	R	Malaysia - Peninsular Malaysia *10249*
V	*Licuala tiomanensis* Furt. *10249*	
	V	Malaysia - Peninsular Malaysia *10249*
R	*Licuala tonkinensis* Becc. *13955*	
	R	*15313* Vietnam *13955*
R	*Linospadix microcarya* (Domin) Burret *20681, 15154*	
	R	*20681* Australia - Queensland *20681*
R	*Linospadix palmeriana* (Bailey) Burret *20681, 15166*	
	R	*20681* Australia - Queensland *20681*
R	*Livistona alfredii* F.Muell. *20681, 15166*	
	R	*20681* Australia - Western Australia *20681*
E	*Livistona carinensis* (Chiov.) Dransf. & Uhl *20884*	
	I	Yemen, Democratic (El Mintaq, Hadramaut)
	E	Djibouti
	E	*20884* Somalia (north) *17950*
V	*Livistona drudei* F.Muell. ex W.Watson *20681, 15166*	
	V	*20681* Australia - Queensland *20681*
R	*Livistona endauensis* Dransf. & K.M. Wong *11389*	
	R	Malaysia - Peninsular Malaysia (Endau-Rompin) *11389*
R	*Livistona exigua* Dransf. *11178*	
	R	Brunei Darussalam *11178*
V	*Livistona lanuginosa* A.N.Rodd ms. *20681*	
	V	*20681* Australia - Queensland *20681*
V	*Livistona mariae* F.Muell. *20681, 15166*	
	V	*20681* Australia - Northern Territory *20681*
I	*Livistona robinsoniana* Becc. *14726*	
	I	*14726* Philippines (Polillo) *14726*
R	*Livistona tahanensis* Ridley *17749*	
	R	Malaysia - Peninsular Malaysia *10249*
R	*Livistona tonkinensis* Magalon *10260*	
	R	Vietnam *8794*
R	*Livistona woodfordii* Ridley *15138*	
	R	*15138* Solomon Is. - South (Nggela Islands) *15138*
V	*Lodoicea maldivica* (J. Gmelin) Pers. *14296*	
	V	Seychelles (granitic) *14296*
E	*Loxococcus rupicola* H. Wendl. & Drude *7956*	
	E	*17945* Sri Lanka *7956*
I	*Lytocaryum hoehnei* (Burret) Toledo *9996*	
	I	*20826* Brazil (Atlantic forest) *8743*
E	*Lytocaryum weddelianum* (H. Wendl.) Tol. *9996*	
	E	Brazil - Espirito Santo *8743*
	E	Brazil - Rio de Janeiro *8743*
V	*Mackeea magnifica* H.E. Moore *20893*	
	V	*20893* New Caledonia *15184*
E	*Marojejya darianii* J. Dransf. & N. Uhl. *10779*	
	E	*20071* Madagascar (Maroantsetra) *20071*
V	*Marojejya insignis* Humbert *11813*	
	V	*17951* Madagascar *20071*
E	*Masoala kona* Beentje *20071*	
	E	*20071* Madagascar (Ifanadiana) *20071*
V	*Masoala madagascariensis* Jum. *11813*	
	V	*17951* Madagascar *20071*

R	*Mauritia carana* Wallace *20883, 8020*	
	R	*20883* Brazil *20883*
	R	*20883* Colombia *20883*
	E	*20883* Peru *20883*
	E	*20883* Venezuela *20883*
I	*Mauritiella cataractorum* Dugand *8020*	
	I	*16853* Colombia *8020*
V	*Maxburretia furtadoana* Dransf. *10517*	
	V	*5929* Thailand (Surat Thani Province: Khao Phra Rahu, K. Changai) *5929*
R	*Maxburretia gracilis* (Burret) Dransf. *10262*	
	R	Malaysia - Peninsular Malaysia (Langkawi) *10262*
E	*Maxburretia rupicola* (Ridley) Furt. *10517*	
	E	*17950* Malaysia - Peninsular Malaysia *10517*
I	*Medemia abiadensis* H.A. Wendl. *10245*	
	I	*5908* Sudan (White Nile) *5908*
E	*Medemia argun* (Martius) Wurtt. ex H.A. Wendl. *11813*	
	Ex/E	*16168* Egypt (Nubian desert) *16168*
	E	*16168* Sudan *16168*
I	*Metroxylon amicarum* (Wendl.) Becc. *14789*	
	I	Micronesia - Caroline Is. (Truk; Ponape)
R	*Metroxylon warburgii* Becc. *15184*	
	R	*17945* Solomon Is. - South *17945*
	R	*15184* Vanuatu *15184*
R	*Moratia cerifera* H.E. Moore *10237*	
	R	*20893* New Caledonia *10237*
I	*Nenga banaensis* (Magalon) Burret *10603*	
	I	*15734* Vietnam (Da Nang: Mt Bana) *10603*
E	*Nenga gajah* Dransf. *10603*	
	E	*17950* Indonesia - Sumatra (c. 800 m) *10603*
	E	*17950* Malaysia - Sabah *14712*
R	*Nenga grandiflora* E. Fernando *10603*	
	R	Malaysia - Peninsular Malaysia (Johor) *10603*
E	*Neoveitchia storckii* (H.A. Wendl.) Becc. *11813*	
	E	*15184* Fiji (Viti Levu) *15184*
V	*Nephrosperma vanhoutteanum* (Wendl. ex Van Houtte) Balf. f. *14296*	
	V	Seychelles (granitic) *14296*
V	*Normanbya normanbyi* (A.W.Hill) L.H.Bailey *20681, 15166*	
	V	*20681* Australia - Queensland *20681*
I	*Oenocarpus balickii* Kahn *20883, 17949*	
	R	*20883* Brazil *20883*
	V	*20883* Colombia *20883*
	R	*20883* Peru *20883*
	E	*20883* Venezuela *20883*
R	*Oenocarpus bataua* (Griseb. & H. Wendl.) Henderson var. *oligocarpa* (Griseb. & H.Wendl.) Balick *20883, 20826*	
	R	*20883* Trinidad & Tobago (Only Trinidad) *20883*
	R	*20883* French Guiana *20883*
	R	*20883* Guyana *20883*
	R	*20883* Suriname *20883*
	R	*20883* Venezuela *20883*
E	*Oenocarpus circumtextus* Martius *20883, 11813*	
	E	*20883* Colombia *20883*
E	*Oenocarpus makeru* Bernal, Galeano, & Henderson *20883*	
	E	*20883* Colombia *20883*
V	*Oenocarpus mapora* ssp. *dryanderae* Karst. *20883*	
	V	*20883* Colombia *20883*

R **Oenocarpus minor** ssp. *intermedius*
Martius *20883*
   R   *20883* Brazil *20883*

E **Oenocarpus simplex** Bernal, Galeano &
Henderson *20883, 20826*
   I   *20826* Colombia *20883*

V **Oncosperma fasciculatum** Thwaites *7956*
   V   *17945* Sri Lanka *7956*

I **Oncosperma platyphyllum** Becc. *14726*
   I   *14726* Philippines (Negros) *14726*

I **Orania decipiens** Becc. var. *mindanaoensis*
Becc. *14726*
   I   *14726* Philippines (Mindanao) *14726*

I **Orania decipiens** Becc. var. *montana*
Becc. *14726*
   I   *14726* Philippines (Mindanao) *14726*

R **Orania longisquama** (Jum.) J. Dransf. & N. Uhl. *11813*
   R   *20071* Madagascar (north-west and east) *20071*

V **Orania ravaka** Beentje. Sp. Nov. *20071*
   V   *20071* Madagascar (north east) *20071*

I **Orania sylvicola** (Griff.) H.E. Moore *10249*
   I   Indonesia - Java *10238*
   I   Indonesia - Sumatra *10238*
   V   Malaysia - Peninsular Malaysia *10249*
   V   *14703* Malaysia - Sarawak (near Kuching) *14703*
   Ex *20099* Singapore *20099*

E **Orania trispatha** (J. Dransf. & N.W. Uhl) Beentje & J. Dransf.
Comb Nov. *20071*
   E   *20071* Madagascar (east) *20071*

E **Parajubaea sunkha** Moraes *21271*
   E   *21270* Bolivia *21271*

E **Parajubaea torallyi** (C. Martius) Burret *20883, 11813*
   E   *20883* Bolivia *20883*

Ex **Paschalococos disperta** Dransfield *14777*
   Ex *14777* Chile - Easter Is. *14777*

R **Pelagodoxa henryana** Becc. *11813*
   R   *19614* French Polynesia - Marquesas Is *19614*

V **Phoenicophorium borsigianum** (K. Koch) Stuntz *14296*
   V   Seychelles (granitic) *14296*

V **Phoenix hanceana** Naudin var. *philippinensis*
Becc. *12804*
   V   Philippines (Batanes Is) *12804*

V **Phoenix rupicola** T. Anders. *14827*
   V   *14827* India - Arunachal Pradesh *10235*
   V   *14827* India - Meghalaya *10235*
   V   *14827* India - Sikkim *10235*

V **Phoenix theophrasti** Greuter *8000, 20171*
   V   *14155* Greece - Crete *8000*
   V   *20731* Turkey *20618*

R **Phoenix zeylanica** Trimen *7956*
   R   *20013* Sri Lanka *7956*

V **Pholidocarpus kingianus** (Becc.) Ridley *19209*
   V   Malaysia - Peninsular Malaysia *19209*
   Ex *20099* Singapore *20099*

V **Pholidocarpus macrocarpus** Becc. *10249*
   E/V   Thailand *10482*
   V   Malaysia - Peninsular Malaysia *19209*

R **Physokentia dennisii** H.E. Moore *15156*
   R   *17945* Solomon Is. - South (Guadalcanal) *15156*

V **Physokentia rosea** H.E. Moore *10242*
   V   *19630* Fiji (Viti Levu, Gau) *19630*

R **Physokentia tete** (Beccari) Beccari *15156*
   R   *15156* Vanuatu (Banks Group) *15156*

R **Physokentia thurstonii** (Becc.) Becc. *10253*
   R   *15184* Fiji (Vanua Levu & Taveuni) *10253*

R **Phytelephas aequatorialis** Spruce *20883, 15728*
   I   *20883* Ecuador (coastal plains up to 1500 m)
             20883

R **Phytelephas seemannii** O.F. Cook *20883, 15728*
   R   *20883* Panama *20883*
   E   *16853* Colombia *8020*

R **Phytelephas tenuicaulis** (Barfod) Henderson *20883*
   E   *20883* Colombia *20883*
   V   *20883* Ecuador *20883*
   V   *20883* Peru *20883*

E **Phytelephas tumacana** O.F. Cook *8020*
   E   *16853* Colombia *8020*

E **Pinanga acaulis** Ridley *11813*
   E   *14701* Malaysia - Peninsular Malaysia *10249*

E **Pinanga adangensis** Ridley *11813*
   E   Thailand (Adang Is.) *8794*
   E   *14701* Malaysia - Peninsular Malaysia *14701*

R **Pinanga albescens** Becc. ex H. Winkler *10525*
   R   *14828* Indonesia - Kalimantan *14828*
   R   *14828* Malaysia - Sabah *14828*
   R   *14703* Malaysia - Sarawak *14703*

R **Pinanga andamanensis** Becc. *14827*
   R   *14827* India - Andaman Is. *13883*

I **Pinanga basilanensis** Becc. *14726*
   I   *14726* Philippines (Basilan) *14726*

R **Pinanga borneensis** Scheffer *14828*
   R   *14828* Indonesia - Kalimantan *14828*

R **Pinanga celebica** Scheff. *14828*
   R   *14828* Indonesia - Sulawesi *14828*

E **Pinanga cleistantha** Dransf. *10534*
   E   *17950* Malaysia - Peninsular Malaysia (Trengganu)
             10534

R **Pinanga cochinchinensis** Blume *10260*
   R   Vietnam *8794*

V **Pinanga dicksonii** Blume *14827*
   V   *14827* India - Kerala (Nilgiri Hills) *10235*
   V   *14827* India - Tamil Nadu (Western Ghats)
             10235

V **Pinanga fruticans** Ridley *10249*
   V   Malaysia - Peninsular Malaysia *10249*

I **Pinanga geonomiformis** Becc. *14726*
   I   *14726* Philippines (Polillo) *14726*

I **Pinanga heterophylla** Becc. *14726*
   I   *14726* Philippines (Rapu-Rapu) *14726*

I **Pinanga isabelensis** Becc. *14726*
   I   *14726* Philippines (Luzon) *14726*

E **Pinanga javana** Blume *10238*
   E   *17950* Indonesia - Java *10238*

R **Pinanga keahii** Furt. *14703*
   R   *14828* Indonesia - Kalimantan *14828*
   R   *14828* Malaysia - Sabah (Kinabalu) *14712*
   R   *14703* Malaysia - Sarawak *14703*

R **Pinanga ligulata** Becc. *14703*
   R   *14703* Malaysia - Sarawak *14703*

I **Pinanga maculata** Porte ex Lem. *14726*
   I   *14726* Philippines *14726*

V **Pinanga manii** Becc. *14827*

V	*13883*	India - Andaman Is. (south)	*13883*
V	*13883*	India - Nicobar Is.	*13883*

I   *Pinanga negrosensis* Becc. *14726*

    I   *14726*   Philippines (Negros) *14726*

R   *Pinanga pachyphylla* J. Dransf. *16088*

    R   *16088*   Malaysia - Sarawak (Bako National Park) *16088*

R   *Pinanga patula* Blume var. *borneensis* Becc. *14828*

    R   *14828*   Indonesia - Kalimantan *14828*

V   *Pinanga pectinata* Becc. *10249*

    V   Malaysia - Peninsular Malaysia *19209*

    Ex   *20099*   Singapore *20099*

V   *Pinanga perakensis* Becc. *10249*

    V   Malaysia - Peninsular Malaysia *10249*

R   *Pinanga punicea* (Blume) Merr. var. *punicea* *14828*

    R   *14828*   Indonesia - Moluccas *14828*

I   *Pinanga rigida* Becc. *14726*

    I   *14726*   Philippines (Luzon) *14726*

I   *Pinanga samarana* Becc. *14726*

    I   *14726*   Philippines (Samar) *14726*

I   *Pinanga sclerophylla* Becc. *14726*

    I   *14726*   Philippines (Mindoro) *14726*

I   *Pinanga sibuyanensis* Becc. *14726*

    I   *14726*   Philippines (Sibuyan) *14726*

V   *Pinanga stricta* Becc. *14703*

    V   *14703*   Malaysia - Sarawak *14703*

V   *Pinanga subintegra* Ridley *10249*

    V   Malaysia - Peninsular Malaysia *10249*

V   *Pinanga subruminata* Becc. *10249*

    V   Malaysia - Peninsular Malaysia *10249*

    Ex   *20099*   Singapore *20099*

R   *Pinanga tenacinervis* Dransf. *10525*

    R   *14703*   Malaysia - Sarawak (G. Mulu NP) *10525*

I   *Pinanga urdanetensis* Becc. *14726*

    I   *14726*   Philippines (Mindanao) *14726*

I   *Pinanga urosperma* Becc. *14726*

    I   *14726*   Philippines (Babuyan) *14726*

I   *Pinanga woodiana* Becc. *14726*

    I   *14726*   Philippines (Luzon) *14726*

R   *Plectocomia billitonensis* Becc. *10631*

    R   *14828*   Indonesia - Sumatra (only Belitung) *10631*

E   *Plectocomia dransfieldiana* Madulid *10631*

    E   *14701*   Malaysia - Peninsular Malaysia *10631*

R   *Plectocomia elmeri* Becc. *10631*

    R   *14726*   Philippines (Mt Apo) *10631*

R   *Plectocomia longistigma* Madulid *10631*

    R   *14828*   Indonesia - Java (east) *10631*

R   *Plectocomia lorzingii* Madulid *10631*

    R   *14828*   Indonesia - Sumatra (Sibolangit) *10631*

V   *Plectocomia microstachys* Burret *10631*

    V   *20756*   China - Hainan Is. *20756*

R   *Plectocomia pygmaea* Madulid *10631*

    R   *14828*   Indonesia - Kalimantan (Sei Poetat: Pontianak) *10631*

V   *Plectocomiopsis wrayi* Becc. *10259*

    E/V   Malaysia - Peninsular Malaysia *19209*

E   *Pogonotium moorei* Dransf. *10669*

    E   *14703*   Malaysia - Sarawak (Gunung Gaharu) *10669*

I   *Prestoea pubens* H.E. Moore var. *pubens* *9150*

    I   *16853*   Colombia (Del Valle) *9150*

V   *Prestoea roseospadix* (L.H. Bailey) H. Moore *20883, 8020*

    V   *20883*   Panama *20883*

R   *Prestoea tenuiramosa* (Dammer) H.E. Moore *8020*

    I   *20826*   Brazil *20826*

    I   *20826*   Guyana *20826*

    R   Venezuela *8020*

Ex/E   *Pritchardia affinis* Becc. *20850, 14209*

    Ex/E   *20850*   U.S. - Hawaii *20850*

E   *Pritchardia aylmer-robinsonii* H. St. John *14209*

    E   *14209*   U.S. - Hawaii (Ni'ihau) *14209*

V   *Pritchardia forbesiana* Rock *14209, 20850*

    I   *20850*   U.S. - Hawaii *20850*

R   *Pritchardia glabrata* Becc. & Rock *14209*

    R   *20828*   U.S. - Hawaii (Maui) *14209*

E   *Pritchardia hardyi* Rock *20850, 14209*

    E   *20850*   U.S. - Hawaii (Kauai) *20850*

E   *Pritchardia kaalae* Rock *20850, 14209*

    E   *20850*   U.S. - Hawaii (Oahu) *20850*

E   *Pritchardia lanigera* Becc. *20850, 14209*

    E   *20850*   U.S. - Hawaii *20850*

Ex/E   *Pritchardia lowreyana* Rock *20850, 14209*

    Ex/E   *20850*   U.S. - Hawaii *20850*

E   *Pritchardia munroi* Rock *20850, 14209*

    E   *20850*   U.S. - Hawaii (leeward Molokai) *20850*

E   *Pritchardia napaliensis* H. St. John *14209*

    E   *20828*   U.S. - Hawaii (Kauai) *14209*

E   *Pritchardia remota* Becc. *20850, 14209*

    E   *20850*   U.S. - Hawaii *20850*

E   *Pritchardia schattaueri* Hodel *20850, 14209*

    E   *20850*   U.S. - Hawaii *20850*

R   *Pritchardia thurstonii* F. Muell. & Drude *10253*

    R   *15184*   Fiji (eastern islands) *10253*

E   *Pritchardia viscosa* Rock *20850, 14209*

    E   *20850*   U.S. - Hawaii (Kauai) *20850*

R   *Pritchardia waialealeana* R.W. Read *20850, 14209*

    R   *20850*   U.S. - Hawaii *20850*

R   *Pritchardia woodfordiana* ined. *15138*

    R   *15138*   Solomon Is. - South (Nggela Island) *15138*

E   *Pritchardiopsis jeanneneyi* Becc. *10237*

    E   *20893*   New Caledonia *10237*

E   *Pseudophoenix ekmanii* Burret *2014*

    E   *8743*   Dominican Republic *8743*

V   *Pseudophoenix lediniana* Read *2014*

    V   *14799*   Haiti *8020*

I   *Pseudophoenix sargentii* H.A. Wendl. ex Sarg. ssp. *sargentii* *8020*

    E   *19002*   U.S. - Florida *8020*

    I   Belize *8020*

    V   *19850*   Mexico - Quintana Roo *9019*

E   *Ptychosperma bleeseri* Burret *20681, 15166*

    E   *20681*   Australia - Northern Territory *20681*

R   *Ptychosperma gracile* Labill. *14790*

    R   *17945*   Papua New Guinea - Bismarck Arch. (incl New Ireland &

Britain) *10242*

R   *Ptychosperma hentyi* Essig *15147*

    R   *15147*   Papua New Guinea - Bismarck Arch. (New Britain) *15147*

R   *Raphia australis* Oberm. & Strey *20604, 10520*

    E   *20745*   Mozambique *20604*

    R   *20604*   South Africa - Natal *20604*

E   *Ravenea albicans* (Jum.) Beentje *20071*

    E   *20071*   Madagascar (north-east) *20071*

V   *Ravenea dransfieldii* Beentje *20071*

    V   *20071*   Madagascar *20071*

V   *Ravenea glauca* Jum. & H. Perrier *10246*

    V   *17951*   Madagascar (Andringitra Mts & Isalo) *20071*

E   *Ravenea hildebrandtii* Bouche ex Wendl. *10246*

    E   *20071*   Comoros *20071*

E   *Ravenea julietiae* Beentje *20071*

    E   *20071*   Madagascar (east) *20071*

V   *Ravenea krociana* Beentje *20071*

    V   *20071*   Madagascar (Andohahela) *20071*

E   *Ravenea lakatra* (Jum.) Beentje *20071*

    E   *20071*   Madagascar (east) *20071*

E   *Ravenea latisecta* Jum. *10246*

    E   *2014*   Madagascar (Andasibe) *20071*

E   *Ravenea louvelii* Beentje *20071*

    E   *20071*   Madagascar (Andasibe) *20071*

R   *Ravenea madagascariensis* Becc. *20071*

    R   *17951*   Madagascar *20071*

V   *Ravenea moorei* J. Dransf. & N.W. Uhl *15145*

    V   *20071*   Comoros (Grande Comore) *20071*

V   *Ravenea musicalis* Beentje *20071*

    V   *20071*   Madagascar (south) *20071*

E   *Ravenea nana* Beentje *20071*

    E   *20071*   Madagascar *20071*

V   *Ravenea rivularis* Jum. & H. Perrier *10246*

    V   *17951*   Madagascar (Mangoky & Onilahy) *20071*

R   *Ravenea robustior* Jumelle & H. Perrier *11813*

    R   *20071*   Madagascar *20071*

V   *Ravenea sambiranensis* Jumelle & H. Perrier *10246*

    V   *17951*   Madagascar *20071*

E   *Ravenea xerophila* Jum. *10246*

    E   *20071*   Madagascar *20071*

I   *Reinhardtia elegans* Liebm. ex Mart. *8020*

    I   *20826*   Honduras *20826*

    R   *19850*   Mexico - Chiapas *20826*

    R   *19850*   Mexico - Oaxaca *20826*

R   *Reinhardtia gracilis* (H. Wendl.) Drude ex Dammer var. *tenuissima* H.E. Moore *8020*

    R   *19850*   Mexico - Oaxaca *20826*

E   *Reinhardtia koschnyana* (H. Wendl. & Dammer) Burret *8020*

    E   *8743*   Costa Rica (Alajuela) *8743*

    E   *20826*   Honduras *20826*

    E   *8743*   Nicaragua (Zelaya) *8743*

    E   *8743*   Panama (Darien) *8743*

    E   *8743*   Colombia (Antioquia and Choco) *8743*

E   *Reinhardtia paiewonskiana* Read, Zanoni & Mejia *10744*

    E   Dominican Republic (Mts.) *10744*

I   *Reinhardtia simplex* (H. Wendl.) Drude ex Dammer *8020*

    E   *8743*   Costa Rica *8743*

    I   *8743*   Honduras *8020*

    I   *8743*   Nicaragua *8743*

    E   *8743*   Panama *8020*

    I   *20826*   Colombia *20826*

R   *Rhapis divaricata* Gagnep. *13955*

    R   *15313*   Vietnam *13955*

V   *Rhopaloblaste augusta* (Kurz) H.E. Moore *10526*

    V   *14827*   India - Nicobar Is. (northern group) *10526*

R   *Rhopaloblaste elegans* H.E. Moore *15138*

    R   *17945*   Solomon Is. - South *15138*

R   *Rhopaloblaste singaporensis* (Becc.) H.E. Moore *14043*

    V   Malaysia - Peninsular Malaysia *10249*

    R   *20099*   Singapore *20099*

R   *Rhopalostylis baueri* (Hook.f.) H.A. Wendl & Drude var. *baueri* *19108*

    R   *19108*   Australia - Norfolk Is. *15184*

R   *Rhopalostylis baueri* (Hook. f.) Wendl. & Drude var. *cheesemanii* (Becc. ex Cheesem.) W.R. Sykes *15184*

    R   *15184*   New Zealand - Kermadec Is. *15184*

V   *Rhopalostylis chathams* *20625*

    V   *20625*   New Zealand - Chatham Is. *20625*

I   *Rhopalostylis sapida* H. Wendl. & Drude *15184*

    I   *15184*   New Zealand *15184*

V   *Roscheria melanochaetes* (H.A. Wendl.) H.A. Wendl. ex Balf. f. *14296*

    V   Seychelles (granitic) *14296*

R   *Roystonea altissima* (Mill.) H.E. Moore *20883, 8020*

    R   *20883*   Jamaica *20883*

R   *Roystonea borinquena* O.F. Cook *20883, 8020*

    I   *20883*   Puerto Rico *20883*

    I   *20883*   USA - Virgin Is. *20883*

V   *Roystonea elata* (Bartr.) F. Harper *20883, 20850, 2014*

    V   *20850*   U.S. - Florida *20850*

    I   *20883*   Cuba *20883*

    I   *20883*   Puerto Rico *20883*

V   *Roystonea princeps* (Beccari) Burret *20883, 8020*

    R   *19890*   Jamaica (west) *20883*

R   *Roystonea regia* (Kunth) O.F. Cook var. *pinguis* L.H. Bailey *9244*

    R   *19105*   Cuba (Guantanamo) *9774*

E   *Sabal allenii* L.H. Bailey *20883*

    I   *20883*   Panama *20883*

E   *Sabal bermudana* L.H. Bailey *14791*

    E   *11813*   Bermuda *14791*

R   *Sabal gretheriae* Quero *15157*

    R   *19850*   Mexico - Quintana Roo (Chiquilá) *15157*

Ex/E   *Sabal miamiensis* Zona *14791*

    Ex/E   *14791*   U.S. - Florida (Miami pinelands) *14791*

R   *Sabal pumos* (Kunth) Burret *14791*

    R   *19850*   Mexico *14791*

R   *Sabal uresana* Trel. *14791*

    R   *19850*   Mexico *8020*

I   *Salacca clemensiana* Becc. *10668*

    E   *14712*   Malaysia - Sabah *14712*

    E   *14712*   Malaysia - Sarawak *14712*

    I   *14726*   Philippines (incl. Sulu Archip.) *10668*

R   *Salacca dolicholepis* Burret *14712*

    R   *14712*   Malaysia - Sabah (Kinabalu) *14712*

R   *Salacca dransfieldiana* Mogea *11177*

	R	*14828* Indonesia - Kalimantan *11177*
R	*Salacca flabellata* Furt. *10249*	
	R	*14828* Malaysia - Peninsular Malaysia *10249*
V	*Salacca graciliflora* Mogea *10674*	
	V	*14701* Malaysia - Peninsular Malaysia *10674*
Ex/E	*Salacca lophospatha* Dransf. & Mogea *10668*	
	Ex/E	*14712* Malaysia - Sabah (type coll. only) *10668*
R	*Salacca minuta* Mogea *10674*	
	R	*14828* Malaysia - Peninsular Malaysia *10674*
E	*Salacca multiflora* Mogea *10674*	
	E	*17950* Malaysia - Peninsular Malaysia *10674*
R	*Salacca palembanica* Mogea *14828*	
	R	*14828* Indonesia - Sumatra *14828*
R	*Salacca rupicola* Dransf. *14703*	
	R	*14703* Malaysia - Sarawak (G. Mulu NP) *14703*
V	*Satakentia liukiuensis* (Hatusima) H.E. Moore *10250*	
	V	Japan (Ryukyu Islands) *10250*
E	*Satranala decussilvae* Beentje & J. Dransf. *20071*	
	E	*20071* Madagascar *20071*
E	*Schippia concolor* Burret *11813*	
	E	*11813* Belize (Cayo) *8743*
	E	*11813* Guatemala (lower Petén) *8743*
R	*Socratea hecatonandra* (Dugand) Bernal *20883, 11813*	
	I	*20883* Colombia (west) *20883*
	I	*20883* Ecuador *20883*
I	*Socratea salazarii* Moore *20883, 15727*	
	E	*20883* Bolivia *20883*
	E	*20883* Brazil *20883*
	R	*20883* Peru (Loreto & Amazonas Depts) *20883*
R	*Syagrus botryophora* (C. Martius) C. Martius *20883, 8020*	
	I	*20883* Brazil *20883*
	V	*19614* Brazil - Bahia (coastal forest) *8743*
	V	*19614* Brazil - Espirito Santo *19614*
	V	*19614* Brazil - Sergipe *19614*
E	*Syagrus cardenasii* Glassman *20883, 8020*	
	E	*20883* Bolivia *20883*
I	*Syagrus duartei* Glassman *8020*	
	I	*20826* Brazil - Minas Gerais *20826*
R	*Syagrus flexuosa* (C. Martius) Becc. *20883, 8020*	
	E	*20883* Bolivia *20883*
	I	*20883* Brazil *20883*
R	*Syagrus glaucescens* Glaziou ex Becc. *8020*	
	R	*19614* Brazil - Minas Gerais *20826*
I	*Syagrus graminifolia* (Drude) Becc. *8020*	
	I	*19614* Brazil *8020*
	E	*20826* Paraguay *20826*
R	*Syagrus harleyi* Glassman *8793*	
	R	*19614* Brazil - Bahia *8793*
Ex/E	*Syagrus leptospatha* Burret *8020*	
	Ex/E	*19614* Brazil - Mato Grosso *8743*
V	*Syagrus macrocarpa* Barb. Rodr. *8020*	
	E	*19614* Brazil - Espirito Santo *19614*
	V	*19614* Brazil - Minas Gerais *8743*
R	*Syagrus microphylla* Burret *8020*	
	R	Brazil - Bahia *20826*
R	*Syagrus orinocensis* (Spruce) Burret *20883, 8020*	
	R	*20883* Colombia *20883*
	V	*20883* Venezuela *20883*
R	*Syagrus picrophylla* Barb. Rodr. *8020*	
	R	*19614* Brazil - Bahia (Serra do Mar) *8020*

	R	*19614* Brazil - Espirito Santo (Serra do Mar) *8020*
	R	*19614* Brazil - Rio de Janeiro (Serra do Mar) *8020*
R	*Syagrus pleioclada* Burret *8020*	
	R	*19614* Brazil - Mato Grosso *19614*
	R	*20827* Brazil - Minas Gerais *20826*
	R	*20827* Brazil - Sao Paulo *20826*
V	*Syagrus pseudococos* (Raddi) Glassman *8743*	
	V	*19614* Brazil - Espirito Santo *19614*
	E	Brazil - Rio de Janeiro *8743*
	E	Brazil - Sao Paulo *8743*
R	*Syagrus ruschiana* (Bondar) Glassman *8020*	
	R	*20827* Brazil - Espirito Santo *20826*
	R	*20827* Brazil - Minas Gerais *20826*
R	*Syagrus smithii* (H.E. Moore) Glassman *20883, 8743*	
	V	*20883* Brazil *20883*
	R	*19614* Brazil - Acre *19614*
	R	*20826* Colombia *20883*
	R	*20883* Peru (Loreto) *20883*
V	*Syagrus stratincola* Wess. Boer *20883, 8679*	
	I	*20826* French Guiana *20883*
	E	*20883* Suriname *20883*
R	*Syagrus werdermannii* Burret *8020*	
	R	*19614* Brazil (Cerrado) *8020*
E	*Tectiphiala ferox* H.E. Moore *10082*	
	E	*20771* Mauritius *10519*
E	*Thrinax ekmaniana* (Burret) Borhidi & Muniz *11813*	
	E	*19105* Cuba (Vila Clara) *5607*
R	*Thrinax excelsa* Lodd. *20883, 8765*	
	R	*20883* Jamaica *20883*
V	*Thrinax parviflora* Sw. *20883*	
	V	*20883* Jamaica *20883*
V	*Thrinax rivularis* (Leon) Borhidi & Muniz var. rivularis *9996*	
	V	*19105* Cuba (Guantanamo; Holguin) *9774*
V	*Thrinax rivularis* (Leon) Borhidi & Muniz var. savannarum (Leon) Borhidi & Muniz *9996*	
	V	*19105* Cuba (Guantanamo; Holguin) *9774*
V	*Trachycarpus nana* Becc. *17617*	
	V	*17617* China - Yunnan *11139*
R	*Trithrinax biflabellata* Barb. Rodr. *20883, 14840*	
	E	*20176* Argentina - Chaco *20176*
	E	*20176* Argentina - Formosa *20176*
	E	*20176* Argentina - Salta *20176*
	V	*20883* Bolivia *20883*
	I	*20883* Paraguay *20883*
V	*Trithrinax brasiliensis* Mart. *14840*	
	E	*19614* Brazil - Parana *19614*
	E	*19614* Brazil - Rio Grande do Sul *8743*
	V	*19614* Brazil - Santa Catarina *19614*
I	*Trithrinax schizophylla* Drude *20883, 8020*	
	E	*14840* Argentina (Jujuy province) *14840*
	R	*20883* Bolivia *20883*
	I	*20883* Brazil *20883*
R	*Veillonia alba* H.E. Moore *10518*	
	R	*15184* New Caledonia *10518*
Ex/E	*Veitchia filifera* (H.A. Wendl.) H.E. Moore *10253*	
	Ex/E	*19630* Fiji (Vanua Levu) *10253*
R	*Veitchia joannis* H.A. Wendl. *10253*	
	R	*15184* Fiji *10253*
R	*Veitchia macdanielsii* H.E. Moore *13954*	
	R	*15184* Vanuatu (Espiritu Santo) *13954*

I	*Veitchia merrillii* (Becc.) Moore *14726*	
	I	*14726* Philippines (Calamianes) *14726*
R	*Veitchia metiti* Becc. *15184*	
	R	*15184* Vanuatu *15184*
E	*Veitchia montgomeryana* H.E. Moore *13954*	
	E	*13954* Vanuatu (Efate) *13954*
E	*Veitchia pedionoma* (A.C. Smith) H.E. Moore *10253*	
	E	*19630* Fiji (Vanua Levu) *10253*
E	*Veitchia petiolata* (Burret) H.E. Moore *10253*	
	E	*19630* Fiji (Vanua Levu) *10253*
V	*Veitchia simulans* H.E. Moore *10253*	
	V	*19630* Fiji (Taveuni) *10253*
E	*Veitchia spiralis* H. Wendl. *14844*	
	E	*17945* Vanuatu *14844*
V	*Veitchia vitiensis* (H.A. Wendl.) H.E. Moore *10253*	
	V	*15184* Fiji (Ovalau, Viti Levu & Kandavu) *10253*
V	*Verschaffeltia splendida* H.A. Wendl. *14296*	
	V	Seychelles (granitic) *14296*
E	*Voanioala gerardii* J. Dransf. *14792*	
	E	*20071* Madagascar (Masoala Peninsula) *20071*
R	*Wallichia triandra* (Joseph) S.K. Basu *14827*	
	R	*14827* India - Arunachal Pradesh (Haylung, Wakroo, Lohit) *11494*
R	*Washingtonia filifera* (L. Linden) H. Wendl. *20883, 20850, 8020, 20171*	
	E	*20850* U.S. - Arizona *20850*
	I	*20850* U.S. - California *20850*
	I	*20850* U.S. - Nevada *20850*
	R	Mexico *20883*
		20883 Bolivia *20883*
R	*Wendlandiella gracilis* Dammer *20883, 8020*	
	E	*20883* Bolivia *20883*
	E	*20883* Brazil *20883*
	R	*20883* Peru *20883*
V	*Wendlandiella gracilis* Dammer var. *gracilis 20883*	
	E	*20883* Brazil *20883*
	V	*20883* Peru *20883*
E	*Wendlandiella gracilis* Dammer var. *polyclada* (Burret) Henderson *20883*	
	E	*20883* Peru *20883*
V	*Wendlandiella gracilis* Dammer var. *simplicifrons* (Burret) Henderson *20883*	
	V	*20883* Bolivia *20883*
	V	*20883* Peru *20883*
R	*Wendlandiella polyclada* Burret *8020*	
	R	*19614* Peru *17955*
I	*Wendlandiella simplicifrons* Burret *8020*	
	I	*19614* Peru *17955*
I	*Wettinia anomala* (Burret) R.Bernal *20826*	
	I	*16853* Colombia *20826*
	I	*20827* Ecuador *20826*
R	*Wettinia augusta* Poepp. & Endl. *20883, 8020*	
	E	*20883* Brazil *20883*
	E	*20883* Colombia *20883*
	R	*20883* Peru *20883*
V	*Wettinia disticha* R.Bernal *20826*	
	V	*16853* Colombia (Cordillera Occidental) *10743*
R	*Wettinia drudei* (O.F. Cook & Doyle) Henderson *20883*	
	E	*20883* Brazil *20883*
	V	*20883* Colombia *20883*
	V	*20883* Ecuador *20883*

	V	*20883* Peru *20883*
I	*Wettinia fascicularis* Burr et H.E. Moore & Dransfield *16853*	
	E	*16853* Colombia *8020*
	I	*20827* Ecuador *20826*
V	*Wettinia hirsuta* Burret *8020*	
	V	*16853* Colombia *8020*
I	*Wettinia kalbreyeri* (Burret) R.Bernal *20826*	
	I	*20826* Colombia *20826*
E	*Wettinia longipetala* A. Gentry *20883, 8801*	
	E	*19614* Peru (Pasco) *20883*
R	*Wettinia maynensis* Spruce *20883, 8020*	
	E	*20883* Colombia *20883*
	R	*20883* Ecuador *20883*
	R	*20883* Peru *20883*
I	*Wettinia minima* R.Bernal *20826*	
	I	*20826* Ecuador *20826*
V	*Wodyetia bifurcata* Irvine *20681, 15153*	
	V	*20681* Australia - Queensland *20681*

Pandanaceae

Number of genera:	3
Number of species:	682-782
Recorded threatened species:	41 (5%)

Old World, especially tropical (Malesia).

I	*Freycinetia auriculata* Merr. *13833*	
	I	*13833* Philippines (low and medium altitudes) *13833*
R	*Freycinetia baueriana* Endl. ssp. *baueriana 19108*	
	R	*14226* Australia - Norfolk Is. *19108*
R	*Freycinetia marginata* Blume *20681*	
	R	*20681* Australia - Queensland *20681*
I	*Freycinetia marquisensis* F. Brown	
	I	French Polynesia - Marquesas Is
V	*Pandanus balfourii* Martelli *14296*	
	V	*19182* Seychelles *14296*
R	*Pandanus barklyi* Belf. F. var. *barklyi 20774*	
	R	*20771* Mauritius *20774*
Ex	*Pandanus barklyi* Balf. f. var. *macrocarpus* Vaughan & Wiehe *20774*	
	Ex	*20771* Mauritius *20774*
R	*Pandanus calcicola* Holttum & H. St. John	
	R	Malaysia - Peninsular Malaysia
I	*Pandanus canaranus* Warb.	
	I	India - Karnataka (Mangalore)
E	*Pandanus carmichaelii* Vaughan & Wiehe *20774*	
	E	*20771* Mauritius *20774*
R	*Pandanus clandestinus* Stone *20893*	
	R	*20893* New Caledonia *20893*
Ex	*Pandanus conglomeratus* Balf. f. *20774*	
	Ex	*20771* Mauritius *20774*
V	*Pandanus decastigma* Stone *20893*	
	V	*20893* New Caledonia *20893*
I	*Pandanus decipiens* Martelli *13833*	
	I	*13833* Philippines (low altitude) *13833*
V	*Pandanus decumbens* (Brongn.) Solms-Laub. *20893*	
	V	*20893* New Caledonia *20893*
Ex	*Pandanus drupaceus* Thouars *20774*	

Ex   20771 Mauritius 20774

R   *Pandanus elatius* Ridley 881
    R   14224 Australia - Christmas Is. 881

V   *Pandanus embuensis* St. John ined. 6073
    V   6073 Kenya 6073

R   *Pandanus eydouxia* Balf.f 20774
    R   20771 Mauritius 20774

R   *Pandanus gemmifer* St.John 20681
    R   20681 Australia - Queensland 20681

V   *Pandanus glaucocephalus* Vaughan & Wiehe 20774, 20771
    V   20771 Mauritius 20774

I   *Pandanus hornei* Balf. f. 14296
    I   19182 Seychelles (granitic) 14296

Ex   *Pandanus iceryi* Horne ex Balf. f. 20774
    Ex   20771 Mauritius 20774

Ex   *Pandanus incertus* Vaughan & Wiehe 20774
    Ex   20771 Mauritius 20774

R   *Pandanus irregularis* Ridley
    R   Malaysia - Peninsular Malaysia

R   *Pandanus julifer* Martelli 16040
    R   16040 Philippines (Camiguin de Misamis) 16040

V   *Pandanus kajui* Beentje ined. 20057
    V   20057 Kenya (central) 20057

E   *Pandanus lacuum* H. St. John 20893
    E   20893 New Caledonia 20893

Ex   *Pandanus macrostigma* Martelli 20774
    Ex   20771 Mauritius 20774

I   *Pandanus merrillii* Warb. 13833
    I   13833 Philippines (Palawan) 13833

E   *Pandanus microcarpus* 20774
    E   20771 Mauritius 20774

R   *Pandanus multidrupaceus* Gagnepain 6057
    R   Vietnam 6057

I   *Pandanus multispicatus* Balf. f. 14296
    I   19182 Seychelles (granitic) 14296

R   *Pandanus nativitatis* Ridley 881
    R   14224 Australia - Christmas Is. 881

Ex   *Pandanus obsoletus* Vaughan & Wiehe 20774
    Ex   20771 Mauritius 20774

I   *Pandanus occulta* Merr. 13833
    I   13833 Philippines (low altitude) 13833

E   *Pandanus palustris* Thouars 20774
    E   20771 Mauritius 20774

R   *Pandanus piniformis* Holttum & H. St. John
    R   Malaysia - Peninsular Malaysia

R   *Pandanus polyglossus* Martelli 16040
    R   16040 Philippines 16040

V   *Pandanus prostratus* Balf.f. 20774
    V   20771 Mauritius 20774

E   *Pandanus pyramidalis* Barkly ex Balf.f. 20774
    E   20771 Mauritius 20774

R   *Pandanus rigidifolius* Vaughan & Wiehe 20774
    R   20771 Mauritius 20774

R   *Pandanus sarasinorum* 16040
    R   16040 Indonesia - Sulawesi 16040

I   *Pandanus sechellarum* Balf. f. 14296
    I   19182 Seychelles (granitic) 14296

Ex   *Pandanus spathulatus* Martelle 20774

Ex   20771 Mauritius 20774

V   *Pandanus sphaeroideus* Thouars 20774
    V   20771 Mauritius 20774

V   *Pandanus spiralis* R.Br. var. *flammeus*
    Stone 20681
    V   20681 Australia - Western Australia 20681

V   *Pandanus vandermeerschii* Balf.f. 20774
    V   20771 Mauritius 20774

E   *Pandanus verecundus* Stone 20893
    E   20893 New Caledonia 20893

Philydraceae

Number of genera: 4
Number of species: 5
Recorded threatened species: 1   (20%)

Australia; western Pacific islands to Japan and mainland Southeast Asia.

R   *Helmholtzia glaberrima* (Hook.f.) Caruel 20681
    I   20681 Australia - New South Wales 20681
    I   20681 Australia - Queensland 20681

Phormiaceae

Number of genera: 7
Number of species: 36
Recorded threatened species: 4   (11%)

Old World tropics especially Australasia and South America.

R   *Dianella fruticans* R.Henderson 20681
    R   20681 Australia - Queensland 20681

I   *Dianella intermedia* Endl. var. *marquisensis* F. Brown
    I   French Polynesia - Marquesas Is

R   *Thelionema grande* (C.White) R.Henderson 20681
    I   20681 Australia - New South Wales 20681
    I   20681 Australia - Queensland 20681

R   *Xeronema callistemon* W. Oliver
    R   New Zealand - North Is.

Pontederiaceae

Number of genera: 9
Number of species: 30
Recorded threatened species: 1   (3%)

Tropical and subtropical; into North temperate region.

R   *Heteranthera mexicana* S.Watson 20883, 20850
    V   20850 U.S. - Texas 20850
    I   20883 Mexico 20883

Potamogetonaceae

Number of genera: 1
Number of species: 100
Recorded threatened species: 9   (9%)

Cosmopolitan.

E   *Potamogeton clystocarpus* Fern. 20850, 14781
    E   20850 U.S. - Texas 20850

E   *Potamogeton floridanus* Small 20850
    E   20850 U.S. - Florida 20850

R   *Potamogeton hillii* Morong 20850, 14352
    V   20850 Canada - Ontario 20850
    E   20850 U.S. - Connecticut 20850
    R   20850 U.S. - Massachusetts 20850

V	20850	U.S. - Michigan *20850*
V	20850	U.S. - New York *20850*
E	20850	U.S. - Ohio *20850*
E	20850	U.S. - Pennsylvania *20850*
R	20850	U.S. - Vermont *20850*
I	20850	U.S. - Wisconsin *20850*

E   *Potamogeton hoggarensis* Dandy *10487*

E	14958	Algeria *10487*

R   *Potamogeton latifolius* (J.W. Robbins) Morong *20850*

I	20850	U.S. - Arizona *20850*
I	20850	U.S. - California *20850*
I	20850	U.S. - Nevada *20850*
I	20850	U.S. - Oregon *20850*
E	20850	U.S. - Texas *20850*
I	20850	U.S. - Utah *20850*

E   *Potamogeton mariannensis* Cham. & Schltr. *18338*

E	18338	U.S. - Guam (Agana springs) *18338*

E   *Potamogeton ogdenii* Hellquist & Hilton *20850*

E	20850	U.S. - Massachusetts *20850*
E	20850	U.S. - New York *20850*
E	20850	U.S. - Vermont *20850*

R   *Potamogeton subsibiricus* Hagstr. *20850, 14352*

I	20850	Canada - New Brunswick *20850*
V	13967	Canada - Mackenzie *13967*
E	20850	Canada - Ontario *20850*
V	20850	Canada - Quebec *20850*
E	20850	Canada - Yukon Territory *20850*
V	20850	U.S. - Alaska *20850*

V   *Potamogeton tennesseensis* Fern. *20850*

E	20850	U.S. - Ohio *20850*
E	20850	U.S. - Pennsylvania *20850*
E	20850	U.S. - Tennessee *20850*
E	20850	U.S. - Virginia *20850*
I	20850	U.S. - West Virginia *20850*

Restionaceae

Number of genera:	30	
Number of species:	400	
Recorded threatened species:	58	(14%)

Widely distributed in Southern Hemisphere, especially Australia and South Africa.

V   *Askidiosperma longiflorum* (Pillans) H.P.Linder *20803*

V	20803	South Africa - Cape Province *20803*

V   *Calopsis impolita* (Kunth) H.P.Linder *20604*

V	20604	South Africa - Cape Province *20604*

R   *Calopsis levynsiae* (Pillans) H.P.Linder *20604*

R	20604	South Africa - Cape Province *20604*

I   *Calopsis monostylis* (Pillans) H.P.Linder *20604*

I	20604	South Africa - Cape Province *20604*

V   *Calopsis rigorata* (Mast.) H.P.Linder *20604*

V	20604	South Africa - Cape Province *20604*

R   *Cannomois aristata* Mast. *20604*

R	20604	South Africa - Cape Province *20604*

I   *Ceratocaryum fistulosum* Mast. *20604*

I	20604	South Africa - Cape Province *20604*

R   *Ceratocaryum pulchrum* H.P.Linder *20604*

R	20604	South Africa - Cape Province *20604*

E   *Chondropetalum acockii* Pillans *20604*

E	20604	South Africa - Cape Province *20604*

V   *Chondropetalum rectum* (Mast.) Pillans *20604*

V	20604	South Africa - Cape Province *20604*

I   *Elegia extensa* Pillans *20604, 3774*

I	20604	South Africa - Cape Province *20604*

Ex   *Elegia fastigiata* Mast. *20604, 3774*

Ex	20604	South Africa - Cape Province *20604*

V   *Elegia fenestrata* Pillans *20604*

V	20604	South Africa - Cape Province *20604*

V   *Elegia prominens* Pillans *20604*

V	20604	South Africa - Cape Province *20604*

V   *Elegia stokoei* Pillans *20604*

V	20604	South Africa - Cape Province *20604*

V   *Elegia verreauxii* Mast. *20604*

V	20604	South Africa - Cape Province *20604*

R   *Hypodiscus alternans* Pillans *20604*

R	20604	South Africa - Cape Province *20604*

R   *Hypodiscus sulcatus* Pillans *20604*

R	20604	South Africa - Cape Province *20604*

V   *Ischyrolepis coactilis* (Mast.) H.P.Linder *20604*

V	20604	South Africa - Cape Province *20604*

V   *Ischyrolepis duthieae* (Pillans) H.P.Linder *20604*

V	20604	South Africa - Cape Province *20604*

R   *Ischyrolepis esterhuyseniae* (Pillans) H.P.Linder *20604*

R	20604	South Africa - Cape Province *20604*

R   *Ischyrolepis fuscidula* (Pillans) H.P.Linder *20604*

R	20604	South Africa - Cape Province *20604*

R   *Ischyrolepis karooica* Esterh. *20604*

R	20604	South Africa - Cape Province *20604*

E   *Ischyrolepis sabulosa* (Pillans) H.P.Linder *20604*

E	20604	South Africa - Cape Province *20604*

R   *Ischyrolepis vilis* (Kunth) H.P.Linder *20604*

R	20604	South Africa - Cape Province *20604*

R   *Ischyrolepis wittebergensis* Esterh. *20604*

R	20604	South Africa - Cape Province *20604*

R   *Lepidobolus desertii* Gilg *20681*

R	20681	Australia - Western Australia *20681*

R   *Lepyrodia valliculae* J.Black *20681*

R	20681	Australia - South Australia *20681*

R   *Platycaulos cascadensis* (Pillans) H.P.Linder *20604*

R	20604	South Africa - Cape Province *20604*

I   *Platycaulos subcompressus* (Pillans) H.P.Linder *20604*

I	20604	South Africa - Cape Province *20604*

E   *Restio abortivus* Nees *20681*

E	20681	Australia - Western Australia *20681*

E   *Restio acockii* Pillans *20604*

E	20604	South Africa - Cape Province *20604*

I   *Restio aureolus* Pillans *20604*

I	20604	South Africa - Cape Province *20604*

R   *Restio brunneus* Pillans *20604*

R	20604	South Africa - Cape Province *20604*

V   *Restio chaunocoleus* F.Muell. *20681, 14223*

V	20681	Australia - Western Australia *20681*

R   *Restio distans* Pillans *20604*

R	20604	South Africa - Cape Province *20604*

R   *Restio dodii* Pillans *20604*

R	20604	South Africa - Cape Province *20604*

V   *Restio festuciformis* Nees ex Mast. *20604*

V	20604	South Africa - Cape Province *20604*

R   *Restio fusiformis* Pillans *20604*

R	20604	South Africa - Cape Province *20604*

V   *Restio harveyi* Mast. *20604*

	V	*20604* South Africa - Cape Province *20604*	

R   *Restio involutus* Pillans *20604*
     R   *20604* South Africa - Cape Province *20604*

V   *Restio longipes* L.A.S.Johnson & O.Evans *20681*
     V   *20681* Australia - New South Wales *20681*

E   *Restio micans* (Kunth) Nees *20604*
     E   *20604* South Africa - Cape Province *20604*

R   *Restio monocephalus* R.Br. *20681*
     R   *20681* Australia - Tasmania *20681*

R   *Restio papyraceus* Pillans *20604*
     R   *20604* South Africa - Cape Province *20604*

V   *Restio scaber* Mast. *20604*
     V   *20604* South Africa - Cape Province *20604*

R   *Restio tuberculatus* Pillans *20604*
     R   *20604* South Africa - Cape Province *20604*

I   *Staberoha multispicula* Pillans *20604*
     I   *20604* South Africa - Cape Province *20604*

R   *Staberoha stokoei* Pillans *20604*
     R   *20604* South Africa - Cape Province *20604*

R   *Thamnochortus acuminatus* Pillans *20604*
     R   *20604* South Africa - Cape Province *20604*

V   *Thamnochortus dumosus* Mast. *20604*
     V   *20604* South Africa - Cape Province *20604*

I   *Thamnochortus ellipticus* Pillans *20604*
     I   *20604* South Africa - Cape Province *20604*

R   *Thamnochortus guthrieae* Pillans *20604*
     R   *20604* South Africa - Cape Province *20604*

V   *Thamnochortus muirii* Pillans *20604*
     V   *20604* South Africa - Cape Province *20604*

R   *Thamnochortus nutans* (Thunb.) Pillans *20604*
     R   *20604* South Africa - Cape Province *20604*

V   *Thamnochortus pellucidus* Pillans *20604*
     V   *20604* South Africa - Cape Province *20604*

V   *Thamnochortus pluristachyus* Mast. *20604*
     V   *20604* South Africa - Cape Province *20604*

R   *Willdenowia purpurea* Pillans *20604*
     R   *20604* South Africa - Cape Province *20604*

R   *Winifredia sola* L.A.S.Johnson & B.G.Briggs *20681*
     R   *20681* Australia - Tasmania *20681*

Ruscaceae

Number of genera: 3
Number of species: 8
Recorded threatened species: 4   (50%)

Macaronesia, Europe, Mediterranean, West Asia.

R   *Ruscus colchicus* Yeo *5942*
     R   Turkey
     I   *5942* Georgia *5942*

V   *Ruscus streptophyllus* Yeo
     V   Portugal - Madeira

R   *Semele androgyna* (L.) Kunth
     R   Portugal - Madeira
     V   Spain - Canary Is.

V   *Semele gayae* (Webb) Svent. & Kunkel *20750*
     V   *20750* Spain - Canary Is. *20750*

Smilacaceae

Number of genera: 12
Number of species: 330
Recorded threatened species: 11   (3%)

Tropical and subtropical, especially Southern Hemisphere; also in parts of North temperate region.

R   *Smilax biflora* Sieb. ex Miq. *11164*
     R   *11164* Japan *11164*

R   *Smilax biltmoreana* (Small) J.B.S. Norton ex Pennell *20850*
     I   *20850* U.S. - Alabama *20850*
     I   *20850* U.S. - Florida *20850*
     R   *20850* U.S. - Georgia *20850*
     I   *20850* U.S. - Kentucky *20850*
     R   *20850* U.S. - North Carolina *20850*
     I   *20850* U.S. - South Carolina *20850*
     V   *20850* U.S. - Tennessee *20850*

R   *Smilax canariensis* Brouss. ex Willd. *20171*
     R   Portugal - Madeira
     V   Spain - Canary Is.

I   *Smilax chiriquensis* Morton *20883, 9006*
     I   *20883* Panama *20883*

R   *Smilax cordato-ovata* Rich. *8679*
     R   French Guiana *8679*

R   *Smilax divaricata* Sol. ex H.C.Watson *20171*
     R   Portugal - Azores

V   *Smilax jamesii* G. Wallace *20850*
     V   *20850* U.S. - California *20850*

V   *Smilax luei* *20854*
     V   *20854* Taiwan *20854*

V   *Smilax nantoensis* *20854*
     V   *20854* Taiwan *20854*

R   *Smilax renifolia* Small *20850*
     R   *20850* U.S. - Texas *20850*

R   *Smilax wightii* A. DC. *11494*
     R   *11494* India - Tamil Nadu (Nilgiri Hills) *11494*

Stemonaceae

Number of genera: 3
Number of species: 30
Recorded threatened species: 2   (6%)

Eastern Asia; Malesia; northern Australia; southeastern United States.

R   *Croomia pauciflora* (Nutt.) Torr. *20850*
     R   *20850* U.S. - Alabama *20850*
     V   *20850* U.S. - Florida *20850*
     E   *20850* U.S. - Georgia *20850*
     Ex/E   *20850* U.S. - Louisiana *20850*

V   *Stemona angusta* Telford *20681*
     V   *20681* Australia - Queensland *20681*

Strelitziaceae

Number of genera: 3
Number of species: 7
Recorded threatened species: 2   (28%)

Tropical.

I   *Strelitzia alba* (L.f.) Skeels *20604*
     I   *20604* South Africa - Cape Province *20604*

R   *Strelitzia juncea* Link *20604*

R   20604 South Africa - Cape Province *20604*

Tecophilaeaceae

Number of genera:	6	
Number of species:	42	
Recorded threatened species:	3	(7%)

Africa, S.America to California.

R   *Cyanella aquatica* Oberm. ex G.Scott *20604*
   R   *20604* South Africa - Cape Province *20604*

R   *Cyanella cygnea* G.Scott *20604*
   R   *20604* South Africa - Cape Province *20604*

Ex   *Tecophilaea cyanocrocus* Leybold *6163*
   Ex   *6163* Chile *6163*

R   *Walleria gracilis* (Salisb.) S.Carter *20604*
   R   *20604* South Africa - Cape Province *20604*

Trilliaceae

Number of genera:	5	
Number of species:	52	
Recorded threatened species:	16	(30%)

North temperate.

R   *Scoliopus bigelovii* Torr. *20850*
   I   *20850* U.S. - California *20850*

I   *Trillium amabile* Miyabe & Tatew. *11164*
   I   *11164* Japan *11164*

R   *Trillium decipiens* J.D. Freeman *20850*
   V   *20850* U.S. - Alabama *20850*
   I   *20850* U.S. - Florida *20850*
   R   *20850* U.S. - Georgia *20850*

R   *Trillium discolor* Wray ex Hook. *20850*
   V   *20850* U.S. - Georgia *20850*
   E   *20850* U.S. - North Carolina *20850*
   I   *20850* U.S. - South Carolina *20850*

R   *Trillium foetidissimum* J.D. Freeman *20850*
   R   *20850* U.S. - Louisiana *20850*
   R   *20850* U.S. - Mississippi *20850*

E   *Trillium govanianum* Wallich ex Royle *11139*
   E   China - Xizang Zizhiqu *11139*

R   *Trillium lancifolium* Raf. *20850*
   V   *20850* U.S. - Alabama *20850*
   V   *20850* U.S. - Florida *20850*
   V   *20850* U.S. - Georgia *20850*
   I   *20850* U.S. - Mississippi *20850*
   E   *20850* U.S. - South Carolina *20850*
   E   *20850* U.S. - Tennessee *20850*
   I   *20850* U.S. - Virginia *20850*

R   *Trillium ludovicianum* Harbison *20850*
   R   *20850* U.S. - Louisiana *20850*
   E   *20850* U.S. - Mississippi *20850*

R   *Trillium nivale* Riddell *14905*
   R   *14905* U.S. - Kentucky *14905*
   V   *14905* U.S. - Michigan *14905*
   E   *14905* U.S. - Pennsylvania *14905*
   E   *14905* U.S. - South Dakota *14905*
   E   *14905* U.S. - Wisconsin *14905*

R   *Trillium parviflorum* Soukup *20850*
   I   *20850* U.S. - Oregon *20850*
   V   *20850* U.S. - Washington *20850*

E   *Trillium persistens* Duncan *20850*
   E   *20850* U.S. - Georgia *20850*
   E   *20850* U.S. - South Carolina *20850*

R   *Trillium pusillum* Michx. *20850*

V   *20850* U.S. - Alabama *20850*
R   *20850* U.S. - Arkansas *20850*
I   *20850* U.S. - Kentucky *20850*
V   *20850* U.S. - Maryland *20850*
E   *20850* U.S. - Mississippi *20850*
V   *20850* U.S. - Missouri *20850*
E   *20850* U.S. - North Carolina *20850*
I   *20850* U.S. - Oklahoma *20850*
I   *20850* U.S. - South Carolina *20850*
V   *20850* U.S. - Tennessee *20850*
V   *20850* U.S. - Texas *20850*
V   *20850* U.S. - Virginia *20850*
E   *20850* U.S. - West Virginia *20850*

R   *Trillium pusillum* Michaux var. *ozarkanum* (Palmer & Steyermark) Steyermark. *20850*
   R   *20850* U.S. - Arkansas *20850*
   E   *20850* U.S. - Kentucky *20850*
   V   *20850* U.S. - Missouri *20850*
   E   *20850* U.S. - Oklahoma *20850*
   E   *20850* U.S. - Tennessee *20850*

V   *Trillium pusillum* Michaux var. *pusillum* *20850*
   V   *20850* U.S. - Alabama *20850*
   E   *20850* U.S. - Kentucky *20850*
   I   *20850* U.S. - Maryland *20850*
   I   *20850* U.S. - Mississippi *20850*
   E   *20850* U.S. - North Carolina *20850*
   E   *20850* U.S. - South Carolina *20850*
   E   *20850* U.S. - Tennessee *20850*

V   *Trillium pusillum* Michaux var. *virginianum* Fern. *20850*
   V   *20850* U.S. - Maryland *20850*
   E   *20850* U.S. - North Carolina *20850*
   V   *20850* U.S. - Virginia *20850*
   I   *20850* U.S. - West Virginia *20850*

V   *Trillium reliquum* J.D. Freeman *20850*
   V   *20850* U.S. - Alabama *20850*
   V   *20850* U.S. - Georgia *20850*
   E   *20850* U.S. - South Carolina *20850*

R   *Trillium rugelii* Rendle *20850*
   V   *20850* U.S. - Alabama *20850*
   R   *20850* U.S. - Georgia *20850*
   V   *20850* U.S. - North Carolina *20850*
   I   *20850* U.S. - South Carolina *20850*
   V   *20850* U.S. - Tennessee *20850*

R   *Trillium simile* Gleason *20850*
   E   *20850* U.S. - Georgia *20850*
   E   *20850* U.S. - North Carolina *20850*
   I   *20850* U.S. - South Carolina *20850*
   I   *20850* U.S. - Tennessee *20850*

V   *Trillium texanum* Buckl. *20850*
   E   *20850* U.S. - Louisiana *20850*
   V   *20850* U.S. - Texas *20850*

Triuridaceae

Number of genera:	7	
Number of species:	70	
Recorded threatened species:	11	(15%)

Tropical and subtropical.

R   *Andruris japonica* (Makino) Giesen *11164*
   R   *11164* Japan *11164*

R   *Lacandonia schismatica* E. Martínez & C.H. Ramos *14293*
   R   *19850* Mexico - Chiapas *14293*

I   *Sciaphila africana* A. Chev. *7926*
   I   Côte d'Ivoire (Bas-Cavally)
   I   *6072* Ghana (Ankasa) *6072*

I	*Sciaphila erubescens* (Champ.) Miers *10252*		
	I	*16162* Sri Lanka *10252*	
I	*Sciaphila inornata* Petch ex Alston *10252*		
	I	*16162* Sri Lanka *10252*	
E	*Sciaphila okabeana* Tuy. *8037*		
	E	*19134* Japan - Ogasawara-shoto *8037*	
I	*Sciaphila secundiflora* Trimen ex Benth. *10252*		
	I	*16162* Sri Lanka *10252*	
R	*Sciaphila takakumensis* Ohwi *11164*		
	R	*11164* Japan *11164*	
E	*Sciaphila thailandica* K. Larsen *19120*		
	E	*19120* Thailand (Chiang Mai) *19120*	
R	*Sciaphila tosaensis* Makino *11164*		
	R	*11164* Japan *11164*	
V	*Seychellaria thomassetii* Hemsley *14296*		
	V	*19182* Seychelles *14296*	

Velloziaceae

Number of genera:	6
Number of species:	250
Recorded threatened species:	5 (2%)

South America; Africa; Madagascar; southern Arabia.

E	*Vellozia panamensis* Standl. *20883, 9006*		
	I	*20883* Panama *20883*	
R	*Xerophyta argentea* (Wild) Loren B. Smith & Agens.		
	R	Zimbabwe	
I	*Xerophyta goetzei* (Harms) L.L. Smith & Ayensu *5926*		
	I	*5926* Tanzania *5926*	
I	*Xerophyta longicaulis* Hilliard *20604*		
	I	*20604* South Africa - Natal *20604*	
I	*Xerophyta nutans* L.B. Smith & Ayensu *5926*		
	I	*5926* Tanzania *5926*	

Xanthorrhoeaceae

Number of genera:	9
Number of species:	15
Recorded threatened species:	3 (20%)

Australia; Tasmania; New Guinea; New Caledonia.

V	*Xanthorrhoea arenaria* Bedford *20681*		
	V	*20681* Australia - Tasmania *20681*	
V	*Xanthorrhoea bracteata* R.Br. *20681*		
	V	*20681* Australia - Tasmania *20681*	
R	*Xanthorrhoea brevistyla* D.Herbert *20681*		
	R	*20681* Australia - Western Australia *20681*	

Xyridaceae

Number of genera:	4
Number of species:	200
Recorded threatened species:	19 (9%)

Tropical and subtropical; a few species in temperate zone.

R	*Abolboda abbreviata* Malme *21283*		
	R	*21283* Brazil *21283*	
R	*Abolboda bella* Maguire *21283*		
	R	*21283* Venezuela *21283*	
R	*Abolboda egleri* Lyman B. Smith & Downs *21283*		
	R	*21283* Brazil *21283*	
R	*Xyris chapmanii* Bridges & Orzell *20850*		
	I	*20850* U.S. - Alabama *20850*	

	E	*20850* U.S. - Florida *20850*	
	I	*20850* U.S. - Georgia *20850*	
	V	*20850* U.S. - Mississippi *20850*	
	V	*20850* U.S. - North Carolina *20850*	
	I	*20850* U.S. - South Carolina *20850*	
	I	*20850* U.S. - Texas *20850*	
R	*Xyris columbiana* Malme *11699*		
	R	*11699* Colombia *11699*	
	R	*11699* Venezuela *11699*	
R	*Xyris contracta* Maguire & Lyman B. Smith *11699*		
	R	*11699* Brazil *11699*	
	R	*11699* Venezuela *11699*	
R	*Xyris drummondii* Malme *20850*		
	E	*20850* U.S. - Alabama *20850*	
	V	*20850* U.S. - Florida *20850*	
	E	*20850* U.S. - Georgia *20850*	
	E	*20850* U.S. - Louisiana *20850*	
	V	*20850* U.S. - Mississippi *20850*	
	V	*20850* U.S. - Texas *20850*	
E	*Xyris ekmanii* Malme *5607*		
	E	*19105* Cuba (Pinar del Rio) *5607*	
V	*Xyris guillauminii* Conert *20893*		
	V	*20893* New Caledonia *20893*	
I	*Xyris intermedia* Malme *5607*		
	I	*19105* Cuba (Pinar del Rio) *5607*	
V	*Xyris isoetifolia* Kral *20850*		
	I	*20850* U.S. - Alabama *20850*	
	V	*20850* U.S. - Florida *20850*	
E	*Xyris longibracteata* Britton & P. Wilson *5607*		
	E	*19105* Cuba (Juventud Is.) *5607*	
V	*Xyris longisepala* Kral *20850*		
	E	*20850* U.S. - Alabama *20850*	
	V	*20850* U.S. - Florida *20850*	
R	*Xyris neblinae* Maguire & Lyman B. Smith *11699*		
	R	Venezuela *11699*	
R	*Xyris nigrescens* Kraal *10128*		
	R	*11699* Costa Rica *10128*	
R	*Xyris rubrolimbata* Heimerl *11699*		
	R	*11699* Colombia *11699*	
	R	*11699* Venezuela *11699*	
R	*Xyris scabrifolia* Harper *20850*		
	E	*20850* U.S. - Alabama *20850*	
	E	*20850* U.S. - Florida *20850*	
	E	*20850* U.S. - Georgia *20850*	
	E	*20850* U.S. - Louisiana *20850*	
	E	*20850* U.S. - Mississippi *20850*	
	V	*20850* U.S. - North Carolina *20850*	
	I	*20850* U.S. - South Carolina *20850*	
	V	*20850* U.S. - Texas *20850*	
E	*Xyris tennesseensis* Kral *20850, 14775*		
	E	*20850* U.S. - Alabama *20850*	
	E	*20850* U.S. - Georgia *20850*	
	E	*20850* U.S. - Tennessee *20850*	
R	*Xyris terrestris* Idrobo & Lyman B. Smith *11699*		
	R	*11699* Colombia *11699*	

Zannichelliaceae

Number of genera:	4
Number of species:	7-8
Recorded threatened species:	1 (12%)

Cosmopolitan.

R	*Zannichellia macrocarpa* *19575*		
	R	*19575* Argentina *19575*	

Zingiberaceae

Number of genera: 47
Number of species: 1,000
Recorded threatened species: 76 (7%)

Tropical regions, especially southern and Southeast Asia.

R	**Achasma triorgyale** (Baker) Holttum	
	R	Malaysia - Peninsular Malaysia
R	**Aframomum alpinum** (Gagnepain) Schumann *7959*	
	R	*5926* Tanzania *7959*
I	**Aframomum laxiflorum** Lock *7959*	
	I	*5926* Tanzania *5926*
I	**Aframomum letestuanum** Gagnep.	
	I	Gabon
R	**Aframomum longiligulatum** Koechlin	
	R	Cameroon
R	**Aframomum usambarense** J.M. Lock *7959*	
	R	*5926* Tanzania *7959*
E	**Alpinia bilamellata** Makino *8037*	
	E	*19134* Japan - Ogasawara-shoto *8037*
R	**Alpinia boninsimensis** Makino *8038*	
	R	*19134* Japan - Ogasawara-shoto (Chichijima; Hahajima) *8038*
I	**Alpinia fax** Burtt & Smith *8021*	
	I	*16162* Sri Lanka (Kalupahana, Tangamalai FoR) *8021*
I	**Alpinia foxworthyii** Ridl. *13833*	
	I	*13833* Philippines *13833*
R	**Alpinia gagnepainii** Schumann *6057*	
	R	Vietnam *6057*
R	**Alpinia hylandii** R.M.Smith *20681*	
	R	*20681* Australia - Queensland *20681*
I	**Alpinia rufescens** (Thwaites) Schum. *8021*	
	I	*16162* Sri Lanka (Dickoya, Kandy) *8021*
I	**Amomum acuminatum** Thwaites *8021*	
	I	*16162* Sri Lanka (Ekneligoda, Ratnapura) *8021*
I	**Amomum benthamianum** Trimen *8021*	
	I	*16162* Sri Lanka (Reigam Korale, Kalutara) *8021*
R	**Amomum dallachyi** F.Muell. *20681*	
	R	*20681* Australia - Queensland *20681*
I	**Amomum echinocarpum** Alston *8021*	
	I	*20013* Sri Lanka (Kandy) *8021*
I	**Amomum fulviceps** Thwaites *8021*	
	I	*20013* Sri Lanka *8021*
I	**Amomum graminifolium** Thwaites *8021*	
	I	*16162* Sri Lanka (Sinharaja) *8021*
I	**Amomum hypoleucum** Thwaites *8021*	
	I	India - Tamil Nadu
	I	*16162* Sri Lanka *8021*
I	**Amomum masticatorium** Thwaites *8021*	
	I	*20013* Sri Lanka *8021*
R	**Amomum microstephanum** Baker *13883*	
	R	*13883* India - Karnataka (Concan) *13883*
	R	*13883* India - Tamil Nadu *13883*
I	**Amomum nemorale** (Thwaites) Trimen *8021*	
	I	*20013* Sri Lanka (Hewessa, Kalutara) *8021*
I	**Amomum palawanense** Elm. *13833*	
	I	*13833* Philippines (low altitude) *13833*
R	**Amomum queenslandicum** R.M.Smith *20681*	

	R	*20681* Australia - Queensland *20681*
R	**Amomum thyrsoideum** Gagnepain *6057*	
	R	Vietnam *6057*
I	**Amomum trichostachyum** Alston *8021*	
	I	*16162* Sri Lanka (Gilimale FoR) *8021*
R	**Amomum vespertilio** Gagnepain *6057*	
	R	Vietnam *6057*
R	**Aulotandra kamerunensis** Loes.	
	R	Cameroon
I	**Boesenbergia albo-lutea** (Baker) Schecht. *7771*	
	I	India - Andaman Is. *7771*
R	**Boesenbergia curtisii** (Hook.f.) Schltr.	
	R	Malaysia - Peninsular Malaysia
I	**Boesenbergia pulcherrima** (Wallich) Kuntze	
	I	India - Karnataka (Western Ghats)
	I	India - Kerala
I	**Cautleya petiolata** Baker	
	I	India - Himachal Pradesh
	I	India - Uttar Pradesh
I	**Curcuma albiflora** Thwaites *8021*	
	I	*16162* Sri Lanka (Kitulgala FoR, Kegalle) *8021*
I	**Curcuma decipiens** Dalz.	
	I	India (Western Ghats)
R	**Curcuma montana** Roxb.	
	I	India - Karnataka
	R	*18228* India - Tamil Nadu *18228*
R	**Etlingera australasica** (R.M.Smith) R.M.Smith *20681*	
	R	*20681* Australia - Queensland *20681*
R	**Geanthus vignaui** (Rech.) Loes. *8006*	
	R	U.S. - American Samoa *8006*
	R	Western Samoa *8006*
R	**Globba albiflora** Ridley	
	R	Malaysia - Peninsular Malaysia
R	**Globba fasciata** Ridl. *19209*	
	R	Malaysia - Peninsular Malaysia (Perak) *19209*
R	**Globba globulifera** Gagnepain *6057*	
	R	Vietnam *6057*
I	**Globba pauciflora** Baker *7771*	
	I	India - Andaman Is. (S. Andaman Is.) *7771*
I	**Hedychium calcaratum** A. Rao & Verma	
	I	India - Meghalaya (Khasi hills)
I	**Hedychium dekianum** A. Rao & Verma	
	I	India - Meghalaya (Khasi & Jaintia hills)
I	**Hedychium gracillimum** A. Rao & Verma	
	I	India - Meghalaya (Khasi hills)
I	**Hedychium gratum** A. Rao & Verma	
	I	India - Meghalaya (Khasi hills)
I	**Hedychium longipedunculatum** Sastry & Verma	
	I	India - Arunachal Pradesh (Subansiri)
Ex	**Hedychium marginatum** C.B. Clarke	
	Ex	India - Nagaland
I	**Hedychium rubrum** A. Rao & Verma	
	I	India - Meghalaya
R	**Kaempferia cochinchinensis** Gagnepain *6057*	
	R	Vietnam *6057*
R	**Kaempferia decora** van Druten	
	R	Mozambique

I   *Kaempferia rotunda* L.
       I   India - Kerala (Trivandrum)

I   *Kaempferia siphonantha* Baker *7771*
       I   India - Andaman Is. *7771*

V   *Mantisia spathulata* Schultes *14872*
       V   *14872*   Bangladesh *14872*

V   *Paracautleya bhatii* Smith *13883*
       V   *13883*   India - Karnataka (South Kanara Dist.,
                  Manipal) *13883*

I   *Renealmia alticola* Maas *9660*
       I   *9660*   Colombia *9660*

R   *Renealmia brasiliensis* K.Schumann *11307*
       R   *11307*   Brazil - Espirito Santo *11307*
       R   *11307*   Brazil - Guanabara *11307*
       R   *11307*   Brazil - Minas Gerais *11307*

R   *Renealmia caucana* Maas *9660*
       R   *9660*   Colombia *9660*

R   *Renealmia chalcochlora* Schumann *9660*
       R   *9660*   Colombia *9660*

E   *Renealmia chiriquina* Standl. *20883, 10125*
       I   *20883*   Panama *20883*

R   *Renealmia chrysotricha* O.G.Petersen *11307*
       R   *11307*   Brazil (Corcovada Mts.) *11307*

I   *Renealmia cuatrecasasii* Maas *9660*
       I   *9660*   Colombia *9660*

E   *Renealmia dressleri* Maas *20883, 10747*
       I   *20883*   Panama *20883*

I   *Renealmia ferruginea* Maas *9660*
       I   *9660*   Colombia *9660*

E   *Renealmia helenae* Maas *20883, 10125*
       V   *9429*   Panama *20883*

I   *Renealmia lucida* Maas *9660*
       I   *9660*   Colombia *9660*

R   *Renealmia oligotricha* Maas *10125*
       R   Ecuador *10125*

V   *Renealmia pallida* Maas *18200*
       V   *12468*   Peru *18200*

R   *Renealmia pirrensis* P. Maas & H. Maas *11310*
       R   *11306*   Panama *11310*

Ex/E   *Renealmia pycnostachys* K.Schumann *11307*
       Ex/E   *11307*   Brazil - Minas Gerais *11307*

R   *Renealmia sylvestris* (Sw.) Horan. *20883*
       R   *20883*   Jamaica *20883*

I   *Renealmia vallensis* Maas *9660*
       I   *9660*   Colombia *9660*

V   *Renealmia wurdackii* Maas *18200*
       V   *12468*   Peru *18200*

R   *Siliquamomum tonkinense* Baillon *6057*
       R   Vietnam *6057*

I   *Siphonochilus aethiopicus* (Schweinf.)
       B.L.Burtt *20604, 15013*
       I   *20604*   Swaziland *20604*
       E   *20604*   South Africa - Natal *20604*
       E   *20604*   South Africa - Transvaal *20604*

I   *Zingiber cernuum* Dalz.
       I   India - Karnataka (Concan)

R   *Zingiber rufopilosum* Gagnepain *6057*
       R   Vietnam *6057*

Zosteraceae

Number of genera: 3
Number of species: 18
Recorded threatened species: 1   (5%)

Subarctic, temperate, subtropical seacoasts.

R   *Phyllospadix serrulatus* Rupr. ex Aschers. *20850*
       I   *20850*   Canada - British Columbia *20850*
       V   *20850*   U.S. - Alaska *20850*
       I   *20850*   U.S. - Oregon *20850*
       I   *20850*   U.S. - Washington *20850*

DATA SOURCES

23 **Lucas, G. Ll. & Synge, H. (comps.). (1978).**
The IUCN Plant Red Data Book. Morges, Switzerland: IUCN.
540 pp.

86 **Williams, G.R. & Given, D.R. (1981).** The Red
Data Book of New Zealand: rare and endangered species of
endemic terrestrial vertebrates and vascular plants.
Wellington, N.Z.: Nature Conservation Council. 175 pp.
Maps.

320 **Leigh, J.H. & Boden, R. (1979).** Australian
flora in the Endangered Species Convention - CITES.
Spec. Publ. No. 3. Canberra, Australian National Parks
and Wildlife Service. 93 pp. Col. illus.

881 **Leigh, J.H., Briggs, J.D., & Hartley, W.
(1981).** Rare or threatened Australian plants. Spec.
Publ. No. 7. Canberra: Australian National Parks and
Wildlife Service. 178 pp. Illus., maps.

1034 **Douglas, G.W., Argus, G.W., Dickson, H.L., &
Brunton, D.F. (1981).** Les plantes vasculaires rares
du Yukon. [The rare vascular plants of the Yukon.].
Syllogeus 61(35):28-64. Maps. Contribution to
Unesco Program on Man and the Biosphere.

1058 **Hunt, D.R. (1982).** The conservation status of
Mexican mammillarias: a preliminary assessment.
Cact. Succ. J.(U.K.) 44(4):87-88.

1144 **Holttum, R.E. (1982).** *Diplazium
prescottianum* (Wall. ex Hook.) Bedd: a Singapore
fern now possibly extinct. *Gard. Bull.
Singapore* 35(1):65-68. Illus.

1170 **Nair, N.C. & Ramachandran, V.S. (1982).** A note
on the rare plant *Oianthus disciflorus* Hook.f.
Bull. Bot. Surv. India 22(1-4):234-235. (1980
publ. 1982).

1172 **Nair, N.C. & Srinivasan, S.R. (1982).**
Rediscovery of *Eugenia discifera* Gamble
(Myrtaceae) and its lectotypification. *Bull. Bot.
Surv. India* 22(1-4):232-233. (1980 publ. 1982).

1746 **Krasnitskii, A.M. (1978).** Osnovye zadachi
spetsializatsii zapovednogo dela. [Foundation problems
of specialization in the nature reserve business.].
In Latvia. Akademiya Nauk Latviiskoi SSR.
Institut Biologii. Rastitel'nyi mir okhranyaemykh
territorii. Riga, Zinatne. 29-33. Rus. Includes nature
reserve organization.

1920 **Anon. (1978).** UNESCO's programmes on natural
resources and environment for 1979-80. *Nat.
Resources* 14(4):13-28.

1975 **Ortuno, F. & Pena, J. de la. (1977).** Reservas
y cotos nacionales de caza: 2. Región Cantábrica.
Colección Naturaleza Española: 3. Madrid, INCAFO. 253p.
Sp. Col. illus., maps.

2014 **Moore, H.E. (1979).** Endangerment at the
specific and generic levels in palms.
Principes 23(2):47-64.

2050 **Holub, J., Procházka, F., & Cerovsky, J.
(1979).** Seznam vykynulych, endemickych a ohrozenych
taxonu vyssich rostlin kveteny CSR (1. verze). [List of
the extinct, endemic and threatened taxa of vascular
plants of the flora of the Czech Socialist Republic
(first draft)]. *Preslia* 51(3):213-237. Cz
(En).

2063 **Maher, R.V., Argus, G.W., Harms, V.L., & Hudson,
J.H. (1979).** Les plantes vasculaires rares de la
Saskatchewan. [The rare vascular plants of
Saskatchewan]. *Syllogeus* 20:55. Maps.

2203 **Kuzmanov, B. (1978).** About the "Red Book of
Rare Bulgarian Plants". *Phytology* 9:17-33.
English summary.

2232 **Ward, D.B. (ed.). (1979).** Rare and endangered
biota of Florida: 5. Plants. Gainesville: University
Presses of Florida. 175 pp. Illus., maps. Series edited
by P.C.H. Pritchard. Reviewed in *Threatened Pl.
Commit. Newsl.*, 7: 23-24 (1981).

2268 **Abraham, Z. & Mehrotra, B.N. (1983).** Some
observations on endemic species and rare plants of the
montane flora of the Nilgiris. South India. *J.
Econ. Taxon. Bot.* 3(3):863-867. 1982 publ. 1983.

2327 **Anon. (1983).** Rediscovered! The black orchid.
S. Afr. Gard. Home April 1983:53,55. Col.
illus. *Disa bodkinii*.

2358 **Lobo, M. da G.A. (1982).** *Sipolisia
languginosa* Glaziou: uma espécie ameaçada de
extinçao. Flora, espécies raras ou ameaçadas de
extinçao: 1. *Cadernos FEEMA Ser. Trab. Techn.*
18:21-24.

2359 **Vianna, M.C. (1982).** *Vochysia
oppugnata* (Vell.) Warm., canela-santa: uma
Vochysiaceae ameaçada. Flora, espécies raras ou
ameaçadas de extinçao: 1. *Cadernos FEEMA Ser. Trab.
Techn.* 18:13-20. Por. Illus.

2383 **Carauta, J.P.P. & Castro, M.W. de. (1982).**
Plantas em perigo de extinçao: *Dorstenia*.
Flora, alguns estudos: 1. *Cadernos FEEMA Ser. Trab.
Tecn.* 1:29-65. Por (En). Illus. 16 spp. of
Dorstenia.

2409 **Casari, M.B. (1982).** Espécies de
Anthurium (Araceae) raras ou ameaçadas no
Estado do Rio de Janeiro. (Rare or endangered
Anthurium (Araceae) species in the State of
Rio de Janeiro.). [Rare or endangered
Anthurium (Araceae) species in the State of
Rio de Janeiro.] Flora, alguns estudos: 1. *Cadernos
FEEMA Ser. Trab. Techn.* 1:17-27. Por (En). Illus.

2457 **Ertter, B. (1983).** Notes on *Ivesia
rhypara*. *Madroño* 30(4):257-258.

2790 **Ayensu, E.S. & DeFilipps, R.A. (1978).**
Endangered and threatened plants of the United States.
Washington, DC: Smithsonian Institution and World
Wildlife Fund Inc. 403 pp. Lists 90 Extinct, 839
Endangered and 1211 Threatened taxa for the continental
U.S. Also covers Hawaii, Puerto Rico and Virgin Is.

2897 **Phillips, B.R. (1980).** Saving an endangered
plant in Bermuda. *Threatened Pl. Committ.*

Newsl. 5:6-7.

3060   Sahni, K.C. & Naithani, H.B. (1979). A rare and spectacular rhododendron from Kameng District. *Indian Forester* 105(1):77.

3064   Maher, R.V., White, D.J., Argus, G.W., & Keddy, P.A. (1978). The rare vascular plants of Nova Scotia. *Syllogeus* 18:1-38.

3119   Sauleda, R.P. & Adams, R.M. (1979). *Encyclia inaguensis* Nash ex Britton and Millspaugh - a rare orchid from the Bahama Islands and the Caicos group. *Bull. Amer. Orchid Soc.* 48(3):257-260. Illus.

3204   Cronk, Q.C.B. (1980). Extinction and survival in the endemic vascular flora of Ascension Island. *Biological Conservation* 17(3):207-219. Illus., map.

3260   Veblen, T.T. (1978). Guatemalan conifers. *Unasylva* 29(118):25-30. Includes conservation.

3374   Kondratiuk, I., Ivashyn, D.S., & Burda, R.I. (1978). Study of the flora and vegetation of the Stanitsa-Lugansk branch of the Lugansk State Reservation. *Introd. Aklim. Rosl. Ukr. Akad. Nauk. URSR* 13:18-22. Uk (Rus).

3434   Jaakkola, E. (1980). Finland's rich forests. *Naturopa* no. 34/35:55.

3774   Hall, A.V., de Winter, M., de Winter, B., & van Oosterhout, S.A.M. (1980). Threatened plants of Southern Africa: a report of the Committee for Terrestrial Ecosystems National Programme for Environmental Sciences. Pretoria: South African National Scientific Programmes Report No. 45. CSIR. 244 pp.

4066   Jermy, A.C. (ed.). (1980). Notulae et novitates Muluenses No. 1. *Bot. J. Linn. Soc.* 81:1-46. En. Illus., map, key. Includes one substantial paper and two short notes on Bornean palms by J. Dransfield.

4115   U.S. Department of the Interior. Fish and Wildlife Service. (1985). Endangered and threatened wildlife and plants: proposal to determine *Coryphantha robbinsorum* (Cochise pincushion cactus) to be a threatened species. *Federal Register* 50(44):9083-9086.

4300   Arora, Y.K. & Gupta, R.K. (1983). Native ornamental orchids: conservation and cultivation of endangered and extinct species. *J. Econ. Taxon. Bot.* 4(2):393-411. Illus.

4321   Day, R.T. (1983). A survey and census of the endangered furbish lousewort, *Pedicularis furbishiae*, in New Brunswick. *Canadian Field-Naturalist* 97(3):325-327. Maps.

4380   Hinds, H.R. (1983). The rare vascular plants of New Brunswick. *Syllogeus* 50:38. En, Fr. Maps.

4480   Aiken, S.R. & Leigh, C.H. (1984). A second national park for Peninsular Malaysia? The Endau-Rompin controversy. *Biological Conservation* 29(3):253-276. Maps.

4650   Popenoe, J. (1984). Threatened plants in the Bahamas. *Threatened Pl. Newsl.* 13:11.

4705   Abeywickrama, B.A. (1983). Threatened or endangered plants of Sri Lanka and the status of their conservation measures. pp. 11-18 *In* Jain, S.K., Mehra, K.L. (eds.). Conservation of tropical plant resources. Howrah, Botanical Survey of India.

4952   Nietschmann, B. (1984). Biosphere reserves and traditional societies. *In* UNESCO-UNEP. Conservation, science and society. Paris, Unesco. 499-508. Contributions to the First International Biosphere Reserve Congress, Minsk, Byelorussia/USSR. 26 September - 2 October 1983. Map.

4988   Jain, S.K. & Sastry, A.R.K. (comps.). (1983). Materials for a catalogue of threatened plants of India. Howrah, Botanical Survey of India. 69 pp.

5042   Rackham, O. et al. (1983). Trees in the 21st century. Berkhamsted, A B Academic Publishers. 133p. Illus., maps.

5170   Powell, D. & Covacevich, J. (1983). Lister's palm, *Arenga listeri*, on Christmas Island: a rare or vulnerable species? *Principes* 27(2):89-93. Illus.

5204   Velchev, V., Kozuharov, S., Bondev, I., Kuzmanov, B., & Markova, M. (1984). Chervena kniga na NR Bulgariya: izcheznali, zastrasheni ot izchezvane i redki rasteniya i zhivotni: tom 1. Rasteniya. [Red Data Book of the People's Republic of Bulgaria: v. 1. Plants]. Sofiya: Izdatelstvo na Bulgarskata Akademiya na Naukite. 447 pp. Bul (En, Rus). Illus., col. illus., maps.

5231   Hore, D.K. & Balakrishnan, N.P. (1984). Orchids of Great Nicobar Island and their conservation. *J. Bombay Nat. Hist. Soc.* 81(3):626-635.

5314   Barreno, E. et al. (1984). Listado de plantas endémicas, raras o amenazadas de España-Islas Canarias. [List of endemic, rare or threatened plants in Spain: Canary Islands]. *Información Ambiental* (Conservacionismo en España) 3:XVIII, XXIV.

5374   Pal, G.D. (1983). *Christensenia aesculifolia* (Blume) Maxon: first report of a poorly known fern from Subansiri District, Arunachal Pradesh, India. *Bull. Bot. Surv. India* 24(1-4):180-182. Illus. (1982 publ. 1983).

5375   Nair, N.C. & Srinivasan, S.R. (1983). On the rediscovery of *Koilodepas calycinum* Bedd. (Euphorbiaceae) and *Holcolemma canaliculatum* (Nees ex Steud.) Stapf. ex Hubbard (Poaceae) from south India. *Bull. Bot. Surv. India* 24(1-4):241-242. (1982 publ. 1983).

5376   Dixit, R.D. & Ghosh, B. (1983). Additional collections of *Lindsaea tenera* Dryand., endemic to India. *Bull. Bot. Surv. India* 24(1-4):240. (1982 publ. 1983).

5379   Henry, A.N. & Swaminathan, M.S. (1983). On the

rediscovery of two rare endemic plants of India. *Bull. Bot. Surv. India* 24(1-4):234-235. Illus. (1982 publ. 1983).

5387 Perring, F.H. & Farrell, L. (1983). British Red Data Book: 1. Vascular plants. (2nd ed.). Lincoln: RSNC. 99 pp. Identifies more than 300 rare and threatened taxa, 17.6% of the native flora, and summarises status of and threats to each species.

5399 Gómez-Campo, C. (ed.). (1985). Plant conservation in the Mediterranean area. Geobotany Series 7. Dordrecht: Dr W. Junk Publishers. 269 pp. Illus., maps.

5403 Gomez-Campo, C. & Malato-Beliz, J. (1985). The Iberian Peninsula. *In* Gomez-Campo, C. (ed.) Plants conservation in the Mediterranean area. pp. 47-70 in (ed.). Dordrecht: Dr W. Junk. Illus. Maps.

5409 Snogerup, S. (1985). The Mediterranean islands. pp. 160-173 *In* Gomez-Campo, C. (ed.). Plant conservation in the Mediterranean area. Dordrecht: Dr W. Junk. Illus. Map.

5410 Leon, C., Synge, H., & Lucas, G.Ll. (1985). The value of information in saving threatened Mediterranean plants. *In* Gomez-Campo, C. (ed.). Plant conservation in the Mediterranean area. Dordrecht, Dr W. Junk. 177-196.

5437 Melville, R. (1970). Endangered plants and conservation in the islands of the Indian Ocean. *In* Papers and proceedings of the IUCN 11th technical meeting, New Delhi, India, 25-28 November 1969. Switzerland, IUCN. 103-107.

5462 Pingitore, E.J. (1981). Espécies vegetales en vias de extinción de la Republica Argentina. *Bol. Soc. Hort. Argentina* 37:10-13. Tentative list of 69 threatened species.

5465 Leigh, J.H., Boden, R., & Briggs, J.D. (1984). Extinct and endangered plants of Australia. Melbourne: Macmillan. 369 pp. Includes detailed case studies of 76 species presumed extinct and 203 which are endangered.

5532 Carvalho, J.C.M. (1968). Lista das espécies de animais e plantas ameaçadas de extinçao no Brasil. [List of plant and animal species threatened with extinction in Brazil]. *Fund. Brasil. Conserv. Natureza, Bol. Inform.* 3:11-16. Por. 13 species listed.

5567 Bouchard, A.D., Barabe, D., Dumais, M., & Hay, S. (1983). The rare vascular plants of Quebec. *Syllogeus* 48:79. En, Fr.

5595 Marticorena, C. (1980). Threatened plants and areas of Chile. Universidad de Concepcion. List of threatened plants of the continent and Islas of Mas a Tierra, Mas Afuera, Santa Clara, San Felix and San Ambrosio.

5598 Schlegel Sachs, F.M. (1982). Espécies Chilenas Amenazadas. Univ. Austral de Chile. List of threatened plants including Ex:9, E:53, V:15, R:42.

5607 Borhidi, A. & Muñiz, O. (1983). Catálogo de plantas Cubanas amenazadas o extinguidas. La Habana: Acad. Ciencias de Cuba. 85 pp. Lists 959 species of gymnosperms and flowering plants threatened or extinct, including 832 endemics, with their distribution by provinces and assignment into categories - noncompatible with IUCN categories.

5642 Jiménez, J. de J. (1978). Lista tentativa de plantas de la República Dominicana que deben protegerse para evitar su extinción. Santo Domingo: Coloquio Internacional sobre la practica de la conservación. CIBIMA/UASD. Lists 133 species of threatened flowering plants, of which 49 are endemic.

5670 Porter, D.M. (1990). Red Data Bulletin: Galapagos Islands. In prep. 232 endemic vascular plant taxa with notes on their distribution and conservation status.

5710 Sastre, C. (1978). Plantes menacées de Guadeloupe et de Martinique. 1. Espèces altitudinales. [Threatened plants of Guadeloupe and Martinique. 1. High altitude species]. *Bull. Mus. Natn. Hist. Nat.* (3 series) 519:65-93. Fr (En). Description of vegetation, sheets on 13 rare and threatened species with illustrations and habitat photographs.

5727 Cook, C.D.K. (1980). The status of some Indian endemic plants. *Threatened Pl. Committ. Newsl.* 6:17-18. Mentions 5 threatened wetland species.

5767 Lee, T.B. (1980). Rare and endangered species in the area of Mt Sorak. *Bull. Kwanak Arbor.* 3:197-201. Mentions 12 taxa with notes on distribution. (Ko).

5815 Given, D.R. (comp.). (1976). Threatened plants of New Zealand: a register of rare and endangered plants of the New Zealand Botanical Region. Christchurch, DSIR. Loose-leaf series of detailed double-paged datasheets with maps on 50 selected threatened species. Supplements in 1977, 1978.

5825 Gjerlaug, H.C. (1975). Liste over truede ogleller sjeldne planter i Norge, karsporeplanter og froplanter. Oslo. (unpublished). No. Includes a list of rare and threatened plants.

5851 Woodbury, R.O. et al. (1975). Rare and endangered plants of Puerto Rico: a committee report. Commonwealth of Puerto Rico: USDA Soil Conservation Service and Dept. of Natural Resources. 85 pp. Lists 515 rare and endangerd species of endemic and non-endemic plants, with their habitat, distribution and threat.

5852 Strahm, W. (1989). Plant Red Data Book for Rodrigues. Königstein: Koeltz Scientific Books. 241 pp. maps, illus. Includes detailed accounts of all endemics and threatened non-endemic species, incl. conservation categories; introduction on geography, botany and conservation problems. Illus., maps.

5908 Wickens, G.E. (1979). Sudan. Part of Appendix to: Possibilities and needs for conservation of plant species and vegetation in Africa. pp. 85-88 *In* Hedberg, I. (ed.). Systematic botany, plant utilization and biosphere conservation. Stockholm: Almqvist & Wiksell International. Contains 258 species and infraspecific taxa.

5914   **Kemp, E.S. (1979).** Swaziland. Part of appendix
to: Possibilities and needs for conservation of plant
species and vegetation in Africa. pp. 101-103
In Hedberg, I. (ed.). Systematic botany, plant
utilization and biosphere conservation. Stockholm,
Almqvist & Wiksell International. Stockholm: Almqvist &
Wiksell International. Contains 155 species and
infraspecific taxa: E:2, V:16, R:137.

5926   **Wingfield, R.C. (1979).** Tanzania. Part of
appendix to: Possibilities and needs for conservation of
plant species and vegetation in Africa. pp. 95-99
In Hedberg, I. (ed.). Systematic botany, plant
utilization and biosphere conservation. Stockholm:
Almqvist & Wiksell International. Contains about 390
endemic species and infraspecific taxa.

5929   **Bain, J. & Humphrey, S.R. (1982).** A profile of
the endangered species of Thailand. Gainesville,
Florida: Office of Ecological Services. 367 pp. Lists 53
plant taxa rare or threatened in Thailand, with 3 data
sheets and 14 dot maps. 2 vols.

5932   **Adams, C.D. & Baksh, Y.S. (1981).** What is an
endangered plant? *Living World*:9-14. Journal
of the Trinidad and Tobago Field Naturalists Club.
Includes distribution tables of 648 threatened
non-endemic species and of 215 endemic species, with
criteria for ranking the selected species.

5942   **Borodin, A.M. et al. (1985).** Krasnaya kniga
SSSR: redkie i nakhodyashchiesya pod ugrozoi
ischeznoveniya vidy zhivotnykh i rastenii. - izdanie
vtoroe [2]: tom pervyi - vtoroi [1-2]. (2nd edition).
[Plant Red Data Book for the USSR]. Moscow: Lesnaya
Promyshlennost. Illus., col., maps. Vol. 1 - Animals;
Vol. 2 - Plants.

6057   **Loc, P.K. (1986).** Lists of rare and endangered
plant species of Vietnam (1986-1988).

6062   **Fukarek, P. (1959).** Arbres et arbustes rares
et menacées de la flore de Yougoslavie. [Rare and
threatened trees and shrubs of Yugoslavia]. pp. 159-165
In IUCN. Animaux et vegetaux rares de la
Région Mediterranéenne. Proceedings of the IUCN 7th
Technical Meeting, 11-19 September 1958, Athens, vol. 5.
Brussels: IUCN.

6072   **Hall, J.B. (1979).** Ghana. Part of appendix to:
Possibilities and needs for conservation of plant
species and vegetation in Africa. pp. 88-91 *In*
Hedberg, I. (ed.). Systematic botany, plant utilization
and biosphere conservation. Stockholm: Almqvist and
Wiksell. Contains 210 species and infraspecific taxa.

6073   **Gillett, J.B. (1979).** Kenya. Part of appendix
to: Possibilities and needs for conservation of plant
species and vegetation in Africa. pp. 93-94 *In*
Hedberg, I. (ed.). Systematic botany, plant utilization
and biosphere conservation. Stockholm, Almqvist &
Wiksell International. Stockholm: Almqvist & Wicksell
International. Examples of taxa threatened in major
vegetation types, and includes E:11, V:20, R:4, I:1.

6074   **Nooteboom, H.P. (1984).** A new *Shorea*
from Java. *Flora Malesiana Bull.* 9(1):44-45.

6086   **Adjanohoun, E.J. (1979).** Benin. Part of
appendix to: Possibilities and needs for conservation of

plant species and vegetation in Africa. pp. 91-92
In Hedberg, I. (ed.). Systematic botany, plant
utilization and biosphere conservation. Stockholm:
Almquist & Wiksell International.

6087   **Gilbert, M. (1979).** Ethiopia. Part of appendix
to: Possibilities and needs for conservation of plant
species and vegetation in Africa. pp. 92-93 *In*
Hedberg, I. (ed.). Systematic botany, plant utilization
and biosphere conservation. Stockholm: Almqvist &
Wiksell International. Contains 29 endemic succulent
taxa - E:1, V:4, R:12, I:12.

6088   **Wild, H. & Müller, T. (1979).** Rhodesia. Part
of appendix to: Possibilities and needs for conservation
of plant species and vegetation in Africa. pp. 99-100
In Hedberg, I. (ed.). Systematic botany, plant
utilization and biosphere conservation. Stockholm:
Almqvist & Wiksell International. Contains 84 species
and infraspecific taxa: E:18, V:26, R:40.

6154   **Steyermark, J.A. (1977).** Future outlook for
threatened and endangered species in Venezuela. pp.
128-135 *In* Prance, G.T., Elias, T.S. (eds.).
Extinction is forever. Proceedings of a symposium at the
New York Botanical Garden, 11-13 May 1976. New York: New
York Botanical Garden. General review of the extent and
occurrence of endemism and floristic relationships in
Venezuela.

6155   **Gentry, A.H. (1977).** Endangered plant species
and habitats of Ecuador and Amazonian Peru. *In*
Prance, G.T., Elias, T.S. (eds.). Extinction is forever.
Proceedings of a symposium at the New York Botanical
Garden, 11-13 May 1976. New York, New York Botanical
Garden. 136-149. Maps. An assessment of threatened and
endangered habitats.

6163   **Muñoz P., C. (1977).** Threatened and endangered
species of plants in Chile. *In* Prance, G.T.,
Elias, T.S. (eds.). Extinction is forever. Proceedings
of a symposium at the New York Botanical Garden, 11-13
May 1976. New York, New York Botanical Garden. 251-253.
Plant list.

6164   **Ravenna, P. (1977).** Neotropical species
threatened and endangered by human activity in the
Iridaceae, Amaryllidaceae and allied bulbous families.
pp. 257-266 *In* Prance, G.T., Elias, T.S.
(eds.). Extinction is forever. Proceedings of a
symposium at the New York Botanical Garden, 11-13 May
1976. Bronx, New York: New York Botanical Garden. Illus.

6165   **Moore, H.E. (1977).** Endangerment at the
specific and generic levels in palms. pp. 267-282
In Prance, G.T., Elias, T.S. (eds.).
Extinction is forever. Proceedings of a symposium at the
New York Botanical Garden, 11-13 May 1976. Bronx: New
York Botanical Garden. Illus.

6180   **Hall, A.V. & Veldhuis, H.A. (1985).** South
African Red Data Book: plants - Fynbos and Karoo biomes.
Pretoria: CSIR. 160 pp. South African National
Scientific Programmes Report No. 117.

6197   **Anon. (1984).** Arnold Arboretum joins forces
with other gardens to save the rarest plants. *Plant
Sciences* 4(3):3.

6295   **Chandrabose, M., Nair, N.C., & Chandrasekaran, V.**

(1982). Two rare and threatened flowering plants of South India: rediscovered. *Indian J. Forest.* 5(2):159-160.

6369 **Klosowski, S. & Checinska-Rybak, A. (1984).** Gozdzikowate. (Carnation family.). *Przyroda Polska* 6:23-25. Pol. Col. illus. Protected plants.

6796 **Cody, W.J. (1979).** Vascular plants of restricted range in the continental Northwest Territories, Canada. *Syllogeus* 23:1-57.

6930 **Takhtajan, A.L. (1981).** Rare and vanishing plants of the USSR to be protected. Leningrad: Nauka. 202 pp.

6936 **Futak, J. (1981).** Endemicke rastliny Slovenska. [Endemic plants of Slovakia.]. pp. 45-47 *In* Holub, J. (ed.). Mizejici flora a ochrana fytogenofondu v CSSR. (The vanishing flora and protection of the gene pool in Czechoslovakia.) Studie CSAV, 20. Prague: Academia. Cz (En).

6951 **Hendrych, R. (1981).** Bemerkungen zum Endemismus in der Flora der Tschechoslowakei. [Observations on endemism in the flora of Czechoslovakia]. *Preslia* 53:97-120. Translated from German.

6963 **Andriamampianina, J. (1979).** Madagascar. Part of appendix to: Possibilities and needs for conservation of plant species and vegetation in Africa. p. 103 *In* Hedberg, I. (ed.). Systematic botany, plant utilization and biosphere conservation: Proc. of a sym. held in Uppsala in commemoration of the 500th ann. of the Univ. Stockholm: Almqvist & Wiksell International.

6966 **Guillarmod, A.J. (1979).** Lesotho. Part of appendix to: Possibilities and needs for conservation of plant species and vegetation in Africa. p. 101 *In* Hedberg, I. (ed.). Systematic botany, plant utilization and biosphere conservation: Proc. of a sympsium held in Uppsala in commemoration of the 500th anniversary of the Univ. Stockholm. 101. Stocklholm: Almqvist & Wiksell.

6968 **Huntley, B.J. (1979).** Angola. Part of appendix to: Possibilities and needs for conservation of plant species and vegetation in Africa. p. 90 *In* Hedberg, I. (ed.). Systematic botany, plant utilization and biosphere conservation: Proc. of a sym. held in Uppsala in commemoration of the 500th ann. of the Univ. Stockholm, Almqvist & Wiksell Int'l. 99. Stockholm: Almqvist & Wicksell.

6987 **Henry, A.N. & Swaminathan, M.S. (1979).** Rare or little known plants from south India. *J. Bombay Nat. Hist. Soc.* 76(2):373-376.

7072 **Lanfranco, E. (1983).** Safeguarding our environment. 3. Malta's plant life. *The Teacher* 3:23. Illus.

7200 **Martinelli, G. & Leme, E. (1986).** Rare bromeliads from Brazil, No. 2 *Vriesea triligulata. J. Bromeliad Soc.* 36(1):18-20.

7201 **Croat, T.B. (1985).** A new collection of the

rare *Alloschemone occidentalis* (Poepp.) Engl. & Krause. *Aroideana* 8(3):80-82.

7389 **Koopowitz, H. & Kaye, H. (1983).** Plant extinction: a global crisis. Washington, DC: Stone Wall Press. 239 pp.

7588 **Lee, Y.-N. (1981).** Plants. *In* Choi, K.-C., *et al.* (eds.). Rare and endangered species of animals and plants of Republic of Korea. Seoul, Korean Association for Conservation of Nature. 154-271, 277-280.

7607 **Kiew, R. (1983).** Portraits of threatened plants. (*Ilex praetermissa* Kiew and *Didymocarpus primulina* Ridley). *Malay. Naturalist* 37(2):6-7.

7609 **Ng, F.S.P. & Low, C.M. (1982).** Checklist of endemic trees of the Malay peninsula. Kepong, Malaysia: Forest Research Institute. 94 pp. Lists 654 trees endemic to the Malay peninsula, including peninsular Thailand; rarity is based on numbers of herbarium specimens.

7730 **van Steenis, C.G.G.J. (1948).** Flora Malesiana. Leiden: Flora Malesiana Foundation. Illus., maps. (20 volumes planned. 8 volumes on flowering plants (Series I) and two volumes on pteridophytes (Series II) published by 1991).

7731 **Hara, H., Stearn, W.T., & Williams, L. (1978-1982).** An enumeration of the flowering plants of Nepal. London, British Museum (Natural History). 3 vols.

7738 **Shrestha, T.B. (1986).** List of endemic plants - Nepal.

7739 **Mukherjee, S.K. (1985).** Systematic and ecogeographic studies of crop genepools: 1. *Mangifera* L. Rome, IBPGR Sec......... .. pp. Tables. Maps. Extensive bibliography.

7747 **Hamann, O. & Wium-Andersen, S. (1986).** *Scalesia gordilloi* sp. nov. (Asteraceae) from the Galapagos Islands, Ecuador. *Nord. J. Bot.* 6:35-38.

7749 **Exell, A.W., Wild, H., Fernandes, A., Brenan, J.P.M., & Launert, E. (eds.). (1960-1995).** Flora Zambesiaca. Volumes published up until 1996. London, Crown Agents.

7750 **Fernandes, R.B. & Fernandes, A. (1976).** Anacardiaceae africanae novae vel minus cognitae III. *Garcia de Orta* 3(1):15-16.

7752 **Wild, H. (1965).** The flora of the great dyke of Southern Rhodesia with special reference to the serpentine soils. *Kirkia* 5(1):49-86.

7753 **Obermeyer, A.A. (1962).** A new *Haemanthus* and a new *Tritonia* from Southern Africa. *Kirkia* 3:22-24.

7754 **Wild, H. (1964).** The endemic species of the Chimanimani Mountains and their significance. *Kirkia* 4:125-157. lists species endemic to

Mozambique and Zimbabwe, with appendix of species endemic on Mount Mulanje, Nyasaland (Malawi).

7755 **Brenan, J.P.M. (1960).** *Triceratella,* a new genus of Commelinaceae from Southern Africa. *Kirkia* 1:14-19.

7757 **Wild, H. (1963).** New and interesting species. *Kirkia* 4:45-73.

7758 **Brenan, J.P.M. (1963).** Santalaceae. *In* Wild, H. The endemic species of the Chimanimani Mountains and their significance. *Kirkia* 4:125-157.

7759 **Peterson, B. (1963).** Thymeleaceae. *In* Wild, H. The endemic species of the Chimanimani Mountains and their significance. *Kirkia* 4:125-157.

7760 **Verdcourt, B. (1960).** New Convolvulaceae from the Flora Zambesiaca area. *Kirkia* 1:26-31.

7761 **Verdcourt, B. (1967).** New Convolvulaceae from the Flora Zambesiaca area II. *Kirkia* 6(1):117-122.

7763 **Reynolds, G.W. (1960).** A new species and a new variety of *Aloe* from Southern Rhodesia. *Kirkia* 1(2):156-159.

7764 **Summerhayes, V.S. (1961).** A new genus of orchids from Southern Africa. *Kirkia* 1(2):88-89.

7765 **Beard, J.S. (1962).** The genus *Protea* in tropical Africa. *Kirkia* 3:138-206.

7768 **Launert, E. (1961).** Some new species of *Eragrostis* from southern tropical Africa. *Boletin da Soc. Brot.* Ser.2 35:15-27.

7769 **Merxmuller, H. (1953).** Neue Sippen aus Sud-Rhodesia. *Mit. Bot. Munch.* 6:196-208.

7771 **Jain, S.K. & Rao, R.R. (1983).** An assessment of threatened plants of India. Proceedings of the seminar held at Dehra Dun, 14-17 Sept., 1981. Howrah, Botanical Survey of India. 334 pp.

7772 **Henderson, R.J.F. (1969).** Contributions from the Queensland Herbarium. No. 2 *Podolepis monticola,* a new species of Compositae from Queensland. Brisbane: Queensland Herbarium. Department of Primary Industries. 9 pp. Illus.

7848 **Oliver, D., Thiselton-Dyer, W.T., Prain, D., & Hill, A.W. (eds.). (1868).** Flora of tropical Africa. Ashford, Kent: English Ministry of thè Colonies. Incomplete; 10 vols - last part 1937.

7849 **Brenan, J. et al. (1953-1954).** Plants collected by the Vernay Nyasaland Expedition of 1946. *Memoirs of the New York Botanical Garden.* Three articles in two successive volumes: 8:191-256, 8:409-506, 9:1-132.

7853 **Wild, H. (1969).** The genus *Nidorella*

Cass. *Bol. Soc. Brot.* 43:209-246.

7855 **Huber, H. (1957).** Revision der gattung *Ceropegia. Memórias Sociedade Bróteriana* 12:1-214. Tables.

7856 **Grey-Wilson, C. (1977).** Studies in African *Impatiens* (Balsaminaceae). Thesis, published by the Reading University. 2 vols. 860 pp.

7858 **Nelmes, E. (1955).** Notes on Cyperaceae XXXVI. *Kew Bull.* 10:91-92.

7859 **Kabuye, C.H.S. & Renvoize, S.A. (1975).** The genus *Aloeochaete,* tribe Danthonieae (Gramineae). *Kew Bull.* 30:569-577.

7860 **Verdcourt, B. (1970).** Studies in the Leguminosae - Papilionoidae for the Flora of Tropical East Africa: I. *Kew Bull.* 24:1-70.

7861 **Gillett, J.B. (1958).** *Lotus* in Africa south of the Sahara and its distinction from *Dorycnium. Kew Bull.* 13:361-381.

7862 **Taylor, P. (1958).** Tropical African Primulaceae. *Kew Bull.* 13:133-149.

7865 **Bally, P.R.O. (1961).** The genus *Monadenium.* Printed in Berne. Illus., maps.

7866 **Blackmoore, S. (1980).** The genus *Kniphofia* (Liliaceae) in Malawi. *Nyala* 6(2):115-124.

7867 **Duviegneaud, P. (1954).** *Humularia.* in Flore Congo Belge, Ruanda, Urundi. 7 volumes by 1958. Published by l'Institut National pour l'Etude Agronomique du Congo Belge.

7869 **Bremekamp, C.E.B. (1953).** Some new species of *Pavetta* L. from Tropical and South Africa II. *Kew Bull.* 8:501-505.

7871 **Bullock, A.A. (1953).** Notes on African Asclepiadaceae III. *Kew Bull.* 8:329-362.

7872 **Bullock, A.A. (1956).** Notes on African Asclepiadaceae VII. *Kew Bull.* 10:611-626.

7874 **Hubbard, C.E. (1957).** Notes on African grasses XXV. *Kew Bull.* 12:51-52.

7875 **Summerhayes, V.S. (1957).** African orchids XXIV. *Kew Bull.* 12:107-126.

7876 **Peterson, B. (1958).** A new species of the genus *Struthiola* (Thymeleaceae). *Kew Bull.* 13:319-320.

7877 **Summerhayes, V.S. (1958).** African orchids XXV. *Kew Bull.* 13:57-87.

7879 **Summerhayes, V.S. (1962).** African orchids XXVIII. *Kew Bull.* 16:253-314.

7881 **Summerhayes, V.S. (1966).** African orchids XXX.

Kew Bull. 20:165-199.

7883 **Bremekamp, C.E.B. (1971).** Tropical African plants XXXI: Rubiaceae. *Kew Bull.* 25:186-188.

7884 **Polhill, R.M. (1974).** A revision of *Pearsonia* (Leguminosae - Papilionoideae). *Kew Bull.* 29:383-410.

7889 **Leach, L.C. & Plowes, D.C.H. (1966).** Stapeliae from South Tropical Africa, II. *Journal of South African Botany* 32:41-60.

7890 **Burtt, B.L. (1962).** Studies in the Gesneriaceae of the Old World XXII. *Notes Royal Bot. Garden Edinburgh* 24:41-49.

7892 **Jonsell, B. (1975).** *Lepidium* L. (Cruciferae) in Tropical Africa. *Botaniska Notiser* 43:20-46.

7895 **Hartley, T.G. (1982).** *Maclurodendron*: A new genus of Rutaceae from Southeast Asia. *Gard. Bull. Sing.* 35:1-19.

7896 **Hartley, T.G. (1974).** A revision of the genus *Acronychia* (Rutaceae). *Journ. Arnold Arb.* 55:470-567. Only part of an article continuing through two hefts.

7897 **Zarzycki, K. & Wojewoda, W. (1986).** Lista roslin wymierajacych i zagrazonych w Polsce. [List of threatened plants in Poland]. Warszawa: Panstwowe Wydawnictwo Naukowe (Polish Scientific Publishers). 128 pp. English summary.

7902 **Mendes, E.J. (1969).** Additiones et adnotationes Florae Mozambicanae - I. *Bol. Soc. Brot.* Ser.2 43:333-339.

7906 **Exell, A.W. & Mendonca, F.A. (1973).** Duas espécies novas de *Teclea* (Rutaceae). *Garcia de Orta* Ser.Bot. 1:93-94. Planches.

7916 **Brenan, J.P.M. (1960).** New and noteworthy *Cassias* from Tropical Africa II. *Kew Bull.* 14:178-188.

7917 **Gillett, J.B. (1970).** Additions to our knowledge of *Indigofera* L. in East Tropical Africa. *Kew Bull.* 24:465-506.

7918 **Verdcourt, B. (1972).** Studies in the Leguminosae - Papilionoideae - Hedysareae (sensu lato) for the 'Flora Zambesiaca': 2. *Kew Bull.* 27:435-445.

7921 **Phipps, J.B. (1964).** Studies in the Arundinellae (Gramineae), I. *Kirkia* 4:87-124.

7922 **Dyer, R.A. & Verdoorn, I. (1969).** *Encephalartos manikensis* and its near allies. *Kirkia* 7(1):147-158.

7923 **Wild, H. (1972).** New and interesting species of Compositae from South Central Africa I. *Kirkia* 8:167-172.

7924 **Müller, T. (1986).** Returned questionnaire: Endemics of Zimbabwe; *Aloes* and *Euphorbias* of Zimbabwe.

7925 **Cox, P.A. (1986).** Returned Questionnaire: American Samoa and Western Samoa.

7926 **Hutchinson, J., Dalziel, J.M., & Hepper, F.N. (1927).** Flora of West Tropical Africa. Published by the English Ministry of State for the Colonies. 3 vols to 1972. 2nd edition.

7927 **Aubreville, A. & Leroy, J.-F. (1961-1995).** Flore du Gabon. Published by the Gabon Government through Muséum National d'Histoire Naturelle, Paris. Incomplete; 34 volumes by 1996.

7954 **Souza, S. de. (1981).** Letter to G. Lucas. Université Nationale du Bénin, Laboratoire de Botanique. Comments on 27 (possibly) threatened plant taxa in Benin.

7955 **Polunin, O. & Stainton, A. (1984).** Flowers of the Himalaya. Oxford, Oxford Univ. Press. 580p. Illus.

7956 **Hooker, J.D. (1872).** Flora of British India. London.

7958 **Bhandari, M.M. (1978).** Flora of the Indian Desert. Jodhpur, Scientific Publishers. 471p.

7959 **Turrill, W.B., Milne-Redhead, E., Hubbard, C.E., & Polhill, R.M. (1952).** Flora of Tropical East Africa. Published by the East African Community. Still being produced (1985) in separate hefts for each (part of a) family.

7961 **U.S. Department of the Interior. Fish and Wildlife Service. (1983).** Endangered and threatened wildlife and plants: proposed endangered status for *Jatropha costaricensis* (Quemador del Pacífico). *Federal Register* 48(137):32525-32526.

7967 **U.S. Department of the Interior. Fish and Wildlife Service. (1985).** Endangered and threatened wildlife and plants: final rule to determine *Zanthoxyllum thomasianum* to be an endangered species. *Federal Register* 50(245):51867-51870.

7983 **U.S. Department of the Interior. Fish and Wildlife Service. (1986).** Endangered and threatened wildlife and plants: proposed endangered or threatened status for seven Florida scrub plants. *Federal Register* 51(69):12444-12451.

7984 **U.S. Department of the Interior. Fish and Wildlife Service. (1985).** Endangered and threatened wildlife and plants: final rule to determine *Buxus vahlii* as an endangered species. *Federal Register* 50(156):32572-32575.

7996 **U.S. Department of the Interior. Fish and Wildlife Service. (1985).** Endangered and threatened wildlife and plants: reopening of comment period on proposed Endangered status for *Cupressus abramsiana* (Santa Cruz cypress). *Fed. Reg.* 50(228):48616-48617.

7999 **U.S. Department of the Interior. Fish and Wildlife**

Service. (1986). Endangered and threatened wildlife and plants: proposed endangered status for *Banara vanderbiltii*. *Federal Register* 51(69):12455-12457.

8000 **Tutin, T.G. et al. (eds.) (1964)**. Flora Europaea. (1st ed.). Cambridge: Cambridge University Press. 5 vols, 1964-1980. 2nd ed. vol 1 1993.

8001 **Komarov, V.L. & Shishkin, B.K. (1933)**. Flora URSS. Jerusalem, Israel: Academy of Sciences of the USSR, Moscow and Leningrad. 30 vols (1933-1964). Program for Scientific Translations. Vols 1-21 and 24 translated into English, 1963-1979, by N. Landau.

8003 **Berhaut, J. (1971)**. Flore illustrée du Sénégal. Gouvernement du Sénégal, Ministère du Développement Rural. 6 vols by 1979.

8006 **Amerson, A.B., Whistler, W.A., & Schwaner, T.D. (1982)**. Wildlife and wildlife habitat of American Samoa. II: Accounts of flora and fauna. Washington, DC, U.S. Fish and Wildlife Service. 151 pp. Annotated list, maps.

8015 **Grey-Wilson, C. (1984)**. Plants in peril: 1. *Kew Mag.* 1(2):92-93. The African Violet, Saintpaulia.

8020 **Glassman, S.F. (1972)**. A revision of B.E. Dahlgren's index of American palms. Cramer. 294 pp. Phanerogamarum Monographiae Tomus VI.

8021 **Dassanayake, M.D. & Fosberg, F.R. (eds.). (1980)**. A revised handbook to the flora of Ceylon. New Delhi: Amerind Publ. Co. 5 vols so far.

8037 **Iwatsuki, K. (1986)**. Annotations to: List of plants in the CMC database for Ogasawara-Gunto.

8038 **Yoshida, A. & Tannawa, T. (1977)**. Endangered plant species of the Ogasawara Islands. *Notes Waimea Arbor.* 3(2):8-12. Tentative list of 31 'endangered', 17 'rare' and 6 'depleted' taxa.

8048 **Woolliams, K.R. (1978)**. Observations on the flora of the Ogasawara Islands. *Notes Waimea Arbor.* 5(2):2-10. Data on 18 mostly threatened plant species.

8049 **Brownlie, G. (1961)**. Studies on Pacific ferns, 4. The pteridophyte flora of Pitcairn Island. *Pacific Science* 15(2):297-300.

8050 **St. John, H. & Philipson, W.R. (1962)**. An account of the flora of Henderson Island, South Pacific Ocean. *Trans. R. Soc. N.Z. Bot.* 1(14):175-194.

8051 **Cheng, Wen-Chun. (1980)**. Sylva Sinica. Flora of Woody Plants in China Committee. 929 pp. Vol. 1 (in Chinese).

8058 **U.S. Department of the Interior. Fish and Wildlife Service. (1985)**. Review of plant taxa for listing as endangered or threatened species; notice of review. *Federal Register* 50(188):39526-39584.

8177 **Given, D.R. (1975)**. Conservation of rare and

threatened plant taxa in New Zealand - some principles. *Proc. New Zealand Ecol. Soc.* 22:1-6. Map. Includes remarks on Philip Island.

8243 **Wang, H. (1986)**. Letter to S. Stuart. Lists five threatened Chinese plants.

8260 **Ng, F. (1984)**. Portraits of threatened plants, 6. *Musa gracilis* Holttum. *Malay. Naturalist* 38(1):9-10. Illus.

8309 **Comber, J.B. (1990)**. Checklist of Javan Orchidaceae. Unpublished list.

8316 **Cheek, M. (1986)**. Annotations to: List of *Nepenthes*.

8318 **Sutter, H. (1986)**. Annotations to: List of plants in the WCMC database for Burma. Includes annotations to list of plants protected in Burma by the 1902 Burma Forest Act as amended to date.

8321 **Blower, J. (1985)**. Conservation priorities in Burma. *Oryx* 19(2):79-85.

8322 **Dray, A.M. (1985)**. Plantas a proteger em Portugal continental. [Protected plants in Portugal]. Serviço Nacional de Parques, Reservas e Conservaçao da Natureza, Lisboa. 56 pp.

8328 **Degener, O. &. I. (1932)**. Flora Hawaiiensis or the new Flora of the Hawaiian Islands. Honolulu, J. Pan-Pacific Research Institute. 7 loose-leaf fascicles.

8477 **Maynard, A.C. (1986)**. Letter to H. Synge. Gives distributions of 2 conifers.

8482 **Wang, S.Y. (1986)**. List of threatened plants of China. 18 pp. List with IUCN categories; endemism not given.

8485 **Croat, T.B. (1984)**. Rediscovery of a rare monstera (*Monstera gracilis*). *Aroideana* 7(1):12-13. Illus.

8489 **Purdie, A.W. (1985)**. *Chordospartium muritai* (Papilionaceae) - a rare new species of New Zealand tree broom. *New Zealand J. Bot.* 23:157-161. Illus., map.

8552 **Nicholls, W.H. (1950)**. Additions to the Orchidaceae of Australia - 3. (Two new species of *Pterostylis* in Victoria). *Victorian Naturalist* 67:45-48. Illus.

8560 **Henderson, R.J.F. (1969)**. *Podolepis monticola*, a new species of Compositae from Queensland. *Contrib. Queensland Herbarium* no. 2:1-9. Illus.

8615 **Fosberg, F.R. & Sachet, M.-H. (1981)**. Polynesian plant studies 6-18. *Smithsonian Contributions* 47:1-38.

8616 **St. John, H. & Philipson, W.R. (1960)**. List of the flora of Oeno Atoll, Tuamotu Archipelago, south-central Pacific Ocean. *Trans. R. Soc. N.Z.* 88(3):401-403.

8617 Fosberg, F.R. (1937). Some Rubiaceae of southeastern Polynesia. *Occ. Papers Bernice P. Bishop Mus.* 13(19):245-293.

8619 Davis, P.H. (1965-1985). Flora of Turkey and the East Aegean Islands. 9 vols. Edinburgh: Edinburgh University Press. Illus., maps.

8622 Iwatsuki, K. (1986). List of endemics to the Bonin and Volcano Islands.

8623 Pignatti, S. (1982). Flora d'Italia. Bologna: Edagricole. 3 vols.

8679 Roosmalen, M.G.M. van. (1985). Fruits of the Guianan flora. Wageningen: Institute of Systematic Botany, Utrecht and Silvicultural Dept of Wageningen Agricultural University.

8743 Johnson, D.V., Read, R.W., & Balick, M.J. (1986). Economic botany and threatened species of the palm family in Latin America and the Caribbean. Part 2. The status of threatened species of the palm family in Latin America and the Caribbean. Mimeo. 30 September 1986. (unpublished). Final report on WWF 3322. Includes Appendix 2, on palms of Atlantic forest. Appendix 1, by H. Balslev on Ecuador, is a separate entry.

8745 Clements, M.A. (1982). Preliminary checklist of Australian Orchidaceae. Canberra: National Botanic Gardens. Lists over 600 taxa.

8751 Ohwi, J. (1965). Flora of Japan (in English). Washington, DC: Smithsonian Institution. 1067 pp. En.

8754 Nasir, E. & Ali, S.I. (1970). Flora of West Pakistan. Islamabad: Pakistan Agricultural Research Council. Continued as Flora of Pakistan, 1980. 57 fascicles so far.

8757 Hillcoat, D., Lewis, G., & Verdcourt, B. (1986). A new species of *Ceratonia* (Leguminosae - Caesalpiniodeae) from Arabia and the Somali Republic. *Kew Bull.* 35(2):261-271. Taxon published in the IUCN Plant Red Data Book as *Ceratonia* sp.nov.

8764 Cadet, Th. (1984). Liste et commentaires sur les plantes en danger des Mascareignes. [An annotated list of plants in danger]. Paris, Mimeo: Conservatoire et Jardins Botaniques de Nancy. 20 pp. Includes notes on local uses.

8765 Read, R.W. (1975). The genus *Thrinax* (Palmae: Coryphoideae). *Smithsonian Contrib. Bot.* 19:1-98.

8766 Correll, D.S. & Correll, H.B. (1982). Flora of the Bahama Archipelago. Vaduz, Liechtenstein: Cramer. 1692 pp. Includes the Turks and Caicos Islands.

8767 Howard, R.A. (ed.). (1974). Flora of the Lesser Antilles: Leeward and Windward Islands. Jamaica Plain, Mass., Arnold Arboretum. 6 vols, 1974-1989.

8777 Granville, J.J. de. (1980). Returned Questionnaire: Palms of French Guiana.

8778 Moore, H.E. (1980). Returned Questionnaire: Palms of Mexico.

8793 Dransfield, J. (1979). Lists and comments on palms, made in 1979. Some written on card index.

8794 Dransfield, J. (1978). Lists and comments on palms, made in 1978. Some written on card index.

8801 Gentry, A.H. (1986). Notes on Peruvian palms. *Ann. Missouri Bot. Gard.* 73(1):158-165. Describes 3 new species, makes 3 new combinations and reports 1 new record for Peru.

8836 Schenk, J.R. (1984). A conservation strategy for forest utilization in Solomon Islands. Solomon Islands, Physical Planning Division. 62p. Illus., maps, forest.

8840 Fosberg, F.R. (1973). On present condition and conservation of forests in Micronesia. *In* Pac. Sci. Assoc. Standing Comm. on Pac. Bot. Symposium: Planned utilization of the lowland tropical forests, August 1971. Bogor, Indonesia.

8895 Zohary, M. et al. (1966). Flora Palaestina. Jerusalem, Israel Academy of Sciences. 3 vols so far.

8896 Shmida, A. (1986). Letter to Steve Davis. Notes on threatened plants of Israel.

8897 Mouterde, P. (1966). Nouvelle Flore du Liban et de la Syrie. Beirut, Dar El-Machreq. 3 vols so far.

8899 Boulos, L. & Al-Eisawi, D. (1978). Returned List: Initial returns for Jordan.

8904 Glassman, S.F. (1979). Re-evaluation of the genus *Butia* with a description of a new species. *Principes* 23(2):65-79. New species is *Butia purpurascens*.

8934 Avishai, M. (1980). A list of oncocyclus *Iris* from the Middle East proposed for inclusion in the threatened plants survey. Includes notes on distribution.

8937 Al-Eisawi, D.M. (1982). List of Jordan vascular plants. Amman. 152 pp. Mimeo.

8941 Phillipps, A. (1987). Letter to Steve Davis. Includes a list of threatened taxa with IUCN categories.

9001 Breedlove, D.E. (ed.). (1981). Flora of Chiapas. California Academy of Sciences. 2 vols so far.

9002 Wiggins, I.L. (1980). Flora of Baja California. Stanford: Stanford University Press. 1025 pp.

9003 Smith, A.R. (1980). New taxa and combinations of Pteridophytes from Chiapas, Mexico. *Amer. Fern. J.* 70(1):15-27.

9004 Standley, P.C., Steyermark, J.A., & Williams, L.O. (1946). Flora of Guatemala. *Fieldiana Bot.* 24. Illus. 13 parts. Complete, 1946-1978.

9006 Woodson, R.E. et al. (1943). Flora of Panama. *Ann. Missouri Bot. Gard.* 30-67. Complete, 1980.

9009 Stolze, R.G. (1976). Ferns and fern allies of Guatemala. *Fieldiana Bot.* 39:1-130.

9012 Seymour, F.C. (1975). *Polypodium* in Nicaragua. *Phytologia* 31(2):129-192.

9015 Sosa, V. (ed.). (1978). Flora of Veracruz. Instituto de Investigaciones sobre Recursos Bióticos. 73 families so far.

9016 Smith, A.R. (1971). Systematics of the neotropical species of *Thelypteris*, Section Cyclosorus. *Univ. Calif. Publ. Bot.* 59:1-143.

9017 Gómez, L.D. (1978). *Thelypteris oroniensis*, a new genus from Costa Rica. *Amer. Fern J.* 68(1):9-10.

9018 Zanoni, T.A. & Adams, R.P. (1979). The genus *Juniperus* (Cupressaceae) in Mexico and Guatemala: synonymy, key and distributions of the taxa. *Bol. Soc. Bot. Mex.* 38:83-121. Maps, illus.

9019 Vovides, A.P. (1981). Lista preliminar de plantas Mexicanas raras o en peligro de extinción. [Preliminary list of 210 rare, threatened and endangered Mexican plant species]. *Biotica* 6(2):219-228. Sp (En).

9020 DeLuca, P., Sabato, S., & Vázquez Torres, M. (1984). *Dioon tomasellii* (Zamiaceae), a new species with two varieties from western Mexico. *Brittonia* 36(3):223-227.

9021 Robert, M.-F. (1978). Un nouveau pin pignon mexicain: *Pinus johannis*. *Adansonia* (sér. 2) 18(3):365-373.

9025 Gómez, L.D. (1984). Plantae Mesoamericanae novae. VI. *Phytologia* 52(3):153-156.

9026 Gómez, L.D. (1983). Plantae Mesoamericanae novae. VIII. *Phytologia* 53(2):97-101.

9027 Perez de La Rosa, J.A. (1985). Una nueva espécie de *Juniperus* de Mexico. *Phytologia* 57(2):81-86.

9034 Palmer, T.C. (1933). Shorter notes. *Amer. Fern. J.* 22:36.

9035 Leonard, E.C. (1950). Five new species of Acanthaceae from Honduras. *Ceiba* 1:103-115.

9036 Wasshausen, D.C. (1975). The genus *Aphelandra* (Acanthaceae). *Smithsonian Contrib. Bot.* 18:1-157.

9037 Standley, P.C. (1937-1939). Flora of Costa Rica. *Field Mus. Nat. Hist., Bot. Ser.* 18(1-4):1-1616. Map. Complete.

9038 Daniel, T.F. (1983). *Carlowrightia*

(Acanthaceae). *Flora Neotropica*, Monograph 34. 116 pp.

9039 Molina, A. (1965). Nuevas fanerógamas de América Central. *Ceiba* 11(1):65-71.

9040 Leonard, E.C. (1959). A new genus of Acanthaceae from Mexico. *Wrightia* 2(1):1-3.

9041 Daniel, T.F. (1980). The genus *Justicia* (Acanthaceae) in the Chihuahuan Desert. *Contr. Univ. Mich. Herb.* 14:61-67.

9042 Daniel, T.F. (1978). A new *Mirandea* (Acanthaceae) from Nuevo Leon, Mexico. *Syst. Bot.* 3(4):428-433.

9043 Daniel, T.F. (1981). *Mexacanthus*, a new genus of Acanthaceae from western Mexico. *Syst. Bot.* 6(3):288-293.

9044 McDade, L.A. (1982). New species of *Justicia* and *Razisea* (Acanthaceae) from Costa Rica, with taxonomic notes. *Syst. Bot.* 7(4):489-497.

9045 Daniel, T.F. (1982). *Anisacanthus andersonii* (Acanthaceae), a new species from northwestern Mexico. *Bull. Torrey Bot. Club* 109(2):148-151.

9046 Daniel, T.F. (1984). New and reconsidered Mexican Acanthaceae. *Madroño* 31(2):86-92.

9048 Daniel, T.F. (1983). Systematics of *Holographis* (Acanthaceae). *J. Arnold Arboretum* 64:129-160.

9049 Leonard, E.C. (1960). A new *Stenandrium* from the state of Durango, Mexico. *Wrightia* 2(2):83-85.

9050 Daniel, T.F. (1984). A revision of *Stenandrium* (Acanthaceae) in Mexico and adjacent regions. *Ann. Missouri Bot. Gard.* 71:1028-1043.

9052 Wasshausen, D.C. (1981). New species of *Justicia* (Acanthaceae). *Phytologia* 49(1):65-68.

9053 Wasshausen, D.C. (1973). New species of *Aphelandra* (Acanthaceae). *Phytologia* 25(7):465-502.

9054 Matuda, E. (1972). Plantas nuevas de Mexico. *An. Inst. Biol. Univ. Nal. Auton. Mexico* 43(1):51-62.

9055 Piña, I. (1980). Rare and threatened Agavaceae and Cactaceae of Mexico. Sociedad Mexicana Cactología.

9057 Gómez-Pompa, A. & Valdés-Reyna, J. (1962). Una especie epífita de *Yucca* de la selva lacandona. *Bol. Soc. Bot. Méx.* 27:43-46.

9058 Miranda, F. (1961). Plantas nuevas del sur de México. *Bol. Soc. Bot. Méx.* 26:120-132.

9061 Standley, P.C. & Williams, L.O. (1952). Ocho géneros de árboles y arbustos nuevos para Centro América. *Ceiba* 3:24-35.

9063 Fryxell, P.A. (1977). New species of Malvaceae from Mexico and Brazil. *Phytologia* 37(4):285-316.

9064 Lundell, C.L. (1976). Studies of American plants, XII. *Wrightia* 5(7):241-259.

9065 Lundell, C.L. (1970). Studies of American plants, II. *Wrightia* 4(4):129-152.

9070 Dressler, R.L. (1978). Two noteworthy ornamentals from the Caribbean coast of Panama. *Selbyana* 2(2,3):300-302.

9071 Madison, M. (1978). The species of *Anthurium* with palmately divided leaves. *Selbyana* 2(2,3):239-282.

9075 Standley, P.C. & Williams, L.O. (1951). Plantae Centrali-Americanae, II. *Ceiba* 1:231-255.

9077 Barringer, K.A. (1984). A new species of *Guatteria* (Annonaceae) from Panama. *Ann. Missouri Bot. Gard.* 71(4):1186-1187.

9078 Croat, T.B. (1983). A revision of the genus *Anthurium* (Araceae) of Mexico and Central America. Part I. Mexico and Middle America. *Ann. Missouri Bot. Gard.* 70(2):211-420.

9079 Gentry, H.S. (1960). A new *Agave* from Oaxaca. *Brittonia* 12:98-100.

9084 Williams, L.O. (1970). Tropical American plants, XI. *Fieldiana Bot.* 32(12):179-206.

9089 Gentry, A.H. (1980). Bignoniaceae Part I. (Crescentieae and Tourrettieae). *Flora Neotropica*, Monograph 25. 131 pp.

9090 Fryxell, P.A. (1969). The genus *Hampea* (Malvaceae). *Brittonia* 21:359-396.

9092 Robyns, A. (1967). Bombacaceae Neotropicae Novae I. New species of *Chorisia* and *Quararibea*. *Ann. Missouri Bot. Gard.* 54:184-186.

9094 Higgins, L.C. (1976). Two new species from the Chihuahuan Desert. *Phytologia* 33(6):411-413.

9096 Gentry, A.H. (1977). New species of *Gibsoniothamnus* (Scrophulariaceae / Bignoniaceae) and *Tournefortia* (Boraginaceae) from eastern Panama and the Chocó. *Ann. Missouri Bot. Gard.* 64:133-135.

9097 Smith, L.B. & Downs, R.J. (1977). Pitcairnioideae, Tillandsioideae, Bromelioideae (Bromeliaceae). *Flora Neotropica*, Monograph 14(1-3).

9098 Hazlett, D.L. (1979). Arboles maderables y otros árboles desconocidos de la Cordillera Nombre de Dios. *Ceiba* 23(2):76-84.

9099 Williams, L.O. (1968). Tropical American plants, X. *Fieldiana Bot.* 32(4):35-61.

9105 Barringer, K.A. (1983). Notes of Central American Aristolochiaceae. *Brittonia* 35(2):171-174.

9110 Stevens, W.D. (1983). New species and names in Apocynaceae, Asclepiadoidea. *Phytologia* 53(6):401-405.

9111 Baker, R.A. & Burger, W.C. (1976). Key and commentary on the species of *Spathiphyllum* (Araceae) in Costa Rica, including *S. silvicola*, sp. nov. *Phytologia* 33(7):447-454.

9114 Vovides, A.P. (1986). Relación de plantas Mexicanas raras o en peligro de extinción. 7 pp. Veracruz: INIREB.

9139 Rathakrishnan, N.C. (1983). Rare and little-known orchids from the erstwhile Presidency of Madras. *Bull. Bot. Surv. India* 23(3-4):237-239. (1981 publ. 1983).

9147 Whistler, W.A. (1986). A revision of *Psychotria* (Rubiaceae) in Samoa. *J. Arnold Arboretum* 67:341-370.

9148 Quero, H.J. & Read, R.W. (1986). A revision of the palm genus *Gaussia*. *Syst. Bot.* 11(1):145-154.

9149 Moore, H.E. (1980). Two new species of *Geonoma* (Palmae). *Gentes Herbarum* 12(1):25-29.

9150 Moore, H.E. (1980). Four new species of Palmae from South America. *Gentes Herbarum* 12(1):30-38.

9155 Lan, K.M. (1984). A new variety of *Amentotaxus argotaenia*. *Acta Phytotaxonomica Sinica* 22(6):492. Ch. Illus.

9157 Chen, S.C. & Tsi, Z.H. (1984). *Paphiopedilum malipoense* sp. nov. - an intermediate form between *Paphiopedilum* and *Cypripedium* with a discussion on the origin of the genus. *Acta Phytotaxonomica Sinica* 22(2):119-124. Ch (En).

9159 Melville, R. & Heybroek, H.M. (1971). The elms of the Himalaya. *Kew Bull.* 26(1):5-28. Illus., maps.

9204 Humphries, C.J. (1977). A new genus of the Compositae from North Africa. *Bot. Notiser* 130:155-161.

9216 Mohanan, M., Henry, A.N., & Nair, N.C. (1982). Notes on three rare and interesting orchids collected from Trivandrum District, Kerala. *J. Bombay Nat. Hist. Soc.* 79(1):234-236.

9228 **Rathakrishnan, N.C. & Saran, R. (1983).** Notes on rare plants from Madhya Pradesh. *J. Bombay Nat. Hist. Soc.* 80(3):665-667. Nine taxa of flowering plants.

9244 **Muñiz, O. & Borhidi, A. (1982).** Catálogo de las palmas de Cuba. *Acta Botanica Academiae Scientiarum Hungaricae* 28(3-4):309-334.

9248 **Mudgal, V. & Jain, S.K. (1982).** *Coptis teeta* Wall. - local uses, distribution and cultivation. *Bull. Bot. Surv. India* 22:179-180. Illus. Medicinal.

9249 **Joseph, J., Abbareddy, N.R., & Haridasan, K. (eds.). (1982).** *Gastrodia exilis* Hook., a rare and interesting orchid from Khasi and Jaintia Hills, Meghalaya. *Bull. Bot. Surv. India* 22:203-205. Illus., map. (1980 publ. 1982).

9250 **Mohanan, M. & Henry, A.N. (1982).** Rediscovery of three rare and endemic plants of India. *Bull. Bot. Surv. India* 22:236-237. (1980 publ. 1982).

9272 **Holttum, R.E. (1964).** A revised Flora of Malaya. Singapore: Gov't Printer. 3 vols. Vol. 1 - Orchids of Malaya; Vol. 2 - Ferns of Malaya; Vol. 3 - Grasses of Malaya, by H.B. Gilliland.

9280 **Parris, B.S. (1986).** Grammitidaceae of Peninsular Malaysia and Singapore. *Kew Bulletin* 41(3):491-517.

9282 **Holttum, R.E. (1986).** A new tree-fern in northern Queensland. *Kew Bulletin* 41(3):532.

9283 **Jermy, A.C. (1986).** Two new *Selaginella* species from Gunung Mulu National Park, Sarawak. *Kew Bulletin* 41(3):547-559. Illus.

9315 **Mohanan, M., Henry, A.N., & Nair, N.C. (1982).** Some rare and fast disappearing plants discovered in Trivandrum District, Kerala. *Bull. Bot. Surv. India* 22(1-4):105-108. (1980 publ. 1982).

9326 **Cribb, P.J. (1983).** A revision of *Dendrobium* sect. Latouria (Orchidaceae). *Kew Bulletin* 38(2):229-306. Illus., col. illus., maps.

9327 **Chandrabose, M. & Srinivasan, S.R. (1981).** Notes on two rare and interesting plants from S. India. *J. Bombay Nat. Hist. Soc.* 78(3):630.

9330 **Henry, A.N. & Swaminathan, M.S. (1983).** Rare or new *Exacum* L. (Gentianaceae) from southern India. *J. Bombay Nat. Hist. Soc.* 80(2):456-459. Illus.

9336 **Vajravelu, E. & Bhargavan, P. (1982).** Notes on some rare plants from south India. *J. Econ. Tax. Bot.* 3(3):969-973. Illus.

9389 **Lawesson, J.E. (1986).** Report on the most threatened endemic plants in Galapagos. Santa Cruz. Charles Darwin Research Station. 10pp Annotated list; maps.

9402 **Bogner, J. (1984).** On *Hapaline appendiculata* and *Phymatarum borneense*, two rare Araceae from Borneo. *Plant Systematics and Evolution* 144:59-66. Illus.

9416 **Hegde, S.N. & Rao, A.N. (1983).** Further contributions to the orchid flora of Arunachal Pradesh - 1. *J. Econ. Tax. Bot.* 4(2):383-392. Annotated list of 30 species, of which 3 are new species, 3 new records for India and 3 new records for N.E. Himalayas. 18 species are noted as rare and/or endangered.

9417 **Burger, W.C. (ed.). (1971).** Flora Costaricensis. *Fieldiana Bot.* 35 & 40. Continued in *Fieldiana Bot., New Series* 4, 13, 18, 28, 33, 35, 36.

9420 **Durkee, L. (1981).** Annotations to: List of threatened plants of Middle America.

9422 **Halbinger, F. (1975).** *Barkeria shoemakeri*, a new orchid from the state of Michoacan. *Orquídea (Méx.)* 4(10):296-297.

9423 **Williams, L.O. (1951).** The Orchidaceae of Mexico. *Ceiba* 2(1):1-321.

9424 **Dodson, C.H. (1974).** *Dressleria* and *Clowesia*: a new genus and an old one revived in the Catasetinae (Orchidaceae). *Selbyana* 1(2):130-137.

9425 **Vovides, A.P. (1982).** Annotations to: List of threatened plants of Mexico.

9426 **Gómez, L.D. (1982).** Annotations to: List of threatened plants of Middle America.

9429 **Maas, P.J.M. (1981).** Annotations to: List of threatened plants of Middle America.

9432 **Rauh, W. (1984).** *Tillandsia ehlersiana*: a remarkable new species from Chiapas, Mexico. *J. Bromeliad Soc.* 34(4):166-169.

9443 **Rodas, J. & Aguilar, J. (1980).** Lista de algunas especies vegetales en via en extinción. INAFOR, Guatemala City, Guatemala. 3p. (unpublished).

9444 **Witsberger, D. (1980).** Tree species of El Salvador and their conservation status. 31 pp. (unpublished list).

9446 **Ferreyra, R. (1977).** Endangered species and plant communities in Andean and coastal Peru. *In* Prance, G.T., Elias, T. *(Eds.)*. Extinction is forever. Bronx, New York: New York Botanical Garden. 150-157 pp. Graphs. Vegetation regions and associated endangered plants.

9482 **Grayum, M.H. (1986).** New taxa of *Caladium, Chlorospatha*, and *Xanthosoma* (Araceae: Colocasioideae) from southern Central America and northwestern Colombia.

Ann. Missouri Bot. Gard. 73(2):462-474.

9484 Kress, W.J. (1986). New heliconias (Heliconiaceae) from Panama. *Selbyana* 9:156-166.

9488 Lott, E.J., Jaramillo, V., & Rzedowski, J. (1984). Un género nuevo de la parte meridional de México: *Gypsacanthus* (Acanthaceae, Justicieae, Odontoneminae). *Bol. Soc. Bot. Méx.* 46:47-51.

9490 Pohl, R. (1986). A new *Papsalum* (Poaceae) from Mesoamerica. *Ann. Missouri Bot. Gard.* 73:501.

9518 Prance, G.T. (1972). Chrysobalanaceae. Supplement to Chrysobalanaceae. *Flora Neotropica*, Monograph 9 (supplement). 406 pp.

9522 King, R.M. & Robinson, H. (1974). Studies in the Eupatorieae (Asteraceae). CXXVIII. Four additions to the genus *Ageratina* from Mexico and Central America. *Phytologia* 28(5):491-493.

9524 Turner, B.L. (1985). *Ageratina gonzalezorum* (Asteraceae - Eupatorieae), a new species from Durango, Mexico. *Phytologia* 58(7):498.

9529 Williams, L.O. (1964). Tropical American plants, VI. *Fieldiana Bot.* 31(2):17-48.

9532 McVaugh, R. (1972). Nomenclatural and taxonomic notes on Mexican Compositae. *Rhodora* 54:495-516.

9550 Paray, L. (1958). Nuevas compuestas de México. *Bol. Soc. Bot. Méx.* 22:1-12.

9553 Sorensen, P.D. (1969). A revision of the genus *Dahlia* (Compositae), Heliantheae - Coreopsidinae. *Rhodora* 71:309-416.

9554 Pippen, R.W. (1968). Mexican "Cacalioid" genera allied to *Senecio* (Compositae). *Contrib. U.S. Nat. Herb.* 34(6):365-447.

9567 Turner, B.L. (1975). Taxonomy of *Haploesthes* (Asteraceae - Senecioneae). *Wrightia* 5(5):108-115.

9571 Torres, A.M. (1968). Revision of *Jaegeria* (Compositae - Heliantheae). *Brittonia* 20:52-73.

9581 Rzedowski, J. (1970). Estudio sistemático del género *Microspermum* (Compositae). *Bol. Soc. Bot. Méx.* 31:49-108.

9582 Rzedowski, J. (1972). Dos especies nuevas del género *Microspermum* (Compositae) del estado de Jalisco (México). *Bol. Soc. Bot. Méx.* 32:77-86.

9586 Dillon, M.O. & D'Arcy, W.G. (1978). New and noteworthy Asteraceae from Panama. *Ann. Missouri Bot. Gard.* 65:764-765.

9593 Gómez, L.D. (1985). Annotations to: List of threatened plants of Middle America.

9595 King, R.M. (1965). *Piqueriopsis*, a new genus of Compositae from southwestern Mexico. *Brittonia* 17:352-353.

9604 Robinson, H. (1976). Three new Asteraceae from Guerrero, Mexico. *Phytologia* 33(5):285-292.

9613 Grashoff, J.L. (1974). Novelties in *Stevia* (Compositae: Eupatorieae). *Brittonia* 26:347-384.

9615 Turner, B.L. (1972). *Strotheria* (Compositae - Tageteae) a new monotypic genus from north-central Mexico. *Am. J. Bot.* 59:180-182.

9618 Cronquist, A. (1965). Studies in Mexican Compositae. I. Miscellaneous new species. *Memoirs of the New York Botanical Garden* 12(3):286-292.

9627 Torres, A.M. (1963). Taxonomy of *Zinnia. Brittonia* 15:1-25.

9628 Funk, V.A. (1982). The systematics of *Montanoa* (Asteraceae, Heliantheae). *Memoirs of the New York Botanical Garden* 36:1-133.

9640 Cuatrecasas, J. (1982). Miscellaneous notes on Neotropical Flora, XV. New taxa in the Asteraceae. *Phytologia* 52(3):166-177.

9641 Cuatrecasas, J. (1982). Studies in Neotropical Senecioneae III. New taxa in *Senecio, Pentacalia,* and *Gynoxys. Phytologia* 52(3):159-166.

9649 Nelson, C. (1984). Una *Ocotea* (Lauraceae), una *Salvia* (Labiatae) y una *Eupatorium* (Compositae) nuevos de Honduras. *Ceiba* 25(2):173-176.

9651 Powell, A.M. & Turner, B.L. (1976). New gypsophilous species of *Pseudoclappia* and *Sartwellia* (Asteraceae) from west Texas and eastern Chihuahua. *Sida* 6(4):317-320.

9657 Myint, T. & Ward, D.B. (1968). A taxonomic revision of the genus *Bonamia* (Convolvulaceae). *Phytologia* 17:121-239.

9658 Austin, D. (1981). Annotations to: List of threatened plants of Middle America.

9659 McPherson, G.D. (1980). Eight new species of *Ipomoea* and *Quamoclit* from Mexico. *Contrib. Univ. Mich. Herb.* 14:85-97.

9660 Maas, P.J.M. (1972). Costoideae (Zingiberaceae). *Flora Neotropica*, Monograph 8. 148 pp.

9661 Calderón de Rzedowski, G. (1974). Adiciones a la flora fanerogámica del Valle de México, II. *Bol. Soc. Bot. Méx.* 33:47-67.

9662   Hunt, D.R. (1985). Annotations to: List of threatened plants of Middle America.

9663   Calderón de Rzedowski, G. (1970). Hallazgo de una especie nueva de *Draba* (Cruciferae) en el Valle de México. *Bol. Soc. Bot. Méx.* 31:109-112.

9664   Rollins, R.C. (1976). Studies on Mexican Cruciferae. *Contrib. Gray Herb.* 206:3-18.

9665   Calderón de Rzedowski, G. (1977). *Mancoa rollinsiana*, una especie nueva de Cruciferas encontrada en el Valle de México. *Phytologia* 36(4):269-273.

9666   Rollins, R.C. (1981). Annotations to: List of threatened plants of Middle America.

9667   Rollins, R.C. (1969). A remarkable new crucifer from Mexico. *Contrib. Gray Herb.* 198:1-8.

9668   Rollins, R.C. (1980). The genus *Pennellia* (Cruciferae) in North America. *Contrib. Gray Herb.* 210:5-21.

9669   Dieterle, J.V.A. (1974). A new geocarpic genus from Mexico: *Apatzingania* (Cucurbitaceae). *Brittonia* 26:120-132.

9670   Dieterle, J.V.A. (1980). Two new Cucurbitaceae from Mexico. *Contr. Univ. Mich. Herb.* 14:69-73.

9672   Harling, R. (1985). Annotations to: List of threatened plants of Middle America.

9674   Hermann, F.J. (1974). Manual of the genus *Carex* in Mexico and Central America. Washington, DC: U.S. Forest Service. 219 pp.

9676   Prance, G.T. (1977). Two new species for the Flora of Panama. *Brittonia* 29:154-158.

9677   Prance, G.T. (1976). *Tapura* (Dichapetalaceae) a genus new to Mexico. *Bull. Torrey Bot. Club* 103:21-22.

9678   Williams, L.O. (1961). Tropical American plants, II. *Fieldiana Bot.* 29(6):345-372.

9679   Kubitzki, K. (1981). Annotations to: List of threatened plants of Middle America.

9681   Carnegie Institution of Washington. (1936). Botany of the Maya Area. Washington, D.C. 802p.

9682   White, F. (1981). Annotations to: List of threatened plants of Middle America.

9683   McVaugh, R. & Rosatti, T.J. (1978). A new species of *Arbutus* (Ericaceae) from western Mexico. *Contr. Univ. Mich. Herb.* 11(5):301-304.

9684   Wells, P.V. (1972). The manzanitas of Baja California, including a new species of *Arctostaphylos*. *Madroño* 21:268-272.

9685   Luteyn, J.L. (1982). Ericaceae - Part 1. *Cavendishia. Flora Neotropica.* Monograph 35. 290 pp.

9686   Luteyn, J.L. (1976). Notes on neotropical Vaccinieae (Ericaceae). I. *Gonocalyx* - a genus new to Central America. *Brittonia* 28(1):37-41.

9687   Williams, L.O. (1965). Tropical American plants, VII. *Fieldiana Bot.* 31(6):167-221.

9688   Luteyn, J.L. & Wilbur, R.L. (1977). New genera and species of Ericaceae (Vaccinieae) from Costa Rica and Panama. *Brittonia* 29:255-276.

9690   Williams, L.O. (1967). Tropical American plants, VIII. *Fieldiana Bot.* 31(10):249-269.

9692   McVaugh, R. (1961). Euphorbiaceae Novo-Galicianae. *Brittonia* 13:145-205.

9695   Molina, A. (1951). Nuevas especies de plantas de la República de Honduras. *Ceiba* 1:255-263.

9700   Huft, M.J. (1982). Annotations to: List of threatened plants of Middle America.

9702   Rogers, D.J. & Appan, S.G. (1973). *Manihot, Manihotoides* (Euphorbiaceae) *in* Flora Neotropica. Monograph 13. 272 pp.

9703   Webster, G. (1981). Annotations to: List of threatened plants of Middle America.

9704   Webster, G. (1967). A remarkable new *Phyllanthus* (Euphorbiaceae) from Central America. *Ann. Missouri Bot. Gard.* 54:194-196.

9706   McVaugh, R. (1974). Flora Novo-Galiciana. Ann Arbor, Michigan: University of Michigan Press.

9707   Martínez, M. (1974). Los enciños de México. *An. Inst. Biol. Univ. Nal. Autón. México Ser. Botánica* 45(1):21-56.

9708   Muller, C.H. (1979). *Quercus deliquescens*, a new species from Chihuahua, Mexico. *Phytologia* 42(2):289-291.

9709   Sleumer, H.O. (1980). Flacourtiaceae. *Flora Neotropica*, Monograph 22. 499 pp.

9710   González-Medrano, F. (1972). Una nueva Frankeniaceae del norte de México. *Bol. Soc. Bot. Méx.* 32:71-76.

9715   Pringle, J.S. (1977). Taxonomy and distribution of *Gentiana* (Gentianaceae) in Mexico and Central America. *Sida* 7:174-218.

9718   Wiehler, H. (1978). Miscellaneous transfers and new species of neotropical Gesneriaceae. *Selbyana* 5(1):61-93.

9719 Skog, L. (1982). Annotations to: List of
threatened plants of Middle America.

9721 Wiehler, H. (1978). The genera
Episcia, Alsobia,
Nautilocalyx, and *Paradrymonia*
(Gesneriaceae). *Selbyana* 5(1):1-60.

9722 Beetle, A.A. (1977). Noteworthy grasses from
Mexico, V. *Phytologia* 37(4):317-407.

9726 Seymour, F.C. (1975). *Panicum* in
Nicaragua. *Phytologia* 32(1):1-30.

9727 Pohl, R. (1981). Annotations to: List of
threatened plants of Middle America.

9730 Nelson, C. (1981). Annotations to: List of
threatened plants of Middle America.

9732 Breedlove, D.E. & McClintock, E. (1976).
Thornea (Hypericaceae), a new genus from
Mexico and Guatemala. *Madroño* 23:368-373.

9733 Molseed, E. (1968). *Fosteria,* a new
genus of Mexican Iridaceae. *Brittonia*
20:232-234.

9736 Cruden, R.W. (1968). Three new species of
Tigridia (Iridaceae) from Mexico.
Brittonia 20:314-320.

9738 Manning, W.E. (1957). The genus
Juglans in Mexico and Central America. *J.*
Arnold Arbor. 38:121-150.

9742 Lavin, M. & Sousa, M. (1987). The Madrensis
group of *Coursetia* (Leguminosae: Robinieae).
Syst. Bot. 12(1):106-115.

9745 Fowlie, J.A. (1987). A contribution to a
monographic revision of the genus *Saphronitis*
Lindl. *Orchid Digest* 51(1):15-34.

9749 Villaseñor, J.L. (1986). A new species of the
Mexican genus *Arnicastrum* Greenm. (Asteraceae:
Heliantheae). *Syst. Bot.* 11(2):277-279.

9751 Warnock, M.J. (1987). Synopsis of
Delphinium (Ranunculaceae) in continental
Mexico. *Rhodora* 89(857):47-74.

9772 Palmberg, C. (1987). Conservation of genetic
resources of woody species. 16 pp. Rome: FAO. Paper
prepared for Simposio Sobre Silvicultura y Mejoramiento
Geneti co. Cief. Buenos Aires, 6-10 April 1987. Includes
lists of commercially exploited timber trees.

9774 Borhidi, A. (1987). Letter to V.H.Heywood, 25
February 1987, and annotations to CMC printout of Cuban
palms. TPU printout dated 2 February 1987.

9775 La Frankie, J.V. (1986). Morphology and
taxonomy of the New World species of
Maianthemum (Liliaceae). *J. Arnold*
Arbor. 67(4):371-439.

9777 Epling, C. & Jativa, C. (1968). Supplementary

notes on American Labiatae. X. *Brittonia*
20:295-313.

9783 Mori, S.A. (1981). Annotations to: List of
threatened plants of Middle America.

9784 Dwyer, J. (1965). Notes on the Lecythidaceae
of Panama. *Ann. Missouri Bot. Gard.*
52:351-363.

9785 Prance, G.T. & Mori, S. (1979). Lecythidaceae
- Part I. The actinomorphic-flowered New World
Lecythidaceae (*Asteranthus,*
Gustavia, Grias, Allantoma
and *Cariniana*). *Flora Neotropica,*
Monograph 21.

9786 Mori, S. (1970). A new species of
Lecythis from Panama. *Ann. Missouri Bot.*
Gard. 57:386-388.

9787 Janzen, D. (1974). Swollen-thorn acacias of
Central America. *Smithsonian Contrib. Bot.*
13:1-131.

9793 Frantz, P.R. (1979). A new species of
Centrosema (Leguminosae) from Nicaragua and a
key to the species in Central America. *Sida*
8(2):152-162.

9794 Espinosa, G.J. (1977). Una nueva especie de
Crotalaria (Leguminosae) de Valle de México.
Phytologia 36(4):265-268.

9798 Arroyo, M.T.K. (1976). The systematics of the
legume genus *Harpalyce* (Leguminosae -
Lotoideae). *Memoirs of the New York Botanical*
Garden 26(4):1-80.

9802 Burger, W.C. (1968). Notes on the Flora of
Costa Rica, I. *Fieldiana Bot.* 31(11):273-275.

9808 Cowan, R.S. (1968). *Swartzia*
(Leguminosae). *Flora Neotropica.* Monograph 1.
227p.

9812 Rogers, C.M. (1968). Yellow-flowered species
of *Linum* in Central America and western North
America. *Brittonia* 20:107-135.

9815 Kuijt, J. (1981). Annotations to: List of
threatened plants of Middle America.

9816 Kuijt, J. (1978). Commentary on the mistletoes
of Panama. *Ann. Missouri Bot. Gard.*
65:736-763.

9817 Graham, S. (1968). New species of
Cuphea (Lythraceae) from Mexico.
Brittonia 20:1-10.

9818 Graham, S. (1971). Three new species of
Cuphea (Lythraceae) from Mexico.
Brittonia 23:227-230.

9821 Fryxell, P.A. (1981). Annotations to: List of
threatened plants of Middle America.

9822 Fryxell, P.A. (1976). Mexican species of *Abutilon* sect. Armata (Malvaceae) including descriptions of three new species. *Madroño* 23:320-333.

9823 Fryxell, P.A. (1980). Three new species of Malvaceae from Mexico. *Phytologia* 46(6):391-399.

9825 Fryxell, P.A. (1978). *Gossypium turneri* (Malvaceae), a new species from Sonora, Mexico. *Madroño* 25:155-159.

9826 Fryxell, P.A. (1977). New species of Malvaceae from Mexico and Brazil. *Phytologia* 37(4):285-316.

9827 Fryxell, P.A. (1979). Una revisión del género *Pavonia* en México. *Bol. Soc. Bot. Méx.* 38:7-35.

9828 Fryxell, P.A. (1974). Revision of *Periptera* DC. (Malvaceae). *Bol. Soc. Bot. Méx.* 33:39-46.

9829 Fryxell, P.A. (1971). A revision of *Phymosia* (Malvaceae). *Madroño* 21:153-174.

9832 Kennedy, H. (1978). Notes on Central American Marantaceae II. New species of *Calathea* from Costa Rica and Panama. *Brenesia* 14/15:349-356.

9833 Kennedy, H. (1976). Notes on Central American Marantaceae. I. New species and records from Panama and Costa Rica. *Ann. Missouri Bot. Gard.* 60:413-426.

9835 Almeda, F. (1981). Annotations to: List of threatened plants of Middle America.

9836 Wurdack, J.J. (1982). Annotations to: List of threatened plants of Middle America.

9837 Almeda, F. (1974). A new epiphytic *Blakea* (Melastomataceae) from Panama. *Brittonia* 26:393-397.

9838 Wurdack, J.J. (1976). New Guatemalan Melastomataceae. *Wrightia* 5(7):226-227.

9839 Almeda, F. (1979). A new Costa Rican species of *Clidemia* (Melastomataceae). *Bull. Torrey Bot. Club* 106:189-192.

9840 Wurdack, J.J. (1978). Vicariads in *Henrietella* (Melastomataceae). *Wrightia* 6(2):21-22.

9841 Almeda, F. (1978). Systematics of the genus *Monochaetum* (Melastomataceae) in Mexico and Central America. *Univ. Calif. Publ. Botany* 75:1-134.

9842 Morley, T. (1976). Memecyleae (Melastomataceae). *Flora Neotropica*. Monograph 15. 295 pp.

9843 Pennington, T.D. (1981). Meliaceae. *Flora Neotropica*. Monograph 28. 470 pp.

9987 Gorts van-Rijn, A.R.A. (1985). Flora of the Guianas. Königstein, W. Germany: Koeltz Scientific Books.

9989 Lorence, D.H. (1981). Annotations to: List of threatened plants of Middle America.

9990 Berg, C.C. (1972). Olmedieae, Brosimeae (Moraceae). *Flora Neotropica*, Monograph 7. 229 pp.

9991 Berg, C.C. (1981). Annotations to: List of threatened plants of Middle America.

9992 Kress, W.J. (1985). Annotations to: List of threatened plants of Middle America.

9993 Gentry, A.H. (1975). Additional Panamanian Myristicaceae. *Ann. Missouri Bot. Gard.* 62:474-479.

9996 Numerous. (1990). Plant name changes. Where the plant name has been changed from an earlier usage in the datafile.

9997 Numerous. (1990). Multiple data sources. Where more than one data source was required to provide the information required.

9998 Numerous. (1990). Assumed data. Where assumptions are made on the data before incorporation.

10001 Dwyer, J. & Hayden, M.V. (1966). Three new species of *Neea* (Nyctaginaceae) from Panama. *Phytologia* 14(3):137-139.

10003 Raven, P.H. (1981). Annotations to: List of threatened plants of Middle America.

10004 Plitman, U., Raven, P.H., & Breedlove, D. (1972). New taxa and recombinations in *Lopezia* (Onagraceae). *Ann. Missouri Bot. Gard.* 59:279-281.

10006 Plitman, U., Raven, P.H., Tai, W., & Breedlove, D. (1975). Cytological studies in Lopezieae (Onagraceae). *Bot. Gazette* 136(3):322-332.

10007 Navarro, A.V. (1982). Annotations to: List of threatened plants of Middle America.

10008 Luer, C.A. (1977). Icones Pleurothallidinarum I and III. *Selbyana* 3(1-4):1-412.

10009 Luer, C.A. (1980). Miscellaneous new species in Pleurothallidinae (Orchidaceae). *Phytologia* 46(6):345-387.

10010 Dodson, C.H. (1982). Annotations to: List of threatened plants of Middle America.

10011 Halbinger, F. (1982). Annotations to: List of threatened plants of Middle America.

10012 Williams, L.O. (1956). An enumeration of the Orchidaceae from Central America, British Honduras, and Panama. *Ceiba* 5:1-256.

10013 Hamer, F. (1974). Las orquídeas de El Salvador. San Salvador, El Salvador: Ministerio de Educación. 800 pp. 2 vols.

10015 Dressler, R.L. (1968). Dos orquídeas nuevas de México occidental. *An. Inst. Biol. Univ. Nal. Autón. México, Ser. Botánica* 39(1):117-120.

10016 Scheeren, W. (1974). A new *Epidendrum* from Oaxaca, Mexico: *Epidendrum gastiferum. Orquídea (Méx.)* 4(5):67-72.

10017 Heller, A.H. & Hawkes, A.D. (1966). Nicaraguan orchid studies - I. *Phytologia* 14(1):1-35.

10018 Heller, A.H. (1968). Three new Nicaraguan Epidendrums. *Fieldiana Bot.* 32(2):7-11.

10020 Dressler, R.L. (1981). Annotations to: List of threatened plants of Middle America.

10021 Hágsater, E. (1981). Annotations to: List of threatened plants of Middle America.

10028 Correll, D.S. (1965). Supplement to orchids of Guatemala and British Honduras. *Fieldiana Bot.* 31(7):177-221.

10030 Dressler, R.L. (1979). An attractive new *Sievekingia* from Panama. *Orquídeología* 13(3):224-229.

10034 Hamer, F. (1983). Orchids of Nicaragua. *Icones Plantarum Tropicarum.* fascicles 7-9, 11-13.

10035 Dressler, R.L. (1975). A new *Mormodes* (Orchidaceae) from Panama. *Ann. Missouri Bot. Gard.* 62:510-511. *Mormodes lancilabris.*

10037 Barringer, K.A. (1985). Three new species of *Elleanthus* (Orchidaceae) from Central America. *Brittonia* 37(3):286-290.

10041 Hágsater, E. (1986). *Oncidium hyalinobulbon* LaLlave & Lexarza and *Ercina echinata* (H.B.K.) Lindley. *Orquídea (Méx.)* 10(1):37-42.

10042 Greenwood, E.W. (1986). *Ponthieva angustipetala* Greenwood, una espécie inesperada del Sur de México. *Orquídea (Méx.)* 10(1):7-21.

10044 Leon, E.A. (1986). *Clowesia dodsoniana:* una nueva *Clowesia* de México. *Orquídea (Méx.)* 10(1):191-200.

10047 Halbinger, F. (1982). *Odontoglossum* y géneros áfines en México y Centroamérica. *Orquídea (Méx.)* 8(2):155-242.

10048 Jones, H.G. (1974). Additions to the orchid flora of Belize (British Honduras). *Adansonia* ser. 2 14(2):299-302.

10049 Dressler, R.L. (1983). Two new *Kefersteinia* from Panama. *Orquideologia* 16(1):56-62.

10059 Wendt, T. (1979). Notes on the genus *Polygala* in the United States and Mexico. *J. Arnold Arbor.* 60(4):504-514.

10060 Gentry, A.H. (1973). A new species of Proteaceae from Panama. *Ann. Missouri Bot. Gard.* 60:571-572.

10061 Johnston, M.C. (1976). *Thalictrum henricksonii* (Ranunculaceae), a new species from the Chihuahuan Desert region. *Wrightia* 5(8):301.

10062 Johnston, M.C. & Johnston, L.A. (1978). *Rhamnus. Flora Neotropica*, Monograph 20. 96 pp.

10063 Blackwell, W.H. (1968). Revision of *Bouvardia* (Rubiaceae). *Ann. Missouri Bot. Gard.* 55:1-30.

10064 Anderson, W.R. (1972). A monograph of the genus *Crusea* (Rubiaceae). *Memoirs of the New York Botanical Garden* 22(4):1-128.

10065 Dempster, L.T. (1970). Three new species of *Galium* (Rubiaceae) from Baja California. *Brittonia* 22:184-190.

10066 Dempster, L.T. (1975). A new species of *Galium* (Rubiaceae) from Coahuila. *Madroño* 23:13-14.

10071 Rzedowski, J. (1975). Tres dicotiledóneas mexicanas nuevas de posible interés ornamental. *Bol. Soc. Bot. Méx.* 35:37-50.

10073 Barringer, K.A. (1983). *Polygala dukei* (Polygonaceae), a new species from Panama. *Ann. Missouri Bot. Gard.* 70(1):203-204.

10075 Dempster, L.T. (1975). A new species of *Galium* (Rubiaceae) from the Sierra Madre Oriental. *Madroño* 23(3):108-110.

10077 Turner, B.L. & Turner, G. (1983). A new gypsophilic species of *Galium* (Rubiaceae) from north-central Mexico. *Madroño* 30(1):31-33.

10081 Wendt, T. (1983). Plantae Uxpanapae 1. *Colubrina johnstonii* sp. nov. (Rhamnaceae). *Bol. Soc. Bot. Méx.* 44:81-90.

10082 Bosser, J., Cadet, Th., Julien, H.R., & Marais, W. (1976). Flore des Mascareignes: La Réunion, Maurice, Rodrigues. The Sugar Research Institute, Mauritius; ORSTOM, Paris; Royal Botanic Gardens, Kew. Multipart Flora, ongoing, much still in manuscript held in Kew (with Keith Ferguson).

10086 Halbinger, F. (1986). *Lemboglossum*

uroskinneri en Chiapas. *Orquídea (Méx.)* 10(1):133-137.

10088 **Hunter, G. (1966).** Mexican and Central American *Saurauia* (Dilleniaceae). *Ann. Missouri Bot. Gard.* 53(1):47-89.

10089 **Holmgren, N.H. (1978).** *Castilleja* (Scrophulariaceae) of Costa Rica and Panama. *Brittonia* 30:182-194.

10096 **McVaugh, R. & Mellichamp, T.L. (1975).** Mexican species of *Pedicularis* (Scrophulariaceae) hitherto confused with *P. tripinnata* Mart. & Gal. *Contr. Univ. Mich. Herb.* 11(2):57-63.

10102 **Waterfall, U.T. (1967).** *Physalis* in Mexico, Central America, and the West Indies. *Rhodora* 69:82-120; 203-239; 319-394.

10104 **D'Arcy, W.G. (1978).** A preliminary synopsis of *Salpiglossis* and other Cestreae (Solanaceae). *Ann. Missouri Bot. Gard.* 65:698-724.

10108 **Correll, D.S. (1961).** Four new Solanums in Section Tuberarium. *Wrightia* 2(3):133-141.

10114 **Almeda, F. (1976).** A new species of *Symplocos* (Symplocaceae) from Mexico. *Madroño* 23:365-368.

10117 **Constance, L. & Bye, R.A. (1976).** New Chihuahuan Umbelliferae. *Bot. Mus. Leaflets (Harv. Univ.)* 24:225-240.

10118 **Maas, P.J.M. et al. (1986).** Saprophytes, pro parte. *Flora Neotropica*, Monograph 40, 41, 42. 189 pp.

10120 **Bye, R.A. & Constance, L. (1979).** A new species of *Tauschia* (Umbelliferae) from Chihuahua, Mexico. *Madroño* 26(1):44-47.

10123 **Croat, T.B. (1976).** Notes on Central and South American *Cissus* (Vitaceae). *Ann. Missouri Bot. Gard.* 63:358-363.

10125 **Maas, P.J.M. (1977).** *Renealmia* (Zingiberaceae - Zingiberoideae). Costoideae (Additions). (Costaceae). *Flora Neotropica*, Monograph 18. 218 pp.

10128 **Kral, R. (1982).** *Xyris nigrescens* Kral, a new species of *Xyris* (Sect. *Nematopus*) from Costa Rica. *Ann. Missouri Bot. Gard.* 69:415-417.

10130 **Almeda, F. (1982).** *Symplocos sousae*, a new species of Symplocaceae from Mexico. *Madroño* 29(4):255-258.

10131 **Wendt, T. (1983).** Plantae Uxpanapae II. Novedades en Violaceae y Scrophulariaceae. *Bol. Soc. Bot. Mexico* 45:133-140.

10141 **Dransfield, J., Comber, J.B., & Smith, G. (1986).** A synopsis of *Corybas* (Orchidaceae) in West Malesia and Asia. *Kew*

Bull. 41(3):575-613. Illus., col. illus.

10149 **Madulid, D.A. (1986).** Additions to: List of plants in the CMC database for the Philippines.

10150 **Subramanian, K.N. & Singh, B.G. (1986).** *Gymnacranthera canarica* (King) Warb. - a tree species on the verge of extinction. Mimeo. 3p. (unpublished). Illus.

10153 **Téllez Valdés, O. (1985).** Two new species and a new combination in *Tephrosia* (Leguminosae). *Isleya* 2(3):101-108.

10155 **Burt-Utley, K. & Utley, J.F. (1987).** Contributions toward a revision of *Hechtia* (Bromeliaceae). *Brittonia* 39(1):37-43.

10160 **Knapp, S. (1986).** Three new species of *Solanum* Section Geminata (G.Don) Walp. (Solanaceae) from Panama and western Colombia. *Ann. Missouri Bot. Gard.* 73:738-744.

10161 **Gentry, A.H. (1986).** New neotropical species of *Meliosma* (Sabiaceae). *Ann. Missouri Bot. Gard.* 73:820-824.

10162 **Sousa, M. (1986).** Adiciónes a las leguminosas de la Flora de Nicaragua. *Ann. Missouri Bot. Gard.* 73:722-737.

10166 **MacDougal, J.M. (1982).** Annotations to: List of threatened plants of Middle America. Added new species.

10167 **Minnich, R. (1986).** Range extensions and corrections for *Pinus jeffreyi* and *P. coulteri* (Pinaceae) in northern Baja California. *Madroño* 33(2):144-145.

10168 **Forman, L.L. (1987).** A new genus of Burseraceae from Mexico. *Kew Bull.* 42(1):262.

10169 **Fosberg, F.R., Sachet, M.-H., & Stoddart, D.R. (1983).** Henderson Island (southeastern Polynesia): summary of current knowledge. *Atoll Res. Bull.* 272:1-53. Illus., maps. Lists native and endemic species.

10171 **Ansari, M.Y. (1983).** The fragrant *Ceropegia* of nineteenth century. *Bull. Bot. Surv. India* 24(1-4):190-192. Illus. (1982 publ. 1983).

10173 **Deb, D.B. & Raghavan, R.S. (1983).** A rare species of *Agapetes* D. Don ex G. Don (Ericaceae). *Bull. Bot. Surv. India* 24(1-4):171-173. Illus. (1982 publ. 1983).

10177 **Balakrishnan, N.P. & Nair, N.G. (1983).** New taxa and record from Saddle Peak, Andaman Islands. *Bull. Bot. Surv. India* 24(1-4):28-36. Illus. (1982 publ. 1983).

10178 **Mohanan, C.N. (1983).** A contribution to the botany of Quilon District, Kerala. *Bull. Bot. Surv. India* 23(1-2):60-64. (1981 publ. 1983). Lists endemic and threatened species.

10181 **Shaw, R. (1987).** The genus *Eriochloa* (Poaceae: Paniceae) in North and Central America. *Sida* 12(1):165-207.

10184 **Henrickson, J. (1987).** Two new species of *Cercocarpus* (Rosaceae) from Mexico. *Syst. Bot.* 12(2):293-298.

10186 **Meerow, A.W. (1987).** New species of *Phaedranassa* and *Eucharis* (Amaryllidaceae). *Sida* 12(1):29-49.

10188 **Constance, L. & Affolter, J. (1987).** A trio of new Tauschias (Umbelliferae) from eastern Mexico. *Syst. Bot.* 12(2):286-292.

10196 **Salgado, E. (1987).** Letter to S. Davis via D.A. Madulid. Comments on Philippine ferns.

10197 **Martorell, L.F., Loigier, A.H., & Woodbury, R.O. (1981).** Catálogo de los nombres vulgares y científicos de las plantas de Puerto Rico. Boletin 263. Universidad de Puerto Rico. Rio Piedras, Puerto Rico. Recinto de Mayaguez, Estación Experimental Agrícola. 231 pp. Sp.

10198 **Eriksson, O., Hansen, A., & Sunding, P. (1974).** Flora of Macaronesia. Check-list of vascular plants. University of Umea, Sweden.

10199 **Nicolson, D.H. (1979).** List of threatened plants of Dominica with IUCN conservation categories. Threatened Plants Committee survey: returned list.

10200 **Nicolson, D.H. (1977).** Endemic species of dicots in Dominica. Pers. comm. An updated list from Bruce E. Weber's 1973 thesis "Dominica National Park", published by the Dept. of Recreation Resources, College of Forestry & Nat. Res., Colorado State Univ., Fort Collins, Colorado.

10232 **Stevens, P.F. (1980).** A revision of the Old World species of *Calophyllum*. *J. Arnold Arboretum* 61:258. Illus., maps.

10235 **Basu, S.K. (1983).** A provisional census of palms of India. Howrah, POSSCEF, Botanical Survey of India. 11p. (unpublished).

10237 **Moore, H.E. (1980).** Lists of palms for Hawaii, Japan, Philippines, Marquesas, Samoa, Tuamotu Islands, New Hebrides, Ryukyu Islands, Marianas, Taiwan, Micronesia and Bonin Islands, New Caledonia, Solomon Islands. Manuscript list, with letter to Hugh Synge, dated 19 February 1980. 5p. (unpublished).

10238 **Dransfield, J. (1976).** Lists of and comments on palms, made in 1976.

10241 **Loc, P.K. & Ban, N.T. (1985).** Annotations to: Preliminary list of candidate species of Vietnam.

10242 **Essig, F.B. (1977).** The palm flora of New Guinea: a preliminary analysis. Lae, PNG, Office of Forests. Botany Bulletin no. 9. 54 pp. Illus., keys.

10245 **Andrews, F.W. (1950).** The flowering plants of the (Anglo-Egyptian) Sudan. Arbroath, Scotland: Buncie. 3 vols. Illus., keys. (1950-1956).

10246 **Humbert, H. (1936).** Flore de Madagascar et des Comores. Paris, Muséum National d'Histoire Naturelle. Multipart work, 132 families written out of 189.

10249 **Whitmore, T.C. (1973).** Palms of Malaya. London: Oxford Univ. Press. 132 pp. Illus., keys.

10250 **Hatusima, S. (1971).** Flora of the Ryukyus (including Amami Islands, Okinawa Islands and Sakishima Archipelago). Okinawa: Study Group of Biological Education. 940 pp. Ja. Revised 1975.

10251 **Sledge, W.A. (1982).** An annotated checklist of the Pteridophyta of Ceylon. *Bot. J. Linn. Soc.* 84(1):1-30.

10252 **Abeywickrama, B.A. (1990).** The threatened plants of Sri Lanka. Sri Lanka: NARESA. Unesco - Man and the Biosphere National Committee for Sri Lanka. 56 pp. Publication No. 16. Annotated checklist.

10253 **Smith, A.C. (1979).** Flora Vitiensis Nova: a new Flora of Fiji. Hawaii, Pacific Tropical Botanic Garden. 5 volumes have been published (Spermatophytes only).

10258 **Dransfield, J. (1984).** The rattans of Sabah. Sabah, Forest Department. Sabah Forest Record no. 13: 182p. Illus., keys.

10259 **Dransfield, J. (1979).** A manual of the rattans of the Malay Peninsula. Malaysia Forest Department. Malayan Forestry Records no. 29. 270 pp. Illus., keys. Checklist and descriptions of 104 species.

10260 **HMSO. (1895-1992).** Index Kewensis plantarum phanerogamarum. Kew: Royal Botanic Gardens. Vols 1-2 published in 1895; 19 supplements up to 1993. CD-ROM version 1993 (Oxford University Press).

10262 **Dransfield, J. (1987).** Lists and comments on palms, made in 1987.

10269 **Tackholm, V. (1974).** *Student's Flora of Egypt.* Cairo University.

10270 **Greuter, W., Burdet, H.M., & Long, G. (eds.). (1984).** Med-Checklist. Vols. 1, 3 & 4. A critical inventory of vascular plants of the circum-mediterranean countries. Secretariat Med-Checklist, Botanischer Garten & Botanisches Museum Berlin-Dahlem. Vol. 1: Pteridophyta (ed 2.), Gymnospermae, Dicotyledones (Acanthaceae - Cneoraceae; Vol. 2 Convolvulaceae - Labiatae; Vol. 3 Lauraceae - Rhamnaceae; Vol. 4.

10276 **Gunatilleke, C.V.S. &. I.A.U.N. (1985).** A conservation and protection plan for the Sinharaja Forest. Draft. Colombo, Ministry of Lands and Land Development and Forest Department and Gland, Switzerland, WWF and IUCN. (unpublished). Includes list of plants and their uses and endemism.

10278 **Tan, B.C., Fernando, E., & Rojo, J.P. (1986).** An updated list of endangered Philippine plants. *Yushania* 3(2):1-5.

10283 Gunatilleke, C.V.S. &. I.A.U.N. (1987). Rare woody species of Sinharaja rain forest in Sri Lanka. *In* Kostermans, A.J.G.H. (ed.). Proceedings of the Third Round Table Conference on Dipterocarps. Jakarta, Unesco-MAB and UNEP. 519-530. Paper presented at conference held at Mulawarman Univ., Samarinda, Kalimantan, April 1985.

10288 Furtado, C.X. (1967). Some notes on *Hyphaene*. *Garcia de Orta* 15(4):427-460. Illus.

10291 Kiew, R. (1976). The genus *Iguanura* Bl. (Palmae). *Gard. Bull. Singapore* 28:191-226. Illus., keys, map.

10292 Kiew, R. (1979). New species and records of *Iguanura* (Palmae) from Sarawak and Thailand. *Kew Bull.* 34(1):143-145.

10293 Dransfield, J. (1972). The genus *Johannesteijsmannia* H.E. Moore jr. *Gard. Bull. Singapore* 26:63-83. Illus., map, keys.

10294 Lundell, C.L. (1969). Studies of American plants, I. *Wrightia* 4(3):97-128.

10295 Lundell, C.L. (1971). Studies of American plants, III. *Wrightia* 4(4):153-170.

10297 Lundell, C.L. (1968). Studies of Tropical American plants. IV. *Wrightia* 4(1):31-51.

10299 Lundell, C.L. (1974). Studies of American plants, VI. *Wrightia* 5(2):23-44.

10303 Lundell, C.L. (1975). Studies of American plants - XI. *Wrightia* 5(6):193-198.

10310 Lundell, C.L. (1961). New species, nomenclatural changes, and new records for trees and shrubs of Mexico and Central America. *Wrightia* 3(1):1-20.

10320 Lundell, C.L. (1978). Studies of American plants, XVI. *Wrightia* 6(1):4-20.

10323 Pipoly, J.J. & Lundell, C.L. (1982). Contributions toward a monograph of *Cybianthus* (Myrsinaceae) II. The systematic position of *Ardisia perpuncticulosa*. *Wrightia* 7(2):52-54.

10337 Iltis, H. (1981). Studies in the Capparidaceae XV: *Capparis panamensis*, n. sp. *Ann. Missouri Bot. Gard.* 68:681-685.

10339 Hunt, D.R. (1981). Annotations to: List of threatened plants of Middle America.

10341 Morton, C.V. (1933). The Mexican and Central American species of *Viburnum*. *Contrib. U.S. Nat. Herb.* 26(7):339-366.

10349 Turner, B.L. & Lanford, G. (1982). A new species of *Ericameria* (Asteraceae-Astereae) from north-central Mexico. *Madroño* 29(4):234-236.

10351 Maguire, B. (1977). Notes on Clusiaceae, chiefly of Panama. I. *Phytologia* 36(4):391-407.

10353 Hamilton, C. (1985). Notes and descriptions of seven new species of Mesoamerican Clethraceae. *Ann. Missouri Bot. Gard.* 72(3):539-543.

10354 McVaugh, R. (1972). Compositarum Mexicanum Pugillus. *Contr. Univ. Mich. Herb.* 9:359-484.

10357 Turner, B.L. (1987). A new species of *Sabazia* (Asteraceae, Heliantheae) from Durango, Mexico. *Phytologia* 63(4):307-309.

10358 Dillon, M.O. (1984). A systematic study of *Flourensia* (Asteraceae, Heliantheae). *Fieldiana Bot.* 16:1-66.

10359 Aguilar, J.M. (1981). Annotations to: List of threatened plants of Middle America.

10360 Seymour, F.C. (1981). Annotations to: List of threatened plants of Middle America.

10368 Jenkins, M.D. (ed.). (1987). Madagascar. An environmental profile. Gland, Switzerland and Cambridge, IUCN/UNEP/WWF. 374 pp. Compiled by IUCN Conservation Monitoring Centre, Cambridge. Maps. French edition in prep.

10370 FAO Forestry Department. (1986). Databook on endangered tree and shrub species and their provenances. Forestry Paper No. 77. Rome: FAO. 524 pp. Datasheets on 81 species.

10379 Fay, M.F. & Muir, H.J. (1987). The role of micropropagation in the conservation of European plants. Kew, Royal Botanic Gardens. 7p. (unpublished). Mimeo. Includes case studies of threatened plants from other areas.

10397 García, R.D. & Olmsted, I. (1987). Listado florístico de la Reserva Sian Ka'an. Puerto Morelos, Quintana Roo, Mexico. 71 pp. Sp. Illus.Inventory of 850 species.

10439 Fu, L.G. & Chen, S.Z. (1981). Discovery and designation of *Cathaya argyrophylla*. *Plant Journal (Zhiwu Zazhi)* 4:1-42. Ch.

10482 Smitinand, T. (1979). Letter to TPC. Details on palms of Thailand.

10483 Rechinger, K.H. (ed.). (1963). Flora Iranica. Austria, Graz. 150 parts published out of a projected 170. Illus. Covers Iranian highlands, parts of Afghanistan, west Pakistan, north Iraq, Azerbaijan and Turkmenistan.

10487 Maire, R. (1952). Flore de l'Afrique du Nord. Paris. Fr. 16 volumes published so far, out of 22 expected; incomplete.

10488 Quezel, P. & Santa, S. (1962). Nouvelle Flore de l'Algérie et des régions désertiques méridionales. Paris. Centre National de la Recherche Scientifique. 2

vols. 1170 pp. Fr. Illus.

10499 **Balakrishnan, N.P. (1982).** Nomenclatural notes on some flowering plants - III. *Bull. Bot. Survey India* 22(1-4):173-177. (1980 publ. 1982).

10504 **Hanelt, P. (1963).** Monographische Übersicht der Gattung *Carthamus* L. (Compositae). *Feddes. Rep.* 67:41-180. Ge. Illus., maps.

10505 **Nair, V.J. & Ramachandran, V.S. (1982).** Five plant records for Kerala. *Bull. Bot. Survey India* 22(1-4):193-194. (1980 publ. 1982).

10506 **Ansari, M.Y. (1982).** *Ceropegia panchangiensis* Blatt. et McCann (Asclepiadaceae) - a little known species, rediscovered. *Bull. Bot. Surv. India* 22(1-4):199-201. Illus. (1980 publ. 1982).

10508 **Nair, N.C., Nair, V.J., & Ansari, R. (1980).** Notes on some rare plants from south India. *Bull. Bot. Surv. India* 22(1-4):205-207. Illus. (1980 publ. 1982).

10511 **Ansari, M.Y. & Kulkarni, B.G. (1982).** A new species of *Ceropegia* Linn. (Asclepiadaceae) from the Western Ghats in Maharashtra State (India). *Bull. Bot. Survey India* 22(1-4):221-222. Illus. (1980 publ. 1982).

10512 **Ansari, M.Y. (1982).** *Ceropegia maccannii* Ansari - a new species. *Bull. Bot. Survey India* 22(1-4):227-229. Illus. (1980 publ. 1982).

10517 **Dransfield, J. (1978).** The genus *Maxburretia* (Palmae). *Gentes Herbarum* 11(4):187-199. Illus.

10518 **Moore, H.E. (1978).** New genera and species of Palmae from New Caledonia. *Gentes Herbarum* 11(4):291-309. Illus.

10519 **Moore, H.E. (1978).** *Tectiphiala*, a new genus of Palmae from Mauritius. *Gentes Herbarum* 2:284-290.

10520 **Obermeyer, A.A. & Strey, R.G. (1969).** A new species of *Raphia* from northern Zululand and southern Mozambique. *Bothalia* 10(1):29-37. Illus.

10523 **Moore, H.E. & Uhl, N.W. (1984).** The indigenous palms of New Caledonia. *Allertonia* 3(5):402. Illus., maps. Includes rediscovery of *Pritchardiopsis jennencyi*.

10525 **Dransfield, J. (1980).** Systematic notes on *Pinanga* (Palmae) in Borneo. *Kew Bull.* 34(4):769-788. Illus.

10526 **Moore, H.E. (1970).** The genus *Rhopaloblaste* (Palmae). *Principes* 14(3):75-92. Illus.

10532 **Moore, H.E., Philipps, R.H., & Vodonaivalu, S. (1982).** Additions to the palms of Fiji.

Principes 26(3):122-125. *Gulubia* sp. nov. and *Alsmithia longipes*.

10534 **Dransfield, J. (1982).** *Pinanga cleistantha*, a new species with hidden flowers. *Principes* 26(3):126-129.

10538 **Tryon, R.M. (1987).** Annotations to: List of threatened plants of Latin America.

10539 **Jiménez, Q. (1986).** Arboles en peligro de extinción para Costa Rica. San José: Fundación de Parques Nacionales, Programa Patrimonio Natural de Costa Rica. 4 pp.

10540 **Castillo, J.A. (1986).** Annotations to: List of threatened plants of Latin America.

10544 **Staples, G. (1987).** Annotations to: List of threatened plants of Latin America.

10545 **Hammel, B.E. (1987).** Annotations to: List of threatened plants of Middle America.

10546 **McDonald, J.A. (1982).** A new species of *Ipomoea* (Convolvulaceae) from southwestern Mexico. *Brittonia* 34(3):336-338.

10553 **Buchholz, J. & Gray, N.E. (1948).** A taxonomic revision of *Podocarpus* II. The American species of *Podocarpus*: Section Stachycarpus. *J. Arnold Arboretum* 29:117-151. Keys.

10557 **Dietrich, W. & Wagner, W.L. (1987).** New taxa of *Oenothera* L. Sect. Oenothera (Onagraceae). *Ann. Missouri Bot. Gard.* 74:144-150.

10558 **Van der Werff, H. (1987).** A revision of *Mezilaurus* (Lauraceae). *Ann. Missouri Bot. Gard.* 74:153-182.

10559 **Daniel, T.F. (1986).** Systematics of *Tetramerium* (Acanthaceae). *Systematic Botany Monographs* 12:1-134.

10567 **Mirov, N.T. (1967).** The genus *Pinus*. New York: Ronald Press Co. 602 pp. Maps, keys, illus.

10569 **Royal Botanic Gardens Kew. (1990).** Herbarium sheets. Kew, Royal Botanic Gardens. Used to determine locality and ecological data.

10570 **Neto, H.M. (1976).** *Pichisermollia* Monteiro Neto um nome novo parc *Gigliolia* Becc. *Rodriguesia* 28(4):195-198.

10571 **Dransfield, J. (1979).** A monograph of *Ceratolobus* (Palmae). *Kew Bull.* 34(1):1-33. Illus.

10572 **Nature Conservation Society of Japan, W. (1987).** The list of plants important for conservation (the primary edition). Angiospermae: Corypetalae. Tokyo: NACS-Japan and WWF-Japan. 27 pp.

10573 **Nature Conservation Society of Japan, W. (1987).** The list of plants important for conservation (the primary edition). Angiospermae:

Sympetalae. Tokyo: NACS-Japan and WWF-Japan. 24 pp.

10582 Fah, L.Y. (1987). A preliminary survey of *Mangifera* species in Sabah. Sandakan, Forest Research Centre. Project No. 3305/MAL 75.

10583 Wickens, G.E. (1971). Tropical African Plants: XXXI. *Kew Bull.* 25(2):173-190. A section of miscellaneous species descriptions.

10584 Polhill, R.M. (1963). Tropical African Plants: XXVII. *Kew Bull.* XVII:161-182. A section of miscellaneous species descriptions.

10592 Guan, S.L. (1987). Conservation of the mango and its relatives in Peninsular Malaysia. Forest Research Institute of Malaysia. World Wildlife Fund Malaysia Project MAL 80/85. 29 pp.

10597 Bompard, J.M. & Kostermans, A.J.G.H. (1985). Preliminary results of an IUCN/WWF sponsored project for conservation of wild *Mangifera* species *in situ* in Kalimantan (Indonesia). Montpellier, Laboratoire de Botanique Tropicale and Bogor, BIOTROP. Col. illus., maps. Mimeo.

10598 Strahm, W. (1986). Mauritius and Rodrigues: Conservation of endemic plants. Progress report of WWF/IUCN Project number 3149 from 1 June 1986 to 31 December 1986. 39p. (unpublished). Includes species lists, tables of population data, habitat descriptions, and details of plant propagation programme.

10600 Rushforth, K. (1986). Mexico's spruces - rare members of an important genus. *Kew Mag.* 3(3):119-124. Illus., maps.

10603 Fernando, E.S. (1983). A revision of the genus *Nenga*. *Principes* 27(2):55-70. Palm genus from S.E. Asia and Indo-China.

10604 Green, P.S. (1986). Notes relating to the floras of Norfolk and Lord Howe Islands, II. *J. Arnold Arboretum* 67:109-122.

10630 Dransfield, J. (1984). The genus *Areca* (Palmae: Arecoideae) in Borneo. *Kew Bull.* 39(1):1-22. Synopsis of all Bornean species; sinks *Pichisermollia*.

10631 Madulid, D.A. (1981). A monograph of *Plectocomia* (Palmae: Lepidocaryoideae). *Kalikasan, Philipp. J. Biol.* 10(1):1-94.

10642 Wang, X., Jin, X., & Sun, C. (1986). *Burretiodendron hsienmu* Chun & How: its ecology and its protection. *Arnoldia* 45(4):46-51. Illus., map.

10667 Dransfield, J. (1984). A note on the genus *Zalacella* (Palmae: Lepidocaryoideae). *Kew Bulletin* 39:797-798. Reduces *Zalacella harmandii* from Laos to *Calamus harmandii*.

10668 Dransfield, J. & Mogea, J.P. (1981). A reassessment of the genus *Lophospatha* Burret. *Principes* 25(4):178-180. Sinks this palm genus into *Salacca*.

10669 Dransfield, J. (1982). *Pogonotium moorei*, a new species from Sarawak. *Principes* 26(4):174-177. Palmae.

10670 Dransfield, J. (1981). A synopsis of the genus *Korthalsia* (Palmae: Lepidocaryoideae). *Kew Bull.* 36(1):163-194.

10672 Benl, G. (1976). Some new and rare ferns from West Tropical Africa. *Nova Hedwigia* XXVII:147-154.

10674 Kiew, R. & Dransfield, J. (1987). The conservation of palms in Malaysia. *Malay. Naturalist* 41(1):24-31. List of palms with conservation categories for Pen. Malaysia; result of WWF 3325.

10678 Tyzack, S. (1987). Notes on Wright's gardenia (*Rothmannia annae*), Aride Island, Seychelles. Results of a population census, with notes on fertilisation, germination, and dispersal. Management recommendations.

10701 Straley, G.B., Taylor, R.L., & Douglas, G.W. (1985). The rare vascular plants of British Columbia. *Syllogeus* (59):165.

10710 Strahm, W. (1987). Conservation of endemic plants of Mauritius and Rodrigues. Report of WWF/IUCN Project No. 3149, January-August 1987. 80p. Mimeo. (unpublished). Includes species lists, population data, habitat descriptions, and management proposals.

10720 Strahm, W. (1985). Preserving rare plants in Mauritius. *WWF Monthly Rep.* June 1985:127-130.

10739 Moore, H.E. (1982). *Geonoma tenuissima*. *Principes* 26(4):204-205.

10740 Galeano-Garces, G. (1986). *Geonoma chlamydostachys*, a new species from Colombia. *Principes* 30(2):71-74.

10741 Galeano-Garces, G. & Bernal-González, R. (1985). *Aiphanes acaulis*, a new species from Colombia. *Principes* 29(1):20-22.

10743 Bernal-González, R. (1986). *Catoblastus distichus*, an interesting new palm from Colombia. *Principes* 30(1):38-41.

10744 Read, R.W., Zanoni, T.A., & Mejia, M. (1987). *Reinhardtia paiewonskiana* (Palmae), a new species for the West Indies. *Brittonia* 39(1):20-25.

10747 d'Arcy, W.G. (1987). Flora of Panama: checklist and index. *Monographs in Systematic Botany* 17*18:1-1000. Part 1: The introduction and checklist. Part 2: Index of 7345 species.*

10759 Kress, W.J. (1984). Systematics of Central American *Heliconia* (Heliconiaceae) with pendent inflorescences. *J. Arnold Arbor.* 65:429-532.

10760 Daniels, G.D. & Stiles, F.G. (1979). The

Heliconia taxa of Costa Rica. Keys and descriptions. *Brenesia* 15(Suppl.):1-150.

10764 **U.S. Department of the Interior. Fish and Wildlife Service. (1987).** Endangered and threatened wildlife and plants; proposal to determine *Hymenoxys acaulis* var. *glabra* (lakeside daisy) to be a threatened species. *Federal Register* 52(160):31048-31050.

10766 **Croat, T.B. (1986).** A revision of the genus *Anthurium* (Araceae) of Mexico and Central America. Part II: Panama. *Monographs in Systematic Botany (Missouri Botanical Garden)* 14. 204 pp.

10777 **Grierson, A.J.C. & Long, D.G. (1983).** Flora of Bhutan: including a record of plants from Sikkim. Edinburgh: Royal Botanic Garden. vols. 1 (3 parts) & 2 (1) published so far.

10778 **Meikle, R.D. (1978).** A key to *Commicarpus. Notes Roy. Bot. Gard. Edinburgh* 36:235-249. Illus.

10779 **Dransfield, J. & Uhl, N.W. (1984).** A magnificent new palm from Madagascar. *Principes* 28(4):151-154.

10794 **Anon. (1987).** Geothermal allocations concern council. *Nature Conservation Council Newsl.* 66:3.

10831 **Beetle, A.A. (1987).** Noteworthy grasses from Mexico, XIII. *Phytologia* 63(4):209-297.

10836 **King, R.M. & Robinson, H. (1987).** The genera of the Eupatorieae (Asteraceae). Lawrence, Kansas: Allen Press Inc. 581 pp.

10868 **Anon. (1987).** Blue Vanda. Conservation of a rare orchid through micropropagation. *Bot. Gard. Conserv. News* 1(1):47-49. Illus.

10900 **Linnington, S. & Smith, R.D. (1987).** Deferred regeneration. A manpower-efficient technique for germplasm conservation. *Pl. Genet. Resource. Newsl.* 70:2-12. Gene bank.

10936 **Strahm, W. (1987).** Annotations to: Full list of species in the WCMC database for Mauritius and Rodrigues.

11027 **York, R.P. (1987).** California's most endangered plants. pp. 109-120 *In* Elias, T.S. (ed.). Conservation and management of rare and endangered plants. Proceedings from a conference, Sacramento, California, 5-8 November 1986. Sacramento: California Native Plant Society. Illus., maps. Data sheets on 12 taxa.

11051 **Norris, L.L. (1987).** Status of five rare plant species in Sequoia and Kings Canyon National Parks. pp. 279-282 *In* Elias, T.S. (ed.). Conservation and management of rare and endangered plants. Proceedings from a conference, Sacramento, California, 5-8 November 1986. Sacramento: California Native Plant Society.

11055 **DeLamater, R. & Hodgson, W. (1987).** *Agave arizonica*: an endangered species, a hybrid, or does

it matter? pp. 305-309 *In* Elias, T.S. (ed.). Conservation and management of rare and endangered plants. Proceedings from a conference, Sacramento, California, 5-8 November 1986. Sacramento: California Native Plant Society.

11059 **Holland, R.F. (1987).** What constitutes a good year for an annual plant? Two examples from the Orcuttieae. pp. 329-333 *In* Elias, T.S. (ed.). Conservation and management of rare and endangered plants. Proceedings from a conference, Sacramento, California, 5-8 November 1986. Sacramento: California Native Plant Society.

11082 **Reid, T.S. & Walsh, R.C. (1987).** Habitat reclamation for endangered species on San Bruno Mountain. pp. 493-499 *In* Elias, T.S. (ed.). Conservation and management of rare and endangered plants. Proceedings from a conference, Sacramento, California, 5-8 November 1986. Sacramento: California Native Plant Society. Maps.

11102 **Adamson, R.S. & Salter, T.M. (eds.). (1950).** Flora of the Cape Peninsula. Cape Town: Juta. 887 pp.

11103 **Kostermans, A.J.G.H. (1973).** A forgotten Ceylonese cinnamon-tree (*Cinnamomum capparu-coronde* Bl.). *Ceylon J. Sci. (Bio. Sci.)* 10(2):119-121.

11110 **Sribhibhadh, P., Juntarogool, R., & Mead, E. (eds.). (1987).** Consider the costs: a position paper on the Nam Choan Dam. Bangkok: Wildlife Fund Thailand. 47 pp. Col. illus., maps.

11117 **Lawesson, J.E., Adsersen, H., & Bentley, P. (1987).** An updated and annotated checklist of the vascular plants of the Galapagos Islands. Aarhus, Denmark: University of Aarhus. Reports from the Botanical Institute No. 16. 74 pp. (Sp).

11119 **Vovides, A.P. (1987).** Annotations to: List of threatened plants of Middle America.

11120 **Berg, C.C. (1988).** Annotations to: List of threatened plants of Latin America.

11121 **Robinson, H. & Brettell, R.D. (1974).** Studies in the Liabeae (Asteraceae). II. Preliminary survey of the genera. *Phytologia* 28(1):43-63.

11123 **Graham, S. (1988).** Annotations to: List of threatened plants of Middle America.

11124 **Andersson, L. (1985).** Revision of *Heliconia* subgen. Stenochlamys (Musaceae - Heliconioideae). *Opera Botanica* 82:5-123.

11125 **Kress, W.J. (1988).** Annotations to: List of threatened plants of Latin America.

11127 **Isley, P.T. (1987).** *Tillandsia*. The world's most unusual air plants. Gardena, California: Botanical Press. 256 pp.

11130 **Ravenna, P. (1983).** A new species and a new subgenus in *Ennealophus* (Iridaceae). *Wrightia* 7(3):232-234.

11131 Molseed, E. (1970). The genus *Tigridia* (Iridaceae) of Mexico and Central America. *Univ. Calif. Publ. Bot.* 54:1-127.

11135 Luteyn, J.L. (1987). New species and notes on neotropical Ericaceae. *Opera Botanica* 92:109-130. Illus., maps.

11136 Ravenna, P. (1987). *Diamena* and *Diora*, two new genera of Anthericaceae from Peru. *Opera Botanica* 92:185-193.

11139 National Environment Protection Bureau. (1987). The list of rare and endangered plants protected in China. Botanical Institute of Chinese Academy of Sciences, Beijing: Academy Press. 96 pp.

11149 Webster, G. & Poveda, L.J. (1987). A phytogeographically significant new species of *Jatropha* (Euphorbiaceae) from Costa Rica. *Brittonia* 30(2):265-270.

11153 Tropical Botanic Garden & Research Institute (TBGT). (1988). Returned questionnaire: rare and threatened plants of various Asian countries.

11163 Nature Conservation Society of Japan, W. (1987). The list of plants important for conservation (the primary edition). Pteridophyta. Tokyo: NACS-Japan and WWF-Japan. 18 pp.

11164 Nature Conservation Society of Japan, W. (1987). The list of plants important for conservation (the primary edition). Angiospermae: Monocotyledonae. Tokyo: NACS-Japan and WWF-Japan. 25 pp.

11169 Mathew, B. (1985). A review of the genus *Tricyrtis*. *The Plantsman* 6(4):192-224. Illus.

11177 Mogea, J.P. (1980). The flabellate-leaved species of *Salacca* (Palmae). *Reinwardtia* 9(4):461-479. Illus.

11178 Dransfield, J. (1977). A dwarf *Livistona* (Palmae) from Borneo. *Kew Bull.* 31(4):759-762. Illus.

11179 Essig, F.B. (1982). A synopsis of the genus *Gulubia*. *Principes* 26(4):159-173. Illus.

11181 Miller, J.S. (1987). Annotations to: List of threatened plants of Latin America.

11182 Webster, G. (1987). Annotations to: List of threatened plants of Latin America.

11183 Standley, P.C. (1920-1926). Trees and shrubs of Mexico. *Contrib. U.S. Nat. Herb.* 232:1-1727.

11184 Meerow, A.W. (1987). Annotations to: List of threatened plants of Latin America.

11185 Pérez-Jiménez, A. (1982). *Jatropha chamelensis* (Euphorbiaceae), nueva especie de costa de Jalisco, México. *Bol. Soc. Bot. Méx.*

42:35-39.

11190 Webster, G., Gillespie, J.L., & Steyermark, J. (1987). Systematics of *Croizatia*. *Syst. Bot.* 12:1-8.

11194 Webster, G. & Armbruster, W.S. (1979). A new euglossine-pollinated species of *Dalechampia* (Euphorbiaceae) from Mexico. *Brittonia* 31:352-357.

11195 Webster, G. (1987). A new species of *Jatropha* (Euphorbiaceae) from Nicaragua. *Ann. Missouri Bot. Gard.* 74:117-120.

11196 Webster, G. (1984). A revision of *Flueggea* (Euphorbiaceae). *Allertonia* 3:259-312.

11197 Webster, G. (1978). A new species of *Phyllanthus* (Euphorbiaceae) with southern hemisphere affinities. *Rhodora* 80:570-574.

11198 Webster, G. (1979). A revision of *Margaritaria*. *J. Arnold Arboretum* 60:403-444.

11202 Meerow, A.W. (1990). Systematics of the Amazon lilies, *Eucharis* and *Caliphruria*. *Ann. Missouri Bot. Gard..*

11203 Meerow, A.W. (1987). Biosystematics of tetraploid *Eucharis* (Amaryllidaceae). *Ann. Missouri Bot. Gard.* 74:291-309.

11205 Meerow, A.W. (1987). A monograph of *Eucrosia* (Amaryllidaceae). *Syst. Bot.* 12:460-492.

11206 Ravenna, P.F. (1980). A new yellow-flowered *Hymenocallis* (Amaryllidaceae) from north Peru. *Bot. Notiser* 133:97-98.

11207 Meerow, A.W. (1987). The identities and systematic relationships of *Mathieua* Klotzsch and *Plagiolirion* Baker (Amaryllidaceae). *Taxon* 36:566-572.

11208 Meerow, A. (1984). Two new species of pancratioid Amaryllidaceae from Peru and Ecuador. *Brittonia* 36:18-25.

11209 Ravenna, P.F. (1972). *Pucara*, género nuevo de Amaryllidaceae del norte de Peru. *Ann. Mus. Nat. Valparaiso* 5:85-89.

11210 Ravenna, P.F. (1971). *Stenomesson mirabile*. *Plant Life* 27:77-79.

11211 Barrington, D.S. (1978). A revision of the genus *Trichipteris*. *Contrib. Gray Herb.* 208:3-93. Illus., maps.

11212 Pipoly, J.J. (1987). Annotations to: List of threatened plants of Latin America.

11213 Stahl, B. (1987). Annotations to: List of threatened plants of Latin America.

11215 **Breedlove, D.E. (1987)**. Annotations to: List of threatened plants of Latin America.

11218 **Witsberger, D. (1981)**. Annotations to: List of threatened plants of Middle America.

11232 **Latiff, A. (1987)**. Portraits of threatened plants: 13. *Pterisanthes pulchra* Ridl. *Malay. Nat.* 41(2):25-26. Illus.

11244 **Holm-Nielsen, L.B. & Haynes, R.R. (1985)**. Two new Alismatidae from Ecuador and Peru (Alismataceae and Zannichelliaceae). *Brittonia* 37:17-21.

11245 **Luther, H. (1987)**. Annotations to: List of threatened plants of Latin America.

11258 **Dixit, R.D. (1987)**. IAP pteridophyte conservation data form: *Holcosorus bisulcatus* (Hook.) Ching. 26 March 1987. (unpublished).

11262 **Dixit, R.D. (1987)**. IAP pteridophyte conservation data form: *Woodsia andersonii* (Bedd.) Christ. 27 March 1987. (unpublished).

11266 **Dixit, R.D. (1987)**. IAP pteridophyte conservation data form: *Coniogramme indica* Fee.

11269 **Salgado, A.E. (1987)**. IAP pteridophyte conservation data form: *Ctenitis dubia* (Copel.) Copel. Unpublished data, 20 January 1987. (unpublished).

11270 **Salgado, A.E. (1987)**. IAP pteridophyte conservation data form: *Ctenitis paleolata* Copel. Unpublished data, 23 January 1987. (unpublished).

11271 **Salgado, A.E. (1987)**. IAP pteridophyte conservation data form: *Platycerium grande* (J. Sm. ex Fee) Presl. Unpublished data, 27 January 1987. (unpublished).

11272 **Salgado, A.E. (1987)**. IAP pteridophyte conservation data form: *Ctenitis mearnsii* Copel. Unpublished data, 23 January 1987. (unpublished).

11273 **Dixit, R.D. (1987)**. IAP pteridophyte conservation data form: *Cyathea albosetacea* (Bedd.) Copel.

11274 **Dodson, C.H. & Dodson, P.M. (1984)**. Orchids of Ecuador. *Icones Plantarum Tropicarum* fascicle 10:901-1000.

11278 **Greenwood, E.W. (1987)**. *Govenia bella*, a new species from Oaxaca, Mexico. *Orquídea (Méx.)* 10(2):273-246.

11279 **Hágsater, E. (1987)**. Epidendra nova et criticae 3: new species of the *Epidendrum arbuscula* group of Mexico and Central America. *Orquídea (Méx.)* 10(2):337-353.

11305 **Tan, B.C. (1988)**. Pers. comm. Unpublished. 12 May 1988. (unpublished). Information on Philippine species.

11306 **Maas, P.J.M. (1988)**. Annotations to: List of threatened plants of Latin America.

11307 **Maas, P.J.M. (1977)**. *Renealmia* (Zingiberaceae-Zingiberoideae) Costoideae (Additions) (Zingiberaceae). *Flora Neotropica*. Monograph 18. 218 pp.

11309 **Fries, R.E. (1931)**. Revision der Arten einiger Annonaceen-Gattungen. II. *Acta Horti Berg.* 10(2):129-341.

11310 **Maas, P.J.M. & Maas, H. (1987)**. Notes on New World Zingiberaceae: III. Some new species in *Renealmia*. *Notes Royal Bot. Gard. Edinburgh* 44(2):237-248.

11311 **Walker, J.W. (1971)**. Validation of *Reedrollinsia* Walker (Annonaceae). *Rhodora* 73(795):461.

11312 **Schatz, G. (1985)**. A new *Cymbopetalum* (Annonaceae) from Costa Rica and Panama with observations on natural hybridization. *Ann. Missouri Bot. Gard.* 72(3):535-538.

11315 **Hágsater, E. (1984)**. *Cypripedium dicksonianum* Hágsater, a new species from Chiapas, Mexico. *Orquidea(Mex.)* 9(2):209-212.

11319 **Hágsater, E. (1984)**. Epidendra Mexicana Pollardiana 10: *Epidendrum dorsocarinatum* Hágsater; a new species from the state of Mexico. *Orquídea (Méx.)* 9(2):318-320.

11320 **Hágsater, E. (1982)**. Epidendra Mexicana Pollardiana 8: *Epidendrum rowleyi, E. longipetalum*, and *E. tortipetalum*. *Orquídea (Méx.)* 8(2):376-384.

11322 **Rosillo de Velasco, S. (1983)**. *Mormodes oceloteoides* Rosillo sp. nov. *Orquídea (Méx.)* 9(1):52-58.

11324 **Cardenas, J., Ramírez, A., & Rosillo, S. (1983)**. *Mormodes pabstiana*, a new species of Jalisco, Mexico. *Orquídea (Méx.)* 9(1):78-82.

11325 **Rosillo de Velasco, S. (1983)**. *Mormodes saccata* Rosillo, a new large flowered species from Jalisco, Mexico. *Orquídea (Méx.)* 9(1):40-46.

11332 **Hágsater, E. & Stermitz, F. (1983)**. *Encyclia oestlundii*, another confused species from Mexico. *Orquídea (Méx.)* 9(1):110-112.

11335 **Halbinger, F. (1984)**. *Lemboglossum*, un nuevo nombre para el complejo *Odontoglossum cervantesii*. *Orquídea (Méx.)* 9(2):347-350.

11336 **Hágsater, E. (1988)**. Annotations to: List of threatened plants of Middle America.

11337 **Balogh, P. (1981)**. Nomenclatural notes on the genus *Schiedeela* Schlechter (Orchidaceae).

Orquídea (Méx.) 8(1):38-40.

11338 Burns-Balogh, P. (1986). A synopsis of Mexican Spiranthinae. *Orquídea (Méx.)* 10(1):76-96.

11344 Halbinger, F. (1974). The genus *Barkeria. Am. Orchid Soc. Bull.* 42:620-626.

11345 Wiard, L. (1987). An introduction to the orchids of Mexico. Ithaca, New York: Comstock. 239 pp.

11347 Dixit, R.D. (1986). IAP pteridophyte conservation data form: *Cyathea nilgirensis* Holtt. 11 September 1986. (unpublished).

11348 Dressler, R.L. & Pollard, G. (1971). Nomenclatural notes on the Orchidaceae - IV. *Phytologia* 21(7):440-443.

11350 Dixit, R.D. (1986). IAP pteridophyte conservation data form: *Isoetes bilaspurensis* Panigr. 11 September 1986. (unpublished).

11351 Harling, G. & Sparre, B. (eds.). (1973). Flora of Ecuador. Stockholm, Sweden: Department of Systematic Botany, University of Goteborg, and the Section of Botany, Riksmuseum.

11352 Dixit, R.D. (1986). IAP pteridophyte conservation data form: *Isoetes dixitii* Shende. 11 September 1986. (unpublished).

11353 Dixit, R.D. (1986). IAP pteridophyte conservation data form: *Isoetes sampathkumarnii* L.N.Rao. 11 September 1986. (unpublished).

11354 Dodson, C.H. & Hágsater, E. (1978). *Oncidium pollardii*, a new species from south central Mexico. *Orquídea (Méx.)* 7(1):16-18.

11355 Dixit, R.D. (1986). IAP pteridophyte conservation data form: *Lindsaea malabarica* (Bedd.) Bak. ex C.Chr. 12 September 1986. (unpublished).

11356 Dixit, R.D. (1990). IAP pteridophyte conservation data form: *Lindsaea tenera* Dryand.

11358 Dixit, R.D. (1986). IAP pteridophyte conservation data form: *Selaginella adunca* A.Br. ex Hieron. 11 September 1986. (unpublished).

11359 Dixit, R.D. (1986). IAP pteridophyte conservation data form: *Selaginella cataractum* Alston. 11 September 1986. (unpublished).

11362 Suro González, J. (1978). How I found *Encyclia pollardiana. Orquídea (Méx.)* 7(1):37-41.

11363 Greenwood, E. & González Tamayo, R. (1978). *Malaxis pollardii* L.O. Williams. *Orquídea (Méx.)* 7(1):48-51.

11364 Pridgeon, A.M. (1978). A revision of the genera *Coelia* and *Bothriochilus*.

Orquídea (Méx.) 7(2):81-94.

11367 Jeffrey, C. (1987). Annotations to: List of threatened plants of Latin America.

11368 Jeffrey, C. (1975). Further notes on Cucurbitaceae: IV. Some New World taxa. *Kew Bull.* 33(2):347-380.

11371 Silverstone-Sopkin, P. & Graham, S.A. (1986). Alzateaceae, a plant family new to Colombia. *Brittonia* 38(4):340-343.

11372 Foster, R.C. (1945). Miscellaneous diagnoses and transfers. *Contrib. Gray Herb.* 155:64-70.

11373 Graham, S.A. (1988). Annotations to: List of threatened plants of Middle America.

11375 Ramamoorthy, T.P. & Zardini, E.M. (1987). The systematics and evolution of *Ludwigia* sect. *Myrtocarpus* sensu lato (Onagraceae). *Systematic Botany Monographs* 19:1-120.

11379 Reznicek, A.A. (1982). Two new species of *Carex* (Cyperaceae) from southern Mexico. *Systematic Bot.* 7(3):340-344.

11380 González Elizondo, S. (1985). 3 nuevas especies mexicanas de Cyperaceae. *Phytologia* 57(6):381-385.

11383 Reznicek, A.A. (1986). The taxonomy of *Carex* sect. Hymenochlaenae (Cyperaceae) in Mexico and Central America. *Syst. Bot.* 11(1):56-87.

11384 González Elizondo, M. (1986). Una nueva especie de *Acourtia* (Asteraceae - Mutisieae) de Durango, México. *Phytologia* 61(2):117-118.

11388 Dransfield, J. (1983). *Kerriodoxa*, a new coryphoid palm genus from Thailand. *Principes* 27(1):3-11. Illus.

11389 Dransfield, J. & Wong, K.M. (1987). A new species of *Livistona* (Palmae) from Peninsular Malaysia. *Malayan Nature J.* 41(2-3):119-123. Illus.

11419 Sánchez-Mejorada, H., Anderson, E.F., Taylor, N.P. &. R. (1986). Succulent plant conservation studies and training in Mexico: Stage 1, Part 1: May-June 1986. Assessment of individual species in northeastern Mexico and initial training of conservation specialists. WWF-U.S. 158 pp.

11494 Nayar, M.P. & Sastry, A.R.K. (eds.). (1987). Red Data Book of Indian plants. Vol. 1. Calcutta: Botanical Survey of India. 367 pp. Illus., col. illus.

11495 Curtis, T.G.F. & McGough, H.N. (1988). The Irish Red Data Book 1: Vascular plants. Dublin: Wildlife Service Ireland. 168 pp. Col. illus., maps.

11496 Gómez-Campo, C. (ed.). (1987). Libro rojo de especies vegetales amenazadas de España peninsular e Islas Baleares. [Red Data Book of vascular plants in the

Balearic Islands and peninsular Spain]. ICONA, Ministerio de Agricultura, Pesca y Alimentación. 676 pp. Col illus., maps.

11502 **Garay, L. (1979).** Systematics of the genus *Stelis. Bot. Mus. Leafl. (Harv. Univ.)* 27(7-9):167-259.

11503 **González Villarreal, L.M. (1986).** Contribución al conocimiento del género *Quercus* (Fagaceae) en el estado de Jalisco. Guadalajara, México: Universidad de Guadalajara. 240 pp.

11504 **Huft, M.J. (1988).** Annotations to: List of threatened plants of Middle America.

11505 **Huft, M.J. (1987).** Four new species of *Sapium* (Euphorbiaceae) from Central and South America. *Phytologia* 63(6):441-448.

11530 **Philcox, D. (1980).** Algumas espécies novas de Escrofulariaceas da Bahia. *Bradea* 3(8):51-56.

11531 **Philcox, D. (1978).** A spectacular *Buchnera* (Scrophulariaceae) from Colombia. *J. Arnold Arboretum* 59(3):289-299.

11532 **Philcox, D. (1972).** A new species of *Buchnera* (Scrophulariaceae) from Brazil. *Kew Bull.* 27(2):333-334.

11533 **Mora-Osejo, L.E. (1988).** Annotations to: List of threatened plants of Latin America.

11534 **Todzia, C.A. (1988).** Chloranthaceae. *Flora Neotropica,* Monograph 48. 140 pp.

11543 **Stace, C. (1988).** Annotations to: List of threatened plants of Latin America.

11546 **Macbride, J.F. (1936).** Flora of Peru. *Field Mus. Nat. Hist., Bot. Ser.* 13(1-5C). Continues in *Fieldiana, Bot. New Series* 5, 7, 9, 10, 11.

11547 **Stiles, F.G. (1980).** Further data on the genus *Heliconia* (Musaceae) in northern Costa Rica. *Brenesia* 18:147-154.

11548 **Andersson, L. (1988).** Annotation to: List of threatened plants of Latin America.

11550 **Daniel, T.F. (1987).** Annotations to: List of threatened plants of Latin America.

11552 **Golovanov, V.D. et al. (eds.) (1988).** Red Data Book of RSFSR, plants. Komarov, Moscow: Academy of Sciences of USSR. Botanical Institut of V.L. Rosagropromizdat. 591 pp. Col. illus., maps.

11558 **Rohwer, J. (1987).** Annotations to: List of threatened plants of Latin America.

11559 **Daly, D. (1988).** Annotations to: List of threatened plants of Latin America.

11560 **Schubert, B.G. (1988).** Annotations to: List of threatened plants of Middle America.

11562 **Bennert, H.W., Rasbach, H., Rashbach, K., & Reichstein, T. (1988).** *Asplenium* x *rosselloi* (= *A. balearicum* x *A. onopteris*; Aspleniaceae), a new fern hybrid from Menorca, Balearic Islands. *Willdenowia* 17:181-192.

11566 **Chase, M. (1986).** A monograph of *Leochilus* (Orchidaceae). *Systematic Botany Monographs* 14:1-97.

11570 **Atwood, J.T. (1987).** A new species and new combination of Costa Rican Orchidaceae. *Selbyana* 10:60-62.

11571 **Atwood, J.T. (1987).** The vascular flora of La Selva Biological Station, Costa Rica - Orchidaceae. *Selbyana* 10(1):76-145.

11572 **Bates, D.M. (1974).** *Fryxellia,* a new genus of North American Malvaceae. *Brittonia* 26:95-100.

11577 **Fryxell, P.A. (1985).** Additional novelties in Mexican Malvaceae. *Syst. Bot.* 10(3):268-272.

11578 **Fryxell, P.A. (1984).** Four new species of Malvaceae from Mexico. *Syst. Bot.* 9(4):415-422.

11581 **Johnston, M.C. (1983).** *Anoda henricksonii* (Malvaceae), a new species from the southern Chihuahuan Desert region. *Phytologia* 53(7):451-453.

11582 **Nelson, C. (1982).** A new *Robinsonella* (Malvaceae) from Honduras. *Phytologia* 51(6):381-383.

11585 **Stutts, J. (1988).** Taxonomic revision of *Veronica* subsect. *Chamaedrys* (Compositae: Vernonieae). *Rhodora* 90(861):37-99.

11589 **Prance, G.T. (1987).** Annotations to: List of threatened plants of Latin America.

11597 **Gibbs, P. (1987).** Annotations to: List of threatened plants of Latin America.

11598 **Fryxell, P.A. (1988).** Annotations to: List of threatened plants of Middle America.

11607 **Benl, G. (1978).** The Pteridophyta of Fernando Po. I. *Acta Bot. Barcinon.* 31:31p.

11610 **Holttum, R.E. (1974).** Thelypteridaceae of Africa and adjacent islands. *Jl. S. Afr. Bot.* 40(2):123-168.

11612 **Holttum, R.E. (1986).** Studies in the fern-genera allied to *Tectaria, Triplophyllum,* a new genus of Africa and America. *Kew Bulletin* 41(2):237-260.

11620 **Wasshausen, D.C. (1987).** Annotations to: List of threatened plants of Latin America.

11630 Fay, J.J. (1987). Notes on taxa on the U.S. List for which authorities are required.

11631 Ake Assi, L. (1988). Espèces rares et en voie d'extinction de la flore de la Côte d'Ivoire. Le cas de *Monanthotaxis capea* (E.G. et A. Camus) Verdc. (Annonaceae). Centre National de Floristique, Universite d'Abidjan. 3 p. (unpublished)6 pp.

11649 Sykes, W.R. & Atkinson, I.A.E. (1988). Rare and endangered plants of Norfolk Island. Wellington: DSIR, Botany Division.

11658 Green, T. (1988). Endangered species: another opinion. *Amer. Orchid Soc. Bull.* 57(1):29-30.

11675 Miller, J. (1988). A revised treatment of Boraginaceae for Panama. *Ann. Missouri Bot. Gard.* 75(2):456-521.

11679 van der Werff, H. (1988). Eight new species and one new combination of Neotropical Lauraceae. *Ann. Missouri Bot. Gard.* 75(2):402-419.

11680 Nevling, L. & Barringer, K. (1988). A new and endangered species of *Daphnopsis* (Thymeliaceae) from Ecuador. *Ann. Missouri Bot. Gard.* 75(2):728-729.

11699 Kral, R. (1988). The genus *Xyris* (Xyridaceae) in Venezuela and contiguous northern South America. *Ann. Missouri Bot. Gard.* 75(2):522-722.

11714 Lellinger, D. (1989). The ferns and fern-allies of Costa Rica, Panama and the Chocó. (Part I: Psilotaceae through Dicksoniaceae). *Pteridologia* 2A:1-364.

11731 Landrum, L.R. (1986). *Campomanesia, Pimenta, Blepharocalyx, Legrandia, Acca, Myrrhinium,* and *Luma* (Myrtaceae). *Flora Neotropica,* Monograph 45. 178 pp.

11733 Loizeau, P. (1988). Annotations to: List of threatened plants of Middle America.

11748 Muñoz Pizarro, C. (1971). Chile: plantas en extincion. Santiago: Editorial Universitaria. 248 pp. Illus., col. illus.

11751 Boudet, G., Lebrun, J.-P., & Demange, R. (1986). Catalogue des plantes vasculaires du Mali. Maisons Alfort, Institut d'Elevage et de Médecine Vétérinaire des Pays Tropicaux. 480 pp.

11793 Sita, P. (1988). Annotations to: Draft IUCN list of plant taxa of Congo.

11813 Johnson, D.V. (1988). Worldwide endangerment of useful palms. *Adv. Econ. Bot.* 6:268-273.

11815 Wu, Z. & Fu, Q. (1988). Second batch precious rare and endangered plants of China from Shaanxi. *Shaanxi Forest Sci. Tech.* 2:19-2.

11840 Jardin Botánico Nacional, Havana, Cuba (HAJB). (1988). Returned questionnaire: rare and threatened plants of Cuba. List has been annotated to show changes in IUCN Red Data Book Categories, deletion of taxa and name changes with a supplementary list dated August 1988.

11878 Croft, L., Hemmes, D.E., & Macneil, J.D. (1976). Puukohola Heiau National Historic Site plant survey. *Newsl. Hawaii. Bot. Soc.* 15(4-5):81-94.

11911 McDonald, A. (1988). Annotations to: List of threatened plants of Middle America. TPU list: 13 October 1988.

11925 Weber, A. (1988). Portraits of threatened plants 14. *Phyllagathis stonei* A. Weber. *Malay. Naturalist* 41(3-4):4-5. Illus.

11926 Weber, A. (1988). Portraits of threatened plants 15. *Phyllagathis magnifica* A. Weber. *Malay. Naturalist* 41(3-4):5. Illus.

11933 Soto Arenas, M.A. (1988). Listado actualizado de las orquídeas de México. [Updated list of the orchids of Mexico]. *Orquídea (Méx.)* 11:233-277. English summary. Lists 918 species, subspecies and varieties in 144 genera.

11938 Soto Arenas, M.A. & Hágsater, E. (1988). Algunas ideas acerca de la conservación de las orquídeas Mexicanas y un listado preliminar de los taxa amenazados. Unpublished. 12 pp.

11967 Stevens, D. (1987). Annotations to: List of threatened plants of Middle America.

11973 Clark, L. (1987). Two new Mesoamericana species of *Chusquea* (Poaceae: Bambusoideae). *Ann. Missouri Bot. Gard.* 74:424-427.

11974 Clark, L. (1985). Three new species of *Chusquea* (Gramineae: Bambusoideae). *Ann. Missouri Bot. Gard.* 72:864-873.

11975 Altieri, M.A. & Merrick, L.C. (1988). Agroecology and *in situ* conservation of native crop diversity in the Third World. *In* Wilson, E.O. (ed.). Biodiversity. Washington, D.C., National Academy Press. 361-369. Crop genetic resources.

11980 Mori, S.A., Prance, G.T., & Zeeuw, C. (1990). Lecythidaceae - Part II: The zygomorphic-flowered New World genera (*Couroupita, Corythophora, Bertholletia, Couratari, Eschweilera,* & *Lecythis*). With a study of secondary xylem of neotropical Lecythidaceae. *Flora Neotropica,* Monograph 21 (II). 376 pp.

11981 Robson, N. (1987). Annotations to: List of threatened plants of Latin America.

11986 Meyer, F. (1951). *Valeriana* in North America and the West Indies (Valerianaceae). *Ann. Missouri Bot. Gard.* 38:377-503.

11988 Stevenson, D.W. (1986). Typification of names

in *Zamia* L. and *Aulacophyllum* Regel (Zamiaceae). *Taxon* 35(1):134-144.

11989 Stevenson, D. (1987). Again the West Indian Zamias. *Fairchild Tropical Garden Bull.* July 1987:23-27.

11990 Williams, L.O. & Allen, P. (1954). A new *Pseudima. Ceiba* 4:224-225.

11992 Grayum, M. (1987). Annotations to: List of threatened plants of Middle America.

11994 Grayum, M. (1988). Annotated list of plants collected from the Manzanillo/Gandoca region.

11995 Hekking, W.H.A. (1988). Violaceae Part 1 - *Rinorea* and *Rinoreocarpus.* *Flora Neotropica*, Monograph 46. 207 pp.

11997 Grayum, M. & Nevers, G. de. (1988). New and rare understory palms from the Peninsula de Osa, Costa Rica, and adjacent regions. *Principes* 32(3):101-114.

11999 Burger, W. (1988). A new genus of Lauraceae from Costa Rica, with comments on problems of generic and specific delimitation within the family. *Brittonia* 40(3):275-282.

12001 Hickey, R. (1988). *Isoetes pallida*, a new species from Mexico. *Am. Fern J.* 78(1):35-36.

12007 Mickel, J. & Beitel, J. (1988). Pteridophyte flora of Oaxaca, Mexico. *Memoirs of the New York Botanical Garden* 46:1-568.

12013 Molina, A. (1984). New records of flowering plants for Honduras. *Ceiba* 25(2):127-133.

12014 MacBryde, B. (1981). Annotations to: List of threatened plants of Middle America.

12015 Green, P. (1980). Letter to Hugh Synge.

12018 Taylor, C. (1984). *Palicourea spathacea* (Rubiaceae), an unusual new species from Costa Rica. *Syst. Bot.* 9(2):226-228.

12020 Wussow, J., Urbatsch, L., & Sullivan, G. (1985). *Calea* (Asteraceae) in Mexico, Central America, and Jamaica. *Syst. Bot.* 10(3):241-267.

12029 Turner, B.L. (1986). A new species of *Galinsoga* (Asteraceae - Heliantheae), a new species from Durango, Mexico. *Phytologia* 59(2):91-92.

12032 Derrick, L.N., Jermy, A.C., & Paul, A.M. (1987). Checklist of European Pteridophytes. *Sommerfeltia* 6:94.

12036 Knapp, S. (1986). A new species of *Solanum* section Geminata (Solananceae) from western Mexico. *Brittonia* 38(1):89-91.

12041 Almeda, F. (1983). Three new Mesoamerican species of *Miconia* (Melastomataceae). *Brittonia* 35(1):42-48.

12042 Prance, G.T. (1983). Additions to neotropical Dichapetalaceae. *Brittonia* 35(1):49-54.

12044 Soderstrom, T. & Zuloaga, F. (1985). New species of grasses in *Arberella*, *Cryptochloa* and *Raddia* (Poaceae: Bambusoideae: Olyreae). *Brittonia* 37(1):22-35.

12046 Wendt, T., Mori, S.A., & Prance, G.T. (1985). A new family for the flora of Mexico. *Brittonia* 37(4):347-351.

12053 Williams, L.O. & Standley, P.C. (1952). *Pentaplaris*, a new genus of Tiliaceae from Costa Rica. *Ceiba* 3:139-142.

12055 Wunderlin, R. (1983). Revision of the arborescent *Bauhinias* (Fabaceae: Caesalpinioideae: Cercideae) native to Middle America. *Ann. Missouri Bot. Gard.* 70:95-127.

12059 Forero, E. (1983). Connaraceae. Flora Neotropica, Monograph 36. 208p.

12065 Hatch, S., Valdes R., J., & Morden, C. (1986). *Stipa hirticulmis* (Poaceae: Stipeae), a new species from Nuevo Leon, Mexico. *Syst. Bot.* 11(1):186-188.

12066 Davidse, G., Soderstrom, T., & Ellis, R. (1986). *Pohlidium petiolatum* (Poaceae: Centotheceae), a new genus and species from Panama. *Syst. Bot.* 11(1):131-144.

12067 Johnston, M.C. (1986). *Phyllanthus barbarae* (Euphorbiaceae), new species from southwestern Tamaulipas, Mexico. *Syst. Bot.* 11(1):35-38.

12068 Huft, M.J. (1985). A new *Syngonanthus* (Eriocaulaceae) from southern Mexico. *Ann. Missouri Bot. Gard.* 72:448-449.

12069 Castillo-Campos, G. & Lorence, D.H. (1985). *Antirhea aromatica* (Rubiaceae, Guettardeae), a new species from Veracruz, Mexico. *Ann. Missouri Bot Gard.* 72:268-271.

12070 Pohl, R. (1985). Three new species of *Rhipidocladum* from Mesoamerica. *Ann. Missouri Bot. Gard.* 72:272-276.

12071 Madrigal-Sánchez, X. & Rzedowski, J. (1988). Una especie nueva de *Diospyros* (Ebenaceae) del municipio de Morelia, estado de Michoacán (México). *Acta Botánica Mexicana* 1:3-6.

12079 Santos, J.U.M. (1987). *Aspilia* Th. *(Compositae - Heliantheae)* espécies Brasileiras ameaçadas de extinçao. *Bot. Mus. Par. Emilio Goeldi, ser. Bot.* 3(2):109-117. Illus.

12107 Taylor, N.P. (1985). The genus *Echinocereus*. Kew, England: Royal Botanic

Gardens. 160 pp. Col. illus.

12111 Lellinger, D. (1988). Annotations to: List of
threatened plants of Latin America.

**12224 Crosby Arboretum, Hattiesburg, Mississippi, USA
(CROS). (1988).** Returned questionnaire: rare and
threatened carnivorous plants of the world. Notes on
status of carnivorous plants in the USA.

12225 Malcomber, S. (1988). Returned questionnaire:
rare and threatened carnivorous plants of the world.
Annotated with status of carnivorous plants in Borneo.

12238 Amoroso, V.B. (1990). Some endangered economic
and endemic ferns of the Philippines. pp. 15-27 in
(unknown published source).

**12249 Wyse Jackson, P.S., Strahm, W., Cronk, Q.C.B., &
Parnell, J.A.N. (1988).** The propagation of
endangered plants in Mauritius. *Moorea*
7:35-45. Map.

12250 Lawesson, J.E. & Adsersen, H. (1987). Notes on
the endemic genus *Darwiniothamnus*
(Asteraceae-Astereae) from the Galapagos Islands.
Opera Botanica 92:7-15. Illus., map. Includes
note on conservation.

12346 Lock, J.M. (1989). Legumes of Africa; a
checklist. Kew: Royal Botanic Gardens. 619 pp. Provides
IUCN conservation status for all taxa [but these
categories are assigned based more on distribution than
on actual conservation criteria].

12349 Holttum, R.E. & Edwards, P.J. (1983). The
tree-ferns of Mount Roraima and neighbouring areas of
the Guayana Highlands with comments on the family
Cyatheaceae. *Kew Bull.* 38(2):155-188. Illus.

**12379 Arce, S.J.P., Estenssoro, C.S., & Ergueta, S.P.
(1987).** Diagnóstico del estado de la flora, fauna y
communidades importantes para la conservación. Bolivia,
La Paz, Centro de Datos para la Conservación. 98 pp.

12382 López, J. & Little, E.L. (1987). Arboles
communes del Paraguay. Washington, DC: Peace Corps. 425
pp.

12437 FLORUTIL. (1988). Threatened Cactaceae of the
U.S./Mexico border states. Phoenix, Arizona, Desert
Botanical Garden. 4 pp.

12468 Centro de Datos para la Conservación. (1986).
Lista preliminar de plantas especiales. Limón, Peru:
Centro de Datos para la Conservación. 19 pp. Unpublished
list. 19 December 1986.

12469 Backeberg, C. (1966). Das Kakteenlexicon:
enumeratio diagnostica Cactacearum. Fischer. 741 pp.
Illus., col. illus., maps.

12470 Luer, C.A. (1987). Icones Pleurothallidinarum
IV. Systematics of *Acostaea,
Condylago, Porroglossum.
Monographs in Systematic Botany* 24:1-91.
Illus.

**12471 Schutzman, B., Vovides, A., & Dehgan, B.
(1988).** Two new species of *Zamia*
(Zamiaceae, Cycadales) from southern Mexico. *Bot.
Gaz.* 149(3):347-360.

12472 Gentry, A.H. (1988). Annotations to list of
threatened plants of Latin America.

12473 Lasser, T. (ed.). (1964). Flora of Venezuela.
Caracas, Instituto Botánico. 13 vols so far.

12476 McPherson, G. (1988). A new species of
Vantanea (Humiriaceae) from Panama. *Ann.
Missouri Bot. Gard.* 75(3):1148-1149.

12477 Zamora, N. & Poveda, L. (1988). Una nueva
especie de *Caryodaphnopsis* Airy Shaw
(Lauraceae) para la región neotropical. *Ann.
Missouri Bot. Gard.* 75(3):1160-1166.

12478 Zamora, N. & Poveda, L. (1988). Una nueva
especie de *Guettarda* L. (Rubiaceae,
Guettardeae) para Costa Rica. *Ann. Missouri Bot.
Gard.* 75(3):1157-1159.

12480 Webster, G. & Huft, M.J. (1988). Revised
synopsis of Panamanian Euphorbiaceae. *Ann. Missouri
Bot. Gard.* 75(3):1087-1144.

12482 Fernández, R. (1986). Propuesta y
actualización de la lista de especies de flora y fauna
silvestre clasificadas con fines de protección.
Unpublished. 16 June 1986.

12491 Jermy, A.C. (1989). Annotations to: New World
tree-fern list.

12495 Thompson, D. (1988). Systematics of
Antirrhinum (Scrophulariaceae) in the New
World. *Systematic Botany Monographs* 22:1-142.

12496 Taylor, N.P. (1988). Supplementary notes on
Mexican *Echinocereus* (1). *Bradleya*
6:65-84.

12497 Hamer, F. (1988). Orchids of Central America.
An illustrated field guide (A-L). *Selbyana*
10(Suppl.):1-430.

12516 Turner, B.L. (1986). Two new species of
Ageratina (Asteraceae - Eupatorieae) from
Durango, Mexico. *Phytologia* 61(2):77-79.

12529 Taylor, N.P. (1989). Annotations to: DS 12437
FLORUTIL (1988). Threatened Cactaceae of the U.S./Mexico
border states.

12544 Latiff, A. & Mat Salleh, K. (1989). Pers.
comm.

12612 Tryon, R. (1976). A revision of the genus
Cyathea. Contrib. Gray Herb.
206:19-98. Illus., maps.

12615 Gastony, G.J. (1973). A revision of the fern
genus *Nephelea. Contrib. Gray Herb.*
203:81-148. Illus., maps.

12616 Tryon, R. (1980). Annotations to: TPU list.

12617 Walker, T.G. (1966). A cytotaxonomic survey of the pteridophytes of Jamaica. *Trans. Roy. Soc. Edinb.* 66:169-237.

12618 Maguire, B. et al. (1978). The botany of the Guayana highland - part X. *Memoirs of the New York Botanical Garden* 29:1-288.

12619 Tryon, R. (1971). The American tree ferns allied to *Sphaeropteris horrida*. *Rhodora* 73(793):1-18. Illus.

12621 Windisch, P.G. (1977). Synopsis of the genus *Sphaeropteris* (Cyatheaceae) with a revision of the neotropical exindusiate species. *Bot. Jahrb.* 98(2):176-198. Illus., maps.

12622 Riba, R. (1967). New taxa in the genus *Alsophila*. *Rhodora* 69(777):65-69. Illus.

12625 Stolze, R.G. (1974). A taxonomic revision of the genus *Cnemidaria* (Cyatheaceae). *Fieldiana (Bot.)* 37:1-98. Illus., maps.

12732 Wycherley, P.R. (1989). Letter to Dr Wyse Jackson. Comments and returned questionnaire on the rare and threatened carnivorous plants of the world in cultivation.

12755 Anon. (1989). Ten-year review proposal to delist *Alocasia zebrina* from Appendix I. Data sheet for CITES.

12756 Anon. (1989). Ten-year review proposal to delist *Alocasia sanderiana* from Appendix I. Data sheet for CITES.

12777 Molau, U. (1988). Scrophulariaceae - Part 1. Calceolarieae. *Flora Neotropica Monograph* No.47.

12779 Catling, P. & Catling, V. (1988). An annotated list of the orchids of Belize. *Orquídea (Méx.)* 11:85-102.

12780 Heinrich, J. & Goldblatt, P. (1990). Mesoamerican Iridaceae I. Unpublished. 31p. For publication in Flora Mesoamericana.

12781 Salazar, C.G. (1988). *Mormodes tuxtlensis*, nueva especie de Veracruz, México. *Orquídea (Méx.)* 11:51-62.

12783 Meerow, A. (1989). Systematics of the Amazon lilies, *Eucharis* and *Caliphruria* (Amaryllidaceae). *Ann. Missouri Bot. Gard.* 76(1):136-220.

12787 Gibson, A. & Horak, K. (1978). Systematic anatomy and phylogeny of Mexican columnar cacti. *Ann. Missouri Bot. Gard.* 65:999-1057.

12788 Castaño, R., Hágsater, E., & Aguirre, L.E. (1984). *Phragmipedium exstaminodium*: a new species from Chiapas, Mexico. *Orquídea*

(Méx.). 9(2):198-202.

12804 Gruezo, W.S. & Fernando, E.S. (1985). Notes on *Phoenix hanceana* var. *philippinensis* in the Batanes Islands, Philippines. *Principes* 29(4):170-176. Illus.

12838 Gunatilleke, I.A.U.N. &. C.V.S. (1991). Threatened woody endemics of the wet lowlands of Sri Lanka and their conservation. *Biological Conservation* 55(1):17-36.

12840 Ekim, T., Koyuncu, M., Erik, S., & Ilarslan, R. (eds.). et al. (1989). Türkiye'nin tehlike altindaki nadir ve endemik bitki turleri. (Serie no: 18). [List of rare, threatened and endemic plants in Turkey prepared according to IUCN Red Data Book categories]. Ankara: Türkiye Tabiatini Koruma Dernegi [Turkish Association for the Conservation of Nature and Natural Resources]. 227 pp. Tu (En).

12844 Anon. (1989). Liste des taxons necessitant une action de protection prioritaire. Mimeo.

12848 FAO Regional Office for Asia and the Pacific. (1985). Dipterocarps of South Asia. Bangkok: FAO. 321 pp. (Rapa Monograph 1985/4).

12850 Kostermans, A.J.G.H. (ed.). (1987). Proceedings of the Third Round Table Conference on Dipterocarps. Jakarta: Unesco. 657 pp. Papers presented at an international conference held at Mulawarman Univ., Samarinda, E. Kalimantan, 16-20 April 1985. Includes conservation.

12921 Latiff, A. (1989). Portraits of threatened plants 19. *Ampelocissus floccosa* (Ridl.) Galet. *Malay. Naturalist* 42(2-3):3-5. Illus.

12936 Kiew, R. (1989). Lost and found - *Begonia eiromischa* and *Begonia rajah*. *Nature Malaysiana* 14(2):64-67. Col. illus., map.

12947 Smitinand, T. & Santisuk, T. (1981). Dipterocarpaceae of Thailand with special reference to silvicultural ecology. *Malaysian For.* 44(2-3):377-385.

12948 White, F. (1988). The taxonomy, ecology and chorology of African Ebenaceae. II. The non-Guineo-Congolian species of *Diospyros* (excluding sect. *Royena*). *Bull. Jard. Bot. Nat. Belg.* 58:325-448.

12983 Erfurth, T. & Rusche, H. (1976). The marketing of tropical wood. C. Wood species from Southeast Asian tropical moist forests. FO: MISC/76/8.

13102 White, F. (1978). The taxonomy, ecology and chorology of African Ebenaceae. I. The Guineo-Congolian species. *Bull. Jard. Bot. Nat. Belg.* 48:245-358.

13153 Packer, J.G. & Bradley, C.E. (1984). A checklist of the rare vascular plants in Alberta. Prov. Mus. Alta. Nat. Hist. Occ. Paper No. 5.

13154 Taylor, R.L., Straley, G.B., & Douglas, G.W. (1985). The rare vascular plants of British

Columbia. *Syllogeus* 59:165.

13294 **Wang, S. et al. (1988).** [The present state of preservation of the precious, rare and threatened plants in Hubei, as well as the proposition for studying further these plants]. *J. Wuhan Bot. Res.* 6(3):285-298. Ch (En).

13336 **Kelly, D.L. (1988).** The threatened flowering plants of Jamaica. *Biological Conservation* 46(3):201-216. Maps. Includes list of threatened species.

13351 **Schembri, P.J. & Sultana, J. (eds.). (1989).** Red Data Book for the Maltese Islands. Malta: Department of Information. 142 pp. Col. illus.

13378 **Given, D.R. (1988).** Rare and endangered plants - protection and conservation. *In* Proceedings of the New Zealand Parks and Recreation Admin. Conference, 1987. 151-165.

13640 **Colorado Native Plant Society. (1989).** Rare plants of Colorado. Estes Park: Colorado, Rocky Mountain National Park. 75 pp. Data on 92 threatened plants; introductory chapters on plant communities and habitats. Col. illus.

13662 **Wraber, T. & Skoberne, P. (1989).** Rdeci seznam ogrozenih praprotnic in semenk SR Slovenije. [The Red List of threatened vascular plants in Socialist Republic of Slovenia]. *Varstvo Narave* 14-15:429. maps.

13712 **Plowman, T. (1987).** Provisional list of endangered species of neotropical *Erythroxylum*. Unpublished list, 4 p. (unpublished).

13713 **Maas, P.J.M. & van Setten, A.K. (1987).** Annotations to: List of threatened plants of Latin America. TPU list: 16 December 1987.

13766 **Simpson, B. (1979).** A revision of the genus *Polylepis* (Rosaceae: Sanguisorbeae). *Smithsonian Contrib. Bot.* 43:1-62.

13769 **Maas, P.J.M. & Westra, L.Y. Th. (1985).** Studies in Annonaceae II. A monograph of the genus *Anaxagorea* A. St. Hil. *Bot. Jahrb. Syst.* 105(2):145-204. Part 2.

13771 **Maas, P.J.M. & Westra, L.Y.Th. (1986).** Studies in Annonaceae. V. Additional notes on *Anaxagorea* A. St. Hil. *Proc. Kon. Ned. Akad. Wetensch. Ser. C.* 89(1):75-82.

13773 **Maas, P.J.M. et al. (1990).** Studies in Annonaceae. IX. New species from the Neotropics and miscellaneous notes. *Proc. Kon. Ned. Akad. Wetensch. Ser. C.*.

13774 **Fries, R.E. (1934).** Revision der Arten einiger Anonaceen-Gattungen, III. *Acta Horti. Berg.* 12(1):1-220.

13776 **Morawetz, W. & Maas, P.J.M. (1984).** Notes on the systematics of the Amazonian genus *Guatteriella* (Annonaceae). *Pl. Syst. Evol.* 148:19-23.

13777 **Fries, R.E. (1939).** Revision der Arten einiger Anonaceen-Gattungen, V. *Acta Horti Berg.* 12(3):289-577.

13780 **Forest Management Bureau. (1988).** Natural forest resources of the Philippines. Department of Environment and Natural Resources, Manila. 62 pp. Report of Philippine-German Forest Resources Inventory Project.

13781 **Fries, R.E. (1937).** Revision der Arten einiger Anonaceen-Gattungen, IV. *Acta Horti Berg.* 12(2):221-288.

13782 **Fries, R.E. (1930).** Revision der Arten einiger Anonaceen-Gattungen, I. *Acta Horti Berg.* 10(1):1-128.

13783 **Fries, R.E. (1957).** New species of Annonaceae from the Upper Amazon Basin. *Ark. Bot. n.s.* 3(18):599-606.

13784 **Maas, P.J.M. et al. (1990).** Monograph of *Rollinia*. To be published in *Flora Neotropica*.

13785 **Fries, R.E. (1941).** Neue amerikanische Annonaceen. *Acta Horti Berg.* 13(3):103-116.

13786 **Westra, L.Y. Th. (1985).** Studies in Annonaceae, IV. A taxonomic revision of *Tetrameranthus* R.E. Fries. *Proc. Kon. Ned. Akad. Wetensch. Ser. C.* 88(4):449-482.

13787 **Maguire, B. et al. (1953).** The botany of the Guyana Highlands. *Memoirs of the New York Botanical Garden.* 12 parts, 1953.

13791 **McDonald, A. (1987).** Revision of *Ipomoea* section *Exogonium* (Choisy) Griseb. (Convolvulaceae). *Brenesia* 28:41-87.

13825 **Judziewicz, E.J. (1989).** Pygmy bamboos: a critically endangered group. *Species* 12:31-32.

13826 **Soderstrom, T. & Zuloaga, F. (1989).** A revision of the genus *Olyra* and the new segregate genus *Parodiolyra* (Poaceae: Bambusoideae: Olyreae). *Smithsonian Contrib. Bot.* 69:1-79.

13827 **Judziewicz, E. & Soderstrom, T. (1989).** Morphological, anatomical, and taxonomic studies in *Anomochloa* and *Streptocaeta* (Poaceae: Bambusoideae). *Smithsonian Contrib. Bot.* 68:1-52.

13828 **Ochoa, C. (1988).** *Solanum bill-hookeri*: new wild potato species from Peru. *American Potato J.* 65:737-740.

13830 **Martinelli, G. & Leme, E. (1989).** Rare bromeliads from Brazil, No. 3: *Lymania corallina*. *J. Bromeliad Soc.* 39(5):217-220.

13831 **Rauh, W. (1989).** *Pitcairnia billbergioides*. *J. Bromeliad Soc.*

39(5):195-196.

13833 **Madulid, D.A. (1987).** A checklist of the rare, endemic and endangered plants of Palawan. *Philippine Scient.* 24:55-66.

13845 **Ashton, P.S. (1990).** Annotations to: conservation status listings for Dipterocarpaceae. TPU printout dated 8 November 1989; annotated on 5 March 1990.

13864 **Mori, S.A. (1977).** *Eschweilera costaricensis* (Lecythidaceae): a new species for the floras of Costa Rica and Nicaragua. *Ann. Missouri Bot. Gard.* 74(2):455-456.

13865 **Fryxell, P.A. (1979).** Taxonomic notes on Chiapas Malvaceae. *Syst. Bot.* 4(3):253-256.

13866 **Miller, J.S. (1987).** Two new species of *Cordia* (Boraginaceae) from Central America. *Ann. Missouri Bot. Gard.* 74:670-673.

13867 **Kelly, D.L. & Burke, D. (1990).** Endemic flowering plants of Jamaica under threat: a fresh report. 30 pp. Map. School of Botany, Trinity College, University of Dublin, Dublin 2, Ireland.

13868 **Malcomber, S. (1989).** Additions to the TPU list of *Nepenthes*, particularly the species of Northern Borneo, based on field knowledge attained between June 1986 and September 1987.

13873 **Ridley, H.N. (1922).** The Flora of the Malay Peninsula. London: Reeve. 5 vols. 1922-1925.

13875 **Benoit, C.I. (ed.). (1989).** Red list of Chilean terrestrial flora. (Part One). Santiago: Chilean Forestry Service (CONAF). 151 pp. Illus., col., map. Book corresponds to an updated edition of the proceedings of the symposium "Chilean Threatened Native Tree and Shrub Flora". Chilean Forest Service. Aug. 27-30, 1985, Santiago, Chile.

13882 **Butt, L.P. (1990).** An introduction to the genus *Cycas* in Australia. Palm and Cycad Society of Australia. 55p. Illus., col. illus.

13883 **Nayar, M.P. & Sastry, A.R.K. (eds.). (1988).** Red Data Book of Indian Plants. Vol. 2. Calcutta: Botanical Survey of India. 268 pp. Illus., col. illus.

13892 **Weeda, E.J., Mayden, R., & Bakker, P.A. van der. (1990).** Floron Lijst van de in Nederland verdwenen en bedreigde planten (Pteridophyta en Spermatophyta) over de periode 1.1.1980-1.1.1990. [FLORON Red Data List 1990. Red Data List of the extinct, endangered and vulnerable plants in the Netherlands in the period 1980-1990]. *Gorteria.* 16(1):26p. Du (En).

13924 **Songwe, C. (1990).** Revised preliminary list of timbers of Cameroon with conservation categories.

13926 **Whitmore, T.C. (1990).** Comments on Draft Listing of Tropical Timbers of Peninsular Malaysia.

13928 **Chudnoff, M. (1984).** Tropical timbers of the world. (Agriculture Handbook no. 607). Forest Products Laboratory Madison, Wisconsin: United States Department of Agriculture. 464 pp. Illus.

13954 **Dowe, J.L. (ed.). (1989).** Palms of the South-West Pacific. Their origin, distribution and description. Milton, Qsd, Australia: The Publication Fund, Palm and Cycad Societies of Australia. 198 pp.

13955 **Nguyen Nghia Thin. (1991).** List of palms rare and endangered species of Indochina.

13967 **Argus, G. & Pryer, K. (1990).** Rare vascular plants in Canada. Our natural heritage. Ottawa: Canadian Museum of Nature. 191 pp. Maps.

13988 **El-Hadidi, M., Batanouny, K., & Fahmy, A. (1991).** The Egyptian plant red data book. Vol. 1: Trees and shrubs. Cairo: UNEP. 226 pp. Illus., map. Lists 36 Endangered, 38 Vulnerable, 8 Indeterminate, 11 Rare and 8 Extinct species.

14000 **ECE. (1989).** Draft European Red List of threatened animals and plants. Addendum 3: Non-endemic vascular plants. 12 pp. With annotations of changes to the draft red list.

14010 **Mabberley, D.J. (1987).** The plant-book. A portable dictionary of the higher plants. Cambridge, England: Cambridge University Press. 707 pp.

14011 **Willis, J.C. (1973).** A dictionary of the flowering plants and ferns. (Eighth ed.). Cambridge: Cambridge University Press. 1245 pp.

14043 **Kiew, R. (1989).** Conservation status of Palms in Peninsular Malaysia. *Malayan Naturalist* 43(1-2):3-15. Illus.

14068 **Lamb, A. (1990).** The conservation of orchids in east Malaysia. Paper presented at the symposium on the 'State of Nature Conservation in Malaysia' August 24-26 1990, Kuala Lumpur. 26 pp.

14071 **Ekim, T. (1990).** Letters to Chris Leon concerning Bern Convention - revision of Appendix I. With data sheets.

14107 **Garnett, W. (1990).** Plants in the national collection of the Center for Plant Conservation growing at Waimea Arboretum and Botanical Garden (endemic to Hawaii unless otherwise stated). *Notes from Waimea Arboretum and Botanical Garden* 17(2):4-10.

14155 **Anon. (no date).** Annotated printout of Bern Convention - revision of Appendix I. 175 pp.

14161 **Caixinhas, M.L., Almeida, M.T., & Vasconcelos, T. (1989).** Letter to Chris Leon concerning Bern Convention - Revision of Appendix I. With a list of plant species 'Vulnerable' in Europe and present in Portugal.

14166 **Anon. (1990).** Revised Appendix I of Bern Convention - working document. Non-endemic taxa.

14177 **Anon. (no date).** Revised Appendix I (Bern Convention) - (working document #2). Endemic taxa.

14182 Whitmore, T.C. & Tantra, I.G.M. (eds.).
(1986). Tree flora of Indonesia. Checklist for
Sumatra. Bogor, Indonesia: Forest Research and
Development Centre. 381 pp. Keys. Illus.

14184 Whitmore, T.C., Tantra, I., & Sutisna, U. (eds.).
(1989). Tree flora of Indonesia. Checklist for
Kalimantan. Part II. 1. Bogor, Indonesia: Forest
Research and Development Centre. 429 pp.

**14185 Whitmore, T.C., Tantra, I.G.M., & Sutisna, U.
(eds.). (1989).** Tree flora of Indonesia. Checklist
for Sulawesi. Bogor, Indonesia: Forest Research and
Development Centre. 204 pp. Keys. Illus.

14188 Yves, J. (1990). Letter to Chris Leon from the
Conservation Botanique de Brest concerning threatened
plants in France. With notes on various French endemics
and subendemics.

**14197 Ekim, T., Koyuncu, M., Guner, A., & Vural, M.
(1990).** Conservation summary. Turkish species.

14198 Pinto da Silva, A.R. (1981). Plantas em perigo
- Jasiones. Boletim da Comissao Nacional do Ambiente,
Ano V, Nr.4 - Anexo.

14209 Wagner, W., Herbst, D., & Sohmer, S. (1990).
Manual of the flowering plants of Hawaii. Honolulu:
University of Hawaii Press, Bishop Museum Press. 1853
pp. 2 vols. Illus.

14220 Coode, M. (1982). Pers. comm., 1982. Kew.

14222 Lesouef, J. (1981). Annotations to BGCCB list
for the South Atlantic.

14223 Briggs, J.D. & Leigh, J.H. (1988). Rare or
threatened Australian plants. Revised Edition.
Australian National Parks and Wildlife Service. 277 pp.
Illus., map.

14224 Powell, D. (1983). Letter to S. Davis. 8th
August. Lists 16 plants endemic to Christmas Island.

14225 Green, P. (1982). Pers. comms. in 1982.

14226 Leigh, J.H. (1982). Letter to TPU, 13 May
1982.

14227 Leigh, J.H. (1980). Annotations to TPU list of
threatened plants for Lord Howe Island.

14229 Broggi, M.F. & Waldburger, E. (1984). Rote
Liste der gefahrdeten und seltenen Gefasspflanzenarten
des Furstentums Liechtenstein. [Red List of rare and
threatened vascular plants of the Principality of
Liechtenstein]. Vaduz: Buch- und Verlagsdruckerei AG. 40
pp. Col. illus.

14230 Meikle, R.D. (1977-1985). Flora of Cyprus.
Kew, UK: Bentham-Moxon Trust, Royal Botanic Gardens,
Kew. 1969 pp. 2 vols.

14233 Coode, M. (1976). Pers. comm., 1976. Kew.

**14234 Dupont, J., Girard, J.-C., & Guinet, M.
(1989).** Flore en détresse: Le Livre Rouge des
plantes indigènes menacées à la Réunion. [Plants in
distress: Red list of threatened plants endemic to the
Reunion]. SREPEN & Région Réunion Conseil Régional. 133
pp. Covers 47 threatened taxa. Col. illus., line
drawings.

14236 Hodel, D.R. (1991). Annotations to: list of
threatened palms of Latin America. TPU list.

14242 Hodel, D.R. (1990). New species and notes on
related taxa in *Chamaedorea* subgenus
Stephanostachys. *Principes*
34(4):160-176.

14244 Moran, R.C. (1995). Flora Mesoamericana.
(Pteridophytes).

14245 Martínez, G.J. & McDonald, J. (1989).
Nowickea (Phytolaccaceae), a new genus with
two new species from Mexico. *Brittonia*
41(4):399-403.

**14247 Bravo-Hollis, H. & Sánchez-Mejorada, H.
(1985).** Notas sobre las Cactáceas de Mesoamérica
XI. *Cact. Suc. Mex.* 30(4):91-96.

**14248 Bravo-Hollis, H. & Sánchez-Mejorada, H.
(1985).** Notas sobre las Cactáceas de Mesoamérica X.
Cact. Suc. Mex. 30(3):67-68.

**14249 Bravo-Hollis, H. & Sánchez-Mejorada, H.
(1985).** Notas sobre las Cactáceas de Mesoamérica
VIII. *Cact. Suc. Mex.* 30(1):12-24.

14252 Lopestri, V. (1984). *Corypantha
robbinsorum* en Mexico. *Cact. Suc. Mex.*
29(4):81-83.

**14253 Bravo-Hollis, H. & Sánchez-Mejorada, H.
(1984).** Datos preliminares acerca de las Cactáceas
en Mesoamérica VII. *Cact. Suc. Mex.*
29(4):88-91.

**14254 Bravo-Hollis, H. & Sánchez-Mejorada, H.
(1984).** Notas sobre las Cactáceas de Mesoamérica
VII. *Cact. Suc. Mex.* 29(3):65-72.

**14255 Bravo-Hollis, H. & Sánchez-Mejorada, H.
(1984).** Datos preliminares acerca de las Cactáceas
de Mesoamérica. *Cact. Suc. Mex.* 29(1):11-12.

14257 Glass, C. & Foster, R. (1974).
Astrophytum myriostigma Lem. var.
cuadricostatum. Cact. Succ. J.(U.S.)
46(3):112.

14258 Kimnach, M. (1959). Icones plantarum
succulentarum: *Disocactus quezaltecus*
(Standley et Steyermark) Kimn. *Cact. Succ.
J.(U.S.)* 31(5):137-140.

**14260 Bravo-Hollis, H. & Sánchez-Mejorada, H.
(1985).** Notas sobre las Cactáceas de Mesoamérica.
Cact. Suc. Mex. 30(2):38-48.

14262 Glass, C. & Foster, R. (1984). Cacti and
succulents for the amateur. *Cact. Succ.
J.(U.S.)* 56(4):158-159.

301-306).

14264 Taylor, N.P. (1984). A review of *Ferocactus* Br. et R. *Bradleya* 2:19-38.

14265 Glass, C. & Foster, R. (1971). *Mammillaria fittkaui*, a new species from the state of Jalisco. *Cact. Succ. J.(U.S.)* 43(3):115-117.

14267 Craig, R.T. (1945). The Mammillaria Handbook. Pasadena, California: Abbey Garden Press. 390 pp.

14269 Fitz Maurice, W.A. (1988). Fieldnotes. *Cact. Succ. J. (U.S.)* 60(2):72-75.

14271 Glass, C. & Foster, R. (1979). New nomenclatural combinations in the Cactaceae. *Cact. Succ. J. (U.S.)* 51(3):123-126.

14273 Glass, C. & Foster, R. (1977). A revision of the genus *Turbinicarpus* (Backbg.) Buxb. et Backbg. *Cact. Succ. J. (U.S.)* 49(4):163-179.

14279 Perry, J.P. (1991). The pines of Mexico and Central America. Portland: Timber Press. 231 pp. Maps, illus.

14280 Glass, C. & Foster, R. (1980). The succulents of San Luis Potosí: the southern edge of the Chihuahuan Desert. *Cact. Succ. J.(U.S.)* 52(1):40-43.

14281 Anderson, E.F. (1986). A revision of the genus *Thelocactus* Br. et R. (Cactaceae). *Bradleya* 5:49-76.

14288 Leigh, J.H., Briggs, J., & Hartley, W. (1981). Rare or threatened Australian plants. Australian National Parks and Wildlife Service. 178 pp.

14290 Puente, M.R. (1992). El género *Opuntia* (Cactaceae) en el Valle de San Luis Potosí, San Luis Potosí. Universidad Autónoma de San Luis Potosí, Escuela de Agronomía, Mexico. 156 pp. Instituto de Investigación de Zonas Desérticas.

14291 Luer, C.A. (1990). Icones Pleurothallidinarum VII. Systematics of *Platystele*. *Monographs in Systematic Botany* (Missouri Botanical Garden) 38:1-135.

14292 Almeda, F. (1989). *Tessmannianthus*, an arborescent genus of Melastomataceae new to Panama. *Ann. Missouri Bot. Gard.* 76(1):1-6.

14293 Martínez, E. & Ramos, C.H. (1989). Lacandoniaceae (Triuridales): una nueva familia de México. *Ann. Missouri Bot. Gard.* 76(1):128-135.

14294 González Elizondo, S. (1991). Annotations to: List of threatened plants of Middle America. TPU list: 10 May 1991.

14296 Robertson, S.A. (1989). Flowering plants of the Seychelles. Royal Botanic Gardens, Kew. 327 pp. Annotated checklist, including gymnosperms. (Manuscript prepared by 1982, later additions in Addenda on pages

14301 Imada, C.T., Wagner, W.L., & Herbst, D.R. (1989). Checklist of native and naturalized flowering plants of Hawai'i. *Bishop Museum Occasional Papers* 29:1-87.

14344 Clark, L. (1989). Systematics of *Chusquea* Section Swallenchloa, Section Verticillatae, Section Serpentes, and Section Longifoliae (Poaceae - Bambusoideae). *Systematic Bot. Monographs* 27:1-127.

14346 Argus, G.W. (1986). *Salix raupii*, Raup's willow, new to the flora of Alberta and the Northwest Territories. *Canadian Field-Naturalist* 100:386-388.

14352 Argus, G.W. & Pryer, D.J. (1982-1987). Atlas of the rare vascular plants of Ontario. 4 parts. Ottawa: National Museum of Natural Sciences.

14354 Argus, G.W. & Steele, J.W. (1979). A reevaluation of the taxonomy of *Salix tyrrellii*, a sand dune endemic. *Systematic Botany* 4:163-177.

14360 Blondeau, M. & Cayouette, J. (1987). Extensions d'aires dans la flore vasculaire du Nouveau-Quebec. *Naturaliste Canadien* 114:117-126.

14362 Boivin, B. (1972). Flora of the prairie provinces. Part III. Connatae. Provancheria 4. Quebec: Université Laval. 224 pp.

14366 Bouchard, A., Brouillet, L., Hay, S., & Saucier, I. (1987). The rare vascular plants of Newfoundland. (Progress report). Quebec: Institut Botanique de l'Université de Montréal. 12 pp.

14393 Catling, P.M. (1987). Preliminary list of the rare vascular plants of Prince Edward Island. Biosystematics Research Centre, Agriculture Canada.

14394 Catling, P.M., Freedman, B., & Lucas, Z. (1984). The vegetation and phytogeography of Sable Island, Nova Scotia. *Proceedings of the Nova Scotia Institute of Science* 34:181-247.

14397 Ceska, O., Ceska, A., & Warrington, P. (1986). *Myriophyllum quitense* and *Myriophyllum ussuriense* (Haloragaceae) in British Columbia, Canada. *Brittonia* 38:73-81.

14409 Douglas, G.W. (1982). The sunflower family of British Columbia. Vol. 1 - Senecioneae. British Columbia Provincial Museum. 180 pp.

14410 Douglas, G.W. & Packer, J.G. (1988). *Erigeron salishii*, a new *Erigeron* (Asteraceae) from British Columbia and Washington. *Canadian Journal of Botany* 66:414-416.

14414 Fabijan, D.M., Packer, J.G., & Denford, K.E. (1987). The taxonomy of the *Viola nutallii* complex. *Canadian Journal of Botany* 65:2562-2580.

14419 **Ford, B.A. & Ball, P.W. (1988)**. A revaluation of the *Triglochin maritimum* complex (Juncaginaceae) in eastern and central North America and Europe. *Rhodora* 90:313-337.

14430 **Gentry, J.R. & Carr, R.L. (1976)**. A revision of the genus *Hackelia* (Boraginaceae) in North America, north of Mexico. *Memoirs of the New York Botanical Garden* 26(1):280-292.

14438 **Harris, J.G. (1985)**. A revision of the genus *Braya* (Cruciferae) in North America. Ph.D. thesis. Edmonton: University of Alberta. 250 pp.

14474 **Klinkenberg, B. (1986)**. Status report on the dwarf hackberry, *Celtis tenuifolia*. Committee on the Status of Endangered Wildlife in Canada. Ottawa: Canadian Wildlife Service. 31 pp.

14480 **Kott, L. & Britton, D.M. (1983)**. Spore morphology and taxonomy of *Isoetes* in northeastern North America. *Canadian Journal of Botany* 61:3140-3163.

14501 **U.S. Department of the Interior. Fish and Wildlife Service. (1991)**. Endangered and threatened wildlife and plants; *Astragalus bibullatus* (Guthrie's ground-plum) determined to be endangered. *Federal Register* 56(187):48748-48751.

14511 **U.S. Department of the Interior. Fish and Wildlife Service. (1991)**. Endangered and threatened wildlife and plants; proposed endangered status for the plant *Isoetes louisianensis* (Louisiana quillwort). Proposed rule. *Federal Register* 58(203):52500-52503.

14512 **U.S. Department of the Interior. Fish and Wildlife Service. (1991)**. Endangered and threatened wildlife and plants; proposed endangered status for the plant *Clematis morefieldii* (Morefield's leather flower). Proposed rule. *Federal Register* 58(203):52503-52506.

14526 **Lahti, T., Kemppainen, E., Kurtto, A., & Uotila, P. (1991)**. Distribution and biological characteristics of threatened vascular plants in Finland. *Biological Conservation* 55:299-314.

14581 **House, D.E. (1987)**. Recovery plan for Navajo sedge (*Carex specuicola* J.T. Howell). Albuquerque, NM: U.S. Fish and Wildlife Service. 39 pp.

14594 **U.S. Department of the Interior. Fish and Wildlife Service. (1991)**. Swamp pink (*Helonias bullata*) recovery plan. Newton Corner, Massachusetts: U.S. Fish and Wildlife Service. 56 pp. Map.

14621 **Poole, J.M. (1987)**. Recovery plan for the ashy dogweed (*Thymophylla tephroleuca*). Approved plan. Albuquerque, NM: U.S. Department of the Interior. Fish and Wildlife Service. 46 pp.

14662 **Center for Plant Conservation (CPC). (1990)**. Printout of CPC's data for North American plants.

14664 **Anon. (no date)**. Fundaçao biodiversitas.

14665 **Johnson, D.V. (ed.). (1991)**. Palms for human needs in Asia. Palm utilization and conservation in India, Indonesia, Malaysia and the Philippines. Rotterdam: A.A. Balkema. 258 pp.

14695 **Hall, A.V., de Winter, M., de Winter, B., & van Oosterhout, S.A.M. (no date)**. Threatened plants of Southern Africa. A report for the Committee for Terrestrial Ecosystems National Programme for Enviromental Sciences. Pretoria: CSIR. South African National Scientific Programmes Report No. 45.

14701 **Kiew, R. (1991)**. Palm utilization and conservation in Peninsular Malaysia. pp. 75-130 *In* Johnson, D. (ed.). Palms for human needs in Asia. Palm ultilization and conservation in India, Indonesia, Malaysia and the Philippines. Rotterdam: A.A. Balkema.

14703 **Pearce, K.G. (1991)**. Palm utilization and conservation in Sarawak (Malaysia). pp. 131-173 *In* Johnson, D. (ed.). Palms for human needs in Asia. Palm utilization and conservation in India, Indonesia, Malaysia and the Philippines. Rotterdam: A.A. Balkema.

14704 **U.S. Department of the Interior. Fish and Wildlife Service. (1991)**. Endangered and threatened wildlife and plants; proposed threatened status for the plant *Thelypteris pilosa* var. *alabamensis* (Alabama streak-sorus fern). *Federal Register* 56(230):60957-60961.

14708 **Dixit, R.D. (1983)**. Rare and interesting Pteridophytes of India. pp. 328-334 *In* An assessment of threatened plants of India. Naba Mudran Private Limited, Calcutta, India: Director, Botanical Survey of India.

14711 **U.S. Department of the Interior. Fish and Wildlife Service. (1991)**. Endangered and threatened wildlife and plants; determination of endangered status for *Scirpus ancistrochaetus* (northeastern bullrush). *Federal Register* 56(88):21091-21096.

14712 **Dransfield, J. & Johnson, D. (1991)**. The conservation status of palms in Sabah (Malaysia). pp. 175-179 *In* Johnson, D. (ed.). Palms for human needs in Asia. Palm ultilization and conservation in India, Indonesia, Malaysia and the Philippines. Rotterdam: A.A. Balkema.

14720 **Mehrotra, A. (1983)**. Studies on endemism and rarity in the family Eriocaulaceae in India. pp. 279-282 *In* An assessment of threatened plants of India. Naba Mudran Private Limited, Calcutta, India: Director, Botanical Survey of India.

14721 **Chandra, V. (1983)**. Notes on endangered species of *Scleria* in India. pp. 276-278 *In* An assessment of threatened plants of India. Naba Mudran Private Limited, Calcutta, India: Director, Botanical Survey of India.

14722 **Agrawal, S. (1983)**. Some rare gentians. pp. 272-275 *In* An assessment of threatened plants of India. Naba Mudran Private Limited, Calcutta, India: Director, Botanical Survey of India.

14723 Bahadur, K.N. & Jain, S.S. (1983). Rare bamboos of India. pp. 265-271 *In* An assessment of threatened plants of India. Naba Mudran Private Limited, Calcutta, India: Director, Botanical Survey of India.

14724 Prakash, V. & Jain, S.K. (1983). Tribe Isacjneae (Poaceae) - its endemism and rarity in India. pp. 256-264 *In* An assessment of threatened plants of India. Naba Mudran Private Limited, Calcutta, India: Director, Botanical Survey of India.

14726 Madulid, D.A. (1991). The Philippines: Palm utilization and conservation. pp. 181-225 *In* Johnson, D. (ed.). Palms for human needs in Asia. Palm utilization and conservation in India, Indonesia, Malaysia and the Philippines. Rotterdam: A.A. Balkema.

14727 Sivadasan, M. (1983). Threatened species of Indian Araceae. pp. 251-255 *In* An assessment of threatened plants of India. Naba Mudran Private Limited, Calcutta, India: Director, Botanical Survey of India.

14732 Sastry, A.R.K. & Hajra, P.K. (1983). Rare and endemic species of Rhododendron in India - A preliminary study. pp. 222-231 *In* An assessment of threatened plants of India. Naba Mudran Private Limited, Calcutta, India: Botanical Survey of India.

14736 Balakrishnan, N.P. & Vasudeva Rao, M.K. (1983). The dwindling plant species of Andaman and Nicobar Islands. pp. 186-202 *In* An assessment of threatened plants of India. Naba Mudran Private Limited, Calcutta, India: Director, Botanical Survey of India.

14750 Prance, G.T. (1991). Annotations to: List of threatened plants in Chrysobalanaceae, Dichapetalaceae, and Lecythidaceae.

14761 Shah, N.C. (1983). Endangered medicinal & aromatic taxa of U.P. Himalaya. An assessment of threatened plants of India. pp. 40-49 *In* Botanical Survey India. Naba Mudran Private Limited, Calcutta, India: Director, Botanical Survey of India.

14768 Dhar, U. & Kachroo, P. (1983). Some remarkable features of endemism in Kashmir Himalayas. pp. 18-22 *In* An assessment of threatened plants of India. Naba Mudran Private Limited, Calcutta, India: Director, Botanical Survey of India.

14774 U.S. Department of the Interior. Fish and Wildlife Service. (1991). Listing proposals - June/July 1991. *Endangered Species Technical Bulletin* 16(7-8):7-9. Illus.

14775 U.S. Department of the Interior. Fish and Wildlife Service. (1991). Final listing action approved for four species. *Endangered Species Technical Bulletin* 16(7-8):11.

14777 Zizka, G. (1991). Flowering plants of Easter Island. Frankfurt am Main, Germany: Palmengarten. 108 pp. Illus., col. illus., map. Includes 5 endemics, 25 natives, 141 introduced (37 established and 74 non-established), 8 doubtfuls.

14781 U.S. Department of the Interior. Fish and Wildlife Service. (1991). Endangered and threatened wildlife and plants; Final rule to list *Potamogeton clystocarpus* (little aguja pondweed) as endangered. *Federal Register* 56(220):57844-57849.

14782 Nayar, M.P. & Sastry, A.R.K. (eds.). (1990). Red Data Book of Indian Plants. Vol. 3. Calcutta: Botanical Survey of India. 271 pp. Illus., col. illus. Covers 195 "threatened" taxa.

14788 Dransfield, J. (1991). *Lemurophoenix* (Palmae: Arecoideae), a new genus from Madagascar. *Kew Bull.* 46(1):61-68.

14789 Rauwerdink, J.B. (1986). An essay on *Metroxylon*, the sago palm. *Principes* 30:165-180.

14790 Essig, F.B. (1978). A revision of the genus *Ptychosperma* Labill (Arecaceae). *Allertonia* 1(7):415-478.

14791 Zona, S. (1990). A monograph of *Sabal* (Arecaceae: Coryphoideae). *Aliso* 12(4):583-666.

14792 Dransfield, J. (1989). *Voanioala* (Arecoideae: Cocoeae: Butiinae), a new palm genus from Madagascar. *Kew Bull.* 44(2):191-198.

14793 Lewis, B.A. (1992). Appendix 1: Threatened orchids from the Solomon Islands.

14794 Lewis, B.A. & Cribb, P.J. (1991). Orchids of the Solomon Islands and Bougainville. Kew: Royal Botanic Gardens. 335 pp.

14795 Lewis, B.A. & Cribb, P.J. (1989). Orchids of Vanuatu. Kew: Royal Botanic Gardens. 171 pp.

14797 Hodel, D.R. & Uhl, N.W. (1990). New species of *Chamaedorea* from Costa Rica and Panama. *Principes* 34(3):120-133.

14798 Hodel, D.R. & Uhl, N.W. (1990). A new species and synopsis of a distinctive and natural subgroup of *Chamaedorea*. *Principes* 34(3):108-119.

14799 Henderson, A., Aubry, M., Timyan, J., & Balick, M. (1990). Conservation status of Haitian palms. *Principes* 34(3):134-142. 13 genera and between 21-24 species of palms occur naturally in Haiti, and up to 1/4 of these species may be endemic to the country.

14800 Wheatley, Jos. I. (1991). Annotations to the Vanuatu Status Report.

14801 Brown, E. (1991). The quest for *Jubaeopsis caffra*, the pondoland palm. *Principes* 35(2):99-101.

14803 Glenny, D. (1991). Annotations to Solomon Island Status Report.

14805 Hodel, D.R. & Grayum, M.H. (1991). Two new species of *Chamaedorea* (Arecaceae) from

Panama. *Principes* 35(3):133-138.

14807 **Endt, D. (1991).** The native palms of Chile: a rare opportunity to visit the private hacienda, Los Palmas, Cocolan. *Principes* 35(2):19-21.

14811 **Hodel, D.R. & Uhl, N.W. (1990).** Two new species of *Chamaedorea* from Mexico. *Principes* 34(2):58-63.

14813 **Hodel, D.R. (1990).** *Chamaedorea amabilis*, an ornamental species from Central America. *Principes* 34(1):4-10. The species is threatened by collectors.

14821 **Anon. (1991).** Proposal to include the genus *Tillandsia* on Appendix II of CITES.

14827 **Basu, S.K. (1991).** India: Palm utilization and conservation. pp. 13-35 *In* Johnson, D. (ed.). Palms for human needs in Asia. Palm utilization and conservation in India, Indonesia, Malaysia and the Philippines. Rotterdam: A.A. Balkema.

14828 **Mogea, J.P. (1991).** Indonesia: Palm utilization and conservation: pp. 37-73 *In* Johnson, D. (ed.). Palms for human needs in Asia. Palm utilization and conservation in India, Indonesia, Malaysia and the Philippines. Rotterdam: A.A. Balkema.

14840 **Pingitore, E.J. (1982).** Rare palms in Argentina. *Principes* 26(1):9-18.

14844 **Hodel, D.R. (1982).** In search of *Carpoxylon*. *Principes* 26(1):34-41.

14845 **U.S. Department of the Interior. Fish and Wildlife Service. (1991).** Osterhout milkvetch (*Astragalus osterhoutii*), Pendland beartongue (*Penstemon penlandii*) draft recovery plan. Grand Junction, Colorado: U.S. Fish and Wildlife Service. 12 pp. Map.

14868 **Bernal, R.G. (1986).** Colombia. The palms of the Colombian Pacific. 27-33 pp. Report of WWF Project 3322 (WWF-US), 30 November.

14871 **U.S. Department of the Interior. Fish and Wildlife Service. (1991).** Endangered and threatened wildlife and plants; final rule to list the plant *Phlox nivalis* ssp. *texensis* (Texas trailing phlox) as endangered. *Federal Register* 56(189):49636-49639.

14872 **Mansur-Azim, N. (1989).** A tentative list of species threatened in Bangladesh (including endemics). (Pteridophytes and Angiosperms). Memo from Michael Green to Vernon Heywood.

14874 **Saunders, R. (1988).** Notes on carnivorous plant questionnaire. Letter from Rod Saunders to P. Wyse Jackson.

14875 **U.S. Department of the Interior. Fish and Wildlife Service. (1991).** Endangered and threatened wildlife and plants; *Conradina verticillata* (Cumberland rosemary) determined to be threatened. *Federal Register* 56(230):60937-60941.

14876 **Parris, B. (1988).** List of ferns in the WCMC database for Peninsular Malaysia with annotations by Barbara Parris.

14905 **Nesom, G.L. & La Duke, J.C. (1985).** Biology of *Trillium nivale* (Liliaceae). *Canadian Journal of Botany* 63:7-14.

14908 **Royal Botanic Gardens Kew. (1991).** Kew Calendar 1992. Royal Botanic Gardens, Kew. The plants featured in this Calendar are all endangered.

14952 **Cohen, O. & Shmida, A. (1990).** Botanical notes. Discoveries of 1989 rare plants survey. *Israel - Land and Nature* 15(4):184.

14958 **Meddour, R. (1988).** Quelques commentaires sur la liste des plantes rares et menacées en Algérie. [Comments on the list of rare and threatened plants in Algeria]. *Ann. Rech. Forest Alg.* 3(3):43-65.

14961 **Chang, C. (1988).** Threatened plants of Botel Tobago. 3 pp.

14964 **Anon. (1991).** Endangered Brazilian cacti. *SSC Newsletter - Cacti & Succulent Group* (2):2.

14965 **Anon. (no date).** Dun - select committee on flora and fauna. List of Sarawak plants recommended for protection.

14980 **Hamann, O. (1991).** Indigenous and alien plants in the Galápagos Islands: problems of conservation and development. pp. 169-192 *In* Heywood, V.H. & Wyse Jackson, P.S. (eds.). Tropical botanic gardens. Their role in conservation and development. San Diego: Academic Press Inc.

14981 **Friedmann, F. (1991).** The threatened plants of the flora of the Seychelles and their conservation. pp. 193-208 *In* Heywood, V.H. & Wyse Jackson, P.S. (eds.). Tropical botanic gardens. Their role in conservation and development. San Diego: Academic Press Inc.

15013 **Cunningham, A.B. (1991).** Development of a conservation policy on commercially exploited medicinal plants: a case study from southern Africa. pp. 337-358 *In* Akerele, O., Heywood, V. & Synge, H. (eds.). Conservation of medicinal plants. Cambridge: Cambridge University Press.

15014 **U.S. Department of the Interior. Fish and Wildlife Service. (1983).** Endangered and threatened wildlife and plants; Proposed endangered status for the plant *Echinacea laevigata* (smooth coneflower). *Federal Register* 56(236):64229-64234.

15015 **Stevenson, D.W. & Osborne, R. (1991).** The world list of cycads. Proc. CYCAD 90. Lists 144 Zamiaceae spp.

15044 **U.S. Department of the Interior. Fish and Wildlife Service. (1983).** Endangered and threatened wildlife and plants; Proposal to list the plant *Spiranthes diluvialis* (Ute ladies'-tresses) as a threatened species. *Federal Register* 55(219):47347-47350.

15046 U.S. Department of the Interior. Fish and Wildlife Service. (1991). Pitcher's thistle, *Cirsium pitcheri*, recovery plan. Technical/Agency draft. Minneapolis, Minnesota: U.S. Fish and Wildlife Service, Region 3. 111 pp.

15079 Tirvengadum, D.D. (1989). *Ramosmania rodriguesii*, nouvelle rubiacée endémique de Rodrigues (Mascareignes). *C.R. Soc. Biogéogr.* 65(1):13-20.

15080 Olivier, L. (1992). Letter to Chris Leon, including list entitled "Proposition de list UICN pour la Corse". 12 pp.

15088 Benoit, C. & Ivan, L. (eds.). (1989). Libro rojo de la flora terrestre de Chile (Primero parte). Santiago: Impresora Creces Ltda. 157 pp. Col. illus. Lists 11 E, 26 V, 32 R.

15100 Vu Van Dung, & Vu Van Can. (1991). Endangered forest plant species in Viet Nam. Ha Noi: Ministry of Forestry. Centre of Technical Scientific and Economical Information. 81 pp.

15104 Melville, R. & Bramwell, D. (1973). Threatened plants of the Canary Islands. 57 pp. Published with the financial assistance of UNESCO.

15105 Anon. (no date). Threatened plants in protected areas of the Canary Islands (Spain). (Presented by the Spanish delegation).

15106 Anon. (no date). Endangered, Threatened, and Recently Extinct Species of Puerto Rico and the Virgin Islands. Contributions from Fosberg et al. listing 102 "Rare" or "Threatened" species.

15107 Anon. (no date). Endemic flora of Puerto Rico and the Virgin Islands. Lists 306 species endemic to Puerto Rico.

15112 Synge, H. (1992). Information collected for Biodiversity Status Report.

15135 Norton, D.A. (1991). *Trilepidea adamsii*: an obituary for a species. *Conservation Biology* 5(1):52-57.

15138 Dowe, J.L. (ed.). (1989). Palms of the Solomon Islands. Milton Qld, Australia: The Palm and Cycad Societies of Australia. 55 pp.

15139 Dowe, J.L. & Uhl, N.W. (1989). *Carpoxylon macrospermum*. *Principes* 33(2):68-73.

15142 Dransfield, J. (1990). Notes on rattans (Palmae: Calamoideae) occurring in Sarawak, Borneo. *Kew Bull.* 45(1):73-99.

15144 Dransfield, J., Shu-Kang, L., & Fa-Nan, W. (1985). *Guihaia*, a new Coryphoid genus from China and Vietnam. *Principes* 29(1):3-12.

15145 Dransfield, J. & Uhl, N.W. (1986). *Ravenea* in the Comores. *Principes* 30(4):156-160.

15147 Essig, F.B. (1987). A new species of *Ptychosperma* (Palmae) from New Britain. *Principes* 31(3):110-115.

15148 Fernandes, H. de Q. B. (1989). Uma nova espécie de *Euterpe* (Palmae - Arecoideae - Areceae) do Brasil. *Acta Bot. Bras.* 3(2):43-49.

15153 Irvine, A. (1983). *Wodyetia*, a new Arecoid genus from Australia. *Principes* 27(4):158-167.

15154 Jones, D. (1984). Palms in Australia. NSW, Australia: Reed Books Pty Ltd.

15155 Kahn, F. & Mejia, K. (1988). A new species of *Chelyocarpus* (Palmae, Coryphoideae) from Peruvian Amazonia. *Principes* 32(2):69-72.

15156 Moore, H.E. (1969). A synopsis of the genus *Physokentia* (Palmae - Arecoideae). *Principes* 13:120-136.

15157 Quero, H.J. (1991). *Sabal gretheriae*, a new species of Palm from the Yucatan Peninsula, Mexico. *Principes* 35(4):219-224.

15160 Loc, P.K. (1992). Conversations with Prof. Phan Ke Loc.

15166 Dowe, J.L. (1991). Global action plan - Australian palms. 6 pp. With added comments from Dennis Johnson.

15184 Dowe, J.L. (1991). Palms of the Southwest Pacific. 5 pp. Annotated list by John Dowe.

15198 Fosberg, F.R. (1988). A review of the natural history of the Marshall Islands. Report prepared for the East West Center/MacArthur Foundation/SPREP Northern Marshall Islands natural diversity and protected area survey. East West Center, Hawaii.

15199 Henderson, A. (1990). Conservation status of Haitian palms. Letter to Dennis Johnson.

15202 Hodel, D.R. (1991). *Chamaedorea* palms. As annotated by D. Hodel. 5 pp.

15206 Seidensticker, J. & Suyono. (1980). The Javan tiger and the Meru Betiri Reserve. A plan for management. Gland: IUCN. 167 pp.

15211 Blouch, R. & Sumaryoto, A. (1979). Proposed Bawean Island Wildlife Reserve management plan. Bogor. 63 pp.

15229 Judd, W.S. (1986). Botany of the National Parks of Haiti. USAID. USAID Report.

15247 Erftemeijer, P., van Balen, B., & Djuharsa, E. (1988). The importance of Segara Anakan for nature conservation. PHPH - AWB/Interwader Report No. 6. Illus. Maps.

15308 Whistler, W.A. (1990). Preliminary key to Palmae of Samoa. 2 pp.

15313 **Thin, N.N. (1992).** List of palms rare and endangered species of Indochina. 1 pp.

15316 **Fay, M.F. & Muir, H.J. (1990).** The rôle of micropropagation in the conservation of European plants. pp. 27-32 *In* Hernández Bermejo, J.E., Clemente, M., Heywood, V. (eds.). Conservation techniques in botanic gardens. Germany: Koeltz Scientific Books.

15358 **Bañares Baudet, A. (1990).** La flora amenazada de los parques nacionales Canarios con especial referencía al Parque Nacional de Garajonay. (The threatened flora of the national parks of the Canary Islands with special reference to Garajonay National Park). pp. 87-90 *In* Hernández Bermejo, J.E., Clemente, M., Heywood, V. (eds.). Conservation techniques in botanic gardens. Germany: Koeltz Scientific Books.

15398 **Blanca, G. & Molero Mesa, J. (1990).** Peligro de extinción en Sierra Nevada (Granada, España). (Dangers of extinction in the Sierra Nevada (Granada, Spain). pp. 97-101 *In* Hernández Bermejo, J.E., Clemente, M., Heywood, V. (eds.). Conservation techniques in botanic gardens. Germany: Koeltz Scientific Books.

15399 **WWF. (1980).** Cagar Alam GN. Tangkoko-Dua Saudara, Sulawesi Utara - Management Plan 1981-1986. A WWF report prepared for the Directorate of Nature Conservation, Directorate-General of Forestry, Republic of Indonesia. Bogor: WWF. Maps.

15534 **Miller, A.G. (1992).** List of Socotran endemics with conservation status. Revised November 1991. 15 pp.

15638 **Dod, D. & Judd, W.S. (1986).** The orchids of the national parks of Haiti. USA: USAID.

15658 **CITES. (1992).** CITES Appendices as of June 1992.

15727 **Henderson, A. (1990).** Arecaceae. Part I. Introduction and the Iriarteinae *in* Flora Neotropica. Monograph 53. New York: New York Botanical Garden. 101 pp.

15728 **Barfod, A.S. (1991).** A monographic study of the subfamily Phytelephantoideae (Arecaceae). *Opera Botanica* 105:1-73.

15734 **Loc, P.K. (1992).** Annotations to: Conservation status listing for Vietnam dated 25 March 1992. 49 pp.

15810 **Barneby, R.C. (1964).** Atlas of North American *Astragalus*. Part II. The Ceridotherix, Hypoglottis, Piptoloboid, Trimeniaeus and Orophaca Astragali. *Memoirs of the New York Botanical Garden* 13:597-1188.

15814 **Bayer, R.J. & Stebbins, G.L. (1987).** Patterns of chromosomal evolution in *Antennaria* (Asteraceae: Inuleae). *Systematic Botany* 12:305-319.

15826 **Wagner, W.H. & Wagner, F.S. (1990).** Moonworts (*Botrychium* subg. *Botrychium*) of the Upper Great Lakes Region, USA and Canada. with descriptions of two new species. *Contributions from the University of Michigan Herbarium* 17:313-325.

15827 **Wagner, W.H. & Wagner, F.S. (1986).** Three new species of moonworts (*Botrychium* subg. *Botrychium*) endemic in western North America. *American Fern Journal* 76:33-47.

15846 **Rivas-Martínez, S., Fernández-González, F., & Sánchez-Mata, D. (1990).** Endemic taxa of the Iberian Central System: distribution and ecology. pp. 179-184 *In* Hernández Bermejo, J.E., Clemente, M., Heywood, V. (eds.). Conservation techniques in botanic gardens. Germany: Koeltz Scientific Books.

15882 **Moss, E.H. (1983).** Flora of Alberta. (2nd ed.). Toronto, Ontario: University of Toronto Press. 687 pp.

15886 **Porsild, A.E. (1964).** Illustrated flora of the Canadian Arctic archipelago. (2nd ed. rev.). National Museum of Canada. 218 pp. Bulletin 146.

15911 **Adams, C.D. (1971).** Miscellaneous additions and revisions to the flowering plants of Jamaica II. *Phytologia* 21(2):65-71.

15914 **U.S. Department of the Interior. Fish and Wildlife Service. (1983).** Endangered and threatened wildlife and plants; Threatened status for three Florida plants. *Federal Register* 57(90):19813-19819.

15915 **U.S. Department of the Interior. Fish and Wildlife Service. (1992).** Endangered and threatened wildlife and plants; Proposed endangered status for three Florida plants of the genus *Conradina*. *Federal Register* 57(98):21369-21374.

15917 **U.S. Department of the Interior. Fish and Wildlife Service. (1992).** Endangered and threatened wildlife and plants; Proposed threatened status for the plant *Pinguicula ionantha* (Godfrey's butterwort). *Federal Register* 57(98):21377-21380.

15918 **Cribb, P.J. (1987).** The genus *Paphiopedilum*. Portland, Oregon: Royal Botanic Gardens, Kew, in association with Timber Press. 222 pp. Col. illus., maps. Kew Magazine Monograph.

15919 **Du Puy, D. & Cribb, P.J. (1988).** The genus *Cymbidium*. London and Portland, Oregon: Christopher Helm and Timber Press. 236 pp. Col. illus., maps.

15922 **Fourie, S.P. (1984).** Threatened Euphorbias in the Transvaal. *The Euphorbia Journal* 2:75-90. Col. illus.

15923 **Kim, Y.S. (1992).** List of rare and endangered plant species in Republic of Korea. 14 pp.

15925 **Boyer, M. (1992).** Technical draft Recovery Plan for Cooley's meadowrue (*Thalictrum cooleyi* Ahles). Atlanta, Georgia: U.S. Fish and Wildlife Service, Southeast Region. 39 pp.

15926 **Anon. (1984).** The succulent Euphorbiaceae. Photographic collection and descriptions. *The*

Euphorbia Journal 2:95-152. Col. illus.

15932 **Hall, H. (1984).** *Euphorbia hallii.*
Notes on some South African Euphorbias. *The*
Euphorbia Journal 2:19-28.

15934 **Grey-Wilson, C. (1988).** The genus
Cyclamen. Portland, Oregon, USA: Timber Press.
147 pp.

15937 **Koutnik, D. (1984).** A brief taxonomy of the
Euphorbia Clava-Loricata complex (Treisia). *The*
Euphorbia Journal 2:39-50. Col. illus.

15943 **Anon. (1992).** Rare durian rescued from
extinction. *Geneflow*:20. Special UNCED
edition: Biodiversity and Plant Genetic Resources.

15947 **Kim, Y.S. (1992).** Rare and threatened plants
of the Republic of Korea. BGCI printout with annotations
by Yong Shik Kim. 5 pp.

15957 **Lee, T.B. (1983).** Endemic plants and their
distribution in Korea. *Bull. Kwanak*
Arboretum:71-113.

15960 **Penafiel, S. (1990).** Annotation to list of
tropical timbers for the Philippines.

15961 **Anon. (1991).** Portrait of threatened plants:
Paphiopedilum niveum. Malayan
Naturalist 45(1 & 2):42.

15964 **Hunt, D.R. (1992).** CITES Cactaceae checklist.
Kew: Royal Botanic Gardens, Kew. 190 pp. Compiled with
the financial assistance of the CITES Nomenclature
Committee and the US Scientific Authority for CITES.

15970 **Hawthorne, W. (1990).** Field guide to the
forest trees of Ghana. Chatham: Natural Resources
Institute, for the Overseas Development Administration,
London. 278 pp.

15976 **Kemp, M. (1985).** *Encephalartos*
longifolius.. Encephalartos. 1(1):6-13. A
translation is located with the article. Includes
description,distribution and conservation details.

15978 **U.S. Department of the Interior. Fish and Wildlife**
Service. (1992). Endangered and threatened wildlife
and plants; Proposed threatened status for the plant
Amaranthus pumilus (seabeach amaranth).
Federal Register 57(101):21921-21925.

15983 **Ricci, M. & Eaton, L. (1992).** The rescue of
Wahlenbergia larrainii in Robinson Crusoe
Island. Illus., map. Manuscript submitted to
Biological Conservation.

16005 **DeLay, L., O'Conner, R., & Ryan, J. (1992).**
Agency draft recovery plan. Pondberry (*Lindera*
mellissifolia [Walt.] Blume). Atlanta, Georgia:
Southeast Region U.S. Fish and Wildlife Service. 62 pp.

16029 **Voorhoeve, A.G. (1979).** Liberian high forest
trees. (2nd ed.). Wageningen, Netherlands: H. Veenman
and Zonan N.V., Wageningen.

16040 **Anon. (1992).** Rare endemic species collected.
Philippine Flora Newsletter:3.

16059 **U.S. Department of the Interior. Fish and Wildlife**
Service. (1992). Agency draft recovery plan for
American hart's-tongue fern (*Phyllitis*
scolopendrium [L.] Newman variety
americana Fernald). Asheville. North Carolina:
U.S. Fish and Wildlife Service. 36 pp.

16067 **Fernando, E.S. (1990).** The genus Heterospathe
(Palmae) in the Philippines. *Kew Bull.*
45(2):219-234.

16073 **Sheng-Ji, P., San-Yang, C., & Shao-Quan, T.**
(1989). New materials of Palmae from China.
Acta Phytotaxonomica Sinica 27(2):132-146.

16087 **Smitinand, T. (1990).** Annotated list of
dipterocarps in Thailand.

16088 **Dransfield, J. (1990).** Notes on
Pinanga (Palmae) in Sarawak. *Kew*
Bull. 46(4):691-698.

16098 **Lapis, A.B. (1989).** An account of taxa related
to *Calamus siphonospathus* complex.
Sylvatrop 12(1/2):61-85.

16110 **Walters, T. & Decker-Walters, D.S. (1992).** In
search of the elusive and endangered Okeechobee gourd.
Plant Conservation 7(1):2.

16120 **Hall, J.B. & Bada, S.O. (1979).** The
distribution and ecology of Obeche *(Triplochiton*
scleroxylon). J. Ecol. 67:543-564.

16162 **Wijesinghe, L.C.A., Gunatilleke, I.A.U.N.,**
Jayawardana, S.D.G., Kotagama, S.W., & Gunatilleke,
C.V.S. (1990). Biological conservation in Sri Lanka
(A national status report). Colombo: Natural Resources,
Energy and Science Authority of Sri Lanka. 64 pp.

16168 **El Hadidi, M., Abdel Ghani, M.M., & Fahmy, A.G.**
(1992). The plant red data book of Egypt. 1. woody
perennials. Cairo: The Palm Press. 155 pp. Maps.

16174 **Gartland, S. (1991).** Letter to Sara Oldfield
listing trees which are probably endangered in Cameroon.

16228 **Dowes, J. (no date).** Pitcairnioideae
(Bromeliaceae). *Flora Neotropica.* Monograph
14.

16273 **Anon. (1991).** Nine species listed.
Oryx (Oct 1991) 25:193.

16283 **Johnson, D.V. (1992).** Annotation to printout:
Palm database changes; New World. Group 3, July 1992. 4
pp.

16294 **Kumar, Y. (1992).** 'Extinct' orchid
rediscovered. *Current Science* 62(8):547-548.
Bulbophyllum rothschildianum rediscovered in
hills of northeast India.

16317 **Asociación Nacional para la Conservación de la**
Naturaleza. (1990). List of threatened and

vulnerable plants of Panama.

16319 Matola, S. (1990). Species discoveries in Belize. *Species* 15:16.

16322 Cabrera, A.L. (1963-1968). Flora de la provincia de Buenos Aires. Buenos Aires: INTA. 6 volumes.

16326 Pennington, T.D. (1990). Sapotaceae. *Flora Neotropica*, Monograph 52. Bronx, New York: The New York Botanical Garden. 770 pp.

16336 Chebez, J.C. & Haene, E. (1989). Lista tentativa de plantas vasculares argentinas en peligro de extinción. [Preliminary list of vascular plants of Argentina in danger of extinction]. 18 pp. Unpublished.

16337 Correa, M.N. (1969). Flora Patagónica. Buenos Aires: INTA. 8 volumes.

16347 Neill, D. & Palacios, W. (1989). Arboles de la Amazonia Ecuatoriana. Lista preliminar de especies. Quito, Ecuador: Dirección Nacional Forestal. 120 pp. Preliminary list of native tree species of Amazonian Ecuador below 600m elevation; includes 1009 species of trees attaining at least 5m in height.

16358 Arosemena, A., Estrada, R., Jurado, C., & Konanz, M. (1989). Orquídeas de la costa del Ecuador. Guayaquil, Ecuador: Asociación Ecuatoriana de Orquídeología. 129 pp.

16360 Secretaría de Desarrollo Urbano y Ecología. (1991). Listado de especies raras, amenazadas, en peligro de extinción, o sujetas a protección especial, y sus endemismos en la República Mexicana. Flora terrestre y acuática. México: Secretaría de Desarrollo Urbano y Ecología. 9-26 pp.

16385 Bravo-Hollis, H. (1978). Las cactáceas de México. México, DF: Universidad Nacional Autónoma de México.

16386 Farjon, A. (1990). Pinaceae. Drawings and descriptions of the genera *Abies, Cedrus, Pseudolarix, Keteleeria, Nothotsuga, Tsuga, Cathaya, Pseudotsuga, Larix* and *Picea*. Königstein, Germany: Koeltz Scientific Books. 330 pp.

16387 Sutton, D. (1988). A revision of the tribe Antirrhineae. Oxford, UK: Oxford University Press. 544 pp.

16388 Withner, C. (1988). The Cattleyas and their relatives. Vol. 1. The Cattleyas. Portland, Oregon: Timber Press. 147 pp.

16389 Kuijt, J. (1991). *Panamanthus*, a new monotypic genus of neotropical Loranthaceae. *Ann. Missouri Bot. Gard.* 78(1):172-176.

16390 Kimnach, M. (1978). *Selenicereus atropilosus*, a new species from Jalisco. *Cact. Succ. J. (U.S.)* 50:268-270.

16396 Ehlers, R. (1988). *Tillandsia klausii*, a new *Tillandsia* from southern Mexico. *J. Bromeliad Soc.* 38:257-260.

16401 Gibbs, P., Semir, J., & da Cruz, N. (1988). A proposal to unite the genera *Chorisia* Kunth and *Ceiba* Miller (Bombacaceae). *Notes Royal Bot. Gard. Edinburgh* 45:125-136.

16402 Stahl, B. (1989). A synopsis of Central American Theophrastaceae. *Nord. J. Bot.* 9(1):15-30.

16430 Ormazabal, C. (1988). Sistemas nacionales de areas silvestres protegidas en América Latina. Santiago: FAO. 205 pp.

16436 Rodríguez, R.R., Matthei, O., & Quezada, M. (1983). Flora Arbórea de Chile. Chile: Universidad de Concepción. 408 pp. 87 species described including their uses; vegetation types and their endemics.

16473 Carauta, J.P.P. (1978). *Dorstenia* L. (Moraceae) do Brasil e países limítrofes. *Rodriguésia* 29(44):71-73.

16585 Ghillány, B.A. de. (1979). The rare *Koellensteinia eburnea* of Brazil. *Amer. Orchid Soc. Bull.* 48(1):14-16.

16686 Leme, E. (1986). Rio-Bahia-Rio. *J. Bromeliad Soc.* 36(6):243-249, 267.

16692 Lewis, G.P. (1987). Legumes of Bahia. Kew, England: Royal Botanic Gardens. 369 pp.

16721 Wurdack, J.J. (1969). Certamen Melastomataceis. XIV. *Phytologia* 19(3):191-197.

16747 Rizzo, J. (1981). Flora do Estado de Goias, Coleçao Rizzo. Goiania.: Universidade Federal de Goias. 4 vols.

16826 Stevens, W.D. (no date). Flora de Nicaragua (in preparation).

16853 Bernal, R. (1989). Endangerment of Colombian palms. *Principes* 33(3):113-128.

16887 Leonard, E.C. (1951-1958). The Acanthaceae of Colombia. *Contr. U.S. Nat. Herb.* 31:1-781.

16890 Lozano-Contreras, G. (1975). Contribuciónes a las Magnoliaceae de Colombia, III. *Caldasia* 11(53):27-50.

16929 Trelease, W. & Yunker, G. (1950). The Piperaceae of northern South America. University of Selenois Press, Urbana. 838 pp. si.

16943 Brandbyge, J. & Holm-Nielsen, L. (1986). Reforestation of the High Andes with local species. *Reports from the Bot. Institute, Univ. of Aarhus* 13(1):114.

16956 Dodson, C.H. & Marmol, P. (1982). Orchids of Ecuador. *Icones Plantarum Tropicarum* 5:401-500. Illus.

16958 Dodson, C.H. & Gentry, A.H. (1978). Flora of the Rio Palenque Science Center. *Selbyana* 4(1-6):1-628.

16963 Dodson, C.H. & Marmol, P. (1980). Orchids of Ecuador. *Icones Plantarum Tropicarum* 1-4:1-400. Illus.

17000 Luer, C.A. (1979). Miscellaneous new species in the Pleurothallidinae. *Selbyana* 5(2):145-194.

17008 Martinelli, G. & Leme, E. (1983). Rare bromeliads from Brazil, No.1: *Vriesea lancifolia* (Parker) L.B. Smith. *J. Bromeliad Soc.* 33(5):195-198.

17014 Martinelli, G. & Leme, E. (1986). *Neoregelia gavionensis*, a new species from Brazil. *J. Bromeliad Soc.* 36(2):71-72.

17079 Sociedade Botânica do Brasil. (1992). Centuria plantarum Brasiliensium extintionis minitata. Sociedade Botânica do Brasil. 175 pp. Data sheets on Brazilian plants.

17203 Werkhoven, M.C.M. (1986). Orchids of Suriname. Paramaribo, Suriname: Vaco. 256 pp.

17208 Centro de Datos para la Conservación. (1986). Ecosistemas criticos en el Peru: Recommendaciones del CDC - Peru et World Resources Institute. Lima: Universidad Nacional Agraria-La Molina. 53 pp.

17248 Teixeira, D.E. (1988). Amazonian timbers for the international market. (ITTO Technical Series 1). Brasilia: Brazilian Institute for Forestry Development & ITTO. 94 pp. Col. illus.

17279 Molau, U. (1992). Scrophulariaceae, Part 1 - Calceolarieae. *Flora Neotropica*, Monograph 47. Bronx, NY: New York Botanical Garden.

17371 Tryon, R.M. & Stolze, R. (1989). Pteridophyta of Peru. Part II. 13. Pteridaceae - 15. Dennstaedtiaceae. *Fieldiana Bot. New Series* 22:1-128.

17435 Beentje, H.J. (1988). Atlas of the rare trees of Kenya. *Utafiti* 1(3):71-125. National Museums of Kenya.

17450 Ng, F.S.P., Low, C.M., & Sanah, M.A.N. (1990). Endemic trees of the Malay Peninsula. Kuala Lumpur: Forestry Department. 118 pp. Col. illus. FRIM Research Pamphlet No.106.

17457 Commission of the European Communities. (1991). CORINE biotopes. The design, compilation and use of an inventory of sites of major importance for nature conservation in the European Community. L-2920 Luxembourg: Commission of the European Communities, Directorate-general, Environment, Nuclear Saftey and Civil Protection. K3-K10 pp.

17458 Matthews, W.S., Van Wyk, A.E., & Bredenkamp, G.J. (1992). Endemic flora of the North-Eastern Transvaal Escarpment, South Africa. *Biological Conservation* 63:83-94.

17459 Jiménez, Q., Poveda, L., Zamora, N., & Sánchez, P. (1988). Arboles amenazados o en peligro de extinción para la Peninsula de Osa. 5 pp.

17462 Erfurth, T. & Rusche, H. (1976). The marketing of tropical wood. B. Wood species from South American tropical moist forests. Rome: FAO.

17466 Schmidt, R. (1989). Current tropical moist forest management activities in Brazil. Report prepared for the government of Brazil. Rome: FAO. 29 pp. FO:MISC/89/4. Map.

17530 Anon. (no date). The Teide National Park. 8 pp.

17534 Bramwell, D. & Perez, J.R. (1982). Prioridades para la conservación de la diversidad genética en la flora de las Islas Canarias. *Botanica Macaronesica* 10:3-17.

17577 Shik, Y. (1992). Conservation Status Listing - Plants of South Korea. Annotations by Yong Shik. 36 pp. TPU printout.

17615 Hodel, D.R. (1992). Chamaedorea palms. The species & their cultivation. Lawrence, Kansas: Allen Press. 338 pp.

17616 Quero, H.J. (1992). Current status of Mexican palms. *Principes* 36(4):203-216.

17617 Fu, L. & Jin, J. (eds.). (1992). China Plant Red Data Book. Rare and endangered plants. Vol. 1. Beijing: Science Press. xviii, 741 pp. Col. illus.; maps. 338 taxa, of which 121 are Endangered, 110 are Rare, and 157 are Vulnerable.

17661 Jain, S.K. & Sastry, A.R.K. (1984). The Indian Plant Red Data Book - I. Botanical Survey of India, Dept of Environment.

17662 Mathew, B. (1992). Annotations to: Conservation status listing: *Sternbergia*.

17663 Mathew, B. (1983). A review of the genus *Sternbergia*. *The Plantsman* 5(1):1-16.

17664 Mathew, B. (1992). Annotations to: Conservation status listing: *Galanthus*. 3 pp. TPU printout.

17665 Walters, S.M. et al. (1986). The European Garden Flora. (1). 318 pp.

17668 Carter, S. (1992). Annotations to: Conservation status listing: *Aloe*. 28 pp. TPU printout.

17671 Kassas, M., Ayyad, M., Springuel, I., & Zahnran, M. (1992). Egypt: Habitat diversity. Plant ecology. 4-113 pp. For the United Nations Environment Programme.

17672 Carter, S. (1992). Annotations to: Conservation status listing: *Euphorbia*. TPU printout.

17673 **Chepstow-Lusty, A. (1992)**. Letter about the conservation status of plants from Henderson Island.

17674 **Madulid, D.A. & Agoo, E.M.G. (1991)**. Status report on rare and endangered Philippine plants II. *Cycas chamberlainii* Br. & Kienh. *The Philippine Scientist* 28:99-112.

17681 **Anon. (1979)**. Prosopis species. pp. 153-161 *In* Tropical legumes: Resources for the future. Washington, DC: National Academy of Sciences.

17685 **Anon. (1979)**. VI Luxury timbers. pp. 211-238 *In* Tropical legumes: Resources for the future. Washington, D.C.: National Academy of Sciences.

17690 **Lewis, B.A. (1992)**. Additions to the orchid flora of Vanuatu in the south-west Pacific. *Kew Bull.* 47(4):685-691.

17694 **Kennedy, K. & Poole, J. (1992)**. Large-fruited sand-verbena (*Abronia macrocarpa*) recovery plan. Albuquerque, New Mexico: U.S. Fish and Wildlife Service, Region 2. 37 pp. Map.

17695 **U.S. Department of the Interior. Fish and Wildlife Service. (1992)**. Hinckley oak (*Quercus hinckleyi*) recovery plan. Albuquerque, New Mexico: U.S. Fish and Wildlife Service, Region 2. 39 pp. Map.

17718 **Boland, D.J., Brooker, M.I.H., Chippendale, G.M., Hall, N., Hyland, B.P.M., Johnston, R.D., Kleing, D.A., & Turner, J.D. (1962)**. Forest trees of Australia. Melbourn: Thomas Nelson & CSIRO. Illus. Maps.

17746 **IBAMA. (1992)**. Lista oficial de espécies da flora Brasileira ameaçadas de extinçao. 4 pp.

17749 **Dransfield, J. & Kiew, R. (1990)**. The palms of Taman Negara. *The Journal of Wildlife and Parks* 10:38-45. A special issue to commemorate the golden jubilee of Taman Negara.

17750 **Anon. (1981)**. Descripción general y anatomica de 105 maderas del grupo Andino. Junac: Junta del Acuerdo de Cartagena. 441 pp.

17762 **Dihoru, G. (no date)**. Proposals for adding to the check list of threatened plants. 15 pp. (Romania) List of species.

17778 **Anon. (1992)**. The endemic flora of Almeria (Southern Spain): a conservation/biosystematic study of the endemic *Rosmarinus* species of southern Spain. 9 pp. Appendix contains list of endemics of the Cabo de Gata area.

17779 **Lapelé, M. & Vaiciúaité, R. (1992)**. Red Data List of Lithuania. Lists plants, including lower plants, and animals.

17781 **Morgan, V. & Leon, C. (1990)**. Bern Convention. Revision of Appendix I (Flora).

17786 **Anon. (1992)**. A Hungarian proposal concerning amendments to the CORINE biotopes project's endangered plant species list. 7 pp.

17788 **Anon. (1988)**. Unique San Bernadino plants focus of research. *Center for Conservation Biology - Update.* (Fall/Winter) 2(2):4-6.

17789 **Anon. (1993)**. 'Extinct' plants rediscovered. *Oryx* 27(1):12.

17796 **Anon. (1991)**. Conservation of the palmate-bracted bird's beak: a most unusual endangerd wetland annual. *Center for Conservation Biology - Update* (Fall/Winter) 5(2):1-2.

17807 **Alexandra, K. (1989)**. Study in populations of rare and threatened plants. 7-14 pp. Presented at the CMEA meeting held in Poland in October 1989.

17809 **Mirek, Z. (1989)**. Extinction of and threat to the vascular flora of the Polish Carpathians. 21-29 pp. Presented at the CMEA meeting held in Poland in October 1989. Illus., maps.

17821 **Anon. (1992)**. The list of threatened plant species of European importance for Czechoslovakia. 1-2 pp. Prepared for the CORINE biotopes project.

17823 **Dihoru, G. (1992)**. Proposals for adding to the check list of threatened plants. Endemics. 2 pp. Produced in 1992 for the CORINE biotopes project for Romania.

17824 **MacDougal, J.M. (1994)**. Revision of *Passiflora* section *Pseudodysosmia*(Passifloraceae). *Systematic Botany Monographs* 41:1-146. (in press).

17832 **Storkersen, O.R. (1992)**. Truete arter i Norge. [Norwegian Red List]. DN-rapport 1992 - 6. Tungasletta 2, N-7005 Trondheim: Directorate for Nature Management. 22-28 pp. List of Vascular plants, fungi, lichens, bryophytes, mammals, birds, reptiles and amphibians, fish, butterflies and moths, beetles, dragonflies and other invertebrates.

17833 **Meléndez, E.N. (1982)**. Plantas medicinales de Puerto Rico. [Medicinal plants of Puerto Rico.]. Universidad de Puerto Rico. 1-498 pp. Illus. Common names included.

17882 **Government of Japan. (1992)**. World Heritage List Nomination. Yakushima (Yaku Island). Environmental Agency. 27 pp. Maps. Slides.

17887 **Delaney, K.R. & Wunderlin, R.P. (1989)**. A new species of *Crotalaria* (Fabaceae) from the Florida Central Ridge. *Sida* 13(3):315-324.

17888 **Anderson, L.C. (1991)**. *Paronychia chartacea* ssp. *minima* (Caryophyllaceae): a new subspecies of a rare Florida endemic. *Sida* 14(3):435-441.

17890 **Wallace, S.R. (1992)**. Conservation status listing: Florida. TPU printout with annotations.

17891 **Anon. (1993)**. Draft Document - Trade status of habitat directive species for inclusion in EC trade regulation.

17908 Morin, N.R. & Unger, J.M. (1992). Botanical News. *Neviusia cliftonii* (Rosacea: Kerrieae), an intriguing new relict species fron California, discovered. *Flora of North America Newsletter* (Winter 1992) 6(4):27.

17912 Zizka, D. (1993). Categories for indigenous plants of Easter Island. 1 pp. Short list of indigenous plants with endemics.

17915 Anon. (1992). Recovery plans. Endangered plants endemic to South Australia. *On the Brink!* 2:10.

17916 Anon. (1992). Endangered plants of northern New South Wales. *On the Brink!* 2:11.

17919 Zizka, G. (1993). Buschmannskerze, Storch-, Reiher-, und Kranichschnabel - Schnabelkräuter im Palmengarten. [cranesbill geraniums in the Palm garden]. *Der Palmengarten - Stadt Frankfurt Am Main* (January):3-10.

17928 Mercier, H. & Kerbauy, G. (1993). Micropropagation of *Dyckia macedoi* - an endangered endemic Brazilian bromeliad. *Botanic Gardens Micropropagation News* 1(6):70-72.

17933 Mallia, A. & Schembri, P.J. (1991). Orobanchaceae. pp. 102-202 in *National Database on Biodiversity. Sample Entries for Evaluation*. Msida - Malta: Department of Biology, University of Malta. (unpublished).

17934 Mallia, A. & Schembri, P.J. (1991). Orchidaceae. *National Database on Biodiversity. Sample Entries for Evaluation* Msida - Malta: Department of Biology, University of Malta. (unpublished)10-82 pp.

17940 Rao, Y.S. (1992). Forest news. Forestry profile: Laos. *Tigerpaper* XIX(4):9-11. information on economics, forest resources etc.

17945 Johnson, D.V. (1992). Additions and corrections to WCMC palm database by John Dowe, Nov. 1992. 5 pp.

17946 Borchenius, F. & Balslev, H. (1989). Three new species of *Aiphanes* (Palmae) with notes on the genus in Ecuador. *Nord. J. Bot.* 9(4):383-393.

17949 Kahn, F. (1990). Las palmeras del Arboretum Jenaro Herrera (Provincia de Requena, Departamento de Loreto, Peru). *Candollea* 45(1):341-362.

17950 Dransfield, J. (1993). Conversation with Dennis Johnson.

17951 Beentje, H.J. (1993). Annotation of conservation status listing of the palms of Madagascar. 6 pp.

17954 Moraes, M. (1992). Bolivian palms. Listing. 6 pp.

17955 Moussa, F., Kahn, F., Henderson, A., Brako, L., & Hoff, M. (1992). Las palmeras en los valles principales de la Amazonia Peruana. [Palms of the major river valleys of Peruvian Amazonia.]. *Bull. Inst. fr. études andines* 21(2):565-597.

18023 Braun, K. (1992). Swaziland flora - species of possibly high conservation priority. 7 pp. Unpublished document, Swaziland National Trust Commission.

18035 Fosberg, F.R., Sachet, M., & Oliver, R. (comps.). (1979). A geographical checklist of the Micronesian Dicotyledonae. *Micronesica* 15(1-2):41-295.

18038 Walter, K.S. (1992). Trip report - Workshop on Biodiversity Data for the GEF Biodiversity Action Plan for China. Beijing, 9-13 November 1992. 9 pp.

18089 Luer, C.A. (1983). Thesaurus masdevalliarum. A monograph of the genus *Masdevallia*. Munich: Helga Koniger. 16 vols. Col. illus.

18102 Nasir, Y. (1991). Threatened plants of Pakistan. pp. 229-234 *In* Plant Life of South Asia, S.J. Ali & A. Ghaffer (eds.).

18105 Dodson, C.H. & Dodson, P.M. (1989). Orchids of Ecuador. Icones plantarum tropicarum, series II. Fascicles 5, 6. St Louis, Missouri: Missouri Botanical Garden. Illus.

18110 Hágsater, E. & Salazar, G.O. (1990). Orchids of Mexico. Icones Orchidacearum. Fascicle 1. Mexico City: Asociacion Mexicana de Orquideologia. 1-100 pp. Illus.

18124 Koopowitz, H. & Kaye, H. (1990). Plant extinction: A global crisis. (2nd ed.). London: Christopher Helm.

18128 Shimizu, Y. (1992). Origin of *Distylium* dry forest and occurrence of endangered species in the Bonin Islands. *Pacific Science* 46(2):179-196. includes maps, figs., photos.

18134 U.S. Department of the Interior. Fish and Wildlife Service. (1993). Endangered and threatened wildlife and plants; Endangered or threatened status for seven central Florida plants. *Federal Register* 58(79):25746-25753. Detailed descriptions of habitat.

18154 Landolt, E. (1991). Rote Liste - Gefährdung der Farn- und Blütenpflanzen in der Schweiz. [Red List - Threatened ferns and flowering plants in Switzerland]. Bern, Switzerland: Bundesamt für Umwelt, Wald und Landschaft. 185 pp.

18176 Boggan, J., Funk, V., Kelloff, C., Hoff, M., Cramers, C., & Feuillet, C. (1992). Checklist of the plants of the Guianas (Guyana, Surinam, French Guiana). Washington, DC: Biological Diversity of the Guianas Program, Smithsonian Institution. 381 pp.

18200 Brako, L. & Zarucchi, J.L. (1993). Catalogue of the flowering plants and gymnosperms of Peru. *Mongr. Syst. Bot.* (Missouri Bot. Gard.) 45:1-1286.

18211 **Radcliffe-Smith, A. (1992).** The Botany of Socotra. pp. 189-205 *In* Doe B. (ed.).Socotra. Island of Tranquillity. London: IMMEL Publishing Limited.

18216 **Ingelög, T., Anderson, R., & Tjernberg, M. (eds.).** **(1993).** Red Data Book of the Baltic Region. Part 1. Lists of threatened vascular plants and vertebrates. Uppsala: Swedish Threatened Species Unit. 95 pp.

18223 **Anon. (no date).** Special flowers of Gibraltar. Gibraltar: Wildlife (Gibraltar) Ltd. In aid of the Gibraltar Botanic Gardens.

18228 **Balakrishna, P. (1993).** Letter to Kerry S. Walter with corrections to Conservation Status Listing for India.

18264 **Conti, F., Manzi, A., & Pedrotii, F. (1992).** Libro Rosso delle piante d'Italia. [Red book of plants in Italy]. Rome: WWF Italia. 637 pp. Illus.

18265 **Dressler, R.L. (1993).** Conversation about orchid conservation and taxonomy.

18270 **Farjon, A., Page, C.N., & Schellevis, N.** **(1993).** A preliminary world list of threatened conifer taxa. *Biodiversity and Conservation* 2:304-326. 416 Threatened, 1 Extinct. IUCN's V & R categories subdivided.

18271 **Anon. (1993).** Distribution of endemic plants of Cyprus. 20 pp. Computer printout with localities for 127 Cyprus endemics, including flower phenology and giant trees.

18289 **Dahlgren, R. & Van Wyk, A.E. (1988).** Structures and relationships of families endemic to or centered in southern Africa. *Monogr. Syst. Bot. Missouri Bot. Gard.* 25:1-94. Illus.

18294 **Supthut, D.J. (1989).** Letter to Sara Oldfield concerning succulents in Madagascar.

18295 **Supthut, D.J. (1992).** Letter to WCMC (Sara Oldfield) concerning international trade in *Aloe*.

18326 **Keay, R.W.J. (1989).** The trees of Nigeria. Oxford: Oxford University Press. 476 pp. Illus.

18329 **Moscoso, R.M. (1943).** Catalogus Florae Domingensis I: Spermatophyta. New York: University of Santo Domingo. xlviii, 732 pp.

18338 **Herbst, D. (1991).** Annotations to WCMC plant list for Guam.

18341 **Balakrishna, P. (1993).** Annotations to WCMC printout entitled "Unresolved India - 534 records". Includes letter to Kerry S. Walter dated 9 Aug 1993 and annotations to list dated 21 Sep 93.

18551 **Little, E.L. et al. (1974).** Trees of Puerto Rico and the Virgin Islands, Second Volume. Agriculture Handbook No. 449. Washington, DC: U.S.D.A. Forest Service. 1024 pp. Second volume to Little & Wadsworth, 1964; includes endemic, rare, and endangered tree species.

18767 **Fuller, D.O. (1991).** Medicine from the wild. An overview of the U.S. native medicinal plant trade and its conservation implications. Washington, DC: World Wildlife Fund. 28 pp.

18799 **Ellshoff, Z.E. (1991).** The rarest Hawaiian members of the *Hibiscus* family. *National Tropical Botanical Garden Bull.* 21(3):7-12.

18826 **Spiller, S.F. (1992).** New list of plant candidates in Arizona approved by the Fish and Wildlife Service.

18996 **Royal Botanic Gardens Kew, & International Institute for Environment and Development. (1993).** Report on sustainable environmental development strategy and action plan for St Helena. Vol. 3. Status of the endemic flora and preliminary recovery programmes. 95 pp. Unpublished report for the St Helena Government.

18997 **Cronk, Q.C.B. (1989).** The past and present vegetation of St Helena. *Journal of Biogeography* 16:47-64.

19001 **Fiard, J. (1992).** Arbres rares et ménacés de la Martinique. (Collection Régionale Connaissance du Patrimoine). Martinique: Société des Galeries de Géologie et de Botanique de Fort-de-France. 152 pp.

19002 **Center for Plant Conservation (CPC). (1992).** Printout of CPC's data for North American plants.

19006 **Jones, D. (1986).** Status of Malaysian Rutaceae (unpublished list). Attached to letter to Steve Davis dated 17 May 1986.

19007 **Katende, A.B. (1993).** Annotations to: TPU conservation status report for Uganda dated 29 Jun 1993. Attached to letter from Derek Pomeroy to Kerry S. Walter. Includes additional taxa to add to TPU database.

19011 **Royal Botanic Garden Edinburgh. (1993).** Living collections database in BG-BASE format.

19034 **Hoffmann, A.E. (1989).** Cactaceas. En la flora silvestre de Chile. Una guía para la identificación de los cactos que crecen en el país. Santiago, Chile: Ediciones Fundación Claudio Gay. 272 pp.

19035 **Carter Holmes, S. (1993).** Annotations to TPU printout: Eurphorbiaceae dated 28 Jun 1993.

19037 **Anon. (1991).** Endangered species and habitats of Thailand. Ecological Research Department, Thailand Institute of Scientific and Technological Research. 239 pp. Col. illus., map. Covers 111 species - 3 plants, 40 mammals, 41 birds, 12 fishes, 12 amphibians and reptiles, 3 insects.

19045 **Hirtz, A. (1993).** Annotated printout (Ecuadorean orchid specimens in herbaria) with conservation status.

19047 **Soepadmo, E. (1991).** Indomalayan wild orchids - their ecological and conservation status. Paper presented at the International Conference and Exhibition on Orchids and Ornamental Plants: Kuala Lumpur 22-28 August, 1990. *Malaysian Orchid Bulletin* 5:63.

19052 **Cortes, John. (1993).** Letter to Kerry S. Walter regarding conservation status of plants in Gibraltar.

19054 **Lucas, J. (1992).** Placement Year Report 1991/1992. Illus. List of Hawaii and species information sheets.

19057 **U.S. Department of the Interior. Fish and Wildlife Service. (1993).** Recovery plan for *Geocarpon minimum* MacKenzie. Atlanta, Georgia: U.S. Fish and Wildlife Service. 34 pp. Prepared by A.B. Pittman.

19090 **Middleton, D.J. & Wilcock, C.C. (1990).** A critical examination of the status of *Pernettya* as a genus distinct from *Gaultheria*. Edinburgh J. Bot. 47:291-301.

19095 **Wagner, W.H. (1993).** Conversation with Kerry S. Walter concerning conservation and distribution of *Botrychium* and *Diellia*.

19102 **Keble Martin, W. (1982).** The concise British Flora. (4). London: Michael Joseph Limited. 247 pp. ill.

19103 **Johansson, D.R. (1978).** Saintpaulias in their natural environment with notes on their present status in Tanzania and Kenya. *Biol. Conserv.* 14:45-62.

19105 **Borhidi, A. (1992).** Letter to Hugh Synge concerning conservation status of Cuban plants. Includes annotations to 27 Aug 1991 TPU printout for Cuba.

19106 **Given, D.R. (1992).** Letter to Hugh Synge concerning conservation status of New Zealand plants.

19108 **Green, P. (1991).** Letter to Hugh Synge concerning conservation status of Norfolk and Lord Howe Islands plants. Includes annotations to 27 Aug 1991 TPU printouts for Lord Howe Island and Norfolk Island.

19109 **Luke, W.R.Q. (1991).** A preliminary list of rare, vulnerable and endemic plants for Kenya (appendix B cntd.). Prepared for National Biodiversity Board. p. 25 in The costs benefits and unmet needs of biological diversity conservation in Kenya. Prepared with assistance from the Overseas Development Administration, UK.

19116 **Ricci, M. (1990).** Programa de conservación y recuperación de plantas amenazadas de Juan Fernandez. (Including annotations by H. Synge). Proyecto CONAF -WWF 3313 Chile. (Technical Report). Ministerid de Agricultura Corporacion Nacional Forestal.

19117 **Zizka, G. (1990).** Changes in the Easter Island Flora. Comments on Selected Families. *Courier (Forschungsinstitut Senckenberg)* 125:189-207.

19118 **Murray, D.F. (1992).** Vascular plant diversity in Alaskan Arctic tundra. *The Northwest Environmental Journal* 8:29-52.

19120 **Anon. (1992).** Annex 1 - Species ecological status by category. pp. 42-59 in UNEP Thailand Country Study on Biodiversity.

19121 **Akeroyd, J.R. (1992).** Annotations to WCMC Conservation Status Listing - Plants of Greece. With particular attention to endemics of Crete.

19123 **U.S. Department of the Interior. Fish and Wildlife Service. (1993).** Endangered and threatened wildlife and plants: Determination of endangered status for the plant Pima pineapple cactus (*Coryphantha scheeri* var. *robustispina*). *Federal Register* 58(183):49875-49880.

19124 **U.S. Department of the Interior. Fish and Wildlife Service. (1993).** Utah reed-mustards: Clay reed-mustard (*Schoencrambe argillacea*), Barneby reed-mustard (*Schoenocrambe barnebyi*), shrubby reed-mustard (*Schoenocrambe suffrutescens*), recovery plan. Denver, Colorado. 20 pp.

19125 **Ricci, M. (1991).** Letter to Hugh Synge concerning conservation status of plants of the Juan Fernandez Islands. Includes annotations to 12 Aug 1991 TPU printout for the Juan Fernandez Islands.

19130 **Burtt, B.L. (1963).** Studies in the Gesneriaceae of the Old World XV: The genus *Saintpaulia*. Notes Roy. Bot. Gard. Edinburgh 22(6):547-568.

19134 **Iwatsuki, K. (1991).** Annotations to TPU printout: Ogasawara-Shoto.

19135 **Iwatsuki, K. (1993).** Annotations to TPU printout: Volcano Islands.

19136 **Kitayama, K. (no date).** Threatened endemic species of the Bonin (Ogasawara) Islands. An airport construction on the island of Anjima. 3 pp.

19140 **Lewis, B.A. (1993).** *Malagasia* refound! 1 pp. rediscovery of *Malagasia alticola* (Capuron) L. Johnson and B. Briggs in Madagascar.

19160 **Ministry of Agriculture, Royal Government of Bhutan. (1993).** Schedule 2: list of totally protected plant species. *J. Roy. Soc. Arts.* Lists 42 totally protected plant species.

19161 **Pradhan, R. (1993).** Annotations to WCMC plant list for Bhutan dated 31 August 1993.

19164 **Akeroyd, J.R. (1992).** Letter to Hugh Synge concerning conservation status of plants of various Mediteranean Islands including: Cyprus, Sicily, Malta, Corsica, Sardinia and the Balearic Islands. Includes annotations to 1991 TPU printouts for the these countries.

19170 **Gardner, D. & Marsh, M. (1993).** Endangered monocots. *Kew Scientist* 4:7. *Gasteria baylissiana* and *Hohenbergiopsis guatemalensis*.

19174 **Iriondo, J.M., De Hond, L.J., & Gómez-Campo, C.**

(1993). Current research on the biology of threatened plant species of the Mediterranean Basin and Macaronesia: a database. (Preliminary Draft). Madrid, Spain: Commission for the Conservation of Plant Resources. Organization for the phyto-Taxonomic Investigation of the Mediterranean Area. (unpublished)209 pp. Includes database printout of 201 threatened species with details of the organisation undertaking research.

19181 Friedmann, F. (1991). *Flore des Seychelles*. (Première partie: Dicotylédons). Manuscrit inédit.

19182 Friedmann, F. (1991). Annotations to Threatened Plant Unit printout for the Seychelles (granitic islands) dated 12 Sep 1991. 6 pp.

19184 Waldren, S. (1993). Annotations and additions to TPU printout of the Pitcairn islands. 7 pp. Includes additions to Oeno.

19185 Waldren, S., Florence, J., & Chepstow-Lusty, A.J. (1995). Rare and endemic vascular plants of the Pitcairn Islands, south-central pacific ocean: a conservation appraisal. *Biological Conservation*.

19186 St. John, H. (1987). An account of the flora of Pitcairn Island with new Pandanus species. Pacific Plant Studies 46. Honolulu, Hawaii.

19187 Fosberg, F.R., Paulay, G., Spencer, T., & Oliver, R. (1989). New collections and notes on the plants of Henderson, Pitcairn, Oeno and Ducie islands. Atoll Research Bulletin 329:1-18.

19209 Said, I.M. & Rozainah, Z. (1992). An updated list of wetland plant species of Peninsular Malaysia, with particular reference to those having socio-economic value. Asian Wetland Bureau. 109 pp. Publication No. 79.

19213 Cronk, Q. C.B. (1991). Letter to Hugh Synge concerning conservation status of plants; includes annotated conservation status listings for St. Helena, Tristan de Cunha and Falkland Islands.

19215 Lamb, A. (1992). Orchid conservation in Sabah (Malaysian Borneo): a list of species of botanical and horticultural importance and interest and their conservation status. *Botanic Gardens Conservation News* 1(10):44-47. Lists accessions of the Tenom Orchid Centre, including IUCN conservation categories.

19216 Jermy, A.C. (1993). An updated and annotated checklist of Pteridophytes.

19218 Balakrishna, P. & Ravishankar, T. (1993). Letter with list of corrections to TPU printout for India.

19221 Adams, C.D. (1972). Flowering plants of Jamaica. Jamaica: University of the West Indies. 848 pp.

19232 Stace, C. (1991). New flora of the British Isles. Bury St Edmunds: Cambridge University Press. 1226 pp.

19257 Phengklai, C. & Khamsai, S. (1985). Some non-timber species of Thailand. *Thai Forest Bulletin (Botany)* 1(15):108-148.

19264 Cunningham, A.B. (1993). African medicinal plants: setting priorities at the interface between conservation and primary healthcare. People and plants working paper - March 1993. Paris: UNESCO. 50 pp.

19266 Tutin, T.G., Burges, N.A., Chater, A.O., Edmondson, J.R., Heywood, V.H., Moore, D.M., Valentine, D.H., Walters, S.M., & Webb, D.A. (eds.). (1993). Flora Europaea Volume 1. (Second edition). Psilotaceae to Platanaceae. Cambridge, UK: Cambridge University Press. 581 pp.

19277 Phuphathanaphong, L. (1985). Studies in Thai flora. 4. Aristolochiaceae. *Thai Forest Bulletin (Botany)* 1(15):29-57. Pics.

19281 Ubolcholaket, A. (1983). Preliminary study on Gentianaceae of Thailand. *Thai Forest Bulletin (Botany)* 1(14):94-127. Maps.

19305 Given, D.R. (1994). Letter to WCMC (Harriet Gillett) concerning threatened plants of New Zealand. Refers to datasource 19303.

19306 Zarzycki, K. & Szelag, Z. (1992). Czerwona lista roslin naczyniowych zagrozonych w Polsce [Red List of threatened vascular plants in Poland]. *in* K.Zarzycki, W.Wojewoda & Z.Heinrich (eds.) Lista roslin zagrozonych w Polsce [List of threatened plants in Poland]. pp. 87-98 in (ed.). Kraków: W. Szafer Institute of Botany, Polish Academy of Sciences. Bilingual - with English.

19321 Maglocky, S. & Feráková, V. (1993). Red List of ferns and flowering plants (*Pteridophyta and Spermatophyta*) of the flora of Slovakia (the second draft). *Biológia* (48) 4:361-385.

19352 Centro de Datos para la Conservación-CDC-CVC. (1980). Lista preliminar de plantas especiales del Centro de Datos para la conservación, CDC-CVC. Cauca, Colombia: Corporación Autónoma Regional del Cauca. 10 pp.

19353 Centro Do Datos Para la Conservacion-CDC-CVC. (1986). Lista preliminar de plantas especiales del centro de datos para la conservacion, CDC-CVC. Cauca, Colombia: Corporacion Autonoma Regional del Cauca.

19354 Estenssoro, S. (1987). Lista preliminar de plantas especiales. La Paz: Centro de Datos para la Conservación. 17 pp.

19358 Mianda-Bungi, N. (1988). Catalogue des plants endémiques du Zaïre. 7 pp. Includes letter from author to Robert Madams.

19366 Kazmierczakowa, R. & Zarzycki, K. (eds.). (1994). Indeks lacinskich nazw opisanych gatunków z podaniem kateforii zagrozenia (synonimy zlozono kursywa) [Index of Latin names of species covered in the "Polish red data book of plants"]. 301-303 pp. Includes threat categories.

19389 Bellingham, P.J. (1993). The effects of a hurricane on Jamaican montane rain forests. Vascular flora of the western Blue Mountains, Jamaica. 41 pp. PhD dissertation, University of Cambridge, Cambridge, UK.

19400 Stehle, H. (1979). Considérations phytogéographiques et écologiques sur des orchidacées des antilles françaises. *C.R.Soc.Biogéogr.* 484:137-144.

19401 Sastre, C. (1979). Considérations phytogéographiques sur les sommets volcaniques Antillais. *C.R.Soc.Biogéogr.* 484:127-135.

19407 Adams, R.P. (1983). The junipers (*Juniperus*; Cupressaceae) of Hispaniola;. Comparisons with other caribbean species and among collections from Hispaniola. *Moscosoa* 2(1):77-89. Maps, illus.

19408 Hartshorn, G. et al. (1981). Natural Vegetation. pp. 13-21 *In* The Dominican Republic, country environmental profile, a field study. Virgina: McLean. Lists 137 threatened species, based on a list prepared by CIBIMA by Dr. José de Jesús Jiménez. Orchid list prepared by D.D.Dod.

19417 Oltean, M., Negrean, G., Popescu, A., Roman, N., Sanda, V., Milhailescu, S., & Dihoru, G. (1994). Lista rosie a speciilor de plante endemice si amenintate din Romania. [Red list of endemic and threatened plant species in Romania]. (Produced for CORINE Biotopes Project for Romania). Includes letter of explanation from Dr. Mircea Oltean to Johanna Sidey.

19420 Vaughan, R.E. (1980). Notes on some aspects of the plant ecology of Mauritius with a census of the Perrier reserve. 33 pp.

19421 Anon. (1986). The Ile aux Aigrettes project. 6 pp. Jointly spons. by Mauritius Wildlife Appeal Fund & Lions Club of Curepipe.

19425 Anon. (1994). List of plant species which are distributed in Bulgaria and are included in CORINE programme. 2 pp. Correspondance to Graham Drucker from Ministry of Environment.

19426 Anon. (1994). Correspondance with WCMC including list of plant species to be added to the CORINE Biotopes Project. Bulgarian Ministry of Environment.

19427 Smith, A.C. (1971). Studies of Pacific Island plants, XXIV. The genus Terminalia (combretaceae) in Fiji, Samoa, and Tonga. *Brittonia* 23(4):394-412. (11 spp described).

19432 Farjon, A. (1993). Letter from Secretary of SSC Conifer group to Harriet Gillett concerning conifer taxonomy.

19434 Burton, F. (1993). Letter to WCMC including list of status of endemic plants in the Cayman Islands.

19435 Adams, C.D. (1994). Letter from C. Dennis Adams to Harriet Gillett. Includes annotations to: List of threatened plants of Jamaica dated 19 January 1994.

19436 Shillinger, G. (1994). Urgent call for research on the wax palm forests of the Colombian

Central Andes. email message on Conslink.

19437 Dodson, C.H. (1986). Orchids of Ecuador. List as of 1986. 117-129 pp.

19446 Procter, J. (1973). A check-list of the native and naturalised orchids of the Seychelles.

19448 Halloy, S. (1994). Annotations to the Argentina WCMC printout dated 17 Jan 1994. 23 pp.

19449 Kucera, B. (1994). Letter to Johanna Sidey concerning the plant checklists for the extension to the PHARE region with specific reference to endemic taxa.

19452 Smith, A.C. (1971). Studies of Pacific Island Plants, XXII. New flowering plants from Fiji. *Pacific Science* XXV(4):491-501.

19453 Smith, A.C. (1969). Studies of Pacific Island plants, XXI. New and noteworthy flowering plants from Fiji. *Pacific Science* XXIII(3):383-393.

19454 Smith, A.C. (1954). Botanical studies in Fiji. *Smithsonian Report*:305-315.

19464 Reifenberger, U. & Reifenberger, A. (1993). Letter to Threatened Plants Committee concerning Sonchus wildpretii U. et A. Reifenberger.

19470 Anon. (1984). Malaysian and Singapore mangrove species at risk. Malayan Naturalist:9. Lists threatened mangrove species and their status from Global status of mangrove ecosystems, Commission on ecology papers Number 3, IUCN 1983.

19471 NEMS. (1993). Cook Islands. National environmental management strategies. South Pacific Regional Environment Programme.

19472 Anon. (1992). Fiji. National Report to UNCED. South Pacific Regional Environment Programme.

19473 Rongo, T. (1993). Cook Islands. State of the environment report. Regional Environment Technical Assistance Project.

19486 Proctor, G.R. (1982). More additions to the flora of Jamaica. Journal of the Arnold Arboretum 63:199-315.

19488 Council of the European Communities. (1992). Couçcil Directive 92/43/EEC of 21 May 1992. on the conservation of natural habitats and of wild fauna and flora. pp. 7-50 in *Official Journal of the European Communities*. Includes annexes II, IV and V of plants of community interest for conservation.

19498 Jeffrey, C. (1961). Aizoaceae *in* Flora of Tropical East Africa. Hubbard, C.E. & Milne-Redhead, E. (eds.). Crown Agents For Oversea Governments And Administrations.

19499 Verdcourt, B. (1971). Annonaceae *in* Flora of Tropical East Africa. Milne-Redhead, E. & Polhill, R.M. (eds.). Crown Agents For Overseas Governments And Administrations.

19501 **Verdcourt, B. (1968).** Aquifoliaceae
in Flora of Tropical East Africa.
Milne-Redhead, E. & Polhill, R.M. (eds.). Crown Agents
For Oversea Governments And Administrations.

19502 **Tennant, J.R. (1968).** Araliaceae *in*
Flora of Tropical East Africa. Milne-Redhead, E. &
Polhill, R.M. (eds.). Crown Agents For Oversea
Governments And Administrations.

19503 **Grey-Wilson, C. (1982).** Balsaminaceae
in Flora of Tropical East Africa. Polhill,
R.M. (ed.). A.A. Balkema/ Rotterdam/ Brookfield.

19508 **Wickens, G.E. (1973).** Combretaceae
in Flora of Tropical East Africa. Polhill,
R.M. (ed.). Crown Agents For Oversea Governments And
Administrations.

19509 **Turrill, W.B. & Milne-Redhead, E. (eds.).**
(1956). Caryophyllaceae *in* Flora of
Tropical East Africa. Crown Agents For Oversea
Governments And Administrations.

19510 **Turrill, W.B. & Milne-Redhead, E. (eds.).**
(1956). Canellaceae *in* Flora of Tropical
East Africa. Crown Agents For Oversea Governments And
Administrations.

19512 **Elffers, J., Graham, R.A., & Dewolf, G.P.**
(1964). Capparidaceae *in* Flora of
Tropical East Africa. Hubbard, C.E. & Milne-Redhead, E.
(eds.). Crown Agents For Oversea Governments And
Administrations.

19514 **Verdcourt, B. (1963).** Convolvulaceae
in Flora of Tropical East Africa. Hubbard,
C.E. & Polhill, R.M. (eds.). Crown Agents For Oversea
Governments And Administrations.

19519 **Jeffrey, C. (1967).** Cucurbitaceae *in*
Flora of Tropical East Africa. Milne-Redhead, E. &
Polhill, R.M. (eds.). Crown Agents For Oversea
Governments And Administrations.

19521 **Breteler, F.J. (1988).** Dichapetalaceae
in Flora of Tropical East Africa. Polhill,
R.M. (ed.). A.A. Balkema/ Rotterdam/ Brookfield.

19522 **Lucas, G. Ll. (1968).** Dilleniaceae
in Flora of Tropical East Africa.
Milne-Redhead, E. & Polhill, R.M. (eds.). Crown Agents
For Oversea Governments And Administrations.

19524 **Radcliffe-Smith, A. (1987).** Euphorbiaceae Part
I *in* Flora of Tropical East Africa.
Polhill,R.M. (ed.). A.A. Balkema/ Rotterdam/ Brookfield.

19525 **Carter, S. & Radcliffe-Smith, A. (1988).**
Euphorbiaceae Part II *in* Flora of Tropical
East Africa. Polhill,R.M. (ed.). A.A. Balkema/
Rotterdam/ Brookfield.

19526 **Sleumer, H. (1975).** Flacourtiaceae
in Flora of Tropical East Africa. Polhill,R.M.
(ed.). Crown Agents For Oversea Governments And
Administrations.

19527 **Bamps, P., Robson, N., & Verdcourt, B. (1978).**

Guttiferae *in* Flora of Tropical East Africa.
Polhill,R.M. (ed.). Crown Agents For Oversea Governments
And Administrations.

19528 **Verdcourt, B. (1971).** Hamamelidaceae
in Flora of Tropical East Africa.
Milne-Redhead, E. & Polhill, R.M. (eds.).

19531 **Gillett, J.B., Polhill, R.M., & Verdcourt, B.**
(eds.). (1971). Leguminosae Part 4: Papilionoideae
(1) & (2) *in* Flora of Tropical East Africa.
Milne-Redhead, E. & Polhill, R.M. Crown Agents For
Oversea Governments adn Administrations.

19532 **Brenan, J.P.M. (1964).** Leguminosae Part 2:
subfamily Caesalpinioideae *in* Flora of
Tropical East Africa. Milne-Redhead, E. & Polhill, R.M.
(eds.). Crown Agents For Oversea Governments And
Administration.

19533 **Brenan, J.P.M. (1959).** Leguminosae Part 1:
subfamily Mimosoideae *in* Flora of Tropical
East Africa. C.E. Hubbard & E. Milne-Redhead (eds.).
Crown Agents for Oversea Governments and
Administrations.

19534 **Schick, M. (1985).** Annotations to the TPU list
of threatened plants of Chile.

19535 **Schlegel, F. (1985).** Threatened Chilean
plants. Valdivia Universidad Austral de Chile. 5pp.

19536 **Marticorena, C. (1986).** Annotations to: the
conservation status listing of threatened plants of
Chile.

19537 **Arnal, H. (1988).** Annotations to: conservation
status listing for Venezuela dated 2 December 1988.

19538 **Wood, J. (1988).** Colombian Acanthaceae - Some
new discoveries and some reconsiderations. Kew Bull.
43(1):1-51.

19539 **Ferrari, J.M. (1982).** Letter to Jane
Villa-Lobos.

19542 **Sullivan, G. (1986).** *Remijia
chelomaphylla* (Rubiaceae), a new species from Peru.
Systematic Botany 11(2):298-301.

19547 **Anon. (1994).** Application form for approval
and grant aid for an overseas expedtion from the Royal
Geographic Society. 2 pp. Concerns *Magnolia
pallescens* and *Pinus occidentalis*.

19549 **Dummitt. (1989).** Letter to Jane Villa-Lobos
concerning threatened plants in Argentina.

19550 **Gilmartin, A. (1982).** Annotations to:
conservation status listing for Ecuador.

19552 **Escobar, L. (1982).** Annotations to: the
conservation status listing for Passifloraceae.

19553 **Lozano, J. (1973).** Annotations to: the
conservation status listing for Colombia.

19555 **Mori, S.A. (1987).** Annotations to: the

conservation status listing: Lecythidaceae.

19556 Norman, E. (1986). Annotations to: the conservation status listing for Ecuador dated 27 May 1986.

19557 Brandbyge, J. (1986). Annotations to: the conservation status listing for Ecuador.

19558 Wurdack, J.J. (1988). Annotations to: the conservation status listing: Melastomataeae.

19560 Rizzini, C. (1982). Letter to Jane Villa-Lobos. 10 March 1982.

19561 Hunt, D.R. (1979). New species and a new combination in the Tradescantieae. American Commelinaceae: VII. *Kew Bull.* 33(3):403-406.

19563 Harley, R. (1981). Letter to Jane Villa-Lobos.

19564 Rizzo, J.A. (1982). Annotations to: the conservation status listing for Goiás, Brazil.

19565 Burkhart, A. (1964). Sinopsis de la especies de *Mimosa* de la serie Lepidotae. Darwiniana 13:379-381.

19566 Kiesling, R. (1986). Annotations to: the conservation status listing for Argentina.

19567 Casari, M.B. (1982). Communication with Jane Villa-Lobos concerning threatened plants in Brazil.

19569 Badillo, V. (1987). Annotations to: the conservation status listing for Ecuador dated February 1987.

19570 Todzia, C.A. (1987). Annotations to: the conservation status listing for Ecuador dated 18 December 1987.

19571 Plowman, M. (1987). Annotations to: the conservation status listing for Colombia and Ecuador dated 8 December 1987. TPU printout.

19572 Simpson, B. (1987). Annotations to: the conservation status listing for Ecuador dated 10 December 1987. TPU printout.

19573 Constance, L. (1986). Annotations to: the conservation status listing for Ecuador dated 19 June 1986. TPU printout.

19574 Covas, G. (1986). Annotations to: the conservation status listing for Argentina dated January 1986.

19575 Halloy, S. (1984). Annotations to: the conservation status listing for Argentina dated October 1994.

19576 Kovács-Láng, E. (1994). Reply to candidate check-list of threatened plants for the PHARE countries of Europe. Additional list of 11 species to be included in the check-list.

19577 Vallester, E. (1983). Annotations to: Conservation status listing of plants of Middle America.

19578 Hoff, M. (1993). Contribution à l'étude des *Turneraceae* des Guyanes: *Turnera rupestris* Aublet, espèce menacée de disparition en Guyane. (Studies on the flora of the Guianas no. 70). *Acta Bot. Gallica* 140(3):291-299.

19582 Metz, G.D. (1993). Proposed rule to reclassify Siler Pincushion Cactus from endangered to threatened status. Includes *Federal Register* publication on the state of *Pediocactus sileri* in the wild.

19588 Jebb, M. (1991). An account of *Nepenthes* in New Guinea. *Science in New Guinea* 17(1):7-49.

19594 Leach, G.J. & Osbourne, P.L. (1985). Freshwater plants of Papua New Guinea. Papua New Guinea: UPNG Press.

19605 Fay, M. (1994). *Cosmos atrosanguineus* a well known but endangered member of the Compositae. *Kew Scientist* 5:8.

19607 Oltean, M. (1994). Letter to Johanna Sidey concerning candidate check-list of threatened plants for the PHARE countries of Europe dated 13 April 1994. Includes list of 59 threatened species suggested for the check-list.

19608 Dihoru, G. (1994). Letter to Johanna Sidey concerning the candidate check-list of threatened plants for the PHARE countries of Europe dated 25 March 1994. Includes list of 34 species suggested for inclusion in the check-list.

19614 Johnson, D.V. (1994). Letter from SSC Palm specialist group to Harriet Gillett with list entitled "Palm database changes/corrections, Group 10, April 1994".

19615 Gajdos, P. (1994). Letter to Johanna Sidey concerning the candidate check-list of threatened plants for the PHARE countries of eastern Europe dated 17 April 1994. Includes comments and a list of taxa proposed for inclusion on the check-list.

19616 Zarzycki, K. (1994). Letter to Johanna Sidey concerning threatened vascular plants in Poland. Includes annotations to check-lists of threatened plants for the PHARE region of Europe.

19618 Granville, J.J. de & Henderson, A. (1988). A new species of *Asterogyne* (Palmae) from French Guiana. *Brittonia* 40:76-80.

19619 Henderson, A. & Steyermark, J. (1986). New palms from Venezuela. *Brittonia* 38:309-313.

19624 Gelderblom, C. (1994). Letter from Caroline Gelderblom to Dr Kerry Walter concerning lists of threatened plants in Southern Africa dated 7 March 1994. Contains comments by Craig Hilton-Taylor on the list for Zambia given by Mike Bingham (DS 19487).

19625 Moya Lopez, C.E. et al. (1991). *Gaussia*

spirituana Moya et Leiva. sp. nov.: una neuva palma de Cuba Central. *Revista Del Jardin Botanico Nacional*(Cuba) 12:15-20.

19629 Simpson, R.B. (1994). Pitchers in trade. A conservation review of the carnivorous plant genera *Sarracenia, Darlingtonia* and *Heliamphora. Kew Conservation Review*:61.

19630 Lear, M. (1994). Letter to Harriet Gillett dated 28 March 1994, enclosing extracts from "Plant Conservation in Fiji" written by Michael Lear and Beverley Woods in March 1992. Includes new draft threatened plant list.

19634 Anon. (1994). Collections of the U.S. National Herbarium, Smithsonian Institution, Washington DC.

19695 Jenkins, M. (1994). Email message to Harriet Gillett concerning re-discoery in the wild in Vietnam of *Paphiopedilum delenatii*. 1 pp.

19698 Kahn, F. & Moussa, F. (1994). Diversity and conservation status of Peruvian palms. *Biodiversity and Conservation* 3:227-241.

19701 Palmer, M. (1994). A strategic framework for the conservation of the native flora of Great Britain and Northern Ireland. Joint Nature Conservation Committee, English Nature, Countryside Council for Wales, Scottish Natural Heritage, Department of the Environment for Northern Ireland. 45 pp.

19703 Mill, R.R. (1994). Annotations to Conifers - taxa listed on BG-BASE - status report as of 2 February 1994.

19704 Edwards, S. & Asfaw, Z. (1992). The status of some plant resources in parts of Tropical Africa. *Botany 2000: East and Central Africa. NAPRECA Monograph Series No. 2.*

19706 Little, E.L., Woodbury, R.O., & Wadsworth, F.H. (1974). Trees of Puerto Rico and The Virgin Islands. Second volume. Washington DC 20250: U.S. Dept. of Agriculture, Forest Service. Agriculture handbook no. 449.

19709 Peev, D. (1993). Convention on the conservation of European wildlife and natural habitats. Threatened plant species in Bulgaria including candidate species for Appendix I of the Bern Convention. Strasbourg: Council of Europe. Standing Committee, 13th meeting.

19710 Sánta, A. (1993). Convention on the conservation of European wildlife and natural habitats. Report on the biogeographical regions of Hungary and its main plant conservation problems and data sheets of species selected. Strasbourg: Council of Europe. 36 pp.

19711 Klaudisova, A. (1993). Convention on the conservation of European wildlife and natural habitats. Threatened plant species in the Czech Republic. Strasbourg: Council of Europe. 32 pp.

19712 Proctor, G.R. (1984). Flora of the Cayman Islands. (Kew Bulletin Additional Series XI). Royal Botanic Gardens, Kew: London, HMSO. 834 pp.

19718 Benson, L. (1982). The cacti of the United States and Canada. California: Stanford University Press. with line drawings by Lucretia Breazeale Hamilton.

19723 Farjon, A. (1994). Annotations to: Conservation status listing of Conifers of the world dated 2 February 1994.

19727 De Laubenfels, D.J. (1988). Coniferales. *Flora Malesiana* series I - spermatophyta, flowering plants 10(3).

19728 Anon. (1994). English translation of the Flora Rei Popularis Sinicae (Flora of China).

19734 Leon, H. & Alain, H. (1953). Flora de Cuba III Dicotiledoneas and Malpighiaceae to Myrtaceae. (No. 13). Contribuciones ocasionales del museo de historia natural de la salle. La Habana.

19737 Godfrey, R.K. (no date). Trees, shrubs and woody vines of northern Florida and adjacent Georgia and Alabama. With the majority of illustrations by Melanie Darst. Athens and London: The University of Georgia Press.

19738 Britton, & Wilson. (1924). Scientific survey of Porto Rico and the Virgin Islands. Volume V Botany of Porto Rico and the Virgin Islands. New York: New York Academy of Sciences. Pandanales to Ylymeleales.

19744 Brown, A. (1994). Letter to Mike Maunder concerning reintroduction of *Calandrinia feltonii* in the Falkland Islands.

19748 White, C.T. (1926). Ligneous plants collected in New Caledonia by C. T. White in 1923. *J. Arnold Arboretum* 7:74-103.

19751 Sicinski, J.T. (1994). Letter to Johanna Sidey with regard to Polish threatened plant species for the CORINE-PHARE extension.

19752 Correll, D.S. (1981). Annotations:List of threatened plants of Middle America. June 29, 1981.

19753 Gentry, H.S. (1981). Annotations: List of threatened plants of Middle America.

19754 Burger, W. (1981). Annotations: List of threatened plants of Middle America.

19755 Rzedowski, J. (1981). Annotations: List of threatened plants of Middle America.

19757 Nauman, L. (1981). Annotations: List of threatened plants of Middle America.

19758 Stolze, R. (1981). Annotations: List of threatened plants of Middle America.

19760 Burt-Utley, K. (1981). Annotations: List of threatened plants of Middle America.

19761 Smith, L.B. (1981). Annotations: List of

threatened plants of Middle America.

19763 **Stevenson, D. (1987).** Annotations: List of threatened plants of Middle America.

19764 **Smith, N.J.H., Williams, J.T., Plucknett, D.L., & Talbot, J.P. (1992).** Tropical forests and their crops. USA: Cornell University. 568 pp.

19766 **Goldblatt, P. & Jenrich, J. (1991).** *Calydorea* Herbert (Iridaceae: Trigridieae): notes on this new world genus and reduction to synonymy of *Salpingostylis, Cardiostigma, Itysa,* and *Catila. Ann. Missouri Bot. Gard.* (78) 2:504-511.

19773 **Meijer, W. & Wong, M. (1993).** *Rafflesia cantleyi* and *R. hasseltii* compared. *Malayan Naturalist* 47(1 & 2):10-12. colour photographs.

19788 **Davidse, G., Sousa S., M., & Chater, A.O. (eds.). (1994).** *Flora Mesoamericana.* México City: Universidad Nacional Autónoma de México. 543 pp. (Vol. 6).

19790 **Utley, J. (1987).** Annotations: List of threatened plants of Middle America. December 17, 1987.

19791 **Plowman, T. (1981).** Annotations: List of threatened plants of Middle America. May, 1981.

19792 **Gómez-Laurito, J. (1982).** Annotations: List of threatened plants of Middle America. July, 1982.

19793 **Holdridge, L. (1982).** Annotations: List of threatened plants of Middle America. March 1982.

19794 **Pringle, J. (1982).** Annotations: List of threatened plants of Middle America. Jan 1982.

19796 **Rudd, V. (1981).** Annotations: List of threatened plants of Middle America. 28 Oct 1981.

19797 **Dempster, L.T. (1981).** Annotations: List of threatened plants of Middle America. November, 1981.

19798 **Kiger, R. (1987).** Annotations: List of threatened plants of Middle America. 14 December 1987.

19800 **Johnston, M.C. (1981).** Annotations: List of threatened plants of Middle America. September 1981.

19801 **Pennington, T. (1982).** Annotations: List of threatened plants of Middle America. January 1982.

19802 **Williams, L.O. (1981).** Annotations: List of threatened plants of Middle America. April 1981.

19803 **Kirkbride, J. (1981).** Annotations: List of threatened plants of Middle America. June 1981.

19804 **Fernández-Pérez, A. (1981).** Annotations: List of threatened plants of Middle America. September 1981.

19805 **Cropper, S.C. (1993).** Management of endangered plants. Victoria, Australia: CSIRO. 182 pp. Includes

case studies of ten species.

19806 **Jermy, A.C. (1994).** Email message from SSC Fern group to Harriet Gillett concerning threat status of *Trichomanes speciosum* in Italy and the Canaries.

19812 **Austin, D.F., de la Puente, F., & Contreras, J. (1991).** *Ipomoea tabascana* an endangered tropical species. *Economic Botany* 45(3):435.

19818 **Hernández-Bermejo, J.E. & Clement Muñoz, M. (1994).** Protección de la flora en Andalucía. Andalucía: Junta de Andalucía, Consejená de Cultura y Medio Ambiente. 217 pp. includes list of endemic and threatened plants, 484 being endemic to Andalucía.

19823 **Soto Arenas, M., Salazar, G., & Rojas, A. (1993).** Nomenclatural changes in *Rhynchostele, Mesoglossum,* and *Lemboglossum* (Orchidaceae, Oncidiinae). *Orquídea*(Méx.) 13(1-2):145-152.

19824 **Cribb, P.J. & Soto Arenas, M. (1993).** The genera *Cypripedium* in Mexico and Central America. *Orquídea* (Méx.) 13(1-3):205-214.

19826 **Teytaud, A.R. (1983).** DRAFT study of management alternatives for the proposed protected areas at Sandy Cay and Norman Island, B.V.I. A report prepared for the BVI Parks and Protected Areas Project. ECNAMP and the Govt. of the British Virgin Islands. 63 pp.

19839 **Dostál, J. (1982).** Seznam. Cévnatych rostlin kveteny Ceskoslovenské. Praha: Prazská Botanická Zahrada Praha-Troja.

19840 **Beldie, A.L. (1977-1979).** Flora Romaniei. Determinator ilustrat al plantelor vasculare. Bucuresti: Editura Acadamiei Repulicii Socialiste România. two volumes.

19841 **Futák, J. & Bertová, L. (eds.). (no date).** Flora Slovenská. Vydavatelstvo Slovenskej. Volume III.

19842 **Hejny, S. & Slavík, B. (eds.). (1988).** Kvetena Ceské Socialistické Republiky I. Prague: Ceskoslovenská Akademie Ved.

19847 **Jordanov, D. (1976).** Flora Reipublicae Populares Bulgarica (Flora of the People's Republic of Bulgaria). Volume VI. Bulgaria: *In* Aedibus Academiae Scientiarum Bulgaricae.

19848 **Organo del Gobierno Constitucional de los Estados Unidos Mexicanos. (1994).** Dario Oficial de la Federación. 3-24 pp. Official list of threatened plants in Mexico.

19850 **Secretaria de Desarrollo Social. (1994).** Las especies y subespecies de flora y fauna silvestres terrestres y acuaticas en peligro de extinción, amenazadas, raras, y las sujetas a protección especial y que establece especificaciones para su protección. Mexico City: Secretaria de Desarrollo Social. Mexican law passed May 16, 1994.

19860 **Puente, R. (1991).** Annotations to: The conservation status listing of threatened plants of

Middle America.

19866 **Hawkes, J.G. (1990).** The potato: evolution, biodiversity and genetic resources. London: Belhaven Press. 259 pp.

19869 **Dressler, R.L. (1993).** Field guide to the orchids of Costa Rica and Panama. Ithaca, NY.: Comstock Publishing Associates. 374 pp.

19873 **Atay, S. (1994).** Annotations to WCMC printout entitled "Turkey - conservation status listing of plants" dated 21 June 1994. Includes list of corrections by Prof.Dr. Neriman Ozhatay.

19874 **Davidse, G. (1994).** Letter to Jane Villa-Lobos dated 4 May 1994.

19878 **Supthut, D. (1994).** Annotations to: conservation status listing of species of Didiereaceae.

19879 **Supthut, D. (1994).** Annotations to conservation status listing of species of Apocynaceae.

19889 **Hodgson, W. (1994).** The Agave Family - information for the SSC Action Plan for Cacti and Succulents.

19890 **Kelly, D.L. (1994).** Systematic list of threatened flowering plant species in the Jamaican flora. List based on the appendix to Kelly, D.L. (1988) The threatened flowering plants of Jamaica. Biological Conservation 46: 201-216.

19893 **Suzan, H., Nabhan, G., & Patten, D. (1994).** Nurse plant and floral biology of a rare night-blooming cereus, *Peniocereus striatus* (Brandegee) F. Bauxhaum. *Biology* 8(2):461-470.

19894 **Patterson, T. (1988).** A new species of *Picea* (Pinaceae) from Nuevo Leon, Mexico. *Sida* 13(2):131-136. Maps.

19904 **Gentry, J.L. & Standley, P.C. (1974).** Solanaceae in Flora of Guatemala. *Fieldiana: Botany.* 24 Part X. Numbers 1 & 2. Field Museum of Natural History.

19907 **Téllez Valdés, O. (1994).** Fax to WCMC containing a preliminary list of *Dioscorea* species from Mexico and Central America dated 14 September 1994.

19909 **Lear, M. (1994).** Fax to Harriet Gillett with additions to the Temperate Tree list dated 22 September 1994.

19911 **Morera, J. & Astorga, C. (eds.). (1993).** II reunion preparatoria para la cracion de la red mesoamericana de recursos fitogeneticos (REMERFI). [Preparatory meeting for the creation of the Mesoamerican Plant Genetic Resources Network REMERFI]. Turialba, Costa Rica: CATIE/IBPGR/IICA. 129 pp.

19915 **Hawkes, J. (1994).** Annotations to WCMC printout entitled "Conservation status listing of *Solanum*".

19919 **Jones, M. (1994).** Letter to Harriet Gillett concerning *Berhautia senegalensis*.

19924 **Barretto, G.D. & Saye, J.L. Y. (1980).** Hong Kong Orchids. Urban Council. 108 pp.

19926 **Meerow, A. (1994).** Annotations to WCMC printout entitled "Threatened Plants of South America".

19932 **Luteyn, J.L. (1994).** Annotations to WCMC printout entitled "List of threatened plants of South America".

19934 **Kraus, F. (1991).** Biodiversity conservation on Guana Island, British Virgin Islands. *Proceedings of the Regional Symposium on Public and Private Cooperation in National Park Development* Road Town, Tortola, British Virgin Islands. 138 pp. British Virgin Islands National Parks Trust.

19937 **Le Sueur, F. (1984).** Flora of Jersey. Jersey, C.I.: Société Jersiaise. 244 pp. maps.

19938 **Roux, J.P., Ryan, P.G., Milton, S.J., & Moloney, C.L. (1992).** Vegetation and checklist of Inaccessible Island, central South Atlantic Ocean, with notes on Nightingale Island. *Bothalia* 22(1):93-109.

19940 **Hammer, M. L.A. (1994).** The status and distribution of *Catharanthus coriaceus* Markgraf (Apocynaceae). *Biodiversity and Conservation* 3:501-511. maps.

19941 **Cooper, J. & Ryan, P.G. (1994).** Management plan for the Gough Island wildlife reserve. Government of Tristan da Cunha. 96 pp. Appendix 5 contains an annotated list of vascular plants recorded from Gough Island.

19943 **Jiménez Madrigal, Q. (1993).** Arboles maderables en peligro de extincion en Costa Rica. San José, Costa Rica: Museo Nacional de Costa Rica. 121 pp.

19947 **Oltean, M. & Negrean, G. et al. (1994).** Lista rosie a plantelor superioare din România. Studii, sinteze, documentatii de Ecologie 1. Bucuresti. 52(2):52.

19949 **Dihoru, G. & Dihoru, A. (1994).** Plante rare, periclitate si endemice in flora Romaniei. Lista rosie Acta Botanica horti Bucurestiensis. 1993-1194 173-197.

19951 **Bertoni, S. et al. (1994).** Flora Amenazada del Paraguay. Ministerio de Agricultura y Ganaderia.

19954 **Cremers, G. (1994).** Annotations to: Threatened plants of French Guiana (South America).

19955 **Dihoru, G. (1994).** Annotations to: Conservation status listing of plants: Romania.

19956 **Dawn, J. (1994).** *Rafflesia* in Temenggor. *Malayan Naturalist* 47(3&4):26-27.

19960 **Soukup, J. (1987).** Vocabulario de los nombres vulgares de la flora peruana y catalogo de los generos. Lima (Peru): Editorial Salesiana. 436 pp.

19961 Encarnación, F. (1983). Nomenclatura de las especies forestales comunes en el Peru. (No.7). Proyecto PNUD/FAO/PERU/81/002. Lima. 147 pp.

19962 Centro de Datos Para la Conservación Peru. (1992). Estado de conservación de la diversidad natural de la región noroeste del Peru. Lima: Universidad Nacional Agraria la Molina. 211 pp.

19964 Centro de Datos para la Conservación Peru. (1991). Plan Director del Sistema Nacional de Unidades de Conservación (SINUC), una aproximación desde la diversidad biológica. Lima (Peru): Universidad Nacional Agraria la Molina. 153 pp.

19965 Tovar, O. (1990). Tipos de vegetación, diversidad floristica y estado de conservación de la cuenca del Mantaro. Lima: Universidad Nacional Agraria La Molina, Centro de Datos para la Conservación Perú. 73 pp.

19966 Tovar, O. (1993). Las Gramineas (Poaceae) del Perú.

19970 Moreno Saiz, J.C. & Sainz Ollero, H. (no date). Atlas corologico de las monocotiledoneas endemicas de la Peninsula Iberica e Islas Baleares. Ministerio de Agricultura Pesca y Alimentacion.

19975 National Research Council. (1989). Lost crops of the Incas: Little known plants of the Andes with promise for worldwide cultivation. Washington D.C.: National Academy Press. 415 pp.

19976 WCMC. (1994). CITES species recorded in TAXATAB.

19977 Vásquez, R. (1989). Plantas utiles de la Amazonia Peruana. (1). Iquitos - Peru. 194 pp.

19997 Cellinese, N., Jarvis, C.E., Press, J.R., Short, M.J., & Viciani, D. (comps.). (1994). Threatened plants of Italy. Interim Report. European Plant Information Centre.

20007 Anon. (1995). Convention on the conservation of European Wildlife and Natural Habitats - Proposal for amendment to Appendix 1 Presented by Cyprus. Strasbourg: Council of Europe. 8 pp. Proposes addition of *Centaurea akamantis*.

20013 Werner, W. (1995). Annotations to WCMC printout entitled "Conservation status listing for Sri Lanka".

20015 Nakaike, T. (1995). Annotations to WCMC printout entitled "Cconservation status listing of tree ferns of Japan".

20016 Osborne, R. (1995). The world cycad census and a proposed revision of the threatened species status for cycad taxa. *Biological Conservation* 71(1):1-12.

20017 Nakaike, T. (1992). New flora of Japan, pteridophytes. 868 pp.

20018 Huang, T.C. (ed.). (1994). Flora of Taiwan (2nd ed.). Pteridophyta Gymnospermae. Taipei: Editorial Committee of the Flora of Taiwan. 1-648 pp. Keys.

20025 Hágsater, E. (1993). The genus *Epidendrum*. Part 1. A century of new species in *Epidendrum*. *Icones Orchidacearum*. Fascicle 2. 1-100 pp.

20035 Smith, A.R. & Grayum, M.H. (1988). *Cyathea stolzei* x *ursina*, a distinctive tree fern hybrid from Costa Rica. *Amer. Fern J.* 78(3):105-108.

20039 Braun, K. (1994). Swaziland National Trust Commission threatened plant database printout. Includes letter from Kate Braun (SNTC) to Harriet Gillett (WCMC).

20041 Reynel, C. & Pennington, T. (1989). Reporte sobre los cedros y su situación en el Perú, una contribucción al conocimiento y la conservación de las Meliáceas peruanas. Lima: Universidad Nacional Agaria La Molina, Centro de Datos Para la Conservación Perú. 100 pp.

20042 Reynel, C. (1986). Aproximación a la taxonomia, distribución y status de las Moráceas peruanas. Lima: Universidad Nacional Agraria La Molina. Facultad de Ciencias Forestales.

20045 Kramer, K.U. & Green, P.S. (eds.). (1990). The families and genera of vascular plants. Volume 1. Pteridophytes and Gymnosperms. Springer-Verlag. 404 pp.

20046 Carpio, C. (1994). Annotations to: Threatened Plants of South America - Peru.

20050 Nelson, C. (1995). Annotations to: Conservation status listing of threatened plants of Honduras returned February 21, 1995.

20051 Leigh, J.H. & Briggs, J.D. (1992). Threatened Australian plants. Overview and Case Studies. Australian National Parks and Wildlife Service. 120 pp.

20057 Beentje, H.J. (1994). Kenya trees, shrubs and lianas. Nairobi, Kenya: National Museums of Kenya. 722 pp. includes IUCN threat category.

20064 Eggli, U. & Taylor, N. (eds.). (1994). List of names of succulent plants other than cacti. Whitstable, Kent: Whitstable Litho. 176 pp. From Repertorium Plantarum Succulentarum (1950-1992).

20065 Lock, J.M. & Heald, J. (1994). Legumes of Indo-China. A checklist. The Royal Botanic Gardens, Kew. 164 pp.

20067 Anderson, E.F., Arias Montes, S., & Taylor, N.P. (1994). Threatened cacti of Mexico. Kew, England: The Royal Botanic Gardens, Kew. 135 pp.

20071 Dransfield, J. & Beentje, H.J. (1995). Palms of Madagascar. Royal Botanic Garden, Kew. 500 pp. Includes IUCN threat categories.

20072 Grubb, P.J. & Tanner, E.V.J. (1976). The montane forests and soils of Jamaica: a reassessment.

Journal of the Arnold Arboretum 57:313-368. maps.

20074 **Gentry, A.H. (1992).** Bignoniaceae - Part II (Tribe Tecomeae). *Flora Neotropica Monograph* No.25(II).

20076 **Ramos Lopes, M.H. & Carvalho, M.L.S. (1990).** Lista de espécies botanicas a proteger em Portugal Continental. [List of botanical species in need of protection in continental Portugal]. Lisboa, Portugal: Ministerio do Ambiente e dos Recursos Naturais. 11 pp.

20078 **U.S. Department of the Interior. Fish and Wildlife Service. (1995).** Memorandum requesting information on Acuña cactus (*Echinomastus erectocentrus*) including a status summary.

20079 **U.S. Department of the Interior. Fish and Wildlife Service. (1993).** Endangered and threatened wildlife and plants. (50 CFR 17.11 & 17.12).

20081 **Pereira Carauta, J.P. (1989).** *Ficus*(Moraceae) no Brazil: Conservaçao e taxonomia. *Albertoa* 2(1):1-350.

20083 **Aronsson, M., Hallingbäck, T., & Mattsson, J.-E. (eds.). (1995).** Rödliste växter i Sverige. [Swedish Red Data Book of plants]. Lists 445 threatened vascular plants.

20084 **Morat, Ph., Deroin, Th., & Couderc, H. (1994).** Présence en Nouvelle-Calédonie d'une espéce endémique du genre *Oryza* L. (Gramineae). *Bull. Mus. Natl. Hist. Nat,* Paris (4) 16(1):3-10.

20085 **Anon. (1994).** Flora Conservation. Revised 1994 CAFF lists of flora at risk in the circumpolar Arctic. Appendix 1. 39 pp.

20087 **Gillett, J.B. (1993).** Annotations to WCMC printout entitled "Kenya Conservation Status Listing of Plants - annotated by Jan B. Gillett". Includes letter to Harriet Gillett with additional comments.

20093 **Zamora, P.M. & Co, L. (1986).** Guide to Philippine flora and fauna. Vol. III. Ecomonic Ferns, Endemic Ferns and Gymnosperms. Quezon City: Ministry of Natural Resources & University of the Philippines. 268 pp.

20099 **Ng, P.K.L. & Wee, Y.C. (eds.). (1994).** The Singapore Red Data Book. Threatened Plants and Animals of Singapore. Singapore: The Nature Society. 343 pp.

20103 **Taylor, P. (1989).** The genus *Utricularia* - a taxonomic monograph. Kew Bulletin Additional Series IV.

20118 **Villasenor, J.L., Dávila, P., & Chiang, F. (1990).** Fitogeografia del Valle de Tehuacán-Cuicatlán. *Biol. Soc. Bot. México* 50:135-149.

20137 **Delucchi, G. & Correa, R.F. (1992).** Situacion ambiental de la Provincia de Buenos Aires. A. Recursos y rasgos naturales en la evaluación ambiental. Las especies vegetales amenazadas de la Provincia de Buenos Aires. La Plata: Provinicia de Buenos Aires Comisión de

Investigaciones Cientificas. 39 pp.

20146 **Ghazanfar, S.A. (1995).** Plant conservation in Oman. Part 1. A study of the endemic, regionally endemic and threatened plants of the Sultanate of Oman. 62 pp. Compiled with Anthony G. Miller, Ian McLeish, Tom A. Cope, Phil Cribb and Salim H. Al Rawahi.

20155 **Norman, E. (1995).** Annotations to: list of threatened plants of Latin America, 9 February 1995.

20162 **Beentje, H. (1995).** Letter to Charlotte Jenkins with information regarding threatened plants in Kenya and threatened palms in Madagascar.

20171 **Tutin, T.G., Heywood, V.H., Burges, N.A., Valentine, D.H., Walters, S.M., & Webb, D.A. (eds.). (1995).** Flora Europaea Vol 1-5. Electronic dataset supplied by R.J Pankhurst, Royal Botanic Garden Edinburgh, May 1995.

20175 **Aronsson, M., Hallingbäck, T., & Mattsson, J.-E. (eds.). (1995).** Rödlistade växter i Sverige 1995. [Swedish red data book of plants 1995]. Uppsala: ArtDatabanken. 271 pp.

20176 **Chebez, J.C. (1994).** Los que se van. Especies Argentinas en peligro. Buenos Aires, Argentina: Albatros. 604 pp. Con ilustraciones de Aldo Chiappe.

20178 **Vangjeli, J., Ruci, B., & Mullaj, A. (1995).** Libri i kuq. Bimët e kërcënuara e të rralla të Shqipërisë. [Red Book of threatened and rare plant species of Albania]. Tirana: Akademia e Shkencave e Republikës Së Shqipërisë & Instituti I Kërkimeve Biologjike Komiteti I Mbrojtjes Së Mjedisit. 169 pp. Lists 320 rare and threatened plants, including 4 extinct and 12 probably extinct species.

20185 **Lorence, D., Flynn, T., & Wagner, W.L. (1995).** Contributions to the flora of Hawai'i III. New additions, range extensions and rediscoveries of flowering plants. *Bishop Museum Occasional Papers* 41:19-58.

20202 **Jacobsen, H. (1970).** Lexicon of succulent plants.

20204 **Ansari, M.Y. (1971).** *Ceropegia media* (Huber) Ansari stat. nov. from Western Ghats (Maharashtra). *Bull. Bot. Survey India* 11:199-201.

20206 **Bally, P.R.O. (1965).** Miscellaneous notes on the flora of tropical East Africa, including descriptions of new taxa, 23-28. *Candollea* 20:13-41.

20207 **Dyer, R.A. (1983).** *Ceropegia, Brachystelma* and *Riocreuxia* in Southern Africa. Rotterdam: A.A. Balkema. 242 pp.

20211 **Albers, F. & Meve, U. (1995).** Annex 2: List of Asclepiadaceae of conservation concern. *In* SSC Action Plan for cacti and succulents. 6 pp.

20212 **Bruyns, P.V. (1989).** The genus *Ceropegia* in Arabia. *Notes Roy. Bot. Gard. Edinburgh* 45:287-326.

20213 Meve, U. & Liede, S. (1994). A conspectus of *Ceropegia*.L (Asclepiadaceae) in Madagascar, and the establishment of C. sect *Dimorpha* (Engl.). *Phyton* 34(1):131-142.

20216 Francisco-Ortego, J., Hawkes, J.G., Lester, R.N., & Acebes-Ginovés, J.R. (1993). *Normania*, an endemic Macaronesian genus distinct from *Solanum* (Solanaceae). *Plant Systematics and Evolution* 185:189-205.

20224 Soerianegara, I. & Lemmens, R.H.M.J. (eds.). (1993). PROSEA 5(1). Timber trees: major commercial timbers. Wageningen: Pudoc Scientific Publishers. 610 pp.

20228 Malaisse, F. & Schaijes, M. (1993). Notes on the Ceropegias of South East Zaire. *Asklepios* 58:21-30.

20263 Ved, D.K. (1995). Plants under threat - New List Forged. (from FRLHT). *AMRUTH* 5:2-3.

20264 Carter, S. (1994). Aloaceae *in* Flora of Tropical East Africa. Rotterdam: A.A. Balkema. 60 pp.

20266 Sane, H.D. & Ghate, V.S. (1993). Range extension of endemic *Ceropegia huberi* Ansari in Maharashtra. *Journal Bombay Natural History Society* 90:126-127.

20271 Friis, I. (1992). Forests and Forest Trees of Northeast Tropical Africa. Their Natural Habitats and Distribution Patterns in Ethiopia, Djibouti and Somalia. Middlesex, UK: HMSO. 396 pp.

20272 Bingham, M. (1995). Letter to Mike Maunder concerning conservation status of *Calandrinia feltonii*.

20273 Albers, F. (1995). Annotations to WCMC printout entitle "Conservation status listing of *Ceropegia*".

20274 Hawthorne, W.D. (1995). Ecological profiles of Ghanaian forest trees. Oxford Forestry Institute. 345 pp. Tropical Forestry Papers 29.

20276 Bruyns, P.V. (1984). *Ceropegia*, *Brachystelma* and *Tenaris* in South West Africa. *Dinteria* 17:3-80.

20283 Govaerts, R. (1994). Checklist of *Quercus* species world wide.

20306 Gerbaulet, M. (1992). Die gattung *Anacampseros* L. (Portulacaceae). Untersuchungen zur systematik. [The genus *Anacampseros* L. (Portulacaceae). Investigations into systematics]. *Bot. Jahrb Syst.* 113(4):477-564.

20308 Rowley, G.D. (1994). *Anacampseros* and allied genera - a reassessment. *Bradleya* 12:105-112.

20310 Reitz, R., Klein, R.M., & Reis, A. (1978).

Projeto Madeira de Santa Catarina. Levantamento das espécies florestais nativas em Santa Catarina com a possibilidade de incremento e desenvolvimento. Itajaí, Santa Catarina: Herbário "Barbosa Rodrigues" - HBR. 320 pp.

20311 Reitz, R., Klein, R.M., & Reis, A. (1983). Projeto Madeira de Rio Grande do Sul. Levantamento das espécies florestais nativas com possibilidade de incremento e desenvolvimento. Herbário "Barbosa Rodrigues" - HBR. 528 pp.

20316 Hill, K. (1994). Extract from Flora of Australia Vol 48 - Gymnosperms. keys.

20318 Stanley, & Ross. (1989). Flora of South Eastern Queensland. Vol.3. Brisbane: Qsld. Dept. Primary Industries. keys.

20326 Allan, H.H. (1961). Flora of New Zealand. (1). Wellington: R.E.Owen, Government Printer. 1085 pp. keys.

20328 Quinn, C.J. (1982). The Taxonomy of *Dacrydium* Sol. ex Lamb emend de Laub (Podocarpaceae). *Australian Journal of Botany* 30:311-320. Keys.

20329 Laubenfels, D.J. de. (1972). Flore de la Nouvelle-Calédonie et Dépendances. (4). Gymnospermes. Paris: Muséum National d'Histoire Naturelle. 167 pp. Maps, illus.

20333 Laubenfels, D.J. de & Silba, J. (1987). The *Agathis* of Espiritu Santo (*Araucariaceae*, New Hebrides. *Phytologia* 61:448-452. Illus.

20337 Silba, J. (1984). An International Census of the Coniferae. *Phytologia* 7:3-79. Checklist.

20342 Page, C.N. (1988). New and Maintained Genera in the Conifer Families Podocarpaceae and Pinaceae. *Notes From the Royal Botanic Garden Edinburgh* 45(2):377-395.

20343 Laubenfels, D. de. (1984). Un neuvo *Podocarpus* (Podocarpaceae) de la Espanola. *Moscosoa* 3:149-150.

20344 McVaugh, R. (1992). Flora Novo-Galiciana. Vol 17 Gymnosperms and Pteridophytes. Ann Arbor, Michigan: University of Michigan Herbarium. 467 pp. Keys, illus.

20346 Morin, N.R. (ed.). (1993). Flora of North America - North of Mexico. Pteridophytes and Gymnosperms Vol 2. New York: Oxford University Press. 475 pp. Keys, maps, illus.

20350 Laubenfels, D. de. (1982). Flora de Venezuela. Podocarpaceae. Caracas: Instito Nacional de Parques, Educacion Ambiental. 71-86 pp. Keys, illus.

20352 Leroy, J. (ed.). (1972). Flore de Madagascar et des Comores. Gymnospermes. Paris: Museum National D'Histoire Naturelle. 25 pp. Keys.

20353 Laubenfels, D. de. (1991). The Podocarpaceae of Costa Rica. *Brenesia* 33:119-121. Keys.

20354 **Killeen, T.J. (1993).** Guia de Arboles de Bolivia. La Paz, Bolivia: Herbario Nacional de Bolivia. Keys.

20356 **Silba, J. (1990).** Supplement to the International Census of the Coniferae II. *Phytologia* 68(1):7-78. Checklist.

20358 **Tripp, K.E. (1995).** *Cephalotaxus* The Plum Yew. *Arnoldia* 55(1):24-40. Illus.

20362 **Laubenfels, D. de. (1985).** Taxonomic Revision of *Podocarpus*. *Blumea* 30(2):251-278. Keys.

20365 **Zanoni, T.A. & Hager, J. (1993).** Le Vegetation Natural de la Republica Dominicana; un Neuvo Classification. *Moscosoa* 3:39-81. Illus.

20366 **Haber, W.A. (1991).** Lista Provisional de las Plantas de Monteverde, Costa Rica. *Brenesia* 34:63-120. checklist.

20367 **Laubenfels, D. de. (1969).** A Revision of the Malesian and Pacific Rainforest Conifers. Parts 1 & 2. *Journal of the Arnold Arboretum* 50:274-369. Keys, maps.

20368 **Staskiewicz, J. (1988).** A taxonomic revision of the genus *Podocarpus* from the Greater and Lesser Antilles. *Fragmenta Floristica et Geobotanica* 33(1-2):71-106. Keys, maps.

20369 **Zanoni, T.A. (1982).** Flora de Veracruz. *Taxodiaceae* Fasc. 25. Xalapa, Veracruz: Instituto Nacional de Investigacions Sobre Recursos Bioticos.

20372 **Kirkpatrick, J. (1989).** The Conservation and Reservation Status of Tasmanian Higher Plants. Wildlife Division Scientific Report No. 91/2. Hobart: Department of Parks, Wildlife and Heritage. Maps.

20374 **Adam, P. (1992).** Australian Rainforests. New York: Oxford University Press. 137-178 pp. Maps, illus.

20376 **Dvorak, W.S. & Donahue, J.K. (1992).** CAMCORE Cooperative Research Review 1980-1992. Forestry Department, North Carolina State University, USA: CAMCORE (La Cooperativa de Recursos de Coníferas de Centroamérica y México). 94 pp. Maps, illus.

20377 **Troupin, G. (ed.). (1982).** Flore des plantes ligneuses de Rwanda. Terverun, Belgium: Musée Royal de L'afrique Central. Keys, illus.

20387 **Thulin, M. (1993).** Flora of Somalia - Vol 1. Surrey: RBG Kew. Keys.

20389 **Barry, J.P. (1970).** Essai de monographie du *Cupressus dupreziana* A.Camus, cyprés endémique du Tassili des Ajier (Sahara Central). *Bull. Soc. Hist. Nat. Afrique Nord Alger* 61:95-178. Maps, illus.

20406 **Ibanez, J. et al. (1989).** Data on a Population of *Tetraclinis articulata* (Vahl) Masters. *Ecologia* 3:99-106.

20409 **Jaffre, T., Veillon, J.M., & Cherrier, J.F. (1987).** on the occurence of two Cupressaceae. *Neocallitropsis pancheri* and *Libocedrus austrocaledonica* in the Mt Paéua area and new sites for the gymnospems in New Caledonia. *Bulletin de Museum National d'Histoire Naturelle Section B Adansonia* 9(3):273-288. Maps.

20416 **Sachsse, H. & Schulte, E. (1987).** Some important wood properties of the Bolivian *Podocarpus parlatorei*. *Holz Als Roh-Und Werkstoff* 45(12):475-480.

20418 **Martinez, P. (1981).** Flora and phytosociology of relict stands containing *Pilgerodendron uviferum* in San Pablode Tregua Farm. *Bosque* 4(1):3-11.

20419 **Silba, M.D.G. (1983).** Flora de Mocambique - 1. Cycadaceae. 2. Podocarpaceae. 3. Cupressaceae. Lisbon: Instituto de Investigaçao Cientifica Tropical. 44 pp. Keys, illus.

20427 **Stein, A.H. (1956).** Natural Forests of Chile. *Unasylva* 10(4):155-161. Maps, illus.

20430 **Houerou, H.N. (1969).** Le Vegetation de la Tunisie Steppique. [Vegetation of the Tunisian Steppe]. *Annales de l'Institut National de la Recherche Agronimique de Tunisie* 42(5):620. Maps, illus.

20437 **Whitmore, T.C. (1977).** A First Look at *Agathis*. Tropical Forestry Papers No. 11 Oxford: Unit of Tropical Silviculture, Dept. of Forestry, Comm. For. Institute. Maps, illus.

20438 **Ntima, O.O. (1968).** The Araucarias - fast growing timber trees of the tropics. Trees of the Lowland Tropcis No. 3. Oxford: Unit of Tropical Silviculture, Dept. of Forestry, Comm. For. Institute. Maps, illus.

20443 **Laubenfels, D. de. (1978).** The Taxonomy of Philippine Coniferae and Taxaceae. *Kalikasan* 7(2):117-152. Keys.

20445 **Birks, J.S. & Barnes, R.D. (1990).** Provenance variation in *Pinus caribbaea*, *Pinus oocarpa* and *Pinus patula* ssp. *tecunumanii*. Tropical Forestry Papers No.21 Oxford: Unit for Tropical Silviculture, Comm. For. Instit., Univ. of Oxford. Maps, illus.

20452 **Whitmore, T.C. (ed.). (1972).** Tree Flora of Malaya - a Manual for Foresters Vol 1. Hong Kong: Longman. 470 pp. Illus.

20454 **Pham-Hoáng, H. (ed.). (1991).** An Illustrated Flora of Vietnam. (3). Saigon: Mekong Press. Illus., keys.

20456 **Little, E.L. & Critchfield, W.B. (1966).** Geographic Distribution of the Pines of the World. USDA Misc. Pub. No. 991 Washington: United States Department of Agriculture. 100 pp. Maps.

20457 **Wolf, C.B. & Wagener, W.W. (1948).** The New

World Cypresses. Vol.1 Pt.1. Anaheim: Rancho Santa Ana
Botanical Garden. 1-248 pp. Maps, illus.

20458 Barnes, R.D. & Styles, B.T. (1983). The Closed
Cone Pines of Mexico and Central America. *Comm.
For. Review* 62:81-84. Maps, keys, illus.

20460 Darrow, W.K. & Zanoni, T.A. (1990).
Hispaniolan *Pinus occidentalis* - a little
known pine of economic potential. *Comm. For.
Rev.* 6969(2

20464 Orchard, A.E. (ed.). (1994). Flora of
Australia. Vol. 49 - Oceanic Islands. Canberra:
Australian Government Publishing Service. Keys, maps.

20465 Bailey, D.K. (1983). A new allopatric
segregate from a new combination in *Pinus
cembroides* Zucc. at its southern limits.
Phytologia 54(2):89-101. Keys, maps.

20468 Styles, B.T. & Hughes, C.E. (1983). Studies of
variation in Central American Pines 3. Notes on the
taxonomy and nomenclature of the pine and related
gymnosperms in Honduras and the adjacent Latin American
Republics. *Brenesia* 21:269-291. Keys, maps.

20471 Styles, B.T. & McCarter, P.S. (1988). The
Botany, Ecology, Distribution and Conservation Status of
Pinus patula ssp. *tecunumanii* in the
Republic of Honduras. *Ceiba* 24(1-2):3-31.
Maps, illus.

20475 Taylor, R.J. & Patterson, T.F. (1980).
Biosystematics of Mexican Spruce species and
Populations. *Taxon* 29(4):421-467. Maps, illus.

20477 Beaman, R.S. & Beaman, J. (1993). The
Gymnosperms of Mt Kinabalu. *Contributions from the
University of Michigan Herbarium* 19:307-341.
Checklist.

20479 Riskind, D.H. & Patterson, T.F. (1975).
Distributional and ecological notes on *Pinus
culminicola. Madrono* 23:159-161. Maps.

20480 Gordon, A.G. (1968). The ecology of *Picea
chihuhuana* Mart. *Ecology* 49:880-896.
Maps, illus.

20481 Tioong, S.K.K. (1984). *Podocarpus
laubenfelsii* ; a new species from Borneo.
Blumea 29:523-524.

20482 Whitmore, T.C. (1980). A monograph of
*Agathis. Plamt Systematics and
Evolution* 135:41-69. Keys, maps.

20485 Yuncker, T.G. (1959). Plants of Tonga.
Bernice P. Bishop Museum Bulletin 220:283.

20487 Hancock, I.R. & Henderson, C.P. (1988). Flora
of the Solomon Islands. research Bulletin No.7. Dodo
Creek Research Station Honiara: Research Department,
Ministry of Agriculture and Lands.

20489 Pisano, E. (1983). The Magellanic Tundra
Complex. Ecosystems of the World 4b: Mires, Swamp, Bog,

Fen and Moor. Amsterdam: Elsevier. 295-328 pp.

20493 Steyermark, J.A. (1986). Speciation and
Endemism in the Flora of the Venezuelan Tepuis. p. 644
in High Altitude Tropical Biogeography. New York: Oxford
Uni. Press.

20495 Ferguson, D.K. (1985). A new species of
Amentotaxus (Taxaceae) from North Eastern
India. *Kew Bulletin* 40(1):115-119.

20496 Ferguson, D.K. (1989). On Vietnamese
*Amentotaxus. Bull. Mus. Natn. Hist. Nat.
Paris* (4) 11.

20497 Kolbeck, J. & Kucera, M. (1989). A Brief
Survey of Selected Woody Species of North Korea.
Pruhonice, Czechoslovakia: Botanical Institute, Czech
Academy of Sciences.

20501 Hayashi, Y. (1952). The Natural Distribution
of Important Trees Indigenous to Japan. Conifers: Report
2. *Bull. Govt. For. Experimental Station*
Tokyo. Maps, illus.

20502 Hayashi, Y. (1951). The Natural Distribution
of Important Trees Indigenous to Japan. Conifers: Report
1. *Bull. Govt. For. Experimental Station*
Tokyo. Maps, illus.

20507 Page, C.N. (1980). *Picea farreri*, a
new temperate conifer from upper Burma. *Notes from
the Royal Botanic Garden Edinburgh* 38(1):129-136.
Maps, illus.

20509 Donahue, J.K. (1995). Observations on
Pinus maximartinezii Rzedowski.
Madrono 42(1):19-25. Maps, illus.

**20511 Taiwan Endemic Species Research Institute.
(1995).** Conservation Status Listing of Plants in
Taiwan (Draft). 79 pp.

20513 Prospect. (1995). Species listing from the
PROSPECT database. Distributions and names of c. 1250
species.

**20528 Olivier, L., Galland, J., & Maurin, H. (eds.).
(1995).** Livre rouge de la flore menacée de France.
Tome 1: Espèces prioritaires. [Red book of threatened
plants of France. Volume 1: Priority species]. Paris:
Muséum National d'Histoire Naturelle. 486 pp.

20556 Knox, E.B. (1995). The List of East African
Plants (LEAP): An electronic database (Draft). 72 pp.

20572 Timberlake, J.R. (1995). Annotations to WCMC
printout entitled "Conservation status listing for
Zimbabwe".

20574 Timberlake, J.R. & Mapaure, I. (1992).
Vegetation and its conservation in the Eastern
mid-Zambezi valley, Zimbabwe. *Transactions of the
Zimbabwe Scientific Association* 66:1-14. maps.

20575 Timberlake, J.R. & Shaw, P. (eds.). (1994).
Chirinda forest - a visitor's guide. Harare, Zimbabwe:
Division of Research & Development, Zimbabwe Forestry

Commission. 158 pp.

20578 **Supthut, D. & Nyffeler, R. (comps.). (1994).**
List of Madagascar succulent plant species. Annex to the
Succulent Action Plan 1995. 11 pp.

20580 **Gioda, A. (1994).** Fax to Gérard Sournia
concerning rediscovery of *Bipinnula*
taltalensis in Chile.

20587 **Wigginton, M. (1995).** British Red Data Books:
vascular plants - draft list. 8 pp. Includes old and new
IUCN categories.

20593 **Lawalrée, A. & Delvosalle, L. (1969).**
Ptéridophytes et Spermatophytes rares, disparus ou
menacées de disparition en Belgique. Delvosale, L.,
Demare, F., Lambinon, J. & Lawalrée Plantes rares,
disparues our menacées de disparition en Belgique:
L'appauvrissement de la flore indigène. Min.V. Landbouw,
Best. V. Watres En Bossen, Dienst Domaniale
Natuurreservaten En Natuurbescherming, Werken Nr.4.
23-96 pp.

20604 **Hilton-Taylor, C. (1996).** Red Data List of
southern African plants. Strelitzia 4. Pretoria, South
Africa: National Botanical Institute. 117 pp.

20609 **Colling, G. & Reichling, L. (1995).** Red data
book of Luxembourg: Pteridophyta and Spermatophyta.
Draft document.

20618 **Guener, A. (1995).** Conservation status of
Turkish woody plants. 12 pp.

20619 **Németh, F. (1995).** Letter to Donna Smith
containing annotations to WCMC list of plants of
Hungary.

20620 **Kuusk, V. (1995).** Annotations to WCMC list of
plants of Estonia, both nationally and globally
threatened.

20625 **Oates, M.R. & de Lange, P.J. (1995).**
Annotations to: Conservation status listing of plants of
New Zealand.

20626 **Ohba, H. (1995).** List of endangered tree
species of Japan. 4 pp.

20627 **Degteva, S. (1995).** Annotations to WCMC list
of plants of the Russian Federation.

20628 **Czerepanov, S.K. (ed.). (1995).** Plantae
vasculares rossicae et civitatum collimitanearum. St
Petersburg: World and Family-95 Ltd. 990 pp. Russian
Edition.

20631 **Sávulescu, T. (ed.). (1952-1970).** Flora
Republicü Populare Române. Bucuresti: Flora Republicii
Sócialist România.

20635 **Dihoru, G. (1987).** Plante endemice in flora
României. Bucuresti: Editura Ceres. 183 pp.

20640 **Korneck, D., Schnittler, M., & Vollmer, I.**
(1995). Rote Liste der Fern- und Blütenpflanzen. in
in Rote Listen Gefährdeter Pflanzen in

Deutschland. - Schr.R. Vegetations Kunde. Germany:
Bundesamt Für Naturschutz. in preparation.

20644 **Schnittler, M. (1995).** Annotations to WCMC
list of plants of Germany, including new list of
datasources for Germany.

20645 **Mavol, J. (1995).** Annotations to WCMC list of
plants of the Balearic Islands, including new list of
datasources for the Balearic Islands.

20647 **Mus, M. (1994).** Conservation of flora in the
Balearic Islands. in *Ecologia Mediterranea*
20(3).

20648 **Castroviejo, S., Lainz, M., Lopez Gonzalez, G.,**
Montserrat, P., Muñoz Garmendia, F., Paiva, J., &
Villar, L. (1993). Flora Ibérica. Plantas
vasculares de la Península Ibérica e Islas Baleares.
Volumes I-IV 1986-1993. Madrid: Real Jardín Botánico.
CSIC.

20649 **Anon. (1936-1965).** Flora of UkrSSR. Kiev:
Publishing House of Academy of Sciences of Ukrssr. vol.
1-12.

20650 **Andrienko, T.L. (1995).** Annotations to WCMC
list of plants of Ukraine, including new list of
datasources for Ukraine.

20651 **Mus, M. (1983).** Plans de Conservació dels
Vegetals Amenaçats de les Balears. I. Mallorca. II
Menorca. III Pitiuses. Palma de Mallorca: Conselleria
d'Agricultura i Pesca. Govern Balear.

20653 **Anon. (1987).** Determinant of higher plants of
Ukraine. Kiev: Naukova Dumka. 546 pp.

20654 **Anon. (1972).** Determinant of higher plants of
Crimea. Leningrad: Nauka. 560 pp.

20655 **Anon. (1994).** Red Book of the Ukraine. Kiev:
Ukrainska Encyclopedia. part 1, animals part 2, plants
in print.

20656 **Rossello, J.A., Cubas, P., & Torres, N.**
(1992). An annotated check-list of the Balearic
vascular flora. I. Pteridophyta-Coniferophytina.
Candollea 47:61-69.

20659 **Mus, M. (1990).** Taxonomia i nomenclatura de
plantes baleàriques. In *Boll. Soc. Hist. Nat.*
Balears 32:153-154.

20660 **Aparicio, A. (1995).** Annotations to WCMC list
of plants of Spain, including new list of datasources
for Spain.

20661 **Rivas-Martinez, S., Asensi, A., Molero, J., &**
Valle, F. (1991). Endemisms vasculars de Andalucía.
Rivaggodaya 6:5-76.

20662 **Castroviejo, S. et al. (1990).** Flora Iberica
II.

20664 **Aparicio, A. (1993).** Plans de separación de
species vegetales avenatodes en el Parque Natural Sierra
de Grazelema (Cádiz-Málaga). *Acta Bot.*

Malacitana 18:199-221.

20665 **Aparicio, A. & Guisande, R. (1995).** Ecologia, Conservación de *Echinospartum algibicum* Talever & Mpauho (Gelinteae, Fabaceae). *Acta Bot. Malacitana* 20. in press.

20671 **Smith, A.C. (1971).** Studies of Pacific Island Plants, XXIII. The Genus Diospyros (Ebenaceae) in Fiji, Samoa, and Tonga. *Journal of the Arnold Arboretum* 52(3):369-403.

20673 **Rassi, P., Kaipainen, H., Mannerkoski, I., & Stehls, G. (eds.). (1992).** Uhanalaisten elinten ja kasvien seurantatoimikunnan mietint. [Report on the monitoring of threatened animals and plants in Finland]. Helsinki: Ministry of the Environment. 328 pp. in Finnish.

20676 **Lemmens, R.H.M.J., Soerianegara, I., & Wong, W.C. (eds.). (1995).** Plant Resources of South-East Asia No 5(2). Timber Trees: Minor commercial timbers. Leiden: Backhuys Publishers. 655 pp.

20677 **Ammann, K., Derron, M., Landolt, E., & Moser, D.H. (1995).** Annotations and additions to WCMC printout entitled "Switzerland - globally threatened taxa. Status report as of 3 October 1995".

20678 **Sunderland, T. & Ndam, N. (eds.). (1994).** Mount Cameroon Project - 1st annual science review. 31 pp.

20681 **Briggs, J.D. & Leigh, J.H. (1996).** Rare or threatened Australian plants. Melbourne, Australia: CSIRO Publications.

20686 **Rakonczay, Z. (ed.). (1990).** Voros Konyu. [Hungarian Red Data Book]. Budapest: Akadémiai Kiadó. 360 pp.

20689 **Nooteboom, H.P. (1985).** Notes on Magnoliaceae with a revision of *Pachylarnax* and *Elmerrillia* and the Malesian species of *Manglietia* and *Michelia*. *Blumea* 31:65-121.

20690 **Laguna, E. (1995).** Annotations to WCMC list of plants of Spain. Report about Valencian exclusive endemics.

20692 **Laguna, E. (comp.). (1994).** Libro de la flora vascular rara, endémica o amenazada de la Comunidad Valenciana. Valencia: Conselleria de Medi Ambient de la Generalitat Valenciana. 275 pp. with 400 colour photographs.

20698 **Güner, A. & Zielinski, J. (comps.). (1995).** The conservation status of the Turkish woody flora. 17 pp.

20699 **Mateo, G. & Crespo, M.B. (1990).** Claves para la flora valenciana. *Del Cenia al Segura*. Valencia.

20700 **Olivares, A., Peris, J.B., Stübing, G., & Martin, J. (1995).** *Cheirolophus lagunae* sp. nov. (Asteraceae). endemismo iberolevantino. *Anales Jard. Bot. Madrid* 53(2):

20701 **Crespo, M.B. (1995).** pers. com. concerning *Limonium scopulorum* from Dr M.B. Crespo of University of Alicante to E. Laguna.

20704 **Carvalho, M.L.S. & Arriegas, P.I. (1995).** Letter to Harriet Gillett concerning endangered plants in Portugal. Includes annotated printouts of Portugal dated 6 October 1995.

20705 **Arriegas, P.I., Carvalho, M.L.S., & Serra, M.G.L. (1992).** Portuguese Plants in the Bern Convention (Appendix I). Systematics and Conservation Evaluation. London: N.H.M. Poster.

20706 **Cotrim, H.M. & Pinto, M.J.G. (1994).** Population distribution and colonisation habitat patterns in southwest Portuguese endemic *Silene rothmaleri* P. Silva. *Journadas de Fitossociologia* XIV.

20709 **Nooteboom, H.P. (1996).** The Magnoliaceae of China (Draft).

20710 **Alziar, G. (1995).** Annotations to WCMC list of plants of Cyprus.

20720 **Tóth, E. (1996).** Letter with Hungarian endemic plant data from literature: "1990 Hungarian Red Book", "Identification Book of the Hungarian vascular flora" and "Save the Wild Flowers".

20726 **Jeanmonod, D. (1996).** Annotations to list entitled "Corsica - all taxa listed in the WCMC plants database".

20727 **Fandos, J. (1996).** Annotations of WCMC list of plants of the Balearic Islands.

20728 **Castroviejo, S. et al. (1986-1993).** Flora Iberica. Plantas vasculares de la Península Ibérica e Islas Baleares. Madrid. vol. 1-4.

20730 **Montmollin, B. de & Kamari, G. (1996).** Annotations to WCMC printout entitled "Crete - nationally threatened taxa listed at WCMC" dated 21 December 1995.

20731 **Tzanoudakis, D. & Montmollin, B. de. (1996).** Annotations to WCMC printout entitled "Greece - nationally threatened taxa listed at WCMC" dated 16 October 1995.

20732 **Bolós, O. & Vigo, J. (1984-1990).** Flora dels Països Catalans. Barcelona. vol. 1-2.

20733 **Katende, A.B. (1995).** Annotations to: WCMC printout of Trees of Uganda dated 23 Nov. 1995.

20736 **Pla, V., Sastre, D., & Llorens, L. (1992).** Aproximació al catàleg de la flora de les Illes Balears. Palma de Mallorca.

20738 **Raimondo, F. (1996).** Annotations to WCMC list - Sicily all taxa listed.

20739 **Chin, S.C. & Kiew, R. (1985).** *Malayan Naturalist* 39(1&2):23.

20740 Jacobsen, N. (1987). *Malayan Naturalist* 40*40(3*

20742 Kiew, R. (ed.). (1991). The State of Nature Conservation in Malaysia. Malaysia: Malayan Nature Society.

20743 Henry, J. & Olivier, L. (1996). Letter to Harriet Gillett including Annotated WCMC printout entitled "France - Conservation Status Listing of Plants" dated 25 October 1995.

20744 Raimondo, F.M., Gianguzzi, L., & Ilardi, V. (1994). Inventario delle specie "a rischio" nella flora vascolare nativa della Sicilia. Quad. Bot. Ambientale Appl. 3 :65-132.

20745 Bandeira, S.O., Marconi, L., & Barbosa, F. (no date). Preliminary study of threatened plants of Mozambique. AETFAT Proceedings (in press):1-9.

20746 Mill, R.R. (1996). Email to Charlotte Jenkins with corrections to the conservation listing for Socotra.

20749 Keay, R.W.J. (1996). Letter to WCMC concerning threatened and endemic tree species in Nigeria.

20750 Gómez-Campo, C. et al. (eds.) (1996). Libro Rojo de Especies Vegetales Amenazadas de las Islas Canarias. [Red List of Threatened Plant Species of the Canary Islands]. Lists 300 threatened species, including island and protected area location.

20751 Meerow, A.W. & Silverstone-Sopkin, P. (1995). The rediscovery of Plagiolirion hormannii Baker (Amaryllidaceae). in *Brittonia* 47(4):426-431. The New York Botanical Garden.

20753 Téllez-Valdés, O. & Martínez-Rodríguez, A.I. (1993). A New Species of *Dioscorea* (Dioscoreaceae) from Mesoamerica. *Novon* 3:204-207. illus.

20756 Kohorn, L.U. (1995). Letter to WCMC with changes to Plant Red Data Book: Chinese Species. IUCN, Action Plan for Plant Conservation in China, Draft.

20757 Skoberne, P. (1995). Annotations to WCMC printout entitled "Slovenia - Globally Threatened Taxa" and dated 3rd October 1995.

20761 Farjon, A. et al. (1996). SSC Conifer Specialist Group.

20765 Téllez Valdés, O. (1996). Letter to Harriet Gillett listing species of *Dioscorea* with distributions in Mexico and Central America.

20767 Burkill, H.M. (1985). The Useful Plants of West Tropical Africa. (2nd ed.). Vol 1: Families A-D. Great Britain: The Royal Botanic Gardens, Kew. 1-960 pp.

20771 Strahm, W.A. (1993). The conservation and restoration of the flora of Mauritius and Rodrigues. PhD Thesis (2 vol.), Reading Uni. U.K.

20773 Hubbard, C.E. & Vaughan, R.E. (1940). The grasses of Mauritius and Rodriguez. London. England: Crown Agents. 1-128 pp.

20774 Vaughan, R.E. & Wiehe, P.O. (1953). The genus *Pandanus* in the Mascarene Islands. *O. Linn. Soc. Bot.* 55:1-32.

20775 Verdcourt, B. (1990). In. Litt. to Wendy Strahm.

20776 Holttum, R.E. (1983). The fern-genera *Tectaria, Heterogonium* and *Ctenitis* in the Mascarene Islands. *Kew Bull.* 38(1):107-130.

20798 Puchalsky, J. (1996). Annotations to WCMC list of plants of Poland.

20799 Figueiredo, E. (1996). Plant Life: *Lasiodiscus*. Gulf of Guinea Conservation Newsletter. No. 3:6. Published by the Gulf of Guinea Conservation Group.

20800 Puchalski, J. & Kazmierczakowa, R. (no date). Threatened Plant Species in Poland, including candidate species for Appendix I of the Bern Convention. 50 pp. Council of Europe, Convention on the conservation of European Wildlife and Natural Habitats.

20802 Bouchet, P., Jaffre, T., & Veillon, J. (1995). Plant extinction in New Caledonia: protection of sclerophyll forests urgently needed. *Biodiversity and Conservation* 4:415-428.

20803 Hilton-Taylor, C. (1996). Annotations and Corrections to the Red Data List of southern African plants.

20804 Garbari, F. (1996). Annotations to WCMC threatened plant list of Italy.

20805 Valsecchi, F., B, C., & Emanuele, B. (1996). Annotations of WCMC list of plants of Sardinia.

20807 Giddy, C. (1996). Letter to J. Sidey referring to the Conservation Status listing of Cycads. New species and annotations.

20808 Montmollin, B. de. (1996). Annotations to WCMC list entitle "Crete - Nationally Threatened Taxa".

20810 Arriegas, P.I. (1996). Letter to members of Habitats Directive Scientific Working Group concerning *Thymus cephalotos*.

20813 Carvalho, M.L.S. & Arriegas, P.I. (1996). Letter to Harriet Gillett including annotated WCMC lists of threatened plants of Portugal and 5 annexes containing references.

20818 Wiles, G.J. (1996). Letter to Julie Reay with annotations to Northern Marianas printout plus additional species.

20819 Rauferson, L. & Rinehart, A.F. (1992). Ferns and orchids of the Mariana Islands. Guam: Rauferson &

Rinehart.

20821 **Bibiloni, G. & Mus, M. (1996).** Annotations to WCMC list of threatened plants of Balearic Islands.

20822 **Islebe, G. (1993).** Will Guatemala's *Juniperus-Pinus* forests survive? *Environmental Conservation* 20(2):167-168.

20825 **Wiles, G.J., Schneinen, J.H., Nafus, D., Jurgensen, L.K., & Manglone, J.C. (1996).** The status, biology, and conservation of *Seranthes nelsonii* (Fabaceae), an endangered Micronesian tree. *Biological Conservation.* in press.

20826 **Henderson, A., Galeano, G., & Bernal, R. (1995).** Field Guide to the Palms of the Americas. New Jersey: Princeton Univ. Press. 352 pp. plus 64 plates.

20827 **Strahm, W. (1996).** Letter to WCMC with annotations concerning Neotropic palm data.

20828 **Johnson, D.V. (ed.). (1996).** Palms: their conservation and sustained utilization. Status survey and conservation action plan. Gland, Switzerland: IUCN. 116 pp. IUCN/SSC Palm Specialist Group.

20831 **Leeuwenberg, A.J.M. (1994).** A revision of *Tabernaemontana*. Two. The New World species and *Stemmadenia*. Royal Botanic Gardens, Kew. 450 pp. Illus.

20832 **Leeuwenberg, A.J.M. (1991).** A revision of *Tabernaemontana*. One. The Old World species. Royal Botanic Gardens, Kew. 205 pp. Illus.

20833 **Pennington, T.D. (1991).** The genera of Sapotaceae. Royal Botanic Gardens, Kew & New York Botanical Garden. 295 pp.

20840 **Nixon, K. (1996).** Comments in an email from Allen Coombes to Sara Oldfield concerning the list of threatened *Quercus*.

20843 **Timberlake, J. (1996).** Letter to Sara Oldfield containing synonymy of plant species in Zimbabwe.

20845 **Florence, J. (1996).** Letter to Harriet Gillet including list entitled "Listes des espèces endémiques de Polynésie Française avec leur répartition géographique et leur statut IUCN, tirée de la banque de données botaniques NADEAUD". [List of endemic species of French Polynesia with IUCN category and distribution, from the database "NADEAUD".

20847 **Giddy, C. (1996).** Fax to J. Sidey listing new taxa in southern Africa with conservation status listing.

20850 **The Nature Conservancy. (1996).** Natural Heritage Central Database. (Status and distribution data on North American plants, developed in collaboration with the Association for Biodiversity Information, U.S. and Canadian Natural Heritage Programs and Conservation Data Centers, and North Carolina Botanical Garden Biota of North America Program.).

20852 **BGCI. (1993).** BGCI list of plants of conservation interest for Hortus Botanicus Universitatis Labacensis, Ljubljana, Yugoslavia (LJU). List of Yugoslavian threatened plants with conservation status listing. 1 pp.

20854 **Yang, J. & Pan, F. (1996).** The current status of native woody vegetation in Taiwan. pp. 89-108 *In* Hunt, D. (Ed.). Temperate Trees Under Threat. International Dendrology Society.

20858 **Hawthorne, W. (1995).** Categories of conservation priority and Ghanaian tree species. WCMC Working Document 4. 1-38 pp.

20874 **Domínguez Lozano, F., Galicia Herbada, D., Moreno Rivero, L., Moreno Saiz, J.C., & Sainz Ollero, H. (1996).** Threatened plants in Peninsular and the Balearic Spain: A Report based on the EU Habitats Directive. *Biological Conservation* 76:123-133.

20883 **The Nature Conservancy. (1996).** Natural Heritage Central Database. (Status and distribution data on Latin American plants, developed in collaboration with Latin American Conservation Data Centers and Missouri Botanical Garden.).

20884 **Thulin, M. (1996).** Annotations to: the conservation listing for trees of Somalia.

20885 **Clarke, G.P. & Lovett, J. (1996).** Data collection forms for tree species of Tanzania.

20886 **Bandeira, S. (1995).** Data collection forms for tree species of Mozambique.

20887 **Aké Assi, L. (1995).** Data collection forms for tree species of Côte d'Ivoire.

20889 **Kiew, B.H., Kiew, R., Chin, S.C., Davison, G., & Ng, F.S.P. (comps.). (1985).** Malaysia's 10 most endangered animals, plants, and areas. *Malayan Naturalist* 38(4):2-6.

20890 **WWF & IUCN. (1994-1997).** Centres of Plant Diversity. A guide and strategy for their conservation. 3 volumes. Cambridge, UK: IUCN Publications Unit.

20891 **Dransfield, S. (1996).** New species of *Dinochloa (Gramineae-Bambusoideae)* in Malesia and notes on the genus. *Kew Bulletin* 51(1):103-117. Illus.

20892 **Dransfield, S. (1996).** Letter to Wendy Strahm containing notes on bamboo species.

20893 **Jaffre, T., Bouchet, P., & Veillon, J.-M. (1996).** Threatened Plants of New Caledonia: Is the system of protected areas adequate? Appendix: Threatened species of the endemic flora of New Caledonia. *Biodiversity & Conservation*:36. submitted.

20894 **Stevenson, D.W. (1996).** Email from Wendy Strahm to Harriet Gillett listing edits from Dennis Stevenson, NYBG to WCMC Cycad list.

20895 **Hilton-Taylor, C. (1996).** Annotations to WCMC list of South African queries.

20899 **Southern Africa Discussion Group. (1996).** Comments on Southern African threatened trees. WCMC/SSC African Regional Workshop, Zimbabwe.

20900 **East African Discussion Group. (1996).** Comments on East African threatened trees. WCMC/SSC African Regional Workshop, Zimbabwe.

20907 **Hedberg, I. & Edwards, S. (eds.). (1989).** Flora of Ethiopia. Volume 3. Pittosporaceae to Araliaceae. Ethiopia & Sweden: The National Herbarium, Addis Ababa & The Department of Systematic Botany, Uppsala. 659 pp.

20909 **Timberlake, J.R. (1996).** Annotations to the conservation listing of trees of Zimbabwe.

20911 **Lovett, J. (1996).** Tanzanian forest trees with a restricted distribution.

20913 **Watt, A. (1996).** Data collection forms for conifers of New Caledonia.

20914 **Téllez Valdés, O. (1996).** Letter to Harriet Gillett containing status listing of threatened *Tephrosia* species of Mexico and Central America.

20915 **Sternberg, G. (1996).** Letter to Charlotte Jenkins concerning oaks of North America.

20916 **Sternberg, G. (no date).** Oak images from Temperate North America. *Journal of the International Oak Society* 6:8-17.

20920 **White, L. (1995).** Réserve de la Lopé. Gabon. Etude de la végétation - raport final. 163 pp.

20921 **Lovett, J. & Friis, I. (1996).** Patterns of endemism in the woody flora of north-east and east Africa. pp. 582-601 In L.J.G. van der Maesen *et al.* (eds.). The biodiversity of African plants. The Netherlands: Kluwer Academic Press.

20922 **Strahm, W. (1996).** Personal communication to WCMC.

20924 **Edwards, S., Tadesse, M., & Hedberg, I. (eds.). (1995).** Flora of Ethiopia and Eritrea. Volume 2, Part 2. Canellaceae to Euphorbiaceae. Ethiopia & Sweden: The National Herbarium, Addis Ababa & The Department of Systematic Botany, Uppsala. 455 pp.

20926 **Kubitzki, K. & Renner, S. (1982).** Lauraceae I (*Aniba* and *Aiouea*). *Flora Neotropica*.

20927 **Rohwer, J.G. (1993).** *Nectandra* (Lauraceae). *Flora Neotropica*.

20928 **Mori, S.A. & Prance, G.T. (1990).** Lecythidaceae. Part II. The zygomorphic-flowered genera. *Flora Neotropica*.

20931 **Sternberg, G. (1996).** Letter to Charlotte Jenkins describing the occurrence of *Quercus inopina* and *Quercus durata*.

20932 **Timberlake, J. (1996).** Notes on possible globally threatened tree species occurring in Africa that have been recorded from Zimbabwe.

20985 **Ministry of Science, Technology and Environment. (1996).** Sach do Viet Nam Phan Thuc Vat. Red Data Book of Vietnam Volume 2. Plants. Hanoi: Science and Technics Publishing House. 484 pp. Lists 356 threatened taxa including fungi.

20990 **Brito, A.A. (1995).** Letter to Wendy Strahm including annotations to: List of threatened trees of Cuba.

20991 **Schmitt, K. (1996).** Botanical survey in the Oban Division, Cross River National Park. 51 pp. Oban Hills Programme, Calabar.

20992 **Pires O'Brien, J. (1996).** Data collection forms for Sapotaceae species in Brazil.

20999 **Spichiger, R. & Loizeau, P.A. (1985).** Trigoniaceae & Vochysiaceae. Flora del Paraguay. Conservatoire et Jardin Botaniques, Ville de Genève & Missouri Botanical Garden.

21001 **de Dios Muñoz, J. (1990).** Anacardiaceae. Flora del Paraguay. Conservatoire et Jardin Botaniques, Ville de Genève & Missouri Botanical Garden.

21002 **Breteler, F.J. (1996).** Conversation with Charlotte Jenkins concerning the occurrence of a new *Xanthocercis* species in Gabon.

21003 **Hess, W. (1996).** Data collection forms for *Quercus* species.

21006 **Stoffelen, P., Robbrecht, E., & Smets, E. (1996).** A revision of *Corynanthe* and *Pausinystalia* (African Rubiaceae-Coptosapelteae). *Botanical Journal of the Linnean Society* 120(4):287-325.

21008 **Liogier, A.H. (1982-1985).** La Flora de la Española. 3 vols. Dominican Republic: Universidad Central Del Este. Centénario de San Pedro de Macoris.

21009 **Maas, P.J.M. & Westra, L.Y.Th. et al. (1992).** *Rollinia*. Flora Neotropica. Monograph 57. New York: New York Botanical Garden. 188 pp.

21011 **Varty, N. (1996).** Data collection forms for Brazilian Atlantic forest species.

21013 **Pires O'Brien, J. (1996).** Data collection forms for Lecythidaceae tree species.

21017 **Jenkins, C. (1996).** Evaluations of *Rinorea* species derived from information in Hekking, W.H.A. (1988) Violaceae Part I - *Rinorea* and *Rinoreocarpus*. Flora Neotropica. New York Botanical Garden.

21018 **Weitzman, A.L. (1995).** Diversity of Theaceae and Bonnetiaceae in the montane Neotropics. pp. 365-375 In Churchill, S.P. *et al.*(eds.). Biodiversity and conservation of neotropical montane forests. New York: New York Botanical Garden.

21019 Rohwer, J.G. (1996). Letter to Sara Oldfield with information on Neotropical Lauraceae.

21020 Rohwer, J.G. (1988). The genera *Dicypellium, Phyllostemonodaphne, Systemonodaphne* and *Urbanodendron* (Lauraceae). *Bot.Jahrb.Syst.* 110(2):157-171.

21021 Corrigan, H. & Sam, C. (1996). Letter regarding conservation status of trees in Vanuatu.

21022 Pereira, J.P., Sastre, C., & Romaniuc, S. (1996). Indice das espécies de Moráceas do Brasil. *Albertoa* 4:77-96.

21025 Molur, S. & Ved, D.K. (eds.). et al. (1995). Conservation assessment and management plan (CAMP) for selected species of medicinal plants of southern India. 108 pp.

21028 Wurdack, J.J., Morley, T., & Renner, S. (1993). Flora of the Guianas. *Melastomataceae.*

21037 Bohs, L. (1994). *Cyphomandra* (Solanaceae). Flora Neotropica. Monograph 63. New York: The New York Botanical Garden. 175 pp.

21038 Du Puy, D.J. & Labat, H. (1996). Data collection forms for Madagascan trees for the Conservation and Sustainable Management of Trees project.

21039 Du Puy, D.J., Phillipson, P.B., & Rabevohitra, R. (1995). The Genus *Delonix* (Leguminosae: Caesalpinioideae: Caesalpinieae) in Madagascar. (Kew Bulletin) 50(3):445-475.

21040 Ashton, P. (1996). Annotations to: Dipterocarpaceae.

21043 Breteler, F.J. (1989). The Connaraceae. A taxonomic study with emphasis on Africa. Wageningen Agricultural University. 403 pp.

21044 Breteler, F.J. (1991). Flore du Gabon. 32. Dichapetalaceae. Paris: Muséum National D'Histoire Naturelle. 221 pp.

21046 Nixon, K., Hess, W., Coombes, A., & Rodriguez, M. (1996). Discussions on the status of *Quercus* species in the Americas. Regional workshop for the Conservation and Sustainable Management of Trees project.

21056 Prado, D.E. (1996). Data collection forms for South American (particularly Argentinian) distributions.

21059 East West Herbs Ltd. (no date). Price List and Catalogue. 5 pp.

21065 Lovett, J. (1996). Completed data collection forms of restricted range trees of Tanzania.

21069 van Gelderen, D.M., de Jong, P.C., & Oterdoom, H.J. (1994). Maples of the World. Hong Kong: Timber

Press Inc. 1-458 pp.

21072 Bridson, D.M. (1994). Additional notes on *Coffea* (Rubiaceae)from Tropical East Africa. *Kew Bull.* 49(2):331-342.

21073 Hallé, N. (1986). Flore du Gabon. Volume 29. Celastraceae Hippocrateoideae. Paris: Muséum National D'histoire Naturelle. 287 pp.

21079 Launert, E. & Pope, G.V. (1991). Flora Zambesiaca. Volume 9. Ulmaceae, Cannabaceae, Moraceae, Cecropiaceae, Urticaceae, Casuarinaceae, Salicaceae, Ceratophyllaceae. London: Flora Zambesiaca Managing Committee. 135 pp.

21082 Van der Werff, H. (1993). *Persea glabra*, a new species of Lauraceae from Bahia. *Kew Bull.* 48(1):25-27.

21089 González Cangas, M. (1996). Chile data collection forms.

21091 Silic, C. (ed.). (1996). The List of the Vegetable Species (Pteridophyta and Spermatophyta) for the Red Book of Bosnia and Herzegovina. Sarajevo: 1996. 20 pp.

21093 Mitre, M.E. (1996). Data collection forms for Panamá.

21094 Barneby, R.C. & Grimes, J.W. (1996). Silk Tree, Guanacaste, Monkey's Earring. A generic system for the synandrous *Mimosaceae* of the Americas. Part 1. *Abarema, Albizia* and Allies. Bronx, New York: The New York Botanical Garden. 1-295 pp.

21097 Friis, I. (1989). A synopsis of Buxaceae in Africa south of the Sahara. *Kew Bulletin* 44:293-299.

21102 Missouri Botanical Garden. (1997). Peru Checklist: Catalogue of the Flowering Plants and Gymnosperms of Peru. World Wide Web http://www.Mobot.Org/MOBOT/Research/peru.html.

21105 Iriondo, J.M., De Hond, L.J., & Gómez-Campo, C. (1994). Current research on the biology of threatened plant species of the Mediterranean Basin and Macronesi: a database. *Bocconea* 4:385.

21107 Bohs, L. (1995). Transfer of *Cyphomandra* (Solanaceae) and its species to *Solanum. Taxon* 44(4):587-593.

21116 Okullo, J.B. et al. (1997). Completed data collection forms for woody plants of Uganda.

21117 Ndjele, M. (1997). Completed data collection forms for tree species of Zaire.

21119 Boratynski, A. (1997). Letter to Sara Oldfield containing information and completed data collection forms on threatened woody species of Poland, Greece and Turkey.

21141 Schouten, R.T. (1986). Revision of

Gymancranthera. Blumea 31(2):455-485.

21143 **de Wilde, W.J.J.O. (1979)**. New account of the genus *Knema* (Myristicaceae). Blumea 25(2):321-478.

21163 **de Wilde, W.J.J.O. (1997)**. Southeast Asian and Malesian *Myristica*. Scheduled for publication in Blumea 42 (1).

21172 **Hou, D. (1996)**. *Caesalpinioideae*. in Flora Malesiana. Leiden: Flora Malesiana Foundation.

21173 **Frodin, D. (1997)**. Conversation with Charlotte Jenkins concerning the taxonomy of *Schefflera* species.

21184 **Soto Arenas, M. (1990)**. Una nuevo orquídea de Morelos, México: *Ponera dressleriana*. *Orquídea (Méx.)* 12(1):117-126.

21185 **García-Cruz, C. (1992)**. *Epidendrum lowilliamsii*, una nueva especie del centro de México. *Orquídea (Méx.). 12(2):131-138.*

21190 Salazar Chávez, G. (1992). Mormodes sotoana, una nueva especie de México y Guatemala confundida con *M. ignea* (Orchidaceae: Catasetinae). *Orquídea (Méx.).* 12(2):261-267.

21196 **Soto Arenas, M. (1993)**. Classificación infraspecífica de *Laelia anceps. Orquídea (Méx.)* 13(1-2):125-144.

21198 **González Tamayo, R. (1993)**. El género *Physogyne* (Orchidaceae, Spiranthinae). *Orquídea (Méx.)* 13(1-2):173-180.

21204 **Vázquez, J., Cuevas, R., Cochrane, T., Iltis, H., Santana, F., & Guzmán, L. (1995)**. Flora de Manantlán. Plantas vasculares de la Reserva de la Biosfera Sierra de Manantlán, Jalisco-Colima, México. *Sida, Botanical Miscellany.* 1-312 pp.

21205 **Evans, R. (1995)**. Systematics of *Cryosophila* (Palmae). *Systematic Bot. Monographs* 46:1-70.

21207 **Luther, H. (1996)**. A checklist of the Bromeliaceae of Costa Rica. *J. Bromeliad Soc.* 45(6):60-63.

21219 **Pupulin, F. & Mora-Retana, D. (1994)**. A revision of the Costa Rican species of *Trichocentrum* (Orchidaceae). *Selbyana* 15(2):87-103.

21220 **. (1995)**. Revision of *Ipomoea* section *Leptocallis* (Convolvulaceae). *Harvard Papers in Botany* 6:97-123.

21221 **Taylor, C., Hammel, B., & Burger, W. (1991)**. New species, combinations, and records in Rubiaceae from the La Selva Biological Station, Costa Rica. *Selbyana* 12:134-140.

21222 **Laferriere, J. (1990)**. The taxonomy and ethnobotany of *Yucca madrensis. Cactus*

and Succulent J. (US) 62:95-96.

21224 **Luteyn, J. (1996)**. New species, new records, and neotypification of some Mesoamerican Eriaceae. *Brittonia* 48(2):241-249.

21227 **Grayum, M. (1995)**. Notes on Costa Rican *Peperomia* (Piperaceae), including four new species. *Phytologia* 79(2):108-113.

21229 **Vázquez-G, J.A. (1994)**. *Magnolia* (Magnoliaceae) in Mexico and Central America: a synopsis. In *Brittonia* 46(1):1-23.

21232 **Daly, D. (1993)**. Notes on *Bursera* in South America, including a new species. Studies in Neotropical Burseraceae VII. In *Brittonia* 45(3):240-246.

21233 **Warford, N. & Harrell, B. (1996)**. *Clowesia dodsoniana* Aguirre L. Its history, pollination, and osmosphores. *Orchid Digest* 60(4):174-179.

21240 **Graham, S. (1990)**. New species of *Cuphea* section *Melvilla* (Lythraceae) and an annotated key to the section. In *Brittonia* 41(1):12-32.

21248 **Lascurain, M. (1996)**. A new species of *Calathea* (Marantaceae) from Veracruz, Mexico. *Novon* 6(4):385-388.

21250 **Reznicek, A. & Camelbeke, K. (1996)**. *Carex porrecta* (Cyperaceae), a distinctive new species from northern South America and Costa Rica. *Novon* 6(4):423-425.

21251 **Stergios, B. (1996)**. Contributions to South American Caesalpiniaceae. II. A taxonomic update of *Campsiandra* (Caesalpinieae). *Novon* 6(4):434-459.

21252 **Knapp, S. (1989)**. Six new species of *Solanum* sect. Geminata from South America. *Bull. Br. Mus. nat. Hist. (Bot.)* 19:103-112.

21253 **Debreczy, Z. & Rácz, I. (1995)**. New species and varieties of conifers from Mexico. *Phytologia* 78(4):217-243.

21254 **Kvist, L. & Skog, L.E. (1992)**. Revision of *Kohleria* (Gesneriaceae). *Smithsonian Contributions to Botany* 79:1-83.

21258 **Mora-Retana, D. & García, J. (1992)**. Lista actualizada de las orquideas de Costa Rica (Orchidaceae). *Brenesia* 37:79-124.

21259 **Luer, C. (1996)**. Nuevas especies de *Restrepia. Orquideologia* 20(2):117-182.

21260 **Kvist, L. & Skog, L.E. (1996)**. Revision of *Pearcea* (Gesneriaceae). *Smithsonian Contributions to Botany* 84:1-47.

21263 **Hernández, H. & Bárcenas, R. (1995)**.

Endangered cacti in the Chihuahuan Desert: I. Distribution patterns. *Conservation Biology* 9(5):1176-1188.

21264 Hágsater, E. (eds.) & Dumont, V. (1996). *Orchids - Status Survey and Conservation Action Plan*. Gland, Switzerland and Cambridge, UK: IUCN. 153 pp.

21265 Salazar, G. & Soto Arenas, M. (1996). El género *Lepanthes* Sw. en México. *Orquidea (Mex.)* 14(1):1-231.

21266 Christenson, E. (1991). Mesoamerican orchid studies I: orchids of Panama. *Lindleyana* 6(1):42-48.

21267 Luer, C. (1991). New species of *Pleurothallis* and a new combination. *Lindleyana* 6(2):94-108.

21268 Albert, V. & Chase, M. (1992). *Mexipedium*: a new genus of slipper orchid (Cypripedioidea: Orchidaceae). *Lindleyana* 7(3):172-176.

21269 Catling, P. (1990). *Lepanthes yuvilensis*, a new species from Oaxaca, Mexico. *Lindleyana* 8(1):25-31.

21270 Kuijt, J. & Kellogg, E. (1996). Miscellaneous mistletoe notes, 20-30. *Novon* 6(1):33-53.

21271 Moraes, M. (1996). Novelties of the genera *Parajubaea* and *Syagrus* (Palmae) from interandean valleys of Bolivia. *Novon* 6(1):85-92.

21272 Ulloa, C. & Jorgensen, P. (1996). A new species of *Mutisia* (Compositae - Mutisieae) from Ecuador. *Novon* 6(1):131-133.

21273 Renner, S. & Hausner, G. (1995). New species of *Siparuna* (Monimiaceae) I. Four new species from Ecuador and Colombia. *Novon* 5(1):61-70.

21274 Grayum, M. (1991). *Chlorospatha kressii* (Araceae), a new compound-leaved species from Chocó Department, Colombia. *Novon* 1(1):12-14.

21275 Londoño, X. & Judziewicz, E. (1991). A new species of *Guadua*, *G. calderoniana* (Poaceae: Bambuseae), with notes on the genus in Bahia, Brazil. *Novon* 1(1):27-32.

21276 Al-Shehbaz, I. (1991). The South American *Dictyophragmus* (Brassicaceae). *Novon* 1(2):71-72.

21277 Lorence, D. (1991). New species and combination in Mexican and Central American *Rondeletia* (Rubiaceae). *Novon* 1(3):135-157.

21278 Pipoly, J. (1993). The genus *Geissanthus* (Myrsinaceae) in the Chocó Floristic Province. *Novon* 3(4):463-474.

21279 Wasshausen, D. (1992). New species and new combinations of *Justicia* (Acanthaceae) from the Venezuelan Guayana. *Novon* 2(1):62-80.

21280 Pipoly, J.J. (1991). Systematic studies in the genus *Myrsine* L. (Myrsinaceae) in Guayana. *Novon* 1(4):204-210.

21281 Seigler, D. & Ebinger, J. (1995). Taxonomic revision of the ant-acacias (Fabaceae, Mimosoideae, *Acacia*, series Gammiferae) of the New World. *Ann. Missouri Bot. Gard.* 82(1):117-138.

21282 Ollgaard, B. (1993). Neotropical Lycopodiaceae - an overview. *Ann. Missouri Bot. Gard.* 79(3):687-717.

21283 Kral, R. (1992). A treatment of American Xyridaceae exclusive of *Xyris*. *Ann. Missouri Bot. Gard.* 79(4):819-885.

21285 Carnevali, G. & Ramírez, I. (1990). New or noteworthy orchids for the Venezuelan Flora. VIII. New species and combinations from Venezuelan Guayana. *Ann. Missouri Bot. Gard.* 77(3):549-558.

21286 Taylor, C.M. (1995). New species and combinations in Rubiaceae from Costa Rica and Panama. *Novon* 5(1):201-207.

21287 Terrell, E. & Koch, S. (1994). A new species of *Bouvardia* (Rubiaceae) from Mexico, and transfer of *Hedyotis xestosperma* to *Bouvardia*. *Novon* 4(2):179-182.

21289 Almeda, F. (1993). *Pilocosta* (Melastomataceae) revisited: a new species, polypoidy, and the base chromosome number of the genus. *Novon* 3(4):311-316.

21290 Mcleisch, I., Pearce, N., & Adams, B. (1995). *Native Orchids of Belize*. Rotterdam, The Netherlands: A.A. Balkema. 278 pp.

21291 Gonzalez Ayala, J. (1992). *Lista Preliminar de Plantas Salvadorenas Amenazadas de Extinción*. San Salvador, El Salvador. 50 pp.

21292 Luer, C.A. (1988). Icones Pleurothallidinarum V. Systematics of *Dresslerella* and *Scaphosepalum*. Addenda to *Porroglossum* (Orchidaceae). *Systematic Botany Monographs (Missouri Botanical Garden)* 26:1-111.

21293 Luer, C.A. (1989). Icones Pleurothallidinarum VI. Systematics of *Pleurothallis* subgenus Ancipitia subgenus Scapula and *Trisetella*. Addendum to *Porroglossum*. *Systematic Botany Monographs (Missouri Botanical Garden)* 31:1-125.

21294 Luer, C.A. (1993). Icones Pleurothallidinarum X. Systematics of *Dracula*. Systematic Botany Monographs (Missouri Botanical Garden) 46:1-244.

21295 Luer, C.A. (1994). Icones Pleurothallidinarum

XI. Systematics of *Lepanthes* subgenus
Brachycladium and *Pleurothallis* subgenus
Aenigma subgenus Elongatia subgenus Kraenzlinella.
Addenda to *Dracula, Lepanthiopsis,
Myoxanthus, Platystele,
Porroglossum,* and *Trisetella.
Systematic Botany Monographs (Missouri Botanical
Garden)* 51:1-137.

21296 **Bennett, D. & Christenson, E. (1996).**
Icones Orchidacearum. Peru: Pastorelli de
Bennett. unpaged pp.

21297 **Christenson, C. (1994).** Annotations to South
American orchid list. 12 September 1994.

21298 **Luer, C.A. (1996).** Icones Pleurothallidinarum
XVIII. Systematics of *Restrepia* (Orchidaceae).
*Monographs in Systematic Botany (Missouri Botanical
Garden)* 59:1-168.

21300 **Anon. (no date).** Data derived from TNC data
(data source 20850).

21301 **Luer, C.A. (1995).** Systematics of
Brachionidium. Addenda to
Dresslerella, Platystele and
*Porroglossum. Monographs in Systematic
Botany (Missouri Botanical Garden)* 57:1-146.

21304 **Emanoil, M. (ed.). (1994).** Encyclopedia of
endangered species. IUCN-The World Conservation Union.
Gale Research International Ltd. 1230 pp.

21305 **Marticorena, C. & Rodríguez, R. (eds.).
(1995).** *Flora de Chile. Vol.1
Pteridophyta - Gymnospermae.* Concepción, Chile:
Universidaad de Concepción. 350 pp.

21306 **Rohwer, J. (1997).** Letter to Charlotte Jenkins
with review notes on the species summaries for
Nectandra.

21307 **Taylor, N. (no date).** *In*: Oldfield,
S.F. (Comp.) Cacti and succulents - status survey and
conservation action plan. (Conservation status given
according to new IUCN categories. Status interpreted as
"I" Indeterminate for inclusion in the 1997 IUCN Red
List of Threatened Plants). in In Press. IUCN, Gland,
Switzerland and Cambridge, UK.

21309 **Talbot, S.S. (ed.). (1997).** Rare Arctic
Endemic Vascular Plants. (Draft 18/2/97 CAFF Plants). 84
pp.

21310 **Chinh, N.N. et al. (1996).** Vietnam Forest
Trees. Hanoi: Agricultural Publishing House. 1-788 pp.

21312 **Rushforth, K. (1996).** Threatened broadleaves.
Aesculus wangii. Broadleaves 3:4.

21313 **Nelson, C.H. (1997).** Threatened Trees of
Honduras. The letter contains all the 1994 IUCN threat
categories.

21316 **Hughes, C. (1997).** Draft chapter on
conservation from "The genus *Leucaena*: a
genetic resource handbook". 12 pp.

21318 **Read, J. & Hope, G.S. (1996).** Ecology of
Nothofagus forests of New Guinea and New
Caledonia. pp. 200-256 *In* Veblen, T.T. *et
Al.* The Ecology and Biogeography of
Nothofagus Forests. Yale University Press.

21323 **Meerman, J. (1997).** List of threatened and
non-threatened *Passiflora* of Belize. 6 pp.

21326 **Meerman, J.C. (ed.). (1996).** Vegetative Key to
the Passionflowers of Belize. *Passiflora*
6(3):25-28.

21329 **Page, W. (1997).** Data collection forms
completed on the threatened tree species of Mauritius.

21343 **Mitchell, J.D. & Daly, D.C. (1993).** A revision
of *Thyrsodium* (Anacardiaceae).
Brittonia 45(2):115-129.

21344 **Mori, S. & Mitchell, J.D. (1990).**
Tapirira bethanniana (Anacardiaceae) and
Eschweilera piresii subsp.
viridipetala (Lecythidaceae), two new taxa
from Central French Guiana. *Memoirs of the New York
Botanical Garden* 64:229-234.

21345 **Mitchell, J.D. & Daly, D.C. (1991).**
Cyrtocarpa Kunth (Anacardiaceae) in South
America. *Annals of the Missouri Botanical
Garden* 78(1):184-189.

21348 **U.S. Fish and Wildlife Service. (1994).**
Endangered and threatend wildlife and plants;
determination of endangered or threatened status for 21
plants from the Island of Hawaii, State of Hawaii.
Federal Register. 10305-10325 pp.

21349 **U.S. Fish and Wildlife Service. (1995).**
Recovery plan for the Kauai plant cluster. Portland,
Oregon: U.S. Fish and Wildlife Service. 270 pp.

21351 **U.S. Fish and Wildlife Service. (1996).**
Endangered and threatened wildlife and plants;
endangered status for the plant *Delissea
undulata. Federal Register.* 53124-53130
pp.

21352 **U.S. Fish and Wildlife Service. (1996).**
Endangered and threatened wildlife and plants;
determination of endangered and threatened status for
nineteen plant species from the island of Kauai, Hawaii.
Federal Register. 53070-53089 pp.

21353 **U.S. Fish and Wildlife Service. (1996).**
Endangered and threatened wildlife and plants;
determination of endangered status for twenty-five plant
species from the island of Oahu, Hawaii. *Federal
Register.* 53089-53108 pp.

21354 **U.S. Fish and Wildlife Service. (1996).**
Endangered and threatened wildlife and plants;
determination of endangered or threatened status for
fourteen plant taxa from the Hawaiian Islands.
Federal Register. 53108-53124 pp.

21355 **U.S. Fish and Wildlife Service. (1996).**
Endangered and threatened wildlife and plants;
determination of endangered status for thirteen plants

from the Island of Hawaii, State of Hawaii. *Federal Register*. 53137-53153 pp.

21356 **U.S. Fish and Wildlife Service. (1996)**.
Recovery plan for the Big Island plant cluster.
Portland, Oregon: U.S. Fish and Wildlife Service. 176 pp.

21357 **U.S. Fish and Wildlife Service. (1996)**.
Recovery plan for Koolau Mountains plant cluster.
Portland, Oregon: U.S. Fish and Wildlife Service. 124 pp.

21358 **U.S. Fish and Wildlife Service. (1996)**.
Recovery plan for Molokai plant cluster. Portland,
Oregon: U.S. Fish and Wildlife Service. 143 pp.

21384 **Hunt, D.R. (1997)**. CITES Cactaceae checklist
(draft). (2). Kew: Royal Botanic Gardens, Kew. 1-190 pp.

21389 **Davis, A.P. et al. (1997)**. CITES Bulb
Checklist (Draft). For the genera: *Cyclamen*,
Galanthus and *Sternbergia*. The Royal
Botanic Gardens, Kew. 1-87 pp.

21390 **Osborne, R. et al. (1996)**. The world list of
Cycads. 1-16 pp.

21391 **Eggli, U. & Carter, S. (1997)**. The CITES
Checklist of Succulent Euphorbia Taxa (Euphorbiaceae).
Draft Version - July 1997. 1-68 pp.

INDEX

Aa	689	*Acranthera*	499	*Aesandra*	536
Abarema	332	*Acridocarpus*	389	*Aeschynanthus*	289
Abatia	280	*Acriopsis*	689	*Aeschynomene*	336
Abelia	118	*Acrocephalus*	307	*Aesculus*	301
Abeliophyllum	437	*Acrocomia*	726	*Aetheolirion*	638
Abies	22	*Acrolophia*	689	*Aethionema*	212
Abrodictyum	13	*Acronema*	585	*Afgekia*	336
Abromeitiella	627	*Acronychia*	523	*Aframomum*	751
Abronia	434	*Acrophyllum*	231	*Afrocarpus*	27
Abrotanella	145	*Acropogon*	575	*Afrothismia*	637
Abutilon	391	*Acrorumohra*	10	*Afrotrilepis*	640
Abutilothamnus	391	*Acrostemon*	244	*Afrovivella*	207
Acacia	332	*Acrosynanthus*	499	*Afzelia*	336
Acaena	490	*Acrotrema*	233	*Agalinis*	548
Acalypha	258	*Acrotriche*	243	*Aganosma*	54
Acamptopappus	145	*Acrymia*	307	*Agapanthus*	608
Acanthaceae	34	*Acsmithia*	231	*Agapetes*	244
Acanthocereus	92	*Actephila*	258	*Agarista*	244
Acanthocladium	145	Actinidiaceae	43	*Agathis*	19
Acanthodesmos	145	*Actinodaphne*	323	*Agathisanthemum*	499
Acantholimon	452	*Actinokentia*	726	*Agathosma*	523
Acanthomintha	307	*Actinolema*	585	Agavaceae	606
Acanthopanax	58	*Actinotus*	585	*Agave*	606
Acanthophoenix	726	*Adamea*	396	*Ageratina*	146
Acanthorrhinum	547	*Adansonia*	78	*Ageratum*	146
Acanthus	33	*Adelia*	259	*Aglaia*	406
Acaulimalva	391	*Adelobotrys*	396	*Aglaonema*	620
Acca	419	*Adenandra*	523	*Agoseris*	146
Acer	42	*Adenanthera*	336	*Agrimonia*	490
Aceraceae	42	*Adenanthos*	471	*Agropyron*	651
Aceratium	242	*Adenia*	445	*Agropyropsis*	651
Achasma	750	*Adenocarpus*	336	*Agrostemma*	119
Achillea	145	*Adenodaphne*	323	*Agrostis*	651
Achlys	74	*Adenodolichos*	336	*Agrostistachys*	259
Achnophora	146	*Adenophora*	108	*Agrostophyllum*	689
Achyranthes	46	*Adenophorus*	11	*Aichryson*	207
Achyrospermum	307	*Adenophyllum*	146	*Ailanthus*	569
Acianthus	689	*Adenoplusia*	89	*Ainea*	673
Acidocroton	258	*Adenopodia*	336	*Ainsliaea*	146
Acidoton	258	*Adenosma*	547	*Aiouea*	323
Acineta	689	*Adesmia*	336	*Aiphanes*	726
Acinos	307	*Adhatoda*	34	Aizoaceae	43
Acioa	137	Adiantaceae	3	*Ajuga*	307
Aciotis	396	*Adiantum*	3	*Akebia*	323
Aciphylla	585	*Adinandra*	579	*Alamania*	689
Acleisanthes	435	*Adolphia*	485	*Alberta*	500
Acmadenia	522	*Adonis*	479	*Albertisia*	409
Acmena	419	*Adromischus*	207	*Albizia*	336
Acmenosperma	419	*Aechmea*	627	*Albolboda*	750
Acmopyle	27	*Aeginetia*	548	*Albuca*	670
Acomis	146	*Aegiphila*	598	*Alcea*	391
Aconitum	478	*Aeonium*	207	*Alchemilla*	490
Acostaea	689	*Aeranthes*	689	*Alchornea*	259
Acourtia	146	*Aerides*	689	*Alchorneopsis*	259
Acradenia	523	*Aerisilvaea*	259	*Aldama*	146
		Aerva	47	*Alectryon*	533

Alepidea	585	*Alzateaceae*	46	*Anacyclus*	146
Alepis	385	*Amaioua*	500	*Anagallis*	468
Aletes	586	*Amana*	684	*Anagyris*	337
Aletris	688	*Amanoa*	259	*Anaphalis*	146
Alfaroa	306	*Amaracarpus*	500	*Anaphyllum*	621
Alisma	607	*Amaracus*	307	*Anarrhinum*	548
Alismataceae	607	Amaranthaceae	46	*Anaxagorea*	50
Alkanna	79	*Amaranthus*	47	*Anaxeton*	147
Allagopappus	146	Amaryllidaceae	616	*Ancana*	50
Allagoptera	727	*Amaryllis*	616	*Anchietea*	601
Alleizettella	500	*Amauropelta*	17	*Anchonium*	214
Allexis	601	*Ambelania*	54	*Anchusa*	79
Alliaceae	608	*Amblystigma*	61	*Ancistrachne*	652
Allium	608	*Ambrosia*	146	Ancistrocladaceae	50
Allocasuarina	131	*Amelanchier*	490	*Ancistrocladus*	49
Allochilus	689	*Amentotaxus*	29	*Ancrumia*	611
Allochrusa	120	*Amesiodendron*	533	*Andrachne*	259
Alloeochaete	652	*Amherstia*	337	*Androcorys*	689
Alloispermum	146	*Ammandra*	727	*Androcymbium*	637
Allolepis	652	*Ammi*	586	*Andrographis*	34
Allophylus	533	*Ammiopsis*	586	*Andropogon*	652
Alloplectus	289	*Ammobium*	146	*Androsace*	468
Alloschemone	620	*Ammopiptanthus*	337	*Androsiphon*	670
Alloschmidia	727	*Ammoselinum*	586	*Andruris*	749
Allowissadula	391	*Amomum*	751	*Andryala*	147
Alloxylon	471	*Amomyrtus*	419	*Aneilema*	638
Alluaudia	233	*Amoora*	406	*Anemia*	17
Alluaudiopsis	233	*Amoreuxia*	143	*Anemone*	479
Almaleea	336	*Amorpha*	337	*Angelica*	586
Alnus	75	*Amorphophallus*	621	*Angelonia*	548
Aloaceae	611	*Amorphospermum*	536	*Anginon*	586
Alocasia	620	*Amparoa*	689	*Angiopteris*	14
Aloe	611	*Ampelocera*	585	*Angkalanthus*	34
Aloinopsis	43	*Ampelocissus*	604	*Angophora*	419
Alonsoa	548	*Amperea*	259	*Angraecum*	689
Alopecurus	652	*Amphianthus*	548	*Aniba*	323
Alphandia	259	*Amphiblemma*	397	*Anigozanthos*	668
Alphitonia	486	*Amphibromus*	652	*Anisacanthus*	34
Alphonsea	50	*Amphicarpaea*	337	*Anisochilus*	307
Alpinia	751	*Amphidasya*	500	*Anisodontea*	391
Alseis	500	*Amphiolanthus*	548	*Anisomeris*	500
Alseodaphne	323	*Amphisiphon*	670	*Anisopappus*	147
Alsinidendron	120	*Amphitecna*	75	*Anisophyllea*	50
Alsmithia	727	*Amphithalea*	337	Anisophylleaceae	50
Alsodeiopsis	304	*Amphoricarpos*	146	*Anisoptera*	235
Alsophila	5	*Amphorogyne*	532	*Anisotes*	34
Alstonia	54	*Amsinckia*	79	*Anisotome*	586
Alstroemeriaceae	616	*Amsonia*	54	*Annamocarya*	306
Alternanthera	47	*Amyema*	385	*Anneslea*	579
Althaea	391	*Amygdalus*	491	*Annesorhiza*	586
Altingia	300	*Amyris*	524	*Annona*	50
Alvaradoa	569	*Anacampseros*	467	Annonaceae	50
Alysicarpus	337	*Anacamptis*	689	*Anoda*	392
Alyssum	213	Anacardiaceae	48	*Anodendron*	55
Alyxia	54	*Anacardium*	48	*Anoectochilus*	689
Alzatea	46	*Anacolosa*	436	*Anogeissus*	143

Anogramma	3	
Anomochloa	652	
Anredera	72	
Antennaria	147	
Anthemis	147	
Anthericaceae	620	
Anthericum	620	
Anthocercis	570	
Anthodiscus	119	
Anthodon	133	
Anthonotha	337	
Anthopteropsis	245	
Anthopterus	245	
Anthospermum	500	
Anthotium	294	
Anthurium	621	
Anthyllis	337	
Anticharis	548	
Antidesma	259	
Antirhea	500	
Antirhoea	500	
Antirrhinum	548	
Antistrophe	415	
Antithrixia	148	
Antonella	652	
Antrophyum	18	
Anulocaulis	435	
Anvilleina	148	
Aotus	337	
Apacheria	212	
Apama	60	
Apassalus	34	
Apatophyllum	133	
Apatostelis	690	
Apatzingania	229	
Apeiba	583	
Apera	652	
Apetahia	108	
Aphanamixis	406	
Aphandra	727	
Aphanes	491	
Aphanisma	135	
Aphanostelma	61	
Aphelandra	34	
Aphragmus	214	
Aphyllorchis	690	
Apiopetalum	58	
Apios	337	
Apium	586	
Apocynaceae	54	
Apocynum	55	
Apodanthera	229	
Apodicarpum	586	
Apodolirion	616	
Apodytes	304	
Apollonias	324	
Aponogeton	620	
Aponogetonaceae	620	
Aporocactus	92	
Aporusa	259	
Appendicula	690	
Appunia	500	
Apterosperma	579	
Apurimacia	337	
Aquifoliaceae	57	
Aquilaria	581	
Aquilegia	479	
Arabidopsis	214	
Arabis	214	
Araceae	620	
Arachniodes	10	
Arachnis	690	
Aralia	58	
Araliaceae	58	
Araucaria	19	
Araucariaceae	19	
Arberella	652	
Arbutus	245	
Arceuthobium	603	
Archangiopteris	14	
Archibaccharis	148	
Archidendron	337	
Archidendropsis	337	
Archineottia	690	
Archontophoenix	727	
Arctomecon	443	
Arctostaphylos	245	
Arctotheca	148	
Ardisia	415	
Ardisiandra	468	
Areca	727	
Arenaria	120	
Arenga	727	
Argemone	443	
Argentipallium	148	
Argophyllum	257	
Argostemma	500	
Argylia	75	
Argyranthemum	148	
Argyreia	203	
Argyrolobium	338	
Argyroxiphium	149	
Argythamnia	259	
Ariocarpus	92	
Arisaema	623	
Arischrada	307	
Aristea	673	
Aristida	652	
Aristocapsa	461	
Aristogeitonia	259	
Aristolochia	60	
Aristolochiaceae	60	
Armeria	452	
Armodorum	690	
Arnaldoa	149	
Arnebia	80	
Arnica	149	
Arnicastrum	149	
Arnoglossum	149	
Arnottia	690	
Arpophyllum	690	
Arrhenatherum	653	
Arrojadoa	92	
Artabotrys	50	
Artemisia	149	
Arthraxon	653	
Arthrocarpum	338	
Arthrocereus	92	
Arthrophyllum	58	
Arthropteris	14	
Artocarpus	411	
Artorima	690	
Arum	624	
Aruncus	491	
Arundinaria	653	
Arundinella	653	
Arytera	533	
Asarum	61	
Ascarina	137	
Asciadium	586	
Asclepiadaceae	61	
Asclepias	61	
Ascocentrum	690	
Ascochilus	690	
Ascyrum	296	
Asimina	50	
Askidiosperma	747	
Aspalathus	338	
Asparagaceae	625	
Asparagus	625	
Asperula	500	
Asphodelaceae	625	
Asphodeline	625	
Asphodelus	626	
Aspidoglossum	62	
Aspidonepsis	62	
Aspidopterys	389	
Aspidosperma	55	
Aspilia	150	
Aspleniaceae	4	
Asplenium	4	
Asplundia	640	
Astartea	419	
Astelia	626	
Asteliaceae	626	
Aster	150	
Asteranthe	50	
Asteranthos	329	

Asteriastigma	280	*Axiniphyllum*	151	*Basiphyllaea*	690
Asteriscium	586	*Axonopus*	653	*Baskervillea*	690
Asteriscus	151	*Ayenia*	575	*Basselinia*	729
Asterogyne	727	*Azara*	280	*Bassia*	135
Asterolasia	524	*Azorella*	586	*Batesimalva*	392
Asteromyrtus	419	*Azorina*	108	*Bathysa*	501
Asterostigma	624	*Aztekium*	92	*Bauhinia*	349
Astilbe	545	*Babiana*	673	*Baumea*	640
Astiria	575	*Baccaurea*	259	*Beaucarnea*	649
Astragalus	338	*Baccharis*	152	*Beauprea*	471
Astrantia	586	*Backhousia*	419	*Beccariella*	536
Astridia	43	*Bacopa*	548	*Beccariophoenix*	729
Astripomoea	203	*Bactris*	728	*Beckwithia*	480
Astrocaryum	727	*Badula*	417	*Begonia*	72
Astroloba	614	*Badusa*	501	Begoniaceae	72
Astronidium	397	*Baeckea*	419	*Behaimia*	349
Astronium	48	*Bafutia*	152	*Beilschmiedia*	324
Astrophytum	92	*Baikiaea*	348	*Beiselia*	89
Astrotricha	58	*Baileyoxylon*	280	*Bejaria*	246
Asyneuma	108	*Bakerella*	385	*Belairia*	349
Atalantia	524	*Bakeridesia*	392	*Bellardiochloa*	653
Atalaya	533	*Balaka*	729	*Bellevalia*	670
Ateleia	348	Balanopaceae	70	*Bellis*	152
Ateramnus	259	*Balanophora*	70	*Bellium*	152
Athamanta	586	Balanophoraceae	71	*Belosynapsis*	638
Athanasia	151	*Balanops*	70	*Bembicidium*	349
Athrixia	151	*Balduina*	152	*Bencomia*	491
Athyrium	18	*Balfourodendron*	524	*Benedictella*	349
Atkinsonia	385	*Ballantinia*	215	*Bensoniella*	545
Atractylis	151	*Ballota*	307	*Bentinckia*	729
Atraphaxis	461	*Baloghia*	260	*Bentleya*	450
Atriplex	135	Balsaminaceae	71	*Berardia*	152
Atropa	570	*Balsamocarpon*	348	Berberidaceae	74
Attalea	728	*Balsamocitrus*	524	*Berberidopsis*	281
Atuna	137	*Balsamorhiza*	152	*Berberis*	74
Aubregrinia	536	*Banara*	280	*Berchemiella*	486
Aubrieta	215	*Banisteriopsis*	389	*Berenice*	108
Audouinia	88	*Banksia*	471	*Bergenia*	545
Auerodendron	486	*Baphia*	348	*Bergerocactus*	92
Aulacospermum	586	*Baptisia*	348	*Bergeronia*	349
Aulomyrcia	419	*Barbarea*	215	*Bergia*	243
Aulotandra	751	*Barbosella*	690	*Berhautia*	385
Aureolaria	548	*Barcella*	729	*Berkheya*	152
Aurinia	215	*Barkeria*	690	*Berlandiera*	152
Australopyrum	653	*Barleria*	35	*Berlinia*	349
Austrobuxus	259	*Barlia*	690	*Bernardia*	260
Austrocactus	92	*Barnadesia*	152	*Bersama*	409
Austrocedrus	20	*Barongia*	420	*Berteroa*	216
Austromuellera	471	*Barrosoa*	152	*Bertiera*	501
Austromyrtus	419	*Bartholomaea*	281	*Bertya*	260
Avellanita	259	*Bartlettina*	152	*Berzelia*	89
Avena	653	*Bartonia*	284	*Beschorneria*	607
Avenula	653	*Bartsia*	548	*Besleria*	289
Avonia	467	*Basananthe*	445	*Besseya*	549
Axinaea	397	*Basedowia*	152	*Beta*	135
Axinandra	229	Basellaceae	72	*Betula*	75

Betulaceae	75	Boraginaceae	79	Bredia	398
Beyeria	260	*Borago*	80	*Bretschneidera*	87
Bhesa	133	*Borassodendron*	729	Bretschneideraceae	87
Bhidea	653	*Borassus*	729	*Breviea*	536
Biarum	624	*Borderea*	647	*Breynia*	260
Bidaria	62	*Boreava*	216	*Brickellia*	154
Bidens	152	*Bornmuellera*	216	*Bridelia*	260
Biermannia	690	*Borodinia*	216	*Brighamia*	108
Bigelowia	153	*Borojoa*	501	*Briquetia*	392
Bignoniaceae	75	*Boronella*	524	*Brodiaea*	611
Bijlia	43	*Boronia*	524	*Brodriguesia*	349
Bikkia	501	*Borreria*	501	*Bromelia*	627
Billardiera	450	*Borya*	620	Bromeliaceae	627
Biophytum	442	*Boscia*	117	*Bromus*	654
Bipinnula	690	*Bosistoa*	524	*Brongniartia*	349
Biscutella	216	*Bossiaea*	349	*Brongniartikentia*	729
Bistorta	461	*Boswellia*	89	*Brosimum*	411
Blachia	260	*Bothriochloa*	653	*Broughtonia*	691
Blakea	397	*Botrychium*	14	*Broussonetia*	412
Blandfordia	627	*Botschantzevia*	216	*Browneopsis*	349
Blandfordiaceae	627	*Bottegoa*	533	*Browningia*	92
Blechnaceae	5	*Bouea*	48	*Brucea*	569
Blechnum	5	*Bourreria*	80	*Brunellia*	87
Blechum	35	*Bouteloua*	653	Brunelliaceae	87
Blennosperma	153	*Bouvardia*	501	*Brunfelsia*	570
Blepharis	35	*Bowiea*	670	*Brunia*	89
Blepharizonia	153	*Bowkeria*	549	Bruniaceae	89
Blephilia	308	*Bowringia*	349	*Brunnera*	80
Bletia	690	*Brachanthemum*	153	*Brunsvigia*	616
Bloomeria	611	*Brachiaria*	653	*Bryonia*	229
Blumea	153	*Brachionidium*	691	*Bubbia*	605
Blutaparon	47	*Brachycereus*	92	*Bubonium*	154
Bobartia	674	*Brachychiton*	575	*Buchanania*	48
Bobea	501	*Brachycome*	153	*Buchenavia*	143
Bocageopsis	50	*Brachycorythis*	691	*Buchlomimus*	654
Bocquillonia	260	*Brachyglottis*	154	*Buchnera*	549
Boea	289	*Brachylophon*	390	*Bucida*	144
Boehmeria	595	*Brachynema*	436	*Buckinghamia*	471
Boerhavia	435	*Brachyotum*	397	*Buckleya*	532
Boesenbergia	751	*Brachypeza*	691	*Budawangia*	243
Boisduvalia	439	*Brachypodium*	653	*Buddleja*	89
Bolandra	545	*Brachyscome*	154	Buddlejaceae	89
Bolanthus	121	*Brachysema*	349	*Buergersiochloa*	654
Bolbitis	13	*Brachysiphon*	446	*Bufonia*	121
Boleum	216	*Brachystachyum*	653	*Buglossoides*	80
Boltonia	153	*Brachystegia*	349	*Bulbine*	626
Bolusiella	691	*Brachystelma*	62	*Bulbinella*	626
Bomarea	616	*Brackenridgea*	436	*Bulbophyllum*	691
Bombacaceae	78	*Brahea*	729	*Bulbostylis*	640
Bombax	78	*Brasilicereus*	92	*Bulleyia*	692
Bonamia	203	*Brassaiopsis*	58	*Bulnesia*	605
Bonania	260	*Brassica*	216	*Bumelia*	536
Bonatea	691	*Braunsia*	43	*Bunchosia*	390
Boninia	524	*Bravaisia*	35	*Bunium*	586
Bonnaya	549	*Braya*	216	*Buphthalmum*	154
Bonnetia	296	*Brazoria*	308	*Bupleurum*	586

Burkillanthus	524	Callitrichaceae	107	*Cancriniella*	155
Burmanniaceae	637	*Callitriche*	107	Canellaceae	117
Burmeistera	108	*Callitris*	20	*Canna*	637
Burnettia	692	*Callopsis*	624	Cannaceae	637
Burretiodendron	583	*Calocedrus*	20	*Cannomois*	747
Burretiokentia	729	*Calochilus*	694	*Canscora*	284
Bursera	89	*Calochortus*	684	*Canthium*	501
Burseraceae	89	*Caloncoba*	281	*Caperonia*	260
Bussea	349	*Calophaca*	350	Capparaceae	117
Butia	729	*Calophyllum*	296	*Capparis*	117
Buxaceae	91	*Calopogonium*	350	Caprifoliaceae	118
Buxus	91	*Calopsis*	747	*Capsella*	217
Byrsonima	390	*Caloscordum*	611	*Capsicum*	570
Byrsophyllum	501	*Calospatha*	731	*Captaincookia*	502
Bystropogon	308	*Calothamnus*	420	*Caragana*	350
Byttneria	575	*Calotis*	155	*Carallia*	489
Cabralea	406	*Calpurnia*	350	*Caralluma*	63
Cacalia	154	*Caltha*	480	*Cardamine*	217
Cachrys	587	*Calvoa*	398	*Cardenanthus*	674
Cactaceae	92	*Calycadenia*	155	*Cardiospermum*	533
Cadaba	117	Calycanthaceae	107	*Carduncellus*	155
Cadellia	578	*Calycanthus*	107	*Carduus*	155
Cadetia	692	Calyceraceae	107	*Carex*	640
Cadiscus	154	*Calycogonium*	398	*Caribea*	435
Caesalpinia	349	*Calycolpus*	420	*Carica*	119
Cailliella	398	*Calycorectes*	420	Caricaceae	119
Cajanus	350	*Calycotome*	350	*Cariniana*	329
Cakile	216	*Calydorea*	674	*Carissa*	55
Caladenia	692	*Calyptranthes*	420	*Carlina*	155
Caladium	624	*Calyptrocarya*	640	*Carlowrightia*	35
Calamagrostis	654	*Calyptrogyne*	731	*Carmichaelia*	350
Calamintha	308	*Calyptronoma*	731	*Carminatia*	155
Calamovilfa	654	*Calystegia*	203	*Carpacoce*	502
Calamus	729	*Calytrix*	421	*Carpenteria*	301
Calandrinia	467	*Camassia*	670	*Carpinus*	206
Calanthe	694	*Camchaya*	155	*Carpotroche*	281
Calathea	688	*Camelina*	216	*Carpoxylon*	731
Calatola	304	*Camellia*	579	*Carronia*	409
Calceolaria	549	*Cameraria*	55	*Carthamus*	155
Calea	154	*Camissonia*	439	*Cartonema*	638
Calectasia	637	*Campanula*	108	*Carum*	587
Calectasiaceae	637	Campanulaceae	108	*Caryocar*	119
Calendula	154	*Campbellia*	552	Caryocaraceae	119
Caliphruria	616	*Campecarpus*	731	*Caryodaphnopsis*	324
Calispepla	350	*Campnosperma*	48	*Caryodendron*	260
Callaeum	390	*Campomanesia*	421	Caryophyllaceae	120
Calliandra	350	*Campsiandra*	350	*Caryopteris*	599
Callianthemum	480	*Camptolepis*	533	*Caryota*	731
Callicarpa	599	*Camptoloma*	552	*Caryotophora*	43
Calligonum	461	*Campylanthus*	552	*Casasia*	502
Callilepis	155	*Campylocentrum*	694	*Casearia*	281
Callirhoe	392	*Campylostemon*	133	*Cassia*	351
Callisia	638	*Canarina*	111	*Cassinia*	155
Callistemon	420	*Canarium*	90	*Cassiope*	246
Callisthene	605	*Canavalia*	350	*Cassipourea*	489
Callistopteris	13	*Canbya*	443	*Cassytha*	324

Castanea	277	*Cephalophyllum*	43	*Charpentiera*	47
Castanopsis	278	*Cephalopodum*	587	*Chaseella*	695
Castela	569	*Cephalostachyum*	655	*Chasmanthe*	674
Castilla	412	*Cephalostigma*	111	*Chassalia*	502
Castilleja	552	Cephalotaxaceae	19	*Chaubardiella*	695
Casuarinaceae	131	*Cephalotaxus*	19	*Chazaliella*	502
Catabrosa	654	*Cerastium*	121	*Cheesemania*	217
Catalpa	75	*Cerasus*	491	*Cheilanthes*	3
Catamixis	156	*Ceratandra*	695	*Cheilophyllum*	553
Catapodium	655	*Ceratanthus*	308	*Cheilotheca*	248
Catasetum	694	*Ceratocaryum*	747	*Cheiranthera*	450
Catesbaea	502	*Ceratolobus*	731	*Cheiridopsis*	43
Catha	133	*Ceratonia*	351	*Cheirodendron*	58
Catharanthus	55	*Ceratopetalum*	231	*Cheirolophus*	160
Cathaya	23	Ceratophyllaceae	135	*Cheirostylis*	695
Cathedra	436	*Ceratophyllum*	135	*Chelone*	553
Catila	674	*Ceratopteris*	15	*Chelonopsis*	308
Catopsis	627	*Ceratostigma*	453	*Chelyocarpus*	733
Cattleya	694	*Ceratostylis*	695	Chenopodiaceae	135
Caulanthus	217	*Ceratozamia*	30	*Chenopodium*	135
Caulostramina	217	*Cerbera*	55	*Chesneya*	352
Cautleya	751	*Cerberiopsis*	55	*Chiangiodendron*	282
Cavendishia	246	*Cercocarpus*	491	*Chigua*	31
Cayaponia	229	*Cereus*	92	*Chiliadenus*	161
Cayratia	604	*Ceropegia*	63	*Chilocarpus*	55
Ceanothus	486	*Ceroxylon*	732	*Chiloglottis*	695
Cecropia	132	*Cestrum*	570	*Chiloschista*	695
Cecropiaceae	132	*Ceterach*	4	*Chimaphila*	248
Cedrela	406	*Chaboissaea*	655	*Chimarrhis*	502
Cedrus	23	*Chaenactis*	160	*Chimonobambusa*	655
Ceiba	78	*Chaenorhinum*	553	*Chingia*	17
Celastraceae	133	*Chaenorrhinum*	553	*Chiococca*	502
Celastrus	133	*Chaerophyllum*	587	*Chionanthus*	437
Celmisia	156	*Chaetanthera*	160	*Chione*	503
Celosia	47	*Chaetocarpus*	260	*Chionochloa*	655
Celsia	553	*Chaetolepis*	398	*Chionodoxa*	670
Celtis	585	*Chaetopappa*	160	*Chionographis*	688
Cenchrus	655	*Chaetotropis*	655	*Chionohebe*	553
Cenia	156	*Chalema*	229	*Chirita*	289
Centaurea	156	*Chamaebatia*	491	*Chlamydocarya*	304
Centaurium	284	*Chamaecrista*	351	*Chloraea*	695
Centaurodendron	160	*Chamaecyparis*	20	Chloranthaceae	137
Centella	587	*Chamaecytisus*	351	*Chloris*	655
Centranthus	598	*Chamaedorea*	732	*Chlorocalymma*	655
Centratherum	160	*Chamaemeles*	491	*Chlorogalum*	670
Centrolepidaceae	637	*Chamaepentas*	502	*Chloroleucon*	352
Centrolepis	637	*Chamaeranthemum*	36	*Chlorophytum*	620
Centrolobium	351	*Chamaesyce*	260	*Chlorospatha*	624
Centronia	398	*Chamarea*	587	*Choerospondias*	48
Centropogon	111	*Chambeyronia*	733	*Choisya*	524
Centrosema	351	*Chamelaucium*	421	*Chomelia*	503
Cephaelis	502	*Changium*	587	*Chondrilla*	161
Cephalanthera	694	*Changnienia*	695	*Chondropetalum*	747
Cephalaria	234	*Chaptalia*	160	*Chondrorhyncha*	695
Cephalocereus	92	*Charadrophila*	553	*Chondrosum*	655
Cephalomappa	260	*Charianthus*	398	*Chordospartium*	352

Choricarpia	421	Citharexylum	599	Cochlospermum	143
Choriceras	261	Citronella	304	Codiaeum	262
Chorisandrachne	261	Citropsis	524	Codonanthe	289
Chorizandra	643	Citrus	524	Codonocarpus	299
Chorizanthe	461	Cladochaeta	164	Codonopsis	112
Chorizema	352	Cladocolea	385	Coelachne	655
Chresta	161	Cladopus	456	Coelia	695
Christella	17	Claoxylon	261	Coelidium	352
Christensenia	14	Clarkeila	503	Coelocarpum	599
Christisonia	553	Clarkia	440	Coelogyne	695
Chromolaena	161	Clausena	525	Coelopleurum	587
Chromolucuma	536	Clausospicula	655	Coelorachis	655
Chronanthus	352	Clavija	581	Coffea	503
Chrysanthemum	161	Claytonia	467	Coilostigma	248
Chrysobalanaceae	137	Claytoniella	467	Coincya	218
Chrysobalanus	137	Cleidiocarpon	262	Cojoba	352
Chrysochamela	217	Cleidion	262	Cola	575
Chrysocycnis	695	Cleisostoma	695	Colchicaceae	637
Chrysoglossum	695	Cleistanthus	262	Colchicum	637
Chrysophthalmum	161	Cleistes	695	Coldenia	80
Chrysophyllum	536	Cleistocactus	93	Colea	75
Chrysoplenium	545	Cleistocalyx	421	Coleactina	503
Chrysopogon	655	Clematis	480	Coleanthera	243
Chrysopsis	161	Cleome	118	Coleanthus	655
Chrysosplenium	545	Cleomella	118	Coleocephalocereus	93
Chrysothamnus	161	Cleretum	43	Coleonema	525
Chunia	300	Clermontia	111	Coleus	308
Chuniophoenix	733	Clerodendrum	599	Colletia	486
Chuquiraga	161	Clethra	143	Collinsia	554
Chusquea	655	Clethraceae	143	Collomia	456
Chysis	695	Cleyera	580	Colobanthus	122
Chytranthus	533	Clianthus	352	Colobogyne	164
Cibotium	10	Clibadium	164	Colpodium	655
Cicer	352	Clidemia	398	Colpothrinax	733
Cicerbita	161	Cliffortia	491	Colubrina	486
Ciceronia	161	Clinopodium	308	Columellia	143
Cicuta	587	Clinosperma	733	Columelliaceae	143
Cimicifuga	480	Clinostigma	733	Columnea	289
Cinchona	503	Clitoria	352	Colutea	352
Cincinnobotrys	398	Cloezia	421	Colysis	16
Cineraria	161	Clowesia	695	Comarostaphylis	248
Cinna	655	Clusia	297	Comastoma	285
Cinnamodendron	117	Clutia	262	Comborhiza	164
Cinnamomum	324	Clypeola	217	Combretaceae	143
Cipocereus	92	Cnemidaria	5	Combretum	144
Cipura	674	Cneoridium	525	Comesperma	459
Circandra	43	Cnesmone	262	Commelina	638
Cirrhopetalum	695	Cnidoscolus	262	Commelinaceae	638
Cirsium	161	Coccinia	229	Commicarpus	435
Cischweinfia	695	Coccocypselum	503	Commidendrum	164
Cissampelos	409	Coccoloba	461	Commiphora	90
Cissus	604	Cocconerion	262	Commitheca	503
Cistaceae	142	Coccothrinax	733	Comnellia	627
Cistanche	553	Cochleanthes	695	Comocladia	48
Cistanthe	467	Cochlearia	217	Comparettia	696
Cistus	142	Cochlospermaceae	143	Compositae	145

Conceveiba	262	*Corylus*	207	*Croizatia*	262
Condalia	487	*Corymbium*	164	*Cronquistianthus*	166
Condaminea	503	*Corymborkis*	696	*Croomia*	748
Congea	599	*Corynabutilon*	392	*Crossopetalum*	133
conifer	19	Corynocarpaceae	207	Crossosomataceae	212
Conimitella	545	*Corynocarpus*	207	*Crotalaria*	352
Coniogramme	3	*Corypha*	734	*Croton*	262
Conioselinum	588	*Coryphantha*	93	*Crotonogyne*	263
Connaraceae	202	*Coryphopteris*	17	*Crucianella*	504
Connarus	202	*Corythophora*	329	*Cruciata*	504
Connellia	627	*Coscinium*	410	Cruciferae	212
Conophytum	43	*Cosmos*	164	*Crudia*	354
Conospermum	471	*Cossinia*	533	*Crusea*	504
Conostegia	399	Costaceae	639	*Cryosophila*	734
Conostephium	243	*Costus*	639	*Crypsinus*	16
Conostylis	668	*Cotoneaster*	491	*Crypsis*	655
Conradina	308	*Cotopaxia*	588	*Cryptadenia*	581
Conringia	218	*Cottendorfia*	627	*Cryptandra*	487
Consolida	480	*Cotula*	164	*Cryptantha*	81
Constantia	696	*Cotyledon*	208	Crypteroniaceae	229
Convallariaceae	639	*Cotylelobium*	235	*Cryptocarya*	324
Convolvulaceae	203	*Couepia*	137	*Cryptocentrum*	696
Convolvulus	204	*Couma*	55	*Cryptochilus*	696
Cooperia	616	*Couratari*	329	*Cryptochloa*	655
Coopernookia	295	*Couroupita*	329	*Cryptocodon*	112
Copaifera	352	*Coursetia*	352	*Cryptocoryne*	624
Copernicia	733	*Cousinia*	164	*Cryptolepis*	65
Copiapoa	93	*Coussapoa*	132	*Cryptomeria*	29
Coprosma	503	*Coussarea*	504	*Cryptosepalum*	354
Coptis	480	*Coutaportla*	504	*Cryptostylis*	696
Corallocarpus	230	*Craibia*	352	*Ctenitis*	10
Corallorrhiza	696	*Craigia*	583	*Ctenium*	655
Corchorus	583	*Crambe*	218	*Ctenopteris*	11
Cordeauxia	352	*Crambella*	218	*Cucumella*	230
Cordia	80	*Cranichis*	696	*Cucumis*	230
Cordyla	352	*Craspedia*	165	*Cucurbita*	230
Cordylanthus	554	*Crassula*	208	Cucurbitaceae	229
Cordyline	607	Crassulaceae	207	*Cuervea*	133
Coreocarpus	164	*Crataegus*	491	*Cuitlauzina*	697
Coreopsis	164	*Craterispermum*	504	*Culcasia*	624
Corethrogyne	164	*Craterosiphon*	581	*Cullen*	354
Coris	468	*Cremanthodium*	165	*Cullenia*	78
Corispermum	136	*Cremastopus*	230	*Cullumia*	166
Cornaceae	206	*Cremnophyton*	136	*Cuminia*	308
Cornus	206	*Cremosperma*	290	*Cunninghamia*	29
Cornutia	599	*Crepidiastrum*	165	*Cunonia*	231
Corokia	257	*Crepidomanes*	13	Cunoniaceae	231
Coronopus	218	*Crepidospermum*	90	*Cupania*	533
Correa	525	*Crepis*	165	*Cupaniopsis*	533
Corryocactus	93	*Crescentia*	75	*Cuphea*	386
Cortaderia	655	*Crinodendron*	242	*Cupheanthus*	421
Corybas	696	*Crinum*	616	Cupressaceae	20
Corycium	696	*Cristaria*	392	*Cupressus*	20
Corydalis	443	*Crithopsis*	655	*Curculigo*	673
Corylaceae	206	*Crocosmia*	674	*Curcuma*	751
Corylopsis	300	*Crocus*	674	*Curroria*	65

Curupira	436	*Cyphostemma*	605	Davidsoniaceae	232
Cuscuta	204	*Cypripedium*	697	*Daviesia*	355
Cusickiella	218	*Cypselea*	44	*Debregeasia*	595
Cuspidaria	75	Cyrillaceae	231	*Decaschistia*	392
Cussonia	58	*Cyrtandra*	290	*Deckenia*	734
Cuviera	504	*Cyrtandroidea*	291	*Dedeckera*	462
Cyananthus	112	*Cyrtanthus*	616	*Deeringothamnus*	51
Cyanastraceae	640	*Cyrtocarpa*	48	*Degeneria*	232
Cyanastrum	640	*Cyrtomium*	10	Degeneriaceae	232
Cyanea	112	*Cyrtorchis*	697	*Degenia*	218
Cyanella	749	*Cyrtostachys*	734	*Dehaasia*	325
Cyanicula	697	*Cystoathyrium*	18	*Deherainia*	581
Cyanotis	638	*Cystopteris*	18	*Deinbollia*	534
Cyathea	5	*Cytisus*	354	*Deiregyne*	697
Cyatheaceae	5	*Daboecia*	249	*Delilia*	166
Cyathobasis	136	*Dacrycarpus*	27	*Delissea*	113
Cyathocline	166	*Dacrydium*	27	*Delonix*	355
Cyathodes	243	*Dacryodes*	90	*Delosperma*	44
Cyathostemma	50	*Dactyladenia*	138	*Delostoma*	76
Cyathula	47	*Dactylanthus*	71	*Delphinium*	481
Cybianthus	417	*Dactylis*	656	*Delpydora*	537
cycad	30	*Dactylorhiza*	697	*Deltaria*	582
Cycadaceae	30	*Daemonorops*	734	*Dendranthema*	166
Cycadopsida	30	*Dahlgrenodendron*	325	*Dendriopoterium*	492
Cycas	30	*Dahlia*	166	*Dendrobium*	697
Cycladenia	55	*Dalbergia*	354	*Dendrocacalia*	166
Cyclamen	468	*Dalea*	354	*Dendrocereus*	94
Cyclanthaceae	640	*Dalechampia*	263	*Dendrochilum*	699
Cyclanthera	230	*Damnacanthus*	504	*Dendroglossa*	16
Cyclea	410	*Damnxanthodium*	166	*Dendromecon*	444
Cyclobalanopsis	278	*Dampiera*	295	*Dendropanax*	58
Cyclogramma	17	*Danaea*	14	*Dendropemon*	386
Cyclophyllum	504	*Danais*	504	*Dendrophthora*	604
Cyclopia	354	*Dansiea*	144	*Dendrophylax*	699
Cyclostemon	263	*Danthonia*	656	*Dendroseris*	166
Cyclotrichium	308	*Danthoniopsis*	656	*Dendrosicyos*	230
Cycnoches	697	*Daphne*	581	*Dendrosida*	392
Cylindrocline	166	Daphniphyllaceae	232	*Denhamia*	133
Cymbalaria	554	*Daphniphyllum*	231	*Dennettia*	51
Cymbidium	697	*Daphnopsis*	582	Dennstaedtiaceae	9
Cymbocarpum	588	*Darlingia*	471	*Deparia*	18
Cymbopetalum	50	*Darniella*	136	*Deppea*	504
Cymbopogon	655	*Darwinia*	421	*Derwentia*	554
Cymopterus	588	*Darwiniothamnus*	166	*Deschampsia*	656
Cynanchum	65	*Dasylirion*	649	*Descurainia*	218
Cynoglossum	82	*Dasymaschalon*	51	*Desmanthodium*	166
Cynometra	354	*Dasynotus*	82	*Desmanthus*	355
Cynorkis	697	*Dasyphyllum*	166	*Desmodium*	355
Cypella	675	*Datisca*	232	*Desmoncus*	734
Cyperaceae	640	Datiscaceae	232	*Desmos*	51
Cyperus	643	*Daubenya*	670	*Desmostachys*	304
Cyphanthera	570	*Daucus*	588	*Deuterocohnia*	628
Cyphia	113	*Davallia*	9	*Deutzia*	302
Cyphokentia	734	Davalliaceae	9	*Deyeuxia*	656
Cyphophoenix	734	*Davidia*	206	*Dialium*	356
Cyphosperma	734	*Davidsonia*	232	*Diamena*	620

Dianella	746	*Digitaria*	656	*Dirca*	582
Dianthoveus	640	*Diglyphosa*	699	*Dirhamphis*	392
Dianthus	122	*Dignathe*	699	*Disa*	699
Diapensiaceae	232	*Digomphia*	76	*Disanthus*	300
Diaphananthe	699	*Dillenia*	233	*Discaria*	487
Diascia	554	Dilleniaceae	233	*Dischidia*	66
Diastella	471	*Dillwynia*	356	*Discocactus*	94
Dicellostyles	392	*Dilomilis*	699	*Discocalyx*	417
Dicentra	444	*Dimeria*	657	*Discocarpus*	264
Dicerandra	308	*Dimocarpus*	534	*Discophora*	304·
Dichaea	699	*Dimorphandra*	356	*Disocactus*	94
Dichanthelium	656	*Dinochloa*	657	*Disperis*	700
Dichanthium	656	*Dinteranthus*	44	*Disporum*	639
Dichapetalaceae	232	*Dioclea*	356	*Dissanthelium*	657
Dichapetalum	232	*Diodia*	504	*Dissochondrus*	657
Dichelostemma	611	*Dionaea*	240	*Dissotis*	399
Dicheranthus	305	Dioncophyllaceae	234	*Distephanus*	166
Dichilanthe	504	*Dionychastrum*	399	*Disterigma*	249
Dichiloboea	291	*Dionysia*	469	*Distichostemon*	534
Dichondra	205	*Dioon*	31	*Distylium*	300
Dichrostachys	356	*Dioscorea*	647	*Dithyrea*	218
Dichrotrichum	291	Dioscoreaceae	647	*Diuris*	700
Dicksonia	10	*Diosma*	525	*Djaloniella*	285
Dicksoniaceae	10	*Diospyros*	240	*Dodecahema*	462
Dicliptera	36	*Dipcadi*	670	*Dodecastigma*	264
Diclis	555	*Diphasiastrum*	1	*Dodecatheon*	469
Dicoma	166	*Diphasiopsis*	525	*Dodonaea*	534
Dicoria	166	*Diplacus*	555	*Doerpfeldia*	487
dicot	34	*Diplandrorchis*	699	*Dolichochaete*	657
Dicraeanthus	456	*Diplazium*	18	*Dolichometra*	504
Dicraeopetalum	356	*Diplobryum*	456	*Dolichos*	356
Dicranolepis	582	*Diplocaulobium*	699	*Doliocarpus*	233
Dicranopteris	11	*Diplocyclos*	230	*Dombeya*	576
Dicranopygium	640	*Diplodiscus*	583	*Domeykoa*	588
Dicrastylis	599	*Diploglottis*	534	*Domingoa*	700
Dictamnus	525	*Diploknema*	537	*Donnellsmithia*	588
Dictyocaryum	734	*Diplomeris*	699	*Doodia*	5
Dictyophragmus	218	*Diplopterys*	390	*Dorema*	588
Dictyosperma	734	*Diplosoma*	44	*Doricera*	504
Dictyospermum	638	*Diplospora*	504	*Doronicum*	166
Dicypellium	325	*Diplostephium*	166	*Dorstenia*	412
Didelotia	356	*Diplotaxis*	218	*Dorycnium*	356
Didiciea	699	*Diplothorax*	412	*Doryopteris*	3
Didiereaceae	233	*Diplycosia*	249	*Dorystaechas*	308
Didonica	249	*Dipodium*	699	*Douglasia*	469
Didymaea	504	*Diposis*	588	*Douradoa*	436
Didymaotus	44	Dipsacaceae	234	*Dovyalis*	282
Didymocarpus	291	*Dipsacus*	234	*Downingia*	114
Didymoplexis	699	*Dipteracanthus*	36	*Draba*	218
Didyplosandra	36	*Dipteranthus*	699	*Drabastrum*	220
Dieffenbachia	624	Dipterocarpaceae	235	*Dracaena*	649
Diellia	5	*Dipterocarpus*	235	Dracaenaceae	649
Dierama	675	*Dipteronia*	42	*Dracocephalum*	308
Diervilla	118	*Dipteryx*	356	*Dracontomelon*	48
Dietes	675	*Diptychandra*	356	*Dracophyllum*	243
Digitalis	555	*Dirachma*	287	*Dracosciadium*	588

Dracula	700	*Echidnopsis*	66	*Elytranthe*	386
Dracunculus	624	*Echinacea*	167	*Elytraria*	36
Drakaea	700	*Echinocactus*	94	*Elytrigia*	657
Drakonorchis	700	*Echinocereus*	94	*Elytropappus*	167
Draperia	302	*Echinochloa*	657	*Embelia*	417
Dregea	66	*Echinodorus*	607	*Embergeria*	167
Dregeochloa	657	*Echinolaena*	657	*Embolanthera*	300
Drejerella	36	*Echinopanax*	59	*Embreea*	701
Dresslerothamnus	166	*Echinophora*	588	*Emmenanthe*	302
Drimia	671	*Echinops*	167	*Emmenopterys*	504·
Drimys	605	*Echinopsis*	96	*Emmenosperma*	487
Droguetia	595	*Echinospartum*	357	*Emorya*	89
Droogmansia	356	*Echiostachys*	82	*Empedoclesia*	249
Drosanthemum	44	*Echium*	82	*Emplectanthus*	66
Drosera	240	*Ectotropis*	44	*Empleurum*	525
Droseraceae	240	*Ectrosia*	657	*Enantia*	51
Drummondita	525	*Edanyoa*	13	*Encelia*	167
Dryadella	701	*Edraianthus*	114	*Enceliopsis*	168
Dryandra	471	*Ehretia*	82	*Encephalartos*	31
Drymaria	124	*Ehrharta*	657	*Encholirium*	628
Drymonia	292	*Eizia*	504	*Encyclia*	701
Drymophloeus	735	*Ekmania*	167	*Endiandra*	325
Drynaria	16	*Ekmanianthe*	76	*Endonema*	447
Dryopteridaceae	10	*Ekmanochloa*	657	*Enemion*	482
Dryopteris	10	*Elachanthus*	167	*Enicosanthum*	51
Drypetes	264	*Elaeagia*	504	*Enkianthus*	249
Dubautia	167	Elaeagnaceae	242	*Ennealophus*	675
Dubouzetia	242	*Elaeagnus*	242	*Entada*	357
Duckeanthus	51	Elaeocarpaceae	242	Epacridaceae	243
Dudleya	208	*Elaeocarpus*	242	*Epacris*	243
Dulacia	436	*Elaeodendron*	133	*Epaltes*	168
Dumasia	356	*Elaeoluma*	537	*Ephedra*	18
Dunnia	504	*Elaeoselinum*	588	Ephedraceae	18
Duranta	599	*Elaphanthera*	532	*Ephippianthus*	701
Durio	78	*Elaphoglossum*	13	*Epiblema*	701
Duroia	504	*Elaterium*	230	*Epidendrum*	701
Dutaillyea	525	Elatinaceae	243	*Epigeneium*	702
Duvalia	66	*Elatine*	243	*Epilobium*	441
Duvaliandra	66	*Elatostema*	595	*Epilyna*	702
Dyckia	628	*Elattostachys*	534	*Epimedium*	74
Dyerophytum	453	*Elegia*	747	*Epinetrum*	410
Dymondia	167	*Eleiotis*	357	*Epipactis*	702
Dypsis	735	*Eleocharis*	644	*Epiphyllum*	96
Dyschoriste	36	*Eleorchis*	701	*Epipogium*	702
Dysophylla	308	*Elephantomene*	410	*Epiprinus*	264
Dysopsis	264	*Elephantopus*	167	*Episcia*	292
Dysosma	74	*Elephantorrhiza*	357	*Epithelantha*	96
Dysoxylum	406	*Eleutharrhena*	410	*Eragrostis*	658
Dyssodia	167	*Elingamita*	417	*Eremalche*	392
Eastwoodia	167	*Elionurus*	657	*Eremanthus*	168
Ebenaceae	240	*Elleanthus*	701	*Eremia*	249
Ebenus	356	*Elliottia*	249	*Eremiella*	249
Ecbolium	36	*Ellipanthus*	202	*Eremocharis*	588
Ecclinusa	537	*Elodea*	673	*Eremocrinum*	620
Echeandia	620	*Elsholtzia*	308	*Eremogone*	124
Echeveria	209	*Elymus*	657	Eremolepidaceae	244

Eremophila	414	
Eremopoa	658	
Eremosparton	357	
Eremostachys	308	
Eremurus	626	
Erepsia	44	
Eria	703	
Eriastrum	456	
Erica	249	
Ericaceae	244	
Ericameria	168	
Erigeron	168	
Erinna	611	
Erinocarpus	583	
Eriocaulaceae	649	
Eriocaulon	649	
Eriochloa	658	
Eriochrysis	658	
Eriodictyon	302	
Eriogonum	462	
Eriolaena	576	
Erioneuron	658	
Eriope	308	
Eriophyllum	170	
Eriosema	357	
Eriosemopsis	504	
Eriosorus	3	
Eriospermaceae	651	
Eriospermum	651	
Eriostemon	525	
Eriosyce	96	
Eriosynaphe	588	
Eriotheca	78	
Erithalis	504	
Eritrichium	83	
Erlangea	170	
Ernodea	505	
Erodium	287	
Erophila	220	
Erucastrum	220	
Ervatamia	55	
Erycibe	205	
Erycina	703	
Eryngium	588	
Erysimum	220	
Erythrina	357	
Erythrocephalum	170	
Erythrochiton	525	
Erythrococca	264	
Erythrodes	703	
Erythronium	685	
Erythrophysa	534	
Erythrospermum	282	
Erythroxylaceae	256	
Erythroxylum	256	
Escallonia	257	
Escalloniaceae	257	
Eschscholzia	444	
Eschweilera	329	
Escobaria	96	
Esenbeckia	525	
Espostoopsis	97	
Etlingera	751	
Eubrachion	244	
Eucalyptus	422	
Euceraea	282	
Euchaetis	525	
Eucharis	617	
Euchorium	534	
Eucnide	384	
Eucomis	671	
Eucommia	258	
Eucommiaceae	258	
Eucrosia	617	
Eucryphia	258	
Eucryphiaceae	258	
Eugeissona	737	
Eugenia	425	
Euhesperida	308	
Euleria	48	
Eulophia	703	
Eulychnia	97	
Euodia	526	
Euonymus	133	
Eupatorium	170	
Euphorbia	264	
Euphorbiaceae	258	
Euphrasia	555	
Eureiandra	230	
Euroschinus	48	
Eurya	580	
Eurycorymbus	534	
Euryodendron	580	
Euryops	171	
Eurystyles	703	
Eurytaenia	589	
Eustachys	658	
Euterpe	737	
Euthamia	171	
Eutrema	221	
Euzomodendron	221	
Evax	171	
Evodia	526	
Evolvulus	205	
Evotella	703	
Evrardiella	685	
Ewartia	172	
Exacum	285	
Excoecaria	270	
Exellodendron	138	
Exocarpos	532	
Exostema	505	
Exostyles	357	
Eysenhardtia	357	
Facheiroa	97	
Fagaceae	277	
Fagara	526	
Fagonia	606	
Fagraea	384	
Fagus	278	
Fahrenheitia	270	
Falcatifolium	27	
Fanninia	66	
Faramea	505	
Farfugium	172	
Faroa	285	
Farrago	658	
Farsetia	221	
Fatsia	59	
Faucaria	44	
Faujasia	172	
Feddea	172	
Felicia	172	
Femeniasia	172	
Fendlera	302	
Fenestraria	44	
fern	3	
Fernandezia	703	
Fernandoa	76	
Fernelia	505	
Fernseea	628	
Ferocactus	97	
Ferraria	675	
Ferreyranthus	172	
Ferula	589	
Ferulago	589	
Festuca	658	
Ficinia	644	
Ficus	413	
Filago	172	
Filipendula	492	
Fimbristylis	644	
Firmiana	576	
Fitchia	172	
Fitzroya	20	
Flacourtiaceae	280	
Flaveria	172	
Fleischmannia	172	
Flemingia	357	
Fleurydora	436	
Flickingeria	703	
Flindersia	526	
Flourensia	172	
Floydia	472	
Flueggea	270	
Foetidia	331	
Fokienia	20	
Fontainea	270	

Fontquera	172	*Galvezia*	556	*Gilbertiodendron*	358
Forchhammeria	118	*Gambelia*	556	*Gilia*	456
Forestiera	438	*Garcinia*	297	*Gilletiodendron*	358
Forsteronia	55	*Gardenia*	507	*Gilliesia*	611
Forsythia	438	*Garnotia*	659	*Gilmania*	465
Fortunella	526	*Garrettia*	599	*Ginalloa*	604
Fosterella	628	*Gasteranthus*	292	*Gingidia*	590
Fosteria	675	*Gasteria*	614	*Ginkgo*	30
Fothergilla	300	*Gastonia*	59	Ginkgoaceae	30
Fouquieria	284	*Gastrochilus*	704	ginkgophyte	30
Fouquieriaceae	284	*Gastrodia*	704	Ginkgopsida	30
Fragaria	492	*Gastrolobium*	358	*Ginoria*	387
Frailea	97	*Gastrolychnis*	124	*Gironniera*	585
Frankenia	284	*Gaudinia*	659	*Githopsis*	114
Frankeniaceae	284	*Gaultheria*	251	*Gladiolus*	676
Franklandia	472	*Gaura*	441	*Glandularia*	599
Franklinia	580	*Gaussia*	737	*Glaucium*	444
Frantzia	230	*Gavilea*	704	*Glaziocharis*	637
Frasera	285	*Gaylussacia*	252	*Gleasonia*	508
Fraxinus	438	*Gayophytum*	441	*Gleditsia*	358
Freesia	675	*Geanthus*	751	*Gleichenia*	11
Fremontodendron	576	*Geijera*	526	Gleicheniaceae	11
Frerea	66	*Geissanthus*	417	*Glenniea*	534
Freycinetia	745	*Geissois*	231	*Glinus*	410
Freylinia	556	*Geissoloma*	284	*Glionnetia*	508
Freziera	580	Geissolomataceae	284	*Glischrocolla*	447
Friesodielsia	51	*Geissorhiza*	676	*Globba*	751
Frithia	44	*Gelasine*	676	*Globularia*	294
Fritillaria	685	*Geniostoma*	384	Globulariaceae	294
Froelichia	47	*Genipa*	508	*Glochidion*	271
Froesia	478	*Genista*	358	*Gloeospermum*	601
Froesiochloa	659	*Genistella*	358	*Glomeropitcairnia*	628
Froriepia	590	*Genistidium*	358	*Glossarion*	172
Fryxellia	392	*Genoplesium*	704	*Glossocarya*	599
Fuchsia	441	*Gentiana*	285	*Glossogyne*	172
Fuirena	645	Gentianaceae	284	*Glossopetalon*	212
Fulcaldea	172	*Gentianella*	286	*Gloxinia*	292
Fumana	142	*Gentianopsis*	286	*Gluema*	537
Fumaria	444	*Genyorchis*	704	*Gluta*	48
Fumariola	444	*Geocarpon*	305	*Glyceria*	659
Furcraea	607	*Geocaryum*	590	*Glycine*	359
Gaertnera	505	*Geonoma*	737	*Glycosmis*	526
Gagea	686	*Geophila*	508	*Glycyrrhiza*	359
Gahnia	645	Geraniaceae	287	*Glyphochloa*	659
Gaillardia	172	*Geranium*	288	*Glyphochola*	660
Gaimardia	637	*Gerbera*	172	*Glyptopetalum*	133
Galactia	357	*Gerrardanthus*	230	*Glyptostrobus*	29
Galanthus	617	*Gesneria*	292	*Gmelina*	600
Galatella	172	Gesneriaceae	289	*Gnaphalium*	172
Galaxia	676	*Gesnouinia*	596	gnetophyte	18
Galega	358	*Gethyllis*	617	Gnetopsida	18
Galeola	703	*Gethyum*	611	*Gochnatia*	173
Galeottiella	703	*Geum*	492	*Goerziella*	136
Galinsoga	172	*Gibbaeum*	44	*Goethea*	392
Galipea	526	*Gibsoniothamnus*	556	*Goetzea*	294
Galium	505	*Gigasiphon*	358	Goetzeaceae	294

Gomortega	294	Grubbiaceae	296	Haemodoraceae	668
Gomortegaceae	294	*Guadua*	660	*Haemodorum*	669
Gomphandra	304	*Guaiacum*	606	*Haenianthus*	438
Gompholobium	359	*Guapira*	435	*Hagsatera*	705
Gomphostemma	308	*Guardiola*	173	*Hakea*	473
Gongora	704	*Guarea*	406	*Halacsya*	83
Gongylosperma	66	*Guatteria*	51	*Halenia*	286
Goniolimon	453	*Guatteriella*	51	*Halesia*	577
Goniopteris	17	*Guatteriopsis*	51	*Halimium*	142
Goniothalamus	51	*Guettarda*	508	*Halimolobos*	221
Gonocalyx	252	*Guibourtia*	359	*Halimolobus*	221
Gonocarpus	299	*Guihaia*	738	*Hallieracantha*	37
Gonocytisus	359	*Guioa*	534	*Halocarpus*	27
Gonolobus	66	*Gulubia*	738	*Halophila*	673
Gonospermum	173	*Gundlachia*	173	Halophytaceae	299
Gonzalagunia	508	*Gunnarella*	704	*Halophytum*	299
Goodenia	295	*Gunnera*	296	Haloragaceae	300
Goodeniaceae	295	Gunneraceae	296	*Haloragis*	300
Goodmania	465	*Gunniopsis*	45	*Haloragodendron*	300
Goodyera	704	*Gustavia*	331	*Halosarcia*	136
Gordonia	580	*Gutierrezia*	173	*Halosciastrum*	590
Gossypium	392	Guttiferae	296	*Hamadryas*	482
Gouania	487	*Guyonia*	399	Hamamelidaceae	300
Govenia	704	*Guzmania*	628	*Hamamelis*	300
Grabowskia	570	*Gyminda*	133	*Hamelia*	508
Graderia	556	*Gymnacranthera*	415	*Hammatolobium*	359
Graellsia	221	*Gymnadenia*	704	*Hampea*	392
Graffenrieda	399	*Gymnema*	67	*Hanabusaya*	114
Gramineae	651	*Gymnigritella*	704	*Hanburia*	230
Grammitidaceae	11	*Gymnocarpium*	18	*Hancockia*	705
Grammitis	12	*Gymnocarpos*	305	*Handeliodendron*	537
Grammosciadium	590	*Gymnocladus*	359	*Hannoa*	569
Grammosolen	570	*Gymnopogon*	660	*Hansteinia*	37
Graptopetalum	209	*Gymnosiphon*	637	*Hapaline*	624
Graptophyllum	36	*Gymnospermium*	74	*Haplocoelopsis*	534
Gratiola	556	*Gymnostachyum*	36	*Haplocoelum*	534
Gratwickia	173	*Gymnostemon*	569	*Haplodictyum*	17
Gravesia	399	*Gymnostoma*	132	*Haploesthes*	174
Greenia	660	*Gynandriris*	678	*Haplopappus*	174
Greenovia	209	*Gynoxys*	173	*Haplophragma*	76
Greenwayodendron	51	*Gynura*	173	*Haplophyllum*	526
Greigia	628	*Gypsacanthus*	36	*Haplorhus*	48
Grevea	411	*Gypsophila*	124	*Haplostachys*	308
Grevillea	472	*Gyranthera*	78	*Haplostephium*	174
Grewia	583	*Gyrocaryum*	83	*Haplostichanthus*	51
Greyia	295	*Gyrostemon*	299	*Haplothismia*	637
Greyiaceae	295	Gyrostemonaceae	299	*Haptanthus*	271
Grias	331	*Gyrotaenia*	596	*Harpagonella*	83
Griffinia	617	*Haageocereus*	97	*Harpalyce*	359
Grimmeodendron	271	*Habenaria*	704	*Harperocallis*	688
Grindelia	173	*Haberlea*	292	*Harrisella*	705
Grisebachia	252	*Habracanthus*	37	*Harrisia*	97
Grisollea	304	*Habranthus*	617	*Hartia*	580
Grosourdya	704	*Hackelia*	83	*Hartwrightia*	174
Grossulariaceae	295	*Haeckeria*	174	*Hasseltia*	583
Grubbia	296	*Haemanthus*	617	*Hasseltiopsis*	583

Hastingsia	671	Henriquezia	509	Hieracium	176
Hatiora	97	Henrya	37	Hierochloe	660
Haworthia	615	Henslowia	438	Hieronima	271
Hazardia	174	Hensmania	620	Hilaria	660
Hebe	556	Heptacodium	118	Hildegardia	576
Hebeclinium	174	Heptanthus	176	Hillebrandia	74
Heberdenia	417	Heptaptera	590	Hillia	509
Hechtia	629	Heracleum	590	Himantoglossum	706
Hedeoma	309	Herbertia	678	Hippeastrum	618
Hederorkis	705	Herissantia	392	Hippocastanaceae	301
Hedinia	221	Heritiera	576	Hippocratea	133
Hedyachras	534	Hermannia	576	Hippocrepis	359
Hedycarya	411	Hermbstaedtia	47	Hiptage	390
Hedychium	751	Hernandia	301	Hiraea	390
Hedyosmum	137	Hernandiaceae	301	Hirschfeldia	222
Hedyotis	508	Herniaria	305	Hirtella	138
Hedysarum	359	Herpetacanthus	37	Hirtzia	706
Hedyscepe	738	Herrania	576	Hladnikia	590
Heisteria	436	Herrickia	176	Hodgkinsonia	510
Helcia	705	Herschelianthe	705	Hoffmannia	510
Heldreichia	221	Hesperaloe	607	Hoffmannseggia	359
Helenium	174	Hesperantha	678	Hohenbergia	629
Helianthella	174	Hesperelaea	438	Hohenbergiopsis	629
Helianthemum	142	Hesperevax	176	Hoita	359
Helianthocereus	97	Hesperis	222	Holarrhena	55
Helianthus	174	Hesperocallis	671	Holboellia	323
Helichrysum	174	Hesperocnide	596	Holcosorus	16
Helicia	473	Hesperolinon	382	Holcus	660
Heliciopsis	474	Hesperomannia	176	Hollandaea	474
Heliconia	669	Hesperoxiphion	678	Hollisteria	465
Heliconiaceae	669	Hessea	618	Holmgrenanthe	556
Helicostylis	413	Hetaeria	706	Holmskioldia	600
Helicteres	576	Heteranthera	746	Holocarpha	176
Helictotrichon	660	Heterocentron	399	Holographis	37
Helietta	526	Heterochaenia	114	Holosteum	124
Heliocauta	175	Heteropappus	176	Holothrix	706
Heliocereus	97	Heteropetalum	51	Holstianthus	510
Heliomeris	175	Heteroplexis	176	Homalium	282
Heliophila	221	Heteropogon	660	Homalomena	624
Heliotropium	83	Heteropteris	390	Homalopetalum	706
Helixanthera	386	Heterospathe	738	Homeria	678
Helleborus	482	Heterostemma	67	Homopholis	660
Helmholtzia	746	Heterotheca	176	Homoranthus	428
Helonias	688	Heterotrichum	399	Hoodia	67
Helosis	71	Heterotropa	61	Hopea	236
Hemandradenia	203	Heuchera	545	Hoplestigma	301
Hemarthria	660	Hexaglottis	678	Hoplestigmataceae	301
Hemiandra	309	Hexalectris	706	Hordeum	660
Hemianthus	556	Hexalobus	51	Horkelia	492
Hemicrambe	222	Hexaneurocarpon	76	Hormathophylla	222
Hemigenia	309	Hexaspora	133	Hornea	534
Hemigraphis	37	Hexastylis	61	Hornschuchia	51
Hemizonia	175	Hibbertia	233	Horridocactus	98
Hemizygia	309	Hibiscadelphus	392	Horsfieldia	415
Henriettea	399	Hibiscus	393	Horstrissea	590
Henriettella	399	Hicksbeachia	474	Hortonia	411

Hosta	670	*Hymenopappus*	177	*Intsia*	361
Hostaceae	670	Hymenophyllaceae	13	*Inula*	177
Houssayanthus	534	*Hymenophyllum*	13	*Inversodicraea*	456
Houstonia	510	*Hymenopyramis*	600	*Iodes*	304
Hovea	359	*Hymenorchis*	706	*Ionactis*	177
Hoverdenia	37	*Hymenostegia*	360	*Ionopsidium*	222
Howea	738	*Hymenostemma*	177	*Iostephane*	177
Howellia	114	*Hymenothrix*	177	*Ipheion*	611
Howelliella	556	*Hymenoxys*	177	*Iphigenia*	638
Hoya	67	*Hyophorbe*	738	*Iphiona*	177
Hubbardia	660	*Hyoseris*	177	*Ipomoea*	205
Hudsonia	143	*Hyospathe*	738	*Ipomopsis*	457
Huernia	67	*Hypagophytum*	209	*Ipsea*	706
Hugonia	383	*Hypecoum*	444	*Irenepharsus*	222
Hulsea	176	*Hyperbaena*	410	*Iresine*	47
Hulthemosa	493	*Hypericum*	297	Iridaceae	673
Humbertochloa	660	*Hypertelis*	410	*Iridodictyum*	678
Humboldtia	359	*Hyphaene*	738	*Iris*	678
Humiriaceae	301	*Hypocalymma*	428	*Iryanthera*	415
Humiriastrum	301	*Hypochoeris*	177	*Isachne*	660
Humularia	360	*Hypodiscus*	747	*Isatis*	222
Hunga	139	*Hypoestes*	37	*Ischaemum*	660
Hunteria	55	*Hypolytrum*	645	*Ischnochloa*	661
Huodendron	578	Hypoxidaceae	673	*Ischyrolepis*	747
Huperzia	2	*Hypoxidia*	673	*Isidorea*	510
Hutchinsia	222	*Hypsela*	114	*Iskandera*	223
Hyacinthaceae	670	*Hypseochloa*	660	*Ismene*	618
Hyacinthella	671	*Hypserpa*	410	*Isocarpha*	177
Hyacinthoides	671	*Hypsophila*	133	*Isocoma*	177
Hyacinthus	671	*Hyptis*	309	*Isodendrion*	601
Hybanthus	601	*Hyssopus*	309	*Isodon*	309
Hydatella	673	*Hysterionica*	177	Isoetaceae	1
Hydatellaceae	673	*Iberis*	222	*Isoetes*	1
Hydnocarpus	282	*Ibervillea*	230	*Isoglossa*	37
Hydnoraceae	301	Icacinaceae	304	*Isolepis*	645
Hydrangea	302	*Ichnanthus*	660	*Isolona*	51
Hydrangeaceae	302	*Ichnocarpus*	55	*Isonandra*	537
Hydrilla	673	*Ichthyothere*	177	*Isoplexis*	556
Hydrobryopsis	456	Idiospermaceae	305	*Isopogon*	474
Hydrobryum	456	*Idiospermum*	305	*Isopyrum*	482
Hydrocharis	673	*Ifloga*	177	*Isotoma*	114
Hydrocharitaceae	673	*Iguanura*	738	*Isotria*	706
Hydrocleys	687	*Ikonnikovia*	453	*Itaobimia*	361
Hydrocotyle	590	*Ilex*	57	*Itaya*	738
Hydrodea	45	*Iliamna*	393	*Iteiluma*	537
Hydrolea	302	Illecebraceae	305	*Iti*	223
Hydropectis	177	Illiciaceae	306	*Itzaea*	206
Hydrophyllaceae	302	*Illicium*	306	*Iva*	178
Hydrophyllum	302	*Ilysanthes*	556	*Ivesia*	493
Hyeronima	271	*Impatiens*	71	*Ixanthus*	286
Hygrophila	37	*Imperatoria*	590	*Ixeris*	178
Hylocereus	98	*Indigofera*	360	*Ixia*	679
Hylomecon	444	*Indopolysolenia*	510	*Ixiolaena*	178
Hylotelephium	209	*Indosinia*	436	*Ixodia*	178
Hymenaea	360	*Indotristicha*	456	Ixonanthaceae	306
Hymenocallis	618	*Inga*	361	*Ixonanthes*	306

Ixora	510	Kendrickia	399	Lacaena	706
Jacaima	67	Kennedia	361	Lacandonia	749
Jacaranda	76	Kentiopsis	739	Laccopetalum	482
Jacksonia	361	Keraudrenia	576	Lachanodes	178
Jacobsenia	45	Kermadecia	474	Lachenalia	671
Jacquemontia	206	Kerriodoxa	739	Lachnaea	582
Jacquinia	581	Keteleeria	23	Lachnocapsa	223
Jaegeria	178	Kickxia	556	Lachnocaulon	650
Jambosa	428	Kingdonia	482	Lacistema	322
Jamesbrittenia	556	Kingiodendron	361	Lacistemataceae	322
Jamesia	302	Kionophyton	706	Lactoridaceae	323
Jamesianthus	178	Kirengeshoma	302	Lactoris	323
Jankaea	292	Kirkia	569	Lactuca	178
Japonolirion	688	Kitaibelia	393	Lactucosonchus	179
Jasione	114	Klattia	680	Lacunaria	478
Jasminocereus	98	Kleinia	178	Ladenbergia	511
Jasminum	438	Knautia	234	Laelia	706
Jasonia	178	Knema	415	Laennecia	179
Jatropha	271	Kniphofia	626	Laetia	282
Jedda	582	Knoxia	511	Lafoensia	387
Jepsonia	546	Koanophyllon	178	Lafuentea	557
Joannesia	271	Kobresia	645	Lagenandra	624
Johannesteijsmannia	739	Kochia	136	Lagenifera	179
Johrenia	590	Kodalyodendron	526	Lagenophora	179
Jollydora	203	Koehneola	178	Lagerstroemia	387
Joosia	511	Koeleria	661	Lagochilus	309
Jordaaniella	45	Koellensteinia	706	Lagoseris	179
Jovibarba	209	Kohleria	292	Lagotis	557
Juania	739	Koilodepas	271	Lambertia	474
Jubaea	739	Kokia	393	Lamium	309
Jubaeopsis	739	Kokoona	134	Lampranthus	45
Juglandaceae	306	Kolkwitzia	118	Lamyropappus	179
Juglans	306	Komarovia	590	Lamyropsis	179
Julbernardia	361	Kopsia	55	Landolphia	55
Julostylis	393	Korthalsella	604	Lannea	48
Jumellea	706	Korthalsia	739	Lantana	600
Juncaceae	683	Kosopoljanskia	590	Lantanopsis	179
Juncaginaceae	684	Kosteletzkya	394	Lapeirousia	680
Juncus	683	Kotschya	361	Laplacea	580
Juniperus	21	Koyamaea	645	Lappula	83
Juno	680	Krameria	307	Lapsana	179
Jurinea	178	Krameriaceae	307	Lardizabalaceae	323
Justicia	37	Krauseola	124	Larix	23
Kaempferia	751	Krigia	178	Laserpitium	591
Kailarsenia	511	Krokia	428	Lasianthaea	179
Kalanchoe	209	Kudoacanthus	39	Lasianthus	511
Kalappia	361	Kundmannia	590	Lasiobema	361
Kalidiopsis	136	Kunkeliella	532	Lasiochlamys	282
Kalimeris	178	Kunstleria	361	Lasiococca	271
Kallstroemia	606	Kuntheria	639	Lasiocorys	310
Kalmia	252	Kunzea	428	Lasiocroton	271
Kalmiella	252	Kyllinga	645	Lasiodiscus	487
Karimbolea	67	Labiatae	307	Lasiopetalum	576
Keenania	511	Labichea	361	Lasiopogon	179
Kefersteinia	706	Labordia	385	Lasthenia	179
Keiskea	309	Labourdonnaisia	537	Lastreopsis	10

Latania	739	*Leontopodium*	179	*Leucothoe*	253
Lateropora	252	*Leopoldia*	671	*Leuzea*	180
Lathraea	557	*Leopoldinia*	739	*Lewisia*	467
Lathyrus	361	*Lepanthes*	707	*Leymus*	661
Launaea	179	*Lepanthopsis*	709	*Liabum*	180
Lauraceae	323	*Lepechinia*	310	*Liatris*	180
Laurembergia	300	*Lepidagathis*	39	*Libertia*	680
Laurentia	114	*Lepiderema*	534	*Libocedrus*	21
Lautembergia	271	*Lepidium*	223	*Libyella*	661
Lavanduia	310	*Lepidobolus*	747	*Licania*	139
Lavatera	394	*Lepidocaryum*	739	*Licaria*	325
Lavoisiera	400	*Lepidocordia*	83	*Licuala*	739
Lavoixia	739	*Lepidolopha*	180	*Ligeophila*	709
Lawrencia	394	*Lepidorrhachis*	739	*Ligularia*	181
Laxmannia	620	*Lepidospartum*	180	*Ligusticum*	591
Layia	179	*Lepidosperma*	645	*Ligustrum*	438
Lazarum	624	*Lepidothamnus*	27	*Lilaeopsis*	591
Leandra	400	*Lepinia*	55	Liliaceae	684
Leavenworthia	223	*Lepisanthes*	535	Liliopsida (monocots)	606
Lebronnecia	394	*Lepisorus*	16	*Lilium*	686
Lecaniodiscus	534	*Leptactina*	511	Limnanthaceae	382
Lecanorchis	707	*Leptinella*	180	*Limnanthes*	382
Lechea	143	*Leptocereus*	98	Limnocharitaceae	687
Lechenaultia	295	*Leptochilus*	16	*Limnophila*	557
Lecocarpus	179	*Leptochiton*	618	*Limnopoa*	661
Lecomtedoxa	537	*Leptochloa*	661	*Limoniopsis*	453
Lecythidaceae	329	*Leptodactylon*	457	*Limonium*	453
Lecythis	332	*Leptodermis*	511	*Limosella*	557
Ledebouria	671	*Leptoderris*	362	Linaceae	382
Ledebouriella	591	*Leptomeria*	532	*Linanthus*	457
Ledermaniella	456	*Leptopteris*	15	*Linaria*	557
Ledodendron	252	*Leptopus*	271	*Lindackeria*	282
Ledothamnus	252	*Leptorhynchos*	180	*Lindelofia*	83
Leea	332	*Leptosema*	362	*Lindenbergia*	558
Leeaceae	332	*Leptospermum*	428	*Lindenia*	511
Leersia	661	*Leptostylis*	537	*Lindera*	325
Legenere	114	*Lepturidium*	661	*Lindernia*	558
Legrandia	428	*Lepturus*	661	*Lindmania*	629
Leguminosae	332	*Lepyrodia*	747	*Lindsaea*	9
Leiospora	223	*Lereschia*	591	*Linnaeopsis*	292
Leitneria	381	*Lesliea*	709	*Linociera*	438
Leitneriaceae	381	*Lespedeza*	362	*Linospadix*	740
Lellingeria	13	*Lesquerella*	224	*Linum*	383
Lembertia	179	*Lessertia*	362	*Liodendron*	271
Lemboglossum	707	*Lessingia*	180	*Liparia*	362
Lemna	684	*Leucadendron*	474	*Liparis*	709
Lemnaceae	684	*Leucaena*	362	*Lipocarpha*	645
Lemurophoenix	739	*Leucanthemum*	180	*Lipochaeta*	181
Lenbrassia	292	*Leucas*	310	*Lippia*	600
Lendneria	557	*Leuchtenbergia*	98	*Liquidambar*	300
Lennoaceae	381	*Leucochrysum*	180	*Liriodendron*	387
Lentibulariaceae	382	*Leucocoryne*	611	*Lisianthius*	286
Leochilus	707	*Leucocroton*	271	*Lisianthus*	287
Leonia	601	*Leucojum*	618	*Lissanthe*	244
Leontochir	616	*Leucopogon*	243	*Listera*	710
Leontodon	179	*Leucospermum*	475	*Litchi*	535

Lithachne	661	Loxogramme	16	Macranthera	558
Lithocarpus	278	Loxsoma	14	Macrocarpaea	287
Lithodora	83	Loxsomataceae	14	Macroclinium	710
Lithophila	47	Loxsomopsis	14	Macrocnemum	511
Lithophragma	546	Lozania	322	Macrohasseltia	583
Lithops	45	Ludwigia	441	Macrolobium	366
Lithospermum	83	Luffa	230	Macromeria	83
Litsea	325	Lugoa	181	Macropiper	447
Livistona	740	Luina	181	Macropteranthes	144
Lloydia	686	Luisia	710	Macrosamanea	366
Loasa	384	Lunania	282	Macrostelia	394
Loasaceae	384	Lunaria	225	Macrostylis	526
Lobelia	114	Lundellianthus	181	Macrotyloma	366
Lobivia	98	Lupinus	364	Macrozamia	32
Lobostemon	83	Luzula	683	Madhuca	537
Lobularia	225	Lycaste	710	Madia	182
Lochia	305	Lychnis	124	Maerua	118
Lockhartia	710	Lychnophora	181	Maesa	417
Lodoicea	740	Lycianthes	570	Magnistipula	142
Loeflingia	124	Lycium	570	Magnolia	387
Loesenera	362	Lycomormium	710	Magnoliaceae	387
Loeseneriella	134	Lycopodiaceae	2	Magnoliopsida (dicots)	34
Loewia	584	Lycopodiella	2	Mahonia	74
Logania	385	Lycopodiopsida	1	Maianthemum	639
Loganiaceae	384	Lycopodium	2	Maingaya	301
Logfia	181	Lycopus	310	Maireana	136
Lolium	661	lycosphen	1	Malacothamnus	394
Lomandra	688	Lygodesmia	181	Malacothrix	182
Lomandraceae	688	Lymania	629	Malagasia	475
Lomariopsidaceae	13	Lyonia	253	Malaisia	413
Lomatia	475	Lyonothamnus	493	Malania	437
Lomatium	591	Lysiana	386	Malaxis	710
Lomatophyllum	615	Lysiclesia	253	Malcolmia	225
Lomatozona	181	Lysimachia	469	Malesherbia	389
Lonchocarpus	362	Lysionotus	292	Malesherbiaceae	389
Lonchostoma	89	Lythraceae	386	Malleola	711
Lonicera	118	Lythrum	387	Mallotus	272
Lopezia	441	Lytocaryum	740	Malmea	51
Lophochlaena	661	Mabrya	558	Malope	394
Lophochloa	661	Macadamia	475	Malouetia	55
Lopholaena	181	Macaranga	271	Malpighia	390
Lophophora	98	Macarthuria	410	Malpighiaceae	389
Lophoschoenus	645	Macbridea	310	Maltebrunia	661
Lophospermum	558	Machaeranthera	181	Malus	493
Lophostachys	39	Machaerina	645	Malvaceae	391
Loranthaceae	385	Machaerium	365	Malvaviscus	394
Loranthus	386	Machaonia	511	Mammea	299
Lordhowea	181	Machilus	326	Mammillaria	98
Lotononis	362	Mackeea	740	Mananthes	39
Lotus	363	Mackenziea	39	Mancoa	225
Loudetia	661	Macleania	253	Mandevilla	55
Lourtella	387	Maclura	413	Mandragora	571
Louteridium	39	Maclurodendron	526	Manettia	511
Lowiaceae	688	Maclurolyra	661	Manfreda	607
Loxococcus	740	Macodes	710	Mangifera	48
Loxodera	661	Macowania	182	Manglietia	388

Manihot	272	Meconopsis	444	Menyanthaceae	410
Manilkara	538	Mecranium	400	Menziesia	253
Mantisia	752	Medemia	740	Merendera	638
Manulea	558	Medicago	366	Meriania	401
Mapania	645	Medicosma	527	Merremia	206
Marah	230	Medinilla	400	Merrilliopanax	59
Marantaceae	688	Medusagynaceae	396	Mertensia	83
Maranthes	142	Medusagyne	396	Merxmuellera	661
Marantochloa	688	Medusandra	396	Meryta	59
Marasmodes	182	Medusandraceae	396	Mesadenus	712
Marathrum	456	Meehania	310	Mesanthemum	650
Marattia	14	Megacarpaea	225	Mesembryanthemum	45
Marattiaceae	14	Megadenia	225	Mesoglossum	712
Marcetella	494	Megalachne	661	Mespilus	494
Marcgravia	396	Megaleranthis	482	Mesua	299
Marcgraviaceae	396	Megalopanax	59	Metalasia	182
Maresia	225	Megalostoma	39	Metaporana	206
Margaritaria	273	Megastylis	712	Metarungia	39
Margyracaena	494	Meineckia	273	Metasequoia	29
Margyricarpus	494	Melaleuca	429	Metathelypteris	17
Maripa	206	Melampodium	182	Meteoromyrtus	429
Mariscus	645	Melampyrum	558	Metharme	606
Markea	571	Melandrium	124	Metrodorea	528
Marlierea	429	Melanochyla	48	Metrosideros	429
Marojejya	740	Melanodendron	182	Metroxylon	740
Marrubium	310	Melanoselinum	592	Mexacanthus	39
Marsdenia	67	Melanospermum	558	Mexicoa	712
Marshallia	182	Melanthera	182	Meximalva	394
Marsilea	14	Melanthiaceae	688	Mexipedium	712
Marsileaceae	14	Melastoma	400	Meziella	300
Martiodendron	366	Melastomastrum	400	Mezilaurus	326
Mascagnia	391	Melastomataceae	396	Michauxia	115
Masdevallia	711	Melhania	576	Michelia	388
Masoala	740	Meliaceae	406	Miconia	401
Mastichodendron	538	Melianthaceae	409	Micraira	661
Mastigostyla	680	Melica	661	Micranthemum	558
Mastixia	206	Melichrus	244	Micrantheum	273
Matayba	535	Melicope	527	Micranthocereus	101
Matelea	67	Melicytus	601	Microberlinia	366
Mathieua	618	Melilotus	366	Microbiota	21
Mathurina	585	Melinis	661	Microcitrus	528
Matisia	78	Meliosma	409	Microcnemum	136
Matthiola	225	Meliosmaceae	409	Micrococca	273
Mattiastrum	83	Mellissia	571	Microcorys	310
Matucana	101	Melocactus	101	Microcycas	33
Matudaea	301	Melochia	577	Microderis	182
Maughaniella	45	Melodinus	55	Microlepia	9
Mauritia	740	Melodorum	51	Microlepidium	225
Mauritiella	740	Melothria	230	Micromeria	310
Maxburretia	740	Memecylon	400	Micromyrtus	429
Maxillaria	712	Mendoncia	39	Micropholis	538
Mayna	282	Meniscogyne	596	Micropyropsis	661
Maytenus	134	Menispermaceae	409	Microschoenus	684
Mazus	558	Menkea	225	Microseris	182
Mecomischus	182	Mentha	310	Microsorium	16
Meconella	444	Mentzelia	384	Microsorum	16

Microspermum	182	Monizia	592	Murdannia	638
Microstaphyla	14	Monnina	459	Muretia	592
Microstrobos	27	Monochaetum	403	Murraya	528
Microtis	712	Monocostus	640	Musa	689
Microtropis	134	monocot	606	Musaceae	689
Mikania	183	Monocyclanthus	52	Muscari	672
Mila	101	Monolena	403	Musineon	592
Miliusa	51	Monolopia	183	Mussaenda	512
Millettia	366	Monopetalanthus	366	Musschia	115
Milligania	626	Monophyllaea	292	Mutisia	183
Miltoniopsis	712	Monopyle	292	Mycetia	512
Mimetes	475	Monotes	237	Myodocarpus	59
Mimosa	366	Monotoca	244	Myonima	512
Mimulus	558	Monotropsis	253	Myoporaceae	414
Mimusops	539	Monsonia	288	Myopordon	183
Minthostachys	311	Monstera	624	Myoporum	414
Minuartia	124	Montamans	512	Myosotidium	84
Mirabilis	435	Montanoa	183	Myosotis	84
Miraglossum	68	Montia	467	Myosurus	482
Mirandea	39	Montiniaceae	411	Myrceugenia	430
Mirbelia	366	Montrouziera	299	Myrcia	430
Miricacalia	183	Monttea	559	Myrcianthes	430
Miscanthus	661	Mora	366	Myrciaria	430
Mischocarpus	535	Moraceae	411	Myriactis	183
Misopates	559	Moraea	680	Myrica	415
Mitella	546	Moratia	740	Myricaceae	415
Mitolepis	68	Moricandia	225	Myricanthe	273
Mitostigma	68	Morina	414	Myriophyllum	300
Mitracarpus	512	Morinaceae	414	Myristica	415
Mitranthes	429	Morinda	512	Myristicaceae	415
Mitrantia	429	Moringa	414	Myrrhidendron	592
Mitrastemon	478	Moringaceae	414	Myrrhinium	430
Mitrephora	51	Mormodes	712	Myrsinaceae	415
Mitrophyllum	45	Mortoniella	56	Myrsine	417
Mitrostigma	512	Mortoniodendron	583	Myrtaceae	419
Moacroton	273	Morus	413	Myrteola	430
Modiolastrum	394	Mosiera	429	Myrtus	430
Moehringia	126	Mosla	311	Myxopyrum	439
Mogoltavia	592	Mossia	45	Nageia	28
Molinaea	535	Mouretia	512	Najas	673
Mollinedia	411	Mouriri	403	Nama	302
Molluginaceae	410	Moussonia	292	Nananthea	183
Mollugo	410	Mozartia	429	Nanothamnus	183
Moltkia	84	Mucoa	56	Napoleonaea	332
Momordica	230	Mucronea	465	Narcissus	618
Monactis	183	Mucuna	367	Nargedia	512
Monadenia	712	Muehlenbeckia	465	Narthecium	688
Monadenium	273	Muellerina	386	Nashia	600
Monanthes	210	Muhlenbergia	661	Nastanthus	107
Monanthotaxis	51	Muilla	611	Nathaliella	559
Monarda	311	Muiria	45	Nauclea	512
Monardella	311	Munnozia	183	Naucleopsis	413
Monechma	39	Munroidendron	59	Naufraga	592
Monimiaceae	411	Munronia	407	Nautilocalyx	292
Monimiastrum	429	Muraltia	459	Navarretia	458
Monimopetalum	134	Murbeckiella	225	Navia	629

Neanotis	512	Nertera	512	Notodon	367
Necepsia	273	Nervilia	713	Notodontia	512
Necranthus	559	Nesaea	387	Notonia	183
Nectandra	326	Nesiota	487	Notoptera	183
Nectaroscordum	611	Nesocaryum	84	Notospartium	367
Neea	435	Nesocodon	115	Notothixos	604
Negria	293	Nesogenaceae	434	Nototriche	394
Neisosperma	56	Nesogenes	434	Nototrichium	47
Nelia	45	Nesohedyotis	512	Notylia	713
Nemacladus	115	Nesoluma	539	Nouelia	183
Nemastylis	681	Neuburgia	385	Nouettea	56
Nematopoa	662	Neuracanthus	39	Nowickea	447
Nemcia	367	Neurachne	662	Nuihonia	253
Nemesia	559	Neurocalyx	512	Nuphar	436
Nenga	740	Neurolaena	183	Nuxia	89
Neoastelia	627	Neuropeltis	206	Nyctaginaceae	435
Neobesseya	101	Neuwiedia	713	Nymphaeaceae	436
Neobolusia	713	Neviusia	494	Nymphoides	410
Neobracea	56	Newcastelia	600	Nyssa	206
Neobuxbaumia	101	Newtonia	367	Oberonia	713
Neobyrnesia	528	Nicolletia	183	Obetia	596
Neocallitropsis	21	Nicotiana	571	Obregonia	102
Neocheiropteris	16	Nidorella	183	Oceanopapaver	118
Neochevalierodendron	367	Niedzwedzkia	76	Ochlandra	662
Neocogniauxia	713	Nierembergia	571	Ochna	436
Neocuatrecasia	183	Nigella	482	Ochnaceae	436
Neofinetia	713	Nigritella	713	Ochreinauclea	512
Neofranciella	512	Nilgirianthus	39	Ochrosia	56
Neogontscharovia	456	Niphogeton	592	Ochrothallus	539
Neohenricia	45	Nipponanthemum	183	Ocimum	312
Neolemonniera	539	Nirarathamnos	592	Ocotea	328
Neolitsea	328	Nissolia	367	Octoknema	437
Neomirandea	183	Nitrophila	136	Oddoniodendron	367
Neomoorea	713	Nivenia	681	Odixia	183
Neoparrya	592	Noahdendron	301	Odontites	559
Neopatersonia	672	Noccaea	225	Odontochilus	713
Neopicrorhiza	559	Nodocarpaea	512	Odontocline	183
Neoporteria	101	Nogra	367	Odontoglossum	713
Neopringlea	283	Nolana	571	Odontonema	39
Neoregelia	630	Nolina	649	Odontophorus	45
Neoroepera	273	Nomosa	84	Oeceoclades	714
Neosprucea	583	Nonea	84	Oecopetalum	305
Neostapfia	662	Normanbya	740	Oedera	184
Neostenanthera	52	Normania	571	Oenanthe	592
Neostrearia	301	Northea	539	Oenocarpus	740
Neottia	713	Notanthera	386	Oenothera	442
Neoveitchia	740	Notechidnopsis	68	Oeoniella	714
Nepenthaceae	434	Notelaea	439	Oerstedina	293
Nepenthes	434	Nothoalsomitra	230	Oianthus	68
Nepeta	311	Nothocestrum	571	Okenia	435
Nephropetalum	577	Nothofagus	278	Olacaceae	436
Nephrosperma	740	Notholaena	3	Olax	437
Nephthytis	624	Nothopegia	48	Oldenburgia	184
Neraudia	596	Nothospondias	569	Oldenlandia	512
Neriacanthus	39	Nothotsuga	23	Olea	439
Nerine	619	Notochloe	662	Oleaceae	437

Oleandra	14
Oleandraceae	14
Olearia	184
Oligoceras	273
Oliniaceae	439
Oliveriana	714
Olmeca	662
Olymposciadium	592
Olyra	662
Omalanthus	273
Omalotheca	184
Omiltemia	513
Omphalea	273
Omphalodes	84
Onagraceae	439
Oncidium	714
Oncodostigma	52
Oncosperma	741
Onobrychis	367
Ononis	367
Onopordum	184
Onoseris	184
Onosma	84
Onosmodium	85
Oonopsis	185
Oparanthus	185
Opercularia	513
Operculina	206
Ophellantha	274
Ophioglossaceae	14
Ophioglossum	15
Ophiopogon	639
Ophiorrhiza	513
Ophrypetalum	52
Ophrys	714
Ophthalmophyllum	46
Opiliaceae	442
Opithandra	293
Oplonia	39
Opuntia	102
Orania	741
Orbea	68
Orbeanthus	68
Orbeopsis	68
Orbexilum	368
Orchidaceae	689
Orchidantha	688
Orchis	715
Orcuttia	662
Oreithales	483
Oreobliton	136
Oreocereus	104
Oreodendron	582
Oreomunnea	307
Oreomyrrhis	592
Oreonana	592
Oreopanax	59
Oreoporanthera	274
Oreopteris	17
Oreorchis	715
Oreoxis	592
Oricia	528
Oriciopsis	528
Origanum	312
Orites	475
Oritrophium	185
Ormenis	185
Ormocarpum	368
Ormosia	368
Ornithoboea	293
Ornithocarpa	225
Ornithocephalus	715
Ornithogalum	672
Ornithoglossum	638
Ornithopus	368
Orobanche	559
Orochaenactis	185
Oropetium	662
Orophea	52
Orostachys	210
Orothamnus	475
Ortegocactus	104
Orthaea	253
Orthocarpus	560
Orthopterum	46
Orthopterygium	48
Orthosiphon	312
Oryctes	571
Oryza	662
Oryzopsis	662
Osbeckia	404
Oschatzia	592
Osmanthus	439
Osmorhiza	592
Osmoxylon	59
Osmunda	15
Osmundaceae	15
Ossaea	404
Osteospermum	185
Ostodes	274
Ostrearia	301
Ostrowskia	115
Ostrya	207
Otacanthus	560
Otholobium	368
Othonna	185
Otiophora	513
Otoba	415
Otocarpus	226
Otophora	535
Otostegia	312
Ottelia	673
Ottoschulzia	305
Ouratea	436
Owenia	407
Oxalidaceae	442
Oxalis	442
Oxandra	52
Oxanthera	528
Oxera	600
Oxyanthus	513
Oxygonum	465
Oxygyne	637
Oxypolis	592
Oxystigma	368
Oxystylis	118
Oxytheca	465
Oxytropis	368
Ozoroa	48
Ozothamnus	185
Pachites	715
Pachyanthus	404
Pachycarpus	68
Pachycereus	104
Pachyctenium	592
Pachycymbium	68
Pachylarnax	388
Pachyphyllum	715
Pachypodium	56
Pachysandra	91
Pachystegia	185
Pachystela	539
Pachystigma	514
Paeonia	443
Paeoniaceae	443
Paepalanthus	650
Paesia	9
Palaeocyanus	185
Palafoxia	185
Palaquium	539
Palaua	395
Palicourea	514
Palisota	639
Palmae	726
Palmeria	411
Palmorchis	715
Pamianthe	619
Panamanthus	386
Panax	59
Pancheria	231
Pancratium	619
Pandanaceae	745
Pandanus	745
Panicum	662
Papaver	444
Papaveraceae	443
Paphinia	715
Paphiopedilum	715

Papperitzia	716	*Patrinia*	598	*Pentaplaris*	583
Parabarium	56	*Pauia*	571	*Pentas*	514
Paraboea	293	*Paullinia*	535	*Pentaschistis*	663
Paracaleana	716	*Paulownia*	560	*Peperomia*	447
Paracalyx	369	*Pauridia*	673	*Peponium*	230
Paracaryum	85	*Pausinystalia*	514	*Peponopsis*	230
Paracautleya	752	*Pavetta*	514	*Pera*	274
Paradrymonia	293	*Pavonia*	395	*Peraxilla*	386
Parafaujasia	185	*Paxistima*	134	*Perebea*	413
Parahancornia	56	*Payena*	539	*Pereskia*	104
Parahebe	560	*Pearcea*	293	*Perezia*	186
Parahyparrhenia	662	*Pearsonia*	370	*Pericallis*	186
Paraixeris	185	*Pectinaria*	68	*Pericampylus*	410
Parajubaea	741	*Pectis*	186	*Perideridia*	592
Paramachaerium	369	Pedaliaceae	446	*Peripentadenia*	243
Paramongaia	619	*Peddiea*	582	*Periptera*	395
Paranephelium	535	*Pedicularis*	560	*Peristeria*	716
Paranomus	475	*Pedilanthus*	274	*Peristrophe*	39
Parantennaria	185	*Pedilochilus*	716	*Peristylus*	716
Paraphalaenopsis	716	*Pediocactus*	104	*Perittostema*	86
Pararistolochia	61	*Pediomelum*	370	*Perityle*	186
Parashorea	237	*Pegolettia*	186	*Persea*	328
Parasicyos	230	*Pelagodoxa*	741	*Persicaria*	466
Parasilaus	592	*Pelargonium*	288	*Persoonia*	476
Paraskevia	86	*Pelea*	528	*Perymenium*	187
Paratecoma	76	*Pelecyphora*	104	*Pescatoria*	716
Parathesis	418	*Peliosanthes*	639	*Petagnia*	593
Paratrophis	413	*Pellacalyx*	489	*Petalonyx*	384
Paravitex	600	*Pellaea*	3	*Petasites*	187
Parentucellia	560	*Pellegriniodendron*	370	*Petchia*	56
Pariana	662	*Pelliciera*	446	*Petelotiella*	596
Parietaria	596	Pellicieraceae	446	*Peteravenia*	187
Parinari	142	*Pellionia*	596	*Peterodendron*	283
Parishella	115	*Peltaea*	395	*Petrea*	600
Parkeriaceae	15	*Peltanthera*	89	*Petrobium*	187
Parkia	369	*Peltariopsis*	226	*Petrocoma*	126
Parkinsonia	370	*Peltoboykinia*	546	*Petrocoptis*	126
Parmentiera	76	*Peltophorum*	370	*Petronymphe*	611
Parnassia	445	Penaeaceae	447	*Petrophile*	476
Parnassiaceae	445	*Penelopeia*	230	*Petrophyton*	494
Parodianthus	600	*Peniocereus*	104	*Petrorhagia*	126
Parolinia	226	*Pennantia*	305	*Petrosimonia*	136
Paronychia	305	*Pennellia*	226	*Peucedanum*	593
Parrya	226	*Pennisetum*	663	*Phacelia*	302
Parsonsia	56	*Penstemon*	561	*Phaeanthus*	52
Parthenice	185	*Pentacalia*	186	*Phaedranassa*	619
Parthenium	185	*Pentachaeta*	186	*Phagnalon*	187
Pasania	278	*Pentachondra*	244	*Phaius*	716
Paschalococos	741	*Pentagonia*	514	*Phalacrocarpum*	187
Paspalidium	662	*Pentagramma*	3	*Phalaenopsis*	716
Paspalum	663	*Pentaloncha*	514	*Phalaris*	663
Passerina	582	*Pentameris*	663	*Phanera*	370
Passiflora	445	*Pentapanax*	59	*Phaseolus*	370
Passifloraceae	445	*Pentapeltis*	592	*Phebalium*	528
Pastinaca	592	*Pentaphragma*	447	*Pheidonocarpa*	293
Pastinacopsis	592	Pentaphragmataceae	447	*Phellodendron*	529

Phenax	596	*Physogyne*	717	*Pittosporum*	450
Phialanthus	515	*Physokentia*	741	*Pityopsis*	187
Phidiasia	39	*Physoplexis*	115	*Pityrodia*	600
Philadelphus	302	*Physoptychis*	226	*Placea*	619
Philbornea	384	*Physostegia*	313	*Placodiscus*	535
Philibertia	69	*Phytelephas*	741	*Pladaroxylon*	187
Philippia	253	*Phyteuma*	115	*Plagianthus*	395
Philodendron	624	*Phytolacca*	447	*Plagiobothrys*	86
Philydraceae	746	Phytolaccaceae	447	*Plagiogyria*	15
Phinaea	293	*Piaranthus*	69	Plagiogyriaceae	16
Phippsia	663	*Picconia*	439	*Plagiolirion*	619
Phlebophyllum	39	*Picea*	23	*Plagiosiphon*	370
Phlegmatospermum	226	*Picramnia*	569	*Plagius*	187
Phleum	663	*Picrasma*	569	*Plakothira*	384
Phlomis	312	*Picris*	187	*Planchonella*	539
Phlox	458	*Picrodendron*	276	Plantaginaceae	451
Phoebanthus	187	*Pieris*	254	*Plantago*	451
Phoebe	328	*Pierreodendron*	570	*Platanthera*	717
Phoenicanthus	52	*Pilea*	596	*Platycalyx*	254
Phoenicophorium	741	*Pilgerodendron*	21	*Platycarpum*	515
Phoenix	741	*Pilocarpus*	529	*Platycaulos*	747
Pholidocarpus	741	*Pilocosta*	404	*Platycerium*	16
Pholidota	717	*Pilopleura*	593	*Platycladus*	22
Pholisma	381	*Pilosocereus*	105	*Platycoryne*	718
Pholistoma	304	*Pilostyles*	478	*Platydesma*	529
Phoradendron	604	*Pimelea*	582	*Platyglottis*	718
Phormiaceae	746	*Pimenta*	431	*Platygyne*	276
Photinia	494	*Pimpinella*	593	*Platylepis*	718
Phragmanthera	386	Pinaceae	22	*Platylobium*	370
Phragmipedium	717	*Pinanga*	741	*Platymiscium*	370
Phreatia	717	*Pinaropappus*	187	*Platysace*	593
Phryna	126	*Pinarophyllon*	515	*Platyspermation*	257
Phrynium	688	*Pinguicula*	381	*Platystele*	718
Phthirusa	386	Pinopsida	19	*Plectocomia*	742
Phycella	619	*Pinosia*	126	*Plectocomiopsis*	742
Phylica	487	*Pintoa*	606	*Plectorrhiza*	718
Phyllacanthus	515	*Pinus*	24	*Plectrachne*	663
Phyllagathis	404	*Piper*	449	*Plectranthus*	313
Phyllanthus	274	Piperaceae	447	*Plectronia*	439
Phyllitis	5	*Piperia*	717	*Plegmatolemma*	40
Phyllopodium	563	*Piptadenia*	370	*Pleiomeris*	418
Phyllospadix	752	*Piptadeniopsis*	370	*Pleione*	718
Phyllostachys	663	*Piptochaetinum*	663	*Pleiospermium*	529
Phyllostegia	313	*Piptochaetium*	663	*Pleiospilos*	46
Phyllota	370	*Piptostigma*	52	*Pleodendron*	117
Phymaspermum	187	*Pipturus*	597	*Pleomele*	649
Phymosia	395	*Piqueriopsis*	187	*Pleopeltis*	16
Physacanthus	40	*Pisonia*	435	*Plethiandra*	404
Physaliastrum	571	*Pisoniella*	436	*Pleurisanthes*	305
Physalis	571	*Pistacia*	48	*Pleurocarpaea*	187
Physaria	226	*Pitardia*	313	*Pleuropappus*	187
Physinga	717	*Pitavia*	529	*Pleuropetalum*	47
Physocalyx	563	*Pitcairnia*	630	*Pleurostylia*	134
Physocardamum	226	*Pithecellobium*	370	*Pleurothallis*	718
Physoceras	717	Pittosporaceae	450	*Pleurothyrium*	328
Physochlaina	571	*Pittosporopsis*	305	*Plicosepalus*	386

Plinia	431	*Polytrema*	40	*Protea*	476
Plinthanthesis	663	*Polyzygus*	593	Proteaceae	471
Pluchea	187	*Pomaderris*	487	*Protium*	90
Plumbaginaceae	452	*Pomatocalpa*	720	*Prumnopitys*	29
Pneumatopteris	17	*Ponera*	720	*Prunella*	314
Poa	663	Pontederiaceae	746	*Prunus*	495
Podadenia	276	*Ponthieva*	720	*Psacalium*	187
Podalyria	371	*Popowia*	52	*Psammisia*	254
Podistera	593	*Populus*	531	*Psammosilene*	126
Podocarpaceae	27	*Porlieria*	606	*Psathura*	515
Podocarpus	28	*Porodittia*	563	*Psathyrostachys*	665
Podolepis	187	*Porophyllum*	187	*Pseudagrostistachys*	276
Podonephelium	535	*Porroglossum*	720	*Pseudanthus*	276
Podonosma	86	*Portlandia*	515	*Pseudarrhenatherum*	665
Podophorus	665	*Portulaca*	467	*Pseudephedranthus*	52
Podostemaceae	456	Portulacaceae	467	*Pseuderanthemum*	40
Poecilanthe	371	*Potamogeton*	746	*Pseuderemostachys*	314
Poeciloneuron	299	Potamogetonaceae	746	*Pseudima*	535
Poellnitzia	616	*Potentilla*	494	*Pseudobaeckea*	89
Pogogyne	314	*Pothos*	624	*Pseudobahia*	187
Pogonotium	742	*Poupartia*	49	*Pseudobombax*	78
Pogostemon	314	*Pourouma*	132	*Pseudocarapa*	407
Pohlidium	665	*Pouteria*	540	*Pseudocarpidium*	601
Poikilacanthus	40	*Pouzolzia*	597	*Pseudocatalpa*	76
Polanisia	118	*Povedadaphne*	328	*Pseudocentrum*	720
Polemoniaceae	456	*Pradosia*	543	*Pseudoclappia*	188
Polemonium	458	*Prangos*	593	*Pseudoconnarus*	203
Polhillia	371	*Prasophyllum*	720	*Pseudocranichis*	720
Polianthes	607	*Pratia*	116	*Pseudocyclosorus*	17
Pollia	639	*Premna*	600	*Pseudodanthonia*	665
Polyalthia	52	*Prenanthes*	187	*Pseudoeugenia*	431
Polybotrya	11	*Prepusa*	287	*Pseudoglochidion*	276
Polycarena	563	*Prestoea*	742	*Pseudolarix*	26
Polycarpaea	126	*Prestonia*	56	*Pseudolmedia*	414
Polycarpon	126	*Primula*	469	*Pseudolysimachion*	563
Polyceratocarpus	52	Primulaceae	468	*Pseudomarrubium*	314
Polyctenium	226	*Primularia*	404	*Pseudomussaenda*	515
Polygala	459	*Prionanthium*	665	*Pseudopanax*	60
Polygalaceae	459	*Prionotrichon*	226	*Pseudophegopteris*	17
Polygonaceae	461	*Priotropis*	371	*Pseudophleum*	665
Polygonatum	639	*Prismatocarpus*	116	*Pseudophoenix*	742
Polygonella	466	*Prismatomeris*	515	*Pseudopyxis*	515
Polygonum	466	*Pristimera*	134	*Pseudorhipsalis*	105
Polylepis	494	*Pritchardia*	742	*Pseudosabicea*	515
Polylophium	593	*Pritchardiopsis*	742	*Pseudosalacia*	134
Polymnia	187	*Priva*	600	*Pseudosciadium*	60
Polyneura	665	*Proatriplex*	136	*Pseudoscolopia*	283
Polyosma	257	*Proboscidea*	446	*Pseudostellaria*	126
Polypleurella	456	*Prockia*	583	*Pseudotaxus*	29
Polypodiaceae	16	*Procopiania*	86	*Pseudotsuga*	26
Polypodium	16	*Procris*	597	*Pseudovesicaria*	226
Polypogon	665	*Pronephrium*	17	*Pseudoxandra*	52
Polyscias	59	*Prosopanche*	301	*Pseuduvaria*	52
Polysphaeria	515	*Prosopis*	371	*Psiadia*	188
Polystachya	719	*Prostanthera*	314	*Psidium*	431
Polystichum	11	*Protarum*	625	*Psiguria*	230

Psilocarphus	188	Purshia	496	Ravenia	529
Psiloesthes	40	Putranjiva	276	Razisea	40
Psilostachys	276	Puya	631	Reaumuria	579
Psilotaceae	2	Pycnandra	543	Rebutia	105
Psilotrichum	47	Pycnanthemum	314	Redowskia	226
Psilotum	2	Pycnarrhena	410	Reedia	645
Psittacanthus	386	Pycnospatha	625	Reediella	13
Psoralea	371	Pycreus	645	Reedrollinsia	52
Psoralidium	372	Pyrenacantha	305	Reevesia	577
Psorothamnus	372	Pyrenaria	580	Regelia	431
Psychilis	720	Pyrethrum	188	Rehderodendron	578
Psychotria	515	Pyrostria	518	Rehia	665
Psydrax	518	Pyrrhocactus	105	Reichardia	188
Psygmorchis	720	Pyrrocoma	188	Reicheia	431
Pteleopsis	144	Pyrrosia	16	Reidia	276
Pteralyxia	56	Pyrus	496	Reinhardtia	743
Pterandra	391	Pyxidanthera	232	Reldia	293
Pterichis	720	Qiongzhuea	665	Relhania	188
Pteridaceae	16	Quaqua	69	Remijia	519
Pteridopsida	3	Quararibea	79	Remusatia	625
Pteridrys	11	Quassia	570	Remya	189
Pteris	16	Quercus	278	Renanthera	721
Pterisanthes	605	Quesnelia	634	Renealmia	752
Pternopetalum	594	Quiina	478	Reseda	485
Pterocarpus	372	Quiinaceae	478	Resedaceae	485
Pteroceltis	585	Quinchamalium	532	Restio	747
Pterocephalus	235	Quintinia	258	Restionaceae	747
Pteroceras	720	Rabiea	46	Restrepia	721
Pteroglossaspis	720	Radermachera	76	Restrepiopsis	721
Pteronia	188	Rafflesia	478	Retama	372
Pterosicyos	230	Rafflesiaceae	478	Retrophyllum	29
Pterospermum	577	Rafnia	372	Reutealis	276
Pterostylis	720	Rahowardiana	571	Revealia	189
Pterostyrax	578	Raillardella	188	Reyemia	564
Pterothrix	188	Raillardiopsis	188	Reynoldsia	60
Pterygodium	721	Rajania	649	Reynosia	488
Pterygota	577	Ramatuela	144	Rhabdodendraceae	485
Ptilagrostis	665	Ramonda	293	Rhabdodendron	485
Ptilimnium	594	Ramorinoa	372	Rhabdosciadium	594
Ptilostemon	188	Ramosmania	518	Rhadamanthus	672
Ptilotrichum	226	Randia	518	Rhagodia	136
Ptilotus	47	Ranunculaceae	478	Rhamnaceae	485
Ptychopyxis	276	Ranunculus	483	Rhamnidium	488
Ptychosema	372	Ranzania	75	Rhamnus	488
Ptychosperma	742	Raoulia	188	Rhamphicarpa	564
Pubistylus	518	Rapanea	418	Rhamphogyne	189
Puccinellia	665	Raphanorhyncha	226	Rhaphidophora	625
Pucciphippsia	665	Raphia	743	Rhaphidophyton	136
Pueraria	372	Raphidophora	625	Rhaphidospora	40
Pulchranthus	40	Raphionacme	69	Rhaphithamnus	601
Pulicaria	188	Raritebe	518	Rhapis	743
Pulmonaria	86	Raspalia	89	Rhaponticum	189
Pulsatilla	483	Rauhia	619	Rhaptopetalum	569
Pultenaea	372	Raulinoa	529	Rhazya	57
Punica	387	Rauvolfia	57	Rheedia	299
Purdiaea	231	Ravenea	743	Rheum	466

Rhexia	404	*Robinsonia*	189	Ruscaceae	748
Rhigiocarya	410	*Robiquetia*	721	*Ruschia*	46
Rhinacanthus	40	*Robynsia*	519	*Ruscus*	748
Rhinanthus	564	*Rochefortia*	86	*Rustia*	520
Rhinephyllum	46	*Rockinghamia*	276	*Ruta*	529
Rhinerrhiza	721	*Rodriguezia*	721	Rutaceae	522
Rhipidantha	519	*Roegneria*	665	*Rutheopsis*	594
Rhipidocladum	665	*Roella*	116	*Rutidosis*	189
Rhipsalis	105	*Roemeria*	445	*Ruyschia*	396
Rhizanthella	721	*Roggeveldia*	681	*Ryania*	283
Rhizobotrya	226	*Rollandia*	116	*Ryparosa*	283
Rhizophoraceae	489	*Rollinia*	52	*Rytidocarpus*	227
Rhodamnia	431	*Romanschulzia*	227	*Rytidosperma*	665
Rhododendron	254	*Romanzoffia*	304	*Rytigynia*	520
Rhododon	315	*Romeroa*	77	*Sabal*	743
Rhodogeron	189	*Romnalda*	688	*Sabatia*	287
Rhodomyrtus	431	*Romneya*	445	*Sabazia*	189
Rhodophiala	619	*Romulea*	681	*Sabia*	531
Rhodothamnus	255	*Rondeletia*	519	Sabiaceae	531
Rhoiptelea	490	*Roridula*	490	*Sabicea*	521
Rhoipteleaceae	490	Roridulaceae	490	*Sabinea*	373
Rhopaloblaste	743	*Rorippa*	227	*Sacciolepis*	665
Rhopalopilia	442	*Rosa*	496	*Saccolabiopsis*	721
Rhopalostylis	743	Rosaceae	490	*Saccolabium*	721
Rhus	49	*Roscheria*	743	*Saccopetalum*	53
Rhynchanthera	405	*Rossioglossum*	721	*Sachsia*	189
Rhynchocalycaceae	490	*Rostellularia*	40	*Sageraea*	53
Rhynchocalyx	490	*Rosularia*	210	*Sagittaria*	608
Rhynchocorys	564	*Rotala*	387	*Saintpaulia*	293
Rhynchoglossum	293	*Rothmaleria*	189	*Sairocarpus*	564
Rhynchosia	372	*Rothmannia*	520	*Salacca*	743
Rhynchosinapis	226	*Roupala*	477	*Salacia*	134
Rhynchospora	645	*Rourea*	203	Salicaceae	531
Rhynchostele	721	*Roussea*	258	*Salicornia*	136
Rhynchostylis	721	*Rousselia*	597	*Salix*	531
Rhynchotheca	289	*Roycea*	136	*Salmea*	189
Rhyticalymma	40	*Roystonea*	743	*Salpichroa*	571
Rhytidocaulon	69	*Ruagea*	407	*Salpinctium*	41
Rhytidophyllum	293	*Rubia*	520	*Salpixantha*	41
Ribes	295	Rubiaceae	499	*Salsola*	136
Richardia	519	*Rubus*	496	*Salvia*	315
Richeria	276	*Rudbeckia*	189	*Sambucus*	119
Ricinocarpos	276	*Rudgea*	520	*Samolus*	470
Ricinocarpus	276	*Ruellia*	40	*Samyda*	283
Ricotia	226	*Rufodorsia*	293	*Sanango*	89
Rindera	86	*Rugelia*	189	*Sanchezia*	41
Rinorea	601	*Ruizia*	577	*Sanctambrosia*	126
Rinzia	431	*Rulingia*	577	*Sandoricum*	407
Riocreuxia	69	*Rumex*	466	*Sanguisorba*	499
Risleya	721	*Rumfordia*	189	*Sanicula*	594
Ristantia	431	*Rumohra*	11	Santalaceae	532
Rivasgodaya	373	*Rungia*	40	*Santalum*	532
Rivea	206	*Rupertia*	373	*Santapaua*	41
Robeschia	226	*Rupicapnos*	445	*Santolina*	189
Robinia	373	*Rupicola*	244	*Saphesia*	46
Robinsonella	395	*Ruprechtia*	466	Sapindaceae	533

Sapindus	535	Schiedeella	722	Scolopia	283
Sapium	276	Schima	580	Scolosanthus	521
Saponaria	126	Schinopsis	49	Scopelogena	46
Sapotaceae	536	Schinus	49	Scopolia	571
Sapphoa	41	Schippia	744	Scopulophila	306
Saprosma	521	Schisandra	547	Scorzonera	190
Sarcanthemum	189	Schisandraceae	547	Scrophularia	564
Sarcanthus	722	Schistocarpha	190	Scrophulariaceae	547
Sarcaulus	543	Schistotylus	722	Scurrula	386
Sarcocapnos	445	Schivereckia	227	Scutellaria	317
Sarcochilus	722	Schizachyrium	665	Scyphochlamys	521
Sarcoglyphis	722	Schizaea	17	Scyphogyne	255
Sarcomelicope	529	Schizaeaceae	17	Scyphostachys	521
Sarcomphalus	489	Schizochilus	722	Scytopetalaceae	569
Sarcopteryx	535	Schizocodon	232	Sebaea	287
Sarcosperma	543	Schizodium	723	Sebastiania	277
Sarcostemma	69	Schizoglossum	69	Secale	666
Sarcotoechia	535	Schizomeria	231	Secamone	69
Sarojusticia	41	Schizostachyum	666	Sechiopsis	230
Sarracenia	544	Schlimia	723	Sechium	230
Sarraceniaceae	544	Schlimmia	723	Secondatia	57
Sartwellia	189	Schlumbergera	105	Securidaca	461
Sasa	665	Schmardaea	407	Securinega	277
Sassafras	329	Schmidtia	666	Seddera	206
Satakentia	744	Schmidtottia	521	Sedella	210
Satranala	744	Schoenobiblus	582	Sedopsis	468
Satureja	316	Schoenocaulon	688	Sedum	210
Satyria	255	Schoenocrambe	227	Selaginella	2
Satyridium	722	Schoenolirion	672	Selaginellaceae	2
Satyrium	722	Schoenorchis	723	Selago	565
Saugetia	665	Schoenoxiphium	646	Selenicereus	106
Saurauia	43	Schoenus	646	Selenipedium	723
Sauropus	277	Schoepfia	437	Selkirkia	86
Saussurea	189	Schrankia	373	Semecarpus	49
Sauvagesia	436	Schrebera	439	Semele	748
Sauvallea	639	Schrenkia	594	Semenovia	594
Sauvallella	373	Schtschurowskia	594	Semiarundinaria	666
Savia	277	Schultzia	594	Semiliquidambar	301
Saxegothaea	29	Schumacheria	234	Semiramisia	255
Saxifraga	546	Schumanniophyton	521	Sempervivum	211
Saxifragaceae	545	Schwalbea	564	Senecio	191
Scabiosa	235	Schwantesia	46	Senna	373
Scaevola	295	Sciadocephala	190	Sequoiadendron	30
Scagea	277	Sciadopitys	30	Serapias	723
Scalesia	190	Sciaphila	749	Serialbizzia	374
Scaligera	594	Scilla	672	Serianthes	374
Scaligeria	594	Scindapsus	625	Sericanthe	521
Scandix	594	Scirpus	646	Sericocalyx	41
Scaphosepalum	722	Scleria	647	Serjania	535
Scariola	190	Sclerocactus	105	Serpyllopsis	13
Scelochilus	722	Sclerocarya	49	Serratula	194
Schaefferia	134	Sclerolaena	136	Serruria	477
Schaffnerella	665	Sclerolobium	373	Sesamoides	485
Schefflera	60	Sclerotheca	116	Sesbania	374
Schickendantzia	616	Sclerotiaria	594	Seseli	594
Schiedea	127	Scoliopus	749	Seshagiria	69

Sesleria	666	Smyrniopsis	594	Sphaerophysa	374
Sessilanthera	682	Smyrnium	594	Sphaerosciadium	594
Sesuvium	46	Sobolewskia	227	Sphalmium	477
Setaria	666	Sobralia	723	Sphenodesme	601
Seychellaria	750	Socotranthus	69	Sphenomeris	9
Shaferocharis	521	Socratea	744	Sphenopus	666
Sherbournea	521	Solanaceae	570	Sphenostemon	574
Shibateranthis	484	Solandra	572	Sphenostemonaceae	574
Shorea	237	Solanum	572	Sphinctanthus	521
Shortia	232	Soldanella	470	Sphyrastylis	723
Shoshonea	594	Solenanthus	86	Sphyrospermum	255
Sibara	227	Solenophora	294	Spigelia	385
Sibbaldia	499	Solenopsis	116	Spiloxene	673
Sibthorpia	565	Solenostemon	318	Spiraea	499
Sicyocaulis	230	Solidago	194	Spiraeanthemum	231
Sicyos	230	Sommera	521	Spiraeanthus	499
Sida	395	Sonchus	195	Spiranthes	723
Sidalcea	395	Sonderothamnus	447	Spirella	69
Sidastrum	396	Sonerila	405	Spirogardnera	532
Sideritis	317	Sonneratia	387	Spirostegia	565
Sideroxylon	543	Sophora	374	Spirotecoma	77
Sievekingia	723	Sophronitis	723	Spirotheca	79
Sigmatostalix	723	Sorbaria	499	Spongiosperma	57
Silene	127	Sorbus	499	Sporobolus	666
Siliquamomum	752	Sorghastrum	666	Sprengelia	244
Silphium	194	Sorghum	666	Spyridium	489
Simaba	570	Sorocephalus	477	Staavia	89
Simaroubaceae	569	Sorolepidium	11	Staberoha	748
Simira	521	Soulamea	570	Stachyanthus	305
Simplicia	666	Souroubea	396	Stachyarrhena	521
Simsia	194	Sowerbaea	620	Stachydeoma	319
Sinapidendron	227	Spachea	391	Stachyphrynium	688
Sinapis	227	Spananthe	594	Stachys	319
Sindora	374	Spaniopappus	196	Stachystemon	277
Sinia	436	Sparattanthelium	301	Stachytarpheta	601
Sinojackia	578	Sparattosperma	77	Stachyuraceae	575
Sinopanax	60	Sparaxis	682	Stachyurus	574
Sinopteris	4	Spatalla	477	Stackhousia	575
Sinowilsonia	301	Spathacanthus	41	Stackhousiaceae	575
Siparuna	411	Spathandra	405	Staehelina	196
Siphocampylus	116	Spathelia	529	Stahlia	374
Siphonochilus	752	Spathiphyllum	625	Stanfordia	227
Siphonoglossa	41	Spathodeopsis	77	Stangea	598
Sipolisia	194	Spathoglottis	723	Stangeria	30
Siraitia	231	Spatholobus	374	Stangeriaceae	30
Sisymbrium	227	Specularia	116	Stanhopea	723
Sisyranthus	69	Speea	611	Stanleya	227
Sisyrinchium	682	Spergula	131	Stapelia	69
Sium	594	Spergularia	131	Stapelianthus	69
Skimmia	529	Spermacoce	521	Stapeliopsis	70
Sloanea	243	Spermolepis	594	Staphylea	575
Smelowskia	227	Sphaeradenia	640	Staphyleaceae	575
Smilacaceae	748	Sphaeralcea	396	Stauntonia	323
Smilacina	639	Sphaerantia	431	Staurogyne	41
Smilax	748	Sphaerolobium	374	Staurogynopsis	41
Smithia	374	Sphaeromeria	196	Stawellia	620

Steenisioblechnum	5	*Stipagrostis*	667	*Swainsona*	375
Stefanoffia	595	*Stirtonanthus*	374	*Swallenia*	667
Steganotaenia	595	*Stoebe*	196	*Swartzia*	375
Steganthera	411	*Stomatium*	46	*Swertia*	287
Steinmannia	611	*Stomatochaeta*	196	*Swida*	206
Steirodiscus	196	*Storckiella*	374	*Swintonia*	49
Stelechocarpus	53	*Storthocalyx*	536	*Syagrus*	744
Stelis	723	*Streblacanthus*	41	*Symphonia*	299
Stellaria	131	*Streblorrhiza*	374	*Symphoricarpos*	119
Stellera	582	*Streblus*	414	*Symphyandra*	116
Stelleropsis	582	*Strelitzia*	748	*Symphyochlamys*	396
Stellilabium	724	Strelitziaceae	748	*Symphytum*	86
Stemmacantha	196	*Strempeliopsis*	57	Symplocaceae	578
Stemmadenia	57	*Streptanthus*	227	*Symplocos*	578
Stemodia	565	*Streptocarpus*	294	*Synadenium*	277
Stemona	748	*Streptocaulon*	70	*Synammia*	16
Stemonaceae	748	*Streptochaeta*	667	*Synaphea*	477
Stemonoporus	239	*Streptolirion*	639	*Synapsis*	77
Stenandrium	41	*Streptopetalum*	585	*Syncarpha*	196
Stenanona	53	*Streptopus*	639	*Syncarpia*	431
Stenanthemum	489	*Striga*	565	*Syncolostemon*	320
Stenia	724	*Strobilanthes*	41	*Syndesmanthus*	255
Stenocactus	106	*Stroganowia*	228	*Syneilesis*	196
Stenocarpus	477	*Strombosia*	437	*Syngonanthus*	651
Stenocereus	106	*Strongylodon*	374	*Synosma*	196
Stenodrepanum	374	*Strophanthus*	57	*Synotis*	197
Stenogramma	17	*Strotheria*	196	*Synsepalum*	544
Stenogyne	320	*Strumaria*	619	*Synthyris*	565
Stenomesson	619	*Struthanthus*	386	*Syntrichopappus*	197
Stenorrhynchos	724	*Struthiola*	582	*Syrenia*	228
Stenosiphonium	41	*Struthiopteris*	5	*Syringa*	439
Stenostephanus	41	*Strychnos*	385	*Syringodea*	682
Stenotaenia	595	*Stryphnodendron*	375	*Systeloglossum*	724
Stenothyrsus	41	*Stuartia*	580	*Systenotheca*	466
Stenotus	196	*Stuhlmannia*	375	*Syzygium*	432
Stephanandra	499	*Stylapterus*	447	*Tabebuia*	77
Stephania	410	Stylidiaceae	577	*Tabernaemontana*	57
Stephanomeria	196	*Stylidium*	577	*Tachigali*	377
Stephanopodium	232	*Stylisma*	206	*Tacinga*	106
Stephanostema	57	*Stylocline*	196	*Tacitus*	212
Steptorhamphus	196	*Stylogyne*	419	*Taeckholmia*	197
Sterculia	577	*Stylosanthes*	375	*Taeniophyllum*	724
Sterculiaceae	575	*Styphelia*	244	*Taihangia*	499
Sterigmostemum	227	Styracaceae	578	*Taiwania*	30
Steriphoma	118	*Styrax*	578	*Talauma*	388
Sternbergia	619	*Suaeda*	136	*Talbotiella*	377
Stevia	196	*Suarezia*	724	*Talinum*	468
Steyerbromelia	634	*Succisa*	235	*Talisia*	536
Steyermarkia	521	*Succisella*	235	Tamaricaceae	579
Stictocardia	206	*Sucrea*	667	*Tamarix*	579
Stigmaphyllon	391	*Suessenguthia*	42	*Tambourissa*	411
Stigmatodactylus	724	*Sullivantia*	547	*Tanacetum*	197
Stilbaceae	577	*Sunipia*	724	*Tangtsinia*	724
Stilbocarpa	60	Surianaceae	578	*Tanquana*	46
Stillingia	277	*Sutera*	565	*Tanulepis*	70
Stipa	666	*Sventenia*	196	*Tapeinidium*	10

Tapeinosperma	419	*Tetramicra*	724	*Thornea*	299
Tapiphyllum	521	*Tetramolopium*	198	*Thottea*	61
Tapirira	49	*Tetraneuris*	198	*Thouinia*	536
Tapiscia	575	*Tetraperone*	198	*Thrasya*	667
Tapura	233	*Tetraplasandra*	60	*Thraulococcus*	536
Taraktogenos	283	*Tetrapteris*	391	*Thrinax*	744
Taraxacum	197	*Tetraria*	647	*Thrixspermum*	724
Tarenna	521	*Tetrasiphon*	135	*Thryptomene*	433
Tasmannia	605	*Tetrastigma*	605	*Thuja*	22
Tauschia	595	*Tetrastylidium*	437	*Thunbergia*	42
Taverniera	377	*Tetrataxis*	387	*Thurovia*	199
Taxaceae	29	*Tetratheca*	584	*Thurya*	131
Taxodiaceae	29	*Tetrathyrium*	301	*Thylachium*	118
Taxodium	30	*Tetrazygia*	405	*Thymbra*	321
Taxus	29	*Tetrazygiopsis*	405	*Thymelaea*	582
Teagueia	724	*Teucrium*	320	Thymelaeaceae	581
Teclea	529	*Thaleropia*	433	*Thymophylla*	199
Tecoma	78	*Thalia*	688	*Thymopsis*	199
Tecomanthe	78	*Thalictrum*	484	*Thymus*	321
Tecophilaea	749	*Thaminophyllum*	198	*Thyrsodium*	49
Tecophilaeaceae	749	*Thamnea*	89	*Thyrsopteris*	10
Tectaria	11	*Thamnocalamus*	667	*Thysanocarpus*	229
Tectaridium	11	*Thamnochortus*	748	*Thysanotus*	620
Tectiphiala	744	*Thamnosma*	530	*Tianschaniella*	87
Tectona	601	*Thayeria*	16	*Tibouchina*	405
Tecunumania	231	Theaceae	579	*Tigridia*	682
Tegicornia	137	*Thecacoris*	277	*Tilia*	583
Teinostachyum	667	*Thelasis*	724	Tiliaceae	583
Telanthophora	197	*Thelesperma*	198	*Tiliacora*	410
Telekia	197	Theligonaceae	581	*Tilingia*	595
Teline	378	*Theligonum*	581	*Tillandsia*	634
Telipogon	724	*Thelionema*	746	*Timonius*	522
Telopea	478	*Thelocactus*	106	*Tinguarra*	595
Temmodaphne	329	*Thelocephala*	106	*Tinospora*	410
Temnopteryx	522	*Thelymitra*	724	*Tipularia*	724
Templetonia	378	*Thelypodiopsis*	228	*Tiquilia*	87
Temu	433	*Thelypodium*	228	*Tmesipteris*	2
Tenicroa	687	Thelypteridaceae	17	*Tococa*	405
Tephroseris	197	*Thelypteris*	17	*Tocoyena*	522
Tephrosia	378	*Themistoclesia*	255	*Todaroa*	595
Tepuia	255	*Theobroma*	577	*Toechima*	536
Terminalia	144	Theophrastaceae	581	*Tofieldia*	688
Ternstroemia	580	*Thereianthus*	682	*Tolpis*	199
Tessmannia	379	*Theriophonum*	625	*Tolumnia*	724
Tessmannianthus	405	*Thermopsis*	379	*Tomanthea*	199
Tetraberlinia	379	*Thesium*	532	*Tonestus*	199
Tetraclinis	22	*Thesmophora*	577	*Topobea*	405
Tetracoccus	277	*Thespesia*	396	*Tordylium*	595
Tetradenia	320	*Thevetia*	57	*Torenia*	565
Tetradymia	198	*Thismia*	637	*Torilis*	595
Tetraena	606	*Thlaspi*	229	*Torreya*	29
Tetragastris	91	*Thomasia*	577	*Torreyochloa*	667
Tetragonia	46	*Thomsonia*	625	*Torularia*	229
Tetragonolobus	379	*Thoracostachyum*	647	*Torulinium*	647
Tetrameranthus	53	*Thoreldora*	530	*Tournefortia*	87
Tetramerium	42	*Thorella*	595	*Tournonia*	72

Toussaintia	53	*Trifolium*	379	*Tromotriche*	70
Tovaria	584	*Triglochin*	684	Tropaeolaceae	584
Tovariaceae	584	*Trigonella*	380	*Tropaeolum*	584
Tovarochloa	667	*Trigonia*	584	*Trophis*	414
Tovomita	299	Trigoniaceae	584	*Tropidia*	725
Tovomitopsis	299	*Trigonidium*	725	*Tropidocarpum*	229
Townsendia	199	*Trigonobalanus*	280	*Trybliocalyx*	42
Toxocarpus	70	*Trigonosciadium*	595	*Trymalium*	489
Tozzia	565	*Trigonospora*	18	*Trymatococcus*	414
Trachelium	116	*Trigonostemon*	277	*Tsuga*	27
Trachelospermum	57	*Trigonotis*	87	*Tsusiophyllum*	255
Trachyandra	626	*Trilepidea*	386	*Tuberaria*	143
Trachycalymma	70	Trilliaceae	749	*Tuberolabium*	725
Trachycarpus	744	*Trillium*	749	*Tubocapsicum*	574
Trachymene	595	*Trimenia*	584	*Tucma*	683
Trachystoma	229	Trimeniaceae	584	*Tuctoria*	668
Tracyina	199	*Trimeris*	116	*Tugarinovia*	199
Tradescantia	639	*Trimezia*	682	*Tulipa*	687
Tragia	277	*Trinia*	595	*Tupeia*	386
Tragopogon	199	*Triniochloa*	667	*Tupistra*	639
Trapa	584	*Triodia*	667	*Turbina*	206
Trapaceae	584	*Triolena*	405	*Turbinicarpus*	106
Trattinnickia	91	*Triopteris*	391	*Turnera*	585
Tremandraceae	584	*Triopterys*	391	Turneraceae	585
Trematolobelia	116	*Triphora*	725	*Turpinia*	575
Trevoria	724	*Triphyophyllum*	234	*Turraea*	409
Trianaeopiper	450	*Triphysaria*	565	*Tuxtla*	199
Trianoptiles	647	*Tripleurospermum*	199	*Tylecodon*	212
Trianthema	46	*Triplophyllum*	11	*Tylophora*	70
Triaristella	724	*Tripogandra*	639	*Tynnanthus*	78
Trias	725	*Tripogon*	667	*Typhonium*	625
Triaspis	391	*Tripsacum*	668	*Uebelinia*	131
Tribonanthes	669	*Tripterococcus*	575	*Uebelmannia*	107
Tricalysia	522	*Tripterospermum*	287	*Uechtritzia*	199
Triceratella	639	*Triscenia*	668	*Ugni*	433
Trichadenia	283	*Triscyphus*	637	*Ulbrichia*	396
Trichanthemis	199	*Trisetaria*	668	*Ulex*	380
Trichanthodium	199	*Trisetella*	725	Ulmaceae	585
Trichilia	407	*Trisetum*	668	*Ulmus*	585
Trichocentrum	725	*Tristania*	433	Umbelliferae	585
Trichocereus	106	*Tristaniopsis*	433	*Umbellularia*	329
Trichocladus	301	*Tristemma*	406	*Umtiza*	380
Trichocline	199	*Triteleia*	611	*Uncaria*	522
Trichodesma	87	*Trithrinax*	744	*Uncinia*	647
Trichodiadema	46	*Triticum*	668	*Ungeria*	577
Trichoglottis	725	*Tritonia*	682	*Ungernia*	620
Trichomanes	13	*Tritoniopsis*	683	*Unona*	53
Trichopilia	725	*Triumfetta*	583	*Unonopsis*	53
Trichosanthes	231	*Triunia*	478	*Urandra*	305
Trichoscypha	49	Triuridaceae	749	*Urbananthus*	199
Trichostema	322	*Trivalvaria*	53	*Urceola*	57
Tricostularia	647	*Trochetia*	577	*Urceolina*	620
Tricyrtis	639	*Trochetiopsis*	577	*Urelytrum*	668
Tridax	199	*Trochocarpa*	244	*Urena*	396
Tridentea	70	*Troglophyton*	199	*Urera*	597
Tridimeris	53	*Trollius*	485	*Urginea*	673

Urmenetea	200	*Veronicastrum*	569	*Watsonia*	683
Urocarpidium	396	*Verreauxia*	295	*Weberbauerella*	381
Urogentias	287	*Verschaffeltia*	745	*Weberocereus*	107
Uromyrtus	433	*Verticordia*	433	*Wedelia*	201
Urophyllum	522	*Vetiveria*	668	*Weigela*	119
Urospathella	625	*Vexatorella*	478	*Weinmannia*	231
Urostachys	2	*Viburnum*	119	*Wellstedia*	87
Ursinia	200	*Vicia*	380	*Wendlandia*	522
Urtica	597	*Victorinia*	277	*Wendlandiella*	745
Urticaceae	595	*Vieraea*	201	*Wercklea*	396
Utleria	70	*Vigna*	381	*Werneria*	201
Utleya	255	*Viguiera*	201	*Westoniella*	201
Utricularia	382	*Villarsia*	410	*Westringia*	322
Uvaria	53	*Vincetoxicum*	70	*Wetria*	277
Uvariodendron	54	*Viola*	602	*Wettinia*	745
Uvariopsis	54	Violaceae	601	*White-sloanea*	70
Vaccinium	255	*Virectaria*	522	*Whiteochloa*	668
Vahlia	598	*Virola*	415	*Whitneya*	201
Vahliaceae	598	Viscaceae	603	*Whyanbeelia*	277
Valantia	522	*Viscum*	604	*Wiborgia*	381
Valdivia	258	*Vismia*	299	*Widdringtonia*	22
Valeriana	598	*Visnea*	581	*Wiesneria*	608
Valerianaceae	598	Vitaceae	604	*Wikstroemia*	583
Valerianella	598	*Vitellaria*	544	*Wilkesia*	201
Vallaris	57	*Vitellariopsis*	544	*Wilkiea*	411
Vallesia	57	*Vitex*	601	*Willbleibia*	668
Vallisneria	673	*Vitis*	605	*Willdenowia*	748
Vanclevea	200	*Vittadinia*	201	*Willisia*	456
Vanda	725	*Vittaria*	18	*Willkommia*	668
Vanilla	725	Vittariaceae	18	*Wimmeria*	135
Vantanea	301	*Vlokia*	46	*Winifredia*	748
Vaseyanthus	231	*Voanioala*	745	Winteraceae	605
Vaseyochloa	668	*Vochysia*	605	*Witheringia*	574
Vateria	239	Vochysiaceae	605	*Witsenia*	683
Vateriopsis	239	*Volutaria*	201	*Wodyetia*	745
Vatica	239	*Votomita*	406	*Wolffiella*	684
Vauquelinia	499	*Voyria*	287	*Wollemia*	19
Vavilova	380	*Vriesea*	636	*Woodia*	70
Veillonia	744	*Vrydagzynea*	726	*Woodsia*	18
Veitchia	744	*Vulpia*	668	Woodsiaceae	18
Velezia	131	*Vvedenskya*	595	*Wormia*	234
Vella	229	*Wagenitzia*	201	*Worsleya*	620
Velleia	295	*Wahlenbergia*	116	*Wrightia*	57
Vellereophyton	200	*Waldsteinia*	499	*Wrixonia*	322
Vellozia	750	*Wallenia*	419	*Wulfenia*	569
Velloziaceae	750	*Walleria*	749	*Wullschlaegelia*	726
Ventenata	668	*Wallichia*	745	*Wurmbea*	638
Ventilago	489	*Walsura*	409	*Wyethia*	201
Vepris	530	*Waltheria*	577	*Xanthocercis*	381
Veratrum	689	*Warburgia*	117	*Xanthophyllum*	461
Verbascum	565	*Warea*	229	*Xanthophytopsis*	522
Verbena	601	*Warneckea*	406	*Xanthorrhoea*	750
Verbenaceae	598	*Warrea*	726	Xanthorrhoeaceae	750
Verbesina	200	*Wasabia*	229	*Xanthosia*	595
Vernonia	200	*Washingtonia*	745	*Xanthosoma*	625
Veronica	568	*Waterhousea*	434	*Xanthostemon*	434

Xantolis	544
Xantonneopsis	522
Xenoscapa	683
Xeronema	746
Xerophyta	750
Xerothamnella	42
Ximenia	437
Xiphidium	669
Xiphopteris	13
Xiphotheca	381
Xylobium	726
Xylocalyx	569
Xylococcus	256
Xylopia	54
Xylopiastrum	54
Xylorhiza	201
Xylosma	283
Xylotheca	284
Xyridaceae	750
Xyris	750
Xysmalobium	70
Yeatesia	42
Yoania	726
Youngia	202
Yucca	607
Yunquea	202
Zaluzania	202
Zamia	33
Zamiaceae	30
Zannichellia	750
Zannichelliaceae	750
Zanonia	231
Zantedeschia	625
Zanthoxylum	530
Zea	668
Zelkova	585
Zenkerella	381
Zephyranthes	620
Zeravschania	595
Zetagyne	726
Zeugites	668
Zeuktophyllum	46
Zeuxine	726
Zeylanidium	456
Zieria	530
Zigadenus	689
Zimmermannia	277
Zingeria	668
Zingiber	752
Zingiberaceae	751
Zinnia	202
Zinowiewia	135
Zizania	668
Ziziphora	322
Ziziphus	489
Zornia	381
Zosteraceae	752
Zuckia	137
Zygogynum	605
Zygophyllaceae	606
Zygophyllum	606